DATE DUE

MR 1 0 '0			

DEMCO 38-296

WORLD HISTORY

WORLD HISTORY

A Dictionary of Important People, Places, and Events, from Ancient Times to the Present

BRUCE WETTERAU

A Henry Holt Reference Book

HENRY HOLT AND COMPANY
NEW YORK

A Henry Holt Reference Book
Henry Holt and Company, Inc.
Publishers since 1866
115 West 18th Street
New York, New York 10011

Henry Holt® is a registered
trademark of Henry Holt and Company, Inc.

Previous edition published by Macmillan and Company in 1983
under the title Concise Dictionary of World History.

Library of Congress Cataloging-in-Publication Data
Wetterau, Bruce.
World history : a dictionary of important people, places, and
events, from ancient times to the present / Bruce Wetterau. —
1st ed.
p.   cm.—(A Henry Holt reference book)
Rev. ed. of: Macmillan concise dictionary of world history. 1983.
1. History—Dictionaries.   I. Wetterau, Bruce.   Macmillan concise
dictionary of world history.   II. Title.   III. Series.
D9.W47   1993   93-34819
903—dc20   CIP

ISBN 0-8050-2350-X

Henry Holt books are available for special
promotions and premiums. For details contact:
Director, Special Markets.

First Edition—1994

Designed by Lucy Albanese

Printed in the United States of America
All first editions are printed on acid-free paper. ∞
3   5   7   9   10   8   6   4   2

Contents

Preface

For historians, these are times that quicken the pulse. Great things are happening in the world: the birth of democracy in the former Soviet Union, the Cold War's sudden end, Germany's reunification, and the near wholesale realignment of Europe itself. Decades of grinding, hopelessly knotted problems disappeared so quickly that it seemed almost as if by magic. But it surely was not.

World History is an up-to-date general reference dictionary for history, which not only provides a clear, easy-to-follow record of events leading up to these most recent triumphs, but also spans the broad run of history back to the beginnings of civilization. With this single volume, the reader gains ready access to a staggering amount of factual information. Virtually all the important people, events, nations, and empires throughout history are included in these pages, plus legions of the lesser known as well.

In all, the book contains nearly 10,000 concisely written text entries, plus approximately 135 historical outlines that include more than 7,000 items altogether. This mix of alphabetically arranged text entries and chronologically arranged historical outlines is what makes the dictionary both versatile and different from other general history references.

Whether it's a matter of exploring new areas of history, reviewing what has already been learned, or just refreshing the memory on specific facts and dates, this dictionary is the first place to turn. Historians and teachers can use it as a handbook when they want to review areas of history outside their own specialities. The outline histories and clear, concisely written text entries are ideal for students reviewing the histories of major nations and empires they are studying. And writers, editors, working professionals, and history buffs can put the dictionary to immediate use as a convenient one-volume sourcebook for checking facts, dates, spellings of names, and the like.

Some readers may notice this book closely resembles the *Concise Dictionary of World History,* first published in 1983. In fact, this is a revised and fully updated edition of that work under a new title. It is worth noting that, as before, the dictionary not only covers world history but also the basic history of individual countries, such as the United States, Britain, France, China, and so on. The twenty or so most important nations are covered in depth, while many others are presented in substantial detail. In that way it continues to serve as a reference for key areas of history in general.

Changes have been made to the plan of the previous edition, however. The coverage is somewhat more focused; entries for mythical and legendary figures were deleted, along with those for most modern cities, to make room for more relevant material.

In all, over 100,000 words of new text have been added, both to update the book and to include the many new entries. In addition, hundreds of existing entries, particularly those for important persons, have been revised and enlarged, providing more detail while maintaining the concise, ready-reference format.

Of the new entries, many were suggested by members of the Board of Academic Review (see page xiv), an academic advisory committee new to this edition. Board members read material in their respective fields, mainly to ensure that the important points of history had been covered. However, in some areas they also suggested changes and additions to make the material conform more closely with what might be taught in a college survey course for undergraduates. For example, survey courses in U.S. and European history these days put greater emphasis on social history, and a number of new entries suggested by reviewers deal with this area.

For college students taking introductory survey courses in U.S., English, French, German, Russian, Spanish, and Chinese history—certainly among the more common history courses—the historical outlines and concise text entries can serve as a helpful study aid. That is not to say they will substitute for actually attending class; no book can match what any professor teaches in a particular course. But when it comes time to review material in these core areas, the historical outlines especially can help students gain a firmer grasp of the subject matter. In a sense, each item in the outline acts like a flash card, challenging students to remember what they know about it.

Much of the new text for this edition went into updating and expanding the historical outlines. Coverage of recent events is routinely more detailed in historical outlines of this type, and this book is no exception. But the complexity and importance of recent events in so many countries demanded even more space be devoted to them. In the case of former Communist states, for example, the historical outlines provide a relatively detailed, blow-by-blow record of the transition from hard-line Communist to democratic governments.

The scope of historical outlines for major nations and empires was also expanded beyond political history to include the most famous writers, artists, inventors, scientists, and other figures who lived and worked within their borders. The reader will notice the biggest change in those major nations and empires that are traditional watersheds of the arts and sciences. Regrettably, space and time limitations prohibited a more systematic inclusion of, for example, major writers of every nation for which there is a historical outline. Nevertheless, for the most important figures in history, the additions create more useful historical outlines and also serve as helpful cross-references to the alphabetically arranged text entries.

Some historical outlines from the previous edition also underwent a more general revamping and enlargement. China and Japan, for example, are significantly larger now and better reflect their long histories as well as their importance in Far Eastern and world affairs. (The transliteration of Chinese names now also follows the new Pinyin system, though cross-references from the old Wade-Giles spelling have been included wherever possible.) Other revamped historical outlines include Canada, Australia, Chile, and Austria, while minor additions were made to numerous others. Elsewhere, new historical outlines were added for the United Nations, the Cold War, the Iran-Iraq War, and the Persian Gulf War.

A word about the book's basic coverage also seems important here. Like most reference books, the dictionary is deliberately weighted to include material of greatest potential value to the average reader. There is, by design, relatively more material on the United States, Great Britain, France, Germany, et cetera—the countries that readers in the United States, the major market for this book, are most likely to look up. Also, these are among the areas of history students most often study in college. That is not to dismiss the history of other, often smaller, nations as unimportant. But in a single-volume reference of such broad scope hard choices had to be made on what to include.

The aim of those choices was to produce a useful general reference for history, one that offers both broad scope and sufficient detail to be of practical value to the great majority of readers.

BRUCE WETTERAU
Charlottesville, Virginia

Acknowledgments

Compiling the second edition was far less complex and time-consuming than the first. Still there was much to be done and, as with the first edition, the help of able free-lancers proved invaluable. Ann Marr, Bill Wenthe, Chris Carruth, Cindy Remington, Cheryl Roach, Ken Whitehead, and Keith Pomeroy helped draft part of the new and updated text. Katherine Somervell and Ann Marr both handled the enormous job of proofreading the computerized manuscript before it was delivered to the publisher, and Mary St. John doubled as researcher and editorial assistant.

The University of Virginia Library proved, as always, an invaluable resource, and the staff deserves thanks for their help with the sometimes knotty research problems created by a project of this type. Bowman Literary Services, of Staunton, Virginia, also should be mentioned for handling the optical scanning of the original text, which converted the bound first edition into electronic form.

My thanks also go to my editor at Henry Holt, Mary Kay Linge, who shepherded the 2,800-page manuscript through the final phases of publication.

I would also like to thank again the academic reviewers for their hard work and valuable contributions, all of which were accomplished despite a tight deadline. In addition to suggesting changes and additions, they also noted errors and inconsistencies that, alas, inevitably creep into a work of this size. Their comments helped improve the accuracy of the book and for that I owe them a special thanks. But it is only fair to point out fact-checking was not their responsibility, and that the burden for any remaining errors rests, as always, with the author.

Lastly, those who labored on the first edition should not be forgotten. Senior editors Ray Hand, Jr., and Kenneth Whitehead took part in various phases of the project, while contributors Lina Accurso, Lilian Barrington, Diana Healy, Constance Murphy, and Linda Palmer helped draft entries. Lilian Brady and Gloria Cestaro served as associate editors; Joy Aquilino, Laura Ball, Roxanne Basmaci, Christopher

Carruth, Karen Cestaro, and Laurie Paleo helped with research. Robinson Mason, Andrew Mason, Ellie Aquilino, Dolores Margarita, and Robin Michelson all served as editorial assistants.

BOARD OF ACADEMIC REVIEW

Notes to the Reader

Two types of entries. Unlike most other history references, this dictionary contains both historical outlines covering broad topics chronologically (like the history of France) and alphabetically arranged text entries that focus on more specific events, famous individuals, places, and the like. The two types complement each other and make this an especially versatile guide to history.

For example, the historical outline for France provides a useful overview of its long history as well as a quick way to review key events in any part of it. But suppose you want more information on the Enlightenment or Louis XV—both being mentioned briefly in the historical outline for France. You have only to look up text entries under either name.

Conversely, if after reading about the French *Camisards* in a text entry, you wonder what else happened in France in their time, just turn to the outline for France and skip to the 18th century.

Cross-references. Virtually every major event and person in history has a separate entry (or historical outline) in this book. For this reason, specific cross-references for every name mentioned within any given entry would be pointless.

At times though, cross-references (*q.v.* and *See also*) have been included to show readers where other potentially useful information is located. Also, when biographical names are mentioned within an entry, the reader will find a separate entry for that person whenever the first initial(s) and last name are given. If the first and last names are given in full, there is no separate entry. (Obviously, this system does not apply to biographical names without first names [i.e., George V], or where first names may not be immediately obvious, as in Chinese and Islamic names.)

Variant names and spellings. Variant names and spellings are given in parentheses immediately following the boldfaced entry name.

Population totals.   When populations are given for countries, they are the latest available (estimated or actual) figures.

Abbreviations.   Only a few simple abbreviations are used. They include:

b.	born
c	circa (approximately)
d.	died
fl.	flourished
m.	married
orig.	originally
pop.	population
pseud.	pseudonym
q.v.	which see

WORLD HISTORY

Aasen, Ivar Andreas 1813–96. Norwegian philologist. He devised (1853) a new Norwegian language (Landsmaal) by standardizing existing dialects.

Abailard, Peter *See* **Abelard, Peter.**

Abano, Pietro d' 1250?–1316? Italian doctor and philosopher. Abano sought to reconcile Arabian medical theory and Greek philosophy in his *Conciliator differentiarum.* Though he established Padua as a center for medical study, he was twice denounced by the Inquisition.

Abbadides (Abbadids) Arab Muslim dynasty that briefly ruled (1023–91) Seville, Spain. They were in power from the collapse of the caliphate of Córdoba to the occupation of Seville by the Almoravides.

Abbas I (~ the Great) 1557–1628? Shah of Persia (1587–1628). He defeated the Uzbeks and Turks, regained Persian territory, and established Isfahan as Persia's capital. Under his reign, the arts, public works, and trade flourished.

Abbas II (~ Hilmi Pasha) 1874–1944. Last Egyptian khedive (1892–1914), successor to his father, Tewfik Pasha. He unsuccessfully opposed British control of Egypt and was deposed at the beginning of WW I, when Britain made Egypt a protectorate.

Abbas, Ferhat 1899–1985. Algerian statesman and nationalist movement leader. He was the first president of the Algerian provisional government (1958) and president of the Constituent Assembly when Algeria gained independence from France (1962–63).

Abba Hilmi Pasha *See* **Abbas II.**

Abbasid Dynasty of Muslim caliphs who ruled the Caliphate (750–1258), successors to the Umayyad caliphs (*q.v.*). The line was established (750) after Abu Muslim revolted and defeated the last Umayyad caliph, Marwan II (*d.* 750). During the reign of the 37 Abbasid caliphs, the capital was moved from Damascus to Baghdad. The caliphs' real power declined, the empire slowly disintegrated into petty kingdoms, and finally fell to the Mongols (1258). The Caliphate was subsequently removed to Egypt. (*See also* Caliphate, Empire of.) *Notable Abbasid caliphs included:* Abu al-Abbas 750–754; al-Mansur 754–775; Harun al-Rashid 786–809; al-Mamun 813–833; and al-Mutasim 833–842.

Abbas the Great *See* **Abbas I.**

abbey Usually a self-contained religious community of monks or nuns, consisting of several buildings, including a church, living quarters, and work spaces. Important to the development of the Benedictine order (*q.v.*), abbeys became centers for learning and the arts, as well as worship, in medieval times.

Abbey Theatre Irish theater and theatrical company formed by the Irish National Theatre Society. The society was founded (1902) by J. M. Synge, W. B. Yeats, and others. Since then many leading actors and playwrights have been associated with the theater.

ABC Powers Collective name for Argentina, Brazil, and Chile, which arose from their joint action on Latin American affairs in the early 20th cent.

Abdali Sultanate Former quasi-independent territory, a part of Yemen (southern) since 1967. The sultanate won its freedom from Yemen in 1728 and was ruled independently until 1839. Thereafter, by treaties with the British, it became part of the Aden Protectorate and ultimately of the former southern Yemen.

Abd al-Kadir 1807–83. Algerian rebel leader. From 1832 to 1844, he struggled against French

1

rule in Algeria. His army was finally driven into Morocco, was defeated (1844) at Isly, Morocco, and forced to surrender (1847).

Abdallah *See* **Abdullah.**

Abd Allah (Khalifa, the) (Abdullah et Taaisha) 1846–99. Sudanese rebel leader. The successor to Muhammad Ahmed, he led Sudanese independence forces to many victories against Egypt. He was decisively defeated by the British at Omdurman (1898).

Abd al-Malik (Abdul-Malik) c646–705. An Umayyad caliph (685–705), successor to his father, Marwan I. He conquered a rival caliph and thus unified Islam. He instituted monetary and postal reforms and made Arabic the official language. *See also* Muslim civil wars.

Abd'al-Medjid *See* **Abdul Mejid.**

Abd-al-Mumin (Abdul-Mumin) 1094?–1163. A Berber Muslim leader, founder of the Almohade Empire. A disciple of Almohade leader Muhammad ibn Tumart, he defeated (1147) the Almoravides, established Marrakesh as his capital, and extended his empire through North Africa and Muslim Spain.

Abd-ar-Rahman *See* **Abd-er-Rahman.**

Abd-el-Krim 1882?–1963. Moorish rebel leader. He successfully fought the French and Spanish in Morocco, only to be defeated by their combined forces (1926).

Abd-er-Rahman (Abdu-r-Rahman) (Abd-ar-Rahman) 1778–1859. Sultan of Morocco and Fez (1822–59). His efforts to expand his influence in Algeria led to defeat in war with France (1844). Activities of Moroccan pirates led to conflict with other European nations.

Abd er-Rahman I (Abd-ar-Rahman I) 731–788. First Umayyad emir of Córdoba (756–788) in Muslim Spain. The only survivor of the Abbasid massacre of his family in 750, he seized power in Córdoba. He later repulsed Charlemagne's invasion at Roncesvalles (778), in defense of his emirate.

Abd er-Rahman III (Abd ar-Rahman) 891–961. Umayyad emir of Córdoba (912–929) in Muslim Spain and its first caliph (929–961). Under his rule, the city's military and cultural importance was greatly enhanced.

Abdul-Aziz 1830–76. Ottoman sultan (1861–76). His repudiation (1875) of the interest on loans from European nations led to foreign takeover of Ottoman finances. Revolts and inde-pendence movements further shook the Ottoman Empire, and he was deposed by Midhat Pasha.

Abdul-Hamid I 1725–89. Ottoman sultan (1774–89), successor to his brother, Mustafa III. During his reign, Ottoman power dwindled through two of the Russo-Turkish Wars (*q.v.*), which established Russian supremacy in the Crimea.

Abdul-Hamid II 1842–1918. Ottoman sultan (1876–1909), successor to Murad V. His reign saw the continuing decline of the Ottoman Empire, the Russo-Turkish War (1897), and Armenian massacres (1894–96). His despotic rule was curbed (1908) by a revolt of the Young Turks.

Abdullah (Abdullah ibn Hussein) 1882–1951. First king (1946–51) of newly independent Jordan. During the Arab-Israeli War (1948–49), he took the West Bank of the Jordan River and subsequently annexed the territory. He was assassinated (1951).

Abdullah et Taaisha *See* **Abd Allah.**

Abdullah ibn Hussein *See* **Abdullah.**

Abdul-Malik *See* **Abd al-Malik.**

Abdul Mejid (Abd' al-Medjid) 1823–61. Ottoman sultan (1839–61), successor to his father, Mahmud II. He introduced short-lived reforms (1839, 1856), ended, with European aid, Muhammad Ali's revolt, and fought Russia in the Crimean War (1853–56).

Abdul-Mumin *See* **Abd-al-Mumin.**

Abdul Rahman, Tunku 1903–73. A Malaysian statesman. He headed the Nationalist party, negotiated Malaysian independence from Britain (Aug. 31, 1957), and became first prime minister (1957–70). The Federation of Malaysia was formed (1963) during his administration.

Abdu-r-Rahman (Abdurrahman) *d.* 732. Governor of Muslim Spain (721–732). He was killed by Charles Martel in the famous Battle of Tours (732).

Abdu-r-Rahman *See also* **Abd-er-Rahman.**

Abelard, Peter (Abailard, ~) (Abeilard, ~) 1079–1142. French theologian and philosopher. A teacher of wide reputation in Paris, he applied Aristotelian logic to questions of faith. He secretly married a student, Héloïse, and was subsequently mutilated by thugs hired by her angry uncle. Abelard then became a monk at Saint Denis and Héloïse became a nun. Then his *Theologica,* an analysis of the Trinity, was condemned as heresy (1121), and he was thereafter hounded by charges of heresy.

Abell, Kjeld 1901–61. Danish playwright noted for his innovations in stage technique.

Abensberg-Eckmuhl, Battles of Victory for Napoleon (Apr. 23, 1809) over Austrian forces during the Napoleonic Wars (1803–15). The Austrians, under Archduke Charles Louis (1771–1847), sought to take advantage of Napoleon's difficulties in the Peninsular War to liberate occupied German states. To that end, Charles launched (Apr. 10) an attack into Bavaria with a force of nearly 200,000 soldiers, while also calling for a general revolt by German states. He was met by nearly 180,000 allied French troops under Napoleon. In the ensuing battles at Abensberg, Eckmuhl, and Landshut (Apr. 19–23), Napoleon split the Austrian force and compelled it to retreat southward. Though he failed to decisively defeat the Austrians, Napoleon nevertheless prevented a general rebellion of German states.

Abercromby, Sir Ralph 1734–1801. British general. He served in the Seven Years' War (1756–63) and distinguished himself in Holland while commanding a British retreat during the French Revolutionary Wars (1792–1802). He was killed while leading an expedition against the French in Egypt.

Aberdeen, George Hamilton-Gordon, 4th earl of 1784–1860. British statesman who served twice as foreign secretary (1834–35, 1841–46), and as prime minister (1852–55). As foreign secretary, he settled two boundary disputes between the US and Canada by concluding the Webster-Ashburton Treaty (1842) and the Oregon Treaty (1846). As prime minister, he was unable to prevent British involvement in the Crimean War (1853–56).

Aberhart, William 1878–1943. Canadian politician who advocated Social Credit, or cash payments to citizens by the government. He helped to organize the Social Credit party in Alberta and served as Alberta's premier (1935–43), but failed to implement his social and economic programs.

Abijah (Abijam) *fl.* c915 BC. Second king of Judah, successor to his father, Rehoboam, and grandson of Solomon. During his brief reign, he warred against Jeroboam I. {2 Chron 13; 1 Kings 15}

Abjuration, Act of *See* Act of Abjuration.

Abo, Treaty of Treaty (Aug. 7, 1743) between Sweden and Russia, following the Russo-Swedish War (1741–43). By its terms, Sweden ceded to Russia part of southeastern Finland.

abolition Worldwide movement for an end to slavery, and an important issue in US history. Abolition was an outgrowth of the concern for human rights that arose during the Enlightenment of the 18th cent. In Britain, the abolition movement began in the late 18th cent. and brought about laws ending slavery throughout the British Empire by the early 19th cent. British abolitionists, such as W. Wilberforce, first won passage of laws (1807) against the trading of slaves and then, by the Abolition Act of 1833, succeeded in having slavery itself abolished throughout the empire. At about the same time in South America, former Spanish colonies were establishing their independence and, as they did so, abolished slavery within their respective borders. In the US, the first efforts at ending slavery came with a 1770 ban on slaveholding by the Quakers (among their followers). Slavery had become an integral part of the Southern plantation economy in the US, however, and more inclusive efforts at abolition (such as during the writing of the Constitution) were stubbornly resisted by Southern states. By 1820, the political debate between anti-slavery (Northern) and pro-slavery (Southern) states had resulted in the Missouri Compromise. This compromise plan sought to keep the number of anti-slavery and pro-slavery states (and thus the number of Senate seats) equal. But keeping the balance was difficult at a time when new states were being added to the Union. The militant abolitionist movement (as distinct from moderate anti-slavery elements) began in the North in the 1830s, through the efforts of such men as C. Finney, T. Weld, and W. Garrison. The movement received its impetus from the religious revivals of the 1820s Great Awakening, which sparked such other crusades as temperance and women's rights. Abolitionists were generally extremists, and, though their fiery campaigns were at first unpopular even in the North, they gained strength and spurred the political debate over abolishing slavery. Garrison started his influential newspaper, the *Liberator,* in Boston (1831), and the Anti-Slavery Society was founded in Philadelphia (1833). The society split in 1840 over various issues, including Garrison's extremism, his opposition to involvement in political action to end slavery, and his insistence on putting women's rights on equal footing with ending slavery. The anti-Garrison faction formed the Liberty Party and put forward presidential candidates (1840, 1844), but the party failed at the polls. Meanwhile, the struggle in Congress between pro-slavery and anti-slavery factions continued. By 1850, the doctrine of maintaining an equal number of anti-slavery and pro-slavery states had proved unworkable. It was replaced by a new compromise formula called Popular Sovereignty (*q.v.*). This doctrine was embodied in two bills, the Compromise of 1850 and the Kansas-Nebraska Act (*q.v.*), and seemed to resolve the issue for a time in the 1850s. But the conflict over slavery only worsened and violence erupted in Bleeding Kansas (where "free soldiers" fought against slavery supporters) and the Harpers Ferry raid (*q.v.*). Finally, the newly formed Republican party adopted a moderate but openly anti-slavery platform. The election (1860) of A. Lincoln, a Republican and anti-slavery moderate, provoked Southern states into secession and civil war. Though it was not without tremendous cost, the American Civil War (*q.v.*) finally ended slavery in the US (formally accomplished by the Emancipation Proclamation and the 13th Amendment). By the end of the 19th cent., the spread of anti-slavery sentiment had resulted in the abolition of slavery in most other parts of the world. Slavery continues to exist in parts of Asia and Africa.

Abominations, Tariff of US protective tariff passed on May 19, 1828. Originally a political ploy to gain support for A. Jackson's presidential candidacy, the bill was designed to force President J. Q. Adams to defeat it and thereby fall into discredit. It passed, however, and Adams signed it into law. The tariff led J. Calhoun to advocate "nullification" by the states.

Aboukir, Battle of (Abukir, ~) 1. (Nile, Battle of the) British naval victory (Aug. 1–2, 1798) over a French fleet during the French Revolutionary Wars (1792–1802). Adm. H. Nelson commanded British forces in this battle at Aboukir Bay, Egypt. 2. Victory for Napoleon (July 25, 1799) over the Ottoman Turks, during the French Revolutionary Wars (1792–1802). Napoleon's army of 7,700 met some 18,000 Turkish troops, led by Mustafa IV, at the village of Aboukir, Egypt. French losses were 900; Turkish were 12,000 killed and 3,000 captured.

Abraham (Abram) Biblical figure, regarded as the father of the Hebrew people. He journeyed from Ur to Canaan to found a new nation. He figures prominently in three religions: Judaism, Christianity, and Islam. [Genesis 11–25]

Absalon (Axel) c1128–1201. Danish archbishop and statesman. An adviser to Danish kings, he helped establish Denmark's independence from the Holy Roman Empire. He also figured in the introduction of canon law into Denmark and in the founding of Copenhagen.

absolutism Government by authority of the king alone. This form of government was prevalent in Europe from the 15th to 18th cents. It evolved gradually as monarchs overcame limits on their personal power (imposed by the church and the nobility). Absolute monarchies, typified by the rule of French king Louis XIV, were largely brought to an end in Europe by the upheavals of the French Revolution and post-Napoleonic years.

abstract expressionism (New York school) Artistic movement. Developed in New York in the 1940s, it was the first major artistic movement in which Americans played a dominant role. Among the early abstract expressionists were M. Rothko, W. de Kooning, and J. Pollock.

Abu-Abdallah *See* **Boabdil.**

Abu al-Abbas (~ as-Saffah) c722–754. Muslim caliph (750–754), founder and first caliph of the Abbasid dynasty. He led the revolt that overthrew the Umayyad caliph (749) and resulted in the massacre of members of the Umayyad family.

Abubacer *See* **Ibn Tufail.**

Abu Bakr 573–634. Father-in-law of Muhammad, and his closest follower. As successor to Muhammad and first caliph (632–634), he began the expansion of the Caliphate (*q.v.*).

Abukir, Battle of *See* **Aboukir, Battle of.**

Abulfaraj *See* **Bar-Hebraeus, Gregorius.**

Abu Muslim, Revolt of Muslim rebellion (747–750) led by Abu Muslim against the Umayyad rulers. This revolt enabled Abu al-Abbas to overthrow the Umayyads.

Abu Nasr al-Farabi *See* **Farabi, al-.**

Abydos Ancient town, now in northwest Turkey. Here Xerxes and his army crossed the Dardanelles on a bridge of boats during an invasion of Greece (480 BC). Abydos is also associated with the legend of Hero and Leander (*q.v.*).

Abydos, Table of Ancient list of kings at the temple of Seti I in Abydos, Egypt. It helped to establish the chronology of the ancient Egyptian kings.

Abyssinia *See* **Ethiopia.**

Academy Ancient Greek school near Athens, founded (c387 BC) by Plato. Here Plato taught, and his followers continued teaching Platonic philosophy for 900 years. The school was finally closed by the emperor Justinian I (529).

Académie Française *See* **French Academy.**

Acadia Former French colony in North America. It included what are now the coastal Canadian provinces of Nova Scotia, New Brunswick, and Prince Edward Island, as well as parts of Maine. The French founded their first permanent settlement at Port Royal (1605) and, soon after, the territory began passing back and forth between France and England. Following the War of Spanish Succession (1701–14), most of the territory came under permanent English control (by the Peace of Utrecht, 1713). British distrust of the French settlers led to mass resettlement (1755, 1758) in other colonies. The last French possessions in Acadia passed to the English by the Treaty of Paris (1763).

Acarya *See* **Bhascara.**

Achaea (Achaia) Historic region of ancient Greece located on the north coast of the Peloponnesus. Though Achaea is said to have once extended over most of the Peloponnesus and southeast Thessaly, it was only a small territory in the north from the 6th to 4th cents. BC. During this period, and near the end of Macedonian domination (4th–3d cents. BC), towns of this region formed the Achaean League. Following the Roman conquest of Greece, Achaea was made part of a Roman province (146 BC). The region later gave its name to that of a Roman province.

Achaean League Two confederations of Greek cities, the second being regarded as an ancient model of federal government. The first (5th–4th cents. BC) was formed by Achaean towns for defense against pirates. The second (280–146 BC) was originally made up of Achaean cities allied to overthrow Macedonian rulers. By 227 BC other Greek cities, including Athens, had joined the league, and in that year Sparta declared war on the league. The league was forced to give up resistance to Macedonian control in return for help against Sparta. During the Macedonian Wars (from 200 BC), however, the league sided with the Romans and subsequently came to control most of the Peloponnesus. However, the Romans became suspicious of Achaean de-

signs and in 146 BC ended the confederation, creating a Roman province in its place.

Achaemenidae (Achaemenids) Ancient Persian dynasty founded in the 7th cent. BC by King Achaemenes. The line included the founder of the Persian Empire, Cyrus the Great, and provided kings of the empire during its ascendancy (from 550 BC). The last king of the dynasty was Darius III, killed during the conquest of Persia by Alexander the Great (330 BC). *Rulers of the dynasty were:* Cyrus the Great 550–529 BC; Cambyses II 529–522; Darius I 521–485; Xerxes I 485–465; Artaxerxes I 465–425; Xerxes II 424; Darius II 424–408; Artaxerxes II 404–359; Artaxerxes III 359–338; Arses 338–336; and Darius III 336–330.

Achaemenids *See* **Achaemenidae.**

Achaia *See* **Achaea.**

Acheson, Dean Gooderham 1893–1971. A presidential adviser and US secretary of state (1949–52) influential in implementing the Marshall Plan and in establishing the North Atlantic Treaty Organization. He also developed the policy of "containment" of Communism.

Achille Lauro Cruise ship hijacked in 1985. Heavily armed Palestinian hijackers boarded the Italian vessel (Oct. 7) off Alexandria, Egypt, holding her passengers captive as they demanded release of Arab prisoners held in Israel. The PLO guerrillas surrendered two days later, but not before killing the wheelchair-bound American passenger Leon Klinghoffer. Egyptian officials gave the hijackers free passage from the country, but US Navy jets forced their plane to land in Sicily where all but their leader, Mohammed Abbas (who managed to escape), were arrested and put on trial.

Achinese War War (1873–1904) between Dutch colonial forces and the Muslim kingdom of Achin in northern Sumatra. By the Sumatra Treaty (1871), the British recognized Dutch hegemony over Sumatra in return for Dutch claims to the Gold Coast, Africa. The Dutch subsequently moved against the Achinese (1873), who had long resisted Dutch control and were actively engaged in piracy. The Dutch defeated the sultan of Achin that year, but local leaders carried on a protracted and costly guerrilla war, which lasted until 1904.

ACLU *See* **American Civil Liberties Union.**

Acre (Akko) City of ancient Palestine, now located in northwest Israel. Founded before 1500

BC, it is mentioned in the Bible and was an important port under the Romans. Conquered by the Arabs (AD 638), it subsequently was held by the crusaders (1104–87, 1191–1291). The Ottoman Turks controlled the city from 1517 to 1918, when it was captured by the British. The Israelis annexed the city (1949) after the Arab-Israeli War (1948).

Acre, Battle of 1. Victory for crusaders (July 12, 1191) during the Third Crusade (1189–92). Acre, defended by Saladin, was forced to surrender after a long siege (1189–91) by Christian forces. English king Richard I massacred nearly 3,000 Muslim prisoners. 2. Muslim victory (May 18, 1291) that marked the end of Christian crusaders' presence in the Holy Land. In April, 1291, Egyptian Mamelukes laid siege (with 160,000 troops) to Acre, then one of the few remaining Christian strongholds. Despite efforts to reinforce the city, it fell, and its surviving defenders were killed. Within a few months, the last of the crusaders had been killed or driven out of the Holy Land.

Acropolis The citadel, or elevated portion, of ancient Greek cities, usually reserved for defensive or religious purposes. The best-known acropolis is the rock outcropping in Athens, on which the Parthenon and other famous buildings were constructed during the 5th cent. BC. Its remains are considered one of the architectural treasures of the world and include such famous buildings as the Parthenon and Erechtheum.

Act in Restraint of Appeals to Rome English law nullifying the pope's authority in England. It was passed (Jan., 1533) by Parliament to permit King Henry VIII to annul his marriage to Catherine of Aragon and to marry A. Boleyn.

Action Française *See* **French Action.**

Actium, Battle of Decisive naval battle fought (Sept. 2, 31 BC) off the west coast of Greece, in which Octavian defeated Antony (with whom he shared control of the Roman Empire) and Cleopatra. By his victory, Octavian became sole ruler of the Roman Empire. Antony's dalliance with Cleopatra, unpopular at Rome, made Antony's position more vulnerable and thus helped bring on the battle, which at bottom was for control of the empire. Though both sides had deployed land and sea forces, Antony engaged Octavian at sea. Routed by Octavian's fleet, Antony and Cleopatra managed to escape and returned to Egypt.

Act of Abjuration Dutch declaration of independence (July 26, 1581). Following years of revolt, the Dutch finally declared their independence from Spain and its Habsburg king, Philip II. The act listed grievances against Philip and asserted that he had forfeited rights to rule the Dutch United Provinces.

Act of Settlement British act (June 12, 1701) establishing line of succession for the crown. Following the death of the last Stuart heir to the throne, Parliament by this act passed the crown to the House of Hanover (to the granddaughter of James I, Sophia, or her heirs). In addition, the act excluded Catholics from succession and further stipulated that the monarch must belong to the Church of England, may not leave Britain without permission from Parliament, may not involve Britain in wars to defend his foreign territories, may not appoint foreigners to government posts, and may appoint judges for life (unless they were found guilty of misconduct).

Act of Six Articles Series of laws passed by the English Parliament (1539), at the instigation of Henry VIII, concerning the doctrine of the Church of England. The acts upheld transubstantiation, condemned clerical marriage and communion under both species, and sanctioned private masses and confession. They were repealed in the subsequent reign of Edward VI.

Act of Supremacy Two acts of Parliament that gave the English king supreme authority over the Church of England and thus broke ties with Rome. The first, in 1534, made Henry VIII head of the church in England, and the second, in 1559, vested this authority in Elizabeth I.

Act of Union 1. Act (effective 1536) that united Wales with England. 2. Act (effective May 1, 1707) that united Scotland with England. 3. Act (effective Jan. 1, 1801) that united Great Britain and Ireland. The union with Ireland was dissolved by Anglo-Irish treaty (Dec. 6, 1921), which gave Ireland dominion status and created Northern Ireland as a separate state under British control. 4. British act (effective 1841) that united Upper and Lower Canada. It preceded the British North America Act (*q.v.*).

Acton, John Emerich Edward Dalberg-Acton, 1st baron 1834–1902. English historian, who planned and began work on the *Cambridge Modern History.*

Acton, Sir John Francis Edward 1736–1811. A Neapolitan statesman. As prime minister of

Naples (1785–1806), he allied it with England and Austria against France. He fled during the French occupation of Naples (1798–99), participated in reprisals against the Parthenopean Republic (*q.v.*), and went into exile after Napoleon captured Naples (1806).

acupuncture Chinese medical technique involving the insertion of fine needles at specified points on the body. This ancient practice was developed by the Chinese before 2500 BC and is still used today to control pain and cure a variety of ailments.

Adams, Abigail Smith 1744–1818. Wife of President J. Adams (*m.* 1764) and mother of President J. Q. Adams. Her letters are a colorful and detailed source of political and social history.

Adams, Brooks 1848–1927. American historian, son of C. F. Adams. He advanced his theory of the growth and decay of civilization according to lines of commerce in *The Law of Civilization and Decay.* He predicted the supremacy of the US and Russia in world affairs.

Adams, Charles Francis 1807–86. American diplomat, son of President J. Q. Adams. He played a key role in maintaining England's neutrality during the American Civil War and in negotiating the Alabama Claims (*q.v.*) with England.

Adams, Henry Brooks 1838–1918. American historian, son of C. F. Adams. His works have earned him a major place in American letters. Among them are: *History of the United States of America, Mont-Saint-Michel and Chartres,* and *The Education of Henry Adams.*

Adams, James Truslow 1878–1949. American historian. Adams wrote many books on American history including *The Founding of New England,* which won the Pulitzer Prize (for history) in 1922, and *The Adams Family.* He was editor of the *Dictionary of American History.*

Adams, John 1735–1826. 2d US president (1797–1801), successor to G. Washington, and 1st vice-president (1789–97). A leading Massachusetts patriot and political theorist in the years before independence, he was a delegate to the First and Second Continental Congresses, recommended G. Washington as commander of the Continental Army, helped draft the Declaration of Independence, carried out diplomatic missions in Europe and helped negotiate the Treaty of Paris (1783), which ended the American Revolution. Serving as Washington's vice-president, Adams aligned himself with the Federalists (*q.v.*), who advocated a strong central government. Adams's term as president saw near war with France, brought about by the American rapprochement with Britain, and a bitter struggle between Federalists and Jeffersonian Republicans. Events during his administration included: the XYZ Affair (1797); the Treaty of 1800 (or Treaty of Mortefontaine, Sept. 30, 1800), which ended the American alliance with France formed in 1778; passage of the Alien and Sedition Acts (1798); the Kentucky and Virginia Resolutions (1798–99), and Fries's Rebellion (1799). Adams was defeated by T. Jefferson in the election of 1800, sometimes also referred to as the Revolution of 1800.

Adams, John Quincy 1767–1848. 6th US president (1825–29), successor to J. Monroe. The son of President J. Adams, he served in various diplomatic posts from 1794, became a Federalist senator (1803–08), helped negotiate the Treaty of Ghent (1814), and became secretary of state (1817–25) under President J. Monroe. In this last post, he was involved in the purchase of Florida from Spain (1819) and was instrumental in formulation of the Monroe Doctrine (1823). Adams won the presidential election of 1824, though the four-way race was decided in the House of Representatives. Outraged Jacksonian Democrats (A. Jackson had won the popular vote) waged a bitter feud with Adams for the next four years and thereby greatly reduced the effectiveness of his administration. He was also involved in a controversy over the American System (*q.v.*) for protective tariffs, which resulted in passage of the Tariff of Abominations and the rise of the nullification controversy. Adams, defeated by Jackson in 1828, served as a congressman (1831–48) and became an anti-slavery spokesman.

Adams, Samuel 1722–1803. American statesman during the Revolutionary War era. Born in Boston and a graduate of Harvard College (1740), he tried unsuccessfully to establish himself in business before turning to politics. By 1764, his polemics against the Sugar Act established him as a leader of opposition in Massachusetts against British colonial authority. By 1769, he was leading the Massachusetts radicals, and at some point between then and 1774 decided that the movement's objective should be full independence from Britain, and not just a political accommodation on British taxation in the colonies. Adams set up the Boston Committee of Correspondence (1772), played a leading role in the Boston Tea Party, and served in the Continental Congress (1774–81). He signed the Declaration of Independence and served as governor of Massachusetts (1794–97).

Adams-Onis Treaty *See* **Transcontinental Treaty.**

Addams, Jane 1860–1935. American social reformer. With Ellen Gates Starr, she founded (1889) Hull House, a settlement house in Chicago and one of the first in the US. A leader of the woman suffrage and pacifist movements, she was awarded the Nobel Peace Prize (with Nicholas Murray Butler) in 1931.

Addison, Joseph 1672–1719. English essayist, poet, and statesman, best known for his contributions to such periodicals as the *Tattler* (founded by R. Steele) and the *Spectator* (founded with Steele). He is noted for the clarity and brilliance of his prose.

Addresses to the German Nation German nationalist speeches. J. Fichte delivered these highly nationalistic lectures at the University of Berlin in 1807–08. He called for an end to French domination of Germany and a regeneration of German spirit.

Aden Protectorate *See* **Yemen.**

Adler, Alfred 1870–1937. Austrian psychiatrist who founded a school of psychiatry based on analysis of an individual's inferiority feelings. An associate of S. Freud from 1902 to 1911, he came to reject Freud's emphasis on sex. Instead, he developed a psychotherapy based on the premise that neurosis develops from feelings of inferiority, brought about by conflict between the environment and the need for self-assertion.

Adler, Felix 1851–1933. American educator and social reformer who founded the New York Society for Ethical Culture (1876) and the Ethical Culture Movement (*q.v.*).

Admiral Graf Spee Famous German pocket battleship of WW II. Operating in South American waters, the battleship was hunted down and engaged in battle by three British cruisers. Later bottled up in Montevideo harbor, it was scuttled by the Germans (Dec. 17 1939).

Admonition to the Parliament, An English Puritan reform proposal. Sent anonymously to Parliament (1572), the proposal urged strict reform of the Anglican church according to Calvinistic doctrines. R. Hooker opposed the reforms, which were not adopted.

Adoptionism Christian heresy, similar to Nestorianism. It originated in the 2d and 3d cents. and reappeared in Spain in 782. Adoptionists maintained that Jesus was born human and assumed divinity only after baptism and "adoption" by God. Adoptionist views were also advanced (12th cent.) by P. Abelard.

Adowa, Battle of Decisive battle (Mar. 1, 1896) fought at Adowa, in north central Ethiopia. The Ethiopian army of King Menelik II defeated Italian forces, thereby halting (for the time) Italy's move toward creating an African colonial empire.

Adrian I *d.* 795. Roman Catholic pope (772–795), successor to Stephen III. He called upon Charlemagne to defeat the Lombards (773), then threatening Rome. Thereafter, the pope maintained a close alliance with Charlemagne, and Charlemagne established a protectorate over papal lands. Adrian confirmed decrees of the Second Council of Nicaea (787).

Adrian IV *d.* 1159. The only English pope (1154–59), born Nicholas Breakspear, successor to Anastasius IV. He crowned Frederick I (1155) Holy Roman Emperor but later came into conflict with him. Adrian's supposed donation of Ireland to Henry II of England is disputed.

Adrianople (*now* Edirne) City located in northwest Turkey. It was founded by Emperor Hadrian (AD c125) and suffered many conquests because of its strategic location. It was variously conquered by the Visigoths, crusaders, and Ottoman Turks, and figured in the Russo-Turkish Wars (captured from the Turks, 1829, 1878) and Balkan Wars (captured from the Turks, 1813). It was restored to Turkey in 1923. *See also* events below.

Adrianople, Battle of (Hadrianople, ˜) 1. Victory (July 3, AD 323, at Adrianople, now in Turkey) for Constantine I, ruler of the Western Roman Empire, during the Roman Civil Wars. Constantine defeated Licinius, emperor of the East. Roughly 50,000 soldiers were involved on each side and some 20,000 were killed. 2. Major Visigoth victory (Aug. 9, AD 378) over the Romans at Adrianople, now in Turkey. The Visigoths, under their chief, Fritigern, routed a force of 30,000 Romans under Emperor Valens. Valens and 20,000 Romans were killed. Emperor Theodosius I was subsequently forced to come to terms with the Visigoths (382).

Adrianople, Treaty of (Edirne, ˜) Treaty (Sept. 14, 1829, at Adrianople, now in Turkey) between

Russia and Turkey, ending the Russo-Turkish War (1828–29). By its terms, Russia won possession of territories along the Black Sea (including the mouth of the Danube); the Dardanelles and other Turkish waters were opened to Russian merchant ships; autonomy was recognized for Serbia, Moldavia, and Wallachia; and Greece was granted almost complete independence.

Adullamites British political faction. The Adullamites were Liberals in Parliament who joined with Conservatives (1866) to defeat the Reform Bill of 1866. The bill would have expanded the electorate and thus stirred fears of the evils of democracy among the Adullamites.

Adventists Protestant churches that preach the second coming of Jesus and the formation of his 1,000-year (millennial) kingdom. The origins of the Adventist churches can be traced to the teachings of an American, W. Miller, who preached the coming of the end of the world in 1843. Miller's followers formally adopted (1845) their belief in the second coming of Christ, and in subsequent years organized various Adventist sects. The largest, the Seventh-Day Adventists, was formed officially in 1863 and is dedicated to missionary work.

Aegates, Battle of *See* **Punic War (1).**

Aegean civilization Name for Bronze Age cultures in the region of the Aegean Sea from c3000 to c1000 BC. Aegean cultures include the Minoan on the island of Crete, the Mycenaean on the Greek mainland, and also that of the inhabitants of the Cyclades. The Minoan culture (*fl.* c3000–c1400 BC) was dominant throughout the Aegean until the conquest of the Minoans (c1400), apparently by the Mycenaeans. The Mycenaean culture then predominated, until it was in turn destroyed by invasions from the north (c1100 BC).

Aegean Sea A part of the Mediterranean Sea, lying between Greece and Asia Minor (west and east) and between Crete and the Dardanelles (south and north). The sea was called Archipelago in ancient times, thus the general term for an island group. Among the many islands within its boundaries are Samos, Lesbos, Thasos, Euboea, the Dodecanese, the Aegean, and the Cyclades.

Aegnina, Paul of *See* **Paul of Aegnina.**

Aegospotami, Battle of The Spartans, under Lysander, defeated the Athenians, under Conan (*d.* c390 BC), in the final naval battle (405 BC)

of the Peloponnesian War. Athens surrendered the next year.

Aeolis (Aeolia) Ancient territory (now in Turkey) surrounding a number of cities on the western coast of Asia Minor. The cities were founded c11th cent. BC by the Aeolians, a Hellenic people.

Aeschylus 525–456 BC. Greek poet of Athens, called the father of Greek tragedy. He is known to have fought at the battles of Marathon and Salamis (490, 480 BC), and later won a prize for his play *The Persians* (c472). Thereafter, he gained a wide reputation and made many important innovations in Greek theater, including the introduction of a second actor and the use of scenery and costumes. Among his other extant works are *Seven Against Thebes, Prometheus Bound,* and the great *Oresteia* trilogy (*Agamemnon, The Libation-Bearers,* and *The Eumenides*).

Aesop *fl.* 6th cent. BC. Famous Greek fable writer and possibly only a legendary figure. Fables attributed to him include *The Fox and the Grapes* and *The Hare and the Tortoise.* His fables are noted for their wit and moral instruction.

aesthetics (esthetics) In philosophy, the study of the nature of beauty in works of art. Ancient Greek philosophers, such as Plato and Aristotle, were concerned with the nature of art and beauty. But aesthetics as a distinct study began about the 15th cent. AD, when art evolved from a craft into a profession. Two basic positions on the nature of beauty are: the objective view, in which beauty is inherent in the work; and the subjective view, in which beauty is a matter of pleasing the individual observer.

Aeterni Patris Catholic encyclical issued by Pope Leo XIII on Aug. 4, 1879. It established the dominance of Thomism, the teachings of Saint Thomas Aquinas, in the Roman Catholic church.

Aethelbald *d.* 757. The king of Mercia (716–757). Aethelbald controlled most of England from the Humber River to the English Channel and styled himself "King of Britain" after 736.

Aethelbert c552–616. King of Kent (c560–616). Aethelbert became Anglo-Saxon England's first Christian ruler after his conversion by Saint Augustine of Canterbury. His legal code is the earliest extant code of Anglo-Saxon laws.

Aethelbert *d.* 865. King of Wessex (860–865). His brief reign was plagued by Danish invasions.

Aethelflaed (Aethelfleda) *d.* 918. Mercian ruler (911–918) called "Lady of the Mercians." With her brother, Edward the Elder, she drove the Danes from eastern England. Mercia was united with Wessex after her death.

Aethelfrith *d.* 616.   King of Northumbria (c593–616). Aethelfrith incorporated the northern kingdoms of Bernicia and Deira into Northumbria, and later warred successfully against both the Scots and the Welsh.

Aethelred *d.* 871.   King of Wessex and Kent (c865–871). He began organizing forces to resist the Danish invaders but died before making significant territorial gains. He was succeeded in the task by his brother, Alfred the Great.

Aethelred c968–1016.   King of England (978–1016). Nicknamed "the Unready," he was unable to stop raids and invasions by the Danes. An invasion by the Danish king Sweyn (1013) forced him to flee to Normandy until 1014. His sons were Edmund Ironside and Edward the Confessor.

Aethelstan   *See* **Athelstan.**

Aethelwulf *d.* 858.   King of Wessex (839–856), successor to his father, Egbert, and father of Alfred the Great.

Aëtius   *See* **Châlons, Battle of.**

Aetolia   Ancient region of west central Greece. Its major cities included Calydon and Thermom, and it became important in Greek history with the formation of the Aetolian League (*q.v.*). It became a Roman possession after the league had collapsed (189 BC).

Aetolian League   Confederation of cities in ancient Greece, similar in nature to the Achaean League. Organized by Aetolian cities in the 4th cent. BC, it resisted Macedonian conquest late in that century. Then, as an ally of Macedonia (280 BC), the league extended its control over central Greece, including Boeotia. Attacks on the Achaean League (220) brought war with Macedonia and defeat of the Aetolians by the Macedonians. The league next sided with the Romans against Macedonia (200–197). A dispute with the victorious Romans, however, led to war (192) and final defeat of the league (189) by the Romans.

Afars and Issas   *See* **Djibouti.**

Affair of the Diamond Necklace   Famous scandal (1785–86) in the court of French king Louis XVI that helped precipitate the French Revolution. A prominent French nobleman, Cardinal de Rohan (1734–1803), was tricked by a young adventuress into believing that Queen Marie Antoinette wanted to purchase an expensive diamond necklace secretly. Hoping to curry favor with the queen, Cardinal de Rohan purchased the necklace on credit and gave it to the adventuress. The scandal broke when the jeweler attempted to collect. The cardinal was eventually acquitted, the adventuress escaped, and the king and queen were thoroughly disgraced by the incident.

Affair of the Spanish Marriages   A political affair surrounding the marriages (1846) of Spanish queen Isabella II (to her cousin Francisco de Asís (1822–1902), duke of Cádiz) and of Isabella's sister Luisa Fernanda (to Antoine, duke of Montpensier (1824–90), son of French Bourbon king Louis Philippe). The marriages violated agreements (1843, 1845) between England and France that Isabella would marry within the Neapolitan and Spanish branches of the Bourbon house and that her sister would not marry a French prince until after Isabella had married and borne children. The matches were a result of Spanish distrust of British intentions in Spain, notably about possible support of the Progresistas, who sought to reinstate the Constitution of 1812. The affair was protested by British viscount H. Palmerston, who declared them contrary to provisions of the Treaty of Utrecht. The marriages caused a serious breach in British-French relations.

affirmative action   Term describing US programs using racial, ethnic, and gender quotas and other means of preferential treatment to overcome the effects of past discrimination. Since the early 1970s, businesses and other organizations receiving federal funds have been required to follow affirmative action guidelines, which are enforced through the Equal Opportunities Act (1972). The constitutionality of such programs was called into question by *Bakke* vs *University of California* (1978), a Supreme Court case concerning the reverse race discrimination caused by giving racial minorities preference in college admissions. The Court found the program unconstitutional but said that race could be a partial factor in determining admissions procedures. In other cases, the Court struck down affirmative action guidelines when determining layoffs of employees but upheld hiring quotas in cases involving previous discriminatory practice.

Affonso *See* **Alfonso.**

Afghanistan Republic (pop. 15,592,000) located in south central Asia. Afghanistan is strategically located on the main route to India and has thus been invaded and conquered many times. Great Britain and Russia vied for control of the region in the 19th cent., with Britain gaining the advantage until 1919, when Britain formally recognized Afghan independence for the first time. In 1978, a Communist government was established by a *coup d'état* and thus fostered close ties with the Soviets. In the late 1970s, the Soviets invaded Afghanistan, ostensibly to support the government. The Soviet occupation led to a prolonged guerrilla war by Afghan rebels, who eventually forced the Soviets to withdraw. Key dates in the history of Afghanistan include:

C6TH CENT. BC   Region conquered by Persian king Darius I.

c330–327 BC   Region conquered by Alexander the Great.

3D CENT. BC–7TH CENT. AD   Afghanistan came under control of various rulers, including the Kusana and Sassanidae.

7TH CENT.   Arabs began conquest of region.

977–1186   Ghaznavids, an Islamic dynasty, ruled vast areas in Afghanistan, Iran, and northern India.

13TH CENT.   Genghis Khan conquered Afghanistan.

14TH CENT.   Tamerlane conquered Afghanistan.

16TH CENT.   Baber conquered Afghanistan, then advanced into India to establish the Mughal Empire.

1730s   Persian leader Nadir Shah conquered Afghanistan.

1747–73   Ahmad Shah became ruler in Afghanistan after death (1747) of Nadir Shah; united Afghan tribes, expanded his domain, and established an independent Afghan state.

1826–63   Dost Muhammad ruled; became emir (1835); conflicts with Britain led to his ouster during first Afghan War (1838–42); restored, he ruled Afghanistan until his death (1863).

1863–79   Shere Ali reigned; policies led to outbreak of second Afghan War (1878–80) with Britain.

1880–1901   Abd ar-Rahman Khan reigned; rule marked by settlement of various border disputes.

1901–19   Habibullah Khan reigned; began program of modernization; kept Afghanistan neutral during WW I.

1907   Anglo-Russian convention ended long rivalry between Britain and Russia for control of Afghanistan.

1919–29   Amanullah Khan reigned; invaded India (third Afghan War, 1919) to end British influence in Afghanistan; secured British recognition of Afghan independence by Treaty of Rawalpindi (Aug. 1919); proclaimed himself king (1926); instituted reform program that led to his overthrow.

1929–33   King Nadir Shah reigned, succeeding after period of turmoil; promoted plan of modernization; assassinated.

1933–73   Muhammad Zahir Shah reigned; maintained Afghan neutrality in WW II.

1947   Relations with Pakistan strained following Afghan support for creation of independent Pathan tribal state within Pakistan.

1956   Government signed agreements with US and Soviet Union for massive economic-aid program.

1963   Government began policy to lessen dependence on US and Soviet Union.

1964   New constitution approved, firmly establishing constitutional monarchy.

1973   King Muhammad Zahir Shah deposed (July 17) in coup led by Muhammad Daud Khan, his brother-in-law.

1973–78   Afghanistan proclaimed a republic; Muhammad Daud Khan in office as president.

1978   Coup, reportedly Soviet-approved, ended in murder of President Muhammad Daud Khan (Apr.).

1978–79   Pro-Communist Nur Muhammad Taraki in power; signed friendship treaty with the USSR (Dec. 1978).

1979   About 5,000 guerrillas reported advancing on capital of Konar province, north of Kabul (Jan.); government sent some 12,000 Afghan troops to check their advance.

1979   Muslim extremists kidnapped US ambassador Adolph Dubs to bargain for release of religious leaders arrested by Taraki regime; Dubs killed (Feb.) in police shootout, which Soviet advisers refused to discourage.

1979   Government accused Iran of sending some 4,000 soldiers, in company with 7,000 Afghan anti-government fighters, into Afghanistan

(Mar.); charged Pakistan with supporting rebels as well.

1979 Hafizullah Amin, former foreign minister, in office as prime minister (Mar. 27); Taraki continued as president, but with little real power.

1979 Guerrilla groups reported in every Afghan province (July).

1979 Guerrillas massacred 30 Soviets at Kandahar (Aug. 12).

1979 Some 1,500 Soviet advisers arrived in Afghanistan (Sept.).

1979 Hafizullah Amin in complete control of the government (Sept.); Taraki ousted in apparent coup (Sept. 14); his death reported (Oct. 9).

1979 Massive airlift of Soviet troops arrived in Kabul (Dec. 25–26); Soviet invasion of Afghanistan under way.

1979 Soviet-directed coup (Dec. 27) put Babrak Karmal in power; Amin killed.

1979–86 Karmal in power; formed government from his Parcham (Flag) party, a faction of the Afghan Communist organization; his Soviet-backed administration was marked by effective guerrilla resistance from the Iranian-backed Muslim Jihad and numerous other guerrilla groups, and by often bloody feuds with the rival Khalq (People's) faction of the Afghan Communist party.

1980 Soviet invasion roundly condemned by UN and governments around the world.

1980 Soviets, now with some 80–90,000 troops in Afghanistan, launched heavily armed sweeps throughout the country; by year's end, some 1.2 million Afghan refugees had fled to Pakistan and about 400,000 to Iran.

1981 Soviet troops, increasingly responsible for the fighting, replaced Afghans guarding Kabul (Apr.); continued stiff guerrilla resistance and wholesale desertions severely weakened the Afghan army.

1981 Karmal resigned as prime minister (June); remained in power as president and general secretary of the ruling People's Democratic Party of Afghanistan (PDPA).

1981–82 Winter offensive mounted by Soviet commanders; aimed at wiping out guerrillas operating along Pakistani border, the operation merely dislodged them until the summer, when they returned to mount hit-and-run attacks; Soviets forced to defensive strategy

of maintaining control of cities and main road links.

1982 UN-sponsored talks between Soviet-backed Afghan government and Pakistani delegation began in Geneva (June); UN-sponsored talks, held between various principals, held every year until Soviet withdrawal.

1983 Soviet troop strength in Afghanistan reached 105,000; casualties and desertions meanwhile slashed the Afghan army from 80,000 in 1979 to 30,000 in 1983.

1983 Major victories over guerrillas in northeast Afghanistan announced by government (Dec.); war effectively stalemated by 1983–84, however, with guerrillas (the Islamic mujaheddin and others) holding the mountains and countryside, and the Soviets and Afghan troops holding large towns and cities.

1984 Government ordered draft of all males 18 and older (Jan.).

1984 UN commission to investigate charges of torture in Afghan prisons.

1985 Soviet troops in Afghanistan increased to 140,000.

1985 Government expanded draft to include males up to age 40.

1985 Heavy fighting reported in rebel stronghold, the Panjshir valley north of Kabul; Soviets also tried cutting rebel supply lines from Pakistan, running through eastern Afghanistan; southern Afghan city of Kandahar heavily bombed by Soviets; rebels nevertheless continued to inflict heavy casualties.

1985 Government called a Loya Jirga, a traditional assembly of Afghan tribal leaders (Apr. 6); assembly duly endorsed Soviet invasion and called on rebels to cease fighting.

1985 Kamal ousted his defense minister and the head of his secret police, and appointed several non-Communists to government posts in unsuccessful effort to make his government more appealing to Afghan people.

1986 Soviets reported seeking politically acceptable way to withdraw from Afghanistan.

1986 Gen. Mohammed Najibullah, head of Afghan secret police and reportedly a more willing servant of Soviet aims, replaced Kamal as head of the ruling Communist party (May 1); Najibullah called for "national reconciliation."

1986 Karmal ousted (with Soviet help) from presidency and other posts (Nov. 21); Najibullah now firmly in control.

1986 US Stinger and British Blowpipe missiles provided mujaheddin with first effective weapon against Soviet bombers and attack helicopters.

1986 Afghan refugees now totaled 3 million in Pakistan and 1.5 million in Iran.

1987 Government proclaimed cease-fire (Jan. 15); rebels ignored it.

1987 Heavy fighting reported in Pakistani border area near Jalalabad.

1988 Geneva accords signed for withdrawal of Soviet troops from Afghanistan (Apr. 14); Afghanistan, Pakistan, USSR, and US all signed agreement; withdrawal to be completed by Feb. 15, 1989.

1988 Elections held (Apr.), with Najibullah's ruling People's Democratic Party of Afghanistan winning control; bicameral National Assembly convened.

1989 Nine-year Soviet military presence in Afghanistan ended with departure of last Soviet soldier on Feb. 15; Soviets continued to supply large amounts of arms to Afghanistan, however; current estimates put Afghan deaths in fighting at 1 million, and some 5 million casualties, including civilians.

1989 Najibullah and Soviets both reported making unsuccessful efforts to negotiate settlement with rival mujaheddin rebel groups, which refused talks with the Communist government.

1990 Troops loyal to Najibullah crushed a military coup attempt (Mar. 6); over 200 reported killed.

1990 Fazl Haq Khaleqiar, not a member of the ruling Communist party, appointed prime minister (May); Najibullah appointed new cabinet, mostly independents and non-Communist party figures, in effort to broaden his political base.

1990 Tribal council, the Loya Jirga, enacted constitutional amendments ending guarantees of Communists' right to rule and establishing multi-party system (May 28–29).

1991 US and USSR agreed to stop supplying arms to combatants in Afghanistan (Sept.).

1992 Najibullah claimed Muslim rebels agreed to end 13-year civil war; would form transitional government until elections could be held.

1992 Najibullah deposed as he tried to flee the country (Apr. 16); reported in hiding as rebel forces continued advance on Kabul; most of the rest of Afghanistan under rebel control.

1992 Muslim rebels seized control of Kabul (Apr. 25); rival rebel factions, the moderate Jamiat-e-Islami group, and the radical fundamentalists led by Gulbuddin Hekmatyar, reported in the city.

1992 Sibghatullah Mojaddidi in office as president of newly formed Islamic government of Afghanistan (Apr. 28).

1992 Skirmishes in Kabul reported with radical fundamentalist rebels; Jamiat-e-Islami leader Ahmad Shah Masoud arrived in city with 10,000 troops to restore order (Apr. 29).

1992 New government banned alcohol, ordered traditional Muslim dress for women, and shut down movie theaters while establishing the new Islamic state.

1992 Mojaddidi relinquished power to council of rebel leaders (June) in the face of continued fighting.

1992 Kabul ravaged as fighting between Iranian-backed fundamentalist guerrillas and other rebel groups intensified.

Afghan Wars *See* **Anglo-Afghan Wars.**

AFL-CIO *See* **American Federation of Labor–Congress of Industrial Organizations.**

Africanus, Sextus Julius *fl.* AD 221. Christian historian, author of a chronology of the world. It covered history from the creation, dated at 5499 BC, to AD 221.

Afrikaans Germanic language spoken in South Africa. It is derived from the Dutch language spoken by 17th-cent. settlers of South Africa and is now considered a separate language.

Afrika Korps German military unit during WW II. Led by Field Marshal E. Rommel, the unit conquered much of North Africa in early 1942. The drive by the Afrika Korps into Egypt was finally turned back (1942) by British Gen. B. Montgomery after the Battle of el-Alamein. The unit finally surrendered (May 1943).

Afrikaner Bond South African political party. The first political party in the (then) colony, it was founded in 1879, sought independence from the British, and backed the Boers in the Boer War. It merged with other parties to form the South African party (1910).

Agade *See* **Akkad.**

Agadir Incident Incident (July, 1911) in which Germany challenged the French hegemony in Morocco by sending the gunboat *Panther* to Agadir harbor. The incident resulted in an accord (Nov., 1911) between the two countries.

Aga Khan Hereditary title of the leader of the Ismaili Muslim sect. Followers of the sect are numerous in India, Pakistan, central Asia, and East Africa. The current leader (since 1957) is Aga Khan IV (1936–).

Aga Khan III 1877–1957. Indian statesman and leader of the Ismaili Muslim sect from 1885. He worked to gain Muslim support for Britain during WW I, played an important role in conferences to reform the constitution of India (1930–32), and became president of the League of Nations General Assembly in 1937.

Aga Muhammad Khan *See* **Agha Muhammad Khan.**

Agassiz, Jean Louis Rodolphe 1807–73. Swiss-born American naturalist, geologist, and educator. His research expeditions, writings, and lectures influenced the development of the natural sciences in the 19th cent. He opposed Darwin's theory of evolution, however.

Agee, James 1909–55. American writer. Agee was an influential film critic and scriptwriter. His novel *A Death in the Family* won a posthumous Pulitzer Prize (1957).

Ager Bruttius *See* **Bruttium.**

Agesilaus II c444–360 BC. Spartan king (399–360 BC), successor to Agis I. Although he was a brilliant soldier, he was unable to thwart the rise of Thebes and the decline of Sparta. His reign saw war against Persia, the Corinthian War (395–387), the King's Peace, and Spartan defeat at the Battle of Leuctra (371).

Agha Muhammad Khan (Aga Muhammad Khan) 1742–97. Shah of Persia (1794–97). He founded the Kajar dynasty, unified Persia, and invaded the Russian province of Georgia (1795). His cruelty in repressing internal dissent led to his assassination.

Agiad dynasty *See* **Agis I.**

Agincourt, Battle of Important English victory over the French (Oct. 25, 1415), at Agincourt, France during the Hundred Years' War (1337–1453). English king Henry V, claiming the French throne, had invaded France and, after some fighting, decided to withdraw to Calais. His force of 14,000 lightly equipped archers was intercepted by the French constable Charles d'Albret and 50,000 heavily armored soldiers. Bogged down by a muddy battlefield, the French became easy targets for the English archers. Losses were 5,000 French to 200 Englishmen. Henry went on to Calais, but the battle opened the way for later English conquests in France.

Agis I c11th cent. BC. King of Sparta and, according to legend, founder of the Agiad dynasty. The Agiad line was one of two (with the Eurypontids) important and simultaneously ruling dynasties of Spartan kings.

Agis II *d.* c399 BC. King of Sparta (c427–399 BC). Agis commanded the Spartan army during the Peloponnesian War (431–404 BC) and won a major victory against Argos at the Battle of Mantinea (418 BC).

Agis IV *d.* c240 BC. Spartan king (c244–240 BC). He attempted to strengthen Sparta through several unsuccessful reforms, for which he was tried and executed.

Agnes, Saint *fl.* 4th cent. AD. Roman Christian girl martyred at 13. She revealed her Christian faith by refusing marriage and was subsequently murdered during persecutions ordered by Diocletian.

Agnew, Spiro Theodore 1918– . An American politician, 39th US vice-president (1969–73). Noted for his speeches attacking radicals and liberals, Agnew was reelected with President R. Nixon in 1972. Amid the Watergate crisis, however, Agnew came under fire for alleged corruption (during his time in Maryland politics). He resigned (Oct. 10, 1973) and pleaded no contest to charges of income tax evasion.

agnosticism Belief that one can never prove or disprove the existence of God. It is distinct from atheism, which rejects the existence of God. The term "agnostic" was coined (1869) by T. H. Huxley and implies a skepticism of human ability to know the true nature of the world. "Agnostic" can also be used in a nonreligious sense. Among proponents of forms of agnosticism were H. Spencer, A. Comte, and I. Kant.

agrarian laws Ancient Roman laws meant to regulate land ownership and ensure just distribution of the considerable public lands that came into Roman hands by conquest. In 367 BC C. Licinius attempted to limit the holdings of any single owner. This law was a dead letter by the time T. and G. Gracchus sought to allow greater ownership by the poor (133–121 BC). The edict of Domitian (AD 82), confirming existing land titles, marked the end of such efforts at distribution of land.

Agrarian party (*now* Center party) Finnish political party. This party was founded (1866) by Count Arvid Posse (1820–1901) to demand new methods of taxation and military quartering.

Agrarian Reform Act (Stolypin Land Reform) Reform measures allowing individual Russian peasant families to own land that formerly belonged to peasant communes (mirs). Decreed by Prime Minister P. Stolypin (Nov. 22, 1906) and confirmed and expanded by the Duma (1910–11), they were designed to create an independent, landowning peasantry that would support the tsarist autocracy.

Agreement of the People *See* **Levelers.**

Agricola (Gnaeus Julius ~) AD c37–93. Roman soldier and statesman, father-in-law of the historian Tacitus. He conquered much of Britain and served as its governor (AD 78?–84?).

Agricola, Georgius (Bauer, Georg) 1494–1555. German mineralogist known as the father of mineralogy for his pioneering work in geology and in classification of minerals.

Agricola, Gnaeus Julius *See* **Agricola.**

Agricola, Johann (or Johannes) 1494–1566. German Protestant reformer. A friend of M. Luther, he played a key role in the founding of Protestantism. From 1536 he opposed Luther by espousing antinomianism (*q.v.*) and helped draw up the Augsburg Interim (*q.v.*).

Agricola, Rodolphus c1443–85. Dutch humanist who helped spread Renaissance ideas in Germany. Agricola completed his university education at Louvain (1465), wrote a book on the life of the Italian scholar Petrarch, and in 1484 became a lecturer at Heidelberg. A believer in individual freedom and the intellectual and physical development of the self, Agricola wrote a book on education called *De formando studio* (1484).

Agrippa, Marcus Vipsanius c63–12 BC. Roman general and close friend of Octavian (later Augustus). Commanding Octavian's forces, he defeated Sextus Pompey (36 BC) and played a major role in Octavian's decisive victory over Antony and Cleopatra at the Battle of Actium (31 BC). Later, during Augustus's reign, Agrippa served him as a loyal ally and married Augustus's daughter Julia, fathering five children by her.

Agrippina I (Agrippina the Elder) *d.* AD 33. Granddaughter of Augustus and wife of Germanicus Caesar. When her husband died (AD 19), she became involved in a struggle with Tiberius. He banished her, and she died of starvation. Her son became the emperor Caligula.

Agrippina II (Colonia Agrippina) *d.* AD 59. Sister of the emperor Caligula. She married her uncle Claudius I and is believed to have murdered him to ensure the ascendancy of her son Nero. Nero, in turn, had her put to death for her intrigues.

Agrippina, Colonia *See* **Agrippina II.**

Agrippina the Elder *See* **Agrippina I.**

Aguinaldo, Emilio 1869–1964. Filipino revolutionary. He led the uprising against Spain (1896–98) and fought against the US (1899–1901) as head of a short-lived Philippine republic. In 1901 he swore allegiance to the US.

Aguirre, Lope de c1508–1561. Spanish adventurer and rebel. He is said to have murdered (1560) the leaders of an expedition in search of El Dorado in South America, to have attempted to usurp Spanish control in Panama, and to have murdered his daughter just before his capture by Spanish authorities.

Ahab Great king (c874–c853 BC) of the north kingdom of Israel, successor to his father, Omri. He was allied with Jehoshaphat, king of the south kingdom of Judah. He succeeded in resisting Assyrians in two wars but was killed in a third against Benhadad. His wife, Jezebel, introduced Phoenician elements to the Hebrew culture, including the worship of Baal. [1 Kings 16–22]

Ahaz *d.* c727 BC. King of Judah (c731–727 BC). He overcame the combined forces of Israel and Syria by allying Judah with Assyria. This action was criticized by Isaiah and cost Judah its independence. [2 Kings 15–17; 2 Chron 28; Isaiah 7]

Ahaziah *d.* c851 BC. 1. King of Israel (c853–851 BC), successor to his father, Ahab. [1 Kings 22; 2 Kings 1; 2 Chron 20] 2. King of Judah (843? BC), slain (with King Jehoram of Israel) by Jehu [2 Kings 8–9; 2 Chron 22].

Ahmad Shah Durrani *See* **Ahmed Shah.**

Ahmed (Ahmad Mirza) 1898–1930. Shah of Persia (1909–25), successor to his father, Muhammad Ali. The last of the Qajar dynasty, he was overthrown by Reza Shah Pahlavi and fled to Paris.

Ahmed I 1589–1617. Ottoman sultan (1603–17), successor to his father, Muhammad III. Under his reign, the Ottoman Empire was weakened by war and uprisings. He signed the

Treaty of Szitvatorok (1606) with Austria, which further diminished Ottoman influence and prestige.

Ahmed III 1673–1736.　Ottoman sultan (1703–30), successor to his brother Mustafa II. He protected Charles XII of Sweden after the latter's defeat at Poltava (1709), and was thus drawn into the Northern War against Russia. Turkish involvement ended favorably with the Treaty of Pruth (1711) Ahmed later seized and lost the Peloponnesus, and signed the Treaty of Passarowitz (1718). Overthrown by the Janissaries, he died in prison.

Ahmed Shah (Ahmad Shah Durrani) c1724–73. Afghan ruler (1747–73), founder of the Durrani dynasty, and considered the founder of Afghanistan. A cavalry commander under Nadir Shah (of Persia), he formed the Afghan kingdom of Kandahar after Nadir Shah's death. He extended his rule over a large area, invaded India several times (1747–69) during his reign, and sacked Delhi (1757).

Ahmose I (Amasis) *d.* c1546 BC.　King of ancient Egypt (c1570–46 BC). He drove the Hyskos from Egypt and established the 18th dynasty. He extended Egyptian control into Nubia and the eastern Nile delta and invaded Palestine.

AIDS　Disease, the cause of a massive epidemic spreading worldwide since the early 1980s. AIDS is the abbreviation for Acquired Immune Deficiency Syndrome, which attacks the human body's immune system. First identified in 1981, the disease caused more than 90,000 cases in the US by the end of the decade (over half have died) and the World Health Organization estimated some 450,000 cases worldwide. An estimated eight to ten million people worldwide were believed infected by this time, but had not yet begun to show symptoms. By the 1990s, no cure had yet been discovered for AIDS.

Aigun, Treaty of　Treaty (May 16, 1858) by which China settled its northeast border with Russia. It gave Russia territory on the Amur River. This agreement was followed by further concessions in the Treaty of Beijing (*q.v.*).

Aiken, Conrad 1889–1973.　American poet and novelist, whose works, such as the short story *Silent Snow Secret Snow* reflect his interest in the workings of the human psyche. His *Selected Poems* (1929) won a Pulitzer Prize (1930).

Ain Jalut, Battle of　*See* **Ayn Jalut, Battle of.**

Aisne, Battle of　*See* **World War I** (Sept. 14, 1914; Apr.–May 1917; May 27, 1918).

Aix, Battle of　*See* **Aquae Sextiae, Battle of.**

Aix-la-Chapelle, Congress of　*See* **Congress of Aix-la-Chapelle.**

Aix-la-Chapelle, Treaties of　Two treaties concluded at Aix-la-Chapelle, now Aachen, Germany.　1. Treaty (May 2, 1668) ending the War of Devolution. It was arranged between France and the nations of the Triple Alliance, including England, Sweden, and the Dutch Republic. By the treaty, France retained conquered towns in Flanders, while returning other territories taken from Spain.　2. Treaty (Oct. 18, 1748), ending the War of Austrian Succession. It provided for mutual restitution of all conquered territories except Silesia (ceded to Prussia) and Parma, Piacenza, and Guastalla (ceded to Spain). The treaty also confirmed the Pragmatic Sanction of 1713 and the succession of the Protestant Hanovers in Britain.

Akbar 1542–1605.　Great Mughal emperor (1556–1605) of India. He subdued revolts and expanded Mughal control over all of north India (by 1592) and, later, into the Deccan. An able administrator, he adopted a policy of tolerating non-Muslims, reformed finances and taxes, and built his capital at Fatehpur Sikri.

Akhenaton (Ikhnaton) (Amenhotep IV) *d.* c1362 BC.　Egyptian pharaoh (c1379–c1362 BC) of the XVIIIth dynasty, successor to his father Amenhotep III. He is renowned for having instituted monotheism in Egypt by forcibly converting his kingdom to the worship of the sun god Aton (*q.v.*). Despite resistance from the priesthood, he attempted to eradicate all reference to other gods, including Amon (*q.v.*), and founded a new capital at Akhetaton (now Tell El Amarna). His conversion sparked revolutionary changes in Egyptian art and literature but Akhenaton's preoccupation with internal affairs resulted in the loss of extensive territory in the provinces. His successor, Tutankhamen, restored worship of the old gods. Akhenaton's reign is referred to as the Amarna Age.

Akkad　Ancient region occupying what was later the northern part of Babylonia and what is now part of Iraq. Akkad rose to prominence in the 3d millennium BC with the conquests of Sargon, who briefly united Akkadian and other cities (notably of Sumer) into an empire. The capital of the empire was Akkad (*anc.* Agade) and the language spoken was Akkadian, a Semitic dialect. The empire declined and fell (3d millennium BC) to invading tribes a century after Sargon's unification.

Akko *See* **Acre.**

Alabama State in the US South, the 22d state. Alabama was first explored by the Spanish under H. de Soto (1540) and first permanently settled by the French at Mobile (1711). The region passed to Britain (1763) and then was divided between Spain and the newly created US (1783). The rest of the territory was obtained as part of the Louisiana Purchase (1803). Alabama became a state (1819) and seceded (1861) during the Civil War. Slavery was abolished in 1865. The present state constitution was adopted in 1901.

Alabama Claims US government claims against Britain. The damages claimed were caused by Confederate cruisers, notably the *Alabama,* that had been built during the American Civil War in neutral Britain. After the Civil War, the US sought payment for damages from Britain for direct and indirect losses caused by the ships. By the Treaty of Washington (1871), the British submitted to arbitration. The tribunal disallowed claims for indirect losses but awarded the US $15.5 million for direct losses (1872). The settlement helped define the role of a neutral.

Alabama Platform Plan advanced by Southern political leader W. Yancey (1848), in opposition to the Wilmot Proviso. It called for protection of slavery in lands ceded to the US by Mexico and would have forbidden territorial legislatures to outlaw slavery.

Alam al-Halfa, Battle of (Alam Halfa, ˜) British victory (Aug. 31–Sept. 4, 1942) in Egypt during WW II. The British, under Gen. B. Montgomery, turned back an attack by German field marshal E. Rommel's Afrika Korps.

Alamanni *See* **Alemanni.**

Alamein, Battles of El 1. WW II battle (July, 1942) in which British forces stopped a German sweep across Egypt (led by Field Marshal E. Rommel from May, 1942) and thereby saved Egypt from German conquest. 2. WW II battle (Oct. 23–Nov. 4, 1942), in which British Gen. B. Montgomery forced the Germans under Rommel to withdraw from Egypt into Libya.

Alamo Historic fort in San Antonio, Texas. Originally a chapel, it became a symbol of resistance in Texas to Mexican domination when fewer than 200 Americans tried unsuccessfully

to defend it against Gen. A. del Santa Anna's army of thousands. The Americans occupied the fort in Dec., 1835, and held out against Santa Anna from Feb. 24 to March 6, 1836. Among the Americans slain there were D. Crockett and J. Bowie.

Alani (Alans) Nomadic people. The Alani were a warlike people thought to have originated in the Black Sea region before the 1st cent. AD. Forced westward by the Huns (4th cent.), many of the Alani joined with the Vandals in their invasions of Gaul and Spain.

Alans *See* **Alani.**

Alarcos, Battle of Muslim victory over Spanish Christians (July 18, 1195). The Almohades, responding to an invasion by Christian forces, decisively defeated Alfonso VIII of Castile in southern Spain. Thereafter the Almohades were able to raid Alfonso's territories without opposition.

Alaric I AD c370–410. King of the Visigoths (AD 395–410), who sacked Rome in 410. Alaric commanded Visigothic troops under Roman emperor Theodosius I and became their king on the emperor's death (395). He invaded Greece, demanded subsidies from Rome, quarreled with Emperor Flavius Honorius, and laid siege to and finally sacked Rome.

Alaric II *d.* 507. Visigoth king (484–507), successor to his father, Euric. He ruled Spain and southern Gaul, and issued the *Breviary of Alaric* (*q.v.*). He was defeated and killed by Frankish king Clovis I at Vouille.

Alaric, Breviary of *See* **Breviary of Alaric.**

Alaska 49th US state. Alaska was first explored (1741) by the Russians under V. Bering, and they established the first settlement on Kodiak Island (c1783). Control of the region was granted to the Russian American Fur Company (1799–1861), and in 1825 the Russians agreed to set the present southern boundary at 54°40′ N latitude. Sec. of State W. Seward arranged (1867) for the US purchase of Alaska (thereafter nicknamed Seward's Folly) for $7.2 million. Largely ignored until the gold rush of the 1890s, Alaska did not become a territory until 1912. Alaska's Aleutian Islands were attacked by the Japanese in WW II. Alaska became a state in 1959, and its constitution dates from 1956. Since the 1970s, it has been an important oil-producing state.

Alaskan boundary dispute US-Canadian border dispute involving Canada's border with Alaska.

A commission established the boundary (1903), in accordance with US claims, at the original boundary line (54°40′ N lat.) set in 1825.

Alaungpaya (Alompra) (Aungzeya) 1711–60. King of Burma (1753?–60) and founder of the Konbaung dynasty, which ruled Burma until the British takeover (1886). He led opposition to domination by the Mon kingdom and created a unified kingdom of Burma.

Alba, Fernando Álvarez de Toledo, duke of (Alva, ˜) 1507?–82. Spanish soldier and statesman, adviser to King Philip II. As governor of the Spanish Netherlands (1567–73), he attempted to put down the Dutch rebellion for independence. His administration was marked by cruelty and was noted for the special court Alba established, called the Court of Blood, which executed thousands. Alba later led the Spanish invasion of Portugal (1580).

Al-Bah-Rayn *See* **Bahrain.**

Albani, Giovanni Francesco *See* **Clement XI.**

Albania (People's Socialist Republic of Albania) Albania is a former Communist republic located on the mountainous western coast of the Balkan Peninsula in southeastern Europe. The population is 3,268,000 and the capital is Tirana. Following WW II a Communist government was established and while remaining within the Communist bloc, the Albanian government broke with the USSR in 1961 and pursued closer relations with Communist China. Chronic economic problems in the 1980s culminated in serious food shortages and unrest and in the early 1990s, following the prodemocracy revolts in the rest of Eastern Europe, the Communists were ousted from power. Key dates in the history of Albania include:

C3D CENT. BC Coastal region dominated by Greek colonies; independent kingdom flourished inland.

1ST CENT. AD Kingdom came under Roman influence; Romans left few lasting marks on Albanian culture.

395 Byzantines dominated region encompassing Albania after the fall of Rome.

1000s Venetians colonized the region.

1082 Normans under R. Guiscard invaded Albania.

1272 Charles I of Naples proclaimed king of the territory, following Naples's rise as dominant power in the region.

1346 Serbian conqueror Stephen Dushan made himself emperor of a short-lived empire that included Serbs, Albanians, Bulgars, and Greeks; empire broke apart following his death in 1355.

1400s Invasions by Ottoman Turks.

1444 Albanian prince named Skanderbeg, now a national hero, organized alliance of Albanian princes to oppose Turkish invasions; from 1444–66 he repulsed 13 Turkish offensives.

1468 Skanderbeg died; alliance of princes broke up and Albania soon fell before invading Turks.

1478–1912 Albania, finally conquered by Turks, made part of the Ottoman Empire; Islam introduced.

1877 Russo-Turkish War; Russian victory resulted in allocation of most Albanian territory to other Balkan nations, by Treaty of San Stefano; settlement reversed by Congress of Berlin in 1878.

1878 Albanian League, first Albanian nationalist group, formed (July 1) to oppose partitioning of Albania; the league was successful in battles against Montenegro (1879, 1880) before being crushed by Turkish troops (1881).

1912 First Balkan War fought; Balkan League (Serbia, Bulgaria, Greece, and Montenegro) conquered most all Ottoman domains in Eastern Europe; creation of Albania confirmed by Treaty of London (May 30, 1913), though Allied forces occupying country remained.

1912 Albania proclaimed its independence (Nov. 28) amid the crisis of the Balkan War; Allied forces meanwhile occupied Albania.

1913 London Conference proclaimed Albania independent (May 30).

1913 Second Balkan War (June–July); Serbia occupied Albania.

1913 European powers restored Albanian autonomy but ceded much territory to Montenegro, Serbia, and Greece.

1914 Prince William of Wied became first king of modern Albania; arrived in Durazzo Mar. 7.

1914 Revolt against the government led by Essad Pasha (May); Essad Pasha arrested and banished but unrest continued.

1914–18 WW I; the outbreak of actual fighting (Aug.) only worsened the turmoil inside Albania; later, Albania became the scene of fighting between rival Balkan states seeking to dismember it, as well as invasions by major European powers.

1914 King William abdicated (Sept. 3) as nation slipped into state of anarchy.

1914–16 Essad Pasha ruled as dictator of Albania.

1915 Italians, Greeks, and Montenegrins occupied parts of Albania (Mar.).

1916 Central Powers overran much of Albania (Jan.–Mar.), though Italy retained control in south.

1917 Italy proclaimed Albania an Italian protectorate.

1918 Albanians formed government at Durazzo (Dec. 25); provisional governments ruled Albania until 1925.

1919 Paris Peace Conference awarded Italy mandate over Albania; Albania's southern region of Epirus awarded to Greece, while territory in the north went to Montenegro (Dec. 9).

1920 Armed clashes with Italian occupation forces (June–July); Italians withdrew from most of Albania.

1920 Albania joined the League of Nations.

1922 Rebels opposed to leadership of Ahmed Zogu captured Tirana; revolt quashed (Apr. 12).

1924 Tirana taken during general uprising (June); Albanian Orthodox bishop, Fan S. Noli, named to head Nationalist provisional government (June 12).

1924 Ahmed Zogu led revolt against Noli government (Dec. 12–25); Tirana occupied and Noli government fled to Italy; Ahmed Zogu became head of government.

1925 National Assembly proclaimed Albania a republic (Jan. 23); Ahmed Zogu elected president (Feb. 1).

1925 Zogu arranged first loan from Italy; marked start of rapidly increasing financial dependence on Italy.

1926 Albania signed treaty setting boundaries with Greece and Serbia.

1928 Albania made a democratic monarchy; Zogu proclaimed himself King Zog I (Sept. 1).

1939 WW II began; Italy occupied Albania (Apr. 7), uniting it with the Italian crown; Zog ousted and exiled.

1940 Albania, under Italian control, declared war on the Allies.

1940–41 Italy launched attack on Greece from Albania; Greece counterattacked into Albania but was finally forced to surrender troops in Albania.

1941 Albanian Party of Labor formed by Albanian partisan fighters; eventually taken over by Enver Hoxha and under his Communist regime gave rise to Albania's sole legitimate party.

1943–44 Hoxha led Communist guerrillas fighting the Italian Fascist occupation.

1944 Germans withdrew from Albania; Hoxha and his Communist partisans established a provisional government.

1944–54 Hoxha in office as prime minister; he established a hard-line Stalinist government and retained a tight grip on the reins of power until his death in 1985.

1946 Albania proclaimed a republic.

1948 Hoxha established close ties with the USSR, thereby bringing Albania under Soviet domination.

1954–81 Former partisan fighter Mehmet Shehu in office as prime minister.

1955 Albania entered Warsaw Pact.

1961 Albania, opposed to Soviet de-Stalinization policy and rapprochement with Tito, broke ties with the Soviet Union; allied itself with Communist China.

1967 Government made practice of religion illegal.

1968 Withdrew from Warsaw Pact.

1971 Resumed relations with Greece and Yugoslavia.

1973–76 Large-scale purge of officials.

1978 Albanian government's open criticism of Chinese government led to break with long-time ally; end of Chinese financial aid marked beginning of Albania's serious economic decline.

1980 Trade agreements concluded with Yugoslavia, making it Albania's chief trading partner.

1980 Yugoslavia accused Albania of helping foment riots (Mar. and Apr.) in the Yugoslav province of Kosovo, populated mainly by ethnic Albanians.

1981 Long-time prime minister Mehmet Shehu committed suicide (Dec. 18) under mysterious circumstances; Hoxha claimed almost a year later that Shehu planned to assassinate him on orders from Yugoslavia.

1982 Adil Çarçani in office as prime minister (Jan.), heading new government.

1982 Ramiz Alia became head of state; government reshuffled (Nov.) to eliminate friends and allies of late Mehmet Shehu.

1983 Undercover purge of party and government officials carried out during the year; reports told of arrests of political, military, and other prominent figures; former ministers of Defense and the Interior believed executed.

1983 Hoxha's 75th birthday celebrated with official government propaganda campaign applauding his leadership; Albania's economy, meanwhile, continued on a downward slide begun soon after Albania lost Chinese aid money; Hoxha's long-standing policy of isolation included prohibitions against foreign investment, despite the desperate need for outside capital.

1984 Government sponsored public celebrations for 40th anniversary of Communist rule in Albania (Nov.).

1984 Frontier with Greece opened (Dec.) for first time since 1940; first road link opened in 1985.

1985 Hoxha died (Apr. 11).

1985 Ramiz Alia succeeded Hoxha as party leader.

1986 Opening of rail line between Shkodër, Albania, and Titograd, Yugoslavia, gave Albania its first link with European rail network (Aug.).

1987 Food shortages becoming more acute; centralized bureaucracy, poor management, corruption, and inefficiency blamed for these and Albania's other economic woes; open demands for change began to mount in 1988, fostered by sweeping reforms in the USSR.

1987 Official end to technical state of war with Greece, declared during WW II (Aug.); Albania signed cooperative agreements with Greece soon after.

1989 Albanian leader Alia rejected demands for sweeping reforms (Dec. 15); began program of permitting some concessions to blunt reformists' demands.

1989–90 Unrest, strikes, and mass demonstrations forced more government concessions; ban on religious "propaganda" ended, and Ministry of Justice reestablished.

1990 Some 4,000 Albanians, seeking escape from their homeland, mobbed West German and other foreign embassies (July); embarrassed government allowed emigration soon after.

1990 Albanian political leader and pro-government author Ismail Kadare fled country (Oct. 25), proclaiming the government would never agree to real reforms.

1990 First Catholic mass since 1967 celebrated in Shkodër (Nov.); Muslims, who make up 70 percent of the population, resumed worship in Tirana mosque (Jan. 1991).

1990 Albania restored diplomatic relations with USSR, ending break that began over Soviet de-Stalinization in 1961.

1990 Worker and student demonstrations demanding multi-party elections in 1991 (Dec.); statues of Stalin in public places removed; Alia fired Communist hard-liners from government and agreed to one opposition party.

1990 Opposition Democratic party legalized (Dec. 19); led by academic Gramos Pashko.

1991 Italy promised $50 million in aid (Jan.).

1991 Flood of Albanian refugees in Italy reaches 20,000 by Mar.; some 17,000 fled to Greece.

1991 Pro-democracy protesters pull down massive statue of Hoxha in Tirana's Skanderbeg Square (Feb. 20); pro-Communists organized counterdemonstrations outside Tirana.

1991 Alia reshuffled his pro-Communist government amid mass pro-democracy protests; named Fatos Nano premier (Feb. 22).

1991 Over 400 political prisoners released (Mar.).

1991 First elections held since 1945 (Mar. 31); ruling Albanian Workers' party remained in power despite high voter turnout.

1991 Widespread protests against election outcome; Interior Ministry troops killed 3 and wounded 30 in Shkodër (Apr. 2).

1991 Alia reelected president (Apr. 30); renounced Communist party affiliation.

1991 Diplomatic relations established with US for first time since 1939 (May 15).

1991 Half of Albania's workers joined strike (May 15) called by Albania's Union of Free and Independent Trade Unions.

1991 Alia's pro-Communist cabinet resigned (June 4) in the face of ongoing unrest.

1991 Pro-Communist Ylli Bufi in office as premier of interim, nonpartisan government; opposition members made up half of cabinet and Communists renounced party membership; new elections scheduled for 1992.

1991   Albanian Workers' party (Communist) renamed itself Albanian Socialist party (June 12) amid growing opposition to Communism.

1991   Albania joined the Conference on Security and Cooperation in Europe (June 19), the last country to do so.

1991   Albania's agricultural industry collapsed following breakup of collectives; US began airlift of emergency food rations (July 20); European Economic Community provided badly needed food shipments as well.

1991   Government arrested Enver Hoxha's widow and other Communist hard-liners to blunt pro-democracy demands (Dec. 4).

1991   Caretaker government dissolved after opposition Democratic party members withdrew from cabinet, blaming Alia government for stalling reforms (Dec. 4).

1991   Mass demonstrations against pro-Communist government (Dec. 9–12); protesters blamed government for food shortages.

1991   Vilson Ahmeti in office as prime minister (Dec. 10).

1992   Albanian economy in near complete collapse; unemployment hit 70 percent and inflation was estimated at 150 percent; gangs roamed cities and countryside sparking wave of violent crime; foreign donations needed to feed population.

1992   Opposition Democratic party soundly defeated pro-Communist ruling party (Mar. 22); Alia resigned (Apr. 4), finally breaking the Communist hold on Albania's government.

Albanian League   Albania's first nationalist group (1878–81). Formed after the Russo-Turkish War of 1877–78, the group sought to block plans by the Congress of Berlin to partition the region among Montenegro, Serbia, and Greece. Negotiations failed and the league took up arms to prevent the annexations (1879). Troops sent by the Ottoman Turks, who controlled the region, crushed the league (1881).

Albany Congress   Meeting held (June 19–July 11, 1754) at Albany, New York, to win the Iroquois Confederacy over to the British side in the impending French and Indian Wars. The meeting, attended by delegates from seven American colonies and by 150 tribal members, failed to produce an effective alliance with the Indians. It

was notable, however, as the forum for B. Franklin's Albany Plan, a planned union of the colonies. The scheme was later rejected by colonial legislatures.

Albany Plan   *See* **Albany Congress.**

Albany Regency   New York State political machine run by Democrats (1820–c1850) and generally regarded as one of the first effective political machines in the US. The organization was developed by M. Van Buren and was centered in Albany, New York. Its decline began in the 1840s with the appearance of factions in the Democratic party, notably the Hunkers.

Albee, Edward Franklin 1928–   . American playwright. Albee is known for such works as *Who's Afraid of Virginia Woolf?, Zoo Story,* and *A Delicate Balance,* for which he won a Pulitzer Prize (1967).

Alberoni, Giullo 1664–1752.   Italian cardinal and statesman. As de facto prime minister of Spain (c1714–19), he arranged the marriage of Philip V to Elizabeth Farnese. His aggressive policies promoting Spanish interests in Italy resulted in formation of the Quadruple Alliance (1718) and a brief war against Spain. He was banished in 1719.

Albert (of Saxe-Coburg-Gotha) 1819–61.   Prince consort of British queen Victoria. At first unpopular, his diligence and diplomatic ability brought him great admiration. His moderating influence in the Trent Affair (1861) may have prevented war between Britain and the US.

Albert I c1250–1308.   German king (1298–1308) a Habsburg and son of King Rudolf I. After Rudolf's death (1291), Adolf of Nassau was made king, in an attempt to keep the crown from becoming a Habsburg title. Albert overthrew him (1298) and was confirmed king (1303) by Pope Boniface VIII.

Albert I 1875–1934.   Belgian king (1909–34), successor to his uncle Leopold II. He led the Belgian army against the Germans in WW I, played a leading role in the reconstruction of Belgium after the war, and instituted such political and social reforms as universal male suffrage.

Albert II 1397–1439.   Holy Roman Emperor (1438–39), successor to his father-in-law, Sigismund. He sought to prevent internal warfare in Germany and to improve its administrative organization, became embroiled in the Hussite Wars, and died while fighting the Turks. He was the first of the Habsburg line of emperors.

Albert of Brandenburg 1490–1568.   First duke of Prussia (1525–68) and last grand master of the Teutonic Knights (1511–25). A Protestant, he heeded M. Luther's advice and created (1525) the secular dukedom of Prussia, ending the Teutonic Knights' rule over the territory. The territory remained under Polish suzerainty.

Albert the Bear c1100–1170.   First margrave of Brandenburg. He led campaigns against the Wends and by treaty inherited (1150) Brandenburg from Prince Pribislav, the last Wendish prince. During his rule he expanded German influence in Eastern Europe by promoting colonization.

Albert the Great, Saint *See* **Albertus Magnus, Saint.**

Alberta   Province in western Canada. Originally inhabited by Indians up to 10,000 years ago, the region was explored by Europeans in the 17th and 18th cents. Included in a land grant by English king Charles II (1670), the area was exploited by fur trappers and traders, and eventually came under the control of the Hudson's Bay Company. The Scottish explorer Sir A. Mackenzie traversed the region in 1793. The following year a fort was built on the site of what is now Edmonton. Included in the Northwest Territories after the government took control of the region in 1870, Alberta became a province in 1905. Population growth began after a railroad was built through the area in the 1880s, and land grants helped fuel a surge in population growth during the early 1900s. Alberta suffered during the 1930s Great Depression, which helped give rise to the Social Credit party and calls for monetary reform. Oil (first discovered there in 1914) helped fuel economic growth in Alberta in the years after WW II.

Albertus Magnus, Saint (Albert the Great, Saint) c1200–1280.   Scholastic theologian and philosopher. He helped introduce the works of Aristotle in Europe, promoted the study of natural science, and advanced the use of the scientific method. One of his students was T. Aquinas.

Albigenses   Christian heretical sect that flourished (12th–13th cents.) in southern France. Named for the city of Albi, the Albigenses were predominantly Cathari (*q.v.*). Extreme ascetics, they believed in the Manichaean dualism of good and evil. The Albigensian Crusade was mounted against them (1208). Following this, the medieval Inquisition was instituted against them and with

it began (1239) a century-long persecution that finally eliminated the sect.

Albigensian Crusade   Crusade (1208–13) against Christian heretics in southern France. The crusade was largely directed against the Cathari and Waldenses, reformist sects that had arisen in opposition to church corruption and that then enjoyed the favor of noblemen in southern France. Pope Innocent III proclaimed the crusade (1208), which amounted to an invasion of southern France by the barons of northern France under S. de Montfort. In 1209 he massacred some 20,000 inhabitants of Beziers and, by his victory (1213) at Muret, broke the power of the heretics. Fighting continued, however, and he died (1218) at the siege of Toulouse. The conquest was completed by French king Louis IX, who, by the Peace of Paris (1229), acquired Toulouse. The subsequent medieval Inquisition eliminated heretical sects in southern France by the 14th cent.

Albion   Ancient name for England, still used in literary references. It is derived from the Latin *albus,* or "white," for the white chalk cliffs of Dover.

Alboin *d.* 572?   Lombard king (c562–572) who greatly expanded the Lombard kingdom. He began by conquering Germanic tribes (Gepidae) to the east of his lands, then located in Austria and western Hungary. He next invaded Italy (568), and eventually took all of northern Italy from the Byzantines.

Albornoz, Gil Álvarez Carrillo de 1310?–67.   A Spanish soldier and cardinal. He restored papal authority over the Papal States through military and diplomatic means, thus allowing return (1368) of the popes from Avignon to Rome. He prepared (1357) a constitution for the Papal States, which remained in effect until 1816.

Albrecht *See* **Albert.**

Albuquerque, Alfonso de 1453–1515.   A Portuguese viceroy of the Indies (1506–15), a principal founder of Portugal's empire in the East. As viceroy, he conquered Goa in India (1510) and made it a center of Portuguese power. He went on to conquer other eastern territories, including Ceylon and Malacca on the Malay Peninsula. He twice took Ormuz (1507, 1515) to control the Arab spice trade.

Alcáçovas, Treaty of   Treaty (Mar. 6, 1479) between Portugal and the kingdom of Castile. By its terms Castile received the Canary Islands, while Portugal was given West Africa and Guinea. Portugal also renounced claim to the Castilian throne.

Alcaeus *d.* c580 BC.   Greek lyric poet. A contemporary of Sappho, he invented Alcaic verse, which was later adapted by Horace. Of his ten books, only fragments survive.

Alcalá Zamora, Niceto 1877–1949.   A Spanish statesman. He led the Spanish revolution (1931) that established the republic, and served as its first president (1931–36). Deposed because of his moderate policies, he died in exile.

Alcamenes *fl.* c440 BC.   Greek sculptor, believed to have been the pupil and later rival of Phidias. His works include the sculptures *Aphrodite of the Gardens* and *Hermes Propylaios.*

Alcazarquivir, Battle of   *See* **Three Kings, Battle of.**

Alcibiades c450–404 BC.   Athenian statesman and military leader, from the same family as Pericles. Regarded as both brilliant and unscrupulous, he rose to prominence during the Peloponnesian War (431–404 BC). Opposing the Peace of Nicias (421), he rallied the Athenians to an alliance against Sparta and a disastrous campaign in Sicily (415). Falsely charged with defacing sacred statues, he fled to Sparta. He aided the Spartans until forced to flee to Persia (411). Recalled to Athens (411), he led the Athenian fleet to victories against the Spartans and recovered Byzantium (408). But when the Athenian fleet was defeated by Lysander (407), he was exiled. He was subsequently killed on Lysander's orders.

Alciphron *fl.* 2d or 3d cent. AD.   Greek writer. He fabricated a series of about 100 letters, supposedly written by the common people. They provide a useful but literary picture of 4th-cent. Athenian life.

Alcmaeonidae   Athenian family. They influenced Athenian politics at intervals from the 7th to 5th cents. BC. Among its members were Cleisthenes, Pericles, and Alcibiades.

Alcott, Louisa May 1832–88.   American novelist. Her best known work is *Little Women.*

Alden, John c1599–1687.   English colonist, one of the Pilgrim founders of Plymouth Colony. According to legend, he courted Priscilla Mullens for his friend M. Standish, though she finally married Alden. Alden was assistant to the governor of Massachusetts (1633–41, 1650–86) and twice deputy governor.

Aldhelm c639–709.   Early Saxon poet and teacher, the abbot of Malmsbury (from c675) in Wessex. A student at the School of Canterbury, he learned Latin and Greek, studied a wide range of subjects, and began writing poetry. As abbot of Malmsbury, he not only attended his religious duties, but also encouraged learning and helped pioneer the writing of poetry in Latin verse among the Saxons of early England. He also wrote prose treatises, one of his most famous being on the science of poetic meter.

Aldobrandini, Ippolito   *See* **Clement VIII.**

Aldrich, Nelson Wilmarth 1841–1915.   American politician and financier. As US senator (1881–1911), he worked for the Aldrich-Vreeland Currency Act of 1908. His study of banking reform helped establish the Federal Reserve System.

Aldrin, Edwin Eugene, Jr. (~, Buzz) 1930–   .   American astronaut. As a member of the Apollo 11 mission (July, 1969), he was the second person to set foot on the moon.

Alekseyev, Konstantin Sergeyevich   *See* **Stanislavsky, Konstantin.**

Alemán, Miguel 1902–83.   Mexican statesman. As president of Mexico (1946–52), he worked to modernize industry and agriculture and to improve living conditions.

Alemanni (Alamanni)   Loose confederation of Germanic tribes that had settled in what is now southwestern Germany and northern Switzerland by the 3d cent. AD. The Alemanni came into conflict with the Romans and by the 5th cent. AD occupied Baden, Alsace, and parts of Switzerland. Frankish king Clovis I defeated them (496), and in the 6th cent. they became subjects of Frankish kings.

Alembert, Jean le Rond d' 1717–83.   A French mathematician and philosopher. A major figure of the Enlightenment in France, he was coeditor, with D. Diderot, of the *Encyclopédie.* His works include an important treatise on dynamics.

Alep   *See* **Aleppo.**

Aleppo (Alep)   Historic city in northern Syria. Founded before the 2d millennium BC, it was on the main caravan route from Syria to Baghdad. It has been under the control of various peoples, including the Persians, Romans, Byzantines, Arabs, and Turks. Its importance declined (19th cent.) with construction of the Suez Canal.

Alessandri Palma, Arturo 1868–1950.   Chilean politician, twice president of Chile (1920–25,

1932–38). He led the Liberal Alliance in Chile and was able in his second term to achieve political and economic reforms. He helped write a new constitution (1925), which included provisions for universal male suffrage.

Alessandri Rodríguez, Jorge 1895–1970. President of Chile (1958–64).

Alexander (Alexander of Battenberg) 1857–93. Prince of Bulgaria (1879–86). With tsarist support, he became first prince of the new autonomous state of Bulgaria. His annexation of Eastern Rumelia led to war with Serbia (1885) and to his forced abdication in 1886.

Alexander 1888–1934. Yugoslavian king (1921–34). He played a major role in unifying Yugoslavia at the end of WW I. The regent of Serbia, he created an unstable kingdom (1918) embracing the rival ethnic groups of Serbs, Croats, and Slovenes. A constitutional monarchy was established in 1921, but increasing disorders forced him to abolish it (1929) in favor of a dictatorship. He instituted a new constitution in 1931. Alexander was assassinated by a Croatian terrorist in 1934.

Alexander 1876–1903. King of Serbia (1889–1903), successor to his father, Milan. His authoritarianism, his suspension (1894) of the liberal constitution, and his scandalous marriage led to his assassination by the military.

Alexander 1893–1920. King of Greece (1917–20), successor to his father, Constantine I, when the latter was forced to abdicate by the Allies during WW I. The government was actually run by Venizelos, his premier.

Alexander I 1078?–1124. King of Scotland (1107–24), successor to his brother Edgar. He ruled the northern part of Scotland, while his brother David ruled the south. He suppressed a clan rebellion (1115).

Alexander I 1777–1825. Russian tsar (1801–25), successor to his father, Paul I. After defeats at Austerlitz and Friedland, he submitted to Napoleon's Continental System, under the Treaty of Tilsit (1807). But he later repulsed Napoleon's invasion of Russia (1812), marched into Paris (1814), and, by his defeat of Napoleon, became one of the most important rulers in Europe. In his early years, he instituted many liberal reforms. After 1814, however, he was influenced by the Pietism of J. Krüdener. This led to his formation of the Holy Alliance and support for conservative

and reactionary policies, especially those of C. Metternich.

Alexander II 1818–81. Russian tsar (1855–81), successor to his father, Nicholas I. Shortly after his accession, he negotiated an end to the Crimean War (1853–56) and instituted many liberal reforms, including the Edict of Emancipation (1861) and the limited local government of the Zemstvo (*q.v.*). His reforms, however, failed to prevent the rise of the populist Narodnik movement in the 1860s, and his attempts to suppress it led to his assassination. During his reign he brutally suppressed a Polish rebellion (1863), formed the Three Emperors' League, extended Russian territories in central Asia, and engaged in the Russo-Turkish Wars (1877–78).

Alexander III *See* **Alexander the Great.**

Alexander III (Orlando Bandinelli) *d.* 1181. Italian-born pope (1159–81), successor to Adrian IV. With help from the Lombard League, he managed to assert papal authority over Holy Roman Emperor Frederick I and forced him to sign the Treaty of Vienna (1177). He also opposed Henry II of England, canonized Thomas à Becket, and received Henry's penance for Becket's murder.

Alexander III 1241–86. King of Scotland (1249–86), successor to his father, Alexander II (1198–1249). He married a daughter of English king Henry III and resisted Henry's attempt to control Scotland. During his reign, Scotland finally won from Norway the permanent control of the Hebrides and the Isle of Man (1266).

Alexander III 1845–94. Russian tsar (1881–94), successor to his father, Alexander II. He became tsar after his father's assassination and instituted reactionary policies that included an increase in police repression and censorship. The power of the Zemstvos was sharply curtailed, national minorities were forced to undergo Russification, and religious minorities were persecuted.

Alexander VI 1431?–1503. Spanish-born pope (1492–1503), successor to Innocent VIII, and a symbol of papal corruption during the Renaissance. A member of the Borgia family, he is said to have won election to the papacy through bribery. As pope, he proclaimed division of Spanish and Portuguese possessions in the New World (1493) (*see* Tordesillas, Treaty of), successfully resisted an invasion of Italy by French king Charles VIII (1494), ordered the execution of

G. Savonarola (1498), and began a censorship of books (1501). Throughout his reign he pursued the aggrandizement of his family's fortunes.

Alexander Balas *d.* 145 BC. King of Syria (150–145 BC), who came to power by slaying Demetrius I, the Seleucid king. He named Jonathan Maccabaeus governor of Palestine and was later killed in battle by Demetrius II, son of Demetrius I.

Alexander, Harold Rupert Leopold George, 1st earl of Tunis 1891–1969. British field marshal who directed the British evacuation at Dunkirk (1940) during WWII. He subsequently led British forces in Burma, North Africa, Sicily, and southern Italy, and was made commander in chief of British Mediterranean forces in 1944.

Alexander Nevsky c1220–63. Russian prince and military hero. He defeated the Swedes at the Battle of the Neva (1240) and the Teutonic Knights at the Battle of Lake Peipus (1242).

Alexander of Battenberg *See* **Alexander.**

Alexander of Hales *d.*1245. English theologian and philosopher. A Franciscan, he taught at the University of Paris. His teachings contained elements of Aristotle's philosophy and influenced Franciscan scholasticism.

Alexander the Great (Alexander III) 356–323 BC. Macedonian king (336–323 BC), successor to his father, Philip II. One of the world's greatest conquerors, he created a vast empire extending from Greece to northern India, and, by his conquests, helped spread Greek civilization throughout the ancient world. Soon after becoming king, Alexander crushed revolts in Thrace, Illyria, and Thebes. His rule in Greece thus established, he began his epic military expedition (334–324 BC) with some 37,000 soldiers and the initial objective of conquering Persia. He met and defeated the Persians at the battles of Granicus (334) and Issus (in Syria, 333), laid siege to and finally took Tyre (332) to complete conquest of Phoenicia, marched unopposed into Egypt (332–331), and there founded the great city of Alexandria (332). He again defeated the Persians at the Battle of Gaugamela (331), sent Persian king Darius III into flight, and sacked the Persian capital of Persepolis (331). He continued eastward to Media (330) and central Asia, where he invaded Scythia (329). Despite open discontent in his army (over his acceptance of Persian manners and increasingly autocratic rule), Alexander invaded India (327). After the Battle of Hydaspes (326), he took control of the Punjab and, his men unwilling to go farther, returned to Persia (324). He subsequently consolidated Macedonian control of his conquests and attempted to integrate Greeks and Persians by, among other things, ordering his soldiers to marry Persian women. The hero of these great conquests, and such legendary feats as cutting the Gordian Knot, died shortly after a prolonged banquet in 323. His conquests created a short-lived empire that imposed a common currency and common system of laws on the diverse cultures it embraced. New roads and increased trade between the various parts of the empire brought a period of prosperity. A builder as well as a conqueror, Alexander built over 70 cities before his death. (*See also* Macedonia.)

Alexandra 1844–1925. Queen consort of English king Edward VII (m. 1863) and mother of King George V.

Alexandra Feodorovna 1872–1918. Last tsarina of Russia, consort of Nicholas II (1894–1918). Her unfailing loyalty to the hated Rasputin and her disastrous meddlings in politics helped bring about the Russian Revolution. A Hessian princess, she came under Rasputin's sway when he seemed able to control her son's hemophilia. While Nicholas was at the front in WW I, she took control of the government (1915) and began replacing government ministers with favorites of Rasputin. This discredited the government and opened the way for the October Revolution (1917). She was shot, with Nicholas and her children, by revolutionaries.

Alexandria Egypt's second largest city and a major center for cotton, manufacturing, and exports. Founded in 332 BC by Alexander the Great, it became one of the largest and greatest cities of antiquity. The Ptolemies (*q.v.*) ruled their Egyptian-based empire from there (323–30 BC), and it became a principal center of both Hellenistic and Jewish culture. It attracted scholars such as Aristarchus of Samothrace, who collated Homer's texts; the geometer Euclid; and the astronomer Claudius Ptolemy, originator of the Ptolemaic System (*q.v.*). The Greek Septuagint (Old Testament) was translated there. Alexandria boasted antiquity's best libraries, as well as the tall lighthouse considered one of the Seven Wonders of the World. The city was captured by J. Caesar (47 BC) and incorporated into the Roman Empire by Augustus (30 BC). In Christian times it was the seat of one of the four major patriarchates, and great churchmen such as Saint Athanasius were bishops there. Alexandria declined after Arab conquerers moved Egypt's capital to Cairo (AD 969). The city was captured in modern times by Napoleon (1798), then by the British (1801), and afterward began to regain its former importance.

Alexandria, Appian of   *See* **Appian of Alexandria.**

Alexandria, Catherine of   *See* **Catherine of Alexandria.**

Alexandria, Clement of   *See* **Clement of Alexandria.**

Alexandria, Hero of   *See* **Hero of Alexandria.**

Alexandria, Saint Cyril of   *See* **Cyril of Alexandria, Saint.**

Alexandria, School of   *See* **Alexandrian School.**

Alexandrian School   Egyptian Christian school. Founded at Alexandria in the mid-2d cent. AD, it was the first Christian institution of higher learning and philosophy. It sought to reconcile Christianity with Greek culture and to advance orthodox Christian teachings.

Alexis 1629–76. Russian tsar (1645–76), successor to his father, Michael. Alexis established a legal code that recognized serfdom, warred against Poland (1654–67) and Sweden (1656–61) (*see* Northern War), acquired part of the Ukraine and Kiev, approved the reforms of Nikon (*q.v.*), and put down S. Razin's peasant revolt (1670–71).

Alexius I Comnenus 1048–1118. Byzantine emperor (1081–1118), successor to Nicephorus III by his overthrow, and first of the Comnenid rulers. Alexius restored the crumbling Byzantine empire that, when he took power, was threatened by invasions and internal dissent. He defended against Norman invasions (1081–85), contained the Seljuk Turks, repulsed invasions by a tribe of nomadic Turks (1091), and put down rebellions in Crete and Cyprus. His request for aid from the West against the Turks resulted in proclamation of the First Crusade (1096).

Alexius III Angelus *d.* 1210. Byzantine emperor (1195–1203) who deposed his brother Isaac II. Following the overthrow, crusaders (*see* Fourth Crusade) attacked the Byzantine capital of Constantinople (1203) and reinstated Isaac II. Isaac's son, Alexius IV, was installed as coemperor, and Alexius III died in exile.

Alexius V *d.* 1204. Byzantine emperor (1204), son-in-law of Alexius III Angelus. He overthrew coemperors Isaac II and Alexius IV. The army of the Fourth Crusade (*q.v.*) deposed him, sacked Constantinople (1204), and established the Latin Kingdom of Constantinople (*q.v.*).

Alfarabius   *See* **Farabi, al-.**

Al Fatah   *See* **Palestine Liberation Organization.**

Alfonsine Tables (Alphonsine ~) Astronomical data on the planets. This updating of Ptolemy's work was commissioned by Alfonso X and was completed in 1252. T. Brahe later proved them incorrect.

Alfonso I 693?–757. Christian king of Asturias (739–757) When the Berbers rebelled (741) in Muslim Spain, Alfonso was able to conquer Galicia, León, and Santander.

Alfonso I (~ the Battler) *d.* 1134. Christian king of Aragon and Navarre (1104–34). Noted for warring against the Moors, he captured Saragossa (1118) and led a raid into Andalusia (1125). He encouraged Christian settlement in his kingdom.

Alfonso I (~ Henriques) 1111?–1185. First king of Portugal (1139–85). The son of Henry of Burgundy, count of Portugal, he engaged in wars (1128–39) against the Moors and rulers of León and Castile to establish an independent kingdom. He was crowned after his victory over the Moors at Ourique (July 25, 1139). He continued fighting and captured Lisbon in 1147.

Alfonso II (~ the Fat) 1185–1223. King of Portugal (1211–23), successor to his father, Sancho I. He helped defeat the Moors at Las Navas de Tolosa (1212). He quarreled with the church and was excommunicated by Honorius III.

Alfonso III (~ the Great) 838?–911? Christian king of Asturias (866–911?), who fought numerous battles against the Moors and greatly extended his kingdom.

Alfonso III 1210–79. Portuguese king (1248–79), successor to his brother, Sancho II. He completed the unification of Portugal by driving the Moors from Algarve (1249). He instituted political, financial, and commercial reforms.

Alfonso IV 1291–1357. King of Portugal (1325–57), successor to his father, Diniz. He aided Alfonso XI of Castile in his victory over the Moors at Tarifa (1340). But his approval of the murder of his son's beloved mistress, I. Castro, led to a revolt by his son (later Pedro I).

Alfonso V (~ the Noble) 994?–1027. Spanish king of León (999–1027), successor to his father

Bermudo II. Under his reign, the city of León passed from Moorish to Spanish control.

Alfonso V (~ the Magnanimous) 1396–1458. King of Aragon and Sicily (1416–58), successor to his father, Ferdinand I. He conquered Naples and made himself its king in 1442. Thereafter, he held court in Naples and became involved in Italian affairs.

Alfonso V (~ the African) 1432–81. Portuguese king (1438–81), husband of Juana la Beltraneja. He won major victories against the Moors in North Africa but failed to advance his wife's claim to Castile. He was decisively defeated by rival claimants, Queen Isabella and King Ferdinand, at the Battle of Toro (1476).

Alfonso VI 1030–1109. Christian king of León (1065–1109) and Castile (1072–1109). His advances into Muslim territories brought about the takeover of Muslim Spain by the Almoravids. The legendary El Cid may have been active during Alfonso's reign.

Alfonso VI 1643–83. Portuguese king (1656–83), successor to his father, John IV. Mentally impaired, he let Count Castelho Melhor rule. He was ousted (1667) by his wife and his brother, later Peter (Pedro) II. During Alfonso's reign, Spain recognized (1668) Portugal's independence.

Alfonso VII 1104–57. King of León and Castile (1126–57). He warred frequently against the Muslims.

Alfonso VIII (~ the Noble) 1155–1214. Spanish king of Castile (1158–1214), successor to his father, Sancho III. In 1195, he was defeated by Muslim Almohades, and Castile was invaded by León and Navarre. He recovered and later led allied Spanish forces to a major victory over the Moors at Las Navas de Tolosa (1212).

Alfonso X (~ the Wise) 1221–84. Spanish king of Castile and León (1252–84), successor to his father, Ferdinand III. He conquered Cádiz and Cartagena from the Moors, sought unsuccessfully to become Holy Roman Emperor (1257–75), and encouraged culture and learning. He promulgated the Siete Partidas, a great compilation of laws.

Alfonso XI (~ the Avenger) 1311–50. Spanish king of Castile and León (1312–50), successor to his father, Ferdinand IV. Made king at age one, he assumed power in 1325. He led the Spanish to victory over the Moors at the Battle of Algeciras, now in Morocco (1344).

Alfonso XII 1857–85. Spanish king (1874–85), son of Isabella II. Forced into exile (1868) by a revolution, he was proclaimed king in 1874. He returned to Spain (1875), restored order, and consolidated the power of the monarchy.

Alfonso XIII 1886–1941. King of Spain (1886–1931), successor to his father, Alfonso XII. His reign was marked by political and social instability. He supported the military coup of Primo de Rivera (1923) and went into exile (1931) with the establishment of the Second Republic.

Alfonso Henriques   *See* **Alfonso I.**

Alfonso the African   *See* **Alfonso V.**

Alfonso the Avenger   *See* **Alfonso XI.**

Alfonso the Battler   *See* **Alfonso I.**

Alfonso the Fat   *See* **Alfonso II.**

Alfonso the Great   *See* **Alfonso III.**

Alfonso the Magnanimous   *See* **Alfonso V.**

Alfonso the Noble   *See* **Alfonso V, Alfonso VIII.**

Alfonso the Wise   *See* **Alfonso X.**

Alfred (~ the Great) 849–899. Saxon king (871–899) of Wessex, England, and successor to his brother Aethelred. He is the hero of English resistance to the Danish invasions in the 9th cent. Following his brother's death in war against the Danes, he at first resorted to payment of Danegeld, then defeated the Danes at Edington (878) and London (886). Alfred repulsed renewed Danish invasions from 892 to 896. During his reign, he brought about a revival of learning, issued a code of laws, and consolidated his powers as monarch.

Algeciras, Battle of   *See* **Alfonso XI.**

Algeciras Conference   Meeting of European powers (Jan.–Apr., 1906) in Algeciras, Morocco. Germany sought unsuccessfully to reduce French and Spanish influence in Morocco. By the agreement here, France and Spain received increased authority and control of Moroccan financial, commercial, and police affairs.

Alger, Horatio 1832–99. American author of more than 100 books for boys, featuring poor youths who, through hard work, clean living, and a stroke of luck, achieve success. His books were immensely popular in the late 19th cent.

Algeria   Republic located in northwest Africa. The population is 25,714,000 and the capital is Algiers. Originally inhabited by Berbers, Algeria successively came under control of the Carthaginians, Romans, Byzantines, and Ottoman Turks. By the 17th cent. it was a center of pirate activity (*see* Barbary States), which continued until the French invaded Algeria and made it a colony. Its Muslim heritage, and rising nationalistic sentiment, contributed to a major struggle in the 1950s between the ruling European colonists and the Muslim majority. It ended with establishment of the Republic of Algeria in 1962. Key dates in the history of Algeria include:

9TH–5TH CENTS. BC Algeria (roughly ancient Numidia) came under domination of Carthage.

206 BC Numidians allied with Romans against Carthage during the Second Punic War; thereafter Rome gradually took control of Numidia.

AD 396–430 Saint Augustine was bishop at Hippo.

AD 429 Algeria devastated by invasion of Vandals from Spain.

6TH CENT. Byzantine Empire established rule over northern Algeria.

7TH CENT. Muslim Caliphate Empire captured region; Berber tribesmen converted to Islam and adopted Arabic language and customs.

10TH CENT. Fatimid Muslim dynasty began its climb to power in northeastern Algeria.

15TH CENT. Spain conquered coastal Algeria; Turkish pirates aided Algerians against the Spanish.

16TH CENT. Turkish pirates, with Ottoman aid, drove out the Spanish; Algeria came under Ottoman rule.

1671 Dey of Algiers became autonomous ruler of Algeria; region became center for piracy and slave trade in the Mediterranean.

1816 Continued acts of piracy led British to bombard Algiers.

1830–37 French invaded Algeria and gained control of coastal Algeria; the Berber leader Abd al-Kadir continued resistance in the country's interior.

1847 Abd al-Kadir forced to surrender to French.

1848 Algeria made French territory; Europeans began large-scale colonial settlement.

1900 Algeria gained self-government in administrative and financial matters; European colonists controlled the government.

1920s–1940s Rise of nationalistic sentiment among discontented Muslims.

1942 Algeria became a center for Allied operations in North Africa during WW II.

1945 Muslim nationalist uprising led to severe repression by French; thousands of Muslims killed.

1947 Statute of Algeria passed by French National Assembly, granting greater autonomy to Algerian Muslims; many of its articles were never implemented.

1954 National Liberation Front (FLN) formed by Muslims; launched (Nov. 1) an armed revolt against French rule.

1957 French military cleared the cities of FLN terrorists; Muslim resistance continued.

1958 Demonstrations against concessions to Muslims staged by French colonials and military in Algeria; this led to political crisis in France and contributed to C. de Gaulle's return to power.

1958 FLN established the rebel Provisional Government of the Algerian Republic (GPRA); F. Abbas named prime minister.

1962 Accord signed by French government and GPRA, calling for cease-fire and eventual Algerian independence under Muslim majority rule.

1962 Secret Army Organization (OAS) formed by elements of French army in Algeria; mounted a brief and unsuccessful terrorist campaign against Algerian independence; European community (some one million persons) left Algeria.

1962 Algerians voted (July 1) for independence; France recognized Algeria as an independent state.

1963 A. Ben Bella became president; consolidating power, he began implementing leftist programs.

1965 Ben Bella deposed by Houari Boumédienne, who established a revolutionary council to govern the country.

1967 Attempted military coup led by Colonel Zbiri fails.

1971 Boumédienne nationalized French petroleum interests in Algeria.

1974–76 Algeria established closer relations with the US; became a major oil and gas exporter to US.

1978 Boumédienne died (Dec.) in office. Chadli Bendjedid, a leading Algerian political official, succeeded to the presidency (1979).

1978–92 Bendjedid in office as president, succeeding Boumédienne; consolidated his power as president and began shift away from strict

Marxist ideology; sought stronger ties with Western countries.

1980 Bendjedid, as part of his reform program, divided state-run Sonatrach corporation, which employed 85,000 workers, into 13 private industries.

1980 Earthquake measuring 7.5 on Richter scale struck (Oct. 10), killing over 10,000 and leaving over 400,000 homeless.

1980–81 Algeria, as intermediary, played a key role in negotiations during the hostage crisis in Iran.

1982 First woman appointed to Bendjedid's cabinet; Bendjedid withdrew a controversial Family Rights Bill, calling for national debate on topic of women's rights.

1984 Bendjedid reelected (Jan.) for five-year term; continued trend toward reducing state control of industry and depoliticizing the armed forces.

1985 Incidents of terrorism sparked by discontent over government austerity measures and unrest among Muslim fundamentalists; austerity measures necessitated by high foreign debt and falling oil prices.

1986 Bendjedid forced passage of revision to National Charter, attempting to simultaneously appease discontent and consolidate his control; opposition to the ruling FLN party increased, culminating (Nov.) in student riots in Constantine.

1986 Algerian economy hard hit by falling oil prices on world market.

1986–87 Algeria improved relations with Libya; entered joint oil exploration venture with Libya.

1988 Algeria reopened border with Morocco (June), signaling improved relations with its western neighbor.

1988 Government reforms, aimed at free-market economy, sparked riots (Oct. 4) in Algiers and other cities; Bendjedid declared a state of siege (Oct. 6–11); 3,743 arrested; deaths estimated in the hundreds.

1988 Bendjedid proposed (Oct. 10) amendments to the constitution in aftermath of riots; would shift power away from presidency to governing body of elected officials; referendum passed overwhelmingly (Nov. 3), opening the way for multi-party system.

1990 First multi-party elections held (June 12); in municipal and provincial elections, the ruling FLN lost much of its power to the Islamic Salvation Front (FIS).

1991 Violent demonstrations by FIS in Algiers (June), protesting redistricting for upcoming parliamentary elections; Bendjedid declared a state of emergency and postponed parliamentary elections; violent incidents continued until Bendjedid lifted state of emergency (July 17).

1991 First free parliamentary elections held (Dec. 26) since national independence in 1962; FIS party won largest block of seats in Parliament.

1992 President Bendjedid resigned (Jan. 11); military council assumed power and voided elections; sparked widespread unrest.

1992 Mohammed Boudiaf, leader of ruling military council, assassinated (June 29); assassin, reportedly a member of his bodyguard, under arrest; widespread unrest by Muslim fundamentalists in following weeks.

Algiers Algerian capital and a major North African port. Founded by Muslims (10th cent.) on the site of a Phoenician city called Icosium, it became important under the Ottoman Turks as a base for the Barbary pirates. Several military expeditions were sent against the city (16th–19th cents.), including an American force under S. Decatur (1815). French conquest of Algeria began there (1830). The city figured in WW II as an Allied headquarters and in the revolt (1958) that ended the French Fourth Republic.

Alhambra Moorish palace and fortress overlooking Granada, Spain, and built during the 13th and 14th cents. The finest example of Moorish architecture in Spain, it was damaged after the Moors were expelled from Spain (1492). Restoration began in 1828.

Ali 600?–661. Fourth Muslim caliph (656–661), successor to Uthman and cousin and son-in-law of Muhammad. He was the husband of Fatima, but his right to succeed to the Caliphate was disputed. This resulted in the great split between Shiite supporters of Ali and the Sunnite Muslims. A devoted follower of Muhammad, he was challenged after his accession by Muawiya and was murdered by a fanatic. (*See also* Muslim Civil Wars.)

Alien and Sedition Acts Four laws passed (1798) by US Congress. Ostensibly passed to control French aliens at a time when the French revolutionary government was becoming increasingly belligerent, the laws were an attempt by the Federalist party to stifle opposition from Jeffersonian Republicans. The Jeffersonians were sympathetic to the French Revolution and relied heavily on votes of recent immigrants. The alien laws raised to 14 years the residence needed for naturalization, and gave President J. Adams power to arrest and deport aliens. The sedition act forbade criticism of the government. It resulted in the conviction of 10 Republicans and precipitated the Kentucky and Virginia Resolutions.

Alien Registration Act of 1940   *See* **Smith Act.**

Alipasha 1741?–1822.   Turkish governor of Janina in Greece (from 1788). Called "The Lion," he conquered much of Albania and was alternately the ally of France and England. His court was described by Lord G. Byron in *Childe Harold's Pilgrimage.*

Aljubarrota, Battle of   Important battle (Aug. 14, 1385) in Portuguese history, in which Portuguese independence from the Spanish kingdoms was confirmed. With the aid of English troops, John I, regent of Portugal, defeated armies under John I of Castile near the village of Aljubarrota, in Portugal.

Al-Khowarizmi   Arab mathematician. The word "algebra" is said to derive from a work of his. His writings, translated into Latin, provided much of medieval Europe's mathematical knowledge.

Al-Kindi   *See* **Kindi.**

Allen, Ethan 1738–89.   American Revolutionary War hero and leader of the Green Mountain Boys. He formed the Green Mountain Boys in the years prior to the Revolution to defend claims of Vermont settlers against rival claims of New Yorkers. During the war he led his unit at the Battle of Ticonderoga (1775) and participated in an abortive mission to take Montreal (1775), during which he was taken prisoner. A deist, he wrote *Reason the Only Oracle of Man* (1784).

Allenby, Edmund   *See* **Megiddo, Battle of.**

Allende Gossens, Salvador 1908–73.   Chilean politician. Allende founded the Chilean Socialist Party (1933) and became the Western Hemisphere's first freely elected Marxist president (1970). Overthrown in 1973, he was said to have committed suicide.

Alliance for Progress   Inter-American economic assistance program. The US established this aid program (1961) to bolster South American countries against Communism and to effect social and economic reforms. Funding was sharply reduced after 1971.

Allied Powers (Allies) WW I and WW II allies. The original Allied Powers in WW I were Britain, France, and Russia, and they opposed the German-dominated Central Powers. As the war progressed, 18 other countries joined the original Allied Powers. In WW II, the principal allies were Britain, the US, France, the USSR, and China and included numerous other countries.

Allies   *See* **Allied Powers.**

All-India Muslim League   *See* **Muslim League.**

Alma, Battle of the   Victory (Sept. 20, 1854) for the French and British over the Russians during the Crimean War (1853–56). The allies threw some 26,000 troops into battle at this river near Sevastopol. Russian losses were 1,200 killed, 4,000 captured, to allied losses of 4,000 casualties. The Russians retreated to Sevastopol.

Almagro, Diego de c1475–1538.   Spanish conquistador, a leading figure in the conquest of Peru (16th cent.). He later fought Pizarro for the city of Cuzco, was defeated and executed.

Almagro, Diego de (the Younger)   *See* **Castro, Cristobal Vaca de.**

al Mansur   *See* **Mansur.**

Almohades (Almohads)   Muslim sect and dynasty of Berber Muslims that ruled Morocco and Muslim Spain (12th–13th cents.). This puritanical sect was founded (c1120) in Morocco by Ibn Tumart (1078?–1130) in opposition to the ruling Almoravides (*q.v.*). By 1147, Ibn Tumart's successors had ousted the last of the Almoravide rulers. The decline of Almohade power began in the 13th cent., when they lost Muslim Spain to the Spanish and Portuguese at the Battle of Las Navas de Tolosa (1212). They were ousted from power in Morocco (1269).

Almohads   *See* **Almohades.**

Almoravides (Almoravids)   Berber Muslim dynasty, rulers of an empire in North Africa and Muslim Spain (11th–12th cents.). The dynasty was founded by Abd Allah ibn Yasin (*d.* 1058?), who began by converting tribesmen in the Sahara to his zealous reform of Islam. The Almoravides attacked Morocco (c1054), and by 1092 they ruled Morocco, parts of Algeria, and Muslim Spain. They established their capital at Marrakesh (1062). The Almoravides were overthrown by the Almohades (*q.v.*) in the 12th cent.

Almoravids *See* **Almoravides.**

Alompra *See* **Alaungpaya.**

Alp Arslan *See* **Seljuks.**

Alphonsine Tables *See* **Alfonsine Tables.**

Alphonso *See* **Alfonso.**

Alsace Region and former province of eastern France. It came under French control by the Treaty of Westphalia (1648) but was annexed (1871) by Germany after the Franco-Prussian War. Returned to France after WW I, it was reoccupied by Germany for the duration of WW II.

Altenheim, Battle of *See* **Sasbach and Altenheim, Battles of.**

Althaus, Johannes *See* **Althusius, Johannes.**

Althing Parliament of Iceland. First convened in 930, it is the oldest parliamentary body in Europe, although it was inactive for a time in the 19th cent. In 1944 it voted for Iceland's independence from Denmark.

Althusius, Johannes (Althaus, ˜) 1557–1638. German jurist. Sometimes called "the father of federalism," he advanced the theory that all human associations (from families to nations) are based on an implied contract made by free peoples.

Altmark, Truce of Treaty (Sept. 25, 1629) between Sweden and Poland, setting up a six-year truce in their long war of succession (1600–60). Poland gave up most of its Livonian and Prussian territories, and Polish king Sigismund III gave up his claim to the Swedish throne.

Altranstadt, Treaties of Two treaties between Poland and Sweden signed in Saxony. In the first (Sept. 24, 1706), Polish king Augustus II was forced to give up the throne to Stanislaus I. In the second (Aug. 31, 1707), Holy Roman Emperor Joseph I granted Protestants of Silesia religious freedom.

Alva, Fernando Álvarez de Toledo, duke of *See* **Alba, Fernando Álvarez de Toledo, duke of.**

Alvarado, Pedro de 1486?–1541. Spanish conquistador, chief lieutenant of H. Cortés in the conquest of Mexico (1519–21). He was in command of Tenochtitlan (now Mexico City) when the Aztecs forced a temporary evacuation of the city (July 1, 1520), an incident called "The Sad Night" (*La Noche Triste*). In 1523 he conquered Guatemala and Salvador for Cortés and was made governor of Guatemala.

Álvarez Quintero, Joaquin and Serafin 1873–1944. Spanish playwright, who collaborated on more than 100 plays with his brother, Serafin Álvarez Quintero (1871–1938).

Alvear, Marcelo T. 1868–1942. Argentine political leader and president (1922–28). A cofounder of the Unión Civica Radical (UCR, 1890), a liberal democratic party, he took part in the revolutions of 1890, 1893, and 1905, and then served in various government posts. As president, he proved a responsible fiscal administrator and promoted construction of roads, schools, and hospitals. Disagreements with UCR leader H. Irigoyen led to a split in the UCR in 1924.

Amadeo, Ferdinando Maria di Savoia *See* **Amadeus.**

Amadeus (Amadeo, Ferdinando Maria di Savoia) 1845–90. Spanish king (1870–73), successor to Isabella II. He came to power at a time of republican-inspired unrest and was forced to abdicate after the outbreak of the Second Carlist War.

Amadeus VIII 1383–1451. Antipope Felix V, the last of the antipopes, and duke of Savoy (1416–51). He was elected antipope (1439) in opposition to Eugene IV by the Council of Basel but resigned in 1449, when Nicholas V became pope.

Amado, Jorge 1912– . Brazilian novelist. A leftist radical, Amado has been imprisoned and exiled for his political activities at various times since the 1930s. A prolific writer (over 20 novels) of international fame, he often writes of city life among the lower classes. Among his works are *Cacau* (1933), *Gabriela, Clove and Cinnamon* (1958), and *Dona Flor and Her Two Husbands* (1969).

Amalasuntha (Amalasontha) *d.* 535. Queen and regent of the Ostrogoths (526–534), daughter of Theodoric the Great. As regent, her policy of friendship with Byzantine emperor Justinian made her many enemies, and she was banished and murdered in 535.

Amalric I (Amaury I) c1135–74. King of the Latin Kingdom of Jerusalem (1162–74), successor to his brother Baldwin III. He sought unsuccessfully to gain control of Egypt.

Amalric II (Amaury II) c1155–1205. King of Cyprus (1194–1205) and of the Latin Kingdom of Jerusalem (1197–1205). He gained the latter by his marriage to Isabella, daughter of Amalric I.

Amana Church Society *See* **Amana colonies.**

Amana colonies Seven communal villages on the Iowa River in east Iowa. Founded (1855) by

German Pietists who emigrated (1842) to escape persecution, the Amana colonies were among the most successful communes in the US. In 1932, religious and business functions were divided. This resulted in the formation of the Amana Church Society and a separate cooperative corporation.

Amanullah Khan (Amanollah ˜) 1892–1960. Amir of Afghanistan (1919–29), successor to his father, Habibullah. He won independence from Britain (1919), but his social reforms, including the emancipation of women, led to his overthrow.

Amasis *See* **Ahmose I.**

Amati Italian family of violin makers from Cremona, whose violins date from 1564. The family includes Andrea (c1520–c1578) and Nicolò (1596–1684), who was a teacher of A. Stradivari.

Amaury I *See* **Amalric I.**

Amaury II *See* **Amalric II.**

Amaziah *d.* c780 BC. King of Judah (c798–c780 BC), successor to his father, Jehoash. He conquered Edom but was defeated and imprisoned after attacking King Jehoash of Israel. [2 Kings 14; 2 Chron 25]

Amboina Massacre Execution (Feb., 1623) of a group of English merchants by Dutch authorities on Amboina, an island in eastern Indonesia. The Dutch governor believed the English were conspiring with Japanese mercenaries to attack the Dutch garrison there.

Amboise, Conspiracy of *See* **Conspiracy of Amboise.**

Amboise, Peace of French religious compromise (1563). French Catholics agreed to allow Huguenots (Protestants) limited rights of worship, specifically in the homes of nobility and in certain towns.

Ambrose, Saint AD 339?–397. Roman bishop of Milan (AD 374–392) and noted opponent of Arianism. He persuaded Gratian, Roman emperor of the West, to ban all heresies (379). In dealing with the emperors Valentinian II and Theodosius (whom he excommunicated in 390), he laid the basis for medieval church-state relations. He wrote many hymns and is credited with introducing Eastern choral music to the Western church (Ambrosian chant). The great Ambrosian library at Milan (founded 1609) is named after him.

Ambrosian library *See* **Ambrose, Saint.**

Ameixial, Battle of Portuguese victory (June 8, 1663) over a much larger Spanish force led by John of Austria. The battle, fought in Portugal, was part of Portugal's successful drive for independence from Spain.

Amenemhet I *d.* c1970 BC. King of ancient Egypt (c2000–c1970 BC), founder of the 12th dynasty. During his reign, trade and art flourished in Egypt. His son, Sesostris I, became co-regent in 1980 BC.

Amenemhet III *d.* c1801 BC. An Egyptian king (1849–01 BC), successor to his father, Sesostris II. He constructed massive irrigation and land reclamation projects and promoted trade, bringing the Middle Kingdom period to a peak of influence and prosperity.

Amenhotep I (Amenophis I) *d.* 1526 BC. King of ancient Egypt (c1546–c1526 BC) and successor to his father, Amasis I. He expanded Egyptian territories in Nubia and invaded Libya.

Amenhotep II (Amenophis II) d 1425 BC. King of ancient Egypt (c1450–c1425 BC), successor to his father, Thutmose III. He led successful campaigns in Asia and maintained Egyptian control over Nubia.

Amenhotep III (Amenophis III) *d.* 1379 BC. King of ancient Egypt (c1417–1379 BC), successor to his father, Thutmose IV. He consolidated gains of previous kings and inaugurated a massive building program at Thebes and elsewhere, including colossal statues ("colossi of Memnon") from his now ruined mortuary temple at Thebes, and additions to the temples at Karnak and Luxor.

Amenhotep IV *See* **Ikhnaton.**

Amenophis I *See* **Amenhotep I.**

Amenophis II *See* **Amenhotep II.**

Amenophis III *See* **Amenhotep III.**

America Name for the two continents of the Western Hemisphere, North America and South America, and used more specifically to refer to the US. The term was coined (1507) by the German teacher Martin Waldseemüller in memory of Amerigo Vespucci.

American Anti-Slavery Society Abolitionist organization founded (1833) by W. Garrison. The group grew rapidly in the North during the 1830s. It split (1839) over Garrison's radical policies, including his denunciation of the US Constitution, though local-level groups carried on into the 1850s.

American Bill of Rights *See* **Bill of Rights.**

American Civil Liberties Union (ACLU) American legal-action group. Founded in 1920, the

ACLU has involved itself in controversial law cases over such civil rights as freedom of speech and assembly. Notable cases include the Scopes Trial and *Brown* v. *Board of Education, Topeka, Kansas.*

American Civil War Sectional conflict (1861–65) in the US, fought between the Southern agricultural states, whose plantation economies were dependent upon Negro slave labor, and the industrial North with its strong anti-slavery sentiment. Many complex issues contributed to the outbreak of war, but chief among them were the question of slavery, the authority of the federal government, and states' rights. (For events leading up to the war, *see* United States, 1820–60.) The war took some 600,000 lives and caused great destruction and hardship. But it forced an end to slavery and preserved the Union. Key events in the Civil War include:

1860   A. Lincoln elected president (Nov. 6).

1860   South Carolina seceded from the Union (Dec. 20) as a result of Lincoln's election.

1861   Crittenden Compromise, a final attempt at preserving the Union, failed.

1861   Confederates fired on Union supply ship, attempting to relieve Fort Sumter in Charleston (South Carolina) Harbor (Jan. 9); Union ship withdrew.

1861   Mississippi seceded (Jan. 9), followed by Florida (Jan. 10), Alabama (Jan. 11), Georgia (Jan. 19), Louisiana (Jan. 26), and Texas (Feb. 1).

1861   A congress convened (Feb. 4) by representatives of seceding states, at Montgomery, Alabama, created provisional government of Confederate States of America and elected J. Davis its president.

1861   Confederate president Davis called for 20,000 volunteers for the Confederate army (Apr. 8).

1861   Confederate forces under Gen. P. Beauregard fired on Fort Sumter, forcing its surrender and opening hostilities of the Civil War (Apr. 12–14).

1861   Lincoln made a call for 75,000 Union volunteers (Apr. 15) and ordered a blockade of ports of the seceding states (Apr. 19); maintained throughout the war, the blockade seriously hampered but never completely stopped the flow of goods from overseas.

1861   Virginia seceded from the Union (Apr. 17), followed by Arkansas (May 6), North Carolina (May 20), and Tennessee (June 8).

1861   Confederate forces under generals Beauregard and J. Johnston routed the Union army at First Battle of Bull Run (July 21), in northern Virginia.

1861   Bull Run dashed Union hopes for a speedy victory; new Union strategy included continuing the naval blockade of the South, taking control of the Mississippi River (to split the Confederacy), and capturing Richmond, the Confederate capital.

1861   Confederates captured Springfield, Missouri, after winning the Battle of Wilson's Creek (Aug. 10).

1861   Gen. G. McClellan named (Nov.) commander of the Union army; he formed the Army of the Potomac.

1861   Trent Affair involving British steamer stopped (Nov. 8) by Union naval ship; US came to brink of war with Britain over seizure of Confederate envoys.

1862   Union campaign in the West began with fight to take key states of Kentucky and Tennessee; Union advance into Kentucky began with victory at Battle of Mill Springs (Jan. 19); Gen. U. S. Grant's forces then captured key Confederate defensive positions of Fort Henry and Fort Donelson (Feb. 6–16), Confederates abandoned Nashville and eventually retreated across Tennessee toward Shiloh.

1862   Legal Tender Act passed for issue of $150 million in greenbacks.

1862   Fight to keep Missouri secure for the Union won at Battle of Elkhorn Tavern, Arkansas (Mar. 7–8), as Union forces continued successful advance; upper Mississippi secured by Union victories at New Madrid (Mar. 13) and Island Number 10 (Apr. 8) in Missouri.

1862   Union ironclad *Monitor* fought Confederate ironclad *Merrimac* to a draw at Hampton Roads, Virginia (Mar. 9); engagement proved the value of ironclad warships.

1862   Grant's forces, pursuing the retreating Confederates in southern Tennessee, were badly bloodied but victorious at the Battle of Shiloh (Apr. 6–7); Confederates lost key leader, Gen. A. Johnston, in the battle; Union forces next captured Corinth, northern Mississippi, and forced the Confederates eastward; Memphis, Tennessee, fell to Union armies next (June 6).

1862 In the east, Union's Peninsular Campaign (Apr.–July) to capture the Confederate capital of Richmond, Virginia, proved unsuccessful; Union troops led by Gen. McClellan reached the outskirts of Richmond but were outmaneuvered by Gen. R. E. Lee's Confederate forces: Lee made commander of the Army of Northern Virginia (June); Union forces withdrawn to Washington.

1862 Admiral D. Farragut's Union fleet captured New Orleans (Apr. 28) from the Confederates; this victory capped a series of successful Union naval operations in which strategic points on the Confederate coastline were captured; fall of New Orleans also meant Confederates along Mississippi could be pressured from both north and south.

1862 New Union army advance toward Richmond defeated at Second Battle of Bull Run (Aug. 29–30), Lee advanced into Maryland and threatened Washington, D.C., until suffering a bloody defeat at the Battle of Antietam (Sept. 17); Lee retreated into Virginia and, after delays, Union armies engaged him at the Battle of Fredericksburg (Dec. 13); Union forces were badly defeated and went into winter quarters.

1862–63 Vicksburg Campaign in Mississippi (Nov.–July); led by Gen. Grant, Union forces captured last Confederate positions on the Mississippi River and thus cut the Confederacy in two; the victory (July 4) marked a major turning point in the war.

1862–63 Also, in the west, Union and Confederate forces fought to a draw at Battle of Murfreesboro, Tennessee (Dec. 31, 1862–Jan. 2, 1863).

1863 Lincoln issued the Emancipation Proclamation (Jan. 1).

1863 New Union advance in the east, led by Gen. J. Hooker, halted at Battle of Chancellorsville, Virginia (May 2–4); Confederate Gen. "Stonewall" Jackson fatally wounded; Union troops retreated to Fredericksburg.

1863 Gen. Lee invaded the North, crossing into Pennsylvania (June).

1863 Battle of Gettysburg, Pennsylvania (July 1–3); Union forces under Gen. G. Meade were victorious in what is considered the decisive

battle of the war; Lee forced to withdraw to Virginia.

1863 Draft riots in New York City (July).

1863 In the west, after Grant's victory at Vicksburg (July 4), fighting was centered around Chattanooga, in eastern Tennessee; Union forces took Chattanooga (Sept. 9) but were defeated at the Battle of Chickamauga, Georgia (Sept. 19–20); forced to retreat to Chattanooga, they were besieged by Confederates under Gen. B. Bragg; but Gen. Grant was finally victorious in the Battle of Chattanooga (Nov. 23–25), thus securing Tennessee for the Union and setting the stage for an invasion of Georgia.

1864 Gen. Grant named commander in chief of all Union armies (Mar.); Gen. W. Sherman made commander in the west; Grant was to attack Lee's army in Virginia while Sherman was to attack Gen. J. Johnston and take Atlanta.

1864 Battle of the Wilderness in Virginia (May 5–6) opened Grant's campaign against Lee; defeated by the Confederates, Grant moved southeastward, where he was again repulsed in bloody fighting at Spotsylvania Courthouse (May 8–21); Grant continued south toward Richmond and again suffered heavy losses at the Battles of Cold Harbor (June 1–12).

1864 Atlanta Campaign; led by Gen. W. Sherman, Union forces invaded Georgia (May 7) and marched for Atlanta; despite delaying tactics of Gen. J. Johnston, Sherman forced the Confederates to give up Atlanta (Sept. 2).

1864 Union troops defeated (June 10) by Confederate raiders at the Battle of Brice's Cross Roads in Mississippi.

1864 Petersburg Campaign begun (June 15) by Gen. Grant; after Cold Harbor, Grant attempted to bypass Lee's army and attack Petersburg, which defended the southern approach to Richmond; Lee was barely able to move to defend Petersburg and the battle degenerated into a 10-month siege by Union armies.

1864 Gen. J. Early dispatched (July) by Lee to conduct raids behind Union lines; Early threatened Washington briefly; Union Gen. P. Sheridan was victorious against Early in battles in the Shenandoah Valley, Virginia, including Winchester, Fisher's Hill, and Cedar Creek (Sept. 19–Oct. 19) Early was thereafter forced to withdraw from the strategic Shenandoah Valley.

1864   Admiral D. Farragut defeated Confederate fleet (Aug. 5) at the Battle of Mobile Bay.

1864   Confederates raided Vermont town of St. Albans from Canada (Oct. 19).

1864   President Lincoln reelected (Nov.), partly because of Sherman's capture of Atlanta.

1864–65   Sherman's March to the Sea (Nov. 15–Dec. 21); leading 60,000 Union soldiers, Sherman marched southeast across Georgia, laying waste to all in his path; Savannah was taken (Dec. 21); Sherman then turned north, took Columbia, South Carolina (Feb. 17, 1865) and Goldsboro, North Carolina (Mar. 19, 1865).

1865   Thirteenth Amendment, abolishing slavery in the US, passed by Congress (Feb. 1); ratified (Dec.).

1865   Hampton Roads Peace Conference (Feb. 3), unsuccessful attempt to negotiate an end to the war.

1865   Lee made overall Confederate commander (Feb. 6).

1865   Final phase of the Petersburg Campaign; Gen. P. Sheridan defeated Confederates at Battle of Five Forks (Apr. 1), crippling Confederate position at Petersburg, Virginia.

1865   Grant captured Petersburg, Virginia (Apr. 2), and occupied Richmond (Apr. 3).

1865   Appomattox Courthouse, Virginia (Apr. 9); pursued by Grant, Gen. Lee was finally surrounded and forced to surrender at Appomattox Courthouse, effectively ending the war.

1865   Lincoln assassinated (Apr. 14).

American Colonization Society   An organization founded in the US (Dec., 1816) to transport Negro freedmen to Africa. The society's colonization efforts led to the founding of Liberia. Organized chiefly by Robert Finley (1772–1817), the society established a successful colony (1821) at what was to become Monrovia, Liberia, and subsequently transported several thousand Negro freedmen to Africa. By the 1830s, however, such resettlement plans had become unpopular in the US and the society declined after 1840.

American Expeditionary Force   The collective name for American soldiers who fought in Europe during WW I. Commanded by Gen. J. Pershing, they entered combat Oct., 1917, and left France Aug., 1919.

American Federation of Labor–Congress of Industrial Organizations (AFL-CIO)   Important US labor-union federation formed by the merger of the AFL and the CIO in 1955. The AFL was formed (1886) as a federation of autonomous national and local craft unions. It opposed the socialism and political activism of the Knights of Labor, and under the leadership of S. Gompers significantly improved the lot of US workers. In the 1930s a split developed over the old system of organizing workers by craft (rather than by industry) and, in 1937, ten unions were expelled from the AFL. These unions formed the CIO, which soon became a powerful new federation of industrial unions. G. Meany was named AFL-CIO president (1955) when the two federations merged.

American Fur Company   Fur company incorporated (1808) by J. J. Astor to compete with British chartered companies in the Great Lakes region, Canada, and the American Northwest. The company helped open the Great Lakes region and the West to settlers and became one of the first American trusts.

American Indians   *See* **separate entries under names of Native American tribes and nations.**

American Labor party   Short-lived US political party founded (1936) in New York by labor leaders and liberals. The party generally supported national and local candidates who favored New Deal social legislation, and until the early 1940s it figured in New York politics. The party split (1944) over its Communist element. The anti-Communist faction formed the Liberal party (1944) and effectively broke the party, which disbanded in 1956.

American party   *See* **Know-Nothing party.**

American Revolution   (War of Independence) Military conflict (1775–83) between Britain and its American colonies that resulted in American independence and creation of the United States. The military phase of this great rebellion was the culmination of a gradual split between Britain and the colonies that had been growing for decades over political and economic issues. (For events leading up to the war, *see* United States 1750–75.) The American victory in the war meant the loss of a major element in the British colonial empire, but Britain compensated for it by gaining control of India. The revolution had far-reaching international repercussions as well. A functioning democracy was established and it thus provided some impetus for other revolutionary struggles, notably in France and later in Spanish America. Key events in the war include:

1775   P. Revere's ride (Apr. 18).

1775   Battles of Lexington and Concord (Apr. 19) outside Boston, the opening hostilities of the American Revolution.

1775   Fort Ticonderoga in New York captured (May 10) by E. Allen and B. Arnold.

1775   Second Continental Congress convened (May 10); appointed (June 15) G. Washington commander of Continental Army.

1775   Battle of Bunker Hill near Boston, first major battle of the revolution (June 17); British took position but at great cost; British failed to break Colonials' siege of Boston.

1775   T. Gage resigned as British commander following the Battle of Bunker Hill, succeeded by Gen. W. Howe.

1775   In Canada, American forces captured Montreal (Nov. 12).

1775–76   Quebec Campaign in Canada; Continental forces unable to capture Quebec.

1776   T. Paine published *Common Sense,* calling for American independence.

1776   American Colonials defeated (Feb. 27) Loyalists in the Battle of Moore's Creek Bridge; British occupation of North Carolina thwarted.

1776   G. Washington took Dorchester Heights overlooking Boston (Mar. 16); Colonial siege finally forced British evacuation (Mar. 17) of Boston.

1776   Battle of Charleston, South Carolina (June 28); Colonials repulsed British attackers.

1776   Declaration of Independence proclaimed (July 4) by Congress; colonies now committed to seeking full independence.

1776   British landed on Long Island, New York; won Battle of Long Island (Aug. 27); Washington retreated to Manhattan.

1776   Battle of Harlem Heights (Sept. 16); Colonials successfully delayed advance of Howe's troops up the Hudson.

1776   Washington forced to withdraw following indecisive Battle of White Plains (Oct. 28); retreated across New Jersey into Pennsylvania.

1776–77   Washington launched his surprise raid into New Jersey; crossed Delaware (Dec. 25) and took 918 prisoners in victory at the Battle of Trenton (Dec. 26); routed a British column at the Battle of Princeton (Jan. 3); took up winter quarters at Morristown, New Jersey, forcing British to withdraw to New York.

1777   British plan to cut the colonies in two during 1777; Gen. J. Burgoyne and Lieut. Col. St. Leger to mount two-pronged attack from Canada linking up at Albany, New York, from the east and west.

1777   Gen. Burgoyne's forces, marching south from Montreal, captured Fort Ticonderoga (July 5); continued southward advance.

1777   Gen. Howe meanwhile left New York (July 23) and struck westward to capture Philadelphia, the Colonials' capital.

1777   Americans halted St. Leger's forces at Fort Schuyler in central New York (Aug. 3–23); St. Leger forced to return to Canada without having linked up with Burgoyne.

1777   Raiding party from Burgoyne's column badly defeated (Aug. 16) at the Battle of Bennington, Vermont.

1777   Battle of Brandywine (Sept. 11) near Philadelphia; Gen. Howe defeated Washington's Colonial forces; British captured Philadelphia soon after (Sept. 26).

1777   First Battle of Saratoga fought (Sept. 19); colonials successful in holding lines against Burgoyne's forces at Freeman's Farm.

1777   Battle of Germantown (Oct. 4), unsuccessful attack by Washington on British near Philadelphia.

1777   Second Battle of Saratoga (Oct. 7); American victory at Bemis Heights ended the British attempt to split the colonies in two; Gen. Burgoyne surrendered (Oct. 17); marked a turning point in the war.

1777   Articles of Confederation passed (Nov. 15) by Congress.

1777–78   Washington wintered with troops at Valley Forge under conditions of severe hardship; Gen. F. von Steuben drilled the soldiers into an efficient fighting force.

1778   American victory at Saratoga convinced French to openly support American cause (from Feb. 1778); troops, supplies, and war fleet to be sent.

1778 Carlisle Commission, unsuccessful British peace mission (Apr. 12).

1778 Sir. H. Clinton became British commander in chief; concerned about the arrival of the French, he evacuated Philadelphia (June 18) and marched for New York City.

1778 Gen. Washington attacked Clinton's troops in New Jersey, but the Battle of Monmouth (June 28) was indecisive, Clinton withdrew to New York City.

1778 Wyoming Massacre (July 3), bloody defeat of American settlers by superior British force in Pennsylvania.

1778 Cherry Valley Raid (Nov. 11) in New York by Tories and Indians.

1778 British shifted their offensive to the south; Savannah, Georgia, captured (Dec. 28).

1779 Spain entered war against Britain (June).

1779 Capt. J. P. Jones captured the British ship *Serapis* (Sept. 23).

1780 British Gen. C. Cornwallis launched Carolina campaign, initially successful attempt to gain control of these southern colonies.

1780 Battle of Charleston, South Carolina (May 12), led to British occupation.

1780 Plot by B. Arnold to turn West Point over to the British uncovered (Sept.); Arnold fled to the British side.

1780 Battle of Camden, South Carolina (Aug. 16), one of the worst American defeats of the war, enabled the British to invade North Carolina.

1780 Battle of Kings Mountain, North Carolina (Oct. 7), victory of American over British troops.

1781 Mutinies by Colonial troops in Pennsylvania and New Jersey put down.

1781 Articles of Confederation ratified (Feb.).

1781 British defeated N. Greene's forces (Apr. 25) at the Battle of Hobkirk's Hill, South Carolina.

1781 N. Greene victorious (Sept. 8) at the Battle of Eutaw Springs; British driven back to Charleston, South Carolina.

1781 Yorktown Campaign (Sept. 28–Oct. 19), final campaign of the war; Continental forces aided by a French fleet trapped British forces under Lord C. Cornwallis at Yorktown, Virginia and compelled Cornwallis's surrender; marked virtual end of military conflict in colonies.

1782 British Parliament sanctioned opening of negotiations (Mar. 5), B. Franklin, J. Jay, and J. Adams negotiated for the Americans and won very favorable terms (Nov. 30) in a preliminary treaty (incorporated in the Treaty of Paris).

1783 Treaty of Paris signed (Sept. 3), formally ending war and recognizing US independence.

1783 British troops evacuated (Nov. 25) from New York City.

American Revolution, Daughters of the *See* **Daughters of the American Revolution.**

American System H. Clay proposed this program (1824) for American economic self-sufficiency and internal improvements. It included road and canal construction, high tariffs to protect American industry from foreign imports, and development of American agriculture. The plan, not adopted at the time, nevertheless had broad appeal and became popular with the Whig party.

Ames, Oakes *See* **Crédit Mobilier of America.**

Amherst, Jeffrey Amherst, 1st baron 1717–97. British general. His campaigns against the French in Canada during the last French and Indian War (1758–60) led to the British conquest of Canada and its incorporation into the British Empire.

Amiens, Mise of *See* **Mise of Amiens.**

Amiens, Treaty of Peace treaty (Mar. 27, 1802) ending the War of the Second Coalition and the French Revolutionary Wars. Signed at Amiens, France, by Great Britain and France (and her allies Spain and the Batavian Republic), the treaty restored all conquered territory except Ceylon and Trinidad. The British, suspicious of Napoleon, eventually refused to return Malta. War resumed in 1803.

Amin, al- *See* **Muslim Civil Wars.**

Amin, Idi 1925– . Ugandan general and dictator. The armed forces commander from 1966, he overthrew the government of President Milton Obote (1925–) in 1971. His dictatorship was marked by extreme cruelty, and in 1972 he ordered the expulsion of Asian residents from Uganda. He was overthrown on Apr. 13, 1979.

amir *See* **emir.**

Amistad Affair Controversy (1841) in which African slaves aboard the Spanish slaver *Amistad* mutinied (1839) and sailed to America. J. Q. Adams successfully defended the mutineers before the Supreme Court as freedmen, not pirates, in a case involving salvage of the *Amistad.*

Amman Jordanian capital city, located in north-central Jordan. Occupied since before the 3d millennium BC, it was once the great capital of the biblical Ammonites and was renamed Philadelphia by Egyptian conquerors. The city disappeared entirely in the 14th cent. and was not resettled until the 19th. It became the capital of Transjordan (1921) and capital of Jordan (1946).

Ammianus Marcellinus c330–c395. Greek soldier in Roman service, and historian. Of his 31-volume history of Rome, only volumes covering AD 353–378 survive. Written in the tradition of Tacitus, they are considered a reliable source.

Ampère, André-Marie 1775–1836. French physicist and mathematician known for his work in electromagnetism. Born in Lyons, Ampère was a child prodigy who mastered all existing mathematical knowledge by age 12. He became a physics and chemistry professor at Bourg in 1801. While a professor of mathematics at the École Polytechnic in Paris, he developed a law of electromagnetism (1809), now known as Ampère's law, to describe mathematically the magnetic force between two electric currents. He also developed a mathematical theory explaining existing electromagnetic phenomena. Ampère was the first to develop techniques for measuring electricity, and he built a crude galvanometer. The ampere, a unit of electric current, is named for him.

Amphictyonic League League of city-states in ancient Greece, originally composed of 12 Greek tribes, including Thessalians, Phocians, Dorians, Ionians, Achaeans, and Boetians. The league met twice a year—at the temple of Demeter (near Thermopylae) in the spring and at the temple of Apollo at Delphi in the fall—and discussed matters relating to the cults. The league, which had the power to declare sacred wars, came under the control of more powerful city-states by the 6th cent. BC and thereafter took on a political as well as religious significance. In the 4th cent. BC, Philip II of Macedon used the league's power to declare sacred wars that advanced his conquest of Greece.

Amphissean War *See* **Sacred War (Fourth).**

Amram ben Scheschna (Amram Gaon) *d.* 875. Jewish scholar. Amram wrote the oldest surviving Jewish prayer book, the *Seder Rab Amram.* He was an expert on Judaic laws and customs.

Amritsar, Massacre of *See* **Massacre of Amritsar.**

Amritsar, Treaty of Treaty (Apr. 25, 1809) between the British East India Company and Sikh leader Ranjit Singh. It defined the territories of each in the Punjab region.

Amundsen, Roald 1872–1928. Norwegian explorer, first to reach the South Pole (on Dec. 14, 1911). Amundsen studied medicine before joining the first expedition to spend a winter in Antarctica (1879). Some years later, from 1903–06, he sailed the Northwest Passage. Deciding to try for the South Pole, Amundsen and four others set out from the Antarctic coast by dog sled on Oct. 19, 1911, and despite the harsh Antarctic weather and hazardous terrain, became the first men to reach the South Pole (Dec. 14). Amundsen's party arrived just ahead of the ill-fated rival expedition led by Englishman R. F. Scott. Amundsen's 1918 Arctic expedition ended in failure, but determined to reach the North Pole, he, L. Ellsworth, and Italian aeronautical engineer Umberto Nobile (1885–1978) passed directly over it in a dirigible in 1926. Amundsen died in 1928 trying to rescue Nobile, whose dirigible had crashed near Spitsbergen.

Anabaptists Christian sects that arose in Europe during the 16th-cent. Protestant Reformation. Anabaptists generally rejected infant baptism in favor of adult baptism, favored separation of the church and state, and opposed the use of force. The movement is said to have begun (c1520) in Zurich, Switzerland, and, despite persecutions by both Catholics and Protestants, spread rapidly. A sect in Moravia gave rise to the Hutterites, and a sect in the Netherlands became Mennonites.

anarchism Theory that advocates complete individual freedom, especially from control by government or other outside authority. Based on the belief that such restrictions corrupt mankind, philosophic anarchism, advanced (19th cent.) by P. Proudhon, seeks nonviolent evolution toward an anarchistic society. Extreme anarchists, beginning with the Russian revolutionary M. Bakunin, have favored terrorism to advance their cause. This violent aspect became commonly associated with anarchism after a series of violent acts (such as the Haymarket Square riot, 1886) and political assassinations, including those of French president M. Carnot (1894), Italian king Humbert I (1900), US president W. McKinley (1901), and Greek king George (1913).

Anastasius I AD c430–518. Byzantine emperor (AD 491–518), successor to Zeno. He drove the Isaurians from Constantinople, built a wall for defense against the Slavs and Bulgars, and instituted tax and social reforms. His adherence to Monophysitism was opposed by Rome.

Anatolia *See* **Asia Minor.**

Anaxagoras c500–428 BC. Greek philosopher who taught in Athens. Among his students were Pericles and, it is believed, Socrates. He was banished for his teachings on the physical nature of the universe.

Anaximander c611–c547 BC. Greek philosopher whose teachings are said to prefigure the development of astronomy and the theory of evolution. One of the earliest Western philosophers, he attempted to provide a systematic explanation of the nature of the universe and all things in it.

Anaximenes *fl.* 6th cent. BC. Greek philosopher. He held that air was the primary substance of the universe and that all matter was composed of air but differed in density. He is considered, with Thales and Anaximander, to be one of the first Western philosophers.

ancien régime Term for the political and social order in France up to the outbreak of the French Revolution, in 1789.

ancient Germans Germanic (or Teutonic) people of uncertain origins who were located in the region encompassing southern Sweden, Denmark, and part of northern Germany at the time of the decline of the Celtic civilization in Europe (1st cent. BC). In subsequent migrations, Germanic peoples spread through Northern, Central, and Western Europe. The Goths settled in southern France and environs (5th cent. AD), the Angles and Saxons in England (5th cent. AD), the Vandals in Spain and North Africa (5th cent.), and the Franks in northern France (5th cent.). The first contact between Germanic tribes and the Romans dates from the 2d cent. BC, and the victory by the Cimbri and Teutones at Arausio (105 BC) notwithstanding, the Roman armies in c102 BC wiped out the two tribes. Thereafter, the various Germanic tribes gained in strength and, by their relentless attacks during the 3d to 4th cents. AD, figured in the fall of the Roman Empire.

Ancients and Moderns, Quarrel of *See* **Perrault, Charles.**

Ancon, Treaty of Treaty (Oct. 20, 1883) between Peru and Chile ending the War of the Pacific. Peru ceded to Chile the provinces of Tarapaca, Tacna, and Arica.

Andalusia Historic region in southern Spain. Originally the kingdom of Tartessus (2d millennium BC), it was conquered by the Phoenicians (480 BC), who had established the colony of Gadir (modern Cádiz) there (c1100 BC). Following Roman conquest (3d cent. BC), it flourished as a cultural center. Under the Moors (AD 711–1492) Andalusia was divided into the kingdoms of Córdoba, Seville, Jaén, and Granada and became a great Muslim center of commerce and culture. Christian kings of Spain completed conquest of the region in 1492.

Andersen, Hans Christian 1805–75. Danish writer, world famous for his fairy tales. Born in poverty, Andersen attended the University of Copenhagen (1828), where he wrote his first successful fantasy tale. He turned next to playwriting, then to novels, before beginning to write the fairy tales for which he famous. His collections of tales included such stories as *The Snow Queen* and *The Little Match Girl.* He is considered Denmark's leading author and storyteller.

Anderson, Carl David 1905– . American physicist noted for discovery (1932) of the positron. He also helped to discover the meson. He was awarded the Nobel Prize in Physics in 1936.

Anderson, Elizabeth Garrett 1836–1917. English physician. Barred from medical schools, she trained with private physicians and was licensed to practice in 1865. She helped open the medical profession to women.

Anderson, Marion 1902–93. American opera contralto and advocate of racial equality. Born in Philadelphia, she became the first black to sing in the White House (for the Roosevelts, 1936) and to sing with the Metropolitan Opera Company (1955). In 1958, she served as an alternate in the US delegation to the UN.

Anderson, Maxwell 1888–1959. An American dramatist best known for his tragedies in verse. Much of his work deals with modern moral and social questions. His dramatic works include *What Price Glory?, Winterset,* and *Barefoot in Athens.* He won the Pulitzer Prize for Drama in 1933.

Anderson, Sherwood 1876–1941. An American writer best known for *Winesburg, Ohio,* a novel dealing with the inhabitants of a small Ohio town.

Andorra Tiny principality (*pop.* 51,000) located in the Pyrenees Mountains, between France and

Spain. The capital is Andorra and the language is Catalan. The principality's origins can be traced back to Carolingian times. Emperor Charles II is said to have granted overlordship (9th cent.) of Andorra to the Spanish bishop of Urgel, a claim contested by French nobles until the present arrangement of joint suzerainty was agreed to in 1278. French king Henry IV inherited French rights to Andorra, which subsequently passed to French presidents. Efforts to modernize Andorran government during the 1980s resulted in enactment of an income tax (1983) and the adoption of a parliamentary government (1993), ending a 715-year-old feudal system of rule.

Andrada e Silva, José Bonifácio de (José Bonifácio) 1763?–1838. Brazilian statesman considered to be the father of Brazilian independence. He supported independence from Portugal and establishment (1822) of a Brazilian monarchy under Pedro I. He served (1822–23) as prime minister.

Andrássy, Count Gyula (Julius) 1823–90. Hungarian statesman and a principal figure in formation of the Dual Monarchy (1867). A leader of the abortive Hungarian revolt against Austria (1848–49), he eventually sought the compromise of the Dual Monarchy and became Hungary's first prime minister (1867–71). Later, as foreign minister of Austria-Hungary (1871–79), he was responsible for the unpopular occupation of Bosnia and Herzegovina (1878) and arranged the Dual Alliance (1879) between Germany and Austria-Hungary. In the latter, he wrested important concessions from Bismarck.

André, John 1751–80. British army officer during the American Revolution. He conspired with B. Arnold to arrange the surrender of West Point to the British. Captured (1780) before the plan could be accomplished, he was hanged as a spy.

Andrew, Saint One of the twelve apostles, brother of Saint Peter. He is said to have been martyred on an X-shaped cross. He is patron saint of Russia and Scotland.

Andrew II *d.* 1235. King of Hungary (1205–35), and son of Béla III. During his reign, he was forced by rebellious nobles to issue the Golden Bull (1222), considered the Hungarian Magna Carta.

Andrews's Raid (Great Locomotive Chase) Raid (Apr. 12, 1862) during the American Civil War (1861–65). Nineteen Union soldiers, led by civilian James Andrews (*d.* 1862), attempted to knock out the railway between Chattanooga, Tennessee, and Atlanta, Georgia. They stole a locomotive in Georgia but were caught by the Confederates after a ninety-mile chase.

Andreyev, Leonid Nikolayevich 1871–1919. A Russian writer. His enormous early popularity declined as his work turned from realism to the metaphysical and symbolic. His works include *The Red Laugh* and *The Seven Who Were Hanged.*

Andropov, Yury Vladimirich 1914–84. Leader of the former Soviet KGB security agency and leader of the former USSR (1982–84). As a youth, Andropov worked in various jobs before completing his university education. He joined the Communist party in 1939 and began to gain notice after joining the party secretariat staff in Moscow (1951). Andropov helped coordinate the invasion of Hungary (1956), which broke the Hungarian Revolution (*q.v.*), and from 1967–82 served as KGB head, where he gained a reputation for repressing dissidents. When the ailing Soviet leader L. Brezhnev died in Nov. 1982, the aging Andropov was chosen as his successor. Within eight months, however, Andropov also became ill and died (Feb. 1984).

Andrusov, Treaty of (Andrussovo, ˜) Treaty (Jan. 20, 1667) concluded between Russia and Poland, ending the Thirteen Years' War (1654–67). The treaty settled the basic issue of control of the Ukraine and, by its terms, Russia won the province of Smolensk and the eastern Ukraine, including Kiev.

Andrussovo, Treaty of *See* **Andrusov, Treaty of.**

Angelico, Fra (Pietro, Guido di) c1400–55. Florentine painter whose works are noted for their religious themes. He joined the Dominican order (c1420–25), and was called Angelico ("the angelic") after his death.

Angelus Byzantine family. This family produced the Byzantine emperors Isaac II Angelus, Alexius III Angelus, Alexius IV Angelus, and their descendant Michael VIII Palaeologus.

Angevin 1. Another name for the Plantagenet kings of England (1154–1399), the first three of whom were also counts of Anjou (thus Angevin). Ties between the French and English lines began with the marriage (1129) of Geoffry IV, count of Anjou, and Matilda, daughter of English king Henry I. Their son became Henry II, king of England and count of Anjou. With this dual title, Kings Henry II, Richard I, and John successfully ruled England and large domains on the

Continent as well. These domains, including Brittany, Normandy, Anjou, Aquitaine, Maine, and Touraine, were almost entirely lost to the French by the end of King John's reign (1216). 2. Name for rulers who were descendants of the French House of Anjou in several collateral lines. They ruled variously over Hungary, Poland, Naples, and parts of France (13th–15th cents.).

Angkor Thom Ancient capital of the Khmer Empire in northwest Cambodia. Constructed (c1200) after the sacking of nearby Angkor Wat, it was the Khmer capital until 1434, when Phnom Penh became the capital.

Angkor Wat Ancient capital of the Khmer Empire in northwest Cambodia, built (12th cent.) by Khmer king Suryavarman II (*d.* c1150). It was sacked and ruined (c1177) and a new capital, Angkor Thom, was established nearby. Its ruins are considered an architectural treasure.

Anglican church *See* **Church of England.**

Anglican Communion A worldwide union of churches that subscribe to the beliefs and liturgy of the Church of England, as defined in the Book of Common Prayer.

Anglo-Afghan Wars (Afghan ˜) 1. First ˜ War (1838–42) in which the British invaded Afghanistan from India, deposed the Afghan ruler Dost Muhammad and installed their own puppet. A rebellion against the British broke out (1841), forced their retreat from Kabul, and ended in a massacre of British troops (1842). Dost Muhammad was restored (1842). 2. Second ˜ War (1878–80) between Britain and Afghanistan. Concerned about Russia's increasing influence in Afghanistan, the British again invaded from India and forced the Afghan ruler to accept the Treaty of Gandamak (1879). A rebellion against the British broke out (Sept. 3, 1879). A new emir quelled the rebellion and, though he did not challenge the 1879 treaty, he continued to counter British influence by befriending Russia. 3. Third ˜ War (May 10–Aug. 8, 1919) in which the Afghans attempted to invade British India. Hoping to end British influence in Afghanistan, Afghan emir Amanullah launched a religious war. His plan to provoke Muslims in India to an uprising against the British failed, and his forces were soon forced out of India. Amanullah succeeded, however, in negotiating the Treaty of Rawalpindi (Aug. 8), by which the British recognized Afghan independence.

Anglo-American Conference *See* **Trident Conference.**

Anglo-Burmese Wars *See* **Burma Wars.**

Anglo-Dutch Wars *See* **Dutch Wars.**

Anglo-Egyptian Condominium Name for the government of eastern Sudan (1899–1956). Britain and Egypt jointly ruled there: Egypt nominated its governor, who was then approved by the British. Egyptian control was only nominal after 1924.

Anglo-Egyptian Sudan *See* **Sudan.**

Anglo-Egyptian Treaty Treaty (Aug. 26, 1936) whereby Britain granted Egypt conditional independence. The agreement created a military alliance between Egypt and Britain and provided for a withdrawal of British troops, except those needed to protect the Suez Canal.

Anglo-Russian Convention Pact (Aug. 31, 1907) between Britain and Russia settling their claims to Tibet, Afghanistan, and Persia. Both nations feared growing German power, and this agreement became a basis for their alliance in WW I.

Anglo-Saxons Germanic peoples that ruled England from 5th cent. AD, following the decline of Rome, to 1066, the time of the Norman conquest. Both the Angles and Saxons were originally located in the region around Schleswig (in north Germany and Denmark). Both arrived in the British Isles late in the 5th cent. and established small kingdoms there. "Anglo-Saxon" has also been used as a general term for the English since the time of the Norman conquest. *See also* Anglo-Saxon Heptarchy.

Anglo-Saxon Heptarchy The seven Anglo-Saxon kingdoms (5th–9th cents.) that arose in England after the Teutonic invasions. Their domains included all of south England (except parts of Wales) by the 8th cent. They were conquered by the Danes (9th cent.). The seven were Essex, Wessex, Sussex, Kent, East Anglia, Mercia, and Northumbria.

Anglo-Soviet Agreement Treaty (May 26, 1942) between Britain and the USSR, a twenty-year agreement uniting the two nations against Nazi Germany and its allies.

Angola (People's Republic of Angola) Angola is an independent state (*pop.* 8,802,000) located in coastal southwest Africa. Its capital is Luanda. Long a Portuguese colony, Angola was once a major source of slaves used in Portuguese Brazil. Significant development of the colony began after WW II and Angola was the last of Portugal's African possessions to win independence (1975). Subsequently a Soviet-backed faction gained control of the country, though guerrilla resistance continued until a peace settlement in 1991 promised the restoration of democratic government. Key dates in the history of Angola include:

1482 Northern coast discovered by Portuguese navigator Diogo Cão.

1575 Permanent colony established by Portuguese at Luanda; region became a prime source of slaves for Portugal's colonies in Brazil.

1641–48 Dutch briefly controlled Angola.

1885 Borders of Portugal's colony established by Treaty of Berlin.

1902 Portugal gained control of the interior by conquering the native Mbundu kingdom.

1951 Angola made a Portuguese overseas province; industrial development and immigration encouraged.

1956 Angolan nationalist group Movimento Popular de Libertação den Angola (MPLA) formed.

1961 Angolan nationalist resistance to colonial government began; various groups engaged in guerrilla warfare and established competing governments in exile.

1962 Nationalist group Frente Nacional de Libertação den Angola (FNLA) organized.

1966 Nationalist group União Nacional para a Independéncia Total de Angola (UNITA) established.

1972 Angola made an autonomous state under Portuguese supervision; guerrilla resistance continued.

1973 Legislative elections for new government held.

1974 New government in Portugal ceased fighting against rebels in Angola; ordered Angolan independence.

1975 Angolan independence declared (Nov. 11); struggle for control of country between dominant MPLA (backed by USSR and Cuba), UNITA (backed by South Africa), and FNLA (backed by US and Zaire).

1975–79 MPLA leader Agostino Neto in office as president of MPLA; proclaimed People's Republic of Angola after Soviet-backed MPLA gained control (with help of Cuban troops, from Oct. 1975); resistance by rival

groups continued, however; Marxist people's republic established.

1976 US military aid to rebel forces in Angola ended.

1977 Failed coup attempt (May); purge of government and MPLA party officials followed; MPLA reorganized as political party, the MPLA-PT.

1977–78 Refugees from Zaire launched invasions from Angola; Soviet-backed regime denied involvement.

1979– MPLA-PT leader José Eduardo dos Santos in office as president, following death of Neto; maintained close ties with USSR.

1980 Legislative assembly established following elections.

1982 MPLA-PT government signed economic cooperation agreement with USSR.

1982 Diplomatic contacts with Western powers (Portugal and US) reported.

1984 FNLA rebels ceased armed resistance; South African-backed UNITA continued determined guerrilla campaign, however; South African troops meanwhile had regularly launched attacks in Angola, claiming to be in pursuit of the Namibian rebel group SWAPO.

1984 South Africa withdrew most of troops occupying Angolan border area; Angola agreed to try to keep SWAPO and Cuban troops out of area; military activity temporarily ended there.

1985 US Congress reversed 1976 Clark amendment (July), banning military aid to UNITA; aid started in 1986.

1987 South African troops again reported inside Angola; South African aid to UNITA publicly confirmed; UN subsequently demanded South Africa's withdrawal from Angola.

1987 Angola applied for IMF membership.

1988 Multi-national, US-brokered peace negotiations begun among Angola, Cuba, and South Africa (May), in attempt to resolve fighting in Angola and Namibia.

1988 Cease-fire in Angola (Aug.); remaining South African troops withdrew from Angolan border areas.

1988 Peace agreements signed in New York (Dec. 22) by Angola, Cuba, and South Africa to end hostilities; the 50,000 Cuban troops to be withdrawn from Angola; Namibia to become independent; South Africa to end aid to UNITA.

1988–91 Ongoing, international efforts at reaching peace settlement between MPLA-PT government and UNITA rebels; UNITA insisted on major reforms, including multi-party political system.

1990 MPLA-PT agreed to major reforms (Oct.), including creation of democratic socialist government (ending Marxist state), multi-party system, and introduction of market economy.

1990 Peace talks between Angolan government and UNITA began in Lisbon, Portugal (Apr.).

1991 MPLA-PT government permitted forming of political parties (Mar.).

1991 Last Cuban troops left Angola (May).

1991 Government and UNITA signed peace agreement at Lisbon, Portugal (May 31).

1991 General amnesty law enacted (May 31).

1992 Democratic elections held; coalition government installed.

Angoulême, Louis Antoine de Bourbon, duke of 1775–1844. Last dauphin of France and eldest son of King Charles X. He failed to stop Napoleon on his return from Elba (1814) and led the French invasion of Spain (1823). He went into exile (1830) after his father was forced to abdicate.

Ångström, Anders Jonas 1814–74. A Swedish physicist noted for his work in spectrum analysis. The angstrom unit, used to measure the wavelength of light, is named after him.

animatism *See* **animism.**

animism Belief that spirits dwell within all things, living and nonliving. Common as a central concept among primitive religions, animism postulates the existence of an individual spirit within each object. This is distinct from *animatism* in what are regarded as earlier, more primitive religions. This form of belief holds that all things share an undifferentiated spiritual power.

Anjala League Conspiracy (1788–89) by Scandinavian nobles and army officers against Swedish king Gustavus III. Opposed to the Russo-Swedish War (1788–90), the conspirators attempted to settle the war themselves by communicating directly with the Russians. The offer was refused, the conspirators were discovered, and most were imprisoned.

Anjou Historic region and former province located in western France. Made a countship (9th cent.) by Charlemagne, it was prominent (10th–12th cents.) as the seat of the Angevin family (*q.v.*). Anjou became a hereditary domain of English Angevin kings (1154–1204), until it was taken by the French king Philip II and made part of French domains.

Anjou, Margaret of *See* **Margaret of Anjou.**

Ankara, Battle of Mongol victory (July, 1402) at Ankara, Turkey, over the forces of Ottoman sultan Bajazet I. Tamerlane led the Mongols in this battle, in which Bajazet was captured.

Anna Comnena 1083–1148? Byzantine princess, daughter of Alexius I. Frustrated in her attempts to obtain the imperial crown, she turned to the writing of the *Alexiad,* a classic on the life of her father.

Anna Ivanovna 1693–1740. Empress of Russia (1730–40), daughter of Ivan V, and successor to her cousin Peter II. Made empress by the supreme privy council, she ruled as an autocrat, and her reign was marked by repression and terror. She relied largely upon Ernst Johann Biron (1690–1772) to rule the country. The War of the Polish Succession and the Russo-Turkish War (1736–39) took place during her reign.

Annam Name sometimes applied to region in central Vietnam. The name was originally used by the T'ang dynasty Chinese after they combined occupied provinces in Vietnam to form the protectorate of Annam (meaning "pacified south"). In the 10th century AD, Tonkin ruler Dinh Bo Linh gained control over the petty kingdoms within Chinese Annam and thereafter won recognition of Vietnamese independence from China. The name Annam was dropped by the Vietnamese. The Chinese briefly regained control of the area (now north and central Vietnam) in 1407, only to be driven out by Le Loi in 1428. Le Loi founded the Le dynasty, which ruled over a unified state until the 1500s. The Champa kingdom to the south was added to these domains in 1471, following protracted warfare. The Le dynasty fell in 1542 and after a decade of unrest, the territory was effectively split into two kingdoms—the north was ruled by the Trinh from Tonkin (modern Hanoi) and the south by the Nguyen from Hue. The Nguyen expanded their domains southward into parts of modern-day Cambodia in the 1700s. Revolts toppled both ruling dynasties in the 18th cent. (Nguyen, 1778; Trinh, 1786). In 1787 Nguyen-Anh (from Hue) gave the French control of Da Nang and certain islands in return for military aid. Nguyen-Anh reunited Vietnam with French help in 1802 and ruled as emperor of Vietnam until his death in 1820. The French later used abuses of French nationals and Christian converts as a pretext for invading and conquering Cochin China, the southern part of Vietnam, between 1858 and 1862. A Frenco-Spanish military expedition to the north in 1873 and a buildup of French troops in northern Vietnam (by 1882) led to the Sino-French War (1883–85) with China, which also laid claims to Vietnam. Both central Vietnam and northern Vietnam (Tonkin to the French) became French protectorates by 1884 (the Chinese later relinquishing their claims), as the French expanded their control over Indochina. In 1887 the protectorates became part of the French Union of Indochina.

Annapolis Convention   US convention (Sept. 11, 1786) at Annapolis, Maryland, attended by delegates from Delaware, New Jersey, New York, Pennsylvania, and Virginia. Called to discuss commercial difficulties created by the Articles of Confederation, the convention led to the Constitutional Convention (1787), which drafted the US Constitution.

Anne 1665–1714.   English queen (1702–07) and queen of Great Britain and Ireland (1707–14), successor to William III. The last Stuart monarch and the daughter of James II, she acquiesced in the overthrow of her father in the Glorious Revolution. Throughout her reign, which saw intense rivalry between Tories and Whigs, she was influenced by Sarah Jennings (1660–1774), duchess of Marlborough, and (after 1710) by A. Masham. During her reign, Great Britain was formed by the Act of Union with Scotland (1707), the succession of the Hanoverian kings was ensured by the Act of Settlement (1701), and England became embroiled in the War of the Spanish Succession (1701–14)

Anne, Saint *fl.* 1st cent. BC.   Wife of Saint Joachim and mother of the Virgin Mary. She is the patron saint of Brittany and of Quebec, Canada, and of women in labor.

Anne of Austria 1601–66.   French queen, wife of King Louis XIII (*m.* 1615), and daughter of Spanish king Philip III. On her husband's death (1643), she became regent (1643–61) for her son, Louis XIV, with Cardinal Mazarin as minister. Her regency was marked by rebellions of the Fronde (*q.v.*).

Anne of Brittany 1477–1514.   Duchess of Brittany and queen consort to French kings Charles VIII (1491–98) and Louis XII (1499–1514). As sole heir to Brittany (1488), she tried desperately to guarantee its independence from France but was forced to marry first Charles, then Louis. During her lifetime she did maintain Brittany's independence, but her daughter's marriage to Francis I finally resulted in its annexation by France (1532).

Anne of Cleves 1515–57.   Fourth queen consort of Henry VIII of England. Henry married her in Jan., 1540, to form an alliance with the Protestant Schmalkaldic League to forestall an attack on England by Catholic powers. The attack failed to materialize, and the marriage was dissolved in July, 1540.

annexation   Act by which a nation or state declares sovereignty over territory formerly outside its borders. Usually accompanied by military conquest or threat of it, annexation is distinct from cession, in which a state acquires territory by treaty or purchase.

Anouilh, Jean 1910–87.   French playwright. Anouilh's internationally popular plays include *Antigone* (1944), *Waltz of the Toreadors* (1952), *Becket* (1959), and *The Lark* (1953).

Anschluss   German term, meaning connection or union. It was used especially to describe the incorporation of Austria into the German Reich on Mar. 11, 1938, a union that had been sought often by German nationalists after WW I.

Anselm, Saint c1033–1109.   Archbishop of Canterbury, Doctor of the Church, and founder of scholasticism (*q.v.*). He advanced a theory of the atonement of Christ and originated the ontological proof of God's existence.

Antarctica   The fifth-largest continent, located almost entirely within the Antarctic Circle. Antarctica was not discovered until modern times. The British captain J. Cook was the first to sail within the Antarctic Circle (1772–75). American, British, and Russian expeditions all claim the first actual sighting (1820) of Antarctica. In subsequent years of the 19th cent., the coastal regions of the continent were explored by many, including the Scotsman J. Ross (1839–43). The Norwegian R. Amundsen reached the South Pole first (Dec. 14, 1911), followed a month later by British R. Scott (Jan. 17, 1912), whose party perished returning. The American admiral R. Byrd conducted important investigations in the 1930s. During the International Geophysical Year (1957–58), scientists from 56 nations exhaustively studied the continent. Twelve nations established stations there, and, in 1959, signed the Antarctic Treaty (*q.v.*).

Antarctic Treaty International agreement (1959) by which twelve nations designated Antarctica an independent, demilitarized, scientific research zone. The US and the USSR were among the signatories of the 30-year treaty. A new international treaty was signed after protracted negotiations during the 1980s.

antebellum period In general, a term used to refer to the period prior to a war. It is often used in connection with the social and political institutions of the US that existed before the American Civil War (1861–65).

Anthony, Marc *See* **Antony.**

Anthony, Saint (Anthony the Great, Saint) AD 251?–c350. Egyptian hermit and monk, also known as Saint Anthony of Egypt. Traditionally the first Christian monk, he organized an eremitic monastic community in Egypt that became a model for later monastic societies in the East. He is regarded as the father of Christian monasticism.

Anthony, Susan Brownell 1820–1906. American reformer and woman-suffrage-movement leader. A pioneering figure in the feminist movement (from c1854), she led the struggle to secure voting rights for women, finally granted by the 19th Amendment (1920).

Anthony of Egypt, Saint *See* **Anthony, Saint.**

Anthony of Padua, Saint 1195–1231. Portuguese monk and noted follower of the Franciscan order. He preached with great ability in France and Italy. He is the patron saint of Portugal and his name is invoked by Roman Catholics to find lost objects.

Anthony the Great, Saint *See* **Anthony, Saint.**

Anti-Comintern Pact Agreement (Nov. 25, 1936) by which Germany and Japan vowed to oppose the Communist International. They were later joined by Italy, Spain, and others.

Anti-Corn-Law League An organization formed (1839) in England to repeal the Corn Laws, grain import duties that kept the price of bread high. Under the leadership of R. Cobden and others, the league organized support among farmers and workers and eventually won Prime Minister R. Peel to their cause. Parliament repealed the Corn Laws in 1846.

Antietam, Battle of (Sharpsburg, ˜) Bloody victory (Sept. 17, 1862) for Union forces during the American Civil War (1861–65). The battle turned back a Confederate invasion of the North that threatened Washington, D.C. The Confederates, numbering 65,000 soldiers under Gen. R.E. Lee, crossed the Potomac into Maryland shortly after the Second Battle of Bull Run. They were defeated (Sept. 17) at Antietam Creek (near Sharpsburg) by 85,000 Union soldiers under Gen. G. McClellan, following preliminary engagements (Sept. 14–15). Union casualties numbered about 12,000, while Confederate losses ranged variously from 9,000–14,000.

Antifederalists In US history, name for those opposing adoption of the Constitution (1787–88). Antifederalists, as they were called by the Federalists (supporters of the Constitution), opposed the strong central government proposed by the newly drafted Constitution. Instead, they sought a stronger role for states and more extensive checks on central government powers in order to preserve democracy. Antifederalists, led by P. Henry, G. Clinton, G. Mason, and others, commanded a majority in at least six of the original thirteen states, but ultimately proved unable to prevent ratification of the Constitution by the required nine states. In fact only North Carolina and Rhode Island actually opposed ratification. Among the factors contributing to their defeat were: momentum in favor of ratification (eight states ratified before Antifederalists began organized opposition); promises for amendments to protect individual liberties (what became the Bill of Rights); the prestige and political skill of Federalists (among them G. Washington); and widespread support of the Constitution in the press. Antifederalists did not continue as a political group (nor did antifederalism remain a coherent philosophy) after ratification of the Constitution. However, in the 1790s Federalists sometimes used the term Antifederalist during attacks on Jeffersonian Republicans (*q.v.*).

Antigonids A dynasty that ruled ancient Macedonia and parts of Greece from 276 to 168 BC. It was established by Antigonus II, a grandson of Alexander the Great's general, Antigonus I. The dynasty prevailed until clashes with Rome resulted in defeat of the last of the dynasty, Perseus, at Pydna (168 BC).

Antigonus I (Antigonus Cyclops) 382?–301 BC. Macedonian general under Alexander the Great, founder of the Antigonids, and important figure in the Wars of the Diadochi (*q.v.*). He was made governor of Phrygia in 333 BC and, after Alexander's death, expanded his domains throughout Asia Minor, Syria, and Mesopotamia. He pronounced himself king (306), and was killed at the Battle of Ipsus (301).

Antigonus II (Antigonus Gonatas) 319?–239 BC. Macedonian king (276–239 BC), grandson of Antigonus I. He seized control of Macedonia (276), withstood attacks by Pyrrhus and Ptolemy II, won the Chremonidean War (266–262), and briefly united mainland Greek territories under Macedonian control.

Antigonus III (Antigonus Doson) *d.* 221 BC. King of Macedonia (227–221 BC). He was regent for Philip V, son of Demetrius II, and in 227 declared himself king. Siding with the Achaean League, he defeated Spartan king Cleomenes III at Sellasia (222). He formed a Hellenic League (224) to further Macedonian hegemony in Greece.

Antigonus Cyclops   *See* **Antigonus I.**

Antigonus Doson   *See* **Antigonus III.**

Antigonus Gonatas   *See* **Antigonus II.**

Anti-Masonic party   First American third party, formed (1826) to oppose election of Freemasons to public office. The disappearance and presumed murder of a writer who was planning to reveal secrets of the fraternal order of Freemasons caused a major scandal. The Freemasons' refusal to cooperate in the investigation resulted in the founding of the Anti-Masonic party in New York, and, in 1832, the party won many congressional seats. By 1834, however, Anti-Masons had been absorbed into the new Whig party. The Anti-Mason national nominating convention at Baltimore (1831) was the first ever held and became the model for such political conventions in America.

Antinoüs   AD c 110–130.   Favorite of Emperor Hadrian and his constant companion. After Antinoüs drowned in the Nile, Hadrian founded the city of Antinoöpolis and built many temples in his honor.

antinomianism   Doctrine that some Christians, by virtue of their special faith, do not have to obey the moral laws of the Old Testament. The Antinomian controversy first appeared during the 16th-cent. Protestant Reformation as a doctrinal dispute involving one of M. Luther's fellow reformers, J. Agricola. Opposed by Luther, Agricola recanted by 1540. Subsequently, some radical Anabaptists and several sects in 17th–18th-cent. England were accused of antinomianism.

Antioch   Historic city in what is now southeast Turkey. Founded by the Syrians (c300 BC), the city was located on important trade routes. It was conquered by the Romans (64 BC), and under them became a cultural center. The city became one of the three original patriarchates and was important in the early history of the Christian church. From the 6th cent. to the 16th, the city was conquered by various powers and figured in the Crusades. When it fell to the Ottoman Turks (1516), it was of little importance. It was made part of Syria in 1920 and was restored to Turkey in 1939.

Antioch, principality of   *See* **Principality of Antioch.**

Antioch, Saint Ignatius of   *See* **Ignatius of Antioch, Saint.**

Antiochus I (~ Soter) c324–c261 BC.   Seleucid king of Syria (280–c261 BC), successor to his father, Seleucus I. His reign was troubled by internal strife, attacks by the Gauls, and the first Syrian War (*q.v.*), in which he lost Phoenicia and other territories. He is noted as a great builder of cities.

Antiochus II c287–247 BC.   Seleucid king of Syria (c261–247 BC), successor to his father, Antiochus I. He waged the second Syrian War (*q.v.*), a continuation of wars against Egypt that began under his father's reign. He secured peace and recovered much lost Syrian territory, however, by marrying Berenice, daughter of his enemy, Ptolemy II.

Antiochus III (~ the Great) 242–187 BC.   Seleucid king of Syria 1223–187 BC), successor to his brother Seleucus III. He waged the fourth Syrian War (*q.v.*), extended the Seleucid Empire eastward into India, but was defeated in a struggle with Rome. After invading Greece, he was defeated by the Romans at Thermopylae (191) and Magnesia (190) and thus lost all territories west of Mount Taurus.

Antiochus IV (~ Epiphanes) *d.* 163 BC.   Seleucid king of Syria (175–163 BC), successor to his brother Seleucus IV. He conquered most of Egypt (169–168) but was forced to withdraw by Rome. His efforts to introduce Greek institutions and religion in Judaea led to the revolt of the Maccabees (*q.v.*).

Antiochus Epiphanes *See* **Antiochus IV.**

Antiochus Soter *See* **Antiochus I.**

Antiochus the Great *See* **Antiochus III.**

Antipater *d.* 319 BC. Macedonian general who served as regent in Macedonia (334–323 BC) during the Asian campaign of Alexander the Great. As regent after Alexander's death, he defeated rebellious Greek city-states in the Lamian War (*q.v.*). He maintained the last vestiges of central authority in the Macedonian Empire until his death, which was followed by the Wars of the Diadochi.

antipope Pope of the Roman Catholic church elected in opposition to the legitimate pope. Antipopes were elected for a variety of reasons, including doctrinal disputes, power struggles between the church and secular rulers, and historic divisions within the church (i.e., Babylonian Captivity, Great Schism). Antipopes were elected as early as AD c217 (Hippolytus) and the last was elected 1439 (Felix V).

Antirent War (Helderberg ~) US rebellion (1839–46) by tenant farmers in upper New York State against a system of perpetual leases (the patroon system). The revolt was provoked by the Van Rensselaer family's attempt to collect $400,000 in back rent and finally resulted in an end to the patroon system.

Anti-Saloon League American temperence organization founded (1893) at Oberlin, Ohio, and established as a national organization in 1895. It sought legislative prohibition of the sale of liquor and became a major factor in the passage of the 18th Amendment.

anti-Semitism Historically persistent prejudice (or open hostility) toward Jews. This prejudice at first stemmed from religious differences between Jews and Christians, but from the late 19th cent. it was largely based on supposed racial differences. Anti-Semitism in this form became the basis for A. Hitler's systematic extermination (1939–45) of six million Jews during WW II. Arab hatred of the Israelis has brought hatred of the Jews into the post-WW II, modern era.

Antisthenes *d.* 365 BC. Greek philosopher. Antisthenes was a follower of Socrates and founded the Greek school of Cynics (*q.v.*).

Antoine, André 1858–1943. French actor, manager, and critic, influential in French theater. He founded the Théâtre Libre in Paris (1887) and there presented naturalistic plays. He also opened the Théâtre Antoine (1897) and later was director of the Odéon in Paris.

Antoine, duke of Montpensier *See* **Affair of the Spanish Marriages.**

Antonescu, Ion 1882–1946. Rumanian general and dictator. Made premier by King Carol (1940), he assumed dictatorial powers and forced Carol's abdication (1940). He allied Rumania with Germany during WW II, declared war on the USSR (1941), and was arrested in a coup in 1944.

Antoninus, Marcus Aurelius *See* **Marcus Aurelius;** *see also* **Caracalla.**

Antoninus Pius (Titus Aurelius Fulvus Boinonius Arrius Antoninus) AD 86–161. Roman emperor (AD 138–161), successor to Hadrian. One of the "five good emperors," he continued the period of general prosperity and built the Antonine Wall.

Antonius, Marcus *See* **Antony.**

Antony (Marcus Antonius) (Marc ~) c83–30 BC. Roman soldier, political leader, and ally of J. Caesar. His love affair with Cleopatra (*q.v.*) is near legendary. A courageous soldier, he served with Caesar in Gaul (54 BC), became a tribune (49), and joined Caesar in the civil war against Pompey (notably at the Battle of Pharsalus [48], in which Pompey was defeated). He became consul with Caesar (44) and, after Caesar's assassination, forced the conspirators to flee Rome. Antony for a time opposed both the Senate and Caesar's heir, Octavian (later Augustus Caesar). But after gaining the support of Lepidus, Antony came to terms with Octavian, and the three (Octavian, Antony, and Lepidus) formed the Second Triumvirate, with Antony ruling Asia. There followed the murders of hundreds of senators and the Battle of Philippi (42), resulting in the deaths of Cassius and Brutus. Antony then began (c42) his affair with Cleopatra, was forced to leave Egypt (40), and at Rome married Octavian's sister. He soon returned to Egypt and Cleopatra, however, and, by his dissolute lifestyle, alienated both Octavian and the Senate. Octavian attacked and defeated Antony at Actium (31), and, when Octavian pursued him to Alexandria, both Antony and Cleopatra committed suicide (30).

Antwerp Belgian city, a commercial center and important European port. A Norman fort in the 9th cent., it was chartered in 1291 and rose to prominence (15th cent.), when it replaced

Bruges as a center for the cloth trade. By the 16th cent., it was the most important commercial and financial center in Europe. By the mid-17th cent., however, the city had suffered a number of reverses, including conquest by Spain and the closing of its port by the Peace of Westphalia (1648), and it declined quickly. Napoleon reopened the port (1795), and in the 19th cent. it again began to prosper. The Germans captured it in WW I (1914–18) and WW II (1940–44).

Anvari (Anwari) c1126–c1189. Persian poet. Anvari was renowned for both his lyric and satirical skills. His works are collected in the *Divan.*

Anvil, Operation (Operation Dragoon) Allied invasion of southern France (Aug. 15, 1944) during WW II. This landing by the American Seventh Army and the French First Army met little resistance and quickly linked up with Gen. G. Patton's forces in Dijon.

Anville, Jean Baptiste Bourguignon d' 1697–1782. French geographer and cartographer whose maps of ancient and medieval geography are noted for their accuracy. His work led to great improvements in mapmaking.

Anwari *See* **Anvari.**

ANZAC Combined Australian and New Zealand Army Corps that saw action during WW I. The unit was noted for its efforts in the Battle of Gallipoli (1915) and in later battles in France.

ANZUS *See* **Australia, 1951.**

Anzio landing *See* **World War II, Jan. 1944.**

Apache Indians American Indian tribes of the US Southwest. Apaches were farmer-warriors and are believed to have migrated to the Southwest from Canada about AD 1000. Some tribes, however, were also driven south from the Midwest plains by the Comanche and Ute as late as the 18th cent. Apaches attacked Spanish colonials from the 17th cent. and engaged in the bloody Apache and Navaho wars against Americans in the 19th cent. The Apaches formerly consisted of many subgroups, including Jicarilla, Chiricahua, Coyotero, and Kiowa.

apartheid Racial segregation policy enforced by the white supremacist government of the Republic of South Africa. White domination of native Africans has been part of government policy since creation of the South African state (1910). But apartheid, aiming at complete physical separation of the races, was articulated by the Afrikaner National party government in 1948. The government subsequently resettled part of the black population in rural "homelands," designated for blacks only, and strictly regulated them. South Africa was forced out of the British Commonwealth (1961) because of its apartheid policies and in the 1980s came under pressure of economic sanctions organized by various nations in the international community opposed to apartheid. In recent years, the government has taken steps to end the policy. *See also* South Africa.

Apelles *fl.* 4th cent. BC. Greek painter, considered the greatest of his time. He was court painter to Philip II and Alexander the Great. None of his works survives and he is known only because of his great reputation.

Apocrypha Collection of 14 books appended to the authorized (King James) version of the Old Testament, considered uncanonical by Jewish and Protestant faiths. They do not appear in the Hebrew version of the Bible but are included in the Septuagint (Greek) and Vulgate (Latin) versions.

Apollinaire, Guillaume 1880–1918. French poet, a leading figure in the Paris avant-garde movement. His poetry was experimental and his only play, *Les Mamelles de Tirésias,* was an early experiment in surrealism.

Apollinarianism Christian heresy that began with Apollinarius of Laodicea (*d.* AD 390?). Apollinarius taught that because of Jesus' divine nature, he was not truly human and therefore did not possess both perfectly human and perfectly divine natures. This heresy was condemned by the Council of Constantinople (AD 381).

Apollodorus *fl.* 5th cent. BC. Athenian painter. He is believed to have introduced the technique of shading light and color in painting. None of his works survives.

Apollonius of Perga *fl.* 3d cent. BC. Greek mathematician. His treatise on conic sections is a major mathematical work of antiquity. It contains first use of the terms "parabola," "hyperbola," and "ellipse."

Apollo program US program to land human beings on the moon. Inaugurated May, 1961, by President J. Kennedy, the program suffered a serious setback in the preparatory phase when a fire broke out in the Apollo 1 space capsule (Jan. 27, 1967) during testing at Cape Kennedy. Three astronauts in the capsule were killed, the first deaths of US astronauts. Preparations for the moon landing included a number of preliminary missions and several moon landings were eventually made. Apollo 8 was the first manned moon orbit (Dec. 1968), and Apollo 11 was the first moon landing (July 20, 1969). In the latter, astronaut N. Armstrong became the first man to walk on the moon. Apollo 17 (Dec., 1972) was the last flight of the program. (*See also* Space Exploration, 1967–72.)

apostle One of the twelve disciples chosen by Jesus to act as the principal missionaries of Christianity. The twelve are Peter, Andrew, John, James (son of Zebedee), James (son of Alphaeus), Philip, Bartholomew, Thomas, Thaddaeus, Matthew, Simon, and Matthias (who replaced Judas Iscariot). Early Christian missionaries, who were primarily responsible for founding the church in a country, are also referred to as apostles. Thus, Saint Patrick is known as the apostle of Ireland.

Apostolic Constitutions A compilation of early Christian ecclesiastical law. At first thought to be the work of the apostles, they are now believed to have been written by a 4th-cent. Syrian author. They provide valuable insight into the practices of the early Christians.

apostolic succession Christian doctrine holding that the special powers of the apostles have passed through each of their successors to the present-day bishops of the church. The doctrine is accepted by the Roman Catholic, Eastern Orthodox, Anglican, and other churches.

Appeals to Rome, Act in Restraint of *See* **Act in Restraint of Appeals to Rome.**

appeasement policy British policy toward Germany after WW I that was originally intended to reintegrate Germany into European affairs. The policy misfired in the face of growing Nazi aggression from 1937 to 1939. During that time, the British under Prime Minister N. Chamberlain, attempted to avoid war by offering Germany territorial concessions. The policy proved both unpopular in Britain and ultimately unsuccessful.

Appian of Alexandria *fl.* 2d cent. AD. Greek-born Roman historian. He wrote a 24-volume history of Roman conquests, from the founding of Rome to the reign of Trajan. Less than half survives.

Appian Way Roman road built (312 BC) to connect Rome with Capua. It was later extended to Brindisi and was over 350 miles long, becoming the main road to the East.

Appleseed, Johnny *See* **Chapman, John.**

Appomattox Courthouse Site in central Virginia where, on Apr. 9, 1865, Gen. R. E. Lee surrendered Confederate forces under his command to Gen. U. S. Grant, thereby effectively ending the Civil War. Lee's westward retreat (after the Battle of Five Forks) had been blocked by surrounding Union armies, forcing the surrender.

APRA (Alianza Popular Revolucionaria Americana; American Popular Revolutionary Alliance) Political party in Peru, originally organized by exiled radicals in 1924. Founded on a patchwork of Marxist-Leninism and other radical principles, the party aroused stiff opposition in Peru, and followers suffered persecutions in the 1920s and 1930s. Party leaders abandoned many of the harshest radical tenets in the 1940s, however, and since that time it has been a powerful political force in Peru. Outlawed by the government in the late 1930s, early 1940s, and early 1950s, the APRA has had legal status as a political party since 1956.

Apries *d.* 569 BC. Egyptian king (c588–570 BC), successor to his father, Psamtik II. He engaged in unsuccessful wars against the Babylonians under Nebuchadnezzar.

April Laws *See* **March Laws.**

April Theses Plan, formulated by the Russian revolutionary N. Lenin, to replace the bourgeois provisional government of Russia with one controlled by Bolshevik-dominated soviets. Having returned to Russia after the March Revolution, Lenin first outlined his plan Apr. 17, 1917. It was adopted by the Bolsheviks after some early resistance and was carried out during the November Revolution. In addition to the takeover of power, the plan called for an end to Russian participation in WW I, distribution of land to peasants, nationalization of banks, and soviet control of manufacturing and distribution.

Apuleius, Lucius (Apuleius of Madaura) *fl.* 2d cent. AD. Latin philosopher and writer whose romance *Metamorphoses,* or *The Golden Ass,* had a major influence on later novelists.

Apuleius of Madaura *See* **Apuleius, Lucius.**

Aquae Sextiae, Battle of (Aix, ˜) Roman victory (102 BC) over invading Gallic tribes, the Teutones. The Romans, under G. Marius, decimated the Teutones at Aquae Sextiae, in what is now southern France, and later defeated the Cimbri, allies of the Teutones.

Aquila Ponticus *fl.* 2d cent. AD. Jewish translator of the Old Testament from Hebrew into

Greek. His literal translation was used by the Jews for centuries.

Aquinas, Thomas *See* **Thomas Aquinas.**

Aquino, Benigno *See* **Philippines, 1983.**

Aquino, Corazon *See* **Philippines, 1986–1992.**

Aquitaine Region of southwestern France. Conquered by J. Caesar (56 BC), it was made a kingdom by Charlemagne. The marriages of Eleanor of Aquitaine (12th cent. AD) resulted in a long struggle between England and France for possession of the kingdom. France acquired complete control by the end of the Hundred Years' War (1337–1453).

Aquitaine, Eleanor of *See* **Eleanor of Aquitaine.**

arabesque Decorative style important in Muslim cultures. Derived by Muslim craftsmen from an earlier Hellenistic decorative style, it is characterized by intricately entwined vines, leaves, and other flowing lines.

Arabia (Arabian Peninsula) Peninsular region in the Mideast. Earliest known civilization in the region centered around the ancient Sabaean, Minaean, and Himyarite kingdoms. The birthplace of Islam (7th cent. AD), Arabia is today one of the world's most important oil-producing regions. It includes the modern countries of Saudi Arabia, Yemen, Oman, Kuwait, United Arab Emirates, Qatar, and Bahrain.

Arabian Peninsula *See* **Arabia.**

Arab-Israeli War 1. First ~ War (1948–49) between Israeli and allied Arab states (Egypt, Syria, Transjordan, Iraq, and Lebanon). War broke out after the creation of the Israeli state (May 14, 1948). The Arabs at first gained territories in the southeast and captured Old Jerusalem. A four-week UN-negotiated truce (June, 1948) was followed by Israeli offensives and finally a cease-fire (Jan. 7, 1949), by which time the Israelis had regained most of the lost territories. Separate armistice agreements (not formal treaties) were negotiated with the Arab states in early 1949. As a result of the war, some 400,000 Palestinian Arabs from the former Palestine fled to neighboring Arab countries. These refugees gave impetus to renewed Arab-Israeli conflicts and creation of the Palestine Liberation Organization. 2. Second ~ War (Oct.–Nov., 1956) between Israel and Egypt. Taking advantage of international tensions created by G. Nasser's nationalization of the Suez Canal (*q.v.*), Israeli forces, led by M. Dayan, invaded (Oct. 29) the Sinai peninsula. In five days of fighting, up

to the Nov. 6 cease-fire, the Israelis captured nearly all the Sinai east of the canal. Under pressure from the US and UN, the Israelis returned the captured Sinai (1957), accepting guarantees of Israeli access to the Gulf of Aqaba. A UN Emergency Force (UNEF) was stationed on the Egyptian border with Israel. 3. Third ~ War (Six-Day War) (June 5–10, 1967) between Israel and the Arab states of Egypt, Syria, and Jordan. Provoked by border incidents and Egypt's closing of Israeli access to the Gulf of Aqaba, the Israelis attacked the Arab countries (June 5). They knocked out the Arab air capability, then took the Sinai, the West Bank, Old Jerusalem, and the Golan Heights. The war ended June 10, though no treaties were negotiated. 4. Fourth ~ War (Yom Kippur War) (Oct. 6–25, 1973) between Israel and allied Arab states (Egypt and Syria, supported by Iraq, Libya, and Jordan). In a surprise move on the Jewish holiday of Yom Kippur the Egyptians attacked across the Suez Canal and the Syrians attacked from the north. The Israelis fell back initially but pushed back the Arabs on both fronts, finally even gaining a foothold on the east bank of the Suez. Though fighting continued sporadically on the Syrian front (ending May 31, 1974), the Israelis agreed (Jan 18, 1974) to limited withdrawal and establishment of a UN peace-keeping force. 5. Fifth ~ War (Lebanese War) *See* Lebanon, 1982.

Arab League Loose alliance of Arab countries founded (1945) to promote Arab unity and interests. Frequently rendered impotent in political matters because of internal divisions, the league has been more successful in economic and administrative affairs. It failed (1948) to prevent formation of Israel, instituted a mutual defense pact (1950), and since then has been largely ineffective in the crises brought on by Arab-Israeli wars. The original members were Egypt, Syria, Lebanon, Jordan, Saudi Arabia, Iraq, and Yemen. Since 1945, other Arab nations and the PLO have joined. Egypt was ousted (Mar., 1979) after signing peace accords with Israel.

Arab Socialist Renaissance party *See* **Ba'th party.**

Arafat, Yasir 1929– . Chairman of the Palestine Liberation Organization (PLO). He became PLO chairman (1968), commander in chief of the Palestine Revolutionary Forces (1971), and head of the PLO political department (1973). Though PLO terrorism continued, he worked to move the organization away from terrorism and toward political persuasion. A split with radical elements in the PLO forced him to move the organization's headquarters from Lebanon to Tunisia (1982), and then to Baghdad (1987). When the PLO unilaterally declared the "State of Palestine" (1988), Arafat was appointed president.

Aragon, Catherine of *See* **Catherine of Aragon.**

Aragon, kingdom of Kingdom in what is now northeast Spain. Created as a kingdom (1035) by Sancho III for his son Ramiro I, Aragon eventually became one of the great medieval Spanish kingdoms. Ramiro and Alfonso I greatly expanded the original domains southward and, in 1137, added Catalonia. Many territories, including Valencia, Sardinia, the Two Sicilies, and Naples, were added from the 13th to 15th cents. It was united with Castile (1479) by Ferdinand V and Isabella I to form the basis of the modern Spanish state.

Arai Hakuseki 1657–1725. Japanese scholar, historian, and philosopher. He was noted for his writings on Confucianism.

Arakcheyev, Aleksey Andreyevich 1769–1834. Russian general. He counseled Tsars Paul I and Alexander I. One of Tsar Alexander's most trusted advisers, he helped to reorganize the Russian army and founded the hated military colonies.

Araki Sadao 1877–1966. Japanese general, war minister (1931–33), and education minister (1937–39). An ultranationalist faction leader, Araki urged Japanese world domination. He was sentenced to life imprisonment as a war criminal after WW II.

Aram Ancient country in what is now Syria. The Aramaean people established a number of kingdoms in the region after 1200 BC. The Aramaeans unsuccessfully attacked Israel during King David's reign and later established themselves as kings of Babylonia. Western Aramaean kingdoms fell to the Assyrians (720 BC), while eastern kingdoms became part of the Chaldean Empire (17th cent.).

Arango, Doroteo *See* **Villa, Francisco.**

Aranjuez, Revolt of Spanish rebellion (Mar. 1719, 1808) at Aranjuez, in central Spain. Rioting here forced the dismissal of Prime Minister M. Godoy and the abdication of Charles IV during Napoleon's invasion of Spain (1807–08).

Araucanian Wars Warfare (16th cent.) between Spanish conquistadors and the fierce Araucanian Indians in Chile. Outbreaks of violence began in

the 1530s, and in 1541 P. Valdivia fended off Araucanian attacks and founded Santiago. The Indians again threatened Santiago after massacring (1553) Valdivia's expedition farther south. Spanish forces ultimately forced the Indians southward but never conquered them. The Araucanians rose again (19th cent.) when settlers threatened these homelands in the south. They were finally defeated (1870) by the Chilean Army.

Ararat Mountain at the eastern frontier of Turkey, traditionally considered the resting place of Noah's Ark. The kingdom of Ararat, roughly equivalent to what became Armenia, flourished from the 9th to 7th cents. BC.

Arausio, Battle of Victory (Oct. 6, 105 BC) for Gallic tribes, the Cimbri and Teutones, over the Romans at this town in what is now southern France. Roman losses were heavy.

Arbela, Battle of *See* **Gaugamela, Battle of.**

Arbogast *d.* AD 394. Frankish general in Roman service. A commander under Theodosius I, he defeated the rebel Maximus (AD 388). He failed in his attempt to install Eugenius as emperor of the West (392), and was defeated by Theodosius at Frigidus River (Sept. 5–6, 394), now in northern Italy.

Arcadia Region of ancient Greece in the central Peloponnesus, largely isolated from the rest of Greece. Its major city was Megalopolis. Arcadian cities sporadically fought against the Spartans and formed the short-lived Arcadian League (370–362 BC), with Theban support, to resist Sparta.

Arcadia Conference First major WW II council involving the US, held in Washington, D.C. (Dec. 22, 1941–Jan. 14, 1942). It was attended by President F. Roosevelt and Prime Minister W. Churchill and resulted in the first UN declaration and plans for coordinating the military effort.

Arcadian League *See* **Arcadia.**

Arcadius AD c377–408. First Roman emperor of the East (AD 395–408). On the death of his father, Emperor Theodosius I, the Roman Empire was permanently divided into Eastern and Western empires. Arcadius's brother, Honorius, ruled the West. Arcadius was an ineffectual ruler, left the government to his ministers (including Rufinus), and was controlled by Eudoxia (*d.* 404), his wife.

Arc de Triomphe de l'Étoile Triumphal arch in Paris at the end of the Champs-Élysées. Built

(1806–36) to commemorate the victories of Napoleon, it is a symbol of French military honor.

Arce, Manuel José 1783?–1847. Central American leader, first president of the Central American Confederation (1825–29).

archaeology The study of past human cultures through the recovery and analysis of material remains. Archaeology is broadly divided into the study of prehistoric and historic cultures and is also divided into particular periods or cultures, such as Egyptian, Greek, and Roman. Archaeology as a science began with the 15th-cent. interest in Greek sculpture. Since then, such important discoveries as Pompeii and Troy, the deciphering of Egyptian hieroglyphics, and the finding of the Dead Sea Scrolls have contributed greatly to archaeologists' knowledge of ancient cultures. Archaeologists now employ sophisticated methods for excavating and dating artifacts and draw on a wide variety of scientific disciplines in the analysis of their finds.

archbishop In Christian ecclesiastical hierarchy, a bishop with certain supervisory powers over the bishops of a province. The title came into use in the Western church during the 7th cent.

archduke Title of nobility, primarily used by the Austrian Habsburgs. It was first conferred (1453) by Habsburg Holy Roman Emperor Frederick III and since then has been a hereditary title of male Habsburg heirs.

Archer, William 1856–1924. A Scottish critic, playwright, and translator. His translations of H. Ibsen's works influenced the development of British and American drama.

Archidamian War War (431–421 BC) between Sparta and Athens. It was the opening phase of the Peloponnesian War (*q.v.*). The war was named after King Archidamus II (*d.* 427 BC), who led the first Spartan invasions of Attica.

Archidamus II *See* **Archidamian War.**

Archimedes 287–212 BC. Greek mathematician and inventor noted for his contributions to the fields of geometry, mechanics, and hydrostatics. Among his discoveries were the principle of buoyancy (Archimedes's Principle), a water pump known as Archimedes's Screw, and the principle of the lever.

archons Magistrates in ancient Greece. Originally they had political, religious, and military powers in the city-states (especially Athens), but by the 5th cent. BC their roles had been reduced to control of judicial functions (while sharing political and religious functions). The first archons were chosen from among the aristocracy. Eligibility was gradually extended to other classes, and, in the 5th cent. BC, all but the poorest citizens were eligible to hold the office. Archons declined in importance after 487, when they were no longer elected, but instead were chosen by lot.

Arctic Region surrounding the North Pole, including northern parts of North America, Europe, and Asia. The first known exploration of the region may have been by the Greek Pytheas (4th cent. BC). Subsequently Irish monks (9th cent. AD) and Norse Vikings (10th cent. AD) were in Iceland. Following the voyages of J. Cabot, European exploration began in earnest, stimulated largely by the search for Northeast and Northwest passages to Asia. Other explorers followed, including M. Frobisher, V. Bering, H. Hudson, J. Franklin, F. Nansen, and R. Amundsen. R. Peary became the first to reach the Pole (1909), and R. Byrd flew over it (1926). In 1958, the nuclear submarine *Nautilus* made the first voyage under the polar icecap.

Ardashir I (Artaxerxes) *d.* AD c241. King of Persia (AD c226–c241), who founded the Sassanidae dynasty. He overthrew the Parthian king, established Zoroastrianism as the state religion, expanded his empire, and warred against Roman emperor Alexander Severus (AD 231–233).

Ardennes, Battle of the *See* **Bulge, Battle of the.**

Arendt, Hannah 1906–1975. A German-born American political scientist. A fugitive from Nazi Germany, she is noted for her studies of totalitarianism. Among her works are *Origins of Totalitarianism, The Human Condition,* and *Eichmann in Jerusalem.*

Areopagus Council in ancient Athens. Formed sometime after 1000 BC and composed of former archons (magistrates) of Athens, the Areopagus functioned as a legislative body and guardian of Athenian laws. Under Draco, the council had judicial powers in murder cases. Solon is sometimes said to have reduced its legislative functions and instituted the Boule, or Council of 400, for these functions. In 462–461, the council lost its powers, which were invested in more democratic bodies. The Areopagus was revived under the Romans.

Argentina Republic located in southern South America. The population is 32,291,000 and the capital is Buenos Aires. First colonized by the

Spanish in the 16th cent., Argentina gained its independence in 1816, overcame years of political turmoil, and by the late 19th cent. had become a leading nation of South America. In the early 1980s, Argentina's military government seized the offshore British possession of the Falkland Islands but following a brief war was forced to surrender the islands. The incident resulted in the ouster of Argentina's military government and election of the first civilian president in some years. Key events in the history of Argentina include:

1516 Río de la Plata, major coastal river delta region, discovered by Juan Díaz de Solís.

1536 Spanish established settlement at what is now Buenos Aires.

1776 Buenos Aires made seat of a viceroyalty that ruled regions of Argentina, Paraguay, Bolivia, and Uruguay.

1806–7 British force attacked and occupied Buenos Aires, forcing the viceroy to flee; Argentine forces expelled the British the following year and repelled a second British force.

1810 Argentine revolutionaries refused to recognize Spanish king Joseph Bonaparte, installed by Napoleon, revolutionaries deposed the viceroy (May 25) and established a ruling junta; the rebels later broke with representatives of deposed King Ferdinand VII, thereby instigating war with the royalists.

1810–13 Revolutionaries tried unsuccessfully to liberate all of viceroyalty; royalist forces retained control of what is now Uruguay, Paraguay, and Bolivia, however.

1816 Congress of Tucumán declared complete independence from Spain (July 9); United Provinces of Río de la Plata formed from liberated territories.

1819–20 Civil war between leaders from Buenos Aires, who wanted strong central government, and leaders from other provinces, who favored federal system of government; political turmoil continued into the 1830s.

1825–27 Argentina successfully aided Uruguayans in war against Brazil; this led to Uruguay's independence.

1835 J. Rosas assumed dictatorial powers as governor of Buenos Aires province; rapidly extended his control over other Argentine provinces through reign of terror; united Argentina under his firm control until 1852.

1852 Rosas overthrown by J. Urquiza.

1853 Argentine constitution adopted; Argentine Republic proclaimed; Urquiza became first president (1854–60).

1854–59 Buenos Aires province seceded from the republic; defeated and forced to return five years later.

1860–62 Santiago Derqui served as president.

1862–68 President Bartolomé Mitre in office as president.

1862 Buenos Aires made capital of Argentina.

1864–70 War of the Triple Alliance with Paraguay.

1868–74 Domingo Faustino Sarmiento served as president; as Argentina's first civilian president, he worked to increase democracy and improve education.

1874–80 President Nicolás Avellaneda in office.

1880–86, 1898–1904 Julio Argentino Roca became president; rapid development of Argentina during his presidencies.

1886–90 President Miguel Juárez Celmán in office.

1890–92 Carlo Pellegrini in office as president.

1892–95 Luis Sáenz Peña served as president.

1895–98 President José Evaristo Uriburu in office.

1902 Long-standing border dispute with Chile settled.

1904–06 Manuel Quintana in office as president.

1906–10 José Figueroa Alcorta served as president.

1910–14 Roque Sáenz Peña served as president.

1914–16 President Victorino de la Plaza in office.

1914–18 Argentina remained neutral during W W I.

1916–22, 1928–30 Radical party, led by President H. Irigoyen, came to power; instituted many reforms but provoked growing opposition.

1922–28 Marcelo Torcuato de Alvear in office as president.

1930 President H. Irigoyen overthrown by conservatives, led by Gen. José Uriburu, as economic problems caused by the Great Depression mounted.

1930–32 Gen. Uriburu served as president.

1932–38 President Augustin Justo in office.

1938 Radicals return to power under President Roberto Ortíz (served 1938–42); kept

Argentina neutral during WW II though Fascist groups were active.

1942–43 President Ramón Castillo in office.

1943 Military coup; ruling military junta included Col. J. Perón.

1943–44 Pedro Ramírez in office as president.

1944–46 Edelmiro Farrell served as president.

1945–52 E. Perón, wife of J. Perón and a popular figure in Argentina, worked for reforms, including voting rights for women; died in 1952.

1946 Perón won national election.

1946–55 J. Perón in office as president, establishing popular dictatorship; regime marked by reduction of civil and political liberties.

1949 Perón secured new constitution allowing him to succeed himself as president.

1952 Women granted right to vote.

1955 Military forced ouster of Perón; new government faced serious economic problems as well as the problem of dealing with Perón's followers (Peronistas).

1955–58 Pedro Eugenio Aramburu served as president.

1958–62 Arturo Frondizi in office as president.

1962–63 José María Guido served as president.

1963–66 Arturo Umberto Illia in office as president.

1966 Military seized power to prevent Peronistas from gaining office; Gen. Juan Carlos Ongania in office as president (1966–70).

1970–71 Roberto Marcelo Levingston served as president.

1971 Ban on political parties (since 1966) ended.

1971–73 Alejandro Agustin Lanusse in office as president.

1972 J. Perón returned to Argentina (Nov. 17) after 17-year exile.

1973 First elections since 1965; Héctor J. Cámpora, a Peronista, won presidency.

1973 President Cámpora resigned (July 13) to allow Perón to run for presidency.

1973–74 President J. Perón in office as elected president; his wife Isabel elected vice-president.

1974 Mass arrests (May) in Tucumán province begun to counter left-wing opposition to the Perón government.

1974 Perón died in office (July); his wife succeeded him as president.

1974 President Isabel Perón declared (Nov.) a state of siege following outbreak of numerous terrorist attacks.

1976 President Perón overthrown (Mar.) and arrested in military coup; Lieut. Gen. Jorge Rafaél Videla became new president.

1976–81 Gen. Videla in office as president.

1976–79 Military junta conducted so-called "dirty war" in which between 6,000 and 15,000 leftists were killed or disappeared ("disappeared ones").

1977 Inflation reported near 350% for previous year.

1980 Military government moved toward return to civilian rule, but with preconditions; economic crisis continued, prompting bank failures and corporate bankruptcies; government devalued the peso.

1981 Gen. Roberto Viola served as president; replaced following a heart attack.

1981–82 Gen. Leopoldo Galtieri in office as president; continued process of liberalizing government begun by Viola; economic crisis continued; austerity measures, which sparked public unrest, introduced.

1982 Falkland Islands War (Apr.–June); Argentine invasion force driven off islands by British troops.

1982 Galtieri ousted (June) after Argentina lost Falkland Islands War; Gen. Reynaldo Bignone appointed president by the army (July, served 1982–83).

1983 Military regime, faced with past failures and chronic economic problems, moved to transfer power to civilian government; meanwhile approved Ley de Pacification Nacional (Aug.), providing amnesty for all military, police, and others who committed political crimes during past 10 years (later repealed).

1983 First elections held since 1973; Dr. Raul Alfonsin of the Radical party (UCR) elected president.

1983–89 President Alfonsin in office; instituted radical reform of military; over half of the senior military officers retired; ordered trials for members of three military juntas that followed 1976 coup; organized commission to investigate dirty war in which thousands were killed.

1985 Inflation rose to over 1000% annually.

1985 Five high-ranking military leaders tried and sentenced for crimes against humanity, including torture and killings of disappeared ones during the reign of the military juntas; former military president Gen. Videla given life imprisonment.

1986 Numerous strikes called during the year.

1986 Former President Galtieri, along with other military leaders, sentenced for negligence in the failed Falkland Islands war; Galtieri pardoned (1989) after serving part of sentence.

1987 Brief mutiny by soldiers protesting continued trials against military for crimes committed during reign of junta; unrest quelled peacefully (May).

1989 Carlos Saul Menem of the Peronist party won presidential election (May); Peronist party also gained control of Chamber of Deputies and most provincial governments.

1989 Government declared state of siege (May 29–June 28) as continuing economic crisis sparked food riots and looting; announced economic reforms (July 9), including privatization of state-owned companies.

1989– President Menem in office (July); confronted worst economic crisis in Argentine history, with inflation rate at 1500% and unrest on the rise.

1989 Menem pardoned military leaders and others (Oct.) punished for their conduct in the "dirty war" of the late 1970's; more pardons announced in Dec., 1990.

1990–92 Government imposed various economic austerity measures; sparked labor unrest and food riots.

Arginusae, Battle of Sea battle during the Peloponnesian War. The Spartan navy, under Callicratidas, was defeated by the Athenians, under Conon, off the Arginusae Islands in the Aegean Sea (406 BC.). Callicratidas was killed and over half of the Spartan ships were sunk.

Argolis Region of ancient Greece in the northeast Peloponnesus. Its most important city was Argos.

Argos City of ancient Greece, in northeast Peloponnesus. Inhabited since the early Bronze Age, it was a major power, and enemy of Sparta, in the Peloponnesus from the 7th cent. BC. It joined the Achaean League in 229 BC and was captured by Rome in 146 BC. Argos was a center of worship of the goddess Hera.

Argyll *See* **Campbell, earls of Argyll.**

Arianism Christian heresy (4th cent. AD) concerning the nature of Christ in relation to God. Arianism was the subject of a great controversy in the East, provoked (c318) by an Alexandrian priest, Arius (*d.* 336). Arius's teachings, which held that Christ was not of the same divine nature as God, were condemned at the First Council of Nicaea (1st ecumenical). The controversy continued, however, and a number of factions arose in opposition to the orthodox Christian Nicene party. These factions were supported by Constantius II, Roman ruler in the East, and, when he became sole emperor (350), he imposed Arianism throughout the empire. The accession of orthodox Christian rulers in the West (Gratian) and East (Theodosius I) brought an end to the controversy within the empire. The First Council of Constantinople (381) was convened and affirmed the Nicene formula. Arianism survived among Germanic tribes until the mid-7th cent.

Arias de Ávila, Pedro (Pedrarias Dávila) (Pedro Arias Dávila) c 1440–1531? Spanish soldier and colonial administrator noted for his cruelty. He replaced V. Balboa as governor in Panama (1514–26) and was involved in Balboa's execution. He expanded Spanish colonial rule and founded Panama City (1519).

Arimathea, Saint Joseph of *See* **Joseph of Arimathea, Saint.**

Ariosto, Ludovico 1474–1533. Italian epic and lyric poet. His major work, the *Orlando Furioso,* an epic based on the story of Roland, is considered a Renaissance masterpiece.

Aristarchus of Samos *fl.* 3d cent. BC Greek astronomer believed to have been the first to maintain that the earth revolves around the sun. He is also said to have deduced that night and day are caused by the earth's rotation.

Aristides *d.* c468 BC. Athenian general and statesman, a commander at the Battle of Marathon. Later ostracized (probably for opposing Themistocles), he returned to fight with Athens at Salamis (480 BC) and Plataea (479). He was a founder with Cimon of the Delian League (478).

aristocracy Government by a special or privileged class of people, often the landed, the very wealthy, or those born into the class, who are considered worthy of ruling or taking part in government. It is distinct from oligarchy, in which a select few, rather than a privileged class, hold the reins of power. In Greek times, the distinction was made on the basis of motives: oligarchs were held to be those who ruled for personal gain, while aristocrats were those few, chosen for their virtue, who ruled in the best interests of the state. In modern times, aristocracy often refers to the privileged class itself. The governments of Athens (to the 5th cent. BC) and England (late 18th and early 19th cents.) are examples of government by aristocrats.

Aristogiton *See* **Harmodius and Aristogiton.**

Aristophanes c448–c388 BC. Athenian dramatist, considered the greatest writer of ancient Greek comedy. Little is known of Aristophanes's life, but his comedies provide a revealing picture of the society, the literature and the politics of his day. His plays range from an attack on the Peloponnesian War to a satire on Socrates. He is believed to have written about 40 plays, of which 11 survive. They include *The Birds, The Frogs, Lysistrata, The Clouds, The Acharnians,* and *The Knights.*

Aristotelianism The great body of Aristotle's teachings and subsequent additions and interpretations that have accrued to it since Aristotle's lifetime (4th cent. BC). Aristotelianism flourished within and greatly influenced many cultures outside Greece. Many of Aristotle's fundamental doctrines continue to be influential in modern times. Aristotelianism spread from Greece to Rome, and, after the fall of Rome, Aristotle's teachings were lost in the West. Aristotelianism flourished (from 9th cent. AD) among the Arabs, however, and was reintroduced to the West by Muslim and Jewish scholars (12th and 13th cents.). Through the works of Saint Thomas Aquinas (13th cent.), who synthesized Aristotelian rationalism and Christian thought, Aristotelianism greatly influenced the course of medieval scholasticism and Roman Catholic theology. (*See also* Aristotle.)

Aristotle 384–322 BC. Greek philosopher and scientist, one of the great thinkers of all time. His works in philosophy, science, ethics, and esthetics had a major influence on the development of civilization in the West. Aristotle studied (367–347 BC) under Plato at the Academy in Athens and later tutored (342–335?) Alexander the Great. Returning to Athens in 335, he opened a school (the Lyceum) and taught there until just before his death. His works, lost in the West after the fall of Rome, were reintroduced by Arab scholars in the 9th cent. and formed the basis of scholasticism (*q.v.*). In his time, Aristotle and his followers, known as Peripatetics, stressed the importance of observation, the necessary correlation of theory to fact, and the value of logic. Aristotle's works, actually compiled from lecture notes two centuries after his death, include *Organon,* on logic; *Nicomachean Ethics,* on moral philosophy; *Metaphysics,* on fundamental metaphysical concepts; *Politics; Poetics,* on esthetics; *Constitution of Athens,* on Athenian government; and works in the sciences. (*See also* Aristotelianism.)

Arius *See* **Arianism.**

Arizona US state in the Southwest. Originally inhabited by Pueblo, Apache, and Navaho Indians, the region was explored by the Spanish in 1539. Although Indians successfully prevented permanent settlements in the region until the 18th cent., it was ruled as part of New Spain (1598–1821) and part of independent Mexico (1821–48). By the Treaty of Guadalupe Hidalgo and the Gadsden Purchase (1848, 1853), it became US territory. The defeat of the Apaches (late 19th cent.) brought a rise in ranching operations there, and in 1912 Arizona became the 48th state. The state constitution was passed in 1911.

Arkansas 25th US state, located in the south-central part of the country. The region was explored by the Spanish (1541), and the first permanent settlement, Arkansas Post (1682), was established by the French. Settled for a time under the Mississippi Scheme (c1720), the region changed hands between the French and Spanish before the US bought it in the Louisiana Purchase (1803). It was established as a separate territory (1819), and then became a state (1836). The region was settled in the early 1800s, and during the Civil War it joined the Confederacy (1861). Resistance to enfranchisement of Negroes held up readmission to the Union until 1868. The current state constitution was passed in 1874.

Arkansas Post *See* **Arkansas.**

Arkwright, Sir Richard 1732–92. English inventor of the cotton spinning frame and other power-driven weaving devices. He was a major figure in the development of the factory system of textile production in England.

Arles, Council of Roman Catholic church council (AD 314). Constantine I convened this council in Gaul to deal with the Donatists (*q.v.*). It again condemned the Donatists and affirmed the supremacy of Rome.

Arlington, Henry Bennet, 1st earl of 1618–85. An English statesman. As secretary of state (1662–74) under King Charles II, he became a member of the Cabal (*q.v.*). In 1674 he was impeached for corruption and Catholicism. Acquitted, he resigned.

Armada *See* **Spanish Armada.**

Armagnacs Faction of French noblemen whose war with the Burgundians (1411–18) for control of France figured in the Hundred Years' War. The Armagnac faction was formed by Bernard VII, count of Armagnac, following the murder of Louis d'Orléans (1407) in a struggle for control of the French throne. A Burgundian, John the Fearless, was in power when civil war broke out (1411) between the two factions. The Armagnacs seized control in 1413 but became embroiled in the defense of France against an invasion by English king Henry V. John the Fearless was subsequently able to regain control of the government (1418) and thereupon massacred the Armagnacs. John was assassinated (1419) and King Charles VII came to power. Charles's alliance with the Burgundians (1435) assured the Armagnacs' final decline. (*See also* Burgundians.)

Armed Neutrality, League of *See* **Copenhagen, Battle of.**

Armenia Region and former kingdom of Asia Minor, located in northeast Turkey and southwest Russia. The Armenian people settled the area before the 6th cent. BC, and then successively fell under the control of the Medes, Persians, Alexander the Great (330 BC), and the Seleucids. They formed an independent kingdom in 189 BC and under Tigranes I gained control over a wide area. The Romans soon conquered the kingdom, however (69–67 BC). Armenia was first to adopt Christianity as a state religion (AD 303), and in the 4th–5th cents. AD suffered persecutions at the hands of the Zoroastrian Persians. Armenia was subsequently conquered by many different peoples (and was devasted by the Mongols in the 13th and 14th cents.) until the Ottoman Turks took over the region in the 16th cent. From 1894 to 1915, Armenians suffered sporadic massacres by the Turks. During WW I, the Turks ordered the relocation of 1.75 million Armenians to Syria

and Mesopotamia, and some 600,000 died during the difficult passage. Russian advances in the region led to establishment of an independent Armenia (1918). By 1921, however, Armenian territory had been divided and annexed by the USSR and Turkey.

Armenia (*formerly* Armenian Soviet Socialist Republic) Independent state and member of the Commonwealth of Independent States, formerly a Soviet republic. It borders on western Turkey and northern Iran. The region came under Soviet control following the partition of Armenia by the Soviets and Turkey, and was made a Soviet Republic on Apr. 2, 1921. Joined with Azerbaijan and Georgia, it became part of the Transcaucasian Soviet Federated Socialist Republic within the USSR (1922). Armenia became a Soviet republic in 1936. Ethnic unrest in Armenia was reported as early as 1987, with Armenians demanding return of an ethnically Armenian region of neighboring Azerbaijan, Nagorny Karabakh. Anti-Armenian riots in Azerbaijan began in 1988, and by 1989, Nagorny Karabakh had become the scene of intense fighting. A severe earthquake struck Armenia (Dec. 1988), killing some 25,000 persons. In 1990, amid continued fighting in Nagorny Karabakh and the pro-democracy movement sweeping the USSR, Armenia declared its independence (Aug.) and laid claim to Nagorny Karabakh. Subsequently, Soviet troops sent to restore order in the disputed region generally backed Azerbaijanis, however. Fighting over Nagorny Karabakh continued into 1992, though both sides had agreed to a cease-fire by mid-year. Armenia followed the other Soviet constituent republics in declaring independence (Sept. 23) following the failed Soviet coup in 1991. Likewise it joined with 11 other former Soviet republics to form the Commonwealth of Independent States on Dec. 21, 1991.

Armenian church (*also called* Gregorian church) Eastern Christian sect and Armenian national church. Founded (AD 303) in the kingdom of Armenia, it was the first Christian state church. It broke with Rome after the Council of Chalcedon (451) in a dispute over Monophysitism. The church, though it has renewed ties with Rome, maintains a largely autonomous status.

Arm-in-Arm Convention *See* **National Union Convention.**

Arminianism Christian theological movement. Begun (c1603) by Dutch religious reformer J. Arminius, the movement opposed Calvinists' extreme belief in predestination. Instead, the Arminians asserted free will was fully compatible with God's sovereignty over man. Arminians issued (1610) the Remonstrance, a statement of their position, and were condemned by the Dutch Synod of Dort (1618–19). Arminianism, however, later influenced J. Wesley and Methodist doctrine.

Arminius *d.* AD c19. Chief of German tribes, once a Roman citizen. He disgraced the Roman Empire when his forces surprised and decimated a Roman army (AD 9) commanded by Varus in the Teutoburg Forest, east of the Rhine River. Arminius was later badly beaten in battle (AD 16) against Germanicus Caesar.

Arminius, Jacobus (Jacob Harmensen) 1560–1609. Dutch theologian who opposed the Calvinist view of predestination and whose doctrines became known as Arminianism (*q.v.*).

armistice A temporary halt in fighting, mutually agreed upon by belligerents. Strictly speaking, a general armistice does not end the state of war. This is technically accomplished by a peace treaty. In fact, however, armistices ended both WW I (Nov. 11, 1918) and the Korean War (July 27, 1953) and each was a form of peace treaty.

Armory Show *See* **Eight, The.**

Armour, Philip Danforth 1832–1901. American meat-packer. He headed the Chicago-based Armour and Company (1875–99) and was responsible for innovations in meat-packing techniques. A noted philanthropist, he was charged in 1898–99 with selling tainted beef.

Arms, Assize of *See* **Assize of Arms.**

Armstrong, John 1758–1843. American general, politician, and diplomat. He authored the *Newburgh Letters* (1783), anonymous letters written during the American Revolution demanding payment of soldiers' back pay. Later, as secretary of war (1813–14), he was blamed for military reverses in the War of 1812, including the British capture of Washington, D.C.

Armstrong, Neil Alden 1930– . American astronaut. On July 20, 1969, Armstrong became the first person to set foot on the moon. As part of the Apollo II flight, he and E. Aldrin remained on the moon's surface for over twenty hours, collecting samples and data.

Army of the Green Standard Army in China established during the Qing dynasty (1644–1912). At one time it numbered 600,000 men (stationed throughout the empire) and acted as a supplementary army to the military force established by the Banner System. It deteriorated in strength, however, and proved ineffective against rebels in the Taiping Rebellion (1860–65).

Arnauld (Arnault) (Arnaut) French family whose members were leaders of Jansenism. They include Antoine Arnauld (1612–94), his sister Jacqueline Marie Arnauld (1591–1661), and his brother Robert Arnauld d'Andilly (c1588–1674).

Arnault *See* **Arnauld.**

Arnaut *See* **Arnauld.**

Arnhem, Battle of German victory (Sept. 17–26, 1944) in WW II. During the Allied drive across Europe, British and Polish airborne troops made a heroic but unsuccessful attempt to seize control of a bridge across the Rhine at Arnhem, the Netherlands.

Arnold, Benedict 1741–1801. US general and notorious traitor during the American Revolution. His brilliant campaigns at Lake Champlain (1776) and at Saratoga (1777) did not earn him the recognition he coveted. Disaffected, he attempted (1780) to surrender West Point to the British. The plot was uncovered; his accomplice, Major J. André, was executed, and Arnold fled to the British.

Arnold, Matthew 1822–88. English poet and critic, one of the great English literary figures of his day. An inspector of schools (1851–86) and an Oxford professor (1857–67), he published his first volume of poetry in 1849. He subsequently published collected works, such as *Other Poems* and *New Poems,* and works of literary and social criticism, such as *Essays in Criticism* and *Culture and Anarchy.* Arnold, an advocate of state-regulated secondary schools, also wrote on education and believed that the welfare of a nation hinged on its intellectual life.

Arnold, Thomas 1795–1842. English educator. His reforms as headmaster of the Rugby School influenced the English system of public education. He was the father of Matthew Arnold.

Arnold of Brescia c1090–1155. Italian monk and religious reformer. Opposed to church wealth and corruption, he supported a republican uprising in Rome, and in 1155 was arrested, tried, and executed.

Arnulf c850–899. King of the East Franks (887–899) and Carolingian emperor (896–99). He overthrew his uncle, Emperor Charles III, and became king of the Germans, defeated the Normans (891), invaded Italy at Pope Formosus' invitation, and captured Rome (1895). He was crowned emperor by the pope (896) and was the last Carolingian emperor.

Aroostook War US-Canadian border controversy. Residents of Maine and New Brunswick were involved in a dispute over rival claims to the Aroostook Valley in 1838–39, though there was no actual bloodshed. The question was settled by the Webster-Ashburton Treaty (1842).

Árpád c840–907. Magyar chief and Hungarian national hero. He led his people from Asia into what is now Hungary (c890) and founded the line of Hungarian kings known as the Árpád dynasty (ruled 997–1301).

Arras, Battle of 1. French victory (Aug. 24–25, 1654) at Arras, France, over Spanish forces in the last years of the Thirty Years' War. The French broke a Spanish siege of Arras, killing some 3,000 soldiers. 2. Unsuccessful British offensive (Apr. 9–May 3, 1917) at Arras, France, during WW I. The offensive, intended to draw German forces northward, was commanded by British field marshal D. Haig. Losses were 75,000 Germans and 84,000 British.

Arras, Treaty of 1. In 1435, French king Charles VII and Philip the Good, duke of Burgundy, concluded a treaty that reconciled the Burgundians with the monarchy and ended the Burgundian alliance with England (under the Treaty of Troyes). 2. In 1482, French king Louis XI signed a treaty with Maximilian I (later Holy Roman Emperor), providing for the marriage of his son to Maximilian's daughter. France got Artois and Franche-Comté, which it returned (1493) when the marriage was called off.

Arriaga, Manuel José de 1842–1917. Portuguese politician. A leader in the revolt (1910) that deposed King Manuel II, he was the first president (1911–15) of the republic. He resigned (1915), following royalist uprisings.

Arsacidae (Arsacids) (Arshakuni) Dynasty of Parthian rulers. Founded by Arsaces I (c247 BC), who overthrew the Seleucids, the dynasty ruled over Persia and Mesopotamia. The Arsacidae kings ruled until the Sassanidae conquest (AD c226). Noted rulers of the dynasty were Mithradates I and II (reigned 171–138 BC, 123–88 BC).

Arsacids *See* **Arsacidae.**

Arshakuni *See* **Arsacidae.**

Artaxerxes *See* **Ardashir I.**

Artaxerxes I *d.* 425 BC. Persian king (465–425 BC), successor to his father Xerxes I. He put down revolts in Egypt and Bactria, and fought the Athenians. He is noted for his toleration toward Judaism.

Artaxerxes II *d.* c359 BC. Persian king (404–c359 BC), successor to his father, Darius II. Under his rule Persia lost control of Egypt, and his brother Cyrus the Younger led an unsuccessful uprising (ending 401 at Cunaxa) against him. Conflicts with the Greek city-states also erupted, and Persian hegemony in Greece was established by the King's Peace (386 BC).

Artaxerxes III *d.* 338 BC. Persian king (c359–338 BC), successor to his father, Artaxerxes II. He won power by murdering many of his relatives and his reign was marked by cruelty and bloodshed. He conquered Egypt (343 BC) and checked the decline of the Persian Empire.

art deco Decorative style. Art deco is the style of art, architecture, and jewelry that developed in the 1920s. It is characterized by a streamlined look, achieved by the use of long, sleek, stylized lines.

Artevelde, Jacob van c1290–1345. A Flemish statesman who, at the outset of the Hundred Years' War between England and France, allied himself with Edward III of England and became ruler (c1337) of the city of Ghent. Though Ghent was dependent on the English wool trade, Artevelde's extreme pro-English policies led to his murder.

art for art's sake *See* **Gautier, Théophile.**

Arthur I 1187–1203? Duke of Brittany. On the death of his uncle, English king Richard I, his claim to the throne was usurped by his uncle, King John. Arthur was imprisoned (1202) by John, who is also believed to have murdered him.

Arthur, Chester Alan 1830–86. US president (1881–85), the 21st, successor to President J. Garfield following his assassination (1881). A prominent New York lawyer, he was early identified as a machine politician because of his association with New York Republican party boss Sen. Roscoe Conkling (1829–88). Although he had been allied with the Stalwarts faction (*q.v.*), Arthur became the Republican nominee for vice-president, as running mate to Garfield, and entered office with him (1881). There was concern Arthur might corrupt the national government with machine politics. But when he became president (Sept. 19, 1881), he reassured an anxious public and governed with integrity throughout his tenure. During his presidency, the Pendleton Civil Service Act (1883) was passed and the Star Route Frauds came to trial. He did not seek reelection and died soon after he left office.

Arthurian legend The exploits of the legendary British King Arthur and his Knights of the Round Table, as developed in medieval romances and adventure stories. Prominent elements of the legend include Arthur's life and conquests; the legend of Merlin; Sir Lancelot's affair with Arthur's wife, Queen Guinevere; the quest for the Holy Grail and the exploits of Sir Galahad, Parsifal, and others; Arthur's death from wounds sustained in battle with Mordred (his nephew and enemy); and the final ruin of Camelot. The legends are thought to derive from Celtic myths. Among the major works in the Arthurian cycle are *Historia Regnum Britanniae* (c1135) by Geoffrey of Monmouth, *Roman de Brut* (c1155) by Wace, works by Chrétien de Troyes, and *Morte d'Arthur* by Sir T. Malory.

Articles of Confederation First constitution of the US (1781–89), which established a confederation of the original thirteen states. Though a central government was created by the articles, real power resided with the states. The ultimate failure of this system led to creation of a strong federal government. The articles were drafted (1776) by J. Dickinson, were passed (Nov. 15, 1777) by the Continental Congress, and became effective Mar. 1, 1781. They kept the Continental Congress as the confederation's central government and theoretically gave it power to control national and international affairs. But the Congress lacked enforcement powers, and by 1786 it was clear a new form of government was needed. The articles were superseded (1789) by the Constitution, drafted at the Constitutional Convention (1787).

Articles of Schwabach Seventeen Protestant articles of faith drawn up (1529) by M. Luther and others at Schwabach, Bavaria. These articles subsequently formed the basis of the Augsburg Confession (*q.v.*).

Artigas, José Gervasio 1764–1850. Uruguayan revolutionary leader and national hero. He fought in the revolution (1811) against Spain and then against the junta governing the United Provinces. Artigas stablished control over areas now in Uruguay and Argentina (1814–20) but was forced into exile by a Portuguese invasion from Brazil.

art nouveau Artistic style. Art Nouveau developed in the late 19th cent. and early 20th cent. as a reaction against the excesses of Victorian art. It emphasized the use of lines, as typified by works of P. Gauguin and H. Toulouse-Lautrec.

Arundel, Thomas Howard, earl of *See* **Howard, Thomas, 13th earl of Arundel.**

Arval Brothers In Roman religion, a college of 12 priests, chosen from the highest Roman families, which presided over rites to promote fertility of the fields.

Aryabhata AD c476–550. Hindu mathematician and astronomer. He was one of the first to use algebra. He also explained solar and lunar eclipses and the earth's rotation on its axis.

Aryan Name once used for the Indo-European peoples who spread through south Asia and northern India in ancient times. J. Gobineau spread (19th cent.) a popular but false notion concerning the existence of a superior Aryan race. This notion later formed the basis for Nazi claims that they were a "master race" and was used to justify programs to exterminate Jews and other "inferior" races.

Asa *d.* 875 BC. Third king of Judah (c915–875 BC), successor to his father, Abijah. He opposed idolatry and recaptured territory from the Israelites. [1 Kings 15; 2 Chron 14–16]

Asante, Empire of *See* **Ashanti, Empire of.**

Asbury, Francis 1745–1816. English-born American Methodist missionary. Asbury came to America (1771) and became the first Methodist bishop in America (1784). He inaugurated the circuit-rider system for frontier missionary work.

asceticism Doctrine that calls for self-denial of material and sensual pleasures in order to develop spiritual or inner powers. It has figured in the development of both philosophy and religion. It was advocated by the Cynics and Stoics in ancient Greece and was important in the development of monasticism.

Asculum, Battle of (Ausculum, ~) 1. Victory (279 BC) for Pyrrhus, king of Epirus, over the

Romans in what is now southeast Italy. Some 40,000 soldiers under Pyrrhus defeated an equal force of Romans at great cost. Casualties numbered 6,000 Epirots to 3,500 Romans, giving rise to the expression "Pyrrhic victory." 2. Victory (89 BC) for Rome in the Social War (*q.v.*). The revolt against Rome led by the Marsi and other tribes centered in the south, at Asculum and was marked by a massacre of Roman citizens there (90 BC). The Romans retook the city (89 BC), exacted retribution, and soon after ended the war by extending citizenship to the rebellious tribes.

Ashanti, Empire of (Asante, ˜) African kingdom in what is now central Ghana. The Ashanti people occupied the region by the 13th cent. and, in the second half of the 17th, King Osei Tutu created the empire, with his capital at Kumasi. The Ashanti continued to expand their empire, supplying (18th cent.) the British and Dutch with slaves from conquered peoples. Wars with the British in the 1820s, 1860s, and 1870s led first to a British takeover (1896), then annexation to the British Gold Coast colony (1901).

Ashikaga period (Muromachi period) In Japanese history, the period in which the Ashikaga shoguns ruled (1338–1578). Their capital was located at Kyōto. Though the era was marked by the rising power of regional warlords and frequent warfare (supporters of two rival emperors warred 1336–92), it nevertheless saw commercial prosperity, increased foreign trade, extensive contacts with China, and the flowering of Zen Buddhist culture.

Ashley, William *See* **Sunday, Billy.**

Ashurbanipal (Assurbanipal) (Asurbanipal) *d.* c626 BC. Last of the great Assyrian kings (c669–c626 BC) and successor to his father, Esarhaddon. He was unable to keep rebellious Egypt (660 BC) within the empire, though he crushed a rebellion in Babylon (c648 BC) and conquered the Elamites. During his reign the empire reached the height of its splendor. At Ninevah Ashurbanipal organized a famous royal library whose 22,000 clay tablets have become a prime source of knowledge about the Mesopotamian world.

Ashurnasirpal II *d.* 859 BC. Assyrian king (884–859 BC). A ruthless conqueror, he greatly expanded his empire, extending it westward to the Mediterranean. He centralized authority by installing governors in conquered lands and moved his capital from Ninevah to Calah.

Asia Minor (Anatolia) Asian section of Turkey, the peninsular region also identified as Anatolia.

asiento de negros Spanish slave contracts. They were drawn up between Spain and a company or nation providing African slaves to Spain's American colonies. The most famous was made with the British South Sea Company (1713) and figured in the outbreak of the War of Jenkins's Ear.

Asís, Francisco de, duke of Cádiz *See* **Affair of the Spanish Marriages.**

Askia Muhammad I *See* **Songhai, Empire of.**

Asoka *d.* c232 BC. Indian emperor (273–232 BC) of the Maurya dynasty. A great conqueror, he unified much of India for the first time, bringing it under his control. Then, remorseful of the suffering he had caused, he converted to Buddhism and did much to ensure its spread throughout India.

Aspern-Essling, Battle of Battle (May 21–22, 1809, near Vienna) during the Napoleonic Wars. Austrian archduke Charles Louis, commanding 80,000 soldiers, defeated Napoleon's army of 80,000 men. Austria lost 24,000 men, the French over 20,000, including Marshal J. Lannes. It was Napoleon's most serious defeat up to that time.

Asquith, Herbert Henry, 1st earl of Oxford and Asquith 1852–1928. British statesman and prime minister (1908–16), successor to H. Campbell-Bannerman. A Liberal member of Parliament from 1886, he became an influential party spokesman and helped return the Liberals to power in 1905. He was chancellor of the exchequer (1905–08). As prime minister, he instituted old-age pensions (1908) and unemployment insurance (1911). Following a crisis over the budget, he won passage of the Parliament Act of 1911, by which the House of Lords lost its veto powers. Asquith's advocacy (1912) of Irish Home Rule precipitated a crisis in Ireland. Britain entered WW I under his guidance but military setbacks led to his ouster in 1916. He continued as Liberal party leader until 1926.

Assad, Hafiz al- 1928– . Syrian general and president (1971–). Assad was a defense minister who became Syria's president (1971) after leading a bloodless *coup d'état*. He sent the Syrian peace-keeping force in Lebanon (1976) and eventually agreed to a peace settlement in the long civil war there. *See also* Syria, from 1971.

Assandum, Battle of Victory (Oct. 18, 1016) for the invading Danes, led by Canute, over the English, led by Edmund Ironside, in what is now Essex, England.

Assassin Member of secret Muslim sect that, by its practice of murdering all enemies of the order, terrorized the Muslim world (11th–13th cents.). It was founded (c1090) by Hasan ibn al-Sabbah (*d.* 1124) after the capture of Almut, a fort in Persia (now Iran). From this base the sect, an offshoot of the Ismaili sect of Islam, spread throughout Persia and into Syria. Its followers in Persia were said to have murdered caliphs, generals, and statesmen of the Abbasid caliphate before the order fell to Mongol invaders (1256). The Syrian branch fell (1272) to the Mamelukes of Egypt.

Assembly of Notables French assembly called (Feb., 1787) in the years prior to the French Revolution (1789–99). It was convoked by Finance Minister Charles Calonne (1734–1802) to approve a land tax needed to keep the government out of bankruptcy. The assembly refused to give its approval, as had the Parliament, and forced Calonne's ouster. The assembly was dissolved May, 1787.

Assideans *See* **Hasidim**

Assisi, Saint Francis of *See* **Francis of Assisi, Saint.**

assize Term meaning a session of a court of law, as in the case of Bloody Assizes (*q.v.*). The term was also used in reference to ordinances, as in Assize of Arms (*q.v.*).

Assize of Arms English ordinance issued by King Henry II (1181), ordering knights and freemen to acquire arms according to income and rank.

Assize of Clarendon English judicial reforms (1166). Henry II instituted these reforms, which included changes in criminal law and established the first organized code for judge and jury selection.

Assurbanipal *See* **Ashurbanipal.**

Assyria An ancient Near Eastern empire that, at its height (9th–7th cents. BC), included lands in present-day Arabia, Egypt, Iran, Iraq, Syria, Palestine, and Turkey. Assyria's original capital, Ashur—named after the city's principal god—was located on the upper Tigris River as early as the 3d millennium BC. From Ashur Assyrians expanded by means of successive military conquests. Innovative and effective soldiers and organizers of what they conquered, they were legendary in antiquity for their cruelty. Their greatest expansion began with Tiglath-Pileser III, who subdued Babylonia. Sargon II defeated Israel (722 BC) and deported the inhabitants. The wars of his successor, Sennacherib, with his vassal, Hezekiah of Judah, are mentioned in the Bible. Under Ashurbanipal, Assyria reached its height (7th cent. BC). The cuneiform library collected about this time, and excavated from the ruins of the Assyrian capital at Ninevah, constitutes one of the best sources of knowledge about the ancient Near East. Early in the reign of Ashurbanipal, Egypt broke away from the empire in a revolt led by Psamtik I. Thereafter the decline was rapid. The Medes and the Babylonians conquered Ninevah itself in 612 BC.

Aston, Francis William 1877–1945. An English physicist. He developed the mass spectrograph and discovered a number of isotopes. He was awarded the Nobel Prize in Chemistry in 1922.

Astor, John Jacob 1763–1848. American merchant, financier, and founder of the Astor family fortune. In 1808, he formed the American Fur Company (*q.v.*), which came to monopolize US fur trade and is considered the first American trust.

Astor, Nancy Witcher Langhorne, viscountess Astor 1879–1964. An American-born British politician. She was the first woman to sit in the House of Commons (1919–45) and was identified with the "Cliveden set," a group of British leaders who sought to appease Fascist powers in the 1930s.

Asturias, kingdom of Former Spanish kingdom (718–910) located in northwestern Spain. Fleeing the Muslim invasion of Spain, Visigothic nobles formed this northern kingdom as the last Christian stronghold in Spain. In succeeding centuries it served as the starting point for the Christian reconquest of Spain and became known as the kingdom of León and Asturias.

Astyages *fl.* 6th cent. BC. Last king of the Median Empire (584–c550 BC). He was overthrown by Cyrus the Great, who thereby founded Persia.

Asurbanipal *See* **Ashurbanipal.**

Atahaulpa *d.* 1533. Last Inca ruler before the Spanish conquest of Peru. He overthrew his brother Huascar (1532) and made himself ruler of the Inca Empire in Peru. He was captured (1532) and executed by the Spanish conquistadors under F. Pizarro.

Atatürk, Kemal 1881–1938. Turkish soldier statesman, and president (1923–38), considered the founder of modern Turkey. He was a leading figure in the Young Turks and other nationalist groups from 1908. By 1921 he headed a nationalist army, which repulsed a Greek invasion (1919–22) and subsequently overthrew the sultan (1922). He abolished the sultanate (Nov. 1, 1922), and, during his long term as president of the republic, he instituted many reforms aimed at westernizing Turkey.

Athaliah *fl.* 9th cent. BC. In the Old Testament the wife of Jehoram and mother of Ahaziah. She succeeded Ahaziah and became queen of Judah, slaying all the royal children but Jehoash. An uprising resulted in her death and the succession of Jehoash.

Athanagild *d.* 567. Visigothic king of Spain (554–567). He became king by an alliance with Byzantine emperor Justinian I and restored peace within his domains by ending persecution of Catholics. He was father of Frankish queens Brunhilda and Galswintha.

Athanasius, Saint AD c293–373. Patriarch of Alexandria (AD 328–373) and Doctor of the Church. He attended the First Council of Nicaea and became the chief defender of Nicene orthodoxy against Arianism. He was several times exiled for his beliefs.

atheism Philosophical doctrine. Atheists deny the existence of God or any other supernatural power. The term was used by the ancient Greeks and the Romans viewed Christians as atheists (because Christians denied the existence of all gods but the one Christian God). Atheism in the modern sense did not become significant in the Western world until the 18th cent. Among the noted exponents of atheism are P. Holbach, L. Feuerback, and R. Ingersoll.

Athelstan (Aethelstan) *d.* 939. Saxon king (924–939), successor to his father, Edward the Elder. He defeated a confederation of his opponents at Brunanburh 937) and became the first Saxon ruler of all England.

Athenian League, Second Another name for the second alliance (378–338 BC) of Greek city-states dominated by Athens.

Athens Historic city and capital of Greece. Athens was a focal point of ancient Greek culture, noted as a center of the arts and learning. Many of the temples and other buildings of the ancient city remain as classic works of architecture. The democratic form of government developed in the city-state of Athens is considered the forerunner of modern democracy. Great philosophers (Socrates, Plato, Aristotle) taught there and the masters of Greek drama (Aeschylus, Sophocles, Euripides, and Aristophanes) were all Athenians. Inhabited before 3000 BC, Athens rose as a dominant city-state in ancient Greece during the 5th cent. BC. Its power was broken by its archrival Sparta, during the Peloponnesian War at the end of the 5th cent. Athens continued for a time as a cultural center, but it never again attained its former greatness. (*See also* Greece.) Key events in the history of Athens include:

c700 BC Athens became leader of 12 towns in Attica.

683 BC Hereditary kingship abolished in Athens; archons to serve one year.

621 BC Draco's law code; first Athenian law code established harsh system of justice.

594 BC Solon made archon amid grave social crisis; Draconian code reformed; involuntary servitude for debt (serfdom) abolished; reforms laid basis for democracy.

561–527 BC Pisistratus in power as tyrant; rapid expansion of city begun; temple construction started.

508 BC Cleisthenes instituted his reforms; established Athenian democracy.

490–479 BC Persian Wars; Athens and the other city-states ultimately repulsed the Persian invaders.

490–480 BC Themistocles in power; built up Athenian navy and (in 478) rebuilt the city's fortifications.

c480–c380 BC Greek drama flourished at Athens during this period.

480 BC Athens destroyed by Persian king Xerxes; rebuilt soon after.

480 BC Athenian navy and allies won a great victory over the Persians at Salamis.

478 BC Delian League formed by Athens to protect against Persians.

462–429 BC Pericles rose to power; fostered Athenian golden age and made Athens the political and cultural center of Greece.

454 BC Treasury of the Delian League transferred to Athens; Athens dominated other city states of the league.

447 BC Construction of the classical temples on the Acropolis began.

431–404 BC Peloponnesian War against Sparta; victorious Spartans forced Athens to tear down its defenses; imposed rule of Thirty Tyrants (404); Athens never regained former power.

403 BC Athenians overthrew the Thirty Tyrants.

399 BC Socrates condemned to poison himself.

395–387 BC Corinthian War.

c387 BC Plato founded the Academy at Athens.

378 BC The Second Athenian Naval League formed by Athens.

357–355 BC Social War; Athens forced to recognize independence of some of the allies it had once dominated.

338 BC Battle of Chaeronaea; Macedonians conquered Athens.

c335 BC Aristotle opened his school, the Lyceum, at Athens.

323–322 BC Lamian War; unsuccessful revolt against Macedonian rule; Athens reduced to a provincial city; became a center of Hellenic culture.

197 BC Athens came under Roman control, after Romans defeated Macedonians.

86 BC Roman general Sulla sacked Athens, after Athenians opposed Rome in the Mithridatic War.

FROM AD 395 Visigoths captured city (395) as Roman power declined; Athens entered a long period of obscurity in which it passed to Byzantines and later the Turks (15th cent.)

1687–88 Parthenon badly damaged in war between Ottoman Turks and Venice.

1834 Athens became capital of independent Greek kingdom; city largely rebuilt in following years.

1941–1944 German occupation of city during WW II.

Athens, Timon of *See* Timon of Athens.

Athos, Mount *See* Mount Athos.

Atkinson, Sir Harry Albert 1831–92. A British-born prime minister (1876–77, 1883–84, 1887–90) of New Zealand. While serving as prime minister and in other government posts, he encouraged local farming and industry, abolished provincial governments, and established a centralized government.

Atlanta, Battle of *See* Atlanta Campaign.

Atlanta Campaign Series of battles (May 7–Sept. 2, 1864) fought by Union forces to capture Atlanta, Georgia, during the American Civil War (1861–65). Atlanta's capture was an important factor in the reelection of President A. Lincoln. Gen. W. Sherman began moving his 100,000-man army from Chattanooga toward Atlanta on May 7. He was opposed in a long series of battles by Gen. J. Johnston (replaced by Gen. J. Hood, July 17), commanding a smaller Confederate force. These battles included engagements at Kennesaw Mountain (June 27), Peachtree Creek (July 20), Atlanta (July 22), and Ezra Church (July 28). Thereafter Sherman began heavy bombardment of the city and gradually extended Union positions around it. Sherman forced Gen. Hood to abandon the city, and occupied it Sept. 2, 1864.

Atlanta Compromise Plan for racial harmony. In a speech given (1895) at Atlanta, Georgia, black spokesman B. T. Washington advocated friendly but separate social existences for America's blacks and whites. Whites applauded the speech, but disapproving blacks later founded the Niagara Movement (1905).

Atlantic, Battle of the Prolonged contest for control of the Atlantic during WW II. The German Navy, far smaller than the British and French navies at the outset of the war, soon resorted to submarine warfare. Allied losses of cargo shipping were heavy during the early part of WW II. But, by mid-1943, the Allies were clearly winning the battle against German submarine wolf packs, by using the convoy system and antisubmarine warfare techniques.

Atlantic Charter WII declaration (Aug. 14, 1941) by British prime minister W. Churchill and US president F. Roosevelt that outlined a program for world peace. The principles of the Atlantic Charter were later incorporated (1942) into the UN Charter. The joint declaration resulted from meetings between the two leaders held aboard naval vessels in the Atlantic. Though the US was still officially neutral, it pledged, with Britain, to: forgo territorial gains; restore sovereignty to governments conquered by force; make basic raw materials available to all nations; promote improvement of economic and social conditions worldwide; ensure freedom from fear and want; maintain freedom of the seas; and work toward eliminating war.

atomic bomb Weapon of great destructive power, using energy that results from the splitting of atoms. It was developed by the US in a crash program (Manhattan Project, from 1940) during WW II. The first atomic bomb was exploded (July 16, 1945) at the New Mexico testing grounds. Two bombs were subsequently dropped on Japan (Hiroshima, Aug. 6, and Nagasaki, Aug. 9, 1945), which forced Japan's surrender and opened the age of nuclear warfare.

atomism Scientific doctrine. Atomism holds that the universe is composed of individual particles that are invisible and indestructible. First put forward by such ancient Greek thinkers as Leucippus and Democritus, the theory gained importance among European scientists from the 17th cent. on.

atomists Early school of Greek philosophy, adherents of atomism (*q.v.*).

Attalid (dynasty) *See* **Pergamum.**

Attalus *See* **Pergamum.**

Attica Region surrounding Athens in ancient Greece, located in what is now east-central Greece. The early history of the region is uncertain. Greek legend tells of the unification of 12 independent Attic towns by Theseus to form the city-state of Athens. From the 13th cent. BC onward, Athens was the preeminent city of Attica and, from the 5th cent. BC, the region came under Athenian control. Other Attic cities include Marathon and Eleusis.

Attila AD 406?–453. King of the Huns (AD 434–453), notorious as the leader of savage barbarian hordes from central Asia that attacked the Roman Empire. Called the "Scourge of God," he became ruler of the Huns with his brother Bleda in 434. Though East Roman emperor Theodosius II had agreed (434) to pay the Huns tribute, Attila and Bleda nevertheless attacked (441) the eastern Roman provinces. They ravaged the countryside and finally agreed (443) to a treaty that trebled monies paid by the Romans. After murdering Bleda (445), Attila became sole ruler of the Huns and again attacked (447–50) the Romans. In 450 Roman emperors Marcian and Valentinian III refused Attila his tribute. Attila, with an army of some 500,000 barbarians, invaded Gaul (451), unsuccessfully laid siege to Orléans, and was defeated (451) at the Battle of Châlons by the Romans and Visigoths. He withdrew to Hungary, then ravaged northern Italy (452), and was forced to break off the invasion before reaching Rome. He died a short time later.

Attlee, Clement Richard, 1st earl 1883–1967. British statesman and prime minister (1945–51). A social worker and member of the Fabian Society in his early years, he headed the British Labour party (1935–55). As prime minister, he instituted many important Socialist reforms, including founding of the National Health Service and nationalization of the Bank of England, utilities, and basic industries. His administration also saw Britain's granting of independence to India (1947), Pakistan (1947), Burma (1948), Palestine (1948), and Ceylon (1948, now Sri Lanka).

Attucks, Crispus *See* **Boston Massacre.**

Auden, W(ystan) H(ugh) 1907–73. A British-born American poet, considered a major 20th-cent. literary figure. During the 1930s, he was one of a group of left-wing writers whose works reflected their concern for social issues.

audiencia Court of Spain during the late medieval period. It had administrative and judicial powers, and figured prominently in Spain's American colonies, where it helped check abuses of authority by colonial government officials.

Audubon, John James 1785–1851. American ornithologist and artist, best known for his drawings of North American birds in *The Birds of America.*

Augsburg, Diet of Meeting convened (Apr. 8, 1530) by Holy Roman Emperor Charles V to convince rebellious Lutheran noblemen to help turn back a Turkish invasion of the empire. The meeting failed to win over the Lutherans. The Augsburg Confession (*q.v.*) was presented during this council. Other diets held at Augsburg include those of 1547–48 (*see* Augsburg Interim) and 1555 (*see* Augsburg, Peace of).

Augsburg, League of Pact formed (July 9, 1686) against France by Holy Roman Emperor Leopold I and his allies prior to the War of the League of Augsburg (1688–97). Leopold entered into the defensive alliance with Holland, Sweden, Spain, Bavaria, the Palatinate, and Saxony. The league was replaced (1689) by the Grand Alliance.

Augsburg, Peace of A convention established (Sept. 25, 1555) at Augsburg, Bavaria, providing for an end to religious conflicts of the Reformation within the Holy Roman Empire. The settlement allowed individual states to decide whether Catholicism or Lutheranism was to be practiced in their territories and determined that Catholics and Lutherans should migrate to states where their faith had been adopted. Though Calvinists were not included in the agreement, the settlement halted religious conflicts in the empire for some 50 years.

Augsburg Confession A statement of the basic doctrines of the Lutheran church, presented (1530) at the Diet of Augsburg. The creed was largely written by P. Melanchthon and remains the authoritative statement of the Lutheran faith. The 28 articles were drawn up to provide a statement of principles that could be accepted by the Holy Roman Empire's Roman Catholics and that would put an end to false claims about Lutheran doctrine.

Augsburg Interim Provisional settlement issued (May 15, 1548) by Holy Roman Emperor Charles V in an unsuccessful attempt to halt disputes between Catholics and Lutherans within the empire. Lutherans, however, objected to the terms and adopted (1548) a counterproposal, the Leipzig Interim.

augur A Roman prophet who interpreted omens and signs believed to be warnings from the gods. Augurs were held in high esteem until Theodosius abolished the College of Augurs (AD c391).

Augusta, Treaty of Treaty (1773) between the colony of Georgia and the Cherokee and Creek Indians. The Indians gave up two tracts of land the sale of which was to pay off debts to white merchants.

Augustan Age Period of great literary flowering in Rome (usually, 27 BC–AD 14; also 43 BC–AD 17). With the preceding Ciceronian Period, it forms the Golden Age of Roman literary history. During this period, many of the greatest figures in Latin literature wrote under the patronage of Emperor Augustus and his adviser Maecenas. Among the classics completed in this age are Vergil's *Aeneid,* parts of Horace's *Odes* and *Epistles,* Propertius's elegies, Livy's *History of Rome,* and Ovid's *Metamorphoses. By* extension, Augustan Age also refers to a literary flowering in other nations (i.e., 18th-cent. England and 17th-cent. France).

Augustine, Saint AD 354–430. Great Christian thinker and a Father of the Church. He first became a follower of Manichaeanism, was converted to Christianity by Saint Ambrose (AD 387), and subsequently became bishop of Hippo in Africa (AD 396). A Neoplationist, he brought together Christian religion and Greek philo-

sophical traditions in his teachings. Among his important works are attacks on Manichaeanism, Donatism, and Pelagianism. His most famous works include *Confessions* and *The City of God.*

Augustine of Canterbury, Saint *d.* c605. Italian, first archbishop of Canterbury, known as the Apostle of England. He and forty other Benedictine monks went to England (597) and there converted King Aethelbert. Augustine established a church and monastery at Canterbury.

Augustinians Broadly, name applied to religious orders in the Roman Catholic church that follow the Rule of Saint Augustine (concerning monastic life). More specifically, it refers to three religious orders: Augustinian Canons, an order of Roman Catholic clerics (formed 11th cent.); Augustinian Hermits, formed (1256) by the unification of autonomous Italian monasteries; and the Augustinian Recollects, a reformist offshoot (16 cent.) of the Augustinian Hermits.

Augustus (*orig.* Gaius Octavius) (*adopted name* Gaius Julius Caesar Octavianus) (*sometimes called* Octavian) Sept. 23, 63 BC–AD Aug. 19, 14. First of the Roman emperors (27 BC–AD 14) and an able administrator who established the structure of Rome's imperial government. A grandson of J. Caesar's youngest sister, he became a favorite of Caesar's and and thereby gained an early entrée into public life. Only 18 when Caesar was assassinated, young Gaius Octavius suddenly learned from Caesar's will that the dictator had adopted him and named him as his heir. Though M. Antony at first forcibly opposed his right of succession, Octavian (as Augustus is usually referred to during this period) won powerful allies in the Senate and soon arranged a settlement with Antony. He, Antony, and M. Lepidus then agreed to share power, forming the Second Triumvirate (Nov. 27, 43) to rule the West (Caesar's assassins held the East). Soon afterward the triumvirs ordered a bloody purge, killing 300 Roman senators and some 2,000 other political enemies (Cicero among them). Octavian and Antony next avenged Caesar's death by defeating M. Brutus and C. Cassius at Philippi (42). Later, by the Treaty of Brundisium (40), Octavian formally took control of the West, Lepidus got Africa, and Antony the East, though he was also obliged to take Octavian's sister, Octavia, for his bride. Octavian strengthened his ties with the aristocracy by marrying the influential Livia Drusilla (38), while Antony's continued dalliance with Cleopatra aroused opposition to him in Rome. Octavian meanwhile further strengthened his position by defeating the rebel S. Pompeius at Mylae and Cape Naulochus, Sicily (36). Then, with the Second Triumvirate (renewed, 37) finally at an end in 32, Octavian's only serious rival for control of the empire was Antony. Capitalizing on accumulated resentment over Antony's affair with Cleopatra, Octavian launched a military expedition against Antony and Cleopatra. His great victory at Actium (31), and the subsequent suicides of Antony and Cleopatra, made Octavian sole ruler of the Roman Empire. The Roman republican government, long in decay, was never to be the same again. While maintaining the outward republican forms, Octavian nevertheless transformed his government into a monarchic regime. Octavian began his rule as "first citizen," though the Senate gave him the title *imperator* (from which "emperor" is derived) in 29, *princeps* (from which "prince" is derived) in 28, and finally *augustus* (meaning reverend or august) in 27. The end of the Roman republic and start of the empire are usually dated from this time in 27 BC. Augustus's reign was marked by prosperity and stability, administrative reforms, consolidation of power in Rome, the establishment of Pax Romana (a long period of relative peace that lasted until c180), and a bloody defeat of a Roman army by the rebel German chieftain Arminius (*q.v.*) in AD 9. Augustus made Egypt a Roman province (30 BC), reduced and dispersed Rome's standing army, formed the Praetorian Guard (27), reduced the size of the Senate from 1,000 to 600 and made himself its president, extended the frontier northward deep into Germany (by 9), evolved the beginnings of an imperial civil service, reformed the financial system, annexed Judaea (AD 6), expanded the network of roads throughout the empire and completed many public buildings. His extensive patronage of the arts (he was patron of Vergil, Livy, Horace, and Ovid) fostered a cultural flowering known as the Augustan Age (*q.v.*). The month of August was named after him. Upon his death, Augustus was succeeded by his stepson Tiberius.

Augustus II (~ the Strong) 1670–1733.   King of Poland (1697–1733) and elector of Saxony

(1694–1733). He provoked the Northern War (1700–21) with Sweden to gain possession of Livonia and, defeated, was forced to abdicate (1706) by the Treaty of Altranstadt. He was restored (1709) after Russia, an ally, defeated Sweden.

Augustus III 1696–1763. King of Poland (1734–63) and elector of Saxony (1733–63), successor to his father, Augustus II. A patron of the arts, he left affairs of state to his ministers. He supported Austria in the War of the Austrian Succession and the Seven Years' War.

Augustus the Strong   *See* **Augustus II.**

Aulic Council   Court and advisory council of the Holy Roman Empire. Established (c1498) by Maximilian I, it was intended to assist the emperor in executive matters. It eventually became a powerful judicial court of appeals, however, and functioned until the fall of the empire (1806).

Aungzeya   *See* **Alaungpaya.**

Aurangzeb (Aurungzebe) 1618–1707. Mughal emperor of India (1658–1707), successor to his father, Shah Jahan. He brought the Hindu-Muslim Mughal empire to the height of its power. Though his reign brought great prosperity and expansion of Mughal domains, his rule was also marked by numerous rebellions among the Sikhs, Rajputs, Jats, and especially the Marathas. The empire broke up shortly after his death.

Aurelian (Aurelianus, Lucius Domitius) AD c212–275.   Roman general and emperor (AD 270–275), successor to Claudius II. One of the great Roman emperors, he briefly restored the disintegrating empire. Though forced to give up Dacia to the Goths, he stopped the barbarian advance at the Danube, reestablished Roman rule in the East (272) by capturing Zenobia and Palmyra, and restored Roman rule over Europe by defeating Tetricus (274), his rival for control of the region. He was assassinated while on a military campaign against the Persians. Aurelian's Wall, a 12-mile-long defensive fortification around Rome, was begun by him.

Aurelian's Wall   *See* **Aurelian.**

Aurelianus, Lucius Domitius   *See* **Aurelian.**

Aurelius, Marcus   *See* **Marcus Aurelius.**

Auriol, Vincent 1884–1966.   French statesman. A Socialist deputy from 1914, he served as first president of the French Fourth Republic from 1947 to 1954.

Aurungizebe *See* **Aurangzeb.**

Auschwitz (*properly,* Auschwitz-Birkenau) Noto-rious German concentration camp established (1940) by the Nazis. Some 4 million people, mostly Jews, are believed to have been extermi-nated there during WW II.

Ausculum, Battle of *See* **Asculum, Battle of.**

Ausgleich Facilitating agreement (Feb., 1867) that created the Austro-Hungarian Dual Monar-chy. Following Austria's defeat in the Austro-Prussian War (1866), negotiations between the two monarchies (in progress since 1864) were stepped up. The compromise agreement was finally reached. By its terms, the two states maintained separate ministries and parliaments, shared military and foreign-policy responsibili-ties and common expenses. Austrian emperor Francis Joseph was crowned king of Hungary (June 8, 1867).

Austen, Jane 1775–1817. English novelist famous for her comedies of manners. Her novels treat the life of the English gentry and are noted for their sharp insights into character and society. Her works include *Sense and Sensibility, Pride and Predjudice, Mansfield Park, Emma,* and *Persuasion.*

Austerlitz, Battle of (The Battle of the Three Emperors) Great victory by Napoleon (Dec. 2, 1805) over the combined Russian and Austrian forces during the Napoleonic Wars. It was the first battle of the War of the Third Coalition. Napoleon, with 68,000 soldiers, engaged the 83,000-man force under Tsar Alexander I and Emperor Francis II near Austerlitz (now Slav-kov). By his brilliant plan and its execution, Napoleon crushed and scattered the superior force. Austro-Russian losses, including prison-ers, were some 26,000 to Napoleon's 9,000 casu-alties. The defeat forced Russia to withdraw from Austria, and Austria to sign the Treaty of Press-burg (1805).

Austin, Stephen Fuller 1793–1836. An Ameri-can pioneer who founded Anglo-American set-tlements in Texas in the 1820s, when the region was under Mexican jurisdiction. He is known as "the Father of Texas."

Australasia Term sometimes used to denote cer-tain islands in the South Pacific, including Aus-tralia, New Zealand, New Guinea, and other islands in the region. It is also used as an equiva-lent term for Oceania.

Australia (Commonwealth of Australia) Aus-tralia is the smallest continent and is located between the Pacific and Indian oceans. The pop-ulation is 16,646,000 and the capital is Can-berra. The Commonwealth is made up of the states New South Wales, Victoria, Queensland, South Australia, Western Australia, and Tasma-nia, and two territories, the Northern Territory and the Australian Capital Territory. Long a member of the British Commonwealth, Aus-tralia was originally settled by the British as a penal colony. Key dates in the history of Aus-tralia include:

c38,000 BC Aborigines believed to have arrived in what is now Australia.

1601 Portuguese sailor Manuel Godhino de Eredia believed to have sighted Australia.

1606 Spaniard Luis Vaez de Torres believed to have sighted Australia.

1606 Dutch explorers aboard the ship *Duyfhen* sighted Queensland.

1606 Dutch explorer Dirk Hartog explored Australia's western coast.

1642 Now famous Dutch navigator A. Tas-man discovered Tasmania (Nov. 24), calling it Van Diemen's Land; later charted Australia's northern coast (1644).

1688 Englishman W. Dampier explored west-ern coast and landed at King Sound.

1770 Captain J. Cook, aboard the *Endeavour,* explored Botany Bay; claimed eastern Aus-tralian coast for Britain.

1788 First British penal colony established at present-day Sydney (Jan. 26); Rose Hill established as colony's farm (Nov.).

LATE 1700s Escaped convicts formed groups of roving bandits called bushrangers; last of bushranger bandit gangs (led by Ned Kelly) killed off or executed by 1880.

1793 First group of settlers who are not con-victs arrived.

1801–03 British navigator Matthew Flinders (1774–1814) completed first circumnaviga-tion of Australia (June 9, at Port Jackson) aboard the *Investigator.*

1803 Founding of first Australian newspaper, *Sydney Gazette and New South Wales Advertiser.*

1804–30 European settlers nearly eliminated Tasmanian aborigines in Black War.

1806–08 W. Bligh, ill-fated captain of HMS *Bounty,* became governor of the colony; removed from office by Rum Rebellion (Jan. 26).

1817   First bank founded in Australia.

1823   Court system and legislative councils established.

1824   Newspaper *Australian* founded by W. Wentworth.

1825   Brisbane founded as a penal colony.

1829–50   Britain claimed entire continent (1829); Australian Colonies Government Act granted limited self-government (1850).

1831   Crown land grants abolished; lands to be sold at auction.

1836   Church of England installed its first bishop in Australia.

1849   Sir H. Parks began his campaign to end transport of British criminals to Australia.

1851   Gold strike in Victoria brought rush of new immigrants and marked beginning of period of rapid development; later gold strikes made in Queensland (1872–82), Western Australia (1892–93).

1854   Eureka stockade; revolt by miners put down.

1854   Service began on country's first railroad, linking Port Melbourne with Melbourne.

1858   Telegraph service established.

1862   Explorer John McDouall Stuart (1815–66) became first to cross the continent.

1866   Public School Act established education system in New South Wales.

1868   Transport of British criminals to Australia ended; last contingent of British troops left Australia two years later.

1880   Telephone service began in major cities.

1890s   Major strikes broke out during this period.

1891–98   Constitution drafted.

1894   Woman suffrage granted for first time in South Australia colony.

1899   Boer War; Australia sent troops to aid British.

1900   British Parliament passed Commonwealth of Australia Constitution Act.

1901   Constitution put into effect; Australian colonies federated as Commonwealth of Australia.

1901–03   Edmund Barton, leading figure in Australia's federation movement, in office as first prime minister; resigned in reaction to partisan politics of new Parliament.

1901   Immigration Restriction Act passed to limit influx of non-Europeans.

1901   National flag adopted.

1902   Woman suffrage granted for all national government elections.

1903–04   A. Deakin in office as prime minister; served again in 1905–08 and 1909–10.

1906   Papua and New Guinea made territories of Australia.

1913   Construction of capital, Canberra, begun.

1914–18   World War I; Australia joined allies and sent troops (from 1914); occupied German New Guinea (1914).

1915   William L. Bragg awarded Nobel Prize for Physics (shared with his father William H. Bragg), the first person born in Australia to win the award.

1917   Transcontinental railroad completed.

1919   Australia joined League of Nations; Australian-occupied German New Guinea made League of Nations mandate under Australia's control.

1922   Australian airline Qantas began first regular service.

1923   Broadcast radio station in operation.

1923–29   Viscount Bruce of Melbourne in office as prime minister.

1927   Government moved capital to Canberra.

1930   Depression hit Australia; government subsequently imposed austerity measures to ease economic ills.

1931   United Australia party formed.

1931–39   J. Lyons in office as prime minister; his term marked by period of economic stability.

1939–41   R. Menzies served as prime minister.

1939–45   World War II; Australia joined the Allies, sending its first troops to Libya (1940); declared war on Japan after Pearl Harbor.

1942   US Gen. D. MacArthur, driven out of Philippines by invading Japanese, arrived in Australia; began to regroup Allied forces in Pacific to halt Japanese advance; Allied victories in Coral Sea and elsewhere forestalled possible invasion of Australia by Japanese.

1944   Menzies organized new Liberal party, succeeding United Australia party.

1945   Australia became founding member of UN.

1948–49   Australian statesman H. Evatt served as UN General Assembly president.

1949–66   R. Menzies, Liberal party candidate, again in office as prime minister; his administration marked by growth of industry (especially in the 1950s), stimulation of foreign investment, and closed ties with Britain and the US.

1950–53 Korean War; Australia sent troops to bolster UN forces.

1951 Joined ANZUS, alliance with US and New Zealand.

1953 Government organized national atomic energy commission.

1954 Australia joined SEATO.

1956 First television broadcasting.

1956 Melbourne hosted Olympics.

1960 Sir Macfarlane Burnet (1899–1985) shared the Nobel Prize for Physiology or Medicine for his work on immune response to transplanted tissue; Australian Sir John Eccles (1903–   ) likewise shared the prize in 1963.

1965–75 Vietnam War; Australian troops joined US and South Vietnamese forces in the fight against the Communist North Vietnamese; Australian combat troops withdrawn in 1971.

1966 Prime Minister Menzies retired, ending the longest unbroken term as prime minister to date in Australian history.

1966 Long-standing exclusion of non-European immigrants effectively ended by immigration law reform.

1969 Equal pay for equal work principle established for women.

1970 Mass demonstrations against Vietnam War held.

1971 First Australian aborigine seated as member of Parliament.

1972 Political crisis over continuing economic problems of inflation and recession.

1972–75 Gough Whitlam in office as prime minister, returning the Australian Labor party to power for first time since 1949.

1972 Government formally recognized Communist China.

1973 Voting age lowered to 18.

1973 Patrick White (d. 1990), leading Australian writer, awarded Nobel Prize for Literature.

1975 Governor General Sir John Kerr dissolved parliament (Nov.) and called for new elections amid continuing fiscal difficulties.

1975–83 Malcolm Fraser in office as prime mimster.

1975 Australian territories of Papua and New Guinea granted independence.

c1975–85 Numerous discoveries of mineral, coal, gas, and precious metal deposits; exploitation of natural resources sparked complaints from environmental interests; income and employment from extracting resources eventually helped improve economy, however.

1978 Vietnamese boat people begin making landfall at Darwin.

1980 Prime Minister Fraser instituted government spending cutbacks and incentives for the private sector; economic problems nevertheless continued into the 1980s.

1982 Australian economy in midst of depression.

1983–91 Robert (Bob) Hawke of Australian Labor party in office as prime minister (Mar.); economy improved under his centrist administration.

1984 Former British colony of Cocos (Keeling) Islands voted to join Australian Commonwealth.

1985–1986 Australia and Great Britain agreed to sever remaining legal ties between them.

1985 Government signed treaty declaring South Pacific a nuclear-free zone.

1986 Separation from UK finalized (Mar. 2, 1986) in Canberra by Queen Elizabeth II, who proclaimed the UK Australia Act law.

1987 Stock market crashes (Oct.), ending period of intense speculation and prompting creation of new securities commission (1990).

1988 Australia celebrated bicentennial of first settlement by Europeans.

1988 Federal, state, and territorial budgets are all balanced for first time in over fifty years.

1990 Hawke's Australian Labor party won elections (Mar. 24), marking the first time Labor formed a fourth consecutive government; economy entered recession, however.

1991– Paul Keating, former national treasurer, in office as prime minister (Dec. 19); announced $1.72 billion government spending program to "kickstart" the economy (Feb. 1992).

Austrasia East Frankish kingdom from 6th to 8th cents., roughly consisting of parts of eastern France, western Germany, and the Netherlands. It was formed (511) when King Clovis I divided Merovingia between his sons. There followed a long series of wars between rulers of Austrasia and neighboring Neustria, especially between queens Brunhilda and Fredegunde, that gradually eroded royal power in Austrasia. Following the reign of Dagobert I, real power rested with the mayor of the palace in the Austrasian capital of Metz. As mayor, Pepin III seized power (751) from the Merovingians and thus founded the Carolingian line of kings.

Austria Republic located in central Europe. The population is 7,595,000 and the capital is Vienna. Austria's history began with Charlemagne's establishment (8th cent.) of an Eastern March (Österreich) in the region. Later elevated to a duchy within the Holy Roman Empire, it came under the rule of the House of Habsburg. Austria dominated the government of the Holy Roman Empire (*q.v.*) from the 15th cent. until its dissolution in 1806. As the Austrian empire (Austria-Hungary after 1867), it remained one of the great European powers. Austria played a pivotal role in the outbreak of WW I, but by that time control over its vast, ethnically mixed empire had greatly declined. The history of modern Austria began at the end of the war, when the empire was dissolved and a republic, greatly reduced in size, was established. **For more on important persons and major events** *see* **entries under specific names.** Key dates in the history of Austria include:

LATE 8TH CENT. Charlemagne established Eastern March in region of what is modern Austria.

1156 Austria made a duchy by Holy Roman Emperor Frederick I.

1282 House of Habsburg gained possession of Austria; Habsburgs greatly increased Austria's power, importance, and holdings.

1438 Albert II, a Habsburg, became Holy Roman Emperor; thereafter, Habsburgs controlled the imperial crown almost without interruption until just before the empire was dissolved (1806).

FROM 1517 Protestant Reformation and attempts to halt its spread resulted in period of instability.

1524–26 Peasants' War sparked by Protestantism.

1526 Austria gained control of Bohemia, a kingdom within the Holy Roman Empire and some of Hungary, which had remained outside the empire.

1529 Ottoman emperor Suleiman the Magnificent laid siege to Vienna for the first time, thus beginning long period of military rivalry with Austria.

1591–1606 Fifteen Years' War fought with the Ottoman Empire.

1618–48 Thirty Years' War.

1648 Peace of Westphalia ended Thirty Years' War and reduced powers of the Holy Roman Emperor over states in the empire; Austria, the collective name for Habsburg lands inside and outside the empire, began its rise as a major power.

1656–1723 J. Fischer von Erlach architect and sculptor lived; introduced baroque style to Austria.

1682–99 Austro-Turkish War fought between Austria and her allies and the Ottoman Empire.

1683 Field Marshal E. von Starhemberg successfully defended Vienna against Turkish attack.

1699 Treaty of Karlowitz ending Austro-Turkish War signed with the Ottoman Turks.

1701–14 War of the Spanish Succession.

1711–40 Austrian Charles VI reigned as Holy Roman Emperor.

1711–94 Statesman W. von Kaunitz lived.

1713 Austria gained control of the Spanish Netherlands by the Peace of Utrecht.

1718 First Quadruple Alliance formed with France, Britain, and the Netherlands against Spain.

1718 Treaty of Passarowitz concluded with Ottoman Empire.

1732–1809 Famed composer F. J. Haydn lived.

1733–35 War of the Polish Succession; Austria gained accession of Frederick Augustus II and Augustus III.

1736–39 Austria joined Russia in Russo-Turkish War.

1739 Treaties of Belgrade concluded with Ottoman Empire.

1740 Maria Theresa succeeded to rule of the Habsburg domains through the Pragmatic Sanction; her succession led to the War of the Austrian Succession (1740–48).

1740–42 First Silesian War fought between Prussia and Austria.

1744–45 Second Silesian War fought between Austria and Prussia.

1745 Treaty of Dresden between Austria and Prussia ended Second Silesian War.

1748 Treaty of Aix-la-Chapelle ended War of the Austrian Succession.

1756 Diplomatic revolution; changed long-established alliances.

1756–63 Seven Years' War.

1763 Treaty of Hubertusburg ended Seven Years' War; Prussia gained Silesia.

1766–1858 Count J. Radetzky, noted Austrian field marshal, lived.

1772, 1793, 1795 Austria annexed much new territory through the Partitions of Poland.

1778–79 War of Bavarian Succession; Prussia prevented Austria from taking over Bavarian lands.

1786 W. Mozart composed *The Marriage of Figaro;* known for his brilliant works in various musical genres.

1787–92 Austrians joined Russians in Russo-Turkish War.

1791 Declaration of Pillnitz issued (Aug. 27) by Austria and Prussia; contributed to outbreak of the French Revolutionary Wars.

1791 Peace of Sistova concluded with Bulgaria.

1792–1815 Austria embroiled in French Revolutionary Wars and Napoleonic Wars.

1797 Treaty of Campo Formio marked Napoleon's victory over Austria and ended the War of the First Coalition.

1797–1828 Composer F. Schubert lived.

1801 Treaty of Lunéville; ended Austria's participation in the French Revolutionary Wars.

1803–53 Physicist C. Doppler lived; noted for work on light and sound waves.

1804 Collapse of Holy Roman Empire imminent; Francis II became the first emperor of Austria, as Francis I, and two years later gave up the imperial crown when the Holy Roman Empire was dissolved.

1805 Treaty of Pressburg with Napoleon I; Austria forced to cede territories.

1809 Peace of Schönbrunn; signed following French victory over Austria at the Battle of Wagram.

1815 Congress of Vienna established Austria as the leading power in the German Confederation, which replaced the Holy Roman Empire.

1815 Holy Alliance formed with Russians and Prussians.

1815 Quadruple Alliance formed with Britain, Prussia, and Russia after Napoleon's defeat.

1815–48 C. von Metternich, Austrian foreign minister, flourished as the leading European statesman; helped promote era of peace, conservatism, and repression of liberal nationalistic movements in post-Napoleonic Europe.

1817 F. Grillparzer wrote his play, *The Ancestress.*

1818 Congress of Aix-la-Chapelle.

1820 Congress of Troppau.

1821 Congress of Laibach.

1822–84 Biologist G. Mendel lived; his studies became basis for modern genetics.

1824–96 Composer A. Bruckner lived.

1842–1925 Physician J. Breuer lived; considered a forerunner of S. Freud by his treatment of mental disorders.

1848 Habsburg rule threatened by revolutions of 1848; Habsburgs were able to restore authority throughout the empire.

1848–52 F. Schwarzenberg served as prime minister.

1848–1916 Francis Joseph reigned as emperor of Austria (and king of Hungary, 1867–1916).

1849–59 A. Bach served as minister of the interior; instituted repressive regime.

1850 Erfurt Parliament; Austria opposed Prussian plan for union of German states.

1860–1911 Composer G. Mahler lived.

1864 Treaty of Vienna with Denmark.

1865 Convention of Gastein (Aug. 14) gave Austria control of Holstein; Prussia got Schleswig.

1866 Austro-Prussian War fought (June 15–Aug. 23); led to Austria's defeat and exclusion from the German Confederation; established Prussia's dominance over German states after long rivalry with Austria.

1866 Treaty of Vienna signed with Italy.

1866 Treaty of Prague; ended the Austro-Prussian War.

1867 Ausgleich agreement made possible the formation of the Dual Monarchy, creating two largely separate kingdoms, Austria and Hungary, under one king-emperor; political unrest within the empire mounted in subsequent years, however.

1867 Composer J. Strauss wrote *The Blue Danube.*

1868–70 Graf von E. Taaffe served as premier; reappointed for 1879–93.

1868 Nagoda compromise; Croatia rejoined with Hungary.

1870–1937 A. Adler, psychiatrist, lived; founded a school of psychiatry based on analyzing feelings of inferiority.

1873–77 Three Emperors' League formed.

1873–1943 Theater director M. Reinhardt lived; originated many modern theater techniques.

1874–1929 H. von Hofmannsthal, poet and dramatist, lived.

1878 Congress of Berlin met to decide matters relating to the Balkan States.

1886–1980 O. Kokoschka lived; known for his expressionist landscapes and dramas.

1889–1951 Philosopher L. Wittgenstein lived; noted for studies of relation of thought and language to real and metaphysical worlds.

1898 Elizabeth, wife of Francis Joseph and empress of Austria, assassinated by Italian anarchist.

1905 Baroness von Suttner, a novelist, became first woman to receive the Nobel Peace Prize.

1908 Bosnian crisis; Austria-Hungary precipitated crisis by annexing Bosnia and Herzegovina.

1914 Archduke Francis Ferdinand, Austrian heir apparent, assassinated by Serbian nationalist at Sarajevo; subsequent Austrian demands on Serbia led to outbreak of WW I.

1914–18 World War I; Austria allied with Germany, Bulgaria, and the Ottoman empire.

1915 F. Kafka published *The Metamorphosis;* his other works published posthumously.

1916 Conservative Prime Minister K. von Sturgkh assassinated by Socialist.

1916–18 Charles I reigned as last Austrian emperor.

1919 Treaty of Saint-Germain concluded (Sept. 10) by Allied powers; established republic of Austria and abolished Austro-Hungarian monarchy; Austrian territory greatly reduced; union with Germany forbidden.

1920 M. Hainisch became first president of the newly formed republic of Austria.

1920s Economic disasters following WW I led to rising political turmoil, notably between Socialists and monarchists; ascendancy of National Socialists began late in the decade.

1921 Composer A. Berg wrote the opera, *Wozzeck.*

1923 Poet R. Rilke wrote *Duino Elegies.*

1932 Engelbert Dollfuss became chancellor; opposed Nazism and union with Germany but adopted elements of fascism in the government.

1933 E. Schrödinger received Novel Prize for Physics; noted for work on subatomic particles.

1934 Dollfuss assassinated by Austrian Nazis.

1934–38 Kurt von Schuschnigg in office as chancellor (1934); unable to resist growing Nazi pressure for Anschluss (union) with Germany; resigned.

1938 German troops occupied Austria (Mar.); Hitler made Austria part of the Third Reich.

1938 S. Freud fled country, seeking refuge in London (June).

1938 Physicist L. Meitner collaborated with O. Hahn and Fritz Strassmann to produce nuclear fission from uranium.

1939–45 World War II.

1945 Soviet troops captured Vienna (Apr.).

1945 Austria occupied by Allied forces at end of WW II and divided into zones of occupation.

1945–50 Karl Renner served as president of the Austrian government.

1947 Austria barred from UN membership by Soviet veto.

1955 Allied occupation ended (May 15) by Austrian State Treaty; Austrian sovereignty recognized by major powers; Austria became a UN member.

1960s Country enjoyed period of economic prosperity.

1970–83 Bruno Kreisky, a Socialist, in office as chancellor; Socialist Party (SPÖ) now dominant party, after long rivalry with conservative People's party; Kreisky established Austrian foreign policy of "active neutrality" during long term of office.

1973 Government passed new liberalized penal code and labor law; in 1974 enacted Radio Law, setting up public broadcast media corporation; right-wing control of radio and television ended.

1973 K. Lorenz shared Nobel Prize for Physiology or Medicine; noted for work on patterns of animal behavior.

1976 Winter Olympics held at Innsbruck (Feb.).

1979 Vienna International Center turned over to UN to house several UN agencies; part of Austrian government program to promote Vienna as a third "UN city."

1980 SPÖ vice-chancellor Hannes Androsch forced to resign (Dec.) following financial scandal involving one of his businesses.

1981 Arab terrorist bomb at Vienna synagogue killed two (Aug. 29); Palestinians responsible were later given life sentences.

1981 Some 30,000 Polish refugees sought refuge in Austria during year; a new influx of Poles arrived in 1984.

1982 50,000 demonstrators protested in Vienna during Peace March (May 15); government voted to block arms sales to nations abusing human rights.

1983 SPÖ member Fred Sinowatz in office as new Austrian chancellor, following resignation of Bruno Kreisky; SPÖ, after losing parliamentary majority in elections (Apr.) formed coalition government with the Freedom Party (FPÖ).

1985 Huge quantities of Austrian wines destroyed after reports an antifreeze-like chemical additive, diethylene-glycol, had been used as a sweetener.

1985 Arab terrorists killed 3 and wounded 40 in bloody attack on Israeli El Al airline counter at Vienna's airport (Dec. 27).

1986 Former UN secretary-general Kurt Waldheim, campaigning for Austrian presidency, became object of scandal concerning his past as a low-ranking German officer during WW II; he denied being involved in Nazi atrocities, but was not finally cleared (by international commission of historians) until 1988.

1986–92 Waldheim in office as president following run-off election; SPÖ member Franz Vranitzky in office as chancellor.

1987 SPÖ negotiated "Grand Coalition" with the People's Party (ÖVP) and formed new government under Vranitzky: new government began austerity program to reduce growing budget deficit; began program to reorganize and partly privatize ailing state-owned industries (such as steel); later introduced tax reform package (1989).

1989 Empress Zita, widow of last Habsburg emperor, dies and is buried in Vienna (Apr.).

1989 Former Chancellor Sinowatz and another high official investigated on criminal charges concerning illegal arms sales to Iran.

1989 Berlin Wall opened in Germany (Nov.); collapse of East European Communist governments sent refugees streaming into Austria in 1990.

1990 Long-time SPÖ political leader Bruno Kreisky died.

1991 Bicentennary of Mozart's death celebrated.

1991 First Austrian in space as part of Soviet crew sent up to *Mir* space station.

1992 Conservative Thomas Klestil in office as president; overwhelmingly defeated Socialist candidate in elections.

Austria, Anne of   *See* **Anne of Austria.**

Austria, Margaret of   *See* **Margaret of Austria.**

Austria, Marie Thérèse of   *See* **Marie Thérèse of Austria.**

Austria-Hungary   *See* **Dual Monarchy.**

Austrian Netherlands   *See* **Netherlands, Spanish and Austrian.**

Austrian State Treaty Treaty (May 15, 1955) between Austria and the WW II Allies. The treaty ended the Allied occupation of Austria and halted discussions on plans for dividing it.

Austrian Succession, War of the (1740–48) This complex war involved the major European powers in a general and largely indecisive conflict. The war broke out after the death of Holy Roman Emperor Charles VI (1740), a member of the powerful Habsburg family. It was fought over succession to the vast Habsburg family domains (centered on Austria), although other political rivalries were involved (notably between France and Britain). Long before his death, Charles had issued the Pragmatic Sanction of 1713, naming his daughter, Maria Theresa, as heir to the Habsburg lands (but not the imperial title). During his lifetime, Charles labored tirelessly to win general support in Europe for her succession. But on Charles's death, Maria was seen as too weak to retain control of the domains, and rival claimants disputed her succession. When war broke out, France, Prussia, Spain, Bavaria, and Saxony took up arms against Austria, ruled by Maria. Britain under George II sided with Austria. An ongoing war between Britain and Spain (War of Jenkins's Ear) merged into the general conflict, which also spread to French and British colonies (King George's War in North America) and later to Britain (second revolt of the Jacobites). Exhaustion, not decisive victory, eventually ended the war. Maria was recognized as heir to Habsburg domains and her husband, Francis I, was elected Holy Roman Emperor. Prussia (the real winner) won Silesia from Austria and emerged as a major power. Key events include:

1740–42 Frederick the Great of Prussia started the war by invading and occupying the Austrian territory of Silesia (First Silesian War).

1741 Charles Albert of Bavaria, a rival claimant to Maria's Habsburg domains, led his forces against Austria and captured Prague in Bohemia.

1741 Charles Albert elected Holy Roman Emperor Charles VII.

1741 Britain, fearing the French would gain control in Europe if Austria collapsed, sided with Austria.

1742 Austria conquered Bavaria and pushed into Bohemia; Prussia withdrew from the war after Austria ceded a large part of Silesia to it.

1743 French retreat (1742–43) was capped by British king George II's victory over the French at the Battle of Dettingen (June 27); Saxony made peace with Austria.

1744–45 King Frederick of Prussia, fearing a too powerful Austria, joined Emperor Charles VII and France against Austria (called Second Silesian War); Prussia soon put on the defensive, however.

1745 Bavaria forced out of war following the death of Emperor Charles VII.

1745 Battle of Fontenoy (May 11) in Flanders; France defeated Austria and her allies and began to invade the Austrian Netherlands.

1745 Britain concluded peace with Prussia; Maria Theresa's husband became Holy Roman Emperor Francis I.

1745 Treaty of Dresden (Dec. 25) ended war with Prussia; Prussia recognized Francis I as emperor and Austria confirmed Prussian possession of Silesia.

1746 Britain forced to withdraw troops to contend with French-backed revolt of the Jacobites; France completed conquest of the Austrian Netherlands.

1748 Treaty of Aix-la-Chapelle signed (Oct.); provided for end of war and mutual restitution of most conquered territory, though Prussia retained Silesia.

Austro-Hungarian Monarchy *See* **Dual Monarchy.**

Austro-Prussian War (Seven Weeks' ~) War (June 15–Aug. 23, 1866) between Prussia (allied with Italy) and Austria (allied with Hanover, Bavaria, and most other German states). The war resulted in Austria's exclusion from the German Confederation (*q.v.*) and thus opened the way to the eventual unification of Germany under Prussian domination. The war was precipitated by Prussian chancellor O. Bismarck to gain those ends for Prussia. Bismarck first provoked a crisis with Austria over administration of the Schleswig-Holstein region in spring 1866 and, claiming Austrian violation of the Convention of Gastein (*q.v.*) sent (June 6) Prussian troops into Holstein. In subsequent fighting, the Italians lost to Austrian forces opposing them in Italy, but the Prussians displayed remarkable military efficiency and quickly defeated Austrian forces in the north. One Prussian army took Hanover (June 27–29) and, on another front in Bohemia, delivered the final crushing blow (July 3) to Austria at the Battle of Sadowa (*q.v.*). The war was formally ended by the Treaty of Prague, which in addition to providing for the North German Confederation, ended Austrian hegemony in Italy.

Austro-Turkish War A war (1682–99) between Austria (and her allies) and the Ottoman Empire. Taking advantage of unrest in Hungarian territories, the Turks invaded Austria and besieged Vienna (July–Sept., 1683). Poland and other states of the Holy League (formed 1684) joined the war against Turkey. Despite reverses, they won notable victories against the Turks, including the Battle of Zenta (1697). The Turks sued for peace and agreed (1699) to the Treaty of Karlowitz (*q.v.*).

authoritarianism Political system based on blind submission of individuals to a central authority, either a single leader or small group of them.

autocracy System of government in which a single ruler has absolute power over the entire government.

auto-da-fé During the Inquisition, a public ceremony in which judges read the sentences imposed on those convicted of religious infidelity. Such ceremonies, often very elaborately staged, were held from 1481 to as late as 1815.

autonomy In politics, a limited form of self-government in which a nation, or some part of one, governs its internal affairs, yet is not entirely free of responsibility to a larger or more powerful political entity. During the decolonization of the British empire, for example, former colonies were granted autonomy, allowing them control over their internal affairs as a step toward full independence. In ancient Greece, autonomy was closely allied with the concept of freedom, including economic self-sufficiency and the right of the *polis* to establish its own constitution, as well as the power to govern internal affairs. The importance of autonomy to the separate city-states in ancient Greece became the chief deterrent to political unity among them.

Autumn Harvest Uprising Chinese peasant revolt inspired by Communist forces (Sept., 1927). Mao Zedong was among the leaders of the revolt, which involved peasants and Communist regulars in the Hunan-Jiangxi region. Though it failed, Mao gained both experience and the conviction that peasant discontent could be of great importance to the Communist movement.

Avars Nomadic Asian peoples. The Avars seem to have come from the Caucasus. They conquered and occupied large areas of Russia and Hungary, forming a powerful empire (c6th to 8th cents.). They were defeated by Charlemagne (805).

Aventine secession Italian political crisis. On June 10, 1924, a group of 150 non-Fascist members withdrew from the Chamber of Deputies to protest B. Mussolini's Fascist government. Reacting to the Matteoti Crisis (*q.v.*), the deputies demanded an end to the use of violence in suppressing dissent.

Avenzoar *See* **Ibn Zuhr.**

Averescu, Alexandru 1859–1938. Rumanian politician and general. Averescu fought against the Ottoman Turks (1877–78) and against the Central Powers during WW I. As prime minister (1918), he conducted Rumania's post-WW I peace negotiations. He was prime minister again in 1920–21 and 1926–27.

Avernus Ancient name for Averno, a small crater lake in southern Italy. Volcanic gases arising from it were said to kill birds flying over it, and ancient Romans believed it to be the entrance to hell.

Avicenna 980–1037. Muslim philosopher and doctor. He authored over one hundred works on medicine and philosophy, including the famous *Canon of Medicine.* His works were influenced by Aristotelian and Neoplatonic teachings.

Avignon City in southeast France. It was the papal see from 1309 to 1378, during the Babylonian Captivity, and served as the seat of rival popes until the end of the Great Schism (1417).

Avignon Papacy *See* **Babylonian Captivity.**

Avila, Saint Theresa of *See* **Teresa of Avila, Saint.**

Ávila Camacho, Manuel 1897–1955. A Mexican general and politician. Ávila fought in the revolution of 1914 and was president from 1940 to 1946. A moderate, he inaugurated a period of consolidation of the social reforms resulting from the Mexican Revolution.

Avogadro, Amadeo 1776–1856. Italian physicist who developed (1811) Avogadro's Law, which holds that equal volumes of gases at the same temperature and pressure contain an equal number of molecules. This concept was a major contribution to the development of chemistry and physics.

Axel *See* **Absalon.**

Axis Powers WW II coalition, headed by Germany, Italy, and Japan, that opposed the Allied powers. The alliance began (Oct. 25, 1936) with a pact between Germany and Italy and the Anti-Comintern Pact (Nov. 25, 1936) between Germany and Japan. The three later signed (Sept. 27, 1940) the Berlin (or Tripartite) Pact.

Ayacucho, Battle of Battle near the city of Ayacucho, Peru. On Dec. 9, 1824, revolutionary forces under A. de Sucre defeated superior Spanish colonial forces, thereby securing the independence of Peru. The Spanish lost 2,000 men.

Aybak *See* **Mamelukes.**

Ayer, Alfred Jules 1910–89. British philosopher. Ayer was an important exponent of logical positivism. He wrote such books as *Language, Truth and Logic; The Foundations of Empirical Knowledge;* and *The Concept of a Person.*

Ayn Jalut, Battle of (Ain Jalut, ˜) Great victory (Sept. 3, 1260, near the Sea of Galilee) for the Egyptian Mamelukes over the invading Mongols. The battle marked the end of the Mongols' westward invasion (under Hulagu). The Mamelukes later captured Syria from them.

Ayub Khan, Muhammad 1907–1974. Pakistani politician, president (1958–69). He encouraged land reform and a system of local governments called "basic democracies." However, an unsuccessful two-week war with India (1965) and internal unrest forced his resignation (Mar., 1969).

Ayyubids Muslim dynasty of Egyptian rulers. A Sunni Muslim dynasty founded (1169) by Saladin, it ruled Egypt, Iraq, Syria, and Yemen until 1250. Under Ayyubite rule, Egypt became the leading Muslim power and successfully opposed the crusaders. The dynasty was overthrown by the Mamelukes.

Ayutthaya *See* **Rama Tiboti I.**

Azaña, Manuel 1880–1940. Spanish statesman. He served as prime minister (1931–33) under Pres. A. Zamora and was president (1936–39) of the republic during the Spanish Civil War.

Azariah *See* **Uzziah.**

Azerbaijan (*formerly,* Azerbaijan Soviet Socialist Republic) Independent republic and member of the Commonwealth of Independent States, located on the northern border of Iran and adjacent to Armenia. A part of Urartu and Medea in ancient times, it came under Persian control and was Zoroaster's birthplace. Contested by the Persians and Ottoman Turks in the 17th cent., it fell to the Persians in 1618. Russia gained control of northern Azerbaijan (the larger part) in the 19th cent. by the treaties of Gulistan (1813) and Turkmanchay (1828). Incorporated into the USSR (1922) as part of the Transcaucasian Soviet Socialist Federated Republic, it became a constituent republic in 1936. Ethnic unrest broke out in 1988 as a result of Armenian demands for return of the Azerbaijani territory of Nagorny Karabakh, which was predominately ethnic Armenian. Protests by Armenians and Azerbaijanis in Nagorny Karabakh escalated and in May 1989, Soviet troops were sent. Nevertheless, full-scale warfare broke out in the disputed region and in 1990, rioting between ethnic groups spread across Azerbaijan. Thousands more troops were sent, and on Jan 19, they reopened the Azerbaijani capital of Baku, which had been taken over by Azerbajani militants. Ultimately the Soviet government backed Azerbaijani control of the region, however, and fighting against Armenian rebels in the disputed region continued into 1992, though a cease-fire was agreed to in mid-year. Azerbaijan followed other constituent republics in declaring independence (Aug. 30, 1991) after the failed Soviet coup, and became a member of the Commonwealth on Dec. 21, 1991.

Aztec Empire Empire of the Aztecs, once located in central Mexico. At the time of the conquest of Mexico by H. Cortés (1519–21), the chief Aztec city was Tenochtitlán (founded c1325). The Aztecs migrated to this region from the north (c11th cent.) and, through a series of alliances and conquests (12th–16th cents.), gained control over neighboring peoples. Their economy was based on the cultivation of corn, they were skilled builders and craftsmen, they had a system of picture-writing, and their religion pervaded all aspects of life. They practiced human sacrifice and their chief god was Huitzilopochtli, a god of war. The Spaniards were able to conquer the numerically superior Aztec forces led by Montezuma because the Spanish possessed guns and horses, because the Aztecs had been weakened by a smallpox epidemic (brought unknowingly from Europe by the Spanish), because the Spanish found willing allies among native peoples of the region, and because the Aztecs regarded the Spanish as descendants of the god Quetzalcoatl. (*See also* Cortés, Hernando.)

Azuchi-Momoyama period *See* **Japan, 1568–1600.**

B

Baal Shem-Tov (Eliezer, Israel ben) c1700–60. Russian-born founder of the Hasidim (*q.v.*), a Jewish sect.

Baashaa *d.* c888 BC. King of Israel (911–*c*888 BC). He gained the throne by murdering Nadab, and made war against Asa of Judah. {1 Kings 15–16; 2 Chron 16}

Ba'ath party *See* **Ba'th party.**

Bab, the (Mirza Ali Muhammad) 1819–50. Arab religious leader. The founder (1844) of Babism, he had a charismatic personality that, with his claims to divinity, led to his execution by the Shi'ite Muslims. He is considered one of the founders of Bahaism.

Babar *See* **Babur.**

Babbage, Charles 1792–1871. English mathematician and inventor. A founder of the Royal Astronomical Society, he spent many years working on a mechanical calculator, the forerunner of modern calculating machines.

Babel, Tower of *See* **Tower of Babel.**

Baber *See* **Babur.**

Babeuf, François Noël 1760–97. French revolutionary of the late 18th cent. whose ideas of economic egalitarianism foreshadowed modern socialism. He is sometimes called the first Socialist theorist. Seeking economic justice, he organized a secret society to overthrow the Directory (1796), but his "conspiracy of equals" was discovered and he was executed.

Babington, Anthony 1561–86. English conspirator. He joined a plot (1586) to murder Queen Elizabeth I and place Mary, Queen of Scots, on the throne. The plot was discovered and Babington was executed. Evidence of Mary's complicity led to her execution.

Babism Originally a sect of Shi'ite Muslims that flourished briefly during the 19th cent. and gave rise to Bahaism (*q.v.*). An ascetic doctrine, it fused elements of various teachings, including Shi'ite, Gnostic, and Sufi doctrines. It spread throughout Persia, following proclamation of the arrival (1844) of the prophet, or Bab, in the person of Mirza Ali Muhammad. Persecution of Babists soon began (1845) and the Babists withdrew from the Islamic fold (1848). Uprisings against the Persian shah finally resulted in a massacre of Babists at Teheran and the execution of the Bab (1850) A successor, Baha Allah, fled Teheran and by 1863 formed Bahaism as an offshoot of Babism.

Babur (Baber) (Babar) (*orig.* Zahir ud-Din Muhammad) 1483–1530. Mongol soldier, poet, and founder of the Mughal empire in India. Descended from Genghis Khan and Tamerlane, he first tried unsuccessfully to take Samarkand from the Uzbeks. He was, however, successful in Afghanistan and established a kingdom there (1504). In 1525–26 he led a small invasion force into India and, following the capture of Delhi (1526), proceeded to conquer most of northern India. These conquests formed the Mughal Empire (*q.v.*).

Babylon Ancient city of Mesopotamia and one of the most important cities of antiquity. Established by the 3d millennium BC, it gained importance in the early 2d millennium BC when Hammurabi made it the capital of the kingdom of Babylonia. During this period, it became the commercial center of the region. Destroyed (c689 BC) by Sennacherib, it was rebuilt and reached its height in the 7th–6th cents. BC, under the rule of Nebuchadnezzar II. Babylon became famous for its splendor, and its Hanging Gardens were one of the Seven Wonders of the World. Babylon fell (538 BC) to the Persians under Cyrus the

Great and was later conquered (331 BC) by Alexander the Great. In the early 3d cent. BC its importance was largely eclipsed by the rise of Seleucia as commercial center of the region.

Babylon, Hanging Gardens of *See* **Hanging Gardens of Babylon.**

Babylonia Term sometimes used collectively to refer to the city-state civilizations that flourished as early as the 3d millennium BC in the valley of the Tigris and the Euphrates. More specifically, it refers to the empires centered on the city of Babylon. The first great empire was that of Hammurabi (c1830–1530 BC), which saw the issuance of the Code of Hammurabi and the appearance of the Babylonian ziggurat, or step-towered temple. Babylonia was then dominated by the Kassites (c1530–1150 BC), the Aramaeans (c1100–1000 BC), and, from the 10th cent., by the Empire of Assyria (*q.v.*). A Babylonian ruler, Nabopolassar, ended Assyrian rule (625 BC) and joined the Medes in the capture of Assyria's capital, Nineveh (612 BC). His son Nebuchadnezzar defeated the Egyptians at the great Battle of Carchemish in 605 BC, and a new Babylonian Empire, sometimes called the Chaldaean Empire, was formed. It included Mesopotamia, Syria, Palestine, and Cilicia. These were the days of legendary Babylonian glory when the Hanging Gardens were built. It was during this period that the Jews were deported from Judah to Babylon (the Babylonian Captivity). Cyrus the Great of Persia began his attacks on Babylonia around 547 BC and Babylon fell to the Persian Empire in 538 BC.

Babylonian Captivity (˜ Exile) (Captivity) Name of important periods in the history of Israel and the Roman Catholic church. 1. In the history of Israel, the mass deportation of prominent Jews to Babylon, following Nebuchadnezzar's conquest of Jerusalem and destruction of the Temple (586 BC) [2 Kings 24–25]. When Cyrus the Great overthrew the Babylonian Empire (c538 BC), he allowed the Jews to return. Many thousands, but not all of them, did so. The end of the 70-year captivity prophesied in the Bible was marked by completion of the new temple (516 BC). [2 Chron 36; Ezra 1; Isaiah 40–48; Daniel 6] 2. In the history of the Roman Catholic church, the Avignon papacy, the period (1309–76) during which the popes resided at Avignon, in what now is France. The first pope to make his residence at Avignon was Clement V, who

sought a better location from which to conduct the papacy. The seventh and last Avignon pope, Gregory XI, left Avignon (1376) to reestablish the papacy at Rome (1377). The Great Schism (*see* Schism) followed.

Bacchylides *fl.* 5th cent. BC. Greek lyric poet. The nephew of Simonides of Ceos, he was a contemporary of Pindar. Fragments of his epicinian odes were first discovered in 1896.

Bach, Alexander 1813–93. Austrian minister of justice (1848) and of the interior (1849–59). He instituted the Bach system of centralized authority, characterized by both police repression and liberal social and economic reforms.

Bach, Karl Philipp Emanuel 1714–88. German composer, son of J. S. Bach.

Bach, Johann Christian 1735–82. German composer, the son of J. S. Bach. Bach's musical style influenced later composers, including W. Mozart.

Bach, Johann Christoph *See* **Bach, Johann Sebastian.**

Bach, Johann Sebastian 1685–1750. German composer, the most illustrious member of a celebrated musical family and one of the great composers of all time. Orphaned by the age of 19, Bach showed his musical talents early under the tutelage of his brother Johann Christoph Bach (1671–1721). After serving variously as an organist concertmaster and musical director, he became musical director of the church and music school of St. Thomas in Leipzig, where he spent the rest of his life. In his lifetime he composed a vast number of works, including instrumental and vocal pieces and a large body of religious compositions. Among his best-known works are *The Well-Tempered Clavier, St. Matthew Passion, Mass in B Minor,* the *Goldberg Variations,* and the *Brandenburg Concertos.*

Bach, Wilhelm Friedemann 1710–84. A German composer. The eldest son of J. S. Bach, he was a celebrated composer and organist in his day, but wrote down few of his compositions.

Bacon, Francis 1561–1626. English philosopher, statesman, and essayist. He is credited with making important advances in inductive logic, which later encouraged the general advancement of science. In his day Bacon was noted for both his meanness and his great intelligence. His public career as a member of Parliament (from 1584) and lord chancellor (1618–21) ended with his conviction for taking bribes. His most important works include *De Augmentis Scientiarum, Novum Organum,* and *The New Atlantis.*

Bacon, Roger 1214?–1294? English philosopher and Franciscan monk. An important proponent of experimental science centuries before it became widely accepted, he wrote many descriptions of experiments, including one that revealed the formula for gunpowder for the first time in Europe (1242). He also proposed making a hot air balloon from thin copper sheets, a mechanical flying machine powered by movable wings, and mechanically powered ships and carriages centuries before anyone tried constructing them. Bacon was born of a well-to-do family, studied at both Oxford and Paris, and lectured at Paris before returning to Oxford to teach, probably in 1247, and where he joined the Franciscan order. At Oxford he became a zealous and celebrated teacher—posthumously known as Doctor Mirabilis, the Admirable Doctor—devoting himself to learning and experimentation in all branches of science known then, including optics, mathematics, astronomy, and alchemy. About 1257 Bacon's health failed and the Franciscans, suspecting his work was heretical, apparently confined him in Paris for ten years. Bacon countered in 1267–68 by writing for Pope Clement IV a summary of his work *Opus majus,* at once a treatise on the importance of scientific study and a valuable encyclopedic work on science as it was then known. That same year Bacon also completed *Opus minus* and *Opus tertium* for Clement. Bacon continued writing, completing *Compendium philosophiae* (1272) and other works before being imprisoned again for heresy by the Franciscans. He died not long after his release and was buried at Oxford.

Bacon's Rebellion Uprising in Colonial Virginia (1676) led by Nathaniel Bacon (1647–76). The rebellion was provoked by Gov. W. Berkeley's colonial policies, including his refusal to protect colonists from attacks by Indians, with whom he had a lucrative fur trade. Bacon raised an army of 300 colonists and defeated the Indians. Declared a rebel by the governor, Bacon marched on Jamestown, captured it, and forced the governor to flee. A short time later, however, Bacon died of malaria and the rebels disbanded. Gov. Berkeley returned to exact a bloody revenge on the colonists, killing 23 of them.

Bactria Ancient country, located in northern Afghanistan and adjacent parts of the former USSR. An important focal point for trade between Western and Eastern civilizations, it was conquered by the Persians c545 BC. Con-

quered next by Alexander the Great (328 BC), it was made part of the Seleucid Empire. It became an independent Greek kingdom (256 BC) and during the next century expanded to include parts of Afghanistan, Pakistan, and central Asia. After 130 BC, Bactria fell to various conquerors and never again rose to power.

Bad Axe River, Battle of *See* **Black Hawk War.**

Baden Former state located in southwest Germany. Baden played a role in the formation of the German Empire.

Baden, Treaty of *See* **Rastatt and Baden, Treaties of.**

Baden-Powell of Gilwell, Robert Stephenson Smyth Baden-Powell, 1st baron 1857–1941. British army officer. He founded (1908) the Boy Scouts and, with his sister Agnes (1858–1945), the Girl Guides (1910).

Badoglio, Pietro 1871–1956. Italian field marshal. As head of a new government after B. Mussolini's fall in 1943, he negotiated an armistice with the Allies, but opposition led him to resign in 1944.

Badr, Battle of Battle (Mar., 624) at Badr, near Medina. Muhammad, leading 300 Muslims, attacked and defeated a Meccan force of 1,000 accompanying a caravan returning from Syria. The raid was Muhammad's first military victory and served to strengthen his movement.

Baduila *See* **Totila.**

Baeda, Saint *See* **Bede, Saint.**

Baedeker, Karl 1801–59. German publisher and founder of the series of Baedeker guidebooks for travelers. His books represented the first recognition of the emerging tourist industry.

Baekeland, Leo Hendrik 1863–1944. American chemist and inventor of Velox photographic paper and Bakelite, the first thermosetting plastic.

Baer, Karl Ernst von 1792–1876. Estonian biologist. A pioneer in the study of embryology, he discovered the mammalian egg and the notochord, and presented a theory of embryonic development.

Báez, Buenaventura c1810–1884. Dominican statesman. Several times president of the Dominican Republic, he sought unsuccessfully to have his country annexed by the U.S. (1869–70).

Bagdad *See* **Baghdad.**

Bagehot, Walter 1826–77. English social scientist, economist, and editor (1860–77) of *The Economist.* He wrote *The English Constitution* (1867), a classic study, and *Physics and Politics*

(1872), which applied physical principles to politics.

Baghdad (Bagdad)　Iraqi capital city. The site of important cities since Mesopotamian times, the present city was founded (763) as the capital of the Abbasid caliphs. During the 8th and early 9th cents., Baghdad reached the height of its commercial and cultural prosperity as one of the greatest Islamic cities. Its decline began in the 9th cent. and was completed by successive conquests. Part of the Ottoman Empire (1534–1917), it was taken by the British (1917) and became the capital of the new kingdom of Iraq (1920). The Iraqi republic was established by a coup in Baghdad in 1958.

Baha Allah (~ Ullah) 1817–92.　Persian religious leader. A disciple of the Bab, he declared himself the Promised One and successor to the Bab, and founded (1863) Bahaism.

Bahaism　Religion founded (1863) by Baha Allah and now practiced throughout the world. Bahaism is an offshoot of Babism, of which Baha Allah was once a follower. After persecution and exile of the Babists by the Persians, Baha Allah declared himself (1863) the Promised One, or manifestation through which men could know God. The religion was spread throughout the world by his son and successors. Among its major tenets are that God is knowable only through his manifestation; the unity of all religions; the need for world peace; and universal government.

Bahamas (*properly* Commonwealth of the Bahamas) Island chain and independent nation (pop. 251,000) in the Atlantic, southeast of Florida. The Bahamas were the site of C. Columbus's first landing (1492) in the New World (probably at San Salvador). The islands were first settled by the English in the mid-1600s. Long a base for pirates such as Blackbeard, the Bahamas were not freed of them until the early 1700s. Spanish claims to the islands were relinquished to England by the Treaty of Paris (1783). The Bahamas were a base for blockade runners during the Civil War and rum runners during Prohibition. The islands were granted independence in 1973. In following years, due to the country's liberal banking laws, the Bahamas became an international banking center. Throughout the 1980s the government struggled with the problem of drug trafficking, the Bahamas being a major conduit for illegal cocaine and marijuana smuggled into the US. More determined enforcement and a cooperative anti-drug program with the US appeared to have significantly reduced drug shipments through the Bahamas by 1990.

Baha Ullah　*See* **Baha Allah.**

Bahrain (Al-Bah-Rayn) (Bahrein)　Sheikhdom (pop. 512,000) in the Persian Gulf with its capital at Manama. An oil-rich archipelago, Bahrain was ruled by the Portuguese from the 1500s to 1602, when it passed into Persian control. Since the late 18th cent., Bahrain has been ruled by the al-Khalifa family (originally from the Saudi tribal federation). Bahrain signed its first treaty with Britain in 1816, at which time it became an informal British protectorate. The protectorate lasted until 1971, when Bahrain became independent. The last British military forces were withdrawn in 1991, following the Persian Gulf War. Subsequently, Bahrain agreed to allow a US regional support base to be sited within its borders.

Baïf, Jean Antoine de 1532–89.　French poet, born in Venice. A learned and imaginative poet, he was one of the seven members of the Pléiade.

Bailey, James A.　*See* **Barnum, Phineas Taylor.**

Bailly, Jean Sylvain 1736–93.　French astronomer and politician, noted for his study of the moons of Jupiter. As mayor of Paris (1789–91), he allowed the national guard to fire on a mob (July, 1791), for which he was later executed.

Bain, Alexander 1818–1903.　Scottish philosopher. He applied scientific principles to the study of psychology and emphasized the importance of the will.

Baird, John Logie 1888–1946.　Scottish inventor and pioneer in television. He demonstrated the first television system in 1926 and demonstrated color television in 1928.

Bajazet I (Beyazid I) 1347–1403.　Ottoman sultan (1389–1402), successor to his father, Murad I. He conquered most of Asia Minor and besieged Constantinople for ten years but was defeated by Tamerlane at Ankara (1402).

Bajazet II (Beyazid II) 1447–1513.　Ottoman sultan (1481–1512), successor to his father, Muhammad II. He fought wars with Venice and Egypt, and completely rebuilt Constantinople after the 1509 earthquake.

Baji Rao I *d.* 1740.　Second Peshwa (1720–40) of the Maratha state of India, successor to his father Balaji Vishvanath (*d.* 1720). He organized the Marathas against Muslims threatening from the north, and formed an alliance with the Rajputs against the Mughal Empire (1739).

Baji Rao II *See* **Bassein, Treaty of.**

Baker, Isaac *See* **Scribner, Charles.**

Baker, Ray Stannard (*pseud.* David Grayson) 1870–1946. American muckraking journalist and author, whose eight-volume biography of W. Wilson (1927–39) won a 1940 Pulitzer Prize.

Baker v. *Carr* US Supreme Court case (1962) concerning the apportionment of seats in state governing bodies. Tennessee was using outdated voting districts which no longer represented the true distribution of its population, especially for minorities and those in rural areas. The Court decided that courts could direct the redrawing of district boundaries to ensure political equality of the voters. The many lawsuits inspired by this decision resulted in the Court's principle of equal representation: one person, one vote.

Baksar, Battle of (Buxar, ˜) Battle (Oct. 23, 1764) at Baksar, India, in which a British and native force of 7,000 defeated a Mughal army of 40,000, thus reestablishing British control in Bengal.

Bakufu (Shogunate) Name for the Japanese military government of a shogun, or supreme military commander. The first shogun came to power in 1192, and successive bakufus, or shogunates, ruled Japan until 1868. Generally, the Japanese emperor held appointive authority over the shogun and his bakufu, but practically those who ran the bakufu held great power because of their influence over warriors throughout the realm.

Bakunin, Mikhail 1814–76. Russian revolutionary and anarchist leader. His views led to his expulsion from the Communist First International in 1872 and caused a rift in the Communist movement.

Balaclava *See* **Balaklava, Battle of.**

Balaji Vishvanath *See* **Baji Rao I.**

Balakirev, Mili Alekseyevich 1837–1910. Russian composer and leader of the group called The Five. His work influenced other composers, including Tchaikovsky.

Balaklava, Battle of (Balaclava) Battle of the Crimean War, fought between allied forces and Russia in Oct., 1854. It is noted chiefly as the site of the British cavalry charge celebrated in *The Charge of the Light Brigade* by A. Tennyson.

Balboa, Vasco Núñez de c1475–1519. Spanish explorer and conquistador. Balboa sought his fortune in the Indies, joining (1500) an exploratory voyage along the coast of what is now Colombia. He later settled in Hispaniola, Haiti, but failed to make a living as a farmer. Anxious to escape his creditors, Balboa stowed away (1510) on another voyage to Colombia, which had been organized to find survivors of a failed colony. Balboa seized command and after finding the settlers, moved them (1511) to what became the first stable settlement on the South American continent, the village of Santa María de la Antigua. Balboa was named interim governor of the colony and immediately began expeditions in search of gold and silver. In Sept., 1513, he first sighted the Pacific Ocean from a mountain peak, claiming the ocean and its shoreline for Spain. Balboa spent several years exploring the Pacific coast but in 1518 was charged with treason and mistreatment of the Indians. He was beheaded in Jan., 1519.

Baldwin I 1058?–1118. Latin king of Jerusalem (1100–18). A leader in the First Crusade, he consolidated and strengthened Latin control in the East.

Baldwin I 1171–1205? First Latin emperor of Constantinople. A leader of the Fourth Crusade, he was proclaimed emperor in 1204 but was defeated by the Bulgarians at Adrianople (1205).

Baldwin II *d.* 1131. Latin king of Jerusalem (1118–31), successor to his cousin Baldwin I. He expanded the strength and territory of Jerusalem.

Baldwin II 1217–73. Last Latin emperor of Constantinople (1228–61), successor to his brother Robert of Courtenay. He fled to Italy when the Greeks under Michael VIII captured Constantinople in 1261.

Baldwin III 1130?–62. Latin king of Jerusalem (1143–62), son of and successor, with his mother, to King Fulk, assuming sole rule c1152. His reign saw the failure of the Second Crusade and the fall of Damascus (1154.)

Baldwin IV (Baldwin the Leper) c1161–85. Latin king of Jerusalem (1174–85), successor to his father, Amalric I. He spent most of his reign in conflict with Saladin.

Baldwin V *d.* 1186. Latin king of Jerusalem (1185–86), successor to his uncle, Baldwin IV. Raymond of Tripoli (c1140–87) acted as his regent.

Baldwin, James (Arthur) 1924–87. American author. Baldwin is noted for his powerful descriptions of the black American experience in such volumes as *Another Country* and *The Fire Next Time.*

Baldwin, Robert 1804–58. Canadian statesman. A Reform party leader in Upper Canada, he supported the union of Canada and responsible government. He formed, with L. Lafontaine, coalition governments in 1842–43 and 1847–51, the latter noted for its numerous reforms.

Baldwin, Stanley 1867–1947.   British statesman. As prime minister (1923–24, 1924–29, 1935–37) he obtained passage of the Trade Disputes Act (1927), which limited the power of unions, and played a role in the abdication of Edward VIII in 1936. He opposed British rearmament in the face of the increasing German military threat.

Baldwin the Leper   *See* **Baldwin IV.**

Balewa, Sir Abubakar Tafawa 1912–66.   Nigerian statesman, the first prime minister of independent Nigeria (1960–66).

Balfour, Arthur James, 1st earl of 1848–1930.   A British statesman, prime minister (1902–05). As foreign secretary (1916–19), he issued the Balfour Declaration (*q.v.*).

Balfour Declaration   British foreign-policy statement issued (Nov. 2, 1917) by A. Balfour and expressing British sympathy for the establishment of a Jewish national home in Palestine. This was a major step in the eventual founding of the State of Israel.

Baline, Israel   *See* **Berlin, Irving.**

Baliol, Edward de (Balliol, ~) *d.* 1363.   King of Scotland and son of John de Baliol. With English support he invaded Scotland (1332), defeated David II, and was made king. He soon after lost his crown, regaining it with the support of Edward III, to whom he ceded several Scottish counties and, in 1356, his title.

Baliol, John de (Balliol, ~) 1249–1315.   King of Scotland (1292–96). Gaining the crown through the support of Edward I, he swore fealty to Edward but later allied with France (1295), renounced his fealty (1296), and was defeated by Edward.

Balkan Entente   Mutual defense agreement (1934) among Greece, Rumania, Turkey, and Yugoslavia, to provide protection from other Balkan countries. It was voided by German aggression in WW II.

Balkan Peninsula   Peninsula in southeastern Europe, roughly bounded by the Adriatic, Aegean, and Black seas. Occupied by Ottoman Turks in the 14th and 15th cents., the area was the site of struggles for independence in the late 19th cent. and was the setting for the Balkan Wars and the events leading to WW I.

Balkan War 1. First ~ War (Oct. 18, 1912–May 30, 1913) between the Ottoman Empire and the Balkan League (Bulgaria, Greece, Montenegro, and Serbia). Taking advantage of Ottoman involvement in war with Italy (Tripolitan War), the Balkan League declared war on the Ottomans and, in a rapid series of victories, overran nearly all Ottoman domains in Eastern Europe. Fighting was halted by an armistice (Dec. 3, 1912), then resumed (Jan., 1913) when peace negotiations broke down. Hostilities continued until early May, and the war was brought to a close by the Treaty of London (May 30, 1913). In the treaty, the Ottomans lost all but a small part of their European territories, which were divided among members of the league and the new state of Albania. The treaty did nothing to ease the international tensions that eventually led to the outbreak of WW I. 2. Second ~ War (June 29–July 30, 1913) between Bulgaria and Serbia (soon joined by Rumania, Greece, and the Ottomans). The Treaty of London left Serbia disgruntled because territories it wanted were joined to the newly formed Albania. Serbia thereupon quarreled with Bulgaria, hoping to gain part of the Macedonian territory awarded to Bulgaria by the treaty. Bulgaria retaliated by launching a surprise attack (June 29, 1913) against Serbia and its ally, Greece. Rumania and the Ottomans entered the brief war and helped to utterly defeat Bulgaria. By the Treaty of Bucharest (Aug. 10, with Serbia, Rumania, and Greece) and by the Treaty of Constantinople (Sept. 29, with the Ottomans), Bulgaria was stripped of most of the territories it had won in the previous war. This war heightened the international tensions that led to WW I.

Balkis   *See* **Sheba.**

Ball, John *d.* 1381.   English priest and social reformer. Excommunicated in 1376, he was a leader in the peasant revolt of Wat Tyler (1381) and was executed.

Ballet Russe   *See* **Diaghilev, Sergei.**

Balliol   *See* **Baliol.**

Balmaceda, José Manuel 1840–91.   Chilean president (1886–91). He instituted wide reforms but caused a civil war between congress and the president. He was ousted and shot himself.

Balsamo, Giuseppe   *See* **Cagliostro, Alessandro, Conte.**

Baltic Entente   Pact (Sept. 12, 1934) signed by Lithuania, Latvia, and Estonia. The three states sought mutual defense against Nazi Germany.

Baltic States Name for the countries of Lithuania, Latvia, and Estonia, located east of the Baltic Sea. The territory was under Russian rule from the 1700s. After WW I and the Baltic War of Liberation, the three independent countries were formed (1918) but were retaken by Russia in 1940 and incorporated into the USSR until 1991. The term "Baltic States" sometimes includes Finland and Poland. *See also* names of individual states.

Baltic War of Liberation War (1918–20) in which the Baltic States (Lithuania, Latvia, and Estonia) repulsed attacks by both the Russians and Germans and thereby maintained their newly won independence. All three Baltic states declared independence from Russia after the revolution of 1917 and soon after became embroiled in warfare. Lithuania declared independence (Feb. 16, 1918) and, with German aid, was able to defeat the invading Bolsheviks. The short-lived Treaty of Brest-Litovsk (Mar., 1918) ended fighting until Germany collapsed at the end of WW I. The Bolsheviks again invaded Lithuania (after Nov., 1918) and were again defeated, this time with Polish aid. By the Treaty of Moscow (1920), Lithuanian independence was recognized. In Latvia, German occupying forces prevented formation of a national government and army immediately after the Russian Revolution. After Germany's defeat in WW I, however, Latvia proclaimed independence (Nov. 18, 1918) and was invaded (Jan., 1919) by the Bolsheviks. The Bolsheviks were soon forced out by a combined German-Latvian force. The Germans then made an unsuccessful attempt to take over and were defeated by Latvian forces. By the Treaty of Riga (1920), Russia recognized Latvian independence. Estonia proclaimed independence (Nov. 28, 1917) and soon came under Bolshevik attack. Germany occupied Estonia (Dec., 1917) to stop the Russian advance and, by the Treaty of Brest-Litovsk (1918), the Russians recognized Estonian independence. At the close of WW I, however, the Germans withdrew (Nov., 1918) from Estonia and the Russians again invaded (Nov. 22, 1918). They were driven out, with British help (Jan., 1919) and, by the Treaty of Tartu (Feb., 1920), Russia recognized Estonian independence.

Baltimore, George Calvert, 1st baron *See* **Calvert, George, 1st baron Baltimore.**

Baltimore Incident US-Chilean incident (Oct. 16, 1891) shortly after the Chilean civil war. Crew members of the USS *Baltimore,* on leave in Valparaiso, were attacked, and two crewmen were killed. Chile agreed to pay an indemnity, and war was avoided.

Balts Peoples of the eastern coast of the Baltic Sea, including the Latvians and the Lithuanians.

Balzac, Honoré de 1799–1850. French writer and one of the world's greatest novelists. He labored in poverty for some ten years before publishing his first successful novel, *Les Chouans* (1829). He wrote voluminously for the next 20 years, though he was never able to elude the debts that plagued him. In 1834 he devised *The Human Comedy,* the overall scheme for his novels, which were collectively to depict human society. Among his masterpieces are *Eugénie Grandet* (1833), *Le Père Goriot* (1834), and *Le Cousin Pons* (1847).

Bamboo Annals Ancient Chinese records. Written on bamboo paper, they date to the Jin state, which was destroyed in the 5th cent. BC. The papers were discovered in AD 281 but have been lost.

Bancroft, George 1800–91. American historian and statesman, and author of the 10-volume *A History of the United States.* As secretary of the navy (1845–46) he established the US Naval Academy at Annapolis.

Bancroft, Hubert Howe 1832–1918. American historian. He compiled a 39-volume history of the Pacific coast of North America, largely the work of assistants.

Bandaranaike, Mrs. Sirimavo *See* **Sri Lanka.**

Bandaranaike, S.W.R.D. *See* **Sri Lanka.**

Bande Nere, Giovanni delle *See* **Medici, Giovanni de'.**

Bandinelli, Orlando *See* **Alexander III.**

Bandung Conference Meeting of 29 African and Asian nations (1955), held at Bandung, Indonesia. Organized by Indonesia, India, Pakistan and others, and including Communist China, it sought to promote mutual friendship and oppose colonialism.

Bangladesh (*formerly* East Pakistan) South Asian republic (pop. 117,976,000) on the Bay of Bengal. With India and Pakistan, it was part of the Mughal Empire (1526–1857), then became a part of British India (1857–1947). In 1947, Bangladesh became East Pakistan, the eastern province of Pakistan. In 1971 East Pakistan declared its independence, which it achieved following war between India and Pakistani forces in East Pakistan (Dec., 1971). Pakistan recognized Bangladesh in 1974. Coups in 1975, 1981, and 1982 shook the government and brought the military to power. The 1972 constitution was finally restored in 1986, though anti-government unrest continued until Hossain Mohammad Ershad (president since 1983) resigned in 1990. Sixteen years of presidential rule was subsequently ended by constitutional amendment, passed in 1991, making the prime minister chief executive. The country's coastal area is periodically hit by fierce storms and flooding in which tens of thousands have been killed.

Bangorian Controversy Religious controversy over powers of the Church of England. The controversy stemmed from a sermon delivered (1717) before King George I by the bishop of Bangor (Wales), Benjamin Hoadly (1676–1761). In it Hoadly challenged the disciplinary and judicial powers of the church. Supporters of the church's authority and Hoadly's defenders published some 200 pamphlets over a period of several years, arguing the issue.

Ban Gu AD 32–92. Chinese historian, writer, and poet. With the help of his father Ban Biao and sister Ban Zhao, Ban Gu compiled the *Hanshu* (*History of the Former Han Dynasty*). The book, written in 100 chapters, influenced later historical writing in China.

Bank of the United States Name of two national banks chartered in early US history (1791–1811; 1816–36). The first, proposed by A. Hamilton, was established (Feb. 1791) with a capitalization of $10 million and a 20-year charter, despite opposition by the Jeffersonians (who questioned its constitutionality and who thought it favored mercantile interests over farmers). Based in Philadelphia, the bank functioned smoothly throughout its 20-year charter, but opposition by state banks and others blocked extension of its charter, forcing its closure in 1811. Congress passed a 20-year charter for the second Bank of the US (1816), with a capitalization of $35 million. After a period of mismanagement (1816–19), the bank operated on sound footing, and the Supreme Court decision *McCulloch* v. *Maryland* settled the issue of its constitutionality (1819). In the 1830s, however, President A. Jackson vetoed a bill to renew the bank's charter (1832), and in 1833 he ordered government deposits withdrawn. The bank closed in 1836 when its charter expired.

Banks, Nathaniel Prentiss 1816–94. American politician and Union general during the Civil War. He commanded Union forces at New Orleans (1862) and captured Port Hudson (1863), thereby helping Gen. U. Grant to open the Mississippi.

Banneker, Benjamin 1731–1806. Black American scientist and writer. Almost entirely self-taught, he compiled an astronomical almanac based on his own calculations (published 1792–1802) and was appointed assistant to the surveyor of the new District of Columbia (1791). His scientific accomplishments were used by abolitionists as proof of the intellectual capabilities of blacks.

Banner System Manchu army system in which tribal warriors were grouped into units under distinctive banners (1601). These companies, stationed all over China, enabled the Manchus to conquer China and establish the Qing dynasty.

Bannockburn, Battle of Battle (June 23–24, 1314) at Bannockburn, Scotland. Here Scottish forces under Robert the Bruce defeated the army of English king Edward II, thereby establishing Scottish independence.

Banting, Sir Frederick Grant 1891–1941. Canadian physician. With John J. R. Macleod (1876–1935) and Charles H. Best (1899–1978), he isolated insulin, for which he and Macleod received the Nobel Prize for Physiology or Medicine (1923).

Bantu A diverse people of Africa, related primarily by similarities in their languages. Bantus occupy almost all of southern Africa below the Congo River. It is believed that Bantus originally occupied homelands in east-central Africa and spread (c1st cent. BC?) south from there. Bantu tribes include Ashanti, Basutos, Kaffirs, Matabele, Swahilis, and Zulus.

Banville, Théodore de 1823–91. A leading French poet of his day and a member of the Parnassian movement. He is said to have influenced later symbolist poets.

Bao Dai (Nguyen Vinh Thuy) 1913–   . Last Vietnamese emperor (1926–45). He initially attempted reform in Vietnam but was thwarted by French colonial rule. Forced to abdicate (1945) by Ho Chi Minh, he returned in 1949 to rule as head of state, but his authority was eclipsed by his weak rule and the growing strength of the Viet Minh. Ngo Dinh Diem replaced him in 1955.

Baptists Protestant Christian denomination. Baptists permit baptism of believers only (as opposed to infant baptism) and generally practice baptism by immersion. The Baptist churches originated within the English Separatist (Independents) movement and began (c1608) with the teachings of John Smyth (c1570–1612). Baptists soon formed two distinct groups: the General Baptists, following the Dutch reformer J. Arminius's doctrines of the general atonement of Christ; and the Particular Baptists, following the stricter teachings of J. Calvin. The two groups merged in 1891. The first Baptist church in America was founded (1639) at Providence, Rhode Island, by R. Williams, who had been banished from Massachusetts for opposing infant baptism. The subsequent spread of Baptist churches in America was greatly accelerated during the Great Awakening. Baptist sects include the Seventh Day Baptists, who observe Calvinist doctrine and celebrate the Sabbath on Saturday.

Bar, Confederation of   *See* **Confederation of Bar.**

Baradaeus, Jacob   *See* **Syrian Orthodox church.**

Barbados   Island nation (pop. 260,000) in the West Indies, off the coast of South America. Believed to have been discovered by the Portuguese (16th cent.), it was first settled by the English (c1627). Under British rule, it was a major producer of sugar until 1834, when slavery was abolished. It was the headquarters of the colonial government of the Windward Islands (1833–85) and gained independence in 1966. Flogging of criminals was reintroduced to combat a wave of violent crime during the 1980s.

Barbara, Saint *fl.* 3d or 4th cent.   Virgin martyr, patron saint of artillerymen. According to legend, her father killed her for professing Christianity, and was then struck down by lightning.

Barbarelli, Giorgio   *See* **Giorgione.**

barbarian   Greek term for a stranger or foreigner, later applied by the Romans to Germanic tribes.

barbarian invasions   Name given to the conquest of portions of the Western Roman Empire by tribes from the north. By the 4th cent. AD Rome's political and militry power had weakened, allowing Germanic tribes to seize and settle in northern Roman provinces. The Visigoths crossed the Danube (AD 376) and, led by Alaric, sacked Rome (410). His successor, Ataulf, sought to fuse Roman elements into a Visigothic kingdom. Rome was nearly sacked (451) by the Huns under Attila, and was sacked (455) by the Vandals under Gaiseric. The Germanic tribes under Odoacer deposed (476) Romulus Augus-

tulus, last Roman emperor of the West, and the Western Empire ceased to exist. Other groups to seize Roman territory included the Ostrogoths, the Burgundians, and the Franks.

Barberini, Maffeo   *See* **Urban VIII.**

Barbarossa II (Khair ed-Din) 1466?–1546. Turkish corsair who seized Algiers (1518) from Spain, conquered Tunis (1534), and raided the coasts of Greece, Spain, and Italy.

Barbary States   Name for the North African states of Tripoli, Morocco, Tunis, and Algeria during the 16th to 19th cents. A notorious center for pirates, the region was also called the Barbary Coast. Despite a major military campaign mounted (1541) by Holy Roman Emperor Charles V, Algeria, Tunis, and Tripoli fell to the Ottoman Turks in the 16th cent. Semi-independent states within the empire, they became a haven for privateers, the Barbary pirates, who raided ships and coastal towns for booty and slaves. Morocco also became a pirate base. Attacks by European powers and the US (*see* Tripolitan War) on the Barbary States brought its decline. Piracy ended with the French conquest of Algeria (from 1830).

Barbizon school   School of realistic French landscape painting (19th cent.) founded by Théodore Rousseau (1812–67) and Jean François Millet (1814–75). It contributed to the development of realism in French painting.

Barbo, Pietro   *See* **Paul II.**

Barbon, Praise-God   *See* **Barebone, Praise-God.**

Barclay de Tolly, Mikhail, Prince 1761–1818. Russian field marshal of Scottish descent, whose policy of retreat before Napoleon's army (1812) proved ultimately a successful tactic. Defeated at Smolensk (1812), he was replaced by M. Kutuzov, who continued his tactic.

Bardeen, John 1908–91.   American physicist, twice co-winner of the Nobel Prize in Physics. He received the prize (1956) with Walter H. Brattain (1902–87) and William Shockley (1910–89) for development of the transistor; and (1972) with Leon N. Cooper (1930–   ) and John Schrieffer (1931–   ) for the theory of superconductivity.

Barebone, Praise-God (Barbon, ˜) 1596?–1679. English preacher and leather merchant. As a member of O. Cromwell's Nominated Parliament (1653), he lent it the nickname Barebones Parliament.

Barebones Parliament (Little Parliament) (Nominated Parliament)   Parliament assembled by O.

Cromwell (July, 1653) following his dissolution of the Rump Parliament. Named after member Praise-God Barebone, it resigned its powers to Cromwell, who established the Protectorate.

Bar-Hebraeus, Gregorius (Abulfaraj) 1226–86. Syrian scholar known best for his chronicle of the world, written in Syriac.

Bari, Council of Religious council called (1098) by Pope Urban II in an attempt to reconcile the Eastern and Western churches.

Baring British banking family, including Sir Francis Baring (1740–1810), chief founder (1763) of John and Francis Baring and Company, which helped to finance British military operations against the French in the Napoleonic Wars. Many family members have also served in government.

Baring, Sir Francis *See* **Baring.**

Barkley, Alben W(illiam) 1877–1956. Vice-president of the United States (1949–53) under H. Truman. A member of the House (1913–27) and Senate (1927–49, 1954–56), he played a major role in forming the New Deal.

Bar Kokhba, Simon (Simon Bar Cochba) *d.* AD 135. Jewish leader who led a major revolt against Roman emperor Hadrian (AD 132–135) until his defeat by J. Severus (AD 135).

Barlow, Joel 1754–1812. American writer and diplomat, one of the Connecticut Wits. Appointed ambassador to France (1811), he was caught in Napoleon's retreat from Moscow and died from exposure.

Barnabas, Saint (*orig.* Joses, or Joseph) *d.* AD c61. Christian apostle from Cyprus. A founder of the church at Antioch, he accompanied Paul on his first missionary journey to Cyprus.

Barnard, Christiaan Neething 1922– . South African surgeon. Barnard introduced open-heart surgery to his country and performed the first human heart transplant (Dec. 3, 1967).

Barnard, George Grey 1863–1938. American sculptor, noted for a controversial statue of A. Lincoln (1917). His private collection of Gothic and medieval art was the foundation for the Cloisters museum in New York City.

Barnard, Henry 1811–1900. American educator. With H. Mann, he led the movement to improve the US educational system and became the first US commissioner of education (1867).

Barnave, Joseph 1761–93. French revolutionary. A Jacobin leader, he helped to return the fleeing King Louis XVI to Paris (1791). Breaking with the Jacobins, he joined the Feuillants, and his advocacy of a constitutional monarchy led to his execution.

Barnburners Radical faction of New York Democrats (1842–48) opposed to their conservative counterparts, the Hunkers. Largely an anti-slavery group, Barnburners supported the Wilmot Proviso. The faction split from the state Democratic party (1847) and, barred from the national convention (1848), it nominated M. Van Buren for president. By splitting the Democratic vote, it helped Z. Taylor to victory. The faction broke up after the election, some members joining the Free-Soil party. Barnburners were named after a legendary farmer who burned his barn to clear it of rats.

Barnet, Battle of Battle (Apr. 14, 1471) fought at Barnet, England, during the War of the Roses. The battle resulted in a major Yorkist victory for Edward IV over the Lancastrians, led by Henry VI.

Barnum, Phineas Taylor 1810–91. American showman. Barnum introduced sensational exhibits to his museum in New York, and with James A. Bailey (1847–1906) formed the Barnum and Bailey Circus (1881).

Baroja y Nessi, Pio 1879–1956. Basque-born writer, one of the major Spanish novelists of the 20th cent.

Baronius, Caesar 1538–1607. Italian ecclesiastical historian, author of *Annales Eccliastici*, a history of the church to the year 1198.

Barons' War Rebellion (1263–67) by English barons against the arbitrary rule of King Henry III. Henry precipitated the uprising by refusing to abide by the Provisions of Oxford and of Westminster. Led by S. de Montfort, the barons at first forced Henry's submission (1263). Fighting was renewed (1264) after the barons rejected the Mise of Amiens, arbitration in favor of Henry. Victorious at the Battle of Lewes (1264), Montfort became virtual ruler of England and summoned (1265) a representative parliament that was a model for the House of Commons. Montfort was defeated and slain by Prince Edward at the Battle of Evesham (1265), and baronial resistance ended in 1267.

baroque Artistic and architectural style, which flourished in Europe and England in the 17th and 18th cents. It was characterized by fluidity of movement and grandness of scale. It arose in Italy (c1600) and thereafter spread throughout

Europe, taking on distinctive national characteristics in each area. Among the leading artists and architects in this period were (in Italy) Caravaggio and G. Bernini; (in France) N. Poussin; (in Flanders) P. Rubens; (in Holland) Rembrandt and Vermeer; (in Spain) Velásquez and (in England) Van Dyck and C. Wren. The term baroque also applies to a musical style developed in this period.

Barrackpore Mutiny Mutiny (Nov. 2, 1824) of Indian troops at Barrackpore, India, during the first Burma War (1824–26). Indian troops, holding serious grievances against British commanders, refused to obey orders and were subsequently fired upon by European troops. The massacre fostered deep resentment that contributed to the Indian Mutiny (1857–58).

Barras, Paul François Jean Nicolas, vicomte de 1755–1829. French revolutionary. An early Jacobin, he helped overthrow M. Robespierre and, with the aid of Napoleon, established the Directory (1795). He was overthrown by Napoleon in 1799.

Barrès, Maurice 1862–1923. French novelist and politician whose influential works reflected his ardent nationalism and individualism.

Barrie, Sir James Matthew 1860–1937. Scottish novelist and dramatist, known best for his play *Peter Pan.*

Barrier Treaty Treaty (Nov. 15, 1715) signed at Antwerp by Great Britain, Austria, and the Netherlands, ceding to the Dutch fortresses along the Belgian frontier with France, for protection from French attack.

Barry, John 1745–1803. US naval officer in the American Revolution. He captured the British tender *Edward,* the first British ship taken by a commissioned American naval vessel.

Bart, Jean 1650–1702. French naval officer and privateer noted for his naval exploits during the War of the Grand Alliance.

Barth, Karl 1886–1968. Swiss theologian. Barth's philosophy, called dialectical theology, stressed the word of God and his revelation in Jesus Christ as the central means of understanding man's relationship to God.

Bartholdi, Frédéric Auguste 1834–1904. French sculptor whose works include the *Statue of Liberty* and the *Lion of Belfort* monument at Belfort, France.

Bartholomew, Saint *fl.* 1st cent. AD. One of the twelve disciples of Jesus Christ, usually identi-

fied with Nathanael. He is believed to have preached in or near India and to have been martyred in Armenia.

Bartók, Béla 1881–1945. Hungarian composer, a major figure in 20th-cent. music. His works, striking and original, reflect his study of Hungarian folk music.

Bartolommeo, Fra (Baccio della Porta) 1475–1517. Italian painter. A master of the Florentine school of Renaissance painting, he was influenced by Raphael.

Barton, Clara 1821–1912. American humanitarian whose nursing services during the Civil War earned her the title "Angel of the Battlefield." She founded the American Red Cross (1881).

Barton, Edmund *See* **Australia, 1901–03.**

Barton, Elizabeth 1506?–34. English servant woman known as the Nun of Kent or the Maid of Kent. Her prophecies warning against Henry VIII's marriage to Anne Boleyn were exposed as fraudulent, and she was executed.

Bartram, John 1699–1777. American botanist. He founded, near Philadelphia, the first botanical garden in the US.

Baruch, Bernard Mannes 1870–1965. US financier and presidential adviser. He made his fortune through stock market speculation and during WW I served as chairman of the US War Industries Board. During WW II he advised President F. Roosevelt on mobilizing the economy for the war effort.

Bärwalde, Treaty of (Brandenburg, ˜) French-Swedish treaty (January 13, 1631) by which French king Louis XIII agreed to pay annual subsidies to Swedish king Gustavus II Adolphus to support an army against the Habsburgs in the Thirty Years' War.

Barzun, Jacques 1907– . American writer and educator whose books include *Darwin, Marx, Wagner* and *The Teacher in America.*

Bascio, Matteo da *See* **Capuchins.**

Basel, Confession of Name of two statements of Reformation doctrine. 1. First ˜. Statement drafted by J. Oecolampadius (1531) and revised by Oswald Mycanius (1488–1552). 2. Second ˜. Name sometimes applied to the first Helvetic Confession, written (1536) by Heinrich Bullinger (1504–75) and others and adopted by the Swiss Reformed church.

Basel, Council of Council of the Roman Catholic church convened (1431–49) at Basel, noted for its struggle with Pope Eugene IV over the issue of conciliarism versus papal supremacy. The council made a number of reforms and by the Compactata of Prague (1436) found a settlement for the Hussite question. Eugene, after attempting to come to terms with the conciliarists by making numerous concessions, summoned the Council of Ferrara-Florence (1437) to deal with other church matters. The few bishops remaining at Basel declared Eugene a heretic and replaced him (1439) with antipope Felix V. The struggle continued until Pope Nicholas V, successor to Eugene, was recognized as the legitimate pope. Felix abdicated (1449) and the council at Basel was dissolved.

Basel, Peace of   *See* **Basel, Treaties of.**

Basel, Treaties of   1. (~, Peace of) Treaty (Sept. 22, 1499) between Holy Roman Emperor Maximilian I and the Swiss Confederation, ending a series of conflicts and effectively granting Swiss independence.   2. Treaty (Apr. 5, 1795) between France and Prussia, ending Prussia's participation against France in the French Revolutionary Wars (1792–1802). France relinquished control of the right bank of the Rhine in return for Prussia's recognition of French claims to the left bank.   3. Treaty (July 22, 1795) between France and Spain, ending Spain's participation against France (1793–95) in the French Revolutionary Wars (1792–1802). France returned conquered territories in exchange for Santo Domingo.

Basil I (~ the Macedonian) c813–86.   Byzantine emperor (867–86). He assassinated (867) his coruler, Michael III, and proclaimed himself emperor. He founded the Macedonian dynasty and his reign marked a golden age in Byzantine history.

Basil II (*surnamed* Bulgaroktonos) c958–1025. Byzantine emperor (976–1025), nominal successor (963) to his father, Romanus II, with his brother, Constantine VIII (960?–1028). Coming to power in 976, he incorporated the kingdom of Bulgaria into the empire (1018) after a series of conflicts with the Bulgarians.

Basil IV Shuisky   *See* **Time of Troubles.**

Basil, Saint (~ the Great, Saint) AD c330–c379. Greek bishop of Caesarea (from AD 370). One of the great fathers of the Greek church, he supported orthodox belief against Arianism. (*See also* Basilians).

Basil the Macedonian   *See* **Basil I.**

Basilians   Members of the religious order founded (AD 358) by Saint Basil the Great and including many of the monks of the Eastern church. A Basilian order was also established in France in 1822.

basilica   In ancient Roman architecture, a large, multi-purpose public hall serving variously as a marketplace, courthouse, or meeting place. A rectangular roofed structure, the Roman basilica enclosed a large hall that ran the length of the building and had a stagelike platform at one, and sometimes both, ends. The early Christians adopted this type of structure for their churches, after Christianity was recognized within the Roman empire.

Basilides   *See* **Gnosticism.**

Baskerville, John 1706–75.   English printer and designer of the Baskerville typefaces.

Basques   An ethnic group inhabiting northern Spain and southern France from ancient times. Converted to Christianity (5th cent.), Basques largely resisted conquest by the Romans, Visigoths, Moors, and Franks. French Basques finally submitted to the Franks (9th cent.). The Basque kingdom of Navarre resisted Spanish kings until 1512. The Spanish Civil War (1936–39) divided the Basques politically, and the region was a site of fierce fighting. The Basque Separatist movement has continued into recent times. *See also* Spain.

Bassein, Treaty of   Anglo-Indian treaty (Dec. 31, 1802).   The Maratha leader Peshwa Baji Rao II (*d.* 1852) entered into an alliance with the British East India Company, trading independence for protection. The treaty gave Britain a foothold in the area and led eventually to the Second Maratha War and the downfall of the Maratha Confederacy.

Bassianus, Varius Avitus   *See* **Heliogabalus.**

Bastian, Adolf 1826–1905.   German anthropologist. His theory, that certain ideas common to all mankind differ in form according to culture, influenced later anthropologists and psychologists.

Bastille   French fortress and later (17th–18th cents.) a notorious prison in Paris, France. Built (c1370) by Charles V, it became a symbol of arbitrary royal powers because prisoners (from 17th cent.) detained by the king's *Lettre de Cachet* were held there. The storming of the prison (July 14, 1789) symbolized the end of the *ancien régime* for French revolutionaries, although the rioters were after munitions stored there, and just seven prisoners were in the jail that day. Bastille Day (July 14) is a French national holiday.

Basutoland *See* **Lesotho.**

Bataan Death March Forced march (beginning Apr. 9, 1942) of 75,000 Americans and Filipinos captured by the Japanese at Bataan, Philippines, during WW II. The brutal conditions were such that only 54,000 survived the 60-mile trek from Mariveles, on the Bataan peninsula, to Camp O'Donnell. The march was commanded by Gen. Masaharu Homma (1888?–1946), who later was hanged as a war criminal.

Batavian Republic Name given to the Netherlands after conquest (1795) by Napoleon in the French Revolutionary Wars. It became the kingdom of Holland in 1806.

Bates, Henry Walter 1825–92. English naturalist and explorer. His study of the effect of natural selection in animal mimicry supported C. Darwin's theory of evolution.

Bathory, Elizabeth *d.* 1614. Hungarian countess, said to have slain more than six hundred young girls and to have bathed in their blood in order to restore her youth.

Bathory, Sigismund 1572–1613. Prince of Transylvania (1581–99). A vassal of Holy Roman Emperor Rudolf II, Bathory provoked a civil war in Transylvania through his policies against the Ottoman Turks.

Ba'th party (Ba'ath ~) (Arab Socialist Renaissance party) Arab political party (founded 1943), especially influential in Syria and Iraq. The party advocates creation of a unified Arab socialist state. In Syria, the party was important in the formation (1958) of the United Arab Republic and Syria's subsequent withdrawal from it (1961). It was involved in coups (Mar., 1963; Feb., 1966), and in the latter radical left-wing Bathists took power in Syria. In Iraq, the party came to power briefly after a coup (Feb., 1963) and returned to power by a coup in July, 1968. Bathist opposition was chiefly responsible for blocking a planned union (1963) among Egypt, Syria, and Iraq.

Batista y Zaldívar, Fulgencio 1901–73. Cuban dictator. He took part in the overthrow of G. Machado (1933) and served as president from 1940 to 1944. In 1952 he seized power and ruled as dictator until overthrown by F. Castro (1959).

Batlle y Ordóñez, José 1856–1929. President of Uruguay (1903–07, 1911–15). A leader of the liberal Colorado party, he introduced numerous political and social reforms and influenced the writing of the Uruguayan constitution of 1918.

Battle Above the Clouds *See* **Chattanooga, Battle of.**

Battle of *See under names inverted, as in* **Atlantic, Battle of the.**

Batu Khan *d.* 1255. Mongol leader, a grandson of Genghis Khan. He established the Kipchak khanate, also known as the Golden Horde (*q.v.*).

Baudelaire, Charles 1821–67. French poet and critic whose writings had a major influence on the development of the symbolist movement. His best-known collection is *Les Fleurs du mal* (1857).

Baudouin I 1930–93. Belgian king (1951–93), successor to his father, King Leopold III.

Bauer, Georg *See* **Agricola, Georgius.**

Bauhaus School of design founded (1919) at Weimar, Germany. Originally headed (1919–28) by architect W. Gropius, the school sought to overcome divisions between the arts, crafts, and modern industry. To do this, students were given multidisciplinary training. The economical, geometric designs that became associated with the school proved unpopular with the Nazis, who closed the school (1933). Gropius and other Bauhaus associates, including L. Mies van der Rohe and L. Moholy-Nagy then carried the Bauhaus movement to the US, where Bauhaus design had been well received.

Baum, Lyman Frank 1856–1919. American writer known best for his book *The Wizard of Oz.*

Bautzen, Battle of Battle (May 20–21, 1813) in the Napoleonic Wars fought at Bautzen (Germany). Napoleon's French army of 140,000 troops defeated a Russo-Prussian army of some 90,000. Though a victory for Napoleon I, French losses were greater than Russo-Prussian casualties.

Bavaria West German state. Originally inhabited by Celts, it was conquered by the Romans (1st cent.), then by Germanic peoples ending with the Franks. In 788 it became part of Charlemagne's empire. One of the main duchies of the Holy Roman Empire in medieval Germany, Bavaria passed in 1180 to the house of Wittelsbach, which held it until 1918. It became a kingdom (1806) under Maximilian I and joined the German empire in 1871. Bavaria became a socialist republic (1918) and joined the Weimar Republic, but lost its independence with the rise

(1933) of Nazi Germany. In 1949 Bavaria became part of the German Federal Republic.

Bavaria, Isabeau of   *See* **Isabeau of Bavaria.**

Bavarian Succession, War of the (Potato War) Dispute (1778–79) in which Prussia prevented Austria from taking over Bavarian lands. Charles Theodore, successor to the extinct line of Bavarian electors of Wittelsbach, precipitated the conflict by ceding Lower Bavaria to Holy Roman Emperor Joseph II of Austria. Frederick II (the Great), however, feared increased Austrian influence in southern Germany, and with Saxony raised an army against the Austrians. There were no major engagements and the brief war was ended by the Treaty of Teschen (1779).

Bayard, Pierre du Terrail, seigneur de c1473–1524. French soldier, called "the knight without fear and without blame." He halted an invasion of central France by Holy Roman Emperor Charles V at Mézières (1521) and distinguished himself in the Italian Wars (1494–1529).

Bayer, Johann 1572–1625. German astronomer and author of the *Uranometria* (1603), the first complete star chart. He also was the first to designate stars by Greek letters according to their magnitudes.

Bayinnaung Burmese ruler (1551–81). A fierce warrior, he conquered much surrounding territory and unified Burma. He twice invaded Siam, and maintained a puppet ruler there for fifteen years.

Bayle, Pierre 1647–1706. French philosopher. An advocate of tolerance and skepticism, he greatly influenced philosophers of the Enlightenment. His major work is the *Dictionnaire historique et critique.*

Bay of Islands War War (1844–47), usually considered part of the first Maori War (*q.v.*), between European settlers and Maori natives in New Zealand. After the massacre of Europeans at Wairu (1843), a native rebellion began (1844) in the Bay of Islands region of northern New Zealand. Led by Maori chief Hone Heka, some 1,000 natives took part in the rebellion, caused by the natives' anger at declining profits from trade. They attacked settlements in the north (from 1845) until their revolt was quashed (1847) by Gov. Sir George Grey (1812–98).

Bay of Pigs Invasion Unsuccessful invasion (1961) of Cuba by Cuban exiles. Organized by the US CIA, the invasion was a major embarrassment to the newly elected Kennedy administration and was an important event leading up to the Cuban Missile Crisis (1962). Planned (from May, 1960) under the Eisenhower administration and approved by President J. Kennedy shortly after his inauguration, the invasion was an outgrowth of worsening relations between the US and Cuba's F. Castro. Bombing of Cuban air bases by rebel planes began on Apr. 15 and the landings began on Apr. 17. Some 1,500 Cuban exiles took part in the invasion (along Cuba's southern coast, mainly at the Bay of Pigs), which was intended to spark a general uprising. The invasion had clearly failed by Apr. 19, in part because Kennedy apparently refused to allow air cover. Many of the invaders were captured, and 1,113 survivors were ransomed back to the US by the Cubans for food and medicine (1962).

Bay Psalm Book First book published in the American colonies. Published in Cambridge, Massachusetts, in 1640, the book is titled *The Whole Book of Psalms Faithfully Translated into English Metre.*

Bean, Roy c1825–1903. American frontier judge, known as the "law west of the Pecos." Bean changed the name of Vinegaroon, Texas, to Langtry in honor of the English actress Lily Langtry (1853–1929). There he dispensed his own form of frontier justice and became a figure of western folklore.

bearbaiting (bullbaiting) Medieval entertainment in which dogs were set upon a bear (or bull) tied to a stake or otherwise made immobile. Popular in England and Europe for centuries, it was outlawed by Parliament in the 19th cent.

Beard, Charles A(ustin) 1874–1948. American historian noted for his emphasis on the importance of economic forces in the shaping of American history.

Beatrix   *See* **Juliana.**

Beauchamp, Thomas de, earl of Warwick *d.* 1401. English statesman. One of the governors of Richard II during his minority, he later opposed Richard and was imprisoned, then exiled. He was restored by Henry IV.

Beauclerc, Henry   *See* **Henry I.**

Beaufort, Margaret, countess of Richmond and Derby 1443–1509. English noblewoman, mother of Henry VII. She founded professorships of divinity at Oxford and Cambridge and endowed Christ's College and St. John's College at Cambridge.

Beaufort, Pierre Roger de   *See* **Gregory XI.**

Beauharnais, Hortense de 1783–1837. French noblewoman. Queen of Holland from 1806–10, she was the wife of L. Bonaparte and mother of Napoleon III.

Beaumanoir, Philippe de Remi, sire de c1246–96. French jurist who wrote *Coutumes de Beauvaisis* (c1283), which codified French law up to that time.

Beaumarchais, Pierre Augustin Caron de 1732–99. French playwright. His comedies *Le Barbier de Séville* (1775) and *Le Mariage de Figaro* (1784) inspired operas by G. Rossini and W. Mozart. He lost his fortune supplying arms to the US during the American Revolution.

Beauregard, Pierre Gustave Toutant 1818–93. Confederate general. He ordered the firing on Fort Sumter in 1861, thus beginning the Civil War, and fought at the First Battle of Bull Run (1861) and at Shiloh (1862).

Beauvoir, Simone de 1908–86. French existentialist writer, long associated with J. Sartre. Her books include *The Blood of Others* and *The Second Sex* (1949).

Beaverbrook, William Maxwell Aitken, 1st baron 1879–1964. Canadian-born financier, British politician, and newspaper magnate. He served in Parliament, and in the cabinets of D. Lloyd George (1918) and W. Churchill (1940–42) advocated free trade within the British Empire.

Bebel, August 1840–1913. German Socialist leader. Drawn to socialism by W. Liebknecht, he helped to found the Social Democratic party of Germany (1869), which he led for many years.

Beccaria, Cesare Bonesana, marchese di 1738–94. Italian writer. His essay opposing capital punishment, *Dei delitti e delle pene* (1764), had a great influence on penal reform in Europe.

Bechuanaland *See* Botswana.

Becket, Thomas à *See* Thomas à Becket.

Beckmann, Max *See* expressionism.

Becquerel, Antoine Henri 1852–1908. French physicist. He discovered radioactivity in uranium (1896) and shared the 1903 Nobel Prize for Physics with P. and M. Curie, who had named and studied the phenomenon. Their work marked the beginning of nuclear physics. He investigated the radioactivity of radium, proving that it is made up of an electron stream (1900). He also demonstrated that radioactivity causes an element to be transformed into another (1900). Becquerel proved that a material's radioactivity can be chemically removed but that the material will subsequently regain its radioactivity.

Bede, Saint (Baeda, ˜) 673?–737. English historian and Benedictine monk, called the Venerable Bede. His *Ecclesiastical History of the English People* is a main source for early English history and covers the period from 55 BC to Saint Augustine's mission to Kent in AD 597. Bede's system of dating events after Christ's birth as AD soon became established practice.

Bedlam English hospital properly named Bethlehem Royal Hospital. Originally a priory (founded c1247) in London, it was later used for confinement of the mentally ill. Its name was slurred in common use to "bedlam," a word now used to describe any scene of uproar. The hospital was one of the first mental institutions in Europe, and the first in England.

Bedouin Arabic-speaking nomadic peoples of the Middle East, constituting about 10 percent of the population of the region. Many Bedouin have been forced by modern events to give up their nomadic way of life.

Beebe, Charles William 1877–1962. American naturalist, explorer, and writer. In 1934 he descended in the sea, using a bathysphere, to a record depth of 3,028 feet (923 meters).

Beecher, Catharine 1800–78. US educator and writer. The daughter of L. Beecher, and older sister of H. B. Stowe, she was well known during the 1840s, promoting women's superiority as teachers and in the family. Beecher wrote on such issues as changes in middle-class life, the role of women in domestic life, and women's social and political contributions. Her works included *Treatise on Domestic Economy* (1843).

Beecher, Henry Ward 1813–87. American Congregational preacher and brother of H. B. Stowe. As pastor (1847–87) of Plymouth (Congregational) Church in Brooklyn, New York, he was an influential opponent of slavery and supporter of woman suffrage and the theory of evolution. A sensational court trial for adultery (1875) tarnished his career, although the evidence was inconclusive.

Beecher, Lyman 1775–1863. American Presbyterian minister, the father of C. and H. W. Beecher and H. B. Stowe. A revivalist clergyman, he had congregations in Connecticut and Massachusetts, and preached in the West. He spoke out against rationalism, Catholicism, and intemperance. Beecher founded the American Bible Society (1816).

Beerbohm, Sir Max 1872–1956.   English writer and caricaturist noted for his humorous parodies, essays, and caricatures.

Beer Hall Putsch   *See* **Munich Putsch.**

Beethoven, Ludwig van 1770–1827.   German composer, one of the greatest composers of all time. Beethoven was tutored first by W. Mozart and then by F. J. Haydn (1792–94) in Vienna, then the center of the music world. Beethoven soon rose to be the preeminent composer of his day. His personal life, however, was marked by the onset of his deafness (c1801) and his stormy relationship with his nephew, then his ward. Beethoven, through his brilliant and emotional compositions, transcended the limitations set by classical style and set the stage for the works of the later Romantic period. Among his greatest works are his nine symphonies, including No. 3, the *Eroica,* originally written to honor Napoleon, and No. 9, which includes a choral finale based on F. von Schiller's *Ode to Joy.* His major works also include the *Moonlight Sonata, Missa Solemnis,* and the opera *Fidelio.*

Beghards   Semimonastic religious associations of Catholic men, similar to the Beguines. They flourished in Europe in the 13th cent. Condemned at the Council of Vienne (1311) as a heretical sect, they gradually disappeared.

Begin, Menachem 1913–92.   Israeli politician and prime minister (1977–83). A member of the right-wing underground military organization Irgun prior to Israeli independence (1948), Begin later led the Herut (Freedom) party, and then the Likud Bloc. A critic of earlier Labor party governments, he nevertheless became the Israeli prime minister who concluded formal peace with Egypt (Mar. 26, 1979). He received the 1978 Nobel Peace Prize along with Egyptian pres. A. Sadat. He was later seriously criticized for air attacks on an Iraqi nuclear reactor and for the annexation (1981) of the Golan Heights (taken from Syria in the 1967 war). The Israelis were also successful in a war against the PLO in Lebanon (1982) during his administration.

beguines   Religious communities of women that flourished in Europe in the 12th and 13th cents. Semimonastic orders, they devoted themselves to charitable works and preaching. Though condemned by the Council of Vienne (1311), they still survive in Belgium and the Netherlands.

Beham, Barthel 1502–40.   German painter and engraver. He was a member of the group of engravers known as the Little Masters, whose works were influenced by A. Dürer.

Beham, Hans Sebald 1500–50.   German painter and engraver, and brother of B. Beham. A member of the Little Masters, he is known for his miniature engravings.

behaviorism   Psychological theory. Introduced by J. Watson (1913), behaviorism maintains that animal and human actions are physical responses to environmental stimuli. Contributors to behaviorist theory include I. Pavlov and B. F. Skinner.

Behistun Inscription (Bisitun Inscription)   Carving in an elevated rock face near Behistun, western Iran. The inscription, ordered (c6th cent. BC) by Persian king Darius I, appears in Assyrian, Old Persian, and Elamite, and greatly facilitated decipherment of ancient Babylonian and Elamite texts.

Behrens, Peter 1868–1940.   German architect noted for his influence on the development of modern architecture and industrial design.

Behring, Emil Adolph von 1854–1917.   German bacteriologist and pioneer in serum therapy. With S. Kitasato he developed antitoxins for diphtheria and tetanus, and in 1901 received the first Nobel Prize in Physiology or Medicine.

Behring, Vitus Jonassen *See* **Bering, Vitus Jonassen.**

Beijing (Peking) (Peiping)   Capital city of the People's Republic of China. The nation's cultural, educational, political, and transportation center, it is located on the site of several earlier cities, dating to the 1st millennium BC. As Cambuluc (Khanbalik), it was Kublai Khan's capital (13th cent.). Renamed Peking, it was China's capital from 1421 to 1912. In 1860 Peking was occupied by British and French troops and in 1900 it was the site of the Boxer Rebellion (*q.v.*). In 1928 its name was changed to Peiping. Occupied by the Japanese (1937–45) before and during WW II, it was capital of a Japanese puppet government. It was taken by the Communists (1949), who reestablished it as China's capital and renamed it Peking. Under the Communists, Peking was greatly expanded and improved. In the 1980s, the English transliteration of the city's name was changed to Beijing. The Forbidden City (*q.v.*), the former imperial residence, is located in the city.

Beijing, Treaty of (Peking, ~) Treaty (Nov. 2, 1860) in which China and Russia settled the frontier border between Xinjiang (Sinkiang) and Turkestan. China also gave Russia a coastal territory, now the site of Vladivostok.

Béjard *See* **Béjart.**

Béjart (Béjard) French family of actors who performed with J. Molière. Its members included Madeleine Béjart (1618–72), Molière's mistress, and Armande Béjart (c1642–1700), Molière's wife. After Molière's death, their company merged with a rival group to become the Comédie Française.

Béla IV 1206–70. King of Hungary (1235–70), successor to his father, Andrew II. During his reign, much of Hungary was devastated by Mongol invasions. Most of his rule was spent in rebuilding and repopulating Hungary, and warring against King Ottocar II of Bohemia.

Belarus *See* **Belorus.**

Belaúnde Terry, Fernando 1912– . Peruvian architect and statesman. As president of Peru (1963–68), he instituted many social and economic reforms, but his pro-US policies led to his ouster (Oct., 1968) in a military coup. Returning from exile in 1976, he was reelected president and served 1980–85.

Belgian Congo *See* **Zaire.**

Belgium Constitutional monarchy located in northwestern Europe. The population is 9,985,000 and the capital is Brussels. Once part of the Roman province of Belgica, the region came under Frankish, Burgundian, Habsburg, Spanish, Austrian, and French control before gaining independence in 1831. Due to its strategic importance, Belgium was guaranteed perpetual neutrality (1839) by the major European nations. Belgium's neutrality was broken twice by Germany, during both world wars. Key events in the history of Belgium include:

3D CENT. AD Franks entered region; Belgian territory eventually became part of Carolingian Empire.

9TH CENT. Belgian lands became part of duchy of Lower Lorraine after division of Carolingian Empire.

12TH–15TH CENTS. Lower Lorraine broke up into small duchies; region became center of wool trade and other commerce.

15TH CENT. Territory came under control of dukes of Burgundy.

1477 Control of region passed to Habsburg family by the marriage of Mary of Burgundy to Maximilian I.

1555 Region passed to Spanish Habsburgs and became part of the Spanish Netherlands.

1578 Revolt of the Netherlands against harsh Spanish rule; southern, predominantly Catholic part (now Belgium and Luxembourg) eventually reconquered by Spain.

1714 Territory passed to Austria by the Peace of Utrecht; constituted part of the Austrian Netherlands.

1794 Austrian Netherlands conquered by French during the French Revolutionary Wars.

1797 France acquired Belgian territories by Treaty of Campo Formio.

1815 Congress of Vienna divided former Austrian Netherlands; Grand Duchy of Luxembourg created from part of territory while remainder was united with the Netherlands.

1831 Revolt in former Austrian Netherlands (1830); independent Belgium created.

1831–65 Leopold I ruled as first king of the Belgians; reign marked by extensive industrial growth.

1839 Belgian neutrality guaranteed by major European powers at the London Conference.

1865–1909 Leopold II reigned; Belgium became major industrial and colonial power; annexed Belgian Congo (1908).

1909–34 Albert I reigned.

1914 Belgium invaded by German forces (Aug. 4) at outbreak of WW I; most of Belgium occupied by Germans by end of Nov.; Belgian resistance hindered German invasion of France.

1925 Locarno Pact guaranteed the post-WW I borders of the Rhineland, Belgium, France, and Germany.

1930 Administrative division of Belgium into Flemish (Dutch-speaking) and Walloon (French-speaking) provinces under different administrations.

1934–51 Leopold III reigned.

1940 Belgium invaded by German forces (May 10) in WW II; Leopold III surrendered (May 28); Belgian government voted to rescind Leopold's power to rule; Belgian government-in-exile established in London (Oct.).

1944 Belgian forces operating with Allies in WW II liberated Belgium (Sept.).

1947   Benelux customs union established by Belgium, the Netherlands, and Luxembourg.

1949   Belgium became founding member of NATO (Apr. 4).

1951   Leopold III abdicated; his son Baudouin I became king.

1957   Belgium became member (Mar. 25) of newly organized European Economic Community.

1960s   Belgian Congo (now Zaire) became independent (1960); Belgium suffered period of political and social turmoil.

1972   Political crisis over readjustment of Fleming and Walloon territories; moves to add Brussels (85 percent francophone) as third region blocked by Flemings, who controlled the government there, until 1980s.

1979–1980   Severe economic problems, including high unemployment, resulted in four successive governments during this period; wage freeze and other austerity measures sparked widespread protest.

1980   Prime Minister Wilfried Martens resigned, after rejection of plan to divide division of Belgium into three administrative regions based on linguistic groups.

1980   Limited autonomy granted (Aug. 5) for Flanders and Wallonia, Belgium's two major linguistic regions.

1981   Mark Eyskens in office as prime minister; Eyskens instituted temporary price freeze.

1981   W. Martens returned to power as prime minister after coalition government of Eyskens collapsed.

1982–86   Martens granted special powers by Parliament; he introduced austerity program including devaluation of Belgian franc, wage and price controls; reduced working hours for employed to open up more jobs for the unemployed.

1984   Terrorist bomb attacks against NATO fuel supply lines in Belgium (Oct.); marked increasing opposition to deployment of NATO Cruise missiles in Belgium.

1986   Police seized arms caches and arrested leading members of the Fighting Communist Cells (CCC) terrorist group.

1987   Martens's government collapsed over long-standing divisions between Flemish and Walloon linguistic communities; country faced political crisis as subsequent elections failed to produce viable government for over four months.

1988   New center-left coalition of Social Christian, Socialist, and Flemish Nationalist (Volksunie) parties took office (May), with Martens as prime minister; regions and linguistic communities to get greater powers and Brussels to have own regional council.

1990   King Baudouin stepped down from throne for several days in order to avoid signing (on religious grounds) an abortion law; law was enacted during his brief abdication.

1991   Martens resigned over continuing problems with new arrangement of linguistic regions; Liberal party, which won Nov. elections, unable to form viable coalition.

1992   Flemish Christian Democrat Jean-Luc Dehaene sworn in as prime minister (Mar.), heading center-left coalition.

1992   Legislature approved Maastricht Treaty on European union (July).

1993   King Baudouin died; succeeded by Albert II.

Belgrade, Treaties of   Two peace treaties (Sept., 1739) by which the Ottoman Empire ended wars with both Russia and Austria. Austria ceded northern Serbia and Little Walachia to the Ottomans, while Russia retained Azov but agreed not to build a fleet on the Black Sea.

Belinsky, Vissarion Grigoryevich 1811–48.   Russian writer. His view that literature had social and political responsibilities greatly influenced the development of Soviet literary criticism.

Belisarius c505–565.   Byzantine general under Justinian I. He suppressed the Nika Riot in Constantinople (532), defeated the Vandals in Africa (533–34), and recaptured parts of Italy from the Ostrogoths (535–40).

Belize (*formerly* British Honduras)   Commonwealth country and former British colony (pop. 180,400) in Central America. Much of its economy is based on forest products (notably mahogany). Originally part of the Mayan civilization, it was settled by English timber cutters from Jamaica (17th cent.). Spain contested English possession until 1798. Guatemala has claimed the territory periodically since the early 19th cent. and in the 1970s a contingent of British troops was stationed in Belize to prevent a possible Guatemalan invasion. Belize was granted internal self-government in 1965 and became an independent commonwealth Sept. 21, 1981. Guatemala officially recognized independent Belize in 1991, though negotiations on its claims to Belize continued.

Bell, Alexander Graham 1847–1922. Scottish-born American audiologist and inventor. His first jobs were teaching music and elocution and in 1864, he began experimenting with sound. Bell's parents became worried about his frail health, however, and the family moved to Canada (1870). There Bell recovered and then became a professor of vocal physiology at Boston College (1873) in the US. Bell and his assistant Thomas Watson then began experimenting with transmitting sound electrically, and long hours of work on a new device, the telephone, finally resulted in Bell's being granted a US patent for his invention (Mar., 1876). Numerous lawsuits for patent infringement followed the commercial application of Bell's telephone, none was successful. In 1877, Bell married a deaf student he had helped years before, Mabel Hubbard. He continued his work with sound communications, inventing a photophone to transmit sound with beams of light, and a graphophone, the earliest sound-recording device. Bell also continued educating the deaf, and in 1898 became president of the National Geographic Institute.

Bell, Andrew 1753–1832. British educator. At Madras, India, he developed the monitorial system, which uses students in the teaching process.

Bell, Sir Charles 1774–1842. Scottish anatomist and surgeon who distinguished between motor and sensory nerves. His works include *The Nervous System of the Human Body.*

Bell, John 1797–1869. American statesman. A Whig leader in Tennessee, he delayed the state's secession from the Union until the beginning of the Civil War. He was an unsuccessful candidate for president on the Constitutional Union party ticket (1860).

Bellamy, Edward 1850–98. American novelist, author of the Utopian romance *Looking Backward, 2000–1887* (1888).

Bellarmine, Saint Robert (*b.* Bellarmino, Roberto Francesco Romolo) 1542–1621. Italian theologian. One of the foremost defenders of the Roman Catholic church in the 16th cent., he played a role in the trial of Galileo.

Bellarmino, Roberto Francesco Romolo *See* Bellarmine, Saint Robert.

Belleau, Rémy 1528–77. French poet and scholar, and member of the literary group known as the Pléiade.

Belle-Isle, Charles Louis Fouquet, duc de 1684–1761. Marshal of France. By supporting the election of Charles Albert of Bavaria as Holy Roman Emperor Charles VII, he helped to involve France in the War of the Austrian Succession (1740–48).

Bellini, Giovanni c1430–1516. Venetian painter. He was a leading Renaissance painter; his religious paintings and landscapes helped make Venice a center of Renaissance art.

Bellow, Saul 1915– . American novelist whose works deal with individuals and their struggles within modern society. He was awarded the Nobel Prize in Literature (1976).

Belorus (Belarus, Byelarus) (*formerly* Belorussian Soviet Socialist Republic; Belorussia; Byelorussia; White Russia) Independent state and member of the Commonwealth of Independent States. Located between the Baltic States and the Ukraine, the state has a population composed largely of White Russians. Minsk is a key city. The region was settled by Slavs from the 5th cent., and came under the control of Kiev in the 9th cent. After Mongol invasions (13th cent.) destroyed the Kievan state, Belorus fell to Lithuanian invaders (14th cent.), and through the union of Poland and Lithuania became part of Poland. Russia next acquired the regions by the Partitions of Poland (1772, 1793, 1795). Subsequently, the region was overrun and ravaged during wars from the 16th to 20th cents., including invasions of Russia by Napoleon and Hitler. During WW I, Belorus briefly enjoyed independence (1918–19) before the Soviets took control in 1919. Poland occupied Belorus during the Russo-Polish War (1919–20), and in 1920 gained control of the western part. The remainder was joined to the USSR in 1922. During the breakup of the USSR, Belorus's president supported the failed coup and was forced to resign in Aug. 1991, after which Belorus declared independence and adopted its current name. It was one of the three original Slavic republics (with the Ukraine and the Russian Federation) to join the Commonwealth of Independent States (Dec. 8).

Below, Count Otto von *See* Caporetto, Battle of.

Bemis Heights, Battle of *See* Saratoga Campaign.

Bemis Heights, First Battle of *See* **Freeman's Farm, Battle of.**

Benavente y Martínez, Jacinto 1866–1954. Spanish dramatist, winner of the Nobel Prize in Literature (1922). His major work, *Los intereses creados,* is in the style of the Italian commedia dell'arte.

Ben Bella, Ahmed 1918– . Algerian statesman. A leader of the Algerian nationalist movement against the French after WW II, he was a founder of the Front Libération Nationale (FLN) in 1954 and became Algeria's first president (1963–65). Ben Bella was overthrown in a coup.

Benchley, Robert Charles 1889–1945. American humorist and journalist whose books include *My Ten Years in a Quandary* and *Benchley Beside Himself.*

Benedek, Ludwig August von *See* **Königgratz, Battle of.**

Benedict XIII (antipope) *See* **Luna, Pedro de.**

Benedict XIV (*b.* Prospero Lambertini) 1675–1758. Italian-born pope (1740–58), successor to Clement XII. He encouraged science, learning, and the arts.

Benedict XV (*b.* Giacomo della Chiesa) 1854–1922. Italian-born pope (1914–22), successor to Pius X. He maintained strict neutrality during WW I, made great efforts to aid war victims, and attempted to mediate an end to the war.

Benedict, Saint *d.* c547. Italian monk. His rule, which he wrote for the monastery at Monte Cassino, became the rule for the Benedictine Order. The Rule of Saint Benedict is the basis of Western monasticism. (*See also* Benedictines.)

Benedict, Ruth Fulton 1887–1948. American anthropologist who stressed the role of culture in personality formation. She studied Indians in the US Southwest, as well as Asian and European cultures, and wrote *Patterns of Culture* (1934) and *The Chrysanthemum and the Sword* (1946).

Benedictines (Order of Saint Benedict) Roman Catholic monks, followers of the Rule of Saint Benedict. Established by Saint Benedict (early 6th cent.), the rule forms a traditional basis for western monasticism. It provides for a practical, well-balanced communal existence, stressing worship, study, and manual labor. Saint Benedict wrote the rule for his now famous monastery founded (c529) at Monte Cassino. Subsequently, Charlemagne tried to make all monasteries in his empire follow the Rule of Saint Benedict, thereby contributing to the spread of Benedictine monasticism in Europe. Benedictine abbeys remained predominant until the 12th cent., declined for a time, and almost disappeared during the Reformation (16th cent.). They were dealt a further blow during Napoleon's reign. Benedictine abbeys in their ascendancy served not only to spread Christianity throughout Europe but also to preserve Latin culture (Benedictines faithfully copied books as part of their duties) in a period of great instability. The Cluniac and Cistercian orders are outgrowths of Benedictine reform movements.

Benelux Name of the European economic union formed (1948) by Belgium, the Netherlands, and Luxembourg.

Beneš, Eduard 1887–1948. Czechoslovakian statesman. A founder of the Little Entente (1920–21), he served as Czech president (1935–38) but resigned after German annexation of the Sudetenland. He headed the Czech government-in-exile during WW II and served again as president (1946–48).

Benét, Stephen Vincent 1898–1943. American poet, short-story writer, and novelist. Interested in military history early in his life, Benét is known best for his narrative poem of the Civil War, *John Brown's Body.* In addition to many volumes of collected poems, Benét wrote novels, such as *Jean Huguenot,* and short stories, such as *The Devil and Daniel Webster.* He was twice awarded the Pulitzer Prize (1929, 1944).

Benét, William Rose 1886–1950. American poet, and brother of S. V. Benét. His volume *The Dust Which Is God* (1941) received the Pulitzer Prize for Poetry (1942).

Bengal Region and former province in northeast India. Once a part of the Mughal empire, it became a presidency (1699) under British control. It was divided between East Pakistan (Bangladesh) and India (1947).

Bengal, Partition of Administrative division of Bengal, India, ordered (July 19, 1905) by the British colonial government. It resulted in widespread protest by Bengalis and marked a turning point in the Indian nationalist movement. British Viceroy of India Lord G. Curzon executed the partition to simplify administration of the region. The partition split Bengal into eastern and western parts, united them with other adjacent areas, and sparked nationalist opposition, which included boycotts and terrorist activities. The partition was rescinded (Dec., 1911) by King George V.

Bengal famine   Indian disaster (1770) in which a famine destroyed one-third of the population of Bengal. Neither the British overseers nor local authorities moved to alleviate the suffering.

Bengali   Indo-Aryan language spoken by people of west Bengal, India, and Bangladesh.

Bengal System   *See* **Cornwallis Code.**

Ben-Gurion, David (*b.* David Grün, or Gruen) 1886–1973.   Israeli statesman and first prime minister (1948–53; 1955–63), remembered as the "Father of the Nation." Born in what is now Poland, he became involved in the Zionist movement early and at age 20 went to Palestine, joining a Jewish agricultural settlement there (1906). After WWI, he began actively promoting Jewish immigration to Palestine to help establish it as a Jewish homeland, and in 1920 founded the Histadrut, a workers' confederation that became the ruling body among Jews in Palestine. Ben-Gurion was named head of the newly founded Israeli Workers' Party (Mapai, 1930) and in 1935, chairman of the Zionist Executive, which coordinated Zionism worldwide. After WWII, Ben-Gurion advocated guerrilla warfare against the British occupation force in Palestine, a move that helped bring about creation of an independent Israel in 1948. As Israel's first prime minister and defense minister (1948–53), he transformed the Zionist guerrilla forces into an effective army and led them to victory in the First Arab-Israeli War (*q.v.*). His first term also saw admission of Israel to the UN and enactment of the Law of Return (1950), granting automatic citizenship to all immigrant Jews. Retiring in 1953, he returned to office again in 1955, and thereafter established close relations with France. Following a secret meeting with French and British officials concerning the Suez Crisis, he ordered the Israeli invasion of the Sinai (Oct. 1956) that began the Second Arab-Israeli War (*q.v.*). Israeli troops in the Sinai were later withdrawn (1956–57) and replaced by UN peacekeeping forces. Resigning a second time (1963), Ben-Gurion continued to serve in the Israeli Knesset until 1970.

Benhadad *d.* c841 BC.   King of Damascus. He repulsed the Assyrian king Shalmaneser III at Karkar (853 BC), killed King Ahab of Israel in battle and was overthrown and murdered by Hazael.

Benin (Republic of Benin) (*formerly* Dahomey)   Small coastal republic in west-central Africa (est.

pop. 4,840,000). In precolonial times, the region was dominated by warring tribal kingdoms, such as Great Ardra, Little Ardra, and Abomey (later called Dahomey). These wars produced, and later were often fought to produce, slaves that were sold to European slave traders. A part of what was called the Slave Coast (*q.v.*), the region was supplying some 20,000 slaves a year by the end of the 17th cent. and continued to be important in slave trade until the 19th cent. The French were firmly established in the region by 1863 and conquered the kingdom of Dahomey (1892–93). Subsequently the French ruled the territory as a protectorate until 1899, when it was made part of French West Africa (*q.v.*). It was made a French overseas territory (1946), an autonomous member state of the French Community (1958), and an independent state (Aug. 1, 1960). The country was torn by social and economic problems as well as by numerous changes of government. A military coup in 1963 was followed by several short-lived governments (1965, 1967, 1969), by two unsuccessful attempts at elections (1968, 1970), and finally by an 11-man military government (after a coup in 1972). Stability was restored with the installation of Lt. Col. Mathieu Kerekou (ruled 1972–91). He renamed the country the People's Republic of Benin in 1975, after establishing a revolutionary socialist government. The country suffered chronic budget and trade deficits, however, and following the pro-democracy revolutions in Eastern Europe, Benin abandoned the Communist system. Nicephore Soglo was elected president (1991) of the new multi-party democracy. Benin's official name was shortened to Republic of Benin.

Benin, kingdom of   Former West African kingdom located in what is now Nigeria. A powerful kingdom even before the advent of Portuguese exploration of Africa (13th cent.), it began trade with Portugal (late 15th cent.) and remained a power in the region until the 18th cent., when it began its decline. The kingdom fell to British control in the late 19th cent.

Benjamin, Judah Philip 1811–84.   American lawyer and politician. He served in the US Senate (1853–61) and in the Confederate cabinet during the Civil War, notably as secretary of state (1862–65). He fled to Britain after the war and later became a queen's counsel (1872). He is considered the most prominent American Jew of his century.

Bennett, James Gordon 1795–1872. American newspaper publisher and editor. He founded (1835) and edited the *New York Herald,* one of the first "penny newspapers," and introduced innovations that greatly influenced modern journalism.

Bennett, Richard Bedford 1870–1947. Canadian statesman and Conservative party leader. As prime minister (1930–35) during the Great Depression, he presided over the Imperial Conference (1932) at Ottawa, which produced a number of preferential trade agreements within the British Empire. The measures, designed to cope with the depression and the adverse effects of the US Hawley-Smoot Tariff, failed to restore Canada's economy and in 1935 the Liberal party returned to power.

Bennington, Battle of Battle of the American Revolution, at Bennington, Vermont (Aug. 16, 1777). Some 1,600 Americans under J. Stark successfully defended the town's military supplies from a British force of 800, thus further hindering British Gen. J. Burgoyne's campaign in the north.

Bentham, Jeremy 1748–1832. English philosopher, jurist, and economist who was a principal figure in the founding of utilitarianism. A qualified lawyer, he chose not to practice but to pursue a scientific analysis of law, ethics, and economics. Out of this came his utilitarian arithmetic for calculating the greatest happiness for the greatest number of people. His theories, as set forth in works such as *Introduction to the Principles of Morals and Legislation,* influenced 19th-cent. legal and political reforms.

Bentley, Richard 1662–1742. English scholar, one of the greatest of classical scholars. His *Dissertation upon the Epistles of Phalaris* is his best-known work.

Benton, Thomas Hart 1782–1858. American politician. As senator (1821–51) and congressman (1853–55), he opposed slavery but supported westward expansion. His support of hard currency earned him the nickname "Old Bullion." His grandnephew, also named Thomas Hart Benton (1889–1975), was a noted painter.

Bentonville, Battle of Civil War battle (Mar. 19, 1865) at Bentonville, North Carolina. Here a Confederate force of about 24,000 under Gen. J. Johnston was defeated by a Union force under Gen. W. Sherman.

Benz, Carl Friedrich 1844–1929. German engineer credited as the builder of the first automobile powered by an internal combustion engine (demonstrated in 1885 and patented in 1886).

Ben-Zvi, Itzhak 1884–1963. Israeli statesman. A founder of Israel (1948), he served as president (1952–63).

Beowulf English epic poem, author unknown, probably composed in the 8th cent. A literary masterpiece, it is based largely on Scandinavian history and mythology.

Béranger, Pierre Jean de 1780–1857. French poet. His lyrics, favoring republicanism, led twice to his imprisonment, but their popularity earned him wide respect.

Berbers Muslim peoples of North Africa, comprising a large part of the populations of Algeria, Libya, and Morocco.

Berceo, Gonzalo de 1180?–1247? Earliest known Castilian poet, noted for his poems on religious themes.

Berchtold, Leopold, count von 1863–1942. Austro-Hungarian statesman. As foreign minister (1912–15), he sent to Serbia (July, 1914) the ultimatum that precipitated WW I.

Berengar II *d.* 966. Italian king (950–961). His intrigues with Pope John XII against Otto I of Germany led to his imprisonment and death in Bavaria.

Bérengar of Tours c999–1088. French theologian noted for his opposition to the doctrine of real presence of the eucharist.

Beresteczko, Battle of Polish-Cossack battle (summer, 1651) at Beresteczko, the Ukraine. Polish forces under King John II defeated the Cossack army of B. Chmielnicki, thereby crippling the Ukrainian struggle for independence and leading eventually to Russian control of the Ukraine.

Berezina River in Belorus. Crossing the Berezina (Nov. 26–29, 1812) under fire, Napoleon lost 20,000 troops but saved his Grand Army from capture by the Russians.

Berg, Alban 1885–1936. Austrian composer and leading figure in 20th-cent. music. A student of A. Schoenberg, he is noted for his successful fusion of atonal and traditional elements in his music. Among his most important works is the atonal opera *Wozzeck.*

Bergara, Convention of *See* **Convention of Vergara.**

Bergerac, Peace of French treaty (Sept. 17, 1577) ending the Sixth War of Religion between the French Huguenots and Catholics. The Huguenots had been defeated but received favorable terms.

Bergerac, Savinien Cyrano de *See* **Cyrano de Bergerac, Savinien.**

Bergson, Henri 1859–1941. French philosopher. His highly imaginative philosophical works challenged scientific determinism and proved very popular. In *Creative Evolution* (1907), his best-known work, he argues that *élan vital* (the life force), not natural selection, provides the basis for evolution. He was awarded the 1927 Nobel Prize in Literature.

Bering, Vitus Jonassen (Behring, ~) 1681–1741. Danish navigator. In the service of Peter the Great of Russia he explored the Siberian coast north to the Arctic and discovered Alaska for the Russians (1741), though he died during the expedition. Bering Sea and Bering Strait are named in his honor.

Bering Sea Dispute Incident (1886) between the US and Canada over pelagic, or open-sea, sealing in the Bering Sea. The US claimed jurisdiction through the purchase of Alaska from Russia, and seized several Canadian ships. An international tribunal (1893) denied the US claim, but an international agreement (1911) prohibited pelagic sealing in the Bering Sea.

Berkeley, George 1685–1753. Irish philosopher and Anglican bishop. He developed a philosophy of subjective idealism based on the principle of *esse est percipi,* the notion that material things exist only in being perceived by the mind. His thinking influenced other important philosophers, such as D. Hume and I. Kant. Among his important works are *Essay Towards a New Theory of Vision* and *Three Dialogues Between Hylas and Philonous.*

Berkeley, Sir William 1606–77. English-born governor of Virginia (1641–c1651, 1660–76). His unpopular policies led to Bacon's Rebellion.

Berkman, Alexander *See* **Goldman, Emma.**

Berlin Capital of Germany, which from 1945–90 was divided into East Berlin and West Berlin. Berlin was formed by the merger (1307) of two Wendish villages, Berlin and Kolln. It became the capital of the German Empire (1871–1918), the Weimer Republic (1919–32), and Nazi Germany (1933–45). After WW II the city was divided into sectors by British, French, American, and Russian occupation forces. Disagreement with Soviet authorities led to division of the city into two districts, the Russian section becoming (1949) East Berlin, and the western section West Berlin (1950). The Cold War division of the city was starkly demonstrated by the Berlin Wall (*q.v.*), which was built by the East Germans in the 1960s to halt the flow of defectors to the West. The tearing down of the wall in 1989, which heralded the reunification of Germany the following year, was celebrated by millions of Berliners.

Berlin, Congress of *See* **Congress of Berlin.**

Berlin, Irving (*b.* Israel Baline) 1888–1989. American songwriter. Among his best-known songs are *Alexander's Ragtime Band* and *God Bless America.*

Berlin, Treaty of *See* **Congress of Berlin.**

Berlin airlift (and blockade) US and British effort to supply the western sectors of Berlin, Germany (June 1948–Sept. 1949) with food and fuel. The airlift broke a Soviet blockade of the city and represented an important victory for the US early in the Cold War. The result of worsening disputes between Soviet and Western powers over administration of divided Germany, the Soviet blockade began as the Western powers instituted programs for monetary reform and integration of their zones of occupation. The airlift began June 26, 1948, and continued until Sept. 30, 1949, although the blockade had been lifted May 4. The airlift delivered over two million tons of supplies to the beleaguered city.

Berlin Conference (Berlin-West Africa Conference) Meeting (Nov. 15, 1884–Feb. 26, 1885) at Berlin to resolve disputes between colonial powers in the Congo region of Africa. Attended by the European powers and the US, the conference was under the leadership of German chancellor O. Bismarck. Representatives agreed on the following for the Congo region: abolition of slavery, freedom of trade and navigation on waterways, designation of the Congo as a neutral region, and principles for partitioning the Congo. The powers also sanctioned what was to become the Congo Free State. As for larger concerns in Africa, the conference set up policies for the conquest and colonization of the continent, setting in motion the scramble by European powers to set up colonies there. Virtually the entire continent was colonized in subsequent years (only Ethiopia being excepted). *See also* Potsdam Conference.

Berlin Decree Order issued (1806) by Napoleon at Berlin, instituting the commercial blockade of Britain and inaugurating the Continental System. Napoleon issued the decree in response to the British blockade of commercial ports under French control. In it he also ordered the arrest of all Englishmen and confiscation of their property within French domains.

Berlin Pact   *See* **Axis Powers.**

Berlin Wall   Fortified wall once dividing East and West Berlin, constructed (Aug., 1961) by the East German government to stop the defection of East Germans to the West. Continuing depressed economic conditions in East Germany, the hard-line Communist government there, and the economic revival in West Germany encouraged over 2 million defections between 1949 and 1960, mainly through divided Berlin, a phenomenon that drained off much-needed skilled workers and embarrassed the Communist government. The East German government first put up a barricade of barbed wire and cinderblocks on Aug. 12, 1961, eventually replacing it with a formidable system of concrete walls, mine fields, and guard towers that stretched over 100 miles around West Berlin, then an island of Western capitalism surrounded by East Germany. The wall quickly became a well-publicized symbol of the ills of Communism and the "Iron Curtain" mentality of Communist governments, and while it markedly slowed them, it did not stop defections to the West. Between 1961 and 1989, some 10,000 East Germans tried to cross the wall, with about half succeeding and half being captured. The official total of those killed in attempted crossings was put at about 200, though a check of East German records in 1992 revealed over 350 had died. Weakened by continued economic strife and the wave of pro-democracy sentiment sweeping through the Communist world in 1989, the East German government finally bowed to political pressure and opened the wall on Nov. 9. The occasion sparked mass celebrations in Berlin, and hordes of East Germans flocked to West Berlin, as more and more holes were opened to allow free travel between divided Germany. The event, vastly important to Germany, signaled not only the coming of German unification (accomplished with a year), but also the collapse of Communist governments throughout Eastern Europe.

Berlin-West Africa Conference   *See* **Berlin Conference.**

Berlioz, Hector 1803–69.   French composer, considered to be the greatest French Romantic composer. His treatise on orchestration influenced later composers.

Bermuda   British crown colony (pop. 59,000), consisting of some 300 islands in the western Atlantic Ocean. Discovered (1515) by Spanish navigator Juan de Bermúdez (*fl.* 16th cent.), Bermuda was first settled by English colonists (1609). Bermuda was granted self-government in 1968. The assassination of governor Sir Richard Sharples (1973) led to a period of political unrest, culminating in serious riots (1977). The government moved to end racial discrimination and began, but did not continue, talks on independence.

Bermúdez, Juan de   *See* **Bermuda.**

Bernadette, Saint (*b.* Marie Bernarde Soubirolls) 1844–79.   French visionary. As a girl she claimed to have seen (1858) visions of the Virgin Mary in a grotto at Lourdes. She was canonized in 1933.

Bernadotte, Count Folke 1895–1948.   Swedish diplomat and humanitarian. He arranged the release of thousands of concentration camp victims during WW II. He was assassinated while serving as UN mediator in Palestine.

Bernadotte, Jean Baptiste Jules   *See* **Charles XIV John.**

Bernanos, Georges 1888–1948.   French novelist and polemicist. His *Diary of a Country Priest* (1936), one of his best novels, reflects his opposition to modern materialism.

Bernard of Clairvaux, Saint 1090–1153.   French cleric, mystic, and in his day one of the most prominent figures in the Roman Catholic church. A Cistercian monk, he founded the monastery at Clairvaux (1115) and spent the rest of his life as its abbot. Nevertheless, he gained great influence in the church by his eloquence, his widespread reputation as a pious and devoted churchman, and his influence with the popes of the day. He opposed the rationalist philosophy of P. Abelard and promoted the Second Crusade. He was canonized in 1174.

Bernardone, Giovanni Francesco   *See* **Francis of Assisi, Saint.**

Bernini, Giovanni Lorenzo 1598–1680.   Italian sculptor, architect, and painter, and the leading figure in Italian baroque art. His works include statues of *David* and *Apollo and Daphne.*

Bernouilli, Jacob   *See* **Bernoulli, Jacob.**

Bernoulli, Daniel 1700–82.   Swiss mathematician and physicist, the most famous of the second generation of the Bernoulli family of mathematicians. In 1738 he wrote his best-known work *Hydrody-*

namica, dealing with the mechanical properties of fluids. The work included Bernoulli's principle, stating that the pressure of a moving gas decreases as its speed increases. Often called the first mathematical physicist, Bernoulli was awarded numerous prizes for his work on astronomy, probability, oceanography, and other areas of science. He shared the 1735 Paris Academy of Sciences prize with his father who, it is said, banished his son from the house in the belief that the prize should have been his alone.

Bernoulli, Jacob (Bernouilli, ~ or Jacques) 1654–1705. Swiss mathematician whose work helped to develop calculus and the theory of probability. The Bernoulli numbers are named after him.

Bernoulli, Jean (~, Johann) 1667–1748. Swiss mathematician noted for his work in integral and exponential calculus.

Bernstein, Eduard 1850–1932. German socialist. After years in exile from Germany, in 1901 he returned to become a leader of revisionism, a movement that focused on improving the welfare of workers rather than Marxist revolutionary ideology. Revisionists, unlike Marxists, believed the capitalist system would remain viable.

Bernstein, Leonard 1918–90. American composer and conductor. His works include the *Mass,* the opera *Trouble in Tahiti,* and the musical *West Side Story.*

Berry, Charles Ferdinand, duke of 1778–1820. French noble, and son of Charles, count of Artois (later Charles X). His assassination led to a royalist reaction against the liberal movement in France.

Bertha of the Big Foot (Bertrada) *d.* 783. Frankish queen, the wife of Pepin the Short and the mother of Charlemagne. She is celebrated in Carolingian legend.

Berthelot, Pierre Eugène Marcelin 1827–1907. French chemist. His research and numerous writings greatly contributed to the development of modern chemistry, especially organic and thermochemistry.

Berthier, Louis Alexandre 1753–1815. Marshal of France. He served as chief of staff under Napoleon (1805–14). Upon Napoleon's return from exile in Elba, Berthier retired from France. He died, perhaps by suicide, shortly therafter.

Bertrada *See* **Bertha of the Big Foot.**

Berzelius, Jons Jakob (~, Johan Jakob) 1779–1848. Swedish chemist. His accurate table of atomic weights and introduction of modern chemical symbols were major contributions to the development of modern chemistry. He also discovered the elements selenium, thorium, and cesium.

Besant, Annie (*b.* Annie Wood) 1847–1933. English social reformer and theosophist. She advocated Fabian socialism and other movements before adopting Theosophy (1889) and moving to India. There in 1916 she founded the Indian Home Rule League.

Bessarabia Region of in the southwest of the former USSR, largely incorporated into what is now Moldova. It has frequently been a path of invasion between Europe and Asia. Contested by Russia and Rumania in the 20th cent., it became part of the former Soviet Union by the Rumanian peace treaty of 1947.

Bessemer, Sir Henry 1813–98. English inventor of the Bessemer process, the first for the economical production of steel (1856). The son of an engineer, Bessemer invented "gold powder" for paint coloring and an improved artillery shell (during the Crimean War). Seeking a stronger iron for artillery barrels, he developed the steel-making process which bears his name. He established a steel plant at Sheffield in 1859 and continued as an inventor, developing a solar furnace, astronomical telescope, and machinery for diamond polishing. He was knighted in 1879.

Betancourt, Romulo 1908–81. Venezuelan politician. Twice president of Venezuela (1945–48, 1959–64), Betancourt instituted such reforms as universal suffrage, land redistribution, and industrial development, while securing greater revenues from oil companies in Venezuela.

Bethlehem Town on the West Bank of the Jordan River, now in Israeli occupied territory. The birthplace of Jesus, it is one of the principal shrines of Christianity. Here Emperor Constantine erected (AD c330) the Church of the Nativity, where Saint Jerome produced the Vulgate version of the Bible. Bethlehem was part of the British Palestine mandate from 1922 to 1948, when it became part of Jordan. It has been occupied by Israel since the 1967 Arab-Israeli War.

Bethlehem, Synod of *See* **Jerusalem, Synod of.**

Bethlen, Gabriel 1580–1629. Prince of Transylvania (1613–29) and king of Hungary (1620–21). He opposed the Holy Roman Empire in the Thirty Years' War.

Bethlen, Count Stephen 1874–1947? Hungarian statesman. As prime minister (1921–31), he sought revision of the Treaty of Trianon, secured a treaty of friendship with Italy (1927), and guided Hungary's economic recovery from WW I.

Bethmann-Hollweg, Theobald von 1856–1921. German statesman. As chancellor of Germany (1909–17), he did not want war, but his policies contributed to the outbreak of WW I. His attempts to bring about a mediated end to the war led to his forced resignation.

Bethune, Mary McLeod 1875–1955. Black American educator, nationally known for her work in advancing education of blacks. The daughter of former slaves, she turned to teaching and opened (1904) a school for black girls that later became Bethune-Cookman College (Daytona Beach, Florida). The founder of the National Council of Negro Women (1935), she was an adviser to President C. Coolidge and director of the Negro Affairs Division under President F. Roosevelt (1936–45).

Betti, Ugo 1892–1953. Italian dramatist and poet. Betti's dramas are ranked in importance second only to those of Pirandello. His plays include *La Padrona, Frano allo scalo nord,* and *Il diluvio.*

bey In the former Ottoman Empire, a provincial ruler. Originally the title was appointive, but by the 18th cent., it had become hereditary.

Beyazid *See* **Bajazet.**

Beyle, Marie Henri *See* **Stendhal.**

Bhagavad-Gita Sanskrit poem, considered a major exposition of Hindu philosophy as well as a literary treasure. An anonymous work, it is a major episode in the Mahabharata (*q.v.*).

Bhascara (Acarya) 1114–c1185. Hindu astronomer and mathematician, noted as the first to make systematic use of the decimal system in a mathematical work.

Bhil People of western India and Pakistan, numbering about two million and speaking Bhili, an Indo-European language.

Bholan Pass *See* **Bolan Pass.**

Bhumibol Adulyade *See* **Chakkri dynasty.**

Bhutan Himalayan kingdom (pop. 1,566,000) northwest of India. Bhutan was conquered by the Tibetans (16th cent.) and the Chinese (1720). The southern part of Bhutan was annexed by the British (1865), who agreed to an annual subsidy to Bhutan for the annexed territory. A hereditary monarchy was established in Bhutan in 1907. From 1949 Bhutan's foreign affairs have been guided by India, which defended the kingdom from Chinese encroachment following China's

occupation of Tibet (1950). The independent status of Bhutan was augmented by its admittance (1971) to the UN. In the late 1970s and early 1980s, the government resolved an ongoing problem of Tibetan refugees in Bhutan by allowing them to become citizens (or return to Tibet). In 1990–91 violent unrest by ethnic Nepalese broke out in southern Bhutan. King Jigme Singye Wangchuk (*b.* 1955) has been head of state since 1972.

Bhutto, Benazir *See* **Pakistan, 1988–1990.**

Bhutto, Zulfikar Ali 1928–79. Pakistani political leader. His policies helped to cause the secession of East Pakistan and the ensuing war (1971). As president (1971–73) and prime minister (1973–77), he opposed secession and the formation of Bangladesh but was forced to recognize its independence (1974).

Biafra Nigerian secessionist state that existed from 1967 to 1970. Its population was largely of the Ibo tribe, which believed it could not survive within Nigeria. The secession, led by Lt. Col. Chukwuemeka Odumegwu Ojukwu (1933–), led to the Nigerian Civil War and was ended by a combination of Nigerian military advances and economic sanctions. It is believed that more than a million Biafrans died of starvation.

Bible *See* **Old Testament, New Testament, Septuagint.**

Bibliothèque Nationale National library of France and its most important library. The origins of the collection date back to the 14th cent. and the royal library of Charles V. This collection of some 900 volumes was successively added to and since 1537 it has received by law a copy of all books published in France. The collection now contains over 6½ million books and manuscripts.

bicameral system Political system by which the legislative branch of a government is divided into two chambers. Examples include the US Congress, divided into the Senate and the House of Representatives, and the British Parliament, divided into the House of Lords and House of Commons.

Bichat, Marie François Xavier 1771–1802. French anatomist and physiologist. His pioneering human tissue studies contributed to the development of modern histology.

Biddle, John 1615–62. English theologian, the founder of English unitarianism. Biddle, frequently imprisoned for heresy, died in jail.

Bidlack Treaty Treaty (1846) between the US and New Granada (later Colombia), guaranteeing New Granada sovereignty over the Isthmus of Panama and granting the US right-of-way across the isthmus. It became important when the US sought to build the Panama Canal.

Biedermeier Artistic style and period in Germany following the Napoleonic Wars. The style became popular among the middle class in the 1820s and 1830s. It emphasized the comforts of middle-class home and family life. Biedermeier furniture was generally of simple, homey design and was made of inexpensive materials.

Bienville, Jean Baptiste le Moyne, sieur de 1680–1768. French colonial governor and colonizer of Louisiana. From 1701 he was leader of the first colonies in Louisiana and founded New Orleans in 1718.

Bierce, Ambrose Gwinnett 1842–1914? American journalist and author, known best for his sardonic short stories. Among his works are the early *The Fiend's Delight* (1872) and his noted *Devil's Dictionary* (1906). Bierce disappeared on a trip to Mexico (1913).

Bierstadt, Albert *See* **Hudson River school.**

Big Black River, Battle of American Civil War battle (May 17, 1863) at the Black River, Mississippi. Here Confederate Gen. John Pemberton (1814–81) sought unsuccessfully to keep his army from being trapped by Gen. U. S. Grant at Vicksburg.

Big Foot, Bertha of the *See* **Bertha of the Big Foot.**

Big Stick Policy Term given to the aggressive foreign policy of President T. Roosevelt, who advocated massive military and naval power as an instrument of foreign diplomacy. It was derived from the saying "speak softly and carry a big stick."

Bilhapur, Battle of Indian battle (Apr. 1, 1731) in which the Maratha Peshwa Baji Rao I (*d.* 1740) defeated his opponents and killed his rival to become virtual ruler in the Maratha kingdom.

Billaud-Varenne, Jean Nicolas 1756–1819. French revolutionary, a Jacobin. A member of the Committee of Public Safety during the French Revolution, he helped institute the Reign of Terror and, later, to overthrow M. Robespierre.

Billings, Warren *See* **Mooney, Thomas J.**

Billings, William 1746–1800. American composer of hymns, one of the earliest American composers. His books included *The New England Psalm Singer.*

Bill of Rights 1. English bill enacted 1689, one of the key documents of English constitutional law. It established the supremacy of Parliament, ending a long struggle for power with the English kings. The bill largely reiterated the terms of the Declaration of Rights (1688), drawn up at the close of the Glorious Revolution and signed by William III and Mary II as a condition for accession to the throne. The provisions stemmed from abuses of royal power under James II and included required parliamentary consent for suspension of laws, raising taxes, and maintaining an army. They also provided for the right to petition the king without reprisal, the free election and operation of Parliament, and a variety of judicial reforms. Royal succession was also established and Roman Catholics barred from the throne. 2. The first ten amendments to the Constitution of the US (all adopted 1791). Concern for the protection of basic rights of individuals sparked strong opposition to ratification of the Constitution, and amendments guaranteeing such rights were promised to win its ratification. Congress submitted (Sept. 25, 1789) twelve amendments, drafted by J. Madison, to the states for ratification and ten were adopted (Dec. 15, 1791). *See also* Constitution of the United States for individual amendments of the Bill of Rights.

Billy the Kid (Bonney, William H.) 1859–81. American outlaw, one of the leading figures in the frontier lore of the American Southwest. A known killer before he reached 16, Bonney led a cattle rustling gang in New Mexico after 1878. He escaped once after being captured by lawmen, and was shot and killed in Fort Sumner, New Mexico, after being tracked down a second time.

bimetallism Monetary system in which two metals, usually gold and silver, were coined without limit and valued at a fixed ratio. Adopted by many countries in the 18th and 19th cents., the system lost favor and was discarded.

Bindusara *See* **Maurya Empire.**

Binet, Alfred 1857–1911. French psychologist. With Théodore Simon (1873–1961), he devised an intelligence test (1905–11) that, with modifications, is widely used today.

Bingham, Hiram *See* **Machu Picchu.**

Birdseye, Clarence 1886–1956. American inventor. He developed the first effective process for quick-freezing food. The company he founded (1924) later became the General Foods Corporation.

Birgitta, Saint *See* **Bridget of Sweden, Saint.**

Biron, Ernst Johann *See* **Anna Ivanovna.**

Biscoe, John *d.* 1848. British navigator. His voyage (1831–32) to Antarctica helped to support British claims in the area.

Bishop Hill American religious and economic colony, founded (1846) in Henry County, Illinois, by Swedish immigrants. It dissolved in 1860.

Bishops' Wars 1. First ~ (1639). Brief war between the Scots and English king Charles I prior to the English Civil Wars (1642–48). Charles's attempt (1637) to force the English liturgy on the Presbyterian Scots resulted in the Solemn League and Covenant (1638) and the seizure of Edinburgh castle (1639). The war was ended much without actual fighting by the Peace of Berwick (1639), in which Charles made concessions to the Scots. 2. Second ~ (1640). Brief war between the Scots and English king Charles I just prior to the English Civil Wars (1642–48). The Presbyterian Scots reaffirmed the covenant and, amid the crisis caused by the Short Parliament in England, the Scots invaded northern England (1640). Following their victory at Newburn on the Tyne (Aug. 28), they occupied Northumberland and Durham. By the Treaty of Ripon (Oct. 26), Charles agreed to make cash payments to sustain the Scottish army. This, however, necessitated calling the Long Parliament (1640), which in turn led to the civil war.

Bisitun Inscription *See* **Behistun Inscription.**

Bismarck, Otto Eduard Leopold von (Iron Chancellor) 1815–98. Prussian statesman, who brought about German unification and became first chancellor of the German Empire (1871–90). A member of the Prussian Diet (1847–50) and Prussian minister to the Diet of the German Confederation at Frankfurt (1851–59), he was made Prussian premier (1862). Thereafter he put into action plans for the unification (by "blood and iron") of Germany under Prussian domination. He precipitated the Austro-Prussian War (1866) and with Austria defeated, created the North German Confederation (1866). To further unification, he provoked (by publication of the Ems Dispatch) the Franco-Prussian War (1870–71) and was named (1871) chancellor of the new German empire under King William I. He subsequently involved Germany in an intricate web of alliances (Three Emperors' League, Dual Alliance, Triple Alliance, Triple Entente) by which he became the leading European statesman. As chancellor, he strove to protect the power of Prussia's agrarian elite while instituting many internal administrative reforms and, in an effort to combat the Socialists, set up the first comprehensive social security plan. He was forced to resign (1890) after the accession of William II.

Bithynia Ancient country located in what is now northwestern Turkey. The territory was originally occupied by Thracian tribes and from the 6th cent. BC it was nominally controlled by Persians and then by Macedonians. An independent kingdom after 297 BC, it flourished briefly with its capital at Nicomedia. Following its decline it became a province of Rome (74 BC).

Bizet, Alexandre César Léopold *See* **Bizet, Georges.**

Bizet, Georges 1838–75. (*b.* Alexandre César Léopold ~) French composer. He is known best for his opera *Carmen* (1875), based on a story by Prosper Mérimée (1803–70).

Bjorko, Treaty of German-Russian agreement. Signed (July 24, 1905) by Kaiser William II and Tsar Nicholas II, it called for mutual military support in Europe should either country be attacked. It was never implemented.

Björnson, Björnstjerne 1832–1910. Norwegian playwright, novelist, and political leader. A major figure in 19th-cent. Norwegian literature, he was awarded the Nobel Prize in Literature (1903).

Björnsson, Sveinn 1881–1952. Icelandic statesman. He was regent of Iceland (1941–44) during the German occupation of Denmark, and became the first president of the Republic of Iceland (1944–52) upon Iceland's independence from Denmark.

Black, Hugo La Fayette 1886–1971. US senator (1927–37) from Alabama and associate justice of the Supreme Court (1937–71). Born in Alabama, Black became a lawyer before serving in the Senate, where he steadfastly supported President F. Roosevelt's New Deal legislation. Appointed to the Supreme Court by Roosevelt, Black joined the Court in reversing previous judicial opinions against New Deal legislation, and later became known as a civil liberties activist, especially in regard to attempts by states to limit individual rights, such as free speech and due process. Black was a leading member of the Court's liberal majority during the 1960s, which struck down school prayer and guaranteed free legal counsel to criminal suspects.

Black and Tans Name applied to members of the British auxiliary police force sent to Ireland (1920) to make reprisals against Irish revolutionaries. Their brutality raised the anger of the Irish and the indignation of the British, and contributed to establishment of the Irish Free State (1921). They derived their name from the colors of their uniforms.

Blackbeard (Edward Teach) (Edward Thatch) *d.* 1718. English pirate. He is believed to have been an English privateer during the War of Spanish Succession (1701–14) and to have subsequently turned to piracy. Commanding five ships and 400 men, he conducted raids from the West Indies to the Virginia coast (1716–18). Blackbeard bought protection for his base in North Carolina by paying the governor a share of his booty, but Virginia governor Alexander Spotswood (1676–1740) sent a British naval detachment against him. Blackbeard was finally killed while trying to elude capture.

Black Code (*Code Noir*) French edict, issued (1685) by King Louis XIV to govern the treatment of slaves and freed blacks in the French holdings in the West Indies.

Black Codes Generally, local laws in the US that from the 17th to 19th cents. regulated the conduct and punishment of Negro slaves; and specifically, laws passed by Southern states immediately after the Civil War to regulate freed blacks. The post–Civil War laws varied, though in general they aimed at maintaining the sharp divisions between blacks and whites. Blacks were permitted to marry and own personal property but land-ownership restrictions, oppressive work laws, mandatory segregation of public facilities, and other provisions effectively blocked their emancipation. In the North the laws were regarded as disguised slavery and helped bring on the programs of Radical Republicans and the Reconstruction era.

Black Death *See* **Black Plague.**

Black Earl *See* **Butler, Thomas, 10th earl of Ormonde.**

Black Flag Army Chinese army that fought against the Manchus in the Taiping Rebellion (1850–64). At the close of the rebellion, the army fled into Indochina, where it later fought the French in the undeclared Sino-French War (1883–85).

Blackfoot Indians American Indian tribes of the Algonquin family, who flourished in the Great Plains region of the US and Canada in the 18th and 19th cents. For a time successful against the encroachments of white civilization, the tribes were eventually forced to sign treaties with the US government. Reduction of the buffalo herds brought mass starvation and near destruction of the Blackfoot tribe in the later 19th cent.

Black Friday US financial panic (Sept. 24, 1869), caused by speculators J. Gould and J. Fisk, who were attempting to corner the gold market. On discovering the scheme, President U. S. Grant flooded the market with government gold to break the corner. This remedy, however, precipitated a panic on the securities market and left thousands ruined. Another day of financial panic (Sept. 18, 1873) is also called Black Friday.

Black Hand Secret criminal society. Organized in Sicily, it flourished there in the late 19th cent. and spread to the US, where it became prominent for a time in the early 20th cent. The society in Sicily was ruthlessly suppressed under B. Mussolini.

Black Hawk War Brief war (1832) between the US and a band of Sac and Fox Indians led by Black Hawk (1767–1838). The conflict arose over the forced cession of Sac and Fox lands in Illinois to the US, called for by a disputed 1804 treaty. Black Hawk refused to leave the lands until forced to move west of the Mississippi in 1831. In 1832 he led a band of 1,000 starving warriors, women, and children back to Illinois and was met by a combined force of militia and US regulars. Pursued into Wisconsin, he was defeated in the Battle of Bad Axe River and all but 150 of his band were massacred.

Black Hole of Calcutta Prison cell for petty thieves in Calcutta, India, that became the scene of a notorious incident. According to a report by an official of the British East India Company, the company's garrison in Calcutta was attacked and taken by native rebels (June 20, 1756). The survivors, supposed to have numbered 146, were locked overnight in the 15 × 18-foot cell. Of them, only 23 were reported to have survived.

The number of men locked in the cell is now believed greatly exaggerated.

Black Hundreds (League of the Russian People) Russian political group which flourished in the early 1900s. Composed of clergy, police, bureaucrats, and the rich, it opposed the growing Russian revolutionary movement, and conducted pogroms against the Jews.

Black Monday US stock market crash of 1987. In a day of frenzied selling (Oct. 19), the Dow Jones industrial average plunged 508.32 points in a single day, by far the largest drop in Wall Street history. The crash marked the end of the bull market which had begun in Aug., 1982, and was at least partly due to the recently installed computerized "program trading" system. The Dow recovered about 300 points the following day, but then turned downward once again. The US government instituted emergency financial measures to help Wall Street brokerages weather the crisis. World financial markets meanwhile followed similar patterns, falling and then rebounding somewhat.

Blackmore, Richard Doddridge 1825–1900. English novelist. His best-known novel is *Lorna Doone,* now a classic.

Black Muslims (Nation of Islam) American racial-religious movement, founded (1930) by Wallace D. Fard (c1877–1934?) to apply the teachings of Islam to black American life. The movement gained many followers through the teachings of Malcolm X.

Black nationalism American black political and social movement, which seeks to encourage a separate national identity among blacks in the US. It stresses the common African heritage and the experiences of American blacks. Rooted in the 19th cent., the movement came to play an important role in the 1960s and 1970s.

Black Panthers American black political movement, founded (1966) by Huey Newton (1941?–89) and Bobby Seale (1936–   ). The movement advocated revolution to achieve equality for blacks. Black Panthers were frequently involved in incidents of violence during the 1960s.

Black Plague (Bubonic Plague) (Black Death) Epidemic disease that ravaged Europe and Asia in the mid-14th cent., so called because it turns the skin of its victims black. It is caused by bacteria infesting rats or other rodents and transmitted to humans by fleas. Epidemics of the plague

occurred in Rome (AD 250–65) and Constantinople (542), killing huge numbers, but the 14th-cent. outbreak was the worst incidence of Black Plague and the deadliest known epidemic of all time. First reports of the plague (in China and India) apparently reached Europe by way of returning sailors in 1346. Then in 1347, an army of the Golden Horde deliberately infected a Genoese trading post in the Crimea during a siege (by catapulting bodies of plague victims into the outpost). The plague then spread quickly that year to Sicily and North Africa, then to southern Italy and the rest of Europe (by 1347–48), including England. The disease cut across all social strata, infecting and killing peasants, noblemen, the learned, and the pious with equal rapidity. By the time it had largely run its course in 1351 (smaller outbreaks continued for years afterward), the Black Plague had killed an estimated one-quarter to one-third of the population in Europe (Eastern Europe was hit less hard). Asian populations were similarly decimated. While many of the social, economic, and cultural changes that appeared after the plague had been under way well beforehand, the devastation undoubtedly accelerated them. Acute shortages of labor caused by the plague, for example, helped emancipate farmers from the bonds of serfdom and led to the first peasant revolts (Jacquerie; Peasants' Revolt). Divisions between classes became less rigid for a time, and a new, moneyed class of enterprising merchants began to replace the old nobility. The psychological impact of such widespread death from (then) unexplained causes was reflected in the morbid overtones appearing in literature and art of the period, in a questioning of fundamental religious values, and in a shift by some to more worldly pursuits. Later Black Plague epidemics struck London (1665), Naples (1672), and the Holy Roman Empire (1711). The last major outbreak of black plague occurred in 1910–13 in India and China, killing millions.

Black Power Slogan that gained prominence in the US during the movement for black equality in the 1960s. It implies a sense of racial pride and an often militant desire to overcome economic and racial barriers through unified black effort.

Blackshirts *See* **SS.**

Blackstone, Sir William 1723–80. English jurist. He is known best for his *Commentaries on the Laws of*

England, which had a major influence on the teaching and practice of law in England and the US.

Black Thursday Name given to Thursday, Oct. 24, 1929, when nearly 13 million shares of stock were sold in a panic on the New York Stock Exchange. It marked the beginning of the prolonged stock market crash (the Crash of 1929) that inaugurated the Great Depression (*q.v.*). The prolonged economic boom of the 1920s had fed a speculative boom on the stock market, with many individuals buying stocks on margin (paying only a small down payment on the share price). The downward plunge begun on Black Thursday suddenly resumed the following Tuesday (Oct. 29) when 16 million shares changed hands, and continued on into Nov. By Nov. 13 some $30 billion in paper value of stocks had disappeared, many individuals and businesses had been wiped out, and the stock market still had not hit bottom. By 1932 an estimated $75 billion in market value had been lost since the 1929 crash began.

Black War Sporadic outbreaks of violence (1804–30) between Europeans and natives of Van Diemen's Land (Tasmania). Clashes between aborigines and European soldiers and convict settlers (sentenced to this British penal colony) began soon after the arrival of the Europeans in 1804. Competition for food and land, atrocities committed by the Europeans, and retaliatory attacks by the natives continued until 1830, by which time the native population had been nearly eliminated. The remaining 200 natives were finally resettled (1835) on Flinders Island.

Black Watch (Royal Highlanders) Distinguished regiment of Scottish infantrymen named for their dark tartan colors. The unit was first organized (1725) to maintain order in the Scottish Highlands. It was formally designated a regiment c1739 and is now the 42d Regiment.

Blackwell, Elizabeth 1821–1910. American physician. She was the first woman to receive a medical degree in the US (1849).

Blaine, James Gillespie 1830–93. American politician. Blaine was an unsuccessful Republican candidate for president in 1884, and was twice secretary of state (1880–81, 1889–92).

Blair, Eric Arthur *See* Orwell, George.

Blair, Francis Preston 1791–1876. American journalist and politician. He was once an influential Democrat and member of President A. Jackson's Kitchen Cabinet. His anti-slavery

beliefs led him to help found the Republican party. He supported A. Lincoln's candidacy (1860) and later, with his approval, arranged the Hampton Roads Conference (1865)

Blake, Robert 1599–1657. English admiral. Considered one of the greatest English admirals, he won naval engagements against the Royalists (1649–51), the Dutch (1652–53), the Barbary pirates (1655), and Spain (1656–57).

Blake, William 1757–1827. Major English poet and artist, and a leading influence in the Romantic movement. Blake, a visionary, created a highly individual style and was largely unrecognized in his time. Born to a prosperous family, he first became an engraver's apprentice (1771). He continued as an engraver, painted, and illustrated books such as Dante's *Divine Comedy.* At the same time he wrote books of poetry, such as *Songs of Innocence* and *Songs of Experience,* and prophetical books such as the *The Marriage of Heaven and Hell.*

Blanc, Louis 1811–82. French Socialist and journalist. He advocated, in *Organisation du Travail,* the establishment of workshops managed by the workers. He was a member of the provisional government set up (1848) after the February Revolution (*q.v.*).

Blanchard, Jean Pierre (˜, François) 1753–1809. French balloonist. After making his first ascent in Paris (1784), he became the first to fly a balloon in England (also 1784) and the US (1793, at Philadelphia). With Dr. John Jeffries (1744–1819), he made the first aerial crossing of the English Channel (Dover to Calais, carrying the first international air mail) on Jan. 7, 1785. He also made successful descents from his balloon with experimental parachutes, before being killed in a ballooning accident.

Blanche of Castile 1187?–1252. Wife of Louis VIII (*m.* 1200) and queen of France during his reign (1223–26). She served twice (1226–36, 1248–52) as regent for her son, Louis IX.

Blanco Fombona, Rufino 1874–1944. Venezuelan poet and essayist who was a leader of the literary movement known as Modernismo.

Bland-Allison Act Act of US Congress (1878) reestablishing the silver dollar as legal tender and providing for minimum government purchases of silver to support market prices. The act was part of the larger free-silver movement sparked by the discontinuation of the silver dollar (known as the Crime of '73). The bill originally proposed by Missouri Rep. Richard P. Bland (1835–99) provided for unlimited silver coinage but was amended to allow for only $2–4 million in monthly silver bullion purchases. The act was superseded by the Sherman Silver Purchase Act (1890).

Blanqui, Louis Auguste 1805–81. French revolutionary. Blanqui figured in the major political upheavals of his day and spent much of his adult life in prison.

Blavatsky, Helena Petrovna 1831–91. Russian Theosophist. She helped to found the Theosophical Society (1875) and expounded Theosophy in such works as *Isis Unveiled* and *The Secret Doctrine.*

Bleeding Kansas Name applied to the US territory of Kansas during the local war (1854–59) between pro-slavery and anti-slavery factions there prior to its admission as a state. The Kansas-Nebraska Act (1854) left to the voters the question of extending slavery into Kansas (Popular Sovereignty). Soon after its passage, Free-Soilers (anti-slavery "Jayhawkers") and pro-slavery men ("Border Ruffians") from Missouri streamed into the state. Violence between the two sides was narrowly averted in the Wakarusa War (Dec. 1855), caused by the murder of an anti-slavery man. However, there followed the sack (May 21, 1856) of Lawrence, Kansas, by pro-slavery men, the Pottawatomie Massacre, and numerous other bloody skirmishes. The violence continued until the Wyandotte Constitution was adopted (1859). Kansas was admitted as a free state (1861).

Blenheim, Battle of Major Anglo-Austrian victory (Aug. 13, 1704) in the War of the Spanish Succession (1701–14). A combined Anglo-Austrian force of 52,000 (under J. Churchill, duke of Marlborough, and Eugene of Savoy) surprised and defeated some 60,000 French and Bavarian troops (under French marshal comte Camille de Tallard, 1652–1728) at the Bavarian village of Blenheim. Anglo-Austrian casualties numbered 12,000. Franco-Bavarian losses were some 15,000 casualties and 13,000 captured. The battle eliminated Bavaria from the war and marked the beginning of France's decline as a military power in Europe.

Blest Gana, Alberto 1830–1920. Chilean novelist. A leading Spanish-American author of the 19th cent., he wrote realistic novels of life in Chile. *Martin Rivas* and *During the Reconquest* are among his works.

Bligh, William 1754–1817. English admiral, remembered as the captain of HMS *Bounty* (*q.v.*) during its famous mutiny of 1789. Bligh and other crewmen set adrift by the mutineers survived a 4,000-mile sea journey, landing in the East Indies in June, 1789. Bligh suffered another mutiny (1797) and later, as governor of New South Wales, his "oppressive behavior" again resulted in a mutiny (1808). Bligh continued to receive promotions, however, eventually attaining the rank of vice admiral.

Bliss, Sir Arthur Edward Drummond 1891–1975. English composer, noted early in his career for his innovative compositions. He became Master of the Queen's Music in 1953.

Bloc National French conservative coalition, which dominated politics in France from 1919–24. It stressed fiscal conservatism and strict German compliance with the Treaty of Versailles.

Blitzkrieg German term, meaning "lightning war," used to describe the German battle tactic in WW II of using massive numbers of airplanes and mechanized forces in sudden assaults on opposing forces.

Bloch, Ernest 1885–1959. Swiss-American composer. His music is based on both classical and Hebraic traditions.

Blois, Charles of *See* **Charles of Blois.**

Blois, Treaties of Several treaties signed at Blois, France, including 1. First ~ (1504), by which Holy Roman Emperor Maximilian I recognized the rule of French king Louis XII in Naples. 2. Second ~ (1505), by which French king Louis XII renounced his claim to Naples, thereby surrendering control to Ferdinand II of Aragon.

Blok, Aleksandr Aleksandrovich 1880–1921. Russian poet, a leader of the Russian Symbolist movement.

Bloodless Revolution *See* **Glorious Revolution.**

Blood Purge ("Night of the Long Knives") Name given the murder (June 30, 1934) of 74 Nazi leaders by order of A. Hitler. Hitler later declared the purge was in response to an alleged plot, but it was actually conducted to eliminate radical elements from the Nazi party, notably Ernst Röhm (1887–1934), leader of the Storm Troopers.

Blood River, Battle of Boer victory (Dec. 16, 1838) in Natal, South Africa, over the Zulu tribe. About 500 Boers under A. Pretorius repulsed an attack of some 10,000 Zulu, killing about 3,000 Zulu warriors. The battle broke

Zulu dominance in the area and secured the Boer position in Natal.

Bloody Assizes Trials conducted in western England after an unsuccessful rebellion (1685) by the duke of Monmouth against King James II. Presided over by Baron G. Jeffreys and four other judges, the trials of Monmouth's followers resulted in over 300 hangings, some 800 deportations to Barbados, and the flogging and imprisonment of many others.

Bloody Mary *See* **Mary I.**

Bloody Omaha *See* **Omaha Beach.**

Bloody shirt American political phrase. Drawn from the saying "waving a bloody shirt," it refers to the post–Civil War techniques used by radical Republicans of stirring up wartime memories and emotions for political gain.

Bloody Sunday Russian massacre (Jan. 22, 1905). Thousands of Russians, marching in St. Petersburg to present a petition of grievances to Tsar Nicholas II, were fired on by tsarist forces. The massacre left more than a hundred dead and several hundred wounded, and led to the Russian Revolution of 1905.

Bloody Week Bloody fighting (May 21–28, 1871) in Paris, France, that marked the downfall of the Commune of Paris (*q.v.*). Parisian rebels had established the Paris Commune (Mar., 1871) by force and taken over the city. On May 21 government forces began a week-long battle to retake Paris and killed about 20,000 Parisian rebels.

Bloomfield, Leonard 1887–1949. American linguist. A specialist in Germanic languages, he was among the first to apply scientific principles to the study of languages.

Bloomsbury group A group of English intellectuals that met for discussions in the Bloomsbury section of London in the early 20th cent. Its members included E. M. Forster, J. Keynes, and V. Woolf.

Blount, William 1749–1800. American political leader. Governor of the territory that became Tennessee (1709–96), he became a senator (1796–97) from Tennessee, but was expelled when it was discovered he had plotted to help the British take over Spain's Florida territory.

Blücher, Gebhard Leberecht von 1742–1819. Prussian field marshal. He played an important role in the defeat of Napoleon at Waterloo (1815).

Blue Laws A term usually applied to laws in the US regulating business and recreational activities on the Sabbath. The term was first used (1781) to describe such laws of the Puritan colony at New Haven, which were printed on blue paper.

Blues and Greens Two Byzantine political factions, important during the 6th cent. They represented divergent popular views on various matters, as in the case of religious doctrine, in which the Blues supported Monophysitism and the Greens supported Christian orthodoxy. Both factions had widespread popular support, though the Blues also claimed the backing of the upper class. Blues and Greens joined forces in the bloody Nika Revolt (532) and in the overthrow of Emperor Maurice (602). By the 9th cent., however, their power was all but broken. The two factions derived their names from racing colors worn by charioteers at Constantinople's Hippodrome.

Blum, Léon 1872–1950. French Socialist and premier. As head of a leftist coalition known as the Popular Front government (1936–37), he instituted many Socialist reforms.

Boabdil (Abu-Abdallah) *d.* 1538. Last Moorish king of Granada (1482–92). His surrender to Castilian forces in 1492 marked the end of Moorish dominion in Spain.

Boadicea (Boudicca) *d.* AD 60. Queen of the Iceni, in what is now Norfolk and Suffolk, England. She led an unsuccessful but bloody rebellion against Roman rule (60).

Boanerges Biblical name given by Jesus to the disciples James and John, and meaning "sons of thunder."

Boas, Franz 1858–1942. German-American anthropologist, considered a leading figure in anthropology in this century. He began his studies of native North American Indians in 1886 and became the first professor of anthropology at Columbia in 1899, a post he held until 1936. Among his works are *The Mind of Primitive Man* (1911) and *Race, Language and Culture* (1940). M. Mead and R. Benedict were students of his.

Boccaccio, Giovanni 1313–75. Italian poet and writer. From 1341 until his death he lived mainly in Florence, and it was there he wrote his best-known work, the *Decameron* (1351–53), a series of folk tales and anecdotes that influenced later literature in Europe.

Bocskay, István 1557?–1606. Hungarian nobleman. He led a rebellion, with Turkish support, in Hungary (1604–06) against the oppressive rule of Holy Roman Emperor Rudolf II. He succeeded in winning treaties that guaranteed constitutional and religious rights for Hungary.

Bodel, Jean c1165–1210. French trouvre (medieval poet). His *The Play of St. Nicholas* (c1200) is believed to be the first miracle play written in French.

Bodin, Jean 1530–96. French political philosopher. His major work, *Les Six livres de la république*, advocated limited monarchy as the ideal form of government and influenced the 17th-cent. philosopher T. Hobbes.

Bodoni, Giambattista 1740–1813. Italian printer. He designed the Bodoni typeface, which is still used today.

Boehme, Jakob (Böhme, ˜) 1575–1624. German theosophist and mystic. His book *Aurora,* condemned as heretical, attempted to explain God and the world in terms of opposing elements, i.e., good and evil. His writings anticipated those of such later philosophers as G. Hegel and B. Spinoza.

Boeotia Ancient region of Greece. It became prominent with the creation of the Boeotian League (c550 BC), which under the domination of Thebes engaged in a power struggle with Athens. The decline of Boeotia's power within the Greek community began with the league's defeat by Philip of Macedon (338 BC). Boeotia was the birthplace of the poets Hesiod and Pindar.

Boeotian League In ancient Greece, a confederacy of city-states of Boeotia. Founded c550 BC, it was dominated by Thebes and ruled by a form of federal government. The league opposed Sparta in the Corinthian War (395–387 BC), was dissolved and later reformed to aid Athens in its defeat of Sparta (379 BC), and suffered in the Third Sacred War (355–346 BC). Defeated with Athens by the Macedonians (338 BC), it was dissolved (335 BC) by Alexander the Great after an unsuccessful revolt.

Boer Name applied to early settlers of South Africa, especially those of Dutch or Huguenot descent. Their descendants are now usually called Afrikaners. The first Boers were settled near the Cape of Good Hope (1652) by the Dutch East India Company. After British annexation of the region (1815), the Boers resisted British authority, abandoned the colony, and set out on what is known as the Great Trek. They fought the British in the Boer War (1899–

1902), but their territories were finally absorbed into the Union of South Africa.

Boer War (South African War) War (1899–1902) between the Boers of the Orange Free State and the South African Republic (Transvaal), and Great Britain. Tensions between the Boers and the British, caused by conflicts of territorial claims in South Africa, were further aggravated by discovery (1886) of gold in the Transvaal and subsequent influx of prospectors and settlers, mainly British subjects. In order to protect their holdings, the Boers passed laws unfavorable to foreigners. The Jameson Raid (*q.v.*) of 1895 led P. Kruger, president of the South African Republic, to conclude a military alliance (Mar. 17, 1896) with the Orange Free State. The situation continued to deteriorate, and the Boers declared war (Oct. 12, 1899). The Boers claimed early victories but in 1900 heavy British reinforcements, under command of Lord H. Kitchener, began to turn the tide. Kruger fled (1900) to Europe to secure intervention on the Boers' behalf, but was unsuccessful. Great Britain annexed the Transvaal (Sept., 1900), but a vicious guerrilla war continued until 1902. The war was ended by the Treaty of Vereeniging (May 31, 1902), by which the Boers yielded to British sovereignty in return for promises of representative government in the future and indemnities for war damages.

Boesky, Ivan 1936– . US stock speculator convicted (1987), fined $100 million, and imprisoned (1988) for insider stock trading. The scandal rocked the Wall Street financial industry, because Boesky and others involved were so high up in US financial circles. Boesky's arrest was just one of a dozen or so on charges of insider trading. Among those also convicted in the scandal was "junk-bond king" Michael Milken, who was fined $600 million and sentenced (1990) to ten years in prison; he was released in 1993.

Boethius, Anicius Manlius Severinus (Boetius) AD c475–c525. Roman philosopher and statesman. His translations of Aristotle kept the study of Greek philosophy alive into the Middle Ages. He wrote *The Consolation of Philosophy* (c524).

Boetius *See* **Boethius, Anicius Manlius Severinus.**

Boganda, Barthelemy 1910–59. African statesman. A major African nationalist leader. Boganda became the first premier of the Central African Republic (1958–59).

Bogomils Slavic religious cult. The Bogomils, extreme ascetics, arose in Bulgaria in the 9th cent. and flourished in the Balkan region until the 15th cent.

Bohemia Historic kingdom, now part of Czechoslovakia. Part of the Moravian Empire, Bohemia came under the rule of the Premysl dynasty (9th cent.) and then became part of the Holy Roman Empire (10th cent.). With the succession (1355) of Holy Roman Emperor Charles IV, Bohemia reached its greatest period. Under Habsburg rule (1526–1918) it gradually lost its independence. After WW I, Bohemia was incorporated into the western part of the new country of Czechoslovakia (*q.v.*).

Bohemond I c1056–1111. Norman nobleman, a son of Robert Guiscard. A leader in the First Crusade, he declared himself prince of Antioch after aiding in its capture (1098).

Böhme, Jakob *See* **Boehme, Jakob.**

Bohr, Niels Henrik David 1885–1962. Danish physicist who made major contributions to the understanding of atomic structure and who pioneered in the development of quantum physics. The son of a physiology professor, Bohr was awarded a gold medal from the Danish Scientific Society at age 22 for determining the surface tension of water. After earning his doctorate in physics at Copenhagen, he began work on atomic structure, first at the University of Cambridge and then at the University of Manchester. By 1911 he had discovered the nucleus of the atom and in 1913 developed the theory of an envelope of electrons orbiting around the nucleus. He also explained the atom's absorption and emission of energy. Bohr became director of Copenhagen's new Institute of Theoretical Physics, which he helped found. When the Germans occupied Denmark in 1940, Bohr joined the resistance, finally escaping arrest (1943) by fleeing the country with his family. In 1944 he worked on the US atomic bomb project at Los Alamos, New Mexico. For almost 50 years Bohr was a leading contributor in the field of quantum physics. He won the Nobel Prize for Physics (1922).

Bohun, Henry de, 1st earl of Hereford 1176–1220. English nobleman. He was among the group of barons who forced King John of England to sign the Magna Carta (1215).

Bohun, Humphrey V de, 2d earl of Hereford and 1st earl of Essex *d.* 1274. English nobleman, son of Henry de Bohun. He joined with the barons in the writing of the Provisions of Oxford (1258) but sided with King Henry III during the Barons' War (1263–67).

Bohun, Humphrey VII de, 3d earl of Hereford and 2d earl of Essex *d.* 1298. English nobleman grandson of Humphrey V. He led the barons who forced King Edward I to reaffirm (1297) the Magna Carta and to agree to limitations on his powers of taxation (1297).

Bohun, Humphrey VIII de, 4th earl of Hereford and 3d earl of Essex 1276–1322. English nobleman, son of Humphrey VII de Bohun. He was one of the 21 barons who forced King Edward II to accept limitations on his powers (1311). He also joined the barons in the execution (1312) of the king's favorite, P. Gaveston.

Bok, Edward 1863–1930. US journalist, editor of *Ladies' Home Journal.* He founded the *Brooklyn Magazine* (1883), which later became *Cosmopolitan* and became editor of *Ladies' Home Journal* in 1889. His innovations helped make the *Journal* the world's largest selling magazine.

Bolan Pass (Bholan Pass) A mountain pass in western Pakistan linking Asia and India. It has long been used as both a trading and invasion route to the Indian subcontinent.

Boleslaus I c966–1025. Polish ruler (992–1025), the first to designate himself Poland's king. He organized Poland's army and internal administration, expanded the kingdom, and waged war with Holy Roman Emperor Henry II.

Boleslaus III 1086–1138. Duke of Poland (1102–38). He fought Holy Roman Emperors Henry V and Lothair II, enlarged his domain, and recaptured part of Pomerania.

Boleslav *See* **Boleslaus.**

Boleslaw *See* **Boleslaus.**

Boleyn, Anne (Anne) (Bullen, Anne) 1507–36. English queen (1533–36), second wife of Henry VIII (*m.* 1533) and mother of Elizabeth I. Her marriage caused England's break with the Roman Catholic church and led to the creation of the Church of England (1534). The daughter of statesman Sir Thomas Boleyn (1477–1539), Anne spent part of her childhood in France before returning to live at the court of King Henry VIII. The king fell in love with her and, anxious for a male heir to the throne, began efforts in 1527 to obtain an annulment from his first wife, Catherine of Aragon. When Pope Clement VII continued refusing his request for six years, Henry finally married Anne secretly in

Jan. of 1533, publicly revealing the union that Easter. On May 23, Henry instructed the archbishop of Canterbury, T. Cranmer, to annul his marriage to Catherine. Ironically, in Sept. Anne gave birth to a girl, none other than the future Queen Elizabeth I. Henry soon began taking up with other women and following a miscarriage and subsequent stillborn birth of a son, Anne was committed to the Tower of London (May 2, 1536). Tried and convicted on the dubious charges of adultery and incest, she was beheaded on May 19.

Bolingbroke, Henry St. John, 1st viscount 1678–1751. British statesman, an influential Tory during the reign of Queen Anne. He was secretary for war (1704–08) during the War of Spanish Succession and later arranged the ouster (1714) of R. Harley as leader of the Tory ministry. He fled Britain on the accession of George I (1714). Returning some years later, he turned to writing and became an associate of A. Pope and J. Swift.

Bolívar, Simón 1783–1830. Venezuelan revolutionary and hero in the South American movement for independence from Spain. The son of wealthy parents, he took an early part in the Venezuelan revolution (1810). Following Spanish victories (1812), he led a military force that briefly recaptured Venezuela (1813). Final success came in the following years. He liberated New Granada (1819) in the Battle of Boyacá, then Venezuela (1821), Ecuador (1822), Peru (1824), and Upper Peru (later Bolívia, so named after him) (1825). In 1819 he was proclaimed president of Great Colombia (eventually including Colombia, Ecuador, and Venezuela). Though his plans for a united South America gave rise to Pan-Americanism, Bolívar was unable to hold Great Colombia together. His assumption of dictatorial powers (1828) failed to prevent secession of Venezuela and Ecuador and in 1830 he resigned.

Bolivia (Republic of Bolivia) Bolivia is an independent state located in west central South America. The population is 6,730,000 and the capital is Sucre. Bolivia was ruled by Indians and Incas until the Spanish conquests in the 1530s. Colonial rule was ended in the 1820s through the efforts of Simón Bolívar, for whom the country is named. Political unrest, rebellions, and coups have plagued Bolivia from the time of its independence. Key dates in the history of Bolivia include:

13TH CENT. Incas conquered region from native Indians.

1538 Incan Empire conquered by H. Pizarro; Bolivia became part of the viceroyalty of Peru.

1545 Silver discovered; native Indians forced to work in mines as colonial settlers rushed to exploit the region.

1776 Region annexed to the new viceroyalty of La Plata.

1809 Uprising in Chuquisaca marked beginning of revolt against Spanish colonial rule.

1824 S. Bolívar and A. de Sucre led successful military campaign against Spanish royalists in Peru and Bolivia; Battle of Ayacucho (near Lima, Dec. 9) ended royalist resistance.

1825 Bolivia declared independence from Spain (Aug. 6).

1826 Constitution drafted by S. Bolívar adopted; Sucre became first president.

1836 Andrés Santa Cruz formed union between Peru and Bolivia; Santa Cruz became leader of new federal republic.

1839 Chile, opposed to the federation, defeated Santa Cruz at the Battle of Yungay (Jan.) and thus ended the federation.

1866–74 Treaties established 24th parallel as Chilean-Bolivian border.

1879–84 War of the Pacific with Chile; Bolivia lost all coastal territories.

1880 New constitution adopted, failed to halt political turmoil.

1890s Future "tin baron" Simón Patiño started exploiting his first mine; with help from foreign investors, he became a leading exploiter of Bolivian tin.

1899 Brazil seized rubber-rich Acre region (in eastern Bolivia) after revolt by Brazilian settlers there.

1903 Brazil received 70,000 sq. mi. of Acre region by the Treaty of Petropolis.

1904 Treaty with Chile granted Bolivia free access to the sea.

1920s Boom in Bolivian tin mining began to play out.

1932–35 Chaco War, undeclared border war with Paraguay over Chaco region.

1934–37 Col. David Toro in power after a series of coups; he seized Standard Oil holdings and mining company profits.

1940 Gen. Enrique Peñaranda elected president under new constitution (adopted 1938);

elections followed short-lived attempt to establish totalitarian state (1939).

1943 Peñaranda joined Allies in WW II; ordered conscription of laborers to work in mines to produce strategic raw materials.

1943 National Revolutionary Movement (MNR) seized power after widespread strikes by workers protesting oppressive working conditions.

1944–46 MNR leader Gualberto Villarroel in office as president; established totalitarian state.

1946–51 Conservative elements seized power; put down MNR-backed rebellions and attempted to prevent duly elected MNR candidate from taking office in 1951.

1952–64 V. Paz Estenssoro, MNR candidate who won elections, in office after MNR seized power.

1952–56 Estenssoro nationalized tin-company holdings, initiated agrarian reforms, and extended civil rights to Indians, and introduced universal suffrage.

1956–60 Dr. Hernan Siles Zuazo, a leading force in the 1952 revolution, in office as president.

1960–64 Estenssoro again served as president; widespread labor unrest led to his ouster in an army coup.

1964 Military coup led by Vice-President Gen. Rene Barrientos Ortuño.

1964–66 Military junta with Barrientos as president ruled Bolivia; left-wing unions and other groups opposed junta; guerrilla uprising in south led by Che Guevara.

1966–69 Barrientos in office as president, following elections.

1967 Government troops, battling guerrilla movement since 1965, killed Che Guevara.

1967 New constitution adopted.

1969 President Barrientos killed in plane crash (Apr.).

1969 Dr. Luis Adolfo Siles Salinas, the vice-president, in office as president; deposed in Sept. by army.

1969–71 Series of coups marked this period of political instability in which right- and left-wing factions vied for control.

1970 Gulf Oil Company holdings nationalized (with compensation).

1971–78 Col. Hugo Banzer Suárez in power; had support of right-wing and of army.

1974 Coup attempts failed (June, Nov.); President Banzer replaced entire cabinet with military personnel.

1978–80 New round of military coups and political unrest followed presidential election.

1980–81 Gen. Luis García Meza seized power (July 17) after presidential elections failed to produce a clear winner; marked 189th coup since independence 154 years before.

1981 Meza's harsh rule resulted in a military takeover (July 31).

1981–82 Gen. Celso Torrelio Villa appointed president by military junta (Aug. 4); promised to restore democracy and began to institute liberal regime.

1982 Gen. Torrelio forced to resign by military junta after he announced elections scheduled for 1983.

1982 Junta appointed more conservative Gen. Guido Vildoso Calderón president; he promptly rejected proposed elections, but was unable to end general strike or restore ailing economy.

1982 Military forced to reconvene Congress (elected in 1980) in wake of continuing unrest, thus reestablishing democratic rule.

1982–85 Dr. H. Siles Zuazo in office as president, after being elected by Congress; US economic aid restored to Bolivia.

1983 Congress balked at austerity plan imposed by government to meet IMF requirements; strikes and unrest by workers continued into 1984.

1984 Government declared moratorium on foreign debt payments while reducing severity of austerity measures to end unrest.

1984 President Zuazo briefly kidnapped (June); two former high officials and 100 army officers arrested; drug lords believed involved.

1985–89 Dr. Paz Estenssoro, member of Historic Nationalist Revolutionary Movement (MNR-H), in office as president; faced continuing economic crisis in which inflation surpassed 20,500 percent; meanwhile, illegal cocaine trade had risen to $2 billion per year.

1985 Indefinite general strike called by unions opposed to new government austerity program (Sept.); government crackdown, including arrests of thousands, broke strike (Oct.).

1985 Contingent of US troops participated in anti-narcotics operation; stirred anti-American sentiment, however.

1986–88 Continued labor unrest over austerity program and other economic problems.

1988 Government stepped up anti-drug campaign; Congress restricted land allowed for legitimate growing of coca and beefed up anti-drug force; leading Bolivian drug lord arrested (July).

1989– President Jaime Paz Zamora in office following elections; promised continued fiscal austerity; inflation dropped to 3 percent and economy posted first growth since 1980.

1989 Government allowed extradition of former Justice and Interior Minister Col. Luis Arce Gómez to US on drug charges (later sentenced to 30 years in prison); constitutional crisis arose after Bolivian Supreme Court charged extradition was illegal and infringed on its powers.

1990 Government decrees advanced rights of indigenous Indian population; set aside northern rain forest as territory for Indians.

1990 Series of terrorist bombings directed against US involvement in Bolivian drug problem.

1991 Supreme Court independence affirmed in pact signed by five largest political parties; headed off major split between government branches.

1991 Amnesty program for drug traffickers instituted (July); seven drug lords reportedly opted for the amnesty, which included guarantee against extradition to US.

1992 Government announced 66 state-owned businesses would be privatized (June).

Bolivian National Revolutionary Movement (MNR) Political group (founded 1941) that fostered a social revolution in Bolivia during the 1950s. Following a general rebellion (Apr. 9–11, 1952), exiled MNR leader V. Paz Estenssoro became president (1952–56) and instituted sweeping economic and social reforms. These included universal suffrage, nationalization of tin mines, land reforms, and disbanding of the army and militia. The reforms bred runaway inflation, however, and by the early 1960s the government abandoned the revolution for a program of fiscal austerity.

Bollandists Name of a group of Belgian Jesuits who are charged with the continuous updating of the *Acta Sanctorum,* the collected lives and legends of the Roman Catholic saints. The group is named after Jean de Bolland (1596–1665), the editor who completed (1643) the first volumes. Except for the period 1794–1837, Bollandists have been revising the great work continuously since 1643.

Bologna, Concordat of *See* Concordat of Bologna.

Bologna, Giovanni 1529?–1628. Flemish sculptor. Among his most famous works are the statues *Flying Mercury* and the *Rape of the Sabines.*

Bolshevik Party Conference Name sometimes used for a congress of the Russian Social Democratic Workers' party, convened (1912) at Prague by N. Lenin. In an effort to maintain the unity of his own Bolshevik faction, Lenin used the occasion to permanently split the party and forced the Menshevik faction to form a separate party organization.

Bolsheviks One of the two important factions of the Russian Social Democratic Workers' party. The faction originated under N. Lenin during the second congress of the Social Democratic Workers' party (1903) at Brussels and London. Generally, the Bolsheviks wanted to establish a dictatorship of the proletariat immediately after the revolution they anticipated would come. Their opponents, the Mensheviks, believed an intermediate stage of bourgeois rule was needed before workers took power. The split subsequently widened and in 1912 Lenin formed the Bolsheviks as a small but distinct revolutionary party. Following the February Revolution and Lenin's return to Russia (1917), the Bolsheviks became increasingly popular with the workers. By controlling the Moscow and Petrograd soviets the Bolsheviks were able to become the ruling power in the government after the October Revolution. Lenin first shared power with other factions but gradually eliminated rival parties. Bolsheviks were officially named Russian Communist party (Bolsheviks) in 1918 and Communist party of the Soviet Union in 1952.

Bonaparte, Charles Lucien Jules Laurent 1803–57. Naturalist, a son of Napoleon's brother Lucien. His best-known work is *American Ornithology.*

Bonaparte, Jérôme 1784–1860. Napoleon's youngest brother. King of Westphalia (1807–13), he fought in Russia and at Waterloo, and served as marshal of France under Napoleon III.

Bonaparte, Joseph 1768–1844. King of Naples (1806–08) and Spain (1808–13). The oldest brother of Napoleon, he was forced to abdicate (1813) after the Peninsular Wars.

Bonaparte, Letizia Ramolino 1750–1836. Corsican matron, the mother of Napoleon.

Bonaparte, Louis 1778–1846. Brother of Napoleon. King of Holland (1806–10), he resisted the Continental System, and was forced by Napoleon to abdicate.

Bonaparte, Lucien 1775–1840. Brother of Napoleon. As president of France's Council of Five Hundred, he helped Napoleon overthrow the Directory and seize power in 1799.

Bonaparte, Mathilde 1820–1904. Daughter of Napoleon's brother Jérôme. She was a noted patron of the arts during the Second French Empire.

Bonaparte, Napoleon See **Napoleon I.**

Bonaparte, Napoléon Eugène Louis Jean Joseph 1856–79. French prince, the son of Napoleon III. He became pretender to the throne on his father's death (1873). He was killed while on a military expedition in Africa.

Bonaparte, Napoléon Joseph Charles Paul 1822–91. Known as Prince Napoleon. He was heir designate to the throne following the death of the son of Napoleon III.

Bonaparte, Pierre Napoléon 1815–81. French politician, son of Napoleon's brother Lucien. He was tried for the murder of a journalist in 1870, but was acquitted.

Bonaventure, Saint (Bonaventura, Saint) 1221–74. Italian theologian. An important church scholar, he was canonized in 1482 and made Doctor of the Church in 1587.

Boniface See **Bonifacius.**

Boniface, Saint c675–754? English Benedictine monk and martyr, originally called Wynfrid or Wynfrith. Called the Apostle of Germany, he is noted for his missionary work among the Germanic tribes.

Boniface VIII 1235?–1303. (Caetani, Benedetto) Italian pope (1294–1303), successor to Celestine V. He fought to maintain supremacy of the church over European kings, notably Philip IV of France. The struggle with Philip eventually resulted in a papal bull (1302) in which Boniface proclaimed supremacy of the pope in temporal and religious matters. An adviser to Philip, who was by then threatening to depose the pope, captured Boniface briefly at Anagni. Though Boniface is said to have stood up to ill treatment, he died shortly after his rescue.

Bonifácio, José See **Andrada e Silva, José Bonifácio de.**

Bonifacius (Boniface) d. AD 432. Roman general. As governor of the Roman province of Africa he became involved in a dispute with Emperor of the West Valentinian III. He was said to have invited the Vandals to aid against the Romans, which led to conquest of Africa by the Vandals under Gaiseric (AD 432).

Bonnard, Pierre 1867–1947. French painter and lithographer, associated with the Nabis and later the Intimists.

Bonney, William H. See **Billy the Kid.**

Bonnie Prince Charlie, the Young Pretender See **Stuart, Charles Edward.**

Bonnivard, François de (Bonivard, ~) c1493–1570. Swiss patriot. Prior of St. Victor, he was imprisoned in Chillon castle for opposing the duke of Savoy in the Revolt of Geneva, and was the subject of Lord G. Byron's poem *The Prisoner of Chillon.*

Bonus Army (~ Marchers) (~ Expeditionary Force) Mass gathering of US WW I veterans (spring-summer of 1932) at Washington, D.C., during the Great Depression. The unemployed and impoverished veterans (estimated variously at 12–20,000) camped in Washington to press their demand for immediate payment of a WW I bonus of about $1,000 each (due to be paid in 1945). The Senate defeated (June 17) a bill for immediate payment and President H. Hoover ordered (July 28) removal of the marchers. US Army troops under Gen. D. MacArthur drove the marchers out and burned their camps. The bonus was finally paid in 1936.

Bonus Expeditionary Force See **Bonus Army.**

Bonus Marchers See **Bonus Army.**

Book of Common Prayer Name of the authorized prayer book of the Church of England and its branches in other countries. Compiled by T. Cranmer (1549), it presented selected and revised versions of Catholic liturgies in English. Made mandatory that year by the Act of Uniformity, it was alternately suppressed and modified in following years. A modern version was adopted in 1928.

Book of Concord Collection (1580) of the major documents of Lutheran faith, including the Apostles' Creed, Nicene Creed, and Augsburg Confession.

Book of the Dead Name given to the collection of ancient Egyptian prayers, formulas, and incantations buried with the dead for use by them in the afterlife.

Boone, Daniel 1734–1820. American frontiersman and folk hero. After leading an unsuccessful attempt to settle in Kentucky (1773, his son James was killed by Indians), he helped blaze the Wilderness Road through Kentucky (1775). That year he moved his family to Boonesborough, one of Kentucky's first settlements. Thereafter he became a noted Indian fighter and hunted and trapped throughout the Kentucky and Missouri region.

Booth, Ballington 1859–1940. English reformer, a son of W. Booth. A commander of the US Salvation Army (1887–96), he left it to found the Volunteers of America (1896).

Booth, Bramwell 1856–1929. British general of the Salvation Army. He succeeded his father W. Booth as general in 1912.

Booth, Charles 1840–1916. English social reformer. His *Life and Labour of the People in London* contributed to the development of the modern social survey method.

Booth, Edwin 1833–93. American actor. Considered one of the great American actors, he is known best for his performances of *Hamlet.*

Booth, Evangeline Cory 1865–1950. British-born daughter of W. Booth. She was commander of the US Salvation Army (1904–34) and general of the international Salvation Army (1934–39).

Booth, John Wilkes 1838–65. American actor who assassinated US president Abraham Lincoln at Ford's Theatre in Washington, D.C., on April 14, 1865. Born into a well-known acting family, Booth showed a talent for acting but did not enjoy success on the stage until he toured the South. He became a staunch supporter of slavery and the South, and later nurtured a deep hatred of Lincoln. After serving as a volunteer in the militia that hanged abolitionist John Brown (1859), he became a Confederate secret service agent during the Civil War and conspired with others to kill Union officers. By 1864, Booth had organized a group of conspirators in Washington, D.C., to kidnap President Lincoln, but his attempts failed and suddenly the war ended. Booth then decided to assassinate Lincoln and on April 14, 1865, just days after the South's surrender, discovered that Lincoln would attend a performance at Ford's Theatre that evening. Entering Lincoln's box during the third act, he shot the President through the back of the head and made a desperate leap to the stage below, breaking his leg in the process. Still, he managed to escape into an adjacent alleyway. Lincoln died early the following day, but a simultaneous attempt to assassinate Secretary of State William Seward by Booth's co-conspirator Lewis Powell failed. The escaping Booth was treated by Dr. Samuel Alexander Mudd (1833–83, later imprisoned for helping Booth) and managed to elude authorities until Apr. 26. Federal troops surrounded a tobacco barn in Virginia where he was believed to be hiding and after firing into the structure, set it ablaze. Booth was either shot or shot himself and his body was later identified by his acquaintances, though rumors did spread that the body was not Booth's. Eight of the nine other suspected conspirators were convicted (four hanged and four sentenced to prison terms).

Booth, William 1829–1912. English minister, the founder (1878) and first general of the Salvation Army.

Booth-Tucker, Emma Moss 1860–1903. English reformer, a daughter of W. Booth. With her husband Frederick St. George de Latour Booth-Tucker (1853–1929), she commanded the US Salvation Army (1896–1903).

bootlegging Usually, illegal trafficking in alcohol, especially in the US during Prohibition (1920–33). Though the illegal manufacture and sale of alcohol were known before Prohibition, it became a burgeoning industry during the Prohibition years. Bootlegging involved smuggling from foreign countries, illegal manufacture within the US, and distribution through illegal "speakeasies." The profits from these lucrative operations helped to establish organized crime in the US and spawned widespread police and political corruption. Activities of bootleggers and the general disregard for dry laws forced the repeal of Prohibition (1933).

Borah, William Edgar 1865–1940. American politician. An isolationist US Senator from Idaho (1907–40), he opposed the Versailles Treaty and US entry into the League of Nations but supported international disarmament and the Kellogg-Briand Pact.

Bordeaux Assembly French National Assembly gathered (Feb. 13, 1871) at Bordeaux, France, following France's defeat in the Franco-Prussian War and the subsequent overthrow of the French Empire.

Borden, Lizzie Andrew 1860–1927. American woman from Fall River, Mass., tried for the brutal ax murders of her father and stepmother

(1892). She maintained her innocence and, after a sensational trial, was acquitted.

Borden, Sir Robert Laird 1854–1937.   Canadian statesman. Conservative party prime minister during 1911–20, he led Canada through WW I, and helped win independent representation for British dominions in the League of Nations.

Border, the   Name given to the border region between England and Scotland. Celebrated in the literature of both peoples, it was the site of many historic battles between the English and Scots until the 17th cent.

Bordet, Jules 1870–1961.   Belgian immunologist, a leader in the study of immune systems. With Octave Gengou he discovered the whooping cough bacillus (1906). For his study of immunity factors in blood he was awarded the Nobel Prize in Physiology or Medicine (1919).

Bordone, Paris 1500–71.   Venetian painter during the Renaissance. A student of Titian, he was noted for his portraits. *Fisherman Presenting the Ring of St. Mark to the Doge* is one of his most famous works.

Borel, Joseph Pierre   *See* **Borel, Petrus.**

Borel, Petrus (~, Joseph Pierre) 1809–59.   French novelist and poet, one of the leading figures of the French Romantic movement. His works include the verse collection *Rhapsodies.*

Borghese, Camillo   *See* **Paul V.**

Borgia, Cesare 1476–1507.   Ruthless, opportunistic Italian soldier and political leader, son of Pope Alexander VI. He is said to have been a model of qualities described in N. Machiavelli's *The Prince.* Educated for a religious career, Borgia showed early signs of a more secular bent and in 1489 entered the University of Perugia to study law. Named bishop of Pamplona (1491), he became a cardinal (1493) following his father's accession to the papacy. Drawn to politics and the military, he resigned his position as cardinal (1498) to become a lieutenant in the papal army. By 1499 Borgia was captain general and to restore control over nobles in the Papal States, began a successful campaign to conquer Romagna and the Marches. Borgia's ruthless opportunism aroused fierce opposition, his critics describing him as a cruel and arrogant monster trying to secure a kingdom of his own before his father's death stripped him of legitimate authority. Murders and political assassinations were ascribed to him, and it is likely he killed his brother-in-law (but probably not his brother). It was in about 1502 that Machiavelli, an

ambassador from Florence, witnessed Borgia's activities first hand. Borgia's father died in 1503 and the newly elected Pope Julius II demanded restoration of cities conquered by Borgia. Borgia fled to Spain, was imprisoned there, escaped (1506), and finally died fighting in Spain for his brother-in-law, the king of Navarre, in 1507.

Borgia, Lucrezia 1480–1519.   Italian Renaissance noblewoman, daughter of Pope Alexander VI, and sister of C. Borgia. Her first marriage was annulled (1497) and she married Alfonso, duke of Bisceglie, to further the Borgia family's alliance with Naples (1498). Fortunes changed, however, and her brother later had Alfonso (1500) murdered. In 1501, she married Alfonso of Este, heir to the duke of Ferrara. As duchess of Ferrara, she devoted herself to religion, education, and charity, becoming a noted patron of the arts and letters.

Borglum, Gutzon 1867–1941.   American sculptor. Among his best-known works is the Mount Rushmore National Memorial, in South Dakota.

Boris I *d.* 907.   Bulgarian ruler (852–89). He converted to Christianity (865) and is credited with introducing and spreading Byzantine Christianity throughout Bulgaria.

Boris III 1894–1943.   King of Bulgaria (1918–43). Possessing virtually dictatorial powers in the last years of his reign, he supported the Axis Powers in WW II. He died under mysterious circumstances shortly after a confrontation with A. Hitler.

Borja, Alfonso de   *See* **Calixtus III.**

Borman, Frank 1928– .   American astronaut. He was a crew member of the Apollo 8 space mission, which made the first manned orbit of the moon (Dec., 1968).

Born, Max 1882–1970.   German-born British physicist noted for his contributions to the theory of relativity and quantum theory. He reformulated the first law of thermodynamics (1921) and later worked on a new quantum theory of atoms, developed an important interpretation of a quantum wave mechanics equation, and helped formulate a theory on forces between atoms. With Walter Bothe (1891–1957) he received the 1954 Nobel Prize in Physics.

Borobudur   A pyramid-like structure in Java, considered one of the greatest of all Buddhist monuments. It was built early in the 9th cent. by adherents of Mahayana Buddhism.

Borodin, Aleksandr P.   *See* **Igor.**

Borodino, Battle of Narrow victory (Sept. 7, 1812) for Napoleon during the Russian invasion of the Napoleonic Wars. In the battle some 120,000 retreating Russian troops under Gen. M. Kutuzov made their last defense of Moscow at the village of Borodino. The Russians managed to hold off Napoleon's force of 130,000 soldiers in the day-long battle but retreated during the night. The French suffered 30,000 casualties and the Russians 45,000. After the battle Napoleon was able to march unopposed into Moscow, but he had lost his chance to destroy the Russian army.

Bosch, Hieronymus (Jerom Bos) c1450–1516. Dutch painter, noted for his images of the bizarre and grotesque. His works include *The Crowning with Thorns* and *The Garden of Earthly Delights.*

Bosnia and Herzegovina Historic region, formerly part of Yugoslavia. Once part of the Roman province of Illyricum, it was settled by Serbs and Croatians (7th cent.). After the 12th cent. it came under Hungarian domination. By the late 15th cent. the region had fallen to the Turks, who controlled it until the Bosnian Rebellion (1875). After the Russo-Turkish War, Austria-Hungary occupied the region (1878), then annexed it (1908), thereby precipitating the Bosnian Crisis. The assassination (1914) of Archduke Ferdinand in Sarajevo led to WW I, after which the territory was annexed (1918) to Serbia. In 1946 it became one of the six constituent republics of Yugoslavia (*q.v.*), and after the collapse of the USSR, declared sovereignty (Oct., 1991) and independence (Feb. 29, 1992). Serbs opposed the move, and Serbian forces engaged Bosnians in a bloody war, which included a prolonged siege of Sarajevo and charges that Serbs had massacred thousands of Bosnians. UN mediation efforts continued into 1993.

Bosnian Crisis International crisis caused by Austria-Hungary's annexation (Oct. 6, 1908) of Bosnia and Herzegovina. The incident contributed to tensions that led to WW I, by straining relations between Austria-Hungary and Russia and by arousing Serbian nationalism. Austria-Hungary had occupied the territories since the Russo-Turkish War (1877–78). When Austria-Hungary announced formal annexation, Russia sided with Serbians in protest. Germany supported Austria-Hungary and threatened war, and Russia, humiliated, backed down.

Bosnian Rebellion Revolt (1875) in Bosnia against Ottoman rule. The uprising, which began in nearby Herzegovina, gained support from Serbia, and culminated in the Serbo-Turkish War of 1876–78.

Bossuet, Jacques Bénigne 1627–1704. French bishop and orator, considered one of the great French orators. He attacked F. Fenelon and quietism, and figured in the Gallican controversy.

Boston, Siege of American military victory (1775–76) during the American Revolution. Shortly after the battles of Lexington and Concord (Apr. 19, 1775), Colonial forces began a siege of Boston, then held by the British. Installation by the Continental Army of artillery on Dorchester Heights (Mar., 1776) forced British evacuation of the city (Mar. 17).

Boston Massacre Incident (Mar. 5, 1770) leading up to the American Revolution (1775–83), in which British troops fired into a crowd of rioting Colonials in Boston. The Townshend Acts, and the quartering of British troops in Boston to enforce them, led to frequent harassment of the soldiers by Boston Colonials. On Mar. 5, a group of nine soldiers was threatened by a crowd of 50–60 angry colonials. The soldiers opened fire and killed five, including Crispus Attucks (1723?–70), who is sometimes called the leader of the mob. The soldiers were later tried and acquitted on charges of murder, though two were found guilty of manslaughter, and most of the Townshend Acts were repealed.

Boston Tea Party Famous incident (Dec. 16, 1773) leading up to the American Revolution. American colonists had protested the tea tax imposed by British Parliament in the Townshend Acts and had blocked delivery of tea at New York and Philadelphia. At Boston, however, Gov. T. Hutchinson demanded payment of the tax. A group of some 50 colonists, disguised as Indians and including P. Revere, boarded three British ships in Boston harbor and threw their cargoes of tea overboard. Parliament responded with the Intolerable Acts, closing the port of Boston.

Boswell, James 1740–95. Scottish author, diarist and famous biographer of S. Johnson. A lawyer from 1776, he sought to befriend the great men of his time and first met Johnson in 1763. He became famous with publication of his *Account of Corsica* (1768) and joined Johnson's literary club (1773). His classic *Life of Samuel Johnson* was published in 1791. Boswell's literary reputation was further strengthened by discovery (1927) of his voluminous journals, in Ireland.

Bosworth Field, Battle of Tudor victory (1485) over the Yorkists, ending the Wars of the Roses in England. Some 5,000 rebel troops under Henry Tudor (later Henry VII) engaged 15,000 Yorkists under King Richard III. Treachery and disorganization led to Richard's defeat and death in battle. Henry thus gained the throne and founded the Tudor dynasty.

Botha, Louis 1862–1919. South African soldier and statesman. A Boer, he was the first prime minister of the Union of South Africa (1910–19).

Bothe, Walter *See* **Born, Max.**

Bothwell, James Hepburn, earl of c1536–1578. Scottish nobleman and third husband of Mary, Queen of Scots (*m.* 1567). Their marriage led to a revolt (1567) of the Scottish nobles. Bothwell fled, dying a prisoner in Denmark.

Botswana (Bechuanaland) Landlocked South African republic (*pop.* 1,300,000). The British occupied Bechuanaland (1884) to prevent incursions from the Boers and Germans, incorporating the southern area into Cape Colony. In the 20th cent. the Union of South Africa sought several times to annex the Bechuanaland protectorate. Britain granted the territory independence on Sept. 30, 1966, and Sir Seretse Khama remained in office as first president from 1966 to 1980. Discovery of major mineral deposits has increased Botswana's strategic and economic importance, and diamonds provide the major share of Botswana's export earnings. During the late 1980s, South Africa launched periodic raids into the country, claiming African National Congress (ANC) guerrillas were operating from there, despite Botswana's long-standing policy against harboring guerrillas.

Botticelli, Sandro (*b.* Allesandro di Mariano Filipepi) c1444–1510. A great Florentine painter of the early Renaissance. He took part in decorating the Sistine Chapel (1481–82) and during his prosperous career enjoyed the patronage of the Medicis, among others. His works include the *Birth of Venus* (c1485), *Primavera* (1478), and illustrations for Dante's *Divine Comedy.*

Boudicia *See* **Boadicea.**

Bougainville, Louis Antoine de 1729–1811. French navigator. He made the first French circumnavigation of the world (1766–69).

Bouillon, Godfrey of *See* **Godfrey of Bouillon.**

Boulanger, Georges Ernest Jean Marie 1837–91. French general and political figure, the instigator of Boulangism, a nationalist movement seeking revenge against Germany. Though for a time he threatened to topple the Third Republic, he was finally forced to flee to Belgium, where he committed suicide.

Boulangism *See* **Boulanger, Georges Ernest Jean Marie.**

Boule *See* **Areopagus.**

***Bounty*, HMS** English ship aboard which occurred the celebrated mutiny on Apr. 28, 1789. The ship, under the command of Capt. W. Bligh, was carrying a cargo of breadfruit trees from Tahiti to the West Indies. Led by the mate Fletcher Christian (*fl.* late 18th cent.), the crew mutinied and set the captain and 18 others adrift. The remainder of the crew is believed by some to have founded a colony at Pitcairn Island.

Bourbon Powerful French royal family whose descendants were rulers of France, Spain, the kingdom of the Two Sicilies, and Parma. The family can be traced back to a 9th-cent. French nobleman, Adhemar (or Aimar). The founder of the royal line was Robert of Clermont (1256–1318), a son of French king Louis IX. Robert married (1272) the Bourbon heiress, Beatrice. The elder line thus formed became extinct (1527) with the death of Charles, duke of Bourbon. But a collateral line, Bourbon-Vendôme, produced Henry IV (ruled 1589–1610), the first of a long line of Bourbon kings of France. King Louis XIV's brother, Philippe, duke of Orléans (1640–1701), founded the Orléans (Bourbon) line and Louis's grandson, Philip, duke of Anjou, founded the Bourbon-Spain line as King Philip V. Bourbon rule of France was uninterrupted until the French Revolution (1789–99), when King Louis XVI was deposed (1792) and guillotined. During the Bourbon Restoration, Louis XVI's brother ruled as Louis XVIII. His successors, Charles X and Louis Philippe (Bourbon-Orléans), were the last Bourbon kings of France. Thereafter claims to the throne by royal pretenders of the Bourbon line continued until extinction of the line with the death (1883) of H. Chambord. Royal claims then passed to the Orléans line. (*See also* Bourbon-Spain, Bourbon-Sicily, Bourbon-Parma.) *Bourbon kings of France were:* Henry IV 1589–1610; Louis XIII 1610–43; Louis XIV 1643–1715; Louis XV 1715–74; Louis XVI 1774–92; Louis XVII 1793–95 (never ruled); Louis XVIII 1814–24; Charles X 1824–30; Louis Philippe 1830–48 (Bourbon-Orléans).

Bourbon, Charles, duke of Bourbon 1490–1527. Constable of France under Francis I. He supported Holy Roman Emperor Charles V against Francis in the Italian Wars.

Bourbon-Parma A branch of the Bourbon family of French royalty. The line was established as a branch of Bourbon-Spain in 1748 when Philip, a son of Spanish king Philip V, was made duke of Parma and Piacenza. The line survived until 1859, when Robert, 5th duke of Parma, lost his title.

Bourbon-Sicily Line of rulers in southern Italy, a branch of the French Bourbon family. Established by Ferdinand I, who was made king of Naples (1759) and ruled the kingdom of the Two Sicilies (1816–25), it lasted until 1860, when the kingdom was incorporated into Italy.

Bourbon-Spain Line of rulers in Spain, a branch of the French Bourbon family. Established with the succession (1700) of King Philip V, the grandson of French king Louis XIV, it has continued, with interruptions, to the present as the royal family of Spain. The rulers are: Philip V 1700–24; Louis I 1724; Philip V 1724–46 (restored); Ferdinand VI 1746–59; Charles III 1759–88; Charles IV 1788–1808; Ferdinand VII 1808; Ferdinand VII 1814–33 (restored); Isabella II 1833–68; Alfonso XII 1874–85; Alfonso XIII 1886–1931; Juan Carlos I 1975– .

bourgeoisie Originally, French merchants and craftsmen in medieval times who, as a class, occupied the economic and social middle ground between landowners and peasants. With the breakup of feudal society, the rise of capitalism and the advent of the Industrial Revolution, the bourgeoisie came to include a wide range of groups of entrepreneurs, such as bankers, factory owners, merchants, and professionals. By K. Marx's theory of class struggle, society consists of the capitalist bourgeoisie pitted against the wage-earning workers, or proletariat (*q.v.*).

Bourges, Pragmatic Sanction of *See* **Pragmatic Sanction of Bourges.**

Bourke-White, Margaret 1904–71. American photojournalist and author. From 1929, as a staff photographer for *Fortune, Time,* and *Life,* she gained a reputation for her photographs of world leaders and photo-essays on such subjects as the American South during the Depression, US and Soviet industry, and WW II.

Bourne, Randolph Silliman 1886–1918. American pacifist and essayist. His articles in opposition to US participation in WW I were collected in *Untimely Papers.*

Bouvines, Battle of Battle (July 27, 1214) at Bouvines, France, in which 10,000 French led by Philip II of France defeated a coalition army of 15,000 led by King John of England and Holy Roman Emperor Otto IV. Philip thus gained control of most of the French lands formerly held by the English (Angevin domains).

Bowditch, Nathaniel 1773–1838. American mathematician and navigator. He corrected and revised J. Moore's *The Practical Navigator* and in 1802 issued his famous *The New American Practical Navigator.*

Bowdler, Thomas 1754–1825. English editor. His expurgated edition of W. Shakespeare's plays, *The Family Shakespeare,* gave rise to the term "bowdlerize."

Bowie, Jim (James) 1799–1836. American frontiersman, credited with invention of the Bowie knife. He died at the Alamo during the Texas war for independence.

Boxer Rebellion Widespread uprising (1900) in northern China against foreigners and foreign influence. Increased foreign domination of China led to the rise of the nationalist, secret organization, the Boxers, and by 1898 the group had the support of the Dowager Empress Cixi. In early June, 1900, rebellion broke out. Some 140,000 Boxers occupied Beijing and began burning foreign buildings and churches and killing Chinese Christians. The Dowager Empress repulsed a small relief force (June 13), declared war, and ordered all foreigners killed. However, a force of 18,000 foreign soldiers finally overcame the Boxers (Aug. 14), and took control of Beijing. China was forced subsequently to make new commercial concessions and to pay reparations, by the Boxer protocol (Sept. 7, 1901).

Boyacá, Battle of Victory (Aug. 7, 1819) for South American revolutionaries fighting for independence from Spain. With Gen. Francisco de Paula Santander (1792–1840), S. Bolívar led some 3,000 rebels across flooded plains and through the high passes of the Andes to surprise a 5,000-man Spanish force outside Bogotá. The engagement near the Boyacá River resulted in the capture of the Spanish commander and 1,800 prisoners, and the independence of New Granada.

Boyar Title given to Russian landowning nobles who were influential in Russia from the 10th to 17th cents. The title was abolished by Peter I.

boycott Concerted refusal by groups or nations to deal economically, politically, or socially with an individual, group, or nation. Its purpose is to protest or change actions or policies.

Boyle, Richard, 1st earl of Cork 1566–1643. English-born Irish administrator, noted for his encouragement of trade and industry in Ireland.

Boyle, Robert 1627–91. Irish-English physicist and chemist, often called "the father of modern chemistry." A graduate of Eton, he established his own laboratories for his researches, first at Oxford (1654–68) and then at London (1668–91). Collaborating with R. Hooke at Oxford to construct a vacuum pump, he used the device in experiments that led to publication (1662) of Boyle's Law, which explains the relationship of pressure and volume in a gas. He established chemistry as distinct from alchemy, rendered the first accurate definitions of a chemical element and reaction, and experimented with acids and bases, calcination of metals, and combustion. Rejecting alchemists' theories on matter in his *The Sceptical Chymist* (1661), Boyle held that a single basic substance made up all matter and that varying clusters (called corpuscles) of this material accounted for differences in all known matter.

Boyne, Battle of the A victory (July, 1690) in Ireland for English king William III over the Jacobite armies of former King James II. Some 35,000 Protestants under William defeated about 25,000 Catholics (French and Irish) at the Boyne River, forcing James to flee to France.

Bozzaris, Marco (˜, Markos) c1788–1823. Greek patriot, an important leader in the War of Greek Independence.

Brabant Revolution Brief rebellion (1789–90) against the rule of Holy Roman Emperor Joseph II in the Belgian provinces of the Austrian Netherlands. The revolt fostered the subsequent drive for Belgian independence.

Bradford, William 1590–1657. English-born American colonist. First elected governor of Plymouth Colony in 1621, he was reelected thirty times. He wrote the *History of Plymouth Plantation.*

Bradford, William 1663–1752. English-born colonial American printer. He published the first *American Book of Common Prayer* and the first New York newspaper, the *New York Gazette.*

Bradley, Omar Nelson 1893–1981. US general. A top commander in North Africa and Europe in WW II, he was made general of the army (1950) and chairman of the joint chiefs of staff (1949–53).

Bradstreet, Anne Dudley c1612–1672. English-born colonial American poet, considered the first important woman writer in America.

Brady, James Buchanan (Diamond Jim ˜) 1856–1917. American financial speculator. A flamboyant, self-made millionaire, he was noted for wearing numerous diamonds and other gems.

Brady, Matthew B. c1823–96. American photographer. A pioneer in photography, he was noted for his many photographs of the US Civil War.

Braga, Teófilo 1843–1924. Portuguese poet and political leader. He was the first president (1910–11) of the new republic of Portugal, and served again in 1915. He wrote an important history of Portuguese literature.

Braganca *See* **Braganza.**

Braganza (Braganca) Ruling house of Portugal (1640–1910) and Brazil (1822–89). The family was founded by Alfonso (*d.* 1451), the illegitimate son of Portuguese king John I. The first member of the royal line was John IV, who ruled the newly independent Portugal (1640–56). The line of rulers lasted until the ouster of Manuel II (1910) and formation of the republic. The Braganza family also provided rulers of Brazil for a time in the 19th cent. They were Pedro I, son of Portuguese king John VI, and Pedro II, who was ousted in 1889. *The Braganza kings of Portugal were:* John IV 1640–56; Alfonso VI 1656–83; Peter II 1683–1706; John V 1706–1750; Joseph 1750–77; Maria I (with Peter III) 1777–86; Maria I 1786–1816; John VI 1816–26; Peter IV 1826; Maria II 1826–28; Miguel 1828–34; Maria II 1834–53; Peter V 1853–61; Louis I 1861–89; Carlos I 1889–1908.

Braganza, Catherine of *See* **Catherine of Braganza.**

Bragg, Braxton 1817–76. Confederate general in the US Civil War. He led Confederate forces to victory in the battle of Chickamauga (1863).

Brahe, Tycho 1546–1601. Danish astronomer. His careful astronomical observations challenged the Aristotelian idea of a fixed universe, and contributed to the growth of modern astronomy.

Brahman (Brahmin) Highest caste of the Hindu religion. Brahmans are by tradition responsible for the study and teaching of the Vedas, and performance of special religious ceremonies. *See also* caste system.

Brahmanism Early phase of Hinduism. Brahmanism derived (1500–700 BC) from the sacred texts of the Vedas and was followed (c500 BC) by the classical period of Hinduism. Brahmanism was developed by the Brahmans, or priests, who oversaw worship according to the Vedic texts. Among its characteristic features were an increasing concern for philosophical speculations (as in the Upanishads), increased elaboration of ceremonies (especially sacrifices), the emergence of the caste system, and development of the concept of transmigration of the soul. The rise of Buddhism and Jainism brought about the evolution of Brahmanism into classical Hinduism.

Brahmin *See* **Brahman.**

Brahms, Johannes 1833–97. German composer of the Romantic period, one of the world's great composers. Brahms rejected what was then the revolutionary romanticism of R. Wagner and F. Liszt and created compositions that combined a restrained romanticism with classical forms. A gifted musician in his youth, Brahms became friends with R. Schumann, who helped establish Brahms's reputation as a composer. Brahms settled in Vienna after 1863 and there composed the bulk of his works, including *German Requiem, Violin Concerto in D,* and his four great symphonies.

Braille, Louis 1809?–52. French teacher and inventor of the Braille system of writing for the blind. Accidentally blinded as a youth, he studied music and from 1824 began working on his system of printing for the blind (published 1829).

Brain Trust (Brains ~) Advisers to F. Roosevelt during his presidential campaign (1932) and the early period of his first administration. The group played a role in formulation of New Deal policies.

Braintree Resolutions Resolutions passed (Sept. 24, 1765) by the town of Braintree, Massachusetts, calling for legal resistance to the Stamp Act.

Bramante, Donato 1444–1514. Italian painter and architect, noted for his buildings in the High Renaissance style. His major work was his plan for the rebuilding of St. Peter's church in Rome.

Brancusi, Constantin 1876–1957. Rumanian sculptor, a leading sculptor of the modern abstract school. His work focused on the simplified forms of objects.

Brandenburg Ancient region divided after WW II between East Germany and Poland. It was conquered by Albert the Bear (12th cent.), whose descendants, the Ascanians, ruled it until 1320. Made an electorate of the Holy Roman Empire, it passed to Frederick I of Hohenzollern. After the Thirty Years' War, it became a military power under the rule (1640–88) of Frederick William, the Great Elector, who conquered East Pomerania and freed Prussia from Polish rule. His son Frederick III took the title Frederick I, King of Prussia (1701), by which name it was known thereafter.

Brandenburg, Albert of *See* **Albert of Brandenburg.**

Brandenburg, Treaty of *See* **Bärwalde, Treaty of.**

Brandt, Willy (Frahm, Karl Herbert) 1913–92. German statesman. Brandt served as mayor of West Berlin (1957–66) and chancellor of the German Federal Republic (1969–74). Brandt modified his country's foreign policy by recognizing the loss of former German territories in Eastern Europe. He was awarded the Nobel Peace Prize (1971) for his work toward reunifying East and West Germany.

Brandy Station, Battle of Battle (June 9, 1863) of the American Civil War. At Brandy Station (now Brandy), Virginia, a force of federal cavalry attacked and was repulsed by Confederate cavalry commanded by Gen. J. Stuart.

Brandywine, Battle of British victory (Sept. 11, 1777) over Colonial forces during the American Revolution (1775–83). The victory led to the capture of the Colonial capital of Philadelphia (Sept. 27). Gen. G. Washington, commanding some 11,000 Colonials, hoped to block the British advance from New York to Philadelphia. He met the British force of some 15,000 soldiers, commanded by Gen. W. Howe, at Brandywine Creek just south of Philadelphia but was eventually forced to withdraw. British casualties were about 600 to American casualties of some 1,000.

Brant, Joseph 1742–1807. Mohawk Indian chief. He joined the British side during the American Revolution and did much to win Indians to their cause. He led Indian forces at the Battle of Oriskany (1777) and in the Cherry Valley Raid (1778).

Branting, Karl Hjalmar 1860–1925. Swedish statesman, a founder of the Swedish Social Democratic party. As premier (1920, 1921–23, 1924–25), he helped to promote social reforms. He was awarded the Nobel Peace Prize (1921).

Braque, Georges 1882–1963. French painter, one of the leading painters of the 20th cent. With P. Picasso he developed cubism.

Braschi, Giovanni Angelo *See* **Pius VI.**

Brasidas *d.* 422 BC. Spartan general who won fame during the Peloponnesian War. He defeated the Athenians under Cleon at Amphipolis, but both he and Cleon were killed during the battle (422 BC).

Bratianu, John (˜, Ion) 1864–1927. Rumanian statesman. Premier of Rumania (1909–11, 1914–18, 1922–26), he brought Rumania into WW I against the Central Powers, and represented Rumania at the Paris Peace Conference (1919).

Brattain, Walter H. *See* **Bardeen, John.**

Braun, Eva 1912–45. German woman, the mistress of A. Hitler. Hitler kept their relationship a secret, and she played no role in his career. She and Hitler were married (Apr. 29, 1945) one day before their joint suicide.

Braun, Wernher von 1912–77. German-American engineer. As director of the Nazi Peenemünde facility, he helped develop the German V rockets during WW II. After the war he went to the US and played a major role in the development of the American space program. He was involved in the launching of Explorer I, the first US satellite (1958), and held important posts at NASA until 1972.

Brazil Republic located in eastern South America. The population is 153,771,000 and the capital is Brasilia. Brazil was colonized and settled by the Portuguese and was seat of the Portuguese monarchy from 1808 to 1821. Brazil became an independent empire in 1822. Development of the country was largely accomplished by slave labor imported from Africa. Although the monarchy established a plan for gradual emancipation, the abolition of slavery (1888) by Isabel, daughter of the emperor, alienated the planters and led to the establishment of the Republic of Brazil in 1889. Key dates in the history of Brazil include:

1500 V. Pinzon, Spanish navigator, explored Brazil's coast and discovered the Amazon estuary.

1500 P. Cabral claimed Brazil for Portugal.

1521–57 Portuguese king John III expanded Portuguese influence in Brazil.

1532 Portuguese admiral, M. Affonso de Sousa, founded first Portuguese settlement in Brazil at São Vicente.

1555 French Huguenot settlement established in Rio de Janeiro Harbor.

1567 Portuguese forced Huguenots out and founded Rio de Janeiro.

1633 Dutch West India Company gained control of northeastern Brazil.

1636–43 John Maurice of Nassau, Dutch general, served as governor of Brazil.

1654 Settlers from Rio de Janeiro forced the Dutch to leave Brazil.

1708–09 War of the Emboabas, civil war between established and new settlers.

1750 Beginnings of Brazil's coffee industry; Pará exported 12 tons of beans to Portugal.

1761 Rio de Janeiro's first coffee seedlings planted.

1763 Rio de Janeiro became capital of Brazil.

1789 Tiradentes Conspiracy, to overthrow Portuguese rule, uncovered.

1807–08 In Europe, Napoleon invaded Portugal in the Peninsular War; Portuguese king John VI fled to Brazil (1807); established Rio de Janeiro as his capital (1808).

1821 John VI returned to Portugal, his son remaining to govern in Brazil; son declared Brazilian independence (Sept. 7, 1822) and became Brazilian emperor Pedro I.

1822–31 Pedro I reigned.

1822–23 J. Andrada e Silva served as prime minister; supported independence from Portugal.

1823–64 A. Gonçalves Dias lived; considered Brazilian national poet.

1824 Pedro I enacted first constitution.

1827 Brazilian troops defeated (Feb. 20) at Battle of Ituzaingo in fight to keep control of Uruguayan territories.

1831–39 Pedro II reigned (initially under a regency; crowned 1841); reign marked by expansion of economy, construction of roads and railroads, and influx of new settlers from Europe.

1839–1908 Great Brazilian novelist J. Machado de Assis lived; wrote *Quincas Borba* and *Dom Casmurro.*

1840s Brazil became world's leading coffee producer; continued expansion of coffee production led to overproduction and economic crisis.

1852 Brazil fought war with Argentina.

1865–70 War of the Triple Alliance against Paraguay.

1887–1959 H. Villa-Lobos, leading Latin composer, lived.

1888–89 Isabel, daughter of Pedro II, abolished slavery in Brazil during the absence of her father (1888); action led to overthrow of the monarchy, and establishment of a republic (1889).

1889–91 M. Fonseca in office as first president.

1890s Coffee ranked as Brazil's leading export by about this time; was also leading source of government revenue.

1891 Fonseca seized power, dissolved Congress, and instituted dictatorship.

1891–94 Floriano Peixoto in power; continued dictatorship.

1893–94 Military revolt against dictatorship; rebellion put down, but was followed by establishment of more democratic, civilian government under Prudente de Morais (served 1894–98).

1898–1902 Manuel Ferraz de Campos Salles in office as president; saved Brazil from financial collapse.

19TH–20TH CENTS. Civilistas, political parties opposed to military government, gained popularity.

1902–06 Francisco de Paula Rodrigues Alves in office as president.

1906 Taubaté Convention; Brazil's coffee-producing states agreed to measures to control production and prices; economic crises of late 1920s ended so-called "valorization" program.

1906–09 Affonso Augusto Moreira Penna served as president.

1909–10 Nilo Peçanha in office as president, following death of Penna.

1910–14 President Hermes da Fonseca in office.

1914–18 Wenceslau Braz Pereira Gomez served as president.

1917 Brazil entered WW I against Germany (Oct.).

1918–19 Francisco de Paula Rodriguez Alves served as president; died in office.

1919–1922 Epitacio da Silva Pessóa in office as president.

1922 Tenentismo social reform movement established; sparked revolts in 1922 and 1924.

1922–26 President Arthur da Silva Bernardes in office; economic boom collapsed, bringing on new economic crisis; government imposed austerity budget and levied income tax.

1926–30 President Washington Luiz Pereira de Souza in office.

1930 Julio Prestes elected to presidency (Mar. 11).

1930 Revolution in Brazil (Oct.) broke out before Prestes's inauguration; Getulio Vargas made acting president; Vargas moved to block Prestes and his supporters, the Paulistas, from gaining power.

1930–45 Vargas in power as president.

1932 Paulistas staged unsuccessful revolt against Vargas's rule.

1933 Government set up National Coffee Department to regulate industry.

1934 Brazilian National Constituent Assembly passed new constitution and made Vargas president.

1937 New constitution issued by Vargas, who took personal control of the government; federal power greatly increased.

1941 Brazil joined Inter-American Coffee Board to control production; dropped its own control in 1946.

1942 Brazil entered WW II on the side of the Allies.

1945 Vargas overthrown (Oct.).

1946 New constitution passed (Sept.).

1946–51 E. Dutra served as president, restoring constitutional democracy.

1951–54 Vargas in office as president; presidency marked by economic and political turmoil; forced to resign.

1952 Brazil's coffee industry again in crisis; Vargas organized the Brazilian Coffee Institute; measures taken to diversify Brazil's economic base.

1954–55 President João Café Filho in office.

1956–61 Juscelino Kubitschek in office as elected president (1955); began the construction of Brasilia.

1960–61 Jánio Quadros in office as president; an anti-Vargas, reformist, he resigned in the face of opposition in Congress; near constitutional crisis averted.

1961–64 João Goulart in office as president; parliamentary government instituted (1961–63) during his presidency but presidential government restored in 1963; military forced Goulart's resignation (1964).

1964–67 Gen. Humberto Castelo Branco served as president; exercised special powers and dissolved all political parties; new constitution passed (1967).

1967–74 Period of political unrest; government dominated by succession of military leaders, outbreaks of terrorism by leftists increased.

1967–69 A. da Costa e Silva headed military regime that led to his dictatorship.

1974–79 Gen. Ernesto Geisel in office as president.

1977 Government canceled US military aid, charging interference in its domestic affairs.

1977 President Geisel suspended Congress to block growing opposition.

1978 Constitutional reforms gave limited freedoms to people, though military government left many restrictions in force.

1979–85 Gen. João Baptista da Figueiredo in office as president; his program of slow liberalization (*abertura*) fostered reappearance of opposition political parties but economic problems plagued his administration.

1980 Pope John Paul II, on 13-city tour, urged the turn toward democratic reform.

1982 Brazil asked foreign banks for moratorium on its rapidly mounting external debt (Dec. 31), thereby technically averting a total default on some $83 billion.

1983 Government imposed strict austerity measures (July); efforts to hold down interest rates forced 25 state banks into insolvency.

1984 Some one million demonstrators rallied (Apr. 10, 16) in favor of proposed constitutional amendment for direct election of president by popular vote; Brazil's Chamber of Deputies defeated the amendment (Apr. 26), letting stand the current system of election by Electoral College.

1985 Tancredo Neves voted president by the Electoral College; the candidate of the opposition Brazilian Democratic Movement Party (PMDB), Neves fell ill and died before taking office.

1985–90 José Sarney, Neves's running mate, in office as president; Sarney faced enormous economic problems, including 200%-plus annual inflation and Brazil's inability to repay foreign debts.

1985 Brazil enacted land reform law (Oct. 10) redistributing 106 million acres.

1986 President Sarney imposed radical economic plan (the Cruzado Plan) to cure Brazil's economic woes (Feb. 28); ordered currency devalued, froze prices, wages, and taxes; plan only temporarily cut inflation; similar anti-inflation plans in 1987 and 1989 also failed.

1988 New constitution adopted (Oct. 5); presidency remained strong with few checks; torture outlawed.

1989 Wave of 300 strikes in Brazil (Mar.–Apr.) as workers demanded wage hikes to offset effects of runaway inflation.

1989 Brazil stopped paying interest on foreign debt (until 1991).

1989 President Sarney unveiled five-year program to protect the Amazon rain forest from destructive development; logging interests, small farmers, and others had been rapidly destroying huge sections of the forest.

1990– Francisco Collor de Mello in office as president, following Brazil's first direct presidential election since 1960.

1990 Brazil, Argentina, Paraguay, and Uruguay formed the Southern Cone Common Market, which, in 1991, sought to reduce trade barriers with the US.

1991 President Collor's privatization program began with sale of state-owned steel plant (Oct.); further sales of state-owned businesses held to raise cash to retire foreign debt.

1991 Government ordered new anti-inflation program; renegotiated overdue debt interest repayment with foreign banks; ordered major devaluation of currency (Nov.).

1992 Special commission found grounds for impeachment of President Collor, saying he used his office for "improper economic benefits" (Aug.); mass demonstrations held by impeachment supporters.

1992 Rate of rain forest destruction reported slowing.

Brazza, Pierre Paul François Camille Savorgnan de 1852–1905. Italian-born French explorer. He established a protectorate over what became the French Congo (1880), founded Brazzaville (1883), and helped expand the French empire in Africa.

Breakspear, Nicholas *See* **Adrian IV.**

Breasted, James Henry 1865–1935. American archaeologist noted for his contributions to the understanding of Egyptian history. His works include *A History of Egypt.*

Brébeuf, Saint Jean de 1593–1649. French Jesuit missionary in Canada among the Huron Indians in New France (1625–29, 1634–49), he was captured and tortured to death in an Iroquois raid.

Brecht, Bertolt 1898–1956. German playwright and poet, and leading figure in 20th-cent. drama. His plays and experimental epic theater emphasized the role of social comment in modern drama. An ardent Communist, he lived in East Germany from 1949. His works include *The Threepenny Opera* (1928), *Mother Courage and Her Children* (1941), and *The Caucasian Chalk Circle* (1955).

Breckinridge, John Cabell 1821–75. American politician. He served as vice-president (1857–61) under J. Buchanan and was an unsuccessful presidential candidate (1860). He served as a Confederate officer and secretary of war (1865) during the American Civil War.

Breda, Compromise of Document signed (1566) by Dutch and Flemish noblemen in the Spanish Netherlands to protest the Inquisition and loss of liberties under Spanish rule. The document is important in the events leading up to the Netherlands revolt against the Spanish. Largely written by Philip van Marnix (1538–98), it was signed by 2,000 Catholic and Protestant noblemen and was presented to Margaret of Parma, the Spanish regent, at Brussels. The nobles, later known as Gueux, were given some satisfaction but sentiment for revolt was only briefly abated.

Breda, Declaration of Document signed (Apr. 4, 1660) by Charles II of England promising to fulfill certain obligations in return for his restoration to the English throne. After the failure of the Protectorate and earlier republican experiments, the Convention Parliament was convened and Charles was invited to return to the throne. He was required only to sign the declaration, which promised amnesty to his former enemies (except the regicides), religious toleration, and back pay owed the army.

Breda, Treaty of Treaty signed (July 31, 1667) by England, the Netherlands, and her allies, France and Denmark, ending the Second Dutch War (1664–67). The English Navigation Acts were changed in favor of Dutch traders and possession of conquered territories by the warring nations was confirmed. The English received the Dutch colonies of New York and New Jersey and regained possessions in the West Indies. The French regained Acadia and retained French Guiana.

Breed's Hill, Battle of *See* **Bunker Hill, Battle of.**

Brehon laws (Feinechus) Ancient Irish legal system, supervised by hereditary judges known as brehons. The system existed in Ireland until the 17th cent., and is noted for its completeness and detail.

Breitenfeld, Battles of Two Swedish victories in the Thirty Years' War (1618–48) at the village of Breitenfeld (now in Germany). 1. In 1631 Swedish king Gustavus Adolphus, leading a 47,000-man army of Swedes and Saxons, defeated Count J. Tilly and his 40,000-man army of the Holy Roman Empire. The battle was the first major Protestant victory and marked the rise of Sweden as a major power. 2. In 1642 the Swedish force invading Saxony under Gen. L. Torstensson surprised and defeated armies of the Holy Roman Empire under Archduke Leopold William (1614–62). Soon after this battle the Swedes captured Leipzig.

Brescia, Arnold of *See* **Arnold of Brescia.**

Brest-Litovsk, Treaty of Short-lived peace treaty signed (Mar. 3, 1918) by Russia and the Central Powers. This treaty ended war between Russia and the German allies but was rendered void by the defeat of Germany and the general armistice ending WW I late in 1918. Russia, weakened by revolution, and now under N. Lenin's leadership, was forced to accept humiliating terms. By the treaty Russia gave up Poland, the Baltic States, and part of Belorus, and recognized the independence of Finland, the Ukraine, and Georgia.

Brétigny, Treaty of (Calais, ˜) Treaty (May 8, 1360) between France and England temporarily ending the Hundred Years' War (1337–1453). The treaty was a result of the French defeat at the Battle of Poitiers (1356), in which French king John II had been taken prisoner. By the treaty John was released on payment of three million gold crowns. France also ceded territories to England, including Aquitane, Gascony, and Calais. In return English king Edward III dropped claims to the French throne. The peace was short-lived and within 13 years France reconquered nearly all territories lost in the treaty.

Breton, André 1896–1966.   French poet, essayist and critic, a founder of the movement known as surrealism.

Breton Succession, War of the   Dynastic struggle in Brittany (1341–65) during the Hundred Years' War. It was ended by the Treaty of Guérande (Apr. 12, 1365), which reestablished rule of the Montfort line in Brittany.

Bretton Woods Conference   Name applied to the United Nations Monetary and Financial Conference, held (July 1–22, 1944) at Bretton Woods, New Hampshire. The conference was called to consider how best to cope with the expected financial problems of the post–WW II world. Its recommendations led to the creation (1945) of the International Bank for Reconstruction and Development, designed for long-term financial aid; and the International Monetary Fund, designed to help stabilize exchange rates and promote international monetary cooperation.

Breuer, Josef 1842–1925.   Austrian physician. He is considered a forerunner of S. Freud. His use of hypnosis and other techniques for the treatment of mental disorders was later developed by Freud and others into psychoanalysis.

Breuer, Marcel Lajos 1902–81.   Hungarian-born American architect and furniture designer. Associated with the Bauhaus, he later worked in partnership with W. Gropius.

Breughel, Jan   *See* **Bruegel, Jan.**

Breughel, Pieter   *See* **Bruegel, Pieter.**

Breviary of Alaric   Compilation of laws, drawn from Roman law and issued (AD 5th cent.) by Visigothic king Alaric II, and binding upon his Roman subjects. Visigoths were ruled by a separate code.

Brewster, William 1567–1644.   English Puritan and an influential leader of the Pilgrims at Plymouth Colony. He helped organize the first party of Pilgrims to sail for America and accompanied them aboard the *Mayflower* (1621).

Brezhnev, Leonid Ilich 1906–82.   Russian Communist leader. He and A. Kosygin became joint leaders of the USSR after the ouster of N. Khrushchev (1964). Brezhnev joined the Communist party in 1931 and later became a protégé of Khrushchev. He was a member of the party Central Committee, first in 1952–53 and again from 1956. He then became chairman of the Supreme Soviet (1960–64), second secretary of the Central Committee (1964), and finally first secretary (Oct., 1964) after Khrushchev's fall

from power. During his term he set forth the Brezhnev Doctrine (1968) in conjunction with the Russian invasion of Czechoslovakia and was instrumental in arranging closer ties with the West, a policy known as détente.

Brezhnev Doctrine   Russian foreign policy statement. Issued (Sept., 1968) by L. Brezhnev, it defended the Russian invasion (Aug., 1968) of Czechoslovakia by stating that Warsaw Pact members had the right to intervene in the affairs of member nations whenever common Socialist interests were threatened.

Brian Boroimhe   *See* **Brian Boru.**

Brian Boru (~ Boroimhe) 926–1014.   Irish king (1002–14). By force of arms he became high king of Ireland, but was killed after his army defeated a coalition of Irish and Danish forces at the Battle of Clontarf (1014).

Briand, Aristide 1826–1932.   French Socialist statesman. Eleven times French premier, and foreign minister from 1925 to 1932, he supported the League of Nations and was a key formulator of the Locarno Pact (1925) and the Kellogg-Briand Pact (1928). He was awarded the Nobel Peace Prize (1926).

Brice's Cross Roads, Battle of   American Civil War battle (June 10, 1864) at Brice's Cross Roads, Mississippi. Some 7,800 Union troops under Gen. Samuel Sturgis (1822–89) were defeated by 3,500 Confederate cavalry under Gen. N. Forrest. Union casualties were 617 dead and wounded, 1,623 captured and Confederates losses were 491.

Bridge of Sighs   Stone bridge in Venice, Italy, connecting the doge's palace, where criminals were tried, with the prison. Built c1600, it received its name from the lamentations of convicted criminals.

Bridger, James (Jim) 1804–81.   American fur trader. One of the Mountain Men, from 1822 he ranged over the Northwest as a trapper, fur trader, and guide and was said to be the first white man to reach the Great Salt Lake, Utah (1824).

Bridget, Saint (Brigid, ~) 453?–523?   One of the three patron saints of Ireland. She founded Ireland's first nunnery at Kildare.

Bridget of Sweden, Saint (Birgitta, ~) 1303?–1373. Swedish visionary and the patron saint of Sweden. Her account of her visions had a wide influence during the Middle Ages.

Bridgewater, Battle of   *See* **Lundy's Lane, Battle of.**

Brienne, John of *See* **John of Brienne.**

Brigid, Saint *See* **Bridget, Saint.**

Brill, Paul 1554–1626. Flemish painter. His landscape paintings influenced the development of Italian art in the 16th and 17th cents.

Brindisi Seaport in southeastern Italy. Mention of the port can be found in Greek legends. After 226 BC it became an important Roman naval station, located at one end of the Appian Way. It later became the port of embarkation for crusaders and was an Italian naval base in WW I.

Brissot de Warville, Jacques Pierre 1754–93. French revolutionary. A leader of the Girondists in the French Revolution, he urged war against Austria (1792). He was executed after a power struggle between the Girondists and the Jacobins.

Britain In modern usage, another name for Great Britain. Britain is the Anglicized form of Britannia, the Roman name for its territories on the British Isles. The term is also specifically applied as a name for the region prior to the Anglo-Saxon invasions of the 5th cent. AD.

Britain, Battle of German bombing raids over Britain (1940–41) during WW II. The raids originally were intended to destroy the Royal Air Force preparatory to the projected invasion of Britain, called Operation Sea Lion. Intensive German air raids began in summer, 1940, and by September the bombing of London and other cities had begun. German aircraft, numbering 1,000 at times, bombed London for 57 consecutive nights. German losses, however, were heavy and by Oct. it became apparent that the Luftwaffe could not gain air supremacy over Britain. By Apr., 1941, the Germans had given up their invasion of Britain and the air raids had tapered off. The battle was the first major German setback and saw the first use of radar in combat.

British Cameroon *See* **Cameroon.**

British Columbia Canadian province on the Pacific coast. Explored and claimed for Great Britain by J. Cook (1778). G. Vancouver mapped the area (1792–94). Explorers such as A. Mackenzie crossed to the Pacific and posts were established in New Caledonia, as the area was known, by fur traders. It became part of Rupert's Land, then controlled by the Hudson's Bay Company (1821). Part of the region, known as the Oregon Country, was ceded (1846) to the US. With the discovery of gold in the Fraser River basin, population increased and it became (1858)

a British crown colony. It became a Canadian province in 1871.

British Commonwealth of Nations Association of Great Britain, its dependencies, and many of its now independent former dependencies. It was established by the Statute of Westminster (Dec. 11, 1931). Its members were originally part of the British Empire but now maintain autonomous governments. The member states enjoy special trade agreements.

British East Africa Collective name of territories once under British control, including Kenya, Uganda, Zanzibar, and Tanganyika. All but Tanganyika became British protectorates between 1890 and 1895. Britain acquired Tanganyika from Germany (1919). The four countries won their independence in the 1960s.

British East India Company British trading company that controlled (18th–19th cents.) commercial and political affairs in India. Chartered (1600) by Queen Elizabeth I to gain a share of the Asian spice trade, the company focused on India after the Amboina Massacre (*q.v.*) in Indonesia (1623). In India, the company defeated the Portuguese (1612) and was granted (1668) political powers by Charles II. It became the United Company (1708) by a merger with a rival British trading company. The French were finally expelled from India (1751–80) by R. Clive and the company became the dominant power in India. British government supervision of the company was effected by the Regulating Act (1773) and the East India Act (1784). The government took over all administrative functions after the Indian Mutiny (1857–58). The United Company was legally dissolved in 1873.

British Empire *See* **Great Britain.**

British Expeditionary Force Name given to British forces sent from England to fight in foreign regions other than those held by the British Empire, and specifically to the British forces in Europe during WW I and WW II.

British Guiana *See* **Guyana.**

British Honduras *See* **Belize.**

British Isles General term for the islands of Great Britain and Ireland, and several thousand small islands, forming an archipelago off western Europe.

British New Guinea *See* **Papua New Guinea.**

British North America Act Legislation (Mar. 29, 1867) by which the British Parliament united Upper and Lower Canada (Ontario and Quebec),

Nova Scotia, and New Brunswick to form the Dominion of Canada. The act also provided a constitutional framework for governing the dominion until Apr., 1982, when constitutional power was formally transferred to Canada.

British Somaliland (Somaliland Protectorate) Former British protectorate in eastern Africa. Under British control from the 1880s, it was joined (1960) with Italian Somaliland to form the republic of Somalia.

Britons Name given to the native Celtic-speaking people who inhabited England at the time of the Roman invasion (1st cent. BC).

Brittany Historic region of northwestern France. Settled (AD c500) by Britons driven from Britain by the Anglo-Saxons, Brittany fought for its independence for centuries, from the Franks, the counts of Anjou, from England, and from France. It was finally united with France through the marriage (1491) of Anne of Brittany to King Charles VIII, and formally incorporated into France in 1532.

Brittany, Anne of *See* **Anne of Brittany.**

Britten, Benjamin 1913–76. English composer, considered the most important British composer since H. Purcell. His works include the operas *Peter Grimes* and *Billy Budd.*

Brock, Sir Isaac 1769–1812. British general. As British military commander in Canada (1806–12), he became famous for capturing Detroit in the War of 1812. He was killed in a later battle.

Brod, Max *See* **Kafka, Franz.**

Broglie, Jacques Victor Albert, duc de Broglie 1821–1901. French historian and statesman. He was twice premier (1873–74, 1877) during the French Third Republic.

Broglie, Victor François, duc de Broglie 1718–1804. French soldier, and marshal of France. He distinguished himself in the War of the Austrian Succession (1740–48) and the Seven Years' War (1756–63), and led the counterrevolutionary army against the French Revolution.

Bronstein, Lev Davidovich *See* **Trotsky, Leon.**

Brontë, Anne 1820–49. English novelist. Her novels were *Agnes Grey* and *The Tenant of Wildfell Hall.*

Brontë, Charlotte 1816–55. English novelist, best known for her novel *Jane Eyre.* A teacher, Brontë returned home after becoming ill and in 1846, collaborating with sisters Anne and Emily, wrote and published a volume of poetry.

The following year her novel *Jane Eyre* became an immediate success. Her other novels included *Shirley* (published in 1849) and *Villette* (1853). She married in 1854 but died just a year later.

Brontë, Emily Jane 1818–48. English novelist and poet, best known for her one novel, *Wuthering Heights.* In 1846, she and her sisters Charlotte and Anne collaborated on a volume of poetry. A year later, she published her novel *Wuthering Heights,* but the book did not meet with immediate success. Brontë died of tuberculosis the next year, never knowing that her novel would eventually be regarded as a classic.

Bronze Age Stage in the development of civilization following the Stone Age when metal replaced stone for tools and weapons. Dating varies according to region and culture. The early part of the Bronze Age is sometimes referred to as the Copper Age and dates from c3500 BC, when copper came into general use in the Near East. Early cultures, such as the Sumerian, Mesopotamian, Minoan, and Mycenaean, developed around the mining, trading, smelting, and casting of metals in following centuries. Bronze did not come into general use until after 2000 BC. The Bronze Age was followed by the Iron Age (*q.v.*)

Brooke, Alan Francis, viscount Alanbrooke 1883–1963. British general. He served with distinction in WW I, and became an expert on artillery and antiaircraft weaponry. During WW II he supervised British defenses during the evacuation at Dunkirk, served as chief of the Imperial Staff.

Brooke, Sir Charles Anthony Johnson 1829–1917. Englishman, the second white rajah of Sarawak, Borneo (1868), and successor to his uncle, J. Brooke. He completed the pacification of native tribes and developed the territory into a prosperous state.

Brooke, Sir James 1803–68. Englishman and first white rajah (1841–68) of Sarawak, a province in Borneo. He was named rajah after helping the Sultan of Borneo to put down a revolt. He created a government for Sarawak, outlawed headhunting and suppressed piracy in the region.

Brooke, Rupert 1887–1915. English poet. The author of two volumes of poetry, he served in the Royal Navy and died during WW I.

Brook Farm Short-lived experimental community, founded (1841) at West Roxbury, Massachusetts, by G. Ripley, and including among its members and guests such notable literary figures as R. Emerson, M. Fuller, and N. Hawthorne.

Brooks, Van Wyck 1886–1963. American critic, biographer, and literary historian. Brooks received a Pulitzer Prize (1937) for *The Flowering of New England,* a volume in his *Makers and Finders* series on American literary history.

Brothers of the Sword, Order of the *See* Livonian Knights.

Broun, Heywood Campbell 1888–1939. American newspaper columnist. He began his liberal column *It Seems to Me* in the 1920s at the New York *World* and continued writing it for other newspapers until his death. He was a founder and first president of the American Newspaper Guild (1933–39).

Browder, Earl Russell 1891–1973. American Communist party leader. A party member from 1919, he was secretary general (1930–44) and candidate for US president (1936, 1940). He was expelled from the party (1946) for supporting free enterprise in the US.

Brown, Charles Brockden 1771–1810. American novelist. The author of *Wieland* and other novels, he is sometimes called the first professional American novelist.

Brown, George 1818–80. Canadian politician and journalist. The founder (1844) of the Toronto *Globe,* he was elected to the Canadian legislature (1851) and led the Clear Grits party. He supported Canadian federation, secularization of the Clergy Reserves, and purchase of what was then the Northwest Territories (Rupert's Land).

Brown, John 1800–1859. American abolitionist. Believing himself divinely appointed to lead southern slaves to freedom, he led the unsuccessful raid on the US arsenal at Harpers Ferry, Va. (Oct. 16, 1859). His composure during his subsequent imprisonment, trial, and execution helped establish him as a leading martyr for the antislavery cause.

Brown, Robert 1773–1858. Scottish botanist. He described Brownian movement, the continuous motion of particles in solution, and discovered the plant cell nucleus.

Browne, Robert *See* Congregationalism; Brownists.

Browning, Elizabeth Barrett 1806–61. English poet, and wife of R. Browning. Her *Sonnets from the Portuguese* is considered her best work.

Browning, Robert 1812–89. English poet, a leading figure in 19th-cent. English poetry. His major work is the four-volume epic *The Ring and the Book.*

Brownists Group advocating separation from the established church in England during the 16th–17th cents. The movement is considered an early form of Congregationalism. Brownists were followers of Robert Browne (c1550–1633), who published tracts (1582) outlining the principles of the movement. The group believed in local, self-governing churches and regulation of their daily lives by covenant. Browne, reconciled to the English church (1591), was denounced by his followers.

Brownson, Orestes Augustus 1803–76. US clergyman and writer. Largely self-educated, he became a Roman Catholic in 1844 and wrote extensively on such subjects as Calvinism, transcendentalism, labor reform, and states' rights. His works included *The Convert* (1857) and *The American Republic* (1865).

Brownsville Affair American racial incident (1906) at Brownsville, Texas. A night shooting raid on the town, resulting in the death of a citizen, was blamed on black soldiers from nearby Ft. Brown. The guilty parties could not be determined, and may not have been the soldiers. Nonetheless, President T. Roosevelt issued a directive giving dishonorable discharges to 167 soldiers. In 1972 the order was reversed by the army and the discharges changed to honorable discharges.

Brown* v. *Board of Education of Topeka, Kansas US Supreme Court decision (May 17, 1954) unanimously overturning an 1896 ruling allowing "separate but equal" facilities for blacks and whites. American public schools thus were forced to integrate racially.

Broz, Josip *See* Tito.

Bruce (Brus) Famous Scottish royal family. The family traces its origins to Robert de Bruce (or Brus) (*fl.* 11th cent.), who helped William I conquer England (1066). The most famous of the family is Robert I (1274–1329), known as Robert the Bruce. The line ended with the death of David II (1371), when the crown passed to the first Stuart king, Robert II.

Bruce of Melbourne, Stanley Melbourne Bruce, viscount 1883–1967. Australian statesman. He served as prime minister (1923–29) and as high commissioner for Australia in London (1933–45).

Bruckner, Anton 1824–96. Austrian composer, known best for his masses and symphonies. He is considered one of the greatest Austrian composers of the 19th cent.

Bruegel, Jan (Brueghel, ˜) (Breughel, ˜) 1568–1625. Flemish painter, called Velvet Bruegel, and known best for his still-life and landscape paintings.

Bruegel, Pieter (˜ the Elder) (Brueghel, ˜) (Breughel, ˜) c1525–69. Flemish painter of landscapes and peasant scenes, considered the greatest of 16th-cent. Flemish painters. He was the head of a long line of painters. His works include *Peasant Wedding* and *Fall of Icarus.*

Brumaire Name of the second month in the French Revolutionary Calendar. On 18 Brumaire (1799) the Directory, composed of revolutionaries, was overthrown and replaced by the Consulate, under Napoleon's control.

Brummell, Beau *See* **Brummell, George Bryan.**

Brummell, George Bryan (Brummell, Beau) 1778–1840. English dandy. Called Beau Brummell, he was a friend of the Prince of Wales (later George IV) and arbiter of English fashion for a time.

Brunanburh, Battle of *See* **Athelstan.**

Brundisium, Treaty of Roman agreement (40 BC), in which M. Antony agreed to rule of the eastern provinces of the Roman Empire, while Octavian ruled the western provinces except for Africa, which remained under control of Lepidus.

Brunechaut *See* **Brunhilda.**

Brunelleschi, Filippo 1377–1446. Florentine architect, one of the greatest of Italian Renaissance architects. His works include the dome for the cathedral at Florence.

Brunei (State of Brunei Darussalam) Independent Muslim sultanate (*pop.* 372,000) in northwest Borneo on the South China Sea. The capital is Bandar Seri Begawan. A powerful sultanate controlling all of Borneo in the 16th cent., it was first visited by Europeans when Magellan's ships arrived in 1521. Military expeditions by Portuguese and Dutch colonial powers quickly reduced Brunei's territories and by the 19th cent. it controlled little more than modern Brunei and Sarawak. Sarawak became a separate sultanate under the British soldier J. Brooke, who quashed a rebellion in Brunei (1841). Brunei became a British protectorate in 1888. Rich oil and gas reserves were discovered there (from 1929), and the country is now one of the world's richest on a per capita basis. A constitution, granted in 1959, returned control of internal affairs to the sultan. Brunei gained independence Jan. 1, 1984.

Brunhilda (Brunechaut) 534?–613. Frankish queen, the wife of Sigebert I of Austrasia (*m.* 561). Her regency of Austrasia (575–613) was marked by a bloody rivalry with Fredegunde (*q.v.*), wife of Chilperic I of Neustria. She seized Neustria, but was defeated and killed by Clotaire II, son of Chilperic I.

Bruning, Heinrich 1885–1970. German statesman. His unpopular policies as chancellor (1930–32) failed to ease Germany's political and economic problems, and he was forced to resign shortly before A. Hitler's rise to power.

Bruno, Giordano 1548–1600. Italian philosopher. His opposition to religious and scientific dogma led to his being burned as a heretic. His ideas influenced later philosophers, notably G. Leibniz and B. Spinoza.

Bruno of Egisheim *See* **Leo IX, Saint.**

Brunswick, Caroline of *See* **Caroline of Brunswick.**

Brunswick Manifesto *See* **French Revolution (1792).**

Brus *See* **Bruce.**

Bruttium (Ager Bruttius) (Calabria) Ancient region located at the southern tip of Italy. It was colonized by the Greeks (8th cent. BC) and conquered by the Romans (3d cent. BC). Renamed Calabria (its modern name) by the Byzantines, who controlled it after the Romans, it became part of the kingdom of Naples (13th cent.) and part of Italy in 1860.

Brutus, Decimus Junius *d.* 43 BC. Roman general. The governor of Gaul, he was, with M. Brutus and others, an assassin of J. Caesar (44 BC). Formerly Caesar's protégé, he nevertheless took part in the assassination and then led a republican army in Cisalpine Gaul against M. Antony. Following reverses, Brutus's troops deserted and he was captured and killed by Gallic tribesmen on Antony's orders.

Brutus, Lucius Junius *fl.* 509 BC. Roman historical figure, said to have led the Romans in driving the Tarquins from Rome and to have founded the Roman republic.

Brutus, Marcus Junius 85–42 BC. Roman soldier and leader. He sided with Pompey in the civil war with J. Caesar, and later joined with Cassius in Caesar's assassination. Defeated by M. Antony and Octavian at Philippi, he committed suicide.

Bryan, William Jennings 1860–1925. American political leader. A gifted orator, he became a leader in the Populist and Free Silver movements and was three times defeated for the presidency of the United States (1896, 1900, 1908). He gave his famous "Cross of Gold" speech at the Democratic convention in 1896. In later years he supported Fundamentalism and was involved in prosecuting the Scopes Trial. Bryan served in Congress (1891–95), and as secretary of state (1913–15) under W. Wilson. Bryan led the prosecution of the Scopes Trial (*q.v.*).

Bryan-Chamorro Treaty US-Nicaraguan treaty (Aug. 14, 1914), by which the US purchased exclusive rights to build a canal across Nicaragua. The canal was never built.

Bryant, William Cullen 1794–1878. American poet and editor. His early poems, such as *Thanatopsis,* made him a leading American poet. Editor and part owner of the New York *Evening Post* (1829–78), he helped to found the Republican party.

Bryce, James Bryce, viscount 1838–1922. British historian and statesman. A leader of the Liberal party, he was a popular and successful ambassador to the United States (1907–13). His works include *The American Commonwealth.*

Buber, Martin 1878–1965. Vienna-born Jewish philosopher. His major works deal with the relationship of man and God, and include *I and Thou.*

Bubonic Plague *See* **Black Plague.**

buccaneers Bands of adventurers of English, French, and Dutch descent that preyed upon the Spanish ships and settlements in the Caribbean and along the South American coast from c1630 to 1690. They became widely known for their exploits under such leaders as H. Morgan. The buccaneers disbanded toward the end of the 17th cent. when many enlisted in the War of the Grand Alliance (1689–97) as privateers.

Bucephalus The favorite horse of Alexander the Great. Alexander built the ancient city of Bucephala, near the present Jhelum, Pakistan, to commemorate the death of the horse (326 BC).

Buchanan, Franklin 1800–74. American naval officer. An organizer and first superintendent (1845–47) of the US Naval Academy, he became the senior naval officer of the Confederacy (1862–64) during the American Civil War. He was captured at the Battle of Mobile Bay (1864).

Buchanan, James 1791–1868. 15th US president (1857–61), successor to F. Pierce. The secession of Southern states began during the last months of his administration. Prior to his election, he was a congressman (1821–31), a senator (1834–45), secretary of state (1845–49) and (variously) a US diplomat. Though personally against slavery, he advocated maintaining the balance between slave and free states. To that end he supported such measures as the Compromise of 1850 and helped formulate the controversial Ostend Manifesto (1854). His part on the latter won him the backing of the South and the presidential election in 1856 as a Democrat. As president he enraged Northern abolitionists by supporting enforcement of the fugitive slave laws and the pro-slavery Lecompton Constitution in the Bleeding Kansas controversy. The Harpers Ferry Raid (1859) increased North-South tensions and, with the Democratic party split, A. Lincoln won the election (1860). In the last months of his administration, Buchanan opposed South Carolina's secession (Dec., 1860) and the seizure of federal forts, but took no decisive action.

Bucharest, Treaties of 1. Treaty (1812) between Russia and Turkey ending the Russo-Turkish War (1806–12). Russia, concerned about the possibility of invasion by Napoleon, sought peace with Turkey. By the treaty's terms, Russia kept Bessarabia and returned Walachia and part of Moldavia. 2. Treaty (1886) ending war between Serbia and Bulgaria over Bulgaria's annexation of Eastern Rumelia. Serbia, defeated, conceded the takeover. 3. Treaty (Aug. 1913) ending Second Balkan War. Defeated Bulgaria received only a small part of territories taken from the Turks in the First Balkan War (1912–13). By the treaty, her former allies, Serbia, Greece, and Rumania, divided most of the territories among themselves. 4. Short-lived treaty (1918) between the Central Powers and defeated Rumania toward the end of WW I. The concessions, including losses of territory and oil leases to the Central Powers, were voided by the Allied victory (1918).

Buchenwald Village in Germany, site of a notorious Nazi death camp. Established after 1933, the camp later became a center for the extermination of Jews and political prisoners. It was captured by American forces in 1945.

Buchman, Frank *See* **Moral Re-armament.**

Buchmanism *See* **Moral Re-armament.**

Buck, Pearl Sydenstricker 1892–1973. American novelist, known best for *The Good Earth* and other novels of life in China. She was awarded a Pulitzer Prize in 1932, and received the Nobel Prize for Literature in 1938.

bucket shop   Name for a type of brokerage house, now illegal, which operated in Britain and the US. The bucket-house operator would delay placing a customer's order, in hopes of making a profit through either the rise or fall of market prices.

Buckingham, George Villiers, 1st duke of 1592–1628.   English statesman. He held great power during the reigns of James I and Charles I, and used it to enrich his relatives. His abuses and disastrous military adventures in Spain and France aroused the wrath of Parliament, which was dissolved by Charles. He was assassinated by a discontented naval officer.

Buckingham, George Villiers, 2d duke of 1628–87.   English courtier and son of James I's favorite, the 1st duke of Buckingham. He supported Charles II in the English Civil Wars (1642–48). After the Restoration (1660–88) he regained the estates he had lost, and became a powerful figure at court and a member of the Cabal ministry.

Buckingham Palace   The British royal family residence in London since 1837. The building originally belonged to the duke of Buckingham and was bought (1761) by George III for his wife. Since the time of Queen Victoria the 600-room building has been designated a royal residence.

Buckle, Henry Thomas 1821–62.   English historian. He completed only two volumes of his *History of Civilization in England,* which influenced the scientific method of writing history.

Budaeus   *See* **Budé Guillaume.**

Buddha c563–c483 BC.   Title (Sanskrit for "enlightened one") of Siddhartha Gautama, the founder of Buddhism (*q.v.*), one of the world's great religions. The son of Suddhodana (*fl.* c6th cent. BC), a king of the Sakya tribe in what is now Nepal, and his wife Mahamaya, Siddhartha at the age of 29 gave up a life of ease to seek the path to enlightenment. After attaining it he spent the rest of his life teaching others.

Buddhism   Religion that originated with the teachings of Buddha in India during the 6th–5th cents. BC. Buddhism arose in opposition to Hinduism, though it shares concepts of bondage in cycles of birth, suffering, and death and escape from this cycle through attainment of nirvana. Many schools of Buddhist thought sprang from Buddha's teachings, though all accept Buddha's

fundamental doctrine of the Four Noble Truths (existence is suffering; suffering has a cause within the self; one may be freed of suffering; following the precepts of the Eightfold Path ends suffering and leads to nirvana). The two main schools of Buddhist thought in modern times arose from a split that developed in the 4th cent. BC. The two schools are Mahayana and Theraveda. Though Buddhism has virtually disappeared in India, it is prevalent in Japan, Korea, China, Tibet, and in Southeast Asia. *See also* Tibetan Buddhism, Pure Land Buddhism, Zen Buddhism. Key events in the spread of Buddhism include:

c528 BC   Buddhism founded; Siddhartha, after six years of wandering in search of spiritual truth, discovered enlightenment (c528 BC) while meditating at Buddha Gaya (now in northeast India); articulated his Four Noble Truths in first sermon soon after; as Buddha, spent the rest of his life spreading his teachings.

c483 BC   Buddha died; his teachings at first spread orally by his followers.

c340 BC   Various factions among the rising Buddhist movement split into two great sects these eventually became the Mahayana (Greater Vehicle) and the Theraveda or Hinayana (Lesser Vehicle), the major divisions of modern Buddhism.

c273–c232 BC   Indian Emperor Asoka promoted the spread of Buddhist teachings; had "Rock Edicts," containing Buddhist principles, engraved on stones and pillars throughout the Mauryan empire; sent Buddhist missionaries to Ceylon and elsewhere.

2D–1ST CENTS. BC   Various Buddhist schools put their own versions of Buddhist teachings in written form; Pali Canon, earliest surviving example of them, written (c29–17 BC) by the Theraveda school in Ceylon.

1ST CENT. BC   Mahayana sutras written, marked rise of Mahayana school.

1ST CENT. AD   Buddhism introduced in China.

4TH CENT. AD   Buddhism spread from China to Korea.

EARLY 5TH CENT. AD   Buddhaghosa, Ceylonese Buddhist scholar, wrote his famous work on Buddhist doctrines, *Way to Purity.*

6TH CENT.   Centers of Buddhism in India destroyed during invasions by White Huns; Buddhism in India began to decline.

6TH CENT. Buddhism spread from Korea to Japan; won only limited following among the nobility until the 12th cent.

6TH CENT. Buddhism introduced in Burma.

6TH CENT. Rise of Zen Buddhism and Pure Land Buddhism in China; eventually became dominant schools of Buddhism there.

7TH CENT. Practices of the Tantra spread among Buddhists; magic, ritual, and spells used to attain various ends, both religious and practical.

7TH CENT. Buddhism introduced in Tibet; rise of Tibetan Buddhism began.

9TH CENT. In China, great persecution of Buddhists ordered (845) by Tang dynasty emperor; restoration of Confucianism (neo-Confucianism) under the Tang emperors further increased opposition to Buddhism in China.

11TH–13TH CENTS. Final decline of Buddhism in India; Buddhism was nearly eliminated in the centuries following absorption by Hinduism, invasions by Muslims of the Ghaznavid dynasty.

12TH CENT. Zen and Pure Land Buddhism became widespread in Japan.

Budé, Guiliaume (Budaeus) 1467–1540. French scholar. A leading Renaissance scholar, he persuaded Francis I to found the Collège de France, and assembled a library that became the Bibliothèque Nationale.

Budge, Sir Ernest Alfred Wallis 1857–1934. English archaeologist who collected and translated many ancient texts and supervised excavations in Egypt, Mesopotamia, and the Sudan for the British Museum.

Buena Vista, Battle of US victory (Feb. 22–23, 1847) over Mexican forces in the Mexican War (1846–48). US forces numbering 5,000 men under Gen. Z. Taylor were met by a Mexican force of 15,000 under Gen. A. de Santa Anna near the hacienda of Buena Vista in northeastern Mexico. In the two-day battle, US forces were hard pressed but eventually won with the aid of artillery barrages. US casualties numbered some 700 to about 1,500 Mexicans.

Buffalo Bill (Cody, William Frederick) 1846–1917. American scout, buffalo hunter, and Indian fighter. His adventures in the West were the subject of numerous dime novels by N. Buntline and others. In 1883 he formed his celebrated Wild West Show and toured the United States and abroad. Cody, Wyoming, stands on the site of his ranch.

Buganda Former East African kingdom, located north of Lake Victoria in what now is Uganda. The leading kingdom of East Africa in the 19th cent., it was the center of a flourishing ivory trade. The kingdom came under the control (1890s) of the Imperial British East Africa Company and was incorporated into Great Britain's Uganda Protectorate. The kingdom continued to exist until 1967, when it became part of the Republic of Uganda and its monarchy was abolished.

Bukhari, al- 810–870. Muslim scholar. His collection of the sayings of the Muslim prophet Muhammad, *al-Sahih,* is regarded by orthodox Muslims as second only to the Koran in religious importance.

Bukharin, Nikolai Ivanovich 1888–1938. Russian Communist party leader. A Bolshevik, he was a member of the ruling Communist Politburo (1924–29). Ousted (1929) from party leadership for opposing Stalin's policy of agricultural reform, he later became a victim of Stalin's Purge Trials and was executed for treason.

Bulfinch, Charles 1763–1844. American architect. As the fourth and last architect of the Capitol building in Washington, D.C., he supervised its completion (1817–30). Among his other buildings are the Massachusetts State House and the Connecticut State House.

Bulganin, Nikolai Aleksandrovich 1895–1975. Soviet political leader. With the support of N. Khrushchev he became premier in 1955. He opposed Khrushchev (1957) and was expelled from the Central Committee and replaced by Khrushchev (1958).

Bulgaria Republic in southeastern Europe, situated on the eastern part of the Balkan Peninsula on the Black Sea. The population is 8,978,000 and the capital is Sofia. Once part of the Roman Empire, Bulgaria was dominated for centuries by the Ottoman Turks. Bulgaria was established as an autonomous principality after the Russo-Turkish War of 1877–78. It fell to the Soviets during WW II and thereafter remained under Soviet domination until economic chaos, coupled with pro-democracy protests in 1989–90, finally brought down the Communist regime. Key dates in the history of Bulgaria include:

6TH CENT. AD Thrace and Moesia (now modern Bulgaria) settled by Slavic tribes.

7TH CENT. Bulgars invaded the region and merged with the other Slavs.

680–1018 First Bulgarian Empire; established by Khan Asparuhk; Bulgarians thereafter repeatedly threatened the Byzantine Empire.

852–889 Boris I ruled; Christianity introduced.

893–927 Empire reached its zenith under Bulgarian tsar Simeon.

10TH CENT. Rise of the heretical Bogomil sect.

969–976 Byzantine emperor John I drove the Russians out of Bulgaria soon after their forces invaded.

1018 Bulgarian Empire made part of Byzantine Empire by Basil II; remained under Byzantines to 1185.

1185–1396 Second Bulgarian Empire; established by Ivan Asen.

1218–41 Ivan II reigned in Bulgaria; conquered much of Balkan Peninsula.

1330 Bulgaria defeated by Serbs; made a tributary.

1389–96 Ottoman Turks invaded and conquered Bulgaria; centuries of Turkish domination followed.

1876 Bulgarians, led by Stefan Stambulov, revolted against Ottomans; Turks killed 15,000 in reprisals (Bulgarian Horrors); Europe aroused against Ottomans.

1877–78 Russo-Turkish War; subsequent Treaty of San Stefano altered by Congress of Berlin.

1878 Congress of Berlin following Russo-Turkish War; autonomous Bulgaria (under Ottoman suzerainty) created, though much smaller than that sought by Russia; Eastern Rumelia (southern part of modern Bulgaria) made autonomous province under Ottoman suzerainty; Macedonia remained under direct Ottoman control.

1879 Russian tsar's nephew, Prince Alexander of Battenberg, made ruler of Bulgaria.

1885–86 Eastern Rumelia annexed by Bulgaria; led to Serbo-Bulgarian War (1885–86) in which Serbia was defeated.

1887–1918 Prince Ferdinand of Saxe-Coburg-Gotha ruled; succeeded following Alexander's abdication (1886).

1908 Ferdinand declared complete independence; made himself tsar.

1912–13 First Balkan War; Bulgaria and allies defeated Ottoman Turks.

1913 Second Balkan War; Bulgaria sought larger share of conquered territories, but was defeated by former allies.

1914–18 WW I; Bulgaria sided with Central Powers (1915) in hopes of regaining territories lost in Second Balkan War; retook Macedonia and Dobruja (1916); forced to sign armistice with allies (1918).

1918–43 Boris III reigned; succeeded on his father's abdication.

1919 Treaty of Neuilly formally ended hostilities of WW I; Bulgaria lost substantial territories.

1920–23 Aleksandr Stamboliski, leader of peasant Agrarian party, in office as premier; overthrown and killed in coup (1923).

1925 Greece invaded Bulgaria but the conflict was ended by the League of Nations.

1935 Boris III assumed dictatorial powers.

1940–45 WW II; Hitler forced Rumania to cede southern Dobruja to Bulgaria (1940); Bulgaria joined Axis Powers and was occupied by Nazis (1941); Boris died under suspicious circumstances after refusing Hitler's demand to break relations with Soviets (1943); Boris succeeded by his son, Simeon II; Soviets invaded Bulgaria and won immediate armistice (1944).

1946 Monarchy abolished and people's republic established (Sept.).

1946 Communist leader Vasil Kolarov became first head of state.

1947 One-party system established; farms collectivized and industry nationalized on Soviet pattern.

1950–56 Valko Chervenkov, the "Bulgarian Stalin" and Bulgarian Communist Party (BCP) leader, in office as prime minister.

1950 Purge of Communist party instituted by Chervenkov.

1951–52 160,000 citizens of Turkish origin deported.

1954–89 Todor Zhivkov (1911–) in power as head of Communist party; he was effective ruler of Bulgaria until his ouster in 1989; kept Bulgaria closely tied to USSR during his long reign.

1955 Entered Warsaw Pact.

1961 Former prime minister Chervenkov expelled from Politburo during anti-Stalin purge; expelled from the party in 1962, he was politically rehabilitated in 1969.

1965   Unsuccessful army coup.

1968   Aided Russian invasion of Czechoslovakia.

1971   New constitution adopted.

1971–81   Stanko Todorov in office as prime minister.

1978   Government instituted New Economic Mechanism program; state-run businesses and organizations to become self-supporting, with aggregate wages tied to performance; ignoring initial lack of success, government in 1980 extended plan to state-run cultural, health, tourist, and even sports organizations.

1980   Former party leader Valko Cherenkov, the "Bulgarian Stalin," died.

1981–86   Grisha Filipov in office as prime minister, replacing Stanko Todorov; Todorov made chairman of National Assembly.

1981   1300th anniversary of Bulgarian state celebrated; 90th anniversary of Bulgarian Communist Party (BCP) also marked.

1982   Bulgarian state security agents linked with attempted assassination of Pope John Paul II in 1981; three Bulgarians indicted in Italy (1984) while embarrassed Bulgarian government denied involvement; suspects eventually acquitted for lack of evidence (1986).

1984   Terrorist bombings reported in Bulgaria, the first incidents of violent opposition to Communist regime in years; 9 killed next year in train bombing.

1985   Brutality and outright killings reported in government's "Bulgarization" program, designed to force country's 10–15% Muslim Turkish minority to abandon Muslim beliefs and customs; government refused to permit emigration.

1985–86   Shortages of energy and other basic goods reported; blamed on inefficiency and mismanagement.

1986   Chernobyl nuclear disaster in USSR; Bulgarian government withheld warnings to citizens about radiation dangers for 11 days.

1986–90   Georgi Atanasov in office as prime minister.

1987   Zhivkov's Bulgarian *perestroika* (restructuring) resulted in outright chaos (Apr.–July); ordered transfer of "socialist properties" to workers' collectives, which were to manage them, but left implementation details unclear; local government system massively reorganized (Aug.).

1987   Zhivkov called to Moscow (Oct. 15) for undisclosed talks, possibly relating to his chaotic reform program.

1987   Government ordered agricultural sector reorganized following disastrous harvest (Dec.).

1988   Government publicly admitted failures in implementing restructuring policies; Zhivkov blamed obstruction by middle-level managers.

1988   Economy now in shambles; chronic shortages worsened and Bulgaria's foreign debt rose sharply; price reform raised 25% of all wholesale prices (Jan.).

1989   Month-long hunger strike by Bulgarian poet Petar Manolov, following police raid on human rights meeting at his apartment (Jan.).

1989   Muslim Democratic League staged relay hunger strikes and street protests in opposition to Zhivkov's forced Bulgarization program (May); police brutality against Muslim protesters sparked mass exodus to Turkey by some 320,000 (May–Aug.).

1989   Long-time party head Zhivkov removed in coup (Nov 10), mounted (allegedly with Soviet approval) by Foreign Minister Petar Mladenov and Defense Minister Dobri Dzhurov.

1989   Berlin Wall, symbol of Communist bloc's hard-line isolationist policies, was opened in Germany (Nov.).

1989   Mladenov in power as head of state and BCP leader; new government promised multi-party democracy and market economy for Bulgaria; ideological police disbanded; free elections promised for June 1990.

1989   Ruling Politburo and National Assembly purged of Zhivkov supporters (Nov.–Dec.); Zhivkov expelled from party and put under arrest on charges of corruption and abuse of power.

1989   Reform BCP government took steps (Dec.) to legalize opposition parties and to dismantle laws guaranteeing the Communist party's role in government; Muslim minority civil rights restored (Dec. 29).

1989   Mass demonstrations against Communist party (Dec.); protesters formed human chain around Parliament.

1990   Andrei Lukanov in office as new BCP prime minister (Feb.); suspended payments on foreign debt as economic crisis worsened.

1990   Some 200,000 attended pro-democracy rally in Sofia (Feb. 25), organized by new opposition party Union of Democratic Forces (UDF).

1990 BCP adopted new name, Bulgarian Socialist Party (BSP) in Apr., following party reorganization along more liberal lines; hardline Communists maintained hold on party, however.

1990 Liberalized BSP won narrow victory in nationwide election (June); protests and political unrest forced President Mladenov to resign (July 6).

1990– Zhelyu Zhelev, UDF leader, in office as president, following split in BSP vote (Aug.); Lukanov formed new BSP government (Sept.).

1990 Rioters burned BSP headquarters in Sofia (Aug. 26).

1990 Food rationing imposed in Sofia (Sept. 1) amid worsening shortages and runaway inflation.

1990 Lukanov resigned (Nov. 29) following renewed student anti-government protests and a general strike by workers.

1990–91 Independent Dimitar Popov in office as prime minister (Dec.); formed three-sided coalition government (UDF, BSP, and BANU, the Bulgarian Agrarian National Union).

1991 Former Communist party boss Zhivkov put on trial (Feb.); convicted in 1992.

1991 US granted Bulgaria most-favored-nation status; marked Bulgaria's pro-West shift.

1991 Coalition government implemented shift to market economy, imposing radical price and interest-rate hikes without public opposition; passed land-reform law to return farms confiscated for Communist collectives.

1991 New democratic constitution promulgated by coalition government (July 12).

1991 Bulgaria negotiated new agreement on repaying its foreign debt.

1991 UDF won parliamentary majority in elections (Oct.); with support from Muslim Movement for Rights and Freedoms (MRF), formed government free of ex-Communists.

1991– UDF leader Filip Dimitrov in office as prime minister; promised program for quick privatization; froze assets of Communist BSP.

Bulgarian Horrors Name applied to the brutal suppression of the 1876 Bulgarian uprising against Ottoman rule. The name was derived from the title of a pamphlet by W. Gladstone which attacked B. Disraeli's pro-Ottoman foreign policy. *See* Bulgaria 1876.

Bulgaroktonos *See* **Basil II.**

Bulge, Battle of the (Ardennes, ˜) Unsuccessful German counterattack (1944–45) on Allied positions in Belgium during WW II. It was the last major German offensive on the Western Front. German armored divisions under Field Marshal G. von Rundstedt launched their surprise attack (Dec. 16) during a period of bad weather in the Ardennes, southern Belgium, in hopes of splitting the Allied forces and of taking the strategic port of Antwerp. They drove 60 miles into Allied territory, creating a "bulge" in the lines. Allied resistance, notably the heroic stand by an American division at Bastogne under command of Gen. Anthony C. McAuliffe (1898–1975), helped to stall the Germans. Improved flying weather allowed Allied air forces to support counterattacks, forcing the Germans to retreat (Jan.).

bull In the Roman Catholic church, a document or pronouncement by the pope, of greater importance than a papal brief or encyclical. Papal bulls deal with such matters as canonizations, pronouncements of church doctrine, and the like. *See also* Golden Bull.

bullbaiting *See* **bearbaiting.**

Bullen, Anne *See* **Boleyn, Anne.**

Bullinger, Heinrich *See* **Basel, Confession of; Helvetik Confession.**

Bull Moose Name given members of the first Progressive party, also known as the Bull Moose party, which was formed in the US (1912–16) to support the presidential candidacy of T. Roosevelt.

Bull Run, Battles of (Manassas, ˜) American Civil War battles fought in northern Virginia. 1. Confederate victory (July 21, 1861) which halted a Union drive, led by Gen. I. McDowell, from Washington toward Richmond. Some 32,000 Confederates under Gen. P. Beauregard forced the 37,000-man Union army to retreat after hard fighting. Casualties were about 3,000 Union to 2,000 Confederate. 2. Confederate victory (Aug. 29–30, 1862). Gen. R. Lee's 56,000-man Confederate force attacked a 70,000-man Union army, led by Gen. J. Pope, at Bull Run and forced Pope to retreat to Washington. Casualties were about 9,000 Confederate to 16,000 Union.

Bülow, Bernhard Heinrich Martin, Fürst von 1849–1929. German statesman. As chancellor of Germany (1900–09) he attempted to strengthen Germany's position as a world power, but instead his policies strengthened the Triple Entente of Britain, France, and Russia.

Bulwer, Sir Henry *See* **Clayton-Bulwer Treaty.**

Buoncompagni, Ugo *See* **Gregory XIII.**

Bunau-Varilla, Philippe Jean 1859–1940. French engineer. Chief engineer of the French Panama Canal project, he worked to sell the project to the US after the French failure (1889), helped instigate the revolution that led to Panamanian independence, and as Panamanian minister negotiated the Hay-Bunau-Varilla Treaty (1903), which gave the US control of the Canal Zone.

Bunche, Ralph Johnson 1904–71. American diplomat. A founder of the United Nations, he worked to negotiate an Arab-Israeli truce in 1949 for which he received the 1950 Nobel Peace Prize.

Bundestag German legislature, the popularly elected lower house of the parliament of Germany. It is responsible for election of the chancellor.

Bunin, Ivan Alekseevich 1870–1953. Russian poet and novelist, author of *The Village.* He was awarded the Nobel Prize in Literature (1933).

Bunker Hill, Battle of (Breed's Hill, ~) Victory (June 17, 1775) for American Colonials over the British early in the American Revolution (1775–83). The first major battle of the war, it proved the Colonial militia could stand up to the British regulars and thus aided the cause of the revolution. The Colonial militia had laid siege to Boston soon after the war began. To block the first British attempt to break the siege, Col. W. Prescott and some 1,000 militiamen were sent (June 16) to fortify Bunker Hill, north of Colonial Boston. The following afternoon, 3,000 British troops, sent by Gen. T. Gage, attacked the fortifications (actually located on nearby Breed's Hill). The Colonials, ordered by Prescott to hold fire until they saw "the whites of the enemy's eyes," withstood two British charges. Out of ammunition, they were forced to retreat on the third. The British sustained heavy casualties (about 1,000 to 450 Americans) and failed to break the siege.

Bunsen, Robert Wilhelm 1811–99. German chemist. With G. Kirchhoff he pioneered spectrum analysis and discovered the elements cesium and rubidium. He introduced the Bunsen burner.

Bunyan, John 1628–88. English preacher and author, whose Christian allegory *The Pilgrim's Progress* is a classic of English literature.

Burbage, James *d.* 1597. English actor. At Shoreditch (now part of London) he built *c*1576 the first English theater, known as The Theatre. It was later moved and rebuilt as the Globe Theatre.

Burckhardt, Jacob Christoph 1818–97. A Swiss historian. His best-known work, *The Civilization of the Renaissance in Italy,* was a model for later works employing a cultural treatment of history.

Burckhardt, Johann Ludwig *See* **Burckhardt, John Lewis.**

Burckhardt, John Lewis (~, Johann Ludwig) 1784–1817. Swiss explorer of Africa and the Middle East. He rediscovered the ancient city of Petra (1812) and traveled to Mecca (1814).

Burger, Warren Earl 1907– . American jurist. Burger was appointed chief justice of the Supreme Court by R. Nixon (1969). Burger was a conservative and his decisions reflected his concern for judicial restraint.

Burgesses, House of American Colonial assembly. Established in Virginia (July 30, 1619), it was the first representative governing body in America.

Burghley, William Cecil, 1st baron (Burleigh, ~) 1520–98. English statesman. Appointed secretary of state (1558) and lord high treasurer (1572), he was chief adviser to Elizabeth I for 40 years and leader of the pro-peace faction in Elizabeth's court.

Burgoyne, John 1722–92. British general and dramatist. He distinguished himself during the Seven Years' War (1756–63), but was defeated at Saratoga (1777) during the American Revolution. He wrote several popular plays, among them *The Heiress* (1786).

Burgundians French political faction that engaged in civil war (1411–18) against the rival Armagnacs for control of France in the 15th cent. The conflict began (1407) when John the Fearless, duke of Burgundy, murdered his rival, Louis, duke of Orléans (brother of the insane French king Charles VI), in a struggle for control of the French throne. John's opponents, the Armagnacs, were so named after their leader Bernard VII, count of Armagnac. He was the father-in-law of Charles, the new duke of Orléans. The conflict led to English intervention (1415) under Henry V, who defeated the duke of Orléans at Agincourt (Oct. 25, 1415) and reconquered Normandy. The civil war thus became part of the Hundred Years' War. The Burgundians captured Paris (1418) and massacred many Armagnacs. John the Fearless was later assassinated (1419) while negotiating with the dauphin (later Charles VII) of France. John's son, Philip the Good, then signed the Treaty of Troyes (1420), allying the Burgundians with the English and declaring English king Henry V regent of France. The ascendancy of the Burgundians came when Philip signed the Treaty of Arras (1435), by which he recognized the new king Charles VII as rightful king of France and allied with him against the English. The power of the Armagnacs declined thereafter.

Burgundy Historic region of eastern France. Settled (AD 5th cent.) by the Germanic Burgundians, it came under the rule of the Merovingians (6th cent.), and was partitioned several times before being reunited (933) as the Second Kingdom of Burgundy. It entered its period of greatest power as a duchy under the rule of Philip the Bold (1342–1404), who received it (1364) from his father John II of France. Philip's descendants greatly increased its territories. After the death of Charles the Bold (1477), most of its possessions passed to the Habsburgs, but the duchy itself was incorporated into France, remaining a province until its division in the French Revolution.

Burgundy, Henry of *See* **Henry of Burgundy.**

Buridan, Jean *d.* c1358. French philosopher. As rector of the University of Paris, he taught nominalism. The allegorical Buridan's Ass, an animal starving between two identical stacks of hay, is identified (incorrectly) with his discussion of the will and moral dilemma.

Burke, Edmund 1729–97. British statesman and political philosopher. He is considered a major British political thinker for his views on Britain's government and its policies toward Ireland, France, India, and the colonies. He became a member of Parliament (1765) in the Whig party, was sympathetic to the cause of American colonials, helped bring about Lord North's resignation, and supported abolition of the slave trade. He opposed the radicalism of the French Revolution in *Reflections on the French Revolution.*

Burke, Martha Jane *See* **Calamity Jane.**

Burkina Faso (*formerly* Republic of Upper Volta) Republic located south of the Sahara Desert on the southern border of Mali in western Africa. Its population is 8,941,000 and the capital is Ouagadougou. The region has been inhabited since Neolithic times and pooples known as the Mossi and Gurma established kingdoms in the region (14th cent.). The French later declared protectorates over the two kingdoms (1895, 1897

respectively). They were created the colony of Upper Volta in 1919 and made an autonomous republic within the French Community in 1958. Independence was achieved Aug. 5, 1960, and beginning in 1966 a long period of instability followed, including coups and unsuccessful attempts at restoring democratic government, that lasted through the 1980s. In 1991 a new constitution was adopted establishing a multiparty democracy. The country's name was changed to Burkina Faso in 1984.

Burleigh, William Cecil, 1st baron *See* **Burghley, William Cecil, 1st baron.**

Burlingame, Anson *See* **Burlingame Treaty.**

Burlingame Treaty Treaty (1868) of friendship between the US and China. It was negotiated by Anson Burlingame (1820–70), a former American diplomat who had become an envoy of the Chinese emperor. By it China recognized Western principles of international law and the US recognized China's territorial sovereignty. The treaty also opened the way for large-scale immigration of Chinese laborers to the US.

Burma *See* **Myanmar.**

Burma War (Burmese ~) (Anglo-Burmese ~) 1. First ~ War (1824–26) brought on by a Burmese invasion (1823) of eastern territories in British India. The British invaded Burma (1824) and took Rangoon easily. Despite stiffening resistance, British forces moved northward and eventually defeated the Burmese army (1825). By the Treaty of Yandabo (Feb. 24, 1826), the Burmese ceded coastal provinces to British India, including Arakan and Tenasserim. 2. Second ~ War (1852) brought on by friction between the Burmese monarchy and British traders in Burma. The British invaded (1852) Burma, captured all of the south, but did not advance to the north. The British annexed (Jan., 1853) the province of Pegu and a revolution in the north brought the accession of King Mindon, who did not challenge the British conquests. 3. Third ~ War (1885–86) in which the British completed their conquest of Burma and ended the rule of the Konbaung dynasty. The invasion of the remaining independent northern territories was provoked by continuing friction between British traders and the Burmese monarch, Thibaw (1858–1916, reigned 1878–85). Thibaw surrendered late in 1885 and the British formally annexed Burma (Jan. 1, 1886), though guerrilla warfare against the British continued for several years.

Burnett, Frances Eliza Hodgson 1849–1924. English-born American writer, known best as author of *Little Lord Fauntleroy.*

Burnham, Daniel Hudson 1846–1912. American architect and city planner. He designed early steel-frame "skyscrapers" such as the Chicago Masonic Temple building (1892) and devised (1907–09) a far-sighted plan for the development of the city of Chicago. He oversaw construction of the World's Columbian Exposition in Chicago (1893).

Burning of the Books Famous incident in ancient China, in which the Qin government under Emperor Shi Huangdi attempted to destroy all writings critical of its authoritarian form of government (213 BC). Huangdi's chancellor, Li Si, led the call for the edict, which effectively imposed his Legalist views on Confucian and other scholars. Some books were burned and several scholars executed.

Burns, John 1858–1943. British labor leader. As president of the Local Government Board (1905–14), he became the first working-class man to serve in a British cabinet.

Burns, Robert 1759–96. Scottish national poet and one of the world's most celebrated poets. He captured and enriched the spirit of Scottish folk tradition. Though raised on a farm, he was well educated and after failing as a farmer he turned (1786) to publishing his poetry. He enjoyed immediate success with *Poems, Chiefly in the Scottish Dialect,* and thereafter devoted himself to writing poems and songs of rural Scotland. He wrote such poems as "Tam o' Shanter" and "The Jolly Beggars" and the ever-popular song "Auld Lang Syne."

Burnside, Ambrose Everett 1824–81. Union general in the US Civil War. He fought in the first battle of Bull Run and Antietam. Succeeding G. McClellan (1862) as commander of the Army of the Potomac, he was relieved following his defeat at Fredericksburg.

Burr, Aaron 1756–1836. US vice-president (1801–05) who was later charged with treason (1807). Once a US senator from New York (1791–97), Burr served as the third US vice-president under T. Jefferson. While in office he killed (1804) his political rival, A. Hamilton, in a duel. His political career finished, he sought to create an independent country in what was then Spanish territory. An associate, Gen. J. Wilkinson, betrayed him and reported that Burr had also intended to encourage the secession of western US territories. Tried (1807) for treason and acquitted, he lived out the rest of his life in obscurity.

Burroughs, Edgar Rice 1875–1950. American author of adventure novels, known best as the creator of the Tarzan stories.

Bursa (Brusa) (Prusa) Turkish city and center of the Turkish silk industry. Founded in the 3d cent. BC, it was the capital of Bithynia and was called Prusa. It was the first capital of the Ottoman Empire (1326–1413).

Burundi Republic (*pop.* 5,647,000) in east central Africa on Lake Tanganyika. The capital is Bujumbura. The country's majority population is Hutu, a people that settled in the region by the 11th cent. The rival Tutsi people arrived in the 14th–15th cents. The territory was later claimed (1890) by Germany as part of German East Africa and was then taken by Belgium in WW I. Incorporated into the League of Nations mandate of Ruanda-Urundi, it became a UN trust territory in 1946. Belgium continued to rule through the native monarchical government until Burundi's independence (1962). Conflict between the country's two major ethnic groups, the Tutsi and Hutu, cost upward of 100,000 lives after establishment of the republic (1966), and in the 1970s the Tutsi emerged as the dominant group within Burundi. Some 20,000 people were killed in new tribal warfare in 1988, after which the Hutus were granted a greater role in the government. Renewed inter-tribal killings (1991) came amid efforts at establishing a new democratic constitution.

Bury, John Bagnell 1861–1927. British historian and authority on the late Roman and Byzantine empires.

Büsching, Anton Friedrich 1724–93. German geographer. His emphasis on the use of statistical data helped to establish geography as a science.

Bush, George Herbert Walker 1924– . Forty-first US president (1989–1993), successor to R. Reagan. One of five children, Bush served as a Navy pilot (1942–45) in the Pacific theater during WW II and earned the Distinguished Flying Cross. After the war, he married Barbara Pierce (1945), graduated from Yale, and established himself as a businessman in Texas. Entering politics as a Republican, he served as a US Congressman (1967–71), as US ambassador to the UN (1971–72), director of the CIA (1976–77), and then as vice-president (1981–89) under R. Reagan. After becoming president, Bush ordered the invasion of Panama to unseat Panamanian strongman M. Noriega and had him brought back to the US for trial on drug charges. Bush's term also saw the unfolding of the savings and loan crisis, and an ill-fated deal with Democrats in Congress, in which Bush broke a campaign pledge and agreed to new taxes in return for limits on government spending. By late 1990, the US slid into a recession, however, and the rest of Bush's term was marked by a weak or slowly recovering economy, with low inflation but high unemployment and an ever-increasing deficit. Bush's greatest successes came in matters of foreign policy. Amid the collapse of Communism in Eastern Europe and the USSR itself, he won important arms and military troop reduction agreements with the Soviets (and their successors) and, with the Soviet leaders, declared an end to the long Cold War. Meanwhile the US under Bush also took the lead in organizing world political and military opposition to Iraqi aggression in the Persian Gulf War (*q.v.*). Hampered by a sluggish economy in 1992 and a third party candidacy mounted by conservative businessman Ross Perot, Bush lost his bid for election to a second term.

Bushidō Term meaning "way of the warrior" and a code of conduct in Japan identified with Samurai warriors. The code developed from feudal times and stressed personal honor and, above all, loyalty to the feudal lord. Formulated during the Tokugawa shogunate (1600–1868), it reflected the values and lifestyles of the daimyo and samurai in the 17th cent. In the 19th cent. the code was made the basis for fierce loyalty to the emperor and influenced Japanese thought and behavior until the end of WW II.

Bushman Member of an ancient indigenous African tribe, living primarily in southern Africa.

Bushnell, David 1742–1824. American inventor, sometimes called the father of the submarine. His submarine, the *Turtle,* invented in 1775, is considered a forerunner of modern submarines.

Bushnell, Horace 1802–76. American Congregational minister. His theological views had a major influence on the growth of religious liberalism. Bushnell wrote *Christian Nurture* (1847), among other works.

bushrangers Australian bandits of the 19th cent. Originally escaped convicts, they terrorized the bush country from the late 1700s to 1880, when the last band was caught and killed. They have become part of Australian folk history.

Busta Gallorum, Battle of (Battle of Taginae) Battle (AD 552) in which Byzantine General Narses defeated the Goths in Italy and killed their leader, Totila. The battle brought much of Italy under Byzantine rule.

Butades of Sicyon *fl.* c600 BC. Greek sculptor who worked at Corinth. He is believed to have been the first to sculpt in clay.

Bute, John Stuart, 3d earl of 1713–92. British statesman who had great influence with King George III early in his reign. As prime minister (1762–63) he negotiated the Treaty of Paris (1763), ending the Seven Years' War (1756–63).

Butler, Benjamin Franklin 1818–93. American politician and Union general in the American Civil War, noted for his harsh measures as military governor of New Orleans (1862). As a Massachusetts representative in Congress (1867–75, 1877–79), he helped lead radical Republicans in adopting reconstruction and impeaching President A. Johnson.

Butler, John 1728–96. Notorious American Loyalist commander during the American Revolution. His mixed force of whites and Indians, called Butler's Rangers, perpetrated the Wyoming Massacre (1778) in Pennsylvania's Wyoming Valley.

Butler, Samuel 1835–1902. An English author of the Utopian satire *Erewhon* and the autobiographical novel *The Way of All Flesh.*

Butler, Thomas, 10th earl of Ormonde (Black Earl) 1532–1614. Irish nobleman. He was noted for serving the English cause in putting down Irish rebellions in 1579 and 1597.

Butler, Walter 1752?–81. Notorious American Loyalist commander during the American Revolution. The son of J. Butler, he commanded Butler's Rangers during the Cherry Valley Massacre (1778).

Buxar, Battle of *See* **Baksar, Battle of.**

Byzacena *See* **Roman Province of Africa.**

Bylini Russian term for the heroic and narrative folk poems of Russian history. Passed down through oral tradition, the Bylini have had a notable influence on Russian literature.

Byng, Julian Hedworth George, 1st Viscount Byng of Vimy 1862–1935. British general. During

WW I he led the Canadian Corps in the celebrated capture of Vimy Ridge (1917), and commanded the British 3d Army (1917–18).

Byrd, Richard Evelyn 1888–1957. American admiral, polar explorer and aviator. A pioneer in polar aviation, he was the first to fly over the North Pole (1926). He established (1928) the Little America base in Antarctica, flew over the South Pole (1929), and headed US expeditions in the Antarctic until the 1950s.

Byrd, William 1542–1623. English composer, a leading composer of English sacred music. Though he was a Catholic, he enjoyed the protection of Queen Elizabeth.

Byron, George Gordon, 6th baron 1788–1824. English poet and satirist, one of the great Romantic poets and a symbol of Romanticism personified. He was born clubfooted. Byron succeeded his eccentric father as baron in 1798. Following publication of a satire, *English Bards and Scotch Reviewers,* he won widespread fame. Divorced in 1816, he left England and lived the rest of his free-spirited life in Europe. He died while aiding Greek insurgents fighting against Turkish rule. His many important works include *A Vision of Judgement, Beppo, Don Juan* and *Childe Harold's Pilgrimage.*

Byzantine Empire The Byzantine Empire was the successor state to the Roman Empire after the fall of the Western Roman Empire (AD 476). It corresponded to the Eastern Roman Empire (created by the division of the Roman Empire into the Western and Eastern empires, AD 395). It became the last bastion of Roman and Hellenic culture. For centuries after the Western Empire collapsed, the Byzantine Empire withstood the onslaughts of such groups as the Vandals, Goths, Persians, and Seljuk and Ottoman Turks, thereby insuring a relatively peaceful period for the reorganization of Europe. It preserved Roman and Greek traditions and contributions, such as the legal code *Corpus juris civilis,* made a lasting imprint on Western civilization. Key dates in the history of the Byzantine Empire include:

AD 330 Roman emperor Constantine I rebuilt city of Byzantium as Constantinople, making it seat of the Roman Empire.

AD 378 Goths victorious against Roman armies at Battle of Adrianople; opened way for their settlement in Byzantine territory.

AD 381 Second Ecumenical Council; established bishop of Constantinople as second in rank only to Rome.

AD 395 Roman Empire permanently divided at death of Theodosius; his son Arcadius succeeded as emperor of the Eastern (or East Roman) Empire.

451 Fourth Ecumenical Council; Constantinople granted patriarchal status and reaffirmed its primacy after Rome; settled religious controversies by refuting Monophysitism and Nestorianism; declared Christ united two natures in one person (diophysite).

453 Attila died, ending the invasion of Europe by the Huns.

476 Fall of Western Roman Empire; Eastern Empire survived as the Byzantine Empire, successor state to Roman Empire.

476–477 Reign of Zeno the Isaurian (474–481) challenged by the usurper, Basiliscus.

6TH CENT. AD Rise of Blues and Greens, rival political factions, within the empire.

527–565 Justinian I reigned; one of the great rulers of the Byzantine Empire; ordered compilation of the legal code *Corpus juris civilis* (529–535); empire reached its height under Justinian including in its domains Italy, part of North Africa, and southern Spain.

529 Ghassanid kingdom, ruled by Arabs on the southeastern frontier of the Byzantine empire, established as phylarchate; served as close ally and buffer state.

532 Constantinople heavily damaged in Nika Riot of Blues and Greens against Justinian; attempt to overthrow Justinian failed.

532 Construction of Hagia Sophia begun; one of the masterpieces of Byzantine architecture, it was but a part of the great building program under Justinian.

533–534 North Africa brought under Byzantine control when Byzantine general Belisarius defeated Vandals.

535 Belisarius began reconquest of Italy (from Ostrogoths), later completed by Narses.

540 Persians invaded Syria.

541 Plague of Justinian; over next few years up to 50 percent of the population in the central empire were killed by the pandemic.

552–554 Byzantine general Narses defeated the Ostrogoths, led by Totila, in Italy; brought Italy under firm Byzantine control.

554 Armenian Monophysite church formally broke ties with Roman Catholic and Orthodox Christian churches.

559 Belisarius repulsed invasion of the Huns and Slavs that had reached the outskirts of Constantinople.

568–571 Lombards invaded northern Italy taking control of all but the Exarchate of Ravenna.

LATE 6TH CENT. Great migration of Slavs into Balkan Peninsula.

584 Southeastern frontier of empire exposed following breakup of Ghassanid phylarchate.

591–593 Invading Avars, threatening Constantinople, driven back.

602–610 Phocas, a soldier, reigned after seizing the throne.

610–641 Heraclius I reigned; assumed power after Phocas was overthrown.

622–627 Heraclius warred against and decisively defeated the Persians, who had intermittently threatened the empire from 540 and who had conquered much of the southern empire from 611.

626 Constantinople successfully resisted attacks by Slavs and Avars.

629 Battle of Mu'ta; Muslims defeated in first fighting between Byzantines and Muslims.

FROM 634 Rise of the Muslim Caliphate; Muslims began rapid expansion of their empire, taking over considerable Byzantine territory.

636 Byzantine power in Syria broken by Muslim Arab victory at Battle of the Yarmuk River (Aug. 20).

637–642 Muslim caliphs continued expanding their empire; Jerusalem fell (637) and Byzantine Egypt was lost (642).

638 Heraclius's attempt to resolve religious controversy over Monophysitism gave rise to new heresy, Monotheletism.

649 Cyprus conquered by Muslims.

654 Muslims broke Byzantine naval supremacy; conquered Aegean islands and Rhodes.

AFTER 656 Muslim forces pushed into what later became Armenia, Azerbaijan, and Georgia.

673–678 Muslim Arab threat to Byzantine Empire reached its height; Constantinople withstood siege by Arabs throughout the period and finally won peace settlement (678).

695–717 Period of anarchy and unrest in which the army gained power and named a succession of emperors; empire raided by Arabs and a new enemy, the Bulgars; order restored by Leo III.

698 Muslim Arab caliphs completed conquest of Byzantine territories in North Africa (begun 647).

711 Muslims conquered much of Spain, continuing rapid expansion of their empire.

717–741 Leo III reigned; put down revolts by army and restored order: founded Isaurian dynasty; began controversy over iconoclasm (726).

741–775 Constantine V reigned; advocated iconoclasm, lost control of Italy; warred against Bulgars (755–764).

751–756 Lombards conquered the Exarchate of Ravenna, Byzantine foothold in Italy; Franks called in by pope to aid against Lombards and thereby began alliance of popes in Rome and European monarchs.

780–797 Irene, mother of Emperor Constantine VI, held real power during his reign; overthrew him (797).

787–843 Iconoclastic controversy; temporarily ended by Council of Nicaea (787), revived again in 815; the ban on icon worship was finally rescinded in 843.

797–802 Irene reigned as first Byzantine empress; refused to recognize Charlemagne's empire as successor state to Western Roman Empire (800).

812 Emperor Michael I recognized Charlemagne's empire as the successor to the Western Roman empire.

813–820 Leo V reigned; repelled Bulgar attack on Constantinople; forced Bulgars to accept peace treaty (817).

826 Muslims took control of Sicily, posing new threat to shipping in Mediterranean; later took Crete as well.

860 Russians launched first attack on Constantinople.

860s Saints Cyril and Methodius began their missionary work among the Slavs; Bulgars accepted Christianity.

869–870 Council of Constantinople; Photius patriarch of Constantinople and leader of Byzantine opposition to the primacy of Rome, was excommunicated by the council;

Ignatius, called to succeed him, attempted to heal growing split between Eastern and Western churches.

867–886 Basil I reigned; founded Macedonian dynasty (867–1057); introduced legal code; his reign marked a golden age in Byzantine history; Basil rebuilt Byzantine military strength; his army and navy generally successful against Muslim Arabs.

886–912 Leo VI reigned; compiled Basilica, the Byzantine legal code; waged war against the Bulgarians (from 889).

900s Rise of feudalism in the empire; feudal revolts against the emperors in this century proved unsuccessful.

913–959 Constantine VII reigned; Bulgarians seriously threatened Constantinople; warfare with Russian princes.

969–976 John I reigned; forced the Russians out of Bulgaria and, advancing against the Muslim Arabs, took parts of Syria.

976–1025 Basil II reigned; won final submission of Bulgarians (1018) after decisive victory against them (1014).

988 Prince Vladimir of Kiev accepted Christianity.

992 Venice granted major trade concession, as reward for providing military aid in Italy.

1042–54 Constantine IX reigned with wife Zoë; Seljuk Turks began to drive Byzantines from Asia Minor; empire began to crumble.

1042 Normans began attacks on Byzantine territories in southern Italy; eventually won control of Sicily and Naples to form Kingdom of the Two Sicilies (1091)

1054 Schism between Roman and Eastern Orthodox churches became permanent.

1071 Normans completed conquest of Byzantine territories in Italy.

1071 Romanus IV defeated by Seljuk Turks at Battle of Manzikert; Byzantine hold on Asia Minor seriously weakened as Seljuks advanced.

1075 Rome recognized Croatia and Zeta as independent; Hungarian tribes continued pushing into former Byzantine territories.

1081–1118 Alexius I Comnenus reigned; established the Comnenian dynasty (1081–1185); defended the empire against Norman invasions led by Robert Guiscard.

1096 Era of the Crusades began; Byzantine emperors, threatened by Seljuk advances, forced to contend with potentially dangerous force of European Christians sent to fight the Seljuks in the Holy Land.

1099 Jerusalem taken by Crusaders.

1143–80 Manuel Comnenus reigned; averted war with Christians on Second Crusade; extended Byzantine hegemony over Hungary, notably after conquering Dalmatia (1168); accepted unfavorable peace after war with Venice (1176); attempted to promote ties with the Western church.

c1167 Serbian Prince Stephen Nemanja founded Serbian state under Byzantine suzerainty.

1181 Hungarians pushed into Dalmatia and Croatia.

1185–95 Isaac II reigned; acceded after leading a revolt; collapse of central authority began as petty nobles gained power; Normans defeated but revolt by Bulgarians resulted in creation of a new Bulgarian kingdom (1185).

1187 Saladin defeated Crusader armies at Battle of Hattin; Jerusalem retaken by Muslims.

1204 Crusaders (on Fourth Crusade) captured Constantinople; Latin Empire of Constantinople established after sack of Constantinople.

1204–05 Baldwin I reigned as first Latin emperor of Constantinople.

1206 Theodore I Lascaris founded the empire of Nicaea after the fall of the empire to the crusaders.

1228–61 Baldwin II reigned as last Latin emperor of Constantinople.

1244 Mongol incursions into Asia Minor began.

1261 Michael VIII Paleologus (ruled 1261–82) reconquered Constantinople, effectively ending Latin Empire of Constantinople; Byzantine Empire reestablished.

1300s Ottoman Turks began their rise to power in northwestern Asia Minor, expanding their empire at the expense of the Byzantines.

1340s Serbs, led by Stephen Dushan, rose to power and threatened the Byzantine Empire.

1341–47 War between John V and John VI for control of the empire; both Turks and Serbs called in to help; war set the stage for the final collapse of the empire; by 1391 the Turks had begun their attacks on Constantinople, the last vestige of Byzantine Empire.

1453 Constantinople fell to the Ottoman Turks; Constantine XI, last Byzantine emperor (1448–53), fell defending the city; Byzantine Empire ceased to exist.

Byzantium Ancient Greek city once located on the site of Constantinople. It gave its name to the Byzantine Empire, of which Constantinople later became capital. Founded 7th cent. BC by Megarian Greeks, it became an important commercial city. It was conquered (AD 196) by the Romans and, by order of Constantine I, the city was later rebuilt (AD 330) as Constantinople.

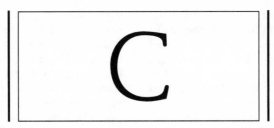

C

Caaba *See* **Kaaba.**

Cabal An unpopular inner group of five advisers that served (1667–73) King Charles II of England. This informal ministry dominated court policy and engaged in various intrigues until Parliament forced its dissolution (1673). Members were: Clifford of Chudleigh; A. Ashley Cooper, Lord Shaftesbury; G. Villiers, the duke of Buckingham; H. Bennet, the earl of Arlington; and J. Maitland, the duke of Lauderdale.

Cabala (Cabbala) A mystical interpretation of the Scriptures that arose among Jews in the 13th cent. and to a lesser degree among Christians in the 15th and 16th cents. Cabalists held that for those who knew the secrets, every word, letter, number, and accent in the Scriptures revealed mysteries about God and the universe. Cabalism influenced the development of Hasidism.

Cabarrus, Jeanne Marie Ignace, Theresa de *See* **Tallien, Theresa.**

Cabbala *See* **Cabala.**

Cabeca de Vaca, Álvar Núñez *See* **Cabeza de Vaca, Álvar Núñez.**

Cabet, Étienne 1788–1856. French Socialist and founder of the Icaria commune in America (c1849).

Cabeza de Vaca, Álvar Núñez (Cabeca de Vaca, ~) c1490–c1557. Spanish soldier and explorer. Tales of his trek through the unexplored American Southwest spurred exploration of the region.

Cabochiens Faction of Parisian tradesmen that sided with the Burgundians in the civil war against the Armagnacs (1411–18). In 1413 Cabochiens rioted and seized control of Paris. Before the uprising was quashed by the Armagnacs, Cabochiens issued their *ordonnance cabochienne,* radical reforms intended to end government corruption.

Cabot, George *See* **Hartford Convention.**

Cabot, John 1450–98. Italian navigator serving England. On a voyage of discovery (1497), he landed at what may have been Cape Breton Island and explored the coastline of Nova Scotia and Newfoundland.

Cabral, Pedro Álvares (Cabrera, ~) c1467–c1520. Portuguese navigator. He explored the Brazilian coast (1500) is disputed.

Cabrera, Pedro Álvares *See* **Cabral, Pedro Álvares.**

Cabrillo, Juan Rodríguez d. 1543. Portuguese soldier and explorer in the service of Spain. During an exploratory voyage, he discovered the California coast (1542).

Cabrini, Saint Frances Xavier 1850–1917. Italian-American founder of Missionary Sisters of the Sacred Heart of Jesus (1880). The first American saint (canonized 1946), she is best known for her work among Italian immigrants in the US.

Caccini, Giulio 1550?–1618. Italian composer and singer. He was a member of a group of Florentine music theorists who composed what are considered the earliest operas.

Cade, John (Jack) *See* **Cade's Rebellion.**

Cade's Rebellion In England, a brief revolt (1450) by small-property owners over political grievances and corruption in King Henry VI's government. Led by John (Jack) Cade (*d.* 1450), some 40,000 rebels took London and executed the king's treasurer, Lord Saye. The rebels disbanded on being promised pardons by the king.

Cadillac, Antoine Laumet de La Mothe 1658–1730. French soldier, explorer, and administrator. Cadillac first traveled to Canada in 1683, where he fought against the Iroquois, lived briefly in Maine, and then served as colonial official in what is now Michigan. Later, after establishing a fur-trading post, he founded Fort-Pontchartrain du Détroit (1701), now the city of Detroit, where he governed until 1710. Forced to relocate to the French colony of Louisiana, Cadillac governed there briefly until recalled to France in about 1717. Cities in Michigan and Maine are named for him.

Cadoudal, Georges 1771–1804. Royalist conspirator during the French Revolution. He was a principal leader of the royalist Chouans (*q.v.*) in revolt against the revolutionary government. He was guillotined after participating in an attempt to overthrow Napoleon I.

Cadwaladr *See* **Cadwallader.**

Cadwallader (Caedwalla) (Cadwaladr) *d.* 664/689? King of the Gwynedd in what is now north Wales.

Caedmon *fl.* 670. Earliest known English Christian poet. He was said to be an illiterate herdsman who discovered his poetic gifts through a vision.

Caedwalla *See* **Cadwallader.**

Caerleon (Caerllion) (Isca Silurum) Now a district in Wales, it was once the site of a major Roman fortress in Britain. It is also considered one of the possible locations of King Arthur's court, the legendary Camelot.

Caerllion *See* **Caerleon.**

Caesar Another name for the famous family of the Julian clan of ancient Rome and, for a time, title of Roman rulers. The line begins with Sextus Julius, who was praetor in 208 BC. Its two most famous members are Julius and Augustus Caesar (whose actual name is Gaius Julius Caesar Octavianus). After AD 68, the name "Caesar," with "Augustus," became a title taken by emperors who were not of the family. This tradition lasted to the time of Hadrian, who adopted only the title "Augustus."

Caesar, Julius c102–44 BC. Great Roman statesman and general. Caesar established himself as sole ruler and dictator of the empire and pacified Italy and the provinces. He extended the empire throughout Gaul and devised the Julian calendar, the basis of the modern calendar. During his early career, Caesar aligned himself with the popular party and, in 60 BC, sought the consulate of Rome. Frustrated by Senate opposition, he formed the First Triumvirate with Crassus and Pompey and thus became consul in 59. He was then named proconsul of Gaul and Illyricum (58) and became a military hero as commander of

Roman armies in the Gallic Wars (58–51). Crassus' death ended the triumvirate (53) and set Pompey, now sole consul, against Caesar. In 49, Caesar led his armies from Gaul against Pompey. Crossing the Rubicon, he marched unopposed to Rome, and was made dictator. Caesar emerged victorious from the ensuing military exploits (49–45) in the provinces against Pompey's army and in 44 was named dictator for life. But his dictatorial powers had aroused bitter resentment in Rome. On the Ides of March (Mar. 15) 44, Caesar was assassinated by a band of conspirators which included Brutus, Cassius, and Casca. (For further details on Caesar's exploits, *see* Rome, 60–44 BC; Gallic Wars.)

Caesarea, Eusebius of *See* **Eusebius of Caesarea.**

Caetano, Marceio José das Neves Alves 1906–80. Portuguese statesman, premier (1968–74), ally of and successor to A. Salazar. Though an extreme conservative, he permitted some moderate reforms before being ousted by the military.

Cagliostro, Alessandro, Conte (*pseud. of* Balsamo, Giuseppe) 1743–95. Italian adventurer. He was a magician and alchemist who was popular in King Louis XVI's court, until he was implicated in the Affair of the Diamond Necklace (1785).

Cagoulards French terrorist group of the 1930s. Named for the hoods worn by the members, the group supported royalist and Fascist tendencies. In Nov., 1937, an armed revolt against the Popular Front government (*q.v.*) was forestalled by discovery of their arms caches.

Cahenslyism Late 19th-cent. movement among European Roman Catholic immigrants in the US calling for appointment of bishops and priests of their own nationality. The movement was named for a German, Peter Paul Cahensly, who with other Europeans pressed the cause at the Vatican.

Caillaux, Joseph 1863–1944. French statesman influential in French politics between 1898 and 1939. He served several times as finance minister and once as premier (1911–12). A pacifist, he was convicted of treason in 1920, but by 1925 he had returned to office as finance minister.

Cairo Egyptian capital city (*pop.* 5,084,500), a port and the largest city in Africa. Founded 969 by the Fatimids as the Egyptian capital, it was taken by Saladin in the 12th cent. Cairo was the capital under the Mamelukes from the 13th to 16th cents. and reached the height of its prosperity before modern times. The Ottoman Turks controlled it from the 16th to 19th cents., and after 1805 Cairo was capital of a quasi-independent country. The British maintained a military presence there from 1882 to 1946.

Cairo Conference Meeting of WW II Allies held (Nov. 22–26, 1943) at Cairo to discuss Far East policies. It preceded the Teheran Conference and was attended by US president F. Roosevelt, British prime minister W. Churchill, and Chinese general Chiang Kai-shek. Afterward, the leaders pledged to continue war against Japan until its surrender, to strip Japan of its island possessions, to grant Korea eventual independence, and to forgo territorial gains by their respective nations.

Cakste, Janis 1859–1927. Latvian statesman. During WW I, he was an important figure in securing independence for and recognition of the Republic of Latvia. He was its first president, elected in 1922 and reelected in 1925.

Calabria See **Bruttium.**

Calais, Treaty of See **Brétigny, Treaty of.**

Calamity Jane (*pseud. of* Burke, Martha Jane) c1852–1903. American frontier heroine. A skilled rider and markswoman who dressed in men's clothing, she gained widespread notoriety in the late 1800s for her exploits in the South Dakota Black Hills.

Calatrava, Knights of See **Knights of Calatrava.**

Calcutta, Black Hole of See **Black Hole of Calcutta.**

Calder, Alexander 1898–1976. American sculptor. He is best known as the originator of mobiles.

Calderón Bridge Bridge in west central Mexico where a rebel force under M. Hidalgo y Costilla was defeated by Spanish royalist forces (Jan. 17, 1811). It marked the end of the first attempt at Mexican independence.

Calderón de la Barca, Pedro 1600–81. Spanish dramatist and poet. He is considered one of Spain's greatest playwrights. *El divino Orfeo* and *La hija del aire* are among the many plays he wrote.

Caldwell, Erskine 1903–87. American author of novels about the rural South. *Tobacco Road* and *God's Little Acre* are among his best-known works.

Caledonia Roman name for the region north of their territories on the British Isles and roughly corresponding to what is now Scotland. In modern usage it refers to Scotland.

Calhoun, John Caldwell 1782–1850. American statesman, vice-president (1825–29, 1829–32), and champion of the Old South. A nationalist and supporter of the War of 1812, he became secretary of war (1817–25) and then served as vice-president under J. Q. Adams and A. Jackson. He became a supporter of states' rights, and, breaking with Jackson over the Eaton Affair (*q.v.*) and nullification (*q.v.*), he resigned the vice-presidency. After winning passage (1832) of the controversial Ordinance of Nullification in South Carolina, he served in the US Senate (1832–43, 1845–50), where he worked to protect the interests of the South and oppose abolition of slavery. His debates with D. Webster are famous.

California US state on the Pacific coast, the 31st state. Spanish explorer J. Cabrillo claimed the lower coast for Spain (1542), and Sir F. Drake claimed the region north of San Francisco (1579) for the English. Gaspar de Portola established a permanent settlement at San Diego (1769), and settlement by Americans did not begin until the 1840s. The Mexican governor of the region was driven out in 1845, and, during the Mexican War (1846–48), the territory was occupied by US troops. It was ceded to the US by the Treaty of Guadalupe Hidalgo (*q.v.*). The gold rush of 1848 increased population, and California became a state in 1850. Its constitution has been in effect since 1880.

Caligula AD 12–41. Roman emperor (AD 37–41), successor to Tiberius and notorious as a despotic ruler. Though his father, mother, and two brothers were rumored to have been put to death by Tiberius, Caligula befriended and ultimately succeeded him. At first a popular figure, he is sometimes said to have gone mad after a serious illness (AD c38). Tales of his subsequent ruthless cruelties and eccentric behavior are legion, and he squandered the great wealth of the treasury. He was assassinated.

caliph Ruler of the Muslim state founded by the prophet Muhammad (7th cent.). The caliphate was established on Muhammad's death (632) and was invested with temporal and spiritual powers. Caliphs reigned over the Caliphate (*q.v.*) from 632 until its conquest by the Mongols in 1258. The first four caliphs were Abu Bakr, Umar, Uthman, and Ali, and are called the Orthodox Caliphs. Their reign was broken in 661 when Muawiya claimed the Caliphate and established the Umayyad dynasty (*q.v.*). The Abbasid line later replaced the Umayyads.

Caliphate Muslim theocracy established in western Arabia (7th cent.) by the prophet Muhammad. After Muhammad's death (632), the original Muslim state was rapidly expanded into a great empire by his successors, the caliphs, who held both temporal and spiritual powers. Two great dynasties ruled this empire, the Umayyads and their successors, the Abbasids. At its greatest extent, the Muslim Empire stretched from Afghanistan in the east, across the Mideast and North Africa, and up into Spain. But divisions among the Muslims over religious and political matters, and strains caused by inclusion of so many diverse peoples within the Muslim world, seriously weakened the empire. These problems set the stage for the empire's final decline and eventual collapse before the invading Mongols (1258). Key events in the history of the empire include:

c612 Muhammad began preaching at Mecca in western Arabia.

622 Hijra (July 15–16), Muhammad's flight from Mecca to escape enemies of his teachings; marked beginning of Muslim era; Muhammad established following at Medina.

624–625 Muhammad's followers defeated a force from Mecca at Badr, but were themselves defeated at Uhud.

628 Muhammad conquered the oasis of Khaibar, which Jews from Medina had held; Muhammad had condemned Jews at Medina because they opposed him.

630–632 Muhammad marched into Mecca with 10,000 followers (632); tradition of Islamic pilgrimage established; Muhammad now secure in his position as prophet; tradition of jihad (holy war) against nonbelievers eventually paved the way for the great expansion of the Muslim state; raids against Byzantines to north conducted.

632 Muhammad died (June 8); Caliphate established.

632–634 Abu Bakr, Muhammad's father-in-law, became first of the four patriarchal caliphs; suppressed revolts and established Muslim military power.

634–644 Umar I, second patriarchal caliph; Persian lands to north (modern Iraq) conquered (c635); Jordan, Palestine, and Syria

taken from Byzantines with Battle of Yarmuk (636); northern advance stopped at edge of Byzantine Anatolia; Byzantine Egypt conquered (640–645).

644–656 Uthman, third patriarchal caliph; completed conquest of Persia (651); launched expeditions to Cyprus and North Africa; discontent within Muslim world led to his assassination.

656–661 Ali, fourth patriarchal caliph and husband of Fatima, Muhammad's daughter; first Muslim Civil War broke out; division of Islam into Shi'ite and Sunni (orthodox) Muslims traditionally dated from this time.

661 Hasan, Ali's son, appointed caliph after Ali was assassinated; Hasan soon after submitted to Muawiya.

661–680 Muawiya reigned as first caliph of the Umayyad dynasty (reigned 661–750); he restored order after civil war and made Damascus capital of the Muslim Empire; great expansion of the empire accomplished by his Umayyad successors.

674–680 Raids against Byzantine Empire became a protracted war in which the Muslims seriously threatened Constantinople.

680–683 Yazid I, Muawiya's son, became caliph; opposition in Arabia to domination by Syrian Muslims provoked Yazid's attacks on Medina and Mecca; set stage for second civil war.

683–692 Second Muslim Civil War.

685–692 Abd al-Malik succeeded as caliph; made peace with the Byzantines and then set about subduing various rebel groups involved in civil war; rival caliph (Ibn az-Zubayr) in Arabia was slain in battle at Mecca (692), thus ending the civil war.

692–705 Remainder of Abd al-Malik's reign marked by his consolidation of power, building of the Dome of the Rock at Jerusalem (691), renewed war with the Byzantines, the capture of Carthage (698), and conquest of Byzantine North Africa.

711–714 Muslims from North Africa raided Visigothic kingdom in Iberia; quickly brought about collapse of the kingdom.

716–717 Arab Muslims mounted their last major attack on Byzantine Constantinople; attackers withdrawn after the death of Caliph Suleiman (reigned 715–717).

724–743 Hisham reigned as caliph; his reign was marked by the end of rapid territorial expansion under the Umayyad dynasty, and general peace and prosperity; Muslim Empire now extended from Afghanistan in the east, across the Arabian Peninsula and North Africa, and into Spain in the west; a Berber revolt (740–742) greatly reduced territories in North Africa that were held by the Arabs; period of decline followed Hisham's reign.

732 Muslims invaded Iberia; Christian kingdoms formed in what became northern Spain; Muslim advance halted by Charles Martel at Battle of Poitiers (in modern France) and never again moved northward from Spain.

747–750 Revolt of Abu Muslim; by taking advantage of discontent among various Arab groups, Abu Muslim succeeded in fomenting a general rebellion that resulted in the overthrow of the Umayyad dynasty; Abbasid dynasty established by Abu-al-Abbas as Saffah (reigned 750–54).

750–1258 Abbasid dynasty reigned; moved government from Damascus to Iraq in 763, eventually founding Baghdad as the capital; period marked by deepening split between Sunni (orthodox) and Shi'ite Muslims, increasing influence of Persians (later Turks) in the Muslim world, and the consequent decline in power of the old Arab ruling class.

750 Abd-ar-Rahman I was the only Umayyad to escape executions that followed the Abbasid takeover; he made his way to Muslim Spain and established (755) the Umayyad line there (ruled until 1031)

754–775 Al-Mansur reigned as caliph, killed Abu Muslim and thus sparked unsuccessful revolts; moved capital to Baghdad (c763), which developed into the leading Muslim city; his reign was marked by stability and prosperity.

786–809 Harun al-Rashid reigned as caliph; luxury of his court immortalized in *Thousand and One Nights;* but rebellion and unrest were common in Syria, Egypt, and in far eastern reaches of empire; Harun issued the Meccan documents (802), which set forth his ill-fated plan to divide the empire in two on his death.

809–813 Muslim Civil War; broke out after Harun's death, between rulers of new eastern and western parts of the empire; Abd Allah al-Mamun emerged victorious.

813–833 Al-Mamun reigned as caliph; golden age of Muslim Arab culture; al-Mamun warred against Byzantines, put down revolts in Egypt, Syria, and Armenia; ordered translation of Greek texts, attempted to heal rift between Sunni and Shi'ite Muslims.

842–847 Al-Wathiq reigned as caliph; unsuccessfully tried to halt rising influence of non-Arabs (Persians, Turks).

861–945 Breakdown of central authority; period of widespread rebellion and unrest; provincial rulers in the east and west became largely autonomous; political and military leadership taken over by the amir (from 936); caliphs reduced to spiritual figureheads largely dependent upon the amirs.

929 Umayyad ruler Abd-ar-Rahman III took advantage of weakened Abbasid caliphate to declare himself caliph.

945–1055 Buyids, a dynasty of Persians, in power as amirs; though they favored the Shi'ite Muslims, they nevertheless maintained the Sunni caliphs as figureheads.

969–1171 Fatimids, a Shi'ite dynasty opposed to the Abbasids, conquered Egypt (969) and established the Fatimid dynasty there; actively attempted to overthrow Abbasids while they remained in power.

998 Rise of the Sunni Muslim Ghaznavid Empire in Afghanistan.

1008–31 Muslim Civil War; fought in Spain, it resulted in the end of the Umayyad dynasty rule there.

1055–92 Seljuk Turks, zealous Sunni Muslims, rose to power as their westward migration increased their numbers in the empire; led by Togrul Beg, the Seljuks ousted (1055) the Buyid amirs from power, restored Sunni power, and themselves assumed temporal powers as sultans; Seljuk power reached its zenith under Malik-shah (1072–92), and thereafter conflicts among the sultans gave increased power to the Abbasid caliphs.

1095–1291 Era of the Crusades, rise of Saladin, who suppressed the Fatimids in Egypt (1171), as the great leader of Muslim forces against the Crusaders.

1258 End of the Caliphate; Mongol conqueror Hulagu Khan overran the empire and destroyed the capital of Baghdad; last reigning caliph, al-Musta'sim (ruled 1242–58), killed.

c1261–1517 Abbasid line lived on in Egypt, but held no real power; line ended by Ottoman Turkish conquest of Egypt (1517).

Calixtines *See* **Utraquists.**

Calixtus II (Callistus II) (*orig.* Guido of Vienne) *d.* 1124. French-born pope (1119–24), successor to Gelasius II. He forced Holy Roman Emperor Henry V to accept the Concordat of Worms (1122) and thereby ended the Investiture Controversy.

Calixtus III (Callistus III) (*orig.* Borja Alfonso de) 1378–1458. Spanish-born pope (1455–58), successor to Nicholas V. He failed in his attempts to raise a crusade against the Turks. Calixtus III was also the name of an antipope to Alexander III (1168).

Callaghan, Leonard James 1912– . British Labour party prime minister (1976–79). A conservative Labourite, he rose in the party through trade union work and served as chancellor of the exchequer (1964–67), home secretary (1967–70), and foreign secretary (1974–76). His term of office was marked by severe economic problems.

Calles, Plutarco Ellas 1877–1945. Mexican revolutionary general and president (1924–28). He joined the revolution against P. Díaz (1910) and, as president, instituted unsuccessful agrarian reforms. He established the National Revolutionary party, and, until his exile in 1936, he virtually ruled Mexico.

Callias *fl.* 449 BC. Athenian statesman. He is believed to have negotiated the Treaty of Callias (449), in which a long period of hostility between the Greeks and Persians was brought to an end. There is doubt that a written treaty ever existed, but the two peoples remained at peace for many years after his mission.

Callias, Treaty of *See* **Callias.**

Callimachus Late 5th-cent. BC Greek sculptor. He is believed to have been an Athenian and the originator of the Corinthian column.

Callistus II *See* **Calixtus II.**

Callistus III *See* **Calixtus III.**

Calmette, Albert Léon Charles 1863–1933. A French bacteriologist. A student of L. Pasteur, he developed, with Camille Guèrin (1872–1961), a vaccine used to inoculate infants against tuberculosis (1908).

Calonne, Charles *See* **Assembly of Notables.**

Calpurnia *fl.* 1st cent. BC. Roman woman, J. Caesar's last wife (from 59 BC). She is said to have tried to prevent his attendance at the Senate on the day of his assassination (44 BC).

Calvert, George, 1st baron Baltimore c1580–1632. British colonizer, whose efforts led to the founding (1632) of the colony of Maryland.

Calvin, John 1509–64. French theologian and, as founder of Calvinism, one of the great figures of the Protestant Reformation. Able at debating, Calvin at first studied law. He became a Protestant (1533), and was forced to leave France because of religious persecution. Later (at Basel, 1536) he completed his great theological work *Institutes of the Christian Religion,* which systemized Protestant dogma. He next went to Geneva (1536) to establish a theocracy according to his Calvinistic doctrines. Expelled from Geneva (1538) and then recalled (1541), Calvin struggled until 1555 to establish his absolute supremacy there. He was involved in noted controversies against the Lutherans and the Anabaptists, as well as in the trial and burning of M. Servetus (1553).

Calvinism 1. The body of religious teachings advanced by J. Calvin and his followers. Calvinism arose during the 16th-cent. Reformation and differed from Lutheranism in placing the church above the state, in emphasizing predestination and the notion of grace, and in developing a theology of the covenant (pact with God). Calvinistic doctrines were important in the development of English Puritanism, Scottish Presbyterianism, and the theocratic communities of early New England Puritans. Other noted Calvinists include J. Knox and J. Edwards. 2. Name for the body of doctrines that form the basis of the Reformed and Presbyterian churches.

Calvo, Carlos 1824–1906. Argentine diplomat and jurist. He is best known for the Calvo Doctrine, advanced in his book *International Law of Europe and America in Theory and Practice.*

Cambacérès, Jean Jacques Régis de 1753–1824. French revolutionary statesman. He was second consul under Napoleon (1799–1804), and, from 1804, archchancellor of the French Empire. He played an important role in formulating the Code Napoléon.

Cambodia (*formerly* Kampuchea) Republic located in Southeast Asia. The population is 6,592,000 (est.) and the capital is Phnom Penh. Cambodia's early history was shaped in part by early Hindu and Buddhist influences. The Khmer Empire flourished in Cambodia from the 6th to 15th cents. and at its peak made Cambodia the leading empire in the region. As the Khmer Empire declined, Cambodia suffered numerous attacks from neighboring states, and finally in the 19th cent. became a French protectorate. After achieving independence (1953), Cambodia became increasingly embroiled in the conflict in Vietnam, its traditional enemy. The Vietnam War had drastic repercussions in Cambodia, and political and social instability culminated in a bloody Khmer Rouge regime, an invasion by Vietnamese forces, and years of guerrilla warfare. A UN-backed peace agreement between opposing factions was agreed to in 1991. Key dates in the history of Cambodia include:

C3D–5TH CENTS. AD   Funan Empire flourished in Cambodia; Hinduism and other elements of Indian culture introduced.

C6TH CENT. AD   Funan Empire overrun by Khmer people from the north; Khmer Empire established in Cambodia.

9TH–13TH CENTS.   Khmer Empire rose to its height; extended its power through much of Southeast Asia.

12TH–13TH CENTS.   Angkor Wat and Angkor Thom built.

13TH CENT.   Buddhism introduced.

13TH–15TH CENTS.   Khmer Empire declined; lost territories during attacks by Siam in the west and Vietnam in the east; collapse came in 15th cent.

1863   French established protectorate over Cambodia.

1887   Cambodia made part of French colonial Indochina.

1941–55   Norodom Sihanouk reigned as king.

1940–45   WW II; Japanese troops entered Cambodia (1940) and held real power there; French Vichy government was allowed to remain until 1945, when the Japanese ousted the French from all Indochina.

1945   French reestablished control in Cambodia following WW II.

1946   Cambodia became autonomous within the French Union.

1953   Cambodia became independent.

1954   Cambodia invaded by Vietminh, Communist forces fighting against French rule in neighboring Vietnam.

1954   French withdrew troops from Indochina at the end of the French Indochina War.

1955   Norodom Sihanouk turned over Cambodian throne to his father, Prince Norodom Suramarit, and became prime minister.

1960   Sihanouk became Cambodian chief of state.

1960–75   Vietnam War; Sihanouk's attempts to keep Cambodia neutral ultimately failed as war spread from Vietnam into Cambodia.

1963–65   Sihanouk, claiming US interference in Cambodian affairs, refused further US aid (1963); diplomatic relations with US ended.

1966–67   Lon Nol became premier under Prince Sihanouk (Aug.).

1969   US began secret aerial bombing of Communist bases in Cambodia; diplomatic relations reestablished with US soon after.

1970   Sihanouk proved unable to dislodge Vietnamese Communist forces from Cambodia; he was overthrown (Mar. 18) in bloodless coup.

1970–75   Lon Nol became chief of state; Cambodian troops began fighting Vietnamese.

1970   South Vietnamese and US forces began offensives (Apr. 29–30) against Communist strongholds in Cambodia.

1970   Cambodian government forces under increasing attacks by anti-government Khmer Rouge and Vietnamese Communists; US air strikes supported government troops.

1970   Cambodian government forces driven out of northeastern provinces by Communists; Premier Lon Nol given wartime powers (June 27).

1970   Republic proclaimed (Oct. 9); monarchy abolished.

1970   Cambodian and South Vietnamese forces began offensive (Nov. 8) south of Phnom Penh.

1971   South Vietnamese began new offensive (July 8) in Parrot's Beak region in Vietnam.

1971   North Vietnamese broke through defenses north of Phnom Penh (Dec. 2).

1972   Lon Nol seized power (Mar. 10); dissolved National Assembly.

1972   Lon Nol elected (June 4) to presidency under new constitution.

1973   Highway 5, last supply route to Phnom Penh cut (Apr. 4) by Khmer Rouge forces.

1973   Direct US participation in fighting ended (Aug. 15).

1975   Evacuation of American personnel (Apr. 11–12).

1975   Gen. Lon Nol fled Cambodia (Apr. 1) as Khmer Rouge forces closed in.

1975   Cambodian government surrendered (Apr. 17) to Khmer Rouge rebels.

1975–78   Rebels, led by Pol Pot, ruled with hard-line Communist regime; instituted reign of terror; forced populace to leave cities for hard labor in miserable conditions in jungles; deaths from executions and hardships estimated at over one million.

1975   Sihanouk named chief of state for life by Khmer Rouge rebels (Apr.).

1975   *Mayaguez* incident (May); crew of US merchant ship seized, then returned after US aircraft began bombing attack.

1978   Vietnamese invasion of Cambodia began after series of border incidents (Dec.).

1979   Phnom Penh captured by Vietnamese regular army troops (Jan. 7); Pol Pot regime fell; resistance by Khmer Rouge troops continued in some areas; famine narrowly averted by aid from Western nations, and especially Thailand.

1979–92   Heng Samrin of People's Revolutionary Party in power as president of Vietnamese-held territories; his administration's chief strength lay in widespread fear of the Khmer Rouge returning to power, but this was counterbalanced by a traditional hatred of the Vietnamese in Cambodia; Vietnamese advisers oversaw all levels of government.

1980   Government reestablished monetary system; refugees began returning to towns.

1982   Major Vietnamese offensive failed to break guerrilla resistance by Khmer Rouge or the non-Communist Khmer People's National Liberation Front (KPNLF); Vietnamese mounted similar unsuccessful dry season offensives in subsequent years, particularly in western Cambodia.

1982   Sihanouk became head of a coalition of guerrilla groups, including the Khmer Rouge, then fighting the Vietnamese-backed regime.

1983   Vietnamese troops attacked Khmer rebel forces in western Cambodia (Jan.); some 30,000 refugees flooded into Thailand.

1984   KPNLF soundly defeated Vietnamese offensive against their base at Amphil (Apr.); guerilla groups, including the Khmer Rouge, KPNLF, and Sihanouk's 7,000-man Armée Nationale Sihuanoukiste (ANS), dominated countryside; cut road and rail links, and raided provincial capitals.

1985   Some 230,000 refugees flooded into Thailand following major offensive by Vietnamese in western Cambodia; Vietnamese forced Cambodian laborers to build defensive fortifications along western border.

1986   Guerrilla coalition launched successful attack on Battambang (Mar.), an important city in western Cambodia.

1986   National Assembly postponed elections scheduled for 1987.

1987   First formal talks (Dec., in France) between Sihanouk and Heng Samrin's Vietnamese-backed government; agreed solution lay in negotiated settlement between various Cambodian factions, and that new government should be independent and democratic.

1987   Drought and continued warfare resulted in danger of serious famine.

1988   Vietnamese began withdrawing troops; concern now turned to fears extremist Khmer Rouge might regain power.

1988   Khmer Rouge announced they would agree to an international peacekeeping force (Oct. 22); Chinese declared they would cut aid to Khmer Rouge and other guerrilla groups proportional to the Vietnamese troop reductions.

1989   Unsuccessful talks between the Vietnamese-backed government, the People's Republic of Kampuchea (PRK), the ANS, KPNLF, and Khmer Rouge at Jakarta (Feb. 19–21).

1989   Vietnamese withdrew virtually all remaining troops in Cambodia (Apr.–Dec.).

1989   Peace talks at Paris (July 30–Aug. 30) stalemated; Khmer Rouge position in future government proved major stumbling block.

1989   Khmer Rouge launched successful offensive in western Cambodia and around Phnom Penh (Oct.–Nov.).

1989   Sihanouk approved Australian plan for Cambodia (Nov.); Cambodia to become UN trusteeship pending free elections.

1990   UN Security Council approved plan in principle (Jan.).

1990   Sihanouk's coalition group renamed the National Government of Cambodia (Feb.), dropping the reference to the Khmer Rouge–inspired name Kampuchea.

1990 Cambodia faced severe economic problems, including falling agricultural production and an inflation rate running over 120 percent per year; Soviets meanwhile declared they would cut financial aid beginning in 1991.

1990 US refused to support any regime that included Khmer Rouge (July).

1990 Australian peace plan accepted by all competing factions in Cambodia during conference at Jakarta (Sept. 10); they agreed to form 12-man Supreme National Council; UN to supervise disarmament of all guerrilla groups.

1991 Heavy fighting in western and northern Cambodia as Khmer and other guerrilla groups sought to improve their positions before implementation of any peace agreement.

1991 Permanent cease-fire agreed to (June 26).

1991 Prince Sihanouk elected chairman of the Supreme National Council (July); Council to relocate to Phnom Penh.

1991 UN Security Council agreed to peace plan (Sept. 30); Cambodia to become multiparty democracy; UN to run country as trusteeship until UN supervised elections in 1993.

1991 Former Vietnamese-backed PRP renamed itself Cambodian People's party (Oct.).

1991 13-year civil war ended by formal peace agreement signed in Paris by all Cambodian factions (Oct. 23).

1992 UN ordered deployment of 22,000 soldiers, police, and officials needed to maintain order in Cambodia (Feb.); biggest UN peacekeeping mission ever, to last 18 months and cost $1.9 billion; UN will also repatriate 360,000 Cambodian refugees in Thailand.

Cambrai, Battle of Inconclusive WW I battle (Nov. 20–Dec. 3, 1917) between the British and Germans. This battle in north France saw the first important tactical deployment of (British) tanks in combat. British losses were 43,000, German 41,000.

Cambrai, League of A short-lived alliance (1508–10) between Holy Roman Emperor Maximilian I, King Ferdinand V of Aragon, King Louis XII of France, and Pope Julius II. The league was formed at Cambrai (Dec. 10, 1508) for the purpose of conquering and dividing up territories of the republic of Venice. The league collapsed (1510), having had only partial success.

Cambrai, Treaty of (Ladies' Peace) (Paix des Dames) Treaty (Aug. 3, 1529) between French king Francis I and Holy Roman Emperor Charles V that briefly halted the Italian Wars (1494–1559). It was negotiated by Francis's mother, Louise of Savoy, and Charles's aunt, Margaret of Austria. By its terms, Charles surrendered claims to Burgundy, and Francis gave up claims in Italy. War soon broke out again, lasting until 1559.

Cambridge Agreement Agreement (Aug. 26, 1629) that transferred the government of the Massachusetts Bay Company from England to the Massachusetts colony. Puritan stockholders had refused to make the journey from England to the Massachusetts colony if this condition could not be met.

Cambridge Platform Essentially a constitution for governing New England Congregational churches, adopted Aug., 1648. The platform was approved as a declaration of principles for church government and doctrine at a church synod held in Massachusetts.

Cambridge Platonists Philosophical school that developed (17th cent.) at Cambridge University, England. Founded by Benjamin Whichcote (1609–83), the school arose in reaction to the teachings of T. Hobbes, and attempted to synthesize the teachings of Plato with Christian doctrine.

Cambuluc *See* **Beijing.**

Cambyses II *d.* 522 BC. Persian king (529–522), successor to his father, Cyrus the Great. He conquered Egypt (525 BC) but was forced to abandon plans for further conquests in Africa by a revolt at home. He died trying to quash the rebellion.

Camden, Battle of British victory (Aug. 16, 1780) over American colonials during the Carolina Campaign (*q.v.*) in the American Revolution (1775–83). One of the greatest disasters in American military history, the defeat led to the British invasion of North Carolina. Lord C. Cornwallis commanding some 2,200 British regulars, opposed a force of about 3,000 American regulars and new recruits, led by Gen. H. Gates. The Americans planning to attack the British-held town of Camden, South Carolina, were routed by Cornwallis. Losses were 2,000 Americans (including Gen. J. Kalb) and 324 British.

Camel, Battle of the (Basra, ˘) Victory (Dec. 9, 656) for the caliph Ali over his opponents during the First Muslim Civil War 1656–661). The rebels, led by Muhammad's widow, Aisha (611–678), his cousin Zobair (*d.* 656), and his companion Talha (*d.* 656), took control of Basra, a port city on the Persian Gulf. Ali, commanding some 29,000 soldiers, attacked the larger rebel force and finally captured Aisha.

Cameronians Scottish religious group. Cameronians were Covenanters and followers of Richard Cameron (*d.* 1681). They organized as the Reformed Presbyterians after 1681. Most Cameronians united with the Church of Scotland (1876).

Cameroon (*prop.* United Republic of Cameroon) (*formerly* Federal Republic of Cameroon) Republic of west central Africa, independent since 1960. The population is 11,900,000 and the capital is Yaoundé. German presence in the region began in the late 19th cent., and by 1902 the territory was a German colony. Conquered by the Allies during WW I, it was divided (1919) by League of Nations mandate into French Cameroon and British Cameroon. These territories became (1946) UN trust territories. French Cameroon became independent (1960) and the south half of British Cameroon was joined to it (1961). The north sector joined Nigeria. The first president of Cameroon, Ahmad ou Ahidjo, served until 1982. His successor, President Paul Biya, held the post into the early 1990s.

Camillus, Marcus Furius *d.* 365? BC. Celebrated Roman general and statesman. He was elected dictator five times between 396 and 367 BC, and captured Veii (396). He is credited with several other important victories.

Camisards Protestant peasants in southern France who rebelled (1702–10) against persecutions by French Catholics. The revolt followed revocation (1685) of the Edict of Nantes by King Louis XIV and his attempts to impose Catholicism on his subjects. Led by the peasant commander J. Cavalier and others, the Camisards burned Catholic churches and used guerrilla tactics against royal armies. The government retaliated by massacring whole villages. The revolt was broken by 1705, though sporadic fighting continued until 1710.

Camoëns, Luk Vaz de *See* **Camões, Luiz Vaz de.**

Camões, Luiz Vaz de (Camoëns, Luiz Vaz de) 1524–80. Considered the greatest Portuguese poet. He is best known for his epic poem *The Lusiads.*

Camorra Secret society of criminals that flourished (19th cent.) in Naples, Italy. Of uncertain origins, the society was known for its involvement in robbery, smuggling, and blackmail by the early 19th cent. The Camorra operated freely under the Bourbon rulers of Naples and eventually gained considerable political power. Following the unification of Italy (1861), the government began a campaign against the Camorra. Manhunts (from 1882) and a sensational murder trial (1911), involving 20 supposed Camorra members, brought about its decline.

Campanella, Tommaso 1568–1639. Italian philosopher and Dominican monk. Imprisoned for 27 years during the Inquisition, he is best known for his work *The City of the Sun.* An account of a utopian society, it parallels Plato's *Republic.*

Campania Historic region in southern Italy noted for its productive farms. Once held by Etruscans and Greek colonists, the region came under Roman control in 340 BC. After the fall of Rome, it changed hands several times, becoming part of the kingdom of Naples (1282) and finally Italy (1861). Among the famous ancient cities in this region were Pompeii, Capua, and Cumae.

Campbell, Archibald, 8th earl and 1st marquess of Argyll 1607–61. Scottish nobleman. A leader of the Covenanters during the English Civil Wars, he was defeated by J. Montrose (1645). He then supported Charles II, and, in 1652, submitted to Cromwell and the Commonwealth. He was beheaded for treason during the Restoration.

Campbell, Archibald, 9th earl of Argyll 1629–85. Scottish nobleman. A Royalist during the English Civil Wars, he fled to Holland (1681) He later returned to take part in the Duke of Monmouth's rebellion (1685).

Campbell, John, 1st earl of Breadalbane 1635–1716. Scottish nobleman. He is said to have taken part in organizing the massacre of the MacDonald clan at Glencoe (1692).

Campbell, John, 2d duke of Argyll and duke of Greenwich 1678–1743. Scottish general. Campbell supported the union of England and Scotland, served in the War of the Spanish Succession (1701–14), supported George I's accession to the throne, and quelled the Jacobite revolt of 1715.

Campbell-Bannerman, Sir Henry 1836–1908. A British statesman. He became Liberal party leader (1899) and British prime minister (1905–08). An opponent of the Boer War, he is noted for permitting self-government for the defeated Orange Free State and the Transvaal (1906–07).

Campbellites *See* **Disciples of Christ.**

Camp David Accords *See* **Israel, 1978.**

Campion, Edmund 1540–81. English Jesuit martyr. He was arrested and tortured after distributing a pamphlet, titled *Ten Reasons* (1581), denouncing the Anglican church. He was executed on spurious charges of treason after he refused to recant.

Campo Formio, Treaty of Treaty (Oct. 17, 1797) between France and Austria ending the War of the First Coalition during the French Revolutionary Wars (1792–1802). The treaty, which marked Napoleon's victory over Austria, was signed at the village of Campo Formio in northern Italy, following the preliminary Peace of Loeben (Apr. 18, 1797). By its terms, France won the Belgian provinces, Lombardy, and the Ionian Islands. Austria received most of the republic of Venice, including the city of Venice, Istria, and Dalmatia.

Camus, Albert 1913–60. French author, one of the major writers of this century. Among his best-known works are *The Stranger* (1942) and *The Plague* (1947). He won the Nobel Prize in Literature in 1957.

Canaan Biblical name for ancient Palestine. In the Old Testament it was the Israelites' Promised Land. Following their exodus from Egypt, the Israelites conquered and settled this region.

Canada Country located in the northern part of North America. The population is 26,660,000 and the capital is Ottawa. Canada was explored and settled by both English and French and its history reflects the influence of both nations, as well as the struggle of French- and English-speaking Canadians to overcome their differences. Canada was invaded by Colonial forces during the American Revolution and again during the War of 1812, but since that time has had peaceful and generally friendly relations with the US. Created by the unification of 4 provinces in 1867, Canada has grown into a federation of 10 provinces. Key dates in the history of Canada include:

c1000   Leif Ericson, Norse explorer, believed to have led Viking expedition that landed on Canadian coast.

c1005   Thorfinn Karlsefni, Islandic navigator, established short-lived colony in North America.

1497   J. Cabot explored Nova Scotia and Newfoundland.

1534–35   J. Cartier discovered Gulf of St. Lawrence, St. Lawrence River; established French claims to the area.

1576–78   English navigator Sir M. Frobisher made three unsuccessful attempts to find a northwest passage through Canada.

1583   Sir H. Gilbert explored Newfoundland, claiming it for England.

1604–08   S. de Champlain explored parts of eastern Canada.

1605   Port Royal, first permanent settlement in Canada, founded by S. de Champlain; French colony of Acadia established in following years.

1608   S. de Champlain founded Quebec City.

1625–29   Jesuit Saint J. de Brébeuf served as missionary to Huron Indians in New France.

1629–32   English captured Quebec (1629); it was returned to France in 1632; fur trade exploited in subsequent years.

1642   Montreal permanently settled by French.

1663   French king Louis XIV dissolved Company of New France and instituted royal government in the colony of New France in Canada.

1663   F. de Laval, French bishop, founded seminary at Quebec, later known as Laval University.

1670   Hudson's Bay Company formed by English for colonization and trade in Canada; was prominent in the early development of Canada.

1682   Explorer R. de La Salle claimed Mississippi Valley for France, calling it Louisiana.

1689–97   King William's War; French and English launched attacks on each other's settlements.

1702–13   Queen Anne's War; British captured Port Royal and other French territories.

1713   Britain acquired most of Acadia, Newfoundland, and territory around Hudson Bay through Peace of Utrecht.

1744–48   King George's War.

1755   French Acadians (in Nova Scotia) deported by British for refusing oath of loyalty to the king.

1756–63 French and Indian War fought; British defeated French on Plains of Abraham (1759) and took Quebec; Montreal fell to British (1760); conflict ended by Treaty of Paris (1763), by which all French territory in Canada passed to Britain.

1774 Quebec Act passed (June 22) by British Parliament, established permanent government in Canada, granted legal and religious concessions to French-speaking people of Quebec.

1775–83 Canada remained loyal to the king during the American Revolution; Canada became a haven for United Empire Loyalists fleeing the US after the Revolution.

1783 Treaty of Paris ended the American Revolution; US–Canadian border left unclear, opening way for the Northeast boundary dispute.

1783 North West Company founded for Canadian fur trade; later rivaled Hudson's Bay Company.

1789 Nootka Sound controversy.

1789–1812 Explorer and fur trader David Thompson (1770–1857) traveled extensively in western Canada; drew up map of Canada and northern US.

1791 Constitutional Act divided Quebec into English-speaking Upper Canada (now Ontario) and French-speaking Lower Canada (now Quebec), but failed to grant self-government.

1792–93 G. Vancouver surveyed northwest coast of North America.

1793 Scottish explorer Sir A. Mackenzie traversed Canada, becoming the first European to cross America north of Mexico.

1812 T. Douglas, 5th earl of Selkirk, established Red River Settlement in Rupert's Land (Manitoba).

1812–15 War of 1812 between the US and Britain; several invasions of Canada repulsed.

1817 Rush-Bagot Convention signed, demilitarizing Canadian border with US.

1818 Convention of 1818 established Canadian–US border east of Lake of the Woods.

1821 North West Company merged with Hudson's Bay Company, ending bitter competition and some violence.

1832 *Wacousta* published by novelist John Richardson; popularized Canadian national historical novel.

1837 Unsuccessful attempt to overthrow the government by W. L. Mackenzie and some 800 followers in Upper Canada; L. Papineau led a revolt in Lower Canada; Mackenzie's escape to the US resulted in the Caroline Affair.

1839 Lord Durham's Report to British Parliament; following revolts in both Upper and Lower Canada for reform, Lord Durham investigated and recommended union of the provinces and establishment of effective government.

1840 Canadian shipowner S. Cunard founded first regular transatlantic steamship line.

1841 Upper and Lower Canada united as Province of Canada; union of francophone and anglophone populations provided opportunity in legislature to gain experience needed for self-government.

1841–42 Canadian explorer G. Simpson made round-the-world overland journey through northern part of the world.

1842 Webster-Ashburton Treaty.

1844 Toronto *Globe* founded by G. Brown.

1845 Explorer J. Franklin, searching for the Northwest Passage, killed after his ships froze in ice.

1846 Oregon Treaty settled Oregon Question, a dispute with US over Canada's boundary in the Oregon Country.

1846–50 Economic depression; Montreal especially hard hit.

1848–51 Clear Grits movement to promote land reform.

1850–54 Arctic explorer R. McClure completed first successful navigation of Northwest Passage.

1851–54 F. Hincks served as premier of the United Province of Canada (modern-day Ontario and Quebec).

1854–66 US-Canadian trade reciprocity treaty; spurred economic growth in Canada.

1852 Historian F. Garneau wrote *History of Canada*.

1854 Clergy Reserves secularized after long controversy; ended practice of setting aside land for Anglican church.

1854 Manorial system (seignorial system) abolished in Canada; first established in 1568.

1864 Charlottetown Conference held to discuss unification of Canada.

1864 Quebec Conference held (Oct. 10–27) by delegates from colonies of British North

America; drafted resolutions that were the basis for establishment of unified Canada.

1865–1924 Noted landscape painter J. W. Morrice lived.

1866–67 Westminster Conference in London laid basis for British North America Act.

1867 British North America Act; provinces of Quebec, Ontario, Nova Scotia, and New Brunswick unified and became the Dominion of Canada.

1867–73 Sir J. A. Macdonald served as first prime minister; guided nation through crucial early years.

1867 Canada First Movement organized to promote Canadian nationalist spirit.

1867–73 Alexander Mackenzie, first Liberal prime minister, in office.

1869–70 Riel's Rebellion in western Canada against the federal government.

1870 Red River Settlement joined Canada as province of Manitoba.

1871 British Columbia became part of the dominion.

1871 Treaty of Washington signed with US.

1871 Bank Act; became basis of Canada's banking regulation.

1873 Prince Edward Island became Canadian province.

1873 Canadian Pacific railroad scandal helped bring down J. Macdonald's Conservative government.

1873–96 Long periods of economic depression, especially in 1873–81.

1875 Supreme Court of Canada established.

1878–91 Macdonald back in office as prime minister; instituted policy of trade protectionism (National Policy) to ease effects of depression; began construction of Canadian Pacific Railway.

1880 Royal Canadian Academy of Arts founded, National Gallery of Canada created.

1884–85 Riel's Rebellion (second) in Saskatchewan against government.

1885 Canadian Pacific Railway completed; east and west coasts linked by rail.

1886 Bering Sea dispute with the US.

1888 Jesuit Estates Act passed.

1890 European immigrants began arriving in large numbers.

1890s Confederation group of Canadian authors active.

1896–1911 Sir W. Laurier served as first French-Canadian prime minister; wheat-producing Prairie provinces settled; economic prosperity restored.

1897 Author C. Roberts wrote his popular *History of Canada.*

1897 Great Klondike gold rush began.

1898 *Black Rock,* first of a series of adventure novels about pioneer life, published by Rev. Charles W. Gordon.

1904–11 A. George, 4th earl of Grey, served as British colonial governor general.

1905 Alberta and Saskatchewan became provinces of Canada.

1907 Poet Robert W. Service published *Song of a Sourdough.*

1908 *Anne of Green Gables* published by Lucy Maud Montgomery.

1910 Writer Stephen Leacock published his collection of humorous stories, *Literary Lapses.*

1911–20 Sir R. Borden served as prime minister; won independent representation for British dominions in the League of Nations (1919).

1914–18 WW I; Canada joined Allies and actively participated in war effort; by war's end the Canadian Corps was commanded by Sir Arthur Currie.

1915 Poet J. McCrae wrote *In Flanders Fields.*

1920 Group of Seven formed; the group was dedicated to painting Canadian landscapes.

1921–30 W. L. Mackenzie King served as prime minister.

1923 Sir F. Banting received Nobel Prize for Physiology or Medicine with Scottish physiologist John Macleod for isolating insulin.

1926 Poet E. J. Pratt wrote his epic *The Titans.*

1927 Old Age Pensions Act; federal government to pay half the cost.

1929 US stock market crash; marked beginning of depression in Canada.

1930–40 Cooperative Commonwealth Federation, Canadian Socialist party, and Social Credit party gained support during the Depression, particularly in Western provinces.

1931 British Commonwealth of Nations created; Canada gained equal status with Britain and other members of the Commonwealth by Statute of Westminster.

1934 Bank of Canada established as reserve bank.

1935   C. Douglas, who devised theory of Social Credit, served as reconstruction adviser to the government of Alberta.

1935–48   Mackenzie King back in office as prime minister.

1939–45   WW II; Canada joined Allies and played an active role in the war effort.

1947   Canadians hereforth called "Canadian citizens" (not British subjects), following legislation passed by Parliament.

1948–57   L. Saint Laurent in office as prime minister.

1949   Newfoundland became Canadian province.

1949   Canada became founding member of NATO.

1950–53   Korean War; Canadian troops part of UN forces fighting in Korea.

1951   Massey Report issued; promoted federal subsidies for scientific research and the arts.

1957–63   John G. Diefenbaker served as prime minister; brought Conservatives to power for first time since 1935.

1957   Hospital Insurance and Diagnostic Services Act enacted; eventually extended health insurance coverage to nearly the entire population.

1959   St. Lawrence Seaway opened.

1963–68   L. B. Pearson served as prime minister; Liberals returned to power.

1964   New national flag introduced, replacing Union Jack.

1967   Canadian M. McLuhan published *The Medium Is the Message: An Inventory of Effects.*

1967   Parti Québécois founded.

1967   Canada celebrated its centenary; Canada Day instituted (July 1).

1968–79   Prime Minister P. Trudeau in office; a Liberal and French-Canadian, he faced a worsening crisis over French separatism in Quebec; favored bilingualism, opposed separatism.

1970s   French separatist movement in Quebec became major political controversy.

1970   Diplomatic relations with China established.

1970   Trudeau utilized (Oct. 16) War Measures Act to halt kidnappings by French-Canadian radicals Front de Libération Québécois.

1975   Prime Minister Trudeau imposed wage and price controls (1975–78) in the face of worsening economic problems.

1979   Economic problems forced Prime Minister Trudeau to dissolve Parliament (Mar. 26) and call for new elections.

1979–80   Joe Clark (Progressive Conservative) in office as prime minister after defeating Trudeau's Liberals in the elections; Clark government, which became shortest in Canadian history (9 months), quickly aroused public resentment by trying to implement controversial election promises.

1980   Novelist Mordecai Richler published *Joshua Then and Now.*

1980–84   Trudeau back in office as prime minister, following elections that ousted the Clark administration; his administration marked by program to increase Canadian ownership of oil industry, by easing of separatist tensions in Quebec, and by enactment of new patriated constitution.

1980   Canadian diplomats helped smuggle six US citizens out of Iran (Jan.), thereby preventing their being seized as hostages by Muslim fundamentalists.

1980   Referendum to implement Quebec separatism defeated (June) in Quebec provincial vote; serious threat to Canadian unity averted.

1980   Discussions between Trudeau government and provinces on new Canadian constitution began; various stumbling blocks arose, including control of resources in the provinces, allocation of federal powers to provinces, and procedures for amending the constitution; talks continued over next year.

1980   Government approved construction of Canadian sections of Alaska oil pipeline (July).

1981   US president R. Reagan visited Canada (Mar.); criticized Canada's Foreign Investment Review Agency as obstacle to US investment in Canada.

1981   Alberta protested national government energy program; government agreed to raise domestic oil and gas prices (Sept.).

1981   Prime Minister Trudeau called new conference of provincial and federal representatives to resolve final difficulties on new constitution (Nov.); French-language rights extended and Charter of Rights and Liberties added; approval of amendments to be by seven of ten provinces (about 50% of the population); Quebec remained only province to reject Constitution Act (1982).

1981 Draft of new constitution approved by Queen Elizabeth (Dec. 8).

1981 Economy in decline; inflation, unemployment, and interest rates all hit new highs; slow recovery began in 1982.

1982 Queen Elizabeth assented to Constitution Act (Apr. 17); provided for legal autonomy of Canada and replaced the British North America Act (1867) as the instrument of Canadian government; constitutional amendment process now entirely within Canadian hands; Canada to remain in Commonwealth and to continue to be a constitutional monarchy.

1982 Federal government adopted anti-inflationary policy; imposed mandatory controls on public service wage hikes (June).

1983 Government signed agreement (Feb. 10) with US allowing testing of US weapons on Canadian soil (except nuclear, chemical, and biological weapons); peace groups protested cruise missile tests in 1984.

1983 Long-time Progressive Conservative party worker M. Brian Mulroney replaced Clark as party head (Jan.); won first elective office as Nova Scotia MP (Aug. 29).

1983 Public employee strike in British Columbia (Nov.).

1983 First amendment to new constitution passed; provided for consultation with native Canadian groups before passing constitutional amendments on their rights.

1983 Trudeau's personal, international "peace crusade" failed to produce new initiatives, despite Trudeau's meetings with world leaders (Nov.–Dec.).

1984 Trudeau resigned as leader of Liberal party (Feb. 29); John Turner, former Trudeau cabinet member, replaced him.

1984 John Turner in office as prime minister.

1984 Supreme Court ruled that Quebec law, establishing French as the official language in schools, violated 1982 Charter of Rights (July); ruled English-speaking children had right to education in English; Quebec government protested the decision.

1984 Liberal party defeated by Progressive Conservative party; Conservatives campaigned on end to confrontational politics, reduction of federal control over economy, and encouragement of private enterprise; Conservatives won 211 of 282 seats in House of Commons.

1984–93 Brian Mulroney in office as prime minister; his first ministry marked by establishment of closer economic ties with US, an improving economy, and continuing efforts to resolve Quebec problem.

1984 International Court of Justice established official maritime boundary between Canada and US in long-disputed area of Gulf of Maine (Oct. 12).

1985 Government dismantled Foreign Investment Review Agency.

1985 US president R. Reagan visited Canada (Mar.); discussed US–Canadian free trade agreement.

1985 Mulroney administration moved to end Trudeau's National Energy Program; ended federal taxes on oil and natural gas production; negotiated Western Accord with provinces, to price Canadian oil in line with world market.

1985 Canada reasserted its claim to sovereignty over Arctic waters (Sept.); announced plans to increase patrols against US intrusion.

1985 Imposed trade sanctions against South Africa to protest apartheid government.

1985 Liberal party in Quebec ousted long-time Parti Québécois separatist government, in power since 1976 (Dec.).

1986 Report on acid rain recommended joint Canadian-US research into ways to make coal-burning facilities less polluting (Mar.).

1986 Negotiations on controversial US-Canadian free-trade agreement began (May).

1987 Free trade agreement between Canada and US adopted (Oct. 3); went into effect Jan. 1, 1989.

1987 Meech Lake Accord (Apr. 30); Prime minister Mulroney negotiated agreement with all 10 provincial premiers for amendments to 1982 constitution that would resolve Quebec's grievances; Quebec to be recognized as "distinct society" with appropriate rights to preserve its French language and culture; and new amendments henceforth to require approval by all 10 provinces.

1987 Quebec became first province to approve accord (June); all other provinces required to approve by June 1990.

1989 Canada joined Organization of American States.

1990 Meech Lake Accord failed (June); endorsement by 8 of 10 provinces and last-minute efforts by Mulroney government were thwarted by parliamentary maneuvering in Manitoba and Newfoundland; separatist sentiments aroused in Quebec.

1990 Government introduced federal goods and services tax.

1991 Persian Gulf War; some 4,000 Canadian troops aided the allied effort to oust Iraqi forces from Kuwait.

1991 Joint US–Canadian treaty to reduce acid rain signed (Mar. 13); sulphur dioxide emissions from coal-fired electrical generating plants to be reduced.

1991 Commission appointed by Mulroney to formulate new plan for constitutional changes that would resolve Quebec question and other difficulties; proposals reported (Sept.) and quickly denounced by Quebec separatists.

1991 Some 70,000 public employees struck to end freeze on wages (Sept.–Oct.); government legislated end to strike.

1992 Government spending freeze announced (Jan.).

1992 Toronto-based international real estate conglomerate Olympia and York reported in serious financial straits.

1992 Charlottetown Accord on proposed constitutional amendments defeated in referendum (Oct.); accord sought to recognize Quebec as distinct society, recognize rights of aboriginal peoples, and create an elected Senate.

Canada Company British land company. At the instigation of author J. Galt, the company was organized (1826) to generate revenue to compensate settlers' losses arising from the War of 1812. The company sold government lands in northern Canada and helped promote colonization there.

Canary Islands Seven islands in the Atlantic Ocean off the northwest coast of Africa (*pop.* 1,275,000) which now make up two provinces of Spain. Once called the Fortunate Isles, they have long been a stopping place for travelers from many parts of the world. In 1402, they were settled by the Spanish kingdom of Castile, and they have remained under Spanish control since then.

Canaveral, Cape US space-program center and principal launch point for US rockets into outer space. Used for rocket testing since 1950, it was the launch site for the first US space satellite (Jan. 31, 1958), the first US manned space flight (May 5, 1961), and the Apollo program (*q.v.*) moon landing (July 20, 1969).

Candragupta *See* **Chandragupta.**

Canetti, Elias 1905– . Bulgarian novelist and playwright. Fascinated by the psychology of crowds, he wrote *Tower of Babel* (1935) to describe the insanity of mob behavior. His numerous plays depict the power of crowds and the position of the individual in society. He won the Nobel Prize for Literature (1981).

Cannae, Battle of Great Carthaginian victory (216 BC) over the Romans during the Second Punic War (218–201 BC). The Carthaginians, led by Hannibal, encircled and decimated a Roman army of some 85,000 men, led by consuls Gaius Terentius Varro and Lucius Aemilius Paulus, near the village of Cannae, in what is now southeast Italy. Roman losses were over 50,000; Carthaginian, fewer than 6,000.

Cannon, Joseph Gurney 1836–1926. American politician. A Republican congressman from N.C. for 46 years between 1873 and 1923, he wielded almost complete control over the House during his term as its Speaker (1903–11).

Cano, Juan Sebastián del *d.* 1526. Spanish navigator. He took command of and completed Magellan's exploratory voyage of 1519, following Magellan's death in the Philippines (1521). He thus became the first man to circumnavigate the earth (1522).

canon law System of regulations for governing the clergy and the church. The Roman Catholic church, the Eastern Orthodox church, the Anglican churches, and independent Eastern Christian churches all have accumulated bodies of canon law. The Roman Catholic canon law is by far the most extensive. It includes laws issued by popes, ecclesiastical councils, and bishops (for local matters). Canon law can be traced back to the early papal decretals (392, Pope Siricius). The subsequent profusion of canon laws led to efforts at systemizing them (from the 6th cent.), including Gratian's works, the corpus of canon law (*Corpus juris canonici,* 1580) and the code of canon law (*Codex juris canonici,* 1917). Canon laws of the Church of England, known as the Constitutions and Canons Ecclesiastical, were issued 1603–04.

(For canon law of the Eastern churches, *see* Oriental canon law.)

Canon law, Oriental   *See* **Oriental Canon law.**

Canopus, Decree of   *See* **Decree of Canopus.**

Cánovas del Castillo, Antonio 1828–97.   Spanish politician and historian. Cánovas was instrumental in restoring Bourbon king Alfonso XII to the throne (1875), and subsequently served as premier intermittently between 1875 and 1897.

Canterbury, Saint Augustine of   *See* **Augustine of Canterbury, Saint.**

Canton   Term for a constituent state in the Swiss Confederation.

Canton   *See also* **Guangzhou.**

Canton Commune   The short-lived government formed by the Chinese Communist party in opposition to Guomindang (*q.v.*) efforts to suppress them. The Communists captured Guangzhou (Dec., 1927), but were quickly and ruthlessly suppressed with much bloodshed.

Canton system   Chinese trade system. From 1759 until the Treaty of Nanjing (1842), foreign merchants were allowed to conduct their trade with China only in the city of Guangzhou (Canton) and were forced to deal with approved merchants.

Canute (Cnut) (Knut) c995–1035.   Danish king of England (1016–35), Denmark (1019–35), and Norway (1028–35). He invaded England (1015), conquered Wessex and Northumbria, and, after pitched battles, divided England with Edmund Ironside. Following Edmund's death (1016), he became sole ruler, and administered his kingdom wisely. He married Aethelred's widow, Emma, and by her had his son Harthacanute. He succeeded his brother to the Danish throne (1019), and, after defeating a Norwegian invasion of Denmark (1026), he conquered Norway (1028).

Canute IV (~ the Saint) *d.* 1086.   Danish king (1080–86). Canute built many churches and cathedrals, and attempted an invasion of England (1085). He was killed by rioters who were enraged over taxes he imposed.

Canute the Saint   *See* **Canute IV.**

Cao Cao (Ts'ao Ts'ao) AD 155–220.   Chinese general. He held real power during the last years of the last Han emperor, Xiandi, and set up the new Wei dynasty in 220.

Cao Xueqin 1715?–63.   Chinese author. Born the son of servants to Kangxi Emperor, he was raised in a world of luxury and royal splendor.

Experiences of growing up in this world formed the backdrop for one of the most popular Chinese novels, *Hongloumeng* (*Dream of the Red Chamber*).

Cape Frontier Wars (Frontier Wars) (Kafir Wars)   Series of wars fought in the 18th and 19th cents. by Dutch, and later British, settlers against natives in South Africa. The major conflict occurred (1850–53) after the British annexed territory to the east of Cape Colony and established British Kaffraria there. The Xhosa were defeated and several years later suffered a famine. Renewed resistance by the Xhosa led to the last Kafir war (1877–78) and their final defeat. In the years following, their territories were absorbed by the Cape Colony.

Cape of Good Hope   Cape at the southern tip of Africa, notorious among sailors for heavy seas. First rounded (1488) by Bartholomeu Dias (1450?–1500). It was an important landmark on the sea trade route between Europe and the East. The cape itself was colonized by the Dutch (1652), passed to the British (1806), and was made part of South Africa (1910).

Čapek, Karel 1890–1938.   Czech playwright, novelist, and essayist. He is best remembered for his play *R.U.R.* (*Rossum's Universal Robots*) from which the term "robot" derives.

Capellari, Bartolomeo Alberto   *See* **Gregory XVI.**

Cape St. Vincent, Battle of   Naval battle (Feb. 14, 1797) off the coast of southern Portugal during the French Revolutionary Wars (1792–1802). The British forces, commanded by Sir John Jervis (1735–1823), defeated a Spanish fleet of almost twice as many ships, which were to have joined the French in an invasion of Britain.

Capet, Hugh   *See* **Hugh Capet.**

Capetians   Dynasty of kings that ruled in France from 987 to 1328. The Capetians were descendants of Robert the Strong (*d.* 866), count of Anjou and Blois, and the first Capetian king was Hugh Capet. He replaced the last Carolingian king in 987, and at that time ruled only a small kingdom around Paris. His successors, however, gradually absorbed the surrounding kingdoms and increased the power of the monarchy, thereby laying the foundations of modern France. The Capetians were succeeded by the collateral lines of Valois and Bourbon. *The Capetian kings were:* Hugh Capet 987–996; Robert II 996–1031; Henry I 1031–60; Philip I 1060–

1108; Louis VI 1108–37; Louis VII 1137–80; Philip II 1180–1223; Louis VIII 1223–26; Louis IX 1226–70; Philip III 1270–85; Philip IV 1285–1314; Louis X 1314–16; John I 1316; Philip V 1317–22; Charles IV 1322–28.

Cape Verde (*properly* Republic of Cape Verde) Republic consisting of 15 islands located off the west coast of Africa. The population is 339,000 and the capital is Praia. First settled by the Portuguese in 1462, Cape Verde subsequently prospered as a Portuguese colony serving the slave trade. The colony's importance declined in the late 19th cent. as the abolition movement ended trafficking in slaves. The islands' position on shipping lanes again brought prosperity after WW II, and in 1951 Cape Verde became an overseas province of Portugal. Nationalist aspirations prevailed, however, and the islands became independent in 1975, with ties to Guinea-Bissau on the Africa mainland. Cape Verde broke with Guinea-Bissau in 1981, adopting its own constitution that year.

capitalism Economic system in which property, means of production, and financial institutions are privately owned and which is driven by the profit motive. Theoretically based on free enterprise and unregulated competition, capitalism can be traced back to the 16th cent., when mercantilism rose to replace feudalism. Capitalism flourished, however, with the coming of the Industrial Revolution (18th cent.) and spawned such notable capitalist theoreticians as A. Smith. Social inequities and theoretical weaknesses perceivied by K. Marx gave rise to Socialism in the 19th cent. By the 20th cent., the archetypal capitalistic notion of unregulated enterprise (never fully realized) had given way to a host of social reforms and regulatory bodies imposed by national governments.

Capitol *See* **Capitoline Hill.**

Capitol Domed building in Washington, D.C., that houses the US Senate and House of Representatives. It is the symbolic center of the federal government. Begun in 1793 from plans submitted by W. Thornton, the unfinished building was burned by the British (1814) during the War of 1812. Work on it began again that year and was finally completed (1830) by C. Bulfinch, the sixth architect involved in its construction. It was subsequently enlarged (1851–65) by Thomas U. Walter (1804–87).

Capitoline Hill (Capitol) One of the seven hills of Rome and the historic center of the city. It is the site of the temple of Jupiter Capitolinus and the Tarpeian Rock, from which criminals were thrown to their death.

capitulations Economic concessions granted by the Ottoman empire to friendly European states. The practice was abolished (1914) on the eve of WW I. Restored after the war, they were again abolished by the Treaty of Lausanne (July, 1923).

Capo d'Istria, Count Giovanni Antonio *See* **Kapodistrias, Count Ioannes Antonios.**

Capone, Al (Alfonse) 1899–1947. Notorious American gangster. He was the leader of Chicago's organized crime underworld from the mid-1920s to 1931, when he was convicted of federal income tax evasion. He subsequently died of an advanced case of syphilis.

Caporetto, Battle of (Isonzo, ˜) Austro-German victory (Oct. 24, 1917) over the Italians during WW I. The battle was a major disaster for the Italians and resulted in reorganization of the army and formation of the Supreme Allied War Council for coordinating the war effort. Fifteen combined Austrian and German divisions, under German general Otto von Below (1857–1944), attacked Italian forces on the Isonzo line at Caporetto (then) in northeast Italy. Italian forces retreated some 70 miles (Oct. 24–Nov. 7), by which time some 300–600,000 Italians had been lost as casualties, prisoners, or deserters.

Capote, Truman 1924–84. Noted American author. Among his novels are *Other Voices, Other Rooms* and *In Cold Blood,* a work he called a nonfiction novel.

Cappadocia Ancient region now located in eastern Turkey. Once a satrapy of Persia (c6th cent. BC), it evolved into an independent kingdom (3d cent. BC). Henceforth it became an ally of the Romans and finally a province (AD 17).

Captivity *See* **Babylonian Captivity.**

Capua Town in southern Italy and once a prosperous city of ancient Rome. Originally an Etruscan town, it fell to the Romans (c340 BC) and prospered following the construction of the Appian Way. The scene of Spartacus's revolt (73 BC), it was destroyed by the Vandals (AD 456) and the Muslims (840). The modern city was built in 856 and was subsequently the scene of many battles, including heavy fighting during WW II (1943).

Capuchins Roman Catholic order of Franciscan monks, properly the Friars Minor Capuchin. The order was established (c1525) in Italy by Matteo da Bascio (c1495–1552) as a movement for reform of the Catholic church. Its friars were expected to live a life of poverty. The movement became widespread, and in subsequent years they rivaled the Jesuits in importance within the church.

Carabobo, Battle of Battle (June 24, 1821) in northern Venezuela that established Venezuelan independence from Spain. A combined force of 6,500 rebels under S. Bolívar and J. Paez attacked and crushed a smaller Spanish force, led by Gen. Miguel de la Torre. Soon afterward, Bolívar liberated the capital, Caracas.

Caracalla (Marcus Aurelius Antoninus) AD 188–217. Roman emperor (AD 211–217), notorious for his ruthless brutality. He and his brother Geta succeeded their father, Septimius Severus. Caracalla, however, killed Geta and ordered a massacre of some 20,000 of his brother's followers (AD 212). He also granted citizenship to all free men within the empire in order, it is believed, to increase tax revenues.

Caractacus (Caratacus) (Caradoc) *fl.* AD 50. British chieftain, a son of Cymbeline. He led the British against Roman invaders (AD 43–50) but was finally defeated and captured by Emperor Claudius's forces.

Caradoc *See* **Caractacus.**

Carafa, Gian Pietro *See* **Paul IV.**

Caratacus *See* **Caractacus.**

Carausius, Marcus Aurelius 245?–293. Roman general. Placed in command of a Roman fleet in Gaul, he revolted and set himself up as emperor in Britain (c287–293). He was killed by one of his ministers during an invasion ordered by Roman emperor Maximian.

Caravaggio (Michelangelo Merisi) 1573–1610. Italian artist who influenced the development of baroque art (*q.v.*) through his naturalistic paintings. His noted works include *Death of the Virgin* (1606) and the *Fortune Teller* (1594).

Carbonari Italian secret society formed in the kingdom of Naples in the early 19th cent. Carbonari groups came to stand for freedom from foreign rule. The lodges first appeared during, and soon opposed, the reign of J. Murat (1808–15), the Neapolitan king installed by Napoleon. The lodges spread throughout Italy

and, in the post-Napoleonic years, opposed Austrian domination. By 1830, however, the Carbonari were drawn into the movement for Italian unification, the Risorgimento, and disappeared. In the 1820s, Carbonari lodges were also active in Spain and France.

Carchemish, Battle of Battle (605 BC) in which Babylonian king Nebuchadnezzar defeated the Egyptian king Necho II along the Euphrates River, in what is now Syria. The defeat cost Egypt its territories in Syria.

Cárdenas, Garcia López de *See* **Coronado, Francisco Vásquez de.**

Cárdenas, Lázaro 1895–1970. Mexican soldier and president (1934–40). Cárdenas fought in the 1913 revolution, and, as president, he aroused much opposition by nationalizing foreign-owned properties (including oil fields) and by breaking up large estates to give land to small farmers. The latter reform established government-owned communal farms (the Ejido system).

Cardigan, James Thomas Brudenell, 7th earl of 1797–1868. British general during the Crimean War (1853–56). He led the now famous charge of the Light Brigade at the Battle of Balaklava (1854). The disastrous cavalry maneuver is said to have been caused by a mixup in orders.

cardinal In the Roman Catholic church, an ecclesiastical rank second only to the pope. Cardinals act as advisers to and emissaries of the pope and, as members of the Sacred College of Cardinals, elect the pope.

Cardozo, Benjamin Nathan 1870–1938. American jurist and associate justice of the US Supreme Court (1932–38). He was an influential jurist, whose wide reputation stemmed from his term as a New York State appeals court judge (1914–28) and his books on jurisprudence.

Carleton, Guy, 1st baron Dorchester 1724–1808. British general and governor of Quebec four times between 1766 and 1796. Commander of British troops in Canada during the American Revolution, he defeated the Americans during the Quebec Campaign (1775–76). He became commander of British forces in America and served to the end of the Revolution (1782–83).

Carlisle Commission (Peace Commission of 1778) British peace overture during the American Revolution (1775–83). Surprised by their defeat at Saratoga (1777), the British sent F. Howard, 5th earl of Carlisle, to America to offer the Colonials a negotiated settlement. On June 17, however, the Continental Congress responded by demanding complete independence and withdrawal of all British forces, and thus rejected the British peace offer.

Carlists Supporters of Don Carlos (1788–1855) and his descendants as rightful heirs to the Spanish throne (after 1833). Carlists represented a conservative element in support of traditional monarchy and the church, and, though greatly diminished in number, they continue to be a factor in rural Spain. The movement known as Carlism began when Don Carlos claimed the throne on the death of his brother, King Ferdinand VII, by the terms of the Salic Law. Ferdinand, however, had set aside (1832) the Salic Law to ensure succession of his daughter, Isabella II. Ferdinand's death thus provoked the Carlist Wars (1833–39, 1873–76) and other lesser Carlist uprisings. The direct line of Carlist claimants ended in 1936, though Carlists supported Don Juan (1913–93), son of Alfonso XIII, as his successor. Don Juan's son, Juan Carlos, became king of Spain on Gen. F. Franco's death (1975).

Carlist Wars 1. Civil War (1833–39) in Spain, the Carlists' rebellion against the government of Queen Isabella II. Supporters of Don Carlos, a rival claimant to the throne, rebelled soon after the accession of Isabella. Their strength lay in northern rural Spain, especially the Basque provinces and Navarre, Aragon, and Catalonia, where opposition to a liberalized and centralized monarchy was strongest. The Carlists' attempt to capture Madrid failed (1837), however, and after a mutiny, the Carlist commander joined (1839) Gen. B. Espartero, commander of government forces. The war ended with the Convention of Vegara and Don Carlos's departure from Spain. 2. Civil war (1873–76) in Spain, a rebellion by Carlists against the newly formed republic. Following abdication of King Amadeus and creation of the republic (1873), Carlists in northern Spain again rebelled. The bloody war involved the Basque Provinces and Catalonia, Aragon, and Valencia, and ended (1876) when Don Carlos VII (1848–1909) fled Spain.

Carloman 751–771. Co-ruler of the kingdom of the Franks (768–71), successor, with his brother Charlemagne, to their father, Pepin the Short. Carloman ruled the eastern half of the kingdom, which, on his death, was seized by Charlemagne.

Carloman 828–880. German king (876–880), son of Louis the German. He was king of Bavaria and Carinthia, and of Italy (877–80), but he failed in his claim to the crown of the Holy Roman Empire.

Carloman *d.* 884. Co-ruler (879–882) of the West Frankish Kingdom. With his brother Louis III, he succeeded his father, King Louis II (the Stammerer), and became sole ruler upon his brother's death (882).

Carlos *See also* **Charles.**

Carlos VII *See* **Carlist Wars.**

Carlos, Don *See* **Carlists.**

Carlos de Austria, Don 1545–68. Spanish prince and son of King Philip II. Accused of conspiring to murder his father, he was tried and died soon afterward in prison. His father was rumored to have murdered him. He is the subject of Schiller's tragedy *Don Carlos.*

Carlotta 1840–1927. Empress of Mexico (1864–67), the wife of Maximilian from 1857. She was sent to Europe (1866) to seek aid for the fight against republican revolutionaries then opposing her husband. She failed, became insane, and was confined in Belgium.

Carlowitz, Treaty of *See* **Karlowitz, Treaty of.**

Carlsbad Congress *See* **Carlsbad Decrees.**

Carlsbad Decrees (Karlsbad ˜) Measures recommended (Aug. 31, 1819) by German ministers for suppression of liberal agitation within the German Confederation. The ministers met at the Carlsbad Congress, convened (Aug. 6) by C. von Metternich, following the murder of the German writer August von Kotzebue (1761–1819) by a student. They resolved on press censorship, supervision of universities to suppress liberal student organizations, and establishment of a central committee to investigate revolutionary conspiracies. The measures failed to check the growth of liberalism.

Carlson, Evans Fordyce 1896–1947. American soldier, WW II leader of Carlson's Raiders, a guerrilla unit famous for attacks (1942) on Makin Island and Guadalcanal.

Carlyle, Thomas 1795–1881. Scottish essayist and historian, one of the most influential social critics of his day. He gave up teaching in 1819 and, after publishing works on the German romantics, wrote *Sartor Resartus,* in which he established his characteristic literary style. He moved to London (1834) and there wrote his great *French Revolution* and other works, including *Chartism,* and *History of Frederick the Great.*

Carman, William Bliss *See* **Confederation group.**

Carmelites One of the four important Roman Catholic orders of mendicant friars. The order was begun (c1155) by a group of European hermits under Saint Berthold on Mount Carmel in Palestine. Approved 1226 by Pope Honorius III, the order moved to Europe after the crusaders were forced out of the Holy Land. There the Carmelites abandoned (13th cent.) hermitism and became mendicant friars. A movement to return to a more rigorously ascetic existence was begun (1562) by Saint Theresa and Saint John of the Cross. In 1593 it became the independent order of Discalced Carmelites.

Carmona, António Oscar de Fragoso 1869–1951. Portuguese president (1926–51). A general, he took part in the military coup of 1926 and became president of the provisional government that year. He was subsequently elected president and established, with A. Salazar as premier, dictatorial control of Portugal.

Carnap, Rudolf 1891–1970. A German-born American philosopher. He is noted as a leading advocate of logical positivism and for his works on the philosophy of language, including *The Logical Syntax of Language, Logical Foundations of Probability,* and *Introduction to Symbolic Logic and Its Applications.*

Carnegie, Andrew 1835–1919. Scottish-born American steel magnate and philanthropist. Between 1873 and 1900 he built the Carnegie Steel Company into one of the country's largest steel manufacturing concerns. Following its sale to US Steel Corporation (1901), he turned to philanthropy and endowed numerous libraries and educational institutions.

Carnot, Lazare Nicolas Marguerite 1753–1823. French revolutionary. He was known as the "Organizer of Victory" for his skills at organizing and directing the army during the French Revolution-ary Wars. He was a member of the Committee of Public Safety and the Directory, and served in various posts under Napoleon.

Carnot, Marie François Sadi 1837–94. French president of the Third Republic (1887–94). His term was marked by troubles with G. Boulanger and the Panama Scandal (1892). He was assassinated by an Italian anarchist.

Carnot, Nicolas Léonard Sadi 1796–1832. French physicist, son of L. Carnot. A pioneer in the science of thermodynamics, he is sometimes referred to as a founder of that field.

Caro, Joseph ben Ephraim (Karo, ˜) 1483–1575. Jewish scholar, an authority on the Talmud. He wrote *Shulhan Aruk,* an important codification of Jewish law and customs.

Carol I 1839–1914. German prince and first Rumanian king (1881–1914). He won Rumania's independence from the Ottoman Turks at the Congress of Berlin (1878) and, on becoming king, instituted programs to modernize the country.

Carol II 1893–1953. Rumanian king (1930–40), successor to his son, Michael. After renouncing his right of succession (1925), he returned to Rumania (1930), ousted his son, and had himself proclaimed king. He contested attempts by the fascist Iron Guard to take control after 1938 but was forced to abdicate in 1940.

Carolina Campaign British campaign (1780–81) to subdue the Carolinas during the American Revolution. A military failure, the campaign contributed to the subsequent final British defeat (1781) at Yorktown (*q.v.*). After the capture (May, 1780) of Charleston, South Carolina, by Sir H. Clinton, British forces under Gen. C. Cornwallis moved north. At Camden, South Carolina, they routed (Aug. 16) Colonial forces under Gen. H. Gates. Gates retreated to North Carolina, but Cornwallis was defeated (Oct. 7) by guerrillas in the Battle of King's Mountain. Gates was replaced as commander in the south by Gen. N. Greene. The British suffered another defeat in the Battle of Gowpens (Jan. 17, 1781), but gained a nominal victory (Feb. 15, 1781) at Guilford Courthouse, and a victory (Sept. 8) at Eutaw Springs. Nonetheless, Cornwallis was obliged to retreat to Charleston and afterward shifted fighting to Virginia, thus setting the stage for the Yorktown Campaign.

Caroline Affair Destruction (Dec. 29, 1837) of an American vessel by Canadian forces during their effort to quash a rebellion by W. L. Mackenzie. Mackenzie and his rebels had retreated to Navy Island in the Niagara River. They were being supplied by American sympathizers via the steamer *Caroline.* On Dec. 29, Canadian forces crossed into US territory and burned the *Caroline,* killing one American. The incident resulted in counterthreats of war by both the US and British governments.

Caroline of Brunswick 1768–1821. Wife of English king George IV. She married George (1795) while he was still a prince, but by the next year the two were separated. She fought successfully George's attempt to end the marriage by divorce, but was nevertheless barred from the coronation. She died a few weeks later.

Carolingians Dynasty of Frankish kings that ruled the Carolingian Empire and successor states until the 10th cent. The line was founded by Pepin of Landen (*d.* 640), who was mayor of the palace of Austrasia for the Merovingian king Dagobert I. Succeeding generations continued to rule as mayors of the palace, though they in fact had the power of kings. It was not until Pepin the Short deposed (751) the last Merovingian that the Carolingians took the title of king. Pepin's son, Charlemagne, vastly expanded Frankish domains and created the Carolingian Empire. Shortly after Charlemagne's death, the empire was divided (843) among his three sons into the west, the east, and Francia Media. By 870 almost all of Francia Media had been absorbed by the east and west kingdoms and the Carolingian family was clearly divided into French and German lines. *Carolingian Mayors of the Palace were:* Pepin of Landen 628–640; Pepin of Herstal 687–714; Charles Martel 715–741; Carloman (with Pepin) 741–747; Pepin the Short 741–751; *Kings of the Empire were:* Pepin the Short 751–768; Charlemagne 768–814; Louis I 814–840; Lothair I (title only) 840–855; Louis II (title only) 855–875; Charles II the Bald (title only) 875–877.

Carondelet, Francisco Luis Héctor, baron de c1748–1807. Spanish colonial governor of Louisiana and West Florida (1791–95) He is noted for having strained relations between the US and Spain by forming alliances with Indians against the US. He also attempted to stir up separatist movements among Kentucky frontiersmen.

Carpenter, Malcolm Scott 1925– . American astronaut. Carpenter was the second American to orbit the earth (May 24, 1962).

carpetbagger In the US South during Reconstruction (1865–77), a derisive term for politicians and adventurers from the North. Carpetbaggers were generally believed to have moved to the South after the Civil War (with no more possessions than fitted into a carpetbag) to take advantage of newly enfranchised Negro voters. Many northerners who went south did so to help Negros through the transition from slavery to freedom. However, numerous unscrupulous opportunists among them helped corrupt Reconstruction governments in the South.

Carpocrates *See* **Carpocratians.**

Carpocratians Gnostic sect founded 2d cent. AD by the Alexandrian philosopher Carpocrates. Carpocratians rejected the divinity of Jesus and believed that all men had once been united with God. They were notorious libertines who argued that religious regulations only hindered them in attaining spiritual perfection. The sect survived to the 6th cent. AD.

Carranza, Venustiano 1859–1920. Mexican revolutionary and political leader. Carranza joined F. Madero in his revolt (1910) against P. Díaz, and then fought V. Huerta when he overthrew Madero (1913). Carranza headed the provisional government (1914–17) and during this time successfully countered uprisings by F. Villa and E. Zapata. He accepted the constitution of 1917, served as president (1917–20), and was killed after trying to prevent A. Obregón from taking office as president.

Carrera, Rafael 1814–65. Guatemalan revolutionist and dictator (1840–65). He brought the Central American Federation to an end by declaring Guatemala's independence (1838), reestablished the power of the church in Guatemala, and dominated the affairs of other Central American states.

Carrhae, Battle of Parthian victory (53 BC) over Roman invaders in northern Mesopotamia. During the wars of the First Triumvirate, Crassus invaded Parthia with a large army. His force was routed and he was killed, leaving Pompey the effective ruler of Rome.

Carrick's Ford, Battle of Union victory (July 14, 1861) in West Virginia during the early skirmishes of the American Civil War (1861–65)

Carroll, Lewis (*pseud. of* Dodgson, Charles Lutwidge) 1832–98. English writer, mathematician. He is best known as the author of two famous children's books, *Alice's Adventures in Wonderland* and *Through the Looking Glass.*

Carson, Kit (*prop.* Christopher) 1809–68. Celebrated American frontiersman. Carson first won notoriety as a guide on J. Frémont's exploratory treks through the West (1842–45). He became a noted Indian fighter and later an Indian agent in the Southwest.

Cartagena Now a Spanish port city and major naval base. Founded (243 BC) by Carthaginian general Hasdrubal, it became the center of Carthaginian power in Spain and later flourished under Roman control (from 209 BC). It was held by the Moors until conquest by the Spanish Christians (13th cent.), and was developed into a major naval base by Spanish king Philip II (16th cent.).

cartel An agreement among manufacturers and suppliers of similar products to fix prices, limit supplies, and otherwise manipulate a market in order to increase profits. A cartel may be either domestic or international in scope. Cartels were important in Germany from the late 19th cent., and especially after WW I. (For domestic cartels in the US, *see* trust.)

Carter, James Earl, Jr. *See* **Carter, Jimmy.**

Carter, Jimmy (~, James Earl, Jr.) 1924– . Thirty-ninth president of the US (1977–81). An Annapolis graduate and navy officer, he was a moderately liberal Georgia legislator (1962–66) and was elected governor of Georgia in 1970. Although almost unknown nationally and without major backing, he managed by a brilliant grassroots campaign to defeat Republican G. Ford in the 1976 presidential election. President Carter tried to project a populist image as president and to add the common touch to the presidency. His major achievement in office was the personally negotiated Camp David Accords that led to the 1979 peace treaty between Egypt and Israel, ending a state of war lasting over 30 years. Important events during the Carter administration included the return of the Panama Canal (*q.v.*) to Panama, the continuing "energy crisis" brought about by the decision of the OPEC nations to raise oil prices (from 1974), the "nuclear accident" caused when radioactive gases escaped from the Three Mile Island plant in Pennsylvania (1978), and the Soviet invasion of Afghanistan (1979), which prompted President Carter to embargo grain and technology exports to Russia and call for US withdrawal from the Moscow Olympic Games. He was criticized for his handling of the Hostage Crisis (*q.v.*) and US Mideast policy suffered as a result of this incident and the Iranian revolution that spawned it. These stresses of the late 1970s, combined with a deteriorating economy, contributed to Carter's defeat on Nov. 4, 1980, by R. Reagan.

Carteret, Philip 1639–82. English colonial governor, the first governor of New Jersey (1665–76). He became governor of East New Jersey (1676–82) after the colony was divided.

Cartesianism Philosophical doctrine first articulated by R. Descartes. It held that there is an absolute division between the mind (thinking) and the material world (matter). Mind, matter, and God were all considered innate. Descartes's mind/matter dualism arose from his famous proposition, "I think, therefore I am." The philosophy was further developed and modified by Nicolas de Malebranche (1638–1715), B. Spinoza, and others.

Carthage Ancient city-state of North Africa, located near modern Tunis. Founded, according to tradition, by Dido of Tyre (9th cent. BC), it rose to prominence in the 6th–5th cents. BC and established control over Sardinia, Malta, the Balearic Islands, and much of North Africa and Sicily. Rivaling Rome for control of the Mediterranean, Carthage engaged Rome in the First Punic War (264–241 BC), by which it lost Sicily. Subsequently conquering much of Spain, under Hamilcar Barca and Hasdrubal, it fought the Second Punic War (218–201 BC), and was defeated by Rome despite the brilliant campaign of Hannibal. The Third Punic War (149–146 BC) brought final destruction of Carthage and razing of the city. A new city founded by J. Caesar rose to become Rome's administrative center in Africa. Captured (AD 439) by the Vandals under Gaiseric, it was recovered (AD 553) by the Byzantines, and destroyed by the Arabs (AD 698).

Carthusians Small order of Roman Catholic monks, founded (1084) in France by Saint Bruno. Belonging to a strict and contemplative order, the monks live in private cells within their monasteries and meet with one another only during worship. Since its founding, the order has never undergone reform.

Cartier, Sir Georges Étienne 1814–73. Canadian statesman. A francophone "father of confederation," he was joint prime minister of Canada (1858–62) with Sir J. Macdonald and later served in the government of unified Canada.

Cartier, Jacques 1491–1557. His discovery and exploration of the Gulf of St. Lawrence and the St. Lawrence River (1534–35) laid the basis for French claims in Canada.

cartouche In ancient Egyptian writing, the oval frame surrounding hieroglyphs of a ruler's name.

The term also applies to the decorative frames around coats of arms and tablets in architectural ornamentation.

Cartwright, John 1740–1824.   English reformer known as "the father of reform." A radical who supported the American colonists, he was noted for advocating parliamentary reform, universal manhood suffrage, and abolition of slavery.

Carver, George Washington 1864–1943.   American agricultural scientist. A former slave, he won a wide reputation as Tuskegee Institute's director of agricultural research. He is noted for discovering new uses for such crops as peanuts, soybeans, and sweet potatoes.

Carver, John c1576–1621.   English Puritan and Pilgrim. He was a prosperous merchant in London who made financial arrangements for the Pilgrim colony in New England. He sailed with the *Mayflower* and became first governor of the colony at Plymouth (1620).

Casablanca Conference   Meeting (Jan. 14–24, 1943) during WW II between US president F. Roosevelt, British prime minister W. Churchill, and others at Casablanca. Held shortly after the city's capture, the meeting resulted in a joint declaration to prosecute the war against the Axis Powers until their unconditional surrender.

Casals, Pablo 1876–1973.   Spanish musician, composer, and conductor who was a world-famous cellist. He was especially noted for his performances of works by J. S. Bach.

Casanova de Seingalt, Giovanni Jacopo 1725–98. Italian adventurer and world-famous womanizer. His autobiography, *Story of My Life,* celebrates his many amorous exploits.

Casca, Publius Servilius *d.* c42 BC.   Roman politician, the first of the group of assassins to stab J. Caesar (44 BC).

Casement, Sir Roger David 1864–1916.   British consular official and Irish revolutionary. He became famous for revealing mistreatment of native workers in the Congo Free State (1904). He was executed during WW I, however, for seeking German help in securing Ireland's independence.

Casimir II 1138–94.   Polish king (1177–94), a member of the Piast family. He established the Polish Senate and instituted laws protecting the rights of peasants.

Casimir III (Casimir the Great) 1310–70.   Polish king (1330–70), successor to Ladislaus I and last ruler of the Piast family. He is noted for having consolidated royal control over the kingdom and for having expanded its territories through peaceful means. He founded the University of Cracow (1364).

Casimir IV 1427–92.   Polish king (1447–92) and ruler of Lithuania (1440–92), successor to his brother Ladislaus III. A member of the Jagiellon family, he emerged victorious from a long war with the Teutonic Knights (1466) and convened the first Polish Diet (1467).

Casimir the Great   *See* **Casimir III.**

Caslon, William 1692–1766.   English type designer. He designed the famous typeface known as Caslon.

Cassander 354?–297 BC.   Macedonian king (305–297 BC), the son of Antipater. One of the Diadochi, who fought for control of the Macedonian Empire after the death of Alexander the Great (323 BC), he became the dominant figure in the struggle by 318, and king in 305. Cassander was responsible for the deaths of Alexander's mother, son, and widow. He rebuilt the city of Thebes.

Cassel, Battle of   Battle (1328) in which French king Philip VI defeated the rebellious communes of Flanders and reestablished French rule.

Cassini, Jean Dominique (~, Giovanni Domenico) 1625–1712.   Italian-born French astronomer. Among his many discoveries concerning the sun and planets was his identification of four moons of Saturn.

Cassirer, Ernst 1874–1945.   German philosopher, a leader of the Neo-Kantian Marburg school. He studied the relationship between culture and man's symbolizing activity.

Cassius (Cassius Longinus, Gaius) *d.* 42 BC.   A principal conspirator against J. Caesar and one of his assassins (44 BC). He killed himself after his armies were defeated by M. Antony at the Battle of Philippi.

Cassius Longinus, Gaius   *See* **Cassius.**

caste system   System for hereditary division and ranking of groups within a society, especially in Hindu India. An individual born into the caste is required to take up the caste occupation (warrior, farmer, priest), and must marry within the caste. The caste system in India dates back to the period of Brahmanism (*q.v.*) and now consists of thousands of castes based on occupation. Four great groups of castes, Brahmans (priests and scholars), Kshatriyas (rulers and warriors),

Vaisyas (farmers and merchants), and Sudras (laborers, servants, and peasants) form the basis of the system. The fifth group, considered to be outside society, was that of the Untouchables (menial laborers and outcasts). The system has thus far resisted forces opposing it, including the rise of Buddhism (a reaction against it), the period of British domination, industrialization, and the efforts of M. Gandhi. Untouchability, however, was abolished by law in 1949.

Castiglione, Baldassare 1478–1529. Italian courtier and diplomat. Castiglione served in the court of Ludovico Sforza, that of the marquis of Mantua, and that of the duke of Urbino, and wrote *The Courtier* (1513–18). The work became one of the century's great books and helped establish the Renaissance ideal for the aristocracy.

Castile, Blanche of *See* **Blanche of Castile.**

Castile, Eleanor of *See* **Eleanor of Castile.**

Castile, kingdom of Spanish kingdom, formed from territories the Christian kings captured from the Moors (8th–9th cents.). After two centuries of claims and counterclaims León was permanently united with Castile (1230). Then, in 1479, Castile was unified with Aragon under Queen Isabella and King Ferdinand. This new kingdom formed the basis of modern Spain.

Castillon, Battle of French victory (July 17, 1453) over the English, ending the Hundred Years' War (1337–1453). French forces, responding to a revolt in Guyenne, laid siege to the town of Castillon in southwest France. English forces, some 6,000, under John Talbot, 2d earl of Shrewsbury (1413–60), were sent by English king Henry VI to take advantage of the revolt. Shrewsbury attacked the French siege force prematurely (July 17), and his army was routed. Guyenne was back in French control by Oct., 1453, the remaining British troops having left France.

Castlereagh, Robert Stewart, 2d viscount 1769–1822. British statesman, noted for his term as foreign secretary (1812–22). He played a major role in organizing the Grand Alliance, which defeated Napoleon and was an important figure in the Congress of Vienna (1814–15), which subsequently carved up the French Empire.

Castracani, Castruccio 1281–1328. Italian nobleman. As the lord of Lucca, he led the Ghibellines of Tuscany in successful battles against Florence. Holy Roman Emperor Louis IV created him a duke in 1327.

Castro, Cipriano 1858–1924. Venezuelan president (1901–08), successor to Ignacio Andrade. Castro seized control of the government (1899). His refusal to honor foreign debts led to a blockade (1902) by Germany, Italy, and France. He was overthrown by J. V. Gómez.

Castro, Cristóbal Vaca de *fl.* 1540–45. Spanish colonial administrator, sent to Peru (1541) to settle the feud between F. Pizarro and Diego de Almagro (1520–42). Finding Pizarro dead, he assumed the governorship and put down Almagro's rebellion. He was succeeded (1544) by N. Vela and then imprisoned for 12 years on false charges of embezzlement.

Castro, Fidel 1926– . Cuban premier (1959–) and central figure in the Cuban Revolution. An opponent of Cuban dictator F. Batista, he led an unsuccessful revolt (July 26, 1953), organized the 26th of July Movement (*q.v.*), and failed again (1956) at a revolt. From his mountain bases, however, he led a guerrilla movement that finally overthrew Batista (Jan. 1, 1959). Thereafter he established a totalitarian government, instituted sweeping economic and social reforms (including nationalization of industry and collective agriculture), entered the Communist sphere, and announced a policy of exporting revolution. His rule has been marked by the Bay of Pigs Invasion, Cuban Missile Crisis, economic failures, a US economic embargo and Soviet subsidies, growing isolation from other Latin American countries, involvement in African and Latin American revolutionary movements, the mass emigration (1980) of Cuban "boat people" to the US, and the determined adherence to the Communist system (to mid-1992) despite the collapse and shift to democratic government by its leading ally, the former USSR.

Castro, Inés de *d.* 1355. Spanish noblewoman. A noted beauty, she was the beloved mistress of Dom Pedro, the future Peter I of Portugal. She was murdered on orders given by his father, King Alfonso IV. The tragic incident is a recurrent theme in Portuguese literature.

Catalan Romance language. Derived from Latin, Catalan is spoken in Andorra and parts of Spain and France. There is a large body of literary works in Catalan.

Catalan Company European mercenary soldiers (14th cent.). Led by R. de Flor, the Catalans were employed by Byzantine emperor Andronicus II to fight Turkish invaders. They defeated the

Turks, then ravaged the country themselves for several years.

Cateau-Cambresis, Treaty of Treaty concluded (1559) between France, Spain, and England. It ended the long struggle for control of Italy (1494–1559). Hostilities began with the Italian Wars (1494–1559) between France and Spain, with England joining the fighting occasionally as Spain's ally. By the treaty, Spain's dominance over Italy was recognized, thus initiating a long period of control by Spain's Habsburg rulers. France also restored Savoy to Spain, agreed to an adjustment in the border of the Spanish Netherlands, and returned Corsica to Genoa. French possession of Calais was confirmed by England.

Cathari Christian heretics of a variety of sects that once flourished in Western Europe (11th–14th cents.). Influenced by the Bogomils (*q.v.*) and Paulicians (*q.v.*), the Cathari were exponents of Manichaean Dualism, in which God ruled over the spiritual world and Satan ruled over the material world. By the mid-12th cent., the Cathari had churches in Italy and France. In southern France, where they were most numerous, they were called Albigenses and were the object of the 13th-cent. Albigensian Crusade (*q.v.*). This and the subsequent persecution of the Inquisition put an end to the heretical sects.

Cathay Name used to refer to China in medieval times. M. Polo established the term in popular usage through descriptions of his journey to the region. The term generally applied to what is now northern China.

Cather, Willa Sibert 1876–1947. American novelist. She is best known for her stories of frontier life, of which *O Pioneers!* (1913) and *My Ántonia* (1918) are noted examples.

Catherine I 1684?–1727. Russian empress (1725–27). The mistress of Tsar Peter I (the Great), she became his second wife (1712). She was crowned empress-consort (1724), and, on her husband's death, she succeeded him on the throne (1725). The government during her reign was dominated by A. Menshikov.

Catherine II (Catherine the Great) 1729–96. German-born Russian empress (1762–96), successor to her husband, Peter III, by his overthrow. An able and ambitious leader, she was an important figure in Russia's emergence as a European power. She conspired with a lover, Gen. Grigori Orlov (1734–83), to usurp and

murder (1762) her unpopular husband. She made many important administrative reforms, but it was her involvement in European wars and politics that most benefited Russia. She won control of Poland by installing a lover as king (Stanislaus II), and then took the lion's share of territory in the Partitions of Poland. With her lover G. Potemkin she devised the Greek Project to dismember the Ottoman Empire. After the Russo-Turkish War (1768–74), she annexed the Crimea (1783). She was a noted patron of the arts and friend of the Encylopedists.

Catherine de Médicis 1519–89. French queen (1547–59) as wife of King Henry II and ruler of France as regent (1560–74) to her second son, King Charles IX. She became regent on the death of her first son, King Francis II (1560), and during the religious conflicts that dominated her regency, alternately allied herself with Protestants and Catholics. She took part in planning the Massacre of St. Bartholomew's Day (1572). Her third son Henry III, succeeded to the throne in 1574.

Catherine of Alexandria, Saint *d.* AD 307? Christian martyr and virgin, of Alexandrian birth. She is said to have been condemned to death by the Roman emperor for professing her Christian faith. In what was considered a miracle, the torture wheel broke and she was beheaded instead.

Catherine of Aragon 1485–1536. Spanish-born English queen. Catherine was the daughter of Ferdinand and Isabella of Spain, wife of Henry VIII (*m.* 1509), and mother of Mary Tudor. Henry's attempt to annul their marriage (from 1527) resulted in a break with the Roman Catholic church, which was then being influenced by Catherine's nephew, Holy Roman Emperor Charles V. This culminated in his marriage to Anne Boleyn (1533) and formation of the Church of England.

Catherine of Braganza 1638–1705. Portuguese princess, wife of English king Charles II (1662–85). A Roman Catholic, she was able but generally unpopular in England and was unjustly accused (by T. Oates) of trying to poison her unfaithful husband (1678). She returned to Portugal some years after her husband's death.

Catherine of Siena, Saint 1347–80. Italian mystic and one of the influential figures of the medieval church. She gained a wide reputation for her dedication to the needy. She is said to have influenced Pope Gregory XI to end the Babylonian Captivity (1376).

Catherine of Valois 1401–37. French noblewoman and wife (*m.* 1420) of English king Henry V. She was mother of Henry VI by the king. After Henry's death (1422) she had a son by a Welsh nobleman, Owen Tudor (*d.* 1461). That son became father of Henry VII, first of the Tudor kings.

Catherine the Great *See* **Catherine II.**

Catherine the Great, Instruction of *See* **Instruction of Catherine the Great.**

Catholic church *See* **Roman Catholic church.**

Catholic Emancipation Movement in Britain to end discrimination against Catholics which was imposed by English law and which included forfeiture of inherited land and exclusion from Parliament. Reform measures were passed in the late 18th cent., and by the Catholic Emancipation Act (Apr. 13, 1829) Catholics were given nearly full equality.

Catholic Emancipation Act *See* **Catholic Emancipation.**

Catholic League (League) (Holy League) League of French Roman Catholics formed (1576) by Henry duke of Guise and aided by Spanish king Philip II to suppress Protestantism during the French religious wars. It opposed the accession of Henry of Navarre to the French throne as Henry IV, but, weakened over the years, was unable to block Henry's coronation (1594).

Catholic Reformation Calls for reform within the Roman Catholic church which began before the Protestant Reformation, were aimed at the spread of corruption and worldly attitudes within the church, and promoted the creation of new groups dedicated to religious renewal (such as the Capuchins, Ursulines, and Jesuits). The official church efforts at reform, the Counter-Reformation, began in the mid-16th cent., as forces within the Roman Catholic church advocating reform began to exert greater influence. Decisive moves toward reform began with the convening (1545) of the Council of Trent by Pope Paul III. The council met in three different sessions (1545–47, 1551–52, 1562–63) to reformulate Catholic doctrine with greater precision and to reform abuses and corruption that had given rise to Protestantism. The council reaffirmed the Roman Catholic teaching on the seven sacraments and on the importance of church tradition alongside the Scriptures. In the practical realm, the council established the modern seminary system for training priests and thus provided the means to eliminate many of the abuses by the clergy. The council's liturgical reforms lasted virtually intact until replaced by those of the Second Vatican Council (1962–65). Great reforming popes of the Catholic Reformation included: Paul III; Paul IV, who thoroughly reformed abuses in the Roman Curia; Pius IV; and Saint Pius V, who reformed the Roman missal and breviary. An important element in the Catholic Reformation was the reform of religious orders, such as that effected by Saint Theresa of Avila and Saint John of the Cross within the Carmelite order, and the founding of new orders, notably the Jesuits. These religious orders, especially the Jesuits, spread the spirit of the Catholic Reformation, founded new schools and helped to wrest converts from Protestantism. The foreign and military policies of Catholic rulers in Europe, such as Holy Roman Emperor Charles V and his son Philip II of Spain, were often conducted according to imperatives inspired by the Catholic Reformation. But the religious and educational reforms that came out of this reform movement had more lasting effects.

Catiline c108–62 BC. Roman politician and conspirator. Barred from the consulship (66 BC) on charges that were later proved false, he was subsequently accused of plotting (65) a rebellion. He was acquitted and ran again (63) for the consulship against Cicero. Defeated, he organized the Conspiracy of Catiline (*q.v.*) in which he met his death.

Catiline, Conspiracy of *See* **Conspiracy of Catiline.**

Cato, Marcus Porcius *See* **Cato the Elder; Cato the Younger.**

Cato Minor *See* **Cato the Younger.**

Cato Street Conspiracy English assassination plot. A. Thistlewood, an anarchist, plotted the murder of British cabinet officers but was captured with accomplices (Feb., 1820) at his arsenal on Cato Street. He was executed for treason.

Cato the Censor *See* **Cato the Elder.**

Cato the Elder (˜ the Censor) (*name of* Marcus Porcius ˜) 234–149 BC. Roman statesman and champion of the traditional way of life in Rome. He resisted the influence of Greek civilization in Rome and promoted a return to the simple, idealistic, and moral life of old Rome. He staunchly opposed the Scipio family, an embodiment of Hellenistic influences, and as censor instituted many measures aimed at reforming Roman life. His public career included terms as consul (195 BC) and censor (184). His repeated demand for an attack on Carthage helped bring about the Third Punic War (149–146).

Cato the Younger (~ Minor) (*name* of Marcus Porcius ~) 95–46 BC. Roman statesman and great-grandson of Cato the Elder. He was a highly regarded leader of the Optimates, conservative aristocrats, and actively opposed J. Caesar and his allies. He joined in the armed resistance to Caesar and killed himself following Caesar's victory at the Battle of Thapsus (46 BC).

Catt, Carrie Chapman 1859–1947. American suffragist. A former superintendent of schools, she joined the women's suffrage movement in the 1880s and helped organize the National American Woman Suffrage Association. She organized political campaigns and spoke extensively on the suffrage movement. After women gained the right to vote (1920), she founded the League of Women Voters (1920).

Catton, Charles Bruce 1899–1978. American historian noted for his works on the American Civil War. He won the Pulitzer Prize (1954) for his book *A Stillness at Appomattox.*

Catullus, Gaius Valerius 84?–54? BC. Roman lyric poet, regarded as the greatest of ancient Rome. He is best remembered for his love poems to a woman he named Lesbia (perhaps Clodia, *q.v.*).

Catulus, Gaius Lutatius *fl.* 3d cent. BC. Roman consul (242 BC) and general. He was commander of the Roman fleet that defeated the Carthaginians off the Aegates islands (241). The action ended the First Punic War (264–241).

Catulus, Quintus Lutatius *d.* 87 BC. Roman general and consul (102 BC). Together with co-consul Marius, Catulus defeated the Cimbri (101 BC). Marius received sole credit, however, and Catulus later supported L. Sulla against him.

Catulus, Quintus Lutatius *d.* c60 BC. Roman politician and consul (78 BC). The son of Q. L. Catulus, he helped Pompey put down a revolt by M. Lepidus (77? BC). An opponent of J. Caesar, he accused Caesar of taking part in the Conspiracy of Catiline. Caesar in turn accused him of embezzlement.

Caucasian 1. Peoples inhabiting the Caucasus region of southwest Russia, including the former Soviet Republics of Georgia, Armenia, and Azerbaijan. 2. Term for the Caucasoid or so-called white race.

caudillo Term for a leader who is a political boss with a strong (often insurgent) military following. It is used especially in reference to such South American leaders as J. de Rosas and P. Díaz.

Caulaincoult, Armand Augustin Louis, marquis de 1772–1827. French diplomat and general. He became Napoleon's aide-de-camp (1802), and served as ambassador to Russia (1807–11) and foreign minister (1813–14, 1815).

Cavaignac, Louis *See* **June Days.**

cavalier 1. A horseman, mounted knight, or cavalryman. 2. Name used by royalist supporters of English king Charles I during the English Civil Wars (1642–48). They opposed the Roundheads, or Parliamentarians. 3. Name of the Royalist party following Restoration (1660–88) of the monarchy in England. "Cavalier" was eventually replaced by "Tory" as the party name.

Cavalier, Jean 1681–1740. French Protestant. He was leader of the Camisards (*q.v.*) during their rebellion (1702–04). He fled the country after the treaty he arranged with the Catholics proved unacceptable to his followers.

Cavalier Parliament Parliament of the English Restoration which sat from 1661 to 1679 and which was overwhelmingly Royalist. The Parliament was responsible for passage of repressive laws (*see* Clarendon Code) directed against Catholics and Nonconformists.

Cavalier poets English literary group. Named for their royalist sympathies, these poets flourished in the 17th cent. and included in their number R. Lovelace, R. Herrick, and J. Suckling.

Cavendish, Henry 1731–1810. French-born English physicist and chemist. Born to a family descended from English nobility, he interited a fortune at the age of 40 but maintained his simple lifestyle. Cavendish is best known for his discoveries in chemistry, namely the properties of air, the nature of hydrogen (which he called inflammable air), and his discovery that water is not an element but a compound. He also experimented with electricity, meteorology, and other applied sciences. His final research, when he was nearly 70 years old, became known as the Cavendish experiment: he calculated the density of the earth using measurements from a sensitive torsional balance.

Cavour, Camillo Benso, count di 1810–61. Italian statesman and one of the most important figures in the Risorgimento, the unification of Italy. As premier (1852–59, 1860–61) of what was then the kingdom of Sardinia, he brought about the union of central Italy with the north (1860), encouraged G. Garibaldi to invade Sicily, and sent troops to occupy the Papal States. The unification of the kingdom of Italy under Victor Emmanuel II was completed just before his death (1861).

Caxton, William c1422–1491. English printer, the first in his country. He learned printing at Cologne (1471–72), printed the first book in English, *The Recuyell of the Historyes of Troye* (1475), while at Bruges. He printed the first book in England (1477) at Westminster.

Ceauşescu, Nicolae 1918–89. Rumanian statesman, party leader, and head of state (1965–89). He pursued a policy of independence from Russia while establishing closer ties with China and the West. He refused to participate in the Warsaw Pact invasion of Czechoslavakia (1968) and later condemned the Soviet invasion of Afghanistan. Economic problems and his authoritarian rule led to his overthrow and execution during the pro-democracy revolts that swept Eastern Europe in the late 1980s. *See also* Rumania, 1965–89.

Celaya, Battle of 1. First victory (Sept. 28, 1810) for Mexican revolutionaries, led by M. Hidalgo y Costilla, over Spanish forces. 2. Decisive victory (Apr., 1915) for forces of provisional Mexican leader V. Carranza over a rebel force led by F. Villa. Carranza's forces were led by A. Obregón.

Celestine I, Saint *d.* 432. Italian-born pope (422–32), successor to Saint Boniface I. He opposed Nestorianism and approved the decision of the Council of Ephesus (431). He is sometimes said to have sent Saint Patrick to Ireland.

Celestine V, Saint (Murrone, Pietro del) 1215–96. Italian-born pope (1294), successor to Nicholas IV. Founder of the Celestine Order (c1254), he resigned after a chaotic five-month reign. He was subsequently imprisoned by his successor, Boniface VIII, to prevent a schism in the church.

Cellini, Benvenuto 1500–71. Italian sculptor, goldsmith, and author during the Renaissance. His autobiography is considered an important account of 16th-cent. life. *Perseus with the Head of Medusa* (1546–54) is among his most famous sculptures.

Celsius, Anders 1701–1744. Swedish astronomer who invented the Celsius thermometer scale (1742?, also called the Centigrade scale). A professor of astronomy at the University of Uppsala, Celsius is known for his observations of the aurora borealis (northern lights), for measuring the distance from the earth to the sun, and for determining the precise shape of the earth. In 1740 he built the Uppsala Astronomical Observatory. Celsius presented his new thermometer scale in 1742 before the Swedish Academy of Sciences.

Celt-Iberian War War (134–133 BC) in which the Romans conquered the Celtiberians, descendants of Iberians and Celtic invaders in Spain. They were decisively defeated by Scipio Africanus the Younger (133 BC).

Celts (Kelts) Ancient people who dominated Western and Central Europe until about the 1st cent. BC. Celtic tribes are believed to have emanated from a region encompassing part of France and southern Germany (before 1200 BC). By the 5th cent. BC, their migrations had carried them into Spain, the British Isles, the Balkan region, and Asia Minor. In the early 4th cent., they even invaded and sacked Rome. The Celts were farmer-raiders with what was primarily a tribal organization. They evolved a well-developed culture (called La Tène) and religion (*see* Druids). By 1st cent. BC, the Celts succumbed to invasions of Germanic tribes and their civilization disappeared as a distinct entity.

Cenci, Beatrice 1577–99. Italian noblewoman whose cruel fate has been the subject of several literary works. Imprisoned and brutalized by her father, she arranged to have him murdered. She and the other members of the family confessed to the plot under torture and, refused leniency, were executed (1599).

censor In ancient Rome (from 443 BC–22 BC), a public official charged with registering citizens and their property, maintaining the senatorial rolls, and punishing breaches of moral conduct. Two censors were always elected for 18-month terms and both were required to agree before a judgment could be passed against an individual. Plebeians were elected censors at least as early as 351 BC and by 339 BC election of at least one plebeian as censor was required by law. Sulla sharply curbed the censors' powers and the office effectively ceased to exist when the Roman emperors assumed their powers (from 22 BC).

Center party German political party that figured in the Kulturkampf (1871–83). Formed to protect interests of Catholics in the newly formed imperial German state, its membership included Catholics from all classes. Though it suffered during Chancellor O. von Bismarck's Kulturkampf (*q.v.*) and was never able to attain a clear majority in subsequent years, the party remained a force in German politics until the 1930s. After WW II, former members became the nucleus of the new Christian Democratic Union.

Center party *See* **Agrarian party.**

CENTO *See* **Central Treaty Organization.**

Central African Republic Republic located in central Africa. The population is 2,879,000 and the capital is Bangui. Inhabited since Paleolithic times, the region was a frequent target of slave raids (16th–18th cents.), which virtually wiped out the original inhabitants. Later explored and occupied (1880s) by the French, it became the French colony of Ubangi-Shari (1894). It was joined (1906) with Chad into an administrative unit and became (1910) part of French Equatorial Africa. In 1920, Chad became a separate colony. Ubangi-Shari became a French territory in 1946, and in 1958 became autonomous as the Central African Republic. The republic became fully independent on Aug. 13, 1960. Its first president, David Dacko, was overthrown (1965) in a military coup headed by Col. Jean-Bédel Bokassa, who made himself emperor. Bokassa's ruthless and arbitrary rule was ended (1979) by another coup, and Dacko was reinstalled as president. Dacko was overthrown in a military coup (Sept. 1, 1981) and Gen. André Kolingba became head of a military government. A new constitution was adopted in 1986, establishing one-party rule, and Kolingba remained in power as president of a largely civilian government. Bokassa, meanwhile, returned in 1986 and was arrested and imprisoned after a trial. Pressure for democratic reforms resulted in adoption of a multi-party system in 1991.

Central America Name of the southernmost region of North America, including part of lower Mexico, Guatemala, Honduras, El Salvador, Nicaragua, Costa Rica, and Belize. Though properly part of South America, Panama is generally referred to as part of Central America.

Central America, United Provinces of *See* **Central American Union.**

Central American Federation *See* **Central American Union.**

Central American States, Organization of *See* **Organization of Central American States.**

Central American Union (Central American Federation) (United Provinces of Central America) Confederation (1823–38) of Central American states, including Guatemala, El Salvador, Nicaragua, Honduras, and Costa Rica. The states were part of the Mexican Empire (1822–23) until A. Iturbide was ousted (Feb., 1823). Soon after the union was formed, civil war broke out between liberals and conservatives, and liberal leader Francisco Morazán (1799–1842) became president (1829). He ruled until Indian rebels, led by R. Carrera, captured Guatemala City (1838) and thereby dissolved the union. Numerous subsequent attempts at reunification have failed.

Central Committee The governing body of the Communist party in the former Soviet Union. The Central Committee was formed (1912) to determine Bolshevik policy. After the Bolsheviks took control of the Russian government, the Central Committee established (1919) the Politburo and the Secretariat as well as the Orgburo (absorbed by the Secretariat, 1952). Although the Central Committee was nominally the highest governing body in the Communist party, policy-making and administrative functions were later largely taken over by the Politburo and the Secretariat. The Central Committee was dissolved with other party organs during the collapse of the USSR in 1991.

Central Intelligence Agency (CIA) US intelligence agency. It was formed (1947) under the National Security Act and replaced the Office of Strategic Services (OSS), organized during WW II. In addition to information gathering, the agency has at times been involved in the internal affairs of foreign countries. These activities became a source of controversy in the 1960s and 1970s and included involvement in the Bay of Pigs Invasion, in the war in Laos, in Chile during Allende's regime, and in Nicaragua during the Contra rebel war against the pro-Communist Sandinista government.

Central Powers Name applied to Germany and its allies during WW I. In addition to Germany, the Central Powers included Austria-Hungary, Bulgaria, and the Ottoman Empire.

Central Treaty Organization (CENTO) International organization formed in 1955 for Mideast defense. Originally known as the Baghdad Pact, it was reorganized in 1959 after Iraq withdrew. Members included Turkey, Great Britain, Pakistan, and Iran. CENTO was dissolved in 1979 after Iran and Pakistan withdrew.

Ceos, Simonides of   *See* **Simonides of Ceos.**

Cernan, Eugene Andrew 1934– . American astronaut. He was a crew member of Apollo 17, the last American mission to the moon (Dec., 1972).

Cerro Gordo, Battle of   US victory (Apr., 1847) and first important engagement of US forces against Mexicans during the Mexican War (1846–48). About 8,500 US troops, under Gen. W. Scott, routed some 12,000 Mexicans, under A. de Santa Anna, near Veracruz, Mexico.

Cervantes Saavedra, Miguel de 1547–1616. A Spanish novelist, poet, and playwright. He is author of *Don Quixote,* a classic novel satirizing the extravagant romances of chivalry popular in his day. Cervantes's early life was turbulent: he lost his left hand in the Battle of Lepanto (1570), was captured and enslaved by the Barbary pirates, and was finally ransomed (1580). He subsequently wrote poems and plays but did not publish Part I of *Don Quixote* until he was in his late fifties. It proved an immediate success.

Cervera y Topete, Pascual   *See* **Santiago, Battle of.**

Céspedes, Carlos Manuel de   *See* **Ten Years' War.**

cession   *See* **annexation.**

Ceylon   *See* **Sri Lanka.**

Cézanne, Paul 1839–1906. French postimpressionist painter who influenced the development of 20th-cent. art. Painting landscapes and still lifes most often, he developed a style in which he emphasized the underlying structure of a subject through his use of geometric patterns and color. His work played an important role in the development of cubism.

Chacabuco, Battle of   Victory (Feb. 12, 1817) for Chilean rebels during the war for Chilean independence from Spain. Rebel forces, led by J. San Martín and B. O'Higgins, defeated the Spanish forces north of Santiago and occupied that city soon afterward. O'Higgins was then named ruler but Chilean independence was not proclaimed until a year later.

Chaco Peace Conference   *See* **Chaco War.**

Chaco War   Bloody war (1932–35) between Bolivia and Paraguay over possession of the Gran Chaco, a lowland plain in central South America.

The war was precipitated by Bolivia's need for a coastal port and the discovery of oil in the Chaco. Sporadic fighting began (1928), and by 1932 fullscale war had broken out. Early gains by the numerically superior Bolivian forces were wiped out by Paraguayan victories under Lt. Col. José Estigarribia (1888–1940). Paraguay declared war formally (1933), and, after heavy fighting (1934), its forces drove (1935) into Bolivian territory. Bolivia rallied to counterattack, regained the initiative, and agreed to a truce (1935). Three years of negotiations at the Chaco Peace Conference resulted in a treaty (1938) by which Paraguay won most of the contested Chaco. Bolivia was granted a corridor to and a port on the Paraguay River. About 100,000 soldiers were killed in the war.

Chad (Tchad)   Republic located in north central Africa. The population is 5,064,000 and the capital is N'Djamena. The region of modern Chad was explored by Arab traders in the 7th cent. The Muslim empire of Kanem, later known as Bornu, was established by peoples from North Africa in the 13th cent. and was dominant in the region until the rise of the rival empires of Wadai and Bagirmi (16th–17th cents.). The French began their conquest of Chad in the early 1890s and made it part of the French Congo in the early 1900s. In 1920, Chad became a separate French colony. It became a French territory in 1946 and voted (1958) for self-rule within the French Community. Chad became independent on Aug. 11, 1960. Muslim tribes in the north began (1966) a guerrilla war that continued until 1973. Chad was severely affected by a drought in the 1960s and 1970s. From 1975, Chad was in a state of turmoil with various groups fighting for control of the government. Libyan troops brought a temporary end to the fighting in 1980, and in 1981 an Organization of African Unity (OAU) peace-keeping force had replaced the Libyans. Following a coup in 1982, renewed civil war broke out. France sent some 3,000 troops (1983) and Libyan troops were again directly involved. By 1987, Libyan troops had been driven out of Chad and a cease-fire was arranged in Sept. 1987. Chad and Libya signed a peace accord in 1989. A new constitution adopted in Dec., 1989, established a one-party government with a powerful presidency. However, in 1990 a rebel group called Mouvement Patriotique du Salut (MPS) invaded Chad from the Sudan and by early Dec., 1990, took control of the government. The rebel leader, Idriss Deby, formed a government, promising to eventually establish a multi-party system and hold elections. Both Libya and the Sudan gave their support to the new government. Rules for establishing political parties were approved in late 1991. An invasion in late 1991 by some 3,000 soldiers loyal to the previous government was defeated in early 1992.

Chaeronea Ancient Boeotian town in what is now Greece. The birthplace of Plutarch, it was the site of two battles important in ancient times. On Sept. 1, 338 BC, Macedonian king Philip II defeated the armies of Athens and Thebes and thereby established Macedonian control over Greece. In 86 BC some 30–40,000 Romans under L. Sulla defeated the 110,000-man army of Mithridates VI during the First Mithridatic War.

Chagall, Marc 1887–1985. French painter. He was regarded as a forerunner of the surrealists. In addition to his paintings, which often drew on Jewish life and folklore, Chagall also created notable murals and book illustrations.

Chaikovsky, Nikolai Vasilyevich 1850–1926. Russian Socialist. Chaikovsky established (1875) an unsuccessful utopian commune in Kansas. Returning to Russia, he opposed the Bolsheviks and headed (1918–20) the counterrevolutionary White Russian government at Archangel.

Chain, Ernst Boris *See* **Florey, Sir Howard Walter Florey, Baron.**

Chakkri dynasty (Chakri ˜) Ruling dynasty of Thailand from 1782. The line was founded by Chao Phraye Chakkri, who was instrumental in repulsing the Burmese invasions of the late 18th cent. and who ruled as King Rama I (1782–1809). The line of Chakkri kings remains unbroken to modern times. Notable rulers of the dynasty include King Mongkut (Rama IV, 1851–68), King Chulalongkorn (Rama V, 1868–1910), and King Prajadhipok (Rama VII, 1925–35), who advocated creation of a constitutional government. The current Thai king is Bhumibol Adulyadej (1927–) (Rama IX, from 1946).

Chalcedon, Council of Fourth ecumenical council (451) of the early Christian church, held in Chalcedon (now in Turkey). Convened by Eastern Roman emperor Marcian, the council reversed the Council of Ephesus, condemned Eutyches and his Monophysitism (*q.v.*), proclaimed the dual nature (human and divine) of Christ as formulated by Pope Leo I, and issued letters against Nestorius.

Chalcis (Chalkis) Greek city. In ancient times it was the most important city on the island of Euboea. It was settled by the Ionians, and later defeated neighboring Eretria in the Lelantine Wars (late 8th cent. BC). Conquered by the Athenians (c506 BC), it remained under their control until 411 BC, and later flourished under the Romans. Chalcis founded many colonies in the 8th–7th cents. BC.

Chaldaea *See* **Chaldea.**

Chaldea (Chaldaea) Originally, the region south of Babylonia. After the Chaldean Empire (second Babylonian Empire) was established (625 BC) by Nabopolassar, Chaldea included the whole of Babylonia. The empire prospered under Nabopolassar's son, Nebuchadnezzar II, and was subsequently conquered by the Persians (538 BC). (*See also* Babylonia.)

Chaldiran, Battle of Victory (Aug. 23, 1514) for the Ottoman Turks, under Selim I, during an invasion of Persia. Selim led his force of 50,000 men into Persia against the Safavid ruler Ismail I. The invasion was part of a holy war proclaimed by Selim I against the heretical Shi'ite Muslim sect.

Chalkis *See* **Chalcis.**

Challenger expedition Great oceanographic survey undertaken (1872–76) by the British. Under the direction of Sir Charles W. Thomson (1830–82) aboard the HMS *Challenger*, the expedition covered nearly 69,000 miles in the Atlantic, Indian, Antarctic, and Pacific oceans. The 50-volume report was a major contribution to the field of oceanography.

Challoner, Richard 1691–1781. English Catholic bishop. His revision of the Douay version of the Bible became the edition used by English Catholics.

Châlons, Battle of One of the decisive battles of history, fought near Châlons-sur-Marne, France, in June, AD 451. The Roman general Aëtius (AD 396?–454), allied with the Visigoths, defeated Attila the Hun and prevented his conquest of Western Europe.

Chamberlain, (Arthur) Neville 1869–1940. British statesman and prime minister (1937–40) in the years leading up to WW II, successor to S. Baldwin. A Conservative member of Parliament from 1918, he at first pursued a policy of appeasement toward the Fascists and Nazis by recognizing Italy's takeover of Ethiopia (1938) and acceding to Hitler in the Munich Pact (1938). He also ordered a speed-up of British rearmament, however, and when Hitler invaded Poland (1939), he declared war on Germany. The British defeat in Norway (1940) forced his resignation.

Chamberlain, Sir Austen 1863–1937. A British statesman, son of J. Chamberlain. As foreign secretary (1924–29) to S. Baldwin, he played a major role in negotiating the Locarno Pact (1925). He won the Nobel Peace Prize in 1925.

Chamberlain, Joseph 1836–1914. British statesman. As colonial secretary (1895–1903), he formulated the policy of imperial preference for colonial trade (1902). His tenure was marked by the Boer War (1899–1902).

Chamberlain's Men British theatrical company. W. Shakespeare wrote for and acted in this troupe, which was organized in 1594. It performed frequently at the Globe Theatre and was designated the King's Men by James I (c1603).

Chambers, Robert *See* **Chambers, William.**

Chambers, Whittaker *See* **Hiss, Alger.**

Chambers, Sir William 1726–96. English architect of the Palladian school. One of the most important English architects of his day, he designed Somerset House (1776) in England and wrote *A Treatise on Civil Architecture.*

Chambers, William 1800–83. Scottish publisher. With his brother, Robert (1802–71), he founded the publishing firm of W.&R. Chambers (after 1832). The company published educational and reference works, among them *Chambers' Encyclopaedia.*

Chambord, Henri Charles Ferdinand Marie Dieudonné d'Artois, count of 1820–83. French nobleman and Bourbon claimant to the throne as Henry V. After the fall of Napoleon III (1871), there was a brief movement toward restoration of the Bourbon monarchy. Chambord's outspoken hatred of the revolution, however, defeated the movement (1874), and the Third Republic was formally instituted.

Chamoun, Camille 1900–87. Lebanese political leader, president (1952–58). He was a Christian and an advocate of pro-West policies. Muslim opposition to his administration resulted in the Lebanese Crisis (*q.v.*).

Champa Ancient kingdom (2d–15th cents.) of the Chams, located in what is now southern Vietnam. Formed (2d cent. AD) during the collapse of the Chinese Han dynasty, the kingdom was known to the Chinese as Lin-yi. Thereafter it adopted many aspects of Indian culture and religion, was reconquered and ruled by China (5th–6th cents.), warred with neighboring Annam (*q.v.*) and the Khmer Empire, and succumbed to the Vietnamese in 1471.

Champion's Hill, Battle of Union victory (May 16, 1863) during the American Civil War (1861–65). Some 15,000 Union soldiers, led by Gen. U. Grant, defeated 17,500 Confederate soldiers, led by Gen. J. Pemberton, at this Mississippi town. Union losses were nearly 2,500, Confederate, 3,800. Grant subsequently advanced to Vicksburg.

Champlain, Samuel de 1567–1635. French navigator and explorer, called the "father of New France." After earlier expeditions to Canada, Champlain founded the settlement of Port Royal in Nova Scotia (1605). In 1608, he founded the city of Quebec and, establishing a lucrative fur trade there, was named commandant of New France. Further explorations took Champlain as far west as Lakes Ontario and Huron and as far south as Massachusetts Bay. He also traveled to Lake Champlain, in New York, which is named for him. Champlain extended French claims to territory as far west as Wisconsin. In 1628, he defended Quebec from English privateers, surrendering his garrison only after running out of food and gunpowder. (The colony was restored to the French in 1632.) Champlain made his last trip to Quebec in 1633, where he died of a stroke in 1635.

Champollion, Jean François 1790–1832. French Egyptologist, the founder of Egyptology. Working with the Rosetta Stone (*q.v.*), he was largely responsible for finding the keys to deciphering Egyptian hieroglyphics (1821).

Chancellorsville, Battle of Confederate victory (May 2–4, 1863) over Union forces during the American Civil War (1861–65). The victory resulted in the Confederate invasion of Pennsylvania and the Battle of Gettysburg. A 130,000-man Union army, under Gen. J. Hooker, advanced (May 1) to Chancellorsville, Virginia, and was defeated there by a 60,000-man Confederate force, led by Gen. R. E. Lee. However, Confederate Gen. Stonewall Jackson was wounded in the battle and died later. Union losses were 17,000, Confederate 12,000.

Chandler, Raymond Thornton 1888–1959. An American author of detective stories, including *The Big Sleep* and *Farewell, My Lovely.*

Chandragupta (Candragupta) *d.* 286? BC. Indian emperor (c322–c297 BC), founder of the Maurya Empire. Through his conquests he created an empire that included most of India. He subsequently turned back an invasion by Seleucus I (305 BC) and established an effective administrative system. He is said to have abdicated in 297 to become a Jain monk.

Chandragupta I (Candragupta I) *d.* AD 330? Indian king (AD 320–330?). He founded the Gupta dynasty, and, through marriage, vastly extended his domains in northern India.

Chandragupta II (Candragupta II) (Vikramaditya) *d.* AD c415. Ruler (AD c380–c415) of the Gupta kingdom in northern India. He extended his domains to the west and south by conquests. His reign marked a high point in the Hindu arts.

Chang Ch'ien *See* **Zhang Qian.**

Chang Hsüeh-liang *See* **Zhang Xueliang.**

Chang Kuo-t'ao *See* **Zhang Guotao.**

Channing, William Ellery 1780–1842. American clergyman and author. A Congregational minister in Boston who preached morality and Christian principles, he became known as "the apostle of Unitarianism" and organized what became the American Unitarian Association (1820). Channing denounced war, slavery, and poverty in his writings and figured in the New England transcendental movement, influencing R. Emerson and W. Bryant.

chapbook Inexpensive pamphlet. Chapbooks contained popular reading material and first appeared in Europe during the late 15th and early 16th cents. They were the forerunners of popular magazines of the 19th cent.

Chapman, John (Johnny Appleseed) 1774–1845. American pioneer and folk hero. A tree nurseryman in Pennsylvania, he sold and gave away seedlings to westward-bound pioneers. From c1800 to 1845 he wandered in the wilderness region as far west as Ohio tending apple-tree nurseries he had planted in the forests and helping settlers with their orchards.

Chardin, Pierre Teilhard de *See* **Teilhard de Chardin, Pierre.**

Chares 3d cent. BC. Greek sculptor. He created the Colossus of Rhodes, one of the Seven Wonders of the World, and is said to be the founder of the Rhodian school of sculpture.

Charge of the Light Brigade *See* **Balaklava, Battle of.**

Charlemagne (Charles the Great) (Charles I) c747–814. King of the Franks (768–814) and emperor (800–814) of the vast Carolingian Empire in Western Europe, united by his conquests. The son and successor of Pepin the Short, he first succeeded (768) with his brother Carloman as co-ruler of the Frankish domains, then became sole ruler (771) on Carloman's death. Thereafter he conquered the Lombards (773–774) in response to Pope Adrian's request for aid against them, subdued the Saxons (772–804), annexed Bavaria (788), and conquered the Avars in the region of the Danube (by 798). He was crowned by Pope Leo III (Christmas Day, 800) as emperor of the (reconstituted) Western Roman Empire in return for preventing the pope's ouster by unruly Romans. However, Byzantine emperor Michael I recognized Charlemagne (812) only as emperor of the Carolingian Empire (and not as Emperor of the Western Roman Empire). Under Charlemagne's rule an effective administrative system was developed, commerce, education, and building were promoted, and his capital at Aix-la-Chapelle became a cultural center.

Charles I (Spanish king) *See* **Charles V.**

Charles I *See* **Charlemagne.**

Charles I (~ of Anjou) 1226–85. French nobleman, king of Naples and Sicily (1266–85), son of French king Louis VIII. He won the throne of Naples and Sicily by conquest and, in subsequent years, vastly extended his territories. His harsh rule, however, led to the Revolt of the Sicilian Vespers (1282).

Charles I 1288–1342. Hungarian king (1308–42), son of Charles II of Naples and founder of the Hungarian Angevin line. He reorganized the army and stimulated trade. Under his rule, Hungary regained its status as a major power.

Charles I 1600–49. English king (1625–49), successor to his father, James I. His firm belief in the divine right of kings and consequent struggles with Parliament resulted in the English Civil Wars (1642–48). Charles's marriage to the unpopular French Catholic Henrietta Maria and his wars against Spain and France only added to his differences with Parliament. The struggle began soon after his accession and was characterized by bold maneuvers on both sides: Parliament refused Charles some money grants until he agreed to end arbitrary practices; Charles briefly relented, agreeing to the Petition of Right (1628), then dissolved Parliament (1629) and ruled without it, raising money by a variety of constitutional but unpopular means. Charles rigorously pursued religious orthodoxy, and his attempt to impose English liturgy in Scotland embroiled him in the Bishops' Wars (1639–40). This crisis prompted calling of the Short and Long Parliaments (1640), which in turn resulted in the English Civil Wars. The defeated Charles was tried and executed (1649).

Charles I 1863–1908.   Portuguese king (1889–1908), successor to Louis I. Charles vied with Britain and Japan for African colonial territories and contended with unrest at home. A revolt (1906) prompted him to grant Prime Minister João Franco (1855–1929) dictatorial powers. This resulted in a revolt (1908) and in his assassination.

Charles I 1887–1922.   Last ruler of the Austro-Hungarian Empire (1916–18), successor to Emperor Francis Joseph. He acceded during WWI and tried to open negotiations for peace (1916). He likewise failed in a plan to keep the dual monarchy united, and in 1918 Hungary and Czechoslavakia declared independence.

Charles II (king of Hungary)   *See* **Charles III of Durazzo.**

Charles II (~ the Bald) 823–877.   King of the West Franks (France) (843–877) and emperor of the West (875–877), a son and successor to Louis I (the Pious). With Louis the German, he made the Oath of Strasbourg (842), and subsequently agreed to redivision of the empire by the Treaty of Verdun (843) and the Treaty of Mersen (870). He then succeeded to the imperial crown (875).

Charles II 1248–1309.   King of Naples (1285–1309), successor to his father, Charles I (1226–85). He was defeated (1302) in the War of the Sicilian Vespers to regain Sicily (begun in his father's reign).

Charles II (~ the Bad) 1332–87.   King of Navarre (1349–87). He was noted in his day as a treacherous intriguer who conspired against his father-in-law, John II, among others.

Charles II 1630–85.   English king (1660–85), successor (after the English Restoration) to his father, Charles I. His restoration (1660) brought a period of relative stability after the fall of the Protectorate. Following the English Civil Wars,

by agreements with the Scots, he was crowned (1651) Charles II, and invaded England. Defeated (1651) by O. Cromwell, he fled to the Continent, where he remained until his restoration. Though he favored Catholicism and religious toleration, he was forced by public sentiment and acts of the Cavalier Parliament to accept strict laws of uniformity (Clarendon Code and Test Act) and to rescind his two declarations of indulgence (1662, 1672). Charles nevertheless continued his efforts in behalf of religious toleration, established his pro-Catholic Cabal (1667–74) ministry, and entered into secret agreements with the French (Treaty of Dover, 1670). The Popish Plot (1678), defaming Catholics, led to an attempt by Parliament to block the succession of Charles's Catholic brother, James II. Charles dissolved Parliament (1681), ruled without it, and, after the Rye House Plot (1683), gained popularity. During his reign, Britain also entered the Triple Alliance (1668) and was involved in the Second and Third Dutch Wars.

Charles II 1661–1700.   Last Spanish Habsburg king (1665–1700), successor to his father, Philip IV. His reign was marked by the continued decline in Spain's power and the War of Devotion (*q.v.*) and the War of the League of Augsburg. Dissatisfaction with his choice of Philip of Anjou (Philip V) as successor led to the War of Spanish Succession (1701–14).

Charles III (~ the Fat) 839–888.   Frankish emperor of the West (881–887) and king of the East (882–887). He briefly reunited Charlemagne's empire (885–887) but proved a weak ruler. His overthrow by Arnulf (887) began the final breakup of Charlemagne's empire.

Charles III (~ the Simple) 879–929.   French king (893–923), proclaimed king in opposition to, and successor to, King Eudes. He ended Norse raids by ceding (911) territory to them (now part of Normandy), and added Lorraine to the French kingdom (911). He was deposed in 923.

Charles III (~ of Durazzo) 1345–86.   King of Naples (1381–86) and Hungary (1385–86) as Charles II. A member of the Angevin line, he succeeded Joanna I in Naples by deposing her and putting her to death. He was assassinated soon after being elected to succeed King Louis I of Hungary.

Charles III 1716–88.   Spanish king (1759–88), successor to Ferdinand VI. An "enlightened despot," he instituted many beneficial administrative reforms. His reign was marked by defeat in the Seven Years' War (1756–63) and Spain's participation in the American Revolution (after 1779).

Charles IV (~ the Fair) 1294–1328.　French king (1322–28), successor to his brother Philip V and last of the Capetian kings. He won (1327) a part of Aquitaine from the English, who then controlled the territory.

Charles IV 1316–78.　Bohemian king (1346–78). Elected Holy Roman Emperor in opposition to Louis IV (1346), he succeeded him (1347) but was not crowned until 1355. He issued the Golden Bull of 1356 and thus established a constitutional basis for his rule of the empire. A noted patron of the arts and sciences, he founded the University of Prague and made the city a showplace of central Europe.

Charles IV 1604–75.　Duke of Lorraine. Charles attempted to resist domination by the French kings by means of plots and intrigues, and thus lost control of his domains several times. He supported Spanish involvement in the Fronde (*q.v.*).

Charles IV 1748–1819.　Spanish king (1788–1808), successor to his father, Charles III. A weak ruler, he relied on M. de Godoy to run the government. His reign was marked by two invasions by the French (1794, 1807) and domination by Napoleon. He was forced to abdicate in 1808.

Charles V (Charles the Wise) 1337–80.　French king (1364–80), successor to his father, John II. As regent for his father (1356–60), he put down the Jacquerie revolt. As king, he ruled France during its recovery from the early phase of the Hundred Years' War (1337–1453) He consolidated the power of the monarchy, strengthened the military, instituted reforms, and regained almost all the territories lost to the English.

Charles V 1500–58.　Spanish king (1516–56, as Charles I, succeeding Ferdinand II) and Holy Roman Emperor (1519–56, as Charles V, succeeding Maximilian I). A Habsburg, he was one of the most powerful European kings, ruling over a vast inherited empire that included much of Europe and all of Spain's New World possessions. Charles's reign was marked by involvement in the Italian Wars (1494–1559) against France and by attempts to stop M. Luther and the Protestant Reformation. In addition to the events of the Italian Wars, Charles's reign saw

the brief Revolt of Communeros (1520–21); his Diet of Worms (1521), banning Lutheranism; rebellions in Germany, such as the Peasants' War (1524–26), and the rise of the Lutheran Schmalkaldic League; war against the Ottoman Turks; the Council of Trent (1545) and the Counter-Reformation; the defeat (1547) of the Schmalkaldic League and the Diet of Augsburg (1547–48); and the unsuccessful Augsburg Interim (1548). Charles abdicated (1556) in Spain to his son Philip II and in the Holy Roman Empire to Ferdinand I.

Charles V (~ Leopold) 1643–90.　Duke of Lorraine. Deprived of his duchy by Louis XIV, Charles became a successful field marshal for the Holy Roman Emperor. He aided the defense of Vienna (1683) and drove the Turks from Hungary (1685).

Charles VI (~ the Well-Beloved) (~ the Mad) 1368–1422.　French king (1380–1422), successor to his father, Charles V. He suffered fits of insanity and could not rule by himself. His reign was marked by war between the Armagnacs and Burgundians, the English invasion of France (1420), and the Treaty of Troyes (1420).

Charles VI 1685–1740.　Austrian Holy Roman Emperor (1711–40), successor to his brother Joseph I and last of the direct Habsburg line. A pretender to the Spanish throne, he precipitated the War of Spanish Succession (1700–14). His accession as emperor (1711) soon ended this conflict, though he again warred against Spain as a member of the Quadruple Alliance (1718–20). In wars with the Ottoman Empire (1716–18, 1736–39), he won and then lost territory in Hungary and Serbia. He lost the War of Polish Succession (1733–35). His attempt to ensure succession of his daughter Maria Theresa to Habsburg domains (by the Pragmatic Sanction of 1713) led to the War of Austrian Succession (1740–48).

Charles VII (~ the Well-Served) 1403–61. French king (1422–61), successor to his father, Charles VI. From the time of the Siege of Orléans (1429) to the Battle of Castillon (1453), he gradually forced the English out of France and thus finally ended the Hundred Years' War (1337–1453). He also issued the Pragmatic Sanction (1438).

Charles VII (~ Albert) 1697–1745.　Holy Roman Emperor (1742–45), successor to Charles VI. On the death of Charles VI, he became embroiled in the War of Austrian Succession (1740–48) and died before peace was restored.

Charles VIII 1470–98.   French king (1483–98), successor to his father, Louis X. He initiated the Italian Wars (1494–1559) with an abortive invasion of Italy, in which he hoped to conquer the kingdom of Naples. He was defeated at the Battle of Fornovo (1495).

Charles IX 1550–74.   French king (1560–74), successor to his brother, Francis II. The Wars of Religion (*q.v.*) began during his reign. Under pressure from his mother, Catherine de Médicis, he ordered the Massacre of St. Bartholomew's Day (1572), in which thousands of Huguenots were killed.

Charles IX 1550–1611.   Regent of Sweden (1592–94, 1599–1604) and king (1604–11). He opposed the Catholic king Sigismund III (of Poland and Sweden), defeated him in battle (1598), and restored Lutheranism in Sweden. He precipitated a long period of wars with Poland (1600–60) and provoked the Kalmar War (1611–13).

Charles X 1757–1836.   French king (1824–30), successor to King Louis XVIII. He took part in the counterrevolutionary Wars of the Vendée. As king he vainly tried to reestablish the ancien régime. His last prime minister, A. de Polignac, provoked the July Revolution (1830).

Charles X Gustavus 1622–60.   Swedish king (1654–60), successor to his cousin Queen Christina. He led Sweden in the First Northern War (1655–60). He died while treaties, advantageous to Sweden, were being concluded.

Charles XI 1665–97.   Swedish king (1660–97), successor to his father, Charles X Gustavus. By the Riksdag of 1682, he established an absolute monarchy in Sweden. His reign was marked by treaties concluding the First Northern War (1655–60) and by Sweden's participation in the Third Dutch War (1672–78).

Charles XII 1682–1718.   Swedish king (1697–1718), successor to his father, Charles XI. He proved himself a brilliant military leader during the Second Northern War (1700–21), but his ambitious plans ultimately cost Sweden its status as a major power.

Charles XIII 1748–1818.   Swedish king (1809–18) and first king of a united Sweden and Norway (1814–18). Successor to his nephew, Gustavus IV, he ruled Sweden under a constitution that limited his powers. During his reign, Finland was ceded to Russia (1809) and Sweden and Norway were united (1814).

Charles XIV John (*orig.* Bernadotte, Jean Baptiste Jules) 1763–1844.   French general and king of Sweden and Norway (1818–44), successor to Charles XIII. A French marshal under Napoleon, he was elected crown prince of Sweden (1810), and from that time virtually ruled Sweden. He turned against Napoleon and helped defeat him at Leipzig (1813). He then forced Norway into union with Sweden (1814). His subsequent reign was marked by a period of relative peace.

Charles XV 1826–72.   King of Sweden and Norway (1859–72), successor to his father, Oscar I. A popular ruler, he supported the creation of a bicameral legislature (1866).

Charles Albert   *See* **Charles VIII.**

Charles Albert 1798–1849.   King of Sardinia (1831–49), a member of the Savoy family. A liberal-minded ruler during the Risorgimento, he warred against Austria twice and was defeated both times, first at Custozza (1848) and again at Novara (1849). He abdicated after his second defeat.

Charles Edward, the Young Pretender   *See* **Stuart, Charles Edward.**

Charles Leopold   *See* **Charles V.**

Charles Louis, Archduke   *See* **Abensberg-Eckmuhl, Battles of.**

Charles Martel (Charles the Hammer) 688–741. Frankish mayor of the palace (c715–741), successor to his father, Pepin of Herstal, and grandfather of Charlemagne. He became mayor of the palace of Austrasia after his father's death (714). He subsequently defeated rulers of Frankish territories, the Spanish Muslims, and a number of German tribes, to reunite the Frankish kingdom. He divided his mayoral office between his sons Pepin and Carloman.

Charles of Anjou   *See* **Charles I.**

Charles of Blois c1319–64.   Duke of Brittany. Charles was the nephew of French king Philip VI. He was a chief figure in the War of the Breton Succession (1341–65), which was ended soon after his death in battle.

Charles of Durazzo   *See* **Charles III.**

Charles of Valois 1270–1325.   French nobleman, son of French king Philip III. Created count of

Valois by his father (1285), he was father of French king Philip VI, the first of the Valois line.

Charles River Bridge v. ***Warren Bridge*** US Supreme Court decision (1837) that encouraged development of public facilities, such as transportation, by state and local government. The Charles River Bridge Company, granted a charter (1785) by the state of Massachusetts to build a bridge and collect tolls, sued when the state built another bridge nearby. The Court determined that the early charter did not guarantee exclusive rights to bridge traffic and further stated that such exclusivity would hinder progress.

Charles the Bad   *See* **Charles II.**

Charles the Bald   *See* **Charles II.**

Charles the Bold 1433–77. Last of the powerful dukes of Burgundy (1467–77), successor to his father, Philip the Good. He was an enemy of French king Louis XI and ambitious to expand his domains. His final defeat at Nancy (1477) marked the end of Burgundy's status as an autonomous state.

Charles the Fair   *See* **Charles IV.**

Charles the Fat   *See* **Charles III.**

Charles the Great   *See* **Charlemagne.**

Charles the Hammer   *See* **Charles Martel.**

Charles the Mad   *See* **Charles VI.**

Charles the Simple   *See* **Charles III.**

Charles the Well-Beloved   *See* **Charles VI.**

Charles the Well-Served   *See* **Charles VII.**

Charles the Wise   *See* **Charles V.**

Charleston, Battle of   1. American victory (June 28, 1776) over the British during the American Revolution (1775–83). American colonel W. Moultrie successfully defended his garrison on Sullivan's Island in the Charleston, South Carolina, harbor during an attack by British warships. 2. Major British victory (May 12, 1780) during the American Revolution (1775–83). Following a six-week siege by some 16,000 soldiers under Sir H. Clinton, the British forced the surrender of Charleston, South Carolina, and some 7,000 American defenders under Gen. B. Lincoln. The British then launched their invasion of the Carolinas. They held the city until Dec. 14, 1782. 3. (Siege of Charleston) Prolonged Union effort to capture this South Carolina city during the American Civil War (1861–65). Following capture of Fort Sumter (*q.v.*) by the Confederacy, Charleston harbor was blockaded by the Union navy and after 1863, was bombarded by Union forces. It did not fall to Union forces (taken Feb. 18, 1865) until Sherman's March to the Sea.

Charlottetown Conference   Preliminary meeting (Sept., 1864) of delegates from Canadian crown colonies to discuss unification of Canada. The conference was followed by the Quebec Conference (*q.v.*). Originally called to discuss federation of the Maritime colony, the conference was attended by delegates of other colonies, who promoted a plan for a general union.

charte constitutionnelle   *See* **Charter of 1814.**

chartered companies   Companies created by special government charter for the purpose of colonization and trade in foreign lands. The companies were especially important (16th–17th cents.) in the creation of Europe's vast overseas colonial empires. Chartered companies were frequently empowered to govern as well as explore and colonize these new lands and thus figured in the early history of the US, Canada, India, and Africa. Their functions, however, were eventually absorbed by the home governments. *See separate entries for the following major trading companies:* British East India Company; Dutch East India Company; Dutch West India Company; French East India Company; Hudson's Bay Company; Massachusetts Bay Company; Muscovy Company; Virginia Company.

Charter of 1814 (*charte constitutionnelle*) Constitution issued (June 14, 1814) by French king Louis XVIII, following his restoration to the throne at the end of the Napoleonic era. Louis promulgated the constitution at the urging of C. Talleyrand and other advisers. It established a constitutional monarchy with a bicameral legislature and guaranteed civil liberties and religious toleration established under Napoleon's reign. Catholicism was made the state religion. The charter was rewritten in 1830.

Charter 77   *See* **Czechoslovakia, 1977.**

Charter to the Nobility   Charter (May, 1785) guaranteeing the rights and prerogatives of the Russian nobility. Issued by Catharine II (the Great), the charter extended these rights to the nobility as a corporate body and eliminated earlier distinctions between old and new nobility. By its terms the nobility were granted the rights of assembly, petition of the monarch, and trial by their peers. It also gave them powers over their serfs, excluded them from mandatory service to the state, and exempted them from personal taxes.

Chartism Mass movement (1838–48) for political reform which arose among workingmen in Britain. The movement was centered around demands for reforms set forth in the People's Charter drafted by William Lovett. They included universal male suffrage, voting by ballot, and elimination of property qualifications for members of Parliament. Spawned by a severe depression and unpopular revisions of the Poor Laws, the movement briefly became nationwide. Chartist petitions were submitted to Parliament (1838, 1840, 1848), and all were rejected. Chartist riots in May, July, and Nov., 1839 resulted in arrests of Chartist leaders and a decline in the movement. It revived briefly in 1848, but a return of prosperity brought the final decline of the movement.

Chase, Salmon Portland 1808–73. American public official and 6th chief justice of the US Supreme Court (1864–73). He was a founder of the Free-Soil and Republican parties and secretary of treasury under President A. Lincoln (1861–64). Chase proposed the plan for the national banking system (1863), presided over the impeachment proceedings against President A. Johnson (1868), and was several times a candidate for president.

Chase, Samuel 1741–1811. American patriot, Supreme Court associate justice (1796–1811), and signer of the Declaration of Independence. T. Jefferson's failed attempt to have him removed from the court for political reasons (1805) helped establish the Court's traditional independence from political influence.

Chateaubriand, François René, vicomte of 1768–1848. French writer and diplomat, a founder of French Romanticism. His life was enmeshed with the upheavals of the French Revolution, and he variously served the monarchists, Napoleon, and the Restoration. His first great literary success, however, came (1802) with publication of *The Genius of Christianity.* His many other works include the novels *Atala* and *René,* and his memoirs, *Mémoires d'outre-tombe.*

Chateauguay, Battle of British victory (Oct. 26, 1813) during the War of 1812. A small contingent of British troops intercepted and defeated the advance party of an American invasion force,

led by Gen. W. Hampton, as it neared its objective of Montreal, Canada. The defeat turned back the American invasion of Canada.

Chattanooga, Battle of Union victory (1863) at Chattanooga, Tennessee, during the American Civil War (1861–65). One of the important Union victories, it was the culmination of the Chattanooga Campaign (1863) and gave the North undisputed possession of that strategic city. The Army of the Cumberland, under Gen. W. Rosecrans, was besieged (Sept., 1863) at Chattanooga by Confederate forces, under Gen. B. Bragg, after the Battle of Chickamauga Creek. By November, Gen. U. Grant had replaced Rosecrans and had mustered some 60,000 men to face Bragg's 50,000. He began the attack late in November with units under Gen. W. Sherman, Gen. J. Hooker, and Gen. G. Thomas. On Nov. 24, Hooker cleared Lookout Mountain (Battle Above the Clouds) of Confederates. On Nov. 25, Thomas moved up Missionary Ridge and routed the Confederates. Bragg was forced to retreat into Georgia and sustained losses of 7,000 men to the Union's 6,000.

Chatterton, Thomas 1752–70. English poet. Recognized as a forerunner of the Romantic movement, he was largely unrecognized in his own time. He committed suicide at age 17.

Chaucer, Geoffrey 1340?–1400. Early English poet, author of *The Canterbury Tales* and one of the most important figures in English literature. Born into a middle-class family, Chaucer won the favor of King Edward III, subsequently held various court-appointed administrative posts, and even undertook a number of diplomatic missions during the 1370s. Chaucer's literary works are usually divided into three periods. The early period (ending 1370) reflects a French influence and includes his first major work, the *Book of the Duchesse.* The middle period shows an Italian influence (Boccaccio, Dante) and includes *House of Fame, Parlement of Foules, Legend of Good Women,* and *Troilus and Criseyde.* The late period (after 1387) includes his masterpiece, *The Canterbury Tales.*

Chaumette, Pierre Gaspard 1763–94. French revolutionary. As a leader in the Commune of Paris, he instituted social reforms, including improvements in hospitals and treatment of the poor. A democratic extremist, he also advocated the anti-Christian cult of reason and helped organize the first ceremony in the worship of the goddess Reason, held at Notre Dame Cathedral (Nov. 10, 1793). Chaumette was executed by M. Robespierre's order.

Chautauqua movement Adult education system. Similar to the Lyceum, it was begun (1873) in Chautauqua, New York, by John Vincent (1832–1920) and Lewis Miller (1829–99). It supported summer lectures and classes in the arts, sciences, and humanities.

Chavez, Cesar 1927–93. American labor leader and director of the United Farm Workers (UFW). Born the son of immigrants, Chavez first began organizing workers in the California grape industry (1962), using nonviolent tactics adapted from the civil rights movement. His union later became the United Farm Workers, and after organizing successful boycotts against lettuce and table-grapes, he brought the UFW into the AFL-CIO organization (1972). His efforts improved the lot of agricultural laborers.

Chazars *See* **Khazars.**

Checkers Speech Emotional television address on Sept. 23, 1952, in which R. Nixon preserved his position as vice-presidential candidate and won new support for the Eisenhower-Nixon ticket. Nixon answered charges that he had benefited from a fund raised by California friends by pointing to his modest personal circumstances, noting his wife's "Republican cloth coat" and his dog, Checkers.

checks and balances The principle of government whereby power is divided among executive legislative, and judicial branches, in order to prevent excesses and abuses of power. The theory of the separation of powers was articulated in Montesquieu's *The Spirit of Laws* (1748) and was applied to government in the US Constitution (*q.v.*) in 1789.

Cheever, John 1912–1982. American novelist and short-story writer whose works depict life in 20th-cent. suburban America. Among his works are *The Wapshot Chronicle* and *Bullet Park.*

Cheka Russian secret police unit. The Cheka was organized in Dec., 1917, to combat counter-revolutionary activity. It was granted power of execution in 1918. After 1922 it was replaced by the GPU (*q.v.*).

Chekhov, Anton Pavlovich 1860–1904. Russian playwright and short-story writer, one of Russia's great literary figures. A practicing physician

until forced to retire by a chronic case of tuberculosis, he first won fame with stories such as *Ward Number Six* and *The Steppe.* From 1898 he began writing plays, which were produced by the Moscow Art Theater and which are now world famous. Among them are *The Sea Gull* (1896), *Uncle Vanya* (1899), and *The Cherry Orchard* (1904).

Chen Duxiu (Ch'en Tu-hsiu) 1879–1942. Chinese scholar and Communist leader. Chen, an advocate of sweeping cultural revolution, was a leader of the May Fourth Movement (*q.v.*) and a principal founder of the Chinese Communist party.

Chénier, André Marie de 1762–94. French poet, sometimes called the greatest of 18th-cent. France. He was guillotined during the Reign of Terror in France and is perhaps best known for his *Elégies.*

Chennault, Claire Lee 1890–1958. American general. He organized (1941) the volunteer air-combat unit called the Flying Tigers, which fought in China, and headed conventional US air combat units there later in WW II.

Ch'en Tu-hsiu *See* **Chen Duxiu.**

Cheops *See* **Khufu.**

Chephren *See* **Khafre.**

Cheribon Agreement *See* **Linggadjati Agreement.**

Chernenko, Konstantin Ustinovich 1911–85. Soviet politician and conservative leader of the USSR (1984–85). Born the son of Siberian peasants, Chernenko joined the Communist party in 1931 and later began working as a propagandist. He ran the Soviet Central Committee proganda arm (1956–60) in Moscow and there befriended L. Brezhnev. Chernenko became Brezhnev's chief of staff in 1964 when the latter became Soviet leader. He then was appointed to the Central committee in 1971, and served as a member of the Politburo from 1977. Though Chernenko was considered Brezhnev's heir apparent, the post of Soviet leader went to Y. Andropov instead, following Brezhnev's death in 1982. When the aging Andropov died unexpectedly in 1984, Chernenko succeeded him as Soviet leader. After only a short term of office, in which he maintained a hard-line policy in (then) chilly East-West relations, Chernenko himself died of old age and poor health. He was succeeded by the younger, more liberal-minded M. Gorbachev.

Cherokee Indians   North American Indian tribe once located in the US Southeast. First visited by the Spanish (mid-16th cent.), they were subsequently friendly with British settlers until the mid-18th cent. The tribal population was cut in half by a smallpox epidemic (c1750), and, after 1760, hostilities against the settlers began. During the American Revolution (1775–83), the Cherokee allied themselves with the British royalists, and engaged in sporadic warfare (1776–81). Their defeat and loss of territories in subsequent treaties began the process of their removal from the Southeast. By the Indian Removal Act, the Cherokee were forcibly removed (1838) to Oklahoma. The long trek under Chief J. Ross cost thousands of lives and was called the Trail of Tears. In Oklahoma the Cherokee became one of the Five Civilized Tribes. The tribe disbanded in 1906.

Cherry Valley Raid   Raid (Nov. 11, 1778) on a village in upper New York during the American Revolution (1775–83). The Iroquois Indians, led by J. Brant, joined with W. Butler and Butler's raiders in this attack, which left the town destroyed.

Chersonese, Tauric   Ancient city in the Crimea, near modern Sevastopol. Founded (6th cent. BC) by the Ionian Greeks, it was an important trading center in ancient times and continued to flourish under the Romans and Byzantines. It fell into ruin in the 14th cent.

Chersonese, Thracian (Chersonesus)   Geographical region, known as the Gallipoli Peninsula, it is located in European Turkey. It was a major grain-producing region in ancient times and was crossed by major trade routes.

Chervenkov, Valko   *See* **Bulgaria, 1950–61.**

Chesapeake   US frigate. On June 22, 1807, the British ship *Leopard* stopped her off the Virginia coast, searched her for British deserters, and forcibly removed four crewmen. This incident, the Chesapeake Affair, increased anti-British sentiment in the US in the years before the War of 1812. When, during the War of 1812, the *Chesapeake* was attacked and boarded (June 1, 1813) outside of Boston harbor by crewmen of the British warship *Shannon,* American commander J. Lawrence uttered his famous cry, "Don't give up the ship!"

Chesapeake Affair   *See Chesapeake.*

Chesterton, G(ilbert) K(eith) 1874–1936.   English author and critic. A prolific man of letters, noted for his mastery of the paradox, he wrote essays, poems, critical works, theological treatises, and even a series of detective novels.

Chevreuse, Marie de Rohan-Montbazon, duchess of 1600–79.   French noblewoman. She was involved in several conspiracies against Cardinal Richelieu and Cardinal Mazarin during their terms as ministers of France. Exiled by Richelieu, she later became Mazarin's ally.

Chevrolet, Louis   *See* **Durant, William Crapo.**

Cheyenne Indians   North American Indian tribe once located in the Great Plains. Pressed by hostilities with other tribes, the Cheyenne migrated from Minnesota and, by the early 1800s, had settled in the Black Hills. By 1851, part of the tribe had moved south, and the Cheyenne were split into northern and southern tribes. Discovery of gold (1858) on tribal lands in Colorado brought on war with the whites. The southern Cheyenne were generally subdued by Gen. G. Custer after his destruction of the Washita River village (1868). The northern Cheyenne and Sioux combined to massacre Custer's forces at Little Bighorn (1876). They surrendered in 1877 and were removed to Oklahoma

Chia-ching   *See* **Jiajing.**

Chia-ch'ing   *See* **Jiaqing.**

Chiang Ch'ing   *See* **Jiang Qing.**

Chiang Chung-cheng   *See* **Chiang Kai-shek.**

Chiang Kai-shek (Chiang Chung-cheng) 1887–1975.   Chinese Nationalist general and leader, who headed the governments of China (1928–49) and of the exiled Nationalists on Taiwan (after 1949). A trained military leader, Chiang took part in the Chinese Revolution of 1911, rebellions against the government of Yuan Shih-kai, and served (from 1918) in Sun Yat-sen's Nationalist Guomindang government. He began the Northern Expedition (1926–28), took control of the Guomindang (Sun had died 1925), broke with the Communists (1927), warred against them in the Chinese Civil War (1927–49), and established the Nationalists as rulers of China (1928–49) until the Communist takeover. He held power under various titles, and, after being seized in the Xi'an Incident (1936), agreed to an alliance with the Communists against the threat of Japanese invasion. He then led a loosely united China during the Sino-Japanese War (1937–45) and WW II, but, after 1945, resumed civil war against the Communists. This time the Communists gained the upper hand, and by

1949 he and his Nationalist government had been forced into exile on Taiwan. Chiang's subsequent fortunes declined with those of his government on Taiwan. After enjoying two decades of US support, his government was expelled (1971) from the UN in favor of the Communist People's Republic of China.

Chiang Kai-shek, Madame *See* **Soong Mei-ling.**

Chiaramonte, Barnaba Gregorio *See* **Pius VII.**

Chicago school American architectural school that pioneered the building of skyscrapers (late 19th cent.). Principal figures in this school were L. Sullivan, F. L. Wright, D. Burnham, and J. Root.

Chicherin, Georgi Vasilyevich 1872–1936. Russian revolutionary and diplomat. He served as foreign commisar (1918–28) after the Russian revolution and won recognition of the new government by Western European countries. He negotiated the Treaty of Rapallo (1922).

Chickamauga Creek, Battle of Battle (Sept. 19–20, 1863) during the American Civil War (1861–65). Some 55,000 Union troops, led by W. Rosecrans, were engaged by 70,000 Confederates, led by B. Bragg, near Chattanooga. Union losses were 16,000, Confederate 18,000, making this one of the war's bloodiest battles.

Ch'ien Lung *See* **Qianlong.**

Chiesa, Giacomo della *See* **Benedict XV.**

Chikamatsu, Monzaemon 1653–1724. Japanese dramatist, sometimes called the "Shakespeare of Japan." He wrote over one hundred plays, most of them for puppet theater.

Childebert I *d.* 558. Merovingian Frankish king (511–558), successor with his three brothers to his father, Clovis I. Childebert received the northwestern part of the Merovingian kingdom (in what is now France), and by various means increased his holdings at his brothers' expense.

Childebert II 570?–595. Frankish king of Austrasia (575–595), successor to his father, Sigebert. From 575 to 585, his mother Brunhilde ruled for him as regent. He subsequently engaged in wars to expand his territories and was defeated in one attempt, by Neustrian king Clotaire II.

Childeric I AD c436–481. Frankish king (AD c457–481), one of the first of the Merovingian dynasty and father of Clovis I. He was successful in ridding his kingdom (now part of Belgium) of Visigoths (by AD 469) and Saxon pirates.

Children's Crusade *See* **Crusade, Children's.**

Chile Republic located on the southwestern coast of South America. The population is 13,000,000 and the capital is Santiago. Chile gained its independence from Spain in 1818 but its growth was slow until the late 19th and early 20th cents., when its rich deposits of nitrates and copper came under the control of foreign companies. Chile's political history has been one of struggle between conservative and liberal factions. The 20th cent. saw the rise of Communist and Socialist organizations as powers on the political scene. In 1970 Salvador Allende Gossens became the first Marxist to be elected chief executive of a government in the Western Hemisphere. He died in 1973 during a military coup and civilian democratic government was not restored until 1990. Key dates in the history of Chile include:

1540s–50s Spanish under Pedro de Valdivia founded Santiago (1541), Concepción (1550), Valdivia (1552), and other settlements in Chile.

16TH CENT. Conquistadors fought Araucanian Wars against native peoples in central Chile.

16TH CENT. Epic poem *La Araucana,* called the "Aeneid of the Chileans," composed by Spanish soldier Alonso de Ercilla y Zúñiga, who fought in the wars.

1810–14 Unsuccessful attempt to establish Chilean independence led by B. O'Higgins and Juan Martínez de Rozas.

1817 Argentine rebel J. de San Martín and the Chilean O'Higgins led rebel force from Argentina into Chile; began expulsion of Spanish royalists from Chile with victory at Battle of Chacabuco (Feb. 12); O'Higgins named director general.

1818 O'Higgins proclaimed Chilean independence (Feb. 12).

1818 J. de San Martín defeated the Spanish in final battle of Maipú (1818). Chilean independence firmly established.

1818–23 O'Higgins governed as dictator in Chile; opposition to his rule led to his resignation.

1820s–1870s Chilean copper industry boomed, as industrialization of Europe created rising demand; by 1860s Chilean copper mines reached a peak 44% share of world production, amounting to over half Chile's exports; depletion of easily mined ores and competition from other producing countries brought sharp drop in world production share by the 1880s.

1823–31 Period of political instability; ten presidents spent time in office; civil war between Conservative and Liberal factions erupted, 1829–30, with the Conservatives gaining control of the government.

1831–41 President Joaquin Prieto, a Conservative, in office.

1833 New constitution adopted; led to eventual establishment of strong, centralized representative government in Chile.

1836–39 Chile opposed confederation of Bolivia and Peru; Chilean forces broke up confederation at Battle of Yungay (1839).

1841–51 Manuel Bulnes, who led Chilean forces at Battle of Yungay, served as president.

1851–61 Manuel Montt in office as president; promoted education and other liberal reforms; revolts by Liberals quashed.

1861–71 Democratic reforms and increased economic development marked this period, the presidency of José Joaquin Pérez; final defeat of Araucanian Indians by Chilean army (1870), ending the Araucanian Wars and paving way for settlement farther southward.

1864–66 War between Peru and Spain, in which Chile sided with Peru.

1871–76 President Federico Errázuriz Zañartu in office; a Liberal, he promoted democratic reforms, anti-clerical policies, and education.

1876–81 Anibal Pinto served as president.

1879–83 Chile emerged victorious in War of the Pacific (1879–83); conflict ended by the Treaty of Ancon (1883); Chile awarded valuable territories from Bolivia and Peru.

1881–86 President Domingo Santa María in office.

1881 Rich nitrate deposits in Atacama desert (won by Chile during the War of the Pacific) came under foreign control; mining of nitrate deposits helped offset decline in copper exports during 1880s.

1883–1929 Tacna-Arica Controversy, prolonged territorial dispute with Peru; ultimately resolved along lines suggested by US Pres. H. Hoover.

1886–91 J. Balmaceda served as president; his liberal reforms caused civil war (1891) and his ouster; parliamentary dictatorship ruled until adoption of 1925 constitution.

1891 Baltimore Incident (Oct. 16) threatened war with US; sparked by supposed US support for Balmaceda.

1891–96 Jorge Montt in office as president; instituted financial reforms and increased powers of local authorities.

1896–1901 Federico Errázuriz Echaurren served as president; disagreement with Argentina over border territory nearly resulted in war.

EARLY 1900s Second boom in Chilean copper industry began; lower grade ores required foreign capital and expertise to mine profitably; Chuquichamata, which became world's largest open-cast mine, began producing in 1915; El Teniente, world's largest underground copper mine, began producing in 1912; Potrerillos, Chile's third great copper mine, started producing in 1926. The three, all foreign owned, accounted for bulk of Chilean copper exports.

1901–06 President Germán Riesco, a Liberal, in office.

1906–10 Conservative Pedro Montt served as president; fostered growth of railroads and production of copper and nitrates.

1907 Widespread strikes quashed by government troops.

1910–15 President Ramón Barros Luco in office.

1914–18 World War I; Chile, which declared neutrality, profited by exporting nitrates to Allies for explosives manufacture; Germans developed synthetic nitrates, however, and as this technology spread after WW I, Chile's share of world nitrate production plummeted from 90% (1919) to 24% (1929).

1915–20 President Juan Luis Sanfuentes served.

1920–21 Economy hit hard by sharp drop in nitrate exports following end of WW I.

1920–24 Reformer A. Alessandri Palma served as president; elected by Liberal coalition, he was forced out of office by a military takeover (Sept. 15, 1924).

1925 Alessandri Palma restored to presidency briefly, following coup against military regime; helped write new constitution (1925), giving president more powers, guaranteeing separation of church and state, and expanding the electorate.

1925–27 President Emiliano Figueroa Larrain in office, following Alessandri's resignation.

1927–31   Carlos Ibáñez del Campo in office as dictator-president; promoted labor and educational reforms.

1930s   Great Depression caused great hardship in Chile; promoted the rise of Socialist and Marxist groups that sought to alter Chilean government and economic system.

1931–32   Period of political instability in which seven different presidents held office.

1932–38   Alessandri Palma again in office as president, this time as head of Liberal-Conservative coalition; his presidency marked by sweeping social reforms, sharply improved economy (after 1933), and rise of Fascist and Communist factions.

1938   Fascist revolt failed.

1938–41   President Pedro Aguirre Cerda, leader of radical leftist coalition (Popular Front), in office; instituted reforms to benefit working class.

1941–42   Gerónimo Méndez served as acting president.

1942   Chile, along with other Latin American nations, declared war on Germany and other Axis Powers.

1942–46   Juan Antonio Rios in office as president; elected by the Radical coalition, he was unable to carry out reforms.

1946–52   Gabriel González Videla served as president; elected as a Radical candidate with Communist support, he tried unsuccessfully to solve Chile's economic ills; turning to the Liberals and Conservatives after 1948, he took measures against Communists; US investment in Chilean copper industry increased substantially from 1945.

1949   Women granted right to vote.

1950–53   Korean War; increased copper exports resulted in period of economic prosperity for Chile.

1952–58   C. Ibáñez del Campo served second time as president; failed to enact significant reforms.

1958–64   Jorge Alessandri Rodríguez served as president; administration marked by continuing economic trouble, including high unemployment and soaring inflation; government instituted massive public works program to ease unemployment.

1964–70   Eduardo Frei Montalvo, a Christian Democrat, served as president; introduced numerous reforms; government took control-

ling interest in US-owned mines in Chile, which had accounted for bulk of copper exports since the 1920s.

1970–73   S. Allende Gossens, a Communist, became president; nationalized copper companies and nitrate industries (1971); sought to institute Socialist program in Chile.

1971   Diplomatic relations established (Jan. 5) with China.

1971   Congress blocked Allende's planned governmental reforms; measures would have created unicameral legislature and increased presidential powers.

1972   Allende imposed martial law (Oct. 12) in 13 provinces to deal with truckers' strike.

1973   Military staged unsuccessful coup (June 29) against Allende government.

1973   Military coup overthrew Allende government (Sept. 11); President Allende died under suspicious circumstances; US CIA implicated in attempts to destabilize the government.

1973–90   Gen. Augusto Pinochet Ugarto served as president (from Sept. 13); instituted right-wing dictatorship firmly opposed to Marxists.

1976   OAS accused military government of police terrorism.

1978   Government lifted state of siege in force since military takeover.

1980   New constitution adopted.

1981   Pinochet elected president under new constitution; civilian president to be elected at close of Pinochet's eight-year term.

1981–83   Strict monetarist policies aggravated the impact of a recession; business failures increased and banks were weakened.

1982   Gen. Pinochet faced overt hostility at the funeral of former President Eduardo Frei Montalvo; economic crisis and continuing human rights abuses led to increased opposition to his government.

1983   Government declared 90-day moratorium on debt repayments, causing a run on the nation's banks; mass demonstrations suppressed by the government.

1984–87   Mass demonstrations, growing number of terrorist attacks, and international criticism undermined Pinochet regime even as the economy began to improve.

1984   Members of Pinochet's family charged with corruption; the Roman Catholic church began to support demonstrations against the government.

1985 Government imposed a 90-day state of siege (May); order lifted after one month in order to reach agreements with creditor banks on loans.

1986 Death of Rodrigo Rojas (July), a 19-year-old who had recently returned from exile in the US; sparked new round of international condemnation of Pinochet regime.

1986 Pinochet survived the first known assassination attempt (Sept.).

1987 Pope John Paul II visited Chile (Apr.), describing the Pinochet regime as "dictatorial" and "transitory"; Gen. Fernando Matthei and other members of the junta called for a return to civilian rule.

1988 Constitutional freedoms granted as the state of emergency and censorship were lifted: political parties were allowed to organize.

1988 Voters rejected Pinochet regime (Oct.); Pinochet to remain in office until March 1990, when a democratically elected president and congress would take office.

1989 Patricio Aylwin Azócar, Christian Democrat, won presidential elections (Dec.); Pinochet attempted to remain as commander in chief of the armed forces in order to guarantee a military role in the new government.

1990– Patricio Aylwin Azócar in office as president; announced an amnesty for nonviolent political prisoners and started investigation of human rights abuses during the Pinochet regime.

1990 Mass graves of political prisoners discovered in the Atacama desert; Pres. Allende reported to have committed suicide during the 1973 coup.

1991 Further investigation of Pinochet regime revealed over 3,000 people had been killed or "disappeared"; financial corruption of Pinochet regime also exposed.

1991 In Santiago, government ordered factories closed and 40 percent of cars off the streets to reduce serious air pollution.

1991 Mass grave of some 120 victims of Pinochet regime opened in Santiago (Sept.)

1992 Chile refused asylum to former East German hard-line leader E. Honecker, then in hiding in Chile's Moscow embassy (Mar.).

Chilpancingo, Congress of *See* **Congress of Chilpancingo.**

Chilperic I *d.*584. Frankish king of Neustria (561–584), whose reign was marked by feuds and warfare against his brother, Sigebert, king of Austrasia. The feud became vicious when Chilperic killed his wife Galswintha, sister of Austrasian queen Brunhilde, and eventually led to Sigebert's conquest of Neustria (575).

Ch'in *See* **Qin.**

Chin *See* **Jin.**

China (People's Republic of China) Communist republic located in east central Asia. The population is 1,130,065,000 and the capital is Beijing. Archaeological evidence indicates China had an advanced civilization as early as the 3d–2d millennia BC, which seems to have spread from the Yellow River valley. Legends tell of great rulers of ancient times, notably: Fuxi (Fu Hsi), the mythical first ruler of China who supposedly taught people how to fish, hunt, and domesticate animals in 2900 BC; Shennong (Shen Nung), the second ruler who taught them farming skills and established an agricultural society; and Huang Di (Huang Ti), the third ruler, who was credited with many innovations, ranging from the introduction of mathematical calculations to the building of boats. The later Xia dynasty of Chinese rulers remains shrouded in legend and it is with the Shang dynasty that the very extensive history of China—backed by significant archaeological evidence—really begins. The current Romanization of Chinese names is used below, though in many cases the earlier (usually Wade-Giles) transliteration appears immediately following in parentheses. **For more on important persons and major events** *see* **text entries under specific names.** Key events in the history of China include:

2 MILLION BC Crude Stone Age tools were in use by early humans in Shanxi (Shensi) province by this time.

c500,000–210,000 BC Beijing Man (*Homo erectus*) lived in limestone caves near Beijing; Beijing Man fossils first discovered in modern times in 1920s.

c200,000–50,000 BC Neanderthaloid man (*Homo sapiens*) established food-gathering culture along the Yellow River.

c6000 BC Neolithic culture typical of East and Southeast Asia (Hoabinhian culture) developed in China by about this time; included farming, weaving (hemp and silk), and pottery making; neolithic cultures in various regions of China apparently developed separately.

5000 BC Clear differences develop between agriculture in cooler, dryer northern China (millet raised) and the wetter, warmer south (wet rice).

c5000 BC Yangshao culture replaced early neolithic cultures; typified by village excavated at Banpo (Shaanxi province) and red and black painted pottery.

c3000–2000 BC Longshanoid horizon; gradual spread of Longshan culture throughout China; featured ritual pottery, use of potter's wheel; metallurgy (first copper and later bronze), fashioning of jade articles, and forming of ruling elite in towns.

3000 BC Sheep and cattle being raised in north; water-buffalo and cattle in south.

c2205–c1767 BC Traditional dates of Xia (Hsia) dynasty, legendary first dynasty of rulers; said to have been founded by Yu the Great.

c2000–1800 BC Palace complexes built at Erlitou in Henan (Honan) province; may be Xia capital or early Shang dynasty palace.

c1554–1045 BC Shang dynasty ruled, the first dynasty identified by archaeological evidence; about 28 or 29 kings ruled as theocratic chieftains, variously controlling the Yellow River plain and outlying areas; developed relatively advanced civilization with extensive farming, spoke-wheeled chariots, and bronze weapons; divination and ancestor worship common; casting of bronze vessels common in this period;

c1200–1180? BC Wu Ding reigned; royal armies numbered 3,000 or 5,000 men by this time; practice of scapulimancy, divination by reading cracks made in cattle and turtle bones, was widespread; frequent sacrifices of animals and humans (involving anywhere from 10 to 300 at a time).

c1150 BC Wen Wang flourished as king of the Zhou, a state on the western frontier; an intelligent and benevolent leader, who became idealized model for later Zhou rulers, greatly extended Zhou domains until Shang rulers recognized him as Count of the West.

c1144 Wen Wang, falsely accused by a jealous nobleman, was imprisoned by Zouxin, the last Shang ruler, for three years; according to

traditional accounts he wrote the classic *I Ching* (Book of Changes) while imprisoned.

1122 BC Wu Wang, Wen Wang's son and ruler of Zhou domains along northwest border of Shang territory, defeated and killed Zouxin after a series of bloody battles; set up a feudal system of government, dividing up his domains among relatives and nobles willing to acknowledge Zhou suzerainty.

1122–221 BC Zhou (Chou) dynasty in power; ruled in west from capital at Hao and in east (over old Shang empire) from Luoyi; ancestor worship and divination practiced; Bronze Age culture reached its height; period also noted for political turmoil and development of Chinese form of feudalism.

771 BC Western capital of Hao abandoned after unrest and barbarian invasion; Zhou rulers moved to Luoyi in east; marked decline of Zhou power and end of Western Zhou.

771–221 Eastern Zhou period (traditionally divided into Spring and Autumn and Warring States periods); produced classical age of Chinese literature in which Confucius, Laozi (Lao-tze), and Mencius flourished; marked by beginning of continuous recorded history of China; rise of Confucianism and Daoism (Taoism), which replaced old religions; important advances in military techniques and technology (introduction of crossbow); introduction of iron and mass production of iron implements.

722–481 BC Period covered by famous chronicle *Spring and Autumn Annals.*

AFTER 700 BC From this time Zhou kings hold little real power, instead depending for defense on a league of nobles, headed by a *ba* (overlord).

c604–531 BC Laozi lived, according to traditional accounts of this widely revered, legendary Chinese philosopher; founded Daoism; believed to have written *Dao-te Ching,* now a sacred Daoist text.

551–479 BC Confucius lived; the teachings of this great Chinese philosopher, first collected by his disciples in the *Analects,* became the basis for Confucianism, which dominated Chinese thought and culture until the 20th century.

470?–391? BC Philosopher Mo-tzu lived; his doctrine of universal love rivaled Confucianism for a time.

453–221 BC Warring States period; empire divided into petty kingdoms, Zhou, Jin, Wei, Han, Zhao, Chu, Yan, and Qi; frequent warfare and corruption characterized the period, which also saw the rise of Confucianism.

371?–288? BC Confucian philosopher Mencius lived; called the second sage after Confucius, he was a key figure in the development of Confucianism; his *Book of Mencius* became a classic Confucian text.

c298–c230 BC Philosopher Xunzi lived; an opponent of Confucianism, he nevertheless systematized the teachings and thereby helped establish the Confucian tradition.

255–210? BC Reign of Shi Huangdi; as ruler of the Qin (Ch'in), a petty kingdom in the northwest, he conquered the warring states, brought the Zhou to an end, abolished feudalism and created (221) the first unified Chinese empire under centralized government; established Legalist system of rewards and punishments; began construction of the Great Wall.

249 BC Shi Huangdi in complete control of Eastern Zhou state; subsequently conquered the remaining warring states, beginning with Han (230) and ending with Qi (221); marked end of Warring States period and start of unified Qin Empire in China.

233 BC Death of Legalist philosopher Han Fei; he believed military power was key to relations between kingdoms.

213 BC Burning of the Books ordered by Emperor Qin Shi Huangdi.

202 BC–AD 220 Han dynasty reigned; restored order after death of Qin Shi Huangdi; empire greatly expanded, especially by Wudi (Wu Ti); Examination System was introduced and Confucianism promoted; Buddhism introduced from India, silk trade developed and many cultural advances made.

2D CENT. BC Explorer Zhang Qian (Chang Ch'ien) traveled through India and Greece; brought back knowledge of these cultures.

180–157 BC Wendi ruled as emperor; consolidated Han dynasty control and later came to be regarded as model ruler.

145–c90 BC Sima Qian, first great Chinese historian, lived; wrote *Shiji.*

AD 9–25 Han dynasty briefly overthrown by Wang Mang, a government official; Wang Mang's attempts at radical reform provoked peasant revolt of Red Eyebrows (AD 18–23), resulting in his assassination by them.

AD c100 First Chinese dictionary compiled.

AD 105 Paper invented.

AD 184–204 Rebellion of the Yellow Turbans; contributed to final overthrow of Han dynasty (AD 220).

220–589 Six Dynasties period followed the collapse of the Han dynasty; each of the dynasties had its capital at Nanjing; period marked by warfare between petty kingdoms, rise of Buddhism and Daoism, significant cultural advances, and a resurgence of feudalism.

220–264 Three Kingdoms period immediately after the fall of the Han dynasty was marked by bloody wars, intrigues, and individual heroism; empire was divided into the Wu, Wei, and Shu Han kingdoms.

265–316 Western Jin period; China briefly reunited under Gen. Sima Yan, Jin dynasty ruler; Revolt of Eight Kings helped bring end to the empire after his death in 290.

304–439 Ascendancy of Sixteen Kingdoms in northern border region; all but three of the kingdoms ruled by non-Chinese.

317–420 Eastern Jin period; Jin rulers, forced to give up north, formed empire in south with capital at Nanjing.

485 Equal-field system established under the Northern Wei ruler to distribute land.

581 Yang Jian conquered Northern Wei; went on to reunify China under Sui dynasty.

589–618 Sui dynasty reigned; reunited China, began construction of Grand Canal, refortified Great Wall.

618–907 Tang dynasty, founded by Li Yuan; Confucianism revived, printing developed, and the civil service system refined.

626–649 Taizong ruled; consolidated Tang control and drove out the Turks.

638–713 Zen Buddhist priest Huineng lived; introduced doctrine of "sudden enlightenment."

684–704 Wu Zhao reigned as empress of China; Korea conquered (655).

c700–762 Poet Li Bai lived; considered one of China's greatest poets.

712–756 Xuanzong reigned as sixth Tang dynasty emperor; instituted reforms and fostered great prosperity; Tang Empire reached its zenith.

712–770   Poet Du Fu lived; one of China's greatest poets, he attacked the luxury enjoyed by those in the royal entourage and deplored hardships of the poor.

755   Tang dynasty nearly overthrown in revolt by An Lushan; rulers never regained former power.

768–824   Han Yu, poet, essayist, and government official, lived; he came to be called the "Prince of Letters."

907–960   Five Dynasties and Ten Kingdoms period; five short-lived dynasties ruled from the end of the Tang to the rise of the Song; marked by chaos.

960–1279   Song dynasty in power; after order was restored, there followed a period of great cultural flowering and such innovations as printing with movable type and first use of gunpowder; commerce flourished; the dynasty finally collapsed before the Mongol invasions, begun by Genghis Khan (c1206) and completed by Kublai Khan.

960–976   Taizu reigned as founder of the Song dynasty; largely completed reunification of China by 976; established capital at Kaifeng; so-called Northern Song period lasted 960–1127.

1019–86   Historian Sima Guang lived; wrote massive history of China covering period 403–959.

1127–1279   Southern Song period; invasions by nomadic Jurchen tribes in the north forced Song rulers to move capital to Lin'an in south.

1130–1200   Neo-Confucian philosopher Zhu Xi lived; noted as one of the most important commentators on Confucianism.

c1180–1224   Painter Xia Gui lived; regarded as master of landscape painting.

c1206–79   Mongol invasions; Mongols brought end to Song dynasty rule in 1279.

1260–1368   Yuan dynasty, founded by Kublai Khan, ruled China; established capital at Beijing, completed Grand Canal and made numerous other advances.

c1275–1292   M. Polo in China during his famous journey.

1368–1644   Ming dynasty in power, last of native Chinese emperors; restored traditional Chinese culture and made many conquests (later lost these territories); Spanish and Portuguese traders entered China; Zeng He expe-

ditions launched, eventually reaching as far as East Africa.

1403–24   Yongle reigned; annexed Annam, moved his capital from Nanjing to Beijing and brought Ming dynasty empire to its zenith.

1472–1528   Neo-Confucian philosopher Wang Yangming lived

1522–67   Emperor Jiajing reigned; China plagued by Mongol invasions, piracy, and revolts; Macao ceded to Portuguese.

LATE 1500s   Epic *Golden Lotus* (*Jin Ping Mei*) written by unknown author.

1644   Qing forces (from Manchuria) seized control of China after they were called in by Ming emperor to put down a rebellion by Li Zicheng.

1644–1912   Qing dynasty (Manchu) in power, last dynasty of emperors; they greatly expanded the empire but during the 19th cent. succumbed to incursions by foreign powers and internal dissent.

1655   Dutch secure limited trading privileges with China; British gain trading rights beginning in 1670.

1662–1722   Kangxi extended China's rule to Taiwan, Tibet, and Outer Mongolia.

1673–81   Revolt of the Three Feudatories against the Manchu dynasty quashed.

1689   Treaty of Nerchinsk; Russians forced to give up outposts in Amur Valley in return for trading rights with China.

1704   Pope intervened in Rites Controversy among Roman Catholic missionaries in China.

1724   Teaching of Christianity banned by imperial edict; most Christian missionaries expelled.

1735–96   Qianlong reigned; brought empire to its greatest extent during his long reign; his successful "10 Great Campaigns" added New Province (modern Xinjiang), secured Qing borders against attack, and strengthened China's hold over the southern and eastern empire; however, the costly military campaigns and rampant corruption in government during the later years of his reign seriously weakened the empire and brought about his downfall.

1750   Qing control of Tibet restored by granting Dalai Lama power to govern, with supervision from two imperial overseers.

1755 Qianlong's army battled Mongols in Ili region; second campaign waged 1756–57 to neutralize Mongol threat of invasion.

1757 Foreign trade restricted to Canton.

1758–59 Emperor's troops conquered Muslims of Chinese Turkestan (modern Sinkiang).

1759 "Guangzhou (Canton) system" established to control activities of foreign traders in China; marked restriction of foreign trade by government that lasted into the next century.

1766–70 Kingdom of Burma brought under Qing control.

1772 Qianlong ordered the *Complete Library in the Four Branches of Literature* compiled, including classical, philosophical, historical, and literary texts.

1773 Opium trade developed in China; addiction spread rapidly among Chinese despite ban on its use (1796).

1788–89 Annam fell to China's imperial army.

1792 Chinese defeated invasion of Tibet by Gurkhas of Nepal; gained control over Nepal.

1795–97 Miao tribes revolted in south-central China.

1796 Qianlong forced to abdicate (Oct. 15) in favor of his son Jiaqing; Qianlong's authority had been undermined by spread of corruption and nepotism orchestrated by emperor's favorite courtier Heshen (Ho-shen); nevertheless he continued to hold real power until his death in 1799.

1796–1804 White Lotus Rebellion; full-scale revolt against Manchu rule by White Lotus Society; contributed to eventual collapse of Manchu dynasty.

1796–99 Unscrupulous courtier and imperial favorite Heshen put in charge of suppressing revolt by White Lotus Society (opponents of "foreign" Manchu rulers) in west and central China; Heshen deliberately prolonged the campaign in order to divert money for army expenses to himself and his cronies; imperial forces began to regain control from 1799.

1799 Former Emperor Qianlong died; Emperor Jiaqing had the corrupt Heshen arrested and forced him to commit suicide.

1807 First Protestant missionary in China arrived in Guangzhou (Canton).

1813 Heavenly Reason Society, secret cult with large following among imperial officials, sparked uprisings in several cities; some 200 rebels unsuccessfully attacked the Forbidden City (Oct. 8), attempting to restore Ming dynasty.

1820 Emperor Daoguang in power following death of Jiaqing; unsuccessfully attempted to restore depleted imperial treasury by reducing government expenses; corrupt government officials continued to drain treasury and weaken imperial authority.

1825–32 Muslims in Chinese Turkestan rebelled; Muslim leader Jehangir captured and executed in 1828, after which imperial forces completed the job of restoring order.

1833 British East India Company charter expired; British government assumed authority for trade with China, appointing superintendent of trade at Guangzhou (Canton); Chinese officials refuse direct contact with British (until 1837), allowing only petition through intermediaries.

1838 Imperial edict imposed death penalty for opium selling and use; foreign trade at Guangzhou (Canton) suspended briefly after Chinese seize opium belonging to British merchant.

1839 Foreign merchants at Guangzhou (Canton) ordered to turn over opium to imperial government and to halt opium trade on pain of death; officials confiscated 20,000 chests of opium and refusing British compromise offer, halted trade; the shooting of a Chinese villager (July 7) by drunken British sailors led to the first armed clashes and finally the outbreak of war.

1839–42 First Opium War fought against Britain; China defeated and, by British-dictated Treaty of Nanjing (Aug. 29), forced to cede Hong Kong, open five ports to trade (Guangzhou [Canton], Xiamen, Fuzhou, Shanghai, and Ningpo), pay a large indemnity, and grant right of equality in diplomatic communication; provision for equitable tariffs marked end of Chinese tribute system on foreign trade; the US and other European powers forced similar concessions (1844) in what were called "unequal treaties."

1841–50 Uprisings became an annual occurrence as corruption, overtaxation, and foreign influence all helped further weaken authority of the government.

1843 Hong Kong declared a British crown possession (June 25).

1843 British wrested supplementary Treaty of Bogue (Oct. 8) from Chinese, which introduced concept of "most favored nation" in trade agreements.

1844 Roman Catholic and Protestant missionaries tolerated by imperial edict (Dec.), ending official ban on Christian missionaries imposed in 1724.

1849 Grand Canal, key artery for rice transport, became impassible for want of repairs; rice shipped by sea, leaving thousands of canal boatmen discontented and without income.

1850–64 Taiping Rebellion, unsuccessful but devastating uprising against Qing rule; even after the revolt had been quelled, the imperial government never again regained effective control over the country, being forced to concede control of provinces to regional military leaders who had captured them from the rebels; the rebellion, with its mixed social and spiritual aims, became model for later Nationalist and Communist revolts.

1851–61 Emperor Xianfeng (1831–61) in power following the death of Daoguang; his reign was consumed by war and revolt, marking the further disintegration of authority at all levels of government in China.

1856–60 Second Opium War; fighting began after Chinese police arrested (Oct. 8) 12 Chinese aboard the *Arrow*, a Chinese-owned sailing ship out of Hong Kong flying a British flag; British and French forces eventually forced Chinese to accept Treaty of Tianjin (Tientsin, June 26, 1858), opening five new treaty ports and the Yangtze River to foreign trade.

1859 Fighting resumed after Chinese refused to honor terms of Treaty of Tianjin; Beijing occupied (Oct. 13) and imperial Summer Palace burned (Oct. 18) by Anglo-French force; new treaties ending the Second Opium War forced further concessions, including the opening of all China to Westerners.

c1861–c74 Self-strengthening movement, unsuccessful attempt to modernize and Westernize China; government established foreign office to promote knowledge of the West and Western diplomacy.

1862–74 Emperor Tongzhi reigned following the death of his father, Xianfeng; his eight-man regency was overthrown (Nov. 1862) by the empress dowager Cixi (Tz'ŭ Hsi, 1835–1908) and co-conspirators, who subsequently oversaw the government.

1865–68 Nien Rebellion by organized bandit gangs in the eastern empire; after an initially unsuccessful campaign the army quashed the revolt in 1868.

1868 Burlingame Treaty with the US (July 28); opened up large-scale immigration of Chinese to the US.

1870 Tianjin Massacre; 21 Frenchmen killed by mob of Chinese (June 21) aroused by rumors of mistreatment of orphans at a Catholic orphanage; marked resurgence of anti-foreign sentiment.

1871–81 Russia occupied Chinese territory in Ili Crisis.

1875–1908 Emperor Guangxu reigned: chosen by his aunt the empress dowager Cixi to succeed her son on his death, he was completely dominated by her; during his reign Japan and European powers began taking direct control of China's outlying territories, while the empress dowager all but stopped efforts at modernization and reform of the crumbling imperial government; meanwhile government finances, hampered by fixed tariffs set by unequal treaties, became steadily more dependent on foreign loans.

1876 China's first railway, a 12-mile link between Shanghai and Woosung, was completed.

1876 Korea declared independence from China; threatened by a Japanese naval force, Korea signed a treaty proclaiming its independence and giving Japan extraterritorality and rights to Korean ports. Western powers soon negotiated treaties of their own.

1876–77 Chinese Turkestan (Xinjiang) restored to imperial control after Muslim uprisings had brought adventurer Yakub Beg (1820–77) to power there; Yakub killed himself after his army was crushed.

1883–85 Sino-French War; French gained control of Vietnam and other Indochina domains once under Chinese domination.

1887 Swollen Huang Ho (Yellow River) broke through a massive dike and suddenly flooded some 10,000 square miles of surrounding countryside, killing an estimated 1.5 million Chinese.

1891 Anti-Christian riots broke out in China; churches attacked; riots occurred again in 1895.

1892 Uprisings in Manchuria and Mongolia.

1894–95 Sino-Japanese War fought with Japan over Korea; China defeated and forced to grant substantial concessions to Japan by the Treaty of Shimonoseki (Apr. 17, 1895), including a large indemnity, control of Taiwan, and further trade privileges.

1895 Sun Yat-sen led an abortive revolution in Guangzhou (Canton).

LATE 1890s Foreign powers, aware China might not long continue as an independent state, established spheres of influence and leased territories in China, effectively dividing the country among themselves.

1898 Short-lived Reform Movement of 1898, the 100 Days, initiated by the emperor to stave off collapse of imperial government; attempt at establishing constitutional monarchy and modernization of government blocked by empress dowager, who staged a coup (Dec. 22) with Yuan Shikai and assumed power herself.

1899–1900 US enunciated Open Door Policy to maintain equal trading privileges between foreign powers operating in China and to guarantee the sovereignty of the Chinese government.

1900–01 Boxer Rebellion against foreign influence; spurred by anti-Christian sentiment and supported by the dowager empress, some 140,000 Boxer secret society members occupied Beijing (June, 1900); 18,000-man foreign army arrived (Aug. 14) and after protracted negotiations, the revolt was formally ended (Sept. 1901).

1901–05 Dynastic reforms; foot-binding of women also abolished.

1905 Chinese Examination System abolished; 2,000-year-old system was cornerstone of traditional Chinese Confucian society; dowager empress forced by events to permit this and other reforms piecemeal.

1907 Dowager empress approved plan to establish representative government over nine-year period.

1908 Britain agreed to limit opium imports from India to China; later agreed to eventual end of opium trade (1911).

1908 Emperor Guangxu, imprisoned by the dowager empress until the very last, died (Nov. 14); dowager empress died the following day.

1908–12 Boy emperor Xuantong reigned: succeeded at age three on death of his uncle, ruling under a regency during the last years of China's imperial government.

1910 Chinese take direct control of Tibetan government; Dalai Lama fled (Feb.).

1910 Constitutional assembly convened; power struggle between provincial delegations and those appointed by imperial government became clear; assembly forced government promise of national parliament by 1913.

1911 Government nationalizes building of all future railroad trunk lines in China; plan designed to speed building of railroads with foreign capital and expertise, while maintaining Chinese control over the lines; provincial Chinese entrepeneurs, angry over loss of potential profits, stir up unrest, notably in Szechwan.

1911 Chinese Revolution of 1911 (Oct.–Dec.) sparked by Sun Yat-sen; revolt by military in Wuhan (Oct. 11) spread through empire, toppling the Manchu government.

1911 Sun named president of new government (Dec. 30).

1912 Boy emperor forced to abdicate (Feb. 7), ending the 267-year rule by the Manchus and the 2,000-year-old Chinese imperial government.

1912 China declared a republic (Feb. 12).

1912 Sun resigned (Feb. 15) to unite country behind new leader, Yuan Shikai; Yuan soon after established a repressive regime.

1912 Woman suffrage was enacted.

1912 China's first trial by jury conducted in Shanghai (May).

1912 Guomindang Nationalist party organized (Aug.).

1913 Chinese Parliament convened (Apr. 8, 1913), with Guomindang as strongest party; Guomindang platform calling for elected government in opposition to Yuan's designs for strengthening his political power; Yuan ordered murder of Guomindang party chairman Sung Chiao-jen (1866–1918).

1913 Guomindang sparked second revolt in southern provinces (July 10), put down by Yuan later that year.

1913 Guomindang party outlawed; Sun later revived party, forming provisional governments at Guangzhou (Canton) from 1917 to 1923.

1914 Parliament dissolved by Yuan (Nov.); new constitution promulgated (1914) but Yuan became virtual dictator of China.

1915 Japan presented its Twenty-one Demands, seeking virtual domination of China; China forced to concede to most of the demands.

1915–16 Yuan failed in attempt to create new imperial dynasty.

1916 Yuan died; new attempt at convening parliament quashed when provincial military governors seized Beijing (1917).

1917–26 Warlord period; central government at mercy of regional military leaders; Sun Yat-sen headed the nationalist Guomindang faction and won control of the southern provinces.

1917 China joined Allies in WW I.

1919 May Fourth Movement; nationalistic demonstrations by thousands of students in Beijing (May 4) were sparked by the Versailles Peace Conference plan to award Japan rights to former German concessions in Shandong; mass protests against Japanese expansionism spread nationwide, eventually forcing the Chinese government's refusal to sign the treaty.

1920 Chinese Communist party organized by C. Duxiu and Li Dazhao, with guidance and financial aid from Russian Communists, who had already publicly condemned foreign intrusion in China and renounced all Russian interests there.

1921 First Congress of the Chinese Communist party held by few dozen members, including Mao Zedong.

1922 Nine-Power Treaty signed following Washington Conference; guaranteed China's sovereignty; separate agreement brought Japanese withdrawal from Shantung.

1923–27 United Front formed; Chinese Communists, on advice from Soviet advisers, join Nationalist Guomindang; Guomindang in turn received guidance and financial aid from Soviets; United Front aims included independence from foreign imperialists and national unification.

1925 Sun Yat-sen, leader of the Guomindang, died; split between Communist left and the right wing within the Guomindang subsequently widened.

1926–28 Chiang Kai-shek, now leader of the Nationalist Guomindang, conducted the successful Northern Expedition against warlords.

1927 Chiang split with the Communists, who had attempted to oust him from the Guomindang; set stage for the long Chinese Civil War between Nationalist Guomindang and Chinese Communists (continuing until 1949).

1927 Autumn Harvest Uprising, unsuccessful Communist peasant revolt (Sept.); short-lived Guangzhou (Canton) Commune, in which Communists seized Guangzhou briefly in Dec., followed soon after.

1928 Northern Expedition against warlords ended in victory; Chiang Kai-shek set up nationalist government at Nanjing.

1928–31 Chiang Kai-shek in power as president of China; resigned office (1931), though he retained his leadership role, notably through his ties with the military.

1931–43 Lin Sen in office as president of Nationalist China; his tenure was marked by continued fighting with the Communists, the Second Sino-Japanese War, and finally the ravages of World War II.

1931 Mukden Incident (Sept. 18); became pretext used by the Japanese to invade and occupy Manchuria (completed by Feb., 1932).

1931–34 Jiangxi Soviet, the Communist opposition government to Chiang Kai-shek's Nationalist Guomindang government, set up in southwest by Mao Zedong and Zhu De (Nov.).

1932 Former Chinese emperor Xuan Tong, now named Henry Puyi, became nominal ruler of Japanese puppet state in Manchuria; ruled until 1945 (1934–45 as emperor).

1932 Japanese troops make first incursions into northern China (Dec.).

1934–35 Long March by Chinese Communists to escape Nationalist Guomindang armies; Mao Zedong became leader of Communist Party (1935); Communists established base in northwest.

1936 Nationalist government introduced income tax.

1936 Chiang Kai-shek seized (Dec. 12) by one of his generals in X'ian Incident; finally agreed to alliance with Communists to fight invading Japanese.

1937 Sino-Soviet treaty of nonagression signed (Aug.) to manifest Soviet opposition to Japanese expansionism.

1937–45 Second Sino-Japanese War; Japanese invasion of China itself; conflict merged into WW II.

1937 Nanjing, China's capital, captured by Japanese troops during their rapid southward drive; Japanese loot city and slaughter some 40,000 civilians; China's capital moved to Chungking.

1940 Mao's *On the New Democracy* proposed Communist-led joint dictatorship by all "revolutionary classes"; claimed a prolonged "bourgeois-democratic" stage of social evolution would allow for existence of private enterprise.

1942–43 Communist Rectification Campaign; Mao instigated harsh purge of party members deemed not loyal enough; many tortured and some driven to suicide.

1943 Chinese Communists began expanding control of countryside in Japanese-occupied northern China; while Japanese held cities, Communists won control of villages, one-by-one, convincing local landlords to reduce rents and redistributing lands of absentee owners; Communists organized local militias to fight Japanese.

1943–49 Chiang Kai-shek back in office as president of Nationalist China, following death of Lin Sen; presided over the fall of China to Communist forces; Nationalist government by this time had become corrupt and ineffective.

1945 Sino-Soviet Treaty, intended to deter future Japanese aggression, signed with USSR.

1945–49 Final phase of civil war between Nationalist Guomindang and Communists broke out soon after WW II ended; Communists, already in control of much of northern China, eventually emerged victorious (1949).

1945 Marshall Mission failed; US Gen. G. Marshall attempted to negotiate (Dec.) postwar settlement between Nationalist and Communist factions to prevent further fighting.

1946 Nationalist government recognized independence of Outer Mongolia.

1946 New constitution for the Chinese republic was issued by the Nationalists.

1947 Fighting in civil war turns in favor of Chinese Communist armies from this time onward.

1949 Chiang Kai-shek, his armies defeated by Communists, withdrew to Taiwan and set up his Nationalist government there; US refused to recognize Communist China.

1949 Mao became chairman of the new People's Republic of China (Sept. 30); subsequently the object of a personality cult, he remained leading power in China until his death.

1949–76 Zhou Enlai in office as premier (Oct. 1); also served as foreign minister (1949–58); gained widespread reputation as able peacemaker in Chinese political circles.

1949 Beijing designated as China's capital.

1949 Chinese People's Political Consultative Conference convened (Sept. 1); laid out course of change in China (Common Program); called for prolonged "New Democratic" phase, with toleration of non-Communist political parties and private enterprise.

1949 People's Republic of China was formally proclaimed (Oct. 1) by Mao in ceremony at Tiananmen Square; Soviet Union recognized new government following day.

1949 Inner Mongolia became part of China.

1949 Mao on state visit to Moscow (Dec., 1949–Feb., 1950); persuaded (then) reluctant Stalin to sign treaty for alliance and economic aid to China (Feb. 14.).

1950 Communist forces occupied Hainan Island (Apr.); planned invasion of Taiwan halted by threat of US action, following outbreak of Korean War (June).

1950–51 Tibet occupied by China; Chinese took control of government, but otherwise allow Tibetan theocracy to continue.

1950–53 Korean War; Chinese entered conflict after UN forces crossed 38th parallel, reacting to what it perceived as a threat to Manchuria, its biggest modern industrial center; began sending troops to aid North Koreans in Oct., 1950; war mentality sparked harsh campaign against "counterrevolutionaries," including mass executions and reign of terror in cities; brought about more radical Communist policy in the government.

1950 Agrarian Reform Law enacted (June 28); redistributed land to peasants and broke power of centuries-old landlord-gentry class;

poor mobilized against landowners in "speak-bitterness" meetings and many instances of arbitrary violence occurred; massive program completed by 1952.

1951–52 Three-Anti Campaign mounted by Communist Party leaders to combat corruption and waste in the bureaucracy.

1952 Five-Anti Campaign (Jan.); campaign against corruption and lawlessness in China's private sector industry and commerce; employees mobilized to criticize and accuse employers; a significant number were jailed or fined, while some others were driven to suicide; old business class virtually eliminated.

1953 General campaign to collectivize agriculture begun; resistance mounted until 1955, when Mao called for full commitment to process; thereafter outright force used to complete program over the next year.

1953–57 Five-Year Plan; featured collectivization of agriculture and heavy emphasis on development of heavy industry (as means of easing urban and rural unemployment); agricultural sector faltered, while rapidly expanding heavy industry failed to ease unemployment and spur more general economic growth; meanwhile resentment at rigid economic management became widespread.

1954 Census put population of mainland China at 583,000,000.

1954 First National People's Congress held (Sept 15–28); new constitution adopted, putting Mao, Zhou Enlai, and Liu Shaoqui at head of government.

1955 Chinese army attacks across Taiwan Strait resulted in US-Taiwan mutual defense pact.

1955 Bandung Conference; Communist China gained international prestige among Asian and African nations by joining conference; aid to developing Third World countries became cornerstone of Chinese foreign policy.

1956 Hundred Flowers Movement (May 1956–June 1957); Mao instigated this reform movement amid climate of liberalization in Communist world (de-Stalinization); Mao quoted (May 2) ancient adage "let a hundred flowers bloom, and a hundred schools contend," and encouraged freedom of debate in arts and even politics; widespread resentment of Communist party's monopoly quickly

became evident; movement spawned strikes and protests for more freedom.

1957 Anti-Rightist Campaign; June 1957, party leaders reacted to upheavals of Hundred Flowers Movement by attacking outspoken critics; banished many to rural areas and imprisoned some others, thus quashing move for liberalization in China.

1958–60 Great Leap Forward; Mao attempted to establish decentralized system of agriculture and industrial production; organized collectives into communes (embracing about 20,000 persons) which would farm land and also manufacture tools, etc.; despite widespread use of outright coercion, system soon failed.

1958 Second Taiwan Strait Crisis (Aug.–Oct.); China's attempt to establish naval blockade of Nationalist-held offshore island broken by US intervention.

1959–61 Bad harvests brought collapse and abandonment of Mao's Great Leap; family farming and private land reclamation now tacitly allowed to increase food production.

1959 Short-lived revolt in Tibet (Mar.) quickly put down by Chinese; Chinese reorganized Tibetan government and economy along Communist lines; thousands of Tibetans fled to India.

1959 Second National People's Congress held (Apr.); Liu Shaoqui, Mao's heir apparent, replaced Mao as party chairman, though Mao retained as party head.

1960 Sino-Soviet split; responding to Soviet criticism and growing mistrust of Soviet motives, Chinese criticized Soviet Communists as revisionists (Apr.); Soviets ended aid to China and withdrew technical experts (June), compounding economic hardships of failed Great Leap.

1961 17 million people reported members of China's Communist party.

1961 Chinese began increasing trade contacts with Japan; Japan eventually became China's major trading partner.

1962 Border war with India; disputed Aksai-Chin plateau (on border with Tibet) became site of first brief Sino-Indian clash (1959); Chinese troops successfully attacked (Oct. 20, 1962) in force as Indian soldiers moved into disputed area in 1962; fighting ended (Nov.), though later talks failed to resolve the issue.

1963 Socialist Education Movement; party campaign mounted (May) to halt corruption and demoralization in rural areas; movement merged with Cultural Revolution (Dec., 1966).

1963 Mao published nine polemics against Soviet revisionism, partly in effort to deflect criticism of the failed Great Leap.

1964 First Chinese atomic bomb exploded.

1965 New Soviet premier A. Kosygin visited China (Feb.); China subsequently continued attacks on Soviet revisionism.

1965 Third National People's Congress held.

1965–69 Cultural Revolution; Mao incited revolt to purge older party leaders (especially those disaffected by failure of Great Leap) and to renew revolutionary zeal in party by encouraging the young to revolt; Red Guard units formed at universities and schools throughout China (from Aug., 1966); revolutionary upheaval resulted in widespread brutality and economic paralysis, forcing party leaders to halt the unrest.

1966 Liu Shaoqui, Mao's heir apparent, fell victim to Cultural Revolution; accused of taking "the capitalist road,: he was publicly humiliated, beaten, and imprisoned; he finally died in prision (1969) and was not rehabilitated by the party until 1980.

1968 Concern over Soviet aggression (notably the invasion of Czechoslavakia) brought Sino-Soviet relations to lowest ebb; paved way for improved relations with US.

1969 Ninth Party Congress held (Apr.); marked beginning of reconstruction after turbulence of Cultural Revolution; new party constitution promulgated, emliminating once-powerful secretariat; Lin Piao, formally designated as Mao's new heir apparent.

1970–71 Party Committees formed in provinces as part of organization rebuilding effort; military men in leadership positions.

1970 China assigned diplomats to overseas embassies; posts vacant since 1967.

1970 China launched its first space satellite (Apr. 24).

1971 US table tennis team visited China (Apr.); marked start of public efforts to normalize US-Chinese relations; US gave China equal trading status with USSR.

1971 50th anniversary of China's Communist party (July 1).

1971 Lin Biao, Mao's heir apparent, killed in a plane crash (Sept. 12); Mao later revealed Lin had plotted to assassinate him and take over government, but had been discovered and forced to flee; Lin wanted to preserve some radical economic themes of Cultural Revolution and opposed ties with US.

1971 Lin publicly denounced and his allies in military purged; more determined shift away from leftist radicalism followed in subsequent years: military representation in government reduced.

1971 Admission of China to UN approved (Oct.); Taiwan expelled.

1971 Chinese develop acupuncture technique that provided successful anesthetic for all types of operations.

1972 US President R. Nixon visited China (Feb. 21–28) as part of effort to normalize relations.

1972 Japanese Premier K. Tanaka visited China (Sept.); trade with Japan, now China's leading trade partner, far above that of other nations.

1972 Examinations in schools, banned since 1966, reintroduced.

1973 Tenth National Party Congress held (Aug.); approved a revised party constitution and elected new Central Committee with Mao as chairman.

1973 28 million reported members of China's Communist party.

1974 Gang of Four (leading radicals including Mao's wife), direct political campaign against widely respected Premier Zhou Enlai, while ostensibly attacking Confucianism; their attacks lasted until his death (1976).

1975 Fourth National People's Congress held (Jan.); adopted new national constitution (superseding that of 1954); gave party Central Committee chairman (Mao) direct command over armed forces; Premier Zhou Enlai reported increases since 1964 of 51 percent in agricultural output and 190 percent in gross industrial output; Four Modernizations development program announced for first time (targeting agriculture, industry, military, science, and technology).

1975 Troops used to end strikes and labor unrest in Hangchow (July); unrest resulted from radical campaign aimed at workers.

1976 Premier Zhou Enlai died (Jan. 8); Hua Kuo-feng, little-known former minister of public security, succeeded him as a compromise between radicals and moderates.

1976 Riot by tens of thousands in Beijing (Apr. 5) following attempt by party officials to suppress memorial for late Zhou Enlai; thousands arrested by militia.

1976 700,000 reported dead in major earthquake in Tangshan, northeast China (July); worst earthquake worldwide in over 400 years.

1976 Mao died (Sept. 9); power struggle among various rival factions led to violent clashes in almost a third of China's provinces.

1976 Premier Hua arrested the so-called Gang of Four, leading radicals Jiang Qing (Mao's widow), party vice-chairman Wang Hungwen, party vice-chairman and vice premier Zhang Chunqiao, and Politbureau member Yao Wenyuan (Oct. 7).

1976 Premier Hua Kuofeng formally became party chairman (Oct. 24), succeeding Mao and ending the power struggles; kept posts already inherited from Zhou Enlai as well; mass demonstrations on Hua's behalf, and against the Gang of Four, held.

1977 Eleventh National Party Congress held; Chairman Hua proclaimed that the Cultural Revolution ended with arrest of Gang of Four.

1978 Fifth National People's Congress (Feb. 26–Mar. 5); new national constitution adopted, restoring legal institutions dismantled by radicals and stating for the first time citizen's basic rights; party leaders now committed to end abuses of revolutionary radicalism and concerted program to modernize China; Vice-Premier Deng Xiaoping soon became a leading figure in the drive toward modernization.

1978 Technical state of war with Japan ended by friendship treaty.

1978–82 Return to individual farming following failure of collectivized agriculture; individual farmers given contracts with state.

1978 Wall poster campaign began in Beijing, calling for increased democracy and redress of other grievances (Nov.).

1978 Deng's reform era began (Dec.); far-reaching changes launched at Third Plenary Session of Eleventh Central Committee.

1979 Full diplomatic relations with US established (Jan. 1).

1979 Troops began limited invasion across border into Vietnam (Feb. 17) to punish the Vietnamese for their invasion of Cambodia; China unilaterally withdrew troops (Mar. 16).

1979 Government officially criticized the Cultural Revolution and, while not denouncing Mao, sought to end cult worship of him.

1980 Central Committee ordered removal of most images of Mao then on public display.

1980 Deng proclaimed "Four Basic Principles" in response to calls for democracy; said changes in the socialist road should be guided by the principles (Communist party leadership, dictatorship of the proletariat, Marxism-Leninism, and the thought of Mao Zedong).

1980 Mao's widow and nine other radicals tried in public show trials (Nov. 20–Jan. 25) as government continued shift from radicalism; collectively the defendants were accused of having "persecuted to death" over 38,000 people; eight admitted their guilt and received long prison terms; Mao's widow and one other got the death sentence (commuted to life imprisonment, 1983).

1981 Party published official assessment of Mao (July), distinguishing between the man and his thought, and noting his mistakes (*i.e.,* the Cultural Revolution) were those of a great proletarian revolutionary.

1981 Hua Kuofeng, Mao's hand-picked successor as party chairman, demoted to lowest-ranking vice-chairman after having been stripped of much of his power the previous year by allies of Deng Xiaoping; Gen. Hu Yaobang named new party chairman.

1982 Census reported (July); mainland population at 1.008 billion people.

1982 US agreed to limit arms sales to Taiwan in order to continue policy of friendly relations toward China.

1982 Twelfth National Party Congress held (Sept. 1–11); approved new state constitution, replacing 1978 version; restored post for official head of state; abolished the commune as the basic political unit, while retaining it for economic purposes; abolished life terms for high political posts; provided for special administrative regions, in the event Taiwan or Hong Kong should join the People's Republic.

1983 Fifth National People's Congress held (June 6–21).

1984 China joined International Atomic Energy Agency (Jan.).

1984 Accord for return of Hong Kong in 1997 signed with Britain (Sept. 26).

1984 Communist leaders approved plan for major reform of urban economic structure (Oct.), similar to successful rural economic reform; urban businesses to get more autonomy and become responsible for wages, profits and losses; businesses to pay taxes instead of turning over profits to state.

1985 Student demonstrations against Japan, resulting from resentment over serious imbalance of Sino-Japanese trade.

1986 Britain's Queen Elizabeth visited China (Oct. 12–18).

1986 Planned one-million-man troop reduction in Chinese army reported complete.

1986 Some 20,000 students involved in demonstrations at various points during the year; protests focused on demands for more democratic freedoms.

1987 Party general secretary Hu Yaobang resigned (Jan.) under pressure following criticism of his handling of the 1986 student unrest; succeeded by Premier Zhao Ziyang.

1987 Thirteenth National Party Congress convened (Oct. 25).

1987– Li Peng in office as China's new premier.

1987 Tibetan monks led mass demonstrations against Chinese rule (Sept. 27); violent clashes with police reported (Oct. 1, 6).

1987 China to regain Portuguese colony of Macao in 1999, by formal agreement with Portugal (Apr. 13).

1987 Seventh National People's Congress convened (Mar.); coverage of differing views at opening session permitted in news media, in keeping with party moves toward greater democracy; the congress approved new laws giving factory managers more control over operations and liberalizing restrictions on joint ventures with foreign businesses; Zhao Ziyang proposed making coastal China a free-trade zone.

1989 Diplomatic relations with Soviet Union normalized; marked formal end to decades-old Sino-Soviet split; relations had been improving since 1982.

1989 Former party secretary Hu Yaobang died (Apr.); students, moved by memory of his liberal reformist sympathies during 1986 unrest, begin demonstrations to honor him.

1989 Some 100,000 students and workers marched in Beijing calling for more democratic freedoms (May 4).

1989 Soviet leader M. Gorbachev on state visit to Beijing (May), amid growing unrest; first visit by Soviet leader since 1959.

1989 Tiananmen Square protests; one million demonstrators packed Beijing's Tiananmen Square calling for more democratic freedoms (May 17); while noting the "good intentions" of demonstrators, party leaders said they must be patient; demonstration persisted into early June, when government sent in troops; hundreds killed and thousands injured when troops opened fire to disperse crowds; some 10,000 demonstrators reported arrested; world opinion sharply critical of harsh measures employed by Chinese government.

1989 Party general secretary Zhao Ziyang ousted; succeeded by Jiang Zemin (June 24).

1989–90 Government reported inflation dropped from 27 to 6 percent in this period.

1990 Government ended martial law restrictions in Beijing (Jan. 11), imposed during Tiananmen Square protests.

1990 Premier Li Peng on state visit to Soviet Union (Apr.); signed agreements on aid and basic principles for reducing troops along common borders.

1990 US extended China's most-favored-nation trading status despite opposition to handling of Tiananmen Square protests; renewed that status again in 1992.

1991 China reestablished diplomatic relations with Vietnam, following resolution of differences over Cambodia.

1992 China exploded 1,000-kiloton nuclear bomb, its biggest to date, in underground test.

1992 Border between Chinese-controlled Tibet and India reopened for first time in 35 years.

1992 14th Party Congress held; leaders vowed to continue Deng's policies; will continue shift toward capitalism while maintaining tight control over political matters.

China, Great Wall of *See* **Great Wall of China.**

China, Nationalist *See* **Taiwan.**

Chindits *See* **Wingate, Orde Charles.**

Chinese Civil War War (1945–49) that culminated a long struggle between Guomindang (Nationalist) Chinese and the Communist Chinese for control of China. The civil war is generally considered to have begun in 1945, soon after the end of WW II. But Communist and Nationalist forces had been fighting in China intermittently since 1927. In 1926–27 the Communists had helped Chiang Kai-shek's Guomindang forces take power from the warlords (provincial military rulers). After his victory in 1927, however, Chiang Kai-shek purged Communists from the Guomindang, formed his Nationalist government, and began military expeditions against Communist strongholds. From 1931, the Guomindang was also forced to contend with Japanese expansionism that later resulted in the Sino-Japanese War (*q.v.*). The Guomindang finally drove the Communists out of the region south of the Yangtze River, precipitating the Communists' famous Long March (1934–35) to strongholds in northwest Shaanxi province. Mao Zedong emerged as the Communist leader during the march. Despite their differences, Guomindang and Communists at times organized a temporary common front against the invading Japanese, notably in 1937 when the Red Army was ostensibly incorporated into the Chinese army. China entered WW II as an ally, but a controversy developed when US Gen. J. Stilwell urged Chiang Kai-shek to commit more of his troops to fighting against the Japanese, instead of the Chinese Communists. At the end of WW II both Guomindang and Communist forces moved to take over territories formerly occupied by the Japanese. US Gen. G. Marshall was dispatched to China to attempt reconciliation between the two forces (Dec., 1945). But by Apr. 1946, widespread fighting had resumed, in which the Guomindang was initially successful. Nationalist victories culminated in the capture of the Communist capital of Yan'an (Mar. 19, 1947), but the tide of the war subsequently turned in favor of the Communists. They gained control of Manchuria by the end of 1947 and captured Beijing on Jan. 15, 1949. The Communists kept up the pressure and by July Chiang Kai-shek was forced to begin withdrawing the remnants of his Guomindang forces to Taiwan.

The Communists proclaimed the People's Republic of China on Oct. 1, 1949, while the Nationalists formally established their government on Taiwan on Dec. 8, 1949.

Chinese Communist party Ruling political party of the People's Republic of China. Founded (1920) by Chen Duxiu and Li Dazhao (Li Ta-chao) (1888–1927), it first joined the Chinese Guomindang government but was expelled (1927) by Chiang Kai-shek. Thus there began the long struggle between the Communists and the Guomindang, the Chinese Civil War (*q.v.*). The party maintained a precarious existence in China and was forced to make the famous Long March into northern China. Led by Mao Zedong (after 1935), it thrived in the north and established its own government. It effected a truce (1936) with the Guomindang in the face of Japanese aggression and conducted a guerrilla war against the Japanese during WW II. In 1945 it resumed war with the Nationalists, and forced them out of the mainland in 1949. Since that time the Communist party has remained the dominant power in China. In recent years the party has experimented with elements of capitalistic free-market economics, and following the collapse of the USSR in 1991, the party vowed to continue these economic reform programs while maintaining tight political control over the country.

Chinese Examination System A system of civil service examinations long in use in the Chinese Empire. Candidates were tested in their knowledge of the Confucian classics. The system began in a very limited way about 124 BC under the Han emperor Wudi, and was expanded in the Tang and Sung dynasties. The system helped maintain the stability of China for over 2,000 years, and was not abolished until 1905 amid a movement to modernize China.

Chinese exclusion acts US legislation passed (1882–94) to prohibit Chinese immigration. Chinese (particularly laborers) began emigrating to the Pacific coastal region by the mid-19th cent. The Burlingame Treaty (1868) further encouraged this influx of cheap labor until resentment among US workers came to a head. Congress passed the first exclusion act in 1882, banning Chinese immigration for 10 years. Subsequent acts (1888, 1892) violated treaties with China, and by a new treaty (1894), immigration was banned for another 10 years. The ban continued until 1924, when new immigration laws shut out all Asians. The exclusion acts were repealed in 1943.

Chinese Revolution of 1911   Uprising that succeeded in overthrowing the last (Qing, or Manchu) dynasty of Chinese emperors and establishing a Chinese republic. The revolution broke out in Wuhan on Oct. 11, 1911, after army officers were implicated in the secret revolutionary alliance *T'ung-meng-hui* (Combined League Society), headed by Dr. Sun Yat-sen. On being discovered, the officers forced their commander to rebel against Manchu troops and the rebellion spread from province to province. The imperial family fled (Dec., 1911), and the boy emperor, Xuantong (Puyi), abdicated on Feb. 7, 1912. The government passed into the hands of a national assembly at Nanjing which had elected Sun the first president of the Chinese Republic (Dec. 30, 1911). China officially became a republic on Feb. 12, 1912. Sun soon resigned (Feb. 15, 1912) in order to unite the country behind Yuan Shikai, a former Manchu military leader who had come to terms with the rebels. In office, however, Yuan sought to increase his power. He was opposed by the (Nationalist) Guomindang party (founded 1912), which favored a parliamentary system with an elected prime minister. Elections established the Guomindang as the strongest party in the parliament (convened Apr. 8, 1913), and when Yuan attempted to consolidate his power, the Guomindang started a second revolution (July 10). Yuan crushed the revolt and, finally, dissolved parliament (Jan. 10, 1914). Yuan ruled until his death (1916), though his power was checked somewhat by provincial military rulers. Following Yuan's death, the military rulers, who came to be called "warlords," vied for control of China. They thus prevented establishment of an effective central government until the rise of the Guomindang, under Chiang Kai-shek's leadership, some years later. (*See also* Chinese Civil War.)

Ch'ing   *See* Qing.

Chinghiz Khan   *See* Genghis Khan.

Ch'in Shih Huang Ti   *See* Shih Huang Ti.

Chippendale, Thomas 1718–79.   Noted English furniture maker. His graceful, neoclassic furniture designs drew from Chinese, Gothic, and French rococo art.

Chippewa, Battle of   US victory (July 5, 1814) over the British during the War of 1812. An invasion force of some 4,000 Americans crossed the Niagara River into southern Canada and defeated a British force of about 2,000.

Chisholm* v. *Georgia   US Supreme Court decision (1793) that affirmed the right of a citizen to sue the government of another state in federal court. The decision was superseded by the 11th Amendment (1798).

Chislieri, Antonio   *See* **Pius V.**

chivalry   Code of moral and ethical conduct that developed during feudal times in Europe (12th–15th cents.). Central to the code was the feudal knight, who exhibited the ideal qualities of piety, loyalty to his feudal lord, courtesy and courtly (platonic) affection for ladies of the court, and valor on the field of battle. Chivalry flourished in the 12th and 13th cents., especially during the Crusades. It declined as an ideal of conduct by the 15th cent., when military campaigns were more openly waged for gain than for reasons of honor or religious duty. The chivalric code was central to the popular medieval romances of the Arthurian legend (*q.v.*).

Chivington Massacre   *See* **Sand Creek Massacre.**

Chlorus, Constantius   *See* **Constantius I.**

Chmelnitsky, Bogdan   *See* **Khmielnicki, Bogdan.**

Chocim, Battles of (Khotin, ˜)   1. Polish victory (Aug.–Sept., 1621) over the Ottoman Turks, ending a brief war between the two (1620–21). The war was sparked by Polish intervention in Moldavia, and, in 1621, the Turks, under Osman II, invaded Poland. Polish forces, raised by Sigismund III, met the Turks at Chocim and successfully withstood Turkish attacks for over a month. 2. Polish victory (Nov., 1673) over the Ottoman Turks, ending a brief war between the two (1672–76). The Turks, allied with Ukrainian Cossacks (then in rebellion against Poland), invaded the Ukraine (1672) and initially forced Poland to negotiate. Polish forces regrouped under John Sobieski (later King John III) and attacked the Turks at Chocim, Moldavia. The Poles largely destroyed the 25,000-man Turkish army garrisoned there and turned the tide of the war.

Chomsky, (Avril) Noam 1928–   . American writer, linguist, teacher, and political activist. Chomsky developed his revolutionary theory of generative grammar in such books as *Current Issues in Linguistic Theory, Cartesian Linguistics,* and *Language and Mind.* An outspoken opponent of US involvement in Southeast Asia, he published books on foreign policy, including *At War with Asia* (1970) and *Toward a New Cold War* (1982).

Chopin, Frédéric François 1810–49. World-famous Polish composer of the Romantic school, noted for his piano compositions. A child prodigy, he composed his first polonaise at age seven and first performed publicly on the piano the following year. Chopin left Poland permanently (1831) for Paris, but always remained a Polish nationalist. During his affair with G. Sand (1836–47), he wrote his 24 piano preludes. Other works included sonatas in B flat minor (1840) and B minor (1845), many nocturnes, etudes, ballades and scherzos, and, celebrating Polish nationalism, numerous mazurkas and polonaises. Many of Chopin's best-known works are written for the piano as a solo instrument; his piano concertos in E minor (1833) and F minor (1836) feature the piano as the dominant instrument. Chopin died in Paris of tuberculosis (1849).

Chou *See* **Zhou.**

Chouan, Jean *See* **Chouans.**

Chouans Peasant bands in western France that rebelled (1793) against the revolutionary government during the French Revolution (1789–99). Named after their leader, Jean Chouan (*pseud. of* Jean Cottereau, 1757–94), they later were led by G. Cadoudal and took part in the Wars of the Vendée (1793–96) and other risings. Though their guerrilla activities were largely suppressed by Napoleon, small uprisings (the "Petite Chouannerie") continued until Napoleon's downfall (1815).

Chou En-lai *See* **Zhou Enlai.**

Chou Hsin *See* **Zhouxin.**

Chou Kung *See* **Zhou Gong.**

Chremonidean War War (c266–262 BC) fought by Athens and Sparta against Macedonian rule. Spurred on by promises of aid from Egyptian king Ptolemy II, the Athenians and Spartans rebelled (266 BC) against King Antigonus II. The Spartans were badly defeated (265), and the Athenians yielded (262) after a two-year siege by the Macedonians. The Macedonians subsequently established new military outposts in the region.

Chrétien de Troyes (Chrestien de Troyes) *fl.* 1164. French poet, one of the great medieval poets of the Arthurian romances. Among his important works are *Erec et Enide, Cligès, Lancelot, Yvain,* and

Perceval. In the latter he introduced the search for the Holy Grail to the Arthurian cycle.

Christ, Churches of *See* **Churches of Christ.**

Christ, Disciples of *See* **Disciples of Christ.**

Christian I 1426–81. King of Denmark and Norway (1450–81) and Sweden (1457–64), founder of the Oldenburg line. He warred against the Swedes (1451–57) to press his claim to the Swedish throne, took possession of Schleswig and Holstein (1460), and was deposed from the Swedish throne (1464). In his last attempt to retake the throne (1471), Christian was repulsed by S. Sture.

Christian II 1481–1559. Danish king of Denmark and Norway (1513–23) and Sweden (1520–23), successor to his father, King John. His reign marked the final breakup of the Kalmar Union (1523). An unpopular king, he at first succeeded in bringing rebellious Sweden back into the Union (1520). He ordered the Stockholm Bloodbath (1520), however, and, by the popular reaction against him, helped bring on Swedish independence (1523). At that time Denmark also rebelled and deposed him.

Christian III 1503–59. King of Denmark and Norway (1534–59). With Sweden, he helped break the power of the Hanseatic League (1536), established the supremacy of the Danish navy in northern Europe, made Lutheranism the state religion in Denmark and Norway (1536), and reduced Norway's status to that of a province of Denmark.

Christian IV 1577–1648. King of Denmark and Norway (1588–1648). He strengthened the navy, industry, and commerce in his kingdom. He successfully waged the Kalmar War (1611–13), but his invasion of Germany during the Thirty Years' War (1618–48) proved disastrous. Following a defeat by the Swedes, he was forced to yield power to the nobility.

Christian V 1649–99. King of Denmark and Norway (1670–99). Popular with his people, he advanced commoners into the ranks of the nobility. Until 1676, he was largely guided by one such nobleman, P. Griffenfeld, who led him into an unsuccessful war (1675–79) with Sweden. The monarchy became absolutist during his reign.

Christian VII 1749–1808. King of Denmark and Norway (1766–1808). He was mentally unstable and his physician, J. Struensee, largely controlled the government until his execution

(1772). Thereafter, other advisers and finally Christian's son, Frederick VI, held power.

Christian VIII 1786–1848. King of Denmark (1839–48). Elected king of Norway (1814), he permitted adoption of a liberal constitution, attempted to break the union of Norway with Sweden, and was forced to abdicate (1814) by the Swedes. As Denmark's king, he reformed the penal system.

Christian IX 1818–1906. King of Denmark (1863–1906), successor to Frederick VII. His war with Austria and Prussia (1864) ended in defeat and loss of the provinces of Schleswig, Holstein, and Lauenburg. His reign was marked by agitation for liberal constitutional reforms.

Christian X 1870–1947. King of Denmark (1912–47), successor to his father, Frederick VIII. He granted women the right to vote (1915), and, by his refusal to flee the invading Nazis in WW II, became a symbol of Danish resistance.

Christian, Fletcher   *See Bounty,* HMS.

Christian Churches   *See* **Disciples of Christ.**

Christianity   General term used to describe the religion that arose in Palestine (1st cent. AD) from the life and teachings of Jesus Christ and that has spread to nearly every part of the world. Historically, it has been the predominant religion in the West for many centuries and had an enormous influence on the development of Western civilization, especially in literature, art, architecture, and music. Christianity is based on the New Testament (*q.v.*), which records the acts and teachings of Jesus, and the Old Testament is regarded as sacred and authoritative Scripture. Christian doctrine was further refined by a series of "creeds" promulgated in the course of early church history. Together, these beliefs attempted to reflect Jesus Christ's own revelations about God and the salvation of mankind. Apostles chosen by Jesus constituted the early leadership of the church, or "assembly" of his followers. The church perpetuated the teachings of Jesus, claimed the authority to interpret them authentically, and administered the sacraments, believed to have been established by Jesus for the spiritual benefit of the faithful. However, disagreements among Christians about Jesus' teachings occurred as early as New Testament times. Major doctrinal crises usually resulted in "little churches" that split from the main church and maintained "heresies," such as Arianism, Mono-

physitism, Nestorianism, Donatism, and so on. These were condemned by the main tradition, and most of the dissident Eastern and African churches had split from the church by the end of the Council of Chalcedon (AD 451). Bitter disputes over such issues as Iconoclasm caused the final split (1054) between the Roman Catholic and Eastern Orthodox churches. Some centuries later, Christianity was again divided by the Protestant Reformation, which followed M. Luther's rebellion (1517) against the authority of the church. Protestantism arose from this split and became, with the Roman Catholic church and the Orthodox Eastern church, one of the three main branches of Christianity. In modern times, especially since the 1920s, adherents of the ecumenical movement have been active in attempting to overcome the differences that separate these three branches. (*See also* Roman Catholic church; Protestantism; Reformation; Orthodox Eastern church; names of sects.)

Christian mysticism   *See* mysticism.

Christian Science (*prop.* Church of Christ, Scientist)   Religion founded (1879) by M. Eddy. Christian Scientists believe the evils of the material world, such as illness, sin, and death, mask the reality of the spiritual universe. Prayer, they believe, can break through the mask and overcome evil. Thus, Christian Scientists have at times gained notoriety by refusing medical help. Eddy experienced a miraculous healing herself (1866), and organized the mother church in Boston (1892). Since then the faith has spread to many countries around the world.

Christian Socialism   Socioreligious movement that began in mid-19th-cent. England. A reaction against the social inequities of capitalism, Christian Socialists were more concerned about the sufferings of the poor in an industrial society than about expropriation of privately owned factories and property. An outgrowth of the failed Chartism movement, this form of Socialism spawned a number of workingmen's associations, cooperative ventures, and some reforms during the 1850s. By the late 19th cent., the movement had spread to the US and Germany. In Germany, Christian Socialist parties became involved in anti-Semitic activities and were officially condemned there by the king (1894).

Christians of Saint John   *See* **Mandaeans**

Christie, Dame Agatha 1890–1976. English writer, one of the most successful mystery writers of all time. Among her works are *Ten Little Indians, The Mousetrap,* and *Witness for the Prosecution.*

Christina 1626–89. Queen of Sweden (1632–54), successor to her father, Gustavus II. An eccentric woman, she abdicated in favor of her cousin Charles X (1654). She was unsuccessful in her attempt to regain the crown after his death in 1660.

Christophe, Henri 1767–1820. Haitian rebel and ruler. Born a slave, he joined the rebellion against French rule led by F. Toussaint L'Ouverture. He became provisional leader of Haiti (1807), and then, in a subsequent civil war, formed a kingdom in the north (1811). Haiti was reunified on his death.

Christopher, Saint 3d cent. AD. Christian martyr whose existence is historically uncertain. He is said to have carried a small child across a river, discovering partway across that he could barely hold up the child. After the crossing, the child revealed himself as Christ, carrying the weight of the world in his hands. Christopher is the patron saint of travelers.

Chrysler's Farm, Battle of (Crysler's Farm,˜) Battle (Nov. 11, 1813) during the War of 1812. British forces defeated a superior American force north of the St. Lawrence and thus halted the American advance against Montreal.

Chrysostom, Saint John AD c347–407. Clergyman and one of the fathers of the Greek church. He became archbishop of Constantinople (AD 398–403) and, for a time, enjoyed wide influence and fame for his eloquence. Popular with the common people, he was banished to Armenia (404).

Chudleigh, 1st baron, Clifford of *See* **Clifford of Chudleigh, 1st baron.**

Chu Hsi *See* **Zhu Xi.**

Chuikov, Vasily Ivanovich 1900–82. Russian general. He commanded the stubborn Russian defense of Stalingrad (1942) during WW II, accepted the German surrender of Berlin (1945), and commanded Russian forces in Germany (1949–53).

Chu-ko Liang *See* **Zhuge Liang.**

Chulalongkorn (Rama V) 1853–1910. King of Siam (1868–1910). Educated by an English governess, he carried out the modernization programs begun by his father, King Mongkut. He abolished slavery (1874), reorganized the government to centralize authority, and managed to maintain Siam's independence by playing the British and French against each other.

Ch'un Chiu *See* **Chunqiu.**

Chung Te (Abahai) 1592–1643. Manchurian ruler (from 1627) and founder of the line that became the Ch'ing dynasty (*q.v.*). He began the Manchu conquest of the Ming dynasty but died before it could be completed (1644).

Chunqiu (Ch'un Chiu) Period in Chinese history (722–481 BC), a subdivision of the Zhou dynasty (*q.v.*). Also called the "Spring and Autumn Period," it was marked by the rise of small, quarreling states.

Churches of Christ American Protestant churches, most numerous in the American South and West. Fundamentalist and evangelical, they are an offshoot of the Disciples of Christ, and broke away from that body c1840.

Churchill, Sir Winston Leonard Spencer 1874–1965. British statesman, author, and prime minister (1940–45, 1951–55). He is regarded as one of the outstanding figures of the 20th cent. for his brilliant leadership of Britain during WW II. A soldier and well-known journalist by the time he was elected to Parliament (1900), he was a Conservative party member throughout most of his career. He served in a variety of government posts, including first lord of the admiralty (1911–15), colonial secretary (1921–22), and chancellor of the exchequer (1924–29). Churchill recognized and spoke out against the threat of Nazi Germany and was next appointed to the admiralty (1939). He became prime minister (1940) when N. Chamberlain's government was ousted for its handling of the war with Germany. During the war years, he rallied the British to the war effort, lobbied for help from the US (then neutral), and helped write the famous Atlantic Charter (1941). Subsequently, he figured in the conferences of the Allies at Casablanca (1943), Quebec (1943), Cairo (1943), Teheran (1943), Yalta (1945), and Potsdam (1945). In the postwar years, Churchill was out of power (1945–51), though he spoke vigorously against the menace of the USSR (coining the phrase "iron curtain"). Prime minister again in 1951, he retired in 1955 but continued as a member of Parliament until 1964. He received the Nobel Prize in Literature in 1953.

Church of Christ, Scientist *See* **Christian Science.**

Church of England (Anglican Church) The Christian, national church of England and mother church of the Anglican Communion. It is headed by the king (or queen) and the archbishops of the two traditional provinces, Canterbury and York. Though the church retains much of the structure and liturgy of the Roman Catholic church (it was united with Rome until the reign of Henry VIII), its doctrines are largely an outgrowth of the Protestant Reformation. These doctrines are set forth in the Book of Common Prayer, the Thirty-Nine Articles, the Catechism, and Books of Homilies. Key dates in the history of the church are:

2D–5TH CENTS. Christianity was established in Britain during the Roman occupation.

5TH CENT. Christianity declined during the Anglo-Saxon invasions that followed the Romans' departure; vestiges of Christianity survived as the Celtic church.

597 Saint Augustine began conversion of the Anglo-Saxons.

601 Saint Augustine became the first archbishop of Canterbury; first cathedral built.

735 York became an archbishopric.

1066 The Norman conquest marked the beginning of closer ties with Rome, the arrival of clerics from continental Europe, and the rise of clerical influence in secular matters.

1170 Thomas à Becket martyred after long struggle with King Henry II to maintain church prerogatives against royal authority.

1378 Great Schism began in Roman Catholic church; intensified anticlericalism in England.

c1380–1401 Lollardy, anticlerical reform movement, flourished in England.

1401 Parliament passed statute for burning of heretics.

1529–34 Henry VIII brought to a head a long struggle for power between the monarchy and the pope; he demanded the pope's assent to his divorce from Catherine of Aragon.

1533 Pope Clement VIII refused his sanction to the divorce and excommunicated Henry; T. Cranmer became first Reformation archbishop of Canterbury.

1534 Henry obtained passage of the Act of Supremacy in Parliament; it named him head of the English church and thus created the Church of England; no doctrinal changes were made.

1536–39 Henry seized the property of the monasteries.

1539 Henry obtained passage of the Act of Six Articles to check the spread of Lutheranism; there followed persecutions of both Lutherans and Catholics, who refused to recognize Henry as head of the Church of England.

1547 King Edward VI repealed the Act of Six Articles and introduced Protestant doctrines in the church.

1549 Book of Common Prayer was issued; revised (1552); first Act of Uniformity passed requiring clergy to conform to rites in Book of Common Prayer; other Acts of Uniformity passed 1551, 1559, and 1662.

1552 The Forty-two Articles, concerning Anglican doctrine, were published by T. Cranmer.

1555–58 Mary I briefly restored Roman Catholicism during her reign; papal authority was reestablished in England; Protestants were persecuted.

1559 Independent national church of England reestablished by Elizabeth I; Act of Supremacy reenacted.

1563 The Thirty-nine Articles of Faith (replacing the Forty-two Articles) were published to complete Elizabeth's refounding of the church; the church thus established was a compromise and incorporated largely Protestant dogma with Catholic structure and liturgy (in English); the reforms failed to satisfy Protestant extremists and gave added impetus to such dissenters as Nonconformists, Puritans, Separatists, Brownists, Presbyterians, and Congregationalists.

1604 Hampton Court Conference (*q.v.*) held.

1611 King James (authorized) version of the Bible was completed.

1625–49 Reign of Charles I; Charles, an absolutist and Arminian, aroused opposition among Puritans and other groups by his high-handed measures, intended to bring about religious uniformity; his attempt to impose episcopacy led to the Solemn League and Covenant (*q.v.*) in Scotland (1638).

1633 W. Laud became archbishop of Canterbury; aroused opposition of Puritans and non-Arminians.

1642–48 English Civil Wars; political and religious struggle between Royalists and Parliamentarians.

1649–60 Victorious Puritan Parliamentarians established the Commonwealth and Protectorate (*q.v.*); the Church of England was disestablished for a time.

1660 Charles II restored to the throne; the reaction against Puritanism was renewed.

1661 Modern version of the Book of Common Prayer adopted.

1661–65 Clarendon Codes, harsh measures to promote uniformity with the Church of England, were enacted, giving new impetus to the Nonconformists.

1673 Test Act; officeholders required to accept communion with the Church of England.

1688 King James II attempted to reestablish Catholicism in England; the archbishop of Canterbury refused to read James's order of toleration in all churches; James was deposed and replaced by the Protestants, William and Mary, in the Glorious Revolution (1688).

1689 English Bill of Rights was passed, with measure excluding Catholics from the monarchy.

1701 Act of Settlement, stipulating that the monarch must belong to the Church of England, was passed.

1709 Sacheverell Case; conviction of clergyman for sedition sparked anti-nonconformist riots.

1717 Bangorian Controversy began (during George I's reign).

c1729 Movement that resulted in the Methodist Church was begun by J. Wesley; the movement arose amid a new concern for evangelicalism in the Church of England (18th cent.).

1751 Bill to naturalize Jews in England sparked riots.

1799 Anglican Church Missionary Society, an outgrowth of evangelicalism, was founded.

1829 Catholic Emancipation Act passed, ending long-standing restrictions on Catholics.

c1833 Rise of the Oxford Movement, which sought a return to Roman Catholic ritual and dogma in the Anglican church.

1870 Education Act passed; diminished church's role in education.

20TH CENT. Rise of the ecumenical movement.

1919 Church Assembly, a church legislative body, was formed.

1982 Pope John Paul II visited Britain; meetings with Anglican church leaders marked significant step in effort to reestablish ties between the English church and Rome.

1992 Church voted to allow women priests.

Church of Scotland National church (Presbyterian) of Scotland. Movement toward a Protestant national church in Scotland began (1557) with the signing of the First Covenant by Scottish nobles. Under the guidance of J. Knox, the movement came under Calvinist influence, and Knox figured in the drafting (1560) of the *Book of Discipline,* which outlined the church's Presbyterian organization. The church's legal position was ratified (1592) by Parliament, but James VI (after 1603, English king James I) and his successors in Scotland sought to reimpose the episcopacy. This led to the resistance by the Covenanters (*q.v.*) during the 17th cent. Existence of the church was guaranteed (1707) by the union of England and Scotland. The church suffered a number of secessionist movements, notably the Free Church of Scotland (1843) and the United Presbyterian Church of Scotland (1847), which merged (1900) into the United Free Church of Scotland. The latter rejoined the Church of Scotland in 1929.

Church of the Brethren *See* **Dunkards.**

Church of the New Jerusalem (New Church) Religious society formed by the followers of E. Swedenborg. The first church appeared in England in 1788. Followers believe in achieving self-realization through an understanding of Swedenborg's commentaries on the Scriptures.

churrigueresque Relating to a Spanish architectural style. Introduced by Charles II's royal architect, Don José Churriguera (1650–1723), it was a highly ornate adaptation of Renaissance and baroque styles.

Chu Teh *See* **Zhu De.**

Cibó, Giovanni Battista *See* **Innocent VIII.**

Cicero, Marcus Tullius (Tully) 106–43 BC. Great Roman orator, statesman, philosopher, and man of letters. His orations, especially the *Orations Against Catiline* and the *Philippics,* are important in the study of Latin. An ardent republican, he was elected consul (63 BC) and exposed the famous Conspiracy of Catiline (63

BC). He was exiled (58) for executions he ordered as a result of the conspiracy, and was then recalled (57). He was a staunch defender of the republic during the Roman Civil Wars and opposed J. Caesar. After Caesar's assassination, he delivered the famous *Philippics* (44–43) against his enemy, M. Antony. He was put to death (43) by Octavian at Antony's insistence.

Ciceronian Period   Latin literary period (70–43 BC). It marked the first great stage of Latin literature and was greatly influenced by the technique and style of Cicero. It was followed by the Augustan Age (*q.v.*).

Cid, the (El Cid) (Cid Campeador) c1040–99. Spanish soldier and hero. His real name was Rodrigo Díaz de Vivar. He fought valiantly in wars between the kingdoms of Castile and Navarre but was banished from Castile (1081). Thereafter, he was a soldier of fortune under the Moors of Saragossa and had many adventures. He conquered Valencia (1094) and ruled it until his death.

Cimabue, Giovanni *d.* c1302. Italian painter. His paintings, mostly on religious themes, reflect the change in Italian medieval painting from the once-dominant formal Byzantine style to the more natural style of later artists. He is said to have been Giotto's teacher.

Cimber, Lucius Tillius   Roman conspirator, one of J. Caesar's assassins (44 BC). He distracted Caesar with a petition and then held him during the stabbing.

Cimbri   Germanic tribe that invaded Rome (late 2d cent. BC) after being forced out of their homelands to the north. They were victorious in several engagements (notably Arausio, 105 BC) before being annihilated by Marius and Q. Catulus at Vercellae (101 BC).

Cimmerians   Ancient people of the northern Black Sea region who flourished briefly in the 7th cent. BC. Mentioned by Homer, they were apparently forced (late 8th cent.) southward by the Scythians into what is now Turkey. There they conquered Phrygia and invaded Lydia (7th cent.). Defeated decisively by the Lydians late in the 7th cent., they disappeared from history.

Cimon *d.* 449 BC.   Athenian soldier-statesman, noted for his victories against the Persians. He distinguished himself at the Battle of Salamis (480 BC). As commander of the Delian League

forces, he won a great victory over the Persians at Eurymedon River (466), in which he defeated both their naval and land forces on the same day. His popularity suffered a temporary setback after he became leader of the pro-Spartan faction in Athens and he was ostracized for a time.

Cincinnatus *fl.* 5th cent. BC.   Roman hero, consul (460 BC) and dictator (458 BC). According to traditional accounts, he was made dictator to rescue the Roman army from annihilation by the Aequi and, once that was accomplished, gave up his power to return to farming.

Cinna, Lucius Cornelius *d.* 84 BC.   Roman consul (87–84 BC) and a leader of the popular party. Elected consul under L. Sulla, he tried to rescind some of Sulla's reforms after Sulla left to fight Mithridates VI in the east. With Marius, he overcame Sulla's supporters at Rome and massacred them. He became sole consul on Marius's death (86 BC), and was murdered by his soldiers shortly before Sulla's return.

Cinq-Mars, Henri Coiffier, marquis de 1620–42. French courtier and conspirator in the court of Louis XIII. Ambitious for power, he plotted against Louis's minister, Cardinal Richelieu. One plan, which involved a secret pact with Spain, was uncovered and ended with his execution.

Cinque ports   Confederation (11th–15th cents.) of English port cities located on the English Channel. The confederation provided ships and personnel to the crown for defense of England. Its importance declined rapidly after the formation of the royal navy (late 15th cent.) under Henry VII. The original five ports were: Hastings, New Romney, Hythe, Dover, and Sandwich.

Ciompi, Revolt of   Revolt (1378) by lower-class workingmen (*ciompi*) in Florence. Government in Florence was dominated by the major guilds, which had successfully excluded such lesser guilds as that of the wool workers. Inequities and economic hardships imposed by this system sparked the revolt (July, 1378). It resulted in formation of a short-lived government in which all guilds were represented. Major guilds regained control by 1382.

Cisalpine Republic   Republic in north Italy set up (1797) and controlled by Napoleon. It included Milan, Modena, Parma, Bologna, Ferrara, Romagna, and later Venetia. It became Napoleon's kingdom of Italy (1805), and was dissolved by the Congress of Vienna (1815).

Cistercians Order of Roman Catholic monks founded (1098) in France by Saint Robert. An outgrowth of the Benedictine order, the Cistercians were reformers. They rebelled against the laxity that had overtaken the Benedictine order by returning to the strict, ascetic life of the first Benedictines. Both Saint Stephen Harding and Saint Bernard of Clairvaux influenced the development of the order, the latter being largely responsible for its rapid spread during the 12th cent. By the 14th cent., however, it weakened and declined, and this set the stage for later reform movements in the order, notably by the Trappists. Begun (1664) at La Trappe, France, this movement fostered still stricter observance of the ascetic life and became a permanent division of the Cistercian order.

Citium, Zeno of *See* **Zeno of Citium.**

Citizen Genêt *See* **Genêt, Edmond Charles Édouard.**

Citizen King *See* **Louis Philippe.**

city-state (*Greek* polis) A city and surrounding lands governed as an autonomous state by its citizens. Though city-states appeared in other civilizations, they were especially important in the history of ancient Greece. Such city-states as Athens, Sparta, and Thebes came to dominate whole regions of Greece. For purposes of mutual defense, the city-states formed confederacies, such as the Delian and Peloponnesian leagues. Ultimately, however, the city-states and their leagues were no match for the centralized power of the Macedonian and Roman empires.

civilistas South American political parties. Active in Peru and Brazil (late 19th–early 20th cents.), the civilistas were primarily made up of merchants, bankers, and landowners who opposed control of their governments by the military. The antimilitary policies of the civilistas were partly responsible for Peru's defeat in the War of the Pacific (1879–84).

Civil Rights Act Name of several US laws. 1. Passed (1866) over President A. Johnson's veto, the act gave Negroes full rights as citizens and was designed to counter Black Codes enacted by Southern states after the Civil War. The constitutionality of the act was questioned, however. Once its provisions had been confirmed by passage of the 14th Amendment, Congress reenacted the bill (1870). 2. Passed (1871) to enforce the 14th and 15th Amendments, particularly in regard to Ku Klux Klan terrorism and discrimi-nation in public establishments. It was ruled (1883) unconstitutional in part. 3. Passed (1875) to require equal accommodations in public facilities. It was struck down (1883). 4. Passed (1957) to establish a civil rights commission to investigate infringements of Negro voting rights. 5. Passed (1964) to end discrimination of all kinds, including religious and sex discrimination. It was a sweeping measure, though it was used first to attain civil rights for blacks. It forbade discrimination in public places, schools, and employment. 6. Passed (1968) to end housing discrimination.

civil rights movement US social reform movement of the late 1950s and early 1960s that secured wide-ranging legal rights for American blacks (and other minorities). Among the federal acts passed as a result of this movement were the landmark Civil Rights Act of 1964, banning discrimination in employment, schools, and public accommodations; the 1965 Voting Rights Act, guaranteeing blacks the right to vote; and the 1968 housing bill, banning discrimination in housing. After the American Civil War and emancipation from slavery, blacks became the object of discriminatory laws (Jim Crow laws, *q.v.*) and practices. The Jim Crow laws created separate white and black societies in the South and elsewhere, despite passage of the 13th, 14th, and 15th constitutional amendments and the civil rights acts of the Reconstruction period. The Supreme Court established the principle of separate but equal facilities by its decision in *Plessy* v. *Ferguson* (1896). The NAACP later pressed the cause of black civil rights but the basic principle of "separate but equal" stood until the 1950s, when the Supreme Court banned school segregation in its decision on *Brown* v. *Board of Education of Topeka, Kansas* (1954). The popular civil rights movement began a year later after a black woman, Rosa Parks (1913–), refused to move to the back of a bus in Montgomery, Alabama (Dec. 5, 1955). Out of this incident came a nonviolent protest movement against discrimination, organized by such groups as Rev. Dr. M. L. King's Southern Christian Leadership Conference (SCLC), the Student Nonviolent Coordinating Committee (SNCC), and the Congress of Racial Equality (CORE). Sit-ins, freedom rides, and other nonviolent protests culminated (1963) in the March on Washington (*q.v.*). In subsequent years these protests, and the commitment of presidents J. F. Kennedy and L. Johnson to civil rights, led to passage of the sweeping civil rights legislation of the 1960s. As this legislation was being passed, however, splits developed within the civil rights movement and began the period of its decline. By 1966 advocates of black power came to the fore to challenge the concepts of nonviolence and racial harmony that had been so important in rallying support among blacks and whites for civil rights. Rioting by blacks in major cities across the country, the assassination of Dr. King (Apr. 4, 1968), and the fanatical militancy of such splinter groups as the Black Panthers ended the organized militant phase of the civil rights movement by the close of the 1960s. In subsequent decades, substantial gains were made by working through the courts and especially the political system, with significant gains being made on both the local and national levels of the political arena.

Civil War *See under country names* (*i.e.,* American, English, Chinese, Russian, Mexican).

Cixi (Tz'ŭ Hsi) 1835–1908.   Dowager empress of China (1861–1908) and regent for most of that period. Originally a concubine, she came to power by bearing the emperor's only son, T'ung Chih. As regent for him and his successors, she steadfastly resisted reforms and played a role in the Boxer Rebellion (*q.v.*).

Clairvaux, Saint Bernard of *See* **Bernard of Clairvaux, Saint.**

Clapham Sect English social reformers. These wealthy, conservative Evangelical Christians were active c1790–1830. They advocated abolition of slavery, prison reform, an end to gambling and brutal sports, and missionary work. W. Wilberforce was a prominent member.

Clare, Gilbert de, 8th earl of Gloucester 1243–95. English nobleman. In the Barons' War he was at first a leader of the barons. He then turned to the royalists and helped defeat S. Montfort at Evesham (1265).

Clare, Gilbert de, 9th earl of Gloucester 1291–1314.   English nobleman who was killed serving Edward II at the Battle of Bannockburn.

Clare, Richard de, 7th earl of Gloucester 1222–62. English nobleman. He was a leader of the barons who forced the Provisions of Oxford on King Henry III (1258).

Clarence, George, duke of 1449–78.   English nobleman. He frequently conspired against his brother, King Edward IV. Edward finally impris-

oned the duke in the Tower of London and executed him.

Clarendon, Assize of *See* **Assize of Clarendon**

Clarendon, Constitutions of *See* **Constitutions of Clarendon.**

Clarendon, Edward Hyde, 1st earl of *See* **Hyde, Edward, 1st earl of Clarendon.**

Clarendon, George William Frederick Villiers, 4th earl of *See* **Villiers, George William Frederick, 4th earl of Clarendon.**

Clarendon Code Four laws enacted (1661–65) during the reign of King Charles II to suppress Nonconformists and other sects dissenting from the established Church of England. The laws were passed shortly after Charles's restoration, during the ministry of E. Hyde, 1st earl of Clarendon, though he personally opposed them. The acts were: Corporation Act (1661), requiring all municipal officers to be members of the established church; the Act of Uniformity (1662), requiring all clergymen to accept and use the Book of Common Prayer, the Conventicle Act (1664), forbidding assembly (of more than five) for worship of faiths other than authorized; and the Five-Mile Act (1665), forbidding Nonconformists to come within five miles of any town. Charles attempted unsuccessfully to moderate the laws by his declarations of indulgence (1662, 1672).

Clark, George Rogers 1752–1818.   American Revolutionary War commander. Clark commanded volunteer units in Kentucky and environs (the Old Northwest) during the American Revolution (1775–83) and secured this frontier against British and Indian attacks. He was a brother of W. Clark.

Clark, Mark Wayne 1896–1984.   American general. He was Fifth Army commander in North Africa and Italy (1943–44) during WW II and commander of UN troops in Korea (1952–53).

Clark, William 1770–1838.   American explorer. With his friend, M. Lewis, he undertook a three-year journey of exploration (1804–06) through the newly acquired lands of the Louisiana Purchase to the Pacific Northwest. The maps and journals compiled by Lewis and Clark contributed greatly to knowledge of the region.

Clarke, John 1609–76.   English-born preacher, one of the founders of Rhode Island. Driven out of Massachusetts Bay Colony for siding with A. Hutchinson and the antinomianism (*q.v.*) cause, he helped found Portsmouth (1638) and Newport (1639). With R. Williams, he returned to England and helped secure a royal charter for Rhode Island.

classical 1. In music, the period from c1750 to c1820. The classic period was presaged by the decline of baroque forms and the appearance of rococo, or preclassical compositions, in the early 18th cent. The classic period saw the development of the sonata form, the rise of instrumental over vocal music, and evolution of the characteristic classical mediums: the symphony, string quartet, instrumental sonata, and solo concerto. Among the many notable composers of this period are W. Mozart, F. J. Haydn and L. van Beethoven. 2. In literature, the body of poetic, dramatic, and prose works written by ancient Greeks and Romans. The classic period in Greece ranges from about the 6th cent. to the 4th cent. BC, and in Rome from the 1st cent. BC to 2nd cent. AD.

classical revival *See* **Neoclassicism.**

classicism Term applied to the imitation of the aesthetic values (such as simplicity, symmetry, and harmony of form) found in the art, architecture, and literature of ancient Greece and Rome. Revival of these values began during the Renaissance and influenced many artists, among them Michelangelo and Raphael. Classicism led to the formation of the 16th-cent. French literary group the Pleiade, and influenced such 16th- and 17th-cent. English writers as J. Dryden and A. Pope. The Napoleonic age saw the growth of classical imitation in the classical revival. Classicism also influenced art and architecture in continental Europe, England, and the US in the 19th cent. It continues to be a force in 20th-cent. architecture and the arts.

Claudian (Claudianus) *d.*408? Alexandrian-born Latin poet. Claudian was the last of the great Latin classic poets. *The Rape of Prosperine* is one of his best-known epic poems.

Claudianus *See* **Claudian.**

Claudius I (Germanicus, Tiberius Claudius Drusus Nero) 10 BC–AD 54. Roman emperor (AD 41–54), proclaimed successor to Caligula. Not considered a strong ruler, he nevertheless added Mauretania (AD 41–42) and Britain (after AD 43) to the Roman Empire.

Claudius II (Claudius, Marcus Aurelius) AD 214–270. Roman emperor (AD 268–270), successor to Gallienus. He led Roman forces in an important victory over invading Goths at Naissus (AD 269).

Claudius, Mareus Aurelius *See* **Claudius II.**

Clausewitz, Karl von 1780–1831. Prussian general and noted writer on military strategy. His famous book *On War* advocated "total warfare" against every possible enemy target, including civilians and private property.

Clausius, Rudolf Julius Emmanuel 1822–88. A German mathematical physicist. He is considered a pioneer in thermodynamics and introduced the concept of entropy.

Clay, Henry 1777–1852. American statesman. Three times an unsuccessful presidential candidate (1824, 1832, 1844), he was a congressman from Kentucky (1811–14, 1815–21, 1823–25), secretary of state (1825–29), and Whig party senator (1831–42, 1849–52). As a congressman he formulated his American System (*q.v.*), helped pass the Missouri Compromise (1820), and was instrumental in J. Q. Adams's election as president. He helped end the Nullification Controversy by the Compromise Tariff of 1833, and, by the Compromise of 1850, tried to prevent civil war.

Clayton, John M. *See* **Clayton-Bulwer Treaty.**

Clayton Antitrust Act US bill passed (1914) to supplement the provisions of the Sherman Antitrust Act (1890). It specified as antitrust violations corporate practices not covered in the previous bill, including rebates, interlocking directorates, intercorporate stock holdings, and price discrimination. The act exempted labor and agricultural organizations from the provisions and also included restrictions on the use of injunctions in labor disputes.

Clayton-Bulwer Treaty Treaty signed (1850) by the US and Britain guaranteeing that neither country would attempt to dominate or colonize the territories of Central America. Negotiated by US secretary of state John M. Clayton (1796–1856) and British diplomat Sir Henry Bulwer (1801–72), the treaty was designed to maintain the neutrality of a proposed canal (later the Panama Canal) through the Central American isthmus. The treaty was both vague and highly controversial, however, and was finally superseded by the Hay-Pauncefote Treaty (1901), which made possible a US-controlled canal.

Clear Grits Political faction (1848–51) in Canada West (now Ontario). Followers demanded legislative representation by population and rejected pro-Catholic policies on the Clergy Reserves (*q.v.*). G. Brown was a leading figure in the party, which eventually merged with other groups to form the Liberal party.

Cleisthenes (Clisthenes) *fl.* 6th cent. BC. Athenian statesman who established democracy in Athens. A member of the politically active Alcmaeonidae family, he was chief archon in 525–524 BC. In 508 BC, despite a struggle with the aristocrat Isagoras, he managed to institute his reforms, which broke the power of the landed aristocrats. His reforms included creation of ten new Athenian tribes (not based on family connection or geographic location); creation of a representative council of 500, chosen from the new tribes; greater powers of government were given to the demes; and establishment of the practice of ostracism.

Clemenceau, Georges 1841–1929. French premier (1906–09, 1917–20). Known as "the Tiger," he rallied French forces in WW I and thereby played an important role in the Allied victory. He took part in founding the French Third Republic (1870), and later was implicated in the Panama Scandal. His first government was ousted over his handling of a miners' strike. His second government fell because he failed to press for harsher terms from Germany in negotiations for the Treaty of Versailles (1919).

Clemens, Samuel Langhorne *See* **Twain, Mark.**

Clement I, Saint (Clement of Rome) AD 30?–100? Pope (AD 90–99 or 88?–97) and first apostolic father. He is one of the earliest popes.

Clement III *See* **Guibert of Ravenna.**

Clement V (Got, Bertrand de) 1264–1314. French-born pope (1305–14). Clement moved the papacy from Rome to Avignon, France, and thus began the Babylonian Captivity (*q.v.*). Under pressure from French king Philip IV, he called the Council of Vienne (1311) and dissolved (1312) the Knights Templars (*q.v.*).

Clement VI (Roger, Pierre) 1291–1352. French-born pope (1342–52) at Avignon, France. Clement's reign was marked by the outbreak of the Black Plague, and he is remembered for his attempts to protect Jews, then being accused of causing the plague.

Clement VII *See* **Robert of Geneva.**

Clement VII (Medici, Giulio de) 1478–1534. Italian-born pope (1523–34). Clement was caught in the power struggle between French king Francis I and Holy Roman Emperor Charles V. In 1527, Charles invaded Italy, sacked Rome,

and imprisoned Clement. Clement also refused (c1527) Henry VIII his divorce from Catherine of Aragon, and thus set the stage for the break between the English church and Rome.

Clement VIII (Aldobrandini, Ippolito) 1536–1605. Italian-born pope (1592–1605). Clement absolved French king Henry IV of excommunication after he rejected Protestantism (1593) and moderated the influence of the Spanish kings on the church.

Clement XI (Albani, Giovanni Francesco) 1649–1721. Italian-born pope (1700–21). Clement condemned Jansenism and, embroiled in the struggle for the Spanish throne, failed to avert the War of Spanish Succession (1701–14).

Clement XIV (Ganganelli, Lorenzo) 1705–74. Italian-born pope (1769–74). To avoid schism with Spain and France, he dissolved (1773) the Society of Jesus (Jesuits), then regarded by the kings as a threat to their power.

Clement, Jacques 1567–89. French monk, a Dominican. Clement assassinated (1589) French king Henry III for choosing a Protestant as his successor.

Clement of Alexandria *d.* AD c215. Greek Christian theologian and teacher at the Alexandrian School. He was the teacher of the Christian philosopher Origen and a prolific writer. He fled Alexandria during the persecution of Christians under Severus.

Clement of Rome *See* **Clement I, Saint.**

Cleomenes I *d.* c489 BC. King of Sparta (c519–491 BC). He is remembered for his interference in Athenian politics (notably his initially successful attempt to oust the Athenian leader Cleisthenes to undo his democratic reforms) and for his cruelty in battle against Argos (c494), during which some 6,000 enemy soldiers were slaughtered.

Cleomenes III *d.* 219 BC. King of Sparta (c235–221 BC). He established the supreme authority of the king by abolishing the Spartan ephorate (five elected magistrates) and enacted other reforms. He was successful in warfare against the Achaean League (227–222) until the league allied itself with Macedon. His subsequent defeat (222) by Antigonus III at Sellasia marked the fall of Sparta to the Macedonians.

Cleon *d.* 422 BC. Athenian politician and soldier. Cleon began his career by opposing Pericles and is generally remembered as a demagogue. He distinguished himself in battles against the

Spartans during the Peloponnesian Wars (431–404 BC) and was killed in battle.

Cleopatra (Cleopatra VII) 69–30 BC.   Queen of Egypt (51–49, 48–30 BC), noted beauty celebrated for her love affairs with J. Caesar and M. Antony. Wedded by custom to her brother, Ptolemy XIII, she was ousted from power by him (49). Caesar, then pursuing Pompey in Egypt, fell in love with her and restored her to power (48 BC). With Ptolemy XIII dead, she nominally married another brother, Ptolemy XIV, and became Caesar's mistress, bore him a son, Cesarion, and lived with Caesar at Rome (from 46) until his assassination (44). She then met and entranced Antony (42) with her charms and they lived together until 40, when Antony was forced to return to Rome and marry the sister of Octavian (later Augustus). Cleopatra by this time had given birth to twins by Antony. Antony and Cleopatra again became lovers in 36 and their affair was unpopular in Rome. Octavian at last sent an army to destroy Antony and Cleopatra. Octavian was victorious at the Battle of Actium (31) and the two lovers fled to Alexandria. There, with Octavian approaching, she is said to have induced Antony to commit suicide. She then tried to captivate Octavian and, seeing he was unmoved and intended to display her in his triumph at Rome, killed herself.

Cleopatra's Needles   Two red granite Egyptian obelisks, incised with hieroglyphs and dating from c1500 BC. They stood first in Heliopolis and then were moved (c14 BC) to Alexandria. Today one stands in London, the other in New York City.

Clergy Reserves   Canadian land grants to the Church of England. The British Constitutional Act (1791) specified that land be set aside for "Protestant" clergy. From the early 19th cent., however, disposition of the lands was disputed by dissenting Protestants. The Church of England claimed all the land for itself, while other Protestant denominations contested the claim. Most of the land was finally allocated to secular use (1854) and large cash payments were made to the churches (including the Roman Catholic church).

Clermont   *See* **Fulton, Robert.**

Clermont, Council of   Church council (1095, at Clermont, France), in which Pope Urban II preached the First Crusade. The Byzantine Empire was at that time being reduced by Muslim conquests and Emperor Alexius I requested aid from the pope. Urban's primary concern was liberating Jerusalem, however. At the council he urged French knights to take up the cause, citing Muslim persecutions, the Muslim capture of the Holy Land, and the possible material gain of such a venture. The response was enthusiastic and Raymond IV accepted the first of the crosses distributed by Urban.

cleruchy   In ancient Greece, a colony in which settlers remained citizens of the mother country. In the 5th and 4th cents. BC especially, colonies of Athenian citizens became an important instrument of Athenian imperialism. Cleruchies were strategically placed in other lands, providing pockets of Athenian citizens that became bases for policing the countryside. As Athenian citizens, cleruchs voted, served in the military, and paid taxes, while generally gaining possession of the best lands in the colony. Cleruchies also helped encourage resettlement by providing land for poor Athenians.

Cleveland, (Stephen) Grover 1837–1908.   (*nicknamed* the Great Obstructionist) 22d and 24th US president (1885–89, 1893–97), successor to C. Arthur, B. Harrison. A former governor of New York and a reform Democrat, he was elected to his first term amid a popular movement to end corrupt government. As president, he opposed political bosses, fought "pork barrel" legislation and implemented the Pendleton Civil Service Act of 1883. The fight for lower tariffs, however, loomed as the major issue of his first administration. He subsequently lost the election (1888) to Harrison over the issue. Reelected (1892) when the Populist party split the vote, Cleveland largely devoted the efforts of his second administration to ending the economic depression that resulted from the Panic of 1893 (*q.v.*). During his second term, Cleveland failed to prevent passage of the Wilson-Gorman Tariff Act (1894, raising tariffs), forced repeal of the Sherman Silver Purchase Act (1893), used federal powers to break the Pullman Strike (1894), became involved in the Venezuela Boundary Dispute (*q.v.*), and expanded powers claimed under the Monroe Doctrine as a result of it. Continuing economic problems and the rising power of the free-silver movement, resulted in his failure to win renomination (1896).

Cleves, Anne of   *See* **Anne of Cleves.**

client   A free man in ancient Rome who acknowledged dependence on and received support from a patron in return for loyalty and such help in public and private life as the patron deemed necessary. The client often received food or the cash equivalent, could not be forced to bear witness against the patron, was required to greet the patron each morning, and was expected to vote according to the patron's wishes at public assemblies. The system of clientage, included in Roman law from the 5th cent. BC, became hereditary by the 1st cent. BC. Because of their dependence upon patrons, clients came to be looked down upon during the empire period, but individual Romans and families nevertheless acquired large numbers of clients, especially in the provinces. With the expansion of the system about this time to include conquered cities, states, and their rulers, clientage became a factor in maintaining Rome's control over the empire.

Clifford of Chudleigh, Thomas Clifford, 1st baron 1630–73. English statesman. A Catholic member of the Cabal ministry under Charles II, he was forced to resign when the Test Act (1673) banned Catholics from holding state office.

Clinton, Bill (William Jefferson) 1946–   .   The 42d US president (1993–   ). An Arkansas native, Clinton graduated from Georgetown University (1968), attended Oxford University as a Rhodes scholar, and graduated from Yale with a law degree in 1973. He married his wife Hillary Rodham, also a Yale law graduate, in 1975. Having worked in Democratic campaign organizations for a number of years, he won election as Arkansas governor (1978–80), becoming one of the youngest governors in the US. After losing a reelection bid in 1980, he retook the governorship in 1982 and served continuously until his election to the presidency in 1992. Widely acknowledged as a skilled politician, he won the Democratic presidential nomination in 1992, despite charges of impropriety in his personal life, and won the presidential race against Republican incumbent G. Bush (and independent Ross Perot) by campaigning on a centrist platform focusing on the poor state of the economy, and by promising change and economic growth. On taking office, he put forward a number of legislative initiatives, most notably on deficit reduction.

Clinton, DeWitt 1769–1828. US political leader who sponsored the Erie Canal construction project. He was a nephew of G. Clinton. During his long career as a New York politician and US senator (1802–03), he sought to promote building of the canal as a commercial link between the Northeast and the Midwest via the Great Lakes. After federal authorities rejected the idea, he won funding from New York State (1816) and as NY governor (1817–23, 1825–28), oversaw the building of the Erie Canal (completed 1825), what was disparagingly referred to as "Clinton's ditch."

Clinton, George 1739–1812.   American statesman and vice-president (1805–1812), Clinton served as first governor of New York (1777–95) and first proposed the Erie Canal. He died during his (second) term as vice-president, under J. Madison.

Clinton, Sir Henry 1738?–95.   British general during the American Revolution (1775–83). He served under Gen. W. Howe early in the war, then succeeded him as British commander (1778–81). He evacuated Philadelphia (1778) and later captured Charleston (1780), but his failure to provide timely support for Gen. C. Cornwallis in the Yorktown Campaign (*q.v.*) was blamed for the final British defeat in the war. He resigned his command (1781) after Cornwallis surrendered in the south.

Clisthenes   *See* **Cleisthenes.**

Clive, Robert, baron of Plassey 1725–74.   British soldier and statesman who helped establish British rule in India. In the service of the British East India Company, he defeated the French in the south, conquered the rulers of Bengal, and established himself as its first British governor (1757–60). He then defeated (1759) the Dutch in India. He again served as the governor of Bengal (1765–67).

Cliveden Set   *See* **Astor, Nancy Witcher Langhorne, viscountess Astor.**

Clodia *fl.*1st cent. BC.   Roman matron, noted beauty and sister of Clodius. She is thought to have been Catullus's lover, immortalized in his poems as Lesbia.

Clodius *d.*52 BC.   Roman tribune and demagogue. He figured in Cicero's exile from Rome (58 BC) and, as a rival of the tribune Milo, led a gang of thugs that tyrannized the city of Rome for several years.

Clontarf, Battle of　Battle (Apr. 23, 1014, near Dublin) in which the Irish, led by King Brian Boru, turned back an attempted invasion of Irish domains by the Danes under Sweyn.

Clotaire I *d.*561.　Merovingian king (558–561). Before his father, Clovis I, died, he divided the Frankish kingdom among Clotaire and his other three sons. From 558 to 561, however, Clotaire reigned as sole king of the Franks. Clotaire's kingdom was divided on his death. One son, Sigebert I, received Neustria and another, Chilperic I, received Austrasia.

Clotaire II 584–629?　Merovingian king (584–629) of Neustria. He put Austrasian queen Brunhilde to death, seized her lands, and reunited the Frankish Empire under his rule (613–629). In 614 he was forced to concede privileges to the nobility and the clergy.

Cloth of Gold, Field of　*See* **Field of Cloth of Gold.**

Clotilda, Saint AD c470–545.　Frankish queen (AD 493–511). Legend says Clotilda converted her husband, Clovis I, to Christianity. After his death (511) she turned to helping the needy.

Clovis I c466–511.　Frankish king (481–511), founder of the Merovingian kingdom. He gained control of northern Gaul by his victory at Soissons (486) and elsewhere. Next he conquered the Thuringians, converted to Christianity after defeating the Alemanni in 496, won notable victories against the Burgundians and Visigoths, and established his capital at Paris.

Clunaic order　Medieval reformist Benedictine monks, founded (910) at Cluny, France. The order sought a return to the earlier, strict observance of the Rule of Saint Benedict, avoided lay control, and rose to great power by the 11th cent. The order declined gradually after the 12th cent.

Cnidus, Eudoxus of　*See* **Eudoxus of Cnidus.**

Cnossus (Knossos)　Ancient city and center of the Minoan civilization (*q.v.*). Occupied before the 3d millennium BC, the city was the site of a splendid palace. The city was destroyed by invaders (probably Mycenaean) about 1400 BC.

Cnut　*See* **Canute.**

Cobbett, William 1763?–1835.　English journalist and reformer. He was a noted advocate of reforms to improve the lot of the industrial working class.

Cobden, Richard 1804–65.　English radical politician. Cobden favored free trade and led the fight to repeal the Corn Laws. Elected to Parliament (1841), he opposed the Crimean War and urged British support for the North in the American Civil War.

Cobden-Chevalier Treaty (Anglo-French Treaty)　Trade agreement (1860) negotiated with France by British politician R. Cobden. The treaty established reciprocal tariffs between Britain and France and ended a period of heightened tensions.

Cochin　*See* **India** (1498).

Cochin China　Historic region in the south of Vietnam embracing the Mekong Delta region, originally settled by Khmer. It was long contested by the Khmer and Champa kingdoms and was finally taken over by the Vietnamese kingdom of Annam (18th cent.). It became part of the French domains in Indochina (c1862–1949) and then was joined to other territories to form Vietnam. Ho Chi Minh City (Saigon) is the major city of the region.

Cochise *d.*1874.　Apache Indian chief in Arizona. He became a leader (after 1861) of Apache raiders who warred against white settlers. His band of 200 braves conducted raids until 1872, when they surrendered voluntarily.

Cockcroft, Sir John Douglas 1897–1967.　English physicist. He and E. Walton shared the Nobel Prize in Physics (1951) for splitting atomic nuclei with accelerated atomic particles.

Cocteau, Jean 1889–1963.　French writer, artist, and film maker. Cocteau was a leader of surrealism and the avant-garde. Among his best-known works are the films *Beauty and the Beast* and *Orphée* and the novel *Les Enfants Terribles.*

Code Civil　*See* **Code Napoléon.**

Code Napoléon (*Code Civil*) (Napoleonic Code)　Compilation of the civil laws of France and its possessions issued by Napoleon (1804). It is still in effect, with modifications, in France today. Following the breakup of the Napoleonic Empire, the code was modified and voluntarily adopted by a number of European countries.

Code of Canon Law (*codex juris canonici*)　Codification of Roman Catholic canon law. Begun (1904) under Pope Pius X, it was completed and promulgated (1917) under Pope Benedict XV. (*See also* canon law.)

Code of Hammurabi　A relatively sophisticated legal code written (c18th cent. BC) by Hammurabi, founder of the Babylonian Empire. One of the earliest known legal codes, it was based on the system of "an eye for an eye" and meted out punishments equal in kind and severity to the injury inflicted. The code was rediscovered in 1901.

codex juris canonici *See* **canon law; Code of Canon Law.**

Codomannus, Darius *See* **Darius III.**

Cody, William Frederick *See* **Buffalo Bill.**

Coeur, Jacques c1395–1456. French merchant and financial adviser to Charles VII. He restored order to the state finances and helped finance the military campaign that finally drove the English from Normandy. He was driven out of France (c1454) on trumped-up charges.

Coeur d'Alene Riots Strikes and riots by union miners in Idaho during the 1890s. Rioting began in 1892, when miners attacked armed guards protecting nonunion lead and silver miners. Sporadic outbreaks of violence continued, and, in 1905, the unrest became a major scandal when the governor of Idaho was murdered. A former miner, who said the union was involved in the murder, was convicted.

Cohan, George Michael 1878–1942. American showman, writer, and composer. He wrote such famous songs as "Over There" and "I'm a Yankee Doodle Dandy" and wrote the shows *Little Johnny Jones, The Tavern,* and *Forty-Five Minutes from Broadway.*

Cohn, Ferdinand 1828–98. German botanist and bacteriologist. Cohn is often called the father of bacteriology. He aided R. Koch in his research on the disease anthrax.

Coin's Financial School Book written by William Hope Harvey (1894), an expression of the free-silver philosophy of currency in the US. Harvey favored free and unlimited coinage of silver, opposing restrictions to bimetallism (use of silver and gold money). He held restrictions would unfairly benefit eastern financiers at the expense of farmers and workers.

Coke, Sir Edward 1552–1634. English jurist, famous in English history as a defender of common law against royal prerogative. He played a major role in formulating the Petition of Right (1628). Notoriously severe as a prosecutor, he tried Sir W. Raleigh and, later, the conspirators in the Gunpowder Plot. As chief justice of common pleas (1606–13) and chief justice of the king's bench (1613–16), however, he became a champion of the supremacy of common law. Returned to Parliament, he became a leader of the opposition to James I and Charles I.

Coke, Thomas *See* **Methodism.**

Colbath, Jeremiah Jones *See* **Wilson, Henry.**

Colbert, Jean Baptiste 1619–83. French statesman. As comptroller of finance to Louis XIV, Colbert supported mercantilism and government economy. His policies helped make France a commercial and naval power.

Colchis Ancient country located near the Black Sea. It was thought to be the mythical land of Medea, where the Golden Fleece, sought by Jason, was kept.

Cold Harbor, Battle of Battle (June 1–12, 1864) during the American Civil War (1861–65). Fought during Gen. U. Grant's drive toward Richmond, the battle pitted over 100,000 Union soldiers against some 59,000 Confederates, led by Gen. R. E. Lee. The Confederates stopped the Union advance in stiff fighting and finally forced Grant to turn away from Richmond toward Petersburg.

Cold War Name for the international rivalry between the US and the USSR from the close of WW II until the collapse of the USSR. The Cold War period saw the division of the world into well-defined Western and Communist spheres of influence, domination of world politics by the US and USSR as superpowers, East-West political and propaganda struggles, the continuing threat of nuclear war (from the 1950s), and outbreaks of limited warfare between pro-Western and pro-Communist forces. Suspicions about Soviet leader J. Stalin's designs for expansion of the Communist world were aroused after WW II by his transformation of Soviet-occupied Eastern Europe into a closed network of Communist satellite states. In a famous speech (Mar. 15, 1946) at Fulton, Missouri, former British prime minister W. Churchill pointed to the "iron curtain" that had descended across Europe. The following year US president H. Truman announced the Truman Doctrine (Mar. 12, 1947) to counter threatened Communist takeovers in Greece and Turkey. This was followed by announcement of the Marshall Plan to provide for the recovery of war-torn Europe and to counter Communist expansionism there. The last years of the 1940s were marked by the US-Soviet confrontation in the Berlin blockade and airlift (from 1948), formation of NATO (1949), and the Communist takeover in China (1949). The 1950s saw increased Communist activity in Southeast Asia, the Korean War, formation of the Communist

Warsaw Pact (1955), a continuing US policy of "containing" Communism, the rise of the nuclear arms race and the threat of "massive retaliation." At the same time, however, possibilities of a "thaw" in Cold War tensions were seen in the death of Stalin (1953), N. Khrushchev's subsequent de-Stalinization policy, the limited successes of the Geneva Summit Conference (1955), and the exchange of official visits in 1959 (Vice-President R. Nixon to USSR; Khrushchev to US). The early 1960s brought renewed tensions, however. The building of the Berlin Wall (1961) and the Cuban Missile Crisis (1962) temporarily halted moves toward better East-West relations. But a trend of more far-reaching importance in the 1960s was the break-up of rigid divisions between pro-West and Communist-bloc countries. The Sino-Soviet split (1960) led to a deep rift in the Communist bloc (later exploited by the US), and the granting of independence to British, French, and Dutch colonies created fertile ground for unrest and competition between the US and USSR. The Vietnam War not only cost the US considerable power and prestige but it also led to divisions among Western nations and especially their Third World allies. The 1970s saw a turning away from the hard-line divisions of the Cold War period in favor of a new policy of détente (*q.v.*). The US opened relations with China, increased trade and other economic ties with the USSR, and entered into nuclear arms limitation talks. Policies of détente by no means eliminated mistrust and competition between the superpowers, however. Events of the late 1970s and early 1980s, such as the Soviet invasion of Afghanistan, the crisis over Solidarity in Poland, and the movement for a military defense buildup in the US marked an end to détente and brought on a marked "chill" in US-Soviet relations. However, the rise to power of M. Gorbachev (1985) marked the beginning of an abrupt change in Soviet policy. Representing a new generation of leadership, he instituted *glasnost* (openness, 1986) and *perestroika* (restructuring, 1987) and set about purging the government of hard-line, old guard Communists. And in a dramatic reversal of the long-time Soviet policy of interventionism, he announced the USSR would no longer interfere with the governments of other Soviet-bloc nations. Without the backing of Soviet troops, old-line Communist regimes in Eastern Europe

soon faced an outpouring of demands for economic and democratic reforms, and in 1989–90 all the old regimes were toppled. Gorbachev likewise faced enormous pressure for democratic reforms, further complicated by ethnic strife and nationalist movements in the Baltic States and elsewhere in the USSR. While trying to balance the need to keep the USSR together against mounting demands for faster reforms, Gorbachev also agreed to major cuts in nuclear weapons, ordered the withdrawal of Soviet troops from Europe, and sought direct aid from the US to help with the transition to a market economy. In 1990, US president G. Bush and Soviet leader Gorbachev jointly pronounced the end of the Cold War. The USSR, however, did not survive long after; in 1991 it collapsed and its constituent republics formed a loose confederation, the Commonwealth of Independent States. With the breakup of the USSR, the US remained as the world's lone superpower. *See also* United States; Commonwealth of Independent States. Key events in the history of the Cold War include:

1944 Soviet armies, driving the Germans westward out of the USSR, crossed the border into Poland (Feb.) and Rumania (Mar.); Allies, stalled in Italy, launched massive Normandy invasion in western France (June) and began pushing eastward toward Germany; necessity of wartime alliance kept in check US and British suspicions about J. Stalin's postwar designs; Stalin meanwhile also seemed to put aside his distrust of his powerful capitalistic allies.

1944 Bretton Woods Conference (July); US, seeking to establish stable world economy at war's end, set up the World Bank and International Monetary Fund; established US dollar as world's reserve currency (other currencies being valued in relation to it); Stalin refused to join the system.

1944 Warsaw Uprising in Poland (Aug.–Oct.); pro-democratic Polish underground briefly seized control of Warsaw, only to be crushed by Germans while Soviet forces awaited the outcome outside the city; Soviets then drove Germans out of Poland and set about installing a Communist regime.

1944 Germans withdrew from Albania; Communist partisans emerged from hiding to establish a pro-Communist Albanian government; their leader, E. Hoxha, led the hard-line Communist regime until 1985.

1944–45 US Manhattan Project reached final stages of building world's first atomic bomb (tested 1945); Soviet government, meanwhile, used its spy network to steal crucial atomic secrets for its own atomic bomb project.

1945 Yalta Conference (Feb.); division of Germany into four occupation zones at war's end set; Allies reluctantly approved Soviet-backed regime in occupied Poland as interim government (pending free-elections).

1945 In Rumania, Soviets installed government dominated by Communists (Mar.).

1945 Yugoslav Communist partisan leader Tito (Josip Broz) installed as premier of his country (Mar. 7), with Communists in key positions.

1945 US president F. D. Roosevelt died in office (Apr. 12); Vice-President H. Truman succeeded to the presidency (1945–53).

1945 President Truman, now deeply concerned about Soviet moves to impose Communist government in Eastern Europe, formally upbraided Soviet foreign minister V. Molotov (Apr. 23).

1945 US, pursuing policy of establishing stable order in postwar world, hosted the San Francisco Conference of Allied powers (Apr.–June), during which the United Nations charter was adopted.

1945 Nazi Germany surrendered (May 7); war in Europe ended.

1945 President Truman halted Lend-Lease aid to the USSR in response to Soviet actions in East Europe; relations with Stalin cooled, though US continued policy of goodwill toward its ally.

1945 US recognized Soviet-backed regime in Poland, after Soviets agreed to include some non-Communists (May).

1945 Potsdam Conference (July); Soviets insisted on exacting heavy war reparations from Germany; controversial questions about makeup of East European governments and administration of occupation zones put off to future meetings; growing rift between USSR and US on plans for postwar world order becoming apparent.

1945 US dropped atomic bombs on Hiroshima (Aug. 6) and Nagasaki (Aug. 9), becoming (for the time) the world's only nuclear power and bringing on the age of nuclear weaponry; Japan, shocked by the awesome power of the bombs, surrendered (Aug. 14), thus ending WW II.

1945 War's aftermath; US and USSR ranked as world's two leading powers; US, only major industrial power undamaged by war, had a powerful conventional military (and the ability to project it worldwide) as well as frighteningly powerful nuclear weapons; USSR boasted an enormous land army (300 divisions) capable of overrunning Western Europe and other neighboring regions; however USSR, like most of Europe, faced enormous job of rebuilding, as well as massive refugee problems and severe shortages of food and other commodities; meanwhile Stalin quickly imposed tight control over Eastern Europe (refusing to even allow in Western journalists), possibly because he feared the newly conquered peoples would not remain loyal to Communist governments.

1945 Soviets signed friendship treaty with Chinese Nationalists (Aug. 14); then reassumed control over Manchuria and systematically stripped region of industrial equipment.

1945 Korea occupied by Soviet troops (Aug., in the north) and US troops (Sept., in the south); de facto partition of Korea (at 38th parallel) soon established, with Communist government in north and pro-Western government in south; meanwhile, Soviets were not allowed to participate in occupation of Japan.

1945 UN Charter ratified (Oct. 24); world's major powers after WW II, including the US and USSR, all became members; UN established as forum for peaceful settlement of international disputes.

1945 US president Truman outlined basic principles of US foreign policy in Navy Day speech (Oct. 27); twelve points included support for right of national self-determination and refusal to recognize governments imposed by foreign powers (as in Eastern Europe).

1946 Five-year plan announced in speech by Stalin (Feb. 9); called for rebuilding of Soviet heavy industry and military, and included blunt statements of hostility toward West; thereafter the Soviets labeled the US as the leader of Western militaristic reactionaries, while billing themselves as progressive and peace-loving.

1946   Long telegram sent from Moscow by US diplomat George F. Kennan (Feb. 22); outlined Soviet leadership's "neurotic" fears about Western ideas as a threat to their power; noted they used Marxist ideology to excuse their unethical behavior and abuses of power; soon after this telegram, Kennan outlined foundations of US Cold War policy in magazine article, suggesting program of "containment" of Communism.

1946   Former British prime minister W. Churchill, speaking at Fulton, Missouri, made reference to the Soviet "iron curtain" surrounding occupied Eastern Europe (Mar. 15); Churchill's speech popularized the term.

1946   US resorted to threats to force Soviet troop withdrawal from Iran (Mar.), in accordance with their previous agreement.

1946   US announced new policy on Germany as cooperation on administration of occupation zones there broke down (Sept. 6); US proposed unification of zones occupied by Western powers, effectively forcing the permanent division of Germany.

1946   In Bulgaria, Communists abolished the monarchy and set up a people's republic (Sept.).

1946   Chinese civil war between Nationalists and Communists resumed (Oct.), after US-brokered negotiations failed; US supplied aid to Nationalists from May 1947.

1946–50   Breakup of the British, French, and Dutch colonial empires; decolonization, begun well before WW II, proceeded rapidly from 1946, creating numerous independent states in the Mideast (including Israel) and the Far East.

1947   Communist takeover in Poland completed; government established as Communist people's republic (Feb.).

1947   US president Truman announced Truman Doctrine (Mar. 12), in response to Communists' attempt to seize power in Greece and move to force concessions from Turkey; US to provide aid to these and other nations threatened by Communist takeovers, as part of broad policy of containing Communism; postwar divisions between the East and West thus hardened further.

1947   President Truman issued Loyalty Order (Mar. 22) as fears about Communist subversives in government began to spread ("Red Scare").

1947   Moscow Conference (Mar.–Apr.); split widened between Soviets and Western powers occupying Germany.

1947   US and British occupation zones in Germany merged (May).

1947   European Recovery Plan (Marshall Plan) proposed by US secretary of state G. Marshall (June); US to fund massive aid plan to help European nations recover from war; USSR and satellites refused to take aid, with Stalin denouncing the plan as capitalist plot.

1947   In the US, National Security Act created the Department of Defense, established the National Security Council, and created the Central Intelligence Agency; Strategic Air Command, whose bombers carried atomic bombs, also created this year.

1947   Soviets organized Cominform to coordinate Communist parties in various nations (Oct., dissolved 1956).

1947   Stalin ordered development of ICBM missiles as means to threaten US from Soviet bases.

1947–49   In Hungary, minority Communist party consolidated its control within the government; aided by Soviet forces, it conducted bloody campaigns against anti-Communists and the church.

1948   Communist takeover in Czechoslavakia (Feb.), ending short-lived democratic government there.

1948   Western powers unified occupation zones in Germany (Mar.); Soviets withdrew from Allied Control Council.

1948   Break in relations between Soviet Union and Yugoslavia (June); popular Yugoslav leader Tito defied Stalin's threats and established independent Communist state; exposed first rift in the monolithic Communist bloc.

1948   Western powers instituted currency reforms (June 18) to economically unify Western zone.

1948   Berlin blockade built by Soviets (from June 24) in retaliation for recent moves in Germany by Western powers; all overland access to West Berlin (well inside Soviet occupation zone) was cut off.

1948 Berlin airlift begun (June 26) by US and Britain to resupply the barricaded city; airlift eventually totaled over 275,000 flights and provided West Berlin with food and fuel until 1949.

1948 Term "cold war" coined (October 28) by US businessman and statesman Bernard Baruch.

1949–50 Frequent border clashes between North and South Korea; several thousand troops killed.

1949–53 D. Acheson served as US secretary of state under Truman; helped promote US policy of containment of Communism.

1949 Soviet Union formed Council for Mutual Economic Assistance (Comecon) to promote economic development of member nations (Jan.); charter members included the USSR, Poland, Hungary, Rumania, Czechoslavakia, and Bulgaria.

1949 V. Molotov resigned as Soviet foreign minister, a post he had held since 1939.

1949 North Atlantic Treaty Organization (NATO) formed (Apr. 4) by nations of Europe and North America; marked response by Western nations to growing threat of Communist aggression.

1949 Soviets lifted blockade of West Berlin (May 12).

1949 Federal Republic of Germany formed (May 23) from Western-occupied zones; Cold War East-West divisions thus became institutionalized.

1949 Soviets exploded their first atomic bomb (Aug.); US no longer world's sole nuclear power.

1949 In Hungary, Communists gained complete control; new constitution adopted (Aug. 10) establishing the Hungarian People's Republic, modeled on Soviet lines.

1949 Communist People's Republic of China declared (Oct. 1) following rout of Nationalist forces by Chinese Red Army; Soviet Union recognized Mao Zedong's government for first time; loss of China proved major blow to US, which refused to recognize Red China, and fueled Cold War fears in the West about the expansion of Communism.

1949 German Democratic Republic established (Oct. 7) by Soviets to govern their Eastern zone.

1949 Greek royalist forces victorious in civil war against Communists (Oct.).

1949 In the US, A. Hiss accused of being a Communist spy; his conviction for perjury (Nov. 17, 1950) marked beginning of furor over subversives in US government.

1950 US Senator J. McCarthy startled Americans by claiming over 200 unnamed officials in State Department were Communists (Feb. 9); McCarthy subsequently exploited fear of communism by unjustly accusing many individuals in the McCarthy hearings (1950–54), including a series of televised hearings in 1953; so-called McCarthyism marked height of Cold War "Red Scare."

1950 Threatened Communist Chinese invasion of Taiwan, the Chinese Nationalist stronghold, blocked by presence of US Seventh Fleet off Chinese coast.

1950 Soviet spy K. Fuchs imprisoned by British for passing US atomic bomb secrets to the USSR (Mar.).

1950–53 Korean War; Communist North Koreans invaded South (June 25, with Stalin's blessings) to start the conflict; US played leading role in what was called UN "police action" and "limited war" but was actually the first major East-West military confrontation of the Cold War.

1950 US agreed to supply troops for NATO defense force in Europe, as fears of Communist expansionism spread (Sept.); Korean War also resulted in US plan to beef up its conventional and nuclear forces.

1950 Prague Proposals advanced by the USSR (Oct.); proposed unified, demilitarized Germany, but with assembly weighted heavily in favor of East Germans; plan failed to gain support.

1951 US formed ANZUS defense pact with Australia and New Zealand.

1951 Defense treaty between US and Japan signed; cemented US defense responsibilities in the Pacific.

1952 British joined nuclear club after exploding atomic bomb (Oct.).

1952 US exploded world's first hydrogen bomb, many times more powerful than atomic bomb (Nov.), thereby temporarily winning technological superiority; Soviets exploded their own H-bomb in Aug. 1953.

1953–61 US president D. Eisenhower in office; J. F. Dulles served as secretary of state (1953–59) and helped shape US Cold War policies during this crucial period.

1953 Stalin died (Mar. 5); policy of government by "collective leadership" to replace Stalin's rule was initially adopted by the USSR; G. Malenkov in office as premier.

1953–56 V. Molotov back in office as Soviet foreign minister.

1953 In Communist East Germany, food shortages sparked riots; Soviet troops restored order; USSR then reduced East Germany's war reparations payments and later cut back exploitation of other East European satellite states.

1953 First successful test of US Intermediate-Range Ballistic Missile (IRBM); missiles, capable of carrying nuclear warheads, soon became key element in Cold War arms race between US and USSR.

1953 J. and E. Rosenberg executed in the US after being convicted of stealing atomic secrets (June).

1953 US President Eisenhower, after hinting the US might use atomic bombs, won negotiated end to Korean War (July 27).

1954 In Guatemala, the US CIA helped block a Communist-backed coup.

1954 Communist victory at Dien Bien Phu (May 7) in Vietnam; French forces, battling Communist rebels since end of WW II, humiliated by the defeat.

1954 Geneva Conference (Apr.–July); French agreed to independence for Laos and Cambodia, and north-south partition of Vietnam, pending elections (set for 1956, but never held); US officials articulated "domino theory," stating that if Vietnam went Communist, the rest of Southeast Asia would also become Communist; US began supporting South Vietnam in wake of French withdrawal from Indochina.

1954 US began crash program to develop the Intercontinental Ballistic Missile or ICBM (June).

1954 Eisenhower, concerned that "brushfire" wars in Asia and elsewhere could sap national strength, shifted US Cold War policy; adopted policy of threatening "massive retaliation" to deter aggression; strengthened US

military's nuclear arm, the Strategic Air Command, while cutting overall defense spending; developed long-range bombers and built US airbases overseas.

1954 Southeast Asia Treaty Organization (SEATO) organized; included US and Australia, New Zealand, Pakistan, the Philippines, Thailand, Britain, and France.

1954 West Germany admitted to NATO.

1955 US formed Baghdad Pact Organization (later called CENTO).

1955 In the USSR, Premier (and effective Soviet leader) G. Malenkov fell from power (Feb.); replaced by N. Bulganin as premier.

1955 Bandung Conference held in Indonesia by newly independent African and Asian nations (Apr.); leaders of Egypt, India, and Indonesia dominated conference, adopting generally anti-West tone; marked emergence of Third World countries, which subsequently became significant force in world politics.

1955 Soviets adopted policy of giving aid to and forming alliances with non-Communist nations.

1955 Warsaw Pact formed between the USSR and Soviet-bloc satellite nations (May); created to counter NATO alliance.

1955 US president Eisenhower proposed "Open Skies" plan (July); proposed exchange of maps of US and Soviet military bases along with agreement for unlimited aerial reconaissance; Soviets rejected the plan.

1955 US established early warning system (DEW line) to detect possible Soviet attack; Strategic Air Command (SAC) kept planes loaded with nuclear bombs airborne at all times for quick response to any attack.

1956 US began U-2 high-altitude reconaissance flights over the USSR.

1956–64 Soviet leader N. Khrushchev in power; presided over period of growing Soviet military power and prestige.

1956 Twentieth Party Congress; Khrushchev made his "Secret Speech" (Feb.) denouncing Stalin; this policy of de-Stalinization, an easing of restrictions, later gave rise to unrest in Poland and Hungary; Khrushchev also noted Soviet's nuclear weaponry now made the USSR an equal of the US and forced an era of "peaceful coexistence; proposed supporting wars of "national liberation" as means of advancing Communism among the many new Third World countries.

1956   Communist Poland hit by strikes and riots during summer; lack of Soviet action encouraged other challenges to Communist authority, notably in Hungary.

1956   Suez Crisis; Egyptian President G. Nasser nationalized the Suez Canal (July 26); Israel, in league with Britain and France, attacked Egypt, igniting the Second Arab-Israeli War (Oct.–Nov.).

1956   Hungarian Revolution (Oct.–Nov.); Soviet troops invaded Hungary and crushed the liberal revolt while Western powers were mired in the Suez Crisis; Soviets subsequently adopted policy of "centralism" for East European satellites and condemned attempts at "revisionism."

1957   Eisenhower Doctrine articulated following Suez Crisis, in response to threat of Communist advance in Mideast (Jan.); Congress authorized both financial aid and use of troops in Mideast, if necessary.

1957   Treaty of Rome signed (Mar. 25), creating Common Market in Europe; marked major step toward integration of West European nations.

1957   Soviet space satellite Sputnik launched (Oct. 4) as world's first man-made earth satellite; Soviets now had important lead in race for technological superiority, while Western powers fretted about "missile gap"; space race began.

1957   Soviet Union tested the first Intercontinental Ballistic Missile (ICBM), posing new threat of massive nuclear attack that could be launched against US in minutes; US tested its first ICBM the following year; both nations began massive buildup of nuclear-tipped ICBMs, and missile attack replaced nuclear bombers as primary weapon in nuclear warfare strategy.

1957   British government shifted its basic military strategy; now to rely mainly on relatively inexpensive nuclear deterrent, instead of its conventional military forces.

1958   US president Eisenhower ordered intermediate-range missiles deployed in Turkey, Italy, and Britain; ordered US weapons development programs stepped up; created the National Aeronautics and Space Administration (NASA).

1958   China's chairman Mao Zedong ordered Great Leap Forward (May); resulted in staggering economic chaos and famine (1960–61) that killed six to seven million Chinese.

1958   Pro-West regime overthrown in Iraq by various factions, including Communists (June); Iraq aligned with anti-West Egypt, Syria, and Yemen; Lebanon hit by unrest next.

1958   US president Eisenhower ordered 5,000 US troops sent to Lebanon to help government restore order (July).

1958   French president C. de Gaulle instituted the French Fifth Republic; subsequently sought to establish France as an independent military and diplomatic power; exploded its first atomic bomb (1960); became an important force in Third World politics.

1959   In Cuba, rebel leader F. Castro seized Havana (Jan.) and set himself up as dictator; declared himself a Communist and nationalized US property there; Castro sought Soviet aid and thereafter became an important Soviet client-state just off the US coast; forced US to reassess Latin American policy.

1959   US vice-president R. Nixon on visit to the USSR; engaged in highly publicized Kitchen Debate with Khrushchev on merits of American and Soviet systems.

1959   Soviet leader N. Khrushchev toured the US (Sept.); hopes raised for Cold War "thaw"; in private talks, Eisenhower sought to halt arms race.

1960   Numerous former colonies in Africa gained independence about this time, providing a new arena for East-West Cold War competition; Congo crisis (from 1960) became the first, and a coup (1963) brought a pro-Communist government to power; thereafter both China and the USSR sought to influence the Congo.

1960   Sino-Soviet split began (July); Maoist China, angered by Soviet refusal to supply it with nuclear weapons and other slights, denounced Soviet "revisionism" of Marxist doctrine; Soviet advisers withdrawn and aid to China ended; USSR now threatened by NATO in West and fanatical Chinese in East; China and USSR thereafter competed for leadership of Communist world.

1960   U-2 Incident; Soviets downed US spy plane over Soviet territory (May 1); Paris summit canceled; new round of Cold War tensions began.

1960 US successfully tested Polaris missile in first underwater launch of IRBM; marked advent of submarine as key weapon in strategy of nuclear warfare; nuclear-powered submarines were constantly on move and hard to track, making it difficult to eliminate their missiles by a preemptive strike.

1960 In South Vietnam, National Liberation Front organized by Communists and other opponents seeking to overthrow the corrupt Diem regime and reunite North and South Vietnam (Dec.); both China and the USSR approved North Vietnam's planned takeover in the South (Dec.); war in South Vietnam now began in earnest.

1961–63 US president J. F. Kennedy in office; promoted "flexible response" to Communist aggression as opposed to "massive retaliation"; increased US defense budget by 30 percent to bolster conventional forces; nevertheless approved nuclear arms strategy based on Minuteman ICBMs, submarines armed with Polaris missiles, and long-range B-52 bombers; raised Cold War tensions over Cuba (1962) to the brink of nuclear war.

1961 US broke diplomatic relations with Cuba (Jan.).

1961 Alliance for Progress established by US president Kennedy to improve relations with Third World countries and combat Communism in South America; US substantially expanded foreign aid to other parts of the world.

1961 Soviet cosmonaut Y. Gagarin became first human to travel in space (Apr. 12); Soviets scored another major coup in the race for technological superiority, gaining international prestige for the Communist cause; US president Kennedy subsequently launched crash program to land humans on the moon by 1970.

1961 Bay of Pigs Invasion (Apr. 17); CIA-backed invasion of Cuba turned into fiasco; US deeply embarrassed by incident, which also brought Soviet pledge to defend Cuba in future.

1961 Vienna summit (June); Khrushchev threatened to give East Germany control over access to West Berlin; determined to defend the city, Kennedy retaliated by calling up US reservists.

1961 Berlin Wall erected (Aug. 13); East German and Soviet troops built the fortified wall to halt politically embarrassing flow of refugees to West Germany; wall soon became symbolic of Communist repression.

1962 American astronaut J. Glenn became the first American to orbit the earth (Feb. 20).

1962 Cuban Missile Crisis (Oct.); US spy planes detected Soviet missiles being installed in Cuba; US imposed naval quarantine of Cuba and threatened nuclear war if missiles were not removed; Soviet leader Khrushchev forced to order missiles removed.

1962 US advisers in Vietnam now numbered 11,000 (Dec.), as President Kennedy committed the US in Vietnam to test counterinsurgency and nation-building concepts.

1963 "Hot-line" telecommunications link between US and USSR installed to prevent a repetition of the Cuban Missile Crisis; Soviets, meanwhile, began massive peacetime military buildup that finally achieved (in the 1970s) nuclear parity with the US and made the USSR a major naval power as well.

1963 US, USSR, and Britain signed Nuclear Test Ban Treaty in Moscow ceremony (Aug. 5); underground testing was allowed, however, and nuclear arms race continued; US sought to maintain "mutual assured destruction," which theoretically made nuclear war unthinkable by both sides.

1963 US president Kennedy assassinated in Dallas, Texas (Nov. 22); years later allegations surfaced that Castro had arranged Kennedy's assassination in retaliation for CIA-backed assassination attempts against him.

1963–69 US president L. Johnson in office, succeeding Kennedy; continued many of Kennedy's policies and sharply increased US commitment in Vietnam War (from 1965).

1963 H. (Kim) Philby, unmasked as a master Soviet spy in Britain, escaped to USSR.

1964 China exploded its first atomic bomb; as new member of nuclear club, China now posed much greater threat to USSR.

1964 Khrushchev ousted from power (Oct. 14–15); fall caused by failure of his agricultural programs (notably the "virgin lands" scheme), Soviet humiliation in the Cuban Missile Crisis, and the Sino-Soviet split.

1964–82 L. Brezhnev became Soviet leader, though "collective leadership" was stressed at first; by early 1970s, era of détente with West brought what appeared to be a halt in the Cold War.

1965–73 US actively involved in Vietnam War; soon after inauguration to his first full term, President Johnson stepped up US involvement in Vietnam; ordered bombing of North (Feb., 1965); sent hundreds of thousands of US troops to Vietnam.

1965 President Johnson ordered US troops sent to the Dominican Republic to block leftist coup attempt; US remained committed to preventing spread of Communism in Latin America.

1965 In Indonesia, Gen. Sukarno approved brutal pro-Communist revolt (Oct., encouraged by China); move backfired, however, resulting in Sukarno's ouster and a bloody purge that included deaths of some 300,000 Communists; Communist movement in Indonesia destroyed.

1966 France, continuing its independent course, withdrew French forces from NATO (July); sought closer relations with USSR.

1966–69 Chinese society torn by radical Communist Cultural Revolution.

1967 Outer Space Treaty signed by US and USSR; banned weapons of mass destruction in space.

1967 Third Arab-Israeli War (June); US backed Israel, and the USSR backed Egypt, which it had been supplying with arms; Israel emerged victorious from the war, while the Soviets gained favor with Arab nations and other Third World states.

1968 Prague Spring (Aug.); Soviets led Warsaw Pact invasion of Czechoslovakia to halt liberalization of government; Soviets issued Brezhnev Doctrine, declaring right of military intervention against "counterrevolutionary" movements in Warsaw Pact nation; Soviet world prestige damaged by invasion of Czechoslovakia.

1968 US forced to begin seeking way out of Vietnam War following success of Tet offensive and widespread protests at home; US power and prestige declined as result of failure in war against Vietnamese Communists.

1969–74 US president R. Nixon in office; gradually effected US withdrawal from Vietnam; promoted détente and cultural exchanges to ease East-West tensions and adjust to reality

of America's declining power; normalized relations with Communist China; provided military support to targeted regional powers, making them local "policemen" and thereby shedding the US role of the "world's policeman."

1969 US landed first human on the moon (July 20); winning of space race reasserted American technological superiority and gave US world prestige a needed boost.

1969 Sino-Soviet tensions reached high point following many border clashes and massive Soviet military buildup (including nuclear weapons) along border with China; helped encourage Soviets to seek better relations with US through détente.

1969 March on Washington, massive anti-war protest (Nov. 15); demanded immediate, not gradual, withdrawal from Vietnam.

1969 Strategic Arms Limitation Talks between the US and the USSR began; Soviets had nearly achieved parity with US, but advent of ABMs and MIRV technology would threaten new arms race in the 1970s.

1969–79 Era of détente; US perceived détente as means of easing Cold War tensions and avoiding further brushfire wars, as well as possibly encouraging some change within the USSR; USSR saw détente, according to one observer, as opportunity to create a "world safe for historical change" (West was obliged to stop fighting Communism, while the Soviets could continue their campaign against capitalism, by supporting wars of liberation); these opposing perceptions eventually brought détente to an end.

1970s Multiple Independently–targetable Re-entry Vehicle (MIRV) developed; single missile now could deliver nuclear warheads to several different targets.

1970s Cuba became fully dependent on the USSR; Soviets subsidized Cuban economy to tune of $3 billion yearly through above-market sugar purchases and other deals.

1970 In Chile, pro-Communist S. Allende elected president; he established close ties with Cuba, but severe economic problems weakened his regime and led to his overthrow by a military coup (1973), in which the CIA was involved.

1970 West Germany, promoting closer relations with Communist Eastern Europe (*Ostpoli-*

tik), concluded treaty with USSR renouncing use of force (Dec.); West Germany later recognized East Germany (1972).

1971 Soviets supported India against US-backed Pakistan in war over Bangladesh; Soviets further cemented relations with India by concluding 20-year friendship treaty.

1971 Ping-Pong diplomacy; responding to US overtures, Chinese invited US table tennis team to play in China (Apr.); secret talks followed, and China was soon admitted to the UN (Nov.).

1972 US president Nixon visited China (Feb. 21–27); process of normalization of relations with China continued as US sought to take advantage of Sino-Soviet split.

1972 President Nixon on historic first presidential visit to USSR (May 22–June 1); signed SALT I agreement, limiting antiballistic missile systems (ABMs) and the number of ICBM missile launchers for both sides; also signed agreements formalizing terms of détente, following negotiations in which Soviets had explicitly refused to stop supporting "wars of liberation."

1972 Relations between Egypt and the USSR soured; Soviet personnel asked to leave country in major setback for Soviet Mideast policy.

1972 SALT II talks began with USSR.

1972 USSR forced to buy grain from the West following bad harvests.

1973 Brezhnev visited US; held talks with US president Nixon.

1973 US involvement in Vietnam War halted by peace agreement signed at Paris (Jan. 27); last US troops withdrawn (Mar.).

1973 Fourth Arab-Israeli War (Oct.); USSR threatened to intervene on behalf of Egyptians; US responded by calling worldwide nuclear alert.

1973 East and West Germany both admitted to the UN.

1973–77 H. Kissinger served as US secretary of state.

1973–74 Nixon-Brezhnev summits failed to produce significant agreements on arms limitation.

1974 Nobel Prize-winning author A. Solzhenitsyn forced to leave USSR as a dissident (Feb.); underscored issue of human rights abuses in the USSR.

1974 Trade agreement with US concluded; Soviet emigration policies eased as part of the deal.

1974 Watergate crisis in US climaxed with President Nixon's resignation (Aug.); crisis resulted in Congressional constraints on presidential powers and furthered decline of US power and prestige.

1974–77 US president G. Ford in office; Congressional opposition to US involvement overseas severely limited Ford's options in containing spread of Communism; meanwhile, in Africa, Communist governments came to power in Ethiopia (1974), Angola (1975–76) and Mozambique (1975).

1975 In Cambodia, Communist Khmer Rouge seized capital (Jan.); instituted reign of terror in which an estimated 1.2 million were killed before an invasion by the Vietnamese toppled the regime.

1975 Last Americans evacuated from South Vietnam (Apr. 29) as North Vietnamese completed successful invasion of South; Vietnam united under Communist rule soon after.

1975 Cambodians captured US cargo ship in *Mayaguez* Incident (May 12).

1975 Helsinki Accords agreed to by USSR and 34 other nations attending Helsinki summit on European affairs.

1976 Chinese Communist leader Mao Zedong died (Sept.); his successors began moving away from radical Communist ideology, eventually even instituting some capitalistic economic reforms.

1977–81 US president J. Carter in office; US foreign policy, stressing human rights issues, seen as weak and vacillating during this period, though Carter administration established full diplomatic relations with China (Jan., 1979) and brokered historic Egyptian-Israeli peace treaty (Sept. 1978).

1978 Research programs for building neutron bomb reported delayed by both US and USSR.

1979 Nuclear accident at Three Mile Island power plant in US (Mar. 28) heightened public awareness of dangers of nuclear power.

1979 US and USSR signed SALT II agreement on arms limitation (June); ratification held up by Senate concern about Soviet expansionism in Third World; both nations informally observed agreement until 1987, when US abandoned deployment limits.

1979–1981 Hostage crisis (Nov.); following ouster of pivotal US ally in Mideast, Shah of Iran, Muslim fundamentalists in Iran seized 52 US embassy workers and humiliated the US by holding them hostage until Jan. 20, 1981.

1979 Soviet invasion (Dec.) of Afghanistan to support puppet regime there; Soviets, unable to defeat Afghan guerrillas, suffered humiliating defeat in which they were obliged to withdraw from Afghanistan (1989).

1979 US agreed to requests from West European governments for deployment of new US missiles (cruise and Pershing II); would balance some 900 new SS-20 missiles deployed by USSR.

1980 US president Carter ordered (Jan. 4) embargo on grain shipments to the Soviet Union in response to Soviet invasion of Afghanistan; promised to defend Persian Gulf nations (Carter Doctrine); détente effectively ended.

c1980 Cruise missiles developed; guided by extremely sophisticated onboard equipment, the missiles achieved astonishing accuracy and could fly in under radar detection systems to deliver conventional or nuclear warheads.

1980–82 Solidarity crisis in Poland; labor unions briefly defied Poland's Communist regime; USSR backed away from threats of invasion.

1981–89 US president R. Reagan in office; promoted buildup of US military and sought to restore US power and prestige in world affairs.

1981 President Reagan ordered economic sanctions imposed against the Soviet Union for its part in the crackdown against Solidarity in Poland.

1981 President Reagan increased US involvement in El Salvador; US, charging Nicaragua with aiding Salvadoran rebels, cut off aid (Jan.); Nicaragua countered (1982) by charging US with supporting Contra rebels seeking overthrow of Sandinista government.

1981 US lifted embargo on Soviet grain purchases (Apr.).

1981 Reagan administration abandoned plans for controversial mobile MX missiles (Oct.).

1982 Demonstration (June 12) in New York City, the largest to date, in which an esti-

mated 750,000 participated, protesting nuclear arms race.

1982 Strategic Arms Reduction Talks (START) began between the US and USSR.

1982–84 Soviet leader Y. Andropov, former KGB head, in power following death of Brezhnev (Nov.); campaigned against production inefficiency and corruption, which had seriously weakened the Soviet economy; died in office (Feb. 1984).

1983 President Reagan proposed his Strategic Defense Initiative (SDI) program, dubbed Star Wars (Mar.).

1983 Soviets shot down South Korean airliner for violating its airspace (Sept.), killing 269 persons; Soviet image abroad badly tarnished by this action.

1983 US invaded Grenada (Oct.) to block takeover attempt by faction of extremist revolutionary Communists with ties to Cuba (Oct. 31); troops withdrawn after restoring previous moderate leftist government.

1984–85 Soviet leader K. Chernenko in power, following death of Andropov (Feb.); continued attempts to end corruption and inefficiency; died in office (Mar.), forcing an unprecedented third major change in Soviet leadership in three years.

1985–91 Soviet leader M. Gorbachev in power; began wide-ranging liberal reform of government (1986); his reforms soon unleashed a torrent of demands for the ouster of Communists and for democratic government, in the end bringing on the collapse of the Communist-bloc governments (1989–90) and finally the USSR itself (1991).

1985 Geneva summit (Nov.) between Reagan and Gorbachev; marked start of good relations between two leaders; they concluded agreement banning chemical weapons and ordered resumption of cultural exchanges (halted in 1979).

1986 Gorbachev, proclaiming need for drastic reform of Soviet society before 27th Congress of the Communist party (Feb.), announced need for *glasnost* (openness) as a key to effecting the changes; era of Gorbachev's liberal reforms began.

1986 Chernobyl nuclear accident (Apr.) in USSR; government withheld public warnings about radioactive fallout resulting from reactor fire; radioactive cloud spread over Ukraine and parts of Europe; Soviet mishandling of the emergency widely criticized.

1986 Iceland summit conference (Oct.); Gorbachev and Reagan discussed disarmament proposals; Reagan refused to reduce US Star Wars (SDI) program, however; no new agreements reached.

1986 In the US, the Iran-Contra scandal broke (Nov.); US foreign policy crippled by controversy (into 1987).

1986 USSR passed laws to foster private enterprise in certain areas of the economy (Nov., to take effect May, 1987); marked first break in state's legal monopoly of economy.

1987 Gorbachev proposed policy of *perestroika* (restructuring), the second key principle (with *glasnost*) of his wide-ranging reform program (Jan.).

1987 USSR and China agreed to negotiate long-standing border dispute (Aug.); marked beginning of improved Sino-Soviet relations.

1987 Civil wars in Nicaragua and El Salvador ended; Nicaragua's pro-Communist government voted out of office in free elections (1990).

1987 Intermediate Nuclear Forces (INF) Treaty signed at Washington, D.C., summit between Reagan and Gorbachev (Dec.); first treaty to eliminate whole class of weapons (all short- and medium-range nuclear weapons).

1988 Moscow summit (May–June); INF treaty formally activated; talks on Strategic Arms Reduction Treaty (START) stalled over question of SDI program in US.

1988 Gorbachev's regime rocked by nationalist unrest in the Baltic States (Aug.) and outbreaks of ethnic violence elsewhere in the USSR.

1989–93 US president G. Bush in office; presided over the end of the Cold War and normalization of relations with the former USSR.

1989 In the USSR, Gorbachev engineered purge of older hard-line Communists (Apr.), replacing them with reformers.

1989 US Strategic Defense Initiative (SDI) space satellite successfully tracked test missiles launched on earth's surface.

1989 USSR-China summit held in Beijing (May); Gorbachev arrived amid demonstrations leading up to Tiananmen Square massacre (May), which severely damaged China's image abroad.

1989 Gorbachev, visiting Germany, publicly reversed long-standing interventionist Brezhnev Doctrine; declared that states have right to political self-determination (June).

1989 President Bush proposed expanding discussions on nuclear weapons to include reductions in conventional forces in Europe (June).

1989 Berlin Wall, long-standing symbol of Cold War East-West divisions, was torn down (Nov.); collapse of all East European Communist governments began as economic ills and pro-democracy demands overwhelmed the hard-line regimes.

1989 Lithuanian Communist party voted to secede from USSR (Dec.); Gorbachev, while upholding right of secession, insisted on preliminary discussions; Baltic liberation movement eventually contributed to collapse of USSR.

1989 Malta summit (Dec.); Bush and Gorbachev discussed 50% nuclear arms reduction, major reductions in US-USSR conventional forces in Europe, trade deals, and the withdrawal of the USSR from Eastern Europe.

1990 Gorbachev elected president by secret ballot in Congress (Mar. 14); election gave Gorbachev mandate for sweeping reforms, as pro-democracy demands mounted in the USSR.

1990 Washington summit (May–June); Bush and Gorbachev declared the Cold War over; discussed Soviet blockade of breakaway Republic of Lithuania; signed trade accord contingent on Soviets' relaxing their emmigration laws.

1990 US and other major Western powers agreed to help USSR shift to market economy (July); promised economic aid and technical expertise.

1990 The USSR, the US, Britain, and France agreed to reunification of Germany (Sept.); Germany formally reunified, resolving a long-standing source of Cold War tensions.

1990 Treaty on Conventional Armed Forces in Europe (CFE) signed in Paris (Nov.) by NATO and Warsaw Pact members; reflected Soviet withdrawal from Eastern Europe; put limits on conventional forces deployed between Atlantic Ocean and Ural Mountains.

1990 Charter proclaiming end to post-World War II era of confrontation in Europe was signed by Bush, Gorbachev, and representatives of 32 other nations (Nov.); set up secretariat for Conference on Security and Cooperation in Europe (CSCE).

1991 Warsaw Pact disbanded (Mar.); Soviet troops to be withdrawn from Germany, Hungary, and Czechoslavakia; US to cut troop strength in Europe by half over next five years (May).

1991 Moscow summit (July 30–31); historic START treaty signed by Gorbachev and President Bush (July 31); called for first-ever reduction in long-range nuclear arms amounting to 30% of stockpiles by 1998; US granted USSR most-favored-nation trading status.

1991 USSR collapsed (Aug.); coup attempt by hard-line Communists failed and the constituent republics declared independence from the USSR; B. Yeltsin emerged as leading political figure; Communist party officially suppressed; republics formed loosely knit Commonwealth of Independent States (Dec.); US now the world's lone superpower.

1991 Independence of Baltic States (Estonia, Latvia, Lithuania) officially approved (Sept. 6).

1991 Gorbachev announced withdrawal of 11,000 Soviet troops from Cuba (Sept.).

1991 US president Bush ended round-the-clock alert for Strategic Air Command (SAC) long-range bombers armed with nuclear weapons (Sept. 27).

1991 Gorbachev formally resigned as USSR president (Dec. 25).

1991 USSR Supreme Soviet voted end to 1922 treaty forming the USSR (Dec. 26).

1992 US president Bush pledged to help finance $24 billion aid package for former Soviet Union (Apr.).

1992 Four newly independent Soviet republics agreed to honor cuts in nuclear missiles agreed to in 1991 US-Soviet treaty (May).

1992 US and Russia agreed to cut long-range nuclear missile arsenals by two-thirds (June).

1992 US completed withdrawal of all tactical nuclear weapons from around the world, in accordance with 1991 agreement (July).

Cole, Thomas *See* **Hudson River school.**

Coleridge, Samuel Taylor 1772–1834. A leading English Romantic poet and critic. Once called a "damaged archangel" by C. Lamb, Coleridge wrote his most important poems dur-

ing his friendship with W. Wordsworth (1797–c1802). Together they published (1798) *Lyrical Ballads,* an important work in the English Romantic movement which contained Coleridge's famous "Rime of the Ancient Mariner." Coleridge also wrote during this period the poems "Kubla Khan," "Christabel," and "Dejection: An Ode." Addicted to opium by 1800, he moved to London (1816), where the habit was brought under control and he completed his notable *Biographia Literaria.*

Colet, John 1467?–1519. British theologian. A leading humanist and scholar, he influenced such scholars as D. Erasmus and T. More, and founded (1509) St. Paul's School in London.

Colette 1873–1954. French novelist, whose works are noted for their minute observation and descriptive intensity. Among her works is the novel *Gigi.*

Coligny, Gaspard de 1519–72. Soldier and prominent French Huguenot. Fearful of Coligny's influence over the young King Charles IX, Catherine de Médicis instigated his murder in the St. Bartholomew's Day Massacre.

Coliseum *See* **Colosseum.**

collectivism Economic system that advocates control of the means of production by groups of workers or the state rather than by the individual.

Collins, Michael 1890–1922. A leader of the Irish Republican Army. A member of the Sinn Fein, he negotiated a treaty (1921) with the British giving Ireland dominion status but was assassinated by extremist revolutionaries.

Collins, Michael 1930– . American astronaut. He guided the command module of the Apollo 11 mission, during which N. Armstrong and E. Aldrin became the first two men to set foot on the moon (July 20, 1969).

Collins, William Wilkie 1824–89. English author, the first Briton to write detective novels. He wrote *The Woman in White* and *The Moonstone.*

Collodi, Carlo (*pseud.* of Carlo Lorenzini) 1826–90. Italian author. A journalist by profession, Collodi wrote many children's tales, including the classic *Pinocchio* (1883).

Colombia Republic located in northwestern South America. The population is 32,598,000 and the capital is Bogotá. Colombia's coast was first explored (1502) by C. Columbus and Spanish settlements were established in the area soon after. In the early 18th cent. the area, known as New Granada, was incorporated into the larger viceroyalty of New Granada and in 1819 was liberated from Spanish rule by S. Bolívar's victory at Boyacá. Much of Colombia's modern history has been marked by conflict between conservative and liberal factions, which have sought to determine the nation's political character. Key dates in the history of Colombia include:

1538 G. Jiménez de Quesada conquered Colombia for Spain, founded Bogotá.

EARLY 16TH CENT. Audencia of New Granada, including area of modern Colombia, established.

1717–39 New Granada joined with areas later forming modern Ecuador, Panama, and Venezuela to form viceroyalty of New Granada.

1780–81 Revolt of the *comuneros* presaged independence movement.

1810 Uprising in Bogotá (July 20); marked beginning of New Granada's war for independence.

1819 S. Bolívar's victory (Aug. 7) in the Battle of Boyacá secured the independence of New Granada Audencia from Spanish rule.

1819 New nation of Greater Colombia (Gran Colombia) proclaimed; included New Granada, Ecuador (after 1822), Panama, and Venezuela.

1821 New constitution adopted; Bolívar became first president of Greater Colombia.

1831 Greater Colombia dissolved (1830); New Granada, including area of modern Panama, became republic of New Granada; struggle began between Conservatives, favoring strong central government and Roman Catholic church, and Liberals, favoring federalism and anticlericalism.

1834 First recorded export of Colombian coffee; coffee industry expanded slowly; coffee did not become important export until late 19th cent.

1851–52 Slavery abolished.

1858 Provinces of New Granada reorganized as independent states within confederation known as Granadina.

1863 Civil war between Liberal and Conservative factions broke out (1861); victorious liberals formed United States of Colombia.

1867–80 Period of civil wars between Liberal and Conservative factions; conflict ended by election (1880) of R. Núñez, a moderate, as president, and formation of a liberal-conservative coalition.

1885 Liberal uprising against federal government defeated.

1886 Republic of Colombia established; abolished sovereign states in favor of central government; Roman Catholic church made state church.

1899–1902 Colombia plunged into civil war; Conservative faction regained power after three years of conflict.

1903 Hay-Herrán Treaty negotiated to establish US control over what was to become the Panama Canal Zone; treaty rejected by Colombian Congress.

1903 Uprising in Panama; US sent troops to aid Panamanians against Colombia; US recognized Panamanian independence and soon after completed treaty with Panamanians for Panama Canal.

1914 Thomson-Urrutia Treaty negotiated; Colombia recognized Panamanian independence and received special privileges in the Canal Zone and an indemnity from the US.

1927 Federacafe organized by government to promote Colombian coffee industry and to support prices.

1930 Liberals in power for the first time in over two decades, held presidency until 1946 though reform programs failed to solve the social and economic problems.

1941 WW II; Colombia joined the Allies.

1948 Liberal leader Jorge Eliécer Gaitán assassinated in Bogotá (Apr. 9); led to violent conflict in Bogotá and elsewhere in Colombia.

1948–58 La Violencia; violence in Bogotá marked the beginning of period of civil unrest and repressive rule that resulted in the deaths of some 200,000 persons.

1950 Liberal party withdrew from presidential election (1949); conservative Laureano Gómez became president.

1953 G. Rojas Pinilla seized power in military coup.

1957 Military junta ousted Rojas Pinilla, ending his brutal and corrupt reign as dictator.

1957 National Front, a Liberal-Conservative coalition, formed; coalition formed to end unrest and was to remain in effect until 1974 with Conservative and Liberal presidents alternating every four years (from 1958).

1962 Colombia joined International Coffee Agreement, international group to set coffee export quotas.

1958   Alberto Lleras Camargo elected National Front president.

1966–70 National Front president Carlos Lleras Restrepo in office; his highly successful administration put through political reforms and greatly improved the economy.

1974–78 Liberal President Alfonso López Michelsen in office following first free elections in over 20 years.

1978   Liberal President Julio César Turbay Ayala in office.

1981   Government captured or killed top leaders of M-19 urban guerrilla group; offer of amnesty for followers failed.

1982–86 Belisario Betancur Cuartas, a Conservative, in office as president.

1984   President Batancur established a Peace Commission to negotiate with guerrilla groups; cease-fire signed (Aug. 24) between Betancur and guerrilla groups M-19 and Popular Liberation Army (ELP); truce broken by M-19 (June, 1985).

1984   Minister of Justice, Rodrigo Lara Bonilla, assassinated by cocaine traffickers (May).

1985   Eruption of volcano Nevado del Ruiz (Nov. 14) caused mudslides that killed over 25,000 persons.

1986–90 President Virgilio Barco Vargas, a Liberal, in office.

1987–88 Competition between Medellín and Cali cocaine cartels escalated into open warfare; some 15 percent of Colombia's population said to be involved in drug trade.

1989   Liberal party presidential candidate Luis Carlos Galan assassinated by Medellín cartel (Aug. 18); Medellín cartel declared "total and absolute war" against the Colombian government (Aug. 24), continuing a wave of bombings, kidnappings, and assassinations.

1990   Guerrilla group M-19 signed new peace treaty with government (Mar. 9); M-19 participated in elections for first time.

1990–   President César Gaviria Trujillo, a Liberal, in office (Aug.).

1990   Constituent Assembly elected to reform constitution of 1886 (Dec. 9).

1991   Leader of Medellín cartel, Pablo Escobar Gaviria, surrendered to authorities (June 19); Escobar incarcerated at special estate-like prison near his hometown of Envigado; government criticized for lenient treatment of Escobar.

1991   Constituent Assembly voted changes in Colombian constitution of 1886 (June 19), banning extradition of Colombian nationals (a ban which encouraged Escobar's surrender), reducing size of legislature, and allowing civil divorce in Roman Catholic marriages.

1992   Escobar escaped from prison (July 22); declared renewed "war" against Colombian government.

colonialism   Policy or program by which a state seeks political or economic control over other territories. In ancient times the Phoenicians, Greeks, and Romans all established colonies to expand their trade and culture, often populating them with their own citizens. In medieval times, especially the 13th cent., Italian city-states such as Venice and Genoa followed the same pattern. During the 15th to 17th cents., Portugal, Spain, England, France, and the Netherlands all established extensive colonial empires, both in the New World and in the East. By the 18th cent., however, Britain had acquired control of India, Canada, and other territories and, despite loss of the American colonies, ranked as the greatest European colonial power. France lost one colonial empire in the 18th-cent. colonial wars with Britain and acquired another empire in Africa in the 19th cent. The efforts of Japan, Germany, and Italy to become colonial powers in the late 19th and early 20th cents. contributed to the outbreak of both WW I and WW II. In the Spanish-American War, the US acquired Caribbean territories and the Philippines. The breakup of the Spanish and Portuguese empires in South America began in the early 19th cent., when most colonies there won independence. The main period of decolonization, however, began after WW I, when colonial rule came to be considered temporary and necessary only for the development of the colony. Decolonization proceded rapidly after WW II, when colonial empires broke up and former colonies gained independence. (*See also* imperialism.)

Colonna, Oddone   *See* **Martin V.**

Colorado   West-central state of the US, the 38th state. The territory was first explored and claimed by the Spanish (18th cent.) and the French. The eastern, French portion, was sold to the US with the Louisiana Purchase (1803), and the rest was ceded by Mexico in the Treaty of Guadalupe Hidalgo (1848). Settlers came in great numbers with the discovery of gold at Cherry Creek (1858). Colorado became a territory (1861), and statehood was granted in 1876.

Colosseum (Coliseum) Amphitheater situated in Rome, the scene of gladiatorial combat and, by tradition, the arena for Christian martyrdom. Completed in AD 80, it could seat about 50,000.

Colossus of Rhodes Massive bronze statue of the sun god Helios that stood in the harbor of Rhodes (Greece) (280–c225 BC). One of the Seven Wonders of the World, it was destroyed by an earthquake.

Colt, Samuel 1814–62. American arms developer who invented (1835) the first successful revolving-magazine pistol, the Colt revolver.

Columba, Saint (Columcille) 521–597. Irish priest and saint. He established a monastery in Scotland (565), from which he spread Christianity throughout central and southern Scotland.

Columbia The world's first reusable space ship, called the "space shuttle." Despite minor malfunctions, it flew into the earth's orbit in both April and November, 1981, and glided back safely, landing at Edwards Air Force Base, California. Further successful flights were made in March and July 1982.

Columbus, Bartholomew *See* **Santo Domingo.**

Columbus, Christopher 1451–1506. Genoese navigator in the service of Spain, credited with the discovery (1492) of America. Though the Vikings are believed to have previously landed (c1000) in North America, it was Columbus' voyage that opened the great epoch of European exploration and colonization in the New World. Columbus became an experienced navigator while serving the Genoese and Portuguese, and his idea of sailing west to Asia was not new. It was not until 1492, however, that the Spanish monarchs Ferdinand and Isabella agreed to support his venture. He left Spain (Aug. 3, 1492) with three ships, (the *Santa María, Niña* and *Pinta*) and landed on the island of San Salvador in the Bahamas Oct. 12, just over two months later. Believing he had reached islands east of Japan, he briefly explored the Caribbean and then returned to Spain later in October. Three other voyages followed (1493, 1498, 1502), on which he discovered other Caribbean islands and reached the South American coast. Unable to adequately administer the Spanish colony in the New World he was removed as governor (1500), and died

shortly after his disastrous fourth voyage (1502–04).

Columcille, Saint *See* **Columba, Saint.**

Comanche Indians North American Indian tribe. A nomadic offshoot of the northern Shoshone Indians, they moved south and established themselves (18th cent.) as the dominant group in the southern Great Plains. Noted for their excellent horsemanship and skill in combat, they successfully defended their lands against settlers for many years. They were finally defeated, and relocated on reservations in Oklahoma after several bloody engagements in the 1870s.

Combes, Émile 1835–1921. French politician. As premier (1902–05), he brought about the separation of church and state.

Combination Acts British antiunion laws. The Combination Acts of 1799 and 1800 outlawed trade unions and punished those who joined or aided them. The laws were repealed in 1824, restored the next year, and then ignored.

Comenius, John Amos 1592–1670. Czech clergyman and noted educational reformer. He is known best for his *Didactica magna*, which sets forth his theory of universal education for men and women.

Commager, Henry Steele 1902– . American historian. Commager's numerous works include *The American Mind, The Era of Reform, The Blue and the Gray,* and *Majority Rule and Minority Rights.*

Committee of Public Safety French revolutionary committee, set up by the National Convention (Apr. 6, 1793) to supervise the executive bodies of the Convention. From July, 1793 to July, 1794, the Committee ruled France, mobilized the nation, and instituted the Reign of Terror under the domination of its principal member, M. Robespierre. Robespierre was overthrown July, 1794, but the Committee continued, much weakened, until establishment of the Directory (1795).

Committees of Correspondence Committees set up (1763–75) by towns, cities, and legislatures in Colonial America. Formed originally to communicate with other American colonies about opposition to British laws (Sugar Act, Stamp Act), they helped promote Colonial unity and organization of the Continental Congress. Notable among them were the Boston committee, formed (1772) by S. Adams; and the Virginia committee (formed 1773), on which T. Jefferson and P. Henry served. The Boston committee directed the Boston Tea Party (1773).

Commodus AD 161–192. Roman emperor (AD 180–192), successor to his father, Marcus Aurelius. On his father's death, Commodus cut short his military campaign against the Germans and began a life of dissipation in Rome. He was strangled by an arena wrestler named Narcissus.

common law Term applied to the legal system prevalent in England and in other countries orginally colonized by England. It is based upon a history of judicial precedent in which court decisions were derived from common custom and reason rather than statutes.

Common Market *See* **European Economic Community.**

Commonweal of Christ *See* **Coxey's Army.**

commonwealth Term for an organized community that exists through consent of the governed. The term was frequently used by such 17th-cent. political theorists as T. Hobbes and J. Locke. In English history, the term "commonwealth" refers to the period (1649–53) when the English monarchy was abolished and England governed as a commonwealth. (*See also* Protectorate.)

Commonwealth of Independent States (*formerly* Union of Soviet Socialist Republics; Russia) Country located in Europe and Asia, extending from Eastern Europe across the entire northern part of the Asian continent to the Pacific Ocean. Its capital is Moscow. Traditionally, the history of the Russian state begins in the 9th cent. with Rurik, a Scandinavian invader who established a petty kingdom at Novgorod in northwestern Russia. It was not until the 14th cent., however, that the Duchy of Moscow began its rise as the nucleus of the modern Russian state. The grand dukes of Moscow steadily added to their domains and in the mid-16th cent. Ivan IV the Terrible became the first to call himself "tsar" of Russia. Thereafter Russian expansionism pushed the borders eastward into Siberia and southward into Persian and Ottoman domains. By the 19th cent. Russia had become a major European power (especially after repulsing Napoleon's invasion) and had acquired vast territories. But late emancipation of serfs (1861), oppressive conditions of the poor, failure to enact reforms, and defeats in WW I led to the spread of radicalism and the Revolution of 1917. The revolution brought the Bolsheviks to power and thereby created the first Communist state. In the years before WW II, Communists sought to consolidate their hold over Russia (renamed Union of Soviet Socialist Republics in 1922) and to rebuild the economy. The Soviets emerged from WW II as a leading world power (with the US). In subsequent years the Soviets engaged the Western powers in the Cold War, a protracted political rivalry. By the early 1970s the USSR and the US began a rapprochement (détente) aimed at easing Cold War tensions through international cooperation. The program was largely successful in the 1970s and cultural and economic relations between Communist and non-Communist nations were significantly improved. However, the Soviet invasion of Afghanistan (1979) and policies toward Poland in the early 1980s soured US–USSR relations, delivering a setback to the policy of détente. Following M. Gorbachev's rise to power in 1985, the USSR entered a new period of liberalization and reform that, coupled with chronic economic problems and the spread of popular pro-democracy movements, led to the fall of Communist governments in Eastern Europe and finally to the collapse of the Soviet Union itself. While proponents for greater democratic freedoms in the USSR had made considerable gains by mid-1991, an attempted coup by hard-line Communists in Aug., 1991 brought on the final collapse of the USSR and the suppression of the Communist party, which had ruled the country since the 1917 revolution. The individual republics making up the USSR proclaimed independence and later in 1991, 11 of the 15 original republics formed a loose federation, the Commonwealth of Independent States. The former Soviet republics were: the Russian Federation (including Siberia), Belorussia, the Ukraine, Georgia, Estonia, Latvia, Lithuania, Moldavia, Armenia, Azerbaijan, Kazakhstan, Turkmenia, Uzbekistan, Tajikistan, and Kirghizia. *See* 1991 in the following chronology for member states of the new federation (CIS). **For more on important persons and major events,** *see* separate entries. Key events in the history of what is now the Commonwealth of Independent States include:

6TH–8TH CENTS. AD Avars, nomadic people from the Caucasus, ruled empire embracing much of what became modern Russia.

9TH CENT. AD Northwestern Russia occupied by the Eastern Slavs, who had long occupied the region; Khazars, a Turkic people, controlled region to the south (from 7th cent AD).

9TH–10TH CENTS. Varangians, Scandinavian conquerors, invaded Rus'.

862 Rurik, a Varangian, established control over Novgorod (near Baltic, in western Russia); founded Rurik dynasty of later Russian rulers.

879–912 Oleg reigned; expanded Varangian domains to include Kiev; moved capital to Kiev (c882); united Eastern Slavs in region and laid foundation of Kievan Rus', which eventually included vast domains lying between the Baltic and Black seas.

911 Oleg concluded commercial treaty with Byzantine Empire; subsequent contact with Byzantines greatly influenced development of Russian culture.

945–972 Sviatoslav reigned as duke of Kiev; greatly expanded domains and brought duchy to height of its power.

980–1015 Vladimir I reigned; made Christianity (Orthodox Eastern) the state religion (c988).

1019–54 Yaroslav reigned; duchy of Kiev divided among his heirs at his death; control of duchy subsequently rotated among heirs; led to period of wars and collapse of Kievan Rus'.

1185 Prince Igor defeated in battle that was celebrated in first work of Russian literature, *The Song of Igor's Campaign* (c1187).

12TH CENT. Autonomous principalities emerged from collapse of Kievan Rus'; Novgorod, Vladimir, Suzdal, Smolensk, and (later) Moscow emerged as powerful cities loosely united by common heritage.

c1147 Moscow founded.

1223 First Mongol invasion; armies of Genghis Khan defeated forces of Russian principalities at battle of Kalka River; Mongols withdrew immediately afterward.

1237–40 Second Mongol invasion, led by Batu Khan; Russian cities in south and west (Kiev among them) taken and destroyed; Novgorod in the north bypassed.

1240 Novgorod attacked by invading Swedes; Alexander Nevsky became Russian national hero by defeating Swedes at the Battle of the Neva.

1240s Poland and duchy of Lithuania expanded into Russian domains, taking control of western parts (what became Belorus and the Ukraine).

1242 Novgorod attacked by Teutonic Knights; Alexander Nevsky defeated them at the Battle of Lake Peipus.

1242 Empire of the Golden Horde established; dominated Russia from the south until 1480.

1246–63 Alexander Nevsky ruled as grand duke of Novgorod; accepted suzerainty of Golden Horde as protection against further invasions.

1300s Rise of Moscow, in the principality of Vladimir, as a powerful city, due partly to its position as a trade center.

1328–41 Ivan I reigned as duke of Moscow; became collector of Russian tribute paid to Mongols and thus gained great wealth; helped make Moscow the residence of the metropolitan see of the Russian church.

1359–89 Dmitry reigned as duke of Moscow; began revolt against Mongol overlords; ceased practice of dividing domains among heirs.

1380 Battle of Kulikovo; Demetrius defeated the Mongols.

1389–1425 Vasily reigned as grand duke of Moscow; struggle for succession broke out on his death.

1392–98 Tamerlane invaded the Empire of the Golden Horde and reached the borders of the Russian principalities; Golden Horde declined steadily thereafter.

1453 Fall of Constantinople to the Ottoman Turks; Moscow proclaimed successor to Rome and Constantinople as new center of the Orthodox church and "Third Rome."

1462–1505 Ivan III the Great reigned; adopted autocratic style of rule; greatly expanded domains and began drive to unite domains of Eastern Slavs; exploited divisions between Tatar khans.

1472 Ivan married Sophia, niece of the last Byzantine emperor; she is said to have convinced him to adopt Byzantine ways of government.

1474 Rostov captured.

1478 Ivan conquered Novgorod and added its extensive domains to the Grand Duchy of Moscow.

1485 Tver, a powerful rival, was conquered by Ivan.

1497 First code of laws promulgated by Ivan.

1497–1502 Period of civil war over right of succession; Vasily III won.

1505–33 Vasily III reigned as grand duke; greatly strengthened the monarchy; continued expansion, adding Pskov (1510), Smolensk (1514) and Riazan (1521); emergence of bureaucracy.

1533–84 Ivan IV the Terrible reigned; both cruel and mentally unstable, he became the first to call himself "tsar" (caesar, 1547); greatly expanded Russian domains and consolidated powers of the monarchy at the expense of the boyars (nobles); instituted reign of terror (from c1565).

1552–56 Tatar khanates of Kazan and Astrakhan conquered (1552, 1556), beginning eastward expansion of Russia.

1558–82 Livonian War fought; Russia ultimately forced to renounce claims to Livonia.

1565 Ivan set up *oprichnina* (crown land) under his direct control.

1566 First national assembly called by Ivan.

1581–82 Conquest of Siberia begun for the tsar by the Cossack chief Yermak; eastward expansion at the expense of the Mongols continued.

1584–98 Fedor I reigned as tsar; the last of the Rurik dynasty; incompetent and unable to rule; government run by Boris Godunov, his brother-in-law.

1589 Orthodox patriarchate of Moscow given formal status.

1591 Death of Dmitry, heir to the throne; Godunov believed to have arranged murder to secure his succession.

1597 Serfdom established by law.

1598–1605 Boris Godunov reigned as tsar; chosen by nobles as tsar; successfully concluded brief war with Sweden; popular distrust of him spread, particularly after famine followed crop failures of 1601–02; Time of Troubles began just before his death.

1604–13 Time of Troubles; period of social and political chaos began with revolt led by pretender, Dmitry, who claimed to be heir to Rurik line; Dmitry, made tsar (1605) after Godunov's death, was murdered by boyars; ensuing period marked by appearance of new pretenders, peasant revolts, and invasions by Sweden and Poland (Moscow occupied 1610–12); Orthodox church headed patriotic movement to drive out Poles; and Michael Romanov elected tsar (1613).

1613–45 Michael Romanov reigned; founded Romanov line; on his accession country was in ruins, with many areas still held by Swedes, Poles, and rebels; order gradually restored and agreements concluded with Sweden (1617) and Poland (1618); government bureaucracy, which had survived Time of Troubles, aided recovery.

1613–1917 Romanov dynasty ruled Russia.

1645–76 Alexis reigned as tsar; reign marked by promulgation of new law code (1648) that continued serfdom and by acquisition of the eastern Ukraine.

1652–66 Nikon reigned as patriarch of the Russian Orthodox church; introduced reforms to bring Russian rites into conformity with Byzantine rite and thus provoked schism and persecution of Old Believers, who favored Russian tradition; attempts to assert supremacy of church over tsar led to his downfall.

1654 Uprising by Zaporozhian Cossacks in Ukraine against Polish rule; Cossacks sought Russian aid.

1654–67 Thirteen Years' War with Poland; Russians, taking advantage of Cossack uprising, gained the eastern Ukraine and Kiev.

1656–61 War with Sweden; Russia failed to gain control of Baltic territories.

1670–71 Revolt by Don Cossacks, peasants, and Old Believers, led by S. Razin; crushed by Tsar Alexis's forces.

1676–82 Fëdor III reigned; ended system of military and civil appointments on basis of social rank; began wars against Ottoman Turks.

1676–81 Russo-Turkish War; Russians gained most of Turkish Ukraine.

1681–1736 Russian Orthodox reformer Feofan Prokopovich lived; aided Tsar Peter the Great in bringing the church under control of the monarchy.

1682–1725 Peter I the Great reigned; made Russia a European power; his reign was dominated by his efforts to modernize and Westernize Russia and by nearly continuous wars; instituted administrative and fiscal reforms; built Russia's first navy.

1689 Peter overthrew the regency of his halfsister Sophia; assumed direct rule.

1695–96 Russo-Turkish War; Peter I captured Azov.

1700S Dukhobors, religious sect, founded; some 7,000 emigrated to Canada in late 19th cent.

1700–21 Northern War with Sweden; Russia broke Swedish power in the Baltic and gained Livonia, Estonia, Ingermanland, and part of Karelia; victory made Russia a European power.

1703 St. Petersburg, built by Tsar Peter, established as Russian capital.

1710–11 Russo-Turkish War; Ottomans attacked Russia, regaining Azov.

1711–65 M. Lomonosov lived; reformed Russian literary language.

1721 Russian Orthodox church put under state control; patriarchate of Moscow abolished.

1721 Tsar Peter formally adopted title Emperor of Russia.

1722 Table of Ranks issued by Tsar Peter; established rigid hierarchy for all government posts; advancement was by merit and seniority.

1725–27 Catherine I reigned; the mistress and second wife (*m.* 1712) of Peter I; A. Menshikov dominated the government.

1727–30 Peter II reigned; manipulated by powerful nobles; A. Menshikov arrested.

1730–40 Anna Ivanovna reigned as tsarina; Baltic Germans gained influential posts.

1733–35 Russia allied with Austria against Poland in War of the Polish Succession; gained accession of Frederick Augustus II as Augustus III.

1736–39 Russo-Turkish War; Russians retook Azov.

1740–41 Ivan VI reigned; succeeded as an infant; overthrown in palace conspiracy.

1741–62 Elizabeth, daughter of Peter the Great, reigned as tsarina; pursued anti-German policy and allied Russia against Prussia.

1741–43 Russia victorious in Russo-Swedish War; gained Finnish territory.

1756–63 Seven Years' War; Russia allied with other European powers against Prussia for most of war; Elizabeth's death ended Russian participation and saved Prussia from defeat.

1762 Peter III reigned; quickly alienated nobles and the church; his decision to withdraw (1762) from Seven Years' War helped bring about his assassination.

1762–96 Catherine II the Great; participated in overthrow of her husband; increased Russian power and prestige in Europe; warred against the Ottoman Turks; instituted administrative reforms and patronized the arts.

1764 Stanislaus II installed as Polish king by Catherine; as Catherine's lover he was dominated by her and Russian interests in Poland.

1766 Instruction of Catherine the Great issued; outlined her liberal political views on a variety of needed reforms (including emancipation of serfs) and was intended to guide commission charged with recommending government reform; commission later failed to produce meaningful reform.

1768–74 Russo-Turkish War; Russians victorious in Crimea and greatly increased influence in region; Russia established as protector of Christians in Ottoman domains.

1768–1844 Noted Russian fabulist I. Krylov lived; his fables proved influential in later Russian culture.

1772 First Partition of Poland; Russia gained Polish territories east of the Dnieper and Dvina rivers.

1773–74 Peasant revolt against serfdom led by Pugachev; new, harsher laws on serfdom promulgated after the rebellion was crushed.

1785 Charter to the Nobility issued by Catherine; guaranteed nobles rights and prerogatives.

1787–92 Russo-Turkish War; Russia generally successful in war caused by its annexation of Crimea (1783).

1790 *A Journey from St. Petersburg to Moscow* published by A. Radishchev; denounced serfdom.

1792–1802 French Revolutionary Wars in Europe.

1793–1856 N. Lobachevsky, Russian mathematician and a founder of non-Euclidean geometry, lived.

1793 Second Partition of Poland; Russia gained Lithuanian Belorussia, the western Ukraine, and other parts of Poland.

1795 Third Partition of Poland; Russia shared (with Austria and Prussia) remaining central core of Polish kingdom; kingdom ceased to exist.

1796–1801 Paul I reigned; reversed many of Catherine's policies and attempted to limit nobles' powers; his inconsistent foreign policy included brief participation in coalition against France (1798) and alliance against Britain after; assassinated.

1801–25 Alexander I reigned; a liberal ruler early in his reign, he supported the conservative movement of the post-Napoleonic period.

1801 Russia annexed Georgia; Russian possession confirmed (1813) after victory in war with Persia (1804–13).

1803–15 Napoleonic Wars; Alexander, defeated by Napoleon in fighting in Europe, submitted to Napoleon by the Treaty of Tilsit (1807); Napoleon later broke the alliance and launched his ill-fated invasion of Russia (1812); Alexander's rout of the invasion force led to Napoleon's downfall and made Russia a leading European power.

1804–57 M. Glinka, lived; founded Russia's nationalist school of composers and wrote the opera *A Life for the Tsar.*

1806–12 Russo-Turkish War; Russia acquired Bessarabia.

1808–09 Russo-Swedish War; Russia gained Finland from Sweden.

1811–48 V. Belinsky, lived; influenced development of Russian literary criticism.

1812–70 Radical writer, A. Herzen, lived; wrote books on socialism and revolution.

1825 Decembrist Conspiracy, abortive revolt (Dec.) by nobles and officers, against accession of Nicholas I.

1825–55 Nicholas I reigned; instituted oppressive rule, though he did attempt to improve the lot of the serfs; revolutionary sentiment began spreading; Russia's expansionist wars against the Ottoman Empire continued; Russian literature flourished.

1826–28 War with Persia; Russia gained part of Armenia.

1826 Convention of Akkerman (Oct. 7); Russians forced agreement on Ottoman Empire; Russia to oversee autonomy of Moldavia and Wallachia.

1828–29 Russo-Turkish War; begun in support of Greek independence; Russia penetrated deep into Balkans; Treaty of Adrianople greatly increased Russian influence in region.

1829–94 Piano virtuoso and composer A. Rubinstein lived.

1830–31 Polish uprising against Russian rule; revolt crushed and Poland lost measure of autonomy gained in 1815.

1831 Romantic poet A. Pushkin wrote *Eugene Onegin* and the play *Boris Godunov* this year.

1837–1910 Composer M. Balakirev lived; his work influenced Tchaikovsky.

1840 *A Hero of Our Time* published by Romantic novelist M. Lermontov.

1842 *Dead Souls* published by founder of Russian literary realism, N. Gogol.

1842–1911 Radical Prince P. Kropotkin lived; became a leader in development of anarchist theory.

1848 *Communist Manifesto,* later a seminal work for Russian Communists, written by Germans K. Marx and F. Engels.

1853–56 Crimean War; with the Ottoman Empire on the verge of collapse at the hands of the Russians, other European powers joined Ottomans against Russia; Russia was defeated and in subsequent years the fate of the Ottoman Empire became a major concern of European powers.

1855–81 Alexander II reigned; instituted liberal reforms but failed to prevent rise of populist Narodniki movement; continued Russian expansion in central Asia and Far East; emancipated the serfs.

1859 Muslim leader Shamyl who battled Russian domination in the Crimean War defeated and captured.

1860 Treaty of Peking; China ceded Ussuri region (north of Amur River) to Russia; these Far Eastern territories included future site of Vladivostok.

1860 Vladivostok founded; became imortant Russian naval base in Far East.

1861 Edict of Emancipation freeing the serfs issued by Tsar Alexander II; one of various reforms proclaimed by the tsar.

1862 *Fathers and Sons,* depicting conflicts between the old Russian aristocracy and the new democratic-minded intelligentsia, written by I. Turgenev.

1863 Polish rebellion suppressed with great brutality.

1864 Zemstvos, local councils, established.

1864–69 L. Tolstoy wrote his masterpiece *War and Peace,* one of the great novels of all time; later wrote *Anna Karenina* (1873–76).

1866–1944 Painter W. Kandinsky, founder of abstract art, lived; he also helped start the Munich-based Blau Reiter group.

1867 Russia sold Alaska to the US.

1868 Opera *Boris Godunov* composed by M. Mussorgsky.

1869 Chemist D. Mendeleev devised the periodic table of elements; completed improved version in 1871, again based on his periodic law.

1870–85 N. Przhevalsky led expeditions to Mongolia and Tibet, greatly expanding geographical knowledge of the regions.

1871–81 Russia occupied Chinese territory in Ili Crisis.

1872 Three Emperors' League formed with Prussia and Austria-Hungary.

1873–1943 S. Rachmaninov, noted Romantic composer and piano virtuoso, lived.

1875 H. Blavatsky helped found the Russian Theosophical Society.

1876 Narodniki, radical populists, formed secret Land and Liberty society.

1877 P. Tchaikovsky composed score for the ballet *Swan Lake;* later did scores for *The Nutcracker* (1892) and *Sleeping Beauty* (1890).

1877–78 Russo-Turkish War; victorious Russians advance to just outside Constantinople.

1878 Congress of Berlin; European powers forced Russia to accept greatly reduced concessions from Ottoman Empire following war of 1877–78.

1879–80 Novelist F. Dostoyevsky published his now classic *The Brothers Karamazov;* previously published *Notes from the Underground* (1864), *Crime and Punishment* (1866), and *The Idiot* (1868).

1880–1921 Leading Russian Symbolist poet, A. Blok, lived.

1881 Alexander II assassinated by "People's Will," a wing of the Land and Liberty Society.

1881–94 Alexander III reigned; instituted reactionary and repressive regime; adopted policies of russification of national minorities by force and persecution of Jews and other religious minority groups; fostered industrialization; miserable conditions of workers helped spread revolutionary movement.

1881 Wave of pogroms conducted against Jews following assassination of Alexander II; continued until outbreak of Russian Revolution.

1887 Reinsurance Treaty concluded with Germany.

1888 Russian nationalist composer N. Rimsky-Korsakov composed music for *Scheherazade.*

1893–1930 Leading poet of Russian Revolution, V. Mayakovsky, lived.

1893–1953 Pioneer Russian film director, V. Pudovkin, lived.

1893 Triple Entente formed with France and Britain.

1894–1917 Nicholas II reigned as last tsar of Russia; an ineffective ruler, he presided over Russian defeats in WW I and was unable to stem the rising tide of revolution and was overthrown.

1896–1905 D. Merezhkovsky published his trilogy of historical novels, *Christ and Antichrist.*

1897 N. Lenin arrested for his radical activities; exiled to Siberia (1897–1900); left Russia for Switzerland (1900).

1898 Moscow Art Theater founded by V. Nemirovich-Danchenko and K. Stanislavsky, "the father of method acting."

1898 Russian Social Democratic Labor party, a Marxist group, founded by radicals at Minsk; group was soon after broken up by police and forced to meet in exile in Europe.

c1900 Marxist revolutionary G. Plekhanov collaborated with N. Lenin; later sided with Mensheviks.

1901 Socialist Revolutionary party formed; a leading revolutionary group, it was an ideological outgrowth of the populist Narodnik movement; group conducted terrorist campaign.

1903 Russian Social Democratic Labor party split into two factions, Mensheviks and radical Bolsheviks; Lenin led the Bolsheviks.

1904–05 Russo-Japanese War; Russia suffered a humiliating defeat in the Far East at the hands of the Japanese; helped to further discredit government.

1904 Zemstvo Congress (Nov.) convened at St. Petersburg; called for end to government repression and creation of a Duma (representative assembly).

1904 A. Chekhov's *The Cherry Orchard* performed; his earlier noted plays included *The Sea Gull* (1896) and *Uncle Vanya* (1899).

1904 L. Andreyev published *The Red Laugh.*

1904 Nobel Prize for Physiology or Medicine awarded to I. Pavlov, famous for his studies on conditioning.

1905 Trans-Siberian railroad completed; fostered colonization of Siberia.

1905 On Bloody Sunday, tsar's troops fired (Jan. 22) on protesters in St. Petersburg; Russian Revolution of 1905 began.

1905 Concessions granted (Mar.) by tsar, amid wave of strikes and unrest; included creation of advisory assembly and religious toleration; concessions failed to halt spreading unrest.

1905 Treaty of Portsmouth signed, ending Russo-Japanese War (Sept. 5).

1905 Nationwide strike (Oct. 20–30) in protest against tsarist government; threat of political collapse forced tsar to make concessions.

1905 First soviet (council) of workers formed (Oct. 26) at St. Petersburg.

1905 Tsar Nicholas issued October Manifesto (Oct. 30) to liberalize government; constitution granted, civil liberties guaranteed, and Duma (with legislative powers) to be created; Count Witte became first prime minister (dismissed May 1906).

1905 Cadet (Constitutional Democratic party) and Octobrist parties formed as liberal moderates split; Cadet party favored progressive government.

1905 Government arrested (Dec. 16) members of the St. Petersburg soviet.

1905 Uprising by Moscow workers (Dec.) suppressed after hard fighting in the streets.

1905–11 Black Hundreds active against revolutionists in the provinces; carried out pogroms against the Jews.

1906 Fundamental Laws issued (May 6) by tsar; limited powers of the Duma and asserted supremacy of tsar over Duma.

1906 First Duma convened (May 10); dominated by Cadet party; openly critical of tsarist government, it was dissolved (July 21).

1906 P. Stolypin named prime minister (June); sought to quench revolutionary ferment by instituting meaningful land reforms; supported constitutional government.

1906 Stolypin land reforms instituted (Nov. 22) to distribute land as private property to peasants; ended system of mirs (peasants' communal land-holding system).

1907 Second Duma in session (Mar.–June); radical membership increased; dissolved (June 16).

1907–12 Third Duma in session; election law favoring conservative elements gave majority of seats to conservatives; order restored in Russia as Prime Minister Stolypin and Duma pressed reform program and suppressed radical unrest.

1907 Anglo-Russian Convention settled disputes with Britain over Persia, Afghanistan, and Tibet; relations strengthened.

1907–19 V. Nijinsky enjoyed international fame as a ballet dancer.

1908 E. Metchnikov, microbiologist studying human immunology, awarded Nobel Prize for Physiology or Medicine.

1909 Ballet Russe founded by S. Diaghilev.

1911–12 Scandal over influence of Rasputin in royal court spread; rumors of Rasputin's corrupt and immoral behavior included purported intimate relationship with Tsarina Alexandra.

1911 Prime Minister Stolypin assassinated (Sept. 14) by revolutionary.

1912–13 First and Second Balkan Wars; Ottomans driven out of Eastern Europe while tensions between Russia and Austria, over respective interests in region, increased.

1912–17 Fourth Duma in session, conservatives again in the majority.

1913 Suprematism school of abstract art founded; later influenced development of modern architecture.

1914 Assassination of Austrian Archduke Francis Ferdinand by Serbian nationalist (June 28); tensions in Eastern Europe mounted as Germany backed Austria against Serbia; Russia backed its ally, Serbia, and was drawn into WW I.

1914–18 WW I; Russian losses in the war further weakened, then brought down, the tsarist government.

1915 Progressive Bloc, alliance of liberals and conservatives in Duma formed (Aug.) to urge reforms; members appointed Provisional Government after fall of imperial government in 1917.

1915 Tsar Nicholas took command (Sept.) of the Russian army following the disastrous defeat of Russian forces in the Galicia campaign (May); Tsarina Alexandra (dominated by Rasputin) left in charge of government.

1916 Russian government near collapse; mismanagement of government by Alexandra and Rasputin combined with severe economic dislocations, including food shortages, caused by ongoing war.

1916 Rasputin assassinated (Dec. 30) by angry noblemen; Rasputin's death failed to halt collapse of government.

1917 Russian Revolution of 1917, wave of strikes and unrest (Mar.) resulted in creation of Provisional Government and abdication of Tsar Nicholas (Mar. 15); Bolsheviks, led by Lenin, seized power (Nov.) and thus established the first Communist state.

1917 Bolshevik government formed (Nov. 7) under Lenin's leadership; L. Trotsky and J. Stalin held high posts; reorganization of Russia along Communist lines begun; banks nationalized and large estates broken up.

1917 Program of establishing worker control of factories begun (Nov. 28); government-controlled unions formed.

1917 Cheka organized to combat counterrevolutionaries (Dec.).

1917 Bolshevik government concluded armistice with Germany (Dec. 5); fighting resumed after Germans demanded Russia cede Poland and other territories in western Russia.

1917 Don Cossacks rebelled against Bolshevik government (Dec. 9); their uprising merged with the other counterrevolutionary warfare of the Russian Civil War.

1917 Church property seized (Dec. 17); suppression of the church begun.

1917 Japanese forces landed at Vladivostok (Dec. 30) and began operations in Far East.

1918–22 Russian Civil War; counterrevolutionary groups, the White Russian Army, and foreign troops attempted to topple the Communists; Red Army, organized by L. Trotsky, was ultimately victorious and regained control over nearly all Russian territory.

1918 Constituent Assembly, elected after Bolshevik takeover, convened (Jan. 18); Social Revolutionary party members held clear majority over Bolsheviks; assembly forced to disband by Red Army troops.

1918 Moscow established as Bolshevik capital (Jan.).

1918 Land nationalized (Feb. 19).

1918 Ukraine declared independence from Russia (Jan. 28); one of several border regions to declare independence in the months after the Bolshevik takeover; included Moldavia, Lithuania, and Transcaucasia.

1918 Treaty of Brest-Litovsk concluded (Mar. 3); in the face of a continuing German advance the Bolsheviks agreed to give up Poland, the Ukraine, and other territories on the western frontier.

1918 Communist party adopted as name of the Bolshevik party (Mar.).

1918–19 British, later joined by French and US troops, occupied Murmansk and Archangel in extreme northwest Russia; fighting with Bolsheviks began; WW I armistice largely ended US and British support and troops were withdrawn (Oct.).

1918 Constitution adopted (July 10); government run by Politburo and Central Committee of the Communist party (sole legal party); hierarchy of local, provincial, and national (All-Russian) soviets established.

1918 Nicholas and royal family executed by Communists (July 16).

1918 Red Terror instituted by Communists after unsuccessful attempt to assassinate Lenin (Aug. 30); widespread killings of all opponents began; murders of prisoners and enemy suspects by both Reds and Whites numbered perhaps 100,000; some two million of bourgeois class fled Russia.

1918 WW I ended by armistice between Germans and Allies (Nov. 11).

1919–20 White Russian offensives launched against Red Army in western Russia; from Siberia, by Adm. Alexander Kolchak; from the Don region in the south, led by Gen. Anton Denikin; from the Baltic region in the extreme west, led by Gen. Nikolay Yudenich; poor communications and other factors led to the failure of the drives against the Red Army in 1920.

1919 Third International organized (Mar. 2); avowed aim was to spark Communist revolutions in countries throughout the world.

1919 Karakhan Manifesto issued (July 15); offered to renounce tsarist interests in China, contributed to subsequent establishment of Chinese Communist party.

1920 Baltic States of Estonia, Latvia, and Lithunania recognized as independent.

1920 Russo-Polish War fought (Apr.-Oct.); war sparked by Polish advances into the Ukraine.

1920 White Army offensive (June-Nov.) from the Crimea, led by Baron Ferdinand von Wrangel; Red Army drove Wrangel's army into Turkey.

1920 Independence of Finland recognized (Oct. 14).

1920 Food levy instituted (Dec. 14) to help supply the Red Army; peasants, required to give government all surplus food, resisted; peasant uprisings and strikes by workers broke out as Russian economy collapsed (1920–21).

1921 Kronstadt Rebellion was a Russian revolt of sailors at the Kronstadt Naval Base (Feb.–Mar.); capped period of growing unrest at collapse of Russian economy and shortages of food; forced Lenin to institute his New Economic Policy (NEP).

1921 Lenin introduced (Mar. 17) his New Economic Policy to revive the economy; faced with economic collapse and internal unrest, Communist party abandoned "war communism"; food levy abolished and replaced by "tax" which took only part of their surplus; limited capitalism reestablished, though state controlled all major industries; full economic recovery achieved by mid-1920s.

1922–53 J. Stalin in office as general secretary of party's Central Committee.

1922 Last elements of White Russian Army driven out of eastern Siberia (into Manchuria) following withdrawal of Japanese from Vladivostok (Oct. 25), Russian Civil War ended.

1922 Treaty of Rapallo signed (Apr. 16) with Germany; this pact for economic cooperation provided Communist Russia with first diplomatic recognition.

1922 Union of Soviet Socialist Republics (USSR) organized (Dec. 30), then including Russia, Belorussia, the Ukraine, and Transcaucasia.

1924 Lenin died (Jan. 21).

1924–53 J. Stalin in power; after the first years of vying for power, Stalin gradually increased his power as dictator; established his "personality cult" in the 1930s, which gave him absolute power; promoted industrialization at the expense of Marxist ideals and developed Stalinist line of "socialism in one country."

1924–26 Stalin's struggle for power; opposed chiefly by Trotsky, who wanted to end the New Economic Policy and return to revolutionary economic policies; Trotsky and his allies expelled from party posts (1926), signaling Stalin's victory.

1927 15th All-Union Congress (Dec.); confirmed Stalin's supremacy by condemning opposition to the party line; Trotsky's faction was expelled from the party.

1928 Five-Year Plan instituted by Stalin (Oct. 1) to replace New Economic Policy; stimulated development of heavy industry and instituted collectivization of agriculture.

1929 Trotsky exiled from USSR (Jan.).

1930s Collectivization of nearly all farmland completed despite widespread opposition by farmers; some five million peasant farms were forcibly confiscated and owners sent to labor camps in Siberia.

1932–33 Widespread famine resulted partly from government's farm policy.

1933 US recognized the USSR.

1933 Communist party purged of about one million members.

1933 Nobel Prize for Literature awarded to poet and novelist I. Bunin.

1934 USSR joined League of Nations; actively participated in disarmament conferences.

1934 Sergei Kirov, close associate of Stalin, assassinated (Dec. 1, probably by agent of Stalin); touched off a new round of purges, which reached height in 1936–38; over one million estimated to have died in Stalin's purges, including purge of the army in 1937–39.

c1935 Stakhavonism movement initiated to increase workers' industrial output.

1935 Alliances with France and Czechoslovakia exacerbated worsening relations with Nazi Germany.

1936–38 Purge Trials; rivals of Stalin eliminated in series of phony trials; led to Stalin's consolidation of power in Russia.

1936–39 Soviets supported loyalists against German-backed nationalists in the Spanish Civil War; relations with Germany worsened.

1936 S. Prokofiev composed *Peter and the Wolf.*

1936 Anti-Comintern Pact concluded (Nov. 25) between Nazi Germany and Japan, USSR threatened now in the East, moved closer to alliance with anti-Fascist democracies.

1936 New constitution adopted; supposedly democratic, it maintained the absolute rule of the Communist party; Presidium and two-chamber Supreme Soviet to run government.

1937 Composer D. Shostakovich wrote his famous *Symphony No. 5.*

1938–56 Biologist T. Lysenko, who claimed to have disproved basic laws of genetics, served as president of the Russian Academy of Agricultural Sciences.

1938 L. Kaganovich, influential ally of Stalin, became member of Presidium.

1938 Fighting between Soviet and Japanese forces along the Siberian border; Soviets supported the Chinese in the Sino-Japanese War.

1938 German invasion of Czechoslovakia; Soviets unsuccessfully sought firm action from European allies against Germany.

1939 V. Molotov suddenly made commissar of foreign affairs (May); Soviets resisted firm alliance with European allies against Germany.

1939 Nonaggression Pact signed (Aug. 23) with Nazi Germany, marking sudden reversal in Soviet policy.

1939–45 WW II: Soviets, initially allied with Nazis, joined the Allies when Germany invaded the USSR (1941); repulsed German invasion at great cost, including over 20 million persons killed and the destruction of much of its industry; participated in "liberation" of Europe; Soviets emerged from the war as a superpower and leading opponent of the US–dominated Western powers.

1939–40 Russo-Finnish War; Russians victorious after hard fighting.

1943 Russian Orthodox Patriarchate formally restored by Stalin.

1943 Third Communist International (Comintern) disbanded.

1944–45 Soviet government reportedly received information about secret US atomic bomb project.

1945 Consolidation of Soviet position begun; by war's end Soviets had occupied Eastern Europe and much of Manchuria and Korea; relations with Allies quickly broke down, especially over joint occupation policies in Germany; Soviets moved to install Communist governments in occupied territories and elsewhere around the world; Allies meanwhile resisted expansion of Soviet influence and the Cold War began.

1945 USSR became a charter member of the UN.

1946 Stalin assumed chairmanship of Council of Ministers, a post he held until his death in 1953.

1946 Five-Year Plan announced by Stalin; aimed at economic recovery from war and rebuilding of Soviet industry; industry was quickly restored but agricultural output remained low.

1946–47 Famine resulted from drought in grain-producing regions.

1947 Communists' unsuccessful attempt to seize power in Greece prompted formulation of Truman Doctrine by US; directed at halting Communist expansionism, the doctrine hardened postwar divisions between the East and West.

1947 USSR and satellites refused to take aid under Marshall Plan.

1947 Cominform organized to coordinate Communist parties in various nations.

1948 Break in relations with Yugoslavia; Yugoslav leader Tito established his independent Communist policies.

1948–49 Berlin blockade and airlift; friction with former Allies led Soviets to establish unsuccessful blockade of West Berlin.

1949 Soviets exploded their first atomic bomb.

1949 Soviets recognized newly established People's Republic of China.

1950–53 Korean War; relations with US worsened as result of the war.

1952 Stalin issued his "Last Testament," calling for completion of drive against economic problems (Oct.).

1952 Party officially named Communist Party of the Soviet Union.

1953 Doctors' Plot revealed (Jan. 13) by Stalin.

1953 Soviets exploded their first hydrogen bomb.

1953 Stalin died (Mar. 5); policy of "collective leadership" to replace Stalin's rule was initially adopted by government,

1953 Failed attempt to seize power made by Lavrenti Beria.

1953 Georgi Malenkov succeeded as premier; N. Khrushchev, as first secretary of the Central Committee, became major rival for power; Malenkov sought increased consumer-goods production and more intensive use of existing agricultural lands; Khrushchev countered by calling for vast expansion of agricultural lands and further development of heavy industry.

1955 Malenkov fell from power (Feb.); replaced by Nikolai Bulganin as premier.

1955 Warsaw Pact formed with satellite nations; created to counter Western NATO alliance.

1955 Soviets adopted policy of giving aid to and forming alliances with non-Communist nations.

1956 Twentieth Party Congress; Khrushchev made his "Secret Speech" (Feb.) denouncing Stalin; de-Stalinization, an easing of restrictions, gave rise to unrest in Poland and Hungary.

1956 Cominform dissolved.

1956 Hungarian Revolution (Oct.–Nov.); Soviet troops used to crush the liberal revolt.

1957 Sweeping reorganization to decentralize economic ministries of government; sparked coalition (Molotov, Malenkov, and Lazar Kaganovich) against Khrushchev; Khrushchev defeated the coalition in a brief power struggle and won their expulsion from party posts.

1957 Soviet satellite Sputnik launched (Oct. 4) as first man-made earth satellite; space race with US began.

1958–64 Khrushchev in office (Jan.) as premier, replacing Bulganin; pursued continuing policy of reform and ongoing Cold War with West, while also accepting principle of peaceful coexistence with West; his attempts to stimulate agricultural production failed and the USSR was forced to import grain in 1963.

1958 B. Pasternak, author of *Doctor Zhivago,* won the Nobel Prize for Literature; Communists comdemned his book.

1959 Premier Khrushchev made historic visit to US (Sept.); marked height of "thaw" in Cold War.

1960 Sino-Soviet split began; Maoist China opposed Soviet "revisionism" of Marxist doctrine; broke with Soviets over implementation of revolutionary Communism; Soviet aid to China ended.

1960–75 Vietnam War; Soviets provided supplies to North Vietnam, but no troops; gained considerable political prestige for Communist movement by the victory over US forces in Vietnam.

1960 U-2 Incident; Soviets downed (May 1) US spy plane over Soviet territory; new round of Cold War tensions began.

1961 R. Nureyev, famous Russian ballet dancer, defected to the West.

1961 Soviets established relations with Cuba following F. Castro's break with US; provided important Communist outpost in Western Hemisphere.

1961 Soviet cosmonaut Y. Gagarin became first man to travel in space (Apr. 12).

1961 Berlin Wall erected (Aug.) by East Germans to halt politically embarrassing flow of refugees to West Germany.

1962 Cuban Missile Crisis (Oct.); Soviets forced to withdraw missiles from Cuba after US president J. Kennedy threatened nuclear war.

1963 "Hot-line" telecommunications link between US and USSR installed.

1963 Nuclear Test Ban Treaty signed.

1963 H. (Kim) Philby, unmasked as a master Soviet spy in Britain, escaped to USSR.

1964 Khrushchev ousted from power (Oct. 14–15); fall caused by failure of his agricultural programs (notably the "virgin lands" scheme), Soviet humiliation in the Cuban Missile Crisis, and the Sino-Soviet split.

1964–82 L. Brezhnev in office as first secretary of the Central Committee; Brezhnev clearly the most powerful member of new government, though "collective leadership" was stressed at first; more orderly course of reform adopted and overt anti-Stalin propaganda halted; by early 1970s, policy of détente with West brought what appeared to be a halt in the Cold War.

1964–80 A. Kosygin in office as premier, replacing Khrushchev in that post.

1965–77 Nikolai Podgorny in office as chairman of the Presidium (president).

1965 Government reestablished 28 economic ministries abolished in Khrushchev era; instituted system whereby individual firms made production decisions on basis of prices and profits; marked radical departure from former close government supervision, though government still controlled basic course of economy; industrial output greatly improved by 1970s.

1965 Nobel Prize for Literature awarded to M. Sholokhov; works included trilogy on Russian life that began with *The Silent Don.*

1968 Five-day, 41-hour work week established for Soviet workers.

1968   Prague Spring; Soviets invaded Czecho-slovakia to halt liberalization of government there.

1968   Brezhnev Doctrine issued defending invasion of Czechoslovakia; declared right of military intervention when order threatened in Warsaw Pact nation.

1969   Border warfare with Chinese; heavy fighting over Damansky Island in Ussuri River.

1970   Official condemnation of agricultural program approved by Central Committee; increased grain and meat production called for.

1970   Leading Soviet dissident A. Solzhenitsyn received the Nobel Prize for Literature.

1971   Soviets supported India against US-backed Pakistan in war over Bangladesh.

1972   US president R. Nixon visited China (Feb.); marked beginning of US alliance with China, which exploited embarrassing ideological rift in the Communist world.

1972   US president R. Nixon in USSR on first visit by US president (May 22–June 1); SALT I agreements signed.

1972   Relations with Egypt soured; Soviet personnel asked to leave country in major setback in Soviet Mideast policy.

1972   SALT II talks with US began.

1972   Soviets forced to buy grain from the West following bad harvests.

1973   Shake-up of the Central Committee Brezhnev's allies, A. Gromyko, Andrei Grechko, and Yuri Andropov installed on the committee.

1973   USSR threatened to intervene in 1973 Arab-Israeli War on behalf of Egyptians; US responded by calling worldwide nuclear alert.

1973   Brezhnev visited US; held talks with US president R. Nixon.

1974   Trade agreement with US concluded; Soviet emigration policies eased as part of the deal.

1974   Nobel Prize–winning author, A. Solzhenitsyn, forced to leave USSR as a dissident.

1975   New Five-Year Plan announced; called for significant increase in agricultural investment.

1977   New constitution adopted (Oct. 4); Communist party specifically named as ruling party of the Soviet Union.

1977   L. Brezhnev replaced N. Podgorny as chairman of the Presidium (president), first Soviet leader to act as both first secretary of Central Committee and chairman of Presidium.

1979   USSR and US signed SALT II agreement on arms limitation (June); US Senate refused to ratify agreement.

1979   Invasion (Dec.) of Afghanistan by Soviet troops ordered to back puppet regime there; Soviets unable to put an end to guerrilla resistance by Afghans.

1980   US imposed embargo on grain shipments to USSR in response to invasion of Afghanistan (Jan. 4); marked continued deterioration of détente.

1980   US called boycott of Olympic Games to be held at Moscow; boycott only partly successful.

1980–81   Relations with US deteriorated over Solidarity crisis in Poland; USSR backed away from threats of invading Poland.

1980   A. Kosygin resigned (Oct. 23) as premier because of ill health; Nikolay A. Tikhonov succeeded him.

1980   Kosygin died (Dec. 18).

1981   US lifted embargo on Soviet grain purchases (Apr.).

1981   Agreement signed (Nov. 20) for construction of natural gas pipeline from Siberia to Western Europe; US attempted to block pipeline construction in retaliation for Soviet handling of the Polish crisis.

1982   Strategic Arms Reduction Talks (START) began with US.

1982   Brezhnev died (Nov. 10); Yuri Andropov, former head of the KGB, succeeded Brezhnev as party leader.

1982–84   Andropov in office as party general secretary; his short term was marked by campaigns against production inefficiency and corruption; influence of M. Gorbachev firmly established by this time.

1984   Andropov, in poor health, died (Feb. 9).

1984–85   K. Chernenko in office as party general secretary; pursued policy of détente; continued attempts to end corruption and inefficiency.

1985   Chernenko, also in poor health, died (Mar.), forcing an unprecedented third major change in Soviet leadership in three years.

1985–91   M. Gorbachev, former Central Committee secretary and Politburo member, in office as party general secretary; began wide-ranging liberal reform of government that over the next few years unleashed a torrent of demands for the ouster of Communists and for democratic government, in the end bringing on the collapse of the Communist-bloc satellite nations and finally the USSR itself.

1985　A. Gromyko, member of the old guard of Soviet leaders and foreign affairs minister since 1957, appointed to largely ceremonial post of Supreme Soviet Presidium chairman; marked beginning of purge, engineered by Gorbachev, of older leaders and their replacement by younger appointees; purge broadened in 1986 to remove corrupt and inefficient officials in the national and regional governments.

1985　Geneva summit (Nov.) between Gorbachev and US president R. Reagan; marked start of good relations between two leaders, who concluded agreement against chemical weapons and ordered cultural exchanges resumed (halted in 1979).

1986　Gorbachev, proclaiming need for drastic reform of Soviet society before 27th Congress of the Soviet Communist party (Feb.), announced need for *glasnost* (openness) as a key to effecting the changes; era of Gorbachev's liberal reforms began.

1986　Chernobyl nuclear accident (Apr.); government withheld public warnings about radioactive fallout resulting from reactor fire; some 200 died in the disaster and radioactive cloud spread over the Ukraine and parts of Europe.

1986　Iceland summit conference (Oct.); Gorbachev and Reagan discussed disarmament proposals; Reagan refused to reduce US Star Wars (SDI) program, however; no new agreements reached.

1986　Legislation passed to foster private enterprise in certain areas of the economy (Nov., to take effect May, 1987); marked first break in state's legal monopoly of economy.

1986　Nuclear physicist Dr. Andrei Sakharov and some other leading dissidents released during the year.

1987　Unrest reported in Baltic States (Estonia, Latvia, and Lithuania), and in Armenia; Armenian protesters wanted Nagorny Karabakh, a part of Azerbaijan since 1923, returned to Armenia.

1987　Gorbachev proposed policy of *perestroika* (restructuring), the second key principle (with *glasnost*) of his wide-ranging reform program (Jan.); would reduce central government control and add small measure of democracy, including multi-candidate elections by secret ballot for local level government and party posts.

1987　New immigration law passed (Jan.), allowing sharp increase in emigration by Soviet Jews; rate jumped from 1,000 in 1986 to 60,000 by 1989.

1987　Soviet Union held first multi-candidate elections for local councils (June 21), implementing part of Gorbachev's *perestroika* policy.

1987　Gorbachev publicly denounced Stalin's bloody purges of the 1930s (July); marked but one of official reassessments of Soviet past announced during year (including mistakes made under Brezhnev), in keeping with new *glasnost* policy.

1987　USSR and China agreed to negotiated resolution of long-standing border dispute (Aug.); marked beginning of improved relations with China.

1987　B. Yeltsin, a Politburo member and the Moscow City Communist party first secretary, ousted for accusing hard-liners in the Central Committee of slowing the pace of reform in Soviet government (Nov.).

1987　Intermediate Nuclear Forces (INF) Treaty signed at Washington, D.C., summit between Gorbachev and Reagan (Dec.); first treaty to eliminate whole class of weapons (all short- and medium-range nuclear weapons).

1988　Anti-Armenian riots reported in Azerbaijan (Feb.) as tensions between Armenia and Azerbaijan increased; Armenian government called for return of Nagorny Karabakh to Armenia (May).

1988　Moscow summit (May–June); INF treaty formally activated; talks on Strategic Arms Reduction Treaty (START) stalled over question of SDI program in US.

1988　Extraordinary party conference approved radical restructuring of national legislature and voting system (June); popularly elected members of Congress of People's Deputies to elect members of Supreme Soviet and its chairman (serving as head of state); one-third of seats in new Congress reserved for Communist party members, the rest to be elected in multi-candidate races; elections to be held in 1989.

1988 Party approved memorial for victims of Stalin's bloody regime.

1988 Unrest by nationalists in the Baltic States (Aug.).

1988 Gorbachev ousted Gromyko (Oct.), taking over as chairman of the Supreme Soviet Presidium; also forced out additional Politburo members connected with Brezhnev regime.

1988 Ethnic unrest reported in Georgia (Nov.); Estonia, followed later by Latvia and Lithuania, asserted primacy of its laws over USSR central government laws.

1988 Gorbachev, speaking at UN, proclaimed end to Cold War; promised USSR would pursue openness (*glasnost*) and vast program of restructuring of Soviet society (*perestroika*).

1988 Earthquake rocked Armenia (Dec.); about 25,000 reported killed.

1989 Khrushchev rehabilitated by Soviet media.

1989 Over 100 older members of the party Central Committee forced to resign during purge engineered by Gorbachev (Apr.); further reorganization in Sept. put reformers in Politburo and Central Committee Secretariat.

1989 Unrest in Georgia turned to demands for independence from USSR (Mar.); Soviet troops killed 19 in fights with demonstrators (Apr.).

1989 Mass protests supporting Yeltsin's candidacy for new Congress were organized in Moscow (Mar.).

1989 Elections for new Congress held (Mar. 26); many Communist party hard-liners defeated in Moscow, Leningrad, and elsewhere to give Gorbachev's reforms a popular mandate.

1989 Soviets began withdrawal of troops from Mongolia (May).

1989 USSR–China summit held in Beijing (May).

1989 Government troops sent to Nagorny Karabakh to halt ethnic unrest there (May); serious ethnic unrest reported in region by Aug.

1989 New Congress convened (May); elected Gorbachev chairman of the Supreme Soviet (head of state); Communist party allocated majority in new Supreme Soviet, however, leaving little room for popularly elected radicals.

1989 Soviet proposal for limited economic autonomy spurned by Estonia (May); Estonia, Latvia, and Lithuania later opted for full independence.

1989 Mass protests organized on behalf of Yeltsin (May), who was not elected to Supreme Soviet; elected delegate turned his seat over to Yeltsin.

1989 Gorbachev, visiting Germany, publicly reversed long-standing Brezhnev Doctrine and declared that states have right to political self-determination (June); later reiterated new Soviet policy of noninterference.

1989 Ethnic unrest spread to Uzbekistan and Kazakhstan (June).

1989 Nikolai Ryzhkov, elected Council of Ministers chairman by Supreme Soviet, instituted massive restructuring of government (June); half of all ministries abolished or combined with others.

1989 US president G. Bush proposed expanding discussions on nuclear weapons to include reductions in conventional forces in Europe (June).

1989 Gorbachev proposed multi-candidate elections for party posts at party Central Committee meeting (July), following criticism of his reforms by leading Politburo conservative, Yegor Ligachev.

1989 Yeltsin formed Inter-Regional Group (July), a coalition of 300 radicals in the Congress of People's Deputies; vowed to oppose conservatives and speed up pace of reforms.

1989 Miners struck in Ukraine and Siberia, demanding better working conditions and a speed up of reforms (July); Gorbachev ended the strikes by promising to meet demands, including reforms allowing right to strike.

1989 Ethnic rioting in Moldavia (Aug.), following effort to make republic's official language Moldavian; unrest over various issues continued 1989–90, including demands for reunification with Rumania, of which it was once a part.

1989 Law adopted which both permitted right to strike in principle and banned strikes in essential industries (Oct.); miners went on strike in defiance of ban (Oct.–Dec.).

1989 Supreme Soviet approved (Oct.) reforms ending bloc of reserved seats in Congress for

Communist party; also provided for direct election of presidents of Soviet republics.

1989   Berlin Wall, long-standing symbol of Cold War East-West divisions, was torn down (Nov.); collapse of East European Communist governments began as economic ills and pro-democracy demands overwhelmed the hard-line regimes.

1989   Presidium of Supreme Soviet ruled invalid all laws in Baltic States that conflicted with Soviet laws (Nov.).

1989   Lithuanian Communist party voted to secede from USSR (Dec.); Gorbachev, while upholding right of secession, insisted on preliminary discussions.

1989   Malta summit (Dec.); Gorbachev and US president G. Bush discussed 50 percent nuclear arms reduction, major reductions in US–USSR conventional forces in Europe, and trade deals.

1989   USSR recorded trade deficit this year, the first in 13 years.

1990   Democratic Platform of the Communist Party, a pro-democracy group, formed by pro-reform Communists from cities across USSR (Jan.).

1990   Two-day riot in Baku, capital of Azerbaijan (Jan.), sparked ethnic fighting throughout Azerbaijan and civil war in Nagorny Karabakh; Soviet troops retook Baku from protesters (Jan. 19).

1990   Mass pro-democracy rally held in Moscow (Feb.); called for ouster of conservatives, end to party privileges, and abolition of Article Six, guaranteeing supremacy of Communist party.

1990   Soviet Communist party ruled declaration of independence by Lithuanian Communists invalid (Feb.); Baltic States demanded negotiations on independence.

1990   Gorbachev proposed new reforms before Central Committee plenum (Feb.), including abolition of Article Six and creation of post of president, to be elected directly by the people; first election for president to be held in 1994.

1990   Soviets agreed to exclude US SDI program from START negotiations (Feb.).

1990   Central Committee approved end to Communist party's constitutional guarantees of supremacy (Article Six) (Mar.).

1990   Lithuania declared full independence (Mar. 11); Soviet troops seized Communist headquarters in Vilnius, following Soviet ruling independence was invalid; Soviets later briefly halted deliveries of oil and natural gas (Apr.) to Lithuania, after which negotiations began.

1990   Estonian Communist party voted for independence (Mar.); adopted gradual approach to secession, as did Latvia in its May 4 declaration.

1990   Congress of People's Deputies approved creation of executive presidency (Mar. 13).

1990   Gorbachev elected president by secret ballot in Congress (Mar. 14); to serve until projected direct popular elections in 1994.

1990   Communist party hit by mass resignations following publication of Central Committee open letter calling for expulsion of Democratic Platform faction members (Apr.).

1990   Georgia's Supreme Soviet ended Communist party monopoly and demanded talks with national government on Georgian independence (Apr.).

1990   Some 30,000 anti-government protesters interrupted Moscow May Day parades; supported Lithuania's declaration of independence.

1990   Washington summit (May–June); Bush and Gorbachev discussed Soviet blockade of break-away republic of Lithuania; signed trade accord contingent on Soviets' relaxing their emmigration laws; declared Cold War was over.

1990   Yeltsin elected chairman of Supreme Soviet of Russian Federation, the largest and most powerful of the Soviet republics (May 30); the Congress of the Russian Federation subsequently voted for the primacy of its laws over those of the USSR (June), a move repeated by all the other republics by October.

1990   Government ended censorship of media and eased restrictions on public and private businesses (June).

1990   Coal miners from across USSR formed first independent union (June).

1990   Moldavia declared 1940 annexation of Moldavia illegal (June, later voided by Soviets); changed name to Moldova; asserted primacy of its laws over those of USSR central government.

1990   Yeltsin quit the Communist party (July), leading a wave of defections by thousands.

1990   Ukraine declared independence (July); claimed right to organized separate military.

1990–91   Persian Gulf War; Soviets sought negotiated solution, but last-minute peace plan, which did not meet UN conditions, was rejected; Soviets acquiesced to use of US–led forces to drive Saddam Hussein out of Kuwait.

1990   Shatalin plan, a radical program for the rapid shift to a market economy promulgated (Aug.); compromise plan sought.

1990   Armenia declared its independence (Aug.); ordered all Communist party property within its borders confiscated; Gorbachev voided order by decree.

1990   USSR, the US, Britain, and France agreed to reunification of Germany (Sept.); Germany formally reunified.

1990   Gorbachev given emergency powers (for 18 months) to reform economy by decree and to maintain law and order (Sept.); economy deteriorated rapidly during the year as productivity continued to fall, budget and trade deficits widened, and inflation hit an official 19 percent during the year.

1990   Party control of police, KGB, and military cut back by Gorbachev decree.

1990   Gorbachev launched compromise plan for shift to market economy (Oct.); foreign ownership to be allowed, commercial exchange rate for ruble set, and interest rates increased.

1990   Supreme Soviet reasserted primacy of national laws over those of republics (Oct.), which had all declared sovereignty; legalized independent political parties and unions; and barred government interference in religious worship.

1990   Treaty on Conventional Armed Forces in Europe (CFE) signed in Paris (Nov.) by NATO and Warsaw Pact members; put limits on conventional forces deployed between Atlantic Ocean and Ural Mountains.

1990   Republican Party of Russia founded by members of the Democratic Platform (Nov.).

1990   Draft of new Union Treaty approved by Supreme Soviet (Dec.); treaty would redefine relationship between national government and republics and, Gorbachev claimed, would end threatened breakup of USSR; Baltic

states, Georgia, Armenia, and Moldavia rejected the treaty out of hand.

1990   Georgia's government proclaimed the Republic of Georgia (Dec.).

1990   Foreign Minister Eduard Shevardnadze resigned, warning of danger of return to dictatorship (Dec.).

1991   Five percent sales tax introduced to raise revenue for national and republican governments (Jan.).

1991   Valentin Pavlov named prime minister (Jan.), succeeding Ryzhkov.

1991   Soviet troops seized buildings in Riga and Vilnius in the breakaway Baltic republics (Jan.); thousands protested the takeovers in Vilnius.

1991   Voters in breakaway Baltic States approved referendums calling for independence (Feb.–Mar.); Gorbachev declared referendums invalid.

1991   Wave of strikes began with coal miners' walkout (Feb.); economy, already in trouble because of declining production and other ills, threatened with major crisis by stoppages; helped force Gorbachev to adopt compromise "anti-crisis" plan.

1991   Yeltsin called on Gorbachev to resign during nationwide TV broadcast (Mar. 9), as power struggle between the two leaders intensified.

1991   Warsaw Pact disbanded (Mar.); Soviet troops to be withdrawn from Germany, Hungary, and Czechoslavakia.

1991   Referendum on future of USSR held (Mar. 17); Soviet republics that participated approved plan to recast USSR as federation of equal, sovereign republics; Estonia, Latvia, Lithuania, Georgia, Armenia, and Moldavia refused participation in vote; direct election of president approved in Russian Federation.

1991   Voters in Georgia approved referendum (99 percent for it) for independence from USSR; Georgian Supreme Soviet voted for complete independence (Apr. 9).

1991   Prime Minister Pavlov introduced "anti-crisis" program; retail price hikes imposed as part of move toward free-market pricing; average 60 percent retail price increase expected by year's end.

1991   "9 plus 1" accord concluded at Novo-Ogarevo (Apr. 23); nine leaders of republics and Gorbachev agreed on plan for major economic and political restructuring; new union treaty to be drafted (for looser federation devolving more powers to republics); strikes to be banned to restore order; price hikes to be moderated; new elections to be held.

1991   Government joined with US in backing Mideast peace talks (Apr.).

1991   Striking miners in Siberia and Ukraine returned to work (May).

1991   In Georgia, Zviad Gamsakhurdia became first-ever elected president of the republic (May 26); his dictatorial style soon aroused resentment and unrest, however.

1991   Yeltsin elected president of Russian Federation (June 12), providing popular mandate for his radical reforms, and for his struggle with Gorbachev over power of republics versus the national government; under Yeltsin's leadership, Russian Federation led other republics in assuming greater powers.

1991   Voters in Leningrad approved measure to readopt city's original name of St. Petersburg (June 12), which had been changed after the Communist Revolution of 1917.

1991   Gorbachev attended Group of Seven (Western industrial powers) summit in London (July 15–17); members agreed to support Soviet shift to market economy.

1991   Legislation passed to denationalize state assets (July); to be 40–50 percent complete by 1992.

1991   Gorbachev announced new union treaty accepted by nine republics (July 24); national government and republics to govern jointly in foreign policy, defense, budgetary matters, and other areas; republics to have control over all others; impending signing of treaty (scheduled for Aug. 20) sparked the failed Soviet coup.

1991   Moscow summit (July 30–31); historic START treaty signed by Gorbachev and Bush (July 31); called for first-ever reduction in long-range nuclear arms amounting to 30 percent of stockpiles by 1998; US granted USSR most-favored-nation trading status.

1991   Soviet coup (*q.v.*) failed (Aug. 18–21); high government officials acting in concert with Communist party leaders unsuccessfully attempted to oust Gorbachev before new Union Treaty, weakening central government, could be signed; failed attempt resulted in suppression of Communist party, collapse of former Soviet Union, and creation of loosely knit Commonwealth of Independent States.

1991   Gorbachev, released from house arrest, returned to Moscow (Aug. 22); resigned as Communist party general secretary and called on Party to dissolve itself (Aug. 24) on learning of party's role in coup.

1991   Collapse of USSR: Ukraine declared full independence from USSR (Aug. 24) in wake of coup attempt; other remaining republics (Baltic republics having already won independence) followed suit and by year's end only the Russian Federation had not formally declared independence.

1991   Belorus president Nikolai Dementei resigned (Aug. 25), after having publicly supported the coup; Belorus declared economic independence.

1991   Moldavia declared independence (Aug. 27); now known as Moldova.

1991   Supreme Soviet suspended Communist party (Aug. 29).

1991   Azerbaijan declared independence (Aug. 30), as did Uzbekistan (Aug. 31).

1991   Supreme Soviet made wide-ranging transfer of powers to republics and approved transition government under Gorbachev (Sept. 5).

1991   Independence of Baltic States (Estonia, Latvia, Lithuanian) officially approved (Sept. 6).

1991   In Georgia, opposition leaders arrested as unrest over Gamsakhurdia administration increased (Sept.); unrest continued, however, and moves to oust the president resulted in civil war in Georgia.

1991   Government announced withdrawal of 11,000 troops from Cuba (Sept.).

1991   Tajikistan voted for independence (Sept. 9), as did Armenia (Sept. 23).

1991   Ukraine declared intention of becoming nuclear-free (Oct.).

1991   Eleven republics agreed to form unified economic community (Oct. 18) to pursue common economic reform program (Russian Federation, Ukraine, Belorus, Moldova, Azerbaijan, Armenia, Uzbekistan, Tajikistan, Turkmenia (Jurkmenistan), Kirghizia (Kyrgyzstan), and Kazakhstan.

1991   Turkmenia voted for independence (Oct. 27).

1991   Yeltsin plan for economic reform approved in Russian Federation (Nov. 1);

called for fiscal austerity and privatization similar to Poland's shock therapy program.

1991   Union treaty approved by nine of former Soviet republics (Nov. 14); provided for directly elected president; republics to retain all powers not specifically delegated to national government.

1991   Russian Federation took over responsibility for finances of national government (Nov. 30).

1991   Voters turned down referendum on proposed union treaty (Dec. 1).

1991   Commonwealth of Independent States (CIS) created by Yeltsin (for Russian Federation) and leaders of the two other Slavic republics (Ukraine and Belorus) during meeting at Minsk (Dec. 8); provided only for single currency, economic unity, and unified command for nuclear arms; USSR declared dissolved; other republics invited to join.

1991   Kazakhstan voted for independence (Dec. 16).

1991   Yeltsin ordered seizure of Kremlin (Dec. 19).

1991   Alma-Ata agreement signed in Kazakhstan (Dec. 21); three Slavic republics, plus all but one of the other republics (Georgia), agreed to recognize sovereignty of other republics, adhere to current borders, respect rights of national minorities, form a single unified economy, and honor treaties signed by former USSR government; members were the Russian Federation, Ukraine, Belorus, Moldova, Azerbaijan, Armenia, Uzbekistan, Tajikistan, Turkmenia, Kirghizia, and Kazakhstan.

1991   Gorbachev resigned as USSR president (Dec. 25).

1991   USSR Supreme Soviet voted end to 1922 treaty forming the USSR (Dec. 26).

1992   Baltic States demanded withdrawal of Commonwealth troops stationed there (Jan. 5); CIS agreed to start pullout (Feb. 1).

1992   In Georgia, President Gamsakhurdia fled capital as opposition forces threatened (Jan.); military council took power as fighting began to diminish.

1992   47-nation conference on aid to CIS held (Jan. 22–23); US to begin airlift of emergency supplies.

1992   Yeltsin promised to end targeting of strategic nuclear weapons at US cities (Jan.

26); later proposed new round of cuts in strategic nuclear weapons (Jan. 29).

1992   Eight republics became UN members (Feb): Kazakhstan, Armenia, Azerbaijan, Kyrgyzstan, Moldova, Tajikistan, Turkmenistan, and Uzbekistan.

1992   Communist party financial aid to Communists in US, France, Israel and numerous other countries revealed (Feb.); aid totaled $200 million over 30-year period.

1992   *Pravda,* former Communist party organ, forced to shut down for lack of sufficient operating funds (Feb.).

1992   Minsk summit of presidents of CIS republics (Feb. 15); three republics refused to maintain unified conventional army.

1992   Russian Federation to sell off about 75 percent of state-owned retail stores by year end (Feb. 29).

1992   Yeltsin began organizing separate military for Russian Federation, following breakdown of efforts to maintain unified CIS military (Mar.); later revealed plans for sharp reduction in troop levels (Apr. 1).

1992   Kiev summit of CIS republic presidents (Mar. 20); failed to resolve key issues, including Russian Federation's claim to all of former USSR assets.

1992   E. Shevardnadze, former Soviet foreign minister, in power as head of provisional government in Georgia (Mar.).

1992   US president G. Bush pledged to help finance $24 billion aid package for former Soviet Union (Apr.).

1992   IMF and World Bank offered membership to most of the former Soviet republics (Apr 27).

1992   Two nuclear weapons missing from Kazahkstan reported to be in Iran (May); Iranians deny charge.

1992   Four newly independent Soviet republics agreed to honor cuts in nuclear missiles promised in 1991 US–Soviet treaty (May); previously agreed to transfer nuclear weapons to Russian Federation for dismantling by July 1992.

1992   Azerbaijan and Armenia signed Iranianbrokered accord to end fighting over Nagorno Karabakh (May 8); some 1,500 killed since 1988.

1992   US and Russia agreed to cut long-range nuclear missile arsenals by two-thirds (June).

1992   In Georgia, government troops thwarted an attempted coup by supporters of ousted President Gamsakhurdia (June 24).

1992   Yeltsin agreed to cut inflation and government deficits to qualify for $4 billion IMF loan (July 5); would cut 15–20 percent per month inflation to below 10 percent.

1992   Yeltsin, speaking before G-7 summit of major industrial powers, offered to swap Russian assets for reduction of $70 billion national debt (July 8); G-7 leaders agreed to $24 billion self-help aid package for Russia.

1992   Moldovan separatists agreed to plan to end fighting in Trans-Dniester region (July).

1992   Productivity in republics reported still declining sharply (July).

1992   Tax cut enacted, reducing income tax from flat 60 percent to sliding scale of 12 to 40 percent (July).

1992   Yeltsin's radical economic reform program continued (Sept.); some 700,000 owned their own apartments by Sept., but four-fold pay increase for workers hardly compared with 2,000 percent inflation; unemployment threatened to increase 20-fold in 1993.

Commonwealth of Nations, British   *See* **British Commonwealth of Nations.**

commune   Term once applied to medieval towns that achieved self-government by rebellion or by charter. Communes were generally formed in areas where royal authority was weak.

Commune of Paris (Paris Commune)   1. Governmental body during the French Revolution (1789–99) Originally formed (1789) as the elected city government of Paris (under Mayor Jean Sylvain Bailly, 1736–93), the Commune became a vehicle for radical extremists in the revolution. Under the leadership of J. Hébert and P. Chaumette, it vied with the Committee of Public Safety and the National Convention for control of the revolutionary government. Executions of its leaders during the Reign of Terror weakened the Commune's power, and it was finally abolished (1794) in the Thermidorian reaction.   2. Short-lived rebel government formed (1871) in Paris. Opposed to policies of A. Thier's Government of National Defense, and particularly the humiliating peace terms accepted after the Franco-Prussian War (1870–71), Parisian workers rose in rebellion (Mar. 18, 1871). A government was formed by the revolu-

tionaries (mostly radical republicans) and enacted some short-lived reforms. Government troops reentered the city and, in what is known as Bloody Week, crushed the revolt by May 28. More than 17,000 men, women, and children were executed and thousands of others were arrested in what amounted to reprisals against the working class by the bourgeoisie and aristocracy.

communism   Political philosophy based upon the principle of collective ownership of both property and means of production. Communists view history from the perspective of class struggle and seek to establish a classless society, in its most ideal form a "dictatorship of the proletariat." The idea of a communal society, a fundamental element of communist thought, dates back to the ancient Greeks and was advanced by Plato in his philosophical work the *Republic*. T. More in his famous work *Utopia* (1516) promoted the idea of a communal society and T. Münzer, leader of the Anabaptists, advanced the ideal of a religious communal society during the unsuccessful Peasants' War (1524–25). The Industrial Revolution (*q.v.*) and the severe economic hardships suffered by workers gave rise to socialism (*q.v.*) in the late 18th and early 19th cents. Modern communism then emerged from the socialist movement, first as a radical wing of socialism and finally (early 1900s) as a separate and distinct ideology of revolution and collective ownership. The fundamental rivalry between communist and capitalist societies has been a factor in world history since the creation of the first Communist state, the USSR, in 1917. After WW II it led to the tensions of the Cold War (*q.v.*). Detente and increasing East-West contacts in the 1970s and 1980s brought an end to the competition, but by the end of the 1980s, Communist governments in Europe and other parts of the world had been seriously weakened by chronic economic problems, corruption, and pro-democracy unrest. Communist governments in Eastern Europe and finally the USSR itself collapsed in rapid succession during 1989–91. China remained as the world's only major power embracing communism. (*See also* Commonwealth of Independent States [from 1917], Marxism, Leninism, Stalinism.) Key events in the history of communism include:

1848   *Communist Manifesto* written by K. Marx and F. Engels; introduced concept of historic necessity of revolution as a result of class struggle; initially a statement of radical Socialist principles, it became the cornerstone of communist ideology.

1864 First International formed at London; a Socialist labor federation, it was split by a power struggle between Marx and the anarchist N. Bakunin (1876).

1870s Spread of Socialist parties in Europe.

1880s–90s Split widened between advocates of gradual ("evolutionary") socialism and exponents of revolutionary socialism (communism).

1889 Second International formed at Paris; federation of Socialist and labor groups committed to eventual social revolution.

1896 Anarchists, extreme radicals, ousted from Second International; Marxist doctrine of inevitable revolution reaffirmed, however.

1898 German evolutionary Socialist E. Bernstein called for a revision of Marxist ideology and denied historical necessity of revolution.

1898 Russian Social Democratic Labor party founded (Mar.) by Russian Marxists at Minsk.

1903 N. Lenin forced Russian Social Democratic Labor party to split into Bolshevik (revolutionary) and Menshevik (gradualist) factions; split led to formation of the Communist party when Bolsheviks seized control of the Russian Revolution (1917).

1914 Second International collapsed as Socialist groups split along nationalist lines at the outbreak of WW I.

1915 Zimmerwald Conference of Socialists denounced WW I as imperialistic; this stand was attacked by Lenin's leftist factions, which wanted to transform the war into a civil war against the bourgeoisie.

1916 Spartacus party formed in Germany; became nucleus of German Communist party after WW I.

1917 Russian Revolution; Lenin's Bolsheviks seized power (Oct.) and thus established Russia as the first Communist state. Communist dictatorship of Russia instituted.

1918 Bolsheviks formed Communist party in Russia; Lenin's ideology dominant under his leadership (to 1924).

1919 Communists formed Third International, or Comintern, to spread Communist revolution worldwide; break between Socialists and Communists complete.

1921 Chinese Communist party founded.

1920s Lenin died (1924); J. Stalin began to consolidate personal power in the USSR; moved party away from ideology of world revolution and began ideological struggle with L. Trotsky.

1922 USSR formally established by treaty.

1925 Patriarch Tikhon, elected in 1918, died; Stalin refused to permit election of new patriarch.

1929–38 Trotsky expelled from the USSR (1929); Stalin concentrated on establishment of model Communist state in the USSR; secured complete control of Communist party in series of purge trials (late 1930s) and thus established his totalitarian state.

1941–45 Soviets joined Allied nations during WW II after Russia was invaded (1941) by Nazi Germany.

1943 Comintern dissolved to promote alliance with Allies during WW II.

1943 Stalin restored patriarchate in Russian Orthodox church.

1945 Relations between the Communists and the West deteriorated at the end of WW II; Soviets established satellite states in Eastern Europe; Cold War began.

1949 Chinese Communists came to power on mainland China, adding another major nation to the Communist bloc.

1950–53 Korean War, first major East-West armed conflict stemming from ideological rivalry.

1956 De-Stalinization; Soviet premier N. Khrushchev denounced Stalinism at 20th Party Congress; attack contributed to uprisings against Communist regimes in Poland and Hungary.

c1961 Cuba established Communist government; became first Communist state in Western Hemisphere, a coup for Soviet Communists and an embarrassment to the US.

1960 Relations between Soviets and Communist China disintegrated; led to major ideological split within Communist world, in which Chinese accused Soviets of revisionism.

1960–75 Vietnam War, second major armed conflict arising from East-West ideological rivalry; Communist North Vietnam won control of South.

1966–69 Cultural Revolution in China; ultraradical Chinese Communist factions sought to impose extremist ideology throughout government and society.

1970s Soviets joined US in promoting détente, policy aimed at lessening tensions between non-Communist and Communist nations; resulted in diplomatic and economic ties between various nations of the two blocs.

1968 Prague Spring; Soviets invaded Czechoslovakia to halt liberalization of Communist government there.

1973 Shake-up of the Central Committee Brezhnev's allies, A. Gromyko, Andrei Grechko, and Y. Andropov installed on the committee.

1977 New Soviet constitution adopted (Oct. 4); Communist party specifically named as ruling party of the Soviet Union.

1979 Soviet troops invaded Afghanistan to back puppet regime there; Soviets unable to overcome Afghan guerrillas, supported by US and others; failed invasion damaged Soviet prestige at home and abroad.

1986 Soviet leader M. Gorbachev, proclaiming need for drastic reform of Soviet society before 27th Congress of the Soviet Communist party (Feb.), announced need for *glasnost* (openness) as a key to effecting the changes; era of Gorbachev's liberal reforms began.

1986 Soviets passed legislation to foster private enterprise in certain areas of the economy; marked first break in the Soviet state's legal monopoly of economy and an important shift from Marxist ideas.

1987 Gorbachev proposed policy of *perestroika* (restructuring), the second key principle (with *glasnost*) of his wide-ranging reform program (Jan.).

1987 Gorbachev publicly denounced Stalin's bloody purges of the 1930s (July); party later approved a memorial for the victims.

1987 B. Yeltsin, a Politburo member and the Moscow City Communist party first secretary, ousted for accusing hard-liners in the Central Committee of slowing the pace of reform in Soviet government (Nov.).

1988–89 Mounting unrest in the USSR forced ruling Communist party to implement some democratic reforms, including election of representatives to national legislature; Communist hard-liners subsequently were defeated at the polls; demands for reform and for a quicker pace of change increased.

1989 Berlin Wall, long-standing symbol of East-West divisions, was torn down (Nov.); collapse of Eastern European Communist governments began as economic ills and pro-democracy demands overwhelmed the hard-line regimes.

1990 Mass pro-democracy rally held in Moscow (Feb.); called for ouster of conservative Communists, end to party privileges, and abolition of Article Six, guaranteeing supremacy of Communist party.

1990 Central Committee approved end to Communist party's constitutional guarantees of supremacy (Article Six) (Mar.).

1990 Gorbachev elected executive president by secret ballot in Congress (Mar. 14); to serve until projected direct popular elections in 1994.

1990 Government ended censorship of media and eased restrictions on public and private businesses (June).

1990 B. Yeltsin quit the Communist party (July), leading a wave of defections by thousands.

1991 Soviet coup (*q.v.*) failed (Aug.); hard-line Communist leaders unsuccessfully attempted to oust Gorbachev to block his reforms; failed attempt resulted in suppression of Communist party, and collapse of former Soviet Union.

1991 Gorbachev resigned as Communist party general secretary following coup; called on party to dissolve itself (Aug. 24) because of its role in coup.

1991 Collapse of USSR, ending existence of first Communist state; republics one-by-one declared independence during late summer and fall.

1991 Supreme Soviet suspended Communist party (Aug. 29).

1991 Gorbachev resigned as USSR president (Dec. 25).

1991 Non-Communist Commonwealth of Independent States formed as loose federation of all but one of the former Soviet republics (by Dec.).

1991 USSR Supreme Soviet voted end to 1922 treaty forming the USSR (Dec. 26).

1992 *Pravda,* former Communist party organ, forced to shut down for lack of sufficient operating funds (Feb.).

Communist Manifesto Fundamental statement of Communist revolutionary doctrine, written

(1848) by K. Marx and F. Engels. It proposed that workers around the world join together and fight to put control of business and government in the hands of the proletariat. These doctrines had few international consequences until the rise of the Russian Communist party during the Russian Revolution (1917).

Communist party (Communist Party of the Soviet Union) Political party that ruled the Soviet Union. It was founded (1903) by N. Lenin at the party congress of the Russian Social Democratic party in London. Lenin headed the Bolshevik (*q.v.*) faction, the radical wing of the party, which stood in opposition to the more moderate Mensheviks. It became the ruling party in Russia following the Russian Revolution and subsequent seizure of power by the Bolsheviks (1917) and remained in power until 1991, when it was disbanded following the failed coup by Soviet hard-liners. (*See also* Commonwealth of Independent States, from 1917; communism.)

Comnenus Family name of a line of Byzantine rulers, who reigned in the 11th and 12th cents. The line was founded by Manuel Eroticus Comnenus (*fl.* 11th cent.), a general under Byzantine emperor Basil II. A branch of the family later ruled the empire of Trebizond. *The Comnenid rulers of the Byzantine Empire were:* Isaac I 1057–59; Alexius I 1081–1118; John II 1118–43; Manuel I 1143–80: Alexius II 1180–83; Andronicus I 1183–85.

Compactata of Prague *See* **Hussite Wars.**

Compact of Iglau (Compactata) Agreement signed (1436), at Iglau (Jihlava), now in Moravia, between the Hussites and German king Sigismund.

Company of the Merchants of the Staple (Merchant Staplers) Association of English merchants who controlled the country's wool exports from the 13th through the 16th cents. Its name came from the practice of gathering all exports into one town, called the "staple," to minimize export duties. Its influence waned when the English began to weave their own cloth. The Merchants Adventurers, who exported finished cloth, eventually rose in their stead.

Compostela, Saint James of *See* **James, Saint "the Greater."**

Compromise of Breda *See* **Breda, Compromise of.**

Compromise of 1850 Series of bills passed (1850) by US Congress to settle the crisis over extension of slavery into new territories. The compromise measures, arranged by H. Clay and S. Douglas and supported by D. Webster, prevented secession of the South for some years but failed to resolve the fundamental question of slavery. The crisis was brought on (1849) by California's petition to be admitted to the union as a "free" state. The compromise, intended to balance the interests of the North and South, included California's admission as a free state, the eventual admission of Utah and New Mexico with the slavery question to be determined by popular sovereignty, the abolition of slave trade in Washington, D.C., and a strict fugitive-slave law. The peace was short-lived. The doctrine of popular sovereignty contributed to the armed conflicts of Bleeding Kansas (*q.v.*) and the fugitive-slave law aroused bitter opposition in the North.

Compromise of 1867 *See* **Dual Monarchy.**

Comstock, Henry Tompkins Paige *See* **Comstock Lode.**

Comstock Lode Site of major US silver deposits near Virginia City, Nevada. It was named for Henry Tompkins Paige Comstock (1820–70), who claimed (1859) sections of the lode but sold his claim before its value was discovered. It produced great amounts of silver and contributed to the settlement of Nevada and California, but was depleted and abandoned by c1898.

Comte, Auguste 1798–1857. French philosopher, founder of positivism and an important figure in the development of sociology. He described his system for attaining a stable society in the modern world in his work *The Course of Positive Philosophy.* Another important work in the development of positivism is his *System of Positive Polity.*

***Comunero* movement** Spanish republican rebellion. The uprising took place (1520–21) in the cities of Castile in reaction to the autocratic rule of Charles V. Though Charles crushed the rebellion, he subsequently modified his policies. Similar *comunero* revolts occurred later in Paraguay (1723–35) and in New Granada (1780–81).

Comyn, John *See* **Robert I.**

conciliarism Medieval religious theory. It held that a general council of the Roman Catholic church possessed greater authority than the pope and had the power to depose him. Both Vatican councils (1870, 1962–65) reaffirmed papal supremacy.

Concini, Concino *d.* 1617. Italian adventurer in France. The favorite of Queen Marie de Médicis he held great influence in the early reign of King Louis XIII and was made marshal of France. His intrigues, however, aroused the wrath of Louis, by whose order he was assassinated.

Concord, Battle of *See* **Lexington and Concord, Battles of.**

concordat Binding treaty between an ecclesiastical authority (usually the pope) and a secular one. It carries the force of international law.

Concordat of Bologna French-papal agreement, (Aug. 18, 1516) by which Pope Leo X ceded to French king Francis I extensive control over the French church.

Concordat of 1801 Agreement between Napoleon and Pope Pius VII ending the break between the Roman Catholic church and the revolutionary government of France. The church was reestablished in France, church property confiscated during the revolution was to remain in private hands, and archbishops and bishops were to be nominated (for appointment by the pope) by the French government. The concordat remained in force until 1905, when anticlericalism in France brought about legal separation of church and state.

Concordat of Worms An agreement concluded (1122) between Holy Roman Emperor Henry V and Pope Calixtus II, to end the Investiture Controversy. By its terms, the power to appoint bishops and abbots was divided between emperor and pope. Elections of German bishops or abbots were to take place in the presence of the emperor or his representative. The emperor was to decide contested elections. Those elected were to be first invested with secular duties and privileges by the emperor, and then consecrated with spiritual rights and obligations by the pope. In Burgundy and Italy, however, investiture by the emperor was to follow consecration by the pope or ecclesiastical authority. Although the concordat gave the pope spiritual authority over the church offices, it did not end the rivalry between the popes and the emperors.

Condé, House of Line of French nobles. A branch of the powerful Bourbons, its members bore the title "prince of Condé," beginning in the 16th cent. with Louis I de Bourbon (1530–69), a leader of the Conspiracy of Amboise. The line became extinct in 1830.

Condé, Louis II de Bourbon, prince de (the great Condé) 1621–86. French general. Though loyal to the court at the outset of the Fronde (*q.v.*), he fell into disfavor. He then led a rebel army during the Fronde of the princes.

Condé, Louis Joseph de Bourbon, prince de 1736–1818. French general and leader of the army of Condé, a corps of French émigrés formed to overturn the French Revolution.

Condorcet, Antoine Nicolas, marquis of 1743–94. French philosopher. His most famous work predicted the perfectibility of mankind. An active supporter of the French Revolution, he died in prison at the hands of the extremist Jacobin faction.

condottieri Italian mercenaries. Employed by medieval Italian city-states in their frequent feuds, they often changed sides to the highest bidder and proved ineffective in combat. Engagements between rival condottieri bands were noted for their lack of bloodshed.

Confederacy (Confederate States of America) Secessionist government of the South during the US Civil War (1861–65). A provisional government was formed (Feb., 1861) shortly after the secessions began, and a permanent government for the eleven states of the Confederacy was installed Feb., 1862. J. Davis was president and A. Stephens vice-president. The Confederate constitution was adopted Mar., 1861, and Richmond was made the capital July, 1861. The Confederacy carried on all domestic and foreign governmental functions for the duration of the war. In the foreign arena, the South failed in its attempt to force European powers into an alliance by withholding cotton exports. The failure of King Cotton as a weapon proved to be a crucial setback. At home, the largely agricultural South was at a disadvantage against the more populous, industrial North. Soon after war began, there developed manpower shortages (even with conscription), material shortages caused by the Union blockade of the South, and serious inflation caused by lack of adequate financial reserves. Despite the Confederacy's determined and often heroic military stand, it was finally forced to surrender to the North at Appomattox Courthouse (Apr., 1865). *The Con-*

federate States, with dates of their secession and reentry to the Union, are:

SOUTH CAROLINA	DEC. 1860–JUNE 1868
MISSISSIPPI	JAN. 1861–FEB. 1870
FLORIDA	JAN. 1861–JUNE 1868
ALABAMA	JAN. 1861–JUNE 1868
GEORGIA	JAN. 1861–JULY 1870
LOUISIANA	JAN. 1861–JUNE 1868
TEXAS	FEB. 1861–MAR. 1870
VIRGINIA	APR. 1861–JAN. 1870
ARKANSAS	MAY 1861–JUNE 1868
NORTH CAROLINA	MAY 1861–JUNE 1868
TENNESSEE	JUNE 1861–JULY 1866

Confederation, Articles of *See* **Articles of Confederation.**

Confederation Government Confederation government of Bolivia and Peru (1836–39). The confederation was opposed by Chile and Argentina and fell after defeat of its forces by Chile at Yungay (Jan. 20, 1839).

Confederation group Canadian literary group of the late 19th cent. Its members were noted for their celebration of Canada's natural beauty, and included the poets William Bliss Carman (1861–1929) and Charles G. D. Roberts (1860–1943).

Confederation of Bar League of Polish nobles formed (1768) at Bar (then in Poland) to oppose Russian domination of Polish internal affairs. The league formed after Polish king Stanislaus II acceded to the wishes of Catherine II of Russia and granted religious equality to Poland's non-Roman Catholic minority. The nobles, among them C. Pulaski, were finally defeated by Russian armies in 1772, despite assistance from Turkey and France. The war with Russia culminated in the first Partition of Poland (1772).

Confederation of Radom League of Polish nobles. Formed (June 23, 1767) with Russia's support, it was a confederation of groups opposed to the reform measures of Polish king Stanislaus II. The league was a contributing factor in events leading up to the first Partition of Poland (1772).

Confederation of the Rhine League of German states (1806–13) organized by Napoleon. He formed the league, after defeating the Austrians at the Battle of Austerlitz (1805), to counter the two major German powers, Austria and Prussia. The league ultimately included almost all the German states except Austria and Prussia. On joining, each of the states gave up its allegiance to the Holy Roman Empire. The major states that joined the league included Bavaria, Württenberg, Baden, Hesse-Darmstadt, and Nassau. The league collapsed after Napoleon's defeat in Russia but nevertheless marked the end of the Holy Roman Empire and played a part in the later unification of modern Germany.

Conference of Genoa Meeting (Apr. 10–May 19, 1922) of 29 European nations and 5 British Commonwealth countries at Genoa, Italy. The conference was held to discuss resumption of trade between Europe and the new Soviet government and plans for financing post-WW I reconstruction. Other questions soon dominated the conference, however, including repayment for foreign property seized by the Soviets during their revolution, repayment of the Russian war debt, and repayment for damages inflicted by the Allied military expedition into Russia after the revolution. The Treaty of Rapallo (1922), a separate pact between Russia and Germany, forced the adjournment of the conference.

Conference of Lausanne 1. Meetings (Nov., 1923–July, 1924) between Allied powers and the Ottoman Empire, leading to the Treaty of Lausanne. 2. Meetings (June–July, 1932) to discuss repayment of war debts from WW I. Attended by Great Britain, France, Belgium, Germany, Italy, and Japan, the conference scrapped the Young Plan for war reparations by Germany, such repayment having been made impossible by worldwide economic depression. The new plan called for repayment of a reduced sum, but was ultimately rejected (1932) by the US Congress. Germany subsequently made no payments and the Nazi government later repudiated the debt.

Conference of San Remo International conference held (Apr. 19–26, 1920) at San Remo, Italy. Representatives of Great Britain, France, Italy, Japan, Belgium, and Greece completed the draft of the later peace treaty of Sèvres with Turkey and created British mandates in Palestine and Iraq, and French mandates in Syria and Lebanon.

Confucianism Chinese moral and ethical philosophy that has played a major role in much of China's history. Confucianism is based on classical writings and precepts dating to the early period of Chinese history. These precepts were systematized by Confucius (551–479 BC) and modified and developed by later Chinese philosophers. Originally an ethical system, Confucianism adopted metaphysical elements from Buddhism, Daoism, and other systems, notably with the advent of Neo-Confucianism (10th–13th cents.). It greatly influenced the Chinese imperial government, and Confucian traditions were perpetuated by the Chinese Examination System (*q.v.*). Confucianism declined with the opening of China to the West (19th cent.) and has been virtually eliminated from political life by the Chinese Communists. Key dates in the history of Confucianism include:

23D–3D CENTS. BC Elements of what became Confucian thought developed during Hsia (23d–18th cents. BC), Shang (18th–12th cents. BC), and Chou (12th–3d cents. BC) dynasties.

8TH–3D CENTS. BC Chou dynasty declined under pressure from barbarian invasions; political disintegration and rise of feudalism altered traditional Chinese life.

551–479 BC Confucius lived; sought to reestablish order through traditional political and moral teachings; believed by tradition to have expanded and ordered such thought in works including *Wu Ching* (Five Classics) and *I Ching* (Book of Changes).

479 BC Confucius died; subsequent scholars compiled aphorisms attributed to him in *Lun y;* some 70 disciples continued his teachings.

372–289 BC Mencius lived; advanced Confucian thought and carried on vigorous debates with opposing philosophical schools.

3D CENT. BC Hsun-tzu lived; opposed Mencius's teaching that humanity's nature was basically good and advocated strong hierarchy of society; contributed to rise of Legalists, whose teachings supported strong imperial rulers.

221–207 BC Confucian thought declined with unification of China under Ch'in dynasty, which drew upon Legalist teachings.

206 BC–AD 220 Confucianism restored during rule of Han dynasty.

156–87 BC Han emperor Wu Ti lived; established Confucianism as official philosophical school. Chinese Examination System, based on knowledge of Confucian thought, adopted for testing civil servants.

C1ST CENT. AD Confucianism split into two schools: the Old Text School, which placed emphasis on the original Classical texts; and the New School, which incorporated later texts and teachings, including Taoist thought.

1ST CENT. AD Shrines to Confucius constructed; Confucius became subject of veneration.

3D CENT. AD Fall of Han dynasty (AD 220); Confucianism declined with rising political disorder in China.

3D–6TH CENTS. AD Buddhism and Taoism gained in importance as Confucianism declined.

581–907 China reunited during Sui (581–618) and T'ang (618–907) dynasties; Confucianism regained its position of importance, new edition of *Wu Ching* issued during early T'ang (7th cent.).

960–1279 Rise of Neo-Confucianism during Sung dynasty; incorporated metaphysical elements from Daoism and Buddhism.

1130–1200 Chu Hsi lived; greatest exponent of Neo-Confucian thought.

1472–1529 Wang Yang-ming lived; developed school of thought emphasizing introspection and intuition which increasingly opposed the rigid institutional form of Confucianism adopted by the Ming dynasty.

19TH CENT. Confucian traditions challenged by Western influences on Chinese life.

1858–1927 K'ang Yu-wei lived; attempted to incorporate Western thought into framework of Confucianism; sought unsuccessfully to modernize China in Hundred Days of Reform (1898).

1905 Chinese Examination System abolished in move toward modernization.

1911–12 Chinese imperial rule ended by Nationalist Revolution; Confucianism as an institution severely crippled.

1949 Communists came to power in China; Confucian teachings suppressed.

Confucius 551–479 BC. Famous Chinese philosopher whose teachings form the basis for Confucianism. Confucius was a social reformer who hoped to create a just society by his teachings on morality and government. Little is known of his life other than that he was born to a poor family in eastern China and his father died when he was very young. Confucius educated himself and became known for his scholarship. He served in an official post for a time and then turned (c495 BC) to travel, and gathered a small circle of disciples. Through them he hoped to bring an end to the constant wars and tyrannical governments so prevalent in his time. Soon after the death of Confucius, the disciples compiled his teachings in the *Analects,* which was studied as a basic text in China for two thousand years.

Congo (Republic of the Congo) (*formerly* People's Republic of the Congo; French Congo) Republic located in Equatorial Africa. The population is 2,305,000 and the capital is Brazzaville. The Congo's coastal region was first explored (15th cent.) by the Portuguese. In the 1870s, the region north of the Congo River was explored by Savorgnan de Brazza (1852–1905), who founded Brazzaville (1880) and established a French claim in the region. The same year he negotiated with the native Bateke and established a French protectorate over the area, which became known as the French Congo and, later, Middle Congo. In 1910, the Congo was made part of French Equatorial Africa. It became (1946) a French overseas territory and was granted autonomous rule (1958). The Congo became independent on Aug. 15, 1960, with Fulbert Youlou in office as its first president. An uprising in 1963 led to a change in government and the introduction of Communist economic and political systems. An army coup brought Maj. Marien Ngouabi to power in 1968. He renamed the country the People's Republic of the Congo and was assassinated in 1977. Col. Denis Sassou-Nguesso became president in 1979 and a new socialist constitution was adopted that year. Though a treaty with the USSR was concluded in 1981, the Congo during the 1980s established closer ties with other Communist and non-Communist nations, particularly France. With the country's economy troubled throughout the decade, Sassou-Nguesso in 1989 abandoned socialism and introduced economic reforms, including privatization and encouragement of private enterprise. Opposition parties were permitted in 1990 and the ruling party officially abandoned Marxist-Leninist ideology in 1991. Also in 1991, a transition government came to power pending free elections, and the country's name reverted to Republic of the Congo. Cuban troops, stationed in the Congo since 1977, were withdrawn in 1991.

Congo, Democratic Republic of the *See* **Zaire.**

Congregationalism System of church organization in which local churches govern themselves. Congregational churches are Protestant and are most numerous in the US and Britain. Congregationalism arose (16th–17th cents.) in Britain as a reaction to the established Church of England and first appeared among the followers (Brownists) of Robert Browne (c1550–1633). Congregationalists in the early 17th cent., then known as Independents, suffered persecutions until 1689, when the Act of Toleration was declared. The movement spread to America (1620) with the Pilgrims, and the first Congregational church was built (1629) at Salem, Massachusetts. Since then Congregationalism in both the US and Britain has undergone periods of expansion and decline. From the 19th cent., groups of these churches have tended to form unions and broad fellowships while maintaining the autonomy of the local congregation. Another group called Independents, not related to the Congregationalists, emerged during the revolutionary Parliaments of the 1640s.

Congress Kingdom of Poland (Congress Poland) Kingdom of Poland created (May 3, 1815) by the Congress of Vienna after Napoleon's fall. The Russian tsar was designated ruler of the kingdom, though Congress Poland was granted a constitution, a legislative diet, and the right to maintain an army. Polish resistance to the tsar's domination led to the November Insurrection (1830–31) and January Insurrection (1863–64). Both revolts were unsuccessful and resulted in severe repression and eventual reduction of the kingdom to a Russian province (1864). Poland was ultimately recreated as an independent state after WW I.

Congress of Aix-la-Chapelle Meeting (Oct.–Nov., 1818) of members of the Quadruple Alliance (Britain, Austria, Prussia, Russia) and France at Aix-la-Chapelle (now Aachen, Germany). The powers resolved (Oct. 9) to withdraw the forces occupying France since Napoleon's defeat and to restore France to full sovereignty. The congress was one of several meetings in which the major powers worked together to shape the stable and conservative policy (as in the Holy Alliance), which prevailed in Europe after the Napoleonic era.

Congress of Berlin Meeting of European powers called (1878) to renegotiate the Treaty of San

Stefano and deal with British and Austro-Hungarian dissatisfaction with terms forced on the Ottoman Empire by Russia after the Russo-Turkish War (1877–78). Headed by O. von Bismarck, the meeting resulted in the Treaty of Berlin (July 13, 1878), which cost Russia much of what it had gained in the earlier treaty. Austria-Hungary was to occupy Bosnia and Herzegovina; Britain was to occupy Cyprus; and Montenegro, Serbia, and Rumania were recognized as independent. An autonomous Bulgaria (much smaller than that sought by Russia) was created under Ottoman suzerainty. Russia gained control over Ottoman territories in Asia and the Balkans.

Congress of Chilpancingo   Mexican revolutionary congress (convened Sept., 1813) at Chilpancingo, Mexico. It declared Mexican independence from Spain (Nov., 1813) and promulgated Mexico's first constitution (Oct. 22, 1814).

Congress of Laibach   Meeting (Jan.–May, 1821) of European powers. A continuation of the Congress of Troppau (1820), it was held at Laibach, Yugoslavia, and was attended by representatives of the Holy Alliance (Austria, Prussia, and Russia), Great Britain, France, and other, lesser states. Despite opposition by the French and British, the congress sanctioned armed intervention (by C. Metternich's Austrian forces) to put down liberal revolutions in Naples and Piedmont. The congress was a victory for Metternich's conservative policies, which supported absolutist monarchies.

Congress of Paris   Conference (Feb.–Mar., 1856) of Austria, France, Great Britain, the Ottoman Empire, Russia, and Sardinia, to end the Crimean War. The congress culminated with the Treaty of Paris (*q.v.*).

Congress of Troppau   Conference (Oct.–Dec., 1820) at Troppau, Austria (now Opava, Czechoslovakia), to consider European action against the uprisings in Spain and the Two Sicilies. The Russian and Austrian emperors attended, the latter accompanied by C. Metternich, but Britain and France sent lower-ranking representatives and refused to subscribe to the protocol threatening armed intervention against insurgents. (*See also* Congress of Laibach.)

Congress of Tucumán   Argentine Congress that met in Tucumán and declared (July 9, 1816) Argentine independence from Spain. The Congress pursued the idea of an independent

South American monarchy but was unable to impose an effective government structure. It was ultimately forced to disband (1820) by local caudillos.

Congress of the United States   The legislative branch of the US government, consisting of the Senate and the House of Representatives. As established by Article I of the Constitution, Congress is empowered to "make all laws" necessary for the execution of the power "vested by [the] Constitution in the government of the United States." The Senate, the upper house, consists of two senators from each state, named by state legislatures until the 17th Amendment provided (1913) for their election by direct popular vote. Senators serve terms of six years and one-third of the members are elected every two years, making the Senate a continuing body. The vice-president of the United States is the presiding officer of the Senate and has a vote in case of a tie. When the vice-president is absent, his place is taken by a president *pro tempore,* who is fourth in line of succession to the US presidency. The House of Representatives, the lower house, consists of 435 members apportioned according to population, each state being entitled to at least one. Representatives serve for two years, and the entire body is elected anew every two years. The House is presided over by a speaker, nominated by the party currently enjoying a majority and elected by the House. The speaker is third in line of succession for the presidency. Legislation must be approved by both houses. Money bills and impeachment proceedings originate only in the House. The Senate confirms presidential appointments (by a simple majority), ratifies treaties (by a two-thirds majority), and tries impeachment cases. Congress is required by the Constitution to hold an annual session which, since the passage of the 20th Amendment (1933), begins on Jan. 3 of each year. Legislation, once it has passed both houses, must be signed by the president within ten days, or it becomes law automatically, unless Congress adjourns in the meantime. Two-thirds majorities are needed in both houses to override a presidential veto. Since 1803 the US Supreme Court has effectively exercised a power implied, but not specified, in the Constitution, of invalidating congressional legislation on grounds that it is unconstitutional. If this occurs, Congress must redraft the bill or initiate a constitutional amendment (which must be approved by three-fourths of the states) to secure the legislation it wishes.

Congress of Verona Conference held (Oct. 20–Dec. 14, 1822) between the major European powers. The congress authorized French intervention in the Spanish revolution against Ferdinand VII, but British opposition led to failure of the congress system.

Congress of Vienna International congress (Sept., 1814–June, 1815) called to reorganize Europe following the fall of Napoleon. The agreements reached at this convention shaped Europe's political structure for much of the 19th cent. Principal nations at the congress were France, Austria, Prussia, Russia, and Great Britain, although numerous smaller nations were represented. Major settlements reached at the congress included establishment of the borders of France and confirmation of the restoration of Bourbon king Louis XVIII to the French throne; confirmation of Ferdinand VII as king of Spain; establishment of the German Confederation from the remnants of the Holy Roman Empire; the reestablishment and enlargement of the Swiss Confederation; and the restoration of the Austrian monarchy. Austria lost Belgium, the Austrian Netherlands, and other territories, but was compensated with new lands, including Lombardy-Venetia, Dalmatia, and the Tyrol. Prussia gained substantial portions of the Rhine and Saxony. Poland was divided among Austria, Prussia, and Russia, and a new Polish kingdom (Congress Kingdom of Poland) was placed under Russian rule. A new kingdom of the Netherlands was established, and the kingdom of Sardinia restored. Sweden received Norway, Russia kept Finland, and Great Britain retained possession of Cape Colony, Ceylon, Malta, and other territories. The Papal States were restored, but the congress did nothing to advance the unification of Italy.

Congress party *See* **Indian National Congress.**

Congress Poland *See* **Congress Kingdom of Poland.**

Congreve, William 1670–1729. English Restoration dramatist who excelled in the comedy of manners. His best-known plays include *Love for Love* and *The Way of the World.*

Connally, John Bowden, Jr. 1917–93. American politician. Connally managed the senatorial campaign (1948) of L. Johnson, served as secre-

tary of the navy under J. Kennedy (1961–62), and as governor of Texas (1963–68). He served as secretary of the treasury (1971–72) and as special adviser to the president (1973–74) under R. Nixon.

Connecticut State in the Northeast US, the fifth state. The first Europeans to explore (1614) and settle (1633) Connecticut were the Dutch. They were follwed by English Puritans from the Plymouth Colony, whose settlements were absorbed by the Massachusetts Bay Company. The Connecticut colonies received a royal charter in 1662 and in 1665, New Haven colony joined the Connecticut colony (1665). Connecticut and other New England colonies were the scene of King Philip's War, in which the Indians were defeated. During the American Revolution, Connecticut became an important source of supplies for the Continental Army but was otherwise not much involved in the fighting. The colony became a state in 1788, relinquished claims to western lands in 1800, became an important center of manufacturing during the 1800s, and abolished slavery in 1848. The state adopted its present constitution in 1965.

Connecticut Compromise *See* **Virginia and New Jersey Plans.**

Connecticut Wits (Hartford ˜) Group of American poets in and around Hartford, Connecticut, who flourished in the years immediately after the American Revolution. Largely composed of Yale instructors and students who were conservative Federalists, they collaborated to produce a number of political satires in verse. Their works, written in the style of earlier British poets, were aimed at the liberalism of Jeffersonian Democrats and included *The Anarchiad* and *The Political Greenhouse.* Leading members included J. Barlow and Timothy Dwight (1752–1817).

conquistadores Spanish military adventurers who led the Spanish exploration and conquest of the New World. Among them were F. Pizzaro and H. Cortés.

Conrad I *d.* 918. Elected German king (911–918). His reign was marked by instability and rebellions inspired by feudal lords.

Conrad II c990–1039. Elected German king and Holy Roman Emperor (1024–39). The first of the Salian emperors, he stabilized and strengthened his domain.

Conrad III c1093–1152. Elected German king (1138–52), first of the Hohenstaufen line. His contest with Lothair II over the crown of the Holy Roman Empire led to struggles between the Guelphs and Ghibellines.

Conrad IV 1228–54. Elected German king (1237–54), son of Emperor Frederick II. One of the last Hohenstaufen rulers, he continued his father's struggle with Pope Innocent IV for control of Italy.

Conrad, Joseph 1857–1924. Polish-born author, considered one of the greatest English novelists. Once a merchant seaman, he wrote stories of adventure reflecting his maritime experiences. Among the best known are *Lord Jim* and *Heart of Darkness.*

Conrad von Hötzendorf, Franz 1852–1925. Austrian count and ruthless military strategist. A staunch conservative and influential propagandist, he planned Austria-Hungary's campaigns during World War I and served as chief of staff (1906–11, 1912–16). He favored attacks on Serbia and Italy, distrusting their expansionist policies, but his invasion of Serbia failed, as did his attacks against Italy (1916) and Russia. The new emperor Charles I dismissed Conrad in 1916 for opposing peace initiatives.

conservatism Belief in preserving the stability of the existing order. Conservatives oppose broad reforms (though not necessarily all reform) that may cause upheavals of the social or political system and thus often oppose liberalism. Conservatism of the 19th cent., a reaction against the French Revolution (1789–99), was articulated in the works of E. Burke and others. It was characterized by support for rule by the king and the propertied class and opposed liberal republicanism of the rising bourgeoisie. In modern times, conservatism has come to favor such things as freedom from the regulation of business and opposes extension of the welfare state.

Conservative party (Canada) *See* **Progressive Conservative party.**

Conservative party Major British political party (formed 1832), a coalition of middle-class interests. Though it represents a conservative viewpoint, the party has traditionally favored moderate social and political reforms. The successor to the Tory party, it was formed after passage of the Reform Bill (1832). Under the leadership of Sir R. Peel, the Conservatives began courting the rising business class, and Peel's Tamworth Manifesto (1834) was written to that end. Peel headed the first Conservative

government of Britain (1834–35), and thereafter Conservatives have been in and out of power up to modern times. *Among the Conservative governments were:* 1841–46 under Peel; 1874–80 under B. Disraeli; 1885–1905 (except 1886, 1892–95) under R. Salisbury and A. Balfour; 1922–29 (except 1924) under A. Law and S. Baldwin; 1935–40 under S. Baldwin and N. Chamberlain; 1940–45 (coalition government) under W. Churchill; 1951–64 under Churchill, A. Eden, H. Macmillan, and A. Douglas-Home; 1970–74 under E. Heath; 1979–90 under M. Thatcher; and 1990– under J. Major.

Conspiracy of Amboise Unsuccessful plot (1560) by French Protestants (Huguenots) to kidnap King Francis II and put an end to the influence of the Catholic Guise family. Led by the Bourbon prince Louis I de Bourbon Condé, they planned to seize the king and members of the Guise family at Amboise. They were discovered, however, and some 1,200 Huguenots were massacred.

Conspiracy of Catiline Abortive attempt (63–62 BC) to overthrow the Roman government during Cicero's consulship. Organized by Catiline after losing his bid (64 BC) for the consulship, the conspiracy was revealed to Cicero by Fulvia, Catiline's mistress. Cicero then denounced Catiline in the Senate in the first of four famous orations against him. Catiline fled Rome and Cicero had those conspirators remaining behind arrested and executed without due process. Cicero was later exiled for this. Catiline and his army of rebels meanwhile were caught trying to make their way to Gaul. The rebels were defeated in battle and Catiline was slain.

Constable, John 1776–1837. Leading 19th-cent. English landscape artist. He strongly influenced the French Romantics.

Constance 1152–98. Wife of Holy Roman Emperor Henry VI (*m.* 1186). By her marriage to Henry, Constance, a Sicilian, gave the German Hohenstaufen family a claim to Sicily. She was empress-consort of the Holy Roman Empire until Henry's death (1191–97) and was also queen of Sicily (1194–98). She served (1197–98) as regent for her son, and assured his accession to the throne as Emperor Frederick II.

Constance, Council of Council (1414–18) of the Roman Catholic church that ended (1417) the Great Schism. The council (part of which is called the 16th ecumenical council) also issued (1415) the Sacrosancta, which confirmed the supremacy of the church council over the pope (Conciliarism). When the council convened, there were three popes—Gregory XII, John XXIII, and Benedict XIII. After issuing the Sacrosancta, it deposed John (1415), negotiated Gregory's resignation, and deposed Benedict (1417), to end the Schism. Martin V was then elected (1417) pope. The council also declared the Hussite movement heretical and had J. Huss and Jerome of Prague burned at the stake (1415, 1416).

Constance, Peace of Peace treaty (June 12, 1446) between Zurich (and its ally, Holy Roman Emperor Frederick IV) and neighboring Swiss cantons, ending a war for control of disputed territories.

Constance, Treaty of Treaty (1183), by which Holy Roman Emperor Frederick I made peace with Pope Alexander III and with the Lombard towns. By its terms the Lombard towns gained virtual autonomy, but Frederick retained nominal suzerainty.

Constans I AD 320 or 323–AD 350. Roman emperor (AD 337–350), successor to his father, Constantine I. After the death (AD 340) of his brother Constantine II, he became sole ruler of the Western Roman Empire.

Constant de Rebecque, Benjamin 1767–1830. A Swiss-born French author and politician. A widely known liberal pamphleteer in France, he wrote *Adolphe* (1815), an early psychological novel.

Constantine 1868–1923. Greek king (1913–17 and 1920–22). His refusal to support the Allies in WW I forced his first abdication, and his disastrous war with Turkey, the second.

Constantine I (the Great) (*orig.* Constantinus, Flavius Valerius Aurelius) AD 280?–337. Roman emperor (AD 306–337) who helped make Rome a Christian state. On the death (306) of Constantinus I, Constantine's father and co-emperor with Galerius, there followed a long struggle among rival claimants to the throne. On the eve of the Battle of Milvian Bridge (312) against his next-to-last rival, Constantine had a vision, accepted Christianity, and by his subsequent victory in battle became emperor in the West. By his Edict of Milan (313) with co-emperor Licinius, he confirmed Christianity as a lawful religion. He later emerged victorious from battle with Licinius (323) and thereby became sole ruler of the Roman Empire. He con-

vened the First Council of Nicaea (325) to resolve the dispute over Arianism and strengthen Christianity. He moved the imperial capital to Byzantium, which he rebuilt (330) as the city of Constantinople.

Constantine II AD 316–340. Son of Constantine I and co-emperor (AD 337–340) of the Roman Empire. He was killed while trying to seize territories controlled by his brother Constans I.

Constantine IV *d.* 685. Byzantine emperor (668–685). He halted Muslim attacks on Constantinople but was forced to give up northern territory to the Bulgars.

Constantine V 718–775. Byzantine emperor (741–775), successor to his father, Leo III. His advocacy of Iconoclasm and opposition to monasticism eventually cost the Byzantine Empire its control over Rome and the rest of Italy.

Constantine VI *b.* c770–797. Byzantine emperor (780–797), successor to his father, Leo IV. His mother, Irene, ruled as regent (780–790) and as coruler (792–97) but deposed and blinded him.

Constantine VII (Porphyrogenitus, Constantine) 905–959. Byzantine emperor (913–959) and scholar, son of Leo VI. His writings concerned the history and politics of his empire. His reign was marked by legal and land reforms, and war with Bulgarians and Russian princes.

Constantine VIII *See* **Basil II.**

Constantine XI (Palaeologus, Constantine) *d.* 1453. Last Byzantine emperor (1449–53), successor to his brother John VIII. He died during the Great Siege of Constantinople, in which the Turks completed their conquest of the Byzantine Empire.

Constantine, Donation of *See* **Donation of Constantine.**

Constantine the Great *See* **Constantine I.**

Constantinople (now Istanbul) Former capital of the Byzantine Empire and of the Ottoman Empire. Located in what now is Turkey, it has been named Istanbul since 1930. Known in ancient times as Byzantium, the city was renamed Constantinople (AD 330) by Constantine the Great, who established it as the capital of the Roman Empire. It became capital of the Byzantine Empire after the fall of the Western Roman Empire (AD 476). The city flourished under Byzantine rule. It was sacked by crusaders (1204) during the Fourth Crusade and became the nucleus of the Latin Empire of Constantinople (*q.v.*). The Ottoman Turks, under Muhammad II, conquered it and thereby overthrew the Byzantine Empire (1453). The city remained capital of the Ottoman Empire through WW I. During the subsequent occupation (1918–23) by Allied forces, the last Ottoman sultan was deposed (1922), and Ankara became capital of the new republic of Turkey.

Constantinople, Councils of **1.** First Council of ~ (AD 381) (2d ecumenical council). Called by Roman emperor Theodosius I, the council condemned Arianism and Apollinarianism, reaffirmed the Council of Nicaea (AD 325) and the Nicene Creed, and issued a doctrinal statement on the Holy Ghost as an equal in the Trinity of the Father, Son, and Holy Ghost. **2.** Second Council of ~ (AD 553) (5th ecumenical council). Convened by Byzantine emperor Justinian I, the council condemned Nestorianism and approved Justinian's edict of 544 on the heresy. **3.** Third Council of ~ (680–681) (6th ecumenical council). Called by Byzantine emperor Constantine IV, the council condemned Monotheletism, issued a doctrinal statement on the existence of separate will and operation in both the human and divine natures of Christ, and condemned Pope Honorius I as a Monothelite. The Quinisext Council is considered part of this council in the West. **4.** Fourth Council of ~ (869–870) (8th ecumenical council in the West). Called at the recommendation of Byzantine emperor Basil I, the council excommunicated Photius, rival of Saint Ignatius of Constantinople for the patriarchy of Constantinople.

Constantinople, Latin Empire of *See* **Latin Empire of Constantinople.**

Constantinople, Saint Ignatius of *See* **Ignatius of Constantinople, Saint.**

Constantinople, Treaty of *See* **Balkan War (2).**

Constantius I (Chlorus, Constantius) AD c250–306. Roman emperor (AD 305–306) and father of Constantine the Great. He put down the rebellion of Allectus in Britain (296) and defeated the Alemanni in Gaul (298).

Constantius II AD 317–361. Roman emperor (AD 337–361), son of Constantine the Great. He fought against the Persians under Shapur II. On the death of his brother Constans I (AD 350), he became sole emperor.

Constantius III *d.* AD 421. Roman emperor of the West (AD 421). A general of Honorius, he defeated the Visigoths, married Honorius's sister (417), and was named co-emperor by Honorius (421).

constitution *See* **Constitution of the United States.**

Constitution, the *See* ***Old Ironsides.***

Constitution Act *See* **Canada (1982).**

Constitutional Convention (Federal Constitutional Convention) (Philadelphia Convention) US convention called (May 25–Sept. 17, 1787) at Philadelphia, Pennsylvania, and presided over by G. Washington. The convention was called by Congress to amend the Articles of Confederation, which had proved ineffective in dealing with the political and economic problems besetting newly independent America. Delegates from 12 states (Rhode Island sent no delegates) drafted and signed (Sept. 17, 1787) the Constitution of the United States of America after much debate (see Virginia and New Jersey Plan). The convention then dissolved and the Constitution was sent to the 13 states for ratification. There ensued a major struggle by supporters of the Constitution, known as Federalists, to secure its enactment into law. This came with ratification (June, 1788) by New Hampshire, the ninth state to do so.

Constitutional Union party American political party. Composed mainly of former Know-Nothings and Whigs, it nominated J. Bell as presidential candidate in the 1860 election. It carried Kentucky, Tennessee, and Virginia, but soon after disappeared as a political force.

Constitution of the United States Document empowering the federal government of the US. In addition to defining the form and system of government, it describes the basic liberties of American citizens and basic laws of the land. Drafted and signed (Sept. 17, 1787) at the Constitutional Convention (*q.v.*), the Constitution was designed to remedy the shortcomings of the Articles of Confederation (*q.v.*), by providing for a strong central government. The Constitution went into effect (Mar. 4, 1789), following ratification by 11 (9 required had ratified by June 21, 1788) of the original 13 states. The Bill of Rights, a set of 10 amendments to the Constitution, was passed (Sept. 25, 1789) and ratified (Dec. 15, 1791). The two remaining states ratified the Constitution after passage of the Bill of Rights. Amendments in the Bill of Rights are listed below. The Constitution consists of a

Preamble, the following seven articles, and the Amendments to the Constitution listed below them.

Article I Describes the organization, powers, and limitations of the legislative branch.

Article II Empowers the president and executive branch (*q.v.*) and describes the duties of the president and means by which he is to be elected.

Article III Empowers the judicial branch (*q.v.*) and defines jurisdictions of the Supreme Court and lower courts.

Article IV Describes the relationship of states to the federal government, as well as to other states.

Article V Describes the method of amending the Constitution.

Article VI Declares the Constitution to be the supreme law of the land, which no state may abridge.

Article VII Describes the ratification process.

AMENDMENTS TO THE CONSTITUTION
Bill of Rights (all adopted 1791)

Amendment I guarantees freedom of religion, speech, the press, petition, and assembly.

Amendment II guarantees the right to bear arms.

Amendment III restricts quartering of soldiers.

Amendment IV protects against illegal search and seizure.

Amendment V guarantees due process and rights of the accused.

Amendment VI guarantees the accused a speedy trial and other rights during trial.

Amendment VII guarantees the right to a jury trial in civil suits.

Amendment VIII protects against imposition of excessive bail and cruel and unusual punishment.

Amendment IX reserves for the people rights not enumerated in the Constitution.

Amendment X reserves for the states or the people powers not enumerated in the Constitution.

Subsequent Amendments

Amendment XI limits the jurisdiction of federal judiciary (ratified 1795).

Amendment XII revises procedures for electing the president and vice-president (ratified 1804)

Amendment XIII abolishes slavery (ratified 1865). This and the following two amendments resulted from the Civil War.

Amendment XIV reaffirms the right of citizens to representation and equal protection under the law. It also bans insurgents (namely Confederates) from government office, and invalidates debts incurred by them (ratified 1868).

Amendment XV guarantees the right to vote, regardless of race or creed (ratified 1870).

Amendment XVI empowers the federal government to collect the income tax (ratified 1913).

Amendment XVII changes the procedure for electing senators from election by state legislatures to direct popular election (ratified 1913).

Amendment XVIII bans alcoholic beverages (ratified 1919). *See also* Prohibition.

Amendment XIX guarantees women the right to vote (ratified 1920). *See also* Woman Suffrage.

Amendment XX revises the term of office for the president, vice-president, and Congress (to eliminate the lame duck Congress (*q.v.*) (ratified 1933). It also fixes the line of succession in the event of the president's death in office.

Amendment XXI repeals Prohibition (ratified 1933).

Amendment XXII establishes the two-term limit on the presidency (ratified 1951).

Amendment XXIII provides for voting and representation rights for the District of Columbia (ratified 1961).

Amendment XXIV bans poll taxes (ratified 1964).

Amendment XXV provides for presidential succession and succession of the vice-president (ratified 1967).

Amendment XXVI lowers the voting age to 18 (ratified 1971).

Amendment XXVII prohibits a sitting Congress from voting itself a pay raise (ratified 1992, over 200 years after J. Madison first proposed the amendment).

Constitutions and Canons Ecclesiastical *See* canon law.

Constitutions of Clarendon Sixteen ordinances issued (1164) by English king Henry II to limit the power of the Catholic church. These measures were opposed by Thomas à Becket, and his murder (1170) by the king's supporters forced Henry to modify the ordinances.

Constitutions of Melfi (Liber Augustalis) Administrative law code given (1231) to the kingdom of Sicily by Holy Roman Emperor Frederick II. One of the important legal documents of the Middle Ages, it established a strong and efficient central, bureaucratic government in the kingdom.

consul Name given the two chief magistrates of the ancient Roman republic. Consuls wielded virtually royal powers although their term of office was limited. The position was the highest achievable by citizens.

Consulate French government (1799–1804) established after overthrow of the Directory in the *coup d'état* of 18 Brumaire. Under the Consulate, three consuls—one of whom was Napoleon—ruled France, until Napoleon's assumption (1804) of the title "emperor."

Continental Army American army during the American Revolutionary War authorized by the Second Continental Congress and placed under the command of Gen. G. Washington on June 15, 1775. This force had arisen spontaneously around Boston following the Battles of Lexington and Concord (*q.v.*). Numbering around 20,000 at its maximum, the army was trained by Washington and led to victory (1781) over the British.

Continental Congress Legislature and interim government (1774–89) for the 13 colonies (later states) during the American Revolution and postwar years until adoption of the Constitution of the United States. The First Continental Congress, brought about by Colonial opposition to the Intolerable Acts (especially among Committees of Correspondence and the Sons of Liberty), was convened (Sept. 5–Oct. 26, 1774) at Philadelphia, with P. Randolph presiding. It opposed J. Galloway's conciliatory plan, created the Continental Association to halt trade with Britain, and sent a list of colonists' grievances to King George III. The Second Continental Congress was convened (May 10, 1775–Dec. 20, 1776) at Philadelphia, with Randolph (and later J. Hancock) as president. The Congress created the Continental Army (May 31, 1775), appointed G. Washington commander (June 15), rejected Lord North's plan for peaceful settlement, opened American ports in defiance of British acts, and adopted the Declaration of Independence (July 4, 1776). During the war, subsequent sessions, held at Philadelphia (except 1776–77, 1777–78), were characterized by disputes between Congress and the military. After adoption of the Articles of Confederation (1781), the inability of the congress to govern effectively led to the Annapolis and Constitutional conventions and eventual adoption of the Constitution.

Continental Divide (Great Divide) Continental barrier marking a division between eastward- and westward-flowing river systems. Specifically, in North America, the term refers to the Rocky Mountain chain.

Continental System French economic plan (1806–12) adopted by Napoleon (in the Berlin Decree) to freeze trade with England during the Napoleonic Wars. Russia's refusal to conform to it led to Napoleon's invasion of Russia (1812). The plan also contributed to outbreak of the War of 1812.

Contreras, Battle of Battle (Aug. 19–20, 1847) of the Mexican War. A decisive victory for American forces under Gen. W. Scott over Mexican soldiers under Gen. A. de Santa Anna, it was fought during the American drive on Mexico City.

Conventicle acts English religious acts (1593, 1664). Created to suppress dissenters within the Anglican church, they were repealed by the Toleration Act (1689).

Convention of Akkerman Treaty (Oct. 7, 1826) forced on the Ottoman Turks by the Russians and signed at Akkerman, Russia. By its terms, the Turks granted Serbia autonomy, gave Russia rights to oversee the autonomy of Moldavia and Walachia, and granted Russia navigation and commercial rights in Turkish domains.

Convention of 1818 US–British border agreement (Oct. 20, 1818) establishing the 49th parallel as the US–Canadian border from the Lake of the Woods to the Rocky Mountains and providing for open occupation of Oregon territory for 10 years.

Convention of Gastein Austro-Prussian agreement (Aug. 14, 1865) settling administration of Schleswig-Holstein, seized (1864) from Denmark. Prussia administered Schleswig and Austria administered Holstein.

Convention of Kloster-Zeven Agreement signed (Sept. 8, 1757) by the duke of Cumberland near Zeven, in Hanover, following his defeat by the French in the Seven Years' War. The convention, allowing French occupation of Hanover, was repudiated by the British government.

Convention of Beijing *See* **Opium War (2).**

Convention of Sintra Agreement (Aug. 30, 1808) between British and French forces in Portugal during the Peninsular War. Much criticized in Britain, it allowed the French to return home with their arms, baggage, and booty.

Convention of Vergara (Bergara, ˜)　Agreement (Aug. 31, 1839) ending resistance by Spanish Carlists to the rule of Queen Isabella II.

Convention Parliament English Parliament (Apr.–Dec., 1660). It restored Charles II and the Stuart monarchy to the English throne, following Charles's signing of the Declaration of Breda (*q.v.*), and thus began the Restoration (*q.v.*) period.

Conway, Thomas　*See* **Conway Cabal.**

Conway, Treaty of　*See* **Llewelyn ab Gruffydd.**

Conway Cabal　American Revolutionary plot. Several dissatisfied American officers, including Gen. Thomas Conway (1735–1800?), sought unsuccessfully to replace G. Washington with H. Gates as head of the Continental Army.

Cook, James 1728–79.　English navigator famed for his exploratory voyages in the Pacific and Antarctic. In command (1768–71) of the ship *Endeavour,* he discovered and charted New Zealand and the eastern coast of Australia, and circumnavigated the globe. On his second voyage (1772–75), commanding the *Resolution* and the *Adventure,* he explored the Antarctic coast and discovered New Caledonia. His third voyage (1776–79), to discover a northwest or northeast passage, ended with his murder by Hawaiian natives.

Cooke, Jay 1821–1905.　American financier. He founded (1861) Jay Cooke and Company, which marketed federal bonds during the Civil War. Its failure (Sept. 18, 1873) caused the Panic of 1873.

Coolidge, (John) Calvin 1872–1933.　The 30th US president (1923–29), successor to W. Harding. Coolidge was governor of Massachusetts (1919–21) when he won national attention by using the state militia to break the Boston police strike (1919). Shortly thereafter he was nominated as the Republican vice-presidential candidate, and entered office with President W. Harding. As vice-president, he was not part of Harding's inner circle and was not involved in the Teapot Dome scandal (*q.v.*). After Harding's death (1923) he became the president and quickly restored public confidence in government. Elected (1924), he refused to run again in 1928. His administration was characterized by pro-business policies; presidential vetoes of farm-relief legislation; conservative fiscal policies stressing economy in government and tax cuts; and encouragement of speculative stock market

booms, which finally resulted in the stock market crash of 1929.

coolie　A Chinese or Indian laborer. Coolies (some of whom were indentured laborers) were sent during the 19th cent. to work in the US, West Indies, and other places where cheap labor was needed for work on projects such as railroads.

Cooper, James Fenimore 1789–1851.　The first major American novelist. A sailor and US naval officer (1806–11), he married (1811) and took up the life of a gentleman. He won fame with publication (1821) of his second book, *The Spy,* and thereafter began his *Leatherstocking Tales* of frontier life. This series included *The Pioneers, The Last of the Mohicans, The Prairie, The Pathfinder,* and *The Deerslayer.*

Cooper, Leon N.　*See* **Bardeen, John.**

Cooper, Leroy Gordon, Jr. 1927–　.　American astronaut. One of the seven original astronauts, he made the last flight of the Mercury program, aboard *Faith* 7 (May, 1963).

Cooper, Peter 1791–1883.　US manufacturer, inventor, and philanthropist. He constructed the early locomotive "Tom Thumb," founded Cooper Union, a college in New York City, and became a financial backer of the project for laying the Atlantic cable.

Co-operative Commonwealth Federation　Canadian political party active in the 1930s and 1940s. Formed (1932) during the Depression, the party advocated creation of a socialist state by democratic means. It was strongest in the western provinces and won control (1944) of the government of Saskatchewan. The party continued to dominate Saskatchewan but declined in the other provinces after WW II. In 1961, it merged with the Canadian Labor Congress, forming the New Democratic Party (NDP). The NDP has since become one of Canada's three major political parties.

Copenhagen, Battle of　British naval victory (Apr. 2, 1801) against the Danish fleet at Copenhagen. The battle stemmed from the French Revolutionary Wars. Denmark had joined (1800) the League of Armed Neutrality along with Russia, Sweden, and Prussia. In addition to proclaiming their neutrality, the four nations also agreed to ignore British rules governing maritime activities of neutrals. Though the British did not declare war, they nevertheless sent a fleet under Lord H. Nelson on a raid against the Danish. The British destroyed the Danish fleet at Copenhagen.

Copernicus, Nicholas 1473–1543. Polish astronomer, considered the founder of modern astronomy. On the basis of his observations and calculations, he advanced the then revolutionary idea that the earth rotated on its axis and that the planets, including the earth, revolved around the sun (the Copernican system). Educated in astronomy at the University of Krakow, he was appointed (1497) canon of the cathedral at Frauenburg, East Prussia. In subsequent years he began to develop his heliocentric theory, opposing the traditional, earth-centered theory. By 1530, he had largely completed his book on the theory, *On the Revolutions of the Celestial Spheres* (*De revolutionibus orbium coelestium*), but delayed the start of publication until 1540. He is said to have received the first bound copy just before his death (1543).

Copland, Aaron 1900–90. American composer. His works, reflecting American themes and traditions, include the ballets *Rodeo* and *Appalachian Spring.*

Copper Age The stage in the development of civilization when pure copper came into use. The Copper Age is considered the early part of the Bronze Age. The earliest known use of copper (c6500 BC) occurred in the Near East, and by c3500 BC copper metallurgy was well known throughout the region. Copper was in general use by c3000 BC, and this is commonly considered the beginning of the Bronze Age. The use of bronze began c2400 BC and became widespread after 2000 BC.

Copperhead Derogatory American political term applied to northern Democrats who either opposed the Civil War or sympathized with the South.

Coptic church Christian church of Egypt. The church has only a small following in a country that has been predominantly Islamic since the 7th cent. Formed in early Christian times, it adheres to Monophysitism and has been independent of the Roman Catholic church since AD 451, when the Council of Chalcedon declared Monophysitism a heresy. A still smaller church, the Catholic Coptic church, rejoined the Roman Catholic church in 1741.

Coral Sea, Battle of the US–Japanese naval and air battle (May 7–8, 1942) in the southwest Pacific during WW II. The US assembled a task force to meet a Japanese fleet involved in a planned invasion of Port Moresby, New Guinea. US carrier planes sank a Japanese carrier the first day. In a battle fought solely by carrier planes the next day, the US sustained heavy losses (including one carrier sunk) but turned back the Japanese for the first time in the war.

Corbeil, Treaty of Treaty (May 11, 1258) signed by French king Louis IX and James I of Aragon. It settled territorial claims of France and Aragon, with terms favorable to France.

Corday, Charlotte 1768–93. Frenchwoman, the assassin of French revolutionary leader J. Marat (July 13, 1793). She stabbed Marat in his bath because of his persecution of the Girondists, with whom she sympathized.

Cordeliers Political club formed (1790) during the French Revolution. Officially known as the Society of the Friends of the Rights of Man and of the Citizen, it was founded to denounce abuses of power. It soon became a formidable political power under the leadership of G. Danton and others. The Cordeliers were involved in the deposing of King Louis XVI, and later, under the more radical influence of J. Hébert and J. Marat, brought down (1792–93) the moderate Girondists. Under Hébert's leadership the club adopted extreme radicalism, and for a time Hébert rivaled M. Robespierre for power. The club dissolved when Hébert was executed (1794) during the Reign of Terror.

Córdoba, Treaty of Treaty (Aug. 24, 1821) signed by Mexican revolutionary forces and Spanish colonial authorities at Córdoba, Mexico. The treaty established Mexican independence.

Corfu Declaration Proclamation (July 20, 1917) calling for creation of Yugoslavia at the end of WW I. Meeting at Corfu, Greece, representatives of the Serbian government-in-exile, the Croats, and the Slovenes put aside long-standing differences and announced a planned union of their states under Serbian king Peter I. Montenegro joined the union (Nov. 26) after the ouster of King Nicholas I, who had opposed it. The new kingdom was formally proclaimed Dec. 4, 1918.

Corinth Ancient Greek city. Settled (9th cent. BC) by Dorians, it became a major city-state in the Peloponnesus and the leading commercial center of Greece. Corinth played a major role in the Persian Wars (499–479 BC) and allied with Sparta against Athens in the Peloponnesian War (431–404 BC). It fought against Sparta in the

Corinthian War (395–387 BC), and became a member of the Achaean League (243 BC). Destroyed (146 BC) by the Romans, it became a Roman colony (44 BC). Subsequently occupied by the Ottoman Turks, the Venetians, and again by the Turks, it was completely destroyed (1858) by an earthquake. Modern Corinth stands northeast of the ancient site.

Corinth, Battle of Battle (Oct 3–4, 1862) of the American Civil War, at Corinth, Mississippi. Union forces under W. Rosecrans defeated Confederate units under S. Price and E. Van Dorn in two days of heavy fighting.

Corinthian order Greek architectural style, the last of the three major styles of classical Greek architecture. An ornate style, it influenced later Roman and Renaissance styles.

Corinthian War War (395–387 BC) against Spartan domination, fought by Athens and her allies (Corinth, Argos, and Thebes). At the instigation of Persia, then at war with Sparta, the allied city-states went to war against Sparta. The Spartans won initial victories—the battles of Nemea and Coronea—but suffered a major defeat at the hands of the Athenians and the Persians in a naval battle at Cnidus (all 394 BC). Subsequently the Spartans convinced the Persians to turn against Athens, and the two powers then dictated the terms of the King's Peace to Athens.

Coriolanus *fl.* 5th cent. BC. Legendary Roman patrician, said to have received his surname by capturing the Volscian city of Corioli. He later led the Volscians against Rome and spared it from destruction only because of the tearful pleas of his wife and mother.

Corneille, Pierre 1606–84. French dramatist, one of the great French tragedians. Educated in law, he worked as a local official in the royal government until 1650. He successfully produced his first play in 1629 (*Mélite*), and as his popularity grew was included among Cardinal Richelieu's group of dramatists, *Les Cinq Auteurs.* Unsuited to the group's collective approach to writing drama, he produced his first tragedy in 1635 (*Médée*). His best-known work, *Le Cid,* was performed in 1637. Called the single most important play in the history of French theater, it marked the starting point of modern French drama. The play also sparked a bitter controversy at the time. With the plays *Horace, Cinna,* and *Polyeucte* (1640–41), Corneille began a period in

which he dominated French theater. From 1651 his popularity declined rapidly, however, and he eventually abandoned the theater.

Cornelia *fl.* 2d cent. BC. Roman matron, the mother of Tiberius and Gaius Gracchus. To a patrician matron discussing jewelry, she is said to have pointed to her sons and said, "These are my jewels."

Cornelius, Pope *See* **Novatian.**

Corn Laws Series of English laws regulating export and import of grain, to maintain a stable supply of domestic grain. Opponents of the laws formed (1839) the Anti-Corn Law League, and in 1846 Parliament, led by R. Peel, repealed the laws.

Cornwallis, Charles, 1st marquess 1738–1805. British general and statesman. Although opposed to the British policies which precipitated the American Revolution, he led British forces in the Carolina and Yorktown campaigns. He is probably best known for his surrender following the disastrous Siege of Yorktown, Virginia (1781), which effectively ended the war. As governor general of India (1786–93, 1805), he established (1793) the Cornwallis Code, the administrative framework for British rule in the colony. Cornwallis also served as viceroy of Ireland (1798–1801) and put down a rebellion in 1798. He supported the granting of political rights to Roman Catholics, and resigned after King George III rejected the proposals. He died (1805) shortly after being reappointed as governor general of India.

Cornwallis Code (Bengal System) Administrative reforms adopted (May 1, 1793) by the British East India Company for the government of Bengal, India. The system, named after Governor General C. Cornwallis, was adopted elsewhere in India and remained in effect until 1833. By the code, administration was separated into commercial, revenue, and judicial departments. Private trade was strictly forbidden, and adequate salaries were paid to administrative personnel. Though the system introduced a measure of stability, it also excluded Indians from important posts.

Coronado, Francisco Vásquez de 1510–44. A Spanish explorer of what became the US Southwest. Seeking treasure cities, Coronado led an expedition (1540–42) north from Mexico into Texas, and from there through Oklahoma to Kansas. García López de Cárdenas led a party of

Coronado's men on a side trip and discovered the Grand Canyon (1540).

Coronea, Battle of   1. Boeotian victory (447 BC) over Athens during the First Peloponnesian War. The Athenian defeat led to reestablishment of the Boeotian League.   2. Battle (394 BC) during the Corinthian War, a Spartan victory over the coalition of city-states allied against it.

Coronel, Battle of   German naval victory (Nov. 1, 1914) off Coronel, Chile, during WW I. The German squadron under Admiral Graf von Spee decisively defeated an inferior British squadron under Sir Christopher Cradock (1862–1914), who went down with his flagship.

corporative state   Economic system, first employed by the Italian Fascist government of B. Mussolini. It involved government control of the national economy while retaining elements of capitalism, and was adopted in part by Nazi Germany and by Spain under F. Franco.

corpus juris canonici   *See* **canon law.**

corpus juris civilis (Justinian Code)   Roman legal code issued (529–535) by order of Byzantine emperor Justinian I. The voluminous work provided a systematic and comprehensive code of Roman law and greatly influenced later European legal systems. It consisted of four major parts: the Codex, a compilation of existing imperial ordinances; the Digesta, or Pandecta, a collection of extracts of written legal opinions on laws; the Institutiones, a manual on Roman law; and the Novellae, a compilation of imperial laws instituted by Justinian.

Corpus of Canon law   *See* **canon law.**

Corradini, Enrico 1865–1931.   Italian journalist and political writer. Born in Tuscany, he was known both as a journalist and for his novels and plays.

Corregidor, siege of   Month-long Japanese siege (Apr.–May, 1942) of Corregidor Island, Philippines, during WW II. After the fall of Bataan, 11,000 US and Filipino troops under Gen. J. Wainwright held out against Japanese attacks, but were forced to surrender (May 6, 1942).

Correspondence, Committees of   *See* **Committees of Correspondence.**

Cortes   Spanish national assembly, which derives its name from the legislative assemblies formed (12th cent.) in various Spanish states.

Cortés, Hernando (Cortéz, ˜) 1485–1547.   Spanish conquistador and conqueror of Mexico (1519–21). He joined with D. Velázquez in con-

quering Cuba (1511), then led a military expedition into Mexico to conquer the Aztec empire of Montezuma for Spain. Setting out (1519) with 600 men and 16 horses, and ignoring Velázquez's orders that he return, he burned his eleven ships on arriving in Mexico, to prevent his men from retreating. After conquering Mayan tribes, he marched to the Aztec capital of Tenochtitlán (later Mexico City). Montezuma received Cortés, believing him to be the descendant of an Aztec god; Cortés immediately took him hostage. After traveling to the coast to defeat forces sent by Velázquez, Cortés returned to the capital to find the Aztecs in revolt. In a famous battle known as *La Noche Triste* ("The Sad Night," 1520), Cortés suffered heavy casualties. Returning a year later, he conquered the city and, with it, the empire. He was, however, replaced (1526) as governor of New Spain. He died (1547) in Spain, disillusioned and embittered.

Cortona, Pietro da 1596–1669   Italian painter and architect and noted master of the baroque style. *Allegory of Divine Providence* is among his works.

Corupedion, Battle of   Battle in the Wars of the Diadochi (*q.v.*) fought in Asia Minor (281 BC). Seleucus I, ruler of the Seleucid Empire, defeated and killed Lysimachus and thus became master of Asia Minor.

Cosa Nostra   *See* **Mafia.**

Cossa, Baldassarre (Cassa, Baltasare) (John XXIII (antipope)) c1370–1419.   Antipope (1410–15) as John XXIII, during the Great Schism. He was elected in opposition to Pope Gregory XII and antipope Benedict XIII. He was deposed (1415) by the Council of Constance.

Cossa, Baltasare   *See* **Cossa, Baldassarre.**

Cossacks   Russian and Ukrainian peasant-soldiers, noted as cavalrymen in the Russian imperial armies. Cossacks in the 15th cent. were escaped serfs from Poland and Russia who formed independent settlements on the Ukrainian frontier. From the 16th cent. Cossack bands were in the service of Polish and Russian sovereigns and by the 18th cent. were under Russian domination. Although they lost their traditional autonomy, they eventually became a privileged military class in the Russian Empire. By the 1900s there were some 12 Cossack units, named for the geographic regions they occupied, including the Don and Kuban Cossacks. Cossacks were frequently used to put down rebellions. Some fought the Bolsheviks during the Russian Civil War (1918–22). Under the new regime they lost their special privileges and their villages were turned into Communist collectives. *See also* Zaporozhe Cossacks.

Costa e Silva, Artur da 1902–69. Brazilian president (1967–69). Head of a military regime that had seized power (1964) in Brazil, he initially attempted reforms but in 1968 dissolved congress and assumed dictatorial powers.

Costa Rica Republic located in Central America, bordered on the east by the Caribbean Sea and the west by the Pacific Ocean. Nicaragua lies to the north and Panama to the south. The population is 3,023,000 and the capital is San José. Originally a Spanish colony, Costa Rica has a democratic constitutional government, and has enjoyed relative political stability throughout much of its history. Key dates in the history of Costa Rica include:

1502 C. Columbus discovered Caribbean coast; named it Costa Rica (rich coast).

c1563 Region subdued and brought under captaincy-general of Guatemala.

1821 Declared independence from Spain (Sept. 15).

1822–23 Forced to join Mexican empire under A. de Iturbide.

1823–38 Iturbide's empire collapsed; Costa Rica joined United Provinces of Central America.

1825 Costa Rica, first of Central America's coffee producers, exported first coffee crop; coffee became leading export in 1829.

1848 Republic declared.

1857 Helped to defeat the filibuster W. Walker in Nicaragua.

1874 Banana cultivation introduced on Atlantic coast; coffee previously dominated agriculture in central highlands.

1896 Disputed territory on boundary with Nicaragua awarded to Costa Rica.

1899 United Fruit Company founded to consolidate the banana trade.

1909 Costa Rica became leading banana producer for a time.

1917–19 Frederico Tinoco in office after overthrowing elected president Alfredo Gonzáles; US opposition brought his overthrow.

1918 Entered WW I on Allied side.

1941 Joined Allies in WW II.

1948 Disputed presidential election between Otilio Ulate and Rafael Calderón Guardia resulted in brief civil war; military junta, led by Col. José Figueres Ferrer seized power; Guardia's attempted invasion failed (Dec.).

1949–53 Ulate in office as president after new constitution was adopted (1949).

1951 Attempted coup by Guardia thwarted.

1951 Costa Rica joined the Organization of American States.

1953–58 Figueres in office as elected president.

1958–62 Mario Enchadi Jiménez in office as president after UN–supervised elections.

1974–78 Daniel Oduber Quirós in office as president; ruling National Liberation Party failed to keep majority in legislature.

1978–82 Coalition leader Rodrigo Carazo Odio in office as president; serious economic problems led to inability to pay foreign debt.

1980 Widespread strike by workers on banana plantations.

1981 Government suspended payments on its $2.6 billion foreign debt, among the highest per capita debts in Latin America.

1982–86 Luis Alberto Monge, National Liberation party member, in office as president; maintained Costa Rica's traditional neutrality despite US pressure to back Nicaraguan Contras; presented "100-day plan" for reviving economy, then faltering before 54 percent inflation, high unemployment, excessive foreign debt, and lack of foreign reserves.

1983 Government signed preliminary agreement for refinancing unpaid foreign debt now estimated at $4 billion.

1986–90 Dr. Oscar Arias, National Liberation party member, in office as president, following elections; resisted US pressure to back Contras; proposed 25-year plan to restructure foreign debt.

1987 Arias lodged formal complaint with US government about US attempts to pressure Costa Rica into joining fight against Sandinista government in Nicaragua (Mar.).

1987 President Arias presented the Arias Plan for peace in Central America before meeting of Central American heads of state (June 25–26); plan called for immediate halt to all fighting, end to aid for guerrilla groups, amnesty for all rebels, and negotiations for permanent peace in all conflicts; plan, adopted unanimously, became basis for subsequent end to fighting in Central America.

1987   Arias received Nobel Prize for Peace.

1988   Government program to increase planting of export crops (and thereby raise needed foreign money) scorned by farmers; they complained that remaining land might not yield enough to meet Costa Rica's domestic need for food.

1989   IMF and World Bank agreed to new debt reduction plan for Costa Rica.

1990–   Rafael Angel Calderón Fournier, member of the opposition Social Christian Unity Party (PUSC), in office as president following elections; imposed austerity program to help ease economic ills.

Coster, Laurens Janszoon *See* **Koster, Laurens Janszoon.**

Côte d'Ivoire (Ivory Coast) Republic located in coastal West Africa. The population is 12,070,000 and the capital is Abidjan. European traders established settlements in the region from the 16th cent. and for a time trade in slaves and ivory flourished. The French made the coastal region a protectorate in 1842 and created the colony of the Ivory Coast (1893), even though native resistance in the interior had not yet been completely broken. Made part of French West Africa (1895), it was held by Vichy government forces in WW II and became a French territory (1946). Ivory Coast next became an autonomous republic (1958) within the French Community. It achieved complete independence (Aug. 7, 1960). Since that time the republic has been under the leadership of President Félix Houphouët-Boigny (1905–), who has maintained a pro-Western policy. Continuing economic problems led to imposition of an austerity program in 1990, which in turn sparked prolonged and widespread unrest. That same year the government approved a multi-party system, and in Oct., 1990, President Houphouët-Boigny was reelected in the country's first contested elections.

Cottereau, Jean *See* **Chouans.**

Cotton, John 1584–1652. English-born Puritan clergyman and grandfather of C. Mather. A leading figure in the Massachusetts Bay Colony, he advocated theocracy and helped to found the Congregational church.

Cotton Famine English industrial crisis (1861–65) caused by the withholding of cotton from English mills by events of the American Civil War. The mill workers of Lancashire were particularly affected, but Britain maintained its support of the Union.

Coty, René 1882–1962. French politician, last president (1954–59) of the Fourth Republic. He retired when C. de Gaulle became president of the Fifth Republic (1959).

Coubertin, Pierre, baron de 1863–1937. French educator who revived the Olympic Games (1894). After touring the US and Greece to study education, he proposed (1892) restarting the Olympics, last held some 1,500 years earlier. In 1894, the proposal was adopted by an international athletic group, and plans were made to begin the games again in Athens in 1896. Coubertin believed the amateur athletic competition would help ease world tensions.

Coué, Émile 1857–1926. French pharmacist and psychotherapist. He introduced (1920) autosuggestion, and is known for his formula "Every day in every way I am getting better and better."

Coughlin, Father Charles E. 1891–1979. Catholic priest and political activist. Coughlin began broadcasting radio sermons in the 1920s to raise money for his church in a suburb of Detroit, Michigan, and quickly garnered not only the funds he sought but enormous public popularity as well. By 1930 his radio sermons commanded an audience of some 40 million listeners. He also voiced extremist views on political issues, however, condemning Wall Street, modern capitalism, and increasingly in the 1930s, President F. Roosevelt and the New Deal. Coughlin lost popularity in the late 1930s soon after advocating anti-Semitism and praising A. Hitler and B. Mussolini. His broadcasts ceased in 1940.

Coulomb, Charles Augustin de 1736–1806. French physicist. He made important discoveries in the areas of electricity, magnetism, and friction. He also invented a magnetoscope, a magnetometer, a compass, and a torsion balance which he used (1777) to show that torsion suspension can measure very small forces. Using his torsion balance in electrical studies, he formulated Coulomb's Law, which deals with electrical charges. The unit of electric charge, the coulomb, was named for him.

council, ecumenical *See* **ecumenical council.**

Council in Trullo *See* **Quinisext Council.**

Council of Four Hundred *See* **Areopagus.**

Council of Ten Venetian tribunal founded (c1310) to investigate plots against the state. It soon gained vast powers in both domestic and foreign matters, and existed until abolishment (1797) of the Venetian state by Napoleon.

Council of the Republic Preparliament Russian provisional government (Oct.–Nov., 1917), headed by A. Kerensky. Largely ineffective, it was swept away by the Bolshevik seizure of power.

count European rank of nobility, equivalent to the German Graf and the English earl. The title derives from the Latin *comes,* originally an official in the Roman republic.

Count's War (Feud of the Counts) War of succession (1533–36) in Denmark. By confirming succession of Christian III, the war confirmed the Protestant Reformation in Denmark-Norway (then united under Christian) and established hereditary succession to the throne. On the death of King Frederick I (reigned 1523–33), Christian, a Lutheran and the legitimate heir, was opposed by Count Christopher of Oldenburg. Christian had the services of the Swedish navy, while Christopher had the support of Danish nobles and populace. The tide of the war turned in Christian's favor by 1535, when Christopher's army and naval forces were destroyed. Christopher finally surrendered (July 28, 1536) at Copenhagen.

coup d'état French term meaning "blow to the state," applied to the seizure by force of political power and the overthrow of the state.

Courtenay, Robert of *See* **Robert of Courtenay.**

Court of Blood *See* **Alba, Fernando Álvarez de Toledo, Duke of.**

Courtrai, Battle of *See* **Golden Spurs, Battle of the.**

Cousteau, Jacques-Yves 1910– . French underwater explorer and co-inventor of the aqualung (1943). The co-author of such books as *The Silent World* and *The Living Sea,* he is one of the world's leading proponents of oceanic exploration and conservation.

Couthon, Georges 1755?–94. French revolutionary. He crushed a counterrevolution in Lyons (1793) and helped M. Robespierre conduct the Reign of Terror. He was guillotined after the *coup d'état* of 9 Thermidor (July 27, 1794).

Covenanters Scottish Presbyterians who, during crises in the 16th–17th cents., were sworn to defend their church by a solemn covenant. The first covenant was signed (1557) when Protestants opposed the Catholics in a struggle for power in Scotland. The National Covenant was signed (1638) to oppose Charles I's episcopal reforms and resulted in the Bishops' Wars (1639–40). By the Solemn League and Covenant (1643), the Scots became allies of the Parliamentarians in the early phase of the English Civil Wars. The Parliamentarians eventually turned against the Scots and defeated them (1650–51). After Charles's restoration (1660), renewed attempts at suppressing Presbyterianism led to rebellions and royal persecutions until the Glorious Revolution (1688).

Coward, Sir Noël 1899–1973. English playwright, actor, and composer. His sophisticated comedies included *Hay Fever, Private Lives,* and *Blithe Spirit.* He also produced the film *Brief Encounter.*

Cowell, Henry Dixon 1897–1965. American composer, one of the leading avant-garde American composers. He introduced the use of "tone clusters," several adjacent piano keys struck simultaneously.

Cowley, Abraham 1618–67. English poet and essayist. One of the leading poets of his day, he also served as royalist agent for English queen Henrietta Maria in France during the English Civil Wars.

Cowpens, Battle of Battle (Jan. 17, 1781) of the Carolina Campaign (*q.v.*), in the American Revolution, near Cowpens, northern South Carolina. Some 1,000 Continental troops under D. Morgan decisively defeated a British force of 1,100 under Col. Banastre Tarleton (1754–1833). The British suffered over 900 dead, wounded, or captured. The Americans lost 12 dead, 60 wounded.

Cowper, William 1731–1800. English poet. A leading poet of the 18th cent., he suffered recurrent bouts of mental illness, but managed to produce such masterpieces as the long poem *The Task* and *The Castaway.*

Cox, Jacob Dolson 1828–1900. American general and politician. Appointed a Union brigadier in the Civil War, he fought at Antietam (1862) and Atlanta (1864). He later served as governor of Ohio (1866–68) and secretary of the interior (1869–70) under President U. Grant.

Coxey, Jacob S. *See* **Coxey's Army.**

Coxey's Army (Commonweal of Christ) Band of unemployed men, led by Jacob S. Coxey (1854–1951), who marched (1894) from Massilon, Ohio, to Washington, D.C., seeking Congressional aid in relieving unemployment. Coxey failed to raise the great number of men he had hoped for, and the movement collapsed when Coxey and others were arrested in Washington (May 1, 1894) for trespassing.

Cradle of Liberty *See* **Faneuil Hall.**

Cradock, Christopher *See* **Coronel, Battle of.**

Craigavon, James Craig, 1st viscount 1871–1940. Irish statesman. An opponent of home rule, he became the first prime minister of Northern Ireland (1921–40).

Crane, Stephen 1871–1900. American writer. One of the pioneers of American realism, he is known best for his Civil War novel *The Red Badge of Courage.*

Cranmer, Thomas 1489–1556. English clergyman. He aided Henry VIII in dissolving his marriage to Catherine of Aragon and was appointed (1533) archbishop of Canterbury. Subsequently, he supported Henry variously as head of the Church of England and in Henry's other divorces. He compiled the *Book of Common Prayer* (1549) and played a major role in writing the Forty-two Articles. On the accession of Catholic Queen Mary he was burned for heresy.

Crashaw, Richard 1612–49. English poet noted for his religious poetry. A convert to Roman Catholicism, Crashaw traveled to France (1644), then to Italy, where he was influenced by the baroque style of art. His works include the volume *Steps to the Temple.*

Crash of 1929 *See* **Black Thursday.**

Crassus, Lucius Licinius 140–91 BC. Roman politician and orator. He sponsored a law banishing those who had not legally attained Roman citizenship. The law was a major cause of the Social War.

Crassus, Marcus Licinius *d.* 53 BC. Roman politician. One of the wealthiest Romans, he suppressed (71 BC) the slave revolt led by Spartacus, and joined with J. Caesar and G. Pompey in the first Triumvirate (60 BC). His death while fighting the Parthians led to a power struggle between Caesar and Pompey.

Crazy Horse *d.* 1877. American Sioux Indian chief of the Oglala tribe. He was a leader in the defeat of Col. G. Custer at the Battle of Little Bighorn (1876).

Creasy, Sir Edward Shepherd 1812–78. English historian. Creasy's major works include *Fifteen Decisive Battles of the World* and *The History of the Ottoman Turks.*

Crécy, Battle of Battle (Aug. 26, 1346) of the Hundred Years' War, at Crécy, France. English king Edward III led a force of some 10,000 to a decisive victory over about 20,000 French led by Philip VI. The English then advanced to besiege Calais.

Crédit Mobilier of America US railroad construction company involved in a major American financial scandal (1872). The scandal revolved around construction of the Union Pacific Railroad (1865–69), partly funded by federal loans and grants and partly by a Union Pacific bond issue. Between 1865 and 1869, directors and principal stockholders of Union Pacific allowed exorbitant payments for construction to be made to Crédit Mobilier, which they owned. Crédit Mobilier in turn paid others for actual construction and thereby realized millions in profits. Union Pacific capital was thus systematically drained off and by 1869 the company was deeply in debt. The scandal broke during the 1872 presidential election campaign, when it was revealed that US congressman Oakes Ames (1804–73) and other politicians were involved in the corrupt dealings.

Creek Indians North American Indian tribe that once inhabited parts of Georgia and Alabama. In Colonial times, the Creek generally fought alongside English settlers in wars against the Spanish and Apache Indians, formed the unsuccessful Creek Confederation, and were defeated in the Creek War (1813–14) They were moved to Indian Territory in the 1830s. There the Creek became one of the Five Civilized Tribes.

Creek War War (1813–14) between the Creek Indians and the US. The Creek, British allies in the War of 1812, were stirred up by the Shawnee chief Tecumseh and began the war by massacring (Aug. 30, 1813) about 500 Americans at Fort Mims, Georgia. Gen. A. Jackson was sent with some 5,000 soldiers to subdue the Creek. After winning initial battles, Jackson put an end to the war by his decisive victory (Mar. 27, 1814) at the Battle of Horseshoe Bend. The Creek subsequently signed the Treaty of Fort Jackson (Aug. 9, 1814), giving up most of their tribal lands.

Crépy, Treaty of (Crespy, ˜) Treaty (Sept. 18 1544, at Crépy, northern France) between Holy Roman Emperor Charles V (also king of Spain) and French king Francis I, ending wars between them (1521–44). By its terms Charles gave up claims to Burgundy, and Francis relinquished claims to Naples, Flanders, and Artois.

Crete Greek island. Crete was the center of the Minoan civilization (*q.v.*) and one of the earliest advanced cultures. By the 16th cent. BC it had spread its culture and influence to the Greek mainland and throughout the eastern Mediterranean and had established dynastic centers at Cnossos and Phaistos, its major cities. After the fall of the Minoans (c1400 BC), Crete was resettled by Dorian Greeks. It became an important commercial center and, in the 3d cent. BC, a haven for pirates. Annexed (67 BC) by Rome, it later became part of the Byzantine Empire, passed to Venice (1204) during the Fourth Crusade, and then to the Ottoman Turks (1715). Rivalry between Greece and Turkey for control of Crete led to the Greco-Turkish War (1897) and establishment (1898) of a semiautonomous state under European occupation. Crete declared its union with Greece (1908) and was officially annexed in 1913. During WW II, it was captured (May, 1941) by the Germans in the first successful major airborne operation.

Crèvecoeur, Michel-Guillaume Jean de (*pseud.* ˜, J. Hector St. John) 1735–1813. French-born American author and agriculturist. He is known best for his *Letters from an American Farmer.*

Crick, Francis Harry Compton *See* **Watson, James.**

Crimea Russian region, now part of the Ukraine. A peninsula extending from the Ukraine to the Black Sea, it has been conquered many times in history. It was the site of the Crimean War (1853–56).

Crimean War War in southeastern Europe (1853–56) fought by Russia against the Ottoman Turks and their allies, France, Britain, and Sardinia. A long series of Russo-Turkish Wars (*q.v.*) had resulted in Russian expansion in southeast Europe at the expense of the Turks. In the 19th cent., European powers became concerned over

the dismemberment of the Ottoman Empire (*see* Eastern Question). Rivalries between France (a long-time ally of the Ottomans) and Russia finally provided the spark that led to war. British and French troops bore the brunt of fighting and the allies were ultimately victorious. The war broke Russian dominance in southeastern Europe. Key events in the Crimean War include:

1851–53 France challenged Russia's position as custodian of Christian holy places within the Ottoman Empire; it sought special considerations for Latin Christian churches from the Ottoman Turks; these were granted (1852) and the Russians, who favored Greek Orthodox Christians, were roused to action.

1853 Russian Tsar Nicholas I delivered ultimatum to Turkish government (May); Russian demands refused; Russian forces occupied (July) Moldavia and Walachia (now in Rumania).

1853 Ottoman Empire declared war on Russia (Oct. 23).

1854 France and Britain declared war on Russia (Mar.).

1854 Russia withdrew from Moldavia and Walachia under pressure from Austria; Austrian army moved into the region (Aug.).

1854 British and French forces landed on the Crimean Peninsula on the north coast of the Black Sea; victorious in the Battle of Alma River (Sept. 20) soon after; Russian forces withdrew to Sevastopol.

1854 Allied forces began siege of Sevastopol, key Russian position on Black Sea (Oct.).

1854 Battle of Balaklava fought (Oct. 25); Russians failed to break siege of Sevastopol but inflicted heavy casualties on the British; this battle inspired Tennyson's famous poem *Charge of the Light Brigade.*

1854 Russians defeated at Battle of Inkerman (Nov. 5); siege of Sevastopol continued.

1854–55 Military action halted during winter; severe conditions suffered by the war casualties led to Florence Nightingale's celebrated nursing efforts.

1855 Sardinia declared war against Russia (Jan.).

1855 Nicholas died (Mar.); Alexander II became Russian tsar; moved to negotiate an end to the war.

1855   Russian forces marching to relieve Sevastopol defeated at Battle of Chernaya River (Aug. 16).

1855   Allied forces besieging Sevastopol captured Malakhov fortress (Sept. 8); Russians forced to evacuate Sevastopol (Sept. 11).

1856   Treaty of Paris (Mar. 30) formally ended hostilities.

Crime of '73   Name for the US government's move (1873) to stop minting the silver dollar. In later years, the action was vigorously attacked by Populists and other advocates of free silver (*q.v.*). The 1878 Bland-Allison Act (*q.v.*) restored the silver dollar as legal tender.

Cripps Mission   Unsuccessful diplomatic mission (Mar. 22–Apr. 12, 1942) to India, in which the British government offered eventual independence in exchange for India's support during WW II. With India in the midst of its long drive for independence and with the Japanese threatening invasion of India from the East, the British sent Sir Stafford Cripps (1889–1952) to negotiate for India's help in fending off the Japanese. Indian leader M. Gandhi opposed the plan for phased independence after the war and the Indian National Congress rejected it (Apr. 11). The Congress later called (Aug. 8) for immediate independence. The subsequent arrest of its leaders resulted in mass demonstrations and an official ban on the Congress.

Crispi, Francesco 1819–1901.   Italian statesman. He aided G. Garibaldi in the conquest of Sicily (1860) and served as Italian premier (1887–91, 1893–96).

Crispin and Crispinian, Saints *fl.* 3d cent.   Christian martyrs, patron saints of shoemakers, whose trade they followed. Said to have been brothers, they were beheaded by order of Roman emperor Maximilian.

Crispus, Gaius Sallustius   *See* **Sallust.**

Cristofori, Bartolomeo di Francesco 1655–1731. Italian harpsichord maker, credited with invention of the hammer action employed in pianos and construction (c1710) of the first piano.

Crittenden, John J.   *See* **Crittenden Compromise.**

Crittenden Compromise   Unsuccessful legislation proposed (Dec., 1860) in a final attempt to avert the US Civil War. Put forward by Kentucky senator John J. Crittenden (1787–1863), the measures attempted to rework the Missouri Compromise (1820). Crittenden sought to continue the fugitive slave laws, uphold the doctrine of Popular Sovereignty in new territories, and sanction slavery in the District of Columbia. The measure was defeated in the Senate by one vote (Mar., 1861).

Croatia   Historic region, formerly a constituent republic of Yugoslavia. Settled by Croats in the 7th cent., it formed a union with Hungary (1102). Its Westernization and acceptance of Roman Catholicism set it apart from the Slavs of Serbia, Bulgaria, and Russia. It was conquered by the Turks (16th cent.) and by Napoleon (1809–13). In 1918, the Serbs, Croats, and Slovenes joined to form Yugoslavia. Periodic agitation in Croatia for greater autonomy culminated in demands for independence during the late 1980s and a civil war against Serb-dominated troops of the now-defunct national Yugoslavian government. Fighting continued into the 1990s. *See also* Yugoslavia, from 1981.

Croato-Hungarian Compromise of 1868   *See* **Nagoda.**

Croce, Benedetto 1866–1952.   Italian philosopher, historian, critic, and statesman. Founder (1903) of the journal *La Critica,* he strongly opposed Fascism and was a leader of the Liberal party after WW II.

Crockett, David (~, Davy) 1786–1836.   American frontiersman and politician. He fought against the Creek Indians in the War of 1812 and was a member of Congress (1827–31, 1833–35). He died at the Alamo.

Croesus *d.*546? BC.   Last king of Lydia (560–546 BC), successor to his father, Alyattes, and famed for his great wealth. He was defeated in battle by Cyrus the Great at Sardis (546).

Croker, Richard 1841–1922.   Irish-born American politician. He was leader (1886–1902) of New York's Tammany Hall.

Cromwell, Oliver 1599–1658.   English soldier and statesman, a hero of the English Civil Wars (1642–48) and head of government during the Commonwealth and Protectorate (1649–58). A leader of the Parliamentarians before the outbreak of war, he later distinguished himself as a military commander (eventually second in command of the New Model Army) at such battles as Marston Moor (1644), Naseby (1645), Preston (1648), and Worcester (1651). He ordered King Charles I's execution (1649), and on formation of the Commonwealth (1649) became its leader. He invaded and subdued Ireland (1649) and Scotland (1650–51). He dissolved (1653) the Rump Parliament and others in following years. After the failure of his Barebones Parliament, he was made (1653) Lord Protector, thus establishing the English Protectorate, but was unable in his last years to form a stable parliamentary government. He failed in his attempts to form an international Protestant league, concluded the first of the Dutch Wars, and added Jamaica and Dunkirk to the English possessions. Two years after his death the Convention Parliament restored (1660) the English monarchy.

Cromwell, Thomas, earl of Essex 1485?–1540. English statesman. He served as secretary to Cardinal Wolsey and later rose to become chief counselor to King Henry VIII. In Henry's service he played a major role in the Protestant Reformation and arranged the king's marriage to Anne of Cleves. Henry's dissatisfaction with the match contributed to Cromwell's downfall and beheading.

Crookes, Sir William 1832–1919. English physicist and chemist. He discovered (1861) the element thallium and invented the Crookes radiometer.

Cross of Gold speech Speech (July 8, 1896) by W. Bryan, a delegate at the Democratic National Convention. His speech, supporting the free-silver movement, contained the words "you shall not crucify mankind upon a cross of gold" and secured for Bryan the presidential nomination.

Croton, Milo of See **Milo of Croton.**

Crouchback, Edmund See **Lancaster, Edmund, earl of.**

Crusade (See also individual crusades.) Principally, the medieval wars undertaken (11th–13th cents.) by European Christians to reconquer the Holy Land from the Muslims. Brought on by Seljuk conquests in the region and by appeals for aid from Byzantine emperor Alexius I, the First Crusade was preached (1095) by Pope Urban II at the Council of Clermont. Thereafter the crusades became a popular vehicle for spiritual and material gain throughout Europe and resulted in nine (including the Children's Crusade) major expeditions against the Muslims. The term "crusade" was later used in reference to military expeditions, sanctioned by the pope, against heretics and others.

Crusade, Children's Ill-fated crusade (1212) by unarmed children to free the Holy Land. Supported by church authorities after the disgrace of the Fourth Crusade, it included contingents from France and Germany. In France, some 30,000 youths, led by the visionary peasant boy Stephen of Cloyes, left by ship (Aug., 1212) from Marseilles. Those who survived passage to Alexandria were sold into slavery. The German group of 20,000 youths, led by the German boy Nicholas of Cologne, marched across the Alps to Italy. Most, however, died or deserted along the way.

Crusade, First Holy war (1096–99) by European Christians to aid the Byzantines in the recapture of the Holy Land from the Muslims (Seljuks). The only successful crusade, it resulted in formation of the Crusader States (see below). Wandering preachers, notably Peter the Hermit and Walter the Penniless, spread the message of the crusade in Europe and raised hordes of peasant followers. These disorganized bands marched (1096) to Constantinople, robbing villages and massacring Jews along the way. They were quickly thrown into battle against the Muslims (and killed) in Asia Minor. Organized contingents of crusader knights arrived at Constantinople (late 1096), where Byzantine king Alexius I demanded an oath of loyalty from them. Fighting against Muslims began the next year and included victories for the crusaders at Nicaea (1097), Dorylaeum (1097), and Antioch (1098). Finally, some 20,000 crusaders marched to Jerusalem, took the city (July 15, 1099), and massacred Muslims and Jews. The crusade ended with the Battle of Ascalon (Aug. 12, 1099), when crusaders defeated an army of Egyptian Muslims near Jerusalem. The crusaders set up the Crusader States, including the Latin Kingdom of Jerusalem, the Principality of Antioch, and the counties of Edessa (under Baldwin, later Baldwin I of Jerusalem) and Tripoli (under Raymond IV).

Crusade, Second Holy war (1147–49) fought by European Christians after the Muslims captured Edessa (1144) from the crusaders. Preached by Saint Bernard of Clairvaux, the crusade involved a combined force of 140,000, led by Holy Roman Emperor Conrad III and French king Louis VII. The Germans and French departed for Constantinople (Apr., 1147), pillaged Byzantine territories along the way, and were quickly sent to Asia Minor by Byzantine emperor Manuel I. The Germans were nearly wiped out in a surprise attack at Dorylaeum (Oct., 1147) and the French were likewise reduced by the Muslims. The remnants of the two forces combined (1148) and unsuccessfully attacked Damascus (1148). They were badly mauled in the ensuing retreat. Conrad left for Europe (1148) and Louis's departure (1149) brought the crusade to an end.

Crusade, Third Holy war (1189–92) fought by European Christians after the capture (1187) of Jerusalem by the Egyptian sultan Saladin. Preached by Pope Gregory VIII, the crusade was led by Holy Roman Emperor Frederick I, English king Richard I, and French king Philip II. Frederick died on the way, and Richard and Philip arrived (1191) to join the siege at Acre (under way since 1189). The city was taken (July, 1191), and after a quarrel with Richard, Philip returned to France. Richard negotiated a truce (1192) with Saladin, in which the Christians retained only a small part of the former kingdom of Jerusalem and access to Jerusalem. The crusade ended with Richard's departure (Oct., 1192).

Crusade, Fourth Holy war (1202–04) fought by European Christians, originally directed against Muslim conquerors of the Holy Land. This crusade brought the crusades into discredit and ended with the formation of the Latin Empire of Constantinople. Preached by Pope Innocent III, the crusade was led by French noblemen. Assembling at Venice (1202), they agreed, in return for passage to the Holy Land, to help Venice capture the city of Zara on the Adriatic. For this they were briefly excommunicated by the pope. The crusaders, promised money and aid, again diverted from their mission and moved to reinstate deposed Byzantine emperor Isaac II (d. 1204). The crusaders arrived at Constantinople and put Isaac (1203) on the throne, only to see him overthrown (1204) by Alexius V. The crusaders thereupon sacked the city and set up the Latin Empire (1204), ending, for a time, the existence of the Byzantine Empire.

Crusade, Fifth Holy war (1218–21) fought by European Christians against Muslim Egypt. Preached by Pope Innocent III, the crusade was led by papal legate Cardinal Pelagius, Hungarian king Andrew II, and John of Brienne. Crusaders attacked (May, 1218) Damietta on the Nile delta and, following a long siege, captured (Nov., 1219) the city. Their long-delayed advance up the Nile (July, 1221) foundered in the rising flood waters of the river, and the crusaders were forced ultimately to evacuate Egypt (Sept., 1221).

Crusade, Sixth Holy war (1228–29) undertaken by Holy Roman Emperor Frederick II. After the failure of the Fifth Crusade, Frederick was obliged to take some action. He set out in 1227, was excommunicated by Pope Gregory IX for delaying, and continued to Acre where he negotiated (1229) a 10-year treaty with the Egyptians without engaging in any hostilities. Despite opposition from Christian factions in Jerusalem, he was crowned king of the city (1229) and returned to Europe. Unrest between these factions ensued and Turkish and Egyptian Muslims retook the city (1244).

Crusade, Seventh Holy war (1248–54) undertaken by French king Louis IX. With the support of Pope Innocent IV, Louis embarked (1248) and attacked Egypt (May, 1249) with a force of 15,000 soldiers. Damietta (on the Nile delta) fell to the Christians again (1249) but further advances toward Cairo (1250) met with disaster. Louis was captured (and later ransomed) and many of his soldiers were massacred. Damietta was evacuated, and Louis spent the next four years in Jerusalem (to 1254) in attempts to gain release of his captured soldiers and to better fortify Christian positions in the Holy Land.

Crusade, Eighth Last of the holy wars (1270), undertaken by French king Louis IX. With the rise of Mameluke sultan Baybars (reigned 1260–77), the Muslims began renewed conquests of Christian territories in the Holy Land. Louis began preparations in 1267 (Antioch fell in 1268) and he departed July, 1270. He landed at Tunis, but his force was struck by disease. Louis died and his army withdrew. Subsequently (in what is sometimes called the Ninth Crusade), England's Prince Edward (later Edward I) landed at Acre (1271), concluded a treaty (1272) with the Muslims, and withdrew. Muslim conquests continued, however, and the last Christian outpost in the Holy Land was lost (1291) at the Battle of Acre. Thereafter crusaders withdrew to Cyprus.

Crusade, Ninth Name sometimes given to the final phase of the Eighth Crusade (q.v.).

Crysler's Farm, Battle of See **Chrysler's Farm, Battle of.**

Crystal Palace Famous English exhibition hall. Constructed of iron and glass, it was built at Hyde Park for the Great Exhibition of 1851, and was reerected near London, where it stood until razed by fire (1936).

Cuba Island republic located in the West Indies. The population is 10,582,000 and the capital is Havana. First discovered (1492) by C. Columbus and colonized by Spain, it became the center for Spanish colonization in the New World and was the last Spanish stronghold to gain independence (19th cent.). Cuba came under increasing US domination after the Spanish-American War, until F. Castro's successful revolution in 1959 turned the island into a strategic Communist stronghold in the West. Following the Cuban Missile Crisis in the early 1960s, Cuba became a base for the promotion of revolutions in Latin America. In the early 1990s Communist Cuba was hard hit by the collapse of the USSR, on which it depended heavily for trade and military and financial aid. Key dates in the history of Cuba include:

1492 C. Columbus discovered Cuba.

EARLY 1500s Spanish began colonization of Cuba; used island as base for colonial expansion in the New World.

1763 British occupied Havana (1762) during Seven Years' War; Spanish control of Cuba restored by Treaty of Paris.

1791 Slave revolt in Haiti; resulted in increased sugar growing in Cuba (using slave labor).

1868–78 Ten Years' War against Spanish rule; revolt ended in failure.

1886 Slavery abolished.

1895 New war against Spanish rule, led by José Martí, began.

1898 US government and citizens outraged by accounts of Spanish brutality in Cuba; war fever reached height with the sinking of US battleship *Maine* in Havana harbor (Feb.).

1898 Spanish-American War; Spain defeated; Cuba placed under US military control.

1901 In US, the Platt Amendment provided for independence under US protection and stated that US could intervene in Cuba militarily.

1902 Estrada Palma became first president of Cuba.

EARLY 1900s Massive US investment in Cuba began; led to uprising in Cuba and US military intervention (1906–09); US again intervened in 1912, 1917.

1925–33 Gerardo Machado served as president; instituted numerous reforms but became increasingly repressive and was overthrown (1933) by Fulgencio Batista.

1933–59 Batista regime; Batista controlled Cuban politics from 1933 to 1952; seized power (1952) and established a dictatorship.

1934 US scrapped unpopular Platt Amendment.

1953 F. Castro staged unsuccessful uprising the year after Batista seized power.

1956 Castro began guerrilla war, centered in Oriente province, against Batista.

1958 US cut off military aid to Cuba.

1959 Batista fled Cuba (Jan. 1); Castro marched triumphantly into Havana, beginning Cuban Revolution.

1959–61 Castro's revolution grew increasingly Communist in orientation; thousands were arrested, many executed; property, notably US holdings, was confiscated (1960); US broke diplomatic relations (Jan., 1961) and established an economic embargo.

1961 Castro openly avowed Communism; Soviet influence over Cuba increased during the 1960s, particularly after the Cuban Missile Crisis; meanwhile, Castro's authoritarian regime expanded health care, housing, and education to the entire population.

1961 Bay of Pigs invasion (Apr.) by US–backed Cuban exiles was crushed.

1962 Cuba expelled from council of Organization of American States.

1962 Cuban Missile Crisis (Oct.); nuclear showdown averted after Soviets agreed to withdraw nuclear missiles from Cuba and US pledged not to invade the island.

1970s Cuba, through above-market-price sugar purchases and other deals with the USSR, became totally dependent on the Soviets; Soviet economic subsidies amounted to some $3 billion a year.

1973 Agreement with US for return of hijackers marked a shift toward better relations with the US.

1975 Cuban troops in Angola to support Marxist regime.

1977 US eased some restrictions on trade and travel to Cuba.

1978 Cuban troops in Ethiopia to aid Marxist regime there.

1978 Castro agreed to allow emigration of political prisoners to US; 50,000 others with relatives outside Cuba also allowed to leave.

1980 Cuban "boat people" (Mariel boat lift); Castro, angered by swarms of refugees anxious to leave Cuba, opened port of Mariel to boats from US; over 120,000 refugees, including Cuban criminals, transported to US (Apr.–Sept.).

1980 Castro freed US citizens jailed in Cuba (Oct. 27).

1981 US president R. Reagan, following break in talks with Cuba, instituted measures against Cuba (tighter economic sanctions; investment in Cuba and travel there made illegal, 1982); shipments of Soviet arms to Cuba continued.

1983 US invaded Grenada; Cuban personnel ousted and Cuban influence curtailed, as relations with US worsened.

1984 Cuba cut troops stationed in Ethiopia by half, bringing level to 5,000 involved in fighting there.

1985 Cuba began establishing closer ties with other Latin American countries from about this time; improved relations with Argentina, Peru, Brazil, and Uruguay.

1985 Cuba accepted return of 2,746 criminals and mentally ill from the US in exchange for 3,000 political prisoners.

1985–87 Sugar and tobacco production dropped sharply because of long drought.

1986 Major shakeup of Communist party leaders; many older veterans of 1956 revolution replaced by younger party members.

1986 Castro introduced austerity measures (Dec.) to deal with economy suffering from effects of continued drought, lowered sugar and oil prices, and foreign trade deficit.

1987 US brought alleged human rights violations by Cuba before the UN; UN condemnation voted down by narrow margin; measure defeated again in 1988, though an inspection team did find violations.

1988 Cuba completed negotiations with Angola and South Africa, setting the stage for withdrawal of Cuban forces from southern Africa.

1989–91 Cuban troops, which had reached a high of 50,000, withdrawn from Angola following peace agreement there.

1989 Soviet leader M. Gorbachev visited Cuba (Apr. 2–5); sought to reduce Soviet aid to Cuba; Castro publicly denounced movement toward democracy and free market in the Communist bloc.

1989 Several senior military men found to be involved in drug trafficking (between Colombia and the US) as well as smuggling in Angola; took bribes from Medellín drug cartel in return for use of Cuban airstrips to refuel planes smuggling drugs to US; 4 senior officers executed, 14 other officials jailed.

1990 Cuba began its first two-year term on the UN Security Council.

1990 Government broke ties with Nicaragua following election defeat of pro-Communist Sandinista government (Feb.).

1990 Castro declared he would cut half the jobs in the Communist party bureaucracy (Oct.).

1990 Rationing imposed on all commodities (Nov.); government warned of possible US attack.

1991 Economic crisis deepened as the Communist USSR collapsed; Castro claimed Cuba lost 85 percent of its trade due to collapse of Communist governments in Eastern Europe and the USSR itself.

1992 Some 1,500 former Soviet troops stationed in Cuba to leave by mid-1993.

Cuban Missile Crisis US–USSR Cold War confrontation (Oct. 22, 1962–Jan. 7, 1963) over installation of ballistic missiles in Cuba. The crisis nearly precipitated nuclear war between the US and the USSR. After the US–backed Bay of Pigs Invasion (1961), Soviet chairman N. Khrushchev authorized installation of the missiles on Cuban soil. US president J. Kennedy proclaimed a naval quarantine of Cuba (Oct. 22, 1962) after learning of the sites and publicly warned that an attack from Cuban bases would mean US retaliation against Russia itself. Khrushchev gave in to US demands for withdrawal of the missiles (Oct. 28) and the US promised not to invade Cuba. The US lifted its quarantine (Nov. 20) and, in a formal note to the UN (Jan. 7, 1963), the US and Russia announced the end of the crisis.

Cuban Revolution Phase of modern Cuban history that began on Jan. 1, 1959, with the overthrow of the regime of F. Batista by F. Castro and his band of insurgents. Castro, heading his 26th of July Movement (*q.v.*), had earlier attempted to invade Cuba with a force of revolutionaries (Dec., 1956), but his forces had been defeated and scattered. A small band hid out in the Sierra Maestra Mountains, conducting guerrilla actions and acquiring new recruits, until Castro was finally able to take over. His immediate efforts to install a socialist government brought quick US reactions in the form of an economic and sugar boycott and, later, the disastrous Bay of Pigs Invasion (*q.v.*). Soviet support of the Cuban Revolution brought about (Oct., 1962) the Cuban Missile Crisis (*q.v.*), when the USSR tried to install offensive missiles there. Cuba became a virtual Soviet satellite, and over the years has pursued a policy of "exporting" revolution by its involvement in political upheavals in Latin America and even Africa (Angola). Castro's style of socialism remained highly personal despite his dependence on the Soviet bloc.

cubism   Artistic movement. A reaction against realism and impressionism, cubism reduced all objects to their basic geometrical shapes. Famed cubists include P. Picasso and G. Braque.

Culpeper's Rebellion   American Colonial uprising (1677–79). Led by John Culpeper (*fl.* 1677), Carolina colonists rebelled against restrictive British trade laws and established their own government (1677–79).

Cult of Reason   Short-lived, extremist anti-Catholic movement during the French Revolution led by P. Chaumette, J. Hébert, and others. Chaumette staged the first worship ceremony for the cult in Notre Dame Cathedral (Nov. 10, 1793) and he later ordered Paris churches closed. The cult was abolished (1794) and its leaders executed by M. Robespierre.

Cultural Revolution   (Great Proletarian Cultural Revolution) Chinese political movement (1966–69) headed by Mao Zedong and intended to help purge the Chinese Communist party of bourgeois or capitalist elements. Implemented by brigades of young people known as Red Guards, the movement spread to touch every facet of life in China and seriously damaged China's cultural, industrial, and political development.

Cumae   Ancient city near Naples, Italy, believed one of the oldest Greek colony in Italy. Founded (c750 BC) by Greek settlers, it became a Roman town (338 BC) and was destroyed AD 1205. Extensive ruins exist on its site.

Cumberland Road   *See* **National Road.**

Cummings, Edward Estlin (e. e. cummings) 1894–1962. American writer and painter noted for his brilliantly unorthodox poetry. His novel *The Enormous Room,* a classic, is based on his experiences in France during WW I.

Cunard, Sir Samuel 1787–1865.   Canadian shipowner and merchant. He established (1839) the first regular transatlantic steamship line, which became the Cunard Line.

Cunaxa, Battle of   Battle (401 BC) at Cunaxa, north of Babylon, in which Cyrus the Younger attempted to overthrow his brother, Persian king Artaxerxes II. Cyrus was killed, and the 13,000 Greek mercenaries in his army began their Retreat of the Ten Thousand, celebrated by Xenophon in his *Anabasis.*

cuneiform writing   Ancient writing system, developed (c4th millennium BC), probably by the Sumerians. Based on wedge-shaped symbols, it was widely used in Asia Minor and included numerous distinct systems, including Babylonian, Elamite, Hittite, and Persian.

curia   Ancient Roman political division. By tradition, Romulus divided Rome into 3 tribes of 10 curiae each. Each curia voted as a unit in the assembly, the Comitia Curiata. The term came to denote the meeting place of such a body as the Roman Senate, etc.

Curie, Pierre 1859–1906 and **Curie, Marie Sklodowska** 1867–1934.   French scientists and co-discoverers of radium and polonium. The Curies were married (1895) and, after A. Becquerel discovered radioactivity, Marie began her own investigations. She was joined by Pierre in 1898, and in that year they jointly isolated radium and polonium. With Becquerel they were awarded the 1903 Nobel Prize in Physics. Following Pierre's death, Marie continued work on radium and received the Nobel Prize in Chemistry (1911).

Curtis, Charles 1860–1936.   American politician, vice-president of the US (1929–33) under President H. Hoover. A Republican, Curtis served in the House of Representatives (1893–1907) and Senate (1907–13, 1915–29).

Curtis, Cyrus Hermann Kotzschmar 1850–1933. American publisher. He established (1890) the Curtis Publishing Company, which published the *Ladies' Home Journal* and the *Saturday Evening Post.*

Curzon, George Nathaniel, 1st marquess Curzon of Kendleston 1859–1925.   He served as viceroy of India (1898–1905) and in the cabinets of H. Asquith and D. Lloyd George during WW I. He instituted the Partition of Bengal (*q.v.*). As foreign secretary (1919–24) he presided over the Conference of Lausanne.

Curzon Line   Armistice line proposed by British foreign secretary G. Curzon during the Russo-Polish War (1920). It was incorporated almost entirely as the Russian-Polish border, by treaty (Aug. 16, 1945).

Cush   *See* **Kush.**

Custer, George Armstrong 1839–76.   American soldier. He distinguished himself as a Union officer in the Civil War but in 1876 led more than 250 men into the Battle of Little Bighorn (*q.v.*). Custer was killed along with his men in this famous massacre.

Custer's last stand   *See* **Little Bighorn, Battle of.**

Custoza, Battles of   1. Battle (July 24, 1848) at Custoza; Italy, in which Austria defeated Italian rebels and Sardinian forces led by Sardinian king Charles Albert.   2. Battle (June 24, 1866) at Custoza, in which Austria decisively defeated Italian forces seeking to liberate Venice from Austria. Nonetheless, Austria ceded Venice to France, and France ceded it (July 3) to Italy.

Cuthbert, Saint c634–687.   English saint, a noted figure in the early Christian church in England. A shepherd in the kingdom of Northumbria, Cuthbert experienced a vision and thereafter entered a monastery (651). After Northumbria adopted Roman Christian traditions (abandoning Celtic Christian practices) at the Synod of Whitby (663–64), Cuthbert served as prior of the Holy Island monastery (664–76, also called Lindisfarne). In 676 he retired to a hermitage at Inner Farne, which he left briefly to serve as bishop (685–86) at Holy Island.

Cutter, Charles Ammi 1837–1903.   American librarian who developed an early system for the classification of books.

Cuvier, Georges Léopold Chrétien Frédéric Dagobert, baron 1769–1832.   French naturalist. He contributed greatly to the development of comparative anatomy and paleontology.

Cuza, Alexander John 1820–73.   First prince of Rumania (1859–66). Elected (1859) prince in both Moldavia and Walachia, he was proclaimed prince of Rumania on unification of the two states (1861). He confiscated and redistributed monastic lands, freed the serfs (1864), and reformed Rumanian legal and educational systems.

Cyclades   Greek islands in the Aegean Sea, so named because they form a circle around the island Delos. Most of the islands were members of the Delian League (5th cent. BC) and its successor, the second Athenian naval league.

Cynewulf (Cynwulf) *fl.* c750.   English poet. Little is known of his life. His surviving works, chiefly religious in nature, are *Juliana, The Ascension, Elene,* and *The Fates of the Apostles.*

Cynics   Philosophical school (4th cent. BC–6th cent. AD) founded in ancient Greece by Antisthenes. Originally the Cynics held that virtue was the only good and, preaching a life of self-sufficiency and ascetic poverty, came to ridicule the conventional way of life. Other famous Cynics included Diogenes of Sinope and Crates.

Cynwulf   *See* **Cynewulf.**

Cyprian, Saint (Cyprianus, Thascius Caecilius) *d.* AD c258.   Bishop of Carthage (AD c248). He opposed Pope Stephen I on the issue of papal authority over other bishops, and disputed the validity of baptisms performed by schismatics.

Cyprianus, Thascius Caecilius *See* **Cyprian, Saint.**

Cyprus   Island republic (*pop.* 630,000) in the Mediterranean, site of Mt. Olympus. Cyprus has been populated since Neolithic times, and its development was strongly influenced after 1500 BC by Greece. Conquered many times, including by the Ottoman Turks (1571), Cyprus was placed under British administration (1878) and was annexed by Britain (1914). It gained independence in 1960. Continuous strife between Greek Cypriots (80 percent of the population) and Turkish Cypriots (18 percent) led to serious clashes between Greece and Turkey. A military coup (July 15, 1974) resulted in the ouster of President Makarios by rebels seeking union with Greece. Turkey invaded Cyprus (July 20) to protect the Turkish Cypriots and took half of the island. Makarios became president again (Dec. 7) and Turkish Cypriots withdrew to a sector in the north, where they established the Turkish Republic of Northern Cyprus in 1983 by declaration. The situation remains unresolved.

Cyrano de Bergerac, Savinien 1619–55.   French satirist and fantasist, known for fighting many duels occasioned by comments about his large nose. He was the subject of the play *Cyrano de Bergerac* by E. Rostand.

Cyrenaics   Ancient Greek philosophical school (4th cent.–c275 BC). They held that pleasure was the highest good, and contributed to development of the philosophy of Epicureanism.

Cyril and Methodius, Saints *d.* 869/885.   Greek brothers who were apostles to the Slavs. They translated the liturgy into Slavonic and are believed to have invented the Cyrillic alphabet, upon which modern Russian and Eastern Slavic languages are based.

Cyril of Alexandria, Saint *d.* AD 444.   Patriarch of Alexandria (AD 412–444) and Doctor of the Church. He expelled the Jews from Alexandria. An opponent of Nestorianism, he presided over the Council of Ephesus (AD 431).

Cyril of Jerusalem, Saint AD 315?–386?   Christian theologian and bishop of Jerusalem (AD c350–386?). He was expelled three times from his see for his opposition to Arianism.

Cyrus the Great *d.* 529 BC.   Persian king (c550–529 BC), founder of the Persian Empire. He overthrew the Median king Astyages (c550 BC), conquered Lydia (c546 BC) and Babylonia (538 BC), and extended his empire into Asia. He freed the Jews in Babylonia, ending the Babylonian Captivity.

Cyrus the Younger *d.* 401 BC.   Persian prince, son of Darius II. After his brother Artaxerxes II became king (404 BC), Cyrus conspired against him. Raising an army against Artaxerxes, he was defeated and killed in the Battle of Cunaxa.

Czechoslovakia (Czech and Slovak Federal Republic)   Country located in central Europe. The population is 15,695,000 and the capital is Prague. Czechoslovakia was formed (1918) during the dismemberment of the Austro-Hungarian Empire at the end of WW I. Though based on the principle of national self-determination, the new state embraced many minorities, and ethnic tensions threatened its stability. Czechoslovakia included the historic regions of Bohemia, Moravia, and Slovakia as well as Ruthenia, which became part of the Soviet Union in 1945. Czechoslovakia was dismembered on the eve of WW II (1938–39) by Germany, Poland, and Hungary and was reestablished (1945) at the end of the war. Czechoslavakia renounced its Communist government during the wave of pro-democracy demonstrations that swept through Eastern Europe and the Soviet Union during the late 1980s. Czech and Slovak leaders failed to resolve fundamental differences between the two constituent regions and in 1993 the Czech and

Slovak states became independent. Key dates in the history of Czechoslovakia include:

1916   Czechoslovak National Council formed (Jan.) for creation of independent nation.

1918   Czech National Council proclaimed itself the government in the Czech lands (Oct. 28) and formed union with Slovakia (Nov. 14); Tomáš Masaryk became first president of Czechoslovakia.

1919   Republic of Czechoslovakia recognized by Allied powers and Austria, by Treaty of St. Germain (Sept.).

1920   Treaty of Trianon (June); Hungary recognized Czechoslovakia, and Ruthenia was added to its territory.

1920–21   Little Entente, defensive pact formed by Czechoslovakia, Rumania, and Yugoslavia.

1930s   In Germany, rise of A. Hitler as dictator coincided with rise of agitation for union with Germany in the Czech border land (Sudetenland), which was heavily populated by Germans.

1935   Masaryk resigned as president; succeeded by E. Beneš.

1938   Hitler's demands in Czechoslovakia led to crisis in Europe; war temporarily averted by Munich Pact (Sept. 29); major European powers agreed to cession of Sudetenland to Germany.

1938   Beneš resigned as president (Oct. 5); succeeded by Emil Hácha; Czechoslovakia reorganized as Federated Republic of Czecho-Slovakia (Nov.).

1938   Poland occupied part of Czechoslovakia (Oct.).

1939   Germany and Hungary completed dismemberment of Czechoslovakia (Mar.); Germany declared protectorate over Bohemia and Moravia, and occupied Slovakia; Hungary annexed Ruthenia, renamed Carpatho-Ukraine.

1940   Beneš established Czech government-in-exile in London during WW II.

1945   Czechoslovakia reconstituted at end of WW II; Ruthenia (Carpatho-Ukraine) incorporated into Soviet Union (July); Beneš again became president of Czechoslovakia (Oct.).

1946   Communist party became leading political party in Czechoslovakian national elections.

1948   Communists secured virtual control of Czech government (Feb.).

1948   Jan Masaryk, non-Communist foreign minister, died (Mar. 10) in fall from window; death called suicide by government.

1949   New constitution establishing Czechoslovakia as a people's democratic republic, modeled on Soviet lines (May 9); Beneš resigned as president (June 7); constitution signed into law (June 8) by his successor, Communist party leader Klement Gottwald.

1950–52   Series of government and party purges instituted to consolidate Communist party control in Czechoslovakia.

1957–68   Antonin Novotný served as president.

1968   Alexander Dubček became Communist party leader (Jan.), replacing A. Novotný; Ludvík Svoboda made president (Mar.); Prague Spring, program of liberalization, began under Dubček's direction.

1968   Warsaw Pact forces led by Soviet army invaded Czechoslovakia (Aug. 20); most of the Prague Spring reforms instituted were reversed.

1969   Self-immolation in Prague by student Jan Palach, protesting Soviet invasion and crushing of Prague Spring.

1969   Dubček ousted as party leader (Apr.); mass purges of reformers in party carried out.

1970   Dubček expelled from Communist party (June).

1975–89   Gustáv Husák in office as president; his administration marked by close relations with the USSR and resolutely hard-line domestic policies, including continued denunciation of Prague Spring, repression of dissent, and refusal to institute needed reforms; by the 1980s the weakened Czech economy, mismanaged and badly in need of reform, became a factor in the fall of the Czech Communist party.

1977   Over 200 Czech intellectuals signed a petition demanding compliance with human rights provisions of the Helsinki Agreement; hundreds of others added their signatures as police began arresting those who signed (Jan. 6); sporadic arrests continued into the early 1980s.

1980   Husák reelected as president; continued as party general secretary.

1981   Set of Measures program instituted to improve widespread inefficiencies in Czech economic planning; program quickly proved ineffective.

1981   Shortages and price increases, notably for oil, reported; Soviet deliveries of oil began falling below specified targets.

1983   World Assembly for Peace held in Prague as antinuclear forum (June); Czech government took leading role in denouncing new deployment of US nuclear missiles.

1983   Deployment of new Soviet tactical nuclear missiles in Czechoslovakia announced (Oct.), to counter planned deployment of US missiles; move sparked Czech antinuclear protests in 1983–84.

1984   Czech poet Jaroslav Seifert awarded Nobel Prize for Literature; Seifert, a signer of the 1977 Charter 77 on human rights, proved an embarrassment to the Communist regime.

1985   Husák in Moscow for meetings following M. Gorbachev's call for reforms (May); in years following, the Czech government, which had long denounced the liberal reforms of Prague Spring, opted for the status quo; successfully resisted pressure for needed reforms until 1989.

1985   Some 150,000 gathered for celebration of 1100th anniversary of Saint Methodius's death (July); marked substantial growth of religious sentiment in Czechoslovakia, despite government efforts to discourage it.

1986   Chernobyl reactor disaster in USSR; Czech government, long committed to development of nuclear power, issued no radiation warnings; radioactive fallout reported over much of Czechoslavakia.

1986   Václav Havel, noted Czech playwright, awarded Erasmus Prize in the Netherlands; forced to remain in Czechoslovakia, Havel sent an acceptance speech that publicly lauded the dissident group Charter 77, of which he was a member.

1987   Central Committee of Communist Party of Czechoslovakia met (Mar.); hard-liners later called Soviet reforms inappropriate to conditions in Czechoslovakia.

1987   M. Gorbachev visited Czechoslovakia (Apr.); general expectation for reform aroused, though Gorbachev's visit failed to bring the needed shakeup in Czech leadership.

1987   Czech actor Miloš Kopeckný, echoing widespread sentiment, publicly declared that real reform would be impossible until current leaders were gone; his comments made in speech before theater and media workers congress (May).

1987   Over 1,000 people demonstrated in Prague on Human Rights Day (Dec. 10); dissident groups, long officially suppressed, becoming stronger and bolder.

1987   Husák turned over leadership of party to Miloš Jakeš, while retaining post as Czech president; Jakeš, another hard-liner, had overseen mass purges of reformers following Prague Spring.

1988   Shortages of consumer goods worsening; government reshuffled industrial organizations.

1988   Government used force to disperse group of religious demonstrators in Bratislava (Mar.); some 600,000 later signed a petition calling for religious freedom.

1988   Communists three times reshuffled government in effort to deflect mounting criticism (Apr., Oct., Dec.); old guard effectively remained in power, however; Ladislav Adamec in office as prime minister.

1988   Some 10,000 demonstrators gathered in Prague to condemn the crushing of Prague Spring; government used force to break up rally (Aug.).

1988   Jamming of Radio Free Europe halted for first time since 1951.

1989   Police used tear gas, water cannon, and dogs to break up anti-government demonstrations by mostly young protesters (Jan.); activist playwright Václav Havel among those arrested in week of protests; police brutality sparked further unrest and formation of dissident groups.

1989   Pro-democracy petition, "Just a Few Sentences," signed by tens of thousands (June), as unrest and pressure for change mounted.

1989   President M. Gorbachev gave Soviet blessings to pro-democracy reforms in Hungary and Poland (July), during speech renouncing the Brezhnev Doctrine; 1968 Soviet invasion of Czechoslovakia subsequently condemned by Poland and Hungary, leaving Husák's Communist regime isolated and embarrassed on the issue.

1989   Anniversary of 1968 Soviet invasion marked by further demonstrations (Aug. 21).

1989   Fall of East German Communist regime (Oct.).

1989   Special police squads, acting on government orders, brutally attacked student demonstrators in Prague (Nov. 17); the injury of 150 students sparked the widespread unrest that finally brought down the Communist government; for seven days Prague and other cities were paralyzed by spontaneous, mass anti-government protests involving hundreds of thousands of Czechs.

1989   Civic Forum established as coordinating group for anti-government activities (Nov. 19); Havel became Civic Forum leader.

1989   Czech Communist Party Central Committee met in stormy session (Nov. 24–25); ruled out massive force to restore order; ordered Prime Minister Adamec to form new government, including some non-Communists.

1989   Some 750,000 demonstrated for democratic change at Prague's Letná parade ground (Nov. 25); two-hour general strike followed on Nov. 27.

1989   Communist-dominated Federal Assembly, responding to mass demonstrations, amended Czech constitution to remove provisions guaranteeing Communist party leadership (Nov. 29); official condemnation of Prague Spring reversed Nov. 30.

1989   Warsaw Pact members officially denounced the 1968 invasion of Czechoslavakia at Moscow meeting (Dec. 4).

1989   Adamec formed new government with five non-Communists (Dec. 3); Adamec's government forced to resign (Dec. 7) after Civic Forum threatened another general strike unless Husák resigned and government with non-Communist majority was formed—by Dec. 10.

1989   Husák swore in new government and resigned on Dec. 10, Human Rights Day.

1989   Marián Čalfa, a Communist and lawyer, in office as prime minister; new government composed of non-Communist majority, including former dissidents; non-Communists also in control of Czech and Slovak regional governments; multi-party elections to be held in mid-1990.

1989   Emergency Czech Communist Party Congress held (Dec. 20–21); former Prime Minister Adamec made party chairman; formally accepted multi-party system; dissolved party People's Militia; formally apologized for damage done to country by Communists.

1989 Hero of Prague Spring, A. Dubček, now filling a vacated seat in Federal Assembly, became speaker of the parliament (Dec. 28).

1989–90 Havel in office as interim president, following election by members of Federal Assembly (Dec. 29) and culminating Czechoslovakia's so-called "velvet revolution"; censorship ended and freedom of religion instituted; Communist party forced to turn over assets to the government; and the army reorganized and reduced in size.

1990 Country formally adopted new name (Apr.), the Czech and Slovak Federal Republic (CSFR); Slovak desire for complete independence quickly threatened to break up the union.

1990 Laws enacted establishing private enterprise (Apr.); laws restoring property seized by Communists and for auctioning off small, government-run businesses passed in Oct.

1990 Multi-party elections held for federal and Czech and Slovak parliaments (June); Communist party, already reduced from 1.7 million to 650,000 members, commanded 14 percent of the vote.

1990–92 Havel in office as president, following election (July); power-sharing agreement between Czech and Slovak republics loomed as potential crisis; negotiated withdrawal of some 75,000 Soviet troops, in Czechoslovakia since 1968, completed by 1991; trade with West was sharply increased and independence of the USSR was firmly established by 1991.

1991 Czechoslovakia became full member of Council of Europe.

1992 Leaders of the Czech and Slovak regions of Czechoslovakia agreed to split the country into two separate nations (June 20); richer Czech region wanted strong federal government and quick shift to capitalism, while poorer Slovak region wanted greater independence; regional parliaments to make formal decision by Sept. 30.

1992 Vladimir Merciar in office as premier of Slovakia (June 24), following elections for the regional government.

1992 Slovaks successfully blocked President Havel's reelection bid (July).

1992 Slovakia's regional parliament declared sovereignty (July 17); federal president Havel announced he would resign.

Czechoslovak National Council Nationalist organization of Czechs and Slovaks. Formed (Jan. 1916) by T. Masaryk, E. Beneš, and others, it became the first provisional Czech government when the republic was established (Nov. 14, 1918).

Czolgosz, Leon *See* **McKinley, William.**

D

Dabrowski, Jan Henryk 1755–1818. Polish general. He participated in the rebellion against Russia (1794) and led the Polish legion under Napoleon.

Dachau German town near Munich, infamous for the Nazi concentration camp opened there in 1933. It operated until the Allied occupation (1945).

Dacia Ancient European region corresponding roughly to modern Rumania. The Dacian, or Getae, people were conquered by the Romans under Trajan, and Dacia was made a Roman province (AD 107). Aurelian surrendered it to the Goths (c270).

Dada (Dadaism) Literary and artistic movement. Dada flourished in Europe at the end of WW I. It stressed the absurdity and unpredictability of life through flamboyant and nihilistic art and literature. It was the forerunner of surrealism.

Dadaism *See* **Dada.**

Dagobert I c612–c639. Frankish king (629–639), son of King Clotaire II. He united Austrasia, Aquitaine, and Neustria, and was the last Merovingian king to rule a united Frankish kingdom.

Daguerre, Louis Jacques Mandé 1789–1851. French scene painter and photography pioneer. He invented the daguerreotype (1839), a process using copper for the photographic plate.

Dahomey, Republic of *See* **Benin.**

Dáil Éireann House of Representatives of the Republic of Ireland. Though elected as members of the British Parliament (Dec., 1918), the representatives met instead at Mansion House, Dublin, proclaimed the Irish Republic, and continued as an illegal body until the establishment of the Irish Free State (1921).

Daimler, Gottlieb 1834–1900. German engineer and pioneer automaker. He developed an internal-combustion engine (1885) and founded the Daimler Motor Company (1890), which eventually became part of Daimler-Benz.

daimyō Japanese feudal lord. From the 8th cent. these lords owned great estates and wielded great political power as independent territorial barons. Brought under the power of the shogunate (1603), they were eventually forced to turn their lands over to the emperor (1869).

Dakota Indians *See* **Sioux Indians.**

Daladier, Édouard 1884–1970. French politician, member of the Radical Socialist party. As premier (1938–40), he signed the Munich Pact (1938) to appease Nazi Germany. He was arrested and interned in Germany during WW II.

Dalai Lama Tibetan Buddhist spiritual leader. The line of Dalai Lamas was begun in the 14th cent., and each one is considered to be the reincarnation of his predecessor. The 14th in the line was installed in 1940, and fled Tibet during the abortive revolt against the Communist Chinese occupation (1959). (*See also* Tibetan Buddhism.)

Daley, Richard Joseph 1902–76. Chicago mayor and political boss. A state representative and senator (1939–46) in Illinois, he became Cook County Democratic chairman in 1953, before serving as Chicago mayor (1955–76). Wielding enormous influence in the state and the Democratic party as a whole, he brought about the rebirth of Chicago at a time when other northern cities were declining. Court rulings against patronage eventually weakened his influence.

Dalhousie, James Andrew Broun Ramsay, 1st marquess of 1812–60. British statesman and governor general of India (1847–56). He annexed the Punjab (1849) and other states, began the Indian telegraph and railway systems, and instituted reforms in Hindu society.

Dali, Salvador 1904–89. Spanish surrealist artist. He painted everyday objects in distorted, nightmare situations (called "paranoiac") based on his study of psychology and dreams. He wrote *The Secret Life of Salvador Dali.*

Dallas-Clarendon Convention *See* **Dallas, George Mifflin.**

Dallas, George Mifflin 1792–1864. US statesman and J. Polk's vice-president (1845–49). As minister to Great Britain (1856–61), he negotiated the Dallas-Clarendon Convention (1856), which helped settle Anglo-American rivalries over Central America, and brought an end to England's claim of a right of search.

Dalmatia Province of Croatia on the Adriatic Sea. Once part of the Roman Empire, it was taken by Slavic tribes (7th cent.) and ruled variously by Venetians, Turks, and Austrians. Italy disputed its award to Yugoslavia after WW I and again after WW II but finally agreed to its cession in the Italian peace treaty (1947).

Dalton, John 1766–1844. English chemist, one of the founders of atomic theory. He studied color blindness, from which he suffered (known for a time as Daltonism), and weather, and developed the law of partial pressures (Dalton's Law). He was credited with bringing order to an inexact science when he formulated the theory that atoms of different elements have different weights (1808) and published a list of elements, each accompanied by a chemical symbol and an atomic weight (some incorrect). His atomic theory held that atoms of any given element are identical but unlike atoms of other elements, and described chemical combinations of different elements, in which respective atoms join together to form "compound atoms" (now called molecules).

Damascus Capital of Syria, and considered the oldest continuously inhabited city in the world. A city before the time of Abraham (c1500 BC), it was held by the Egyptians, Israelis, Hittites, Persians, Greeks, and Romans and, in AD 635, was captured by the Arabs. It was ruled by the Ottoman Turks for some 400 years (from 1516). It was occupied by the British and Arabs (1918) and then was capital of the French mandate. In 1941, it became capital of independent Syria.

Damascus, Saint John of *See* **John of Damascus, Saint.**

Damien, Father (Veuster, Joseph de) 1840–89. Belgian Catholic missionary. Ordained in Honolulu (1864), he worked with the lepers of Molokai, Hawaii, from 1873 until his death from the disease.

Damocles Courtier of the tyrant Dionysius the Elder of Syracuse (4th cent. BC). After praising the tyrant, he was invited by Dionysius to a banquet. Damocles was seated beneath a sword hanging by a single thread, signifying the precariousness of power.

Dampier, William 1652–1715. English buccaneer and explorer. He was a pirate (1678–91) in Spanish-American waters, chiefly on the west coast of South America. He published his *New Voyage Round the World* in 1697, and, two years later, discovered the Dampier Archipelago and straits.

Damrosch, Walter 1862–1950. German-American conductor and composer. He formed the Damrosch Opera Company, specializing in German works, and composed the opera *Cyrano de Bergerac* (1913). He was the conductor of the New York Symphony (1903–27).

Dana, Charles Anderson 1819–97. Crusading American journalist. After five years at Brook Farm (*q.v.*), and 15 years as New York *Tribune* editor, he became part-owner and editor of the New York *Sun,* where he became involved in exposing government corruption.

Dana, James Dwight 1813–95. American geologist and mineralogist. He was a scientist on C. Wilkes's Antarctic and South Seas expedition, wrote *A System of Mineralogy,* and co-edited the *American Journal of Science.*

Dana, Richard Henry 1815–82. American lawyer and author of the novel *Two Years Before the Mast.* He also wrote *The Seaman's Friend,* a manual on the legal rights of seamen.

Danbury Hatters' Case US Supreme Court decision (1908). The United Hatters of North America boycotted a nonunion firm. Under the Sherman Antitrust Act, the union was declared in restraint of trade, the first time the act was applied to a labor combination.

Dandolo, Enrico c1108–1205. Doge of Venice (1192–1205), who led the crusaders in the capture of Constantinople (1203–04) on the Fourth Crusade. Earlier he was ambassador to the Byzantine court (1173) and was blinded there by order of the Emperor Manuel.

Danegeld Medieval English land tax used to buy off Danish raiders, especially under King Ethelred (978–1016). It was revived under the Normans (12th cent.) who created the Domesday Book (*q.v.*), partly to facilitate the levy of this tax.

Danelaw Region of Anglo-Saxon England settled by the Danes (19th cent.). It extended north from the Thames, along the east coast, and Danish laws obtained there.

Danes *See* **Norsemen; Denmark.**

Daniel An Old Testament prophet, taken captive to Babylon (605 BC). He interpreted dreams for Nebuchadnezzar, became an official, and had to be delivered from the lion's den where he had been thrown by Darius for disobeying an edict.

Daniels, Josephus 1862–1948. American statesman and journalist. He was editor of the Raleigh, N.C. *News and Observer,* secretary of the navy under W. Wilson, and ambassador to Mexico under F. Roosevelt.

Danilo I 1677–1735. Montenegrin leader, the last elected prince-bishop of Montenegro. The post was made hereditary to the prince-bishops' nephews thereafter. He formed a military alliance with Russia in order to help preserve Montenegrin independence against the Turks.

Danilo II 1826–60. Montenegrin prince-bishop. Danilo secularized his post, retaining his princely title but transferring his religious duties to an archbishop. His internal reforms provoked dissent and he was assassinated.

D'Annunzio, Gabriele 1863–1938. Italian poet, dramatist, novelist, and soldier. His poetry was richly sensual; in other writings he espoused Fascism. He was an Italian hero in WW I and afterward occupied Fiume for Italy (1919–21) in defiance of the Treaty of Versailles.

Dante Alighieri 1265–1321. Italian poet, and author of *The Divine Comedy* (1321), one of the greatest masterpieces of Western literature. Dante, through his works, helped to establish the Italian vernacular as the literary language of Italy. Raised in Florence, he was exiled (1302) after a factional struggle among the Guelphs, of which he was a member. He wandered through various Italian cities until sometime after 1313, when he settled in Ravenna. *The Divine Comedy,* partly inspired by a continuing romantic devotion to a woman thought to be Beatrice Portinari, consists of three parts: Hell, Purgatory, and Paradise. In this epic poem, he journeys to each

of the three, guided through the first two by Vergil (*q.v.*), and through heaven by Beatrice.

Danton, Georges Jacques 1759–94. A leading figure in the French Revolution, Danton was noted as a powerful orator and has been portrayed variously as a great patriot and an unscrupulous politician. He was a leader of the Cordeliers (founded 1790), and vigorously supported wars of national defense against foreign powers while serving in the Legislative Assembly (1791–92). He claimed to have played a role (nature uncertain) in the storming of the Tuileries Palace (Aug. 1792) and subsequent overthrow of the monarchy, then arose as a leading figure in the new government. He was elected to the new National Convention (1792), voted for the execution of Louis XVI, and became leader of the Jacobin Club (Mar., 1793). He was a leader of the Committee of Public Safety (Apr.–July, 1793) and was in power when the Girondists (June) were expelled from the Convention. Excluded from the new Committee of Public Safety (soon dominated by M. Robespierre), Danton became a leader of forces (later called Indulgents) seeking to moderate radicalism of the revolution and excesses of the Reign of Terror. He was finally arrested by Robespierre and guillotined (Apr. 5, 1794).

Daoism (Taoism) Major Chinese religious and philosophical system. Daoism was, by tradition, founded by Laozi in the 6th cent. BC. But the book upon which the system is based, *Dao-te Ching,* appears to have been written in the 3d cent. BC. According to Daoism, human beings can find Dao (the Way) by following a policy of nonaction, or passivity. The Way is the natural course of all events in the world, and the human path to happiness is through elimination of desire, ambition, and struggle, which go contrary to all nature. Daoism was in part a reaction to the organized system of ethical conduct advanced by Confucianism. By the 5th cent. AD, it was an organized religion. A hierarchy of gods was developed and ways to increase longevity and achieve immortality were sought. Daoist religion has been an important influence in China, especially in the arts. Although it was suppressed by the Chinese Communist government, Daoism is still practiced in China.

Dardanelles (Hellespont) Narrow strait between the Aegean and Marmara seas that controls navigation between the Mediterranean and Black seas.

Important in both ancient and modern times, it was called the Hellespont by the Greeks and was celebrated in the legend of Hero and Leander. Ancient Troy was located on its western shore and it was the site of famous crossings during invasions by Xerxes I (480 BC) and Alexander the Great (334 BC). In the 19th cent., it was the object of the Straits Question (*q.v.*) and during WW I the scene of the Gallipoli Campaign (*q.v.*).

Dardanelles Campaign *See* **Gallipoli Campaign.**

Dare, Virginia *b.* 1587. First child of English parents born in America. She was born in Sir Walter Raleigh's Roanoke Island colony; the island was found deserted in 1591.

Darien Scheme Abortive Scottish attempt at colonization on the Isthmus of Panama (1698–1700). Directed by W. Paterson, it failed with enormous losses to investors.

Dario, Ruben (Sarmiento, Felix Ruben García) 1867–1916. Nicaraguan-born poet and journalist. A leader of *Modernismo,* he strongly influenced modern Spanish-language writers with works such as *Azul* (1888).

Darius I (˜ the Great) c549–486 BC. Persian king (521–486 BC) and successor to Cambyses II, after defeating a false claimant, Magian Gomates. Darius, a member of the Achaemenid (*q.v.*) dynasty, proved a great ruler. He extended the Persian Empire into northern India and Europe, and in battle against the Scythians he invaded Macedonia and Thrace (1515). He was, however, unsuccessful in his efforts against the Greek city-states during the Persian Wars (*q.v.*). Noted as a great builder and administrator, he created an effective administrative organization based on a system of satrapies.

Darius II (˜ Nothus) *d.* 404 BC. Persian king (423–404 BC), illegitimate son of Artaxerxes. He spent much time suppressing revolts, formed an alliance with Sparta against Athens (c412 BC), and lost Egypt (410 BC).

Darius III (˜ Codomannus) *d.* 330 BC. Last king (336–330 BC) of Persia's Achaemenid (*q.v.*) dynasty. He was defeated by Alexander the Great at Granicus (334), Issus (333), and Gaugamela (331). He fled, only to be murdered by one of his satraps, Bessus.

Darius Codomannus *See* **Darius III.**

Darius Nothus *See* **Darius II.**

Dark Ages A period of European history between the decline of Roman civilization and the rise of medieval Christian civilization. It is often dated from AD 476–800, or, more generally, between AD c500 and c1000. (*See also* Middle Ages.)

Darlan, Jean François 1881–1942. French admiral, member of H. Petain's cabinet in the Vichy government (*q.v.*). He negotiated an armistice with the Allies in North Africa independently of Vichy (1942) and then was assassinated by an anti-fascist.

Darnley, Henry Stuart, lord 1545–67. Scottish lord. Darnley was the second husband of Mary, Queen of Scots, and father of James I of England. After his implication in the murder of Mary's secretary David Rizzio (1533?–66), he was himself assassinated.

Darrow, Clarence Seward 1857–1938. American lawyer. He was defense counsel in controversial trials such as that for US Socialist E. Debs in the 1894 Pullman strike (*q.v.*); for Chicago thrill killers Leopold and Loeb (1924); and in the 1925 Scopes Trial (*q.v.*) on the teaching of evolution, where he was opposed by W. J. Bryan.

Dartmouth College Case US Supreme Court decision (1819). The Court ruled that New Hampshire could not forcibly alter the charter or character of Dartmouth College. This ruling applied the sanctity-of-contracts principle to a state-issued charter and powerfully reinforced the Constitution's contract clause as a protection of private property against state encroachment.

Darwin, Charles Robert 1809–82. English naturalist, who established Darwinism (*q.v.*) as the reigning scientific theory of biological evolution. Though he did not originate the concept of evolution, his many observations and explanations of the mechanisms of natural selection provided the first widely accepted basis for the theory. A grandson of E. Darwin, he first became convinced of gradual evolution while serving (1831–36) as a naturalist aboard HMS *Beagle.* He subsequently began a long period of research and observation. Prodded by the work of A. Wallace, who had reached (1858) the same conclusions independently, Darwin published (1859) his famous *On the Origin of Species by Means of Natural Selection.* He supplemented this with many other works, notably *The Descent of Man.*

Darwin, Erasmus 1731–1802. English physician and grandfather both of C. Darwin and F. Galton. In his writings such as *Zoonomia* (1794–96), he anticipated later evolutionary principles.

Darwinism Theory of biological evolution developed by C. Darwin (mid-19th cent.) and now accepted, with some modifications, as the reigning scientific theory of evolution. Though the idea of evolution was not new, Darwin's theory explained the mechanisms which established it in the scientific community. The theory posed radical implications for religious thinkers and philosophers. Darwinism supplanted the then widely accepted theory of a special creation of each species. It postulated three mechanisms: heredity, by which features of a species are passed to succeeding generations; variety (now understood as mutation), the process by which new features are developed; and natural selection (later dubbed "survival of the fittest"), through which new characteristics become dominant by being tested in the environment.

Daudet, Alphonse 1840–97. French writer. He was noted for his gentle, humorous portrayal of provincial life in the south of France, as in *Lettres de Mon Moulin* (1869).

Daudet, Léon 1867–1942. French writer and journalist, son of A. Daudet. He co-founded the royalist paper *L'Action Française* (1907) and was known for his polemics against his times, which he considered decadent.

Daugherty, Harry Micajah 1860–1941. American politician and US attorney general (1921–24) under W. G. Harding. He was tried but not convicted of a conspiracy to defraud the US government (1927) because of his alleged involvement in the Teapot Dome (*q.v.*) and other scandals.

Daughters of the American Revolution (D.A.R.) Patriotic society organized in 1890 in Washington, D.C. Its members are women who are descendants of those who aided the Revolution.

Daumier, Honoré 1801–79. French caricaturist, painter, and lithographer. His work satirized the bourgeoisie, and he was briefly imprisoned for depicting King Louis Philippe as Gargantua, but he is considered a major realistic artist.

Daun, Leopold, Graf von 1705–66. Austrian soldier. Field marshal during the Seven Years' War (1756–63), he twice defeated Frederick the Great's Prussian army (1757 and 1758) but was defeated at Torgau (1760). He advocated a classic war of maneuver.

dauphin Title of the heir to the French throne. It was first given to the future Charles V by his grandfather Philip VI (1350) when the latter acquired the southeastern province of Dauphiné from which the title was taken.

Dauphiné Former French frontier province in the southeast. Its capital was Grenoble. Formerly ruled by the counts of Vienne, it was purchased by the French crown in the mid-14th cent.

David *d.* c973 BC. Second king of Israel (c1013–c973 BC), one of the great figures in the Old Testament, and an ancestor of Jesus. A heroic figure for both Christians and Jews, David is the subject of such famous biblical narratives as the David and Goliath story. Many of the psalms are also attributed to him. David succeeded Saul as king of the Hebrews, after first serving and then warring against him. As king, David forged the confederation of Hebrew tribes into a unified kingdom and took Jerusalem as his capital. [1 and 2 Samuel; 1 Kings 1–2]

David I 1084–1153. King of Scotland (1124–53) son of Malcolm III and Saint Margaret. He defended his niece Matilda's claims to the English throne against Stephen, but was defeated in 1138 at the Battle of the Standards. He introduced the Anglo-Norman feudal system into Scotland and founded many monasteries.

David II (David Bruce) 1324–71. King of Scotland (1329–71). Son of Robert the Bruce. When Scotland was successfully invaded by E. de Baliol, he was exiled to France (1334–41). He tried to invade England (1346) after regaining the throne but was routed at the Battle of Neville's Cross (*q.v.*), captured, and held prisoner until 1357. Most of the rest of his reign was spent trying to pay off his ransom.

David, Jacques Louis 1748–1825. French painter, founder of the French classical school. He was court painter to Louis XVI but then supported the French Revolution. Later he was Napoleon's court painter. One of his best-known works is *The Assassination of Marat* (1793). He dominated French painting for a generation.

David, Saint *d.* 588? Patron saint of Wales. He founded many churches and monasteries and moved the seat of ecclesiastical government to Mynyw (Menevia), today Saint David's. The national Welsh festival is still celebrated on his feast day of Mar. 1.

David Bruce *See* **David II.**

Dávila, Pedrarias *See* **Arias de Ávila, Pedro.**

Dávila, Pedro Arias *See* **Arias de Ávila, Pedro.**

Davis, David 1815–86. American jurist and statesman. Davis was frequently presiding judge when A. Lincoln practiced law, and was named by him to the US Supreme Court (1862). He later served as US senator from Illinois.

Davis, Jefferson 1808–89. American soldier, statesman, and president of the Confederacy (1861–65) during the US Civil War. A US senator from Mississippi (1847–51) and soldier in the Mexican War, he became US secretary of war (1853–57). Again in the Senate (1857–61), he led the Southern bloc until Mississippi seceded. As Confederate president (provisional, 1861, and elected 1862), he attempted to form a strong central government. This policy and his attempts to manage the army personally led to many disputes within the Confederate government. Davis was captured (1865) by Union soldiers after R. E. Lee's surrender and was imprisoned for two years.

Davis, John (Davys, ˜) c1550–1605. English navigator who made three voyages (1585–87) in search of the Northwest Passage (*q.v.*) during which he discovered Davis Strait. He discovered the Falkland Islands in 1592. He was killed by Japanese pirates while sailing near Singapore.

Davis, John William 1873–1955. American lawyer and politician. He was a West Virginia congressman (1911–13), US solicitor general (1913–18), and ambassador to England (1918–21). In 1924, he was the Democratic compromise candidate for president, chosen on the 103d ballot after a deadlocked convention; but he was easily defeated by C. Coolidge in the election.

Davis, William Morris 1850–1934. American geographer and geologist. He formulated the theory of land change through cycles of erosion, introduced the term "peneplain" to describe a rolling lowland, and wrote *The Coral Reef Problem* (1928).

Davout, Louis Nicolas 1770–1823. French general. He fought successfully for Napoleon at Austerlitz (1805), Auerstedt (1806), and Wagram (1809), and joined the Russian campaign (1812–13). He was Napoleon's minister of war during the Hundred Days (1815).

Davy, Sir Humphry 1778–1829. English chemist and physicist. He is best known for his discoveries of the elements sodium and potassium (1807). He also isolated barium, boron, calcium, strontium, and magnesium (1808) through his research in electrochemistry. He studied the effects of nitrous oxide (laughing gas) in 1799, showing that breathing the gas causes intoxication and theo-

rized that hydrogen is the element common to all acids. He discovered and named chlorine (1810) while doing research on hydrochloric acid. Davy determined the relative atomic masses of several elements including hydrogen and potassium. He also invented a safety lamp for miners (1815) which would burn safely even when in contact with methane gas.

Dawes, Charles Gates 1865–1951. American statesman and vice-president (1925–29) under C. Coolidge. As head of the post-WW I reparations commission, he authored the Dawes Plan (*q.v.*), which temporarily stabilized European finances. He was a co-winner of the Nobel Peace Prize, 1925.

Dawes Act US law (1887) that sought to integrate American Indians into the national life. Sponsored by Massachusetts senator Henry L. Dawes (1816–1903), it conferred citizenship on civilized Indians and gave land individually to those renouncing tribal holdings.

Dawes Plan Post-WW I reparations agreement. American banker C. Dawes played a central role in introducing a new schedule for gradual German war reparations of almost 20 billion marks to the Allies. Though accepted in 1924, Germany failed to meet its terms and the plan was replaced by the Young Plan in 1929.

Day, Benjamin Henry 1810–89. American journalist. He founded the first American penny newspaper, the New York *Sun* (1833), the first newspaper to employ newsboys; and *Brother Jonathan* (1842), the first illustrated weekly in the US.

Dayan, Moshe 1915–81. Israeli general and statesman. Dayan was a brilliant military strategist as chief of staff in the Sinai Conflict (1956) and minister of defense in the Six-Day War (1967). He also served as agriculture minister and again as defense minister.

Daye, Stephen c1594–1668. English-born American printer. He had the first printing press in the colonies, in Cambridge, Massachusetts. The first piece he issued was a broadside, *The Freeman's Oath* (1639), followed by the famous *Bay Psalm Book* (1640), the first book printed in the American colonies.

D-Day June 6, 1944, the start of the WW II Normandy Invasion (*q.v.*). Beginning at 6:30 AM, Allied forces landed on five beaches codenamed Omaha and Utah (Americans) and Gold, Juno, and Sword (British and Canadians). The worst channel weather in 25 years caused a one-day postponement of the landing from the planned June 5 disembarkment.

deacon Christian clerical rank. In the Roman Catholic Church, the deaconate is the first rank in Holy Orders and can be held by both single and married men, though only the single can advance to the priesthood. In Protestant churches, deacons serve various religious and administrative functions.

Dead Sea Scrolls Ancient manuscripts discovered (from 1947) in caves above the Dead Sea. Written between the 1st cent. BC and the first half of the 1st cent. AD, they were left by the ancient Jewish sect of Essenes and include material on their life and practices. There are fragments from nearly every book of the Old Testament—in a few cases complete books, such as the Isaiah scroll. These scrolls contain texts virtually identical to the received biblical texts, and are nearly a thousand years older than the earliest texts previously available to scholars. The Dead Sea Scrolls are considered one of the most valuable and significant archaeological finds of all time.

Deák, Francis 1803–76. Hungarian statesman. He advocated recognition of Hungarian rights within the union with Austria. After the failure of the 1848 Hungarian Revolution, he became acknowledged leader of his country. He restored the constitution (1867) and supported the dual Austro-Hungarian monarchy.

Deakin, Alfred 1856–1919. Australian statesman. He was the first Australian attorney general (1901) and three times prime minister (1903–04, 1905–08, 1909–10). He was an advocate of the federation of Australian states.

Deakin, Arthur 1890–1955. British trade union leader. Deakin led England's powerful Transport Workers Union and later the World Federation of Trade Unions (1945–49). He withdrew from the latter because of its Communist sympathies and helped found the International Confederation of Free Trade Unions.

Deane, Silas 1737–89. American Revolutionary politician; the first US foreign diplomat. He successfully negotiated aid for the Revolution, recruited C. Pulaski, Baron F. W. von Steuben, and the Marquis de Lafayette, but was later accused of profiteering and died in exile.

Dearborn, Fort *See* **Fort Dearborn.**

Dearborn, Henry 1751–1829. American soldier and statesman. Dearborn fought in the American Revolution, most notably at Bunker Hill and Quebec. He was T. Jefferson's secretary of war, but had to be relieved of his command in the War of 1812. Fort Dearborn was named for him.

Debs, Eugene Victor 1855–1926. US Socialist leader. He helped direct the 1894 Pullman strike (*q.v.*) and ran for president as a Socialist five times (1900–20). He was imprisoned during WW I under the Espionage Act (1918–21).

Debussy, Claude 1862–1918. French composer of impressionistic works such as *Prelude to the Afternoon of a Faun, Nocturnes,* and *La Mer.*

Decadents Name applied to 19th-century poets and authors who felt that art should be above conventional morality; they included P. Verlaine, S. Mallarmé, and O. Wilde.

Decalogue *See* **Ten Commandments.**

Decatur, Stephen 1779–1820. US naval officer in the Tripolitan War (1801–05) and the War of 1812 (1812–14) and the US punitive expedition of 1815 against Algiers. He is remembered for his toast: "Our country! In her intercourse with foreign nations may she always be in the right; but our country, right or wrong."

Deccan Term used to describe peninsular India. It is mostly segmented, hilly tableland. It was the region of Dravidian populations not reached by the Aryan invasions (1500–800 BC) and the scene of the British-French struggle for control of India (mid-18th cent.).

Decembrist Conspiracy The first modern revolutionary uprising in Russian history. Following the death of Tsar Alexander I (*q.v.*) the Decembrists staged an uprising in St. Petersburg (Dec., 1825) to try to prevent the accession of Nicholas I (*q.v.*) and secure a constitution. Most of the conspirators were nobles and officers. Their uprising was easily quelled and 121 went on trial, of which 5 were executed, 31 were imprisoned, and the rest were exiled to Siberia. Although they failed, the Decembrists had established a revolutionary "tradition" which had profound effects on later Russian history.

Decius AD 201–251. Roman emperor (249–251). Sent by the emperor Philip the Arabian to put down a mutiny, he was compelled by his soldiers to become emperor, and they deposed Philip. During his brief reign he inaugurated the greatest persecution of Christians in antiquity.

Decker, Thomas　*See* **Dekker, Thomas.**

Declaration of　*See under names inverted, as in* **Independence, Declaration of.**

Declaratory Act　*See* **Stamp Act Congress.**

Decree of Canopus (Table of Tanis)　Ancient Egyptian decree, written (238 BC) in Greek, demotic script, and hieroglyphs. Discovered in 1866, it provided translators with an important key to deciphering Egyptian writings, second only to the Rosetta Stone (*q.v.*).

decuriones　Members of the governing council in municipalities and colonies in ancient Rome. Appointed for life, they controlled the local government and were responsible for collecting taxes paid to the central government. Former local magistrates and other appointees of suitable wealth and rank could become decuriones, and their number in any given community varied with its size. Decuriones suffered during the later Empire period when the economy declined and imperial demands for tax money increased, because decuriones were personally liable when taxpayers defaulted. The position finally became hereditary and mandatory, and decuriones, reduced from a ruling class to a corps of tax collectors, then formed the class known as curiales.

Deere, John 1804–86.　US manufacturer of agricultural implements. In partnership, he made the first steel plow. He formed the manufacturing firm Deere & Company (1868) in Moline, Illinois.

Defence of India Act　British legislation. The act was first passed in 1915 to quell nationalist revolts in India during WW I. When it was extended after the war, M. K. Gandhi began his Noncooperation Movement.

Defenestration of Prague　An incident (May 23, 1618) in which Bohemian Protestants threw two imperial regents from the window of Hradčany Castle in Prague, to protest the closing of Protestant chapels. The two escaped with their lives, but the incident signaled the beginning of Bohemian revolt against Habsburg rule. This marked the beginning of the Thirty Years' War.

Defoe, Daniel 1660–1731.　English author. Defoe went bankrupt as a merchant and later as a pamphleteer, and was imprisoned (1702–03) for offending the queen. He subsequently turned to journalism and became involved in a number of publications. He did not begin writing novels until his late fifties and thereafter wrote such famous works as *Robinson Crusoe* (1719) and *Moll Flanders* (1722).

Degas, (Hilaire Germain) Edgar 1834–1917. French artist. He is best known for his impressionistic pastels and paintings of dancers and women at their toilette, such as *The Chrysanthemums* (1865) and *The Rehearsal* (1877).

De Gasperi, Alcide 1881–1954.　Italian statesman. During WW II, he organized the Christian Democratic party. He was premier (1945–53) and led Italy into NATO (1951).

de Gaulle, Charles 1890–1970.　French general and first president (1959–69) of the Fifth Republic. A WW I veteran and a brigadier general, he opposed the armistice (1940) with Germany after the fall of France and organized the Free French forces in London (1940). He became co-president (1943) with H. Giraud of the French Committee of National Liberation at Algiers and, by mid-1944, had made himself sole president. He returned to France (Aug., 1944) amid the Allied victories and served briefly as president of the provisional French government (Nov., 1945–Jan., 1946). He was recalled (May, 1958) to lead France out of the crisis over Algerian independence, and after passage (Nov. 1958) of a new constitution created the Fifth Republic, he was elected president. He supported Algerian independence, though rebellions by the French in Algeria delayed it until 1962. During his long tenure, de Gaulle sought to restore France's waning prestige. He ended French participation in NATO (1966), developed a French nuclear-weapons program, blocked Britain's entry into the Common Market, and pursued an independent foreign policy that included establishing closer ties with China and Russia. His government survived serious student and labor unrest (May, 1968) but he was forced to resign (1969) after his referendum on political reforms was defeated.

Deists　Enlightenment school of religious thought. Deists believe that God exists because of the existence of the universe, nature, and reason. They eschew formal religions, revelation, and belief in miracles. Famous Deists include F.M.A. de Voltaire, J.-J. Rousseau, and T. Jefferson.

Dekker, Thomas (Decker, ˜) 1572?–1632.　English Elizabethan dramatist and pamphleteer. He wrote *The Shoemaker's Holiday* and other satiric accounts of London life.

De Kooning, Willem 1904– . Netherlands-born US artist. A leader of the abstract expressionism movement (*q.v.*), he painted, notably, a series entitled *Woman*.

Delacroix, Ferdinand Victor Eugène 1798–1863. French artist, considered the leader of the Romantic school. He painted many scenes from literature and history such as *Dante and Vergil* (1821) and *The Massacre at Chios* (1824).

Delany, Martin Robinson 1812–85. American black leader. He founded the newspaper *Mystery* (1843) to publicize his people's problems, became a medical doctor (graduated from Harvard), advocated emigration to Africa, and served as an army physician during the American Civil War.

Delaroche, Hippolyte Paul 1797–1859. French painter of portraits and historical subjects such as *Death of Queen Elizabeth* and *Children of Edward.*

Delaware US state in the Middle Atlantic region; the first state. Originally inhabited by the Delaware Indians, the area was explored by H. Hudson in 1609 and was settled by the Dutch (1631) and the Swedes (1638). The English took control of the region in 1664 and it was granted to W. Penn as part of Pennsylvania (1682). Delaware broke ties with Pennsylvania and became an independent state (1776) and was the first state to ratify the US Constitution (1787). Its constitution was adopted in 1897.

Delaware Indians American Indian tribe. A branch of the Algonquins, they lived mainly in the New York–New Jersey–Pennsylvania area. They were conquered by the Iroquois (1720) and later driven westward by settlers.

De la Warr, Thomas West, baron 1577–1618. The first English governor of Virginia (1610). Delaware Bay and the state of Delaware are named for him.

Delcassé, Théophile 1852–1923. French foreign minister (1898–1905, 1914–15). He contributed to the Entente Cordiale (*q.v.*) with England and the establishment of other European alliances in the years before WW I.

De Leon, Daniel 1852–1914. US Socialist leader and writer. He was the Socialist Labor party candidate for New York governor (1891) and edited its journal, *The People.* He was a doctrinaire Marxist and, in 1905, helped found the Industrial Workers of the World (*q.v.*).

Delescluze, Louis-Charles 1809–71. French radical and journalist. He participated in the February Revolution of 1848, and later opposed Napoleon III. A leader of the 1871 Paris Commune (*q.v.*), he died fighting on the barricades.

Delhi (Old Delhi) Indian city in north central India, surrounded by the city of New Delhi. Delhi came to prominence when Shah Jahan made it the capital of the Mughal Empire (1638). Extensive construction followed, including the Red Fort, within which was the famed Peacock Throne. Delhi was sacked (1739) by the Persian Nadir Shah, who removed the Peacock Throne. Occupied (1803) by the British, Delhi was a center for the Sepoy uprising of 1857. It served as the capital of India (1911–31) until the inauguration of New Delhi.

Delhi Pact 1. British-Indian agreement. On March 5, 1931, M. K. Gandhi agreed to discontinue Indian civil disobedience against Britain and join in the Round Table Conferences in return for the release of nonviolent political prisoners. 2. (Nehru-Liaqat Pact) An agreement between India and Pakistan concluded on April 8, 1950, whereby refugees were allowed to move back and forth to settle property, abducted women and loot were restored, forced conversions were canceled, and minority rights guaranteed.

Delhi Sultanate The first Muslim Empire in India (1192–1398). It was established by the conquest of Delhi by Mohammed of Ghor (1192). His general Qutb ud-Din Aibak, established the "slave dynasty" (so called because he and some of his successors were former military slaves) that ruled until 1290. It was succeeded by the Khalji Dynasty, which ruled until 1320, brought almost the entire subcontinent under the Delhi sultanate's sway and steadily repulsed the Mongols. Revolts and a loss of territory began in the Tughluq dynasty (1325–98). With the capture of Delhi by Tamerlane (1398) the sultanate disintegrated. Only local rulers remained until the establishment (16th cent.) of the Mughal Empire.

Delian League League of Greek city-states constituted (478 BC) to oppose the threat of invasion of Greece by the Persian Empire. The league's headquarters and treasury were on the island of Delos, but Athens maintained its leadership in the league, which at its height included about 140 members. It was slowly transformed into an Athenian empire in which members attempting to secede, such as Naxos (c470 BC), were subdued by Athenian forces. The league's treasury was eventually transferred to Athens

(454 BC). The league came to an end with the decisive defeat of Athens (404 BC) by Sparta in the Peloponnesian War (*q.v.*). Athens also led a later naval league, the Athenian confederacy of 378 BC, which was destroyed by Philip of Macedon's defeat of Athens (338 BC).

Delisle, Guillaume 1675–1726.   French cartographer. Delisle is often called the father of modern cartography. His maps corrected many long-standing errors, and he was appointed court geographer by Louis XV.

Della-Cruscans   Members of an English poetical movement. These English poets lived in Italy in the late 18th cent., publishing highly romantic, sentimental verse under Italian pseudonyms.

Della Robbia, Luca 1400?–1482.   Italian Renaissance sculptor. A Florentine, Della Robbia was greatly admired for his sculpture gallery of boys and angels (*cantoria*) in the Florence cathedral. He founded a family studio famous for enameled terra cotta works.

Delorme, Philibert 1510?–1570.   French Renaissance architect. He designed the Château d'Anet for Diane de Poitiers, the great gallery of Chenonceaux, and the Tuileries, commissioned by Catherine de Médicis.

Delos   Greek island in the Aegean Sea and legendary birthplace of Artemis and Apollo. Delos was the center of the Delian League until 454 and was a commercial center until conquered by Mithridates VI (88 BC) and subsequently abandoned.

Delphi   A town in Phocis, Greece, at the foot of Mount Parnassus. It was the seat of the Delphic oracle, which prophesied from the 7th cent. BC until it was silenced by the Christian Roman emperor Theodosius (4th cent. AD). The oracle was believed to speak for the god Apollo through a priestess in a trance.

demagogue   In ancient Greece, a leader of the popular party or cause of the common people. In modern times, it refers to any political leader who plays upon the passions of the masses for personal gain.

deme   Athenian territorial division during ancient times in Greece. A deme was a village.

Demetrius   *See also* **Dmitri.**

Demetrius I c337–283 BC.   King of Macedon (294–288 BC), a son of Antigonus I. He commanded his father's army and helped to rebuild his empire during the wars of the Diadochi (*q.v.*). Finally driven out by Lysimachus and Pyrrhus,

he had to surrender to Seleucus I (285). His son, Antigonus II, later regained Macedon.

Demetrius I (~ Soter) c187–150 BC.   King of Syria (162–150 BC). During the reign of his father, Seleucus IV, he lived in Rome as a hostage. He escaped and took the throne after killing his cousin Antiochus V, whose father, Antiochus IV, had usurped the throne from Seleucus; but he was defeated by another usurper, Alexander Balas, in league with the Maccabees.

Demetrius II *d.* 229 BC.   King of Macedon (239–229 BC). Macedon was seriously weakened by his constant and losing warfare with the Aetolian League and the Achaean League. Antigonus III succeeded him.

Demetrius II (~ Nicator) *d.* c125 BC.   King of Syria (145–139 and 129–125 BC). The son of Demetrius I, he deposed Alexander Balas, who had previously deposed his father. He was captured (139 BC) and held by the Parthians for 10 years, but was released and resumed his reign. He reaffirmed Judaean independence, freeing the Jews from Syrian taxation.

De Mille, Cecil Blount 1881–1959.   American motion-picture producer who made the first US feature film, *The Squaw Man* (1913). He also produced film epics such as *The Ten Commandments* (1923, remade 1956).

democracy   Form of government based on rule by the people, though that rule may be exercised in various ways. The classic example of early democracy is that of the ancient Greek city-state Athens. It was a direct democracy, in which all male citizens participated in government by their vote. That system worked because the total number of citizens was small and a large part of the populace (slaves and women) was denied citizenship. Athenian democracy represented short-lived experiments in government by the people, and it was not until the 18th–19th cents. that the democratic form of government began to flourish. Social and political concepts (representative assemblies, natural rights, and the social contract) developed from the Middle Ages onward and contributed to the development of modern democracy. The gradual ascendancy of parliamentary government in Britain, the American Revolution, and the French Revolution were important in its implementation and rapid spread during the 18th to 20th cents. Modern democracy is generally a representative democracy: government is run by representatives of the people, elected and fully accountable to them. This form of government is often accompanied by a constitution that empowers the government and enumerates the rights of the people (constitutional democracy). In the West, notions of personal freedoms and individual rights are fundamental elements of the concept of democracy. The so-called peoples' democracy of Communist countries, however, is based on the contention that economic democracy (economic equality, collective ownership) is of overriding importance.

Democratic Centralists Opposition group that attempted to check the growth of bureaucratization and authoritarianism within the Russian Communist party after the Russian Revolution. The 7th Soviet Congress (Dec., 1919) ostensibly endorsed the group's aims. But when no progress was realized, Centralists presented a Declaration of Forty-six to the Politburo (Oct. 15, 1923). However, J. Stalin subsequently defeated all further opposition at the 15th Party Congress (Dec., 1927).

Democratic League Chinese political group. Founded in 1941, it sought a middle ground between the Chinese Communists and Nationalists. After WW II, its membership divided between the two groups.

Democratic party One of the two major American political parties. It was founded (1792) by T. Jefferson under the name of Democratic Republicans. It adopted its present name with the popular victory (1828) of President A. Jackson. Badly split over the slavery issue, it lost its dominant position and became the minority party from 1860 until the election (1912) of W. Wilson, except for the elections (1884, 1892) of G. Cleveland. The election (1932) of F. D. Roosevelt inaugurated a long period of Democratic dominance that usually included its control of one or both houses of Congress, even under Republican presidents. The party originally favored limited federal government and state and local rights, but this policy was completely reversed in the 20th cent., when it became the party of federal intervention and "big government." The party has been consistent throughout its history, however, in favoring populism, low tariffs, cheap money, and the perceived interests of the common people, while opposing big business, industrial concentrations, and rigid monetary and fiscal standards.

Democratic Republicans *See* **Democratic party.**

Democritus c460–c370 BC. Ancient Greek materialistic philosopher who expanded on the atomic theory of his teacher Leucippus. He held that everything is composed of indestructible atoms of matter whose motion explained the creation of the universe.

Demosthenes 384?–322 BC. Athenian and the greatest Greek orator. A professional speech writer, he turned to politics in 355 BC. By his speeches he warned the Athenians against King Philip of Macedon, who was becoming a threat to their liberty. Later he struggled against the pro-Macedonian faction in Athens. He poisoned himself after taking part in an unsuccessful revolt (323) against Macedonian rule. His speeches include the three *Philippics* (against King Philip, from 351–341), the *Olynthiacs,* and *On the Crown.*

Deng Xiaoping (Teng Hsiao-p'ing) c1902– . Chinese Communist leader who in the late 1970s and 1980s introduced facets of the free enterprise system in Communist China. As general secretary of the Chinese Communist party (1956–67) he worked closely with Mao Zedong. Purged (1967) during the Cultural Revolution, he was rehabilitated (1973) and became first deputy prime minister (1977). In subsequent years he established himself as China's most influential leader and ruled by compromise and persuasion; he instituted wide-ranging reforms of China's economic and political systems, including decentralization of economic management, shifting control over farming to individual peasants, and opening up China's businesses to foreign investment. Though he stepped down from his political posts in 1987, he remained a major figure in the Chinese Communist party. His power and his reforms appeared to have remained intact following the upheavals of the Tiananmen Square massacre.

Denikin, Anton Ivanovich 1872–1947. Russian general. He succeeded General L. G. Kornilov (1918) as supreme commander of the White Army which unsuccessfully fought the Bolshevik forces until its defeat in 1920.

Denis, Maurice 1870–1943. French artist. He was a leader of the Symbolist movement and a member of the Nabis group (*q.v.*) of painters, and is especially known for his religious works and murals and book illustrations.

Denis, Saint 3d cent.? Patron saint of France and traditional first bishop of Paris. He was said to have been martyred by decapitation on Montmartre during the persecution by Roman emperor Valerian, and is represented in traditional Christian art carrying his head in his hands.

Denmark Constitutional monarchy located on the northern coast of Europe. The population is 5,134,000 and the capital is Copenhagen. The region was inhabited by Scandinavian peoples (Norse) from prehistoric times and a ruling dynasty emerged at the end of the 8th cent. The Danes were subsequently involved in invasions of England (9th–11th cents.), helped colonize Greenland, Iceland, and Atlantic Islands, and were for a time united with neighboring Sweden and Norway. A constitutional monarchy was established in Denmark in the mid-19th cent. Key events in Denmark's history include:

9TH–11TH CENTS. Danes participated in Viking raids on Western Europe; invaded England in the reign of King Alfred (reigned 871–99).

c910–c985 Harold Bluetooth reigned; first Christian king of Denmark (after 960), who claimed to have unified kingdom.

1013 Conquest of England, by Sweyn, son of Harold Bluetooth.

1018–35 Denmark, Norway, and England united under King Canute the Great.

1080–86 Canute IV reigned; attempted an invasion of Norman England (1085).

1157–82 Waldemar I (the Great) reigned; he overcame rival claimants to the throne and restored order after a period of civil war; began eastward expansion of Danish empire at the expense of the Wends (Slavs).

1202–41 Waldemar II reigned; extended Danish control over northern Europe to Estonia in the east; initiated many domestic and legal (Jutland Code) reforms and strengthened the monarchy; divided Denmark into great feudal estates.

1282 Eric V forced by nobles to accept the Great Charter and share his power with annual parliaments and a Council of Nobles.

1320–26 Christopher II reigned; nobles forced him to agree to further limitations of royal powers.

1340–75 Waldemar IV reigned; restored Denmark as a leading power; forced to submit to the Treaty of Stralsund (1370), granting the Hanseatic League extensive commercial rights.

1380 Iceland united with Denmark.

1397 Kalmar Union formed by Queen Margaret; united Denmark, Norway, and Sweden under the Danish crown.

1448–81 Christian I founded the Oldenburg dynasty; the present ruling family traces descent to him. He united Schleswig and Holstein with the Danish crown.

1513–23 Christian II reigned; notoriously cruel, he ordered Stockholm Bloodbath of Swedish nobles; driven out of Sweden (1521) and deposed (1523) by Danes.

1523 Sweden won independence from Denmark.

1533–36 Counts' War, war of succession confirming the Protestant Reformation in Denmark-Norway.

1535–39 Christian III reigned; Lutheranism established as state religion.

1611–13 Denmark defeated Sweden in the Kalmar War.

1618–48 Thirty Years' War; Sweden rose as the dominant Scandinavian power and acquired Danish territory.

1648–70 Frederick III reigned; Denmark badly defeated in renewed war with Sweden (1657–60); in the (first) Northern War forced to accept Treaty of Copenhagen (1660), settling modern boundaries of Denmark, Sweden, and Norway; in subsequent years, Frederick instituted absolute monarchy in Denmark.

1665 P. Griffenweld wrote the King's Law, justifying absolute monarchy.

1700–21 Northern War.

1788 Serfdom abolished, and peasant ownership promoted thereafter.

1803–15 Napoleonic Wars; Denmark sided with Napoleon; lost Norway to Sweden and Pomerania to Prussia (1815).

1848–63 Frederick VII reigned; liberal movement, gaining support since the 1830s, ascendant during his rule.

1848–51 War with Prussia over status of Schleswig; Denmark forced to agree to make no efforts to increase ties with region.

1849 Liberal constitution enacted; constitutional monarchy established.

1863–1906 Christian IX reigned; liberals lost power to conservatives; industrialization begun in 1850s proceeded rapidly and, along with agrarian reforms, brought Denmark a period of great prosperity.

1864   War with Prussia and Austria; Denmark annexed Holstein (1863) and thus abrogated agreement of 1851; defeated soon after war broke out (1864), Denmark lost Schleswig and Holstein by the Treaty of Vienna.

1866   New constitution promulgated; gave conservatives more power by increasing the power of the upper house (Landsting), which became more powerful than the lower house (Folketing).

1912–47   Christian X reigned.

1914–18   Denmark neutral in WW I.

1915   Constitutional reforms enacted.

1918   Universal suffrage enacted.

1918   Iceland granted independence, though Danish monarch continued as titular head of state.

1920   Denmark joined the League of Nations.

1920   Northern part of Schleswig united with Denmark following a plebiscite.

1939   Denmark signed nonaggression pact with Nazi Germany.

1939–45   WW II; Denmark occupied by Germans (1940); Danish underground actively resisted Nazis; Danish minister in Washington put Greenland under US protection; Denmark liberated by British (1945).

1944   Iceland voted for independence from Denmark, ending a union that began in 1380.

1945   Joined UN.

FROM 1945   Social Democratic party became the leading political force in Denmark.

1947–72   Frederick IX reigned.

1949   Became founding member of NATO (Apr. 4).

1953   New constitution; established constitutional monarchy with unicameral legislature (Folketing); constitution amended to allow succession of female heir.

1972   Denmark joined the Common Market.

1972–   Margrethe II reigned as Danish queen, succeeding Frederick IX.

1973–75   Social Democrats out of power; election defeat resulted from voter reaction to high taxes.

1975–82   Anker Jorgensen, a Social Democrat, in office as prime minister.

1982–   Poul Schlüter, Conservative party leader, in office as prime minister.

1983   Prime Minister Schlüter resigned after Folketing defeated 1984 Finance Bill (Dec.

15); Schlüter returned as prime minister after elections (1984).

1985   Massive strikes paralyzed Danish economy (Mar. 24–Apr. 1); settlement imposed (April 1) by Folketing.

1985   Greenland withdrew from European Community following disagreements over questions of fishing rights and other matters.

1986   Denmark banned all trade with South Africa (May 30) to protest apartheid system.

1987   Schlüter resigned (Sept.) after failing to create a new coalition majority; returned to office next day after reestablishing previous four-party coalition.

1991   Denmark and Sweden agreed to construct railroad and highway bridge to connect the two countries (Mar.).

1992   Voters rejected the Maastricht Treaty on European union (June).

Deogaon, Treaty of   Indian-British treaty. In it on Dec. 17, 1803, Raghuji Bhonsla II of Maratha ceded much of his land, and almost all his power, to the British East India Company.

Depression   *See* **United States (1929–39).**

Depretis, Agostino 1813–87.   Italian statesman and premier. Following Italy's political unification (1861), he served as minister of public works (1862), minister of the navy (1866), and minister of finance (1867). He first became premier in 1876, a post he held, with some interruptions, for eleven years. His administration was toppled by a scandal (1878), but he returned to power the same year. He died in office in 1887. His government is remembered for its extension of suffrage (1882), from two to seven percent of the Italian population.

De Quincey, Thomas 1785–1859.   English writer famous for his essays. He wrote, notably, *Confessions of an English Opium Eater.*

Derby, Edward George Geoffrey Smith Stanley, 14th earl of 1799–1869.   English statesman. He supported national education for Ireland, abolished West Indian slavery as colonial secretary (1833), became a leader of the Conservative party, and was three times prime minister (1852, 1858–59, 1866–67).

Derrida, Jacques 1930–   .   French philosopher and critic of Western philosophy. Derrida taught philosophy at the Sorbonne (1960–64) and the École Normale Supérieure (1965–   ) in Paris.

He opposes the search for metaphysical certainty (or meaning), central to most modern philosophies. He seeks through "deconstruction" to make such metaphysical assumptions explicit in his analysis of philosophical writings. He is known for such works as *Speech and Phenomena* (1967) and *Margins of Philosophy* (1972).

dervish The friar, or male religious, of Islam. Although they form religious communities or fraternities—which were very important in the Middle Ages—they do not take vows. Some dervishes, such as howling or whirling dervishes, favor extreme practices. Others favor mystical practices.

Desargues, Gérard 1593–1662. French mathematician and a founder of modern geometry. He worked on conic sections and developed the theorem on the perspective of two triangles that is named for him.

Descartes, René 1596–1650. French philosopher, mathematician, and scientist who is called the father of modern philosophy. By his famous proposition, "I think, therefore I am (*Cogito, ergo sum*)," he oriented philosophy toward problems of epistemology and formulated a philosophical dualism of mind and body. His thinking greatly influenced rationalist philosophers and spawned Cartesianism. In mathematics, Descartes is said to have founded analytic geometry and developed the Cartesian coordinates and Cartesian curves. His most important works are *Discourse on Method* (1637), *Meditations* (1641), and *The Principles of Philosophy* (1644).

Desiderius *d.* after 774. Last Lombard king of Italy. Pope Adrian I requested aid from Charlemagne after Desiderius threatened Rome. Desiderius was defeated at Pavia (774) by Charlemagne, who assumed the title "King of the Lombards" and sent Desiderius to a monastery. This event strengthened ties between the Roman Catholic church and the Frankish kings.

Desiderius Erasmus *See* **Erasmus.**

De Smet, Pierre Jean 1801–73. French Jesuit missionary who won the trust of Indians in the American Midwest and later served as a mediator in disputes between Indians and settlers.

Desmond, earls of Title of Irish nobility first given to Maurice Fitzgerald (1329). The title was last borne by Gerald Fitzgerald, the 15th earl, who rebelled against Queen Elizabeth (1579), was at large for some four years but was finally captured and killed (1583).

Desmoulins, Camille 1760–94. French revolutionist and journalist. His speech of July 12, 1789, roused the crowd to attack the Bastille two days later. He published two notable revolutionary newspapers, but during the Reign of Terror (*q.v.*), he failed to support M. Robespierre completely, and he was guillotined, with G. J. Danton, as a moderate.

De Soto, Hernando c1500–42. Spanish explorer. De Soto explored what is now the southern United States and is believed to be the first white man to cross the Mississippi River. He died of fever and was buried in the river.

Despenser, Hugh Le *d.* 1265. Medieval justiciar, or high royal judicial officer, of England. Despenser sided with the barons in the Barons' War (*q.v.*) against Henry III (1263). He was killed at the battle of Evesham. His namesake son and grandson both served the king against the barons.

Despenser, Hugh Le (*called* ˜ the Elder) 1262–1326. English adviser to King Edward II, created earl of Winchester. He and his son dominated the king until the uprising of the barons under R. de Mortimer and Queen Isabella. They were then hanged for rapacity.

Despenser, Hugh Le (*called* ˜ the Younger) *d.* 1326. English courtier. He and his father supported Edward II and both were banished (1321). Upon their return, Hugh continued to provoke quarrels with R. de Mortimer and Queen Isabella and was hanged after the latter came to power.

Dessalines, Jean Jacques c1758–1806. Emperor of Haiti (1804–06). Born a slave, he fought in the insurrection under F. D. Toussaint L'Ouverture (1791). He expelled the French with British help (1803) and declared himself Emperor Jacques I (1804). He was assassinated because of his cruelty.

de-Stalinization USSR political program instituted (Feb. 24–25, 1956) by N. Khrushchev at the Communist party's 20th Congress. In his now famous Secret Speech, Khrushchev denounced the excesses of J. Stalin's regime, particularly the political purges of the 1930s, and called for moderation in party rule and an end to the political terrorism identified with Stalin's rule. The campaign destroyed the cult image of Stalin as the all-wise leader of international communism and helped spark the outbreak of political and intellectual turmoil in Hungary and Poland in 1956.

détente French term meaning "relaxation," adopted as an English word in the late 1960s to describe efforts to ease Cold War tensions between the US and USSR. The Strategic Arms Limitation Talks (SALT) that began in Nov., 1969, and the resulting treaties, were major initiatives that fostered détente. The heyday of détente was 1972–78. US-Soviet relations cooled after the Soviet invasion of Afghanistan in Dec., 1979, and the repression by the Polish government in Dec., 1981, which threatened to revive the Cold War (*q.v.*).

Deulino, Truce of A treaty concluded in the winter of 1618–19 that brought about a 14-year truce in the fighting that broke out during Russia's Time of Troubles (*q.v.*). The Polish king Sigismund III had taken advantage of the troubles to try to place his son on the throne of Muscovy. By this treaty, Poland retained Smolensk, while Russia received back important hostages. No final settlement was reached until the Treaty of Polianov (1634), when Poland recognized Michael Romanov as the legitimate tsar.

Deuteronomic Reform Religious reform movement in the kingdom of Judah (c621 BC). The movement was begun by King Josiah after a law code, believed to be that contained in the biblical book of Deuteronomy, was found in the temple at Jerusalem. Reforms included elimination of pagan worship in rural areas and centralization of worship in Jerusalem.

Deuteronomy In the Bible, the last of the five books of the law (the Pentateuch). It contains a summary of the history of God's dealings with Israel; of the law believed delivered to Moses, including the Ten Commandments (*q.v.*), songs and speeches of Moses, and the account of his death.

Deutsch-Wagram *See* **Wagram, Battle of.**

De Valera, Eamon 1882–1975. Irish statesman. He was the president of Sinn Fein (1917–26), founded the extreme republican group Fianna Fáil (1924), was prime minister (1937–48, 1951–54, 1957–59) and president (1959–73) of Ireland.

Devolution, War of War (1667–68) in which the French king Louis XIV attempted to conquer the Spanish Netherlands, later the Netherlands (*q.v.*). The war stemmed from Louis's marriage to Marie Thérèse, daughter of the Spanish king Philip IV. When Philip failed to pay her dowry, Louis claimed the Spanish Netherlands as his wife's rightful inheritance. His claim was made on the basis of an old law of "devolution." Louis's armies, under H. Turenne, overran (1667) the Spanish Netherlands and Franche-Comté. The Netherlands organized the Triple Alliance (*q.v.*) in 1668 and forced Louis's armies to retire by the Treaty of Aix-la-Chapelle (*q.v.*). The French, however, again invaded the Netherlands in the Third Dutch War.

Devonshire, Spencer Compton Cavendish, 8th duke of 1833–1908. British statesman. Originally a Liberal, he broke with W. E. Gladstone over Irish Home Rule (*q.v.*), and led Parliament in defeating that issue on several occasions.

Dewar, Sir James 1842–1923. British chemist and physicist. He invented the Dewar flask, which prevented heat loss, and studied the properties of matter at low temperatures. He liquefied (1898) and solidified hydrogen (1899).

De Wet, Christiaan Rudolph 1854–1922. Boer general. He wrote *The Three Years' War* (1902) about his service in the Boer War of 1899–1902 (*q.v.*). In 1914, he led a rebellion against South Africa's entrance into WW I.

Dewey, George 1837–1917. American admiral who defeated the Spanish squadron in Manila Bay during the Spanish-American War (1898). Only eight Americans were wounded, while eight Spanish ships were destroyed.

Dewey, John 1859–1952. American philosopher and educator. A professor at Columbia and other American universities in the years from 1888 to 1930, he was an early and important exponent of pragmatism (*q.v.*). In addition, his theories on education had an important influence on the progressive-school movement. He was a prolific writer; his works include *Essays in Experimental Logic, Experience and Nature,* and *Art as Experience.*

Dewey, Melvil 1851–1931. US librarian who founded the Dewey Decimal System for the classification of library books. This system classifies subjects using numbers from 000 through 999, designating more specific subjects with decimal points.

Dewey, Thomas Edmund 1902–71. American politician. He was governor of New York (1942–54) and ran as Republican candidate for president in 1944 and 1948, when he unexpectedly lost to H. Truman.

Dewey Decimal System *See* **Dewey, Melvil.**

dharma Hindu religious principle. Dharma expresses the religious, philosophical, ethical, and moral laws that govern the behavior and duties of each individual. In essence, it is equivalent to virtue, or right conduct. It is sacred to Hinduism, Buddhism, and Jainism (*q.v.*).

Dharma-sastra Sanskrit legal books. From the 1st cent. BC through the 6th cent. AD, these basic books of Hindu law were written in verse by the Brahmans.

Diadochi Macedonian generals who, as successors of Alexander the Great, battled each other in the wars of succession (323–281 BC) that broke up the Macedonian empire. Called the Wars of the Diadochi, these hostilities began with a struggle for the regency and quickly became battles for the throne itself. They were continued by succeeding generations of the generals and, by 281 BC, resulted in the formation of distinct empires under the Seleucids (*q.v.*) in Asia Minor, the Ptolemys (*q.v.*) in Egypt, and Antigonids (*q.v.*) in Macedonia. Among the Diadochi were Perdiccas, Antipater, Craterus, Seleucus I, Ptolemy I, Antigonus I, Eumenes, Demetrius I, and Lysimachus.

Diaghilev, Sergei Pavlovich 1872–1929. Russian ballet producer. He founded the Ballet Russe (1909), which revolutionized the dance by integrating music and scene in its productions and worked with artists such as the composer I. Stravinsky and the dancer and choreographer V. Nijinsky.

dialectical materialism Doctrine of Marxism, or communism, which holds that all reality is independent of the human mind and is reducible to matter. History proceeds through the clash of opposing forces that become resolved into new syntheses. All human history is a class struggle characterized by exploitation on the part of those who own the means of production; but the dialectical movement of history, it is held, will eventually result in the overthrow of capitalism by the proletariat of workers, and a classless society will ensue. This philosophy was expounded through the writings of K. Marx and F. Engels.

Diamond Jim Brady *See* **Brady, James Buchanan.**

Diamond Necklace, Affair of the *See* **Affair of the Diamond Necklace.**

Diane de Poitiers 1499–1566. Mistress of Henry II of France. She became his mistress while he was still dauphin (1536) and had greater influence than his wife, Catherine de Médicis. Noted for her beauty, she was a patroness of (and inspiration for) the arts.

diarchy *See* **dyarchy.**

Dias, Bartholomeu *See* **Cape of Good Hope.**

Díaz, Porfirio 1830–1915. Mexican soldier and president (1877–80, 1884–1911). Born of poor parents, he served in the Mexican War (*q.v.*), the War of Reform (1857–60), and the wars against Maximilian. In subsequent years, he led rebellions against the elected government and, after overthrowing S. Lerdo de Tejada, was elected president. In his long term of office, he established firm control over political machinery, used harsh measures to suppress insurrections, and opened Mexico to foreign exploitation. He was overthrown (1911) by F. Madero.

Dickens, Charles 1812–70. English novelist and one of the world's great writers. Dickens had a difficult childhood, being forced to work in a factory at age 12 after his father was consigned to debtors' prison. Ambitious and a hard worker, he eventually found work as a journalist. He began writing short fictional sketches in 1833 and became famous (1837) with publication of installments of *The Posthumous Papers of the Pickwick Club* in a London newspaper. Among his many famous novels are *Oliver Twist* (1837–39), *A Christmas Carol* (1843), *David Copperfield* (1849–50), and *A Tale of Two Cities* (1859).

Dickinson, Emily 1830–86. One of the great American poets. The daughter of a Massachusetts lawyer, she spent much of her life as a recluse in her father's house. She devoted herself to writing letters and poems, ultimately completing over 1,000 poems. Of these, she allowed fewer than a dozen to be printed in her lifetime. Her genius was recognized with the posthumous publication of her poems, beginning in 1890.

dictator Term applied in modern times to authoritarian leaders who assume extraordinary powers, with or without legislative sanction, such as A. Hitler. In ancient Rome, dictators were chosen by the consuls of the Roman Republic (*q.v.*) in times of emergency. They wielded great power but were limited to six-month terms and were held accountable for their decisions. Their subordinates were called the masters of the horse.

Diderot, Denis 1713–84. French Enlightenment philosopher, editor of the great French *Encyclopédie,* and man of letters. As editor of the *Encyclopédie* (1745–72), he arranged for contributions from all the important French writers (later known as the Encyclopedists (*q.v.*) of his day and created one of the chief works of the *philosophes* (*q.v.*). He was also a novelist (*Rameau's Nephew*), dramatist, and innovative critic of art. His philosophical works include *Thoughts on the Interpretation of Nature* and *Elements of Physiology.*

Diem *See* **Ngo Dinh Diem.**

Diemen, Anton van 1593–1645. Governor general of the Dutch East India Company (1636–45). He took Ceylon and Malacca from the Portuguese and extended Dutch influence in the East Indies.

Dien Bien Phu, Battle of Vietnamese victory over France (May 7, 1954) during the Indochina war. The battle concluded with the surrender of the French fortified outpost at Dien Bien Phu in a northwestern valley of Vietnam. Hoping to lure the guerrilla forces of the Vietminh (*q.v.*) into a pitched battle in which artillery would be decisive, the French general Henri Navarre concentrated some 15,000 men in a fortified camp. But the Vietnamese general V. Nguyen Giap surrounded it with some 40,000 troops, brought up his own artillery, and, after a long siege (Nov., 1953–May, 1954), left 2,293 dead, 5,134 wounded, and took more than 10,000 prisoners in all. The French were compelled to leave Indochina after a big-power conference at Geneva in July, 1954, which partitioned Vietnam along the 17th parallel. This battle is considered one of the greatest victories ever won by a former colony over a colonial power.

Dieppe raid An experimental commando attack by the Allies during WW II (Aug. 19, 1942) on the French coastal town of Dieppe. More than two-thirds of the mostly Canadian troops were lost.

Diesel, Rudolf Christian Karl 1858–1913. German inventor and engineer. Diesel invented an internal-combustion engine (1892) and the refined diesel engine (1896) which bears his name.

Diet The legislature of Japan, composed of two houses. The term was once used more generally in Europe in reference to a council.

Diet of *See under names inverted, as in* **Worms, Diet of.**

Digby, Sir Kenelm 1603–65. English diplomat, courtier, and author. He supported Charles I during the English Civil Wars (*q.v.*) and was chancellor to Queen Henrietta Maria in France after the Restoration (1660–64).

Diggers Groups of communal farmers who flourished (1649–51) briefly in England. Spurred on by high food prices after the English Civil Wars (*q.v.*), a band of agitators led by Ger-

rard Winstanley (1609–52) occupied and cultivated common lands in Surrey. The Diggers, Puritan extremists who called themselves True Levellers, wanted to end private ownership of land. Opposition soon mounted, however, and in 1650 they were suppressed. Several other Digger communes were likewise dispersed.

Dillinger, John 1902–34. American bank robber. Dillinger roamed Depression-era mid-America robbing banks and allegedly murdering 16 people. Declared "public enemy number one," he was killed by the FBI in a Chicago shoot-out.

Dingley Tariff American protective tariff. This law, sponsored by Maine's Republican congressman Nelson Dingley (1832–99), imposed a high protective tariff on foreign imports from 1897 to 1909.

Ding Ling (*pseud. of* Chiang Wei-chih) 1904–86. A leading 20th-cent. Chinese author whose novels explored the role of women in Chinese society. She began writing in the 1920s after becoming involved with her lover, a young leftist. She joined the Communist party in 1933 after his capture and execution by the Nationalists, and thereafter became a leading writer of proletarian themes. Though her criticisms of communism (such as those on women's rights) made her unpopular with the government, she nevertheless wrote the first Chinese novel to win the Stalin Prize (1951), *The Sun Shines Over the Sang-kan River.* Thrown out of the party in 1957, she was restored in 1979.

Dinh Bo Linh (Dinh Tien Hoang) *d.* 979. Vietnamese emperor. Dinh Bo Linh was an able soldier and organizer who created (968) a reunified empire in Vietnam, ending a period of anarchy and established independence from China.

Dinh Tien Hoang *See* **Dinh Bo Linh.**

Diniz 1261–1325 King of Portugal (1279–1325), son of Alfonso III. He encouraged agricultural improvements, founded the University of Coimbra (1290), negotiated the first commercial treaty with England (1294), and founded the Portuguese navy (1317).

Dio Cassius AD c155–235? Greek-born Roman historian. Cassius held many high Roman civilian and military offices, but was best known for his 80-volume *History of Rome,* written in Greek, of which 19 books survive intact.

Diocletian AD 245–313. Roman soldier and emperor (AD 284–305), successor to Numerian

(Emperor of the East) in 284 and Carinus (Emperor of the West) on the latter's death in 285. Diocletian instituted military, financial, and administrative reforms, (including the division of the empire (AD 293) into four parts (the East; Italy and Africa; Gaul, Spain, and Britain; Illyricum and the Danube region). During his reign Britain was again made part of the empire, the Persians were conquered, and the last serious persecutions of Christians began (303). He brought a measure of stability to the empire but did not reverse Rome's decline.

Dio Cocceianus *See* **Dion Chrysostom.**

Diodorus Siculus *d. after* 21 BC. Sicilian-born Greek historian who wrote a world history, starting with the creation and extending to Caesar's Gallic Wars.

Diogenes *d.* c320 BC. Greek Cynic philosopher. He rejected the comforts of life, living in a tub; he is known for going about with a lantern "looking for an honest man."

Diogenes Laërtius *See* **Zeno of Citium.**

Dion Chrysostom (Dio Cocceianus) *d. after* AD 112. Greek philosopher and rhetorician. He was banished from Rome by Emperor Domitian but returned under Nerva and Trajan. Of his orations, 80 still exist.

Dion of Syracuse 409?–354? BC. Syracusan philosopher and politician. He tried to set up a government according to the teachings of Plato under his nephew Dionysius the Younger but failed. He became ruler himself (356 BC) but was assassinated shortly afterward.

Dionysius of Halicarnassus *fl.* 1st cent. BC. Greek historian who came to Rome in 29 BC and wrote a 20-volume history of Rome, *Roman Antiquities,* of which only the first nine are extant.

Dionysius the Areopagite, Saint *fl.* 1st cent. AD. Athenian Christian converted by the apostle Paul. Tradition says he was the first bishop of Athens. In the Middle Ages, several mystical treatises that greatly influenced scholasticism (*q.v.*) were mistakenly attributed to him. These writings were actually composed around the 5th cent., and are today attributed to Pseudo-Dionysius.

Dionysius the Elder 430–367 BC. Tyrant of Syracuse (405–367 BC). He led two successful wars against Carthage (398–392) and made Syracuse the major power in Greek Italy. Later wars with Carthage were failures.

Dionysius the Younger *fl.* 368–344 BC. Tyrant of Syracuse, son of Dionysius the Elder. His uncle, Dion of Syracuse, with Plato's backing, tried to make him into a philosopher-prince but failed. He was expelled by Dion (356) and again by Timoleon (344) after the former's assassination.

Diophantus 3d cent. AD. Greek mathematician. He introduced a type of indeterminate algebraic equation into his work *Arithmetica;* 6 of the 13 books of this earliest-known work on algebra are extant.

Diori, Hamani 1916–89. The first president of Niger (1960–74). Diori led his country to complete independence from France (1960). He supported economic growth and mediated in the Biafran War but was overthrown by a military coup.

Dioscorides, Pedanius 1st cent. AD. Greek physician. While serving as surgeon with Nero's Roman army, he collected the pharmacological information used in his text *De Materia Medica,* used for 1,500 years.

diplomatic revolution (reversal of alliances) European foreign-policy conditions leading to the Seven Years' War (*q.v.*) also brought about (1756) changes in long-established alliances. The year preceding the war saw the alliance of France with Austria and Russia, and of Britain with Prussia, and the estrangement of Britain from Russia, which fought on the side of Austria and France in the war.

Dirac, Paul Adrien Maurice 1902–84. English physicist. He developed a version of quantum mechanics and shared a Nobel Prize in Physics with E. Schrödinger (1933). He and E. Fermi developed the Fermi-Dirac statistics.

Directory Executive body (1795–99) of the French First Republic during the French Revolution. It consisted of five directors nominated by the Council of Five Hundred (*q.v.*) and elected by the Council of Ancients. Embroiled in struggles with the councils and plagued with infighting among the directors, the Directory succumbed first (1797) to the *coup d'état* of 18 Fructidor and finally (1799) to the coup of 18 Brumaire, in which Napoleon took power. The Directory was then replaced with the Consulate.

Dirksen, Everett McKinley 1896–1969. American statesman. Dirksen served Illinois as a Republican congressman (1933–49) and senator (1951–69). Generally a conservative, he nevertheless led Democratic President L. Johnson's fight for the Civil Rights and Voting Rights acts.

disappeared ones *See* **Argentina, 1976–78.**

Disarmament Conference International conference held in Geneva (1932–37) for the purpose of preventing general rearmament. It was attended by members of the League of Nations as well as by the United States and USSR. Deadlocks ensued over the definitions of war materials and over refusal of various countries to accept parity. France refused to accept limitations. Germany, already limited in armaments by the Treaty of Versailles (*q.v.*), contended that it had a right to rearm unless other nations disarmed to an equivalent level. The conference adjourned for five months (1933). When it reassembled, Germany had passed under Nazi control and withdrew (Oct. 14) from the conference and the League of Nations. The conference was thenceforth without significance, though it met sporadically until May, 1937.

Disciples of Christ (Campbellites) American Protestant body, founded by former Presbyterians Thomas and Alexander Campbell c1810. They preached unity among all Christians, with the Bible as their only guide. They became known as the Christian Churches and officially adopted this name in 1957.

Disney, Walt 1901–66. American movie producer. He created the cartoon character Mickey Mouse (1928) and produced full-length animated and other popular films such as *Snow White and the Seven Dwarfs* (1938).

Disputations Debates in medieval universities. Students were required to defend views against attacks on them. They evolved into the modern examination system whereby degree aspirants are required to defend original theses before examining professors.

Disraeli, Benjamin, 1st earl of Beaconsfield 1804–81. British author, statesman, and Conservative prime minister (1868, 1874–80), succeeding (respectively) E. Derby and W. Gladstone. A controversial figure, Disraeli pursued an aggressive foreign policy in the interests of British imperialism. He was a noted author when he became (1837) a member of Parliament and there became a leader of the young Conservative (Tory) faction. He aggressively opposed the prime minister and member of his own party, Sir R. Peel, on the repeal of the Corn Laws (*q.v.*) in 1846 and thereby helped bring down Peel's government. He subsequently served as chancellor of the exchequer (1852, 1858–59), worked for passage of the Reform Bill of 1867 to enfranchise a large bloc of working-class voters, and served briefly as prime minister (1868). Though many social reforms were instituted, Disraeli's second term as prime minister (1874–80) was dominated by foreign-policy matters. These included formal annexation of Fiji (1874) and the Transvaal (1877), purchase of controlling interest in the Suez Canal (1875), the Anglo-Afghan War (1878–79), and involvement in the continuing power struggle between the Ottoman Empire and Russia in the eastern Mediterranean. Among the novels Disraeli wrote were *Sybil* (1845) and *Tancred* (1847).

District of Columbia US federal district coextensive with the city of Washington, on the Potomac River between Virginia and Maryland. Established by congressional acts (1790–91), the region was chosen by G. Washington as the seat of the federal government. The government moved there (June 10, 1800) from Philadelphia during the presidency of J. Adams. The town of Georgetown was consolidated with Washington (1878), which is governed by a presidential commission. Residents of the district won the right to vote in presidential elections (1961) by the 23d Amendment and the right to elect their own mayor by adopting a new charter (1974).

Divine, Father c1882–1965. American black religious leader. Born George Baker, he founded the Peace Mission movement in the Harlem section of New York City.

divine right Political doctrine asserting that a king's power came from God and that he was accountable only to God, not to the people he ruled. It reached its height in Europe in the 17th cent. It was largely ended by England's Glorious Revolution and the French Revolution.

Divines at Westminster, Assembly of *See* **Westminster Assembly.**

Dix, Dorothea Lynde 1802–87. American social reformer. She crusaded for more humane treatment for the insane and the imprisoned, and was superintendent of women nurses during the American Civil War.

Dixie Name applied to the US Southern states. The origin of the term is obscure, and has been attributed to memories of a kind slaveholder of that name as well as to the Mason-Dixon line (*q.v.*). A song, *Dixie,* composed (1859) for a minstrel show by Daniel Decatur Emmett (1815–1904) became the song of the Confederacy and later of the South generally.

Dixiecrats (States' Rights Democrats) American political group. In 1948, Southern Democrats refused to support their party's civil rights program, and formed their own group. Their presidential candidate was Governor Strom Thurmond of South Carolina, who carried four Southern states against H. Truman.

Dixon, Jeremiah *See* **Mason-Dixon line.**

Djibouti (*formerly* Afars and Issas, French Territory of the; French Somaliland) Independent country in East Africa. The population is 530,000 and the capital is Djibouti. Held by the French from 1862, it was a colony (French Somaliland) from 1896 until 1946, when it became a territory in the French Union. In 1958 it entered the French Community. It was renamed Afars and Issas in 1967 and became independent on May 8, 1977. Gouled Aptidon Hassan was first president (in office 1977–   ). An underdeveloped nation with an agricultural economy, it is strategically located at the entrance to the Red Sea. Refugees flooded into the country during the Ethiopian conflict in the 1970s. The US was granted rights to establish military bases there (1980) after unrest in Ethiopia threatened Djibouti's stability. Universal suffrage was enacted in 1981. President Gouled was elected to a new term, after which a one-party system was established. Intertribal tensions increased in the late 1980s, and a full-scale revolt by Afar groups broke out in the north (Nov. 1991).

Dmitry (Demetrius) 1582–91. Name of the son of Ivan IV, child heir to the Russian throne, who was murdered (1591), possibly by B. Godunov. Dmitry was also the name of three claimants (false Dmitrys) to the throne who appeared shortly after Godunov succeeded to the throne. They created what is called the Time of Troubles (1604–13). The first false Dmitry appeared c1600 and may have been Yury Otrepyev, a Russian nobleman. He ruled for less than a year, after Godunov died (1605), before being assassinated. The second Dmitry (the Thief of Tushino) was active from 1607 to 1610, and the third (the Thief of Pskov) was active from 1611 until his execution in 1612.

Dobson, Frank 1888–1963. English sculptor. He developed a modernistic, non-naturalistic style, and did many female nudes and sculpted portraits.

Docetism Early heresy in Christianity, which claimed that Jesus did not take a true human form on earth but was a phantasm. It was a form of Gnosticism (*q.v.*).

Doctors' Plot Russian Stalinist conspiracy. On Jan. 13, 1953, J. Stalin announced that 10 prominent Russian doctors were American agents who were plotting to murder Communist leaders. Stalin died before the trials, and most of the accused were released.

Doctrinaires French royalist political writers who gave their name to any abstract, dogmatic thinker by the manner in which they defended the restored French monarchy (1815–30). They included, notably, F. Guizot.

Doctrine of Lapse One of the policies used by the British East India Company (19th cent.) to justify annexation of native kingdoms in India. By it, a failure in the direct royal line of succession meant that direct control of the state passed to the company. Parts of the Maratha states were annexed in this way. This doctrine was used in conjunction with the doctrine of paramountcy, by which the company justified interference in states that were being misgoverned.

Dodecanese Islands Greek island group in the Aegean Sea. It belonged to the Ottoman Empire (16th cent. to 1912), then to Italy until 1947, when it was ceded to Greece. Rhodes is the administrative center.

Dodgson, Charles Lutwidge *See* **Carroll, Lewis.**

Dondona Village in Epirus, Greece, site of the oldest of the ancient Greek oracles. It was dedicated to the chief god, Zeus.

Doenitz, Karl 1891–1980. German admiral. He supervised (1930s) the creation of the new German submarine fleet, contrary to Versailles Treaty (*q.v.*) prohibitions against rearming, commanded it from 1936, and became commander-in-chief of the navy (1943–45). As A. Hitler's designated successor in the closing days of the war, he ordered Germany's surrender (May 7, 1945). Sentenced at the Nürnberg war trials (1946), he served 10 years in prison.

doge Chief office in the one-time Italian republics of Genoa and Venice. The Venetian doge was the chief magistrate from 697 until 1797, though his real power was curtailed after the establishment of the Council of Ten in 1310.

Dogen 1200–1253. Japanese philosopher and teacher. Dogen was a Buddhist monk who studied Zen Buddhism (*q.v.*) in China and helped introduce it to Japan through his Soto School.

Doheny, Edward L. *See* **Teapot Dome.**

Dole, Sanford Ballard 1844–1926. Hawaiian statesman. He served as the first president of the Republic of Hawaii (1894–1900) and as governor of the US Territory of Hawaii (1900–1903) when it was annexed.

Dolet, Étienne 1509–46. French scholar and printer of Lyons called "the martyr of the Renaissance." He was executed for heresy after publishing a work allegedly denying the soul's immortality.

dollar diplomacy Diplomatic expression. In general, this term refers to the policy of buying another country's support with loans or aid. Specifically, it refers to the foreign policy of W. H. Taft and P. C. Knox, who sought to increase US trade by supporting US enterprises abroad.

Dollfuss, Engelbert 1892–1934. Austrian statesman. He became chancellor in 1932 and declared a dictatorship along Italian Fascist lines (1934). He was assassinated by Austrian Nazis attempting a takeover.

Döllinger, Johann Joseph Ignaz von 1799–1890. German theologian and historian. Excommunicated for opposing the doctrine of papal infallibility as promulgated by the First Vatican Council (1869–70), he became a member of the Old Catholics (*q.v.*).

Domenico Veneziano c1400–1461. Italian Renaissance painter who created the *St. Lucy Altarpiece* in the Uffizi Palace at Florence.

Domesday Book The record of a survey ordered by William the Conqueror (1086) to determine economic conditions in England and the ownership of land for taxation purposes.

Dominic, Saint 1170?–1221. Spanish Catholic who founded the Dominicans (*q.v.*) in 1216, a religious order that emphasizes study and preaching. He was a Castilian; his full name was Dominic Guzmán.

Dominican Republic Independent state located on the eastern part of the Caribbean island of Hispaniola, adjacent to Haiti. The population is 7,253,000 and the capital is Santo Domingo. The island was governed by Spain until it was ceded to France in 1795. The republic was established in 1844 and long periods of internal dis-

order ensued. Key events in the Dominican Republic's history include:

1492   C. Columbus discovered island of Hispaniola; claimed it for Spain; named it La Española; later established his son Diego as viceroy.

1496   Santo Domingo established.

1697   Western part of the island, a haven for buccaneers, ceded to France.

1795   In the Treaty of Basel, Spain ceded La Española to France.

1801   Haitian black slaves, under Toussaint L'Ouverture, revolted; conquered island; French forces subsequently defeated Toussaint.

1808–09   Successful revolt against the French.

1814–21   Spanish again ruled; finally expelled (1821).

1822   Eastern part of island conquered by Haitians, led by J. Boyer.

1844   Haitian rule overthrown on east part of island; Pedro Santana established the Dominican Republic; became first president.

1861–65   Became Spanish province, after long period of unrest and frequent attacks by Haiti.

1865   Spain withdrew forces; second Dominican Republic declared (Feb.); unrest became chaotic.

1869   President Buenaventura Báez attempted annexation with US; US Senate refused to ratify treaty.

1882–99   Gen. Ulíses Heureaux served as president; was assassinated.

1905   Government finances near collapse; control of customs department turned over to US.

1916–24   US sent marines to quell civil disorders (1916); military government established.

1922   Partial restoration of civilian government.

1930–61   Rafael Trujillo Molina in power after overthrowing Horacio Vásquez (1930); began long dictatorship.

1937–38   Border dispute with Haiti; Trujillo expelled Haitians in Dominican Republic, during which 10,000 of them were killed (1937); dispute settled (1938).

1947   Election held; Trujillo curbed opposition party, was reelected "overwhelmingly."

1947   Trujillo charged that Cuban Communists were plotting invasion.

1949 Uprising quelled; Trujillo blamed Cubans and others for revolt.

1959 Abortive coup by exiled Dominicans living in Cuba.

1960 OAS charged Trujillo with involvement in plot to kill Venezuelan president R. Betancourt; sanctions imposed.

1960 Trujillo named Joaquin Balaguer president.

1961 Trujillo assassinated (May 30); Balaguer subsequently attempted democratic reforms.

1962 Balaguer forced out of office by civil unrest.

1962–63 Leftist Juan Bosch in office as elected president; Bosch overthrown (Sept.) by right-wing military coup; civilian triumvirate ruled afterward.

1965 Leftist revolt (Apr.); US president L. Johnson sent 25,000 US troops, who effectively supported anti-Bosch forces, to occupy the country; OAS arranged a cease-fire.

1965 Hector García Godoy became provisional president (Sept.).

1966 Balaguer elected president; OAS forces withdrawn; Balaguer was subsequently reelected, until 1978.

1978–82 Antonio Guzmán, Dominican Revolutionary Party (PRD) leader, in office as president; instituted land reform program.

1979 Coup attempt failed (Sept.).

1982–86 Salvador Jorge Blanco, ruling PRD party candidate, in office as president following elections; his administration was marked by severe economic problems brought on by a foreign debt crisis.

1984 Three-day riot sparked by 50% price hikes (Apr.); 80 dead, 400 injured, and 5,000 arrested as military restored order; US provided $18 million in food, distributed free to poor.

1984 Pope John Paul II visited the country (Oct.).

1985 Steep price hikes on food and other necessities implemented by government in order to qualify for International Monetary Fund (IMF) loans; government rolled back some hikes and increased minimum wage following strikes and rioting (Jan., Feb., June, July).

1986– Balaguer, Christian Social Reformist Party (PRSC) member, again in office as president following elections; aging Belaguer now serving his fifth term as president.

1986 Former president Blanco under investigation for misappropriating public funds while in office; left for US for medical treatment following alleged heart attack (1987); sentenced to 20 years in prison in 1991.

1987 Government negotiated deal to sell USSR sugar following cutback in US sugar quota.

1990 Two-day riot followed new round of government imposed price hikes (Aug.).

1991 Some 2,000 Haitian workers deported (July); thousands of others reportedly left voluntarily.

1991 IMF granted new loans subject to continued austerity program.

Dominicans (Order of Preachers) Important order of Catholic friars founded (1216) in France by Saint Dominic. Sanctioned the same year by Pope Honorius III, the order began as an attempt to convert the Albigenses (*q.v.*). Since then the order has retained its evangelical character and is also characterized by devotion to theological studies, preaching, and teaching. The order was greatly influenced (13th cent.) by its member Saint Thomas Aquinas and since then has also been dedicated to promoting Thomism (*q.v.*). The order was in charge of the Inquisition (*q.v.*) and actively engaged in missionary work. Other noted Dominicans include Albertus Magnus and Savonarola. With the Franciscans (*q.v.*), it is one of the two principal Catholic orders of friars.

dominion Former name of a country in the British Commonwealth (*q.v.*). Prior to 1939, "dominion" referred to a self-governing country, such as Canada, which still retained ties to the British Empire. The term was abandoned because of its implied inferior status.

Domitian (Domitianus, Titus Flavius) AD 51–96. Roman emperor (81–96), son of Vespasian, successor to his brother Titus. The cruelty of his later years led to his assassination in a plot led by his wife, Domitia. Nerva succeeded him.

Domitianus, Titus Flavius *See* **Domitian.**

Donatello c1386–1466. Italian Renaissance sculptor. A founder of realistic sculpture, as seen in his bronze *David* (1430–32, Bargello Palace, Florence), he was the first sculptor since antiquity to do freestanding statues independent of their surroundings.

Donation of Constantine Grant of land supposed to have been made to the papacy by the

Emperor Constantine. The document asserting the alleged grant was probably forged in the mid-8th cent. to bolster papal claims of temporal power over central Italy. The demonstration of this forgery in the Renaissance (1440) by a papal secretary, L. Valla, was one of the first successful uses of historical critical methods that later became standard.

Donation of Pepin *See* **Pepin the Short.**

Donatism North African schismatical movement (4th cent. AD). The Donatists believed that only the "pure" were true members of the church and that sacraments administered by priests who had sinned were invalid. They were condemned by the Synod of Arles (314) and declined definitively after the formidable attack on their doctrines launched by Saint Augustine in the early 5th cent.

Donatus *fl.* AD 333. Roman teacher of grammar and rhetoric. He taught Saint Jerome and wrote the *Ars grammatica,* a Latin textbook used throughout the Middle Ages.

Don Carlos *See* **Carlist Wars; Carlists.**

Don Cossacks Cossacks (*q.v.*) who settled along the lower course of the Don River and founded a semi-independent republic under the suzerainty of the Russian tsars (16th cent.). They lost their autonomy after a revolt (1707–08) and became a special military caste (1835). They were used by the tsars to suppress revolutionary movements after 1886.

Donelson, Fort *See* **Fort Donelson.**

Doniphan, Alexander William 1808–87. American soldier. As commanding officer of a unit in the Mexican War, he led his troops in a brilliant long march by land and sea from New Mexico to Chihuahua (Dec., 1846–Mar., 1847). He fought two victorious battles along the way, losing few of the nearly 1,000 men under his command.

Donizetti, Gaetano 1797–1848. Italian opera composer of *Lucia di Lammermoor* (1835) and other Romantic operas.

Donne, John 1572–1631. English poet, the foremost of the Metaphysical poets (*q.v.*). Donne was for a time an adventurer, a public official and, finally, was ordained as an Anglican priest (1615). Though his poetry was later neglected (until the 20th cent.), both his poetry and sermons were well recognized in his day. He is noted for his use of imagery and paradox; his works include *Songs and Sonnets,* his two *Anniversaries, Devotions upon Emergent Occasions,* and his many sermons.

Donnelly, Ignatius 1831–1901. American author and reformer. He was congressman (1863–69) from Minnesota and a founder of the Populist party (1892). He tried to prove that F. Bacon wrote W. Shakespeare's plays in *The Great Cryptogram* (1888).

Donner party Group of emigrants to California (1846–47) who were trapped all winter by snow in the Sierra Nevadas. Out of 87, 47 survived only by recourse to cannibalism.

Donnybrook Irish town and county. Now part of Dublin, Donnybrook was famous for its annual fair (1204–1855) in which drunken brawling was an expected part of the festivities, making the word "donnybrook" synonymous with a brawl.

Don Pacifico Affair Incident (1850) in which the British government seized Greek ships in Piraeus (Athens) harbor in support of the claims of a British subject, David Pacifico, against the Greek government. It was considered an extreme example of the bellicose foreign policy of Lord Palmerston, who was obliged to promise Queen Victoria that he would inform her of his actions after the French and Russians protested the incident.

Doolittle, Gen. James H. 1896– . American aviator and war hero, who led the first US bombing raid against Tokyo during WW II (Apr. 18, 1942), following the Japanese attack on Pearl Harbor. He also commanded US air forces during the North Africa invasion and in Europe.

Doppler, Christian Johann 1803–53. Austrian physicist. He discovered that the frequency of light and sound waves seems to vary according to the distance of the source from the observer, a phenomenon now called Doppler's Principle.

Doria, Andrea 1468–1560. Genoese admiral of an ancient Genoese princely family. He fought for Francis I of France between 1522 and 1528, but then switched allegiance to the emperor Charles V. He established a virtual dictatorship over Genoa (1529), and fought sea battles in alliance with the empire against both Turks and Barbary pirates. He was one of the great Italian seamen. The ocean liner *Andrea Doria* (sunk [1956] in the Atlantic) was named after him.

Dorians People of ancient Greece who settled in the Peloponnesus (c1100 BC), replacing the Achaean Greeks. They established colonies in Crete, Italy, Sicily, and Asia Minor.

Doric order Greek architectural style. Doric is the earliest style of Greek art and architecture (7th cent. BC). Its columns, which had no base, were marked by 20 sharp-edged flutes, culminating in a characteristic curved-mold capital. Doric columns predominated in such ancient structures as Greek temples during the archaic period, as well as the Parthenon (*q.v.*).

Dornier, Claudius 1884–1969. German aircraft designer and builder. He initiated all-metal airplanes and made seaplanes such as the *Do X* (1929) which carried 169 passengers from Germany to New York on its maiden flight (1931). Dornier bombers were Luftwaffe standards in WW II.

Dorr, Thomas Wilson 1805–54. American crusader for universal manhood suffrage. During the agitation against the Rhode Island Charter, which restricted the franchise to property-owners, both Dorr's followers and their rivals called their own constitutional conventions and set up rival governments of Rhode Island (1841–42). Even after the adoption of a new constitution, Dorr was sentenced to life imprisonment for treason but was later pardoned.

Dort, Synod of *See* **Arminianism; Remonstrants.**

Dorylaeum, Battle of 1. First ˜. Crusader victory over the Seljuk Turks fought at Dorylaeum (near modern Eskişehir Turkey) on July 1, 1097, during the First crusade (*q.v.*). The first column of the Crusader army, consisting of some 10,000 men under Bohemond, was attacked by a huge Turkish army. Reinforcements arrived and the Turks were routed, suffering some 30,000 casualties to about 4,000 Crusader casualties. 2. Second ˜. Turkish victory over a German army led by Conrad III of Hohenstaufen in Oct., 1147, during the Second Crusade (*q.v.*). Only Conrad and some knights were able to fight their way out of an ambush in which the Crusader army was decimated by Turkish archers. The defeat contributed to the failure of the Second Crusade.

Dos Passos, John Roderigo 1896–1970. American realistic author of the trilogy *U.S.A.* (1937), made up of *The 42d Parallel, 1919,* and *The Big Money.*

Dost, Muhammad 1793–1863. Emir (ruler) of Afghanistan (1826–63). His attempts to play off the Russians against the British embroiled him with the latter in the first of the Afghan Wars (1839–42), but an accommodation with the British was finally reached in 1855.

Dostoyevsky, Feodor Mikhailovich (Dostoevsky, ˜) 1821–81. Russian novelist and one of the world's great writers. His *The Brothers Karamazov*

(1879–80) is a classic. He first gained recognition (1846) as a writer with *Poor Folk* but was exiled (1849) to Siberia for his association with a radical group. On returning (1859) from Siberia, he again took up writing and completed his most important works. Among them are *Notes from the Underground* (1864), *Crime and Punishment* (1866), *The Idiot* (1868), and *The Possessed* (1871–72).

Doubleday, Abner 1819–93. Reputed originator of the game of baseball and Civil War officer. A 1908 commission concluded that he indeed invented baseball as we know it, in 1839, at Cooperstown, New York, but its conclusions are still disputed by some.

Doughty, Charles Montagu 1843–1926. English traveler and author. He published the classic *Travels in Arabia Deserta* (1888), based on his original observations of Arab life.

Doughty, Thomas *See* **Hudson River school.**

Douglas Noble family prominent in Scottish history for more than 700 years. The family figured in the border wars between Scotland and England and members were variously earls, marquises, and dukes of Douglas, Angus, Hamilton, Queensberry, and Morton. The origins of the family are uncertain, though the Douglases were among the ancestors of the Stuart (*q.v.*) line of Scottish kings. In modern times, a descendant of the Douglas family, Sir A. Douglas-Home, was British prime minister (1963–64). Among the prominent members of the family were: William of Douglas (*d.* 1298), 1st lord of Douglas, a leader of J. de Baliol's forces; Sir James Douglas, lord of Douglas (1286–1330), great commander under Robert I the Bruce; William Douglas, 1st earl of Douglas (c1327–84), engaged in border wars with the English; James Douglas, 2d earl of Douglas and Mar (c1358–88), raided across English border, was killed at the battle of Otterburn; Archibald Douglas, 3d earl of Douglas (c1328–1400), made the family the most powerful in Scotland; Archibald Douglas, 4th earl of Douglas (c1369–1424), who joined the French against the English in 1423; Archibald Douglas 5th earl of Douglas (c1391–1439), who rose to great power under James II; William Douglas, 6th earl of Douglas (1423–1440), beheaded with his brother by James II to break the family's power; William Douglas, 8th earl of Douglas (c1425–52), murdered by James II after regaining some family lands; James Douglas, 9th earl of Douglas (1426–88), rebelled against James II and thus lost family lands to the Angus line; Archibald Douglas, 5th earl of Angus (c1449–1514), opposed James III and became chancellor under James IV; Archibald Douglas, 6th earl of Angus (c1489–1557), married Scottish dowager queen, Margaret Tudor, and for a time gained control of Scotland; Archibald Douglas, 8th earl of Angus (1555–88), joined an English-backed invasion of Scotland and forced James to restore his family lands.

Douglas, Clifford Hugh 1879–1952. English engineer and economist. He authored the theory of Social Credit (*q.v.*) and served as reconstruction adviser to the government of Alberta, Canada (1935), which was dedicated to his theories.

Douglas, David 1798–1834. Scottish botanist. He traveled early throughout North America studying its plants. The Douglas fir which he observed (c1825) is named for him.

Douglas, Gawin 1474?–1522. Scottish poet and bishop of Dunkeld. He is known for doing the first English translation of the *Aeneid* and is considered one of the greatest early Scottish poets.

Douglas, Sir James 1803–77. Canadian colonial governor. He built Fort Victoria on Vancouver Island (1843), where he became governor (1851). He was also appointed governor of British Columbia (1858–1863).

Douglas, Stephen Arnold 1813–61. American statesman, a great orator and central figure in the national debate over slavery in the years prior to the American Civil War. A Democrat from Illinois, he was a congressman (1843–47) and senator (1847–61). As a senator he was a proponent of expansionism and became chairman of the Committee on Territories. He thereby held an important position in the North-South struggle over slavery, then centered on the question of extending slavery to new US territories. He formulated the doctrine of Popular Sovereignty, was instrumental in passage of the Compromise of 1850 (*q.v.*), and proposed what became the 1854 Kansas-Nebraska Act (*q.v.*). He engaged in the notable Lincoln-Douglas debates during the senatorial election (1858), when he defeated Lincoln, but was narrowly defeated by Lincoln in the presidential election (1860).

Douglas, William Orville 1898–1980. US Supreme Court justice (1939–75). Douglas was appointed to the Supreme Court by F. D. Roo-

sevelt. He was consistently liberal on most matters, such as civil rights, the First Amendment, civil liberties, and the environment.

Douglas-Home, Sir Alexander Frederick 1903– . British statesman. He entered Parliament as a Conservative (1931), was secretary to N. Chamberlain (1937–39), foreign secretary (1960–63). On becoming prime minister (1963–64), replacing H. Macmillan, he had to renounce his Scottish peerage.

Douglass, Frederick 1817–1895. American abolitionist who escaped slavery in 1838. Taught to read by a former owner, he lectured in the US and Britain, edited an abolitionist newspaper, organized two regiments of Massachusetts Negroes in the American Civil War, and finally wrote *Life and Times of Frederick Douglass* (1882).

Douhet, Giulio 1869–1930. Italian general. He was an early advocate of strategic bombing and an independent air force whose theories influenced German and Italian tactics in the Spanish Civil War (*q.v.*).

Doumer, Paul 1857–1932. French statesman. He was president of the French Third Republic (1931–32) until his assassination by the insane Russian émigré P. Gorgoulov. A. Lebrun succeeded him.

Doumergue, Gaston 1863–1937. French politician. He was first elected to the Chamber of Deputies (1893) as a Radical-Socialist, served in several ministries, and was elected president of the Third French Republic (1924–31). He later served briefly as a "strong man" premier (1934) as a result of the turmoil surrounding the Stavisky Affair (*q.v.*).

Dover, Treaty of Anglo-French secret treaty. On May 22, 1670, Charles II of England secretly agreed to aid French king Louis XIV in his plans for expanding French domains. In return, Louis was to provide money that would free Charles from financial dependence on Parliament. By this agreement, Louis XIV broke up the Triple Alliance (*q.v.*) against him and paved the way for the Third Dutch War (*q.v.*).

Dow, Herbert Henry 1866–1930. American chemist. Dow patented many chemical processes, including the extraction of bromine and magnesium from brine. He founded the Dow Chemical Corporation.

Dowie, John Alexander 1847–1907. Scottish founder of what he called the Christian Catholic church (1896). He preached faith healing and, in 1901, established Zion City in Illinois, where he ruled his followers as a benevolent despot until deposed (1905).

Dowland, John 1562–1616. English composer, a leading composer of secular music in the Elizabethan and Jacobean periods.

Dowson, Ernest Christopher 1867–1900. English poet. One of the Decadents (*q.v.*), he is remembered for the lines, "I have been faithful to thee, Cynara, in my fashion."

Doyle, Sir Arthur Conan 1859–1930. English author who created the famous detective character Sherlock Holmes. The first Holmes book was *A Study in Scarlet* (1887); it introduced his friend, Dr. Watson, and his home on Baker Street.

Dózsa Rebellion Hungarian peasant revolt (1514). György Dózsa led 100,000 peasants against the taxes and oppression of the nobility (1514). The revolt was crushed, the peasants condemned to servitude, and Dózsa executed.

Draco (Dracon) *fl.* 621 BC. Athenian lawgiver and politician. His laws were very severe, death being prescribed for most crimes. He also transferred responsibility for punishment of murder from the victim's family to the state. The adjective "draconian" refers to him.

Dracon *See* **Draco.**

Draft riots Mass rioting (July 13–16, 1863) in New York City during the American Civil War (1861–65). The riots were provoked by a new and unpopular draft act for Union armies. Laborers especially resented a provision that allowed the rich to buy deferments and also feared that newly freed blacks would take their jobs. The rioters, mostly foreign-born Americans, ransacked draft stations, burned buildings, looted stores, and attacked Negroes. Police and state militia finally quelled the riots but not before some 500–1,000 people had been injured and $1.5–2 million worth of property was damaged.

Drago, Luis *See* **Drago Doctrine.**

Drago Doctrine International law proposal advanced by Luis Drago (1859–1921) at the Hague Conference (1907). It forbade the use of military force by one country to recover debts owed by another, but was not accepted.

dragoon European soldier of the late 16th to early 20th cents. Dragoons were trained as both cavalry and foot soldiers.

Drake, Edwin Laurentine 1819–80. American oilman. He drilled the first oil-producing well in the US, at Titusville, Pennsylvania (1859).

Drake, Sir Francis 1540?–1596. English navigator and adventurer, regarded as the greatest of the Elizabethan seamen. From 1572, Drake undertook a number of raiding missions against Spanish colonies in the Americas, which made him rich and famous. On one such expedition (1577–80), to raid Spanish colonies on the Pacific coast of South America, he captured great riches and by his westward return became the first Englishman to circumnavigate the earth. In 1588 he served as vice-admiral against the Spanish Armada. His invasion of Portugal (1589) failed, and he died during a raid on the West Indies.

Drang nach Osten (Drive to the East) German phrase describing Germany's historic desire to expand eastward. It was last cited by A. Hitler to justify his aggression toward such countries as Poland, Czechoslovakia, and, ultimately, Russia.

Dravidians Group of people, living primarily in southern India, who speak Dravidian languages (Telugu, Tamil, Kannada, and Maliyali).

Drebbel, Cornelis Jacobszoon 1572–1634. Dutch inventor. He designed the first navigable submarine (1620).

Dred Scott Case US Supreme Court case (1857) involving Dred Scott, a slave taken from Missouri, a slave state, to Illinois, a free state, and then to a free territory. Scott argued that his residence in the free state and territory made him a free man. The Court decided against Scott, stating that slaves had no legal standing in court, and that the Missouri Compromise (*q.v.*) (1820) was unconstitutional.

Dreiser, Theodore 1871–1945. American novelist noted for such naturalistic novels as *Sister Carrie* and *An American Tragedy.*

Dresden, Battle of Battle (Aug. 26–27, 1813) of the Napoleonic Wars, at Dresden, Germany. Napoleon's last major victory in Germany, it caused 10,000 French casualties to the allies' (Austrians, Prussians, Russians) 38,000 casualties.

Dresden, Treaty of Treaty (Dec. 25, 1745) between Austria and Prussia, ending the Second Silesian War. Frederick the Great of Prussia gained control of much of Saxony, retained much of Silesia, and acknowledged Francis I as Holy Roman Emperor.

Dresden Codex Mayan hieroglyphic text, one of the few pre-Columbian manuscripts to survive the Spanish conquest. It is kept in the state library at Dresden, Germany.

Drew, Daniel 1797–1879. American railway speculator. A director of the Erie Railroad, he allied successfully with J. Fisk and J. Gould in the "Erie War" (1866–68) against C. Vanderbilt, but later went bankrupt in the Panic of 1873.

Dreyer, John Louis Emil 1852–1926. Danish astronomer. His *New General Catalogue of Nebulae and Clusters of Stars* is a standard reference.

Dreyfus Affair Controversy over the French army's refusal to recognize the false conviction of Capt. A. Dreyfus for treason. The affair destabilized French political life from Dreyfus's conviction (1894) to his final exoneration (1906). Dreyfus, an Alsatian of Jewish background, was convicted on the evidence of a document supposedly written by Dreyfus, offering military intelligence to the German military attaché. Later it was discovered that Major F. Esterhazy had written the document. Esterhazy was acquitted by a court-martial (1898), prompting É. Zola, a supporter of Dreyfus, to publish his open letter *J'Accuse,* accusing the judges of acquitting Esterhazy in order to protect the army. In 1898 it was learned that another document apparently incriminating Dreyfus was in fact forged by Major Hubert Henry (1846–98), who confessed to the forgery and committed suicide. Dreyfus was retried, but, incredibly, was once again convicted. In order to settle the matter, President É. Loubet pardoned Dreyfus (Sept., 1899), and in 1906 a court of appeals exonerated Dreyfus. He was reinstated in the army. The affair polarized French society for more than a decade. Traditionalists and Catholics tended to support the army, as did anti-Semites. Dreyfus gained the support of liberals such as É. Zola and G. Clemenceau. As a result of the affair, the anticlerical Radical party came to power in France.

Drive to the East *See* **Drang nach Osten.**

Droysen, Johann Gustav 1808–84. German historian and politician. He urged the unification of Germany under Prussia and wrote a 14-volume political history of Prussia.

Druids Ancient Celtic priests and teachers. Knowledge of them comes chiefly from Roman writers, notably J. Caesar.

Drury Lane Theatre London theater. The oldest English theater still in use, its original building opened in 1663. Its current building dates to 1812.

Druses (Druzes) Middle Eastern religious sect, an offshoot of the Ismailis, whose members live largely in the mountain regions of Syria and Lebanon. They believe in the divinity of the sixth Fatimid caliph, al-Hakim (985–1021) and in his second coming. Their opposition to Christians, notably the Maronites, in the 19th cent. brought French intervention in the region.

Drusus Caesar *d.* AD 23. Roman soldier. The son and heir of Roman emperor Tiberius, he suppressed a serious mutiny in Pannonia (AD 14). He was poisoned by his wife Livilla and her lover Sejanus, the emperor's favorite.

Drusus, Marcus Livius *d.* 109? BC. Roman politician. Made tribune (122 BC) with C. Gracchus he successfully undermined the liberal reforms sought by Gracchus by proposing, but failing to implement, even more liberal reforms.

Drusus, Marcus Livius *d.* 91 BC. Roman politician, son of the elder M. Drusus. Made tribune (91 BC), he attempted to introduce a sweeping reform program, which included enfranchisement of the Italians, but was assassinated.

Drusus Germanicus, Nero Claudius 38–9 BC. Roman soldier. The brother of Roman emperor Tiberius and father of the emperor Claudius, he was acclaimed for his successful campaigns in Germany.

Druzes *See* **Druses.**

Dryden, John 1631–1700. English poet, dramatist, and critic. He first gained recognition (1659) with *Heroic Stanzas,* and in 1668 became poet laureate. His conversion to Catholicism (1685) and the accession (1688) of the Protestant monarchy under William and Mary, ultimately cost him the laureateship. Among his poems are *Religio Laici, The Hind and the Panther,* and *Alexander's Feast.* His many dramatic works include *All for Love, Absalom and Achitophel,* and *Marriage à la Mode.*

dualism In philosophy and religion, the division of the world into two separate components such as mind and matter in Cartesianism, and good and evil in religion and some systems of ethics.

Dual Monarchy (Austro-Hungarian Monarchy) System established (1867) by the Ausgleich (*q.v.*), whereby the Austrian Empire was divided into Austrian and Hungarian kingdoms. The two states were united in the person of the Austro-Hungarian emperor, who ruled through ministries in Austria and Hungary. Ministries of war, foreign affairs, and finance were combined, however. The system was largely worked out by F. Deák, and in accordance with it Austrian emperor Francis Joseph was crowned king of Hungary on June 8, 1867.

Duane, James 1733–97. American politician. As a member of the Continental Congress (1774–83), he helped draft the Articles of Confederation.

Duarte 1391–1438. Portuguese king (1433–38), successor to his father, John I, and father of Alfonso V. Called the "philosopher king," he is noted chiefly for his aid to and encouragement of his brother, Henry the Navigator.

Du Barry, Marie Jeanne Bécu, countess 1743–93. French mistress of King Louis XV. Though not greatly involved politically, she held a position of influence in Louis's court. She was guillotined during the French Revolution.

Dubček, Alexander 1921–92. Czechoslovakian political leader whose liberal reforms led to the Soviet-sponsored invasion of Czechoslovakia (1968). Dubček fought with the Slovakian Resistance forces against the Germans in WW II. After the war he rose through Communist party ranks and in Oct., 1967, became first secretary of the party. His subsequent easing of censorship, rehabilitation of political prisoners, and program of democratization alarmed the Soviet Union, which with other Warsaw Pact countries invaded Czechoslovakia (Aug. 20–21, 1968). Dubček was forced to make political concessions to the Soviets and his reform program was gradually dismantled. Dubček became (Jan., 1970) ambassador to Turkey, and soon after disappeared from the political scene until the fall of the Czech Communist government in 1989.

Du Bois, W(illiam) E(dward) B(urghardt) 1868–1963. American writer, educator, and civil rights leader. An opponent of B. T. Washington's accomodationist views, Du Bois was a founder (1909) of the National Association for the Advancement of Colored People (NAACP). He wrote *The Souls of Black Folk* (1903) and edited the NAACP magazine *Crisis* (to 1932). A proponent of pan-Africanism in later years, he moved to Ghana in the 1960s.

Duccio di Buoninsegna 1255?–1319? Italian artist. He founded the Sienese school of art. His major work is the *Maesta* altarpiece in the Siena Cathedral.

Duchamp, Marcel 1887–1968. French-born American artist. A founder of Dada, he was also associated with cubism and other art movements of the 20th cent. He is known best for the cubist *Nude Descending a Staircase.*

Duchesne, André 1584–1640. French historian noted for his compilations of the sources of French and Norman histories.

Dudley, John, duke of Northumbria *See* **Edward VI.**

Dudley, Thomas 1576–1653. Colonial governor of Massachusetts (1634–35, 1640–41, 1645–46, 1650–51). His strict orthodoxy led to conflict with other Puritan leaders, notably J. Winthrop.

Duer, William 1747–99. American Revolutionary leader and financier. He served in the Continental Congress (1777–79) and as assistant secretary of the treasury (1789) under A. Hamilton. His imprisonment (1792) for debt is said to have contributed to the financial Panic of 1792.

Dufay, Guillaume c1400–74. Flemish composer, the leading Burgundian composer of his day. He is noted for his innovations in four-part music and musical notation, and use of counterpoint.

Dufour, Guillaume Henri 1787–1875. Swiss general. He served in the French army under Napoleon, and later led Swiss forces against the Sonderbund (1847). He helped to found the Red Cross.

Du Fu (Tu Fu) 712–770. Chinese poet. Sometimes considered the greatest of all Chinese poets, he wrote pessimistic lyrics attacking court luxury and deploring hardships of the poor.

Dufy, Raoul 1877–1953. French artist. Associated for a time with the fauvists, he developed his own personal style, produced many fabric designs, and illustrated books for such writers as G. Apollinaire and A. Gide.

Du Guesclin, Bertrand c1320–1380. French soldier and constable of France. He was called the "eagle of Brittany" for his daring exploits against English forces during the Hundred Years' War, while in the service of French kings John II, Charles V, and Henry II.

Duhamel, Georges 1884–1966. French author. His background as a surgeon was reflected in his novels *Vie des Martyrs* and *Civilisation.*

Dukas, Paul 1865–1935. French composer. His best-known work is *The Sorcerer's Apprentice* (1897).

Dukhobors (Doukhobors) (Christian Community of Universal Brotherhood) (*since 1939, Union of Spiritual Communities of Christ*) Religious sect that originated in southern Russia during the 18th cent. Made up largely of peasants in Russia, the sect refused to recognize the authority of church or state and believed in individual revelation. They developed flourishing communes in the 19th cent. but were several times forcibly moved eastward in conflicts with the tsarist government. Some 7,000 Dukhobors were allowed to emigrate (1898–99) to western Canada, where their eccentric beliefs (including refusal to pay taxes) caused sporadic confrontations with government authority.

Dulles, John Foster 1888–1959. US secretary of state (1953–59). A prominent international lawyer and diplomat, he was appointed secretary of state by President D. Eisenhower. Thereafter he promoted, and was identified with, America's Cold War policies. He was a proponent of collective security agreements (Southeast Asia Treaty Organization) and massive nuclear retaliation to counter the threat of Communism. He also backed the Chinese Nationalists and helped formulate the Eisenhower Doctrine.

Duluth, Daniel Greysolon, Sieur (Dulhut ˜) 1636–1710. French explorer in North America. He explored the Lake Superior region (1678) and northern Minnesota (1680), where the city of Duluth is named for him.

Duma Russian legislative body. Created by Tsar Nicholas II after the 1905 revolution, the Duma served as the lower house of the Russian legislature until the revolution of 1917. Nicholas dissolved it several times. (*See also* Commonwealth of Independent States, 1905–17).

Dumas, Alexandre (Dumas père) 1802–70. French novelist and dramatist, author of such popular historical novels as *The Three Musketeers* and *The Count of Monte Cristo.* A clerk in Paris in his early years, he first gained recognition (1829) with his historical plays, including *Henri III,* but it was his novels that won him enduring fame. From the 1840s on, he wrote voluminously and produced (frequently in collaboration with others) his most famous works.

Dumas, Alexandre (Dumas fils) 1824–95. French novelist and dramatist, the illegitimate son of Alexandre Dumas père. He was the author of the novel *La Dame aux Camélias* (1848), which he adapted for his play *Camille* (1852).

Du Maurier, Daphne 1907–89. English author. Her novels include *Rebecca, Frenchman's Creek,* and *My Cousin Rachel.*

Dumouriez, Charles François 1739–1823. French general during the French Revolutionary Wars (1792–1802). At first successful against Prussia and Austria, he joined Austria after his defeat at Neerwinden (1793).

Dunant, Jean Henry 1828–1910. Swiss philanthropist, the moving force behind the establishment (1864) of the Red Cross. He was corecipient of the first Nobel Peace Prize (1901).

Duncan, Isadora 1878–1927. American dancer whose interpretive dancing and unconventional personal life greatly influenced the development of modern dance.

Dundee, John Graham of Claverhouse, 1st viscount c1649–1689. Scottish soldier, known as Bonnie Dundee. He led his forces against William of Orange in an attempt to restore James II to the throne, but was killed at Killiecrankie.

Dunes, Battle of the Battle (June 14, 1658) of the Fronde, near Dunkirk, now in France. The Spanish army under Don John of Austria and Louis II de Condé was decisively defeated by the French under Vicomte H. de Turenne.

Dunkards (Church of the Brethren) (Dunkers) (Tunkers) German Baptist sect, so called for their baptismal practice of immersion. Originating in Germany (1708), they were forced by persecution to move to America (1719).

Dunkirk Seaport on northern coast of France near the Belgian border. It was the site of the heroic evacuation (May 29–June 4, 1940) of some 340,000 British and French troops trapped by the advancing Germans early in WW II. The two-pronged German invasion of Belgium (May) encircled the British and French divisions by May 20 and an attempted Allied breakout to the south (May 21–23) was defeated. With the Germans closing in and their only escape being to cross the English Channel, the British organized (May 29) what became a makeshift armada of transports and civilian craft, and every available boat was pressed into service. The success of the evacuation was in large part due to the Royal Air Force, which provided air cover for the evacuation. Though the evacuation proved a remarkable feat, huge stores of heavy equipment and material had to be left behind.

Dunois, Jean, comte de c1403–68. French general, natural son of Louis, duke of Orléans. During the Hundred Years' War, he served the Dauphin (later Charles VII), defended Orléans until relieved by Joan of Arc (1429), and helped to capture Paris (1436).

Duns Scotus, John *d.* 1308. Scottish philosopher and theologian. He founded Scotism, a school of scholasticism frequently opposed to the speculative theology of T. Aquinas.

Dupin, Amandine Aurore Lucie *See* **Sand, George.**

Dupleix, Joseph François, marquis 1697–1763. French colonial administrator. As governor of French India (1742–54), he sought to establish French supremacy in India but was thwarted by the English under R. Clive.

Duplessis, Maurice Le Noblet 1890–1959. Canadian politician. He was a founder of the Union Nationale party, which advocated Quebec's autonomy. He was attorney general and premier of Quebec (1936–39, 1944–59).

Du Pont, Eleuthère Irénée (du Pont, ~) 1771–1834. American industrialist. His gunpowder plant, built (1802) near Wilmington, Delaware, was the foundation for the E. I. Du Pont de Nemours & Co. industrial complex.

Du Pont, Pierre Samuel (du Pont, ~) 1870–1954. American industrialist. He was a director of E. I. Du Pont de Nemours & Co., established by his great-grandfather, E. I. Du Pont.

Du Pont, Samuel Francis (du Pont, ~) 1803–65. American naval officer. He commanded the South Atlantic fleet of the federal blockade against the South during the Civil War but was relieved of command after the Union defeat at Charleston, South Carolina (1863).

Du Pont de Nemours, Pierre Samuel (du Pont de Nemours, ~) 1739–1817. French economist. An adviser in the treaty negotiations following the American Revolution (1783), he participated in the French Revolution but was forced to flee (1799) to the US.

Dupplin Moor, Battle of Battle (Aug. 12, 1332) of the Scottish Civil War. Edward de Baliol, claimant to the Scottish throne, defeated Donald, earl of Mar, regent for Scottish king David II. Baliol was soon after crowned king of Scotland.

Durand, Asher Brown 1796–1886. American painter and engraver. A founder of the Hudson River school, he is noted for his engraving of J. Trumbull's painting *Signing of the Declaration of Independence.*

Durand Line Boundary line established (Nov. 12, 1893) to divide Afghanistan from British territories in India. It later became the border between Afghanistan and Pakistan.

Durant, Ariel *See* **Durant, Will.**

Durant, Will (William James) 1885–1981. American philosopher and historian. With his wife Ariel (1898–1981) he wrote the 11-volume *The Story of Civilization.*

Durant, William Crapo 1861–1947. American industrialist. He founded General Motors (1908) and the Chevrolet Motor Company (1911), the latter with Louis Chevrolet (1879–1941).

Dürer, Albrecht 1471–1528. German artist, considered one of the great artists of the German Renaissance. He adapted styles of the Italian Renaissance painters and was noted for his use of classical forms and for his technical mastery. He was famed for his woodcuts and engravings as well. Among Dürer's famous works are: the paintings *Adam and Eve* and *Four Apostles;* the altarpieces *Feast of the Rose Garlands* and *Adoration of the Trinity;* the copper engravings *Knight, Death and Devil* and *St. Jerome in His Study;* and the woodcuts *Apocalypse* and *Passion of Christ* (two cycles).

Durham, John George Lampton, 1st earl of 1792–1840. English statesman. As governor general of Canada (1838, for about five months) he investigated the causes of the rebellions of 1837 and sought solutions to the problems giving rise to the unrest. His decision to send many of those believed involved in the rebellions to Bermuda prompted his recall to England for overstepping his authority. While aboard ship bound for England, he drafted the Durham Report, which resulted in the Act of Union uniting Upper and Lower Canada. Durham died soon after reaching England. His report not only advocated the union and a measure of self-government for Canada, but also recommended measures to eliminate the use of the French language and to eliminate francophone political activity.

Durkheim, Émile 1858–1917. French sociologist, considered a founder of modern sociology. His works include *The Division of Labor in Society* (1893).

Dürnkrut, Battle of *See* **Marchfeld, Battle of.**

Durrell, Lawrence George 1912–90. British writer, known best for his tetralogy of novels *The Alexandria Quartet.*

Duryea, Charles Edgar 1862–1938. American inventor and manufacturer. Duryea built one of the first successful automobiles (1892) and introduced the spray carburetor and pneumatic tires.

Dust Bowl US region in the southern Great Plains, famous during the Great Depression. Once a fertile prairie region, the area was ravaged in the early 1930s by great dust storms that stripped off the topsoil and made farming impossible. Brought on by a combination of severe drought, poor farming practices, and the prevailing high winds in the region, the dust storms forced thousands of farmers in parts of Kansas, Oklahoma, Texas, New Mexico, and Colorado to desert their farms. Conservation measures have since greatly reduced the area susceptible to dust storms.

Dutch East India Company Dutch colonial trading company (1602–1798) that advanced and protected Dutch commercial and colonial interests from the Cape of Good Hope to the Strait of Magellan.

Dutch Guiana *See* **Suriname.**

Dutch Wars Three wars (1652–54, 1664–67, 1672–78) conducted principally by England and France against the United Provinces (later the Netherlands). The cause of the first two wars was the trade rivalry between England and the Dutch. The third war was the result of the expansionist aims of French king Louis XIV and ultimately involved several European powers. The war ended with the United Provinces intact and the acquisition of territories from Spain and others. Key dates include:

1652–54 First Dutch War.

1651 Navigation Act passed by English Parliament to curtail Dutch trade with English colonies; led to outbreak of war.

1652 English fleet under R. Blake engaged the Dutch (May), marking the opening of the first Dutch War.

1652 Dutch defeated the English at Dungeness (Nov.), thereby gaining control of the English Channel.

1653 Dutch concluded (Jan.) treaty with Denmark, effectively ending English trade in the region.

1653 English fleet victorious over the Dutch at Portland (Feb.); Dutch fleet withdrew.

1653 English defeated the Dutch at Gabbard's Shoal (June) and began blockade of Dutch ports.

1653 Dutch Admiral Maarten Tromp attempted unsuccessfully to break English blockade off Texel (July 31) and was killed.

1654 Treaty of Westminster signed (Apr.) between England and the United Provinces, thus ending the first Dutch War; England won favorable terms, including payment for losses.

1664–67 Second Dutch War.

1664 English attacked Dutch possessions in Africa and the North American colony of New Netherland, thus opening hostilities of the second Dutch War.

1665 England declared war on the United Provinces (Mar.).

1665 English forces defeated the Dutch at Battle of Lowestoft (June).

1666 French declared war on England (Jan.) but made little effort to support the Dutch.

1666 Dutch were victorious over the English fleet at the Battle of the Downs (June 1–4).

1666 English fleet victorious over the Dutch (Aug.); began to sink Dutch merchant shipping.

1667 Dutch destroyed English fleet docked on Thames River (June); followed outbreak of plague (1665) and Great Fire of London (1666).

1667 Treaty of Breda signed (July 31), ending the second Dutch War; provisions largely favorable to the Dutch, but the English gained the colonies of New Netherland.

1672–78 Third Dutch War.

1670 Treaty of Dover concluded between English king Charles II and French king Louis XIV, thus preparing the way for third Dutch War.

1672 France invaded the United Provinces (May) from the south, opening hostilities of the third Dutch War.

1672 Dutch opened the dikes at Amsterdam, flooding the region and halting French advance.

1672 Dutch fleet victorious over the English and French at Battle of Southwold Bay.

1672 William of Orange became leader of the United Provinces after an uprising against the government.

1673 Spain, the Holy Roman Empire, and Lorraine joined the war against France (and its ally Sweden); French driven out of the United Provinces by year's end.

1674 England ceased hostilities against the Dutch; France continued the war and gained several victories.

1675 France recovered Alsace region by Marshal Turenne's victory at the Battle of Turckheim (Jan. 5).

1675 Swedes defeated in the Battle of Fehrbellin (June 28).

1675 Austrians defeated French at the battles of Sasbach and Altenheim, near the Rhine (July 27–Aug. 1); French marshal Turenne killed. French retreated across the Rhine.

1676 Dutch and Spanish fleets defeated in battles in the Mediterranean.

1678 French captured Ghent and Ypres.

1678–79 Treaties of Nijmegen signed, ending the war; terms generally favorable to France; United Provinces gained back all its territory.

Dutch West India Company Dutch colonial trading organization (1621–1791). It fought the Portuguese for Brazil but was driven out (1654), and ten years later the company lost New Netherland (modern New York–New Jersey) to the English (1664). Reorganized (1674), the company was never successful.

Dutra, Eurico Gaspar 1885–1974. Brazilian soldier and statesman. As president (1946–51), he restored Brazil to a constitutional democracy and improved relations with the US.

Duvalier, François (Papa Doc) 1907–1971. Haitian dictator. Elected president (1957), he declared himself president for life (1964) and suppressed all opposition through terrorism.

Dvaravati Ancient kingdom which flourished from the 6th–13th cents. AD in what now is Thailand. It was instrumental in spreading Indian culture and Buddhism throughout mainland Southeast Asia.

Dvořák, Anton 1841–1904. Czech composer noted for his use of Slavic folk material in his compositions. He is known best for his symphony *From the New World.*

dyarchy (diarchy) Governmental system introduced in India by the British (1919). A modification of India's colonial government, it was designed to gradually develop India's capacity for self-rule. The system divided governments of India's provinces into executive councilors responsible to the British crown and ministers responsible to the provincial legislature. Much criticized and successful in only some provinces, dyarchy was replaced by complete provincial autonomy in 1935.

Dyrrhachium, Battle of Setback for J. Caesar (48 BC) during his campaign against Pompey. Caesar met a far superior army under Pompey at Dyrrhachium, in what is now Albania. After waiting some months for reinforcements, battle was joined and Caesar was defeated, at a cost of 1,000 men.

Eadgar *See* **Edgar.**

Eakins, Thomas 1844–1916. American artist, one of the great artists of the 19th cent. His works are in the realistic style and include *The Gross Clinic.*

Earhart, Amelia 1898–1937? Noted American aviator, first woman to fly solo across the Atlantic (1932) and first person to fly solo from Hawaii to California (1935). Her disappearance in an apparent crash somewhere over the Pacific (1937) remains a mystery.

earl British title of nobility. The oldest English noble rank, it dates from the reign of Danish king Canute. It is hereditary and ranks below duke and marquess. It corresponds in rank to a count.

Early, Jubal Anderson 1816–94. Confederate general in the American Civil War. He led the Southern forces in the Shenandoah Valley (1864–65) and almost reached Washington, D.C. His eventual defeat by Gen. P. Sheridan resulted in his loss of the command and cleared the way for the Union drive toward Richmond.

East Africa Geographical area comprising the modern countries of Uganda, Kenya, and Tanzania. (Ethiopia and Somalia, and, farther south, Mozambique, are sometimes also included.) The name came into use before WW II to designate the Uganda protectorate, the Kenya colony and protectorate, and the Tanganyika territory, all under British administration.

East Anglia Early English kingdom, located in what are now Norfolk and Suffolk counties. It was one of the kingdoms of the Anglo-Saxon heptarchy (*q.v.*) and its first known king was Raedwald (6th cent.). It was conquered by the Anglo-Saxon kingdom of Mercia (7th cent.) and passed to the Danish conquerors in 878.

Easter Island Chilean island in the eastern Pacific, noted for the gigantic carved stone statues found there. Since the island was discovered (1772), numerous theories have been developed concerning the origins of the statues.

Eastern Chin *See* **Jin.**

Eastern Jin *See* **Jin.**

Eastern Empire *See* **Roman Empire; Byzantine Empire.**

Eastern Orthodox church *See* **Orthodox Eastern church.**

Eastern Question Broad term referring to the series of international conflicts and crises (19th–20th cents.) brought on by the breakup of the Ottoman Empire. Control of the Eastern European territories of the Ottoman Empire was of key importance to various European powers, notably Russia, whose interest in the region dated from the late 16th cent. In the 19th cent., competing interests and growing instability of the region led to a series of shifting alliances among European powers to take over or prevent the takeover of various parts of the region. At various times the countries involved included Russia, Austria, Prussia, Britain, France, and, later, Germany. The crises were numerous and included the Russo-Turkish Wars, the War of Greek Independence, the Crimean War, the Bosnian Rebellion, the Bosnian Crisis, and the Balkan Wars. The Eastern Question ended with WW I and the collapse of the Ottoman Empire, although the region remained unstable.

Eastern Roman Empire *See* **Roman Empire; Byzantine Empire.**

Eastern Solomons, Battle of Naval battle (Aug. 23–25, 1942) in which the Americans defeated the Japanese during WW II. It was part of the battle for Guadalcanal (*q.v.*).

Easter Rebellion Revolt in Ireland (Apr. 24–May 1, 1915) against British rule. Led by P. Pearse, the rebellion broke out in Dublin, spread to other parts of Ireland, and was suppressed only after bitter fighting in the streets. The subsequent execution of Pearse and others helped bring down the H. Asquith government and paved the way for creation of the Irish Free State (*q.v.*).

East Germany *See* **Germany.**

East Goths *See* **Ostrogoths.**

East India Act *See* **British East India Company.**

East India Company, British *See* **British East India Company.**

East India Company, French *See* **French East India Company.**

East Indies In modern usage, the islands of the Malay Archipelago, including Indonesia, Borneo, Sumatra, and New Guinea.

Eastman, George 1854–1932. American inventor and industrialist. He developed a process for making photographic dry plates (1880), produced the Kodak camera (1888), and founded the Eastman Kodak Company.

East Pakistan *See* **Bangladesh.**

East Prussia Historic region in Eastern Europe and the homeland of the Prussians. It was conquered by the Teutonic Knights (13th cent.), accepted Polish suzerainty (16th cent.), and became part of the independent kingdom of Prussia (*q.v.*) in 1701.

Eaton, John Henry 1790–1856. American politician. He was a senator from Tenn. (1818–29) and secretary of war (1829–31) under President A. Jackson. The refusal by Washington society to accept his second wife led to the Eaton Affair (*q.v.*) and his resignation.

Eaton, Theophilus 1590–1658. American Colonial governor. He was a founder of New Haven Colony and its first governor (1639–58). He also drafted a code of laws for the colony (1656).

Eaton, William 1764–1811. US army officer. During the Tripolitan War (1801–05), he led a small American-backed force that sought to end the war by restoring Hamet Pasha to power. The war ended before the scheme could be completed.

Eaton Affair Incident in which US secretary of war J. Eaton was forced to resign (1831) because Washington society refused to accept his new wife, Margaret O'Neale Eaton (1799–1879). The recent widow of a local innkeeper, she married Eaton (1828) shortly before he became secretary of war. Washington socialites, led by Vice-President J. Calhoun's wife, snubbed Mrs. Eaton. Though Eaton had President A. Jackson's support, he eventually resigned.

Eban, Abba Solomon 1915– . Israeli statesman. Eban was Israel's first UN representative and first ambassador to the US. He was foreign minister (1966–74) under Prime Minister G. Meir. He lost his seat in the Knesset in the 1989 elections.

Ebert, Friedrich 1871–1925. German politician. As first president of the German republic (1919–25), he worked for acceptance of the Weimar constitution and put down uprisings (1919, 1920) from the left (Spartacus party) and right (Kapp Putsch).

Éboli, Ana de Mendoza de la Cerda, princesa de 1540–92. Spanish noblewoman and mistress of King Philip II. She was involved in court intrigues and is a character in J. Schiller's *Don Carlos.*

ecclesiastical courts Courts established by the church to judge and punish offenses against religious or canon law. During the Middle Ages, these courts came to rival the imperial or royal courts, since they had jurisdiction over all clerics; over wills; over all sacramental matters, which by extension included marriages, separation, legitimacy, etc.; and over widows, orphans, and other wards of the church. It was this broad responsibility of the ecclesiastical courts that made possible establishment of the Inquisition (*q.v.*). The power of the courts declined after the Reformation.

Eck, Johann Maier von 1486–1543. German Roman Catholic theologian, an opponent of M. Luther and the Lutheran reform movement. He was instrumental in having Luther excommunicated (1520).

Eckehart, Meister *See* **Eckhart, Meister.**

Eckhart, Meister (Eckehart, ˜) c1260–c1328. German Dominican mystic, founder of German mysticism. Though he was accused of heresy (1327) and his teachings were condemned by Pope John XXII (1329), he nevertheless influenced later religious and philosophical movements.

Eckhout, Gerbrand van den *See* **Eeckhout, Gerbrand van den.**

eclecticism Philosophical doctrine that advocates the taking of usable elements from various philosophical systems, without concern for contradictions between the systems. Eclecticism arose among Greek philosophers as early as the 2d cent. BC. Cicero was among its most famous practitioners.

Ecuador   Republic located on the west coast of South America. The population is 10,506,000 and the capital is Quito. The country has a history of political instability and has had nearly 50 presidents since it gained independence in the 19th cent. There has been a long-standing rivalry between Ecuador's two principal cities, Quito in the highlands and Guayaquil on the coast. Quito is the traditional center of the conservative faction, which favors landowners and the church. Guayaquil is home of the liberals and radical revolutionaries. Key events in the history of Ecuador include:

1000   Indian kingdom of Quito formed; later absorbed into the Inca Empire of Peru (c15th cent.).

1532   Spanish conquistador F. Pizarro conquered region.

1534   Spanish conquistador P. de Alvarado attempted unsuccessfully to conquer Ecuador, as discord among Spanish broke out.

1540   Pizarro's brother, Gonzalo, rebelled against Spain, ruled independently for nine years.

1548   Spanish forces reconquered the territory; executed Gonzalo Pizarro.

1563   Became a presidency (administrative district) of the Viceroyalty of Peru.

1809   First unsuccessful revolt against Spain.

1822   Guayaquil Conference (July 26–27); rebel leaders S. Bolívar and J. San Martín discussed joining forces, but abandoned plan.

1822   Rebel commander A. de Sucre decisively defeated Spanish forces at the Battle of Pichincha; Ecuador gained independence; region made part of S. Bolívar's Great Colombia.

1830   Ecuador became an independent state after the breakup of Great Colombia.

1830–35   Juan José Flores, a conservative, in office as president; civil war broke out between liberals and conservatives (1833).

1832   War with Colombia; Ecuador failed to gain Colombian border territories it sought; border disputes with Colombia and Peru persisted for more than a century after.

1895   Revolution of 1895; conservatives ousted and liberals began long period of control of government; many liberal reforms enacted.

1907–11   Liberal constitutional reforms made during the second presidency of Eloy Alfaro (1907–11).

1916–20   Alfredo Moreno in office as president.

1925   Military takeover; inaugurated a series of regimes headed by rival military juntas.

1931–40   Period of continuing political turmoil; 12 presidents were in office during this time.

1932   Some 500 people killed during failed military coup (Aug.).

1933   United Fruit Company set up banana plantation in Ecuador.

1934   Ecuador became member of League of Nations.

1940–44   Carlos Arroyo del Rio ruled as dictator; brought period of relative domestic political calm while becoming entangled in border war with Peru.

1941   Border war with Peru, dispute resolved by arbitration; Peru awarded most of the territory by treaty (1944).

1944   Revolution in Guayaquil returned to office Dr. José María Velasco Ibarra (who had been deposed as president by the military in 1935); he remained in office until 1947.

1945   Ecuador joined the UN.

1948–52   Galo Plaza Lasso, a former ambassador to the US, in office as president, following free elections; economy remained underdeveloped.

1951   Ecuador became the leading banana producer, outpacing Honduras.

1956–60   Camilo Ponce Enriquez in office as president; first conservative in power in over half century.

1960   Ecuador repudiated treaty (made in 1944) awarding Peru border territory.

1963   Military coup; military junta in power.

1963   Communist party banned.

1966   Military junta removed from power; civilian government to be installed.

1968–72   Velasco Ibarra in office as president, ending period of military rule; his fifth time in office (from 1934).

1970   President Velasco Ibarro assumed dictatorial powers amid prolonged fighting between students and police.

1970s   Ecuador claimed 200-mile limit on its territorial waters; seized several US fishing boats; US cut off aid.

1972 President Velasco Ibarra deposed by military to prevent holding of elections scheduled for June (Feb. 15).

1972–76 Guillermo Rodríguez Laura in power; resigned in 1976.

1975 Right-wing military coup attempt crushed (Sept. 1).

1976–79 Military junta ruled.

1977 Striking sugar cane workers rioted; 220 killed.

1978 New constitution restored civilian government.

1979–81 Jaime Roldós Aguilera in office as president.

1981 Two-month border war with Peru broke out (Jan. 28).

1981 US tuna boat seized for violating Ecuador's claimed 200-mile territorial limit; it was released after one month.

1981–84 Osvaldo Hurtado Larrea in office as president, after President Aguilera was killed in a plane crash (May 24).

1983 Hurtado devalued currency and introduced austerity measures in response to falling oil prices and rising foreign debt (Mar.); violent protests ensued; three major labor unions began indefinite strike (Mar. 23).

1984–88 León Febres Cordero, Social Christian party candidate, in office as president, following elections; Febres increasingly advocated a free market economy.

1985 President Febres personally directed attempted rescue of banker kidnapped by Alfaro Vive terrorists; banker and four terrorists killed (Sept.).

1986 Former head of joint chiefs of staff led short-lived revolt after being ousted over corruption charges (Mar.).

1987 Government suspended payments on foreign debt as financial crisis worsened.

1987 Trans-Andean oil pipeline destroyed by earthquakes (Mar. 5); oil exports halted until May 9.

1987 Week-long student riots in Quito.

1988–92 Rodrigo Borja Cevallos, member of Democratic Left party, in office as president; announced emergency economic package, favoring strong government control of economy.

1990 Former President Febres formally charged with embezzling public funds.

1991 Alfaro Vive guerrilla group disbanded; joined Democratic Left party.

1992– Sixto Duran in office as president (July); planned free market economic reforms.

ecumenical council In the Roman Catholic church, a general council called by the pope (before 1123, called by the emperor) to decide doctrinal questions and other church matters. The council's decisions must be approved by the pope before the council is considered ecumenical and its findings become binding. Of the 21 councils recognized by the Roman Catholic church as ecumenical, the Orthodox Eastern church recognizes only 7 of the councils (excluding the Fourth Council of Constantinople) held before the schism of 1054. The ecumenical councils are the councils of: 1. Nicaea, First (AD 325); 2. Constantinople, First (381); 3. Ephesus (431); 4. Chalcedon (451); 5. Constantinople, Second (553); 6. Constantinople, Third (680–681); 7. Nicaea, Second (787); 8. Constantinople, Fourth (869–870); 9. Lateran, First (1123); 10. Lateran, Second (1139); Lateran, Third (1179); Lateran, Fourth (1215); Lyons, First (1245); Lyons, Second (1274); Vienne (1311–12); Constance (1414–18); Basel & Ferrara-Florence (1431–45); Lateran, Fifth (1512–17); Trent (1545–63); Vatican, First (1869–70); Vatican, Second (1962–65).

ecumenical movement Movement seeking the unification of all the Protestant churches in the world and, eventually, the unification of all Christians. Its origins date to the 19th cent. and the formation of such groups as the Evangelical Alliance (1846). The movement became international with the establishment of the World Missionary Conference (1910), and gained momentum with the founding of the International Missionary Council (1921) and the Universal Christian Conference on Life and Work (1925). The leading force for ecumenism today is the World Council of Churches, which held its first assembly in 1948 and merged (1961) with the International Missionary Council. In the US, a number of Protestant groups have merged to form the United Church of Christ. Further dialogue among Christian churches, aimed at final reunification, was encouraged by the Second Vatican Council.

edda Ancient Icelandic literary works (13th cent.) in two parts. The *Prose Edda,* by Snorri

Sturluson, is a textbook of Icelandic poetry. The *Poetic Edda* is a valuable collection of poems giving the text of Scandinavian myths.

Eddy, Mary Baker 1821–1910. American religious leader and founder of the Christian Science church (*q.v.*). She wrote *Science and Health with Key to the Scriptures* and the *Church Manual* and founded the *Christian Science Monitor* (1908).

Eden, Robert Anthony, 1st earl of Avon 1897–1977. British statesman. He served as foreign minister under N. Chamberlain (1935–38, resigned to protest appeasement policy) and under W. Churchill in 1940–45 and 1951–55. He was prime minister (1955–57), but was forced to resign after he ordered military intervention in the Suez Canal Crisis (1956).

Edgar (Eadgar) 943?–975. King of the English (959–975), son of Edmund I. He supported reforms of the English monasteries which brought about a return to strict observance of the Benedictine rule. He was formally crowned king (973, at Bath) in the first coronation for a king of all England.

Edgar Atheling 1050?–1130? English prince, grandson of Edmund Ironside. Chosen king after the defeat of King Harold at the Battle of Hastings, he was forced to submit to William the Conqueror (1066). After taking part in unsuccessful rebellions, he made peace (1074) with William.

Edict of Emancipation Edict issued in Russia (Mar. 3, 1861) by Alexander II, freeing the serfs. By its terms, serfs (about one-third of the Russian population) were granted personal freedom and rights to an allotment of land, to be paid for over a 49-year period. Failure of this land-allotment system helped foment the Russian Revolution. The author of the edict is believed to have been Vasily Drosodov Philaret (c1782–1867), long an advocate of the abolition of serfdom.

Edict of January *See* **L'Hôpital, Michel de.**

Edict of Milan Decree (AD 313) that granted religious toleration of Christians within the Roman Empire. Issued by Constantine, emperor of the West, and Licinius, emperor of the East, it established a lasting policy of toleration within the empire. It also ordered restoration of property confiscated from Christians.

Edict of Nantes Declaration of religious toleration in France (Apr. 13, 1598) at the close of the Wars of Religion. King Henry IV attempted to restore peace between the Protestant Huguenots and Catholics by granting Protestants greater freedom. By the edict, Huguenots were allowed the same civil and social rights as Catholics, though they were not allowed to hold religious services in Paris. The edict was denounced by the Catholics. The eventual revocation of the Edict of Nantes by Louis XIV (Oct. 18, 1685) stripped Protestants of all rights and resulted in a mass emigration of Protestants to other European countries and to America.

Edinburgh, Philip Mountbatten, duke of 1921– . Consort of British queen Elizabeth II. They were married Nov. 20, 1947, and he was made a prince in 1957.

Edinburgh, Treaty of Treaty (July 6, 1560) between England, France, and Scotland, signed to ease the strife between Protestants and Catholics in Scotland. It provided for a withdrawal from Scotland of both French troops (supporting the Catholics) and English troops (supporting the Protestants).

Edington, Battle of Battle (878) in which Alfred the Great, Anglo-Saxon king of Wessex, decisively defeated the invading Danes. Wessex thus remained the only Anglo-Saxon kingdom to resist the Danes successfully and became the center from which the Anglo-Saxon kings would reconquer England (10th cent.).

Edirne *See* **Adrianople.**

Edison, Thomas Alva 1847–1931. Famous American inventor, one of the great inventors of the modern world and holder of 1,069 US patents. Raised in Michigan, Edison was an industrious youth with no formal education. By age 10, however, he had a laboratory in the basement of his home and by age 12 he was out selling newspapers. Between 1862 and about 1867, he worked as a railroad telegraph operator and during this time took out his first patent (1866), for an electric vote recorder. Soon afterward he invented the stock ticker, the sale of which financed a research laboratory in Newark, New Jersey. Following Bell's invention of a practical telephone, Edison contributed a crucial improvement, the carbon granule microphone. That invention paid for Edison's move to Menlo Park, New Jersey, which subsequently remained his home and chief research center. In 1877 he invented a crude phonograph, thereby ushering in the era of recorded sound, and in 1879 demonstrated the first practical light bulb, using a carbonized cotton filament mounted in a glass vacuum chamber. To create the market for his light bulb, Edison worked to make a commercial electric distribution system possible, focusing his attention on the development of improved generators (raising their efficiency from 40% to over 90%), and the design and building of power generating stations, cables, and meters to measure the flow of electricity. In 1888, Edison turned his attention to the possibilities of motion pictures, developing a high-speed camera and kinetograph (peep show viewer). His discovery of the Edison effect led to the creation of the electron tube, and the many companies Edison formed during his prosperous career eventually became the General Electric Company. Among his last projects was an unsuccessful attempt to develop a battery-powered car that could compete with the gasoline-powered models of his day.

Edmund, Saint 1170?–1240. English archbishop of Canterbury (1233–40). Involved in struggles with King Henry III, he managed to force concessions and reforms from Henry for a time. Ultimately, however, Henry prevailed, and Edmund resigned as archbishop (1240).

Edmund Ironside *d.* 1016. King of the English (1016), successor to his father, Ethelred the Unready. After his father's death, he led the resistance against the invading Danes under King Canute. Edmund was killed at the Battle of Assandun (1016).

Edo *See* Tokyo.

Edo period *See* Japan, 1600–1868.

Edom Biblical region, between the Dead Sea and the Gulf of Aqaba in what is now Jordan. It was inhabited by the descendants of Esau.

Edrisi *See* Idrisi.

Edward I 1239–1307. English king (1272–1307), successor to his father, Henry III. He consolidated the power of the crown at the expense of the barons and the clergy, annexed Wales, and engaged in wars for control of Gascony and Scotland. Crowned (1274) after his return from the Ninth Crusade, he conquered and annexed Wales by the Statute of Wales (1284). From 1290 until his death, he was involved in wars to control Scotland (against J. de Baliol, W. Wallace, and Robert Bruce). He established (1303) English claims to Gascony by a treaty with Philip IV. By various statutes, he limited the authority of

church courts to clerical matters, and, by the Statutes of Westminster (1275–90), he limited the power of the feudal lords. He also convened (1295) the Model Parliament.

Edward II 1284–1327. King of England (1307–27), successor to his father, Edward I. He was a weak ruler whose favorites (notably P. Gaveston) angered the barons, and he was defeated in wars for control of Scotland by Robert Bruce at the Battle of Bannockburn (1314). His wife, Isabella, with R. de Mortimer, deposed him.

Edward III 1312–77. English king (1327–77), successor to his father, Edward II. He usurped (1330) the regency controlled by his mother and R. de Mortimer, 1st earl of March, and began the long series of wars with France known as the Hundred Years' War (1337–1453). He also engaged in indecisive wars against Scotland. His reign saw the rising power of the Commons in Parliament, the ravages of the Black Plague (1348–49, 1362, 1369), the resultant labor shortages that helped end serfdom, and enactment of laws to curb papal authority over the English church.

Edward IV 1442–83. King of England (1461–70, 1471–83), successor to Henry VI. He led the Yorkist party against the Lancastrians in the Wars of the Roses (1455–85), and, after being forced to flee England (1470), returned to depose Henry VI. Both Henry and the Lancastrian leader R. Neville, earl of Warwick, were put to death.

Edward V 1470–83. King of England (1483), successor to his father, Edward IV. He was arrested and believed murdered by his uncle, the duke of Gloucester. The duke thereupon succeeded him as Richard III.

Edward VI 1537–53. English king (1547–53), successor to his father, Henry VIII. Administration was left to his regents, E. Seymour and John Dudley (1532?–88), duke of Northumbria, who ousted Seymour in 1549. During Edward's reign, Protestant reforms were introduced to the newly created Church of England by publication of the Forty-Nine Articles (1553) and the first Book of Common Prayer (1549). Dudley arranged for Edward to name Lady J. Grey to succeed him.

Edward VII 1841–1910. English king (1901–10), successor to his mother, Queen Victoria. As king he promoted Anglo-French relations (1904).

Edward VIII 1894–1972. King of England (1936), successor to his father, George V. Edward abdicated the throne when objections within the government to his proposed marriage with the twice-divorced Wallis Warfield Simpson threatened a constitutional crisis. Thereafter known as the duke of Windsor, he married Mrs. Simpson (1937).

Edwards, Jonathan 1703–58. American Congregationalist theologian, who initiated the Great Awakening (*q.v.*) revival movement in America. He wrote *Freedom of the Will* (1754).

Edward the Black Prince 1330–76. Son and heir of Edward III of England. During the Hundred Years' War (1337–1453), he defeated and captured French king John II at the Battle of Poitiers. He subsequently ruled Aquitaine (1363–72), and died before his father.

Edward the Confessor *d.* 1066. King of England (1042–66). Raised among the Normans, he nevertheless succeeded his Danish half-brother, Harthacanute. He struggled with the Dane Godwin (*q.v.*) because he favored the Normans during his reign. On Edward's death, Norman claims to the throne resulted in the Norman Conquest (*q.v.*).

Edward the Elder *d.* 924. Anglo-Saxon king of Wessex (899–924), successor to his father, Alfred the Great. He largely completed a campaign, begun (917) with his sister, Aethelflaed, to drive the Danes from England. At his death he controlled Mercia, East Anglia, and Northumbria.

Edward the Martyr *d.* 978. Anglo-Saxon king of the English (975–78), successor to his father, Edgar. He was said to have been murdered by his stepmother, Aelfrida.

Eeckhout, Gerbrand van den (Eckhout, ⁀) 1621–74. Dutch artist, pupil of Rembrandt. He was noted for biblical scenes and portraits.

Egbert *d.* 839. King of Wessex (802–839). By his victory over Mercia (825) at Ellendune, he ended Mercia's domination of Wessex and thus initiated the rise of Wessex as the dominant power in England. At his death he was recognized as overlord of Kent, Surrey, Sussex, Essex, East Anglia, and Northumbria.

Eginhart *See* **Einhard.**

Egmont, Lamoral, count of 1522–68. Flemish statesman and hero. With Count P. Hoorn, he opposed persecutions of Protestants in the Spanish Netherlands by Spanish king Philip II. Both were subsequently executed, which resulted in the outbreak of the revolt against Spanish rule in the Netherlands.

Egypt (Arab Republic of Egypt) Country located in northeastern Africa. The population is 54,139,000 and the capital is Cairo. The Nile River flows (south to north) through Egypt to the Mediterranean Sea. Civilization developed in the fertile Nile valley in extremely ancient times and had reached a high degree of organization by 3100 BC. At that time a unified kingdom was created by joining Lower Egypt (essentially, the region of the Nile delta in the north) and upper Egypt (the region south of Cairo). Ancient Egyptian civilization flourished for nearly two millennia thereafter (about 2700–1000 BC) before beginning the period of final decline. Egyptian history (up to Alexander's conquest in 332 BC) is generally divided into 30 dynasties, corresponding to the ruling dynasties reckoned to have been in power during each period. Dates, especially before 2000 BC, are at best approximations. Alexander the Great's conquest of Egypt (332 BC) marked the beginning of continuous domination by foreign powers that lasted into the 20th cent. During that time the Egyptians absorbed first Hellenic Greek, then Roman, Muslim and British cultural influences from their foreign overlords. Muslim culture, which was brought to Egypt by Arab conquerors (7th cent. AD), remains dominant in modern Egypt, which is Arabic-speaking. Modern Egypt has played an important role in Mideast affairs. Until the late 1970s it was the leading center of Arab unity and of implacable opposition to Israel. Then in 1978–79 Egypt became the first Arab nation to establish diplomatic relations and enter into formal peace agreements with Israel. Since then Egypt has continued to back Mideast peace efforts. **For more on important persons and major events** *see* **separate entries under names.** Key events in the history of Egypt include:

c3400 BC Egyptians began using primitive hieroglyphic writing.

c3100 BC Menes united Upper and Lower Egypt under his rule; built Memphis as his capital; founded 1st dynasty.

c3100–c2890 BC 1ST DYNASTY.

c2890–c2700 BC 2D DYNASTY, little-known period in which Hetepsekhemui reigned as first king; advances in technology, government, and the arts continued, setting the stage for the Old Kingdom; last king of dynasty, Khasekhemui, reunified Egypt after period of struggle.

c2700–c2200 BC Old Kingdom Period; first period of Egyptian greatness and the age during which the pyramids were built.

c2700–c2613 BC 3D DYNASTY; founded by Nebka, of whom little is known.

c2650? Zoser flourished as king; Imhotep, his minister, credited with directing the construction of the first step pyramid (of cut stone) outside Memphis; Zoser's reign also marked by advances in government and first cultural flowering; southern border established at First Cataract on the Nile.

c2613–c2500 BC 4TH DYNASTY; founded by Snefru. This was the dynasty of kings who built the first true pyramids.

c2613–c2589 BC Snefru reigned; government administration reached high degree of refinement; raids conducted into Nubia and Libya, and the Sinai said to have been conquered, pyramid construction techniques were refined and first true pyramid built at Dashur, near Cairo.

c2589–c2566 BC Khufu reigned; he built the Great Pyramid at Giza, the largest of all pyramids; his reign marked a high point in the power of Egyptian kings and he was revered as both king and god.

c2558–c2533 BC Khafre reigned; built second great pyramid at Giza; great Sphinx believed to have been carved in Khafre's image during this period.

c2500 BC Menkaure reigned; traditionally regarded as a just ruler; Menkaure's reign is believed to mark the beginning of the decline of the king's power; he built the smallest of the three pyramids at Giza; sculpture reached high degree of refinement.

c2500–c2345 BC 5TH DYNASTY; rise of sun worship, centered on shrine of sun god, Ra, at Heliopolis; during this period, central authority of the king weakened as provincial rulers gained power; scribes active and papyrus scrolls indicate detailed administrative orga-

nization of temples; Pyramid texts date from this time.

c2345–c2200 BC 6TH DYNASTY; founded by King Teti; powerful local rulers continued to rise; this led to the breakup of the Egyptian kingdom at the end of the dynasty.

c2343?–c2294 BC Pepi I reigned; the son of Teti, Pepi was forced to fight a rival for the throne he sent military expeditions to Nubia and Palestine; extensive trade with Byblos (in modern Lebanon).

c2294–c2200 BC Pepi II reigned; he succeeded to throne at age six and ruled for 94 years, according to tradition; kingdom, weakened by rise of provincial nobles, collapsed soon after his death, bringing an end to the Old Kingdom Period.

c2200–c2040 BC First Intermediate Period; kingdom divided among local rulers, who vied with one another to expand their domains, centers of power established at Heracleopolis (Middle Egypt) and Thebes (Upper Egypt), resulting in the ascendancy of Thebes and reunification of Egypt under its rulers.

c2200–c2130 BC 7TH–10TH DYNASTIES.

c2130–c2000 BC 11TH DYNASTY; kings ruled from Thebes and gradually expanded their power; Mentuhotep II began final struggle with Heracleopolis and by his victory (c2040 BC) reunited Upper and Lower Egypt.

c2040–c1786 BC Middle Kingdom Period; kings ruled as feudal lords over the powerful nobles; period marked by Golden Age of Egyptian literature and art, and flourishing commerce; hieroglyphic writing system refined.

c2000–c1786 BC 12TH DYNASTY.

c2000–c1970 BC Amenemhet I reigned; founded 12th dynasty by seizing power from Mentuhotep III in about 2000 BC; established capital at Ithtowe, near Memphis, conquered lower Nubia, advancing border of Egypt to Second Cataract of the Nile; developed contacts with Asiatic peoples.

c1970–c1926 BC Sesostris I reigned; crushed an attempted takeover in which his father Amenemhet I, was killed; waged successful campaigns in Nubia and Libya; brought about a period of prosperity.

c1926–c1897 BC Amenemhet II reigned; mines in Nubia and Sinai yielded gold and copper; contacts with Greek culture on Crete established.

c1897–c1878 BC   Sesostris II reigned; reclamation of the Fayyum depression (south of Cairo) began; later became one of Egypt's most fertile agricultural regions.

c1878–c1849 BC   Sesostris III reigned; a powerful ruler, he instituted administrative reforms and curbed the power of the nobles; built fortifications at Second Cataract to secure Egypt's southern border.

c1849–c1801 BC   Amenemhet III reigned; prosperity reached its zenith and the arts flourished; reclamation of the Fayyum continued; extensive trade with foreign lands brought influx of foreign peoples.

c1786–c1570 BC   Second Intermediate Period (13TH–17TH DYNASTIES); the end of the 12th dynasty (c1786 BC) marked the rise of the vizier, the king's chief officer of state, as the real ruler of Egypt; the viziers continued in power until the rise of the Hyksos, an Asiatic people that had gradually settled parts of Egypt; Hyksos ruled as kings of the 15th and 16th dynasties.

c1650–c1570 BC   17TH DYNASTY; this dynasty arose at Thebes and gradually restored control of Egypt to native rulers, thus ending the Second Intermediate Period; the final reunification of Egypt under native rule was completed by Ahmose, founder of the 18th dynasty.

c1570–c1085 BC   New Kingdom Period (18–20TH DYNASTIES); last period of Egyptian greatness, in which the ancient empire reached its height; it was marked by the building of magnificent temples, and the great military conquests.

c1570–c1320 BC   18TH DYNASTY, the greatest of all Egyptian dynasties.

c1570–c1546 BC   Ahmose reigned; expulsion of the Hyksos was completed (1570) and Egypt was again united under a single native ruler; Ahmose wed his sister, following practice established by previous dynasty.

c1546–c1526 BC   Amenhotep I reigned; extended Egyptian territories southward into Nubia and sent military expeditions into Asia; began New Kingdom practice of burial in the Valley of the Tombs of the Kings.

c1526–c1512 BC   Thutmose I reigned; extended Egyptian control to the Fourth Cataract of the Nile in the south and sent a military expedition deep into Syria.

c1512–c1504 BC   Thutmose II reigned; married his half-sister, Hatshepsut, who wielded real power during his reign; she later became regent to Thutmose III.

c1504–c1450 BC   Thutmose III reigned; his conquests in Syria and the Sudan greatly increased Egyptian power and wealth.

c1450–c1425 BC   Amenhotep II reigned; led successful campaigns to maintain Egypt's hold on Syria.

c1425–c1417 BC   Thutmose IV reigned; conducted successful military expeditions into Nubia and Syria.

c1417–c1379 BC   Amenhotep III reigned; built temples at Thebes and elsewhere; married Tiy, a commoner; military gained considerable influence during his reign.

c1379–c1362 BC   Akhenaton reigned; during his reign he instituted monotheistic worship of the god Aton and attempted to eliminate the traditional worship of Amon; change sparked a cultural revolution, though worship of Amon was restored soon after Akhenaton's death.

c1361–c1352 BC   Tutankhamen reigned; the boy king restored Amon worship; the religious center of Egypt was reestablished at Thebes; Tutankhamen's tomb, containing great riches, was discovered virtually intact in AD 1922.

c1348–c1320 BC   Horemheb reigned; appointed military men to government posts; appointed Ramses I his heir.

c1320–c1200 BC   19TH DYNASTY.

c1320–c1318 BC   Ramses I reigned; founded the 19th dynasty.

c1318–c1304 BC   Seti I reigned; conquered Libyans and invaded Syria in an attempt to check the advance of the Hittites.

c1304–c1237 BC   Ramses II reigned; his long reign was marked by prosperity and unsuccessful campaigns against the Hittites; he was a noted temple-builder and was probably the king who enslaved the Hebrews.

c1288–c1299 BC   Battle of Kadesh, inconclusive attack by Ramses II on Hittites in Syria.

c1236–c1223 BC   Merneptah reigned; defeated attacks by the Libyans and Sea Peoples; records of his reign contain the earliest mention of Israel, and many believe him to have been king at the time of the Hebrew Exodus from Egypt.

c1210–c1200 BC Seti II reigned; came to the throne after period of rule by a usurper; period of anarchy followed his death.

c1200–c1085 BC 20TH DYNASTY; founded by Setnakht (ruled c1200–c1198 BC), who restored order.

c1198–c1167 BC Ramses III reigned as the last of the great Egyptian kings; successfully defeated attacks by Libyans and seaborne assaults by the Sea Peoples; other groups of Sea Peoples (Philistines) settled in Palestine, then Egyptian territory; economic decline began in Ramses' reign and, combined with the increasing power of Theban priests, helped erode the power of subsequent kings in the dynasty.

c1085–332 BC Period of decline and foreign domination followed the end of the New Kingdom Period (c1085 BC).

c1085–c945 BC 21ST DYNASTY; called the Tanite dynasty; the capital was located at Tanis in the Nile delta region; priests at Thebes gained great power, and consequently little is known of the kings that reigned in this period; Egypt lost control of its Asian empire and of Nubia.

c945–c745 BC 22D DYNASTY; called the Libyan dynasty, it was founded by Sheshonk I, member of a Libyan family in Egypt; the capital was at Tanis; attempts to foster relations with priests at Thebes were only partly successful.

c745–c712 BC 23D–24TH DYNASTIES; period of civil war and political chaos; 23d dynasty (in south) recognized by Thebes; Libyans attempted to establish control over south, invasion by Piankhi (c730 BC), a Kushite, and his withdrawal; Libyans again controlled north, maintaining capital at Sais (24th Saite dynasty) until c712.

c712–c663 BC 25TH DYNASTY; called the Ethiopian Dynasty, it was founded by Shabaka, who conquered all Egypt; the Ethiopian kings had only nominal allegiance of the Libyan and Egyptian nobles in the north, however, and could not meet the rising threat of the Assyrians.

c689–c663 BC Taharka reigned; gave support to Palestine in its revolt against Assyria; defeated (671 BC) by Esarhaddon, who drove him out of Egypt; Taharka managed to regain

the south (as far as Thebes) and held it against attack by the Assyrian Ashurbanipal.

c663–c525 BC 26TH DYNASTY, also called Saite period.

c663–c609 BC Psamtik I reigned; appointed governor by the Assyrians, he launched a successful rebellion and regained Egyptian independence; established his capital at Sais, in the delta region, and reunited Egypt; encouraged influx of Greeks and thereby established Greek influence in Egypt.

c609–c593 BC Necho II reigned; he took advantage of the collapse of Assyrian Empire (at the hands of the Babylonians) to conquer Syria and Palestine; Necho was, however, defeated by the Babylonian Nebuchadnezzar II at Carchemish (605 BC) and thereafter withdrew to Egypt.

c588–c570 BC Apries reigned; he warred unsuccessfully against the Babylonians in Syria; an unsuccessful campaign in Libya led to a period of civil war and the overthrow of Apries.

c525–c404 BC 27TH DYNASTY; Egypt conquered by Persian king Cambyses (c525 BC), who founded the 27th dynasty; Egypt administered as a Persian satrapy (province).

c486 BC Egyptians in delta region rebelled against Persian rule; Persian king Xerxes I broke the revolt and reduced Egypt's status within the empire.

c465–c450 BC New revolt in delta region; Egyptians, with aid from Greeks, held out for some years.

404–399 BC 28TH DYNASTY; formed by successful revolt after death of Persian king Darius II; capital established at Sais.

399–380 BC 29TH DYNASTY; new dynasty came to power through power struggle; capital established at Mendes.

380–343 BC 30TH DYNASTY, founded by Nekhtnebf I, after he seized power (380 BC); he succeeded in turning back an invasion by Persia (374 BC); Persian King Artaxerxes III reconquered Egypt (343 BC) and put an end to the dynasty.

332 BC Alexander the Great conquered Egypt; Egypt began period of rule by Macedonian Greeks.

332 BC Alexandria founded by Alexander the Great; city later became a leading center of Hellenistic culture.

323 BC Ptolemy, one of Alexander's generals, became governor of Egypt on Alexander's death; friction between Alexander's successors, among whom the Macedonian empire had been divided, led to the Wars of the Diadochi; as the wars continued, the heirs gradually assumed the role of kings in their respective domains.

321 BC Ptolemy defeated Perdiccas in the wars and thereby strengthened his position as ruler of Egypt.

312 BC Ptolemy defeated Antigonus I, his former ally, in the Wars of the Diadochi.

306 BC Demetrius defeated Ptolemy in a naval battle off Salamis, but his ally Antigonus I failed in his land invasion of Egypt.

305–285 BC Ptolemy I reigned over Egypt, Libya, and other lands after proclaiming himself king; founded the great library of Alexandria and made the city a center of Hellenistic culture and trade; founded Ptolemaic dynasty.

301 BC Battle of Ipsus; Antigonus's defeat and death in battle, in which Ptolemy I did not participate, ended serious threat to Ptolemy's rule in Egypt.

285–246 BC Ptolemy II reigned; he enlarged the museum at Alexandria, continued to foster the arts and learning, and commissioned the translation of the Hebrew Old Testament into Greek (Septuagint); revived earlier Egyptian rulers' practice of marrying their sisters.

276–272 BC First Syrian War; Ptolemy II defeated the Seleucids under Antiochus I.

260–255 BC Second Syrian War.

246–222? BC Ptolemy III reigned; dynasty at the height of its power, with the Egyptian navy controlling the eastern Mediterranean.

245–241 BC Third Syrian War; Ptolemy gained Mediterranean coastal domains in Syria and southern Asia Minor.

221–205 BC Ptolemy IV reigned, the decline of the dynasty began with his rule.

221–217 BC Fourth Syrian War; Ptolemy IV defeated Seleucids under Antiochus I and gained Coele Syria.

205–181? BC Ptolemy V reigned; possessions in the eastern Mediterranean coastal region lost to Syria in the fifth Syrian War (201–195 BC).

180–145 BC Ptolemy VI reigned; unable to halt an invasion (170 BC) by Antiochus IV of Syria he was forced to share power with his wife, Cleopatra, and his brother (later Ptolemy VII); a war between Ptolemy VI and his brother brought the first intervention by Rome in Egyptian affairs.

145–116 BC Ptolemy VII reigned; he seized power from Ptolemy VI, married, then drove off the widow of Ptolemy VI; after putting down a revolt led by her (130–127 BC), he ruled with great cruelty and drove the scholars out of Alexandria.

116–107 BC Ptolemy VIII reigned; he was driven out of Egypt by his brother and co-ruler, Ptolemy IX; Roman influence over Egypt growing by this time.

107–88 BC Ptolemy IX reigned; he held power after driving Ptolemy VIII out of Egypt; was himself overthrown by Ptolemy VIII (88 BC).

88–81 BC Ptolemy VIII reigned after regaining the throne from Ptolemy IX.

80 BC Ptolemy X; deposed by a mob at Alexandria after he murdered his stepmother (who was also co-ruler).

80–51 BC Ptolemy XI reigned; an ineffective and hated ruler, he was deposed by rebellious Alexandrians (58 BC); he was restored by the Romans (55 BC).

51–47 BC Ptolemy XII reigned; Ptolemy XI left Egypt to his children, Ptolemy XII and Cleopatra (VII); Ptolemy XII deposed Cleopatra (49 BC).

48 BC Cleopatra began her famous love affair with Caesar, then in Egypt; he undertook the Alexandrine War to restore her to the throne, and in the fighting her brother, Ptolemy XII, was killed (47 BC).

47–44 BC Ptolemy XIII reigned; he was married to his sister, Cleopatra, and installed on the Egyptian throne by Caesar.

44 BC Cleopatra had Ptolemy XIII murdered so that her son by Caesar could become king.

44–30 BC Ptolemy XIV reigned; he was co-ruler with his mother, Cleopatra, until he was slain by Octavian.

42–30 BC Cleopatra, hoping to advance Egypt's fortunes, pursued her love affair with Marc Antony; the liaison was unpopular in Rome, especially after Antony was married to Octavian's sister; friction between Antony and Octavian (later Augustus) mounted and led to inevitable conflict between the two leaders of the Roman world at the Battle of Actium.

31 BC   Octavian defeated Antony and Cleopatra at Actium; Antony and Cleopatra committed suicide (30 BC).

30 BC   Ptolemy XIV killed by Octavian; Egypt became a Roman province.

30 BC–AD 639   Egypt under Roman rule; as a major source of Rome's grain supply, Egypt retained a special status within the empire; local government remained in hands of Egyptian bureaucrats and Egypt enjoyed relative peace and prosperity, even as Rome suffered political upheavals.

2D CENT. AD   Alexandrian School founded.

AD c185–c254   Origen lived; became leading theologian of the early Greek church.

c3D CENT. AD   Spread of the Coptic language among Egyptians; use of Greek alphabet and borrowed Greek words to replace some earlier Egyptian words.

AD c293–373   Saint Athanasius, an Egyptian, lived; led struggle against Arianism in the Christian church.

4TH CENT. AD   Land gradually became concentrated in large estates, as a result of excessive taxes imposed by Romans.

4TH CENT. AD   Christianity became dominant religion of Egypt.

AD c375–444   Saint Cyril of Alexandria lived; figured prominently in struggle against Nestorianism.

AD 395   Permanent division of the Roman Empire into Eastern and Western empires; Egypt administered as part of the Eastern Empire.

AD 476   Fall of the Western Roman Empire; Roman domination of Egypt continued under the Byzantine (Eastern Roman) rulers; Christianity flourished.

616   Egypt conquered by Persians under Khosru II; reverted to Byzantines on the death of Khosru II (628).

639–642   Muslim conquest of Egypt.

642–1882   Muslim rule of Egypt began under the Arab caliphs of the Caliphate; during this period Egypt gradually adopted Arab language, Islamic religion and culture.

661–750   Umayyad caliphs ruled Egypt as part of the Caliphate; colonization by Arabs and incentives for those who adopted Islam gradually reduced following of Christian church.

706   Arabic made official language of Egypt, replacing Coptic language.

747–750   Revolt of Abu Muslim; general rebellion in the Caliphate; brought the Abbasid dynasty of caliphs to power.

750–969   Abbasid caliphs ruled over Egypt.

829–830   Unsuccessful rebellion by Copts and others against Abbasid rule; subsequent repressive measures against Copts spurred conversion to Islam.

868–905   Tulunid dynasty in power; Ahmad ibn Tulun, a Turk, made governor by the Abbasid caliph; ibn Tulun quickly asserted autonomy of Egypt and took control of Syria; Egypt prospered.

905   Muslim caliphs restored their control over Egypt.

935–969   Ikhshidid dynasty of governors reigned; reasserted Egyptian autonomy; internal unrest in Egypt beginning in 968 paved the way for the Fatimid conquest.

969–1171   Fatimid rule in Egypt; Fatimids, a Shi'ite sect of Islam, had already gained control of most of North Africa before taking Egypt; they subsequently attacked the Abbasid caliphs and took control of Syria and part of Mesopotamia.

969   Cairo founded by Fatimids; made Egypt a center of Islamic religion.

FROM 1047   Breakup of the Fatimid empire; territories in east and west gained independence.

1099   Jerusalem captured by Christians on First Crusade; marked further decline of Fatimid power.

1167–69   Syrian armies invaded Egypt to aid Fatimids in regaining control; Saladin, a Syrian commander, made vizier of Egypt by Fatimids.

1169–93   Saladin reigned in Egypt; in 1171 he ended Fatimid rule and restored Egypt to the Abbasid caliphs; founded Ayyubid dynasty in Egypt; asserted Egyptian autonomy after 1174 and brought under his control Syria, part of Mesopotamia, Yemen, the Hejaz, and after 1187 much of the Holy Land.

1169–1250   Ayyubid dynasty in power in Egypt; Saladin divided his empire among his heirs at his death; this resulted in breakdown of central authority; to meet challenge of Christian Crusaders, last of Ayyubid rulers purchased Turkish slaves, Mamelukes, to fight in his army; Mamelukes seized power in 1250.

1187   Saladin conquered Jerusalem in his campaign to drive Christians from Holy Land; this prompted the Third Crusade by Christians.

1189–92   Third Crusade; Christians ultimately negotiated truce with Saladin, in which they were granted access to Jerusalem.

1217–21   Fifth Crusade; Christian forces attacked and invaded Egypt; withdrew following defeat in attack on Cairo.

1228–29   Sixth Crusade; Egyptians concluded treaty with Holy Roman Emperor Frederick II, giving him control of Holy Land (1229).

1244   Egyptians and Turks reoccupied Jerusalem.

1248–54   Seventh Crusade; Christians invaded Egypt and were routed during advance on Cairo.

1250–1517   Mamelukes reigned in Egypt; Mamelukes, Turkish slaves in Egyptian army, took advantage of power struggle among Ayubbids to seize power; with the subsequent collapse of the Caliphate (1258) before the Mongol invasions, Mameluke Egypt became a Muslim center.

1260–77   Baybars I reigned as Mameluke sultan of Egypt.

1260   Mamelukes defeated (Sept. 3) the Mongols at the Battle of Ayn Jalut, checking their western advance.

1261   Abbasid caliphs permitted to establish themselves in Cairo, following the Mongol conquest of the Caliphate.

1270–72   Eighth Crusade; prompted by Mameluke conquests in the Holy Land, it ended in negotiated settlements (1271–72).

1291   Mameluke armies won the Battle of Acre, driving the last of the Crusaders from the Holy Land.

1293–1341   al-Malik an-Nasir reigned as sultan; Mamelukes concluded treaty with the Mongols (1323); period of general peace and prosperity ensued; Mameluke decline began after death of al-Malik.

1517   Ottoman sultan Selim I conquered Egypt.

1517–1882   Ottomans ruled Egypt; Egypt, reduced to a province, was exploited and declined; Mamelukes continued to wield power as beys (local rulers) under the Ottoman viceroy; the beys of Egypt gained power and eventually asserted the autonomy of Egypt.

1768–73   Ali Bey in power; called himself sultan and secured Ottoman recognition of his autonomy.

1786–87   Ottoman troops sent to Egypt to reassert control over the Mameluke beys; troops withdrawn after failing to break power of beys.

1798–1801   Napoleon launched French invasion of Egypt during the French Revolutionary Wars; campaign, which ended in disaster, had been calculated to disrupt British colonial trade and threaten India; French driven out by combined British and Ottoman force.

1799   Napoleon's troops discovered Rosetta stone.

1801–05   Ottomans failed in their attempt to reassert control in Egypt; soldier, Muhammad Ali, became viceroy after a revolt (1805) against the Ottoman viceroy.

1805–49   Muhammad Ali reigned as virtually independent viceroy of Egypt; instituted sweeping reforms, undertook economic development (beginning industrialization), and laid foundations of modern Egyptian state.

1811   Muhammad Ali ordered massacre of Mameluke leaders to break the power of this faction.

1811–18   Muhammad Ali's Egyptian troops defeated the Wahhabi sect; restored the Hejaz and central Arabia to Ottoman control.

1820–21   Northern Sudan conquered; Egyptian control in region expanded under Muhammad Ali's successors.

1825–28   Egyptian forces fought against rebels in Greece, following request from the Ottoman sultan for aid; Egyptian successes in campaign brought European intervention; Egyptians forced to withdraw.

1831–40   Egyptians occupied Syria; declining Ottoman Empire unable to repel invasion; European powers, concerned about the collapse of the Ottoman Empire, forced Egyptians to withdraw (1840).

1841   Hereditary right to rule Egypt granted to Muhammad Ali by the Ottoman sultan.

1848–54   Abbas I reigned in Egypt; halted Westernization policy and opposed European influence.

1854–63   Muhammad Said Pasha reigned; instituted many reforms to modernize Egypt; construction of Suez Canal began (1859); reforms and canal proved costly and later ruined Egyptian finances; first foreign loan arranged through British.

1863–79 Ismail Pasha reigned; attempted to finish modernization program; undertook extensive building and floated huge loans, creating massive government debt; completed the ruin of Egypt's finances; campaign against Ethiopia failed; hired Europeans to command military campaigns to hold on to the Sudan (1870s).

1869 Suez Canal completed.

1875 Ismail Pasha, confronted with Egypt's worsening financial situation, was forced to sell Egypt's shares in the Suez Canal to the British, who thereby gained major interest.

1876 Debt commission established by British and French to manage Egyptian finances; Ismail Pasha forced to submit to this intervention by Europeans.

1878 Europeans appointed to head some government ministries.

1879 Ismail Pasha deposed, largely through influence of French and British.

1879–92 Tewfik Pasha reigned; European control firmly established, and French and British remained in government posts; nationalist uprisings against Europeans led to establishment of direct British administration of Egypt (1882).

1881–82 Nationalist uprisings led by Urabi Pasha.

1882 Nationalist riots at Alexandria (June 12); British bombarded Alexandria (July) and landed troops; nationalists defeated and Cairo occupied (Sept.); British began occupation of Egypt.

1883–1907 Evelyn Baring, 1st Earl Cromer, served as consul general; his long administration came to be called the "veiled protectorate" because he ruled Egypt's indigenous rulers.

1883–98 Messianic revolt in the Sudan, led initially by Muhammad Ahmed al-Mahdi (the Mahdi) wrested control of the Sudan from Egypt; Sir C. Gordon's forces massacred at Khartoum (1885); the Mahdi and successor Khalifa Abdallahi ruled the Sudan until the Anglo-Egyptian reconquest by British Gen. H. Kitchener (1896–98).

1888 Suez Canal Convention signed by European powers to guarantee neutrality of Suez Canal.

1892–1914 Abbas II reigned; failed in attempt to break British control (1893); during his reign, the nationalist movement reasserted its opposition to both British occupation and rule of Abbas II.

1898 Fashoda Crisis with France; British, completing conquest of Sudan, encountered French in region (1898); French and British subsequently reached agreement defining spheres of influence in region.

1899 Anglo-Egyptian condominium established joint British-Egyptian rule in the Sudan until (1956).

1902 Aswan Dam completed.

1914–18 WW I; war declared against Ottoman Empire; British declared Egypt a protectorate (1914) and deposed Abbas II.

1917–22 Fuad I reigned; made major gains in freeing Egypt of British rule.

1918 Nationalist Wafd party founded by S. Zaghlul and others.

1919 Nationalist revolt, fueled by harsh British administration during WW I; British troops used to quell revolt.

1921 Nationalist unrest; nationalist leaders deported as talks on Egyptian independence continued.

1922 British unilaterally declared Egyptian independence (Feb. 28, subject to major restrictions), after Anglo-Egyptian talks broke down; British presence (including troops) to continue pending negotiations.

1922 Fuad I proclaimed king of Egypt (Mar. 15); reigned to 1936.

1923 Constitution issued (Apr. 19) establishing bicameral legislature.

1924 Zaghlul, leader of Wafd nationalists in office as first premier; his brief term was ended by conflict with Britain over the Sudan (resigned when British sought harsh reprisal against the Sudan for assassination of British military commander there); political situation remained unstable while negotiations continued with British, who maintained their dominating presence in Egypt.

1928 Religio-political Muslim Brethren movement founded by Hasan al-Banna.

1936–52 Farouk I reigned.

1936 Anglo-Egyptian treaty signed (Aug. 26); British troops to be withdrawn to Suez base.

1938 King Farouk dissolved Wafd-dominated parliament; new elections returned majority of supporters of his government.

1939–45 WW II; Egypt remained neutral; nevertheless became important base of British operations and site of battles in the North Africa Campaign; British imposed Wafd government on King Farouk.

1945 Egypt became a member of the UN.

1945 Egypt played leading role in forming Arab League.

1946 Anglo-Egyptian talks broke down (Oct.) as Egypt demanded control of the Sudan and withdrawal of British troops.

1948–49 First Arab-Israeli War; Egypt joined other Arab states against newly created state of Israel; Egypt signed armistice (Feb. 24) but not permanent treaty with Israel.

1950 Wafd party gained control of elected government as political unrest increased.

1950–52 M. Nahas Pasha, Wafd leader, became premier; sought immediate withdrawal of all British forces; anti-British unrest increased and Egypt abrogated 1936 treaty (Aug. 6, 1951); British refused to withdraw and violence in Cairo between nationalists and British broke out (1952); King Farouk dismissed the Wafd government (Jan. 27, 1952) as violence increased.

1952 Army coup (July 23) led by Gen. M. Naguib but under command of G. Nasser; Farouk forced to abdicate in favor of Ahmad Fuad II, his infant son.

1952 Agrarian reforms enacted.

1953 Treaty with Britain signed (Feb. 12) granting right of self-determination in Sudan; Sudan to decide on whether to establish ties with Egypt.

1953 Republic declared (June 18); monarchy abolished.

1953–54 Gen. Naguib in office as first president.

1954 Treaty with Britain signed (Oct.); British to withdraw forces from Suez Canal within 20 months; British permitted to send troops under specified conditions.

1954–70 Nasser in office as president (from Nov.); during his long tenure, he restored political stability and became a leading exponent of Arab nationalism.

1956 New constitution adopted.

1956 Suez Crisis; Nasser was refused loan (by US) to build Aswan High Dam, and thereupon nationalized Suez Canal (July 26); Israel, responding to long series of border clashes with Egypt launched (Oct. 29) invasion of Egypt, beginning the Second Arab-Israeli War; Israelis captured Sinai (as far as the Suez Canal).

1956 British and French troops entered fighting to take canal (Oct. 31).

1956 Cease-fire arranged (Nov. 6).

1956 UN forces occupied the canal zone (Dec.), ending Suez Crisis.

1957 Israeli forces withdrawn from Egyptian territory.

1958–61 United Arab Republic; Egypt and Syria united, with Yemen joining soon after; Nasser elected president; program of nationalization in Egypt began (largely complete by 1962).

1960 Construction of Aswan High Dam begun with massive Soviet aid.

1961 Syria withdrew from the UAR following disputes with Egypt; Egypt dissolved union with Yemen.

1964 New constitution adopted.

1967 Third Arab-Israeli War (June 5–10); Israelis pushed to east bank of Suez Canal in six days; Suez blocked by wrecks, and Egyptian losses in armament were heavy; Soviets provided massive aid to Egypt to rebuild army.

1967 UN Security Council passed Resolution 242, calling for Arab recognition of Israel, pending Israel's return of occupied territories.

1969–70 "War of Attrition"; armed clashes between Egypt and Israel resulted in Soviet military intervention on Egypt's behalf; US-brokered cease-fire agreed to in July 1970.

1970 Nasser died (Sept. 28).

1970–81 A. Sadat in office as president; after years of hostility with Israel, Sadat reversed Egyptian policy and entered in historic treaty with Israelis (1979).

1971 Aswan High Dam dedicated.

1971 Sadat crushed coup attempt (May 14).

1972 Sadat ousted (July 18) Soviet military advisers and took over Soviet bases in Egypt.

1973 Sadat took over (Mar. 26) duties of premier; made himself military governor-general of Egypt.

1973 Fourth Arab-Israeli War (Oct. 6–25); Egypt and Syria launched attacks against Israel; Israelis occupied part of west bank of Suez; Arab nations imposed oil embargo on US and other Israeli allies; cease-fire halted fighting; US secretary of state H. Kissinger negotiated pull-back from Suez Canal by both sides (Jan., 1974) and thereafter Kissinger sought to further negotiations through "shuttle diplomacy."

1974 Full diplomatic relations, broken after the 1967 Arab-Israeli War, reestablished with the US (Feb. 28).

1974 Treaty with US signed; US to provide nuclear technology for peaceful purposes.

1974 Premiership restored (Sept.); Abdel Azziz Heqazi assumed duties.

1975 Suez Canal reopened (June).

1976 Sadat announced an end to friendship treaty with the Soviets (Mar.).

1977 Food riots in Cairo killed 44 (Jan.).

1977 Cease-fire (July) ended series of border clashes with Libya.

1977 Sadat made historic state visit to Israel (Nov. 19–21) in the first of a series of peace initiatives between the two nations.

1977 Tripoli Declaration issued (Dec. 5) by Arab opponents of Sadat's peace initiatives; diplomatic relations with Egypt frozen.

1977 Israeli prime minister M. Begin visited Egypt (Dec. 24–26) to continue discussion of possible peace settlement.

1978 Sadat signed (Sept. 17) the Camp David Accords, providing a framework for peace with Israel.

1979 Sadat signed (Mar. 26) historic formal peace treaty with Israel; Israelis to pull out of Sinai in phases; Egypt and Israel to establish diplomatic relations.

1979 Arab League imposed sanctions against Egypt to protest Egyptian-Israeli treaty (Mar. 31).

1980 Israeli El Al airline began service to Cairo.

1980 Sadat publicly opposed Soviet invasion of Afghanistan; Egypt trained Afghan guerrillas and provided arms.

1980 Constitutional amendments approved by referendum (May); parliament to have second chamber and restrictions on president's term to be dropped.

1980 Sadat appointed himself as prime minister (May); ordered new economic policy formulated in face of 25% inflation rate.

1980 Former Iranian shah (Mohammad Reza Pahlavi), in Egypt since Mar., died of cancer in Cairo hospital (July).

1980 Work on Suez Canal completed (Dec.), allowing passage of supertankers.

1981 Egypt ratified the Nuclear Nonproliferation Treaty (Feb.); closed deals for 8 nuclear powered electrical generating plants with US, West Germany, and France.

1981 Egypt resumed diplomatic relations with Sudan (Mar.).

1981 Riots between Muslims and Copts left 14 dead (June), as Muslim fundamentalist fanaticism increased in Egypt; authorities began mass arrests (Sept.), jailing 1,500 in three days.

1981 Sadat assassinated in Cairo by Muslim fundamentalists (Oct. 6) while reviewing a massive military parade; the assassins, Egyptian Muslim fundamentalist soldiers, dismounted from a vehicle during the parade and attacked the reviewing stand with grenades and automatic weapons, killing Sadat and 10 others; all the attackers were arrested, tried, and 5 Muslims implicated in the plot were executed (1982).

1981– H. Mubarak, Sadat's vice president, in office as president; continued Sadat's policies and did not make new cabinet appointments; his administration was plagued by a continuing foreign debt crisis and a rising tide of Muslim fundamentalist unrest during the 1980s; he reintegrated Egypt with the Arab world, but his efforts as a Mideast peacemaker were less than successful.

1982 Egypt began shipments of Soviet arms to Iraq, then embroiled in war with Muslim fundamentalist Iran; over one million Egyptians working in Iraq, and 15,000 Egyptian soldiers were fighting in support of Saddam Hussein's regime.

1982 Phased Israeli withdrawal from occupied Egyptian territory in the Sinai completed (Apr. 25), in accordance with treaty; meanwhile the Israeli invasion of Lebanon and Jewish settlements in occupied territories cooled relations between Egypt and Israel; Egypt began rapprochement with Arab neighbors and to lesser degree with USSR.

1982 Egypt faced serious financial problems as oil revenues and other income sources declined; as the world's 10th largest debtor ($16 billion in foreign debt), Egypt was ill-prepared for the sharp drop now occurring in its balance of trade; national budget further burdened by inflated bureacracy of 11 million and government subsidies of consumer goods.

1983 Sadat's brother sentenced to prison on corruption charges; released after serving only a few months.

1983 Reconstituted Wafd party recognized by government (Oct.).

1983 US aid to Egypt now totalled over $2 billion.

1984 Libyan ship believed responsible for laying mines in Red Sea (Aug.); 17 ships sustained minor damage from mine explosions.

1984–85 Kamal Hasan Ali, Mubarak's foreign minister, in office as prime minister.

1984 Riots in industrial town of Kafr al Dawar followed cuts in government food subsidies (Sept.).

1985 Egypt, now facing $30 billion in foreign debts, asked US for $915 million more in financial aid (Jan.), but received only $500 million; meanwhile Egypt temporarily abandoned efforts for IMF loan credits because of required harsh economic reforms; government cut bread subsidy and raised gas prices by 30 percent.

1985–86 Ali Lutfi in office as prime minister (appointed Sept.).

1985 Egyptians helped negotiate end to *Achille Lauro* hijacking (Oct.) after Palestinian hijackers sailed the Italian cruise liner to Egypt; US authorities, angered at Egypt's plan to simply release the four terrorists (who had killed a Jewish American), forced the Egyptian plane carrying them to Tunis to land in Italy and began extradition proceedings.

1985 Libyan agents attempted to kidnap and kill exiled Libyans living in Egypt (Nov. 2).

1985 Terrorists hijacked Egyptian airliner on Athens-to-Rome flight (Nov. 23); Egyptian commandos stormed plane after it landed in Malta and terrorist began shooting at passengers; over 60 killed in the incident.

1986 Riot in Cairo by some 17,000 conscript policemen (Feb. 25); strikes and riots by dis-satisfied textile and railway workers also broke out during the year.

1986 Egypt, in line with Arab governments, denounced US air attack on Libyan bases (Apr.).

1986 Muslim fundamentalist stronghold of Asyut torn by riots (Oct., Dec.).

1986 Muslim plot to burn video shops and take over radio station in Alexandria broken up (Oct.); Islamic Jihad group accused of plotting a military coup (Dec.).

1986 Atif Sidqi in office as prime minister, following Mubarak's abrupt firing of Ali Lutfi (Nov.).

1987 PLO broke relations with Egypt (Apr.).

1987 Arab summit effectively ended ostracism of Egypt imposed after Israeli-Egyptian peace treaty; Arab nations to decide individually whether reestablish relations; all but Syria, Lebanon, and Libya resumed relations by 1988.

1987 IMF, following protracted negotiations on needed economic reforms, granted Egypt much needed loan credits (May 15); Egypt, staggering under $40 billion foreign debt and 20% inflation rate, thus averted major financial crisis; imposed a 60% currency devaluation, began unifying exchange rates, and promised to cut energy subsidies.

1987 Egypt negotiated new agreements on outstanding loans to the Paris Club ($12 billion), the US, USSR, and European countries (Mar.–Dec.).

1987 Mubarak, head of ruling National Democratic party, reelected to new five-year term (Oct.).

1987 Muslim fundamentalists, becoming increasingly fanatical, failed in three separate assassination attempts (May–June), including one on US diplomats.

1987 Khalid Abdul Nasser, Nasser's son, fled Egypt after being accused of involvement in Muslim assassinations; later cleared of charges (1991).

1988 Egypt, along with other Arab nations, recognized Palestinian statehood.

1988 Government, fearing serious unrest, failed to implement all promised economic reforms and thereby lost IMF loan credits for the year; ensuing financial crisis left Egypt unable to pay for food imports, and sparked unrest over shortages and increasing prices.

1988 Egyptian novelist Naguib Mahfouz received the Nobel Prize for Literature.

1989 Egypt readmitted to Arab League (May 22).

1989 Hundreds of thousands of Egyptian workers left Iraq for Egypt following dispute with Iraqi government over limits on how much of their wages could be sent home.

1989 Police fired into rioting mob of Muslim fundamentalists in Assiut (June); one person killed; riots at Assiut University broke out in Dec.

1989 Sit-in at Helwan steel plant (Aug.); one killed and 600 arrested.

1988 US sent $230 million in financial aid to ease Egypt's ongoing financial crisis; agreed to delay in payments of military debts.

1990 PLO terrorists launched bloody attack on Israeli tourist bus in Egypt (Feb. 4); Mubarak, who had been promoting talks between the US and PLO, was politically embarrassed by the attack and quickly condemned it.

1990 Police killed 15 Muslim fundamentalists during riot in Fayyum region (Apr.).

1990 Mubarak on official visit to Syria (May), first presidential visit since 1977.

1990 Government imposed steep price hikes on consumer goods.

1990 Mubarak, seeking peaceful settlement of Iraq-Kuwait crisis, publicly claimed his long-time ally, Iraq, would not invade Kuwait (July); Mubarak subsequently led Arab efforts against Iraqi occupation of Kuwait and sent some 35,000 troops to join Operation Desert Storm.

1990 Rifa'at Mahjuh, the president of Parliament, shot and killed by unidentified assassins in Cairo (Oct. 13).

1990 US forgave $7 billion in Egyptian military debts in return for Egypt's participation in Persian Gulf War; by 1991, $13 billion in foreign debts had been canceled by the US and other nations.

1991 IMF granted Egypt standby loan (Apr.); other foreign loans rescheduled; Egypt to impose sales tax, minimum income tax, and 30% hike in energy prices, and to minimize state interference in management of state-owned enterprises.

1991 Boutros Boutros Ghali, Mubarak's deputy prime minister, elected UN secretary-general (Dec.).

1992 Muslim militants attacked a Christian village (May), killing 14 persons.

Egyptian-Israeli Peace Treaty Treaty signed (Mar. 26, 1979) by Egyptian president A. Sadat and Israeli prime minister M. Begin. The agreement formally ended the state of war that had existed between the two countries for some 30 years and established diplomatic relations. The treaty followed the signing (Sept. 17, 1978) of the Camp David Accords by the two leaders. This agreement culminated a 13-day conference among US President J. Carter, Sadat, and Begin and provided for a "framework for peace" in the Mideast. Both the Camp David Accords and the peace treaty were actively opposed by other Arab countries.

Eichmann, Adolf 1906–62. German Nazi official, a principal figure in the Nazi program to exterminate Jews during WW II. He escaped to Argentina after the war, was brought back to Israel (1960), tried, and hanged.

Eiffel Tower Paris landmark, built for the Paris Exposition of 1889 in the Champ-de-Mars. Designed by Alexandre Gustave Eiffel (1832–1923), it is 984 feet high.

Eight, The Group of American artists who exhibited together in New York (1908). They advocated a realistic view of their surroundings, as opposed to academism. They became part of the "ashcan" school, and were involved in the famous Armory show (1913), at which European modern art was introduced to America.

1800, Treaty of *See* **Adams, John.**

1814, Charter of *See* **Charter of 1814.**

1812, War of War (June 18, 1812–Jan. 8, 1815) between the US and Britain, largely provoked by British harassment of US shipping. During the prolonged conflict between Britain and Napoleonic France, both sides set up naval blockades and American trade suffered badly. While the Chesapeake Affair (*q.v.*) and other incidents turned Americans against the British, US response was limited to a series of ineffective trade embargo measures, including the Nonimportation Act (1806), the Embargo Act (1807), and the Nonintercourse Act (1809). Widespread suspicion that the British had provoked Indians to attack Americans at the Battle of Tippecanoe (1811) and subsequent efforts by "war hawks" (*q.v.*) in Congress led to a declaration of war by President J. Madison (June 18). There followed a three-pronged attack on Canada. This initial attack failed and resulted in the surrender of Detroit (Aug. 16, 1812) by Gen. W. Hull. The

American navy succeeded in capturing the British warships *Guerrire* and *Macedonian,* among others, in 1812, though the British soon regained control of the seas. But on Lake Erie, Commodore O. Perry captured a British fleet (Sept., 1813) and thereby made possible the American victory at the Battle of the Thames (Oct. 1813) and the burning of Toronto. In 1814, American victories at the battles of Chippawa and Lundy's Lane in Canada and an abortive British invasion of New York under Sir G. Prevost (*see* Battle of Plattsburgh) ended in retreat behind the respective borders. The British amphibious invasion (Aug.–Sept., 1814) in the South resulted in the capture and burning of Washington, D.C. But again, after failing to capture Fort McHenry (*q.v.*) in nearby Baltimore (Sept. 14), the British withdrew. Meanwhile, dissatisfaction with the war on both sides led to negotiations and the Treaty of Ghent (*q.v.*), officially ending the war (Dec. 24, 1814). News of the treaty, however, arrived only after A. Jackson's decisive victory over the British at the Battle of New Orleans (Jan 8, 1815).

Eighth Crusade *See* **Crusade, Eighth.**

Eighth Route Army Chinese Communist army, formed in 1937 and led by Zhu De. It engaged in guerrilla warfare against the Japanese invaders (1937–45) in China and worked in collaboration with the Nationalist government. The unit became part of the Communist People's Liberation Army after the war.

Einaudi, Luigi 1874–1961. Italian statesman and economist. An anti-Fascist, he was exiled (1943–45), became minister of the budget (1947), and was elected first president of the Italian republic (1948–55).

Einhard (Eginhart) c770–840. Frankish historian. He was a favorite in the court of Charlemagne and wrote the biography *Life of Charlemagne.*

Einstein, Albert 1879–1955. German-born American theoretical physicist, one of the most important scientists of all time, who developed the theory of relativity and made important contributions to the quantum theory. While earning a doctorate (1905) at the University of Zurich and working (1902–09) in a Swiss patent office, Einstein formulated three great theories: the special theory of relativity, in which he postulated the equivalence of mass and energy ($E = mc^2$); his theory of Brownian motion; and his theory on the photoelectric effect. He developed his general theory of relativity (1913–16), and achieved wide recognition (1919) when part of the theory was confirmed by independent observation. Forced to leave Germany (1933), he emigrated to the US, and was for the remainder of his life a member of the Institute for Advanced Study at Princeton, New Jersey. He was awarded the Nobel Prize in Physics in 1921.

Einthoven, Willem 1860–1927. Dutch physiologist. He developed the electrocardiograph (1903). He was awarded the Nobel Prize in Physiology or Medicine in 1924.

Eisenhower, Dwight David 1890–1969. Thirty-fourth US president (1953–61), succeeding H. Truman, and supreme commander of Allied forces during WW II. Eisenhower's two terms as president were marked by a period of general peace and prosperity, his conservative domestic policies, the Cold War, and a US policy aimed at "containment" of communism. Once an aide to D. MacArthur, Eisenhower rose quickly during WW II to become US commander in North Africa (1942), Allied commander in North Africa (1942–43), and supreme commander of Allied forces in Europe (1943–45). A brilliant organizer of military forces, he commanded the massive Normandy invasion (1944) and subsequent Allied drive across Europe, which brought an end to the war in Europe. In the postwar years he served in various military posts and, as first NATO commander (1950–52), organized these forces. In 1952 he ran for the presidency as a Republican and, during his first term (1953–57), ended the Korean War (1953), organized SEATO (1954), and attended the Geneva Conference (1955). His second term (1957–61) was marked by the rise of the civil rights movement (federal troops forcibly desegregated schools in Little Rock, Arkansas, in 1957), the Eisenhower Doctrine (*q.v.*), the Lebanese crisis (1958), the Cuban Revolution (1959), and the U-2 crisis (1960).

Eisenhower Doctrine Statement of US foreign policy articulated (Jan. 5, 1957) by President D. Eisenhower in the wake of the Suez Crisis. In it he offered economic and military assistance to any Mideast country in need of aid to resist Communist aggression.

Eisenstein, Sergei Mikhailovich 1898–1948. Russian film director, considered a pioneer in film technique. Among his classics are *The Battleship Potemkin, Ten Days That Shook the World,* and *Alexander Nevsky.*

Eisner, Kurt 1867–1919. German Socialist. He organized the revolution that overthrew the monarchy in Bavaria (1918) and became prime minister of the short-lived Bavarian republic. He was assassinated soon afterward.

ejido system *See* **Cárdenas, Lázaro.**

Elam Ancient country located in present-day Iran. Its capital was Susa. Its turbulent history as an independent, warlike state extends from the 4th millennium BC to 640 BC, when it was absorbed into the Assyrian Empire.

elastic clause Name of a clause in Article I, Section 18, of the US Constitution. It gives Congress the power to make all laws necessary to execute powers specifically enumerated in the Constitution. It therefore allows Congress to decide what other powers (not set forth) are needed (thus, the "elastic" clause).

El Cid *See* **Cid, the.**

El Dorado Legendary country of great riches sought, but never found, in South America by adventurers such as F. Pizarro (1539) and Sir W. Raleigh (1595).

Eleanor of Aquitaine 1122?–1204. Queen consort of Louis VII of France (1137–52) and Henry II of England (1152–89). For supporting her sons in revolt against Henry, she was put into confinement by Henry (1173–85). She was adviser to her sons King Richard I and King John of England. She was an important patron of literature.

Eleanor of Castile *d.* 1290. Queen consort of English king (*m.* 1254) Edward I and daughter of Ferdinand III of Castile. She joined Edward on a crusade (1270–72) and there prevented his death.

Eleatic school One of the important pre-Socratic schools of philosophy. It is believed to have been founded (late 6th cent. BC) by Parmenides, and was centered at Elea, a Greek colony in Italy. The Eleatics denied conventional notions of reality, believing instead in an infinite, invisible, changeless "Being." Principal exponents of Eleaticism were Parmenides, Zeno of Elea, Melissus of Samos (*fl.* 5th cent. BC).

electoral college In the US, the body of electors chosen from each state to select the next president. Though they usually vote for the candidate who won the majority of popular votes in their state, they are not constitutionally obliged to do so, and presidents have won elections with less than the majority popular vote. Various plans have been advanced to change the system, including election by direct popular vote.

electors Ecclesiastical and secular German princes. From the 13th cent. to the collapse of the Holy Roman Empire (1806), these princes of various German states elected the king of Germany, who then became the Holy Roman Emperor. From the late 13th cent. the electors were seven in number (confirmed by the Golden Bull of 1356).

Eleusinian Mysteries In ancient Greece, an important secret religious ritual honoring Demeter and Persephone. The ritual originated in Eleusis and was celebrated there. Initiation into the mysteries eventually became open to all Greek citizens. The ritual itself was divided into two parts: the Lesser Mysteries, honoring the return of Persephone, were celebrated each year in February; and the Greater Mysteries, honoring Demeter, were held once every five years in early fall. Celebration of the Greater Mysteries involved a mass procession from Athens to Eleusia, where a secret ritual, still unknown today, was performed.

Elgar, Sir Edward William 1857–1934. English composer. His best-known works are *Dream of Gerontius* and the five *Pomp and Circumstance* marches.

Elgin, James Bruce, 8th earl of 1811–63. British statesman. He was governor of Jamaica (1842–46) and then governor general of Canada (1847–54). In the latter post, his conduct became a model for subsequent governors general. He supported the Rebellion Losses Act of 1849 (*q.v.*), despite rioting in which Parliament buildings in Montreal were set on fire. Elgin maintained good relations with elected administrations in Canada and helped with the Reciprocity Treaty with the US (1854). Later he served in various posts in England and abroad in China, before taking on his last as viceroy of India (1862–63).

Elias *See* **Elijah.**

Eliezer, Israel ben *See* **Baal Shem-Tov.**

Elijah (Elias) *fl.* c875 BC. Biblical Hebrew prophet. He worked to end worship of the god Baal during the reign of King Ahab and his wife Jezebel. [1 Kings 16–21; 2 Kings 1–2]

Elijah ben Solomon 1720–97. Lithuanian Jewish scholar. Elijah opposed Hasidism (*q.v.*) as unscholarly and divisive. His teachings include commentaries on the Old Testament, Talmud, Mishnah, Midrash, cabala, and halakah.

Eliot, Charles William 1834–1926. American educator president of Harvard University (1869–1909), and editor of the *Harvard Classics.*

Eliot, George (Evans, Mary Ann) 1819–80. English novelist. Her psychological novels, considered among England's greatest, include *Adam Bede, The Mill on the Floss,* and *Silas Marner.*

Eliot, Sir John 1592?–1632. English parliamentary leader. Eliot championed free speech and other liberties in Parliament, brought impeachment charges against the duke of Buckingham, the king's favorite, and promoted the Petition of Right (*q.v.*). Charles I imprisoned him.

Eliot, John 1604–90. English Colonial missionary. His work with Indians in Massachusetts led to his translation of the Bible into their native language. It was the first Bible printed (1661) in North America.

Eliot, Thomas Stearns 1888–1965. American-born English poet, dramatist, and critic who was a leading modernist and one of the great poets of this century. He settled in London (1914) and there began writing his early poems while working as an editor. He became a British subject in 1927. His works include poems, such as *The Waste Land, Ash Wednesday,* and *Four Quartets;* plays; and critical works. He was awarded the Nobel Prize in Literature in 1948.

Elisha (Eliseus) *fl.* 875 BC. Biblical Hebrew prophet who succeeded Elijah in the task of ending the worship of Baal. By his use of moderate and diplomatic means, Elisha was able to gain many disciples for the worship of God. [1 Kings 19; 2 Kings 2–9, 13]

Elizabeth *See* **Isabeau of Bavaria.**

Elizabeth 1596–1662. Queen of Bohemia (1619–20) as wife of Frederick the Winter King (*m.* 1613). She was noted for beauty and for the misfortunes she suffered after Frederick was deposed.

Elizabeth (Petrovna, Elizabeth) 1709–62. Empress of Russia (1741–62) by her overthrow of young Ivan VI. Advised by her chancellor, Bestuzhev-Ryumin, she rid Russia of German influence and opposed Prussia in the Seven Years' War.

Elizabeth 1837–98. A Bavarian princess, she was empress of Austria (1854–98) and queen of Hungary (1867–98) as wife of Emperor Francis Joseph (*m.* 1854). Elizabeth was assassinated by an Italian anarchist.

Elizabeth 1843–1916. Queen of Rumania (1881–1916), wife of Carol I (*m.* 1869). Using the pseudonym Carmen Sylva, she wrote books in four languages, including *Penses d'une reine* and *The Bard of Dimbovitza.*

Elizabeth I 1533–1603. English queen (1558–1603), successor to Mary I. Elizabeth's reign saw a period of increasing commercial activity, England's rise as a naval power, the beginnings of English exploration and colonization in the New World, and a period of great literary activity. The dominant aspect of her reign, however, was the restoration of Protestantism and her struggle with Catholics at home and abroad. She reestablished the Church of England by winning passage of the Act of Supremacy and the Act of Uniformity (1559) and promulgated (1563) the Thirty-Nine Articles (*q.v.*) of the Anglican faith. The subsequent Catholic rebellions and plots against Elizabeth resulted in increasingly repressive measures against them, as well as in the execution (1587) of the Catholic Mary, Queen of Scots, whose accession the conspirators sought. Though Elizabeth agreed with France to a mutual military withdrawal from Scotland by the Treaty of Edinburgh (1560), she nevertheless supported Protestants against the Catholics there. Likewise, she offered support to French Protestant Huguenots and help to Protestants in the revolt of the Netherlands against Spain. Her anti-Catholic policies and encouragement of raids by English privateers on Spanish shipping finally provoked Philip II of Spain to mount an unsuccessful attempt to invade England and end Protestantism there (*see* Spanish Armada). The last years of her reign were marked by a revolt led by her favorite, R. Devereaux, 2d earl of Essex. (*See also* Great Britain, 1558–1603; Elizabethan Age.)

Elizabeth II 1926–   . British queen (1952–   ), successor to her father, George VI. She entered the direct line of succession upon abdication of her uncle, Edward VIII (1936), married (1947) Philip Mountbatten (1921–   ), duke of Edinburgh, and was crowned June 2, 1953. Though her role is largely symbolic and ceremonial, Elizabeth remains popular with her subjects. For more on political events during her reign, *see* Great Britain, 1952–   .

Elizabeth, Saint 1207–31. Hungarian princess, daughter of King Andrew II, and wife of Louis IV of Thuringia. She devoted herself to the poor and sick and was canonized in 1235.

Elizabethan Age Period of English history, specifically the reign of Elizabeth I (1558–1603). England enjoyed many years of general peace and prosperity and rose as a great naval power during this period. But it was most remarkable as a golden age of English literature. W. Shakespeare, E. Spenser, and C. Marlowe all belong to this time. Early 17th-cent. literature, produced during the reign of James I, is sometimes included in this period, though it is more specifically called Jacobean. Parliamentary politics also became increasingly more important during the period.

Elizabeth of Valois 1545–68. Spanish queen (1559–68), daughter of French king Henry II. She married (1559) Philip II, though she was originally intended for his son Don Carlos.

Elkhorn Tavern, Battle of (Battle of Pea Ridge) American Civil War battle (Mar. 7–8, 1862) in northwestern Arkansas, a victory for Union forces.

Elkins, Stephen Benton 1841–1911. American statesman. He was secretary of war under President B. Harrison (1891–93) and senator from West Virginia (1895–1911). He authored the Elkins Act (1903) against railroad rebates.

Elkins Act of 1903   *See* **Elkins, Stephen Benton.**

Ellenborough, Edward Law, earl of 1790–1871. British statesman, president of the Board of Control of the East India Company and governor-general of India (1841–44). He annexed Sind (1843).

Ellesmere, Thomas Egerton, baron c1540–1617. English jurist, statesman, and adviser of both Elizabeth I and James I. He participated in the trials of Mary, Queen of Scots (1586) and the 2d earl of Essex (1601), and was a champion of royal prerogative.

Ellington, Duke (˜, Edward Kennedy) 1899–1974. Black American composer and jazz musician. Having composed his first piece of music at age 16, he moved to New York, where he appeared in Harlem's Cotton Club and established a nation-wide reputation through radio broadcasts and records. He regularly toured the US and Europe (from the 1930s), became known for his contributions to American jazz music, and composed in all some 1,500 works.

Ellis, Henry Havelock 1859–1939. English physician and author. He advocated sex education and wrote *Studies in the Psychology of Sex.*

Ellis, William 1794–1872. English missionary in the South Sea Islands (1816–24). He set up the first printing press in the South Pacific.

Ellora Village in west central India, site of Buddhist, Hindu, and Jain cave temples dating from the 2d cent. BC. The most outstanding is the Hindu Kailasa temple (8th cent.).

Ellsworth, Lincoln 1880–1951. US explorer and engineer. With R. Amundsen and Umberto Nobile, he was on the first flight across the North Polar Basin in the dirigible *Norge* (1926). In 1935, he became the first to fly across Antarctica.

Ellsworth, Oliver 1745–1807. American statesman and jurist. As delegate to the Constitutional Convention, he co-authored the Connecticut Compromise (*see* Virginia and New Jersey Plans) (1787). He was the third chief justice of the US (1796–1800).

El Salvador Republic located in western Central America on the Pacific Coast. The population is 5,221,000 and the capital is San Salvador. The country was ruled by Spain until 1821. Densely populated and primarily agricultural, the country has a history marked by considerable internal strife. Key dates in El Salvador's history include:

1524–25 Spanish conquistador P. de Alvarado began conquests of El Salvador during his invasion of Central America; area later included in the captaincy general of Guatemala.

1821 Independence from Spain (Sept. 15).

1821–23 Became part of A. de Iturbide's Mexican Empire.

1823–39 Joined Central American Federation after collapse of Iturbide's empire.

1839 Republic established; thereafter revolutions regularly broke out.

1860s Commercial coffee production begun; most coffee plantations later came under control of "fourteen families."

1886 Constitution enacted.

1931–44 Gen. Maximiliano Hernández Martínez in power as dictator; he overthrew (1931) the first freely elected president in 20 years.

1939 New constitution adopted.

1944 Martínez fled as unrest spread (1944); turmoil continued in subsequent years; Maj. Oscar Osorio in power (1949–56) after military coup.

1962–67   Julio Adalberto Rivera in office after period of continuing instability; free elections restored.

1969   Soccer War (q.v.) fought with Honduras.

1970   Demilitarized zone established along border with Honduras.

1972–77   National Conciliation party candidate Arturo Armando Molina in office as president; was appointed by National Assembly after elections produced no clear winner.

1977–79   Gen. Carlos Romero in office as president, despite violence and charges of voting fraud during elections.

1979   Violence between government forces and leftist rebels flared; 23 killed when police fired on demonstrators outside a cathedral in San Salvador (May 8).

1979   Romero declared state of siege, constitution suspended (May 24).

1979   Romero deposed (Oct. 15) by civilian and military junta; junta failed in attempt to end violence and came under attack by both leftist and rightist extremists.

1980   Civilian junta members resigned (Jan. 2); new junta formed with military and Christian Democrats (PDC), following military promises for reform; right-wing violence subsequently increased.

1980   Peaceful mass demonstration fired on by troops (Mar. 18); 48 killed.

1980   San Salvador archbishop Oscar Romero shot and killed in church while conducting funeral mass for a slain demonstrator (Mar.); gunmen later killed 39 others attending archbishop's funeral.

1980   Four American women missionaries murdered (Dec. 4); US suspended aid pending investigation; five National Guard soldiers arrested for murders (1982).

1980–82   José Napoleón Duarte, leader of the Christian Democrats, in office as president, following US-backed shakeup (Dec.) of junta; US aid restored; his term marred by ongoing civil war between leftist and right-wing terrorist and government forces.

1981   Rebel FMLN (Farabundo Martí Liberation Front) launched its so-called "final offensive" (Jan.); offensive failed to make significant gains; both FMLN and government refused offers of talks.

1981   US president R. Reagan sent military advisers; increased military and economic aid.

1981   New FMLN offensive sought to disrupt electric service and communications (July–Aug.); rebels destroyed Golden Bridge, disrupting road transport between two halves of country.

1981   Grisly massacre of up to 1,000 Salvadoran men, women, and children at remote town of El Mozote and surrounding hamlets; government troops blamed for massacre.

1981   Warfare disrupted national economy; inflation hit 50 percent and unemployment posted sharp rise.

1981   Unofficial count put death toll during year at about 13,000 people; another 2,000 disappeared; 300,000 had been driven out of their homes; and over 200,000 had fled the country.

1982   Four Dutch TV journalists murdered in Chalatenango province (Mar. 17).

1982   Right-wing National Republican Alliance (ARENA, Alianza Republicana Nacionalista) gained majority in Constituent Assembly during elections; US pressured ARENA into including Christian Democrats in ruling coalition.

1982   Alvaro Alfredo Magaña named president; his administration marked by amnesty offer to rebels and halt in land reform program, which was to have converted some 329 estates into cooperative farms.

1982   Unofficial estimate of death toll in civil war put at 30,000 by year's end; some 5,000 civilians killed in 1982 alone.

1983   Pope John Paul II visited El Salvador (Mar.); during visit to tomb of slain archbishop Romero, Pope called for end to violence.

1983   US president Reagan sharply increased military aid to El Salvador (Mar.).

1983   Government forces launched major offensive against rebels (June).

1983   US envoy met with Salvadoran guerrilla representatives in Colombia (Aug.).

1984–89   Former president Duarte again in office as president, following elections (Mar., May) generally accorded as free and fair; despite continued efforts at negotiations, his administration proved unable to end the civil war; by 1988, with Duarte dying of cancer, power effectively passed to the military.

1984   President Duarte met with guerrilla leaders for face-to-face talks (Oct. 15); civil war meanwhile remained stalemated.

1985 Government launched offensive in Chalatenango province (Jan.); FMLN meanwhile aimed at disrupting the Mar. parliamentary and municipal elections.

1985 Duarte's Christian Democrats won clear majority in National Assembly and in municipal races (Mar.).

1985 FMLN terrorist attack on San Salvador restaurant killed 13, 4 of them US marines (July 19); terrorists arrested.

1985 Duarte imposed unpopular war tax and import controls in effort to shore up economy (Aug.); businesses shut down in protest.

1985 FMLN guerrillas kidnapped President Duarte's daughter (Sept. 10), demanding release of 34 prisoners; she was released unharmed 44 days later.

1986 Government troops defeated rebels on Volcán de Guazapa and attacked strongholds in Chalatenango and Morazán; rebels refused to attend new round of peace talks (Sept.).

1986 San Salvador wrecked by severe earthquake (Oct. 10); 1,500 dead and 10,000 injured; government forced to rely on donated aid.

1987 Supreme Court ruled against Duarte's war tax (Feb. 24), precipitating a government financial crisis.

1987 FMLN rebels overran military base in Chalatenango province (Mar. 31); 42 government troops killed; rebel attack on another base (May) also succeeded.

1987 Central American summit in Guatemala approved the Arias Plan for peace in Central America (June 25–26); set deadlines for halt in all wars, for end to aid to rebel groups, for instituting general amnesty, and for start of negotiations.

1987 Duarte restarted talks with rebels.

1988 State monopoly for marketing coffee disbanded; Congress transferred its authority to Salvador Coffee Council, a coffee growers' group.

1989 FMLN again unsuccessfully attempted to disrupt elections.

1989 Rebels made failed attempt to kill vice-president elect, and assassinated the minister of justice (Apr.), following win by ARENA party in the national elections.

1989– Alfredo Cristiani, a coffee grower and member of the right-wing ARENA party, in office as president.

1989 Bloody FMLN offensive began (Nov. 11); over 1,200 people killed in 12 days of fighting; government imposed news blackout as guerrillas temporarily gained control of Escalón district in San Salvador (Nov. 22–23).

1989 Six Jesuit priests killed by uniformed death squad (Nov. 16); eight soldiers arrested; news of killings aroused outrage worldwide.

1990 Spokesman for FMLN kidnapped and killed (Jan. 12).

1990 Government and FMLN representatives agreed on outline of new government structure (Apr.); talks broken off (Sept.).

1990 Military bases throughout country attacked in major FMLN offensive (Nov.); rebels used Soviet-made SAM missiles to knock down fighter plane.

1991 FMLN shot down US helicopter (Jan. 2); executed crewmen.

1991 Talks with rebels resumed (Jan.).

1991 Ruling ARENA party lost its majority in National Assembly following March elections.

1991 Government and rebels agreed on changes to the constitution (Apr.).

1991 UN sent observers to monitor human rights violations (July).

1991 Cease-fire instituted by rebels (Nov. 16).

1991 Negotiations at UN resulted in phased peace program to be fully implemented by Oct. 1, 1992.

1992 World Court ended century-old border dispute between El Salvador and Honduras (Sept.); awarded two-thirds of disputed territory to Honduras; territorial dispute had sparked 1969 Soccer War.

Elsevier, Louis *See* **Elzevir, Louis.**

El Supremo *See* **Francia, José Gaspar Rodríguez.**

Éluard, Paul 1895–1952. French poet, a founder of surrealism. He participated in the French Resistance. Among his works are *Poésie et vérité* and *Au rendez-vous allemand.*

El Zanjón, Peace of *See* **Ten Years' War.**

Elzevir, Louis (Elsevier, ~) 1540–1617. One of a Dutch family of book publishers. He founded the business in Leiden in 1583 and it continued until 1712.

Emancipation, Edict of *See* **Edict of Emancipation.**

Emancipation Proclamation Famous proclamation issued (Sept. 22, 1863) during the American Civil War by President A. Lincoln. It declared all slaves in the Confederacy to be free (as of Jan. 1, 1863) and was issued by Lincoln as a wartime measure in his capacity as commander in chief of the military. It did not apply to slaves outside territories held by rebels (ultimately freed by other legislation), but nevertheless granted theoretical freedom to some three million Negroes. The proclamation, brought about partly by pressure from Northern abolitionists, marked a change in Lincoln's policy from simple restoration of the Union (and maintenance of the status quo on slavery) to a more definitive anti-slavery policy. Formal abolition of slavery in the US was finally accomplished by adoption (1865) of the 13th Amendment.

Emanuel I *See* **Manuel I.**

Embargo Act US legislation (Dec. 22, 1807) halting all exports from the US. During the Napoleonic Wars (1803–15), both Britain and France declared blockades of each other and thereby interfered with American commerce. The Embargo Act was President T. Jefferson's attempt to use economic pressure to force both Britain and France to recognize the neutral shipping rights of American merchants. The act, even with additional legislation passed in 1808 and 1809, proved both unenforceable and economically disastrous for the US. Britain and France were largely unaffected. With New England nearing open rebellion, the Nonintercourse Act was passed (1809), resuming all foreign trade except that with Britain and France. Legislative trade restrictions were effectively ended with Macon's Bill No. 2 (Mar. 23, 1810).

Emboabas, War of the Brief civil war (1708–09) in eastern Brazil. Established settlers, called *paulistas,* fought European newcomers, called *emboabas,* who flocked to the area during a gold rush. When the *emboabas* won, the *paulistas* moved westward, and discovered new gold deposits.

Emerson, Ralph Waldo 1803–82. American poet, essayist, and lecturer who greatly influenced American thought. A Harvard student at age 14, he later traveled in Europe (1832–33), where he met such leading Romantic poets as Coleridge and Wordsworth. Returning to the US, he began writing actively (1835). He soon published his essay *Nature,* which established him as a leading exponent of Transcendentalism.

In following years, he wrote, lectured widely, and was a member of the Massachusetts literary circle that included H. Thoreau and N. Hawthorne. He gained widespread recognition in the 1840s with his two volumes of essays, which included the celebrated *Self-Reliance.*

Emigrant Aid Company New England company (*active* 1854–57) formed to promote settlement of Kansas territory by anti-slavery settlers. Organized (1854) just before passage of the Kansas-Nebraska Act, the company was designed to ensure that Kansas would not become a slave-holding state, an issue to be decided by a popular vote (*see* popular sovereignty). The company sent over 1,000 abolitionist settlers to Kansas, who later figured in the Bleeding Kansas (*q.v.*) incident.

émigrés French royalist sympathizers who fled France during the Revolution. Many joined Prince L. de Condé in setting up court at Koblenz, and most returned on restoration of the monarchy (1814).

Emin Pasha, Mehmed (Schnitzer, Eduard) 1840–92. German explorer. Named governor of a province in the Sudan by C. Gordon (1878), he was rescued by Sir H. Stanley during an uprising (1885) by the Mahdists.

emir (amir) Muslim title that was used variously for a military or naval commander, provincial governor, or other official. Though emirs who were provincial governors usually had administrative powers under the caliph, they sometimes had sufficient power to rule as virtually independent sovereigns. Muslim caliphs adopted the title amir almuminin, or "commander of the faithful."

Emmanuel Philibert 1528–80. Duke of Savoy (1553–80). He regained his duchy from the French by the Treaty of Cateau-Cambrésis (1559). He instituted much-needed reforms to revitalize the economy and eliminated foreign influence there.

Emmet, Robert 1778–1803. Irish nationalist leader. The uprising in Ireland he had planned with French help failed in 1803 and he was hanged for treason.

Emmett, Daniel Decatur *See* **Dixie.**

Empedocles c490–430 BC. Greek philosopher from Sicily. He taught, as earlier Greeks had, that all things were composed of the elements earth, water, fire, and air, but unlike Parmenides, claimed that harmony and discord caused them to variously combine and separate.

emperor   Title, derived from the Latin *imperator,* a title given to victorious generals. J. Caesar and Augustus both adopted the title to mean supreme ruler, and from the time of Nero, it came into continuous use in the Roman Empire. Charlemagne reestablished use of the title in the West (9th cent.).

Empire of   *See names inverted, as in* **Ashanti, Empire of.**

Empire style   French decorative style, a neoclassic style introduced in France during Napoleon's reign. It was marked by emphasis on classic forms and imperial grandeur. Adapted variously in other countries, it spread throughout Europe and to the US.

empiricism   A school of philosophy holding that all valid human knowledge is derived from experience. Although the concept of empirical knowledge has been known since ancient Greek times the school began its classical development in Britain (18th cent.), especially in the writings of J. Locke, G. Berkeley, and D. Hume. Empiricists oppose rationalism, with its defense of intuition, innate ideas, or *a priori* knowledge. Some form of empiricism lies at the base of most modern philosophies of science.

Empson, William   1906–84.   English poet and critic. He wrote an influential critical work, *Seven Types of Ambiguity.* His poetry, known for its wit and intellect, includes *The Gathering Storm.*

Ems Dispatch   Telegram sent to Prussian chancellor O. von Bismarck by King Wilhelm I of Prussia (later German emperor Wilhelm I) on July 13, 1870. The French ambassador had sought assurances from Wilhelm that no member of his family would seek the Spanish throne. Wilhelm refused to give such an assurance and then telegraphed a report of his conversation with the ambassador to Bismarck. Bismarck, however, wanted a test of strength with France. He edited the telegram to make it appear that France had been insulted and published it. Predictably, France then declared war on July 19, thus beginning the Franco-Prussian War (*q.v.*).

Enabling Act   *See* **Germany, 1933.**

enclosure   Process by which common lands shared by peasants were converted to privately ownership. In England over 50 percent of the enclosures were in place by 1600, but the process was also widespread on the Continent and in Scandinavia.

encomienda   System for supplying Indian laborers in Spanish colonial America (16th–18th cents.). The encomienda (entrustment) specified that a Spanish settler would receive a certain number of Indian laborers, in return for which he would protect them and instruct them in Christianity. The system resulted in great hardships for the Indians despite attempts at reform (16th cent.).

Encyclopédie   *See* **Encyclopedists; Diderot, Denis.**

Encyclopedists   (Encyclopédistes) Name of group of writers who produced the *Encyclopédie,* a great French encyclopedia of science, arts, and trades, which was important in advancing the ideas of the Enlightenment (*q.v.*). The work was edited by J. d'Alembert and D. Diderot in France (1745–72), and contained articles by many noted writers of the Enlightenment (Rousseau, Voltaire, Montesquieu, Quesnay, J. Turgot, and others), who subsequently became known as Encyclopedists. The first volume was published in 1751, followed by 27 others published by 1772, some of which sparked heated controversy. Seven additional volumes, including indexes and plates, were published between 1776 and 1780.

Endecott, John   (Endicott,~) c1588–1665.   English colonist. He was a founder of the Massachusetts Bay Colony and its first governor (1629–30).

Enders, John   *See* **Robbins, Frederick Chapman.**

Enesco, Georges   1881–1955.   Rumanian violinist, composer, and conductor known for his Rumanian folk themes. He was a teacher of Yehudi Menuhin (1916–   ).

Engels, Friedrich   1820–1905.   German Socialist philosopher who, as a collaborator with K. Marx, helped found modern communism. The son of a factory owner, he managed the family's English factory and spent much of his life (especially after 1850) in England. Engels was a leading figure at the First International and Second International, and collaborated with Marx to write the *Communist Manifesto* (*q.v.*). By his continuing collaboration with Marx, Engels greatly influenced Marxism and the theory of Dialectical Materialism. He edited the last two volumes of *Das Kapital* (after Marx's death), and his own work, *The*

Origin of the Family, Private Property, and the State, is said to have influenced N. Lenin.

Enghien, Louis Antoine Henri de Bourbon-Condé, duke of 1772–1804. French prince, son of émigré leader L. de Condé. He was kidnapped on Napoleon's orders, accused of a conspiracy with G. Cadoudal to overthrow Napoleon, and executed.

England Constituent unit of the United Kingdom of Great Britain and Northern Ireland. It is the administrative and economic center of the United Kingdom and has the largest population. For the history of England, *see* Great Britain.

England, Church of *See* **Church of England.**

England, Mary of *See* **Mary of England.**

English Bill of Rights *See* **Bill of Rights.**

English Civil Wars (Great Rebellion) Armed conflict (1642–48) between forces of the English Parliament and those of King Charles I. The war was caused by a complex of political, economic, social, and religious problems. The policies of King Charles (and of James I before him) brought an ongoing struggle for power between the king and Parliament to a head. Attempts to impose religious uniformity aroused Puritans and Independents against the government as well. In general, Charles was supported by older aristocratic families, Catholics, and by people living in the north and west, while the parliamentary stronghold lay in the south and southeast. A substantial portion of the population, especially among the lower classes, remained neutral in the conflict, however. During the wars O. Cromwell emerged as the leading figure of the parliamentary army and the army became a stronghold of Puritan sentiment. Cromwell became leader of the Commonwealth and Protectorate (*q.v.*) government created after the monarchy was abolished. The monarchy was reestablished in 1660. (*See also* Great Britain.) Key events include:

1625 Charles I succeeded to the throne; his belief in divine right of kings led to a continuation of struggle between king and Parliament which had troubled the reign of his predecessor, James I.

1626 Parliament dissolved by Charles because it had limited his right to collect customs duties and had impeached his favorite, G. Villiers, duke of Buckingham.

1628 Charles I convened a new Parliament in order to raise needed money.

1628 Petition of Right presented to Charles by Parliament; listed his abuses of power; Charles agreed to demands to get money.

1629 Charles again dissolved Parliament; step taken after Parliament continued protests against taxation, the Spanish war, and toleration of Catholics.

1629–40 Charles ruled without Parliament for 11 years.

1634 Charles extended ship-money tax, a device for raising money without Parliament, from coastal towns to entire kingdom.

1638 Solemn League and Covenant signed by Scottish Presbyterians after Charles attempted to impose English liturgy in Scotland.

1639 First Bishops' War; Charles warred with Scotland over his attempt to impose English liturgy there; Charles forced to reconvene Parliament to get funds for war.

1640 Short Parliament convened; dissolved by Charles after it demanded reforms.

1640 Second Bishops' War with Scotland; Charles was defeated and forced to agree to monetary payments to Scots.

1640 Long Parliament convened, brought about by Charles's need for money and the Scottish crisis; Parliament passed numerous fundamental reforms, including law prohibiting dissolution of Parliament without its consent; Charles agreed to some reforms.

1641 Grand Remonstrance issued against Charles by Parliament; Parliament demanded control over the army, church reform, and appointment of royal ministers acceptable to it.

1642 Charles tried to have J. Pym and other leaders of parliamentary opposition arrested (Jan.); break between Parliament and Royalists nearly complete.

1642 Nineteen Propositions issued (June) by Parliament and rejected by Charles; preparations for war began on both sides, with Royalists generally concentrated in north and Parliamentarians in the south.

1642–46 First Civil War.

1642 Battle of Edgehill (Oct. 23) fought; first major battle of war proved indecisive.

1643 Parliament secured an alliance with Scotland by promising to establish Presbyterianism as the state church in England (Sept.); Scottish troops then joined fighting.

1644   Battle of Marston Moor (July 2); O. Cromwell and his regiment (called Ironsides) inflicted a stinging defeat on the Royalists.

1645   Self-Denying Ordinance passed; all members of Parliament (except Cromwell) resigned their commands in army (Apr.).

1644–45   Parliamentary army reorganized into the New Model Army; Puritan influence became predominant in the army.

1645   Cromwell victorious over Charles in the Battle of Naseby (June 14); Royalist resistance nearly broken.

1646   Battle of Stowe-on-the-Wold (Mar. 26); Royalists beaten in this battle of the First Civil War.

1646   Charles surrendered himself to the Scots (May 5).

1647   Charles turned over to Parliament by the Scots (Jan.).

1647   Growing independent and Puritan religious opinion in the army made consensus impossible on the parliamentary side; Presbyterians began to turn back to Royalist cause.

1647   Army refused order by Parliament to disband; seized King Charles (June 4); Cromwell joined rebelling army faction, which then attempted to negotiate with Charles; army occupied London (Aug. 6) to impose policies on Presbyterian members of Parliament.

1647   King Charles escaped to the Isle of Wight (Nov.); concluded agreement with Scotland, now disaffected by the radicalism of the English Parliamentarians; Scottish armies to fight for Royalist cause.

1648   Second Civil War, brief but complex struggle; pitted Scotland against England, Parliament against the Royalists, and Independents against Presbyterians.

1648   Parliamentary forces quelled uprisings in various parts of the kingdom.

1648   Battle of Preston; Cromwell and his parliamentary army defeated the invading Scottish army (Aug. 17–19); marked end of fighting in the Second Civil War.

1648   King Charles again seized by the army (Dec.).

1648   Pride's Purge; parliamentary army, under Cromwell's control, expelled pro-Royalist Presbyterians from Parliament (Dec.); remaining members constituted Rump Parliament.

1649   Instrument of Government (temporary) issued by army (Jan. 20).

1649   King Charles beheaded after trial (Jan. 30); monarchy abolished and Commonwealth proclaimed the day of Charles's execution; Cromwell became head of state.

enlightened despot Monarch whose power, though absolute, was theoretically based on the rule of reason. The doctrine of enlightened despotism arose during the 18th cent. Enlightenment.

Enlightenment (Age of Reason) Intellectual movement of the 18th cent., centered in France but extending throughout Europe and to America. Characterized by an abiding belief in rationalism, science, and natural laws, it fostered radically new views that challenged accepted religious, political, and social doctrines. The Enlightenment was an outgrowth of the 17th-cent. advances in science and philosophy (especially the work of J. Locke, I. Newton, and R. Descartes), and many of the ideas of the Enlightenment were embodied in the American and French revolutions. The Encyclopedists (*q.v.*), *philosophes* (*q.v.*), physiocrats (*q.v.*), and numerous individual literary and intellectual figures were important to the Enlightenment. Commonly associated with the Enlightenment were: (*in France*) J.-J. Rousseau, F. Voltaire, D. Diderot, and C. Montesquieu; (*in Britain*) A. Smith, J. Bentham, D. Hume, and E. Gibbon; (*in Germany*) G. Lessing, M. Mendelssohn, and J. von Herder; (*in America*) T. Paine, T. Jefferson, and B. Franklin. (*See also* deists.)

Ennius, Quintus 239–169? BC. Roman poet called the father of Latin literature. He wrote, among other works, a history of Rome in the epic poem *Annales.*

Enragés During the French Revolution, a group of extremists who called for social justice and economic programs (including price controls and assistance to the poor) to benefit the common people. Enragés were active in the unrest in Paris (Feb.–Mar., 1793) that helped bring about the ouster of the moderate Girondist faction. The group exacted further concessions from the revolutionary government before the Committee of Public Safety ordered its leaders arrested (Sept.).

entente Agreement or understanding between two nations on matters of policy.

Entente Cordiale The "cordial understanding" reached between Britain and France (Apr. 8, 1904). By the agreement, France was given a free hand in Morocco, while British control of Egypt was recognized. Spheres of influence in Africa, Thailand (Siam), and the Pacific were better defined. Russia later joined the pact (1907), making it the Triple Entente (*q.v.*).

Enver Pasha 1881–1922. Turkish general. A Young Turk (*q.v.*), he was a leader in the 1908 revolt to restore the liberal 1876 constitution. He became minister of war, helped bring the Ottoman Empire into WW I as a German ally, and, during the war, became virtual ruler of the Ottoman Empire. He fled the empire after the war.

Epaminodas *d.* 362 BC. Theban general and noted tactician. He led the Boeotians to victory over Sparta at Leuctra (371 BC), thus breaking Spartan power. He was killed in battle during a later invasion of the Peloponnesus.

Épée, Charles Michel, Abbé de l' 1712–89. French teacher. He devised a one-hand system of communication for deaf-mutes and founded a school for them in Paris.

Ephesus Ancient Greek seaport, once located near what is now Smyrna, Turkey. A leading Ionian city of great wealth in classical Greek times, it passed first to the Persians and then to the Romans. Under the Romans it prospered as the leading city of the Asian province until it was sacked by the Goths (3d cent. AD).

Ephesus, Council of Third ecumenical council called (AD 431) by Roman emperors Theodosius II (Eastern) and Valentinian III (Western) to resolve the controversy over Nestorianism (*q.v.*). The council, under Saint Cyril, condemned Nestorius's teachings, but did so before the arrival of the Eastern bishops, who supported him. A controversy resulted and was not settled until Pope Celestine I upheld the council, excommunicated Nestorius, and won the support of Theodosius.

ephor Name for a magistrate of Sparta and other Dorian cities. A board of five ephors was elected annually, and, though functions changed over the centuries, they were primarily elected as overseers of the dual kings of Sparta. Ephors figured in Spartan government from the 8th cent. BC. Eliminated (c227 BC) by Cleomenes III, the office was later restored.

Ephorus c405–330 BC. Greek historian who wrote a universal history of Greece, arranged by topics. Only fragments remain, but he was the chief source for the historian Diodorus of Sicily, much of whose work survives.

Epictetus (Flavius Arrian) AD 55?–135?. Greek Stoic philosopher. A freed slave, Epictetus taught that salvation lay in acceptance of God's will and concern for the common welfare. He wrote nothing, and his teachings were set down by his pupil Flavius Arrian.

Epicureanism Greek school of philosophy founded (after 306 BC) by Epicurus. It held that the chief aim of life was to experience pleasure and avoid pain. Epicurus himself taught that such an end was to be achieved by prudence and moderation, but this aspect of his teaching was not always observed by his followers. Epicureanism anticipated both modern materialism and modern utilitarianism.

Epicurus 341–270 BC. Greek philosopher who taught that happiness and pleasure are the supreme moral good. However, he also advised honor and restraint, principles that were overlooked by his enthusiastic followers.

Épinay, Louise de la Live d' 1726–83. French literary figure during the Enlightenment. She was a friend and patroness of D. Diderot, J.-J. Rousseau, and others.

Epiphanes, Ptolemy V *See* **Ptolemy V.**

Epirus Ancient Greek country on the Ionian Sea in what is now northwest Greece and southern Albania. It reached the height of its power under King Pyrrhus (3d cent. BC), but fell to the Romans in the third Macedonian War (171–168 BC).

Episcopal church, Protestant *See* **Protestant Episcopal church.**

Epoch of Civil Wars In Colombian history, a period (1867–80) of civil war between liberals, who sought a democratic federal government free of clerical domination, and conservatives, who advocated a strong central government and a prominent position for the church. The struggle ended (1880) with the election of Rafael Núñez (1825–94), who formed a coalition of conservatives and moderates. As president (1880–82, 1884–94), he at first introduced liberal reforms, but he also strengthened the central government and the church's position within it.

Epstein, Sir Jacob 1880–1959. American-born sculptor. His works are massive and were often controversial; his *Strand Statues* were removed

(1937) from the British Medical Building in London.

equal-field system Chinese system for land distribution and taxation established in 485 BC and later also adopted in Japan. Each adult peasant was allotted a specified amount of land, most of which reverted to the government on his death. The system disappeared in China and Japan by the 8th cent. AD.

Equal Rights Amendment *See* **feminism.**

Equatorial Africa, French *See* **French Equatorial Africa.**

Equatorial Guinea (*formerly* Spanish Guinea) West African republic (*pop.* 360,000) whose agricultural economy is based primarily on cocoa and coffee. The capital is Malabo. Discovered by the Portuguese in 1471, the area was ceded to the Spanish in 1778. The British later settled some freed slaves there, and the Cubans set up a penal colony (19th cent.). A Franco-Spanish treaty defined the boundaries (1900) of this Spanish possession. Independence was proclaimed on Oct. 12, 1968, and subsequently President Francisco Marcias Nguema instituted a harsh dictatorship. Lt. Col. Teodoro Obiang Nguema Mbasogo seized power (Aug. 3, 1979) and suspended the Constitution. A new constitution was adopted in 1982, as part of a move toward eventual civilian government. Opposition to Obiang Nguema's government and attempted coups continued through the 1980s, and in 1991 a new constitution provided for formation of political parties. However, provisions also allowed for the indefinite extension of the president's term.

equites Originally, the Roman cavalry. The "equites" came to be the designation for the wealthiest members of Roman society who were also politically inactive and, after the 1st cent. BC, formed a distinct class charged with administrative and financial matters. By the 1st cent. BC, equites performed some political tasks, such as serving on juries, and during the early empire, their role in government was greatly expanded.

ERA *See* **feminism.**

era of good feeling In US history, a term used to describe the period 1817–24, when, with the decline of the Federalist party, the Democratic Republican policies went unchallenged and sectionalism decreased. J. Monroe was president during this period.

Erasmus (Desiderius ˜) 1466?–1536. Dutch theologian and one of the great humanist scholars.

Ordained a Roman Catholic priest (1492), he soon came to oppose the pedantry of scholastic theologians. He traveled widely throughout Europe (settling in Basel after 1521) and, through his critical and satirical works, became a leading figure among the circle of humanist thinkers there. He remained within the Catholic church, however, and, after refusing to join M. Luther's movement for radical reforms, came to oppose him openly. Among Erasmus's many important works are his edition of the *New Testament,* editions of Latin and Greek classics, and his critical pieces, including *The Praise of Folly* and *Colloquies.*

Erastianism *See* **Erastus, Thomas.**

Erastus, Thomas 1524–83. Swiss physician and theologian. A supporter of Zwingli during the Protestant Reformation, Erastus opposed Calvinists' efforts to impose their system of church government at Heidelberg (in modern Germany) and was excommunicated for two years. He wrote a paper (published posthumously) arguing for secular punishment of sins (as opposed to divine excommunication), which gave rise to a movement called Erastianism in the 17th cent. This movement advocated supremacy of the state over the church.

Erato In Greek religion, the Muse of erotic poetry.

Eratosthenes c275–c195 BC. Greek scientist, astronomer, and poet. He was the first to measure the earth's circumference and tilt of its axis.

Erebus In Greek religion, son of Chaos, husband of Night, and father of Day. He was darkness personified.

Erech (Uruk) Ancient Mesopotamian city located in what is now Iraq. Founded about 5000 BC, it was the site of temples of the Sumerian goddess Inanna and the god Anu.

Erechtheum Ionic temple on the Athenian Acropolis. Built between 421 and 405 BC, and designed by Mnesicles, it is known for its complexity of design and the technical mastery of its detail.

Eretria Ancient Greek city, once located on the island of Euboea, Greece. Eretria was destroyed by Darius (490 BC) for supporting the Ionian revolt in the years leading up to the Persian Wars (*q.v.*). Though resettled by Athens, it never regained its previous influence.

Erfurt Parliament Meeting (Mar. 20, 1850) between Prussia and a number of lesser German states to consider Prussia's plan for a union of German states, dominated by Prussia and Austria. Austria opposed the plan, however, and Prussia was forced by threat of war to withdraw it. The withdrawal was made in the "Punctation {or humiliation} of Olmütz" (Nov. 29, 1850). This was a formal agreement signed by Prussia accepting the existing German Confederation (dominated by Austria).

Erhard, Ludwig 1897–77. German statesman. He planned for the postwar economic recovery in West Germany and became its economics minister (1949). He succeeded K. Adenauer as chancellor (1963–66) and established a policy of assuring social welfare of all citizens while actively promoting private enterprise.

Eric VII (Eric of Pomerania) c1381–1459. King of Norway (1389–1439), Sweden (1412–39), and Denmark (1412–39). He ruled in a period of internal unrest and was deposed in all three countries (1439).

Eric IX *d.* 1160. King of Sweden (1150–60). He led a crusade against Finland (1157) to force the Finns to accept baptism. He was killed while there and later became patron saint of Sweden.

Eric XIV 1533–77. King of Sweden (1560–68), successor to his father, Gustavus I. An ineffective ruler, he was deposed and imprisoned by his brother, John.

Eric of Pomerania *See* **Eric VII.**

Ericson, Leif *See* **Leif Ericson.**

Ericsson, John 1803–89. Swedish engineer. He invented the screw propeller (1836) and built the Union ironclad *Monitor,* which fought (1862) the Confederate ironclad *Merrimac* during the American Civil War.

Eric the Red *fl.* 10th cent. Norse explorer. On being exiled from Iceland, he explored Greenland and founded the first colony there (c986), near the modern Julianehaab.

Eridu Ancient Sumerian city, south of Ur in modern Iraq. It was founded between 7000 and 5000 BC and is considered the oldest known city in Sumer. It was the seat of the water god Ea.

Erie Indians North American Indian tribe. They inhabited the Lake Erie region in the present states of New York, Pennsylvania, and Ohio. In 1656 the Erie were almost annihilated by the Iroquois, the survivors being assimilated into the Iroquois tribes.

Ermak *See* **Yermak.**

Ernest Augustus of Hanover *See* **George V.**

Ernst, Max 1891–1976. German artist. He was a follower of the Dada movement and a founder of surrealism, known for his work in collage and other mediums.

Erskine, Thomas, 1st baron 1750–1823. Scottish jurist, noted defense counsel during a wave of treason and sedition trials in Britain brought on by upheavals of the French Revolution. T. Paine was among his clients (1792).

Erzberger, Matthias 1875–1921. German statesman and leader of the Catholic Center party. He led the delegation that signed the armistice ending WW I (1918). He was assassinated by nationalists.

Esarhaddon King of Assyria (681–669 BC), Successor to his father, Sennacherib. He conquered the Chaldaeans and the Egyptians (c670 BC) and built the great palace at Ninevah.

Eskimo (Inuit) A people who are the chief inhabitants of the Arctic regions in northeast Siberia and from the Bering Sea to Greenland. They are of uncertain, but likely Asian, origin, and had ranged as far east as Greenland by the 13th cent.

Espartero, Baldomero 1792–1879. Spanish general and statesman. He won important victories for Isabella II in the Carlist War (1833–39), became regent (1841–43), and was prime minister (1854–56).

Esperanto Artificial international language. Esperanto was invented (1887) by Ludwig Zamenhof (1859–1917). It has its roots in the Romance languages, its words are spelled phonetically, and it utilizes a simple grammatical structure.

Espy, James Pollard 1785–1860. American meteorologist. In *Philosophy of Storms* he advanced what is said to be the first valid explanation of cloud formation.

Essad Pasha 1863–1920. Albanian political leader. He joined the Young Turks and was Albanian deputy in the Turkish Parliament. During WW I, he was dictator (1914–16) of newly created Albania. He fled the country after being defeated by the Austrians in the war.

Essex, Robert Devereux, 2d earl of 1567–1601. English courtier and favorite of Elizabeth I. He was a commander in the fighting that led to the sack of Cádiz (1596). Sent to Ireland (1599) to put down a rebellion by the earl of Tyrone, he concluded a truce (against the queen's wishes) and suddenly found himself in disfavor. He made a rash attempt (1601) at ousting the queen's ministry by force, but the plot was uncovered and he was executed.

Essex Junto Extremist faction of the American Federalist party, so nicknamed by J. Hancock because most of its members came from Essex County, Massachusetts. It was prominent in the calling (1814) of the secessionist Hartford Convention (*q.v.*).

Estaing, Charles Hector, comte d' 1729–94. French admiral. He commanded a French fleet (1778–80) in support of the colonists during the American Revolution (1775–83), and was guillotined during the French Revolution (1789–99).

Este Italian princely family that ruled Ferrara (1240–1597) and Modena (1288–1796). They were noted patrons of the arts. Azzo d'Este II (996–1097) was the founder of the line, which ended with the death of Ercole III Rinaldo (1727–1803).

Esterházy Hungarian noble family. Ferenc Zerházy (1563–94) took the name when he became baron of Galantha, and the line includes soldiers, art patrons, and diplomats. Prince Nikolaus Joseph (1714–90) was patron to J. Haydn for 30 years.

Esterhazy, Ferdinand Walsin 1847–1923. French army officer involved in the Dreyfus Affair (*q.v.*). He sold military documents to the Germans, for which a French Jew, Capt. A. Dreyfus, was convicted. Esterhazy confessed in 1899.

esthetics *See* aesthetics.

Estienne, Henri II 1531?–98. French-born Swiss printer. Estienne continued his family's successful printing business. A distinguished scholar, he was renowned for his editing of classical works particularly *Thesaurus Graecae linguae.*

Estienne, Robert 1498?–1559. French printer and scholar. Robert headed the family printing business and was royal printer to Francis I. He was especially noted for his Bibles and his editions of Greek and Roman classics.

Estigarribia, José *See* Chaco War.

Estonia (Republic of Estonia) Independent state and formerly a constituent republic of the USSR, located on the Baltic Sea. The population is 1,600,000 and the capital is Tallinn. The Danes conquered Estonia (1219), and the Teutonic Knights ruled it from the 14th to the 16th cents. Sweden subsequently controlled the region until 1721, when Estonia passed to Russia. It became an independent republic (Feb. 24, 1918) amid the upheavals of the Russian Revolution and

WW I, and established its independence following the Baltic Wars of Liberation (*q.v.*), when the USSR recognized Estonian independence by the Treaty of Tartu (Feb. 2, 1920). Economic problems brought on by the Great Depression and reduced trade with the USSR brought unrest and a coup in Mar., 1934, but in 1938 a presidential system of government was established. The 1939 pact between the USSR and Germany contained a secret provision for the reoccupation of Estonia and Latvia and a month later Estonia was forced to allow stationing of Soviet troops in the country. Estonia was reannexed by the USSR (Aug. 3, 1940). The Soviets instituted a harsh regime and began deporting huge numbers of Estonians to Siberia (over 10,000 were arrested for deportation on the night of June 14, 1941 alone). Nazi Germany occupied Estonia 1941–44, and the USSR quickly reestablished authoritarian control over the region after the German surrender. The "Forest Brethren," armed guerrillas, fought against the Soviets until the 1950s. During the 1940s and 1950s heavy industry was developed in the region. By the 1970s environmental issues had become a focus of opposition to Soviet rule, and Soviet leader M. Gorbachev's policy of openness resulted in increasing public protest and support for anti-Soviet opposition during the 1980s. Then in Dec., 1988, the Estonian Supreme Soviet declared its sovereignty, restating its position after the USSR voided the declaration. In 1990 Estonia declared that the transition period to Estonian independence had begun (Mar.), held elections for a prime minister (Apr.), and adopted the country's current name (May). As the USSR attempted to reestablish control in Lithuania and Latvia, Estonian voters overwhelmingly approved a referendum on independence. During the Soviet coup (Aug., 1991), Soviet troops occupied parts of Tallinn, but the Estonian government declared immediate independence nevertheless (Aug. 20). The crumbling USSR government recognized Estonian independence (Sept. 6). Estonia joined the UN in Sept., 1991.

Estonian Revolt of 1343 *See* Saint George's Day Revolt.

Estrées, Gabrielle d' 1573–99. Mistress of King Henry IV of France. Their three children were legitimized and became the founders of the Vendôme line.

Ethelred *See* Aethelred.

Ethical Culture movement   A nonsectarian movement founded by F. Adler (1876) in New York City. It seeks the advancement of moral systems based on ethics rather than on religious doctrine.

ethics   Branch of philosophy concerned with good and evil as they relate to human conduct. Among the ancient Greeks, Socrates equated virtue with knowledge, while both Plato and Aristotle grounded it in the nature of humanity. Aristotle further held that virtue contributed to achievement of man's proper end and advocated following the "golden mean" to attain it. The Judeo-Christian tradition equated the good with the will of God, and, in the teachings of such philosophers as Saint Thomas Aquinas (13th cent. AD), its attainment was linked with the realization of humanity's proper end. I. Kant (18th cent.), with his categorical imperative, tried to establish an absolute ethical standard independent of religion. Philosophers of the rationalist school grounded ethics in the human conscience, while empiricists tied it to human experience.

Ethiopia (*formerly* Abyssinia)   A Socialist state located in northeast Africa, and bordered on the north by the Red Sea. The population is 51,375,000 and the capital is Addis Ababa. Ethiopia has one of Africa's longest recorded histories; by tradition Ethiopia traces its government back to about the 11th cent. BC and to the rule of King Menelik I, believed to be the son of Solomon and Sheba. The region was early dominated by Egypt and, in the 8th cent. BC, Ethiopians conquered much of Egypt and controlled it to about the 7th cent. BC. In modern times Ethiopia has been ravaged by famine and a prolonged civil war. A UN-backed peace agreement was agreed to in 1991. Key dates in Ethiopia's history include:

1ST CENT. AD   Kingdom of Aksum flourished in region; recorded history of Ethiopia began.

4TH CENT. AD   Bishop Frumentius introduced Christianity.

6TH CENT. AD   Conquered what is now Yemen in Arabia; period of commercial prosperity and cultural flowering followed.

650   Muslims drove Ethiopians from Arabia; cut off from rest of world by Muslim conquest of North Africa, Ethiopia sank into obscurity for a thousand years.

1520   Portuguese visited Ethiopia.

1530–43   Portuguese aided Ethiopians in repulsing invasion by Somalis.

1855   Ethiopia reunified by King Theodore II.

1868   King Theodore imprisoned British diplomats; British invaded, Theodore committed suicide.

1889–1911   Menelik II reigned; expanded borders of Ethiopia.

1889   Addis Ababa became capital.

1895–96   Italy invaded in the Ethiopian War; Menelik defeated Italy, and Ethiopian independence was recognized.

1916–30   Zauditi, Menelik's daughter, became empress; her cousin Ras Tafari ruled as regent.

1930   Zauditi died; Ras Tafari crowned Emperor Haile Selassie I.

1931   Haile Selassie granted country a constitution and a parliament.

1934–35   Italy invaded and conquered Ethiopia in Italo-Ethiopian War; League of Nations unable to halt Italy's aggression.

1936   Haile Selassie forced into exile.

1936   Ethiopia annexed to Eritrea and Italian Somaliland to form Italian East Africa.

1941   WW II; British forces captured Ethiopia (1941); Haile Selassie restored.

1952   UN placed Eritrea (eastern coastal region) under Ethiopian rule.

1955   New constitution adopted.

1960   Coup attempt (Dec.); Haile Selassie restored by the army.

1969   Eritrean Liberation Front started violent campaign for secession of Eritrea.

1970   Guerrilla activity in Eritrea resulted in declaration of state of emergency.

1973–74   Severe famine resulted from prolonged drought.

1974   Serious unrest caused by famine; resignation of the cabinet; Haile Selassie named a moderate, Endalkachew Makonnen, prime minister; agreed to call constitutional convention.

1974   Army took control of Addis Ababa (June).

1974   Makonnen overthrown (July), arrested, later executed; succeeded by Michael Imru.

1974   Haile Selassie peacefully deposed (Sept. 12); placed under palace arrest; US military aid halted.

1974   Armed forces committee proclaimed Ethiopia a Socialist state with one political party, the Supreme Progressive Council (Dec. 20).

1974–75 All lands and businesses nationalized.

1975 Haile Selassie died (Aug. 27).

1975 Government troops battled Eritrean guerrillas as fighting intensified.

1977 Gen. Teferi Benti, chairman of Provisional Military Council, shot and killed during a council meeting; Lt. Col. Mengistu Haile Mariam became head of state.

1977–90 Mengistu in power as head of state; his regime eventually brought about a short-lived Marxist-Leninist state that collapsed in the face of widespread famine and a successful challenge by separatist and anti-government rebel forces.

1977 American diplomats ordered to leave.

1977 Heavy fighting between government troops and ethnic Somalis in southeastern Ethiopia; Somalia charged with aiding rebels.

1977 Russia ended (Oct.) military aid to Somalia, backed Ethiopia in border war.

1978 Somalis defeated (Mar.) in southeast, Ogaden region; Cuban troops aided Ethiopian victory; government reported successes against guerrillas (pro-Communist) seeking independence of northwestern region of Eritrea.

1978 Friendship treaty signed with the Soviets.

1979 Government forces badly defeated by Eritrean rebels, Eritrean People's Liberation Front (EPLF), at Nacfa in north (Dec.).

1980 Government victory at Assab in Eritrea (Apr.) and in southern Ogaden (July).

1980–81 Major government offensive against EPLF stronghold at Nacfa stalled; heavy fighting reported in Tigré province (south of Eritrea) by Tigré People's Liberation Front (TPLF).

1982 Red Star offensive in Eritrea by some 100,000 government troops failed (Feb.–May); rebels inflicted 30–40,000 casualties.

1983–85 Widespread famine caused by drought and ongoing civil war; estimated 7.5 million received emergency food and some 750,000 reportedly died of hunger; massive relief effort by Western nations (from Oct., 1984) stabilized situation by Dec., 1984, despite interference from government and (later) outright attacks on relief workers by rebel groups; adequate rains in 1984–85 significantly eased problem of hunger.

1983 Controversial resettlement program begun by government to move people out of drought-prone areas; by 1986 about 600,000 people had been relocated to south and west in Ethiopia.

1983 Cuban troops in Ethiopia, once numbering 12,000, reported leaving country.

1984 Compulsory military service introduced.

1984 Disastrous train crash near Awash killed 392 and injured 370 (Jan.).

1984 Government stronghold at Barentu (western Eritrea) recaptured (Aug. 25) soon after EPLF forces took it; new offensive against rebel-held Nacfa (Oct.) stalled.

1984–85 Some 25,000 Ethiopian Jews airlifted to Israel.

1985–90 Villagization program begun to consolidate scattered rural homesteads into villages; seen as preliminary step toward collectivization of farming by many; some 100,000 fled to Somali Republic in first year; government moved over 12 million people before end of program.

1987 New constitution adopted (Feb.) after national referendum; established Ethiopia as People's Democratic Republic of Ethiopia, a Marxist-Leninist state with a national soviet.

1987 Mengistu Haile Mariam, effective ruler of Ethiopia since 1977, in office as president.

1987 Sudan accused Ethiopia of aiding rebel Sudan People's Liberation Movement.

1987–88 New severe famine narrowly averted by established relief mechanisms and unexpectedly improved harvest.

1988 EPLF rebels routed 18,000-man government force, taking government base at Afabet in north (Mar.); government pulled out of surrounding area; TPLF rebels in neighboring Tigré likewise made significant gains (Mar.–Apr); by May, government troops had recaptured most of the rebel gains.

1988 Some 750,000 refugees flooded into Ethiopia to escape famine and warfare in Sudan and Somalia.

1989 TPLF captured key town of Enda-Selassie in Tigré province (Feb. 22); government quickly abandoned whole region.

1989 Attempted coup by senior military officers crushed; 54 of the officers, trying to impose a political solution to the Eritrean wars, were killed outright and 12 others executed (1990) after trial; military severely weakened as a result.

1989 Peace talks with EPLF held in US (Atlanta, Georgia) in June, and again in Nairobi (Nov.); fighting in Eritrea at standstill.

1989 TPLF rebels meanwhile moved to within 90 miles of Addis Ababa; began peace talks with government (Nov.).

1990 EPLF forces captured key northern port of Massawa (Feb.); 100,000-man Ethiopian army, effectively encircled, resupplied by air.

1990 President Mengistu, in desperate bid to hold on to power, announced end to Marxist-Leninist orientation of Ethiopian government (Mar. 5); collective farms abandoned and land turned over to farmers.

1991 TPLF-led coalition of rebels advanced through western Ethiopia, meeting little government resistance (Feb.–Apr.); EPLF forces drove southward from Massawa in Eritrea to port of Assab (Apr.); TPLF coalition next moved in on Addis Ababa (May).

1991 President Mengistu fled country for Zimbabwe (May 21); rebel forces took Addis Ababa (May 28).

1991– Meles Zenawi in power as president of Ethiopia; promised elections in 1993; maintained state ownership of industry and agriculture; made no attempt to assert sovereignty over EPLF-held Eritrea.

1991 Isayas Afewerki, EPLF leader, in power as head of provisional government in Eritrea (May 30); agreed to two-year delay of independence referendum.

1992 Government and leftist guerrillas signed formal peace treaty ending 12-year civil war (Jan. 16).

Etruria   *See* **Etruscans.**

Etruscans Ancient people who established a flourishing civilization in northern Italy (Etruria) between the 8th and 4th cents. BC. They are believed to have emigrated to Italy from the Near East around the 12th cent. BC. They initiated trade with the Greeks, and their navy virtually dominated the Mediterranean for two centuries (7th–6th cents.). They ruled in Rome (6th cent.) as the legendary "Tarquin kings," but were expelled around 509 BC, according to tradition, after the king's son raped the Roman matron

Lucretia. The Romans subsequently defeated the Latins decisively in the Battle of Lake Regullus (496 BC), and began the gradual subjugation of Etruscan cities (completed by 282 BC). The Romans borrowed freely from Etruscan civilization, and the toga, curule chair, and the Latin alphabet are all derived from the Etruscans.

Euboea Island on the east coast of Greece. Important ancient towns were Chalcis and Eretria. Dominated by Athens (5th cent. BC) and Macedon (from 4th cent.), it was taken by Rome (196 BC). The island passed to various conquerors after Rome's fall and was annexed to Greece in 1830.

Eubulus c405–c335 BC. Greek statesman who restored the finances of Athens. Following years of warfare that brought Athens near bankruptcy, Eubulus became Theoric Commissioner (355 BC) and thereafter gained control of all Athenian finances. By his astute financial management, he built up a surplus of public monies (without raising taxes) and fostered a period of general economic prosperity. Eubulus, who generally sought to limit Athenian involvement in major wars, lost power with the rise of Demonthenes and those calling for war against Philip of Macedon (342).

Euclid *fl.* c300 BC. Greek mathematician famous for his fundamental contribution to the study of geometry and the development of mathematics. Details of his life are uncertain, but it is known that he taught at the great school of Alexandria in Egypt and that he wrote the celebrated mathematical treatise *Elements.* The work included a systematic presentation of plane geometry, which long served as the basic text for its study, and treatments of number theory and solid geometry. It was not until the 19th cent. that fundamental departures from his system of plane geometry began to be presented.

Eudes (Odo) c860–898. French king (888–898), successor to Charles III (the Fat) in the West Frankish Kingdom. He defended Paris against the Norsemen and was succeeded by his rival, Charles III (the Simple).

Eudes of Lagery *See* **Urban II.**

Eudoxus of Cnidus 390?–340 BC. Greek astronomer and mathematician known for his invention of the theory of proportion and his explanation of the motion of the planets and calculation of the length of the solar year.

Euergetes, Ptolemy III   *See* **Ptolemy III.**

Eugene III (Montemagno, Bernardo dei Paganelli di) *d.* 1153. Italian-born pope (1145–53) who was driven from Rome by Arnold of Brescia, the reformer. He preached the unsuccessful Second Crusade (1147–49) while in France.

Eugene IV (Gabriele Condulmaro) 1383–1447. Italian-born pope (1431–47), successor to Martin V. His reign was marked by his dispute with the Council of Basel (*q.v.*) over conciliarism. He convened the Council of Ferrara-Florence (*q.v.*) in its stead. His opponents unsuccessfully tried to depose him and elected the antipope Felix V.

Eugene of Savoy, Prince 1663–1736. Great French-born general. A brilliant strategist in service of the Holy Roman Empire, he defeated the Turks at Vienna and later drove them from Hungary. He commanded the imperial armies during the wars of the Spanish Succession (1701–14) and the Polish Succession (1733–35). Among his many victories were the battles of Zenta and Blenheim.

Eugénie (*in full*, Eugénia Marie de Montijo de Guzmán) 1826–1920. Empress of France (1853–70) as wife of Napoleon III. She fled to England when the empire fell (1870).

Euhemerus *fl.* c330 BC. Greek mythographer whose novelistic work *Sacred History* sought to prove that mythological beings were based on events of historical fact.

Eulenspiegel, Till *fl.* 14th cent. German folk hero, a peasant and prankster who played wicked, often obscene, tricks on the arrogant. His escapades are the subject of numerous literary and musical works.

Euler, Leonhard 1707–83. Swiss mathematician. Called the most prolific mathematician of all time, he produced works that treated all major branches of mathematics.

Eumanes II *See* **Pergamum.**

eunuch Male court official who has been castrated. Eunuchs were variously employed as harem guards, political advisers, and military leaders in many Middle Eastern, Asian, and Oriental states.

Euphrates *See* **Tigris and Euphrates.**

Euric *d.* AD c484. King of the Visigoths (466–484), younger son of Theodoric I. Under Euric, the Visigothic kingdom reached its greatest extent. He ruled most of Spain and southern Gaul and established his capital at Toulouse. He promulgated the first Visigothic law code.

Euripides 480?–406 BC. One of the three great tragic poets (with Sophocles and Aeschylus) of ancient Greece. He spent the greater part of his life in Athens, and there entered his tragedies in the annual competition of the festival of Dionysus. He is said to have written 92 plays (of which 18 definitely attributed to him survive) but won first prize in only 4 competitions. His writing is generally considered more realistic in tone then that of the other great tragic poets. Among his extant works are *Cyclops, Orestes,* and *Electra.*

European Economic Community (E.E.C., Common Market) West European economic association. It was formed in 1957 and its original members were Belgium, France, Italy, Luxembourg, the Netherlands, and West Germany. Its goals were to establish the economic union of member nations and eventually to bring about political union. It has sought to eliminate internal tariffs, institute a uniform external scale of tariffs, achieve free movement of labor and capital from one nation to another, abolish obstructions to free competition, and establish collective trade and transportation policies. In 1973, Great Britain, Ireland, and Denmark joined the organization. Since then new members have included Greece (1981), Portugal (1986), and Spain (1986). Greenland withdrew in 1985. The European Community (EC), formed by a merger of the EEC, European Coal and Steel Community, and European Atomic Energy Community (1967), established the European Monetary System (1979), and after passage of the Single European Act (1987), made major strides toward economic unification of Western Europe. After the collapse of Communism in East Europe, East European states also took steps toward becoming members of the EEC.

European Free Trade Association (EFTA) Trade group organized (1959) by nations outside the European Economic Community (EEC) to remove barriers to free trade of industrial goods between member nations. Established by the Stockholm Convention (1959), the group originally consisted of Great Britain, Denmark, Austria, Sweden, Norway, Switzerland, and Portugal. Finland joined in 1961 and Iceland became a member in 1970. Britain and Denmark withdrew (1973) to join the EEC, as did Portugal (1986). The group succeeded in generally eliminating import duties between members on manufactured goods (1966) and in 1977 concluded trade pacts with the EEC that established free trade between members of the two groups. Unlike the EEC, which is part of a long-range program aimed at European unification, the EFTA is concerned only with commercial trade policy.

European Parliament Legislative arm of the European Community (EC). Organized in 1958, the Parliament seats over 500 representatives, who are directly elected by voters in member nations. Representatives meet for several weeks each year in either Luxembourg or Strasbourg to take up matters of concern to the EC and its subordinate organizations, including economic, political, and social affairs. Members of the Parliament elect a president and 12 vice-presidents to head up the assembly.

European Recovery Plan *See* **Marshall Plan.**

Eurymedon River, Battle of *See* **Cimon.**

Eusebius of Caesarea (Eusebius Pamphili) AD c263–339? Greek theologian and historian. He became bishop of Caesarea in Palestine (AD c314) and wrote on early Christian history in *Chronicle* and *Ecclesiastical History.*

Eusebius Pamphili *See* **Eusebius of Caesarea.**

Eustachio, Bartolomeo (Eustachio, Bartolommeo) *d.* 1574. Italian anatomist who described the Eustachian tube connecting the ear to the pharynx, as well as other organs of the body.

Eutaw Springs, Battle of American Revolutionary War battle (Sept. 8, 1781), part of the Carolina Campaign (*q.v.*). Some 2,300 Americans under N. Greene narrowly defeated 2,500 British troops under Col. Alexander Stewart, forcing them to retire to nearby Charleston, South Carolina. American casualties were 400, British 693.

Eutyches AD c378–c452. Archimandrite of the Eastern church in Constantinople. He founded Eutychianism, an early and extreme form of Monophysitism (*q.v.*), in reaction to Nestorianism. He was condemned for heresy, excommunicated, and banished (AD 451).

Eutychianism *See* **Eutyches.**

Evangelical Alliance Association of Protestant evangelical Christians of various denominations founded in 1846. The alliance originated in reaction to the Oxford Movement (*q.v.*) in the Church of England and was formed during a London convention attended by some 800 delegates from evangelical churches in Europe and America.

Branch organizations were created in various countries with the aim of promoting unity and the doctrines of evangelicalism. The importance of the alliance has declined in this century.

evangelicalism A term used to describe churches and groups within the Protestant fold that emphasize a strict and literal biblical faith, personal conversion experiences, and pietistic practices. Originally the Lutherans were known as Evangelicals, as distinguished from the Calvinists, who were called "Reformed." But the term was later applied to the new Protestant sects that arose (18th cent.) from Pietism (*q.v.*) in Europe, Methodism (*q.v.*) in Britain, and the Great Awakening (*q.v.*) in the United States. Today such conservative Protestant groups as the Fundamentalists prefer to be called Evangelical rather than Protestant.

Evans, Mary Ann *See* **Eliot, George.**

Evarts, William Maxwell 1818–1901. American lawyer and statesman. He was counsel for A. Johnson in the impeachment proceedings (1868) and for the Republican party in the Hayes-Tilden dispute over the election of 1876.

Evatt, Herbert Vere 1894–1965. Australian statesman. He was justice of the high court of Australia (1930–40) and led the Australian delegation to conferences on formation of the UN. He served as president of the UN General Assembly (1948–49).

Evelyn, John 1620–1706. English author. His *Diary* (1640–1706) is considered an important source regarding late 17th-cent. English politics and religion.

Everest, Sir George 1790–1866. British surveyor general of India (1830–43) for whom Mount Everest is named.

Evesham, Battle of Decisive battle (Aug. 4, 1265) that all but ended armed resistance in the Barons' War (1263–67). Edward (later Edward I) defeated and captured S. de Montfort near this town in central England and thereby restored his father, King Henry III, to power.

evolution Biological theory holding that living things have developed gradually from earlier forms. The concept appears in ancient Greek writings by Thales, Aristotle, and others. Scientific advances (17th–19th cents.) tended to support it, but it was C. Darwin's great work *On the Origin of Species* (1859) that eventually brought about its acceptance. The biological theory of evolution is opposed by supporters of the religious concept of special creation, which stipulates that God created each species separately. The dispute gave rise to the Scopes Trial (1925) and continues to the present day.

Ewald, George Heinrich August von 1803–75. German Orientalist and theologian. He is best known for his *Hebrew Grammar* and *History of Israel.*

Ewell, Richard Stoddert 1817–72. Confederate general during the American Civil War (1861–65). He served under Gen. Stonewall Jackson and lost a leg at the Second Battle of Bull Run (1862). Taking over Jackson's command after Jackson was killed in battle, Ewell led R. E. Lee's invasion of Pennsylvania and commanded units in the Battle of Gettysburg, the Wilderness campaign, and the Petersburg Campaign.

Exarchate of Italy *See* **Exarchate of Ravenna.**

Exarchate of Ravenna (Exarchate of Italy) The part of Italy controlled by the Byzantines (6th–8th cents.), mainly a strip of territory in north-central Italy but also including isolated pockets under their control in southern Italy. Ravenna was the administrative capital, and the chief Byzantine official was called an exarch. The Lombards gained control of Ravenna (752).

executive branch The branch or department of modern government, notably in the US, that executes or carries out the laws, as distinguished from the legislative branch, which enacts them and the judicial branch, which interprets them. These distinctions stem from the theory of checks and balances (*q.v.*), or separation of powers, whereby absolute power is denied to any single organ of government. In the US, the Constitution grants the president executive powers. However, it specifies only that he shall be commander in chief of the armed forces, that he may make treaties and appoint officers of the government (by and with the consent of the Senate, generally), and that he must report to Congress from time to time on "the state of the union." From this bare outline of presidential executive authority, the development of the power of the modern presidency has been considerable. The president and his administration now command an enormous apparatus of state that makes it possible for him to intervene effectively in nearly every aspect of the society. Presidents H. Truman and L. Johnson were even able

to make war without the express consent of Congress—in Korea and Vietnam respectively—by calling these wars "police actions" or by securing only concurring "resolutions" about them from Congress. The 1970s and 1980s have witnessed a trend, arising from Vietnam and the Watergate controversies, toward curbing presidential powers.

Exile *See* **Babylonian Captivity.**

existentialism Modern school of philosophy concerned with human beings' relationship to the world around them and which teaches that the actual existence of humanity holds the clue to the meaning of being. Existentialism stems from S. Kierkegaard's revolt against the rationalism of G. Hegel. His work was subsequently built upon by two noted philosophers, M. Heidegger and J. Sartre.

Exodus The escape (c13th cent. BC) by the Jews from their enslavement in Egypt. It is an event of great significance in biblical history and is described in the second book (Exodus) of the Old Testament. The book narrates the flight from Egypt under Moses' guidance and includes the crossing of the Red Sea, the trek through the wilderness, and the giving of the Ten Commandments on Mt. Sinai.

Expedition of the Thousand A daring military campaign (Apr.–Oct., 1860) in which G. Garibaldi, with an army of some 1,000 scarcely trained, idealistic volunteers, conquered the Bourbon kingdom of Naples. Garibaldi undertook the campaign in the name of a unified Italian state. Impatient with the cautious diplomatic efforts at unification by Victor Emmanuel II of Piedmont-Sardinia and his minister C. Cavour, Garibaldi landed his force in Sicily on his own and conquered the island (by Aug. 20) after defeating a force of some 20,000 Bourbon troops there. He then crossed to the mainland and marched triumphantly into Naples (Sept. 7). He was prevented from marching on Rome itself by the intervention of the army of Victor Emmanuel II, and soon after turned over conquered Bourbon territories to Emmanuel.

expressionism Twentieth-cent. movement in art and literature that sought to express an inner vision or the essence of a subject by exaggerating or distorting its characteristics. The movement flourished before and after WW I, especially in Germany. The German Max Beckman (1854–

1950), Austrian O. Kokoschka, Frenchman G. Rouault, and Lithuanian Chaim Soutine (1894–1943) were all considered notable expressionist painters. In literature, the Irish novelist J. Joyce, the German writer F. Kafka, and, in some of his plays, the American playwright E. O'Neill, were considered expressionist writers. The movement, though itself short-lived, was immensely influential in the subsequent development of painting and writing.

Eyck, Hubert van c1366–1425.   Flemish painter, believed to be the older brother of Jan van Eyck. Little is known of his life. He is thought to have painted the altarpiece at Ghent.

Eyck, Jan van c1390–1441.   Flemish painter. Van Eyck was a master of realism, rendering minute detail with great accuracy. His most famous work is *Giovanni Arnolfini and His Bride* (1434).

Eylau, Battle of   Battle (Feb. 8, 1807) during the Napoleonic Wars (1803–15). Napoleon fought this indecisive battle against the combined forces of Russia and Prussia at Eylau (in the Baltic coastal region). Heavy snow contributed to the confusion of battle. France suffered 15,000 casualties, the allies 18,000.

Ezra   Hebrew scribe and priest (5th cent. BC). He became a leader in Jerusalem after the Jews returned from the Babylonian Captivity. [Ezra and Nehemiah]

Ezra Church, Battle of   *See* **Atlanta Campaign.**

Ezzelino da Romano 1194–1259.   Ghibelline leader. The son-in-law of Holy Roman Emperor Frederick II, Ezzelino aided him against the Lombards and became the most powerful man in northern Italy. His rule there was remembered for its cruelty.

F

Fabian Society English Socialist society, founded (1883) by Frank Podmore (1855–1910) and Edward Pease (1857–1955) to gradually advance the Socialist cause from within the existing government framework. Fabians did not advocate revolutionary methods for change. They helped organize a labor-oriented committee (1900), which later became the British Labour party, with which Fabians are affiliated today. Prominent Fabians include G. Shaw and S. Webb.

Fabius Maximus Rullianus, Quintus (Fabius Maximus Rullus, Quintus) *d.* c290 BC. Roman general, consul (five times between 322 and 295 BC) and dictator (315 BC). He won an important victory at Sentinum (295 BC) in the third Samnite War.

Fabius Maximus Verrucosus, Quintus (Cunctator, or the Delayer) *d.* 203 BC. Roman general, consul (five times between 233 and 209 BC), and dictator (217 BC). The leader of Roman forces at the outset of Hannibal's invasion during the Second Punic War, he is remembered for delaying tactics in which he harassed but did not directly engage the enemy. The strategy was unpopular but was proved correct after his replacement (216) and the subsequent Roman defeat at Cannae (216).

Facta, Luigi *See* **March on Rome.**

Fahrenheit, Gabriel Daniel 1686–1736. German physicist noted for the invention of the Fahrenheit temperature scale and introduction of the mercury thermometer.

Faidherbe, Louis Léon César 1818–89. French colonial governor of Senegal (1854–61, 1863–65) and soldier. He strengthened and expanded the colony during his administration.

fair Gathering of merchants and consumers. The fair had its origins in the public marketplaces of ancient Greece and Rome. It grew to be a large periodic event and the major vehicle for trade before the development of transportation. Fairs were often tied to religious festivals and occasions and became so important to both church and state that they were given special powers and privileges. With the rise of commerce and industry in the 17th and 18th cents. and the increasing ease with which people could find things to buy, fairs lost their importance. They have continued into the present in somewhat modified form.

Fair Deal Name given (1949) by President H. Truman to the domestic program of his administration. It called for legislation to increase jobs, improve civil rights, create new housing, establish a national medical plan, and repeal the Taft-Hartley Act.

Fairfax of Cameron, Thomas, 3d Baron 1612–71. English general, a leader of the Parliamentarians during the English Civil Wars. He succeeded R. Devereaux, earl of Essex, as commander (1645), organized the New Model Army (1645), and won several important victories, including the Battle of Naseby. He resigned (1650) after formation of the Commonwealth, refusing to invade Scotland.

Fair Labor Standards Act (Wages and Hours Act) American labor law (1938), the first attempt to regulate the wages and working hours of American laborers. It fixed minimum-wage and overtime rates and established child-labor age limits.

Fair Oaks, Battle of *See* **Seven Pines, Battle of.**

Fair of Lincoln *See* **Lincoln, Battle of.**

Faisal c1906–75. Saudi Arabian king (1964–75), successor to his brother King Saud. A leading figure in the Arab world, he supported Yemeni royalists in their unsuccessful fight against the republicans, joined other Arab countries in the 1967 Arab-Israeli War and organized the 1973 Arab oil embargo. He was assassinated by his nephew.

Faisal I (Faysal I) (Feisal I) 1885–1933. King of Syria (1920) and Iraq (1921–33). A leader of the Arab nationalist movement, he was a key figure in the Arab revolt against Ottoman rule during WW I. Crowned king of Syria (1920), he was deposed by the French in the same year but became king of Iraq with support of the British.

Faisal II (Faysal II or Feisal II) 1935–58. Last king of Iraq (1939–58), successor to his father, Ghazi I. He was killed during the revolution that ended the monarchy in Iraq.

Falange Spanish political party that became the ruling party of Spain under Gen. F. Franco. Organized (1933) by José Antonio Primo de Rivera (1903–36), it became the party of Spanish Fascism. Falangists took part in the Spanish Civil War (1936–39), and, after 1937, the group was taken over by Franco. Franco turned the party to his own ends, making it the official party under his dictatorship. Though its ideology was significantly altered, the party continued in power until recent times.

Falier, Marino *See* **Faliero, Marino.**

Faliero, Marino (Falier or Falieri, ˜) 1274–1355. Doge of Venice (1354–55). Involved in a conspiracy by plebeians to assassinate the patricians, or nobles, he was executed after a trial by the Council of Ten.

Falkenhayn, Erich von *See* **World War I (Sept. 10, 1914).**

Falkland, Lucius Cary, 2d viscount c1610–43. English writer and Royalist during the English Civil Wars. A member of the Short and Long parliaments (1640), he failed in his attempts to head off the civil war. He served with Charles I, and, despairing of the war, is said to have welcomed his own death in battle.

Falkland Islands British crown colony, located southeast of Argentina. Believed to have been discovered (1592) by British navigator J. Davis, they were settled (18th cent.) by the British and French. French and British possessions were taken over by Spain, though Britain retained formal sovereignty. The islands were then claimed (early 19th cent.) by Argentina after it gained independence from Spain. Britain retook control of the islands (1833). During WW I the British

destroyed a German fleet under Graf von Spee near here (Dec., 1914). Argentina unsuccessfully challenged British sovereignty over the islands in the 1982 Falkland Islands War (*q.v.*).

Falkland Islands, Battle of Naval engagement (Dec. 8, 1914) between British and German fleets, near the Falkland Islands during WW I. The battle led to the destruction of the German fleet and the death of its commander, Graf von Spee.

Falkland Islands War Brief war (1982) between Argentina and Britain over possession of the Falkland Islands. Following years of unsuccessful negotiations with Britain for possession of the islands, the Argentines invaded (Apr. 1–2, 1982) and took control of the islands. A British naval task force arrived off the islands some weeks later and the first British landings began in June. The British took several Argentine strongholds on the islands and, after surrounding the main Argentine contingent at Stanley, forced the nearly 10,000 Argentine troops to surrender (June 14).

Fall, Albert Bacon 1861–1944. US senator from New Mexico (1912–21) and secretary of the interior (1921–23). He was convicted (1929) of receiving bribes in return for leases to oil lands in the Teapot Dome scandal.

Fallen Timbers, Battle of Battle (1794) between American forces under Gen. A. Wayne and Indians of the Northwest Confederation. Fought near present-day Toledo, Ohio, it was a decisive defeat for the confederation and ended concerted Indian resistance to settlement by whites.

Fallières, (Clément) Armand 1841–1931. French statesman. He was president of the Third Republic of France (1906–13).

false decretals Forged ecclesiastical papers. Decretals are religious letters outlining binding church decisions. In the 9th cent., several anonymous French clergymen sought to end Carolingian interference in church affairs by falsifying several documents and inserting into them legitimate decretals. The false decretals, supposedly advancing religious independence from civil authority, were largely believed until the 17th cent.

False Dmitris *See* **Dmitri; Time of Troubles.**

Family Compact Name of a wealthy group of Canadians who dominated the government in Upper Canada between the late 1790s and 1830s. This group controlled both the government ministries and the Legislative Council. Popular reaction to their control centered on questions of patronage, land grants, control of the judiciary, and support for the Anglican church. Following a period of legislative conflict and the Act of Union (1840), reformers won the government. A comparable group in French Lower Canada was called the Château Clique.

Family Compact Name of three treaties between the Bourbon rulers of France and Spain. 1. The first ~ (1733) was concluded to counter British commercial supremacy and to check Austrian designs on Italy. 2. The second ~ (1743) provided for continuation of the 1733 alliance. 3. The third ~ (1761) was the most important of these treaties. It brought Spain into the Seven Years' War against Britain. Spain's participation (after 1762) was minimal, however.

Faneuil, Peter *See* **Faneuil Hall.**

Faneuil Hall (Cradle of Liberty) Historic public market- and meeting place, in Boston, Massachusetts. The original hall, built (1740–42) by Peter Faneuil (1700–43), burned in 1761. Rebuilt (1763), it was the site of meetings of American revolutionaries.

Fanfani, Amintore 1908– . Italian statesman. A left-wing Christian Democrat, Fanfani held numerous government positions and was a leading force in Italian politics in the 1950s and 1960s. He was three times prime minister (Jan., 1954, 1958–59, 1960–63) and was elected life senator (1972).

Fannin, James W. *See* **Goliad Massacre.**

Farabi, al- (Alfarabius) c870–c950. Muslim philosopher. He is remembered chiefly as an influential exponent of Artistotle's teachings in the Islamic world.

Faraday, Michael 1791–1867. British physicist and chemist, known for his contributions to the study of electricity and magnetism. Beginning his career as assistant to Sir H. Davy (1813), he went on to make the basic discoveries concerning electricity and the nature of magnetism and light. He invented the electric motor (1821), electric generator (1831), and the transformer (1831). In 1825, he discovered the compound benzene. He demonstrated the principle of electromagnetic induction (1831) and formulated Faraday's Laws of electrolysis (1834). A scientific genius, he is often regarded as the greatest experimental scientist of his time. The farad, an elec-trical unit of capacitance, and the Faraday constant used in electrolysis are named for him.

Fard, Wallace D. *See* **Black Muslims.**

Far East Term that generally refers to the eastern portion of the Asian continent. It includes eastern Siberia, Mongolia, China, Korea, and Japan and is sometimes also meant to include the countries of Southeast Asia.

Far Eastern Territory Former Russian administrative region on the Pacific Ocean from the Arctic Ocean to Korea. Organized as the Far Eastern Republic (1920), it became (1922) part of the Russian SFSR, was reorganized (1926) as the Far Eastern Territory, and was subdivided (1938).

Fargo, William George 1818–81. American pioneer in express delivery. A founder (1850) of the American Express Company, he and other partners set up the Wells, Fargo and Company (1852), linking California with the East.

Farigoule, Louis *See* **Romains, Jules.**

Farley, James Aloysius 1888–1976. American politician. He played a major role in the presidential election campaigns (1932, 1936) of F. Roosevelt and served under Roosevelt as postmaster general (1933–40).

Farmer-Labor party Short-lived minor US political party (1919–24). Founded as the National Labor party, it became the Farmer-Labor party in 1920 and advocated a policy of nationalization. It ran a third-party presidential candidate (1920), fell to Communist control (1923), and disappeared after 1924. A Minnesota party of the same name (1918–44) supported F. Roosevelt in 1932 and 1936.

farmers-general French financiers who in pre-revolutionary France bought the right to collect taxes from the citizenry. Their unscrupulousness contributed to the French Revolution.

Farnese Italian family that ruled the duchy of Parma and Piacenza from 1545 to 1731. It was founded by Alessandro Farnese, who, as Pope Paul III, established (1545) the duchy for his natural son, Pier Luigi Farnese (1503–47). Other members included A. Farnese (*q.v.*).

Farnese, Alessandro *See* **Paul III.**

Farnese, Alessandro 1545–92. Italian soldier, duke of Parma and Piacenza (1586–92), and celebrated general in the service of Spanish king Philip II. He was appointed (1578) governor of the Netherlands, and his victories over the Dutch rebels helped ensure Spain's control in the region.

Farnese, Elizabeth 1692–1766.   Spanish queen, wife of Philip V (*m.* 1714). For a time the virtual ruler of Spain, she used strategems enabling her son Charles III to become king of Naples and Sicily.

Farnese, Pier Luigi   *See* **Farnese.**

Farouk I (Faruk I) 1920–65.   Egyptian king (1936–52), successor to his father, Fuad I. His unpopular policies and Egypt's defeat by Israel in 1948 led to his overthrow by M. Naguib and G. Nasser in 1952.

Farragut, David Glasgow 1801–70.   American naval officer during the US Civil War. He led the Union navy to major victories at New Orleans (1862) and Mobile Bay (1864). At the latter he uttered his famous "Damn the torpedoes." He was the US Navy's first vice-admiral (1864) and admiral (1866).

Farrell, James Thomas 1904–79.   American novelist, known best as author of the Studs Lonigan trilogy.

Faruk I   *See* **Farouk I.**

fascism   Political movement for totalitarian government that began in Italy (c1919) under the leadership of B. Mussolini. Fascism is sometimes used more restrictively to refer to the Italian movement, the parallel German movement being distinguished as National Socialism (Nazism). Fascism is characterized by subservience of the individual to the state (in the person of an exalted leader), extreme nationalism, elitism (and especially in Nazism, anti-Semitism), formation of the corporative state (*q.v.*), militarism, and imperialism. Fascism in Italy was born amid the post-WW I chaos bred by labor unrest and attempts at Communist and Socialist takeover. Mussolini organized (c1919) bands of thugs, later called Blackshirts, and, with police backing, brutally suppressed labor agitation in northern Italy. He then created the Fascist party (1921) with the backing of many conservative elements, and took control of the Italian government (Oct. 29, 1922) after the famous March on Rome (*q.v.*). Thereafter the Fascist party remained the ruling party of Italy until the close of WW II. (For the rise of fascism in Germany, *see* National Socialism; in Spain, *see* Falange.)

Fashoda Incident   Diplomatic crisis (1898) between Britain and France over claims to the Sudan. Both countries sought to link their colonies on the African continent by continuous corridors of land. The Sudan represented an intersection of their aims. Defying British claims, the French sent a military contingent from the Congo and occupied Fashoda (now Kodok). The British, under Lord H. Kitchener, arrived two weeks later. The French government, fearing all-out war, withdrew its forces a month and a half later, and subsequently dropped claims to the region (1899) in return for British concessions in the Sahara.

Fastolf, Sir John   *See* **Herrings, Battle of the.**

Fathers of the Church   Term applied to the early Christian writers whose interpretations of Christian doctrine are generally considered definitive by the church.

Fatima 606?–632.   Daughter of Muhammad and wife of Ali. An important figure in Islamic religion, she is claimed to be the forebear of the Fatimid dynasty.

Fatimid (Fatimite)   Muslim dynasty that ruled (909–1171) an empire in North Africa. Members of the Ismaili sect, the Fatimids claimed descent from Muhammad through his daughter Fatima. The dynasty began its rule in North Africa and Sicily (909) and ruled there in opposition to the Abbasid caliphs. The Fatimids subsequently reached their greatest power under el-Muizz (reigned 953–975). He conquered Egypt, Palestine, and part of Syria, and built Cairo, which he made his capital. The empire began to disintegrate after his reign, giving way to internal stresses, Norman invasions, the Crusades (11th cent.), and the Ayyubids under Saladin.

Fatimite   *See* **Fatimid.**

Fauchard, Pierre 1678–1761.   French dentist considered a founder of modern dental practices. He wrote *The Surgeon Dentist* (1728), which became a standard work in the field.

Faulkner, William 1897–1962.   American novelist. One of the great American writers of the 20th cent., he is celebrated for his novels chronicling life in the imaginary Yoknapatawpha County, Mississippi. Among his best works are *The Sound and the Fury, As I Lay Dying,* and *Absalom, Absalom!* He was awarded the Nobel Prize in Literature (1949) and twice was awarded the Pulitzer Prize for Fiction (1955, 1963).

Faure, Félix 1841–99.   French statesman. As president (1895–99), he improved French relations with Russia but came into conflict with

Britain over the Fashoda Incident. The Dreyfus Affair occurred during his presidency, and his refusal to reopen the case contributed to friction between pro-Dreyfus and anti-Dreyfus factions.

Faust *fl.* 16th cent. German doctor who acquired the reputation of a magician who had sold his soul to the devil (Mephistopheles) for knowledge and power. His legend is the basis for numerous literary works, notably the dramatic poem *Faust* by J. Goethe.

Faust, Johann *See* **Fust, Johann.**

Fausta, Flavia Maximiana *d.* AD c326. Roman empress, wife of Constantine I (the Great), and mother of Constantine II, Constantius II, and Constans I. She is said to have been put to death by her husband after causing him to kill his oldest son, Crispus, because of her false accusations.

Faustin I *See* **Soulouque, Faustin Élie.**

Faustina the Younger AD c125–176. Roman empress, daughter of Antoninus Pius, and wife of Marcus Aurelius. She accompanied her husband on many campaigns, thus earning the title "Mother of the Army."

fauvism Brief French artistic movement (1905–08) characterized by bold use of color and expressionist approach. Its adherents included H. Matisse and G. Rouault, and it influenced the development of later movements, notably cubism.

Favre, Gabriel Claude Jules 1809–80. French statesman. He was leader of the republican opposition to Napoleon III's Second Empire. As vice-president and foreign minister of the Government of National Defense (1871), he negotiated the disadvantageous Treaty of Frankfurt, ending the Franco-Prussian War.

Fawcett, Dame Millicent Garrett 1847–1929. English feminist. An advocate of peaceful means to gain woman's suffrage, she opposed the militant Pankhursts.

Fay, Sidney Bradshaw 1876–1967. American historian, known best for his work on the causes of WW I, *The Origins of the World War.*

Faysal *See* **Faisal.**

February Manifesto Russian proclamation (Feb. 15, 1899) declaring that the tsar had the right to overrule Finland's constitution and rule by edict. Up to that time Finland was ruled as an autonomous duchy within Russia The manifesto was revoked by Tsar Nicholas II (Nov., 1905) during the Russian Revolution of 1905.

February Revolution 1. Revolution in France (1848) that brought about the abdication of King Louis Philippe and creation of the short-lived Second Republic. The king's increasingly reactionary policies, opposition to his unpopular minister F. Guizot, and widespread unemployment caused by a severe economic slump resulted in the revolt which was precipitated by the banning (Feb. 22, 1848) of an antigovernment banquet. Rioting broke out that day, and the revolution began the next, when government troops fired on demonstrators. The king abdicated (Feb. 24), and the republic was immediately proclaimed. The provisional government was a coalition of moderate republicans, led by A. de Lamartine, and Socialist republicans, led by L. Blanc. It subsequently recognized "the right to work," created (Feb. 26), the national workshops to ease unemployment, and proclaimed universal male suffrage (Mar. 2). The workshops soon failed, however, and mass demonstrations by Socialist republicans aroused fears of a Communist takeover. Moderates were thus victorious in elections for the new National Assembly, and, in the face of new unrest, moved (Mar. 15) to dissolve the national workshops. This precipitated the bloody uprising known as June Days (*q.v.*). Gen. L. Cavaignac was installed as dictator and restored order. The assembly promulgated a new constitution (Nov. 20), and Louis Napoleon (later Napoleon III) was elected president. Soon after taking office, Napoleon seized power and founded the Second Empire (1852). 2. ~ (March Revolution) The beginning phase of the Russian Revolution (*q.v.*) in 1917. It was precipitated by bread riots in Petrograd and resulted in the abdication of Tsar Nicholas II on Mar. 12, 1917 (old-style dating, Feb. 27). The February Revolution was followed by the October Revolution (*q.v.*), in which Bolsheviks seized power.

Federal Constitutional Convention *See* **Constitutional Convention.**

federalism The system of government whereby states or entities unite under a centralized (federal) government, while retaining a measure of autonomy. The federalist system established by the US Constitution (1789) placed foreign affairs, common defense, interstate commerce, and the like under a strong federal government. Existing autonomous governments in the various states that joined the federal union continued to function, though with reduced powers.

Federalist Papers American political essays. They were a series of 85 essays written (1787–88) by A. Hamilton, J. Madison, and J. Jay which urged the ratification of the United States Constitution and expressed the need for a strong central government. Originally written for New York State newspapers, they were collected (1788) as *The Federalist.* They were an important formative influence in the early years of America's government.

Federalist party American political party, considered America's first organized political party. Formed in the 1790s, it was led by A. Hamilton. The Federalists espoused a strong central government and a pro-British, anti-French foreign policy. They were opposed by T. Jefferson's Democratic Republicans. G. Washington, though officially neutral, frequently sided with the Federalists. J. Adams, the second US president, was the last Federalist party member to gain the presidency. The party's power declined rapidly after the Hartford Convention (*q.v.*) of 1814–15.

Fëdor I (Feodor or Fyodor) 1557–98. Russian tsar (1584–98), successor to his father, Ivan the Terrible, and last tsar of the Rurik dynasty. He was incompetent, and the government was run by his brother-in-law, B. Godunov.

Fëdor II 1589–1605. Russian tsar (1605), successor to his father, B. Godunov. He ruled only briefly before being killed in a riot provoked by the nobles, the boyars. He was succeeded by a pretender to the throne, the first of the false Dmitris.

Fëdor III (Feodor or Fyodor) 1656–82. Russian tsar (1676–82), successor to his father, Alexis. Under his reign the system of appointing noblemen to military and civil positions on the basis of social rank was abolished (1681 or 1682).

Feinechus *See* **Brehon Laws.**

Feisal *See* **Faisal.**

Felix V (antipope) *See* **Amadeus VIII.**

Fellini, Federico 1920–93. Italian film director noted for his innovative film techniques and his juxtaposition of realism and fantasy. His films include *La Strada* and *La Dolce Vita* (1959).

Felton, Rebecca Latimer 1835–1930. American writer and reformer. She was the first woman to serve in the Senate, serving Oct.–Nov., 1922, as interim appointee from Georgia.

feminism Women's movement to secure political, economic, and social equality with men. Though the concern for equality for women dates back to ancient times, feminism as a movement is rooted in the 18th and 19th cents. Mary Wollstonecraft's *Vindication of the Rights of Women* (1792) is considered a germinal work, and feminism as an organized movement began at a women's convention at Seneca Falls, New York (July, 1848). The feminist cause, especially in the area of woman suffrage (*q.v.*), was subsequently carried forward in the US by the National Woman Suffrage Association (led by S. Anthony and E. Stanton) and eventually spread to Europe. By the early 1900s, feminists had gained considerable improvement in the status of women, most notably in achieving the right to vote. A resurgence of feminism in the US occurred in the 1960s, when the movement became known as Women's Liberation. The National Organization for Women (NOW) was formed in 1966 and the late 1960s and early 1970s saw the rise of militant feminism. Though feminists brought about reforms in such areas as abortion and sex discrimination in employment, their campaign in the late 1970s and early 1980s centered on the drive to ratify the Equal Rights Amendment (passed by Congress, 1972). The amendment failed to win ratification in the required number of states by the June, 1982, cutoff date.

Fénelon, François de Salignac de la Mothe 1651–1715. French theologian and writer. His support of quietism led to the condemnation (1699) by Pope Innocent XII of Fénelon's *Explanation of the Sayings of the Saints.*

Feng Yuxiang 1882–1948. Chinese general. Called the "Christian General," he supported Chiang Kai-shek and the Guomindang in the 1920s but later opposed Chiang's policies.

Fenian movement Irish nationalist movement. A secret revolutionary group organized (c1858) to achieve complete Irish independence from Britain, it included groups in both Ireland and America. It actively harassed the British in Britain, Ireland, and America in the 1860s and 1870s. Its activities were frequently betrayed by spies planted within the organization's ranks. It was eventually replaced by the Sinn Fein movement.

Feodor *See* **Fëdor.**

Ferber, Edna 1887–1968. American novelist and short-story writer. Among her novels are *So Big* and *Show Boat*. She was awarded the Pulitzer Prize for Fiction in 1925.

Ferdinand 1861–1948. First tsar of Bulgaria (1908–18). He proclaimed Bulgaria's independence from the Ottoman Empire and fought against it in the Balkan Wars. Ferdinand's alliance with the Central Powers and Bulgaria's subsequent defeat in WW I forced his abdication in 1918.

Ferdinand 1865–1927. Rumanian king (1914–27). By siding with the Allies in WW I, he was able to double Rumania's size through postwar peace treaties. He introduced voting and agrarian reforms.

Ferdinand I (Ferdinand the Great) *d.* 1065. Spanish king of Castile (1035–65) and León (1037–65). He brought much of Spain under his control, but divided his kingdom among his three sons at his death.

Ferdinand I 1345–83. Portuguese king (1367–83), successor to his father, Peter I. He waged three successive wars to gain the Castilian throne and each time suffered a humiliating defeat.

Ferdinand I 1503–64. Holy Roman Emperor (1558–64), successor to his brother Charles V. He negotiated the Peace of Augsburg (1555) and reformed the Aulic Council (1559).

Ferdinand I 1751–1825. King of the Two Sicilies (1816–25). As king of Naples, Ferdinand had been forced to flee (1799) when Napoleon established the Parthenopean Republic. Reinstated by the British (1815), he became king of the unified Kingdom of the Two Sicilies (1816). His reactionary rule led to serious turmoil (1820) and the granting of constitutional government, which he soon abrogated.

Ferdinand II 1578–1637. Holy Roman Emperor (1619–37), king of Bohemia and Hungary, successor to his cousin Matthias. His reign was marked by the Thirty Years' War, in which he attempted to put down a series of rebellions by Protestants which began just after his succession to the Bohemian throne (1618).

Ferdinand II 1810–59. King of the Two Sicilies (1830–59), successor to his father, Francis I. His harsh rule earned him the enmity of many. A revolt (1848) in Palermo led to his approval of a constitution, which he soon ignored. He later bombarded the cities of Palermo and Massina, then in rebellion, and earned the name "King Bomba."

Ferdinand II 1816–85. Titular king of Portugal (1837–53). He became king consort by his marriage (1836) to Maria II, and on her death became regent to his sons Pedro V (1853–55) and Louis (1861).

Ferdinand III 1199–1252. King of Castile (1217–52) and León (1230–52). Ferdinand united Castile with León and recaptured most of Spain from the Moors. He was canonized in 1671.

Ferdinand III 1608–57. Holy Roman Emperor (1637–57), successor to his father, Ferdinand II. A series of defeats at the hands of Protestants forced him to agree to the Peace of Westphalia (1648), ending the Thirty Years' War.

Ferdinand IV 1285–1312. Spanish king of Castile and León (1295–1312), successor to his father, Sancho IV. During his reign, Gibraltar was retaken from the Moors (1309).

Ferdinand V (Ferdinand the Catholic) 1452–1516. Spanish king, king of Aragon (1479–1516), king of Castile and León (1474–1504), and regent of Castile (1504–16). Through marriage and conquest, Ferdinand pursued the unification of Spanish kingdoms into what is now modern Spain. He married Isabella I of Castile (1469) and from 1474 they ruled Castile jointly. He succeeded his father, John II, as king of Aragon (1479), and subsequently conquered Granada from the Moors (1492). He began the Italian Wars against France, conquered Naples (1504), and annexed most of the kingdom of Navarre (1512). His reign saw the voyage of C. Columbus (1492) and the acquisition of rich possessions in the New World. With Isabella, he also instituted the Inquisition and expelled the Jews (1492) and the Moors (1502). Following Isabella's death (1504), he ruled Castile as regent.

Ferdinand VI 1712?–59. Spanish king (1746–59), successor to his father, Philip V. He enacted numerous domestic reforms and ably kept Spain from involvement in the Seven Years' War.

Ferdinand VII 1784–1833. Spanish king (Mar.–May, 1808, 1814–33), successor to his father, Charles IV. He was prevented from having real power by M. de Godoy. Ferdinand forced his father's abdication (1808) but was in turn forced from the throne by Napoleon and imprisoned until 1814. Ferdinand resumed control after Napoleon's ouster from Spain, but his rule was harsh and repressive. His repeal of the Salic Law in favor of his daughter Isabella II led to the first Carlist War. During his reign, Spanish power declined and Spain lost all its possessions in the Western Hemisphere except for Cuba.

Ferdinand, archduke *See* **Francis Ferdinand.**

Ferdowsi *See* **Firdausi.**

Ferlinghetti, Lawrence 1919– . American poet. Owner of City Lights bookshop and founder of City Lights Books (publishers), both in San Francisco, he was a leading figure in the Beat movement of the 1950s, and published the works of A. Ginsberg and others. His collections include *A Coney Island of the Mind.*

Fermat, Pierre de 1601–65. French mathematician. He is considered the founder of the modern theory of numbers.

Fermi, Enrico 1901–54. Italian-American physicist who made major contributions to the then emerging science of nuclear physics and who worked on construction of the atom bomb. During experiments in 1934 to 1937, Fermi became the first to split uranium atoms with neutrons, though he did not know it at the time. In 1938 other scientists found that he had actually split atoms and thus discovered the previously unknown process of nuclear fission. Fermi became part of the secret Manhattan Project in the US during WW II and in Dec., 1942, produced the first controlled nuclear chain reaction. He received the Nobel Prize in Physics in 1938.

Fernández, Manuel Félix *See* **Guadalupe Victoria.**

Ferrar, Nicholas 1592–1637. English theologian who established (1626) a small utopian community at Little Gidding. Although initially successful, it was disbanded by Parliament (1647).

Ferrara-Florence, Council of Roman Catholic church council (1438–45) convened to end the schism between the Latin and Greek churches. An extension of the Council of Basel, it was opened at Ferrara but was moved to Florence (1439) because of the plague. Agreement was reached (1439) on the use of the Latin term "Filioque" (*q.v.*), on the use of unleavened bread in the Eucharist, on the Latin definition of purgatory, and on papal supremacy. Union of the two churches was announced (1439), though many Greeks refused to recognize the union and the schism ultimately continued.

Ferraro, Geraldine 1935– . US congresswoman and Democratic candidate for vice-president (1984). A teacher and law school graduate, she served in Congress from 1979 to 1985. In 1984 she became the first woman nominated as a vice-presidential candidate by a major political party, running with W. Mondale in the unsuccessful Democratic presidential campaign that year.

Ferry, Jules 1832–93. French statesman and public official during the Government of National Defense. His education bill (1882) established the French system of public education, free of religious influence. As premier (1880–81, 1883–85) he greatly expanded the French colonial empire in Africa and Indochina.

Fersen, Hans Axel, count 1755–1810. Swedish soldier and marshal of Sweden. He helped in the unsuccessful attempt to get King Louis XVI and Marie Antoinette out of France at the outset of the French Revolution. Later, as marshal under Gustavus IV, he took part in the wars against Napoleon.

Fertile Crescent Ancient Middle Eastern region stretching from the Nile to the Euphrates in parts of modern Egypt, Israel, Lebanon, Syria, Jordan, and Iraq. The site of some of the earliest settlements, the region has been conquered numerous times.

Fes *See* **Fez.**

Festus, Sextus Pompeius *fl.* 2d cent. AD. Roman lexicographer. His abridgment of a major glossary of Latin words by Marcus Verrius Flaccus is a primary source for the study of Roman civilization.

Fetterman Massacre Massacre of 80 US soldiers (1866) in Wyoming during the Sioux Wars. Led by Col. William Judd Fetterman (1833?–66), the soldiers ventured off a safe trail and were ambushed by a band of Chief Red Cloud's warriors.

Feud of the Counts *See* **Count's War.**

feudalism Social system that was prevalent in medieval Europe (8th–14th cents.). By this system, a lord granted vassals lands (fiefs) within his domains and guaranteed them protection from attack. In return, the vassals swore their loyalty to the feudal lord and provided a specified number of warriors for his army. Vassals, in turn, subdivided their fiefs (subinfeudination), and thus became lords to vassals of progressively smaller fiefs. At the bottom of this complex structure was the feudal manor, which was tenanted by serfs (*q.v.*), and which by its agricultural output provided the economic base for the feudal system. The feudal system is generally thought to have arisen in Europe in the Frankish kingdom of Charlemagne (8th–9th cents.). From there, it was spread by Frankish conquests to Spain, Italy, and Germany. It was transplanted to England by the Normans under William the Conqueror and to the Holy Land by rulers of the Crusader States. Though the feudal society at its height (13th cent.) provided a viable means of protection from outside attack, there were inherent weaknesses in the system. Hardships suffered by the serfs were legion. The system of subinfeudination fragmented authority, put the reigning king at the mercy of his vassals, and, by creating a multitude of largely independent petty kingdoms, fostered warfare among them. The rise of powerful monarchs and the growth of a new middle class (merchants and officials), among other factors, helped bring about a gradual decline of feudalism. By the 14th cent., it had largely disappeared, though European society retained vestiges of the system for centuries. Other cultures also experienced periods of feudalism, notably Japan (10th–19th cents.).

Feuerbach, Ludwig Andreas 1804–72. German philosopher. Once a student of G. Hegel, he became a proponent of naturalistic materialism. He held that God was a projection of man's inner nature.

Feuillants French political club during the French Revolution. The Feuillants, including A. Barnave, the Marquis de Lafayette, and E. Sieyès, favored a constitutional monarchy but after 1792 were suppressed by the Jacobins.

Fez (Fes) Moroccan city, a Muslim holy city. Founded (790) by Idris I, it rose in power as the capital of early sultans. At the height of its power in the 14th–15th cents., it declined after Marrakesh became the capital.

Fianna Fáil Irish political party. Organized under the leadership of E. de Valera in 1926, it was formed to oppose the Irish Free State (est. 1921) and to win complete independence from Britain. It has largely controlled the Irish government since 1932, though its major rival, Fianna Gael, has been in power for short periods. As of 1992, Fianna Fáil headed the government.

Fichte, Johann Gottlieb 1762–1814. German philosopher. An influential proponent of transcendental idealism in his day, he is also remembered for his patriotic discourses, *Addresses to the German Nation.*

Ficino, Marsilio 1433–99. Italian philosopher and translator of Greek classics into Latin. He was an important exponent of Platonism in his day.

fief In feudalism, land granted by a lord to a vassal in return for the vassal's knightly service and allegiance. The fief was the cornerstone of feudal society.

Field, Stephen Johnson 1816–99. American jurist, associate justice of the Supreme Court (1863–97). A conservative, he was largely responsible for early interpretations of the 14th Amendment which blocked government regulation of business for many years.

Fielding, Henry 1707–54. One of the greatest of English novelists. He is known best for his classic novel *Tom Jones.*

Field of Cloth of Gold Name given the place, near Calais, France, where in 1520 English king Henry VIII met French king Francis I to propose an alliance. Little was accomplished.

Fieschi, Sinibaldo de' *See* **Innocent IV.**

Fifteen Years' War War (1591–1606) between Austria and the Ottoman Empire. After initial Turkish advances against the Austrians, S. Báthory, prince of Transylvania, allied (1595) with Holy Roman Emperor Rudolf II. The Turks invaded Transylvania but were driven out. The Habsburgs occupied Hungary, but then S. Bocskay, with Turkish aid, fomented a revolt in Transylvania and drove the Habsburgs from Hungary (1604–06). The war marked the ascendance of Transylvania as a political power, and demonstrated a decline in Ottoman imperial power in Europe.

fifth column Term for subversives who work from within to undermine a nation. During the Spanish Civil War, the Fascist Gen. Gonzalo Queipo de Llano (1875?–1951), advancing on Madrid with four military columns, is said to have referred to supporters within the city as his "fifth column."

Fifth Crusade *See* **Crusade, Fifth.**

Fifth Monarchy Men Puritan extremists in England active during the mid-17th cent. This sect of millenarians derived its name from belief in a fifth kingdom mentioned in the Book of Daniel. Its followers held that Jesus would return to rule this kingdom (fifth after Assyrian, Persian, Greek, and Roman empires) and that they were appointed to establish the kingdom for him by any means, including force. They rebelled briefly (1657, 1661), but the sect died out following the execution of their leader.

Fifth Republic Name given the new government of France established with the election (Dec., 1958) of C. de Gaulle as president.

Fifty-four forty or fight Slogan used by Americans who in the 1840s sought annexation of all of the Oregon Territory up to latitude 54°40′ North, then jointly occupied by Britain and the US. It was used by the Democrats during the successful presidential campaign of J. Polk (1844).

Fiji Island group and republic in the South Pacific. Discovered (1643) by A. Tasman, the islands became a British colony (1874), were granted a constitution (1937), and became an independent republic (Oct. 10, 1970). Fiji was a strategic supply link in Allied operations during WW II.

filibuster Prolonged political debate used by legislators to obstruct passage of bills they oppose but lack the strength to defeat. In the 19th cent. the term was applied to armed adventurers who led private expeditions to Central and South American nations.

filioque Latin term meaning "and from the Son," added by the Latin church (6th cent.) to the Nicene Creed. It provoked a bitter controversy and was a main cause of the schism between the Eastern and Western churches.

Filippi, Allesandro di Mariano *See* **Botticelli, Sandro.**

Fillmore, Millard 1800–74. Thirteenth US president (1850–53), successor to Z. Taylor. A political leader in New York State, Fillmore served as US congressman (1833–35, 1837–43), and joined the Whig party in 1834. He became vice-president (1849) under Taylor, the Whig candidate, and president on Taylor's death in office (July 9, 1850). During his administration, Fillmore attempted to steer both his policies and the Whig party on a middle course in the intensifying debate over abolition of slavery. He supported passage of the Compromise of 1850 (*q.v.*) and thereby helped delay civil war. But he raised a storm of protest among Northern abolitionists when he sought to enforce the Fugitive Slave Act (*see* **Fugitive Slave Laws**), which was part of the compromise. The Whig party was badly split over the slavery issue during the election of 1852. Fillmore failed to win the nomination, and the party disintegrated soon after the election. Fillmore subsequently retired from politics except for a brief reappearance (1856) as the Know-Nothing party's presidential candidate.

Fink, Mike 1770?–1823? American frontiersman and folk hero. A celebrated Indian fighter, marksman, and brawler, he was at one time a keelboatman on the Mississippi and Ohio rivers.

Finland Republic located in northern Europe. The population is 4,977,000 and the capital is Helsinki. Finns took over the region by about the 8th cent. Finland came under Swedish control in the 12th cent. and remained subject to the Swedish kings until the Russians conquered the territory during the Napoleonic Wars. Russian control was ended by a successful drive for independence that coincided with the Russian Revolution of 1917. Since that time the neighboring Soviet Union has been a major factor in Finnish history. The Soviets influenced Finnish politics in the years after WW II, but the Finnish government successfully maintained a neutral stance during the Cold War years. The collapse of Communist governments in Eastern Europe and the USSR hurt Finland's economy through loss of trade. Key events in the history of Finland include:

7TH–8TH CENTS. Finns, migrating to Finland from the south, forced Lapps to move to far northern region.

1157 Territory conquered by Sweden's king Eric IX, who introduced Christianity; area ruled as part of Sweden until early 19th cent.

c1550 Protestant Reformation; Lutheranism spread throughout the country.

1581 Finland made a grand duchy; Swedish language and culture continued to dominate.

1700–21 Great Northern War; Sweden ceded parts of eastern Finland to Russia.

1802–84 E. Lönnrot, philologist, lived; collected oral folklore in *Kalevala.*

1802–04 Romantic poet J. Runeberg lived.

1807 Treaty of Tilsit; France agreed not to oppose Russian conquest of Finland.

1808–09 Russia, as an ally of Napoleon, invaded and conquered Finland during the Napoleonic Wars; Russians allowed Finns considerable autonomy thereafter.

1812 Helsinki became the capital of Finland in place of Turku.

1849 Second edition of *Kalevala,* national epic of Finland, compiled by Lönnrot.

1863 Finnish nationalist feelings began to rise in the early 19th cent.; Finnish language finally achieved official status.

1866 Agrarian political party founded by Count Arvid Posse.

1899 J. Sibelius composed *Finlandia.*

1899 Tsar Nicholas II initiated policy to Russify Finland; constitution suspended by the

February Manifesto (Feb. 15); Russia henceforth ruled Finland by edict.

1903–04 Russian governor-general of Finland granted dictatorial powers as Finns resisted Russification (1903); governor-general assassinated (1904).

1905 Finns joined in general strike as Revolution of 1905 broke out in Russia; Tsar Nicholas II granted many concessions, including limited self-government.

1917 After the outbreak of the Russian Revolution, the Finnish Parliament declared the country's independence (Dec. 6).

1918 Finnish War of Independence; anti-Communist Finns defeated Bolshevik Finns (Jan.–May).

1919 Republic established, Kaarlo Juho Ståhlberg in office as first president (1919–1925).

1923 Finnish Communist party outlawed.

1932 Lapua Movement, fascist group, formed in 1929, attempted coup (1932); suppressed by government thereafter.

1932 Nonaggression treaty signed with USSR as part of Finnish foreign policy of maintaining neutrality.

1939–40 Russo-Finnish War broke out as WW II began; Russians victorious after hard fighting and heroic Finnish resistance; Finland forced to give up territories in the east.

1941 Germany invaded USSR; Finland aligned itself with the Germans in the hope of regaining territories lost to the USSR.

1944 Finland again defeated by Soviets; forced to make further concessions and join in effort to drive Germans out of Finland.

1944–46 Baron C. Mannerheim served as president.

1946–56 Juho Kusti Passikivi in office as president; believed appeasement of the Soviets was essential for Finnish independence.

1947 Post-WW II treaty confirmed loss of eastern territories to the USSR.

1948 Treaty of cooperation signed with Soviets; power of Finnish Communist party began to decline.

1955 Joined the UN.

1956–81 Urho Kekkonen in office as president; maintained a policy of judicious neutrality, the "Paasikivi-Kekkonen line," in dealing with neighboring USSR and Western nations.

1966 Finnish Communists participated in coalition government.

1970 Finland concluded trade agreements with both the European Economic Community (Common Market) of the West and the Council for Mutual Economic Assistance (Comecon) of the Eastern Communist countries.

1975 Helsinki the site of the signing of a European security agreement by 35 heads of government; established procedures for seeking international peace.

1980 Export income (increasing to West and decreasing to USSR over next decade) fueled economic growth, and 11 percent inflation rate; Finnish markka revalued.

1981 Crisis over indexing in national wage negotiations; Prime Minister Mauno Koivisto rejected ultimatum by President Kekkonen to reach consensus or resign (Apr. 2) and by his stand won compromise.

1981 Long-time president Urho Kekkonen resigned because of ill health; Koivisto became acting president; Kekkonen died in 1986.

1982– Koivisto, a Social Democrat, in office as president following elections.

1982–87 Prime Minister Kalevi Sorsa led center-left coalition government.

1984 White collar union ordered strikes by teachers, social workers, doctors, and others as government tried to ease inflationary pressures by moderating wage increases in central wage agreements.

1985 Finland's Communist party, long split between majority and minority factions, formally divided; reunited (1990) in the Left League.

1986 Chernobyl nuclear disaster in the USSR; government criticized for failing to promptly alert the public to radiation dangers.

1987–91 Harri Holkeri, Conservative party leader, in office as prime minister; formed new coalition government following election that produced largest non-Socialist majority since 1930.

1987 Constitutional reform approved, allowing for conditional direct elections; electoral college to meet only if presidential candidate fails to win over 50 percent of popular vote.

1988 President Koivisto returned to office following electorial college vote.

1988 Government began partial privatization program (Oct.) with three state-owned companies; reformed tax system (cut top rate to 44%) and increased legal rights of employees.

1989 Nation's largest private shipbuilding company bankrupt (Oct.); reorganized with government aid.

1989 Soviet president M. Gorbachev on state visit; gave first-ever explicit Soviet recognition of Finland as a "neutral Nordic country"; signed new five-year trade agreement, even as Soviet trade with Finland continued declining to new lows.

1990 Finland negotiating for entry into EEC.

1990 Government proclaimed restrictions on Finland's military, set by Paris Peace Treaty of 1947, were no longer valid.

1991 Trade with USSR put on hard currency basis, ending long-standing barter agreement (Jan.).

1991– Esko Aho, Center party leader, in office as prime minister.

1991 Serious recession hampered economy; interest rates reached 30 percent, the markka was devalued, and unions agreed to a 22-month wage freeze.

1992 Finland applied for EEC membership.

Finlay, Carlos Juan (~, Charles John) 1833–1915. Cuban physician who discovered (1881) that yellow fever was transmitted by mosquitoes. His findings were confirmed (1900) in experiments by a US Army commission.

Finlay, Charles John *See* **Finlay, Carlos Juan.**

Finney, Charles Grandison 1792–1875. American evangelist. A lawyer turned Presbyterian minister (1924), he became famous for his highly successful revival meetings.

Finnish War of Independence Civil war (Jan.–May, 1918) fought by anti-Communist Finns with German help. The Finnish Bolsheviks were defeated and the former Russian province aligned itself with Germany in the last months of WW I.

Firdausi (Firdusi) (Ferdowsi) (Firdousi) (*pseud. of* Abul Kasim Mansur) c940–1020. Persian poet, author of the *Book of Kings,* the Persian national epic. The narrative poem covers Persian history to AD 651 and the conquest by the Muslims.

Firdousi *See* **Firdausi.**

Firdusi *See* **Firdausi.**

fire-eaters Pejorative term applied by Americans in the North to Southern extremists who advocated secession to preserve slavery.

Firestone, Harvey Samuel 1868–1938. American rubber manufacturer. He founded the Firestone Tire and Rubber Co. (1900) and built it into one of the largest rubber companies in the US.

First Coalition Alliance of European nations against France that opposed the French Revolution. It was formed in 1792 and its major members included Austria, Prussia, Russia, Britain, and Spain. (*See also* French Revolutionary Wars.)

First Crusade *See* **Crusade, First.**

First Helvetic Confession *See* **Basel, Confession of.**

First Punic War *See* **Punic War, First.**

First Republic Spanish republic (1873–74). It was formed following the abdication of Spanish king Amadeus I but was soon overthrown, and Alfonso XII was proclaimed king.

Fischer von Erlach, Johann Bernhard 1656–1723. Austrian architect and sculptor who introduced the baroque style to Austria.

Fish, Hamilton 1808–93. American statesman. He served as governor of New York (1849–50) and US senator (1851–57). As secretary of state (1869–77) under President U. Grant, he negotiated settlement of the Alabama Claims with Britain.

Fish, Hamilton 1849–1936. American politician. A son of H. Fish, he was assistant US treasurer under T. Roosevelt (1903–08) and congressman (1909–11).

Fisher, Saint John 1459–1535. English Catholic bishop and martyr. He was beheaded for refusing to acknowledge King Henry VIII as head of the church in England under the acts of Succession and Supremacy.

Fisk, James 1834–72. American financier, a flamboyant personality and unprincipled financial manipulator. In his most infamous scheme, he attempted, with D. Drew and J. Gould, to corner the gold market (1869). This resulted in the financial panic called Black Friday.

Fitch, John 1743–98. American inventor. He is considered the inventor (before R. Fulton) of the first American steamboat (1787) although he failed to establish it commercially.

Fitzgerald, Edward *See* **Omar Khayyam.**

Fitzgerald, Lord Edward 1763–98. Irish revolutionary. He unsuccessfully sought aid from revolutionary France for his uprising (1798) against British rule. Wounded in battle, he died in prison.

Fitzgerald, F. Scott (~, Francis Scott Key) 1896–1940. American novelist and short-story writer, one of America's great writers. Fitzgerald has gained a place in American literature as the chronicler of the post-WW I "Jazz Age." His novels include *This Side of Paradise, The Beautiful and Damned, The Great Gatsby, Tender Is the Night,* and *The Last Tycoon.* Among his short-story collections are *Tales of the Jazz Age* and *All the Sad Young Men.*

Fitzgerald, Gerald, 15th earl of Desmond d. 1583. Irish nobleman. He rebelled against Queen Elizabeth's attempts to take over Irish lands. Declared a traitor, he was hunted down and killed.

Fitzgerald, James, 10th earl of Kildare and 1st duke of Leinster 1722–73. Irish nobleman. A member of the Irish Parliament, he is remembered for blocking a plan to hand over surplus revenues from Ireland to the British crown.

Fitzgerald, Maurice d. 1176. Soldier of Welsh and Norman heritage. He helped the king of Leinster, D. McMurrough, in his invasion of Ireland (1169) and thus acquired the Fitzgerald family holdings there.

Fitzgerald, Thomas, 10th earl of Kildare (*called* Silken Thomas) 1513–37. Irish nobleman. When his father, the lord deputy of Ireland, was rumored to have been executed by Henry VIII, Fitzgerald led the Irish in rebellion against the king (1534). He surrendered the following year, and was eventually hanged.

Five Civilized Tribes Five American Indian tribes forcibly removed from their lands in southeastern US to the West after passage of the Indian Removal Act (1830). The tribes were the Cherokee, Chickasaw, Choctaw, Creek, and Seminole.

Five Dynasties Chinese historical period between the end of the Tang dynasty (907) and the beginning of the Sung (960). Five successive short-lived dynasties tried but failed to establish authority. Corruption and anarchy reigned instead, and northern China also suffered famine and floods. The unsuccessful dynasties were the Later Liang (907–923), Later Tang (923–936), Later Jin (936–946), Later Han (947–950), and Later Zhou (951–959). Their capitals were located near the present-day Kaifeng, Honan province.

Five Forks, Battle of Union victory (Apr. 1, 1865) in the American Civil War, at Five Forks, near Richmond Virginia. Union forces under Gen. P. Sheridan defeated the Confederate troops of Gen. G. Pickett. The battle led to the Union capture of Petersburg and (Apr. 3) Richmond.

Five Hundred, Council of Ancient Athenian representative government. Established (508 BC) by Cleisthenes, it consisted of 50 representatives from each of 10 tribes.

Five Nations, League of *See* **Iroquois Confederacy.**

Five-Power Constitution Chinese governmental system advanced by Sun Yat-sen to replace the Chinese imperial order. It called for government by five departments—executive, legislative, judicial, examination, and control—and was implemented (1928) nominally by Chiang Kai-shek upon his accession to power.

Five-Year Plan In the former USSR, name given economic programs designed to increase industrial and agricultural growth through establishment of quotas or goals. The first plan was established (1928) by J. Stalin.

Fizeau, Armand Hippolyte Louis 1819–96. French physicist. He made (1849) the first measurement of the speed of light at the earth's surface. He also studied the spectrum of the sun and applied the Doppler effect to the motion of the stars.

Flaccus, Aulus Persius *See* **Persius.**

Flaccus, Quintus Horatius *See* **Horace.**

flagellants Christian sects originating in 13th-cent. Europe and practicing self-punishment (whipping) as a means to avoid God's wrath. The movement was largely suppressed by the 15th cent., but flagellant sects have continued sporadically to the present.

Flagg, Ernest 1857–1947. American architect. He designed the Singer Building in New York City, which at its completion (1908) was the tallest building in the world (612 ft.).

Flaherty, Robert Joseph 1884–1951. American movie director, explorer, and writer. He directed *Nanook of the North* (1922), generally considered the forerunner of documentary motion pictures.

Flaminian Way One of the great Roman roads. Begun in 220 BC, it extended for 209 miles between Rome and Cisalpine Gaul, ending at what is now Rimini, in northern Italy.

Flamininus, Titus Quinctius c230–174? BC. Roman general and statesman. During the second Macedonian War, he defeated Macedonian king Philip V (197 BC) and subsequently declared (196 BC) Greece independent of Macedonian rule.

Flaminius, Gaius (or Caius) *d* 217 BC. Roman statesman and general. As censor (220 BC) he undertook construction of the Flaminian Way and the Circus Flaminius. He was killed at Lake Trasimene leading Roman forces against Hannibal's invasion of Italy.

Flamsteed, John 1646–1719. English astronomer. The first astronomer royal (appointed 1675), he compiled a major star catalogue, the posthumously published *Historia Coelestis Britannica.*

Flanders Historic county located along the North Sea coast and now divided between Belgium and France. Flanders became a countship in 862 and though dominated by French monarchs, enjoyed a great deal of autonomy in subsequent centuries. Flanders became the leading center of the cloth industry in Europe (13th cent.), and its major cities (Ghent, Ypres, and Bruges) prospered as free communes in manufacturing and trade. Industrialization and prosperity during the 13th and 14th cents. brought a period of rebellion against French domination, alliance with England during the Hundred Years' War, and conquest by the dukes of Burgundy. Flanders passed to the Habsburgs (1477), came under control of the Spanish Habsburg kings (1506), and unsuccessfully rebelled (1576–84) against Spanish rule during the revolt of the Low Countries. After 1714, parts of Flanders passed to various powers until 1830, when the final disposition between Belgium and France was completed. Flanders was the scene of heavy fighting during WW I and the British retreat at Dunkirk during WW II.

Flanders, Henry of *See* **Henry of Flanders.**

Flaubert, Gustave 1821–80. French writer, considered a master of the realistic novel. His masterpiece, *Madame Bovary* (1856), resulted in his prosecution on moral grounds, but he was acquitted.

Flavian Family of Roman emperors that ruled in the 1st cent. AD. The Flavian emperors were Vespasian and his sons Titus and Domitian.

Flavius Arrian *See* **Epictetus.**

Fleet Prison Notorious English jail in London. Its inmates included religious martyrs and victims of the Star Chamber, and it later became known as a debtors' prison. Several times destroyed, it was permanently demolished in 1845–46.

Fleming, Sir Alexander 1881–1955. Scottish bacteriologist. He was codiscoverer, with Sir H.

Florey, of penicillin, and was corecipient of the Nobel Prize in Physiology or Medicine in 1945.

Flemish school Term applied to the tradition of art and architecture that originated in Flanders before the 12th cent. and achieved great influence in European art (15th–17th cents.). The introduction by H. and J. van Eyck of improved techniques in oil painting (15th cent.) revolutionized painting in Europe and helped make Flanders a center of artistic activity. Other notable 15th-cent. Flemish artists included H. Bosch and P. Brueghel the Elder. Flemish art again flourished in the 17th cent. with the work of P. Rubens, A. Van Dyck, and J. Brueghel.

Fleurus, Battles of Three battles fought near Fleurus, Belgium. **1.** Victory (Aug. 9, 1622) of Protestant forces over an allied Catholic army of Spanish and Bavarians during the Thirty Years' War. **2.** Victory (July 1, 1690) of French king Louis XIV over allied forces during the War of the League of Augsburg. **3.** French victory (June 26, 1794) over Austria during the French Revolutionary Wars. Some 70,000 French troops defeated a force of 50,000, mostly Austrians. The battle marked a turning point in France's struggle against the First Coalition.

Fleury, André Hercule de 1653–1743. French statesman and Roman Catholic cardinal. A trusted adviser to Louis XV, he effectively ruled France from 1726 to 1743.

Flexner, Abraham 1866–1959. US educator. Flexner published an evaluation of American educational institutions (1908), followed by a critical study of US and Canadian medical schools that helped bring about needed reform in medical education. Becoming secretary to the General Education Board of the Rockefeller Foundation (1913), he directed huge private donations into American medical education. Later he founded the Institute for Advanced Study in Princeton, New Jersey.

Flinders, Matthew *See* **Australia, 1801–03.**

Flodden, Battle of Battle fought (Sept. 9, 1513) at Flodden, northern England. Some 20,000 English soldiers under T. Howard, 2d duke of Norfolk, defeated an invading Scottish army of 30,000 led by King James IV. James was killed and his army was crushed, with losses put at 10,000.

Flor, Roger de *d.*c1306. Italian-born mercenary. He entered the service of the Byzantine emperor Andronicus II (c1303), but the brutal practices of his army and his apparent intention to set up his own kingdom led to his assassination.

Floréal, Coup of 22 *See* **French Revolution** (1798).

Florence Historic city located in central Italy. In the 14th and 15th cents. Florence was not only a great center of Renaissance art and humanist studies but also a leading banking center. In ancient times Florence was first an Etruscan, then a Roman town, and rose to importance in the 12th cent., when it became an autonomous commune. Florence was ruled by the famous Medici (*q.v.*) family between 1434 and 1737, except for such brief interregnums as the short-lived, puritanical republic established under G. Savonarola (1494–98). In 1737, the Habsburg-Lorraine family succeeded the Medici and ruled Florence until it was absorbed into the unified kingdom of Italy (1860). Florence served briefly as capital of the kingdom (1864–71). The city was home at one time or other for some of the world's greatest literary, intellectual, and artistic figures, including Dante, L. da Vinci, Galileo, N. Machiavelli, G. Boccaccio, Michelangelo, Raphael, B. Cellini, Donatello, Massacio, and S. Botticelli. Among its many landmarks are the Uffizi, the Pitti Palace, and the Cathedral of Santa Maria del Fiore (begun 1296) with its octagonal cupola (by F. Brunelleschi, 1434), campanile (by Giotto, 1387), and famous bronze doors (by A. Pisano and L. Ghiberti, 1330–1447). Florence's many art treasures generally survived WW II, but floods in 1966 caused considerable damage.

Flores, Venancio *See* **Triple Aillance, War of the.**

Florey, Sir Howard Walter 1898–1968. British pathologist. With Ernst Boris Chain (1906–79), he purified penicillin and succeeded in producing enough for practical use. With Chain and A. Fleming (*q.v.*), who discovered penicillin, Florey was awarded the Nobel Prize in Physiology or Medicine in 1945.

Florida US state, on the Atlantic Ocean and the Gulf of Mexico, the 27th state. Ponce de León discovered the region and claimed it for Spain (1513). Colonization began with the founding (1565) of St. Augustine. Britain gained Florida in the Treaty of Paris (1763), but it was returned to Spain in 1783. After years of conflict, it was ceded to the US (1819). Granted statehood in 1845, Florida seceded from the Union (1861)

and joined the Confederacy in the US Civil War. It was readmitted in 1868, and its present constitution was adopted in 1885.

Floridablanca, José Moñino y Redondo, conde de 1728–1808. Spanish statesman. He was premier of Spain (1776–92), and president of the Central Junta (1808), the Spanish government during the French invasion of Spain in the Peninsular War.

Floyd, John Buchanan 1806–63. US secretary of war (1857–60) and Confederate general. He resigned as secretary of war under suspicion of having mismanaged finances, and subsequently became a Confederate general. He was relieved of command after his defeat at Fort Donelson (1862).

Foch, Ferdinand 1851–1929. French general and in 1918, commander of Allied armies in WW I. He fought at the battles of the Marne (1914) and Somme (1916) and was largely responsible for the final defeat of the Germans in 1918.

Fokine, Michel 1880–1942. Russian-born American choreographer, considered the father of modern ballet.

Fokker, Anthony Herman Gerard 1890–1939. Javanese-born aircraft manufacturer. Fokker manufactured airplanes for Germany in WW I. He later emigrated to America, became a US citizen, and designed both commercial and military aircraft in the US.

Folger, Henry Clay 1857–1930. American businessman, known best as founder of the Folger Shakespeare Library in Washington, D.C. The library is based on his personal collection of Shakespeareana.

Folk High School *See* **Grundtvig, Nikolai Frederik Severin.**

Fonseca, Manuel Deodoro da 1827–92. Brazilian general and first president of Brazil (1889–91). He took part in overthrow of the monarchy and establishment of the republic (1889).

Fontaine, Pierre François Léonard 1762–1853. French architect. He and Charles Percier (1764–1838), his associate, were two of the leading architects of the Empire period. He was architect for Napoleon and, later, for kings Louis XVIII and Louis Philippe.

Fontainebleau Name applied to a school or group of artists who, in 16th-cent. France, largely during the reigns of kings Francis I and

Henry II, decorated the royal palace at Fontainebleau.

Fontainebleau, Treaty of Treaty (Oct. 27, 1807) between Napoleon and Spanish king Charles IV dividing Portugal between Spain and France. The treaty was just a step in Napoleon's campaign to bring the Iberian Peninsula under French control.

Fontana, Domenico 1543–1607. Italian architect. He designed the Lateran Palace (1588) and parts of the Vatican (1588). He also was responsible for setting up the Egyptian obelisk in front of St. Peter's.

Fontenelle, Bernard Le Bovier de 1657–1757. French man of letters. His works, many of which dealt with scientific subjects, helped set the stage for the Enlightenment.

Fontenoy, Battle of Battle (May 11, 1745) of the War of the Austrian Succession, at Fontenoy, near Tournai, Belgium. French count M. de Saxe, leading 50,000 French troops, defeated an equivalent force of English, Dutch, Hanoverians, and Austrians under the British duke of Cumberland. It was the last British campaign of the war.

Foote, Andrew Hull 1806–63. American naval officer. As commander of Union naval operations on the upper Mississippi in the Civil War, he distinguished himself in operations against Fort Henry, Fort Donelson, and Island No. 10.

Foot Resolution Resolution introduced (1829) into the US Congress by Samuel A. Foot calling for limitation of sale of public lands. The resolution led to the famous debate (1830) between D. Webster and R. Hayne concerning states' rights and nullification.

Foraker, Joseph Benson 1846–1917. American politician. An Ohio political boss, he was US senator (1897–1909) until a scandal involving payments from the Standard Oil Co. ended his political career.

Forbidden City Chinese fortress city located within the city of Beijing, so-called because most Chinese were forbidden to enter. It was the site, from 1421 to 1911, of the emperors' palaces. After China's fall to the Communists (1949), the palaces were opened to the public as museums.

Force Bill Name given to several pieces of American legislation. 1. Bill passed (Mar. 2, 1833) to reinforce the Tariff of 1832 over the nullification efforts of South Carolina. 2. Bill passed (May 31, 1870) to aid in reconstruction of the South and to protect the rights of newly freed slaves. 3. Bill passed (Apr. 20, 1871) aimed at suppression of the Ku Klux Klan. 4. Bill, also called the Lodge Election Bill, introduced into Congress (1890) to establish federal control of national elections for the further protection of black voters. This bill never cleared the Senate.

Ford, Edsel Bryant 1893–1943. American auto manufacturer, son of H. Ford. He was president of Ford Motor Co. (1919–43).

Ford, Ford Madox (Hueffer, Ford Madox) 1873–1939. English novelist, poet, and critic. As editor of the *Transatlantic Review* and *English Review,* he published works by the major writers of this century. Among his own works are *The Good Soldier* and *Parade's End.*

Ford, Gerald Rudolph, Jr. (*orig.* King, Leslie Lynch, Jr.) 1913– . Thirty-eighth US president (1974–77), successor to R. Nixon. Ford, noted for his integrity and his loyalty to the Republican party, was a US congressman from Michigan (1949–73) and House minority leader (1965–73). Appointed (Dec. 6, 1973) to replace Vice-President S. Agnew who resigned amid the emerging Watergate Scandal (*q.v.*), he became president (Aug. 9, 1974) when Nixon was forced to resign. During his brief tenure as president, Ford issued (Sept. 8, 1974) Nixon a full pardon for charges arising from Watergate, presided over the final evacuation of US personnel from Saigon (Apr. 29, 1975), and ordered a rescue operation in the Mayaguez Incident (*q.v.*). Ford failed to win election to a full term in 1976, in part because of widespread reaction to Watergate and the Republican party.

Ford, Henry 1863–1947. American auto manufacturer who pioneered the assembly-line techniques that revolutionized modern mass production. With others he organized (1903) the Ford Motor Co., and by 1907 had won sole control of it. He introduced to America (1908) the Model T, an inexpensive car, which was produced until its replacement (1928) by the Model A.

Ford, John 1586–c1640. English dramatist, considered the major English dramatist during the reign of Charles I. His works include *'Tis Pity She's a Whore, The Broken Heart,* and *Love's Sacrifice.*

Ford, Worthington Chauncey 1858–1941. American statistician, historian, and editor. He edited the writings of G. Washington and J. Q. Adams, and was chief of the manuscript division of the Library of Congress (1902–09).

Foreign Legion   French volunteer army unit composed mainly of foreigners. Established (1831) by King Louis Philippe to secure French control in Algeria, the legion fought in wars throughout the French colonial empire and served with distinction in WW I and WW II. Its headquarters were moved from Algeria to France in 1962.

Foreign Ministers, Council of   Council of the foreign ministers of the major Allied powers, called together (1945) at the end of WW II to formulate peace settlements with nations that had been allied with the Axis. It included ministers from the US, Great Britain, the USSR, and (from 1946) France.

Foreign Wars, Veterans of   *See* **Veterans of Foreign Wars.**

Forester, Cecil Scott 1899–1966.   British writer known best for his series of novels featuring Horatio Hornblower, a fictional naval hero of the Napoleonic era.

Formigny, Battle of   Battle (Apr. 15, 1450) of the Hundred Years' War, at Formigny, northern France. A decisive French victory over the English, it marked the end of English resistance to the French recapture of northern France. Some 4,000 of the 5,000-man English force were slaughtered.

Formosa   *See* **Taiwan.**

Forest Cantons   *See* **Four Forest Cantons.**

Fornovo, Battle of   French victory (July 6, 1495) over the forces of the League of Venice during the French invasion of Italy (1494–95) by Charles VIII during the Italian Wars (*q.v.*).

Forrest, Edwin   *See* **Macready, William Charles.**

Forrest, Nathan Bedford 1821–77.   Confederate general during the American Civil War. Considered a great military strategist, he led many important calvary raids behind enemy lines (1862–64). He is said to have ordered the Fort Pillow Massacre (1864).

Forrestal, James Vincent 1892–1949.   American public official. He was secretary of the navy (1944–47) under President F. Roosevelt and the first secretary of defense (1947–49) upon the organization of the Department of Defense.

Forster, Edward Morgan 1879–1970.   English novelist, essayist, and critic. One of the major authors of the 20th cent., he wrote, among other works, *Howards End* and *A Passage to India.*

Fort Clatsop   *See* **Lewis and Clark Expedition.**

Fort Dearborn   American army post, established (1803) on the Chicago River and named for Secretary of War H. Dearborn. Destroyed during the War of 1812, it was rebuilt (1816–17), and, with other communities, became the city of Chicago.

Fort Donelson   Confederate stronghold during the American Civil War, located on the Cumberland River at Dover, Tennessee. Its fall (Feb. 16, 1862) to Union forces under Gen. U. Grant, aided by a gunboat flotilla under Commodore A. Foote, allowed the Union army to advance on Nashville. Here Grant issued his famous reply to a request for surrender terms: "No terms except unconditional and immediate surrender can be accepted."

Fort McHenry   US fort at the entrance to Baltimore Harbor. Its bombardment (Sept. 13–14, 1814) by the British during the War of 1812 inspired F. Scott Key to write *The Star-Spangled Banner.*

Fort Pillow Massacre   Infamous racial incident in the US Civil War, at Fort Pillow, on the Mississippi, north of Memphis, Tennessee. The fort was stormed (Apr. 12, 1864) and taken by Confederate forces under Gen. N. Forrest, and many of its defenders, half of whom were black, were killed. Forrest was accused of allowing his men to massacre the black Union troops after they had surrendered.

Fort Stanwix, Battle of   Siege (Aug. 2–23, 1777) during the American Revolution. At Fort Stanwix near Rome, New York, 750 Americans successfully withstood a siege by a British force of 1,700 led by Gen. B. St. Leger. The relief of the fort by B. Arnold contributed to the subsequent British defeat at Saratoga.

Fort Sumter   Fort in the harbor of Charleston, South Carolina, site of the first military action of the American Civil War. Following the secession of South Carolina (Dec., 1860), state officials demanded the evacuation of some 100 US Army soldiers garrisoned in the fort. When President A. Lincoln signaled his intent to resupply the fort (Apr., 1861), Confederate forces, under Gen. P. Beauregard, shelled it (Apr. 12–14) and forced its evacuation. The fort was not recaptured until 1865.

forty-niners   Name given to the American gold prospectors who traveled by thousands to California in 1849 after hearing that gold had been discovered (1848) on J. Sutter's land.

Forty-two Articles *See* **Thirty-nine Articles.**

forum Roman meeting place. Similar to the Greek agora, it was a large, centrally located, open-air place in which Roman citizens would gather for festivals, speeches, elections, or other public events.

Fosdick, Harry Emerson 1878–1969. American Baptist minister. A well-known leader of modernists within the church, he became embroiled in controversy with the fundamentalists in the 1920s. His sermons were aired in a national radio program (1926–46).

Foster, Stephen Collins 1826–64. American song writer. His minstrel songs and ballads, such as *Oh! Susannah, Camptown Races,* and *My Old Kentucky Home,* are among the best known of popular American songs.

Foster, William Zebulon 1881–1961. American Communist party leader and presidential candidate (1924, 1928, 1932). A labor agitator, he headed the party from 1921 to 1930 and from 1945 to 1957.

Foucault, Jean Bernard Léon 1819–68. French physicist. He developed a method to measure accurately the speed of light (1850), demonstrated the earth's rotation by means of "Foucault's pendulum" (1851), and invented the gyroscope (1852).

Foucault, Michel 1926–84. French structuralist philosopher. The son of a physician, Foucault at first studied the history of mental illness. His interests then focused on ways in which societies operate, specifically the social mechanisms of exclusion. He is known for such writings as *Madness and Civilization* (1961) and *Discipline and Punish: the Birth of the Prison* (1975).

Fouché, Joseph 1763?–1820. French revolutionary and famed minister of police. As untrustworthy as he was shrewd, he alternately helped and intrigued against French leaders in the tumultuous years between 1792 and 1815. As police minister (1799–1802, 1804–10), he organized the French police and created a notorious spy network.

Foucquet *See* **Fouquet.**

Fouqué, Friedrich Heinrich Karl, Baron de la Motte 1777–1843. German Romantic novelist and poet. He is known best for his story *Undine.*

Fouquet, Jean (Foucquet, ~) c1415–c1480. French painter. A leading painter in his day, he

was court painter to Louis XI and Charles VII. Among his works are the illuminations in the *Book of Hours.*

Fouquet, Nicolas (Foucquet, Nicholas) 1615–80. French superintendent of finance (1653–61) to King Louis XIV. He enriched himself and others at the expense of the royal treasury and was finally tried for embezzlement (1661–64) and sentenced to life imprisonment (1664).

Fouquier-Tinville, Antoine Quentin 1746–95. French revolutionary. Prosecutor for the Revolutionary Tribunal (1793–94) during the Reign of Terror, he himself fell victim to the guillotine.

Four Forest Cantons The first four Swiss cantons (Uri, Schwyz, and Unterwalden in 1291, Lucerne in 1332) to break away from Habsburg domination. They formed the foundation of the Swiss Confederation.

Four Freedoms American policy objectives as stated by President F. Roosevelt in his State of the Union message (1941). The freedoms, to be enjoyed by the world, were: freedom of speech, freedom of worship, freedom from want, and freedom from fear.

Fourier, Charles 1772–1837. French social philosopher. He advocated the organization of society based on the phalanx, a communal unit of 1,620 people. His philosophy fostered numerous attempts at communal societies, including the Brook Farm experiment in the US.

Fourier, Jean Baptiste Joseph, baron 1768–1830. French mathematician and physicist noted for his contributions in the field of mathematical physics.

Fournier, Pierre Simon 1712–68. French type designer and founder. He designed many new type faces and wrote the *Manuel typographique.*

Four Noble Truths *See* **Buddhism.**

Four-Power Pacific Treaty International pact (Dec. 13, 1921) by which the US, Great Britain, France, and Japan agreed to respect each other's Pacific territorial rights and to confer peacefully in case of disagreement.

Fourteen Points American peace proposals advanced (Jan. 8, 1918) by US president W. Wilson as a foundation for a lasting peace after WW I. They were: the abolition of secret diplomacy; freedom of the seas; equality of trade among peaceful nations; mutual reduction of armaments; peaceful mediation of colonial disputes; self-determination for USSR possessions restoration of Belgium; restoration of French territory in Alsace-Lorraine;

readjustment of the Italian border; autonomy for the national populations within Austria-Hungary; restoration of Serbia, Montenegro, and Rumania; establishment of an independent Poland; self-determination for Turkish possessions and the internationalization of the Dardanelles; and the creation of a "general association of nations" to mediate future disputes. Many of the points as enumerated by Wilson were altered or ignored by the Treaty of Versailles (*q.v.*), but the 14th point was the foundation for the League of Nations.

Fourth Crusade *See* **Crusade, Fourth.**

Fourth Republic Name given the French government established (1946) after WW II. It lasted until 1958. (*See also* France, 1946–58.)

Fowler, Henry Watson 1858–1933. English lexicographer. He compiled the classic reference work *A Dictionary of Modern English Usage.*

Fox, Charles James 1749–1806. British statesman. Acclaimed for his oratory, the liberal Fox supported both American and Irish independence and the French Revolution. He argued for religious toleration and an end to the slave trade.

Foxe, John 1516–87. English Protestant clergyman. He wrote the widely read *Book of Martyrs,* which recounted (though not always accurately) the persecution of Protestant reformers up to his time.

Fox Indians *See* **Sac and Fox Indians.**

Frahm, Karl Herbert *See* **Brandt, Willy.**

France (French Republic) Republic located in Western Europe. The country's population is 56,184,000 (est.) and the capital is Paris. France evolved from the West Kingdom of the Franks, which was formed by the divisions of Charlemagne's empire (843–871). Development of a powerful French monarchy began in the 10th cent. and culminated in the absolutism of Louis XIV in the 17th–18th cents. By then France had also become a major European power. A flourishing culture developed in France in the 12th cent. and it has significantly influenced modern civilization in the West, notably in literature and the arts. The French Revolution, which began as an experiment in liberal republicanism, ended with Napoleon's rise to power. Under Napoleon, France briefly controlled nearly all of continental Europe. By the time of Napoleon's fall in 1815, the spirit of the French Revolution had been spread throughout Europe and gave rise to liberal, nationalistic movements that flowered in the mid-1800s. France led

Europe in becoming a democracy and a republic, but declined as a military power. Since WW II France has followed a relatively independent foreign policy, cultivating relations with Third World countries and, in more recent years, with (then) Soviet-bloc countries. (*See also* French Revolution, French Revolutionary Wars, Napoleonic Wars.) **For more on important persons and major events** *see* **entries under specific names.** Key events in the history of France include:

c600 BC Celts settled in Gaul (region roughly that of modern France).

c600 BC Marseilles founded by Ionian Greeks as a trading colony.

58–51 BC Romans, led by J. Caesar, conquered Gaul; prospered in subsequent years as a Roman province.

52 BC Gallic village of Paris conquered by Caesar.

1ST CENT. AD Christianity introduced in Gaul.

3D CENT. Saint Denis, patron saint of France, lived; martyred by Roman emperor Valerian on Montmartre.

3D CENT. AD Invasions of Gaul by Franks and other barbarian peoples began.

FROM 428 AD Salian Franks gradually took control of northern France.

481 AD Clovis I became leader of the Salian Franks; this marked the beginning of the Merovingian kingdom in Gaul.

486 AD Battle of Soissons; Clovis I defeated armies of the last Roman governor of Gaul.

496 AD Clovis defeated the invading Alemanni; converted to Christianity and thereafter became a staunch opponent of Arianism.

500 Clovis attacked but did not conquer Burgundy.

507 Visigoths defeated by Clovis in battle at Vouillé.

511–687 Merovingian kingdom divided; on the death of Clovis (511) there followed nearly two centuries of wars and divisiveness; two Frankish kingdoms, Austrasia and Neustria, emerged but their kings had been weakened by the constant wars; the mayors of the palace, who served them, held real power.

c534 Burgundy conquered.

575–91 Saint Gregory of Tours wrote *History of the Franks.*

687 Pepin of Heristal, as mayor of the palace of Austrasia (1687–714), conquered Neustria;

he thus united the Merovingian kingdom under his rule, though the kings remained in title; Pepin was the first of the Carolingians.

8TH–14TH CENTS. Feudalism established as dominant social system in France other European countries.

715–741 C. Martel, Pepin's son, became Austrasian mayor of the palace; subdued Neustria and began series of conquests that expanded Frankish domains.

732 Battle of Poitiers; C. Martel won famous victory over Muslim force advancing from Spain; victory increased his power.

751 Carolingian kingdom founded; Pepin the Short, mayor of the palace from 741, overthrew the Merovingian king and took the crown for himself (751).

754–756 Donation of Pepin; in return for papal sanction for his overthrow of the Merovingians, Pepin aided the pope against Lombards in Italy, donated lands conquered from them to the church.

768–814 Charlemagne reigned; by his conquests brought the Carolingian kingdom to its greatest extent, including most of modern France, Germany, northern Italy, and the Low Countries.

800 Charlemagne crowned emperor of the (reconstituted) Western Roman Empire by Pope Leo III; coronation, granted in return for aiding pope, strengthened ties between Rome and the European monarchs.

814–840 Louis I (the Pious) reigned as the last ruler of a unified Carolingian Empire.

843 Treaty of Verdun; empire divided into three parts by Louis's heirs: West Frankish kingdom (roughly modern France), East Frankish kingdom (roughly modern Germany), and a narrow middle kingdom that included Italy; middle kingdom (except Italy) largely absorbed by other two in following years.

870 Treaty of Meersen; middle Frankish kingdom (except Italy) divided between West and East Frankish kingdoms.

843–877 Charles the Bald reigned as king of the West Franks; Charles held the imperial crown as (titular) ruler of the Carolingian Empire from 875.

877–879 Louis II (the Stammerer) reigned.

879–884 Louis's heirs, Louis III (ruled 879–882) and Carloman (ruled 879–884), reigned in the West Frankish kingdom.

881 Louis III defeated Norse raiders at Saucourt.

881–887 Charles III (the Fat) reigned; he briefly reunited West and East Frankish kingdoms (882–887) but was overthrown; final breakup of the Carolingian Empire.

888–898 Eudes and Charles III (the Simple) chosen as rival kings of the west; Eudes was forced to defend Paris against Norse raiders and fight a civil war with Charles.

898–923 Charles III king in the west; after Eudes's death (898) he ended Norse raids by ceding parts of Normandy to their leader, Rollo (911); deposed by rebellious nobles (923).

910 Clunaic order founded at Cluny as reformist branch of Benedictine order.

922–923 Robert I, a Capetian, named king in opposition to Charles during the revolt; he was killed in battle.

923–936 Rudolph reigned; central authority further weakened by renewed fighting against Norsemen and rivals, as well as against Magyar invaders.

936–954 Louis IV reigned; embroiled in wars with Hugh the Great, a leader of the nobles who was aided by German king Otto I; Louis finally emerged victorious in 950.

954–986 Lothair reigned; wars with the nobleman H. Capet and Holy Roman Emperors Otto II and Otto III (over Lorraine) reduced royal power to almost nothing.

987–996 H. Capet reigned, founding the Capetian line of French kings; his domains consisted of the region around Paris; as king of the West, he held only nominal rule over the feudal principalities that then comprised France (including Normandy, Brittany, Burgundy, and Aquitaine).

996–1031 Robert II reigned; excommunicated by Pope Gregory V for marrying (996) widow of Eudes; brought Burgundy under the control of French kings (1015).

11TH–12TH CENTS. Romanesque style art and architecture, centered in France, reached its height.

11TH–13TH CENTS. Troubadours flourished in southern France.

1031–60 Henry I reigned; embroiled in various wars to maintain his domains and opposed interference by the church.

1060–1108 Philip I reigned, increased royal domains at the expense of feudal lords; unsuccessfully attempted to separate Normandy from English control (after 1066); opposed the reforms of Pope Gregory VII.

1108–37 Louis VI (the Fat) reigned; warred with King Henry I of England over English domains on the Continent; repulsed an invasion by the Holy Roman Emperor Henry V (1124); issued royal charters to towns then beginning a period of rapid growth.

1095 First Crusade preached at Council of Clermont, held in France; French nobleman, Raymond IV, count of Toulouse, organized the crusade.

12TH–13TH CENTS. The trouvére, lyric poets and musicians, flourished in northern France.

12TH CENT. Gothic style in art and architecture originated in France at this time.

1115 Saint Bernard of Clairvaux founded his monastery at Clairvaux.

1121 P. Abelard's book, *Theologica,* condemned as heresy; his romance with Héloïse and subsequent misfortunes, later became the subject of literature.

1137–80 Louis VII reigned; forced to submit to the pope (1144); took part in the unsuccessful Second Crusade; rivaled English for control of Continental domains.

1144 Geoffrey Plantagenet, count of Anjou, gained Normandy by his marriage to Matilda; later gave this powerful duchy to his son, Henry of Anjou (later Henry II of England).

1152 Louis VII annulled his marriage to Eleanor of Aquitaine; she later married Henry of Anjou and when Henry became king of England, he laid claim to Anjou, Normandy, and Aquitaine.

c1164 Great medieval poet of Arthurian romances, C. de Troyes, flourished.

1180–1223 Philip II reigned; by his conquests, doubled French domains; conquered northeastern territories from feudal lords and captured Normandy, Brittany, Anjou, Maine, and Touraine from the English (1204); central government underwent tremendous expansion.

1200 University of Paris founded; in following years Paris became a medieval center of learning; Albertus Magnus and Saint Thomas Aquinas did highly influential work in theology there.

c1200 Poet J. Bodel wrote *The Play of St. Nicholas,* believed the first French miracle play.

1208–13 Albigensian Crusade against heretics in southern France.

1214 Battle of Bouvines; Philip emerged victorious from this battle against English king John and Holy Roman Emperor Otto IV; established France as a major power.

1216 Saint Dominic founded Dominican order of Catholic friars; order subsequently in charge of Inquisition and actively pursued missionary work.

1223–26 Louis VIII reigned; launched unsuccessful invasion of England to aid barons' revolt (1216–17); resumed fighting against Albigensians.

1226–70 Louis IX reigned; considered the ideal medieval monarch, he brought medieval France to its height; instituted administrative reforms.

1229 Raymond of Toulouse, who had supported the Albigensians, submitted to the crown; his lands, comprising much of southern France, added to royal domains.

1231–32 Medieval Inquisition began.

1242 Unsuccessful rebellion by nobles in southern France, aided by invasion by English king Henry III.

1248–54 Louis's participation in the Seventh Crusade proved ruinous; captured and ransomed back to France.

1259 Treaty of Paris, settling territorial disputes with English king Henry III; included renunciation of former English territories and French suzerainty over Aquitaine.

1270–85 Philip III reigned.

1285–1314 Philip IV reigned; his attempt to tax clergy grew into dispute with the pope.

1294–98 War with England; Philip failed in his effort to take the English-held duchy of Guienne.

1302–03 Philip called the first States-General (council of nobles) in connection with his dispute with the pope.

1302 Battle of the Golden Spurs (July 11); Flemish towns opposing French annexation decisively defeated French troops.

1305 Philip secured election of Pope Clement V, a supporter of his cause.

1309 Pope Clement V moved the papacy to Avignon (Babylonian Captivity), increasing Philip's control of church.

1312 Pope Clement V condemned the Knights Templars at King Philip's urging;

Philip then confiscated the order's considerable wealth.

1314–16 Louis X reigned.

1316 John I reigned.

1316–22 Philip V reigned; Salic Law invoked to justify his succession and thus established its use in France.

1322–28 Charles IV (the Fair) reigned as last of the Capetian kings.

1328–1589 Valois dynasty reigned; founded by Philip VI.

1328–50 Philip VI reigned; the Salic Law was invoked to allow for his succession.

1337–1453 Hundred Years' War; long rivalry for control of English domains on the Continent ended when French drove out all English forces (1453); victory gained at great cost, with France laid waste and its nobility decimated; the monarchy became significantly stronger, however.

1341–65 War of the Breton Succession, dynastic struggle in Brittany.

1348–49 Black Plague spread to France.

1350–64 John II reigned; was captured during the Hundred Years' War (1356); Battle of Poitiers fought (1360).

1358 Jacquerie, group of French peasants, revolted against increased war taxes.

1364–80 Charles V (the Wise) reigned; regained much territory from England, instituted reforms, consolidated power of the monarchy, strengthened the military.

1380–1422 Charles VI reigned; suffered fits of insanity and was unable to rule; civil war between Burgundians and Armagnacs broke out (after 1407) over which faction was to control the regency of Charles; Burgundians became allies of English; Battle of Agincourt fought (1415).

c1415–80 Noted painter J. Fouquet lived; served as court painter to Louis XI and Charles VII.

1422–61 Charles VII reigned; English controlled north of France at outset of his rule; not crowned until after Joan of Arc inspired French troops to lift siege of Orléans; his reign saw the end of the Hundred Years' War (1453) and the capture of virtually all English territory on the Continent.

1429 Joan of Arc lifted siege of Orléans during Hundred Years' War, a feat that made her a French heroine; she was later burned at the stake by the Burgundians (1431).

1431–1463? F. Villon, great French lyric poet, lived.

1438 Pragmatic Sanction of Bourges; issued by Charles VII to limit papal powers; asserted powers of French king in France and declared pope subject to general council (conciliarism).

1440 Praguerie, revolt by nobles against Charles VII.

1461–83 Louis XI reigned; overcame rebellious nobles and laid the basis for absolute monarchy in France.

1465 League of the Public Weal, rebel alliance formed by nobles against King Louis XI.

1467–1540 Leading French Renaissance scholar, G. Budé, lived.

1477 Louis defeated Charles the Bold, duke of Burgundy; Burgundy, until then autonomous state, joined to French crown.

1480 House of Anjou became extinct; Louis added its territories (Provence, Anjou, Maine, and Bar) to possessions of French crown.

1470–98 Charles VIII reigned; his attempt to conquer Naples brought on the long Italian Wars.

1494–1559 Italian Wars; fought for control of Italy; Spanish Habsburgs emerged victorious after years of sporadic warfare.

1498–1515 Louis XII reigned; he was unsuccessful in the Italian Wars.

16TH CENT. Pleiad, a group of seven French Renaissance poets, flourished; led by P. de Ronsard.

16TH CENT. Fontainebleau school of French artists did decorative painting at royal palace at Fontainebleau.

1520 Treaty of Cambrai (Ladies' Peace) with Holy Roman Emperor Charles V; it briefly halted the Italian Wars.

1515–47 Francis I reigned; continued Italian Wars against Holy Roman Emperor Charles V; his reign marked by flowering of the French Renaissance and by beginnings of Protestantism in France.

1516 Concordat of Bologna; Pragmatic Sanction of Bourges rescinded.

1520 Field of Cloth of Gold; Francis attempted to form alliance with English King Henry VIII.

1532–64 F. Rabelais wrote *Gargantua and Pantagruel.*

1533–92 Essayist M. de Montaigne lived.

1534–35 Discovery and exploration of St. Lawrence River in North America by J. Cartier.

1537 Law passed requiring that copy of all books published in France be donated to national library, Bibliothèque Nationale; collection begun with royal library of Charles V (14th cent.).

1546 Scholar É. Dolet, called "martyr of the Renaissance," executed for heresy.

1547–59 Henry II reigned; ended Italian Wars and began persecutions of French Protestants (Huguenots); increased royal powers.

1547 Brittany united to French crown.

1556–58 War between Valois and Habsburg families won by Spanish Habsburgs at the Battle of Gravelines, northern France.

1558 Calais captured by French; was last English territory in France.

1559–60 Francis II reigned; Catholic Guise family rose to power and dominated his reign; used their power to severely persecute Protestants.

1560 Conspiracy of Amboise, Protestant plot to break power of Guise family; foiled, it led to massacres of Protestants.

1560 Treaty of Edinburgh signed with England and Scotland; led to withdrawal of French and English troops from Scotland to ease conflict between Catholics and Protestants there.

1560–74 Charles IX reigned; he was dominated by his mother, Catherine de Médicis, throughout his reign.

1562–98 Wars of Religion; series of wars stemming from persecution of French Protestants by Catholics and complicated by struggles for political power.

1574–89 Henry III reigned; helped plan the Massacre of St. Bartholomew's Day (1572) during the continuing Wars of Religion; the last of the Valois line, he was assassinated.

1589 Henry III assassinated by French Dominican monk, J. Clement for having chosen Protestant successor.

1589–1610 Henry IV reigned; the leader of French Protestants, he converted to Catholicism (1593) to win support for his accession; he founded the Bourbon line.

1589–1792 House of Bourbon in power.

1598 Edict of Nantes established toleration of Protestants and ended Wars of Religion.

17TH CENT. Painter N. Poussin became leading force in French classicism.

1601–65 Mathematician P. de Fermat lived; founded modern theory of numbers.

1603 French explorer Samuel de Champlain voyaged to Canada; later founded Quebec.

1610–43 Louis XIII reigned; dominated by his mother, Marie de Médicis, until 1617 and thereafter relied on his ministers.

1613–80 Writer of maxims, F. de La Rochefoucauld, lived.

1618–48 Thirty Years' War.

1619–55 Satirist Cyrano de Bergerac lived; later made subject of E. Rostand's play of that name.

1624–42 Cardinal Richelieu in power as chief minister to Louis XIII; promoted concentration of power in monarchy at expense of nobles; helped make France the dominant European power.

1632 Company of New France formed; promoted French colonization of Acadia in eastern Canada until English permanently took over in 18th cent.

1637 Philosopher R. Descartes published his *Discourse on Method,* one of his most important works; later published *The Principles of Philosophy* (1644).

1637 Dramatist P. Corneille wrote his tragedy *Le Cid.*

1642–44 Scientist B. Pascal invented first digital calculator.

1642–61 Cardinal Mazarin in power as chief minister; succeeded Richelieu and remained in office under Louis XIV; continued Richelieu's policies; broke remaining power of nobles and helped make France leading power.

1643–1715 Louis XIV reigned; absolutism reached its height in France while his extravagance and expansionist wars wrecked French finances; built Palace of Versailles.

1648 Alsace controlled by France after the Treaty of Westphalia ending the Thirty Years' War.

1648–49 Fronde of the Parlement, unsuccessful rebellion against Louis's rule.

1650–53 Fronde of the Princes, unsuccessful rebellion by nobles led by the Prince de Condé.

1657–1757 Scholar B. Le Bovier de Fontenelle lived; his ideas helped shape those of the Enlightenment.

1659 Peace of the Pyrenees ended hostilities with Spain that continued after the Thirty Years' War; border established.

1662–90 Charles Le Brun dominated French art as court painter to Louis XIV.

1664 French East India Company, colonial trading organization, formed to develop trade with India.

1664 Playwright Molière wrote his famous comedy *Tartuffe;* later wrote *Le Misanthrope* (1666).

1667–68 War of Devolution; first of Louis's expansionist wars and directed at acquiring the Spanish Netherlands.

1668–94 Poet Jean de La Fontaine wrote *Fables choises, mises en vers,* a literary masterpiece.

1668–1747 A. Lesage, French writer, lived.

1671–84 Astronomer J. Cassini discovered four moons of Saturn.

1672–68 Dutch War; Louis XIV sought to expand French domains and commerce at the expense of the Netherlands.

1673 French explorer J. Marquette charted course of the Mississippi River in North America with L. Jolliet.

1675–1726 Father of modern cartography, G. Dalisle, lived.

1675–1755 Memorist L. Saint-Simon lived.

1677 J. Racine, great dramatist, wrote *Phèdre;* two years later completed *Iphigénie en Aulide.*

1677 Theologian F. Fénelon embroiled in controversy over quietism.

c1680 Poison Affair; Louis XIV's mistress accused of obtaining potions to kill rivals.

1682 Gallican Articles approved by French clergy, an important document in French movement called Gallicanism, which sought greater independence of the French church from the pope.

1682 Explorer R. La Salle laid claim to Mississippi valley in North America, naming it Louisiana.

1683–1764 Composer, J. Rameau, lived.

1684–1721 Rococo painter, J. Watteau, lived.

1685 Revocation of the Edict of Nantes; toleration of French Protestants ended, resulting in mass emigration of Protestants from France.

1685 Saint John Baptist de la Salle founded first normal school to train teachers to work with poor children.

1688 Author J. La Bruyère wrote *Les Caractères ou les moeurs de ce siècle,* a classic in French literature.

1688–97 War of the League of Augsburg, Louis's third expansionist war.

1695–1702 Author J. de la Motte Guyon imprisoned in the Bastille for advocating religious movement called quietism.

1697 French poet C. Perrault published the Mother Goose fairy tale collection.

1700s Enlightenment, great intellectual movement, rooted in the scientific revolution and devoted to rationalism, emerged in France and spread through Europe and America.

1700s Rococo style in the arts originated in France.

18TH–19TH CENTS. Romantic movement in art and literature emerges in response to theories of the Enlightenment and classicism.

1701–14 War of the Spanish Succession; France gave up claims to Spanish throne and lost all but small part of colonial possessions in Canada.

1702–10 Revolt of the Camisards, Protestant peasants.

1715–74 Louis XV reigned; a weak and unpopular ruler, he was dominated by his mistresses; financial difficulties of his reign helped bring on French Revolution.

1720 Mississippi Scheme uncovered; financial scandal involved government.

1723–89 Baron d'Holbach, Enlightenment philosopher, lived.

1728 Dentist P. Fauchard wrote *The Surgeon Dentist,* which became a standard work.

1733–35 France supported Poland in War of the Polish succession; occupied duchy of Lorraine (1733).

1736–1806 Physicist C. Coulomb lived.

1740–48 War of the Austrian Succession; France mainly fought England in the colonies.

1741–1828 Master of portrait sculptures, J. Houdon, lived.

1744–1829 Biologist J. de Lamarck lived.

1745–1826 P. Pinel, French physician, lived; revolutionized treatment of mentally ill.

1748 Political philosopher C. de Montesquieu wrote his masterwork, *The Spirit of Laws.*

1749–1827 Mathematician P. de Laplace lived.

1751–72 Great work of the Enlightenment, the *Encyclopédie,* compiled by scholar D. Diderot.

1756 Diplomatic Revolution ended long-established European alliances.

1756–63 Seven Years' War; France lost most of colonies in India and Canada to England by the Treaty of Paris.

1758 F. Quesnay, leader of Physiocrats, completed his *Tableau Économique.*

1760–1825 C. Saint-Simon, social thinker who formulated early form of scientific socialism, lived.

1762 Philosopher J.-J. Rousseau wrote *The Social Contract.*

1766–69 Navigator L. de Bougainville completed first French circumnavigation of the world.

1766–1831 Composer R. Kreutzer lived.

1768–1830 J. Fourier, mathematician and physicist, lived.

1771 Parlements (courts) dissolved by Louis XV to check their growing power; restored (1774) after move proved unpopular.

1771–1802 M. Bichat, anatomist and physiologist, lived.

1774 Chemist A. Lavoisier explained the role of oxygen in combustion, thus disproving the phlogiston theory.

1774–92 Louis XVI reigned; tried to rule as an enlightened despot but attempts to put forward badly needed reforms failed and led to the French Revolution.

1774–76 A. Turgot, minister of finance, started ambitious program of tax and other reforms but was dismissed before it was completed.

1775 Playwright P. de Beaumarchais wrote *The Barber of Seville;* completed *The Marriage of Figaro* in 1784.

1777–81 J. Necker in power as finance minister; enacted some reforms and was ousted (1781); he then made public the precarious state of the treasury.

1778–83 French aided colonists in American Revolution, thus further depleting royal treasury.

1780 French government sent Gen. J. comte de Rochambeau and some 6,000 French troops to aid the Colonial cause in the American Revolution.

1780–67 J. Ingres, a leading 19th-cent. French classicist painter, lived.

1783 Inventor J. Mongolfier constructed first practical hot-air balloon.

1783–87 C. de Calonne in office as finance minister; devised plan to save France from financial disaster by reforming land tax; plan bitterly opposed by anstocrats.

1785 Affair of the Diamond Necklace; Queen Marie Antoinette tied to a sexual and financial scandal, which only increased popular dislike of her.

1785 Balloonist J. Blanchard completed first aerial English Channel crossing.

1787 Assembly of Notables convened to save the monarchy from bankruptcy (Feb.); Calonne's land-tax reform submitted to it to circumvent opposition from the Parlements (courts); assembly dismissed without accomplishing reform (May).

1787–88 E. Loménie de Brienne in office as finance minister; continued to press for Calonne's reforms and met continuing opposition from the aristocracy; forced decision to call States General; resigned (Aug.).

1788–89 Necker recalled as finance minister; States-General convened (1789) and thus began the revolution.

1789 Journalist C. Desmoulins gave speech (July 12) that rallied crowd to storm the Bastille (July 14).

1789 H. de Mirabeau, leading figure of early French Revolution, elected to States-General; unsuccessfully advocated moderate course of establishing constitutional monarchy.

1789 M. Lafayette, then vice-president of the National Assembly, drafted the Declaration of the Rights of Man.

1789–99 French Revolution; France plunged into several years of turmoil and experimentation with republican government; Napoleon emerged as the leader of revolutionary France and established first the Consulate (1799) and then the empire (1804) under his imperial control.

1791 Erotic writer Marquis de Sade wrote *Justine.*

1792 Army engineer C. Rouget de Lisle wrote French national anthem, *La Marseillaise.*

1792–1802 French Revolutionary Wars; other European powers, opposed to the revolutionary government, warred against France.

1793 Radical revolutionary J. Hébert arrested in early attempt to oust moderate Girondists (May); he helped overthrow the Girondists and institute the Reign of Terror later in 1793.

1793 French queen Marie Antoinette, wife of Louis XVI, guillotined (Oct.).

1793 Girondist leader J. de Warville executed after takeover by radical Jacobins.

1793 J. David, founder of French classical school, painted *The Assassination of Marat*.

1794 Philosopher A. Nicolas, marquis of Condorcet, executed by Jacobin extremists.

1794 Radical revolutionary G. Couthon guillotined following the end of the Reign of Terror.

1794 Elegaic poet A. de Chénier guillotined.

1796–1832 Pioneering thermodynamics physicist, N. Carnot, lived.

1797 XYZ Affair, attempted bribing of American diplomats by French officials, led to undeclared naval war with US.

1799–1802 J. Fouché served as minister of police; organized French police forces in France and again served as minister 1804–10.

1799–1804 Government of the Consulate in power; Napoleon seized power by the Coup of 18 Brumaire (Nov. 9); he established the Consulate with himself as dictator, restored order, and instituted reforms.

1799 Constitution of the Year VIII (Dec. 29); formally established government of the Consulate and instituted efficient administrative system.

1800 Treaty of San Ildefonso concluded between Spain and France; Spain retroceded Louisiana territory to France.

1800s Various movements arose in 19th-cent. France, including the Symbolists and Parnassians; this period also saw the rise of the Barbizon school of realistic landscape painting and the spread of the Empire style.

1801 Napoleon restored relations with the Roman Catholic church, severed since the early days of the Revolution.

1801 J. Jacquard built the first loom to weave patterns.

1801–79 Caricaturist H. Daumier lived.

1802 French Revolutionary Wars ended; terms favorable to France.

1802 Napoleon made consul for life (Aug. 2).

1802 Writer F. Chateaubriand, published *The Genius of Christianity*.

1803–15 Napoleonic Wars; Napoleon's conquests gave France control of much of continental Europe for a time.

1803–69 Great Romantic composer H. Berlioz lived.

1804 Assassination plot against Napoleon discovered (Feb.); G. Cadoudal, a conspirator, executed; Napoleon used incident to justify creation of the empire.

1804 Napoleon proclaimed emperor (May 18) by Senate and Tribunate of the Consulate.

1804–14 Empire period; Napoleon crowned (Dec. 2); Napoleon created a new nobility and installed rulers in conquered territories within the empire; period marked by expansion of the empire throughout Europe during the Napoleonic Wars.

1804 Napoleon issued the famous Code Napoléon.

1804–69 Literary critic C. Sainte-Beuve lived.

1804–76 Writer G. Sand lived.

1805–81 Revolutionary activist H. Blanqui lived; spent much of his life in prison.

1807 Napoleon issued the Commercial Code.

1808–15 Napoleon's friend and ally, Marshal J. Murat, reigned as king of Naples.

1808 Social philosopher, C. Fourier, wrote *The Social Destiny of Man*, proposing existence of natural social order of man.

1809 A. Ampère, physicist and mathematician, developed his law of electromagnetism, Ampère's law.

1809 Chemist J. Gay-Lussac developed law of combining volumes for gases.

1810 Penal code issued by Napoleon.

1810 Napoleon married Marie Louise, daughter of Austrian emperor Francis I, after divorcing Josephine.

1810 Napoleon ordered destruction of book *De l'Allemagne*, written by G. de Staël.

1814 Napoleon's first abdication (Apr. 6), following occupation of Paris by allied forces.

1814–30 Restoration period.

1814–24 Louis VIII reigned; restored to power (Apr. 6); issued Declaration of Saint-Ouen (May) as basis for new constitution.

1814 Treaty of Paris (first, May 30); returned France to boundaries of 1792.

1814 Charter of 1814 issued (June 4) as new constitution for France; retained some freedoms gained by revolution.

1815 Hundred Days; Napoleon returned from exile and entered Paris (Mar. 20); reestablished as emperor, he was defeated at Waterloo and again abdicated (June 22).

1815 Chamber Introuvable established (Aug.); ultraroyalists dominated Chamber of Deputies as persecutions of former revolutionaries and Bonapartists reached height; Chamber finally dissolved (Sept., 1816) and replaced by moderates.

1815 Treaty of Paris (second, Nov. 20); imposed harsher terms, including payment of war indemnity and military occupation by allies for three years.

1815 B. Constant de Rebecque completed early psychological novel *Adolphe.*

1816 Physician R. Laënnec invented the stethoscope.

1818 Military occupation of France ended after the Congress of Aix-la-Chapelle.

1819 Anti-classical artist J. Géricault painted his famous work, *The Raft of the Medusa.*

1820 Comte de Villèle established ministry of ultraroyalists; marked victory of ultraroyalists in struggle with moderates and liberals; ministry instituted reactionary policies.

1820 Poet A. de Lamartine, first true French Romantic poet, published *Méditations poétiques,* which established him.

1820s–1860s Greatest of French Romantic artists, F. Delacroix, painted his most famous works during this period.

1822 French intervention in the liberal revolt in Spain approved at the Congress of Verona; Spanish monarchy restored (1823).

1824–30 Charles X reigned; vainly tried to reestablish *ancien régime* and thereby provoked growing hostility of liberal factions; decision to install ultraroyalist ministry under A. de Polignac led to revolution.

1828–93 H. Taine, noted figure in 19th-cent. positivism, lived.

1829 L. Braille began publicizing his system of writing for the blind.

1829 H. Balzac published his first successful novel, *Les Chouans.*

1830 Algeria occupied by French.

1830 July Revolution (July–Aug.) ended in victory for bourgeois liberals; Charles abdicated and a parliamentary monarchy was assured by revision of the Charter of 1814.

1830 Play *Hernani* by V. Hugo, precipitated riots between classicists and romanticists; Hugo wrote such classic novels as *The Hunchback of Notre Dame* and *Les Misérables.*

1830–48 Louis Philippe ("Citizen King") reigned, installed by the Chamber of Deputies, he was head of the Orléanist branch of the Bourbon family; his reign was marked by economic instability and growing power fro the bourgeoisie.

1830–1903 Impressionist painter Camille Pissarro lived.

1832 P. Borel, leading Romantic poet and novelist, wrote his *Rhapsodies.*

1835 T. Gautier wrote *Mademoiselle de Maupin.*

1835–39 A. de Tocqueville published *Democracy in America.*

1835–75 G. Bizet composed the opera *Carmen.*

1839 Photography pioneer L. Daguerre invented the daguerreotype.

1840 Socialist L. Blanc published *Organization of Work.*

1841 Balzac designated the body of his work, past and future, as *The Human Comedy.*

1844 A. Dumas (père) wrote *The Three Musketeers* and *The Count of Monte Cristo.*

1844–96 Poet P. Verlaine lived.

1846 Astronomer U. Leverrier, with Englishman J. C. Adams, discovered planet Neptune.

1848 February revolution broke out; forced King Louis Philippe to abdicate (Feb. 24) and led to establishment of Second Republic.

1848–52 Second Republic.

1848 June Days, bloody revolt by workers in Paris (June 23–26).

1848 New constitution (Nov.) created government by strong president and unicameral legislature.

1848–51 Louis Napoleon, nephew of Napoleon I, in office as elected president.

1849 Physicist A. Fizeau measured the speed of light at earth's surface for the first time.

1850 Novelist Stendhal published *The Red and the Black.*

c1850 Socialist theorist, P. Proudhon, advocated "mutualism."

1851   Coup by Louis Napoleon (Dec. 2); he proclaimed himself Emperor Napoleon III (1852).

1852   A. Dumas (fils) completed *La Dame aux Camélias,* later dramatized as *Camille.*

1852   Physicist J. Foucault invented the gyroscope.

1852–60   Second Empire period.

1852–70   Napoleon III reigned; promulgated imperial constitution (Jan. 15, 1852); promoted industrialization and economic growth.

1854   Philosopher A. Comte, founder of positivism, published his *System of Positive Polity.*

1854–56   Crimean War; France opposed Russian expansion into domains of the Ottoman Turks.

1856   Novelist G. Flaubert wrote *Madame Bovary.*

1857   Poet C. Baudelaire wrote *Les Fleurs du mal.*

1858   Attempt to assassinate Napoleon III by Italian nationalist Felice Orsini (Jan. 14); precipitated Napoleon to help Italian nationalists drive Austrians out of Italy (from May, 1859).

1860   Napoleon agreed (Nov.) to more liberal government to counter mounting opposition to his rule; legislature given new powers.

1860s   Chemist L. Pasteur developed pasteurization.

1861   French intervened in Mexico; established Mexican empire under Maximilian I, which lasted until just after French troops were forced to withdraw (1866).

1863   É. Manet, the originator of impressionism, by this time had painted *Olympia,* one of his greatest works.

1865   É. Zola published his first novel, *Le Confession de Claude.*

1866–68   Frenchman M. Garnier explored and mapped Indochina.

1869   *Germinie Lacerteaux* written by the Goncourt brothers, pioneers of the Naturalism movement.

1869   Writer A. Daudet portrayed French provincial life in *Lettres de Mon Moulin.*

1870   New constitution creating parliamentary empire forced on Napoleon by growing movement for liberalization (Apr.).

1870–71   Franco-Prussian War; France was quickly defeated and occupied, marking end of French hegemony on the Continent.

1870   Reverses in Franco-Prussian War led to political unrest; Napoleon III overthrown (Sept.).

1870   J. Verne wrote the early work of science fiction, *Twenty Thousand Leagues Under the Sea.*

1870–71   Government of National Defense formed (Sept. 4); capitulated to Germans (Jan. 28, 1871).

1870–1940   Third Republic.

1871–73   A. Thiers in office as head of state (Feb.) with legislative assembly (Bordeaux Assembly).

1871   Commune of Paris, revolt by radicals in Paris (Mar.–May).

1871   Treaty of Frankfurt (May 10) ended the Franco-Prussian War; France lost territory in Alsace and Lorraine.

c1872–1886   Impressionism, influential French school of art, flourished.

1873   Symbolist poet A. Rimbaud wrote *A Season in Hell.*

1873–79   M. MacMahon in office as second president of the republic; his unsuccessful attempt to name a royalist ministry over objections of the Chamber of Deputies established power of chamber over ministry (1877).

1875   New constitution formally established republic after attempts to restore monarchy failed to gain support.

1876   Leading symbolist poet S. Mallarmé wrote *Afternoon of the Faun.*

1876   Impressionist P. Renoir painted the popular *Girl with Watering Can.*

1876   Postimpressionist painter P. Cézanne began to evolve his geometric style about this time, and thereby helped lay the foundation for cubism.

1877   Impressionist E. Degas painted *The Rehearsal.*

1877   Composer C. Saint-Saëns composed the opera *Sampson and Delilah.*

1879–87   J. Grévy in office as president.

1880–1918   Poet G. Apollinaire, an early surrealist, lived.

1880s   Avant-garde composer E. Satie began writing his unconventional musical compositions.

1880s   Expansion of the French colonial empire in Indochina and North Africa began.

1883–85   Sino-French War; France won control of Vietnam as it expanded its control in Indochina.

1880 Explorer P. de Brazza established French protectorate over the Congo; established colony there from 1883.

1880 Physician C. Laveran discovered parasite that causes malaria; awarded Nobel Prize for Physiology or Medicine (1907).

1880 Composer J. Offenbach died, leaving his opera *Tales of Hoffmann* unfinished.

1880 A. Rodin sculpted *The Thinker.*

1880–81, 1883–85 J. Ferry in office as premier; oversaw expansion of the French colonial empire in Africa and Indochina.

1881–1955 Artist F. Léger lived; pioneered "machine art."

1884 Trade unions legalized; labor movements and socialism on the rise.

1884 Composer J. Massenet wrote *Manon.*

1885 Writer, H. Guy de Maupassant published *Bel-Ami.*

1885 Pasteur devised vaccination against rabies.

1886 Neoimpressionist painter G. Seurat completed *Sunday Afternoon on the Island of La Grande Jatte,* a notable example of the pointillistic technique he developed.

1886 *Statue of Liberty,* created by French sculptor F. Bartholdi, erected in New York Harbor.

1887 V. Sardou wrote the play *La Tosca.*

1887 Actor A. Antoine founded the Théâtre Libre in Paris.

1889 Boulanger Crisis; Gen. G. Boulanger, widely popular since 1886, came close to seizing power as dictator (Jan. 1889); fled France soon after.

1889 Engineer P. Bunau-Varilla, in charge of the French Panama Canal project, persuaded France to sell project to United States.

1890 Novelist A. France published *Thaïs.*

1890s Group of French artists called Nabis formed.

1891 Impressionist C. Monet painted *Haystacks.*

1891 H. de Toulouse-Lautrec painted *Le Moulin de la Galette.*

1891 Great postimpressionist painter H. Gauguin moved to Tahiti; his works figured in the development of modern art.

1892 Panama Scandal rocked French government.

1893 E. Durkheim, a founder of sociology, wrote *The Division of Labor.*

1894 C. Debussy composed *Prelude to the Afternoon of a Faun.*

1894 Bacteriologist A. Yersin discovered the black plague bacillus, simultaneously with S. Kitasato.

c1894–1902 Dreyfus Affair, French army captain falsely accused of treason; prolonged crisis brought moderate leftists to power and advanced anticlericalism.

1895 L. and A. Lumière invented cinematograph.

c1895 Removable pneumatic tires for autos developed by Michelin brothers.

1896 Scientist A. Becquerel discovered radioactivity in uranium.

1897 P. Dukas composed *The Sorcerer's Apprentice.*

1897 Playwright E. Rostand wrote *Cyrano de Bergerac.*

1898 Extreme conservatives founded the French Royalist party called French Action.

1898 Fashoda Incident, with Britain, resulting from French and British expansion in Africa.

1898 Scientists P. and M. Curie isolated radium and polonium; shared 1903 Nobel Prize for Physics for their work.

1898–1905, 1914–15 T. Delcassé served as French foreign minister.

c1900 Artist A. Mailiol began sculpting; became famous for his massive statues of female nudes.

1900 Leading Symbolist H. de Régnier wrote his novel *La Double Maîtresse.*

1901 First Nobel Peace Prize awarded to French economist F. Passy and Swiss philanthropist J. Dunant.

1901 First Nobel Prize for Literature awarded to poet R. Sully-Prudhomme.

1904 Entente Cordiale, informal understanding with Britain, reached to counter growing power of Germany.

1905 Separation of church and state by law.

1905 Fauvist H. Matisse exhibited his painting *Woman With the Hat.*

1905 Moroccan Crisis, resulting from colonial rivalry with Germany.

1905–08 Fauvism, short-lived French artistic movement, ascendant; influenced later development of modern art.

1905–11 Psychologist A. Binet developed his system of intelligence tests.

1906–13 Clément Armand Fallières served as president; his term marked by rise of nationalism and spread of labor troubles.

1907　L. Daudet, writer and journalist, co-founded royalist paper *L'Action Française.*

1908　G. Braque painted his *Nude,* which illustrated a stage in the development of cubism.

1908　Theologian A. Loisy, founder of Modernism in the Catholic Church, excommunicated.

1908　Philosopher G. Sorel published *Reflections on Violence.*

1908　A. Calmette, bacteriologist, developed tuberculosis vaccine.

1908–14　So-called "White period" of painter M. Utrillo, in which his best-known works were produced.

1909　C. Pathé pioneered the film newsreels.

1910　Primitivist H. Rousseau painted *The Dream.*

1910　Sculptor H. Gaudier-Brzeska, who later led the movement called vorticistism, began his career in sculpting.

1911　Agadir Incident, renewed troubles with Germany over Morocco.

1913–20　Raymond Poincaré in office as president; led France through war years.

1914–18　World War I; France, the primary battleground, devastated by the war; after the war, gained left bank of the Rhine, as well as mandates in Syria and Africa.

1913–1927　Novelist M. Proust published his masterpiece, *Remembrance of Things Past,* a novel in seven parts.

1915　Nobel Prize in Literature awarded to R. Rolland, author of *Jean Christophe.*

1917　Poet P. Valéry wrote *La Jeune Parque.*

1917　Infamous Dutch spy, Mati Hari, executed in France.

1919–24　Bloc National, a conservative coalition, dominated national politics.

1921　Writer A. France received Nobel Prize in Literature.

1923　D. Milhaud, pioneering composer, wrote *Creation of the World.*

1923–25　France occupied the Ruhr district when Germany failed to make war reparations payments.

1924–34　Poet A. Breton, a founder of surrealism, wrote his manifestos for surrealism.

1924–26　Crisis of the franc.

1925　Locarno Pact signed with Germany, restoring relations.

1927　Architect Le Corbusier completed the first building, a villa, built according to his revolutionary new style of design.

1927　Philosopher H. Bergson, who wrote *Creative Evolution,* received Nobel Prize for Literature.

1927　G. Marcel, first French existential philosopher, published his *Metaphysical Journal.*

1928　M. Ravel composed the ballet *Boléro.*

1930s　Economy hit by worldwide Great Depression.

1931　Composer A. Roussel wrote the ballet *Bacchus and Ariane.*

1931–40　A. Lebrun in office as president.

1932–46　J. Romains published his 27-volume novel *Men of Good Will.*

1933　Visionary Saint Bernadette canonized.

1933　A. Malraux wrote *Man's Fate.*

1934　Stavinsky Affair; the financial scandal resulted in a political crisis and rise of French fascism.

1935　Concessions in Africa made as government followed policy of appeasement toward fascist Italy.

1936　Expressionist G. Rouault painted *The Old King.*

1936　G. Bernanos wrote his novel *Diary of a Country Priest.*

1936–38　Popular Front formed governments in France under L. Blum; front was a coalition of Socialists, Radicals, and Communists led by Blum; instituted social reforms.

1937　Filmmaker J. Renoir directed *La Grande Illusion.*

1937　Composer F. Poulenc wrote his *Mass in G.*

1938　Munich Pact signed to appease Nazis.

1939–45　World War II; the French, quickly defeated and occupied, nevertheless continued to resist Germans; much of France damaged in Allied drive across Europe at end of war.

1940　Third Republic ended; Vichy government under French marshal H. Pétain established in unoccupied France (June).

1940　C. de Gaulle set up Free French government in London.

1942　Vel d'Hiv roundup of 16,000 Jews by French police (July); Jews subsequently deported to Nazi death camps.

1942　Vichy government superseded following complete German occupation of France.

1943   J.-Y. Cousteau, famous French underwater explorer, co-invented aqualung.

1943   Famed existentialist J. Sartre published *Being and Nothingness.*

1943   A. de Saint-Exupéry wrote the fable *The Little Prince.*

1944–46   De Gaulle established provisional government at Paris (Aug.); Vichy collaborators purged; nationalization of financial industry and utilities (1945–46).

1945   Women gained right to vote.

1945   France joined the UN.

1945   Novelist Colette wrote *Gigi.*

1945   J. Cocteau directed the noted film *Beauty and the Beast.*

1946   France received massive US aid to rebuild war-torn economy.

1946–58   Fourth Republic; government formed with weak executive; colonial empire reorganized as the French Union.

1946–54   Indochina War; France unsuccessfully tried to reestablish its control over the region.

1947   A. Gide received the Nobel Prize for Literature.

1947   Statesman J. Monnet drafted the Monnet Plan for reconstructing postwar French economy.

1947–54   Vincent Auriol in office as first president; French politics marked by rivalries between the Popular Republican Movement (MRP, moderate), Socialists, and Communists.

1949   France became founding member of NATO.

1949   S. de Beauvoir published *The Second Sex.*

1949   C. Lévi-Strauss, social anthropologist, wrote his first major work, *The Elementary Structure of Kinship.*

1951   S. Weil, philosopher and religious mystic, wrote *Waiting for God.*

1952   Nobel Prize for Literature awarded to author F. Mauriac.

1952   J. Anouilh wrote *Antigone.*

1954   Rebellion against French rule in Algeria broke out (Nov. 1); followed France's defeat in Indochina that year.

1954–59   R. Coty in office as last president of the Fourth Republic.

1956   Suez Crisis; France joined with Britain in opposing Egyptians.

1956   J. Genet, leader of the Theater of the Absurd.

1957   France became founding member of European Economic Community.

1957   Nobel Prize for Literature awarded to A. Camus, who wrote *The Stranger* and *The Plague.*

1958   De Gaulle recalled to power (June 1) as continuing crisis in Algeria threatened to topple French government; de Gaulle given extraordinary powers and mandate to write new constitution.

1958   Fifth Republic formed; new constitution established strong presidency; French Community replaced French Union of overseas territories.

1958–69   De Gaulle in office as first president; achieved granting of Algerian independence; pursued independent foreign policy and established strong Gaullist constituency; presided over period of economic growth.

1959   Philosopher P. Teilhard de Chardin published *The Phenomenon of Man.*

1959   Director F. Truffaut completed his film *The 400 Blows.*

1959   Playwright E. Ionesco wrote *Rhinoceros.*

1960   France exploded its first nuclear device.

1962   Algerian independence granted despite terrorist campaign by Secret Army Organization in France and Algeria.

1964   France recognized Communist China.

1966   France withdrew from NATO; US and others forced to withdraw military forces from France.

1968   Student riots (May) sparked a national political crisis; subsequent elections gave de Gaulle an absolute majority; education system reformed.

1969   De Gaulle resigned (Apr.) after his program for regional reform was rejected by voters.

1969–74   G. Pompidou in office as president; largely continued de Gaulle's policies, though he ended French opposition to Britain's membership in the Common Market.

1970   Pompidou signed agreement for political and economic cooperation with USSR.

1974   President Pompidou died in office (Apr. 2).

1974–81   Valéry Giscard d'Estaing in office as president; continued Gaullist independent foreign policy.

1979 Strikes and rioting broke out after government subsidies to industry were cut.

1981– F. Mitterrand, a Socialist, in office as president; his election victory over the Gaullist coalition marked a sharp leftward shift in French politics; left-wing government formed, with four Communists being named to cabinet posts; after an initial period of rapid social and economic reform, the pace of change was markedly slowed by increased opposition from the right and by an economic recession.

1981 President Mitterrand began implementing his Socialist program; minimum wage raised 10 percent and new taxes of business and the wealthy promised.

1982 Nationalization of selected major industries became effective (Feb. 11).

1982 French territory of Corsica granted greater autonomy to elect territorial assembly; move opposed by Corsican separatists, who continued campaign of terrorist attacks throughout the 1980s.

1982 French troops took part in operation to oversee evacuation of PLO from Beirut, Lebanon; French troops later made up largest portion of UN peace-keeping forces in Lebanon.

1983 Government imposed budget cuts and other deflationary measures to combat recession.

1983 French troops sent to Chad to help fight Libyan-backed rebels there; additional troops sent in 1987.

1983–84 Wave of terrorist attacks by Basque separatists in southwestern France; government subsequently stopped granting asylum to Spanish Basque separatists and began cooperating with Spain in effort to halt their terrorist activities.

1985 New proportional representation system introduced for electing National Assembly members; voters throughout a department (province) to choose from alternate lists of party candidates representing the department; former system of voting for a single member representing district within a department restored for 1988 election.

1985 French secret service agents blew up Greenpeace trawler *Rainbow Warrior* in New Zealand harbor, killing one aboard; boat had been engaged in protest against French program of atomic tests in South Pacific.

1986 Mitterrand's left-wing government lost legislative majority to center-right coalition; Mitterrand named Jacques Chirac, leader of Gaullist Rassemblement pour la République (RPR) prime minister; Chirac formed predominately center-right government, serving under Socialist President Mitterrand.

1986 Government ordered 65 state-run companies privatized (July).

1986 Terrorist bombing campaign in Paris sparked enactment of stiffer anti-terrorist measures.

1986 French struck deal with Iran, settling on repayment of $1 billion loan made to former shah of Iran and ousting anti-Iranian mujahidin group from France; French hostages held in Lebanon by pro-Iranian terrorists released in 1987–88, amid charges government had made secret arrangement with Iran.

1987 Scandals over French arms illegally supplied to Iran, and embezzlement of French foreign-aid money.

1988 Mitterrand reelected president in decisive win over divided rightist opposition; Socialist Michel Rocard formed minority left-wing coalition government "opening to the center"; government fell into pattern of collapsing before increasingly frequent public protests and unrest on a variety of issues; continued fostering close ties with USSR and East European nations.

1988 Wave of strikes followed government attempt to cut budget by holding down public service workers' wages.

1989 Berlin Wall opened (Nov. 9), heralding end of Cold War division of Europe; subsequent unification of Germany forced major foreign policy shift for France; French opted for encouraging greater integration among European nations as means of containing unified Germany's political and economic power.

1990 Assembly passed legislation reforming scandal-ridden party financing practices (including kickbacks and fake invoices); law criticized for allowing prosecution of only those outside political office, and not the politicians themselves.

1990 France to cut military by 35,000 men and scale back weapons procurement programs (July); to withdraw all 50,000 troops now stationed in Germany (Sept.).

1990–91 Persian Gulf War; France, long-time ally of Iraq and home to a large Muslim population, nevertheless sent troops for coalition force to oust Iraqis from Kuwait.

1990 Government enacted stiffer penalties for anti-Semitic and similar acts after flurry of racist incidents; some 200,000 had marched in Paris against racism and anti-Semitism.

1990 Mass demonstration by some 200,000 secondary school students; protests turned violent, resulting in worst Paris riots since 1968; government increased education budget.

1990 Corsica to be granted greater autonomy under Joxe Plan (Nov.); separatist protested plan with terrorist bombings and assassinations (1990–91); Joxe Plan enacted in Apr., 1991.

1990 Treaty on Conventional Armed Forces in Europe (CFE) signed in Paris (Nov.) by NATO and Warsaw Pact members; put limits on conventional forces deployed between Atlantic Ocean and Ural Mountains.

1991 Prime Minister Rocard's government dissolved (May); Edith Cresson, France's first female prime minister, formed new government; promised more control over economy and industry, but her popularity quickly fell amid unrest and general disenchantment with government; Mitterrand, meanwhile, sought to slow entry of former Communist-bloc nations to EC.

1991 Prime Minister Cresson established emergency job training program for youths, in response to wave of violence in urban areas with high immigrant populations (June–July).

1991 Stricter rules on immigration (July) and political asylum (Oct.) established; employers of illegal immigrants to be punished.

1991 Maastricht summit on unification of Europe (Dec.); France promoted adoption of European political and economic union.

1992 Investigation into political party financing scandals yielded recommendation for prosecution of 11 politicians, including members of the ruling PS party.

1992 Prime Minister Cresson's government dissolved following major local and regional election losses for Socialists; former Finance Minister Pierre Beregovoy named prime minister; he promised to ease unemployment by spurring economic growth.

1992 Legislature voted to amend constitution to meet requirements of Maastricht Treaty on political and economic union; amendments allowed adoption of single European currency, free circulation of European Community citizens in France, and gave them right to vote in elections in France.

1992 EC agricultural ministers agreed to mandate farm subsidy cuts in the member countries (July); French government supported the reform despite blockades and other protests mounted by farmers in France (June).

France, Anatole (*pseud. of* Jacques Anatole Thibault) 1844–1924. French author. One of the leading literary men of his day, he wrote *Thaïs* and *The Red Lily,* among other works. He was awarded the Nobel Prize in Literature in 1921.

France, Battle of German offensive (May 10–June 16, 1940) against France during WW II. After defeating the Belgian and Allied armies in Belgium and forcing them to evacuate at Dunkirk, the Germans turned to the destruction of the French army. Outflanking the Maginot Line (*q.v.*), the Germans moved south, taking Paris on June 14 and Verdun one day later. On June 16, French premier P. Reynaud resigned and was replaced by Marshal H. Pétain, who immediately called for an armistice. France formally accepted Germany's armistice terms (June 22, 1940) at Compiègne, in the same railway car the Germans had accepted armistice terms in WW I.

Franche-Comté Name given to the French county of Burgundy (as distinct from the duchy of Burgundy). It became a possession of the Habsburgs (16th cent.), and was annexed by France (1678).

Franchia Media *See* **Lotharingia; Verdun, Treaty of.**

Francia, José Gaspar Rodríguez (El Supremo) 1761?–1840. Dictator of Paraguay (1814–40). Joining the government after the bloodless revolt against Spain (1811), he became dictator (1814) and thereafter freely exercised his harsh personal rule.

Francis I 1494–1547. French king (1515–47), successor to his father-in-law, Louis XII. Much of his reign was spent in conflict with Holy Roman Emperor Charles V. He failed to gain the support of English king Henry VIII at the Field of Cloth of Gold (1520) and eventually engaged Charles in four wars, largely unsuccessful. During his reign the French Renaissance flowered and J. Cartier explored North America.

Francis I 1708–65. Holy Roman Emperor (1745–65). As duke of Lorraine (1729–37), he ceded his duchy to Poland to end the War of the Polish Succession. His marriage (1736) to Maria Theresa, a stronger personality and Habsburg heiress, led to his accession as coregent of Austria and Holy Roman Emperor during the War of the Austrian Succession (*q.v.*). The Seven Years' War (1756–63) was fought during his reign.

Francis I 1777–1830. Italian king of the Two Sicilies (1825–30), successor to his father, Ferdinand I. His reign was marked by corruption and repressive policies.

Francis I (of Austria) *See* **Francis II.**

Francis II 1453–88. Duke of Brittany (1458–88), successor to his father, Arthur III. Francis struggled to remain independent of France. He joined (1465) the League of the Public Weal against Louis VI and unsuccessfully rebelled against Charles VIII, whom his daughter, Anne of Brittany, later married.

Francis II 1544–60. French king (1559–60), successor to his father, Henry II. The Guise family effectively ruled France during his short reign and used their power to persecute the Huguenots (Protestants). The unsuccessful attempt to break their power was called the Conspiracy of Amboise (*q.v.*).

Francis II (˜ I of Austria) 1768–1835. Last Holy Roman Emperor (1792–1806) and king of Bohemia and Hungary, successor to his father, Leopold II. He was also first emperor of Austria (Francis I, 1804–35). A determined opponent of the French Revolution and of Napoleon, he was several times defeated by the French in battles between 1793 and 1806. In 1806 he was compelled to sign the Treaty of Pressburg, which dissolved the Holy Roman Empire. In domestic politics he stood for tightly centralized rule and repression of dissent.

Franciscans Originally a religious order founded in Italy (1209) by Saint Francis of Assisi and now three separate orders: Friars Minor, Friars Minor Conventual, and Friars Minor Capuchin. The order was founded on rules written by Saint Francis stressing a life of poverty, religious devotion, and dedication to helping others. Francis subsequently rewrote and modernized the rules following the rapid spread of his order. These new rules were formally approved by Pope Honorius III (1223). By the 16th cent. the order had split between the Conventuals, who adhered to the communal life, and the zealously ascetic Observants. The Observants became an independent order (1517) and subsequently gave rise to the Capuchins (1525), whose order was founded on still stricter devotion to the ascetic life. The Franciscans have been prominent in missionary and educational work.

Francis Ferdinand 1863–1914. Austrian archduke (1875–1914). The nephew of Austrian emperor Francis Joseph I, he became heir after the death (1889) of Crown Prince Rudolf. The assassination of Francis and his wife at Sarajevo (June 28, 1914) touched off WW I.

Francis Joseph 1830–1916. Emperor of Austria (1848–1916) and king of Hungary (1867–1916), the younger brother of Francis Joseph. An absolutist, Francis was forced to yield to constitutional reform (1861) and creation of the Dual Monarchy (1867, *q.v.*) after a series of military reversals. He allied himself with Germany in WW I.

Francis of Assisi, Saint (*b.* Giovanni Francesco Bernardone) 1182–1226. Italian monk, founder of the Franciscans and one of the great saints of the Christian church. The son of a merchant, he converted to a life of poverty and religious devotion while still in his twenties. He began preaching as a layman in 1209, and in that year, with permission from Pope Innocent III, founded the Franciscan order based on his teachings. He made a pilgrimage to Palestine (1219–20) during the Fifth Crusade, and in 1221 gave up leadership of the Franciscans. Following a 40-day fast (1224) at Mount Alverno, he miraculously received the "stigmata," wounds likened to those suffered by Jesus at the Crucifixion. Francis died with the wounds, said to be the first instance of such stigmata. He was canonized in 1228.

Francis of Sales, Saint 1567–1622. French Roman Catholic bishop, Doctor of the Church. He is known for his work in converting French Calvinists and for founding the Order of the Visitation for women.

Franck, César Auguste 1822–90. Belgian-French organist and composer of the Romantic school. His best-known work is his *Symphony in D minor.*

Franco, Francisco 1892–1975. Spanish general and dictator. Made army chief of staff (1934), he took part in the military revolt (1936) at the outset of the Spanish Civil War. Later that year he became leader of the rebel government and, with the aid of German and Italian troops, brought the civil war to an end (1939). Despite the Fascist origins of his ruling Falange party, Franco kept Spain neutral during WW II and maintained a pro-Western policy in the years afterward until his death.

Franco, João *See* **Charles I (1863–1908).**

Franconia One of the five historic duchies of medieval Germany (with Saxony, Lotharingia, Swabia, and Bavaria), located in what is now west central Germany. Originally part of the Frankish kingdom, it became the basis for the East Frankish kingdom on the division of the Carolingian Empire (843). It was partitioned (939), creating the duchies of Rhenish Franconia and Eastern Franconia. In subsequent centuries the duchies were further fragmented and divided. The name Franconia now survives as the name of three modern German provinces in Bavaria: Lower, Middle, and Upper Franconia.

Franco-Prussian War War (1870–71) between France and Prussia (with allied German states). The war brought about the unification of the German states under Prussian domination and thus achieved the long-sought goal of Prussian minister O. von Bismarck. Following the Austro-Prussian War (1866), France aggressively sought an opportunity to check the rising power of Prussia. Bismarck, on the other hand, was near to completing the unification of German states. Only the southern states remained outside the North German Confederation (*q.v.*) and Bismarck hoped to play on anti-French sentiment to bring them into the fold. With both sides thus primed, war was almost inevitable and fighting broke out in Aug., 1870. France suffered a humiliating defeat soon after. Consequences of the war were far-reaching: France rebelled against the monarchy and established the Third Republic (1870); Germany was unified (1871); and French hegemony over Continental Europe was ended. Key dates in the war include:

1870 Prince of Prussia's ruling house (Hohenzollern-Sigmaringen) offered Spanish throne; France, concerned about growing Prussian power, threatened war if the prince took the throne; Prussians declined the throne (July 11).

1870 France demanded apology and assurances from Prussian king William I against further consideration of taking the Spanish throne; William I refused (July 13).

1870 Ems Dispatch released (July 13) by Prussian minister O. von Bismarck, contributing to tensions that ended in outbreak of war; Bismarck revised the dispatch, sent to him by King William, to help provoke war.

1870 France declared war on Prussia (July 19).

1870 France mobilized some 200,000 troops, Prussia more than 450,000; southern German states joined Prussian cause against France, as Bismarck had expected (July); Prussians invaded Alsace (Aug. 4).

1870 The Prussians defeated the French in major battles at Weissenburg (Aug. 4), at Worth (Aug. 6), and at Spichern (Aug. 6).

1870 French armies led by Marshal A. Bazaine bottled up at Metz by two German armies; attempts to break out were defeated at Vionville (Aug. 16) and Gravelotte (Aug. 18).

1870 Marching to relieve Metz, the French under Marshal M. de MacMahon and Emperor Napoleon III were surprised by the Germans and driven northward toward Sedan (late Aug.).

1870 Battle of Sedan (Sept. 1), northern France, ended in surrender of French army and downfall of the Emperor Napoleon III.

1870 Paris rebelled upon the news of defeat at Sedan; France declared a republic; Paris surrounded and besieged by the Germans (Sept. 19).

1870 Marshal Bazaine surrendered his garrison of nearly 180,000 men at Metz (Oct. 27); Paris continued to resist despite worsening famine.

1871 German states formally unified (Jan. 18) into the German Empire; William I of Prussia became king of Germany; these events marked culmination of Bismarck's long effort to achieve unification.

1871 Paris surrendered to Germans (Jan. 28).

1871 French named A. Thiers as head of state (Feb.); preliminary peace treaty approved (Mar. 1).

1871 Commune of Paris, bloody revolt by Paris radicals (Mar.–May) against new government; loyal French troops retook city and inflicted severe reprisals.

1871 Final peace treaty signed at Frankfurt (May 10); France ceded Alsace and part of Lorraine to the German Empire and agreed to pay five billion francs in reparations.

Frankfurt, Council of Ecclesiastical meeting. Called (794) by Charlemagne, with the approval of Pope Adrian I, to consider the acts by the Second Council of Nicaea, it condemned Adoptionism as well as the worship of graven images and carried out reforms of the Frankish church.

Frankfurt, Treaty of French-German treaty (May 10, 1871) ending the Franco-Prussian War. France was forced to yield disputed territories in Alsace and Lorraine, to pay a 5-billion-franc indemnity, and to suffer German occupation until these terms were met.

Frankfurter, Felix 1882–1965. Austrian-born American Supreme Court justice. Appointed (1939) by F. Roosevelt, he followed a policy of judicial restraint, particularly in criminal and civil liberties cases.

Frankfurt Parliament *See* **Revolutions of 1848.**

Franklin A short-lived, self-governing US state (1784–88) in what is now eastern Tennessee. The lands were ceded by North Carolina to the US government in 1784, but settlers in the territory were determined to enter the Union as a state. They established a government (1785), with J. Sevier as president, and until 1788 continued to press for recognition as a state. The territory was again ceded to the US (1790), and became the state of Tennessee (along with additional lands to the west) in 1796.

Franklin, Benjamin 1706–90. American publisher, author, scientist, statesman, and diplomat, whose wit and wisdom made him one of the most widely known figures of Colonial America. Largely self-educated (he left school at 10), he owned his own newspaper in Philadelphia by 1730 and there published the internationally famous *Poor Richard's Almanack* (1732–57). He subsequently invented the Franklin stove (c1744), conducted his famous experiment with lightning by means of a kite (1752), and invented bifocal eyeglasses (1784). During this period he became widely known in scientific circles for his researches and also served as deputy postmaster general for the American colonies (1753–74). He was a delegate (1754) to the Albany Congress (*q.v.*), and, after 1757, spent a great deal of time in England serving as an agent on various matters. He returned to America (1775) just prior to the outbreak of the American Revolution, was a delegate to the Second Continental Congress, and helped draft the Declaration of Independence, which he also signed. Sent to France (1776) to win recognition for the republic, he gained a wide following there. He was in England again (1781) to help with peace negotiations to end the Revolutionary War. Once again in America, he helped arrange the compromise at the Constitutional Convention (1787) which resulted in the writing of the Constitution. The complete version of his *Autobiography* was published in 1868.

Franklin, Sir John 1786–1847. English explorer of the North American Arctic. His expedition (1845) in search of the Northwest Passage ended in disaster and his death when his ships became icebound.

Franks Germanic confederation that formed a powerful kingdom in Gaul after the fall of the Roman Empire. Believed to have originated along the Rhine River, the Franks by the 3d cent. AD had gained in strength and numbers and began a series of invasions into Gaul. Clovis I united the several Frankish tribes (5th cent. AD), adopted Christianity, and conquered northern Gaul from the Romans. He established a united Frankish kingdom, which flourished under the Merovingian dynasty and later the Carolingian. The Franks reached their height under the rule of Charlemagne (9th cent.), whose empire was divided and eventually became France and Germany. France derives its name from the Franks.

Fraser, James Earle 1876–1953. American sculptor. His best-known works are *The End of the Trail* and the Indian and buffalo on the US nickel.

Frazer, Sir James George 1854–1941. Scottish classicist and anthropologist. He is known best for his work *The Golden Bough.*

Fredegund *d.*597. Frankish queen. The mistress of King Chilperic I of Neustria, she convinced the king to kill his wife, Galswintha (567), and make her queen. Galswintha, however, was sister of Brunhilda, queen of Austrasia, and the murder of Galswintha caused a long war between Neustria and Austrasia, in which Austrasia was finally victorious.

Frederick I (˜ Barbarossa) c1123–90. Holy Roman Emperor (1155–90), prominent member of the Hohenstaufen family and successor to Conrad III. His reign was marked by attempts to pacify warring German nobles and by several unsuccessful attempts to gain control over Lombardy. He died during the Third Crusade.

Frederick I 1372–1440. Elector of Brandenburg (1417–40) and first of the Hohenzollern line. Made elector (1417) by Holy Roman Emperor Sigismund, he secured the future of the Hohenzollern family (*q.v.*).

Frederick I 1657–1713. First Prussian king (1701–13), son of Frederick William and his successor as elector of Brandenburg (1688–1713). By promising Prussian military aid in the oncoming War of the Spanish Succession, he won permission from Leopold I to create the kingdom of Prussia (1701).

Frederick II 1194–1250. Holy Roman Emperor (1220–50), king of Germany (1212–20), Sicily (1197–1250), and Jerusalem (1229–50). A Hohenstaufen, he was a grandson of Frederick Barbarossa, whose antipapal policies he continued. He was excommunicated several times, once for seizing the Papal States. His attempts to unify Italy and Germany, largely unsuccessful, were opposed vigorously by the Lombard League. While conducting the Fifth Crusade, he crowned himself (1229) king of Jerusalem. He later frequently referred to himself as "lord of the world." Because of his unceasing struggles with the papacy, the strength of both the Hohenstaufen family and the German nation were weakened.

Frederick II (˜ the Great) 1712–86. Prussian king (1740–86), successor to his father, Frederick William I. Under Frederick's leadership, Prussia evolved from a small Germanic state into an international power. A brilliant military tactician, Frederick seized portions of Silesia in the War of the Austrian Succession. Almost defeated in the Seven Years' War (1756–63), Frederick emerged victorious when his admirer Peter III assumed the Russian throne and took Russia out of the war. Frederick promulgated civil, legal, and penal reforms and internal improvements such as roads and canals. A patron of the arts, he enjoyed a long correspondence with Voltaire. Frederick increased Prussian domains through the First Partition of

Poland (1772) and engaged in the War of the Bavarian Succession (1778–79) to prevent Prussia's rival, Austria, from gaining power within the Holy Roman Empire.

Frederick III 1415–93. Holy Roman Emperor (1452–93) and king of Germany (1440–93). Frederick set the stage for future Habsburg domination by marrying (1477) his son Maximilian I to Mary of Burgundy, whereby Burgundy and the Netherlands (through Burgundian claims) came under Habsburg rule. He swore German allegiance to Rome, a move that infuriated German nobility.

Frederick III (˜ the Wise) 1463–1525. Elector of Saxony (1486–1525). He founded the University of Wittenberg (1502), where M. Luther and Melanchthon became professors. He later became Luther's protector (1521) after the Diet of Worms.

Frederick III (˜ the Pious) 1515–76. Elector palatine (1559–76). A convert to Lutheranism (1546) and then Calvinism (1561), he became a leading figure in the latter movement. He published the Heidelberg Catechism (1563).

Frederick III 1609–70. King of Norway and Denmark (1648–70). Frederick was forced to cede much of his territory to Swedish king Charles X following a war (1657–60). A coalition of burghers and clergy then united to curb aristocratic power, strengthen the monarchy, and help Denmark regain its vitality.

Frederick III 1831–88. Emperor of Germany and king of Prussia (1888). A liberal, Frederick ruled for only 99 days before succumbing to throat cancer.

Frederick IV 1574–1610. Elector palatine (1592–1610). An ardent Lutheran, he helped found (1608) the Protestant Union of Evangelical States and was chosen its first leader.

Frederick IV 1671–1730. King of Norway and Denmark (1699–1730). Frederick was unsuccessful in his attempts to regain southern Sweden. He established an educational system and abolished serfdom.

Frederick V 1723–66. King of Denmark and Norway (1746–66). He took little interest in state, leaving it to his foreign minister. During his reign, trade with Asia and the Americas greatly increased and his kingdom's financial affairs flourished.

Frederick VI 1769–1839. King of Denmark (1808–39) and Norway (1808–14). Frederick's alliance with Napoleon against Britain, resulting largely from the British bombardments (1801, 1807) of Copenhagen, led to the loss of Norway to Sweden through the Treaty of Kiel (1814).

Frederick VII 1808–63. Danish king (1848–63), successor to his father, Christian VIII. His reign was marked by the adoption of a constitution and creation of a constitutional monarchy. He also incorporated into Denmark much of Schleswig-Holstein (1863), thereby precipitating war with Prussia.

Frederick VIII 1843–1912. Danish king (1906–12), successor to his father, Christian IX. He served in the war against Prussia (1864) and had an uneventful reign.

Frederick IX 1899–1972. Danish king (1947–72). Frederick and his father, Christian X, imprisoned (1943–45) by the Nazis in WW II, became symbols of Danish resistance to German occupation.

Frederick Augustus I (~ the Just) 1750–1827. First king of Saxony (1806–27) and elector of Saxony (1763–1806). Defeated by Napoleon (1806), he concluded a separate peace and, as a result, became king. After Napoleon's final defeat, however, the Congress of Vienna (1815) ceded the major part of his kingdom to Prussia.

Frederick Augustus the Just *See* **Frederick Augustus I.**

Frederick Barbarossa *See* **Frederick I.**

Frederick Henry 1584–1647. Prince of Orange and stadholder of the United Provinces (1625–47). He regained many Dutch cities from Spain and finally negotiated an advantageous treaty with that country (1647).

Fredericksburg, Battle of Battle (Dec. 13, 1862) of the American Civil War at Fredericksburg, Virginia. Some 78,000 Confederate troops under Gen. R. E. Lee decisively defeated an assault by 120,000 Union troops under command of Gen. A. Burnside, halting Burnside's advance on Richmond. Confederate casualties were 5,000, Union casualties 12,000. Burnside was relieved of command. The battle was as much a boost to Confederate hopes as it was a defeat for Union arms and morale.

Frederick the Fair c1286–1330. German king (1314–22) and Austrian duke (1306–30). A disputed election (1314) for the German crown led to war between Frederick and Louis IV of Bavaria. The conflict ended in Frederick's defeat (1322) and retirement to Austria.

Frederick the Great *See* **Frederick II.**

Frederick the Great Elector *See* **Frederick William.**

Frederick the Pious *See* **Frederick III.**

Frederick the Winter King 1596–1632. King of Bohemia (1619–20) and elector palatine (1610–20). The Protestants of Bohemia, refusing to accept the Catholic Ferdinand II as their king, chose Frederick instead. He was quickly defeated and exiled. He was son-in-law to English king James I and grandfather of George I.

Frederick the Wise *See* **Frederick III.**

Frederick William (~ the Great Elector) 1620–88. Elector of Brandenburg (1640–88). Frederick negotiated an armistice to the Thirty Years' War and built a strong army in the interim, ensuring him fair treatment in the Peace of Westphalia. He unified Prussia and secured its sovereignty through a treaty (1657) with Poland.

Frederick William 1771–1815. Duke of Brunswick (1813–15). After Napoleon seized his duchy (1806), he formed the Black Brunswickers in a brave but unsuccessful attempt (1809) to drive out the French. He finally succeeded (1813) but was killed soon after.

Frederick William I 1688–1740. Prussian king (1713–40), successor to his father, Frederick I. Considered a strong ruler, he instituted many reforms and built the Prussian army into a powerful fighting force.

Frederick William II 1744–97. Prussian king (1786–97), successor to his uncle Frederick II. Though he was not considered an exceptional leader during his reign, Prussia continued its territorial expansion, notably at the expense of Poland through the partitions of Poland.

Frederick William III 1770–1840. King of Prussia (1797–1840). A weak king, he was dominated by Napoleon, but he allied himself with Russia and declared war (1813) on France. After the Congress of Vienna he alienated his people by joining the reactionary Holy Alliance.

Frederick William IV 1795–1861. Prussian king (1840–61), successor to his father, Frederick William III. His reign was marked by a brief rebellion (1848) and by his involvement in unsuccessful plans to unify Germany. (*See* Revolutions of 1848).

freedmen Term applied to former slaves who were released from bondage. In ancient Rome, freedmen were accorded varying degrees of civil rights.

Freedmen's Bureau US government bureau (1865–72) formed during Reconstruction to help former black slaves and oversee abandoned lands after the Civil War. Headed by Gen. O. Howard, the bureau provided food, medical attention, some semblance of protection, and, later, educational institutions for newly freed slaves in the war-torn South. It failed, however, in its aim to resettle blacks on the abandoned lands. Unpopular among white Southerners, it was finally disbanded in 1872.

free enterprise Economic doctrine based on the action of private individuals and companies operating in the marketplace free of government control. It is strongly identified with capitalism.

Free French Name given the military wing of the French Committee of National Defense. It was formed (June 23, 1940) in London by C. de Gaulle to continue French opposition to German occupation after the fall of France (1940) during WW II.

Freeman's Farm, Battle of 1. (Saratoga, First Battle of) First engagement (Sept. 19, 1777) of the Saratoga Campaign during the American Revolution. Continental forces under Gen. H. Gates repulsed British forces under Gen. J. Burgoyne, thereby delaying the British advance on Albany. 2. (Saratoga, Second Battle of) (Bemis Heights, Battle of) Battle fought (Oct. 7, 1777) by a British reconnaissance party under Burgoyne and Colonials under Gen. B. Arnold at Bemis Heights, near Freeman's Farm. The Americans were victorious.

Freemasons Secret fraternal order, one of the largest in the world. Though the order claims ancient origins, it seems to have developed from fraternities of English and Scottish stonemasons in the Middle Ages. The modern history of the organization dates from the formation of the Grand Lodge in England (1717). The movement spread rapidly throughout Europe and reached America in 1730 or 1733. Today there are independent national Masonic organizations in many countries throughout the world. In addition to their vow of secrecy, Masons generally adhere to a liberal philosophy of equality and religious toleration. They are generally opposed by the Catholic church. In America a reaction against them gave rise to the Anti-Masonic party. Many prominent people have been Freemasons, including 13 US presidents.

free silver American currency-reform movement. Adherents of free silver advocated unlimited coinage of silver as a way to increase the supply of money. Free silver was espoused by populists, progressives, and farmers, and was opposed by Eastern financiers, who favored the single gold standard. This controversy led to adoption of the Bland-Allison Act (1878) and the Sherman Silver Purchase Act (1890). The free-silver movement figured in American politics in the last half of the 19th and early 20th cents. W. Bryan based his unsuccessful presidential campaigns of 1896 and 1900 on the advocacy of free silver.

Free-Soil party Short-lived US political party (1848–54) organized to oppose extension of slavery into new US territories. Following the defeat of the Wilmot Proviso in Congress, antislavery Whigs, disaffected Democrats called Barnburners, and members of the Liberal party met in Buffalo (1848) and formally organized the party. Their presidential candidate, M. Van Buren, failed to win (1848) but proved to be a decisive factor in the election of President Z. Taylor, because they split the Democratic vote in the North. Following the Compromise of 1850, the party began to dissolve, and in 1854 it became part of the newly formed Republican party.

Free Territory of Trieste Territory created (1947) after WW II. It divided the Adriatic city of Trieste and environs into zones administered by Britain and Yugoslavia. It was abolished (1954) and its holdings divided between Italy and Yugoslavia.

freethinker Term applied to one whose religious and philosophical opinions are freely arrived at by use of reason, rather than through ecclesiastical authority. The term came into use in the 18th cent. with the rise of deism.

free trade Term applied to commerce conducted without governmental interference in the form of import and export regulations. A. Smith's *Wealth of Nations* was a strong argument for free trade, which developed as a movement in the 17th and 18th cents.

free will Philosophical concept that holds that man can choose, through his own will, a given action. The concept has long been a subject of both philosophical and religious debate. It opposes the concept of determinism.

Frei Montalva, Eduardo 1911–82. Chilean president (1964–70). He was a founder of the Christian Democratic party (1957) and as president introduced democratic and economic reforms.

Freising, Otto of *See* **Otto of Freising.**

Frémont, John Charles (The Pathfinder) 1813–90. American explorer, soldier, and an unsuccessful presidential candidate of the new Republican party (1856). He led expeditions in the Rockies (1842) and in Oregon and California (1843–44). In 1845 he took part in the revolt by Californian settlers against Mexico and set up the Bear Flag State. He subsequently became a leader in the conquest of California during the war with Mexico. He made a fortune when gold was discovered on his California property in the 1840s but eventually lost it all in unsuccessful railroad ventures. He served as commander in the West during the Civil War but was removed because of his actions regarding slavery. He was governor of the Arizona Territory (1878–83).

French, Daniel Chester 1850–1931. American sculptor known best for his statue of A. Lincoln in the Lincoln Memorial, Washington, D.C.

French, Sir John *See* **World War I (Aug. 7, 1914).**

French Academy (Académie Française) French cultural society. Dating from the early 1630s and a small informal group of scholars who met weekly to discuss intellectual matters, it was formally established (1835) by Cardinal Richelieu to regulate French language and literature.

French Action (Action Française) French Royalist party. Organized (1898) by extreme conservatives, it supported H. Pétain's government during WW II. Postwar charges of collaboration with the Germans resulted in its decline.

French and Indian War War (1754–63) in North America that became part of the larger European conflict known as the Seven Years' War. The French and Indian War was the last in a series of wars between the British and French for control of territory in what are today Canada and the United States (For more on the earlier wars, *see* **King William's War, Queen Anne's War, King George's War.**) The war was sparked by rivalry over the upper Ohio Valley region. The French in the late 1740s sought to link their Canadian and Louisiana possessions by taking control of the Ohio Valley region. This, however, blocked any future westward expansion of the British colonies along the American coast and thus roused the colonists to action.

Ultimately, France lost all its Canadian colonies to Britain. The war also gave American colonists a sense of being able to defend themselves and contributed to their growing feelings of independence from the British crown. Key dates in the war include:

1748   Ohio Company formed by Virginians to explore Ohio Valley territory to west of American colonies.

1748–49   French built a string of forts in Canada and the Ohio Valley to secure their control of the region.

1753   French commander Marquis Duquesne led force of French troops to occupy the Ohio Valley; G. Washington sent by Virginians to tell them to leave region.

1754   French built Fort Duquesne (at modern Pittsburgh).

1754   G. Washington on military expedition from Virginia against French; built Fort Necessity but was forced to surrender it soon after.

1754   Albany Congress held (June) to coordinate defense plans to deal with French expansion in the western region.

1755   Campaign against French in the Ohio Valley (and Canada) began under British Gen. E. Braddock.

1755   Braddock was defeated and later died after attack on Fort Duquesne (July 9).

1756   Seven Years' War began in Europe.

1756   French under Gen. L. de Montcalm took British forts Oswego and George.

1757   British Fort William Henry taken by French.

1758   Gen. de Montcalm repulsed British attacks (July) on Fort Ticonderoga.

1758   British captured Louisburg (July 26) in eastern Canada.

1758   Fort Duquesne captured from the French (Nov. 25); renamed Fort Pitt.

1759   Fort Ticonderoga fell to British forces.

1759   Battle of the Plains of Abraham in Canada (Sept. 13); decisive engagement of the war; de Montcalm killed in battle; British captured Quebec (Sept. 18) soon after.

1760   Montreal captured (Sept. 8), ending the war in the Americas.

1763   Treaty of Paris; British possession of French territory in Canada confirmed.

French and Swedish War War (1635–48) conducted by France and Sweden against the forces of the house of Habsburg and the Holy Roman Empire. The last phase of the Thirty Years' War (1618–48), it was ended by the Peace of Westphalia (1648).

French Cameroon *See* **Cameroon.**

French Community Organization of French states, overseas departments, and former territories created by the constitution of the Fifth Republic (1958). Among its members are France, Corsica, French Polynesia, French Guiana, and others. It promotes economic, technical, and cultural exchanges.

French Congo Former French possession, now known as French Equatorial Africa (*q.v.*).

French East India Company French colonial trading organization established (1664) by J. Colbert to protect French trade interests. It was successful for a time in India under J. Dupleix, less so in America, and was abolished in 1769.

French Equatorial Africa Former federation of French colonies in west central Africa, with its capital at Brazzaville. The first French settlements were established on the Gabon River (1839). French claims were extended by exploration, military ventures, and agreements with other colonial powers until 1887, when the approximate borders of what was then known as the French Congo were established. The federation of French Equatorial Africa was formed (1910), and during WW II it supported the Free French forces. The territories in the federation voted for independence (1958), and in 1960 they became the Central African Republic and the republics of Chad, Gabon, and the Congo.

French Guiana Overseas department (*pop.* 63,000) of France, located on the northeast coast of South America. The first permanent settlement was established (1604) at Cayenne, by the French. The colony was captured (1676) briefly by the Dutch during the Dutch Wars, and by 1713 boundary disputes with the neighboring Portuguese were settled. In the 18th cent., Jesuits were expelled, some 14,000 Europeans died in an unsuccessful attempt to establish a new colony, and the colony saw an influx of deportees from France (many of whom died) during the French Revolution. France briefly lost the colony (1809–17) to British and Portuguese forces, and, after abolition of slavery (1848), the colony entered a period of economic decline. It was in 1852 that the first of the penal colonies was established, the most notorious of them, Devil's Island, continuing in use until 1951. The colony was made an overseas department in 1946.

French Guinea *See* **Guinea.**

French Indochina *See* **Indochina, Federation of.**

French Indochina War *See* **Indochina War.**

French Morocco Former French protectorate in northwestern Africa. Occupied by the French in the early 1900s, the region became a French protectorate (1912). It was incorporated (1956) with Spanish Morocco and Tangier into the kingdom of Morocco.

French Polynesia French Pacific territory consisting of over one hundred Pacific Ocean islands, the largest of which is Tahiti. Acquired during the 19th cent., the islands were placed under central administration in 1903.

French Revolution Prolonged political and social struggle (1789–99) in France that surrounded the overthrow of the monarchy and establishment of the First Republic. The revolution was caused by a number of factors, chief among them resentment against the *ancien régime,* the old social order dominated by the king and his nobles, and a prolonged crisis over government finances. The ideas of the Enlightenment (*q.v.*) and the recent success of the American Revolution also helped provide a climate for the Revolution. The Revolution began as an attempt to create a constitutional monarchy and in this early phase the moderate bourgeoisie dominated the Revolution. But by late 1792 the demands for long-overdue reforms and the sheer inertia of revolution resulted in proclamation of the republic. The republic was consumed by the violence of the revolution. Attacks by other European nations (*see* French Revolutionary Wars) only multiplied effects of the bitter factional struggles, riots, and counterrevolutionary uprisings. The chaos helped bring the extreme radicals to power and touched off the bloody Reign of Terror. The French succeeded in mustering powerful armies and were victorious against their foreign enemies. However, a succession of attempts to form a stable republican government failed and ended in creation of the Consulate, a dictatorship led by their great military leader, Napoleon. (*See* *also* France, Napoleon.) Key events in the Revolution include:

1789   States-General convened (May 5); representatives of the three estates (clergy, nobility and commoners) met at Versailles; its intended purpose (to enact fiscal reforms) dwarfed by strong sentiment for sweeping political and social reform.

1789   Jacobins, a political club (faction) formed by delegates to the States-General.

1789   Third estate (commoners) insisted it alone represented France; voted to constitute itself as the National Assembly (June 17) after a deadlock developed in the States-General over voting procedures.

1789   Tennis Court Oath taken (June 20) by members of the National Assembly after they had been locked out of their meeting hall; meeting in a tennis court, they vowed not to disband until France had a constitution; individual members of other estates joined third estate.

1789   Louis XVI yielded to the National Assembly and ordered that all members of the remaining two estates should join it (June 27).

1789   King Louis concentrated troops around Paris and Versailles; Louis dismissed (July 11) his popular minister, J. Necker, and this along with fears that Louis might disband the National Assembly led to unrest in Paris.

1789   Rioting began in Paris (July 12).

1789   Paris Commune formed (July 13) as revolutionary sentiment spread in French cities; new militia formed in Paris (National Guard) and elsewhere; Marquis de Lafayette commanded the Paris National Guard.

1789   Storming of the Bastille (July 14), an arsenal and prison; the Great Fear (of reprisals by royalist armies) spread through countryside as peasants refused to pay taxes and attacked estates of noblemen (July–Aug.).

1789   Feudal structure in France abolished by National Assembly (Aug. 4); legal and fiscal equality proclaimed.

1789   Declaration of the Rights of Man adopted by the National Assembly (Aug. 26).

1789   National Assembly wrote a new constitution providing for a constitutional monarchy (Sept. 10); king's powers sharply limited, unicameral legislature provided for.

1789   Paris mob, consisting mostly of women, stormed the royal palace of Versailles (Oct. 5–6); angered by high bread prices and the king's resistance to Assembly legislation, they forced the king's removal to Paris; National Assembly removed to Paris.

1789   National Assembly confiscated church lands to overcome financial crisis (Nov. 2); issued *assignats,* notes backed by these public lands.

1789   Public opinion swayed in favor of revolutionary action by rise of clubs such as the Jacobins and publication of inflammatory political newspapers such as J. P. Marat's *L'Ami du Peuple.*

1790   Cordeliers, political club formed to prevent abuses of power; J. P. Marat and G. Danton became leaders.

1790   Civil Constitution of the Clergy (July 12); Roman Catholic church reorganized, and clerics to be paid by the state.

1790   King Louis approved the new national constitution creating a constitutional monarchy (July 14).

1790   Assembly imposed (Nov. 27) requirement of oath by clerics as resistance to Civil Constitution of the Clergy mounted; church split over oath and many clerics who refused suffered persecutions.

1791   Reacting to rising revolutionary tide, Louis XVI attempted to flee abroad with the royal family (June 20–21); apprehended at Varennes (June 25) and brought back to Paris a virtual prisoner.

1791   Feuillants, political club formed by moderate Jacobins (June) who opposed abolition of the monarchy.

1791   Paris republicans demanded the king be deposed; massed on the Champ-de-Mars (July 17), they were fired on by the National Guard (on Lafayette's order) and were dispersed.

1791   Declaration of Pillnitz (Aug. 27); Prussia and Holy Roman Empire agreed to war against France to restore the monarchy, if other powers joined them; declaration angered French and paved the way for war.

1791   Constitution put in force by the Assembly (Sept. 3); King Louis swore to uphold it (Sept. 14).

1791–92   Legislative Assembly in power; convened (Oct. 1), it was initially dominated by moderate Girondists; radical Jacobins among the groups opposed to the Girondists.

1792 Legislative Assembly under Girondist influence declared war on the Austrians (Apr. 20), inaugurating the French Revolutionary Wars. French armies quickly put on defensive by Austrians.

1792 Fall of Girondist ministry (June 13); rapid spread of unrest.

1792 Austro-Prussian armies crossed into France (July 11); radicalism increased in Paris.

1792 Brunswick Manifesto (July 27); Austro-Prussian commander threatened to destroy Paris if the king was harmed; Parisians angered by manifesto.

1792 Storming of Tuileries (Aug. 10); mob instigated by radicals killed the king's Swiss Guard; Legislative Assembly "suspended" the king and formed provisional government headed by G. Danton; new assembly, the National Convention, to be formed.

1792 Lafayette, then in command of units in the revolutionary army, defected (Aug. 19) to the Austrians to escape trial by radicals.

1792 September Massacres (Sept. 2–6) in Paris; prisoners in Paris jails slaughtered as hysteria mounted over approach of Austro-Prussian armies; soon after, French armies turned tide against the enemy.

1792–95 National Convention in power; convened (Sept. 21); dominated first by Girondists, then by Jacobins.

1792 First Republic proclaimed (Sept. 22) by National Convention; monarchy abolished (Sept. 21).

1793 Louis XVI guillotined (Jan. 21) after being tried for treason by the National Convention.

1793 Britain entered war against France (Feb.) and French armies soon after again suffered reverses.

1793 Counterrevolutionary rebellion in the Vendée (western France) began (Mar.).

1793 Émigrés, French royalists who had fled revolutionary France, declared "civilly dead" by Convention; (Mar. 28) émigré property confiscated.

1793 Committee of Public Safety established by National Convention (Apr. 6); at first had limited executive functions.

1793 J. Hébert arrested (May 24) for leading disorders; arrest instigated by Girondists.

1793 Insurrection of radical *Enragés;* Convention forced to arrest 31 Girondist deputies; this gave the "Mountain" (Jacobins and other left radicals) control of the Convention (June 2), and marked fall of Girondists (moderates) from power.

1793 Girondist deputies sparked revolts in the provinces after being forced to flee Paris (June); revolutionary government restored order by year's end.

1793 New Republican constitution proclaimed (June 22); it did not really take effect because extraordinary power remained in hands of the Committee of Public Safety.

1793 Committee of Public Safety gained dictatorial powers, taking on powers from the Convention and the Paris Commune (July); the Committee thus effectively became ruling body of revolutionary France. M. Robespierre became Committee member July 27.

1793 C. Corday killed J. P. Marat (July 13) for his persecution of the Girondists.

1793 Universal conscription of males ordered (Aug. 23) as internal revolts and advances of the armies of the First Coalition threatened the revolutionary government; an army of nearly a million men created.

1793–94 Reign of Terror instituted (Sept.) after sansculottes (radical workers and shopkeepers) invaded the Convention and demanded it do more to prevent counterrevolutionary activities; thousands of royalists, counterrevolutionaries and others were ultimately killed.

1793 Convention formally suspended constitution (of 1793); Committee of Public Safety to head revolutionary government until end of wars with foreign powers; Robespierre, a member of the committee since July 27, gradually took control of it by eliminating his opponents.

1793 Execution of Queen Marie Antoinette (Oct. 16).

1793 Principal Girondists guillotined (Oct. 31); executions averaged 60 per month thereafter.

1793 First Cult of Reason ceremony held (Nov. 10); Hébertists led anti-Christian movement and proclaimed "Cult of Reason."

1793–1805 French Revolutionary Calendar put in effect (Nov. 24); remained in use to 1805.

1793 Revolutionary dictatorship of France set up by Committee of Public Safety (Dec. 4); committee took power to appoint and dismiss even local officials.

1793 New victories by French armies drove enemy back out of France (Dec.).

1794 J. Hébert, radical leader of the anti-Christian movement, guillotined (Mar. 24) on orders from Robespierre; Hébert was a major opponent of Robespierre, who wanted a more moderate policy on religion.

1794 J. Danton, another leader of opposition to Robespierre, guillotined (Apr. 5) along with his followers; Robespierre leading power of government.

1794 Cult of the Supreme Being proclaimed by Robespierre (June), after the Convention instituted a civic religion recognizing a Supreme Being (May 7).

1794 Law of 22 Prairial passed (June 10); allowed only acquittal or death in trials and eliminated most rights of accused; executions increased markedly and aroused sentiment against Robespierre.

1794 *Coup d'état* of 9 Thermidor (July 27); Convention impeached Robespierre; he was beheaded (July 28) along with his followers; moderates took power and the Thermidorian Reaction began. Terror ended and persecution of the Jacobins began; more radical revolutionary measures rescinded.

1794 Paris Commune abolished (July 27).

1794 Jacobin club closed in Paris (Nov. 12).

1795 Riots over food prices and attack on National Convention (Apr. 1) suppressed by National Guard; reprisals against radical leaders.

1795 New attack on National Convention and riots among workers in Paris (May 20) put down by National Guard; reprisals against suspected Jacobins spread (White Terror).

1795 Churches reopened (May 30).

1795 Revolutionary Tribunal, the court of the Terror, abolished (May 31); justice courts empowered to try treason.

1795 Constitution of 1795 (Aug. 22); executive power rested with five-man Directory, Council of 500 and Council of Elders established.

1795 Insurrection against the Directory suppressed (Oct. 5) by troops commanded by Gen. Napoleon Bonaparte; Napoleon named commander of the Army of the Interior.

1795–99 Directory in power; convened Nov. 2, it presided over the last years of the revolution and pursued a generally moderate course.

1796 Counterrevolutionary uprising of the Vendée and elsewhere again suppressed (Feb.).

1796 Napoleon given command of French armies in Italy; his success in the Italian campaign (from Apr.) made him a national hero.

1797 F. Babeuf executed (May 17); had led (1796) conspiracy of former Jacobins and advocates of what became Socialist doctrines.

1797 Coup of 18 Fructidor (Sept. 4) by the republicans; Directory took on dictatorial powers.

1797 Treaty of Campo Formio (Oct. 17); War of the First Coalition ended, though Britain continued hostilities.

1798 Napoleon given approval to begin what became his disastrous campaign against Egypt (beginning in May).

1798 Coup of 22 Floréal (May 11); election of new council members nullified to block seating of Jacobins; opposition to the Directory, which arranged the nullification, spread.

1799 Coup of 30 Prairial (June 18); Councils, bolstered by newly elected Jacobin members, forced the ouster of three directors; censorship of press ended and radicalism again flourished.

1799 Napoleon returned to Paris (Oct. 16) after leaving his army behind in Egypt.

1799 Coup of 18 Brumaire (Nov. 9); Napoleon, with the aid of directors E. Sieyès and Pierre Roger Ducos, and his brother Lucien, engineered the overthrow of the Directory; established Consulate under his control.

French Revolutionary Calendar Calendar established during the French Revolution, used in France from Nov. 24, 1793, to Dec. 31, 1805. It reorganized the calendar into 12 months of 30 days each. The months were divided into three 10-day "decades" instead of weeks and the five days (or six in a leap year) at the end of the year were holidays. The names of the months were: Vendémiaire; Germinal; Brumaire; Floréal;

Frimaire; Prairial; Nivôse; Messidor; Pluviôse; Thermidor; Ventôse; Fructidor.

French Revolutionary Wars Series of wars (1792–1802) between France and various European powers, notably Austria and Britain. (The wars against France between 1803 and 1815 are called the Napoleonic Wars.) The French Revolutionary Wars were sparked by the European monarchs' disapproval of the new revolutionary government, by attempts to restore the monarchy in France, and by the desire of some revolutionary factions to demonstrate the strength of their new government. To defend France, the revolutionary government created what became a powerful army and the wars quickly became a vehicle for the expansion and aggrandizement of France. Britain, which became France's most stubborn enemy, retained supremacy of the seas. The wars brought Napoleon (a hero of the conflict) to power in France, gained France considerable territory and influence in Europe, and brought on the final collapse of the Holy Roman Empire (1806). (*See also* French Revolution, Napoleon, Napoleonic Wars, France.) Key dates in the wars include:

1791 Declaration of Pillnitz (Aug); Holy Roman Empire and Prussia said they would restore French king Louis XVI, if the other powers would join them.

1792 Girondists, who favored war, gained control of the government (Mar.).

1792–97 War of the First Coalition; Austria, Prussia, Britain, Spain, the Netherlands, and others joined in war against France.

1792 France declared war on Austria (Apr. 20).

1792 Brunswick Manifesto issued (July 27) by the commander of the Austro-Prussian forces; promised destruction of Paris if King Louis was harmed; increased radical sentiment against monarchy.

1792 Austrian and Prussian armies advanced against French armies; reverses aroused mobs in Paris and King Louis was "suspended" (Aug. 10).

1792 Battle of Valmy (Sept. 20), French revolutionaries defeated combined Austrian and Prussian force; first important battle of the war.

1792 French republic declared (Sept. 22); French armies advanced into foreign territories.

1792 France defeated Austria at Jemappes and occupied Austrian Netherlands (Belgium, Nov. 6).

1792 France issued (Nov.) a declaration of willingness to assist all peoples fighting for liberty.

1793 Louis XVI executed (Jan. 21); other powers of First Coalition joined the fighting soon after.

1793 French forces defeated in Holland by the Austrians (Mar. 18) and at Mainz by the Prussians (July 23).

1793 Counterrevolution in Vendée began (Mar.), increasing troubles of revolutionary government.

1793 Committee of Public Safety formed (Apr. 6) as crisis deepened; Reign of Terror began some months later.

1793 Armies of the coalition advanced into French territory (July); French revolutionary government declared (Aug.) universal conscription to deal with invasion and internal revolt.

1793 British captured Toulon (Aug. 29).

1793 Inexperienced French forces defeated Austrians at the Battle of Wattignies (Oct. 15–16), forcing them to retreat.

1793 Revolt of the Vendée put down (Oct.); harsh reprisals by revolutionary government followed.

1793 Toulon recaptured from British (Dec. 19); French armies reentered German territory soon after.

1794 Spain invaded by French forces (May).

1794 French forces defeated Austria at the Battle of Fleurus (June 26); Austrian Netherlands recaptured (July) and United Provinces invaded.

1794 Robespierre executed (July); Reign of Terror ended.

1795 Batavian Republic created (May 16) by victorious French, who joined conquered territories of the Austrian Netherlands and the United Provinces.

1795 Peace agreements (*see* Basel, Treaties of) forced on Prussia (Apr. 5) and Spain (July 22).

1795 French forces repulsed invasion (July) by British seeking to aid royalist Chouans.

1795 French mounted three-pronged attack in an effort to knock Austria out of the war; two armies attacked German states while Napoleon led southernmost army against Austrians in northern Italy.

1796 French armies advanced against German states until the new Austrian commander, Archduke Charles, turned the tide (Aug.–Sept.) and drove them back across the Rhine.

1796 Napoleon advanced through Nice to Piedmont (Apr.); Savoy and Nice ceded to France.

1796 Napoleon victorious against the Austrians at the Battle of Lodi, in Italy (May 10).

1796 Napoleon created the Lombard republic after conquering much of Lombardy (May) from the Austrians.

1796 Treaty of San Ildefonso concluded (Aug. 19); Spain formally allied with France against Great Britain.

1796–97 Siege of Mantua, Italy, conducted by Napoleon I; Austrian surrender gave Napoleon mastery of Italy (Feb.).

1797 British defeated a French and Spanish naval force (Feb. 14) in the Battle of Cape Saint Vincent.

1797 Treaty of Tolentino concluded (Feb. 19) between Napoleon and Pope Pius VI; pope sought to halt French advance on Rome and ceded territories to France.

1797 Fighting with Austria halted by Peace of Leoben (Apr. 18).

1797 French invaded and occupied Venice (May).

1797 Cisalpine Republic created (July) from conquered territories in northern Italy.

1797 Treaty of Campo Formio (Oct.); formally ended war between Austria and France; France gained Austrian territories in the Netherlands and Italy, and the left bank of the Rhine; Austria gained part of Venice; treaty ended war of the First Coalition, though Britain continued fighting against France.

1798 French created Roman Republic (Feb.) after taking pope captive.

1798 French invaded Switzerland (Apr.) to enforce creation of the Helvetic Republic.

1798 Napoleon, now a hero to the French, began his attack on the British Empire by way of Egypt (July); government gave him permission for operation in part to get him out of country.

1798 Napoleon advanced in Egypt, captured Alexandria (July 2) and routed the Egyptian Mamelukes at the Battle of the Pyramids (July 21).

1798 Battle of the Nile; British fleet under Adm. H. Nelson destroyed Napoleon's fleet (Aug. 1).

1798 War of the Second Coalition; Russia, Britain, Austria, Ottoman Empire, Portugal and Naples joined to oppose Napoleon (Dec. 24); Russians and Austrians to attack in Italy, Austrians to attack in Germany and Switzerland, British and Russians to attack in the Netherlands.

1799 French proclaimed the Parthenopean Republic (Jan. 23) after capturing Kingdom of Naples.

1799 Napoleon attacked the Ottoman Empire in Syria (Feb.); forced to withdraw to Egypt (Mar. 20).

1799 Battle of Stockach (Mar 25); Austrians defeated French and forced them back across the Rhine.

1799 Austrians and Russians successful in northern Italy; defeated French at Magnano (Apr. 5), Cassano (Apr. 271, Trebbia (June 17–19), and Novi (Aug. 15).

1799 Battle of Zurich (June 4–7); Austrians briefly successful in Switzerland; Zurich lost to French in following Sept.

1799 Parthenopean Republic overthrown (June 20) and monarchy restored.

1799 In Egypt, Napoleon defeated Ottoman Turks at the Battle of Aboukir (July 25); situation remained hopeless for French, since they were cut off from France by the British; Napoleon returned to France (Aug. 24), leaving subordinates to extricate the army.

1799 Russians forced into retreat after being defeated by the French at Zurich (Sept. 26).

1799 Convention of Alkmaar (Oct. 18); British agreed to withdraw from the Netherlands following their unsuccessful campaign there.

1799 Russia, defeated and disgruntled with its allies, withdrew from the coalition. (Oct. 22).

1799 Napoleon seized power in France (Nov. 9); became first consul; after consolidating his position, he returned to the war.

1800 Battle of Marengo (June 14) in Italy; Napoleon defeated the Austrians and reestablished French control in Italy.

1800 British occupation of Malta (Sept.).

1800 In north, Austrians defeated at the Battle of Hohenlinden (Dec. 3); Second Coalition collapsed, though Britain carried on fighting.

1801 Treaty of Lunéville (Feb. 9) ended Austrian participation in war against France.

1801 Peace treaty with Naples (Mar. 18).

1801 Battle of Copenhagen (Apr. 2), British naval victory against the Danish fleet at Copenhagen.

1801 British forced French to surrender Egypt (Aug).

1801 War of the Oranges; France and Spain conquered and divided Portugal (Sept.).

1802 Treaty of Amiens (Mar. 27) between Britain and France, ending the war of the Second Coalition and the French Revolutionary Wars; Britain agreed to restoration of conquered territories.

French Somaliland *See* **Djibouti.**

French Union French political organization (1946–58) that replaced the colonial system. Established by the constitution of the Fourth Republic, it brought France and its overseas territories and protectorates into a loose federation. Former colonies were granted semiautonomous status and had limited representation in the French government. In 1954, Vietnam, Laos, and Cambodia broke away from the union, and in 1958 the union was reorganized into the French Community.

French West Africa Former federation of French West African territories that included Dahomey, French Guinea, French Sudan, Ivory Coast, Mauritania, Senegal, Niger, and Upper Volta. Established in 1895, the territories became autonomous republics in 1958, and the federation was abolished in 1959.

Fréron, Louis Marie-Stanislas 1754–1802. French revolutionary. A zealous participant in the Reign of Terror, he was a leader in the successful conspiracy against M. Robespierre (1794) and took part in subsequent Thermidorian reaction against the Jacobins.

Freud, Sigmund 1856–1939. Austrian neurologist and founder of psychoanalysis. Freud pioneered the use of free association in the treatment of psychological problems and explored the effect of childhood impressions and repressed feelings on later behavior. His theories had a major influence on other scientists working in the field, including A. Adler and C. Jung. Both Adler and Jung, however, disagreed with Freud's emphasis on the importance of sexuality as a motivating force in behavior, and they devel-

oped their own followings. Freud, however, remains a major force in psychoanalysis. Among his many writings are *The Ego and the Id, Totem and Taboo,* and *A General Introduction to Psychoanalysis.*

Friar Lands Question US-Filipino land controversy. The Catholic church, which had been involved in Spanish rule in the Philippines, owned almost one-tenth of its improved lands. After the American takeover (1898), the US bought 410,000 acres from the church (1903), to be resold to Filipino farmers.

Friars Minor Capuchin *See* **Capuchins; Franciscans.**

Frick, Henry Clay 1849–1919. American industrialist, a key organizer of the Carnegie Steel Company (1889) and the US Steel Corporation (1901).

Friedan, Betty 1921– . Writer, feminist leader, and founder-president of the National Organization for Women (NOW, 1966). She wrote *The Feminine Mystique* (1963), theorizing that middle-class American women were not fulfilled by their traditional domestic roles. She was instrumental in NOW's support for the Equal Rights Amendment and legalized abortion. In 1981 she published *The Second Stage.*

Friedland, Battle of French victory (June 14, 1807) over Russia in the Napoleonic Wars. Some 86,000 French troops defeated a Russian force of 46,000 at Friedland (now Pravdinsk, Russia). The battle led to the Treaty of Tilsit.

Friedman, Milton 1912– . American economist. A prolific writer, he is a noted advocate of laissez-faire capitalism. He won the Nobel Prize for Economics (1976) and served as a policy advisor to President R. Reagan (1981–88).

Friends, Society of *See* **Society of Friends.**

Fries, John *See* **Fries's Rebellion.**

Fries's Rebellion An abortive revolt (1799) by Pennsylvania German-Americans opposed to a new federal property tax levied for a potential war with France. Led by John Fries (c1750–1818), the rebels briefly took up arms against the assessors and collectors. All were eventually pardoned by President J. Adams.

Friuli Historic region in what is now northeastern Italy and northwestern Slovenia. Subjected to Roman rule (2d cent. BC), it became a Lombard duchy (6th cent. AD), then passed to the Franks (8th cent.). Thereafter it changed hands several times and was subsequently divided and fragmented. The final disposition of the region between Italy and Yugoslavia was made in a treaty (1947) following WW II.

Frobisher, Sir Martin 1535?–94. English navigator. He led three exploratory voyages (1576, 1577, 1578) to Canada's northeastern coast in unsuccessful attempts to find a northwest passage.

Froebel, Friedrich Wilhelm August 1782–1852. German educator. The founder of the kindergarten system, he opened the first such school (1837) at Bad Blankenburg, Germany.

Frohman, Charles 1860–1915. American theatrical manager. He built a powerful syndicate of theaters and was noted for his ability to develop the talent of his performers. He died aboard the *Lusitania.*

Froissart, Jean 1333?–1400? French courtier and chronicler. His chronicles of the 14th cent. provide a valuable and lively account of the times.

Fromm, Erich 1900–1980. German-born American psychoanalyst. He is known especially for his books dealing with the isolation of man in modern society. Among his works are *Escape from Freedom* and *The Sane Society.*

Fronde Two major rebellions by French noblemen, brought about for the most part by their opposition to the growing power of the monarchy. 1. Fronde of the Parlement (Aug., 1648–Apr., 1649). The government's need for more income led the French minister, Cardinal J. Mazarin, and Anne of Austria, regent for young King Louis XIV, to seek approval of a drastic revenue measure. The Parlement of Paris, a special court, rejected the measure, which included forfeiture of magistrates' salaries. Parlement then proposed new limitations on royal authority. This the government answered by arresting some members of Parlement, an act that provoked a popular uprising in Paris (Aug. 26, 1648). The government, then embroiled in the last months of the Thirty Years' War, acknowledged the protest and released the members. With the Thirty Years' War over however, the government turned against the rebellious nobles. Troops under Louis II de Bourbon, prince de Condé, blockaded Paris (Jan., 1649), but he was unable to break the rebellion. The government therefore accepted (Apr. 1, 1649) the Peace of Rueil, ending the Fronde of the Parlement. 2. Fronde of the Princes (Jan., 1650–Sept.,

1653). The prince de Condé, leader of the government troops in the Fronde of the Parlement, soon fell out with the government and was arrested (Jan. 18, 1650). The nobles united for his release, however, and engaged in fighting with government troops in various provinces. Though the government succeeded in putting an end to armed resistance, an alliance of Condé's supporters in Paris won the ouster (Feb., 1651) of the hated minister, J. Mazarin, and obtained Condé's release. However, the intrigues of Anne of Austria, regent to King Louis XIV, soon provoked him to war against the government (Sept., 1651). Condé was unsuccessful in battle and was rescued from total defeat when his army was allowed to enter the city of Paris (July, 1652). Unable to win over the Parlement in Paris, and with support for the Fronde waning, Condé fled France. King Louis returned to Paris (Oct. 21, 1652), recalled Mazarin (Feb., 1653), and crushed the last of the rebels by Sept., 1653. The Fronde of the Princes was the nobles' last major rebellion against the monarchy.

Frondizi, Arturo 1908– . Argentine radical politician and president (1958–62). As a Radical party congressman (1946–51), Frondizi gained fame for publicly attacking abuses of the Peronist regime. He became president during the period of instability that followed the ouster of President J. Perón, and survived over 30 attempted military coups. His administration succeeded in revitalizing the country's oil industry and instituted an economic austerity program (1959). He was ousted in a military coup after trying to bring the banned Peronistas back into national politics.

Frontenac, comte de Palluau et de (Louis de Buade) 1620–98. French governor of New France (1672–82, 1689–98). He defeated the warring Iroquois Confederacy (1696), and during the war between England and France he successfully defended the colony against British attack.

Frontier Wars *See* **Cape Frontier Wars.**

Frost, Robert Lee 1875–1963. One of the best-known American poets in the 20th cent., famous for his deeply symbolic poems of rural New England life. He was born in San Francisco and lived with his family in New England from age 10. In his early years he worked at a number of trades before leaving for England (1912). Following the immediate popularity of his first collections of poetry, *A Boy's Will* and *North of Boston,* he returned to New England. He continued to write poetry, completing several additional collections, including *Mountain Interval* and *New Hampshire,* and taught at various universities. He received the Pulitzer Prize for Poetry in 1924, 1931, 1937, and 1943.

Fructidor, Coup of 18 *See* **French Revolution (1797).**

Fuad I (Ahmed Fuad Pasha) 1868–1936. Egyptian king (1922–36), the first to reign after Egypt's nominal independence from Britain. He was made sultan (1917) and became king when Egypt was declared nominally independent (1922). Later faced with strong opposition from the Wafd party (*q.v.*), he twice dissolved the parliament (1928, 1930).

Fuchs, Klaus Emil 1911–88. German-born British physicist and spy for the Communists. He worked in the US on the atomic bomb project (1943–46) and thereafter continued his work in nuclear research in Britain. Exposed as a spy (1950), he admitted passing information to the Soviets from 1943.

Fugger Family of German bankers and merchants who dominated and influenced European trade and finance from the 15th to 17th cents. Their interests included the collection of church indulgences; mercury, copper, and silver mines; shipping and real estate. Their influence and fortunes declined after their constant loans of money to finance various unsuccessful wars for the Habsburgs.

fugitive slave laws American slave laws. Passed in 1793 and 1850, they made mandatory the return of runaway Southern slaves. Frequent Northern disobedience of the laws was a contributing factor to the Civil War.

Fu Hsi *See* **Fuxi.**

Fujiwara family Family of Japanese nobles that virtually ruled Japan from the 8th to 12th cents. Founded by Kamatari, it rose to power under Fuhito in the early 8th cent. and gained dominance as the regents' line under Yoshifusa Fujiwara (804–872). The family's influence was diminished by the rise of the military government (Bakufu) in the 13th cent.

Fujiwara, Michinaga 966–1027. Japanese regent (998–1027). Michinaga was the most powerful of the Fujiwara family, having married daughters to four emperors and served as regent for all of them.

Fujiwara, Nakatomi *See* **Fujiwara family.**

Fujiwara, Yoshifusa *See* **Fujiwara family.**

Fukuzawa, Yukichi 1834–1901. Japanese author, educator, and journalist. He became one of his century's most influential proponents of Westernization in Japan.

Fulbright, James William 1905– . US senator (1945–75). A Democratic senator from Arkansas, he was the widely known chairman of the Foreign Relations Committee from 1959 to 1974 and a strong opponent of US military intervention.

Fulk V the Young 1092–1143. Count of Anjou (1109–31) and king of Jerusalem (1131–43). He married (1129) the daughter of Baldwin II, upon whose death (1131) he became king of Jerusalem. He halted the advance of Zangi. His grandson became English king Henry II.

Fuller, Melville Weston 1833–1910. American jurist and eighth chief justice of the US Supreme Court (1888–1910). He was a skilled administrator and is considered one of the ablest chief justices in the Court's history.

Fuller, Richard Buckminster 1895–1983. American architect and engineer. Fuller is noted for his use of geodesic domes in building design.

Fuller, Thomas 1608–61. English clergyman, author, and noted wit. He wrote the *History of the Worthies of England,* a valuable source of biographical information.

Fulton, Robert 1765–1815. American inventor who built the first commercially successful steamboat in America. In 1802 he contracted with R. Livingston to build a steamboat for use on the Hudson River. The *Clermont* was completed and launched in 1807 and subsequently went into regular service on the river. He later designed the *Fulton,* the first steam-powered warship (1814).

Fulvia *d.* 40 BC. Wife of M. Antony (from 44 BC). After Antony became enamored of Cleopatra, she instigated a revolt (41 BC) against Octavian in hopes of drawing him back to her. Spurned by Antony, she died a short time later.

Fundamentalism American Protestant movement originating in the early 20th cent. Fundamentalists adhere to traditional interpretations of the Bible. Among its members was W. Bryan, who defended Fundamentalism in the famous Scopes evolution trial.

Funk, Casimir 1884–1967. Polish-born American biochemist. He is credited with the discovery of vitamins.

Fust, Johann (Faust, ˜) 1400?–66. German moneylender and partner (1450?–55) of J. Gutenberg. He gained possession of Gutenberg's press on dissolution of their partnership and went into the business of printing books with his son-in-law.

futurism Italian artistic and literary movement. expressed the turbulent nature of the 20th cent. Its glorification of war and destruction was a precursor of Fascism.

futwa *See* **mufti.**

Fuxi (Fu Hsi) *fl.* c2800 BC. Legendary Chinese emperor. He is said to have invented writing and formulated the diagrams upon which the *I Ching* is based and to have instituted the first marriage rites and laws in China.

Fyodor *See* **Fëdor.**

G

Gabon (Gabon Republic) Independent state located in west central Africa, on the Atlantic coast. The population is 1,069,000 and the capital is Libreville. Gabon's history prior to the Portuguese exploration (15th cent.) is largely unknown. Gabon's principal industries revolve around exploiting its rich oil, uranium, iron ore, and manganese deposits, and it has maintained close ties with France. Key events in Gabon's history include:

15TH CENT. Portuguese navigator Diego Cam explored region, which became a center of the slave trade (to 19th cent.)

1839 French established their first settlement.

1849 Libreville founded.

1889–1904 Governed by French as part of French Congo.

1910–57 Governed as part of French Equatorial Africa.

1913 A. Schweitzer established hospital in region soon after control of the interior was established.

1940 Free France captured Gabon from the Vichy government during WW II.

1946 Became French overseas territory.

1958 Given status as autonomous republic within the French Community.

1960 Gabon established as independent republic (Aug. 17); Leon Mba in office as first president (1960–67).

1964 President Mba deposed in military coup; restored by France.

1967 President Mba died.

1967– President Omar Bongo in office; pursued policies to speed exploitation of natural resources, making oil a leading export commodity; resisted calls for multi-party system until the 1990s.

1973 President Bongo converted to Islam.

1973 Bongo, candidate of Gabon's only legal party, Parti Démocratique Gabonais (PDG), is re-elected president without opposition.

1978 "Bongo Plan," government-imposed fiscal austerity measures, instituted in the face of rapidly rising foreign debt and budget deficits; steep rise in oil prices (from 1978) aided government's program.

1980 President Bongo reelected unopposed; again elected unopposed for five-year term in 1986.

1981 Bongo reportedly concerned by election of Socialist President F. Mitterrand in France; believed Socialists opposed to his regime.

1981 Opposition unrest at university in Libreville (Dec.); sparked demands for multi-party system.

1982 Suspected members of the illegal opposition party, Mouvement de Redressement Nationale (MORENA), were tried and convicted for involvement in unrest at Libreville; 13 of the teachers, journalists, and others given 20-year sentences.

1983 French president Mitterrand visited Gabon (Jan.) in attempt to ease tensions with Bongo to protect extensive (and lucrative) French interests in Gabon; the following year France promised to give Gabon a nuclear reactor.

1985 Air force captain executed for plotting coup against Bongo (Aug.).

1986 New link of Trans-Gabonais railway completed; connected central Gabon with Franceville in southeast.

1987 Ruling PDG put up candidates in local elections for first time.

1989 Exiled MORENA opposition party leader Father Abessole Mba returned to Gabon; he advocated multi-party system.

1990 Pro-democracy protests, sweeping across Africa, broke out in Gabon; multi-party system for Gabon approved (Apr.).

1990 Riots broke out in Port-Gentil (May) after death of opposition leader there; French troops intervened to restore order on Bongo's request.

1990 Ruling PDG won slim majority in first multi-party elections (Sept.).

Gabriel, Jacques Ange 1690–1782. French architect. One of the greatest French architects of his century, he became royal architect to Louis XV (1742) and designed additions to palaces and public buildings.

Gabrieli, Andrea and Giovanni c1510–86, 1557–1612. Italian organists and composers at Saint Mark's in Venice. Giovanni became first organist at the church on his uncle's death. Both wrote masses and other choral works in addition to works for the organ.

Gadsden Purchase Treaty between the US and Mexico for the purchase of a strip of territory in northern Mexico (1853). The 30,000-square-mile strip was an important part of a projected southern transcontinental railroad route, but the Mexican War had left the boundary with Mexico unsettled. The purchase of the land for $10 million was negotiated by James Gadsden (1788–1858) and narrowly approved by the Senate (1854).

Gaelic Language of Celtic origins that is spoken in the Scottish Highlands, Ireland, and on the Isle of Man. In 19th-cent. Ireland, a "Gaelic Revival" attended the discovery of the means to translate Ireland's early Gaelic literature.

Gaeta, Giovanni da *See* **Gelasius II.**

Gaffar Khan *See* **Red Shirt Movement.**

Gagarin, Yuri Alekseyevich 1934–68. Soviet astronaut and national hero. The first man to travel in space (Apr. 12, 1961), he orbited for about one and a half hours aboard his spacecraft, *Vostok 1,* and reached a maximum orbit of 188 miles above the earth. He died in a plane crash.

Gage, Thomas 1721–87. British general during the American Revolutionary War. Appointed commander of British forces in North America

(1763), he replaced T. Hutchinson as governor of Massachusetts in 1774. The colony was then on the verge of revolt and, when he ordered the munitions at Concord seized (1775), the full-scale revolution began. He resigned his command after Bunker Hill (*q.v.*) in 1775.

gag rules Rules of legislative procedure designed to prevent consideration of or debate on certain issues. Gag rules were important in US history from 1836 to 1844, when they were used to block consideration of numerous anti-slavery petitions in the House of Representatives. J. Q. Adams was a leading figure in the successful drive to repeal the gag rules.

Gainsborough, Thomas 1727–88. English portrait and landscape painter, considered the most original and versatile 18th-cent. English artist. After studying under a French engineer in London, Gainsborough returned to his hometown of Sudbury (1745). Later he moved to Bath (1759) where he began doing portraits for well-to-do clients. He exhibited his work regularly in London (from 1761), painted the most fashionable of London's society (including the royal family, 1781), and was elected a member of the Royal Academy (1768). Among his many famous works are *The Blue Boy* (c1770), *The Watering Place* (1777), and *The Mall* (1783).

Gaiseric (Genseric) AD c390–477. King of the Vandals (*q.v.*) and Alani (*q.v.*) (AD 428–477). After leading his people from Spain to Africa (429), he proceeded to conquer the Roman province of Africa and from there won Sardinia, Corsica, and Sicily. In 455 he sacked Rome.

Gaitskell, Hugh Todd Naylor 1906–63. British statesman and Labour party leader (1955–63). The most serious challenge to his leadership came in 1960 when he managed to reverse a party conference vote in favor of unilateral nuclear disarmament.

Gaius 2d cent. AD. Roman jurist. He wrote a voluminous legal text, *Institutes,* which formed the basis for the later *Institutes* of Justinian I.

Galatia Ancient region of central Asia Minor, located in area around modern Ankara, Turkey. It was named for the Gauls, who took it in the 3d cent. BC. Their expansion was stopped by Attalus I. The Romans conquered the area in 189 BC. It became a Roman province in 25 BC.

Galba, Servius Sulpicius 3 BC–AD 69. Roman emperor (AD 68–69), successor to Nero. A provincial governor, he was proclaimed emperor by his troops after an uprising against Nero (AD 68). A short time later he was killed in a rebellion (AD 69) led by his successor, Otho.

Galbraith, John Kenneth 1908– . Canadian-American economist. An influential proponent of Keynesian economics, he was an adviser to President J. Kennedy, and US ambassador to India (1961–63). Among his writings are *The Affluent Society* and *The New Industrial State.*

Galen (Galenus, Claudius) AD c130–c200. Greek physician (court physician to Marcus Aurelius) who wrote some 500 treatises on medicine and philosophy. His medical works drew on past medical knowledge, his own experimentation, and on dissection of animals. He made significant additions to understanding of human anatomy. Sometimes considered the founder of experimental physiology, he was regarded as the undisputed medical authority well into medieval times, which unfortunately hindered further progress in medicine during that time.

Galenus, Claudius *See* **Galen.**

Galerius (Gaius Galerius Valerius Maximinianus) *d.* AD 311. Roman emperor (AD 305–310) of the Eastern Empire, successor with Constantius I (in the West) to Diocletian. A zealous persecutor of Christians, he granted an edict of toleration just before his death.

Galicia Historic region in Eastern Europe, now divided between Poland and the former USSR. The cities of Cracow and Lvov are located within the region. Galicia gained independence for a time in the 12th cent. and became part of Poland by 1360. The region was annexed by Austria during the first Partition of Poland. The USSR and Poland divided up Galicia after WW II.

Galicia, kingdom of Spanish kingdom, located in northern Spain. It was an independent kingdom of the German Suevi in the 5th and 6th cents. AD. It was conquered in turn by Visigoths and Moors before becoming linked to Castile and León.

Galician Offensive *See* **June Offensive.**

Galilee The northern region of ancient Palestine in what is now northern Israel. It is mentioned frequently in the Bible as Jesus' homeland. [Mark 1:9; Luke 2:4; John 1:46] After the Romans destroyed Jerusalem (AD 70) it became a stronghold of Judaism. The region was resettled by Zionists late in the 19th cent. and was entirely absorbed by Israel after the Arab-Israeli War (*q.v.*) of 1948–49.

Galilee, Judas of *See* **Judas of Galilee.**

Galileo (*properly,* Galileo Galilei) 1564–1642. Italian mathematician, physicist, and astronomer. One of the world's great scientists, he is regarded as the founder of the experimental method, which is the cornerstone of modern science. Born at Pisa, he discovered the law of pendulums as a student and first won notice by his invention of the hydrostatic balance (c1586). He later experimented (c1589–92) with falling bodies (not, as in the popular legend, by dropping objects from the tower of Pisa) and disproved the Aristotelian theory that objects of different weights fall at different speeds. This revelation (which aroused great hostility in the scholarly community), his observation of the parabolic path of a projectile, and other discoveries foreshadowed the universal laws of motion formulated by I. Newton. After constructing (c1610) and perfecting a telescope (invented earlier by the Dutch), Galileo discovered that the moon shines by reflected light, that the Milky Way is composed of individual stars, and that Jupiter was orbited by 4 moons (12 are now known). His researches confirmed his belief in the Copernican theory (*q.v.*) and he openly supported (1613) this heliocentric theory. It was condemned by the church (1616) as dangerous and Galileo was warned by church authorities against supporting it. Nevertheless, he published (1632) his *Dialogue Concerning the Two World Systems,* openly supporting Copernican theory. He was subsequently tried and sentenced to house arrest by the Inquisition. He continued his scientific work, however and discovered the librations (oscillations) of the moon before his death.

Gall c1840–94. American Indian, a Sioux war chief. He was a leader under Sitting Bull during the massacre of G. Custer and his men at the Battle of Little Bighorn (*q.v.*) in 1876. He ended his war with the whites in 1881.

Gallas, Matthias, graf von 1584–1647. Imperial general (1634–45) of the Holy Roman armies during the Thirty Years' War (*q.v.*). A commander under A. von Wallenstein, Gallas was involved in his removal (1634) and then succeeded him (1634) as overall commander. His drunkenness and several disastrous defeats finally led to his own removal in 1645.

Gallatin, Albert 1761–1849. Swiss-American US secretary of the treasury (1801–14). Through his insistence on sound fiscal policies he managed a significant, though temporary, reduction in the national debt. The reduction was wiped out by the War of 1812. He played a major role in negotiating the Treaty of Ghent (*q.v.*) in 1814, which ended the conflict.

Galle, Johann Gottfried 1812–1910. German astronomer who discovered the planet Neptune (1846).

Gallegos, Rómulo 1884–1969. Venezuelan novelist and president (1948). A teacher, he published his first novel, *El Ultimo Solar* in 1920, and later completed his best-known work, *Doña Bárbara* (1929). The leader of the radical Acción Democratica party, he was elected president in 1947, but was ousted in a military coup a few months after taking office (Nov., 1948).

Gallican Articles *See* **Gallicanism.**

Gallicanism Movement among French Catholics for greater independence from papal authority. Gallicanism can be traced back to the Great Schism (14th cent.) and involved both secular and ecclesiastical matters. The famous Gallican Articles, issued by Louis XIV (1682) and approved by the French clergy, represent the clearest statement of Gallican aims. They proclaimed that the king was not subject to the pope, that the pope was subject to ecumenical councils, that the traditions and customs of the French church were outside the pope's authority, and that the pope's authority in doctrinal matters was binding only with approval of the whole church. Gallicanism was seriously compromised by the state's attack on the church during the French Revolution. Later, the First Vatican Council (*q.v.*) of 1870 confirmed the opposing philosophy of Ultramontanism and firmly established papal authority. Gallicanism subsequently ceased to be an active movement.

Gallic Wars Series of campaigns conducted by J. Caesar (58–51 BC) leading to the Roman conquest of Gaul. The wars began when Caesar moved against the Helvetii, who attempted to move into southern Gaul. Caesar then defeated (57 BC) the tribes in what is now Belgium, defeated the Veneti (56) in Brittany, and conducted a punitive invasion (55) into Germany. In 54 he invaded Britain (for the second time, the first being in 55) and defeated the Britons under King Cassivellaunus but returned to Gaul soon after. He subsequently put down a rebellion of all Gaul (52), led by Vercingetorix, and the following year reduced all resistance to Roman

authority in Gaul. The campaigns gave Caesar immense power and prestige. As commander of a strong army he was able to contest Pompey's authority as leader of Rome. The main source for information on the campaigns is Caesar's own *De bello Gallico.*

Gallieni, Joseph Simon 1849–1916. French soldier and colonial governor. He played an important role in pacifying the French Sudan and Madagascar (1870–1905). During WW I he played a critical role in the victory of the First Battle of the Marne (*q.v.*) in 1914.

Gallienus, Publius Lucinius Valerianus Egnatius *d.* AD 268. Roman emperor, co-ruler with his father Valerian (AD 253–260) and successor to him (260–268). His reign was marked by the widespread revolts of the Time of the Thirty Tyrants (*q.v.*).

Gallipoli Campaign (Dardanelles ˜) Allied military operation in Turkey during WW I. The Allies attempted to wrest control of the Dardanelles (*q.v.*) from the Ottoman Empire in order to better supply Russia. The campaign was backed by D. Lloyd George and Lord H. Kitchener, and commenced on Feb. 19, 1915. After an unsuccessful naval attempt to force the Straits, British and French troops were landed on both sides of the Straits, notably on the Gallipoli Peninsula. The operation became a disaster in which 55,000 Allied troops were lost before the evacuation (Dec., 1915–Jan., 1916). Churchill, who was linked with the failed campaign (though he is now said to have favored a Baltic campaign instead), was obliged to resign as first lord of the admiralty.

Gallitzin, Demetrius Augustine 1770–1840. American Roman Catholic clergyman born a Russian prince. From 1795 to 1840 he was a widely known frontier missionary to settlers in southwestern Pennsylvania.

Galloway, Joseph c1731–1803. American loyalist leader during the American Revolutionary War. As a delegate to the Continental Congress (*q.v.*) in 1774–75, he proposed a plan for peaceful settlement with Britain. His plan was narrowly defeated, and he later joined the British, becoming superintendent of the Philadelphia port under Gen. W. Howe.

Gallup, George Horace 1901–84. American public opinion expert. He developed the Gallup poll, a survey of public opinion. The poll first gained wide notice when Gallup successfully predicted the reelection of President F. Roosevelt in 1936.

Galsworthy, John 1867–1933. English novelist and dramatist. Born of a wealthy family, he is best known for *The Forsyte Saga,* a series of novels about a well-to-do family in the late 1800s and early 1900s. He also wrote successful plays, including *Strife* and *Loyalties.* He won the Nobel Prize in Literature in 1932.

Galt, Sir Alexander Tilloch 1817–93. English-born Canadian politician and speculator. A member of the Province of Canada legislature from 1849 to 1872, he became an important advocate of confederation of the provinces. Following the 1867 British North America Act (*q.v.*), he served briefly as finance minister (1867–68) of the newly created dominion.

Galt, John 1779–1839. Scottish novelist. He is best known for his tales of Scottish country life.

Galton, Sir Francis 1822–1911. English scientist. In *Hereditary Genius,* he argued that talent is an inherited characteristic. A grandson of E. Darwin and cousin of C. Darwin, he founded— and coined the term for—the science of eugenics.

Galuppi, Baldassare 1706–85. Italian composer of light operas who is credited with the development of the *opera buffa* style. His best-known opera is *Il Filosofo di Campagna.*

Galvani, Luigi 1737–90. Italian physiologist. His controversy with A. Volta over the source of the electricity which induced muscle contractions in frogs' legs through use of dissimilar metals stimulated important research into the nature of electricity. Some terms dealing with electricity are named after Galvani.

Gálvez, Bernardo de c1746–86. Spanish colonial governor. As Spanish governor of Louisiana (1777–83), he was largely responsible for Spain's acquisition of British territory in Florida (1783). He became viceroy of New Spain in 1785.

Gálvez, José, Marqués de la Sonora 1720–87. Spanish colonial administrator. As inspector general to New Spain (1765–72), he instituted important reforms in the administration of the colonies.

Gama, Vasco da c1469?–1524. Portuguese navigator who first made the sea voyage from Europe to India. His voyage and the trade it opened up with India provided the foundation for the Portuguese Empire. Chosen by King Manuel I to find a route to India, he sailed with four ships in 1497. He rounded the Cape of Good Hope (already explored by 1488) and after enduring both storms and mutinies he reached Calicut in India (1498). He subsequently commanded a fleet of 20 ships on a second voyage to India (1502–03). This time he founded the Mozambique and Sofala colonies on the African coast and, after leading a naval attack, established Portuguese rule over Calicut. Sent to India as a viceroy in 1524, he died soon after his arrival.

Gamaliel 1. Jewish rabbi, *d.* about AD 50. A prominent Pharisee who taught Saint Paul [Acts 22] and advised against persecuting the Apostles. [Acts 5] 2. ~ of Jabneh. Jewish rabbi, *d.* AD 115? A grandson of Hillel, and a leader of his people recognized by the Romans, he helped establish the Passover Seder ritual that was substituted for the former Temple sacrifice, interrupted by the destruction of the Temple in AD 70.

Gambetta, Léon 1838–82. French political leader. After the fall of the Second Empire (*q.v.*) in 1870, he organized a provisional government of national defense, dramatically escaped from Paris in a balloon, and was virtual dictator of France for five months (1870–71). One of the founders of the Third Republic (*q.v.*) and shapers of its constitution (1875), he served briefly as premier (1881–82).

Gambia (*properly* The ~) West African republic. The smallest African nation, it extends in a narrow strip from the Atlantic along both sides of the Gambia River for about 200 miles. The population is 860,000 and the capital is Banjul. Peanuts are the primary product. It was discovered by the Portuguese (1455) and used by the British as an anti-slave-trade base (1800s). The Gambia became a British crown colony in 1843. Periodically governed by Sierra Leone, it became independent in 1965. President Dawda Kairaba Jawara, in office since 1970, was elected (1982) in The Gambia's first direct presidential elections. A confederation with Senegal was effected Feb. 1, 1982, but was dissolved Sept., 1989, following disagreements over final stages of the merger.

Gamow, George 1904–68. Russian-American nuclear physicist and author of popular books on science. He is noted for his work in explaining stellar evolution through principles of nuclear physics.

Gandamak, Treaty of Treaty signed by Amir Yakub of Afghanistan with the British on May

16, 1879, concluding the Second Afghan War (*q.v.*). By it the British agreed to pay the amir an annual subsidy for their occupation of the Khyber Pass (*q.v.*), the amir agreed to conduct his foreign relations only through the government of India, and British trade was to be free.

Gandhi, Indira 1917–84. Indian prime minister (1966–77, 1980–84) and daughter of J. Nehru. She succeeded President Lal Bahadur Shastri (1904–66) and presided over India's defeat of Pakistan (1971). Facing a challenge to her 1972 election, she declared a state of emergency (1975) and suspended the 1976 election. She was unseated as prime minister the following year (July 25, 1977) but after new elections she was returned to power in 1980. She served from 1980 until her assassination by Sikhs in her own bodyguard (Oct., 1984), who sought retaliation for her use of troops in putting down a Sikh revolt. *See also* India, 1966–77 and 1980–84.

Gandhi, Mohandas Karamchand 1869–1948. Indian political leader and national hero who became a symbol of nonviolent protest and of India's independence movement. Educated in both India and Britain, he remained overseas until 1914. On his return, he supported the British government in India during WW I, though he took an increasing interest in Indian home rule. Meanwhile he took up the life of an ascetic and began advocating abolition of the caste system (*q.v.*) in India. His nonviolent campaigns of civil disobedience (called *satyagraha*) against various laws soon propelled him to the leadership of the movement for Indian home rule, as well as the Congress party (*q.v.*). Arrested for organizing a protest against the government salt monopoly, he was released to take part (1931) in the Round Table Conference (*q.v.*). During the 1930s, the pattern of Gandhi's mass nonviolent protests and subsequent arrests continued. But Gandhi only gained prestige (he was called Mahatma, or "great soul"), and he was able to wrest major concessions from the British rulers of India. During the early part of WW II, he began demanding India's complete independence from Britain. This he tried to achieve by refusing Indian support for the British war effort against the Japanese, a tactic that resulted in his internment until 1944. He vigorously supported Britain's postwar plans to grant India's independence, though he was unsuccessful in opposing

the partition of India and creation of Pakistan (1947). He was assassinated (Jan. 30, 1948) by a Hindu fanatic during a time of disturbances between Muslims and Hindus.

Ganganelli, Lorenzo *See* **Clement XIV.**

Gang of Four Four leading figures of the Cultural Revolution (*q.v.*) in China in 1966–69 who were put on trial (Nov. 20, 1980) along with other radicals. They were charged with a variety of abuses during the Cultural Revolution, including the deaths of some 34,000 people. The leading figure among the four was Jiang Qing, Mao Zedong's wife; the trial marked her fall from power.

Gaodi (Kao Tsu; Liu Bang; Liu Pang) 256–195 BC. Chinese emperor (202?–195 BC), founder of the Han dynasty. Originally a petty official named Liu Bang, he came to power as the king of a new independent state of Han (206), following the collapse of the Qin dynasty. Soon after he became a rival of Xiang Yu (*d.* 202), an aristocrat then in control of the kingdom of Chu, and the story of their fight for supreme power became the subject of later Chinese literature. Liu Bang and his supporters emerged victorious, and after capturing the former Qin seat of government, he proclaimed himself the first Han emperor (posthumously known as Gaodi).

Gao Gang (Kao Kang) c1902–55. Chinese Communist leader. He was one of the most powerful political figures in the Communist government until his purge (Apr., 1955) from the party and subsequent suicide.

Gaozu *See* **Li Yuan.**

GAR *See* **Grand Army of the Republic.**

Garamond, Claude *d.* 1561. French type designer. His Roman type faces supplanted the Gothic type faces then in use and helped establish the Roman style as the standard in printing.

García Íñiguez, Calixto 1836–98. Cuban revolutionary. A commander in the rebellion called the Ten Years' War (*q.v.*) of 1868–78, he led Cuban forces against the Spanish in the Spanish-American War (1898).

García Lorca, Federico 1898–1936. Spanish poet and dramatist. He was one of the most important Spanish poets of this century. His works include *Gypsy Ballads* and *Lament for the Death of a Bullfighter.*

García Márquez, Gabriel 1928– . Colombian novelist and short-story writer. A journalist during the 1950s, he began writing fiction in the late 1940s, enjoyed his first literary successes in the 1950s, and went on to become a leading writer in the "magical realism" movement in Latin America. He won the Nobel Prize for Literature in 1982. His best-known novel is *One Hundred Years of Solitude* (1967).

Garcilaso de la Vega 1539?–1616.   Peruvian historian, best known for his commentaries on the life of the Incas and the conquest of Peru.

Garfield, James Abram 1831–81.   Twentieth US president (1881), successor to R. Hayes. A former teacher, lay preacher, and Ohio state senator, Garfield distinguished himself as a Union army major general during the American Civil War (1861–65) and served as a Republican US congressman (1863–80). He became the Republican presidential candidate (1880), breaking a deadlock between supporters of J. Blaine and U. Grant at the party convention. On taking office (Mar. 4, 1881), Garfield initiated a political struggle with a Republican faction called the Stalwarts (*q.v.*) by naming Blaine as secretary of state and initiating action on the Star Route Frauds. After only months in office, Garfield was mortally wounded (July 2, 1881) by a disgruntled office-seeker, Charles J. Giteau, and died Sept. 19.

Garibaldi, Giuseppe 1807–82.   Italian soldier and hero of the Risorgimento (*q.v.*), or unification of Italy. While in his twenties, he was involved in an unsuccessful revolt (1835) in Italy and fled to South America. He became famous there as a leader of rebel forces in Uruguay (1842–46). Garibaldi returned to Italy and joined his friend G. Mazzini in establishing a revolutionary republic at Rome (1849). He became a hero for his leadership of rebel forces against the pope's armies, but was ultimately forced to retreat and flee Italy. Having given up his hopes for an Italian republic he was willing (1860) to serve the interests of Victor Emmanuel II to further the unification of Italy. That year he undertook his famous conquest of the Kingdom of the Two Sicilies with the Expedition of the Thousand (*q.v.*). In 1861 Victor Emmanuel became king of a united Italy, except for the Papal States. Garibaldi made two reckless and abortive attacks on the Papal States (1862, 1867). In 1874, he became a member of the Italian parliament.

Garigliano, Battles of   Battles fought near the strategic Garigliano River in south central Italy. 1. On Dec. 28, 1503, 15,000 men under Ferdinand V decisively defeated a French invasion force under Louis XII, forcing the latter to accede to Spanish rule over Naples. 2. From Nov., 1943, to May, 1944, there was heavy fighting here in WW II during the Allied drive on Rome, including the battle for Cassino.

Garneau, François Xavier 1809–66.   French-Canadian historian. Considered the earliest important francophone historian, he wrote the *History of Canada.*

Garner, John Nance 1868–1967.   US vice-president (1933–41). A Democratic congressman from Texas (1903–33), he served under President F. Roosevelt during his first two terms.

Garnier, Marie Joseph Francis 1839–73.   French explorer in Indochina. He played a major role in an expedition that ranged from Cambodia and Laos to Yunnan in China (1866–68), accurately mapping territory unknown to geographers.

Garrison, William Lloyd 1805–79.   American abolitionist. An uncompromising and often abrasive publicist for the anti-slavery cause, he published (1831–65) the *Liberator,* a newspaper he made famous with his views and which he continued until the abolition of slavery.

Garter, Order of the   *See* **Order of the Garter.**

Garvey, Marcus Moziah 1887–1940.   Jamaican-born American black nationalist. Through his Universal Negro Improvement Association (from 1914), Garvey advocated the worldwide union of blacks, rejected integration, and championed a "Back to Africa" movement.

Gary, Elbert Henry 1846–1927.   American lawyer and business executive. He was one of the principal organizers of the US Steel Corp. (1901) and served as its chairman (1903–27). Gary, Indiana, was named for him.

Gascoigne, George 1525?–77.   English poet, essayist, and dramatist, noted for his experimentation with literary forms. He was author of *Certain Notes of Instruction,* considered the first essay by an Englishman on writing verse.

Gasparri, Pietro 1852–1934.   Italian cardinal. Under Pope Pius X, he was responsible for organizing the Code of Canon Law (1904–07), a codification of the law of the Roman Catholic church. He also played a major role in negotiating the Lateran Treaty (*q.v.*) of 1929.

Gaspee A British revenue cutter that was burned by rebellious Rhode Islanders on June 10, 1772. The names of the perpetrators were concealed and they went unpunished. Britain passed the Intolerable Acts (*q.v.*) partly in retaliation.

Gastein, Convention of *See* **Convention of Gastein.**

Gates, Horatio 1728?–1806. American general in the American Revolutionary War. As commander of an army in the north, he defeated the British Gen. J. Burgoyne in an important victory at Saratoga, which turned the tide of the war in the Americans' favor. Subsequently embroiled in the Conway Cabal (*q.v.*), he was transferred to the south and was disgraced in the Carolina Campaign (1780).

Gates, Sir Thomas *d.* 1621. English Colonial governor of Virginia. Named in the Virginia colony charter (1606), he twice served as governor (1610, 1611–14).

Gatling, Richard Jordan 1818–1903. American inventor. He invented the Gatling gun (1861), a crank-operated forerunner of the machine gun.

gauchos Nomadic horsemen and cattlehands who roamed the vast grasslands (*pamapas*) of Argentina and Uruguay from the 18th cent. to the 19th cent. Gauchos were men of mixed breed (*mestizo*), usually of European and Indian or African and Indian parentage, who rose to importance as the Argentine cattle industry and trade in hides grew. Their unfettered, roving lifestyle has been preserved and romanticized as part of the Argentine cultural heritage in, among other works, the epic poem *Martin Fierro* (1879) by José Hernández and the novel *Don Segundo Sombra* (1926) by Ricardo Güiraldes. Gauchos were reduced to the role of farmhands in the late 19th cent., by which time the vast grasslands had been fenced off into large livestock raising estates. The term gaucho has also been applied more broadly to rural farmers, drifters, and thieves.

Gaudier-Brzeska, Henri 1891–1915. French sculptor. He was the leading sculptor in the movement known as vorticism (*q.v.*).

Gaugamela, Battle of (Arbela, ˜) Decisive Macedonian victory (Oct. 1, 331 BC) over the Persians during Alexander the Great's wars of conquest. The battle marked the beginning of the decline of the Persian Empire. Alexander's 47,000 Macedonian troops defeated some 250,000 soldiers under Darius III on the plain of Gaugamela in the territory of ancient Assyria. Losses were 40–90,000 Persians to only 100–500 Macedonians.

Gauguin, Eugène Henri Paul 1848–1903. Famous French painter, a postimpressionist and a principal figure in the development of modern art. He did not begin painting full time until age 35, before then dividing his time between his work as a stockbroker and painting. He was associated with the impressionists until 1888, when he developed his own characteristic style, synthetism. Instead of imitating nature, he created abstracted figures from the primitive subjects and bright colors he used. Despairing of modern civilization, Gauguin went to Tahiti (1891) and thereafter lived in the South Pacific (excepting 1893–95). Among his many famous works are: *The Yellow Christ* (1889), *Where Do We Come From? What Are We? Where Are We Going?* (1898), and *Two Tahitian Women* (1899).

Gaul Ancient name for the area once inhabited by Celts, roughly comprising modern France. Roman Gaul included also parts of northern Italy (Cisalpine Gaul). By the time of J. Caesar, Rome already ruled the part of Transalpine Gaul that is today Provence. Caesar conquered the rest of Gaul for Rome in the Gallic Wars (*q.v.*) of 58–51 BC, immortalizing in his account of the wars Gaul's division into "three parts"—Aquitania, Gallia, and Belgica. Gaul flourished as a center of Roman civilization until the collapse of the Western Empire (AD 476) and thereafter came under control of the Franks. Gaul formed the nucleus of the Frankish Merovingian and Carolingian empires.

Gaullists French political term. Gaullists were the supporters of the nationalistic policies of French general (later president) C. de Gaulle. The term was employed to describe de Gaulle's followers during the period of his leadership of the Free French (*q.v.*) and it was retained to describe the political party organized after 1945 and dominant after the foundation of the Fifth Republic (*q.v.*).

Gaunt, John of *See* **John of Gaunt.**

Gauss, Karl Friedrich 1777–1855. German mathematician. He is regarded as one of the greatest of all mathematicians. He had begun producing notable work by the time he was 22 and went on to formulate important theories in mathematics (especially number theory), physics, and astronomy.

Gautier, Théophile 1811–72.   French poet and novelist. He was an exponent of pure aestheticism and coined the term "art for art's sake" in the preface to his famous story *Mademoiselle de Maupin* (1835).

Gaveston, Piers *d.* 1312.   English nobleman, a favorite of King Edward II of England and regent during his absence. An enemy to the barons by his manner and his position, he was several times exiled for short periods. On his return in 1312, however, the barons revolted and executed him.

Gay, John 1685–1732.   English dramatist and poet, best known for his work *The Beggar's Opera.*

Gay-Lussac, Joseph Louis 1778–1850.   French chemist and physicist known for important contributions to the study of gases. He formulated the law of expansion of gases (1802), demonstrating that as temperature rises, all gases expand by the same fraction of their volume. Setting a record for altitude during a balloon ascent which stood for 50 years (1804), he also demonstrated the constant composition of air at heights of more than 7,000 meters above sea level. Working with A. Humboldt, he accurately established the proportions of hydrogen and oxygen in water. He is best known for the law combining volumes (1808), which states that gases combine in simple proportions by volume.

Geary, John White 1819–73.   American politician and Union general. He was governor of Kansas (1856–57) during the period when it was called Bleeding Kansas (*q.v.*), proved an able commander during the American Civil War, and later served as governor of Pennsylvania (1867–73).

Geber   *See* **Jabir Ibn Hayyan, Abu Musa.**

Geddes, Sir Patrick 1854–1932.   Scottish biologist and sociologist noted for his work in the field of town planning. His works include *City Development* and *Cities in Evolution.*

Geiger, Abraham 1810–74.   German rabbi and scholar. He was an early leader of Reform Judaism (*q.v.*).

Geiger, Johannes Wilhelm 1882–1945.   German physicist and inventor, with W. Müller, of what is now known as the Geiger counter (1928), a device for measuring radiation.

Gelasius I *d.* AD 496.   Pope (AD 492–496).   He was important in the formulation of the doctrine of papal primacy in controversies with the Byzantine emperor. His strictures against Cae-

saropapism helped lead to the later Western idea of the separation of church and state.

Gelasius II (Gaeta, Giovanni da) *d.* 1119.   Italian-born pope (1118–19), successor to Paschal II. Gelasius opposed Holy Roman Emperor Henry V in the ongoing investiture controversy (*q.v.*). When Henry set up antipope Gregory VIII, Gelasius excommunicated them both. Gelasius was subsequently driven out of Rome by Henry and died at Cluny, France.

Gellius, Aulus *fl.* 2d cent. AD.   Roman author of *Attic Nights,* a book containing extracts of many ancient works that are now otherwise lost.

Gelon *d.* 478 BC.   Greek ruler. He made himself master of Syracuse and much of Sicily. He crushed the Carthaginians at Himera (480 BC).

Gempei War   Japanese civil war (1180–85) that led to the downfall of the Taira clan as military allies of the Retired Emperor. The Taira had increased their influence over the imperial court in Kyōto from 1158. In 1159, they defeated the rival general Yoshitomo. In 1180 his son, Yoritomo, organized dissident Taira clan members and the remainder of the Minamoto clan for a rebellion against the Taira military power. The war culminated in the naval battle of Dannoura (1185), in which the Taira were crushed. Yoritomo became the leading general and commander of warriors in Japan, and in 1192 was appointed shogun by the emperor. The Kamakura shogunate was thereby established and continued to rule Japan until 1333.

Generation of '98   Spanish intellectual movement. Spain's 1898 defeat in the Spanish-American War fostered an introspective period among Spanish writers and philosophers that ultimately enriched Spanish literature. They included Miguel Unamuno y Jugo (1864–1936), José Martínez Ruiz (1874–1967), and José Ortega y Gasset (1883–1955).

Genêt, Edmond Charles Édouard (Citizen ˜) 1763–1834.   French diplomat. He was sent to the US to win its support in the French revolutionary government's war against Britain. He was unable to sway President G. Washington from a neutral policy and, when he attempted to rally popular support, Washington had him recalled.

Genet, Jean 1910–86.   French dramatist. Genet was a leading proponent of the Theater of the Absurd, portraying social outcasts in such plays as *The Maids* (1948), *The Balcony* (1956), and *The Blacks* (1958).

Geneva, Robert of *See* **Robert of Geneva.**

Geneva Conferences International meetings. This name refers to several peace-keeping conferences held in the Swiss city. A 1927 meeting tried but failed to achieve a reduction of naval armaments. The Disarmament Conference, held primarily between 1932 and 1934, also failed to restrict offensive weaponry and fell apart when A. Hitler withdrew. A 1954 meeting discussed a Korean War armistice and partitioned Indochina, while a 1955 summit meeting among the US, France, Britain, and Russia sought to end the Cold War. A 1958 US-British-Russian meeting was the first of several held to discuss the banning of nuclear tests and nuclear arms limitation.

Geneva Conventions International agreements. From 1864 through 1949, a series of international agreements was reached at Geneva, Switzerland, to regulate and prevent abuses of war and the treatment of prisoners of war. Initiated by the Red Cross, signatory nations agreed to provide humane treatment for all prisoners as well as medical attention for the sick and wounded. Because of WW II abuses, the four conventions signed in Aug., 1949, concerning the sick and wounded, prisoners of war, and civilians in time of war are considered especially important.

Geneva Protocol League of Nations agreement. On Oct. 2, 1924, the assembly of the League of Nations unanimously agreed to make arbitration of disputes mandatory for member nations. However, the protocol became a dead letter when the British cabinet rejected the idea several months later and failed to ratify the protocol.

Geneviève, Saint c422–c500 or 512. Patron saint of the city of Paris. She is said to have predicted correctly that Paris would remain unscathed by an impending attack by Attila the Hun (451).

Genghis Khan (Jenghiz ⁓) (Chinghiz ⁓) (*orig. name* Temujin) 1167?–1227. Mongol conqueror, who, as leader of notoriously savage Mongol armies, created a vast Asian empire. Named chief of a Mongol tribe while still a youth, he succeeded in conquering other Mongol tribes and in organizing them (1206) into a confederacy. With his capital at Karakorum (*in modern* Mongolian People's Republic), he invaded (1213–18) and conquered northern China. From 1218 to 1224 he extended his empire in the west, conquering parts of what are now northern India, Iran, Iraq,

and southern Russia. By the time of his death, the empire extended from the Korean Peninsula in the east to the Black Sea in the west. The empire was subsequently divided among his sons, including Ogadai and Jagatai, and their descendants, including Batu Khan, Hulagu Khan, and Kublai Khan.

Genoa, Conference of *See* **Conference of Genoa.**

Genseric *See* **Gaiseric.**

Gentili Alberico 1552–1608. Italian jurist who is regarded as one of the earliest writers on international law. He is noted for his works on laws for the conduct of war.

Gentlemen's Agreement Accord (Feb. 24, 1907) between the US and Japan halting the immigration of Japanese laborers into the United States. By this agreement, brought about by pressure from West Coast states, Japan promised to stop further emigration and the US agreed to stop anti-Japanese discrimination.

Gentz, Friedrich von 1764–1832. Prussian political theorist in the Austrian service. He was influential in the realignment of the European powers after the Napoleonic Wars (*q.v.*), and was chief secretary at the Congresses (*q.v.*) of Vienna (1814–15), Aix-la-Chapelle (1818), Troppau (1820), and Verona (1822).

Geoffrey IV (Geoffrey Plantagenet) 1113–51. Count of Anjou. He laid claim to and conquered Normandy (1135–44). In 1150 he turned the duchy over to his son, the future English king Henry II.

Geoffrey of Monmouth c1100–54. English clergyman and writer. He was author of *Historia Regum Britanniae* (c1135), a fanciful account of British kings that contained the first account of the legendary King Arthur and widely influenced British literature.

Geoffrey Plantagenet *See* **Geoffrey IV.**

George I 1660–1727. German-born elector of Hanover and king of Great Britain and Ireland (1714–27), the first of the Hanoverian kings and successor to Queen Anne. An unpopular king, he succeeded under the 1701 Act of Settlement (*q.v.*). Under his reign Britain entered into the Quadruple Alliance (*q.v.*) and concluded the 1713 Peace of Utrecht. The king himself was implicated in the South Sea Bubble scandal (*q.v.*). He was the great-grandson of James I.

George I 1845–1913. Greek king (1863–1913), elected successor to Otto I. His reign was marked by the adoption of a constitution (1864), the acquisition of new territories in Thessaly and Epirus, and an unsuccessful war with the Ottoman Turks (1896–97) over Crete (Greco-Turkish War, *q.v.*).

George II 1683–1760. German-born elector of Hanover and king of Great Britain and Ireland (1727–60), a member of the Hanover family, and successor to his father, George I. Under his reign Britain saw the last of the Jacobite rebellions (1745–46), the ouster of Sir R. Walpole, and the beginning of the Seven Years' War (1756–63).

George II 1890–1947. Greek king (1922–23, 1935–47), successor to his father Constantine I. He was forced to leave Greece (1923) and shortly thereafter a republic was proclaimed (1924). Recalled in 1935, he acquiesced to the dictatorship of J. Metaxas (1936) and, in 1941, fled from the invading Germans. He was restored to the throne in 1946, and was succeeded by his brother Paul I (1901–64).

George III 1738–1820. King of Great Britain and Ireland (1760–1820), a member of the Hanoverian family, and successor to his grandfather, George II. Under his reign Britain enjoyed a period of economic prosperity and cultural activity. At the same time the king's policies led to political instability at home and the American Revolution (*q.v.*) abroad. By 1784, however, he achieved his goal of breaking Whig control in Parliament with a general Tory victory in the elections. His reign also saw Britain's participation in the French Revolutionary and Napoleonic Wars (*q.v.*), the union of the Irish and English kingdoms (1801), and the War of 1812 with the US. George refused to permit Catholic Emancipation (1801). Suffering what was believed a hereditary disease, he became insane (1810). He was elector and later king of Hanover but never visited it.

George IV 1762–1830. King of England and Ireland (1820–30), a member of the Hanover family, successor to his father George III. He became regent for his insane father (1810) and under him the Tory party continued in power. His reign saw a marked decline in the influence of the monarchy thanks to his dissolute ways and to the scandals that surrounded his married life. He was succeeded by his brother William IV.

George V 1819–78. German king, the last king of Hanover (1851–66) and successor to his father Ernest Augustus (1771–1851). He allied himself

with Austria during the Austro-Prussian War (*q.v.*) and following the Prussian victory his kingdom was taken over and annexed by Prussia. His father, a son of George III of England, had acceded to the throne of Hanover in 1837 when Hanover was separated from Britain at the accession of Victoria.

George V 1865–1936. King of Great Britain (1910–36), successor to his father, Edward VII. He played a moderating role in the crises during his reign and guided Britain through WW I. Among the events of this period were the 1916 Irish Sinn Fein Rebellion (*q.v.*), the 1922 Irish Free State (*q.v.*) settlement, the formation of the "national" government (1931) and the 1935 Government of India Act (*q.v.*). A popular monarch, he changed the royal family name from Saxe-Coburg-Gotha to Windsor during WW I.

George VI 1895–1952. King of Great Britain and Northern Ireland (1936–52), successor to his brother Edward VIII. He is noted for his efforts to shore up British morale during WW II. During his reign, India was granted independence (1947). He was succeeded by his daughter Elizabeth II.

George, Henry 1839–97. American economic reformer. He developed the idea of the single tax (1871). Under this system, designed to eliminate poverty, the government would abolish all taxes except that on land itself.

George, Saint 4th cent.? Patron saint of England. A saint of the Eastern church, he may have been martyred in Palestine around AD 250 or during the great persecutions by Diocletian on Apr. 23, 303. Because of the association of his name with chivalric legends during the Middle Ages, particularly the one about his slaying of the dragon, he became very popular in story and art, was made patron of soldiers and adopted as patron by England, Aragon, and Portugal.

George of Podebrad 1420–71. Bohemian king (1458–71). A leader of the Utraquists (*q.v.*) in the Hussite Wars (*q.v.*), he took Prague (1448) and became first regent to King Ladislaus (1453–57) and then king of Bohemia. He successfully resisted a challenge to his throne by the Hungarian king Matthias Corvinus (1469).

Georgia Historic region and now an independent state, located on the eastern shore of the Black Sea. Georgia was formerly a constituent republic of the USSR, and Stalin was a native of the region. In ancient times the region was known as Colchis (*q.v.*) and Iberia, and was part of the Roman Empire from 65 BC. In AD 337 the region was converted to Christianity and thereafter suffered in wars between the Byzantines and Persians. Muslims gained control of Georgia from 654, while the unification of the Georgian kingdom began in the 8th cent. Invasions by Mongols and Timurs and wars between the Turks and Persians brought about the kingdom's decline (from 13th cent.). From 1801 to 1864 Russia annexed Georgian lands and, after a brief period of independence (1918–21) following the Russian Revolution, Georgia was made a republic within the USSR (1922). In recent years, Georgia became the scene of, first, ethnic unrest (1988) and then violent demands for independence (Apr.). In 1990, Georgia's Supreme Soviet demanded talks with the national government on independence (Apr.) and in 1991, Georgian voters overwhelmingly approved a referendum on independence. The Georgian legislature voted for the measure (Apr. 9) and on May 26, Zviad Gamsakhurdia became first-ever elected president of the republic (May 26). His dictatorial style soon aroused resentment and unrest, however, and by late 1991 attempts to oust him resulted in a civil war. Georgia, in a state of turmoil, did not join the Commonwealth of Independent States, the only one to do so outside of the Baltic States. President Gamsakhurdia was driven from the capital in early 1992 and a military council took power as fighting began to diminish. Civilian rule was restored when E. Shevardnadze, former Soviet foreign minister, became the provisional head of state (Mar.).

Georgia US state and one of the original Thirteen Colonies (*q.v.*). Georgia was first explored by the Spanish under H. de Soto (1540). The first town, Savannah, was founded (1733) by J. Oglethorpe for the English. Rival claims to the region were settled when Oglethorpe defeated the Spanish at the Battle of Bloody Marsh (1742). Georgia was made a colony in 1754 and ratified the Constitution in 1788. Amid the Yazoo Land Claims (*q.v.*) controversy, Georgia turned over its western lands to the federal government and established its current boundaries (1802). The Creek and Cherokee Indians were forced to leave the state in the 1830s. The state was ravaged by Sherman's March during the US Civil War and afterward the great plantations were replaced by tenant farmers and sharecroppers. Blacks voted in the Democratic primary for the first time in 1946 and were integrated with whites in the schools after 1961. The state adopted a new constitution in 1945.

Georgian style English architectural style. This formal, neoclassic style, characterized by red brick with white woodwork, was popular in England c1715–1820. From there the style spread to Colonial America.

Gerhardsen, Einar Henry 1897–1987. Norwegian statesman. Gerhardsen was a labor leader who was held hostage by the Nazis during WW II. He was the first (1945–51) post-liberation Norwegian prime minister, a post he held twice more (1955–63, 1963–65).

Géricault, Jean Louis André Théodore 1791–1824. French painter who rebelled against the classical school and became an important figure in the transition to Romanticism in French painting. *The Raft of the Medusa* (1819) is among his most famous paintings.

German Confederation A loose confederation (1815–66) of 35 independent German kingdoms and 4 free cities formed largely for mutual defense. It was dominated by Austria, and its history was marked by a growing rivalry between Austria and Prussia. Following the destruction of the Holy Roman Empire (*q.v.*) by Napoleon and the subsequent fall of his French-based empire, the German states were left largely unprotected. The German Confederation was therefore created at the Congress of Vienna (*q.v.*) in 1815 and a German diet under Austrian presidency was formed. The diet, briefly supplanted (1848–50) by the Frankfurt Parliament, survived until the Austro-Prussian War (*q.v.*) of 1866 and the formation of the North German Confederation (*q.v.*).

German East Africa Name of a former German colony in East Africa. The region was first explored by the Germans in 1884 and was declared a protectorate in 1885. In 1891 the German government took direct control of the colony, overcame native rebellions and developed it. Following WW I, it was divided (1919) between Britain and Belgium, becoming Tanganyika (now Tanzania) and Ruanda-Urundi (now Rwanda and Burundi respectively).

Germanic laws German tribal laws. These were the unwritten, customary laws of the Germanic peoples prior to their contact with Rome. They dealt predominantly with family and property rights and codes of justice and punishment, and were regarded as personal and tribal law, not territorial.

Germanicus, Tiberius Claudius Drusus Nero *See* **Claudius I.**

Germanicus Caesar 15 BC–AD 19.   Roman general and consul whose uncle was Emperor Tiberius. As commander of Roman armies on the Rhine, he defeated Arminius (AD 16) and his German tribes. Tiberius is said to have become jealous of his fame and, after sending him to the East, to have finally instigated his murder.

German Nation, Addresses to the *See* **Addresses to the German Nation.**

German New Guinea *See* **Papua New Guinea.**

Germans, ancient *See* **ancient Germans.**

Germantown, Battle of Battle (Oct. 4, 1777) during the American Revolution. Gen. G. Washington attacked this British stronghold near Philadelphia. Though it failed, it was a daring raid and, together with the Colonial victory in the Saratoga Campaign, helped convince the French to send aid to the Americans.

Germany Country located in central Europe. The population is 79,070,000 and the capital is Berlin. The unified German state was formed (19th cent.) from the petty German states that were once part of the Holy Roman Empire. (*For history of Germany prior to 1801, see* Holy Roman Empire.) By the end of the 19th cent., Germany had emerged as a major military and industrial power. It was deeply involved in the complex series of events that led to WW I and played a major role in the fighting against the Allied powers. Germany was defeated and the subsequent social, economic, and political instability in Germany created the climate that brought A. Hitler to power. Germany was once again defeated in WW II and the victorious Allies, determined to prevent another war, divided Germany into zones of occupation. Cold War tensions between the Soviet Union and the Western powers hardened the divisions. In the late 1940s the occupation zones of Western powers became West Germany (Bonn as capital) and the Soviet zone became East Germany (East Berlin as capital). Divided Germany became a focal point for East-West tensions in subsequent years, until finally the nation was reunified in 1991. **For**

more on important persons and major events, *see* separate text entries by name. Key events in German history include:

1801   Treaty of Lunéville (Feb. 9); Austria and other states of the Holy Roman Empire consented to treaty after being defeated by France; treaty effectively ended the Holy Roman Empire.

1801–58   Physiologist J. Müller lived.

1801–59   K. Baedeker, publisher, lived; founded travel guidebook series.

1803   Austria and German states formally accepted Napoleon's plan to begin reorganization of the 300 petty states that made up the Holy Roman Empire.

1803–73   Chemist Baron von Liebig lived.

1804–72   Philosopher L. Feuerbach lived.

1805–15   Napoleonic Wars; German states suffered much destruction in the wars; French occupation introduced liberalism and aroused German nationalism.

1806   Confederation of the Rhine created (July 12) by Napoleon; completed reorganization of German states; included Bavaria, Baden, Württemberg, and Hesse-Darmstadt.

1806   Holy Roman Empire formally dissolved (Aug. 6) by Holy Roman Emperor Francis II; he became Austrian Emperor Francis I.

1807–08   Addresses to the German Nation nationalistic lectures delivered by J. Fichte.

1809–47   Composer J. Mendelssohn lived.

1810–56   Romantic composer R. Schumann lived; wrote *Spring* and *Piano Concerto in A minor.*

1810–82   Physiologist T. Schwann lived; isolated first enzyme (pepsin) from animal tissue.

1811–99   Chemist R. Bunsen lived; introduced Bunsen burner.

1812–87   A. Krupp, steel magnate, lived; began casting of artillery barrels, for which Krupp became famous, at family steelworks.

1813–83   Romantic composer R. Wagner lived; wrote operas *The Ring of the Nibelung, Lohengrin,* and others.

1814–15   Congress of Vienna; Austria gained control over other German states as leader of a new confederation; Prussia and Bavaria enlarged by new territories.

1815–66   German Confederation; German states now reduced to about 40, united under the leadership of Austria; C. von Metternich, Austrian statesman, dominated the Confederation until mid-century and imposed his conservative policies.

1817–88 H. Storm, author noted for haunting realism, lived; wrote *The Rider of the White Horse.*

1818–24 Historian L. von Ranke wrote his early work, *History of the Latin and Teutonic Nations.*

1819 Carlsbad Decrees; were measures recommended for suppression of liberal agitation within the German Confederation.

1819 Zollverein, a customs union, established under the leadership of Prussia; by 1830 it included nearly all the German states except Austria and strengthened Prussia's position as leader of the states.

1820s–1830s Biedermeier period of artistic style gained popularity.

1821–94 H. von Helmholtz, physiologist and physicist, lived.

1821–1912 Pathologist R. Virchow, a founder of cellular pathology, lived.

1822–88 R. Clausius, mathematical physicist, lived; introduced concept of entropy in physics.

1822–90 Archaeologist H. Schliemann lived; discovered and excavated ruins of ancient Troy.

1824–87 Physicist G. Kirchhoff lived.

1826–66 Mathematician G. Riemann lived; made important contributions to science of geometry.

1827 Poet H. Heine published *The Book of Songs,* which established his international reputation.

1828 Chemist F. Wöhler synthesized first organic compound from inorganic materials.

1828–1870 Ophthalmologist A. von Gräfe lived; known for developing treatments for glaucoma and cataracts.

1828–98 F. Cohn, a founder of bacteriology, lived.

1830 Liberal revolt broke out, sparked by July Revolution in France; liberals suppressed by Metternich, with Prussian aid.

1830s–1840s Young Germany literary movement reached its height.

1832 Federal Diet of Confederation given greater powers by Six Articles; included tighter controls on press and assembly within the states.

1832–1920 W. Wundt, founder of experimental psychology, lived.

1833 Abortive plot to seize Federal Diet at Frankfurt and create liberal, unified German state.

1833–97 Composer J. Brahms lived; wrote *Requiem, Violin Concerto in D,* and his four great symphonies.

1834–96 Historian H. von Treitschke lived.

1837–51 Ernst Augustus succeeded to the throne of Hanover; abolished liberal constitution (1840) and established absolute monarchy.

1840–61 Frederick William IV reigned in Prussia; increased Prussia's role as leader of German Confederation.

1846 Astronomer J. Galle discovered planet Neptune.

1847 United Diet of Prussia convened by Frederick IV; aroused hopes for constitutional reforms among liberals elsewhere in the Confederation.

1848 Revolutions of 1848; Metternich fell from power (Mar. 13) and Austria was preoccupied with revolts in domains outside the Confederation; King Frederick of Prussia appeased rebels by embracing German nationalism and granting liberal constitution; other German states did the same.

1848 K. Marx published *The Communist Manifesto* with F. Engels; the work established them as leading advocates of Communist ideology.

1848–50 Frankfurt National Assembly convened (May 18); dominated by middle class, this parliament replaced the Diet of the Confederation and sought to form a national government of Germany.

1848–51 War over Schleswig-Holstein, Prussians intervened at the request of the Frankfurt Assembly to prevent Danish troops from occupying region, which had large German-speaking population.

1849 Frankfurt Constitution drawn up (Mar. 27) by Frankfurt Parliament; named Prussian king Frederick emperor of a unified German state; Frederick demurred, then refused the crown and offered his own scheme, the Prussian Union.

1850 Erfurt Parliament met (Mar.); Prussian Union accepted.

1850   Austria, having quelled the liberal revolts within its domains, countered by reconstituting the German Confederation (May); threatened Prussia with war if it went ahead with the Prussian Union.

1850   Punctation of Olmütz (Nov. 29); Prussia, humiliated by Austria, agreed to reestablishment of the German Confederation.

1850–53   Prussia successfully resisted Austria's efforts to join the Zollverein and thus maintained Prussia's economic hold over the German states; period of rapid industrialization began.

1854–1902   F. Krupp, industrialist, lived.

1857–1933   Feminist C. Zetkin lived; helped found Communist party.

1858–1938   Philosopher E. Husserl lived; founder of phenomenology.

1858–1942   German-American anthropologist F. Boas lived.

1860–62   Crisis over reorganization of the Prussian army; liberals feared that abolition of the National Guard would undermine their standing and that a large standing army would give the king too much power; reorganization carried through.

1861–71   William I reigned as king of Prussia.

1862   O. von Bismarck came to power in Prussian government with promises of carrying through army reforms; a conservative, he ultimately succeeded in uniting Germany (1871).

1863   Social Democratic Party of Germany founded.

1863   Prussians again succeeded in blocking Austrian entry to the Zollverein.

1864   War over Schleswig-Holstein; Denmark annexed the duchies, violating agreement of 1851; Prussia defeated Denmark, which ceded Schleswig-Holstein to Austria and Prussia.

1864–1920   M. Weber, sociologist and political economist, lived; wrote *The Protestant Ethic and the Spirit of Capitalism.*

1864–1949   Composer R. Strauss lived; wrote operas *Salome* and *Der Rosenkavalier.*

1866   Austro-Prussian War; Bismarck helped provoke war over Schleswig-Holstein; Prussians won control of both duchies by their victory and organized a new confederation of German states in the north.

1866–71   North German Confederation;

ship of Prussia; was nucleus of subsequent German Empire.

1869   German Social Democratic Workingmen's party formed.

1870   France opposed offer of Spanish crown to Prussian prince Leopold of Hohenzollern-Sigmaringen; after winning refusal, sought to humiliate Prussia and thereby helped bring on war.

1870   Bismarck revised and released (July 13) Ems Dispatch and thereby increased tensions with France.

1870–71   Franco-Prussian War; Bismarck, hoping to bring southern German states into the North German Confederation, helped provoke war with France; the war united the German states and ended in defeat of France.

1870–1950   G. Krupp, industrialist and manufacturer of armaments, lived; made Krupp leading arms manufacturer during WW I; supported A. Hitler.

1871   Germany unified (Jan. 18); William of Prussia created king of united Germany, Alsace and Lorraine added to German territories after war with France.

1871–88   William I reigned as German emperor; Bismarck became chancellor and leading figure of the government of the German Empire.

1871   Imperial constitution accepted by the Reichstag (Apr. 14); framed by Bismarck, it established Prussian kings as hereditary emperors of Germany; Bundestag (upper house) and Reichstag (lower house, elected by manhood suffrage) formed; monarchy and wealthy elite retained control of state through three-class voting system.

1871–87   Bismarck instituted the Kulturkampf, cultural struggle against the Catholic church in Germany.

1871   Center party organized to protect interests of Catholics.

1872   Bismarck arranged the Three Emperors' League (between Germany, Russia, and Austria-Hungary) to isolate France.

1873   Financial crisis; economic depression lasting some years followed.

1874–1945   Philosopher E. Cassirer lived.

1875   Socialists met at Gotha (May); marked rise of Socialism in Germany, groups united, adopted nonviolent Socialism of Ferdinand Lassalle.

1875 Central bank (Reichsbank) formed.

1876 Bacteriologist R. Koch isolated bacteria causing anthrax.

1878 Emperor William escaped two assassination attempts.

1878 Reichstag dissolved after Bismarck blamed Social Democrats for attempts on the emperor; Socialists suppressed (1878–90).

1879 Alliance with Austria marked restoration of relations with that state.

1879 Protective tariff enacted, ending free-trade policy; meanwhile, period of rapid industrialization and commercial prosperity also began about this time.

1880–1936 O. Spengler, historian and philosopher, lived; wrote *The Decline of the West.*

1880–1938 Artist E. Kirchner lived; became a leading figure in German expressionism.

1882 Triple Alliance with Italy and Austria.

1882 German Colonial League formed to promote colonial expansion.

1882 Koch discovered organism causing tuberculosis.

1882–1936 Philosopher M. Schlick, a logical positivist, lived.

1883–89 Model social security laws enacted as Bismarck attempted to counter Socialist influence.

1883–1969 Philosopher K. Jaspers lived; noted German existentialist.

1884 South-West Africa made a German protectorate.

1884 Togoland and the Cameroons became German colonies.

1885 Germany declared German East Africa a protectorate.

1885 Congress of Berlin organized by Bismarck; established ground rules for division of Africa by European colonial powers.

1885 Engineer G. Daimler developed an internal combustion engine; later founded Daimler Motor Company.

1885–1973 Conductor O. Klemperer lived.

1886 C. Benz, engineer, patented first automobile powered by internal combustion engine.

c1886 Physicist H. Hertz discovered radio waves.

1887 Reinsurance Treaty, secret agreement with Russia to maintain neutrality in each other's wars with other states.

1888 Frederick III reigned briefly before his death.

1888–1918 William II reigned as last of the German emperors; first sought to appease Socialists by instituting labor and other social reforms, then became increasingly conservative.

1890 Bismarck resigned over differences with new emperor and rising power of the Socialists.

1891 Erfurt Congress of Socialists; German Socialists adopted Marxian principles.

1891–1976 Artist M. Ernst lived.

1893–1947 Sociologist K. Mannheim lived; wrote *Ideologie und Utopie.*

1895 Physicist W. Roentgen discovered X-rays.

1895–1963 Composer P. Hindemith lived; composed opera *Mathis der Maler.*

1896 R. Diesel perfected the diesel engine.

1897 German naval expansion began with emperor's appointment of Alfred von Tirpitz as marine minister.

1900 Second Navy Bill passed by Reichstag; backed by rye producing Junker aristocracy and iron and steel industrialist ("rye and iron" alliance), the bill ordered construction of German battleship fleet, which eventually would threaten British naval supremacy.

1900 Physicist M. Planck postulated modern quantum theory, subsequently revolutionizing physics; won Nobel Prize for Physics (1918).

1900–09 Count von Bülow in office as chancellor; considerable social legislation enacted.

EARLY 1900s Expressionist movement in art and literature popular in Germany.

1901 Nobel Prize in Physics awarded to W. Roentgen.

1901 Bacteriologist E. von Behring received first Nobel Prize for Physiology or Medicine; earlier devised antitoxins for diphtheria and tetanus.

1901–76 Physicist W. Heisenberg lived; contributed to Quantum Theory.

1902–09 Great German-born theoretical physicist A. Einstein formulated his theories of relativity; later received Nobel Prize for Physics (1921).

1905 Moroccan crisis with France.

1906–12 Archaeologist H. Winckler excavated Hittite capital at Bogazköy, Turkey.

1907–67 Industrialist A. Krupp lived.

1908–09 Crisis over Austrian annexation of Bosnia and Herzegovina; Germany forced Russia to accept the annexation.

1910–12 Psychologist M. Wertheimer researched theory of perception of motion; led to development of Gestalt psychology.

1911 Alsace and Lorraine made a German state.

1911 Agadir Incident, crisis with France over Morocco; France ceded Congo territory to Germany to avert war.

1912 Socialists became the largest single party in the Reichstag, though it remained a minority; victory came after adoption of moderate (revisionist) Socialist principles.

c1912 Psychologist K. Koffka co-founded school of Gestalt psychology with W. Köhler and M. Wertheimer.

1912 G. Hauptmann, received Nobel Prize for Literature; known for *Before Dawn* and *The Weavers*.

1914 Murder of Austrian Archduke Francis Ferdinand by a Serbian nationalist (June); Austria, backed by Germany, declared war on Serbia; Russia backed Serbia and declarations of war followed; Germans put Schlieffen Plan into motion, beginning war with attack on France via Belgium (Aug. 4).

1914–18 World War I: Germany, the leader of the Central Powers, suffered heavy losses in the war and though it was victorious over Russia and not yet invaded in the west, it was forced to accept an armistice (Nov. 11, 1918).

1917 Field Marshal P. von Hindenburg and Chief of Staff E. Ludendorf overthrew Chancellor T. von Bethmann-Hollweg; held power to 1918.

1918 Treaty of Brest-Litovsk; forced on the new Communist government of Russia, the (short-lived) treaty briefly gave Germany control over Eastern Europe.

1918 Mutiny at Kiel began among German navy men (Oct. 28) and quickly became nationwide uprising; Emperor William fled to Holland (Nov. 9) and a republic was proclaimed.

1918 Socialists took control of government (Nov. 10); struggle between Social Democrats and Spartacists (Communists) began.

1918 Armistice to end the war accepted by Germans (Nov. 11).

1919 Spartacist uprisings in Berlin, led by Communists, crushed (Jan.–Mar.); Communist leaders were executed.

1919 Allies demanded $33 billion in war reparations.

1919 Treaty of Versailles; accepted by German government (June 23) after futile attempt to modify harsh terms; Germany stripped of colonies, forced to cede Alsace-Lorraine to France, north Schleswig to Denmark, and Polish Corridor to Poland; forced to agree to heavy war reparations and restrictions on rearmament; terms bitterly resented in Germany and contributed to outbreak of WW II.

1919–33 Weimar Republic, established by constitution (adopted July 31), it was governed by a chancellor and two houses, the Reichstag and Reichsrat; women given the right to vote.

1919–25 F. Ebert in office as first president of the new republic.

1920 Kapp Putsch, unsuccessful attempt to reestablish monarchy (Mar 13–17).

1920 Spartacist uprising in the Ruhr crushed.

1920 Center party gained control of the government in Reichstag elections.

1921 A. Hitler reorganized German Workers' party into Nazi party; his appeal to German nationalism, hatred of Jews, and fear of Communists gradually won him a sizable following in subsequent years; Nazi storm troops used brutal force to advance party cause.

1921 Drop in value of German mark began (Aug.); passed level of 88 marks to US dollar.

1922 Germany beset by severe economic troubles; mark dropped to 2,000 per US dollar on currency market; hyperinflation (1922–23) created tremendous economic, political, and social stresses.

1922 Treaty of Rapallo (Apr. 16) canceled war indemnities and normalized relations with USSR.

1923 German mark plummeted on currency market to 3.3 million per US dollar (Aug.); war reparations payments halted but slide continued; by Nov. 4 trillion marks worth one US dollar and sugar was selling for 250 billion marks a pound.

1923 Hitler instigated the abortive Munich Putsch (Nov. 9).

1923–30 Ruhr district occupied after Germany defaulted on war reparations.

1923 Hyperinflation halted by drastic austerity budget; measures plunged Germany into depression between 1925 and 1926.

1923–30 Financial expert H. Schacht served as president of Reichsbank; slowed runaway inflation of 1920s and helped stabilize growth in early Nazi Germany.

1924 Dawes Plan for war reparations accepted.

1925–34 P. von Hindenburg in office as president.

1925 Locarno Pact signed; marked rapprochement with Germany by European powers.

1925 Hitler published *Mein Kampf.*

1926 Germany admitted to League of Nations.

1927 Von Hindenburg denied German responsibility for war (Sept. 18) that was stipulated in Treaty of Versailles.

1927 Philosopher M. Heidegger published *Time and Being.*

1928 Physicist J. Geiger invented Geiger counter with W. Müller.

1928 B. Brecht wrote the play *The Threepenny Opera,* his first major dramatic success.

1929 Kellogg-Briand Pact for renunciation of war accepted.

1929 Young Plan revising war reparations payments adopted.

1929 Great Depression caused severe economic problems in Germany, which had just recovered from the postwar inflation and depression.

1929 Novelist E. Remarque published *All Quiet on the Western Front.*

1929 Novelist T. Mann received Nobel Prize for Literature; wrote *Death in Venice* and *Doctor Faustus.*

1930 President Hindenburg dissolved the Reichstag (July 16) after his budget bill was turned down.

1930 Nazi party made significant gains in elections for new Reichstag; Nazis increased their power in subsequent elections and blocked creation of effective government; violence by Nazi storm troops.

1930s Admiral K. Doenitz supervised creation of new submarine fleet; subsequently commanded it and the navy.

1931 Banks closed in financial crisis (July 14).

1931 Seaplane, built by C. Dornier, completed maiden flight from Germany to New York.

1933 Hitler named chancellor (Jan. 30) after his Nazi party effectively paralyzed government; Von Hindenburg reluctantly made appointment after being convinced Hitler could be controlled.

1933 Reichstag Fire (Feb. 27); Hitler blamed Communists and used incident to assume dictatorial powers.

1933 Enabling Act passed (Mar. 23) by Reichstag alliance of Nazis, conservatives, and Center party; established Hitler's corporative state and his dictatorship.

1933–45 Third Reich; Hitler in power to last days and National Socialist party was only legal party; Hitler's militarism led to world war; Jews and others persecuted in the Holocaust.

1933 Gestapo (secret police) organized by Hitler lieutenant, H. Göring, and run by H. Himmler after 1934; terrorized populace, arrested political opponents, Jews, and members of other "inferior races" for transport to concentration camps; Holocaust began.

1933–45 Dachau, the first of the notorious Nazi concentration camps, in operation.

1933 Germany withdrew from League of Nations.

1934 New highway building program announced by Hitler (Mar.); planned to greatly expand existing 900 miles of four-lane highways (autobahns) to nationwide network.

1934 Hitler ordered end to payments on foreign debt (June 14).

1934 Blood Purge of Nazi party leaders ordered by Hitler (June 30, "Night of the Long Knives"); eliminated all opposition to his rule.

1934 Austrian Chancellor E. Dollfuss killed in unsuccessful Nazi takeover attempt (July).

1934 Nazi J. Ribbentrop admitted publicly that Germany was rearming (Oct.).

1935 Hitler attacked Treaty of Versailles provision on disarmament of Germany (Mar. 16).

1935 Locarno Pact denounced; Rhineland reoccupied (Mar.) by German military.

1935 Nazis instituted (Sept. 15) Nürnberg Laws against Jews.

1936 Pact concluded with Fascist Italy (Oct.).

1936 Anti-Comintern Pact with Japan marked expansion of Axis alliance.

1936 Hitler instituted his four-year plan to turn economy into a war machine; Göring was head of program.

1936 Nazis sent combat troops to Spain, then embroiled in Spanish Civil War.

1938 Anschluss; Germans invaded and annexed Austria (Mar. 12–13).

1938 German occupation of the Sudetenland; Munich Pact (Sept. 29) was move by European powers to appease Hitler and allowed him to occupy region; resulted in complete dismemberment of Czech state, however.

1938 Field Marshal W. Keitel became chief of staff of Nazi high command; served throughout WW II.

1939 Pact of Steel with Italy (May 22) cemented Rome-Berlin Axis.

1939 Nonaggression pact with the USSR (Aug.); paved way for attack on Poland.

1939 Germans invaded Poland (Sept. 1); WW II began.

1939 Hitler escaped assassination attempt unscathed (Nov. 8); bomb planted at Munich beer hall (site of the failed putsch) exploded 15 minutes after Hitler had left.

1939 Aircraft manufacturer E. Heinkel built first turbojet aircraft, the He-178.

1939 German fighter Me-109, designed by W. Messerschmitt, set world speed record, reaching 435 mph.

1939–45 World War II; Hitler briefly established a German empire that included nearly all of Europe, but ultimately suffered total defeat; Germany devastated by Allied drive to crush Nazi war machine.

1940 Some 100 German cities hit by RAF bombing attacks (July); more intensive bombing raids begun on Germany cities 1942–43, with US participation beginning in early 1943.

1944 Nobel Prize for Chemistry awarded to O. Hahn, who demonstrated nuclear fission.

1945 Hitler committed suicide (Apr. 30), as Soviets advanced through streets of Berlin; Adm. K. Doenitz succeeded him.

1945 A. Jodl signed Germany's unconditional surrender (May 7–8); German war machine dismantled and Germany divided into four occupation zones, each administered separately (by US, Britain, France, and USSR); Danzig and territory beyond Oder and Neisse rivers ceded to Poland; Soviets got northern part of East Prussia.

1945 Potsdam Conference, Allies set postwar policies (July–Aug.).

1945–46 Nürnberg Trials held to judge leaders of Nazi party for war crimes.

1945–47 War's aftermath; food shortages and severe economic conditions prevailed; 10 million Germans migrated from Soviet-occupied zones to Western zones; local administration by Germans set up; Socialist Unity Party (SED), a Communist organ, dominated politics in the Soviet (Eastern) sector; Christian Democrats, Social Democrats, and others arose in the Western zones.

1945–46 East German government nationalized industry and large agricultural estates.

1946 Nobel Prize for Literature awarded to famed novelist and poet H. Hesse, who wrote *Siddhartha* and *Steppenwolf.*

1947 Moscow Conference; split developed between Soviets and Western powers occupying Germany (Mar.–Apr.).

1948 Western powers instituted currency reforms (June 18) to economically unify Western zone; Soviets reacted by blockading Berlin.

1948–49 Berlin blockade and airlift, major test of strength in emerging Cold War.

1949 Federal Republic of Germany formed (May 23) from Western-occupied zones; Grundgesetz (provisional constitution) adopted; Theodore Heuss became first president (1949–59), formalized division of Germany.

1949–63 K. Adenauer in office as first West German chancellor; oversaw rapid rebuilding of West Germany; maintained close relations with the West.

1949 German Democratic Republic established (Oct. 7) by Soviets to govern their Eastern zone; Wilhelm Pieck named president (1949–60).

1950s Soviet Union exploited East Germany economy in order to rebuild its own war-ravaged economy; by 1960s, however, East German economy began to grow.

1950 East German government accepted Oder-Neisse line as boundary with Poland.

1950 Western powers eased controls imposed in West by occupation statute.

1950 In East Germany, hard-line Communist W. Ulbricht became secretary-general of the ruling SED party.

1952 Bonn Convention signed; West Germany granted nearly complete sovereignty.

1953 Soviets turned control of East Germany over to a civilian commissioner; granted complete sovereignty Mar. 27, 1954.

1953 Food shortage in East Germany and growing resentment over Soviet-style government sparked strikes and unrest (June); Soviet troops used to put down the protests.

1953 *Counterpoint,* by composer K. Stockhausen, first performed.

1955 West Germany gained full independence (May 5), though troops of occupying powers remained; joined NATO; armed forces created.

1955 East Germany entered Warsaw Pact.

1950s West German economy boomed as its industry completed recovery from war; East Germany continued to stagnate under Soviet system.

1957 Saarland turned over to West Germany by France.

1957 West Germany became charter member of the Common Market.

1957 West German legislature (Bundestag) designated Berlin Germany's official capital; Bonn to serve as government seat.

1959 Novelist G. Grass wrote *The Tin Drum.*

1960–71 In East Germany, W. Ulbricht in office as chairman of council of state; won Soviet recognition for East German republic; economy prospered and became strongest in Eastern Europe; adopted hard-line policy against West Germany to force recognition of East Germany.

1961 Berlin Wall erected by East Germans to stop the flow of refugees to the West.

1963 West Germany signed friendship treaty with France.

1963–66 L. Erhard (Christian Democrat) in office as West German chancellor; poor economy and other problems forced his resignation.

1966–69 K. G. Kiesinger (Christian Democrat) in office as West German chancellor; formed coalition government with Christian Socialists and Social Democrats; opened relations with East European nations.

1968 East German troops participated in the Warsaw Pact invasion of Czechoslovakia.

1968 New East German constitution adopted.

1969–74 In West Germany, W. Brandt (Social Democrat) in office as chancellor; his *Östopolitik* resulted in formal treaties with the Soviets and their European satellite nations.

1970 West German chancellor W. Brandt and East German premier W. Stoph at first meeting between leaders of these two states (Jan. 19).

1970 East Germans formally recognized cessation of territories beyond the Oder and Neisse rivers to Poland.

1970 East Germans halted traffic (Dec. 18–22) between West Berlin and West Germany for four days.

1971–89 In East Germany, Erich Honecker in office as chairman of the council of state; relations with West Germany significantly improved.

1973 Treaty signed (June 6) to normalize relations between East and West Germany.

1973 West and East Germany admitted to the UN.

1974 Chancellor Brandt of West Germany resigned (May 6) after one of his aides was exposed as an East German spy.

1974–82 Helmut Schmidt (Social Democrat) became West German chancellor.

1974 East Germany established diplomatic relations with US (Sept.).

1974 East Germany adopted new constitution.

1976 Communist summit held (June) in East Berlin; Soviet domination in Communist countries opposed.

1978 East German troops involved in fighting in Angola.

1980 East Germany closed border with Poland (Oct.) as crisis over Solidarity movement mounted.

1981 East German head of state, E. Honecker, spoke on possible reunification of Germany, thus reversing party line (Feb.).

1981 Controversy in West Germany over stationing of US nuclear missiles there; Chancellor Schmidt threatened to resign (May) over issue, but won approval.

1982–91 H. Kohl, leader of coalition of Christian Democratic Union and Christian Social Union, in office as West German chancellor; would oversee unification of divided Germany and become its first chancellor.

1983 Mass antinuclear demonstration in West Germany (Nov.), sparked by deployment of US nuclear missiles there; Soviets increased nuclear missiles stationed in East Germany.

1984 Strike by metal industry and engineering workers in the West lasts for seven weeks (May–June).

1986 Terrorist bomb exploded at West Berlin nightclub frequented by US servicemen (Apr. 4); 1 American killed, 50–60 wounded; incident became basis for US bombing raid on Libya, which was suspected of aiding the terrorists.

1986 Refugees from Third World countries allowed to cross into West Berlin by East German government.

1986 Ecological disaster threatened Rhine River in Germany; 1,000 tons of toxic chemicals accidentally spilled into river during a chemical plant fire upstream in Switzerland (Nov.).

1987 Germans celebrated 750th anniversary of Berlin's founding.

1987 East Germany's E. Honecker on first visit to West Germany (Sept.).

1989 Soviet leader M. Gorbachev, visiting Germany, publicly reversed long-standing Brezhnev Doctrine and declared that states have right to political self-determination (June); later reiterated new Soviet policy of noninterference.

1989–90 Refugees from East Germany, Poland, Hungary, and Czechoslavakia flooded into West Germany as East European Communist governments collapsed amid widespread unrest; Hungary became conduit for escaping East Germans when it began allowing refugees to cross its border without exit visas (Sept.).

1989 New Forum, East German pro-democracy opposition group, gathered 100,000 signatures for petition (Oct.); group was legalized in early Nov.

1989 East German government celebrated 40th anniversary (Oct.); Gorbachev attended; demonstrations and unrest followed ceremony in East Berlin, spreading to other cities.

1989 Honecker forced to resign his posts (Oct.) by continuing demonstrations and widespread resentment over use of force to halt them.

1989 Egon Krenz in office as East German head of state; attempted to mollify opposition groups by holding talks; granted amnesty for protesters and those caught trying to leave country.

1989 Mass demonstrations continued, notably in Liepzig and elsewhere (Oct.–Nov.); 500,000 in East Berlin joined protest (Nov.).

1989 East German Council of Ministers resigned in face of continuing pro-democracy demonstrations (Nov. 7); ruling SED party Politburo also quit, leaving the party free to reorganize along more liberal lines.

1989 Berlin Wall opened by East German government (Nov. 9, along with other border crossings to West Germany); mass celebrations held in Berlin as some two million East Germans crossed into West Berlin; subsequent dismantling of Berlin Wall heralded coming end to East-West Cold War.

1989 Chancellor Kohl put forward 10-point unification plan (Nov.); united Germany to accept post-WW II borders; West German Bundestag approved plan.

1989 East German assembly ended Communist party's constitutional guarantee of supremacy (Dec.); government began investigation of former hard-line Communist leaders for corruption and abuse of power.

1989 Chancellor Kohl on first state visit to East Germany; Kohl and East German prime minister Hans Modrow set plans for joint commissions to promote closer ties.

1989 Demonstrations continued in East Germany, now driven by revelations about abuses by the secret police (Stasi) and later by demands for unification with West Germany (ongoing into 1990).

1989 East Germany's Krenz and leadership of SED forced to resign by ongoing political unrest; Dr. Manfred Gerlach named acting head of state (Dec.); SED later renamed Party of Democratic Socialism (PDS).

1990 East German prime minister Modrow introduced four-point plan for unification with West (Feb.).

1990 Soviet leader Gorbachev reportedly approved idea of unification during meeting with Chancellor Kohl (Feb.); US president G. Bush later reasserted that united Germany should be NATO member.

1990 Trustee agency formed in West Germany to supervise privatization of 8,000 state-run businesses in East Germany (Mar.); by late 1991 over half had been privatized and most were taken over by companies in former West Germany.

1990 Two-plus-four negotiations on German unification held (May, June, July, Sept.); foreign ministers of the two Germanys met with counterparts from four nations that occupied Germany after WW II, US, USSR, Britain, and France; resolved questions concerning international implications of reunification.

1990 Treaty for monetary, economic, and social union of the two Germanys took effect (July 1).

1990 Soviet President Gorbachev agreed unified Germany could decide to join NATO; promised to withdraw 370,000 Soviet troops from East Germany within four years (July).

1990 East German legislature (Volkskammer) reestablished five former states (Länder, abolished after WW II)—Brandenburg, Mecklenburg-Western Pomerania, Saxony, Saxony-Anhalt, and Thüringen (July).

1990 Treaty for the Establishment of German Unity signed by two governments (Aug. 31); unification to take place Oct. 3; unified country to be called Federal Republic of Germany; capital to be Berlin, while seat of government to be decided later.

1990 East Germany formally withdrew from Warsaw Pact (Sept.).

1990 Germany formally granted full sovereignty by four occupying powers (US, USSR, Britain, and France) during ceremonies at New York (Oct. 1).

1990 Germany unified (Oct. 3); became NATO member.

1990 First session of enlarged Bundestag of united Germany (Oct. 4); set new national elections for Dec.

1990 Germany and Poland signed treaty recognizing post-WWII border at Oder and Neisse rivers (Nov.).

1990 Christian Democratic Union (CDU) won national parliamentary elections (Dec.); Kohl subsequently reelected as chancellor.

1990 Some 800,000 immigrants and refugees entered West Germany during the year.

1991– Kohl in office as chancellor of united Germany (Jan.); named just three former East German leaders to his government.

1991 Mass protests against impending use of force against Iraq in Persian Gulf War (Jan.); German government nevertheless supported action, contributing money and assistance but no troops, since action was technically outside NATO area.

1991 Former East German leader E. Honecker reported in USSR seeking medical treatment (Mar.); Honecker later reported seeking asylum in Chilean embassy at Moscow (Dec.).

1991 Terrorist Red Army Faction assassinated head of German trustee agency, which supervised privatization of government-run businesses in former East Germany (Apr.).

1991 Bundestag voted to make Berlin seat of government within 10 years (July).

1991 In former East Germany, economic problems helped spark attacks by right-wing neo-Nazis on foreign workers and refugees in temporary shelters (Oct.); sporadic attacks continued into 1992.

1991 Maastricht summit (Dec.); Germany urged creation of federal system for a unified Europe; backed agreement for monetary union.

1991 German Bundesbank raised its interest rate to 9.5%; forced other European nations to raise their rates, despite recession.

1991 Some 500,000 immigrants and refugees entered the country during the year; unemployment in former East Germany hit 12% as result of program to establish market economy there (Dec.); crime rate also rose sharply.

1992 Former East German leader E. Honecker arrested for his role in deaths of those trying to escape to West Germany (July); to be tried on charges.

1992 Government began destroying tanks and other heavy weapons in compliance with newly ratified Conventional Forces in Europe Treaty (Aug.); became first of 29 signatories to begin reducing stockpiles of conventional weapons to prescribed limits.

1992 Completion of Rhine-Main-Danube canal, 2,170-mile network of waterways connecting North Sea to Black Sea (Sept.); took over 30 years to complete.

Geronimo 1829–1909. Celebrated Apache Indian chief who steadfastly resisted attempts to confine his people to Indian reservations. He led groups of Indians away from reservations in the Southwest several times between 1876 and 1886, raiding white settlements and eluding capture. He surrendered for the last time in 1886 and was eventually settled at Fort Sill, Oklahoma (1887).

Gerry, Elbridge 1744–1814. American states-man, US vice-president (1813–14) and signer of the Declaration of Independence. He was a dele-gate to the Continental Congress (1776–85), a US congressman (1789–93) and was involved in the 1797 XYZ Affair (*q.v.*). While governor of Massachusetts (1810–12), he was accused of rear-ranging election districts to his party's advantage, a tactic now known as "gerrymandering."

Gerrymanding *See* **Gerry, Elbridge.**

Gershonites *See* **Levites.**

Gershwin, George 1898–1937. American com-poser. He was one of the great American com-posers of the 20th cent. His many popular songs contained elements of folk and jazz music. His works range from songs like *Swanee* and *Summer-time* to his famous opera, *Porgy and Bess,* and his *Piano Concerto in F Major.*

Gerson, John (Jean de Charlier de Gerson) 1362?–1428. French theologian and church statesman. An advocate of conciliarism (*q.v.*), he helped to end the Great Schism (*q.v.*) in the West-ern church at the Council of Constance (1414) with the election of a new pope, Martin V.

Gesenius, Wilhelm 1786–1842. German bibli-cal scholar. He wrote what are considered impor-tant pioneer studies of Hebrew grammar.

Gessner, Salomon 1730–88. Swiss poet and landscape painter. He is best known for poems such as *Daphnis* and *The Death of Abel.*

Gestalt Name of a school of psychology which holds that humans perceive sights, sounds, etc., as an organized or structured whole and not as a series of individual sensations. The school had its beginnings in the experimental work of M. Wertheimer (from 1912). His work was car-ried forward by colleagues and students.

Gestapo Notorious Nazi secret police organiza-tion officially responsible for internal security within the Third Reich. Formed in 1933, the Gestapo had the power to arrest enemies of the state without judicial review. The Gestapo ter-rorized the German populace and became a pri-mary element in A. Hitler's persecution of the Jews, sending millions of them to concentra-tion camps where they were systematically murdered.

Gettysburg, Battle of Union victory (1863) at Gettysburg, Pennsylvania, during the American Civil War. The series of battles (July 1–3) between some 88,000 Union and 75,000 Con-federate soldiers is considered the turning point of the war. Gen. R. E. Lee was forced to break off his invasion of the North (in Pennsylvania since June 17) to meet the threat of the Army of the Potomac under Gen. G. Meade. Advance ele-ments of the two forces met accidentally just outside Gettysburg (July 1) and Union forces were pushed back to Cemetery Hill. Confederate forces did not attack again until late July 2, giv-ing Meade time to position his army on Ceme-tery Ridge. Following several indecisive battles, Lee ordered a massive attack on the Union cen-ter. About 15,000 Confederates led by Gen. G. Pickett attacked Cemetery Ridge in this famous charge (July 3). The failure of this charge and the defeat of J. Stuart's cavalry marked the close of the battle. Lee began his retreat to Virginia late July 4 and Meade did not immediately order his forces to pursue. Casualties were about 23,000 Union soldiers and 20,000 Confederates.

Gettysburg Address Celebrated speech delivered by President A. Lincoln (Nov. 19, 1863) to ded-icate a new national cemetery at Gettysburg, Pennsylvania. The speech was delivered just five months after the famous Battle of Gettysburg (*q.v.*) and begins with the famous "Four score and seven years ago our fathers brought forth on this continent a new nation, conceived in liberty . . ." and ended with the now classic characterization of the US government as a "government of the people, by the people, for the people."

Ghana (Republic of Ghana; *formerly* Gold Coast) Independent state located in western Africa on the Gulf of Guinea. The population is 15,310,000 and the capital is Accra. It was fre-quently visited (after the 15th cent.) by naviga-tors and traders from many European countries and became a center of the slave trade. Domi-nated by Britain from the 19th cent. until 1960, the country has since experienced considerable political turmoil. Key events in Ghana's history include:

1482 Portuguese established first European settlement at Elmina; rich slave and gold trade soon attracted other European powers.

16TH CENT. Traders from Britain and the Netherlands arrived.

1640 Swedish traders arrived.

1821 Britain began its rule over parts of the Gold Coast.

1850–74 End of slave trade, and warfare with the Ashanti tribes, brought withdrawal of Danish and Dutch. Britain allied with the native Fanti states to defeat the Ashanti tribe (1874).

1874 British established Gold Coast as a colony, separating it from other territories it held in the region.

1896–1901 Britain again fought Ashanti tribe.

1951 Britain granted Gold Coast a new constitution.

1951 Kwame Nkrumah of the Convention People's party elected first prime minister.

1957 Ghana became independent member of the British Commonwealth.

1957 British Togoland voted to become part of Ghana.

1960 Ghana declared a republic (July 1); Nkrumah named himself president for life.

1960–66 First republic.

1961 Nkrumah organized Union of African States with Guinea and Mali.

1964 Opposition parties banned by referendum; Nkrumah arrested opponents.

1966 Nkrumah overthrown (Feb.) by military coup of Gen. Emmanuel Kotoka; National Liberation Council (NLC) ruled.

1967 New military coup averted, but Kotoka killed (Apr.).

1969 NLC transferred power to civilian government of Kofi Busia; new constitution established.

1969–72 Second republic of Ghana.

1972 Col. I. K. Acheampong overthrew Busia as economic problems worsened; constitution suspended, National Redemption Council (NRC) governed.

1978 Lt. Gen. Frederick Akuffo ousted Acheampong; economic problems continued.

1979 Akuffo overthrown (June 4) by Lt. Jerry Rawlings; elections promised; former leaders of government executed on charges of corruption.

1979 Return to civilian government; Hilla Limann of People's National party elected president.

1979–81 Third republic of Ghana; Linmann in office as president; economy weakened by falling cocoa prices on world market, rising inflation (112 percent in 1980), high foreign debt, and shortages of food and basic consumer goods.

1981 Limann overthrown (Dec. 31) in military coup directed by Jerry Rawlings, hero of 1979 coup; parliament dissolved and political parties banned.

1981– Rawlings in power as military dictator; IMF economic austerity program implemented, which by the end of the decade had cut inflation and restored Ghana's economy.

1981 Tribal warfare between the Konkomba and Nanumba left over 600 dead (May, June); army restored order.

1982 Failed coup attempt by local garrison of troops (Nov. 23); 20 arrested.

1983 New attempted coup against Rawlings failed (June 19); and again in 1984 (Mar. 23), after which 10 conspirators were executed.

1983 Ghana's three universities closed following student protests over budget; reopened in 1985.

1985 Assassination plot against Rawlings uncovered (Jan.); five executed after a trial.

1985 Nigeria deported about 300,000 Ghanaians, who had already been expelled once before in 1983.

1985 Rawlings reshuffled his ruling Provisional National Defense Council (PNDC), naming civilians to many posts; government continued to put off return to democracy; meanwhile, in 1986–87, arrests of suspected dissenters increased.

1986 Band of armed Ghanaian rebels arrested after they infiltrated country from Togo (May 28); seven executed.

1988 Elections held for local government; Ghana's three universities closed after student protests over food allowances.

1989 14 officers arrested in attempted assassination of Rawlings (Oct.).

1989 National economy showing signs of improvement as result of austerity program; government showed a budget surplus, export of cocoa and gold were up, and inflation had been brought under control.

1990 Rally by pro-democracy group in Kumasi broken up by riot police acting on government orders (Sept. 17).

1990 Ghana sent troops to Liberia (Aug.), as part of peace-keeping force led by Nigeria.

1991 Ghana's three universities closed after students protested living conditions (June).

1991 Protesting against high prices, 150 women marched naked through the capital.

1992 Voters overwhelmingly approved new constitution that would establish multi-party democracy (Apr.).

Ghazali, al- 1058–1111. Islamic theologian, philosopher, and Sufi mystic. One of the greatest Islamic theologians, he did much to establish Sufism (*q.v.*) as part of Islamic orthodoxy. He opposed rationalistic philosophy that undermined orthodox doctrine and did all he could to reconcile philosophy with theology.

Ghazan, Mahmud 1271–1304. Mongol ruler of Persia (1295–1304). Ghazan was the first Mongol ruler to convert to Islam, which he made the state religion of Persia. He extended his domains to include Syria.

Ghaznavids Central Asian Turkic dynasty that ruled vast areas in modern Afghanistan, Iran, and northern India from 977 to 1186. The most notable Ghaznavid sultan was Mahmud (reigned 998–1030). The dynasty's capital was at Ghazni, in modern Afghanistan. Conquests by the Seljuk Turks (1040) brought on the decline of this empire.

Ghent, Pacification of *See* **Pacification of Ghent.**

Ghent, Treaty of Treaty (Dec. 24, 1814) ending the War of 1812 between the US and Great Britain. The British gave up all territory in the Northwest, US-Canadian boundary disputes were referred to arbitration, and both nations agreed to seek an end to the slave trade. The US failed to gain any concessions on neutral rights, a chief reason for its declaration of war. However, the British withdrawal from the Northwest opened the area to settlement.

Gheorghiu-Dej, Gheorghe 1901–65. Rumanian statesman and Communist party leader from 1945. He served as prime minister (1952–55) and then as president of the State Council (1961–65).

Ghibellines *See* **Guelphs and Ghibellines.**

Ghiberti, Lorenzo c1378–1455. Florentine sculptor, a major figure in the early Renaissance. His famous bronze doors of the Baptistry of the Cathedral of Florence show his development of perspective and naturalistic forms.

Giap, Vo Nguyen *See* **Vo Nguyen Giap.**

Gibbon, Edward 1737–94. British historian. Gibbon's *The History of the Decline and Fall of the Roman Empire* is still consulted as a major historical and literary reference work dealing with that period.

Gibbons v. Ogden Supreme Court decision (1824) which strengthened the federal government's right to regulate interstate commerce. The case, which overturned a state-sanctioned monopoly, involved two ferry services operating between New Jersey and New York. Chief Justice J. Marshall delivered the Court's decision, stating that national law was superior to state law, making the case for a future basis for federal legislation regarding all interstate commerce.

Gibraltar (Rock of Gibraltar) One of the ancient Pillars of Hercules, it is a British crown colony and strategic fortress at the western approach to the Mediterranean. Taken by the Moors (711), it was reconquered by the Spanish (1462). The English captured it (1704) during the War of Spanish Succession (*q.v.*) and have held it ever since. It was last besieged by a combined force of the Spanish and the French (1779–83) and was bombed but not seriously damaged in WW II. Beginning in 1966, Spain began calling upon Britain to return Gibraltar, and a UN General Assembly resolution to that effect was adopted in 1969. But a popular referendum (1967) favored continued British rule.

Gibran, Kahlil (Jibran, ˜) 1883–1931. Arab-American poet and mystic. The highly romantic Gibran, who wrote in both Arabic and English, is known for such books as *The Prophet, The Forerunner,* and *Jesus, the Son of Man.*

Gide, André 1869–1951. French writer. A controversial author, he was a co-founder of the journal *Nouvelle Revue Française* (1909). His novels include *The Immoralist* and *The Counterfeiters.* He received the Nobel Prize in Literature (1947).

Gideon v. Wainwright US Supreme Court decision (1963) establishing the right of all defendants in felony trials to legal representation. Clarence Gideon, accused of committing a felony in Florida, was denied an attorney, defended himself, and was convicted. The Court found that the Fourteenth Amendment guarantee of "due process" applied to state as well as federal proceedings. Justice H. Black wrote the majority opinion, asserting that all defendants are equal before the law.

Gilbert, Sir Humphrey 1539?–83. English navigator and soldier. He reached Newfoundland (1583) on an exploratory voyage to North America and claimed it for England.

Gilbert, William 1540–1603. English scientist and physician, court physician to Queen Elizabeth I. He was first to describe the earth's magnetic field (1600), and devised the terms "electricity," "electric force," and "electric attraction." He published his studies of magnetism in *De Magnete.*

Gilbert, Sir William Schwenck 1836–1911. English playwright. He is best known for his long collaboration with Sir A. Sullivan, in which he wrote librettos for such popular operettas as *H.M.S. Pinafore, The Pirates of Penzance,* and *The Mikado.*

Gilded Age American post-Civil War historical period. Extending from approximately 1869 to 1877, this era was characterized by conspicuous materialism, dubious business and political ethics, and unbounded self-confidence. It took its name from a critical novel (1873) by Mark Twain and US man of letters Charles Dudley Warner (1829–1900).

Gilgamesh Legendary king important in Babylonian mythology who, on the death of his friend Enkidu, sought a plant that would make him immortal. The king's exploits are recounted in the *Epic of Gilgamesh.* One version was unearthed from the ruins of the library of Assyrian king Ashurbanipal, who ruled in the 7th cent. BC. This written version of the legend is thought to date from c2000 BC, and has attracted special interest because of its account of a universal flood that supposedly once engulfed mankind, similar to the one in the Biblical story of Noah.

Gilman, Charlotte Perkins 1860–1935. US feminist and writer. She wrote *Women and Economics* (1898), asserting that society should incorporate "feminine values" of life-giving and nurturing. She believed that if society was to flourish, the current imbalance between genders would have to be righted.

Ginsberg, Allen 1926– . American poet and leading member of the Beat movement. He is best known for his 1956 poem *Howl.*

Giolitti, Giovanni 1842–1928. Italian statesman. He was five times premier between 1892 and 1921 and universal male suffrage (1912) was among the liberal social reforms he fostered. Willing to make alliances with any group that supported his election, he provided the Fascists a firm foothold in the government (1921).

Giorgione (Giorgio Barbarelli) c1478–1511. Venetian painter. He was a predominant force in 16th-cent. Venetian painting. Among his works are *The Three Philosophers* and the *Tempesta.*

Giotto (~ di Bondone) 1266?–1337. Celebrated Florentine painter, sculptor, and architect. One of the greatest painters of the 14th cent., he departed from the traditional Byzantine forms to create a more powerful style of his own, foreshadowing the Renaissance. Among his many famous works are the frescoes in the Arena Chapel in Padua, including *Life of Christ, Life of the Virgin,* and the *Last Judgment.*

Girardin, Émile de 1806–81. French author, journalist, and politician. Born the illegitimate son of a French count, he founded several French periodicals, becoming known as the Napoleon of the press for his ability to publish inexpensive, widely circulated newspapers. Girardin was best known for *La Presse* (1836), a conservative newspaper he priced well under his competitors'. He served in the Chamber of Deputies (1834–51, 1877–81).

Giraud, Henri Honoré 1879–1949. French general. During WW II, he was commander (1942) of French forces during the Allied operations to secure North Africa. Following the Casablanca Conference (*q.v.*), he became co-president (with Gen. C. de Gaulle) of the French Committee of National Liberation (1943). Differences with de Gaulle, however, forced his retirement (1944).

Girondists French political group that figured prominently in the early stages of the French Revolution (*q.v.*). Composed of well-educated, moderate republicans, the group dominated the Legislative Assembly (1791–92). The decline of the Girondists began with the overthrow of the constitutional monarchy (1792) and the formation of the revolutionary National Convention (*q.v.*). The Convention was dominated by radical Jacobins, called Montagnards, who had the support of the working class. The Girondists' moderate policies and open opposition to the Montagnards put them in disfavor with the populace. Hostility toward Girondists culminated in the execution of many of the party's leaders, including J. Brissot de Warville and P. Vergniaud, at the outset of the Reign of Terror.

Girtin, Thomas 1775–1802. English painter. He was one of the early masters of watercolor painting and his landscapes helped establish watercolor as a distinct artistic medium.

Giscard d'Estaing, Valéry 1926– . French political leader. Giscard d'Estaing served as finance minister for C. de Gaulle and G. Pompidou before becoming president (1974). He was defeated in 1981 by Socialist F. Mitterrand. He was reelected to the National Assembly in 1984.

Giullano, Pedro *See* **John XXI.**

Giza, Pyramids of Egyptian pyramids. These three pyramids (*q.v.*), built c2613–c2500 BC, are located near the city of Giza on the western bank of the Nile. They are included among the ancient Seven Wonders of the World (*q.v.*). Khufu built the oldest (and largest, over 480 feet high), Khafre the second (over 470 feet high), and Menkaure the third (over 355 feet high).

Gizycka, Eleanor M. *See* **Patterson, Eleanor Medill.**

gladiators Professional fighters of ancient Rome who were pitted against one another (or wild animals) in armed combat, often to the death. Gladiators provided a popular form of entertainment in the Roman world from about 264 BC to about AD 405 and fights were performed in arenas before large crowds. Gladiators took part in the Servile Wars (*q.v.*).

Gladstone, William Ewart 1809–98. One of the greatest British statesman of his century and prime minister (1868–74, 1880–85, 1886, 1892–94). The son of a Liverpool merchant, he entered Parliament (1833) as a Conservative. He held a number of government posts as a Conservative before changing his affiliation and becoming Liberal party leader (1867). He was embroiled in controversies in subsequent years, including attacks on the Disraeli government for complacence in the Belgian Horrors, the failure of his own government to relieve Gen. C. Gordon at Khartoum, and the Irish Home Rule question. His many accomplishments included civil service reform, an end to paid military commissions, institution of the secret ballot, a system of national public education, and Irish land reforms.

Glass, Carter 1858–1946. American politician, US congressman from Va. (1902–18), US secretary of treasury (1918–20), and US senator (1920–46). A framer of legislation creating the Federal Reserve System (1913), he was an outspoken opponent of President F. Roosevelt's New Deal.

Glencoe, Massacre of *See* **Massacre of Glencoe.**

Glenn, John Herschel, Jr. 1921– . American astronaut in the Project Mercury program. He was the first American to orbit the earth (Feb. 20, 1962), aboard the spacecraft *Friendship* 7. Glenn has served as a US senator from Ohio

(1975–) and campaigned unsuccessfully for the Democratic presidential nomination (1984).

Glidden, Carlos *See* **Sholes, Christopher Latham.**

Glinka, Mikhail Ivanovich 1804–57. Russian composer. He is considered the founder of Russia's nationalist school of composers. He is known best for his opera *A Life for the Tsar.*

Globe Theatre London theater where, after 1599, W. Shakespeare's plays were performed. Built by the actor Richard Burbage (1567?–1619) and others, it was octagonal in shape. It was rebuilt after a fire (1613) and demolished by the Puritans (1644).

Glorious Revolution (Bloodless Revolution) In English history the period (1688–89) that saw the overthrow of King James II, the crowning of William of Orange and his wife Mary II, and the final recognition of parliamentary supremacy. James II's Catholicism and the birth (1685) of his Catholic son and heir, James Edward, aroused a united Whig and Tory opposition to his rule. Seven of its leaders offered the English throne to the Dutch prince William and his wife Mary, James II's Protestant daughter. William landed at Torbay in England (Nov. 5, 1688) and James fled to France (Dec. 22) after his forces deserted him. The throne was offered to William and Mary under conditions set forth in the Declaration of Rights (1689). These conditions, later embodied in the Bill of Rights (*q.v.*), which assured parliamentary supremacy, were accepted and the two were crowned as joint rulers (1689).

Gloucester, Gilbert de Clare, 8th earl of *See* **Clare, Gilbert de, 8th earl of Gloucester.**

Gloucester, Gilbert de Clare, 9th earl of *See* **Clare, Gilbert de, 9th earl of Gloucester.**

Gloucester, Humphrey, duke of 1391–1447. English nobleman, youngest son of Henry IV. Noted as a patron of the Humanists, he was arrested (1447) after a long struggle for power with H. Beaufort, and died a few days later.

Gloucester, Richard de Clare, 7th earl of *See* **Clare, Richard de, 7th earl of Gloucester.**

Gloucester, Robert earl of *d.* 1147. English nobleman and illegitimate son of Henry I. Made earl by his father (1122), he supported Matilda in her fight against Stephen to succeed Henry I.

Gloucester, Thomas of Woodstock, duke of 1355–97. English nobleman. A son of Edward III, Gloucester took control (1386) of Richard II's government. Richard asserted his authority

(1389). Richard later placed Gloucester under charge of Thomas Mowbray (1366?–99), who was suspected of Gloucester's murder.

Gluck, Christoph Willibald 1714–87. German-born opera composer. He broke with the dominant Italian opera style to create operas in which words and music worked together for dramatic effect. He employed this radical new approach in such operas as *Orfeo ed Euridice* and *Iphigénie en Aulide.*

Gneisenau, August, Graf Neithardt von 1760–1831. Prussian general. The chief strategist during Prussia's war of liberation from Napoleonic France (1813–15), he played an important role in the battles at Leipzig (1813) and Waterloo.

Gneist, Rudolf von 1816–95. German jurist and politician. He was a member of the Prussian Diet (1858–93) and the German Reichstag (1867–84).

Gnosticism Religious movement, important in the early history of Christianity, which promised personal salvation through revelation of mystical knowledge. Gnosticism fused elements of many religious, philosophical, and mythical systems of the ancient world and, though the many Gnostic sects varied widely in their beliefs, they generally believed in a world-creator, religious dualism, and Docetism. Gnostic sects had incorporated many Christian ideas by the 1st cent. AD and flourished in the 2d cent. AD. Gnosticism came to be regarded as a heresy by the Christian church and by the 6th cent. most Gnostic sects had disappeared. Major Gnostic sects included those formed by Valentinus (*fl.* AD c135) and Basilides (*d.* AD c140). Important texts of the Mandaean and Coptic Gnostics were found in Egypt in the mid-20th cent.

Goa *See* Portugal, 1510.

Gobelins *See* Le Brun, Charles.

Gobineau, Joseph Arthur, count of 1816–82. French diplomat and writer. He was an early advocate of the racial supremacy of the Aryans. His *Essay on the Inequality of Human Races* is thought to have influenced both F. Nietzsche and A. Hitler.

Go-Daigo 1287–1339. Japanese emperor (1318–19). Go-Daigo was exiled (1319) for attempting to restore power to the monarchy by overthrowing the shoguns, or military rulers. Returned to the throne after a revolt, he was again ousted (1336). He then set up a rival government near Nara that survived until the end of the 14th cent.

Goddard, Robert Hutchings 1882–1945. American physicist, sometimes called "the father of modern rocketry." Goddard designed and built early high-altitude rockets, the first liquid-fuel rockets, and guidance devices.

Gödel, Kurt 1906–78. Czech-American mathematician. He formulated an important theorem (1931), which states that a mathematical system can give rise to propositions that cannot be proved by the system.

Godfrey of Bouillon 1061?–1100. French crusader. A leader of the First Crusade, he became the first Latin ruler of Palestine after the fall of Jerusalem and the battle of Ascalon (1099).

Godfrey of Strasbourg *See* Gottfried von Strassburg.

Godiva, Lady *fl.* c1040–80. Englishwoman renowned for her legendary ride through Coventry. She is said to have ridden naked through the town on a white horse in order to convince her husband, Earl Leofric, to lower an unfair tax. The story of Peeping Tom is generally regarded as a later (17th cent.) addition to the legend.

Godoy, Manuel de 1767–1851. Spanish statesman. He was twice prime minister (1792–97, 1801–08). His policies proved disastrous for Spain. The decisive defeat of the Spanish navy at Trafalgar (1805) and the furor aroused by the Treaty of Fontainebleau (1807) finally led King Charles IV to abdicate (1808).

Godunov, Boris 1551–1605. Russian tsar (1598–1605). A courtier to Ivan the Terrible, he gained the tsar's favor and became regent for the tsar's slow-witted son Fëdor, after the boy became tsar in 1584. Godunov thereafter warred against the Swedes, repulsed a Tatar attack on Moscow, and promoted new efforts to colonize Siberia. In 1598 Fëdor died leaving no heirs (it is said that Godunov had Ivan's other son Dmitri killed), and Godunov was elected tsar, despite considerable opposition among the boyars. Despite his otherwise capable rule, the boyars' opposition and his attempts to reduce their power helped weaken his position. Finally, after a famine in 1602–04, a pretender claiming to be Ivan's son Dmitri invaded Russia. Godunov died the following year and his son Fëdor II ruled only briefly before being killed by a mob.

Godwin (Godwine) *d.* 1053. English nobleman, earl of Wessex. He helped Edward the Confessor gain the throne (1042) but was later exiled by him in a dispute (1051). Godwin launched a successful invasion of England (1052), forcing Edward to restore his lands.

Godwine *See* **Godwin.**

Goebbels, Paul Joseph 1897–1945. German propaganda minister in A. Hitler's Third Reich. A loyal ally to Hitler from 1926, Goebbels was instrumental in his rise to power. As propaganda minister (1933–45), he skillfully manipulated the mass media to maintain Hitler's power and to forward the planned extermination of millions of Jews.

Goering, Hermann Wilhelm *See* **Göring, Hermann Wilhelm.**

Goethals, George Washington 1858–1928. American army engineer who, as chief engineer (1907–14), supervised the completion of the Panama Canal.

Goethe, Johann Wolfgang von 1749–1832. German poet, dramatist, novelist, and scientist, and one of the great figures in Western literature. A genius of great breadth, he wrote treatises on botany, biology, and physics. But it was in the field of literature that he attained his greatest fame. Early influenced by the Sturm und Drang movement, he gained his early fame (1773) with a play, *Götz von Berlichingen* and the novel *The Sorrows of Young Werther.* From 1775 he held offices in the court of Saxe-Weimar, where he met Charlotte von Stein. One of the many women with whom he was romantically involved, she became the inspiration for many of his poems. He maintained an active friendship with F. Schiller. Goethe completed two of his most famous works, *Wilhelm Meisters Lehrjahre* and *Faust,* in his later years.

Gogh, Vincent van 1853–1890. Dutch painter, one of the greatest. A postimpressionist, he greatly influenced expressionism. After failures in both life and love, he took up painting (1880). He painted in the Netherlands until 1886, then lived in Paris with his beloved brother Theo until 1888. In that year he took a house at Arles and there developed his characteristic style. At Arles and after a fight with P. Gauguin, he suffered (1889) the first of what became continuing fits of insanity and cut off his ear. He was committed to the asylum at St.-Rémy (1889–90) and then lived outside Paris for three months before his suicide. Among his many famous works are *The Potato Eaters, Sunflowers, The Chair and Pipe, Starry Night,* and *Crows Over the Wheat Fields,* his last.

Gogol, Nikolai Vasilievich 1809–52. Ukrainian novelist, short-story writer, and dramatist. Considered the founder of realism in Russian literature, he is known best for his novel *Dead Souls* (1842).

Gogunda, Battle of (Haldishat, Battle of) Battle (June, 1576) fought in Rajasthan, northwestern India, between the army of Mughal emperor Akbar and the much smaller army of Rajput leader Pratap Singh of Mewar. The Mughals defeated the Rajputs, but the latter continued their gallant resistance for decades.

Goldberg, Arthur Joseph 1908–90. US statesman. Born the son of immigrant Jews from the Ukraine, he became an influential labor negotiator. He served as secretary of labor under J. Kennedy (1961) and associate Supreme Court justice in 1962. In 1965, he resigned from the Court to become UN ambassador and unsuccessfully sought to negotiate an end to the Vietnam War.

Gold Coast *See* **Ghana.**

Golden Age Historical term given by the ancient Greeks and Romans to the earliest period of the world, during which mankind was peaceful and innocent and warfare nonexistent.

Golden Bull Royal edict, deriving its name from the Latin *bulla aurea* and bearing a gold seal. It was frequently used by Byzantine and Holy Roman Emperors. Notable Golden Bulls included that of 1222, issued by Hungarian king Andrew II to establish the rights of nobles and powers of the monarchy; and the Golden Bull of 1356 (*q.v.*), issued by Holy Roman Emperor Charles IV.

Golden Bull of Rimini Edict (1226) by which Holy Roman Emperor Frederick II granted sovereignty over Prussia to the Teutonic Knights. He incorporated the Knights into his plans and reorganized them into agents of both Christianity and German culture.

Golden Bull of 1356 Document important in the history of the Holy Roman Empire. Issued by Emperor Charles IV, it reformed procedures for electing the emperor (to a majority of seven electors), eliminated involvement of the papacy in selecting the emperor, and formally acknowledged the relatively independent status of princely states within the empire. This framework remained relatively unchanged until the empire was dissolved in 1806.

Golden Circle, Knights of the *See* **Knights of the Golden Circle.**

Golden Fleece, Order of the *See* **Order of the Golden Fleece.**

Golden Horde (Kipchak Khanate) Mongol khanate formed by Batu Khan, a grandson of Genghis Khan and conqueror of the western Russian territories it embraced. Formed in the mid-13th cent., it included Kiev, Moscow, and Novgorod. Russian rulers were kept in power as vassals and were forced to pay heavy taxes to the khans. The khans adopted the Muslim religion and remained in power until 1395, when Tamerlane conquered the region. The empire subsequently broke up into the khanates of Crimea, Kazan, and Astrakhan.

Golden House Roman palace. After the fire of AD 64, Nero seized many acres of land in Rome to build this magnificent palace, which included an artificial lake within its walls. Little of it remains today, but its wall paintings inspired Renaissance artists.

Golden Spurs, Battle of the (Courtrai, Battle of) (Kortruk, Battle of) Flemish-French battle (July 11, 1302) near Courtrai, Belgium, in which untrained Flemish townsmen defeated the professional soldiers of French king Philip the Fair. The craftsmen were opposing the French annexation of Flanders (1301). The battle was so named because after the fighting the field was littered with the gilt spurs of the French.

Goldfish, Samuel *See* **Goldwyn, Samuel.**

Goldman, Emma 1869–1940. Notorious Russian-American anarchist. She became associated with the anarchist movement shortly after her arrival in the US (1886) and was arrested in New York City (1893) for inciting a riot. She and fellow anarchist Alexander Berkman (1870–1936) were deported to Russia (1919) for obstructing the draft.

Goldmann, Max *See* **Reinhardt, Max.**

gold rush Term applied to the waves of prospectors and others who travel to a new region upon discovery of gold. Notable gold rushes occurred in California (1849), Australia (1850s), South Africa (1884), and the Klondike (1897–98).

Goldsmith, Oliver 1728–74. British playwright, poet, and novelist. He is known best for his play *She Stoops to Conquer* and his novel *The Vicar of Wakefield.*

Goldwyn, Samuel (Goldfish, Samuel) 1882–1974. Polish-American film producer. With C. De Mille he produced his first film (1913), *The Squaw Man,* and later formed a production company that became part of Metro-Goldwyn-Mayer (1925). He went on to produce many major motion pictures including *All Quiet on the Western Front.*

Goliad Massacre Massacre (Mar. 27, 1836) at Goliad, Texas, of some 350 Texan fighters during the Texan war for independence (1836). The force, under Col. James W. Fannin (1804?–36), had surrendered as prisoners of war, but were executed by order of Gen. A. de Santa Anna. The massacre served to further inflame the Texan spirit for independence.

Gömbös, Julius 1886–1936. Hungarian premier (1932–36) who promoted fascism in Hungary.

Gómez Castro, Laureano Eleuterio 1889–1965. Colombian politician. Earlier exiled for supporting A. Hitler and F. Franco, as president (1950–51) he declared martial law, suspended parliament, and was deposed.

Gómez, Juan Vicente 1857–1935. Venezuelan dictator (1908–35). A mestizo who made himself rich first as a cattle driver then as a cattle rustler, Gómez supported a successful revolt by C. Castro and thereafter served in a number of government posts. When President Castro's health failed, Gómez took control of the government and thereafter ruled the country. While maintaining strict control over the press and all opposition, he transformed the army into a modern fighting force, created an oil boom by inviting foreign companies to exploit Venezuela's oilfields, and undertook a major public works program. He controlled the government until his death in 1935.

Gompers, Samuel 1850–1924. British-born American labor leader. One of the leading figures of the labor movement in his day, he was a founder and president (1886–1924, except 1895) of the American Federation of Labor.

Gomulka, Wladyslaw *See* **Poland (1956).**

Gonçalves Dias, Antonio 1823–1864. Brazilian poet, considered the national poet of Brazil. Of mixed racial origin, he glorified Indians and the "common people."

Goncourt, Edmond Louis Antoine and Jules Alfred, Huot de 1822–96, 1830–70. French authors and brothers who were famous for their collaboration on such novels as *Renée Mauperin, Germinie Lacerteux,* and *Madame Gervaisais.* Edmond's will established the Goncourt Academy, which awards the Goncourt Prize for fiction.

Góngora y Argote, Luis de 1561–1627. Spanish poet. His elegant style attracted a following of imitators. Their florid attempts at recreating his style became a movement called Gongorism.

Gonzaga Family of Italian noblemen which ruled Mantua and surrounding territories from 1328 to 1708. Established by Luigi Gonzaga (1267–1360), the family ruled as dukes after 1530. The direct line of succession ended in 1627 and competing claims to the dukedom resulted in the War of Mantuan Succession (1628–31). Following the death (1708) of the last of the Gonzaga line, Carlo IV, the duchy was divided and absorbed by Austria and Savoy.

Gonzaga, Luigi *See* **Gonzaga.**

Good Emperors, the Name given to the Roman emperors who reigned during the years AD 96–180. They were Nerva, Trajan, Hadrian, Antoninus Pius, and Marcus Aurelius.

Good Neighbor Policy US policy for improved relations with Latin America, developed during President F. Roosevelt's administration. It ended the policy of US military intervention and established greater economic cooperation and mutual defense agreements.

Good Parliament English Parliament (1376), which attempted to reform the political abuses of Edward III and John of Gaunt. Its reforms were nullified by the Parliament of 1377.

Goodyear, Charles 1800–60. American inventor. He discovered the process for vulcanizing rubber (1839) but failed to capitalize on it and died in debt.

Gorbachev, Mikhail Sergeyevich 1931– . Soviet official, general secretary of the Communist party (1985–91), and president of the USSR (1990–91). Raised the son of a peasant, he joined a Communist youth group in 1946 and later graduated from Moscow State University with a law degree (1955). A Communist party member from 1952, he rose through the ranks of regional party organizations and was named first to the Soviet Central Committee in 1971 and the Politburo in 1979. Following the death of K. Chernenko, Gorbachev became Communist party general secretary and effective head of the USSR. Confronted by a stagnating economy and a bloated government bureacracy dominated by hard-line conservative Communists, Gorbachev embarked on a program of sweeping reforms. Consolidating his position by ousting older leaders in the government and party hierarchy, Gorbachev organized a widespread shakeup of corrupt and inefficent officials in 1986. In 1987, he declared his policy of *glasnost* (openness) as the key means to addressing the ills of Soviet society and in 1988 added a second principle, *perestroika* (restructuring), to his program. In June, 1989, amid growing discontent in Communist-dominated Eastern Europe, Gorbachev announced the abandonment of the Brezhnev Doctrine and maintained the USSR would not interfere with other nations' right to self-determination. Lacking direct Soviet support, Communist governments in Eastern Europe collapsed in 1989–90, falling before a popular pro-democracy movement. Meanwhile, Gorbachev pursued a policy of reform in the USSR, hoping to guide the nation to a more democratic and economically viable system with the Communist party still in power. Ethnic unrest, demands for independence by the Baltic States and other Soviet republics, and demands for quicker and more radical reforms (led by rival B. Yeltsin), all forced Gorbachev to adopt more radical policies than he or his Communist party colleagues originally wanted. Given broad powers in the newly created post of executive president (1990), Gorbachev sought to guide the divergent forces demanding change to a workable compromise that would preserve the Soviet Union, but events overtook him. Responding to demands for greater freedom by the Soviet republics, Gorbachev won agreement for a new union treaty in mid-1991, which would have created a looser federation of constituent republics. That, however, was opposed by a group of hard-line Communist officials, who staged the unsuccessful Soviet coup (*q.v.*) to oust Gorbachev. With the Communist party thoroughly discredited after the failed coup, Gorbachev resigned as general secretary, after which the party was officially suppressed. In addition to presiding over the end of the Communist party's 74-year rule, Gorbachev saw his own power eclipsed by Yeltsin and the ultimate collapse of the USSR itself. He resigned as president in Dec., 1991, shortly after most of the individual republics agreed to form the loosely federated Commonwealth of Independent States. In addition to his leadership role in transforming the USSR to a freer, more open society, Gorbachev also became a leading force in promoting world peace. He withdrew Soviet troops from Afghanistan (1988–89), ending the unpopular and unsuccessful effort to prop up a Soviet-puppet government there, and in 1987 signed an agreement with US president R. Reagan for the destruction of intermediate range nuclear missiles. Further treaties bringing about massive cuts in nuclear arms and conventional forces in Europe were negotiated and these treaties, along with the new Soviet foreign policy and unprecedented reforms of Soviet government, enabled Gorbachev and US president G. Bush to jointly proclaim an end to the Cold War. Gorbachev was awarded the 1990 Nobel Prize for Peace.

Gorboduc Name of the first English play in blank verse (1561), written by T. Sackville and Thomas Norton (1532–84).

Gorchakov, Aleksandr Mikhailovich, Prince 1798–1883. Russian statesman and diplomat. As foreign minister (1856–78) he nullified terms of the Treaty of Paris (1871), imposed after the Crimean War, and was unable to prevent the Russo-Turkish War (1877–78).

Gordian I AD 158–238. Roman co-emperor with his son, Gordian II, for three weeks. He and his son succeeded the tryannical Maximinus. Gordian killed himself on learning of the death of his son in battle.

Gordian II AD 192–238. Roman co-emperor with his father, Gordian I. He was slain in battle after ruling only three weeks.

Gordian III (Gordianus Pius) AD c224–44. Roman emperor (238–44). He succeeded co-emperors Balbinus and Pupienus, who were assassinated shortly after replacing his uncle, Gordian II and grandfather Gordian I. He attacked the Persians (242) but was later assassinated by his soldiers.

Gordon, Charles George 1833–85. British soldier and colonial administrator. He became famous as a military commander in China during the Taiping Rebellion (1860–65) and gained further honors in pacifying the Sudan (1873–80). In 1874 he was sent back to the Sudan and was killed in the Battle of Khartoum.

Gordon, John Brown 1832–1904. American politician and Confederate general in the American Civil War. He served with distinction during the war, then became US senator from Georgia (1873–80, 1891–97) and governor of Georgia (1886–90).

Gordon Riots (No Popery Riots) Mass anti-Catholic riots in London, England (1780). The riots began after a crowd said to number 50,000

persons was led by Lord George Gordon (1751–93) to the House of Commons to demand repeal of the Catholic Relief Act of 1778. There followed a week of destructive riots in which the London prisons were forced open. Catholic churches were burned, and some 400–800 persons were killed or injured. Though a number of rioters were executed, Gordon was acquitted.

Gorges, Sir Ferdinando c1566–1647. English promoter of colonies in North America and proprietor of Maine. Though he never set foot in America, he was involved in many unsuccessful schemes to promote colonization. He eventually received a royal charter to Maine, which his grandson sold for £1,250.

Göring, Hermann Wilhelm (Goering, ⁀) 1893–1946. German military and political leader, one of A. Hitler's chief lieutenants. A hero of the WW I air war, he joined Hitler in the Munich Putsch (1923), and became president of the Reichstag (1932). When Hitler came to power (1933) he was made prime minister and air minister, set up the Gestapo and concentration camps, and in the late 1930s mobilized Germany for war. He was designated Hitler's successor until 1943, when his Luftwaffe proved unable to prevent Allied air attacks on Germany. Tried for war crimes at Nürnberg (1945–46), he committed suicide just before his scheduled execution.

Got, Bertrand de *See* **Clement V.**

Gotham Originally, a village in England. To avoid the expense of an impending visit by King John, the townspeople made themselves appear as complete fools and thus put off the royal party. The name has since been applied to New York City.

Gothic Medieval artistic and architectural style in Europe from the 12th–15th cents. Originating in France, it supplanted the Romanesque style. Gothic art was flowing, mystical, individualistic, and tended toward the naturalistic. Architecture (and allied decorative arts) dominated the movement. Gothic architecture was characterized by height, high vaulted ceilings, tracery between large (often stained glass) windows, and flying buttresses. There was increasing emphasis on decorative detail toward the end of the movement. The most famous example of Gothic architecture is the Cathedral of Notre Dame in Paris. The Gothic styles gave way to the Renaissance forms.

Gothic revival American and British architectural movement of the 19th cent. It revived elements of the Gothic style of architecture.

Goths Germanic tribes. An ancient Teutonic peoples, they included the Ostrogoths and the Visigoths (*qq.v.*). The Ostrogoths established an empire in the region of the Ukraine. After the fall of their empire (AD c370) to the Huns, they joined the Huns in conquest. After the Huns were forced back, the Ostrogoths, when they traveled westward, invaded Italy and overthrew Odoacer (493). The Visigoths moved into the Roman Empire (4th cent. AD), sacked Rome (410), then turned westward to Gaul and Spain. In Gaul they were defeated by the Frankish king Clovis (507) and were defeated in Spain (711) by Muslim invaders from North Africa.

Gottfried von Strassburg (Godfrey of Strasbourg) *fl.* 13th cent. German poet. Considered one of the most important poets of medieval Germany, he wrote a famous version of *Tristan und Isolde.*

Gould, George Jay 1864–1923. American railroad magnate, son of J. Gould. He inherited his father's railroading interests (1892), but lost them following the Panic of 1907.

Gould, Jay 1836–92. American financier and railroad magnate. A ruthless businessman, he was involved with J. Fisk and D. Drew in their scheme to comer the gold market. Following the Black Friday panic (1869) that resulted from the scheme, he bought up railroads and became a major operator in the Southwest.

Government of India Acts British laws passed by Parliament (1773–1935) to govern India. The first acts (1773–1830), also known as the East India Company Acts, regulated the British East India Company. Later acts transferred (1858) power to the crown, and finally paved the way for Indian self-government.

Government of National Defense Interim French government established (Sept., 1870) during the Franco-Prussian War, following the defeat of Napoleon III at Sedan (*q.v.*) and subsequent overthrow of his government. This government continued the futile war until Jan. 28, 1871, when it surrendered. Following the peace settlement, the uprising of the Paris Commune (*q.v.*), and attempts at restoring the monarchy, the French Third Republic was formally established by adoption of the Constitution of 1875.

Gower, John *d.* 1408. English poet. Friend and contemporary of Chaucer, he was considered, with Chaucer, a leading poet in his day. His works include *Confessio Amantis,* a collection of tales.

Gowon, Yakubu 1934– . Nigerian general. Made head of the military government following two 1966 coups, he defeated the secessionist Biafrans and reunited the country (1970), but was deposed in 1975.

Goya y Lucientes, Francisco José de 1746–1828. Spanish artist, considered one of the greatest painters of his century. He began as a designer of royal tapestries and by 1786 was court painter to Spanish king Charles III. Thereafter he enjoyed widespread fame and the favor of the rulers of Spain, and painted portraits of many Spanish notables. After an illness left him deaf in 1793, he also began to do satirical and sardonic works on social evils, including *The Caprices* and *The Disasters of War.* Late in his life he produced such macabre scenes as *Saturn Devouring His Children* and a series of lithographs that included several famous bullfight scenes.

Gozzi, Carlo, Count 1720–1806. Italian dramatist. He is remembered as the author of dramatic "fairy tales" that provided the basis for later works by J. Goethe, F. Schiller, and others.

GPU Soviet secret police. Established (Feb., 1922) to replace the Cheka, it ruthlessly quelled all opposition to government policy. It was renamed OGPU in 1923 and in 1934 its functions passed to the NKVD (1934–46). After that, secret police activities successively passed to the MGB (1946–53), the MVD (1953–54), and finally the KGB (*q.v.*).

Gracchus, Caius Sempronius *d.* 121 BC. Roman tribune (123, 122 BC). Elected tribune ten years after the death of his brother, Tiberius Gracchus, he continued the agrarian reforms begun by his brother. The reforms aroused opposition among the nobility and he was killed following his defeat for a third term as tribune.

Gracchus, Tiberius Sempronius *d.* 133 BC. Roman tribune (133 BC). As tribune he formulated the Sempronian Law, designed to eliminate the widespread poverty of Romans by redistributing public lands to them. Subsequent opposition to his plan in the Senate resulted in a riot in which he was killed.

Gräfe, Albrecht von (Graefe, ~) 1828–70. German ophthalmologist, sometimes called the founder of modern ophthalmology. He developed new treatments for glaucoma (1857) and cataracts (1867).

Graham, Billy (~, William Franklin) 1918– . American evangelist. A widely known preacher, he has organized highly successful revivalist crusades in the US and abroad since 1949.

Graham, Martha 1893–1991. American dancer, choreographer, and teacher who greatly influenced modern dance. Among her highly individualistic works are *Deaths and Entrances, Appalachian Spring,* and *Phaedre.*

Graham, William Franklin *See* **Graham, Billy.**

Granada, Kingdom of Located in southern Spain, this kingdom was part of domains held by the Muslims during medieval times. By 1238, Spanish Christians had conquered most of the Muslim territories and the kingdom of Granada was the last remaining Muslim stronghold on the Iberian Peninsula. Spanish king Ferdinand I finally conquered Granada in 1492 and added these lands to his domains.

Gran Colombia *See* **Great Colombia.**

Grand Alliance, War of the *See* **League of Augsburg, War of the.**

Grand Army Name given the combined French armies (1805–12) under Napoleon. Its great size, excellent training, and organization made Napoleon master of Europe. It was virtually destroyed (1812) during Napoleon's retreat from Russia.

Grand Army of the Republic (GAR) Organization of US Civil War veterans who had served in the Union army or navy. Founded by J. Logan, Richard J. Oglesby (1824–99), and others (1866), the group held its first national encampment at Indianapolis, Indiana, later that year. The group, dedicated to promoting fraternal ties, passage of legislation for veterans' benefits, and service to needy veterans, reached its greatest membership of 400,000 by 1890. It was until 1900 a powerful political bloc within the Republican party, after which time its membership and influence rapidly dwindled. The group's last national encampment was held in 1949 and the organization was dissolved in 1956.

Grand Canal Canal in China. Begun in the 6th cent. BC to facilitate grain transport, it was completed 2,000 years later and is the world's longest canal, extending over 1,000 miles from Beijing to Hangzhou (Hangchow).

grandee Spanish honorary title, dating to the 13th cent. A title held by the highest rank of Spanish nobility, it conferred various privileges, with the right to wear headgear in the presence of the king becoming characteristic of the rank.

grandfather clause Constitutional clause instituted around the turn of the 20th cent. by Southern states to circumvent the 15th Amendment to the Constitution, guaranteeing suffrage to newly freed blacks. The clause limited voting privileges to those who could vote as of Jan. 1, 1867, and their descendants, thus effectively disenfranchising blacks, who did not have the vote in 1867. The clause was declared unconstitutional in 1915.

Grand National Consolidated Trades Union Short-lived English labor organization formed in 1834. Amid the general dissatisfaction among workers and the sudden spread of unions at this time, social reformer R. Owen campaigned strenuously for even greater participation in the movement. Subsequently the Grand National Consolidated Trades Union was formed (1834) to organize a broad range of workers. Its leaders adopted the goal of mounting a general strike for an eight-hour work day. Some 500,000 workers joined, but the union was shut down within months as a result of government repression.

Grand Rebel *See* **Sivaji.**

Grand Remonstrance In English history, a list of grievances presented by the Long Parliament (Dec. 1, 1641) to King Charles I. Charles did not accept them and, in Jan., 1642, he unsuccessfully attempted to arrest leaders of the opposition in the Commons. The Remonstrance widened the rift between king and Parliament and hastened the coming of the English Civil Wars.

Granger movement US agrarian movement of the 19th cent., an outgrowth of a farmers' organization called the National Grange of the Patrons of Husbandry (founded 1867). Grangers sought to redress farmers' economic grievances through cooperative ventures and political pressure on state legislatures. By the time the movement began to decline (after 1876), they had established many farmers' cooperatives and won passage of Granger laws in Midwest farm states. The laws, designed to control railroads and their shipping rates, led to the famous Granger case, *Munn* v. *Illinois* (1876).

Granicus, Battle of the Battle (334 BC) at the Granicus River, now in Turkey. There Alexander the Great won his first major victory against the Persian emperor Darius III.

Grant, Ulysses S. (*baptized* Hiram Ulysses Grant) 1822–85. Commander in chief of Union armies (1863–65) during the American Civil War and

18th president of the US (1869–77), succeeding A. Johnson. He became a colonel in the Illinois volunteers (1861) at the outbreak of the Civil War and soon distinguished himself in battle. He won increasingly important commands, broke Confederate control of the Mississippi, and cut the Confederacy in half by his victory at Vicksburg (1863). Soon afterward he was named commander in chief and, by his war of attrition, forced R. E. Lee's surrender at Appomattox (1865). Joining the Radical Republicans (*q.v.*), Grant won the presidential election of 1868 easily and was elected to a second term in 1872. He was a popular and personally honest president, but his term of office was marked by the turmoil of Reconstruction (*q.v.*) and by the many scandals of the Gilded Age, notably the Crédit Mobilier scandal (*q.v.*), the Whiskey Ring (*q.v.*), and the Black Friday (*q.v.*) financial panic.

Granvelle, Antoine Perrenot de 1517–86.   Frenchman in the service of King Philip II of Spain. As prime minister in the Netherlands (c1560–64), he aroused hostility to the Spanish rule there by persecuting Protestants. He relinquished his post on the advice of the king.

Granville, John Carteret, 1st earl 1690–1763. English statesman. A member of the House of Lords (1730–42), he led the opposition against R. Walpole and finally secured his fall (1742). As chief minister (1742–44) he himself fell from favor after supporting Maria Theresa in the War of the Austrian Succession.

Grass, Günter 1927–   .   German writer. He is known best for his first novel, *The Tin Drum* (1959), a milestone in the development of post-WW II German literature.

Grasse, François Joseph Paul, comte de 1722–88. French admiral. Commanding French fleet sent to aid Colonial forces during the American Revolution, he succeeded in trapping Gen. C. Cornwallis at Yorktown and contributed to the American victory in the Yorktown Campaign.

Gratian (Flavius Gratian) AD 359–383.   Roman emperor of the West (AD 367–383) with his brother Valentinian II. With Saint Ambrose as his adviser, he made himself unpopular by persecuting pagans. He was defeated by the usurper Maximus and was put to death.

Gratian *fl.* 1140.   Italian monk and scholar, regarded as the founder of the science of canon law. He compiled the great collection of canon law, the *Decretum Gratiani.*

Grattan, Henry 1746–1820.   Irish statesman and leader in the fight for Ireland's independence from England. He won legislative independence for Ireland's parliament (1782), fought for Catholic emancipation, and eloquently opposed the Act of Union that joined England and Ireland (1801).

Gravelines, Battle of   Spanish victory (July 13, 1558) over the French, the deciding battle in the dynastic wars known as the Valois-Habsburg Wars. Some 2,000 French troops were killed. The battle led to the Treaty of Cateau-Cambrésis (1559).

Graves, Robert Ranke 1895–91.   English poet and novelist. He published collections of his poetry, novels such as *I, Claudius,* and critical works.

Gray, Thomas 1716–71.   One of the great English poets of his century and author of *Elegy Written in a Country Churchyard.*

Gray Eminence   *See* **Joseph, Father.**

Grayson, David   *See* **Baker, Ray Stannard.**

Great Awakening   Religious revival movement in the American colonies c1720–60. The American counterpart of the European quietism and pietism movements, this evangelical movement largely affected the Calvinist sects. Revivalist preachers such as J. Edwards and G. Whitefield gained many converts by mid-century and their teachings led to splits in the established congregations between factions known as "old lights" and "new lights."

Great Awakening, Second   Religious revival movement of the early 19th century. Beginning with a frontier revival movement sparked by evangelical Protestant preachers, the Second Great Awakening spread through the Southwest and West and from there to the East. Opposed to Calvinist beliefs about predestination, preachers like C. Finney taught their followers that they could choose to do good (moral "free will"), and therefore could obtain salvation if only they committed themselves to seeking it. While the movement reached a peak in the late 1820s and 1830s, its teachings gave impetus to a variety of secular reform movements, including abolition, temperance, and women's rights.

Great Britain (United Kingdom of Great Britain and Northern Ireland)   Kingdom located in western Europe. It includes England, Scotland, Wales and Northern Ireland. The population is 57,121,000 and the capital is London. The rise of Britain as a modern state dates from the Norman Conquest (1066), and by the late 16th cent. Britain had become a major European power. From the 17th cent. to 19th cent., it acquired a vast colonial empire, gave birth to the Industrial Revolution, and became the world's leading military and commercial power. Though Britain maintained its preeminence in the early 20th cent., competition from other industrialized nations (US, Germany, Japan), the breakup of its worldwide colonial empire, and the two world wars brought an end to its dominance as a world power. Britain played a crucial role in the Allied victories during WW I and WW II. In the years after 1945, Britain divested itself of almost all its remaining colonial territories. (*See also* Scotland, Wales, colonialism). **For more on important persons and major events** *see* **separate entries under names.** Key events in Britain's history include:

5TH CENT. BC   Celts invaded British Isles.

55–54 BC   J. Caesar led Roman military expeditions to British Isles, which he called Britannia.

AD 43–84   Roman conquest of Britain; Caractus led revolt against Roman invaders (43–50); Queen Boadicea led another unsuccessful revolt; Roman soldier Agricola conquered north part of England (from AD 78).

AD c120–136   Hadrian's Wall built across Britain to protect flourishing Roman towns from attacks by tribes from the north (Scotland).

AD 410   Romans completed their withdrawal from British Isles, troops needed elsewhere to defend empire against barbarian attacks.

418   Heretic monk Pelagius excommunicated for advancing his theory that baptism was unnecessary for salvation.

5TH CENT. AD   Celtic culture flourished after the Roman withdrawal; attacks by Picts from north resisted; invasions by Saxons, Angles, and Jutes (Germanic tribes from the Continent) forced Celtic inhabitants westward into what is now Wales.

6TH CENT.   Welsh poet Taliesin lived; said to have written *Book of Taliesin*.

6TH–8TH CENTS.   Rise of the Anglo-Saxon Heptarchy, group of seven small kingdoms formed by invading Anglo-Saxons; included Northumbria, Mercia, Wessex, Essex, Kent, Sussex, and East Anglia; Northumbria (founded c547) and Mercia (founded c582) chief among them. Period marked by frequent wars between the rival kingdoms.

?–588?   Saint David, patron saint of Wales, lived.

597   Saint Augustine began Christianization of England; soon after his arrival converted Ethelbert, king of Kent; Ethelbert became first Christian Anglo-Saxon ruler in England.

664   Synod of Whitby; called to decide between Celtic Christianity, then on the rise, and Roman Christianity; decision favored Roman Christianity and thus fostered ties with Christians on the Continent.

c665   Saint Wilfrid served as Bishop of York.

670   Caedmon, earliest-known English Christian poet, flourished.

673–737   Saint Bede, historian and Benedictine monk, lived; wrote *Ecclesiastical History of the English People.*

8TH CENT   *Beowulf,* epic poem by unknown author, composed.

c750   Poet Cynewulf flourished; known for religious works.

787   First raids by the Danes.

802–839   Egbert became king of Wessex; ended supremacy of Mercia by his decisive victory in 825; accepted as king by other kingdoms in the Anglo-Saxon Heptarchy, he was the first to unify what later became modern England.

856–878   Danes launched major invasions of England.

871–899   Alfred the Great became king of Wessex; led resistance against invading Danes; revived learning; issued code of laws and consolidated his powers.

878   Alfred defeated the Danes at the Battle of Edington and thereby halted their advance in England; divided England with Danes and gave them the north part, called Danelaw.

899–921   Conquest of the Danelaw by Alfred's descendants.

925–939   Athelstan became first king to effectively rule a united England; defeated confederation of opponents at Battle of Brunanburh (939).

959–975   Edgar reigned as king of the English; crowned formally (973) at Bath in first coronation ceremony ever held for king of united England.

994–1012 Invasions by Danes, led by Sweyn, renewed; King Ethelred (reigned 978–1016) at first paid them tribute, then ordered execution of all Danes (1002); Sweyn conquered England (1012) and became king.

11TH CENT. Beginnings of the manorial system.

1013–15 King Athelred forced to flee to Normandy (1013–14); launched invasion of England and drove out Danes (1015).

1016 Danes returned under Canute; Canute defeated Ethelred's son, King Edmund Ironside, at the Battle of Assandun.

1016–35 Canute reigned as king of England; ruled England wisely, inherited Danish crown (1018) and gained control of Norway (1028); his descendants ruled England to 1042.

c1040–80 Legendary Lady Godiva lived; said to have ridden naked through town to protest high taxes.

1042–66 Edward the Confessor reigned; succeeded the last Danish king and thus restored Anglo-Saxon rule; however, he was raised in Normandy and appointed many French-speaking Normans to his court.

1053 Revolt led by earl of Godwin forced exile of Edward's Norman appointees.

1063–65 Harold subjugated Wales for Edward (1063); ended rebellion in Northumbria (1065).

1066 Edward at his death named Harold his successor, though his cousin, Duke William of Normandy, claimed the crown.

1066 Battle of Hastings fought (Oct. 14); William the Conqueror defeated and killed English king Harold II; Norman Conquest largely completed.

1066–87 William the Conqueror reigned; crowned king of England in London (Dec. 25); William killed or disenfranchised Anglo-Saxon nobles, replacing them with Normans; instituted feudal system in England.

1085 William ordered compilation of Domesday Book.

1100–35 Henry I reigned; defeated attempt by older brother Robert to take throne (1101); captured Normandy from him (1106), bringing it back under English control.

1135–54 Civil war broke out after Henry's death over his successor; proved economically ruinous; Henry II chosen successor (1154).

c1135 Geoffrey of Monmouth wrote the first account of the Arthurian legend in *Historia Regnum Britanniae.*

1154–89 Henry II reigned; restored order; by his inheritance of Anjou and Normandy (and Aquitaine by marriage) established the Angevin Empire on the Continent; began Plantagenet line of English kings.

1164 Henry II issued Constitutions of Clarendon, limiting power of the Catholic church in England.

1166 Henry II instituted the Assize of Clarendon, noteworthy judicial reforms.

1170 Thomas à Becket; murdered, this capped a long struggle with King Henry II over his attempts to limit church powers in England.

1171 Henry began conquest of Ireland by English.

1181 Henry II issued the Assize of Arms ordering citizenry to procure weapons.

1189–99 Richard I reigned; led unsuccessful Third Crusade to retake Jerusalem.

1190 W. of Longchamp, prelate and chancellor, ruled the country while Richard I was on Third Crusade.

1199–1216 King John reigned; rule marked by struggle with pope and rising power of the barons.

c1200 Middle English poet Layamon flourished; wrote *Brut,* which made first mention of Arthurian legend in English.

1204 War with Philip II of France; King John lost Normandy and other English possessions on the Continent.

1209 King John excommunicated by Pope Innocent III in controversy over investiture of archbishop of Canterbury.

1213 King John forced to accept sovereignty of the pope by Innocent III.

1214?–1294? R. Bacon, philosopher and Franciscan monk, lived; wrote *Opus Majus.*

1215 King John forced to sign Magna Carta by his barons.

1216–72 Henry III reigned; his incompetence finally aroused the barons against him.

1217 Nobles who supported succession of a Frenchman (later Louis VIII of France) defeated at Battle of Lincoln.

1233–40 Saint Edmund served as archbishop of Canterbury; struggled with King Henry III.

1235–53 R. Grosseteste, theologian and scholar, served as bishop of Lincoln.

c1253 Historian M. Paris wrote *Historia Anglorum.*

1258 Henry III compelled to accept Provisions of Oxford, series of reforms imposed by barons.

1264 Mise of Amiens annulled (Jan. 23) Provisions of Oxford.

1264–67 Barons' War; S. de Montfort, baronial leader, virtually ruled England during war.

1272–1307 Edward I reigned; consolidated the power of the crown at the expense of the barons and the clergy.

1275, 1285, 1290 Statutes of Westminster promulgated by King Edward I to reform civil and criminal laws.

1284 Statute of Wales enacted (Mar. 19); Wales annexed.

c1285–1349 W. of Ockham, Franciscan philosopher, lived; devised "Ockham's Razor."

1295 Model Parliament convened, a forerunner of modern British Parliament.

1307–27 Edward II reigned; unpopular, he appointed Piers Gaveston to official post and thereby aroused the barons against him; deposed by the queen and nobles.

1311 Twenty-one barons forced limitations on Edward II's powers; he did not break the barons' power until 1322.

1314 Robert I the Bruce defeated Edward at the Battle of Bannockburn and thereby ended English overlordship of Scotland.

c1320–84 Reformer J. Wycliffe lived; his attacks on church doctrine set the stage for Protestant Reformation.

1327–77 Edward III reigned; usurped (1330) the regency controlled by his mother and R. de Mortimer, 1st earl of March.

1337–1453 Hundred Years' War with France.

1348 Black Plague reached England; combined with ravages of Hundred Years' War to bring about major social changes, including end of feudalism; rise of Lollardry, and Peasants' Revolt (1381).

1350 Order of the Garter formally established.

1376 Good Parliament unsuccessfully attempted to reform abuses by Edward III.

c1377 W. Langland believed to have written poem *The Vision of Piers Plowman.*

1377–99 Richard II reigned; period marked by conflicts with barons.

1381 First Navigation Act passed; government unable to implement it.

c1387–1400 G. Chaucer wrote his masterpiece, *The Canterbury Tales.*

1388 Merciless Parliament impeached five of Richard II's followers for treason; action influenced Richard to more moderate course.

c1393 Poet J. Gower wrote *Confessio Amantis.*

1399–1413 Henry IV reigned; rebelled (1399) against Richard II, defeating him and establishing the House of Lancaster.

1407 Merchants Adventurers trading company formed for English woolen cloth trade.

1413–1422 Henry V reigned; continued fighting in the Hundred Years' War; concluded Treaty of Troyes (1420).

1422–61 Henry VI reigned; rule marked by loss of all English possessions on the Continent at the end of the Hundred Years' War (1453) and prolonged unrest.

1450 Cade's Rebellion.

1455–85 Wars of the Roses, complex dynastic struggle between the House of York and House of Lancaster; ended with accession of Henry VII.

1460 R. Plantagenet, 3d duke of York, recognized as heir apparent to Henry IV; subsequently killed at the Battle of Wakefield.

c1469 Sir T. Malory wrote *Morte d'Arthur.*

1477 W. Caxton printed the first book in England.

1485 Battle of Bosworth Field; Henry Tudor's army defeated supporters of Richard III, the last Yorkist king (killed in battle); battle often seen as end of baronial warfare in England.

1485–1509 Henry VII reigned; marked beginning of reign of Tudor kings; he suppressed Yorkist plots, promoted trade, and restored the royal treasury.

1488–1561 Prophet Mother Shipton lived; said to have predicted date of the Great Fire of London.

1492 Treaty of Étaples; ended war with France; Henry VII renounced claims to all territory on the Continent (except Calais); war with France ended.

1497 Navigator J. Cabot explored coastline of Nova Scotia and Newfoundland.

1499 P. Warbeck, Flemish imposter and pretender to the English throne, executed.

1509 J. Colet, theologian, founded St. Paul's school in London.

1509–47 Henry VIII reigned; attempt to secure a male heir brought conflict with Catholic church.

1513 Scottish invasion force crushed at the Battle of Flodden, northern England.

1515–29 T. Wolsey served as lord chancellor of England under Henry VIII.

c1522 J. Skelton wrote his poem, *Why Come Ye Not to Court.*

1525 W. Tyndale published his translation of the New Testament in English.

1529 Henry sought divorce from his childless wife, Queen Catherine of Aragon, to marry Anne Boleyn; permission refused by pope.

1529–32 Sir T. More served Henry VIII as lord chancellor.

1533 Act in Restraint of Appeals to Rome passed by Parliament; Pope's authority nullified in England; Henry now able to marry A. Boleyn.

1534 First Act of Supremacy passed by Parliament; created Church of England with Henry VIII as head of the church; Henry sought to maintain Catholic character of church.

1535 Sir T. More executed for refusing to endorse Henry VIII's Act of Supremacy.

1535 Catholic bishop Saint John Fisher martyred for refusing to acknowledge Henry VIII as head of church.

1536 Pilgrimage of Grace, uprising caused by suppression of papal authority in England; second uprising (Jan., 1537) led to martial law in northern England.

1536 Wales formally united with England.

1537–1619 N. Hilliard lived; painted miniatures for Queen Elizabeth's court.

1539 Henry had Parliament pass Act of Six Articles to oppose doctrines of the Protestant Reformation.

1544–46 England joined Holy Roman Emperor Charles V in war against France.

1545 Kett's rebellion in Norfolk.

1547–53 Edward VI reigned; favored Protestantism; first Book of Common Prayer authorized for Church of England (1549); first Act of Uniformity passed (1549).

1549 T. Cranmer compiled Book of Common Prayer; later burned at stake for heresy.

1552?–1616 Geographer R. Hakluyt lived; helped promote English exploration of North America.

1552?–1618 Courtier Sir W. Raleigh lived.

1553 Lady Jane Grey reigned nine days as England's queen; was overthrown and later executed.

1553–58 Mary I reigned; reinstated (1555) Catholicism and ties with Rome; persecuted Protestants.

1554?–1600 R. Hooker, theologian, lived; wrote *Of the Laws of Ecclesiastical Polity.*

1555 Muscovy Company founded for Russian trade; first joint-stock company.

1555 H. Latimer, Protestant martyr, burned at the stake for heresy, under Mary Tudor's reign.

1558?–92 Playwright R. Greene lived.

1558–1603 Elizabeth I reigned; rule marked by England's rise as a commercial, colonial, and naval power; Elizabethan Age marked cultural flowering in England, and increasing importance of the House of Commons.

1559 Second Act of Supremacy passed by Parliament; reestablished Church of England and named Elizabeth I head of the church.

1560 Treaty of Edinburgh signed with France and Scotland; led to withdrawal of English and French troops from Scotland, to ease conflict between Catholics and Protestants there.

1562 J. Hawkins became first Englishman to engage in the slave trade.

1563 Thirty-nine Articles outlined theology and devotional practices of Church of England.

1567–1601 Dramatist and satirist T. Nashe lived.

1568–87 Mary, Queen of Scots, imprisoned by Elizabeth; finally executed after being implicated in plot by Catholics against England.

1571 Thirty-Nine Articles on doctrines of Church of England promulgated.

c1576 J. Burbage, actor, built first English theater, known as The Theatre; later rebuilt and called the Globe Theatre.

1576–78 Sir M. Frobisher explored Canada's northern coast, seeking a northwest passage.

1577–80 Sir F. Drake became first Englishman to circumnavigate the earth.

1582 Tracts promoting separation from Church of England published by Brownists.

1583 Newfoundland discovered and claimed.

1584–1654 Scholar, jurist, and Parliamentarian, J. Selden, lived.

1585 First colonists transported to Roanoke Colony in America.

1587 Mary, Queen of Scots, executed on orders of Elizabeth I.

1588   Spanish Armada destroyed by English fleet; fighting with Spain resulted from England's support for revolt of the Netherlands.

1590   E. Spenser published his epic poem, *Faerie Queene.*

1591   Naval hero Sir R. Grenville, commanding the lone raider *Revenge,* killed in famous battle against 15 Spanish warships.

1592   Navigator J. Davis discovered Falkland Islands.

1592   Dramatist T. Kyd wrote *The Spanish Tragedy.*

1593–1633   Metaphysical poet G. Herbert lived.

c1594–1616   W. Shakespeare flourished as an established playwright.

1594   *Romeo and Juliet* performed; W. Shakespeare later wrote *The Merchant of Venice* (1596), *Hamlet* (1600–01), and *Macbeth* (1606).

1594   Chamberlain's Men, theatrical group which included W. Shakespeare, organized; performed frequently at Globe Theatre.

1595   Sir P. Sidney wrote prose essay, *The Defense of Poetry.*

1598   Playwright B. Jonson wrote *Every Man in His Humour;* later wrote *Volpone,* and *The Alchemist.*

1600   British East India Company formed to gain a share of spice trade; company defeated the Portuguese in India (1612) and gradually expanded its interests there.

1600   Scientist W. Gilbert first described earth's magnetic field; also devised the term electricity.

1600   Dramatist T. Dekker wrote *The Shoemaker's Holiday.*

1600s   Metaphysical lyric poets and the Cavalier poets flourished.

1601   Marlowe's *Dr. Faustus* only now entered on Stationer's Register; performed 1588.

1603–25   James I reigned; first of the Scottish Stuart line; his accession personally united crowns of England and Scotland; his rule marked by efforts to accommodate modern Puritans and Catholics, and by some success in addressing Parliamentary grievances, especially in foreign affairs, religion, and taxation.

1603   Bye Plot to force religious reforms.

1604   Hampton Court Conference called; failed to settle differences between Puritan members of the Church of England over liturgy and theology.

1605   Gunpowder Plot, conspiracy by English Catholics to blow up Parliament and the king.

1605   Treaty of Madrid signed, ending Anglo-Spanish War from the 1580s; restored trade with Iberia.

1607   Jamestown (Virginia) founded (May 14) as first permanent English settlement in North America.

1610   H. Hudson discovered and explored what became Hudson Bay.

1611   King James Bible issued.

1612   Prince Henry, heir to English and Scottish thrones, died; had championed reformed Protestantism.

1615–62   Theologian J. Biddle, founder of English unitarianism, lived.

1616   Architect I. Jones, who introduced Renaissance Palladian style in England, completed the Queen's House in Greenwich.

1616–1703   Mathematician J. Wallis lived; contributed to development of calculus.

1618–67   A. Cowley, poet and essayist, lived.

1620   Pilgrims, seeking to escape persecution of religious dissenters in England, founded Plymouth Colony in New England; opened way for settlement by English.

c1623   T. Middleton wrote the play *The Changeling* in collaboration with another noted playwright of his time, W. Rowley.

1624   J. Donne, Metaphysical poet, wrote *Devotions upon Emergent Occasions;* also known for *Death Be Not Proud.*

1624–89   Noted physician T. Sydenham lived; introduced use of quinine for malaria and initiated medical use of opium.

1625–49   Charles I reigned; his arbitrary rule and chronic need for money led to prolonged conflict with Parliament and Scotland, and finally civil war in both kingdoms.

1625–30   War with Spain sparked by commercial rivalry, anti-Catholic sentiment in Parliament, and failed negotiations for marriage agreement with Spain.

1625–41   Arminianism favored by King Charles; aroused resentment in Parliament and the kingdom generally and thereby helped set the stage for a revolt.

1626–29   Unsuccessful war against France.

1627   Philosopher F. Bacon wrote *The New Atlantis.*

1627   J. Ford, dramatist, wrote *'Tis Pity She's a Whore.*

1628   Petition of Right, grievances issued by Parliament and presented to Charles I (May).

1628   Physician W. Harvey published first correct identification of heart function and blood circulation.

1629   Charles dissolved Parliament and ruled for 11 years without it.

1632–1723   Architect Sir C. Wren lived; designed St. Paul's Cathedral.

1637   Charles attempted to force Anglican liturgy on Scotland; Scottish Presbyterians rebelled.

1637   Sir J. Suckling wrote his famous poem, *Why So Pale and Wan, Fond Lover?*.

1637   Parliamentarian J. Hampden challenged right of Charles I to levy ship-money taxes.

1639–40   Bishops' Wars fought by Charles against Scottish Covenanters.

1640   Short Parliament convened by Charles I; refused Charles aid for war against Scottish Covenanters; Long Parliament convened.

1642   Charles I refused to accept Parliament's Nineteen Propositions.

1642–48   English Civil Wars; forces of Parliament defeated royalists and soon established Commonwealth.

1643   Westminster Assembly convened to fix doctrine and liturgy of Church of England; members all Calvinist.

1646   R. Crashaw, metaphysical poet, wrote *Steps to the Temple.*

1648   R. Herrick, poet and clergyman, published *To the Virgins, to Make Much of Time.*

1649   Commonwealth proclaimed (Jan. 30) after end of the English Civil Wars and King Charles's execution; O. Cromwell, leader of the victorious Parliamentarians, became head of state; Rump Parliament sat after Pride's Purge (1648).

1649–52   Revolts by Scots and Irish suppressed by Cromwell; Irish harshly treated.

1651   Navigation Act passed to increase British shipping and trade at the expense of Dutch merchantmen, who dominated the Western European carrying trade; resulted in first Dutch War.

1651   Philosopher T. Hobbes wrote *Leviathan.*

1653   Rump Parliament dissolved; "Barebones Parliament" convened by O. Cromwell.

1653   Protectorate established by new Instrument of Government; first, and only, detailed written constitution in English history; Cromwell given broad powers as Lord Protector.

1657   Humble Petition and Advice drawn up by Parliament (Mar.); modified and superseded Instrument of Government; O. Cromwell continued as protector.

1658–60   Cromwell died (1658); dissatisfaction with government of Protectorate (and Puritan reforms enacted) brought England to near anarchy by 1660.

c1660   R. Hooke discovered law of elasticity in solids, called Hooke's Law; also first to use the biological term "cell."

1660   Charles II restored to throne by Parliament; Convention Parliament convened.

1660–69   S. Pepys wrote his diary, now an important source of information on life during English Restoration period.

1660–85   Charles II reigned; marked beginning of English Restoration period (1660–88).

1661–79   Royalist Cavalier Parliament convened; rise of Whig and Tory factions.

1661–65   Clarendon Code passed; four harsh laws designed to suppress any religious sects dissenting from the established Church of England.

1662   Physicist R. Boyle postulated Boyle's Law on gases.

1662–1742   R. Bentley, classical scholar, lived; known for *Dissertation upon the Epistles of Phalaris.*

1664   Navigation Act passed to control passage of goods to English colonies through England; led to great unrest and eventually contributed to American Revolution.

1664–66   Sir I. Newton discovered laws of motion and universal gravitation, calculus, and the variations of the light spectrum.

1665–67   Second Dutch War.

1667   Poet J. Milton, while blind, dictated his masterpiece *Paradise Lost,* followed in 1671 by *Paradise Regained.*

1668   England joined Triple Alliance against France.

1668   J. Dryden became poet laureate; known for *The Hind and the Panther, Religio Laici,* and *All for Love.*

1670   Charles II signed the secret Treaty of Dover with France.

1670   Hudson's Bay Company founded; did much to promote colonial and commercial development of Canada, especially after 1763.

1672–78 Third Dutch War.

1672 Declaration of Indulgence issued by Charles II; granted religious toleration to certain Nonconformists; voided by Parliament, suspicious of heir James's Catholic religion.

1675 J. Wilmot, 2d earl of Rochester, wrote his poem, *A Satire Against Mankind.*

1675 J. Flamsteed appointed first astronomer royal.

1678 Fictitious Popish Plot; revelations resulted in hysteria and persecution of Catholics.

1678 W. Wycherley wrote his satirical play, *The Plain Dealer.*

1678 J. Bunyan wrote allegorical *Pilgrim's Progress.*

1681 W. Penn obtained rights to Pennsylvania in America; later planned Philadelphia.

1683 Rye House Plot, abortive Whig plan to assassinate King Charles II and James, duke of York.

1685–88 James II reigned; his unconstitutional rule and Catholicism led to his overthrow.

1685 Protestant duke of Monmouth's revolt; James captured him at Battle of Sedgemoor.

1685–1731 Mathematician B. Taylor lived; helped found differential calculus.

1687 Declaration of Indulgence issued by James II; granted toleration to Nonconformists and Catholics; aroused widespread sentiment against James.

1688 Glorious Revolution; James deposed; Protestants William and Mary became rulers of England (he reigned 1689–1702) after agreeing to abide by provisions of the Declaration of Rights.

1689 English Bill of Rights enacted; established supremacy of Parliament, ameliorating the power struggle with monarchy.

1689 Nonconformists granted religious freedom by Act of Toleration.

1689–97 War of the Grand Alliance fought to oppose expansionism of Louis XIV; American phase called King William's War.

1690 James's attempt to retake the throne, with French and Irish aid, defeated by King William at the Battle of the Boyne.

1690 Philosopher J. Locke published *Essay Concerning Human Understanding.*

1691–1781 Catholic bishop R. Challoner lived; revised Douay Bible.

1694–95 W. Paterson founded and directed the Bank of England.

1694 Bank of England instituted.

1700 Playwright W. Congreve wrote *The Way of the World.*

18TH–19TH CENTS. Romantic movement in arts and literature began in Germany and England.

1700s Enlightment, intellectual movement centered in France, spread to England; A. Smith, J. Bentham, D. Hume, and E. Gibbon identified with the movement in England.

1700s Empirical school of philosophy arose in Britain particularly through writings of J. Locke, G. Berkeley, and D. Hume.

1701 Act of Settlement passed by Parliament; provided for royal succession and limited royal powers.

1701–14 War of the Spanish Succession, fought on the Continent and in the colonies (as Queen Anne's War).

1704 Gibraltar taken from Spain.

1702–14 Queen Anne reigned; last of Stuart monarchs.

1705 Astronomer E. Halley accurately calculated return of a comet, which was later named after him.

1707 Act of Union politically uniting England and Scotland as Great Britain (May 1).

1709–11 Sir R. Steele wrote essays with J. Addison for *The Tatler.*

1713 Treaty of Utrecht, ending War of the Spanish Succession; Britain gained considerable colonial territories from France, including Acadia, Newfoundland, and much of Hudson Bay region.

1714 A. Pope wrote poem *The Rape of the Lock;* also known for his later work *Essay on Man.*

1714–70 G. Whitefield, evangelist, lived; helped establish Methodism.

1714–27 George I reigned; founded the Hanoverian line of English monarchs (reigned to 1837); his rule marked by rise of prime minister as leader of government and by dominance of Whig party.

1715 Revolt of the Jacobites, supporters of deposed King James and his heirs, failed.

c1715–1820 Georgian style of architecture popular.

1716 Septennial Act passed by Parliament; extended life of a Parliament from three to seven years.

1717 Grand Lodge of the Freemasons, a secret fraternal order, organized.

1718   Britain joined the Quadruple Alliance.

1718   Blackbeard killed while trying to elude capture after years of piracy.

1718–79   T. Chippendale, famous furniture maker, lived.

1719   Revolt of the Jacobites put down.

1719–20   D. Defoe wrote his classic novel *Robinson Crusoe.*

1720   South Sea Bubble, stock scheme involving the South Sea Company; its collapse ruined thousands and led to Sir R. Walpole's ministry.

1721–42   R. Walpole in power; usually regarded as first prime minister.

1726   J. Swift wrote his classic *Gulliver's Travels.*

1727–60   George II reigned; Walpole continued in office until 1742.

1727–97   J. Wilkes, journalist and politician, lived; championed freedom of the press.

1728   Dramatist J. Gay wrote *The Beggar's Opera.*

1728   Artist W. Hogarth painted *Beggar's Opera.*

1729   Methodist religious movement begun in Oxford, England, by J. Wesley and his brother Charles.

1730–95   J. Wedgwood, pottery manufacturer, lived.

1731–1810   H. Cavendish, physicist and chemist, lived; known for discovering composition of air and water, and the properties of hydrogen.

1733   J. Kay invented the flying shuttle, an important advance in mechanical weaving.

1736–1819   J. Watt, Scottish inventor, lived; invented numerous improvements to the steam engine, thereby laying the foundation for the Industrial Revolution.

1739   War of Jenkins's Ear (with Spain) broke out.

1740–48   War of Austrian Succession; colonial rivalry with France continued, in North America as King George's War.

1742   G. Handel composed his masterpiece, the oratorio *Messiah.*

1742   E. Hoyle, authority on games, wrote *Short Treatise on the Game of Whist;* later expanded to include other games.

1745–46   Jacobite revolt led by Charles Edward (Bonnie Prince Charles); last serious Jacobite rising, it ended in failure.

1749   H. Fielding wrote his classic novel *Tom Jones.*

c1751   Poet T. Gray wrote *Elegy Written in a Country Churchyard.*

1751–1806   T. Sheraton, furniture maker, lived.

1752–70   Poet T. Chatterton lived; became favorite of later English Romantic poets.

1754–1827   Pottery manufacturer J. Spode lived.

1755   S. Johnson compiled his *Dictionary of the English Language.*

1756   Diplomatic Revolution ended long-established alliances in Europe.

1756–63   Seven Years' War; war in America called French and Indian War.

1759–1833   W. Wilberforce, humanitarian and philanthropist, lived; led British movement to abolish slavery.

1760–1820   George III reigned; often controversial, he became insane in his later years.

MID-1700s   Industrial Revolution began; starting in Britain, it later spread to other European nations.

1763   Treaty of Paris ending Seven Years' War; Britain gained mastery of Canada and India; treaty marked Britain's rise as the dominant colonial power.

1763   J. Wilkes published famous issue No. 45 of *The North Briton;* this and subsequent issues attacking the royal government helped establish freedom of the press.

1763?–1835   W. Cobbett, journalist and social reformer, lived.

c1764   J. Hargreaves invented the spinning jenny.

1765   Stamp Act and Quartering Act passed by Parliament; resulted in opposition in American colonies.

1765   H. Walpole wrote his Gothic novel *The Castle of Otranto.*

1765–69   Sir W. Blackstone published *Commentaries on the Laws of England,* influential in teaching and practice of law in England.

1766–1844   J. Dalton, scientist, lived; devised Dalton's Law on gas pressure and developed atomic theory of matter.

1767   Townshend Acts passed to reassert authority in American colonies; led to increased resistance to English rule.

1768   L. Sterne's (unfinished) novel *Sentimental Journey* published.

1768–71   J. Cook discovered and chartered New Zealand and the eastern coast of Australia; on a later voyage he explored the Antarctic coast and discovered New Caledonia.

1769 Sir R. Arkwright patented his water-powered cotton spinning frame.

1770 T. Gainsborough painted *The Blue Boy.*

1773 Playwright O. Goldsmith wrote *She Stoops to Conquer.*

1774 Second Quartering Act passed by Parliament after Boston Tea Party.

1775–1802 T. Girtin flourished; helped establish watercolor painting as a distinct medium.

1775–83 American Revolution broke out in the colonies; resulted in loss of America, a major part of Britain's colonial empire; American colonies replaced by expansion of British interests elsewhere, notably India.

1776 Economist A. Smith wrote *Wealth of Nations.*

1776–88 E. Gibbon wrote *The History of the Decline and Fall of the Roman Empire.*

1776–1837 J. Constable, leading landscape artist, lived.

1780 Gordon Riots led by Lord George Gordon to protest for repeal of the Catholic Relief Act of 1778.

1781 Astronomer W. Herschel discovered Uranus.

1783–1801 W. Pitt the Younger served as prime minister; strengthened office of prime minister and led Britain through the long wars with France; a revived Tory party coalesced around his leadership.

1785 Poet W. Cowper wrote his masterpiece, *The Task.*

1789 Utilitarian philosopher J. Bentham published *Introduction to the Principles of Morals and Legislation.*

1789 Captain W. Bligh set adrift following mutiny aboard the HMS *Bounty.*

1789 Poet W. Blake wrote *Songs of Innocence,* followed in 1794 by *Songs of Experience.*

1793–1802 Britain joined in French Revolutionary Wars against France.

1796 E. Jenner developed technique of vaccination.

1798 Count B. T. Rumford, American-born British physicist, theorized that heat is caused by the motion of particles.

1798 W. Wordsworth, Romantic poet, published *Lyrical Ballads.*

1798 Poet S. T. Coleridge published *Lyrical Ballads* with W. Wordsworth.

1799–1800 Combination Acts banning trade unions and guilds passed.

1800s Gothic revival movement in architecture.

1800–54 Historian T. Macaulay lived; wrote *The History of England from the Accession of James the Second.*

1801 Act of Union; Great Britain and Ireland united, creating the United Kingdom (Jan. 1).

1803–15 Napoleonic Wars; Britain played a leading role in the wars against Napoleon; immediate postwar years marked by severe economic problems and social unrest.

1807 Britain abolished slave trade.

1807–08 Scientist Sir H. Davy isolated many chemical elements through his research in electrochemistry.

1809 Lord G. Byron wrote *English Bards and Scotch Reviewers,* which brought him fame; later works include *Childe Harold's Pilgrimage* (1816–18) and *Don Juan* (1819–24).

1811–16 Rise of the Luddites, bands of workingmen angered by low wages and unemployment.

1811–20 Regency period; George, Prince of Wales, ruled as regent for his father, King George III.

c1812 Inventor C. Babbage devised early mechanical calculating machine.

1812–15 War of 1812 fought with US.

1812–89 Historian Sir E. S. Creasy lived.

1813 J. Austen published her novel *Pride and Predjudice.*

1813–97 Sir I. Pitman lived; invented shorthand system.

1814–99 Surgeon Sir J. Paget lived; discovered trichinosis parasite.

1815 Corn Law passed; prevented import of foreign grain and thereby raised price of bread; working classes especially hard hit.

1818–89 Physicist J. Joule lived; formulated law of conservation of energy.

1819 Peterloo massacre; British cavalry attacked demonstrators seeking reforms.

1819 Romantic poet J. Keats wrote both *To a Nightingale* and *On a Grecian Urn* this year.

1820 Cato Street Conspiracy, an anarchist assassination plot against cabinet officers, uncovered.

1820 Poet P. B. Shelley wrote *Prometheus Unbound.*

1820–30 George IV reigned; proved an incapable ruler.

1821   T. De Quincey wrote *Confessions of an English Opium Eater.*

1821–22   W. Hazlitt published his collected essays, *Table Talk.*

1822–1911   Scientist F. Galton lived; coined the term for the science of eugenics.

1823   C. Lamb, essayist, poet, and critic, wrote *Essays of Elia.*

1824   Combination Acts, banning unions, repealed; later restored, then ignored.

1825   G. Stephenson built a locomotive for England's first railroad.

1825–95   T. H. Huxley, outspoken proponent of Darwinism, lived.

1827–64   Explorer J. G. Speke lived; discovered Lake Victoria, a source of the Nile River.

1829   Catholic Emancipation Act removed most penalties imposed on English Catholics (by Penal Laws); Catholics finally readmitted to Parliament.

1829   Scotland Yard, the first London Metropolitan Police headquarters, established on a street named Scotland Yard.

1830–37   William IV reigned.

1831   Scientist M. Faraday demonstrated principal of electromagnetic induction.

1832   Reform Bill of 1832 passed; doubled size of electorate and extended power to industrialized cities; reforms marked the end of the Tory party, which was reformed as the Conservative party (1832).

1832–1917   Anthropologist Sir E. B. Tylor lived; called the founder of cultural anthropology.

1833   Oxford Movement within the Church of England begun by sermon delivered by J. Keble at Oxford.

1833   Slavery abolished throughout the British Empire.

1837   C. Dickens established his reputation by publishing *The Posthumous Papers of the Pickwick Club;* later published *A Christmas Carol* in 1843, and *A Tale of Two Cities* in 1859.

1837   Sir C. Wheatstone, physicist and inventor, patented an early telegraph with W. Cooke; also invented the stethoscope and Wheatstone bridge.

1837–1901   Victoria reigned; British Empire reached its zenith; period of her reign known as the Victorian Age.

FROM 1837   Victorian style of architecture became popular during Queen Victoria's reign.

1838–48   Rise of Chartism, mass movement among workingmen for effective political reform.

1839–42   First Opium War in China; Britain won trading concessions in China.

1841   J. H. Newman, churchman, wrote *Tract 90;* in 1845 he converted to Catholicism.

1841–46   R. Peel served as prime minister; brought his newly formed Conservative party to power and effected repeal of the controversial Corn Laws.

1842   Reformer A. A. Cooper introduced Coal Mines Act in the House of Commons.

1842–1900   Sir A. Sullivan lived; known for his collaborations with Sir W. Gilbert, including *The Pirates of Penzance* and *The Mikado.*

1843   T. Hood wrote his poem, *The Song of the Shirt.*

1846   Corn Laws repealed; seen as great victory for liberal middle class.

c1847   Sir J. Franklin's expedition in search of Northwest Passage ended in disaster when his ships became icebound in the Arctic.

1847   Novelist A. Brontë wrote *Agnes Grey.*

1847   C. Brontë wrote her classic novel, *Jane Eyre.*

1847   E. Brontë wrote *Wuthering Heights.*

1847–1929   Feminist M. Fawcett lived.

1848   W. M. Thackeray wrote his famous novel, *Vanity Fair.*

1848–53   Pre-Raphaelite school of painters and poets flourished; included D. G. Rossetti and J. Millais.

1849, 1854   Navigation Acts repealed.

1850   Don Pacifico Affair with Greece.

1850   Poet E. B. Browning wrote *Sonnets from the Portuguese.*

1850–54   Sir R. McClure commanded first successful expedition through the Northwest Passage.

1851   Great Exhibition of 1851; monumental Crystal Palace designed by J. Paxton.

1851–53   Critic J. Ruskin wrote *The Stones of Venice.*

1852   P. M. Roget, physician and lexicographer, published *Thesaurus of English Words and Phrases.*

1853–56   Crimean War.

1854   A. Tennyson, 1st baron Tennyson, wrote *The Charge of the Light Brigade;* later works included *Idylls of the King.*

1856   Sir H. Bessemer invented process for economical production of steel.

1856–60   Second Opium War with China; Britain won further trading privileges and forced China to legalize opium trade.

1857   A. Trollope wrote *Barchester Towers.*

1857–59   Indian Mutiny; native revolt against British East India Company rule resulted in transfer of governing authority to the British crown.

1858   W. Morris published his collection of poems, *The Defence of Guenevere and Other Poems.*

1859   G. Meredith published his novel, *The Ordeal of Richard Feverel.*

1859   C. R. Darwin published his *On the Origin of Species by Means of Natural Selection,* establishing Darwinism as prevailing scientific theory of biological evolution.

1859   J. S. Mill, philosopher and political economist, wrote *On Liberty.*

1860   W. Collins wrote the early detective novel *The Woman in White.*

1861   G. Eliot wrote her novel *Silas Marner.*

1861   Trent Affair with US; brief dispute that stemmed from the American Civil War.

1861   Sir W. Crookes discovered the element thallium.

1861–1947   A. N. Whitehead, mathematician and philosopher, lived; collaborated with B. Russell on *Principles of Mathematics.*

1862   C. G. Rosetti wrote *Goblin Market and Other Poems.*

1865   Poet A. C. Swinburne wrote *Atalanta in Calydon.*

1865   L. Carroll published *Alice's Adventures in Wonderland.*

1865   J. Lister developed use of carbolic acid as antiseptic.

1865–1945   A. Symons, poet and critic, lived; helped introduce Symbolist movement to Britain.

1867   Reform Bill of 1867; doubled electorate and redistributed parliamentary seats.

1867   Parliament passed British North America Act, establishing Canada as a self-governing dominion; marked start of Britain's withdrawal from direct rule within the colonial empire.

1868   B. Disraeli served as prime minister.

1868–69   R. Browning wrote his four-volume epic, *The Ring and the Book.*

1868–94   W. Gladstone rose to power; served as prime minister during much of this period as a Liberal party leader; considered one of Britain's great statesmen, he instituted many reforms.

1869   Novelist R. Blackmore wrote *Lorna Doone.*

1869   M. Arnold published *Essays in Criticism.*

1872   San Juan Boundary Dispute with US settled; US awarded San Juan Islands southeast of Vancouver, B.C.

1873   W. H. Pater, critic and essayist, wrote *Studies in the History of the Renaissance.*

1874–80   B. Disraeli again served as prime minister; his term marked by an aggressive foreign policy.

1874–1936   G. K. Chesterton, author and critic, lived.

1875   Disraeli negotiated purchase of Suez Canal stock; British thereby gained controlling interest and began involvement in Egypt.

1877   Radical Charles Bradlaugh and A. Bessant published pamphlet on birth control to test courts on the issue; their case thrown out on technical grounds.

1878   W. Booth founded the Salvation Army and served as its first general.

1878–80   Second Anglo-Afghan War; Britain invaded Afghanistan from India to check rise of Russian influence there.

1879   Lexicographer J. Murray became editor of *The Oxford English Dictionary.*

1882   Phoenix Park murders by Irish extremists opposed to British rule.

1884   Reform Bill of 1884 established virtual universal male suffrage.

1885   Battle of Khartoum (Sudan); famous battle in which Lord C. Gordon was defeated and killed.

1886   Unsuccessful attempt to pass Home Rule Bill for Ireland; sentiment for bill had been building in the 1880s as other attempts at reform failed to appease the Irish; Gladstone backed the bill and was forced out of office (until 1892) in the controversy.

1886–1957   Author P. W. Lewis founded the vorticist magazine *Blast.*

1887–1915   Scientist H. Moseley lived; noted for work on atomic structure.

1888   Jack the Ripper brutally killed women in London; was never apprehended.

1887 Sir A. C. Doyle published the first Sherlock Holmes book, *A Study in Scarlet.*

1891 T. Hardy published *Tess of the D'Urbervilles.*

1892 Physician W. Osler published *Principles and Practice of Medicine,* a standard in the field.

1893 G. B. Shaw wrote his play *Mrs. Warren's Profession;* subsequent plays included *Major Barbara* and *Pygmalion.*

1896 Philosopher H. Spencer completed his *Synthetic Philosophy.*

1896 A. E. Houseman published his collection of poetry, *A Shropshire Lad.*

1897 B. Stoker published the novel *Dracula.*

1898 H. G. Wells published his famous novel, *The War of the Worlds.*

1898 Fashoda incident.

1898 Henry James published *Turn of the Screw.*

1898 Sir J. Dewar first liquefied hydrogen; later succeeded in solidifying it.

1899 Venezuela boundary dispute with US.

1899–1902 Boer War; ruinous conflict in South Africa won by Britain at great cost.

1900 Labour party founded by coalition of Socialists and trade unions; named Labour party in 1906.

1900–74 Philosopher G. Ryle lived; known for *The Concept of Mind.*

1900s American and English school of poetry called Imagists became popular.

1901–10 Edward VII reigned.

1901 Ruling in Taff Val case; held company could sue union for damages resulting from strike; case helped spur growth of Labour party as unions sought remedy through Parliament (1906 legislation nullified ruling).

1901–07, 1930 Sir E. W. Elgar composed the five *Pomp and Circumstance* marches.

1902 B. Potter published her classic children's story, *The Tale of Peter Rabbit.*

1903 Philosopher B. Russell co-wrote *Principles of Mathematics.*

1903 S. Butler wrote his autobiographical novel, *The Way of All Flesh.*

1903 Feminist E. G. Pankhurst founded the militant Women's Social and Political Union.

1903–75 Sculptor J. Hepworth lived.

1904 Entente Cordiale, informal understanding with France, reached to counter growing power of Germany.

1904 Sir F. Younghusband secured a treaty opening Tibet to Western trade.

1905–15 Liberals in power; many reforms enacted, notably under Prime Minister H. Asquith.

1906 Sir J. J. Thomson, noted for his work on the electron, received Nobel Prize for Physics.

1906–21 J. Galsworthy published his novels, titled *The Forsyte Saga.*

1907 Anglo-Russian Convention settled disputes with Russia over Persia, Afghanistan, and Tibet; strengthened relations.

1908–16 H. Asquith in power as prime minister, succeeding H. Campbell-Bannerman.

1908 Scientist E. Rutherford, noted for his work on radioactivity and atomic structure, won the Nobel Prize in Chemistry.

1910 Novelist E. M. Forster wrote *Howards End;* in 1924 wrote *A Passage to India.*

1910–36 George V reigned.

1911 Parliament Act passed eliminating House of Lords' veto power over parliamentary legislation.

1912 British ocean liner *Titanic* sank (Apr. 14).

1914–18 World War I; Britain played a major role in opposing the Central Powers.

1915 Easter Rebellion in Ireland against British rule.

1915 Novelist W. S. Maugham wrote *Of Human Bondage.*

1915 G. Holst composed the orchestral suite *The Planets.*

1915 F. M. Ford wrote *The Good Soldier.*

1916–22 D. Lloyd George (Liberal) in office as prime minister.

1917 Balfour Declaration supported creation of a Jewish state.

1918 Women over 30 granted right to vote; gain equal status with men in 1928.

1918 Poet E. Sitwell wrote *Clown's House.*

1919 Third Anglo-Afghan War.

1920 Britain became a founding member of the League of Nations; awarded mandates over Iraq and Palestine (formerly part of the Ottoman Empire) and over South-West Africa and German East Africa.

1920 Government of Ireland Act created Northern Ireland and provided for Irish Home Rule.

1921 Irish Free State formed after Home Rule failed to end unrest in Ireland.

1922 Protectorate over Egypt ended, though British involvement in Egypt continued.

1922 Poet T. S. Eliot wrote *The Waste Land.*

1922 F. Aston awarded the Nobel Prize in Chemistry; developed the mass spectrograph.

1924 J. R. MacDonald served briefly as prime minister; marked first time Labour party held power.

1925 P. G. Wodehouse wrote *Much Obliged, Jeeves.*

1926 A. A. Milne wrote the famous children's story *Winnie-the-Pooh.*

1926 General strike, marked by violence.

1926 Soldier T. E. Lawrence wrote *The Seven Pillars of Wisdom.*

1928 Writer D. H. Lawrence published his novel, *Lady Chatterley's Lover.*

c1928 Sculptor H. Moore began to develop his characteristic organic forms.

1929 Great Depression began; Britain suffered during the worldwide economic crisis; abandoned the gold standard (1931).

1929 Novelist V. Woolf wrote *A Room of One's Own.*

1931 British Commonwealth of Nations formed (Dec. 11) by Statute of Westminster.

1931–35 MacDonald again served as prime minister.

1932 Author A. L. Huxley published *Brave New World.*

1932 E. Waugh wrote his satirical novel, *A Handful of Dust.*

1933 P. Dirac, noted for his work on quantum mechanics, shared Nobel Prize for Physics.

1934–61 A. J. Toynbee wrote *A Study of History.*

1935 Author R. Graves published his novel *I, Claudius.*

1935 C. S. Forester published the *African Queen.*

1936 Edward VIII reigned; abdicated soon after his succession to marry American divorcee Wallis Warfield Simpson.

1936 A. J. Ayer, proponent of logical positivism, wrote *Language, Truth and Logic.*

1936–52 George VI reigned.

1937–39 British prime minister N. Chamberlain pursued policy of appeasement toward Nazi Germany; Munich Pact concluded (1938); preparations for war begun.

1938 Novelist D. Du Maurier published *Rebecca.*

1939–45 World War II; Britain suffered heavy losses, both through combat and through extensive German air attacks on its cities (Battle of Britain).

1940–45 W. Churchill served as prime minister; led Britain through most of WW II and became a national hero for his determined resistance to the powerful Nazi war machine.

1940–70 C. Percy, baron Snow, published his series of novels called *Strangers and Brothers.*

1942 G. M. Trevelyan published *English Social History.*

1942 C. S. Lewis published *The Screwtape Letters.*

1943 Physicist K. Fuchs began passing atomic secrets to Soviets; exposed as a spy in 1950.

1944 Allied Normandy Invasion launched from Britain.

1945–51 C. Attlee (Labour) in office as prime minister; many Socialist reforms insituted; industry nationalized, socialized medicine introduced (1948); rapid postwar withdrawal from colonialism began as former colonies were granted independence.

1945 Britain became a founding member of the UN.

1945 Opera *Billy Grimes* composed by B. Britten.

1947 Independence granted to India and Pakistan.

1948 Britain accepted US aid through Marshall Plan to rebuild war-torn economy.

1948 Burma, Ceylon, and Palestine granted independence.

1950 D. Lessing wrote *The Grass Is Singing.*

1951 Scientist Sir J. D. Cockcroft received Nobel Prize in Physics with E. Walton for splitting atomic nuclei.

1951–55 W. Churchill (Conservative) served second term as prime minister; denationalized industries and Bank of England; Conservatives held power to 1964.

1952– Queen Elizabeth II reigned.

1952 *The Mousetrap* published by A. Christie.

1953 Sir H. Krebs awarded Nobel Prize for Physiology or Medicine for his studies of metabolic processes.

1953 Sir A. Bliss became Master of the Queen's Music.

1954 Physicist M. Born shared the Nobel Prize for Physics; he contributed to theory of relativity and quantum theory.

1954 Poet D. Thomas published *Under Milk Wood.*

1956 J. R. R. Tolkien completed his trilogy, *Lord of the Rings.*

1956 Suez Crisis; British troops joined fighting to retake the Suez Canal.

1957 Conservative prime minister A. Eden (1955–57) forced to resign over British intervention in Suez Crisis.

1957 Playwright J. Osborne wrote *Look Back in Anger.*

1957–60 Four novels by L. G. Durrell, *The Alexandria Quartet,* published.

1957–63 M. H. Macmillan in office as prime minister; Conservatives retained power.

1959 Anthropologist M. Leakey discovered Zinjanthropus fossil remains in Tanzania; later found *Homo habilis* fossil remains (1961).

1964–70 H. Wilson (Labour) in office as prime minister; first Labour government since 1951; his attempts to join EEC frustrated by C. de Gaulle.

1963 Nuclear Test Ban Treaty signed (Aug. 5).

1963 Soviet spy H. (Kim) Philby escaped to the USSR; had been spy since 1933.

1965 Racial discrimination in public places banned.

1965 Rhodesia unilaterally declared its independence, thereby beginning the protracted Rhodesian crisis.

1967 Steel industry nationalized.

1969 Violence in Northern Ireland between Roman Catholics and Protestants, increasing since 1966, reached serious proportions.

1970–74 E. Heath (Conservative) in office as prime minister; strikes (dock, 1970; postal, 1971; coal, 1974) worsened Britain's growing economic problems; violence in Northern Ireland continued.

1970 Britain admitted to Common Market; became full member 1973.

1971 Decimal currency system instituted.

1971 British troops sent to Northern Ireland to reinforce security forces and maintain border controls.

1972–74 Direct British rule imposed in Northern Ireland; Ulster Parliament ordered suspended.

1973 Britain proclaimed state of emergency to counter economic difficulties resulting from labor disputes, trade deficits, and fuel shortages.

1974–76 H. Wilson (Labour) in office as prime minister.

1974 Three-day work week and state of emergency ended.

1974 IRA bomb damaged Houses of Parliament (June 17); 11 injured.

1974 Anti-terrorist laws enacted following rise in terrorism; IRA outlawed.

1975 First oil pumped from North Sea oil fields.

1976–79 J. Callaghan (Labour) in office as prime minister.

1976 Government imposed new austerity measures in the face of continuing economic crisis.

1978 First "test-tube" baby born, in Lancashire.

1979 Voters in Scotland and Wales rejected referendum for home rule.

1979–90 M. Thatcher (Conservative) in office as Britain's first woman prime minister; served unprecedented 11-year term, longest in this century; she sought to curb Britain's worsening economic crisis by tough deflationary policies; encouraged private enterprise, returning 45% of state-run industry to private sector by 1989; promoted cuts in social spending; increased defense expenditures; curbed power of labor unions; maintained close ties with the US.

1979 Representatives to European Parliament chosen by popular vote for first time (June).

1979 IRA terrorist bomb killed British WW II hero, Lord Mountbatten.

1980 Rhodesian crisis resolved through intervention of British government.

1980 Labour party formally adopted position of calling for unilateral nuclear disarmament.

1981 Marriage of Prince Charles and Lady Diana Spencer (July 20); television coverage transmitted worldwide by communications satellites.

1981 Belize, former British colony became independent member of the Commonwealth (Sept.).

1982 Falkland Islands War against Argentina; Argentine invasion force driven off islands by British.

1982 Pope John Paul II made historic visit to Britain; marked major step in efforts to reestablish ties between the Church of England (independent national church since 1534) and Rome.

1982 IRA terrorist bombs exploded in London (July); 10 persons killed.

1982 King Henry VIII's flagship *Mary Rose*, priceless relic of Tudor era, raised intact (Oct.), 437 years after it had sunk off Portsmouth, England.

1983 Demonstrators protested arrival of US cruise missiles (Nov.), to be sited in Britain as part of NATO response to Soviet buildup of nuclear weapons.

1984 London policewoman killed by shots fired from Libyan embassy (Apr.); gunman had been aiming at protesters demonstrating against Khadafy government; Libyan embassy expelled from Britain.

1984 Government signed agreement with China providing for return of Hong Kong in 1997 (Sept. 26); China agreed to maintain free enterprise system for 50 years.

1984 Thatcher and most cabinet members escaped IRA bomb explosion during conference at Brighton hotel (Oct.).

1985 One-year strike by coal miners ended (Mar.); walkout had been called over decision to close inefficient mines.

1985 Mass demonstration by some 100,000 protesters against nuclear arms race held in London (Oct.).

1985 Ulster Plan approved by Parliament (Nov.); allowed Ireland consultative role in Northern Ireland.

1986 British and French governments agreed to construction of high-speed rail tunnel under the English Channel (Feb.); project to be completed by 1993.

1986 Prince Andrew married Sarah Ferguson (July).

1987 Thatcher reelected following Conservative win in general elections; promised continued privatization, tax and spending cuts, health and education reforms, and program to revitalize inner cities.

1987 Government, concerned about revealing official secrets, tried to block publication of *Spycatcher*, book by former British counter-intelligence agent; book published in Australia.

1987 INF treaty signed by US and USSR (Dec.), eliminating intermediate range nuclear missiles; US cruise missiles to be pulled out of the UK by 1988.

1988 Thatcher pressed for continued nuclear capability at meeting of NATO ministers (Sept.).

1988 Book *Satanic Verses* published by British author Salman Rushdie (Sept.); denounced as offensive by Muslims, the book prompted Iranian fundamentalist leader Ayatollah Khomeini to call for Rushdie's death (Feb. 1989); Rushdie went into hiding.

1988 Pan Am passenger jet crashed at Lockerbie, Scotland (Dec.) when terrorist bomb exploded aboard plane; 259 passengers killed.

1988 Government enacted tax cut, dropping top rate to 40% (from 60%) and bottom rate to 25% (from 27%).

1989 IRA launched new wave of terrorist bomb attacks against targets in Britain; some 20 attacks killed 15 by close of 1991.

1989 Controversial "poll tax" introduced in Scotland (Apr.); introduced in England and Wales (Apr., 1990); measure designed to compensate for reduced central government payments to localities, and recent imposition of a cap on property taxes imposed by localities ("domestic rates"); all residents over 18 to pay single, flat rate.

1989 Thatcher reluctantly approved full membership in European Monetary Union and agreed to work toward EC goal of full economic union (June); UK joined EC exchange rate stabilization system (Oct. 1990).

1989 Government reluctantly agreed to joint Commonwealth statement urging continuation of current sanctions against South Africa to protest apartheid policies (Oct.); Thatcher would subsequently relax UK sanctions in response to reforms effected by South African government (Feb., 1990).

1989 Government plan to allow Hong Kong citizens right of residence in Britain, after Hong Kong reverts to China (1997), sparked controversy (Dec.).

1989 Labour Party adopted position calling for multilateral nuclear disarmament, abandoning earlier demand for unilateral approach.

1989 Thatcher's popularity reported slipping; stemmed from economic factors (high inflation, trade deficit, high interest rates) and controversies over poll tax, proposed National Health Service reforms, and educational reforms.

1989 Soviet abandonment of interventionist policy in Eastern Europe and collapse of Communist governments there prompted review of UK defense policy; UK later decided to reduce size of its conventional military; US to reduce military bases in UK.

1990 Diplomatic relations with Argentina renewed (Feb.).

1990 Protests against poll tax turned violent (Mar.); demonstrations sparked when localities set tax at higher rate than proposed by national government.

1990 Mass rally in London against poll tax turned into riot (Mar.).

1990 NATO future discussed at conference between Thatcher, US president G. Bush, and French president Mitterrand (Apr.); Thatcher called for continued NATO nuclear capability and for NATO membership for united Germany.

1990 IRA car bomb killed Ian Gow, member of Parliament and adviser to Prime Minister Thatcher (July).

1990 Divided Germany formally reunited (Oct.).

1990 EC summit at Rome (Dec.); EC delegation ignored Thatcher's stiff opposition to 1994 as date for implementing single European currency and complete economic union.

1990 Thatcher's opposition to EC union sparked resignation of deputy prime minister (Nov.).

1990 Thatcher, dubbed Britian's "Iron Lady," bowed to growing unpopularity and resigned as prime minister (Nov.).

1990 J. Major (Conservative) in office as prime minister, ending Thatcher's unprecedented 11-year term (Nov.); reformed unpopular poll tax system; confronted growing economic problems (increasing inflation and unemployment) and in 1991, a recession.

1990 Persian Gulf War; British condemned invasion of Kuwait and sent some 42,000 troops to join the US–led multinational force that drove Iraq out of Kuwait; 26 British soldiers killed in war.

1990 Cold War officially proclaimed over at Paris summit (Nov. 19–21); US president Bush, Soviet leader Gorbachev, and leaders of NATO and Warsaw Pact countries signed historic Treaty on Conventional Armed Forces in Europe (Nov. 19), limiting troops and equipment in Europe; leaders then signed (Nov. 21) Charter of Paris, declaring Cold War over and calling for new era of democracy and unity.

1990 Inflation rate hit 9.5% for year; had been 7.8% for most of 1980s.

1991 IRA terrorists hit the prime minister's residence with three mortar rounds (Feb.); no injuries reported.

1991 One person killed by IRA bombs planted at two London railroad stations (Feb.).

1991 Poll tax abandoned (Mar.); government reverted to property tax, with lower rate for one occupant dwellings (council tax system); later increased national value-added tax by 2.5% to lessen local tax burden.

1991 Government began restructuring National Health Service (Apr.).

1991 Queen Elizabeth, on visit to US, gave first-ever address of a British monarch to US Congress (May).

1991 NATO restructuring approved by defense ministers (May); to include force reductions and creation of all-German force in former East Germany.

1991 Bank of England governor, acting in concert with numerous other nations, shut down British offices of Bank of Commerce and Credit International (BCCI) for alleged illegal activities (July).

1992 Prime Minister Major returned to office by unexpected Conservative win in elections (Apr.), despite continuing recession.

1992 House of Commons named Betty Boothroyd speaker of the House, the first woman named to the post in 700 years; Boothroyd, a Labour party member, won with backing of Conservatives.

1992 Princess Anne filed for divorce from her estranged husband Mark Phillips (couple had separated in 1989), ending 15-year marriage.

1992 Prime Minister Major made first official acknowledgment that British intelligence service exists (May); promised to reform British laws on secrecy.

1992 Britain withdrew from EC exchange rate stabilization system.

Great Colombia (Gran Colombia) Former South American republic. Established (1822) by S. Bolívar, it consisted of parts of modern Colombia, Panama, Venezuela, and Ecuador. It lasted until 1830, when Venezuela and Ecuador established their independence.

Great Company, the   *See* **Hudson's Bay Company.**

Great Condé   *See* **Condé, Louis II de Bourbon, prince of Condé.**

Great Depression   Name given the worldwide economic collapse following the US stock market crash of 1929. The stock market failure of 1929 marked the end of the US economic boom of the 1920s, and led to mass failures of businesses and the simultaneous rise of vast unemployment both in the US and in Europe. In the US the Depression reached its lowest point in the early 1930s, and slackened with the New Deal (*q.v.*) reforms inaugurated by President F. Roosevelt. Full economic recovery did not occur until the opening of WW II. In Europe, the economic failure contributed to the rise of the Nazi party in Germany. (*See also* United States (1929–39).)

Great Exhibition of 1851   British industrial exhibit in London. The exhibition was a showcase for advanced machines and products of the day and was housed in the Crystal Palace, a huge building constructed of iron and glass.

Great Fear   Name given to panics (July–Aug., 1789) among the peasants in France during the early phase of the French Revolution (1789–99). Peasants, who had stopped paying taxes to local landed aristocrats, were overcome by unfounded rumors that the aristocrats had hired brigands to attack them. This prompted a series of peasant revolts that allowed the revolution in Paris to succeed.

Great Fire of London   *See* **London.**

Great Interregnum   *See* **Interregnum, The Great.**

Great Leap Forward   Chinese Communist campaign (1958–59) to increase agricultural and industrial output by reorganizing the populace into communes. The government hoped to take advantage of China's great manpower reserves by this new system. The program ended in failure (1960).

Great Moravia   *See* **Moravia.**

Great Peloponnesian War   *See* **Peloponnesian War.**

Great Proletarian Cultural Revolution   *See* **Cultural Revolution.**

Great Rebellion   *See* **English Civil Wars.**

Great Schism   *See* **Schism.**

Great Society   Name for the legislative program adopted by President L. Johnson during his elected term (1965–69). This program of liberal social reforms included his "war on poverty," civil rights reforms, and federal educational, medical, and housing programs.

Great Trek   Emigration (1835–40) by 14,000 Afrikaners (Boers) from Cape Colony into the African interior. Opposed to British policies, especially those favoring natives, the Afrikaners moved northward, battled with native peoples, and finally established the Afrikaner republic of Natal (1839).

Great Wall of China   Celebrated defensive wall begun (214–204 BC) by Qin dynasty emperor Shi Huangdi and added to by succeeding dynasties. Huangdi connected a number of shorter earthen walls erected during the Warring States period, hoping to counter threatened invasions by the Xiongnu. The Ming dynasty built the latest of the walls, using stone to create a 1,500-mile-long, 25-foot-high defensive barrier against potential invaders.

Greco, El (*pseud. of* Domenicos Theotocopoulos) c1514–1614.   Greek-born Spanish painter, one of the great painters of all time. A student of Titian, he was in Toledo, Spain, by 1577, and there became an artist of some reputation. His characteristically distorted figures and use of color, however, did not receive wide recognition until this century. Among his many famous works are *Assumption of the Virgin, Burial of Count Orgaz, Crucifixion, Resurrection,* and *View of Toledo.*

Greco-Turkish Wars   1. War (Apr.–May 1897) between Greece and Turkey over control of the island of Crete, then under Turkish rule. A rebellion on Crete (1896) and a call for union with Greece led to Greek military intervention (1897) on the island. Halted by a blockade established by the European powers, Greece then attacked Turkey (Apr., 1897). After one month of war and several severe defeats, Greece accepted an armistice.   2. War (1921–22) between Greece and Nationalist Turks, led by Kemal Atatürk, who refused to recognize terms of the Treaty of Sèvres (1920) between Greece and the Ottoman Turkish government. Greece invaded Anatolia and, after initial Greek victories, the Turks under Atatürk drove the Greeks out. The war was ended by the Treaty of Lausanne (1923). Greece gave up eastern Thrace, and the two countries exchanged minority populations.

Greece (Hellenic Republic) Country located in southeastern Europe and occupying the southern part of the Balkan Peninsula. The population is 10,088,000 and the capital is Athens. Greece is divided into two geographic regions: northern mainland Greece and the southern Peloponnesus. The two are connected by a narrow isthmus. The culture of ancient Greece, which flourished during the 1st millennium BC, has had enormous impact on the development of Western civilization. Greek philosophers, poets, dramatists, scientists, artists, and architects made many fundamental contributions to their respective fields and are still admired in modern times. These great accomplishments were made despite the nearly constant wars between the many Greek city-states that evolved in ancient Greece. These rivalries, notably between Athens and Sparta, finally cost the Greeks their independence, however. A period of decline, and then foreign domination, began with the conquest of Greece by the Macedonians in the late 4th cent. BC and lasted until the 19th cent. AD, when the modern Greek state was created. Key events in Greek history include:

3000–1000 BC Aegean civilizations flourished.

c2200–c1400 BC Minoan civilization flourished on the island of Crete.

c1600–c1200 BC Mycenaean civilization flourished on mainland Greece.

14TH–13TH CENTS. BC Achaeans arrived in the Peloponnesus.

c1200 BC Trojan War, legendary conflict recounted in Homer's *Iliad,* fought with Troy.

11TH CENT. BC Dorians invaded the Peloponnesus; Aeolians and Ionians consequently established colonies in western Asia Minor.

c800 BC Sparta, in extreme southeastern Greece, gained hegemony over surrounding region, Laconia.

c800 BC Corinth, on the eastern coast between Sparta and Athens, developed a thriving commerce.

8TH–6TH CENTS. BC Period of colonization; Greeks established colonies in southern Italy, Sicily, North Africa, and Spain.

AFTER 8TH CENT. BC Rise of the Greek city-states.

776? BC First Olympic Games held at Olympia.

c750 BC Homer believed to have lived; *Iliad* and *Odyssey* attributed to him.

735–715 BC First Messenian War; Sparta conquered Messenia, to the west.

c700 BC Hesiod lived.

c700 BC Athens, on the eastern coast of the Greek mainland, gained control over the surrounding region, Attica.

7TH CENT. BC The city of Argos briefly dominated the Peloponnesus.

7TH CENT. BC Use of infantry formation called phalanx became widespread in ancient Greece.

7TH CENT. BC Legendary poet Arion, reputed inventor of dithyramb, said to have flourished at this time.

c650–c620 BC Second Messenian War; Sparta put down a revolt by the Messenians.

c636–c546 BC Thales, one of the Seven Wise Men of Greece, lived.

625–585 BC Periander, one of the seven sages, reigned as tyrant of Corinth.

c621 BC Draco established severe laws, the Draconian Code, in Athens.

c611–c547 BC Anaximander, early philosopher, lived.

c600 BC Dorian lyric poet Stesichorus flourished.

c600 BC Butades of Sicyon flourished; thought to be first sculptor to use clay.

c600 BC Thebes, in region of Boeotia (north of Attica), formed Boeotian League.

6TH CENT.? BC Lycurgus reformed Spartan society; created rigid, militaristic system to produce warriors.

6TH CENT. Philosopher Anaximenes lived; believed that air was primary substance of universe.

6TH CENT. BC Lyric poet Sappho lived.

6TH CENT. BC Legendary fable writer Aesop believed to have lived at this time.

6TH CENT. BC Philosopher and poet Xenophanes flourished.

6TH CENT. BC Both Orphic and Eleusinian mysteries emerged about this time.

6TH CENT. BC Ionic style of architecture emerged in Greece.

6TH–5TH CENTS. BC Ionian school of philosophy ascendant in Ionia.

6TH–4TH CENTS. BC   Classical period of Greek literature.

594 BC   Solon instituted his reforms at Athens amid grave social crisis; reforms laid basis for democracy.

c590   First Sacred War fought by league of city-states to protect the shrine at Delphi.

c582–507 BC   Pythagoras lived; founded school at Crotona, Italy; famed as mathematician.

c580 BC   Alcaeus, lyric poet, lived; invented Alcaic verse.

561–527 BC   Peisistratus in power as tyrant of Athens; began temple construction and rapid expansion of the city.

MID 6TH CENT. BC   Sparta formed the Peloponnesian League, consisting of most of the city-states on the Peloponnesus (Argos not a member).

c546 BC   Persians conquered Croesus of Lydia, taking over from him the domination of Ionian city-states in western Asia Minor.

c535–c475 BC   Philosopher Heraclitus lived; early proponent of metaphysical philosophy.

534 BC   Thespis, poet, flourished; thought to be originator of tragic drama.

520–490 BC   Cleomenes reigned in Sparta; maintained Sparta's position as dominant power in the Peloponnesus; intervened in Athenian politics.

c518–438 BC   Great poet Pindar lived.

c512–476 BC   Athenian playwright Phrynichus flourished; first to put women characters in Greek plays.

508 BC   Cleisthenes instituted his reforms; established Athenian democracy.

507 BC   Spartans invaded Attica in order to oust Cleisthenes and restore the aristocracy in Athens; Athenians drove off the Spartans.

506 BC   Athens, in war with Boeotian League, defeated Thebes and Euboea.

5TH CENT. BC   Eleatic school of philosophy founded by Parmenides.

5TH CENT. BC   Greek poet Ion lived.

5TH CENT. BC   Myron lived; sculpted statue called *Discus Thrower.*

5TH CENT. BC   Sculptor Paeonius flourished; said to have sculpted statue of Nike (*Winged Victory*).

5TH CENT. BC   Sophist philosophers flourished from this time.

5TH CENT. BC   Painter Zeuxis flourished; known for using shading to produce realism.

5TH CENT. BC   Eleatic philosopher Zeno of Elea flourished; first to use dialectical method of reasoning.

5TH CENT. BC   Timon of Athens, lived; W. Shakespeare's play, *Timon of Athens* based on him.

5TH CENT. BC   Sculptor Callimachus lived; thought to have originated Corinthian column.

c500–428 BC   Philosopher Anaxagoras lived; thought to have taught Socrates.

c500–c432 BC   Phidias, Athenian sculptor, lived.

499–493 BC   Ionian Greek colonies rebelled unsuccessfully against Persian rule; Athenians and Eretrians sent aid, thus provoking the Persians to invade Greece later (490).

c496–c406 BC   Sophocles, one of the greatest of tragic poets, lived.

490–480 BC   Themistocles in power in Athens; built up Athenian naval strength.

c490–430 BC   Philosopher Empedocles lived.

490–479 BC   Persian Wars: Greek city-states successfully resisted large-scale invasions by Persians; noted Battle of Marathon fought (490).

484?–425 BC   Herodotus, the "father of history," lived.

c480–410 BC   Sophist philosopher Protagoras flourished; believed "man is the measure of all things."

478 BC   Delian League formed mainly by Athenians, Ionians, and islanders to oppose invasion by Persia; became basis of Athenian power in Greece.

470?–399 BC   Socrates, one of the great philosophers of ancient Greece, flourished.

466 BC   Cimon, Athenian statesman and military leader, won Battle of Eurymedon River in new fighting against Persians.

462–429 BC   Pericles rose to prominence as a leading figure in Athenian politics; Athens underwent great cultural flowering and became intellectual and political center of Greece.

461–446 BC   Peloponnesian War (first); Athenians engaged in war with the Peloponnesian League, and at the same time aided a revolt against the Persians in Egypt.

c460–400 BC   Thucydides, great historian of ancient Greece, lived.

c460–c370 BC Hippocrates, father of medicine, lived.

c460–c370 BC Materialistic philosopher Democritus lived; advanced early atomic theory of matter.

c459–c380 BC Orator Lysias lived.

458 BC Athenians defeated the Peloponnesians and captured Aegina.

458 BC Aeschylus, Athenian dramatist, completed his famous *Oresteia* trilogy.

457 BC Sparta took active role with Peloponnesians in war against Athens; invaded Boeotia, defeating Athens at the Battle of Tanagra; withdrew from Boeotia, leaving it to Athens.

c457 BC Defensive walls built between Athens and the Pireus.

446 BC Athenians captured Achaea, on the northern part of the Peloponnesus by this time.

454 BC Athenian forces routed in Egypt by the Persians.

454 BC Treasury of Delian League transferred to Athens; marked ascendancy of Athens in Greece.

451 BC Athens and Sparta agreed to five-year peace.

449 BC Peace of Callias ended hostilities with Persia.

448 BC Second Sacred War.

c448–c388 BC Great dramatist Aristophanes flourished; wrote *The Birds* and other plays.

447 BC Pericles began the construction of the magnificent Athenian acropolis.

447 BC Boeotia rebelled and withdrew from the Delian League.

446 BC Revolt by Euboea and Megara; Athens put down the rebellion after reaching an agreement with the Peloponnesian League, which had invaded Attica.

445 BC Thirty Years' Peace ended the first Peloponnesian War.

440–439 BC Athenians subjugated rebellious Samos.

436–338 BC Isocrates, orator and rhetorician, lived.

c434–c355 BC Xenophon, historian, lived.

431–404 BC Peloponnesian War (*q.v.*); Athens ultimately defeated by Sparta and never regained former power in Greece; Spartans briefly ascendant in Greece.

413 BC Great tragic poet Euripides wrote the play *Electra*.

408?–355? BC Eudoxus of Cnidus, astronomer and mathematician, lived; known for explaining motion of planets and calculating length of solar year.

404 BC Athenians forced by victorious Spartans to accept rule of Thirty Tyrants.

403 BC Athenians overthrew the Thirty Tyrants.

401 BC March of the Ten Thousand; Greek mercenaries fought in support of Cyrus against Persian King Artaxerxes.

4TH CENT. BC Apelles, court painter to Philip II and Alexander the Great, lived.

4TH CENT. BC Sculptor Lysippus lived; changed Greek style of rendering human body.

399 BC Socrates, renowned philosopher, condemned to poison himself at Athens.

396–314 BC Xenocrates, one of Plato's disciples, flourished.

395–387 BC Corinthian War was fought against Spartan domination by Athens and her allies, Corinth, Argos, and Thebes.

c387 BC Plato, great philosopher of ancient Greece, founded his Academy at Athens.

384?–322 BC Great orator Demosthenes flourished.

377 BC Naval League formed by Athens; warred against Sparta until 371.

c372–c287 BC Philosopher Theophrastus lived; succeeded Aristotle as head of Peripatetics.

371 BC Thebes defeated Sparta at the Battle of Leuctra.

370 BC Arcadian League formed by Epaminondas of Thebes; Thebes ascendant on Greek mainland until second Battle of Mantineia (362).

c370–c339 BC Great classical artist Praxiteles lived; known for his nude, *Aphrodite of Cnidus.*

?–365 BC Philosopher Antisthenes lived; founded school of Cynics.

359 BC Philip II became king of Macedon in northern Greece; in subsequent years subdued rebellious peoples of Macedon and then extended his control over Greece.

355–346 BC Third Sacred War; in the general war between Greek city-states, Philip gained control over a large part of the Greek mainland.

342?–291? BC Comic dramatist Menander lived.

339–338 BC Fourth Sacred War; by his victory at Chaeronea, Philip of Macedon gained control over all Greece; formed League of Corinth under Macedonian hegemony.

336 BC Alexander the Great became king of Macedon; put down revolt by Greek city-states, destroying Thebes (335).

c336–264 BC Zeno of Citium lived; established Stoicism as philosophical school.

335–322 BC Aristotle, one of the greatest thinkers of all time, opened the Lyceum school in Athens.

c335 BC Lyceum founded at Athens by Aristotle, one of the world's greatest philosophers.

334–324 BC Alexander's epic journey of conquest began with conquest of Persia, and soon after a vast, but short-lived, empire was created that stretched from India to Greece and Egypt; Macedonian conquests spread Greek culture, inaugurating the Hellenistic Age.

332 BC Alexandria founded in Egypt by Alexander; later became center of Hellenistic culture.

c330 BC Mythographer Euhemerus flourished; wrote *Sacred History.*

323 BC Alexander died; breakup of the empire came with Wars of the Diadochi (321–281).

323–322 BC Lamian War, unsuccessful attempt by Athens and other city-states to overthrow Macedonian rule.

321–281 BC Wars of the Diadochi (Alexander's generals); resulted in partition of the empire, creation of dynasties of Macedonian rulers in each, and spread of Hellenistic influence; Antigonus ruled in Macedonia, the Ptolemies in Egypt, and the Seleucids in Syria and Mesopotamia.

c320 BC Diogenes, Cynic philosopher, died.

306 BC Epicurean school of philosophy founded by Epicurus.

301 BC Battle of Ipsus; death of Antigonus; Diadochi, after some years of war, agreed to partition of the empire; Macedon fell to Cassander, son of Antipater.

300 BC Anatomist Herophilus flourished; known for his work on human anatomy.

c300 BC Protogenes, famous painter, lived.

c300 BC Mathematician Euclid flourished; famous for his contributions to geometry and study of mathematics.

c300 BC Voyages of Pytheas to British Isles and possibly Iceland.

c300 BC Stoicism established at Athens by Zeno.

3D CENT. BC Astronomer Aristarchus of Samos flourished; believed first to hold that the earth revolves around the sun.

3D CENT. BC Sculptor Chares lived; created Colossus of Rhodes, one of the Seven Wonders of the World.

3D CENT. BC Apollonius of Perga lived; noted for his mathematical work on conic sections.

3D CENT. BC Poet Theocritus lived; originated pastoral poetry.

290 BC Aetolian League formed in west part of Greek mainland.

287–212 BC Archimedes lived; discovered Archimedes's Principle of buoyancy and Archimedes's screw.

280–146 BC Second Achaean League; gradually gained control of the Peloponnesus.

279–276 BC Gauls (Celts) invaded northern Greece, ravaging Macedon.

276 BC Antigonus II Gonatus gained control of Macedon; founded Antigonid line of Macedonian kings and warred against Pyrrhus of Epirus.

c275–c195 Scientist Eratosthenes lived; first to measure earth's circumference and tilt of its axis.

c266–262 BC Chremonidean War fought by Athens and Sparta against Macedonian rule.

235–222 BC Cleomenes III reigned in Sparta; instituted much needed reforms and abolished ephors.

222 BC Antigonus III defeated Sparta and forced it to become an ally; Cleomenes driven out and ephors restored.

221–179 BC Philip V reigned as king of Macedon.

211–205 BC Macedonian king Philip V relatively successful in First Macedonian War against Rome.

203?–c120 BC Historian Polybius lived.

200–197 BC Second Macedonian War; Macedonia forced to pay Rome tribute.

2D CENT. BC Astronomer Hipparchus lived.

171–168 BC Third Macedonian War with Rome; Macedonia defeated and divided into four republics.

149–148 BC Fourth Macedonian War; Macedonia defeated and reduced to a Roman province.

146 BC Rome dissolved the Achaean League; Greece thereafter administered by Roman governor of Macedon.

146 BC–AD 395 Greece under Roman rule; economy generally declined though Hellenistic culture continued to flourish and influence Roman culture.

c135–c51 BC Stoic philosopher Poseidonius lived.

1ST CENT. BC Historian Dionysius of Halicarnassus lived; wrote 20-volume history of Rome, *Roman Antiquities.*

88–85 BC Greece invaded by Romans under Sulla after supporting Mithridates in the Mithridatic War; Greece ravaged.

65–8 BC Great lyric poet Horace lived; known for *Satires* and *Ars Poetica.*

63 BC–AFTER AD 21 Geographer Strabo lived; wrote *Geographica.*

1ST CENT. AD Saint Dionysius the Areopagite flourished; apostle Paul converted him to Christianity.

1ST CENT. AD Hero of Alexandria invented crude steam engine, the *aeolipile.*

AD 46?–c120 Biographer and essayist Plutarch lived; wrote biography *Parallel Lives.*

AD 55?–135? Epictetus, Stoic philosopher, lived.

AD 67 Nero granted Greece independence; move rescinded by his successors.

2D CENT. Satirist Lucian lived; wrote *Dialogues of the Gods,* and *Dialogues of the Dead.*

AD 117–138 Revival in Greece fostered by Roman emperor Hadrian, who rebuilt many Greek cities.

AD c130–c200 Physician Galen flourished; his works remained medical authority into medieval times.

AD 174 Geographer Pausanias flourished; noted for *Descriptions of Greece.*

AD c213–273 Philosopher Longinus lived.

AD c217 Philostratus, sophist, flourished; wrote *Life of Apollonius.*

AD c233–304 Porphyry, Neoplatonic philosopher, lived; wrote *Adversus Christianos.*

AD 267–268 Goths invaded Greece; repulsed by Romans.

AD 370 Saint Basil became bishop of Ceasarea.

AD c393 Olympic Games abolished by the Romans.

AD 395 Roman Empire permanently divided into Western and Eastern (Byzantine) empires.

AD 395–1204 Greece under Byzantine control; general decline of Greece.

AD 395–396 Greece ravaged in new invasions by Goths.

AD 398–403 Saint J. Chrysostom served as archbishop of Constantinople.

529 Nine-hundred-year-old Greek Academy closed by Justinian I.

6TH–8TH CENTS. Slavs invaded northern regions of Greece.

1204 Byzantine Empire conquered by Christians on Fourth Crusade; Latin Empire of Constantinople created; Greece divided into feudal duchies, including French-controlled duchy of Athens; Venetians took control of islands and some Greek coastal regions.

1261–1453 Byzantines reestablished their empire; reconquered part of Greece; duchy of Athens and other territories remained under European control.

1456–1829 Ottoman Turks controlled Greece; their rule over the territory was challenged variously in wars with Venice, Austria, and Russia; Greece in period of decline.

1566 Ottomans captured island of Chios from Genoa.

1571 Battle of Lepanto; European Christians defeated Ottoman fleet in battle for Cyprus.

1669 Ottomans captured Crete from Venice.

1718 Treaty of Passarowitz, ending Austro-Turkish War and war with Venice; Ottoman control of Greece recognized in exchange for other territories.

1769 Unsuccessful revolt against Ottoman rule led by Russian Count Orlov.

1797 Ottomans took Ionian islands from Venice.

1815 Friendly Association, secret society founded by Greek nationalists.

1821 Abortive revolt led by the Alexander Ypsilanti; sparked general uprising.

1821–32 War of Greek Independence fought led to Greek independence from Ottoman Empire.

1824–26 Muhammad Ali, Ottoman viceroy of Egypt, invaded Greece to reestablish Ottoman control.

1827 European powers became involved in conflict over Greek independence; Russians subsequently waged Russo-Turkish War (1828–29).

1829 Treaty of Adrianople; treaty ended Russo-Turkish War and Ottomans relinquished control of Greece.

1830 London Protocol (Feb. 3); Europeans established Greece as a kingdom, much smaller than that sought by nationalists.

1831 Assassination of Greek President J. Kapodistrias.

1832 Otto I named king by London Conference; instituted autocratic and unpopular rule; financial problems of new kingdom increased in subsequent years and led to increasing involvement by European powers.

1843 Otto forced to grant constitution; bicameral legislature set up.

1850 British blockaded coast in Don Pacifico Affair.

1862 Otto I deposed.

1863–1913 George I reigned.

1864 New constitution adopted by King George I.

1897 Greco-Turkish War fought (Apr.–May) with Ottoman Turks over control of Crete; Greece, defeated in several engagements, accepted an armistice.

1912–13 Balkan Wars; Greece participated in the wars and gained much of Macedonia and Thrace, former Ottoman domains.

1913 Crete united with Greece.

1913–17 Constantine I reigned.

1914–18 WW I; Greece became a battleground in the Salonica campaign; gained additional territories at end of war.

1917 Constantine refused to support Allies in WW I; was forced to abdicate.

1917–20 Alexander reigned.

1920–22 Constantine I restored to Greek throne.

1921–22 Greco-Turkish War fought with Turkey after Greek invasion of Anatolia; Kemal Atatürk drove the Greeks from Anatolia.

1922–23 George II reigned; forced to abdicate.

1923 Greek republic proclaimed.

1934 Greece joined Balkan Entente, reversing former anti-Turkish policy.

1935 Monarchy reinstated in Greece after years of economic problems and political chaos.

1935–41 George II reigned after restoration of the monarchy.

1936–41 J. Metaxas established as dictator with support of king.

1939–45 WW II; Italian invasion from Albania repulsed (1939–40); occupied by Nazi Germans (1941–44), Greece fell into economic ruin; beginning of civil war between pro-royalists and pro-Communist guerrilla groups; British restored Greek government (1944).

1944–49 Greek Civil War; British and American aid helped Greek government put down Communist insurrection.

1946–47 George II restored to the throne.

1947–64 Paul I reigned as king, succeeding after George died.

1947 Truman Doctrine announced by US president H. Truman to provide aid against Communists in continuing Greek Civil War.

1951 New constitution adopted; marked return to political stability.

1951 Greece joined NATO.

1955–63 National Radical Union party in power under Constantine Karamanlis; period marked by economic recovery and rising tensions over Cyprus.

1964–73 Constantine II reigned; political unrest mounted during his reign.

1967 Military coup (Apr. 21) by right-wing military officers following a succession of political crises; repressive regime instituted, ostensibly to prevent Communist takeover.

1967 Constantine left Greece; military officer made regent.

1968 New constitution adopted; increased powers of prime minister at the expense of the monarchy.

1970 Relaxation of government controls imposed in 1967; some constitutional rights restored.

1973 Unsuccessful coup by navy (May).

1973 Greece proclaimed a republic (June 1); monarchy abolished.

1973 Georgios Papadopoulos made first president of new Greek republic.

1973–74 President Phaidon Gizikis in office following a bloodless coup (Nov. 25).

1974 Military junta resigned (July 23) after Turkey invaded Cyprus; civilian government to be formed.

1974–81 Prime Minister C. Karamanlis in office after being reinstated; new constitution adopted.

1974 Leaders of the 1967 coup, including ex–prime minister G. Papadopoulos, exiled.

1974 Radical Socialist party, Panhellenic Socialist Movement (Pasok), formed.

1974 Greece withdrew from NATO to protest Turkish invasion of Cyprus.

1975 Widely known Greek shipping magnate, Aristotle Onassis, died.

1975–80 Constantine Tsatsos in office as president.

1980–85 C. Karamanlis, former prime minister and New Democratic party candidate, in office as president.

1980–81 New Democratic party candidate George Rallis in office as prime minister; his administration marked by worsening economy, with rising inflation and unemployment.

1980 Greece rejoined NATO.

1981 Greece admitted to Common Market (Jan.).

1981–89 Andreas Papandreou, leader of the radical Panhellenic Socialist Movement (Pasok), in office as prime minister; heading first Socialist government in Greek history, he promised to "socialize" the economy but was restrained by a worsening economic downturn; his administration was marked by an increase in terrorism, by strained relations with Turkey and the US, and by major scandals.

1981 Palestine Liberation Organization granted full diplomatic status.

1981 Government ended political censorship and simplified accent system in written Greek language.

1982 Government imposed wage freeze to combat 22 percent inflation rate; created state-owned drug firm.

1982 New laws allow civil marriages and divorce by consent, and to end the dowry system; Communists who fled Greece during 1946–49 civil war allowed to return.

1983 Government agreed to extend leases on US military bases in Greece to 1988.

1983 Greeks outraged by creation of independent Turkish Republic of North Cyprus (Nov. 15).

1983 US naval attaché murdered by left-wing terrorists (Nov.).

1985– Christos Sartzetakis, Socialist Pasok candidate, in office as president.

1985 Prime Minister Papandreou survived serious election challenge (June); election charac-

terized as "confrontation between two worlds," in which Papandreou's Socialist slate was returned to office, despite worsening economy.

1985 TWA airliner out of Athens hijacked by terrorists (June).

1985 Papandreou introduced new, tougher austerity program aimed at reducing inflation, budget deficits, and trade deficits (Oct.); sparked widespread strikes by workers and professionals in 1986–87.

1986 Brief border clash between Greek and Turkish forces (Dec.).

1987 Technical state of war with Albania, dating from 1940, ended.

1987 Government nationalized church property; Greek Orthodox church excommunicated seven government leaders.

1988 "No war agreement" acceded to by both Greek and Turkish governments (Jan. 31); established hotline and promised annual meetings to discuss differences.

1988 US naval attaché murdered by November 17 terrorist group (June 28); terrorists killed 11 and wounded 52 in terrorist hijacking (July 11).

1988 Financial scandal, called worst ever in Greek history, began unfolding (Oct.); Papandreou administration accused of delaying investigation of over $200 million embezzlement at Bank of Creteus; scandal widened to include wrongdoing in government-run arms industry.

1989 Socialist Pasok party alleged to have received part of money embezzled from Bank of Cyprus.

1989 Tzannis Tzannetakis, New Democracy candidate, in office as prime minister; formed (June) short-lived caretaker coalition government with Communists during investigation of scandals; investigators recommended indictment of Papandreou and five other ministers.

1989 Xenophon Zolotas in office as prime minister (from Nov.), following new national elections; formed new coalition government.

1990– C. Karamanlis, New Democracy candidate, in office as president, following Apr. elections.

1990 Konstantinos Mitsotakis, New Democracy candidate, in office as prime minister; introduced new austerity program, ending wage indexing, and began planning for privatization of failing state-run industries.

1991 Trial of Papandreou and other Pasok ministers began (Mar.); Papandreou cleared but two ex-ministers were convicted (1992).

1991 Terrorist bombings, shootings, and rocket attacks occurred throughout the year.

1992 Maastricht Treaty on European Unity approved (July).

Greece, Seven Wise Men of *See* **Seven Wise Men of Greece.**

Greek Civil War Civil war (1944–49) between Communist and rightist factions in Greece. Following the withdrawal of Nazi occupation forces (fall, 1944), Communist guerrillas attacked both rightist guerrilla forces and the British occupation army. By the Varkizoi Agreement (Jan. 14, 1945), a short-lived government was established. Government instability and widespread unrest, however, led to new fighting (May, 1946). The Communist faction was finally defeated, with American and British aid, by Oct., 1949.

Greek fire Flammable substance used by the Byzantines in warfare from the 7th cent. This secret mixture ignited on contact with water and was used effectively against Arab fleets in naval battles.

Greek Independence, War of The Greek revolt (1821–32) against the Ottoman Empire. After centuries of Turkish domination, Greeks in the Peloponnesus rebelled (Mar. 25, 1821) and proclaimed Greek independence (Jan., 1822). The revolt spread, attracting popular support in Europe and such volunteers as Lord G. Byron, and the Turks were forced to seek aid from Egypt (1824). The Egyptians and Turks soon occupied much of the southern Peloponnesus, but their advance was slowed by intervention of European powers: first at the Battle of Navarino (Oct., 1827), in which the Egyptian naval forces were routed; then by the outbreak of the Russo-Turkish War (1828–29). The London Conference (1830–31) of European powers set the final terms of Greek independence in the London Protocol (Feb. 3), and Otto I was designated king (1832) by the Treaty of London. The Ottoman Turks recognized the independent kingdom of Greece by the Treaty of Constantinople (1832).

Greek Project Secret plan formulated (1782) by Russia's Catherine the Great for the conquest and dismemberment of the Ottoman Empire. Part of the plan called for creation of a new kingdom of Dacia out of Ottoman domains. The plan won Austrian approval but was never implemented.

Greeley, Horace 1811–72. Celebrated American newspaper editor. He founded the *New York Tribune* (1841) and wielded great influence as its editor. After 1850 he became an outspoken critic of slavery. Following the American Civil War he was an unsuccessful opponent of U. Grant in the 1872 presidential elections. He is often remembered for the expression "Go west, young man" and as an advocate of a variety of reforms.

Green, Duff 1791–1875. American journalist. As owner of the *United Telegraph,* a Washington, D.C., newspaper, he backed A. Jackson for president (1828) and became a member of the Kitchen Cabinet. He later broke with Jackson and supported H. Clay for president (1832).

Green, Hetty 1835–1916. American financier. Green inherited $10 million and increased it to $100 million through astute management. She was considered the wealthiest woman in the world.

greenback Nickname for legal-tender notes issued by the US government during the American Civil War (1861–65). It was not backed by gold and contributed to inflation during the war years. Greenbacks were backed by gold reserves after 1879. (*See also* Greenback party.)

Greenback party US political party (1874–88) made up largely of farmers who opposed a return to the gold standard. Greenbackers feared that discontinuation of legal-tender notes (greenbacks) and resumption of the gold standard would mean deflation and financial hardship. The party formed after the Panic of 1873 and ran presidential candidates in 1876, 1880, and 1884, though only once polled more than a million votes. With resumption of the gold standard (1879), Greenbackers joined the Free Silver movement and the party declined rapidly.

Greene, Graham 1902–91. English novelist and playwright. He is the author of both thrillers and more serious novels, of which *Orient Express* and *The Power and the Glory* are examples.

Greene, Nathanael 1742–86. American general in the American Revolution. A strategist considered by many to be second only to G. Washington, he figured in the battles at Trenton (1775), Brandywine (1777), and Germantown (1777).

From 1780, he was commander in the south. After reorganizing the army there, he led it to victory in the Carolina Campaign.

Greene, Robert 1558?–92. English dramatist, a contemporary of Shakespeare, who wrote a variety of plays, including the comic romance *Friar Bacon and Friar Bungay.*

Greenland (Kalaallit Nunaat) World's largest island, located in northeastern North America and nominally controlled by the Danish government. The population is (1989 est.) 55,400, the capital is Nuuk, and fish is the main export. Greenland was discovered (c982) and colonized by the Norseman Eric the Red. Later, his son Leif Ericsson probably visited North America (Vinland) while sailing to Greenland (c1000). Between the 12th and 16th cents., a European colony flourished there and became a Catholic bishopric (c1100). The colony subsequently declined and colonists merged with the Eskimo (Inuit) population. Greenland was recolonized from 1721 by the Norwegians and Danes. Denmark got possession of the colony at the Congress of Vienna (1815) and subsequently took greater interest in developing the island. The US established bases there during WW II (some still remain) and in 1953 Greenland was given representation in the Danish parliament. Greenland subsequently won the right of home rule (May 1, 1979) and organized its own parliament.

Green Mountain Boys American Colonial militia unit first organized by E. Allen (1770) to protect settlers in the Green Mountains (now Vermont) from speculators who held British grants to their land. From 1775 on, they figured in the Revolution. They captured Ticonderoga (1775) and won the Battle of Bennington (1777).

Greens, Blues and *See* **Blues and Greens.**

Green Standard, Army of the *See* **Army of the Green Standard.**

Gregorian calendar Reformed calendar, instituted by Pope Gregory XIII (Oct., 1582). A reformation of the Julian calendar, it established the 365-day year with a leap year of 366. Its effective date of Oct. 5, 1582, according to the Old Style (Julian), thus became Oct. 15, 1582, by the New Style.

Gregorian church *See* **Armenian church.**

Gregorian Reform Term applied to the program of Roman Catholic religious reform advanced by Pope Gregory VII. The reforms notably included attempts to halt lay investiture, the granting of ecclesiastical authority by temporal rulers, and to generally improve clerical morality. Gregory's policies brought him into fierce conflict with Holy Roman Emperor Henry IV.

Gregory I, Saint (Gregory the Great) c540–604. Italian-born pope (590–604), successor to Pelagius II. A Doctor of the Church, he was a celebrated church administrator, noted for his reforms in both church organization and liturgy. He promoted spiritual supremacy of the pope, sent missionaries to southern Britain (597), and encouraged the spread of monasticism. The Gregorian chant is traditionally ascribed to him.

Gregory VII, Saint (*orig.* Hildebrand) c1020–1085. Italian-born pope (1073–85), successor to Alexander II and one of the great church reformers. In the face of powerful opposition, Gregory undertook reforms to end widespread church corruption. In 1073 he called reform synods, condemned clerical marriage and simony, and appointed legates to oversee enforcement of church laws. His battle for reform focused on lay investiture, which he banned in 1075 and which set German emperor Henry IV against him. He twice excommunicated Henry. In retaliation, Henry appointed antipope Clement III, attacked Rome (1081–83), and forced Gregory to retreat to Salerno (where he died).

Gregory IX (Segni, Ugolino di) 1147?–1241. Italian-born pope (1227–41), successor to Honorius III. A pope of forceful disposition, he twice excommunicated Holy Roman Emperor Frederick II (1227, 1239), organized the office of the Inquisition (1233), and ordered the collection of the *Decretals,* which furthered codification of canon law.

Gregory XI (Beaufort, Pierre Roger de) 1330–78. French-born pope (1370–78), successor to Urban V. The last of the French popes, he ended the Babylonian Captivity by moving the papacy from Avignon to Rome (1377).

Gregory XII (Correr, Angelo) c1327–1417. Venetian-born pope (1406–15) during the Great Schism in the Western church, successor to Innocent VII. He was elected to oppose antipope Benedict XIII and was deposed at the Council of Pisa (1409). He resisted the deposition until after the Council of Constance (1415) was convened and Martin V was elected pope.

Gregory XIII (Buoncompagni, Ugo) 1502–85. Italian-born pope (1572–85), successor to Saint

Pius V. He reformed the Julian calendar, establishing the modern Gregorian calendar (*q.v.*) in its place, and promoted education of the clergy.

Gregory XVI (Capellari, Bartolomeo Alberto) 1765–1846. Italian-born pope (1831–46), successor to Pius VIII. He was a conservative and proponent of Ultramontanism. He put down a rebellion by the Carbonari (1832) within the Papal States.

Gregory Nazianzus, Saint (Gregory Theologus) AD c329?–389. Cappadocian theologian and bishop. One of the four fathers of the Eastern church, he is remembered for his discourses on the Holy Trinity.

Gregory of Nyssa, Saint *d.* AD 394. Cappadocian theologian and bishop. One of the four Fathers of the Eastern church, he was a leading proponent of orthodoxy at the first Council of Constantinople (AD 381).

Gregory of Tours, Saint 538?–93. French historian and bishop. He wrote the *History of the Franks* (c575–91), still regarded as an important historical resource.

Gregory the Great *See* **Gregory I, Saint.**

Gregory Theologus *See* **Gregory Nazianzus, Saint.**

Grenada Island nation located just north of the Venezuelan coast. The Western Hemisphere's smallest independent state, Grenada's population is just 84,000 and its capital is St. George's. Sighted by C. Columbus (1498), Grenada was first settled by the French in 1650. The British took control of the island in 1762 (affirmed in the 1783 Treaty of Paris) and established it as a colony. Grenada achieved full independence as a British Commonwealth nation on Feb. 7, 1974. Left-wing leader Maurice Bishop came to power in 1979 following a bloodless coup. Though Grenada remained within the Commonwealth, Bishop soon established ties with Cuba and the Soviet Union. Bishop himself was overthrown and executed (along with five others on Oct. 19, 1983) by the People's Revolutionary Army, which established a more repressive regime. The Organization of Eastern Caribbean States asked the US for help in intervening, however, and soon after 1,900 US troops landed on Grenada (Oct. 25), aided by 300 troops from other Caribbean nations. After several days of fighting, US soldiers prevailed and forced the Cubans on Grenada to return home. The peace-keeping force withdrew gradually (1983–85) and a cen-

trist coalition government took office following elections in 1984.

Grenville, George 1712–70. British statesman. As chief minister (1763–65) under King George III he put through the Revenue Act of 1764 and the Stamp Act of 1765, both of which served to stir up sentiment for rebellion in the American colonies.

Grenville, George Nugent Temple, 1st marquess Buckingham 1753–1813. British statesman, son of G. Grenville. He was lord lieutenant of Ireland (1782–83, 1887–89).

Grenville, Sir Richard 1541?–91. Celebrated English naval hero. His ships carried the first colonists to Roanoke Colony (1585), but he is best remembered as captain of the *Revenge.* During an abortive raid on Spanish treasure ships off the Azores, the *Revenge* battled against 15 Spanish warships for a full day before being taken. Grenville died of wounds after the battle.

Grenville, William Wyndham, baron 1759–1834. British statesman, a son of G. Grenville (1712–70). A leading advocate of Catholic Emancipation, he organized the coalition government known as the Ministry of All Talents (1806–07). British slave trade was abolished under this ministry (1807).

Grévy, Paul Jules 1807–91. French statesman and president (1879–87) during the Third Republic, successor to M. Macmahon. He was forced to resign because of a scandal that broke shortly after his election to a second term.

Grey, Albert Henry George, 4th earl 1851–1917. British colonial administrator. He was administrator of Rhodesia (1896–97) and governor general of Canada (1904–11).

Grey, Charles, 2d earl 1764–1845. British statesman. He was a Whig party leader in the House of Commons and prime minister (1830–34). He obtained passage of the Reform Bill of 1832.

Grey, Sir George *See* **Bay of Islands War.**

Grey, Lady Jane 1537–54. English queen for nine days (1553), successor to Edward VI. Soon after being crowned, she acceded to Mary I's claim to the throne and was later sentenced for treason. She was executed after her father, H. Grey, duke of Suffolk, took part in Sir T. Wyatt's rebellion.

Grey, Zane 1875–1939. American author who wrote many popular western novels, including *Riders of the Purple Sage.*

Grey of Fallodon, Edward Grey, 1st viscount 1862–1933. British statesman. A liberal member of Parliament (1885–1916), he served as foreign secretary (1905–16) and helped guide Britain through the early phase of WW I. He arranged completion of the Triple Alliance (1907) and the Treaty of London (1915).

Grieg, Edvard Hagerup 1843–1907. Norwegian composer who created a distinctive national style.

Grierson, John 1898–1972. British film producer, noted as a leading figure in British documentary films.

Griffenfeld, Peder Schumacher, count 1635–99. Danish statesman. He wrote the King's Law (1665), which justified Denmark's absolute monarchy, and under Christian V he became chancellor of Denmark (1673–76).

Griffith, Arthur 1872–1922. Irish statesman and president of the Irish Republic (1922). He founded the Sinn Fein (1902) and was a leader in negotiations to establish the Irish Free State (1921).

Griffith, D.W. (David Lewelyn Wark) 1875–1948. American movie director, a pioneer in the field. He introduced many new techniques and was a founder of United Artists (1919). *The Birth of a Nation* and *Intolerance* are among his most important films.

Grillparzer, Franz 1791–1872. Austrian dramatist and poet, sometimes called Austria's greatest playwright. *The Ancestress* and *A Dream Is Life* are among his successful plays.

Grimké, Sarah Moore and Angelina Emily 1792–1873, 1805–79. American abolitionists and advocates of women's rights. The daughters of a Southern slaveholder, they first spoke out against slavery in 1835 and for women's rights in 1838. They are sometimes regarded as the first to raise the issue of women's rights in America.

Grimm, Jakob and Wilhelm 1785–1863, 1786–1859. German folklorists and philologists. Though they did much original work in the study of the Germanic languages and folklore, they are best known for their collection of tales, *Grimm's Fairy Tales.*

Grimoard, Guillaume de *See* **Urban V.**

Grivas, Georgios Theodoros 1898–1974. Greek Cypriot general. Grivas headed EOKA, which led the struggle for freedom from Britain. However, he opposed independence and sought union with Greece. He fled Cyprus when his troops killed several Turkish Cypriots (1967).

Groiler de Servières, Jean, vicomte d'Aguisy 1479–1565. French bibliophile. He collected what became a famous library of 3,000 specially bound books. The collection was finally broken up in 1675.

Gromyko, Andrei Andreyevich 1909–89. Soviet foreign minister (1957–85) and member of Soviet Central Committee (1956–89). He became a diplomat (1939) following Stalin's purges and was appointed ambassador to the US (1943–46). In 1946 Gromyko was appointed deputy foreign minister and delegate to the UN. As foreign minister, he earned a reputation as a skilled negotiator and advanced Soviet Cold War policies against Western powers. During the 1970s he played an important part in the Nixon-Brezhnev summit talks. Under M. Gorbachev, he served as president of the Supreme Soviet (1985–88), a prestigious position with little power. Following purges of the Politburo, he resigned the presidency (1988) and was removed from the Central Committee (1989).

Groote, Gerhard (Groot, ~) 1340–84. Dutch religious reformer and preacher who opposed scholastic theologians and founded the Roman Catholic order Brethren of the Common Life (c1374).

Gropius, Walter 1883–1969. German-American architect, a famous exponent of modern architectural style and founder of the Bauhaus school (*q.v.*).

Grosseteste, Robert c1175–1253. English theologian and scholar. A teacher at Oxford (R. Bacon was a student of his) and later its rector, he founded the Oxford Franciscan school and helped make the university an influential center of scholarship. He was a prolific writer on scholarly subjects, and as bishop of Lincoln (1235–53) he both defended church privileges against Henry III and criticized corruption within the Curia. Grosseteste translated into Latin (and wrote commentaries on) many important Greek and Arabic writings on science and philosophy, thus introducing such seminal works as Aristotle's *Ethics* into the Christian world and helping lay the foundation for scholasticism (*q.v*).

Grote, George 1794–1871. English historian. His 12-volume *History of Greece* is considered a classic.

Grotefend, Georg Friedrich 1775–1853. German philologist who became famous for deciphering the Persian cuneiform script.

Grotius, Hugo 1583–1645. Dutch jurist. He wrote *On the Laws of War and Peace* (1625), generally considered to be the foundation of international law. In it he contends that nations, as well as individuals, are subject to natural law.

Grouchy, Emmanuel, marquis de 1766–1847. French general. Sometimes said to be responsible for Napoleon's defeat at Waterloo (1815), he failed to keep the main Prussian force from reaching Waterloo.

Groves, Leslie R. *See* **Manhattan Project.**

Gruen, David *See* **Ben-Gurion, David.**

Grundtvig, Nikolai Frederik Severin 1783–1872. Danish educator, theologian, and writer. He founded the Danish Folk High School (1844), a system of adult education that briefly became popular in European countries.

Grünewald, Mathias (*pseud. of* Neithart, Mathias Gothardt) *fl.* 1500–30. German artist, sometimes considered the greatest of the German Gothic painters. The Isenheim altarpiece is among his greatest works.

Guadalajara, Battle of Battle (Mar., 1937) during the Spanish Civil War (1936–39). Spanish Nationalists with a large contingent of allied Italian troops (some 50,000 soldiers in all) began a drive toward Guadalajara in an effort to surround nearby Republican-held Madrid. In subsequent fighting (Mar. 15–18), the Italians were routed by Spanish Republican armies and the Nationalist offensive was halted.

Guadalcanal, Battle of First major Allied counteroffensive (Aug., 1942–Feb., 1943) against the Japanese during WW II. The battle, fought by both land and sea forces, began with the landing of some 16,000 US marines (Aug. 7, 1942) and establishment of a beachhead on the island of Guadalcanal, in the Solomon Islands. Bloody fighting on the island at times saw the marines outnumbered 10 to 1, as the Japanese poured reinforcements into the fighting. The naval battles, fought to stem the tide of these reinforcements, continued from Aug. 9 to Nov. 30, when the Allies established naval supremacy. The battle for Guadalcanal ended when the Japanese evacuated some 14,000 troops from the island (Feb. 7–9). Japanese losses were 23,000 dead or missing and 1,000 captured. US losses were 1,600 killed and many thousands more, casualties of battle and disease.

Guadalupe Hidalgo, Treaty of Treaty concluded (Feb. 2, 1848) between the US and Mexico ending the Mexican War (1846–48). According to the treaty, signed at the Mexican town of Guadalupe Hidalgo, the US paid $15 million in return for what was then roughly half of Mexico. It set the US boundary at the Rio Grande and included what are now Texas, California, Arizona, New Mexico, Nevada, Utah, and western Colorado. In ratifying the treaty (1848), the Senate rejected a move to add the Wilmot Proviso (*q.v.*) and thereby fueled the growing debate over the extension of slavery.

Guadalupe Victoria (*b.* Fernández, Manuel Félix) 1786?–1843. Mexican general, the first president of Mexico (1824–29). He supported the government of A. de Iturbide and the Plan of Iguala (1821), by which Mexico became independent, but in 1823 joined A. de Santa Anna's revolt against Iturbide.

Guangxu (Kwang Hsu) 1872–1908. Emperor of China (1875–1908), successor to his aunt, Cixi. After assuming authority (1889), he issued several edicts to institute reform in China during the "hundred days of reform." His aunt soon resumed the regency, ending his rule.

Guangzhou (Canton) Chinese port city, now an important trading and industrial center. The city became part of the Chinese Empire in the 3d cent. AD and the first port opened to European trade (16th cent.). It remained China's only port of foreign trade until 1842. It was the seat of the nationalist rebellion (1911) and was occupied by the Japanese (1938–45) in WW II. Guangzhou was seized (1949) by the Communists, who undertook the modernization and development of the city.

Guarantees, Law of Italian law (May 13, 1871) which attempted to establish the relationship between the Italian government and the papacy. It guaranteed religious and diplomatic freedom to the papacy, and established an annual income for the pope, but did not restore papal authority to the territories that had been incorporated into Italy. Pope Pius IX did not accept it, and relations between Italy and the papacy were not formalized until the promulgation of the Lateran Treaty of 1929.

Guatemala (Republic of Guatemala) Independent state located in western Central America on the Pacific coast. The population is 9,340,000 and the capital is Guatemala City. Guatemala was the home of the ancient Mayan-Quiché civilization, which was conquered by Spain (1523–

24). Since its independence in 1821, Guatemala has had a history marked by military dictatorships, coups, border warfare, poverty, and natural disasters. Key events in Guatemala's history include:

1523–24 P. de Alvarado conquered region during military expedition from what is now Mexico; captaincy general of Guatemala established, including most of Central America.

1821 Guatemala declared independence from Spain (Sept. 15).

1821–23 A. de Iturbide made Guatemala part of his Mexican Empire.

1823 Guatemala joined Central American Federation.

1838 R. Carrera declared independence from Central American Federation.

1840–65 R. Carrera reigned as dictator.

1859 Treaty set boundary with British Honduras, but Guatemala later disputed terms and laid claim to that territory.

1870s Commercial coffee production began.

1873–85 Justo Rufino Barrios became president; invaded El Salvador to reestablish Central American Federation; was killed.

1898–1920 Manuel Estrada Cabrera reigned as dictator.

1906 Gen. Manuel Barillas revolted against Cabrera; embroiled most of Central America in warfare; armistice arranged by T. Roosevelt and P. Díaz.

1920 Revolution broke out, forcing Cabrera's resignation; unrest continued over next decade.

1931–44 Gen. Jorge Ubico ruled as dictator; ruled repressively, but ended peonage of Indians and campaigned successfully against corruption.

1945–51 Leftist Dr. Juan José Arévalo in office as president; implemented land and labor reform.

1945 Guatemala renewed its long-standing claims to British Honduras.

1951–54 Jacobo Arbenz Guzmán in office; expropriated large estates, including those of the United Fruit Company.

1954–57 Col. Carlos Castillos Armas in office after leading revolt with secret US help; Arbenz fled to Cuba.

1957 Castillo assassinated; series of coups followed in 1960s.

1960–61 Cuban exiles, to be used later at Bay of Pigs, trained in Guatemala.

1967 Leftist and rightist factions instituted campaign of terrorist violence.

1968 US Ambassador John Gordon Mein killed.

1970–74 Conservative Col. Carlos Araña Osorio in office as president; imposed state of siege to deal with terrorists.

1974–78 Gen. Kjell Laugerud García in office as president.

1976 Almost 100,000 killed or injured in major earthquake (Feb. 4).

1977 Britain offered independence to Belize (formerly British Honduras); Guatemala threatened invasion to make good its claim to this territory in long dispute over 1859 treaty.

1978–82 Gen. Fernando Romeo Lucas García in office as president; instituted corrupt and brutal regime; US military aid halted (1978).

1979 Unofficial estimate put death toll this year from terrorism and counterterrorism at 3,200.

1981 US military aid resumed; warfare with left-wing guerrillas and rightwing "death squads" killing estimated 600 per month.

1981 Guatemala agreed to recognize independent Belize and negotiate territorial claims.

1982–83 Gen. José Efraín Ríos Montt in power following bloodless military coup (Mar. 23); Montt began brutal war against leftist Indian guerrillas; about 2,600 killed in government counterterror campaign.

1983 Pope John Paul II, on visit to Guatemala, urged Indians to stand up for their rights non-violently (Mar.).

1983 Montt overthrown in military coup by the defense minister (Aug. 8).

1983–86 Gen. Oscar Humberto Mejia Victores, the coup leader, in power as head of state; death squad killings continued.

1984 Elections held for Constituent Assembly (July 1); work began on new constitution, completed by June 1985.

1986 Outgoing military government, replaced by first elected civilian president in 16 years, pardoned all abuses by military since 1982.

1986 Vinicio Cerezo Arévalo, a Christian Democrat, in office as president; arrested 115 from secret police staff (Feb.); replaced the chief of police; began peace negotiations (1987) with Guatemalan National Revolutionary Unity (URNG), which represented the leading guerrilla groups.

1987 Right-wing death squads resumed killings.

1987 Central American summit in Guatemala approved the Arias Plan for peace in Central America (June 25–26); set deadlines for halt in all wars, for end to aid to rebel groups, for instituting general amnesty, and for start of negotiations.

1988 Failed coup attempt by military (May 11).

1989 Failed military coup by opponents of negotiated settlement with guerrillas (May 9).

1990 UN-mediated preliminary agreement signed by government reconciliation commission and URNG (June 1).

1990 Troops shot into crowd of 1,500 at Santiago de Atitlán (Dec. 2); 11 people killed.

1991– Jorge Serrano Elías, a businessman and member of Solidarity Action Movement, in office as president, following elections.

1991 First charges of human rights violations lodged against military personnel (Aug.).

1991 Government granted full diplomatic recognition to Belize.

Guayaquil Conference Strategy meeting (July 26–27, 1822) between leaders of the South American independence movement. S. Bolívar and J. San Martín met at this Ecuadorian coastal city to discuss joining forces against Spain. They failed to reach an agreement and Bolívar continued to fight alone.

Guelphs and Ghibellines Two opposing political factions prominent during the struggle for control of northern and central Italy (13th–15th cents.). The Guelphs supported the pope and the Ghibellines the German Holy Roman Emperors. The rivalry led to numerous local wars during this period and in Florence a long civil war that ended (1266) with the expulsion of the Ghibellines. By the 14th cent., after the power of Holy Roman Emperors declined in Italy and the papacy was removed to France, the rivalry was important only in local political struggles. (*See also* Welf.)

Guérande, Treaty of *See* **Breton Succession, War of the.**

Guèrin, Camille *See* **Calmette, Albert Léon Charles.**

Guerrero, Vicente 1783?–1831. Mexican revolutionary and president (1829). From 1810 he led revolutionary forces and became a celebrated guerrilla fighter. After 1822, he joined forces with A. Santa Anna in toppling A. de Iturbide and became vice-president under Guadalupe Victoria. Guerrero was overthrown (1829) by his vice-president, Anastasio Bustamente.

Gueux Dutch revolutionaries. In 1566, Dutch and Flemish nationals petitioned (1566) the ruling Spanish government for redress of grievances by the Compromise of Breda (*q.v.*), but were dismissed as "ces gueux" (beggars). Adopting the name "Gueux" as a badge of pride, they organized under William the Silent and successfully harassed Spanish shipping, notably at the siege of Leiden (1574).

Guevara, Che (Guevara de la Serna, Ernesto) 1928–67. Argentinian-born Communist revolutionary leader. An important figure in F. Castro's Cuban revolution (1959), he became a renowned example for revolutionary movements in Latin America. He was captured and killed while leading a guerrilla war in Bolivia (1966–67).

Guevara de la Serna, Ernesto *See* **Guevara, Che.**

Guggenheim, Simon 1867–1941. American philanthropist and US senator from Colorado (1907–13). He founded the John Simon Guggenheim Memorial Foundation (1925), which provides fellowships in the arts.

Guibert of Ravenna (Clement III) *d.* 1100. Italian antipope (1080–1100) to Gregory VII. He was enthroned when Henry IV captured Rome (1084) and in turn crowned Henry Holy Roman Emperor.

Guicciardini, Francesco 1483–1540. Italian historian and statesman. He wrote *Storia d'Italia,* which is considered the most important history written in the 16th cent.

Guido Aretinus *See* **Guido d'Arezzo.**

Guido d'Arezzo (~ Aretinus) c990–1050. Italian Benedictine monk who made important modifications in the system of musical notation. He is said to have developed the musical staff.

Guido of Vienne *See* **Calixtus II.**

guilds (gilds) Medieval European merchant and craft associations. Guilds originated in Europe (11th cent.) as merchants' associations, formed to protect traveling merchants from bandits. Merchants' guilds became powerful, both economically and politically (12th–13th cents.). They were completely displaced, however, by the rise of the craft guilds and disappeared by the 14th cent. The craft guilds, composed of workers in a particular craft, declined in the 15th cent. as a result of internal disputes and other problems. They disappeared with the rise of capitalism (16th–17th cents.).

guild socialism Movement, centered in Britain, advocating state-owned, worker-controlled industry. It arose briefly in Britain during the early 20th cent. and called for creation of national guilds. Through these guilds, workers were to operate companies while the government was to retain actual ownership. The movement declined rapidly in the early 1920s.

Guilford Court House, Battle of American victory (Mar. 15, 1781) over the British during the Carolina Campaign (*q.v.*) of the American Revolution (1775–83). The battle was fought at Guilford, North Carolina, between some 4,400 Americans under Gen. N. Greene and 2,200 British under Gen. C. Cornwallis. Losses were light in the five-hour battle, but the engagement is said to have led Cornwallis to abandon the Carolinas to the Americans.

Guinea Name once used by Europeans to refer to the western coastal region of Africa.

Guinea (Republic of Guinea) (*formerly* French Guinea) Republic located on the coast of West Africa. The capital is Conakry and the population is 7,269,000. In pre-colonial times, the region was divided variously between tribal states, including empires of Mali, Ghana, and Fulani. Portuguese explorers arrived in the 15th cent., and in subsequent centuries the region supplied slaves to the Portuguese, British, and French. In the 19th cent., the French sought to protect trade in agricultural products and declared a protectorate (1849) over part of the region. They gradually expanded their control and established it as a separate colony (1891), though fighting with natives continued until the end of the century. From 1893 to 1895, the colony was known as French Guinea and after 1895 it was administered as part of French West Africa. Then a major bauxite producer, it became an overseas territory of France (1946) and, after voting against joining the French Community (*q.v.*) in 1958, it achieved full independence. Under Sékou Touré (1922–84), the first president of Guinea after its independence, Guinea first pursued closer relations with Russia and then with the Western powers (from late 1960s). In 1970, Touré successfully repulsed an invasion, launched from Guinea-Bissau, aimed at his over-

throw. Following Touré's death in 1984, the military seized power and ruled until 1990, when a new constitution was approved and a transition government (to civilian democratic government) was installed (1991).

Guinea-Bissau (*formerly* Portuguese Guinea) Coastal West African country. The population is 998,000 and the capital is Bissau. First discovered (1446) by the Portuguese, the region became a center for the slave trade in the 17th and 18th cents. It came under Portuguese control, and its boundaries were established through agreement with France (1886). An independence movement began in Portuguese Guinea in the early 1960s under the leadership of A. Cabral. Rebel forces gained control of parts of the country and in 1973 declared the independence of Guinea-Bissau. Portugal granted independence Sept. 10, 1974. The government was overthrown in a military coup (Nov. 14, 1980), led by João Vieira. The legislative branch was reestablished in 1984 and duly elected Vieira as president. The country's one-party system was abolished in 1991.

Guinegate, Battle of *See* **Spurs, Battle of the.**

Guiscard, Robert *See* **Robert Guiscard.**

Guise French Roman Catholic family that played a major role in French politics (16th and 17th cents.). It was founded by Claude de Lorraine (1496–1550), 1st duke of Guise. His daughter, Mary of Guise, was the mother of Mary, Queen of Scots. His sons François de Lorraine (1519–63), 2d duke of Guise, and Charles de Guise (1524–74) gained great power in France under Francis II. Their persecution of the Huguenots (Protestants) and rivalry with the Bourbons led to the Conspiracy of Amboise (1560), which they ruthlessly suppressed. Their massacre (1562) of Huguenots at Vassy led to the Wars of Religion (1562–98). François's son, Henri de Lorraine (1550–88), 3d duke of Guise, aided in planning and execution of the Massacre of St. Bartholomew's Day (1572) and formed the Catholic League (1576), which continued persecution of the Huguenots. The line ended with François Joseph de Lorraine, 7th duke of Guise (*d.* 1675).

Guise, Charles de, cardinal of Lorraine 1524–74. French Catholic cardinal, son of Claude I, 1st duke of Guise. He and his brother, François, 2d duke of Guise, were the most influential men in the court of Francis II. He is said to have brought the Inquisition to France and is noted for persecution of Protestants.

Guise, Claude de Lorraine, 1st duke of 1496–1550. French Catholic nobleman and soldier. He founded the Guise family, which rose to power in France during the 16th cent. He was created duke of Guise by Francis I in 1527.

Guise, François de Lorraine, 2d duke of 1519–63. French Catholic nobleman and soldier, son of Claude I, 1st duke of Guise. He shared the power of government under Francis II with his brother Charles de Guise and took part in the persecution of French Protestants (Huguenots). Following Catherine de Médicis's rise to power, he joined with others in opposing tolerance toward the Huguenots. His troops are said to have sparked the Wars of Religion by a massacre of Huguenots at Vassy (1562).

Guise, François Joseph de Lorraine, 7th duke of *See* **Guise.**

Guise, Henri de Lorraine, 3d duke of 1550–88. French Catholic nobleman and soldier, a son of F. de Lorraine. He fought the Huguenots in the Wars of Religion, took part in planning the massacre of St. Bartholomew's Day (1572), and formed the Catholic League (1576).

Guise, Henri de Lorraine, 5th duke of 1614–64. French Catholic nobleman, a grandson of H. de Lorraine. He joined the opposition to Cardinal Richelieu (1641) and was forced to flee France until 1654.

Guise, Louis II de Lorraine 1555–88. French cardinal. Louis was the younger brother of H. de Lorraine. He was assassinated by the Royal Guard.

Guise, Mary of *See* **Mary of Guise.**

Guizot, François Pierre Guillaume 1787–1874. French statesman and historian. After 1840 he became chief minister in the government of Louis Philippe, formed after the July Revolution (1830). He was ousted during the February Revolution (1848).

Gujrat, Battle of Battle (Feb. 21, 1849) between British troops under Lord Gough, and some 50,000 Sikhs, led by Sher Singh. The British victory ended the Second Sikh War and resulted in annexation of the Punjab by the British.

Gulf of Tonkin Resolution Resolution passed by the US Congress (Aug. 7, 1964) in support of President L. Johnson's involvement of US military forces in Vietnam. It came as a direct result of the Gulf of Tonkin incident, in which North Vietnamese PT boats attacked (Aug. 4) US destroyers in the gulf. The US retaliated by bombing North Vietnam, and Johnson, requesting congressional approval for such attacks, won passage of the resolution.

Gulistan, Treaty of Treaty (Oct. 12, 1813) between Russia and Persia, at Gulistan, now in Azerbaijan. Persia ceded to Russia much of what became Azerbaijan, and gave up claims to Georgia, Dagestan, and other areas in the region.

Gundahar *See* **Gunther.**

Gundicar *See* **Gunther.**

Gundicarius *See* **Gunther.**

Gunnar *See* **Gunther.**

Guntharius *See* **Gunther.**

Gunpowder Plot Conspiracy by English Catholics to blow up Parliament and King James I (1605). Angered by King James's failure to order greater religious toleration of Catholics, five initial conspirators planned to provoke a general Catholic uprising. They hid barrels of gunpowder in a basement under Westminster Hall in anticipation of the day the king was to attend Parliament. The plot was discovered and one conspirator, Guy Fawkes, was caught in the cellar. The four accomplices, and others who had been involved, were captured and executed.

Gunther (Gundahar) (Gundicar) (Gundicarius) (Gunnar) (Guntharius) *d.* AD 437. Burgundian king (AD 413–437). Gunther was the first king of Burgundy. He led his people across the Rhine (413) to establish his kingdom and later died in battle against Attila.

Guomindang (Kuomintang) Chinese Nationalist political party, the ruling party in China from 1928 to 1949. Following the Communist takeover (1949) on the mainland, the Guomindang formed the opposition government in Taiwan. Organized (1912) as a political party after the Chinese Revolution of 1911 it was led by Sun Yat-sen and called for parliamentary government. Banned (1913), the party organized (1917–23) opposition governments under Sun and then joined (1923) with the Chinese Communist Party (CCP). The Guomindang launched (1926) the Northern Expedition and, by 1928, after breaking with the CCP (1927), took control of the government. Civil war between the Nationalists and the Communists raged almost continuously thereafter until the CCP expelled the Guomindang in 1949.

Gupta dynasty Dynasty of rulers of India (AD c320–550). Guptas ruled over an empire that at one time included northern and parts of central India. The dynasty was founded by Chandragupta I and the empire was greatly expanded by Samudragupta. Chandragupta II was the greatest of all Gupta rulers, and during his reign Indian art and commerce flourished.

Gurkhas *See* **Nepal.**

Gustavian Enlightenment *See* **Swedish Enlightenment.**

Gustav line In WW II, the German line of defense in southern Italy, stretching from Pescara to Gaeta. The Allies finally broke through it during their attack on Rome (May 1944).

Gustavus I 1496–1560. Swedish king (1523–60), first of Vasa dynasty. Following the Stockholm Bloodbath, he raised an army of Swedes against the Danish rulers of Sweden and defeated them. He was elected king (1523) and the Kalmar Union (*q.v.*) was dissolved. He consolidated the power of the monarchy and in 1544 royal succession was made hereditary.

Gustavus II (Gustavus Adolphus) 1594–1632. Swedish king (1611–32), successor to his father, Charles IX. With help from his chancellor, A. Oxenstierna, he pacified the nobles and restored order to the Swedish government. He ended the Kalmar War (1613), successfully waged wars against Russia (1613–17) and Poland (1621–29), and proved a skilled leader of Protestant troops in the Thirty Years' War. He was killed at the Battle of Lutzen (1632).

Gustavus III 1746–92. Swedish king (1771–92). His reign is sometimes referred to as the Swedish Enlightenment. He renewed the authority of the monarchy and restored order, instituted important reforms, and entered into a costly war with Russia (1788–90).

Gustavus IV (Gustavus Adolphus) 1778–1837. Swedish king (1792–1809), successor to his father, Gustavus III. He was an unpopular ruler, and his foreign policies proved disastrous for Sweden. He lost Finland to Russia (1808) and was finally overthrown (1809). His heirs were forbidden to succeed him.

Gustavus V 1858–1950. Swedish king (1907–50), successor to his father, Oscar II. He proved to be a popular and able constitutional monarch who maintained Sweden's neutrality through WW I and WW II.

Gustavus VI 1882–1973. Swedish king (1950–73), successor to his father, Gustavus V. During his reign the Swedish Riksdag passed legislation reducing the king's role to that of a figurehead.

Gutenberg, Johann c1400–68?. German generally regarded as the inventor (in the West) of the method of printing with movable type. Few details of Gutenberg's life are certain but he is thought to have invented his printing method (c1438) while living in Strasbourg. Later, in Mainz, he entered a partnership (1450) with a goldsmith, J. Fust, and began printing the Mazarin Bible. He lost his press and type following a suit by Fust (1455). It is believed that Chinese and Korean printing techniques, invented earlier and similar to Gutenberg's, were unknown to Europeans.

Guyana (*formerly* British Guiana) Independent republic in northeast South America. The population is 765,000 and the capital is Georgetown. The Dutch founded the first settlement (c1620) at Essequibo and in the following century both Britain and France founded colonies there. During the Dutch Wars, England captured the region, but the Dutch regained possession by the Treaty of Breda (1667). The region changed hands frequently during the French Revolutionary and Napoleonic Wars, though Britain ultimately gained control of it at the Congress of Vienna (1815). British Guiana was formally created in 1831 and the discovery of gold (1879) there led to an international controversy, known as the Venezuela Boundary Dispute (*q.v.*), over claims to part of the territory. The movement for independence began after WW II, and a constitution, providing for elections, was adopted in 1952. Britain suspended the constitution (1953) when a pro-Communist government was elected, but new elections in 1957 returned a more moderate government. Despite unrest during the 1960s, elected governments remained in power, and full independence was granted May 26, 1966. A major crisis was averted (1970) when a 12-year truce was negotiated with Venezuela and Surinam over claims to territory in Guyana. Guyana became a republic that same year. Repressive measures by the government and a worsening economy resulted in unrest during the early 1980s. Following the death of President Forbes Burnham (in office 1980) in 1985, Desmond Hoyte became president. By 1989 economic problems forced the government to adopt a severe austerity program, which sparked widespread labor unrest. In 1990 mass demonstrations for democratic reforms also broke out. The government later agreed to electoral reforms, but delayed new national elections into 1992.

Guyon, Jeanne Marie de la Motte 1648–1717. French mystic and author. An important figure in the religious movement known as quietism, she became embroiled in the controversy surrounding it. She was eventually imprisoned in the Bastille (1695–1702) for her writings.

Guzmán Blanco, Antonio 1829–99. Venezuelan dictator. He was vice-president (1863–68) and following overthrow of the government, he led a counterrevolution. He was subsequently elected president (1870) and, until his overthrow in 1888, he ruled with dictatorial powers.

Gwinnett, Button c1735–1777. American patriot and signer of the Declaration of Independence. He was a delegate to the Continental Congress (1776–77) and was president of the state of Georgia (1777).

Gwyn, Nell (˜, Eleanor) (Gwynn, Eleanor) 1650–87. English actress and mistress to Charles II (after 1669). A lively and spirited lady of humble background, she was a popular public figure in her day.

Gwynn, Eleanor *See* **Gwyn, Nell.**

Gypsies (Roma) Nomadic people of uncertain origins who are today found throughout the world. Gypsies speak a language called Romani and are thought to have originated in northern India. They appeared in Persia as a nomadic people (c1000), in Europe (c1500) and in North America (late 1800s). Traditionally Gypsies are craftsmen, entertainers, or fortune-tellers and travel in caravans. As outsiders in settled lands, they have been the object of persecutions, most notably the execution of 400–500,000 of them in A. Hitler's concentration camps.

H

Haakon I (Haakon the Good) c914?–61. Norwegian king (c935–961). An able ruler, he attempted to introduce Christianity to Norway.

Haakon IV (Haakon the Old) (Haakon Haakonsson) 1204–63. Norwegian king (1217–63). Under his reign medieval Norway began its golden age. He added Greenland and Iceland to his realm, made important legal reforms, and encouraged the arts.

Haakon VII 1872–1957. Norwegian king (1905–57), a son of Danish King Frederick VIII. He was elected king by parliament on the dissolution of the union between Norway and Sweden. He ruled in exile at London during the Nazi occupation (1940–45).

Haakon Haakonsson *See* **Haakon IV.**

Haakon the Good *See* **Haakon I.**

Haakon the Old *See* **Haakon IV.**

habeas corpus Writ issued by a court to one who has imprisoned another, calling for the person detained to be produced before the court for a specific purpose. It is used largely to prevent false imprisonment.

Habibullah Khan 1872–1919. Amir of Afghanistan (1901–19). He established friendly relations with the British in India, maintained neutrality in WW I, and introduced many reforms.

Habsburg (Hapsburg) One of the major dynasties of European rulers (13th–20th cents.), members of the Habsburg house became rulers of Austria, the Holy Roman Empire, and Spain. The line can be traced back to the 11th-cent. counts of Habsburg, and in 1273 Rudolf I founded the imperial line. Elected king of the Germans in 1273, he acquired Austria (1278) and made it a hereditary possession (1282). The Habsburgs ruled as kings of the Germans (rulers not crowned as "emperor" by the pope) with interruptions until 1452, when Frederick III was crowned Holy Roman Emperor. Thereafter the title remained in the family until the empire succumbed to Napoleon (1806). By advantageous marriages and inheritance of family domains, Habsburg rulers vastly increased their holdings and reached the height of their power (16th cent.) under Emperor Charles V, who was also Spanish King Charles I. The Habsburg line was divided on his death into Spanish (rulers 1504–1700) and Austrian lines. The Austrian line (known as Habsburg-Lorraine after 1740) ruled the Holy Roman Empire to 1806 and Austria, Hungary, and Bohemia until 1918. *Habsburg Kings and Holy Roman Emperors:* Rudolf I 1273–91; Albert I 1298–1308; Albert II 1438–39; Frederick III 1440–93; Maximilian I 1493–1519; Charles V 1519–56; Ferdinand I 1556–64; Maximilian II 1564–76; Rudolf II 1576–1612; Matthias 1612–19; Ferdinand II 1619–37; Ferdinand III 1637–57; Leopold I 1658–1705; Joseph I 1705–11; Charles VI 1711–40. *Habsburg-Lorraine Holy Roman Emperors:* Francis I 1745–65; Joseph II 1765–90; Leopold II 1790–92; Francis II 1792–1806 (Francis II becomes Francis I of Austria, 1804). *Spanish Habsburg Monarchs:* Holy Roman Emperor Charles V, as Charles I 1516–56; Philip II 1556–98; Philip III 1598–1621; Philip IV 1621–65; Charles II 1665–1700. *Austrian Habsburg Monarchs:* Maria Theresa 1740–80; Joseph II 1780–90; Leopold II 1790–92; Francis II 1792–1804; Francis II, as Francis I 1804–35; Ferdinand I 1835–48; Francis Joseph I 1848–1916; Charles I 1916–18.

Habsburg, Rudolf of *See* **Rudolf I.**

Habsburg-Lorraine *See* **Habsburg.**

Hadith Muslim term, meaning "tradition," applied specifically to stories of the life and technique of Muhammad. They are sacred to Islam.

Hadrian AD 76–138. Roman emperor (AD 1171–38). An energetic ruler, Hadrian fortified the empire's boundaries, built Hadrian's Wall in Britain, and suppressed the revolt of Bar Kokba.

Hadrianople, Battle of *See* **Adrianople, Battle of.**

Hadrian's Wall Defensive wall of stone and wood built by the Romans to protect the northern border of their territories in Britain against invading tribes. Built (139) largely under the reign of Emperor Hadrian, it stretches 73.5 miles across a narrow point in the island of Britain. Large sections of the wall are still standing.

Haeckel, Ernst Heinrich 1834–1919. German biologist and evolutionist. His speculations on biological evolution, based on Darwin's theory, stimulated interest in evolutionary theory.

Hafiz (*pseud. of* Shams ud-din Muhammad) *d.* 1389? One of the greatest of Persian poets, he was a member of the Sufi sect and is perhaps most widely known for his collection of poetry, the *Divan.*

Hagia Sophia (Santa Sophia) Former cathedral at Constantinople, considered a masterpiece of Byzantine art and one of the world's most magnificent buildings. Built as a Christian church by Byzantine emperor Justinian I, it became a mosque (1453) after the Turks conquered Constantinople and now is a museum.

Hague Conferences (˜ Conventions) 1. First ˜ (International Peace Conference of 1899), held at The Hague in the Netherlands (May 18–July 29, 1899). Called by Russia, it was attended by 26 countries, including the US. Though the major question of arms limitations went unresolved, the conference set up the Hague Tribunal (Permanent Court of Arbitration), and banned poison gas, "dumdum" (expanding) bullets, and aerial bombing from balloons. 2. Second ˜ (International Peace Conference of 1907) held at The Hague (June 15–Oct. 18, 1907). Convened by Russia, it was attended by 44 countries. Again the conference made no resolution on arms limitation, though agreement was reached on rights of neutral shipping, general conventions on land and sea warfare, and a ban on submarine mines. The outbreak of WW I forced cancellation of a third conference (1915), but the conferences nevertheless laid the basis for such international organizations as the League of Nations and the United Nations.

Hague Conventions *See* **Hague Conferences.**

Hague Tribunal Permanent Court of Arbitration, an international court. Established (1899) at The Hague, the Netherlands, as a forum to settle international disputes, it was superseded by the World Court (1921).

Hahn, Otto 1879–1968. German scientist. In 1938, with Fritz Strassmann, he demonstrated nuclear fission by bombarding uranium with neutrons. He received the Nobel Prize for Chemistry (1944).

Haidar Ali *See* **Mysore Wars.**

Haig, Douglas, 1st earl 1861–1928. British field marshal in WW I who commanded British forces in France after 1915. His strategy of fighting a "war of attrition" cost the British heavy casualties and aroused a public controversy. Nevertheless, he led the Allied assault that finally broke German resistance (1918).

Haile Selassie (Tafari Makonnen) (Ras Tafari) 1891–1975. Emperor of Ethiopia (1930–74) who worked to modernize his country and bring it into the world political arena. He led the unsuccessful defense against the invading Italian army (1935) and with British help regained his throne (1941). He was deposed (1974) in a military coup.

Hainisch, Michael Arthur Josef Jakob 1858–1940. Austrian statesman. Though he favored union with Germany, he was elected first president of the newly formed Federal Republic of Austria (1920–28).

Haiti Republic in the West Indies on Hispaniola Island. The population is 5,852,000 and the capital is Port-au-Prince. Latin America's most densely populated nation, it was ceded by Spain to France (1697), and in the late 18th and early 19th cents. was the scene of numerous revolts against French rule, notably that of Toussaint L'Ouverture. Haiti became independent (1804), and its history became one of frequent political turmoil. It was occupied (1915–34) by US marines. Haiti's recent history was marked by conflict with the neighboring Dominican Republic and the tyrannical rule (1957–71) of François ("Papa Doc") Duvalier. Duvalier's son, Jean-Claude ("Baby Doc"), succeeded in 1971. Continued economic problems led to the exodus of Haitian "boat people" to the US in 1980. Widespread unrest over poverty and corruption in 1985–86 forced Duvalier from office (he fled to France in 1986). Subsequently the government was rocked by coups (Feb., Sept., 1988; Jan., Sept., 1991), as well as civil unrest and continuing economic problems. The US began repatriating Haitian refugees fleeing the current military regime after Sept., 1991.

Hakka Chinese people living in southern China. A distinct group, their name means "guest people." It is believed they migrated (12th–13th cents.) from northern China.

Hakluyt, Richard 1552?–1616. English geographer. His many books on voyages of discovery helped promote exploration and colonization of North America by the English.

Haldighat, Battle of *See* **Gogunda, Battle of.**

Haldimand, Sir Frederick 1718–91. British general and administrator. During the French and Indian War he served in the Montreal expedition (1760) led by J. Amherst. He served as governor of Quebec province during the American Revolution.

Hale, Edward Everett 1822–1909. American author and clergyman, known best for his short novel *The Man Without a Country.*

Hale, George Ellery 1868–1938. American astronomer. He organized and directed the Yerkes and Mount Wilson observatories and is noted for discovering magnetic fields in sunspots.

Hale, Nathan 1755–76. American Revolutionary War officer and hero who is said to have spoken the famous words "I only regret that I have but one life to lose for my country." Originally a Connecticut militiaman, he volunteered for a dangerous spy mission behind British lines on Long Island. He was caught while returning and was hanged as a spy the next day.

Halepa, Pact of *See* **Pact of Halepa.**

Hales, Alexander of *See* **Alexander of Hales.**

Haley, Alex 1921–92. Black American author who wrote *The Autobiography of Malcolm X* and *Roots,* which became a widely acclaimed television miniseries.

Half-Breeds US political term applied in the 1870s and 1880s to Republicans who sought to end the GOP association with the Civil War and Reconstruction in favor of business and economic interests. They were opposed within the Republican party by the conservative Stalwarts.

The Half-Breeds' leaders included J. Blaine and J. Garfield.

Half-Way Covenant A church doctrine formulated by Puritans in New England in the mid-17th cent. Originally a personal experience of conversion was required for full membership in the Congregational church, though children of members were baptized and enjoyed nearly all church privileges. A controversy arose over the question of baptizing (and admitting to membership) the offspring of these children, many of whom had grown up without a conversion experience. The doctrine of extending privileges to these offspring was adopted at a church synod (1662), but the issue remained highly controversial.

Halicarnassus, Dionysius of *See* **Dionysius of Halicarnassus.**

Halidon Hill, Battle of English victory (July 19, 1333) over the Scottish forces of King David II. English king Edward III, besieging Berwick for E. de Baliol, decisively defeated a Scottish relief force led by Sir A. Douglas, regent for David II.

Halifax, Charles Montague, earl of 1661–1715. English statesman. A Whig party member, he instituted borrowing schemes that created the British national debt (1692), and adopted plans that created the Bank of England (1694).

Halifax, Edward Frederick Lindley Wood, 1st earl of 1881–1959. English statesman. He was viceroy of India (1926–31), foreign secretary (1938–40), and ambassador to the US (1941–46). As foreign secretary he was a staunch supporter of N. Chamberlain's appeasement policy toward the Nazis.

Hall, Charles Martin 1863–1914. American chemist who discovered the first practical process for manufacturing aluminum (1886). With the backing of the Mellon family, he founded a company that eventually became the Aluminum Company of America.

Hall, Granville Stanley 1844–1924. American psychologist and educator. Sometimes called the founder of educational and child psychology, he also originated the *American Journal of Psychology* (1887) and wrote *Adolescence* (1904).

Halleck, Henry Wager 1815–72. Union general in the American Civil War. Although an able administrator, he was an indecisive strategist. He served as general in chief of all Union armies (1862–64) until replaced by U. Grant.

Haller, Albrecht von 1708–77. Swiss physiologist, anatomist, and botanist. Sometimes called the father of experimental physiology, he is known best for his *Physiological Elements of the Human Body.*

Halley, Edmund 1656–1742. English astronomer and mathematician. Though noted for a variety of discoveries relating to heavenly bodies, he is known best for calculating accurately the return (1758) of the comet now named after him.

Hals, Frans c1580–1666. Dutch painter, now ranked among the great portrait painters of his time. He painted both group and individual portraits and during his career developed a characteristic looseness and freedom of style. Among his works are *Banquet of the Officers of the St. George Militia, The Governors of the Almshouse,* and *Lady Regents of the Almshouse.*

Halsey, Bull *See* **Halsey, William Frederick, Jr.**

Halsey, William Frederick Jr. (~, Bull) 1882–1959. American admiral in WW II. An aggressive commander of carrier task forces, he was an important figure in many of the island campaigns against the Japanese. He became commander of South Pacific naval forces (1942–44) and commander of the US Third Fleet (1944–45).

Hamilcar Barca *d.* 229 or 228 BC. Carthaginian general, father of Hannibal. He fought ably in Sicily during the First Punic War, put down a revolt by mercenaries at Carthage (241–238 BC), and made extensive conquests in Spain.

Hamilton, Alexander 1757?–1804. American statesman and a leading Federalist in the early years of the republic. A delegate to the Continental Congress (1782–83), he worked to establish a strong, centralized federal system of government. At the Annapolis Convention (1786), he proposed the convening of the Philadelphia Convention (1787). He made major contributions to the Federalist Papers, which played an important role in gaining ratification of the Constitution. As first US secretary of the treasury (1789–95), he formulated fiscal policy and established the Bank of the US (1791). A leader with J. Adams of the Federalists in their opposition to the Jeffersonian Republicans, he came to oppose Adams. His political maneuvering against his enemy A. Burr led to the famous duel in which he was shot and killed by Burr.

Hamilton, James, 2d baron Hamilton and 1st earl of Arran *See* **Hamilton family.**

Hamilton, James, 2d earl of Arran *See* **Hamilton family.**

Hamilton, James, 3d earl of Arran *See* **Hamilton family.**

Hamilton, James, 3d marquess and 1st duke of 1606–49. Scottish nobleman. A royalist, he led a 24,000-man army against the Parliamentarians during the English Civil Wars. Defeated by O. Cromwell at Preston, he was hanged shortly thereafter.

Hamilton, John, 1st marquess of 1532–1604. Scottish nobleman. A supporter of Mary, Queen of Scots, he participated in the murder of J. Stuart and fled to England.

Hamilton, William, 2d duke of *See* **Hamilton family.**

Hamilton, Sir William 1788–1856. Scottish philosopher, noted for his work in the fields of metaphysics and logic.

Hamilton family Noble family prominent in Scottish history for more than 300 years. Members of the family were variously barons, earls, dukes, and marquesses of Hamilton, Arran, Belhaven, Claneboye, Haddington, and Orkney. Among the prominent members of the family were: James Hamilton, 2d baron Hamilton and 1st earl of Arran (1477?–1529), member of the council of regency during the minority of James V; James Hamilton, 2d earl of Arran (*d* 1575), regent to Mary, Queen of Scots, during her minority; James Hamilton, 3d earl of Arran (1530–1609), proposed as suitor to both English queen Elizabeth I and Mary, Queen of Scots, later confined for insanity; and William Hamilton, 2d duke of Hamilton (1616–51), supported Charles II in the English Civil Wars.

Hamlin, Hannibal 1809–91. American statesman. An opponent of slavery, as a member of the US House of Representatives from Maine (1843–47) he supported the controversial Wilmot Proviso (1846). He also served in the Senate (1848–57, 1869–81), was an early member of the Republican party, and was 15th vice-president of the US (1861–65) under President A. Lincoln.

Hammarskjöld, Dag 1905–61. Swedish statesman and UN secretary general (1953–61). He held various posts in the Swedish government (1930–53) and (1951–53) was a delegate to the UN. Noted as an able and active peacemaker, he played an important role in easing the Suez Crisis (1956) and in maintaining Mideast stability during the crisis in Lebanon (1958). He was killed in an airplane crash while attempting to mediate an end to the civil war that broke out (1960) in the Congo.

Hammerstein, Oscar 1847–1919. American operatic manager. He arranged the first American appearances of many noteworthy European opera productions and singers in the early 1900s.

Hammerstein, Oscar 2d 1895–1960. American lyricist and librettist. He is known best for his collaboration with R. Rodgers, on such hit musicals as *Oklahoma!, The King and I,* and *The Sound of Music.*

Hammett, (Samuel) Dashiell 1894–1961. American author, noted as the originator of the hard-boiled detective novel. His works include *The Maltese Falcon* and *The Thin Man.*

Hammond, James Henry 1807–64. American statesman. An early supporter of Southern secession, he served in the US House of Representatives (1835–36) and as governor of South Carolina (1842–44). A member of the Senate (1857–60), he delivered a celebrated speech in which he declared that "cotton is king." (*See* King Cotton.)

Hammurabi *fl.* c1792–50 BC. Babylonian king. Credited with bringing Mesopotamia under one rule, he is known best for his comprehensive legal code covering economic, familial, criminal, and civil codes of conduct. Considered advanced, humane, and civilized for its era, the code was discovered in 1901.

Hammurabi, Code of *See* **Code of Hammurabi.**

Hampden, John 1594–1643. English parliamentary leader. He became a hero of Parliamentarians when he challenged the right of King Charles I to levy ship-money taxes (1637). His near arrest along with four other members of Parliament (1642) helped bring on the English Civil Wars.

Hampton, Wade 1818–1902. American statesman and Confederate general in the American Civil War. A wealthy planter, he raised "Hampton's Legion" and served well in many important battles. After the war, he became a noted South Carolina politician, elected governor (1876–79) and senator (1879–91).

Hampton Court Conference English religious conference (Jan., 1604) called by King James I to consider Puritan reforms of doctrine and liturgy in the Church of England. The chief results were the King James Bible and improvement in the quality of the clergy.

Hampton Roads Peace Conference American Civil War peace conference (Feb. 3, 1865) aboard the steamer *River Queen* near Hampton Roads, Virginia. The conference failed to negotiate an end to the war.

Hamsun, Knut (*pseud. of* Knut Pedersen) 1859–1952. Norwegian novelist. An influential naturalist writer in the early 20th cent., he is known best for *Hunger* and *The Growth of the Soil.* He was awarded the 1920 Nobel Prize for Literature.

Hancock, John 1737–93. American Revolutionary War patriot, first signer of the Declaration of Independence. A Boston merchant, Hancock became involved in opposition to British taxation when his ship was seized in the Liberty Affair (1768). He served as president of the Provincial Congress (1774–75), a member of the Continental Congress (1775–80), and as its president (1775–77).

Hancock, Winfield Scott 1824–86. Union general and unsuccessful Democratic presidential candidate in 1880. He fought well in several major battles, notably at Gettysburg. His even-handed treatment of Southerners after the war helped him win the Democratic nomination against J. Garfield.

Hand, Learned 1872–1961. US Federal Court of Appeals judge. As US district judge (1909–24) and appellate court judge (1924–51), he was a widely respected jurist.

Handel, George Frederick 1685–1759. German-born English composer, one of the foremost baroque composers. He produced his first operas in Hamburg, next went to Italy (1707–09), and made his first visit to London (1710). He became a British subject (1726). In England he composed his many famous Italian operas, oratorios, concertos, and occasional pieces. Among his works are the operas *Berenice* and *Serse,* the oratorio *Messiah,* the orchestral piece *Water Music,* and what is now the British coronation theme, *Zadok the Priest.*

Handy, W(illiam) C(hristopher) 1873–1958. American composer and bandleader. He popularized the blues idiom in American jazz music and is perhaps best known for his *St. Louis Blues.*

Han dynasty Chinese dynasty. Founded by Liu Bang (later known as Gaodi, *d.* 195 BC), it succeeded the Qin dynasty and ruled China from 202? BC to AD 220. Many characteristic features of Chinese culture were established in this period. The Han unified China, repealed many harsh laws established under the Qin (but kept many Qin government institutions), promoted education and culture, and spread Confucianism. A paid bureaucracy and the Chinese Examination System were instituted during this period, and a distinctive artistic style also emerged. The Han dynasty came to power during the civil war at the end of the Qin dynasty. Liu Bang, king of Han, a petty state in the west, overcame rival kings and conquered Qin and in 202 BC proclaimed himself emperor, thus establishing the Han dynasty. Gaodi, as he was later called, made his capital at Chang'an (*modern* Xi'an) eliminated potential opponents, extended central government control, and set up a system of taxation on grain and other goods. His immediate successors continued policies of consolidation, which marked the early years of the Former (or Western) Han period (202 BC–AD 9). All that changed under Emperor Wudi (reigned 141–87 BC), when he launched attacks against the Xiongnu and rapidly expanded the empire into what are modern Vietnam and Korea. Under Wudi, China also established the Silk Roads (trading routes to central Asia and, later, beyond). The end of Wudi's reign, however, was marked by military reversals and internal dissent that halted further expansion. Han rulers grew steadily weaker until Wang Mang, regent of the last Former Han emperor, seized power (AD 9) and established the short-lived house of Xin (AD 9–23). Wang Mang's attempted radical reforms sparked a peasant revolt (Red Eyebrows, AD 18–23) and in AD 23 he was captured and killed by them.

Han Fei (Han-fei-tzu) *d.* 233 BC. Great Chinese Legalist philosopher. His teachings advocating authoritarianism and complete obedience to the emperor were adopted by the Qin dynasty. While maintaining the importance of governing internally through laws and efficient administration, Han Fei believed military power was the key to relations between kingdoms. A student of Hsün-tzu, he was later remembered for his strong opposition to Confucianism.

Han-fei-tzu *See* **Han Fei.**

Hanging Gardens of Babylon Ancient gardens built (probably in the 6th cent. BC) at Babylon. A series of terrace gardens, they were one of the Seven Wonders of the World.

Hanna, Marcus Alonzo (˜, Mark) 1837–1904. American businessman and politician. A success-ful Ohio businessman and a power in the Republican party, he played a key role in W. McKinley's successful campaigns for governor of Ohio (1891, 1893) and for president (1896).

Hanna, Mark *See* **Hanna, Marcus Alonzo.**

Hannibal 247–182? BC. Carthaginian general during the Second Punic War (218–201 BC). The son of Hamilcar Barca, he became (221) commander of Carthaginian forces in Spain and, by his attack on a city allied to Rome, precipitated (218) the Second Punic War. In one of history's most celebrated military maneuvers, he led an army of 40,000 soldiers (with a supply train of elephants) out of Spain and across the Alps to invade Rome itself. He gained major victories over the Romans at Lake Trasimeno (217) and Cannae (216) but was unable to take the city. Recalled (203) to defend Carthage from Roman attack, he was defeated at Zama (202). He later joined Syrian king Antiochus in wars against Rome, but was defeated (182) and poisoned himself.

Hanno *fl.* 5th cent. BC. Carthaginian navigator who led a fleet of ships along the west coast of Africa for the purpose of establishing new colonies. He eventually founded seven colonies and may have reached Sierra Leone.

Hannover, House of *See* **Hanover, House of.**

Hanover, House of (Hannover, ˜) German ruling family of Hanover. Descended from the Guelphs, the line acceded to the British throne, through the Act of Settlement (1701), through George I. Succeeding Hanoverian rulers of England were George II, George III, George IV, and William IV. Upon the accession (1837) of Queen Victoria the two kingdoms were separated, Victoria not being allowed by Hanoverian law to accede to the Hanoverian throne.

Hanseatic League Once powerful federation of cities (13th–17th cents.), mainly located in what is now northern Germany. It sought to establish trade monopolies and protect its concerns against piracy, robbery, and intervention by foreign governments. The cities of Lübeck and Hamburg founded (1241) the league. It eventually included over 100 others and virtually controlled trade in the Baltic and North Sea regions. The league established great trading depots, including the Steelyard in London, Bruges, Bergen, and Novgorod. The league reached the zenith of its power with conquest of the Danes and the Treaty of Stralsund (1370). The league gradually declined thereafter, due to being unable to resist the Dutch in the Baltic region, the growing power of other European kingdoms, internal struggles among member cities, and the change in trading patterns brought about by the discovery of the New World. The last meeting of the league was held in 1669.

Hansen, Hans Christian Svane 1906–60. Danish statesman. As foreign minister (1953–60) and prime minister (1955–60) he played a key role in Denmark's economic growth and in its emergence as a major force within NATO.

Hanson, John 1721–83. American Revolutionary War patriot and political leader. Sometimes referred to as the first US president, he was actually a presiding legislative officer called the "president" (1781–82) under the Articles of Confederation.

Hansson, Per Albin 1885–1946. Swedish statesman. As prime minister (1932–46) in the critical Depression and WW II years, he encouraged public works, agricultural projects, and social welfare, and kept Sweden neutral during the war.

Han Wên-kung *See* **Han Yu.**

Han Yu (Han Wên-kung) 768–824. Chinese official, essayist, and poet. A Confucian, he was an outspoken critic of Daoism and Buddhism, and was once exiled from the emperor's court for his views. His writings earned him the title "Prince of Letters."

Hara, Kei (Hara, Takashi) 1856–1921. Japanese statesman and prime minister (1918–21). He built his Seiyukai party into a Western-style political machine and became the first Japanese prime minister to form a cabinet according to parliamentary principles.

Hara, Takashi *See* **Hara, Kei.**

Hardecanute *See* **Harold Harefoot.**

Hardenberg, Prince Karl August von 1750–1822. Prussian statesman. As chancellor from 1810, he guided Prussia through the turbulent years of the Napoleonic Wars and was responsible for many political and social reforms.

Harding, Warren Gamaliel 1865–1923. Twenty-ninth US president (1921–23), successor to W. Wilson. Harding's administration was notorious for the Teapot Dome (*q.v.*) scandal. A newspaper publisher and Republican politician in Ohio, he later became a US senator (1915–21). His term as senator was undistinguished, though his congenial manner won him influential friends. Finally at the deadlocked Republican convention

of 1920, Harding was nominated as the compromise candidate for president. He campaigned on a return-to-"normalcy" platform that gained wide appeal in post-WW I America and he won the election easily. Though he was personally an honest man, he surrounded himself with political appointees who proved to be unscrupulous and corrupt. The first years of his administration were marked by a single major administration initiative, the convening of the Washington Conference (1922) for international reduction of naval armament. But in 1923 rumors of scandal began to spread. Harding died while on a tour of the West (Aug. 2, 1923), apparently after receiving reports of the impending revelations. In following months, his appointees in various departments, including Interior, Justice, the Veterans' Bureau, and others, were charged with corruption and negligence. Of the scandals uncovered, Teapot Dome was the worst.

Hardy, Thomas 1840–1928. English novelist and poet, a leading author of the 19th cent. Among his best-known works are *Tess of the D'Urbervilles* and *Jude the Obscure.*

Harmehab Egyptian pharaoh (c1350–1315 BC) and last king of the 18th dynasty. He finalized the return to the worship of the traditional polytheistic religion begun under Tutankhamen and brought about a return of prosperity.

Hargreaves, James *d.* 1778. English inventor who devised the spinning jenny (c1764).

Harlan, John Marshall 1833–1911. Associate justice of the US Supreme Court (1877–1911). A noted dissenter and considered a strict constructionist, he dissented in the Supreme Court's decision (1896) upholding "separate but equal" treatment of blacks.

Harlem Heights, Battle of Series of skirmishes (Sept. 16, 1776) in northern Manhattan, New York, during the American Revolution. The skirmishes slowed the British advance north after the Battle of Long Island, and helped Colonial forces to prepare for the coming Battle of White Plains.

Harley, Robert, 1st earl of Oxford 1661–1724. British statesman and leader of the Tory ministry (1710–14) under Queen Anne. As speaker of the House (1701–05) and secretary of state (1704–08) he exercised considerable influence in the government, and with others oversaw British involvement in the War of Spanish Succession. He was made leader of the Tory ministry (1710) by the queen's favor and during his time in power concluded the Peace of Utrecht (1713). Harley was finally ousted through the efforts of his rival, Henry St. John, 1st Viscount Bolingbroke. (*See also* South Sea Bubble.)

Harmodius and Aristogiton *d.* c514BC. Athenian tyrannicides. They attempted to assassinate the tyrant Hippias and his brother Hipparchus. The plot failed, though Hipparchus was killed. Harmodius was killed immediately and Aristogiton was killed later. Hippias continued his rule for several years more, but after his overthrow Harmodius and Aristogiton were honored.

Harmonists *See* **Harmony Society.**

Harmony Society (Harmonists) 19th-cent. Protestant religious sect. Founded in Germany by George Rapp (1757–1847), it practiced celibacy, asceticism, and communal sharing. It founded the villages of Harmony, Pennsylvania (1806), and New Harmony, Indiana (1814). In 1825 it sold its Indiana holdings to R. Owen and moved back to Pennsylvania. It was disbanded in 1906.

Harmsworth, Alfred Charles William, 1st viscount Northcliffe *See* **Harmsworth, Harold Sidney, 1st viscount Rothermere.**

Harmsworth, Harold Sidney, 1st viscount Rothermere 1868–1940. English publisher. With his brother, Alfred Charles William, 1st Viscount Northcliffe (1865–1922), he built a newspaper publishing empire in Britain that included the *Evening News,* the *Daily Mail,* and the *Daily Mirror.*

Harnack, Adolph von 1851–1930. German theologian. An important church historian, he wrote the influential work *The History of Dogma.*

Harold I (Harold the Fair-haired) c850–c933. Norwegian king (c860–c933). Son of Halfdan the Black, Harold conquered much of Norway and became its first king. During his reign large numbers of Norsemen migrated to Iceland.

Harold II 1022?–66. Last Saxon king of England (1066). Chosen heir by Edward the Confessor, Harold ruled less than a year before his defeat by William, duke of Normandy, at the Battle of Hastings, in which he was killed.

Harold III (Harold the Stern) (Harold Hardrada) *d.* 1066. Norwegian king (c1047–66), successor to Magnus I. He joined with Earl Tostig in an invasion of northern England (1066) and fell with him in battle at Stamford Bridge.

Harold Bluetooth *d.* c985. Danish king. Harold attempted to impose Danish suzerainty over Norway but was defeated. Forced to accept Christianity, he introduced it to Denmark. He was killed in battle by his son Sweyn I.

Harold Hardrada *See* **Harold III.**

Harold Harefoot *d.* 1040. English king (1037–40). The illegitimate son of King Canute, he spent much of his reign fighting Canute's legitimate son Hardecanute (1019?–42) for the throne.

Harold the Fair-haired *See* **Harold I.**

Harold the Stern *See* **Harold III.**

Harpers Ferry Raid Raid (Oct. 16–18, 1859) on a federal arsenal at Harpers Ferry, Virginia (now West Virginia), carried out by J. Brown and 21 other abolitionists. Brown and his men captured the arsenal as part of a plan to start a general slave uprising in the South. Their base at Harpers Ferry was to be the nucleus of a new state in the surrounding mountains, where escaping slaves could find refuge. In fact, the raid was a failure and the arsenal was easily recaptured by combined federal troops and local militia. Brown and six of his followers were hanged. However, the incident had a profound effect on the South, which became convinced the abolitionists would stop at nothing, especially in light of captured documents that showed abolitionists had helped finance the raid. Even though his direct action was generally disapproved, Brown became a martyr of the anti-slavery cause, as attested by the marching song, *John Brown's Body.* The incident was a contributing factor in the election of A. Lincoln, the subsequent secession of the slave states of the South and thus the American Civil War.

Harriman, Edward Henry 1848–1909. American railroad magnate and financier. Once a New York City stockbroker, he built a combination of western railroad lines that made him one of the most powerful men in 19th-cent. American railroading.

Harriman, William Averell 1891–1986. American statesman and diplomat, son of E. H. Harriman. He served in various diplomatic posts since the early 1940s and was chief US negotiator of the Nuclear Test Ban Treaty (1963). Harriman also served as governor of New York (1955–58).

Harrington, Michael 1928–89. Writer and prominent Socialist in the US. He became an adviser to M. L. King, Jr., and was an ardent critic of the Vietnam War. His book, *The Other America* (1962), attracted national attention to the plight of millions of Americans living in poverty.

Harris, Joel Chandler 1848–1908. American writer and humorist famous for his Uncle Remus stories.

Harris, Roy 1898–1979. American composer whose symphonies are noted for their American themes.

Harris, Townsend   *See* **Harris Treaty.**

Harrison, Benjamin 1833–1901. Twenty-third US president (1889–93), successor to G. Cleveland. The grandson of President W. H. Harrison, he was a Union officer during the American Civil War and a US senator from Indiana (1881–87). The Republican presidential nominee in 1888, he defeated G. Cleveland in the electoral college, though Cleveland had almost 100,000 more popular votes. During his administration, the US expanded its influence abroad while at home the economy weakened, setting the stage for the financial Panic of 1893. The first Inter-American Conference was held (fostering the Pan-American movement), and the US participated in the Berlin Conference (1889). Legislation affecting the economy at home included the Sherman Antitrust Act (1890), the high, protective McKinley Tariff Act (1890), and the inflationary Sherman Silver Purchase Act (1890).

Harrison, William Henry 1773–1841. Ninth US president (Mar. 4–Apr. 4, 1841), successor to M. Van Buren. Harrison, who caught pneumonia at his inauguration ceremony, was the first president to die in office. He was a leading figure in the development of the Old Northwest (*q.v.*) and served as governor of the Indiana Territory (1800–12). Harrison became a national figure by defeating Indian chief Tecumseh, then at war against white settlers, at the famous Battle of Tippecanoe (1811). Later, in the War of 1812, he took command of the Old Northwest and reestablished American control of the region, by recapturing Detroit (Sept., 1813) and by his victory at the Battle of Thames River (1813). He then became a US congressman (1816–19), US senator (1825–28), and finally Whig party candidate for president (1840). His successful campaign, which incorporated the slogan "Tippecanoe and Tyler Too," evaded the issues and instead promoted Harrison as the image of a rugged Westerner.

Harris Treaty   Treaty between the US and Japan signed on July 29, 1858. It provided for unsupervised trade and residence at five Japanese ports, a tariff, and the prohibition of imports of opium. It was negotiated by Townsend Harris (1804–78), first US consul general (1855), and later minister (1859), to Japan.

Harsa, Harshavardhana   *See* **Harsha.**

Harsha (Harsa, Harshavardhana) 590?–647?. Indian ruler (606–47). An able commander, he united all of northern India into an empire that lasted throughout his reign.

Hart, Lorenz (~, Larry) 1895–1943. American lyricist noted for his collaboration with R. Rodgers on such popular Broadway shows as *A Connecticut Yankee, The Boys from Syracuse,* and *Pal Joey.*

Hart, Moss 1904–61. American playwright. His many successful productions included the musical *Lady in the Dark.* He frequently collaborated with G. Kaufman. Their comedy *You Can't Take It with You* was awarded the 1937 Pulitzer Prize for Drama.

Harte, Francis Bret(t) 1836–1902. American writer, known best for his vivid sketches of California life.

Hartford Convention   Meeting of New England Federalist party members held (Dec. 15, 1814–Jan. 4, 1815) in Hartford, Connecticut, during the War of 1812. The convention was brought on by widespread dissatisfaction with the war in New England. Presided over by George Cabot (1752–1823), the meeting was held in secrecy and included delegates from Massachusetts, Connecticut, New Hampshire, Vermont, and Rhode Island. Though the convention rejected outright secession, its final report generally adopted a states' rights position and attacked President J. Madison's policies on trade embargoes and the war. The air of secrecy and the timing of the convention (the war ended soon afterward) aroused popular suspicions of treason and thereby contributed to the downfall of the Federalist party.

Harun al-Rashid (Harun ar-Rashid) c764–809. Fifth Abbasid caliph (786–809) and most famous of the dynasty. A son of al-Mahdi, he reigned during the height of the Islamic Empire, which then included southwestern Asia and northern Africa. His exploits and the splendor of his court at Baghdad are celebrated in *The Thousand and One Nights.*

haruspices Etruscan diviners who practiced in ancient Rome from about the late 6th cent. BC. An haruspex interpreted omens, especially those believed to appear in the entrails of sacrificial animals and in natural phenomena and other unusual happenings. Important during the early republic, the practice continued during the empire but always remained outside the bounds of Rome's state religion.

Harvey, William 1578–1657. English physician who was first to identify correctly the function of the heart and blood circulation. He published his findings in 1628.

Hasan (Hassan) c624–c669. Islamic ruler, the 5th caliph (661), and a grandson of Muhammad. He was proclaimed caliph on the death of his father Ali but soon relinquished the title to Muawiya, who challenged his succession.

Hasan Ibn al-Sabbah *See* **Assassin.**

Hasdrubal *d.* 207 BC. Carthaginian general, son of Hamilcar Barca and brother of Hannibal. As commander in Carthaginian Spain he fought against the Romans. He was killed while trying to join his forces with those of Hannibal in Italy.

Hasdrubal *d.* 221 BC. Carthaginian general. Son-in-law of Hamilcar Barca, he succeeded Barca as commander in Spain and added to Carthaginian conquests there.

Hasidim (Assideans) Name given to members of two specific movements in Jewish history. **1.** Group (also known as Assideans) which flourished c300–175 BC. It strictly observed the Talmud and rejected the influence of other cultures. **2.** Group which evolved in Poland c1750, led by Israel ben Eliezer (or Ba'al Shem Tov). Followers believed in miracles as manifestations of God's love and presence, and felt that goodness of heart was more important than scholarship. The sect continues today.

Hasmoneans *See* **Maccabees.**

Hassan *See* **Hasan.**

Hassan II 1929– .Moroccan king (1961–). Hassan suspended Morocco's constitution and assumed dictatorial powers after riots in Casablanca (1965) but continued unrest forced him to yield to reforms (1971) and a larger role for the parliament. Following renewed unrest, he appointed a coalition government under a prime minister (1984).

Hastings, Battle of English-Norman battle (Oct. 14, 1066) in which English king Harold II was defeated and killed by the invading forces of William (the Conqueror), duke of Normandy. William moved on to London, where he was crowned king (Dec. 25). This battle is widely regarded by historians as the most important event in British history, marking the start of Norman influence in England.

Hastings, Warren 1732–1818. British colonial governor. As governor general of India (1774–84), Hastings successfully protected and expanded British interests. Upon his recall to England he was impeached for extortion and mismanagement, but was eventually acquitted.

Hatch Acts American laws (1939, 1940). Proposed by Senator Carl Hatch (1889–1963), they limited campaign contributions from individuals and committees and forbade federal employees from campaigning for candidates.

Hatshepsut *d.* c1481 BC. Egyptian queen, wife of Thutmose II and daughter of Thutmose I. A woman of unusually great power, she ruled Egypt during the reign of her husband, and also as regent for Thutmose III. She brought a period of peace to Egypt.

Hauptmann, Bruno Richard 1899–1936. German-American carpenter, convicted kidnapper of C. Lindbergh's baby son. Arrested (1934) after passing some of the $50,000 ransom money paid two years earlier, Hauptmann was convicted after a sensational trial, and was electrocuted (1936).

Hauptmann, Gerhart 1862–1946. German dramatist, novelist and poet, considered a leading figure in German literature. His many works include the plays *Before Dawn* and *The Weavers*. He was awarded the 1912 Nobel Prize for Literature.

Hausa States (Haussa ~) Group of former African states located in what now is northern Nigeria. Conquered many times during their history, they were taken over (early 20th cent.) by the British and incorporated into the Protectorate of Nigeria.

Haushofer, Karl 1869–1946. German geographer and leading exponent of geopolitics. His theories had an early influence on A. Hitler and Haushofer later became a political adviser to Hitler.

Haussmann, Georges Eugène, baron 1809–91. French official and city planner who, under Napoleon III, redesigned the city of Paris.

Hawaii US island state, the 50th state. First settled (c8th cent.) by Polynesians, the islands were discovered by Capt. J. Cook (1778) and called the Sandwich Islands. The accession (1810) of Hawaiian king Kamehameha I was accompanied by increased foreign trade and growing Western influence. The islands' last ruler, Queen Lili-uokalani, was deposed in 1893 and Hawaii was annexed to the US in 1898. The surprise attack (Dec. 7, 1941) on the US naval base at Pearl Harbor led to US entry into WW II. Hawaii became a state in 1959.

Hawkesbury, baron *See* **Liverpool, Robert Banks Jenkinson, 2d earl of.**

Hawkins, Sir John (Hawkyns, Sir John) 1532–95. English seaman and admiral. The first Englishman to engage in the slave trade (1562), he directed reconstruction of the English fleet and took part in battle against the Spanish Armada.

Hawkyns *See* **Hawkins, Sir John.**

Hawthorne, Nathaniel 1804–64. American novelist and short-story writer, one of the first great American authors. After 12 years of working in enforced seclusion (from 1825), he produced an unsuccessful first novel and a number of short stories (collected as *Twice-Told Tales*) that won him some recognition. He married (1842) and thereafter completed his most famous novels, *The Scarlet Letter* and *The House of the Seven Gables. The Scarlet Letter* is considered the first American psychological novel.

Hay, John 1838–1905. American statesman and author. Private secretary to A. Lincoln (1861–65), he was secretary of state under presidents W. McKinley and T. Roosevelt (1898–1905). He is chiefly remembered as negotiator of the Open Door Policy and the Hay-Pauncefote Treaty.

Haya de la Torre, Victor Raúl 1895–1979. Peruvian political leader and founder (1924) of the Apra party, a popular radical party in Peru. He was twice an unsuccessful presidential candidate (1931, 1962).

Hay-Bunau-Varilla Treaty The treaty concluded (Nov. 18, 1903) between the US and newly independent Panama, establishing the US-controlled Panama Canal Zone. Shortly after Colombia rejected (Aug. 12, 1903), the Hay-Herrán Treaty, Panamanian rebels declared Panama's independence (Nov. 3) from Colombia. Two weeks later the US concluded the treaty for the Canal Zone. Terms, negotiated by US secretary of state J. Hay, were nearly the same as had been offered to Colombia, including a $10 million payment and $250,000 annuity.

Haydn, Franz Joseph 1732–1809. Austrian composer, one of the most important masters of classical music. He made fundamental advances in the symphonic form, the string quartet, and the sonata and thereby profoundly influenced the development of classical music. He wrote most of his great works under the patronage (1761–90) of the Austrian noble House of Esterhazy, and gained recognition throughout Europe. Haydn was known to have influenced his friend W. Mozart and taught L. Beethoven. He wrote over 100 symphonies, including his great *Symphony No. 102 in B Flat Major,* numerous string quartets, operas, piano concertos, and masses.

Hayes, Rutherford Birchard 1822–93. Nineteenth US president (1877–81), successor to U. Grant. He distinguished himself in the American Civil War and became a congressman (1865–67), governor of Ohio (1868–72), and Republican presidential candidate in 1876. The election, which saw the return of former Confederate states to participation in national politics, appeared to favor Hayes's opponent, S. Tilden. Disputes over returns in four states, however, put the election in the hands of a congressional electoral commission, which ultimately decided the election in Hayes's favor. (*See also* United States (1876).) Once in office, Hayes worked to end Reconstruction (1865–77). He removed the remaining federal troops from Southern states, appointed Southerners to government posts, and generally adopted a policy of reconciliation. His attempts at ending civil service corruption embroiled him in a bitter feud with the Stalwart (*q.v.*) Republican Senator Roscoe Conkling. In the controversy over silver coinage, (*see* free silver), Hayes attempted to block passage of the Bland-Allison Act (*q.v.*), but his veto was overridden (1878).

Hay-Herrán Treaty Treaty negotiated (1903) between Colombia and the US to establish control over what was to become the Panama Canal Zone. Colombia, then in control of the region, ultimately refused (Aug. 12, 1903) to ratify the treaty. Terms of the treaty negotiated by US secretary of state J. Hay, included a $10 million payment and a $250,000 annuity in return for rights over the canal route. The US soon afterward concluded the Hay-Bunau-Varilla Treaty with the newly formed independent Panamanian government.

Haymarket Square riot American labor riot (May 4, 1886) in Chicago, Illinois. A bomb, exploding at a labor demonstration, killed 7 policemen and 4 civilians, and wounded over 100 others. Eight anarchists were convicted in connection with the bombing. Four were hanged and one committed suicide, and the remaining three were pardoned in 1893.

Hayne, Robert Young 1791–1839. US senator from S.C. (1823–32) and spokesman for the South. He was D. Webster's opponent in the famous debate (1830) over issues then dividing the North and South.

Hay-Pauncefote Treaty Treaty signed (Nov. 18, 1901) by the US and Britain, which enabled the US to control the proposed Panama Canal. The treaty superseded the Clayton-Bulwer Treaty (1850) with Britain in which the US agreed to joint control of such a canal. Negotiated by US secretary of state J. Hay, the treaty provided for a canal under US jurisdiction and equal treatment for shipping of all nations, and tacitly permitted fortification of the Canal Zone by the US.

Hays, Arthur Garfield 1881–1954. American lawyer, noted as defense attorney in civil liberties cases. He was defense counsel in the Scopes Trial and in the Sacco-Vanzetti case.

Hazael *fl.* 840 BC. King of Damascus who, according to biblical accounts, killed Benhadad and succeeded him. He later conquered Israel and Judah. [1 Kings 19; 2 Kings 8–10]

Hazlitt, William 1778–1830. English essayist and critic. He was an important literary critic and a master of the essay. Among his best-known works are the collected essays *Table Talk* and *The Plain Speaker.*

Hearn, Lafcadio 1850–1904. Greek-born writer who became an American (1869) and then Japanese (1895) citizen. He is known best for his books on Japanese culture.

Hearst, William Randolph 1863–1951. American newspaper publisher. He built a newspaper and magazine publishing empire using the sensationalism and mass-appeal journalism for which he is best remembered.

Heath, Edward Richard George 1916– .British politician. A Conservative, Heath entered Parliament (1950) and held a variety of posts in the governments of A. Eden, H. Macmillan and A. Douglas-Home. As prime minister (1970–74), he succeeded in gaining British entry into the Common Market (1972). However, increasing economic troubles and conflict in Northern Ireland led to his defeat.

Hébert, Jacques René 1755–94. French journalist and revolutionary. A leader of the sansculottes after his political newspaper became popular with the lower classes, he was involved in the storming of Tuileries Palace (1792) and the overthrow of the monarchy. Soon after he became a member of the Commune of Paris, and was arrested (May, 1793) for aiding the radical movement to oust the (moderate) Girondists from the National Convention. His sansculotte supporters won his release soon after, however, and in June, 1793 Hébert was involved in the riot by radicals that forced the expulsion of Girondists from the National Convention. With the Jacobins now in power, Hébert attempted to force the revolution into ever more extreme measures through his influence over the sansculottes, who had forced (Sept., 1793) institution of the Reign of Terror. Hébert, with P. Chaumette, was a leader in the radical de-Christianization program and establishment of the Cult of Reason. He was opposed (from mid-1793) by G. Danton and M. Robespierre, and in Mar., 1794, Hébert was arrested and guillotined along with other Hébertists.

Hebron City in western Jordan, since 1967 part of the Israeli-occupied West Bank. A holy city for both Jews and Muslims, it was settled even before biblical times. It was capital of David's kingdom before Jerusalem and is the burial site of Abraham, Isaac, and Jacob.

hedonism Philosophical doctrine, derived in part from the Greek Cyrenaics, that holds that human pleasure is the highest good. Today it implies the gratification of all sensual desires.

Hedwig *See* **Jadwiga.**

Heem, Jan Davidszoon de (~, Johannes de) 1606–1683 or 1684. Dutch artist, considered one of Holland's greatest still-life painters.

Hegel, Georg Wilhelm Friedrich 1770–1831. German idealistic philosopher, one of the most influential 19th-cent. thinkers. He was a professor at Jena, Heidelberg, and, from 1818, at Berlin. Hegel held ultimate reality to be absolute spirit or mind, and hence held that "whatever is rational is real and whatever is real is rational." All things tend to the complete and perfect design of mind by a logical process which Hegel called the "dialectic." In this process an original tendency, or "thesis," gives rise to its opposite tendency, an "antithesis." Both are then resolved into a higher unity, a "synthesis." Hegel analyzed all reality in terms of this dialectic, and it became a favorite tool of subsequent philosophers. K. Marx and F. Engels rejected Hegel's idealism in favor of materialism but nevertheless based Marxism (*q.v.*) on Hegelian dialectic. Many other philosophers retained Hegel's idealism, however. Hegel's philosophy is set forth in such works as *Phenomenology of Mind* and, especially, *Encyclopedia of the Philosophical Sciences.* Hegel's thought was sometimes used by disciples to support a philosophy of extreme German nationalism.

hegira   *See* **hijra.**

Heian-kyo   *See* **Kyoto.**

Heian period   Period of Japanese history (794–1185) marked by the rise of new Buddhist sects, development of the manorial system, and unbroken control of the imperial court by the Fujiwara regents.

Heidegger, Martin 1889–1976.   German philosopher. Influenced by E. Husserl and S. Kierkegaard, he published (1927) his important work *Being and Time,* in which he discussed the meaning of "being." Though he denied any connection to existentialism, his investigations of the sense of being, and his identification of the loss of it as the central problem of Western civilization, greatly influenced the existential philosopher J. Sartre.

Heidelberg Catechism   Calvinist document. Written (1563) at the request of elector Frederick III the Pious, it was widely adopted by Reformed churches.

Heike   *See* **Taira family.**

Heine, Heinrich 1797–1856.   German lyric poet. After briefly trying careers in business and law, he turned to poetry and established (1827) an international reputation with publication of *The Book of Songs.* Soon afterward he was forced (1831) to leave Germany because of his liberal social ideals and settled in Paris. There he became identified with the Young Germany literary movement and, in addition to his poems, wrote prose satires. His poems were frequently set to music by such noted composers as R. Schumann, F. Schubert, and F. Mendelssohn. The best-known of them is *Die Lorelei.*

Heinkel, Ernst Heinrich 1888–1958.   German aircraft manufacturer and engineer who built the first turbojet aircraft (1939), the He-178.

Heisenberg, Werner 1901–76.   German physicist who made major contributions to the quantum theory. He formulated the matrix theory of quantum mechanics and the uncertainty principle.

Hejaz   Historic region in western Saudi Arabia. It lies on the Red Sea coast and was occupied as early as Babylonian times.

hejira   *See* **hijra.**

Helderberg War   *See* **Antirent War.**

Helena, Saint AD c248–c328.   Mother of Constantine I. She was said to have discovered, while on a pilgrimage to Jerusalem (AD c327), the cross upon which Jesus Christ was crucified.

Helgoland Bight, Battle of (Heligoland Bight, ˜)   British naval victory over Germany (Aug. 27, 1914) in WW I, the first major naval engagement of the war. Meeting the German fleet off the coast of northwestern Germany, the British fleet sank three cruisers and one destroyer and severely damaged three other cruisers, losing no ships of its own.

Heliodorus *fl.* 175 BC.   Ancient Syrian statesman. He was treasurer of Seleucus IV, murdered him (175 BC), and unsuccessfully attempted to take the throne. According to the Bible, he entered the Temple at Jerusalem but was prevented from carrying away the treasure by three angels.

Heliogabalus (Bassianus, Varius Avitus) AD 204–222.   Roman emperor (AD 218–222), successor to Caracalla. Proclaimed emperor by the soldiers, he was killed after a short reign marked by debauchery.

Heliopolis (*biblical* On)   Ancient Egyptian city, located north of present-day Cairo. It was the seat of worship of the sun god Ra in earliest times and a center of learning until eclipsed by Alexandria (332 BC). Cleopatra's Needles were located there.

Hellenism   Name applied to the borrowing or imitation of the culture of the ancient Greeks, especially that of Athens at its height (5th cent. BC). It is usually applied to the works of those who later adopted Greek values and principles. The Hellenistic Age, a time when Greek culture spread throughout the eastern Mediterranean, is generally dated from the death of Alexander the Great to the Roman conquest of Greece in 146 BC.

Hellespont   *See* **Dardanelles.**

Hellman, Lillian 1905–84.   American playwright whose works include *The Children's Hour, The Little Foxes,* and *Watch on the Rhine.*

Helmholtz, Hermann, Ludwig Ferdinand von 1821–94.   German physiologist, physicist, and mathematician. Much of his work was connected with sense perception. He is noted for his study of the conservation of energy.

Helmont, Jan Baptist van 1577?–1644.   Flemish chemist, physicist, and physician. He discovered carbon dioxide and introduced the term "gas" into scientific vocabulary.

helots   Spartan slaves. Considered state property, they were assigned to both agricultural and well-supervised military tasks. Because of their huge numbers, helot revolts were greatly feared by the Spartans.

Helvetia   Roman term for a region in what is now western Switzerland. The name comes from the Celtic people (Helvetii) who occupied the region in J. Caesar's time and is sometimes used to refer to Switzerland.

Helvetic Confession   1. First ~. *See* Basel, Confession of (second).   2. Theological statement written (1562) by Heinrich Bullinger (1504–75) and considered one of the most important statements of Reformation doctrine. It was adopted (1566) by the Swiss cantons and was well received elsewhere in Europe.

Helvetius, Claude Adrien 1715–71.   French philosopher. His book *De l'esprit* contended that all human actions are based on self-interest.

Hemingway, Ernest 1898–1961.   American novelist and short-story writer, a leading American writer of this century. He is noted for his terse literary style and the recurrent themes of courage and virility that pervade his works. After graduation from high school (1917), he became a newspaper reporter and later an ambulance driver in WW I. He worked in Paris as a correspondent after the war and established himself with publication (1926) of *The Sun Also Rises*. Thereafter he wrote such major works as *A Farewell to Arms, For Whom the Bell Tolls,* and *The Old Man and the Sea.* He was awarded the Nobel Prize for Literature in 1954.

Henderson, Arthur 1863–1935.   British statesman. A leader and organizer of the Labour party, he played a leading role in British politics from 1903. He was awarded the Nobel Peace Prize in 1934.

Henri, Robert 1865–1929.   American painter. One of the original members of The Eight or "ash-can school," he was an influential teacher of art in the US.

Henrietta Maria 1609–69.   French wife (*m.* 1625) of King Charles I of England, and daughter of French king Henry IV and Marie de Médicis. Both her Roman Catholic faith and intrigues with foreign governments on her husband's behalf were factors in the outbreak of the English Civil Wars.

Henry I (~ the Fowler) 876?–936.   German king (919–936), successor to Conrad I and founder of the Saxon line. He added Lotharingia (Lorraine) to the German kingdom (925), warred against the Magyars, and reasserted the authority of the monarchy.

Henry I 1008–1060.   Capetian king of France (1031–60). He put down various rebellions and later warred unsuccessfully against William, duke of Normandy.

Henry I (~ Beauclerc) 1068–1135.   King of England (1100–35), successor to his brother, William II. Henry obtained the crown while his older brother, Robert, duke of Normandy, was away on crusade. Henry subsequently defended the crown against an invasion (1101) of England by Robert and later took Normandy from Robert (1106). As king, Henry became embroiled in the investiture controversy (*q.v.*) with Saint Anselm, and a compromise was reached (1107). Henry's efforts to arrange the succession of his daughter, Matilda, resulted in a civil war during the reign of his successor, Stephen.

Henry II 973–1024.   Holy Roman Emperor (1014–24) and German king (1002–24). The last Saxon emperor, he recaptured most of the German land taken by Polish king Boleslaus I and extended his influence throughout Italy. He was canonized (1146).

Henry II 1133–89.   King of England (1154–89), successor to King Stephen. The grandson of Henry I, son of Matilda and husband of Eleanor of Aquitaine, Henry founded the Plantagenet line. He restored order to strife-torn England, reformed its laws, and established the supremacy of royal courts over local justices. He defined church-state relations with the Constitutions of Clarendon but his arguments with Thomas à Becket led indirectly to the latter's murder. Henry consolidated English holdings in northern England, Ireland, and Scotland. He was the father of Richard I and John I.

Henry II (~ of Trastamara) 1333?–79.   King of Castile and León (1369–79). The illegitimate son of Alfonso XI, he fought his half-brother

Peter the Cruel for the throne, and ultimately killed Peter (1369). Henry supported the French in the Hundred Years' War.

Henry II 1519–59. King of France (1547–59), son of and successor to Francis I. Regarded as a weak ruler, he instituted repressive measures against Protestants, added Calais to French domains (1558), and negotiated an end to the Italian Wars.

Henry III (~ the Black) 1017–56. German king (1039–56) and Holy Roman Emperor (1046–56), son and successor of Conrad II. His reign marked the height of the Holy Roman Empire's power, but Henry's efforts at church reform fell short. After succeeding to the German throne, Henry established control over Bohemia and Moravia, and despite losses to raiding Magyars, established the borders of Austria and Hungary (1043). He maintained royal authority in Saxony, but nobles in Lorraine mounted revolts after 1044. From 1043 Henry's main concern was church reform (he denounced payments by new bishops to the king as simony), and arriving in Italy in 1046, forced the appointment of Clement II as pope. Clement in turn crowned him Holy Roman Emperor. The four popes Henry named during his reign helped restore the papacy, but his support for harsh treatment of heretics and efforts at promoting monastic reform movements (notably the Clunaic order) fostered resentment in the church and among the general populace as well.

Henry III *See* **Great Britain, 1216–72.**

Henry III 1551–89. French king (1574–89), successor to his brother Charles IX. As duke of Anjou, he aided his mother Catherine de Médicis in planning the Massacre of St. Bartholomew's Day (1572). His reign was marked by the Wars of Religion that raged in France between the Catholics and Huguenots, and by the War of the Three Henrys (1585–89).

Henry IV 1050–1106. Holy Roman Emperor (1056–1106), successor to his father, Henry III. His reign was marked by a long and unsuccessful struggle with the pope over lay investiture. On gaining his majority (1065), Henry moved to restore authority of the crown in the duchies (notably Saxony). His struggle with the church began (1075) when he appointed the archbishop of Milan. Condemned by Pope Gregory VII for the action, Henry declared the pope deposed (1076), only to be himself declared deposed by

the pope. Faced with a rebellion against the crown, Henry was forced to submit to the pope and was absolved after doing penance at Canossa (Jan., 1077). However, the German nobles elected Rudolf of Swabia as king (antiking) and a civil war ensued (1077–80), from which Henry emerged victorious. Gregory in the meantime again deposed Henry, who in turn made Clement III pope (antipope). Henry then invaded Italy (1081–83) and drove Gregory into exile, where he died. The reforming popes who succeeded Gregory supported revolts against Henry (from 1093). In one, Henry was entrapped (1105) by his rebellious son (later Henry V), but he escaped and died the next year. (*See also* Investiture Controversy.)

Henry IV (~ of Bolingbroke) (~ of Lancaster) 1367–1413. English king (1399–1413), a son of John of Gaunt and the first of three kings of the House of Lancaster. He led a successful rebellion against King Richard II (1399), after which he claimed the crown for himself. His reign was marked by rebellions, including those in Wales and Scotland, and the crown's worsening financial troubles.

Henry IV 1553–1610. First Bourbon king of France (1589–1610), successor to Henry III. His reign marked the end of the Wars of Religion (1562–98). Henry was raised a Protestant and, as Henry of Navarre, became nominal leader of the Protestants (Huguenots) in the Wars of Religion after 1569. His subsequent marriage (1572) to Margaret of Valois, sister of Catholic King Charles IX, during a brief peace in the wars nearly proved disastrous. The marriage was opposed by both sides and only days afterward there occurred the Massacre of St. Bartholomew's Day (*q.v.*) against Protestants. Henry, who thereupon renounced Protestantism to prevent his own death, was confined at Charles's court (1572–76) until he could effect an escape. Afterward he resumed command of Protestant forces and, in 1584, he became heir to the French throne (by the accession of Henry III and death of his heir). However the Catholic League (*q.v.*) bitterly opposed the possible accession of a Protestant, and provoked the War of the Three Henrys (*q.v.*). Henry was successful in this war and, in 1589, became king by the death of Henry III. The Catholic League warred against him, however, and by its alliance with Spain ultimately forced Henry to once again embrace

Catholicism (1593). With that, opposition to Henry began to dissolve and he entered Paris in 1594. He then instituted a policy of reconciliation that resulted (1598) in the Edict of Nantes (*q.v.*), establishing religious toleration. Henry's subsequent reign was marked by a period of general stability and rebuilding.

Henry V 1081–1125. Holy Roman Emperor (1106–25), successor to his father, Henry IV, and last of the Salian dynasty. After leading a near-successful revolt against his father, Henry succeeded him and began to consolidate his power in the empire. But he soon fell out with Pope Paschal II over the Investiture Controversy (*q.v.*), which had plagued his father's reign. In 1111 he captured pope and cardinals at Rome and thereby forced the pope to grant him the right of investiture. The struggle over investiture continued, however, and when Henry lost the support of his bishops, as well as the nobles, he was forced to accept (1122) a compromise measure, the Concordat of Worms (*q.v.*).

Henry V 1387–1422. English king (1413–22). Allying England with the Burgundians, Henry reopened the Hundred Years' War and led the English to victory in the Battle of Agincourt (1415). He conquered Normandy and Rouen and concluded the Treaty of Troyes (1420), by which he agreed to marry Catherine of Valois, daughter of French king Charles VI. Charles acknowledged him rightful heir to the French throne.

Henry VI 1421–71. King of England (1422–61, 1470–71), the last Lancastrian king of England. Henry, while still an infant, succeeded his father Henry V as king of England and his maternal grandfather Charles VI as king of France. Completely unfit to rule, he lost all English territories in France except for Calais. A period of insanity (1453–54) led to the appointment of Richard, duke of York, as lord protector, and his recovery led to the long struggle for the throne between the houses of York and Lancaster, the Wars of the Roses (*q.v.*). Richard succeeded in defeating Henry and imprisoning him, and in being named heir apparent to the throne (1460). Richard was killed soon after and his son claimed the throne as Edward IV. Henry fled to Scotland but was restored briefly (1470–71). Captured by Edward's forces, he was imprisoned in the Tower of London, where he was murdered.

Henry VII (*orig.* Henry Tudor) 1457–1509. English king (1485–1509), founder of the Tudor dynasty, and successor to Richard III. During the period of civil war called the Wars of the Roses, Henry went into exile (1471) in Brittany. The succession (1483) of the unpopular Yorkist, Richard III, made Henry (of the House of Lancaster) a leading contender for the throne. Henry landed in England (1485), defeated Richard at Bosworth Field, and was crowned (1486). By his marriage (1486) to Edward IV's daughter, Elizabeth, he united the houses of York and Lancaster and founded the Tudor line. This also ended the Wars of the Roses. Thereafter Henry foiled Yorkist plots by Margaret of Burgundy, L. Simnel, and P. Warbeck and, despite several attempts at rebellion, generally restored peace after the civil wars. His reign saw the beginnings of English overseas exploration led by J. Cabot and institution of Poyning's Law (1495).

Henry VIII 1491–1547. English king (1509–47), successor to his father, Henry VII. The early years of Henry's reign were marked by participation with the Holy League (from 1511) in war against France and by the defeat of invading Scottish armies at the Battle of Flodden (1513). When relations with Holy Roman Emperor Charles V soured, Henry briefly attempted reconciliation with the French at the Field of Cloth of Gold (*q.v.*). But by 1522 Henry was back at war with France. In the meantime, Henry received (1521) the title "Defender of the Faith" from Pope Leo X for his book, written in answer to M. Luther and the emerging Protestant movement. By 1529 however, Henry fell afoul of the church through his efforts to first annul his marriage to, and to divorce his first wife, Catherine of Aragon. The struggle continued for some years and included Henry's secret marriage to his new love, A. Boleyn (1533), Henry's excommunication (1534), and finally passage of the Act of Supremacy (*q.v.*), creating the Church of England. In subsequent years, Henry dealt ruthlessly with any opposition, Catholic or Protestant, to his position as supreme head of the church in England. Events of this period included the beheading of his former minister, Sir T. More, and many others, confiscation of monastery lands, suppression of the Pilgrimage of Grace (*q.v.*), and passage of the Act of Six Articles (*q.v.*). Events of Henry's later reign included the continuing struggle with the French, a defeat of Scottish forces that resulted in the death of King James V, and a series of new wives that brought the total to six by the time of his death. Edward VI, Elizabeth I, and Mary Tudor were his children.

Henry, Joseph 1797–1878. American physicist. He built the first electric motor (1829) and discovered electrical induction independently of M. Faraday. The henry, the electrical unit of inductance, is named for him. Henry also served as the first director of the Smithsonian Institution.

Henry, O. (William Sydney Porter) 1862–1910. American short-story writer whose stories are noted for their use of irony and surprise endings.

Henry, Patrick 1736–99. American Revolutionary War patriot and orator famous for the words "Give me liberty or give me death," uttered in a speech (Mar., 1775), urging colonists to prepare defenses. A delegate to the Continental Congress (1774–76) and twice governor of Virginia (1776–79, 1784–86), he was an ardent supporter of individual liberties. He played a major role in winning passage of the Bill of Rights.

Henry of Bolingbroke *See* **Henry IV.**

Henry of Burgundy *d.* 1112 or 1114. French nobleman and father of Alfonso I, first king of Portugal. He was made count of Portugal by Alfonso VI of León and Castile in return for his help in fighting the Spanish and the Moors.

Henry of Flanders c1174–1216. Second Latin emperor of Constantinople (1205–16), successor to his brother, Baldwin I. Considered the most competent of the Latin emperors, he defeated invading Bulgarians.

Henry of Lancaster *See* **Henry IV.**

Henry the Black *See* **Henry III.**

Henry the Fowler *See* **Henry I.**

Henry the Lion 1129–95. German prince, duke of Saxony and Bavaria. With the aid of Holy Roman Emperor Frederick I, he recovered Bavaria (1155) and other family territories taken by the Hohenstaufens. When he refused to help Frederick (1176) in a war against the Italians, Frederick stripped him of his holdings.

Henry the Navigator 1394–1460. Portuguese prince who sponsored early voyages of discovery along the west coast of Africa. The son of King John I, he established a court at Sagres (1419) composed of cartographers, navigators, shipbuilders, and seamen. Under his direction the Portuguese caravel was developed, mapmaking was refined, and other advances important to voyages of discovery were made. Though he never sailed himself, Henry organized the expeditions that rediscovered the Madeira Islands (1418), and by degrees ranged southward along, but never quite rounded, the Horn of Africa. In 1441 his ship came back laden with gold dust and slaves, thus providing the means for financing further expeditions. To oversee the burgeoning slave trade, Henry built the first European trading post overseas (1448), a fort on Arguin Island off the Horn of Africa. Later, his captains rounded Cape Verde (1444) and voyaged down the coast as far as present-day Sierra Leone (1460). The voyages to Africa sponsored by Henry began the age of discovery, and laid the foundation for the Portuguese colonial empire.

Henry the Proud c1108–39. Duke of Bavaria (1126–38) and Saxony (1137–38). Henry aided his father-in-law, Holy Roman Emperor Lothair II against the Hohenstaufens. After Conrad of Hohenstaufen succeeded Lothair as Conrad III (1138), Henry lost his duchies. He reconquered Saxony but died soon after.

Henry Tudor *See* **Henry VII.**

Hepburn Act US law (June 29, 1906) empowering the Interstate Commerce Commission to regulate railroad rates. It allowed the commission to lower excessive rates and prohibited certain practices.

Hepworth, Dame Jocelyn Barbara 1903–75. English sculptor. She is considered an influential nonfigurative sculptor.

Heraclea Ancient Greek city located in what is now southern Italy. Site of a battle from which the expression "Pyrrhic victory" derives. Here (280 BC) and at Asculum (279 BC) King Pyrrhus of Epirus was victorious in battle with the Romans, but with such heavy losses that the victory was questionable.

Heraclitus c535–c475 BC. Greek philosopher, an early proponent of a metaphysical philosophy. He believed permanence an illusion and the only reality was constant change.

Heraclius I c575–641. Byzantine emperor (610–41) who deposed the tyrant Phocas. During his reign the empire came under attack from several quarters. He defeated the Avars and Bulgars, and then the Persians (622–627), but lost Syria and Egypt to the Muslims (636–642).

herald Name applied to an officer of a medieval court who was charged with delivering messages (such as declarations of war or peace) from one military commander or sovereign to another.

heraldry Medieval system involving the display of a hereditary symbol, or charge, on shields for purposes of identification. Dating to the 12th cent., the practice soon spread throughout Europe.

Herbert, George 1593–1633. English poet and clergyman. He was one of the metaphysical poets.

Herbert, Victor 1859–1924. Irish-born American composer and conductor. He is known best for his many operettas, which include *Babes in Toyland* and *Naughty Marietta.*

Hercules, Pillars of *See* **Pillars of Hercules.**

Herder, Johann Gottfried von 1744–1803. German critic, clergyman, and philosopher. He played an important role in the Sturm und Drang (*q.v.*) literary movement in Germany.

Heredia, José-María de *See* **Parnassians.**

Heristal, Pepin of *See* **Pepin of Heristal.**

Herkimer, Nicholas *See* **Oriskany, Battle of.**

Hermandad In Spain, local organizations with police powers. Originating in the 12th cent., these units were raised by federations of towns in the kingdoms of Castile, Aragon, and León and provided protection against petty criminals and lawless noblemen. King Ferdinand and Queen Isabella organized (1496) the Holy Hermandad (Santa or Nueva ~), which eventually became a national police unit. The Hermandad had the power to arrest, try, and penalize criminals. It was eventually replaced by a civil guard, though local units survived to 1835.

Hermetic Books Ancient Egyptian texts dealing with such subjects as astronomy, astrology, and magic. They were said to have been written by Thoth, the god of wisdom.

Hermitage Russian museum, located in St. Petersburg. Constructed (1765) as a palace by Catherine II, it contains one of the largest collections of art treasures from all nations and periods.

Herndon, William Henry 1818–91. American lawyer and biographer. A. Lincoln's law partner, he wrote a biography of Lincoln that gave rise to the legendary Ann Rutledge romance.

Hero *See* **Hero of Alexandria.**

Herod Antipas *See* **Salome.**

Herodotus 484?–425 BC. Greek historian. Herodotus traveled widely throughout the known world, settling in southern Italy. He is known best for his richly detailed history of the Persian Wars, and is often called the "father of history."

Herod the Great 73?–4 BC. King of Judaea (37–4 BC), son of Antipater and best known of the Idumaean rulers (reigned 1st cent. BC–1st cent. AD). Herod was made king of Judaea by the Roman M. Antony in 39 BC and took possession of the kingdom two years later. He put down revolts in the early part of his reign and in succeeding years Judaea enjoyed a period of great prosperity. He constructed many public buildings and, though he had converted to Judaism, he promoted Hellenism. Suffering fits of insanity, he became tyrannical and notoriously brutal toward the end of his reign. According to the New Testament [Matthew 2], he was in power at the time of Jesus' birth and ordered the massacre of the Innocents.

Hero of Alexandria (Heron) *fl.* 1st cent. AD Greek mathematician and inventor. He devised a formula to find the area of a triangle and invented a crude steam engine, the *aeolipile.*

Herophilus *fl.* 300 BC. Greek anatomist at Alexandria. Sometimes called the father of anatomy, he dissected and described many organs of the body.

Herrick, Robert 1591–1674. English clergyman and poet. One of the Cavalier poets, he is remembered for the simplicity and sensuousness of his poetry.

Herrings, Battle of the Incident during the English siege of Orléans in 1429. The French attacked an English supply column, led by Sir John Fastolf (1378?–1459), and, in turning back the enemy, the English fought from behind barrels of herring that were among the supplies.

Herriot, Édouard 1872–1957. French statesman. He headed the Radical (Socialist) party from 1919 until his death and was premier three times (1924–5, 1926, 1932).

Herschel, Sir John Frederick William 1792–1871. English astronomer, son of Sir W. Herschel. He continued his father's work, discovered numerous celestial bodies, and made advances in applying photography to astronomy.

Herschel, Sir William 1738–1822. English astronomer. He discovered Uranus (1781), using a reflecting telescope of his own devising, and catalogued hundreds of new double stars, nebulae, and star clusters.

Hersey, John 1914–93. American author. His best-known books include *A Bell for Adano* and *Hiroshima.* He was awarded the Pulitzer Prize for Fiction in 1945.

Hertz, Heinrich Rudolf 1857–1894. German physicist best known for his discovery of radio waves. He began his career as assistant to H. Helmholtz (1880–83), then became professor of physics at several universities. He worked to confirm J. Maxwell's electromagnetic theory of light and heat (1885) and realized that the theory suggested that electric waves could be made to travel through the air. He confirmed his theory (1888), thus discovering the electromagnetic waves later called radio waves. He went on to demonstrate the nature of the waves and their characteristics, *i.e.* that they could be reflected, refracted, and polarized like light. The hertz, a unit of frequency, was named for him.

Hertzog, James Barry Munnik 1866–1942. Boer War guerrilla leader and premier of South Africa (1924–39). His policies included independence from Britain and increased racial segregation.

Herzegovina *See* **Bosnia and Herzegovina.**

Herzen, Aleksandr Ivanovich 1812–70. Russian radical and writer. Living outside Russia after 1847, he published journals and wrote books on socialism and revolution.

Herzl, Theodor 1860–1904. Austrian-born founder of modern Zionism. It was once held that the Dreyfus case convinced Herzl that acceptance of Jews in Europe was impossible, but scholars now believe the rise of anti-Semitism in his Austrian homeland forced Herzl to that conclusion. He subsequently wrote *The Jewish State,* a pamphlet in which he advocated creation of a separate Jewish state.

Heshen (Ho-shen) 1750–99. Powerful and corrupt courtier under the aging Chinese emperor Qianlong. The emperor's favorite, Heshen led imperial forces against the White Lotus Rebellion (*q.v.*), but diverted money for the war to himself and his friends, and then deliberately prolonged the campaign as part of the scheme. He was reputed to have amassed a personal fortune worth $1.5 billion before his death. His actions helped weaken imperial power, and following the emperor's death (1799), he was ousted and forced to commit suicide.

Hesiod *fl.* c8th cent. BC. One of the great early Greek poets. He is known best for two works, *Theogony* and *Works and Days.* The Hesiodic school of ancient Greek poetry is named after him.

Hess, Rudolf 1894–1987. German Nazi leader and A. Hitler's confidant. He created a sensation in 1941 when on his own initiative he flew to Scotland apparently for the purpose of negotiating peace between Britain and Germany. He was sentenced to life imprisonment during the Nürnberg trials.

Hesse West German state. In 1567, the lands of Philip of Hesse were divided among his four sons and eventually formed the two holdings of Hesse-Kassel and Hesse-Darmstadt. Hessian mercenaries came from these regions. Hesse-Kassel became Electoral Hesse and was annexed by Prussia (1868). Hesse-Darmstadt joined the German Empire in 1871 and the republic in 1918. These two regions form the basis of modern Hesse.

Hesse, Hermann 1877–1962. German novelist and poet. He was noted for his interest in human conflicts, psychology, and Oriental mysticism, expressed in such novels as *Demian, Siddhartha,* and *Steppenwolf.* He was awarded the 1946 Nobel Prize for Literature.

Heuss, Theodor 1884–1963. West German politician and publisher, and first president of the German Federal Republic (1949–59). As leader of the Free Democratic party after WW II, he was instrumental in the creation of West Germany's new constitution.

Heyerdahl, Thor 1914– . Norwegian anthropologist and adventurer. His *Kon-Tiki* expedition (1947), in which a balsa raft was used to cross the Pacific, showed that Polynesians could have migrated from South America.

Heyrovsky, Jaroslav 1890–1967. Czech chemist. He is best known for his discovery and development of polarography, a means of chemical analysis, for which he won the Nobel Prize for Chemistry in 1959. His polarograph (first demonstrated in 1924) analyzed chemicals to determine the presence of reducible or oxidizable substances and was widely used within ten years.

Hezekiah 740?–692? BC. King of Judah (720?–692? BC), successor to his father Ahaz. His reign was marked by reforms in religious practices and by two invasions by the ruling Assyrians.

Hickok, James Butler (Wild Bill ˜) 1837–76. American soldier, scout, and deputy US marshal. Known as "the fastest gun in the West," he was noted for his gunfight with the McCanles gang

(1861) and for cleaning up the Kansas frontier towns of Hays (1869) and Abilene (1871). He was shot and killed by Jack McCall during a poker game.

Hickok, Wild Bill   *See* **Hickok, James Butler.**

Hicks, Elias 1748–1830. American Quaker preacher and early abolitionist. His opposition to evangelicalism led to a split (1827) within the Society of Friends. His followers were called Hicksites.

Hidalgo y Costilla, Miguel 1753–1811. Mexican priest and national hero. He organized and led (1810–11) an army of Mexicans in a nearly successful rebellion against Spanish rule (defeated at Calderón Bridge). His revolt marked the opening of the Mexican struggle for independence.

Hideyoshi (Toyotomi, ˜) 1536?–98. Japanese general who completed the unification of Japan and leader of the warlords. He instituted numerous civil reforms, and launched an unsuccessful invasion of China (1592). (*See also* Japan, 1582–98.)

Hiero I (Hieron I) *d.* 466 BC. Greek tyrant of Syracuse, successor to his brother Gelon. He ruled as a despot, defeated the Etruscans at Cumae (474), and was a patron of literature.

Hiero II (Hieron II) *d.* c215 BC. Greek tyrant of Syracuse (c270–215 BC). He concluded a treaty with Rome which recognized his rule over southeast Sicily. In return he supplied Rome with money and soldiers during the First and Second Punic Wars.

hieroglyphic writing A system of picture-writing used by the ancient Egyptians from c3400 BC. Hieroglyphic writing died out by AD 500, and its meaning was lost until discovery (1799) and decipherment (early 19th cent.) of the Rosetta Stone.

Hieron I   *See* **Hiero I.**

Higginson, Thomas Wentworth 1823–1911. American author and Unitarian minister. He was an early abolitionist and commanded the first black regiment during the Civil War.

Highlands, The (Scottish ˜) The mountainous northern region of Scotland where the Gaelic language and customs survive even today. Highland clansmen played an active role in the Jacobite rebellions of 1715 and 1745.

hijra (hegira) (hejira) Name for Muhammad's forced departure (622) from Mecca and journey to Medina, a pivotal event in the history of Islam. Under a system developed by Omar, 2d caliph, all events of the Muslim era are dated from the beginning of the lunar year (July 16, 622) in which the hijra occurred. Muhammad fled from Mecca after opposing the local polytheistic religion and, once in Medina, established himself in that city. (*See also* Muhammad.)

Hilbert, David 1862–1943. German mathematician. His work included important advances in the theory of numbers, theory of invariants, and the axiomization of geometry.

Hildegard, Saint 1098–1179. German mystic. Born into a noble family, she experienced visions from her childhood onward, but it was not until she reached middle age that their authenticity was confirmed by church theologians. With help from a monk, she recorded 26 prophetic and religious visions in *Scivias* (completed 1152). She also founded a convent (1147) and wrote on a variety of subjects, including natural history and medicine.

Hilgard, Ferdinand Heinrich Gustav   *See* **Villard, Henry.**

Hill, Ambrose Powell 1825–65. Confederate general during the American Civil War. His infantry unit figured in the Seven Days' Battles, Second Battle of Bull Run, Antietam, and Gettysburg. He was killed in the Petersburg Campaign.

Hill, Daniel Harvey 1821–89. Confederate general in the American Civil War. He fought in several Virginia campaigns and commanded a corps at Chickamauga.

Hill, James Jerome 1838–1916. American railroad builder. As president of the Great Northern Railway (1882–1907), Hill directed most of the US and Canadian northwestern rail traffic. He was called "the Empire Builder."

Hillary, Sir Edmund Percival 1919– . New Zealand mountain climber. With the Sherpa Tenzing Norgay (c1914–86), he was the first to climb Mount Everest (1953).

Hillel *fl.* 30 BC–AD 9. Jewish scholar born in Babylonia, considered one of the great interpreters of the Hebrew scriptures.

Hilliard, Nicholas 1537–1619. First important English miniature painter. He did portraits of many in Queen Elizabeth's court.

Hillman, Sidney 1887–1946. American labor leader. One of the founders of the Congress of Industrial Organizations (CIO), he helped extend the scope of union benefits.

Himera, Battle of Battle (480 BC) between Carthage and Syracuse in Sicily. Carthage, responding to requests from the Sicilian city-state Himera for aid against Agrigentum, was decisively defeated by Agrigentum's ally Syracuse. The Carthaginian general Hamilcar was killed.

Himmler, Heinrich 1900–45. German National Socialist leader and one of the most powerful men in A. Hitler's Third Reich. Notorious for his ruthlessness and cruelty, he headed the SS (state police unit) and the Gestapo (secret police) and ran the concentration camps in which millions died.

Hinckley, John W., Jr. *See* **Reagan, Ronald Wilson.**

Hincks, Sir Francis 1807–85. Irish-born Canadian journalist and politician. As premier of united Canada (1851–54), he helped secure a reciprocal trade agreement with the US and pushed for railroad construction.

Hindemith, Paul 1895–1963. German composer and violist. One of the leading composers of the 20th cent., he is known best for his opera *Mathis der Maler.*

Hindenburg German dirigible that caught fire and crashed at Lakehurst, New Jersey, on May 6, 1937. Built and promoted by the Nazi government of Germany, the dirigible used highly flammable hydrogen for lift, because access to non-flammable, and strategically important helium gas had been cut off by nations concerned about the Nazis' militaristic policies. The *Hindenburg* burst into flames (beginning at the tail section) while docking at Lakehurst, possibly as a result of atmospheric static electricity or a spark from the dirigible's engines. There was also speculation about possible anti-Nazi sabotage, but the actual cause of the crash has never been determined. Of the 97 persons aboard, 35 were killed.

Hindenburg, Paul von 1847–1934. German field marshal and president of the Weimar Republic (1925–34). The commander of German armies during WW I, he emerged as a national hero despite Germany's defeat. In failing health by 1933, he appointed A. Hitler as his chancellor and thus opened the way for Hitler's takeover of the German government.

Hindi Indo-Aryan language. A written variation of Hindustani, Hindi is, with English, one of the official languages of India and is spoken by more than 280 million people. It has an extensive literature.

Hinduism Religion practiced by the majority of the people of India. Hinduism in its modern form evolved in stages from ancient Vedism (c1500 BC) to Brahmanism, and finally (c2d cent. BC) to Vedantic Hinduism. During its long development Hinduism has absorbed doctrines, rites, and practices from numerous other religions and sects and has spawned a great number of Hindu sects. Generally, however, Hinduism is characterized by acceptance of the Vedas (sacred texts), by adherence to the caste system (*q.v.*), by belief in cycles of life, death, and rebirth of the individual, and by the promise of escape from this cycle through enlightenment. Key dates in the development of Hinduism include:

c2300–1700 BC   Harappa civilization flourished in Indus Valley; developed early religious traditions later incorporated into Vedism, Brahmanism, and ultimately Hinduism.

c1500 BC   Aryans invaded India from region of Iran; brought new elements to traditional Indian religion and began Vedic period (1500–700 BC).

c900 BC   Rig-Veda, compiled over a long period, reached its final form; became a sacred Hindu text.

c800–500 BC   Upanishads composed over extended period; these philosophic texts advanced concepts of reincarnation and karma.

c700–c500 BC   Rise of Brahmanism; priestly class of Brahmins gained power; promoted elaborate rituals, philosophical speculations, and eventually the caste system.

c600–100 BC   Sutras written, established rigid order of conduct and religious ritual and divided society into four major groupings: caste system arose during this period.

c500 BC   Buddhism, Jainism, and various sects emerged to challenge traditional Brahmanism, which had lost its hold on the populace; in reaction, elements of Brahmanism, Jainism, and Buddhism were merged, concept of four stages of life introduced during this period.

c500 BC–AD c100   Mahabharata and Ramayana, great Hindu epics, composed (exact dates unknown); period marked beginning of Hinduism as distinct from earlier Brahmanism.

3D–2D CENTS. BC   Mauryan Empire flourished; Buddhism spread at the expense of Brahmanism.

2D CENT. BC Beginnings of Hinduism; rise of sects revering Vishnu and Shiva (Siva) as devotional deities.

4TH CENT. AD Hinduism began period of growth with rise of Gupta Empire.

4TH–8TH CENTS. AD Puranas, verse texts dedicated to devotion of individual deities, composed during Gupta rule.

7TH–11TH CENTS. Growth of sects devoted to Shiva and Vishnu (devotional Hinduism) contributed to decline of Buddhism in India.

C788–C820 Sankara, considered leading Hindu philosopher, lived; his teachings formed basis of modern Hinduism.

FROM C12TH CENT. Muslim incursions into India brought new Islamic influence on region; Hindu philosophy greatly influenced development of Islam in India.

C13TH–15TH CENTS. Bhakti, a movement marked by emotional devotion to a personal deity, arose.

19TH CENT. Western influence on Hinduism began as British East India Company took control of India.

1897 Ramakrishna Mission founded by Vivekenanda, a disciple of Ramakrishna; mission advanced a simplified form of Hinduism that encouraged social reform and denied the caste system.

1869–1948 M. Gandhi lived; merged traditional Hindu concepts and values into rising Indian nationalist movement; became the leading symbol of Hindu religion in the 20th cent.

1947 India became independent; government of India instituted numerous reforms in subsequent years, among them the outlawing of the caste system.

Hindustan Term meaning "land of the Hindus" and sometimes used to refer to all of India. More often, however, it means the northern part of India. "The Deccan" refers to the southern portion of India.

Hindustani Language group that includes the spoken languages of India (Hindi) and Pakistan (Urdu).

Hipparchus (Hipparchos) *fl.* 2d cent. BC. Important early Greek astronomer. He is believed to have compiled the first star catalogue and discovered subtle changes in the equinoxes caused by the wobble in the earth's rotation. Hipparchus also estimated the sizes of the sun and moon (and their distance from the earth) and investigated parallax.

Hippias 6th–5th cents. BC. Tyrant of Athens (527–510 BC). After the murder (514 BC) of his brother Hipparchus by Harmodius and Aristogiton, Hippias became an even more repressive ruler. He was overthrown (510 BC) by the Alcmaeonidae and exiled to Persia. Hippias then led the Persians in their first invasion of Greece (at Marathon) during the Persian Wars.

hippies Young nonconformists of the youth counterculture in the US during the 1960s. They claimed to be searching for a nonmaterialistic way of life and experimented with unconventional dress and behavior to set themselves apart from the American middle class. Characteristic of the hippie lifestyle were worn and flamboyant clothing, long hair, use of marijuana and other drugs, and belief in free love and communal living.

Hippocrates c460–c370 BC. Greek physician frequently called the "father of medicine." Though little is known of his life, Hippocrates appears to have been a medical writer and teacher of great scientific skill and high moral standards. The Hippocratic Oath, still administered to all new physicians, reflects his medical ethics.

Hippodamus (Hippodamus of Miletus) *fl.* 5th cent. BC. Greek architect. He planned Pireaus and the city of Rhodes.

Hippolytus, Saint (~ of Rome) AD c160–235. Italian theologian, martyr, and the first antipope. He broke with Rome over the question of heresy and became antipope (AD 217–235). *The Refutation of All Heresies* is his most important work. The *Canons of Saint Hippolytus* is believed to be a later revision of his *Apostolic Tradition* by an unknown author.

Hippolytus of Rome *See* **Hippolytus, Saint.**

Hiram (Huram) 989?–936 BC. Phoenician king of Tyre. A friend of David and Solomon, he helped with the construction of the Temple at Jerusalem.

Hirohito 1901–89. Emperor of Japan (1926–89), the son and successor to Taisho. His reign was marked by wars against China from the 1930s and Japan's participation in WW II. He accepted unconditional surrender to the US (1945) and a new constitution making him constitutional monarch (1946).

Hiss, Alger 1904– . US State Department official accused of spying for the Russians. Named by former Communist party member Whittaker Chambers (1901–61) as a conspirator in a Russian spy ring, Hiss was tried and convicted for perjury (1950). R. Nixon figured prominently in the Hiss investigation and the sensational trial was exploited by Senator J. McCarthy.

historiography The study of methods of historical investigation and of writing history.

Hitchcock, Alfred Joseph 1899–1980. British-American film director, famous for such suspense thrillers as *North by Northwest, Psycho,* and *The Birds.*

Hitler, Adolf 1889–1945. Austrian-born German dictator (1933–45) and founder of the National Socialist party (Nazis). Hitler's perverse schemes for German world domination and creation of an ethnically pure "master race" resulted in the outbreak of WW II and the extermination of millions of Jews and other minority groups. A failed artist, Hitler served in WW I and later joined (1919) the German Workers' party in Bavaria, Germany. He reorganized it (1921) into the National Socialist German Workers' party (*q.v.*) and turned it into a nationalistic, paramilitary group. He failed (1923) in his attempt to seize power in Bavaria (Munich Beer Hall Putsch) and, during his short term in prison, started writing *Mein Kampf* (*q.v.*), in which he outlined his plans for the Nazi party. The party grew rapidly during the Great Depression, largely because Hitler's nationalism appealed to the many groups hurt by inflation and economic dislocation. His attacks on Communists and Jews also played an important role in his growing support. The party's strength in the Reichstag increased greatly as a result, though Hitler lost the 1932 presidential election to P. von Hindenburg. Hindenburg named Hitler (Jan. 30, 1933) as his chancellor, however, and Hitler soon after began to consolidate his power. He succeeded in gaining emergency powers, and in banning the Communists, by blaming the Reichstag Fire (*q.v.*) on them. He then won passage of the Enabling Act (Mar. 23, 1933), which established the Third Reich (*q.v.*). Following Hindenburg's death (1934), Hitler became sole ruler of Germany and embarked on his program of expanding German power. He occupied the Rhineland (1936), annexed Austria (1938), occupied Czechoslovakia (1939), and invaded Poland (1939). The last action provoked the outbreak of WW II (*q.v.*). Despite his remarkable early successes, the tide of the war was clearly against him by 1944. With the Russians entering Berlin the following year, he committed suicide (Apr. 30, 1945) with his wife and former mistress, E. Braun.

Hitotsubashi *See* **Tokugawa Keiki.**

Hittite Empire Once powerful kingdom in Asia Minor (c1600–c1200 BC). The Hittites are believed to have discovered the technique of tempering iron and thus figure in the beginnings of the Iron Age (*q.v.*). The Hittite peoples first appeared (c1800 BC) in what is now central Turkey in a migration from the east. They established the Old Kingdom (1600–1400) and during this period Hittite rulers gradually expanded their domains throughout Turkey and into northern Syria. The Hittite ruler Mursilis I even attacked Babylon (c1590) and thereby ended the rule of the Amorite kings. The empire reached its greatest power (especially under Suppiluliumas I, c1380–c1340) during the New Kingdom (1400–1200), when it dominated Asia Minor. Toward the end of this period, Hittites under Muwatallis (c1306–c1282) engaged the Egyptians for control of Syria. This resulted in the famous Battle of Kadesh (1288) and a treaty. Sometime around 1200 invasions by Phrygian, Thracian, and Assyrian peoples caused the sudden collapse of the Hittite empire. By c700 the Assyrians had absorbed the last vestiges of the Hittite empire.

Hoban, James c1762–1831. Irish-American architect. He designed and built the White House and was a supervisor in the construction of the U.S. Capitol building.

Hobbes, Thomas 1588–1679. British philosopher. A theorist in both natural and political philosophy, he was a friend of such notables as Galileo and B. Jonson. He formulated a mechanistic view of human actions, and his writings on free will, the social contract, and political absolutism had an enormous influence on the development of political philosophy. His works include *Human Nature* and *Leviathan.*

Hobkirk's Hill, Battle of Battle of the American Revolution (Apr. 25, 1781) in which a force of 900 British troops defeated some 1,500 Americans under Col. N. Greene, near Camden, South Carolina.

Ho Chi Minh (*pseud. of* Nguyen That Thanh) 1890?–1969. Vietnamese Communist leader, one of the foremost Communists of the 20th cent. He left Vietnam in 1911 and until WW II stayed variously in the US, Britain, France, China, and the USSR. He founded the Indochinese Communist party (1930) and was sought by the French soon thereafter as a leader of revolutionary Vietnamese nationalists. During WW II he organized the Viet Minh movement for Vietnamese independence and his guerrilla units fought the Japanese. After the war he proclaimed (1945) Vietnam a republic, of which he became president (1945–54). He was soon embroiled in the Indochina War (1946–54) and the republic was divided into South and North Vietnam. President of the northern sector (1954–69), he organized the National Liberation Front and the Vietcong guerrilla armies, which fought in the south during the protracted Vietnam War (1960–75).

Ho Chi Minh Trail Network of jungle and mountain trails connecting North Vietnam with South Vietnam, Laos, and Cambodia during the Vietnam War. Much of the network came into use from WW II on, in fighting against the Japanese, French, and the Americans and South Vietnamese. Neither land assaults nor strategic bombing of segments (from 1965) succeeded in preventing the use of the trail to supply the North Vietnamese–Vietcong war effort.

Hofer, Andreas 1767–1810. Austrian patriot. Attempting to keep his native Tyrol under Austrian rule, he led a peasant rebellion that withstood Bavarian and French forces from 1809 to 1810. He was executed by order of Napoleon.

Hoffmann, Ernest Theodor Amadeus 1776–1882. German author and composer, known best for his Gothic horror stories.

Hofmannsthal, Hugo von 1874–1929. Austrian poet and dramatist, famous for his librettos to R. Strauss operas, including *Der Rosenkavalier* and *Electra.*

Hogarth, William 1697–1764. English painter and engraver. He is known best for "morality pictures," of which *Marriage à la Mode* is considered his masterpiece.

Hōgen War *See* Japan, 1156.

Hohenheim, Theophrastus Bombastus von *See* **Paracelsus.**

Hohenlinden, Battle of Battle (Dec. 3, 1800) of the French Revolutionary Wars, at Hohenlinden, southern Germany. Some 110,000 French troops led by J. Moreau defeated an Austrian

force of 130,000 under Archduke John, brother of Holy Roman Emperor Francis II. The last major engagement of the War of the Second Coalition, it left only England in opposition to Napoleon.

Hohenstaufen Family of German nobles and rulers of the Holy Roman Empire (1138–1254). The family originated in the 11th cent. with a Swabian count, Frederick (*d.* 1105). The first Hohenstaufen emperor was Conrad III, crowned 1138. The Hohenstaufen rulers were opposed by the Guelphs and, by their involvement in Italy, eventually brought about the downfall of the family. The family became extinct by the death (1254) of Conrad IV, the execution of Conradin (1268), and the execution of Frederick's illegitimate son, Enzio (1272). *Hohenstaufen rulers of the Holy Roman Empire:* Conrad III, king of the Germans 1138–52; Frederick I Barbarossa, emperor 1155–90; Henry VI, emperor 1191–97; Philip of Swabia, king of the Germans 1198–1208; Frederick II, emperor 1220–50; Conrad IV, king of the Germans 1250–54.

Hohenzollern Family of German nobles that provided rulers of Prussia (1415–1871), brought about a united Germany (1871–1918), and created a line of Rumanian kings (1866–1947). The family was begun by the 11th-cent. counts of Zollern. Following the death of Frederick of Hohenzollern (c1200), the family split into Franconian and Swabian lines. The fortunes of the Franconian line grew around control of Brandenburg, of which Frederick I became elector (1417). Thereafter the line increased its power and domains and in 1701 Frederick I was crowned king of the new kingdom of Prussia. After the unification of Germany (1871), the Franconian rulers ruled as German kaisers until establishment of the Weimar Republic (1918). The Swabian line, later split into the Hohenzollern-Hechingen and Hohenzollern-Sigmaringen lines. The latter division produced princes and then kings of Rumania (1866–1947). *German Kaisers:* William I 1871–88; Frederick III 1888; William II 1888–1918. *Rumanian Kings* Carol I prince 1866–81, king 1881–1914; Ferdinand I 1914–27; Michael 1927–30, 1940–47; Carol II 1930–40.

Hōjō Family of Japanese nobles. As regents for a line of weak shoguns and puppet emperors, they were in effect the rulers of the shogunate and the warrior estate in Japan between about 1219 and

1333. Among their leaders were Hōjō Yasutoki (1183–1242), who consolidated power in the regency, and Hōjō Tokimune (1215–84), who repulsed invasions of Japan by Kublai Khan (1270s–1280s).

Hōjō Tokimune *See* **Hōjō.**

Hōjō Yasutoki *See* **Hōjō.**

Hokusai (Katshushika Hokusai) 1760–1849. Japanese artist, considered one of the great color-print designers. A prolific artist, he produced many works, including the 15-volume *Ten Thousand Sketches.*

Holbach, Paul, Henri Thiry, baron d' 1723–89. French philosopher. An outspoken materialist and naturalist, he attacked religion in several philosophical works.

Holbein, Hans, the Elder 1465–1524. German portrait and religious painter, known especially for his altarpieces and for his silverpoint drawings.

Holbein, Hans, the Younger 1497–1543. German Renaissance portrait and religious painter. The most famous of a family of painters, he is known for his altarpieces, portraits done as court painter to English king Henry VIII, and paintings of religious subjects.

Holberg, Ludvig, baron 1684–1754. Norwegian-born Danish poet, playwright, historian, and philosopher. His collected works are regarded as the foundation of Danish literature.

Hölderlin, Friedrich 1770–1843. German poet. A protégé of F. von Schiller, Hölderlin combined classical Greek form with the energy of the Sturm und Drang movement. He is considered a bridge between the classic and Romantic schools of poetry.

Holland Former county of the Holy Roman Empire that is now divided into two provinces of the Netherlands. Established in 1018, it passed to the House of Wittelsbach (14th cent.) and then to Burgundy (1433). Holland was a leader in commerce, shipbuilding, and the cloth industry in the 16th cent. and led in the fight for Dutch independence.

Holmes, John Haynes 1879–1964. American clergyman and writer. He championed many social causes and was a founder of both the American Civil Liberties Union and National Association for the Advancement of Colored People.

Holmes, Oliver Wendell, Sr. 1809–94. American poet, writer, physician, and father of O. W.

Holmes, Jr. He is known best for his poems *Old Ironsides* and *The Chambered Nautilus* and his series of prose works called the "Breakfast-Table" sketches.

Holmes, Oliver Wendell, Jr. 1841–1935. American jurist and US Supreme Court associate justice (1902–32). Appointed to the court by T. Roosevelt, he became known as the "Great Dissenter" for his dissenting opinions in cases in which the Court struck down new laws passed by Congress. Despite his advocacy of such judicial restraint, he developed the "clear and present danger" concept in regard to restrictions on freedom of speech.

Holmes, Sherlock *See* **Doyle, Sir Arthur Conan.**

Holocaust Name given to the Nazis' systematic persecution of European Jews and other groups between 1933 and 1945, culminating in the barbaric extermination of millions of persons in concentration camps during WW II. Persecution of the Jews and others began weeks after A. Hitler took power in Germany (1933), starting with anti-Semitic laws that became steadily harsher over the years. By 1935, for example, the Nürnberg laws barred German Jews from marrying other Germans and stripped them of their German citizenship. During the 1938 *Kristallnacht* pogrom (Nov. 9–10), virtually all synagogues in Germany were destroyed. Soon after the Nazis began confiscating property owned by Jews and imprisoning Jews in concentration camps. After the outbreak of WWII in 1939, Jews not in concentration camps were herded into ghettos and required to wear a yellow star insignia. Hitler's organized program to strip Jews of their property and even their most basic rights was exported to conquered nations as well as to Allied nations; Jews thus suffered in France, Italy, and Denmark, as well as in the nations of Eastern Europe. Originally the Nazis sought to impose forced deportation of Jews from Germany and conquered territories, but these programs failed. Meanwhile in Poland (and later the USSR) special SS death squads began rounding up and exterminating Jews, Gypsies, and others in conquered cities and towns. Concern about opposition to the mass killings resulted in the Wannsee Conference (Jan. 20, 1942), at which the SS official Reinhard Heydrich discussed the "final solution" to the problem of the Jews. At this meeting, the Nazis decided on evacuating Jews from all occupied territories to concentration camps, where they would be systematically killed or used as slave laborers. Among the camps hastily organized that year were Bergen-Belsen, Sobibor, Auschwitz, Treblinka, and Maidanek. Auschwitz became the main extermination center (up to 10,000 victims were gassed daily), and ultimately some 4 million of the estimated 6 million Jews killed by the Nazis died in these death camps. Some Jews attempted to resist, most notably in the Warsaw ghetto where about 60,000 revolted against the Nazis for a few months (1943), but for the most part hunger, systematic privation, and outright brutality brought about their submission. It is estimated that in all the Nazi camps during WWII (including POW camps) some 18 to 26 million persons died.

Holowczyn, Battle of Battle (July 4, 1708) in the Northern War at Holowczyn, Russia. The Swedish army under Charles XII defeated the Russian army under Gen. A. Menshikov during the Swedish invasion of Russia. The Russian scorched-earth policy, however, forced Charles to abandon his march east and move south to the Ukraine.

Holst, Gustav 1874–1934. English composer. He was inspired by such European composers as R. Strauss and I. Stravinsky. His works include the orchestral suite *The Planets.*

Holy Alliance League formed (Sept. 26, 1815) by Russian tsar Alexander I, Austrian king Francis I, and Prussian king Frederick William III. The league was largely an agreement in which the monarchs swore to uphold Christian principles in their kingdoms. A part of the general European realignment after the fall of Napoleon's empire, it was eventually joined by all Christian European rulers except British king George IV. The alliance itself had little direct impact, but it became a symbol of conservative reactionary policies by which monarchs maintained social order and which characterized European politics until the mid-19th cent.

Holy Land Name applied to the middle, eastern region of Palestine. It is so called because of its historical associations with the Christian, Islamic, and Jewish religions.

Holy League 1. Holy League of 1495 formed to repel an invasion (1494) of Italy by French king Charles VIII. Joined by Pope Alexander VI, Holy Roman Emperor Maximilian I, Ferdinand and Isabella of Spain, and the cities of Venice and Milan, the league forced Charles to retreat (1496) from Naples. 2. Holy League of 1511 formed to drive French king Louis VII out of Italy during the Italian Wars. It was joined by Pope Julius II, English king Henry VIII, Spanish king Ferdinand V, and the city of Venice, and succeeded in expelling (1512) the French from Milan. The French persisted, however, and the allies eventually made separate peace agreements with France. 3. Holy League of 1526 formed to force Holy Roman Emperor Charles V out of Italy. It was joined by Pope Clement VII, French king Francis I, and the cities of Venice and Milan, and was defeated by Charles. 4. Holy League of 1538 formed to oppose the Schmalkaldic League. It was joined by Holy Roman Emperor Charles V and other German Catholic noblemen. 5. Holy League of 1576 (Catholic League) formed to oppose Protestantism in France during the Wars of Religion. It was first proclaimed by Henri, 3d duc de Guise, in protest to concessions granted the Protestants by King Henry III. Disbanded by Henry after a Protestant uprising, it was re-formed (1585) to oppose Protestant heir to the throne, Henry IV. During the War of the Three Henrys the league controlled France's cities, and, on Henry III's assassination (1589), Henry IV was forced to accept Catholicism (1593) to end the league's resistance.

Holy Roman Empire Political entity in central Europe from the 10th to 19th cents., which gave rise to the modern states of Germany and Austria. Its history is complex and begins with the Carolingian Empire of Charlemagne. Charlemagne's empire was (from 800) considered the successor state to the Western Roman Empire (defunct since 476) and embraced much of Europe. But it was divided in 843 and central authority soon died out in the two major divisions, the eastern kingdom (roughly, modern Germany) and the western kingdom (roughly, modern France). Otto I restored control in the east and in 962 was crowned emperor of the Romans by the pope. The Holy Roman Empire was thus founded as the reconstituted Western Roman Empire. Otto's coronation also marked the beginning of the often troubled alliance between the emperors and the Roman Catholic popes. In subsequent centuries the empire was torn by struggles with the popes and by the rising power of the princes. In the 13th cent. the Holy Roman Emperors gave up their claims to control Italy and in the 14th cent. they lost effective control over the princely states within the empire. They had direct rule over only their personal domains, though in the case of the Habsburg emperors (ruled from the 15th cent.) this amounted to considerable territory. The Protestant Reformation, wars with the Ottoman Turks and with France further weakened the empire in the next centuries. Its final collapse was brought on by the French Revolutionary Wars at the end of the 18th cent. (*For subsequent history of the region, see* Germany, Austria, Reformation.) **For more on important persons and events** *see* **entries under specific names.** Key events in the history of the Holy Roman Empire include:

768–814   Charlemagne reigned as king of the Franks, asserted Frankish control in Italy and expanded the Carolingian Empire eastward, subduing the German tribes.

800   Charlemagne crowned emperor by Pope Leo III; this was taken as revival of the Western Roman Empire, which had collapsed in 476.

814–840   Louis I (the Pious) reigned over the empire; his heirs began struggle that would lead to division of empire.

840–855   Lothair I reigned as emperor; though he retained title of emperor, the Carolingian Empire was divided soon after his accession.

843   Treaty of Verdun; Carolingian Empire divided; Louis the German gained the East Frankish Kingdom, Charles the Bald gained the West Frankish kingdom, and Lothair received the imperial title (with no sovereignty over other kingdoms), and a narrow middle section of the Carolingian domains.

843–876   Louis the German reigned over the East Frankish kingdom (roughly modern Germany).

855–875   Imperial crown passed to Louis II, son of Lothair I; he inherited direct control over Italy only.

870   Treaty of Mersen; Louis the German and Charles the Bald divided the middle kingdom (except Italy), thus bringing East and West Frankish kingdoms to a common border.

875–877   Imperial crown passed to the West Frankish king, Charles II (the Bald), on the death of Louis II.

876   Louis the German died; his East Frankish kingdom divided among his heirs.

881–887   Charles III (the Fat) reigned as imperial emperor, succeeding after period of strife; reunited east under his rule (882).

884–887   Charles III (the Fat) next succeeded (884) to West Frankish throne; Carolingian Empire thus briefly reunited; Charles unable to repulse invasion by Norsemen; deposed in east and west.

887   Arnulf deposed Charles III in the east.

887–899   Arnulf reigned as king of the East Franks; repulsed invasions by Norsemen and Slavs.

896–899   Arnulf reigned as emperor; crowned after pacifying Italy (895) at the pope's request; was last of the Carolingian line of emperors, and no emperor was crowned again until 962.

899–911   Louis the Child reigned as king of the East Frankish kingdom; Magyar raids (from 900) broke down central authority and increased power of feudal lords.

911–918   Conrad I reigned as elected king of the east; continuation of Magyar raids, and feuds and rebellions by feudal lords nearly caused complete breakup of eastern kingdom; Lorraine became part of the western kingdom.

919–936   Henry I (the Fowler) reigned as elected king of the eastern kingdom; as duke of Saxony he had been an archfoe of the king; but during his reign he reestablished royal authority in the east; regained Lorraine and decisively defeated the Magyars (933).

936–973   Otto I reigned as German king; completed reestablishment of central authority; regarded as first emperor of the Holy Roman Empire (after 962).

951   First invasion of Italy by Otto; he assumed the title of King of the Lombards.

955   Otto I decisively defeated the Magyars at the Battle of Lechfeld.

960   Otto I subdued the Slavs.

961   Second invasion of Italy by Otto I; he quickly defeated Italian king Berengar II at the request of Pope John XII.

962   Otto crowned emperor by the grateful pope; this marked the beginning of the Holy Roman Empire and the second revival of the Western Roman Empire.

962   Privilegium Ottonianum, agreement concluded (Feb. 13) between Otto and the pope to regulate relations between them; marked the beginning of the long, often troubled rela-

tionship between Holy Roman Emperors and the popes.

963 Pope John deposed by Otto; Leo VIII installed in his place.

965 John XIII named pope by Otto after Leo VIII died; Romans refused to accept him.

966–972 Otto invaded Italy a third time; subdued the Romans and had some successes against the Byzantines in southern Italy.

973–983 Otto II reigned; imperial control in Italy weakened; Danes revolted in the north and Slavs launched invasions of the empire.

974–978 Revolt by Bavaria (led by Henry the Wrangler); Otto ultimately defeated Henry.

980 Otto defeated French king Lothair, who was attempting to take the duchy of Lorraine.

981–982 Campaign by Otto against Arabs in southern Italy failed.

983–1002 Otto III reigned; installed two popes (Gregory V and Sylvester II) and tried to make Rome capital of the empire; driven out by rebellious Romans in 1001.

1002–24 Henry II reigned as last of the Saxon emperors; crowned 1014; warred against King Boleslaus of Poland and reasserted control over Italy (1021–22).

1024–39 Conrad II reigned as first of the Salian rulers, elected German king after the extinction of the Saxon line, he was forced to put down revolts in Germany and Italy; crowned emperor (1027).

1024–1125 Salian dynasty of emperors in power.

1039–56 Henry III reigned; crowned emperor 1046; imperial power at its height; established border with Hungary that remained fixed for centuries; supported the Cluniac Order and failed in his attempt to reform the church.

1046 Synods of Sutri and Rome; Henry reasserted imperial right to nominate popes and named Clement II in place of three rivals claiming papacy.

1056–1106 Henry IV reigned, crowned emperor 1084; his reign marked the beginning of the Investiture Controversy and the rise of the power of the popes.

1075–76 Reformer Pope Gregory VII condemned Henry for appointing a number of bishops, thus beginning the Investiture Controversy; Henry deposed the pope (1076), while the pope deposed Henry.

1077 Henry forced to submit to the pope and do penance at Canossa to avoid revolt within the empire.

1077–80 Civil war within the empire; Henry victorious against the antiking Rudolf of Swabia.

1081–84 Henry marched against Rome as struggle with Pope Gregory was renewed; crowned emperor by antipope Clement III, whom he installed; Normans, allies of pope, drove Henry out of Rome.

1106–25 Henry V reigned, crowned emperor (1111); he accepted the Concordat of Worms (1122) which ended the Investiture Controversy but not the rivalry between popes and the imperial emperors.

1125–37 Lothair II reigned; elected king (with support of clergy) over rival claimant with hereditary ties to royal line.

1125–35 Civil war between the Welfs (Lothair's supporters) and Waiblingers (supporters of the Hohenstaufen family, which claimed the throne on the basis of heredity); the war, won by Lothair, marked the beginning of the long struggle between these factions for control of the throne.

1133 Lothair II crowned emperor after invading Italy (1132–33) to support Pope Innocent II against a rival.

1138–52 Conrad III reigned as first king of the Hohenstaufen line; elected king by German nobles, he was never crowned emperor.

1138–42 Civil war between Conrad and the Welfs; defeated Welfs agreed to peace, but rivalry between Welf and Waiblinger factions continued throughout century.

1147–49 Conrad joined in the Second Crusade; meanwhile the struggle with the Welfs spread disorder throughout the German domains.

1152–90 Frederick I Barbarossa reigned; crowned emperor 1155, he opposed the growing power of the papacy and sought to reimpose imperial control over Italy (launched six invasions of Italy); attempted to check the power of the princes in the empire.

1155 Holy Roman Empire made official name of empire by Frederick.

1156 Austria created as an independent duchy.

1167 Lombard League formed by Lombard cities in northern Italy against Holy Roman Emperor Frederick I.

1189–90 Frederick joined the Third Crusade and died in Asia Minor.

1190 Order of Teutonic Knights formed at Acre during Third Crusade; later became a power in Prussia.

1190–97 Henry VI reigned; crowned emperor 1191; his reign was marked by continuing struggles with the Welfs and by restoration of order in Sicily.

1192–94 English king Richard I held captive by Henry; Richard forced to accept suzerainty of Holy Roman Empire over England and pay a large ransom to obtain his release.

1197–1211 Civil war over succession; Waiblinger Philip of Swabia and Welf Otto IV vied for control; Philip killed (1208) and Otto was deposed after a brief reign.

1212–50 Frederick II reigned; as member of Hohenstaufen line, he opposed the Welfs and continued the struggle with the papacy; imperial control of northern Italy declined.

1214 Battle of Bouvines; Frederick, allied with French king Philip II, defeated the Welf leader Otto IV and John of England.

1226 By issuing the Golden Bull of Rimini, Frederick II granted the Teutonic Knights sovereignty over Prussia.

1246 Antiking of Germans named by Pope Innocent IV, who sought to break power of Hohenstaufens and gain control of Italy; warfare in Italy and Germany followed.

1250–54 Conrad IV succeeded his father, but was never crowned emperor, continued struggle with Innocent IV and died as he was about to renew war in Italy.

1254–73 Great Interregnum followed death of Conrad IV; nobles gained power; no recognized German king during this period.

1273–91 Rudolf I reigned as king; he ended the Great Interregnum and founded the Habsburg line; never crowned emperor; imperial powers declined sharply.

1278 Rudolf defeated Bohemian king Ottocar II and thereby gained core of Habsburg domains (Austria, Styria, Carniola) that remained in family until the 20th cent.

1279 Papal sovereignty over Papal States recognized by Rudolf; followed recognition of papal sovereignty in southern Italy (1275).

1291 Four Forest Cantons formed league against the Habsburgs and thus began the struggle for independence of Switzerland.

1292 Adolph of Nassau elected king of the Germans to prevent crown from becoming hereditary Habsburg title.

1300s Rise of the Hanseatic League, a league formed by German towns to safeguard and promote commerce as imperial authority declined; league remained powerful until the 15th cent.

1314–47 Louis IV reigned; fought Frederick the Fair (1314–22) for German crown.

1327–30 Louis intervened in Italy, declared emperor by Roman laity (1328).

1338 Declaration at Rhense; German electors eliminated papal confirmation for naming of emperor; declared election of German king by them automatically conferred imperial crown; practice of papal confirmation nevertheless continued.

1347–78 Charles IV reigned; received papal confirmation in 1355 and brought end to long struggle with papacy over Italy.

1348 Black Plague began spreading throughout the empire.

1356 Golden Bull of 1356 issued by Charles; formal constitution for empire which confirmed decentralization of authority and created a federation of sovereign states; emperors never again exercised real control over empire, only personal domains; papal confirmation of election of emperor effectively eliminated.

1376–88 First Swabian League formed by German principalities to oppose Charles's increased taxes on cities.

1378–1400 Wenceslaus reigned as king; he was a weak ruler; his reign was marked by warfare between the princes and the imperial cities; deposed in favor of Rupert (ruled 1400–10).

1410–37 Sigismund reigned; was also king of Hungary (1387–1437).

1410 Battle of Tannenberg fought; victory of Polish and Lithuanian forces, who halted eastern advance of Teutonic Knights.

1414–18 Council of Constance convened at Sigismund's urging; brought Great Schism to an end (1417).

1415 Bohemian religious reformer J. Huss executed for heresy.

1419–34 Hussite Wars, struggle between followers of J. Huss and imperial forces.

1428 Sigismund's campaign failed against the Turks advancing in the east.

1438–39 Albert II reigned; following his election as emperor, the imperial crown became hereditary in the Habsburg family.

1440–93 Frederick III reigned; last emperor crowned at Rome (1452); obtained Burgundy by marrying his son, Maximilian, to Mary of Burgundy (1477) and thus set stage for great expansion of Habsburg hereditary domains.

1488–1534 Second Swabian League formed by German principalities.

1493–1519 Maximilian reigned; greatly expanded Habsburg domains, often at the expense of the empire; attempts to reform administration of empire proved only partly successful as princes sought to maintain their power.

1494–1559 Italian Wars; Maximilian involved the empire in wars there; fought France to regain Burgundian territories in Italy, which he had inherited.

1495 Diet of Worms instituted limited constitutional reforms.

c1498 Aulic Council, emperor's personal council, established by Maximilian I.

1499 Switzerland gained independence from the empire.

1508 Maximilian joined the League of Cambrai in war against Venice, gaining some of its territory.

1513 Maximilian joined Holy League against France.

1516 Hungary and Bohemia added to Habsburg domains through marriage.

1516 Maximilian's grandson succeeded to the Spanish throne, thus adding Spain and the New World to Habsburg domains.

1517 Reformation began (Oct.) when M. Luther posted his demands for church reform.

1519–58 Charles V reigned; as king of Spain and Holy Roman Emperor he ruled vast domains but continuing Italian Wars and revolts connected with the Reformation diminished his power.

1521 M. Luther called before imperial Diet of Worms; refused to recant his Protestant teachings.

1522–23 Knights' War, unsuccessful rebellion by knights to ensure ancient privileges against the Reformation.

1524–25 Peasants' War, unsuccessful uprising of peasants and townsmen; denounced by M. Luther and crushed.

1525 Teutonic Knights dissolved by Grand Master Albert of Brandenburg.

1526–29 War with advancing Ottoman Turks, who were successful in Hungary and laid siege to Vienna (1529).

1531 Schmalkaldic League formed by Protestant nobles to oppose the emperor's threats to end Lutheranism by force.

1532 Religious Peace of Nürnberg.

1535 Charles successfully attacked Turkish-held Tunis.

1544–47 Schmalkaldic War against German Protestant powers.

1545–63 Council of Trent; marked beginning of the Counter-Reformation.

1548 Augsburg Interim proclaimed by Diet of Augsburg; Charles V attempted to force a settlement of strife between Catholic and Protestant nobles in the empire.

1555 Peace of Augsburg provided formula for ending conflict between Catholics and Protestants within the empire.

1556 Charles V abdicated Spanish throne to his son Philip.

1556 Charles V abdicated German throne in favor of his brother Ferdinand; Ferdinand subsequently lost control of much of Hungary to the Turks.

1568 Truce concluded with Ottoman Turks by Emperor Maximilian II (reigned 1564–76); emperor agreed to pay tribute to Turks in return for control of part of Hungary.

1576–1612 Rudolf II reigned; Catholic Reformation actively supported, opening way to Thirty Years' War.

1604–06 Hungarians, led by I. Bocskay, revolted against attempts to impose Catholicism in Hungary.

1608–21 Protestant Union formed by Protestant princes to prevent imperial government from reimposing Catholicism.

1612–19 Matthias reigned; failed to ease conflicts between Catholics and Protestants; outbreak of Thirty Years' War.

1618–48 Thirty Years' War; Emperor Ferdinand II (reigned 1619–37) unable to put down revolt by Protestant nobles in Bohemia; war became general European war of religion that seriously weakened the Holy Roman Empire.

1648 Treaty of Westphalia ending the war; Emperor Ferdinand III (reigned 1637–57) forced to agree to terms that effectively ended central authority of imperial crown; thereafter emperors really controlled only hereditary Habsburg domains.

1658–1705 Leopold I reigned; empire embroiled in wars.

1672–78 Third Dutch War; Leopold joined coalition against French King Louis XIV.

1682–99 Austro-Turkish War; Ottoman Turks forced to withdraw from almost all of Hungary.

1689–97 War of the League of Augsburg against France.

1701–14 War of the Spanish Succession over claims to the Spanish throne; French Bourbon line succeeded in Spain; Austrian Habsburgs gained the Austrian Netherlands and Spanish territories in Italy.

1701 Frederick I created the Kingdom of Prussia.

1711–40 Charles VI reigned; tried to ensure succession of his daughter, Maria Theresa, to Habsburg domains; wars with Turks proved indecisive.

1713 Emperor Charles VI issued the Pragmatic Sanction of 1713 to ensure succession of his daughter, Maria Theresa.

1733–35 War of the Polish Succession.

1740–48 War of the Austrian Succession; Maria Theresa ultimately retained Habsburg domains and her husband became Holy Roman Emperor Francis I (reigned 1745–65); Prussia, under Frederick II (the Great), emerged as a major power during the war.

1756–63 Seven Years' War; Austrian Habsburgs failed to regain territories from Prussia while Prussian power increased in Europe.

1765–90 Joseph II reigned; an enlightened despot, he attempted to institute reforms, but many proved to be short-lived.

1778–79 War of the Bavarian Succession; Joseph thwarted in plan to annex Bavaria to Austria.

1781 Serfdom abolished.

1781 Edict of Toleration issued by Joseph.

1787–92 Austrian participation in the Russo-Turkish War proved fruitless.

1790–92 Leopold II reigned; repealed many of Joseph's reforms.

1792 Declaration of Pillnitz; Leopold joined Prussia in this proclamation against revolutionaries in France.

1792–1806 Francis II reigned as the last emperor of the Holy Roman Empire.

1792–1802 French Revolutionary Wars; Emperor Francis defeated by French.

1801 Treaty of Lunéville, ending wars between the Holy Roman Empire and France; Francis forced to consent to the virtual dissolution of the empire and reorganization of German states.

1804 Francis II became Austrian emperor Francis I.

1804–15 Napoleonic Wars; Austria quickly defeated by Napoleon and forced to consent to the Treaty of Pressburg (1805).

1806 Holy Roman Empire formally dissolved.

Holy Sepulcher Church in Jerusalem built over what are traditionally believed to be the sites of Jesus's crucifixion and tomb. Completed in AD 336, the building was originally a rotunda. It has been destroyed, rebuilt, and remodeled several times. The modern structure dates from 1810.

holy war A war fought for the advancement or defense of a religion, such as the Crusades, or, in Islam, a Jihad. The Jihad provided the impetus for conquest (of nonbelievers) that led to the rapid expansion of the Muslim Caliphate in the 7th cent.

Homer Ancient Greek poet who is generally regarded as the author of two of the greatest epic poems in Western literature, the *Iliad* and the *Odyssey*. Homer was revered in ancient times though the details of his life are largely a matter of legend and conjecture. Even his authorship of the two great epics has been contested (the "Homeric question"). He is thought to have lived in a Greek colony in Asia Minor in the 8th cent. BC and, according to one legend, was blind. What is certain, however, is that the two epics profoundly influenced ancient Greek culture and the subsequent development of Western literature.

Homer, Winslow 1836–1910. A leading American artist, he is known best for his paintings of the sea.

Home Rule Irish movement for self-government. Formed (1870) by Isaac Butt (1813–79) and led by C. Parnell (to 1890), the movement included demands for a separate Irish parliament and land reform (*see* Irish Land Acts). Two Home Rule bills (1886, 1893) were backed by W. Gladstone's British Liberal party, but they failed to overcome Conservative opposition in Parliament. A third Home Rule bill was finally passed (1912), but implementation was delayed by the outbreak of WW I. During the war, radical Irish Republicans came to the fore, and, with the declaration of Irish independence by the Dáil Éireann (1918), the Irish Republican Army went into armed rebellion against the British government. The Irish Free State (later the Republic of Ireland) was created in 1921.

Homestead Act US law (passed 1862). The act granted 160 acres of public land to a settler after a five-year occupancy. The movement for land grants to settlers gained momentum after 1835, when land sales were no longer needed to eliminate the public debt. Of great interest to the developing Western states, such land grants were promoted by the Free-Soil party and opposed by the South. By the 1850s the issue of land grants had become related to extension of slavery in the new Western territories. It was not until after the secession of Southern states and the outbreak of the Civil War (1861–65) that the act passed Congress.

Homestead strike Famous US labor dispute (1892). Following the breakdown of wage negotiations with the Carnegie Steel Company at Homestead, Pennsylvania, members of the Amalgamated Association of Iron and Steel Workers went on strike. Company manager H. Frick, however, hired strikebreakers and some 300 Pinkerton detectives to protect them. Strikers shot at the detectives (July 6), and a gun battle broke out in which several were killed and wounded. The state militia was called out to restore order, and the plant was reopened. The strike was officially ended Nov. 20.

Homily of Obedience Homily included in the 1547 edition of the *Book of Homilies* that Queen Elizabeth I ordered read annually. She favored the homily as a clear reminder of the proper hierarchy of subjects in the realm.

Homma, Masaharu *See* **Bataan Death March.**

Homo habilis *See* **Leakey, Louis Seymour Bazett.**

Honduras (Republic of Honduras) Independent state located in northern Central America. The population is 5,281,000 and the capital is Tegucigalpa. A Mayan culture once flourished in the area (from 4th cent. AD) but by the time Columbus discovered Honduras (1502) it had already declined. Like other Central American republics, Honduras has experienced considerable political turmoil since gaining independence from Spain in 1521. There have been well over 100 coups since that time. Key dates in the history of Honduras include:

1502   C. Columbus was first European to sight coastal region of Honduras.

1524   P. de Alvarado established coastal settlements.

1539   Honduras became part of the captaincy general of Guatemala.

1821   Honduras proclaimed independence from Spain.

1821–23   Became part of A. Iturbide's Mexican Empire.

1825–38   Joined Central American Federation.

1838   Became a republic; subsequent history marked by political instability, the struggle between liberals and conservatives, and interference by neighboring countries.

1860   American adventurer and filibusterer William Walker captured in Honduras while on an expedition aimed at Nicaragua.

1863   Alliance with Nicaragua and El Salvador ended in warfare with them.

1874–83   Marco Aurelio Soto in office as president (except 1876); his administration marked by stable government and enactment of reforms.

1883–1911   Long period of unrest and revolution; US Marines finally intervened (1911) during a revolt, led by Manuel Bonilla, and restored order.

1924   Civil war broke out after liberal president López Gutiérrez (1919–24) attempted to hold office after his term; US intervened.

1933–49   Tiburcio Carías Andino in office as president; rebellion put down (1937).

1940s   Honduras became leading banana producer (until the 1950s).

1949–54   Juan Manuel Gálvez in office as president.

1954–56   Julio Lozano Díaz served as president.

1957   New constitution promulgated.

1957–63   Liberal leader Ramón Villeda Morales in office as president.

1961   Dispute over southeastern border with Nicaragua settled by International Court of Justice.

1963 Villeda Morales overthrown by military junta led by Osvaldo López Arellano.

1963–65 Honduras ruled by military junta.

1965 Twelfth constitution adopted.

1965–71 Military leader López Arellano in office as elected president.

1969 Soccer War fought with El Salvador.

1971–75 Ramón Ernesto Cruz elected president (1971); López Arellano ousted Cruz (1972) and held power to 1975.

1975 Bloodless coup (Apr. 22) by Col. Juan Alberto Melgar Castro followed bribery scandal.

1975–78 Melgar in power as head of state.

1978 Military coup (Aug. 7), by Gen. Policarpo Paz García, ousted Melgar.

1980 Military allowed election of a Constitutional Assembly (Apr.); Paz formally transferred power to the Assembly (July).

1980–82 Paz served as interim president following election by Parliament; planned land reform and program to promote literacy.

1981 Honduran troops attacked Salvadoran refugees streaming across border with El Salvador.

1981 National elections held.

1982 Paz relinquished power to elected president, ending military rule.

1982–86 Roberto Suazo Córdova, a member of Partido Liberal (PL), in office as president.

1982 Nicaragua charged Honduras with aiding guerrilla invasions; US promised to help Honduras fight terrorist attacks.

1983 Big Pine II, military exercise involving US naval forces and thousands of US troops, staged in Honduras; exercise intended to threaten Sandinista regime in Nicaragua.

1984 Government ended program for training of Salvadoran soldiers on Honduran soil.

1984 Honduran military officers exiled for involvement in disappearance of 114 people.

1985 Honduran jet fighters provided air support for guerrilla attack inside Nicaragua; government blamed Nicaraguan provocation.

1985 Honduras, along with other Central American nations, signed agreement denouncing terrorism and calling for removal of all foreign military personnel from the area.

1986–90 José Azcona Hoyo, a member of the Liberal party, served as president; first time in 50 years one civilian president replaced another in Honduras; Azcona agreed to allow Nicaraguan Contra rebel bases to remain in Honduras.

1986 Over $1 million in US humanitarian aid to Contras diverted to Honduran military men, according to report by US investigators.

1987 Contra rebels ordered out of Honduras by June 15.

1987 Honduras, along with other Central American nations, approved the Costa Rican Arias Plan for peace in the region (June 26); plan sought to halt all civil wars by immediate cease-fire, by ending aid to all guerrilla forces, and by starting negotiations between all combatants.

1988 Plan for Central American Parliament approved by Honduras.

1990– Rafael Leonardo Callejas, member of the National Party (PN), in office as elected president; his harsh austerity plan, calling for 42 percent cut in government spending, sparked waves of crippling strikes.

1991 US canceled $430 million in Honduran foreign debt.

1992 World Court ended century-old border dispute between Honduras and El Salvador (Sept.); awarded two-thirds of disputed territory to Honduras; territorial dispute had sparked 1969 Soccer War.

Hong Kong British crown colony (*pop.* 5,700,000) in southeastern China, comprised of Hong Kong Island, Kowloon Peninsula, and the New Territories. Victoria, its capital, is site of one of the world's best harbors. Hong Kong is a major trade and commercial center in the Far East. China ceded Britain the island (1841) and the peninsula (1860), and leased it the New Territories for 99 years (1898). Hong Kong was occupied by the Japanese during WW II. In 1984, Britain and China signed an accord for the return of Hong Kong to China in 1997. The capitalist system was to be maintained in Hong Kong for 50 years after the reversion.

Hong Xiuquan *See* **Taiping Rebellion.**

Honorius I *d.* 638. Italian pope (625–638), successor to Boniface V. His failure to condemn Monothelitism outright as heresy led to his own posthumous condemnation as a heretic at the Council of Constantinople (680). This in turn led to a controversy over papal infallibility.

Honorius II (Scannabechi, Lamberto) *d.* 1130. Italian pope (1124–30), successor to Calixtus II. As cardinal, he brought an end to the Investiture Controversy by the Concordat of Worms (1122).

Honorius III (Savelli, Cencio) *d.* 1227. Roman pope (1216–27), successor to Innocent III. Considered an able administrator, he confirmed the orders of the Dominicans (1216), the Franciscans (1223), and the Carmelites (1226).

Honorius, Flavius AD 384–423. Roman emperor of the West (AD 395–423). A weak ruler, he inherited the western half of the Roman Empire on the death of his father, Theodosius I. During his reign his empire was invaded by Visigoths, who captured Rome (AD 409).

Hood, Thomas 1799–1845. English poet. Though he wrote much in a humorous vein, he is perhaps best remembered for such serious poems as *The Song of the Shirt* and *The Bridge of Sighs*.

Hooke, Robert 1635–1703. British physicist and inventor who did notable work in a variety of scientific fields. His law of elasticity (1678) demonstrated that the stress on an elastic body is in direct proportion to the stress produced. He studied gravitation and maintained a long-standing rivalry with I. Newton; both claimed credit for discoveries in gravitation. Hooke suggested that an orbiting body is pulled toward the center of a larger, central body (1664) and also that the force of gravity follows an inverse square law (1679). These hypotheses later proved important to Newton's law of universal gravitation (1687). Hooke published *Micrographia* (1665), the first major work on microscopy, and (1667) coined the biological term "cell." In his studies of geology, he maintained that fossils were remains of plants and animals from the past and rightly insisted that their study would reveal important knowledge about the earth. Hooke's inventions included a spiral spring for watches, a perfected air pump, the wheel barometer, a weather clock, and the universal joint.

Hooker, Joseph 1814–79. Union general in the American Civil War. Nicknamed "Fighting Joe," he succeeded (1863) A. Burnside in command of the Army of the Potomac. Following a major defeat at Chancellorsville (1863) and only days before the Battle of Gettysburg, Hooker resigned as commander of the army.

Hooker, Richard 1554?–1600. English theologian. An Anglican clergyman, he wrote *Of the Laws of Ecclesiastical Polity*, a closely reasoned defense against the arguments of Catholics and Puritans.

Hooker, Thomas 1586–1647. Puritan clergyman born in England. One of the founders of Hartford, Conn. (1636), he was pastor of the colony until his death.

Hoorn, Philip de Montmorency, count of (Horn, ~) 1518–68. Flemish nobleman and soldier. Though loyal to the Spanish rulers of the Netherlands, he opposed the Inquisition and was beheaded.

Hoover, Herbert Clark 1874–1964. Thirty-first US president (1929–33), successor to C. Coolidge. A mining engineer by profession, he became known for his work as head of the US-backed relief agencies in Europe during and after WW I. He next served as US secretary of commerce (1921–29) and in that capacity brought about construction of the Hoover Dam and St. Lawrence Seaway. Picked by the Republican party to succeed Coolidge, he defeated the Democratic contender, A. Smith, in the 1928 election. Only months after he took office, however, inherent weaknesses in the US economy, fostered by his predecessor's policies, culminated in the stock market crash of Oct., 1929 (Black Thursday). As the economic crisis widened into the Great Depression, Hoover maintained an abiding faith in business to restore the economy and private charity to aid the needy. This policy was both unsuccessful and much criticized as the number of unemployed grew to unprecedented proportions. Though Hoover firmly opposed direct federal aid to the unemployed and public works programs, he nevertheless did institute the Federal Farm Board and the Reconstruction Finance Corporation (1932). The failure of his policies to check the worsening depression, his expulsion of the Bonus Army (*q.v.*) from Washington, and the rising tide of bankruptcies, mortgage foreclosures, and bank failures contributed to his defeat by F. Roosevelt in 1932. Thereafter he remained out of politics until after WW II, when he headed two Hoover commissions (1947–49, 1953–55) to investigate government inefficiency.

Hoover, J(ohn) Edgar 1895–1972. American public official. A sometimes controversial director of the Federal Bureau of Investigation (from 1924 to his death), Hoover is credited with turning it into a model law enforcement agency.

Hoover Commission *See* **Hoover, Herbert Clark.**

Hopi Indians (Moki) Tribe of Pueblo Indians (*q.v.*) located in northeastern Arizona.

Hopkins, Gerard Manley 1844–89. English poet and Jesuit priest whose poetry has had an important influence on the poets of the 20th cent.

Hopkins, Johns 1795–1873. American financier and philanthropist. Originally a grocer, he amassed a large fortune in banking and left $3 million to found Johns Hopkins University in Baltimore, Md.

Hopkins, Stephen 1707–85. American politician and signer of the Declaration of Independence. He served as Colonial governor of Rhode Island six times from 1755 to 1768 and was a member of the Continental Congress (1774–76).

Hopkinson, Francis 1737–91. American patriot, writer, musician, and signer of the Declaration of Independence. His pamphlets and songs helped win support for the American Revolution. He was a delegate to the Continental Congress in 1776.

hoplites Heavily armed foot soldiers in ancient Greece. From c8th cent. BC, these soldiers were used as infantry, marching into battle in phalanxes and fighting hand-to-hand in close formation. Hoplites wore helmets, breastplates, and greaves of bronze and carried a bronze shield, a short sword, and a thrusting spear. Though slow-moving and especially vulnerable in rough terrain, massed hoplites fighting in compact formation proved a formidable military force.

Horace (Flaccus, Quintus Horatius) 65–8 BC. Roman poet, one of the great lyric poets of all time. His works reflect the temper of the Augustan Age and his mastery of poetic form. A freedman's son, he was schooled in Rome and Athens. After the Roman Civil War, in which he participated, Horace worked under the patronage of his friend Maecenas. By 35 BC he had produced his first book of *Satires* and thereafter wrote his *Odes, Epistles, Ars Poetica,* and other works.

Horney, Karen 1885–1952. American psychiatrist. She broke with Freudian doctrines on the causes of neuroses, emphasizing environmental and social factors instead of biological drives.

Horseshoe Bend, Battle of *See* **Creek War.**

Horthy, Nicholas (Miklós von Nagybánya) 1868–1957. Hungarian admiral (in the Austro-Hungarian navy) and Hungarian head of state (1920–44). He defeated the Communist revolutionaries and was named regent to the deposed emperor Charles I. Horthy later refused to allow

Charles to retake the throne and himself ruled Hungary until he was arrested by A. Hitler.

Hoshea Last king of Israel, son of Elah. He assassinated and succeeded Pekah (732? BC). His alliance with Egypt against the Assyrians led to the conquest of Israel by the Assyrians (722? BC). [2 Kings 15–17]

Ho-shen *See* **Heshen.**

hostage crisis (American hostage crisis) International crisis (from Nov. 4, 1979) in which Iranian militants seized the US embassy in Teheran, Iran, and held 52 Americans hostage for 444 days. Following the overthrow (Jan., 1979) of Mohammad Reza Shah in the Iranian revolution, anti-American sentiment in Iran was whipped to a fever pitch. The embassy seizure itself was sparked by the shah's arrival in the US for medical treatment. Militants, suspecting a plot to return the shah to power, captured the embassy (Nov. 4) and took 90 hostages. They later released all but 52 Americans. Their demands included return of the shah and his wealth to Iran, and they threatened to try the hostages as spies. President J. Carter ordered the freezing of Iranian assets in the US (Nov. 14). The seizure had the support of Ayatollah R. Khomeini, who used the incident to consolidate his control over the revolution and publicly humiliate the US. Carter was thwarted in attempts to negotiate the hostages' release, and a military rescue attempt (Apr. 24, 1980) failed, leaving eight US servicemen dead. The shah died (July 27), and negotiations dragged through the 1980 presidential election. Negotiators finally reached an accord (Jan. 19, 1981), but the hostages were not released until a few minutes after R. Reagan was sworn in as US president (Jan. 20).

Hottentots A South African people who controlled a large part of South Africa before the arrival of European settlers. They now are divided among several tribes, and their pastoral culture is largely dispersed.

Houdini, Harry (*pseud.* of Ehrich Weiss) 1874–1926. American magician who became world famous for his escape tricks.

Houdon, Jean Antoine 1741–1828. Leading 18th-cent. French sculptor. He is considered a master of portrait sculptures.

Houphouët-Boigny, Félix *See* **Côte d'Ivoire.**

House, Edward Mandell 1858–1938. American diplomat and President W. Wilson's adviser. Known as "Colonel" House, he helped Wilson negotiate terms for the Treaty of Versailles and the Covenant of the League of Nations at the close of WW I.

House of *See under family names, as in* **Bourbon; Habsburg.**

Housman, A(lfred) E(dward) 1859–1936. English poet and classical scholar, known best for his collection of poetry *A Shropshire Lad.*

Houston, Samuel 1793–1863. American frontiersman, soldier, and political official who played a major role in the Texas war for independence. A US congressman (1823–27) and Tennessee governor (1827–29), he lived (1829–33) with the Cherokee Indians after his wife left him. By 1835, however, Houston had become involved in the struggle between American settlers and the Mexicans for control over what is now Texas. As commander of American forces, he eventually routed the Mexicans at San Jacinto (1836) and thereby won Texas's independence. He was president of the territory (1836–38, 1841–44) and, after statehood (1845), became senator (1846–59). Elected governor (1859), he opposed secession and was forced out of office (1861).

Howard Leading English family of noblemen. The duke of Norfolk, who heads the family, is hereditary earl marshal and premier duke of England. The family has a number of cadet branches, including earldoms of Arundel, Northampton, Nottingham, Suffolk, Surrey, Norwich, and Carlisle. The line was founded by William Howard I (*d.* 1308) and gained title (1483) to Norfolk through the marriage of Robert Howard (*d. before* 1436) to the daughter of T. Mowbray, the first duke of Norfolk. Members of the family became leaders of English Roman Catholics after the Reformation. Prominent members of the family include: John Howard, 1st duke of Norfolk; Thomas Howard, 2d duke of Norfolk; Thomas Howard, 4th duke of Norfolk; Henry Howard, 1st earl of Northampton; Charles Howard, 1st earl of Nottingham; Charles Howard, 1st earl of Carlisle; Frederick Howard, 5th earl of Carlisle.

Howard, Bronson Crocker 1842–1908. American playwright whose successes helped spark the development of American drama. Among his best-known plays are *Saratoga* and *Shenandoah.*

Howard, Catherine 1521?–42. Fifth queen of English king Henry VIII. Married to the king shortly after his divorce from Anne of Cleves

(1540), she was convicted of adultery the following year and was beheaded.

Howard, Charles, 1st earl of Carlisle 1629–85. English statesman. A supporter of O. Cromwell, he nevertheless continued to serve after the Restoration of Charles II (1660).

Howard, Charles, 1st earl of Nottingham 1536–1624. English nobleman. He served as ambassador to France (1559), lord high admiral (1585–1618), and lord lieutenant general of England (1599–1619). He was in command of the expedition that defeated the Spanish Armada (1588).

Howard, Sir Ebenezer 1850–1928. English city planner. He was the leading founder of the English garden city movement, which aimed at relieving urban congestion by building self-sufficient towns surrounded by open spaces.

Howard, Frederick, 5th earl of Carlisle 1748–1825. English statesman. Howard was unsuccessful in his attempt to reconcile the American colonies (1778). He later served as viceroy of Ireland (1780–82) and as guardian to Lord G. Byron, the poet.

Howard, Henry, earl of Northampton 1540–1614. English noble. He served as lord privy seal under King James I and was a commissioner at the trials of W. Raleigh and G. Fawkes.

Howard, Henry, earl of Surrey c1517–47. English poet. Howard translated two books of Vergil's *Aeneid,* thus introducing blank verse to England. He also introduced the Petrarchean sonnet.

Howard, John, 1st duke of Norfolk 1430?–85. English noble. John served under Edward IV and Richard III. He died fighting for Richard at the Battle of Bosworth Field.

Howard, Oliver Otis 1830–1909. Union general in the American Civil War. A capable military leader, he is better known as chief commissioner of the Freedmen's Bureau (1865–74) and as a founder and president of Howard University (1869–74).

Howard, Robert *See* **Howard.**

Howard, Thomas, 2d duke of Norfolk 1443–1524. English noble. The son of J. Howard, he was wounded in the Battle of Bosworth Field (1485) and was imprisoned. He later defeated the Scots at Flodden Field (1513) and his father's lands and titles were restored to him.

Howard, Thomas, 4th duke of Norfolk 1536–72. English noble. Queen Elizabeth I placed him in charge of investigating Mary, Queen of Scots, but he was imprisoned for planning to marry her. His plot to aid Spanish king Philip II in an invasion led to his execution.

Howard, Thomas, 13th earl of Arundel c1586–1646. British art patron, noted for his great art collection, particularly his ancient statuary, the Arundel marbles.

Howard, William *See* **Howard.**

Howe, Julia Ward 1819–1910. American author and social reformer. She is known best as the author of *The Battle Hymn of the Republic.*

Howe, William, 5th viscount Howe 1729–1814. English commander of British forces (1775–78) during the American Revolution. He played an important role in the Battle of Bunker Hill and soon after succeeded Gen. T. Gage as overall commander in America. In subsequent battles he occupied New York City (1776) and Philadelphia (1777) but failed to capture Gen. G. Washington's army. This led to the major British defeat at Saratoga (1777) and his subsequent resignation.

Howells, William Dean 1837–1920. American novelist and literary critic. Sometimes called the champion of realism in literature, he is said to have influenced S. Crane, M. Twain, H. James, and others. He wrote *A Modern Instance* and *The Rise of Silas Lapham.*

Hoxha, Enver 1908–85. Ruler of Communist Albania from the end of WW II until his death (1946–85). Hoxha became a Communist while studying in France during the 1930s and in 1941 became secretary general of the Albanian Labor party, a group formed by partisans following Italy's occupation of Albania. A rigid Stalinist, he became prime minister of a Communist-ruled Albania following WW II. Then from 1953 until his death he ruled Albania as first secretary of the ruling Communist party. During his long regime, Hoxha at first established close ties with the USSR, then shifted his alliance to Communist China (after 1961) in reaction to the Soviet de-Stalinization movement. Hoxha broke with the Chinese in 1978, cutting off much-needed foreign aid and effectively isolating Albania. The last years of Hoxha's ruthless and bloody regime were marked by the collapse of Albania's economy and growing resentment toward Communism.

Hoyle, Edmond 1672–1769. English writer and authority on games. His *Short Treatise on the Game of Whist,* published in 1742, was gradually expanded to include many other games and established him as an authority on game rules.

Hsia *See* **Xia.**

Hsia Kuei *See* **Xia Gui.**

Hsiang Army *See* **Hunan Army.**

Hsiung-nu *See* **Xiongnu.**

Hsüan tung *See* **Xuantong.**

Hsün-tzu *See* **Xunzi.**

Huang Ti *See* **Huang Di.**

Huang Di (Yellow Emperor) (Shen Yen Huang Ti) (Huang Ti) The third of China's legendary early emperors who, according to tradition, reigned in the 3d millennium BC. Many fundamental elements of China's civilization are credited to him, including mathematical calculations, the calendar, money, the use of bamboo, and the study of medicine, among others. He is, with Lao-tze, considered the founder of Daoism, and his wife is believed to be the discoverer of the uses of the silkworm.

Huascar *d.* 1533. Emperor of the Incas in Peru. On his father's death (1525), he succeeded to the larger portion of an empire divided between his brother Atahualpa and himself. He lost the empire to his brother (1532) and was later secretly murdered by him.

Huayna Capac *See* **Inca.**

Hubertusburg, Treaty of Treaty (Feb. 15, 1763) between Prussia and Austria ending the Seven Years' War. It guaranteed Prussia's possession of Silesia and its role as a major power in Germany.

Hudaybiyah, Pact of al- Treaty (628) between Muhammad and the rulers of Mecca permitting Muhammad and his followers to enter Mecca for the rite of 'umrah (pilgrimage).

Hudson, Henry c1565–1611? English navigator and explorer. He first led two unsuccessful expeditions for the English (1607, 1608) to discover a northwest passage through the Arctic Ocean to Asia. During a third such expedition, while in Dutch service, he sailed from Holland (1609) aboard the *Half Moon* and explored about 150 miles of the Hudson River, establishing extensive Dutch claims to the area. On his last voyage (1610), again in English service, he sailed aboard the *Discovery* and explored Hudson Bay, which he hoped would lead to the Pacific Ocean. After being forced to spend the winter in Hudson Bay, the crew mutinied and abandoned Hudson, his son, and seven crewmen aboard a small boat (1611). Hudson and the others were never seen again.

Hudson River school Group of American landscape painters and an early school of painting native to America. The school, which stemmed from the European Romantic movement, flourished from 1825 to 1875. It is characterized by but not limited to the dramatic landscapes of the Hudson River region. Among the artists of this school are Thomas Cole (1801–48), Albert Bierstadt (1830–1902), and Thomas Doughty (1793–1856).

Hudson's Bay Company (The Great Company) Chartered corporation (from 1670) that figures prominently in the early development of Canada. Licensed for trade, settlement, and exploration of a vast and vaguely specified region surrounding Hudson Bay, the company eventually expanded its holdings to the Pacific coast. It had governmental control and a monopoly over the lucrative fur trade in its domains. Early clashes with the French traders ended with recognition of British sovereignty in Canada (Treaty of Paris, 1763), and bloody conflicts with the rival British North West Company were ended by a merger of the companies (1821). In 1869, following the unification of Canada, nearly all the company territory was turned over to the Canadian government, and the company thereafter became a powerful retail and manufacturing concern. It was broken up into Canadian and British organizations in 1930.

Hueffer, Ford Madox *See* **Ford, Ford Madox.**

Huerta, Victoriano 1854–1916. Mexican general who overthrew President F. Madero and became military dictator (1913–14). After seizing power, Huerta was faced with numerous attempts at counterrevolution as well as the opposition of US president W. Wilson. Huerta finally fled Mexico and was later jailed in the US.

Hugh Capet c938–96. French king (987–996), son of Hugh the Great and first of the Capetian kings. Inheritance of his father's extensive territories (956) gave him great power, and, after the death of King Louis V, last of the direct Carolingian line, he was elected king.

Hughes, Charles Evans 1862–1942. American statesman and jurist. An associate justice of the Supreme Court (1910–16), he was narrowly defeated by W. Wilson for president (1916).

He thereafter served as secretary of state (1921–25) and chief justice of the Supreme Court (1930–41).

Hughes, Howard Robard 1905–76. Controversial American businessman and reclusive billionaire. Hughes built his financial empire around his father's company, the Hughes Tool Company, and eventually held interests in airplane manufacturing, motion pictures, a major airline, and gambling casinos.

Hugh of Avalon *See* **Hugh of Lincoln, Saint.**

Hugh of Lincoln, Saint (Hugh of Avalon) 1135–1200. English bishop. A Carthusian monk, he is noted for his skill and courage in defending church prerogatives against the designs of English monarchs.

Hugh of Saint Victor 1096?–1141. French or German scholar and mystical theologian. Under his guidance the monastery school of Saint Victor in Paris became one of medieval France's most important intellectual centers.

Hugh the Great *d.* 956. French duke, son of Robert I and father of Hugh Capet. Excluded from the succession, he supported the succession of the Carolingian king Louis IV and attempted to rule through him.

Hugo, Victor 1802–85. French writer. Hugo's poetry, plays, and novels occupy a major place in French Romantic literature. His drama *Hernani* caused riots between classicists and romanticists in 1830, but today he is best remembered for his novels *The Hunchback of Notre Dame* (1831) and *Les Misérables* (1862). A political republican and member of the National Assembly, Hugo was forced into exile by Napoleon III but returned to Paris in triumph after Napoleon's ouster (1870).

Huguenots French Protestants, important in French history during the 16th and 17th cents. Followers of J. Calvin, Huguenots first suffered persecution at the hands of the French Catholic monarchy shortly after the beginning of the Protestant Reformation (1517). Despite executions and massacres, the movement spread to the French nobility, where it became interrelated with the struggle for political power. Bitter rivalry led to such events as the Conspiracy of Amboise (1560), the St. Bartholomew's Day Massacre (1572), and the Wars of Religion (1562–98). A period of toleration followed the Edict of Nantes (1598) and ended with Huguenot uprisings in the 1620s when King Louis XIII attempted to suppress Protestantism.

By the Peace of Alais (1629), Huguenots lost their political power, and, under Louis XIV, the Edict of Nantes was revoked (1685). This led to a mass exodus of most Huguenots from France. Civil rights of Huguenots were not restored until 1787. By the Declaration of the Rights of Man (1789) they were granted religious equality.

Huineng 638–713. Chinese priest and sixth patriarch of Zen Buddhism. He is known for his introduction of the doctrine of satori, or "sudden enlightenment."

Hukbalahap Rebellion Revolt (1946–54) by Communist-led guerrillas in the Philippines. The Hukbalahap, or People's Anti-Japanese party, proved a highly successful resistance group during the Japanese occupation, and after WW II went into open rebellion against President M. Roxas's government. Their guerrilla war grew into a widespread peasant rebellion by 1950 that finally ended with the surrender of guerrilla leader Luis Taruc in 1954.

Hulagu Khan (Hulegu or Hulaku) 1217–65. Mongol ruler, grandson of Genghis Khan and founder of the Il-Khan dynasty. Sent to put down a revolt by the Persians, he defeated and executed Caliph Mustasim, destroyed the Islamic capital of Baghdad (1258), and set up his khanate, which lasted until 1335.

Hull, Cordell 1871–1955. American statesman and US secretary of state (1933–44). As President F. Roosevelt's secretary of state, he did much to stimulate trade with other nations through reciprocal trade agreements and played an important role in establishing the UN. He was awarded the Nobel Peace Prize in 1945.

Hull, William 1753–1825. American general and governor of the Michigan Territory (1805–12). During the War of 1812, he was in command of Detroit, and surrendered it to the British without resistance (1812). He was court-martialed for cowardice, but his death sentence was commuted.

Hull House *See* Addams, Jane; Kelley, Florence.

humanism Philosophy or attitude that places humankind and human values, welfare, and creativity at the center of consciousness. Humanism was the philosophy that, beginning in the 14th cent., was a central feature of the Renaissance (*q.v.*) in Italy, and spread over the rest of Europe in the following three centuries. It represented a shift from the medieval view of the world as an adjunct to God's creation and fostered a new emphasis on the study of man and the world as objects in themselves. It favored a new Platonism (*q.v.*) over Aristotelianism (*q.v.*) and Scholasticism (*q.v.*). It also looked to Greek and Roman models in art, literature, and thought. One of the major results of the early Renaissance in Italy was an intensive search for and study of ancient manuscripts. The Turkish conquest of Constantinople (1453), which drove many Greek-speaking scholars to seek refuge in Italy, gave added impetus to this interest in the ancient world. The great early Renaissance humanists included F. Petrarch, G. Boccaccio, L. Valla, and the host of Italian painters led by Michelangelo and L. da Vinci. Erasmus and T. More were outstanding later humanists. In modern times, humanism has come to mean an agnostic philosophy that regards man as "the measure of all things," as opposed to religious beliefs.

Human Rights, Universal Declaration of *See* **Universal Declaration of Human Rights.**

Humbert I (Umberto I) 1844–1900. Italian king (1878–1900) who succeeded his father, Victor Emmanuel II. Under his reign Italy joined in the Triple Alliance (1882) and prosecuted the Ethiopian War (1887–96).

Humbert II (Umberto II) 1904–83. Last king of Italy (1946), successor to his father, Victor Emmanuel III. A referendum held shortly after his succession created a republic and stripped him of his powers.

Humble Petition and Advice English document advanced (Mar., 1657) by Parliament during the Protectorate. Superseding the Instrument of Government (*q.v.*), the original version established an upper house of Parliament and sought to name O. Cromwell king, with the power to choose his successor. Cromwell declined to be named king, and, after subsequent modifications, the Humble Petition was passed. Cromwell remained lord protector.

Humboldt, Baron Alexander von 1769–1859. German geographer and explorer. From 1799 to 1804, he explored vast areas in South America in company with French botanist Aimé Bonpland (1773–1858). They trekked over more than 6,000 miles, exploring the Orinoco River, the sources of the Amazon, the Andes Mountains, and much of Mexico. Throughout the expedition, financed by Humboldt himself, they compiled accurate maps and kept careful records of local geological climate, measurements of the earth's magnetic field, and the vast array of flora and fauna they encountered. Humboldt published a 30-volume work, *Voyages of Humboldt and Bonpland* (1805–34), which contributed to the sciences of physical geography and meteorology and speculated about the relationships between a region's geography and its flora and fauna. Humboldt returned to Berlin in 1827 and in 1849 led an expedition to central Asia under Russian auspices. The Humboldt current in the Pacific was named for him.

Hume, David 1711–76. Scottish philosopher and historian. Hume developed a skeptical philosophy that restricted knowledge to actual experience and rejected most theology as an unprovable matter of belief. Among his many writings are *An Enquiry Concerning Human Understanding* and *History of England.* The latter was long a major reference work. (*See also* empiricism.)

Humiliation of Olmütz   *See* **Erfurt Parliament.**

Humphrey, Hubert Horatio 1911–78.   US vice-president (1965–69). As a Democratic senator from Minnesota (1949–65), he was a noted orator, liberal leader, and staunch defender of civil rights. While serving as vice-president under L. Johnson, Humphrey defended escalation of the Vietnam War. This was a contributing factor in his narrow loss to R. Nixon in the presidential race of 1968. He was reelected to the Senate (1970) and tried unsuccessfully to win the Democratic presidential nomination in 1972.

Hunan Army (Hsiang Army)   Chinese regional army organized (1852) in the province of Hunan by Zeng Guofan. Its purpose was to help bring an end to the Taiping Rebellion. At its peak the force numbered approximately 125,000 men.

Hundred Days   1. Period in French history (Mar. 20–June 28, 1815) during which Napoleon returned from exile and attempted to reestablish his empire. Escaping exile on the island of Elba, he landed in the south of France (Mar. 1, 1815) and marched north with a small force. By the time he reached Paris (Mar. 20, 1815), he had rallied France behind him and forced King Louis XVIII to abdicate. Once again emperor, he was opposed (from Mar. 25) by a new coalition of nearly all the other European nations. Following the coalition victory over J. Murat at Tolentino (May 3) and subsequent capture of the kingdom of Naples, Napoleon

launched an attack (June 14) into Belgium. Napoleon's forces were victorious in the battles of Ligny and Quatre Bras (June 16), but were completely crushed at the great Battle of Waterloo (June 18). Soon after, Napoleon surrendered to the British, and King Louis was restored (June 28), ending the Hundred Days period. (*See also* Waterloo; Napoleonic Wars.)   2. Period in US history (from Mar. 4, 1933) marking the first months of President F. Roosevelt's administration. Roosevelt was inaugurated (Mar. 4) during the Great Depression, amid economic disaster, great unemployment, and numerous bank failures. During the Hundred Days period his administration initiated much of the legislation for his first New Deal (*q.v.*) program. The term "Hundred Days" has also been applied to the early months of other presidential administrations.

Hundred Years' War   Series of related wars (1337–1453) between England and France. The conflict stemmed from English claims to the French throne (based on descent from the Norman conquerer, William I) and the long rivalry over territories on the Continent that were then English possessions. Just before war broke out, France and England were vying for the lucrative wool and cloth trade of Flanders, and English king Edward III was concerned about protecting the English-held duchy of Guienne (in modern France). Edward touched off the war by invading France to take the crown by force. The protracted war that followed was fought mainly in France and devastated the country. The outbreak of the Black Plague only added to the loss of life on both sides. The consequences of the war were far-reaching: English presence on the Continent was all but ended; and the ravages of war contributed to the decline of feudalism, the rise of a middle class, and the emergence of a strong monarchy. Key dates in the history of the war include:

1337   English king Edward III proclaimed himself king of France in opposition to French king Philip VI.

1339   English invaded France through the Low Countries; land war indecisive.

1340   English gained control of the Channel by their victory (June 24) in the naval battle of Sluis.

1345   New English invasion of northern France began.

1346   Battle of Crécy fought (Aug. 26); major English victory over the French.

1346–47   English besieged and captured Calais; victory followed by lull in fighting (to 1355).

1355   English forces led by Edward the Black Prince conquered Bordeaux in southwest France; raids conducted in southern France.

1356   Battle of Poitiers (Sept. 19); English routed French forces and captured King John II, who had succeeded to the French throne.

1358   Jacquerie revolt.

1360   Treaty of Brétigny, ending first period of the Hundred Years' War; England gained Calais and much of Aquitaine from France; French king John returned for a large ransom.

1369–86   Fighting resumed; new French king Charles VI attacked English (1369) using guerrilla war tactics; by 1386 the French had retaken much of the territory held by England.

1396   England and France agreed to a truce, to last for 30 years.

1415   English king Henry V resumed the war by invading France; France embroiled (from 1407) in civil war between Burgundians (pro-English) and Armagnacs over control of the French throne; subsequent alliance between Burgundians and English seriously weakened French position.

1415   Henry V defeated French at Battle of Agincourt; French suffered heavy losses.

1415–19   Normandy conquered; Rouen captured (1419); English gained control of most of northern France.

1420   Treaty of Troyes signed (May 20); by its terms French king Charles VI accepted English king Henry V as heir to the French throne.

1422   Both Henry and Charles died; the French dauphin, Charles's son, declared himself French king Charles VII; the English held that Henry's son, Henry VI, was king; Henry VI controlled the north, Charles VII the south.

1428   English invaded southern France, laid siege to French stronghold of Orléans (Oct.).

1429   French fortunes at low ebb; young visionary Joan of Arc convinced Charles VII to give her command of force to relieve Orléans.

1429   Joan's forces lifted (May) siege of Orléans; tide of war turned in favor of the French; English forces pushed northward.

1429   French won major victory at Battle of Patay (June 18); La Hire routed Shrewsbury's English troops in northern France.

1429   Charles VII crowned (July 17) at Rheims after being encouraged by Joan of Arc.

1430   Joan of Arc captured by Burgundians (then allied with the English); ransomed to the English, she was burned at the stake (1431) as a witch.

1435   Treaty of Arras signed between France and Burgundy, ending the alliance between Burgundy and England and greatly strengthening the French position.

1436   French forces captured Paris from the English; lull in fighting ensued.

1444   Truce of Tours (May 28); fighting halted until 1449.

1449   French began final offensive of war; attacked English in Normandy and Guienne.

1450   Battle of Formigny in northern France (Apr. 15), a decisive French victory.

1450   French completed reconquest of Normandy.

1451   French took duchy of Guienne, except for Bordeaux, from the English.

1453   French captured Bordeaux, marking end of the war; English territories on the Continent (once extensive) now reduced to the city of Calais, which England held until 1558.

Hungarian Revolution of 1956   Brief but bloody rebellion (Oct. 23–Nov. 14, 1956) against Russian domination in Hungary. The revolt was caused by a series of factors, including the movement for reform in Poland, the denunciation of Stalinism by N. Khruschchev, and the Soviet-aided ouster (July, 1956) of the repressive regime of Mátyás Rákosi in Hungary. The revolt was sparked (Oct. 23) when Hungarian forces fired on people demonstrating in Budapest in support of Polish reform and in opposition to Soviet presence in Hungary. Soon the entire country was in revolt. I. Nagy, who as premier had earlier (1953–55) introduced reforms in Hungary, was restored to power (Oct. 24), and János Kádár (1912–89) became new head of the Communist party. Nagy immediately instituted liberal reforms, called for Soviet withdrawal from Hungary, took Hungary out of the Warsaw Pact, and sought aid from the UN to secure Hungary's neutrality. Meanwhile Kádár formed a countergovernment and called for Soviet assistance. Russian forces entered Hungary and on Nov. 4 began operations against the revolt. The rebellion was crushed by Nov. 14 and Kádár was installed as the new head of the government. Nagy and others, tricked by promises of safe conduct, were captured, sent to Rumania, and executed.

Hungary Republic located in Eastern Europe. The population is 10,546,000 and the capital is Budapest. The region of present-day Hungary was part of the Roman provinces of Pannonia and Dacia and was subsequently occupied by Germanic tribes, Huns, Avars, and ultimately the Magyars (9th cent.), who profoundly shaped the history of Hungary. A kingdom from the early 11th cent., Hungary later fell under Ottoman and Austrian Habsburg domination. Hungarian resistance to Austrian hegemony led to formation (1867) of the Dual Monarchy, or Austro-Hungarian Monarchy. Hungary finally became independent with the collapse of the Austro-Hungarian Empire at the end of WW I and, in 1949, became a people's republic, modeled along Soviet Communist lines. In 1989–90, widespread dissatisfaction over continuing economic decline, and the wave of pro-democracy sentiment sweeping through the Communist world, brought about the collapse of the Communist government in Hungary. Key dates in the history of Hungary include:

2D CENT. AD   Germanic tribes invaded region; later displaced by the Huns.

5TH–8TH CENTS. AD   Avars occupied region.

c890   Arpád led Magyars from Asia to Hungary; established Arpád dynasty.

955   Holy Roman Emperor Otto I defeated the Magyars on the Lechfeld; marked the end of Magyars' westward expansion.

1001–38   Stephen I reigned as first crowned king of Hungary; established Christianity in the kingdom.

1077–95   Ladislaus I, a national hero, reigned; conquered Croatia.

1222   King Andrew II (reigned 1205–35) issued the Golden Bull, known as the "Magna Carta of Hungary"; marked rise of powerful magnates (nobles).

1235–70   Béla IV reigned; rule marked by devastating Mongol invasion (1241) and conflict with Austria.

1301   Andrew III, last of the Arpád dynasty, died; period of unrest and civil war.

1308–42   Charles Robert of Anjou reigned as Hungarian King Charles I; strengthened the monarchy, curbed the power of the nobles, and founded the Angevin line in Hungary.

1342–82   Louis I (the Great) reigned; conducted wars against Venice (1346, 1357–58, 1381) and by the Treaty of Turin (1381) gained all of Dalmatia; succeeded to the Polish throne (1370) and thereby made Hungary one of the largest kingdoms in Europe; promoted administrative reforms and commercial prosperity.

1387–1437   Sigismund reigned; began period of rule by foreign kings; his crusade against the Ottoman Turks advancing on fringes of the kingdom failed (1396); elected emperor of the Holy Roman Empire (1411); suppressed the Hussites.

1456   J. Hunyadi, Hungarian hero, ended Ottoman siege of Belgrade.

1458–90   Matthias Corvinus reigned; successful against the Turks; conquered Bohemia, Lusatia, Moravia, and Silesia, reorganized the government, and made Hungary the dominant power in central Europe.

1490–1526   Period of unrest followed death of Matthias Corvinus; nobles sought to regain power; Zápolya family gained control of Transylvania; Doza Rebellion by peasants broke out (1514); kingdom unable to check continuing advance of Turks.

1526   Battle of Mohacs, Turkish victory over Louis II of Hungary; led to more than 150 years of Turkish domination of central Hungary, Habsburg domination in the west, and ascendancy of noblemen in Transylvania.

1572–1608   Rudolph II (later Holy Roman Emperor) reigned as king of Hungary; Protestantism had spread among Magyars as a result of the Reformation (especially in Transylvania) and Rudolph began imperial policy of imposing the Catholic Counter-Reformation in Hungary and elsewhere.

1604–06   I. Bocskay led rebellion against Habsburgs of Holy Roman Empire, then controlling western Hungary; won constitutional and religious rights for Protestants by Peace of Vienna.

1618–48 Thirty Years' War; Hungarian nationalists used opportunities to oppose domination by Habsburg Holy Roman Empire.

1682–99 Austro-Turkish War; Austrian Habsburgs gradually pushed Turks out of Hungary, their claim to the Hungarian throne recognized by Hungarian nobles (1687); finally won control of Turkish domains in Hungary (then including Transylvania).

1703–11 Francis Rákóczy led unsuccessful rebellion against Habsburg rule in Hungary; Habsburgs then promoted settlement of Hungary by Germans and Slavs.

1740–48 War of Austrian Succession; magnates supported claims of Maria Theresa to Habsburg domains, accepting her as queen of Hungary.

1780–90 Joseph II reigned as sole ruler of Habsburg lands; his efforts at radical reforms were widely opposed.

1806 Holy Roman Empire dissolved as a result of defeat in Napoleonic Wars; power of Austrian Habsburgs reduced in subsequent post-Napoleonic period; Austrian Habsburgs retained control over Hungary.

FROM 1815 Rise of liberal nationalist movement began in the post-Napoleonic period.

1848–49 March Laws instituted autonomous constitutional monarchy under Habsburg sovereignty following outbreak of Revolutions of 1848 in Europe, Austrian troops sent into Hungary; L. Kossuth proclaimed Hungary a republic (Apr., 1849).

1849 Austrians victorious (with Russian aid) at the Battle of Temesvar (Aug. 9); battle ended short-lived Hungarian Republic.

1866–67 Austrian power seriously weakened by Austro-Prussian War (1866); Magyar nationalists forced compromise agreement, Ausgleich, establishing Dual Monarchy of Austria-Hungary (1867).

1867–1916 Francis Joseph reigned as emperor of Austria and king of Hungary; Austria and Hungary theoretically equal under separate governments; unrest grew among the Hungarian national minorities (Croats, Slovaks, Serbs, and Rumanians).

1873 The cities of Buda and Pest were united.

1914–18 WW I; Hungary, as part of the Austro-Hungarian Empire, fought with the Central Powers; hardships of war aroused discontent and brought collapse of the Dual Monarchy (Nov. 11, 1918).

1918 Hungarian People's Republic proclaimed (Nov. 16) at close of WW I; Michael Károlyi became first president.

1919 B. Kun seized power after new government proved unable to check unrest among minorities; he established short-lived, Communist soviet republic of Hungary. (Mar. 21–Aug. 1); invasion by Czechs and Rumanians ended the Soviet government.

1920–44 Nicholas Horthy (M. de Nagybánya) in power as regent of a vacant monarchy; harsh reprisals against leftists (White Terror) began.

1920 Treaty of Trianon signed (June 4) by Allied Powers after WW I, established new Hungarian state but greatly reduced territory; this later led to alliance with Fascist Germany in effort to regain lands.

1932–36 Premier J. Gömbös in office; promoted Fascism.

1939–45 WW II; Hungary became an ally of Germany; Germany occupied Hungary when it attempted to end participation in war (1943); Soviet forces drove out Germans and occupied the country (Oct., 1944–Apr., 1945) after hard fighting.

1946 Following national elections (1945), a new constitution was adopted.

1947–49 Minority Communist party consolidated its control within the Hungarian government; aided by Soviet forces, it conducted campaigns against anti-Communists and the church.

1948 Cardinal Mindszenty, Roman Catholic primate of Hungary, arrested and convicted in trial staged by Communists; imprisoned until 1956.

1949 Communists gained control of Hungarian government; new constitution adopted (Aug. 10) establishing the Hungarian People's Republic, modeled on Soviet lines.

1949–53 Mátyás Rákosi ruled as premier; his pro-Stalinist policies caused wide unrest and political and economic turmoil.

1950 US froze Hungarian assets.

1953–55 I. Nagy made premier; moderated Hungary's economic programs but was removed from office.

1955 Hungary joined Warsaw Pact (May 14).

1955–56 Rákosi back in power.

1956 Hungarian Revolt (Oct. 23–Nov. 14), unsuccessful uprising against Russian domination; I. Nagy led new government; declared Hungarian neutrality and withdrew it from Warsaw Pact; revolt crushed by invasion of Russian and other Warsaw Pact forces.

1956 Cardinal Mindszenty, released from prison during revolt, took refuge in US embassy until 1971, when he was allowed out of Hungary.

1956–65 János Kádár in power as premier; led opposition to liberal government of Hungarian Revolution; instituted reforms and purged Stalinist party leaders; Kádár remained in power as acknowledged leader of Hungary until his ouster in 1988.

1958 Nagy executed.

1964 Kádár established agreement with Roman Catholic church to improve relations.

1965 Gyula Kallai became premier; Kádár remained in power as secretary of the Hungarian Socialist Workers party; policies of reform and relaxation of controls continued; over next decades Kádár regime enforced policy of discouraging popular interest in politics and encouraging economic productivity.

1968 Economic reforms established more liberal economic policies and led to increases in production; Hungary eventually developed a flourishing export trade with Western nations.

1975–87 György Lázár in office as premier.

1978 WW II war-debt claims with US settled; US authorities returned Saint Stephen's Crown and other national treasures to Hungary.

1979 Government imposed austerity program in face of steadily declining economy; exports to West declined sharply as recession slowed demand in non-Communist world; by early 1980s Hungary's inflation rate hit double digits, trade deficit widened, and foreign debt was mounting rapidly.

1980 Foundation for the Support of the Poor (SzETA, not officially sanctioned) organized to aid an estimated 30 percent of population living in poverty.

1981 Price increases on foods, gasoline, telephones, and other items.

1981 Five-day work week introduced to prevent worker unrest in Poland from spreading to Hungary; workers angered on discovering output quotas would remain same and that they were to continue working 44 hours a week.

1982 Hungary admitted to International Monetary Fund and World Bank; new loan credits enabled Hungary to avert near bankruptcy over financing its rapidly growing foreign debt.

1982 Steep price hikes in bread and other foods, rents, and transportation to help ease worsening economic situation; price increases continued in 1983, 1984.

1983 Kádár successfully defended his program of conservative reforms during meeting with Soviet officials in Moscow (July).

1984 Government enacted major new reform; elected councils to manage major state-run businesses and have control of business assets.

1985 13th Congress of the ruling Hungarian Socialist Workers' party held; long established conservatism of Kádár and other party heads serving him effectively stifled any consideration of much-needed, major reforms.

1985 Parliamentary elections held under new system requiring at least two candidates for each seat (except for 35 reserved seats); efforts by fledgling democratic opposition forces to nominate candidates stymied when ruling Communists packed nomination meetings.

1985 Rare meeting of opposition leaders held outside Budapest; representing a variety of viewpoints, the 47 sought to create a common front.

1986 Students demonstrated against government (Mar. 15) during Hungary's national day; police used force to break up protest.

1986 Radical reform—involving real redistribution of power—put forward as solution to Hungary's growing economic and political crisis; suggested reform included in *Turning Point and Reform,* a discussion paper written by the People's Patriotic Front, a Communist umbrella organization for all social organizations in Hungary, led by party reformer Imre Pozsgay; paper published in 1987.

1986 Hungary's Writers' Union Congress elected governing presidium devoid of any Communists or Communist supporters (Dec.); government threatened to dissolve union to no avail and finally pro-Communist writers walked out.

1987 Radical intellectuals, called Populists, met at Lakitelek outside Budapest to discuss need for major reforms and to establish Democratic Forum; meeting attended by party reformer Imre Pozsgay.

1987 Democratic opposition forces published their *Program of Democratic Change* in one of Hungary's unofficial journals (a *samizdat*); called for moderate reforms, including subjecting Communist party to rule of law and allowing established opposition parties.

1987–88 Károly Grósz in office as prime minister (June); long-time prime minister Lázár ousted as government sought to blunt growing unrest by reshuffling personnel.

1987 Letter, signed by 100 intellectuals and calling for pro-democracy reforms, sent to all members of Parliament.

1988 Aging Kádár, head of Hungary's Communist government for 36 years, removed from office during conference of Hungarian Socialist Workers' party; installed Grósz as party leader, heading a coalition of party reformers and conservative modernizers.

1988 Miklós Németh in office as prime minister; his government faced $18 billion foreign debt—the Communist world's highest per capita—and mounting unrest, but offered no major reforms.

1988 Opposition groups flourished by year's end; Hungarian Democratic Forum and Alliance of Free Democrats among them.

1989 Reformers in ruling Hungarian Socialist Workers' Party (HSWP) won party vote (May) to end party's control over all government appointments (called *nomenklatura* system); effectively broke Communist party's stranglehold over government.

1989 Ruling HSWP voted itself out of existence (Oct.); reestablished itself as the Hungarian Socialist party.

1989 Former parliamentary speaker Mátyás Szürös in office as acting president; Parliament approved establishment of his transitional government (Oct. 17–20), pending elections.

1989 Szürös proclaimed the Hungarian Republic to replace the former Communist people's republic; change effected on Oct. 23, the anniversary of the 1956 Hungarian Revolution.

1989 National referendum led to further dismemberment of Communist party structure

(Nov. 26); voters approved proposals requiring dissolution of party cells in factories, disbanding of party's private army, and for an accounting of party assets.

1990 First free, multi-party national elections held since establishment of Communist regime (Mar.–Apr.).

1990– József Antall, former historian and leader of Hungarian Democratic Forum (HDF), in office as prime minister; his non-Communist government formed by parliamentary coalition of HDF, Christian Democrats, and the Smallholders party; his government proved both indecisive and hesitant about introducing major reforms.

1990 Taxi drivers' blockade (Oct.); taxi drivers paralyzed traffic in Budapest by blocking intersections to protest a government-imposed 75 percent increase in gasoline prices; blockades sprang up in cities across Hungary that same day; government effected compromise on issue.

1990 Hungary became full member of the Council of Europe.

1991 Kupa Plan for economic restructuring announced by government (Feb.); government meanwhile proceeded slowly toward privatization.

1991 Monetary system reform gave national bank relative independence from government control (Nov.).

1991 Inflation rate reported falling, though unemployment, already at 7.3 percent, was rising (Dec.).

1992 Privatization of 278 medium-sized state-owned businesses announced.

Hunkers Faction of New York State Democrats in the 1840s, conservatives who opposed the radical faction called the Barnburners. They followed a line consistent with President J. Polk's policies, favored chartering of state banks and opposed agitation against slavery. They split openly with the Barnburners in the 1846 gubernatorial election. In the 1848 presidential election, anti-slavery Barnburners joined with the Free-Soil party to support M. Van Buren. This split the Democratic party vote and helped Z. Taylor win the presidency.

Huns Nomadic people of Asia, notorious for their military skills and savagery, who for a time (5th cent. AD) threatened the Roman Empire.

The Huns, of uncertain origins, were at times identified with Hsuing-nu, White Huns, Magyars, and others. Skilled horsemen and archers, they appeared in Eastern Europe (AD c370) and, fighting in roving bands (hordes), they conquered the Alani, Ostrogoths, and Visigoths. Victories over the latter two peoples caused great migrations eastward. In the 5th cent. AD the Huns occupied Eastern and Central Europe and had reached the borders of the Eastern Roman Empire. By 432 a single king of the Huns, Rugilas (Rua or Roas), was exacting tribute from the Romans. His successor, Attila the Hun, launched three invasions into the empire (441, 447, 451). On the first he advanced into the Eastern Empire and threatened Constantinople. On the second he again attacked the Eastern Empire and passed through the Balkans into Greece. On the third he attacked the Western Empire and unsuccessfully attempted to take Gaul. After he was defeated by a combined force of Romans and Visigoths at the Battle of Châlons (451), however, he invaded and briefly ravaged Italy. His death (453) was soon followed by disintegration of his kingdom and the Huns as a unified people.

Hunter's Lodges Paramilitary organizations established (1837–38) in the US along the border with Canada, to overthrow British rule in Canada. They made two notable raids (Prescott, Upper Canada, Nov. 11, 1838; Sandwich, Ontario, Dec. 4, 1838) but were quickly repulsed.

Huntington, Collis Potter 1821–1900. American railroad magnate. He and his business partners made the first transcontinental railroad possible by organizing and building the Central Pacific Railroad (1863–69). He later became president of the Southern Pacific (1890), a railroad he helped form.

Hunyadi, John (~, János) c1387–1456. Hungarian general and hero of the resistance to Turkish conquest. He defeated the Turks in many battles, including his "Long Campaign" (1443–44) and the storming of Belgrade (1456). He also served as elected governor of Hungary (1446–52).

Huram *See* **Hiram.**

Huran ar-Rashid *See* **Harun-al-Rashid.**

Huron Indians A group of North American Indian tribes that, in the 17th cent., were located in the Great Lakes region. Bitter enemies of the Iroquois Confederacy, the Huron were mercilessly attacked (1648–50) and nearly wiped out

by the Iroquois. Some of the surviving Huron settled in Ohio, where they sided with the British in the Revolutionary War and the War of 1812. They were subsequently resettled in Oklahoma.

Husayn ibn-'Ali *See* **Husein ibn-Ali.**

Husein ibn-Ali (Husayn ibn-'Ali) 1856–1931. Arabian king (1917–24). Amir of Mecca (1908–16) under the Ottoman Turks, he led the Arab revolt against them (1916) during WW I and proclaimed himself king of Arabia in 1917. He was defeated in a war with Ibn Saud (1924) and went into exile.

Hu Shi 1891–1962. Chinese philosopher and statesman. He was a primary advocate of the change from classical written Chinese to the vernacular as the written language in China.

Huss, John (Hus, Jan) 1369–1415. Czech religious reformer. A Catholic priest, he was excommunicated and later burned at the stake for advocating the teachings of J. Wyclif. His death led to Hussite Wars (1415–36).

Hussar Name given to units of light cavalry in European armies of the 18th and 19th cents. They were named after the Hungarian cavalry corps organized (15th cent.) by King Mathias Corvinus.

Hussein (Husayn ibn 'Ali) c626–680. Shi'ite Muslim martyr, a son of the fourth caliph 'Ali, and Fatima, daughter of Muhammad. He is revered by the Shi'ites as a true heir of the prophet Muhammad. He was killed (680) while trying to claim the Caliphate after Muawiya's death.

Hussein, Saddam 1937– . Iraqi strongman and president (1979–). Born into a peasant family, he joined the Ba'ath Socialist party (1957) and in 1959 fled the country after attempting to assassinate the Iraqi head of state. Returning to Iraq some years later, he was jailed (1964–66) for another attempt at revolt. Then in 1968 he played a key role in the successful overthrow of the civilian government. On becoming chairman of the ruling Revolutionary Council and president in 1979, he quickly consolidated his control of the government by purging the opposition. In subsequent years he instituted a ruthless, cold-blooded regime while tenaciously clinging to power, surviving several attempted coups (including 1979, 1983, 1989). A fanatical militarist, he embroiled Iraq in bloody wars for nearly all his term as president (into the early

1990s), first in the protracted Iran-Iraq War (1980–90) and then the disastrous Persian Gulf War (1990–91), which he provoked by invading Kuwait. Following the destruction of much of his armed forces in the Persian Gulf War, he was forced to accept humiliating peace terms, including the UN supervised dismantling of all Iraqi weapons of mass destruction (including chemical weapons and equipment for building nuclear weapons). Having failed in battle against foreign opponents and having wrecked the Iraqi economy, Hussein nevertheless succeeded in defeating offensives (1991) by opposition groups within Iraq, notably the Kurds and Shi'ite Muslim rebels. *See also* Iraq, 1968–92.

Hussein ibn Talal 1935– . Jordanian king (1953–), successor to his father, King Talal. During his reign he has maintained a generally moderate stance in the Arab-Israeli conflicts, though he joined with the Arabs in the war of 1967. He successfully put down a revolt by Palestinian guerrillas in Jordan (1970–71), survived an assassination attempt (1972), largely kept Jordan out of the Fourth Arab-Israeli War (1973), condemned the Egyptian-Israeli Treaty, backed Iraq in the Iran-Iraq War (1980–90) and the Persian Gulf War (1990–91), and joined in US–backed Mideast peace talks (1991). *See also* Jordan, 1953– .

Husserl, Edmund 1858–1938. German philosopher who founded the school of thought called phenomenology.

Hussites Followers of J. Huss in Bohemia and Moravia who were involved in a 15th-cent. rebellion against the authority of the Roman Catholic church. Following the execution (1415) of Huss as ordered by the Council of Constance, Hussites split into two groups: the moderate Calixtines, or Utraquists, and the radical Taborites. Despite differences they were allied in seeking approval of the Four Articles of Prague, which called for freedom to preach, communion in both bread and wine, the expropriation of church property, and punishment of mortal sins by civil authorities. They fought together in the Hussite Wars (1415–36) until the church won over the Utraquists with promises of concessions. After the defeat of the Taborites (1434), Utraquiests were granted reforms in an agreement known as the Compactata of Prague (1436). The Utraquists eventually split (16th cent.), with one faction joining the evolving Lutheran church and the other the Roman Catholic church.

Hussite Wars Series of wars (1415–36) fought between Hussites and forces of the Holy Roman Empire. Precipitated by the death (1415) of J. Huss and the succession (1419) of the German Holy Roman Emperor Sigismund as king of Bohemia, the wars involved Hussite demands for religious reforms and Bohemian nationalism. Led by J. Zizka, Hussite forces defeated the emperor's armies (1420, 1422). He was succeeded by Procopius the Great (1424), who led the successful resistance to the crusades against them (1426, 1427, 1431) and commanded invasions into Silesia and Saxony (1425–26) and into Franconia (1429–30). The rift between Utraquists (*q.v.*) and Taborites widened during the wars, however, and in 1433, Utraquists opened negotiations with the Catholic church at the Council of Basel. Utraquists turned against the Taborites (led by Procopius), who refused concessions offered by the church, and civil war broke out in Bohemia. The Taborites were completely defeated (1434) at the Battle of Lipany, ending the wars. Concessions granted to the Hussites were formalized (1436) in the Compactata of Prague, which granted Utraquists the right to communion in both kinds, the right to retain church lands, and the establishment of a separate Bohemian church.

Hutchinson, Anne c1591–1643. English-born American religious reformer. Expelled (1637) from Massachusetts Bay Colony by the Puritans, who accused her of antinomianism, she became one of the founders of Rhode Island.

Hutchinson, Thomas 1711–80. Unpopular Colonial governor of Massachusetts (1771–74). His rigorous enforcement of Colonial laws, notably the Stamp Act, led to the Boston Tea Party (1773). He was replaced by Gen. T. Gage in 1774.

Hutten, Ulrich von 1488–1523. German poet, humanist, and patriot. His satiric *Little Conversation Book* was written to aid M. Luther.

Hutterian Brethren *See* **Hutterites.**

Hutterites (Hutterian Brethren) Communal sect with Anabaptist roots which adheres to the primitive-communist doctrine. It was founded by the Tyrolian Jacob Hutter (*d.* 1536), and its members endured persecution until their settlement in the US in the 19th cent.

Hutton, James 1726–97. Scottish geologist. He developed the theory of uniformitarianism

(1785), which holds that the same geological processes have been at work throughout much of the earth's history. The theory is fundamental to modern geology.

Huxley, Aldous Leonard 1894–1963. English author. Among his many works is the widely read *Brave New World.*

Huxley, Thomas Henry 1825–95. English biologist. An outspoken critic of nonscientific thought, he became the leading advocate of Darwinism in England. He also advocated educational reforms, especially in the area of science.

Huygens, Christiaan 1629–95. Dutch physicist, mathematician, and astronomer. He developed highly improved telescope lenses through which he discovered Titan (1655), the largest of Saturn's satellites, and correctly calculated its period of rotation. He was also the first to understand and explain the ring structure around Saturn (1655), previously believed to be "arms" of the planet. He developed the first pendulum clock (1657), an important accomplishment for its use in navigation. He is perhaps best known for his wave theory of light (1678), which states that light is transmitted as a moving wave of constant vibrations, each separate wave displacing the one before it.

Hydaspes, Battle of the (Jhelum, ˜) Last battle fought (326 BC) by Alexander the Great during his campaign in Asia. Alexander defeated the Indian king Porus near the Hydaspes, now the Jhelum, a tributary of the Indus. Indian losses were 12,000, compared to 980 Macedonian dead.

Hyde, Edward, 1st earl of Clarendon 1609–74. English statesman and historian. As a member of Parliament, he originally opposed, then joined Charles I during the period of the English Civil Wars. He later helped to restore Charles II. His *History of the Rebellion and Civil Wars in England* is still considered an invaluable historical document.

Hyksos Name for rulers of Egypt who were of a Semitic people (sometimes also called Hyksos) that invaded and conquered Egypt after the Middle Kingdom. They ruled c1675–c1550 BC and introduced the horse and chariot to Egypt. The Hyksos kings were finally defeated (c1570 BC) by Ahmose I.

Hypatia *d.* AD 415. Neoplatonic philosopher, mathematician, and celebrated beauty. A teacher of philosophy at Alexandria, she was cruelly murdered by rioting monks, said to be instigated by Saint Cyril, archbishop of Alexandria.

I

Iamblichus *d.* c330. Syrian philosopher, and leading figure in the development of Neoplatonism (*q.v.*). He combined the teachings of Plato and Pythagoras with mystical and magical ideas into a religious type of philosophy.

Iasi, Treaty of *See* **Jassy, Treaty of.**

Ibáñez (del Campo), Carlo 1877–1960. President of Chile (1927–31). He was popular in the pre-Depression era for implementing labor and education reforms.

Iberia 1. Ancient name for Spain, after the Iberian people who once dwelled there. The Iberian Peninsula, occupied by Spain and Portugal, is named for them. 2. Ancient country. Iberia was located in what is now eastern Georgia in the USSR. The Iberians were allied with Rome and later became part of the Byzantine Empire.

Iberian Gates Mountain pass in the Caucasus mountains. It has been an invasion route since ancient times, and is also called the Daryal Pass.

Iberville, Pierre le Moyne, sieur d' 1661–1706. A French-Canadian explorer who led raids against British fur trading posts (1686–97) and who founded the first permanent settlement in the Territory of Louisiana (1699), near present-day Biloxi, Mississippi.

Ibn al-'Arabi 1165–1240. Spanish-born Muslim mystical philosopher and poet. He joined Muslim religious teachings with uplifted mystical expression in such works as *The Meccan Revelation* and *The Interpreter of Desire.*

Ibn Batuta 1304?–78? Muslim traveler and writer. He visited countries from Morocco (his birthplace) to China from around 1325, describing his travels in detail in his book *Rihlah (Travels)*. He is considered one of the most reliable authorities on his times.

Ibn Khaidun 1334–1406. Arab historian, philosopher, and statesman. Born in Tunis, he served as a Muslim judge in Cairo. Considered the greatest of the Arab historians, he provided a description of Arab culture in his *Muqaddimah* (*Introduction*), as well as a philosophy of history explaining the rise and fall of civilizations.

Ibn Saud c1880–1953. Saudi Arabian king and founder (1932) of the modern Saudi state. Raised in exile with his family in Kuwait, he began (c1900) his campaign to reconquer the family domains in the Nejd. By 1922 he had firm control of the Nejd and then conquered the Hejaz (1924–25), of which he became king in 1926. In 1932 he changed the name of this kingdom to Saudi Arabia. He introduced a stable, nationalistic form of government and put an end to tribal wars. His decision to open the country to oil exploration led to the discovery of one of the world's largest oil fields.

Ibn Taymiyah 1263–1328. Arab Islamic theologian. An ardent conservative and traditionalist, he suffered imprisonment (1306–07) as a result of his teachings, which were thought to be too anthropomorphic.

Ibn Tufail (Abubacer) 12th cent. Arab philosopher and physician, born in Spain. He was the author of a Romantic philosophical work, *The History of Havy Ibn-Yaqzan,* about a hermit on an island who attained knowledge of the divine.

Ibn Tumart (Muhammad ~) 1078?–1130. Arab reformer. He founded the Almohade (*q.v.*) sect among Berber tribes in North Africa.

Ibn Zuhr (Avenzoar) c1090–1162. Islamic physician, born in Seville, and a leading medical authority of his day. His writing, translated into Hebrew and Latin, attempted to combat quackery.

Ibrahim Pasha 1789–1848. Egyptian general. He was the conquerer of Arabia and Syria for his father Muhammad Ali, the ruler of Egypt; but was obliged to evacuate some of his conquests when Western powers came to the aid of a faltering Ottoman Empire (*q.v.*). He briefly succeeded his father as viceroy of Egypt before his death.

Ibsen, Henrik 1828–1906. Norwegian writer. Ibsen was a poet and playwright whose dramas established him as one of the world's foremost realistic writers. He explored the depth of emotions beneath society, and his opinions were often far in advance of his time. Among his major works are *The Wild Duck, A Doll's House, Hedda Gabler,* and *An Enemy of the People.*

Iceland (Republic of Iceland) Island republic (*pop.* 259,000) located in the North Atlantic near the Arctic Circle. Capital is Reykjavik. Iceland was settled (9th cent.) by Norsemen. A legislative assembly, the Althing, was established (930), Christianity was introduced (c1000), and Iceland recognized Norwegian suzerainty (1264). Iceland then came under Danish control (by the union of Denmark and Norway) in 1380 and, in the mid-16th cent., the Danes imposed Lutheranism. Iceland declined in the 17th and 18th cents., suffering economic exploitation, pirate raids, and a series of volcanic eruptions. It revived in the following century and an independence movement, led by J. Sigurdsson, eventually (1874) resulted in the granting of a constitution and some home rule. Sovereignty was granted in 1918, though by the terms of the Act of Union Iceland remained in personal union with the king of Denmark. The collapse of Denmark in WW II brought occupation by the British and the Americans and, on June 17, 1944, Iceland became an independent republic. In subsequent years, Iceland joined the UN (1946), concluded an agreement (1951) allowing the US to maintain bases there, and engaged in disputes with Britain over fishing rights and territorial waters (1958–61, 1973–76). In 1980 President Vigdis Finnbogadóttir took office, becoming the world's first directly elected female head of state (in office to 1982). A constitutional amendment in 1991 reformed the Althing into a single house legislature. The government declared Iceland a nuclear-free zone in 1985 and Iceland hosted a US–Soviet summit in 1986.

Ickes, Harold Le Claire 1874–1952. American politician and social reformer of President F. Roosevelt's New Deal (*q.v.*) era. He was secretary of the interior (1933–46).

Iconoclastic Controversy Religious dispute. The Iconoclasts of the Byzantine Empire opposed the use of images (icons) in religious worship (sanctioned 7th cent.), on the grounds that icons were sacrilegious. Emperor Leo III denounced the use of icons (726) and in subsequent years icon worshippers and Iconoclasts were alternately persecuted. The controversy raged throughout the 8th and 9th cents., and was denounced (787) by the Second Council of Nicaea (*q.v.*), which decreed that icons could be venerated but not worshipped. The controversy was ended (843) with the restoration of icon worship during the reign of Emperor Michael III.

Ictinus Highly acclaimed Greek architect of the 5th cent. BC. He was a chief designer of the Parthenon (*q.v.*).

Idaho Northwestern state of the US, the 43d state. White men first entered the region with the Lewis and Clark Expedition (*q.v.*) of 1805, and the fur traders soon followed. Idaho was held jointly by the US and Great Britain until 1846, and it became part of the Oregon Territory in 1848. The discovery of gold (1860) and silver (1863) brought many settlers who built up what are ghost towns today. The Idaho constitution was adopted in 1889, and statehood came in 1890. The state is famous for its potatoes, grown in the arid but fertile plateau watered by federal reclamation projects on the Snake River.

idealism Term in ethics, art, and philosophy. In ethics it is a doctrine that recognizes moral or intellectual ideals as superior to materialistic concerns and seeks perfection in attaining these ideals. In art the aesthetic ideal, the way the subject should appear, is the standard of perfection, and not the mere copying of reality. In philosophy, it refers to schools of thought in which the real world is believed to be nothing more than ideas perceived by the intellect. It is opposed to materialism (*q.v.*). Idealism has been espoused in one form or another since the time of Plato. Plato held that the ideas were an unchanging reality that existed independently of one's mind. In more recent times, it was held that these ideas (and thus the real world) were created by the mind itself. Noted proponents of idealism in various forms were Plato, G. Berkeley, I. Kant, and G. Hegel.

Ides of March March 15 by the Roman calendar. J. Caesar was assassinated on this day in 44 BC.

Idris I 1890–1983. The king of Libya from its independence (1951) until he was deposed by a *coup d'état* in 1969. He was a leader of the Senussi sect in Cyrenaica before being made king.

Idrisi (Edrisi) *b.* 1099? Arab scientist and geographer at the court of Roger II of Sicily, the compiler of one of the most significant works of medieval geography (1154).

Ieyasu *See* **Iyeyasu.**

Ifni Former Spanish territory, now part of southwest Morocco, and noted for its fisheries. Ceded by Morocco to Spain in 1860, it was returned to Morocco in 1969.

Iglau, Compact of *See* **Compact of Iglau.**

Ignatius of Antioch, Saint *d.* AD c107. Syrian Catholic bishop. Ignatius was sent to Rome for execution. En route he wrote seven letters which defined and clarified Catholic beliefs, and are invaluable testimonies to early Christian beliefs. His writings contain history's first mention of the name "Catholic church," which he describes as ruled by bishops.

Ignatius of Constantinople, Saint 800–877. Greek Catholic patriarch. Ignatius, son of Emperor Michael I, opposed the Iconoclasts in the Iconoclastic Controversy (*q.v.*). He was ousted by Photius but restored by the Fourth Council of Constantinople (*q.v.*).

Ignatius of Loyola, Saint 1491–1556. Spanish religious leader. Of noble birth, he entered military service, and was wounded at Pamplona (1521). While convalescing he conceived (from reading lives of the saints) the idea of becoming a soldier for Christ. At the University of Paris he formed the nucleus of the Jesuits, or Society of Jesus (*q.v.*), a religious order for men organized along military lines. After approval by the pope (1540), the Jesuits with Ignatius as their first general organized the most effective Catholic response to the Reformation (*q.v.*), dominated and revolutionized European education, and became the largest religious order of modern times.

Igor c877–945. Prince of Kiev (912–45), succeeding Oleg. He was the son of Rurik, founder of the first dynasty of Rus' princes. He concluded a treaty with Byzantium (945) after his attempt at conquest was thwarted. His wife Olga (c890–969), regent of Kiev, converted to Christianity.

Igor 1150–1202. Rus' prince and legendary hero. His defeat in a battle in 1185 inspired the first work of Russian literature, *The Song of Igor's Campaign* (c1187), rendered in a modern English translation by V. Nabokov (1960). It also inspired the famous opera *Prince Igor* (1869) by Russian composer Aleksandr P. Borodin (1834–87).

Iguala, Plan de *See* **Plan de Iguala.**

IGY *See* **International Geophysical Year.**

Ikeda, Hayato 1899–1965. Moderate Japanese statesman who was prime minister (1960–64). He played a large part in Japan's amazing economic recovery following WW II.

Ikhnaton *See* **Akhenaton.**

Île-de-France *See* **Mauritius.**

Île-de-France French region and former province located around Paris. It was the center of the French monarchy's lands from which the modern nation of France evolved.

Iliad* and *Odyssey Two celebrated Greek epic poems, believed to have been written (c750 BC) by Homer. In ancient Greece they were revered as sources for moral and spiritual guidance. In modern times they are considered among the greatest masterpieces of Western literature. The *Iliad* tells the story of the Trojan War (*q.v.*), fought to return Helen to her husband, the Spartan king Menelaus. The *Odyssey* narrates the adventures of Odysseus, a Greek hero, "a man who was never at a loss," during his return to Ithaca after the Trojan War.

Ili crisis Dispute between Russia and China, centering on Ili province in Chinese Turkestan. Russia invaded Ili (1871) to control the advance of a local ruler, Yakub Beg (1820–77). After Yakub Beg's death, Russia restored most of Ili to China (1881), through the Treaty of St. Petersburg.

Il-Khan Mongol dynasty that reigned (1258–1353) in Persia (modern Iran). Between 1253 and 1258, the Mongol Hulagu Khan conquered this territory, including the Islamic capital of Baghdad, and founded the Il-Khan dynasty. The dynasty reached its height under Mahmud Ghazan (1295–1304), who became the first Mongol to convert to Islam (Sunni). In subsequent years internal unrest broke the Il-Khan's power and brought their rule to an end by 1353.

Illinois State in the north-central US, the 21st state. French explorers, J. Marquette and L. Jolliet, first explored the region (1673), and in 1680 R. La Salle built Fort Crèvecoeur. The French ceded the area to Great Britain in 1763 after the French and Indian Wars (*q.v.*). In 1787, the region became part of the Northwest Territory. Illinois became a state in 1818, and the Indians were driven out after the 1832 Black Hawk War (*q.v.*). The present state constitution was adopted in 1970. The capital is at Springfield. The state's prairie lands constitute one of the country's agricultural heartlands, but it is also one of the principal industrial states.

Illuminati Rationalistic type of religious society founded in Bavaria in 1776 by Adam Weishaupt (1748–1830). It claimed enlightened religious views, but was banned in Bavaria in 1785. The term "illuminati" was also used for other rationalistic-type and anticlerical religious sects from the 16th to 18th cents.

Illyria and Illyricum Illyria was an ancient region on the Adriatic coast, roughly corresponding to parts of Yugoslavia and Albania. The early Illyrians frequently practiced piracy, until they were conquered by the Romans (between 2d and 1st cents. BC). The Romans established it as the province Illyricum, which eventually sent many legionnaires and emperors (Claudius II and Diocletian) to Rome. Illyricum was divided into the provinces of Dalmatia (*q.v.*) and Pannonia after AD 9.

Illyrian Wars Two successful wars fought by the Romans (229–28, 219 BC) to suppress Illyrian pirates. In gratitude the Greeks admitted the Romans to the Eleusinian Mysteries and Isthmian Games, marking the official recognition by the Greeks of Rome as a civilized power.

Illyricum *See* **Illyria and Illyricum.**

Imagists American and English poetry school. These early 20th-cent. poets opposed the excessive sentimentality of the 19th cent. They stressed clearly defined images and verbal precision, and included E. Pound, D. H. Lawrence, and A. Lowell.

imam Islamic leader. "Imam" is a term of high respect in Muslim countries, although the actual duties and honor attached to the name vary. Most typically, the imam leads the Friday prayers at the mosque.

Imhotep c2980–2950 BC. Egyptian sage. Imhotep was revered as the architect of the step pyramid of Zoser, as a doctor, and adviser to 3d-dynasty kings. He was elevated to deity status after his death.

Immigration Restriction Act Legislation passed in 1901 by the Commonwealth of Australia restricting the immigration of non-Europeans into the country. One of the first pieces of Australian legislation, it remains in effect but with notable modifications since WW II.

impeachment Process of formal accusation of public officials for misconduct in office. Developed from the 14th cent. in the English system, the right of impeachment in the US is vested in the Congress by the US Constitution. President A. Johnson and Supreme Court associate justice S. Chase were impeached but subsequently acquitted. A congressional committee voted to ask Congress to impeach President R. M. Nixon over Watergate (*q.v.*) but he resigned first.

Imperial Conferences Meetings of delegates from dominions within the British Empire (and later, the Commonwealth) held variously between 1907 and 1937. The conferences were called to discuss economic and mutual-defense concerns, though their resolutions were nonbinding until enactment of the 1931 Statute of Westminster (*q.v.*). After WW II the formal conferences were replaced by policy meetings between prime ministers of Commonwealth countries. Imperial Conferences were held 1907, 1911, 1917–18, 1921, 1923, 1926, 1930, 1932, 1936, 1937. Before 1907 such meetings were called Colonial Conferences and were held 1887, 1897, 1902.

imperialism In general, the rule over or control of one state by another. More specifically, "imperialism" is used in either of two ways, referring to ancient and modern forms. Ancient imperialism is the process by which early empires were created. This involved military conquest and, to one degree or another, political domination. Ancient imperialism led to creation of the Macedonian, Persian, Roman, Chinese, and numerous other empires. Modern imperialism is the policy by which nations built colonial empires (beginning in 15th–16th cents.). Modern imperialism was at first spurred on by the rewards of increased trade and mineral riches in the Americas, the Indies and later Africa. However, the industrial age brought new motivations. The great colonial empires of the 18th and 19th cents. were exploited for raw materials and also served as ready markets for the vast quantities of finished goods produced by the industrial nations. Competition between the great colonial powers, notably the British, French, Dutch, Portuguese, and later the Germans, led to instability and frequent wars during the 19th cent. In the 20th cent., however, the rise of nationalism brought new resistance to this form of imperialism and resulted in independence movements within the colonies. The years after WW I, and especially those following WW II, saw the breakup of colonial empires as most former colonies won their independence.

impressionism French school of painting (c1872–1886) whose radical innovations profoundly influenced the development of the visual arts. Reacting against then current standards regarding the primacy of subject matter in painting, a small group of French painters led by E. Manet and C. Monet began experimenting with new techniques. Though members of the group developed highly individualistic styles, they generally created works in which color and form, not the subject matter, predominated. Impressionists exhibited as a group eight times (1874–86) before disbanding and remained out of favor in established art circles until the 1920s. Among the impressionists were E. Manet, C. Monet, C. Pissaro, A. Renoir, and E. Degas.

Inca South American Indian people and their vast empire in the Andes region, which at the time of the Spanish conquest (16th cent.) extended from Ecuador to northern Chile. According to legend, the empire was founded (AD c1100) by Manco Capac at what is now Cuzco, Peru. It expanded slowly until the early 15th cent. when a period of rapid conquests began. The empire reached its zenith under the rule of Huayna Capac (1493–1525), who divided the empire between his sons, Atahualpa (*q.v.*) and Huáscar (*q.v.*). The two subsequently warred against each other and, when the Spanish conquistador F. Pizarro arrived in South America (1532), Atahualpa had just defeated his brother. After being received by Atahualpa on friendly terms, Pizarro captured and executed him (1533), entered Cuzco, and with his small force easily subjugated this empire of 10–12 million people. At the time of the Spanish conquest the Incas had a well-advanced civilization organized in a rigid hierarchy, over which the emperor ruled with absolute (and divine) authority. Inca society was based on agricultural production and its religion centered on sun worship. They were great builders and constructed magnificent cities, such as Machu Picchu, and a system of roads, irrigation, and mountainside terraces. There were also extensive mining and advanced metallurgy. Under the Spanish, the Inca religion was forcibly suppressed, a colonial government was installed, and the native population was drawn away from agriculture for work in the mines and colonial towns.

incunabula Bibliographical term. Taken from the Latin word for "cradle," the term refers to the earliest of printed books, those dating from before 1500. They include books from the presses of J. Gutenberg, W. Caxton, and so on.

Independence, Declaration of The document in which the 13 American colonies proclaimed their freedom from Britain. Following the initial battles of the American Revolution, it became clear to members of the Second Continental Congress that a negotiated settlement with Britain was no longer feasible. Consequently, R. H. Lee called on the Congress (June 7, 1776) to adopt a statement proclaiming independence. Largely drafted by T. Jefferson, it was formally adopted by Congress on July 4, 1776 (having already been passed on July 2). J. Hancock, president of the Congress, was first of the 56 delegates to sign the document. The day of adoption (July 4) is celebrated as US Independence Day.

Independence, War of *See* **American Revolution.**

Independence Hall Building in Philadelphia from which, on July 4, 1776, the Declaration of Independence was proclaimed. Both the Continental Congress (*q.v.*) and the US Constitutional Convention met there. It is now a museum.

Independents (Separatists) 17th-cent. term given to those English Christians who believed that local congregations should have control of their own church affairs, free from civil or ecclesiastical authority. The Pilgrims (*q.v.*) who founded Plymouth in Massachusetts (1620) were Independents. The Puritans who founded the Massachusetts Bay (*q.v.*) Colony (1630) became Separatists in New England after they abandoned their attempts to reform the Church of England. Both groups eventually espoused Congregationalism (*q.v.*). In England, Independents enjoyed their greatest influence during the Commonwealth and Protectorate.

Independent Treasury American treasury system, adopted in 1846, by which public revenues were kept at and disbursed from the treasury and subtreasury buildings, without using private or state banks. The system ended with passage of the Federal Reserve Act (1913).

India (Republic of India) Country located on the Indian subcontinent in southern Asia. The population is 844,000,000 and the capital is New Delhi. India has one of the world's oldest cultures, and such religions as Hinduism, Buddhism, and Jainism were begun in India. India was first unified (4th cent. BC) under the Mauryan dynasty and later empires under the Guptas (4th–6th cents. AD), the Delhi Sultanate (13th–14th cents.), and the Mughals (16th–18th cents.) also brought much of India under one ruler. Except for these periods, Indian history was characterized by disunity and warfare between regional states, a fact that helped the British to gain control over the Indian subcontinent in the 18th–19th cents. The movement for independence from Britain began in the late 19th cent. After nonviolent protest campaigns led by M. Gandhi, India became independent in 1947. Conflicts between the Hindu majority and the considerable Muslim population, however, resulted in creation of two separate states (India and Pakistan) when independence was granted. Key dates in the history of India include:

c2500–c1500 BC Indus Valley civilization flourished along the Indus River in the northwest (modern Pakistan).

c1500–800 BC Aryans invaded India; first settled in northern Punjab region and along northern Ganges River.

1500–700 BC Vedic period; Vedism, the religion of the Aryans, was evolved and refined; the Rig-Veda, which later became sacred Hindu text, reached final form.

c1500–c500 BC Brahmanic period; priestly Brahmans gained hold over religious community; promoted elaborate rituals, philosophical speculations, and eventually the establishment of the caste system.

c800–c500 BC Upanishads composed; advanced such fundamental religious doctrines as reincarnation and karma.

C6TH–C5TH CENTS. BC Period of social, religious ferment; rise of new religions and sects in opposition to Brahmanism, which was losing its hold on the populace.

C6TH–2D CENTS. BC Sutras composed; established rigid order of conduct and religious ritual and divided society into four classes, consolidating the caste system.

6TH CENT. BC Magadha kingdom founded in northeastern India as first important Aryan state; became nucleus of later Mauryan kingdom.

557 BC Vardhamana Mahavira achieved enlightenment, founded Jainism; Jainism arose in opposition to Brahmanism in the period of ferment, 6th–5th cents. BC.

c528 BC Gautama Buddha achieved spiritual enlightenment at Boddh Gaya, in northeastern India; Buddhism founded.

517–509 BC Persians under Darius I conquered the Punjab region in the northwest.

327–326 BC Alexander the Great conquered northwestern region that had fallen to Persians; Battle of Hydaspes River.

c322–c185 BC Mauryan Empire; first great Indian empire, founded in northeastern India, it eventually included nearly all of India and part of Afghanistan; classical Indian culture flourished.

c322–297 BC Chandragupta reigned; seized power (c322) in Magadha, drove out the Macedonian Greeks, united the north and created the great Mauryan Empire.

c305 BC Chandragupta defeated Seleucus I Nicator; extended empire westward into modern Afghanistan.

302 BC Alliance concluded with Seleucids; thereafter Greek culture had influence in northwestern India.

297–273 BC Bindusara reigned over the Mauryan Empire; conquered Deccan (southern India).

273–232 BC Asoka reigned in Mauryan Empire; brought empire to its greatest extent (including most of India); then renounced conquest by force; converted to Buddhism, and promulgated a state religion combining elements of both Buddhism and Jainism.

2D CENT. BC Beginnings of Vedantic Hinduism; earlier Brahmanism adopted elements of Buddhism, Jainism, and other competing religious systems; Hinduism eventually became the dominant religion of India.

185–73 BC Sunga dynasty ruled northern India; Mauryan dynasty overthrown, Hinduism became state religion; Jains and Buddhists were persecuted.

FROM C185 BC Tamil kingdoms ascendant in the south; included Chola, Pandyas, and Ceras; conducted trade with the Romans and peoples of Southeast Asia, spreading Hindu culture among them.

C128 BC–AD 450 Yueh-chih people controlled an empire in the northwest.

C50 BC–AD 450 Kushan kingdom, descendants of Yueh-chih, ruled a kingdom in northwestern India that eventually included Afghanistan and parts of central Asia; traded with Rome and spread Buddhism to central Asia and China.

AD 320–C500 Gupta Empire in northern India; eventually included north, parts of central and western India; period of peace and prosperity; golden age of Indian culture; Hinduism enjoyed period of growth.

AD 320–330 Chandragupta I reigned; founded Gupta dynasty after conquering states surrounding the Magadha kingdom.

AD 330–C380 Samudragupta reigned; completed conquest of the north.

AD C380–413 Chandragupta II reigned; an able ruler, he extended the empire westward and southward; classical Indian cultural flowering; science and mathematics reached their height.

AD 405–411 Fa-hsien, Chinese Buddhist pilgrim, visited India.

LATE 5TH–6TH CENTS. White Huns invaded India and occupied northern India; Gupta Empire collapsed; Huns' power finally broken in wars against Turks and Sassanids.

606–647 Harsha reigned; reunited northern India under one ruler; his empire disintegrated into petty states at his death, period of warfare and disunity followed.

7TH CENT. Rise of the Rajput warrior class in northwestern India; they remained powerful until the 16th cent.

888–1267 Chola dynasty, ruling in southeast India, became a major power in the south; Rajaraja I (ruled 985–1014) gained hegemony over Deccan; Chola rulers invaded Sri Lanka (11th cent.) and much of Southeast Asia (hence such names as Indo-China and Indonesia).

977–1186 Rise of the Muslim Ghaznavid dynasty in Afghanistan; raids by Muslims into India began.

1186–94 Muhammad of Ghor, a Muslim, destroyed the Ghaznavids and conquered northern India (by 1194).

1192–1398 Delhi Sultanate, first Muslim kingdom in India established after capture of Delhi by Muslims (1192); Muhammad of Ghor and succeeding rulers (Slave dynasty) conquered most of India; standardized revenue system gradually established.

1398–99 Tamerlane the Mongol conqueror invaded India; Delhi Sultanate ended after Tamerlane sacked Delhi and massacred citizens.

1414–51 Sayyid dynasty ruled the kingdom of Delhi.

1451–1526 Lodi dynasty; Bahlol, an Afghan, deposed the Sayyid rulers, took Delhi, and founded the Lodi dynasty; domains expanded beyond immediate area of Delhi.

1498 Portuguese explorer V. da Gama reached India; first European fort in India established on southwest coast at Cochin (near Bombay) in 1503.

1510 Portuguese established headquarters at Goa, on southwest coast.

C1520 Sikh faith founded by Nanak in the northwest Punjab region.

1526–1724 Mughal Empire; Muslim rulers established control over much of India, uniting it for the first time in centuries; Mughal rulers proved able administrators and sought to integrate Muslim and Hindu peoples; distinctive Mughal culture evolved.

1526–30 Babur reigned as first Mughal emperor; defeated Lodi ruler at Battle of Panipat (Apr. 20, 1526); completed conquest of kingdom of Delhi in north.

1556–1605 Akbar reigned as Mughal emperor; subdued revolts in Punjab, Rajputana, and Gujarat; added Bengal, Kashmir, Sind, and parts of the Deccan, creating a strong Indian empire.

1613 British East India Company established trading colony at Surat after defeating Portuguese.

1628–58 Shah Jahan reigned as Mughal emperor; Mughal culture reached its zenith; Taj Mahal built (1632–53).

1658–1707 Aurangzeb reigned as Mughal emperor; world economic conditions and internal dissention weakened Mughal power in India.

1661 British East India Company gained control of Bombay.

1664 Maratha Confederacy founded in western India and later expanded into central India; led by Sivaji, a champion of Hinduism, the Marathas created a large realm; warred against Mughal emperor Aurangzeb.

1674 Pondicherry established by French on extreme southeastern coast of India; became center of French domains in India.

1691 Calcutta founded by British.

1707 Death of Aurangzeb; Mughal Empire split up; Marathas expanded into central India and dominated much of the south as the most powerful single kingdom.

1708–12 Religious order of Sikhs transformed to military order; defeated by Bahadur Shah, ruler of the crumbling Mughal Empire, who drove them into the mountains in the north (1712).

1724 Hyderabad established as independent kingdom in south central India; came under rule of Nizam during the decline of Mughal Empire (of which it was part).

1739 Persians under Nadir Shah invaded India and sacked Delhi; invaders withdrew, taking fabulous wealth with them, including Peacock Throne and Koh-i-noor diamond.

1746–63 Rivalry between British and French for control of India.

1746–48 French, led by J. Dupleix, captured Madras (1746) from British while War of the Austrian Succession raged in Europe; Madras restored (1748).

1751 British soldier R. Clive successfully resisted French siege of Arcot in ongoing rivalry for control of southern India.

1756 Black Hole of Calcutta incident followed capture of British-held Calcutta by Nawab of Bengal (eastern India); British recaptured Calcutta (1757).

1756–63 British successful in fighting against French in India as Seven Years' War raged in Europe; Clive's victory in Battle of Plassey (1757) gave British control of Bengal.

1756–64 Afghan emir Ahmad Shah invaded India; captured Delhi; Marathas and Sikhs defeated in third Battle of Panipat (1761);

after Afghans withdrew, surviving Indian kingdoms were unable to resist expansion of British power.

1761 Muslim leader Haidar Ali seized power in Mysore (south central India).

1764 British, by defeating puppet Mughal emperor Awadh Nawab Shuja-ud-daula and Bengal Nawab Qasim Ali Khan in the Battle of Baksar, gained hegemony in northern India.

1765–67 R. Clive served as administrator of Bengal; began expanding British control over Indian states.

1767–69 Haidar Ali conducted first Mysore War against British East India Company.

1770 Bengal famine killed one-third of population; British authorities made no attempt to help and enforced high agrarian revenues.

1773 Regulating Act, reorganizing British East India Company, passed; first British government intervention in rule of India.

1774 Rohilla War conducted by the Nawab of Oudh against the Afghan Rohillas; war instigated by the British East India Company.

1775–82 First Maratha War; led to British acquisition of Salsette Island.

1780–84 Haidar Ali conducted second Mysore War against British.

1790–92 Tipu Sultan, son of Haidar Ali, defeated in third Mysore War against British; forced to cede half his territory.

1798 Ceylon (now Sri Lanka) became a British colony.

1799 Tipu Sultan defeated and killed in fourth Mysore War; British restored Hindu Wodeyar monarchy in Mysore.

1803–05 Second Maratha War fought between British and Maratha Confederacy.

1806 Vellore Mutiny against British by Sepoy troops (Indian troops led by European officers).

1809 Treaty of Amritsar defined spheres of British and Sikh influence in the Punjab.

1814–16 War with the Nepalese Gurkhas.

1817–18 Third Maratha War fought between British and Marathas, resulted in destruction of Maratha Confederacy and British domination of most of India; Sind and Punjab still independent.

1824 Barrackpore Mutiny among native Indian troops quashed by British; set stage for 1857 mutiny.

1824–26 First Burma War; British gradually increased control over Burma through a series of wars.

1829 British banned practice of suttee.

1833 British East India Company lost China trade monopoly by revision of charter.

1839–42 First Anglo-Afghan War; British attached the Afghan state from India, marked first in series of wars for control of Afghanistan.

1843 Sind armies defeated by small British force at the Battle of Miani, in modern Pakistan.

1843 Britain annexed Sind.

1845–46 British victorious in First Sikh War in the northwest Punjab region.

1848–49 British victorious in Second Sikh War; annexed Punjab (1849).

1848–56 Unpopular Doctrine of Lapse used by governor general, Earl of Dalhousie, to acquire direct control of native kingdoms.

1852 Second Burma War.

1857–59 Indian Mutiny, major revolt by Indian troops (Sepoys) against British rule; surviving puppet ruler of the Mughal dynasty deported to Rangoon.

1858 British government took direct control of administration of India, ending British East India Company involvement (Sept. 1); numerous reforms enacted.

1861 Indians appointed to legislative and executive councils.

1877 Queen Victoria crowned Empress of India.

1878–81 Second Anglo-Afghan War.

1885 Third Burma War; British gained all of Burma.

1885 Indian National Congress party formed; Indian nationalists used as a vehicle for the Indian independence movement; failed to gain support of most Muslims and thus became Hindu nationalist movement.

1905–11 Partition of Bengal by British viceroy, Lord G. Curzon (ruled 1898–1905); created Muslim majority in East Bengal and sparked protest and violence among nationalists.

1906 Muslim League founded to advance interests of Muslims.

1909 Indian Councils Act; legislation increased Indian self-government.

1914–18 WW I; many Indian troops used by British in fighting Central Powers; war weakened British control in India.

1915 Defence of India Act passed in Britain to quell wartime native revolts; its extension after the war sparked Gandhi's Noncooperation Movement.

1917 Montagu Declaration promised development of self-government in India.

1918–19 Millions died in influenza epidemic.

1918 Montagu-Chelmsford Report promised limited self-government; inadequacies of plan attacked by Indian National Congress.

1919 Rowlatt Acts passed (Feb.) extending British government's wartime powers; Gandhi led protest against the acts.

1919 Amritsar Massacre (Apr.); British troops fired on unarmed protesters in the Punjab, killing 379; anti-British sentiments intensified.

1919 Government of India Act (Dec. 23); Britain instituted system of dyarchy as step toward self-rule for India.

1920–22 Noncooperation Movement (*satyagraha*) organized by Gandhi to protest British rule.

1927 Simon Commission formed by British to study working of Indian constitution; its 1930 report boycotted by Indian National Congress.

1930–31 Gandhi launched second noncooperation campaign after British announced willingness to discuss dominion status for India (1929); radicals wanted full independence.

1930 Red Shirt Movement, anti-British movement supporting Indian National Congress, launched in northwestern India by A. Khan.

1931 Gandhi agreed (Mar.) to Delhi Pact, ending second noncooperation campaign.

1935 Government of India Act; provided for creation (in 1937) of elected provincial legislatures and a federal legislature.

1937 Constitution and government established by Government of India Act (1935) in effect.

1939–45 WW II; British viceroy declared war on Axis powers without consulting Indian leaders; radicals thereupon demanded complete independence as price for their support.

1940 Gandhi began another noncooperation campaign; thousands arrested in 1940 and 1942, especially during "Quit India" activity.

1942 National Congress party suppressed.

1942 Cripps Mission; unsuccessful attempt by British to offer eventual Indian independence in exchange for support during WW II.

1944   Brief, unsuccessful Japanese invasion of India (from Burma).

1945   India became member of the UN.

1945–46   British government first offered, then insisted on complete independence for India; plan for independent government held up by disagreements between Hindu Indian Nationalist Congress and Muslim League (which wanted separate Muslim state); clashes between Hindus and Muslims increased.

1947   India gained formal independence (Aug. 15) as a British dominion, partitioned into India proper and West and East Pakistan (in north), where Muslims were concentrated; independence followed by violence between Hindus and Muslims and migrations by millions between Hindu and Muslim territories.

1947   Punjab partitioned; Muslim west joined to Pakistan; Hindu east joined to India.

1947–64   J. Nehru in office as India's first prime minister.

1947–48   Lord L. Mountbatten served as last British viceroy.

1948   Gandhi assassinated (Jan.) by Hindu fanatic as disorders continued.

1948   Hyderabad, princely state in central India, forced (by military occupation) to join in dominion of India.

1948–49   India-Pakistani War over Kashmir.

1950   India became a republic (Jan. 26), ending ties with British; Rajendra Prasad in office as first president (1950–62); Nehru continued as prime minister.

1956   Government acquired French settlement of Pondicherry.

1961   India annexed Portuguese settlements (Goa and others).

1962   Chinese invaded (Oct.) northeastern border region and occupied territory disputed since 1957.

1965–68   India-Pakistani conflict over Rann of Kutch.

1966–77   Indira Gandhi in office as prime minister.

1969   Indian National Congress party split after suffering election reverses; I. Gandhi formed New Congress party (Congress (I)) and won major victory in 1971 elections.

1970   I. Gandhi dissolved Parliament (Dec.) after it opposed her reform measures.

1971   India-Pakistani War (Dec.) over Bangladesh independence.

1973   Agreement for cooperation (Nov.) with USSR signed.

1974   India exploded its first nuclear device.

1975   Prime Minister I. Gandhi convicted (June) of election fraud; her resignation called for.

1975   Gandhi declared (June) state of emergency; ordered mass arrest of opponents; press censorship imposed.

1976   Constitutional rights suspended (Jan.) and elections postponed; Prime Minister Gandhi given new powers.

1976   Diplomatic relations resumed with Pakistan.

1977   Gandhi's Congress party defeated (Apr.) in elections; Morarji Desai, Janata party leader, became prime minister.

1977   Gandhi arrested (Oct.) on charges of corruption.

1979   Charran Singh (d. 1987) in office as prime minister following Morarji Desai's resignation.

1979   Political crisis continued; Singh resigned.

1980   Gandhi returned to power as prime minister after her Congress (I) party won decisive victory in the Jan. elections.

1980–85   Gandhi in office as prime minister; her administration marked by continued close relations with the USSR; increasing unrest in Assam and the Punjab; and a slow decline in the economy.

1980   Steep price increases for basic commodities; inflation rate reported at 25%.

1980   Sanjay Gandhi, the prime minister's younger son, killed in plane crash (June 23).

1980   IMF granted India loans to help offset trade deficit caused by rising price of imported oil (July).

1980   India launched its first rocket into space (July).

1980   Disturbed Areas Act passed by government (Aug. 27), granting national government special powers of search and arrest in any state suffering outbreaks of unrest.

1981   Census put India's population at 685 million, nearly a 25% increase over 1971.

1982   Police riot in Bombay (Aug. 18); army called in to restore order.

1982   Face-to-face talks between Gandhi and Pakistani president Zia-ul-Haq held (Nov.); first such meeting in 10 years produced mutual cooperation agreement.

1983 Some 5,000 killed in election riots in Assam; the strife, caused by religious and ethnic hatred, forced some 300,000 from their homes.

1983–84 Unrest in Punjab, dominated by Sikh extremists, continued; some 400 killed and 2,000 injured by mid-1984.

1985 Army attacked Sikh strongholds, the Golden Temple at Amritsar and other such temples (June 5–6), striking a major blow against extremists; rioting by Sikhs followed the attacks.

1985 Prime Minister I. Gandhi assassinated by two Sikhs among her bodyguard (Oct. 31); some 2,000 killed during anti-Sikh riots in New Delhi.

1985–89 Rajiv Gandhi, I. Gandhi's son, in office as prime minister; his administration marked by declining popularity of the Congress (I) party following its landslide victory in late 1985; trade with US increased sharply while India's economic situation worsened.

1985 Disastrous Bhopal gas leak killed over 2,500 people (Dec. 3); Union Carbide pesticide plant at Bhopal leaked toxic chemicals killing people in surrounding towns.

1986 Sikh sepratists occupied Golden Temple in Amritsar and proclaimed creation of Sikh state (Apr. 29); government troops quickly reestablished order.

1986 Mizoram, former territory in northeast, made India's 23d state (Aug.).

1987 Teachers' strike became nation's longest nationwide walkout after lasting 70 days (Aug.).

1987 Gandhi government hit with charges of widespread scandal (Apr.); Gandhi reshuffled his cabinet while Parliament began an investigation.

1988 Sikh unrest in Punjab again increasing; over 1,500 deaths attributed to unrest during 1988, some 1,200 being innocent victims of terrorist acts.

1988 Prime Minister Gandhi on official visit to China (Dec.), first visit by Indian prime minister since 1954.

1988–89 Heavy imports, and resulting worsening trade deficit, strained the economy.

1989 Gandhi administration accused of corruption in government report on arms deal with Swedish firm, Bofors (July); Gandhi refused to resign, prompting opposition representatives to withdraw from India's lower house; Gandhi denied later news reports linking a family trust with Bofors bribes (Oct.).

1989 National Front, opposition coalition, won elections; brought first-ever minority government to power.

1989–90 V. P. (Vishwanath Pratap) Singh in office as prime minister; unsuccessfully sought solution to Sikh problem; proved unable to halt unrest spreading rapidly throughout much of India.

1990 National government imposed president's rule in Punjab (Apr.), and Jammu and Kashmir (July).

1990 Singh announced (Aug.) government would fully implement recommendations of 1982 Mandal Commission, calling for additional 27% of government jobs to be reserved for members of India's disadvantaged, lower castes; jobs to be in addition to 22.5% already reserved for disadvantaged castes and tribes.

1990 Some 890 people killed in nearly four months of Hindu-Muslim riots in Uttar Pradesh.

1990 Widespread unrest resulted from Mandal decision; Singh government lost vote of confidence (Nov.).

1990–91 Chandra Shekhar in office as prime minister, having formed a coalition with Congress (I) party.

1991 Prime Minister Shekhar resigned (Mar.) over strained relations with coalition partner Congress (I) party; headed caretaker government pending elections.

1991 Former Prime Minister Rajiv Gandhi assassinated by bomb at campaign rally in Tamil Nadu (May 21); 15 bystanders also killed; ringleader, a member of Liberation Tigers of Tamil Eelam, committed suicide to evade police capture (Aug. 20).

1991– P. V. Narasimha Rao, Congress (I) party leader, in office as prime minister, following June elections; his administration, committed to restoring the economy, instituted austerity measures and devalued the rupee.

1991 Population put at 844 million, according to latest census; at current rate of increase, India to have world's largest population by 2011.

1992 Four top officials of Indian branches of British-owned bank put on leave following revelations of $1.1 billion financial scandal.

Indiana State in the north-central US, the 19th state. The area was explored by the French, including R. La Salle, who arrived in 1679. Vincennes was the first settlement. In 1763, the Treaty of Paris ceded the territory to England as part of the Northwest Territory (*q.v.*). After the Revolutionary War (1783), it was ceded to the US, which began to force the Indians out of the region. It became a state in 1816 and adopted its constitution in 1851.

Indian Councils Act British reform act for the government of India enacted on Nov. 15, 1909. It provided for increased Indian self-government in the form of a representative legislature. An earlier act of the same name (1861) reorganized India's executive administration.

Indian Mutiny (Sepoy Rebellion) Widespread revolt (1857–58) by Indian troops (sepoys) serving in the British East India Company army. The revolt brought about the transfer of authority in India from the company to the British crown (Sept. 1, 1858) and later became a symbol for Indian nationalists. Resentment against East India Company rule had been building for some time, particularly over the company's annexation of native lands and its failure to respect native customs. Hindus and Muslims alike were offended by the introduction of cartridges greased with cow and pig fat and this sparked the mutiny. Indian troops rebelled (May 10, 1857) at Meerut and the bloody revolt (involving massacres of British army officers, European civilians, and rebels) spread rapidly throughout northern and central India. British forces retook Delhi (Sept., 1857) and Lucknow (Mar., 1858). The revolt was effectively crushed in 1858, though some fighting continued into 1859. As a result of the uprising, the (titular) ruler of the Mughal Empire, Bahadur Shah II, was banished by the British. This formally ended the existence of the Mughal Empire.

Indian National Congress (Congress party) Political party in India. Founded in 1885, it became a vehicle for the Indian independence movement in the early 20th cent. The party was taken over (1917) by militants such as B. Tilak and A. Besant and, under the leadership of M. K. Gandhi, it organized the passive-resistance campaigns (*satyagraha*) against British domination that continued to the 1940s. The party became the ruling party of independent India in 1947. It

was led (1947–64) by J. Nehru until his death and continued as the ruling party under his daughter I. Gandhi. Opposition to I. Gandhi, however, finally split (1969) the party into the New Congress party, supporting I. Gandhi, and the Old Congress party, supporting Morarji R. Desai (1896–   ), who succeeded Mrs. Gandhi as prime minister between 1977 and 1980 under the banner of a new Janata party. In 1980, Mrs. Gandhi was returned to power as prime minister, at the head of her faction of the Congress party.

Indian Removal Act US law (1830) implemented by President A. Jackson. It called for the removal of Indian tribes east of the Mississippi and their resettlement in the western territories. During the 1830s some 60,000 Indians were forced to move. Those who resisted were marched under such conditions that, of some 11,000 Cherokees moved, over 4,000 died (1838).

Indian Reorganization Act (Wheeler-Howard Act) US legislation enacted (1934) to improve the economic conditions on American Indian reservations and promote their assimilation into the American mainstream.

Indians, American *See under tribal names.*

Indian Territory US lands set aside (1834) for resettlement of Indian tribes in the West. It once occupied nearly all of what is now Oklahoma. Government policy of removing Indian tribes from the US Southeast was formalized by the Indian Removal Act (*q.v.*) of 1830. By the Indian Intercourse Act (1834) the western territories were set aside for them. Though the territory became the home of a number of tribes displaced by white settlers, westward expansion eventually forced the government to open even this territory to settlers. The western part was opened in 1889 and, on the admission (1907) of Oklahoma as a state the territory was abolished.

India-Pakistani Wars Conflicts between India and Pakistan in the years after the British partition of the Indian subcontinent (Aug. 15, 1947). 1. Kashmir clashes. Partition brought on both rival claims to Kashmir and armed conflict. A UN cease-fire negotiated on Jan. 1, 1949, gave India two-thirds, Pakistan one-third, of Kashmir. 2. Rann of Kutch clashes. Fighting in 1965 along the West Pakistan–Gujarat border led to an international arbitration commission award of 90 percent of the Rann of Kutch to India, 10 percent to Pakistan, on Feb. 19, 1968.

3. India-Pakistani War of 1971. Indian aid to East Pakistan's successful effort to achieve independence as Bangladesh (*q.v.*) led to a full-scale war between India and Pakistan that broke out on Dec. 3, 1971. Pakistan agreed to a cease-fire in the east on Dec. 16, and in the west on Dec. 17. On July 3, 1972, the two countries signed a treaty providing for withdrawal of troops and a commitment to seek peaceful solutions.

Indochina, Federation of (French Indochina) Former federation of states in Southeast Asia including Cochin China, a French colony, and the French protectorates of Annam, Cambodia, Laos, and Tonkin. France had originally gained control in these areas between 1863 and 1894. The Japanese took control during WW II and the French tried to reestablish sovereignty from 1945. However, nationalist groups in Annam, Cochin China, and Tonkin sought independence as the republic of Vietnam from 1945, and plunged the area into war (Indochina War, *q.v.*). The Geneva Conference (*q.v.*) of 1954 marked the end of the federation, since it marked the end of French control of the area.

Indochina War (French Indochina ˜) War (1945–54) fought by Vietnamese Communists and nationalists against occupying armies, most notably the French. Following the Japanese defeat (1945) in WW II, British and Chinese forces occupied the region. At the same time, however, Communist nationalist leader Ho Chi Minh proclaimed the Democratic Republic of Vietnam and began a war against the British and Chinese. French troops reoccupied Indochina (1946) and, after the breakdown of an agreement granting the Vietnamese republic a large measure of autonomy, fighting resumed (late Dec., 1946). This time it was between the French and the Communist nationalist (Vietminh) forces under Vo Nguyen Giap. Heavy fighting continued through 1947. After failing to come to terms with Ho Chi Minh, the French supported creation of an independent Vietnam (within the French Union) with Bao Dai as emperor (Mar. 8, 1949). The Vietminh continued fighting, however, drove the French from northern Vietnam (Oct., 1950), conquered parts of Laos (1953), and broke French military strength (1954) at Dien Bien Phu (*q.v.*). Geneva Conference accords (signed July 21, 1954) ended the war, provided for partition of Vietnam, and promised elections

for reunification by 1956. The US, which had been aiding the Bao Dai regime since 1950, did not sign the accord and thus opened the way for its involvement in the Vietnam War (*q.v.*), sometimes called the Second Indochina War.

Indo-European Name applied to the large family of languages of Europe and southern and southwestern Asia, believed to have evolved from a common parent language, Proto-Indo-European, spoken sometime before 2000 BC. Indo-Iranian languages such as Persian and Sanskrit are members, as well as the Celtic, Germanic, Greek, Romance, and Slavic languages of Europe.

Indonesia (Republic of Indonesia, formerly Dutch East Indies) Country consisting of islands (Sumatra, Borneo, Java, and others) in the Malay Archipelago in the southwest Pacific. The population is 191,266,000 and the capital is Jakarta (on Java). Most Indonesians are descended from Malay peoples. The islands were long under the influence of other cultures, notably Indian, and Muslim (from 14th–15th cents.). The period of European colonial domination began with the arrival of the Dutch in the 17th cent. Modern Indonesia has the largest Islamic population of any nation in the world. Key dates in the history of Indonesia include:

16TH CENT. Portuguese traders arrived to exploit the spice trade; established trading posts (from 1511).

1596–1600 Dutch and English traders arrived.

EARLY 17TH CENT. Dutch succeeded in driving out Portuguese and English; Dutch East India Company controlled region for next three and one-half centuries.

1623 Amboina Massacre; English traders executed by Dutch authorities.

1799 Dutch government assumed control of colony from the Dutch East India Company.

1811–16 British seized Java and part of Sumatra during the Napoleonic Wars; restored to Dutch control afterward.

1916 Volksraad, an advisory council, formed by Dutch colonial government.

1922 Indonesia incorporated into the Dutch kingdom.

1927 Indonesian Nationalist party formed under Sukarno; marked rise of nationalist movement.

1942–45 WW II; Japan occupied Indonesia; nominal self-government.

1945 Sukarno took control (Aug.) of islands of Sumatra and Java; he and Muhammad Hatta proclaimed independent republic.

1945–49 War for independence.

1949 Dutch agreed to creation of the Republic of Indonesia; Sukarno elected president, Hatta premier.

1949 Independence granted (Dec. 27).

1956 Hatta fought with Sukarno and resigned.

1958 Unsuccessful revolts in Sumatra, Sulawesi, and other islands.

1960 Sukarno dissolved Parliament, took firm control of government.

1962 Sukarno seized control of Dutch New Guinea; UN negotiated transfer pending referendum.

1963 Dutch New Guinea transferred to Indonesia as West Irian.

1963–66 War with newly formed Federation of Malaysia; Sukarno launched sporadic guerrilla raids into territory.

1965 Indonesia withdrew from UN as Sukarno developed closer ties with Communist countries; Communist party in Indonesia gained strength.

1965 Communist coup attempted (Sept.) against army, which had powerful voice in government; Gen. Suharto blocked the coup and began taking control of government; relations with West later reestablished.

1965 Widespread massacres of Communists; hundreds of thousands killed (Oct.–Dec.).

1967 Sukarno forced out of office (Mar.) by National Assembly.

1967 Suharto began long term as president; restored order and began aggressive program to rebuild Indonesian economy; his pro-West policies resulted in substantial foreign aid.

1969 West Irian formally annexed.

1976 Pertamina, state-owned oil company, went bankrupt as Indonesian economic problems worsened.

1977 Release of 10,000 political prisoners jailed in 1965.

1978 Government crackdown against opposition criticism (Jan.); newspapers closed, university activity restricted.

1978 Suharto elected to third five-year term as president.

1979 Indonesia established center for Vietnamese "boat people"; provided services on temporary basis only.

1980 Corruption scandal in state-owned Pertamina oil corporation; company officials reportedly received large commissions and may have funneled some of the money to Indonesian officials.

1980 Petition of 50 submitted to Parliament (Dewan Perwakilan Rakyat, DPR); President Suharto's unfavorable reaction to criticism sparked this petition, expressing the "disappointment" of the 50 prominent Indonesians who signed it.

1981 More than 50 judges and 15 prosecutors fired or reprimanded in continued government campaign against corruption.

1981 Government banned television advertising and gambling in an effort to appease large Indonesian Muslim population.

1982 Government deported Soviet officials charged with spying (Feb.).

1982 International convention, The Law of the Sea, signed; affirmed Indonesian claims to sovereignty over straits and seas around the Indonesian archipelago.

1983 Suharto elected to fourth term as president (Mar.)

1983 Faced with a sluggish economy and declining revenues, government introduced austerity measures, including wage freeze for public employees and end to subsidies on rice and other consumer products.

1983 Military reported sporadic clashes with bands of independence fighters in East Timor.

1984 Muslim political organization, United Development Party (PPP) acceded to government's ongoing campaign for adoption of Pancasila, or state ideology, by all social, religious, and political groups; nevertheless, the campaign outraged some Muslims, provoking bombing and arson incidents in 1984–85.

1984 Some 10,000 ethnic Papuans fled from the Indonesian territory of West Irian to Papua New Guinea after a local man, arrested by Indonesian authorities, was killed.

1985 Arrests and trials of suspected opposition figures sparked by terrorist bombings; prominent officials, including some who signed Petition of 50, given long jail terms.

1985 Government ordered thousands of workers, believed former members of Communist trade unions, fired.

1985 Some 6,000 customs workers put on indefinite leave (May) in government bid to end corruption and inefficiency in Indonesian ports; private Swiss company to handle customs inspections.

1985 Substantial surpluses in rice crop resulted from improvements in agriculture instituted just a few years earlier.

1986 Some import monopolies abolished following criticism of business ventures owned by Suharto's family and friends (Oct.).

1987 Commercial regulations reformed; cut red tape for import-export trade, simplified foreign investment in Indonesian business ventures, and reduced regulations on stock market.

1988 Indonesia briefly closed Lombok and Sunda Straits (Sept.), provoking international protest over apparent violation of 1982 Law of the Sea Convention.

1989 Some 300 Muslims, determined to set up Islamic state, attacked provincial police outposts in Sumatra (Feb.); government troops later killed 27 and arrested 19.

1989 Suharto on official visit to USSR, first high-level meeting since 1964.

1990 Suharto decreed that leading businesses should turn over a quarter of company shares to employees and cooperatives.

1990–91 Bands of anti-government rebels reported operating in northern Sumatra; government appeared to have the situation under control by 1991.

1990 Indonesia reestablished diplomatic relations with China, ending break that followed 1965 attempted Communist coup.

1991 Anti-government demonstrators in East Timor province shot and killed by soldiers (Nov.); 50 reported dead.

indulgence Catholic theological term for the pardon and remission of temporal punishment due to sin. In the early church, severe penances were imposed upon penitent sinners. As time went on, the church relaxed the actual penalty, granting an "indulgence" instead by which the penitent received the same merit as if he had actually performed the penance. The church claims to be able to do this by drawing upon the storehouse of merit already acquired in the sight of God by the sacrifice of Jesus and by the virtue and penances of the saints. Indulgences are now granted for specific good works performed or prayers said. Abuses which crept into the granting of indulgences, specifically the buying and selling of them, was one of the issues which led to the revolt of M. Luther (1517) at the time of the Reformation (q.v.).

Indulgence, Declaration of 1. A proclamation (1672) by the English king Charles II granting religious toleration for Nonconformists (q.v.). Parliament, however, refused to accept terms of the declaration and voided it. 2. Proclamation (1687) by the English king James II granting religious toleration for Catholics as well as Nonconformists. The resentment this proclamation aroused was one of the causes of the Glorious Revolution (q.v.) of 1688.

Indus Main river of Pakistan, rising in the Himalayas in Tibet and flowing southwest across Pakistan to the Arabian Sea. The use of its waters has been the cause of conflict between India and Pakistan. The prehistoric Indus Valley civilization grew up along its banks.

Indus civilization (Mohenjo-daro civilization) Ancient civilization that flourished in the Indus River valley (c2500 BC–1500 BC). Excavations at Mohenjo-daro and Harappa in modern Pakistan have revealed a civilization as advanced as those of ancient Egypt and Mesopotamia.

Industrial Revolution Period that saw industry become the predominant force in European economic and social life (18th–19th cents.). This era was marked by the shift from agricultural and cottage-industry forms of production to the factory system, the great increase in the use of machinery for production, a population shift that created great urban centers, and the marked dependence of laborers on their employers. The Industrial Revolution began in the British cotton textile industry and is generally dated from 1750 to 1850. Though the use of machinery was not unknown and though some factories were operating before 1750, this period saw the gradual changeover to an industrial society in Britain. Traditionally, certain inventions are associated with the beginning of industrialism, including J. Watt's steam engine, J. Kay's flying shuttle, J. Hargreaves's spinning jenny, S. Crompton's spinning mule, and Edmund Cartwright's power loom (all between 1733 and 1785). In succeeding years the Industrial Revolution spread to other countries: France after 1830; Germany after 1850; and the US principally after 1860.

industrial union A union or workers' organization known as a "vertical" union because of its acceptance of all types of workers in a given industry, whether skilled or unskilled, and regardless of specialization. Previously unions of a particular craft such as carpenters or fitters had been the norm. Industrial unions developed in Britain in the latter half of the 19th cent.

Industrial Workers of the World (IWW) (Wobblies) Radical labor union active mainly in the US. Founded (1905) in Chicago to promote syndicalism (*q.v.*), the union was dedicated to the overthrow of capitalism and advocated general strikes and other tactics to gain this end. Composed largely of unskilled industrial workers, it conducted some 150 strikes in the early 1900s. The union's radical aims and opposition to US participation in WW I led to federal government prosecutions (1917–18) and to harassment during the Red Scare (1919). The organization ceased to be important in the 1920s, when its major concern was opposition to the new US Communist party. Leaders of the IWW included E. Debs, William ("Big Bill") Haywood (1869–1928), and D. De Leon.

Ingersoll, Robert Green 1833–99. An American humanistic philosopher, politician, and orator. He was a leading proponent of agnosticism and a critic of the Bible and Christianity.

Ingres, Jean Auguste Dominique 1780–1867. A French painter, one of the leading figures in French classical painting in the 19th cent.

Inkerman, Battle of Battle of the Crimean War (*q.v.*), fought on Nov. 5, 1854, at Inkerman, east of Sevastopol. There the English and French defeated the Russians, who had unexpectedly attacked the English camp.

Inner Mongolia (Inner Mongolian Autonomous Region) Autonomous region of the present People's Republic of China, located in the steppe region of northeastern China. It is the traditional home of nomadic Mongol tribes. *See* Mongolia.

Inner Mongolian Autonomous Region *See* **Inner Mongolia.**

Inness, George 1825–94. American landscape painter, whose works were influenced by the

Hudson River and Barbizon schools of painting (*qq.v.*).

Innocent I, Saint *d.* 417. Italian pope (401–417), who upheld Saint John Chrysostom and condemned Pelagianism (*q.v.*). Rome was sacked by Alaric I during his pontificate (410).

Innocent II (*orig.* Papareschi, Gregorio) *d.* 1143. Roman pope (1130–43). Elected by a minority of cardinals to succeed Honorius II, he was forced to flee Rome. He regained his office in 1138, convened the Second Lateran Council (*q.v.*) of 1139, and condemned P. Abelard and Arnold of Brescia.

Innocent III (*orig.* Lotario di Segni) 1161–1216. Italian-born pope (1198–1216), successor to Celestine III. Under Innocent's reign, the papacy achieved its greatest power. Continuing the policies of Gregory VII regarding supremacy of the pope over secular rulers, Innocent became involved in struggles with European kings to enforce his authority. He vied with Holy Roman Emperor Otto IV, excommunicated him (1210), and finally crowned Frederick II in his place (1215). In England, he forced acceptance of his favorite as archbishop of Canterbury and thereby began a struggle with King John. He excommunicated John (1209), ultimately forcing John in 1213 to accept the suzerainty of the pope and to agree to pay him tribute. In addition to asserting papal authority over these and other European sovereigns, Innocent also preached the Fourth Crusade (*q.v.*), which resulted in the creation of the Latin Empire of Constantinople (*q.v.*); promoted the Albigensian Crusade (*q.v.*); called the great Fourth Lateran Council (*q.v.*); and gave papal approval to the missions of both the Franciscans and Dominicans.

Innocent IV (*orig.* Fieschi, Sinibaldo de') *d.* 1254. Pope (1243–54), who convened the First Council of Lyons (*q.v.*) in 1245 and fought to maintain papal sovereignty distinct from the Holy Roman Empire and the Hohenstaufen (*q.v.*) emperors.

Innocent VIII (*orig.* Cibó, Giovanni Battista) 1432–92. Pope (1484–92), who authorized the Inquisition to bring charges against witches in Germany (1484). He maintained peace with the Ottoman Empire and temporarily halted the Turkish advance into Europe by keeping the brother and rival of Sultan Beyazid II prisoner.

Innocent XI (*orig.* Odescalchi, Benedetto) 1611–89. Pope (1676–89). Personally saintly, Innocent quarreled with Louis XIV of France over the latter's claim to be able to administer vacant church sees. As a result, the king convoked a synod and issued (1673) the famous four articles on Gallicanism (*q.v.*). The two also clashed over the king's 1685 revocation of the Edict of Nantes, since Innocent believed that the Protestants had to be tolerated. He also condemned quietism (*q.v.*).

Inquisition   Name of two historic Roman Catholic tribunals.   1. The medieval Inquisition was established (1233) by Pope Gregory X in response to the spread of heretical sects, such as the Albigenses and Waldenses in northern Italy, southern France, and Germany. Judges of the Inquisition were chosen from among the Dominicans to try and judge cases of heresy, then considered intolerable by civil and ecclesiastical authorities alike. If found guilty of heresy, the heretic was turned over to secular authorities for punishment. Though burning at the stake was the ultimate penalty for unrecanted heresy, this penalty was uncommon in medieval times. The usual punishment was penance, fine, or imprisonment. Torture was used in the civil courts of the time and was also admitted in trials for heresy by Innocent IV (1252), despite earlier papal denunciations of torture. During the Catholic Reformation, the functions of the medieval Inquisition were assigned to the Holy Office (1542). Called the Roman Inquisition, it was active against Protestantism and heard charges of heresy against Galileo in what became a famous trial. Its typical function in modern times was the examination of theological writings. The Holy Office was replaced by the Roman Congregation for the Doctrine of the Faith in 1965.   2. Spanish Inquisition. This was a quasi-ecclesiastical tribunal established in 1478 by King Ferdinand and Queen Isabella primarily to examine converted Jews, and later converted Muslims, and punish those who were insincere in the conversion. Pope Sixtus IV reluctantly approved the Spanish Inquisition, which was largely controlled by the Spanish monarchs. The Grand Inquisitor was always a Dominican, however, and the first and most notorious was T. de Torquemada. The Spanish Inquisition was much harsher than the medieval Inquisition and the death penalty was more often exacted, sometimes in mass *autos-da-fé*. It judged cases of bigamy, seduction, usury, and other crimes, and was active in Spain and her colonies. Estimates of its victims vary widely, ranging from less than 4,000 to more than 30,000 during its existence. By the 17th cent. the harshness of the Inquisition was greatly reduced and it was abolished altogether in 1834.

Instruction of Catherine the Great (Nakaz)   Document written (1767) by Catherine the Great of Russia, containing her political views, largely borrowed from C. de Montesquieu, to guide a commission convened (1768) to reform the Russian government. The commission did not produce any meaningful reforms.

Instrument of Government   English constitution under which O. Cromwell ruled England as lord protector between Jan., 1654, and May, 1657. It vested executive authority in the lord protector and a council of state, created a unicameral Parliament, and disenfranchised all Catholics and rebels. The unwillingness of Parliament to ratify it led to its replacement by the Humble Petition and Advice (*q.v.*), but it is notable as the first written constitution of a modern European state.

Insull, Samuel 1859–1938.   English-born American public-utilities magnate. He worked as secretary to inventor T. A. Edison, and later managed Edison's growing electrical equipment empire. He headed a giant Midwest utility complex until 1932, when economic reverses caused its collapse.

integration   *See* **segregation.**

intelligentsia   Term applied to the group of 19th-cent., middle-class Russians who were educated and influenced by Western ideas, and who sought social and political reform. The intelligentsia influenced the development of 20th-cent. revolutionary movements in Russia.

International   1. First (1864–81): Socialist labor federation (founded at London, Sept. 28, 1864) that quickly came under the domination of K. Marx. It was called the International Workingmen's Association. While its express purpose was to foment a Socialist workers' revolution, it failed to play an active role in labor unrest of the period. Split (1876) by a power struggle between Marx and the anarchist M. Bakunin, it was largely defunct by 1881.   2. Second (1889–1914): Loose federation of Socialist groups and labor unions (founded at Paris, 1889). Though committed to an eventual Socialist revolution, the group generally supported parliamentary democracy. The anarchists were formally ousted (1896). The chief aim of the international, however, was its opposition to war, and the outbreak of WW I split the organization along national lines. **3.** Third (Communist International) (Comintern) (1919–43): Organization of Communist parties (founded at Moscow, Mar., 1919), following the Russian Revolution. Formed by Russian Communist leader N. Lenin, the group was intended to oppose other Socialist factions and to foment worldwide revolution. The Comintern, under Soviet domination, became involved in ideological struggles and, in 1943, J. Stalin dissolved the Comintern to ensure Allied support in the fight against Nazi Germany.

International Confederation of Free Trade Unions *See* **labor unions.**

International Court of Justice UN judicial body organized in 1945 and superseding the Permanent Court of International Justice, the judicial arm of the League of Nations. The idea for an international court stemmed from the Permanent Court of Arbitration, set up (1899) at the Hague Conference (*q.v.*), to provide a peaceful means for settling international disputes. A number of cases were settled by the organization in the years prior to WW I, and in 1921 the Permanent Court of International Justice (World Court) was organized under the auspices of the League of Nations. This court was created to exercise judicial functions (albeit limited by consent of the nations involved) rather than simply offering a forum for negotiation and arbitration. The International Court of Justice replaced this court (1945) after the UN was created and is likewise referred to as the World Court. The court is based at The Hague and consists of 15 judges selected by the UN Security Council and the General Assembly.

International Federation of Trade Unions *See* **labor unions.**

International Geophysical Year (IGY) Eighteen-month period from July, 1957, through Dec., 1958, devoted to the cooperative study of the earth and its environment by some 66 participating nations. During the IGY, the USSR launched its first satellite, the Van Allen radiation belt was discovered by a US satellite, and important discoveries about the ocean floor were made, as were many new discoveries about Antarctica (*q.v.*). A 12-nation cooperative agreement on Antarctica was signed as a result of the IGY.

International Monetary Fund (IMF) International organization conceived in 1944 at the Bretton Woods Conference (*q.v.*) and associated with the United Nations as a specialized agency (1945). The IMF was created to help provide stability of international exchange rates and aid member nations in international transactions by reducing the dependence on gold transfers, and by providing short-term liquidity and ready access to foreign currencies. Based in Washington, D.C., the IMF is funded by member nations and has steadily expanded both its services and its influence in the world of international finance. New services added over the years included: Standby Arrangements (1952) to establish credit for anticipated needs; General Agreements to Borrow (1961) for standby credit; Compensatory Financing of Export Fluctuations (1963) for developing countries; and Special Drawing Rights (SDR, 1969), which effectively expanded international liquidity. A special lending pool for the poorest of the developing nations was set up jointly (1986) by the IMF and the International Bank for Reconstruction and Development.

International Peace Conference of 1899 *See* **Hague Conferences.**

International Peace Conference of 1907 *See* **Hague Conferences.**

International style Architectural movement. Popular in Europe and America in the 1920s, it employed modern materials, emphasized smooth, light lines and walls of glass with steel supports. Among its adherents were W. Gropius and Le Corbusier.

International Workingmen's Association *See* **International (First).**

Interregnum, The Great The period in the history of the Holy Roman Empire between the death of the last Hohenstaufen (*q.v.*) emperor, Conrad IV, in 1254, and the election of the first Habsburg (*q.v.*) emperor, Count Rudolf of Habsburg, in 1273. There was no recognized ruler of Germany during this period, and it was characterized by a growth in the power of the princes.

Intolerable Acts Restrictive acts passed by the British Parliament in 1774 in retaliation for the Boston Tea Party (*q.v.*). Four acts closed Boston harbor until restitution had been made for the tea destroyed; revoked the Massachusetts charter and established military government; removed British Colonial officials from the jurisdiction of Colonial courts; and provided for the quartering of British troops in occupied dwellings. A fifth act, the Quebec Act, which had been under consideration before, placed the territory between the Ohio and the Mississippi under the jurisdiction of the province of Quebec. These Intolerable Acts led directly to the convening of the First Continental Congress (*q.v.*) later in the same year.

Inukai, Ki Tsuyoshi 1855–1932. Japanese politician, president of the Seiyukai party (1929–32), and prime minister (Jan.–May, 1932). His assassination marked the rise of military and end of party control of Japanese government.

Investiture Controversy Power struggle (11th–12th cents.) between the Holy Roman Empire and the papacy. The controversy centered on the rift (from 1075) between Emperor Henry IV and Pope Gregory VII over "lay investiture" and was not finally settled until issue of the Concordat of Worms (*q.v.*) of 1122. At the time of the controversy, bishops and other clerics had both secular and clerical powers over ecclesiastical domains. Both the emperor and the pope were involved in the installation (investiture) of these clerical officials, and involvement by the emperor and other secular leaders was known as "lay investiture." The practice led to abuses of the clerical offices and, reacting to a movement for reform, Pope Gregory abolished (1075) lay investiture. In the struggle that followed, Henry was excommunicated, civil war between factions of rebellious nobles broke out (over this and other issues) within the Holy Roman Empire, and Henry attacked Rome (1081–82). Under Emperor Henry V, the controversy continued until a compromise was finally arranged (1122) with Pope Calixtus II in the Concordat of Worms.

Invincible Armada *See* **Spanish Armada.**

Ion *fl.* 5th cent. BC. Greek poet. Only fragments of his poems and plays remain, but he was once awarded third prize in a drama competition won by Euripides.

Ionesco, Eugène 1912– . Rumanian-born French playwright. In plays such as *The Bald Prima Donna* (1950) and *Rhinoceros* (1959) he is considered to have written the purest and most characteristic works in the modern Theater of the Absurd (*q.v.*).

Ionia Ancient district of Asia Minor on the Aegean Sea in modern western Turkey. Colonized by the Ionian Greeks (c1000 BC), it was taken by Croesus (6th cent. BC) and then by the Persians under Cyrus the Great. The Ionian revolt against Persia contributed to the outbreak of the Persian Wars (*q.v.*). The Ionian cities fell to Alexander the Great (334 BC) and later to Rome, and were destroyed as Greek cities by the Ottoman conquest (15th cent. AD).

Ionian school Early school of Greek philosophy, composed of philosophers who were active (6th–5th cents. BC) in Ionia. They held divergent views, though in general they attempted to explain the world around them in terms of matter and physical forces. Among the thinkers of this school were Thales, Anaximander, Anaximenes, Anaxagoras, Heracleitus, and Diogenes of Apollonia.

Ionic order Greek architectural style. The Ionic is one of the major styles of early Greek architecture. It is characterized by slender fluted columns topped by a scroll-shaped capital, and had developed by the 6th cent. BC.

Iowa State in the north-central US, the 29th state. Originally inhabited by the Sioux Indians, the area was explored by J. Marquette, L. Jolliet, R. de La Salle, and J. Dubuque (1762–1810), after whom the first settlement, Dubuque, was named in 1833. Iowa was acquired by the US in the Louisiana Purchase (*q.v.*) of 1803 and became the Iowa Territory in 1838. The rich prairie soil attracted many settlers, and Iowa became a state in 1846. The state constitution was adopted in 1851. Iowa is noted for its abundant corn and other grains. Des Moines is the capital and largest city.

Ipsus, Battle of Battle fought at Ipsus, in Phrygia, Asia Minor, in 301 BC, in which Antigonus I was slain by Lysimachus and Seleucus. The battle marked the end of Alexander's empire.

Iqbal, (Sir) Muhammad 1873–1938. Indian poet, philosopher, and political leader. He urged the establishment of an independent Muslim state, and is considered the spiritual father of modern Pakistan (*q.v.*).

IRA *See* **Irish Republican Army.**

Irala, Domingo Martínez de *d.* 1556 or 1557. Spanish soldier and first governor of Paraguay (1537–42, 1544–56). He was the first governor in the Americas elected by a free vote of the colonists.

Iran Republic, located in the Mideast between Iraq and Afghanistan. The population is 55,647,000 and the capital is Teheran. "Iran" is the modern name of Persia (since 1935) and its emergence as a modern nation may be said to have begun with the overthrow of the Qajar dynasty (1925) by Reza Shah Pahlavi. Iran inherited Persian cultural traditions and has long been a center of the Shi'ite sect of the Islamic religion. Under the Pahlavi dynasty, programs to modernize Iran were actively pursued. However, the pace of modernization, as well as discontent with repressive rule by the shahs, led to the Iranian revolution of 1979. Radical Muslim fundamentalists seized control of the government, attacked Western and modernist influences, and revived the traditional Muslim society. Soon after Iran became embroiled in the bloody Iran-Iraq War. (For history prior to 1925, *see* Persia.) Key events in Iranian history include:

1921 Reza Khan, a soldier, took power in a coup ending British control over Iran (then a League of Nations mandate); led military dictatorship.

1925 Reza Khan elected hereditary shah as Reza Shah; founded Pahlavi dynasty (in power 1925–79).

1925–41 Reza Shah in power; instituted reforms, promoted industrialization and advance of education.

1935 Name of the country officially changed from Persia to Iran by Reza Shah.

1936 Modernization begun; shah's wife and daughters appeared in public without veils, breaking tradition.

1941–45 WW II, Iran occupied by Britain and USSR.

1941 Reza Shah, forced out because of his German ties, abdicated in favor of his son Mohammad Reza Shah (Sept. 16).

1941–79 Mohammad Reza Shah reigned.

1943 Teheran Conference (Nov.); US, USSR, and Britain agreed to guarantee independence of Iran after the war.

1945–46 Short-lived Soviet republics formed in Azerbaijan and Kurdistan, as a result of agitation by USSR.

1946 Soviet troops withdrawn from Iran, following Iranian demands at the UN for their departure.

1951 Premier Gen. Ali Razmara, an opponent of movement to nationalize oil industry, assassinated (Mar. 7); succeeded by Muhammad Mosaddegh.

1951 Premier Mosaddegh, with aid of his National Front movement, nationalized oil industry (Apr.); created National Iranian Oil Company (NIOC).

1952 British blockade nearly brought NIOC operations to a halt; Mosaddegh first ousted, then returned to power, whereupon the shah fled, leaving Mosaddegh in control.

1953 Mosaddegh ousted (Aug.) with help from US CIA; shah returned with aid of Western powers; operation of the NIOC placed in the hands of a Western consortium.

1955 Joined Baghdad Pact, organized against Soviet expansion; received considerable US aid during 1950s and 1960s.

1960s Shah instituted White Revolution reform movement; aimed especially at land reform.

1960 Iran became a founding member of OPEC.

1963 Shah's modernization plans approved in a referendum; women received right to vote; unrest among some religious groups, alienated by reform movement.

1965 Attempted assassination of the shah (Jan. 1).

1969 Iran renounced 1937 treaty with Iraq as tensions mounted between the two countries; border clashes occurred sporadically.

1971 Program to bolster Iran's military capabilities began after Britain withdrew from Persian Gulf (1971); US and British aid increased and soon made Iranian military strongest in Mideast.

1971 2,500th anniversary of Persian Empire celebrated at Persepolis in Iran (Oct. 12).

1973 Shah fully nationalized oil industry in Iran (Mar 20); Western consortium agreed in return for long-term oil contracts (May).

1973 Iran did not participate in Arab oil embargo; used increased profits to finance modernization.

1975 Algiers accord defined boundary with Iraq in disputed Shatt al-Arab waterway at the confluence of the Tigris and Euphrates rivers.

1976 Iran became a leader of OPEC members that raised oil prices.

1978 Muslim fundamentalists, opposed to government reforms, sparked riots in Teheran; called for removal of shah (May 11).

1978 Martial law was imposed in many cities (Sept. 8).

1978 Shah yielded to continuing unrest; named Shahpur Bakhtiar prime minister of a civilian government (Dec. 27); opposition by Muslim fundamentalists continued.

1979   Shah fled Iran, leaving behind Bakhtiar's caretaker government (Jan. 16).

1979   Ayatollah R. Khomeini, leader of the Muslim fundamentalist rebels, returned to Iran after 15-year exile (Feb. 1).

1979   Khomeini formed opposition government in defiance of Prime Minister Bakhtiar (Feb. 5).

1979   Khomeini supporters toppled the Bakhtiar government after days of armed clashes; imperial palace invaded and some army officers executed (Feb. 11).

1979   Khomeini instituted puritanical and repressive Islamic fundamentalist regime; industry and financial institutions nationalized; Islamic traditions revived and most Western cultural influences banned.

1979   Unrest among the Kurds in northwestern Iran; Khomeini government granted concessions to Kurds (Mar. 18).

1979   Khomeini government executed 21 officials accused of plotting against the government (Aug. 8).

1979   Exiled shah arrived in US for medical treatment (Oct. 22).

1979–81   Hostage Crisis; self-styled Iranian "students" seized US embassy and held Americans as prisoners; radical elements in the government exploited the incident to force out moderates and and thus strengthen their position.

1979   Mehdi Bazargan, head of provisional government, pledged to establish an Islamic republic, resigned.

1979   Islamic constitution adopted; Shi'ite Islam became state religion and Ayatollah Khomeini was designated religious and political leader (Dec. 3); Khomeini remained the ultimate authority in Iran until his death.

1979   Exiled shah left the US for Panama (Dec. 15).

1980   UN voted economic sanctions against Iran (Jan.), after UN efforts to mediate the American hostage crisis failed.

1980–81   Abolhassan Bani-Sadr in office as first president elected under the Islamic regime (Feb.); a moderate, he was systematically undermined and then ousted by more radical Muslim elements associated with the ayatollah.

1980   Exiled shah left Panama for Egypt (Mar. 23); died of cancer in an Egyptian hospital (July 27).

1980   Orthodox Muslims in Kurdestan revolted against domination by Shi'ite ayatollahs; Iranian army launched offensive in Kurdestan (Apr.), forcing rebels into mountain strongholds.

1980   Iranian-backed guerrillas attempted to assassinate Iraqi deputy prime minister (Apr.); tensions between Iraq and Iran increased.

1980   US military mission to rescue hostages failed (Apr. 25); Iranians scattered hostages throughout country to block further attempts.

1980   Iraq deported some 40,000 Iranians within its borders.

1980   Street battles in Teheran (June) between extremists in the ruling Islamic Republican Party (IRP) and members of other factions, including the Hezb Allahi and Mujaheddin-i Khalq; marked effort by IRP extremist fundamentalists to purge leftist and moderates from power.

1980   Coup by air force officers based at Hamadan foiled (July 10); 500 arrested.

1980–90   Iran-Iraq War began; months of Iranian-Iraqi border clashes led to an all-out attack by Iraq on Iranian airfields; Iraq advanced across Shatt al-Arab in the Gulf area toward Abadan (Sept. 22); refineries and pipelines hit; Abadan refinery destroyed; Iraqi advanced halted by Dec., with artillery battles between defensive positions ensuing; war dragged on through 1980s with Iraqis gradually gaining the initiative.

1980   Parliament set terms for release of American hostages (Nov. 2); called for release of Iranian assets seized by US, abandonment of all US claims against Iran, return of former shah's assets, and promised not to intervene in Iranian affairs.

1981   American hostages released (Jan. 20), following agreement on return of Iranian assets.

1981   Bloody street battles between Bani-Sadr supporters and more the radical IRP (Mar.).

1981   Khomeini ousted President Bani-Sadr, as tensions increased between moderates and radical Muslim fundamentalists (June 22); Bani-Sadr went into hiding in Iran.

1981   Top officials of new Islamic government killed by bomb in Teheran (June 28); 72 killed; bomb planted by rebel Mujaheddin group, then mounting terrorist campaign of bombings and political assassinations against extremist fundamentalists.

1981   Bani-Sadr escaped from Iran (July 29) and was granted asylum in France.

1981   Bomb explosion killed the newly elected president, Muhammad Ali Raja'i, the prime minister, and three other top government officials (Aug. 30); Mujaheddin blamed; mass arrests of suspected Mujaheddin supporters followed; over 2,200 believed executed.

1981–89   Hajatoleslam Ali Khameni in office as president (Oct. 2), second president in three months; his term was marked by continuing internal strife and ongoing devastation of the Iran-Iraq War, the wrecking of Iranian oil facilities and attendant economic hardship, and the eventual moderation of the fundamentalist revolt in Iran.

1982   Iranian head of Mujaheddin killed in Iran; some 15,000 Mujaheddin supporters believed imprisoned or executed during year.

1982   Coup attempt by former ayatollah associate uncovered (Apr.); 70 air force officers executed for involvement in plot.

1982   Iraqi offer to end war rejected by Iran (July); Ayatollah reported demanding Iraqi leader Saddam Hussein's ouster as well as war reparations.

1983   Iranian government ordered conscription of men aged 19–23.

1984   UN pressured Iran and Iraq into halting bombing attacks on civilian targets (June).

1985   War of the Cities (Mar.–July); Iraqis started new round of air attacks on Iranian cities, including repeated bombing of Teheran; Iranians mounted artillery barrages against Iraqi border cities (notably Basra) and bombarded Baghdad with missiles before the exchange finally ended.

1985   Iranian opposition to war mounted; Freedom Movement, group embracing both clerics and secular supporters, reported calling for end to war and return to democracy.

1986   Iraqis stepped up air attacks against Iranian oil facilities, including loading terminals south of Kharg Island, refineries, and Iranian shuttle tankers; Iranians attempted retaliation by missile attacks on Baghdad.

1986   Secret deal by US to supply arms to Iran revealed (Nov.); revelations resulted in US Iran-Contra scandal.

1986   Iranians reportedly massed million-man army for "final" offensive during the year; offensive never materialized.

1986   Drop in Iranian oil output and fall in world prices resulted in severe economic decline in Iran.

1987   Islamic Republican party dissolved (June); Ayatollah Khomeini reported distancing himself from direct control of government.

1987   Anti-Saudi mobs attacked Saudi embassy in Teheran, following bloody fight between Iranian pilgrims in Mecca and Saudi police (July 31).

1987   UN passed Resolution 598 calling for cease-fire in Iran-Iraq War (July 20); USSR vetoed US–proposed arms embargo against Iran and Iraq (Sept.).

1988   Iraq launched destructive missile barrages against Teheran (Feb. 29 and afterward); people fled city in large numbers.

1988   Mujaheddin's National Liberation Army advanced inside Iranian border at Khuzestan (Mar. 28).

1988   Iraqi offensive regained further Iranian-held territory east of Basra (May); Iran lost other hard-won Iraqi territory in both north and south in June.

1988   *USS Vincennes,* pursuing Iranian gunboats that had been harassing Gulf shipping, mistakenly shot down Iranian airbus flying nearby (July 3); 290 civilians killed.

1988   President Ali Khamenei, acting for war-weary Iran, accepted UN cease-fire in writing (July 18).

1988   UN cease-fire in Iran-Iraq War (Aug. 20) set; peace talks began.

1988   Iran helped arrange for release of French hostages held in Lebanon (May); French restored diplomatic relations with Iran (Aug.).

1989   Ayatollah Khomeini called for death of British author Salman Rushdie after pronouncing his book *The Satanic Verses* blasphemous; British broke diplomatic relations with Iran (Feb.).

1989   Khomeini's heir apparent, Ayatollah Montazeri, publicly attacked by Khomeini (Mar.), as part of drive against "liberals" in the Iranian regime; many executions reportedly carried out during this period.

1989   Abadan refinery back in operation after extensive repairs (Apr.); Kharg Island terminal also in operation.

1989   Ayatollah Khomeini, head of the revolutionary fundamentalist regime in Iran, died (June 3); former president Khameni named *rahbar* (religious leader) to replace him.

1989–   Hashemi Ali Akbar Rafsanjani in office as president, following July elections; promised to restore Iran's shattered economy; he represented more moderate elements, and by 1990 had reduced radicals' influence in government.

1989   Iran signed economic agreement with USSR (Aug.), beginning an Iranian move toward better relations with the Soviets.

1990   Severe earthquake struck northern Iran (June 21); estimated 25,000 dead; Iran accepted outside aid during crisis.

1990   Iraq invaded Kuwait (Aug. 2); Iran followed other nations in condemning invasion.

1990   Iraq formally accepted Iranian terms for formal end to Iran-Iraq War (Aug. 16); agreed to withdrawal from all Iranian lands, to exchange prisoners, and to accept 1975 Algiers accord on Shatt al-Arab waterway.

1991   Iran attempted to convince Iraq to withdraw from Kuwait through diplomatic means (Jan.); effort failed.

1991   Over one million Iraqi refugees flooded into Iran following Persian Gulf War (Apr.); both Kurds and Shi'ites reported among them.

1991   Anti-government protests reported in Teheran (Oct.).

1992   US accused Iran of printing billions of counterfeit US $100 bills, in effort ease its foreign debt and to destabilize the American economy (July).

Iran-Contra scandal   Complex US political scandal (1986–91), by far the most damaging to the R. Reagan administration in its two terms of office. In 1985 US National Security Council (NSC) adviser Robert MacFarlane arranged to sell Iran antitank and antiaircraft missiles (with President Reagan's approval), believing the sale would improve relations with Iranian moderates and thereby hasten release of US hostages being held by pro-Iranian terrorists in Lebanon. The weapons sales in 1985–86, which contravened US policies against bargaining with terrorists and against aiding Iran in its war against Iraq, were first revealed in Nov., 1986. Part of the $48 million from Iran, it then came out, had been

diverted by NSC adviser Adm. John Poindexter and NSC staffer Lt. Col. Oliver North to the Contras in Nicaragua (without, apparently, Reagan's direct knowledge). However, the Boland Amendment (passed by Congress in 1984 and reversed by it in 1986) was in effect then and prohibited military assistance to the Contras, a US–backed guerrilla group fighting Nicaragua's pro-Communist government. Amid the resulting furor in Congress, Reagan fired both North and Poindexter and appointed the Tower Commission to investigate. In Dec. a House-Senate investigation began and conducted televised hearings (May–Aug., 1987). The congressional report (Nov. 1987) was far more critical of Reagan than the earlier Tower Commission report and held him responsible for questionable and possibly illegal acts by his subordinates in the affair. Both North and Poindexter (indicted 1988) were found guilty on some charges (primarily relating to attempts to cover up the scandal). Both were acquitted of all charges on appeal in 1991, however. Efforts by an independent counsel to prosecute others in the case continued into 1993, though further investigation officially ended as of Sept. 1992.

Iranian revolution   *See* **Iran** (1978).

Iran-Iraq War   War (1980–90) between Iran and Iraq. Following the Iranian revolution of 1979 and establishment of Iran's fanatical Shi'ite Muslim regime, tensions with neighboring Iraq increased quickly. Border clashes flared into all-out war when Iraq invaded Iran in Sept., 1980. After initial Iraqi successes, Iranian troops slowly drove out the Iraqis and in turn gained some Iraqi territory. Soon afterward, the war dissipated into virtual stalemate, however, with Iraq having a superiority in arms (it enjoyed virtually total domination of the air later in the war) and Iran fielding huge armies of fanatical troops. Iran, maintaining its threat to export the Muslim fundamentalist revolution and opposed to all but fundamentalist regimes, effectively isolated itself from the world and more importantly, from a military viewpoint, virtually all sources of military supplies. Iraq meanwhile became a focal point for worldwide opposition to the Iranian revolutionary regime, receiving not only the support of Iran's frightened Arab neighbors, but also Soviet and Western aid. The war further degenerated into one of attrition; Iran sustained huge numbers of casualties for temporary territorial gains, while the Iraqi air force raided Iranian oil facilities and cities with impunity. A cease-fire was declared in 1988 and Iraq accepted all Iran's conditions for a formal end to the war in 1990, just after invading Kuwait. Key events in the war include:

1980 Iranian-backed guerrillas attempted to assassinate Iraqi deputy prime minister (Apr.); tensions between Iraq and Iran increased.

1980 Iraq deported some 40,000 Iranians within its borders.

1980–90 Iran-Iraq War began; months of Iranian-Iraqi border clashes led to an all-out attack by Iraq on Iranian airfields; Iraq advanced across Shatt al-Arab in the Gulf area toward Abadan (Sept. 22); refineries and pipelines hit; Abandan refinery destroyed; Iraqi advance halted by Dec., with artillery battles between defensive positions ensuing.

1980 Iraq advanced into Iran's northern provinces, invading Iranian Kurdistan (Dec. 26).

1981 Iranian army mounted a counteroffensive against Iraq (Jan. 5) near Ahwaz (Jan.); limited gains made with great loss of life and equipment during other Iranian offensives in 1981; both sides meanwhile mounted air attacks on each other's oil facilities.

1982 Iranian head of Mujaheddin, fierce opponents of ayatollah's regime, killed in Iran; some 15,000 Mujaheddin supporters believed imprisoned or executed during year.

1982 Iranian offensive begun (Mar. 21); pushed Iraqis out of Khuzestan province; by May, Iraqis driven out of all Iranian territory but city of Khorramshahr, which fell after two-day battle.

1982 Iranian troops invaded Iraq northeast of Basra (July 14); attack failed with huge Iranian losses; Iranians shifted to attacks on other border areas in north and central Iraq, with little success.

1982 Iraq began to dominate in air war; Iran unable to procure much-needed spare parts to keep its planes flying.

1982 Iraqi offer to end war rejected by Iran (July); Ayatollah reported demanding Iraqi leader Saddam Hussein's ouster as well as war reparations.

1983 Iranian government ordered conscription of men aged 19–23.

1983 Iranian offensives into Iraq launched along northern front (Feb., Apr., July); small gains made with large losses in men and materiel, in part because of Iraqi air superiority; Iraqis began more frequent bombing attacks on targets in Iran.

1984 Iranians captured strategic points in Darbandi Khan region (Feb. 13).

1984 Iranian offensive in Iraq's central and southern sectors (Feb.); attacks on wide front, including amphibious invasion of marsh area at Majnoon oilfield, all defeated by Iraqi counterattacks.

1984 Iranians deployed newly raised army of almost 250,000 on southern front, intending massive "final" offensive, which was never launched.

1984 Iraqis began attacking tankers heading for Iranian terminal at Kharg Island (Apr.); Iran's attempts to retaliate by attacking Arab shipping (Kuwait and Saudi) in Persian Gulf blocked first by Arab, then later US, naval warships.

1984 Iraqis took delivery on advanced, long-range Mirage jets from France; Soviets, reacting to Iran's systematic execution of leaders of the Communist Tudeh party, sent Iraq long-range missiles capable of hitting targets deep in Iran; Soviets began to increasingly supply military and economic aid.

1984 UN pressured Iran and Iraq into halting bombing attacks on civilian targets (June).

1984 US restored diplomatic relations with Iraq as part of program to increase support for Arab states opposed to Iran.

1985 Iranian offensive launched (Mar. 11), spearheaded by amphibious attack in Hawizah marshlands; Iranians broke Iraqi defensive lines, pushing beyond the west bank of the Tigris River; Iraqi counterattacks drove Iranian forces back across the border by Mar. 21.

1985 War of the Cities (Mar.–July); Iraqis started new round of air attacks on Iranian cities, including repeated bombing of Teheran; Iranians mounted artillery barrages against Iraqi border cities (notably Basra) and bombarded Baghdad with missiles before the exchange finally ended.

1985 Iraqi air force launched sustained attacks on Iran's Kharg Island oil terminal and tankers using it (from July 15); Iran forced to relocate oil export facilities farther south.

1985 Iranian opposition to war mounted; Freedom Movement, group embracing both clerics and secular supporters, reported calling for end to war and return to democracy.

1986 Iranian troops pushed across the Shatt al-Arab to capture Iraqi town of Fao (Feb. 10); Iraqi counterattacks failed, with heavy losses, though they effectively contained the Iranian advance.

1986 Iraqis, driving into Iran, captured and then lost town of Mehran (May 17–18).

1986 Iraqis stepped up air attacks against Iranian oil facilities, including loading terminals south of Kharg Island, refineries, and Iranian shuttle tankers; Iranians attempted retaliation by missile attacks on Baghdad.

1986 Secret deal by US to supply arms to Iran revealed (Nov.); revelations resulted in US Iran-Contra scandal.

1986 Iranians reportedly massed million-man army for "final" offensive during the year; offensive never materialized.

1986 Drop in Iranian oil output and fall in world prices resulted in severe economic decline in Iran.

1987 Karbala 5 offensive; Iranians in south broke through Iraqi defenses (Jan. 10), pushing westward to threaten Basra; northern offensive pushed into Iraqi Sumar region; Iraqi counterattacks (Feb.) regained most of the territory in north and south, killing some 50,000 Iranians.

1987 US reflagged Kuwaiti tankers (July) following attacks by amphibious Revolutionary Guard units; US Navy warships began regular convoy escort duty in Persian Gulf for ships into and out of Kuwait; US Navy reestablished strong American presence in Gulf.

1987 UN passed Resolution 598 calling for cease-fire in Iran-Iraq war (July 20); USSR vetoed US–proposed arms embargo against Iran and Iraq (Sept.).

1987 US Navy warship sank Iranian vessel caught laying mines in Persian Gulf (Sept. 21).

1988 Iraq launched destructive missile barrages against Teheran (Feb. 29 and afterward); people fled city in large numbers.

1988 Mujaheddin's National Liberation Army advanced from Iraq to inside Iranian border at Khuzestan (Mar. 28).

1988 Iraqis overran Iranian-held port of Fao (Apr. 15); Iranians offered only weak resistance.

1988 US Navy destroyed Iranian oil platforms in Gulf (Apr. 18) after one of its ships hit a mine; two Iranian frigates and four gunboats also sunk during this action.

1988 Iraqi offensive regained further Iranian-held territory east of Basra (May); Iran lost other hard-won Iraqi territory in both north and south in June.

1988 *USS Vincennes,* pursuing Iranian gunboats that had been harassing Gulf shipping, mistakenly shot down Iranian airbus flying nearby (July 3); 290 civilians killed.

1988 President Ali Khamenei, acting for war-weary Iran, accepted UN cease-fire in writing (July 18).

1988 Cease-fire declared in Iran-Iraq War (Aug.); negotiations began, though disputes soon halted progress on key points.

1990 Iraq formally accepted Iranian terms for formal end to Iran-Iraq War (Aug. 16); agreed to withdrawal from all Iranian lands, to exchange prisoners, and to accept 1975 Algiers accord on Shatt al-Arab waterway.

Iraq (Republic of Iraq) Country located in the Mideast, north of Saudi Arabia, between Syria and Iran. The population is 18,782,000 and the capital is Baghdad. Modern Iraq occupies roughly the region of ancient Mesopotamia, known as the "Cradle of Civilization." The Sumerian, Akkadian, Babylonian, and Assyrian cultures all arose in this region. Later, the area was famous as a center of Arab Muslim civilization and Baghdad became the capital of the Caliphate (*q.v.*) under the Abbasid dynasty. The region was controlled by the Ottoman Turks in the 16th–20th cents. Iraq became a British mandate after WW I and began the exploitation of Iraq's oil resources, eventually making the country one of the world's major oil producers. Following the bloody Iran-Iraq War, Iraq invaded and annexed neighboring Kuwait, thereby precipitating the Persian Gulf War. Iraq lost much of its considerable military during the brief and disastrous war with the US–led UN force. Key events in Iraqi history include:

1831 Ottoman empire established direct control over region, subdividing into the three vilayets of Mosul, Baghdad, and Basra.

1869–72 Midhat Pasha served as governor of Baghdad; instituted reformist administration.

1904–14 Negotiations on exploitation of oil resources; resulted in formation of multinational oil company, what became Iraq Petroleum Company.

1914–18 WW I; British invaded and occupied region of Iraq during war with Ottoman Empire.

1920 Iraq made a British League of Nations mandate at San Remo Conference (Apr.).

1920 Armed rebellion against British rule (July); quelled at great cost.

1921 Organized as a kingdom; Faisal I confirmed as king in a plebiscite (Aug.); Faisal was son of Sharif Husayn of Hijaz who cooperated with British in earlier Arab revolt.

1921–33 Faisal I reigned as king in Iraq.

1924 Twenty-year treaty of alliance signed between Iraq and Britain (Oct.), providing for continued British bases.

1925 First Iraqi parliamentary elections (Mar).

1930 Treaty of alliance with Britain for 25 years; Britain to support Iraq's admission to the League of Nations.

1931 Iraq Petroleum Company, a consortium of American, British, Dutch, and French interests, obtained concession to exploit Mosul oil fields; pipeline to the Mediterranean opened three years later.

1932 Iraq became a member of the League of Nations (Oct.).

1933–39 King Ghazi I reigned; succeeded following death of his father, Faisal I.

1936–41 Period of political turmoil; seven coups staged.

1939 King Ghazi killed in an automobile accident (Apr.); succeeded by his infant son, Faisal II, under a regent.

1939–58 Faisal II reigned.

1941 Rashid Ali al-Gailani, leader of a pro-Nazi group, seized power (Apr. 4); routed by British troops, he fled and British control was restored (May 31).

1943 Rise of Ba'ath ("Renaissance"), Arab nationalist-Socialist party.

1944 Pro-British premier, Gen. Nuri es-Said, proposed "Greater Syria," union to be made up of Iraq, Jordan, Palestine and Syria (Aug.).

1945 Iraq joined the Arab League.

1948 Arab-Israeli War; Iraq joined in Arab attack on newly created Israeli state (May 15); Iraq declined to sign armistice with Israel.

1954 All political parties dissolved by Nuri es-Said.

1955 Baghdad Pact signed, forming alliance that later became the Central Treaty Organization.

1958 Arab Union formed (Feb.); Iraq and Jordan joined in federation.

1958 Republic declared after coup (Feb. 14); King Faisal II killed and Arab Union dissolved.

1958–63 Gen. Abdul Karim Kassem, leader of the coup, in power as premier; established ties with Soviets, pressed Iraqi claim to Kuwait and Shatt al-Arab, bordering Iran.

1959 Iraq withdrew from Baghdad Pact.

1961 Neighboring Kuwait, formerly a British protectorate, gained independence; Iraq claim to sovereignty over the country resulted in British troops being stationed there; Iraq formally recognized Kuwait as an independent, sovereign nation in 1963.

1962 Kurdish revolt led by Mustafa al-Barzani gained control of much of northern Iraq; autonomous Kurdistan sought; fighting continued sporadically in the 1960s and 1970s.

1963 Overthrow and execution of Kassem by Ba'ath-dominated coup led by Col. Abdul Salam Aref (Feb.); Aref later instituted purely military rule (Nov.).

1966 President Abdul Salam Aref killed in an airplane crash; succeeded by his brother Abdul Rahman Aref (Apr.).

1967 Arab-Israeli War; Iraq declared war but did not actually engage in the fighting.

1967 Iraq broke diplomatic relations with the US.

1968 President Abdul Rahman Aref forced out by Gen. Ahmad Hassan al-Bakr in a bloodless coup (July).

1968–79 Ahmad Hassan al-Bakr in power.

1970 Right-wing coup attempt blocked by government (Jan. 20).

1970 Kurdish Autonomous Region formed; offered limited self-government for some 2.5 million Kurds in Iraq; Kurdish anti-government rebellion continued however.

1972 Treaty of friendship with USSR signed.

1972 Iraq Petroleum Company nationalized by government (June 1).

1973 Unsuccessful coup attempt.

1973 Fourth Arab-Israeli War fought between Israel and allied Arab states (Oct.); Iraq joined in oil embargo against Israel's allies.

1974 Border war with Iran.

1974 Kurdish rebels took control of territory along border with Turkey.

1975 Algiers accord; defined boundary with Iraq in disputed Shatt al-Arab waterway at the confluence of the Tigris and Euphrates rivers.

1975 Government troops crushed revolt by Kurds (Mar. 22) after withdrawal of Iranian support.

1979 Muslim fundamentalist revolt overthrew government in neighboring Iran; while Iran threatened to export its radical revolt, the movement failed to spread to Iraq's massive Shi'ite population (about 60% of Iraqis; leaders of Sunni Muslim-dominated government nevertheless remained suspicious.

1979 Bombing of Kurdish villages in Iran in retaliation for continued resistance against the central government.

1979– Saddam Hussein in office as president, after ill health forced Ahmad Hassan al-Bakr to resign (July 16); Saddam Hussein, while maintaining a thin veneer of representative government, steadily consolidated his control over the government; fear and distrust of radical Muslim fundamentalists provoked the long Iran-Iraq War, while the massive Iraqi foreign debt created by it sparked the Kuwaiti invasion and the Persian Gulf War.

1979 Coup attempt, launched days after Saddam Hussein became president, failed; some members of ruling Revolutionary Command Council executed.

1979 Iraqi Communists charged ruling Ba'ath party with mounting a reign of terror.

1980 Members for new National Assembly elected (June) in first elections since 1958; members of Legislative Council for Kurdish Autonomous Region also held.

1980 Iranian-backed guerrillas attempted to assassinate the Iraqi deputy prime minister (Apr.).

1980 Border incidents with Iran increased tensions; Iranians refused to negotiate Iraqi demands for changes in the 1975 Algiers accord.

1980–90 Iran-Iraq War; full-scale war with Iran broke out as Iraqi troops crossed border into Iran (Sept. 22); initial Iraqi gains wiped out by Iranian counterattacks and war soon bogged down into war of attrition; Iraq gradually gained upper hand, though, enjoying virtually unchallenged air superiority.

1981 Israeli aircraft destroyed a nuclear reactor being constructed near Baghdad (June 7).

1982 Iraqi troops driven out of Iran (May) by Iranian counteroffensive in the Iraq-Iran War; Iranian advance into Iraq (July) halted by Iraqi resistance; war subsequently stalemated.

1982 Saddam Hussein purged government, consolidating his control.

1983 Ceasefire in ongoing Kurdish rebellion; government began negotiations (Dec.) with rebel group Patriotic Union of Kurdistan (PUK); fighting resumed Jan. 1985 after negotiations broke down.

1983 Failed coup attempt (Oct.); Saddam Hussein's half-brother and senior army officers executed.

1984 US restored diplomatic relations with Iraq (Nov.), following a 17-year break.

1984 Balance of power in Iran-Iraq War shifted to Iraqis as both USSR and US openly supported them with arms and aid; Iran's continuing promotion of revolutionary Muslim fundamentalism isolated it from all but Syria and Libya.

1985 Kurds rejected Saddam Hussein's proposed amnesty for rebels; Iranian troops reported aiding Kurdish raids on targets inside Iraq.

1988 Iraqi troops used chemical weapons in attack against Halabja, a rebel-held Kurdish town (Mar.).

1988 Iraqi offensive launched into Iran (July) during the closing weeks of the Iran-Iraq War; tide of war clearly in Iraqi favor; Iran accepted terms of UN cease-fire (July).

1988 Cease-fire declared in Iran-Iraq War (Aug.); negotiations began, though disputes soon halted progress on key points.

1988 Government troops launched offensive against rebel Kurds (Aug.–Sept.); some 200,000 Kurds fled to Iran and Turkey as Iraqis reportedly again used chemical weapons; government meanwhile evacuated some 300,000 Kurds from border area to create "security zone" along Iranian and Turkish borders (Aug.–Oct.).

1988–89 Iraq sought to undermine Syrian domination in Lebanon by supporting Lebanese Christians with weapons and money; eventually became leading arms supplier for Lebanese army.

1989 Saddam Hussein announced plans to introduce multi-party system in Iraq (Jan.), in effort to blunt criticism of his autocratic regime.

1989 Coup attempt by military failed (Feb.).

1989 International concern mounting about Iraq's massive military buildup; US banned weapons sales to Iraq (July, 1990).

1990 National Assembly approved draft constitution (July); Consultative Assembly (50% of members appointed by president, 50% elected) and National Assembly to form legislative branch; multi-party system to be established; Saddam Hussein to be elected president for life by special amendment to draft constitution.

1990 Iraqi government complained about production in excess of OPEC quotas by Kuwait and United Arab Emirates; charged Kuwait with exploiting Iraqi oil reserves along border; declared Kuwait should forgo debts owed by Iraq.

1990 Iraq organized military buildup on frontier with Kuwait as OPEC meeting began (July); Kuwait agreed to lower its oil output.

1990 Talks begun with Kuwait (July) to resolve territorial disputes and the disposition of Iraq's substantial debt to Kuwait; negotiations broke down.

1990–91 Persian Gulf War (*q.v.*); Iraqi forces invaded (Aug. 2) and occupied Kuwait; Iraqi government suddenly acceded to Iranian demands in Iran-Iraq War negotiations; Iraq, saddled with some $75 billion in foreign debt from Iran-Iraq War, steadfastly refused all subsequent diplomatic efforts aimed at ending the occupation of oil-rich Kuwait; this eventually provoked first UN sanctions, then a US–led allied buildup (Operation Desert Shield) and allied offensive (Desert Storm) that crushed Iraqi forces in Kuwait and on Iraqi soil as well; Saddam Hussein forced to accept very harsh terms for peace.

1991 Saddam Hussein reshuffled his cabinet in bid to remain in power after humiliating loss in Persian Gulf War (Mar.); named loyal supporters and family members to key posts.

1991 Shi'ite Muslim rebels captured Basra and other cities in southern Iraq (Mar.), taking advantage of central government's weakness at the time; government troops, regrouped after their defeat in the Persian Gulf war, soon regained control in the south.

1991 Kurdish guerrillas, some 100,000-strong, expanded their control throughout much of Kurdistan (Mar.); captured city of Kirkuk (Apr.).

1991 Saddam Hussein reportedly agreed in principle to implement 1970 agreement on Kurdistan autonomy (Apr.); talks later bogged down over inclusion of Kirkuk in autonomous zone; Saddam Hussein later cut off all services to zone to force acceptance of terms (Oct.).

1991 Various Kurdish guerrilla factions joined in May to form the Kurdistan Iraqi Front (KIF), seeking full implementation of 1970 agreement on Kurdistan autonomy.

1991 Iraqi army mounted counteroffensive against Kurds (May–June); over one million Kurds fled to Iran and Turkey as Iraqi troops advanced (June); UN-supervised "safe havens" established for Kurds returning to Iraq (June).

1991 Multi-party political system established (Sept.); parties to be strictly controlled, however.

1991 Economy continued to falter after having been wrecked by two wars and the resulting accumulated debt estimated at some $200 billion (including war reparations); inflation rate reported as high as 2,000% for 1991; about one-third of available food came from emergency rations; industrial output declined sharply as result of war damage and continuing UN embargo; refineries, heavily damaged in war, remained at only a fraction of former capacity.

1991–92 UN teams searched for and destroyed Iraqi weapons of mass destruction, in accordance with surrender terms accepted by Iraq; Iraqis hindered teams at various times during this period.

1992 Major Iraqi nuclear complex at al-Atheer destroyed under UN supervision (Apr.).

1992 Mass arrests reported as Saddam Hussein cracked down on suspected dissidents (June).

1992 US fighter jets began enforcing "no-fly zone" over southern Iraq (Sept.) to halt Iraqi air attacks on Shi'ite Muslims, who had revolted against Hussein in 1991.

Ireland (Republic of Ireland; *formerly* Irish Free State, Eire)   Independent country located in the western part of the British Isles and occupying all but the northeastern section (Northern Ireland) of a large island. The population is 3,557,000 and the capital is Dublin. Invaded by the Celts in the 4th cent. BC, Ireland was subjected to raids by the Norsemen from the 9th–11th cents. The English took control of Ireland in the 12th cent. and thus began the long struggle between the Irish and their English overlords. The Irish finally gained independence from Britain in 1922. However, the long-standing resentment over British domination has found new expression in the movement to unite Protestant Northern Ireland (created in 1920) with the Catholic Republic of Ireland. The movement began in the 1960s and since then the Irish Republican Army (IRA) has waged a brutal terrorist campaign aimed at Irish Protestants and the British. Key dates in the history of Ireland include:

c400 BC   Ireland inhabited by Celtic tribes.

AD c430   Saint Patrick introduced Christianity.

c500–800   Golden Age of Irish culture; native Gaelic arts and literature developed; Gaelic culture spread to Scotland; monasteries established and Irish missionaries sent abroad.

c524–528   Saint Bridgit of Ireland founded the first nunnery at Kildare.

9TH–11TH CENTS.   Norse invasions.

1002–14   B. Boru ruled as high king of Ireland.

1014   B. Boru defended Dublin and destroyed the power of the Norse invaders at the Battle of Clontarf (Apr. 23).

11TH–12TH CENTS.   Period of warfare between rival clans.

1142   Church reformer Saint Malachy established Mellifont, first Cistercian abbey in Ireland.

1155   Henry II of England authorized to take possession of Ireland by order of papal bull; document may have been forged.

1166   Rory R. O'Connor seized high kingship; reigned as last high king of Ireland.

1169   English conquest of Ireland began; soldiers sent to restore deposed Irish king of Leinster.

1171   Henry II led a large army into Ireland; his overlordship recognized by some; began period of English rule, based at Dublin; feudalism introduced; wars with Irish opposed to British rule began.

13TH CENT.   An Anglo-Irish Parliament established; native Irish were excluded from it.

1204–1855   Donnybrook held its annual fair, which became famous for rowdyness and brawling.

1315   Scots invaded Ireland; led by Edward Bruce, they allied with local chieftans; undermined English rule.

14TH–15TH CENTS.   English power effectively limited to an area around Dublin called the Pale (where Irish law and customs were forbidden).

1455–85   Anglo-Norman noblemen of the Pale of Ireland participated in Wars of the Roses; their power in Ireland further weakened by the wars.

1494   Tudor king Henry VII renewed efforts to control Ireland; sent a new English governor, Sir Edward Poynings.

1495   Poyning's Law passed by Irish Parliament; Irish Parliaments thereafter to be subject to English Parliament.

1534   T. Fitzgerald, 10th earl of Kildare, led rebellion against the king.

1541   Henry VIII created a Protestant "Church of Ireland," but most of the inhabitants remained Catholic; Catholic monasteries abolished.

1579   T. Butler, 10th earl of Ormonde, helped English put down revolt in Ireland; and again in 1597.

1581–1656   J. Ussher, scholar and archbishop, lived.

1583   G. Fitzgerald, 15th earl of Desmond, killed after rebelling against English rule.

16TH–17TH CENTS.   Penal laws passed to prohibit practice of Roman Catholicism in Britain and Ireland.

16TH–17TH CENTS.   Large-scale colonization of Ireland by Protestants; many Catholics driven off their lands; confiscation of Irish lands during 17th cent. created Irish tenant farm system, with lands held by absentee landlords.

17TH CENT.   Belfast became center for linen industry.

1603   Tyrone's rebellion crushed; Ulster and Munster counties devastated.

1650   O. Cromwell ruthlessly crushed an Irish rebellion that had begun in 1641; many thousands killed; more Irish lands confiscated.

1662   Scientist R. Boyle discovered the relationship between the pressure of a gas and its volume.

1687–90   Jacobite R. Talbot served as lord deputy of Ireland.

1690   Battle of the Boyne near Dublin; English king James II, a Catholic who was deposed during the Glorious Revolution (1688), was defeated by his successor, William III; James was supported by French and Irish Catholics.

1709   Philosopher G. Berkeley wrote *Essay Towards a New Theory of Vision.*

1746–1820   H. Grattan lived; remembered as a leader in fight for Irish independence.

c1760   Whiteboys, a peasant group, formed to harass landlords, tax collectors, and Protestant clergy.

1782   H. Grattan won independence for Ireland's Parliament with repeal of Poyning's Law but Catholics were denied the right to hold office.

1790–1856   Temperance missionary T. Mathew lived.

1791   United Irishmen founded; became underground movement opposing British rule.

1795   Protestant political group, the Orangemen, founded to maintain Protestant domination over the Catholics.

1798   Rebellion by Irish Protestant Wolfe Tone; revolt failed despite aid from revolutionary France.

1801   George III and Prime Minister W. Pitt promoted the Union of Ireland and England to solve Irish problem; abolition of the Irish Parliament and legislative union in a United Kingdom of Great Britain and Ireland effected.

1801   Act of Union formally united Great Britain and Ireland.

1828   D. O'Connell elected to Parliament; sparked passage of Catholic Emancipation Act.

1829   Catholic Emancipation Act; penal laws directed against Catholics repealed.

1845–49   Great Potato Famine; hundreds of thousands starved to death; nearly two million emigrated to the US.

1848   Unsuccessful revolt by W. O'Brien.

c1858   Fenian movement organized, attempted to secure Irish independence; eventually superseded by Sinn Fein.

1869   Anglican church in Ireland formally dissolved.

FROM 1870   Rise of the Home Rule movement for self-government: Home Rule became a major controversy (from late 1800s); opposed by Irish Protestants.

1870–1903   Irish Land Acts passed by British Parliament to aid tenant farmers.

1875   C. Parnell elected to Parliament as an Irish Home Rule advocate.

1891   Author O. Wilde wrote the novel *The Picture of Dorian Gray.*

1902   Sinn Fein, nationalist political party, founded by A. Griffith to secure Irish independence.

1902   Abbey Theatre company founded by J. M. Synge, W. B. Yeats, and others.

1903–66   Writer F. O'Connor lived.

1907   Playwright J. M. Synge wrote *The Playboy of the Western World.*

1916   Irish Republican Army (IRA) formed.

1916   Easter Rebellion broke out; suppressed after fierce fighting; leaders executed, but rebellion led to fall of the government of H. Asquith and eventual establishment of the Irish Free State.

1916   R. Casement executed for seeking German aid in establishing Irish independence.

1918   Dáil Éireann (Irish assembly) created by Sinn Fein members who had been elected to British Parliament and who had refused to take their seats; Irish republic proclaimed.

1918   Irish nationalist countess Markiewicz became first woman elected to British Parliament, but she declined the post.

1919–21   Guerrilla war between Irish rebels and British government forces.

1920   British Black and Tans employed brutal measures against Irish revolutionaries.

1921   IRA leader M. Collins negotiated a treaty with the British giving Ireland dominion status.

1922   Irish Free State established (Jan.) as dominion in the British Commonwealth; northern counties of Ulster remained united with Britain.

1922   Author J. Joyce wrote his monumental novel *Ulysses.*

1922–32 William T. Cosgrave in office as first president of the executive council.

1923 Dramatist S. O'Casey wrote the play *The Shadow of a Gunman.*

1923 Poet W. B. Yeats awarded Nobel Prize for Literature.

1925 Dramatist G. B. Shaw received the Nobel Prize for Literature; noted for plays *Major Barbara* and *Pygmalion,* as well as other works.

1926 Fianna Fáil party founded to sever all ties with Britain.

1937 Independence (as Eire) declared, though ties with the British Commonwealth were retained.

1937–48 E. de Valera in office as first prime minister of Eire.

1939–45 WW II; Eire remained neutral.

1949 The Republic of Ireland proclaimed, replacing Eire; withdrawal from the British Commonwealth and final independence from Britain (Apr. 18).

1955 Ireland joined the UN.

1959–73 E. de Valera served as president of Ireland.

1960s IRA terrorism began in earnest in an effort to unite Northern Ireland to the Republic of Ireland.

1966–73 John Lynch, member of Fianna Fáil party, in office as prime minister; moved against IRA terrorists.

1972 Emergency powers for government approved by legislature in face of increased terrorism in Ireland (Dec. 2).

1973–77 Liam Cosgrave in office as prime minister, heading a coalition government between Fine Gael and the Labor Party.

1976 More stringent anti-terrorist laws passed by the republic after the assassination of the British ambassador.

1977–79 Lynch in office as prime minister; maintained improved relations with British; advocated unification with Northern Ireland (1978).

1979 Lord Mountbatten, British admiral of the fleet, murdered by IRA terrorists (Aug.); simultaneously IRA terrorists massacred 18 British soldiers in Northern Ireland.

1979–81 Charles J. Haughey, Fianna Fáil party member, in office as prime minister, following resignation of John Lynch (Dec.).

1981 IRA prisoners in Northern Ireland's Maze Prison began fasts to the death in order to dramatize the cause of Irish unity.

1981 Anglo-Irish Intergovernmental Council established (Nov.) to formalize regular official contacts between Irish and British governments.

1981–82 Garret FitzGerald, Fine Gael party member, in office as prime minister.

1982 Haughey returned to office as prime minister; failing economy soon brought his government down, however.

1982–87 FitzGerald back in office as prime minister.

1983 Constitutional amendment banning abortion approved by referendum.

1985 Anglo-Irish Agreement signed (Nov.); established Irish government participation in Northern Ireland's political, legal, and security matters; Irish government promised to take steps to deter IRA cross-border raids into Northern Ireland.

1986 Irish government signed European Convention on the Suppression of Terrorism (Feb.).

1986 IRA political wing, Sinn Fein, ended long-time policy of refusing to attend Parliament (since 1922); failed to win even one seat in elections in 1987.

1987–92 Haughey back in office as prime minister, heading a minority government; imposed severe, but successful, austerity program to counter ongoing economic problems.

1988 Irish Supreme Court ruled government cannot refuse extradition of IRA terrorists who claim their crimes were for a political cause.

1989 Government announced policy favoring reduced income tax rates and creation of more jobs.

1990 Death penalty, not invoked since 1954, banned.

1990 Irish Supreme Court ruled on first IRA terrorist extradition case arising from 1986 European convention on terrorism (July); terrorist ordered extradited to Britain.

1990– Mary Robinson, a lawyer and independent, in office as Ireland's president, following elections.

1991 Financial scandal involving government officials rocked the Haughey government (Oct.); Haughey later forced out of office.

1991 Government signed Maastricht Treaty on European union (Dec.); union seen as leading to Ireland's economic development; Irish voters approved the treaty in 1992.

1992– Albert Reynolds, member of Fianna Fáil, in office as prime minister; installed new cabinet.

Ireland, John 1838–1918. US Catholic leader and first archbishop of St. Paul, Minn. (1888–1918). Ordained in 1861, he became a spokesman for Catholic immigrants, encouraging their integration and westward migration. He favored government support for Catholic schools, and was a spokesman for liberal Catholicism.

Ireland, William Henry 1777–1835. English forger of documents and manuscripts of W. Shakespeare. His forgeries were discovered (1796), and he admitted to the hoax.

Irenaeus, Saint AD 125–c202. Early Catholic theologian. Irenaeus was bishop of Lyons and a Father of the Church. He opposed Gnosticism (*q.v.*) eloquently in his work *Against Heresies,* one of the earliest Christian writings to treat doctrine systematically and one of the most important early witnesses to the ancient primacy of Rome over other Christian churches.

Irene c752–803. Byzantine empress. She served as regent for her son Constantine VI from 780 to 790 and in 797 deposed him and had him blinded. She opposed the Iconoclasts, and restored use of icons in the Eastern church. She was deposed in 802.

Ireton, Henry 1611–51. English soldier and Parliamentarian. The son-in-law of O. Cromwell, Ireton signed Charles I's death warrant. He later assisted Cromwell in dispossessing the Irish and establishing English settlers.

Irigoyen, Hipólito 1850?–1933. Argentine political leader. As head of the Radical party, he worked for electoral reform and served as president from 1916 to 1922. Reelected in 1928, he was overthrown in 1930.

Irish Free State Name used by the Republic of Ireland from 1922 to 1937; that is, during the period that Ireland had dominion status within the British Empire. (*See also* Ireland, 1922–1937).

Irish Land Acts Legislation passed (1870–1903) for the benefit of Irish tenant farmers. The acts initiated by W. E. Gladstone, were designed to curtail landlord abuse and provide incentives for peasant proprietorship.

Irish Republican Army (IRA) Irish nationalist organization dedicated to the creation of a single unified Irish state. Organized from the elements dispersed during the Easter Rebellion (*q.v.*) of 1916, it became the political arm of the Sinn Fein (*q.v.*) party, and opposed dominion status after the creation of the Irish Free State in 1922. It declined after its former supporter E. de Valera took over the Irish government and because of its opposition to the Allies in WW II, and was eventually outlawed by both Irish governments. In 1969, it launched new terrorist measures in Northern Ireland which the British government was not able to quell after a dozen years. However, the IRA was by then split into "officials," advocating a Socialist Ireland by democratic means, and the "provisionals," advocating terrorism.

Iron Act British law passed (1750) to limit the growth of the iron industry in the American colonies. It prohibited construction of slitting and plating mills and steel furnaces. It aimed to increase the export of iron ore from the colonies to Britain but had only a limited success.

Iron Age Period in the development of human culture in which iron came to be used predominantly for making tools and weapons. The Iron Age, which succeeded the Bronze Age (*q.v.*), began at various times in various locations. Widespread use of iron is generally thought to have begun in the Near East and it is the Hittites (*q.v.*) who are credited with discovering the technique of tempering iron. Following the breakup of the Hittite Empire (c1200 BC), ironworking techniques were spread through Europe and Asia Minor. By the 5th cent. BC, the use of iron was well established in Europe.

Iron Chancellor *See* **Bismarck, Otto Eduard Leopold von.**

ironclad Warship built during the mid-19th cent. fitted with iron plates. This type of ship was first used by the French during the Crimean War and later employed by both sides in the US Civil War. Ironclads were replaced at the end of the century by all-metal warships.

iron curtain Name once applied to the former Soviet Union's policy of limiting Western information and influence within its borders and those of its Eastern European satellites after

WW II. The term was coined by W. Churchill and used in a speech at Fulton, Missouri (Mar. 6, 1946). The policy of isolation was eroded by increasing East-West contacts during the 1970s and 1980s and had been abandoned even before the collapse of the USSR itself.

Iron Guard Rumanian Fascist group, founded 1924. Organized in military fashion by Corneliu Zelea-Codreanu (1899?–1938), the group assassinated the Rumanian premier (1933). Officially banned thereafter, it continued as the "All-for-the-Fatherland" party. In 1938 King Carol II arrested Zelea-Codreanu and other leaders. The group then helped I. Antonescu take power (1940) in Rumania, but they soon turned against him and rebelled (1941). Following suppression of the group by Antonescu and the fall of Germany in WW II, the group disappeared.

Iroquois Confederacy (Iroquois League) (League of Five Nations) Confederation of Indian tribes important in US Colonial history. It was composed of five tribes (a sixth, the Tuscarora, joined c1722) which occupied Northeast woodlands from Maine to the Great Lakes region. Formed sometime in the 16th cent., the Confederacy was well organized and proved highly effective in warfare. In the 17th cent., it drove off rival tribes, including the Huron, Neutral Nation, and Erie (*qq.v.*). In the French and Indian Wars (17th–18th cents.) they generally served British interests against the French. During the American Revolution, the Confederacy split, with most tribes taking the British side. They took part in the Battle of Oriskany, the Wyoming Massacre, and the Cherry Valley Raid (*qq.v.*), but were finally defeated (1779) in New York by an American retaliatory force. Thereafter the Confederacy ceased to be important. The six tribes of the Confederacy were: Mohawk, Seneca, Onondaga, Oneida, Cayuga, and Tuscarora.

Iroquois League *See* **Iroquois Confederacy.**

irredentism Originally an Italian nationalist movement that aimed to add to Italy all territories inhabited by Italian-speaking people not included at the time of the unification of Italy (1870–71). This was considered *terra irredenta* ("unredeemed land"), and included Trentino, Trieste, Istria, Fiume, and parts of Dalmatia, most of which Italy finally acquired after WW I. But the term "irredentism" has since been applied to any nationalist movement seeking to incorporate territory on the basis of historical, ethnic, and geographic considerations.

Irving, Edward 1792–1834. Scottish minister, whose writings and religious teaching led to the establishment of what he called the Catholic Apostolic Church (Irvingites), which sought to prepare for the second coming of Christ.

Irving, Washington 1783–1859. American author. Irving was one of the first native American writers, and is often called the inventor of the short-story form. His *History of New York by Diedrich Knickerbocker* was one of America's first comic works. His *Sketchbook* includes the famous short stories "Rip Van Winkle" and "The Legend of Sleepy Hollow."

Irvingites *See* **Irving, Edward.**

Isaac I (Isaac Comnenus) c1005–61. Byzantine emperor (1057–59), successor to Michael VI, whom he deposed. He abdicated in 1059 because of ill health and retired to a monastery. He was the first of the Comnenid emperors.

Isaac II (Isaac II Angelus) Byzantine emperor (1185–95) and co-emperor (1203–04). He was deposed and blinded in 1195 by his brother, who became Alexius III, but his son, later Alexius IV, appealed to the Latins of the Fourth Crusade, and the two were briefly restored as co-emperors. Their overthrow by Alexius V led to the storming and sacking of Constantinople by the Crusaders (1204).

Isaac Comnenus *See* **Isaac I.**

Isaac II Angelus *See* **Isaac II.**

Isabeau of Bavaria (Elizabeth) 1371–1435. French queen (1389–1422?). When her husband Charles VI became insane (1392), Isabeau ruled as regent. She sided with the British in the Hundred Years' War and promoted the Treaty of Troyes (*q.v.*). She was the mother of Catherine of Valois, who married Henry V of England.

Isabel 1846–1921. Princess and regent of Brazil. Her abolition of slavery in 1888 helped lead to the fall of the Brazilian Empire in 1889 by alienating the large slave-holding landowners. She followed her father Pedro II into exile.

Isabella 1292?–1358. French-born queen of England. With her lover, R. de Mortimer, she ousted her husband Edward II (1327) and installed her son Edward III. She had her husband murdered; later her son executed Mortimer and jailed her.

Isabella I (Isabella the Catholic) 1451–1504. Queen of Spain. Queen of Castile, with her husband Ferdinand V (*q.v.*), she united most of Spain, instituted the Spanish Inquisition, expelled the Jews (1492), and drove the Moors from Granada (1492). She financed the expedition of C. Columbus that discovered the New World (1492).

Isabella II 1830–1904. Queen of Spain (1833–68), successor to her father Ferdinand VII. Her succession over her uncle, Don Carlos, led to rebellion by the Carlists, who refused to recognize any female succession. Her policies caused political turmoil and she was deposed in 1868.

Isabella the Catholic *See* **Isabella I.**

Isaiah (Isaias) *fl.* 8th cent. BC. Hebrew prophet who began to prophesy in the reign of King Uzziah (c740 BC) and continued to c701 BC. Considered one of the great prophets, he warned against entangling alliances, preached redemptive suffering, prophesied the fall and later redemption of Israel, and proclaimed the coming of a Messiah. Most scholars consider Chapters 40–55 of the Book of Isaiah to have been written by later exilic prophets whom they designate Deutero-Isaiah, and Chapters 56–66 to a post-exilic prophet.

Isaias *See* **Isaiah.**

Isauria Ancient district in south central Asia Minor. Its warlike people were legendary, though defeated by Servilius in 76 BC; it became part of the Roman province of Galatia. It was the birthplace of the Byzantine emperor Zeno, among others.

Isaurian Dynasty of Byzantine emperors that ruled from 717 to 802. The line was founded by Leo III and the last reigning member of the line was the empress Irene, who was forced to abdicate in 802. *The Isaurian rulers were:* Leo III 717–741; Constantine V 741–775; Leo IV 775–780; Constantine VI 780–797; Irene 797–802.

Isca Silurum *See* **Caerleon.**

Isidore of Seville, Saint c560–636. Bishop of Seville (600–636) and prolific writer. His *Etymologiae,* especially *De Natura Rerum,* and other works were very influential. His encyclopedic learning was the means of transmitting much classical learning to the Middle Ages.

Islam One of the world's three great monotheistic religions, with Christianity and Judaism. Islam is the newest of the three and was founded by the prophet Muhammad (*q.v.*) in the 7th cent.

AD. Muslims believe Muhammad was the last of the prophets (including Adam, Noah, Abraham, Moses, and Jesus) sent by Allah (God). They exult in their submission to and praise of Allah. The Islamic faith, which owes much to the earlier Judaic and Christian faiths, is based on the Koran (*q.v.*), the revelations of Allah to Muhammad; the Sunna, collections of sayings of Muhammad (compiled in the 9th cent.); and the principle of Ijma or consensus of the Muslims or Muslim scholars. The prophet Muhammad during his lifetime laid the foundations of the great Muslim theocratic state, the Caliphate (*q.v.*). After his death, the empire was rapidly expanded to include domains stretching from India, across the Mideast, and into North Africa and served to spread the Muslim faith throughout these regions. A dispute over the succession to the caliph (ruler of the Muslim theocracy) in the 7th cent. gave rise to the two main divisions in the Muslim world: the Sunni (orthodox) and Shi'ite sects (*qq.v.*). The Shi'ites gave rise to other sects, including the Assassins, Karmathians, and Druses (*qq.v.*). For more on early Islamic history, *see* Caliphate.

Ismail I 1486–1524. Shah of Persia, 1501–24, founder of Safavid dynasty. Established the Shi'ite form of Islam as the state religion, thus incurring the special enmity of the Sunni Turks and Uzbeks, with whom he warred unceasingly. Succeeded by his son Tahmasp I, father of Ismail II.

Ismail Pasha 1830–95. Egyptian ruler under Ottoman suzerainty (1863–79). The Suez Canal was completed during his rule, but his improvement schemes plunged Egypt into debt, and he was forced to sell his canal shares to Britain (1875) and put Egypt's finances under the control of foreign bondholders (1876). Also known as the Khedive Ismail, he was ousted in 1879 by the Ottoman sultan, who willingly responded to pressure for the dismissal by the British and French.

Isocrates 436–338 BC. Athenian orator and rhetorician. A pupil of Socrates, he was perhaps the leading teacher of his day. He systematized the education of rhetoric, had many famous students, and was a leading exponent of Pan-Hellenism. His 21 surviving discourses are valuable sources of information about Greek life.

isolationism Policy of noninvolvement in the affairs of other nations. In the US, isolationists often cited the warning of G. Washington (in his farewell address) against "entangling alliances." Isolationist policies generally prevailed in the US during the 19th cent., and especially between WW I and WW II. Enough senators favored isolationism to prevent Senate ratification of the Treaty of Versailles (*q.v.*), which would have meant an active US role in the League of Nations (*q.v.*), as proposed by W. Wilson. International aggression, however, forced the US to abandon isolationist policies even before the country's entry into WW II.

Isonzo, Battle of *See* **Caporetto, Battle of.**

Israel Republic (*pop.* 4,371,000) located on the eastern Mediterranean coast. Its capital is Jerusalem. The history of modern Israel begins with its creation in 1948, but the movement to establish a Jewish state in Palestine dates to the late 19th cent. and the beginnings of the Zionist movement. Since 1948, Israel has had to contend with hostile Arab neighbors, frequent wars, and in more recent years terrorist attacks by guerrillas of the Palestine Liberation Organization (PLO). Friction between Arabs and Israelis has been one of the chief factors contributing to Mideast instability. US efforts to settle the differences bore first fruit with the normalization of relations between Egypt (first Arab state to do so) and Israel in the 1970s. A new round of peace initiatives began immediately after the Persian Gulf War (1991). (For history of the region prior to 1948, *see* Palestine; Israel, kingdom of; Judah.) Key dates in the history of modern Israel include:

1897 T. Herzl led first Zionist council at Basel, Switzerland, marking the beginning of the movement for independent Jewish state.

1917–18 British occupied Palestine, defeating the Ottoman army during World War I.

1917 Balfour Declaration (Nov. 3) announced British support for a Jewish "National Home" in Palestine; population in Palestine at this time predominately Arab.

1920 Conference of San Remo in Italy; began creation of British mandates in Palestine.

1921–22 Violent anti-Zionist riots by Arabs in Palestine broke out.

1922 League of Nations made Palestine a mandated territory of Britain; Britain set immigration quotas in attempt to limit influx of Jews.

1929 C. Weizmann founded the Jewish Agency, which oversaw settlement of Jews in Palestine.

1929 Renewed anti-Zionist rioting by Arabs in Palestine; and again in 1936.

1930s Persecution of Jews by Nazis in Germany increased immigration to Palestine.

1933 Beginning of Holocaust in Nazi Germany; some six million Jews were brutally killed before Nazi defeat in WW II.

1933 Jews in Palestine rioted in protest against British attempts to restrict immigration of Jews there.

1936–39 Arab Palestinians rebelled against British control and immigration of Jews.

1937 British proposed dividing Palestine into separate Jewish and Arab states; Arabs opposed the plan; fighting between Jews and Arabs in Palestine flared.

1945 Holocaust revealed; enormity of mass killings of some six million Jews by Nazis shocked world; atrocity helped solidify international support for Jewish homeland.

1945–47 Attacks on British occupation forces by Palestinian Jewish groups seeking Jewish homeland.

1947 UN Special Committee on Palestine issued plan to divide Palestine into separate Arab and Jewish states and establish Jerusalem and environs as an international zone; plan passed (Nov. 29) by UN General Assembly but was rejected by Arabs.

1948 Israeli state created (May 14) according to plan for partitioning Palestine; Tel Aviv became capital; some 400,000 Palestinian Arab refugees fled to neighboring states before Israeli statehood; hundreds of thousands of others followed later.

1948–52 C. Weizmann served as first president of Israel.

1948–53 D. Ben-Gurion served as Israel's first prime minister.

1948–49 Arab-Israeli War broke out upon creation of the Israeli state (May 14); additional territory conquered during war gave Israel about three-quarters of Palestine; Jordan held the rest (the West Bank).

1949 Israel admitted to UN (May 11).

1950 Jerusalem officially became capital of Israel (Jan. 23).

1950 Law of Return enacted, provided for automatic citizenship for all immigrant Jews.

1952–63 I. Ben-Zvi served as president.

1955–63 Ben-Gurion in office as prime minister.

1956 Arab-Israeli War (Oct.–Nov.); Israelis invaded Egypt amid Suez Crisis, captured Sinai territory.

1956 Israeli forces withdrew from the Sinai Peninsula (Nov.); UN peace-keeping forces were subsequently moved into area.

1957 Israeli forces completed withdrawal from Gaza Strip (Mar.); UN forces moved into area.

1963–69 Levi Eshkol in office as prime minister.

1964 PLO organized; dedicated to reclaiming lands occupied by Israel.

1966–74 A. Eban served as foreign minister under G. Meir; also became Israel's first UN representative and ambassador the US.

1967 Egyptian president G. Nasser mobilized Egyptian forces (May) and blocked Israeli access to the Gulf of Aqaba.

1967 Arab-Israeli War (June 5–10); Israelis victorious in Six-Day War; Sinai recaptured and the West Bank and Golan Heights taken.

1969 Prime Minister L. Eshkol died (Feb. 26).

1969–74 G. Meir in office as prime minister.

1972 Palestinian terrorists killed 11 members of the Israeli Olympic team (Sept. 25) in attack on Olympic Village at Munich, West Germany.

1973 Arab-Israeli War (Oct. 6–25); Israelis repulsed attacks by Egyptians and Syrians.

1974 Israel agreed to partial withdrawals from captured territories following US–brokered accords with Egypt and with Syria; UN forces established a buffer zone.

1974–77 Yitzhak Rabin in office as prime minister.

1976 Entebbe Raid (July 3–4) in Uganda to rescue passengers in airliner hijacked by Palestinans.

1977–83 M. Begin in office (June 21) as prime minister.

1977 Egyptian president Sadat made an historic state visit to Israel (Nov. 19–21) in the first of a series of peace initiatives between the two nations.

1977 Begin visited Egypt (Dec. 24–26) to continue discussion on possible peace settlement.

1978 Prime Minister Begin and Egyptian president Sadat signed Camp David Accords (Sept. 17), providing a framework for peace with Egypt.

1979 Begin signed historic formal peace treaty with Egypt (Mar. 26); Israelis to pull out of occupied Sinai in phases (completed 1982).

1980 Israeli Knesset (legislature) approved declaration that Jerusalem would remain unified and the capital of Israel for all time.

1981 Israeli fighter planes sent into Iraq (June 7) to destroy a nuclear reactor under construction near Baghdad.

1981 Government extended Israeli law to occupied territory of the Golan Heights (Dec. 14).

1982 Lebanese War; Israelis invaded Lebanon (June 6); PLO pushed north and was encircled in Beirut; some 14–15,000 encircled; PLO withdrew to various Arab countries (Aug.).

1982 Beirut massacre; Lebanese Christian militia killed hundreds of Palestinian refugees slain in two Beirut Palestinian refugee camps; failure of Israeli occupation force to prevent massacre caused political crisis in Israeli government; Defense Minister Gen. Ariel Sharon was ultimately forced to resign (1983).

1983 Israel signed agreement with Lebanon ending the Lebanese War (May); Syria rejected clause requiring all foreign forces to be withdrawn in three months, whereupon Israeli forces remained in southern Lebanon.

1983–84 Yitzhak Shamir in office as prime minister, succeeding Begin as head of Likud coalition.

1984–86 Shimon Peres, Labor party leader, in office as prime minister, heading a Labor-Likud coalition government.

1985 Israeli army pulled back to within a few miles of Lebanon's southern border (June).

1986 Palestinian guerrillas, again moving southward in Lebanon, renewed rocket attacks on Israeli border towns; Israeli air force thereafter made periodic attacks against PLO targets in southern Lebanon.

1986–92 Shamir returned to office as prime minister.

1987 Arab *intifada* (uprising) began in Gaza strip and spread to Arab communities throughout Israeli-occupied territories; marked start of continuing demonstration against poor living conditions and opposition to rule by Israelis; Israeli use of force to halt protests criticized.

1988 PLO declared independent Palestinian state encompassing Israeli-occupied West Bank and Gaza Strip (Nov.); PLO chairman Y. Arafat explicitly accepted Israel's existence;

Prime Minister Shamir, continuing Israeli policy of refusing to negotiate with terrorist PLO, responded by offering Palestinians of West Bank and Gaza limited self-rule.

1989   Shamir made new peace offer (Apr.); proposed free elections for Palestinian delegates in West Bank and Gaza; delegates would then negotiate self-rule while remaining within Israeli state.

1990   Shamir hard-line policy statement held Jews had right to settle in occupied territories, opposed formation of Palestinian state, and stood by his decision against negotiating with PLO.

1990   US president G. Bush, opposed to new Jewish settlements in Israeli-occupied territory, held up $400 million loan to Israel for new housing for Jewish immigrants from USSR (Mar.).

1990   Violent clashes between Arabs and Israelis increased in occupied territories and Israel proper (May).

1990–91   Persian Gulf War; Arab unrest in occupied territories increased, while attempts by Iraq to link withdrawal from Kuwait with Israeli withdrawal from occupied territories failed; similarly, Iraqi Scud missile attacks on Israel also failed to draw Israel into the conflict.

1990   Palestinians attacked Jewish worshipers at Jerusalem's Temple Mount (Oct.); Israeli police killed 17 Palestinians.

1991   US secretary of state James A. Baker 3d declared building of new settlements in Israeli-occupied territories was main roadblock to Mideast peace (May).

1991   US–Soviet-brokered Mideast peace conference opened in Madrid, Spain (Oct.); subsequent sessions to mid-1992 failed to break deadlock on fundamental issue, the future of Israeli-occupied West Bank and Gaza.

1992   Estimated 350,000 Russian Jews immigrated to Israel by this time (Jan.).

1992   Israeli troops raided Shi'ite Muslim Hezbollah positions in southern Lebanon (Feb.).

1992   Labor leader Yitzhak Rabin in office as prime minister; promised efforts to speed up Mideast peace talks; visited Egypt (July) for talks with President H. Mubarak; froze construction of new settlements in occupied territory.

Israel, kingdom of   Originally, the Old Testament kingdom of the Hebrews ruled by Saul, David, and Solomon. Following the rebellion (c933 BC) by Jeroboam I, the kingdom was divided. The northern part, which was thereafter called Israel, included lands of the 10 northern tribes. [1 Kings; 2 Chron] The southern part, called Judah (*q.v.*), included the lands of the tribes of Benjamin and Judah. The kingdom of Israel was overrun (c721) by Assyrians (*q.v.*) under Sargon II, and many of the inhabitants were carried off. [2 Kings 17] They became known as the Ten Lost Tribes (*q.v.*).

Issus, Battle of   Decisive victory (333 BC) for Alexander the Great over the Persians under Darius III during the Macedonian conquest of the Persian Empire. In an effort to check the invasion, Darius led an unsuccessful attack upon the Macedonians on the Issus plain in present-day southern Turkey. The Macedonians reputedly lost 450 men versus tens of thousands of slain Persians.

Isthmian Games   Greek athletic events. These games were held on the Isthmus of Corinth from 582 BC to the 4th cent. AD in honor of Poseidon. They consisted of both athletic and musical competitions.

Itagaki, Taisuke   1837–1919. Japanese statesman. He played a major role in the 1868 Meiji Restoration (*q.v.*), founded the Jiyuto (Liberal) party, and worked to bring constitutional reforms to the government.

Italian East Africa   Italian African colonies. This was the name given (1936) to the federation of Italian-controlled colonies in Africa composed of Eritrea, Ethiopia, and Italian Somaliland. Italy lost them after WW II.

Italian Wars   Series of destructive wars (1494–1559) for control of Italy. The wars, largely fought by France and Spain, resulted in the domination of Italy by the Spanish Habsburgs. Fighting began with an invasion (1494) of Italy by French king Charles VIII. He took Naples but was forced out of Italy by an alliance of the Holy Roman Empire, Spain, and the pope. French king Louis XII launched another invasion (1499) and took Milan, Genoa, and Naples but was driven out of Naples (1503) by the Spanish. Pope Julius II then organized (1508) the League of Cambrai (*q.v.*) against Venice. By 1510, however, he had turned against France and formed the Holy League (*q.v.*) against it. Following some years of fighting, a peace was arranged (1516) by which the French held Milan and Spain kept Naples. Fighting again erupted (1521) between Holy Roman Emperor Charles V and the new French king, Francis I. In the course of battle, Francis was captured (at the Battle of Pavia) and forced to sign the Treaty of Madrid (1526). On being freed, Francis renounced the treaty and formed a new alliance with England, the pope, Venice, and Florence. In this phase of the wars, Charles sacked Rome (May 1527) and forced the pope to come to terms, the French failed in their siege of Genoa, and Francis finally gave up all claims to Italy in the Treaty of Cambrai (1529). Francis fought two other unsuccessful wars against the Spanish outside Italy. By the Treaty of Cateau-Cambrésis (1559), Spain was confirmed as the dominant power in Italy.

Italo-Ethiopian War War (1935–36) in which Italy took control of the independent African state of Ethiopia. It contributed to international tensions that led up to WW II. Following a border incident (Dec. 5, 1934) between Ethiopia and Italian Somaliland, the Italian dictator B. Mussolini ordered an invasion (Oct. 2, 1935). Ignoring calls for arbitration as well as League of Nations sanctions, the Italians advanced slowly against the Ethiopians in the rough terrain. After taking the fortress of Makallé (Nov. 8), they advanced to the capital, Addis Ababa. Troops under Gen. P. Badoglio took the capital (May 5, 1936) and thus ended the war. Italy's disregard for the League of Nations sanctions, and France's and Great Britain's failure to back the sanctions, severely damaged the League's prestige.

Italo-Turkish War (Tripolitan ~) War (1911–12) in which Italy established a Libyan colony on the North African coast. As part of its policy of colonial expansion, Italy sought a North African colony and had won approval of its plans from major European powers. In the wake of the Moroccan Crisis (*q.v.*) of 1911, Italy declared war (Sept. 29, 1911) on the Ottoman Empire and invaded the province of Tripoli. Tripoli and other coastal towns were taken quickly by forces under Gen. Carlo Caneva (1845–1922), but resistance by the Libyans forestalled a complete conquest. The Italian navy carried hostilities to other Ottoman possessions in the Mediterranean, closing the Dardanelles (Apr.–May) and taking Rhodes (May 16) and the Dodecanese Islands

(May). Threat of war in the Balkans forced the Ottomans to negotiate and, by the Treaty of Lausanne (*q.v.*, 1912), the war was ended (Oct. 18) in Italy's favor.

Italo-Yugoslav Treaty Agreement between Italy and Yugoslavia concluded Jan. 27, 1924. By its terms, the city of Fiume (Rijeka), constituted a free city by the Treaty of Rapallo (1920), was incorporated into Italy. Yugoslavia occupied the city in 1945 and Italy ceded it to Yugoslavia in 1947.

Italy (Italian Republic) Country (*pop.* 57,657,000) located in southern Europe on the Mediterranean Sea. Its capital is Rome. Italy's history begins with the Romans and for centuries it was the center of their vast empire. After the fall of the Western Roman Empire (5th cent. AD), the Italian Peninsula suffered many centuries of divisiveness, wars, and foreign domination. It nevertheless gave birth to the great flowering of Western civilization, the Renaissance. Rome, as the seat of the Roman Catholic popes, was also the spiritual center of Europe for many centuries. The movement for unification of Italy (Risorgimento) began early in the 19th cent. and in 1861 the modern state of Italy achieved unification. Italy fell under the sway of Fascism in the 1920s and was defeated by the Allies in WW II. Italy since the war has had numerous governments and the 1960s and 1970s saw the rise of leftist and Communist factions among Italian voters. (For the history of Italy before the 5th cent., *see* Rome.) **For more on important persons and major events listed below, *see* separate entries.** Key events in Italian history include:

AD 476–493 Odoacer ruled Italy; deposed last Western Roman emperor, Romulus Augustus (476); ruled until his assassination; Ravenna the capital.

AD 489 Theodoric the Ostrogoth invaded Italy, slew Odoacer, and ruled until his death in 526.

6TH CENT. Breviary of Alaric issued by Visigothic King Alaric II.

535 Byzantine emperor Justinian I sent forces (led by Belisarius and Narses) to expel the Goths from Italy.

c547 Saint Benedict died; he was founder of the Benedictine order.

552 Byzantines defeated Goths in Italy at Battle of Busta Gallorum; Goth king Totila killed and Byzantines briefly ruled Italy.

554–567 Narses served as Byzantine prefect of Italy.

556–61 Pelagius I became pope; Justinian gave him temporal control over Rome.

568 Invasion of Italy by the Lombards, another Germanic people, who conquered much of northern Italy; Byzantines held Exarchate of Ravenna, Rome, Naples, and some other parts of Italy; Lombards did not take Rome.

568–774 Italy under the Lombards; Lombards allowed bishops temporal powers in localities; meanwhile the split between the Eastern church and Rome grew; the Byzantines renewed attempts to drive the Lombards from Italy.

c590–604 Saint Gregory I served as pope; noted as church reformer who encouraged monasticism.

712–744 Lombard king Lituprand reigned; brought Lombard kingdom to its height.

751 Lombards captured the Byzantine capital of Ravenna.

752–757 Stephen II served as pope; first temporal ruler of the Papal States (from 756).

753 Lombards threatened Rome; seeking to consolidate their hold on Italy, they advanced on Rome; Pope Stephen II appealed to the Frankish ruler Pepin the Short for aid against the Lombards.

754–756 Pepin the Short invaded Italy and defeated the Lombards.

756 Donation of Pepin; Pepin gave the pope lands around Ravenna that he had conquered from the Lombards; the donation became the basis of the Papal States.

773 Pope Adrian I called on Frankish king Charlemagne to defeat the Lombards, then threatening Rome.

774 Charlemagne conquered the Lombards, who had again threatened Rome; Charlemagne became king of the Lombards after Desiderius surrendered at the siege of Pavia.

795–816 Leo III reigned as pope; he crowned Charlemagne as emperor.

800 Pope crowned Charlemagne emperor of the Romans, thereby reconstituting the Western Roman Empire under Carolingian rule; thus formed alliance between European monarchs and popes.

844–875 Louis II reigned as Frankish king of Italy.

872–882 John VIII reigned as pope; paid tribute to Muslims to protect Rome.

9TH CENT. Carolingian Empire divided by Treaties of Verdun and Mersen; two great Frankish kingdoms created, East (German) and West (French); a third part, including Italy, was later further divided.

9TH–10 CENTS. Control of Italy passed to weak rulers; rise of petty states and cities and frequent wars between them.

917 Arab Muslims conquered Sicily and pillaged Italy.

961–962 Otto I, then asserting his rule over the German states, aided Pope John XII against King Berengar II.

962 Otto I crowned emperor by the pope; Holy Roman Empire (eastern part of former Carolingian Empire) then became the successor state to the Western Roman Empire; alliance formed between Otto I and the pope led to years of struggle between emperors and the popes.

c990–1050 Monk G. d'Arezzo, lived; influenced musical notation and probably originated the musical staff.

11TH CENT. Normans conquered southern Italy and Sicily from the Byzantines and Arabs; these lands, later known as the Kingdom of the Two Sicilies, remained under relatively strong rule thereafter and developed independently of the north; northern Italy, ravaged by wars, broke up into petty kingdoms and city-states.

1073 Pope Saint Gregory VII called reform synods in attempt to end church corruption and end lay investiture.

1075–1122 Investiture Controversy, long struggle between reforming popes and the emperors of the Holy Roman Empire; ended by Concordat of Worms.

1081–83 Rome attacked by Holy Roman Emperor IV, who opposed Pope Gregory over the Investiture Controversy.

1084 Rome sacked by Robert Guiscard's troops.

1190 Hohenstaufen rulers of the Holy Roman Empire gained control of southern Italy as successors to the Normans.

12TH CENT. Florence became autonomous commune; marked its rise to importance.

1106 Venice largely destroyed by two successive fires.

1118–19 Gelasius II reigned as pope; opposed Henry V in the Investiture Controversy.

1122 Holy Roman Emperor Henry V forced to accept the compromise Concordat of Worms in Investiture Controversy.

1130–43 Innocent II pope; forced to flee Rome, he returned in 1138.

1130–54 Roger II reigned in the south; consolidated conquered lands, adding Capua, Naples and the Abruzzi; ruled one of the most advanced unified kingdoms of the time; feudal system firmly established there, but not in northern Italy.

1139 Second Lateran Council convened by Pope Innocent II.

1154 Idrisi, Arab scientist at Roger II's court, compiled a medieval geography.

1155 Monk Arnold of Brescia executed for supporting a republican uprising in Rome.

1169 Mount Etna erupted explosively after having been dormant for centuries; some 15,000 persons killed.

1177 Pope Alexander III forced Emperor Frederick I to sign Treaty of Vienna.

1183 Lombard League forced the church and Holy Roman Emperor to recognize its autonomy by the Treaty of Constance.

1185 Sicilian king William II launched unsuccessful invasion of the Byzantine Empire.

1190–94 Tancred ruled as king of Sicily.

1198–1216 Innocent III reigned as pope; brought papal power to its height; asserted supremacy over European kings, including Holy Roman Emperor Otto IV and English king John.

1209 Saint Francis of Assisi founded the Franciscan order.

13TH–14TH CENTS. Struggle between Guelphs (supporters of papal control in Italy) and Ghibellines (supporters of Hohenstaufen Holy Roman Emperors); strife led to breakdown of central authority in north and central Italy, and the rise of local rulers in the cities; coincided with struggle between popes and Hohenstaufen emperors.

1220–84 Italian sculptor N. Pisano, lived; his school at Pisa later influenced Renaissance art.

1227–41 Gregory IX reigned as pope, during which time he excommunicated Holy Roman Emperor Frederick II twice.

1231 Constitutions of Melfi; law code, regarded as important medieval legal document, established efficient central government in Sicily.

1233 Office of the Inquisition organized by Pope Gregory.

1245–1314 G. Pisano, son of sculptor N. Pisano, lived.

1250?–1316? Physician Abano d' Pietro lived; established Padua as center of medical study.

1255?–1319? Founder of the Sienese school of art, Duccio di Buoninsegna, lived.

c1265–74 Saint Thomas Aquinas wrote *Summa Theologica;* his writings later officially adopted by the Roman Catholic church.

1266 Charles of Anjou, brother of France's king Louis IX, conquered territory that later became the Kingdom of the Two Sicilies.

1279 German king Rudolf I, a Habsburg, ended long struggle between popes and Holy Roman Empire over papal sovereignty in Italy; recognized papal sovereignty in Papal States and in south.

1282 Angevin rule overthrown by the Sicilian Vespers and Sicily came under the power of the Spanish House of Aragon.

14TH CENT. Babylonian Captivity (1309–78); papacy removed to Avignon, France; control of the Papal States broke down; French and Spanish warred for control in the south.

14TH–15TH CENTS. Ruling families came to power in northern Italian cities—Medici in Florence, Visconti and Sforza in Milan, Este of Ferrara, Gonzaga of Mantua, Scala of Verona, etc.; their patronage helped foster the Renaissance, which began in Italy.

c1302 G. Cimabue died; his paintings reflected the movement toward a more natural style.

1304–74 F. Petrarch lived; great lyric poet who influenced Renaissance poetry.

1321 Literary masterpiece, *The Divine Comedy* published by Dante.

1347–80 Mystic, Saint Catherine of Siena, lived; noted for helping the needy.

1348 The Black Death (bubonic plague), introduced by Genoese sailors returning from the East, ravaged Italy and spread to the rest of Europe.

1351–53 *Decameron* written by Boccaccio.

1357 Soldier G. Carrillo de Albornoz wrote constitution for Papal States; restored papal authority there.

1360–1429 G. de' Medici founded the Medici family fortune, which later financed the family's extensive art patronage.

1367–70 Pope Urban V returned the papacy to Rome, until forced back to Avignon by unrest.

1369–1424 Mercenary M. Sforza, lived; founder of the Sforza family.

1377–1446 Renaissance architect F. Brunelleschi lived.

1380–1459 Poggio, Renaissance humanist, lived; rediscovered manuscripts of many Roman authors.

c1400–1461 Domenico Veneziano, Renaissance artist, lived; painted *St. Lucy Altarpiece* in the Uffizi Palace.

1400?–1482 L. Della Robbia, Renaissance sculptor, lived.

1401–28 Renaissance painter Massacio lived; his works later influenced Michelangelo and Raphael.

c1406–69 Painter F. Filippo Lippi, lived.

c1407–57 L. Valla, who uncovered the fraud of the Donation of Constantine, lived.

1413 King of Naples, Ladislaus, sacked Rome.

1430–32 Donatello, sculpted the bronze *David,* one of the first free-standing statues done since antiquity.

1431–1506 Painter A. Mantegna lived; noted for frescoes.

1433–99 M. Ficino, philosopher and translator of Greek classics, lived.

1434–1737 Famous Medici family ruled in Florence.

1442 Spanish House of Aragon won complete control of southern Italy (Sicily and kingdom of Naples) after driving out the French.

1444–1514 Renaissance architect D. Bramante lived.

1450–66 Francesco I Sforza ruled in Milan, founding dynasty that ruled there for almost a century.

1454 Peace of Lodi; Francesco Sforza won succession to duchy of Milan; marked beginning of 40-year peace in Italian peninsula.

1454–1512 Navigator A. Vespucci lived.

1463–94 Renaissance philosopher G. Pico della Mirandola lived.

1466 Artist P. della Francesca painted the series *The Story of the True Cross.*

1474–1533 L. Ariosto, author of the epic *Orlando Furiso,* lived.

1475 First secular play in Italian written by classical scholar A. Politian.

1475–1517 Florentine painter F. Bartolommeo lived.

1476–1507 Soldier and political opportunist C. Borgia lived.

1478 Pazzi Conspiracy, abortive attempt to depose L. de Medici from power in Florence.

1480–1519 Noblewoman L. Borgia, lived; renowned for her patronage of the arts, as well as her involvement in family crimes.

1482 Church scholar Saint Bonaventure canonized.

1483–1520 Noted Renaissance artist Raphael lived; painted *School of Athens* and *Disputa.*

1483–1540 F. Guicciardini, lived; wrote most important history of the 16th cent., *Storia d'Italia.*

1490s First outbreak of syphillis epidemic occurred in Italy; epidemic, which ravaged Europe during next century, may have been caused by virulent form of disease brought back from New World by sailors aboard Columbus's ships.

c1492–1546 Artist G. Romano lived; originated mannerism.

1494–98 Savonarola established short-lived republic at Florence.

15TH–18TH CENTS. Popes gradually established their authority over the Papal States and extended domains to include most of central Italy.

1494 Charles VIII of France invaded the peninsula, marking the beginning of the Italian Wars.

1494–1559 Italian Wars fought for control of Italy; Spanish Habsburgs won after years of sporadic warfare.

1503 L. da Vinci painted the *Mona Lisa;* a multifaceted "Renaissance man," da Vinci was also an architect, military engineer, and student of human anatomy.

1503–13 Julius II reigned as pope; a patron of the arts, he comissioned the building of St. Peter's and Michelangelo's frescoes in the Sistine Chapel.

1508–10 League of Cambrai formed by Holy Roman Empire, Spain, France, and the pope to conquer the Republic of Venice.

1508–12 Michelangelo painted the Sistine Chapel; earlier completed the *Pietà.*

1508–80 A. Palladio lived; created the Palladian style in architecture.

1511 Holy League of erstwhile enemies, Spain, Venice, and the pope, founded to drive Louis XII of France out of Italy.

1511–1537 A. de Medici lived; as duke of Florence, he was hated for his tyranny.

1515 *Sacred and Profane Love* painted by Titian; he later painted *Rape of Europa* in 1562.

1517 *The Prince* written by N. Machiavelli.

1521 Pope Leo X excommunicated M. Luther, thereby helping spark the Protestant Reformation.

1525–74 Anatomist B. Eustachio lived; discovered Eustachian tube.

1527 Pope Clement VII refused Henry VIII a divorce from Catherine of Aragon; set stage for break of the English church from Rome.

1528–88 Painter P. Veronese, famous for his use of color, lived.

1529 In the Peace of Cambrai, France renounced all territorial claims in Italy.

1529 Italian admiral A. Doria became virtual dictator of Genoa.

1544–95 Poet T. Tasso, best known for *Jerusalem Delivered,* lived.

1546–54 B. Cellini sculpted *Perseus with the Head of Medusa.*

1547 Tintoretto, leader of the Mannerist school, painted *Last Supper.*

1550?–1618 Composer G. Caccini lived; became member of Florentine music group that composed the earliest operas.

1552–1608 A. Gentili lived; became early writer on international law.

1555–59 Pope Paul IV reigned; organized the Roman Inquisition and established the Jewish ghetto in Rome.

1559 By the Treaty of Le Cateau-Cambrésis, Spain gained control of both Milan and the Kingdom of the Two Sicilies.

1567–1643 Composer Claudio Monteverdi lived; his works were important in the early history of opera.

1568–1639 Dominican monk T. Campanella wrote *The City of the Sun.*

1572–85 Pope Gregory XIII reigned; introduced the modern Gregorian calendar.

1575–1642 Artist G. Reni lived; painted *Aurora and the Hours.*

1585–90 Sixtus V reigned as pope; restored the Papal States and did much to rebuild Rome.

1588 Architect D. Fontana designed the Lateran Palace.

1594 *Fortune Teller* painted by Caravaggio.

1596–1669 Painter P. da Cortona, lived; became master of baroque style.

c1597 *Dafne,* considered the first true opera, written by Jacopo Peri.

1600 Philosopher G. Bruno burned as a heretic.

1608–47 E. Torricelli, inventor of the barometer, lived.

1618–48 Thirty Years' War fought.

1623 *David* sculpted by baroque artist G. Lorenzo Bernini.

1626 Naples leveled by powerful earthquake (July 30); some 70,000 killed; another Naples earthquake killed 93,000 in 1693.

1626–98 Naturalist F. Redi lived; disproved theory of spontaneous generation.

1628–31 War of the Mantuan Succession.

1632 Galileo published his *Dialogue Concerning the Two World Systems* supporting the heliocentric Copernican theory; this and his other work did much to advance science.

1644–1737 Famed violin maker, A. Stradivari, lived.

c1658–1725 Composer A. Scarlatti lived; influenced development of opera.

1668–1744 G. Vico lived; advanced theory of history's cyclical nature.

1669 Worst eruption of Mount Etna hurled 300-pound boulders for miles and flooded surrounding area with molten lava (Mar. 11); 20,000 killed.

c1675–1741 A. Vivaldi, composer of *The Four Seasons,* lived.

1685–1757 G. Scarlatti lived; known for his harpsicord sonatas.

1696–1770 G. Tiepolo lived; noted for his frescos.

1701–14 War of the Spanish Succession.

1706–85 Composer B. Galuppi lived; wrote operas *Il Filosofo di Campagna.*

c1710 B. Cristofori built the first piano.

1720 Kingdom of Sardinia created; formed by Savoy, Piedmont, and island of Sardinia under House of Savoy.

1720–1806 Count C. Gozzi, dramatist, lived; known for dramatic "fairy tales."

1725–98 G. J. Casanova de Seingalt, adventurer and womanizer, lived; wrote *Story of My Life.*

1737–90 Physiologist L. Galvani lived.

1745–1827 Physicist A. Volta lived; invented the voltaic pile, the first electric battery.

MID-18TH CENT. Naples, Sicily, Parma, and Piacenza passed to Spanish Bourbons; Milan, Mantua, Tuscany, and Modena, to Austria.

1764 C. Bonesana, marchese di Beccaria, wrote his essay opposing capital punishment titled *Dei delitti e delle pene.*

1782–1840 Violinist and composer N. Paganini lived.

1785 Conte A. Cagliostro, magician and alchemist, implicated in the Affair of the Diamond Necklace.

1792–1802 French Revolutionary Wars; Italy, scene of much fighting, fell to Napoleon.

1797 By the Treaty of Campo Formia, Napoleon established the Cisalpine Republic (Milan) and the Ligurian Republic (Genoa).

1798 Pope Pius VI taken to France as prisoner on Napoleon's orders.

1798–99 Roman Republic, a short-lived republic established at Rome.

1799 F. Cardinal Ruffo led revolt in Naples against the Napoleonic regime.

1805 Napoleon, crowned emperor in 1804, made himself king of an "Italy" consisting of the Cisalpine Republic, Emilia-Romagna, and Venetia.

1806 Joseph Bonaparte made king of Naples.

1808 Joachim Murat, Napoleon's brother-inlaw, succeeded as king of Naples.

1808–30 Rise of the Carbonari society in Naples to oppose French domination; later became early supporters of liberal nationalist movement.

1809 Napoleon annexed the Papal States to France.

1811 Physicist A. Avogadro developed his law relating to the volume and pressure of different gases.

1815 Congress of Vienna after Napoleon's fall; Papal States restored; Spanish and Austrian rule restored in other parts of Italy.

1815–61 Rise of the nationalist movement (Risorgimento) for unification of Italy.

1816 Kingdom of the Two Sicilies formally created by unification of Sicily and Naples under one crown.

1816–25 Ferdinand I ruled as king of the Two Sicilies; established the Bourbon-Sicily line of rulers.

1821 Revolt against Victor Emmanuel I, king of Sardinia; forced his abdication.

1824 G. Leopardi wrote his poem, *Canzoni.*

1829 G. Rossini composed the opera *William Tell;* also wrote *The Barber of Seville.*

1831 Young Italy movement formed by Italian nationalist G. Mazzini.

1832 Pope Gregory XVI suppressed rebellion by the Carbonari in the Papal States.

1835 G. Donizetti composed *Lucia di Lammermoor.*

1846 Pius IX elected pope; began a series of reforms in the Papal States.

1846–78 Pope Pius IX reigned, the longest in Catholic history; he defined the dogma of the immaculate conception and presided over the First Vatican Council.

1848–49 Revolutions of 1848; abortive revolts in Rome, Venice, Florence, Naples, and Savoy.

1848–49 D. Manin served as president of the Venetian Republic; Venice fell to Austria in 1849.

1849 Sardinian king Charles Albert abdicated after being defeated twice in battle by Austria.

1849–61 Victor Emmanuel II reigned as king of Sardinia, which became the nucleus of the unified Italian state.

1851 G. Verdi composed the opera *Rigoletto;* also composed *La Traviata* (1853).

1852 Count C. Cavour became Sardinian prime minister.

1859–60 King Victor Emmanuel II, with French aid, drove Austrians out of Lombardy in north; he gained Lombard territories but ceded Savoy and Nice to France.

1860 G. Garibaldi and his Expedition of the Thousand conquered the Kingdom of the Two Sicilies (May–Sept.); territory turned over to Victor Emmanuel II in the name of a united Italy.

1861 Kingdom of Italy formally proclaimed (Mar 17).

1861–78 Victor Emmanuel II reigned as first king of a united Italy; Venetia, Rome, and part of Papal States still outside the Italian kingdom in 1861.

1861 First Italian parliament convened in Turin by Victor Emmanuel II.

1863–1938 G. D'Annunzio, writer and soldier, lived.

1866   Austro-Prussian War; Italy joined Prussia and thereby gained control of Venetia, formerly Austrian domain.

1870   Victor Emmanuel II seized Rome, then in pope's control; beginning of Roman Question; Italian unification substantially completed.

1870–1952   Educator M. Montessori lived; originated the Montessori system of children's education.

1878–1900   Humbert I reigned as king of Italy.

1883   C. Collodi wrote the famous story of *Pinocchio.*

1884–1920   A. Modigliani, modernist painter and sculptor, lived.

1887–91   F. Crispi served as premier; served again 1893–96.

1891–1979   Architect P. Nervi, lived; pioneered use of steel reinforced concrete.

1892–1921   G. Giolitte served as premier five times in this period.

1892–1953   Dramatist U. Betti lived; wrote *La Padrona.*

1893–1964   P. Togliatti lived; led the Italian Communist party.

1895–96   Italy prosecuted the Ethiopian War, establishing an East African colony.

1896   G. Puccini composed his opera, *La Bohème;* also wrote *Madama Butterfly.*

1898–1907   A. Toscanini, conductor, directed music at La Scala.

1900–46   Victor Emmanuel III reigned as king of Italy.

1901   Physicist G. Marconi transmitted radio signals across the Atlantic.

1903   Philosopher B. Croce founded the journal *La Critica.*

1908   City of Messina in Sicily demolished by earthquake (Dec. 28); over 160,000 killed.

1911–12   Italo-Turkish War; Italy established a Libyan colony on the North African coast.

1912   Universal male suffrage granted.

1915   Italy entered WW I after gaining territorial concessions in the secret Treaty of London.

1917–19   V. Orlando served as premier.

1919   Italy gained control of former Austrian domains at the end of WW I; was awarded Trieste, southern Tyrol, Istria, and other territories.

1919   Versailles Treaty signed.

1921   Fascist party organized by B. Mussolini.

1921   L. Pirandello wrote his play, *Six Characters in Search of an Author.*

1922   March on Rome conducted by Fascist followers of B. Mussolini; failure of King Victor Emmanuel III to oppose the movement led to Mussolini's rise to power.

1922   B. Mussolini and Fascist party took control of the Italian government (Oct. 29).

1922   Italian government voted B. Mussolini dictatorial powers for one year to restore order (Nov. 25).

1924   Matteotti Crisis resulted in the Aventine Secession by non-Fascist deputies (June 10); Mussolini suspended constitution and further consolidated power.

1924   O. Respighi composed *The Pines of Rome.*

1926   Mussolini instituted the Corporative State in Italy.

1929   Lateran Treaty; agreement between Italy and the papacy settling the Roman Question; created Vatican City as an independent enclave under direct papal control.

1934–37   Italian-American physicist E. Fermi conducted experiments in which he unknowingly split atoms.

1935–36   Italo-Ethiopian War; Italy took control of the independent African state of Ethiopia.

1936   Mussolini formally annexed Ethiopia in defiance of League of Nations efforts to secure Italian withdrawal.

1936   Italy established an alliance with Germany, the Rome-Berlin Axis (July).

1937   Italy, Germany and Japan in the Anti-Comintern Pact (Sept.).

1938   Munich Pact; agreement providing for the German annexation of the Czechoslovakian territory of Sudetenland.

1939   Pact of Steel concluded, cementing Italy's alliance with Germany (May 22); followed by Italian occupation of Albania.

1939–45   WW II; Italy joined the fighting on the side of the Axis Powers (1940); unsuccessfully attacked Greece (from Albania), lost Ethiopia and Italian Somaliland to British (1941), and lost Libya to Allied forces (1942); these military reverses led to Mussolini's overthrow (1943) as Allies invaded Italy.

1943   King Victor Emmanuel ousted Mussolini; Fascist government dissolved (July); Italian resistance fighters joined Allies.

1943 Italy signed armistice (Sept.), and joined Allies against Germany; Germans in Italy thereafter occupied the country and opposed the Allied advance up the Italian peninsula.

1943–44 Field Marshal P. Badoglio headed government after Mussolini's fall; negotiated armistice with the Allies.

1945 German troops in Italy surrendered (Apr.).

1945 Mussolini and his mistress captured by partisans and summarily executed (Apr.).

1945–53 A. De Gasperi served as premier.

1946 Humbert II became last king of Italy; monarchy abolished and republic established shortly thereafter (June 10).

1946–48 Enrico de Nicola in office as first president.

1947 Formal treaty ending the war; Italy lost some territory to Yugoslavia and all control over its colonial domains.

1947 Writer A. Moravia wrote *The Woman of Rome.*

1948 New republican constitution in effect (Jan. 1).

1948 Christian Democrats won control of government, defeating leftist coalition led by Communists; Christian Democrats (DC) dominated postwar Italian politics until 1963.

1948–55 L. Einaudi in office as first president of the new Italian republic; administration marked by rapid industrial expansion.

1949 Italy became founding member of NATO (Apr 4).

1950 Former Italian Somaliland, now a UN mandate, put under Italian administration; territory later merged with British Somaliland as Somalia (1960).

1954 Trieste divided between Italy and Yugoslavia.

1954 A. Fanfani served as premier for first time; also served 1958–59 and 1960–63.

1955 Italy joined UN.

1957 Became a member of newly organized European Economic Community.

1959 S. Quasimodo received Nobel Prize for Literature.

1959 Director F. Fellini completed the movie *La Dolce Vita;* he became known for his surrealistic techniques.

1962 A. Fanfani inaugurated first of several Christian Democratic governments "opening to the left" in alliance with Socialists, as support for Christian Democrats waned; there followed a succession of political crises and new governments in the 1960s and 1970s.

1963–68 A. Moro premier.

1972 Left-wing Christian Democrat A. Fanfani elected life senator.

1972–73 G. Andreotti formed government after political crisis.

1974 Italian voters supported continuation of divorce law (May 13).

1974 Political crisis ended when A. Moro formed minority government (1974–76).

1976–79 Andreotti again in power as premier; governed with support of growing Communist faction; severe austerity measures imposed.

1976 Communist gains in Italy; party member named speaker of the Chamber of Deputies (July 5).

1976 Renato Curcio, leader of terrorist Red Brigade arrested.

1977 Roman Catholicism no longer state religion of Italy by new agreement between government and Vatican.

1978 Former premier A. Moro kidnapped and eventually killed by terrorists (Mar. 16).

1978–85 Alessandro Pertini in office as Italy's first Socialist president.

1979–80 Francesco Cossiga, Christian Democrat, in office as premier; government collapsed after Communists were barred from government posts.

1979 Palace of Senators in Rome badly damaged by terrorist bomb (Apr. 20).

1980 Terrorist bomb exploded at Bologna railway station (Aug. 2), killing 84 persons; right-wing extremists convicted.

1980 Some 2,500 killed by earthquake in southern Italy (Nov. 23); 150,000 homeless.

1980–81 Arnaldo Forlani, Christian Democrat, in office as premier.

1981 Hundreds of government officials named as members of a secret Masonic lodge (P-2) seeking to undermine the parliamentary government; Premier Arnaldo Forlani's coalition government collapsed as a result of the scandal (May 26).

1981–82 Giovanni Spadolini (Republican party) became new premier following the scandal (June 28); ended long rule by Christian Democrats; Spadolini unable cure Italy's worsening economy.

1981 Terrorists kidnapped (Dec. 17) US Gen. James Dozier, a NATO commander; he was freed unharmed (Jan. 28) during raid by anti-terrorist police; 150 terrorists later arrested.

1982 Banco Ambrosiano, major Italian bank, went bankrupt and its president was murdered; P-2 lodge head Licio Gelli, leading financier Carlo De Benedetti, and others charged in the bank's collapse (1989–90).

1982–83 A. Fanfani again in office as premier; promised increased taxes and reduced government spending to cure economy.

1983–87 First Socialist premier, Bettino Craxi, in office; formed coalition government and promised economic reforms.

1983 Sicily, firmly in grip of Mafia, by this time had become international drug and arms trafficking center; some 1,700 members of the Mafia, Camorra, and other criminal groups arrested during massive police sweep in Italy.

1984 Government decreed reduction in automatic wage indexing as means to halt rising inflation (Feb.).

1984 Terrorist bomb blew up train (Dec.), killing 16 and wounding 266; neo-Fascists and prominent Mafia members convicted (released 1989 on legal technicality).

1985–92 Francesco Cossiga in office as president; the government continued to sink deeper into debt despite strong economic growth in the late 1980s, because taxes and other revenue failed to keep pace with public spending; attempts to deal with economic problems often hampered by politics of Italy's coalition governments.

1985 PLO terrorists hijacked Italian cruise ship *Achille Lauro* (Oct.); plane bearing PLO terrorists, freed by Egypt, forced to land in Sicily by US fighter planes; US requested extradition of terrorists, but government claimed right of prosecution and later convicted terrorists directly involved.

1986 Premier Craxi's government collapsed (June); marked end of Italy's longest continuous government since WW II; Craxi returned to form new government (July).

1987–88 Period of instability in which governments were formed and dissolved over proposed measures to deal with the continuing economic crisis.

1987–88 Mass trials of Mafia suspects ended with 468 convictions, as government attempted to crack down on Mafia.

1988 Christian Democrat Senator Roberto Rufilli assassinated by Red Brigade terrorists (Apr.); nine terrorists later given life sentences.

1988–89 Christian Democrat Ciriaco De Mita in office as premier (Apr.); won end to secret ballot in Parliament (1988), as remedy for one cause of Italy's political instability.

1989 Forty Mafia suspects convicted in mass trial (Apr.), but 82 were acquitted (including the Sicilian Mafia boss).

1989 Some 16 million workers joined general strike against proposed charges for health care (May).

1989 Ongoing kidnappings in Calabria (in south) sparked protest resignations by 42 mayors of region.

1989 Italy's leading Mafia fighter, Giovanni Falcone, escaped assassination attempt (June); some 2,000 killed by Mafia and other secret crime organizations in 1990, as wave of violence spread.

1989 Andreotti in office as premier for sixth time (July).

1989 Italian Communist Party (PCI, Partito Communista Italiano) voted for transformation from Communist to mass social democratic party (Nov.), as East European governments began renouncing Communism; renamed itself Democratic Party of the Left.

1990 Terrorists involved in 1985 *Achille Lauro* hijacking released from prison.

1990 Government decree restricted immigration for first time (Feb.).

1990 Iraq invaded Kuwait (Aug.); Italy sent ships and planes but no ground troops for Allied effort to drive Iraq out of Kuwait.

1990 Operation Gladio, secret anti-Communist defense organization set up by NATO in 1950s, revealed; President Cossiga came under attack as former official connected with organization; Gladio officially terminated (Nov.).

1991 Government anti-Mafia group estimated over 50 percent of local politicians in Naples were targets of criminal investigations; nationwide average was 15 percent.

1991 Public outcry over release of convicted Mafia members on technicality (Feb., Mar.);

government decree returned many of them to jail.

1991 Civil war broke out in neighboring Yugoslavia; Italy bolstered military forces in border areas.

1991 About 24,000 Albanians flooded into Italy to escape repressive government and crumbling economy.

1991 Voters approved referendum on election reform (June), aimed at curbing Mafia influence in politics.

1991 Imprisoned Red Brigade leader Renato Curcio pardoned by President Cossiga as symbolic gesture marking "end of terrorism" (Aug.).

1991 Government began taking new steps to reduce public spending; reform of state pension system among them.

1992 Autonomy granted (Jan.) to Alto Adige region (on Austrian border).

1992 President Cossiga and Premier Amato resigned (Apr.).

1992 Oscar Scalfaro in office as president; named Giuliano Amato (a Socialist) as premier.

1992 Top Mafia-fighter Giovanni Falcone assassinated by powerful bomb blast in Palermo (May 23); some 7,000 government troops sent to Sicily to enforce anti-Mafia crackdown (July).

Ito, Hirobumi, Prince 1841–1909. Japanese statesman and premier (1886–88, 1892, 1898, 1900–01). He tried to introduce Western ideas learned while on government missions to the US and Europe, and drafted the constitution of Japan in 1889. He was assassinated while serving as resident-general in Korea.

Iturbide, Agustín de 1783–1824. Mexican military leader. He led in the Mexican independence movement and, as Agustín I, ruled as emperor from May, 1822, to March, 1823.

Ituzaingo, Battle of Decisive Argentine-Uruguayan victory over Brazil, fought in what is now northeastern Argentina on Feb. 20, 1827. Both Argentina and Brazil had claimed what is now Uruguay when they became independent from Spain and Portugal respectively. As a result of this battle, Uruguay was founded as an independent buffer state (1828).

Ivan III (~ the Great) 1440–1505. Grand duke of Moscow (1462–1505). He broke the power

of Novgorod, exploited divisions between the Tatars of the Golden Horde (*q.v.*), and captured part of the Ukraine from Lithuania. He laid the groundwork for a strong Russian monarchy.

Ivan IV (~ the Terrible) 1530–84. Grand duke of Moscow (from 1533) and first tsar of Russia (1547–84). Notorious for cruelty and erratic behavior later in his reign, he nevertheless greatly expanded Russian domains and consolidated the power of the monarchy at the expense of the Boyars. He succeeded (1533) his father, Vasily III, as grand duke and ended his regency (1547) by taking the title of tsar. He summoned (1566) the first national assembly, began Russia's expansion to the east by conquering Kazan (1552) and Astrakhan (1556), taking them from the Tatars, and engaged in the long, unsuccessful Livonian War (*q.v.*) of 1557–82. Siberia was also conquered (1581–83). In 1565 he split the empire, taking part of it as his personal domain (the *oprichnina*), and then instituted a reign of terror. He executed and exiled Boyars, led a massacre of the inhabitants of Novgorod (1570), and murdered his own son Ivan (1580).

Ivan V 1666–96. Tsar of Russia (1682–96). Physically and mentally unfit to rule, he was nominal coruler with Peter I under his sister Sophia's regency. He retained his title after Peter's succession (1689) but never actively ruled.

Ivan VI 1740–64. Tsar of Russia (1740–41). A nominal ruler, he was deposed as an infant by Elizabeth, daughter of Peter I, and imprisoned until his assassination more than 20 years later.

Ivan the Great *See* **Ivan III.**

Ivan the Terrible *See* **Ivan IV.**

Ives, Charles 1874–1954. American composer. While working in the insurance business, he composed music for many years without gaining recognition. Finally in 1939, his *Concord Sonata* (written in the 1920s) won him a nationwide reputation. He was awarded a Pulitzer Prize for his *Third Symphony* (1947).

Ivory Coast *See* **Côte d'Ivoire.**

Iwo Jima, Battle of US conquest (Feb.–Mar., 1945) of the principal island of the Volcano Islands, during WW II. Three US Marine divisions assaulted the entrenched Japanese on Feb. 9 after heavy bombardment and killed some 21,000 of them, taking 1,259 prisoners when the fighting ended on Mar. 17. Americans killed totaled 4,189 and there were 15,749 wounded. The raising of the flag on Mount Suribachi on Feb. 23 was considered one of the most memorable incidents of the war in the Pacific.

IWW *See* **Industrial Workers of the World.**

Iyeyasu (Tokugawa, ˜) (Ieyasu) 1542–1616. Japanese soldier and ruler. Iyeyasu aided Hideyoshi's unification of Japan. He subsequently made himself daimyo and shogun, and virtual ruler of Japan. He was the founder of the Tokugawa (*q.v.*) shogunate, which ruled Japan until 1867.

J

Jabir ibn Hayyan, Abu Musa (Geber) c721–c815. Arab alchemist and physician. Numerous writings attributed to him, on the nature of matter, influenced the development of medieval alchemy and chemistry.

Jabneh, Gamaliel of *See* **Gamaliel.**

Jackson, Andrew 1767–1845. Seventh US president (1829–37), successor to J. Q. Adams. A military hero, frontiersman, and populist, he became the symbol of the movement known as Jacksonian Democracy. A Tennessee lawyer, he rose to prominence as a military commander in the War of 1812. He defeated the Creek Indians in the Battle of Horseshoe Bend (Mar., 1814) in Alabama and won (1815) a decisive victory over the British at the Battle of New Orleans (*q.v.*). Later, commanding a military force in the first Seminole War (1817–18), he crossed into Spanish-held Florida and provoked an international incident. He served in the US Senate, first in 1797 to 1798, and then from 1823 to 1825. During the latter term, he was an unsuccessful presidential candidate (1824), but by 1828 he had gained sufficient strength to win election to two terms (1828, 1832). Jackson's administration was marked by the rise of the Kitchen Cabinet (*q.v.*) and the Eaton Affair that helped break it up; opposition to a protective tariff (favoring the Eastern industrialists), which resulted in the nullification doctrine and the resignation (1832) of Vice-President J. Calhoun; the retiring of the public debt (1835); and Jackson's opposition to the Bank of the United States. In this last struggle, Jackson vetoed (1832) a bill rechartering the bank. On retaking office, he ordered transfer (1833) of federal funds from the central bank to designated state banks. This fueled a land speculation boom in the West. Jackson tried to curb it by ordering (1836) the purchase of all public lands in gold and silver. But the resultant drain on the banks, and mistrust of their bank notes already in circulation, finally led to the financial Panic of 1837.

Jackson, Robert Houghwout 1892–1954. American jurist, who served from 1941 to 1954 as associate justice of the US Supreme Court. He also served as US counsel at the Nürnberg Trials (*q.v.*).

Jackson, Stonewall *See* **Jackson, Thomas Jonathan.**

Jackson, Thomas Jonathan (~, Stonewall) 1824–63. Confederate general and noted strategist during the American Civil War. Made a brigadier general (May, 1861) under Gen. J. Johnston; Jackson's steadfastness earned him his nickname at the First Battle of Bull Run (1861). He further distinguished himself in fighting in the Shenandoah Valley (1862) and then served under Gen. R. E. Lee in the Seven Days' Battles, the Second Battle of Bull Run, and Antietam. Made lieutenant general, he fought at Fredericksburg and Chancellorsville (*q.v.*). He was accidentally shot by his own troops at Chancellorsville, and died eight days later.

Jacksonian Democracy Term applied to the political developments accompanying the presidency of A. Jackson (1829–37), including the spoils system (*q.v.*), universal white male suffrage, and party conventions.

Jack the Ripper *fl.* 19th cent. English murderer who killed six or seven women in London between Aug. and Nov., 1888. The murders caused a sensation and, despite an exhaustive investigation, the killer's identity has never been satisfactorily proven.

Jacobins Political club that rose to prominence as a faction during the French Revolution (1789–99). Centered in Paris, the club at its height of power (1793) had hundreds of branch groups throughout France. Under the leadership of M. Robespierre, the group dominated the revolutionary government for a time (1793–94) and was responsible for the Reign of Terror. The club began (1789) as a group of moderate deputies to the National Assembly, though by 1790 bourgeois moderates had swelled their ranks and made the club an important pressure group. Following the overthrow of the king (1792), the club admitted Montagnards (*q.v.*), and began to espouse more democratic, then radical, revolutionary aims. They opposed and ousted (1793) the Girondists (*q.v.*) over the prosecution of the French Revolutionary Wars, set up the revolutionary dictatorship, and oversaw the Reign of Terror. The Jacobins fell from power with Robespierre's overthrow on 9 Thermidor (July 27, 1794) and thereafter the club was suppressed.

Jacobite church *See* **Syrian Orthodox church.**

Jacobites Supporters of the exiled English king James II (and his heirs in the Stuart line) after the Glorious Revolution (*q.v.*) of 1688. Considerable support for James remained after his deposition (1688) and was kept alive (1688–1746) by Roman Catholics and disaffected Tories. Jacobites were especially active in Scotland and two unsuccessful rebellions were organized there (1715, 1745). The first Jacobite rebellion ("the fifteen") broke out when George I succeeded to the English throne. Led by J. Erskine, 6th earl of Mar, the Jacobites hoped to install James's son, James Francis Edward Stuart (the Old Pretender), but they were soundly defeated. The second Jacobite rebellion was led by James's grandson, Charles Edward Stuart (Bonnie Prince Charlie), and was aided by the French, then the enemy of Britain in the War of Austrian Succession (*q.v.*). After early victories, Charles's advance into England stalled. His subsequent retreat turned into a rout of the Jacobites at Culloden Moor (Apr. 16, 1746) and thus ended Jacobite resistance.

Jacquard, Joseph Marie 1752–1834. French weaver and inventor. He invented the Jacquard loom, the first machine to weave in patterns.

Jacquerie Revolt (May–June, 1358) by French peasants during the Hundred Years' War (1337–1453). Peasants in northern France rebelled when French nobles demanded increased taxes despite the fact that the countryside had recently been pillaged by English mercenary soldiers. Led by Guillaume Cale (*d.* 1358) and E. Marcel, the peasants sacked and burned castles. They were defeated less than a month later, however, and thousands were massacred by the vengeful nobles.

Jadwiga (Hedwig) 1371–99. Queen of Poland (1384–99). She inherited Poland (and her sister received Hungary) from her father, Louis I. She married Jagiello, grand duke of Lithuania, uniting the two kingdoms. She is a canonized Catholic saint.

Jaffna, kingdom of Former Tamil kingdom in northern Sri Lanka (Ceylon). It was well established by the 14th cent. and lasted until it was conquered by the Portuguese in the 17th cent. The Tamils, a Dravidian people from India, had settled on the island as early as c200 BC.

Jagatai *d.* 1242. Mongol conqueror and a son of Genghis Khan. He joined in his father's great wars of conquest and, following the death of Genghis Khan, did not oppose the succession of his younger brother, Ogadai, as grand khan. In the division (1227) of the Mongol Empire among the heirs of Genghis Khan, Jagatai gained vast domains corresponding roughly to Turkistan and Afghanistan.

Jagiello (Jagello) (Jagellon) Dynasty that ruled in Bohemia, Hungary, Lithuania, and Poland in the 14th–16th cents. (in Poland from 1386 to 1572). The dynasty was founded by Jagiello, duke of Lithuania, who took the name Ladislas II of Poland and was a major force in European affairs.

jagirdar system Indian bureaucratic system introduced (16th cent.) by the Mughals in which officials received the right to collect revenues from estates in lieu of salaries.

Jahn, Friedrich Ludwig 1778–1852. German teacher and nationalist who founded the Turnverein gymnastic movement, through which he sought to free Germany from Napoleonic rule and instill in young Germans a sense of strength and national identity.

Jainism Indian religion. Arising in the 6th cent. BC as a reaction to the rigidity of the Vedic religion, Jainism was by tradition established by 24 saints, or religious figures, the last being Vardhamana Mahavira. It taught a rigid form of asceticism; a reverence for all living things expressed in ahimsa, or nonviolence; and the performance of good acts as means for escaping the cycle of rebirth and achieving Nirvana. At first quite distinct from Hinduism, Jainism eventually incorporated elements of Hinduism. Today many prominent Indians practice Jainism.

Jajau, Battle of Battle fought (June 12, 1707) at Jajau, India, by Bahadur Shah and his brother Azam Shah, over succession to the Mughal throne in India. Bahadur Shah was victorious, and his brother was killed in battle.

Jalal ad-Din ar-Rumi c1207–1273. Great Persian Sufi (mystical) poet and founder of an order of dervishes. In the West, his disciples were called whirling dervishes.

Jamaica Island republic in the West Indies, noted as a tourist attraction and source of bauxite. The population is 2,513,000 and the capital is Kingston. Jamaica was discovered by C. Columbus in 1494 and controlled by Spain until captured by the British in 1655. Sugar was a major product until the abolition of slavery (1833). Independence was finally gained Aug. 6, 1962. From 1972–80, Prime Minister Michael Manley pursued a policy of instituting a socialist economy, which threw the country into near bankruptcy. The election of Edward Seaga (1980), following a violent election campaign, brought a return to pro-West, capitalistic orientation. Steep price rises and violence arising from increased drug trafficking marked the mid-1980s in Jamaica, and in 1988 Hurricane Gilbert inflicted the worst damage in the island's history. Diplomatic relations with Cuba were established in 1990.

James I (James the Conqueror) 1208–76. King of Aragon (1213–76). James conquered the Balearic Islands (1229–35), drove the Moors from Valencia (1238), and enabled Castile to recapture Murcia from the Moors (1266).

James I 1394–1437. King of Scotland (1406–37), successor to his father, Robert III. By breaking the power of the nobility and the Highland clans, James established strong monarchical rule in Scotland. He was assassinated by a group of nobles.

James I (James VI) 1566–1625. Scottish king of England (1603–25), successor to Elizabeth I and first of the Stuart line in England. James first succeeded (1567) his mother, Mary, Queen of Scots, to the Scottish throne (under a regency) and then succeeded to the English throne. During his reign in England, war with Spain was ended, the Hampton Court Conference (*q.v.*) was called (1604), the Gunpowder Plot (*q.v.*) was exposed (1605), and relations between James and the Parliament deteriorated seriously. This last helped bring on the English Civil Wars some years later during the reign of his son, Charles I. In addition, English colonies at Jamestown and Plymouth were founded in America (1607, 1620) and the King James Bible was commissioned (1604). The throne of England passed to him by virtue of his descent from Margaret Tudor, daughter of Henry VII.

James II 1430–60. King of Scotland (1437–60), successor to his father, James I. He reestablished the strong monarchy created by his father and attacked English outposts (1460).

James II 1633–1702. English king (1685–88), successor to his brother Charles II. His overthrow during the Glorious Revolution (*q.v.*) of 1688 established the supremacy of the Parliament in England. James served under his brother Charles after the restoration (1660) and converted to Catholicism (1668). Shortly after being crowned, he put down a rebellion by the Protestant duke of Monmouth (1685) and instituted the Bloody Assizes (*q.v.*). His autocratic methods and efforts to promote Catholicism, notably his declarations of indulgence (*q.v.*), prepared the way for the Glorious Revolution. But it was the birth (1688) of his son and (Catholic) heir that finally precipitated the revolt. James was succeeded by his daughter Mary and her Protestant husband, William III. His attempt to retake the throne was foiled at the Battle of the Boyne (*q.v.*) in 1690, though Jacobites (*q.v.*) carried on the cause for him and his heirs until 1746.

James III 1451–88. King of Scotland (1460–88), successor to his father, James II. A weak ruler, he was unable to control his nobles, who rebelled. They defeated and killed James at Sauchieburn.

James IV 1473—1513. King of Scotland (1488–1513), successor to his father, James III. He unified Scotland and allied it with France against Henry VIII of England. He and many of his nobles died in the Battle of Flodden (*q.v.*).

James V 1512–42. King of Scotland (1513–42), successor to his father, James IV. Assuming power after 1528, he supported Catholicism in Scotland and allied himself with France against his uncle Henry VIII.

James VI *See* **James I.**

James, Epistle of *See* **James, Saint, "the Lesser."**

James, Henry, Sr. 1811–82. American philosophical and theological writer and the father of novelist H. James, Jr., and philosopher W. James.

James, Henry 1843–1916. American author, who lived most of his adult life in England. His novels reflect the impact of the older, more sophisticated European society, as in *The American, The Ambassadors,* and *The Golden Bowl.*

James, Jesse Woodson 1847–82. American outlaw leader of a legendary gang of train and bank robbers in the 1860s and 1870s. James was murdered by Robert Ford, a gang member, for the reward.

James, Saint, "the Greater" *d* AD c44. One of the apostles, brother of John and son of Zebedee. He and his brother were called "Sons of Thunder" because of their zeal. Traditionally he preached Christianity in Spain, where he is venerated as Saint James of Compostela, whose feast (July 25) has for centuries been one of Europe's greatest festivals. According to tradition, he returned to Judaea, where he was martyred.

James, Saint, "the Lesser" *d.* AD c62. One of the apostles, traditionally identified as the kinsman of Jesus, who became bishop of Jerusalem and is supposed to have been the author of the Epistle of James in the New Testament. According to Josephus, he was stoned to death.

James, William 1842–1910. American philosopher and psychologist, brother of H. James. He published his major work, *The Principles of Psychology,* in 1890. He was an advocate of the theory of pragmatism (*q.v.*) and a member of the Harvard faculty until 1907. His other important works include *The Will to Believe* (1897) and *The Varieties of Religious Experience* (1902).

Jameson, Sir Leander Starr *See* **Jameson Raid.**

Jameson Raid Unsuccessful attempt to overthrow (1895) the Boer government of the Transvaal. Led by Sir Leander Starr Jameson (1853–1957), the controversial raid was part of a broader scheme to bring all of South Africa under British control. The plan was hatched by C. Rhodes and Jameson and counted on starting a general uprising of Uitlanders, non-Boer foreigners, in the Transvaal. To that end Jameson and some 500 armed men invaded the Transvaal (Dec. 29, 1895). They were quickly overpowered by Boer forces at Krugersdorp, however, and surrendered (Jan. 2, 1896).

James the Conqueror *See* **James I.**

Jamestown First North American permanent British settlement. Situated in Virginia on the James River, the former village was founded by the London Company on May 14, 1607. Although repeatedly ravaged by fire, Jamestown was the capital of Virginia until 1699.

Jami 1414–92. Persian poet, considered the last great Persian poet and noted for his writings on Sufi philosophy.

Jammu and Kashmir *See* **Kashmir.**

Janáček, Leoš 1854–1928. Czech composer whose works reflect his intense interest in Czech folk music. His best-known work was his opera *Jenufa.*

Janissaries (Janizaries) An elite corps of the army of the Ottoman Empire, noted for its military successes (15th–16th cents.). Members of the corps were procured by taking the children of Ottoman Christian subjects and training them. By the 18th cent. they had become involved in Ottoman politics. Opposing reform, they revolted (1826), were defeated, and the organization was dissolved.

Janizaries *See* **Janissaries**

Jansen, Cornelius 1585–1638. Dutch bishop and theologian. His four-volume work *Augustinus* (1640) was a major influence in the development of Jansenism.

Jansenism Religious movement (*fl.* 17th–18th cents.) in the Roman Catholic church, centered in France. Characterized by its emphasis on the doctrines of divine grace and predestination and by its opposition to the Jesuits, Jansenism sought a return to the severity of early Christianity. The movement stemmed from the posthumous publication (1642) of *Augustinus,* a controversial work by C. Jansen based on the teachings of Saint Augustine. Papal condemnation of Jansenist doctrines began (1653) with Innocent X, and thereafter defense of the movement became a facet of the larger conflict, known as Gallicanism (*q.v.*), between the pope and French Catholics. Jansenists were finally suppressed (1730) in France, however, when Louis XIV joined the pope in opposing them. Noted

Jansenists were A. Arnauld, B. Pascal, and P. Quesnel.

January Insurrection (Second Polish Revolution) Revolution by Poles (1863–64) against Russian domination of the Congress Kingdom of Poland. Despite the liberalization of Russian rule in Poland by Tsar Alexander II, Polish radicals (mainly students) continued political agitation. When the Polish government sought (Jan., 1863) to draft them into the Russian army, they fled to the countryside and began an armed insurrection. Although badly outnumbered and poorly armed, they gained popular support through their promises of land reform. The revolt thus spread to Lithuania and Belorussia. Receiving only some diplomatic support from European powers and unable to institute their reforms, the rebels soon lost popular support. Russia crushed the insurrection, reinstituted direct administration of Poland, and reintroduced harsh measures that effectively terminated the Congress Kingdom.

Japan Island country located off the east coast of Asia. The population is 123,778,000 and the capital is Tokyo. Throughout much of its early history, Japan was strongly influenced by Chinese culture. By the 15th cent., Japan evolved a system of government by indirect rule, in which the emperors were reduced to figureheads and shoguns (military leaders) or others within the shogunate held real power. That system continued in one form or another well into the 19th cent. With the 19th-cent. Meiji Restoration, the emperor again held real power and the warrior-bureaucrat system was abolished. Under the guidance of the imperial government, Japan modernized rapidly and, by the beginning of the 20th cent., had already become a major industrial and military power. Militarists, promoting war and expansionism in China, gained control of government in the 1930s, however, and Japan joined the Axis Powers in WW II. Japan brought the US into WW II by attacking Pearl Harbor, and despite early successes, suffered enormous losses as its attempt at imperialistic military aggrandizement failed. Left as the last combatant in WW II by the surrender of its Axis allies, Japan was finally forced to an unconditional surrender. In the postwar era, Japan's war-ravaged economy quickly recovered and the nation again rose as an industrial power. Today Japan ranks among the leading industrial nations and as such has played an increasingly important role in world affairs. Key events in Japanese history include:

c28,000 BC Archeological evidence indicates habitation of the Japanese archipelago by Stone Age humans from this time or earlier; lowered sea levels periodically exposed land bridges from Korea and the Chinese mainland (especially 20,000–18,000 years ago).

c10,750–10,250 World's oldest-known pottery produced at this time in western Japan.

c10,000–c300 BC Jōmon period; hunter-gatherer way of life dominant; clay figures and pottery with Jōmon cord markings were produced; deep-sea fishing and shellfish gathering became important food sources; global warming trend, from c10,000 BC, caused sea levels to rise and closed off land bridges.

c3500–c2000 BC Village way of life fairly well established by this time; use of storage jars and grinding stones in evidence; from c2000 BC equipment and techniques for deep-sea fishing significantly refined.

1000 BC Spread of Kamegaoka pottery style; marked significant advance in ceramic arts.

660 BC Legendary Emperor Jimmu supposedly founded Japanese Empire at about this time; all Japanese emperors traditionally believed descended from him.

c300 BC Wet rice cultivation introduced on island of Kyūshū from the mainland; marked major advance in Japanese agriculture.

c300 BC–AD c300 Yayoi period; agricultural society, especially dependent on rice cultivation, emerged; regional political systems developed; bronze (and later iron) weapons, iron-edged tools, and water-control systems appeared.

c300 BC–AD 710 Kofun period, protohistoric to early historic period in Japan, during which regional chieftaincies gave way to more centralized government; Chinese writing adapted; tomb mounds for rulers appeared (AD c250–300), indicating established class divisions between rulers and ruled.

AD c100 Chinese chronicle *Han shu* provided earliest written reference to Japan in account of Chinese Han dynasty; mentioned tribute being paid by 100 small principalities.

AD c250 Chinese Wei dynasty history *Wei zhi* written; described Japanese culture of this time, including existence of small kingdoms and wars between them; noted ceremonial use of bronze bells and imported bronze mirrors.

AD 360 Legendary Empress Jingo supposedly led an army to invade Korea; documented contacts with the mainland stimulated the development of Japanese civilization.

FROM 5TH CENT. Parts of Japan ruled under family-centered confederacy; Chinese cultural influence strong; horse-trappings began to appear in tombs from this time.

c500 Emperor Keitai reigned at about this time; after his reign, emperors won stronger role in selecting successor; traditional imperial regalia (curved jewels, sword, mirror) established.

6TH CENT. Yamato Sun line of rulers established as "emperors" from this time; emerged as dominant line from serveral lineages (uji); subordinate uji chiefs organized into hereditary occupations (be) that provided the imperial court with goods and services.

539?–571 Emperor Kimmei reigned.

c550–710 Asuka period; Asuka area became site of palaces and place where Buddhism was introduced; period marked the beginning of historic period in Japan.

c552 Buddhism brought to Japan from Korea; tomb building declined from this time, as interest shifted to temple building; Korean kingdom of Paekche asked for Japanese military aid against Kingdom of Silla; over next decades Paekche sent craftsmen and artisans to Japan.

572–585 Emperor Bidatsu reigned.

585–587 Emperor Yōmei reigned.

587–592 Emperor Sushun reigned.

587 Mononobe, a powerful family opposed to Buddhism, defeated in battle by forces of Soga family, which supported Buddhism; Soga Prince Shōtoku thereafter actively promoted spread of Buddhism.

593–628 Empress Suiko reigned; probably the first of the imperial line to practice Buddhism.

604 Prince Shōtoku issued set of moral and religious instructions for government officials.

629–641 Emperor Jomei reigned.

642–645 Emperor Kōgyoku reigned.

643 Revolt against powerful Soga family, which sought to have Prince Shōtoku's son named emperor; Shōtoku's son murdered;

incident led to transfer of capital to Naniwa (on Osaka Bay) to break Soga family influence over imperial court (645).

645–654 Emperor Kōtoku reigned.

646 Emperor issued Taika Reforms; sought to increase imperial authority and to reduce influence of powerful families (uji) over the court; set up system of land allotments and taxation to finance imperial government; tomb building limited to only the highest-ranking persons.

655–661 Empress Saimei reigned.

661–672 Emperor Tenji reigned; moved imperial palace to Ōtsu; promulgated Ōmi law code (668); ordered first census; established Council of State.

663 Battle of Hakusukinoe; Japanese fleet destroyed in battle against Silla off Korea's coast; Japanese colony on Korean peninsula lost to Silla and allied Chinese forces; Japan cut contacts with China.

672 Jinshin war of succession, following death of Emperor Tenji; a claimant, Prince Otōmo committed suicide during battle; centuries later he was designated as Emperor Kōbun (reigned 672).

672–686 Emperor Temmu reigned; began construction of new capital city of Fujiwara; ordered compilation of new law code; imposed dress code and other regulations affecting daily life; ordered use of coins for transactions.

684 Eight-rank system imposed by Emperor Temmu in radical restructuring of political hierarchy; two top ranks made up imperial family's closest allies, thus further concentrating power in emperor's hands.

686–697 Empress Jitō reigned; promulgated law code begun under her husband, Emperor Temmu (689).

693–775 Scholar Kibi No Makibi lived; on returning from cultural mission to China (735), he set up training program for government officials.

694 Fujiwara, first permanent palace and capital city, built near Asuka in Yamato plain (southern Honshu).

697–707 Emperor Mommu reigned; Taihō law code issued (701), which further concentrated power in emperor's hands (Ritsuryō system); standardized weights and measures (702); re-established relations with T'ang China, and the seven missions to China (from 701–777) resulted in influx of Chinese culture to Japan.

707–715 Empress Gemmei reigned; construction of private Buddhist temples limited (710), some 483 Buddhist temples having been built between c552 and 710; empress moved capital to Nara (710).

708 First Japanese coins minted; until this time, coins had been imported.

710–794 Nara period; began with transfer of capital to Nara by Empress Gemmei.

712 First history of Japan, *Kojiki,* written.

715–724 Emperor Genshō reigned.

724–749 Emperor Shōmu reigned; ordered building of many magnificent Buddhist temples and statues (Tempyō culture).

737 Smallpox epidemic.

743 Population increases forced government to actively encourage opening of new lands for rice cultivation; granted permanent ownership to those who opened the lands.

746 Gembō, Buddhist priest and court official, died; a member of the 717 mission to China, he had brought back to Japan some 5,000 scrolls on Buddhist teachings.

749–758 Empress Kōken reigned.

c750? *Man'yōshū,* poetic anthology compiled; regarded as masterpiece of Tempyō culture.

752 Giant statue, Great Buddha of Tōaiji, completed.

754 Chinese monk Ganjin arrived in Japan; spread teachings of Ritsu sect.

757 Attempted coup against leader of government, Fujiwara no Nakamaro, failed; Nakamaro later ousted by empress and was replaced by Buddhist priest Dōkyō (764).

764 Revolt by Nakamaro failed.

764–770 Empress Kōken reigned again (under name Shōtoku).

770 Buddhist priest Dōkyō banished; Momokawa, leader of the Fujiwara family branch, secured the banishment and also helped enthrone Emperor Kōnin.

770–781 Emperor Kōnin reigned; sought to curb abuses by monks and government officials, and to cut government spending; implemented program to aid large numbers of peasants forced off their land by excessive debts; despite the reforms, tax revenues and central government power continued to decline.

774–835 Buddhist priest and scholar, Kūkai, lived; evolved "True Word" Buddhist philosophy.

781–806 Emperor Kammu reigned; founded Kyōto.

794–1185 Heian period; capital moved to what became Kyōto (794), in part to escape influence of Buddhists; feudal pattern gradually undermined imperial power (ritsuryō system), as provincial warrior class emerged during period; early on, the Fujiwara family dominated government as regents, furthering a pattern of indirect rule common in Japanese history; next retired emperors, and finally the warrior class prevailed; shōen (private landed estates) became widespread and eroded imperial control of lands; period seen as high point of Japanese aristocratic age; arts and literature (especially poetry) flourished as truly Japanese national culture emerged.

794 Kyōto made imperial residence; remained capital for almost entire period to 1869.

806 Priest Saichō, returned from a mission to China, founded the Tendai Buddhist sect in Japan.

806–809 Emperor Heizei reigned.

c806 Shingon Buddhist sect in Japan founded by Kūkai.

809–823 Emperor Saga reigned.

823–833 Emperor Junna reigned.

833–850 Emperor Nimmyō reigned.

838 Last Japanese mission to China.

842 Jōwa Conspiracy; plot by Fujiwara family member, in which false accusations against rivals in the imperial court were used to bring about the rivals' downfall.

850–858 Emperor Montoku reigned.

858–876 Emperor Seiwa reigned.

866 Ōtemmon conspiracy; this plot also figured in Fujiwara family's rise to power.

876–884 Emperor Yōzei reigned.

884–887 Emperor Kōkō reigned.

887 Akō incident; Fujiwara family member Fujiwara No Mototsune successfully challenged Emperor Uda; gained virtual complete control of imperial government as regent.

887–897 Emperor Uda reigned.

891–930 Post of regent allowed to remain vacant.

897–930 Emperor Daigo reigned; ruled without Fujiwara regent; attempted to control growth of shōen (private estates); reformed tax system, basing it on the land rather than on people.

903–972 Priest Kūya lived; helped popularize Pure Land Buddhism in Japan.

c905 *Kokinshū,* one of the greatest Heian period poetry anthologies, compiled.

930–946 Emperor Suzaku reigned.

942–1017 Genshin lived; wrote *Essentials of Pure Land Rebirth;* his works influenced the development of Pure Land Buddhism in Japan.

946–967 Emperor Murakami reigned.

949–967 Post of regent again remained vacant.

c950 *Tales of Ise (Ise Monogatari),* a Japanese literary classic, was written.

967–969 Emperor Reizei reigned; Fujiwara no Saneyori served as regent (967–970) and regency never again allowed to become vacant.

967–1068 Regency Government; emperors during this period all born to Fujiwara mothers and raised in Fujiwara households; Fujiwara no Michinaga, greatest of the Fujiwaras, dominated this period as grandfather of three emperors; regency considered classical period of Japanese literature and culture.

969 Courtier Minamoto Takaakira exiled; rival Fujiwara family thus gained complete control of imperial court.

969–984 Emperor Enyū reigned.

c978–c1031 Writer Murasaki Shikibu lived; wrote the Japanese classic, *Tale of Genji.*

984–986 Emperor Kazan reigned.

986–1011 Emperor Ichijō reigned.

c990 Courtier Sei Shōnagon wrote the *Pillow Book,* a collection of anecdotes; also developed short essay genre, *Zuihitsu.*

c1000 Rise of Bushidan, large bands of mercenaries.

1011–16 Emperor Sanjō reigned.

1016–36 Emperor Go-Ichijō reigned.

1036–45 Emperor Go-Suzaku reigned.

1045–68 Emperor Go-Reizei reigned.

1068–73 Emperor Go-Sanjō reigned; Fujiwara regency's absolute control over imperial line ended; in subsequent years succession of former emperors dominated imperial government.

1073–87 Emperor Shirakawa reigned.

1087–1107 Emperor Horikawa reigned.

1107–23 Emperor Toba reigned.

1123–42 Emperor Sutoku reigned.

1142–55 Emperor Konoe reigned.

1155–58 Emperor Go-Shirakawa reigned.

1156 Hōgen War; Minamoto and Taira generals fought on both sides of the succession dispute; warrior-courtier Taira no Kiyomori subsequently rose in the court after helping the imperial cause in the Hōgen War.

1158–65 Emperor Nijō reigned.

1160 Heiji disturbance; Taira no Kiyomori defeated attempt to seize control of the government.

1165–68 Emperor Rokujō reigned.

1168–80 Emperor Takakura reigned.

1173–1263 Shinran lived; founded the Buddhist Jōdo Shin sect of Pure Land Buddhism.

1175 Hōnen founded the Buddhist Jōdo sect.

1180–85 Emperor Antoku reigned.

1180–85 Gempei War, civil war that led to downfall of Taira clan and rise of Minamoto clan; warrior government (Bakufu); final defeat of the Taira came at Battle of Dannoura (1185).

1183–98 Emperor Go-Toba reigned.

1185–1333 Kamakura period; military government at Kamakura in eastern Japan ascendant following Minamoto victory in Gempei War; Yoritomo's appointment as shogun (1192) began; power shift to military government from imperial court at Kyōto; warrior class, the new military aristocracy, took control of many private estates (under stewards called jito) and succeeded in improving productivity; popular sects of Buddhism spread; in literature, military epics became popular.

1191 Eisai returned from visit to China at this time; subsequently introduced Zen Buddhism and tea drinking to Japan.

1192 Victorious Minamoto clan leader, Yoritomo, formally given the title of shogun, following his conquest of northern Honshū (all of Japan united for first time); by 14th cent. warrior government established as dominant power in Japan while emperors continued as nominal rulers; system of government continued to 1867.

1199–1333 Hōjō family members served as virtual rulers of Japan (in post of shogunal regent), following Yoritomo's death; Yoritomo's widow Hōjō Masako became first such regent.

1200–53 Dogen, philosopher and teacher, lived; founded Sōtō sect of Zen Buddhism in Japan (1227).

1205 Famous anthology, *New Collection of Ancient and Modern Times (Shin Kokinshū)* begun.

1212 *The Ten Foot Square Hut,* memoirs of an imperial courtier, written.

1221 Jōkyū revolt; Hōjō regency crushed rebellion by retired emperor Go-Toba; installed deputy shoguns (tandai) in Kyōto to maintain direct control over imperial government.

1226 Move toward conciliar organization in shogunal government at Kamakura (under Hōjō leadership).

1232 Shogun issued Goseibai Shikimoku, legal code outlining duties and responsibilities of the Bakufu retainers.

1244–1317 Chinese Zen master Issan Ichinei brought Buddhist texts and practices to Japan; also helped spread Neo-Confucian thought.

1249 Shogunal high court established to help settle lawsuits over land.

c1250? Military epic *Tale of the Heike (Heike Monogatari)* written.

1260 Buddhist priest Nichiren predicted a foreign invasion of Japan if his teachings went unheeded; founded the Nichiren sect.

1274 Mongols, sent by Mongol leader Kublai Khan, briefly invaded Japan; fleet carrying 40,000-man force was destroyed by sudden storm after only one day of fighting.

1281 Mongols again launched invasion of Japan; fleet carrying some 150,000 men arrived off Japanese coast and began fighting; two months later, fleet broken up by typhoon, gaving rise to tradition of kamikaze ("divine wind"); despite victory, power of Hōjō Regency declined afterward, however, because it failed to make good on land grants promised to warriors during the battle.

1307 Noted memoirs of courtier, *Confessions of Lady Nijō,* written.

1320–88 Nijō Yoshimoto, courtier poet, lived.

1331–33 Emperor Go-Daigo defied the Hōjō regency; Ashikaga Takauji, sent to reestablish shogunal authority, instead joined Go-Daigo and allowed him to remain on throne; Hōjō regency then sent Nitta Yoshisada, who likewise joined forces with the emperor; Hōjō

family forced to commit suicide, thus ending 150-year Kamakura regime; Ashikaga family subsequently ruled as shoguns at Kyōto.

1333–36 Kemmu Restoration; Go-Daigo tried to rule directly as emperor; Ashikaga Takauji finally captured Kyōto (1336), deposed and sequestered Go-Daigo, and installed Emperor Kōmyō (reigned 1336–48); Go-Daigo soon escaped, however, and set up rival court in the south.

1333–1578 Ashikaga period; Ashikaga shoguns ruled with their capital at Kyōto, forming a coalition government with powerful provincial military governors (shugo); period marked by frequent wars and the rise of local warlords; Zen Buddhism became powerful religious and cultural force, while popular forms (Pure Land and Nichiren) also became widespread; Nō theater, Kyōgen, and linked verse (renga) developed as arts flourished; rise of local warlords (daimyō) and building of castle towns (from late 15th cent.) brought on commercial prosperity and rise of merchant class; craftsmen formed guilds (za).

1333–84 Nō theater dramatist Kan'ami lived.

1336 Ashikaga Takauji issued legal and political code for his Ashikaga regime, the Kemmu Shikimoku.

1336–1405 Zen Buddhist master Zekkai Chūshin lived.

1336–92 Sporadic fighting in war between Northern Court (Ashikaga-backed) and Southern Court (Emperor Go-Daigo and successors).

1338 Ashikaga Takauji appointed shogun; ruled until 1359.

1359–68 Shogun Ashikaga Yoshiakira in power, second of Ashikaga line.

1363–1443 Zeami lived; became famous Nō theater actor and playwright who established Nō as classical art form.

1369–95 Shogun Ashikaga Yoshimitsu in power; built first Ashikaga palace in Muromachi district north of Kyōto (1378, Palace of Flowers); ended civil war between Northern and Southern courts (1392), reunifying imperial line (emperor and his successors kept economically dependent on shoguns from this time); Yoshimitsu, meanwhile, curbed power of the provincial military governors by requiring them to live in Kyōto; became active patron of the arts; began trade with China.

1390–91 Yoshimitsu quashed revolt by two shugo families.

1395–1423 Ashikaga Yoshimochi in office as shogun, though his father Yoshimitsu continued to wield real power until his death in 1408; ended trade with China; power of shogunate subsequently declined.

1399–1400 Shugo revolt again crushed.

15TH CENT Uesugi family rose to power in eastern Japan.

15TH–17TH CENTS. Kanō family of painters dominated Japanese art; Kanō Masanobu and Kanō Motonobu became masters of ink painting during the early Muromachi period.

1415–99 Rennyo lived; under his leadership Jōdo Buddhist sect became a powerful religious and military force.

1417 Shogun Yoshimochi quelled revolt by the powerful Uesugi family.

1420–1506 Landscape painter Sesshū lived; he was a key figure in secularization of painting (previously dominated by Zen Buddhist painters) during the Muromachi period.

1421–1502 Muromachi renga poet Sōgi lived.

1423–25 Boy shogun Ashikaga Yoshikazu ruled briefly.

1429–1441 Shogun Ashikaga Yoshinori in power; briefly reestablished power of shogunate through his ruthless rule; broke revolt in eastern Japan and strengthened control of that region.

1441 Assassination of Shogun Yoshinori by disgruntled warlord; power of shoguns over provincial warlords effectively broken from this time.

1449–74 Shogun Ashikaga Yoshimasa in office; his weak and vacillating rule provoked unrest and helped set the stage for the Ōnin War.

1467–77 Ōnin War; Kyōto destroyed and Yoshimasa forced to resign; subsequent shoguns, named by Hosokawa family, reduced to mere figureheads; military governors, meanwhile, were also ousted by local military warlords, Sengoku daimyo, who seized control of the countryside during the late 15th cent. and built castle towns; subsequent century of unrest called Warring States period.

1488–1532 Sōchō, noted renga poet, lived.

1524–1602 Last master of linked verse (renga) poetry, Satomura Jōha, lived.

1532–36 Lotus Uprising; Nichiren sect Buddhists took control of Kyōto during this time.

1533–1615 Kaihō Yusho lived; became great Azuchi-Momoyama period painter.

1539–1610 Painter Hasegawa Tōhaku, major figure in Azuchi-Momoyama period, lived.

1542 Portuguese made first contact with Japanese; soon established trade; introduced firearms in Japan.

1547–1565 Shogun Ashikaga Yoshiteru in power in name only.

1547–1618 Unkoku Tōgan, important Azuchi-Momayama period painter, lived.

1549 Saint Francis Xavier began Christian missionary work in Japan.

1558–1637 Hon'ami Kōetsu, a leading Azuchi-Momoyama period artist and calligrapher, lived.

1565 Assassination of Shogun Yoshiteru.

1566 Painter Kanō Eitoku created what became known as the flamboyant Azuchi-Momoyama artistic style, while decorating Zen Buddhist monastery; this and subsequent masterpieces made him the greatest painter of the age.

1568–82 Oda Nobunaga, warrior claiming descent from the Taira clan, captured Kyōto (1568) ostensibly to assure succession of Ashikaga Yoshiaki; Nobunaga took control of the government, however, forcing Shogun Yoshiaki into exile (1573); and broke the power of the Buddhist church.

1568–1600 Azuchi-Momoyama period; heralded transformation of Japanese culture from medieval to early modern as the country was reunified politically for first time in century; called the Age of Grandeur, it saw a flourishing of the arts and culture, accompanied by a rapid influx of European influences and the emergence of more cosmopolitan atmosphere in Japan; European traders and Christian missionaries active at this time.

1569–70 Oda Nobunaga issued orders effectively stripping the shogun of key powers; promoted concept of "commonweal" or public welfare as basis for his own authority.

1571–1653 Poet Matsunaga Teitoku lived; figured in development of the haiku, or 17-syllable poem.

1573 Shogun Yoshiaki mounted attack against Nobunaga; Nobunaga destroyed much of

Kyōto and drove Yoshiaki into exile, effectively ending Muromachi shogunate and bringing medieval period to close; Nobunaga thereafter ruled directly, and from 1573 began series of great military campaigns to reduce those daimyo and armed leagues of commoners who tried to resist him; these campaigns began process of reunification of Japan.

1575–76 First provincewide Sword Hunt conducted in recently conquered Echizen province to disarm the populace; farmers forbidden to take part in military activities, a policy that became a hallmark of the new government.

1576 Nobunaga began building sumptuously decorated castle at Azuchi; this and other extravagant castles became symbol of the Azuchi-Momoyama period.

1580 Jesuits granted judicial control in Nagasaki, the key Portuguese trading city in Japan.

1582 Okuni, a 10-year-old girl, performed a dance that became enshrined as the kabuki dance; eventually this dance became extravagant and erotic art form, popular in the Edo period.

1582 Honnōji incident; Nobunaga, then in control of central Japan (about a third of all provinces), assassinated; Azuchi castle destroyed.

1582–98 Toyotomi Hideyoshi, Nobunaga's successor, in power; fought for right of succession and then continued campaigns to unify Japan; continued Nobunaga's policies and systematized Shokuhō system; instituted extensive land surveys (Tailkō kenchi) and established uniform system of taxation; established samurai class as warrior bureaucrats, required to reside in castle towns; encouraged commerce; promoted Nō drama, using heroic treatments of his military exploits as propaganda vehicle.

1582 Battle of Yamazaki; Hideyoshi defeated and killed Nobunaga's assassin.

1587 Grandiose tea ceremony staged by Hideyoshi, who invited the populace to 10-day event in Kyoto; extravagant ceremony ended after only one day.

1588 Hideyoshi ordered nationwide Sword Hunt to disarm village samurai; later forbade change in status from farmer, samurai, or merchant.

1588 Exiled Yoshiaki finally resigned post as shogun.

1590–91 Rebellions in troubled northern province; Hideyoshi crushed the revolts (1591), completing the work of reunification of Japan; daimyo now subordinated to his rule.

1592, 1596 Hideyoshi twice invaded Korea, planning to conquer both Korea and China; Korea devastated, but Japanese forced to withdraw after Hideyoshi died (1598).

1596 Jesuit missionaries published Christian devotional *Imitation of Christ* in Japan; other Western classics published in Japan about this time.

1597 Hideyoshi ordered first persecution of Christians; so-called Twenty-Six Martyrs crucified.

1598 Hideyoshi died; his subordinates began fighting for right to succeed him.

1600 Battle of Sekigahara; Tokugawa Ieyasu, leader of daimyo from central and eastern Japan, won signal victory in the great struggle for succession and thereby established himself as the ruler of Japan.

1600–1868 Edo (Tokugawa) period; Tokugawa Ieyasu founded the Tokugawa shogunate (1603); capital moved from Kyōto to Edo (modern Tokyo); rigid, authoritarian government of the military aristocracy (samurai) instituted; shoguns maintained strong control of local military lords (daimyo); influence of Confucian social ideas mounted and China's four-class model adopted by government (warrior, farmer, artisan, merchant); period saw policy of National Seclusion and over two centuries of peace (Great Peace, from 1638–1864); power of Buddhist establishment curbed; rapid growth of cities; commercial prosperity and the rise of the merchant class.

1603–05 Tokugawa Ieyasu ruled as shogun, after emperor conferred title of shogun; Ieyasu laid the groundwork for Tokugawa system of government (Bakuhan system), in which emperor was excluded from politics and the local military lords (daimyo) were kept under tight shogunal control; shogun made ultimate owner of all land, giving him right to take or grant lands of any daimyo.

1605–23 Tokugawa Hidetada ruled as shogun, following Ieyasu's retirement; Hidetada continued Ieyasu's policies and continued work of institutionalizing the Bakuhan system of government.

1607 First Confucian adviser to the shogun appointed; system of advisers helped put stamp of Confucian thinking on subsequent shogunal laws.

1612 First anti-Christian regulations issued.

1615 Osaka fortress captured and destroyed by Ieyasu, eliminating the last rival to Tokugawa shoguns, the Toyotomi family.

1615 Laws Governing the Imperial Court and Nobility issued by shogun; emperor forbidden to take part in politics.

1615 Shogun issued Regulations for the Military Houses; regulated affairs of daimyo and required daimyo to reside in Edo (or to leave families as hostages in Edo when the daimyo visited home territories).

1616 Ieyasu died.

1620 Writer (and former Christian) Fucan Fabian published *Deus Destroyed*, a harsh criticism of Christianity; work became cornerstone of subsequent anti-Christian thinking.

1622–85 Confucian scholar Yamaga Sokō lived.

1623–51 Tokugawa Iemitsu ruled as shogun; initiated policy of National Seclusion.

1630 Founding of Shōheikō school by scholar Hayashi Razan; school funded by shogun.

1635 Shogunal authority explicitly extended to local territories of daimyo at this time, though daimyo were expected to govern their own domains.

1635 National Seclusion policy begun; shogun outlawed travel abroad; foreigners excluded from Japan in 1639; policy remained in effect for two centuries.

1637–38 Shimabara Rebellion by Japanese Catholics; pushed shogun, already concerned about political dangers of Christianity, into radical anti-Christian (and anti-foreign) measures.

1639 Tokugawa regime limited diplomatic and commercial relations to China, Korea, and the Netherlands, thus ending long-standing Portuguese trade; sought to secure its control over foreign affairs and commerce.

1640 Members of diplomatic mission from Portuguese Macao, seeking reversal of edict limiting Japan's diplomatic and commercial relations, executed by shogun; all 61 killed in shogun's show of resolve.

1642–93 Popular short-story writer Ihara Saikaku lived.

c1643 Last great master artist of Azuchi-Momoyama period, Tawaraya Sōtatsu, died; noted for his elaborately decorated scrolls of courtly poetry, produced in collaboration with artist Kōetsu.

1644–94 Poet Matsuo Bashō lived; his work established the haiku as a highly refined Japanese poetic art form.

1651–80 Shogun Tokugawa Ietsuna ruled; a boy of 10, he was dominated by senior councilors in government; key devices for shogun's control of daimyo eliminated; Confucian notion of scholar-officials ascendant.

1653–1724 Dramatist M. Chikamatsu lived; called "Shakespeare of Japan."

1657–1725 Arai Hakuseki, noted Confucian scholar, lived; as adviser to the shoguns (1709–16), he became noted proponent of Confucian scholar-official ideal.

1657 Mito school began work on *History of Great Japan.*

1670 *Comprehensive History of Japan,* produced by the Hayashi school.

1680–1709 Shogun Tokugawa Tsunayoshi in power; relied on inner chamber of officials to blunt authority of senior councilors; bankrupted the shogunate by his extravagant spending; issued edicts against killing dogs (thus the "dog shogun").

1694 Hishikawa Moronobu died; noted for his woodblock prints.

1709–13 Tokugawa Ienobu ruled as shogun.

1713–16 Tokugawa Ietsugu in power as shogun.

1716–45 Shogun Tokugawa Yoshimune ruled; chosen shogun (1716) after main Tokugawa line failed; instituted Kyōhō reforms to revamp the bureaucracy and government finances; first of three such attempts by shoguns.

1720 Ban on European books ended, subsequent years marked by increasing contact with Europeans.

1721 National census put Japan's population at about 30 million.

1721 Merchant guilds and merchant monopolies legalized; great merchant houses, such as Kōnoike, Sumitomo, and Mitsui, ascendant as merchant class became increasingly important in Japanese economy.

1730–1801   Scholar Motoori Norinaga lived; became a leading proponent of school of National Learning, in which Japanese studies were emphasized over Chinese studies.

1745–60   Tokugawa Ieshige, a weak ruler, in power as shogun.

1760–1849   Woodblock artist Katsushika Hokusai lived.

1760–87   Shogun Tokugawa Ieharu ruled; a weak ruler, he was manipulated by his corrupt favorite, Tanuma Okitsugu; silver coins minted in effort to expand currency; shogun attempted to use his power to engage directly in private commercial sphere; policies reversed on Ieharu's death.

1767–1848   Writer Takizawa Bakin lived; wrote historical novels.

1782–87   Crops failed, causing Temmei famine; meanwhile financial troubles plagued the shogunate and most daimyo.

1782–1863   Scholar Aizawa Seishisai lived; postulated Japan as superior "land of the gods."

1787–1837   Tokugawa Ienari in power as shogun; Kansei reforms carried out by his advisers early in his regime, but proved unsuccessful; later, after Ienari gained control (1817), he embarked on policy of free spending.

1787   Three-day riot in Edo, as economic and social problems sparked unrest.

1797–1858   Andō Hiroshige lived; became famous Edo period woodblock artist.

c1800   Population of Edo, largest of Japan's "castle towns," put at nearly one million; reflected rapid rise of cities during Edo period.

1834–1901   Author Y. Fukuzawa lived; became leading proponent of Westernization.

1836   Serious farmers' revolt broke out as domestic unrest increased.

1837   Unsuccessful rebellion in Osaka led by a petty official.

1837–53   Tokugawa Ieyoshi ruled as shogun.

1838–1922   Prince A. Yamagata lived; helped modernize the army and establish Japan as a world power.

1841–43   Tempo Reforms introduced by Tokugawa shogunate in unsuccessful attempt to reform economy and to restore shogunal political power; abolished guilds and merchant monopolies; attempted to order transfer of daimyo lands; most reforms rescinded.

1847–1934   Admiral H. Togo lived; became famous as commander who defeated the Russians at Port Arthur.

1853–58   Tokugawa Iesada ruled as shogun.

1853–54   US commodore M. Perry arrived in Japan; forced Japan to officially end isolation and sign Treaty of Kanagawa (Mar. 3); exposed failing power of Tokugawa shogunate (based on decentralized balance of power between shoguns and daimyo) and helped seal its fate.

1858–66   Tokugawa Iemochi ruled as shogun.

1858   Harris Treaty signed, opening five ports to US trade (July 29); commercial treaties with other foreign powers followed quickly, further demonstrating shogun's lack of power.

1859–1954   Statesman Y. Ozaki lived; a leading liberal, he eventually served in every Diet from 1890–1952.

1860   Shogunate's strongman assassinated.

1867   Imperial courtiers allied with certain daimyo forced resignation of last shogun (Tokugawa Hitotsubashi, ruled 1867), who stepped aside for new coalition government.

1868   Courtiers and daimyo captured the boy emperor (Jan.) and formally "restored" him to power; thus began the direct rule of the boy emperor Meiji, or Mutsuhito (reigned 1868–1912); armed resistance to restoration began in late Jan., Edo was captured without loss of life (Apr., Edo then renamed Tokyo), and final pacification of north followed in June, 1869).

1868–1912   Meiji Restoration; power of emperor restored after centuries of rule by shoguns; period of modernization, and Westernization in Japan, during which time Japan rapidly developed its industry and became a world power.

1868   Charter Oath issued by imperial government; made sweeping commitment to reform, including establishment of deliberative assemblies, an end to past evil customs (notably feudal systems) and class divisions, and the seeking of knowledge of the outside world.

1868   Constitution of 1868 sought to implement basic promises in the Charter Oath.

AFTER 1868   Rise of the zaibatsu, family-controlled cartels.

1869   Daimyo returned their domains to the imperial government, accepted imperial control, and were in turn named governors to their former territories.

1870s Government sponsored construction of railways and steamship lines, along with construction of pilot factories.

1871 Former daimyo formally dismissed by emperor; their domains were reorganized into prefectures, thus ending last vestige of daimyo system.

1871–73 Iwakura Mission; court officials traveled to various parts of the world seeking knowledge, as promised in the Charter Oath.

1870–71 Laws regulating commoners revoked.

1872 Class equality declared, effectively ending old class system.

1872 Education Order issued; aimed at achieving universal literacy.

1872 Military conscription law enacted to build modern army.

1872 National population put at 33.1 million.

1873 Modern property tax system established; Western calendar replaced Japanese calendar.

1874 Samurai revolt sparked by government decision against military expedition to Korea.

1876 Samurai warrior class abolished by imperial decree after system of universal military service was established.

1876 Samurai revolts against government's modernization program.

1877 Satsuma Rebellion (Jan.–Sept.); noted leader Saigō Takamori led unsuccessful revolt by samurai warriors against modernization program.

c1880 Runaway inflation threatened to wreck the economy.

1881 Military police organized to keep watch on political activity.

1881 First national political party, Jiyūtō, organized.

1882 Bank of Japan founded; this and other aspects of modern financial infrastructure established by Matsukata Masayoshi, finance minister.

1884–1943 Admiral I. Yamamoto lived; led attack on Pearl Harbor (1941).

c1885 Incidents of unrest in rural areas caused by political activity.

1885 Grand Council of State replaced by cabinet system in the imperial government.

1888–1960 Christian evangelist T. Kagawa lived; noted figure in labor and social welfare movements in 1920s and 1930s.

1888 Prince Ito Hirobumi in office as first prime minister; succeeded by Kuroda Kiyotaka (1888–89).

1889 Constitution of 1889; emperor accepted the constitution, drafted by Prince Ito Hirobumi; document established limited constitutional monarchy with bicameral legislature (Diet); power resided in executive, with emperor retaining full sovereignty; ownership of private property and other basic rights recognized.

1892 Marquis S. Okuma founded Waseda University.

1894 S. Kitasato, physician and bacteriologist, isolated the bacillus causing bubonic plague.

1894 Aoki-Kimberley treaty signed with Britain; ended British rights to extraterritoriality and most-favored nation status; preferential trading rights of other nations also ended by treaties concluded soon after 1894.

1894–95 Sino-Japanese War fought over control of Korea; Japan emerged victorious and gained substantial Chinese concessions, including treaty-power rights and control of Taiwan; marked beginning of Japanese imperialism.

1895 Greek-born Lafcadio Hearn became Japanese citizen; noted for books on Japanese culture.

1898 Family system formally adopted for Japanese way of life; samurai family taken as model for the people, and the nation as a whole was seen as a "family state"; meanwhile, reverence for the emperor by the populace reached new extremes.

1899 Rights of extraterritoriality in Japan abandoned by major powers.

1900 Friends of Constitutional Government party formed by Ito.

1900 Boxer Rebellion in China; Japanese troops joined allied expedition to rescue diplomats trapped by Boxers in Beijing.

1901–05 Prime Minister Katsura Tarō in office; elder statesmen (genrō) system came into being as Meiji leaders withdrew from top political posts; retained significant power as advisers to government leaders, however.

1904–05 Russo-Japanese War fought; war sparked by threat of Russian expansion into Korea; victorious Japan emerged as a world power; marked first defeat of European by an

Asian power; war also spurred rapid development of Japan's heavy industry.

1905 Treaty of Portsmouth ended the Russo-Japanese War (Sept. 5); Japan maintained foothold in Manchuria.

1906–08 Prince K. Saionji served first term as prime minister; served second term from 1911–12.

1907 "Gentlemen's Agreement" with US by which Japan restricted emigration of laborers.

1908 Root-Takahira Agreement between US and Japan concluded; this, along with similar agreements with France and Russia, helped establish Japanese sphere of influence in northeast Asia.

1909 Prince Ito, recently retired as Japanese resident-general of Korea, assassinated by Korean patriot.

1910 Japan annexed Korea (Aug.).

1911–40 Rapid growth during this period increased Japan's GNP threefold.

1912–13 Political crisis over continuing interference of genrō in political matters; influence of emerging political parties and popular movements began to be felt.

1912–26 Emperor Taisho reigned.

1913 T. Kato organized and headed the conservative Kenseikai party.

1914–18 WW I; Japan, which joined Allies, occupied Tsingtao and the German-held Marshall, Caroline, and Mariana islands; war stimulated an economic boom in Japan; Japan became a major participant in Versailles Peace Conference.

1915 Twenty-one Demands presented to China; sought virtual control of China; aroused widespread resentment among Chinese nationalists over imperial Japan's interference in China.

1918–21 Hara Takashi named prime minister; he organized first cabinet with officials drawn from political parties; previously genrō had forced appointment of only nonparty members.

1918 Rice riots; anger over rapidly rising rice prices sparked unrest in both the countryside and the cities.

1918 Japanese forced Chinese to agree to allow stationing of Japanese troops in China; Japanese established ties with local warlords in China.

1918–22 Japanese forces played major role in Allied military expedition against revolutionary Red Army in Siberia during Russian Civil War.

1919 Japan became member of the League of Nations.

1920s Rise of radical political movements, including Communists, anarchists, and syndicalists.

1920 Severe recession, following end of wartime boom in Japan.

1921 Prime Minister Hara assassinated; genrō reverted to system of filling cabinets with nonparty appointments.

1921 Four-Power Treaty signed.

1921 Japan Federation of Labor organized.

1922 Nine-Power Treaty signed.

1922 Communist Party of Japan founded.

1923 Tokyo destroyed by massive earthquake and resulting firestorm; over 100,000 killed.

1924–26 Prime Minister Kato Takaaki in office; party members again filled cabinet posts; period of so-called "normal" constitutional government began (1924–32).

1925 Price of raw silk, a key product in Japanese economy, began to decline; drop brought on by increasing use of US-made artificial fabric and by excess supplies of raw silk on market.

1925 Universal manhood suffrage instituted.

1925–70 Author Mishima Yukio lived; wrote novel, *The Sea of Fertility.*

1926–89 Emperor Hirohito reigned.

1927 Minseito political party formed from Kenseito party.

1927 Financial panic brought on by failure of minor Tokyo bank.

1927–29 Baron G. Tanaka served as prime minister.

1928 Communists and other subversives arrested in March 15 incident; in subsequent years radical leftist groups effectively suppressed.

1929–30 Japan hard hit by Great Depression but growth resumed sooner than in other nations; economic problems encouraged militarist movement demanding colonial expansionism.

1930s Strong growth of economy (5.7% per year, 1931–37); growth supported rise of zaibatsu (industrial combines) in heavy industry during the 1930s; pace of population shift to cities increased.

1931 Japan overran Manchuria following the Mukden Incident, deliberately provoked by its army there (Sept. 18); soon after, created puppet state of Manchukuo.

1931–33 Araki Sadao served as war minister; led ultranationalist faction and urged worldwide domination.

1932 Prime Minister T. Inukai assassinated; end of government by party members and rise of militarists in the Japanese government.

1933 Japan withdrew from League of Nations after a commission criticized its Manchurian takeover.

1936 Anti-Comintern Pact signed; Japan allied with Germany through agreement to oppose the Communist International.

1936 Militarists staged unsuccessful attempted coup (Feb.) by seizing downtown Tokyo for three days; military subsequently given increased role in government.

1937–45 Second Sino-Japanese War, which merged with larger conflict of WW II; Japanese armies overran much of China.

1937–39 Prince F. Konoye served as prime minister; helped form 1940 Axis alliance.

1938 National Mobilization bill passed; gave government control over industry and finance; created Japanese war machine.

1939 World War II began in Europe.

1940 Political parties dissolved, following period of increasing police repression.

1940 Tripartite Pact; Japan joined the Rome-Berlin Axis (Sept.).

1940 "Greater East Asia Co-Prosperity Sphere" proclaimed; Japanese troops dispatched to occupy French Indochina.

1941 Neutrality pact signed with Soviets (Sept.).

1941 Japanese troops occupied southern Indochina (July); US froze Japanese assets in the US and imposed oil embargo.

1941 Imperial war conference (Sept. 6); Japanese officials decided on war with US if negotiations on sanctions failed; by Oct., Japanese became convinced negotiations would be fruitless and began secretly preparing for war.

1941–44 Gen. H. Tojo in office as prime minister (and war minister) from Oct.; militarists thus gained complete control of the government, with Tojo overseeing the war effort.

1941–45 Japan a major participant in WW II; engaged US and other Allied forces in Pacific theater, beginning with Pearl Harbor attack (Dec. 7); after initial gains in Pacific, China, and Southeast Asia, the Japanese were slowly driven back, sustaining heavy losses of men and materiel in what became a fanatical stand against overwhelming odds; the last Axis combatant remaining in the war, Japan was forced to accept unconditional surrender in 1945.

1942 First bombing raid against Tokyo by US planes (Apr. 18).

1944 Bombing of Japanese mainland by US B-29s; daylight bombing of Tokyo begun later in year as US air attacks intensified.

1944 Tojo forced to resign following losses in war (notably defeat in Marianas).

1945 Government ordered into war-related service everyone over age six, as Allied invasion of Japanese mainland appeared imminent (Mar.).

1945 Germany surrendered, formally ending war in European theater (May 7).

1945 Allied forces completed capture of Okinawa (June), south of the Japanese mainland.

1945 Japan, now facing certain defeat, rejected Allied surrender ultimatum (July).

1945 US dropped atomic bombs on Hiroshima (Aug. 6) and Nagasaki (Aug. 9); Japan surrendered to Allies.

1945 Japan surrendered (Aug. 14); agreed to US military occupation and relinquished control over outer islands.

1945–52 American occupation; forces under Gen. D. MacArthur in complete control; instituted a demilitarization and democratization process; economy recovered slowly.

1945–46 Kijurō Shidehira in office as prime minister.

1946 Emperor publicly announced centuries-old tradition concerning emperor's divinity was a "false conception" (Jan.); urged Japanese people to forge new state based on "democracy, peace, and rationalism."

1946 Emperor Hirohito acceded to a new constitution and the role of constitutional monarch (May).

1946–47 Shigeru Yoshida in office as prime minister.

1947 General strike by newly legalized labor unions blocked by US occupation authority (Feb.); strikes by public employees later banned.

1947 Democratic constitution became effective (May); formally ended long-standing traditional belief in emperor's divinity.

1947–48 Tetsu Katayana in office a prime minister.

1948 War crimes trials of militarists concluded; Tojo executed by hanging.

1948–54 Shigeru Yoshida back in office as prime minister.

1949 Japanese women reported adopting Western dress.

1949 H. Yukawa awarded Nobel Prize in Physics.

1950–53 Korean War; economic boom resulted from US purchases of war materiel in Japan; Japan subsequently enjoyed economic growth rate of about 9 percent throughout the 1950s.

1951 Peace treaty concluded at San Francisco between Japan and most wartime enemies, including the US (Sept.).

1951 Security treaty with the US (renewed 1960, 1970); US to defend Japan against attack; allowed US troops to be stationed there.

1951 Tokara Archipelago restored to Japan (Dec.).

1952 Japan regained full sovereignty (Apr 28).

1953 Amami Islands restored to Japan (Dec.).

1954–56 Ichirō Hatoyama served as prime minister.

1955 Liberal Democratic party formed from coalition of conservative groups; party remained in power continuously into the early 1990s.

1956 Japan became a member of the UN.

1956–57 Tanzan Ishibashi in office as prime minister.

1957–60 Nobusuke Kishi served as prime minister.

1960 Widespread protest against US-Japanese security treaty (ratified June) forced Kishi to resign.

1960–64 Hayato Ikeda served as prime minister; resigned in 1964.

1963 Some 100,000 demonstrators protested visit by US nuclear sub (Sept.).

1964–72 Prime Minister Eisaku Sato in office; served longest term in history of Japanese prime ministers.

1964 New underwater communications cable in service between US and Japan (June).

1964 Japan hosted the Olympics (Oct.).

1965–70 Continued economic growth now topped 13% per year during this period.

1968 Bonin Islands restored to Japan by the US (June).

1970s Japan became world's largest manufacturer of televisions, radios, and ships; second-leading car manufacturer (first from 1981).

1970 Novelist Yukio Mishima committed suicide (Nov.); his works had celebrated Japan's past militant, imperial glory.

1972 US restored Okinawa to Japan (May 15).

1972 Agreement signed in China formally ended state of war between Japan and China (begun Sept. 25, 1937); diplomatic relations with China resumed, those with Taiwan cut.

1972 Population hit 107.5 million, making Japan the world's seventh-largest country by population.

1973 Oil embargo threatened to strangle Japanese manufacturing economy; Japan, which imported virtually all its oil, eventually forced to reorient its foreign policy and to develop strategy for future growth of manufacturing sector.

1974 Liberal Democrat Kakuei Tanaka resigned as prime minister (in office 1972–74).

1974 Statesman E. Sato received Nobel Peace Prize.

1974–76 Takeo Miki served as prime minister.

1976 Tanaka jailed for accepting money in Lockheed scandal; Liberal Democratic party narrowly retained control of government; lost majority in lower house of Diet.

1976–78 Prime Minister Takeo Fukuda in office; Japan entered period of economic prosperity; began negotiations with US and other countries to reduce her trade surplus.

1978 New trade agreement signed with US (Jan.).

1978–80 Masayoshi Ohira in office as prime minister; economic prosperity continued; proposed tax increase and other government legislation stalled by increasing opposition and lack of majority in the lower house.

1978 Peace and friendship treaty signed with China.

1980–82 Zenko Suzuki in office as prime minister, successor to Ohira, who died in office (June 12); Suzuki resigned over economic ills and factionalism within the Liberal Democratic Party (LDP).

1982–87 Prime Minister Yasuhiro Nakasone in office; increased spending on defense, urged greater participation in world affairs, and sought close relations with US.

1982 US demanded easing of Japan's restrictions on foreign imports and limits on Japan's auto exports to US; Japan meanwhile enjoyed continuing economic growth (averaging over 4% during all of 1980s) and ongoing trade surplus.

1983 Former Prime Minister Kakuei Tanaka convicted of taking bribes in Lockheed scandal (1976); sentenced to four-year prison term and payment of fine; his leadership of Tanaka faction of LDP remained secure, however.

1983 Nakasone survived election challenge, despite severe defeat by his party; formed coalition government; Nakasone proposed policy of "Three Reforms" (reform of administrations of state-run enterprises, reform of government spending to balance the budget, and liberal educational reforms).

1984 Government introduced strict austerity budget.

1986 LDP won majority of seats in lower house of Diet following elections; voter support for LDP highest since 1960s.

1986 Japanese officials in Beijing to discuss reduction of Japan's hefty trade surplus with China.

1986 Japan recorded highest-ever trade surplus; government eased domestic austerity program; increased spending on defense from 1% of gross national product.

1986–90 Government introduced measures to stimulate imports to help reduce trade imbalance; Japan's hefty trade surplus continued throughout the period, however.

1987 National railway system privatized (Apr.).

1987–89 Noburu Takeshita in office as prime minister; promised continuation of Nakasone's policies, liberalization of financial sector, reduction of trade surplus; his government was soon brought down by the Recruit scandal.

1988 LDP proposal for tax reforms, including 3% general consumption tax, met stiff opposition; tax reforms tabled as Recruit scandal unfolded.

1988 Recruit scandal began (June); Prime Minister Takeshita, former Prime Minister Nakasone, and other LDP leaders including Shintaro Abe and Kiichi Miyazawa indirectly involved in questionable trading of shares of the Recruit Cosmos Company; charges later included bribery and other abuses.

1988 Government announced it would make massive loans to China in the period 1990–95.

1988 Plan approved for special investigative committee to look into Recruit scandal (Nov.); three ministers in Takeshita government and Democratic Socialist party head all forced to resign over allegations in scandal (Dec., 1988–Feb., 1989).

1988 Tax reform, most important in 40 years, passed by legislature (Dec.).

1989 Emperor Hirohito died (Jan.), ending Showa era (1926–89).

1989– Emperor Akihito, Hirohito's son, reigned; his era entitled "achievement of universal peace" (Heisei); official coronation ceremony held Nov. 1990.

1989 Takeshita resigned (Apr.); Recruit company reportedly funneled over 150 million yen to him.

1989 Eighteen indicted in Recruit scandal, following investigation by special committee (May); 5 charged with accepting bribes, 13 with offering them.

1989 Former Prime Minister Nakasone admitted profiting from sale of Recruit shares; resigned all LDP posts, but kept seat in the Diet.

1989 Sosuke Uno, the LDP foreign affairs minister, in office as prime minister (June); formed new government to replace Takeshita's scandal-ridden ministry, but included key Takeshita aide in high post; sought tighter controls on political funding.

1989 Sex scandal rocked Uno administration (June); allegations of extramarital affairs appeared to confirm public suspicion about rampant corruption in male-dominated political arena; LDP suffered serious setback in July parliamentary elections, losing upper house majority for first time in party history.

1989 Diet elected two candidates for prime minister for first time in over 40 years (Aug.); upper house chose Takako Doi, a woman and leader of the Japan Socialist party; lower house chose LDP candidate and former education minister Toshiki Kaifu; following constitutional guidelines, lower house vote was adopted.

1989– Toshiki Kaifu in office as prime minister (from Aug.), ending immediate crisis in national government; promised changes in unpopular consumption tax, and electoral and fund-raising reforms; appointed two women to cabinet.

1989 Structural Impediments Initiative (SII), bilateral talks between US and Japan, began (Sept.); sought to remove barriers to marketing of imported goods in Japan and thereby reduce Japan's trade surplus.

1990 General election held (Feb.); LDP scored surprising gains; Kaifu formed new cabinet, excluding any LDP member tainted by Recruit scandal; called for swift conclusion of negotiations with US over reducing Japan's huge trade surplus.

1990 Prime Minister Kaifu formally apologized for Japan's past colonial aggression in Korea (May).

1990 Government agreed to contribute $4 billion to US–led effort against Iraq's invasion of Kuwait (Sept.); LDP withdrew proposed legislation to allow sending of 2,000 noncombatants to Persian Gulf.

1990 Five-day riot broke out in Osaka (Oct.), following arrest of police officer on corruption charges.

1990 Stock market crash (Oct.); Tokyo Nikkei Index dropped to low of 20221.86; total decline for year to date (from 1989 year-end all-time high) amounted to 48 percent; drop in market blamed on high interest rates and fears of banking crisis.

1990 First conviction in Recruit scandal (Oct.); former Nippon Telegraph and Telephone Corp. chairman sentenced to two years in prison.

1990 LDP delegate to lower house, Toshiyuki Inamura, resigned from party after being implicated in new stock manipulation scandal; convicted and sentenced for tax evasion (Nov. 1991).

1990 Government, responding to reduced Soviet threat, announced defense spending cutback (Dec.); Japan to pay greater share of cost for maintaining US troops in Japan.

1990 Government dropped tariffs on over 1,000 imported goods to stimulate imports; trade surplus increased sharply, however, reversing three-year decline.

1990 Stock market closed year down 39 percent from 1989 all-time high, having recovered to 23,848.71 from October crash low of 20221.86.

1991 US criticized Japanese *keiretsu* (groups of corporations) as impediment to marketing of imported goods in Japan (Jan.).

1991 Government increased contribution to Gulf War effort to $9 billion, in response to US pressure (Jan.).

1991 Prime Minister Kaifu's proposed election reforms rejected by LDP, his own party (June); Kaifu resigned pending election of new prime minister.

1991 Scandal broke over irregularities at major Japanese financial institutions (Oct.); Finance Minister Ryaturo Hashimoto forced to resign.

1991– Kiichi Miyazawa, a former LDP finance minister who had resigned during the Recruit scandal, in office as prime minister (Nov.).

1991 Proposed law to allow Japanese troops to be used in UN peace-keeping actions tabled in upper house (Dec.), despite passage by lower house.

1991 Final draft of Uruguay round of GATT (General Agreement on Tariffs and Trade) issued (Dec.); Japan, refusing to end rice import limitations, opposed the proposed agreement.

1991 Kyowa affair (Dec.); Fumio Abe, an LDP party official, resigned after being accused of having been bribed through Kyowa steel company campaign donations and is arrested (Jan. 1992); hearings on scandal to be held by Diet.

1991 Japan's long-sustained high economic growth began to slow during the year, in response to high interest rates and other factors.

1991–92 Japan's surplus in trade with US increased; led to increased tensions between the two governments and greater consumer resistance to Japanese products in US market.

1992 US president G. Bush in Japan for trade talks (Jan.); Japanese agreed to only minor trade concessions.

1992   Prime Minister Miyazawa formally apologized (Jan.) for abuse of Korean women and girls during Japan's WW II occupation of Korea; army had forced the women to serve as prostitutes for its soldiers.

1992   New scandal broke over billions in donations allegedly made for political favors (Feb.); police reported investigating some 280 politicians in case involving trucking company, Sagawa Kyubin; Shin Kanemaru, key figure in LDP, resigned after admitting he received improper $4 million contribution from firm (Aug.).

1992   Government authorized $83 billion in public spending to halt economic downturn resulting from falling prices on stock and real estate markets; Tokyo stock market had hit 6½-year low.

Jaques-Dalcroze, Émile 1865–1905.   Swiss composer. He developed eurhythmics, the expression of musical rhythms through bodily movement.

Jason of Pherae *fl.* 4th cent. BC.   In ancient Greece, the tyrant of Pherae (c385–370 BC) who united all Thessaly under his rule (by 374). Jason sought to further expand his control over all Greece, and in 370 he mobilized the army of Thessaly but was assassinated before his actual objective became known. Thessaly's ascendancy under Jason was short-lived and by 344 Thessaly had surrendered to Philip of Macedon.

Jaspers, Karl 1883–1969.   German philosopher and psychopathologist and a leading figure in the modern existential movement of philosophy.

Jassy, Treaty of (Iasi)   Agreement signed between Russia and Turkey on Jan. 9, 1792, at the end of the Russo-Turkish War (1787–92). The Ottomans regained Moldavia, Walachia, and Bessarabia, while Russia gained a portion of the Black Sea coast and saw her annexation of the Crimea recognized.

Jaurès, Jean 1859–1914.   French Socialist leader who helped to found the unified French Socialist party (1905). He opposed the imminent French-German military confrontation of WW I and was assassinated by a fanatical nationalist.

Java Sea, Battle of the   Japanese naval victory (Feb. 27–Mar. 1, 1942) during WW II over an Allied force in the Java Sea. A fleet of 14 Dutch British, Australian, and American ships, under Dutch command, was routed by a superior Japanese force. The Japanese sank all Allied ships but four American destroyers and sustained minimal losses. The victory opened the way to their subsequent conquest of Java.

Jay, John 1745–1829.   American Founding Father. He was president of the Continental Congress (1778). With B. Franklin and J. Adams, he negotiated peace with Britain after the American Revolutionary War. He favored a strong central government and was one of the authors of the Federalist Papers (*q.v.*). As the first chief justice, he held the states to be subordinate to the federal government in *Chisholm* v. *Georgia* (1793), a decision that provoked the passage of the 11th Amendment, denying authority to the federal courts in suits brought by citizens against states. He negotiated Jay's Treaty (*q.v.*), the unpopularity of which ruined his chances for the presidency. He later served two terms as governor of New York (1795–1801).

Jayewardene, Junius Richard   *See* **Sri Lanka.**

Jay's Treaty   Treaty concluded Nov. 10, 1794, between the US and Great Britain. Though the US won most of the important concessions it sought, the treaty nevertheless aroused a heated controversy in the US and was denounced as a surrender to the British. Negotiated by J. Jay (US) and Lord Grenville (Britain), the treaty was intended to forestall another war with Britain. It provided for British evacuation of the Northwest Territory, settlement of boundaries between the US and British holdings in North America, compensation for attacks on US shipping, and removal of most restrictions on US commerce within British territories. Restrictions on US trade with the British West Indies were among the provisions that fueled the controversy.

Jeanne d'Arc   *See* **Joan of Arc.**

Jeans, Sir James Hopwood 1877–1946.   English mathematical physicist and astronomer. He contributed to the dynamical theory of gases and the tidal theory of planetary evolution and wrote many popular books on astronomy.

Jefferson, Thomas 1743–1826.   Third US president (1801–09), successor to J. Adams. His administration, a victory for the Jeffersonian Republicans, saw the decline of the Federalist party. Earlier, Jefferson was active in the events leading up to the American Revolution. He was a leader in the House of Burgesses (*q.v.*) in Virginia, helped organize the Committees of Correspondence (*q.v.*), was a delegate to the Second Continental Congress (1775–76), and wrote the draft of the Declaration of Independence (*q.v.*). In following years he served as governor of Virginia (1779–81), delegate to the Continental Congress (1783–84), and as secretary of state (1790–93). In the latter post, he became the center of mounting opposition to the financial program of A. Hamilton. Support for his opposition faction, which came to be called the Jeffersonian Republicans, grew in intervening years, and in 1796 Jefferson was elected vice-president (1797–1801). During this period he drafted the Kentucky and Virginia Resolutions (*q.v.*) in response to passage of the Alien and Sedition Acts, which were at least partly directed at Jeffersonian Republicans. His support increased, and he became president (election decided in House of Representatives) in 1801 and was reelected in 1804. His term was marked by US participation in the Tripolitan War (*q.v.*), the Louisiana Purchase (*q.v.*), the Lewis and Clark expedition (*q.v.*), prohibition of the slave trade in the US, A. Burr's trial on charges of treason, and conflicts with Britain over attacks on US shipping. Incidents such as that involving the *Chesapeake* (*q.v.*), were an outgrowth of war between Britain and Napoleon, and Jefferson tried unsuccessfully to impose trade embargoes (*see* Embargo Act) to put a stop to them. The failure of these measures later contributed to the outbreak of the War of 1812 with Britain.

Jeffersonian Republicans First opposition political party in US history and direct ancestor of the present Democratic party (*q.v.*). Organized in the 1790s around opposition to Federalism (*q.v.*), it held power nationally between 1801 and 1825 under the presidencies of T. Jefferson, J. Madison, and J. Monroe. It advocated limited government.

Jeffreys of Wem, George Jeffreys, 1st baron 1645?–1689. English judge under James II, notorious for his vicious prosecution of rebels during the Bloody Assizes, following the 1685 rebellion of James Scott, duke of Monmouth.

Jeffries, Dr. John *See* **Blanchard, Jean Pierre.**

Jehoahaz (Joahaz) *d.* c804 BC. King of Israel, son and successor to Jehu. The Bible reports that under him the northern kingdom reached one of its lowest points because he did what was evil. [II Kings 13:1–9]

Jehoash (Joash) 1. King of Judah (837?–798? BC). Rescued from death at the hands of Jehu and made king at seven, he reigned 40 years before being assassinated. [2 Kings 11–12] 2. King of Israel (800?–785? BC). He was son and successor to Jehoahaz, and his reign was supported by the prophet Elisha. At Beth Shemesh he defeated and reduced Judah to vassalage. [2 Kings 13–14]

Jehoiachin *fl.* c598 BC. King of Judah, successor to his father, Jehoiakim. He ruled only a few months before being captured (597?) by Nebuchadnezzar, carried to Babylon with 10,000 of his people, and imprisoned until the emperor's death. [2 Kings 24–25]

Jehoiakim *fl.* c600 BC. King of Judah (609–598) and son of Josiah. He deposed his brother with the support of Pharaoh Necho. He later rebelled against the Babylonian Nebuchadnezzar, and died before the Babylonian capture of Jerusalem. Jeremiah prophesied the destruction of Jerusalem and the Temple during his reign. [2 Kings 23–25]

Jehoram (Joram) *d.* c843 BC. King of Israel and son of Ahab. With aid from the king of Judah, he suppressed a revolt in Moab. The death of Jehoram and his family at the hands of Jehu marked the end of the family of Ahab. [2 Kings 1–3]

Jehoshaphat (Josaphat) *fl.* 9th cent. BC. King of Judah, successor to his father, Asa. He allied himself with Ahab, king of Israel, and was killed in the latter's expedition to capture Ramoth-Gilead from Syria. [1 Kings 15–22]

Jehovah's Witnesses Religious sect founded in the US by Charles Taze Russell (1852–1916) during the late 19th cent. The Witnesses are noted for their belief in Christ's imminent Second Coming and in their rejection of national allegiances. The members promote their views through the publications *The Watchtower* and *Awake!*

Jehu King of Israel (842–815 BC) and legendary chariot driver. He led the revolt against Ahab and his wife, Jezebel, which resulted in their murder because they introduced Baal worship. He also slew kings Jehoram and Ahaziah of Israel and Judah, and was anointed king of the former by the prophet Elijah. [2 Kings 9]

Jellicoe, John Rushworth Jellicoe, 1st earl 1859–1935. British naval officer who led the British fleet against the German navy at the WW I Battle of Jutland (*q.v.*) in 1916.

Jemappes, Battle of Battle of the French Revolutionary Wars (*q.v.*), fought on Nov. 6, 1792, at Jemappes, in southern Belgium. The French defeat of the Austrian army led to French occupation of Belgium.

Jena-Auerstedt, Battles of French victories in related battles fought on Oct. 14, 1806, in the Napoleonic Wars. 1. At Jena, Napoleon flanked and defeated several Prussian and Saxon forces totaling some 48,000 men, with his army totaling some 56,000. Napoleon lost about 5,000 men and pushed on to Weimar; German casualties were 11,000 killed and wounded and 15,000 captured. 2. North, in Auerstedt, on the same day, a 26,000-man French force under Marshal L. N. Davout assaulted a 63,000-man Prussian force. The French lost 8,000 men but killed or wounded 12,000 of the enemy.

Jenghiz Khan *See* **Genghis Khan.**

Jenkins's Ear, War of War (1739–c1743) between England and Spain. The war was soon absorbed by the larger conflict of the War of the Austrian Succession (*q.v.*). Exclusion of English traders from Spain's American colonies led to smuggling and to a growing resentment against the Spanish. Matters came to a head (1738) when Capt. Robert Jenkins (*fl.* 1731–39) appeared before Parliament. There he exhibited the remains of his ear, which he claimed the Spanish had cut off (1731) after boarding his ship in the West Indies. War was declared (1739), despite Sir R. Walpole's reluctance. In addition to English attacks (1739–40) on Spanish settlements in the Caribbean, there were two attacks (1740, 1743) on St. Augustine (Florida), led by J. Oglethorpe, and a Spanish attack (1742) on Georgia. By 1743, however, hostilities in the Americas had become part of King George's War (*q.v.*), which was itself a part of the War of the Austrian Succession.

Jenner, Edward 1749–1823. British physician, a pioneer in the science of immunology. Following a smallpox epidemic (1788), he noted that people who previously suffered cowpox were immune to smallpox. He experimented (1796) with a patient, James Phipps, innoculating him with cowpox. The boy developed an immunity to smallpox, following this first successful vaccination (from "vaccinia," the medical term for cowpox) against the dreaded disease. Jenner published the results of his experiment (1798) and within a few years vaccination had become widespread. He went on to improve vaccination methods and to discover ways of preserving the live vaccine. During the course of his research, he coined the term "virus."

Jennings, Sarah, duchess of Marlborough *See* **Anne.**

Jeremiah (Jeremias) c650–c570 BC. In the Bible, one of the major Hebrew prophets, whose activities and prophecies are recorded in the Old Testament book named for him. He claimed to have received a divine call to be a prophet in the 13th year of King Josiah (627–626 BC). He preached social justice, warned against Egypt, and counseled the leaders of Judah to accept Babylonian vassalage. He prophesied the fall of Jerusalem and the Temple in the reign of King Jehoiakim (609–598 BC), ascribing these coming calamities to the people's apostasy from God. After the Babylonian Captivity (586 BC) he was taken to Egypt, where he died. A personal feature of the prophecies of Jeremiah are his laments at being obliged to preach a message so unpopular that he was constantly threatened with imprisonment and death.

Jeremias *See* **Jeremiah.**

Jericho Ancient city in Palestine, west of the Jordan River. It was captured and destroyed (c1400–1200 BC) by the Israelites under Joshua, according to the Bible. [Joshua 6] Modern archaeological excavations have shown that the city was several times destroyed and rebuilt during a history of continuous occupation dating back to c8000 BC.

Jeroboam I *fl.* 10th cent. BC. First king of the divided northern kingdom of Israel. He is noted for encouraging idolatry in his kingdom, after successfully leading the revolt against Solomon's successor, Rehoboam (933 BC), which left only the southern kingdom to the house of David. [1 Kings 11–14; 2 Chron 10–13]

Jeroboam II *fl.* 8th cent. BC. King of Israel, successor to his father, Jehoash. He was the last great king of an independent Israel. The prophets Amos and Hosea appeared during his reign. [2 Kings 14, 23–29]

Jerom Bos *See* **Bosch, Hieronymus.**

Jerome, Saint AD c347–419? Christian scholar and monastic leader. After retreating to the desert for study, he was ordained in 378 and became secretary to Pope Saint Damasus (382).

From 386, he lived in a Bethlehem monastery, where he wrote several theological works, corresponded with Saint Augustine and other church leaders and did his monumental translation of the Bible from the original Greek and Hebrew into Latin. This Latin version of the Bible, called the Vulgate (*q.v.*), remained the official version of the Bible in the Western Catholic church until it was finally replaced by an updated Latin version in 1979.

Jerome of Prague c1365–1416. Czech religious reformer who supported the doctrines of J. Wyclif and defended J. Huss at the Council of Constance (*q.v.*). He was burned as a heretic.

Jerusalem Israeli capital city, located in central Israel. Historically, it is important to the Jewish people as the capital of their ancient kingdom of Israel; to the Christians as the site of the Last Supper, the crucifixion, and the resurrection of Christ; and to the Muslims as the place where Muhammad ascended to heaven. Inhabited from the 2d millennium BC (and perhaps earlier), the ancient city was conquered [2 Samuel 5] by King David (c1000 BC) and became the capital of his kingdom of Israel (*q.v.*). His son, King Solomon, extended the city and built the Temple (c970 BC) [1 Kings 3] and thereby established the city's importance to the Jewish religion. In 586 BC, Babylonian king Nebuchadnezzar took the city, destroyed the Temple, and instituted the Babylonian Captivity (*q.v.*). Persian king Cyrus returned the city to the Jews some years later, and the Temple was rebuilt by 515 BC. From the 2d cent. BC, under the Maccabees (*q.v.*), the city rose to great prominence, and, after the Roman conquest in 65 BC, the city flourished as the capital of the Roman client king, Herod the Great. This early period of Roman control was marked by the crucifixion of Christ, the Jewish Revolts (*q.v.*), destruction of the city and Temple by the Romans (AD 70), and the rebuilding of the city by Emperor Hadrian. With toleration of Christianity established within the empire, Jerusalem became a Christian center (4th cent.). It was conquered (637) by the Muslims (who constructed the Dome of the Rock mosque, *q.v.*), by the crusaders (who made it the capital of the Latin Kingdom of Jerusalem (*q.v.*), and by the Muslim conqueror Saladin (1187). Thereafter the city declined until the 19th cent. During WW I, it was captured (1917) by the British and made the capital of their territory of Palestine. The UN plan for creation of the Israeli state set Jerusalem aside as an internationally administered city, but, during the 1948 Arab-Israeli War, the Arabs occupied the Old City and the Israelis took the New City (made the Israeli capital in 1950). In the 1967 Arab-Israeli War, the Israelis occupied the Old City and annexed it (June, 1967).

Jerusalem, Council of Conference convened by the Apostles in Jerusalem (AD c50) concerning the rights of gentile Christians. In the interests of church harmony, it was ruled that the gentiles were exempted from the Mosaic Law observed by the Judaic Christians. Paul and Barnabas pleaded for exemption for the gentile Christians, and Peter agreed. The entire proceedings are described in Acts 15.

Jerusalem, Latin Kingdom of *See* **Latin Kingdom of Jerusalem.**

Jerusalem, Saint Cyril of *See* **Cyril of Jerusalem, Saint.**

Jerusalem, Synod of (Bethlehem, ˜) Council held in Bethlehem (1672) by the Eastern Orthodox church to denounce Calvinist and Lutheran doctrine and defend the memory of Cyril Lucaris (1572?–1638), patriarch of Constantinople (1621), from the accusations of Protestantism lodged against him.

Jervis, Sir John *See* **Cape Saint Vincent, Battle of.**

Jesuit Estates Act Law passed in 1888 by the Quebec legislature; this law was controversial because of Protestant objections. The act awarded the Society of Jesus $400,000 as partial restitution for property appropriated by the British government following temporary suppression of the Jesuit order (1773).

Jesus (Jesus Christ) c8/6 BC–AD 29. Founder of Christianity, recognized by Christians as the Son of God and the Messiah whose coming was prophesied. His life, as set forth in the four Gospels, began with his miraculous birth (celebrated Dec. 25) to Mary at Bethlehem. Jesus was a Jew and was raised in his father's trade of carpentry. He grew up in a period of unrest among the Jews, then chafing under Roman rule. Following his baptism by John the Baptist (*q.v.*), Jesus realized his divine calling and retired into the wilderness to meditate. Gathering his disciples about him, Jesus then undertook missions to

Galilee. The success of these and other missions, the power of his miracles, and his attacks on the Pharisees made Jesus a threat to the governmental and religious authorities of Jerusalem. Thus, when he went to Jerusalem for the last time and created a sensation by ousting the money-changers from the Temple, the authorities sought to eliminate him. After the Last Supper (*q.v.*), Jesus was betrayed by Judas Iscariot, arrested, and crucified. Blame for the death of Jesus has been a major controversy within the Christian church, some holding the Jewish people accountable, while others (especially in recent times) believe it was the Roman officials. He was entombed that day, and some days later his resurrection (celebrated as Easter) became known in Jerusalem. Thereafter, Christ's disciples went forth to spread his teachings, and thus began the Christian era.

Jesus, Society of *See* **Society of Jesus.**

Jewish Agency An international political group evolved from the World Zionist Organization. Founded by C. Weizmann (1929), the agency was the primary institution responsible for the establishment of a Jewish state in Palestine (1948). It sought world support and oversaw the settlement of Jews in Palestine and functioned as a quasi-government of the Jews settled there, dealing with authorities administering the territory under the British mandate.

Jewish Revolts Revolts against Roman rule by Jews in ancient Palestine. 1. The first revolt (AD 66–70) resulted in the capture of Jerusalem and the destruction of the Jewish Temple by the Roman general (later emperor) Titus in AD 70. 2. The second revolt (AD 132–135), led by Simon Bar Kokhba, was bloodily suppressed by Hadrian, who refounded Jerusalem as Aelia Capitolina and forbade any Jew to live in it.

Jews Term generally used to refer to individuals who are either of Jewish parentage or who are followers of the Judaic religion. Within the Jewish community some groups apply stricter limitations on the use of the term. "Jew," "Hebrew," and "Israelite" are frequently used interchangeably, but these terms properly refer to peoples of specific historic periods. "Hebrew" usually refers to the nomadic people who are ancestors of the Jews. "Israelite" refers to the Hebrews and their descendants who inhabited the Holy Land. It applies to these peoples in the period from their entry into the Holy Land until the end of the

Babylonian captivity in 538 BC. Judeans who survived the Captivity are called Jews, and this applies to their descendants into modern times. (For history, *see* Palestine, Judaism, Israel.)

Jezebel *fl.* 9th cent. BC. In the Bible, Phoenician princess who became the wife of King Ahab of Israel. She encouraged the worship of Baal and was a bitter opponent of the prophet Elijah, who prophesied her downfall. This in fact came about when Jehu triumphed over the house of Ahab; Jezebel was thrown from her window and killed, and her body was eaten by dogs. [1 Kings 16–21; 2 Kings 9] Her name has been used to describe any wicked woman.

Jhelum, Battle of *See* **Hydaspes, Battle of the.**

Jiajing (Chia-ching) 1507–66. Chinese emperor (1522–67). During his reign, China was plagued by Mongol invasions, raids by Japanese pirates, and rebellions. He ceded Macao to Portugal (1557).

Jiang Qing (Chiang Ch'ing) 1914?–90. Chinese Communist political leader and the third wife of Mao Zedong. In 1966 she became a leading figure in the Cultural Revolution (*q.v.*), and remained an important political figure into the 1970s. Following Mao's death, she fell from power and was finally put on trial (Nov. 20–Dec. 29, 1980) with the Gang of Four (*q.v.*) for abuses during the Cultural Revolution. She received a suspended death sentence, which was later commuted to life imprisonment.

Jiangxi soviet (Kiangsi ˇ) Independent Chinese Communist government set up (1931) in Jiangxi province after the split between Nationalists and Communists. It was from Jiangxi that the Long March (1934) to Shanxi province began.

Jiaquing (Chia-ch'ing) 1760–1820. Unpopular Chinese emperor (1796–1820), successor to his father, Qianlong. He put down the White Lotus Rebellion and suppressed piracy, but his measures to replenish the treasury proved unpopular.

Jibran, Kahlil *See* **Gibran, Kahlil.**

Jihad *See* **holy war.**

Jim Crow laws Laws passed by states in the US South legalizing racial segregation. In the 1880s, following Reconstruction (*q.v.*), statutes were devised separating blacks from whites in transportation facilities and excluding blacks entirely from specific establishments (housing, schooling, etc.) serving whites. In 1896, the US Supreme Court, in *Plessy* v. *Ferguson,* ruled separate but equal facilities constitutional, and the

Jim Crow laws were not successfully challenged until after WW II. It wasn't until the ruling in the 1954 *Brown* v. *Board of Education of Topeka, Kansas,* case (*q.v.*) declaring separate educational facilities to be unconstitutional that the doctrine began to be reversed. In 1963, the March on Washington (*q.v.*) helped lead to the civil rights acts (*q.v.*) of the 1960s, which effectively outlawed Jim Crow laws and customs. The name is believed to have been taken from a character in a popular minstrel show.

Jiménez de Cisneros, Francisco (Ximenes, Cardinal) 1436–1517. Spanish prelate and statesman. An austere Franciscan, he was confessor to Queen Isabella (1492) and later archbishop of Toledo (1495) and cardinal. He was regent of Spain after the death of Ferdinand (1516) and faced down the nobles while preparing for the accession of Charles I (later the emperor Charles V). A patron of learning, he founded the University of Alcalá (1508) but was also a severe inquisitor general (named 1507).

Jiménez de Quesada, Gonzalo c1500–79. Spanish conquistador who conquered Colombia and founded Bogotá (1538).

Jimmu Tenno *fl.* 660 BC. Legendary first emperor of Japan. Believed to have been a direct descendant of the Sun Goddess, he is regarded as founder of the dynasty of Japanese emperors that still reigns today.

Jin (Chin; Tsin) Name of Chinese dynasty (AD 265–420). It was founded by General Sima Yan (236–290), who briefly united China after the period of the Three Kingdoms. After his death, the empire was destroyed by the Revolt of Eight Kings and by foreign incursions. The period up until the outbreak of the revolts is called the Western Jin (265–316). The subsequent period, Eastern Jin (317–420), saw establishment of the capital at Nanjing and creation of a kingdom in southern China. The north during this period was generally ruled by barbarian invaders.

jingoism Term used to describe advocates of extreme nationalistic fervor. It was first applied to those who wanted Britain to intervene on the side of Turkey in the Russo-Turkish War of 1877–78 and came from a line in a popular song: "We don't want to fight, but, by jingo, if we do, we've got the ships, we've got the men, we've got the money too."

Jinnah, Muhammad Ali 1876–1948. Indian Muslim statesman. He served as head of the Muslim

League from 1934 to 1948, led the struggle to establish Pakistan (*q.v.*), and served as its first governor general (1947–48).

Jin Shengtan *d.* 1661. Chinese author. Drawing on the extensive literature concerning the *Shuihuzhuan* (*The Water Margin*)—a short-lived revolt by Song Jiang (1120–21)—Jin Shengtan wrote a highly popular shortened version of the tales (1644) that remained the standard up to modern times.

Joachim, Joseph 1831–1907. Hungarian violinist and composer, noted for his interpretation and performance of works for violin.

Joahaz *See* **Jehoahaz.**

Joanna II 1371–1435. Last Angevin queen of Naples. Her reign (1414–35) was marked by numerous intrigues and love affairs and a power struggle between the houses of Anjou and Aragon for control of Naples.

Joan of Arc (Jeanne d'Arc) c1412–31. French saint and heroine during the Hundred Years' War (*q.v.*). A visionary, the young girl became convinced she had a divine mission to aid the French dauphin Charles (later Charles VII) against his opponents, the English and the Burgundians. After persuading Charles to give her troops, she raised the Siege of Orléans (*q.v.*) in 1429 and won the Battle of Patay (*q.v.*). Shortly after Charles's coronation, however, she failed in her siege of Paris and was captured by the Burgundians. Turned over to an ecclesiastical court, she was tried as a heretic and was burned at the stake (May 30, 1431). She was canonized in 1920.

Joash *See* **Jehoash.**

Jodl, Alfred 1890–1946. German general. Jodl was A. Hitler's chief of the armed forces operation staff and a key adviser. He was condemned to death at the Nürnberg Trials (*q.v.*) for his shooting of hostages and prisoners of war.

Joel c5th cent. BC. Old Testament prophet. One of the minor prophets, he foretells the establishment of Jerusalem as a fertile, holy city upon the people's full acceptance of God.

Joffre, Joseph Jacques Césaire 1852–1931. French general and marshal of France. He was commander in chief of the army in WW I (1914–16), and his tactics led to the French victory at the 1914 Battle of the Marne (*q.v.*).

Johanan ben Zaccai *fl.* 1st cent. AD. Leader of the Pharisees at Jerusalem. After the destruction of Jerusalem by the Romans (AD 70), he founded the academy at Jabne (Jamnia), thus assuring the survival of traditional Judaism.

John 1167?–1216. King of England (1199–1216). The youngest son of Henry II, he succeeded his older brother, Richard I. He quarreled with the church and saw his kingdom placed under a papal interdict in 1208. He abused feudal custom and was forced by his barons to sign the Magna Carta (*q.v.*), England's first grant of general liberties, in 1215. During his reign England lost most of its domains on the Continent (Angevin Empire).

John I (˜ I Tzimisces) c925–976. Byzantine emperor (969–976). He recaptured Bulgaria from the Russians and extended Byzantine rule over parts of Muslim Syria.

John I (˜ the Posthumous) 1316. King of France and posthumous son of Louis X. He lived only five days and was succeeded by Louis's brother, Philip V.

John I 1350–95. King of Aragon (1387–95), successor to his father, Peter IV. He was a patron of education, and he adopted a friendly policy toward French politics and customs.

John I (˜ the Great) 1357–1433. Portuguese king (1385–1433), successor to his half-brother Ferdinand I, and an illegitimate son of Pedro I. He opposed Castilian claims to the Portuguese throne during the interregnum (1383–85) that followed Ferdinand's death. Following an invasion (1384) by Castilian armies, John was crowned (1385) and went on to win the Battle of Aljubarrota (*q.v.*) in 1385. This victory marked the turning point in the hostilities (ended formally, 1411) and thus secured Portugal's independence. During his subsequent reign, John concluded an alliance with England (1386) and began the period of Portuguese overseas colonization. One of John's sons was Prince Henry the Navigator.

John I 1358–90. Spanish king of Castile and León (1379–90). He had to defend his throne against a claim by John of Gaunt and ended up marrying off his son and successor to the latter's daughter. He tried to unite the Portuguese and Castilian crowns but was twice defeated by the Portuguese, notably at the Battle of Aljubarrota (*q.v.*) in 1385.

John I (˜ Zápolya) 1487–1540. King of Hungary (1526–40) and governor of Transylvania (1511–26). His reign as king was marked by conflict with Ferdinand of Austria, who claimed the throne.

John II (˜ Comnenus) 1088–1143. Byzantine emperor (1118–43). John occupied himself with regaining lost Byzantine lands and influence. He was successful against the Magyars, Serbs, Petchenegs, and Roger II of Sicily, but was forced to yield trading privileges to Venice.

John II (˜ the Good) 1319–64. King of France (1350–64), successor to his father, Philip VI. Captured by the English in the Battle of Poitiers (1356) during the Hundred Years' War, he was released in return for hostages. When one hostage escaped, John returned voluntarily to England, where he died.

John II 1397–1479. King of Aragon (1458–79) and Navarre (1425–79), successor in Aragon to his brother Alfonso V. His reign was troubled by civil war and rebellion.

John II 1405–54. Spanish king of Castile (1406–54), successor to Henry III. A patron of the arts, he left governing to a favorite. He was the father of Isabella I.

John II (˜ the Perfect) 1455–95. King of Portugal (1481–95), successor to his father, Alfonso V. He curbed the power of the nobility, made peace with Spain, and sponsored colonizing expeditions. Bartholomeu Díaz rounded the Cape of Good Hope (1488) during his reign.

John II 1609–72. King of Poland (1648–68). His reign was called "the Deluge" because of incessant warfare with the Cossacks, Russia, and Sweden. In 1655, Charles X of Sweden nearly overran Poland. After ceding the Ukraine to Russia, John retired to a monastery.

John III (˜ Ducas Vatatzes) *d.* 1254. Byzantine emperor of Nicaea (1222–54). John was left only the region of Nicaea by his father-in-law and predecessor, Theodore I Lascaris. John managed to recapture much lost territory but could not regain Constantinople from the Latins.

John III (˜ the Fortunate) 1502–57. King of Portugal (1521–57). Portuguese influence in Brazil, India, Macao, and the Spice Islands was expanded during John's reign. Domestically, he instituted the Inquisition and involved the Jesuits in higher education. The Portuguese overseas empire reached its apogee during his reign.

John III (˜ Sobieski) 1624–96. King of Poland (1674–96). John was commander in chief of the

Polish army prior to his election as king. His reign was marked by constant warfare with the Turks. For raising the Turkish siege of Vienna (1683) he became known as the champion of Christendom.

John IV *d.* 1656.　King of Portugal (1640–56). John expelled the Spanish from Portugal (1640) and became king. He also ousted the Dutch from Brazil (1654) and allied himself with France against Spain in order to protect his interests. He was the first king of the Braganca (*q.v.*) line.

John V (~ Palaeologus) 1332–91.　Byzantine emperor (1341–47; 1355–76; 1379–91), successor to his father, Andronicus III. He recognized the suzerainty of the Ottoman Turks, who had captured large parts of the empire. He tried to heal the Christian schism between East and West in order to secure Western help against the Turks.

John V 1689–1750.　King of Portugal (1706–50). John inherited the War of the Spanish Succession (*q.v.*), but eventually made peace with France and Spain. Enriched by gold from Brazil, his court was an elegant center of culture. He increased Catholic influence in secular affairs.

John VI (~ Cantacuzenus) 1292–1383.　Byzantine emperor (1347–54). He was chief adviser to Andronicus III and claimed the regency after the latter's death (1341). He fought and later became co-regent with John V through the aid of the Ottoman Turks, thus helping the Turks to gain more power over the empire. He abdicated (1354) and retired to a monastery, where he wrote a history of the period.

John VI 1769–1826.　King of Portugal (1816–26). Regent from 1799 for his insane mother, Maria I, he was forced to rule from Brazil (1807–21) because of the Napoleonic Wars and French occupation. He was also forced to recognize Brazilian independence (1825) under his son Dom Pedro I.

John VIII *d.* 882.　Pope (872–882). John opposed Ignatius of Constantinople and supported Photius. He allowed the Slavs to use their own languages in liturgy. He was forced to pay tribute to the Saracens for Rome's protection. He was murdered in Rome.

John VIII (~ Palaeologus) 1390–1448.　Byzantine emperor (1425–48). John was left only the city of Constantinople at his accession. He unsuccessfully sought to safeguard his remaining

domains by agreeing (1439) to a union of Eastern and Western churches at the Council of Florence.

John XII (Octavian) c937–964.　Pope (955–964). He crowned Otto I Holy Roman Emperor (962), and, after conspiring against him, was deposed by a synod of 50 German and Italian bishops organized by Otto.

John XXI (Giuliano, Pedro) *d.* 1277.　Pope (1276–77). John was the only Portuguese pope. He was the author of both medical and scholastic philosophical texts, including the *Compendium of Logic*.

John XXII (Duise, Jacques) 1244–1334.　Pope (1316–34), who reigned at Avignon. He condemned the spiritual Franciscans, improved church administration, and struggled with Holy Roman Emperor Louis IV over papal authority in the empire.

John XXIII (Roncalli, Angelo Giuseppe) 1881–1963.　Italian pope (1958–63), successor to Pius XII and a highly popular figure in the history of the modern church. Born to a poor family, he was ordained (1904) and later served in Vatican diplomatic posts. As pope, he was noted for promoting peace and social reforms to aid the poor, especially in such acclaimed encyclicals as *Mater et Magistra* and *Pacem in Terris* (both 1961); seeking cooperation with other religious denominations; and convening the Second Vatican Council (*q.v.*).

John XXIII (antipope)　*See* **Cossa, Baldassarre.**

John, Saint *fl.* 1st cent. AD.　One of the Apostles. Brother of James, he was, with Peter, closest to Jesus and was the "disciple whom Jesus loved." Traditionally held to be the author of the fourth Gospel, three epistles, and the Book of Revelation, he was also held to have lived to an advanced age in Ephesus, dying there AD c100.

John Baptist de la Salle, Saint 1651–1719.　French priest and educator and founder of the Christian Brothers teaching order. He spent his life teaching the children of the poor. In order to train his teachers, he founded (1685), at Rheims what is considered the first normal school.

John Birch Society　US organization devoted to exposing Communist subversion in the US and abolishing liberal legislation. Founded in 1958, it was briefly one of the foremost right-wing groups operating in the US.

John Cantacuzenus　*See* **John VI.**

John Capistran, Saint (~ of Capistrano, Saint) 1385?–1436.　Italian Franciscan priest. John preached against the Hussites (*q.v.*) in Germany and unsuccessfully led a band of crusaders to Belgrade in order to try to oust the Turks.

John Comnenus *See* **John II.**

John Damascene, Saint *See* **John of Damascus, Saint.**

John Ducas Vatatzes *See* **John III.**

John Frederick I (~ the Magnanimous) 1503–54. Elector (1532–47) and duke (1547–54) of Saxony, last elector of the Ernestine branch of the house of Witten. A leader of the Schmalkaldic League (*q.v.*), he warred against Emperor Charles V, and lost his electorship.

John Frederick the Magnanimous *See* **John Frederick I.**

John Maurice of Nassau 1604–79. Dutch general and colonial governor. John conquered much of Brazil from Portugal for the Dutch West India Co. (*q.v.*) and seized Portuguese settlements on the coast of Guinea. He was governor of Brazil (1636–43).

John Mark *See* **Mark, Saint.**

John of Austria 1547–78. Spanish soldier and naval hero who led Spanish forces to victory over the Turks in the 1571 Battle of Lepanto (*q.v.*). He was the natural son of Emperor Charles V.

John of Austria 1629–79. Spanish general, illegitimate son of Philip IV of Spain. He served as prime minister to Charles II from 1677 to 1679, having overthrown the regency of the Queen Mother Maria.

John of Brienne c1148–1237. French crusader. A leader in the Fifth Crusade (*q.v.*), he became titular king of Jerusalem (1210–25) and regent and co-emperor of Constantinople (1228–37) during the minority of Baldwin II.

John of Capistrano, Saint *See* **John Capistran, Saint.**

John of Damascus, Saint (Saint John Damascene) c675–749. Syrian theologian and Doctor of the Eastern Church, noted especially for his theological work *The Fountain of Wisdom* and for his writings against iconoclasm.

John of Gaunt 1340–99. Duke of Lancaster (from 1362) and son of Edward III of England. In effect, he ruled in England during the last years of his father's reign and during the early reign of Richard II. He was the ancestor of the Tudor (*q.v.*) kings.

John of Lancaster 1389–1435. English nobleman. John, son of Henry IV and brother of

Henry V, was regent of France for his infant nephew, Henry VI. He attempted to solidify English rule in France, but his allowance of Joan of Arc's execution helped undermine his support.

John of Leiden c1509–36. Dutch leader of the Anabaptists (*q.v.*), who led a rebellion in Münster in 1534 and ruled briefly as "king." The lawlessness of his reign harmed the Anabaptist movement.

John of Salisbury c1115–80. English scholastic writer and philosopher. He served as bishop of Chartres (1176–80), wrote books on the church and Aristotelian philosophy, and was author of a biography of his friend Thomas à Becket.

John of the Cross, Saint 1542–91. Spanish mystic and poet, Doctor of the Church and cofounder of the Discalced Carmelites (with St. Teresa of Avila). His works are considered masterpieces of Spanish literature as well as of Catholic mystical theology.

John Palaeologus *See* **John V.**

John Palaeologus *See* **John VIII.**

John Paul II (*b.* Wojtyla, Karol) 1920– . Polish-born pope (1978–), successor to John Paul I, who died after only 34 days in office. John Paul II was the first non-Italian pope to be elected since the 1500s. A strong proponent of traditional Roman Catholic Church positions on divorce, contraception, ordination of women as priests, and other social issues, he has made notable journeys abroad, including the first papal visit to England (May 28, 1982) since the Church of England split from the Roman Catholic church in 1534. He was wounded in an assassination attempt (May 14, 1981) at St. Peter's Square, Rome, by a Muslim fanatic named Mehmet Ali Agca. Three Bulgarians suspected of conspiracy in the plot were later acquitted.

John Sobieski *See* **John III.**

Johnson, Andrew 1808–75. Seventeenth US president (1865–69), successor to A. Lincoln on his assassination. A political leader in Tennessee, Johnson became a US congressman (1843–53) and senator (1857–62) and was the only Southern senator to remain loyal to the Union during the American Civil War. In return, President A. Lincoln first appointed him military governor of Tennessee (1862–64) and then made Johnson his running mate in 1864. Johnson served as vice-president from March to April, 1865, when Lincoln was assassinated. A war Democrat, with no formal schooling, Johnson was unpopular in Congress from the outset. His attempts to promote a conciliatory Reconstruction program in the South, however, inflamed radical Republicans in Congress. Seeking to ensure equal rights still being denied Negroes in parts of the South, Congress passed the Civil Rights Act of 1866 (*q.v.*) over Johnson's veto. Then, in a bitter war against him, Congress passed other acts of Reconstruction despite his vetoes. Finally, when Johnson ousted his secretary of war, E. Stanton, radical Republicans won a House resolution for his impeachment (Feb. 24, 1868). The Senate tried Johnson (Mar. 5–May 26, 1868) on charges that his dismissal of Stanton violated the Tenure of Office Act (passed over his veto) but failed by a slim margin to convict him. Johnson did not seek reelection.

Johnson, Guy c1740–88. Irish-born American Loyalist leader. Johnson was England's superintendent of Indian affairs. He organized the Indians against the American colonists during the American Revolution.

Johnson, Hiram Warren 1866–1945. American political leader and governor of California (1910–17). He helped to found the Progressive party (1912) and ran unsuccessfully as vice-presidential candidate with Theodore Roosevelt. As US senator (1917–45), he was a leading isolationist.

Johnson, James Weldon 1871–1938. American poet. The first black admitted to the Florida bar (1897), Johnson helped to found and was secretary (1916–30) of the National Association for the Advancement of Colored People.

Johnson, Lyndon Baines 1908–73. Thirty-sixth US president (1963–69), successor to the presidency on J. Kennedy's assassination. His administration was marked by the passage of wideranging social legislation, ill-fated involvement in the Vietnam War (*q.v.*), and major outbreaks of social and political unrest. A Democrat and New Deal supporter, Johnson rose under the influence of President F. Roosevelt. He became US congressman from Texas (1937–49) and senator (1949–61). As Senate majority leader (from 1955), he demonstrated great political skill and was elected vice-president (1960) under Kennedy. On Kennedy's assassination (Nov. 22, 1963), he assumed office and was subsequently

elected president by a wide margin in 1964. In the first years of his presidency, Johnson oversaw passage of bills instituting sweeping social reforms. In 1964, he won passage of legislation advanced under Kennedy, including the Civil Rights Act of 1964 (*q.v.*) and a major tax cut. He pressed for and got legislation for his Great Society (*q.v.*) program, which included the Voting Rights Act, aid to education, funding for antipoverty programs, and a Medicare program. His involvement in the Vietnam War, which increased dramatically after the 1964 elections, undermined his social programs, however. Antiwar protests as well as race riots in cities across America increased to fever pitch by 1968, and Johnson declined to run for another term. (*See also* United States, 1963–69.)

Johnson, Reverdy 1796–1876. American lawyer and politician. He served as counsel for the defense in the Dred Scott Case (*q.v.*), helped to keep his native Maryland in the Union during the Civil War, and supported the Reconstruction policies of President A. Johnson.

Johnson, Richard Mentor 1780–1850. Vice-president of the United States (1837–41) under M. Van Buren. Johnson was the first vice-president to be chosen by the Senate, following a deadlock in the electoral college.

Johnson, Samuel 1709–84. English literary figure who was renowned for his conversation as well as for his writings. After a brief career as a teacher, he went to London in 1737 and began writing journalistic works. His pioneering *Dictionary of the English Language* was published in 1755. In 1763, he began his association with his most famous biographer, J. Boswell.

Johnson, Sir William 1715–74. British Colonial merchant and landowner whose friendly relations with the Mohawk Indians and the Iroquois nation greatly helped the British during the French and Indian Wars (*q.v.*).

Johnson, William 1771–1834. American jurist, who served as associate justice of the US Supreme Court (1804–34).

Johnston, Albert Sidney 1803–62. Confederate general in the American Civil War. An able general, he led Confederate forces against U. S. Grant at the Battle of Shiloh (*q.v.*), in which he was killed.

Johnston, Joseph Eggleston 1807–1901. Confederate general in the American Civil War. He was one of the most able officers of the Confederacy, but his policy of defensive warfare during Sherman's Atlanta Campaign angered J. Davis, who relieved him of command. He was restored to command by Gen. R. E. Lee toward the end of the war.

John the Baptist, Saint *d.* AD c30. Jewish prophet who claimed to be the forerunner of Jesus Christ. He baptized his followers, including his kinsman Jesus, but indicated that he merely anticipated the Messiah "who is to come." He denounced the tetrarch Herod Antipas for incestuously marrying his own niece, Herodias, daughter of his brother's wife. Herodias's revenge came when her daughter Salome pleased Herod with dancing and was told she could have whatever she desired. At Herodias's instigation, Salome asked for the head of John the Baptist on a platter. The incident of John's meeting his end in this manner has been a favorite theme of Christian art. [Matthew 3; Mark 1; Luke 3; John 1]

John the Fortunate *See* **John III** (1502–57).

John the Good *See* **John II** (1319–64).

John the Great *See* **John I** (1357–1433).

John the Perfect *See* **John II** (1455–95).

John the Posthumous *See* **John I** (1316).

John Zápolya *See* **John I** (1487–1540).

Joinville, Jean, sire de 1224?–1317? French historian whose biography of Louis IX of France is a valuable account of the life of Louis and of the Seventh Crusade (*q.v.*).

Jolliet, Louis *See* **Marquette, Jacques.**

Jones, Alfred Ernest 1897–1958. Welsh psychoanalyst. An associate and biographer of S. Freud, Jones played a key role in the introduction of psychoanalysis to Britain, Canada, and the US.

Jones, Inigo 1573–1652. English architect. He introduced the Renaissance Palladian (neoclassical) style into England in such buildings as the Queen's House in Greenwich (1616) and the Banqueting Hall in Whitehall (1619–22).

Jones, John Paul 1747–92. Scottish-born American naval hero. John Paul added "Jones" to his name and settled in America to avoid a trial springing from his improper handling of a ship's mutiny. During the American Revolution he plagued British shipping off the coasts of both England and North America. His most famous victory (1779) was aboard the *Bonhomme Richard*. Ordered to surrender by the British ship *Serapis*, he replied, "I have not yet begun to fight."

Jones, Sir William 1746–94. English Orientalist and jurist who was influential in fostering the study of Oriental literature and language in Western Europe. He was the first to point out the resemblance of Sanskrit (*q.v.*) to Latin and Greek (1787).

Jonestown Former communal settlement founded by the Rev. Jim Jones and followers of his US–based People's Temple cult. Over 900 persons died in Guyana (Nov. 19, 1978) after Jones ordered a mass suicide of his followers.

jongleurs French medieval entertainers. The jongleurs were wandering minstrels whose specialties were comic songs and stories, juggling, and acrobatics.

Jonson, Ben 1572–1637. English Elizabethan playwright, critic, and poet. Considered to be the second-ranking English playwright after his friend W. Shakespeare, Jonson was also England's first unofficial poet laureate. Among his many satiric, innovative plays are *Every Man in His Humour, Every Man Out of His Humour, Volpone,* and *The Alchemist.*

Joram *See* **Jehoram.**

Jordan Kingdom located in the Middle East. The population is 3,065,000 and the capital is Amman. Formerly known as Transjordan, it became part of Great Britain's League of Nations mandate territory of Palestine after WW I. The history of modern Jordan began in 1946 when it became independent as the Hashemite Kingdom of Transjordan. (For history of the region prior to 1946, *see* Palestine.) Key dates in the history of Jordan include:

1920 Transjordan became part of British mandate territory of Palestine.

1921 Transjordan made separate from Palestine; Abdullah ibn Hussein became ruler in Transjordan under British control.

1946 Transjordan granted independence (May 25) as Hashemite Kingdom of Transjordan.

1948–49 First Arab-Israeli War broke out after creation of Israeli state; Jordanian forces seized territory on West Bank of Jordan River.

1949 Transjordan became known as Jordan (Apr.).

1950 Jordan annexed territory on West Bank of Jordan River occupied during 1948–49 war.

1951 King Abdullah was assassinated; succeeded by his son Talal.

1952 Talal removed as mentally unfit; his son Hussein became king.

1953– King Hussein ruled as king; his long reign to date has been marked by a generally moderate stance on Mideast problems, ongoing efforts to resolve the thorny Palestinian question, the maintaining of a delicate balance in international policy between his Arab neighbors, the US, and the USSR, and a relatively stable economy (until the late 1980s).

1958 Jordan joined (Feb.) with Iraq to form Arab Federation; revolution in Iraq overthrew the Iraqi monarchy (July) and Jordan withdrew from the federation (Aug.).

1967 Third Arab-Israeli War (Six-Day War) fought between Israel and Arab states (June 5–10); Israelis drove Jordanian forces across Jordan River and occupied West Bank.

1968 Palestine Liberation Organization (PLO) guerrillas in Jordan clashed with government troops; PLO sought West Bank as nucleus of new Palestinian state, while King Hussein wanted it restored to Jordan.

1970 Renewed fighting between PLO and government troops (Sept.), sparked by PLO fears of an Arab-Israeli settlement ignoring their interests; Syrian troops crossed into Jordan to aid PLO, but withdrew after Israel threatened intervention; fighting between government and PLO continued.

1971 Government troops attacked PLO commando bases in north (July); PLO bases destroyed; Palestinian guerrillas driven out of Jordan to Lebanon, where they established new bases.

1971 PLO guerrillas assassinated Jordanian prime minister Wasfi al-Tal (Nov. 28).

1972 Hussein wounded in unsuccessful assassination attempt (Dec.) by Palestinian.

1973 Fourth Arab-Israeli War fought (Oct. 6–25) between Israel and allied Arab states; Jordan remained effectively neutral, but sent some units to fight in Syria.

1974 Hussein joined in Arab summit resolution backing the PLO as the sole representative of Palestinians and calling for independent Palestinian state.

1976–79 Mudar Badran in office as prime minister.

1979 King Hussein and PLO leader Y. Arafat issued joint statement condemning imminent peace settlement between Egypt and Israel (Mar. 17).

1980 National Consultative Assembly convened for two-year period to consider reforms; its term extended in 1982.

1980–84 Mudar Badran back in office as prime minister (Aug.), following death of Sharif Abdul Hamid Sharaf.

1980–90 Iran-Iraq War; Jordan, dependent on trade with Iraq, backed Iraq in the war; Iraqi imports channeled through Jordan as war restricted access to Iraqi ports; relations with neighboring Syria meanwhile were strained, as Syria became one of the few nations to side with Iran.

1982 Terrorist bomb exploded in Amman (Jan.); Syrian-backed terrorists blamed as relations with pro-Iranian Syrians worsened.

1982 Israeli invasion of neighboring Lebanon, aimed at driving PLO out of Lebanon.

1982 Hussein approved of new US–sponsored Mideast peace plan (Sept.), which gave Jordan role in peace process and would link liberated Palestinian state (West Bank territory) with Jordan; Hussein called on PLO to recognize Israel (Nov.).

1983 Talks with PLO chief Y. Arafat on linking Jordan and a liberated West Bank failed (Apr.), as opposition to plan mounted within PLO.

1983 Syrian-backed Abu Nidal terrorist group stepped up terrorist campaign against Jordanians; included several bomb explosions in Amman and attacks aimed at Jordanians abroad.

1984 Parliament recalled (Jan. 16) for first time since 1974; marked beginning of slow trend toward greater freedoms.

1984 Jordan broke relations with Libya (Feb.) following attack on Jordanian embassy in Tripoli.

1984–89 Amad Obaidat, once head of security, in office as prime minister; greater Palestinian representation reflected in new cabinet; Jordan's first female minister among appointees.

1984 Women voted for first time in East Bank elections (Mar.).

1984 King Hussein criticized the US for bowing to Israeli influence; relations with US worsened as US balked at supplying arms to Jordan.

1984 Jordan resumed diplomatic relations with Egypt, broken after the Egyptian-Israeli treaty.

1985 Amman agreement (Feb.); King Hussein and PLO chief Arafat reached formal agreement on terms for further international negotiations on Palestinian question; PLO refused to condemn terrorism or recognize Israel, however.

1986 King Hussein publicly broke with PLO (Feb.) over its failure to abide by Amman agreement; PLO expelled from Jordan.

1987 Iran-Contra scandal in US; Jordanian relations with US hurt by revelations US supplied arms to Iran in Iran-Iraq War.

1988 King Hussein formally cut all ties with the occupied West Bank (July), as the Palestinian uprising there continued against the Israelis; marked end of proposed plan to link Palestinian-controlled West Bank with Jordan.

1988 Jordan imposed first austerity measures as economy began slide into recession; Jordan's foreign debt mounted, as impact of falling oil prices hit its oil-rich Mideast trading partners.

1989 Government closed nation's free currency market, hoping to halt financial crisis; suspended payment on one foreign loan.

1989 Government imposed IMF–recommended price increases.

1989 Sharif Zaid ibn Shaker in office as prime minister (Apr.).

1989 First general elections for parliament held since 1967; continuing ban on political parties forced candidates to campaign as individuals.

1989–91 Mudar Badran back in office as prime minister.

1990–91 Persian Gulf War; Jordanian government tried to remain neutral, seeking negotiated solution to crisis; reluctantly bowed to UN embargo against trade with Iraq; hundreds of thousands of refugees, fleeing the Iraqi invasion, meanwhile sought safety in Jordan.

1991 King Hussein approved new National Charter ending ban on political parties (Jan.).

1991 Tahir al Masri in office as prime minister (June).

1991 Jordan accepted invitation to US–brokered Mideast peace conference; widespread opposition led to protests by high officials and resignation of prime minister (Oct.–Nov.); Jordanian delegation attended conference.

1991– Sharif Zaid ibn Shaker, king Hussein's cousin, again in office as prime minister.

Joseph *See* **Barnabas, Saint.**

Joseph 1715–77. King of Portugal (1750–77). Joseph was completely dominated by his chief minister, the marquês de Pombal, who reformed the government and expelled the Jesuits.

Joseph c1840–1904. American Indian chief of the Nez Percé Indians (*q.v.*), who, in 1877, led his people on an unsuccessful retreat toward Canada after being forced to give up tribal lands.

Joseph I 1678–1711. Holy Roman Emperor (1705–11), successor to his father, Leopold I, and king of Hungary (1687–1711). In the War of the Spanish Succession, he successfully fought France but lost his bid to support the claim of his brother Charles (later Charles VI) to the Spanish throne.

Joseph II 1741–90. Holy Roman Emperor (1765–90), successor to his father, Francis I, and first of the Habsburg-Lorraine line. An enlightened despot, Joseph initiated many social and administrative reforms, although most did not last beyond his reign. Dominated by his mother, Maria Theresa, during the first years of his reign, he undertook a broad plan to modernize the empire after her death (1780). He abolished (1781) serfdom and granted peasants basic rights; abolished monasteries, reduced the clergy, and issued (1781) the Edict of Toleration; and attempted to centralize government of the diverse territories within the empire. This last reform led to revolts in Hungary and the Austrian Netherlands. His reign also saw the War of the Bavarian Succession, territorial acquisitions from the first Partition of Poland, and participation of Austrian forces in the Russo-Turkish War of 1787–92 (*q.v.*).

Joseph, Father (Gray Eminence) (*b.* François Leclerc du Tremblay) 1577–1638. French Capuchin monk, religious reformer, and confidential agent of Cardinal Richelieu. His activities as Richelieu's agent helped lead France into the Thirty Years' War.

Joseph, Saint *fl.* 1st cent. AD. New Testament figure. Joseph was a Galilean carpenter, descendant of King David and husband of Mary. He was regarded as the young Jesus' earthly protector.

Joséphine (Marie Joséphine Rose Tascher de la Pagerie) 1763–1814. Empress of France and wife of Napoleon Bonaparte (1796–1809).

Joseph of Arimathea, Saint Secret follower of Jesus who received Jesus' body after the crucifixion and buried it in his own tomb. He figures in many later stories.

Josephus, Flavius c37–c100 AD. Jewish historian and soldier, noted for his works on Jewish history, including *The History of the Jewish Wars,* an account of the revolt of Judaea (AD 66–70), in which the Jewish Temple was destroyed.

Joses *See* **Barnabas, Saint.**

Josiah (Josias) *d.* c609 BC. King of Judah, successor to his father, Amon. He led religious reforms that made Jerusalem the center of worship of Yahweh. The great event of his reign came in its 18th year when the "book of the law," apparently the Book of Deuteronomy, was discovered in the Temple.

Josquin des Prés c1445–1521. Flemish composer, considered the greatest Renaissance composer of his day. He is noted for his masses, motets, and chansons.

Jouhaux, Léon 1879–1954. French Socialist and trade union leader long associated with the International Labor Organization. He was awarded the Nobel Peace Prize in 1951.

Joule, James Prescott 1818–1889. British physicist, noted for his discovery of the law of conservation of energy. This great discovery was based on his studies (1843–47) on the relationship between electrical, mechanical, and chemical effects and heat to determine the amount of work necessary to produce a unit of heat. He also developed Joule's Law, which states that the amount of heat produced by an electric current running through resistance is proportional to the current's square. Working with William Thomson (later Lord Kelvin), he discovered (1852) the Joule-Thomson effect, the cooling of a gas when it expands due to the molecules' moving apart. The electrical unit of work, the joule, is named for him.

Jourdan, Jean Baptiste 1762–1833. French revolutionary marshal of France. He gained a decisive victory over the Austrians in the 1794 Battle of Fleurus (*q.v.*), and introduced the first law that allowed general conscription (1798).

Jovian (Jovianus, Flavius Claudius) AD c331–364. Roman emperor (363–364), successor to Julian the Apostate. He made an unpopular treaty with the Persians, and restored Christianity to the position granted by Constantine and annulled by Julian.

Jovianus, Flavius Claudius *See* **Jovian.**

Jowett, Benjamin 1817–93. English classical scholar, noted for his translation of the *Dialogues of Plato* (1871) and, as master of Balliol College, Oxford, for his influence on education.

Joyce, James 1882–1941. Irish author whose novel *Ulysses* (1922), with its innovative style, is considered a 20th-cent. literary masterpiece. Joyce left Ireland in 1904 and lived as an expatriate on the Continent. Two of his works are the semiautobiographical *A Portrait of the Artist as a Young Man,* published in 1916, and *Finnegans Wake,* a vast experimental novel, published in 1939.

Juan Carlos I 1938– . Spanish king (1975–), successor to Gen. F. Franco. The son of the Carlist (*q.v.*) pretender Don Juan, he was designated (1954) by Franco as the next ruler of Spain. Juan Carlos succeeded to the throne Nov. 22, 1975, after Franco's death. He withstood an attempted military coup (Feb. 23–25, 1981), in which Spanish civil guardsmen stormed the Parliament and took many of the country's leaders hostage. Subsequent years of his reign during the 1980s were marked by labor unrest and outbreaks of terrorist attacks by Basque separatists. *See also* Spain, 1975– .

Juana la Beltraneja 1462–1530. Castilian princess and daughter of Henry IV of Castile. She contested the throne of Castile with Isabella. After Isabella's succession (1479), Juana retired to a convent.

Juárez, Benito 1806–72. Mexican national hero and president (1858–61, provisional; 1861–72), successor to I. Comonfort. He took part in the overthrow of A. Santa Anna, and, as minister of justice, reduced the power of the church and army in what is called the *Ley Juárez.* He became acting president on Comonfort's resignation and emerged victorious in the War of the Reform (1858–61). He then led the opposition government during the brief reign of Emperor Maximilian (1864–67) and, after Maximilian's fall, he was elected president (1867–72) twice. Juárez died while a revolt by P. Díaz was under way.

Juba I c85–46 BC. King of Numidia. He supported Pompey against J. Caesar in North Africa. Defeated, he committed suicide.

Juba III *d.* AD c20. King of Numidia. Protégé of Augustus, he married Cleopatra Selene, daughter of Antony and Cleopatra. He was made king of Numidia and then Mauretania, and was a noted historian.

Judaea (Judea)   Roman name for the southernmost division of ancient Palestine, called Judah (*q.v.*) in the Old Testament.

Judah   Fourth son of Jacob and Leah. His name was given to one of the Twelve Tribes of Israel (*q.v.*) and to the area of southern Palestine in which two of the tribes settled.

Judah   Southern part of the kingdom of Israel, a separate Israelite kingdom after the northern part seceded (c933 BC). The tribes of Judah and Benjamin had originally settled this southern region of the kingdom of Israel. In the unstable period after King Solomon's death, the north revolted against King Rehoboam and broke away. Jerusalem then became the capital of Judah. Judah became the sole Jewish national state after the Assyrians conquered the northern kingdom (c721) and dispersed many of its inhabitants. Judah also came under Assyrian domination, then passed to the Egyptians and finally to the Babylonians. Revolts against the Babylonians brought harsh reprisals by King Nebuchadnezzar (586), marked by the destruction of the Temple at Jerusalem and the Babylonian Captivity (*q.v.*). After the Persians conquered Babylon, the Jews were allowed to return to Jerusalem and rebuild the Temple (516). Alexander the Great's conquests ended Persian rule and Judah, after a short rule by the Ptolemies, subsequently passed to the Seleucids. The Jews successfully rebelled (168–142) against the Seleucids (*see* Maccabees), and a new independent Jewish kingdom, Judaea, was established (142). Independence was short-lived, however, and after a period of religious strife between Pharisees and Sadducees Judaea came under Roman control (from 63). Revolts against Roman rule led to the destruction of Jerusalem in AD 70. (*See also* Palestine.)

Judah I   AD c135–c220.   Patriarch of the Jews in Palestine and president of the Sanhedrin. He compiled the Mishna (*q.v.*), a compendium of religious and social law.

Judaism   One of the world's three great monotheistic religions. Modern Judaism is actually rabbinic Judaism, which developed (from 1st cent. AD) from the religion of the Jews of ancient Palestine. This forerunner of Judaism also gave rise to Christianity. Rabbinic Judaism arose after the destruction of the second Temple at Jeru-

salem (AD 70). Rabbis (teachers) replaced the priests as religious leaders, the autonomous synagogues replaced the Temple as the center of worship, and prayer and study of the Torah were substituted for the sacrificial rites of the Temple. The Judaic tradition evolved by the rabbis governed both religious and secular life and preserved Jewish culture during the many centuries in which the Jews were dispersed in various foreign lands. (*See also* Palestine; Israel.) Key dates in the history of Judaism include:

C26TH?–13TH CENTS.? BC   Hebrews arrived in Palestine; practiced polytheistic religion; era of the patriarchs, Abraham, Isaac, and Jacob, and acceptance of Yahweh (Jehovah).

C13TH CENT. BC   Exodus from Egypt under the guidance of Moses; Ark of the Covenant, the Law, given to Moses; Israelites settled in Palestine.

c940 BC   First Temple constructed at Jerusalem under King Solomon; practices of sacrificial worship.

8TH CENT.? BC   Period of the prophets, including Isaiah, Jeremiah, Elijah, Amos, Hosea, and Micah; opposed the priests and worship of false gods.

722 BC   Deportation of many of the inhabitants of the northern kingdom of Israel after the Assyrian conquest.

c622? BC   Deuteronomic reform; foreign cults purged, Temple dedicated solely to worship of Yahweh, and worship concentrated at the Jerusalem Temple.

586 BC   Babylonian conquest of the kingdom of Judah; first Temple at Jerusalem destroyed; beginning of the Babylonian Captivity.

586–538 BC   Babylonian Captivity; Israelites conducted prayer meetings to maintain their faith during foreign captivity.

538 BC   Return to Palestine began; building of the second Temple completed (516), reestablishing a center of worship.

FROM 5TH CENT. BC   Ezra began period of religious reforms; introduced the Torah (written Law), formalizing religious doctrine and observances; scribes (Sopherim) assumed leadership from priests; beginnings of oral Law as exposition of written Law; Babylonian prayer meetings outside the Temple continued, laying basis for synagogues.

5TH–2D CENTS. BC The Hebrew Bible ("the Christian Old Testament") compiled from sacred writings, divided into the Law (Torah), the Prophets, and the Writings; exact versions edited by scholars called Masoretes.

FROM 2D CENT. BC Rise of the Sadducees (priestly class adhering strictly to the written Law) and Pharisees (adhering to the written Law and oral Law).

FROM 63 BC Palestine under Roman rule; Great Sanhedrin (Jewish court with religious and political functions) at the Temple in Jerusalem (until AD 70).

30 BC–AD 9 Hillel flourished; great biblical commentator and interpreter of Jewish tradition; devised "Seven Rules of Hillel" for interpreting the Bible.

AD 70 Second Temple at Jerusalem destroyed by Romans; from this time began the development of modern Judaism, with the ascendancy of the rabbinic tradition and decentralized worship in the synagogues; sacrificial worship replaced by prayer service and study.

C1ST CENT. AD Gamaliel lived; as president of the Sanhedrin, he provided leadership following destruction of the Temple by the Romans; he also unified religious laws and rituals.

AFTER AD 70 Johanan ben Zakkai flourished; a noted sage, he set up an academy after the destruction of the Temple and helped lay the foundations of rabbinic Judaism.

AD 40–135 Akiba ben Joseph lived; a chief founder of rabbinic Judaism.

AD 2D CENT. Jews, exiled from Jerusalem after the second Jewish Revolt (132–135), began to disperse to other areas of Near East; rabbinic Judaism devoted to preserving Jewish community and eventual return to promised land.

AD 3D CENT. Mishna codified in final form; collection of oral Laws begun in time of Ezra.

AD 500 Talmud, a collection of the opinions and decisions of the rabbis, compiled; with the Torah (Law), the Talmud became one of the twin pillars of Judaism.

C6TH–C10TH CENTS. Masora, Hebrew text of the Old Testament compiled by Hebrew scholars.

9TH CENT. Seder Rab Amram, oldest surviving prayer book, written.

10TH CENT. Religious study centers, originally founded in Babylon, moved to Spain.

1040–1105 Rashi lived; famous for his commentaries on the Bible and Talmud.

1135–1204 Maimonides lived; the leading figure in medieval Judaism, he compiled a great code of Jewish Law and wrote important philosophical works.

1160?–1235? Hebrew scholar D. Kimhi lived; wrote important grammar and lexicon.

12TH CENT. Yiddish language developed from High German and elements of Hebrew and Slavic.

13TH CENT. Rise of Cabala, a form of Jewish mysticism.

1455–1522 J. Reuchlin, German humanist scholar, lived; defended study of Hebrew writings before the Inquisition.

18TH CENT. Systematic modern study of rabbinic literature introduced by Elijah ben Solomon of Wilna.

1720–97 Elijah ben Solomon lived; noted authority on Jewish culture; opposed Hasidism.

c1740 Hasidim movement founded in Poland; emphasized a mystical approach to God; opposed to rigorous doctrinal literalism; founded by Baal Shem Tov.

1783 Plea for religious tolerance advanced by Enlightenment philosopher M. Mendelssohn.

19TH CENT. Rise of Reform Judaism, movement to make Judaism compatible with the modern world.

1810–74 A. Geiger lived; principal leader in the Reform Judaism movement.

1819–1900 I. Wise, American rabbi, lived; founded many Reform Jewish institutions in US.

19TH CENT. Haskala movement among Jews of Eastern and Central Europe; called for assimilation of Jews into European culture through reform of Jewish traditions and breakup of the Jewish ghettos.

19TH CENT. Orthodox Judaism reaffirmed its rigorous adherence to the totality of Jewish law and tradition; Rabbi Samson Raphael Hirsch among noted leaders.

19TH CENT. Conservative Judaism arose as middle position between Reform and Orthodox Judaism; divisions between various groups continue to present day.

1897 Zionism founded by Theodore Herzl; Zionists sought restoration of Jewish homeland in Palestine.

1948 Israel created; Jewish national state re-established in Palestine for the first time in many centuries.

Judas of Galilee *fl.* AD 6. Ancient Jewish zealot leader. He fomented a revolt against the Roman census for taxation purposes in AD 6 on the grounds that only God was the rightful ruler of Israel. He was killed for his part in this revolt. [Acts 5:37]

Judea *See* **Judaea.**

judicial branch Branch of government vested with authority to interpret the laws and administer the courts. Based on the theory of the separation of powers, Article III of the US Constitution vests judicial power in a Supreme Court and lower courts established by Congress. Although not specifically provided for in the US Constitution, the power of judicial review of executive and legislative acts has become a marked feature of US government. Judicial review is considered to have started with the 1803 decision of the Supreme Court in *Marbury* v. *Madison* (*q.v.*), in which the Court claimed power to invalidate acts of Congress.

judo *See* **jujitsu.**

Jugurtha *d.* 104 BC. King of Numidia (118–104 BC), successor to his uncle, Micipsa. Jugurtha's reign was marked by conflict with Rome. He was eventually captured and put to death in Rome.

jujitsu Oriental weaponless system of defense that aims to utilize an opponent's weight and strength against him by applying pressure to sensitive parts of his body, often by means of blows with the side of the hand (an allied system was developed as karate). Jujitsu was developed over a period of some 2,000 years by Buddhist monks in Japan, China, and Tibet as a means of self-defense not in conflict with nonviolent religious principles. Judo was created in the late 1880s in Japan by modifying jujitsu holds too dangerous to be used in sport.

Julia *d.* 54 BC. Daughter of J. Caesar and wife of Pompey, who helped maintain peace between the two leaders while she lived.

Julia 39 BC–AD 14. Roman matron. Julia was the daughter of Augustus and wife of both Agrippa and Tiberius, but she was banished by her father for her infidelities, and died of starvation soon after Tiberius became emperor.

Juliana 1909– . Queen of the Netherlands (1948–80), successor to her mother, Queen Wil-

helmina. She stepped down in favor of her daughter Beatrix (1938–), who became queen in Apr., 1980.

Julian calendar Calendar instituted (46 BC) by J. Caesar, dividing the year into 12 months and making it 365 days, 11 hours in length. It was superseded by the Gregorian calendar (*q.v.*) in most of Europe in 1582, although the change was not made in England until 1752 and in Russia until after 1917.

Julian the Apostate AD 331?–363. Roman emperor (AD 361–363), successor to Constantius II. Raised a Christian, he converted to paganism and unsuccessfully sought to restore it in the empire; hence his name.

Julius I, Saint *d.* AD 352. Pope (AD 337–352), successor to Pope Saint Mark. He supported Athanasius against the followers of Arianism by convoking a synod at Rome (AD 340), which cleared Athanasius of all the Arians' charges against him. Julius explicitly claimed jurisdiction over the other churches.

Julius II 1443–1513. Pope (1503–13), successor to Pius III. He returned the Papal States to church control and joined in the Holy League against France. He was a great patron of the arts, commissioning his own portrait by Raphael, the initial building of St. Peter's (1506) by Bramante, and the Creation frescoes on the ceiling of the Sistine Chapel (*q.v.*) by Michelangelo.

July Offensive *See* **June Offensive.**

July Revolution Revolt (July, 1830) in France that resulted in the forced abdication of Charles X and the crowning of Louis-Philippe. A victory for the upper bourgeoisie over the aristocracy, the rebellion was brought about by Charles's attempt to restore the absolutist *ancien régime* (*q.v.*). It was sparked by his selection of the unpopular Ultraroyalist J. de Polignac to head the government. To overcome opposition to Polignac in the Chamber of Deputies, Charles issued the July Ordinances (July 26), dissolving the chamber, changing the electoral system (to his advantage), and imposing press censorship. Riots broke out in Paris (July 27–29), Charles abdicated, and Louis-Philippe was chosen king (Aug. 9) by the deputies. The reign of Louis-Philippe was thus called the July Monarchy after the revolt.

June Days Revolt (June 23–26, 1848) by workers in Paris, France, during the early months of the Second Republic (*q.v.*). Though workers had supported the February Revolution (1848), unemployment and failure of the work-relief program (national workshops) failed to ease the workers' discontent. A mass protest in which workers briefly took over (May 15) the National Assembly, resulted in the decision to dismantle the national workshops. The ensuing revolt engulfed Paris in bloody street fighting and brought down the interim government. Gen. Louis Cavaignac (1802–57) was granted dictatorial powers to restore order, and finally put an end to the fighting.

June Offensive (July ˜) (Summer ˜) (Kerensky ˜) (Galician ˜) Russian offensive (June–July, 1917) during WW I. After the overthrow of the tsar in the February Revolution (1917), the provisional government, headed by A. Kerensky, continued to prosecute the war and launched a major offensive in Galicia (July 1). After initial gains, the offensive came to a standstill, and Russian forces were routed by the German counterattack (July 19). The failure of the offensive caused mass desertion and contributed to the Bolshevik seizure of power in Nov., 1917.

Jung, Carl Gustav 1875–1961. Swiss psychiatrist. One of his early works, *The Psychology of Dementia Praecox* (1906), led to a collaboration with S. Freud. Jung broke with Freud in 1913 after publishing *The Psychology of the Unconscious* in 1912. He developed the theory of personality types, extroverted and introverted, and of the collective unconscious.

Junges Deutschland *See* **Young Germany.**

Junius, Franciscus 1589–1677. German-born scholar, noted for his studies of ancient, Anglo-Saxon, and Gothic literature.

junta Governmental committee. A junta is a council that exercises administrative powers, usually in a political emergency or after the overthrow of a government. From Spanish *juntar,* "to join."

Jurchen *See* **Sung.**

Justin I AD c450–527. Byzantine emperor (AD 518–527), successor to Anastasius I and uncle of Justinian I. Justin established close ties with the church in Rome, persecuted Monophysitism (*q.v.*), and relied largely upon others to govern the empire.

Justinian I AD 483–565. Byzantine emperor (AD 527–565), successor to his uncle, Justin I. One of the great rulers of the late empire, he is especially remembered for the legal codex, *Cor-*

pus Juris Civilis (*q.v.*), compiled at his direction. His reign was marked by the conflict between the Blues and Greens in the Nika Riot (532); his call for the Second Council of Constantinople (553) and his involvement in the controversy over Monophysitism (*qq.v.*); and his expansion of the empire, including reconquest of Africa from the Vandals (533–548) and Italy from the Ostrogoths (535–554). Many public buildings were constructed during his reign, including the Hagia Sophia (*q.v.*).

Justinian II (Justinian Rhinotmetus) c669–711. Byzantine emperor (685–795, 705–711). The last of the Heraclian dynasty, he was successful in wars against the Slavs, but lost Armenia to the Arabs. Strongly Orthodox, he rejected Monotheletism and persecuted the Paulicians. He convened the Quinisext Council (691), though its canons proved unacceptable to Rome. Resentment over his ruthless practices and heavy taxation resulted in his overthrow (695, during which his nose was cut off) and exile to the Black Sea. Justinian retook the throne (705), but when his obsession with revenge against his enemies culminated in mass executions, he was overthrown and killed.

Justinian Code *See* **Corpus Juris Civilis.**

Justin Martyr, Saint AD c100–165. Christian religious philosopher and apologist who combined Christian belief with Platonic philosophy. He was one of the first intellectual apologists for Christianity and is an invaluable source for our knowledge of early Christian doctrines.

Jutes Ancient Germanic people from Jutland, in Denmark, who invaded England in the 5th cent. AD and settled in Kent and on the Isle of Wight.

Jutland, Battle of (Skagerrak, ˜) Indecisive WW I naval battle (May 31–June 1, 1916) off the coast of Denmark. It was the only important sea battle between the British and German navies during the war. The German High Seas Fleet, under Admiral R. Scheer, was lured into battle (May 31) with the superior force of the British Grand Fleet, under Admiral J. Jellicoe. Though outnumbered, the Germans inflicted the greater losses on the British before managing to escape the trap. The Allied North Sea blockade, however, was not tested again by German surface warships.

Juvenal (Decimus Junius Juvenalis) 60?–140 AD. Roman satiric poet. Born to a wealthy family, Juvenal embarked on a career as an officer in the army of Emperor Domitian. Apparently disaffected by his failure to receive a promotion, he wrote a satire that earned him banishment to Egypt. Returning to Rome after Domitian's assassination in 96, he spent the remaining years of his life there. His 16 satires attacked the corruption of Roman society as well as the brutalities of all mankind. Many notable epigrams and phrases from his *Satires,* such as "slow rises worth, by poverty oppressed" and "bread and circuses" are remembered today. He is considered the most powerful of Roman satiric poets and established a model for satirical writing.

Juvenalis, Decimus Junius   *See* **Juvenal.**

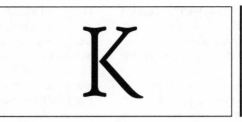

Kaaba (Caaba) Sacred shrine in the Great Mosque at Mecca and the major site of pilgrimage for the followers of Islam. Muslims face toward it when praying.

Kabuki *See* **Japan, 1582.**

Kádár, János *See* **Hungarian Revolution of 1956.**

Kadesh, Battle of Inconclusive battle (c1288 BC) between the Egyptians under King Ramses II and the Hittites. The Egyptians launched the attack on Kadesh, in Syria, in an attempt to halt the Hittite encroachment on the Egyptian Empire.

Kadet (Constitutional Democratic party) Russian political party founded in 1905. A party of moderation, it was continually undermined by more radical groups and ceased to function after 1917.

Kaffirs *See* **Kafirs.**

Kafirs (Kaffirs) Term originally applied by Muslims to all unbelievers. Adopted by the European settlers of South Africa, it was applied to the Bantu-speaking native peoples of the area.

Kafir Wars *See* **Cape Frontier Wars.**

Kafka, Franz 1883–1924. Czech-born Austrian author. Kafka published little in his lifetime and supported himself by working in an insurance office. His friend Max Brod (1884–1968) published his three novels, *The Trial, The Castle,* and *Amerika* posthumously. These works on the alienation of modern man greatly influenced later existentialist authors and marked Kafka as one of the great writers of the 20th cent.

Kaganovich, Lazar Moiseyevich 1893–1991. Russian Communist leader who was instrumental in Stalin's rise to power. A former Communist leader in Turkistan who was elevated to party posts in Moscow by Stalin, Kaganovich from 1924 controlled assignments of party members to posts, government jobs, and positions in industry and labor organizations. Using that power to put Stalin's supporters in positions of power, Kaganovich assured Stalin's success against his opponents following Lenin's death. Kaganovich became a full member of the Central Committee (1924) and the Politburo (1930). He played a key role in the development of Russian transportation and heavy industry and remained a loyal supporter of Stalin until the dictator's death in 1953. Kaganovich lost power following Khrushchev's rise to power in the 1950s and joined other high officials opposed to de-Stalinization who unsuccessfully attempted to oust Khrushchev in 1957. Stripped of his party posts after 1957, Kaganovich was also expelled from the party (belatedly announced in 1964).

Kagawa, Toyohiko 1888–1960. Japanese Christian evangelist, social reformer, and writer. He was prominent in the Japanese labor and social-welfare movements of the 1920s and 1930s.

K'ai Feng Jews Religious group that practiced Judaism at K'ai Feng, Honan province, China, from about the 12th to 19th cents.

Kaiser-Wilhelmsland *See* **Papua New Guinea.**

Kalb, Johann 1721–80. German officer in the French army. As a general in the Continental Army during the American Revolution, he served with G. Washington at Valley Forge (1777), and was killed in the Carolina Campaign.

Kalevala National epic of Finland. It was compiled and edited (1835, enlarged 1849) by E. Lönnrot, who used Finnish folk verses to produce a unified work.

Kalidasa *fl.* AD 5th cent. Indian dramatist, considered to be the greatest Sanskrit writer and perhaps the greatest writer in India's history. His drama *Sakuntala* is his best-known work.

Kalinin, Mikhail Ivanovich 1875–1946. Russian politician. Official head of the Soviet Union from 1919 to 1946, he was chairman of the Soviet central executive committee (1919–38) and of the Presidium (1938–46).

Kalmar Union Scandinavian union (1397) of Denmark, Norway, and Sweden, joined under one crown at Kalmar, Sweden. Sweden withdrew (1523) with the accession of Gustavus I, though Denmark and Norway remained united until 1814.

Kalmar War War (1611–13) between Sweden and Denmark for the possession of Norway's north coast and the dominance of the Baltic. Danish king Christian IV defeated Sweden under Charles IX. Denmark achieved a position of dominance over Sweden and exacted a tribute for the return of the port of Älvsborg.

Kalmucks (Kalmycks) Nomadic people of Mongolian stock occupying the region of the lower Volga River in the former USSR. The Kalmucks migrated to the region (17th cent.) from Chinese Turkistan and were at first allies of the expanding Russian empire. In the 18th cent. they were made vassals, however, and Russian oppression forced the bulk of the Kalmucks into their disastrous journey back to China (1771). Of the 300,000 that began the trek, the majority were killed in attacks by Russians and the Kazakh and Kirghiz peoples. Those that reached Chinese Turkistan were settled in Sinkiang, northwestern China. The remaining Kalmucks in Russia were exiled to Siberia after WW II for collaborating with the Germans. They were released from exile in 1957.

Kamakura shogunate Period in Japanese history (1192–1333) when the Kamakura shogunate ruled Japan as shoguns. Yoritomo, operating from Kamakura (east of Kyōto) crushed the rival clans of Taira (1185) and was named shogun by the emperor in 1192. Yoritomo thus established the institution of the shogunate, and the long period of rule by the shoguns and the warrior class (to 1868). Imperial administration was quickly undermined during the Kamakura period, with the imperial court depending increasingly on the shoguns to control warriors throughout the realm. Following Yoritomo's death in 1199, however, the Hojo clan assumed increasing control as regents of the shogun. After the early 1200s, shoguns themselves had no real power. The Hojo clan (and the Kamakura shogunate) remained in power until Emperor Go-Daigo led a successful revolt (1333) in which his warriors overthrew the Kamakura rule. Go-Daigo reigned until 1336, when he in turn was ousted and the Ashikaga shoguns came to power. During the Kamakura period, the system of warrior government was established (formalized by the Joei Formulary, 1232 and subsequent ad hoc orders), foreign trade flourished, the Zen sect of Buddhism was introduced to Japan, and there was a cultural flowering as well. The No theater was developed during this period.

Kamehameha I (~ the Great) 1758?–1819. Hawaiian king who united and ruled all the Hawaiian Islands (1810–19) and established the Kamehameha dynasty of Hawaiian rulers.

Kamehameha the Great *See* **Kamehameha I.**

Kamenev, Lev Borisovich 1883–1936. Russian Communist leader. He was a member, with J. Stalin and G. Zinoviev, of the triumvirate that succeeded N. Lenin and opposed L. Trotsky. He was executed (1936) in the Stalinist purge of the 1930s.

Kamiakin *See* **Yakima Indian Wars.**

Kamikaze Japanese word meaning "divine wind." It was originally applied to the typhoon that destroyed (1281) a Mongol invasion fleet. In WW II it was applied to the Japanese suicide pilots who tried to fly their bomb-loaded planes into US ships.

Kammu 737–806. Emperor of Japan and founder of Kyōto, the capital of Japan until 1868. A strong ruler, he diminished the power of the Buddhists and brought peace to Japan's northern borders.

Kanagawa, Treaty of (Perry Convention) Treaty (Mar. 31, 1854) between Japan and the US. The treaty was secured by Commodore M. Perry, who had sailed to Japan (1853–54) with a fleet of US warships to end Japanese isolationism. It secured good treatment for US sailors, opened two ports to US trade, and established a US consulate at Shimoda. It was the model for later treaties with other Western powers.

Kandinsky, Wassily 1866–1944. Russian painter and theorist, considered the founder of abstract art. He was a founder of the influential Munich art group, the Blau Reiter.

Kandy, kingdom of *See* **Sri Lanka.**

Kanem-Bornu African empire that flourished in the region around Lake Chad from the 9th to 19th cents. It reached its height in the 16th–17th cents.

K'ang-hsi *See* **Kangxi Emperor.**

Kang Sheng 1899–1975. Chinese political leader. An active Communist since the 1920s, he was a member of the Central Committee and the Politburo and was one of the most powerful leaders in China.

Kangxi, Emperor 1654–1722. Chinese emperor (1661–1722). He extended China's rule to Taiwan, Tibet, and Outer Mongolia, and encouraged the teaching of Western mathematics and astronomy.

Kang Youwei *See* **Reform Movement of 1898.**

Kanishka *See* **Kaniska.**

Kaniska (Kanishka) AD 78?–103? Chinese ruler of northern India and founder of the Kusana empire (*q.v.*). He was an ardent Buddhist and may have introduced the belief to China. Trade with the Romans was fostered during his reign.

Kano Japanese family of painters who dominated art in Japan between the 15th and 17th cents. For seven generations they set painting style and their influence persisted well into the 19th cent.

Kansas Central US state, the 34th state. First explored (1541) by the Spanish explorer Francisco Coronado (1510–54), it was later claimed by France and acquired by the US in the Louisiana Purchase (1803). Kansas was at first considered too barren for settlement, but the controversy between pro- and antislavery groups seeking to establish a majority increased the population and led to passage of the Kansas-Nebraska Act (*q.v.*) and the civil war known as Bleeding Kansas (*q.v.*). Kansas became a state in 1861.

Kansas-Nebraska Act US bill enacted (May 30, 1854) to establish Kansas and Nebraska as separate territories and, more important, to provide a compromise on the extension of slavery into the territory acquired in the Louisiana Purchase. Sponsored by Senator S. Douglas, the act helped bring on the American Civil War. Slavery had been barred from the region by the Missouri Compromise (1820), but Douglas' bill introduced the doctrine of Popular Sovereignty, by which inhabitants of the region would decide the issue of slavery. Unpopular with anti-slavery groups, the act fostered creation of the anti-slavery Republican party and led to Bleeding Kansas (*q.v.*).

Kant, Immanuel 1724–1804. German philosopher. As a teacher at Königsberg University, he began his writings partly in reaction to his studies of G. Leibniz. His metaphysical work *Critique of Pure Reason* expressed his theories of what man could know. His *Critique of Practical Reason* (1788) gave his ethical beliefs, and his *Critique of Judgment* (1790) combined and completed his philosophies. Kant's writings have established him as one of the great philosophers of all time. He engineered a revolution in philosophy by focusing on what the human mind could subjectively know rather than upon what was objectively "out there."

Kao Kang *See* **Gao Gang.**

Kao Tsu *See* **Gaodi.**

Kapodistrias, Ioannes Antonios, Count (Capo d'Istria, Giovanni Antonio) 1776–1831. Greek president (1828–31). A former adviser to Russian tsar Alexander I, he supported Greek independence. His high-handed measures made him an unpopular president, however, and he was assassinated.

Kappel, Battle of *See* **Kappel Wars.**

Kappel Wars Name applied to two wars (1529, 1531) between Swiss Protestants and Catholics during the Swiss Reformation. During the second, the Swiss religious reformer H. Zwingli was killed at the Battle of Kappel (Oct. 11, 1531).

Kapp Putsch Unsuccessful reactionary uprising in Berlin (1920), named after its leader, Wolfgang Kapp (1858–1922). It sought to overthrow the Weimar Republic and restore the German monarchy.

Karadžić, Vuk Stefanović (Karajich, ˜) 1787–1864. Serbian scholar. He developed a simplified Cyrillic alphabet to reflect the Serbian language more closely and compiled collections of Serbian folk songs and tales.

Karageorge (*b.* George Petrović) 1766?–1817. Serbian patriot who led the Serbian uprising against the Turks (1804). He was named hereditary leader of the Serbs (1808), and founded the Karageorgevich dynasty.

Karageorgevich Serbian dynasty, descended from the patriot leader Karageorge. It ruled Serbia from 1842 to 1858, and the kingdom of Serbs, Croats, and Slovenes (later Yugoslavia) from 1903 to 1945.

Karaites Jewish religious sect, said to have been founded in Persia in the 8th cent. It rejected Talmudic interpretation of the Bible and accepted only the Bible as the source of religious law. Its importance declined after the 12th cent., but it has inspired much biblical scholarship.

Karajich, Vuk Stephenovich *See* **Karadžić, Vuk Stefanović.**

Karakhan, Lev *See* **Karakhan Manifesto.**

Karakhan Manifesto Russian manifesto issued (July 15, 1919) by Lev Karakhan (1889–1937), then a member of the newly formed foreign ministry of the USSR. The manifesto renounced tsarist rights and privileges in China. It made a tremendous impression in China as the first such renunciation by a former imperialist power and helped lead to the foundation of a Chinese Communist party (1921).

Karamanlis, Constantine 1907– . Greek statesman and prime minister (1955–63, 1974–80). He was instrumental in resolving the crisis in Cyprus in 1960. Karamanlis was returned to power in 1974, following the collapse of the military junta that had taken control in 1967, and served as president from 1980 to 1985.

karate *See* **jujitsu.**

Karens Members of several ethnic groups living in southern Burma and constituting a substantial minority. The Karens have resisted Burmese political rule since Burma's independence in 1948.

Karlowitz, Treaty of (Carlowitz, ˜) Treaty (Jan. 26, 1699) between the Ottoman Turks and Austria and her allies of the Holy League (Poland, Russia, and Venice) ending the Austro-Turkish War (1682–99). The treaty's provisions made Austria the major power in Eastern Europe. By its terms Austria gained most of Hungary, Transylvania, Croatia, and Slavonia. Poland won Podolia, and Venice received Dalmatia and Morea. Russia continued hostilities until it gained Azov.

Karman, Theodore von 1881–1963. American aeronautical engineer noted for his contributions in the field of mathematics to the development of aerodynamics.

Karmatians Muslim reformist sect prominent from the 9th to 10th cents. The sect was centered in lower Mesopotamia and set up a communistic community there. From this base they fostered wars and rebellions against the Abbasid Caliphate, and in the 10th cent. conquered Yemen. In c930 the Karmatians attacked Mecca and carried off the sacred Muslim Black Stone of the Kaaba. They ransomed it back (952); thereafter their power declined.

Karnak Egyptian village. Karnak occupies the northern half of the ancient site of Thebes; Luxor, the southern half. Karnak is famed for its ancient ruins and temples, especially the Temple of Amon, with its vast hall containing 134 massive columns arranged in 16 rows, the finest construction of the 19th dynasty.

Karo, Joseph ben Ephraim *See* **Caro, Joseph ben Ephraim.**

Károlyi, Mihály, Count 1875–1955. Hungarian statesman who sought Hungarian autonomy within the Austro-Hungarian Empire. After World War I, he briefly served as president of the Hungarian republic (1919) before the rise of B. Kun.

Kashmir (Jammu and Kashmir) Former princely state, now divided between Pakistan and India. It includes the Indian state of Jammu and Kashmir (54,000 sq. mi.) and Pakistani-controlled Azid Kashmir (32,000 sq. mi.). It was included in the Mughal Empire in 1587, and, after changing rulers several times, became part of British India in 1846. There was a Muslim revolt there after the 1947 partition of India and unrest has continued there to the present day. India and Pakistan have both made claims on the entire territory.

Kassem, Abdul Karim 1914–63. Iraqi political and military leader. After leading a successful revolt (1958) to overthrow the Iraqi monarchy, he became the first premier of the Iraqi republic, but was overthrown and executed by the Baath party in Feb., 1963.

Kassites Ancient people, possibly originating in western Iran, who conquered Babylonia and ruled there from the 18th to 12th cents. BC.

Kastrioti, George *See* **Scanderbeg.**

Kato, Takaakira (Katō, Kōmei ˜) 1860–1926. Japanese statesman, and foreign minister when Japan presented the Twenty-One Demands (*q.v.*) to China (1915). He organized and headed the conservative Kenseikai party (1913).

Katyn Village near Smolensk in the western part of the Russian Federation. The nearby Katyn Forest was the site where Soviets massacred some 15,000 Polish officers in 1940. The mass grave was discovered (1943) by the Nazis during their invasion of the Soviet Union. Soviet authorities consistently blamed the Germans for the killings, but in 1952 a US congressional investigating committee claimed to have established that the massacre was carried out under Soviet auspices. In 1990, the Soviets finally admitted J. Stalin had been responsible for the massacre.

Kaufman, George S. 1889–1961. American playwright, collaborator on many very popular musicals and plays, including the Pulitzer Prize-winning *Of Thee I Sing* (1931) and *You Can't Take It with You* (1936).

Kaunda, Kenneth (David) 1924– . Zambian political leader who led the Zambian independence movement and became Zambia's first president (1964–). He was elected chairman of the Organization of African Unity in 1970 and 1980.

Kaunitz, Wenzel Anton, Fürst von 1711–94. Austrian statesman. In the so-called Diplomatic Revolution, he allied Austria with France and Russia in a coalition against Prussia that led to the Seven Years' War (*q.v.*). He was Austria's leading statesman during his lifetime.

Kautsky, Karl Johann 1854–1938. German Socialist leader and Marxist theorist. He was the main contributor to the Erfurt program, which committed the German Social Democratic party to a Marxist program.

Kay, John 1704–64. English inventor of the flying shuttle (1733), a major advance in the development of mechanical weaving.

Kazakhstan (*formerly* Kazakh Soviet Socialist Republic) Independent state extending from the Caspian Sea to China in central Asia. It is a member of the Commonwealth of Independent States. The region was invaded by Mongols in the 13th cent. and became part of the empire of the Golden Horde. Russia retook it between 1730 and 1853, and after the Russian Revolution, it passed from an autonomous republic (from 1920) to a constituent republic (1936). Kazakhstan appeared to have suffered relatively little ethnic unrest in the late 1980s. Its government waited until Dec. 16, 1991, to declare independence after the USSR collapsed and joined the Commonwealth of Independent States just days later.

Kean, Edmund 1789–1833. English actor whose dynamic performances in such roles as Iago, Shylock, and Othello revolutionized English acting style and made him famous as one of England's greatest actors.

Kearny, Philip 1814–62. American Union general. A nephew of S. W. Kearny, he fought in the Mexican War and with the French in Europe. He was a dashing commander in the Peninsular Campaigns and was killed in action reconnoitering Confederate lines.

Kearny, Stephen Watts 1794–1848. American general in the Mexican War. He captured New Mexico, established a civil government there, and helped to capture California, where he was military governor for a time.

Keats, John 1795–1821. English poet, considered one of England's greatest Romantic poets. He gave up a career as a medical student in 1816 to write poetry. Despite his tragically short life and the lack of recognition of his work, Keats produced a number of works renowned for their sensuous imagery. Among his best-known poems are the odes *On Melancholy, To a Nightingale, On a Grecian Urn,* and *To Psyche.*

Keble, John 1792–1866. English clergyman and poet whose sermon *National Apostacy* is considered the origin of the Oxford movement within the Anglican church.

Keita, Modibo *See* **Mali.**

Keitel, Wilhelm 1882–1946. German field marshal and chief of staff of the German high command during WW II. He was convicted at Nürnberg for war crimes and was executed.

Keith, George 1693?–1778. Scottish Jacobite leader. A brother of J. Keith, he took part in the abortive Jacobite uprising of 1715, and then escaped to the Continent, where he eventually rose high in the service of Prussia.

Keith, James Francis Edward 1696–1758. Scottish Jacobite leader in the Jacobite rebellion of 1715. He later served as field marshal in the Prussian army during the Seven Years' War.

Keller, Helen Adams 1880–1968. American author and public figure. Blind and deaf from infancy she overcame her handicaps and became a noted writer and lecturer.

Kellermann, François Christophe 1735–1820. French general and marshal of France, his defeat of the Prussian army at the Battle of Valmy (1792) saved the revolutionary government in France.

Kelley, Florence 1859–1932. US social reformer. The daughter of Quaker parents, she became active in Hull House, one of the first US settlement houses, and from 1898 until 1932 headed the National Consumers' League, which among other things promoted legislation to protect women and children in the workplace.

Kelley, Oliver Hudson 1826–1913. American agriculturalist. He was one of the founders (1867) of the National Grange and became a leader of the Granger movement.

Kellogg, Frank Billings 1856–1937. American statesman. As US secretary of state (1925–29), he formulated the Kellogg-Briand Pact, for which he received the Nobel Peace Prize in 1929.

Kellogg-Briand Pact (Pact of Paris) International agreement (Aug. 27, 1928) declaring an end to war as an instrument of national policy. Initiated by US secretary of state F. Kellogg and French foreign minister A. Briand, the pact was originally signed at Paris by 15 nations and ultimately was subscribed to by 62. The pact was rendered ineffective by the lack of means of enforcement and by provisions that allowed defensive wars and wars to defend allies. In the following years it was ignored by the Japanese (Manchurian invasion, 1931) and others.

Kelts *See* **Celts.**

Kelvin, Lord (Thomson, William) 1824–1907. Scottish mathematician and physicist, noted for his work in the areas of heat, electricity, and magnetism. He proposed a scale of absolute temperature (1848), the Kelvin scale, which is named for him. He devised the second law of thermodynamics (1851), which states that heat flows naturally only from a hot body to a cooler body, and introduced a theory (1853) of oscillating electrical circuits which was subsequently used in producing radio waves. Working with J. Joule, he discovered (1852) the Joule-Thomson effect, which holds that expanding gases cool due to the movement of their molecules. His expertise in electrical science was in large part responsible for the first successful transatlantic telegraph cable (1866). Inventions by Kelvin also included an absolute electrometer (1870).

Kendall, Amos *See* **Kitchen Cabinet.**

Kennedy Prominent American political family from Massachusetts. The founder, Joseph P. Kennedy (1888–1969), acquired a large fortune and served as F. Roosevelt's ambassador to London (1937–40). Three of his sons have gained prominence as American political leaders: J. Kennedy; R. Kennedy; and Edward Kennedy (1932–), US senator and liberal Democratic leader from Massachusetts since 1962.

Kennedy, Edward M. *See* **Kennedy.**

Kennedy, John Fitzgerald 1917–63. Thirty-fifth US president (1961–63), successor to D. Eisenhower. A Democrat and US congressman from Massachusetts (1947–53), he served in the Sen-

ate from 1953 to 1960 and there established himself politically. In the 1960 elections he successfully opposed R. Nixon and became the youngest president (and first Catholic) ever elected to the office. As president, he sought enactment of legislation, which became stalled in Congress, for his New Frontier (*q.v.*) program; instituted the Alliance for Progress (1961) program; and started the Peace Corps program. Kennedy put the federal government squarely behind the civil rights movement in the South and used both federal troops and federal pressure to promote school desegregation there. In foreign affairs, Kennedy quickly became embroiled in a series of clashes with the Communists, including the embarrassing failure of the Bay of Pigs Invasion (*q.v.*), the crisis over the Berlin Wall (*q.v.*), the Cuban Missile Crisis (*q.v.*), and increasing involvement in the war against the Communists in Vietnam. He also concluded the Nuclear Test Ban Treaty of 1963. Kennedy was assassinated (Nov. 22, 1963) in Dallas, Texas, by Lee Harvey Oswald (1939–63). Oswald was in turn shot and killed by Jack Ruby (1911–67), a local citizen. Despite findings of the Warren Commission that Oswald acted alone, rumors of a second gunman and of various conspiracies persisted for years.

Kennedy, Joseph P. *See* **Kennedy.**

Kennedy, Robert F. 1925–68. American politician, younger brother of President J. Kennedy. He was attorney general under presidents Kennedy and L. Johnson (1961–64). As US senator from New York (1964–68), he ran for the Democratic presidential nomination in 1968 but was assassinated on June 5, 1968.

Kennedy Round Series of tariff negotiations conducted (1964–67) by 50 countries responsible for 80 percent of world trade. They agreed to tariff reductions of up to 50 percent on many industrial goods and to substantial reductions on other tariffs.

Kennesaw Mountain, Battle of *See* **Atlanta Campaign.**

Kensett, John Frederick 1818–72. American painter, one of the group of painters known as the Hudson River school.

Kensington Rune Stone Controversial stone found (1898) on a farm near Kensington, Michigan. It bears runic inscriptions supposedly carved by Norse explorers in 1362.

Kent, kingdom of Ancient English kingdom. Founded by the Jutes (5th cent. AD), it rose to power (6th cent.) under Aethelbert, but in the 9th cent. became part of the kingdom of Wessex. The kingdom contained the bishopric of Canterbury, established during Aethelbert's rule.

Kent State Massacre Incident at Kent State University in Kent, Ohio, on May 4, 1970. Ohio National Guardsmen called out against a Vietnam War protest rally fired on protesters, killing four students. The incident provoked a nationwide protest against repression and redoubled sentiment against the war.

Kentucky Central state of the US, the 15th state. Kentucky was first settled in the 1760s. D. Boone opened the Wilderness Road from Tennessee to Kentucky and founded the first settlement, Boonesborough (1775). Made a county of Virginia (1776), Kentucky was the first territory west of the Appalachians to become a state (1792). Federal adoption of the Alien and Sedition Acts (1798) led to passage of the Kentucky and Virginia Resolutions. Kentucky was a border state during the American Civil War. Although it remained in the Union, many Kentuckians fought for the Confederacy.

Kentucky and Virginia Resolutions Resolutions passed (Nov., Dec., 1798) by legislatures in the two states to oppose the Alien and Sedition Acts (1798). The ideas these resolutions put forward laid the basis for states' rights and the nullification controversy. Written by T. Jefferson (Kentucky) and J. Madison (Virginia), the resolutions amounted to a reply by Jeffersonian Republicans to the Federalist party interpretation of federal government powers. Essentially, Jefferson put forward the idea of a compact between the federal government and states established by the Constitution. Further, the states had the power to nullify federal laws they deemed unconstitutional.

Kenya (Republic of Kenya, *formerly* British East Africa) Republic located on the east coast of Africa. The population is 25,393,000; the capital is Nairobi. The region of Kenya was early dominated by the Arabs. Control then passed to the Portuguese, back to the Arabs, and finally to the British. Kenya became independent in 1963. Key dates in the history of Kenya include:

8TH CENT. Arabs settled coast, establishing autonomous colonies.

c1000 Bantu tribes arrived in region.

16TH CENT. Portuguese arrived (from 1498) and gradually gained control of Kenyan coastal region.

1729 Arabs drove out Portuguese and took control of region.

1886 Britain and Germany set up "spheres of influence" in region; most of Kenya went to Britain.

1888 British East Africa Company given royal charter.

1895 British government took control; East Africa Protectorate established.

FROM 1903 European settlers arrived, taking control of highlands region.

1920 Kenya divided into British crown colony (coast) and protectorate (interior).

1952–56 Native Mau-Mau uprising against European domination.

1961 Black Africans gained majority control in Kenya's legislative council for the first time; Jomo Kenyatta, nationalist leader, freed from exile.

1963 Independence declared (Dec. 12); unicameral legislature established by constitution; Kenya African Union became sole political party.

1963–68 Border war with Somali Democratic Republic.

1964 Republic declared; Kenyatta first president (in office 1964–78).

1967 Kenya, Uganda, and Tanzania established East African trading community; disbanded in 1977.

1969 Tom Mboya, Kenyatta's probable successor, assassinated.

1976 Hostilities with Uganda ended by formal peace agreement.

1978 Kenyatta died (Aug. 22).

1979– Daniel Arap Mori in office as president, following elections; quickly consolidated his position and instituted harsh regime which included arrest and torture of opponents; maintained pro-West foreign policy; meanwhile the country was beset by economic problems and widespread corruption that persisted into the 1980s.

1980 Government forced to import maize to feed populace, following food shortage caused by 1979 government program to encourage export of maize reserves.

1981 IMF granted standby loan credit as Kenya's balance of payments deficit rose.

1981 Nationwide strike by hundreds of government doctors (May); after granting some concessions, government broke strike by arresting 20 doctors.

1982 Constitutional amendment establishing one-party system in Kenya approved by parliament (June); Kenya African National Union (KANU) to be ruling party.

1982 Failed coup attempt by low-ranking members of the air force (Aug. 1); some 160 killed and some 800 members of the air force were court-martialed; government disbanded entire air force, reforming it as the "82 Air Force."

1983 Moi, the sole candidate for president, reelected (Sept.).

1983 Queen Elizabeth on official visit (Nov.).

1984 Drought in parts of Kenya resulted in famine; government sought emergency aid from foreign relief agencies.

1986 Anti-government unrest at Kenyatta University (Mar.); government arrested several professors and shut down university, while secret left-wing group, Mwakenya, circulated pamphlets criticizing government; government began program of arrests aimed at breaking up Mwakenya; by 1987, torture was reported being used on suspects who had been arrested.

1986 Government seized 1,000 ivory tusks taken illegally by big game poachers; later issued shoot-to-kill order against poachers.

1986 Constitutional amendment, giving President Moi greatly expanded powers, approved (Dec.).

1987 Former vice-president Oginga Odinga publicly criticized gradual imposition of dictatorship (Apr.); later called for return to multi-party system.

1987 Student protests at University of Nairobi (Nov.); four foreign journalists among those arrested and severely beaten by police.

1988 President and police given more powers by new constitutional amendment (Aug.); Moi now able to fire judges.

1989 Noted palaeontologist Dr. Richard Leakey named head of Kenya's Wildlife Services agency (Apr.).

1989 President Moi, seeking to blunt international criticism on human rights abuses, released all remaining political prisoners (June).

1989 Somali bandits killed famed wildlife conservationist George Adamson in Kenya (Aug.).

1990 Kenya's foreign minister, who had publicly asked for investigation of government corruption, found murdered (Feb.); death sparked anti-government riots; government kept report on killing secret.

1990 Four-day riot in Nairobi and elsewhere (July), following arrest of those advocating return to multi-party system; 20 people killed.

1990 Kenyan researchers discovered Kemron, a drug reportedly effective against AIDS symptoms.

1991 Forum for the Restoration of Democracy (FORD) organized by middle-class professionals in Kenya who sought return to democracy; government stepped up arrests of critics and banned pro-democracy demonstrations.

1991 Two high government officials named as suspects in official inquiry into 1990 murder of Kenya's foreign minister (Nov.); one later was charged with the murder.

1991 New constitutional amendment restored multi-party system (Dec.).

1992 Severe drought reported in Kenya and surrounding countries.

Kenyatta, Jomo c1894–1978. Kenyan political leader and statesman. He was a leader in the Kenyan independence movement and became first president of the Republic of Kenya (1964–78).

Kepler, Johannes 1571–1630. German astronomer, perhaps best known for his laws of planetary motion. After publishing accurate calculations of planetary distances from the sun (*Mysterium Cosmographicum,* 1596), he worked as assistant to T. Brahe (1600), succeeding him as court mathematician to Holy Roman Emperor Rudolph II. His first two laws of planetary motion were described in his *Astronomia Nova* (1609); the first describes the elliptical orbits of the planets, and the second explains the planets' faster motion when near the sun. Kepler's third law states that planets' velocities are directly related to their solar distance. In 1627, he completed the Rudolphine Tables, begun by Brahe, which enabled scientists to determine planetary positions at any time, past, present, and future. He wrote the first science fiction story (1631), about a trip to the moon. A noted supporter of the Copernican heliocentric view of the solar system, Kepler developed astronomical theories that became the basis for work by I. Newton and others.

Kerensky, Aleksandr Feodorovich 1881–1970. Russian revolutionary. He took part in the February Revolution (1917) that toppled the tsarist government, and served as premier of the Provisional Government from July until the Bolshevik October Revolution.

Kerensky Offensive *See* **June Offensive.**

Kern, Jerome 1885–1945. American composer noted for his scores for many musicals. His *Show Boat* had a major influence on later musicals.

Kerouac, Jack (~, Jean-Louis) 1922–69. American novelist. A leader of the Beat movement, Kerouac is known best for his novel *On The Road.*

Kesselring, Albert 1887–1960. German field marshal, one of A. Hitler's top commanders. He led air operations in Poland, Russia, and the West, and was commander in chief of operations in Italy (1943) during WW II.

Kett's Rebellion Brief revolt (1549) near Norwich, England. Driven by the staggering economic inflation, Robert Kett led a short-lived agrarian revolt that was brutally suppressed. About 1,000 rebels were executed.

Key, Francis Scott 1779–1843. American poet, author of *The Star-Spangled Banner.* Key's poem, inspired by the British attack on Ft. McHenry (1814) during the War of 1812, was set to music and became the US national anthem (1931).

Keynes, John Maynard, 1st baron of Tilton 1883–1946. British economist whose views have influenced the economic policies of many governments. He wrote *The General Theory of Employment, Interest, and Money,* which advocated government intervention in solving the unemployment problem. A delegate to the Bretton Woods Conference (1944), he played a key role in establishing the International Monetary Fund.

KGB Russian political security police force. Created in 1954, it functioned as an espionage agency as well as a force against internal subversion and domestic dissidence in the former USSR. (*See also* GPU.)

Khafre (Chephren) c2558–2533 BC. Ancient Egyptian king of the 4th dynasty. He built the second pyramid at Giza and the Sphinx.

Khair ed-Din *See* **Barbarossa II.**

Khalifa, the *See* **Abd Allah.**

Khalji Dynasty *See* **Delhi Sultanate.**

Khan *See* **Mongol Empire.**

khanate of Khiva Former khanate in south-central Asia, ruled by the Uzbeks. It flourished from the 16th cent. until its conquest by Russia (1873). The area is now part of Turkmenia and Uzbekistan.

Khanbalik *See* **Beijing.**

Khartoum, Battle of Battle (1885) between British forces and the forces of the Mahdi, at Khartoum, Sudan. The British were besieged at Khartoum and were finally (Jan. 26) overwhelmed, and British general C. Gordon and all his garrison were killed. The battle is one of the great military engagements of British history.

Khazars (Chazars) Turkic people who ruled a powerful empire (c6th–10th cents.) located west of the Volga and north of the Black Sea in what is now southeastern USSR. With its capital at Itil, at the mouth of the Volga, the Khazar Empire controlled trade between Byzantium and the East and between the Arab Empire and Slavic peoples to the north. By the 8th cent., the Khazar ruling class had embraced Judaism and entered into close relations with the Byzantines. The empire fell (965) to invading Russian armies of Sviatoslav, duke of Kiev, and thereafter ceased to be a power.

Khedive Ismail *See* **Ismail Pasha.**

Khmielnicki, Bogdan (Chmelnitsky, Bogdan) 1593–1657. Zaporozhe Cossack leader. He led the rebellion of the Ukrainians against Polish domination (1648–54). With Russian aid, he successfully resisted Polish armies, and, in 1654, the Ukraine was declared an autonomous Russian protectorate.

Khmer Empire Ancient empire of southeast Asia located in what are now Cambodia, Thailand, and Laos. Established in the 6th cent., it rose to prominence in the 9th to 15th cents., during which time Buddhism, Hinduism, Sanskrit literature, and other elements of Indian culture flourished in the region. The empire reached its height in the 12th and 13th cents., when the cities of Angkor Wat and Angkor Thom were built. Its decline began (14th cent.) with repeated invasions by Chams and Thais. The capture (1432) of Angkor Thom by the Thais marked the end of Khmer power in the region.

Khmer Rouge (Red Cambodians) Cambodian Communists. Supported by the Vietcong, the insurgent group overthrew the government of Lon Nol (1975), and, after a bloody rule, was in turn overthrown by a Vietnamese-backed faction (1978–79).

Khomeini, Ruhollah, Ayatollah 1900–89. Iranian religious leader, a Muslim fundamentalist, and virtual dictator of Iran from Jan. 31, 1979 as a result of the Iranian revolution. Long exiled in Iraq and France during the regime of Shah Muhammad Reza Pahlavi, he returned to tumultuous popular acclaim in Iran after nearly a year of massive violent protests had resulted in the shah's abdication and departure (Jan. 16, 1979). It soon became clear that successive governments and officials acted only on the sufferance of the Ayatollah, even when pledged to the idea of an Islamic republic. He instituted a puritanical and repressive regime opposed to all Western influence and increasingly dominated by religious leaders. Declining to take responsibility for actual government, even though his power was absolute, he contributed to increasing turmoil and chaos, especially after Iraq's military attack on Iran on Sept. 22, 1980. In addition, mob violence led to the seizure by Iranian militants of the US embassy (Nov. 4, 1979) and the resulting hostage crisis (*q.v.*), which was actively exploited by the Khomeini government. Khomeini refused peace overtures in the bloody Iran-Iraq War, despite heavy Iranian losses and economic hardship, until 1988. Then just before his death in 1989, he sparked an international controversy by calling for the death of author Salmon Rushdie for writing *The Satanic Verses,* a book Khomeini believed offended Muslims.

Khorezm Region of ancient Persia, now part of Turkmenia and Uzbekistan. Once part of Cyrus the Great's empire, it became independent in the 12th cent. It was conquered by Genghis Khan (1220), Tamerlane (1378), and by the Uzbeks (16th cent.), who established an independent Uzbek state called the khanate of Khiva (*q.v.*).

Khosru I *d.* 579. Persian king (531–579). He expanded his empire east to the Indus River, and conquered parts of the Byzantine Empire. He encouraged culture and instituted reforms.

Khosru II *d.* 628. Persian king (590–628). After being usurped, Khosru regained the throne with the aid of Byzantine emperor Maurice. After Maurice's murder (602), Khosru turned against the Byzantines, but was defeated by Heraclius I.

Khrushchev, Nikita Sergeyevich 1894–1971. Russian Communist leader, first secretary of the Communist Party of the Soviet Union (1953–64) and premier (1958–64). He joined (1918) the Communist party and rose through the ranks to serve J. Stalin in the Great Purge. A member of the ruling Politburo from 1959, he won the power struggle that erupted after Stalin's death (1953) and that year replaced G. Malenkov as the party's first secretary. His long tenure during the Cold War era was marked by his de-Stalinization program (1956), Russian intervention in the Hungarian Revolution (1956), erection of the Berlin Wall (1961), the U-2 incident, failed Five-Year Plans, and the Cuban Missile Crisis (1962). His ouster (Oct., 1964) was brought on by failures in the Cuban crisis and agricultural production, as well as deteriorating relations with China.

Khufu (Cheops) c2589–c2566 BC. Ancient Egyptian king of the 4th dynasty. He built the great pyramid at Giza.

Khwarazm *See* **Khorezm.**

Khyber Pass Steep mountain pass on the border of Pakistan and Afghanistan. It has long been a commercial route to India as well as an invasion route for such conquerors as Alexander the Great and Tamerlane. It also was used by British forces during the Anglo-Afghan Wars.

Kiangsi soviet *See* **Jiangxi soviet.**

Kickapoo Indians North American Indian tribe, once located in the northern Midwest. After the massacre (c1765) of the Illinois Indians, in which the Kickapoo took part, they occupied lands in Illinois. They aided the British in the American Revolution, fought with Chief Tecumseh against the Americans in the War of 1812, and, after ceding their lands to the US, took part in the Black Hawk War (1831–32). Forced to leave Illinois, they resettled in Kansas.

Kid, Thomas *See* **Kyd, Thomas.**

Kidd, William c1645–1701. British privateer and pirate, known as Captain Kidd. Through numerous legends and stories he has come to be a prominent figure in pirate lore.

Kido Koin (ˉ, Takayoshi) 1833–77. Japanese statesman. He helped to overthrow the Japanese shogunate (1868) and restore imperial rule. He subsequently helped to end feudalism in Japan and institute constitutional government.

Kiel, Treaty of Peace settlement (Jan. 14, 1814) between Denmark and Sweden during the Napoleonic Wars. Denmark, an ally of France, was forced to surrender Norway to Sweden, thus further declining as a European power.

Kierkegaard, Sören 1813–55. Danish philosopher and religious writer whose works had a tremendous influence on the development of modern existentialism. Kierkegaard opposed the philosophical system of the dialectic advanced by G. Hegel and held that man's existence must be governed by his own conscious choice. He also advanced the theory that in religion "truth is subjectivity." His works include *Either/Or, Philosophical Fragments,* and *Works of Love.*

Kiesinger, Kurt Georg 1904–88. German politician. As chancellor of West Germany (1966–69), he continued the pro-West policies of K. Adenauer and L. Erhard.

Kimhi, David 1160?–1235? Jewish scholar believed to have lived and died in Narbonne, France. His grammar and lexicon were the leading works in their field for centuries.

Kim Il-sung (~ Song Ju) 1912– . Resistance leader during the Japanese occupation of Korea and leader of the Democratic People's Republic of Korea (North Korea) since 1948. He served first as premier (1948–72) and then president (1972–). *See also* Korea, 1948– .

Kimitake Hiraoka *See* **Mishima, Yukio.**

Kim Song Ju *See* **Kim Il-sung.**

Kindi (Al-Kindi) *fl.* 9th cent. Arab philosopher. He translated Aristotle's work into Arabic and attempted to reconcile Aristotelian and Neoplatonist thought. His extensive writings dealt with medicine, astrology, and mathematics.

king Designation given to the male ruler of a nation or state. The title is generally hereditary.

King, Ernest 1878–1956. US chief of naval operations during WW II, naval strategist, and often considered the greatest naval commander of the 20th century. A graduate of the US Naval Academy (1901), King served on the staff of the commander in chief of the Atlantic Fleet during WW I. During the 1930s, he became a leading proponent of naval aviation and helped bring about the rapid expansion of the navy's air arm, including the aircraft carriers and planes that played such an important role in WW II. Named commander in chief of the Atlantic Fleet (1940), King became commander in chief of the US Fleet (1941) and chief of naval operations (1942). As such he played a leading role in the US Navy's successful fight against the Japanese in the Pacific, in the Allied naval war against German U-boats in the Battle of the Atlantic, and in the development and use of the Navy's amphibious fleet in the Pacific and European theaters. King retired in 1945, though he continued to serve in an advisory capacity.

King, Martin Luther, Jr. 1929–68. American civil rights leader renowned for his use of nonviolent resistance in the fight for racial equality. A minister in Montgomery, Alabama, he led a successful boycott opposing segregated city buses (1956), and organized the Southern Christian Leadership Conference. One of the leading figures in the black civil rights movement, he led the massive March on Washington, D.C. (1963). King was awarded the Nobel Peace Prize in 1964. He was assassinated Apr. 4, 1968 in Memphis, Tennessee.

King, William Lyon Mackenzie 1874–1950. Canadian Liberal party leader and prime minister (1921–26, 1926–30, 1935–48). A specialist on labor, he was first elected to Parliament in 1908 and became Liberal party leader in 1919. During his long tenure as prime minister, he guided Canada through WW II, entered into defense alliances with the US by the Ogdensburg Declaration (1940) and Hyde Park Declaration (1941), and took part in the United Nations Charter conferences (1945).

King Cotton Term once used in the US South to express the value, both political and economic, of the southern cotton crop in the years before the American Civil War. Believers in the notion of King Cotton held that the importance of cotton to Britain would guarantee the South's success if it were ever forced to secede from the Union. Senator J. Hammond made it the subject of a famous speech before the US Senate (Mar. 4, 1858).

kingdom of *See under names inverted, as in* **Castile, kingdom of.**

King George's War (1744–48). American phase of the War of the Austrian Succession in Europe. It was an outgrowth of colonial rivalries between France and Britain, both of which then had interests in North America, and it was the third of four so-called French and Indian Wars (*q.v.*). The French began hostilities by capturing a British fort located off Nova Scotia. Spurred on by colonists in Massachusetts, the northern

British colonies mustered an army of 4,000 militiamen. With the aid of British warships, they captured the heavily defended French fort at Louisburg, Nova Scotia (1745). Two subsequent attempts (1746, 1747) by French fleets failed to retake Nova Scotia. The French and their Indian allies launched raids into the British colonies, while the British were successful against the French in the West Indies. The war was ended by the Treaty of Aix-la-Chapelle (1748), which restored conquered territories.

King Philip's War   War (1675–76) between New England colonists and Indian tribes in the region. The bloody war cost the lives of hundreds of colonists and resulted in the dispersal of New England tribes to the West. Relations between colonists and Indians were seriously eroded by the Pequot War (1637) and expansion of white settlements on Indian lands. The Indians formed a confederacy under King Philip, son of the Indian leader Massasoit, but they maintained peaceful relations until Colonials executed three Wampanoag tribesmen. War broke out with an Indian raid (June, 1675) on a border settlement. Thereafter dozens of Colonial settlements from Connecticut to Maine were raided and burned. The Colonial militia retaliated in kind against Wampanoag, Narragansett, and Nipmuck villages. The war ended with the death (Aug., 1676) of King Philip.

King's law *See* **Griffenfeld, Peder Schumacher, Count.**

Kingsley, Charles 1819–75.   English author and clergyman whose novels reflected his concern for social issues of the day. He was a leading figure in the Christian Socialism movement.

King's Men *See* **Chamberlain's Men.**

Kings Mountain, Battle of   Battle (Oct. 7, 1780) of the Carolina Campaign (*q.v.*) in the American Revolution, at Kings Mountain, South Carolina. A decisive American victory over Loyalist forces, it contributed to the final British defeat.

King's Peace (Peace of Antalcidas)   Peace agreement (387 BC) between Sparta, Persia, Athens, Corinth and others. Sparta, simultaneously fighting a war against Persia and against an alliance of Greek city-states (Corinthian War, 395–387 BC), negotiated this peace with Persian king Artaxerxes II. By its terms, Greek cities in the west were declared to be autonomous, while those in Asia Minor were to belong to Persia, with Sparta enforcing the terms of the peace. Persia forced (386) Athenian acceptance of the peace by a naval blockade, and thereafter dominated the region as it had before the Corinthian War. This led to new rebellions and Sparta's eventual defeat (371) by Thebes.

King William's War   American colonial war (1689–97) fought by Britain against France in North America. An extension of the War of the League of Augsburg against French king Louis XIV, it is considered the first of the French and Indian Wars. War began with a naval attack on Quebec (1690) by the British. The French and their Indian allies, led by Count Frontenac, then launched attacks on Schenectady, New York, Salmon Falls, New Hampshire, and Casco Bay, in Maine. The New England colonies in turn raised a militia, led by Sir W. Phips, which captured (May 11, 1690) Port Royal in French Acadia. British colonists subsequently attacked Quebec, but were unable to take it. Thereafter, the French and British and their respective Indian allies conducted raids on border settlements. The Treaty of Ryswick ended the war and provided for restoration of all conquered territories.

Kinsey, Alfred Charles 1894–1956.   American zoologist, known best for his studies of human sexual behavior.

Kioto *See* **Kyōto.**

Kipchak khanate *See* **Golden Horde.**

Kipling, Rudyard 1865–1936.   English author, one of England's leading writers in the late 19th and early 20th cents. Much of his work reflects England's history as a colonial empire. His works included *Barrack-Room Ballads* (1892, collected poems), *The Jungle Book* (1894), and *Kim* (1901). Kipling was the first English writer awarded the Nobel Prize for Literature (1907).

Kirby-Smith, Edmund *See* **Smith, Edmund Kirby.**

Kircher, Athanasius 1601?–80.   German Jesuit and scientist. His work with microscopes led him to believe that disease was caused by invisible bodies. He is credited with the invention of the magic lantern, an early slide projector.

Kirchhoff, Gustav Robert 1824–87.   German physicist, noted for his contributions to spectrum analysis, thermodynamics, and electricity. With R. Bunsen, he discovered the elements cesium and rubidium.

Kirchner, Ernst Ludwig 1880–1938. German painter and graphic artist. He was one of the founders of Die Brücke, a German expressionist art movement.

Kirghizia (*formerly* Kirgiz Soviet Socialist Republic) Independent state located on China's western border and now a member of the Commonwealth of Independent States. Nomadic Kirghiz, a people of Mongolian stock, inhabited the region from the 7th cent. Russia annexed Kirghizia as part of Russian Turkistan (1864) and between 1917 and 1921, the inhabitants fought against the Bolsheviks. A famine in 1921–22 killed a half million Kirghiz, and in 1924 Kirghizia was made part of the Soviet Union. It became an autonomous republic (1926) and a constituent republic (1936). Ethnic violence erupted in Osh, which has a predominately Uzbek population, during June 1990 and spread to the capital (Frunze) soon afterward. Troops were called in, but the ethnic violence continued. Following the failed Soviet coup, Kirghizia declared its independence and joined the Commonwealth of Independent States (Dec. 21, 1991).

Kirke, Sir David 1596?–1654? English trader and adventurer. He captured Quebec (1629) and served as governor of Newfoundland.

Kirov, Sergei Mironovich 1888–1934. Russian Communist leader. His assassination marked the beginning of the Stalinist purges of the 1930s.

Kisfaludy, Károly 1788–1830. Hungarian dramatist, considered the founder of Hungarian national drama. Among his best-known works is the play *Tatars in Hungary.*

Kish Ancient Mesopotamian city in Iraq, east of Babylon. According to ancient legend, it was the site of the first Sumerian capital after the Great Flood.

Kishi Nobusuke 1896–1987. Japanese prime minister (1957–60). His support of a controversial US–Japanese security treaty caused widespread protest and led to his resignation.

Kissinger, Henry Alfred 1923– . German-American political scientist, US secretary of state (1973–77) under presidents R. Nixon and G. Ford. He figured prominently in the Nixon administration's efforts to find a solution to the Vietnam War. Following the Arab-Israeli War (1973), Kissinger instituted his so-called shuttle diplomacy, in which he traveled between the Egyptian and Israeli capitals in an attempt to negotiate an agreement between the two countries. He was awarded the Nobel Peace Prize in 1973.

Kitasato, Shibasaburo 1852–1931. Japanese physician and bacteriologist. He developed an antitoxin for tetanus (with E. Behring) and identified, independently of A. Yersin, the bacillus causing bubonic plague (1894).

Kit-Cat Club London club of the early 18th cent. It was founded by leading Whigs and included well-known literary personages among its members.

Kitchen Cabinet Group of unofficial advisers to US president A. Jackson during his first term of office (1829–33). Composed of editors of important newspapers and Jackson's political associates, the group came to replace regular cabinet officers and advisers in formulating Jackson's policies. Of diminished importance after the cabinet reorganization (1831), the group included among others Amos Kendall (1789–1869), Francis P. Blair (1791–1876), Duff Green (1791–1875), John H. Eaton (1790–1856), and M. Van Buren.

Kitchen Debate Widely publicized exchange between US vice-president R. Nixon and Soviet premier N. Khrushchev that took place (1959) while the two men were visiting an American exhibit of a model American kitchen. The two vigorously argued the merits of the American and Soviet systems before the accompanying reporters and media representatives. Nixon later cited this impromptu "debate" as proof of his ability to deal with the Soviets.

Kitchener, Horatio Herbert Kitchener, 1st earl 1850–1916. British field marshal and statesman. He conquered the Sudan and reoccupied Khartoum (1898), and was chief of staff in the South African War. As secretary of war (1914–16), he greatly expanded Britain's military forces.

Kittredge, George Lyman 1860–1941. American scholar and educator. An authority on Shakespeare, Chaucer, and Malory, he taught at Harvard (1888–1936) and had a great influence on the teaching of English.

Kitty Hawk Village in northeastern North Carolina. Nearby is Kill Devil Hill, where the Wright brothers made their first successful powered flight (1903).

Kléber, Jean Baptiste 1753–1800. French general. He campaigned in the French Revolutionary Wars, suppressed the Royalist rebellion in the Vendée (1793), and commanded French forces in Egypt.

Klee, Paul 1879–1940. Swiss abstract artist, whose many works are noted for their innovative style, subtle humor, and use of color.

Kleist, Heinrich von 1777–1811. German poet and dramatist, considered one of the great German dramatists of the 19th cent.

Klimt, Gustav 1862–1918. Austrian painter, founder of the Vienna Secession school of painting. His early works typified late 19th cent. academic painting, but a bolder style emerged later. He founded the Vienna Secession (1897), a group of artists who rejected accepted art forms, preferring an Art Nouveau style of decorative painting.

Klondike Region of the Yukon Territory in northwestern Canada. Discovery of gold here in 1896 led to the gold rush (1897–99).

Kloster-Zeven, Convention of *See* **Convention of Kloster-Zeven.**

Kluck, Alexander von *See* **Marne, Battle of the.**

KMT *See* **Guomindang.**

Knickerbocker American Colonial term for Dutch colonists in New York State. They were so named after the Harmen Knickerbocker family, which settled near Albany (c1674).

Knights Hospitalers (Knights of St. John) (Knights of Jerusalem) (*in full* Order of the Hospital of St. John of Jerusalem) Important religious and military order founded (c1099) in Jerusalem. The order was created by Gérard de Martignes and confirmed (1153) by Pope Eugenius III. Dedicated to the healing and protection of pilgrims to the Holy Land, the order grew rich and powerful during the Crusades. Grateful knights, healed at the order's hospital, made bequests of money and land, while the knights of the order undertook military operations in its name. The misfortunes of the Crusades and the rise of Turkish power, however, forced the order to relocate several times after the fall of Jerusalem (1187): to Acre (1189); to Cyprus (1291); to Rhodes (1310), which they conquered; and to Malta (1530). The order declined in importance after being driven out of Rhodes. Napoleon's conquest of Malta (1798) effectively brought the order to an end. In 1879 it was reorganized and revived as a charitable organization.

Knights of Calatrava Oldest Spanish military and religious order. Established by Cistercian monks to protect the city of Calatrava against the Moors (1158), the order subsequently gained control of large territories. It remained powerful until King Ferdinand and Queen Isabella took it (1493) under the authority of the crown.

Knights of Jerusalem *See* **Knights Hospitalers.**

Knights of Labor US labor organization, founded (1869) in Philadelphia. Originally a secret organization under the leadership of Uriah S. Stephens (1821–82), it included workers of all kinds (as opposed to craft organizations) and sought to replace capitalism with workers' cooperatives. Secrecy was abolished (1881), and under the leadership of Terence V. Powderly (1849–1924) the group reached its greatest membership, some 700,000. In 1886, after a wave of strikes in the US and the disastrous Haymarket Square Riot, membership in the group began a rapid decline. By the end of the century, it was largely replaced by the American Federation of Labor, and was disbanded in 1917.

Knights of Saint Crispin Early US trade union. Founded (1867) to organize shoemakers, a major union in the US. By 1878, however, most of its members had joined the Knights of Labor.

Knights of St. John *See* **Knights Hospitalers.**

Knights of the Golden Circle Secret order of supporters of the South during the American Civil War. Founded (1854) in Ohio as a pro-slavery group, it turned to supporting the Confederacy after the outbreak of war. Active mainly in Ohio, Illinois, Indiana, Missouri, and Kentucky, the group was composed largely of Democrats who wanted to end the war (called Copperheads). In 1864, the group became known as the Sons of Liberty.

Knights of the Temple of Solomon *See* **Knights Templars.**

Knights Templars (Templars) (Knights of the Temple of Solomon) Important religious military order founded (c1119) during the Crusades. Organized by Hugh de Payens at Jerusalem to protect Christian pilgrims from Muslim attacks, the order was confirmed (1128) by Pope Honorius III. It subsequently grew into a powerful army in service against the Muslims and, through bequests, gained considerable wealth and lands in Europe. After the failure of the Crusades, the Templars became a powerful banking group and thereby aroused opposition by the European nobility. French king Philip IV, with consent of Pope Clement V, began persecutions

(1307) of the Templars. By 1314, their property had been confiscated, and the order ceased to exist.

Knights' War Unsuccessful rebellion of German knights (1522–23) during the Reformation. The knights, led by F. von Sickengen, supported the Reformation and sought to ensure their ancient privileges.

Knossos *See* **Cnossus.**

Know-Nothing party (American party) Short-lived US political party active in the mid-1800s. Originally a secretive group, members answered questions about its activities by saying they knew nothing (hence the name). Its major aim, however, was promotion of American nativism, in reaction to the rising tide of European immigration. The party became a national organization (1845) and made significant gains in the 1854 elections in New York, Massachusetts, and other states. The secretive elements were abolished in 1855, but the party split the same year over the slavery issue. It declined rapidly during the remainder of the decade, and its presidential candidate, M. Fillmore, carried only Maryland in 1856. In the North, many party members subsequently became Republicans.

Knox, Frank (˜, William Franklin) 1874–1944. American newspaper publisher. He was an unsuccessful Republican vice-presidential candidate (1936), but served as US secretary of the navy (1940–44) under President F. Roosevelt in a Democratic administration.

Knox, Henry 1750–1806. American officer in the American Revolution. He directed the removal of artillery from Fort Ticonderoga to Boston, where it was used to force British evacuation. Knox served as first US secretary of war (1785–94).

Knox, John c1514–72. Scottish reformer and founding father of the Church of Scotland. After the execution (1546) of his mentor, G. Wishart, he joined a group of Scottish Presbyterian conspirators who had avenged Wishart's death. Eventually captured by Catholic forces, he was rescued from slavery and thereafter served the Protestant cause in England and on the Continent. With the beginning of the Scottish Reformation (1557), Knox returned to Scotland (1559) to lead the fight against Catholic armies. Following the establishment of the Church of Scotland, Knox and others wrote the *First Book of Discipline,* setting forth the basic organization of the church.

Knox lost many supporters with the accession (1561) of Mary, Queen of Scots. He continued to uphold his beliefs and resolutely opposed Mary. His efforts were rewarded when the Protestant nobles forced her abdication (1567).

Knox, Philander Chase 1853–1921. American politician. As US attorney general (1901–04), he led government prosecution of trusts. As secretary of state (1909–13), he defended American financial interests abroad through what has been termed "dollar diplomacy."

Knox, William Franklin *See* **Knox, Frank.**

Knut *See* **Canute.**

Kobo-Daishi *See* **Kukai.**

Koch, Robert 1843–1910. German bacteriologist, a leading figure in the founding of bacteriology. His contributions include the discovery of the organisms causing anthrax (1876) and those causing tuberculosis (1882).

Kodály, Zoltán 1882–1967. Hungarian composer and expert on folk music. After studying music in Budapest, he traveled throughout the country collecting folk music. With B. Bartók, he amassed thousands of folk songs and dances, publishing them between 1906 and 1921. He was also widely acclaimed as a composer and a music educator.

Koffka, Kurt 1886–1941. German psychologist. With W. Köhler and M. Wertheimer, he founded the school of Gestalt psychology.

Koguryŏ Ancient Korean kingdom, founded c2d–1st cents. BC. In 668 BC, it was overrun by the Chinese T'ang and Korean Silla dynasties, and was incorporated into the kingdom of Silla.

Kohathites *See* **Levites.**

Kohl, Helmut 1930– . Chancellor of the Federal Republic of Germany (1982–90) and first chancellor of united Germany (1990–). After serving in West Germany's state legislature (from 1959), Kohl was elected chairman of his party, the Christian Democratic Union (1973). He became chancellor of West Germany (1982) and worked to reduce government spending while strengthening ties to NATO. As Communist governments began to collapse in Eastern Europe (1989–90), Kohl pushed for the rapid reunification of East and West Germany. In the first parliamentary elections following German reunification, Kohl was elected chancellor (Dec. 1990).

Köhler, Wolfgang 1887–1967. Estonian-born psychologist who, with K. Koffka and M.

Wertheimer, founded the Gestalt school of psychology.

Kokoschka, Oskar 1886–1980.   Austrian painter and writer and leading figure in expressionism. He is noted for his expressionist landscapes and dramas.

Kolchak, Aleksandr Vasilyevich 1874–1920. Russian admiral and leader (1918–20) of anti-Bolshevik forces in Siberia during the Russian civil war.

Kolin, Battle of Austro-Prussian battle (June 18, 1757) during the Seven Years' War, at Kolin, now in Czechoslovakia. A force of 53,000 Austrians under L. von Daun defeated some 60,000 Prussians under Frederick the Great, raising the Prussian siege of Prague and forcing Frederick to evacuate Bohemia.

Konbaung dynasty *See* **Alaungpaya; Burmese War (third).**

Königgrätz, Battle of (Sadowa, ˜)   Decisive battle (July 3, 1866) near Königgrätz, now in Czechoslovakia, ending the Seven Weeks' War between Prussia and Austria. Prussian troops commanded by H. von Moltke defeated the Austrian army under Ludwig August von Benedek (1804–81). Austrian casualties were about 40,000, compared to Prussian losses of fewer than 15,000. The victory gave Prussia dominance over Germany.

Königsmark, Countess Maria Aurora 1668?–1728. Swedish noblewoman, mistress of King Augustus II of Poland and Saxony, and mother of Maurice, comte de Saxe.

Konoye, Fumimaro, Prince 1891–1945.   Japanese statesman. As premier of Japan (1937–39, 1940–41) he helped to form the Axis alliance with Germany and Italy.

Koowescoowe *See* **Ross, John.**

Koran (Qur'an)   The sacred book of Islam. A compilation of the revelations received by Muhammad, it is one of the world's most influential books and the major unifying force in the Islamic religion. The authorized text was written down (c650) by Muhammad's secretary, Zaid ibn Thabit, by order of the caliph Uthman. Divided into 114 chapters (suras), the Koran sets forth religious doctrine and codes concerning conduct of the followers of Islam. Accepted as the word of God, the Koran is above doubt or criticism in the Islamic world.

Korea Country occupying a large peninsula in eastern Asia, divided after WW II into North

Korea (Democratic People's Republic of Korea, capital at Pyongyang) and South Korea (Republic of Korea, capital at Seoul). The population of the North is 23,059,000 and the South is 43,919,000. Korea has been influenced by neighboring China since ancient times and was reduced to a Chinese vassal state in the 17th cent. Japan colonized Korea in the early 1900s and held it until the end of WW II. The Soviets and the US established zones of occupation in 1945 and North and South Korea have been under separate governments ever since. Since the Korean War (*q.v.*) there have been talks on reunification, but as of 1992 no agreement had been reached. Key events in the history of Korea include:

12TH CENT. BC   Ki Tse, Chinese feudal lord, founded first known kingdom in Korea; had fled China after overthrow of Shang dynasty.

1ST CENT. BC–7TH CENT. AD   Three Kingdoms period: rise of three separate native kingdoms (Koguryo, Silla, Paekche) on Korean Peninsula.

4TH CENT. AD   Buddhism introduced.

670–935   Kingdom of Silla gained control over peninsula and formed first unified Korean kingdom; Confucianism and other elements of Chinese culture introduced.

935–1392   Koryo kingdom established control over Korea; distinct Korean culture developed.

13TH CENT.   Korea invaded by Mongols from China; Mongols gained control over Korea.

1392   Yi Songgye founded Yi dynasty in Korea (ruled until 1910); established capital at Seoul, ended Mongol control, and established Confucianism.

1592–98   Japanese emperor Hideyoshi unsuccessfully attempted to conquer Korea; Koreans drove out Japanese with Chinese help.

1637   Chinese reduced Korea to vassal state following series of invasions.

17TH–19TH CENTS.   Korea entered period of extreme isolationism; Hermit Kingdom, as it was called, permitted only Chinese influence.

1876   Japan forced Korea to agree to a commercial treaty, thus ending period of Korean isolation; opened Korea to trade agreements with US and other Western nations.

1894–95   First Sino-Japanese War fought with China; led to increasing Japanese influence over Korea; concluding treaty of Shimonoseki forced China to recognize Korean independence (now increasingly under Japanese influence).

1904–05 Japanese forces occupied Korea during Russo-Japanese War, thus increasing Japan's hold on Korea.

1905 Korea declared a Japanese protectorate.

1910–45 Korea part of Japanese empire; annexed in 1910, it was thereafter exploited by Japanese; underwent rapid industrialization.

1919 Japanese resorted to harsh measures to quell rebellion in Korea (Apr.); afterward shifted from military to civilian government in Korea, promising greater autonomy.

1945 Korea divided at end of WW II into two sectors; Soviet troops occupied sector north of 38th parallel; US forces occupied territory in south and suppressed a revolutionary movement there; plans called for reunification within five years.

1948 Soviet opposition to moves for reunification resulted in establishment (May 1) of People's Republic of Korea in north and (Aug. 15) Republic of Korea in south; neither North nor South joined UN.

1948–60 Syngman Rhee in office as first elected president of Republic of Korea, following UN–supervised elections.

1948–72 Kim Il-sung (Kim Song Ju) premier in North Korea.

1949 US and Soviets withdrew troops from Korea.

1950 North Korean forces invaded south (June 25), instigating Korean war (1950–53).

1953 South Korea signed mutual defense treaty with US.

1958 Chinese completed withdrawal of troops from North Korea.

1960 Protest march (Apr. 19) in South Korea led to bloodbath as police shot at student demonstrators; civil unrest spread throughout South Korea, forcing Syngman Rhee to resign.

1961 Military junta seized power (May) in South Korea in bloodless coup; Gen. Park Chung Hee became leader of military government.

1963–79 Park Chung Hee president in South Korea; fostered economic growth (based on exports) and buildup of military.

1968 North Koreans seized US intelligence ship *Pueblo* (Jan. 23), provoking international incident.

1971 First talks between North and South Korean Red Cross societies; by 1972 both sides agreed to seek reunification through negotiations; talks suspended in 1973.

1972 President Park imposed martial law in South Korea (Oct. 17); National Assembly dissolved; political activities banned.

1972 Constitutional revisions adopted (Nov. 21); gave President Park unlimited power and term of office.

1972 Kim Il-sung elected president of North Korea (Dec. 28); remained in office into early 1990s, grooming his son Kim Jong Il as his successor; new constitution promulgated.

1974 President Park ordered measures to stifle growing opposition (Jan 8) in South Korea.

1974 Unsuccessful assassination attempt against President Park in Seoul (Aug.).

1974 First North Korean tunnel under the demilitarized zone discovered; two others discovered by 1978.

1977 US announced intention of withdrawing US troops from Korea; opposition to move later ended in reversal of plan.

1977 North Koreans shot down US helicopter that had accidentally crossed over into the north.

1977 South Koreans implicated in scandal involving bribery of US congressmen.

1979 Talks on reunification with north held (Jan.–Mar.), though little progress was made.

1979 Riots broke out after opposition leader expelled from Assembly (Oct.).

1979 South Korean president Park assassinated (Oct. 26) by head of the Korean intelligence agency; martial law imposed.

1979–80 Choi Kyu Hah installed as South Korean president; some political restrictions rescinded; Choi forced to resign (1980) as unrest mounted.

1980 Antigovernment unrest resulted in imposition (May 18) of total martial law in south.

1980 South Korean troops crushed antigovernment revolt by students and dissidents in city of Kwangju (June 21); some 200 persons killed.

1980 Major purge of government officials (July 9) directed at ending corruption in South Korea.

1980–88 Gen. Chun Doo Hwan in office (Sept. 1) as president of South Korea; his administration saw much of the decade-long period of high economic growth in South, during which the South rose to world's 12th largest trading nation.

1980 New constitution approved by South Korean voters (Oct. 22); would limit presidential powers and lift ban on political parties.

1981 Martial law lifted in South (Jan. 24) by President Chun Doo Hwan.

1983 South Korean airliner shot down by Soviets after straying over top secret military facility at Sakhalin Island off Siberian coast (Sept.).

1983 Bomb blast killed 17 South Korean officials in Rangoon, Burma (Oct.); North Korea blamed; Burma broke diplomatic relations with North over incident.

1985– Sporadic talks between North and South Korea held on reunification and various other issues from 1985; North often used annual US–South Korean military maneuvers as excuse for suspending talks, and actual progress on the central issue of reunification was slow through 1992.

1985–92 Escalating unrest in South Korea, as students, workers, and other groups protested with increasing frequency and violence.

1985 New Korea Democratic Party (NKDP) became South Korea's first major opposition party, following elections to new National Assembly; forced discussions with ruling Democratic Justice Party (DJP) on constitutional reforms.

1986 Possible coup attempt in North (Nov.); false reports of Kim Il-sung's assassination interpreted as possible sign of failed takeover.

1987 Massive protest against slow pace of constitutional reform in South (June); tens of thousands marched nationwide; talks on reform resumed.

1987 Constitutional reforms enacted in South (Oct.); provided for direct election of president, limited president to one term and curbed presidential powers, and banned military personnel from simultaneously holding public office.

1987 South Korean airline blew up in flight; 115 persons killed; South Korea blamed North, producing confession by alleged North Korean agent.

1988– Roh Tae-Woo, member of DJP, in office as South Korean president, following elections; his term marked by worsening unrest and end of South's economic boom.

1988 Protest demonstrations by students (May–Aug.).

1988 Talks between legislatures of North and South held at Panmunjom (Aug.); US meanwhile eased sanctions against North in effort to promote further talks.

1988 Olympics held in Seoul, South Korea (Sept.–Oct.); North boycotted the games.

1988 Former South Korean President Chun offered during nationwide TV address to repay public funds he misappropriated while president (Nov.).

1989–90 Former Communist-bloc nations in Eastern Europe established relations with South; relations with North cooled.

1989–90 Demonstrations, sometimes violent, by students, farmers, industrial workers, and others in South Korea during year.

1990 North denied reports it had program to build nuclear weapons (Feb.).

1990 South Korea's ruling DJP renamed Democratic Liberal Party (DLP) after merger with other parties (Feb.).

1990 New North Korean tunnel under DMZ found (Mar.).

1990 Kim Il-sung reelected president in North (Mar.).

1990 Antigovernment protest rally in Seoul joined by some 200,000 (July).

1990 Japanese government apologized to South Korean government for abuses during 1910–45; apologized to North in 1991, adding offer of reparations for abuses.

1990 South Korea's decade-long high growth rate halted by worldwide recession; South posted first trade deficit in five years.

1991 North and South Korea joined the UN (Sept.).

1991 North Korea reported developing atomic weapons (Oct.).

1992 Diplomatic ties established between South Korea and China.

1992 North and South Korean officials agreed to establish transportation links between their countries.

Korean War War (1950–53) between the North Koreans, backed by the Communist Chinese, and the South Koreans, backed by UN peace forces (principally US troops). Korea was ravaged by the war and there were some 4 million casualties (2 million of them civilians). The war was caused by various factors, including the Communists' desire to reunite Korea under their rule and the rise of Cold War tensions between Communist and non-Communist nations. Korea had been divided at the end of WW II, with Soviet forces occupying the territory north of the 38th parallel, and US forces to the south of it. Plans to reunite the country were never instituted. A Communist government was established in the north and a pro-Western government evolved in the south. Thus the Communist invasion of the south in 1950 became a part of the larger Cold War (*q.v.*) between the Communists and the US and its Western allies. In this context the war was a major test of the US policy of "containing" Communism. Key events in the war include:

1950   Communist forces from North Korea mounted full-scale invasion of south (June 25); UN called for measures to aid South Korea against the invasion.

1950   President H. Truman ordered US military to aid South Korea as part of UN police action (June 30).

1950   South Korean and US forces driven to small zone around Pusan, southeastern Korea (early Sept.).

1950   US Gen. D. MacArthur, commander of UN forces, launched amphibious landing at Inchon (Sept. 15), well to the north; forced North Koreans to retreat.

1950   Seoul retaken by UN forces (Sept. 26).

1950   UN forces followed retreating North Korean forces across 38th parallel; captured Pyongyang, North Korean capital (Oct. 19).

1950   UN forces occupied most of Korea and advanced to Yalu River, Korean border with China, despite warnings by Chinese; Chinese launched invasion into Korea (Nov. 26).

1951   Chinese forces captured Seoul (Jan. 4).

1951   UN forces recaptured Seoul (Mar. 14) after Communist advance faltered.

1951   Communists pushed back to lines roughly along the 38th parallel; Gen. MacArthur openly advocated new invasion across 38th parallel, and was removed (Apr. 11) as supreme commander by President Truman; MacArthur was succeeded by Gen. M. Ridgway.

1951   Communist spring offensive (from May 15) failed.

1951   Peace talks began (July 10) at Kaesong; reconvened at Panmunjom (Oct. 25).

1953   Armistice signed (July 27).

Kornilov, Lavr Georgyevich 1870–1918. Russian general, made commander in chief by A. Kerensky after the February Revolution (1917). He was dismissed, then arrested, for sending troops against Kerensky, and later led anti-Bolshevik forces.

Kortruk, Battle of *See* **Golden Spurs, Battle of the.**

Koryo Korean kingdom (935–1392) from which the name Korea is derived. During its existence the Korean Peninsula was unified and its capital established at Songjong (modern Kaesong).

Korzybski, Alfred (Habdank) 1879–1950. Polish-born American scientist who founded the linguistic system known as general semantics.

Kosciusko, Thaddeus 1746–1817. Polish general and champion of Polish independence. He fought with distinction against the British in the American Revolution, then fought unsuccessfully in Poland against the Russians (1792–93). After the second Partition of Poland (1793), he led a rebellion (1794) against both Russian and Prussian forces. This led to the third Partition of Poland and his imprisonment (1794–96). Thereafter he lived in the US, France, and Switzerland.

Kosovo, Battle of 1. Battle (June 20, 1389; by tradition, June 15) at Kosovo, in which the Ottoman forces of Murad I defeated a confederation of Slavic forces under Serbian prince Lazar I (*d.* 1389). Both Murad and Lazar were killed. 2. Battle (Oct. 16–17, 1448) at Kosovo, in which the Ottoman forces under Murad II defeated the Hungarian army of J. Hunyadi.

Kossuth, Lajos *See* **Kossuth, Louis.**

Kossuth, Louis (~, Lajos) 1802–94. Hungarian revolutionary, a radical leader in the Hungarian Revolution of 1848. He led the republic of Hungary briefly (1849), but was forced to resign in the face of Russian and Austrian intervention. He later continued revolutionary agitation while in exile.

Koster, Laurens Janszoon (Coster, ~) c1370–c1440. Dutch sexton, credited by some as being the inventor of printing with movable type. The controversy over whether he or J. Gutenberg first used movable type continues.

Kosygin, Aleksey Nikolayevich 1904–80. Russian statesman who succeeded N. Khrushchev as premier (1964–80). He joined the Communist party in 1927 and held various government positions under J. Stalin and Khrushchev. He played a major role in Soviet economic planning. As premier, he shared power with L. Brezhnev for a time but was gradually overshadowed.

Kowait *See* **Kuwait.**

Krebs, Sir Hans Adolf 1900–81. German-born English biochemist. With Fritz Albert Lipmann, he received the Nobel Prize in Physiology or Medicine in 1953 for his studies of the metabolic reaction process known as the citric acid, or Krebs, cycle.

Kremer, Gerhard *See* **Mercator, Gerardus.**

Kremlin Triangular citadel in Moscow, once a fortress and now the seat of the government of Russia. Originally constructed in 1156 and modified considerably thereafter, the Kremlin is surrounded by a wall topped by twenty towers. Inside are numerous buildings that were once churches, armories, and palaces, most of which are now used for government purposes (some of the churches are again in use). The center of tsarist government until 1712, when Peter the Great made St. Petersburg the capital, it became the seat of the revolutionary government in 1918. Within the Kremlin walls is the famous Great Bell (Tsar Bell), the world's largest. Red Square is located on the east side of the Kremlin.

Kreuger, Ivar 1880–1932. Swedish financier who attempted to build a world monopoly of the production of matches. The worldwide Great Depression caused his speculative venture to fail, and he committed suicide.

Kreutzer, Rodolphe 1766–1831. French composer and violinist noted for his 40 etudes for the violin. L. Beethoven dedicated his *Kreutzer Sonata* to him.

Krishnamurti, Jiddu 1895–1986. Indian religious philosopher. With Annie Besant, he founded the World Order of the Star, in which he was proclaimed the incarnation of the messianic Buddha. He renounced the claim and dissolved the order. From 1969 until his death he headed the Krishnamurti Foundation.

Kroeber, Alfred Louis 1876–1960. American anthropologist and authority on the Indians of southwestern US, Mexico, and Peru. His work is a major contribution to modern anthropology.

Kronstadt Rebellion Russian revolt (Mar., 1921), the first major revolt against Bolshevik rule after the Russian civil war. Headed by sailors from the Kronstadt naval base near Leningrad, it sought measures to ease the economic hardships caused by the civil war and Bolshevik rule. Though suppressed, it led to the institution of the New Economic Policy.

Kropotkin, Peter Alekseyevich, Prince 1842–1921. Russian anarchist and author, a leading figure in the development of anarchist theory.

Krüdener, Barbara Juliane von, Baroness 1764–1824. Russian novelist and mystic who for a time had great influence over Tsar Alexander I. She claimed to have inspired Alexander to conclude the Holy Alliance.

Kruger, Oom Paul *See* **Kruger, Stephanus Johannes Paulus.**

Kruger, Stephanus Johannes Paulus (~ Oom Paul) 1825–1904. South African statesman. Leader of the Transvaal independence movement, he served as president of the Transvaal (1883–1900) until the Boer defeat in the Boer War.

Kruger telegram Communication (Jan. 3, 1896) from German kaiser William II to Paulus Kruger, president of the Transvaal Republic, congratulating him on his victory over the British in the Jameson Raid (*q.v.*). The telegram greatly angered the British people.

Krupp, Alfred 1812–87. German steel magnate. He introduced modern production methods to Germany and manufactured heavy guns for Prussia in the Franco-Prussian War.

Krupp, Alfred Krupp von Bohlen und Halbach 1907–67. German industrialist, son of G. Krupp. During WW II, he employed concentration-camp victims as slave labor in Krupp factories, and confiscated property in the Nazi-occupied nations. He was imprisoned after the war (1948–51).

Krupp, Friedrich 1787–1826. German steel manufacturer. He founded the steel works at Essen (c1810) which later grew into the massive Krupp armaments and munitions empire.

Krupp, Friedrich Albert (Fritz) 1854–1902. German industrialist, son of A. Krupp. He greatly expanded the scope of Krupp interests.

Krupp, Gustav Krupp von Bohlen und Halbach 1870–1950. German industrialist. He adopted the name Krupp upon his marriage to Bertha Krupp, daughter of F. Krupp. He made Krupp the leading armaments manufacturer during WW I, supported the rise of A. Hitler, and helped Germany to rearm for WW II.

Krutch, Joseph Wood 1893–1970. American author and critic, noted for his drama criticism and for his writing on nature.

Krylov, Ivan Andreyevich 1768–1844. Russian fabulist. His fables in verse satirized contemporary Russian figures and attitudes and have had a lasting influence on Russian culture.

Kshatriya caste *See* **caste system.**

Kubitschek, Juscelino 1902– . Brazilian president (1956–61). A founding member of the Partido Social Democrático (PSD, Social Democratic party), he helped draft Brazil's 1946 constitution. Promising "fifty years of progress in five," he became president in 1956 and fostered a period of rapid economic growth and development. Under Kubitschek new highways were built and steel, oil, and electric power production all increased markedly, but with the cost of high inflation, increased foreign debt, and widespread corruption. His most ambitious project was the building of Brasilia, the country's new capital.

Kublai Khan c1215–94. Mongol emperor (1260–90), successor to his brother Mangu Khan, and grandson of Genghis Khan. He was founder of the Mongol Yuan dynasty in China. Following his election as emperor, he attacked northern China, and thus completed (1279) Mongol conquest (and reunification) of China. With his capital at Khanbalik, or Cambuluc (modern Beijing), he ruled China and nominally controlled a vast Mongol empire that stretched across Asia. His military expeditions against Korea and Burma were successful, but he failed in his attacks on Japan (1274–81) and Java (1293). He was a great builder, and the splendor of his court was recorded by M. Polo.

Kuchuk Kainarji, Treaty of Treaty (July 21, 1774) between Russia and the Ottoman Empire, ending the Russo-Turkish War of 1768–74. The treaty gave Russia Black Sea ports in the Crimea, opened Turkish waters to Russian ships, and gave Russia rights to represent Christians within the Ottoman Empire. The latter provision allowed Russia to proclaim itself protector of orthodox Christians there and facilitated the eventual takeover of Ottoman territories. In addition to ceding Crimean territories to Russia,

the treaty made the Ottoman khanate of Crimea independent, and restored Walachia and Moldavia to the Ottomans.

Kufa Former Arab city located south of Baghdad. Founded (638) by Caliph Omar I, it became seat of the Abbasid caliphate for a time (8th cent.) and was a major seat of Muslim culture. Repeatedly attacked from the 10th cent. on, it had practically disappeared by the 14th cent.

Kukai (Kobo-Daishi) 774–835. Japanese Buddhist priest and scholar. Kukai evolved the "True Word" Buddhist philosophy. He is credited with inventing the style in which Japanese is written.

Ku Klux Klan Secret terrorist organization formed (1867) in the US South to oppose Reconstruction and maintain white supremacy. The Klan originated in Tennessee under the leadership of Gen. N. Forrest and later was responsible for attacks on blacks and carpetbaggers. Forrest disbanded the Klan (1869), and the Force Bill (1870, 1871) effectively suppressed it. Reformed (1915) by William J. Simmons, the new Klan promoted anti-Catholic, anti-Semitic and white supremacist views and after WW I rose to power in many states, including those outside the South. The Klan declined (after 1925) and died out during the Depression. Revived again (1960s) under Robert Shelton, the Klan carried out attacks on civil rights workers in the South.

Kulikovo, Battle of Russian victory (Sept. 8, 1380) over forces of the Golden Horde. Though the Tatars later reconquered the Russians, the battle marked the turning point in the struggle against Tatar domination (from 1240). The Russians, led by Dmitri Ivanovich, prince of Moscow, met the Tatars, led by Mamay, leader of the western part of the Golden Horde, at Kulikovo, on the upper Don River. There were great losses on both sides, but the Tatars were forced to retreat, and did not return until 1382.

Kulturkampf German chancellor O. Bismarck's struggle (1871–83) to assert government control over the Roman Catholic church. Precipitated by the declaration (1870) of papal infallibility (which expanded papal powers at the expense of secular leaders), conflict between the church and state governments broke out in Germany and other European countries. In Germany, Bismarck had, by 1872, taken steps to limit Catholic influence, including expulsion of the Jesuits. He instituted the May, or Falk, Laws (May, 1873), which further limited church powers, and then mandated (1875) civil marriage services. Resistance by German clergymen and the Catholic Center party's 1878 election victory forced Bismarck to moderate. Some years after the death of Pope Pius IX (1878), he reached an accommodation with Pope Leo XIII.

Kun, Béla 1886–c1939. Hungarian Communist leader who briefly headed a soviet republic in Hungary (1919). Later a leader of the Comintern, he became a victim of the Stalinist purges of the 1930s.

Kunersdorf, Battle of Austro-Russian victory (Aug. 12, 1759) over Prussia during the Seven Years' War, at Kunersdorf, Poland. The battle left the Prussian army of Frederick the Great in complete disarray, but the allies failed to follow up their victory.

Kuomintang *See* **Guomindang.**

Kurdistan Mountain region including parts of Iran, Iraq, Syria, Turkey, and Soviet Armenia. Inhabited primarily by Kurds, it has been conquered successively by the Arabs, Seljuk Turks, Mongols, and Ottoman Turks. After WW I, the region was taken from Ottoman rule, and the Treaty of Sèvres (1920) called for establishment of a new Kurdish state. The Treaty of Lausanne (1923), which superseded the Treaty of Sèvres, made no such provision, and the region has since been the site of several Kurdish revolts.

Kurds *See* **Kurdistan.**

Kuropatkin, Aleksey Nikolayevich 1848–1925. Russian general. He fought in the Russo-Turkish War of 1877–78, served as minister of war (1898), and unsuccessfully commanded Russian troops in Manchuria (1904–05) in the Russo-Japanese War.

Kusana (Kushana) (Kushan) Descendants of the Yüeh-chi, who established a ruling dynasty over much of northern India, Afghanistan, and territories to the north from AD c78–220. They declined at about the time of the rise of the Sassanidae.

Kush (Cush) Egyptian name for an ancient African kingdom, located near the modern-day border between Sudan and Egypt. Founded at least as early as 2000 BC, this African kingdom came under Egyptian influence by c1500 BC, but with the decline of the Egyptian empire (8th cent. BC), armies from Kush overran Egypt. Kush then ruled Egypt until the mid-7th cent. BC, when Assyrian invaders took control of it.

Kush thereafter declined as a military power, but became a center of trade and culture.

Kutuzov, Mikhail Ilarionovich 1745–1813. Russian field marshal who commanded Russian forces during Napoleon's invasion of Russia (1812–13). He fought the French at Borodino, and defeated Napoleon through a policy of retreat and minor engagement.

Kuwait (Kowait) Independent Arab emirate, at the head of the Persian Gulf between Saudi Arabia and Iraq. The capital is Kuwait, the population is 2,024,000. The region camed under nominal Ottoman rule (16th to early 19th cent.) and Arab tribes migrated into the area during the 18th century. By agreement with the sheik of Kuwait (Jan. 23, 1899), it became a British protectorate, remaining so until its independence (June, 1961). The border with Saudi Arabia was negotiated by the British in 1922. Oil was discovered in Kuwait (1938, at the Burgan oil field), and the emirate has become a major exporter of oil, especially since the 1960s. Kuwait supported its Arab neighbors in the 1967 Arab-Israeli War, joined in the Arab oil embargo of the early 1970s, and condemned the Egyptian-Israeli treaty. The current emir, Sheikh Jaber al-Ahmad as Sabah, succeeded to the throne in 1977. The country suffered a serious financial crisis after an unofficial Kuwaiti stock exchange collapsed in 1982 and opposition to the government mounted until 1988 when the emir dissolved the National Assembly and began ruling by decree. Public pressure for return to a more democratic government continued into 1990. Meanwhile, Iranian terrorists engaged in a terror bombing campaign within Kuwait (1983–87) because of Kuwait's support for Iraq in the Iran-Iraq war. In 1987, US and British warships began operating in the Persian Gulf as convoy escorts after a series of Iranian attacks on Kuwaiti tankers. Then in July 1990, the Iran-Iraq war over, Iraqi President Saddam Hussein began making accusations against Kuwait and demanded monetary compensation. Ignoring attempts at a negotiated settlement, Iraq invaded Kuwait and began the Persian Gulf War (*q.v.*). The emir established a government-in-exile in Saudi Arabia, and on Aug. 8, Iraq formally annexed Kuwait. Iraqi occupation forces reportedly committed numerous human rights abuses and also systematically looted the country. In Nov. 1990, the UN adopted Resolution 678 authorizing the use of force if a peaceful withdrawal from Kuwait could not be negotiated. The US–led multinational force invaded Kuwait Feb. 24, completing the defeat of Iraqi forces by Feb. 28. The Kuwaiti government returned to a war-ravaged Kuwait on Mar. 4. Hundreds of oil wells, deliberately set afire by retreating Iraqis, belched a dense black smoke that in places completely obscured daylight and burned for months before experts were able to extinguish the blazes. The government imposed martial law for three months and arrested some 900 persons suspected of collaborating with the Iraqis. Some of those arrested were reportedly tortured. Meanwhile, pressure on the government for democratic reform continued, leading to an end of press censorship (1992, though controls on electronic media continued).

Kwang Hsu *See* **Guangxu.**

Ky, Nguyen Cao *See* **Nguyen Cao Ky.**

Kyd, Thomas (Kid, ͡) 1558–94. English dramatist, whose play *The Spanish Tragedy* was the model for the Elizabethan revenge tragedy. He may also have written an earlier version of *Hamlet*.

Kyōto (Kioto) Japanese city. Founded (794) as Heian-kyo and made capital of Japan, it was the imperial residence until 1868, when Tokyo became the capital. It is a major center of Japanese art and culture.

L

labor unions Organizations of workers for improvement of pay, benefits, and working conditions. Unions are the chief manifestation of the labor movement, which rose in response to the new economic and social order brought about by the Industrial Revolution. Early unions in Europe date from the 18th cent. and were at first suppressed by law. During the 19th cent., unions generally won legal recognition and greatly increased their memberships. In 1901, the first international labor union federation, what became known as the International Federation of Trade Unions (IFTU), was formed by the Second Socialist International. By 1919, the IFTU included about half the world's union members, but splits caused by formation of a separate Communist union federation (1921) and internal disputes resulted in the breakup of the IFTU (1945). It was replaced (1945) by the World Federation of Trade Unions (WFTU), with Communist unions participating. By 1949, however, the WFTU split along Communist/non-Communist lines, and in that year the non-Communist unions organized the International Confederation of Free Trade Unions (ICFTU). Since then, both the ICFTU and WFTU have been active in promoting union growth in underdeveloped countries. In the US, the union movement began in earnest with formation of the first national federation of unions, the National Labor Union (1866–72), which was followed by the Knights of Labor (1869–1917) and the American Federation of Labor (1886–1955). The late 1800s saw a period of major strikes and attempts to suppress unions by violent means. The early 1900s were marked by the activities of the militant Industrial Workers of the World (IWW). Nevertheless union membership steadily increased and important benefits were won. The New Deal legislation of the Depression years included many acts favoring both labor and unions. A longstanding division in the US labor movement, the rivalry between the American Federation of Labor and the Congress of Industrial Organizations, was ended (1955) by a merger in which the AFL-CIO was formed.

Labour party British political party, founded (1900) by a coalition of trade unions with participation by members of the Fabian Society (*q.v.*). Though openly committed to Socialist ideals since 1918, the party has traditionally favored specific legislative programs over ideology. The party formed its first government (1922–24) under R. MacDonald, who again led the government (1929–31). The Labour party joined the coalition government under W. Churchill during WW II and, after a major victory at the polls in 1945 formed the government of C. Attlee (1945–51). During Attlee's ministry, major Socialist programs were enacted, including nationalization of railroads, banks, mines, and utilities, and establishment of a national health plan. Ousted by the Conservatives, the Labour party returned to power under H. Wilson (1964–70, 1974–76) and under J. Callaghan (1976–79).

Labrador Largely unpopulated peninsular region in northeastern Canada. It was explored by Norsemen and rediscovered by J. Cabot (1497). Labrador is now part of the province of Newfoundland.

La Bruyère, Jean de 1645–96. French writer, known for his moralistic work *Les Caractères ou les moeurs de ce siècle* (1688), considered a classic of French literature.

Lacan, Jacques 1901–81. French psychoanalyst and writer, who interpreted S. Freud's work. A practicing psychoanalyst in Paris for most of his life, he founded the Freudian School of Paris (1964), then disbanded it (1980) because it failed to reflect strict Freudian principles. He is best known for his reinterpretations of Freud's work in light of structural linguistic theory developed in France.

Lacedaemon *See* **Laconia.**

La Chaise, François d'Aix de 1624–1709. French Jesuit priest. From 1675 until his death he was the confessor of Louis XIV and wielded great influence.

Laclede, Pierre c1724–78. French fur trader and pioneer in America. The trading post and village he founded along the Mississippi (1764) became St. Louis, Missouri.

Laconia (Lacedaemon) In ancient Greek geography, a region in the southeastern Peloponnesus. Its capital and chief city was Sparta, which was for years involved in a struggle with Athens for leadership in Greece.

Ladies' Peace *See* **Cambrai, Treaty of.**

Ladislaus (Lancelot) c1379–1414. King of Naples (1386–1414), successor to his father, Charles III of Anjou. He warred (1387–99) against his rival for the throne, Louis II, and sacked Rome (1413).

Ladislaus I 1040–95. King of Hungary (1077–95). One of Hungary's national heroes, he defended the country against the Poles, Russians, and Tatars and conquered Croatia. He was canonized as a Catholic saint.

Ladislaus I 1260–1333. Duke (1306–20) and king (1320–33) of Poland. He restored the Polish kingdom, which had been divided (1305–12). He took Danzig as the ally of the Teutonic Knights but later fought and won a six-year war against the order.

Ladislaus II (~ Jagiello) 1350?–1434. King of Poland (1386–1434). Ladislaus, grand duke of Lithuania, married the Polish queen Jadwiga, became king, and thereby founded the Jagiello dynasty. During his reign, he warred against the Teutonic Knights and, by his victories (notably the Battle of Tannenberg, 1410), made Poland a great power.

Ladislaus II c1456–1516. King of Bohemia (1471–1516) and Hungary (1490–1516). A weak and vacillating ruler, he was notable for signing a treaty (1515) with the Habsburgs, which, after his son Louis II died without issue, added Bohemia and Hungary to the Habsburg domains.

Ladislaus III 1424–44. King of Poland (1434–44) and of Hungary (as Ladislaus V, 1440–44). He led two crusades against the Turks. The first won him Walachia (1443). He was killed in battle at Varna (in Bulgaria) during the second.

Ladislaus V (~ Posthumus) 1440–57. King of Hungary (1444–57) and Bohemia (1453–57). Prevented from leaving the court of his guardian, Holy Roman Emperor Frederick III, until 1452, he was then unable to wrest power from his regents, J. Hunyadi (Hungary) and George of Podebrad (Bohemia).

Ladislaus Jagiello *See* **Ladislaus II.**

Ladislaus Posthumus *See* **Ladislaus V.**

Laënnec, René Théophile Hyacinthe 1781–1826. French physician. He invented the stethoscope and made major contributions to the diagnosis of chest diseases.

La Farge, John 1835–1910. American artist, noted for his murals and stained-glass windows, many of which were executed for churches and chapels.

Lafayette, Marie Joseph Paul Yves Roch Gilbert du Motier, marquis de (La Fayette, ~) 1757–1834. French soldier and political leader, a hero of the American Revolution and the early French Revolution. A volunteer general in the American Revolution, he distinguished himself at the battles of Brandywine (1777) and Yorktown (1780) and convinced the French to aid the American cause. During the French Revolution, he was a prominent member of the moderate faction; served in the Assembly of Notables (1787), the States-General (1789), the National Assembly (vice-president, 1789); and drafted the Declaration of the Rights of Man (1789). He fell from prominence when, frightened by the growing extremism of the revolution, he ordered the Paris National Guard to fire on a mob (July 17, 1791). Under threat of trial for his opposition to radical republicanism, he defected (1792) to Austria. Returned to France (1799) by Napoleon, he lived quietly until the July Revolution (1830), when he helped install King Louis Philippe.

Laffite, Jean (Lafitte, ~) c1780–1826? French privateer and smuggler. He and his men helped the Americans defeat the British in the Battle of New Orleans (1815), during the War of 1812.

La Follette, Robert Marion 1855–1925. American politician, US senator (1906–25), and a leader of the Progressive party. He was the unsuccessful Progressive candidate for president in 1924.

LaFontaine, Jean de 1621–95. French poet, author of *Fables choises, mises en vers* (1668–94), consisting of more than 200 fables in verse and considered a literary masterpiece.

LaFontaine, Sir Louis Hippolyte 1807–64. Canadian politician who served as joint prime minister with R. Baldwin of a united province of Canada (1842–43, 1848–51). Their ministries introduced reforms and established responsible parliamentary government in Canada.

Lagash (Shirpurla) Ancient city in Sumeria, located in southern Mesopotamia between the Tigris and Euphrates rivers. Inhabited as early as the 6th millennium BC, the city rose to importance in the 3d millennium BC and was conquered by the Akkadian ruler, Sargon, during this period.

Lagos, Battle of Naval battle (Aug. 7–18, 1759) of the Seven Years' War. A British fleet under Admiral Edward Boscawen (1711–61) defeated a French naval force off Lagos, Portugal, and thus headed off a major French invasion of England.

Lagrange, Joseph Louis, Comte 1736–1813. French mathematician, considered the leading mathematician of his day. His major work was *Mécanique analytique,* a mathematical analysis of mechanics.

La Hire (*pseud. of* Vignoles, Etienne de) c1390–c1443. French commander during the Hundred Years' War (1337–1453). He was a loyal companion of Joan of Arc and helped her defeat the English at Orléans and Patay. He continued in command during the decade following her death.

La Hogue, Battle of *See* **League of Augsburg, War of the.**

Laibach, Congress of *See* **Congress of Laibach.**

laissez-faire Economic theory popular during the 18th and 19th cents., which assumed an underlying natural order in economic systems. Thus, it was believed, individuals left to their own initiative (i.e., free from government regulation) would naturally produce the greatest good for themselves and society as a whole. The theory was advanced by the French Physiocrats (*q.v.*) (15th cent.) as a reaction against mercantilism (*q.v.*) and they emphasized the basic tenet of freedom from government regulation. A. Smith (the "invisible hand" of unregulated competition)

and J. S. Mill became the leading exponents of the doctrine in Britain, where it appealed to the commercial interests of the Industrial Revolution. The laissez-faire doctrine was also applied to politics, in a more limited fashion. The doctrine was largely out of favor by the end of the 19th cent.

Lake Chudskoye, Battle of *See* **Peipus, Battle of Lake.**

Lake Regullus, Battle of *See* **Etruscans.**

Lally, Thomas Arthur, comte de 1702–66. French general, who led a French expeditionary force in India during the Seven Years' War. His forced surrender to the British at Pondicherry (Jan., 1761) marked the end of French power in India and led to his execution by French authorities for treason.

Lama A Tibetan Buddhist holy man. (*See* Tibetan Buddhism.)

Lamar, Lucius Quintus Cincinnatus 1825–93. American statesman. He supported the Confederacy during the American Civil War (1861–65) and later served as congressman and senator from Mississippi (1873–75), as secretary of the interior (1885–88), and as associate justice of the Supreme Court (1888–93).

Lamarck, Jean Baptiste Pierre Antoine de Monet, chevalier de 1744–1829. French biologist. He is known for his theory of evolution (proved incorrect by C. Darwin), which held that acquired characteristics are hereditary.

Lama rebellion *See* **Mongolia (the republic).**

Lamartine, Alphonse Marie Louis de 1790–1869. French poet and politician. He is known best for his volumes of poetry, the first of which was *Méditations poétiques* (1820). He has been called the first true French Romantic poet.

Lamb, Charles 1775–1834. Great English essayist, poet, and critic. Among his noted works were *Essays of Elia* and (written with his sister Mary) the children's book *Tales from Shakespeare.*

Lambertini, Prospero *See* **Benedict XIV.**

lame duck An officeholder who has failed to be reelected but who remains in office until a successor is sworn in. The 20th Amendment to the US Constitution (Jan. 23, 1933) abolished the former lame duck sessions of Congress by requiring a new Congress to convene on Jan. 3 after the November in which it was elected.

Lamennais, Félicité Robert de (La Mannais, ~) 1782–1854. French priest and liberal Catholic writer. He promoted both papalism and Christ-tian democracy in France. He broke with church authorities on doctrinal issues and died an unrepentant excommunicate.

Lamian War (Greek ˜)   War (323–322 BC) against Macedonian rule in Greece, fought after the death of Alexander the Great. Athens, at the head of a league of Greek city-states, waged war against the Macedonian general Antipater and succeeded in besieging him at the city of Lamia. The arrival of Macedonian reinforcements (322 BC) broke the siege and allowed Antipater to defeat Athens and its allies. He then imposed an oligarchical government (controlled by him) on Athens.

Lancaster   English noble family founded (1267) by E. Lancaster, second son of Henry III. Lancastrian kings of England were Henry IV, Henry V, and Henry VI. Lancastrians warred against the Yorkists in the War of the Roses (*q.v.*).

Lancaster, Edmund, earl of (Crouchback, ˜) 1245–96.   Second son of Henry III of England, brother of Edward I. He held the title King of Sicily (1255–63), fought in the crusades (1271), and founded the House of Lancaster.

Lancaster, John of   *See* **John of Lancaster.**

Lancaster, Thomas, earl of c1277–1322.   English nobleman, leader of the barons who opposed Edward II and his favorites, notably P. Gaveston and the Despensers. Though he gained great power under Edward for a time, he was eventually defeated and beheaded during warfare against the king.

Lancelot *See also* **Ladislaus.**

Land, Edwin Herbert 1909–91.   American inventor and physicist, inventor of the Polaroid camera. He also devised range-finders, night-sight lenses, and anti-aircraft sights for use in WW II.

Land Acts, Irish   *See* **Irish Land Acts.**

Landen, Pepin of   *See* **Carolingians.**

Landon, Alfred Mossman 1887–1987.   American politician. A banker and oil executive, Landon was governor of Kansas (1933–37). The Republican presidential candidate in 1936, he was soundly defeated by F. Roosevelt.

Landsmaal   *See* **Aasen, Ivar.**

Landsteiner, Karl 1868–1943.   Viennese-born American pathologist. He won the Nobel Prize for Physiology or Medicine (1930) for his discovery of human blood types, and later identified the Rh Factor (1940).

Lane, Sir Ralph c1530–1603.   English adventurer and governor of the ill-fated Lost Colony (*q.v.*) at Roanoke Island, Virginia.

Lanfranc *d.* 1089.   Italian priest who became archbishop of Canterbury (1070–89) during the reign of William I. He served as adviser to the king and crowned his successor, William II (1087).

Langdon, John 1741–1819.   American Revolutionary War leader. He provided financial backing for the New Hampshire militia, and was president of New Hampshire (1785–86, 1788–89), a delegate to the Constitutional Convention, and US senator (1789–1801).

Lange, Dorothea 1895–1965.   American documentary photographer. She is best known for her evocative photographs of common people, notably migrant workers, the homeless and unemployed following the 1929 stock market crash, and Japanese-Americans in US internment camps.

Langland, William c1330–1400.   English author, believed to have written the allegorical poem *The Vision of Piers Plowman*. It is considered a classic of medieval literature.

Langtry, Lily   *See* **Bean, Roy.**

Lannes, Jean 1769–1809.   French marshal. He served under Napoleon in the Italian (1796) and Egyptian (1798–99) campaigns, won an important victory at Montebello (1800), and was killed in the battle at Essling.

La Noche Triste   *See* **Alvarado, Pedro de.**

Lansdowne, Henry Charles Keith Petty-Fitzmaurice, 5th marquis of 1845–1927.   British statesman. He was governor general of Canada (1883–88) and of India (1888–94), secretary of war (1895–1900) during the Boer War, and foreign secretary (1900–05).

Lao Country   *See* **Pathet Lao.**

Laodicean War   *See* **Syrian War (third).**

Lao Dong (Vietnam Workers party)   Vietnamese Communist party established in 1951 by Ho Chi Minh. It succeeded the Viet Minh as the ruling political party of the Democratic Republic of Vietnam.

Laos (Lao People's Democratic Republic)   Communist state located in Southeast Asia, on the northwest Indochina Peninsula. The population is 4,024,000 and the capital is Vientiane. The people are believed to be descendants of the Thai. Long dominated by France, Laos was (after 1950) torn by a bitter struggle between the Western-backed royalists and the Vietnamese- and Communist-backed Pathet Lao. The Pathet Lao gained complete control in 1975. Key dates in the history of Laos include:

MID-14TH CENT. Lan Xang kingdom founded by Fa Ngoum; Buddhism introduced.

17TH CENT. Lan Xang kingdom extended control over much of central Indochina.

1707 Lan Xang kingdom divided into Luang Prabang and Vientiane kingdoms; constant warfare for next century.

1778–1893 Siam dominated region.

1860s French arrived in region.

1893 Laos became French protectorate, incorporated into French Indochina.

1942–45 WW II; occupied by Japan, which held real power there though French Vichy government was allowed to remain; Japanese encouraged Laotians to declare independence from France under rule of king of Luang Prabang.

1946 France reestablished control; made king of Luang Prabang constitutional monarch.

1949 Laos granted semiautonomous status within French Union.

1950 Nationalist, Communist Pathet Lao formed by Prince Souphanouvong to oppose French domination.

1953 Vietnamese Communist Viet Minh and Pathet Lao power established in north as French Indochina War spread to Laos.

1954–55 Geneva agreement gave northern provinces to Pathet Lao, remainder to royalists.

1954 Laos gained full sovereignty (Dec. 29).

1957 Prince Souvanna Phouma, neutralist premier, and Pathet Lao leader Souphanouvong (his half-brother) formed unified government.

1959–62 Civil war resumed, soon becoming conflict between Communists, neutralists, and pro-West factions; neutralist Souvanna Phouma driven into Cambodia.

1962 Geneva Conference arranged for unified coalition government under Souvanna Phouma.

1963 Renewed civil war with Pathet Lao, aided by North Vietnam.

1964 Right-wing military coup attempt against Souvanna Phouma.

FROM 1965 Vietnam War intensified; North Vietnamese established Ho Chi Minh Trail through eastern Laos and gradually increased troop strength there.

1970 Laotian government troops lost Plain de Jarres to North Vietnamese.

1970 CIA activity in Laos revealed.

1971 South Vietnamese troops backed by US air support invaded southern Laos (Jan.–Mar.) as Vietnam war spread to region.

1971 North Vietnamese and Pathet Lao forces advanced against government positions.

1973 Pathet Lao and Souvanna Phouma concluded (Feb. 21) peace agreement.

1973 Government and Pathet Lao reached (July 29) general agreement on political and military settlement.

1973 Right-wing military coup put down (Aug.).

1974 Coalition government formed with Pathet Lao; Souvanna Phouma remained as premier, Souphanouvong as president of National Political Council.

1975 Pathet Lao abolished coalition government and monarchy (Dec. 2); government established along Vietnamese Communist lines.

1975–86 Souphanouvong (b. 1909) in office as president of new government; Vietnamese maintained strong military presence in Laos well into the 1980s, effectively controlling the government.

1975–91 Kaysone Phomvihan (b. 1920) in office as prime minister.

1979 Vietnamese and Laotian forces invaded Cambodia from Laos and overthrew Pol Pot regime.

1979 Prime Minister Phomvihan's official report (Dec. 26) noted that the Communist program to socialize Laos had failed; collectivization subsequently halted and government began promoting private enterprise to restore the Laotian economy.

1980 Abandonment of farming collectives began.

1980 Government reacted to resentment over Vietnamese control of country by large-scale arrests; China reported aiding Laotian anti-Vietnamese groups; Lao People's National Liberation United Front formed by anti-Vietnamese groups (Sept. 15).

1980 Border incident resulted in Thailand's briefly closing the frontier with Laos (June).

1981 Agricultural output rebounded sufficiently by 1981 to end rice imports, following halt in collectivization.

1984 Laotian anti-government guerrillas attacked forestry complex in jungles outside

Vientiane (Mar.); valuable equipment destroyed.

1986 Government cooperated with US mission searching for US servicemen missing in action during Vietnam War.

1986–91 Phoumi Vongvichit in office as president.

1986 Prime Minister Phomvihan announced plans to seek better relations with China, the US, and Thailand, while preserving ongoing relations with Vietnam and the USSR (Nov.).

1986 Government moved to decentralize economic decision-making and to end support of failing economic enterprises.

1987 Terrorist bomb exploded outside Soviet office in Vientiane, marring visit by Soviet foreign minister (Mar.).

1987 US agreed to resume humanitarian aid to Laos (Aug.).

1987 Diplomatic relations reestablished with China (Nov.), ending 8-year hiatus.

1987–88 Border clashes with Thailand over disputed area (Dec.–Feb.); ceasefire ended fighting.

1988 Vietnamese troop level in Laos, previously estimated at over 40,000, sharply reduced.

1988 Provincial secretary of Laotian Communist party among 48 people convicted of involvement in heroin trade (Aug.).

1988 Government sought to further improve economy by allowing state-run businesses to set wages and prices, and by liberalizing foreign investment laws.

1989 Elections for National Assembly held (Mar.); some non-Communist candidates allowed (and were seated), though opposition party candidates were banned outright.

1990 National Assembly passed legislation establishing a national bank, as well as laws regulating property ownership and inheritance.

1990 Japan agreed to provide $11 million in economic aid.

1991 Soviet economic aid ended.

1991 New constitution enacted, establishing the Lao People's Democratic Republic (Mar.).

1991– Kaysone Phomvihan, prime minister since 1975, in office as president.

1991– Gen. Khamtay Siphandon in office as prime minister.

1991 IMF approved restructuring loan (Apr.).

1991 Laos signed agreement on border with Thailand; also agreed to start planning for return of some 60,000 Laotian refugees in Thailand.

Lao-tze *See* **Laozi.**

Lao tzu *See* **Laozi.**

Laozi (Lao-tze; Lao-tzu) c604–531 BC. Chinese classical philosopher and quasi-legendary figure worshiped as a divinity by some. Considered founder of Daoism (*q.v.*), he preached conformity to the Dao, or eternal way of right conduct, and is considered one of the great figures of Chinese history. What little is known about his life came primarily from a book by the 1st cent. BC historian Sima Qian. Laozi was born in Henan province and eventually became part of the royal Zhou court as a *shih* (lowest level of the nobility, who served as astrologer and keeper of sacred books). Two incidents, probably apocryphal, from Laozi's life have been widely repeated and debated. In one, the aging Laozi met Confucius and upbraided him for being proud and ambitious. In the other, Laozi journeyed to the West and on reaching the state of Qin, was asked to write a book. Laozi supposedly responded by writing the *Dao-te Ching,* now among the most famous of all ancient Chinese texts and a summation of Laozi's thinking on the Dao (the Way) and virtue. He then continued his journey and completely disappeared. Scholars believe the *Dao-te Ching* as a whole was written about 300 BC, however, by someone else, perhaps a later royal astrologer named Tan. By the Later Han dynasty, Laozi was already being worshiped by the populace.

La Pérouse, Jean François de Galup, comte de 1741–c1788. French navigator. He explored the Pacific islands while searching for the Northwest Passage and discovered La Pérouse Strait (1787).

Laplace, Pierre-Simon (marquis de) 1749–1827. French astronomer and mathematician who made important discoveries about the motions of comets, planets, and the moon. With J. Lagrange, he helped confirm theories about the permanence and stability of the solar system, scientifically explaining many inconsistencies and irregularities of planetary orbits. He theorized (1787) that the moon's orbit around the earth was influenced by gravitational attraction from the sun. From

1799–1825, he wrote *Trait de Mécanique Céleste,* describing the general principles of motion and equilibrium, thus deriving the earth's law of gravitation. He went on to discover and describe the ebb and flow of tides, as well as the procession of the equinoxes. His *Exposition du Système du Monde* (1796) presented his nebular theory of the origin of the solar system, which was widely accepted until the end of the 19th cent.

Lapland   North European region that lies almost entirely within the Arctic Circle and is divided among Norway, Sweden, Finland, and Russia. Its indigenous inhabitants, the Laplanders, are nomadic.

Lapse, Doctrine of   *See* **Doctrine of Lapse.**

Lapua movement   Fascist organization (1929–32) in Finland. Strongly opposed to Russia and communism, the group rose to power briefly and forced a government ban on the Communist party. However, an attempt (1932) to overthrow the government, led by Gen. Kurt M. Wallenius, miscarried and resulted in a ban on the Lapua movement.

Lardner, Ringgold Wilmer (~, Ring) 1885–1933. American writer. He was known for his humorous short stories about ordinary people. His works include *You Know Me, Al* and *How to Write Short Stories.*

Largo Caballero, Francisco 1869–1946.   Spanish Socialist leader whose radical polemics helped bring on the Spanish Civil War (1936–39). He served briefly as prime minister and war minister (1936–37) before being ousted by the Communists.

La Rochefoucauld, François, duc de 1613–80. French writer famous as the author of maxims, such as those collected in *Réflexions ou sentences et maximes morales.*

Larousse, Pierre Athanase 1817–75. French grammarian, lexicographer, and encyclopedist, who compiled a number of the leading reference works of 19th-cent. France, including the *Grand Dictionnaire universel du XIX siècle.*

Larsa   Ancient city of Babylonia, near what is now Uruk, Iraq. It is mentioned in the Bible (Genesis) and flourished under the Elamites from c2000 BC to 1760 BC.

La Salle, René-Robert Cavelier, sieur de 1643–87. French explorer in North America. Arriving in Canada in 1666, he established Fort Frontenac on Lake Ontario (1672), controlled the region's fur trade, and held the local Indian population in check. After sailing across the Great Lakes, he explored the Illinois and Mississippi rivers, eventually travelling all the way to the Gulf of Mexico (1682). He claimed the Mississippi Basin for French king Louis XIV (1682), naming the region Louisiana and thus acquiring for France the most fertile land on the North American continent. A later expedition, planned to invade and conquer parts of Mexico (1687), was plagued with piracy, shipwrecks, and disease. La Salle was finally murdered in a mutiny somewhere along the Texas coast.

Lascaris, Theodore   *See* **Nicaea, Empire of.**

Las Casas, Bartolomé de 1474–1566.   Dominican Spanish missionary and historian. He worked to improve the treatment of American Indians by the Spanish, helped bring about the New Laws (1542), and wrote the *Historia de las Indias.*

Lassalle, Ferdinand 1825–64.   German Socialist and labor leader. He participated in the Revolution of 1848 and was a founder of the German Social Democratic party. Within the party, his reformist ideals vied with those of Marx's revolutionary ideology.

Lasso, Orlando di (*orig.* Roland Delattre) c1530–94.   Belgian composer. He is considered one of the greatest Renaissance composers and is especially noted for his motets. As a youth he was kidnapped three times for choirs because his voice was so beautiful.

La Tène culture   *See* **Celts.**

Lateran   Name of a complex of church buildings in southeastern Rome, built on land donated to the Catholic church by Emperor Constantine. Among them are the Basilica of St. John Lateran, the cathedral church of Rome, and the Lateran Palace (16th cent.).

Lateran Councils   Councils of the Roman Catholic church at Rome. 1. First (9th ecumenical): Convened by Pope Calixtus II (1123), it reaffirmed decisions of the Concordat of Worms (*q.v.*) regarding the Investiture Controversy (*q.v.*). It was the first church council convened in the West. 2. Second (10th ecumenical): Convened (1139) by Pope Innocent II, it ended the schism created by election of antipope Anacletus II (reigned 1130–38), condemned the teachings of Arnold of Brescia, and forbade marriage by monks, nuns, and other clerics.   3. Third (11th ecumenical): Convened (1179) by Pope Alexander III, it came after restoration of peace between the pope and

Holy Roman Emperor Frederick I. The council ordered that the pope be elected solely by the college of cardinals (by a two-thirds majority) and proclaimed the Albigensian Crusade (*q.v.*). 4. Fourth (12th ecumenical): Convened (1215) by Pope Innocent III, it is considered one of the great councils. It instituted many lasting organizational and procedural reforms, proclaimed the crusades (*q.v.*) to recover the Holy Land, defined the doctrine of transubstantiation, and established the Easter Duty. 5. Fifth (18th ecumenical): Held (1512–17) under popes Julius II and Leo X, the council opposed attempts to revive conciliarism (*q.v.*) and issued the Concordat of 1516, providing for a settlement of disputes between the pope and French king Louis XII.

Lateran Synod Roman Catholic synod (1059) that established the procedure by which the pope was to be elected. It called for election by a college of cardinals, thus eliminating the powers of both the Holy Roman Emperor and the Roman clergy in the selection of popes.

Lateran Treaty Agreement (Feb. 11, 1929) between Italy and the papacy, settling the Roman Question. During the unification of Italy (Risorgimento), the kingdom of Italy seized control of the Papal States and the city of Rome (1860, 1870). The new government offered (Law of Guarantees, 1871) the pope compensation for the territories taken and rights to the Vatican and Lateran. But the pope refused and thus created the Roman Question. Negotiations began in 1926 and the final agreement was signed by B. Mussolini, for King Victor Emmanuel III, and Cardinal P. Gaspari, for Pope Pius XI. It provided for creation of Vatican City as an independent state, establishment of Roman Catholicism as the state religion in Italy, and a large financial compensation to the church for loss of the Papal States.

Lathyrus, Ptolemy VIII *See* **Ptolemy VIII.**

Latimer, Hugh c1485–1555. English Protestant martyr. He supported King Henry VIII in his divorce from Catherine of Aragon, then opposed by the Roman Catholic church, and actively preached the Reformation. Under Catholic Mary Tudor, however, he and other celebrated martyrs were convicted of heresy and burned at the stake in the so-called "Smithfield fires."

Latin America Term used to refer to the Spanish- and Portuguese-speaking countries south of the southwest border of the US, including Mexico and the nations of Central America and South America. (*See individual countries.*)

Latin Empire of Constantinople Feudal empire centered at Constantinople (1204–61). It was established by leaders of the Fourth Crusade (*q.v.*), after they captured the Byzantine capital of Constantinople (1204) and divided various Byzantine lands among themselves and their Venetian bankers. Viewed as a Western intrusion, in Eastern lands, it began to decline soon after its creation. The empire suffered the hostility of the local population, incursions of the Bulgars and Turks, and resistance by the Byzantine emperors, who retired across the Bosporus to form the empire of Nicaea. The empire lapsed after Byzantine emperor Michael VIII retook Constantinople in 1261. However, some Greek islands remained in Venetian hands, Athens passed under Catalan rule, and part of mainland Greece remained in the Frankish Villehardouin family for a longer period.

Latin Fathers *See* **Fathers of the Church.**

Latin Kingdom of Jerusalem Kingdom established (1099) in Palestine and Syria by leaders of the First Crusade (*q.v.*). A feudal kingdom, it included the cities of Jerusalem, Acre, and Tyre and controlled Antioch, Edessa, and Tripoli. Among its rulers were Baldwin I, Baldwin II, Fulk, Amalric I, and Baldwin V. Subsequent crusades were unsuccessful against the Muslims, and Jerusalem fell (1187) to Saladin. Thereafter Muslim armies made further conquests and expelled the last Christian forces from the region by the capture (1291) of Acre. Although the kingdom itself ceased to exist in fact, the title "King of Jerusalem" continued in use for centuries.

Latins Ancient people that inhabited Latium, a plain in what is now central Italy. Romans were Latins and Rome was one of the early Latin cities established in the region (as were Alba Longa, Tusculum, and others). The cities formed confederations to resist the Etruscans and Samnites (Samnite Wars, *q.v.*), and Rome gradually emerged as the dominant power. Rome established complete control by her victory in the Latin Wars (340–338 BC).

Latin Wars Wars (340–338 BC) in which a number of Italian cities sought equality with Rome. With their defeat by Rome, some of these states were made into colonies, others into states dependent upon Rome, and others ceded land for settlement by the Romans.

La Tremoille, Louis de la *See* **Novara, Battles of.**

Latrobe, Benjamin Henry 1764–1820. American architect. He introduced the Greek Revival style in America and directed the rebuilding of the Capitol after it was burned by the British in 1814.

Latter-Day Saints, Church of Jesus Christ of *See* **Mormons.**

Lattimore, Owen 1900–89. American Orientalist and writer. He spent many years overseas in China and served as the US political adviser to Chiang Kai-shek. He was unjustly charged (1950) by Senator J. McCarthy with being a major Communist spy in the US and was not completely cleared until 1955.

Latvia (Republic of Latvia) Historic region and independent state, formerly a constituent republic of the USSR. Latvia is located along the Baltic Sea. The population is 2,700,000 and the capital is Riga. Taken by the Livonian Brothers of the Sword (13th cent.), the area was subsequently divided and controlled variously by Poland, Sweden, and Russia. Latvia gained independence during the Baltic Wars of Liberation and adopted its first constitution in 1922. In 1939, however, Nazi Germany and the USSR agreed that Latvia would become part of the USSR. On July 21, 1940, Latvia's legislature duly ratified the inevitable by voting to become part of the USSR. During WW II, Nazi Germany occupied Latvia from 1941–44, and after the war the Soviets reimposed control over the region. In the 1980s, increasing nationalist sentiment and Soviet leader M. Gorbachev's new policy of openness combined to produce a movement, first for greater Latvian autonomy and then for complete independence. Beginning with open anti-Soviet demonstrations in 1986–87, Latvian nationalism fostered creation of groups dedicated to complete independence in 1988. Then as Lithuania and Estonia challenged Soviet authority, Latvia's Supreme Soviet followed suit by declaring sovereignty (July 28, 1989). Constitutional guarantees of Communist party supremacy were abolished (Jan. 1990), and in May Latvia's 1940 union with the USSR was declared illegal. Gorbachev voided the action (May) and in Jan. 1991 Soviet Interior Ministry troops seized some buildings in Riga. Subsequently a referendum on independence was overwhelmingly approved by voters and on Aug. 21, following the Soviet coup, the Latvian legislature declared full independence. The Communist party was banned

two days later and on Sept. 6, 1991, the USSR officially recognized independent Latvia.

Laud, William 1573–1645. Archbishop of Canterbury (1633–45). He persecuted the Puritans and Calvinists and supported Charles I in his conflict with Parliament. Impeached by the Long Parliament (1640), he was beheaded.

Lauderdale, John Maitland, duke of 1616–82. Scottish statesman. As secretary of state for Scotland and member of the Cabal (*q.v.*) ministry, he was notorious for his harsh rule in Scotland.

Laudon, Gideon Ernst Freiherr von (Loudon, ~) 1717–90. Austrian field marshal. He fought in the service of the Habsburgs and distinguished himself in the War of Austrian Succession, the Seven Years' War, and the Austro-Turkish War.

Laura de Noves 1308?–40. Woman believed to be the inspiration for Petrarch's love poems.

Laurens, Henry 1724–92. American statesman, president of the Continental Congress (1777–78). He was captured (1780) by the British while taking a proposed treaty to the Netherlands. The treaty later precipitated war between England and the Netherlands.

Laurier, Sir Wilfrid 1841–1919. Canadian statesman and first French-Canadian prime minister (1896–1911). A leader of the Liberal party, he worked to develop the Canadian west and to establish Canada's place in the British Empire.

Lausanne, Conference of *See* **Conference of Lausanne.**

Lausanne, Treaty of 1. Treaty (Oct. 18, 1912) concluding the Italo-Turkish War. The treaty called for Turkey's withdrawal from Tripoli. 2. Treaty (July 24, 1923) that formally ended hostilities of the Greco-Turkish War (1920–22) and modified terms of the Treaty of Sèvres (*q.v.*). By it Turkey regained control of the Dardanelles, eastern Thrace, and other territories, including Smyrna.

Laval, François Xavier de (Laval-Montmorency, François Xavier) 1623?–1708. The first French Catholic bishop in Canada. He founded the seminary of Quebec (1663), which became Laval University.

Laval, Pierre 1883–1945. French politician. As premier of the Vichy government during WW II (1942–44), he instituted forced labor and other harsh measures in France. He was executed for treason after the war.

Lavalleja, Juan Antonio c1786–1853. Uruguayan revolutionary. He led a group, known as the

Thirty-three Immortals, and declared Uruguayan independence from Brazil (1825). He later led the Blancos party in Uruguay.

Laval-Montmorency, François Xavier *See* **Laval, François Xavier de.**

Laveran, Charles Louis Alphonse 1845–1922. French physician. He discovered the parasite that causes malaria (1880). Awarded Nobel Prize (Physiology or Medicine) in 1907.

Lavoisier, Antoine Laurent 1743–94. French physicist and chemist, considered the founder of modern chemistry. In his early career, he improved the preparation of saltpeter (potassium nitrate) in making gunpowder (1775) and set up a model farm (1778) to apply modern scientific principles to agriculture. He was a member of the commission set up (1790) to oversee the French system of weights and measures, which eventually led to the establishment of the metric system. He published classifications and analyses of chemical substances, thus contributing to modern chemical nomenclature and classification. By correctly explaining the role of oxygen in combustion (1774), he discredited the phlogiston theory. He performed extensive research on respiration, describing the role of oxygen in breathing and the presence of carbon dioxide and water as natural by-products. Despite the importance of his work, Lavoisier fell afoul of French Revolutionaries and was tried, convicted, and guillotined by a revolutionary tribunal in 1794.

Law, Andrew Bonar 1858–1923. British statesman. He succeeded A. Balfour as Conservative party leader in the House of Commons (1911–15), where he opposed Irish Home Rule. He became prime minister (1922–23).

Law, John 1671–1729. Scottish financier. He organized the ill-fated Mississippi Scheme (*q.v.*) in France for the exploitation of Louisiana colonies.

Law of Guarantees *See* **Guarantees, Law of.**

Lawrence, Abbott 1792–1855. US manufacturer and politician. He was a founder of the textile city Lawrence, Massachusetts, and was US minister to Great Britain (1849–52).

Lawrence, Amos Adams 1814–86. American philanthropist. He supported abolitionist movements and contributed to the establishment of a college in Lawrence, Kansas, that became the University of Kansas.

Lawrence, Charles 1709–60. British general and governor of Nova Scotia (1755–60). He was responsible for the deportation of French colo-

nials from Acadia (in Canada) after the British captured this French colony.

Lawrence, D(avid) H(erbert) 1885–1930. British author. Lawrence was one of the most influential writers in the 20th cent. His work includes the novels *Sons and Lovers, Women in Love, The Rainbow,* and *Lady Chatterley's Lover.*

Lawrence, Ernest Orlando 1901–58. American physicist. Lawrence invented the cyclotron. He also introduced the use of neutron beams in cancer treatment and patented a color television tube. Awarded Nobel Prize in Physics 1939.

Lawrence, James 1781–1813. American naval officer. He commanded the *Hornet* and the *Chesapeake* (*q.v.*) during the War of 1812. It was aboard the latter that he uttered his famous cry "Don't give up the ship!"

Lawrence, Sir Thomas 1769–1830. English painter, the leading portrait painter of his day. Among his works is the noted portrait of Queen Charlotte.

Lawrence, T(homas) E(dward) (Lawrence of Arabia) 1888–1935. British soldier and author. During WW I, he led the Arab troops of Faisal I in revolt against the Ottomans and described his adventures in *The Seven Pillars of Wisdom (1926).*

Lawrence of Arabia *See* **Lawrence, Thomas Edward.**

Laxness, Halldór Kiljan 1902– . Icelandic novelist. His works include *The Weaver of Cashmere* and *Independent People.* He received the Nobel Prize in Literature in 1955.

Layamon *fl.* c1200. Middle English poet whose work, *Brut,* makes the first mention in English of the Arthurian legend and introduced Lear, Cymbeline, and Merlin.

lay investiture *See* **Investiture Controversy.**

League *See* **Catholic League.**

League of *See also under names inverted, as in* **Nations, League of.**

League of Augsburg, War of *See* **Grand Alliance, War of.**

League of the Russian People *See* **Black Hundreds.**

Leahy, William Daniel 1875–1959. American naval officer. He served in the Spanish-American War and in WW I. He became chief of staff under President F. Roosevelt (1942) and continued in that post under President H. Truman until 1949.

Leakey, Louis Seymour Bazett 1903–72. British archaeologist and anthropologist. He is noted for his controversial interpretations of extremely ancient humanoid fossils, which indicated that forerunners of *Homo sapiens* were much older than previously thought. His wife, Mary Leakey, (1913–), discovered (1959) the noted Zinjanthropus fossil remains (believed 1,750,000 years old) in the Olduvai Gorge, Tanzania. Leakey subsequently discovered (1961) what he called a more direct ancestor of humans, the *Homo habilis.*

Leaning Tower of Pisa Tower constructed (1174–1350) at Pisa, Italy. It leans about 17 feet from the perpendicular due to settling, and is a noted attraction for tourists. Numerous attempts have been made to halt the settling, which threatens to topple the structure.

Lebanese Crisis US intervention in a Lebanese civil war. US marines were landed in Lebanon by President D. Eisenhower (July, 1958), in pursuance of the Eisenhower Doctrine (*q.v.*), after opposition to the pro-Western government of C. Chamoun broke out into open rebellion. The marines helped to stabilize the situation. The crisis was resolved by the election of Gen. Fuad Chebab, who had refused to commit the Lebanese army to either side during the fighting.

Lebanese War *See* **Lebanon (1982).**

Lebanon (Republic of Lebanon) Country located in the Mideast and occupying the mountainous coastal region of the eastern Mediterranean. The population is 3,340,000 and the capital is Beirut. The Lebanese coast was originally the home of Phoenician traders, and from the 6th cent. BC various powers had control of the region. Later the mountains of Lebanon offered refuge to religious groups seeking to escape persecution. The Maronite Christians arrived first (7th cent. AD) and were followed by the heretical Muslim sect, the Druses. Orthodox Muslims also arrived in the region. In modern times, Lebanon (as part of Syria) was established as a French mandate (1920) following the collapse of the Ottoman empire and was organized as a separate state by the French in 1926. During WW II, British and Free French troops occupied Lebanon, ousting the Vichy French government there. Lebanon (and Syria) then gained autonomy in stages, though complete independence was not achieved until French troops were forced to withdraw by nationalist unrest (1946). Since then, conflict between the diverse religious factions has resulted in instability and war, notably a brief civil war in 1958, ended by US intervention. Civil war again broke

out in 1975, and traditional Christian-Muslim rivalries were further complicated in the 1970s as Palestine Liberation Organization (PLO) guerrillas, Syrian troops, and UN peace-keeping forces occupied various parts of the country. Effective control of the country became virtually impossible. The Israeli invasion of Lebanon (1982) seriously weakened the PLO position in Lebanon and after the Israeli withdrawal, Syria became the leading force in the war-ravaged country. Efforts at establishing a peaceful settlement continued through the 1980s and culminated in an agreement (1989) to end hostilities. Key events in Lebanese history include:

C25TH–6TH CENTS. BC Phoenicians controlled region; established cities in coastal region (modern Sidon, Tyre, Beirut, and others) which served as a base for their commercial empire.

6TH–4TH CENTS. BC Persians took control of territory.

4TH–1ST CENTS. BC Alexander the Great conquered the area (332) and thereafter the area was controlled by successor states in the region.

64 BC Romans took control of area; Christianity later introduced.

5TH CENT. AD Byzantines maintained control over area after the collapse of the Western Roman Empire.

7TH CENT. AD Maronite Christians established themselves in the Lebanese mountains seeking refuge from persecution by the Byzantine emperor.

7TH CENT. Arab Muslim conquest; Maronites in mountain regions resisted Islam and thus began the historic split between Christians and Muslims in surrounding territories.

11TH CENT. Members of the Muslim Druse sect, fleeing Orthodox Muslim persecution, established an emirate in southern Lebanon.

16TH–20TH CENTS. Ottoman Empire controlled region; Lebanon enjoyed considerable autonomy.

FROM 1516 Maronites in religious communion with the Catholic church in Rome.

1788–1840 Bashir Shihab II reigned as emir.

1831–40 Lebanon (and Syria) ruled by Egyptians.

1860 Druse massacre of Christians led to active French intervention.

1861–1914 European influence in region increased; Ottoman rulers forced to accept establishment of autonomous government in region of Mount Lebanon; region to have non-Lebanese, Christian governor and council with Christian, Muslim, and Druze representatives.

1861–1914 Greater Lebanon, governed by a Christian, created by Ottomans; made relatively autonomous under Ottoman control.

1916 Secret Sykes-Picot agreement between Britain and France; anticipating the breakup and partition of the crumbling Ottoman empire.

1920 France given League of Nations mandate over Syria (including Lebanon).

1920 French established borders of modern Lebanon by adding Bekaa Valley and coastal region to Mount Lebanon.

1926 Lebanese Republic organized by French as separate from Syria.

1941 Vichy forces ousted by Allies during WW II; Free French declared Lebanon independent (1941), though troops remained to 1946.

1943 National Compact; Maronite Christians agreed to cut ties with France and align Lebanon with Arab states; Muslims agreed to maintain Lebanon as separate state and not seek union with other Arab state; earlier Christian-Muslim agreement allotted Lebanese presidency to a Maronite Christian; prime minister to be a Sunni Muslim, assembly speaker a Shi'ite Muslim, foreign minister an Orthodox Christian, etc.; seats in legislature to be allocated on religious basis.

1943–52 Sheikh Bishara el-Khoury in office as first president.

1945 Became a member of the UN.

1945 Joined the Arab League.

1946 French, who resisted granting full independence to Lebanon (and Syria) pending treaty protecting their interests, forced to withdraw troops (Mar.) because of nationalist agitation; Lebanon now completely independent.

1948–49 Arab-Israeli War; Lebanon joined in Arab attack on newly created Israeli state; many Muslim refugees from this and subsequent wars settled in southern Lebanon, changing the balance between Christian and Muslim communities.

1952–58 C. Chamoun served as president; established relations with Western powers; granted women the vote.

1958 US marines landed in Lebanon (July) to halt civil war by Muslims against pro-Western Maronite government of C. Chamoun; crisis ended with election of Gen. Fuad Chebab; US troops withdrawn (Oct.).

1958–64 Chebab in office as president; fostered closer relations with Arab states.

1962 Military coup attempt crushed.

1964–70 Charles Hélou in office as president.

1964 Palestine Liberation Organization (PLO) founded; established headquarters in Beirut (until 1982); conducted raids into Israel from southern Lebanon.

1967 Lebanon did not participate in Arab-Israeli War.

1968 Israelis raided Beirut airport (Dec.), retaliating for terrorist attack on Israeli airliner.

1969 Fighting broke out (Oct.) between PLO guerrillas and Lebanese troops.

1970s Muslims now constituted majority population in Lebanon.

1970–76 Suleiman Franjieh in office as president; PLO guerrillas, driven out of Jordan, established headquarters in Lebanon; tensions with Israel increased as PLO guerrillas launched attacks on Israelis.

1971 PLO, driven out of Jordan, shifted to Lebanon.

1972 PLO guerrillas and Lebanese troops clashed.

1973 Lebanese prime minister Saeb Salam resigned (Apr.) after Israelis raided PLO buildings in Beirut.

1973 Lebanon neutral in fourth Arab-Israeli War.

1974–76 Lebanese civil war pitted Muslims allied with Palestinians and PLO against the Phalangists, a military organization of the Maronites, which dominated the other Christian forces.

1976 Cease-fire agreement reached (Jan.) through Syrian involvement; Muslims gained greater voice in government.

1976–82 Elias Sarkis elected to presidency by parliament (May), after the ouster of Franjieh.

1976 15,000 Syrian troops entered Lebanon to help halt the civil war (May).

1976 Syrian troops occupied Beirut (Nov. 10) as part of Arab League plan to restore peace there.

1978 Israelis invaded southern border region (Mar.) to clear out PLO guerrilla strongholds there; turned over many strategic points to Christian militia as they withdrew to Israel.

1981 Fighting broke out (Apr. 2) in Beirut and surrounding area; Syrian troops involved in the fighting against Christian militia while Israeli jets attacked Syrians.

1981 Syrian antiaircraft missile emplacements moved into Bekaa Valley after Israeli air attacks.

1981 Downing of Israeli aircraft by Syrian antiaircraft missile led to Israeli demand to withdraw emplacements (May).

1981 Special envoy Philip C. Habib dispatched to Middle East by US President R. Reagan to arrange peace settlement.

1981 Israeli air raids conducted in Lebanon in retaliation for PLO attacks on Israel; US suspended shipment of aircraft to Israel (July 20).

1981 Cease-fire between Israelis and the PLO in Lebanon arranged by US special envoy P. Habib (July 24).

1981 Bomb explosions kill dozens in Sidon (Sept. 1) and in Beirut (Oct. 1).

1982 Lebanese War; major invasion of Lebanon by Israel began (June 6); Israelis said they would halt advance at 25 miles into Lebanon.

1982 Syrian antiaircraft missile sites in Bekaa Valley destroyed by Israeli air attacks.

1982 Israeli forces drive to Beirut (June 10); PLO trapped in Beirut between Israelis and Phalangists.

1982 Siege of Beirut (June–Aug.); Israelis gradually advanced and surrounded over 6,000 PLO fighters in west Beirut; began shelling and bombing of sector as negotiations with PLO and others were continued by US envoy P. Habib.

1982 PLO agreed in principle to evacuate Beirut; President Reagan declared end to violence was crucial (Aug. 2) as conditions in west Beirut worsened.

1982 Habib plan for evacuation accepted by Israel (Aug. 15); US, France, and Italy agreed to contribute troops to oversee evacuation of PLO forces, thus ending Israeli siege of Beirut (Aug. 19); multi-national peacekeeping force stationed in Beirut.

1982 Last PLO guerrillas evacuated from Beirut (Aug. 21–Sept. 1).

1982 President-elect Bashir Gemayel and other Christian Phalangists killed by terrorist bomb (Sept. 14).

1982 Beirut Massacre revealed (Sept.); hundreds of Palestinians massacred in refugee camp by Christian militiamen; Israeli occupation forces criticized for failing to prevent massacre.

1982–88 Amin Gemayel, brother of assassinated president-elect, named president (Sept.).

1983 Lebanon and Israel signed agreement declaring end to hostilities and calling for withdrawal of all foreign troops from Lebanon (May); Syria, with 40,000 troops in Lebanon, rejected agreement; Israel consequently kept its troops in the south.

1983 US military headquarters attacked by Muslim extremists (Oct.); 241 marines killed; 58 French soldiers killed in another bombing that day.

1983 PLO leader Y. Arafat and 4,000 PLO supporters forced to evacuate Tripoli stronghold (Dec.), following loss in war with rival, Syrian-backed PLO faction.

1984 US, British, Italian and French peacekeeping troops withdrawn as fighting in Beirut intensified (Feb.–Mar.).

1984 President Gamayel, with his forces controlling only part of Beirut, turned to Syrians for help in restoring order (Mar.).

1984 Syrian-backed security plan put into effect in Beirut (July); reorganized Lebanese army failed to gain control of city, however.

1985 Israeli troops withdrawn from Lebanon; Syria reduced troops in Lebanon to about 25,000.

1986 PLO guerrillas again started launching rocket attacks against Israel from southern Lebanon.

1986 Shi'ite Amal militia, seeking to block resurgence of PLO in Lebanon, cut off food and supplies to Palestinian refugee camps in Beirut and other cities (Oct.); international pressure forced militia to allow essential supplies in (Feb. 1987).

1987 Syrians deployed some 7,500 troops in Beirut to halt fighting between various militias (Feb.).

1988 Siege of Palestinian refugee camps lifted by Shi'ite Amal militia (Jan.).

1988 Iraq, no longer embroiled in the Iran-Iraq war, began to expand its influence in Lebanon.

1988 President Gemayel, his term expired, appointed interim military government after failed attempts to hold presidential election (Sept.); Muslims refused to participate in this government, however; general collapse of government followed and by Oct. only central bank was still intact.

1989 Intense fighting between Christian and Muslim factions (Mar.).

1989 Tripartite Arab Committee on Lebanon met (May); leaders of Morocco, Algeria, and Saudi Arabia unsuccessfully sought to arrange ceasefire; in following months Syria was increasingly blamed as main obstacle to peace plans.

1989 New Tripartite Arab Committee peace plan ("Taif agreement") accepted by all parties, including Syria (Sept.); ceasefire effected Sept. 23.

1989 Lebanese National Assembly met (Oct., in Saudi Arabia); approved Taif agreement; transferred power from presidency to executive cabinet, with equal numbers of Muslim and Christian members; militias to disband; Syrian army to help maintain security for two years.

1989 Christian René Mouawad in office as president, after being elected by the Assembly (Nov.); assassinated 17 days later.

1989– Elias Hrawi in office as president, succeeding Mouawad.

1990 Fighting between Christian factions, provoked by renegade former Lebanese army commander, broke out in Beirut's Christian sector (Jan.–Mar.).

1990 Muslims gained more representation in government following approval of constitutional amendment by National Assembly (Aug.).

1990 Second Lebanese Republic established by approval of constitutional amendments (Sept. 21).

1990 All militias withdrawn from Beirut as specified in Taif agreement (Oct.–Dec.); Lebanese army assumed control in city.

1991 Lebanese army deployed in southern Lebanon (Feb.), establishing degree of government control there.

Lebrun, Albert 1871–1950. French statesman, last president of the Third Republic (1931–40). He surrendered to Marshal H. Pétain, head of the pro-German Vichy government.

Le Brun, Charles 1619–90. French artist. Court painter to King Louis XIV (from 1662) and thereafter he dominated French art. He was director of the Gobelins, a company producing furnishings for French royalty, and designed much of the interior at Versailles, including the Galerie des Glaces.

Lechfeld, Battle of Decisive victory (Aug. 10, 955) over the Magyars by Otto I, German king (later emperor). The battle, which took place near Augsburg, Germany, put an end to the Magyars' westward expansion.

Leclerc, Charles Victor Emmanuel 1772–1802. French general, Napoleon's brother-in-law. He died of yellow fever contracted while putting down a revolt in Haiti led by P. Toussaint L'Ouverture.

Leclerc, Jacques Philippe 1902–47. French general during WW II. He led a force of Free French troops stationed in Equatorial Africa on a 1,500-mile march to join the British in Tripoli (1942–43). He was also a commander in the Normandy invasion.

Lecompton Constitution Proslavery constitution adopted (1857) by the Territory of Kansas prior to its admission as a state. S. Douglas led congressional opposition to acceptance of the constitution and admission of Kansas as a proslavery state. This forced a vote (1858) by inhabitants of Kansas, and the Lecompton Constitution was rejected. Kansas was admitted (1861) as a free state.

Leconte de Lisle, Charles *See* **Parnassians.**

Le Corbusier (*pseud. of* Jeanneret, Charles Édouard) 1887–1965. Swiss-born French architect whose work helped revolutionize 20th-cent. architectural design. He pioneered the use of ferroconcrete and modular housing designs and was an advocate of artistic purism.

Ledru-Rollin, Alexandre Auguste 1807–74. French politician. He took part in the Revolution of 1848 and advocated universal suffrage. After an unsuccessful insurrection against Louis Napoleon (1849), he fled to England.

Le dynasty Vietnamese dynasty (1428–1788). Le Loi restored the independence of Annam (*q.v.*) by driving out the Chinese in 1428. The dynasty ruled over a unified Vietnam until its fall in 1542, after which the kingdom was effectively divided in two. Succeeding rulers continued to reign in the Le dynasty name until 1788.

Lee, Ann 1736–84. English mystic. Called Mother Ann, she became a leader of the Shaking Quakers and introduced the Shaker sect to the US (1774) at Watervliet, New York.

Lee, Arthur 1740–92. American diplomat. In France with B. Franklin and S. Deane to obtain aid for the Colonials during the American Revolution, he became involved in disputes with Deane and Franklin. Both Deane and Lee were eventually recalled.

Lee, Charles 1731–82. English-born American army officer during the American Revolution. As second-in-command to G. Washington, he constantly criticized and disobeyed him. He conspired with Lord Howe; prevented an American victory at Monmouth, New Jersey (1778); and was ousted in disgrace (1780).

Lee, Fitzhugh 1835–1905. Confederate general in the American Civil War, nephew of R. E. Lee. A cavalry commander, he figured in battles at Antietam, Chancellorsville, and Gettysburg and in the Wilderness and Shenandoah Valley campaigns. He later became governor of Virginia (1886–90).

Lee, Francis Lightfoot 1734–97. American Revolutionary War leader. He was a delegate to the Continental Congress (1775–79) from Virginia and signed the Declaration of Independence.

Lee, Henry (˜, Light-Horse Harry) 1756–1818. American Revolutionary cavalry officer, father of R. E. Lee. He was a member of the Continental Congress (1785–88) and governor of Virginia (1792–95). He eulogized G. Washington as "first in war, first in peace, and first in the hearts of his countrymen."

Lee, Light-Horse Harry *See* **Lee, Henry.**

Lee, Richard *d.* 1664. English colonist in Virginia. A wealthy landowner, he held various public offices and founded the Lee family, which was prominent in Virginia.

Lee, Richard Henry 1732–94. American statesman and signer of the Declaration of Independence, which he vigorously supported in the Continental Congress. He helped arrange the Committees of Correspondence (*q.v.*) and was a Virginia delegate to the Continental Congress (1774–79, 1784–89). His opposition to a strong federal government created by the Constitution helped bring about passage of the Bill of Rights.

Lee, Robert E(dward) 1807–70. Confederate commander during the American Civil War (1861–65) and military hero of the Confederacy. A Virginian and West Point graduate, he distinguished himself during the Mexican War (1846–48), served as a cavalry commander in

Texas (1857–61), and led federal troops (1859) against J. Brown in the Harpers Ferry Raid (*q.v.*). He resigned from the military (1861) when Virginia seceded from the Union, and organized Virginia's military forces. He then served as J. Davis' military adviser (1861–62) and in mid-1862, took command of the Army of Northern Virginia. It was in this command that Lee proved his brilliance as a military commander and seriously challenged the better-equipped Union armies. He blocked a Union drive toward Richmond (1862), launched a Confederate invasion of the North (checked at Antietam, 1862), turned back new Union offensives at Fredericksburg and Chancellorsville (1862, 1863), and began his second invasion of the North. Badly defeated at Gettysburg (1863) in this campaign, he skillfully conducted defensive operations (1864–65) against U. Grant's forces for the remainder of the war. Named overall Confederate commander (Feb. 6, 1865), he was at last forced to surrender at Appomattox Courthouse (Apr. 9, 1865) and thereby effectively ended the Civil War.

Lee, William 1739–95. American diplomat. His proposed commercial treaty between the American colonies and the Netherlands was discovered by the British and became the cause of war between England and the Netherlands (1780).

Lee Kuan Yew 1923– . First prime minister of the Republic of Singapore (1965–90). Lee helped negotiate an end to British colonial rule in the late 1950s, and led the country into a short-lived union, the Federation of Malaysia (1963). After Singapore was forced out (1965) over ethnic tensions, the republic was formed and Lee became its prime minister. During his long tenure, Singapore has enjoyed economic prosperity and an effective, democratic government.

Leeuwenhoek, Anton van 1632–1723. Dutch scientist famous for his detailed observations of microscopic organisms. He built more than 247 single-lens microscopes and ground more than 400 lenses with magnifying powers of up to 300 times an object's actual size. He discovered protozoa (1674), which he called "animalicules" and calculated their sizes. He was probably the first to observe bacteria and published the first known drawings of them (1683). The first microscopist to describe spermatozoa (1677), he also discovered parthenogenesis in plants and studied the structure of the lens in the human eye. He provided the first accurate descriptions of red blood corpuscles (1684), noting their different shapes in different animal species.

Lefèvre de'Étaples, Jacques c1455–1536. French theologian whose works anticipated the Protestant Reformation. A humanist, he sought to separate religious studies from the realm of Scholasticism; his *Psalterium quinuplex* (1509) and commentary on the letters of St. Paul (1512) were said to have influenced Martin Luther. Among his other works was a translation of the Vulgate Bible into French.

Legalism Philosophical school in China. Legalism arose amid the instability of the Warring States period (5th–3d cents. BC) and its proponents held that people were by nature bad (as opposed to the Confucian philosophers, who believed them essentially good). Legalists believed in absolutist governments and the imposition of a rigid system of laws to promote obedience and correct behavior, especially that which enhanced the power of the state. Legalism, the chief exponent of which was Han Fei Tzu, served as the ruling philosophy of the Qin dynasty, but opposition to the authoritarianism it encouraged in government eventually brought about the overthrow of the Qin. Han emperor Wuddi banned Legalist philosophers.

Legal Tender Act US congressional act (1862) authorizing the issue of $150 million in paper (greenback) notes without gold backing to help finance the Civil War. After the war the act was declared unconstitutional by the Supreme Court (1870). The court reversed itself in 1871.

Léger, Fernand 1881–1955. French artist, noted for his use of modern industrial images in his "machine art."

legion Standard unit of the Roman army, composed of about 4,000–6,000 soldiers. The legion was made up primarily of heavily armed foot soldiers (with thrusting spears and swords), supported by light infantry and cavalry contingents. There were 28 legions in the Roman army during the early empire, a number that remained fairly constant until barbarian invasions brought about the creation of additional legions. Tactically, legions proved more flexible than other mass formations of the day (such as the Greek phalanx), but the emphasis on heavy infantry left them vulnerable to attack by cavalry (notably horse-mounted barbarian soldiers), archers, and free-roaming guerrilla bands.

Legislative Assembly Name of the national representative body of revolutionary France (Oct. 1, 1791–Sept. 20, 1792). Dominated by the moderate Girondists, it was replaced by the National Convention after the overthrow of the monarchy. During the Second Republic, the name was revived for the assembly, which sat for two years (1849–51). It was dissolved by Napoleon III as a prelude to the dissolution of the Second Republic itself.

legislative branch Name for the branch of government that makes or changes laws. It is generally representative and is often composed of two houses (upper and lower). (*See also* Congress of the United States.)

Legitimists In French history, the supporters (19th cent.) of the head of the senior Bourbon line as rightful French king. They opposed the claims of the Orléanists and the Bonapartists.

Leguia, Augusto Bernardino 1863–1932. President of Peru (1908–12, 1919–30). He settled longstanding disputes with Bolivia, Brazil, and Chile. Though he encouraged modernization, his ruthless treatment of opponents led to his ouster in 1930.

Leibniz, Gottfried Wilhelm, baron von (Leibnitz, ˜) 1646–1716. German philosopher and mathematician. Leibniz developed new notations for calculus and a theory of infinitesimal calculus that predated I. Newton's findings by three years. He actively sought a reconciliation of Catholicism and Protestantism and professed an optimistic belief in a divine plan of the universe that was ridiculed by Voltaire in *Candide.* Leibniz' work influenced, among others, I. Kant and B. Russell.

Leicester, Robert Dudley, earl of 1532?–88. English courtier who won the favor of Queen Elizabeth I but did not succeed in marrying her. A member of the Puritan sect, he opposed Catholics in England and advocated war with Spain.

Leiden, John of *See* John of Leiden.

Leif Ericson (˜ Ericsson, Erikson, Eriksson) *fl.* 1000. Norse explorer, son of Eric the Red. Raised among the Norse colonists in Greenland, he was converted to Christianity while visiting Norway. Sent back to Greenland to convert the colonists, he apparently went off course and landed somewhere in North America, which he called Vinland. He wintered there and then went on to Greenland. By another account, he first went to Greenland and then sailed westward on a voyage of discovery.

Leipzig, Battle of (Nations, ~) Major defeat (Oct. 16–19, 1813) for Napoleon during the Napoleonic Wars. The battle resulted in the loss of Germany and Poland. Prior to the battle, the allies forced Napoleon to concentrate his 180,000-man army at Leipzig and, after a preliminary battle (Oct. 16), massed some 300,000 troops to oppose him. The main attack was launched (Oct. 18) and included Austrian, Russian, Prussian, and Swedish troops. By the early hours of Oct. 19, Napoleon's retreat was under way. Allied losses were 55,000. The French lost 38,000 and some 30,000 were taken prisoner.

Leipzig Debate Famous debate (July 1519) between M. Luther and J. Eck held in Leipzig, Germany. Luther was called upon to defend his then emerging Protestant doctrine and his opposition to indulgences (*q.v.*). Both Luther and Eck, a Catholic theologian, claimed to have won.

Leipzig Interim *See* **Augsburg Interim.**

Leisler, Jacob *See* **Leisler's Rebellion.**

Leisler's Rebellion Insurrection (1689–91) in the British colony of New York. The proscription of the Catholics and accession of Protestant King William (1688) precipitated uprisings in the colonies against Catholic officials. Jacob Leisler (1640–91) set himself up as governor of southern New York in one such outbreak. In 1691, his supporters skirmished with British troops sent to restore order, though Leisler surrendered later that year. He was executed.

Lemaître, Georges 1894–1966. Belgian astrophysicist who postulated the "big bang" theory of the creation of the universe.

Lemercier, Jacques c1585–1654. French architect. Royal architect (from 1618), he completed the Louvre and designed the Sorbonne and the Palais Richelieu (which became the Palais Royal).

Lenclos, Ninon de 1620?–c1705. French courtesan whose lovers included La Rochefoucauld and the Great Condé. Her salon attracted the leading society of her day.

lend-lease Program used by the US during WW II to provide Allies with war materials and supplies. Congress narrowly passed (Mar. 1941) the Lend-Lease Act prior to US entry into the war, initially to aid Britain. This aid was soon extended to China, Russia, and by war's end, some 35 other allied nations. A reverse lend-lease program was set up in 1942, by which nations could repay lend-lease debts by providing US forces with supplies and services. When the program ended (Aug. 1945), some $50 billion in aid had been provided.

L'Enfant, Pierre Charles 1754–1825. French-born American architect and engineer. He drew up plans for the capital city of Washington, D.C., but was dismissed in 1792. His plans were ignored until 1901, when they were used in the remodeling of the city.

Lenin, Nikolai (*pseud. of* Ulianev, Vladimir Ilich) 1870–1924. Russian Communist leader, a central figure in the Russian Revolution, and founder of the Bolsheviks (*q.v.*). Lenin embraced Marxism in 1889 and was eventually arrested and exiled to Siberia (1897–1900). Leaving Russia, he became prominent in the Social Democratic Labor party and, at a party meeting (1903), began the division of the group into two factions, the Mensheviks and (his) Bolsheviks. On the outbreak of the Russian Revolution of 1917, Lenin's return to Russia in the famous "sealed train" (Apr.) was arranged by the Germans, who were counting on the revolution to eliminate Russia from participation in WW I. In Russia, Lenin opposed the provisional government, advocating instead a dictatorship of the proletariat. Lenin's Bolshevik faction gradually gained control of the Soviets in ensuing months and finally ousted the provisional government (1917) in the October Revolution (*q.v.*). Lenin became dictator and, aided by J. Stalin, L. Trotsky, and others, arranged the Treaty of Brest-Litovsk (1918) with Germany, turned Russian factories over to workers, ended private ownership of land, nationalized banks, and introduced other radical reforms. Consolidating his position, Lenin successfully opposed attempts at counterrevolution (1918–21) and crushed his political opponents. He established (1919) the Third International (*q.v.*) and introduced (1921) his New Economic Policy (*q.v.*) to revive the economy. By the time of his death in 1924, he ruled virtually without opposition and had succeeded in laying the foundations of the Russian Communist state.

Leninism Term applied to the political, economic, and social theories advanced by N. Lenin. His theories were built on the teachings of K. Marx and included a new perception of imperialism. Lenin held that imperialist powers would, in their exploitation of underdeveloped regions, come into conflict with each other and thereby sow the seeds of their own destruction. Leninism was also marked by its authoritarian temper, especially in its concept of the revolutionary party as an elite, highly disciplined organization.

Lenôtre, André (Le Nôtre, ˜) 1613–1700. French landscape architect who designed the gardens of Versailles, Chantilly, Fontainebleau, and others.

Leo I *d.* AD 474. Roman emperor of the East (457–474), successor to Marcian. He organized the disastrous attack on the Vandals, under Gaiseric, in North Africa (468).

Leo I, Saint AD c400–461. Italian-born pope (440–461), one of the important popes of the early church. He actively opposed heresy, including Manichaeanism, Pelagianism, Nestorianism, and Eutychianism. His doctrines regarding the two natures of Jesus in one person were adopted at the Council of Chalcedon (*q.v.*). Pope Leo was the greatest early advocate of papal primacy.

Leo III, Saint *d.* 816. Italian-born pope (795–816), successor of Adrian I. He crowned Charlemagne as Roman emperor in 800, thus recreating the Roman Empire in the West and establishing the tradition by which the pope conferred imperial authority on the emperor.

Leo III (˜ the Isaurian) c680–741. Byzantine emperor (717–41) and founder of the Isaurian dynasty. He defeated the last Arab siege of Constantinople (717–18) and began the long controversy over iconoclasm (726).

Leo V *d.* 820. Byzantine emperor (813–20), successor to Michael I. He halted the Bulgar attacks on Constantinople. He also precipitated a resurgence of the iconoclastic controversy and deposed the patriarch Nicephorus.

Leo VI (˜ the Wise) (˜ the Philosopher) 866–912. Byzantine emperor (886–912) whose compilation of imperial law, the *Basilica,* was adopted as the Byzantine Empire's legal code.

Leo IX, Saint (Bruno of Egisheim) 1002–54. German-born pope (1049–54). A clerical reformer. He sought unsuccessfully to regain control of Italy from the Normans in Sicily and to impose the Latin religious practices in Italy (Orthodox practices were widespread there at the time). The latter endeavor led to quarrels with and excommunication (July 16, 1054) of the patriarch of Constantinople. This in turn precipitated the Schism (*q.v.*) between the Eastern and Western churches.

Leo X (Medici, Giovanni de) 1475–1521. Italian-born pope (1513–21), successor to Julius II. His main interest was in the arts. He excommunicated M. Luther (1521) for initiating a protest against the sale of indulgences (1517) during his reign and thus figured in the beginning of the Protestant Reformation.

Leo XIII (Pecci, Gioacchino) 1810–1903. Italian-born pope (1878–1903), successor to Pius IX. He helped end the anti-Catholic Kulturkampf (*q.v.*) in Germany and worked to end friction between the papacy and secular governments elsewhere. He supported the scientific and religious theories of T. Aquinas and pointed out flaws in both capitalism and socialism in his *Rerum novarum* (1891).

Leo Africanus c1485–c1554. Arab traveler and author. Captured by pirates and sold as a slave to Pope Leo X, he converted to Christianity and wrote his famous work, *Description of Africa.*

Leonardo da Vinci 1452–1519. Italian painter, sculptor, architect, engineer, and scientist who was one of the greatest figures of the Renaissance and who is today remembered as the archetypal "Renaissance man" for his multifaceted genius. Born in Florence, he studied art as an apprentice and in 1481 began his early masterpiece *Adoration of the Magi* (never finished). Thereafter he enjoyed the patronage of a succession of nobles, including Ludovico Sforza at Milan (1482–99), Cesare Borgia (1502) at Florence, Louis XII of France (1506), and Francis I (from 1516). During his lifetime he completed such famous works as the *Last Supper* (1497), *Madonna and Child with St. Anne,* the *Mona Lisa* (1503), and *St. John the Baptist* (1512). He is considered an influential pioneer in Renaissance painting and is noted as a master of light and shade and for his technique of sfumato, by which he added a delicately hazy quality to the blending of color. None of his sculptures survive, but he is known to have worked on, among others, a monument to Francesco Sforza. In his lifetime, Da Vinci was also employed as an architect and military engineer and was deeply involved in studies of human anatomy (especially as it related to art) and the natural world. The full extent of his interests, however, was revealed only in his notebooks, which range from details of his scientific investigations to drawings of a man-powered flying machine.

Leonidas *d.* 480 BC. King of Sparta (c491–480 BC), successor to his half-brother Cleomenes I.

He became a Spartan hero when he led the unsuccessful defense of the pass of Thermopylae (480 BC) against invading Persians during the Persian Wars. He and his force of 300 Spartans were killed in the battle.

Leopardi, Giacomo 1798–1837. Italian poet. An invalid from his youth, he became a leading Italian lyricist. His poems, pessimistic in tone, include *Canzoni* and *Canti.*

Leopold I 1640–1705. Holy Roman Emperor (1658–1705), successor to his father Ferdinand III. His reign was marked by participation in the Austro-Turkish War (1682–99), the War of the Grand Alliance (1689–97), the third Dutch War (1672–78), and the start of the War of the Spanish Succession (1701–14).

Leopold I 1676–1747. Prince of Anhault-Dessau (1693–1747). Leopold served Prussia as a field marshal in the War of the Spanish Succession (1701–14) and the War of the Austrian Succession (1740–48).

Leopold I 1790–1865. First king of independent Belgium (1831–65). He refused the Greek throne before finally accepting that of Belgium. He was noted for his diplomacy, and his reign was marked by a period of peace and stability.

Leopold II 1747–92. Holy Roman Emperor (1790–92), successor to his brother, Joseph II. An enlightened despot, he repealed many of his brother's reforms, which were then precipitating rebellion in Habsburg domains. He subsequently joined Prussia in the Declaration of Pillnitz (*q.v.*) a cause of the French Revolutionary Wars (1792–1802). He died just before war began.

Leopold II 1835–1909. King of the Belgians (1865–1909), successor to his father Leopold I. He sent explorer H. Stanley to the Congo, which he later used to base his claim on the region. The Congo Free State was recognized to be under his personal control (1885) until reports of his ruthless exploitation of the natives forced the Belgian government to take it over (1908).

Leopold III 1901–83. King of the Belgians (1934–51), successor to his father, Albert I. He led the Belgian Army against the German invaders during WW II, surrendered (May 28, 1940), and was held prisoner until 1945. Opposition to his restoration after the war forced his abdication (1951).

Leo the Isaurian *See* **Leo III.**

Leo the Philosopher *See* **Leo VI.**

Leo the Wise *See* **Leo VI.**

Leovigild *d.* 586. Visigothic king of Spain (568–86), successor to his brother, Athanagild. He warred successfully against the Suevi in the north and the Byzantines in the south and thus came to control most of what became modern Spain.

Lepanto, Battle of Naval victory (Oct. 7, 1571) for Christian allies of the Holy League over the Ottoman navy. Little more than a temporary setback for the Ottoman Turks, the battle marked the first major defeat of the Turks by Christian forces. The allied Christian fleet was formed after the Turks invaded (1570) Cyprus, controlled by Venice. It consisted of some 200 ships sent by Spain, Venice, and the pope. The fleet, commanded by John of Austria, engaged the Ottoman navy of some 200 ships, commanded by Ali Pasha, off Lepanto, Greece. In a matter of hours the Ottoman navy was destroyed and only about 40 ships escaped capture or sinking. The Turks rapidly rebuilt their navy (by 1572) and ultimately took Cyprus (1573).

Lepidus, Marcus Aemilius *d.* 77 BC. Roman statesman and consul (78 BC). As consul he opposed Sulla's reforms and tried unsuccessfully to reverse them. He marched on Rome (77) after being denied the consulship for 77 and, after losing in battle at Milvian Bridge, was decisively defeated by Pompey.

Lepidus, Marcus Aemilius *d.* 13 BC. Roman statesman. With Marc Antony and Octavian, a member of the second triumvirate (43–36 BC) that ruled Rome after the assassination of J. Caesar. He was forced from power (36 BC) after attempting a revolt (in Sicily) against Octavian.

Lerdo de Tejada, Sebastian 1825–89. President of Mexico (1872–76). He succeeded B. Juárez as president and was overthrown by P. Díaz.

Lerma, Francisco Gómez de Sandoval y Rojas, duque de 1552?–1625. Spanish politician. Lerma was prime minister (1598–1618) to Philip III, over whom he exerted great influence. He expelled the Moriscos and was finally driven from office for financial corruption.

Lermontov, Mikhail Yurevich 1814–41. Russian poet and novelist. An influential Romantic, he is known for his novel *A Hero of Our Time* (1840) and such poems as *The Demon, Borodino,* and *Ismail-Bey.*

Lesage, Alain René 1668–1747. French novelist and dramatist, an exponent of realism noted as the author of the novel *Gil Blas* (1747) and the play *Turcaret* (1708).

Lesbos   Greek island, located in the Aegean Sea. A Bronze Age civilization flourished there and the island was later settled by Aeolians (end of 2d millennium BC). It rose as a center of Greek culture (7th–6th cents. BC) and was home to the poets Sappho and Alcaeus and the philosopher Theophrastus.

lèse-majesté (lese majesty)   A crime against the state or the ruler of a state. Important in medieval times, the concept can be traced back to the Roman republic, when it was used to refer to violations of basic laws of the state. During the time of the Roman Empire, the term was extended to cases involving acts against the emperor himself.

Lesotho (*formerly* Basutoland)   Kingdom in southern Africa, lying within the borders of the Republic of South Africa. The population is 1,757,000 and the capital is Maseru. The kingdom was formed (c1800) by elements of various Bantu peoples forced out of their homelands by the Zulus. These peoples defended the kingdom against the Zulus and later the Boers. It became a British protectorate in 1868 and a colony in 1884. After successfully resisting annexation by South Africa, Lesotho became an independent kingdom (Oct. 4, 1966). King Moshoeshoe II (reigned 1965–90) became head of state, though from 1970–86 he was specifically forbidden to take part in politics. In the early 1980s, tensions with neighboring South Africa increased over suspicions ANC rebels were operating out of Lesotho. Cross-border raids, threatened economic sanctions, and other actions by South Africa continued through the mid-1980s, until finally in 1986 a coup installed a military government (with the king as executive head of state). The new government adopted an aggressive policy against ANC rebels and sought closer relations with South Africa, on which Lesotho's economy was dependent. Following a power struggle within the military, King Moshoeshoe was exiled (1990) and removed from power. His son was elected king (as Letsie III). A coup within the military government (1991) resulted in new leadership and promises that elections would be held. A ban on political activity (since 1986) was rescinded.

Lespinasse, Julie de 1732–76.   Hostess of a noted Parisian salon. She began in the literary salon of Madame Du Deffand and then opened her own (1764) with the philosopher J. d'Alembert as her leading guest.

Lesseps, Ferdinand Marie, vicomte de 1805–94. French diplomat and engineer. He originated the idea of the Suez Canal and directed its construction (1859–69). His Panama Canal project (begun 1881) ended in scandal and a French government inquiry.

Lessing, Doris 1919– .   British author. Lessing's work, which reflects the political and social upheaval of the modern era, includes *The Grass Is Singing, The Children of Violence,* and *The Golden Notebook.*

Lessing, Gotthold Ephraim 1729–81.   German critic, philosopher, and dramatist. Lessing introduced Shakespeare to German literature, assisted in the formation of the German national theater, published theological essays espousing freedom of thought, and wrote the plays *Miss Sara Sampson, Minna von Barnhelm,* and *Nathan the Wise. Laokoon* is among his critical works.

Le Tellier, Michel 1603–85.   French statesman. As minister of war (1643–66), he organized the first French royal army and was appointed chancellor (1677–85) by Louis XIV.

lettres de cachet   French warrants. These secret letters were used to imprison or exile personal enemies of the king or nobility (from 17th cent.). They were outlawed by the National Assembly (1789).

Leucippus 5th cent. BC. Greek philosopher, thought by some to have originated the theory of atoms, usually credited to his pupil Democritus.

Leuctra, Battle of   Battle (371 BC) in which the Spartans were decisively beaten by the military tactics of the Thebans, led by Epaminondas. The battle marked the beginning of the brief Theban ascendancy over Greece.

Leutze, Emanuel 1816–68.   American painter, known for his *Washington Crossing the Delaware.*

Levant   Term used for those countries on the eastern shore of the Mediterranean, from Egypt to Greece. It sometimes also refers to the former French Levant states, Syria and Lebanon.

Levellers   Extremist English Protestant sect and political group active (c1647–50) during the English Civil Wars and Commonwealth. Levellers favored total religious and political equality and advocated a written constitution, universal male suffrage, an end to the monarchy, and abolition of economic and social privileges.

Unable to advance their cause in the Long Parliament (*q.v.*), Levellers organized followers in O. Cromwell's New Model Army. In the Putney debates (Oct. 1647), Levellers forced the army command to consider a proposed constitution, called *Agreement of the People.* It was rejected by Gen. H. Ireton and later mutinies (1649) by Levellers resulted in suppression of the group. Prominent Levellers included J. Lilburne, Richard Overton (*fl.* mid-17th cent.), and William Walwyn (*fl.* mid-17th cent.).

Leverrier, Urbain Jean Joseph 1811–77. French astronomer who, along with the Englishman J. C. Adams, discovered the planet Neptune (1846).

Lévi-Strauss, Claude 1908– . French social anthropologist famous for his works defining structural anthropology. His first major work was titled *The Elementary Structures of Kinship* (1949).

Levites Ancient Hebrew religious functionaries. Drawn from the male population of the tribe of Levi, Levites were originally temple servants and later became teachers of the Law. The tribe of Levi is sometimes said to be named after Jacob's third son, by Leah. Three families make up the tribe of the Levites: the Gershonites, Merarites, and Kohathites.

Lewes, Battle of Battle (May 14, 1264) during the Barons' War (*q.v.*). The barons, led by S. de Montfort, defeated the royal army, captured both King Henry III and Prince Edward (later Edward I), and thereby forced concessions from the king.

Lewes, George Henry 1817–78. English philosopher, critic, and author. He founded *The Fortnightly Review* and wrote the *Life of Goethe* (1855). He lived with G. Eliot from 1854.

Lewis, Clive Staples 1898–1963. English author of *The Screwtape Letters* and the children's fantasies the *Chronicles of Narnia.*

Lewis, John Llewellyn 1880–1969. American labor leader. He was president of the United Mine Workers of America (1920–60) and cofounder of the Committee for Industrial Organization (CIO) in 1935.

Lewis, Meriwether 1774–1809. American explorer. With W. Clark, he led the famous Lewis and Clark expedition (*q.v.*) to the Pacific Northwest.

Lewis, Percy Wyndham 1886–1957. British author and artist. He founded the vorticist magazine *Blast* (1914) with E. Pound, wrote satirical and autobiographical novels, and painted works in a variety of styles.

Lewis, (Harry) Sinclair 1885–1951. American author, the first to win a Nobel Prize for Literature (1930). His satiric novels of American provincialism include *Main Street, Babbitt, Arrowsmith, Elmer Gantry,* and *Dodsworth.*

Lewis and Clark expedition Famous overland expedition (1804–06) in the US Far West. The expedition charted an overland route to the Pacific and provided valuable scientific and practical information about the largely unexplored region. Initiated by T. Jefferson and sponsored by the government, the expedition consisted of about 40 men under the leadership of M. Lewis and W. Clark. The party left from St. Louis (May 14, 1804) and followed the Missouri River to its headwaters (recruiting the Indian guide Sacajawea along the way), crossed the Continental Divide, and then followed in succession the Clearwater, Snake, and Columbia rivers to the Pacific Ocean. They built Fort Clatsop on the coast and, after spending the winter there, returned (Sept. 23, 1806) to St. Louis.

Lexington and Concord, Battle of Opening hostilities (Apr. 19, 1775) of the American Revolution (1775–83). The British governor of Massachusetts, Gen. T. Gage, sparked the battle by sending a column of infantrymen from Boston to destroy a Colonial supply depot at Concord, Massachusetts. Word was sent ahead of the British, however, by P. Revere and others. The British were met at Lexington Green by 50 Colonial militiamen (minutemen), under Capt. John Parker (1729–75), and eight Americans were killed in a brief battle. The British continued to Concord and destroyed what supplies remained there. Part of the British force was attacked at Concord bridge by some 400 minutemen, and the British began their retreat to Boston. Along the way the minutemen, using guerrilla tactics, harried the British column and eventually killed 273. American losses were 95.

Lex Hortensia See **Rome, 287 BC.**

Ley Juárez See **Reforma, La.**

Ley Lerdo See **Reforma, La.**

Leyte Gulf, Battle of (Philippine Sea, ˜) Major WW II victory for the US in battle against the Japanese (Oct. 23–25, 1944). Considered one of the greatest sea and air battles, the victory enabled the US to reconquer the Philippines.

The battle was provoked by US landings (Oct. 20) on Leyte, in the Philippines. The Japanese (in "Sho-Go," or Victory Operation) planned to draw the US Third Fleet northward by means of a decoy fleet and to crush the US landing force in a three-pronged attack. One of the three Japanese attack elements was located and damaged (Oct. 23) by US submarines. On Oct. 25, all three of the attack elements were engaged by naval and air units of the US Seventh Fleet and were largely destroyed.

L'Hôpital, Michel de (L'Hospital, ~) c1505–73. French statesman, until 1568 chief counselor to Catherine de Médicis. He urged a policy of religious tolerance toward Protestants (Huguenots), won passage of the Edict of January (1562) granting them religious freedoms, and was dismissed (1568) during the Wars of Religion (1562–98).

Liang Qichao 1873–1929. Chinese scholar and intellectual who figured in efforts to modernize Chinese society. Liang reinterpreted Confucian classics in an attempt to harness tradition as an agent for changing Chinese society. Both Liang and his mentor, Kang Youwei, figured in the emperor's abortive effort at modernizing Chinese society in 1898 (Hundred Days of Reform, *q.v.*). Exiled (1898–1912) after the Dowager Empress intervened, Liang returned when the republic was formed. Originally a supporter of President Yuan Shikai, Liang blocked Yuan's attempt to make himself emperor.

Liao-yang, Battle of Japanese victory in battle (Aug. 25–Sept. 3, 1904) during the Russo-Japanese War (1904–05). The Russian Gen. A. Kuropatkin was forced to retreat after bitter fighting near this town in northeastern China.

Liaquat Ali Khan 1895–1951. The first prime minister (1947–51) of newly formed Pakistan. He was assassinated.

Li Bai (Li Po; Li Tai Po) c700–762. Chinese Tang dynasty poet, considered one of China's greatest. A romantic, he is said to have gotten drunk, reached for the moon's reflection in a river, and drowned.

Libby, Willard Frank 1908–80. American chemist who developed the radioactive carbon-14 dating method, an important research tool for archaeologists, anthropologists, and historians. He received the Nobel Prize in Chemistry in 1960.

Libby Prison Notorious Confederate prisoner-of-war camp in Richmond, Virginia, originally a tobacco warehouse. Conditions were bad, and many captured Union soldiers died there between 1863 and 1865.

liberalism Generally, a philosophy that advocates maintaining the freedom of individuals from outside restraints. It is characterized by a belief in the fundamental goodness and rationality of humankind, and belief in continuing change as a means to perfect the order of things. Thus it often arises in opposition to conservatism. Fueled by ideas of the Enlightenment, liberalism flourished in the 18th–19th cents. as a movement toward greater personal liberty, toward restrictions on government powers, and toward such persuasive doctrines as laissez-faire economics. By the 20th cent., however, the focus of liberalism had been changed by disparity between industrialists' wealth and the lot of the worker. Thus in modern times, liberalism became concerned with freeing the individual from economic and social restraints. To do this, liberals have sought to institute government programs to provide basic protections for the individual, such as social security, welfare, and other minimum-maintenance programs. (*See also* Liberal party.)

Liberal party   1. British party that, with the Conservative party, was one of the two major parties in that country between 1832 and 1931. Formed from the Whig party after the Reform Bill of 1832, the Liberal party embraced many progressive social-reform causes including extension of the franchise and Home Rule for Ireland. At the same time, it favored laissez-faire capitalism and free trade. The party placed many prime ministers in office, such as W. Gladstone, H. Asquith, and, during WW I, D. Lloyd George. The party declined from the 1920s vis-à-vis the Labour party because of its adherence to laissez-faire doctrines. It finally split in 1931 and thereafter became a minor party. A revival in the 1970s brought back to it the votes of about 15 percent of the electorate.   2. New York State party founded (May, 1944) by elements of the American Labor party, who charged that the latter had become Communist-dominated. It has sometimes held the balance of power in elections between the major parties. From around 1970 it has been counterbalanced by the New York Conservative party.   3. Name given to a number of continental parties generally believing in laissez-faire capitalism and opposed to growing trends toward government regulation of the economy.

Liberal Republican party Short-lived party created (1872) by insurgent Republicans. It was formed largely in reaction to corruption in President U. Grant's first administration, and the party platform included civil service reform and a more moderate program of Reconstruction in the South. The party nominated (1872) H. Greeley for president and, though it had the support of the Democratic party, Greeley was easily beaten by U. Grant in his bid for a second term. The party disappeared shortly thereafter. Leaders included C. Sumner, C. Schurz, and C. F. Adams.

Liberal Union British political party formed (1886) by disaffected members of the Liberal party. They opposed the policies of W. Gladstone.

Liberia (Republic of Liberia) Republic located in coastal West Africa. The population is 2,644,000 and the capital is Monrovia. Liberia was founded (1821) as a home for freed slaves by the American Colonization Society (*q.v.*). Between 1822 and the beginning of the American Civil War (1861–65), thousands of American Negro colonists were transported there and in 1847 Liberia became an independent republic. The country's subsequent history in the 19th cent. was marked by clashes with native populations in the interior, loss of territory to European powers colonizing West Africa, a rebellion that resulted in overthrow of the government (1871), and a growing national debt. The government finally went bankrupt in 1909, though in following years new foreign loans and leases to the Firestone Company for a vast rubber plantation helped the national economy. In 1930, confirmed reports of slavery in Liberia forced the resignation of the government, though by 1936 slavery was effectively eliminated. During the long tenure (1944–71) of President W. Tubman, Liberia was opened to foreign investment, and exploitation of its natural resources was begun. William Tolbert, Jr., served as president (1971–80) until his overthrow by army sergeant Samuel Doe (Apr., 1980). Doe suspended the constitution and established military rule. Following adoption of a new constitution (1984), a multi-party system was instituted and Doe was elected president (1985). Discontent with Doe's regime culminated in an armed revolt (Dec. 1989) in the northeast. Hundreds of thousands of refugees fled to neighboring Guinea and Côte d'Ivoire. By mid-1990 the rebels had entered Monrovia and besieged President Doe in the presidential palace. An African peacekeeping force of some 4,000 troops (initially) was sent, but fighting soon turned into a three-way battle between loyalists and two competing rebel factions. Doe was captured and killed by rebels (Sept. 1990) and after failing to win a ceasefire agreement, the peacekeeping forces went on the offensive in Monrovia (Oct.). Late in the year a ceasefire was agreed to and all rebel soldiers withdrew from Monrovia by Jan. 1991. An interim government was established and a peace plan was agreed to in Sept. 1991, though fighting continued into Dec. An interim government was established (Jan. 1992) and in May peacekeeping troops began disarming rebels. However, rebel leader Charles Taylor refused to disarm and soon gained control of much of the countryside. By Oct. 1992 he was able to threaten Monrovia.

Liberius *d.* AD 366. Italian-born pope (AD 352–366), successor to Julius I. He was banished by Emperor Constantius II (355) for his stand against Arianism (*q.v.*), returned in 358 and later reaffirmed the Nicene faith.

liberty Freedom from restraint of choice or limitation of action, especially in reference to an individual. It is generally conceded that complete personal freedom (anarchy) is untenable and that, in a society, some restraints must be imposed on individuals by government or other outside authority. However, the character of government and the balance between restraints and liberties has been a cause of debate and rebellion throughout the evolution of human civilization. The Magna Carta, Declaration of Independence and Declaration of the Rights of Man, among others, are all expressions of the drive toward individual liberty, as are the philosophical writings of J. Locke and J. Rousseau.

Liberty, Sons of *See* **Sons of Liberty.**

Liberty, Statue of *See* **Statue of Liberty.**

Liberty Affair Incident in Boston Harbor in which British customs officials seized (June 10, 1768) J. Hancock's sloop, *Liberty,* which was smuggling Madeira wine. The popular outcry caused the officials to take refuge and call for infantry support.

Liberty Bell Bell, symbolic in American history, which hung in Independence Hall, Philadelphia, from 1753. According to traditional accounts, it was rung on the signing of the Declaration of

Independence (July 4, 1776) in Philadelphia. It cracked beyond repair in 1846.

Liberty Poles (Liberty Trees) In Colonial America, poles erected (1765–66) as symbols of opposition to unpopular British policies and officials. The first Liberty Pole was located in Boston.

Liberty party First US political party (1840–48) organized to promote abolition of slavery. Led by James G. Birney (1792–1857) and Gerrit Smith (1797–1874), the party was formed (1840) in New York by members of the American Antislavery Society, who were opposed to the society's policy against political action. It nominated Birney as its presidential candidate (1840, 1844). In 1844 it indirectly helped elect J. Polk to the presidency by splitting antislavery support for the Whig party candidate, H. Clay. The party merged (1848) with antislavery Whigs and Democrats prior to the 1848 presidential election, forming the Free-Soil party (*q.v.*).

Liberty Trees *See* **Liberty Poles.**

liberum veto *See* **Sejm.**

Liberty League American organization established (1934) to oppose policies of President F. Roosevelt. Backed financially by conservative industrialists like the du Ponts, the league supported anti–New Deal candidates in the 1934 congressional elections and published pamphlets denouncing the Roosevelt administration as extravagant, socialistic, and dictatorial. The movement failed to win grass-roots support, however, and faded by 1936.

Libya Republic located in northern Africa, bordering Egypt on the west. The population is 4,280,000 and the capital is Tripoli. The region comprising modern Libya came under Ottoman control in the 16th cent. but maintained relative autonomy during the period 1711–1835. The Italians seized control of the region during war with the Ottomans in the early 1900s. After WW II Libya came under UN control and gained independence in 1951. Since 1969, when M. al-Quaddafi seized power, Libya has been a radical and revolutionary influence in the Middle East. Key dates in the history of Libya include:

7TH CENT. BC Phoenicians founded colonies in Tripolitania; region later became eastern part of Carthaginian domains.

7TH CENT. BC Cyrenaica settled by Greek colonists.

1ST CENT. BC Cyrenaica passed to Romans; made a province with Crete.

46 BC Romans conquered Tripolitania during Numidian War; annexed it to African province.

7TH CENT. AD Tripolitania and Cyrenaica overrun by Arab Muslims.

16TH CENT. Tripolitania and Cyrenaica conquered by Ottomans and merged into administrative regency of Tripoli.

1711 Ahmad Karamanli became dey of Tripoli; killed Ottoman governor and secured the governorship, thus established hereditary Karamanli rule of Tripoli (until 1835).

18TH–19TH CENTS. Tripoli became center for pirates, chief source of revenue for the dey; led to Tripolitan war with US (1801–05) and operations by European countries to destroy the pirates; Ottoman Empire resumed governorship of Tripoli (1835).

1840s Sanusiyya brotherhood established in Libya by religious leader Ali al-Sanusi; movement became important social and political force in Cyrenaica and Fezzan.

1911–12 Italo-Turkish War; Italy occupied northern Tripolitania.

1912–14 Italy conquered the rest of Tripolitania.

1930s "Demographic colonization" of Libya promoted by Italian leader Mussolini; arrival of Italian settlers spurred development projects for their benefit.

1940–43 WW II; Libya was site of fierce fighting during North Africa campaigns; after Axis forces were defeated (1943) in region, Libya came under Allied administration.

1949 Administration of Libya passed to UN, which called for Libyan independence by 1952.

1951 Independence granted (Dec. 24); Libya became United Kingdom of Libya, a federated state composed of Cyrenaica, Tripolitania, and Fezzan, a southwest desert region.

1951–69 Idris I reigned as king of Libya.

1953 Libya joined the Arab League.

1953–54 Treaties for establishment of British and US military bases signed.

1955 Became member of the UN.

1958 Oil discovered in Libya; economic situation improved in following years.

1963 Government reorganized by royal decree; provincial governments abolished in favor of central government.

1964 Treaty with Britain terminated; British troops to be withdrawn.

1969 Military coup; M. al-Quaddafi seized power (Sept. 1) from King Idris I.

1969– Quaddafi in power as head of state; though he later relinquished some government posts, he retained ultimate control and aligned Libya with radical elements in Mideast and elsewhere.

1969 Unsuccessful attempt to overthrow Quaddafi (Dec.).

1970 Libya closed US bases; confiscated Italian and Jewish property.

1970 Unsuccessful attempt to overthrow Quaddafi (July).

1973 Quaddafi instituted purge of political opponents (Apr. 15).

1973 Quaddafi signed (Aug. 29) agreement with Egypt providing for unification of the two countries in prearranged stages; plan never enacted.

1973 Libya nationalized majority holdings of foreign oil companies in the country (Sept. 1).

1973 Libya occupied the Aozou strip in northern Chad.

1975 Major arms sale secured from Soviet Union; Russia agreed to supply Libya with nuclear reactor.

1977 Four-day border war with Egypt broke out (July 21); cease-fire arranged through mediation of Algerian President Houari Boumediène (July 24).

1979 Libyan troops sent in unsuccessful attempt to aid Ugandan dictator Idi Amin; Amin granted asylum in Libya.

1980 Formal agreement signed calling for unification of Libya and Syria (Sept. 10); plan subsequently tabled.

1980 Libyan troops intervened in Chad to end civil war there (Dec. 16).

1981 Libyan diplomats expelled (May) from the US for supporting terrorist activities.

1981 Two Libyan fighters shot down (Aug. 19) in dogfight with US fighters off the Libyan coast.

1982 US banned all imports of Libyan products (Mar.); called for general boycott.

1983 Quaddafi sent troops to Chad to support Goukouny Oueddeye (June).

1983 France deployed 3,000 troops in Chad at the request of Chadian president Hissène Habré (Aug.).

1984 Britain severed diplomatic relations with Libya following terrorist bombings in Manchester and London, which were aimed at Libyan dissidents (Apr.).

1984 France and Libya agreed to withdraw forces from Chad (Sept.); many Libyan troops remained in Chad.

1984 Libya and Morocco signed a treaty of union (Aug.); Morocco later reneged on the treaty.

1985 Libya expelled over 120,000 foreign workers, mostly Egyptian (July) and Tunisian (Aug.) nationals.

1985 Quaddafi drew "line of death" across the Gulf of Sirte in dispute with the US over navigational rights (Dec.).

1986 Two American fighter aircraft attacked by Libyan forces in the Gulf of Sirte (Mar.); US responded with Libya bombing raid; attacked military installations, airports, and suspected terrorist training camps in Libya (Apr.).

1987 Libyan diplomats were expelled from many countries, including Kenya, Switzerland, and Italy.

1987 Chad invaded the Aozou strip and occupied the town of Aozou; Libya bombed towns in northern Chad and recaptured Aozou.

1988 Quaddafi implemented political and economic reforms in order to blunt domestic unrest and criticism from abroad.

1988 Chad and Libya restored diplomatic relations (Oct.).

1988 US imposed trade and economic sanctions in the wake of the Pan Am crash at Lockerbie, Scotland (Dec.); Libyan involvement suspected in planting of terrorist bomb that caused crash.

1989 Two Libyan fighter aircraft shot down over the Mediterranean by US fighters (Jan. 4).

1989 Islamic fundamentalists blamed for antigovernment riots in Tripoli (Feb.).

1990 Libya and Sudan signed an "integration" pact (Mar.), as a step toward possible union.

1990–91 Persian Gulf War; Libya opposed deployment of the multinational force for the defense of Saudi Arabia and Kuwait.

1991 France, Britain, and the US demanded extradition of Libyans involved with the bombings of the Pan Am flight over Lockerbie, Scotland, and a French airliner over the Sahara in 1989; Libya denied involvement in the incidents.

1992 PLO leader Y. Arafat survived plane crash during sandstorm in Libyan desert (Apr.).

1992 UN enacted limited sanctions against Libya after it failed to extradite two intelligence agents allegedly involved with attacks on airliners.

Libya Bombing Air attack on targets in Libya (1986). American warplanes, flying from British and Mediterranean locations, bombed several targets in Tripoli and Benghazi (Apr. 14). The air strikes were ordered by US President R. Reagan in retaliation for the recent terrorist bombing of a West German discothèque in which an American serviceman was killed and more than 200 people were injured. Reagan warned of further strikes if Libyan leader M. al-Quaddafi continued supporting anti-American terrorism abroad.

Lichnowsky, Karl Max, Fürst von 1860–1928. German diplomat. Unauthorized publication of a pamphlet he wrote describing his vain efforts to prevent the outbreak of WW I resulted in his ouster (1918) from the Prussian legislature.

Licinian Rogations *See* **Licinius Calvus Stolo, Caius.**

Licinius *d.* AD 325. Roman emperor (AD 308–24) who ruled jointly with Galerius (AD 308–11) and who defeated Emperor Maximinus (314), thereby taking control of the East. He was defeated by Constantine (AD 324), exiled, and executed.

Licinius Calvus Stolo, Caius *fl.* 375 BC. Roman tribune. He is said to have introduced the Licinian-Sextian Rogations, which advanced rights of the plebeians.

Lidice Village in Czechoslovakia, near Prague. It was "liquidated" by the Germans (1942) in reprisal for the assassination of the Nazi governor, Reinhard Heydrich.

Lie, Jonas Lauritz Idemil 1833–1908. Norwegian novelist. His novels treat Norwegian life in a realistic way, as in *The Pilot and His Wife* and *The Family at Gilje.*

Lie, Trygve Halvdan 1896–1968. Norwegian statesman. The first secretary-general of the United Nations (1946–52), he resigned because of Russian objections to his support for UN participation in the Korean War.

Liebig, Justus, baron von 1803–73. German chemist. He established the first chemical teaching laboratory and was a founder of agricultural chemistry.

Liebknecht, Wilhelm 1826–1900. German Socialist and journalist. After participating in the Revolution of 1848, he lived in exile in England (1849–62) and worked with K. Marx. In 1869 he founded the Social Democratic Labor party.

Liechtenstein Small European principality located in the Alps between Austria and Switzerland. The population is 28,000 and the capital is Vaduz. The principality was created in 1719 by the joining of Schellenberg and Vaduz counties in the Holy Roman Empire. It became independent of the German Confederation in 1866 and is a member of a Swiss customs union (1924). Liechtenstein joined the Council of Europe in 1978, the UN in 1990, and the European Free Trade Association in 1991. Women were granted the vote in national elections (1984; local elections in 1986). Prince Franz Josef, head of state since 1938, died in 1989 and was succeeded by his son, Prince Hans-Adam II.

Light Brigade, Charge of *See* **Balaclava, Battle of.**

Ligne, Charles Joseph, prince of 1735–1814. Austrian field marshal. An adviser of Holy Roman Emperor Joseph II and friend of Catherine II of Russia, he is chiefly noted for his correspondence with European dignitaries. He is also remembered for his comment that "the Congress [of Vienna] dances but does not get anywhere."

Ligny, Battle of Early battle (June 16, 1815) of the Waterloo Campaign, fought in Ligny, Belgium, during the Napoleonic Wars (1803–15). Napoleon defeated the Prussian force under Marshal G. Blücher.

Liguria Historic region in northwestern Italy along the Ligurian Sea and including the Italian Riviera, the Maritime Alps, and the Ligurian Apennines. Conquered by the Romans (2d cent. BC), the region eventually came under Genoese control (by 16th cent.) and became part of Italy during its unification (1860).

Ligurian Republic French satellite state. Napoleon gave this name to the republic of Genoa in 1797 and incorporated it into France in 1805. It became part of Sardinia after Napoleon's fall.

Li Hongzhang (~ Hung-chang) 1823–1901. Chinese statesman. He commanded forces against the Taiping Rebellion (1861–64), founded the Chinese navy, and became the dominant figure in Chinese foreign affairs (from c1872). He worked to improve relations with the West and to modernize China.

Li Hung-chang *See* **Li Hongzhang.**

Lilburne, John 1614?–57. English leader of the Leveller (*q.v.*) faction. Though imprisoned several times, he continued to distribute pamphlets and agitate for civil and religious reform. In 1655, while in prison, he became a Quaker.

Li Lisan 1896–1967. Chinese Communist leader. He dominated the Chinese Communist party during the late 1920s. He was eventually replaced by Mao Zedong when his strategy of inciting urban labor rebellions (Li Li-san line) failed.

Liliuokalani 1838–1917. Queen of the Hawaiian Islands (1891–93). She succeeded her brother King Kalakaua and was deposed for trying to resist changes in the constitution.

Lima, Saint Rose of *See* **Rose of Lima, Saint.**

Liman von Sanders, Otto 1855–1929. German general. He commanded the Turkish armies at Gallipoli (1915) and forced the Allied withdrawal. As German commander in Palestine, he was defeated in 1918.

limes In ancient Rome, a fortified line set up on a border frontier of the empire. Frontier garrisons, watch towers, and earth and stone barriers (from the time of Hadrian) were used variously to control the frontiers in Germany, Britain, and elsewhere.

Lin Biao (Lin Piao) 1907–71. Chinese Communist general and politician. After the Long March (1934–35), he became commander of Communist forces in the northeast against Chiang Kaishek's Nationalist army. He became heir apparent to Mao Zedong after replacing Liu Shaoqui (1966) as second-in-command of the Chinese Communist party. He died in a plane crash under suspicious circumstances.

Lincoln, Abraham 1809–65. American national hero, 16th US president (1861–65), successor to J. Buchanan, and Union leader during the American Civil War (*q.v.*). Born to a poor family and raised on the Illinois frontier, he educated himself, worked at various jobs (his rail-splitting days are often remembered), and became a lawyer in 1836. Though he had been involved in politics in the 1830s and 1840s (and as Whig Congressman [1847–49] opposed to the Mexican War), his rise to prominence did not begin until he became embroiled in the slavery question (1850s). As a Republican (from 1856), he unsuc-

cessfully opposed S. Douglas for the US Senate (1858). But in the seven now famous Lincoln-Douglas debates, held during that campaign, Lincoln established himself as a leader of the moderate opposition to slavery. Lincoln became the Republican presidential candidate (1860) and, with the Democratic party split over slavery, won the election. Southern states began seceding soon after his election and just over a month after he took office, hostilities between the North and South broke out at Fort Sumter and the Civil War began. In succeeding years, Lincoln instituted wartime measures, some of which were challenged; meddled in military matters and went through a succession of commanders, finally settling on U. Grant (1863); and maintained his steady, moderate course despite reverses in the war and bitter disputes between radical abolitionists and conservative factions. However, the Emancipation Proclamation (*q.v.*) and the Gettysburg Address (*q.v.*) are by far the best-known events connected with Lincoln's wartime administration. With the war going in the North's favor, Lincoln won reelection to a second term in 1864. Then came R. Lee's surrender and an end to the war. But, tragically, less than a week afterward Lincoln was shot and killed (Apr. 15, 1865) at Ford's Theatre by J. Booth (*q.v.*).

Lincoln, Battle of (Fair of Lincoln) Royalist victory (May 20, 1217) which ended a rebellion by English barons in alliance with Prince Louis of France, pretender to the English throne. Some 400 knights led by the regent of King Henry III, William Marshal (earl of Pembroke), defeated approximately 600 Frenchmen and barons at the town of Lincoln.

Lincoln, Benjamin 1733–1810. American Revolutionary War army officer. He was forced to surrender Charleston, South Carolina, to the British (1780), served as secretary of war (1781–83), and put down Shays' Rebellion (1787).

Lincoln, Mary Todd 1818–82. Wife of A. Lincoln (*m.* 1842). After losing three of her four sons and seeing her husband shot, she was committed (1875) to an asylum. She was released the next year.

Lincoln, Robert Todd 1843–1926. American lawyer, son of A. Lincoln. He was secretary of war (1881–85), US minister to England (1889–93), and president of the Pullman Company (1897–1911).

Lincoln, Saint Hugh of *See* **Hugh of Lincoln, Saint.**

Lindbergh, Ann Spencer Morrow 1906– . American author, wife of C. A. Lindbergh (*m.* 1929). Among her works are *North to the Orient, Gift from the Sea,* and *The Unicorn and Other Poems.*

Lindbergh, Charles Augustus 1902–74. American aviator, the first man to fly alone and nonstop across the Atlantic Ocean (May 20–21, 1927). Virtually unknown when he left the US aboard his plane *Spirit of St. Louis,* he was an international celebrity by the time he reached Paris. He married Anne Morrow (1929) and they lived quietly until their child was kidnapped and murdered (1932) in one of the most sensational crimes of this century. The public later turned against Lindbergh, however. An isolationist, he was convinced of the invincibility of Nazi air power and his speeches for the America First Committee against US intervention in WW II were called pro-Nazi. During the war, however, he distinguished himself by flying combat missions with the US air force.

Lindsay, (Nicholas) Vachel 1879–1931. American poet. After studying art in Chicago and New York, he turned to poetry and began living on what he could earn by reciting his work. Later he published such volumes of poetry as *Rhymes to Be Traded for Bread* (1912) and *The Congo and Other Poems* (1914). His work and his popularity declined in the 1920s, and Lindsay poisoned himself in 1931.

Lines of Torres Vedras Three lines of defensive fortification in Portugal, extending from the Tagus River to the ocean. They were constructed to protect allied forces, under the Duke of Wellington, from French attack during the Peninsular War (1808–14). The lines were never seriously attacked and thereby halted the French invasion of Portugal.

Linggadjati Agreement (Cheribon ˜) Agreement (Nov. 25, 1946) in which the Netherlands formally recognized Indonesia as the de facto government of Java, Sumatra, and Madura.

Linlithgow, Victor Alexander John Hope, 2d marquess of 1887–1952. British statesman who, as viceroy of India (1936–43), maintained British authority in India during the crucial early years of WW II.

Linnaeus, Carolus (*orig.* Linné, Carl von) 1707–78. Swedish botanist. Linnaeus is considered the father of modern botany, primarily for his system of classification and nomenclature of plants and animals. He published over 180 works during his lifetime; among them were *Flora Lapponica, Systema Naturae,* and *Species Plantarum.*

Lin Piao *See* **Lin Biao.**

Linton, Ralph 1893–1953. American anthropologist, author of *The Study of Man, The Cultural Background of Personality,* and *The Tree of Culture.*

Li Po *See* **Li Bai.**

Lippi, Fra Filippo c1406–69. Italian Renaissance painter. He was under the patronage of Cosimo de Medici and did the frescoes in the cathedral choir at Prato.

Lippmann, Walter 1899–1974. US journalist and author. He wrote the influential political column *Today and Tomorrow* (1931–67) and several books, including *Public Opinion.*

Li Si *See* **Qin.**

Lister, Joseph 1st baron 1827–1912. English surgeon, founder of antiseptic surgery. After studying Pasteur's theories on bacteria, he developed (1865) the use of carbolic acid as an antiseptic.

Liszt, Franz 1811–86. Hungarian composer and pianist, foremost concert pianist of his day. He originated the symphonic poem form, of which *Les Préludes* and *Mazeppa* are examples. He revolutionized the sonata form by introducing the device of the leitmotiv. Among his many works for the piano are his Hungarian rhapsodies.

Li Tai Po *See* **Li Bai.**

Lithuania (Republic of Lithuania) Independent state and former Soviet republic in the Baltic Sea region. The population is 3,700,000 and the capital is Vilnius. Organized as a duchy (13th cent.) to resist attacks by the Livonian Brothers and the Teutonic Knights, Lithuania for a time became a powerful medieval state with domains extending to the Black Sea. It came into personal union with Poland (1386) by royal marriage and was forced by the threat of Russian domination (under Ivan IV) to accept the Union of Lublin (1569) with Poland. Russia gained control of Lithuanian territories by the three Partitions of Poland (18th cent.). Lithuania was occupied by Germany during WW I (from 1915) and amid the chaos of the war and the Russian revolution, proclaimed independence (Feb. 16, 1918). The USSR recognized Lithuanian independence following the Baltic Wars of Liberation (*q.v.*), by the Treaty of Moscow (July 12, 1920). Lithuania established a democratic government after adopting a constitution (1922), but it was overthrown in a military coup (Dec. 17, 1926). This government remained in power until the Soviet takeover in 1940. Secret provisions of the 1939 pact between Nazi Germany and the USSR originally provided that Germany would control Lithuania, but a subsequent agreement gave Lithuania to the Soviets (Aug.). Two months later Soviet troops were stationed in Lithuania and the following year the USSR made the country a republic within the USSR (Aug. 3, 1940). Nazi Germany occupied Lithuania 1941–44 and during that time killed almost a quarter of a million people (165,000 Jews among them). After Germany's surrender, the Soviets reestablished their harsh regime, deporting some 350,000 Lithuanians and forcibly collectivizing agriculture. The postwar years also saw the industrialization of the country. Opposition groups were organized as early as the 1960s in Lithuania, and during the 1980s Soviet leader M. Gorbachev's policy of openness led to increasing support for opposition on the environment, cultural issues, and for independence (from 1987). In May 1989, the Lithuanian Supreme Soviet declared sovereignty, and in Dec. Lithuania's Communist party declared its independence from the Soviet party. The government declared full independence and adopted the country's current name on Mar. 11, 1990. The USSR condemned the declaration, ordered troops to occupy Communist party buildings, and then instituted an economic embargo (Apr.–June). The embargo was lifted with the start of short-lived talks between the USSR and Lithuania, and in Jan. 1991, after talks broke down, Soviet troops began attacking and occupying additional buildings in Vilnius. Voters overwhelmingly approved a referendum on independence, however (Feb.), and in following months sporadic clashes with Soviet troops led to several deaths. Following the collapse of the Soviet coup, the USSR formally recognized Lithuanian independence on Sept. 6, 1991. Lithuania became a UN member Sept. 17, 1991. Withdrawal of Soviet troops from the country began Mar. 1992.

Little, Malcolm   *See* **Malcolm X.**

Little America   US base in the Antarctic, on Ross Ice Shelf. It was established by R. E. Byrd (1928–30) as a base for his Antarctic exploration. He reestablished the base (1933, 1939) during subsequent expeditions.

Little Bighorn, Battle of (Custer's last stand) Famous massacre (June 25, 1876) of Gen. G. Custer and his cavalry unit by Sioux and Cheyenne Indians. Custer, leading the advance element of a large cavalry force sent against the Sioux, discovered an Indian camp on the Little Bighorn River near what is now Hardin, Montana. He launched an immediate attack on what he thought was a small force but the Indians, led by Chief Sitting Bull, had hidden the bulk of their warriors. When Custer advanced, they surrounded and massacred the entire force of over 250 men.

Little Entente   Alliance between Czechoslovakia, Rumania, and Yugoslavia formed by treaties (1920–21). The major aim of the alliance was to maintain boundaries of the three countries (as set by treaties after WW I) against German or Hungarian encroachments. The alliance proved ineffectual against the expansionist designs of A. Hitler, however. It ended when Germany, by the terms of the Munich Pact (1938), was permitted to occupy the Czechoslovakian territory of Sudetenland.

Little Parliament   *See* **Barebones Parliament.**

Littre, Maximillen Paul Émile 1801–81.   French philosopher and lexicographer, a leader of the positivist school. He is known for his *Dictionary of the French Language.*

Liturgical movement   Movement among Christian churches to develop new interest for the church liturgy among their followers. Though rooted in the 19th cent., the movement in the Roman Catholic church was greatly advanced by the Second Vatican Council (1962–65), which introduced use of vernacular translations of Latin texts and fostered greater involvement in the services by the laity. Among Protestant churches, the movement focused on revising texts to eliminate archaic expressions and on changing the form of services.

Litvinov, Maxim Maximovich 1876–1951. Russian Communist diplomat. As commissar of foreign affairs (1930–39), he sought cooperation with Western nations against the Axis Powers. He was ambassador to the US (1941–43).

Li Tzu-ch'eng   *See* **Li Zicheng.**

Liu Bang   *See* **Gaodi.**

Liu Shaoqui (˘ Shao-ch'i) 1898–1974. Chinese Communist leader. A recognized authority on party organization, he was head of state (1959–68) and heir apparent under Mao

Zedong. He was ousted during the Cultural Revolution.

Liutprand *d.* 744. Lombard king (712–744). His reign brought the Lombard kingdom to its greatest power. He centralized authority, instituted a just code of law, and conquered Byzantine territories in Italy.

Live-Aid Concert 1985. Benefit concerts to raise money for African famine relief. The Sahel region, a desert-like area in the northern part of Africa, was hard hit by drought in the early 1980s, and the resulting famine which threatened millions gained worldwide attention through television coverage. In 1985, two simultaneous rock concerts were held in Philadelphia and London (July 13) to raise private funds for emergency food and supplies for starving Africans. While tens of thousands of rock fans actually attended the concerts, the event was more remarkable for its worldwide broadcast by satellite and the resulting outpouring of international concern for the crisis in Africa.

Liverpool, Robert Banks Jenkinson, 2d earl of (Hawkesbury, Baron) 1770–1828. English statesman. He was prime minister (1812–27) during the War of 1812 with the US and the last phase of the Napoleonic Wars.

Livia Drusilla c55 BC–AD 29. First Roman empress, wife of Augustus. She married Octavian (Augustus) in 38 BC, before he became emperor. She had two sons, Tiberius and Drusus (Germanicus) by her previous marriage, and she later conspired to ensure Tiberius' succession as emperor.

Livingston, Edward 1764–1836. American lawyer and statesman. A noted jurist in his day, he was secretary of state (1831–33) under President A. Jackson and formulated the president's reply (1832) to the nullification doctrine.

Livingston, Philip 1716–78. American Revolutionary War leader and philanthropist. A moderate, he opposed the Stamp Act, signed the Declaration of Independence, and was a member of the Continental Congress from New York.

Livingston, Robert 1654–1728. Colonial leader in New York. Livingston had extensive land holdings, served in the New York provincial assembly (1709–11, 1716–25), and was secretary of Indian affairs (1695–1728).

Livingston, Robert R. 1746–1813. American statesman. A New York delegate to the Continental Congress, he served on the committee that drafted the Declaration of Independence. As

President T. Jefferson's ambassador to France, he helped negotiate the Louisiana Purchase. He later financed R. Fulton's steamboat, the *Clermont.*

Livingston, William 1723–90. American Revolutionary leader. Livingston served in the Continental Congress and became the first governor of independent New Jersey (1776), a post he held until his death.

Livingstone, David 1813–73. Scottish missionary and explorer. Arriving in Africa as a medical missionary (1841), Livingstone explored its interior, and his discoveries included Victoria Falls and the Zambezi River. He was feared lost on an 1866 expedition to the source of the Nile River. Found by H. Stanley (1871), he refused to leave Africa and died of disease while continuing his search for the Nile headwaters.

Livius Andronicus *fl.* 3d cent. BC. Roman poet, known as the founder of Roman drama. A freed Greek slave, he translated the *Odyssey* and Greek plays into Latin.

Livland *See* Livonia.

Livonia (Livland) Former state located on the east shore of the Baltic Sea. Beginning in the early 13th cent., the Germanic Livonian Knights conquered the region from the native people, the Livs. These Christian knights formed a confederation out of their domains that flourished during the 15th cent. However, internal struggles among the knights and the spread of the Protestant Reformation weakened the state and, during the Livonian War (1558–83), the order disbanded (1561). Portions of the territory passed to or were conquered by Lithuania, Denmark, Poland, Sweden, and Russia. Russia gradually gained control of the region through conquests in the Second (Great) Northern War (1700–21) and Partitions of Poland (18th cent.).

Livonian Knights (Brothers of the Sword, Order of the) German religious order founded (1202) to conquer and Christianize Baltic lands. The order created Livonia (*q.v.*) from conquered territories. The order disbanded (1561) after being defeated by the Russians during the Livonian War (*q.v.*).

Livonian War Unsuccessful war (1558–82) waged by Russian Tsar Ivan IV for control of Livonia and access to the Baltic Sea. Russian attacks against Livonia first led to the dissolution (1561) of the ruling order, the Livonian Knights (*q.v.*). Livonia was then divided among Poland, Lithuania, Sweden, and Denmark, but Russia continued its attempt to conquer the region. Initially successful, it suffered a series of losses to Poland's king, Stephen Bathory, and ultimately was forced (1582) to accept a peace settlement by which it renounced its claims over Livonia.

Livy 59 BC–AD 17. Great Roman historian. Sponsored by Emperor Augustus, Livy wrote the collection of 142 books known as the *Ab urb condita,* which cover the history of Rome from its founding in 753 BC to 9 BC. Thirty-five books are extant and fragments and summaries of all but two remain.

Li Yuan (Gaozu) 565–635. Chinese emperor (618–26) and founder of the Tang dynasty. An official in the Sui dynasty government, he led a revolt (617) that put him in power.

Li Zicheng (~ Tzu-ch'eng) 1605–45. Chinese rebel leader instrumental in the collapse of the Ming dynasty (1644). He organized a rebel government, took Beijing, and forced the remaining Ming forces into an alliance with the Manchus. The Manchus first defeated his forces and then took control of China for themselves.

Llewelyn ab Gruffydd *d.* 1282. Welsh prince and ruler (1246–82), nephew and successor of David II. Though he sided with S. de Montfort in the unsuccessful Barons' War (1263–67), he nevertheless came to control most of Wales during Henry III's reign. Wars with Edward I, however, led to subjugation of Wales by the Treaty of Conway (1277).

Lloyd George, David, 1st earl of Dwyfor 1863–1945. Controversial, Welsh-born, British statesman and Liberal prime minister (1916–22). He first entered Parliament (1890) as a Liberal. As chancellor of the exchequer under H. Asquith, he proposed (1909) his famous People's Budget which provided social insurance by taxing the wealthy. The bill brought on a major political crisis and cost the House of Lords its veto power (by the Parliament Act of 1911). In 1911 he sponsored legislation for health and unemployment insurance programs. After ousting Asquith, he became prime minister and, during his term of office, helped bring the US into WW I, played a major role in negotiating the Treaty of Versailles (1919), and set up the Irish Free State (1922).

Lloyd's Famous London insurance corporation founded in the late 17th cent. Its main business is marine insurance but it handles many other types of insurance risks on an international basis.

Lobachevsky, Nikolai Ivanovich 1793–1856. Russian mathematician. He was a founder of non-Euclidean geometry.

Lobengula *See* **Matabele War.**

Locarno Pact Agreement signed (Oct. 16, 1925) at Locarno, Switzerland, by Germany and other European powers, guaranteeing the post-WW I borders of the Rhineland (and its demilitarization), Belgium, France, and Germany. A major step in Germany's reentry to postwar world affairs, the agreement was preceded by several treaties between individual signatories and eventually led to Germany's acceptance into the League of Nations. The pact was denounced by A. Hitler and was finally broken when the Germans remilitarized (Mar. 7, 1936) the Rhineland. Other signatories of the pact were Britain, France, Italy, Belgium, Czechoslovakia, and Poland.

Lochner* v. *New York US Supreme Court decision (1905) ending state restrictions on ordinary workers' hours. The 5-4 decision struck down a New York law which limited the working hours of bakers based on health concerns. A dissenting opinion written by Justice O. Holmes, Jr., claimed that the decision supported capitalism under the guise of the 14th Amendment.

Locke, John 1632–1704. English philosopher who founded British empiricism. His doctrines on natural rights influenced the writing of the Bill of Rights, the Declaration of Independence, and the Constitution of the United States. In his *Essay Concerning Human Understanding,* he described the human mind and the process by which it acquires knowledge through the five senses. Natural rights, he believed, included the rights of property, the pursuit of happiness, and religious toleration. Locke held that governments involved social compacts and should be based on natural laws. His philosophy greatly influenced the thinking of the 18th-cent. Enlightenment and provided a philosophical basis for the American and French revolutions.

Locofoco party *See* **Locofocos.**

Locofocos (Locofoco party) Nickname for a faction (and short-lived party) of radical Jacksonian Democrats that appeared (1835) in the US. Largely a phenomenon of the Northeast, the Locofocos advocated an end to the national bank and other monopolies. Locofocos split (1835) with regular Democrats in New York and formed (1836) the Equal Rights party. President M. Van Buren eventually took up many of their policies and the Locofocos rejoined the Democratic party (by 1838).

Lodge, Henry Cabot 1850–1924. American politician. He served as senator from Massachusetts (1893–1924) and, as a leading isolationist, headed opposition to US entry to the League of Nations.

Lodge, Henry Cabot, Jr. 1902–85. American politician. He was senator from Massachusetts (1937–44, 1947–53), US representative to the UN (1953–60), and made an unsuccessful bid for the vice-presidency, running with R. Nixon (1960).

Lodi, Battle of French victory (May 10, 1796) over the Austrians in Italy, during the French Revolutionary Wars (1792–1802). Napoleon, commander of the French forces, distinguished himself during the battle and was nicknamed the "Little Corporal." In the battle, Napoleon attacked Lodi Bridge with 5,000 soldiers and forced the 10,000 Austrian defenders to retreat.

Loeben, Peace of *See* **Campo Formio, Treaty of.**

Logan, John Alexander 1826–86. Union general in the American Civil War, senator from Illinois (1871–77, 1879–86), and founder of Memorial Day (1868).

Logos Greek philosophical term used to describe the force of reason and order in the cosmos. The concept, advanced by Heraclitus (6th cent. BC), came to represent a link between God and man.

Loisy, Alfred Firmin 1857–1940. French theologian who founded Modernism in the Catholic church. He was excommunicated for his views in 1908.

Lollardry (Lollardy) English church reform movement that began (14th cent.) at Oxford. Some Lollard doctrines are said to have presaged those of the Reformation. Formed (late 14th cent.) by J. Wycliffe at Oxford, the movement spread throughout England. Persecutions began (1399) under Henry IV and, after two rebellions were suppressed (1414, 1431), the movement went underground, surviving until the rise of the 16th-cent. Reformation. Lollard doctrines, as set forth in their *Twelve Conclusions* (1395) and elsewhere, include: condemnation of the papacy; belief in primacy of the Scriptures; denial of transubstantiation; opposition to war; and condemnation of sacramentals, confession, pilgrim-

ages, clerical celibacy, and other practices of the Catholic church.

Lollardy *See* **Lollardry.**

Lombard League Alliance formed (1167) by Lombard cities in northern Italy against Holy Roman Emperor Frederick I (Barbarossa). Following attempts by Frederick to enforce his authority over the cities, they formed the league (with the support of Pope Alexander III) and successfully resisted Frederick's armies. By the Peace of Constance (1183), Frederick guaranteed the cities their freedom and the league ceased to be important. It was reactivated (1226) to defend against attacks by Holy Roman Emperor Frederick II. Cities in the league included Milan, Venice, Mantua, Padua, and Brescia.

Lombardo Italian architects and sculptors. Pietro Lombardo (c1435–1515) and his sons Antonio (c1458–1516) and Tullio (c1455–1532) worked on such noted Venetian structures as the Doge's palace, Dante's tomb, and the Church of Santa Maria dei Miracoli.

Lombards, Kingdom of Kingdom in Italy formed (6th cent.) by Germanic tribes known as the Lombards. Led by Alboin, these tribes migrated south and conquered (568–572) most of the north and parts of central and southern Italy. After a period of initial instability, the kingdom flourished (7th–8th cent.) with its center at Pavia. Frankish conquest of the kingdom was provoked by Lombard invasions of the Papal States. The Franks, under Pepin the Short, invaded Lombard domains (755, 756) to aid Pope Stephen II. When Lombard King Desiderius again attacked Rome (772), Charlemagne completely conquered the Lombard kingdom and ended its existence as an independent state.

Lombardy Leading industrial region of modern Italy. Once a Roman province, it became the center of the Lombard kingdom (*q.v.*). It passed to Charlemagne (774) and, in medieval times, its cities flourished as independent communes (*see* Lombard League). The region eventually came under control of the duchy of Milan (14th cent.) and was controlled by various powers before being absorbed into the unified kingdom of Italy (19th cent.).

Lombroso, Cesare 1835–1909. Italian educator and criminologist. A professor of psychiatry throughout most of his career, he revolutionized accepted practices in criminology with his views, now mostly discredited, about the scientific characteristics of criminals. He believed that some individuals were born criminals and that a criminal could be identified by distinctive physical characteristics.

Loménie de Brienne, Étienne Charles 1727–94. French statesman and ecclesiastic. As minister of finance, he convoked the States-General of 1789. He died in prison during the French Revolution.

Lomonosov, Mikhail Vasilyevich 1711–65. Russian scientist and author. He reformed the Russian literary language, bringing to it a more energetic, idiomatic style.

London Great Britain's capital city, located in southeastern England. One of the world's greatest cities, it is Britain's cultural and commercial center. London's history dates from Roman times and, in AD c60, the Roman settlement was attacked by Queen Boadicea (*q.v.*). After the fall of Rome, London received (AD 597) the Christian missionary Saint Augustine. It was established as a city of some importance by AD 886, when Alfred the Great took it from the Danes and refortified it. London's growth began in the centuries following the Norman Conquest (1066) and, during the reign of Elizabeth I (16th cent.), it prospered as a commercial (with the rise of trading companies), political, and cultural center. The city later figured as a stronghold of Parliamentary forces in the English Civil Wars (1642–48), suffered the ravages of plague (1665), and was largely destroyed in the great fire of London (Sept. 2–5, 1666). Rebuilt, it rose to worldwide prominence as the seat of Britain's great colonial empire. Though it suffered some raids during WW I, London was a chief objective of German airborne raids in the Battle of Britain (*q.v.*) in WW II. Today London is the site of such famous structures as Westminster Abbey (*q.v.*), Buckingham Palace (*q.v.*), and the Tower of London (*q.v.*). (*See also* London, Treaties of, and London conferences.)

London, Declaration of Proposed (1909) international regulations for naval warfare. The declaration was a result of the London Naval Conference (1908), attended by Great Britain and other European powers, the US, and Japan. It attempted to formalize wartime conventions for blockades, war prizes, contraband, and other matters. The declaration failed to win ratification by the participating nations and an attempt to gain voluntary compliance during WW I was rejected.

London, Jack (˜, John Griffith) 1876–1916. American author of adventure stories, such as *Call of the Wild, The Sea-Wolf,* and *White Fang.*

London, John Griffith *See* **London, Jack.**

London, Tower of *See* **Tower of London.**

London, Treaties of 1. Treaty (Mar. 17, 1824) between the Netherlands and Britain defining their respective spheres of influence in Malaysia. The British gained control of Malacca. 2. Treaty (July 6, 1827) between Britain, France, and Russia, in which they agreed to force the Ottoman Turks and Greek independence fighters to accept mediation. The powers used military force to intervene after Turkey rejected the plan. 3. Treaty (Nov. 15, 1831) between major European powers, settling matters relating to the Belgian war for independence from the Netherlands. 4. Treaty (1832) between Britain, France, and Bavaria, granting the newly created Greek throne to Otto I. 5. Treaty (May 11, 1867) between major European powers, establishing Luxembourg as an independent and neutral state. 6. Treaty (Mar. 13, 1871) in which signatories to the Treaty of Paris (1856) acceded to Russian demands to end the neutral status of the Black Sea. 7. Treaty (May 30, 1913) ending the First Balkan War. It stripped Turkey of its domains on the Balkan Peninsula. Disputes among Balkan states over division of this territory resulted in the Second Balkan War. 8. Secret treaty (Apr. 26, 1915) between Italy, Britain, France, and Russia, granting Italy territorial concessions in return for its entry in WW I. The lands included Trieste, south Tyrol, and part of Dalmatia.

London Bridge Bridge over the Thames River in London, England. Once a structure complete with stores and houses, it was damaged, redesigned, and rebuilt many times between 1176 and 1831. It was rebuilt again in the 1960s.

London Company *See* **Virginia Company.**

London conferences Meetings between representatives of international powers, held in London (19th–20th cents.). These conferences included that of 1830–31, which established Greek independence (1831) and attempted to resolve the war between the Belgians and Dutch over Belgian independence; 1838–39, which settled the division of the Netherlands and newly independent Belgium; 1852, which attempted to resolve conflicts between the Danes and the German Confederation over administration of Schleswig-Holstein; 1908, which resulted in the Declaration of London (*q.v.*) on naval armament; 1930 (London Naval Conference), which established regulations on submarine warfare and limited construction of new battleships; 1933, which unsuccessfully attempted international financial reforms to end the Great Depression; 1945, which saw the beginnings of the postwar rift between Russia and the other WW II Allies.

Long, Crawford Williamson 1815–78. American physician. He was the first physician to use ether in surgery (1842).

Long, Huey Pierce 1893–1935. Notorious American politician (called "the Kingfish"). He was governor of Louisiana (1928–31) and US senator (1931–35) and was known as the leader of a corrupt political machine that controlled his state. He gained nationwide attention with his "Share-the-Wealth" plan and aspired to the presidency. Dr. Carl Weiss assassinated him in Baton Rouge, Louisiana (Sept. 10), however. Weiss was shot and killed by Long's bodyguards.

Longchamp, William of *d.* 1197. English prelate and statesman. As chancellor to Richard I, he ruled the country while the king was on the Third Crusade (1190). Unpopular, he was ousted by Richard's brother, John (1191).

Longfellow, Henry Wadsworth 1807–82. Famous American poet who wrote about the history and legends of America. Among his many popular poems are *The Wreck of the Hesperus, The Village Blacksmith, Evangeline, The Song of Hiawatha, The Courtship of Miles Standish,* and *Paul Revere's Ride.* He also wrote a translation of Dante's *Divine Comedy.*

Longinus c213–273. Greek philosopher. He advised Queen Zenobia, ruler of the eastern kingdom of Palmyra, to revolt against Rome. When the revolt failed, he was executed by Emperor Aurelian as a traitor. Longinus was long thought to be the author of *On the Sublime,* one of the first serious works of literary criticism.

Long Island, Battle of British victory (Aug. 27, 1776) over the Americans during the American Revolution. After evacuating Boston, the British (under Gen. W. Howe) occupied Staten Island. Intending to take New York City, some 20,000 British landed (Aug. 22) at Gravesend, on Long Island. After several days' delay, they engaged and defeated an equal number of American soldiers under G. Washington, at Brooklyn Heights, Long Island. Washington withdrew (Aug. 29), first to Manhattan and then northward toward White Plains.

Long March Heroic march (1934–35) by the remnants of the Chinese Communist army during the Chinese Civil War. When Chinese Nationalists surrounded their base in southeast China, about 100,000 Communist soldiers broke out of the trap (Oct. 15, 1934). During their subsequent 6,000-mile march to a new base in Shaanxi province (northwest China), the Communists crossed rugged terrain and were harried by Nationalist forces. Mao Zedong became leader of the Chinese Communist party during the march (at Tsunyi, Jan., 1935), and, by the time the Communists reached Shaanxi (Oct., 1935), over half had died or been killed.

Long Parliament Name for the English Parliament that sat (Nov. 3, 1640–Mar. 16, 1660) during the English Civil Wars and Interregnum. Called by Charles I to raise money, the Parliament refused, and civil war broke out soon after. After Charles's defeat, the Parliament became the object (1648) of Pride's Purge (*q.v.*). Reduced to 60 members, it thereafter became known as the Rump Parliament. Later Charles I was tried and executed by the Parliament, which was twice dissolved for intervals by O. Cromwell and was succeeded by the Convention Parliament (*q.v.*).

Long Parliament of the Restoration *See* **Cavalier Parliament.**

Longstreet, James 1821–1904. Confederate Army general in the American Civil War. His slowness to attack at Gettysburg (1863) is generally considered the reason for that Confederate defeat.

Longworth, Nicholas 1869–1931. American legislator. A congressman from Ohio, Longworth was Speaker of the House from 1925 to 1931.

Lon Nol 1913–85. Cambodian military leader. He was premier (1966–67) and took control of the government after overthrowing Prince Sihanouk (1970). Reverses in the civil war with Communist Khmer Rouge guerrillas eventually drove him from office (1975).

Lönnrot, Elias 1802–84. Finnish philologist who gathered the oral folklore of his country and published it in the *Kalevala.*

López, Francisco Solano 1826?–70. Dictator of Paraguay (1862–70). He warred unsuccessfully against Brazil, Argentina, and Uruguay in the War of the Triple Alliance (*q.v.*) and was killed during the fighting.

López, Narciso 1798–1851. Spanish-American soldier and revolutionary. He led three unsuccessful military expeditions against Spanish Cuba (1849, 1850, 1851), and was killed in the third.

López de Legaspi, Miguel *d.* 1572. Spanish explorer. He conquered the Philippines for the Spanish (1564) and founded the city of Manila (1571).

Lord Dunmore's War War (Jan.–Oct., 1774) between Shawnee Indians and the Virginia militia. It was prompted by white encroachments on Indian lands and Virginia's seizure of western Pennsylvania. The war, culminating in the Shawnees' defeat at the Battle of Point Pleasant (Oct. 10), opened Kentucky and the Ohio Valley to Colonial expansion.

Lorentz, Hendrik Antoon 1853–1928. Dutch physicist. He and Pieter Zeeman received the Nobel Prize in Physics in 1902 for their explanation of the Zeeman Effect, concerning electromagnetic radiation.

Lorenz, Konrad 1903–89. Austrian zoologist. Lorenz established the discipline of ethology, the scientific study of patterns of animal behavior, especially as related to aggression. With Karl von Frisch and Nikolaas Tinbergen, he was awarded the Nobel Prize in Physiology or Medicine in 1973.

Lorenzini, Carlo *See* **Collodi, Carlo.**

Los Alamos *See* **Manhattan Project.**

Lost Battalion American army unit in WW I. Several American companies, led by Major Charles Whittlesey, were cut off by German forces in the Argonne Forest (Oct., 1918). They were rescued after heroically resisting German attacks for five days.

"lost colony" (Roanoke Colony) English settlement established (July, 1587) on Roanoke Island (now in North Carolina). The 117 colonists vanished mysteriously, leaving behind only the carved word "Croatan." The cause of the disappearance has never been discovered.

Lost Dauphin *See* **Louis XVII.**

"lost generation" Name applied to a group of American writers whose lives and works were greatly influenced by the events of WW I. Among them were F. S. Fitzgerald and E. Hemingway. The term derives from G. Stein's

remark, "You are all a lost generation," which Hemingway used as the epigraph to his novel *The Sun Also Rises.*

Lost Tribes of Israel Considered to be ten tribes of Israel that were exiled from there by the Assyrian king Sargon (c722 BC) [2 Kings 17; 1 Chron 5; Isaiah 11]. Their fate is unknown, but several speculations assert that they became the ancestors of various peoples, including the Anglo-Saxons, American Indians, and Ethiopians. The ten tribes were those of Asher, Dan, Ephraim, Gad, Issachar, Manasseh, Naphtali, Reuben, Simeon, and Zebulun. (*See also* Twelve Tribes of Israel.)

Lotario di Segni *See* **Innocent III.**

Lothair 941–986. Carolingian king of France (954–986), successor to his father, Louis IV. He was dominated throughout most of his reign by Hugh the Great and later by Archbishop Bruno of Cologne. His efforts to obtain control of Lorraine led to conflict with Holy Roman Emperor Otto II.

Lothair I 795–855. Carolingian emperor (840–855), a successor to his father, Louis I, and grandson of Charlemagne. His defeat at Fontenoy (841) marked the end of his attempts to reunite the Carolingian Empire under his rule. By the Treaty of Verdun (843), he became ruler of the middle portion of the divided empire.

Lothair II 835–869. Carolingian king of Lotharingia (855–869). The son of Lothair I (emperor of the West), he became involved in a lengthy dispute with Pope Nicholas I over his divorce and subsequent marriage to his mistress in order to secure an heir.

Lothair II 1075–1137. Holy Roman Emperor (1133–37). He was elected to succeed Henry V, and his was the first case in which an elective monarch came to power over a rival, hereditary claimant.

Lotharingia Kingdom that arose from the division of the Carolingian Empire into three parts. The kingdom, which included the Carolingians' ancestral lands in Austrasia, was the middle of the three kingdoms established by the Treaty of Verdun (843) and was first ruled by Emperor Lothair I. At its greatest extent, it included what are now the Netherlands, Belgium, Luxembourg, the region of Lorraine in France, and Italy. On the death of Lothair I (855), his realm was divided among his sons, with Lotharingia (what became Lorraine) going to Lothair II. Lotharingia was further divided by the Treaty of Meersen (870, *q.v.*).

Loudon, Gideon Ernst, Freiherr von   *See* **Laudon, Gideon Ernst, Freiherr von.**

Louis I (Louis the Pious) 778–840. Carolingian emperor (814–840), successor to his father, Charlemagne. His reign was marked by revolts by his sons over his plans to divide the empire among them. They deposed (and later restored) him twice, once in 830 and again in 833. His reign marked the end of the unified Carolingian Empire.

Louis I (Louis the Great) 1326–82. King of Hungary (1342–82) and Poland (1370–82). Louis conducted several wars against Venice, acquiring control of Dalmatia. He also drove the Turks and Tatars from his lands.

Louis I 1339–84. King of Naples (1382–84). Louis was the son of French king John II. Joanna I of Naples made Louis heir to Naples. He was overthrown by a rival claimant, Charles of Durazzo (Charles III).

Louis I 1786–1868. King of Bavaria (1825–48), son of Maximilian I. He made Munich a cultural center, but his conservative policies and his liaison with L. Montez led to his forced abdication during the Revolution of 1848.

Louis I 1838–89. Portuguese king (1861–89), successor to his brother Peter V. His reign was marked by political unrest and numerous changes of ministries. Under his rule, slavery was abolished in Portuguese colonies (1868).

Louis II *d.* 875. Frankish king of what is now Italy (844–875), nominal emperor of the Carolingian empire. Louis spent most of his reign holding the invading Arabs in check in southern Italy.

Louis II (Louis the Stammerer) 846–879. Frankish king (877–879) of the West (France) Frankish kingdom, successor to his father, Charles II (the Bald).

Louis II 1377–1417. Claimant to the throne of Naples. The son of Louis I, he inherited his father's claim to the kingdom, though he actually held it only from 1390 to 1399. He was driven out by Lancelot.

Louis II 1506–26. King of Hungary and Bohemia (1516–26). Louis was the last of the Jagiello dynasty. He was unable to prevent the Turkish conquest of his Hungarian lands, and died at the Battle of Mohács.

Louis II 1845–86. King of Bavaria (1864–86), successor to his father, Maximilian II. He was the patron of R. Wagner, and he built extravagant palaces. Declared insane in 1886, he drowned himself.

Louis III c863–882. Frankish king (879–882) of the West (France), a son of Louis II. He ruled jointly with his brother Carloman, and turned back the Norman invasion at Saucourt (881).

Louis III 1403–34. Rival for the throne of Naples (1417–34). The son of Louis II, he fought Joanna II and her ally Alfonso V of Aragon for the throne. When Alfonso fell out with Joanna, she made Louis her heir (1421) instead.

Louis IV (Louis d'Outremer) 921–954. King of France (936–954), son of Charles III (the Simple) and successor to Rudolph. His reign was marked by strife with his vassal Hugh the Great.

Louis IV (Louis the Bavarian) 1287?–1347. Holy Roman Emperor (1328–47). Louis fought Frederick the Fair (1314–22) in order to secure his claim. Following defeat of Frederick, Pope John XXII still refused Louis the imperial crown. Pope John steadfastly opposed Louis in ensuing years, and in 1338 the German electors ruled against the papacy. They declared that their election of the emperor automatically conferred the imperial crown.

Louis V 967–987. King of France (986–987), successor to Lothair. The last Carolingian king of France, he was succeeded by Hugh Capet, founder of the Capetian (*q.v.*) line.

Louis VI (Louis the Fat) 1081–1137. King of France (1108–37), successor to his father, Philip I. He fought several wars with King Henry I over English territories on the Continent and strengthened royal authority.

Louis VII (Louis the Young) c1120–80. King of France (1137–80), successor to his father, Louis VI. He annulled his marriage to Eleanor of Aquitaine (1152), who subsequently married Henry II of England. This gave rise to Henry's claims to Aquitaine and a long series of wars between Louis and Henry. Louis aided Henry's sons in a revolt against their father (1173–74) but gained no territories from it.

Louis VIII 1187–1226. King of France (1223–26), successor to his father, Philip II. He invaded England at the invitation of the barons, then rebelling against King John (1216), but withdrew (1217) after the accession of Henry III eroded his support among them.

Louis IX (Saint Louis) 1214–70. King of France (1226–70), successor to his father, Louis VIII. His mother, Blanche of Castile, was his regent (to

1234) and, later, his close adviser. He was defeated and captured on the Seventh Crusade (q.v.) and settled territorial disputes with Henry III of England (by the Treaty of Paris, 1259). His reign was marked by a period of peace and prosperity.

Louis X 1289–1316.   King of France (1314–16), successor to his father, Philip IV. He was forced to grant charters to the nobles to gain their support. He was dominated by Charles of Valois.

Louis XI 1423–83.   French king called Louis the Spider (1461–83), successor to his father, Charles VII. As king, he succeeded in overcoming the rebellious nobles and thereby laid the basis for an absolute monarchy in France. Louis engaged in many revolts against his father, notably the Praguerie (1440), and, as king, succeeded in putting down a revolt (1465) by the League of the Public Weal (q.v.). He took Normandy from his brother Charles. In 1467 he began a long war with Charles the Bold (duke of Burgundy) and his allies Francis II (duke of Brittany) and English king Edward IV. Louis ultimately won Burgundy by the Treaty of Arras (1482), and, with the extinction of the Anjou line, also acquired their territories for the crown.

Louis XII 1462–1515.   King of France (1498–1515), successor to his cousin Charles VIII, known as "the Father of the People" for his benevolent rule. His foreign policy was dominated by attempts to conquer parts of Italy in the Italian Wars (q.v.).

Louis XIII 1601–43.   French king (1610–43), successor to his father, Henry IV. His reign was marked by the strong leadership of his ministers, Cardinals de Richelieu and J. Mazarin, who centralized royal authority and laid the foundation for absolutism in France. Rebellions by French Protestants (Huguenots) were quelled and France joined in the Thirty Years' War (from 1635).

Louis XIV (The Sun King) 1638–1715.   French king (1643–1715), successor to his father, Louis XIII. Louis' reign marked the height of absolutism in France, and, by his expansionist policies, he embroiled the country in a costly series of wars. During Louis' minority, France was weakened by the ongoing Thirty Years' War (1618–48) and rebellions known as the Fronde (1648–53). Louis took power (1661) on the death of the powerful minister Cardinal Mazarin, continued the process of centralizing authority in his own hands, and fostered a period of com-

mercial prosperity. With the royal finances restored and the army strengthened, Louis set out on the first of his wars to enlarge French domains, the War of Devolution (1667–78). This was followed by the Third Dutch War (1672–78), the War of the Grand Alliance (1689–97), and, finally, the War of Spanish Succession (1701–14). This last war left France seriously weakened financially. Within France, Louis' reign was marked by his arbitrary use of the *lettres de cachet* (q.v.), his growing intolerance of Protestants (Huguenots), which ended in his revocation (1685) of the Edict of Nantes (q.v.), and his support of Gallicanism (q.v.). Louis was a lavish patron of the arts, and his reign is sometimes referred to as the Augustan Age of French literature. He likewise maintained a splendid court (in part to keep the nobles in check) and built the magnificent palace of Versailles.

Louis XV 1710–74.   French king (1715–74), successor to his great-grandfather, Louis XIV. Louis was a weak and (at his death) unpopular ruler. The financial difficulties that arose during his reign helped bring on the French Revolution (1789–99). Made king at five, he attained his majority in 1723. The government, however, was largely run (1726–43) by A. Fleury. Thereafter Louis was influenced by a succession of mistresses, notably Mmes. de Pompadour and Du Barry. Louis' reign was marked by: the War of Polish Succession (1733–35), acquisition of the duchy of Lorraine (1735); the War of Austrian Succession (1740–48); the disastrous Seven Years' War (1756–63), which cost France her Canadian and Indian colonies; suppression of the Jesuits (1764); dissolution of Parlement (1771); and a belated attempt at fiscal and legal reforms.

Louis XVI   French king (1774–93), successor to his grandfather, Louis XV. He was overthrown during the French Revolution. Louis was an ineffective ruler and failed in attempts at fiscal and administrative reform, put forward by such ministers as A. Turgot and J. Necker, and was often opposed by Queen Marie Antoinette and the royal court. The extravagance of the court and French support (1778–81) for the American Revolution helped bring the government to near bankruptcy. Thereafter, Louis' reign was swept up in the events of the French Revolution, including: convening of the Assembly of Notables (1787) to approve new taxes; convening of the States-General (1789); legislative rebellion by the third estate and creation of the National Assembly (1789); storming of the Bastille (1789), provoked by the king's ouster of Necker; transfer (1789) of the king and family from Versailles to Tuileries Palace in Paris; unsuccessful attempt at escape (1791) by the king and family; institution (1791) of a constitutional monarchy; establishment (1792) of the republic; trial and execution (1793) of Louis for suspected conspiracy with foreign powers.

Louis XVII 1785–95? Titular king of France during the French Revolution. The son of Louis XVI, he was imprisoned with the royal family in 1792. After his father's execution, Louis was for a time the symbol of royalist hopes. He died in prison.

Louis XVIII 1755–1824. French king (1814–24), crowned after the fall of Napoleon. Following the outbreak of the French Revolution, he fled France (1791) and actively promoted counterrevolutionary plots. He was made king of France (1814), partly through the efforts of C. Talleyrand. His reign began the Restoration (1814–30) and included such events as the Hundred Days (1815) and the rise of the Ultraroyalists (*q.v.*).

Louis, Saint *See* **Louis IX.**

Louis de Bourbon *See* **Condé.**

Louis de Buade *See* **Frontenac, comte de Palluau.**

Louis d'Outremer *See* **Louis IV.**

Louise 1776–1810. Queen of Prussia, wife of Frederick William III. She is remembered for her courage in the face of Prussian defeats in the Napoleonic Wars.

Louise of Savoy 1476–1531. Mother of French king Francis I and regent during her son's Italian expeditions (1515–16 and 1525–26). In 1529, she negotiated the Treaty of Cambrai.

Louisiana State in the US South, the 18th state. Louisiana and environs were claimed for France by R. La Salle in 1682. The first settlement in Louisiana was New Orleans (founded 1718), and Louisiana passed to the US by the Louisiana Purchase of 1803. The Territory of Orleans became the state of Louisiana in 1812. Louisiana seceded (1861) from the Union during the Civil War, and was readmitted in 1868. The present state constitution was passed in 1921.

Louisiana Purchase US acquisition (May 2, 1803) of French-held territory extending westward from the Mississippi River to the Rocky Mountains. The purchase doubled the size of the US and guaranteed use of the commercially important Mississippi River. The territory (at first French, then Spanish) reverted to French control (1800) after Napoleon conquered Spain. US president T. Jefferson, fearful that Napoleon might close New Orleans to US commerce, sent (Apr., 1803) R. Livingston to France to buy the city. Some weeks later, with J. Monroe taking part, negotiations were opened by French minister C. Tallyrand for the purchase of the whole Louisiana territory (over 800,000 sq. mi.). The agreement was signed in May (dated Apr. 30, 1803), and the total price, with interest, came to just over $27 million.

Louis Philippe (Citizen King) 1773–1850. King of the French (1830–48), successor to Charles X by the July Revolution (1830). Once a liberal supporter of the French Revolution, Louis Philippe lived in exile (from 1793) until the Restoration (1814–30). He joined the liberal opposition to the monarchy, and was later chosen king by A. Thiers, M. Lafayette, and other bourgeois leaders of the July Revolution. Though he began his rule in a liberal spirit, he did resort to repressive measures to silence opposition. Workers' rebellions, demands for enfranchisement of the lower bourgeoisie, and the struggles between Legitimists and Bonapartists eventually culminated in the February Revolution (1848). The king abdicated (Feb., 1848) and fled to England.

Louis the Bavarian *See* **Louis IV.**

Louis the Child 893–911. Frankish king (899–911) of the East (Germany), successor to Arnulf. Louis was the last German Carolingian ruler. Invasions by the Magyars from the east eventually broke down the authority of the monarchy in the east.

Louis the Fat *See* **Louis VI.**

Louis the German c804–876. Frankish king (843–876) of the East (Germany). He was allotted a portion of the divided Carolingian Empire by his father, Louis I. Louis joined with his brother, Charles the Bald, to block Lothair I's attempt to reunite the Carolingian Empire under his rule. Louis and Charles forced Lothair to accept the divided empire by the Treaty of Verdun (843).

Louis the Great *See* **Louis I.**

Louis the Pious *See* **Louis I.**

Louis the Stammerer *See* **Louis II.**

Louis the Young *See* **Louis VII.**

Louis the Younger *d.* 882. Frankish king (876–882) of the East (Germany), successor to his father, Louis the German. He expanded his domains by conquering western Lotharingia from Charles the Bald (876). He later acquired eastern Lotharingia.

Lourdes Town in southwestern France famous for its shrine at the spot where Saint Bernadette was said to have seen visions of the Virgin. Millions make pilgrimages there each year.

Louvois, Michel Le Tellier, marquis de 1639–91. French war minister. Under Louis XIV, he instituted reforms that made the French army the most powerful in Europe, encouraged and ruthlessly enforced the revocation of the Edict of Nantes (*q.v.*), and became notorious for the destructiveness of his armies during the War of the Grand Alliance.

Louvre Museum in Paris, France. The original structure was started by Francis I in 1546 and was added to by succeeding rulers. The vast art collection includes the *Mona Lisa* and the *Venus de Milo.*

Lovejoy, Elijah Parish 1802–37. American journalist and abolitionist martyr. He was killed in Alton, Illinois, defending his printing press against a proslavery mob. His death increased sympathy for the abolitionist cause.

Lovell, James Arthur, Jr. 1928– . US astronaut, crew member on the first manned flight to orbit the moon, the Apollo 8 mission (launched Dec. 21, 1968). He was also aboard the Gemini 7 and Gemini 12 missions and commanded the ill-fated Apollo 13 moon flight, aborted because of equipment malfunction.

Low Countries *See* **Netherlands, Spanish and Austrian.**

Lowell, Amy 1874–1925. American poet and critic, a leader of the imagists. Her most famous poems are *Lilacs* and *Patterns.*

Lowell, Francis Cabot 1775–1817. American textile manufacturer. He was a founder of the Boston Manufacturing Co. (1812), the first factory to convert raw cotton into finished cloth.

Lowell, James Russell 1819–91. American poet, essayist, and critic. He was editor of the *Atlantic Monthly* and the *North American Review* and was an influential figure in 19th-cent. New England literary circles. Among his many works was *The Biglow Papers.*

Lowell, Percival 1855–1916. American astronomer. He founded (1894) the Lowell Observa-

tory in Flagstaff, Arizona, and predicted the discovery of the planet Pluto.

Lowell, Robert Traill Spence 1917–77. American poet. His works include *In Lord Weary's Castle, Life Studies, The Dolphin,* and *Near the Ocean.*

Lower Canada Name applied (1791–1841) to the Canadian region comprising present-day Quebec. Settled primarily by the French, it was joined with Upper Canada by the Act of Union (1840, effective 1841) and became known as Canada East. With the confederation of Canada (1867) it became the Province of Quebec.

Lower Egypt Region of Egypt usually considered to include the Nile delta and valley that lie roughly north of Cairo (north of latitude 30 degrees North). A rich, fertile region, it was united with Upper Egypt by Egyptian king Menes (c3100 BC). In ancient times it was symbolized by a red crown and papyrus plant.

Lowie, Robert Harry 1883–1957. American anthropologist. He studied North American Indians and wrote the influential *Primitive Society* and *Social Organization.*

Loyalists (Tories) American colonists who remained loyal to Britain during the American Revolution (1775–83). Loyalists, often government officials and professionals, were centered in New York, Pennsylvania, Georgia, and the Carolinas. Loyalist raids, notably those by W. and J. Butler, roused bitter hatred toward them among the Colonial patriots and led to passage of laws confiscating their property. A large number of the Loyalists, seeking the protection of the British, migrated to Canada.

Loyola, Saint Ignatius of *See* **Ignatius of Loyola, Saint.**

Lublin, Union of Agreement (July 1, 1569) between Poland and Lithuania, merging the two kingdoms into a federated state under a single monarch. King Sigismund II, king of Poland and Lithuania, pressured Lithuanian nobles into accepting formal unification, which lasted to the end of the 18th cent.

Lucan AD 39–65. Roman poet who wrote *Bellum Civile* (often called *Pharsalia*), on the civil war between Caesar and Pompey. He was compelled to kill himself when his part in a conspiracy against Nero was discovered.

Lucania Ancient region of southern Italy. Once inhabited by Greeks and Lucanians, it was devastated by wars with Rome in the 3rd cent. BC.

Lucaris, Cyril of *See* **Jerusalem, Synod of.**

Luce, Clare Boothe 1903–87. American playwright and politician. Her plays include *The Women* and *Kiss the Boys Goodbye*. She served as congresswoman from Connecticut (1943–47) and was ambassador to Italy (1953–56).

Luce, Henry Robinson 1898–1967. American publisher. He cofounded the weekly news magazine *Time* (1923), then founded *Fortune* (1930), *Life* (1936), and *Sports Illustrated* (1954).

Lucian *fl.* 2d cent. AD. Greek satirical author whose many works include *Dialogues of the Gods* and *Dialogues of the Dead.*

Lucillius, Caius (Lucilius, Gaius) c180–102? BC. Latin poet. As the originator of Latin satire, he influenced Horace, Persius, and Juvenal.

Luckner, Felix, graf von 1886–1966. German naval officer. He was known as the "Sea Devil" for his raids on commercial vessels during WW I. He destroyed more than $25 million worth of Allied shipping.

Lucretia *See* **Etruscans.**

Lucretius (Titus Lucretius Carus) c99–c55 BC. Roman poet. Lucretius is renowned for his work *On the Nature of Things,* which is a poetic treatment of the philosophies and scientific theories of Epicurus and Democritus.

Lucullus c110–56 BC. Roman general. Serving under Sulla, he defeated Mithridates VI and made other conquests in Asia Minor. Lucullus later retired from public service (59) and lived a life famous for its luxuriance.

Luddites Bands of workingmen in England who attempted (1811–12, 1816) to destroy textile machinery. Fostered by low wages and unemployment, the movement began (1811) in Nottingham with night raids on textile factories to destroy equipment. The movement spread to other industrial areas, supposedly under the leadership of a mythical King Ludd (or Ned Ludd), and in 1812 harsh repressive measures were enacted to put an end to it. A brief resurgence of the movement was similarly dealt with.

Ludendorff, Erich von 1865–1937. German general. He was P. von Hindenburg's chief of staff during WW I and became the most powerful man in Germany by 1917. His attempt to increase war production at all costs weakened the national economy and helped bring on Germany's defeat in WW I. He participated in A. Hitler's "beerhall putsch" (1923) and was a fanatic in his Aryan racist views.

Ludford Bridge, Battle of *See* **Roses, Wars of the.**

Lukács, György 1885–1971. Hungarian philosopher, writer, and literary critic. Born to a wealthy Jewish family, he was a lifelong proponent of Marxism, becoming well known for his writings. A member of Hungary's parliament (1945), he took part in the 1956 uprising, for which he was arrested and deported to Rumania. Returning to Budapest (1957), he spent the rest of his life at work on literary criticism and philosophical research. He wrote *History and Class Consciousness* (1923) and *The Destruction of Reason* (1954).

Luke, Saint Traditionally, author of the Third Gospel and the Acts of the Apostles. He is thought to have been a physician and was a companion of Saint Paul.

Lull, Ramon (Lully, Raymond) c1236–c1315. Catalan mystic and philosopher. He tried to convert the Muslims of North Africa to Christianity, and was said to have been stoned to death at Bougie.

Lully, Jean Baptiste 1632–87. French composer. He was composer to King Louis XIV and head of the Académie Royale de Musique. He developed the French overture form.

Lully, Raymond *See* **Lull, Ramon.**

Lumière, Louis Jean and Auguste Marie Louis Nicolas 1864–1948, 1862–1954. French brothers who invented the cinematograph for photographing and projecting movies (1895).

Lumumba, Patrice Hemery 1925–61. Political leader of Zaire (then called the Congo). He worked for its independence from Belgium and was its first prime minister (1960). He was murdered after being deposed in the unrest that followed independence.

Luna, Pedro de 1328–1423. Spanish ecclesiastic, antipope as Benedict XIII at Avignon (1394–1417) during the Great Schism. He proved able but was unwilling to relinquish his office to end the Great Schism. He was deposed (1417) by the Council of Constance (*q.v.*).

Lundy's Lane, Battle of (Niagara, ˜) (Bridgewater, ˜) Bloody but indecisive battle (July 25, 1814) during the War of 1812. Some 2,000–3,000 Americans, under Gen. W. Scott, advanced into southern Ontario, Canada, and at Lundy's Lane met 4,500 British soldiers, under Gen. Gordon Drummond. The battle raged into the night, when, with both sides exhausted, the Americans withdrew to Fort Erie.

Lunéville, Treaty of Agreement (Feb. 9, 1801) between Austria and France, ending Austria's participation in the French Revolutionary Wars. It provided for the division of territories in Italy. It also restored Pope Pius VII to Rome and Ferdinand IV to Naples.

Lupescu, Magda (Wolff, ~) 1896?–1977. Rumanian mistress of King Carol II. Married to an army officer, she began an affair with then Prince Carol in the early 1920s. Carol, unwilling to end the affair, gave up his right of succession and went into exile (1925). He returned to his wife and the throne (1930), but kept Lupescu at his side. She was widely criticized for her powerful influence over the king and for her Jewish origins. Carol abdicated in 1940 and the two left the country. They married in 1947.

Lusitania Ancient Roman province, including what is modern Portugal and part of western Spain. It was named for the Lusitani people, who resisted the Romans (2d cent. BC).

Lusitania British ship that was torpedoed and sunk by a German submarine (May 7, 1915), with a loss of 1,195 lives. This incident was a factor in the US entry into WW I.

Lutetia (~ Parisiorum) Roman name for what is now Paris, France.

Luther, Martin 1483–1546. German religious leader, father of the Protestant Reformation (*q.v.*) and founder of Lutheranism (*q.v.*). An Augustinian friar, he was ordained (1507), and subsequently was a professor (1511–46) at the University of Wittenberg, in Saxony. In ensuing years, he arrived at his fundamental doctrine of personal salvation through faith alone. This doctrine ultimately put him in conflict with the church practice (then widespread) of selling indulgences (*q.v.*), and, on Oct. 31, 1517, he nailed his famous Ninety-five Theses (*q.v.*) to the door of the church in Wittenberg to protest the practice. Thereafter Luther found wide support for his protest, refused to recant (1518), debated the Catholic J. Eck (1519) in the famous but inconclusive Leipzig Debate, burned a papal bull condemning his views (1520), was thereupon excommunicated, and was called (1521) before the Diet of Worms (*q.v.*). During this period, he expanded the scope of reforms he sought, as set forth in three treatises: *Address to the Christian Nobility of the German Nation,* calling for German control of the German church; *The Babylonian Captivity of the Church,* attacking papal authority and denying the office of the priesthood as a link between God and man; and *The Freedom of a Christian Man,* reaffirming the doctrine of justi-

fication by faith alone. After the Diet of Worms ordered his arrest, Luther was given protection (1521–22) by the Elector Frederick III. He returned to Wittenberg, however, to try to prevent splits within the growing Reformation movement. The remainder of his years were spent in voluminous writing and in disputes with leaders of new sects spawned by his beliefs, including H. Zwingli and J. Calvin.

Lutheranism The branch of Protestant Christianity based on the teachings of M. Luther. Lutheranism stems from Luther's famous Ninety-five Theses (*q.v.*), which sparked the Protestant Reformation, though its doctrine is more conservative than that of Calvinist Reformed churches. Luther's doctrine stressed that man's salvation comes from faith alone, through the redeeming sacrifice of Jesus Christ; that the Scriptures constitute the one necessary guide to truth; and that the sacraments are valid only as aids to faith. The principal Lutheran statements of faith were the Augsburg Confession (*q.v.*), and Luther's two catechisms. These and other Lutheran documents were collected in the definitive Book of Concord (1580). Luther denied the sacrificial character of the Catholic Mass, and the Lutheran churches formed according to his doctrines abolished clerical celibacy, had communion administered (under both kinds, bread and wine), and retained only the two sacraments of Baptism and the Lord's Supper. The Lutheran churches, organized around individual local congregations, were at first established state churches in the German principalities. Lutheranism also became the established church in Denmark, Finland, Norway, and Sweden. The Prussian state attempted to merge Lutheran churches forcibly with Reformed churches and this led to the first free Lutheran church (1817). This was the typical form Lutheranism assumed in North America, where it was first brought to Manhattan by Dutch settlers (1625) and to Fort Christina (modern Wilmington, Delaware) by Swedish settlers (1638). (*See also* Luther, Martin; Reformation.)

Lutzen, Battle of 1. Swedish victory (Nov. 16, 1632) in Saxony during the Thirty Years' War (1618–48). Swedish king Gustavus II, in an effort to aid German Protestant allies, attacked and defeated the army of the Holy Roman Empire, led by Count A. Wallenstein. Gustavus was killed in the battle. 2. Inconclusive battle (May 2, 1813) in the Napoleonic Wars

(1803–15). Napoleon forced the allies to withdraw but did so at a cost of 20,000 casualties.

Luxembourg (Luxemburg) European grand duchy lying between Belgium, France, and Germany. The population is 369,000 and the capital is Luxembourg. Once a county of the Holy Roman Empire, it was made a duchy (1354) by Emperor Charles IV. It was subsequently ruled by the Spanish and Austrian Habsburgs, was occupied by France (1794), and became a part of the Netherlands by the Congress of Vienna (1815). In 1867, it was declared a neutral, independent territory, although the Germans occupied it during WW I and WW II. Constitutional revisions (1948) ended Luxembourg's official neutral status. Grand Duke Jean has ruled since 1964. The government in 1989 introduced banking reforms to block money laundering in Luxembourg banks by drug traffickers. The following year, the Luxembourg registered Bank of Credit and Commerce International (BCCI) came under fire in the US and elsewhere for illegal activities (including money laundering and fraud), and in 1991 the entire worldwide BCCI organization was liquidated.

Luxembourg, François Henri, duke of 1628–95. French general. He served under his cousin, the Great Condé, in the Fronde and led successful campaigns in Flanders during the War of the Grand Alliance (*q.v.*), defeating William of Orange at Steenkerke (1692) and Neerwinden (1693).

Luxemburg *See* **Luxembourg.**

Luxemburg, Rosa 1870?–1919. German revolutionary and critic of Lenin's centralized Communist party. She was a founder of the Spartacus party (*q.v.*), which became the German Communist party. Arrested after WW I, she was murdered by soldiers.

Lu Xun (*pseud. of* Chou Shu-jen) 1881–1936. Chinese author, considered the greatest of this century. While studying medicine, Lu Xun published what quickly became a famous Western-style short story criticizing traditional Confucian society, *A Madman's Diary* (1918). Similarly, *The True Story of Ah Q* (1921) also criticized China's old order, here focusing on the tendency to rationalize to such an extent that defeat could be seen as a "spiritual victory." His *Call to Arms* (1923) established him as a major writer, and during the upheavals of the Chinese Civil War in the 1930s, he became an active Communist sympathizer, though he never joined the party. In addition to

numerous other works of fiction, he also wrote the scholarly *Outline History of Chinese Fiction.*

Luynes, Charles d'Albert, duke of 1578–1621. French statesman. He was the favorite and chief adviser of Louis XIII and conspired with him to kill C. Concini and to exile Louis's mother, Marie de Medici. He worked to check the influence of nobles and Protestants.

Lvov, Prince Georgi Yevgenyevich 1861–1925. Russian statesman. A member of the first Duma (1905), he was head of the revolutionary Provisional Government from March to July, 1917. He resigned in favor of A. Kerensky.

Lyautey, Louis Hubert Gonzalve 1854–1934. French statesman and marshal. He was resident general of Morocco (1912–16, 1917–25), holding it against the Germans in WW I.

Lyceum Ancient Athenian school where Aristotle taught (founded 335 BC). He and his students were called Peripatetics because they strolled about the school grounds during lessons. The school declined soon after Aristotle's death.

Lycurgus In Greek tradition, the Spartan leader whose reforms of Spartan government and society created the characteristically militaristic Spartan way of life. He may have ruled in the 7th cent. BC.

Lydia Ancient country of Asia Minor in what is now northwest Turkey. The tyrant Cyges founded the Mermnadae dynasty (685–546 BC), which built a powerful Lydian empire of great wealth. The Lydians are believed to have originated the use of coined money during this time. Croesus, the last ruler of independent Lydia, was defeated by Cyrus the Great of Persia (546 BC). Lydia later became a province under the Romans.

Lyell, Sir Charles 1797–1875. English geologist. He wrote *Principles of Geology* and *Elements of Geology* and was a leading exponent of uniformitarianism, the doctrine that the earth's surface was shaped by processes that continue to the present day.

Lyons, Councils of 1. First (13th ecumenical council): Called (1245) by Pope Innocent IV during his struggle with Holy Roman Emperor Frederick II. With Rome under siege by Frederick, the pope used the session to excommunicate and depose Frederick. 2. Second (14th ecumenical council): Called (1274) by Pope Gregory X to act on a pledge by Byzantine emperor Michael VIII to unite the Eastern church with the West. After concessions on the Filioque were made by delegates from the Greek church, the union was proclaimed. It was largely ignored, however, and was later repudiated by Andronicus II. The council also established procedures for election of the pope by cardinals, and ended the Interregnum by recognizing Rudolf I as Holy Roman Emperor.

Lyons, Joseph Aloysius 1879–1939. Australian statesman. He was a founder of the United Australia party (1931), and as prime minister (1931–39) brought about a period of economic stability.

Lysander *d.* 395 BC. Spartan military leader. He was admiral of the Spartan fleet that defeated Athens at Notium (407 BC) and that ended the Peloponnesian War by taking Athens in 404 BC. He was a proponent of Spartan imperialism and hoping to become king of Sparta, proposed ending the hereditary succession of the Spartan monarchy.

Lysenko, Trofim Denisovich 1898–1976. Russian agronomist and biologist. As president of the Academy of Agricultural Sciences (1938–56, 1958–62), he tried to develop high-yield crops and to advance his unorthodox views of genetics.

Lysias c459–c380 BC. Greek orator and speech writer. His simple, unembellished and yet effective style had an important influence on Attic Greek prose.

Lysimachus c355–281 BC. Macedonian general under Alexander the Great. After Alexander's death, he took part in the Wars of the Diadochi (*q.v.*) and thereby became ruler of Thrace (and later Macedonia). He was killed in battle against Seleucus.

Lysippus (Lysippos) Greek sculptor in 4th cent. BC who changed the style of rendering the human figure, making the head smaller and the body more slender. He was a favorite of Alexander the Great.

M

Mabillon, Jean 1632–1707. French scholar. A Benedictine monk, he wrote *De re diplomatica,* which established the science of diplomatics, the study of historical sources.

Mabovitch, Goldie *See* **Meir, Golda.**

Macao (Macau) Portuguese province at the mouth of the Guangzhou (Canton) River in China. Settled by Portugal (1557), it was a major port until the rise of Hong Kong (19th cent.). In 1987, Portugal agreed to return Macao to China in 1999, and in return the Chinese Communist government agreed to maintain the capitalist system in Macao for a period after that time.

McAdoo, William Gibbs 1863–1941. American politician. As US secretary of the treasury (1913–18), he founded and was first chairman of the Federal Reserve Board (1913).

MacArthur, Douglas 1880–1964. American general. He was Allied commander of the Southwest Pacific during WW II and administrator of the Allied occupation of Japan. He was dismissed as commander of the UN forces in Korea by President H. Truman (1951) after he publicly advocated a second drive into North Korea.

Macau *See* **Macao.**

Macaulay, Thomas Babington 1800–54. English historian. His best-known work is *The History of England from the Accession of James the Second.*

McAuliffe, Anthony C. *See* **Bulge, Battle of the.**

Macbeth *d.* 1057. Scottish king (1040–57). He killed his cousin Duncan to gain the throne and was himself killed and succeeded by Duncan's son Malcolm Canmore. His story was the basis for W. Shakespeare's play.

Maccabees (Hasmoneans) Family of Jewish rulers and patriots that ruled Palestine (2d–1st cents. BC), and as described in two biblical books bearing their name. In reaction to suppression and persecution of Jewish religious observances by Seleucid king Antiochus IV, a Jewish priest named Mattathias (*d.* c166 BC) began (c168) a guerrilla war called the Revolt of the Maccabees. His third son, Judas (*d.* c161 BC), to whom the name Maccabeus was applied, defeated Seleucid armies and expelled them (164) from Jerusalem. He then rededicated the Temple (commemorated by Hanukkah) and was killed during a subsequent Seleucid invasion. He was succeeded by his brother, Jonathan (*d.* 143 BC), who was successful against the Seleucids and became the Jewish high priest. Killed by the Seleucids, he was succeeded by Simon (*d.* 135 BC), who negotiated (142) independence for Judaea (southern Palestine) and was made high priest and governor. He was assassinated, and was succeeded by John Hyrcanus (*d.* 104 BC), his son, under whose rule Judaea reached its height. Later Judaean history was marked by the religious struggle between the Sadducees and the Pharisees. The last Maccabees to rule were the brothers Hyrcanus II (*d.* 30 BC) and Aristobulus II (*d.* 48 BC), who engaged in civil war against each other. The war was ended by the Roman general Pompey the Great, who conquered Jerusalem (63 BC), reduced Hyrcanus to religious rule, and established Roman political control over Judaea.

McCarthy, Eugene (Joseph) 1916– . US senator (1959–71). An opponent of the Vietnam War, he made an unsuccessful bid for the Democratic presidential nomination (1968).

McCarthy, Joseph Raymond 1909–57. American politician. US senator from Wisconsin (1947–57). As chairman of the Senate's Government Operations Committee, he ruined many careers by accusing government officials (and others) of Communist affiliations. He was censured by the Senate in 1954. His tactics gave rise to the term "McCarthyism."

McClellan, George Brinton 1826–85. Union general in the American Civil War. Made commander in chief (Nov., 1861), he stopped the Confederate advance at Antietam but was removed from command (Nov., 1862) because of his reluctance to engage the enemy. In 1864 he was an unsuccessful Democratic candidate for the presidency.

Macleod, John *See* **Banting, Sir Frederick Grant.**

McClernand, John Alexander 1812–1900. Union general in the American Civil War. He fought at the Battle of Shiloh and commanded the Vicksburg Campaign (1863) until superseded by Gen. U. Grant, and relieved of command for insubordination.

McClure, Sir Robert John Le Mesurier 1807–73. British naval officer. As commander of a ship in an Arctic expedition (1850–54), he was the first to complete a Northwest Passage, culminating the long search for a sea route from the Atlantic to the Pacific Ocean by way of the Arctic.

McClure, Samuel Sidney 1857–1949. American editor and publisher. He established the first US newspaper syndicate (1884) and founded (1893) *McClure's Magazine.*

McCormick, Cyrus Hall 1809–84. American inventor and manufacturer. He designed the McCormick reaper (1831). His company merged with others to form the International Harvester Company.

McCormick, Robert Rutherford 1880–1955. American editor and publisher. As editor and publisher of the *Chicago Tribune* (1920–55), he became a leader in conservative journalism. He opposed labor unions, the New Deal, and international involvement.

McCormick, Ruth Hanna 1880–1945. US politician. The daughter of M. Hanna, she served as Republican national committeewoman (1924–28) and congresswoman from Illinois (1929–31).

McCrae, John 1872–1918. Canadian physician and poet. A surgeon in the British Army in WW I, he wrote the famous poem *In Flanders Fields* (1915).

McCulloch v. *Maryland* US Supreme Court decision (1819) confirming the powers of Congress to establish a federal bank. Chief Justice J. Marshall's ruling enhanced the powers of the federal government.

Macdonald, Alexandre 1765–1840. French general. He fought in the French Revolutionary Wars and was made marshal by Napoleon. He later served Louis XVIII.

Macdonald, Flora 1722–90. Scottish Jacobite heroine. She aided in the escape of Prince Charles Edward Stuart after his defeat at Culloden Moor (1746).

Macdonald, (James) Ramsey 1866–1937. English statesman, first British Labour party prime minister (1924, 1929–31, 1931–35).

Macdonald, Sir John Alexander 1815–91. Canadian statesman. He played a major role in the federation of the Canadian provinces (1867) as the Dominion of Canada and was its first prime minister (1867–73, 1878–91).

Macdonough, Thomas 1783–1825. American naval officer. He defeated a superior British fleet (Sept. 11, 1814) on Lake Champlain in the War of 1812. His victory remains one of the great events of US naval history.

McDougall, Alexander 1731–86. American Revolutionary War general. He distinguished himself in the battles of White Plains and Germantown, and became commander of West Point (1780) after B. Arnold's plot to surrender West Point to the British failed. He was a member of the Continental Congress (1781–82, 1784–85).

MacDowell, Edward Alexander 1861–1908. American composer, known best for his symphonic poems and piano pieces.

McDowell, Irvin 1818–85. Union general in the American Civil War. He commanded at the First Battle of Bull Run (1861) and was superseded by Gen. G. McClellan. He was relieved of command after the Second Battle of Bull Run (1862).

Macedonia European region on the Balkan Peninsula consisting of parts of Greece, Yugoslavia, and Bulgaria. Under Philip II (359–336 BC), ancient Macedon came to dominate Greece. Seat of the Macedonian Empire under Alexander the Great, it later was conquered by the Roman, Byzantine, and Ottoman empires. Various claims to the region led to the Balkan Wars (1912–13) and the division of the region, largely between Greece and Yugoslavia. For more on the former Yugoslav republic of Macedonia and now an independent state, *see* Yugoslavia.

Macedonia, Kingdom of Ancient country located in northern Greece. Though the region was colonized by Greeks in the 8th cent. BC, Macedonia did not become a major power until the 4th cent. BC, when Philip II (*q.v.*) united his kingdom and made it the dominant power in Greece. His conquests set the stage for the spectacular reign of his son, Alexander the Great (*q.v.*), who created a vast, but short-lived, Hellenistic empire (4th cent. BC) that extended as far east as India. Following Alexander's death (323), his generals fought against each other in the Wars of the Diadochi (*q.v.*) and eventually carved up that empire into a number of successor states. Macedonia proper, weakened by the wars, was restored (3d cent. BC) during the reigns of Cassander, Antigonus II, and Antigonus III. Under Philip V, however, it was defeated by Rome in the first two Macedonian Wars (*q.v.*). After the Third Macedonian War Rome divided up the kingdom and, in 146 BC, made it part of the first Roman province.

Macedonian Wars Four wars between the Kingdom of Macedonia (*q.v.*) and Rome that resulted in the complete domination of Greece by Rome. **1.** First (211–205 BC): King Philip V (*q.v.*) allied himself with Carthage against Rome during the Second Punic War, and the resultant conflict with Rome was the First Macedonian War. The war ended to Philip's advantage. **2.** Second (200–197 BC): This war was brought on by Philip V's attempts to expand his domains. The terms imposed by the victorious Romans were harsh and included subjugation by Rome and payment of tribute. **3.** Third (171–168 BC): Philip's son, Perseus, provoked the third war with Rome by trying to expand Macedonian control in Greece. Rome defeated him and divided Macedonia into four republics. **4.** Fourth (149–148 BC): The Romans this time put down a Macedonian revolt against their rule. Macedonia was thereafter reduced to a Roman province.

McGillivray, Alexander 1759–93. American Indian chief. A leader of the Creek Indians, he supported the British during the American Revolution. Later, with Spanish assistance, he successfully resisted American claims to Creek lands.

McGovern, George Stanley 1922– . American politician, US congressman (1957–61) and senator (1963–81) from South Dakota. A leader of the movement to end the Vietnam War, he was unsuccessful Democratic candidate for president (1972).

McGuffey, William Holmes 1800–73. American educator. He compiled the famous McGuffey Eclectic Readers, which were used in American schools for generations.

McHenry, Fort *See* **Fort McHenry.**

Machado, Gerardo 1871–1939. Cuban political leader. As Cuba's president (1925–33), he attempted internal reforms, but his brutal suppression of opposition led to his downfall.

Machado de Assis, Joaquim Marie 1839–1908. Brazilian author, considered Brazil's greatest writer. His novels include *Memórias póstumas de Braz Cubas, Quincas Borba,* and *Dom Casmurro.*

Machiavelli, Niccolo 1496–1527. Italian statesman, author, and philosopher. A Florentine diplomat, he was imprisoned briefly by the Medici when they regained power (1512). After his release he turned to writing. His best-known work, *The Prince* (1517), contains Machiavelli's thoughts on the methods by which a prince may acquire and make use of political power. It is thought that he used C. Borgia as the model for his cynical, ruthless prince.

Machu Picchu Ancient Incan city, located in the Andes mountains of Peru. First discovered (1911) by Hiram Bingham (1875–1956), it is one of the major pre-Columbian archaeological sites.

Mackenzie, Sir Alexander 1764?–1820. Canadian explorer. He charted the course of the Mackenzie River (1789) and made a transcontinental journey across Canada (1793).

Mackenzie, William Lyon 1795–1861. Canadian journalist and political insurgent. He led an unsuccessful rebellion (1837) to take over the government of Upper Canada at York (Toronto).

McKinley Tariff Act *See* **Harrison, Benjamin.**

McKinley, William 1843–1901. Twenty-fifth US president (1897–1901), successor to G. Cleveland. He distinguished himself in the American Civil War, became a Republican congressman (1877–83, 1885–91) from Ohio and championed the establishment of high protective tariffs. He secured passage of the McKinley Tariff Act of 1890 but was defeated for reelection. Returning to Ohio, McKinley received the support of M. Hanna and the Ohio Democratic party, and became governor (1892–96). Chosen the Republican presidential candidate in 1896, he supported the party's gold platform and defeated the Democratic candidate, W. Bryan, who campaigned for free silver (*q.v.*). During McKinley's first term the US engaged in the Spanish-American War (*q.v.*), from which it emerged a world power and gained possession of Cuba and the Philippines. McKinley also presided over the annexation of Hawaii, and supported the Open Door policy in China. McKinley again opposed Bryan in the 1900 election and was reelected. He altered his stand on tariffs and began to support commercial reciprocity. He spoke on the subject at the Pan-American Exposition in Buffalo (Sept. 5, 1901), and the next day was shot by an anarchist, Leon Czolgosz. He died Sept. 14 and was succeeded by his vice-president, T. Roosevelt.

Mack von Leiberich, Baron Karl *See* **Ulm, Battle of.**

MacLeish, Archibald 1892–1982. American poet, three times winner of the Pulitzer Prize (1933, 1953, 1959). He served as an adviser to President F. Roosevelt and as librarian of Congress (1939–44).

McLuhan, (Herbert) Marshall 1911–80. Canadian educator and author. He is noted for his books on the effects electronic media have on society. Among them are *Understanding Media: The Extensions of Man* and *The Medium Is the Message: An Inventory of Effects.*

MacMahon, Marie Edmé Patrice Maurice de 1808–93. French marshal and statesman. A monarchist, he was the second president (1873–79) of the French Third Republic (1870–1940).

Macmillan, Daniel and Macmillan, Alexander 1813–57; 1818–96. Scottish booksellers and publishers. They founded (1844) the publishing firm of Macmillan and Company.

Macmillan, (Maurice) Harold 1894–1986. British statesman. He entered politics after WW I, and was a member of the House of Commons from 1924 (1924–29, 1931–64). He served in various posts under Prime Minister A. Eden, notably as chancellor of the exchequer (1955–57), and became prime minister after Eden was forced out over the Suez crisis. In office (1957–63), Macmillan sought to improve relations with the US after the Suez Canal crisis, but failed to gain Great Britain's entry into the Common Market because of poor relations with France (which vetoed Britain's entry). During his term Macmillan also dealt with the African independence movement and with economic problems (from 1961). Scandals, including the Vasall spy case (1962) and the Profumo scandal (1963), and austerity measures necessitated by the weakened economy cost him popularity. Despite Britain's successful participation in negotiations (with the US and USSR) for the Nuclear Test Ban Treaty, Macmillan was forced to resign in 1963.

McNaughton, Andrew George Latta 1887–1966. Canadian army general. He was a commander of Canadian forces in Europe during WW II.

Macon, Nathaniel 1758–1837. American politician, US congressman (1791–1815) and senator (1815–28) from North Carolina. He was a strong supporter of T. Jefferson and states' rights.

Macon's Bill No. 2 *See* **Embargo Act.**

Macready, William Charles 1793–1873. English actor and manager of Covent Garden Theatre (1837–39) and of Drury Lane (1841–43). His rivalry with American actor Edwin Forrest (1806–72) sparked violence (May 10, 1849) at New York's Astor Place opera hall. In the ensuing riot more than 20 were killed.

McReynolds, James Clark 1862–1946. American jurist. Appointed associate justice to the Supreme Court (1914–41) by President W. Wilson, he was a strong opponent of the New Deal legislation.

Macrobius *fl.* AD c400. Latin author and philosopher. He wrote the *Saturnalia,* a series of dialogues.

Madagascar (Democratic Republic of ˜; *formerly* Malagasy Republic) Island republic (*pop.* 11,802,000) located off the southeast coast of Africa. Capital is Antananarivo. First settled by Africans and Indonesians, Madagascar was discovered by the Portuguese (1500), and the French established tentative settlements on the island (1642 to late 18th cent.). Several independent kingdoms were once formed on Madagascar, but in the 18th cent. the Merina people began to establish their control over the island with British aid. During this period Christian missionaries and foreign trade were alternately encouraged and opposed by Merina rulers, until the reign (1868–83) of Queen Ranavalona II, who converted to Christianity. The last Merina ruler was Queen Ranavalona III (reigned 1883–96). The French declared a protectorate over Madagascar (1882), which was recognized by Britain and Germany (1890). The Merina resisted, heavy fighting broke out (1894–96), and the monarchy was abolished (1897). Madagascar was occupied by the British (1942) during WW II. In 1958 it became the Malagasy Republic, an autonomous state within the French Community, and on June 26, 1960, it became independent. Following the resignation of the president (1975) over continuing economic problems, Commander Didier Ratsiraka was installed (June, 1975) as president. The country's name was changed to its current form, and Ratsiraka then began a program of nationalization. Food shortages and other problems resulted in outbreaks of violence in 1986–87, and demands for political change forced the end (1989) of constitutional guarantees for the supremacy of the ruling National Front (socialist) party. Multi-party politics resumed and press censorship was ended in 1990. Demonstrations demanding a new constitution and President Ratsiraka's ouster culminated in the deaths of demonstrators outside the presidential palace (Aug. 1991) when troops opened fire. Soon after the government was dissolved, though Ratsiraka remained as head of a transitional government pending elections. The National Forum convened in 1992 and completed the draft of a new constitution in Apr.

Madero, Francisco Indalecio 1873–1913. Mexican president (1911–13). He was a leader in the revolution (1911) against President P. Díaz. Unsuccessful as a reform president, he was arrested and murdered by order of V. Huerta.

Madison, Dolley 1768–1849. Wife of President J. Madison and famous Washington, D.C., hostess. She married Madison (1794) a year after the death of her first husband, and served as White House hostess for the widowed President T. Jefferson, as well as during her husband's presidency. Her letters and memoirs are a valuable source for early US history.

Madison, James 1751–1836. Fourth US president (1809–17), successor to T. Jefferson. An early opponent of British colonial policies, Madison served in the Virginia Convention (1776) and in the Continental Congress (1780–83), then served in the Virginia legislature (1784–86). As a delegate to the Annapolis Convention (*q.v.*) in 1786 he supported the call to convene the Federal Constitutional Convention (1787). There he became, with A. Hamilton, the leading force in the drafting of the Constitution. After the convention, he joined Hamilton and J. Jay in

writing the Federalist Papers, which argued for adoption of the Constitution. As a congressman from Virginia (1789–97), he next supported establishment of the Bill of Rights and opposed the conservative policies followed by Hamilton and others. With T. Jefferson, he drafted the Virginia Resolutions (*see* Kentucky and Virginia Resolutions) in response to the Alien and Sedition Acts (*q.v.*). On Jefferson's election as president, Madison became secretary of state (1801–09). His support of a trade embargo against Britain (*see* Embargo Act) contributed to the outbreak of the War of 1812, which was fought during his terms as president (1809–17). Discontent with Madison's policies and his conduct of the war led in New England to the Hartford Convention (*q.v.*).

Madison, Marbury v.   *See* **Marbury** v. **Madison.**

Madjapahit Empire   *See* **Majapahit Empire.**

Mad Parliament   *See* **Provisions of Oxford.**

Madrid, Treaty of   Treaty (Jan. 14, 1526) between Habsburg emperor Charles V and his prisoner, French king Francis I, temporarily ending the Italian Wars (*q.v.*) between France and Spain. The treaty was never ratified, and Francis subsequently renounced its provisions.

Maecenas   *d.* 8 BC.   Roman statesman. He was adviser to Emperor Augustus and a noted patron of the arts. Among his friends were Horace and Vergil.

Maerlant, Jacob van c1235–c1300. A Flemish poet. He wrote didactic poetry, the most famous being *Spiegel Historael,* an adaptation of Vincent of Beauvais' *Speculum Historiale.*

Maeterlinck, Maurice 1862–1949. Belgian symbolist poet and dramatist. His play *Pelléas et Mélisande* (1892) was the inspiration for C. Debussy's opera. He was awarded the Nobel Prize for Literature in 1911.

Mafia (Cosa Nostra) Notorious crime organization that originated in Sicily. Currently active in the US, South America, and elsewhere, the group is involved in illegal and quasilegal business ventures. The Mafia dates from the 13th cent. and operated in Sicily (18th–19th cents.) as autonomous bands of criminals. Noted for their use of terrorism, bloody vendettas and vows of secrecy, the Mafia bands resisted government campaigns to suppress them (late 19th, early 20th cent.). The group spread to the US in the last years of the 19th cent. Using tactics of their forebears and aided by widespread evasion of the law during Prohibition, organized Mafia "families" built a nationwide crime syndicate that now dominates organized crime in the US.

Magdeburg, sack of Destruction (May 20, 1631) of the city of Magdeburg, Germany, during the Thirty Years' War. Imperial forces under J. Tilly successfully stormed the city and killed its defenders. Fires broke out, and virtually the whole city was destroyed.

Magellan, Ferdinand c1480–1521. Portuguese navigator and explorer, leader of the first voyage circumnavigating the world. Sponsored by Spanish king Charles I (later Holy Roman Emperor Charles V), Magellan set out (1519) to find a western sea route to the Molucca Islands (Spice Islands). He sailed the strait that bears his name, and discovered the Philippines. Though he died in the Philippines (1521), his expedition continued west, under J. Cano, becoming the first to circumnavigate the globe.

Magenta, Battle of French-Piedmontese victory (June 4, 1859) over Austria near Milan, Italy. The Austrian loss advanced the cause of Italian unity.

Magi Members of a priestly caste in ancient Persia. They became priests of the Zoroastrian religion and were considered wise men. The word "magic" comes from "magi." In Christian tradition, the Magi (or Three Kings) brought gifts to the newborn Jesus Christ. The three were Caspar, Melchior, and Balthazar.

Maginot, André See **Maginot Line.**

Maginot Line Network of fortifications on the French-German frontier. Named for war minister André Maginot (1877–1932), who supervised its construction, it was supposedly impregnable to any German assault. During WW II the Germans bypassed the line, attacking through Belgium's Ardennes Forest and thus rendering the line useless.

Magliabechi, Antonio 1633–1714. Italian bibliophile. He was court librarian (1673–1714) to Cosimo III de Medici, grand duke of Tuscany. His 30,000-volume library is now part of the National Library in Florence.

Magna Carta (Magna Charta) English charter, important in the development of British constitutional law and a symbol (mainly by later interpretations) of basic liberties. Angered by King John's heavy taxation and abuses of power, the barons and the church united to force him (by threat of civil war) to sign the document at Run-

nymede on June 19, 1215. Originally written to guarantee rights of the nobility, it contained provisions for church freedom, trial by jury, habeas corpus, and matters of minor import. John later attempted to void the charter and died in the resulting civil war. However, it was reaffirmed by his son, Henry III, in 1216, 1217, and 1225.

Magna Graecia Area of southern Italy, named for its ancient Greek colonies. Established in the 8th cent. BC, they thrived in the 7th and 6th cents. BC. Subsequently they became increasingly isolated from Greece and suffered internal strife, conquest by the Romans, and encroachment by the Carthaginians (in Sicily).

Magnentius See **Mursa, Battle of.**

Magnesia, Battle of See **Antiochus III.**

Magnus I (Magnus the Good) 1024–47. King of Norway (1035–47) and Denmark (1042–47), son of Olaf II. He succeeded Danish king Harthacanute (1042), thereby joining Norway and Denmark. He attempted to press Harthacanute's claim to the English throne but was unsuccessful.

Magnus VI 1238–80. Norwegian king (1263–80), son of Haakon IV. He established a comprehensive system of law in Norway.

Magnus VII 1316–73. King of Sweden (1319–63) and Norway (1319–55), successor to his grandfather Haakon V. A weak ruler, he lost the Norwegian crown to his son Haakon VI and the Swedish throne to his nephew Albert, duke of Mecklenburg (1340?–1412), who ruled as Albert III.

Magnus the Good See **Magnus I.**

Magruder, John Bankhead 1810–71. Confederate general in the American Civil War. He defeated Gen. B. Butler at Big Bethel, Virginia (June 1861), and later commanded Confederate forces in the Peninsular Campaign (1862).

Magyars Ethnic name for the people, living primarily in Hungary, who speak the Hungarian language of the Finno-Ugric family. Descended from nomadic peoples who migrated from the Urals (5th cent.), they also include groups living in Rumania, the former Yugoslavia and Czechoslovakia, and the Ukraine.

Mahabharata One of the two great Sanskrit epics (with the Ramayana) of ancient India. The 18-book poetic work, composed between 200 BC and AD 200, is a complex merging of Indian history and Hindu religious lore. The Mahabharata contains the *Bhagavad-Gita,* the most important single religious text in Hinduism.

Mahamaya *See* **Buddha.**

Mahan, Alfred Thayer 1840–1914. Historian and naval strategist. His book *The Influence of Sea Power Upon History, 1660–1783,* which stressed the importance of a strong navy (built around powerful battleships), helped shape military strategy and foreign policy in the late 19th and early 20th centuries. Mahan's thinking on naval strategy, spelled out in numerous subsequent books, helped promote the building of the United States' "Great White Fleet" of steam-powered battleships before WW I, and sparked the naval armaments race between Britain and Germany in the years leading up to WW I.

Maharashtra, Kingdom of *See* **Maratha Kingdom.**

Mahavira (Vardhamana) c599–527 BC. Last of the 24 tirthankaras (saints) who founded the Indian religion of Jainism. He established a monastic order that practiced asceticism and respect for all life.

Mahayana A leading form of Buddhism, practiced in China, Japan, Korea, and Tibet, and noted for its more liberal treatment of Buddhist doctrine.

Mahdi In Islam, a leader who will appear at the end of the world to save true believers. Although this is not mentioned in the Koran, there have been several claimants to the title.

Mahdi, Muhammad Ahmed 1843?–85. Muslim leader who claimed he was the Mahdi. He led a successful revolution against the Egyptian occupation of the Sudan, and defeated the British at Khartoum (1885).

Mahican Indians (Mohican ~) North American Indian tribe that lived in the upper Hudson Valley. They were dispersed in the mid-17th cent. as a result of wars with the Mohawks. A number of Mohicans settled in Stockbridge, Mass.

Mahler, Gustav 1860–1911. Austrian composer and conductor. In his long career, Mahler served as artistic director of the Vienna Court Opera (1897–1907) and directed the Metropolitan Opera and the New York Philharmonic. He is known best for his choral works, nine completed symphonies, and his unfinished tenth.

Mahmud II 1784–1839. Ottoman sultan (1808–39). During his reign, territory was lost to Russia, Syria was ceded to Egypt, and Greece became independent.

Mahone, William 1826–95. Confederate general in the American Civil War and US politi-

cian. As US senator from Virginia (1881–87), he was a powerful leader in Virginia politics after Reconstruction.

Mahrattas, Kingdom of *See* **Maratha Kingdom.**

Maida, Battle of Battle (July 4, 1806) at Maida, southern Italy, during the Napoleonic Wars. Some 5,000 British troops under Gen. John Stuart defeated a French force led by Gen. Jean Reynier (1771–1814), thereby halting the French advance south.

Mailer, Norman 1923– . American writer, noted for his incorporation of factual material within a fictional framework. Among his books are *The Naked and the Dead, The Deer Park, The Armies of the Night,* and *The Executioner's Song.*

Mailiol, Aristide 1861–1944. French artist. Originally a painter and tapestry designer, he became famous for his massive statues of female nude figures.

Maimonides (Maimun, Moses ben) 1135–1204. Spanish-born Jewish philosopher, considered one of the greatest influences on Jewish thought. He wrote a commentary on the *Mishna,* the *Mishneh Torah,* and *A Guide for the Perplexed.*

Maimun, Moses ben *See* **Maimonides.**

Maine Northeastern US state, the 23d state. The Maine coast had long been known to mariners of various countries, and the entire region was granted to the Plymouth Company in 1606. The first English settlement failed (1607), but there were several successful settlements by the time Maine was annexed to Massachusetts (1652). Conflict with the French and Indians slowed the area's development, and there was dissatisfaction with Massachusetts rule. Maine was admitted to the Union in 1820. The Aroostook War (*q.v.*) led to the Webster-Ashburton Treaty settling the US boundary with Canada.

Maine US battleship whose destruction in the harbor of Havana (Feb. 15, 1898) precipitated US entry into the Spanish-American War.

Maintenon, Françoise d'Aubigné, marquise de 1635–1719. Second wife of King Louis XIV of France. She was governess for his illegitimate children and married him morganatically (1685?).

Maipu, Battle of Battle (Apr. 5, 1818), near Santiago, Chile. Here J. de San Martín defeated Spanish royalist forces and gained independence for Chile.

Maitland, William 1528?–73. Scottish statesman. A supporter and adviser of Mary, Queen of

Scots, he worked for the unification of England and Scotland under her rule.

Majapahit Empire (Madjapahit ˜) (Modjopahit ˜) Hindu kingdom that flourished in Java (13–15th cents.). The Majapahit period is regarded as a golden age in the history of Java. The kingdom was centered in eastern Java, though its extent at the height of its power is uncertain. Founded (1292) by King Vijaya, the kingdom reached its zenith under Vijaya's grandson, King Hayam Wuruk (1350–89), and his minister Gajah Mada. Muslim states that emerged in northern Java conquered the Majapahit kingdom in the late 15th cent.

Major, John 1943– . British prime minister (1990–). Born the son of a circus performer, Major became a member of Parliament (1979) and served in various government posts in the Thatcher administration (from 1981). In 1987 he became treasury chief secretary and in 1989 foreign secretary—briefly—before becoming chancellor of the exchequer that same year. Major became prime minister upon M. Thatcher's resignation, which came amid mounting economic problems and the furor over the poll tax. Major did away with the unpopular tax, wrestled with an economic recession (from 1991), became the target of an IRA attack on his residence (1991; no one was injured), and initiated an overhaul of the National Health Service. In foreign policy, he continued close relations with the US, committed British forces to the allied cause in the Persian Gulf War, joined other nations in signing the historic Treaty on Conventional Armed Forces in Europe (1990), and pulled Britain out of the European Community exchange rate stabilization program. *See also* Great Britain, 1990–92.

Majorian *d.* AD 461. Roman emperor of the West (AD 457–461). He became emperor with the support of Ricimer and worked to reform tax laws. After his defeat by Gaiseric (AD 460), he abdicated and was murdered on Ricimer's orders.

Makarios III (Mouskos, Mihail Christodoulou) 1913–77. Archbishop of the Orthodox Church of Cyprus. A leader in the enosis movement for union with Greece, he became first president of independent Cyprus (1959–77). His ouster in 1974 was followed by the crisis in Cyprus (*q.v.*) and his return to power that year.

Malacca (Melaka) Malayan state. Malacca was in turn ruled by the Portuguese, Dutch, English, and Japanese and was a major trading center from 1400 to 1511. It became part of Malaysia in 1963.

Malachy, Saint 1095–1148. Irish archbishop and church reformer. He established territorial hierarchy in the Irish church and founded (1142) Mellifont, the first Cistercian abbey in Ireland.

Malagasy Republic *See* **Madagascar.**

Malan, Daniel François 1874–1959. South African statesman. As prime minister (1948–54), he established apartheid laws for the separation of the races.

Malatesta Italian family which ruled Rimini and the area around it from the 13th to 16th cents. Prominent members were Malatesta da Verucchio (*d.* 1312), a leader of the Guelphs, and Sigismondo Pandolfo Malatesta (1417–68).

Malatesta, Sigismondo Pandolfo *See* **Malatesta.**

Malawi (Republic of Malawi; *formerly* Nyasaland) Republic in southeast Africa. The population is 9,080,000 and the capital is Lilongwe. First explored (1859) by D. Livingstone, the region was annexed by Britain (1891) as the British Central African Protectorate. Renamed Nyasaland, it became (1953) part of the Federation of Rhodesia and Nyasaland. Opposition to the Federation formed in Nyasaland, and it was abolished (1963). Nyasaland became independent as Malawi (1964) and became a republic (1966). Dr. Hastings Banda served as president (1964–) of a one-party government. Made president for life in 1971, he instituted a repressive regime, dealing harshly with sporadic outbreaks of resistance to his rule. Malawi entered into agreements with neighboring Mozambique (1984, 1986) to block operations by Mozambican rebels based inside Malawi. Ongoing unrest in Mozambique forced an estimated 800,000 Mozambican refugees to flee to Malawi by 1991.

Malaya Peninsula of Southeast Asia, now divided between Malaysia and Singapore.

Malaysia Constitutional monarchy located in Southeast Asia. It is divided into two parts: West Malaysia, on the Malay Peninsula, and East Malaysia, on the island of Borneo. The population is 17,053 and the capital is Kuala Lumpur. Key dates in the history of Malaysia include:

1400 Malacca founded.
1511 Portugal occupied Malacca on the Malay Peninsula.

1641 Dutch captured Malacca.

1786 British East India Company given rights to the island of Penang.

1800 Sultan of Kedah gave British rights to Province of Wellesley on the mainland.

1816 Kingdom of Siam (Thailand), extending control into region.

1819 Britain founded Singapore.

1821 Siam acquired Kedah.

1824 Treaty of London defined British and Dutch spheres of influence; Britain acquired Malacca; Straits Settlement created joint administration for Penang, Malacca, and Singapore.

1874 Pankor Engagement; marked beginning of British domination of Malay states following period of unrest and civil wars.

1896 Federated Malay States created, British resident general named.

1909 Britain gained control of additional territory from Siam.

1942–45 Japan occupied Malaya for duration of WW II.

1946–48 Britain resumed control, created unpopular Malayan Union (1946); replaced (Feb. 1, 1948) by Federation of Malaya.

1948–MID 1950s Communist insurrection ("The Emergency"); 500,000 Chinese residents resettled because most Communists involved were Chinese.

1957 Malaya gained independence (Aug. 31); joined the British Commonwealth; admitted to UN.

1957–70 Tunku Abdul Rahman, who negotiated with Britain for independence, in office as prime minister.

c1960 Remnants of outlawed Communist Party of Malaya fled to southern Thailand.

1963 Singapore, Sabah, and Sarawak joined Malaya (Sept. 16), establishing Federation of Malaysia; federation opposed by Indonesia, which mounted guerrilla war (1963–65).

1965 Singapore (with large ethnic Chinese population) seceded from the federation.

1969 Violence followed Chinese electoral gains (May); parliament suspended; Prime Minister Tunku Abdul Rahman resigned (1970).

1970–76 Tun Abdul Razak in office as prime minister.

1971–90 Government instituted New Economic Policy in effort to give native Malays greater share in economy; included hiring quotas and a target of 30% of corporate assets to be held by Malays.

1976–81 Datuk Hussein bin Onn in office as prime minister; resurgence of terrorist attacks by Communist guerrillas (1976–78), until joint Malaysian government forces began joint military operations with Thailand in border areas.

1977 Muslim unrest in Malaysian state of Kelantan; state of emergency declared.

1978 "Boat people" fleeing Vietnam poured into Malaysia; by 1989 some 230,000 Vietnamese refugees had passed through country on way to resettlement in other nations.

1978 Official ban on "boat people" ended (Nov.) when several hundred drowned off Malaysian coast.

1980–86 Malaysia posted trade deficit each year during this period, until commodity prices began to rebound on world market in mid-1980s.

1981– Datuk Seri Mahathir bin Muhammad in office as prime minister; oversaw privatization program of state-run businesses that began in mid-1980s.

1987 Government arrested over 100 opposition politicians, lawyers, and journalists, ostensibly to head off race riots between Malays and Chinese; all released by Jan. 1989.

1988 Supreme Court chief ousted after he publicly opposed constitutional amendments that curtailed judicial powers (Aug.).

1989 Remnants of outlawed Communist Party of Malaya agreed to peace settlement with government.

1989 Government began turning back Vietnamese refugees.

1989 Banking and finance reform enacted.

1990 Official discussions begun with Vietnam on trade agreement.

1990 Parti Bersatu Sabah (PBS) withdrew from ruling Barisan Nasional (BN) party; PBS leaders accused of trying to take state of Sabah out of Malaysian federation.

1991 Pairin Kitingan, president of PBS, arrested on corruption charges; other PBS officials detained on suspicion of plotting to take Sabah out of the federation.

1991 Government announced New Development Policy, replacing former New Economic

Policy to reallocate economic resources to native Malays; new plan to emphasize education and training, in place of hiring quotas.

Malchus *See* **Porphyry.**

Malcolm III (~ Canmore) *d.* 1093. Scottish king (1057–93), successor to Macbeth whom he killed in battle. He gave refuge to Edgar the Aetheling and married Edgar's sister, Saint Margaret. He was killed on a raid into England.

Malcolm Canmore *See* **Malcolm III.**

Malcolm X (Little, Malcolm) 1925–65. American black leader. A militant Black Muslim, he preached separation from whites, but later came to believe that blacks and whites might be able to live together. He became involved in a struggle within the Black Muslim movement and was assassinated.

Malebranche, Nicolas de *See* **Cartesianism.**

Malenkov, Georgi Maksimilianovich 1902–88. Soviet statesman and Communist leader. Joining the Communist party in 1920, Malenkov rose quickly and became a close ally of J. Stalin. Malenkov was a key figure in Stalin's purges in the 1930s, played an important role in the Soviet war effort during WW II, and was made a member of the Politburo in 1946. After Stalin's death he became prime minister (1953–55) and party secretary (1953) but was forced out of the latter post in favor of N. Khrushchev. As prime minister he sought to improve the lot of collective farmers, stimulate production of consumer goods, and cut back spending on arms, but these programs only provided ammunition that opposition leaders (N. Khrushchev and others) used to secure his ouster in 1955. After joining the attempt to depose Khrushchev in 1957, he was stripped of his remaining posts and expelled from the party.

Malevich, Casimir *See* **suprematism.**

Mali (Republic of Mali; *formerly* French Sudan, Sudanese Republic) Independent republic located in western Africa. The population is 9,182,000 and the capital is Bamako. Many early African empires flourished in the region, including the Mali Empire, which reached its peak in the 14th cent., and the Songhai Empire of the 15th and 16th cents. A period of warfare and invasion ensued until the rise of new Muslim states (19th cent.). The French conquered much of the region by 1898, and Mali, as French Sudan, became part of French West Africa. Ris-

ing nationalism in the 20th cent. led to formation of the Sudanese Union, which soon became Mali's leading political party. Under Modibo Keita (1915–   ) the party campaigned for independence. In 1958 French Sudan became autonomous, within the French Community, as the Sudanese Republic, and in 1960 it became independent as the Republic of Mali. Keita, its first president, followed a Socialist course until his overthrow (1968). Gen. Moussa Traoré subsequently became head of state (1968–91). Severe drought and famine struck the region in 1969–74, 1979, and 1985–86, and refugees fled the country in large numbers. Locust plagues in 1986 and 1988 only added to the problems of famine, disease, and political unrest. Pressure for democratic reforms began in 1990 and following a violent protest (Mar. 1991) in which 112 persons were killed, Traoré was ousted in a military coup (Mar. 26). Elections were held in early 1992 and Alpha Oumar Konaré became president. Meanwhile in 1990, ethnic unrest among Tuaregs in the north resulted in fighting and a flood of refugees seeking safety in neighboring countries. However, a ceasefire was arranged in early 1992.

Malik Shah *See* **Seljuks.**

Malinowski, Bronislaw 1884–1942. Polish-born anthropologist. He formulated the functional theory of social anthropology.

Mallarmé, Stéphane 1842–98. French poet. He was an early symbolist. His best-known poem, *L'Aprés-Midi d'un faune,* inspired C. Debussy's musical composition of the same name.

Mallon, Mary *See* **Typhoid Mary.**

Malone, Edmund 1741–1812. English scholar and editor. He produced an important chronology of the works of W. Shakespeare and exposed the Shakespearean forgeries of W. Ireland.

Malory, Sir Thomas *d.* 1471. English author of the medieval prose romance *Morte d'Arthur.* This account of King Arthur and his Round Table is considered one of the greatest prose works in the English language and is one of the first longer works printed in England by W. Caxton.

Malpighi, Marcello 1628–94. Italian physician noted for his studies of anatomy and his early use of the microscope for animal and plant study.

Malplaquet, Battle of Battle (Sept. 11, 1709) of the War of the Spanish Succession. The allied army of English, Dutch, and Austrians under J. Churchill, duke of Marlborough, and Prince

Eugene of Savoy, forced the French to withdraw. Casualties were so heavy, however, that the allies were obliged to halt their advance on Paris.

Malraux, André 1901–76. French author and political figure. Active in the political struggles of his time, he used his experiences in such novels as *La Condition humaine* and *L'Espoir.* He was the French minister of cultural affairs from 1958 to 1968.

Malta Independent island state in the Mediterranean, comprising the islands of Malta, Gozo, and Comino, and several islets. The population is 354,900 and the capital is Valletta. Occupied by the British from 1800, it was the scene of fierce bombing by the Germans and Italians during WW II. It became independent in 1964 and a republic (Dec. 13, 1974), within the British Commonwealth. British military presence was ended in 1979. The government has sought non-aligned status and maintains close relations with Libya and Italy, as well as other states.

Malthus, Thomas Robert 1766–1834. English economist who pioneered the study of population and society. His *An Essay on the Principle of Population* contended that population would always increase faster than means of subsistence.

Malvinas Islands Argentine name for Falkland Islands (*q.v.*).

Mamelukes Warrior class that provided rulers of Egypt from 1250 until the conquest by Ottoman Turks (1517). Of Asian stock, Mamelukes were first used as slaves and then as warriors by the Muslim rulers of Egypt. The Bahrite dynasty of Mameluke sultans (1250–1382) was founded by Aybak (*d.* 1257), and their rule was characterized by internal dissent and frequent rebellions. Nevertheless, the Bahrite Mamelukes halted the Mongol advance (1260) in Syria and crushed the powerful Assassin sect. During the bloody reign of the Burjite dynasty of Mamelukes (1382–1517), the Egyptians warred against Tamerlane, expelled Christian knights from Cyprus, and finally succumbed (1517) to the Ottoman Turks under Selim I. Under the Turks, the Mamelukes retained their lands and many government posts and eventually regained considerable autonomy. They retained power in Egypt until 1811, when they were virtually exterminated by the Egyptian ruler Muhammad Ali.

Mamun, al- 786–833. Seventh Abbasid caliph (813–33), son of Harun ar-Rashid and successor to his brother al-Amin after defeating him. His reign was marked by a cultural flowering and an interest in science. Al-Mamun established the "House of Wisdom" in Baghdad for the express purpose of translating into Arabic the works of the Greeks.

Manassas, Battle of *See* **Bull Run, Battle of.**

Manchester school Group of British laissez-faire economists, influenced by the ideas of D. Ricardo, who were active between 1820 and 1850. Led by R. Cobden and J. Bright, they advocated freedom of trade and minimal governmental interference in economic affairs.

Manchu *See* **Qing.**

Manchukuo Puppet state established (1932) in Manchuria by the Japanese. Its nominal ruler was Henry Puyi, last Qing emperor. It ceased to exist (1945) when Manchuria was returned to China after WW II.

Manchuria Major industrial region, northeastern China. Home of the Manchus, who established the Manchu (Ch'ing) dynasty in China (1644–1912), it has been the object of struggles between China, Russia, and Japan. Russia and Japan fought for control of it in the Russo-Japanese War (1904–05). Japan occupied Manchuria (1931–32) and set up the puppet state of Manchukuo (1932–45). Returned to China (1945), it became a Chinese Communist stronghold by 1948.

Mancini, Pasquale Stanislao 1817–88. Italian political leader. A liberal and anticlerical, he introduced numerous reforms. As minister of foreign affairs (1881–85) he negotiated the Triple Alliance (1882) with Austria and Germany.

Manco Capac *d.* 1544. Inca ruler. Kept prisoner by F. Pizarro, he escaped (1536), raised an army, and laid siege to Cuzco. Defeated, he continued to fight in the mountains, but was murdered by followers of another rebel leader, D. de Almagro.

Mandaeans (Christians of Saint John) Religious group of Iran and Iraq. They revere John the Baptist and place emphasis on the rite of baptism and fertility worship.

Mandarin Formerly, a Chinese imperial official. The dialect spoken by Chinese officials was known as Mandarin Chinese and in its modern form is the most widely used dialect in China.

mandate Designation for a colonial territory placed under the control of another power by the League of Nations. The system of mandates was used after WW I to provide for those former German and Turkish territories (including Iraq,

Palestine, Syria, and Southwest Africa) that were deemed unable to govern themselves. Mandates still in effect in 1946 became UN trusteeships.

Mandela, Nelson Rolihlahla 1918– . Black South African political leader, an important figure in the anti-apartheid movement. Joining the opposition to South Africa's white-ruled government, Mandela helped found the African National Congress Youth League (1944) and in 1952 organized the Defiance Campaign, a peaceful protest against the government's apartheid policies. Abandoning nonviolent tactics, Mandela organized the military arm (Spear of the Nation, 1961) of the banned African National Congress. In 1964, he was jailed for life on sabotage and conspiracy charges, but his imprisonment helped make him an internationally known symbol of the struggle against apartheid. After UN–backed economic sanctions helped bring a reformist government to power in South Africa, Mandela was released from prison (1990). Elected deputy president of the African National Congress, Mandela subsequently played a key role in negotiations to determine the role of the black majority in South Africa's government. Mandela's wife Winnie was convicted of kidnapping charges (1991), which stemmed from activities while Mandela was in prison.

Mandeville, Sir John *fl.* 14th cent. English author. He wrote *The Travels of Sir John Mandeville,* a romanticized travel account that gained great popularity. It was based largely on the travels of such figures as M. Polo. Little is known of the author.

Manet, Édouard 1832–83. French artist. His paintings, such as *Déjeuner sur l'herbe,* influenced the development of impressionism. Manet painted realistic subject matter and developed a characteristic use of color and brush technique that challenged the then conventional academic style. His first showings met with protest and criticism from established art circles, but he was soon joined by other emerging impressionist painters of his day. His other noted works include *Olympia, Bar at the Folies-Bergère,* and *At the Café.*

Manfred c1232–66. Sicilian king (1258–66), natural son of Holy Roman Emperor Frederick II. He opposed papal authority over Sicily, but was killed in battle against the forces of Charles of Anjou, who claimed the throne.

Manhattan Project US project inaugurated (1942) to develop the atomic bomb during WW II. Placed (Aug., 1942) under command of Gen. Leslie R. Groves (1896–1970), the project scientists created the first self-sustaining nuclear chain reaction (at Chicago, Dec. 2, 1942) and exploded the first nuclear device (July 16, 1945) at the Los Alamos facility near Alamogordo, New Mexico. The project produced the bombs dropped on Hiroshima (Aug. 6) and Nagasaki (Aug. 9). By hastening the Japanese surrender it saved countless American lives, but its success ushered in a new age, in which total war is unthinkable.

Manichaeanism *See* **Manichaeism.**

Manichaeism (Manichaeanism) Religious sect founded in 3d cent. AD Persia, on the teachings of Mani (*fl.* 3d cent.). It drew on Gnosticism, Zoroastrianism, and Christianity. Manichaeism was a dualistic religion which held the universe was divided into the forces of God and light and the forces of Satan and evil. Man had both, the spirit being light and goodness, the body itself being evil. The sect spread rapidly for a time, though by the 6th cent. it had largely disappeared in the West.

Manifest Destiny Historical expression used to justify US expansion in the 1840s. It held that America was chosen by God to establish its dominion from sea to sea, and was used to support American annexation of Texas and territories in the West and Mexico.

Manila Bay, Battle of US naval victory (May 1, 1898) during the Spanish-American War, at Manila. The US fleet under Commodore G. Dewey completely destroyed the Spanish Pacific fleet, thereby securing the Philippines from Spanish control.

Manin, Daniele 1804–57. Venetian statesman. He helped to free Venice from Austrian rule. Made president of the Venetian republic (1848), he unsuccessfully opposed union with Sardinia. He led a valiant but fruitless struggle against Austrian forces until Venice's fall (Aug., 1849).

Man in the Iron Mask Anonymous French prisoner, held captive and masked in the Bastille from 1698 until his death in 1703. His identity remains unknown.

Manitoba Canadian province. First settled (17th cent.) by the Hudson's Bay Company, it was contested by the British and French in the French and Indian Wars, and was ceded to Britain by the

Treaty of Paris (1763). It became a province in 1870.

Maniu, Iuliu 1873–1951. Rumanian statesman. Leader of the Rumanian National Peasants' party and prime minister (1928–30, 1932–33), he was convicted of treason (1947) by the Communists and died in prison.

Manlius Capitolinus, Marcus *d.* 384? BC. Roman consul (392 BC). Awakened one night by the cackling of geese, he discovered and repulsed an attack on Rome by the Gauls (390).

Manlius Torquatus, Titus *fl.* 4th cent. BC. Roman dictator and consul. He fought against the Gauls and Latins, and put his son to death for disobeying orders not to engage the enemy in single combat.

Mann, Horace 1796–1859. American educator. As the first secretary of the Massachusetts state board of education (1837–48), he developed theories and practices that greatly influenced the development of public education in the US.

Mann, Thomas 1875–1955. German novelist, considered one of the preeminent writers of the 20th cent. Awarded the Nobel Prize in 1929, Mann was forced to flee Germany (1933) by the rise of A. Hitler. He became a US citizen in 1944. Among his works are *Death in Venice, The Magic Mountain,* and *Doctor Faustus.*

Mann Act US law (1910) which prohibits the transportation of women across state lines for immoral purposes.

Mannerheim, baron Carl Gustav Emil von 1867–1951. Finnish military leader and statesman. He established the Mannerheim Line (*q.v.*) and commanded Finnish forces in the Russo-Finnish War. He later served as president of Finland (1944–46).

Mannerheim Line Finnish fortification across the Karelian Isthmus. Built under the direction of C. Mannerheim to prevent Soviet aggression, it fell to Russian forces (1940) in the Russo-Finnish War.

mannerism European art style of the 16th cent., characterized by exaggeration, and the disconcerting use of color, form, and spatial relationships. Arising as a reaction to High Renaissance art, it was in turn replaced by the baroque style.

Mannheim, Karl 1893–1947. German sociologist. His book *Ideologie und Utopie* explored the role of individual thought processes and their relation to social conflict.

manorial system (Seigniorial system) Medieval economic system in which a lord gave a peasant the right to tend land on his estate in return for a fixed payment. The system, derived from feudalism, flourished in Europe in the 11th–15th cents., and similar systems arose elsewhere, notably in Japan.

Mansard, François *See* **Mansart, François.**

Mansart, François (Mansard, ˜) 1598–1666. French architect. He is noted for his incorporation of classical elements into baroque architecture. The mansard roof is named after him.

Mansfeld, Peter Ernst, graf von 1580?–1626. Mercenary in the Thirty Years' War (1618–48). He supported the Protestants, notably Elector Palatine Frederick V.

Mansur (Al Mansur) *d.* 775. Second Abbasid caliph (754–75), successor to his brother Abu al-Abbas. He founded the city of Baghdad (762).

Mansur (al-Mansur) 934–1002. Regent of Córdoba under the caliph Hisham II. Assuming complete control, he led many victorious campaigns against Christian cities, and temporarily restored Ummayyad influence in Spain.

Mantegna, Andrea 1431–1506. Italian painter. One of the greatest artists of his day, he is especially noted for his frescoes in Padua, Milan, and Verona.

Mantua, Siege of French campaign (July, 1796–Feb., 1797) of Napoleon Bonaparte against an Austrian army besieged at Mantua, Italy. Napoleon held off four separate Austrian relief attempts, and Mantua ultimately surrendered (Feb. 2), leaving Napoleon virtual master of Italy.

Mantuan Succession, War of the Conflict (1628–31) during the Thirty Years' War in which France and the Habsburgs both sought control of the Italian duchy of Mantua. The Treaty of Cherasco (Apr. 26, 1631) awarded the duchy to Charles of Nevers, a member of the French branch of the Gonzaga family.

Manuel I (Manuel I Comnenus) 1120–80. Byzantine emperor (1143–80) successor to his father John II. He hoped to rebuild the Roman Empire but was defeated by the Turks at Myriocephalon (1176).

Manuel I (Emanuel I) 1469–1521. Portuguese king (1495–1521), successor to John II. During his reign, Portugal became a major commercial power through the voyages of discovery of V. da Gama and P. Cabral.

Manuel I Comnenus *See* **Manuel I.**

Manuel II Palaeologus 1350–1425. Byzantine emperor (1391–1425), successor to his father John V Palaeologus. He sought aid from the kingdoms of Europe to fight the Turks but was unsuccessful. In 1422 he was forced to pay tribute to Murad II.

Manuel II 1889–1932. Portuguese king (1908–10), son of Charles I. He succeeded to the throne after his father and brother were assassinated and was deposed by the republican revolution.

Manx Language of the Goidelic group of the Celtic subfamily, once spoken on the Isle of Man but now practically extinct.

Manzikert, Battle of Byzantine-Turkish battle (1071) at Manzikert, now in Turkey. Some 70,000 Seljuk Turks destroyed an army of 40,000 under Byzantine emperor Romanus IV. The battle led to the fall of Asia Minor to the Turks.

Maoism Ideology of revolutionary communism developed by Mao Zedong. Mao's thinking is generally considered allied with, but distinct from, Russian communism. Mao early on perceived the value of mobilizing China's peasant class, ignored by Soviet Marxists in favor of the proletariat as a source of revolution. By arousing a martial spirit (a fundamental element of Maoist doctrine), Mao succeeded in bringing Chinese peasants to revolution. Once in power, Mao turned away from the traditional Communist pathway to economic development. He opposed formation of a bureaucratic elite and instituted his Great Leap Forward (*q.v.*), which fostered labor-intensive, backyard industries. When this program failed, he again resorted to the martial spirit to purge the party of bureaucrats and elitists, this time with the disastrous Cultural Revolution (*q.v.*).

Maori Wars Wars (1860–72) between Maoris, native inhabitants of New Zealand, and British settlers seeking Maori lands on the North Island of New Zealand. As a result of the Maori King Movement, the natives on the North Island elected a king (1858) and adopted a general policy of refusing to sell native-owned lands to the settlers. A breach of that policy resulted in the first phase of the Maori Wars (1860–61), which ended in a truce. Officials of the British government provoked the second phase of fighting (1863–64), which embroiled the whole North Island in war. The settlers emerged victorious, only to find themselves in another war (1864–72) against more fanatical elements of the Maori tribes. Peace was finally established (1872), with large portions of Maori lands in the possession of the settlers. An earlier uprising (1843–48) is sometimes called the First Maori War.

Mao Tse-tung *See* **Mao Zedong.**

Mao Zedong (˜ Tse-tung) 1893–1976. Chinese Communist leader, founder and first chairman (1949–59) of the People's Republic of China. Born to a peasant family in Hunan province, Mao became a founding member of the Chinese Communist Party. After the split between the Nationalist Guomindang and the Communists, Mao led an abortive peasant revolt known as the Autumn Harvest Uprising (1927). Continuing to oppose the Guomindang, Mao helped to set up the Jiangxi Soviet (*q.v.*) in southeastern China and became its chairman (1931). Nationalist military successes against the Communists forced the Red Army to make its famed Long March (*q.v.*) of some 6,000 miles to Shaanxi province in northwestern China (1934–35). There, Mao established Communist control in the region and began the long struggle against nationalist Guomindang (*see* Chinese Civil War) and the invading Japanese (1937–45) during WW II. The last phase of the civil war with the nationalists broke out soon after WW II, and in 1949 the Communists established control over China. Mao, who had become chairman of the Chinese Communist Party (CCP) in 1935, became chairman of the new People's Republic of China (1949). In following years Mao sought to establish communism in China independently of the Russian model and sought to adapt Marxist ideology to Chinese society. During this period China entered the Korean War (*q.v.*). In order to build the Chinese economy, Mao instituted the Great Leap Forward (1958), a disastrous economic experiment that led to the rise of Liu Shaoqui (*q.v.*) as chairman of the republic. Mao retained his position as chairman of the CCP. The struggle between Liu and Mao led to the Cultural Revolution (*q.v.*) in 1966, and by 1970 Mao was once again undisputed leader of China, remaining so until his death. Mao's writings, especially those dealing with the revolutionary movement and guerrilla tactics, achieved a tremendous influence in China and in other countries, especially among radicals in the developing nations.

Maquis French guerrilla forces that fought against German occupation forces during WW II.

Mar, John Erskine, 1st earl of *d* 1572. Scottish noble. He served as guardian of James VI, son of Mary, Queen of Scots.

Mar, John Erskine, 2d earl of 1558–1634. Scottish noble. He succeeded his father as guardian of Scottish king James VI (James I of England) and was treasurer of Scotland (1616–30).

Mar, John Erskine, 6th earl of 1675–1732. Scottish noble, known as "Bobbing John" for his changes of allegiance. He led the unsuccessful Jacobite rebellion of 1715, which sought to secure the English throne for James, the Old Pretender.

Marat, Jean Paul 1743–93. French Revolutionary leader. He abandoned his medical practice as the French Revolution began in 1789, edited the journal *L'Ami du peuple,* in which he waged a verbal war against the moderate Girondists, and was forced to flee to England in 1790 and 1791. Later, as a member of the Convention, Marat supported the Jacobins in their opposition to the Girondists. Girondist C. Corday stabbed him to death in his bath.

Maratha Kingdom (Mahrattas ˜) (Maharashtra ˜) Kingdom in west-central India that rose to power in the period between the fall of the Mughal Empire and British conquest of India (c18th–19th cents.). Once a small part of the Mughal Empire, the kingdom was founded and greatly expanded by the conquests (1647–80) of Sivaji. Following the death (1707) of the Mughal emperor Aurangzeb, the Marathas extended their control in the southern peninsula. Under Baji Rao, they defeated Mughal armies and (after 1739) took control of the government of the failing empire. With the death (1740) of Baji Rao, central control of the empire declined rapidly. From 1772, it was ruled by five chieftains in what was known as the Maratha Confederacy. The confederacy fell to the British (1818) in the Third Maratha War.

Maratha Wars Series of three wars (1775–1818) in India between the British and the Maratha Confederacy, resulting in the fall of the Maratha Confederacy and British domination in India. 1. The first war (1775–76, 1778–82) was ended by the Treaty of Salbai (1782), by which the British gained Salsette Island, near Bombay. 2. The second war (1803–05) was sparked by the granting of British protection to Peshwa Baji Rao II through the Treaty of Bassein (1802). 3. The third war (1817–18) was sparked by a British invasion of the Maratha Confederation in an attempt to defeat the Pindari tribes, which had been raiding the British territories. The war ended (1818) with the defeat and dissolution of the Maratha Confederation.

Marathon Long fertile plain northeast of Athens, Greece, and connected to Athens in ancient times by a main road. Marathon was the site of the famous Battle of Marathon (490 BC) during the Persian Wars. The distance between the battleground and Athens (just over 26 miles), run in 490 by a messenger bearing news of the Greek victory to Athens, was later adopted for the long-distance race called the marathon.

Marathon, Battle of Battle (490 BC) in which Athenian and Plataean forces under Miltiades defeated the Persian army of Darius I. This great battle of the Persian Wars (*q.v.*) ended the first Persian expedition against the Greek mainland.

Marbury v. *Madison* US Supreme Court decision (1803). Handed down by Chief Justice J. Marshall, it was the first decision to declare an act of Congress to be unconstitutional. It helped to establish the Supreme Court's right of judicial review over acts of Congress.

Marc Antony *See* Antony.

Marcel, Étienne *d.* 1358. French leader. As provost of the merchants of Paris, he secured expanded powers for the States-General from King John II in exchange for funds to continue the Hundred Years' War. After John's capture by the English, he allied with Charles the Bad of Navarre against the dauphin (later Charles V), but was assassinated.

Marcel, Gabriel Honoré 1889–1973. French philosopher and writer, considered an early existentialist. His philosophy held that experience is more important than metaphysics.

Marcellus, Marcus Claudius c268–208 BC. Roman general. Five times consul of Rome, he was called "the sword of Rome." He conquered Syracuse (212 BC), and died while fighting against Hannibal.

Marches, the Mountainous region in central Italy. The region passed (8th cent.) to nominal papal control, but by the 10th cent. independent imperial provinces (marches) were established. Eventually (14th–17th cents.) restored to the Papal States, it joined the kingdom of Italy (1860).

Marchfeld, Battle of (Dürnkrut, Battle of) Battle (1278) at Dürnkrut, on the Marchfeld, Austria. Here Rudolf I, count of Habsburg, defeated the Bohemian king Ottokar II.

March Laws (April Laws) Hungarian reform measures adopted during the 1848 Revolution. They provided for establishment of an autonomous Hungarian state under only nominal Austrian control. Austria refused to recognize the March Laws after it defeated the revolutionaries.

March on Rome Fascist insurrection (Oct.–Nov. 1922) led by B. Mussolini, by which Fascism came to power in Italy. Fascist forces threatened to seize power in Rome and elsewhere and began massing their followers for the insurrection, planned for Oct. 28. After King Victor Emmanuel III refused to declare martial law, Prime Minister Luigi Facta (1861–1930) resigned, crippling the Italian government. Mussolini then was asked (Oct. 29) to form a government by the king to avert a civil war. Mussolini's new government gave him (Nov. 25) dictatorial powers until Dec. 31, 1923.

March on Washington 1. Mass civil rights demonstration (Aug. 28, 1963). Some 200,000 blacks and their supporters, led by Dr. M. King, rallied in Washington, D.C., to press their demands for equal rights. During the rally, Dr. King uttered his famous words "I have a dream. . . ." 2. Mass antiwar demonstration (Nov. 15, 1969) held in Washington, D.C. Led by a coalition of moderate and radical antiwar groups, some 250–400,000 protesters gathered for a largely nonviolent demonstration to press their demands for an end to the Vietnam War. The demonstration marked the high point of Vietnam antiwar protest in the US.

March Revolution *See* **February Revolution.**

Marcian AD c390–457. Eastern Roman emperor (AD 450–57), successor to Theodosius II. He refused to pay tribute to Attila the Hun, avoided wars, and assembled the Council of Chalcedon (451).

Marcion *fl.* AD 144. Early Christian who founded (AD 144) the heretical Marcionite sect. He said there were two Gods and rejected the Old Testament.

Marconi, Guglielmo 1874–1937. Italian physicist. Born to a wealthy Bolognese family, he began the study of radio transmission while still living on his father's estate. There he made important discoveries about long-distance transmission of signals and invented receivers and transmitters. He moved to England and after obtaining a patent for his new equipment, founded the first commercial wireless telegraph service (1897). Marconi later became the first to send and receive transatlantic wireless signals (1901) and won the 1909 Nobel Prize for Physics for his work. During WW I he developed equipment for very short radio waves and later discovered microwave radiation (1932), which led to the development of radar.

Marcos, Ferdinand Edralin 1917–89. President of the Philippines (1966–86). Pursuing a policy of close ties with America and hostility to Communism, he declared martial law (1972) and maintained a repressive, authoritarian regime until his overthrow in 1986. Marcos then fled to Hawaii with his wife Imelda (c1930–   ). However he, his family, and friends were suspected of diverting billions in Philippine government funds, and Marcos and his wife were eventually indicted in the US on racketeering charges. Marcos died in 1989, and Imelda was finally acquitted in 1990.

Marcus Antonius *See* **Antony.**

Marcus Aurelius (*orig.* Marcus Aurelius Antoninus) AD 121–180. Roman emperor (AD 161–80) and famous exponent of Stoicism. Though he ordered persecutions of Christians, his rule was otherwise considered wise and humane. He ruled (161–169) with his brother Lucius Verus (*d.* 169) and was sole emperor thereafter. His reign was marked by his successes against rebellions and barbarian invasions (by Parthians, Germans, and others). In one such victory (AD 174) a German tribe was confused by a fierce thunderstorm and thus fell to the emperor's troops, thereafter called the "Thundering Legion." Marcus Aurelius is known best, however, for his great philosophical work, *Meditations.*

Marcuse, Herbert 1898–1979. German-born American political philosopher, known best for his studies of the failings of modern industrial society. An advocate of radicalization, dissent, and resistance, Marcuse became popular with leftist radicals in the US and Europe during the late 1960s. His works, which contain elements of Freudian, Marxist, and Hegelian thought, include *One-Dimensional Man* (1964) and *Counterrevolution and Revolt* (1972).

Marcy, William Learned 1786–1857. American politician. As US senator from New York (1831–32) he made the remark "to the victor belong the spoils of the enemy" in defense of patronage. This gave rise to the term "spoils system."

Marengo, Battle of Battle (June 14, 1800) in which the French under Napoleon defeated the Austrians under Baron Michael von Melas (1729–1806) at Marengo, Italy. The victory secured northern Italy for France during the French Revolutionary Wars.

Mareth Line German defensive line in Tunisia during WW II. Established by Field Marshal E. Rommel after the 1,500-mile retreat of the Afrika Korps across Libya, it was overcome by Allied forces (Mar., 1943).

Margaret 1353–1412. Queen of Denmark, Norway, and Sweden, daughter of Danish king Waldemar IV. She married (1363) Norwegian king Haakon VI, overthrew Swedish king Albert (1389), and established (1397) the Kalmar Union. Though her nephew Eric VII of Pomerania (ruled 1389–1429) was nominal king, she held the power.

Margaret Maid of Norway 1283–90. Queen of Scotland (1286–90), and successor to Scottish king Alexander III. She was betrothed to Edward, son of English king Edward I. Her death resulted in civil war and Edward I's claim to the rule of Scotland.

Margaret of Angoulême *See* **Margaret of Navarre.**

Margaret of Anjou 1430?–82. Queen consort to English king Henry VI (*m.* 1445). She was a leader of the Lancastrians against the Yorkists during the Wars of the Roses.

Margaret of Austria 1480–1530. Habsburg princess, daughter of Emperor Maximilian I. She was regent of the Netherlands (1507–15, 1519–30) for her nephew Charles (later Holy Roman Emperor Charles V).

Margaret of Navarre (Margaret of Angoulême) 1492–1549. Queen consort (*m.* 1527) of King Henry II of Navarre and sister of French king Francis I. She took an active interest in religious reforms and the arts and was the author of the *Heptaméron.*

Margaret of Parma 1522–86. Natural daughter of Holy Roman Emperor Charles V and mother of A. Farnese. She served ably as regent of the Netherlands (1559–67).

Margaret of Scotland, Saint *d.* 1093. Queen consort (m. c1070) of Scottish king Malcolm III and sister of Edgar Aetheling. She helped to advance Roman Catholic church practices in Scotland.

Margaret of Valois 1553–1615. Queen of Navarre, daughter of French king Henry II, and wife (*m.* 1572) of Henry IV of France. Her marriage was annulled (1599), allegedly because of her promiscuity.

Margaret Tudor 1489–1541. Queen consort of Scottish king James IV (*m.* 1503) and daughter of English king Henry VII. Temporarily regent for her son James V, she lost the regency through her marriage (1514) to A. Douglas, 6th earl of Angus.

Marggraf, Andreas Sigismund 1709–82. German chemist. His discovery of sugar in beets (1747) contributed to the formation of the sugar industry.

Maria I 1734–1816. Portuguese queen (1777–1816), daughter of Portuguese king Joseph I, and wife (*m.* 1760) of Peter III. She and Peter secured the downfall of the hated minister S. Pombal and released many prisoners of his rule. She fled to Brazil (1807) after Napoleon's invasion of Portugal.

Maria II (Maria da Gloria) 1819–53. Portuguese queen (1826–28, 1834–53), daughter of Brazilian king Pedro I. Her reign was marked by civil strife, including civil war and the usurping of the throne by Miguel.

Maria Christina 1806–78. Queen consort of Spanish king Ferdinand VII. She prompted her husband to allow their daughter, Isabella, to succeed him, thus causing the Carlist Wars.

Maria Christina 1858–1929. Queen consort (*m.* 1879) of Spanish king Alfonso XII. While she served as regent (1886–1902) for their son Alfonso XIII, Spain lost the last of its empire in the Americas during the Spanish-American War.

Maria da Gloria *See* **Maria II.**

Maria Luisa 1751–1819. Spanish queen, wife (*m.* 1765) of Spanish king Charles IV. She and her lover M. de Godoy actually ruled the country, ruined its finances, and set the stage for Napoleon's takeover (1808).

Mariamne *d.* 29 BC. Jewish princess, wife of Herod. She was executed by Herod after being falsely accused of adultery by Salome.

Mariátegui, José Carlos 1895–1930. Peruvian Marxist, writer, and cofounder of Peru's first

Socialist party (1928), which soon split into separate Socialist and Communist parties (1930). During his most active years (1923–30), Mariátegui became Peru's leading proponent of Marxism, founded a socialist journal (1926), and published his best-known work, *Seven Interpretive Essays on Peruvian Reality* (1928).

Maria Theresa 1717–80. Austrian archduchess and queen of Hungary and Bohemia (1740–80), consort (*m.* 1736) of Holy Roman Emperor Francis I. She succeeded her father Charles VI as ruler of Austrian Habsburg domains by the law of pragmatic sanction. Her succession resulted in the War of the Austrian Succession (1740–48).

Marie 1875–1938. Rumanian queen (1914–27), granddaughter of English queen Victoria, and wife (*m.* 1893) of Rumanian king Ferdinand I. She helped persuade Ferdinand to join the Allies in WW I.

Marie Antoinette 1755–93. French queen (1774–93), wife of King Louis XVI (*m.* 1770), and an important figure in events leading to the French Revolution. She was the daughter of Austrian Holy Roman Emperor Francis I. Her unpopularity in France helped undermine the credibility of the monarchy. This was due in part to her Austrian heritage, her extravagance, her association with dissolute courtiers, and her influence over her indecisive husband. Her reputation became notorious in the prerevolutionary times, and scandals, often exaggerated or untrue, surrounded her (such as her supposed remark, "If they have no bread, let them eat cake," and involvement in the Affair of the Diamond Necklace). Removed (1789) with Louis from Versailles to the Tuileries Palace, she was taken prisoner during the storming of the Tuileries (1792). She was guillotined (Oct. 16, 1793) some nine months after Louis.

Marie de France *fl.* 12th cent. French poet, France's first known woman poet. Little is known about her except that she wrote verse narratives and fables and probably was residing in England at the time. Her works included *L'Espuratoire Seint Patriz* and *Eliduc.*

Marie de Médicis 1573–1642. Queen consort (*m.* 1600) of French king Henry IV of France and regent (1610–17) for their son, Louis XIII. She depleted the treasury and formed an alliance with Spain before being exiled by her son.

Marie Louise 1791–1847. Empress of France (1810–15), second wife (*m.* 1810) of Napoleon I, mother of Napoleon II, and daughter of Holy Roman Emperor Francis II.

Marie Thérèse of Austria 1638–83. Queen consort (*m.* 1660) of French king Louis XIV. Daughter of Spanish king Philip IV, she renounced her claim to the Spanish throne in return for a substantial dowry. Louis, claiming never to have received it, seized part of the Spanish Netherlands in the War of Devolution.

Marignano, Battle of Battle (Sept. 13–14, 1515) during the Italian Wars, at Marignano, Italy. Here the Franco-Venetian forces under French king Francis I defeated the forces of the Swiss Confederation, forcing the Swiss to retreat. The victory led to the French conquest of Milan.

Marinetti, Filippo Tommaso 1876–1944. Italian author. Considered the founder of futurism, he also supported fascism.

Marion, Francis c1732–95. American Revolutionary general, known as the Swamp Fox for his guerrilla tactics against the British in South Carolina.

Maritime Provinces Name for the Canadian Atlantic provinces of New Brunswick, Nova Scotia, and Prince Edward Island. The region, with the addition of Newfoundland, has been called Atlantic Canada since 1949.

Maritime Territory (Primorski Krai) Easternmost territory of the former USSR. Vladivostok, its capital, is eastern terminus of the Trans-Siberian railway.

Maritsa River, Battle of the Decisive Ottoman victory (Sept. 26, 1371) over Serbia, at Maritsa River, near Adrianople. A force of 70,000 Serbs led by King Vukâsin attempted to halt Turkish expansion in the Balkans, but were overwhelmed by an inferior Turkish force, under Murad I.

Marius, Gaius c155 BC–86 BC. Roman general and the first of his family to serve as consul. He fought with distinction in Africa and in Gaul (defeating the Cimbri and Teutones), instituted important reforms of the army, and became the first to ever serve as consul seven times (between 108 and 101). He enjoyed previously unheard of popularity, though his later years were troubled by, among other things, a rivalry with Sulla, who had once served under him in the army.

Mark, Saint (John Mark) Apostle and traditional author of the Second Gospel. He was a companion to saints Paul and Barnabas.

Markiewicz, Constance Georgine Gore-Booth, countess 1876–1927. Irish nationalist. Sentenced to death for her role in the Easter Rebellion (1916), she was released in 1917. The first woman to be elected to the British Parliament (1918), she declined her seat, and later served in the Dáil Éireann.

Marlborough, John Churchill, 1st duke of 1650–1722. English general, noted for his victories during the War of the Spanish Succession. Instrumental in putting down the rebellion by the duke of Monmouth (1685), he shifted his allegiance from James II to William III during the Glorious Revolution (1688) and commanded William's forces against rebels in Ireland (1689–91). Out of favor (1692), he was restored under Queen Anne, who was an intimate friend of his wife, the duchess of Marlborough. He won great fame for his service in the War of the Spanish Succession, notably in the battles of Blenheim (1704), Ramillies (1706), Oudenarde (1708), and Malplaquet (1709). Out of favor again (1711) when Queen Anne switched allegiance to A. Masham, he was again in favor under King George I.

Marlowe, Christopher 1564–93. English dramatist and poet, considered England's greatest pre-Shakespearean playwright. The son of a shoemaker, he obtained a formal education, receiving a master of arts in 1584, but his life remained one of unconventional and at time reckless behavior. His literary work was another matter, however. He introduced blank verse in drama, often wrote plays around heroic themes, and is considered the leading Elizabethan playwright before Shakespeare. Among his plays are *Tamburlaine, Dr. Faustus, The Jew of Malta,* and *Edward II.* Marlowe also appears to have written parts of W. Shakespeare's *Titus Andronicus* and *Henry VI.* He wrote numerous poems, among them "The Passionate Shepherd to His Love." Marlowe was killed in a dispute in a tavern.

Marmont, Auguste Frédéric Louis Viesse de 1774–1852. Marshal of France who served with Napoleon. His surrender of Paris (1814) forced Napoleon to abdicate.

Marmousets Advisers to French king Charles V, who, though reliable, were unpopular with the nobility because of their humble origins. They also served for a time under Charles VI.

Marne, Battle of the 1. Allied victory (Sept. 5–9, 1914) over German forces advancing on Paris during WW I. The battle marked the failure of the German Schlieffen Plan. The Germans, commanded by Gen. Alexander von Kluck (1846–1934), marched toward Paris with little opposition until they reached the Marne River. French Gen. J. Joffre rushed his troops out of Paris to the river and there attacked the Germans. Though the battle itself was indecisive, the Germans ultimately withdrew. 2. Allied victory (July 15–Aug. 7, 1918) over German forces during WW I. The battle marked the turning point of WW I in favor of the Allies. German forces, under Gen. E. Ludendorff, attacked (July 15) Allied positions near Reims and crossed the Marne River to the west of it. French Gen. F. Foch counterattacked (July 18) and forced the Germans to retreat.

Marnix, Philip van *See* **Breda, Compromise of.**

Marprelate Controversy Pamphlet war (1588–89) waged by anonymous Puritans against the Anglican church. The original pamphlets were directed against Bishop John Whitgift (1530?–1604) and the authoritarianism of the Anglican church. They were attributed to a pseudonymous author, "Martin Marprelate," and were not sanctioned by Puritan leaders. The Anglicans replied with pamphlets of their own, and in the early 1590s government suppression of the Marprelate pamphleteers succeeded in ending the controversy. The author (or authors) of the pamphlets is still unknown.

Marquand, J(ohn) P(hillips) 1893–1960. American author, noted for his novels dealing with upperclass life in New England. His novel *The Late George Apley* was awarded a Pulitzer Prize (1938).

Marquette, Jacques Père 1637–75. French missionary explorer. He and Louis Jolliet (1645–1700) discovered and charted the course of the Mississippi River (1673).

Marsaglia, Battle of *See* **League of Augsburg, War of the.**

marshal Military rank. Marshal denotes the highest army rank in such countries as Britain, France, Germany, Russia, and China. It derives from the Frankish word for the keeper of the king's horses.

Marshall, George Catlett 1880–1959. American general and statesman. He was army chief of staff during WW II. As secretary of state (1947–49) he originated the postwar European Recovery Program (Marshall Plan). He was awarded the Nobel Peace Prize (1953).

Marshall, James Wilson 1810–85. American pioneer. His discovery (Jan. 1848) of gold at

J. Sutter's mill in California led to the Gold Rush of 1849.

Marshall, John 1755–1835. American jurist. A Federalist, and one of the American diplomats involved in the XYZ Affair, he was elected to Congress (1799) and served as secretary of state (1800–01). He was appointed by J. Adams to the Supreme Court as chief justice (1801–35). Marshall's decisions in such cases as *Marbury* v. *Madison* and the Dartmouth College Case helped to establish the Supreme Court's right of judicial review and also helped to strengthen the authority of the federal government.

Marshall, Thomas Riley 1854–1925. American politician, vice-president of the US (1913–21) under W. Wilson. He is remembered for his remark, "What this country needs is a really good five-cent cigar."

Marshall, Thurgood 1908–93. American jurist. As head of the legal staff of the NAACP, he successfully argued before the Supreme Court the landmark civil rights case *Brown* v. *Board of Education of Topeka, Kansas* (1954). He became the first black to be appointed to the Supreme Court (1967–91), where he upheld fair and equal treatment of minorities.

Marshall Islands Pacific islands, since 1947 part of the US Trust Territory of the Pacific Islands. Scene of heavy fighting during WW II, they were later the site of US nuclear weapons tests.

Marshall Plan (European Recovery Program) US program (1948–52) that successfully aided the recovery of Western European nations after WW II. Outlined (1947) by US secretary of state G. Marshall, the program provided massive economic aid (more than $12 billion) and a basis for integration of European economies. The program, also aimed at containing the rising influence of Communist parties in war-torn Europe, was accepted by Western European nations (also Turkey and Iceland). The US Congress, by the Foreign Assistance Act of 1948, created the Economic Cooperation Administration (ECA) to administer the program. The participating countries in turn created (1948) a coordinating agency, the Organization for European Economic Cooperation (renamed the Organization for Economic Cooperation and Development). The program was completed in 1952.

Marsilius of Padua *d.* c1342. Italian political philosopher. His *Defensor pacis* held that political

(and ecclesiastical) power comes from the people. This concept had an immense influence on medieval political philosophy.

Marston Moor, Battle of First significant victory (July 2, 1644) of the Parliamentary forces over the Royalists during the English Civil Wars. The Royalists under Prince Rupert were decisively defeated by forces under O. Cromwell, T. Fairfax, and others, near York.

Martel, Charles *See* **Charles Martel.**

Martens, Frederick (~, Fyodor Fyodorovich) 1845–1909. Russian diplomat. An authority on international law, he served as arbitrator at many conferences, including the Hague Conferences. He was awarded the Nobel Peace Prize (1902).

Martens, Fyodor Fyodorovich *See* **Martens, Frederick.**

Martí, José 1853–95. Cuban writer and patriot. Founder (1892) of the Cuban Revolutionary party, he spent many years as an exile in the US and was killed by Spanish forces after he returned to Cuba.

Martial AD c40–c104. Roman poet. He is noted for his witty epigrams, which became the models for the contemporary epigram.

Martignac, Jean Baptiste Sylvère Gay, vicomte de 1778–1832. French statesman. He was minister of the interior (1828–29) under French king Charles X, but his policies of compromise with liberals alienated the king. He was replaced by Charles with the royalist J. Polignac.

Martin I, Saint *d.* 655. Pope (649–55). He convoked the Lateran Council (649), which condemned Monothelitism. For opening the controversy to debate he was banished to the Crimea by Byzantine emperor Constans II.

Martin IV (Simon de Brie) *d.* 1285. Pope (1281–85). His excommunication of Byzantine emperor Michael VIII caused a break between the Eastern and Western churches.

Martin V (Colonna, Oddone) 1368–1431. Catholic pope (1417–31). Martin's unanimous election at the Council of Constance ended the Great Schism. He was less successful in his reconciliation attempts with the Eastern church and in controlling the Hussites.

Martin, Saint AD 335–397? Bishop of Tours (c371) in Roman Gaul (now France), and patron saint of France. He cofounded the first monastery in Gaul and established the important monastery at Marmoutier.

Martin v. Hunter's Lessee   See **Story, Joseph.**

Marvell, Andrew 1621–78.   English poet. One of the leading satirists of his day, he is known for his wit and lyricism as in *To His Coy Mistress.*

Marx, Karl 1818–83.   German economist and philosopher, considered the founder and premier theorist of modern socialism and international communism. Marx studied at the universities of Bonn and Berlin but abandoned law to take up the study of history and philosophy. Adopting elements of the philosophies of G. Hegel and L. Feuerbach, among others, Marx became an ardent supporter of socialism. He became editor of the *Rheinische Zeitung* in 1842, but his radicalism led to the paper's suppression (1843). Moving to Paris, Marx met F. Engels, who became his friend and collaborator, and with whom he wrote *The German Ideology,* which dealt with Marx's concept of dialectical materialism (*q.v.*) as the operating human force in human history. Joining the Communist League (1847), Marx wrote (with Engels) what has become known as the *Communist Manifesto.* The failure of the 1848 revolutions in Europe led Marx to move to London (1849), where he spent the remainder of his life in poverty, only partly eased by the efforts of Engels and others. Marx made a prodigious study (at the British Museum) of the principles of capitalism and wrote his massive work, *Das Kapital,* which remained unfinished at his death. Marx was a leading figure in the establishment of the First International (*q.v.*). His writings, especially the *Communist Manifesto* and *Das Kapital,* greatly influenced the radical movements of the late 19th and early 20th cents., notably the Russian Communist movement headed by N. Lenin and most Socialist parties of the time as well. His writings formed a theoretical foundation for modern Communist ideology and embodied an important and controversial system of political and economic thought.

Marx, Wilhelm 1863–1946.   German statesman. As chancellor (1923–24) he supported acceptance of the Dawes Plan for war reparations. He served again as chancellor (1926–28).

Marxism   Collective term applied to the political, economic, and social theories advanced by K. Marx and F. Engels in such works as the *Communist Manifesto* and *Das Kapital.* Marx's theories greatly influenced the Socialist movement of the late 19th cent. and are considered the theoretical foundation for modern international Communism. In his writings, Marx advanced the doctrine of dialectical materialism, the idea that the history and structure of civilization have been determined by economic systems operating during each stage of development. As each system developed, he asserted, new economic forces arose and inevitably led to the system's replacement. Thus feudalism was replaced by capitalism, and capitalism was fated to be replaced by Socialism and, ultimately, Communism. A key element of Marxist doctrine is the view of all history as the history of class struggle, of the ruling elite pitted against the working class. According to Marx, this would eventually lead to crisis, in which the working class would rise up against the capitalist order, seize the means of production, and establish communal ownership through a "dictatorship of the proletariat." With the abolishment of the ruling class, all class struggle, hence all history, would come to an end. Finally, when a rational economic system was evolved, the structure of the political state would wither away. Marx's theories had a profound influence on the development of Socialist movements and were the basis for the Bolshevik political movement led by N. Lenin. The Bolsheviks' success in establishing the first Communist state in Russia (1917) contradicted Marx's conviction that the first Communist uprising would take place in a modern industrialized nation. The massive political bureaucracy created under Lenin, and J. Stalin, also contradicted Marxist doctrine. Subsequent modifications of capitalism, such as the workers' vastly higher standard of living and the rise of a managerial class, have also brought some of Marx's principal tenets into question. However, Marxism as a body of political thought remains, in name if not in practice, the official political dogma of Communist nations.

Mary   Mother of Jesus and principal saint of the Roman Catholic church. There are many biblical references to her and these include: her betrothal to Joseph, a carpenter of Nazareth; the annunciation of the birth of Jesus; Mary's visit to her cousin, Elizabeth, mother of John the Baptist; the birth of Jesus and purification at the Temple; the arrival of the Magi and the journey to Egypt; and her presence at the crucifixion. Roman Catholic dogma relating to Mary includes the doctrines of Mary, the Virgin Mother; Mary, the Mother of God; Mary's freedom from original sin (Immaculate Conception); and Mary's assumption directly into heaven.

Mary *See* **Mary, Queen of Scots.**

Mary 1867–1953. Queen consort (*m.* 1893) of English king George V. She was the mother of kings Edward VIII and George VI.

Mary I (Tudor, ~) (Bloody ~) 1516–58. English Queen (1553–58), daughter of Henry VIII and Catherine of Aragon. Her marriage (1554) to Spanish King Philip II caused great opposition. She briefly reestablished Roman Catholicism in England (1555–59) and persecuted Protestants.

Mary II 1662–94. English queen (1689–94), daughter of James II. After James was forced into exile by the Glorious Revolution (1688), Mary became joint sovereign with her husband William of Orange (William III).

Maryland US Middle Atlantic state, the 7th state. English king Charles I granted the colony to G. Calvert, 1st Baron Baltimore (1632), and it was first settled (1634) by Catholics and Protestants seeking religious freedom. Its northern border is the Mason-Dixon line drawn (1767) to settle a boundary dispute with Pennsylvania. During the US Civil War Maryland remained in the Union but its citizens fought on both sides. One of the war's major engagements was fought here at Antietam (1862).

Maryland, McCulloch v. *See McCulloch* v. *Maryland.*

Mary of Burgundy 1457–82. Duchess of Burgundy, daughter of Charles the Bold and heiress to the Netherlands. Her marriage (1477) to Maximilian of Austria (later Holy Roman Emperor Maximilian I) gave the Habsburgs control of The Netherlands.

Mary of England (~ of France) (~ Tudor) 1496–1533. Queen consort (1514–15) of French king Louis XII and daughter of English king Henry VII. She was the grandmother of Lady Jane Grey.

Mary of France *See* **Mary of England.**

Mary of Guise 1515–60. Queen consort (*m.* 1538) of Scottish king James V. The daughter of C. de Lorraine, 1st duke of Guise, she was regent (1554–59) for her daughter Mary Queen of Scots. She successfully allied Scotland with France in war against England, but her attempt to suppress the Protestant movement in Scotland

led to an uprising, sparked by John Knox, and her removal as regent.

Mary of Modena 1658–1718. Queen consort (*m.* 1673) of English king James II of England. The birth (1688) of her son, James Francis Edward, ensured a Catholic succession and provoked the Glorious Revolution.

Mary, Queen of Scots (Stuart, ~) 1542–87. Scottish queen (1542–67), a Catholic of the Stuart family and a celebrated beauty. Her life was marked by controversy and intrigue. She was named queen shortly after birth. Her early life was spent in France. She returned (1561) to Scotland and married (1565) her unpopular cousin, Lord Darnley, to strengthen her claims to the English throne. The couple became disaffected and, after her husband's murder, generally attributed to the earl of Bothwell, she married Bothwell (1567). This led to a Scottish revolt, Mary's forced abdication (June 15, 1567), and her escape to England (1568). As an heir to the throne and a threat to Queen Elizabeth, Mary was kept under guard in England. After several plots by Catholics to overthrow Elizabeth in favor of Mary, Mary was implicated in a scheme by A. Babington and was beheaded. Mary's son became King James I of England.

Mary Tudor *See* **Mary I.**

Masaccio 1401–28 Italian painter, one of the leading figures in Italian Renaissance painting. His works influenced many later artists, including Michelangelo and Raphael.

Masada Israeli fortress on a mountain overlooking the Dead Sea. It was the last Zealot stronghold against Rome (AD 66–73). Here the Zealots withstood a two-year Roman siege, but faced with imminent defeat, virtually all chose death over capture by the Romans.

Masaniello 1620–47? Neapolitan insurrectionist. A fisherman, he led a successful revolt against Spanish rule in Naples. He was murdered soon after.

Masaryk, Jan 1886–1948. Czech statesman and diplomat. He became (1940) foreign minister in the government in exile in London during WW II, and remained in office after the Communist takeover (1948). Soon afterward, he allegedly committed suicide.

Masaryk, Thomas Garrigue 1850–1937. A founding father of Czechoslovakia and its first president (1918–35). He was a leader of pro-Slovak interests in the Austro-Hungarian Empire and fled the country at the outbreak of WW I. With E. Beneš, he organized a de facto government of Czechoslovakia, which won the support of the Allies. When independent Czechoslovakia was formed after WW I, Masaryk was elected president (1918, 1920, 1927, 1934) and instituted a major land-reform program.

Masinissa c238–149 BC. Numidian king in East Africa. He switched allegiance (c206 BC) from Carthage to Rome in the Second Punic War and was rewarded with Carthaginian territory.

Maskelyne, Nevil 1732–1811. English astronomer. He published the *Nautical Almanac* and introduced the determination of longitude by the moon's position.

Mason, Charles *See* **Mason-Dixon line.**

Mason, George 1725–92. American Revolutionary statesman. A member of the Constitutional Convention (1787), he refused to sign the Constitution because of its compromise on slavery and its provision for strong federal government. The changes he called for influenced the drafting of the Bill of Rights.

Mason, John 1586–1635. English colonist. A founding member (1629) of the Laconia Company, he founded New Hampshire.

Mason-Dixon line Boundary line between Maryland and Pennsylvania surveyed (1763–67) by Charles Mason (1730–87) and Jeremiah Dixon (*fl.* 1763–67). Once the line between free and slave states, it is now the traditional border between the North and South.

Masora (Massorah) Vocalized and accented Hebrew text of the Old Testament. Compiled (mainly c6th–c10th cents.) by Jewish scholars (Masoretes), the work represents an effort to standardize the Hebrew Old Testament in its original form. The Masora contains critical notes and a system for the proper pronunciation of the text.

Maspero, Gaston 1846–1916. French Egyptologist. He established the French Institute of Oriental Archaeology, discovered the royal mummies at Dayr al-Bahri (1881), and directed many excavations.

Massachusetts Northeast US state, the 6th state. The first permanent settlement was founded by the Pilgrims at Plymouth (1620). The Massachusetts Bay Company governed the colony (1629–84), which included the province of Maine. In the mid-1700s, the colony was heavily engaged in seagoing trade, especially the "triangular trade" involving slaves, rum, and molasses. Massachusetts became a leader in the Colonial resistance to British rule and was the site during the American Revolution of the battles of Lexington, Concord, and Bunker Hill (1775). The state constitution was adopted in 1780 and Massachusetts became a state in 1788. Industrialization (especially the textile industry) began after the Revolution, and Massachusetts eventually became a leading center of manufacturing and industry.

Massachusetts Bay Company English colonizing company chartered (1620) by English king Charles I. Originally intended for trade, it was used by the Puritans to establish a theocracy in Massachusetts. Its charter was annulled (1684).

Massacre of Amritsar Massacre (Apr. 13, 1919) at Amritsar, India. There, troops under British command fired on unarmed Indian nationalist protesters, killing 379 and wounding about 1,200. The massacre did much to strengthen the anti-British movement in India.

Massacre of Glencoe Massacre (Feb. 13, 1692) of the Scottish Macdonald clan by the rival Campbell clan. The Campbells, led by J. Campbell and J. Dalrymple, 1st earl of Stair, were sent to Glencoe to secure the Macdonalds' oath of allegiance to English king William III. Instead, the Campbells killed some 38 Macdonalds.

Massacre of Saint Bartholomew's Day Massacre of French Protestants (Huguenots) that started in Paris (Aug. 24, 1572) and marked the beginning of renewed fighting in the Wars of Religion (*q.v.*). The massacre was a result of the continuing religious and political rivalry between Protestants and Catholics (led by the Guise family). The Guise family and Catherine de Médicis, mother of King Charles IX, sought to check the rising influence of Adm. G. Coligny, a Protestant. When an attempt to assassinate Coligny failed (Aug. 22), Catherine persuaded King Charles to order the death of Huguenot leaders then in Paris for the wedding of Henry of Navarre (later Henry IV). Following the initial bloodshed (Henry of Navarre and prince de Condé escaped death), a general massacre of Protestants broke out in Paris and spread to the countryside. Thousands were killed by the time the persecution was halted in October.

Massacre of the Innocents *See* **Palestine (4 BC).**

Massacre of Vassy *See* **Guise, François of Lorraine, 2d duke of Guise.**

Massasoit c1580–1661. Chief of the Wampanoag Indians. He signed (1621) a treaty of friendship with the Plymouth colonists and aided the settlers in their first years in New England. His son was King Philip.

Massena, André 1758–1817. French general. He served under Napoleon Bonaparte. His defeat of the Russians at Zurich (1799) saved France from invasion.

Massenet, Jules 1842–1912. French composer. He is known best for his operas *Manon* and *Le Cid.*

Mastai-Ferretti, Giovanni M. *See* **Pius IX.**

Masters, Edgar Lee 1879–1950. American poet, known best for his *Spoon River Anthology,* a collection of epitaphs exploring the lives of the former residents of a small Midwestern town.

Masudi *d.* 956. Arab historian. He wrote the 30-volume *Annals,* a history of the world. It was abridged as *Meadows of Gold and Mines of Gems.*

Matabele War Brief war (July 1894–Jan. 1895) between British colonial forces in South Africa and the Matabele tribes. The Matabele, an offshoot of the Zulu tribes, had settled in their Rhodesian homelands by c1837. Hostilities with white settlers broke out into open war (July 1894) between the British South Africa Company and the Matabele, led by Lobengula (1870–94). The British quickly won the war and thereafter governed the Matabele territory. One final rebellion by the Matabele in 1896 was unsuccessful.

Mata Hari (Zelle, Margaretha Geertruida) 1876–1917. Dutch dancer and spy. She was executed by the French after being found guilty of spying for the Germans during WW I.

Match King *See* **Kreuger, Ivar.**

Mater et Magistra *See* **John XXIII.**

materialism Philosophical doctrine. Materialism as a theory has existed in various forms from ancient times among the Greek Epicureans to present-day Communism (dialectical materialism). Essentially, materialism argues that all aspects of reality (including consciousness) can be explained in terms of bits of matter, or their motion. It is opposed to philosophical idealism and is often in conflict with religion, because it places "matter" over "mind." Materialist philosophers include D. Diderot, T. Hobbes, K. Marx and F. Engels.

Mather, Cotton 1663–1728. American Puritan minister and author, son of I. Mather. One of the leading religious and intellectual figures of his day, he is noted for his involvement in the Salem witchcraft trials (1692), which he defended. Mather wrote *The Wonders of the Invisible World* (1693) among other works.

Mather, Increase 1639–1723. American Puritan minister, son of R. Mather. He was pastor of North Church, Boston (1664–1723) and president of Harvard College (1685–1701). His *Cases of Conscience Concerning Evil Spirits* helped to stem the witchcraft hysteria of the 1690s.

Mather, Richard 1596–1669. English Puritan minister. He emigrated to Massachusetts in 1635 and was the pastor of Dorchester until his death. He helped to draft the Cambridge Platform (1648).

Mathew, Theobald 1790–1856. Irish temperance missionary. A Capuchin priest, he campaigned for temperance in Ireland, England, and the US.

Mathura (Muttra) This city, located in north-central India, is the reputed birthplace of Krishna. It is one of the seven sacred Hindu cities.

Matilda 1046–1115. Countess of Tuscany, a supporter of the papacy in its conflict with the Holy Roman Emperors. It was at her castle that Holy Roman Emperor Henry IV did penance to Pope Gregory VII (1077).

Matilda (Maud) 1102–67. Holy Roman Empress, as wife (*m.* 1114) of Henry V. Daughter of English king Henry I, she was, by her second husband Geoffrey of Anjou (*m.* 1128), the mother of the English king Henry II.

Matisse, Henri 1869–1954. French artist, considered one of the greatest artists of the 20th cent. A leader of the art movement known as fauvism, he is noted for his use of bold primary colors, which he began using from 1905 (*The Green Line*). Among his other works were *The Blue Nude* (1907), *Acrobats in the Circus* (1918), and *Sorrows of the King* (1952).

matriarchy Social system in which family descent is traced through the mother's lineage. Such societies have been observed in Pacific islands, African tribes, and in some American Indian cultures.

Matsuoka, Yosuke 1880–1946. Japanese statesman. As foreign minister (1940–41) he helped establish the Axis alliance with Germany and Italy (1940).

Mattanlah *See* **Zedekiah.**

Matteo da Bascio *See* **Capuchins.**

Matteotti Crisis Crisis (1924) that marked the beginning of B. Mussolini's Fascist dictatorship in Italy. The incident began with a stinging denunciation of the Fascists (May 30) before the Chamber of Deputies, delivered by Socialist deputy Giacomo Matteotti (1885–1924). Matteotti was then kidnapped (June 10) and killed by Fascist thugs. A massive popular reaction against Fascists ensued and opposition deputies walked out in protest (the Aventine Secession). The deputies, however, proved unable to oust Mussolini. He thereupon seized the opportunity to establish the political controls by which he became dictator.

Matthew, Saint One of the twelve Apostles of Jesus. He was originally a tax collector, but little else is known of his life. He is the traditionally acknowledged author of the First Gospel.

Matthew of Paris *See* **Paris, Matthew.**

Matthias 1557–1619. Holy Roman Emperor (1612–19), son of Maximilian II and successor to his brother Rudolf II. His failure to establish an accord between Catholics and Protestants resulted in the Thirty Years' War.

Matthias, Saint Christian apostle. Matthias was chosen by lot to replace Judas Iscariot as one of the twelve Apostles of Jesus.

Matthias Corvinus 1431–90. Hungaran king (1458–90). He waged war against the Turks and Holy Roman Emperor Frederick III, and was a patron of Renaissance culture.

Maud *See* **Matilda.**

Maugham, W(illiam) Somerset 1874–1965. English author, known best for his novels and short stories. His novels include *Of Human Bondage* and *The Moon and Sixpence.*

Maupassant, Henri René Albert Guy de 1850–93. French author, considered a master of the short story, who wrote *The Necklace* and *The Piece of String.* He also wrote novels, including *Bel-Ami* (1885).

Maupeou, René Nicolas de 1714–92. French chancellor (1768–74) under Louis XV. In an attempt to reform the government, he dissolved the Parlement (1771), but it was restored under Louis XVI.

Maurepas, Jean Frédéric Phélippeaux, comte de 1701–81. French statesman, minister of state under French king Louis XV. He was banished (1749) for offending Mme. de Pompadour. He returned (1774) under Louis XVI and aided the American colonies against Britain during the American Revolution.

Mauretania (Mauritania) Ancient region of northwest Africa, comprising parts of present-day Morocco and Algeria. It fell under Roman influence and was formally annexed (AD 42). It fell to the Vandals AD c429.

Mauriac, François 1885–1970. French author. He is known best for his novels dealing with Roman Catholicism, among them *The Desert of Love* and *Thérèse Desqueyroux.* He was awarded the Nobel Prize for Literature (1952).

Maurice c539–602. Byzantine emperor (582–602), successor to Tiberius II. An able and successful ruler, he made peace with Persia and defeated the Avars but was murdered by mutinous troops under Phocas.

Maurice 1521–53. Duke (1541–47) and elector (1547–53) of Saxony. He gained the electoral title by aiding Holy Roman Emperor Charles V against the Schmalkaldic League. He later supported the German Protestant princes against Charles.

Maurice of Nassau 1567–1625. Prince of Orange (1618–25), son of William the Silent. He drove the Spanish from the United Provinces and concluded (1609) a 12-year truce with Spain.

Mauritania (Islamic Republic of Mauritania) Independent state located in northwest Africa on the Atlantic coast. The population is 2,038,000 and the capital is Nouakchott. Mauritania is largely a desert region, and many of its people (among them Arabs, Berbers, and Moors) are nomadic. It gained independence in 1960 after nearly a hundred years of French rule. Key dates in the history of Mauritania include:

11TH CENT. Almoravide movement established among the Muslim Berbers.

14TH–15TH CENTS. Mali Empire dominated southeast Mauritania.

15TH CENT. Portuguese navigators explored coast.

FROM 17TH CENT. European traders active in region.

1860s France gained control of southern Mauritania.

1903 Became French protectorate ruled by colonial government in Senegal.

1904 Became part of French West Africa.

1920 Became a colony of French West Africa, separate from Senegal.

1946 Became French overseas territory.

1957 Nouakchott became administrative center.

1958 Became autonomous republic within the French Community.

1960 Fully independent under Makhtar Ould Daddah (Nov. 28).

1961 Joined UN; Morocco, which claimed Mauritania, objected. Mauritania occupied the southern part of Spanish Sahara (Morocco took the north); the Polisario Front, a Saharan independence group, opposed takeover.

1978 Bloodless coup ousted longtime president Makhtar Ould Daddah; military provisional government set up.

1979 Lt. Col. Muhammad Mahmoud Ould Louly installed as head of state.

1979 Fighting with Morocco, over part of former Spanish Sahara, ended (Aug.); Mauritania withdrew from the region.

1980s Severe drought during the decade resulted in famine conditions by mid-decade, when about 70 percent of Mauritania's population lived on emergency food donations.

1980 Lt. Col. Mohamed Khouna Ould Haidala in power as head of state, following coup (Jan. 4).

1980 Government formally ended slavery; racially mixed former Arab slaves granted rights.

1980–81 Sid Ahmed Ould Bneijara in office as prime minister (Dec.), heading a government made up almost entirely of civilians; two attempted coups failed before President Haidalla dissolved the civilian government (Apr. 1981) and formed a new, all-military government.

1981 Mauritania broke diplomatic relations with Morocco over its alleged involvement in the second attempted coup against the Bneijara government.

1982 Former president Mohamed Ould Salek and former prime minister Sid Ahmed Ould Bneijara imprisoned for mounting an unsuccessful coup attempt (Feb.).

1984 Military ousted President Haidalla (Dec. 12) in bloodless coup; installed Col. Maaoya Sid'Ahmed Ould Taya, a former prime minister; he ruled as president, prime minister, and defense minister.

1986 *Manifesto of Oppressed Black Mauritanians* circulated (Apr.), leading to arrest and conviction of 20 leading blacks (Sept.) for sedition; called attention to racial tensions between light-skinned Moors who dominated government and dark-skinned Mauritanians living in the Senegal River region.

1986 Race riot in Nouadhibou (Nov.), Mauritania's second largest city.

1987 Black Mauritanians, 3 officers and 18 soldiers, convicted following failed coup attempt on Oct. 22; government accused them of planning to set up independent republic in the Senegal River region.

1988 Heavy rains ended drought; hordes of locusts swept across the country.

1988 Tené Youssouf Gueye, a famous black writer, died while imprisoned in one of Mauritania's most notorious prisons; he had been arrested in 1986 as the author of the *Manifesto of Oppressed Black Mauritanians.*

1988 Pro-Iraqi Baathist army officers mounted unsuccessful coup attempt.

1989 Some 450 people killed in rioting.

1990 About 60 army and navy personnel arrested for plotting a coup (Nov.).

1991 Government legalized opposition parties (July).

Mauritius (Île de France) Island country in the Indian Ocean. The population is 1,141,900 and the capital is Port Louis. Discovered (16th cent.) by the Portuguese, the island was held in turn by the Dutch (1598–1710), French (1715–1810), and British (1810–1968). Mauritius gained independence on Mar. 12, 1968. In 1986–87, nine members of the legislature were accused of involvement in drug trafficking following a government investigation. The country became a republic within the Commonwealth on Mar. 12, 1992.

Maurocordátos, Aléxander *See* **Mavrocordátos, Aléxander.**

Maury, Matthew Fontaine 1806–73. American naval officer and hydrographer. He charted the Atlantic, Pacific, and Indian oceans and wrote *Physical Geography of the Sea,* the first modern oceanographic work.

Maurya Empire Ancient Indian empire (*fl* 4th–2d cent. BC) of the Maurya rulers. The first great Indian empire, it united nearly the whole Indian subcontinent (and part of Afghanistan) and promoted a flourishing Indian culture. The empire was founded by Chandragupta I, who overthrew (c322 BC) the ruler of the Magadha kingdom in eastern India and conquered (c305) domains of Seleucus Nicator to the west. The kingdom reached its greatest expansion under the rule of Asoka, who added to conquests made by his predecessor, Bindusara (*d.* c272). Asoka established a special, almost secular form of Buddhism as the state religion. Following his reign, the empire entered into decline and by c185 had broken up into petty kingdoms. (*See also* India, 322–185 BC).

Mausolus *d* 353 BC. Persian satrap, ruler of Caria (376–353 BC). He is known for his monumental tomb at Halicarnassus, known as the Mausoleum.

Mavrocordátos, Aléxander (Maurocordátos, ˜) 1791–1865. Greek statesman. He was a leader in the revolution against the Ottoman Turks (1821), president of the first national assembly (1822), and twice premier.

Maxentius *d.* AD 312. Roman emperor (AD 306–312). Maxentius became emperor after his father, Emperor Maximian, and Emperor Diocletian abdicated. Maximian supported him against Severus. After a quarrel, however, Maximian refused to help him against Constantine, who defeated him in battle (312) at Milvian Bridge (*q.v.*).

Maximian *d.* AD 310. Roman emperor with Diocletian (AD 286–305). He ruled the empire in the West until his abdication (305). He later helped his son Maxentius to become emperor, then broke with him and supported Constantine.

Maximilian 1832–67. Austrian archduke and emperor of Mexico (1864–67). Unpopular with the Mexicans, he was opposed by B. Juárez. Supported for a time by French troops sent by Napoleon III he refused to abdicate after their withdrawal (1867), and was captured and shot.

Maximilian I 1459–1519. Holy Roman Emperor (1493–1519), successor to his father Frederick III. He greatly expanded the hereditary Habsburg domains, often at the expense of the interests of the Holy Roman Empire. Prior to his accession, he added Burgundian lands (Burgundy, the Netherlands, and Luxembourg) to Habsburg possessions by his marriage (1477) to Mary of Burgundy. Burgundy was lost (by the Treaty of Arras, 1483) in wars with the French, and Maximilian undertook the Italian Wars (1494–1559) to regain Burgundian lands there. Though Switzerland was able to win (1499) independence from the empire, Maximilian added Hungary and Bohemia to the Habsburg

possessions by the marriage (1516) of his grandson and granddaughter to heirs of King Ladislaus II. He also ensured Habsburg succession in Spain by the marriage of his son Philip to heiress Joanna (Charles V was their son).

Maximilian I (Maximilian the Great) 1573–1651. Duke (1597–1651) and elector (1623–51) of Bavaria. He was a key founder (1609) of the Catholic League, which opposed the Protestant Union in the Thirty Years' War (1618–48).

Maximilian I 1756–1825. King (1806–25) and elector (1799–1806) of Bavaria. He gained the crown by allying himself with Napoleon and ruled as an enlightened monarch. He championed Bavarian independence and opposed the unification of Germany.

Maximilian II 1527–76. Holy Roman Emperor (1564–76), successor to his father, Ferdinand I. A nominal Catholic, he was tolerant of the Protestants in his realm. He concluded a truce (1568) with Turkish sultan Selim II.

Maximilian II 1811–64. Bavarian king (1848–64), successor to his father, Louis I. His reign was liberal and devoted to the arts and learning. He tried to form a union of small German states led by Bavaria to balance the influence of Austria and Prussia.

Maximilian the Great *See* **Maximilian I.**

Maximin *d.* AD 238. Roman emperor (AD 235–238). He spent much of his reign campaigning against the invading Germans. He was assassinated by his own soldiers.

Maximin *d.* AD 313. Roman emperor (AD 308–313). He persecuted the Christians and attempted to revitalize paganism. He was defeated by Licinius.

Maximus *d.* AD 388. Roman emperor of the West (AD 383–388). He defeated Gratian and drove Valentinian II from Italy. He was defeated and put to death by Eastern emperor Theodosius I.

Maxwell, James Clerk 1831–79. British physicist, considered the greatest 19th cent. theoretical physicist. He studied the rings of Saturn (1855–59), which he found to be made of many small particles. In color vision, he showed that mixtures of three primary colors, red, blue, and green, can produce all colors, and that the human eye has receptors sensitive to the primary colors. Maxwell produced (1861) the first color photograph to use a three-color process. But his best-known work was the electromagnetic theory of light (1864), which held that light is made up of electromagnetic waves. He also established a kinetic theory of gases (from 1860).

Maya Group of related Central American Indian tribes, living in the Yucatán Peninsula, southern Mexico, Guatemala, and Belize. The origin of the Maya is uncertain, but by the 1st millennium BC they had already begun to establish an advanced culture. The Mayan civilization was based on agriculture, and each community retained political independence under the rule of a local hierarchy of priests and political chieftains. Mayan cities centered around royal houses and religious temples built on pyramidal structures. The Maya devised an extremely accurate calendar, a vigesimal (base 20) number system, a complex pantheon of gods and religious ceremonies, and a system of hieroglyphic writing. Their culture is noted for its advances in the arts, architecture, astronomy, and mathematics. Their cities included Chichén Itzá, Uxmal, and Mayapán, which formed the League of Mayapán (13th cent AD). The league was rent by civil war, and the cities eventually abandoned. Mayan civilization had passed its peak by the time of the Spanish conquest (16th cent.) The Spanish accelerated the Mayan decline, abolished much of the Mayan religion, and destroyed virtually all of the Mayan records. A few survive, such as the Dresden Codex (*q.v.*) and the Popol Vuh (*q.v.*), a later text based on original Mayan sources.

Mayaguez Incident Seizure (May 12, 1975) of the US cargo ship *Mayaguez* by Cambodian authorities. Within two weeks after US forces were evacuated from Vietnam, Cambodians boarded the *Mayaguez* and took 39 crewmen hostage. President G. Ford ordered their rescue, during which 38 Americans were killed.

Mayakovsky, Vladimir 1893–1930. Russian poet, leading poet of the Russian Revolution. Among his best-known poems are *A Cloud in Trousers* and *The Backbone Flute,* both written before the revolution.

Mayapán, League of *See* **Maya.**

Mayenne, Charles de Lorraine, duc de 1554–1611. French general, brother of Henry of Guise. He headed the Catholic League against French king Henry IV but refused to place the Spanish Catholic infanta Isabella on the throne.

Mayer, Louis B. 1885–1957. Russian-born US movie producer. Fascinated by the advent of nickelodeons, he capitalized on a single theater

in Massachusetts, building that into a New England theater chain, and then founding Metro Pictures Corporation in New York. Moving to Los Angeles, he eventually merged his company with Metro Pictures and the Goldwyn Company to form MGM (1924). Under the leadership of Mayer and I. Thalberg, MGM became the most profitable studio in motion picture history.

Mayflower English ship upon which the Pilgrims sailed from England to Plymouth, Massachusetts (Sept.–Nov. 1620). The Pilgrims arrived off Cape Cod in November, and landed at Plymouth Dec. 26. (*See also* Pilgrims.)

Mayflower Compact An agreement, signed (Nov. 21, 1620) by the Pilgrims aboard the ship *Mayflower.* By it the settlers agreed to form a "civil body politic," which would form a government with binding laws. It was the basis for the government in Plymouth.

May Fourth Movement Mass movement in China (early 20th cent.) sparked by intellectuals who sought government reform and modernization of Chinese society. The movement, beginning as early as 1915, was precipitated by the government's inability to check Japanese expansionism. But among intellectuals it fostered a broad attack on traditional Chinese society and culture and helped to introduce Western ideologies. The intellectual movement was translated to mass protests by the events of 1919. The post–WW I Versailles Peace Conference transferred (Apr. 28) German concessions in Shantung province, China, to Japan. Some 3,000–5,000 students in Beijing began (May 4) a series of mass protests against the decision, and over the weeks these spread to other cities and spawned a boycott of Japanese goods. China subsequently refused to sign the Treaty of Paris, but more important results were the rising political power of intellectuals, the further decline of traditional culture, the spread of the vernacular in written Chinese, and greater freedoms for women. Among the leading figures in the movement were Ch'en Tu-hsiu and Hu Shih.

Mayo, Charles Horace and William James 1865–1939, 1861–1939. American surgeons. They established the Mayo Clinic in Rochester, Minnesota, and founded (1915) the Mayo Foundation for Medical Education and Research.

Mazarin, Jules (Mazarini, Giulio) 1602–61. French cardinal and statesman. He succeeded

(1642) Cardinal Richelieu as minister of France under King Louis XIII and remained powerful during the regency of Anne of Austria.

Mazarin Bible First known book printed (c1455) from movable type. Printed by J. Gutenberg, it was so named for its discovery (1760) in the library of Cardinal Mazarin.

Mazarini, Giulio *See* **Mazarin, Jules.**

Mazepa, Ivan Stepanovich 1644?–1709. Cossack hetman (leader) in the Russian Ukraine. He fought with the Swedes under Charles XII against Russia, but was defeated at Poltava (1709).

Mazurian Lakes, Battles of the Military campaigns on the Russian front during WW I. 1. Battle (Sept. 9–14, 1914) in which the Germans drove the Russians from East Prussia, inflicting casualties of 125,000 (against some 10,000 German casualties). 2. Battle (Feb. 7–21, 1915) in which the Germans attempted a knockout blow at Russia. They inflicted 200,000 Russian casualties, but without decisive results.

Mazzini, Giuseppe 1805–72. Italian revolutionary and political writer. He campaigned for a united Italy under a republican government, founded the Young Italy Movement (1831), and was a leader in the short-lived Roman republic of 1849. He aided Garibaldi in his efforts to unify Italy and later refused to take part in the monarchical government established in 1861.

Mboya, Thomas Joseph *See* **Mboya, Tom.**

Mboya, Tom (˜, Thomas Joseph) 1930–69. Kenyan political leader. A leader in the Kenyan independence movement, he held several ministerial positions in the government of J. Kenyatta before being assassinated.

Mc *For names beginning with Mc, see under* **Mac.**

Mead, George Herbert 1863–1931. American philosopher. He emphasized the importance of language in social interaction. His *Mind, Self, and Society* was published posthumously.

Mead, Margaret 1901–78. American anthropologist, noted especially for her studies of the people and cultures of Oceania. Her books included *Coming of Age in Samoa, Growing Up in New Guinea,* and *Male and Female.*

Meade, George Gordon 1815–72. Union general in the American Civil War. He fought with distinction at Antietam (1862), Fredericksburg (1862), and Chancellorsville (1863), and defeated Gen. R. E. Lee at Gettysburg (1863).

Meany, George 1894–1980. US labor leader. Originally a plumber, he rose to become (1952) president of the American Federation of Labor (AFL) and of the AFL-CIO (1955).

Mecca Saudi Arabian city, the birthplace of Muhammad (570?) and one of the holy cities of Islam. It is the site of the Sacred Mosque and the Kaaba. Mecca was conquered by the Ottoman Turks (1517), the Wahhabis (1803–13), and Ibn Saud (1924), who refounded Saudi Arabia. (*See also* Muhammad.)

Mechnikov, Élie (Metchnikoff, ˜) 1845–1916. Russian microbiologist and zoologist. He discovered that certain blood cells engulf foreign bodies, a process called phagocytosis. For his work in immunology he was awarded, with P. Ehrlich, the Nobel Prize for Physiology or Medicine (1908).

Mecklenburg Former East German state (until 1952) and historic region on the Baltic. First settled in the 6th cent. it became (14th cent.) a duchy within the Holy Roman Empire. Divided (1701) into Mecklenburg-Schwerin and Mecklenburg-Strelitz, it was reunited (1934).

Mecklenburg Declaration of Independence American declaration (May 20, 1775) severing ties with Britain, said to have been made by the citizens of Mecklenburg, North Carolina. Although these citizens did adopt anti-British resolutions around that time, the declaration is probably not authentic.

Media Ancient Asian country of indeterminate boundaries in what is now roughly northwestern Iran. Under Cyaxares, Media won its independence from the Assyrian Empire, taking much of its territory. The Persian king Cyrus conquered (c550 BC) Media from Astyages, and it remained a part of the Persian Empire until the time of Alexander the Great.

Medici Italian family, rulers of Florence (15–18th cents.) and world-famous patrons of the arts who transformed Florence into a treasure house of European art. Though the family can be traced back to the 12th cent., the huge family fortune was founded by Giovanni di Bicci de' Medici (1360–1429). From his sons stem the two major branches: the Elder Branch, by Cosimo (1389–1464); and the Younger Branch, by Lorenzo (1395–1440). The Elder Branch controlled Florence by means of influence until 1531, when Alessandro (1511–37) became hereditary duke.

On his death the extinct Elder Branch was replaced by the Younger. It ruled Florence until the death of Gian Gastone (1671–1737). Prominent members of the family include Pope Leo X, Pope Clement VII, Pope Leo XI, Catherine de Médicis, and Marie de Médicis.

Medici, Alessandro de' 1511–37. Duke of Florence (1532–37). Made duke by his father-in-law Holy Roman Emperor Charles V, he was hated for his tyrannical rule. His assassination by L. de' Medici ended the Elder Branch of the Medici line.

Medici, Cosimo de' 1389–1464. Florentine ruler and banker. He used his wealth and influence to encourage the arts and scholarship.

Medici, Cosimo I de' 1519–74. Duke of Florence (1537–69). Although a cruel ruler, he increased the wealth and size of his territories, and defeated and incorporated Siena (1555). He was made duke of Tuscany (1569).

Medici, Cosimo II de' 1590–1620. Grand duke of Tuscany (1609–21), successor to his father, Ferdinand I de' Medici. He was a patron of Galileo.

Medici, Ferdinand I de' 1549–1609. Grand duke of Tuscany (1587–1609). He strengthened the duchy.

Medici, Gian Gastone de' 1671–1737. Grand duke of Tuscany (1723–37). He was the last male member of the Medici family. After his death the now impoverished duchy passed to Francis of Lorraine, later Holy Roman Emperor Francis I.

Medici, Giovanni Angelo de' *See* **Pius IV.**

Medici, Giovanni de' (Bande Nere, Giovanni delle) 1498–1526. Italian general known as John of the Black Bands. He fought for both sides in the Italian Wars and was mortally wounded in battle.

Medici, Giovanni de' *See* **Leo X.**

Medici, Giulio de' *See* **Clement VII.**

Medici, Ippolito de' 1511–35. Italian cardinal. He and his cousin, Alessandro de' Medici, ruled Florence under Pope Clement VII. While on a mission to Holy Roman Emperor Charles V he died, possibly poisoned by order of Alessandro.

Medici, Lorenzo de' 1449–92. Florentine statesman known as "the Magnificent." Son of P. de' Medici, he ruled Florence (1478–92) and was a noted writer and patron of the arts.

Medici, Lorenzo de' 1492–1519. Duke of Urbino (1516–19) and son of P. de' Medici. His tomb in Florence was created by Michelangelo. He was the father of Catherine de Médicis.

Medici, Piero de' 1414–69. Florentine merchant prince, successor to his father, C. de' Medici, as ruler of Florence. The father of L. de' Medici, he was known as "the Gouty" because of his ill health.

Medici, Piero de' 1471–1503. Florentine merchant prince, son of L. de Medici (the Magnificent). He ruled Florence (1492–94) until expelled by Savonarola during the invasion of Tuscany by French king Charles VIII.

medieval *See* **Middle Ages.**

Medieval Inquisition *See* **Inquisition** (1).

Medina Saudi Arabian city. It holds the tomb of Muhammad and is Islam's second most holy city. Muhammad made his hijra (flight) here from Mecca in 622. It was ruled successively by the Ottoman Turks, Wahhabis, Egyptians, and again by the Ottomans until taken by Ibn Saud (1924).

Medina-Sidonia, duke of *See* **Spanish Armada.**

Mediterranean Sea World's largest inland sea, between southern Europe, North Africa, and western Asia. A number of the world's oldest civilizations developed in the Mediterranean region.

Meersen, Treaty of Treaty (870) dividing Lotharingia, one of the three kingdoms formed by division of the Carolingian Empire in 843. The treaty, formulated on the death (869) of Lotharingian king Lothair, was signed by Charles II ("the Bald") and Louis the German. Lotharingia lay between Charles' kingdom of the Western Franks and Louis' kingdom of the Eastern Franks, and the two monarchs divided the territory between themselves. Thus a common border was established between the two kingdoms, later to become the states of France and Germany.

Megalopolis Ancient Greek city. Founded (c370 BC) in Arcadia as an anti-Spartan outpost, it was destroyed (222 BC) by Cleomenes III.

Megarian school of philosophy A Greek philosophy founded by Euclid of Megara. It held that good was a single quality, though known by different names.

Megiddo, Battle of Battle (Sept. 19, 1918) of WW I at Megiddo, now in Israel. Here the British under Gen. Edmund Allenby (1861–1936) defeated the Ottoman Turks and began their northward thrust through Palestine. The Ottomans were forced to sign an armistice the next month.

Mehemet *See* **Muhammad.**

Meiji *See* **Mutsuhito.**

Meiji restoration Period of modernization and Westernization in Japan (1868–1912). During this period Japan developed its industry and became a world power. The period began with restoration of power to the emperor, Mutsuhito (reign name, Meiji), after the centuries-long rule by Tokugawa shoguns. The emperor abolished feudalism (1868–69), made Tokyo capital (1869), modernized government administration (1885), and acceded to a new constitution (1889). The government thereafter consisted of an upper and lower (elected) house, a premier, and a group of elder statesmen (Genro). During this period, which ended (1912) with Meiji's death, Japan engaged in the Sino-Japanese War (1894–95) and Russo-Japanese War (1904–05).

Mein Kampf Political publication by A. Hitler. Written by Hitler during his imprisonment after the Munich Putsch, it outlined National Socialism and its program for German expansion and world domination.

Meir, Golda (Mabovitch, Goldie) (Myerson, Goldie) 1898–1978. Israeli political leader and prime minister (1969–1974). She was a founder of Israel, and as prime minister she actively sought a peaceful solution to problems in the Middle East. Her efforts were halted by the Fourth Arab-Israeli War (1973), during which Israel was caught unprepared by a surprise attack. She resigned the following year as her support in the Knesset declined.

Meitner, Lise 1878–1968. Austrian physicist. With O. Hahn she discovered protoactinium, and accomplished uranium fission (1938) with Hahn and Fritz Strassmann (1902–80).

Melaka *See* **Malacca.**

Melanchthon, Philip 1497–1560. German religious scholar. He worked with Luther, published the *Loci Communes* (1521), setting forth Reformation principles, and wrote the Augsburg Confession. He attempted to moderate differences between Catholics and Protestants in order to avoid war and played a significant role in reforming the German educational system.

Melas, Baron Michael von *See* **Marengo, Battle of.**

Melbourne, William Lamb, 2d viscount 1779–1848. British statesman. As prime minister (1834, 1835–41) he was a friend and adviser to the young Queen Victoria. His wife, Lady Caroline, had an affair with Lord G. Byron.

Melchites Christian group of the Middle East headed by the patriarch of Antioch. They are in communion with the pope, but their rites are performed in Arabic.

Melfi, Constitutions of *See* **Constitutions of Melfi.**

Méline, Félix Jules 1838–1925. French statesman and premier (1896–98). Elected to the National Assembly in the 1870s, he served as agriculture minister, became president of the Chamber of Deputies (1888), and later the premier. He opposed Gen. G. Boulanger and helped write legislation designed to protect French industries.

Melissus of Samos *See* **Eleatic school.**

Mellon, Andrew William 1855–1937. American financier. As secretary of the treasury (1921–32), he introduced (1920) tax reforms that helped reduce the national debt. He donated his art collection and gave funds to form the National Gallery of Art.

Melville, Andrew 1545–1622. Scottish Presbyterian scholar and successor to J. Knox. He improved the Scottish universities, wrote much of the *Second Book of Discipline,* and was sent to the Tower of London (1607–11) by English king James I for his criticisms of the Anglican church.

Melville, Herman 1819–91. American author, known best for his classic novel *Moby Dick* (1851). Raised in a well-to-do family, he went to sea after the death of his father in 1832. Melville used his experiences as a seaman (1841–44) in such books as *Typee* (1846), *Omoo* (1847), *Mardi* (1849), and *White Jacket* (1850). After a period of popularity and literary success, Melville drifted into a life of anonymity and spent his later years as a customs official in New York City (1866–85). He died virtually unknown, but today is considered one of America's great writers.

Memphis Capital of the Old Kingdom of ancient Egypt, located at the apex of the Nile delta. It was said to have been established by Menes and was dedicated to the god Ptah. Memphis remained the capital from the New Kingdom to the Third Intermediate period, though during the New Kingdom, Thebes rose as the theocratic capital (the center for religious and administrative functions).

Menahem *d.* c738 BC. King of Israel (c744–738 BC). He killed Shallum for the throne and ruled cruelly. He paid tribute to Assyria for protection. [2 Kings 15]

Menander 342?–291? BC. Greek comic dramatist. He was considered the best of the New Comedy writers and wrote more than 100 plays, which were based on sentimental themes.

Mencius 371?–288? BC. Chinese Confucian philosopher who had a major role in the development of Confucianism. He is called the second sage, after Confucius. Mencius was born to a well-to-do family and his father died when he was just three. His mother, according to tradition, was very careful about his upbringing and one account tells of her moving the family to be near a school for the boy (she has been considered the model mother in China). Mencius pursued his studies and having had Confucius's grandson as his mentor, eventually became a teacher of Confucian thought. He traveled for a time, preaching his message of humane government, concern for the common man, welfare for the old and sick, etc., to rulers of the Warring States, but failed to win them over. Finally he returned home and devoted himself to teaching. The *Book of Mencius,* written by Mencius's disciples, recorded his teachings and became a classic Confucian text.

Mencken, H(enry) L(ouis) 1880–1956. American journalist and critic noted for his iconoclastic criticisms of literature and middle-class American life. Among his works is the classic study *The American Language.*

Mendel, Gregor Johann 1822–84. Austrian biologist. An Augustinian monk, he conducted his experiments on hybrid plants in his monastery garden. He formulated Mendel's Law on dominant and recessive genes, and discovered the male cell's role in fertilization. His studies were published in 1866, but were ignored in his lifetime. Later rediscovered, they now form the basis for modern genetics.

Mendeleev, Dmitri Ivanovich (Mendeleyev, ~) 1834–1907. Russian chemist. He formulated the periodic law and devised the table for the classification of the elements in 1869 (improved version 1871).

Mendelssohn, Jakob Ludwig Felix (Mendelssohn-Bartholdy, Felix) 1809–47. German composer, grandson of M. Mendelssohn. One of the leading composers of the 19th cent., he wrote his first important work when he was seventeen years old. His works include his Violin Concerto in E (1844), five symphonies (including the *Scottish Symphony*), and works for the piano.

Mendelssohn, Moses 1729–86. German Jewish philosopher. He advocated assimilation of the Jews into the German culture and was the model for G. Lessing's play *Nathan the Wise.*

Mendes-France, Pierre 1907–82. French statesman. A Radical Socialist, he was premier (1954–55) when France declared an armistice with Indochina. He was forced from office because of his liberal policy toward Algeria.

Mendoza, Antonio de 1490?–1552. Spanish colonial administrator and first viceroy of New Spain (1535–50). His 15-year administration was just and fair to the Indians and helped stabilize the Mexican territory.

Mendoza, Pedro de 1487?–1537. Spanish soldier and explorer. Commissioned by Holy Roman Emperor Charles V to colonize the Rio de la Plata area, he founded Buenos Aires (1536).

Menelik II 1844–1913. Ethiopian emperor (1889–1913). He crushed an Italian invasion attempt (1895–96), expanded Ethiopia's territory, and worked to modernize his empire.

Menéndez de Aviles, Pedro 1519–74. Spanish sailor and colonizer. Menendez founded St. Augustine, Florida (1565), and led the massacre (1565) of French Huguenot colonists at Fort Caroline, Florida.

Menes *fl.* 3100 BC. Egyptian king. He united Upper and Lower Egypt and founded the 1st dynasty. He also is said to have founded the ancient capital of Memphis.

Menkaure (Mycerinus) *fl.* c2500 BC. Egyptian king of the 4th dynasty. He built the smallest of the three major pyramids at Giza.

Mennonites Protestant Christian sect. Mennonites, now most numerous in the US and Canada, believe in adult baptism, refuse to bear arms, and seek a simplified existence free of worldly concerns. The sect originated in Europe as an outgrowth of the Anabaptists and was largely formed around the work of the Dutch reformer Menno Simons (1496–1561), for whom it is named. The elements of the Mennonite doctrine were set forth (1632) in the Dordrecht Confession of Faith. Mennonite settlements were founded in America as early as 1683. The Mennonite church has split into many smaller sects, including the Amish sects.

Menotti, Gian-Carlo 1911– . Italian composer. His operas have been extremely popular in the US, to which he emigrated in 1927. He is twice winner of the Pulitzer Prize for Music (1950, 1955).

Mensheviks Russian revolutionary party. The Mensheviks, opposed to N. Lenin's Bolsheviks, sought to form a party of the masses (rather than a revolutionary elite), believed there was a necessary transition period before creating the Socialist state, and were willing to work with bourgeois elements during this time to achieve their goal. The Mensheviks were formed by a split (caused by N. Lenin, 1903) in the Russian Social Democratic Workers' party and were first led by L. Martov (1873–1923). The Social Democratic party was permanently split into two factions in 1912 and thereafter the Mensheviks were often divided by internal dissent. They dominated the provisional government of Russia after the February Revolution of 1917 (*q.v.*), were ousted from power by the Bolsheviks in the October Revolution (*q.v.*), and were officially suppressed by the Bolsheviks after 1922.

Menshikov, Aleksandr Danilovich 1672–1729. Russian field marshal and statesman. Adviser to Peter the Great, he helped secure the throne for Peter's widow, Catherine I. He ruled Russia during her reign.

Mentuhotep II (Nebhapetre) Egyptian king (2060–10 BC), a ruler of the 11th dynasty. His reign marked the ascendancy of Thebes and under his leadership Upper, Middle, and Lower Egypt were reunited (c2039 BC).

Menzies, Robert Gordon 1894–78. Australian statesman. As prime minister (1939–41, 1949–66) he followed a pro-American, anti-Communist policy.

Merarites *See* **Levites.**

mercantilism Economic policy and theory that dominated European financial and governmental thinking from the 16th–18th cents. It argued that governmental regulation of a nation's industry and trade was necessary; that exports were preferable to imports or to equal trade; that large populations and armies were beneficial to a nation; that a country's true wealth was determined by its possession of gold and silver. Mercantilism was attacked by Adam Smith in *Wealth of Nations* (1776), a book advocating the laissez-faire (*q.v.*) doctrines that replaced mercantilism in the 18th cent.

Mercator, Gerardus (Kremer, Gerhard) 1512–94. Flemish cartographer. He invented the Mercator projection (1568) for navigator's maps and started work on a great atlas, which was finished (1594) by his son.

Merchants Adventurers English company (1407–1807) established by merchants dealing in foreign trade. Their major market, until 1564, was in the Spanish Netherlands, where finished English cloth was in demand.

Merchants of the Steelyard In medieval England, German merchants of the Hanseatic League (*q.v.*). They conducted their trading operations out of the Steelyard, a section of London along the Thames that served as English headquarters of the league. Special privileges granted these merchants (by royal order) aroused resentment among the English. But the privileges were continued because the trade was economically valuable. With the rise of the English carrying trade in the 16th cent., the German merchants ceased to be important and Queen Elizabeth expelled them (1598).

Merchant Staplers *See* **Company of the Merchants of the Staple.**

Mercia, kingdom of Ancient Anglo-Saxon kingdom comprising much of central England. Settled (6th cent.) by Angles, it was overcome and divided (886) by invading Danes in the east and Alfred of Wessex in the west.

Mercier, Ernest 1878–? French industrialist and engineer. Born in Algeria, he played an important role in setting up power companies in French cities, notably in Paris.

Merciless Parliament (Wonderful Parliament) In English history, the parliamentary session (1388) which impeached five supporters of King Richard II on broadly construed charges of treason. The incident stemmed from Richard's ongoing struggle for power with Parliament and forced him to take a more moderate course for some years.

Meredith, George 1828–1909. English novelist, noted for his intellectual and psychological novels. Among his best-known novels are *The Ordeal of Richard Feverel, The Egoist,* and *The Amazing Marriage.*

Merezhkovsky, Dmitri Sergeyevich 1865–1941. Russian novelist and critic. He wrote the trilogy of historical novels *Christ and Antichrist,* and was an influential figure in the Russian religious and intellectual movements of the early 20th cent.

Mergenthaler, Ottmar 1854–99. German-born American inventor of the Linotype machine.

Patented in 1884, it greatly advanced the printing industry.

Mérimée, Prosper *See* **Bizet, Georges.**

Mermaid Tavern Historical English meeting place in London. The Friday Street Club regularly gathered there. Its members included W. Shakespeare, B. Jonson, and J. Donne.

Merneptah *d.* c1223 BC. Ancient Egyptian king (c1236 BC–c1223 BC), successor to his father Ramses II. He repelled an invasion by the Libyans. The earliest mention of Israel is on one of the steles commemorating this victory. It is thought the Exodus (*q.v.*) occurred during his reign.

Merovech *See* **Merovingians.**

Merovingians Frankish dynasty (481–751) in Western Europe. The dynasty was founded (5th cent.) by the kings of the Salian Franks, one of whom was Merovech (reigned 448–457). The rise of the Merovingians from their kingdoms along the Rhine and in modern Belgium and the Netherlands began with the rule of Clovis I (481–511). He united the Salian and Ripuarian Franks, accepted Christianity (496), and, by his conquests, created a vast kingdom that included most of Gaul. His kingdom was divided by his four sons at his death, united again by Clotaire I (reigned 558–561) and redivided into Austrasia (*q.v.*), Neustria (*q.v.*), and Burgundy (under Austrasian control). Merovingian territories were briefly united again under the rule of Clotaire II and Dagobert I (613–639, inclusive). Already weakened by the many bitter internal wars, the Merovingian rulers after Dagobert lost real power to the noblemen. The mayors of the palace (supposedly in the king's service) held actual power. Charles Martel greatly expanded his power as mayor of the palace, and his son, Pepin the Short, finally overthrew the last Merovingian king, Childeric III, in 751. He thus founded the Carolingian dynasty (*q.v.*). (*See also* France, 481–751).

Merrimack *See* *Monitor* and *Merrimack.*

Mesolithic *See* **Stone Age.**

Mesopotamia Historic region located in what is now Iraq. An important center of early civilization, the area is the fertile plain surrounding the Tigris and Euphrates rivers. The earliest towns in the region were located in the north (5th millennium BC), though the first important cultures eventually rose in the south, notably Sumer (*q.v.*). There followed the dynasty of Ur (*q.v.*), the

Akkadian Empire (*q.v.*), the first and second Babylonian Empires (*q.v.*), and the Assyrian Empire (*q.v.*). Thereafter the region succumbed to other powers, beginning with the Persians, Macedonians, and Romans.

Messenia Ancient Greek region in the Peloponnesus, and site of the present Messinias. Its citizens frequently rebelled against Sparta's domination, notably in the Messenian Wars (*q.v.*). Eventually freed by Epaminondas of Thebes (369), Messenia's freedom heralded the end of Sparta as an important political power.

Messenian Wars Two wars (c735–c715 BC, c650–c620 BC) waged by Sparta against Messenia. The first led to Spartan victory over Messenia. The second, prompted by an uprising in Messenia, was a prolonged struggle and ended with complete Spartan domination of Messenia and the enslavement of its population.

Messerschmitt, Willy 1898–1978. German aviation designer and manufacturer. He founded the Messerschmitt aircraft manufacturing works and built planes for the Luftwaffe during WW II.

Messiaen, Olivier-Eugène-Prosper-Charles 1908–92. French composer and organist. His work is noted for its originality and religious mysticism.

Messiah (Messias) In religion, especially Christianity and Judaism, a redeemer who would come from God to save humanity. In Islam, the Mahdi is a messianic figure.

Messina Italian city, capital of Messina province, Sicily. Founded (8th cent. BC) by settlers from Chalcis, it was destroyed by the Carthaginians (396 BC) and later rebuilt by rulers of nearby Syracuse. Thereafter, it figured in the struggles between the tyrants of Syracuse and the Carthaginians. Messina allied itself with Rome (264 BC) and this brought on the First Punic War between Rome and Carthage. It was later taken by the Goths, Byzantines, and Arabs, before being taken by the Normans, who made it part of their kingdom of Sicily. Centuries later, the capture of Messina during WW II marked the fall of Sicily to the Allies (1943).

Metacomet *See* **Philip** (*d.* 1676).

Metaphysical poets Group of 17th-cent. English lyric poets whose works were noted for their contrasting imagery and intellectual brilliance or wit. The term was coined by S. Johnson, and a leading figure of the group was J. Donne.

Metaurus, Battle of the Battle (207 BC) of the Second Punic War, at the Metaurus River, northeast of Rome. Roman forces under the consuls Marcus Livius Salinator and Claudius Nero decisively defeated the Carthaginians under Hasdrubal, thus saving Rome from invasion and assuring Hannibal's eventual defeat.

Metaxas, John (~, Yanni) 1871–1941. Greek general and statesman. A royalist, as premier (1936–41) he assumed dictatorial powers. He repelled the Italian invasion of Greece (1940) during WW II.

Metaxas, Yanni *See* **Metaxas, John.**

Metellus Macedonicus, Quintus Caecilius *d.* 115 BC. Roman general. He gained Roman victories in Macedonia and Spain. As censor (131 BC), he advocated compulsory marriage to increase the birthrate.

Metellus Numidicus, Quintus Caecilius *d.* 91? BC. Roman general. He defeated the Numidians under Jugurtha (109 BC) but was forced to relinquish command to Marius. In 100, he was exiled for opposing the agrarian reforms of Lucias Appuleius Saturninus.

Metellus Pius, Quintus Caecilius *d.* c63 BC. Roman general who served under Sulla, and son of Metellus Numidicus. He was commander of the war in Spain against Sertorius and consul (80 BC) with Sulla.

Methodism Protestant Christian religious movement in Britain and America, based largely on the teachings of J. Wesley. The movement began (1729) in Oxford, England, when Wesley, his brother Charles (1707–88), G. Whitefield, and others began to hold meetings for religious study. Adopting elements advanced by the Moravian church, the group began a program of evangelism, and by their actions were barred from participation within the Church of England. Whitefield, opposing Wesley's support of the doctrines of J. Arminius, separated from the group (c1741) and formed the Calvinistic Methodists. In 1784 Wesley ordained Thomas Coke (1747–1814) and F. Asbury superintendents of the movement in America, which had grown steadily through the 18th cent. After Wesley's death (1791), the movement in Britain formally separated from the Church of England as the Wesleyan Methodist church. In the US, missionaries called circuit riders spread Methodism throughout the rapidly expanding western frontier in the early 1800s. Methodist factions formed in both Britain and America in the 19th cent. (in the US, the church was split over the

slavery issue), and some subsequently were rejoined. A merger of churches in the US (1939) formed the Methodist church. This in turn joined (1968) with the Evangelical United Brethren church to form the United Methodist church, the largest Methodist group in the world.

Methodius, Saint *See* **Cyril and Methodius, saints.**

Methven, Battle of *See* **Robert I.**

metics In ancient Greece, resident foreigners (including freed slaves) who were often skilled workers and therefore important in commerce and industry. Most Greek city-states had them, but metics were concentrated in Athens. There metics were required to have a sponsor and had limited rights and certain duties, giving them a status above that of a visiting foreigner, but below that of a citizen.

Metternich, Prince Klemens Wenzel Nepomuk Lothar von 1773–1859. Austrian statesman, the leading European statesman (1815–48), whose conservative policies helped maintain political stability in post-Napoleonic Europe. As Austrian foreign minister (1809–48), he helped form the Quadruple Alliance, which finally defeated Napoleon (1813). Thereafter he sought to maintain the balance of power in Europe and to preserve the stability of the monarchies against liberal movements. He made Austria the dominant power in the German Confederation, helped create the Holy Alliance, took part in formulating the Carlsbad Decrees, and was a leading figure at the congresses of Vienna (1814–15), Troppau (1820), Laibach (1821), and Verona (1822). Metternich was forced out of power by the liberal revolutions of 1848, brought on in part by the repressive measures he advocated to maintain order.

Mexican Revolution Period of political and social turmoil in Mexico following the overthrow (May, 1911) of P. Díaz by F. Madero. Madero subsequently headed a popular movement that sought to implement reforms in Mexico. But his rule was ineffective and he was in turn overthrown and murdered (Feb., 1913) by Gen. V. Huerta. Huerta's reactionary rule led to revolts headed by V. Carranza, F. Villa, and E. Zapata, and he was forced from office (1914). Carranza became president, though his rule was challenged by Villa and Zapata, who continued armed resistance. Villa's raid into the US (Mar.

1916) provoked a US expedition into Mexico, headed by Gen. J. Pershing, but Villa successfully evaded it. Under Carranza, Mexico established the Constitution of 1917, which called for separation of church and state, agrarian reform, and nationalization of foreign holdings and mineral rights. Reform came slowly, however, and Mexico remained politically volatile for many years.

Mexican War War (May, 1846–Feb., 1848) between the US and Mexico. It resulted in US acquisition of vast territories in the West, including California, Nevada, Utah, New Mexico, and Arizona. The war was a result of US expansionist policies and accumulated tensions between the two countries. Following admission (1845) of Texas (which had rebelled against Mexican rule) to the Union, relations with Mexico became strained. The US attempted to buy California and New Mexico, but J. Slidell's mission failed. President J. Polk then ordered US troops into disputed territory along the Rio Grande (July, 1845). The Mexicans responded in kind and, on Apr. 25, 1846, fighting broke out between the two armies. The US declared war (May 12, 1846), but by this time US forces under Gen. Z. Taylor had already forced the Mexicans to retreat across the Rio Grande. Gen. S. Kearny invaded New Mexico (June–Aug. 1846), secured it for the US, and then entered California (Dec., 1846), which had already been taken over for the US by Pacific Naval Commander John Drake Sloat (1781–1867) and Capt. J. Frémont. Meanwhile US forces under Taylor and others pushed into Mexico. Taylor won an important victory over A. de Santa Anna (now Mexican president) at the Battle of Buena Vista (Feb., 1847). Gen. W. Scott landed some 12,000 US troops at Vera Cruz (Mar., 1847), took the city, and began the march to Mexico City. Scott won a rapid succession of victories at Cerro Gordo, Contreras, and Chapultepec (a fortress defending Mexico City), and entered Mexico City on Sept. 14, 1847. The Treaty of Guadalupe Hidalgo (*q.v.*) brought the war to an end and, among its other provisions, provided for the purchase of captured Mexican territory for $15 million.

Mexico Republic, the southernmost country of North America. The population is 88,335,000 and the capital is Mexico City. The region comprising Mexico saw the rise and development of a number of indigenous civilizations, among them the Toltec, Maya, and Aztec. Conquered (16th cent.) by the Spanish and made the center of the viceroyalty of New Spain, Mexico became independent in 1821. Since then its history has been marked by periods of political struggle, notably the Mexican Revolution (*q.v.*), which laid the basis for modern Mexican society. Key dates in the history of Mexico include:

600–900 Ancient Mayan city of Uxmal flourished.

8TH–11TH CENTS. Toltecs flourished in central Mexico.

14TH–15TH CENTS. Aztecs flourished in Mexico.

c1325 Aztec city Tenochtitlán founded.

c1479–c1548 F. de Montejo, Spanish conquistador, lived; joined Cortés in conquest of Mexico.

16TH CENT. *Repartimiento* system established: Spaniards given title to vast tracts of lands and native Indian peoples living on them; gave rise to oppressive system of forced labor and helped preserve social divisions between Spanish landowners, Indians, and mestizos (racially mixed persons).

16TH CENT. Popol Vuh, Quiché Indian manuscript, written; described ancient Mayan mythology and culture.

c1502–20 Aztec emperor Montezuma ruled.

1517 Francisco Fernández de Córdoba explored Yucatán; was first European to explore region.

1519–21 H. Cortés conquered territory of Mexico.

1523 Conquistador P. de Alvarado conquered Guatemala and Salvador for Cortés.

1528 Juan de Zumarraga became first bishop of Mexico; in subsequent years the Roman Catholic church forcibly Christianized native Indians and gained great landholdings in Spanish Mexico.

1535 Viceroyalty of New Spain created; Mexico City established as capital amid ruins of Aztec capital of Tenochtitlán.

1535–50 A. de Mendoza served as first viceroy of New Spain.

1539–1617? L. de Velasco lived; served Spain as viceroy of Mexico and Peru.

1540–42 Spanish explorer F. de Coronado led expedition from Mexico into American West.

1540s Spanish explored and laid claim to modern US Southwest region, including California, Arizona, New Mexico, and Texas.

1541   Mixton War, unsuccessful Indian revolt against Spanish rule.

1550?–1624?   J. de Oñate, Spanish explorer, lived; claimed much of American Southwest for Spain.

1680   Pueblo Rebellion, Indian revolt in New Mexico that halted Spanish colonization in that region for a decade.

1765–1815   Priest J. Morelos y Pavón lived; helped lead movement for independence from Spain.

1786   Reforms enacted by Viceroy José de Gálvez to end long-standing corruption and abuses of power by Spanish colonial government.

1807–08   French emperor Napoleon's armies invaded and occupied Spain; Spain's hold on its South American colonies weakened by the upheavals in Europe.

1810   Miguel Hidalgo y Costilla issued (Sept. 16) the *Grito de Dolores,* a call to rebellion to secure social and economic equality; Indians and mestizos rose in revolt.

1810   Hidalgo y Costilla marked his first victory at the Battle of Celaya.

1811   Rebel force under Hidalgo y Costilla crushed by Spanish royalists at Calderón Bridge (Jan. 17).

1813–14   Congress of Chilpancingo proclaimed (1813) a constitutional republic; main rebel forces defeated (1814) by royalist general A. de Iturbide; V. Guerrero carried on guerrilla war.

1820   Spanish Revolution of 1820; conservatives in Mexico (former royalists) decided in favor of independence from Spain.

1820s   American S. Austin helped settle Texas.

1821   Guerrilla leader V. Guerrero and conservative general A. de Iturbide formulated (Feb.) Plan of Iguala, calling for Mexican independence as a monarchy.

1821   Spain recognized Mexican independence by the Treaty of Córdoba (Aug. 24).

1822–24   De Iturbide seized power and declared himself emperor (1822); overthrown (1823) by Antonio López de Santa Anna; republic declared and Guadalupe Victoria became its first president (1824–29).

1833–36   Santa Anna in office as president.

1836   Santa Anna humiliated by Texas revolution, lost the presidency.

1836   Mexican soldiers captured the Alamo.

1838   Pastry War: brief conflict with France.

1839–44   Santa Anna returned to power.

1845–48   Mexican War fought against US; defeated, Mexico lost California and the Southwest to US, Santa Anna ruled and commanded armies (1846–47).

1848   Treaty of Guadalupe Hidalgo; ended the Mexican War.

1853–55   Santa Anna ruled as dictator; overthrown by a liberal revolution (begun 1854) led by Benito Juárez and others.

1854–76   *La Reforma,* period of liberal reforms.

1857   New liberal constitution adopted.

1858–61   War of Reform; Juárez served as provisional president; nationalized church property (1859) and began policy of reform in Mexico.

1861   Juárez elected president; policies of reform led to resentment by conservatives and European intervention; France moved to establish colonial empire in Mexico.

1863   French invaders defeated Mexican forces at the Battle of Puebla (May 17); Mexico City captured soon after.

1864–67   Austrian archduke Maximilian ruled as emperor of Mexico.

1865–67   French withdrew troops from Mexico (1865); Juárez forces launched successful campaign against Maximilian, who was captured and executed.

1867–72   Juárez in office as president; put down revolts; succeeded at his death by Sebastian Lerdo de Tejada.

1872–76   S. Lerdo de Tejada served as president.

1876   P. Díaz overthrew S. Lerdo de Tejada.

1876–1911   Díaz in power (except 1880–84); promoted economic development, but favored rich landowners at expense of poor; peonage increased and church again came back in favor.

1883–1949   Painter J. Orozco flourished; noted for his murals and frescoes.

1886–1957   Artist D. Rivera lived; known for his murals on the life and history of Mexico.

1889–1959   Poet A. Reyes lived; wrote the poem *Visión de Anáhuac.*

1898–1974   Artist D. Siqueiros lived; known for painting murals such as *March of Humanity.*

1911   Mexican Revolution began (May) with overthrow of P. Díaz by F. Madero.

1913   F. Madero overthrown and murdered (Feb.) by Gen. V. Huerta.

1914 Vera Cruz incident; US Marines occupied the city (Apr.–Nov.).

1914 V. Huerta forced from office by uprisings led by V. Carranza, F. Villa, and E. Zapata.

1914–20 Carranza served as president; restored order but there was continued resistance by F. Villa and E. Zapata.

1915 Gen. A. Obregón defeated F. Villa at the Battle of Celaya.

1916 F. Villa's raid on Columbus, New Mexico, led to US military expedition into Mexico; Villa evaded capture.

1917 Constitution established; provided for separation of church and state; communal lands restored to Indians; labor and other reforms.

1920–24 Gen. A. Obregón overthrew Carranza (1920) and served as president.

1924–28 Plutarco Elias Calles served as president.

1928 Obregón reelected president; assassinated before he could take office.

1929 Calles founded National Revolutionary party, Mexico's most powerful political party.

1934–40 L. Cardenas served as president; instituted many reforms; improved lot of Indians, distributed lands under ejido system, nationalized railroads, and expropriated foreign oil holdings.

1940–46 Manuel Ávila Camacho served as president; followed more conservative domestic policy; brought Mexico into WW II against the Axis (1942).

1945 Became a member of the UN.

1946 National Revolutionary party renamed the Institutional Revolutionary party.

1946–52 M. Alemán served as president; worked at modernization of agriculture and improvement of living conditions.

1948 Became a member of OAS.

1950 O. Paz published his book of essays, *El laberinto de la soledad.*

1952–58 Adolfo Ruiz Cortines in office as president.

1958–64 Adolfo López Mateos in office as president.

1964–70 Gustavo Díaz Ordaz in office as president; reforms enacted to aid poor, including seizure of some large estates.

1970–76 Luis Echeverría Álvarez in office as president; promoted ties with underdeveloped Third World countries.

1976–82 José López Portillo in office (Dec. 1) as president; publicly backed left wing regimes in Cuba and elsewhere while maintaining (sometimes strained) relations with US; drastically increased Mexican oil output, making Mexico world's fifth largest producer and thereby easing its economic problems; world oil glut in 1981 brought new economic crisis, however.

1980 Ixtoc I oil well capped (Mar.), ending disastrous spill into Gulf of Mexico; some 3 million barrels of oil discharged during 9-month effort to cap well.

1980 Mexico began enforcing 200-mile limit on tuna fishing off its coasts; US retaliated by banning imports of Mexican tuna (lifted in 1986).

1981 López met with US President R. Reagan to discuss growing problem of illegal Mexican aliens in US; new US immigration program to be established.

1982 López devalued the peso as economic problems worsened; government imposed austerity program.

1982 Mexican-owned banks nationalized (Sept.) as economic crisis worsened; inflation hit 70 percent and thousands of small businesses near bankruptcy.

1982 Mexico defaulted on its $80 billion foreign debt (Dec.).

1982–88 Miguel de la Madrid Hurtado, member of ruling PRI (Partido Revolucionario Institucional) party, in office as president following elections; notwithstanding his promises to clean up rampant corruption born of the 1977–81 oil boom, the new president's party was charged with election fraud in nearly every election held from 1985 onward; meanwhile, the country's finances floundered in the massive foreign debt crisis.

1983 Mexico negotiated new $5 billion loan through US banks (Mar.); talks with other creditors on rescheduling Mexico's debt continued.

1983 Price of tortillas rose 41 percent in July alone; meanwhile, right wing opposition group won sweeping victories in state and municipal elections.

1983 Senator and former director of Pemex, Mexico's state-run oil corporation, arrested for fraud involving some $34 million; some 89 public officials eventually held on corruption charges.

1984 Debtors' Summit attended by Mexico, which had a strong hand in organizing the meeting (July); participants called on US to reduce high interest rates.

1985 Ruling PRI party swept mid-term elections (July), winning every contest; widespread reports of vote fraud sparked riots, but results were not overturned.

1985 US Drug Enforcement Administration agent kidnapped and killed in Guadalajara (Feb. 7); US pressured government to identify and arrest killers.

1985 IMF refused Mexico's loan request (Sept.).

1985 Mexico City devastated by earthquake measuring 7.5 on Richter scale (Sept. 19); some 300 hotels and public buildings collapsed in downtown area; over 7,000 were killed and over 100,000 left homeless.

1986 Mexicans illegally crossing border into US in rapidly increasing numbers as government imposed new austerity measures; US, faced with huge numbers of illegal aliens, eventually had to take drastic steps.

1986 IMF granted $10 billion loan package to help Mexico refinance its foreign debt (July).

1987 Mexico negotiated deal with US Treasury for debt reduction (Dec.).

1988 New charges of election fraud following PRI party victory in national elections (July); PRI extended its 59-year domination of Mexican government, but lost its majority in the Chamber of Deputies.

1988– Carlo Salinas de Gortari, ruling PRI party member, in office as president (Dec.).

1989 Opposition party won race for governorship of Baja California Norte; marked first loss by ruling PRI party in a governor's race in 60 years.

1989 Government negotiated new debt reduction package with commercial banking creditors (July).

1990 Militant activists staged sit-ins at town halls in Guerrero (Mar.), charging PRI with election fraud; seven killed and hundreds wounded as police resorted to force to end demonstrations.

1990 Government to divest majority share in 19 banks nationalized in 1982 (May).

1991 Worsening air pollution in Mexico City forced government to shut down city's biggest—and government-owned—oil refinery (Mar.).

1991 Mexico signed a free-trade agreement with Chile (Sept.).

1992 Sewers exploded in Guadalajara, Mexico's second largest city (Apr. 22); 184 killed; explosions caused by leaking gasoline pipeline owned by state-run oil corporation, Pemex.

1992 World Bank approved $80 million to help clean up air and water pollution in Mexico City (Apr.).

1991 Privatization of state-owned banks started (June).

1991 Government signed free-trade pact with Colombia and Venezuela (July).

1992 North American Free Trade Agreement (NAFTA) set (Aug 12); Mexico, US, and Canada to eliminate tariffs and other trade barriers.

Meyer, Adolf 1866–1950. Swiss-born American psychiatrist. He originated the term "mental hygiene" and held that the cure of mental illness lay in dealing with the whole personality.

MGB *See* **GPU.**

Miani, Battle of British victory (Feb. 17, 1843) over the forces of the mirs of Sind. The British victory led to annexation of most of Sind into British India.

Michael 1596–1645. Russian tsar (1613–45), founder of the Romanov dynasty. His election ended the Time of Troubles. During his reign, Russia made peace with Sweden and Poland.

Michael 1921– . Rumanian king (1927–30, 1940–47), son of Carol II. He overthrew the dictatorship of I. Antonescu (1944) and supported the Allies in WW II. He was forced into exile by the Communist takeover (1947).

Michael I (~ Rhangabe) *d.* c845. Byzantine emperor (811–813). He supported the orthodox faith against the iconoclasts.

Michael I Rhangabe *See* **Michael I.**

Michael II *d.* 829. Byzantine emperor (820–829). He took the throne after his supporters assassinated his predecessor, Leo V. He was tolerant of both sides in the religious dispute between iconoclasts and orthodoxy.

Michael III 839–867. Byzantine emperor (842–867), last of the Amorian-Phrygian line. The controversy over iconoclasm was ended during his reign (843). He warred successfully against the Arabs and Slavs.

Michael VIII (~ Palaeologus) 1224–82. Byzantine emperor (1259–82). He recovered Constantinople (1261) from the Latins and formed a union with Pope Gregory X against Charles of Anjou. Its failure led to the massacre called the Sicilian Vespers (1282).

Michael Psellus 1018–1096. Byzantine philosopher, writer, and statesman. He served in imperial posts under emperors Michael V and Constantine IX and helped foster the study of Greek classics, notably Plato and Homeric literature, at the new imperial university. He served as prime minister under Empress Theodora (1055–56) and was virtual head of state during the reign of Michael VII Ducas (1071–78). He wrote voluminously on a variety of scholarly subjects, and his *Chronographia*, a chronicle of his times, is recognized as the best history of the period.

Michael the Brave *d.* 1601. Rumanian prince of Walachia (1593–1601). He captured and declared himself prince of Transylvania (1599) and Moldavia (1600), thereby uniting Rumania under his rule. His realm was divided after his death, but he is considered a Rumanian national hero.

Michel, Clemence Louise 1830–1905. French anarchist. She was a proponent of revolutionary socialist ideals and advocated violence and class war. She joined the fighting against government troops to defend the Paris Commune (1871) and was later court-martialed and imprisoned. Released in 1880, she continued to advocate revolution and was imprisoned again for inciting a riot. After her release she spent several years in exile in London, and then returned to France, spending the rest of her life lecturing.

Michelangelo (Michelangelo di Lodovico Buonarroti Simoni) 1475–1564. Italian artist, one of the towering figures of the Italian Renaissance. A gifted poet, painter, and sculptor, he is celebrated for such masterpieces as his statues of David and Moses, and the *Pietà* (1497). His painting of the Sistine Chapel took four years to complete (1508–12).

Michelet, Jules 1798–1874. French historian. He wrote the *Histoire de France*, an emotional and nationalistic work.

Michelin, André and Édouard 1853–1931; 1856–1940. French industrialists. Brothers, they invented and produced removable pneumatic tires and established the Michelin tire company.

Michelson, Albert Abraham 1852–1931. American physicist. He measured the speed of light, using an interferometer of his own design. The results of the Michelson-Morley experiment, conducted with Edward Williams Morley (1838–1923), contributed to A. Einstein's theory of relativity. He was awarded the Nobel Prize (1907).

Michener, James Albert 1907– . American author. He was awarded a Pulitzer Prize (1948) for his *Tales of the South Pacific* (1947). Among his novels are *Hawaii* (1959), *Centennial* (1974), and *Texas* (1985).

Michigan State in the north-central US, the 26th state. Michigan was first explored and settled by the French (17th cent.). It was ceded to Britain after the French and Indian War (1754–63), and was scene of the Indian revolt known as Pontiac's Rebellion (1763–66). It was ceded to the US (1783) and became part of the Northwest Territory (1787). After settlement of a boundary dispute with Ohio, Michigan became a state in 1837.

Mickiewiez, Adam 1798–1855. Polish poet. A romantic and patriot, he is known best for the epic *Pan Tadeusz.*

Micon *fl.* c460 BC. Greek painter and sculptor. He collaborated with Polygnotus on *The Greeks and the Amazons* and the mural on the Stoa Poikile at Athens.

Middle Ages Period in European history (c5th–15th cents.) between the fall of the Roman Empire and the discovery of the New World by Columbus (1492). It was the transition period from the ancient cultures to those of the modern world, and its beginning phase is sometimes referred to as the Dark Ages (*q.v.*). The Middle Ages were marked by the rise of the church, by the spread and collapse of feudalism, and by the formative stages of many of the modern European states.

Middle East Term denoting the countries of southwestern Asia and northeastern Africa, including parts of Turkey, Syria, Israel, Jordan, Iraq, Iran, Lebanon, all of the Arabian Peninsula, Egypt, and Libya.

Middle English Name given the language of medieval England and also a period in English literature (c1100–c1500). Middle English language replaced Old English and can be divided into three developmental periods: Early Middle English (c1100–c1250); Central Middle English (c1250–c1400); and Late Middle English (c1400–c1500). Middle English literature includes works by W. Langland, Sir T. Malory, G. Chaucer, and J. Gower.

Middle Kingdom Period in ancient Egyptian history, lasting from the latter half of the 11th dynasty through the 12th dynasty (c2000 BC–c1786 BC). It followed the First Intermediate Period, began with the rule of Amenemhet I and ended with the rule of Amenemhet IV. Egypt enjoyed commercial prosperity during this period, which also saw rule of the pharaohs as feudal lords, the transfer of the capital from Memphis to Itchtowe, the conquest of Lower Nubia, and a golden age of Egyptian literature and arts. The Middle Kingdom was followed by the Second Intermediate Period and the coming of the Hyksos.

Middleton, Thomas 1570?–1627. English dramatist. He wrote tragedies and satirical comedies on the mores of his time, usually in collaboration. Among his works are *Women Beware Women* and *The Changeling*.

Middle West (Midwest) American geographical designation, the collective name for the north central states of the US.

Midhat Pasha 1822–84. Turkish statesman. As grand vizier (1872, 1876–77), he was instrumental in obtaining the first constitution (1876) for the Ottoman Empire.

Midrash An interpretation of Hebrew Scriptures, using rabbinical commentaries.

Midway, Battle of US naval victory over the Japanese (June 3–6, 1942), during WW II. The battle was fought by carrier-based planes on both sides and marked the turning point for the US in the Pacific War. A Japanese task force, assembled to take US–held Midway Island, was intercepted (June 3) off Midway by aircraft of a US carrier force. The Japanese counterattacked with their aircraft, and the battle raged until June 6. Japanese losses included three carriers, 275 planes, one heavy cruiser, and three destroyers. US losses included one carrier, 150 planes, and a destroyer.

Mieris, Frans van 1635–81. Dutch painter known for his small genre and portrait paintings.

Mies van der Rohe, Ludwig 1886–1969. German-American architect. He was director of the Bauhaus in the 1930s. As professor of architecture (1938–58) at the Illinois Institute of Technology, he pioneered construction of functional glass-and-steel buildings.

Mifflin, Thomas 1744–1800. American Revolutionary leader. He was quartermaster general in the Revolutionary army and was involved in the Conway Cabal. He was first governor of Pennsylvania (1790–99).

Miguel 1802–66. Pretender to the Portuguese throne, son of John VI. An absolutist, he contested the succession of his brother Pedro, and later of Pedro's daughter Maria. He renounced his claim in 1834 after having ruled from 1828. (*See also* Portugal, 1828–33.)

Mikhailovich, Draja 1893?–1946. Serbian soldier. He led a guerrilla force against German occupation during WW II, then fought against the Communists. He was executed by Tito's forces.

Mikoyan, Anastas Ivanovich 1895–1978. Russian Communist statesman. A member of the Central Committee (1923–78), he held cabinet positions under J. Stalin and N. Khrushchev and was chairman of the Presidium of the Supreme Soviet (1964–65).

Milan 1854–1901. Prince (1868–82) and king (1882–89) of Serbia. By allying with Russia in the Russo-Turkish Wars, he gained Serbia's independence (1878) from the Ottoman Empire.

Milan, Edict of *See* Edict of Milan.

Milan Decree Decree issued (Dec. 17, 1807) by Napoleon, as part of the Continental System. It stated that ships trading with Great Britain lost their neutrality.

Mile End Concessions *See* Peasants' Revolt.

Miletus Ancient Greek city in Caria, now in Turkey. Once a prosperous Ionian seaport, it led in the Ionian revolt against Persia (499–94 BC). The Persians sacked the city (494 BC).

Milhaud, Darius 1892–1974. French composer, a pioneer in the use of polytonality. His works include the opera *Christophe Colomb* and the ballet *La Création du Monde* (1923).

military-industrial complex Collective term for the US defense establishment, including arms development, manufacturing and procurement. At the end of his term of office, President D. Eisenhower warned against its growing power and it continues to wield great influence, especially in promoting costly new weapons systems. During the Vietnam War the military-industrial complex was the target of numerous protests. The end of the war and the cutback in defense contracts during the late 1970s curtailed its power for a time.

Militia Ordinance Bill passed (1642) by the English Parliament that aggravated relations between Parliament and King Charles I, shortly before the start of the English Civil Wars (1642). Following Charles' attempt (Jan., 1642) to seize five members of the House of Commons, Parliament passed the Militia Ordinance, giving it control over the militia. Charles rejected (Mar.) the measure, and his supporters in Parliament joined him at York. The Parliament at London then delivered (June 2) its Nineteen Propositions, which included the ordinance, to the king.

Mill, James 1773–1836. British philosopher, historian, and economist. He adopted and contributed to the principles of his friend J. Bentham, the founder of utilitarianism. He wrote a *History of British India.*

Mill, John Stuart 1806–73. British philosopher and political economist, son of J. Mill. He further developed the utilitarian doctrines established by J. Bentham and the elder Mill, and formulated principles of inductive reasoning. His works include *A System of Logic* and *On Liberty.*

Millais, Sir John Everett 1829–96. English painter. He was a founder (1848) of the Pre-Raphaelite brotherhood. His works include the controversial *Christ in the House of His Parents.*

Millay, Edna St. Vincent 1892–1950. American poet, one of the leading poets of the 20th cent. She was awarded the Pulitzer Prize (1923) for *The Ballad of the Harp Weaver.*

millennialism Christian belief in the millennium, a period of 1,000 years before the end of the world during which Christ and the saints will rule on earth.

millennium Period of one thousand years. In Christianity, the millennium refers to the time when Jesus will reappear and rule on earth.

Miller, Arthur 1915– . American playwright, twice winner of the Pulitzer Prize (1950, 1956). His plays include *Death of a Salesman, The Crucible,* and *A View from the Bridge.*

Miller, Henry 1891–1980. American author. His books *Tropic of Cancer* and *Tropic of Capricorn,* banned in the US until the 1960s because of their sexual content, influenced the development of modern literature and helped to break traditional literary barriers.

Miller, William 1782–1849. American religious leader. As founder of the Second Adventists, or Millerites, he predicted the Second Coming of Christ in 1843. His movement evolved into the Adventist church (*q.v.*).

Millerand, Alexandre 1859–1943. French statesman. He was minister of war (1912–13, 1914–15) and president of France (1920–24). He was forced from office by a coalition of the political left.

Milligan, ex parte US Supreme Court decision (1866) that military tribunals could judge civilians only in the absence of civil courts. The decision limited presidential, congressional, and military powers over civilians in wartime.

Millikan, Robert Andrews 1868–1953. American physicist, noted for his work on the photoelectric effect and for measuring the charge on the electron. He was awarded the Nobel Prize (1923) and discovered cosmic rays (1925).

Mill Springs, Battle of Union victory (Jan. 19, 1862) over the Confederates in the American Civil War, at Mill Springs, Kentucky. The battle was the first major Union victory in the West.

Milne, A(lan) A(lexander) 1882–1956. English author, famous for his children's books, *Winnie-the-Pooh* and *The House at Pooh Corner.*

Milner, Alfred Milner, 1st Viscount 1854–1925. British statesman. He was a high administrator in South Africa (1897–1905), and his inflexible stand furthered tensions leading to the South African (Boer) War (1899–1902).

Milo 95–47 BC. Roman politician. His rivalry with Clodius led to Clodius' murder and Milo's exile to Massilia. Milo's advocate, Cicero, too afraid to speak at his trial, later published his oration *Pro Milone.* Later returning from exile, he was killed during the civil wars.

Milo of Croton (Milon) *fl.* late 6th cent. BC. Greek athlete, renowned for his wrestling skill and feats of strength at the Olympic and Pythian games.

Milosh (~ Obrenovic) 1780–1860. Serbian prince (1817–39, 1858–60) and founder of modern Serbia. He led the revolt against the Turks and was named hereditary prince (1827). He founded the Obrenovic dynasty.

Milosz, Czeslaw 1911– . Polish-American poet, author, and critic. After serving in diplomatic posts for the Polish government, he defected to France in 1951 and then moved to the US. In addition to poetry, he has published collected essays, such as *The Captive Mind* (1953). Milosz won the Nobel Prize for Literature in 1980.

Miltiades *d.* 489 BC. Athenian general of the aristocratic Philaid family. As one of the commanders of the Athenian forces, he defeated the Persians at Marathon (490 BC).

Milton, John 1608–74. English poet. Milton began his career as a poet while still at Cambridge University. Acclaimed for his pastoral poem *Lycidas,* he nevertheless devoted himself to writing essays supporting the movement to reform the Church of England. His defense of the Commonwealth haunted him after the Restoration. Though blind from 1652, Milton dictated the works for which he is known best, *Paradise Lost* and *Paradise Regained.*

Milvian Bridge Roman bridge, constructed (109 BC) over the Tiber as part of the Flaminian Way. Here Constantine defeated Maxentius (AD 312) and thus became sole ruler in the Western Roman Empire. Here too, according to tradition, he saw the vision of a cross in the sky that led him to adopt Christianity. Constantine soon after brought about toleration of Christianity in the empire.

Minden, Battle of Battle (Aug. 1, 1759) between the French and allied Prussian and British troops during the Seven Years' War (1756–63). Some 45,000 Prussian and British soldiers routed 60,000 French soldiers in this battle at Minden (now located in West Germany).

Mindon Min 1814–78. Burmese king (1853–78) and founder of Mandalay. During his reign he was forced to grant large concessions to the British.

Mindszenty, József 1892–1975. Hungarian Roman Catholic clergyman, primate of Hungary (1946–74). Arrested (1948) for treason, he was freed during the 1956 revolution, then took asylum in the US embassy until 1971, when he left Hungary.

Ming Dynasty of native Han emperors (1368–1644) who greatly expanded the Chinese Empire. Under its rulers the empire came to include all or parts of Vietnam, Burma, Turkistan, Korea, and Mongolia. Hongwu, founder of the dynasty, came to power (1368) and ousted (by 1371) the Mongols of the Yuan dynasty. During the long reign of the Ming emperors the Chinese civil service system was reinstituted; Confucian-

ism was state-supported; exploratory voyages (1405–33) as far west as Arabia were made; European settlements were established (16th cent.) at Canton and Macao; Christian missionaries arrived; and the arts, especially ceramics and architecture, flourished. A succession of weak rulers, heavy taxes, and dissent among factions in government led to peasant revolts and the fall of the dynasty (1644) to the Qing (Manchu) dynasty.

Ministry of All Talents *See* **Grenville, William Wyndham.**

Minnesota North-central US state, the 32d state. First explored by the French (17th cent.), it became an important fur-trading region. The part of Minnesota east of the Mississippi was part of the Northwest Territory, and that west of the Mississippi was ceded to the US by the Louisiana Purchase (1803). Minnesota was admitted to the Union (1858) and fought for the Union in the Civil War. It was a center for the growth of the Granger movement, and also for the Populist party movement of the 1890s.

Minoan civilization Bronze Age culture that developed on Crete (c3000 BC–1000 BC). One of the ancient Greek Aegean civilizations, it was for a time a major maritime power in the Mediterranean. By 1500 BC the Minoans had a well-developed written language and had become skilled in working ceramics and bronze. The Minoan capital at Cnossus, with its luxurious palace, was twice destroyed (and rebuilt) in the second millennium BC, possibly by earthquakes and/or invasions by the Myceneans. The palace was destroyed a last time (c1400) and, soon after, the Minoan civilization disappeared. This civilization is generally divided into three periods: Early Minoan (c3000 BC–c2200 BC); Middle Minoan (c2200 BC–c1500 BC); and Late Minoan (c1500 BC–c1000 BC). The Mycenaean civilization predominated after the fall of the Minoans.

Minseito Japanese political party formed in 1927. A centrist party, it had ties with Japanese business interests and sought better relations with the West. The Minseito, formed from the earlier Kenseito party, was a major party in the years before WW II. The party was dissolved in 1940 after the militarists came to power. A new Democratic party formed after WW II absorbed much of the Minseito party's membership.

minstrel In medieval Europe, a musician, singer, juggler, or other kind of entertainer. While many traveled, others were employed as court entertainers.

Minuit, Peter c1580–1638.   Dutch colonial governor of New Netherland who purchased Manhattan Island from the Indians for $24 worth of trinkets in 1626. He founded New York City (then New Amsterdam) by building a fort at the south end of the island. Later, in Swedish service, he founded New Sweden (1638) on the Delaware.

minutemen   Colonial militia volunteers before and during the American Revolution. The Massachusetts provincial congress organized the volunteers in 1774 and they eventually fought the British at Lexington and Concord (1775), the opening skirmish of the Revolution. Minutemen were absorbed into the regular Colonial army soon after. Early in the Revolution other colonies also formed militias of minutemen, so-called because they were to be ready for duty with only a minute's notice.

mir   Peasant community in Russia. The mir was self-governing until the 17th cent. and thereafter controlled peasant lands in its locality. The mirs were abolished (1917) after the Russian Revolution.

Mirabeau, Honoré Gabriel Riquetti, comte de 1749–91.   French revolutionary politician. Imprisoned by his father during his reckless youth, he later became a popular and powerful orator in the early days of the Revolution. Elected to the States-General (1789) and later president of the National Assembly (1791). He advocated establishment of a constitutional monarchy.

Mirabeau, Victor Riquetti, marquis de 1715–89. French political economist, father of H. Mirabeau. His physiocratic philosophy was set forth in *The Friend of Man, or Treatise on the Population.*

Miramón, Miguel 1832–67.   Mexican general. Miramón opposed the leader of liberal forces, B. Juárez, and served as chief marshal to Emperor Maximilian, with whom he was captured and executed.

Miranda, Francisco de 1750–1816.   Venezuelan revolutionary. He fought the Spanish, briefly gained Venezuelan independence (1810), and ruled with dictatorial powers. He was forced to surrender to the counterattacking Spanish (1812) and died in prison.

Miranda v. *Ferguson*   US Supreme Court decision (1966) establishing an individual's rights during a police arrest. The suspect named Miranda had

confessed during police questioning without having been informed of his right to have an attorney present. The Court decision held that the Constitution's Fifth Amendment protects individuals from self-incrimination even when they are in police custody, and ordered that a suspect's rights must be read to him before questioning. The ruling has been limited by subsequent court decisions.

Miró, Joan 1893–1974.   Spanish artist. A surrealist painter, he used pure colors and abstract shapes in his fantasies, such as *Dog Barking at the Moon.*

Mirza Ali Muhammad   *See* **Bab, The.**

Mise of Amiens   Arbitrated agreement by which the Provisions of Oxford (*q.v.*) were annulled (Jan. 23, 1264). English king Henry III, after disputes with his barons, took the question of the provisions to French king Louis IX for mediation. Louis ruled in favor of Henry.

Mishima, Yukio (Kimitake Hiraoka) 1925–70. Japanese writer best known for his novels concerning the conflict between Eastern and Western cultural influences in Japanese life. The decline of Japanese values and traditions is the major theme of his last work, *The Sea of Fertility.*

Mishna   Collection of Jewish oral laws, divided into six orders: seeds (Zeraim), festivals (Moed), women (Nashim), damages (Nezikim), sacrifices (Kodashim), purifications (Tohorot). With commentaries included in the Gemara, it constitutes the Talmud (*q.v.*).

Mississippi   US state in the Southeast, the 20th state. The first settlement was established at Biloxi by the French in 1699. The area was held by the British and the Spanish after 1763 and was ceded to the US in 1783. The Mississippi Territory was created in 1798 and included the present states Mississippi and Alabama. The western section became the state of Mississippi in 1817, and its constitution was adopted in 1890. It was the second state to secede in the American Civil War (1861) and was readmitted in 1870. Mississippi was a focal point of the drive to win civil rights for blacks during the 1960s.

Mississippi Bubble   *See* **Mississippi Scheme.**

Mississippi Scheme (~ Bubble)   Plan to exploit the lower Mississippi valley and other French colonial territories. French comptroller general J. Law bought up (1717) colonization rights to the Mississippi Territory and in subsequent financial manipulations won control over other

French possessions. His Mississippi Company, which attempted to finance the French national debt in 1720, promoted a speculative boom that ended in financial disaster (Oct., 1720).

Missouri State in the central US, the 24th state. J. Marquette and Louis Jolliet first explored the area (1673, 1683), which was claimed by the French as part of the Louisiana Territory. In 1803, it became part of the US by the Louisiana Purchase (*q.v.*), and the Missouri Territory was created in 1812. The dispute over whether to admit territories as slave states resulted (1820) in the Missouri Compromise (*q.v.*), and Missouri was admitted as a slave state in 1821. The present constitution was adopted in 1945.

Missouri Compromise US legislation passed (1820–21) to maintain the balance between slaveholding and free states. This compromise between the proslavery South and the abolitionists in the North was largely engineered by Rep. H. Clay. It remained in force until replaced (1850) by the Compromise of 1850, which established the doctrine of popular sovereignty (*q.v.*). The issue was first raised (1819) when Missouri applied for admission to the union as a slave state. With states then equally balanced (11 each) between slave and free, the Senate rejected the measure (Feb., 1819). The final compromise measure (passed Mar., 1820), however, provided for the admission of Maine as a free state, Missouri as a slave state, and banned slavery in the Louisiana Purchase territory north of Arkansas. Separate legislation requiring the Missouri constitution to guarantee rights of Negro freedmen (Mar., 1821) held up admission of Missouri until Aug., 1821.

Mistral, Frédéric 1830–1914. French poet. He was a founder of the Félibrige, an association for the promotion of the Provençal language, and wrote a Provençal-French dictionary.

Mistral, Gabriela (*pseud.* of Godoy Alcayaga, Lucila) 1889–1957. Chilean poet. The first Latin American woman to win the Nobel Prize for Literature (1945), she was also a teacher and cultural ambassador to the League of Nations and United Nations. Among her works are *Ternura* (*Tenderness,* 1924), *Tala* (*Destruction,* 1938), and *Lagar* (*The Wine Press,* 1954).

Mitchell, Margaret 1900–49. American novelist, who wrote one book, *Gone with the Wind,* an immediate and lasting success. She won the Pulitzer Prize (1937).

Mitchell, (Billy) William Lendrum 1879–1936. American army general and pilot. He advocated creation of an independent air force and increased use of air power in wartime. He was court-martialed (1925) for his criticism of military leadership.

Mithradates VI (Mithridates ˜) c131 BC–63 BC. King of Pontus (120–63 BC). He waged the three Mithradatic Wars (*q.v.*) against the Romans and was finally defeated by Pompey.

Mithradatic Wars 1. First (88–84 BC). War between Mithradates VI, king of Pontus, and Rome. Taking advantage of unrest in the Roman province of Asia and the upheavals brought about by the Social War (91–88 BC), Mithradates overran the province. While the struggles for power continued at Rome, Roman armies, under L. Sulla, met Mithradates' armies (87) in Greece. By the battles of Chaeronea (86) and Orchomenos (85), Sulla forced the invaders out of Greece and later (84) forced Mithradates to give up all his conquests. 2. Second (83–81 BC). War between Mithradates VI and Rome. The Romans, under Murena, attacked Cappadocia and Pontus. It ended with the restoration of territories Mithradates lost during the war. 3. Third (74–63). War between Mithradates VI, his son-in-law, and Rome. Mithradates' son-in-law, Armenian king Tigranes I, took over Cappadocia and Syria. Roman consul L. Lucullus won early victories against Mithradates and Tigranes (73) but was forced to break off fighting (68) when his troops mutinied. Under command of Pompey (66–63), the Romans completed the conquest and annexed Pontus to the Asian province.

Mithraism Major religion of the ancient world, widespread within the Roman Empire shortly before adoption of Christianity (4th cent. AD). Roman Mithraism, which in some ways resembled Christianity, was concerned with the battle between good and evil, and held out the promise of immortality to its followers. Worship of the god Mithras flourished in Persia (5th cent. BC) and subsequently spread throughout the Mediterranean world. In Rome it flourished by the 2d cent. AD. With the official adoption of Christianity by the late 4th cent., Mithraism was suppressed in the Roman empire and soon disappeared.

Mithridates VI *See* **Mithradates VI.**

Mitre, Bartolomé 1821–1906. Argentine statesman and general. Mitre helped to overthrow

J. de Rosas (1861) and became president (1862–68). He succeeded in uniting the country and brought about a period of prosperity.

Mitterrand, François 1916– . French president (1981–). A Socialist, Mitterrand at first installed a left-wing government (including four Communists) and implemented a Socialist reform program. He increased taxes on business and the wealthy, raised the minimum wage by 10 percent, and began nationalization of selected industries. Rightist opposition and an economic downturn forced him to install a center-right government (1986) and to privatize scores of state-run companies. Reelected in 1988, Mitterrand again installed a leftist government. Domestically, his administration was marked by increasing unrest by labor, students, and other groups and by installation of France's first female prime minister (1991–92). In foreign policy, his government supported German unification, promoted the Maastricht Treaty on European unification, joined the Allied coalition (albeit reluctantly) in the Persian Gulf War, and maintained friendly relations with the USSR and East European nations (and their successor states).

Moabites Ancient Semitic people from the Transjordan plateau east of the Dead Sea. Their kingdom, Moab, is often mentioned in the Old Testament [Gen 19:37; Exodus 15:15]. It ceased to exist after conquest by the Assyrians (8th cent. BC).

Moabite Stone Ancient inscription. This ancient slab dates from 850 BC. Written by the Moabite Mesha in Moabite, a dialect of Hebrew, it describes his victory against Israel.

Mobile Bay, Battle of Union victory (Aug. 5, 1864) in a naval battle during the American Civil War (1861–65). Seeking to neutralize the Confederate port at Mobile Bay, Union land forces attacked (Aug. 3) and captured forts at the entrance to the bay. The Union fleet, commanded by Admiral D. Farragut, then broke through a minefield, entered the bay (Aug. 5), and forced the Confederate fleet to surrender. It was during this battle that Farragut uttered his famous order to continue the attack, "Damn the torpedoes."

Mobutu Sese Seko (Mobutu, Joseph Désiré) 1930– . President (1965–) of the Republic of Zaire (formerly the Congo).

Moctezuma *See* **Montezuma.**

Model Parliament Two representative bodies that figured in the development of the British Parliament. 1. Assembly convened (1265) during the Barons' War (1263–67) by S. de Montfort. Present were two citizens (burgesses) from each city and two knights from each shire in England. 2. Assembly convened (1295) by King Edward I. Representatives of the higher clergy, knights, burgesses, and lower clergy attended.

Modena, Mary of *See* **Mary of Modena.**

modern art Revolution in Western art that began in the late 19th cent. with impressionism (*q.v.*) and continues into the present with such schools as abstract expressionism (*q.v.*) and Op art (*q.v.*). The art is generally characterized by the unconventional use of color, imagery, spontaneity, and the artist's personal vision of the subject matter.

Modernism Modern religious movement (19th–20th cents.) that interpreted traditional Christian doctrines in a way believed more compatible with the teachings of modern philosophy and the findings of modern science. A school of thought of this name among Roman Catholics was condemned as heretical by Pope Pius X (1907).

Modernismo Movement among Spanish poets. It began in Latin America (late 19th cent.) with publication of Azul (1888), a collection by R. Dario. The movement that grew out of this work was largely a rebellion against the Romantic and naturalistic traditions in Spanish poetry and involved exotic imagery and unconventional meter and rhythm.

Modestinus, Herennius *fl.* c250 BC. Roman jurist. Modestinus was a student of Ulpian and was one of Rome's most distinguished and influential judges.

Modigliani, Amedeo 1884–1920. Italian modernist painter and sculptor. He is known for his characteristic elongation of form and use of muted color in his paintings.

Modjopahit Empire *See* **Majapahit Empire.**

Moesia Ancient province of the Roman Empire (from AD 15), situated in what is today southern Serbia and northern Bulgaria. It was later divided into Upper and Lower Moesia.

Mogal *See* **Mughal.**

Mohács, Battle of Battle (Aug. 29, 1526) in which Suleiman I of Turkey defeated and killed Louis II of Hungary. This led to more than 150 years of Turkish domination in Hungary.

Mohammed *See* **Muhammad.**

Mohegan Indians North American Indian tribe important in Colonial New England. Following the Pequot War (*q.v.*), the Mohegans became a powerful tribe in southern New England. The tribe gradually sold off its lands to white settlers and thereafter lived on a reservation in Connecticut.

Mohican *See* **Mahican Indians.**

Moholy-Nagy, László 1895–1946. Hungarian painter, designer, photographer, and teacher. He taught at the Bauhaus school (1923–29) in Germany and founded a school of design in Chicago (1939).

Moki *See* **Hopi Indians.**

Molay, Jacques de 1243?–1314. Last grand master of the Knights Templars (*q.v.*). Philip IV of France had de Molay and his followers arrested (1307) for heresy in a move to break the order's power. Under torture, de Molay confessed, then recanted, and was burned at the stake.

Moldavia Historic former principality now located in modern Rumania. Moldavia won independence from the Hungarian monarchy (c1349) and resisted the Ottoman Turks until the 16th cent. Thereafter it remained under their control until the Russo-Turkish War (1828–29). By the Treaty of Adrianople, Moldavia came under the protection of Russia, though it continued to recognize Turkish suzerainty. Following the Crimean War (1853–56), Moldavia became largely independent and, in 1861, it formally united with neighboring Wallachia to form the modern state of Rumania. For more on the early history of Moldavia, *see* Rumania.

Moldova (*formerly* Moldavian Soviet Socialist Republic) Independent state located between Rumania and the Ukraine and now a member of the Commonwealth of Independent States (CIS). The original autonomous Soviet republic was formed from lands along Rumania's eastern border in 1924 and in 1940 was created the Moldavian Soviet Socialist Republic, with the addition of much of Bessarabia. The Rumanians captured the territory in 1941, holding it until the Soviets, pushing Axis armies westward, reoccupied Moldavia in 1944. Moldavia was among the first republics to push for independence from the USSR. Unrest over efforts to make Moldavian the republic's official language (1989–90) culminated in a declaration that the 1940 annexa-tion of Moldavia, which made it a constituent republic, was illegal. The USSR central government voided the decree, but Moldavia subsequently refused to consider looser federations proposed by Soviet leader M. Gorbachev. Just days after the failed Soviet coup, Moldavia declared its independence (Aug. 27), changed its name to Moldova, and joined the CIS on Dec. 21. Meanwhile, ethnic Russians and Ukrainians who make up the majority population in the Trans-Dniester region of eastern Moldavia, voted to secede from Moldova in Dec., because they feared Moldova would soon merge with Rumania. Fighting continued into 1992, though by mid-year a ceasefire plan had been agreed upon. *See also* Commonwealth of Independent States, 1989–92.

Molière (*pseud.* of Jean Baptiste Poquelin) 1622–73. Great French playwright. Originally an actor, Molière headed his own touring company. However, he is remembered for his brilliant comedies that satirized the characters and society of his times. Among his many works are *Tartuffe, The School for Husbands, The School for Wives, The Doctor in Spite of Himself,* and *The Misanthrope.*

Molina, Luis 1535–1600. Spanish Jesuit who wrote *Concordia liberi arbitrii cum gratiae donis.* In it he articulated his doctrine of Molinism, which sought to reconcile free will and divine grace.

Molinism *See* **Molina, Luis.**

Molinos, Miguel de 1640–97. Spanish priest who founded quietism (*q.v.*), spiritual passiveness. In 1685, he was condemned by the Inquisition and died in prison.

Molly Maguires Irish-American terrorist group active (1860s–70s) in the Pennsylvania coalmining regions. Reacting against poor working and living conditions there, this secret group intimidated and murdered mine company officials and engaged in acts of sabotage. Pinkerton detectives suppressed the group in 1877.

Molnár, Ferenc 1878–1952. Hungarian novelist and playwright. He wrote the novel *The Paul Street Boys* and the plays *Liliom* and *The Swan.*

Molotov, Vyacheslav Mikhailovich (*orig.* Skriabin, ˜) 1890–1986. Soviet statesman. An active member of the Bolsheviks from 1906, he was appointed to the party Central Committee (1921) after the revolution. Supporting Stalin after Lenin's death, Molotov was rewarded by being made a member of the Politburo in 1926.

He served as prime minister (actually, chairman of a ruling council) from 1930–41, and as foreign minister from 1939–49 (and again 1953–56). During WW II, he played an important role in the Soviet war effort, in addition to lending his name to the Molotov cocktail, a bottle of flammable liquid. As foreign minister, he was chief Soviet spokesman for international affairs during WW II and the early Cold War years. A hard-line Stalinist, he joined others who tried unsuccessfully to depose N. Khrushchev (1957). Khrushchev then appointed him ambassador to Outer Mongolia and later expelled him from the Communist party (1964). Molotov was reinstated in 1984.

Moltke, Helmuth von 1800–91. Prussian field marshal. As chief of the general staff (1858–88), he was responsible for Prussian successes in the war against Denmark (1864), the Austro-Prussian War (1866), and the Franco-Prussian War (1870–71).

Moltke, Helmuth von 1848–1916. German army chief of general staff (1906–14). He changed the Schlieffen Plan (q.v.) at the outbreak of WW I, which some believed weakened the offensive against France and prolonged the fighting. The success of the original plan was by no means certain, however.

Mommsen, Theodor 1817–1903. German historian known for his *History of Rome.* He received the Nobel Prize for literature in 1902.

Monaco Independent principality located near the border between France and Italy on the Mediterranean coast. The population is 29,000 and the capital is Monaco-Ville. Believed to have been settled by the Phoenicians, Monaco became an independent state in the 13th cent. and has been ruled by the Grimaldi dynasty since 1297. It was annexed by France (1793–1814), came under the protection of Sardinia (1815–60), and was ceded back to France (1860), which restored its sovereignty under French protection (1861). A constitution was promulgated in 1911 and the current one was adopted in 1962. The principality has been ruled by Prince Rainier III (1923–   ) since 1949.

monarchianism Christian heresy (2d–3d cents. AD). It held that God the Father and Jesus are one, as opposed to two persons in one being. Two forms of monarchianism developed, dynamic and modalistic, both of which were opposed by the church.

monasticism Religious movement in which individuals seek spiritual perfection by living apart from the general society. Monks generally live communally in their monasteries (though in some monastic movements they live as hermits). Their lives are strictly regulated by the monastic rule (often ascetic) and in some monastic traditions worship is the central focus of their existence. Monasticism has been a part of various religions, including Christianity (Western and Eastern), Hinduism, Buddhism, Islam, and Jainism. In the Western Christian church, monasticism generally arose (6th cent.) and the teachings of Saint Benedict were influential in establishing its characteristic form. Thereafter, monasticism spread throughout Europe and spawned many important orders (*see* Benedictines, Carthusians, and Cistercians). Further, these orders were of great importance as centers of learning in an otherwise unstable medieval European society and, by their work as copyists, preserved many of the ancient classics.

Monck, George, 1st duke of Albemarle (Monk, ⁀) 1608–70. English general. A Royalist at the outbreak of the English Civil Wars, he was captured by the Parliamentarians (1644). After the death of Charles I, he served under O. Cromwell in fighting in Ireland and Scotland. He later played a central role in effecting the restoration of the monarchy under Charles II.

Mondale, Walter Frederick 1928–   . US vice-president (1977–81) under President J. Carter. He was early identified with liberal Democratic politics in Minnesota and became US senator (1964–77) from the state. Mondale failed in his 1984 bid for the presidency.

Mondrian, Piet 1872–1944. Dutch artist. He was a founder of the De Stijl movement in abstract art and developed an abstract style called neoplasticism.

Monet, Claude 1840–1926. French artist, a founder of impressionism (q.v.). Noted especially for his many landscapes, Monet developed a characteristic style using color to emphasize the effects of light. Among his many important works are *Water Lilies* (1906), *Haystacks* (1891), and *Rouen Cathedral.*

Mongkut *See* Chakkri dynasty.

Mongol Empire Great Asian empire founded (13th cent.) by the Mongol conqueror Genghis Khan (q.v.). After uniting the Mongol tribes under him (1206), Genghis Khan invaded northern China and subdued Korea. He next led his fierce bands westward, conquered Khorezm, the region of modern Iran and Iraq, and part of Russia, and raided northern India. On his death in 1227, Genghis' son Ogadai became the imperial ruler (great khan), and each of his other sons ruled a part of the empire (khanate). In the west, Mongols under Batu Khan conquered Russia and there established (1241) the Khanate of the Golden Horde (*q.v.*), or Kipchak Empire, that ruled Russia until the 15th cent. In Persia, the Mongol conqueror Hulagu Khan established the Il-Khan dynasty which ruled there (1258–1353). Kublai Khan became great khan in 1260 and moved the Mongol capital to China, where he built a splendid city. He founded the Yuan dynasty, which ruled China until the rise of the Ming dynasty (1368). Under Tamerlane (reigned 1360–1405), the Mongols of the Timurid (*q.v.*) Empire, in central Asia, rose to importance for a time. Finally the Mongol conqueror Baber established the Mughal (*q.v.*) dynasty in India (1526–1707). From the 15th cent., however, the history of the empire was one of decline and power struggles between tribal factions. Finally Mongolia itself was conquered by the Manchus (17th–18th cents.).

Mongolia Historic region located in east-central Asia, to the north of China proper. It is divided today between the Mongolian People's Republic (Outer Mongolia) and Inner Mongolia, now part of China. From ancient times it was the home of nomadic peoples who regularly threatened the Chinese Empire from the north. The region rose to prominence in the 13th cent. as the seat of Genghis Khan's Mongol Empire (*q.v.*). The decline of the Mongol Empire brought Chinese control over both Inner (southern) and Outer (northern) Mongolia (by the 17th cent.). Outer Mongolia regained its independence (1921) as the Mongolian People's Republic (*q.v.*). The Japanese captured parts of Inner Mongolia in the 1930s, during the Second Sino-Japanese War, but these territories were restored to China following WW II.

Mongolia (*formerly* Mongolian People's Republic; Outer Mongolia) Republic located between north-central China and the USSR, in east-central Asia. The population is 2,185,000 and the capital is Ulan Bator. This part of the historic region of Mongolia (*q.v.*) became an independent kingdom during the Chinese Revolution of 1911. The Chinese reoccupied the territory (1919) but

were driven out by White Russians (1921) at the close of the Russian Civil War. Russian Communist troops in turn drove out the White Russians, and Mongolia was proclaimed an independent state under the Living Buddha. After the death of the Living Buddha, Mongolia was proclaimed a republic (1924) and came under the control of Communists, through the Mongolian People's Revolutionary Party (MPRP). Imposition of the Communist system and persecution of Buddhist priests resulted in the exodus of priests, leading thousands of followers, and much livestock, to China (Lama Rebellion, 1932). Mongolia entered into a formal alliance with the USSR in 1936 and remained a Soviet satellite state until recent times. It was admitted to the UN in 1961 and supported the Soviets in their ideological conflict with the Chinese (1960s–80s), though relations with China improved as Sino-Soviet relations thawed in the 1980s. A 20-year friendship treaty with the USSR was signed in 1966 and an agreement for Soviet economic aid was completed in 1970. The USSR withdrew a fifth of its troops from Mongolia in 1987, and in 1989 began withdrawing most of those remaining there. By an agreement concluded in 1990, all remaining Soviet troops were to be withdrawn by 1992. Economic stagnation and increased opposition to Mongolia's Communist government mirrored events in East Europe, and 1989–90 was marked by unrest and mass demonstrations for political reform. Constitutional guarantees of supremacy for the ruling MPRP were abolished in 1990. Pressure for reform continued, however, and a presidential system of government with multiple political parties was adopted. A new constitution was adopted (Jan. 1992). It established a unicameral legislature (Great Hural) and shortened the country's name to Mongolia.

Mongols Nomadic Asian people. They rose to importance in the 13th cent. under Genghis Khan who founded the vast Mongol Empire (*q.v.*). His descendants founded successor states, such as those of the Chinese Yuan dynasty, the Russian Golden Horde, the Timur Empire and the Mughal Empire. Present-day Mongolia is divided between Russia (Outer Mongolia) and China (Inner Mongolia).

Monitor* and *Merrimack Two ironclad warships during the American Civil War that fought the first battle (Mar. 9, 1862) between armored warships. The Union *Monitor,* commanded by Lt.

John L. Worden (1818–97), and the Confederate *Merrimack,* then named the *Virginia* and commanded by Lt. Catesby Jones (1821–77), engaged in battle at Hampton Roads, Virginia. After an inconclusive battle, both ships withdrew and never fought again. The *Monitor* foundered and sank (Dec., 1862) and the *Merrimack* was destroyed (May, 1862) to prevent its capture.

Monmouth, Battle of (Monmouth Courthouse, ~) Indecisive battle (June 28, 1778) during the American Revolution (1775–83). British troops, then retreating from Philadelphia under Gen. H. Clinton's command, were being pursued by Gen. G. Washington's forces. Washington ordered an attack on the British rear at Monmouth, New Jersey. But the action was mishandled by Gen. C. Lee and only the arrival of Washington's main force prevented defeat. That night the British withdrew and eventually arrived safely in New York. Casualties numbered 300 to 400 on both sides.

Monmouth, James Scott, duke of 1649–85. English nobleman, illegitimate son of Charles II and rival of the duke of York (later James II) for the throne. The favorite of anti-Catholic factions in England, he became involved in the Rye House Plot (*q.v.*). After the accession of James II, Monmouth attempted a rebellion against him. Monmouth's makeshift force was defeated at Sedgemoor (July 16, 1685) and he was beheaded.

Monmouth Courthouse, Battle of *See* **Monmouth, Battle of.**

Monmouth's Revolt *See* **Monmouth, James Scott, duke of.**

Monnet, Jean 1888–1979. French political economist and statesman. He drafted the Monnet Plan (1947) for the rebuilding of postwar French economy, the Schuman Plan that resulted in the European Coal and Steel Community, and headed the Action Committee for the United States of Europe (from 1956).

Monocacy, Battle of American Civil War battle (July 9, 1864) fought near Frederick, Maryland. Some 6,000 federal troops, under Gen. L. Wallace, were defeated by the 14,000-man army of Gen. J. Early. The action, however, delayed Early's advance on Washington and thus gave Gen. U. Grant time to strengthen the capital's defenses.

Monophysitism Controversial doctrine of the early Christian church contending that Jesus had

but one nature (divine) and not two (human and divine). The concept had its beginnings in 4th cent. Apollinarianism and developed as a reaction to the extreme dualism of Nestorianism. Monophysitism was denounced as a heresy by the Council of Chalcedon (AD 451), though the council's attempt to formulate a compromise doctrine failed. Proponents of Monophysitism, such as Eutyches, continued the dispute and a schism soon developed between the Western church and the Monophysite Eastern Church. The schism was officially ended (519) by Emperor Justin I, who upheld the Council of Chalcedon. Nevertheless Monophysites persisted and, though persecuted, eventually formed the Coptic, Jacobite, and Armenian churches (all Monophysite).

monotheism Religious doctrine. Monotheism holds that there is only one God, as opposed to polytheism or henotheism, which recognize many gods. For the history of the world's major monotheistic religions, *see* Judaism, Christianity, and Islam.

Monothelitism Controversial doctrine of the Christian church contending that Jesus had two natures (human and divine) but only one will (divine). It was put forward (622) and promulgated (638) as official doctrine within the Byzantine Empire by Heraclius I. An attempt to provide an acceptable compromise to the dispute over Monophysitism, it created a furor instead. Opposed by popes in the Western church, Monothelitism was condemned (649) by a Lateran Council called by Pope Saint Martin I. Emperor Constans II seized and exiled the pope in retaliation and it was not until the accession of Constantine IV (668) that attempts were made to settle the controversy. Constantine called the Third Council of Constantinople (680), which subsequently denounced the doctrine as a heresy. Monothelitism, though briefly revived (711–13), thereafter died out.

Monroe, James 1758–1831. Fifth US president (1817–25), successor to J. Madison. Monroe distinguished himself during the American Revolution and he was wounded in the Battle of Trenton. After the war he was elected to the Virginia legislature (1782) and the Continental Congress (1783–86). A supporter of states' rights, he opposed the centralized government set up by the Constitution. As US senator (1790–94), he supported T. Jefferson against the Federalists. He served (1794–96) as US minister to France and as governor of Virginia (1799–1802). Appointed (1802) special envoy to France, he helped R. Livingston negotiate the Louisiana Purchase (1803). He served as secretary of state (1811–17) and of war (1814–15) under President J. Madison, and succeeded Madison as president (1817). He was reelected handily in 1820. His terms in office saw the Seminole War, US acquisition of Florida from Spain (1819) passage (1820) of the Missouri Compromise (*q.v.*), and issuance (1823) of what is now called the Monroe Doctrine (*q.v.*). His years as president were called the Era of Good Feeling (*q.v.*) and were marked by significant westward migrations. Monroe supported the colonization of Liberia, whose capital, Monrovia, is named for him.

Monroe Doctrine Guiding principle of US foreign policy in North and South America (19th–20th cents.). Enunciated by President J. Monroe (Dec. 2, 1823), the new policy declared that the US would henceforth oppose European powers in any attempt to colonize or interfere with affairs of states in the Americas. It also restated the US policy of nonintervention in European affairs (and existing European colonies). The declaration was prompted by Russian expansionist policies in Alaska and the possible takeover of newly independent South American states. Restated by Pres. J. Polk (1845, 1848), the doctrine was largely ignored by European powers in the 19th cent. Pres. T. Roosevelt added the Roosevelt Corollary (1904) in response to the Venezuela Claims (*q.v.*) incident, thus including possible US intervention to maintain the peace in any South American country. Increasing resentment by South American nations toward US domination in the 20th cent. has led to greater US involvement in such multilateral organizations as the OAS. Exceptions to this trend include the Cuban Missile Crisis and US intervention in the Dominican Republic (1965).

Montagnards *See* **Mountain, the.**

Montaigne, Michel Eyquem de 1533–92. Great French essayist. A courtier to French king Charles IX and once the mayor of Bordeaux, Montaigne was noted for his three books of essays. In them he revealed a spirit of humanism, skepticism of knowledge, and mastery of style. He greatly influenced French and English literature.

Montalembert, Charles Forbes, count of 1810–70. French political leader and historian. A leader of liberal Catholics, he was editor of the newspaper *L'Avenir* and an opponent of Emperor Napoleon III.

Montana State in the US Northwest, the 41st state. Montana was acquired (1803) by the US in the Louisiana Purchase (*q.v.*) and first explored by Lewis and Clark in their expedition of 1804–06. Fur traders set up trading posts in succeeding years, and the discovery of gold in 1852 resulted in several mining settlements. In 1864, the Montana Territory was organized, and after wars with the Sioux Indians (including the Battle of Little Bighorn) the territory saw an increase in ranching. The coming of the railroads brought new settlements and, in 1889, Montana became a state. A new constitution was adopted in 1973.

Montanism Christian movement (2d cent. AD), which was started in Phrygia by Montanus (*fl.* 2d cent.) and his followers, the illuminati. Extreme ascetics who said the end of the world was near, Montanists believed Montanus' teachings to be divine prophecies and held their sect to be superior to the orthodox church. The movement was largely suppressed in the 2d cent., though it persisted until the 9th cent. in some areas.

Montcalm, Louis Joseph de 1712–59. French general. He was commander of the French forces in Canada during the French and Indian Wars (*q.v.*). He successfully defended French territories against the British until his defeat and death at the Battle of the Plains of Abraham.

Monte Caseros, Battle of *See* **Rosas, Juan Manuel de.**

Monte Cassino *See* **Benedictines.**

Montecuccoli, Raimondo, count of *See* **Montecucculi, Raimondo, count of.**

Montecucculi, Raimondo, count of (Montecuccoli, ~) 1609–80. Italian-born general of the Holy Roman Empire. A brilliant tactician, he was successful in the Thirty Years' War and against the Turks (1664) and the French (1672–75).

Montefiore, Sir Moses Haim 1784–1885. British Jewish leader and philanthropist. He was sheriff of London (1837) and traveled throughout Europe and the Middle East trying to alleviate the oppression of Jews.

Montejo, Francisco de c1479–c1548. Spanish conquistador who took part in the conquest of Mexico under H. Cortés.

Montemagno, Bernardo dei Paganelli di *See* **Eugene III.**

Montenegro Former independent kingdom located in what was southern Yugoslavia and now allied with Serbia in the Yugoslav successor state. A mountainous region, it was first settled by Serbs (1389) after their homelands were conquered by the Turks. They warred against the Turks in the 18th and 19th cents. (allied with Russia) and after the Russo-Turkish War (1876–78) secured recognition of independence. Montenegro figured in the Balkan Wars (*q.v.*), supported Serbia in WW I, and joined the Kingdom of Serbs, Croats, and Slovenes after WW I. It was a center of resistance under Marshal Tito during WW II and became part of Yugoslavia in 1946. During the unrest and breakup of Yugoslavia after the fall of the Communist regime, Montenegro joined with Serbia to form the Yugoslav successor state. *See also* Yugoslavia, from 1981.

Montesquieu, Charles de Secondat, baron de la Brède et de 1689–1755. French political philosopher. His most important work was *The Spirit of Laws,* which theorized on the way external conditions determine the form government takes and advocated the balance of power between government and individuals.

Montessori, Maria 1870–1952. Italian educator. She was the first woman recipient of a medical degree in Italy and originated the Montessori system of children's education (based on self-motivation and spontaneity).

Monteverdi, Claudio 1567–1643. Italian composer. His first madrigals were published when he was 15, and he went on to compose works that are important in the early history of opera. Among them are *Orfeo* and *L'Arianna.*

Montez, Lola 1818–61. Irish adventuress. As mistress of Louis I of Bavaria, she antagonized the Jesuits with her liberalism and was forced to leave (1848). She died in the US.

Montezuma (Moctezuma) 1480?–1520. Aztec emperor (c1502–20). A despotic and unpopular ruler, he was taken hostage by the Spanish under H. Cortés. He was killed during the Aztec uprising against the Spanish (June, 1520).

Montfort, Simon de c1160–1218. Norman crusader. He led the Albigensian Crusade (*q.v.*) in southern France and was killed at the siege of Toulouse.

Montfort, Simon de, earl of Leicester 1208–65. English statesman and soldier. Formerly an adviser to Henry III and leader of his forces during revolts in Gascony, Montfort broke with the king and became leader of the barons during the Barons' War (*q.v.*). Following his victory at Lewes (1264), he became virtual ruler of England and summoned the Model Parliament (*q.v.*). He was finally defeated and captured at the Battle of Evesham (*q.v.*).

Montgolfier, Jacques Étienne 1745–99. French inventor. He and his brother, Joseph Michel (1740–1810), designed and constructed the first practical balloon. It was inflated with hot air and first ascended (unmanned) in 1783.

Montgomery, Bernard Law, 1st viscount Montgomery of Alamein 1887–1976. Noted British field marshal during WW II. He defeated E. Rommel's forces at El Alamein in Africa (1942) and forced their surrender (1943), took part in the invasion of Sicily (1943) and Italy, and played a major role in the Normandy invasion (1944) and subsequent Allied drive to Germany.

Montgomery, Richard 1738–75. Irish-American Revolutionary War general. He was second-in-command of the Montreal expedition and was killed while attacking Quebec.

Monticello T. Jefferson's Virginia estate located near Charlottesville. Designed by Jefferson, it was completed in 1772. He and his family are buried here. It became a national monument in 1926.

Montini, Giovanni Battista *See* **Paul VI.**

Montmorency, Anne, duke of 1493–1567. Marshal (1522) and constable of France (1537). He served in the Italian Wars under Francis I. Under Charles IX, he fought in the Wars of Religion and was killed in battle.

Montmorency, Mathieu, baron of c1174–1230. Constable of France (1218). He served under Philip II and under Louis VIII against the English and supported the regency of Blanche of Castile.

Montpensier, Louise d'Orléans, duchess of 1627–93. French princess and soldier. Niece of Louis XIII, she commanded rebel troops in the Fronde of the Princes (*q.v.*) and saved the Great Condé's army at the Battle of the Faubourg Saint Antoine (1652).

Montreux Convention Agreement (July 20, 1936) revising the Straits Convention of 1923. It abolished the International Straits Commission and gave Turkey authority to close the Dardanelles to shipping during wartime.

Montrose, James Graham, 5th earl and 1st marquess of 1612–50. Scottish general. Originally a Covenanter, Montrose supported Charles I during the English Civil Wars (1642–48). He won important victories in Scotland before being decisively defeated at Philiphaugh.

Monts, Pierre du Guast, comte de 1560–1630. French explorer. Monts was S. de Champlain's patron. Together they explored the St. Lawrence River and the American coast to Cape Cod. Monts founded the first French colony in Canada at Port Royal (1605, in modern Nova Scotia).

Mooney, Thomas J. 1883–1942. American radical labor leader. Mooney and Warren Billings (1893–1973) were convicted for the bombing at the San Francisco Preparedness Day Parade (July 22, 1916) in which ten were killed. His death sentence was commuted (1918) and both were pardoned (1939).

Moore, George Edward 1873–1958. British philosopher. A friend of B. Russell, Moore was a realist whose major work, *Principia Ethica,* opposed philosophical idealism.

Moore, Henry 1898–1986. British artist and sculptor, he is internationally known, noted for the characteristic organic form of his sculptures. He also completed a famous series of drawings of bomb shelter scenes during WW II.

Moore, Sir John 1761–1809. British general, noted for his service during the Peninsular War (1808–14). He led his troops on a famous retreat through the mountains to La Coruna, where he defeated the French. He was mortally wounded in the battle.

Moore's Creek Bridge, Battle of Battle (Feb. 27, 1776) during the American Revolutionary War, fought near Wilmington, North Carolina. Colonial patriots defeated a Loyalist force of 1,800 men and thereby checked British plans for occupation of North Carolina.

Moors Originally, a mixed Arab and Berber people living in the Roman province of Mauretania. They became (8th cent. AD) zealous converts to Islam and, led by Tarik (ibn Ziyad), invaded the Iberian peninsula (711). There they conquered the Visigoths and ranged into France, where their advance was checked (732) by C. Martel at Poitiers. All of Spain, save the northern Christian part, was subsequently constituted as a Muslim caliphate under Abd ar-Rahman I. With its capital at Córdoba, the caliphate prospered and many centers of commerce and Muslim culture were established. The government, however, was weak and fell to the Almoravids (1086) and then

the Almohads (1174). The Moors were slowly driven from the Iberian peninsula in the Reconquista, the Christian reconquest (11th–15th cents.), and many Moors resettled in (North) Africa. Those that remained in Spain were persecuted under the Inquisition and were finally expelled (1609). The term "Moors" sometimes refers to Muslims in general.

Moral Re-Armament (Buchmanism) (Oxford Group) International evangelistic organization begun by Frank Buchman (1878–1961) in 1922. The movement is nondenominational and aims at a spiritual revitalization of the individual and attainment of the four moral absolutes: purity, unselfishness, honesty, and love. The movement has been most successful among Protestant denominations.

Morat, Battle of Battle (June 22, 1476) in the war between the Swiss Confederation and Burgundy (1474–76). Some 35,000 Swiss infantrymen routed 20,000 mercenaries in the service of Charles the Bold of Burgundy at this town (now in western Switzerland). Charles was forced to retreat.

Moravia Historic region and former kingdom, located in what is now central Czechoslovakia. Moravia was settled by the Slavs (6th cent.), rose to become a powerful kingdom (Great Moravia) in the 9th cent., and was converted to Christianity by Cyril and Methodius (863). It was taken by the Magyars (10th cent.) and then became part of the kingdom of Bohemia, ruled by the Habsburgs. In 1918 it was made part of Czechoslovakia and, with Silesia, formed the province of Moravia and Silesia (1927). Taken by Germany during WW II, the region was restored in 1945.

Moravia, Alberto (Pincherle, ˜) 1907–90. Italian writer, Moravia's novels of alienation in the modern world include *The Indifferent Ones, The Conformist,* and *The Woman of Rome.*

Moravian church (Renewed Church of the Brethren) (Unitas Fratrum) A small Protestant evangelical denomination founded (c1457) by a group of Hussites. Persecution of the Unitas Fratrum, as it was first called, began (c1460) and eventually drove its members out of Bohemia and Moldavia. But a few of the Moravians were left when, in 1727, the church was revived in Saxony. From this new Moravian community at Hermhut, the church began sending out missionaries to the Americas, Africa, and Asia. From

1735, they founded new Moravian settlements in America. Most members of the church now live in the US.

Moray, James Stuart, 1st earl of *See* **Murray, James Stuart, 1st earl of.**

Morazan, Francisco *See* **Central American Union.**

More, Sir Thomas 1478–1535. English author, statesman, and Roman Catholic saint. More wrote his famous *Utopia* and served as lord chancellor (1529–32) to Henry VIII. His refusal to endorse Henry's Act of Supremacy (*q.v.*), naming the English monarch as the head of the Church of England, led to his resignation and eventual execution.

Morea *See* **Peloponnesus.**

Moreau, Jean Victor 1763–1813. French general. He supported Napoleon in the coup of 18 Brumaire and, as one of Napoleon's generals, won the signal victory at the Battle of Hohenlinden (1800). Napoleon grew jealous and had him banished in 1804. Moreau died fighting for the Royalist cause against Napoleon.

Morelos y Pavón, José María 1765–1815. Mexican priest and hero of the movement for independence from Spain. He fought under and then succeeded M. Hidalgo y Costilla and was successful in his early campaigns against the Spanish. He was later captured and shot, however.

Moreno, Mariano 1778–1811. Argentine revolutionary and intellectual leader. His publications attacking the Spanish colonial administration set the stage for the revolution (May, 1810) that ousted the Spanish viceroy. As a member of the revolutionary government, he established the national library and the government newspaper.

Morfontaine, Treaty of *See* **Adams, John.**

Morgan, Daniel 1736–1802. American Revolutionary War general. Morgan defeated the British at the Battle of Cowpens (1781). After the war, he quelled the Whiskey Rebellion (1794) and served in Congress (1797–99).

Morgan, Sir Henry 1635?–88. Welsh buccaneer. Morgan was a privateer in English service; his daring acts of piracy had the tacit approval of the English government and included brutal attacks on Spanish possessions in the Caribbean. He became lieutenant governor of Jamaica in 1674.

Morgan, John Hunt 1825–64. Confederate general. Morgan was known for his daring raids (1862) behind Union lines in Kentucky, Indiana, and Ohio. Finally captured, he escaped and was later killed at Greenville, Tennessee.

Morgan, John Pierpont 1837–1913. American financier and a leading figure in the early 20th-cent. financial world. The son of J. S. Morgan, he reorganized some of the major US railroads, took over US government financing after the Panic of 1873, and in 1901 financed formation of the United States Steel Corporation. He became the target of congressional investigations into money trusts in 1912.

Morgan, Junius Spencer 1813–90. American financier. Morgan's British-based firm, J. S. Morgan and Company, lent $50 million to France during the Franco-Prussian War.

Morgan, Thomas Hunt 1866–1945. American scientist. Hunt won the Nobel Prize in Physiology or Medicine in 1933 for his work with the fruit fly (Drosophila), which confirmed the action of chromosomes and genes in heredity.

Morgarten, Battle of Decisive victory (Nov. 15, 1315) of the Swiss Confederation over the Austrian Habsburgs. The Austrians, under Leopold I, invaded the canton of Schwyz, a member of the confederation. They were ambushed in Morgarten Pass and some 1,500 Austrians were killed.

Morgenthau, Henry, Jr. 1891–1967. US statesman. As treasury secretary (1934–45) under President F. Roosevelt, he supervised America's WW II economy, including massive taxation and government spending programs.

Moriscos Moriscos were Moors in Spain who were forcibly converted to Catholicism after 1492. Many practiced Islam secretly, however, and all were deported in 1609.

Morison, Samuel Eliot 1887–1976. American historian, writer, and teacher. Morison won Pulitzer prizes for *Admiral of the Ocean Sea* and *John Paul Jones.* Among his many other works is *The Growth of the American Republic* (with H. Commager).

Morley, Edward Williams *See* **Michelson, Albert Abraham.**

Mormons (Latter-Day Saints, Church of Jesus Christ of) Religious denomination founded (1830) in New York. Mormonism is characterized by an emphasis on revelation, the interdependence of spiritual and daily life, and concern for the church community. Mormons were noted as polygamists until the practice was banned

(1890). The church was founded by J. Smith after he translated into the Book of Mormon the golden tablets he said were delivered to him in a revelation. In 1831 Smith moved the church to Ohio, then to Missouri (1831), and was driven to Illinois (1839). There Smith was killed (1844) by an angry mob. Under B. Young the Mormons moved west and settled (1847) in Salt Lake City, Utah. After Utah became a US territory (1850), friction between Mormon and non-Mormon settlers developed and led to the Mormon War (1857). Mormons, however, were in firm control of the territory when it became a state (1896) and since then have spread their faith worldwide.

Mormon War (Utah War) Hostilities (1857–58) between Mormon settlers in Utah and US government troops. When a non-Mormon was appointed by the US government as governor of the Utah Territory (1857), Mormon governor B. Young instituted martial law. US troops, sent there to restore order, were fired upon by Mormons in sporadic raids that lasted until a peace was negotiated (June, 1858). The federal appointee then replaced Young as governor.

Mornay, Philippe de, seigneur du Plessis Marly 1549–1623. French diplomat and Protestant (Huguenot) leader during the Wars of Religion. Mornay wrote tracts in support of the Protestant cause and reconciled the Protestant leader, Henry of Navarre (later Henry IV), with the Catholic king Henry III.

Morny, Charles, duc de 1811–65. French statesman. He helped organize the coup (Dec. 1851) that made his half-brother, Napoleon III, emperor of France.

Moro, Aldo 1916–78. Italian statesman and prime minister (1963–68). As prime minister, he formed a coalition government with the Socialists, though Italy's serious economic problems prevented him from instituting reforms he wanted. He was premier (1974–76) and was kidnapped (Mar., 1978) and killed by left-wing terrorists.

Morocco Kingdom located on the northwest coast of Africa at the entrance to the Mediterranean Sea. The population is 26,249,000 and the capital is Rabat. In the 8th cent. Morocco was the base for the Arab conquest of Spain. After the Moors were expelled from Spain (15th cent.), Morocco came under attack by Spain and Portugal. In the late 19th cent., Morocco became the object of rivalry among the European imperial powers, and both Spain and France established (1912) protectorates there. Morocco was reestablished as an independent kingdom in 1956. Key dates in the history of Morocco include:

1ST CENT. BC Kingdom of Mauretania in region of modern Morocco constituted as Roman province of Mauretania.

5TH CENT. AD Vandals conquered region.

LATE 7TH CENT. Arabs entered Morocco; introduced Islam to Berbers in region.

8TH CENT. Berbers and Arabs launched invasion of Spain.

c788–900 Idris I and descendants established Morocco as unified and independent kingdom.

11TH CENT. Almoravides conquered region, ending period of tribal rule and strife between Umayyad and Fatimid Muslim factions.

12TH CENT. Almohades conquered the Almoravides.

16TH CENT. Spain and Portugal conquered coastal Morocco.

1554 Saadian (first Sherifian) dynasty founded in Morocco.

1578 Portuguese ended attempts to conquer Morocco following defeat in Battle of the Three Kings (Aug. 4).

1660 Alawite (second Sherifian) dynasty founded.

17TH–19TH CENTS. Alawites reconquered much of Morocco; kingdom became center for Barbary pirates.

1822–59 Abdu-r-Rahman reigned; attempted to expand influence into Algeria; was defeated by French, who had invaded Algeria.

1860 Spain invaded Morocco.

1880 Madrid Conference; major powers agreed to respect Morocco's independence; agreement proved short-lived as commercial rivalries intensified.

1906 France and Spain received authority over Moroccan internal affairs at the Algeciras Conference (Jan.–Apr.).

1911 Germany challenged French hegemony in Morocco in the Agadir Incident (July); forced to concede French and Spanish hegemony.

1912 France and Spain established protectorates over Morocco; France received the bulk of the territory (Mar. 30); Spain established (Nov. 27) Spanish Morocco and a Southern Protectorate that became part of Spanish Sahara; Tangier became an international zone.

1921–26 Rif War, unsuccessful revolt against colonial rule, led by Abd-el-krim.

1936 In Spanish Morocco, F. Franco began revolt that marked the beginning of the Spanish Civil War.

1937 Unsuccessful nationalist revolt against French rule.

1942 WW II; Morocco occupied (Nov.) by Allies.

1952 Nationalist Istiglal party declared illegal by French authorities.

1953 Sultan Sidi Muhammad, who supported the Moroccan nationalist movement, deposed by the French.

1955 Sidi Muhammad restored as sultan by the French as unrest spread in Morocco.

1956 France gave up its protectorate (Mar.); Spain renounced its protectorate over Spanish Morocco (Apr.); Morocco was awarded international zone of Tangier (Oct.).

1957 Sidi Muhammad became Moroccan King Muhammad V.

1958 Spain surrendered its Southern Protectorate to Morocco.

1961 King Muhammad V died (Feb. 26).

1961– King Hassan II reigned, succeeding his father.

1962 Hassan II issued constitution establishing parliamentary government in Morocco.

1965 Political turmoil in Morocco came to a head; Hassan II declared state of emergency (June) and assumed personal rule.

1969 Ifni ceded to Morocco by Spain.

1970 New constitution approved (July 25); five-year state of emergency ended.

1971 Unsuccessful attempt to overthrow government (July 10).

1972 King Hassan's proposed constitution approved in nationwide vote (Mar. 1).

1972 Unsuccessful assassination attempt against Hassan II (Aug.).

1975 Some 350,000 Moroccans took part in a march into Spanish Sahara (Nov. 6–9) to press claim that northern section belonged to Morocco; fighting between Moroccans, Mauritanians, and Algerians over region continued; cease-fire established in 1981.

1976 Spain formally renounced control of Western Sahara (Feb. 28); Moroccan troops moved in to fight the Polisario Front, a nationalist movement.

1976 Mauritania and Morocco agreed on a division of Western Sahara (Apr.).

1977 New Chamber of Representatives elected (June), ending twelve years of personal rule by King Hassan.

1977–78 Moroccan troops fought in Zaire against guerrilla forces.

1979 Mauritania renounced its claim to Western Sahara and signed a peace treaty with the Polisario Front there (Aug.); Hassan II announced the annexation of Mauritania's share.

1980 Sahrawi Arab Democratic Republic (SADR), the government-in-exile of the Western Sahara Polisario Front, applied for membership in the Organization of African Unity as a sovereign nation (July); SADR eventually recognized by many countries.

1981 Rioting and general strikes broke out after food prices rose sharply (June).

1984 About 110 people killed in rioting that broke out after rumors of new food price increases (Jan.).

1984 King Hassan and Muammar al-Quaddafi signed the Arab-African Federation Treaty (Aug. 15); Libya ends support for the Polisario Front in Western Sahara.

1984 Legislative elections held (Sept.); center-right parties win the majority of seats in the Chamber of representatives; Muhammad Karim Lamrani appointed Prime Minister.

1986 Israeli Prime Minister S. Peres met with King Hassan in the first official visit between Arab and Israeli heads of state since 1978 (July); Syria severed relations with Morocco.

1986 Hassan rejected the union with Libya (Aug.).

1987 Morocco's application for EEC membership rejected (Oct.).

1987 Diplomatic ties with Egypt reestablished (Nov.).

1988 New round of fighting in Western Sahara as the Polisario Front launched offensive (Jan.).

1988 Fighting reported between students and government forces in Fez (Jan.).

1988 Hassan agreed to meet with officials of the Polisario Front and its government-in-exile, SADR (Dec.).

1989   Diplomatic relations with Syria restored (Jan.).

1989   Trade pact signed (Feb.), creating the economic Union of the Arab Mahgreb (UMA, including Morocco, Algeria, Libya, Mauritania, and Tunisia.

1989   Polisario Front declared ceasefire in Western Sahara (Feb.); Hassan rejected official negotiations with the SADR (Sept.); the Polisario Front renewed attacks.

1990   Islamic fundamentalist movement, Adl wa Alihsane, banned; its leaders imprisoned (Jan.).

1990   General strike and riots in Fez (Dec.); protesters demanded wage increases to keep up with price hikes; some 1,500 people arrested.

1990   Ceasefire in Western Sahara; UN to supervise referendum in Western Sahara on its future; UN authorized mission (Apr. 1991).

1990–91   Persian Gulf War; Morocco initially condemned Iraq and sent troops to Saudi Arabia; however, popular demonstrations and a general strike held in support of the Iraqi people, despite government attempts to discourage them.

1991   Some 200,000 marched in joint demonstration by Morocco's two leading trade unions (May); demands for greater democracy voiced.

1991   Two key political parties, Istiqlal and Union Socialiste des Forces Populaires, joined forces to promote establishment of democratic government in Morocco (Dec.).

Morrill, Justin Smith 1810–98. American legislator. Morrill was a founder of the Republican party in Vermont, served 43 years (1855–98) in both houses of Congress, and established land grant colleges by the Morrill Act (1862).

Morrill Act *See* **Morrill, Justin Smith.**

Morris, Gouverneur 1752–1816. American statesman. Morris was a member of the Continental Congress (1778–79) and the Constitutional Convention (1787), and put the draft of the Constitution in final form. He planned the decimal system of coinage used in America and was minister to France (1792–94).

Morris, Lewis 1671–1746. Colonial jurist and statesman. Morris was chief justice of New York, was instrumental in the separation of New York and New Jersey (1738) into two colonies, and served as New Jersey's first governor (1738–46).

Morris, Robert 1734–1806. American financier and patriot. A signer of the Declaration of Independence, he was called the "financier of the Revolution." He controlled government financing efforts, including those for the army. He later served as a US senator (1789–95) and died in debt.

Morris, William 1834–96. English poet, Socialist, and decorative artist who was an important figure in the Victorian era. Early in his career he was active in the decorative arts and crafts. His major collections of poetical works include *The Defence of Guenevere and Other Poems, The Life and Death of Jason, The Earthly Paradise,* and *Three Northern Love Songs.* He also wrote prose romances, such as *News from Nowhere* and *The Well at the World's End.*

Morse, Jedidiah 1761–1826. American geographer. Morse was a minister whose geography textbooks earned him the name "father of American Geography." His son was S. Morse.

Morse, Samuel Finley Breese 1791–1872. An American painter and inventor. Morse was a portrait painter who developed the telegraph (from 1832) and the Morse code.

Mortimer, Edmund de, 3d earl of March and 1st earl of Ulster 1351–81. English nobleman. Edmund's marriage to Philippa, daughter of Edward III's son, formed the basis to the York (*q.v.*) family claim to the English throne.

Mortimer, Edmund de, 5th earl of March and 3d earl of Ulster 1391–1425. English nobleman. Edmund was heir presumptive of Richard II. He was jailed after Henry IV took the throne. Released by Henry V, Mortimer served Henry faithfully, resisting plots to put himself on the throne.

Mortimer, Roger de, 1st earl of March 1287?–1330. English nobleman. Roger and Queen Isabella, his lover, deposed (1327) and murdered her husband, Edward II, and ruled England together. Isabella's son, Edward III, had him tried and executed.

Mortimer, Roger de, 4th earl of March and 2d earl of Ulster 1374–98. English nobleman. The son of E. de Mortimer, he was declared heir presumptive by the childless Richard II, but died in battle. His great-grandson became Edward IV.

Mortimer's Cross, Battle of   Battle (Feb. 2, 1461) during the Wars of the Roses (*q.v.*), Edward, Duke of York, defeated the House of Lancaster. He proclaimed himself king as Edward IV, though the Lancastrians continued to contest his power.

mortmain From the French word for "dead hand," mortmain implies perpetual ownership of land, especially by a church. Such land was exempt from taxes and, from feudal times in England, efforts were made to limit or ban such holdings and figured in the conflict between church and state.

Morton, James Douglas, 4th earl of c1516–81. Scottish nobleman. Morton was lord chancellor (1563–66) to Mary Queen of Scots. He participated in the deaths of her secretary David Rizzio (1566) and her husband, Lord Darnley. He later forced her abdication (1567) and flight to England.

Morton, Thomas *fl.* 1622–47. English colonial trader. Morton was an Anglican and a fur trader who came into conflict with the early Puritan settlers in New England. They had him arrested and exiled several times.

Morton, William Thomas Green 1819–68. An American dental surgeon. Morton demonstrated the use of ether for surgical anesthesia (1846) and gained general acceptance for its use in medicine. C. Long was the first to use ether in surgery (1842).

Mosaddegh, Muhammad 1880–1967. Iranian statesman. As premier (1951–53), he nationalized Iran's oil industry (1951). This move alienated the West. Amid a major political crisis in Iran, he forced (1953) the shah to flee the country. However, the shah had Western support and soon forced Mosaddegh out of power.

Mosby, John Singleton 1833–1916. Confederate ranger. During the American Civil War Mosby led a small group called "Mosby's Rangers." They specialized in swift, daring raids behind Union lines, and effectively harassed Union military operations.

Moscow Capital city of the Commonwealth of Independent States (CIS) and located in west-central Russia. One of the world's major cities, it is the largest city in the CIS and its commercial and cultural center. Inhabited from Neolithic times, Moscow was first mentioned as a site of a village in 1147. It became the seat of the grand dukes of Moscow and was, from the 14th cent., seat of the metropolitan (later the patriarch) of the Russian Orthodox church. Moscow was destroyed several times by the Tatars but rose to defeat the Tatars and gain dominance over all of Russia. In 1547, Grand Duke Ivan IV first took the title "Tsar of Russia." Tsar Peter I moved Russia's capital to St. Petersburg in 1712. Moscow was virtually destroyed by fire (1812) during Napoleon's occupation and subsequent retreat. It became capital after the Russian Revolution, and was the prime objective of the German invasion (1941) during WW II. The city became the scene of mass pro-democracy demonstrations in the early 1990s and a dramatic standoff between pro-democracy leader B. Yeltsin and leaders of the Soviet coup (*q.v.*), who unsuccessfully sought to seize power in the former USSR.

Moscow Conferences World War II meetings between the Allies (Britain, Russia, and the US) to discuss war and postwar strategies. In the first (1941), America and Britain agreed to lend-lease aid for Russia, and in the second (1942) they discussed the creation of a second European theater of war. At the third meeting (1943), they agreed to the formation of the United Nations, and at the fourth (1944) they discussed the problems of Poland, Bulgaria, and Yugoslavia. A 1947 conference (including France) was less successful in deciding the postwar status of Germany.

Moscow Declaration Agreement (Oct. 30, 1943) by the Soviet Union, Britain, the United States, and China on the need to establish an international peace-keeping organization. It was one of the preliminary agreements that led to formation of the UN.

Moseley, Henry Gwyn Jeffreys 1887–1915. English physicist. By his research on the X-ray spectra of elements, he made important discoveries concerning atomic structure, including the link between atomic number and the charge of its nucleus.

Moses *fl.* c14th–13th cent. BC. Great Hebrew prophet and religious leader. Knowledge of his life is derived from biblical accounts, according to which he was raised in the Egyptian court. He fled Egypt after intervening between an Egyptian and a Hebrew slave and, after becoming a shepherd, received his call from Yahweh (God) to rescue the Hebrews. He returned to Egypt and, demanding that the pharaoh (possibly Ramses II) release his people, caused the plagues of Egypt. Moses finally led his people out of Egypt (*see* Exodus) and across the desert to Mt. Sinai, where he received the Ten Commandments. He then led the Hebrews on the 40-year journey to the Holy Land (Canaan), during which there was much hardship and dissent. When the Hebrews reached the edge of the Holy Land at the Jordan river, Moses climbed Mt. Pisgah to view it and then disappeared. Moses is traditionally regarded as the author of the first five books of the Old Testament (Genesis, Exodus, Leviticus, Numbers, and Deuteronomy), known collectively as the Pentateuch or Torah, of which the last four relate to the period of his life.

Moses, Anna Mary Robertson (~, Grandma) 1860–1961. American painter. She took up painting in her seventies and quickly established herself as an American folk artist.

Moses, Grandma *See* **Moses, Anna Mary Robertson.**

Moses, Robert 1888–1981. Noted US state and municipal official, responsible for major reconstruction projects and city planning in New York City. He supervised the building of parks, 35 highways, 12 bridges, Shea Stadium, numerous housing projects, and the 1964 World's Fair.

Moslem *See* **Islam; Caliphate.**

Mosley, Sir Oswald Ernald 1896–1980. British politician. He founded (1932) the British Union of Fascists. He conducted an anti-Jewish campaign and supported the Nazis, which resulted in his confinement from 1940 to 1943.

mosque Islamic temple, traditionally built facing Mecca and generally including an open courtyard and a minaret (tower). The first mosques were patterned after Muhammad's courtyard at Medina. Among the famous mosques is the Blue Mosque in Istanbul.

Mosquera, Tomás Cipriano de 1798–1878. Colombian statesman, a moderate progressive, and president (1845–49, 1861–67). Born to a prominent family, Mosquera rose through the ranks in the military before entering politics. A Conservative when he became president of New Granada (now Colombia) in 1845, he nevertheless instituted many economic, political, and educational reforms, thereby making his administration the most progressive in 19th-cent. Colombian politics. When civil war between Liberals and Conservatives broke out (1860), Mosquera led Liberal forces to victory (1861) and again became president, this time instituting sweeping anticlerical reforms that effectively broke the economic power of the Catholic church in Colombia. His administration also saw the adoption of a new constitution (1863), for what then became known as the United States of Colombia.

most-favored-nation clause Provision in treaties for international trade. It stipulates that the two participating nations will grant each other all commercial concessions (such as favorable import duties) that have been extended to other nations.

Most Serene Republic of San Marino *See* **San Marino.**

Mother Lode Popular name of the gold-bearing region located in the western Sierra Nevada Mountains of California.

Mo Ti *See* **Mo-tzu.**

Mott, Lucretia Coffin 1793–1880. American feminist and abolitionist. Together with E. Stanton she organized the first US women's rights convention at Seneca Falls, New York (1848).

Mo-tzu (Mo Ti) 470?–391? BC. Chinese philosopher who taught during the tumultuous Warring States period. Mo-tzu taught that people should love each other as they love their own families, and for a time, his doctrine of universal love rivaled the popularity of Confucianism. Widely read in the Chinese classics, Mo-tzu believed Confucianism overburdened with ritual formalities and lacking in religious teaching. Living a simple life, he taught and traveled widely in China, urging an end to offensive war, a return to the old forms of religion, and the spread of universal love. A church organized after Mo-tzu's ideas survived only a few decades, though Moism continued as a leading school of Chinese thought until the 2d cent. BC.

Moultrie, William 1730–1805. American Revolutionary War general. Moultrie defeated a British attack at Sullivan's Island (now Fort Moultrie) and was taken prisoner in the fall of Charleston (1780). He later served as governor of South Carolina.

Mountain, the (Montagnards) French extremist faction in the National Convention (*q.v.*) during the French Revolution. They were so named because they occupied a raised part of the legislative hall. They opposed (and eventually defeated) the more moderate Girondists (*q.v.*). They eventually took control of the Jacobins and became the controlling force behind the Reign of Terror (*q.v.*). Principal figures in the group were M. Robespierre and G. Danton.

Mountain Meadows Massacre Massacre of 137 settlers (Sept., 1857) in Utah, provoked by disputes between Mormon and non-Mormon settlers in Utah. Mormons were charged with inciting the attack, carried out by a mixed band of Paiute Indians and white settlers, apparently led by Mormon John D. Lee (1812–77). Their victims were only passing through Utah on their way to California, and only a few children were spared. Lee was tried and executed (1877).

Mount Athos Mountain located in northeastern Greece. It is noted as the site of numerous monasteries of the Orthodox Eastern church, the first of which was founded there c963.

Mountbatten, Louis, 1st earl Mountbatten of Burma 1900–79. British admiral and statesman. As supreme Allied commander in Southeast Asia (1943–46), Mountbatten defeated the Japanese in Burma. He was last viceroy of India (1947) and chairman of the chiefs of defense staff (1959–65). He was assassinated by Irish terrorists.

Mount Rushmore Mountain in the Black Hills of western South Dakota. The heads of T. Jefferson, A. Lincoln, G. Washington, and T. Roosevelt, carved out of the face of the mountain by G. Borglum, are a national monument.

Mount Sion *See* **Zion.**

Mount Vernon Virginia estate of G. Washington from 1747 until his death in 1799. It is the burial place of the Washington family and is located near Alexandria, Virginia.

Mouskos, Mihail Christodoulou *See* **Makarios III.**

Moussorgsky, Modest Petrovich *See* **Musorgsky, Modest Petrovich.**

Mozambique (Republic of ~, *formerly* Portuguese East Africa) Independent state located in coastal southeast Africa. The population is 14,718,000 and the capital is Maputo. It gained independence in 1975 after nearly five centuries of Portuguese colonial rule. Key dates in Mozambique's history include:

10TH CENT. Arabs and Swahili traders settled coastal region.

1498 Vasco da Gama visited region.

1505 Portuguese began colonization.

16TH–17TH CENTS. Portuguese gradually took control of the interior; *prazeros* (owners of large estates) forced natives to work lands.

FROM MID-17TH CENT. Slave trade flourished.

1752 Colonial government established.

1891 Treaty established border between Mozambique and British territories.

1910 Status changed from province to colony.

1917 Firm control by Portugal over native population secured after nearly two decades of fighting.

1951 Mozambique became a Portuguese overseas province.

EARLY 1960S Reform laws passed, ended forced labor and improved conditions for native blacks.

1963 National Front for the Liberation of Mozambique (FRELIMO) organized.

1964–74 War for independence; FRELIMO guerrillas slowly gained control of much of Mozambique.

1974 New Portuguese military government arranged cease-fire in Mozambique (July); agreed to independence for Mozambique.

1975 Independence granted (June 25).

1975–86 President Samora Moises Machel, a Maoist, in office; Marxist government established; mass exodus by Portuguese left many shops and businesses abandoned; "re-education camps" and policy of clustering people in rural areas into communal villages aroused considerable resentment against new government.

1976 Mozambique Resistance Movement (MNR) set up by Rhodesian Central Intelligence organization to gather intelligence information; later began guerrilla operations against Mozambique government.

1976 Mozambique closed border with white-ruled Rhodesia; Rhodesian troops launched numerous raids into Mozambique over next years.

1980 Reopened border after native blacks came to power in Zimbabwe (Rhodesia).

1980 MNR support base moved from Zimbabwe (formerly Rhodesia) to South Africa; MNR, now at least nominally anti-Communist, stepped up recruitment and anti-government activities in Mozambique.

1981 South African commandos killed twelve African National Congress (ANC) members living in Maputo suburb (Jan. 29); President Machel angrily denounced South Africa, which was suspected of aiding MNR guerrillas in Mozambique.

1981 Mozambique established cooperative agreement with Portugal (May).

1982 MNR estimated to have some 3,000 trained guerrilla fighters, now active in seven of eleven provinces; armed bands frequently resorted to murder, rape, beatings, mutilations, and massacres as warfare continued throughout the 1980s.

1983–84 Famine claimed an estimated 100,000 lives.

1984 Nkomati Accord signed by President Machel and South African prime minister P. W. Botha (Mar. 16); South Africa agreed to end support for MNR, while Mozambique agreed to stop harboring ANC guerrillas; MNR reportedly had other sources of support, including former Portuguese citizens now living outside Mozambique.

1984 President Machel replaced two notorious hard-liners in attempt to ease popular resentment against government over such policies as forced "villagization" in countryside and expelling of unemployed from cities.

1985 Guerrilla attacks now reached suburbs of capital.

1986 Government estimated some 4 million threatened by famine; national economy in shambles following years of warfare.

1986 President Machel killed in plane crash in South Africa (Oct. 19), while returning from conference in Zambia; crash apparently an accident despite suspicions of South African involvement.

1986– Joaquim Chissano in office as president; seeking an end to war with the MNR, Chissano oversaw the transition from Marxist to free, multi-party democratic government.

1987 Guerrillas massacred 380 civilians in the town of Homoine (July); attacks on convoys left over 400 others dead (Nov., Dec.).

1988 Pope John Paul II visited the country (Sept.).

1989 Government stated it would offer amnesty to rebels if they ceased fighting (Mar.); refused to share power with them, however.

1990 Direct talks between government and MNR rebels held (July); President Chissano publicly underscored point that MNR was free to become political party once it ceased fighting.

1990 Government adopted new constitution, providing for multi-party democracy (Nov.); changed name of country, dropping People's Republic for Republic of Mozambique.

1990 Partial ceasefire agreed upon (Dec. 1).

1991 Mozambique's first coup attempt broken up by timely arrests (June).

1991 Government and MNR agreed on protocols to take force after fighting stopped (Nov.); MNR, however, stepped up fighting soon after agreeing to protocols.

1992 First opposition party registered (Mar.).

1992 Drought throughout Southern Africa reported causing food shortages in Mozambique.

1992 Truce agreed to by leftist and rightist factions (Aug. 7), halting 16-year civil war; some 600,000 killed in fighting over the years.

Mozarabs Christians in Muslim Spain (8th–11th cents.) who adopted the Arabic language and culture while retaining their Christian faith. They lived in largely autonomous communities.

Mozart, Wolfgang Amadeus 1756–91. Great Austrian musical genius of the classical period who composed works in every genre. He began composing when he was five and went on a concert tour through Europe at age six. His most famous operas are *The Marriage of Figaro* and *Don Giovanni.* In spite of the brilliance of his many symphonies, concertos, and his last opera, *The Magic Flute,* he died in poverty.

Muawiya *d.* 680. He once served as Muhammad's secretary and later became governor of Syria. In the first Muslim Civil War (*q.v.*), he contested the succession of Ali to the caliphate and, after Ali's death (661), claimed the caliphate. Muawiya thus founded the Umayyad (*q.v.*) dynasty.

Mubarak, Hosni 1929– . Egyptian president (1981–), successor to A. Sadat on his assassination. By his visit (June, 1982) to Saudi Arabia, Mubarak established the first high-level contact with that country since the split between Egypt and its Arab neighbors over the Camp David accords. His administration (to 1992) saw the return of Israeli-held Egyptian lands in accordance with the 1979 treaty, increasing Muslim fundamentalist unrest, serious financial problems, continuing rapprochement with Arab neighbors, and participation by Egyptian troops in ousting the Iraqis from Kuwait during the Persian Gulf War. *See also* Egypt, 1981–92.

muckrakers In US journalistic history, reporters who exposed corruption in business and politics during the early 1900s. They included I. Tarbell, L. Steffens, and U. Sinclair.

Mudd, Samuel Alexander *See* **Booth, John Wilkes.**

Mudejar Name for the Spanish Muslims (later called Moriscos) who were allowed to remain in Spain after the Christian reconquest of Muslim territories there. They lived in protected communities and developed a unique artistic style, which influenced Spanish architecture. They were forced to leave Spain in 1609.

mufti Muslim lawyers who advise judges on Islamic law. Their opinion papers are called *futwa* and are binding in matters of marriage, divorce, and inheritance.

Mughal (Mogul) Muslim dynasty that ruled in India from the 16th to 19th cents. The Mughal empire was at its height from the 16th to the early 18th cents. and was noted for its efficient administrative organization and for its great contributions in the fields of art, architecture, and literature. The empire was founded by Babur, who established Mughal power in India by victory in the battle of Panipat (1526). Babur (ruled 1526–30) was succeeded by his son Humayun (ruled 1530–56). Other notable Mughal rulers were Akbar (ruled 1556–1605), who greatly expanded Mughal power; Jahangir (ruled 1605–27), his son; Shah Jahan (ruled 1628–58), who expanded Mughal power into the Deccan and who built the Taj Mahal at Agra; and Aurangzeb (ruled 1658–1707), under whose rule the empire reached its height and began its decline. Aurangzeb, embroiled in other crises, was unable to halt the rising strength of the Marathas, and after his death (1707) the empire began to divide into a group of provinces. Its last ruler, Bahadur Shah II (ruled 1837–57) was emperor in title only. After the failure of the Indian Mutiny (1857), he was deposed by the British and the empire ceased to exist.

mugwumps In US history, Republicans who deserted (1884) party presidential candidate J. Blaine to support Democrat candidate G. Cleveland, who was subsequently elected.

Muhammad (Mohammed) 570?–632. Arabian prophet and religious leader, founder of Islam (*q.v.*). The son of Abdallah, a merchant of Mecca, Muhammad was raised by his uncle after his father's early death. At the age of 24, Muham- mad married Khadija, a prosperous widow many years his senior; of their children only one, Fatima, had children. Muhammad became a successful merchant in Mecca. However, he came to feel called upon by God to preach among the Arabian people, to dispel their ignorance and superstition, and to provide the Arab world with its own prophet. According to Islamic teaching, he was favored by a revelation from God through the angel Gabriel. At first Muhammad preached only to a small circle, including members of his family, Ali, his son-in-law, and Abu Bakr, his friend. He taught that there was one true God, and that key elements of the struggle toward God's mercy were fasting, almsgiving, and prayer. After several years he felt called upon to preach in public, but his exhortations against the pagan rituals practiced in Mecca made him many enemies. An attempt on his life was planned in 622 but Muhammad was warned and fled to Yathrib, later called Medina. This flight, known as the Hijira, traditionally marks the beginning of the Muslim era. At Medina, Muhammad found increased support and made many new converts. He continued to elaborate his teachings and accounts of his revelations, which formed the basis of the Koran (*q.v.*). However, the growing strength of Islam brought Muhammad into conflict with the Meccans. Muhammad's followers defeated a superior Meccan force at Badr (624) but were defeated at Uhud (625). The strength of Islam continued to rise, however, and in 630 Muhammad marched into Mecca leading 10,000 faithful. He spent his last years at Medina in the company of his several wives, among them his favorite, Aisha (Ayeshah), daughter of Abu Bakr. By his death virtually all of Arabia had come under the control of Islam and the theocratic state (*see* Caliphate) he had established.

Muhammad II 1430–81. Ottoman sultan (1451–81), called the Conqueror, successor to his father, Murad II. He captured Constantinople (1453), bringing the Byzantine Empire to an end. He made Constantinople his capital, and took Greece, most of Serbia, and the Aegean Islands.

Muhammad IV 1641–92. Ottoman sultan (1648–87), son of Sultan Ibrahim, who had been deposed and murdered. Order was restored under the viziers of the Kuprili family (after 1656). He was unable to prevent Algerian independence

(1669), however, and he was deposed after military reverses in the Austro-Turkish War (*q.v.*).

Muhammad V 1844–1918. Ottoman sultan (1909–18). He succeeded his brother, Abdul-Hamid II, who was overthrown by the Young Turks. Muhammad's reign saw the loss of most of the Ottoman Empire's European possessions in the Balkan Wars (*q.v.*) and its ruinous WW I alliance with the Central Powers.

Muhammad VI 1861–1926. Last Ottoman sultan (1918–22), successor to his brother, Muhammad V. He came to power at the close of WW I, submitted to the harsh terms of the Treaty of Sèvres (*q.v.*), and was deposed (Nov. 3, 1922) by the Turkish nationalist K. Atatürk, who established the republic.

Muhammad Ahmad *See* **Mahdi, Muhammad Ahmed.**

Muhammad Ali (Mehemet Ali) (˜ Ali Pasha) 1769–1849. Egyptian viceroy (1805–48), considered the founder of the modern Egyptian state. After unsuccessfully opposing Napoleon in Egypt, he became viceroy of Egypt, then under Ottoman rule. He massacred Mameluke (*q.v.*) leaders in Egypt and thereby established undisputed power, defeated the Wahabis in Arabia (by 1818), invaded the Sudan, sent troops to aid the Ottoman sultan in the War of Greek Independence (*q.v.*), and went to war against the sultan (in Syria). By his victories against the sultan, he gained (1841) virtual independence for Egypt under nominal Ottoman suzerainty. The viceroyalty of Egypt was made hereditary.

Muhammad Ali Basha *See* **Muhammad Ali.**

Muhammad Iqbal *See* **Iqbal, Muhammad.**

Muhammad of Ghor *See* **Taraori, Battles of.**

Muhammad Reza Shah Pahlavi 1919–80. Shah of Iran (1941–79), successor to his father, Reza Shah Pahlavi. He succeeded after his father was deposed by British and Soviet military intervention and, amid nationalist unrest, was forced to leave the country briefly in 1953. He was restored with US and British help and subsequently attempted to promote social and economic reforms. Criticized for his pro-Western policies and brutal treatment of dissenters, he was forced out of Iran (Jan. 16, 1979) by a Muslim fundamentalist revolution in Iran that brought Ayatollah Khomeini to power. In ill health and resisting attempts to return him to Iran for trial (notably the hostage crisis), the former shah died in exile in Egypt.

Muhlenberg, Frederick Augustus Conrad 1750–1801. American clergyman, a son of Heinrich Melchior Muhlenberg. Muhlenberg served in the Continental Congress (1779–80) and was a member (1789–97, from Pennsylvania) and first speaker of the House of Representatives.

Muhlenberg, Heinrich Melchior 1711–87. German-American clergyman. He organized (1748) the first Lutheran synod in America and is regarded as the founder of American Lutheranism.

Muhlenberg, John Peter Gabriel 1746–1807. American clergyman, soldier, and politician, a son of H. Muhlenberg. Muhlenberg served as brevet major general in the American Revolution, and was later a congressman and senator from Pennsylvania.

Mukden Incident Incident (Sept. 18, 1931) used by Japan as a pretext for its invasion of Manchuria. Following an attempt to sabotage the Japanese-controlled South Manchurian Railway, Japanese troops occupied (Sept. 18) nearby Mukden. With the arrival (Sept. 21) of more troops from Korea, the Japanese army began to actively take over the territory. Chiang Kaishek's Nationalist armies, then occupied in civil war with the Communists, were unable to oppose the Japanese, and by Feb. 1932 conquest of Manchuria was complete. Thereupon the Japanese created (Feb. 18) the puppet state of Manchukuo (*q.v.*).

Müller, Hermann 1876–1931. German statesman and political leader in the Weimar Republic. He was chancellor (1920, 1928–30) and, during his second term, negotiated the Young Plan (*q.v.*) and brought an end to French occupation of the Rhineland (1929).

Müller, Johannes *See* **Regiomontanus.**

Müller, Johannes Peter 1801–58. German physiologist and anatomist. Muller was famed for research in such fields as physiology, pathology, and comparative anatomy.

Muller v. *Oregon* US Supreme Court decision (1908) upholding 1903 Oregon legislation that limited the working hours for women in some commercial businesses. The law was defended by attorney Louis Brandeis, who presented what became known as the "Brandeis brief," using sociological and medical data in support of worker rights.

Mumford, Lewis 1895–1990. American educator, author, and social critic. Mumford's works range from city planning to cultural history and treat the larger thesis that humanity must counter dehumanizing tendencies of the modern technological world. This is to be accomplished by restoring cultural emphasis on human and moral values. Among his notable works are *Technics and Civilization, The City in History,* and *The Pentagon of Power.*

Munda, Battle of Battle (Mar. 17, 45 BC) that marked the end of resistance within the Roman Empire to J. Caesar's rule. Following Caesar's victory at Thapsus, Pompey's sons, Gnaeus Pompey (75?–45 BC) and Sextus Pompey (75–35 BC), organized a rebellion against Caesar in the Roman province of Spain. Though outnumbered, Caesar met and defeated the rebel force at Munda, an ancient town in southern Spain. It was Caesar's last military victory.

Munich Agreement *See* **Munich Pact.**

Munich Pact (˜ Agreement) Pact (Sept. 30, 1938) between Germany and other European powers providing for the German annexation of the western Czechoslovakian territory of Sudetenland. A. Hitler had entered into a dispute with Czechoslovakia earlier in 1938 over the territory, which was populated predominantly by ethnic Germans. After several months of negotiations between the major powers, a complex plan for the phased occupation of the territory was worked out and agreed to (at Munich) by Germany, France, Great Britain, and Italy. The pact was rendered meaningless when Hitler invaded (Mar., 1939) Czechoslovakia.

Munich Putsch (Beer Hall Putsch) A. Hitler's unsuccessful attempt (Nov. 9, 1923) to seize power in Bavaria and, ultimately, to take control of the Weimar Republic. As leader of the National Socialist (Nazi) party, Hitler joined with the extremist Gen. E. Ludendorff in a badly organized attempt to incite a right-wing revolution in Munich. Hitler had hoped to capitalize on Germany's severe economic crisis, but his plan soon failed. Arrested and tried, Hitler was sentenced to five years in prison. He served only eight months and during this time wrote his seminal work, *Mein Kampf (q.v.).*

municipium In ancient Rome, a community that enjoyed complete autonomy, except in matters of foreign policy. The municipium supplied troops for the Roman army, but residents could only become Roman citizens by permanently settling in Rome. Councils and magistrates governed the municipia. Willing allies became the first Italian municipes (c338 BC, in Campania and Volscium), but later the system was applied in lands that had been conquered. Following the Social War, the system was applied to all Italian and Latin communities.

Muñoz Marín, Luis 1898–1980. Puerto Rican statesman and governor (1948–64). He founded (1938) the Popular Democratic party and, as the first elected governor, implemented social and economic reforms.

Munsey, Frank Andrew 1854–1925. American publisher, who bought and consolidated competing newspapers and magazines. Among his holdings were the *New York Sun* and the *New York Herald.*

Munster, Sebastian 1489–1552. German theologian and geographer. Munster edited a Hebrew Bible and wrote (1544) *Cosmographia,* the first detailed geography of the world written in the German language.

Münzer, Thomas c1489–1525. German radical reformer, often considered to be among the Anabaptists *(q.v.).* Münzer saw the Protestant Reformation as a social and political revolution, as well as a religious revolt. He broke with M. Luther and became a leader in the Peasants' War *(q.v.).* He was captured and beheaded.

Murad I 1326?–89. Ottoman sultan (c1360–89). By his conquests, he made the Byzantine Empire a vassal state, consolidated Ottoman control over Anatolia, extended Ottoman domains into the Balkans, and established (1362) the Ottoman capital at Edirne (formerly Adrianople). He laid the foundations of the administrative system of the later Ottoman Empire and formed the military corps known as the Janissaries *(q.v.).*

Murad II 1403–51. Ottoman sultan (1421–51). He overcame rival claimants to the throne and, by 1425, had firm control of the empire. He took Salonica (1430) in northern Greece during a war with Venice and won important victories at Varna (1444) and Kosovo (1448) in fighting against the Hungarians and Poles.

Murad IV c1612–40. Ottoman sultan (1623–40). By means of brutal force, he broke the power of rebellious military leaders (including those of the Janissaries), restored the authority of the central government, and successfully concluded a war with Persia, in which he captured Baghdad (1638).

Murad V 1840–1904. Ottoman sultan (1876), successor to his uncle, Abd al-Aziz. He was declared insane after three months and was deposed in favor of his brother Abd al-Hamid II.

Murasaki Shikibu c978–c1031. Japanese writer. She wrote *Tale of Genji,* the first great novel written in Japanese.

Murat, Joachim 1767–1815. French marshal and king of Naples (1808–15). Murat was one of Napoleon's most able cavalry commanders and distinguished himself in Napoleon's Italian, Egyptian, Peninsular, and Russian campaigns. He helped Napoleon seize power in the coup of 18 Brumaire and again joined him in the Hundred Days' campaign.

Muratori, Ludovico Antonio 1672–1750. Italian historian. As archivist and librarian at Modena, he discovered early Christian writings (AD 2d cent.) that listed the books of the New Testament.

Murdoch, Jean Iris (Bayley, Mrs. J. O.) 1919– . British novelist and philosopher. Murdoch's writings include the novels *A Severed Head* and *The Flight from the Enchanter.*

Muret, Battle of Victory for the French Catholic nobles (Sept., 1213) during the Albigensian Crusade (*q.v.*). Forces of the noblemen of northern France, led by S. de Montfort, decisively defeated those of the Albigensian leader Raymond VI at this town in southern France. Raymond's ally, King Pedro II of the Spanish kingdom of Aragon, was killed in the battle. Spanish influence in southern France was thus ended.

Murfreesboro, Battle of *See* **Stones River, Battle of.**

Murillo, Bartolomé Esteban 1617?–82. Spanish baroque painter. Murillo was noted for his portraits and religious subjects, including the *Vision of St. Anthony.* He was a founder and first president of the Seville Academy (1660).

Muromachi shogunate *See* **Ashikaga period.**

Murphy, Frank 1893–1949. American politician and associate justice of the Supreme Court (1940–49). Known for his liberalism, he delivered a dissenting opinion opposing the confinement of Japanese-Americans during WW II.

Murray, James 1722–94. British general and colonial administrator. He distinguished himself in the Seven Years' War (1756–63), and served as governor of Quebec (1760), Canada (1763–66), and Minorca (1774–82).

Murray, Sir James Augustus Henry 1837–1915. Scottish-born English lexicographer. Murray became editor (1879) of the Oxford English Dictionary (completed 1928), editing over half of it himself and establishing its organization.

Murray, James Stuart, 1st earl of (Moray, ˜) c1531–70. Scottish nobleman. A Protestant, he at first supported the rule of his sister, the Catholic Mary Queen of Scots. Later, however, his support of the Calvinist J. Knox resulted in a break with Mary and Murray's unsuccessful attempt (1565) at rebellion. After Mary's fall from power (1567), he became regent, resisted her attempts to regain power, and promoted the Protestant Reformation in Scotland.

Murrone, Pietro del *See* **Celestine V, Saint.**

Murrow, Edward Roscoe 1908–65. Noted American broadcast journalist. Murrow was renowned for his vivid WW II radio reports from England. He pioneered television journalism with his programs *See It Now* and *Person to Person.*

Mursa, Battle of Battle fought (Sept. 28, AD 351) during the Roman civil wars. Roman emperor Constantius II, with an army of 40,000, defeated the usurper Magnentius, leading some 50,000 troops, in a bloody battle at Mursa (now in Croatia). Combined losses totaled 54,000 men.

Mursilis I *See* **Hittite Empire.**

Muscovy Company (Russia Company) English joint-stock trading company founded in 1555. The company enjoyed a monopoly on the Russian trade until 1698.

Musil, Robert 1880–1942. Austrian novelist. He is best known for his classic three-volume novel, *The Man Without Qualities,* written between 1930 and 1933.

Muslim civil wars Political upheavals that significantly altered the course of Muslim history. The first (656–61) was caused by the assassination of Uthman, the third caliph, and involved a struggle for the caliphate between Ali (600?–661), fourth caliph, and among others, Muawiya leader of the Umayyads (*q.v.*). Ali was assassinated and Muawiya established the Umayyad dynasty of caliphs. This event marked the beginning of the long Umayyad rule and also caused the fundamental schism within the Islamic world: the Shi'ites (*q.v.*) were those who supported Ali (and his successors) as the only rightful heirs to the caliphate, while the orthodox Sunni (*q.v.*) Muslims did not. The second (683–

92) was caused when Abd Allah ibn az-Zubayr sought the caliphate after the death of Yazid I (*d.* 683). The civil war ended with the defeat and death of Ibn az-Zubayr and the rise of Abd al-Malik as unchallenged leader of the Muslim world. Another civil war divided the Abbasid caliphate after the death (809) of Harun al-Rashid. The struggle was initiated by his son al-Amin (785?–813), his designated successor, and another son, Abd Allah al-Mamun (786–833), who was proclaimed caliph in Persia. The war ended (813) with al-Amin's defeat and death and the ascendancy of al-Mamun. A final civil war (1008–31) in Córdoba, Spain, ended with the elimination of the Umayyad caliphate in Spain (1031).

Muslim League (*orig.* All-India Muslim League) Political organization founded (1906) in India. Formed by Aga Khan III and other noted Muslims for the protection of Muslims' rights, the group broke away from the predominantly Hindu Indian National Congress and demanded (1940) a separate Muslim state. Led by (Muhammad Ali) Jinnah, it won the creation (1947) of Pakistan and became the dominant political party in the new state. The league had split into factions by the 1960s and declined after the 1970 elections.

Muslims *See* **Islam; Caliphate.**

Mussolini, Benito 1883–1945. Italian Fascist dictator and WW II ally of A. Hitler. The pre-eminent leader of Italian Fascism, he organized the first Fascist group (1919) and party (1921). He orchestrated the Fascist militia's march on Rome (Oct. 1922) and by it became head of the Italian government. Thereafter his rule was marked by the institution of his dictatorship and the following events: the Matteoti Crisis (1924); abolition of parliamentary government (1928), the Lateran Treaty (1929); the Italo-Ethiopian War (1935–36); intervention in the Spanish Civil War; occupation of Albania (1939); and participation and defeat in WW II. Ousted from power (1943), he headed a German-backed opposition government until his execution in 1945.

Mussorgsky, Modest Petrovich (Moussorgski, ~) 1839–81. Russian composer. He is best known for his opera *Boris Godunov* (1868) and his piano suite *Pictures at an Exhibition* (1874).

Mutanabbi, al- 915–965. Great Arab poet, author of collected poems known as the *Divan.*

Mutsuhito (*reign name,* Meiji) 1852–1912. Japanese emperor (1867–1912), successor to the shogun rulers of Japan. His reign is known as the Meiji Restoration (*q.v.*). It saw the end of feudalism and the transformation of Japan into a modern industrial state. He introduced many reforms, including a judicial code, a constitution (1889, providing for a legislature), and the Western calendar (1873). In addition to extensive Westernization, his reign was marked by the Satsuma Rebellion (1877), the Sino-Japanese War (1894–95) and the Russo-Japanese War (1904–5).

Muttra *See* **Mathura.**

Muwatallis *See* **Hittite Empire.**

MVD *See* **GPU.**

Myanmar (Union of ~) (*formerly* Socialist Republic of Burma) Republic located on the Bay of Bengal in Southeast Asia. The population is 41,279,000 and the capital is Yangon. Dominated for centuries by Britain, Myanmar finally achieved independence from Britain in 1948. Key dates in its history include:

3D CENT. AD Burmese people emigrated from Tibet.

1044 Smaller Burmese states were consolidated; Buddhist monarchy established by King Anawratha at Pagân.

1287 Mongol dynasty of China conquered Burma and then withdrew; Thai Shan princes ruled kingdom at Ava.

1519 Portuguese traders arrived in region.

c1550–1600 Toungoo kingdom overthrew Ava; ruled unified empire in Burma (now called Myanmar).

1612 British East India Company established posts near Rangoon (now called Yangon).

1753–60 Alaungpaya founded modern Burmese state; also founded Konbaung dynasty, last dynasty of Burma; expanded empire into India and Thailand.

1824–26 First Burma War initiated by Burmese invasion of eastern territories in British India.

1826 Treaty of Yandabo; Burma ceded Tenasserim and Arakam, gave up claims on Assam and Manipur, and paid indemnity.

1852 Second Burma War; brought on by dissension between Burmese monarchy and British traders; south part (lower Burma) came under British control.

1885–86 Third Burma War; conquest of Mandalay by Britain; marked end of Konbaung dynasty and independent Burma.

1886 Burma annexed (Jan.) by colonial government of British India.

1937 Britain separated Burma from India (Apr. 1); granted it new constitution; Burma became semi-autonomous crown colony.

1937–39 Ba Maw in office as Burma's first prime minister.

1940–42 Ba Maw, having joined with Aung San and other nationalists, jailed for sedition; released after Japanese invaded Burma.

1941 "Thirty Comrades," 30 nationalist opposition leaders including Aung San, Ne Win, and others, went to Taiwan for military training offered by Japanese.

1941–45 WW II; Burma Road, vital Allied supply line to China, made Burma a major battleground; Japanese invaded Burma (1941) and cut Burma Road (1942); Anti-Fascist People's Freedom League, led by Aung San, at first aided Japanese and then (1944) began resistance against them; Allied forces retook Burma (Apr., 1945).

1943–45 Ba Maw in office as head of Japanese puppet government of Burma.

1947 Anglo-Burmese agreement; provided for elections to decide future status of Burma; Aung San's Freedom League party won elections and he became premier.

1947 Aung San and other officials assassinated (July 19); political rival U Saw later executed for planning the killings; Thakin Nu formed new council.

1948 Independence from Britain (Jan. 4).

1950 Freedom League government confronted by uprisings by Communists and by Karen people fighting for independent state.

1950–53 Chinese Nationalists fled to Burma to escape Chinese Communist armies; UN finally ordered Nationalists to leave Burma.

1958 Political crisis within Freedom League party; Premier Nu asked Gen. Ne Win to take over government.

1960 Civilian government restored after Nu's faction won elections; dissent among factions of Nu's followers led to political unrest and threat of civil war.

1962 Gen. Ne Win overthrew civilian government (Mar.); suspended the constitution and established military dictatorship, ruling through the Revolutionary Council.

1962–88 Gen Ne Win in power; nationalized industry and set up socialist state; drove out some 300,000 foreigners, thereby breaking longstanding control of Burmese economy by Chinese and Indians; pursued policy of isolation; kept rebel ethnic groups in check though they remained active.

1974 People's Assembly formally empowered (Mar. 2) under new constitution creating socialist republic; 12-year rule by military coalition ended; Ne Win remained in power as chairman of the ruling state council; his Burma Socialist Program Party (BSPP) held nearly all seats in Burma's unicameral legislature.

1977 Burmese Communist Party saw its support from China sharply reduced; turned to drug smuggling in the 1980s to gain revenue.

1980 Former prime minister Nu, who left Burma in 1969, returned to Burma following government's new policy of reconciliation with opposition leaders.

1981 Brig. Gen. U San Yu named president (Nov.), replacing the aging Ne Win; Ne Win remained in power as chairman of the Burma Socialist Program Party (BSPP), Burma's one legal party.

1981 Rice harvest this year 50 percent greater than that of 1975, as a result of new crop strains and economic incentives to farmers.

1983 South Korean president narrowly escaped assassination (Oct. 9) while visiting Burma; bomb explosion killed South Korean and Burmese dignitaries attending ceremony; North Korean army officers captured and convicted of plot (Nov.).

1985–87 Army variously mounted sustained offensives against Karens and Mons along Thai border, against Kachin, Shan, and Communist rebels along the Chinese border, and against Naga rebels along the Indian border; Karen and Mon rebels successfully frustrated government attacks until 1990, when they were forced out of their strongholds.

1986 Government asked UN for "least developed country" status to qualify for emergency aid (Nov.); national economy now in shambles; socialist Burma suffered shortages, falling factory and agricultural output, mounting trade deficit, runaway inflation, and mounting foreign debt.

1987 Ne Win ordered demonetization of bank notes without compensation (Sept.), thus wiping out individual savings; student riots broke out (Sept.).

1988 Street riots broke out in Rangoon following incident of police brutality (Mar.); soon after, widely circulated letters criticizing the Ne Win regime's handling of the economy sparked protests and riots across the nation; death toll rose into the thousands as police fired into crowds.

1988 BSPP convened emergency congress to discuss reforms (July 23); Ne Win and President San Yu resigned; party recommended greater private enterprise and reduced government controls but no major political reforms.

1988 Gen. Sein Lwin in office as president (July) and chairman of the BSPP; declared martial law and jailed opposition leaders.

1988 Protests and general strike against Gen. Sein crippled Burma's economy; Sein resigned (Aug. 12).

1988 Dr. Maung Maung, a civilian leader of the BSPP, in office as president (Aug. 19); lifted martial law, freed political prisoners, and promised free elections.

1988 Former Defense Minister Gen. Saw Maung in power as president following military coup (Sept. 18); abolished legislature and promised multi-party elections after order was restored; troops again began shooting at protesters.

1989 Burma's name (in English) changed to Myanmar by military government (June 19); capital similarly changed from Rangoon to Yangon.

1989 Anti-government rally in Yangon drew some 10,000 persons (July 5–7); government massed thousands of troops in capital to block further demonstrations.

1989 Government crackdown against dissenters began (July 20), resulting in arrest of thousands; key opposition leader Aung San Suu Ky among those arrested.

1990 First multi-party election held in Myanmar (May) since 1962; military's strongest opponent, National League for Democracy, won clear majority of seats in new People's Assembly; pro-government National Unity Party (descended from the BSPP) won only 10 seats.

1990 Military refused to transfer power to elected government; arrested some 50 legislators and forced others to flee the country.

1991 Opposition leader Aung San Suu Ky, still under arrest, awarded Nobel Peace Prize (Oct.).

1991 Military government rebuked by UN for resisting transfer to elected civilian government (Nov.).

1992 Some 60,000 Muslims fled to Bangladesh to escape repression under the military regime (Jan.–Feb.).

1992 Gen. Than Schwe president.

Mycale, Battle of Greek naval victory (Sept., 479 BC) over the Persians in the Aegean. With the victory at Plataea it was instrumental in ending the Persian invasion of Greece.

Mycenae Ancient Greek city, once located in northeastern Greece. It was a center of the Mycenaean civilization (*q.v.*) and was excavated by H. Schliemann.

Mycenaean civilization Ancient Aegean civilization that flourished on the Greek mainland (c1600–1200 BC). The Mycenaeans entered Greece from the north in c2000 BC. They were in regular contact with Minoans (*q.v.*) on Crete, and they incorporated many elements of Minoan civilization into their own culture. The period of their cultural and commercial domination of the region lasted from 1400 to 1100 BC, when the Dorian Greeks displaced the Mycenaeans. The epics of Homer may reflect elements of Mycenaean civilization.

Mycerinus *See* **Menkure.**

Myconius, Oswald *See* **Basel, Confession.**

Myerson, Goldie *See* **Meir, Golda.**

Mylae, Battle of Important Roman victory in a naval battle (260 BC), off southern Italy against the Carthaginians in the First Punic War (264–241 BC).

Myrdal, Gunnar 1898–1987. Swedish economist and sociologist. Myrdal's *An American Dilemma* (1944) was an important study of racial problems and their effect on American democracy. He received the Nobel Prize in Economic Science in 1974.

Myriocephalon, Battle of Decisive battle (1176) in wars between the Byzantines and Seljuk Turks. Byzantine forces under Murad I Comnenus attempted to recapture territory then occupied by the Turks. The Turks, under Kilij Arslan II, overwhelmed them at a mountain pass near the Myriocephalon fortress in Phrygia. The victory established the Turks in Anatolia.

Myron 5th cent. BC.   Greek sculptor. Myron was renowned for his statues of athletes in action, the most famous of which was his *Discus Thrower* (*Discobolus*).

Mysia *See* **Pergamum.**

Mysore Wars Series of four wars (1767–99) fought in India against British rule. In 1761 the Muslim leader Haidar Ali (1722–82) seized power in Mysore and began to increase his control over the region. He waged the first war (1767–69) against the East India Company, but gained little. In the second war (1780–84), he fought the British with French aid. Upon his death (1782) his son Sahib Tipu (*d.* 1799) became ruler and continued the struggle. In the third war (1790–92), Tipu was defeated by the British under Lord C. Cornwallis and lost half his territory. The fourth war (1799) ended in the death of Tipu and restoration of the Hindu monarchy in Mysore.

Mysteries Ancient religious cults that supplemented the official Greco-Roman paganism. The best-known Mystery cults were the Eleusinian (*q.v.*), Orphic (*q.v.*), and Dionysiac. They usually included initiation into secret "knowledge," including rites of purification and the reenactment of sacred dramas.

mysticism Religious doctrine. Mysticism is the belief that a person can attain direct communication with God through spiritual, intuitive, or transcendental means. This communion of a person's spirit with God results in a feeling of being at one with the universe and is often accompanied by spiritual ecstasy. Mysticism has been an element in many religions, including Christianity.

N

Nabataeans Ancient Arabian people. The Nabataeans were a Semitic people who lived on the trade route between Syria and Arabia. This strategic position enabled them to become wealthy by charging trade duties. The Roman emperor Trajan put an end to Nabataean autonomy in AD 105 and formed the Roman province Arabia Petraea.

Nabis Group of French artists of the 1890s, including Pierre Bonnard (1867–1947), J. Vuillard, and M. Denis, who derived their name from the Hebrew word for prophet. They are characterized by their use of bold colors over flat areas and a common dislike of impressionism (*q.v.*).

Nabokov, Vladimir 1899–1977. Russian-born American writer. Nabokov is best known for his novels *Lolita* (1955) and *Pale Fire* (1962), his vivid and expressive style, and his often bizarre subject matter.

Nabonidus *d.* 583? BC. Last king of Babylonia (c556–538 BC). Nabonidus coruled with his son Belshazzar. He allied himself unsuccessfully with Croesus of Lydia against Cyrus the Great of Persia.

Naboplassar *fl.* 7th cent. BC. Babylonian king (625–605 BC). He ended Assyrian control of Babylonia and thus founded (625) the Chaldaean Empire. He warred against Necho II of Egypt.

Nader, Ralph 1934– . US lawyer and consumer advocate. His publication *Unsafe at Any Speed* (1965), attacking the auto industry, not only prompted legislation on auto safety but launched him on a highly active career as a consumer advocate and critic of government. He and his associates (Nader's Raiders) published numerous consumer-oriented studies on such diverse subjects as baby food, insecticides, and radiation dangers.

Nader Shah *See* **Nadir Shah.**

Nadir Shah (Nader ~) 1688–1747. Shah of Persia (1736–47). Originally a soldier, he usurped the throne, successfully warred with the Turks, sacked Delhi and Lahore, and seized the Koh-i-noor diamond and the Peacock Throne. He is considered the last of the great Asian conquerers.

Näfels, Battle of Battle in the Austrian-Swiss Wars, fought on April 9, 1388. The Swiss ambushed and defeated the much larger Austrian invasion force at this central Swiss town. It helped lead to a 20-year truce that virtually assured the independence of the Swiss cantons under the Holy Roman Empire.

Nagano, Osami 1880–1947. Japanese admiral. Nagano ordered and organized the 1941 Japanese attack on Pearl Harbor (*q.v.*), which brought America into WW II. He was indicted as a war criminal and died while on trial.

Nagarjuna AD c150–c250. Indian Buddhist philosopher. Nagarjuna founded the Madhyamika (Middle Path) school of Buddhism, and was especially noted for his concept of "emptiness."

Nagoda Compromise agreement (Sept., 1868) by which Croatia was rejoined with Hungary in the Austro-Hungarian Dual Monarchy. Croatia, independent of Hungary since 1848, was granted a large measure of autonomy in return for accepting union with Hungary and a governor named by Hungary. The agreement remained in force until WW I.

Naguib, Muhammad 1901–84. Egyptian general and political leader. He took part in the Egyptian revolution (July 23, 1952) that deposed King Farouk I and became premier of the new, military regime. In 1954 he was removed from power and replaced by G. A. Nasser.

Nagy, Imre 1896–1958. Hungarian Communist premier. Nagy was premier (1953–55) but was forced out by Soviet pressure. He was recalled during the 1956 Hungarian Revolution (*q.v.*) but was executed when the USSR put down the rebellion.

Nagyvarad, Peace of Short-lived agreement concluded on Feb. 24, 1538, dividing Hungary between Ferdinand of Habsburg and John Zápolya, who contended for the Hungarian throne following the death of King Louis II (1526) at the Battle of Mohács.

Nahas Pasha, Mustafa el- 1876–1965. Egyptian politician. He led the nationalist Wafd party (*q.v.*) and was prime minister five times between 1928 and 1952.

Naismith, James A. 1861–1939. American athletic director. While a physical education instructor, Naismith invented the game of basketball in 1891.

Namibia (*formerly* South-West Africa) Independent country, located in the extreme southwestern portion of Africa on the Atlantic Coast. The population is 1,372,000 and the capital is Windhoek. The area was claimed by the Portuguese, Dutch, and British before becoming a German colony. South Africa administered the territory as a mandate until 1990, when Namibia became independent. Key dates in the history of Namibia include:

15TH CENT. Portuguese discovered region.

18TH CENT. Portuguese, British, and Dutch explored region.

MID-19TH CENT. British and German missionaries arrived.

1884 Region made a German protectorate.

1904–08 Nama and Herero tribes revolted; Germans put down the revolt, in which thousands were killed.

1908 Diamonds discovered; Europeans began immigrating to South-West Africa.

1915 WW I; South African forces, led by Louis Botha and J. C. Smuts, captured land from Germany.

1920 Treaty of Versailles made territory a South African League of Nations mandate.

1921–22 South Africa crushed Nama revolt.

1946 UN General Assembly rejected South Africa's application for incorporation of the area; asked to make trusteeship application instead.

1947 Smuts, prime minister of South Africa, announced that South-West Africa would continue to be administered under mandate; refused to make region UN trust territory.

1949 Region granted representation in South African parliament as step toward annexation.

1951 UN-South African negotiations over status of South-West Africa ended in failure.

1951–52 South African delegate boycotted UN General Assembly.

1966 UN General Assembly terminated old League of Nations mandate.

1968 Area renamed Namibia.

1971 International Court ordered South Africa to end its control of South-West Africa; South Africa refused.

1974 UN ordered South Africa to turn South-West Africa's government over to native Namibians.

1975 South Africa proclaimed itself willing to grant Namibian independence, but refused to deal with South-West African People's Organization (SWAPO), which had been waging a guerrilla war in Namibia.

1977 South Africa agreed to negotiate with SWAPO.

1978 UN passed Resolution 435 calling for free elections and self-determination for Namibians.

1978 South Africa agreed to Namibian independence after period of transition; Marthinus Steyn named to head interim government.

1980 Windhoek established as capital; territorial army established.

1980 South African army forces launched operation Smokeshell (June); army penetrated deep inside Angolan territory to attack SWAPO bases.

1980 Ministers' Council of the National Assembly took control of Namibia's internal affairs (July 1); South Africa appointed administrator-general.

1981 Conference at Geneva failed to reach agreement on Namibia (Jan.); South African negotiators reported deliberately drawing out negotiations.

1981 Administration of US president R. Reagan actively sought settlement in Namibia; US stepped up involvement in negotiations; presence of Cuban troops in Angola, which Angolans claimed were necessary for defense, became sticking point when South Africa demanded withdrawal of the Cubans before granting Namibian independence.

1981 South African troops again invaded Angola in Operation Protea (Aug.); towns and villages reported devastated in the attack on suspected SWAPO bases.

1983 South African army invaded southern Angola; troops remained inside Angola's borders.

1984 South Africa agreed to plan for withdrawal of its troops from Angola (Feb.); halted withdrawal just inside Angolan border, however.

1984 South Africa and SWAPO met for face-to-face talks.

1985 Transitional government set for Namibia (June 17); South Africa declared the interim government would be in office for two years; SWAPO refused offer to participate.

1985 Angola complained that South African troops had again moved into its southern territory.

1987 SWAPO declared itself ready to negotiate with South African government without preconditions.

1987 Namibia's interim government adopted constitution creating independent, non-racial government.

1988 South Africa unexpectedly offered new peace plan (Aug.); declared ceasefire in Namibia (Aug. 8); said that SWAPO government in Namibia would be acceptable provided Cuban troops left Angola.

1988 US–brokered talks between South Africa, Cuba, and Angola carried out in Brazzaville; set Apr. 1, 1989, as start of respective troop withdrawals.

1989 SWAPO won majority of seats in Namibia Constituent Assembly, following elections held Nov. 7–11; began work on drafting constitution for parliamentary democracy.

1989 SWAPO leader Sam Nujoma in office as president of provisional government.

1990 Namibia gained full independence (Mar. 21).

1990 Constituent Assembly approved constitution, which included a bill of rights and independent judicial branch.

1992 Food shortages reported as a result of drought throughout Southern Africa.

Namur, sieges of Important battles fought at Namur in south-central Belgium, at the confluence of the Meuse and Sambre rivers. 1. In the War of the League of Augsburg (*q.v.*), Namur resisted for 26 days before surrendering on June 5, 1692, to a French force that lost 2,600 men against twice that number of casualties in the city. On Sept. 1, 1695, the Dutch retook Namur after a two-month siege, losing 18,000 men to half that number of French casualties. 2. In WW I, 37,000 Belgian defenders held out for five days against 100,000 Germans before surrendering on Aug. 25, 1914.

Nanak 1469–1539. Indian religious leader and founder of the Sikhs (*q.v.*). Born a Hindu, he came to regard some Hindu practices and beliefs as superstitious, especially when compared to those of the Muslims, by whom he was influenced. After an extended journey (probably to Hindu and Muslim centers), he returned to the Punjab in 1520 and there began to spread his teachings. The Sikh religion he founded sought to bridge differences between the Hindu and Muslim religions.

Nanjing, Rape of *See* **China, 1937.**

Nanjing, Treaty of *See* **Opium War (1); treaty ports.**

Nanking *See* **Nanjing.**

Nansen, Fridtjof 1861–1930. Norwegian explorer and statesman who promoted the separation of Norway from Sweden. His Arctic expeditions furnished much valuable information about the North Pole. He won the Nobel Peace Prize in 1922 for Russian relief work.

Nantes, Edict of *See* **Edict of Nantes.**

Napier, John 1550–1617. Scottish mathematician. Napier invented the logarithm. He introduced Napier's rods for use in counting and decimal points for writing fractions.

Napier of Magdala, Robert Cornelis, 1st baron 1810–90. British soldier. Napier fought in the Sikh Wars (*q.v.*) and the Indian Mutiny, captured Magdala in Ethiopia, and was commander in chief in India (1870–76).

Naples, kingdom of Former kingdom in Italy. The kingdom of Naples, often united with Sicily, dominated southern Italy from the Middle Ages until 1860. Roger II unified the region and declared himself king of Sicily and Apulia (1130). Because the area was of strategic naval and commercial importance, it became the focus of frequent power struggles. At various times the region was ruled by the Normans, the Hohenstaufens, the Angevins, the Spanish, and the Bourbons. Napoleon overthrew the latter, renaming Naples the Parthenopian Republic (1799). The Bourbons were restored by Admiral H. Nelson later that year but were routed again by Napoleon in 1806. The Bourbons again resumed the throne in 1816, renaming it the Kingdom of the Two Sicilies (*q.v.*). The area was united with the rest of Italy by G. Garibaldi (1860).

Napoleon I (~ Bonaparte) 1769–1821. Emperor of the French (1804–14). One of the great conquerors of all time and a gifted administrator as well, Napoleon created a short-lived French empire that included virtually all of continental Europe. By his conquests, he helped to spread liberal reforms instituted in France and thereby affected the subsequent development of modern Europe. Napoleon was born in Corsica, became an artillery officer in the French Army (1785), and served with the republican army during the French Revolutionary Wars (*q.v.*). Napoleon was given command of the republican army in Italy (1796). He quickly reorganized the units under his command into an effective fighting force, and his Italian campaign (1796–97) was overwhelmingly successful. Napoleon's campaign in Egypt (1798–99) proved disastrous. At the same time, France's armies on the Continent suffered serious reverses, and the revolutionary government was on the verge of collapse. Napoleon returned to France and, with the aid of his brother, L. Bonaparte, and J. Sieyès, overthrew the Directory (Nov. 9, 1799). Napoleon was given dictatorial powers as head of the Consulate (*q.v.*). He consolidated his position and from 1800 to 1802 brought the French Revolutionary Wars to a successful conclusion. In following years he instituted reforms in education, law—notably the Code Napoléon (*q.v.*)—and government. He also restored relations with the church (1801), severed during the French Revolution. Napoleon seized on the opportunity presented (1804) by an assassination plot against him (by G. Cadoudal and others) and made himself emperor. He was crowned by the pope (Dec. 2) at Paris. With the empire (*q.v.*) thus established, Napoleon set about creating a nobility and a court. He ultimately named rulers to various states (notably Spain, Holland, Naples, and Sweden). But when he made himself king of Italy (1805), the British

(already at war with him) and other powers organized against him and the Napoleonic Wars (*q.v.*) broke out. Napoleon enjoyed his greatest military successes during these wars (notably at the Battle of Austerlitz), and by about 1808 he had extended French control throughout the Continent. But his invasion of Russia proved disastrous. Napoleon marched into Russia (June, 1812) with some 600,000 troops and hardly managed to escape (Nov., 1812) with fewer than 30,000 troops. The defeat cost Napoleon his empire. One by one former allies joined the coalition of powers against him and by Mar., 1814, the Napoleonic Wars had come to a close. Napoleon abdicated (Apr. 11, 1814) and was exiled to the island of Elba. Napoleon's final defeat did not come until 1815, however. In that year he returned to France and triumphantly entered Paris (Mar. 20). Thus began his famous Hundred Days (*q.v.*) in which he attempted to reestablish his empire. Defeated utterly at Waterloo, Napoleon again abdicated (June 22, 1815) and lived out the rest of his life in exile on the island of St. Helena.

Napoleon II 1811–32. Titular king of Rome. He was the son of Napoleon and Marie Louise. After his father's 1815 abdication, he was brought to his mother's land, Austria, where he remained a virtual prisoner until he died of tuberculosis. He was used as a pawn by C. von Metternich in bargaining with France.

Napoleon III 1808–73. Emperor of the French, nephew of Napoleon I and son of L. Bonaparte. After two unsuccessful attempts to seize power, he was elected French president in 1848. He proclaimed himself emperor in 1852 and inaugurated the Second Empire (*q.v.*). His foreign and domestic policies were popular until 1860, when he was forced to liberalize his government. He was captured during the Franco-Prussian War (1870–71), deposed, and died in exile.

Napoleonic Code *See* **Code Napoléon.**

Napoleonic Wars Wars fought (1803–15) by Napoleon I of France against various European powers. The Napoleonic Wars followed an earlier series of wars (1792–1802), the French Revolutionary Wars (*q.v.*). The French Revolutionary Wars had helped bring Napoleon to power and made France the most powerful nation on the European continent. But Napoleon was unable to match the British navy, and the British remained a continuing threat to his dominance of Europe.

Mutual distrust finally resulted in declaration of war (1803) between France and Britain and, in the years following, various coalitions of European states tried unsuccessfully to defeat Napoleon. Napoleon soon extended his French empire across nearly all of continental Europe. But his ill-fated invasion (1812) of Russia, a former ally, proved to be his undoing. Defeated (1814), Napoleon was forced into exile. He returned to power briefly during his famous Hundred Days (*q.v.*), only to meet his final defeat at Waterloo. Key events in the Napoleonic Wars include:

1803   Britain and France again at war (May); British, suspicious of Napoleon's designs, refused to evacuate Malta (by the Treaty of Amiens) and thus provoked war.

1803   British, with superior navy, captured French overseas colonies; Napoleon, with superior land army, cut British trade with continental Europe and began assembling forces to invade Britain.

1804   British secured informal agreement with Russia for coalition against Napoleon.

1804   French Empire proclaimed; Napoleon crowned himself emperor (Dec 2).

1805   Napoleon proclaimed himself King of Italy and annexed Genoa and the Ligurian Republic; brought Austria into coalition against France.

1805   Third Coalition formed; Russia joined Britain (Apr. 11) and Austria then joined both (Aug. 9); Spain allied itself with France.

1805   Battle of Trafalgar: Adm. H. Nelson destroyed (Oct. 21) the 33-ship combined Spanish-French fleet; Nelson killed but Napoleon's invasion of Britain henceforth impossible.

1805   Battles of Ulm (Oct. 20) and of Austerlitz (Dec. 3): Napoleon crushed superior Austrian-Russian forces.

1805   Treaty of Pressburg: Austria yielded Venice and Dalmatian coast to France, and Tirol and Vorarlberg to Bavaria (Dec. 26); Austria forced out of the coalition.

1806   Joseph Napoleon installed as king of Naples (southern Italy); former Bourbon rulers forced to flee to Sicily, where the British gave them protection.

1806   Confederation of the Rhine, composed of German states organized by Napoleon, formally ended the Holy Roman Empire.

1806   Napoleon created the kingdom of Holland.

1806   British halted attempted French invasion of Sicily at the Battle of Maida (July 4).

1806–12   Russo-Turkish War; Ottoman Turks turned against the Russians at French urging.

1806   Fourth Coalition: Prussia, now allied with Russia, declared war on France (Oct. 8).

1806   Napoleon was victorious over superior Prussian armies at Jena-Auerstadt (Oct. 14); Napoleon occupied Berlin, the Prussian capital.

1806–12   Napoleon instituted Continental System, forbidding all to trade with Britain; established by Berlin Decree (Nov. 21, 1806).

1807   Battle of Eylau proved inconclusive (Feb. 8) as Russians attempted to aid Prussia.

1807   Napoleon defeated a large Russian force at the Battle of Friedland in East Prussia; victory led to the Treaties of Tilsit. (June 14).

1807   Treaties of Tilsit; Russia made an ally of France, and Prussia forced to join Continental System (July 7–9), among other concessions.

1807   Grand Duchy of Warsaw created by Napoleon.

1807   Napoleon created the kingdom of Westphalia from Prussian and Hanoverian lands.

1807   British attacked Copenhagen (Sept.); Denmark declared war against Britain.

1807   Treaty of Fontainebleau (Oct. 27); Spanish government allowed French troops to cross Spain to invade Britain's ally Portugal.

1807   Portugal occupied by French; Portuguese court removed to Brazil (Nov.).

1807   Orders in Council issued (Nov.–Dec.) by British, instituting a blockade of Napoleonic Europe.

1807   Milan Decree issued (Dec. 17) by Napoleon; ships that dealt with Great Britain lost their neutrality.

1808   Revolt by Spanish at Aranjuez (Mar.) led to dismissal of Godoy and abdication of Charles IV (May).

1808   Napoleon appointed his brother, Joseph, king of Spain (June); French troops occupied Madrid (July 20); Spanish rebelled and sent the French into retreat.

1808   Congress of Erfurt (Sept.); meeting between Napoleon and Russian tsar Alexander I to reaffirm alliance.

1808–14   Peninsular War; Napoleon led a new invasion of Spain, while the British invaded

Portugal; in the long campaign that followed, the French were finally driven out of Portugal and Spain.

1809   Fifth Coalition; Austria, allied with Britain, renewed the war on land in the east (Apr.).

1809   Napoleon defeated Austrian forces at Battle of Abensberg-Eckmühl (Apr. 23).

1809   Napoleon annexed the Papal States.

1809   Napoleon suffered his first major military defeat at the Battle of Aspern-Essling in Austria (May 21–22).

1809   Napoleon victorious in the bloody Battle of Wagram in Austria; prevented formation of new coalition against him (July 5–6).

1809   Pope Pius VII arrested (July) by Napoleon; the pope had excommunicated him for annexing the Papal States.

1809   Peace of Schönbrunn concluded by Napoleon with Austria; France gained some 32,000 square miles of Austrian territory (Oct. 14).

1810   Napoleon married Marie Louise, daughter of Austrian emperor Francis II, after divorcing Josephine.

1810   Napoleon annexed Holland.

1810   Tsar Alexander I withdrew from the Continental System (Dec. 31).

1812   War of 1812, between the US and Britain, broke out (June 18); US commerce had suffered as a result of French and British harassment of neutral shipping; war against Britain lasted to 1815.

1812   Napoleon assembled some 600,000 men in the Grand Army and invaded Russia (June 24); Russians, led by M. Kutuzov and Prince Barclay de Tolly, adopted scorched-earth policy as they retreated eastward before Napoleon's army.

1812   Battle of Borodino (Sept. 7); narrow victory for Napoleon; enabled Napoleon to march unopposed into Moscow (Sept. 14).

1812   Russians burned Moscow (Sept. 15–19).

1812   Napoleon remained at Moscow (Sept.–Oct.), waiting for Russians to come to terms; his overtures rejected.

1812   Napoleon ordered the retreat from Moscow (Oct. 19); Grand Army harassed by Russian forces throughout the retreat.

1812   Onset of the Russian winter hampered French retreat; cold weather, constant attacks by Russians, and lack of supplies seriously weakened Napoleon's army; French suffered heavy losses.

1812   Berezina River Crossing (Nov. 26–28); Napoleon's forces suffered heavy losses while crossing this Russian river; French retreat became a rout. Napoleon abandoned his troops and made for Paris (Dec. 5); only some 30,000 of his troops survived his retreat.

1813–14   War of Liberation; Prussia, Russia, Sweden, Austria, and Britain eventually participated in defeating Napoleon.

1813   Prussia, again allied with Russia, declared war on France (Mar.).

1813   Napoleon defeated (May 2) Prussians and Russians at the Battle of Lutzen, in Saxony.

1813   Battle of Bautzen; Russians and Prussians defeated by Napoleon (May 20–21).

1813   Sixth Coalition; Austria joined allies (Aug. 12); for the first time, Napoleon now faced Austria, Britain, Prussia, and Russia at the same time.

1813   Napoleon won his last major battle, at Dresden; fought against allied Austrian, Russian, and Prussian troops (Aug. 27).

1813   Battle of the Nations: the allies defeated Napoleon at Leipzig (Oct. 16–19).

1813–14   Invasion of France by the allies (Dec.); Paris occupied (Mar. 31).

1814   Napoleon abdicated (Apr. 11); Louis XVIII restored to French throne; Napoleon exiled to Elba.

1814   Treaty of Paris formally ended hostilities after Napoleon's defeat; terms not harsh (May 30); boundaries restored to what they were in 1792; some colonies restored.

1814–15   Congress of Vienna in session; restored legitimate monarchs in Austria, Prussia, Spain, and in Italian kingdoms; created the kingdom of The Netherlands, kingdom of Poland (ruled by Russia), and the German Confederation; reestablished independent Switzerland; reached agreement to hold regular congresses to maintain peace.

1815   Hundred Days; Napoleon returned to Paris (Mar. 20) from exile and attempted to reestablish his empire (Mar.–June).

1815   King Louis XVIII fled and the French rallied to Napoleon; Napoleon instituted a liberal constitution; forced to fight by a new coalition against him, he invaded Belgium (June).

1815   French forces victorious at the Battle of Quatre Bras (June 16).

1815 Battle of Waterloo fought; marked Napoleon's final defeat (June 18).

1815 Abdication of Napoleon (June 22); Napoleon exiled to St. Helena in the south Atlantic; Louis was restored.

1815 Treaty of Paris formally ended hostilities after Napoleon's defeat, France submitted to loss of territories, payment of an indemnity, and occupation by allied armies (Nov. 20).

Nara Japanese city and prefecture, located on Honshu just north of Osaka. Nara is one of Japan's most historic and religious centers and was the first permanent capital of Japan. It has a 53-foot-high statue of Buddha, the largest in the world, and is also the resting place of Jimmu Tenno, the first Japanese emperor.

Narodniki (Populists) Members of the Russian populist movement of the 19th century that advocated land for the peasants. Prevented by the police from active work in the villages, adherents of the movement formed a secret Land and Liberty society in 1876; the latter became dominated by its terroristic wing, the People's Will, which, in 1881, assassinated Tsar Alexander II.

Narottama *See* **Norodom.**

Narragansett Indians North American Indians whose language was of the Algonquian-Wakashan stock and who occupied present-day Rhode Island. One of their chiefs sold R. Williams the land on which he founded Providence. They were allied with the colonists in the 1637 Pequot War (*q.v.*) but declined in power along with other Indians after the 1638 King Philip's War (*q.v.*).

Narses AD c478–c573. Byzantine general and statesman. Narses conquered the Ostrogoths (*q.v.*) under Totila in AD 552. He served as prefect of Italy from 554 to 567, when he was removed by Justin II.

Narváez, Ramón María 1800–68. Spanish general and statesman. He was a strong military supporter of Isabella II against the Carlists, and later overthrew B. Espartero. With brief intervals, he served as Isabella's premier from 1844 to 1851 and several times thereafter.

Naseby, Battle of English Civil War battle fought near Naseby in central England on June 14, 1645. Charles I's army of around 7,000 engaged the Parliamentarians' newly organized New Model Army (*q.v.*) of about 14,000 men, commanded by Sir T. Fairfax, with O. Cromwell commanding the cavalry. The Parliamentarians

routed the Royalists, of whom some 3,500 were killed or captured.

Nash, Ogden 1902–71. American writer. Nash was best known for his humorous and satirical verses and for the lyrics of the Broadway musical *One Touch of Venus.*

Nash, Thomas *See* **Nashe, Thomas.**

Nashe, Thomas (Nash, ~) 1567–1601. English dramatist and satirist, a master of scurrilous invective, Nash's anti-Puritanism plunged him into the Marprelate Controversy (*q.v.*). He and co-writer B. Jonson were imprisoned for their play *The Isle of Dogs.*

Nashville, Battle of American Civil War battle. On Dec. 15–16, 1864, the Union army of Gen. G. Thomas defeated the Confederates, in the last major battle of the Civil War. Union losses were 400 killed and 1,740 wounded against total Confederate losses of around 15,000.

Naso, Publius Ovidius *See* **Ovid.**

Nassau Former German duchy. Nassau occupied parts of the present Hesse and Rhineland-Palatinate. It contributed future rulers to the Netherlands and Luxembourg, including the line of William I (the Silent) of Orange, who was also the ancestor of kings of England. Nassau was incorporated into Prussia (1866) after the Austro-Prussian War (*q.v.*).

Nassau, John Maurice of *See* **John Maurice of Nassau.**

Nassau, Maurice of *See* **Maurice of Nassau.**

Nasser, Gamal Abdel 1918–70. Egyptian statesman. Nasser led the 1952 *coup d'état* that ended the monarchy. He also ousted Gen. M. Naguib (1954), naming himself prime minister. He was elected and served as president of Egypt (1956–58) and of the United Arab Republic (1958–70). Strongly Muslim and nationalistic, he nationalized the Suez Canal (1956) provoking the Suez Crisis (*q.v.*), established an alliance with the USSR, and fought the June, 1967, war against Israel. During his tenure he was the foremost symbol of Arab nationalism and resistance to Western domination.

Nast, Thomas 1840–1902. German-born American political cartoonist. Arriving in the US in 1846, Nast grew up in New York City in the years leading up to the Civil War. His rise to fame was linked with the emerging success of illustrated magazines (first at *Frank Leslie's Illustrated Newspaper,* from 1855; then *Harper's Weekly,* from 1857), and his best work concerned the Civil War and Reconstruction. He was also noted for his cartoons attacking Boss Tweed and as the creator (or popularizer) of such enduring symbols as the Democratic donkey and the Republican elephant.

Natal South African province, located in the eastern coastal region. Inhabited by the Zulus, the first European to sight it was V. da Gama, in 1497; and was settled by the Boers in 1837 after their Great Trek. It became a British colony (1843) and, after the Boer War, it became part of South Africa (1910).

Nation, Carry 1846–1911. American temperance crusader. Brandishing an ax, she smashed saloons, and endured countless beatings and over thirty arrests for her temperance movement activities (*q.v.*).

National Assembly The deliberative assembly into which the States-General constituted themselves June, 1789, during the French Revolution. The aim was to prepare a constitution (hence it is also called the Constituent Assembly). The National Assembly ultimately brought about creation of a constitutional monarchy (1791) and was superseded by the Legislative Assembly. (*See also* French Revolution [1789–91].)

National Association for the Advancement of Colored People (NAACP) US organization formed in 1910 to counteract the lynching of blacks by whites. Its first black leader was W. E. B. DuBois. Today it conducts legal and political civil rights activities. In the 1970s, with a membership of more than 400,000 in more than 1,500 local units, it maintained its position as the leading US civil rights organization. It was primarily responsible for bringing about the landmark 1954 US Supreme Court antisegregation decision *Brown* v. *Board of Education of Topeka, Kansas* (*q.v.*).

National Convention French legislative body (Sept. 21, 1792–Oct. 25, 1795), successor to the Legislative Assembly (*q.v.*) during the French Revolution. Convened after the suspension of King Louis XVI, the National Convention established the republic and condemned Louis to death. It came under the control of the Jacobins, and then of M. Robespierre, who promoted the Reign of Terror (*q.v.*). The Thermidorian reaction in the Convention brought this bloody period to an end. The National Convention was replaced by the Directory (*q.v.*).

National Covenant Bond or engagement instituted by Scottish Presbyterians (Feb. 28, 1638)

to observe and maintain their 1581 Confession of Faith. It was the result of efforts by England's King Charles I to impose the English liturgy upon the Scots. (*See also* Covenanters.)

National Front for the Liberation of the South *See* **National Liberation Front.**

nationalism Political or social movement in which an individual's primary loyalty is given to the state. Arising with the formation of modern nation-states, nationalism became a major influence in the history of Europe in the 17th and 18th cents. Later it became a driving force in movements by national groups against imperial rule, such as in Ireland (19th cent.) and colonial states in Africa and Asia (20th cent.). Extreme nationalism also contributed to the rise of Fascism in Italy and National Socialism (Nazism) in Germany.

Nationalist China *See* **Taiwan.**

National Labor Union *See* **labor unions.**

National Liberation Front (~ Front for the Liberation of the South) (NLF) Political and military organization formed (Dec. 20, 1960) to overthrow the South Vietnamese government and reunite North and South Vietnam. Reacting to abuses under the Diem regime in the South, both Communist and non-Communist Vietnamese joined the NLF, though the organization was clearly dominated by Communists. During the Vietnam War (*q.v.*), the NLF military forces, the Vietcong, proved highly successful in guerrilla operations against US and South Vietnamese forces. The NLF established a provisional rebel government in June, 1969, and secured the final conquest of the South in 1975.

National Prohibition Act *See* **Volstead Act.**

National Republican party US political party (c1825–c1836). National Republicans were supporters of J. Q. Adams and nominated him in 1828 to oppose A. Jackson. In 1832, the party nominated H. Clay to oppose Jackson, and, after Clay's defeat, it went into decline. Party members included those connected with business, farm, and labor interests who supported high tariffs and a national bank. By 1836 they had merged with other anti-Jackson forces to create the Whig party (*q.v.*).

National Road (Cumberland ~) Major US highway to the Old Northwest, linking Cumberland, Maryland, and St. Louis, Missouri. Construction began with federal financing in 1811 and by 1833 the road extended to St. Louis. The highway was of major importance in settlement of the American West.

National Security Act   US legislation enacted on July 24, 1947 (and amended on Aug. 10, 1949) that unified the US armed services, with joint chiefs of staff, under a single department headed by a secretary of defense at cabinet level. It established within the executive office of the president the National Security Council, with the president, vice-president, and secretaries of state and defense as members. And it authorized and established the US Central Intelligence Agency (CIA).

National Socialism (Nazism)   Political movement in Germany, the German counterpart of fascist movements that arose in Europe and elsewhere after WW I. National Socialism shared with other fascist movements the characteristics of extreme nationalism, militarism, determination to create a totalitarian state, formation of an elitist class, unswerving obedience to a single leader, and nationalistic expansionism. A. Hitler, leader of the German fascists, outlined many of the doctrines of National Socialism in his book, *Mein Kampf.* Racism was a particularly strong element in the German movement and centered on a fanatical belief in the existence of a "master race," composed of Germanic peoples. It was the duty of the master race, Hitler preached, to dominate the world and eliminate so-called inferior races (particularly Jews and blacks). Hitler and others used this master race theory skillfully to play on popular fears (of Jews, of Communists) and to arouse German nationalistic spirit at a time when Germany was in the midst of political and economic crisis. Indeed, Hitler's fanatical rhetoric (and effective political organization) won a large following for the National Socialism movement and gave Hitler control of the government. But his fanaticism had horrifying consequences. His militant nationalism led directly to WW II and the loss of millions of lives in bloody combat. His attempts to impose the "final solution" to purify the races led to mass extermination of millions of Jews and others (*see* Holocaust) in concentration camps. Germany's defeat in WW II effectively ended the National Socialism movement. (*See also* Nazi party; Fascism.)

National Socialist German Workers' party   *See* **Nazi party.**

National Union Convention (Arm-in-Arm Convention)   Meeting (Aug. 14–16, 1866) in Philadelphia of supporters of US president A. Johnson

to organize opposition to Radical Republicans (*q.v.*). Its candidates were soundly defeated by Radical Republicans in the 1866 congressional elections.

National Woman's Party   Women's rights group formed (c1920) to promote total equality of women. Following passage of the 19th Amendment granting women the vote, militant suffragette Alice Paul and others split with the Congressional Union group, of which they had been members, over future goals of the women's movement. The NWP launched an unsuccessful campaign for an Equal Rights Amendment in 1923. The amendment was opposed by other more moderate women's groups, notably the League of Women Voters.

National Workshops   *See* **February Revolution.**

Nation of Islam   *See* **Black Muslims.**

Nations, Battle of   *See* **Leipzig, Battle of.**

Nations, League of   International organization (1919–46) formed to maintain peace and security in the post-WW I world. Though the league generally failed in its aims during the 1930s, it provided a foundation for the UN organization that succeeded it. Provided for by the Paris Conference of 1919 (largely due to US president W. Wilson's efforts) and the Treaty of Versailles (1919), the league consisted of a secretariat, council, assembly, and the Permanent Court of International Justice. Original members included the WW I Allies and neutral nations, which were later joined by other nations. The US, however, did not join because of isolationist sentiment in Congress. This and the provision for unanimous assent in both the assembly and council seriously weakened the league. Though it was generally successful in social and economic matters, it failed to effectively promote disarmament. Then, beginning with Japan's occupation of Manchuria (1931), the inability of the league to prevent armed aggression became apparent. Other wars of aggression by Japan, Italy, and Germany followed in the 1930s and with the outbreak of WW II, the league collapsed. It was officially dissolved Jan., 1946.

naturalism   Modern philosophical movement that seeks to explain all phenomena in natural, empirical terms, rejecting any metaphysical or supernatural causality. The literary movement of the same name aims to present human life in similar objective, empirical terms, rejecting free will and spiritual factors, and is best exemplified in the novels of É. Zola.

natural rights Philosophical concept. Natural rights are inherent rights that cannot be taken away by a government. They are expressed in the Declaration of the Rights of Man and the Declaration of Independence (*qq.v.*), and in the writings of such thinkers as J. Locke and T. Paine.

Navaho Indians (Navajo ~) American Indian tribe of the Athapascan family of Indian languages. Originally nomadic, they settled in the American Southwest in the 17th cent. They pillaged settlements until subdued by K. Carson (1863–64), who destroyed their sheep and fruit trees. They were granted a 3.5 million-acre reservation in Arizona, New Mexico, and Utah in 1878. By the 1970s they numbered more than 120,000 and hence were America's largest Indian tribe.

Navarino, Battle of Naval battle in the Greek War of Independence, fought on Oct. 20, 1827, in the Peloponnesian harbor of Navarino (now Pylos). Britain, France, and Russia sent 24 ships to the aid of Greece after the Turkish sultan Mahmud II had secured the help of an Egyptian fleet under Ibrahim Pasha to help quell the Greek revolt. The Egyptian-Turkish ships were bottled up in the harbor and more than 50 were sunk, with an allied loss of only 300 men against defenders' casualties of over 4,000. This was the last pitched battle fought between wooden sailing ships.

Navarre, kingdom of Spanish province. It was originally a Basque kingdom on both sides of the Pyrenees; the Spanish portion was annexed by Ferdinand the Catholic in 1515, while the French part was incorporated into France when Henry III of Navarre became Henry IV of France (1589). The historic kingdom reached its apex when its king, Sancho III, married the heiress of Castile and ruled over most of Christian Spain (1000–35).

Navarre, Margaret of *See* **Margaret of Navarre.**

Navas de Tolosa, Battle of Las Important victory (1212) for the Spanish over the Almohads (North African Muslims) during the Christian reconquest of Spain. The Spanish, led by King Alphonso VIII of León and Castile, overwhelmed the Almohads on the plain of Las Navas de Tolosa in southern Spain.

Navigation Acts English legislation (14th to 19th cents.) designed to limit carrying trade to ships of England and English colonies. The first Navigation Act was passed in 1381 but could not be implemented because of a lack of ships. The era of an effective act dates from 1651, when a law aimed primarily at Dutch shipping began the practice of "enumerating" goods that could be shipped to England or its possessions only in their own ships. It contributed to the outbreak of the first Dutch War (1652–54). Enforcement of the acts, especially the 1664 act, by which English colonies could receive European goods shipped only via England, also contributed to unrest in the American colonies. These laws were especially effective during the 17th and 18th cents., and English carrying trade tonnage increased during this period. The acts were all eventually repealed (1849 and 1854).

Nayler, James 1618–60. English Quaker leader. His followers acclaimed him in the words, "Holy, holy, holy, Lord God of Israel," as he rode into Bristol (1656). He was then imprisoned, pilloried, whipped, and branded for blasphemy (1656) in spite of his explanation that they were only worshiping the "Christ within him."

Nazi party (National Socialist German Workers' party) German political party, the instrument of A. Hitler's rise to power and the organ through which he exercised totalitarian control of the German state (1933–45). Founded (1919) as the German Workers' party, it was renamed and reorganized by Hitler along paramilitary lines (by creating Nazi storm troops). He took complete control of it in 1921, and, with the aid of H. W. Göring, R. Hess, and (later) P. J. Goebbels, began to establish the Nazi themes (*see* National Socialism) of belligerent nationalism, anticommunism, and anti-Semitism. Hitler's first attempt (1923) to take power, the Munich Putsch (*q.v.*), failed, and, after a short jail term, he returned to lead the party. The decisive factor in the rise of the Nazi party was the economic collapse and Depression that began in 1929. The Nazis made significant gains in the Reichstag elections of 1930 and 1932, and, in Jan., 1933, Hitler was appointed chancellor. The Reichstag Fire (*q.v.*), in Feb. 1933, gave Hitler the pretext to suppress the Communists and other opponents. In late 1933, Hitler established the corporative state and made the Nazis the official ruling party. Then, by his Blood Purge (*q.v.*) of certain elements of the Nazi party, he established (1934) totalitarian control of the party and the state. Thereafter the party's history, marked by its involvement in WW II and the staggering loss of human life, was that of Germany until 1945. Among the organs of the Nazi party were the SS (Schutzstaffel); the SD (Sicherheitsdienst), for espionage and control of the concentration camps; the Gestapo (*q.v.*); and the Hitler Youth organization.

Nazism. *See* **National Socialism.**

Nearchus *fl.* 324 BC. Macedonian general. Nearchus was a friend of Alexander the Great and commanded a fleet of his on a voyage from the Indus River to the Persian Gulf in 325–324 BC. He later wrote an account of his journey.

Near East Term sometimes applied to the areas around the eastern Mediterranean, the southwestern parts of Asia, and northeast Africa. Today it is more often designated as the Middle East (*q.v.*).

Nebhapetre *See* **Mentuhotep II.**

Nebraska State in the central US, the 37th state. The Spanish and French first visited the area, which was included in the Louisiana Purchase (*q.v.*) of 1803. M. Lewis and W. Clark explored the region, and fur traders set up the first settlements. It became a territory through the Kansas-Nebraska Act (*q.v.*) in 1854, and obtained its present boundaries in 1863. The Homestead Act (1862) and the railroad brought settlers and farmers, and, in 1867, it was admitted as a free state. The state constitution was adopted in 1875.

Nebuchadnezzar c630–562 BC. King of Babylon (605–562 BC), successor to his father, Nabopolassar. In 586 BC, he destroyed Jerusalem while putting down a revolt there and exiled most of its inhabitants to Babylon (Babylonian captivity, *q.v.*). He rebuilt most of the temples in his land and made Babylon, with its Hanging Gardens (*q.v.*), one of the most beautiful cities in the ancient world.

Necho II *d.* 593 BC. Egyptian pharaoh (609–593 BC) of the 26th dynasty. After the fall of Nineveh (612 BC), he sought to aid the Assyrians against the Babylonians and conquered Syria and Palestine, defeating Josiah at Megiddo (609 BC). But he was himself defeated by Nebuchadnezzar II at Carchemish in 605 BC. His defeat spelled the doom of Assyria. Forced to retire to Egypt, he repulsed an attempted invasion and later commissioned a Phoenician naval expedition that apparently circumnavigated Africa.

Necker, Jacques 1732–1804. Swiss-born French statesman and financier. As director of finances

and the treasury in prerevolutionary France he tried but failed to restore fiscal soundness to the old regime. He was one of those who recommended calling the States-General (*q.v.*), and his dismissal by Louis XVI was one of the causes of the seizure of the Bastille on July 14, 1789. His daughter was the writer Mme. G. de Staël.

Neerwinden, Battle of *See* **League of Augsburg, War of the.**

Nefertiti c1372–50 BC. Egyptian queen. She was the wife of Akhenaton and supported his religious reforms. A famous limestone bust depicting her head, found in 1912, is now in the Berlin Museum.

Negro Ethnic and racial term. Negro, meaning "black," is the name given by ethnologists to the brown-skinned peoples who originated in the regions of Africa south of the Sahara. From the 16th to 19th cents., European colonial powers used Negroes taken from Africa as slaves in their colonies. The movement to end slavery (*q.v.*) began in the late 17th cent. and was largely completed in the 19th cent. (*see* abolition). During the civil rights movement (*q.v.*) of the 1960s in the US, the term "black" came into general use in preference to "Negro."

Nehemiah *fl.* 5th cent. BC. Ancient Jewish leader. He obtained permission from the Persians as governor extraordinary of Judaea to rebuild the walls of Jerusalem (444 BC). He also instituted religious reforms that became characteristic features of postexilic Judaism, as recounted in the Old Testament Books of Ezra and Nehemiah.

Nehru, Jawaharlal 1889–1964. Indian statesman, a leader in the movement for India's independence, and India's first prime minister (1947–64). Nehru studied in England and was admitted to the bar (1912). Returning to India, he joined (1919) the nationalist movement for Indian independence from Britain led by M. Gandhi. With Gandhi's help, he became president (1929) of the Indian National Congress, and was reelected three times. During WW II he refused to support the British war effort and was imprisoned. When Indian independence was granted (1947), he became prime minister and minister of foreign affairs. He adopted a policy of nonalignment in international matters and promoted a domestic program of industrialization and socialization. He sought reorganization of the separate Indian states along linguistic lines. His administration was marked by conflict with

Pakistan over Kashmir and by a Chinese invasion of India (1962).

Nehru-Liaqat Pact   *See* **Delhi Pact.**

Nekhtnebf I (Nectanebo)   Ancient Egyptian pharaoh (380–361 BC) and founder of the 30th dynasty. He decisively repelled a Persian invasion force (374 BC) and made substantial additions to the temple of Amon at Karnak.

Nelson, Horatio 1758–1805.   English admiral, lord, and national hero. His ships destroyed the French fleet (1798) at the Battle of the Nile (*q.v.*), stranding Napoleon's army in Egypt. At Trafalgar (*q.v.*), in 1805, his fleet annihilated a numerically superior French-Spanish fleet, ending Napoleon's hopes of subduing Britain. Nelson was killed at Trafalgar. He is celebrated by the Nelson Column in Trafalgar Square, London.

Nemea, Battle of   *See* **Corinthian War.**

Nemean Games   Athletic games held in ancient Greece (from c573 BC) celebrating the god Zeus. A major panhellenic festival, the games were conducted by Argos (after c460 BC) and were similar to the Olympic Games. The Nemean games were held in the second and fourth years of the four-year Olympiad (the period between Olympic Games).

Nemirovich-Danchenko, Vladimir Ivanovich 1858–1943.   Russian author and director. Together with K. Stanislavsky, he founded the Moscow Art Theater, which influenced European and American as well as Russian theater standards.

neoclassicism (classic revival)   Artistic and architectural movement. The classic revival centered in Europe and America in the late 18th and early 19th cents. It was based on a reappreciation of the cultures of Greece and Rome. Examples of its architecture are the Washington Monument and the US Capitol.

Neolithic   *See* **Stone Age.**

Neoplatonism   Philosophical school developed especially by Plotinus in Alexandria and Rome in the 3rd cent. AD. Based on Plato's teachings and containing elements of Oriental philosophy and mysticism, it was the last of the great pagan schools of thought. It taught belief in the One, a comprehensive deity, who gave the Logos (divine word) to individuals through emanation. Porphyry and Iamblichus were important exponents of Neoplatonism. Its influence declined after Justinian closed the Academy at Athens in AD 529, but it influenced both medieval and modern philosophy.

Neo-Pythagoreanism   Philosophical movement that developed in the 1st cent. AD. It incorporated elements of the philosophy advanced (6th cent. BC) by Pythagoras, greatly emphasizing the mystical elements while borrowing from Jewish and Hellenistic philosophy.

Nepal   Independent Himalayan kingdom situated between Tibet in the north, and India in the south and west. The population is 19,158,000 and the capital is Kathmandu. Located in Nepal is Mt. Everest, the highest peak in the world. Nepal's population includes a number of ethnic groups, among them the Sherpas, noted as mountain climbers and guides, and the Gurkhas, who became renowned as fighters in the British army. The Gurkhas gained prominence in Nepal, and in the 18th cent. invaded Tibet. Their invasion was defeated (1792) by the Tibetans and Chinese, and a subsequent treaty favored Tibet. A Gurkha invasion of India led to war (1814–16) with Great Britain. Again defeated, the Gurkhas were obliged by treaty to withdraw to roughly what has become Nepal's southern border. Great Britain affirmed Nepal's independence by treaty (1923). Nepal was ruled by a monarchy until 1951, when a constitutional monarchy was established. India maintained considerable influence in Nepal until the 1960s, when Nepal began to establish relations with China as well. A Sino-Nepalese treaty (1961) defined Nepal's border with Tibet. The country has been ruled since 1972 by King Birendra Bir Bikram Shah (1945–). Tension with India increased in 1989 (possibly because Nepal had purchased arms from China), and India halted all trade and transit to land-locked Nepal, causing shortages of food and basic goods. The disagreement was resolved following negotiations in mid-1990. Opposition to Nepal's repressive government reached significant proportions early in 1990 and culminated in a massive demonstration near the royal palace (Apr.), in which troops fired on the crowd, killing over 50 people. Two days later the king legalized political parties (outlawed for 30 years), and in July issued further liberalizing reforms. A new constitution was enacted (Nov. 9), providing for a constitutional monarchy with limits on royal powers and guarantees of basic democratic rights and freedoms. The first free elections in 50 years were held in 1991.

Nerchinsk, Treaty of   Agreement signed in 1689 between tsarist Russia and the Manchu Empire of China involving trade concessions and territorial disputes. Russia gained trade access to Beijing but lost her Amur Basin trading outposts. It was China's first settlement with a European power, and it governed basic Russo-Chinese relations until the mid-19th cent.

Nero (Claudius Caesar) AD 37–68. Roman emperor (AD 54–68), successor to Claudius I, who had married Nero's mother, Agrippina II, great-granddaughter of Augustus. His reign went well until his cruelty, vanity, and instability surfaced and he murdered his mother (AD 59) and his wife (AD 62). He blamed the Christians for the fire that destroyed much of Rome (64) (for which he was popularly believed responsible), and he began their persecution. He rebuilt the city, creating the mammoth Golden House (*q.v.*) as his palace. A plot against Nero (Pisonian conspiracy led by Gaius Piso) was uncovered in AD 65 and led to widespread executions, resulting in the deaths of Seneca and Lucan, among others. In 68, the legions and the Praetorian Guard revolted, and Nero committed suicide.

Neruda, Pablo 1904–73. Chilean poet and diplomat. A surrealist, he was an influential Spanish-language poet. Among his works are *Twenty Love Poems and a Song of Despair, A New Decade,* and *Toward the Splendid City.* He was awarded the Nobel Prize in Literature in 1971.

Nerva AD c30–98. Roman emperor (AD 96–98). He was consul in AD 71 and 90, was banished by Domitian, but succeeded to the throne after the latter's murder. He was a just ruler who accomplished reforms in laws and taxation; he adopted Trajan to be his successor.

Nervi, Pier Luigi 1891–1979. Italian architect and engineer. Nervi pioneered the use of "ferrocement," concrete reinforced with steel. Among his many well-known designs are the UNESCO building (Paris), the George Washington Bridge Bus Terminal (New York), and the Olympic Stadium (Rome).

Nesselrode, Karl Robert, Count 1780–1862. Russian statesman and diplomat. Guiding tsarist foreign policy for some 40 years, he strongly favored the Holy Alliance (*q.v.*). He dispatched Russian troops to crush the Hungarian revolt of L. Kossuth (1849), but was unable to avert the Crimean War (*q.v.*).

Nestorianism Christian movement (5th cent. AD) that held Jesus Christ had two distinct personalities—divine and human—linked by a moral union. Advanced by Nestorius, this view was condemned by the Council of Ephesus (AD 431), which held that Jesus had both human and divine natures but was one person. Though Nestorianism declined in the West, it spread through the Middle East, Persia, India, and China, and there reached its height (7th–10th cents.) in the form of the Nestorian church. The church rapidly declined in these regions (13th and 14th cents.) following the failure of the Crusades and the ensuing persecution by Tamerlane of Christians in the East. Some Nestorians rejoined the Roman Catholic church (16th cent.) and became known as Chaldaeans.

Netherlands, the (Kingdom of the Netherlands) Country located in northwestern Europe on the coast of the North Sea. The population is 14,864,000 and the capital is Amsterdam; its seat of government, The Hague. Originally part of the Carolingian Empire, the region of the Netherlands first passed to the Holy Roman Empire, and then to the personal domains of the Habsburg family. The Netherlands at this time formed the northern part of the Low Countries (*q.v.*). The Netherlands gained independence (as the United Provinces) in the 16th cent. and in the 17th cent. presided over a great commercial empire. Dutch culture also flourished in this period. In the 18th cent., Dutch power declined as a result of rivalries and wars with England and France. The modern kingdom of the Netherlands was created in 1815. **For more on important persons and major events** *see* **entries under specific names.** Key dates in the history of the Netherlands include:

4TH–8TH CENTS. Area subdued by the Franks; conversion to Christianity under Charlemagne.

9TH CENT. Break-up of the Carolingian Empire; area passed into the eastern (German) possessions of Lothair I, and hence eventually became a part of the Holy Roman Empire.

1018 Holland established as country within the Holy Roman Empire.

1277 Low-lying country around the Zuider Zee flooded by severe storm.

14TH–15TH CENTS. Low Countries, including present-day Belgium, Luxembourg, and the Netherlands, came under the rule of the dukes of Burgundy; land reclamation and dike-building already extensive by this time.

c1370–c1440 Dutch sexton, L. Koster, lived; some claim he invented movable type before Gutenberg.

c1374 Religious reformer G. Groote founded Roman Catholic order Brethren of the Common Life.

1421 Over 100,000 killed when dikes protecting area around Dort burst; 72 villages leveled by deluge.

c1450–1516 Artist H. Bosch lived; painted *The Crowning with Thorns* and other works.

1477 Marriage of Mary of Burgundy to Archduke Maximilian of Austria (May); this brought the Low Countries under the control of the Habsburg family.

1480–1530 Margaret of Austria, Habsburg princess, lived; served twice as regent of the Netherlands.

1509 Scholar Erasmus wrote *The Praise of Folly.*

1530 Hundreds of thousands believed killed when storm broke dikes in Holland; another disastrous flood in 1570 killed an estimated 50,000.

1534 John of Leiden led short-lived revolt by Anabaptists in Münster.

1555 Habsburg Holy Roman Emperor Charles V presented the Low Countries to his son King Philip II of Spain.

1550s–60s Calvinism began to make inroads in the prosperous northern provinces—the area of the present-day Netherlands.

1560s Spanish attempted to impose Inquisition and thereby gain firm control over Low Countries, then agitating against Spanish rule.

1560–1609 Theologian J. Arminius lived; his opposition to Calvinism became known as Arminianism.

1566 Compromise of Breda; this document signed by Dutch and Flemish to protest the Inquisition.

1568 Revolt, led by William I the Silent, broke out in the northern provinces.

1572–74 Spanish driven out of the Low Countries.

1574 Spanish siege of Leiden broken when storm (Oct. 1–2) burst nearby dike, flooding Spanish army's lowland encampment; some 20,000 Spaniards killed.

1576 Pacification of Ghent; Low Countries united under William I's leadership.

FROM 1578 Spanish reconquered southern provinces of the Low Countries and reestablished Catholicism there.

1579 Union of Utrecht brought together the seven northern provinces (most of the present-day territory) as the United Provinces of the Netherlands; southern provinces became the Spanish Netherlands.

c1580–1666 F. Hals lived; famed for his portrait paintings.

1581 Dutch declared independence from Spain by the Act of Abjuration (July 26).

1583 L. Elzevir founded famous book publishing business in Leiden.

1584 William of Orange assassinated; succeeded by his son Maurice of Nassau.

1585 England joined the United Provinces in the struggle against Spain.

1597–1653 M. Tromp lived; became famous Dutch naval commander.

17TH CENT. Golden Age of Dutch culture, especially art and philosophy.

1602 Dutch East India Company founded as a colonial trading company that would be the basis of the Dutch overseas empire.

1604–79 General John Maurice of Nassau conquered much of Brazil from Portugal for the Dutch West India Co.

1606–69 Rembrandt lived; famed for paintings *Two Philosophers, Aristotle Contemplating the Bust of Homer,* and others.

1606–1683/84 J. Heem lived; considered one of Holland's greatest still-life painters.

1607–76 M. Adriaanszoon de Ruyter lived; became naval commander who established Dutch navy as a rival to English navy, for a time.

1609–22 Twelve Years' Truce concluded with Spain; assured *de facto* independence to the United Provinces.

1610 Dutch Protestants known as Remonstrants presented their Calvinist views to the States-General; later were persecuted (until 1625).

1619–67 Dutch took control of Cape of Good Hope, Java, Sumatra, and the other islands of the Malay Archipelago (modern Indonesia).

1620 C. Drebbel invented the first crude but navigable submarine.

1621 Dutch West India Company founded for colonizing and trade in the New World.

1621–74 Artist G. van den Eeckhout, Rembrandt's pupil, lived.

1624 Dutch colony of New Amsterdam (later New York) settled from this time; taken by British in 1664, however.

1625 Jurist H. Grotius wrote *On the Laws of War and Peace*.

1625–47 Frederick Henry served as stadtholder of the United Provinces.

c1628–82 J. van Ruisdael, baroque painter, lived; noted for his mastery of landscape painting.

1632–75 Baroque artist J. Vermeer lived; painted *Girl Asleep, Soldier*, and other works.

1632–1723 Scientist A. van Leeuwenhoek lived; first to accurately describe cells and other microscopic organisms.

1635–81 Painter F. van Mieris lived.

c1636 Dutch seized Ceylon and Malacca from the Portuguese.

1636–45 A. van Diemen acted as governor general of the Dutch East India Company; extended Dutch influence in East Indies.

1640 C. Jansen, Dutch theologian, wrote *Augustinus;* also influenced development of Jansenism.

1642 Navigator A. Tasman discovered Tasmania and New Zealand.

1648 Treaty of Westphalia; Spain recognized the independence of the United Provinces at the end of the Thirty Years' War; retained southern territory, however (roughly modern Belgium).

1652–54 First Dutch War with England, stemming from commercial rivalries.

1652–72 J. de Witt served as head of state.

1655 Physicist C. Huygens discovered Saturn's rings; later discovered polarization of light and formulated a wave theory of light.

1664–67 Second Dutch War with England; colony of New Amsterdam (later New York City) was lost but possession of Surinam was confirmed.

1667–68 War of Devolution, the Netherlands invaded by France; Netherlands joined Triple Alliance (with England and Sweden) against Louis XIV of France, thereby forcing Louis to end the War of Devolution.

1670 B. Spinoza, rationalist philosopher, wrote *Treatise of Religion and Political Philosophy.*

1672–78 Third Dutch War; Louis XIV of France invaded the United Provinces; his French advance was halted when Dutch opened dikes around Amsterdam (1672); French driven out by 1673.

1672 William III of Orange made stadtholder of the United Provinces during the Third Dutch War; came to power after J. de Witt was murdered for attempting to negotiate with French invaders.

1688–97 War of the League of Augsburg; Dutch opposed France.

1689 William III of Orange became king of England.

1701–14 War of the Spanish Succession; Dutch opposed France.

1713 Remaining part of Spanish Netherlands ceded to Austria.

1718 Netherlands joined the Quadruple Alliance against Spain.

1747 William IV of Orange became hereditary stadtholder, displacing Republican party that had ruled from 1702.

1794 United Provinces overrun by French during French Revolutionary Wars.

1795–1806 Batavian Republic established by French revolutionaries.

1806–10 Kingdom of Holland established by Napoleon, who made his brother Louis its king.

1810 All Dutch territory annexed by France after King Louis was overthrown.

1815 Kingdom of the Netherlands formed by the Congress of Vienna; House of Orange elevated to the rank of kings; part of Austrian Netherlands (roughly modern Belgium) joined to kingdom; the other part became the Grand Duchy of Luxembourg.

1815–40 William I reigned.

1824 Treaty of London; defined Dutch and British spheres of influence in Malaysia.

1830–31 Revolt in former Austrian Netherlands (1830); independent Belgium created, which William refused to recognize until the London Conference.

1839 London Conference of great powers; recognized Belgian independence and permanent neutrality.

1840–49 William II reigned.

1848 New liberal constitution promulgated.

1848–1935 Botanist H. de Vries lived; rediscovered principle of heredity.

1849–90 William III reigned; rapid industrialization of the Netherlands and spread of unions accompanied period of commercial prosperity.

1872–1934 Astronomer W. de Sitter lived; advanced theory of expanding universe.

1872–1944 Artist P. Mondrian lived; developed style of abstract art called neoplasticism.

1873–1904 Achinese War; Dutch colonial forces pacified northern Sumatra.

1880 V. van Gogh took up painting after years of personal troubles and failures; became one of the great Dutch painters.

1890–1948 Wilhelmina reigned.

1899 First International Peace Conference held at The Hague; convened to resolve rules of war and the question of arms limitations.

1899 Hague Tribunal (International Court of Arbitration) established at The Hague.

1902 H. Lorentz shared Nobel Prize in Physics with Pieter Zeeman for work on electromagnetic radiation.

1903 Physiologist W. Einthoven developed the electrocardiograph.

1907 Second International Peace Conference; unsuccessful in resolving arms limitation; agreements reached on other aspects of land and sea warfare.

1914–18 WW I; Netherlands remained neutral.

1916 Dikes broken by unusually high tides (Jan.); some 10,000 drowned in the flooding.

1940 WW II; German surprise invasion (May); Rotterdam destroyed by air attacks.

1940–45 German occupation; reign of terror instituted by Germans; mass executions used in retaliation for resistance by Dutch underground; nearly all Dutch Jews killed in concentration camps.

1945 The Netherlands became a member of the UN.

1948–80 Queen Juliana reigned, following abdication of her mother, Queen Wilhelmina.

1949 The Netherlands became founding member of NATO.

1949 Indonesia granted its independence after a four-year war.

1954 Surinam and Netherlands Antilles granted political equality with the Netherlands.

1957 Became a member of newly organized European Economic Community.

1963 Dutch ceded the western half of New Guinea ("West Irian") to Indonesia.

1975 Surinam granted independence (Nov. 25), leaving the Netherlands Antilles as the only remaining possession of the once vast Dutch Empire.

1976 Queen Juliana's husband, Prince Bernhard, disgraced in scandal over dealings with Lockheed Aircraft Corp.

1977–82 Andries A.M. van Agt (*b.* 1931), a Christian Democrat, in office as prime minister.

1979 Government agreed to allow NATO missiles to be based within its borders.

1980 Queen Beatrix crowned (Apr. 30), following the abdication of her mother, Queen Juliana.

1980 New development of 300 houses at Lekkerkerk found to have been built on site of toxic chemical landfill; government forced to raze houses and remove contaminated soil for treatment.

1980–81 Economy slipped into recession.

1981 Elections held; Christian Democrats posted gains at expense of Labor; van Agt remained as prime minister, heading coalition government.

1981 Law passed to legalize abortion.

1982– Ruud Lubbers, a Christian Democrat, in office as prime minister, following new coalition between Christian Democrats and Liberal party; new government proposed wage freeze as recession worsened; introduced austerity program in 1983.

1983 Public employees went on strike against wage cuts.

1984 Economy posted strong gains; unemployment remained high, however.

1984 Mass demonstrations against proposed deployment of NATO cruise missiles in the Netherlands; government deferred final decision.

1985 Netherlands foreign minister on official visit to USSR (Apr.); stated that without reduction in Soviet SS-20 missiles, Netherlands would have to allow basing of cruise missiles.

1985 Pope John Paul II on visit (May); his tour marred by demonstrations against papal domination of Dutch Catholic church.

1986 Parliament approved deployment of NATO cruise missiles (Feb.).

1986 Elections held, in which recent immigrants were allowed to vote for first time; Christian Democrats gained at expense of Liberal party; Lubbers remained as prime minister.

1987 Labor disputes erupted at Rotterdam, world's largest port, over move to reduce work force; government helped win settlement (Aug.).

1990 Persian Gulf War; Dutch navy frigates sent to Gulf in support of UN sanctions against Iraq.

1991 Government introduced austerity program to reduce budget deficit; mass strikes called by both public and private sector workers, but government kept to its program.

1991 Eco-tax imposed on gasoline, natural gas, and electricity.

1991 The Netherlands hosted Maastricht conference on European unity.

1992 The Netherlands signed the Maastricht Treaty on European union (Feb.).

Netherlands, Spanish and Austrian Region corresponding approximately to modern Luxembourg and Belgium. The region came under control (15th cent.) of the Habsburgs as part of their domains known as the Low Countries (Netherlands, Belgium, and Luxembourg). The northern provinces of the Low Countries gained independence as the United Provinces (later called the Netherlands) during the revolt of 1581. The southern part remained under control of the Spanish Habsburgs and thenceforth became known as the Spanish Netherlands. In 1714, however, the area was ceded to Austria by the Peace of Utrecht. It was called the Austrian Netherlands from that time until it was conquered by the French (1794), during the French Revolutionary Wars. In 1815, after Napoleon's downfall, the Grand Duchy of Luxembourg was created from a part of this territory and the remainder was united with the Netherlands. But the union was short-lived and, following a rebellion against the Netherlands, independent Belgium was formed (1831).

Neuilly, Treaty of This treaty between Bulgaria and the Allies was signed Nov. 27, 1919, after WW I. Bulgaria ceded lands to Yugoslavia, Greece, and Rumania, paid reparations, and limited its army to 20,000 men.

Neumann, John von 1903–57. Hungarian-born American mathematician. Neumann worked on the atomic bomb, designed computers, and cowrote *The Theory of Games and Economic Behavior.*

Neustria Western part of the Merovingian Frankish kingdom, located in what is now north-western France and including Paris. Formed by Clovis I (6th cent.) when he divided his domains among his descendants, Neustria was involved in dynastic wars with the neighboring Frankish kingdom of Austrasia (*q.v.*). The continuing struggle between the monarchs permitted the mayors of the palace and factions of nobles to exercise real power, and, in 687, the Austrasian mayor of the palace, Pepin of Herstal, permanently united Neustria with Austrasia. (*See also* Merovingians.)

Neutrality Act Act of the US Congress approved on August 31, 1935, and amended in 1936, 1937, and 1939. The aim of this legislation was to keep the US out of war by prohibiting the sale or transport of war goods or the travel of Americans in belligerent countries or on belligerent carriers. These acts had become a dead letter even before the US entry into WW II in 1941.

Neutral Nation North American Indians inhabiting the northern shore of Lake Erie. This branch of the Iroquois peoples attempted to remain neutral in the Huron-Iroquois War. But in 1649, when some Hurons joined them, the Iroquois Confederacy destroyed them all.

Neuve-Chapelle, Battle of British offensive (Mar. 10–13, 1915) on the Western Front during WW I. Under the over-all command of British field marshal Sir John French, the British unleashed one of the war's first mass artillery barrages against German positions around the town of Neuve-Chapelle in northern France. British forces then took the town, but their offensive was soon contained by the Germans.

Neva, Battle of the Battle fought July 15, 1240 on the Neva River, near what is now St. Petersburg, in which Alexander, prince of Novgorod, decisively defeated a Swedish invasion. For this he received the surname Nevsky.

Nevada US western state, the 36th state. Although the area was crossed by many Americans on their way to California, it was first really explored by J. C. Frémont (1843–45). It was ceded to the US by Mexico (1848) after the Mexican War (*q.v.*) and became part of the Utah Territory (1850). The discovery of gold and silver in the Comstock Lode resulted in several new settlements, and Nevada became a separate territory in 1861. In 1864, it adopted its present constitution and was admitted to the Union. Mostly semi-arid, the state is noted for its mineral wealth and legalized gambling.

Neville, Ralph, 1st earl of Westmorland 1364–1425. English nobleman. Neville supported his brother-in-law Henry IV against Richard II (1399) and put down the revolts of H. Percy, in 1403, and Richard Scrope (1350–1405), in 1405. His grandsons were kings Edward IV and Richard III.

Neville, Richard, earl of Warwick 1428–71. English nobleman, grandson of Ralph Neville. Called "the Kingmaker," he aided the Yorks in the Wars of the Roses (*q.v.*), but turned against Edward IV. He was killed aiding George, duke of Clarence.

Neville's Cross, Battle of English victory in the English-Scottish wars, fought near Durham, England, on Oct. 17, 1346. David II of Scotland invaded England while Edward III was in France, but the English overwhelmed the invaders with archers and spearmen. David himself was captured and held for ransom.

Nevsky *See* **Alexander Nevsky.**

New Amsterdam Dutch colonial settlement in present-day New York State. The Dutch colonized the area at the mouth of the Hudson River (1624–64). It served as the capital of New Netherland until it was captured by Britain (1664) and renamed New York.

Newburgh Letters *See* **Armstrong, John.**

New Brunswick Eastern Canadian province, one of the Maritime Provinces. Although explored in 1525 by the Portuguese, it was settled by the French under S. de Champlain and the Sieur de Monts in 1604–05. Under the French, the area was called Acadia (*q.v.*), and when the British gained control after the French and Indian Wars (*q.v.*), the territory was known as Nova Scotia. Many Loyalists from New England settled there after the American Revolution, and it became a separate crown colony in 1784. In 1867, it joined with three other provinces to form the Dominion of Canada. The province is known for its agriculture, forests, and fishing.

Newcastle, Thomas Pelham-Holles, duke of 1693–1768. English prime minister. Newcastle's weakness during the Seven Years' War (*q.v.*) with France forced his resignation in 1756, but he returned the next year in a political coalition with W. Pitt. He was ineffective in office but skilled in the use of patronage in gaining majorities for Pitt, R. Walpole, and others.

New Church *See* **Church of the New Jerusalem.**

New Deal Name for the program of sweeping social and economic reforms initiated (1933–39) by US president F. Roosevelt during the Depression years. The fundamental premise of the New Deal, that federal government intervention to protect the social and economic welfare of the people was justified, represented a major shift in US government policy and resulted in a trend toward social reform legislation that continued long after the Depression years. Nevertheless, the rapidly worsening Depression demanded new solutions. When Roosevelt took office (1933), he called a special session of Congress which (during Roosevelt's famous Hundred Days) enacted a plethora of reform legislation. Among the measures passed were the Emergency Banking Relief Act (Mar. 9), to prevent the complete collapse of the US banking system; the act creating the Civilian Conservation Corps (CCC) (Mar. 31), to provide 250,000 jobs; the act abandoning the gold standard (Apr. 19); the Agricultural Adjustment Act (AAA) (May 12), to provide farm subsidies; the act creating the Tennessee Valley Authority (TVA) (May 18); the Home Owners Refinancing Act (June 13); and the National Industrial Recovery Act (NIRA) (June 16), to aid business and labor. Reform measures passed after the Hundred Days included the repeal of Prohibition (Dec. 5, 1933); the act creating the Securities and Exchange Commission (SEC) (June 6, 1934); and the act creating the Federal Housing Authority (FHA) (June 28, 1934). This completed what is traditionally considered the First New Deal (1933–34). Roosevelt's Second New Deal (1935–39) was marked by still more reform legislation and by growing judicial and political opposition to his programs. The Supreme Court struck down some of Roosevelt's programs (AAA, NIRA) in the years 1935 to 1937 and this gave rise to Roosevelt's abortive plan to "pack" the court with his appointees (1937). But the great bulk of New Deal legislation remained in force. Among the reforms of the Second New Deal were the act creating the Works Progress Administration (WPA) (Apr. 8, 1935), that ultimately employed 8.5 million Americans; the National Labor Relations Act (July 5, 1935), guaranteeing workers the right to organize and bargain collectively; the Social Security Act (Aug. 14, 1935); and the Fair Labor Standards Act (June 25, 1938), guaranteeing a 40-hour work week and minimum wage. Despite initial opposition, much of the New Deal legislation has survived and has been added to in succeeding generations. The impact of these reforms on modern American society and politics has been enormous.

New Economic Policy Russian Communist economic policy that allowed limited free enterprise such as small businesses and sale of surpluses by peasants. Instituted by N. Lenin in Mar., 1921, to relax tensions and gain support for the regime, it followed the earlier period of "war communism" characterized by forced requisitions of goods, confiscation of capital, nationalization, etc. The NEP was replaced by the first Five-Year Plan (*q.v.*) in 1928.

New Empire *See* **New Kingdom.**

New England Name given to the northeastern area of the United States. It includes the states of Maine, Vermont, New Hampshire, Massachusetts, Connecticut, and Rhode Island.

New England Confederation Confederation formed in 1643 between the colonies of Massachusetts Bay, Plymouth, Connecticut, and New Haven. It was formed to provide for common interests and defense. The first experiment in federation in America, it was dissolved with the revocation of the Massachusetts charter in 1684.

Newfoundland Island off the eastern coast of Canada, which with Labrador forms the tenth Canadian province. It was discovered in 1497 by J. Cabot and became the major fishery, which it remains today. It became a province in 1949.

New France North American territory colonized by France (c1600–1760). The major settlements were in Canada, along the St. Lawrence, with Montreal, Quebec, and Three Rivers as the principal ones. Part of Maine and sections along the Mississippi and Great Lakes basins were also settled and claimed.

New Freedom US political term. It was coined for the presidential campaign of W. Wilson, the winning candidate (1912). It called for a renewed emphasis on individual economic initiative and competition.

New Frontier US campaign term employed by J. F. Kennedy during his presidency (1961–63) to encourage a spirit of challenge and greater opportunity to the American people.

Newgate Once a London guardhouse, Newgate became a famous prison and an execution site from the 15th cent. It was the scene of many riots and fires before it was demolished in 1902.

New Granada New Granada was a Spanish colonial viceroyalty in South America. It included what is now Colombia, Equador, Panama, and Venezuela. Originally part of the viceroyalty of Peru, it was created as the separate viceroyalty of New Granada in 1717 and was eventually divided into Colombia and Panama after independence was won from the Spanish.

New Guinea, Territory of *See* **Papua New Guinea.**

New Hampshire Northeastern US state. One of the New England states, the 9th state. It was originally explored by Martin Pring (1603); the first settlements were at Dover and Portsmouth. The area was governed by Massachusetts (1641–43), and, even when made a separate colony (1679), New Hampshire was under the Massachusetts governor until 1741. In 1782, it gave up its claim to Vermont, and the population increased as lumber camps were established. The first colony to declare its independence, New Hampshire became a state in 1788 and adopted its constitution in 1792. It was one of the cradles of the Industrial Revolution in the US. Its early presidential primary makes the state an important arena for aspiring presidential candidates, and national electoral trends often become evident there.

New Hampshire Grants Land claimed by both New York and New Hampshire colonies. E. Allen and his Green Mountain Boys (*q.v.*) established its independence as Vermont in 1777.

New Harmony *See* **Harmony Society.**

Ne Win (Thakin Shu Maung) 1911– . Burmese military and political leader. As a military commander he played a leading role in achieving Burma's independence from Britain (1948). In 1962 he overthrew the government of U Nu and established a military junta that dominated Burmese politics in the next decades. He remained officially in power until 1981 and maintained his influence even after leaving office.

New Jersey US eastern state, the 3d state. The Dutch and Swedes established the first colonies in the region, which was taken by the English in 1664. It was under proprietary rule until it was made a royal province in 1702. It was ruled by the governor of New York until 1738. In 1776, New Jersey declared itself a state and was the scene of several important battles in the American Revolution, especially at Princeton and Trenton. It ratified the US Constitution in 1787 and adopted its present state constitution in 1947. It is a major industrial region and transportation hub.

New Jerusalem, Church of the   *See* **Church of the New Jerusalem.**

New Kingdom (~ Empire) Period of ancient Egyptian history (1580–1085 BC), which included the 18th–20th dynasties. The New Kingdom began after the overthrow of the Hyksos (*q.v.*). Thebes became prominent as the religious-administrative center, the theocratic capital (while Memphis remained the political capital). The pharaohs centralized power in their own hands and by their conquests brought the Egyptian empire to its greatest extent (parts of Asia included). During this period such pharaohs as Thutmose I and Thutmose III proved themselves great conquerors. Many temples were built and the pharaoh Akhenaton briefly established a monotheistic religion in Egypt. After the reign of Ramses III (c1198–67), the priests at Thebes gained power and thus brought about ancient Egypt's decline. The New Kingdom was followed by a period of domination by various foreign peoples that led finally to the reduction of Egypt to a Roman province. (*See also* Egypt, 1580–1085 BC.)

New Left   Movement in the US, centered mainly among college students, during the 1960s. The New Left emerged from opposition to the Vietnam War and a reaction to civil rights abuses and poverty, and called for free speech and political activism to change unacceptable values of "the establishment." The first important New Left group was Students for a Democratic Society (SDS, formed 1962), but many other local and national groups sprang up in following years. The New Left gave birth to the free-speech movement at the University of California at Berkeley (1964) and numerous and increasingly radical protests against the Vietnam War, including demonstrations at the Pentagon (1967), Columbia (1968), Chicago Democratic National Convention (1968), Washington, D.C. (1969, 1970, 1971), and Kent State (1970). The violence of later demonstrations (in both the peace movement and civil rights), the close of the Vietnam War, and other factors effectively ended the movement in the 1970s.

Newman, John Henry 1801–90.   English churchman and writer. He was a founder of the Oxford movement (*q.v.*), which sought closer correspondence between the beliefs and practices of Christian antiquity and those of the Church of England. He held in his *Tract 90* (1841) that the Thirty-Nine Articles (*q.v.*) of the Church of England were consistent with Catholicism. His own bishop repudiated this position, however, and Newman converted and was received into the Catholic church (1845). His spiritual autobiography, *Apologia pro vita sua* (1864), is considered a masterpiece both of Christian apologetics and English literature. He was made a cardinal in 1879.

New Mexico   US state in the Southwest, the 47th state. Originally inhabited by the Pueblo and Apache Indians, the area was first explored by the Franciscan missionary Fray Marcos de Niza (*d.* 1558) in 1539 and then by Francisco Vásquez de Coronado (1510–54), who discovered the Grand Canyon while in search of a fabled golden city, Quivira. The early Spanish settlements were destroyed by the Indians but reestablished by 1692. The region was a province of Mexico until it was ceded to the US (1848) in the Treaty of Guadalupe Hidalgo (*q.v.*). Terminus of the Santa Fe Trail (*q.v.*) and later the railroad, it became a territory in 1850 but remained troubled by the Indian conflict and disputes between ranchers and homesteaders. It became a state and passed its constitution in 1912. In 1943 the US established its atomic research facility at Los Alamos, and the first atomic bomb was exploded at the White Sands Proving Ground on July 16, 1945.

New Model Army   English parliamentary army that successfully fought the English Civil Wars. It was originally commanded by Sir T. Fairfax but later came under the leadership of O. Cromwell. It was organized by Parliament (1645) to replace the private armies of parliamentarians. By the Self-Denying Ordinance of Apr. 1645, parliamentary leaders were denied commands. Cromwell was the notable exception and, in fact, by its success the highly trained New Model Army became his power base, eclipsing even Parliament.

New Nationalism   US political ideology promoted by T. Roosevelt during his unsuccessful presidential campaign against W. Wilson (1912). Emphasizing a paternalistic approach, Roosevelt's program called for a strong federal government to institute social reforms and protect human rights.

New Netherland   Dutch colony in America. Captured by the British in 1664, it was divided into

New York and New Jersey. The first permanent Dutch settlement was Fort Orange on the Hudson (now Albany, New York), established in 1624; New Amsterdam (later New York City) was founded soon after.

New Orleans, Battle of American victory in the War of 1812 (*q.v.*), fought near New Orleans on Jan. 8, 1815, two weeks after the Treaty of Ghent (*q.v.*) ended the war. Gen. A. Jackson, unaware the war had been ended, lost only eight killed and thirteen wounded in the battle, while killing over two thousand British, including their commander, Sir Edward Pakenham (1778–1815). The battle restored American prestige and vaulted Jackson to fame.

New Spain Spanish viceroyalty (1535–1821) consisting of Mexico, what is now the US Southwest, and Central America south to Costa Rica. Spain's possessions among the Caribbean islands, Florida, and the Philippines were also once administered as part of the viceroyalty. New Spain ceased to exist after Mexico won its independence (1821).

New Sweden Swedish colonial settlement. New Sweden was Sweden's only American colony. It was located in present-day Pennsylvania, New Jersey, and Delaware. Founded in 1638, it was absorbed by the Dutch (1655), after its conquest by P. Stuyvesant.

New Testament The Christian portion of the Bible, relating to the life and teachings of Jesus Christ and the activities and teachings of some of the apostles chosen by Jesus to carry on his work. It consists of 27 books: 4 accounts of the life of Jesus, called "Gospels" ("good news"), ascribed to Matthew, Mark, Luke, and John; an account of the activities of the apostles, especially Paul; 21 epistles, or letters, written in apostolic times and ascribed to Paul, Peter, James, John, and Jude; and an apocalypse, or The Book of Revelations, ascribed to John. The earliest books of the New Testament are thought to have been written around AD 50. Although some say that parts were written later, current scholarship tends to accept the tradition that all of the books were written in the second half of the 1st cent. The canon, or list of approved New Testament books, was not approved by the Catholic church until the 4th cent. A festal epistle of Saint Athanasius of Alexandria (AD 367), as well as a contemporary decree of Pope Saint Damasus in Rome (381), constitute the evidence that the canon had finally been fixed in its contemporary form. Although the New Testament authors wrote according to no established plan, Christians have traditionally believed they were inspired and divinely protected from error in what they wrote.

New Thought American philosophical and religious movement. "New Thought," an outgrowth of transcendentalism (*q.v.*), was popular in America in the late 19th and early 20th cents. It stressed optimism, idealism, and the mind's creative power.

Newton, Huey *See* **Black Panthers.**

Newton, Sir Isaac 1642–1726. English mathematician and physicist. During much of 1664–66, his university, Cambridge, was closed because of plague, and Newton in this time discovered laws of motion and universal gravitation, the calculus, and the variations of the light spectrum. His findings were published in *Principia* (1687) and *Opticks* (1704). Today Newton and Leibniz share the credit for the discovery of the calculus, but Newton's laws of motion and universal gravitation are considered among the greatest syntheses in the history of human thought. They dominated science until replaced by the theory of A. Einstein in the 20th cent. Newton was the greatest and culminating figure of the 17th-cent. scientific revolution, and was president of the Royal Society from 1703 until his death. In his last years he turned to theology and alchemy.

New York Middle Atlantic state of the US and the 11th state. Originally inhabited by the Algonquian and Iroquois Indians, the area was explored (1524) by Giovanni da Verrazano (1485–1528) and H. Hudson (1609). The Dutch established the New Netherland colony (1624), which was taken by the English in 1664 and granted to the duke of York. During the American Revolution, the British held New York City, and several important battles were fought in the territory. New York became a state in 1788 and adopted its current constitution in 1894. Called the Empire State, New York is highly industrialized throughout, yet has a rich agriculture with orchards and vineyards. The completion of the Erie Canal (1825) as well as the building of railroads (from 1831) made New York the principal locus of east-west travel and commerce in the 19th and early 20th cents.

New York City US port city in southeastern New York State, one of the world's great cities. The area was visited by H. Hudson (1609), and the city's history began with the establishment (1624) of the Dutch colony of New Netherland. New Amsterdam, at the tip of Manhattan Island, was its capital. Manhattan was, according to traditional accounts, bought by P. Minuit for $24 in trinkets (1626). During the Dutch Wars, the British captured the colony (1664) and renamed it New York, after the duke of York. Development of the city (given a royal charter, 1686) began under British rule. However, local government was at times harsh and provoked unrest, including Leisler's Rebellion (*q.v.*) of 1689–91. During the American Revolution, the British captured (1776) New York City and used it as a base of operations until the end of the war. The city was nearly destroyed by fires during the occupation, but by 1790 it had been rebuilt and was again growing. New York City was first capital of the US (1785–90) and President G. Washington was inaugurated there (Apr. 30, 1789). The opening of the Erie Canal (1825) made the city a center of transportation to the Great Lakes region and, although much of the city was destroyed by fire in 1835, it underwent a new period of growth. By the mid-1800s it was the nation's leading port. During the American Civil War it was the scene of bloody Draft Riots (1863). After the war, New York City was rapidly industrialized and became the port of entry for millions of immigrants (arriving until the early 1900s), many of whom stayed in the city's slum districts (such as Hell's Kitchen) and worked in its factories. In 1898 the city limits were expanded beyond Manhattan to include the boroughs of the Bronx, Brooklyn, Queens, and Richmond (Staten Island). The early 1900s marked the beginning of the construction of the modern city. The first skyscrapers went up, bridges were constructed, and work on the vast subway system began. By the 1920s New York City was not only a booming commercial and financial center but was also being transformed into a world metropolis.

New York school *See* **abstract expressionism.**

New Zealand Island country in the South Pacific composed of North Island, South Island, and numerous smaller islands. The population is 3,397,000 and the capital is Wellington. Sighted (1642) by the Dutch captain A. Tasman, it was visited several times (1769–77) by J. Cook, and the first European settlers were the

British (1840). That year saw the signing of the Treaty of Waitangi (Feb. 6, 1840), by which the Maoris maintained possession of their land but acknowledged British sovereignty. Friction between the colonists and Maoris led to the Maori Wars (*q.v.*) and subjugation of the Maoris in the 1870s. In 1852 New Zealand was divided into six provinces and granted self-government. It became a dominion (1907), and by the Statute of Westminster (1931) became independent. However, New Zealand did not ratify the statute until 1947. New Zealanders distinguished themselves in combat during WW I, WW II, and the Vietnam War. In 1972, after a period of prosperity, the first Labor government came to power since the 1950s. It was soon confronted by an energy crisis (1973–74), a trade deficit, and recession. The National party regained power in 1975. Tight budgetry and monetary measures were adopted to deal with the continuing weak economy and the government introduced a controversial open shop law (1984). That helped bring Labor back to power. Labor thereupon began a policy of barring all ships either carrying nuclear weapons or having nuclear power plants (1984). The following year, the Greenpeace antinuclear flagship *Rainbow Warrior* was blown up in Auckland harbor by French secret service agents (July 1985; the agents were sentenced to 10 years in prison). Privatization of state-run enterprises began in 1987. The National Party returned to power in 1990 and proposed drastic spending cuts, particularly in areas of social welfare such as education, healthcare, and pensions. Protest demonstrations against the cut were held in 1991.

Ney, Michel 1769–1815. French marshal. Ney, long a supporter of Napoleon, urged him to abdicate after the disastrous losses of the Napoleonic Wars. After briefly serving Louis XVIII, Ney again joined Napoleon during the Hundred Days, was defeated with him at Waterloo (*q.v.*), and was executed.

Nez Percé Indians American Indian tribe of the Sahaptin-Chinook linguistic family. They occupied the northwestern part of America before they were overrun by gold prospectors in the 1860s and 1870s. This led to an unsuccessful revolt by their Chief Joseph in 1877.

Ngo Dinh Diem 1901–63. Vietnamese political leader and prime minister (1954–63). Following the French defeat in Indochina, he emerged as the strong man in South Vietnam, and seemed to have built a solid regime as virtual dictator, enjoying US support. But his authoritarianism and favoritism to Catholics rather than Buddhists led to growing unrest among Communists and non-Communists alike in South Vietnam. He was overthrown in a military coup in 1963 that was engineered with apparent US complicity. He was murdered after being overthrown.

Nguyen Cao Ky 1930– . South Vietnamese military and political leader. He served as commander of the US–backed South Vietnam air force (1963–65). In 1967 he became vice-president under Nguyen van Thieu, whom he ran against in the 1971 elections. He emigrated to the US after South Vietnam's defeat (1975).

Nguyen dynasty Vietnamese dynasty, founded (1802) by Nguyen Anh (*d.* 1820). The dynasty nominally ruled after the French occupation of Indochina, until 1945. An earlier Nguyen line ruled the southern part of divided Annam (*q.v.*) from the 1500s to 1778.

Nguyen That Thanh *See* **Ho Chi-minh.**

Nguyen van Thieu 1923– . South Vietnam (Republic of Vietnam) political leader. President (1967–75) during the years of major US involvement in the Vietnam War, he was unable to check the Communist advance following the US withdrawal in 1973. He resigned and went into exile after the fall of South Vietnam.

Niagara, Battle of *See* **Lundy's Lane, Battle of.**

Niagara movement Organization of American black intellectuals and professionals, organized (1905) by W. E. B. Du Bois and others to advance black civil rights. Largely ineffective, the movement dissolved in 1910, and some members, including Du Bois, joined in forming the NAACP.

Nian Rebellion (Nien ˜) Revolt in China. The Nian, a secret society of rebel guerrillas, staged uprisings from 1853 against the Qing dynasty during and after the Taiping Rebellion (*q.v.*). They were destroyed in 1868.

Nibelungenlied Middle High German epic poem (early 13th cent.) by an unknown author. It is taken from the oral tradition of Siegfried and involves the gold of the Nibelungen, an evil family. The modern operatic tetralogy, the *Ring,* by R. Wagner, is based on the saga.

Nicaea Ancient city. Nicaea, now Iznik, Turkey, was founded in the 4th cent. BC. Across the Bosporus from Constantinople, it was the site of

important Catholic church councils (AD 325 and 787) before its capture by the Turks (1330).

Nicaea, Councils of Councils of the Catholic church, both held in the ancient city of Nicaea, across the Bosporus from present-day Istanbul. **1.** (1st ecumenical): Convened in AD 325 by the Roman emperor Constantine, it condemned Arianism (*q.v.*) and established the Nicene Creed (*q.v.*). **2.** (7th ecumenical): Convened by the Byzantine empress Irene (AD 787) to consider the question of Iconoclasm, raised when her predecessor, Leo III, issued a decree forbidding the "worship" of images (726). The council decided that images could be venerated but not worshiped. It was the last council recognized as ecumenical by both Eastern and Western churches.

Nicaea, Empire of State founded (1206) by Theodore Lascaris (*d.* 1222) to the southeast of Constantinople and lasting until 1261. It was one of the small states formed by the Byzantines after the crusaders conquered Constantinople and set up the Latin Empire of Constantinople (*q.v.*). It was from Nicaea that the Byzantines launched the successful military conquest of the Latin Empire (1261). The Byzantine Empire was reestablished under Michael VIII.

Nicaragua Independent state located in Central America. The population is 3,606,000 and the capital is Managua. Nicaragua's main exports are cotton, coffee, and sugar. It is Central America's largest, but most sparsely populated, country and has a long history of dictatorship and political repression. The recent war between the Communist-backed Sandinista government and US-backed Contra rebels ended in 1987, with agreement on the Arias peace plan. Key dates in Nicaraguan history include:

1522 First visited by Spaniards under Gil González Dávila; settlements established.

16TH–19TH CENTS. Ruled under captaincy general of Guatemala.

1821 Declared independence from Spain.

1821–25 Became part of De Iturbide's Mexican empire.

1825–38 Joined Central American Federation.

1838 Liberals (based in the city of León) and conservatives (in Granada) fought for control; liberals declared Nicaraguan independence and withdrew from the federation.

1848 Britain seized San Juan del Norte in move to control Mosquito Coast.

1855 Capital established at Managua, between León and Granada.

1855 American filibuster William Walker was employed by liberals to head army; captured and sacked Granada.

1856 Walker became president of Nicaragua.

1856–57 Walker seized holdings of C. Vanderbilt in Nicaragua; Vanderbilt backed conservatives, forcing Walker to flee.

1863–93 Conservatives in control of the government.

1893–1909 Liberal revolt brought José Santos Zelaya to power; ruled as dictator.

1907 Zelaya attempted to revive Central American Federation; warred against Honduras and El Salvador; Central American Conference ended hostilities.

1909 Conservatives overthrew Zelaya with US support.

1912 Unsuccessful coup; US marines occupied Nicaragua (1912–25).

1927–33 Marines reoccupied Nicaragua after internal strife resumed (led by Augusto César Sandino); compromise negotiated between factions ended immediate crisis.

1937–56 Anastasio Somoza García, National Guard general, overthrew the government and established military dictatorship.

1939 Constitution revised; Somoza, reelected, visited US and obtained aid.

1947 A. Somoza defeated in elections by Leonardo Arguello; but Somoza became chief of National Guard and forced Arguello to resign.

1956–67 Luis Somoza ruled after his father was assassinated.

1960 Border dispute with Honduras settled; International Court of Justice ruled against Nicaragua.

1967–72 Maj. Gen. Anastasio Somoza-Debayle became president following the death of Luis Somoza.

1972 Somoza-Debayle resigned (May 1) from presidency; interim government to rule until 1974 elections; Somoza retained control of the country.

1972 Earthquake devastated (Dec. 23) Managua.

1973 Somoza-Debayle declared martial law after leftists kidnapped 14 officials.

1974 Somoza-Debayle resigned from army; won presidential election.

1978 Widespread rioting (Jan. 10) in Managua after leading opponent of Somoza-Debayle was assassinated.

1978 National strike (Jan. 23–30) renewed anti-government unrest.

1978 Sandinista guerrillas seized (Aug. 22) National Palace.

1979 Sandinista guerrillas began (May) civil war; Somoza-Debayle ordered massive bombings, alienating many civilians; resisted American and OAS appeals to step down.

1979 Somoza-Debayle resigned, fled country (July 17); Sandinista guerrillas entered Managua, took control of government, capping seven-week civil war.

1979 Country ruled by five-member junta, including two non-Sandinistas.

1980 State of emergency ended, but promised elections delayed until 1985.

1980 Sandinista government nationalized some 60 percent of country's arable land, domestic banks and other economic organizations.

1980 Deposed president Somoza-Debayle, now in Paraguay, killed by unknown gunmen (Sept.); Sandinista government denied involvement.

1981 Nicaragua charged with supplying arms to Salvadoran rebels; US president R. Reagan suspended aid (Jan.).

1981 Nationalization program greatly expanded (July), despite crumbling economy; state of emergency declared, outlawing strikes; government pursued rapid buildup of Sandinista forces, aided by influx of arms from Soviet bloc.

1982 Sandinista government accused US of coordinating guerrilla attacks in Nicaragua; declared new state of emergency.

1983 Sandinista counter-insurgency forces criticized for brutalizing Miskito Indians.

1983 US–backed Contra rebels launched major offensive (Aug.); Sandinista government menaced by US Naval task force doing maneuvers off Nicaraguan coast.

1984 Contra rebels (Nicaraguan Democratic Front) launched attacks on oil installations (Feb.); mined two key ports with support from US CIA (Feb. 25); US vetoed UN resolution against the mining, charging Nicaragua with "exporting revolution."

1984 US Senate voted to halt aid to Contras (June); US Congress later overturned aid cutoff.

1984 Sandinista government lifted harsh emergency laws (Aug. 6), in bid to blunt criticism of regime.

1985 Sandinista leader Daniel Ortega in office as president, following election, apparently fair but marred by some irregularities; offered amnesty to rebels but refused to negotiate with them.

1985 Ortega in inconclusive talks with US secretary of state George Shultz (Mar.).

1985 Sandinista offensive crushed guerrilla group Democratic Revolutionary Alliance (May).

1986 Sandinista troops crossed into Honduras to attack Contra bases (Mar.); US reacted by pledging new aid to Contras (June).

1986 World Court ruled on case brought by Nicaragua against US (June 27); US ignored order to halt aid to Contras.

1986 US supply plane shot down over Nicaragua; pilot provided information on US involvement with Contras.

1986 First revelations in US concerning Iran-Contra scandal.

1987 Contras' spring offensive failed.

1987 Honduras ordered Contras out of the country by June 15.

1987 Central American summit in Guatemala approved the Arias Plan for peace in Central America (June 25–26); set deadlines for halt in all wars, for end to aid to rebel groups, for instituting general amnesty, and for start of negotiations.

1987 Ortega, complying with Arias Plan, offered to negotiate with Contras; Contras accepted and fighting began to taper off.

1988 Government instituted severe austerity program, including end to subsidies and wage freeze; inflation rate hit 3,000 percent.

1988 Nicaragua devastated by hurricane Joan (Oct.); some 321,000 left homeless and food crops heavily damaged; worsened already severe economic ills.

1989 Ortega ordered new austerity measures, including defense spending cuts; released some political prisoners in compliance with Arias Plan.

1989 Sandinistas agreed to free elections in Feb. 1990; granted amnesty for rebels.

1990– Violeta Barrios de Chamorro, member of National Opposition Union party, in office as president, following Feb. elections; ended civil war with Contras and sought reconciliation with leftist Sandinistas; began process of reversing Sandinista program of nationalization.

1990 Ceasefire with Contras set (Apr. 19).

1990 UN supervised final demobilization of the nearly 20,000 Contra rebels, completed in June.

1990 National Workers' Front staged massive strike (May) against government plans to revoke rights of public service employees.

1990 Sandinista officers smuggled 28 Soviet anti-aircraft missiles to rebels in El Salvador (Oct.); move revealed in 1991.

1990 Inflation rate hit 13,000 percent.

1991 Sandinista troops gave formal oath of allegiance to government (Jan. 10).

1991 Land reform law enacted, allowing for partial return of nationalized land, amounting to $11 billion worth.

1992 Chamorro administration hit by bribery scandal; top aide reportedly implicated in attempt to bribe members of parliament.

Nicator, Demetrius *See* **Demetrius II.**

Nicene Creed (Niceno-Constantinopolitan ~) A summation of the basic tenets of Christianity, accepted by Roman Catholicism, Eastern Orthodox, Anglican, and most other Protestant churches. It was drawn up at the Council of Nicaea (AD 325) in order to state the true faith of the church as against the beliefs advanced by Arianism (*q.v.*). But a few elements were added later by the First Council of Constantinople (381) when it assumed substantially the form in which it is recited today. The *filioque* clause (*q.v.*) was added still later in the West (from the 9th cent.). Though sanctioned by the authority of the Roman Catholic church, the *filioque* has always been rejected by the Eastern church.

Niceno-Constantinopolitan Creed *See* **Nicene Creed.**

Nicephorus I *d.* 811. Byzantine Emperor (802–811). He deposed the empress Irene, whom he had served as treasurer. He arranged boundary treaties with Charlemagne (803, 810) establishing the boundaries between the Eastern and Western empires. He was killed by invading Bulgarians.

Nicephorus II (Nicephorus II Phocas) c913–969. Byzantine emperor (963–969). His continuous warfare and heavy taxes made him unpopular. He was murdered by his wife, Theophano, and her lover, his nephew John Tzimisces, who succeeded him as John I.

Nicephorus II Phocas *See* **Nicephorus II.**

Nicholas I, Saint c825–867. Pope (858–867). Nicholas mediated both secular and religious matters. He prevented the divorce of Lothair of Lorraine and supported Saint Ignatius of Constantinople against Photius for the see of Constantinople. He upheld the right of bishops to appeal to Rome over their archbishops. He was one of the two popes traditionally called "the Great" (with Gregory I).

Nicholas I 1796–1855. Tsar of Russia (1825–55). Acceding despite the Decembrist Conspiracy (*q.v.*), Nicholas suppressed the Polish uprising (1830–31) and helped Austria subdue Hungary (1849). His attempt to expand into Ottoman domains led to the Crimean War (*q.v.*).

Nicholas I 1841–1921. Prince and king of Montenegro. He obtained European recognition of Montenegro's independence in the 1878 Treaty of Berlin. He opposed the union of Montenegro with Serbia into Yugoslavia and was deposed in 1918.

Nicholas II 1868–1918. Last Russian tsar (1894–1917), successor to his father, Alexander III. An ineffective and autocratic ruler, Nicholas was greatly influenced by his wife Alexandra, who was in turn dominated by Rasputin (*q.v.*). Russia's defeat in the Russo-Japanese War (1904–05) led to the Revolution of 1905 (*q.v.*), and Nicholas was forced to establish a duma (1906). He took command of the army in WW I (1915), leaving Alexandra (with Rasputin) to govern. Under Alexandra, government at home became chaotic and this, with failures in the war, led to the Russian Revolution of 1917 (*q.v.*). Nicholas and his family were shot by revolutionaries (1918).

Nicholas III (Orsini, Giovanni Gaetani) *d.* 1280. Pope (1277–80). Nicholas successfully managed to keep civil rulers such as Charles I of Anjou and Rudolf I of Germany from interfering in church affairs. His efforts to effect a reunion with Constantinople ultimately failed.

Nicholas V (Parentucelli, Tommaso) 1397–1455. Pope (1447–55). Nicholas ended a schism when antipope Felix V submitted to him. He was a patron of the arts and is the virtual founder of the Vatican library.

Nicholas V (antipope) *See* **Rainalducci, Pietro.**

Nicholas, Saint *fl.* 4th cent. Catholic bishop of Myra in Lycia. Though little is known of his life, he is the subject of many legends and is the patron of Russia, Greece, Sicily, children, and sailors. Legend has transformed his generosity into the Christmas character "Santa Claus," a corruption of his name.

Nicholas of Cusa 1401–64. German humanist and scholar, and from 1448 Roman Catholic cardinal. He worked for monastic reform, and carried out extensive diplomatic missions for Nicholas V. He proposed the hypothesis that the earth revolves around the sun before Copernicus and calendar reform a century before the Gregorian reform. He attacked decadent scholasticism in *De Docta Ignorantia*, "Of Learned Ignorance" (1440).

Nicias *d.* 413 BC. Athenian statesman and general during the Peloponnesian War. Nicias defeated the Spartans and Corinthians (427–426 BC) in some minor skirmishes and was an important supporter of the peace with Sparta (421) that bears his name. He opposed the siege of Syracuse (415) but was made commander along with Alcibiades and Lamachus. The expedition proved a disaster, and he was captured by the Syracusans and executed.

Nicopolis, Battle of Decisive victory (Sept. 25, 1396) by Ottoman Turks over a European army of crusaders. King Sigismund of Hungary organized the crusaders in a response to the Turkish threat to Constantinople. The Turks, under Sultan Bayazid I, overwhelmed the crusaders at Nicopolis in Bulgaria, thus ending any effective European resistance to Ottoman expansion. Thousands were killed and some 10,000 taken prisoner. Only Tamerlane's invasion saved Europe from further Turkish conquests at this time.

Niebuhr, Reinhold 1892–1971. American Protestant theologian. He advanced his theory of applied Christianity in such books as *Moral Man and Immoral Society* and *The Nature and Destiny of Man.* Niebuhr preached "conservative idealism" against facile American optimism, emphasizing the reality of sin in human affairs.

Niemcewicz, Julian Ursyn 1757–1841. Polish writer and patriot. He aided T. Kosciusko in the 1794 Polish revolt and was jailed with him. He was exiled in 1831 for additional revolutionary activity.

Niemoller, Friedrich Gustav Emil Martin 1892–1984. German anti-Nazi theologian. Originally a Nazi advocate, he opposed A. Hitler's takeover of the Lutheran church. He spent the years 1937–45 in a concentration camp.

Nien Rebellion *See* **Nian Rebellion.**

Nietzsche, Friedrich Wilhelm 1844–1900. German philosopher who proposed new values in place of what he regarded as the decadent slave morality of Christianity in *Beyond Good and Evil* (1886). One of his new values involved the "superman" who would achieve by asserting a "will to power." Nietzsche developed this idea in *Thus Spake Zarathustra* (1883–85). He predicted the "death of God" in his *Joyful Wisdom* (1910), among other works. His ideas influenced the Nazis, although Nietzsche was an anti-state individualist and not anti-Semitic.

Niger (Republic of ˜) Independent state located in west-central Africa in the Sahara region. The population is 7,691,000 and the capital is Niamey. The country is largely arid, and most of the population is engaged in subsistence farming. A drought (1968–75) almost devastated the country. Key events in the history of Niger include:

16TH CENT. Songhai Empire controlled large parts of the territory.

16TH CENT. Bornu Empire established by Berbers after the fall of the Songhai Empire.

19TH CENT. Fulani tribe gained southern part.

1884–85 Conference of Berlin placed Niger within French sphere of influence.

1893 Sudanese warriors destroyed Bornu Empire.

1896 Became part of French West Africa.

1922 Established as separate colony within French West Africa.

1926 Niamey replaced Zinder as capital.

1946 Joined the French Union; gained limited self-government.

1958 Became an autonomous republic in the French Community.

1959 Constitution adopted.

1960 Withdrew from French Community, proclaiming complete independence (Aug. 3).

1960–74 Hamani Diori in office as first president.

1968–75 Drought brought famine and severe economic problems; US emergency aid (1974) helped bring about recovery.

1974 Military coup (Apr. 15); Lt. Col. Seyni Kountché suspended constitution, ruled by decree.

1976 Kountché formed civilian-dominated government with himself as head of government.

1976–87 Kountché in power as president.

1980 Government, fearing Libyan invasion to secure Niger's uranium deposits (largest in Africa), promoted demonstrations against Libya by Niger's trade unions.

1981 Libya invaded Chad; raised new concern in Niger about Libyan expansionism, until Libya withdrew in Oct.

1983 Failed coup attempt (Oct.) by president's adviser, Oumarou Adamou (called Bonkano).

1984 Drought affecting much of Africa's sub-Sahara region hit Niger; food shortages continued into 1985, when annual rains returned and produced good harvest.

1985 Anti-corruption campaign launched by government; death penalty to be imposed in some cases.

1985 Niger celebrated 25 years of independence (Aug.); government marked anniversary by starting major program to reforest rural areas.

1987 Gen. Kountché died of brain tumor.

1987– Col. Ali Saibou, Kountché's cousin and Niger's military leader, in office as president; continued rule by minority ethnic group, the Djerma, over the more populous Hausa ethnic group; promised return to constitutional government.

1988 National Movement for a Developing Society founded as Niger's sole political party.

1990 Government used force to break up student march as pro-democracy protests spreading through Africa reached Niger (Feb.); action sparked violent demonstrations; government closed down colleges.

1990–91 Persian Gulf War; 500 troops from Niger joined in allied effort against Iraq.

1992 Short-lived mutiny by government troops demanding back pay (Feb.); government reported two months behind in pay to all government employees.

Nigeria (Federal Republic of ˜) Independent state located in western Africa on the Gulf of Guinea. The population is 118,865,000 and the capital is

Lagos. The land is rich in oil, which for a time made Nigeria among the wealthiest of African nations. Originally populated by such tribes as the Hausa, Fulani, Yoruba, and Ibo, Nigeria was for many years a British colony, which finally gained independence in 1960. Key dates in Nigerian history include:

15TH CENT. Portuguese visited region; slave trade established.

1795–96 Mungo Park explored the Nigerian interior.

1830–31 Richard and John Lander explored the interior.

1861 Britain took control of Lagos; began expanding control in region.

1886 Royal Niger Company chartered; gained control of all trading companies on the Niger River and in the north.

1885 Britain established supremacy over southern Nigeria at the Conference of Berlin.

1897 Kingdom of Benin added to Nigeria.

1900 Protectorate established over southern Nigeria; northern sector pacified and established as a separate protectorate.

1914 Colony and protectorate of Nigeria established by British; economic development began.

1947 Britain granted constitution giving native Nigerians more involvement in government.

1954 New constitution granted after 1947 and 1951 constitutions proved unworkable.

1960 Nigeria became independent (Oct. 1); Abubaka Tafawa Balewa became prime minister (1960–66).

1963 Nigeria became a republic.

1963–66 Bitter disputes between tribal groups and regional governments.

1966 Balewa and other officials killed (Jan.) in coup by Ibo army; Major Gen. Johnson Ironsi became head of military government; abolished constitution.

1966–75 Lt. Col. Gowon in power after coup (July) by Hausa army; Supreme Military Council reigned.

1966 Muslim Hausa tribe massacred (Sept.) Christian Ibos in the north; Ibos fled to eastern region.

1967 Eastern region withdrew (May) from the Federation of Nigeria to become Biafra; bloody civil war ensued.

1970 Biafra surrendered (Jan. 12) to Nigerian government troops, ending nearly three years of war.

1973–74 Famine devastated the area.

1975 Increasing unrest resulted (July 29) in bloodless coup; Muritala Rufai Muhammad installed as head of government.

1976 Muhammad assassinated by seven officers who failed in coup attempt; Supreme Military Council chose Lt. Col. Olusegun Obasanjo as president.

1977 Local government councils elected National Constituent Assembly.

1978 Ban on political parties, in effect since 1966, lifted.

1979–83 Alhaji Shehu Shagari, a member of the National Party of Nigeria, in office as president; as first civilian president in over a decade, he attempted to govern by consensus, but eventually was perceived as weak and ineffective; widespread corruption in government continued despite Shagari's personal crusade against it; his administration was also marked by mounting economic problems and unsuccessful efforts to prevent civil war in Chad.

1980 Bloody riots by radical Muslims in Kano; troops used lethal force to halt unrest; estimated over 4,000 killed.

1980 Okigbo Commission's recommendations of distribution of federal revenue accepted by government; states to get 34.5 percent and national government to retain 55 percent, with the rest going to localities; passed into law in 1981.

1981 Nigerian troops sent to Chad as part of OAU peacekeeping force.

1981 Huge steel producing facility at Ajaokuta completed.

1982 Former Biafran secessionist leader Ojukwu pardoned; returned to Nigeria.

1983 Some 2.2 million citizens of Ghana residing in Nigeria without legal papers were expelled; Nigerian government embarrassed by worldwide publicity given the mass deportation.

1983 President Shagari, confronting a drastic loss in revenue caused by falling prices for Nigeria's exported oil, ordered sharp cut in imports to slow mushrooming foreign debt; resulting shortages of needed goods caused economic chaos; public service workers went unpaid for months.

1983 Military coup overthrew Shagari government; coup blamed on mounting economic ills which were reducing once wealthy Nigeria to status of poor nation.

1983–85 Major Gen. Muhammed Buhari in office as head of state, the leading figure of the new military-led government; government imposed severe austerity program, including mass layoffs and wage freezes (1983–84) to reverse economic decline; imposed harsh program to instill discipline in Nigerian daily life.

1983 Former Nigerian leader Yakubu Gowon, pardoned by former President Shagari in 1981, returned to Nigeria (Dec.).

1984 Nigerian secret police arrested in London while trying to kidnap former minister of transport; tried to drug the former minister, wanted in Nigeria on corruption charges, and smuggle him home in a crate.

1985 Nigerian poet Wole Soyinka joined denunciation of government's public execution of convicted drug traffickers; broad imposition of death penalty only part of "corrective" measures military regime introduced; military decrees also forbade discussions of politics and allowed jailing of journalists.

1985 Bubari government overthrown by military in bloodless coup (Aug. 26); Armed Forces Ruling Council took control.

1985– Gen. Ibrahim Babangida in office as head of state; promised return to more humane government; began releasing political prisoners; his administration marked by continuing efforts to resolve economic problems and by steps toward return to civilian rule.

1986 Poet Wole Soyinka awarded Nobel Prize for Literature.

1987 Government allowed the Nigerian naira to float on currency market, resulting in drastic devaluation; ban on imports lifted and wage freeze ended.

1987 Return to civilian government delayed to 1992; ban on political activity continued.

1987 Number of states increased to 21, following creation of Katsina and Akwa Ibom by dividing up two existing states.

1987 Five AIDS cases reported.

1988 Government privatized most government-run businesses.

1988 World Bank categorized Nigeria among poor nations; Nigeria now qualified for special development loans.

1989 Nigeria rescheduled payment on much of its foreign debt.

1989 High inflation and a sharp increase in domestic fuel price sparked unrest in cities (May); universities closed down to halt unrest among students.

1989 Ban on political activity ended after six years; government created two parties, the Social Democratic Party and the National Republican Convention.

1990 Attempted military coup failed (Apr. 22); 19 killed during attempt; 49 convicted in plot executed (Aug., Sept.).

1991 Riots broke out in Lagos when government wrecked shops belonging to those trading illegally.

1991 States total 30 after government created nine new ones (Aug. 27).

1991 Muslim riots in Kano claimed over 100 lives (Oct.).

1991 Seat of government relocated to newly built capital of Abuja (Dec. 12).

1992 Nigeria's central bank took over country's oldest Nigerian-owned commercial bank (Jan.), the failing National Bank of Nigeria.

Nightingale, Florence 1820–1910. English nurse. Born in a well-to-do family and largely educated by her father, she had a religious experience in 1837 and thereafter became a nurse. Later, as a nursing supervisor, Nightingale introduced strict standards of sanitation to army hospitals during the Crimean War (*q.v.*) and founded a training school for nurses. She was the first woman to receive the British Order of Merit.

nihilism Nineteenth-century movement among the Russian intelligentsia that advocated the overthrow of all order and authority. Given its name in the novel by I. Turgenev, *Fathers and Sons* (1861), the movement embraced both those who wanted to overthrow existing governments by force and terror and those who sought to throw off personal moral restraints.

Nijinsky, Vaslav 1890–1950. Russian ballet dancer and choreographer. Nijinsky revolutionized dance as a member of S. Diaghilev's Ballet Russe. He choreographed such classics as *The Afternoon of a Faun* and *The Rite of Spring*.

Nijmegen, Treaties of Series of European treaties. France ended the Dutch Wars (1672–78) with the Netherlands and Spain by these treaties, signed in the Dutch town of Nijmegen (1678–79). The Netherlands regained all its conquered territories, while France gained Franche-Comte, Artois, and towns in Flanders from Spain.

Nika Riot Riot and abortive revolt (532) in Constantinople. The Blues and Greens (*q.v.*), two popular parties in the Byzantine Empire, were normally opposed to each other. But they united to demand that Emperor Justinian oust two hated officials. Justinian complied but this failed to appease what had become an angry mob. In the ensuing riot, Constantinople was burned, the empress Theodora thwarted an attempt to overthrow her husband, and the emperor's general, Belisarius, restored calm by slaughtering some 30,000 rioters. The incident marked the end of popular party power in the empire.

Nikolsburg, Treaty of Treaty concluded on Dec. 12, 1621, between Ferdinand II of Austria and Gabriel Bethlen, king of Hungary (1619–21) during the Thirty Years' War (*q.v.*). Hungarian Protestants' rights were guaranteed by the Habsburgs, and Ferdinand regained the Hungarian crown, renounced by Bethlen.

Nikon 1605–81. Russian patriarch. Nikon was patriarch of the Russian Orthodox church (1652–66). His reforms and resistance to state interference led to widespread opposition and to his removal. Nikon's reforms were eventually adopted by the church, but many refused to conform to them (and became known as the Old Believers).

Nile, Battle of the *See* **Aboukir, Battle of.**

Nimitz, Chester William 1885–1966. American five-star admiral. Nimitz commanded the US Pacific Fleet during WW II and received the Japanese surrender aboard his ship, the battleship *Missouri.* He was chief of naval operations (1945–47).

Nin, Anaïs 1903–77. American writer. Nin was famed for her letters and diaries as well as such fiction as *Under a Glass Bell* and *Ladders of Fire.*

Nine-Power Treaty Two treaties resulting from the Washington Conference (Nov. 12, 1921–Feb. 6, 1922). The first (Feb. 4, 1922) guaranteed China its territorial sovereignty. The second (Feb. 6, 1922) gave it authority to set trade tariffs. The conference was attended by the US, Britain, France, Belgium, the Netherlands, Portugal, Italy, Japan, and China.

Nineteen Propositions Demands presented (1642) by the Long Parliament (*q.v.*) to Charles I of England. Charles rejected these demands, designed to limit his rule, and this helped provoke the English Civil Wars (*q.v.*). The propositions included demands that the Parliament be allowed to choose royal councilors, control the army, and enforce the laws against Catholics.

Ninety-five Theses Martin Luther's historic document posted on the church door in Wittenberg, Germany, on Oct. 31, 1517, a date that is now considered the beginning of the Protestant Reformation. The theses not only protested the selling of indulgences in the Roman Catholic church, but advanced Luther's opinions on doctrines of the faith, which proved to be unacceptable to church authority. Originally the theses were posted only to invite debate from other Catholic theologians.

Nineveh Ancient city. Nineveh was the capital of the Assyrian empire, located near modern Mosul, Iraq. Sennacherib and Ashurbanipal greatly contributed to its glory by their buildings and sculptures. The fabulous royal library of Nineveh was organized by Ashurbanipal (*q.v.*). The city fell to a coalition of Babylonians, Medes, and Scythians in 612 BC. Its fall is celebrated in the Old Testament book of the prophet Nahum.

Ninth Crusade *See* **Crusade, Ninth.**

Nirvana In Buddhism and Hinduism (*qq.v.*), Nirvana represents the final state of bliss and freedom to which all aspire. In Hinduism it involves release from the perpetual cycle of rebirths. In Buddhism it is the state achieved by enlightenment (knowledge) in which the individual is released from all desire, anger, or pain. Some sages hold it to be equivalent to extinction or annihilation of the personality. The Sanskrit word refers to the going out of a flame after the exhaustion of its fuel.

Nixon, Richard Milhous 1913– . Thirty-seventh US president (1969–74), successor to L. Johnson. After practicing law for five years, Nixon served in the navy during WW II. He began his political career in 1946 with his election as a Republican to Congress. As a member of the House Committee on Un-American Activities, he gained national attention through the investigation of A. Hiss. In 1950 he was elected to the Senate and in 1952 was elected vice-president under D. Eisenhower. As vice-president (1953–61) he made numerous trips abroad. In Venezuela (1958) he was nearly trapped in violent demonstrations, and while visiting Russia (1959) he participated in the Kitchen Debates (q.v.) with N. Khrushchev. Chosen Republican candidate for president (1960), he was defeated by J. Kennedy and, following his defeat (1962) for the governorship of California, he retired to private life. In 1968 he again received the Republican presidential nomination, this time defeating the Democratic candidate (H. Humphrey). As president, Nixon began the withdrawal of US troops from Vietnam, but the order to invade Cambodia (1970) and Laos (1971) provoked widespread protest. In foreign policy, Nixon sought to ease tensions between the West and the Communist bloc through a policy of détente (q.v.), and he visited China in 1972 to mark the US rapproachment with the Communist state. That year he was reelected, defeating the Democratic candidate G. McGovern in a landslide. Nixon obtained a cease-fire with North Vietnam (1973) effectively ending US participation in the Vietnam War (q.v.). Soon after his reelection, however, revelations concerning the Watergate Scandal (q.v.) began to emerge. His vice-president, S. Agnew, was forced to resign (1973) and was succeeded by G. Ford. Nixon was in turn forced to resign (Aug. 9, 1974) under threat of impeachment. He was succeeded by Ford, who granted him a pardon. (See also United States, 1968–74.)

Niza, Fray Marcos de   See **New Mexico.**

Nkrumah, Kwame 1909–72.   Ghanaian statesman. Nkrumah led strikes against British domination of Ghana, which achieved independence under his leadership. He later became its first prime minister (1951) and president (1960).

NKVD   See **GPU.**

NLF   See **National Liberation Front.**

Noailles, Maurice, duc de 1678–1766.   Marshal of France under Louis XV. He distinguished himself in the wars of the Austrian, Polish, and Spanish succession (qq.v.).

Nobel, Alfred Bernhard 1833–96.   Swedish inventor and industrialist. Nobel invented dynamite, though he was a pacifist. With his fortune he established the coveted Nobel prizes, awarded yearly to scientists, economists, writers, and peacemakers.

Nobile, Umberto   See **Amundsen, Roald.**

nobiles   See **patricians.**

Nobility, Charter to the   See **Charter to the Nobility.**

Nogi, Maresuke, Count 1849–1912.   Japanese general. He fought in the Sino-Japanese War (q.v.), captured Port Arthur in the Russo-Japanese War (q.v.), and outflanked the Russians at Mukden.

nominalism   Philosophical doctrine, important in medieval times, which held that universals (abstractions) do not exist and that only specific objects have real existence (ie., a man exists but humanity, the abstract concept of all humans, does not or is unknowable). Nominalists thus opposed the scholastic philosophers and challenged fundamental tenets of Christian theology (ie., the Holy Trinity was unknowable). The philosopher Roscellinus (d. after 1220) is said to have held the nominalist view in the extreme form. An intermediate position (Conceptualism) held that universals exist in the mind as concepts but have no substantive reality in the world outside the mind. This middle position was adopted by William of Ockham (q.v.).

Nominated Parliament   See **Barebones Parliament.**

Nonconformists   Term used to describe those who decline to subscribe to the established state religion. It came into use in English history to describe those Protestants who rejected the established Church of England, particularly those who separated from it around the time of the 1660 Restoration (q.v.) of the monarchy and passage (1662) of the Act of Uniformity (q.v.). It has been applied to Baptists, Congregationalists, Presbyterians, Methodists, and Unitarians, as well as independent groups such as the Brownists, Quakers, and Plymouth Brethren. In Scotland this term, or "dissenters," was used to refer to those who separated from the established Presbyterianism, and included the Anglicans.

Noncooperation movement   Indian protest movement organized between Sept. 1920 and Feb. 1922 by M. K. Gandhi as a reaction to the Massacre of Amritsar (q.v.) by British troops in 1919. The movement involved boycotting British institutions and goods. An outbreak of violence brought the movement to an end, though Gandhi later used nonviolent protests (satyagraha) against the British to gain India's independence.

Nonpartisan League US alliance of farmers formed in 1915. Its purpose was to apply political pressure to achieve the farmers' demands for state control of storage and distribution centers. It spread rapidly through the wheat belt from Wisconsin to Washington and the Southwest. It declined after WW I.

Nonproliferation Treaty Treaty (July 1, 1968) in which nuclear powers agreed to prevent the spread of nuclear-weapons technology to nations that did not then possess such capabilities. The treaty was signed by the US, Britain, USSR, and numerous other nonnuclear countries. Reports of new weapons-development programs persist, however, notably in Pakistan, Libya, and South Africa.

Nootka Sound controversy In 1789 Spain and Britain almost went to war over Nootka Sound, a natural harbor on the coast of Vancouver Island. The Nootka Sound Convention of 1790 granted both nations fishing and settlement rights and ended Spain's exclusive claims to the west coast of North America.

No Popery Riots *See* **Gordon Riots.**

Nordenskjöld, N.A.E. *See* **Northeast Passage.**

Nordlingen, battles of 1. Decisive victory for the Holy Roman Empire (Sept. 5–6, 1634) during the Thirty Years' War (1618–48) (*q.v.*). A combined force of Imperial and Spanish troops, led by Archduke Ferdinand (later Ferdinand III), routed a Swedish force near this Bavarian town. The victory forced France to join the war (May, 1635) and ended Swedish influence in southern Germany. 2. Victory for the French (Aug. 3, 1645) during the Thirty Years' War. French troops, led by the Great Condé, defeated a combined force of the Holy Roman Empire and Bavaria at Nordlingen. The victory was gained at great cost, however, and brought about a lull in fighting.

Norfolk, Thomas Mowbray, 1st duke of c1366–99. English nobleman. Norfolk was a "lord appellant" who dominated Richard II from 1387 to 1389. Uneasy after Richard regained power, he quarreled with Bolingbroke (later Henry IV) and both he and Bolingbroke were banished.

Noriega, Manuel 1938– . Panamanian military leader and strongman. A career military officer, Noriega aided the US intelligence service (beginning in the Nixon years), despite reports of his apparent involvement in drug trafficking.

Following the death of Omar Torrijos (1981), which Noriega was rumored to have engineered, he unified the country's military forces (1983) and thereby strengthened his position. Following revelations about his illicit activities, he successfully resisted attempts at his ouster. However, Noriega was indicted by US grand juries (1988) for drug trafficking and was brought to trial in the US after being captured in the invasion of Panama (1990). He was convicted (1992) and sentenced to forty years in US federal prison.

Norman Conquest English historical period inaugurated in 1066. One of the formative eras in English history, it began with the defeat of the English king Harold II by William the Conqueror, duke of Normandy, at the Battle of Hastings (*q.v.*). Thereafter the customs, laws, and language of the Normans were introduced in England. William replaced the English nobles with his Norman followers and established the feudal system in England.

Normandy Historic region of France on the English Channel. The Norseman Rollo was proclaimed the first duke of Normandy by Charles III of France (911). Duke William (the Conqueror) united Normandy with England by his conquest of England in 1066. It was taken by France under Philip II in 1204, retaken by England in 1417, and again by France in 1450. The beaches of Normandy were the scene for the Allied invasion during WW II (1944). Rouen is the historic capital.

Normandy invasion (Operation Overlord) World War II Allied invasion. On D-Day, June 6, 1944, Allied land, naval, and air troops invaded the northern shores of Nazi-held France. They established beachheads (Utah, Omaha, Gold, Juno, Sword) in five key areas by the next day, opening the area for other Allied troops. The invasion signaled the beginning of the end of the Nazi war effort. The invasion, the largest amphibious landing in history, was overseen and executed by Gen. D. Eisenhower, and some 800,000 combat troops had been massed in Britain for the operation. Over 4,000 ships, under the command of British admiral Sir Bertram Ramsay, were used in the invasion; and about 5,000 fighters and almost 6,000 bombers were used to provide air support. British field marshal B. Montgomery was in command of Allied ground forces during the invasion.

Normans *See* **Norsemen.**

Norodom 1834–1904.   Cambodian king (1860–1904) who brought an end to his country's independence by accepting a French protectorate (1864).

Norodom Sihanouk 1922–   .   Cambodian king (1941–55). Following the French withdrawal from Indochina (1954), he established the People's Socialist Community, abdicated the throne in favor of his father (Prince Norodom Suramarit) and became prime minister. He became head of state again after his father's death (1960) but was unsuccessful at maintaining neutrality during the Vietnam War and was overthrown in 1970 by a US–supported rightist coup. Following the Khmer Rouge takeover in Cambodia, he returned from exile only to be put under house arrest (1975). Released in 1979, he condemned Vietnam's invasion of Cambodia and became president of a coalition government in exile (1982–88). After the Vietnamese withdrawal (1989), he played an active role in negotiations that resulted in a UN–backed transition government in Cambodia. *See also* Cambodia, 1989–92.

Norris, Frank 1870–1902.   American writer. Norris was a naturalist and was influenced by É. Zola. His works include *McTeague, The Octopus,* and *The Pit,* and often intended to expose corruption and exploitation.

Norris, George William 1861–1944.   American legislator from Nebraska. Norris was both a congressman (1903–13) and senator (1913–43). He opposed US entry into WW I, established the Tennessee Valley Authority (*q.v.*), and introduced the 20th (Lame Duck) Amendment to the Constitution, which was enacted in 1933.

Norsemen (Northmen) (Normans)   Scandinavian Vikings who, from the 8th cent., raided and colonized such diverse territories as England, Ireland, France, and Russia. Vikings also colonized Iceland and Greenland and even visited "Vinland" (North America). Norseman from what is now Denmark were called Danes and attacked England as early as 787. The major assault by Norsemen on France came c845. In 912, French king Charles III gave the Norseman Rollo the area around Rouen. This was the beginning of the duchy of Normandy. Later, Christianized Normans of Normandy established (10th cent.) kingdoms in southern Italy and Sicily and, under William the Conqueror, invaded and conquered England (1066). In Russia, the Norsemen were known as Varangians, and one of them, Rurik, established at Novgorod (862) the dynasty that ruled in Russia until 1598. In the same period, strong rulers such as Harold I and Canute began to organize Norse homelands into the Scandinavian nations of Norway, Denmark, and Sweden.

North, Frederick, 2d earl of Guilford and 8th baron North 1732–92.   English statesman. Lord North was George III's prime minister (1770–82) during the American Revolution. His acquiescence to the king's harsh policies in the years leading up to the American Revolution led to the loss of the American colonies. He did not fully support the war and remained in office at the king's insistence until 1782 and the British defeat at Yorktown.

North Africa   Geographical designation. This term identifies the African countries south of the Mediterranean and north of the Sahara. It generally includes Morocco, Algeria, Tunisia, Libya, and, sometimes, Egypt.

North Africa Campaign   Series of military actions in North Africa (1940–43) during WW II. Following Italy's entry into the war (1940), Italian forces began an invasion of Egypt (Sept., 1940). The British counterattacked (Dec.) and drove them back some 500 miles into Libya (Feb., 1941). This brought German intervention and two major German offensives. Gen. E. Rommel, commanding the Afrika Korps, attacked the British (Apr., 1941) and advanced into Egypt. The British counterattacked and drove Rommel back through Libya to El Agheila (Jan., 1942). Rommel opened a new counteroffensive (May, 1942) and again pushed into Egypt. The turning point came (Oct., 1942) in the Battle of El Alamein (*q.v.*). The British, now under command of B. Montgomery, forced Rommel to retreat. Outwitting British attacks, he fell back to southern Tunisia. New Allied forces, commanded by Gen. D. Eisenhower, landed in the west (Nov., 1942) in Morocco and Algeria. They pushed into Tunisia and guaranteed the German defeat, but only after heavy fighting. When the Axis forces finally surrendered (May, 1943) more than 250,000 troops were taken prisoner. The Axis defeat in North Africa was a major victory for the Allies.

Northampton, Battle of   *See* **Roses, Wars of the.**

North Atlantic Treaty Organization (NATO)   Alliance formed after WW II by the Atlantic nations of Europe and North America to counter potential Soviet bloc threats. The treaty was originally signed Apr. 4, 1949, and members included Belgium, Canada, Denmark, France, Great Britain, Iceland, Italy, Luxembourg, the Netherlands, Norway, Portugal, and the United States. Greece and Turkey joined in 1952 and West Germany in 1955.

North Carolina State, in the US Southeast, the 12th state. Sir W. Raleigh's colony on Roanoke Island (1580s) was unsuccessful, and the region was granted by Charles II to eight members of his court. It reverted to the court in 1729 and became a royal colony. During the American Revolution, the Mecklenburg Declaration of Independence (*q.v.*) was drawn up (1775) calling for independence. North Carolina was the scene of fighting in the American Revolution and ratified the US Constitution in 1789 and relinquished its claims to Tennessee in 1790. During the Civil War, it seceded in 1861 and rejoined the Union in 1868. The present amended state constitution was adopted in 1868. North Carolina leads the nation in the production of tobacco, textiles, and furniture.

Northcliffe, Alfred Charles William Harmsworth, viscount 1865–1922. English journalist and publisher. He was considered the most successful publisher in English history, having either founded or salvaged such papers as the *Daily Mail,* the *London Observer* and the London *Times.*

North Dakota North-central US state, the 39th state. The French explorer Pierre de la Verendrye and his sons explored the region in the mid-1700s, and the fur trade brought in others. The US acquired half of the area with the Louisiana Purchase (1803) and the other half from the British in 1818. In 1861, the Dakota Territory was formed, including North Dakota, South Dakota, Montana, and Wyoming, but it was sparsely settled until the late 1800s because of the conflict with the Indians. North Dakota adopted its constitution and became a state in 1889. It is one of the world's premier wheat-growing regions.

Northeast Boundary Dispute US–Canadian border controversy. Due to the vagueness of the 1783 Treaty of Paris, the border between Maine and New Brunswick was unclear. Several points were clarified in the Jay Treaty and the Treaty of Ghent (*qq.v.*) After the Aroostook War (*q.v.*), America and Britain decided to settle the matter permanently through the Webster-Ashburton Treaty of 1842 (*q.v.*).

Northeast Passage Sea route to the Pacific along the northern coasts of Russia and Siberia. Navigators attempted to open such a route from the 16th cent. but it was not opened until 1878–79, when N.A.E. Nordenskjöld (1832–1901) of Sweden accomplished this. The Soviet Union today maintains the route with the help of ice-breakers and patrol planes.

Northern Expedition Military campaign in China (1926–28) conducted by the Nationalist Guomindang and led by Chiang Kai-shek. Planned by Sun Yat-sen, the operation was launched (1926) to overcome the warlords, local military rulers who were preventing establishment of an effective central government. The Nationalists quickly won control of the south and, as the campaign proceeded, the historic purge of Communists from the Guomindang began (Apr. 1927). Beijing was captured (June 1928) and, with the capital secured, Chiang Kai-shek became ruler of a unified China. His authority was never secure, however, and after the Chinese Civil War (*q.v.*) the Communists finally gained control of China (1949).

Northern Ireland (Ulster) Division of the United Kingdom, located in northeastern Ireland. The population is 1,578,000 (1988 est.) and the capital is Belfast. It includes six of the nine counties of the historic English province of Ulster and hence is frequently called Ulster. The English seized much of the land in the area (17th cent.) after suppressing a rebellion in Ireland (1649). Ulster was settled by English and Scottish Protestants. The modern-day political rivalry between Catholics and Protestants (the latter comprising the majority of the population) dates back to the 19th cent. and W. Gladstone's proposal for Home Rule (*q.v.*) in Ireland. The Protestants, fearing Catholic domination from the south, opposed Home Rule. The Government of Ireland Act (1920) established Northern Ireland as a separate province, but the Republic of Ireland refused to acknowledge the division. Frequent clashes continued which, in the late 1960s, erupted into civil war between a wing of the IRA and a Protestant group, the Ulster Defense Association. In 1972 Britain assumed control of government in Northern Ireland. Subsequently, a coalition of Northern Ireland's Social Democratic and Labour parties gained control of a reconstituted assembly, formed an 11-member Northern Ireland Executive, and planned a

Council of Ireland, which would seek cooperation between Catholic and Protestant factions. Continued terrorism by both the IRA and Protestants hampered efforts to resolve the conflict, and a general strike in Ulster (May, 1974) led to resumption of governmental control by Britain. The bloody terrorist war continued in the 1980s and 1990s.

Northern Rhodesia (Zambia) Former African colony. Located in south-central Africa, this was the name of Zambia from 1911 to its establishment as a republic (1964). The name comes from the British empire-builder C. Rhodes.

Northern Sung *See* **Sung.**

Northern Territories Australian region. This is a sparsely settled area of northern Australia bounded by the Timor and Arafura seas on the north and Queensland on the east. Its chief industries are mining and cattle raising.

Northern War (First) War (1655–60) between Sweden and Poland and its allies (Austria, Denmark, and Russia) sparked by Sweden's attempt to expand its Baltic domains. Swedish king Charles X invaded Poland and won a major victory at Warsaw (1656) before being forced to withdraw. In 1658, Charles invaded Denmark and nearly captured Copenhagen. The war with Poland was formally ended (1660) by the Treaty of Oliva (*q.v.*) and the Treaty of Copenhagen with Denmark, in which Sweden gained Danish territory in southern Sweden.

Northern War (Great ~) War fought (1700–21) by Sweden under Charles II and Russia under Peter I (the Great). Russia was supported by Denmark, Saxony, Poland, Prussia, and Hanover. The original belligerents (Russia, Poland, and Denmark) sought to break Swedish hegemony in the Baltic region. Charles prolonged the war by proving a far better warrior than expected, but Sweden was ultimately defeated. The Northern War, concurrent with the War of the Spanish Succession in southern Europe, marked the rise of Russian power in the Baltic.

North German Confederation An alliance of 22 German states north of the Main River under the leadership of Prussia. Formed (1866) after the Austro-Prussian War (*q.v.*), it succeeded the German Confederation (*q.v.*) which had been dominated by Prussia's rival, Austria. The new confederation lasted between 1866 and 1871, when Prussian minister O. von Bismarck achieved his goal of creating a unified empire of all German states under Prussian domination (and excluding Austria). Bismarck thereby created the modern German state.

Northmen *See* **Norsemen.**

Northumberland, earls of *See* **Percy.**

Northumberland, John Dudley, duke of c1502–53. English soldier and politician. He ruled England during the minority of Edward VI and persuaded him to transfer the throne from Mary and Elizabeth I to his own daughter-in-law, Lady Jane Grey. He was subsequently beheaded.

Northumbria, kingdom of Anglo-Saxon kingdom of England, formed by uniting the kingdoms Deira and Bernicia. During the 7th cent., the kingdom accepted Christianity and became the major power in England. Mercia gradually became more powerful, but the entire York area was overrun and ruled by the Danes, until they were beaten by Harold II of England (1066).

North West Company Canadian fur-trading company founded in 1783. It carried on a vigorous and often violent competition with the Hudson's Bay Co. until a merger of the two in 1821.

Northwest Ordinances US legislation passed (1784–87) under the Articles of Confederation to settle the state of western territory (the Northwest Territory, *q.v.*) ceded to the central government by the states after the American Revolution. The principal ordinance was passed on July 13, 1787, and is sometimes called the Ordinance of 1787; it established territories and provided the conditions under which they could become states. It also provided for education, religious freedom, and land division, and it prohibited slavery in the territories as well. This legislation was the most significant accomplishment of the government under the Articles of Confederation.

Northwest Passage Sea route from the Atlantic to the Pacific through the Arctic above North America. From the 16th cent. on, the quest for such a passage gave enormous impetus to the exploration of the North American Arctic, but the actual existence of such a route was not demonstrated until the 1850s, and it was not traversed by a commercial ship until the ice-breaking tanker *USS Manhattan* accomplished the feat in 1969.

Northwest Rebellion *See* **Riel's Rebellion.**

Northwest Territory (Old ~) Region that was the first US territory, comprised of the present states of Ohio, Indiana, Illinois, Michigan, Wisconsin, and part of Minnesota. The area was explored by French traders and missionaries and was taken by the British in the French and Indian Wars (1763). The Treaty of Paris (1783), ending the American Revolution, gave the land to the US. Territorial government was established by the Northwest Ordinance (1787) and the area was divided (1800) into the Indiana Territory and Northwest Territory (including then only Ohio and some adjoining regions).

Norton Thomas *See* **Sackville, Thomas, 1st earl of Dorset.**

Norway (Kingdom of ˜) Kingdom located in northern Europe and occupying the western part of the Scandinavian Peninsula. The population is 4,214,000 and the capital is Oslo. Long a seafaring people, Norwegians were among the Scandinavian Norsemen who raided Europe and colonized Iceland and Greenland between the 9th and 11th cents. Norway was united with neighboring powers for much of its history. From the 14th to 19th cents. it was under Danish control and during the 19th cent. it passed to Sweden. Norway gained independence in 1905 and today possesses one of the world's great merchant marine fleets. Key dates in Norwegian history include:

9TH CENT.   Mountain valleys and fjords of Norway divided into local *fylker* (counties) ruled by petty kings.

860–933   Harold I (the Fairhaired) reigned; conquered and unified most of Norway by 872 and became its first king; also conquered Orkneys and Shetlands.

860–1000   Vikings from Norway intensified seaborne conquests; colonization of Iceland (874), Normandy (911), and Greenland (974).

935–961   Haakon I reigned; briefly reunited kingdom, divided since Harold's death.

995–1000   Olaf I reigned; Christianity introduced; defeated and killed at Svöld in fighting against Sweden and Denmark.

1000   Norway divided between Denmark and Sweden after Olaf's defeat.

1016–28   Olaf II reigned after ending foreign rule; Christianity established; aroused opposition of nobles.

1028   King Canute (of England and Denmark), aided by disaffected nobles, conquered Norway.

1035–47   Magnus I reigned, following Canute's death; ruled as king of Norway and Denmark (from 1042).

1047–66   King Harold III reigned.

1184–1202   Sverre reigned in Norway; gained throne after period of dynastic warfare; created strong monarchy with support of peasants; asserted supremacy of monarchy over church and thereby provoked Crosier War (1196–c1202) against bishops and followers.

1217–63   Haakon IV reigned; Norway enjoyed peace and prosperity; Greenland and Iceland united with crown (1262).

1263–80   Magnus VI reigned; prosperity continued; Magnus instituted administrative and ecclesiastical codes.

14TH CENT.   Black Death (plague) ravaged Norway.

1319–43   Magnus II of Sweden inherited Norwegian throne; forced to abdicate in 1343.

1343–80   Haakon VI reigned.

1380–87   Margaret of Denmark, Haakon's wife, exercised real power in Norway as regent for her son, Olaf V.

1387–97   Margaret held power in both Norway and Denmark after her son died without heirs.

1389–97   Margaret conquered Sweden with the aid of disaffected nobles.

1397   Kalmar Union formed; united Denmark, Norway, and Sweden under one crown; Norway subsequently dominated by Denmark.

1439   King Eric VII of Norway, Sweden, and Denmark was deposed in all three countries.

1523   Sweden withdrew from Kalmar Union; for the next three centuries, Norway was governed as a Danish province.

1534–59   Christian III of Denmark reigned. Lutheranism introduced as Norwegian state religion.

1808–45   Writer H. Wergeland lived; led nationalist movement.

1814   King Christian VIII of Denmark elected king of Norway; attempted to break the union of Norway with Sweden and was forced to abdicate the same year by the Swedes.

1814   King Charles XIV John of Sweden forced Norway into union with Sweden.

1814   Treaty of Kiel; Denmark, an ally of the defeated Napoleon, was forced to cede Norway to Sweden.

1815   Swedish army forced Norway to accept Sweden's Charles XIII, but Norway was recognized as an independent kingdom united with Sweden through the king.

1821 Norwegian Storting (parliament) abolished the Danish-created nobility.

1844–59 Oscar I reigned as king of Norway and Sweden.

AFTER 1850 Golden Age of Norwegian literature and music, with such writers as H. Ibsen and K. Hamsun and such composers as E. Grieg.

1853 Philologist I. Aasen devised Landsmaal, a new Norwegian language.

1877 J. Lie's novel *The Pilot and His Wife* translated into English.

1884 Norwegian government made responsible to the Storting, despite Swedish opposition.

1905 Union with Sweden dissolved by Storting (Aug.) after conflict over separate consular service to assist growing Norwegian merchant fleet; ratified by Sweden (Oct.).

1905–57 Haakon VII reigned as king of Norway.

1911 Explorer R. Amundsen led expedition that was first to reach South Pole (Dec. 14).

1914–18 Norway neutral in WW I.

1920s Labor party (Socialist) rose as dominant power in Norwegian politics; much social legislation passed in 1930s.

1922 F. Nansen, explorer and statesman, awarded the Nobel Peace Prize for Russian relief work.

1940 WW II; Nazi Germany invaded and occupied Norway (Apr. 8–9), a neutral.

1940–45 German occupation; V. Quisling, head of Norwegian Nazis, took over government while the king set up government in exile in Britain.

1945 Norway became charter UN member.

1945–51 E. Gerhardsen (Labor party) in office as prime minister; brought about Norway's rapid postwar economic recovery.

1946–52 T. Lie served as first secretary-general of the United Nations.

1947 Anthropologist T. Heyerdahl crossed the Pacific aboard a primitive raft named the *Kon-Tiki,* to show that primitive South Americans could have reached Pacific islands.

1949 Norway became founding member of NATO.

1955–65 Gerhardsen again in office as prime minister; retirement and social welfare programs instituted.

1957–91 King Olaf V reigned.

1965 Labor party out of power in Norway for first time in three decades.

1971 Scandal forced resignation of prime minister Per Borten's government (Mar.).

1972 Entry into the EEC rejected by voters.

1972 Lars Korvald installed as new prime minister; government crisis over rejection of European Economic Community (EEC) membership ended.

1973 Prime Minister Trygve Bratteli installed following resignation of Lars Korvald.

1976 Government set up national oil company in the wake of North Sea oil discoveries.

1980 Mobile offshore drilling rig collapsed in North Sea (Mar.), killing 123.

1980 Plan to stockpile US military equipment in Norway approved (Dec.).

1981 Gro Harlem Brundtland, a Labor party member, in office as first woman prime minister of Norway.

1981 Price freeze imposed to control inflation (Aug.).

1981–86 Käre Willoch, a Conservative Party member, in office as prime minister, following ouster of the Labor party; sought tax cuts, reduced subsidies, and lessened government regulation of the economy; Conservatives' minority position in parliament made such major reforms unlikely, however.

1983 Conservatives, heretofore a minority government, formed new government based on coalition with Christian People's party and the Center party.

1984 Norwegian diplomat Arne Treholt arrested as Soviet spy (Jan.); sentenced to 20 years in prison (1985).

1984 Statoil, Norway's state-owned oil company, reorganized to increase government revenues and its control over operations; North Sea oil and gas now accounted for 30 percent of Norway's exports.

1986 Strikes and lockouts involving some 100,000 workers in various industries, including oil (Apr.); week-long strikes were worst in decades.

1986–89 Brundtland in office as prime minister; quickly introduced austerity measures, including tax increases, to offset downturn in state revenues resulting from sharp drop in oil prices in 1986; economic turnaround did not come until 1989, however.

1986 Norway to develop extensive Troll and Sleipner gas fields, after winning long-term agreement with European energy consortium for purchase of gas.

1987 Scandal broke over revelations that Kongsberg Våpenfabrikk, a state-run weapons firm, exported technologically advanced equipment to the USSR.

1988 New, temporary wage freeze imposed to help control inflation; became necessary despite 17 percent interest rates.

1989 Jan P. Syse, Conservative party member, in office as prime minister; formed coalition with Center and Christian People's party; began privatization program for state-run businesses; announced tax-reform plan to encourage business and private savings.

1990 Center Party withdrew from coalition over attempt to ease government regulations on foreign ownership in Norway; Conservative government collapsed.

1990– Brundtland back in office as prime minister; publicly supported move to repeal regulations on foreign ownership.

1991 King Harald V crowned king of Norway (Jan.), following death of his father, King Olav V.

1991 Sweeping tax reform approved (June); tax rates lowered.

1991 Government provided massive infusion of capital to head off collapse of national banking system (Oct. 17), following insolvency of nation's second-largest bank, Christina.

1992 Norway (and Iceland), in defiance of 1985 moratorium, to resume commercial whaling (June).

Noske, Gustav 1868–1946. German Social Democratic politician. As minister of defense he suppressed many radical insurrections, most notably the Berlin Spartacus Revolt (1919). He resigned after the 1920 Kapp Putsch (*q.v.*).

Nostradamus (Notredame, Michel de) 1503–66. French physician and astrologer. His symbolic rhymes have come to be regarded by some as prophecies for the world's future and its ending.

Notredame, Michel de *See* **Nostradamus.**

Notre Dame de Paris Cathedral begun in 1163 regarded as a classic example of Gothic architecture. One of the best-known churches in the world, its twin towers were completed around 1245, and it was finally completed in the 14th cent. and restored in the 19th. V. Hugo used it as the setting of his famous romantic novel of the same name (1831).

Novara, Battles of 1. Battle in which a 13,000-man Swiss army, fighting on behalf of the League of Cambrai (*q.v.*), defeated (June 6, 1513) a 10,000-man French army commanded by Louis de la Tremoille (1460–1525). Fighting near Novara in the Italian Piedmont, the Swiss pikemen suffered heavy casualties but inflicted 50 percent casualties on La Tremoille. The defeat forced French king Louis XII to withdraw from Italy. 2. Battle in which 100,000 raw troops of Sardinia-Piedmont were defeated (Mar. 23, 1849) by a numerically inferior but better trained army of Austrian regulars near Novara. The battle was fought during the Italian War of Independence. Field Marshal J. Radetzky inflicted the crushing defeat that led to Charles Albert's abdication and saddled Piedmont-Sardinia with a 65-million-franc indemnity.

Nova Scotia One of the Maritime Provinces of eastern Canada. Originally inhabited by Algonquian Indians, the area may have been explored by J. Cabot (1497). The French founded the first European settlement in 1605, but there was constant conflict with the English for control of the area known as Acadia (*q.v.*). In 1755, England gained control and expelled the French Acadians; the incident was described in H. W. Longfellow's *Evangeline.* Many US Loyalists and Scottish immigrants settled there, and the colony of Nova Scotia entered the Canadian Confederation in 1867. The province is noted for fishing, forestry, mining, tourism, and Scottish cultural celebrations.

Novatian *fl.* AD 250. Early Christian heresiarch and antipope. A Roman priest, he denied that those Christians who had lapsed during the persecution of Decius (AD 250) could be readmitted to the church. When Pope Cornelius (251–53) decreed indulgence toward the lapsed, Novatian started his own rigorist sect that lasted until the 6th cent.

November Insurrection Unsuccessful Polish rebellion (1830–31) against Russian domination of the Congress Kingdom of Poland (*q.v.*). It began (Nov. 29, 1830) after the French July Revolution and rebels seized control of Warsaw.

Tsar Nicholas was deposed as king of Poland (Jan. 25, 1831) and the numerically superior Russian army advanced into Poland (Feb.). The Russians attacked Warsaw (Sept.) after several battles and the Polish army withdrew to Prussia, where it surrendered (Oct. 5).

November Revolution *See* **October Revolution.**

Novgorod Russian city. Novgorod, located in northwest Russia, is one of Russia's oldest cities. Its position on the trade route from Scandinavia to Byzantium made it a major commercial and cultural center. The foundation of the Russian state dates from 862 when the inhabitants of Novgorod asked Rurik to rule them. At its height in the 14th cent., Novgorod boasted rich fairs, factories, and churches. It came under the control of Moscow in 1478. It was a member of the Hanseatic League (*q.v.*). Its churches and museums suffered at Nazi hands in WW II.

novus homo During the Roman republic, term for the first man within a family who became a member of the Senate. During the republic this feat was not particularly unusual and could be accomplished by virtue of military or oratorical prowess, through the efforts of a well-placed patron, and other means. The term was also used in a far rarer situation, when a man from outside the Senate won the consulate. This happened about fifteen times in the mid-to-late republic, and among these ambitious and particularly able individuals were Cato, Marius, and Cicero. During the empire, the rapid rise of a novus homo became more common.

Noyes, John Humphrey 1811–86. American religious reformer. In 1848, Noyes established the Oneida Community (*q.v.*), which believed in the "perfectionism" of humanity through communion with Jesus and communal living.

Nubia Ancient region of northeastern Africa (southern Egypt and northern Sudan) that was for many centuries ruled by Egypt. By the 8th century BC, Nubia had become independent and conquered Egypt. The Negro tribe Nobatae formed the next powerful kingdom of the area and converted to Christianity. After the Muslim takeover (14th cent.), the area became divided into small states.

Nuclear Nonproliferation Treaty *See* **Nonproliferation Treaty.**

Nuclear Test-Ban Treaty Treaty signed in Moscow (Aug. 5, 1963) between the US, Britain, and the USSR, banning nuclear-weapons tests in the atmosphere, in outer space, and underwater. It provided for no international enforcement machinery, nor, since France did not sign, did it include all nuclear powers.

nullification The states' rights doctrine in US history holding that a state had the authority to remedy federal abuses of power by nullifying federal laws within its borders. The Kentucky and Virginia Resolutions (*q.v.*) of 1798–99 had argued that the union was a voluntary compact and that the federal government had no authority not specifically delegated to it by the Constitution. The issue of a protective tariff, which hurt the South, brought the conflict to a head in the 1820s, and the theory of nullification was articulated (1828) by J. C. Calhoun. His home state, South Carolina, passed an Ordinance of Nullification (1832), declaring the federal tariffs of 1828 and 1832 inoperative within its borders. A. Jackson obtained a force bill allowing him to use military force to collect the tariff in Charleston but through the efforts of H. Clay, sought a compromise tariff. South Carolina then rescinded its nullification (1833). The issue was not raised again until 1861, when South Carolina seceded from the Union, precipitating the American Civil War (*q.v.*). The Union victory in the war ultimately settled the issue by establishing federal supremacy over the states.

Numa Pompilius C715–672 BC. Legendary second king of Rome. Numa is thought to have succeeded Romulus, to have established religious laws and the religious calendar, and to have been loved for his wisdom.

Numidia Ancient North African country, situated roughly in modern Algeria. Masinissa became ruler after allying himself with Rome in the Punic Wars (*q.v.*) and was the leader during Numidia's golden age. Under King Juba I, Numidia fell to Rome (46 BC) but enjoyed a long period of prosperity until the invasion of the Vandals in 428. It was later conquered by the Muslims.

Núñez, Rafael 1825–94. Controversial Colombian president, 1880–82, 1884–88. He entered politics as a liberal in the 1850s and served in various cabinet posts before being elected president (1879). In his first term, he oversaw creation of a national bank and repealed anticlerical measures. Reelected with Conservative support in 1883, he was viewed with increasing distrust by Liberals, who rebelled in 1885–86. Núñez then abolished the liberal constitution of 1863, replacing it with the authoritarian Constitution of 1886. Though elected to a new six-year term, he retired in 1888.

Núñez Vela, Blasco *d.* 1546. First Spanish viceroy of Peru (1544–46), sent to enforce the "New Laws" of B. de Las Casas. He antagonized nearly everybody and a revolt against the "New Laws" led by G. Pizarro brought about an altercation in which the viceroy murdered a man. He was arrested, and executed when he tried to raise forces to quell the rebellion and avoid trial in Spain.

Nuremberg *See* **Nürnberg.**

Nurhachi 1559–1626. Manchurian tribal chief and founder of China's Qing (Manchu) dynasty (1644–1912). After uniting Manchuria, he began the conquest of the Chinese empire, which his son, Dorgon, completed.

Nürnberg, Religious Peace of *See* **Religious Peace of Nürnberg.**

Nürnberg Laws Two racial laws passed by the German Nazi party on Sept. 15, 1935. German Jews were denied German citizenship and forbidden to marry or have sexual relations with non-Jews.

Nürnberg Standstill *See* **Religious Peace of Nürnberg.**

Nürnberg Trials War-crimes trials held after WW II in Nürnberg, Germany, for the purpose of trying leaders of the Nazi party. Authorized by the Allies' London Agreement (Aug. 8, 1945), the trials were conducted by a special international tribunal. Twenty-four Nazi leaders were indicted, including H. Göring, W. Keitel, J. von Ribbentrop, A. Rosenberg, R. Hess, and H. Schacht. The tribunal held 403 public sessions (Nov. 20, 1945–Oct. 1, 1946), heard hundreds of witnesses, and utilized captured German documents to prove the charges of war crimes and crimes against peace and humanity (notably the slaughter of the Jews). Twelve defendants were sentenced to be hanged, while the others were either imprisoned or acquitted. Two defendants, including H. Göring, committed suicide. The trials were controversial, but the tribunal argued that all the violations were of international laws recognized prior to WW II and that Nazi crimes against the Jews required a unique response.

Nyasaland *See* **Malawi.**

Nyerere, Julius 1922–   . First president of the United Republic of Tanzania (1964–85). He founded the Tanganyika National Union political party (1954), became the first prime minister and then president when Tanganyika became independent (1961), and effected the union of Tanganyika and Zanzibar as Tanzania (1964). Discouraged by persistent economic problems following war with Uganda's I. Amin, he resigned the presidency but retained the leadership of his party.

Nyssa, Saint Gregory of *See* **Gregory of Nyssa, Saint.**

Nystad, Treaty of Treaty concluded between Russia and Sweden in 1721 ending the Northern War (*q.v.*). Sweden retained Finland but ceded Livonia, Estonia, Ingria, and part of Karelia to Russia, and Russia obtained a "window" on the Baltic.

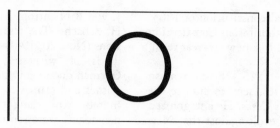

OAS *See* **Organization of American States.**

Oates, Titus 1649–1705. English clergyman who caused a flurry of anti-Catholic hysteria and judicial murder of 35 Catholics with his fabricated story of the Popish Plot (*q.v.*) to kill Charles II so the Catholic James II could succeed. He was convicted of perjury in 1685 and imprisoned, but was freed and pensioned after the Glorious Revolution (*q.v.*) in 1688.

Oath of Strasbourg Oath sworn (842) by Charles II (the Bald) and Louis II (the German) confirming their joint alliance against their brother, Emperor Lothair I. One of the versions in which this oath was recorded is considered to be the earliest written example of the French language.

OAU *See* **Organization of African Unity.**

Obote, Milton *See* **Uganda, 1966–71, 1980–85; Amin, Idi.**

Obregón, Álvaro 1880–1928. Mexican general and president (1920–24). Obregón supported V. Carranza against V. Huerta, F. Villa, and E. Zapata, but eventually deposed Carranza. As president, he advocated education and land reforms and improved relations with the US.

O'Brien, William Smith 1803–64. Irish revolutionary. The Protestant O'Brien first supported the cause of Irish independence in Parliament. When his Young Ireland group later failed in an 1848 insurrection, he was sentenced to death, but was banished instead.

O'Casey, Sean 1884–1964. Irish playwright. O'Casey is best known for his satiric tragicomedies written for the Abbey Theatre (*q.v.*). They include *The Shadow of a Gunman, Juno and the Paycock,* and *The Plow and the Stars.*

Occam, William of *See* **Ockham, William of.**

O'Connor, Sandra Day 1930– . Associate justice of the US Supreme Court, the first woman to serve on the Court. A former Arizona state senator and judge, O'Connor was appointed to the Court by President R. Reagan (1981). During the 1980s, she proved to be a judicial moderate, usually ruling with the majority and sometimes providing the extra vote needed for a majority opinion when the Court was divided.

occultism Supernatural belief in unseen, extraordinary forces that cannot be explained by ordinary scientific means. Occult fields include astrology, alchemy, spiritualism, and theosophy.

Oceania (Oceanica) Pacific Islands. This is the collective name for the thousands of islands in the central and South Pacific Ocean. Ethnically they are divided into Australasia, Melanesia, Micronesia, and Polynesia.

Ochs, Adolph S. 1858–1935. American publisher. Ochs fought yellow journalism (*q.v.*) in his newspapers the *New York Times,* which he converted into a world-famous newspaper dedicated to objective reporting, the Chattanooga *Times,* and the Philadelphia *Times Ledger.* He financed the *Dictionary of American Biography.*

Ockham, William of (Occam, ˜) c1285–c1349. English Franciscan philosopher. He opposed the Aristotelian realism of T. Aquinas, holding that universal ideas exist only in the thinking mind. He is remembered for his principle of economy in thought, called "Ockham's Razor." In philosophy he was a nominalist whose ideas contributed to the decline of scholasticism (*q.v.*) and eventually to the Protestant Reformation.

O'Connell, Daniel 1775–1847. Irish political leader. Nicknamed "The Liberator," O'Connell attempted to gain Irish freedom through political agitation. He founded the Catholic Association (1823) and was first Catholic lord mayor of Dublin (1841) since the reign of James II. His election to Parliament in 1828 provoked the passage of the Catholic Emancipation Act (*q.v.*) to enable him to take his seat without the usual oaths. He supported the Whigs in Parliament and tried to break up the union of Britain and Ireland. Losing support in later years, he died a broken man in Italy.

O'Connor, Frank (O'Donovan, Michael) 1903–66. Irish writer. O'Connor's short stories illuminate many aspects of Irish life. He directed for the Abbey Theatre and translated Gaelic literature into English.

O'Connor, Rory Roderick 1116?–98. Last high king of Ireland (1166–75). O'Connor was king of Connaught before he seized the high kingship (1166). He was forced to submit (1175) to Henry II of England in the Treaty of Windsor (*q.v.*).

Octavia *d.* 11 BC. Roman matron. Octavia was the beautiful and virtuous sister of Augustus and wife (from 40 to 30 BC) of Marc Antony, and kept peace between them for a time. Antony deserted her for Cleopatra.

Octavia AD 42–62. Roman empress. Octavia was the daughter of Claudius and the wife of Nero, who divorced her. She was exiled and executed because of the jealousy of Nero's third wife, Poppaea.

Octavian *See* **Augustus.**

Octavian *See* **John XII.**

Octavianus, Gaius Julius Caesar *See* **Augustus.**

Octavius, Gaius *See* **Augustus.**

October Manifesto Manifesto issued on Oct. 30, 1905, by Russian tsar Nicholas II. Issued in response to the Russian Revolution of 1905 (*q.v.*), it guaranteed civil liberties and called for establishment of a duma, which would have the power to confirm all legislation. The manifesto would have turned the Russian government into a constitutional monarchy, but it was only partially enacted.

October Revolution (November ˜) The *coup d'état* of Oct. 24–25, 1917 (new style, Nov. 6–7), by which the Bolsheviks (*q.v.*), under the leadership of N. Lenin, took control of the Russian Revolution (*q.v.*). The revolution began with the February Revolution (*q.v.*), the abdication of Tsar Nicholas II (March 15, 1917), and the formation of a provisional government dominated by Socialists (eventually headed by A. Kerensky). In April, however, Lenin and other Bolshevik leaders returned to Russia. They called for Russia's

withdrawal from WW I and establishment of a program of land distribution, and managed to gain increasing support. On the night of Nov. 6–7 (old style, Oct. 24–25), supported by Red Guards and the sailors of Kronstadt, the Bolsheviks, led by L. Trotsky, seized all government buildings and the Winter Palace in St. Petersburg. The Council of People's Commissars was then set up, with Lenin as chairman and the Communist regime in Russia began. (*See also* Commonwealth of Independent States, 1917; Russian Revolution.)

Octobrists (Union of October 17) Russian conservative political party. It sought enactment of constitutional reforms based on the October Manifesto (*q.v.*) issued by Tsar Nicholas II. Formed in 1906, the party was dissolved during the 1917 Russian Revolution.

Oda Nobunaga 1534–82. Japanese military leader, son of a warlord family. He was the first Japanese commander to arm his troops with muskets. He unified one-third of Japan before his death in 1582. His successors, Hideyoshi and later Tokugawa, completed the unification. *See also* Japan, 1500s.

Oder-Neisse Line Polish-German frontier established by the USSR, Great Britain, and the US at the 1945 Potsdam Conference (*q.v.*). Poland was compensated at Germany's expense for the Soviet acquisitions on her eastern border. These controversial borders were not recognized by West Germany until 1971.

Odescalchi, Benedetto *See* **Innocent XI.**

Odets, Clifford 1906–63. American playwright. Odets reflected a strong social conscience in such plays as *Waiting for Lefty, Awake and Sing, Golden Boy,* and *The Country Girl.*

Odo *See* **Eudes.**

Odoacer (Odovacar) AD c435–493. German chieftain and mercenary in Roman service who deposed the last Western Roman emperor, Romulus Augustus, in AD 476. A member of the Sciri or Rugian tribe, he was the virtual ruler of Italy until assassinated by an Ostrogothic king, Theodoric, acting for the Byzantines.

O'Donnell, Leopoldo 1809–67. Spanish general and statesman. O'Donnell supported Isabella II against the Carlists (*q.v.*), overthrew B. Espartero, and served several times as premier.

O'Donovan, Michael *See* **O'Connor, Frank.**

Odo of Lagery *See* **Urban II.**

Odovacar *See* **Odoacer.**

Odyssey *See* ***Iliad*** and ***Odyssey***.

Oecolampadius, Johannes 1482–1531. German theologian and reformer. He helped D. Erasmus edit the Greek New Testament, but came under M. Luther's influence (1522). He carried the Reformation to Basel, later siding with U. Zwingli. He drafted the First Confession of Basel (1531).

Offa *d.* 796. King of Mercia (757–796). Offa made his kingdom the most powerful in Anglo-Saxon England. He introduced the coinage system used in England for centuries thereafter, and negotiated (with Charlemagne) the first commercial treaty in English history. He also ordered the building of the extensive earthwork known as Offa's dike.

Offenbach, Jacques 1819–80. German-born French composer. Offenbach created a popular, elegant style of French operetta, but is today best remembered for his full-scale opera *Tales of Hoffmann.*

Ogadai 1185–1241. Mongol ruler (1229–41), successor to his father, Genghis Khan. He conquered northern China (1234) and sent armies under Batu Khan westward into Russia, where they sacked Kiev (1240) and thereby ended Russian resistance. The armies then overran Poland and Hungary, and only Ogadai's death prevented their advance into Western Europe. Ogadai built the Mongol capital city of Karakorum.

Oglesby, Richard J. *See* **Grand Army of the Republic**.

Oglethorpe, James Edward 1696–1785. English philanthropist. Oglethorpe was involved with penal reform and the treatment of debtors. He founded the American colony of Georgia (1733) primarily as an asylum for debtors.

OGPU *See* **GPU**.

O'Higgins, Bernardo 1778–1842. Chilean soldier and statesman. He became leader of the revolutionary forces in Chile (1813) and helped defeat the Spaniards at Chacabuco (*q.v.*) in 1817. He was named supreme dictator and proclaimed Chilean independence on Feb. 12, 1818. He was the first president of Chile, until 1823, when he was deposed for his reforms. He died in exile in Peru.

Ohio State in the north-central US, the 17th state. Prehistoric Mound Builders inhabited Ohio, and the Erie and Iroquois Indians were later major tribes there. R. La Salle claimed the region for France, but the British gained control in the French and Indian Wars (1754). It was ceded to the US after the American Revolution in the Treaty of Paris (1783). Ohio became part of the Northwest Territory in 1787, and Marietta was its first settlement (1788). It became a state in 1803 and adopted its present constitution in 1851.

Ohio Company Organization of Virginia and Maryland colonists interested in western settlement. A British royal charter in 1749 granted it 200,000 acres around the forks of the Ohio River. Activities of the company helped provoke the French and Indian Wars (*q.v.*), since it encroached on territory then claimed by France. The company was the first organized American Colonial effort to settle territory west of the Alleghenies.

Ohio Company of Associates American Colonial settlers. New Englanders formed this settlement group in Boston (1786). The next year they purchased and colonized the land that became the city of Marietta, Ohio, under the Northwest Ordinance of 1787.

Ohm, Georg Simon 1789–1854. German physicist best known for Ohm's Law, the basic law of current flow. Educated in science by his father, a master locksmith, he worked as a schoolteacher before deciding to devote himself to research in physics. He began the studies leading to the formulation of his law in 1825 and discovered that the force of a current traveling through a conductor is a measure of the current. The resulting Ohm's Law was the earliest theoretical study of electricity. The unit of resistance (ohm) and unit of conductivity (mho—ohm spelled backward) are named for him.

Ojibwa Indians North American Indian tribe. Also called the Chippewa, the Ojibwa were a major branch of the Algonquian Indians, and lived in the Great Lakes region. They supported the French in their many colonial wars against the English, but sided with Britain against America in the American Revolution and the War of 1812. They were known for their pictograph form of writing.

Okinawa Japanese island. Okinawa was the scene of a bloody WW II battle between America and Japan (Apr. 1–June 21, 1945). The US won despite casualties of some 48,000, one-third of them fatal. The Japanese lost some 110,000 of their 120,000-man garrison before surrendering on June 21, 1945. Okinawa remained under US military control until May, 1972, when it was returned to Japan.

Oklahoma US state in the Southwest, the 46th state. Originally inhabited by various tribes of Plains Indians, the area was explored by the Spanish and French, beginning in the 16th cent. It became part of the US with the Louisiana Purchase of 1803 and, as the Indian Territory (*q.v.*), was made the home of displaced Indians. Agitation by land-hungry settlers opened the territory for settlement in 1889. The Indian Territory and the western section known as the Oklahoma Territory merged to form the state of Oklahoma in 1907, and the state constitution was adopted in that year.

Okubo, Toshimichi 1832?–78. Japanese statesman. Okubo, a member of the Satsuma clan, played a major role in restoring the emperor (1868) (Meiji Restoration) and westernizing Japan. He opposed his kinsmen's 1877 Satsuma rebellion and was assassinated by them the next year.

Okuma, Shigenobu, Marquis 1838–1922. Japanese statesman. Okuma opposed the feudal aristocracy of H. Ito, supported constitutional reforms, served as prime minister (1898, 1914–16), and founded Waseda University (1892).

Olaf I c963–1000. King of Norway (995–1000). He tried to convert Norway to Christianity, and commissioned Leif Ericson to carry Christianity to Greenland. He was killed in battle against the Danes and the Swedes, who then divided his lands.

Olaf II c995–1030. King of Norway (1015–28). Olaf attempted to unite Norway religiously and politically but provoked internal dissension instead. He was deposed and killed at the Battle of Stiklestad. He is the patron saint of Norway, and completed the Christianization of the country begun by Olaf I.

Olaf V 1903–91. King of Norway (1957–91). Olaf served as commander in chief of the Norwegian armed forces against the Nazi occupation of Norway in WW II. He returned to Norway in 1945.

Old Believers Russian religious dissenters within the Russian Orthodox church who opposed the liturgical reforms made by Nikon, patriarch of Moscow (1652–58). Persecuted through the 17th, 18th, and 19th cents., they split into many sects, some of which still exist and are now officially recognized.

Oldcastle, Sir John *d.* 1417. English soldier and leader of Lollardry (*q.v.*) He performed valuable military service for Henry IV in Wales. His devotion to the teachings of J. Wycliffe led to his condemnation for heresy. W. Shakespeare's character Sir John Falstaff may have been modeled on him.

Old Catholics Schismatic Catholic sect that was formed in Germany in protest against the dogmatic definition of the pope's infallibility issued in 1870 by the First Vatican Council (*q.v.*). The group acquired a bishop consecrated by a Dutch Jansenist bishop in Holland. Mass was said in the vernacular and priests were allowed to marry. The Old Catholics established intercommunion with the Church of England in 1931.

Old Delhi *See* **Delhi.**

Oldenbarneveldt, Jan van 1547–1619. Dutch statesman. Oldenbarneveldt aided William the Silent in driving Spain from the Netherlands and helped negotiate the Treaty of Utrecht (*q.v.*). He was executed by religious opponents.

Old English Language of the early period (5th–11th cents.) in the development of modern English. It was essentially the language of the 5th-cent. Teutonic invaders of England (Celtic influence was minimal) and had four dialects: Northumbrian, Mercian, Kentish, and West Saxon. The literature of the Old English period is predominantly West Saxon and dates primarily from the reign of Alfred the Great. The best-known work from this period is the epic poem *Beowulf.*

Old Ironsides (*Constitution*) Famous US warship, a 44-gun frigate. Built (1798) for service against French privateers, it saw action during the Tripolitan War and during the War of 1812. In the latter war, the ship was victorious in battle against the British ships *Guerrière* (Aug. 19, 1812) and *Cyane* and *Levant* (Feb. 20, 1815). The ship was rebuilt in 1833, 1877, and 1925 and was the subject of O. W. Holmes's poem *Old Ironsides.*

Old Kingdom (Pyramid Age) One of the three great divisions of ancient Egyptian history (with the Middle and New kingdoms), the period during which most pyramids were built. Generally this period may be taken to include dynasties 3d–6th, though sources vary. Dates vary as well, though c2700–c2200 BC is a good guideline. The Egyptian capital was at Memphis. Among the notable rulers of this period are Zoser, Snefru, Khufu, Menkaure, and Pepi.

Old Northwest *See* **Northwest Territory.**

Old Testament Christian term for the older, Hebrew portion of the Bible. It begins with an account of the creation of the world, recounts the calls by God to such figures as Abraham, Isaac, Jacob, Moses, and David, and through them treats the covenant established by God with the Jewish people. It also promises the coming of the Messiah. The Jews adopted the present canon of approved books (considered inspired) around AD 100. They divided them into: 1. The Law, consisting of the Pentateuch, or first five books: Genesis, Exodus, Leviticus, Numbers, and Deuteronomy. 2. The Prophets, another group of books: Joshua, Judges, I and II Samuel, I and II Kings, Isaiah, Jeremiah, Ezekiel, and the Twelve (Minor) Prophets. 3. The Writings (Hagiographa), consisting of heterogeneous books: Psalms, Proverbs, Job, Song of Solomon, Ruth, Lamentations, Ecclesiastes, Esther, Daniel, Ezra, Nehemiah, and I and II Chronicles. This Jewish version was based on the Masora (*q.v.*). The Christians used a different canon, based on a 3rd-cent. BC Greek translation called the Septuagint (*q.v.*). They considered the following additional books (regarded by the Jews only as pious writings) to be inspired Scripture: Tobias, Judith, Wisdom, Ecclesiasticus, Baruch, and I and II Maccabees. The Christian canon was approved in the 4th cent. AD and stabilized in the Latin Vulgate (*q.v.*). At the Reformation, the books not included in the Jewish canon were set aside by the Protestants as uninspired Apocrypha (*q.v.*). The so-called higher criticism of the 19th cent. tended to impugn both the authorship and historicity of the books of the Old Testament. Later research, including archaeological evidence, goes further toward confirming religious traditions, but there is no general agreement concerning Old Testament authorship and chronology. A series of editors and sacred authors from the 10th cent. BC no doubt composed the books from written and oral traditions. However, in both Christian and Jewish religious traditions, the belief is that God protected them from error in communicating these texts.

Oleg *d.* 912. Early ruler of Rus'. He was a Viking (Varangian) leader and the reputed founder of Kievan Rus'. Oleg expanded his realm of Novgorod, inherited from Rurik, to include Kiev, which then became the capital of a Kievan-Novgorodian state (882). His treaties with the Byzantine Empire (907, 911) opened Rus' to Greek Christian, and cultural penetration.

Oliva, Peace of Treaty between Poland and Sweden (May 3, 1660) ending the First Northern War. King John II of Poland renounced his claim to the Swedish throne and ceded Livonia. West Prussia was confirmed as Polish, but the sovereignty of the elector of Brandenburg over it was recognized.

Olivares, Gaspar de Guzmán y Pimental, Conde-duque 1587–1645. Spanish statesman. He was prime minister to Philip IV (1621–43), but his policies of constant warfare and heavy taxation led to revolts by Catalonia and Portugal, and he was removed.

Ollivier, Émile 1825–1913. French statesman. Napoleon III called upon him to help create the "Liberal Empire," which instituted many reforms. However, Ollivier's decision to lead France into the Franco-Prussian War (1870) forced his dismissal.

Olmütz, Punctation of *See* **Erfurt Parliament; Revolutions of 1848.**

Olney, Richard 1835–1917. American statesman. As attorney general (1893–95), he broke the Pullman strike (*q.v.*), and, as secretary of state (1895–97), he declared that America had the right to arbitrate the Venezuela Boundary Dispute (*q.v.*).

Olympia Ancient Greek plain. Olympia was a religious center and site of festivals and athletic contests honoring Zeus. It was the site of the Olympic games (*q.v.*), and its statue of Zeus by Phidias was one of the ancient Seven Wonders of the World (*q.v.*).

Olympiad Greek time measurement. An Olympiad was the four-year period between Olympic games, each Olympiad being marked from the beginning of the games. The first Olympiad was reckoned to have begun in 776 BC.

Olympias *d.* 316 BC. Macedonian queen. She was the wife of Philip of Macedon, and the mother of Alexander the Great, over whom she had great influence. She executed Alexander's successor Antipater, and was in turn executed by Antipater's son, Cassander.

Olympic Games Religious athletic games. These ancient Greek games were held (776 BC–AD 393) at Olympia once every four years and the cycle was called an Olympiad (*q.v.*). They were revived in 1896, and are now held in a different world city every four years.

Omaha Beach (Bloody Omaha) WW II beachhead. One of the five landing points used during the Allied invasion of France on D-Day (June 6, 1941. The American forces landing at this point suffered the fiercest resistance.

Oman Oil-rich Middle Eastern sultanate (*pop.* 1,305,000) on the southeastern Arabian Peninsula, on the Arabian Sea. The capital is Muscat. Oil is Oman's chief export. The area was ruled by the Portuguese (1508–1648) and by the Turks (1659–1741) before being taken by Ahmed ibn Said, the founder of the present ruling family. Oman occupied Zanzibar in 1730, developed strong ties with Great Britain (18th cent.), and was the most powerful Arab state in the early 19th cent. Exploitation of oil deposits began in the 1960s. Sultan Qabus bin Said deposed his father in 1970, promising to use oil revenues for modernization. Oman's position opposite Iran at the mouth of the Persian Gulf, through which pass tankers carrying much of the world's oil, has increased its strategic importance and in 1980 Oman signed a defense pact with the US, allowing the US military use of ports and airbases. Following the Iraqi invasion of Kuwait (1990), Oman supported the US–led military effort against Iraq.

Omar (Umar) 581–644. Second Muslim caliph. A father-in-law of the prophet Muhammad, he at first opposed Islam, but was converted by 618. He chose Abu Bakr as the first caliph to succeed to the authority of the prophet (632) and succeeded him (634). During his caliphate, Arab armies advanced into Syria, Egypt, and Persia. He established the administration and taxation of the subsequent empire.

Omar Khayyám *fl.* 11th cent. Persian poet, astronomer, and mathematician. Khayyám reformed the Muslim calendar and wrote an algebra textbook. However, he is best known for his epigrammatic poems *The Rubáiyát,* especially as translated into English (1859) by Edward FitzGerald (1809–83).

Omdurman, Battle of British defeat and capture of the Mahdist capital at Omdurman, in the central Sudan (Sept. 2, 1898). An Anglo-Egyptian force of about 26,000, led by Sir (later Lord) H. Kitchener, defeated a poorly armed Mahdist force of 40,000 and destroyed the state estab-

lished by the Mahdi (*q.v.*) in 1881. It began British dominance in the Sudan.

Omri *d.* c874 BC. King of Israel (887–875 BC). Omri moved the capital of Israel to Samaria and had close ties to the Syrians. He married his son Ahab to Jezebel, a Phoenician. [1 Kings 16–20]

On *See* **Heliopolis.**

Oñate, Juan de *d.* 1624? Spanish explorer. Oñate took possession of much of the American Southwest for Spain, and was first governor of what is now New Mexico.

Oneida Community Religious commune in America in 19th cent. It was established by J. H. Noyes, a Perfectionist, in New York State (1847). It practiced communal living, and permitted polygamy. In 1881, it was reorganized as a joint stock company and its social experiments were abandoned.

O'Neill, Eugene Gladstone 1888–1953. American playwright. O'Neill won the Nobel Prize in Literature (1936). *Beyond the Horizon* won the first of his three Pulitzer Prizes. Other works include *Anna Christie, Long Day's Journey into Night,* and *The Iceman Cometh.*

O'Neill, Shane c1530–67. Irish chieftain. O'Neill fought for the chieftainship against his British-backed illegitimate half-brother, Matthew. Though Shane won acknowledgment from Elizabeth I, he turned against England, was defeated, and was slain by a rival clan.

Ontario East-central Canadian province. The area was first explored by the French (early 17th cent.), although settlement (by Britain and France) was delayed because of wars with the Iroquois Indians. British claims to the region were upheld by the Treaty of Paris (1763), and the region was included in the crown colony of Quebec (1774). Loyalists from the US settled there following the American Revolution, and battles were fought there during the War of 1812. Ontario entered the Dominion of Canada as a separate province in 1867.

Op art (optical art) Artistic style of the 20th cent. characterized by repetition of form and specific color combinations to create the illusion of movement.

OPEC *See* **Organization of Petroleum Exporting Countries.**

Open Door International diplomatic term applied to the policy of a country that trades with all other nations on an equal basis. The term was first used in the 1890s by the US, which sought to trade with China at a time when such nations as Britain, Russia, France, Japan, Italy, and Germany all demanded special trade concessions from the Chinese. The policy was advanced (1899–1900) to the major nations by US secretary of state J. Hay. Hay declared it to be in effect in 1900.

Operation Dragoon *See* **Anvil, Operation.**

Operation Overlord *See* **Normandy Invasion.**

Operation Sea Lion *See* **Britain, Battle of.**

Opium War Name given two 19th-cent. wars between China and European powers. 1. The first war (1839–42) began when China attempted to enforce its ban on the importation of opium and seized British-owned opium in Guangzhou (Canton). Britain soon defeated China and forced it to cede Hong Kong to Britain, open several ports to British trade, and pay an indemnity. 2. The second war (1856–60) began after Chinese boarded the British ship *Arrow*. France joined Britain in a new war against China. Soon defeated, China agreed to the Treaty of Tianjin (1858), which opened a number of new ports to European trade and secured rights of interior travel in China, rights for Christian missionaries, residence in Beijing for foreign diplomats, and legalization of the opium trade. China's opposition to the agreements led to new conflict and the occupation (1860) of Beijing and burning of the imperial summer palace. The conflict ended with the Conventions of Beijing (1860), which granted still further concessions.

Oppenheimer, J. Robert 1904–67. American physicist. He was a leading figure in the Manhattan Project (*q.v.*) and made important contributions to the construction of the first atomic bomb, but after WW II he became a leading advocate of civilian and international control of atomic energy.

oprichniki *See* **Ivan IV.**

optical art *See* **Op art.**

Optimates *See* **Cato the Younger.**

oracle In ancient Greece, "oracle" referred to the answer given by a god to a question posed by a human, or to the place where such responses were given. The most famous Greek oracle was dedicated to Apollo at Delphi. During the Roman period, the most famous oracle was that of Apollo at Klaros.

Orange Free State South African province. First settled (1820s) by the Boers, it was annexed by Britain (1848). It became independent (1854), but continued conflict in the region led to the Boer War (1899–1902) and its reannexation. It became part of the Union of South Africa in 1910.

Orangemen Irish Protestant political group. It was founded in 1795, and its members sought to maintain Protestant dominance over the Catholics in Ireland.

Oranges, War of the Brief war (1801) in which France and Spain invaded and defeated Portugal. After Portugal's surrender, the country was divided between France and Spain.

Order of Preachers *See* **Dominicans.**

Order of Saint Benedict *See* **Benedictines.**

Order of the Garter Order of knighthood in England founded by King Edward III and formally established in 1350. The order was originally limited to 26, including the king, but its membership was enlarged by later kings. According to tradition, its motto, *Honi soit qui mal y pense* (roughly, Shame on him who thinks evil of it) is a remark attributed to Edward III. While dancing with a countess, he picked up a garter she had dropped, and, returning it to her, made the comment to bystanders.

Order of the Golden Fleece Order of knighthood founded (1430) by Philip the Good, duke of Burgundy. Through intermarriage with the Habsburg family, the order passed to Spain and Austria. It takes its symbol from Jason and the Argonauts.

Order of the Hospital of St. John of Jerusalem *See* **Knights Hospitalers.**

Ordinance of 1787 *See* **Northwest Ordinances.**

ordonnance cabochienne *See* **Cabochiens.**

Oregon US state in the Northwest, the 33d state. It was first explored (16th cent.) by Spanish, British, and Russians, who set up fur-trading posts along its coast. Robert Gray (1755–1806) claimed the area along the Columbia River for the US (1792), and the Lewis and Clark expedition explored farther inland in 1805. As part of the Oregon country, it was held jointly by England and the US from 1818 until England gave up its claims (1846). Oregon's constitution was adopted in 1857, and it was admitted to the Union in 1859.

Oregon Question Dispute between Britain and the United States over the northwest border with Canada. The Convention of 1818 had provided for joint occupation west of the Rockies between

42° and 54° 40′ N. The Oregon Treaty (June 1846) established the border along the 49th parallel.

Oregon Trail American pioneer route stretching from Independence, Missouri, to the Columbia River in Oregon. It was one of the main paths of pioneer travel to the West from the 1840s to the 1870s and extended for some 2,000 miles through the wilderness.

Orestes *d.* AD 476. Roman general. He used barbarian help in deposing (AD 475) Western Roman emperor Julius Nepos and installing his own son Romulus Augustulus, the last emperor of the Western Roman Empire.

Organization of African Unity (OAU) Organization of independent African states, established (1963) to promote African unity and mutual cooperation in defense and development.

Organization of American States (OAS) International organization, founded (1948) to promote military, economic, and cultural cooperation. Its member nations include the United States and most of the nations of Latin America. Cuba was expelled from the OAS in 1962.

Organization of Central American States Central American association, organized (1951) to promote regional and economic unity. Its member states include Costa Rica, El Salvador, Guatemala, Honduras, and Nicaragua.

Organization of Petroleum Exporting Countries (OPEC) International group formed (1960) to promote the interests of countries that supply the world market with oil. When the group was founded, member nations were largely at the mercy of the great international oil companies, which controlled all-important (in times of plentiful supply) systems of distribution and marketing. But as oil consumption began to outstrip production in the late 1960s, producing countries began to get the upper hand. By cutting back their production, OPEC members found they could effectively force the great industrial powers to pay any price for oil they demanded. The huge price increases it put into effect (Dec., 1973) signaled the ascendancy of OPEC as a dominant force in the world oil industry. Membership now includes oil-producing countries in the Middle East, Africa, and South America. An oversupply of oil developed in the early 1980s forced OPEC members to agree to reduced prices and production quotas. Despite temporary disruptions in supply caused by the Iran-Iraq War

and the Persian Gulf War, oil supplies remained relatively plentiful during the 1980s and early 1990s.

Orgetorix *d.* 60? BC. Helvetian chieftain at the time of J. Caesar's Gallic Wars (*q.v.*).

Oriental canon law Ecclesiastical laws concerning the government of Eastern Christian churches. Rudimentary collections of such laws can be traced back to the 5th cent. AD, and a major compilation, important to the canon law of the Eastern Orthodox church, was completed by Photius c880. The various churches in the East do not share a common code of canon law.

Origen AD 185?–254? Christian philosopher. Origen wrote over 800 works seeking to explain and justify Christianity in terms of Greek thought, especially Neoplatonism and Stoicism. He instituted biblical textual criticism at his famous school in Alexandria.

Oriskany, Battle of Battle (Aug. 6, 1777) of the American Revolution, in northern New York State. American militiamen under Gen. Nicholas Herkimer (1728–77) were ambushed and defeated by British troops led by Barry St. Leger (1737–89) as the Americans were attempting to relieve Fort Stanwix (now Rome, New York).

Orlando, Vittorio Emmanuele 1860–1952. Italian statesman. As premier (1917–19), he was one of the "Big Four" at the Paris Peace Conference (1919), which formally ended WW I.

Orléanists French supporters of King Louis Philippe of the Orléans branch of the Bourbon line. Louis Philippe came to the throne after the July Revolution (1830). The Orléanists supported his monarchy against both republican and Bonapartist forces.

Orléans The cadet (younger) branch of the French Valois and Bourbon royal houses. The line has played a leading role in French history. The title "duke of Orléans" was first given (1344) to Philippe (1336–75), son of Valois French king Philip VI. In 1392, King Charles VI gave the title to his brother Louis, a key figure in the struggles between the Armagnacs and Burgundians (*q.v.*). Other members included Charles of ~, a co-commander at the Battle of Agincourt (*q.v.*) and father of French king Louis XII; Philippe I of ~, son of King Louis XIII and brother of King Louis XIV; his son, Philippe II of ~, regent of France during the minority of King Louis XV; Louis Philippe Joseph of ~, who sided with the revolutionists during the French

Revolution; and his son, French king Louis Philippe. Louis Philippe Albert of ~ (1838–94) became count of Paris; and his son, Louis Philippe Robert of ~, became pretender to the French throne upon extinction (1883) of the elder Bourbon lme.

Orléans, Charles, duke of 1391–1465. French prince and poet, son of Louis, duke of Orléans. He tried to avenge the murder of his father by joining the Armagnacs against the Burgundians. He was captured in the Battle of Agincourt (1415) and taken to England. Ransomed in 1440, he spent the rest of his life as a literary personage.

Orléans, Gaston, duke of 1608–60. French prince, son of French king Henry IV and younger brother of Louis XIII. He was involved in several unsuccessful conspiracies against Cardinal Richelieu, and was exiled (1652) from Paris for leading the Fronde.

Orléans, Louis, duke of 1372–1407. French nobleman, chief counselor to his brother, French king Charles VI. Louis's conflict with his uncle, Philip the Bold of Burgundy, precipitated the long power struggle between the Armagnacs and the Burgundians. He was killed by Philip's son John the Fearless.

Orléans, Louis Philippe Albert, duke of *See* **Orléans.**

Orléans, Louis Philippe Joseph, duke of 1747–93. French revolutionary. In 1789, he and other liberal nobles joined the third estate. He changed his title to "Citizen Égalité," and voted for the execution of his cousin Louis XVI. His son became King Louis Philippe.

Orléans, Louis Philippe Robert, duke of 1869–1926. French nobleman, pretender to the French throne during the Third Republic.

Orléans, Philippe I, duke of 1640–1701. French nobleman and soldier. The brother of King Louis XIV, he fought in the Dutch Wars and won the Battle of Cassel. He founded the House of Bourbon-Orléans.

Orléans, Philippe II, duke of 1674–1723. French nobleman and soldier. He was successful in the War of the League of Augsburg and the War of the Spanish Succession. As regent for King Louis XV (1715–23), he presided over the failure (1720) of the Mississippi Scheme (*q.v.*).

Orléans, Siege of Historic siege of Orléans, France (Oct., 1428–May, 1429) by the English during the Hundred Years' War. The English,

supporting the claims of English king Henry VI to the French throne, laid siege to Orléans, controlled by the supporters of the French dauphin Charles VII. The English brought the city to near surrender when Joan of Arc, who had gained the permission of Charles to raise an army, entered the city and lifted the siege. The English defeat marked the turning point in the Hundred Years' War.

Orléans, Territory of *See* **Territory of Orléans.**

Orlov, Grigory *See* **Catherine II.**

Ormonde, James Butler, 2d duke of 1665–1745. Anglo-Irish soldier. A grandson of the first duke, he served as lord lieutenant of Ireland and as commander in chief (1711–14) during the War of the Spanish Succession. Impeached (1715) under George I, he fled to the Continent and joined the Jacobites.

Ormonde, James Butler, 12th earl and 1st duke of 1610–88. Anglo-Irish statesman. He was the principal Irish supporter of the Stuarts during the English Civil Wars and was twice lord lieutenant of Ireland after the Restoration.

Orozco, José Clemente 1883–1949. Mexican painter, considered one of the 20th-cent. masters of the mural and fresco. Many of his works depict scenes from the Mexican Revolution.

Orphic Mysteries Ancient Greek cult. Dating to the 6th cent. BC, it was said to have been founded by Orpheus. Its adherents followed an ascetic code of life.

Orsini Roman family that from the 12th cent. held great political and religious power in Rome and Italy. Its members included popes Celestine III, Nicholas III, and Benedict XIII. It supported the Guelph faction in the long struggle between the Guelphs and Ghibellines (*q.v.*).

Orsini, Giovanni Gaetani *See* **Nicholas III.**

Ortega y Gasset, José 1883–1955. Spanish philosopher and writer. His books made him the most influential author of pre-Franco Spain. One of his best-known works is *Revolt of the Masses*. He was a member of the Generation of '98.

Orthodox Church of Russia Largest of the Orthodox Eastern churches. The origins of the Russian church go back to the introduction of Christianity in Kievan Rus' by Byzantine missionaries. Christianity was made the state religion of Kiev in 988 and the church was governed from Constantinople. In 1439 the Union of Florence briefly reunited Russian Christians with the Roman Catholic church; soon after failure of the union, the Russian church declared itself autocephalous (autonomous and independent). The patriarchate of Moscow was given formal status in 1589, but in 1721 Tsar Peter the Great abolished the patriarchate and put the church under strict state control. The patriarchate was reestablished just before the Russian Revolution of 1917 but, during both Lenin's and Stalin's regimes, the church suffered severe persecutions. In 1943, as part of Stalin's new policies during WW II, the church was revived and encouraged to expand. The church endured yet another period of persecutions (1959–64) under N. Khrushchev. In the 1960s, the church opened relations with the Roman Catholic church (following the Second Vatican Council) and joined the World Council of Churches.

Orthodox Eastern church Collective name for the family of Christian churches that exist largely in the Middle East, Eastern Europe, and Russia. All the Orthodox churches accept the authority of the first seven ecumenical councils of the Catholic church but do not accept later councils. They also do not recognize the authority of the Roman Catholic pope as supreme head of the church nor the practice of mandatory celibacy for priests. The origins of the Orthodox church can be traced to the late Roman Empire. As the empire weakened and was divided into the Western Empire and the Eastern Empire, so too did the early Christian church suffer a growing division. The Western church developed along Latin lines and adopted Roman political and civil patterns, while the Eastern church retained a traditional Greek heritage. The separation between the two parts of the Christian world occurred slowly from the 5th to 11th cents. and became a complete schism in 1054, when Pope Leo IX excommunicated Michael Cerularius, patriarch of Constantinople, and all his followers. The primary disagreement between the Eastern and Western churches was the incorporation of the term *filioque,* meaning "and from the son," into the Nicene Creed. The introduction of the *filioque* occurred in the Western church after centuries of controversy over the nature of the Holy Trinity, the supremacy of the Father, and the nature of the Son as a being with a divine and human nature. The Eastern churches also refused to accept the spiritual supremacy of the pope, as they do not recognize one person as the leading spiritual figure. Eastern churches are largely autonomous, and the major divisions of the church are known as patriarchates. Chief among these are the patriarchates of Constantinople, Alexandria, Antioch, and Jerusalem, all formed in the early history of the Christian church. From these, through missionary work and emigration, sprang numerous other Orthodox churches in Eastern Europe. The greatest of these was the Orthodox church of Russia (*q.v.*), which was originally governed through the patriarchate of Constantinople. It became an independent patriarchate in 1589. In recent years there have been renewed efforts at reconciling the Roman and Orthodox churches, and several Orthodox representatives were invited as observers to the Second Vatican Council (*q.v.*). (*See also* Roman Catholic church, for history to 1054.)

Orwell, George (Blair, Eric Arthur) 1903–50. British novelist, essayist, and critic, one of the leading political writers of his day. He is known best for his novels *Animal Farm* and *1984.*

Osborne, John James 1929–   . English playwright, considered the leading "angry young man" of British drama. His plays include *Look Back in Anger* and *The Entertainer.*

Osborne, Thomas, 1st earl of Danby 1631–1712. English statesman. He served under King Charles I, but his staunch Anglicanism led him to oppose James II. He helped to arrange the marriage of Princess Mary to William of Orange.

Oscar I 1799–1859. King of Norway and Sweden (1844–59) Oscar pursued liberal policies. He championed fiscal and penal reforms and freedom of the press.

Oscar II 1829–1907. King of Sweden (1872–1907) and Norway (1872–1905). During his reign, Norway severed its union with Sweden (1905). Oscar was a noted writer and a patron of the arts.

Osceola c1800–38. Seminole Indian leader. He conducted a successful guerrilla campaign against US forces in the Second Seminole War (1835–37). Arriving for a truce talk, he was arrested and imprisoned. He died soon after.

Osei Tutu d. 1712. West African leader, founder and first ruler of the Ashanti nation. The nation was created from a confederacy of West African kingdoms in what is now Ghana.

Osler, Sir William 1849–1919. Canadian-born British physician, noted for his studies of blood platelets and his numerous books on medical history. His *Principles and Practice of Medicine* has long been a leading reference work.

Osman I (Othman ˜) 1259–1326. Turkish leader, founder of the Ottoman Empire. Declaring himself emir (c1299), Osman greatly extended his holdings, largely through conquest of territory from the Byzantine Empire.

Osmeña, Sergio 1878–1961. Filipino statesman. Osmeña was vice-president (1935–44) when the Philippines fell to Japan in WW II. He fled with President M. Quezon, whom he succeeded as president (1944–46).

Ostend Manifesto Document formulated (Oct., 1854) at Ostend, Belgium, calling for US acquisition of Cuba. Drawn up by the US ministers to France (John Y. Mason, 1799–1859), Great Britain (J. Buchanan), and Spain (P. Soule), it suggested that Cuba should be taken by force if necessary. It caused such an uproar that Secretary of State W. Marcy disavowed it.

ostracism Political banishment imposed by Athenian Greeks on those disrupting Athens' political stability. The banishment lasted ten years, though rights of property and citizenship were retained. The last known ostracism was that of Hyperbolus (418 BC).

Ostrogorsky, Moisey 1854–1919. Russian political scientist. Educated in Russia and abroad in the US and Britain, he wrote a pioneering study of political parties, *Democracy and the Organization of Political Parties* (1902).

Ostrogoths (East Goths) Germanic tribe. The Ostrogoths were the eastern tribes of the Goths, the Visigoths being their western counterparts. They were believed to have originated in southern Scandinavia. After being conquered by the Huns in Russia (AD c370), they joined with them against the Visigoths and pushed southwest into the Roman Empire. After Attila's death (AD 453), many Ostrogoths settled in Hungary and the Balkans. Others under Theodoric were called into Italy to defeat Odoacer. But after eliminating Odoacer, Theodoric made himself king (493). They were finally subjugated by the Byzantine general Narses (552) and were absorbed into other cultures.

Oswald, Lee Harvey *See* **Kennedy, John F.**

Oswiu *See* **Oswy.**

Oswy (Oswiu) d. 670. Northumbrian king (c642–670). By war or marriage, he united most of England under him. He advanced Christianity in England and, at the Synod of Whitby

(*q.v.*), favored Roman religious practices over the Celtic.

Othman I *See* **Osman I.**

Otho I *See* **Otto I.**

Otho, Marcus Salvius AD 32–69. Roman emperor (AD 69). Otho helped Galba overthrow Nero. Subsequently he overthrew Galba and proclaimed himself emperor. After ruling for three months, he was in turn defeated by Vitellius.

Otis, James 1725–83. American Colonial statesman. Otis resigned his office of advocate general in Massachusetts (1756–61) after refusing to enforce the Writs of Assistance. He later served in the Stamp Act Congress.

Ottawa Indians North American Indian tribe. A branch of the Algonquian linguistic family, they lived north of the Great Lakes. They sided with the French in the French and Indian Wars, and later with the British in the American Revolution and the War of 1812. The Indian leader Pontiac was an Ottawa Indian.

Otterburn, Battle of *See* **Douglas.**

Otto I (˜ the Great) 912–973. German king (936–973) and Holy Roman Emperor (962–973). Otto became king at the end of a period in which the east Frankish kingdom—created by the Treaty of Verdun (*q.v.*)—had broken up into petty states. Central authority was then beginning to reemerge under the leadership of the duchy of Saxony. As German king, Otto succeeded in extending his authority over rebellious German dukes by force of arms and by using the church to strengthen his rule ("Ottonian" system). He further reinforced his position by defeating the invading Magyars (955) and by subduing the Slavs (960). He intervened in the west Frankish kingdom (France) over possession of Lorraine and in 951 marched into Italy and assumed the title king of the Lombards. In 961, he again invaded Italy to aid Pope John XII against Berengar II. The pope crowned Otto emperor (962), a title that had lapsed at the end of the 9th cent., and concluded an agreement to regulate relations between the pope and the emperor. Otto's coronation is thus usually taken as the beginning of the Holy Roman Empire (*q.v.*) and its long, often troubled alliance with the church. In 963, Pope John turned against Otto, fearing he had become too powerful. Otto deposed John, installed Leo VIII as pope, and soon after suppressed a revolt by the Romans. After Leo's death in 965, the Romans again revolted and Otto was forced to invade Italy again (966–972).

Otto I (Otho ˜) 1815–67. Greek king (1832–62). The son of Louis I of Bavaria, he was selected to be the king of Greece by the London Conference, after the War of Greek Independence. Autocratic and ambitious, he was unpopular and was finally deposed.

Otto I 1848–1916. Bavarian king (1886–1913), successor to his brother Louis II. He became insane in 1872, and his uncle Luitpold served as his regent (1886–1912). He was deposed by parliament and Luitpold's son became Louis III.

Otto II 955–983. Holy Roman Emperor (973–983) and German king (961–983), successor to his father, Otto I. He repulsed attacks from Bavaria and Denmark but was badly defeated by the Arabs in southern Italy (982). Married Byzantine princess Theophano.

Otto III 980–1002. Holy Roman Emperor (996–1002) and German king (983–1002), successor to his father, Otto II. He installed his cousin as Pope Gregory V and his tutor as Pope Sylvester II. He attempted to make Rome his capital but was forced out. He was preparing to retake the city when he died. He promoted a brilliant cultural revival during his reign.

Otto IV 1182?–1218. Holy Roman Emperor (1209–15) and German king. He contested the throne with Philip of Swabia, and became emperor after Philip's death. He was excommunicated for attacking Italy, and Frederick II was made rival king (1212). Otto was defeated by French king Philip II at Bouvines (1214), and was deposed (1215).

Ottocar I (˜, Premysl I) (Ottokar I) *d.* 1230. Bohemian king (1198–1230). Ottocar won Bohemia's autonomy from Philip of Swabia (1198).

Ottocar II (˜, Premysl II) (Ottokar II) *d.* 1278. Bohemian king (1252–78). He added Austria, Styria, Carinthia, and Carniola to his empire but failed to become Holy Roman Emperor. He opposed Holy Roman Emperor Rudolf I and was defeated and killed at the Battle of Marchfeld.

Ottocar, Premysl *See* **Ottocar I** and **II.**

Ottokar *See* **Ottocar.**

Ottoman Empire Former empire established in the 13th cent. by the Osmanli (Ottoman) Turks. Formed from the territories once ruled by the Seljuk Turks, the empire expanded its holdings at the expense of the Byzantine Empire. The Ottoman conquest of Constantinople (1453) marked the end of the Byzantine Empire. The Ottomans then advanced into Europe, creating an empire that stretched from the Balkans (southeast Europe), across the Near East and into North Africa. By the early 18th cent. the empire began to disintegrate, and during the 19th cent. the Eastern Question (*q.v.*) became a major concern of European powers. The empire was finally dismembered at the end of WW I. (For subsequent history, *see* Turkey.) Key dates in the history of the Ottoman Empire include:

c1299–1326 Osman I reigned; founded Ottoman Empire in northwest Anatolia by absorbing neighboring states as the power of the Seljuk Turks declined; attacked domains of Byzantine Empire.

1326 City of Bursa, conquered by Osman, became first capital of Ottoman Empire.

1326–59 Orkhan reigned as second Ottoman ruler, expanded control over western Anatolia, taking Byzantine and neighboring Turkmen states; began Ottoman expansion in the Balkans (southeast Europe).

1359–89 Murad I reigned; empire rapidly expanded eastward into Byzantine domains and westward into Balkans; Byzantines forced to recognize Ottoman suzerainty.

1361 Ottomans conquered Adrianople; city subsequently became capital of the empire.

1371 Murad I decisively defeated the Serbs (Sept. 26) at the Battle of Maritsa River, near Adrianople.

1386 Battle of Konya; Turkmen states, allied to halt Ottoman expansion eastward, defeated by Murad I.

1389 Christian Slavs defeated (June) at the Battle of Kosovo, now in southern Yugoslavia; Ottoman advance in Balkans continued.

1389–1403 Bajazet I reigned; continued Ottoman advance in Balkans, arousing Europeans against him; his annexation of Turkmen states in Anatolia ended in ruinous conflict with Tamerlane.

1391–98 Bajazet blockaded Constantinople.

1394 Salonika captured.

1395–96 Bajazet invaded Hungary; defeated force of Hungarian, French, English, Polish crusaders at Nicopolis (1396), in Bulgaria.

1402 Tamerlane invaded the empire; Bajazet defeated at the Battle of Ankara (July) and taken captive.

1413–21   Muhammad I reigned after struggle to reunite empire.

1421–51   Murad II reigned: expansion of empire renewed.

1444   Battle of Varna fought (Nov. 10); Murad II destroyed invading Hungarian army, thus maintaining control of Eastern Europe.

1451–81   Muhammad II reigned; called "the Conqueror," he greatly expanded Ottoman domains.

1453   Ottomans captured Constantinople and thus ended the Byzantine Empire; Ottomans made Constantinople their capital.

1456   Ottoman siege of Belgrade lifted after victory by Hungarian J. N. Hunyadi.

1456–58   Serbia subjugated and annexed to empire.

1461   Trebizond Empire, a remnant of Byzantine Empire in Greece, conquered; Ottomans extended control over Greece.

1463–79   First major war with Venice, which the Turks won.

1468   Albania conquered after series of defeats at the hands of Scanderbeg.

1475   Tatar khanate of Crimea forced to recognize Ottoman suzerainty.

1480   Ottomans established foothold in southern Italy with capture of Otranto.

1480–81   Siege of Rhodes, last Christian stronghold in eastern Mediterranean; Turks repulsed.

1512–20   Selim I reigned; in addition to his conquests, Selim I proclaimed himself successor to the Muslim Arab caliphs; Ottomans thus became leaders of the Muslim world.

1514   Selim I victorious (Aug. 23) over a Persian army at the Battle of Chaldiran in Armenia.

1515   Selim annexed parts of Persia.

1516   Syria conquered.

1517   Selim I conquered Egypt.

1518   Algiers conquered.

1520–66   Suleiman I reigned; made notable legal reforms, encouraged arts and greatly expanded empire; also built up Ottoman navy.

1521   Belgrade conquered.

1522   Rhodes conquered.

1526   Battle of Mohacs; Ottoman victory over Hungarian king Louis II; eventually led to Ottoman domination of Hungary.

1529   Ottomans laid siege to Vienna; forced to withdraw.

1530s   Ottomans conquered Iraq and other territories from Persia.

1535   Alliance with France against Habsburgs formed; continued in subsequent centuries.

1540   Ottoman control extended into southern Hungary.

1541   Buda taken; much of Hungary fell under Ottoman rule.

1551   Ottomans conquered Tripoli.

1566–74   Selim II reigned; Cyprus conquered and Tunisia reconquered; reign marked by beginning of decline in sultan's powers as the Muslim clergy and Janissaries gained strength.

1571   Battle of Lepanto, victory of the Christian Holy League over the Ottoman navy; marked first check of Ottoman expansionism.

1571   Cyprus conquered from Venice.

1574–95   Murad III reigned; parts of Armenia conquered, taken from Persia.

1591–1606   Fifteen Years' War fought with Austria.

1603–17   Ahmed I reigned; empire weakened by Treaty of Szitvatorok (1606); commercial concessions granted to European powers.

1605–23   Persians warred against Ottomans, finally capturing Baghdad.

1620–21   Poles victorious at Battle of Chocim.

1623–40   Murad IV reigned; reconquered territories lost to Persia and captured Baghdad (1638); decline of empire, due to corruption, maladministration, and internal unrest, accelerated after his death; grand viziers rose to power.

1645–64   War with Venice in which weakness of Ottoman Empire was revealed.

1656–61   Köprülü Mehmed Pasha ruled as grand vizier; repulsed Venetian invasion (1657) and put down a revolt two years later.

1661–76   Köprülü Fazil Ahmed ruled as grand vizier; reasserted Ottoman power; warred against Austria (won Transylvania and Hungary), captured Crete, and launched unsuccessful attack on Poland.

1676–81   Russo-Turkish War; Russians gained most of Turkish Ukraine.

1682–99   Austro-Turkish War fought; Ottomans lost Hungary, Transylvania, Croatia, Slavonia, Dalmatia, and Podolia.

1695–96   Russo-Turkish War; Russians captured Azov.

1710–11 Russo-Turkish War; Ottomans attacked Russia, regaining Azov as the Northern War raged in the Baltic region.

1736–39 Russo-Turkish War; Russians retook Azov.

1743–46 War with Persia proved indecisive; earlier success of Persia in Transcaucasus (1730).

1768–74 Russo-Turkish War; Russians victorious and greatly increased influence in Crimea; Russians established as protectors of Christians in Ottoman domains; war ended by Treaty of Kuchuk Kainarji.

1787–92 Russo-Turkish War; Russia generally successful in war, caused by its annexation of the Crimea (1783).

1789–1807 Selim III reigned; forced to abdicate during a revolt caused by his attempts at reform.

1806–12 Russo-Turkish War; Russia acquired Bessarabia.

1808–39 Mahmud II reigned; attempted to reestablish power of sultanate.

1821–31 Greek War of Independence; Ottomans lost Greek domains.

1826 Convention of Akkerman signed (Oct. 7), Serbia granted autonomy; Russia to oversee autonomy of Moldavia and Walachia.

1826 Revolt of the Janissaries quashed; their power broken.

1828–29 Russo-Turkish War; Russia penetrated deeply into the Balkans.

1831–33 War with Egypt; Muhammad Ali of Egypt gained Syria; European powers intervened to halt further conflict.

1839–61 Abdul-Mejid reigned; his reforms were opposed by Muslim reactionaries; continued existence of Ottoman state largely dependent on European powers.

1839–40 Ottomans unsuccessfully attacked Egyptians in Syria; Europeans forced Egyptian ruler Muhammad Ali to return Syria to Ottomans; Muhammad Ali made hereditary ruler of Egypt, under Ottoman suzerainty.

1853–56 Crimean War; European powers opposed Russia's expansion into Ottoman domains; Eastern Question became major diplomatic concern in following years.

1861–76 Abd-al-Aziz reigned, liberal movement led by Midhat Pasha gained momentum during his rule; Midhat played key role in his overthrow.

1875 Bosnia and Herzegovina rebelled against Ottoman rule; uprisings led to Serbo-Turkish War (1876–78).

1876 Bulgarian Horrors; Christians massacred.

1876–78 Serbo-Turkish War; Serbs joined rebels in Bosnia and Herzegovina and declared war on the Ottomans; conflict merged with the Russo-Turkish War.

1877 Midhat Pasha secured passage of constitution establishing parliamentary rule in the empire; parliament soon dissolved by sultan Murad V.

1877–78 Russo-Turkish War; victorious Russians advanced to just outside Constantinople.

1878 Congress of Berlin; Russian gains in Russo-Turkish War reduced but Ottomans nevertheless lost much of the Balkans.

1883 British took control of Egypt.

1894–96 Massacres of rebellious Armenians.

1897 Greco-Turkish War fought (Apr.–May) with Greece over control of Crete; Ottomans gained several victories and Greece accepted an armistice.

1908 Rebellion by Young Turks forced restoration of constitutional government.

1908 Bulgaria became independent; Bosnia and Herzegovina passed to Austro-Hungarian Empire.

1911–12 Italo-Turkish War; Italy gained Tripoli and the area that became Libya.

1912–13 Balkan Wars; Ottoman rule in Europe virtually ended.

1913 Young Turks, led by Enver Pasha, seized control of government.

1914–18 Ottomans joined Central Powers during WW I; Arab revolts and Allied drive from Egypt through Palestine further reduced Ottoman power; Allied victory guaranteed the ultimate dissolution of the empire.

1915 Massacre of some 1.5 million Armenians in northern Anatolia.

1918–22 Muhammad VI, last Ottoman sultan, reigned.

1920 Treaty of Sèvres signed with Allies; formally ended existence of Ottoman Empire; nationalists refused to recognize treaty.

1922 Muhammad VI overthrown by nationalists; Republic of Turkey established.

Otto of Freising *d.* 1158. German historian and bishop of Freising. The uncle of Holy Roman

Emperor Frederick I, he is known best for *The Two Cities,* a history of the world to the year 1146, which was inspired by Augustine's *City of God.*

Otto the Great   *See* **Otto I.**

Oudenaarde, Battle of (Audenarde, ˜)   Allied victory over the French (July 11, 1708) during the War of the Spanish Succession, at Oudenaarde, now in Belgium. Some 80,000 allied troops under J. Churchill, duke of Marlborough, and Prince Eugene of Savoy defeated about 100,000 French under the command of Louis Joseph, duke of Vendôme.

Ourique, Battle of   *See* **Alfonso I, king of Portugal.**

Outer Mongolia   *See* **Mongolia.**

Outer Space Treaty   Treaty sponsored (1966) by the UN. Signed (1967) by more than sixty nations, it sought to control the use of outer space for military purposes and promoted international cooperation in space activities.

Overland Trail   Name applied to any of several routes used by American pioneers to travel to the West from the Mississippi in the 19th cent. It applies especially to the Oregon Trail (*q.v.*).

Overton, Richard   *See* **Levelers.**

Ovid (Naso, Publius Ovidius) 43 BC–AD 18. Roman poet, considered one of the great poets of antiquity. Though he studied at Athens for a career in law, Ovid decided instead to become a poet and returned to Rome. He gained early success with *Amores,* a series of light love poems, and went on to demonstrate his gift for psychological insight in later works. Among his many works are *The Art of Love, Metamorphoses,* considered his greatest work, and *Fasti.* After his banishment by Augustus (AD 8, for an unknown offense), he wrote *Tristia,* poems of exile.

Owen, Robert 1771–1858. British manufacturer and reformer. A successful textile manufacturer, he advocated reforms in child employment, education, health, and hygiene. His progressive ideas were adopted by several experimental communities, including one at New Harmony, Indiana (*q.v.*).

Owens, Jesse 1913–80.   American athlete, a black who won four gold medals for the US at the 1936 Olympics at Berlin. His outstanding performance was a severe blow to A. Hitler's myth of Aryan supremacy.

Oxenstierna, Count Axel Gustavsson 1583–1654. Swedish statesman. He virtually ruled Sweden for King Gustavus II during the Thirty Years' War, and served as guardian for Queen Christina.

Oxford, Provisions of   *See* **Provisions of Oxford.**

Oxford and Asquith, Herbert Henry, 1st earl of   *See* **Asquith, Herbert Henry, 1st earl of Oxford and Asquith.**

Oxford Group   *See* **Moral Re-Armament.**

Oxford movement   Movement among 19th-cent. Anglican clergymen at Oxford University to renew the faith and worship of the Church of England (*q.v.*) by returning to early Christian sources. The movement sought to establish that the Anglican church was a branch of the ancient undivided Catholic church by virtue of apostolic succession, and did not derive ecclesiastical authority from king or parliament. It also sought to revive ancient Catholic teachings. The movement is usually dated from 1833, when J. Keble preached an Oxford sermon on England's "national apostasy." J. Newman edited and wrote many of a series of pamphlets, *Tracts for the Times,* propagating the movement's ideas and inspiring the name Tractarians for its adherents. The third principal leader was E. Pusey, who inspired another name, Puseyites, for the group. The movement is considered to have ended (1845) with the conversion of Newman and some other members to Catholicism, but its main themes and ideas have continued to influence the Church of England.

Oxmal   *See* **Uxmal.**

Ozaki, Yukio 1859–1954.   Japanese statesman. A newspaper editor and leading liberal, he was elected to every Diet between 1890 and 1952. He advocated universal suffrage and opposed militarism and was jailed during both world wars.

P

Paasikivi, Juho Kusti 1870–1956. Great Finnish statesman, prime minister (1918, 1944–46) and president (1946–56). As both prime minister and president he pursued a policy of appeasement toward Russia as the only way to ensure Finnish independence.

Pacem in Terris *See* **John XXIII.**

Pachomius c290–346. Egyptian who founded the communal (cenobitic) monastic movement in the early Christian church. Beginning about 314 he began living as a hermit near Thebes and then joined a colony of Christian solitaries living nearby. Sometime thereafter he built the first ever communal living quarters for the solitaries and developed a daily regimen of prayer and work (in support of communal needs). This first communal Christian monastery served as the pattern for 10 other monasteries founded by Pachomius.

Pacific, War of the War (1879–84) between Chile and the neighboring states of Bolivia and Peru. The war erupted over disputed coastal territories located along the border between Chile and Bolivia. Chile first occupied the Bolivian coastal province of Antofagasta (from Feb. 14, 1879), and then Peru was drawn into the conflict. Chile declared war on them both (Apr., 1879) and, after completing its occupation of Bolivia's coastal territory, attacked Peru. Chile made extensive conquests in Peru and finally occupied the capital city of Lima in Jan., 1881. With the Peruvian government on the verge of collapse, Peru and Chile signed (1883) the Treaty of Ancon (*q.v.*), by which Chile won mineral-rich Peruvian lands. Chile and Bolivia then signed the Treaty of Valparaiso (Apr. 4, 1884), by which Bolivia ceded its entire coastline to Chile.

Pacification of Ghent Religious truce and union (Nov. 8, 1576) agreed to by Protestant and Catholic provinces of the Spanish Netherlands, then in rebellion against rule by the Spanish Habsburgs. The agreement was intended to put aside religious differences between the Calvinist (northern) provinces and the Catholic (southern) provinces for the purposes of driving out Spanish troops sent to put down their revolt. This document was followed (1879) by the Union of Utrecht (*q.v.*), by which the northern provinces declared complete independence.

Pacific Islands, Trust Territory of the UN trust territory administered by the US. Capital is Saipan. It consists of the Caroline, Marshall, and Mariana (except Guam) island groups. German possessions until WW I, the islands became Japanese territories by League of Nations mandate (1922). They were taken by the US during WW II and became US trust territories in 1947.

Pacific Scandal Canadian political scandal (1873). Prime Minister J. Macdonald was charged with awarding the construction contract for the Canadian Pacific Railway to a syndicate headed by Sir Hugh Allan, in return for campaign contributions by Allan. The scandal caused the downfall of Macdonald's Conservative administration.

Pacific Treaty, Four-Power *See* **Four-Power Pacific Treaty.**

pacifism Ethical, philosophical, or moral opposition to war or violence. Pacifism may take the form of either individual or organized action. Its development has been greatly influenced by religion, and doctrines of nonviolence may be found in the teachings of Buddhism, Christianity, and Judaism, as well as in the tenets of such sects as Quakers and Mennonites. In modern history, pacifism was a factor in M. Gandhi's policies of nonviolent resistance against British rule in India, in the civil rights movement in the US (1950s and early 1960s), and, for a time, in the opposition to the US conduct of the Vietnam War.

Pact of Halepa (Khalepa, Treaty of) After quelling an insurrection in Crete, the ruling Turks through this pact granted (Oct., 1878) Greek Christians on the island a majority of seats in the assembly, as well as a large measure of self-government.

Pact of Paris *See* **Kellogg-Briand Pact.**

Pact of Steel Treaty (May 22, 1939) between Germany and Italy, confirming the German-Italian alliance. The treaty obligated each to enter any war in which the other was engaged. Thus Italy joined A. Hitler in WW II (June 10, 1940) and ultimately broke the treaty by reaching a separate peace with the Allies on Sept. 3, 1943.

Paderewski, Ignace Jan 1860–1941. Polish pianist, composer, and patriot. A world-famous pianist, Paderewski donated much of his fortune made from piano concerts to Polish charities. He served briefly as Poland's prime minister in 1919 and died in exile in the US.

Padilla, Juan de 1490–1521. Spanish revolutionary. Padilla led a revolt by the Communeros (*q.v.*) against Holy Roman Emperor Charles V but was captured and executed.

Padua, Marsilius of *See* **Marsilius of Padua.**

Padua, Saint Anthony of *See* **Anthony of Padua, Saint.**

Paeonius *fl.* 5th cent. BC. Greek sculptor. Paeonius is thought to have sculpted the famed statue of Nike (*Winged Victory*) that was discovered in 1875.

Páez, José Antonio 1790–1873. Venezuelan revolutionary and statesman. He aided S. Bolívar in the fight for South American independence from Spain. Later, however, he led the movement to separate (1831) Venezuela from Bolívar's Great Colombia (*q.v.*). Páez was president (1831–35, 1839–43) and dictator (1861–63) of Venezuela.

Paganini, Niccolò 1782–1840. Great Italian violinist and composer. Paganini revolutionized violin technique, making extensive use of harmonics.

Pagerie, Marie Joséphine Rose Tascher de la *See* **Joséphine.**

Paget, Sir James 1814–99. British surgeon. He discovered the parasite that causes trichinosis and was noted for his work on cancers and bone diseases.

Pahlavi (Pehlevi) Iranian branch of the Indo-European languages. Pahlavi was the middle stage (3d–10th cents. AD) in the evolution from the old to modern Persian language and was the official language of the Sassanid dynasty.

Paine, Thomas 1737–1809. English-born American patriot, pamphlet writer, and political theorist. He emigrated to America in 1774 and quickly became active in the revolutionary cause. His famous pamphlet *Common Sense* (Jan. 1776) argued for independence from Britain and his series of pamphlets, *The Crisis* (1776–83), advanced the patriot cause during the war years. Returning to England, he wrote *The Rights of Man* in support of the French Revolution. Convicted of treason in England, he went to France and took part in the Revolution, until he was imprisoned (1793–94) during the Reign of Terror. While there he wrote *The Age of Reason,* promoting deism (*q.v.*). Returning to the US (1802), he was met with disfavor and died in obscurity.

Painlevé, Paul 1863–1933. French mathematician and statesman. Painlevé promoted aviation in France and served twice as premier (1917, 1925). He was renowned for his writings on higher mathematics.

Paiute North American Indian tribe, a branch of the Shoshone tribe. They were divided into the northern Paiute (in parts of California, Oregon, and Nevada) and the southern Paiute (in parts of Nevada, Utah, and Arizona). The Ghost Dance religion arose among the Paiutes during the late 19th cent.

Paix des Dames *See* **Cambrai, Treaty of.**

Pakenham, Sir Edward *See* **New Orleans, Battle of.**

Pakistan (Islamic Republic of Pakistan) Muslim state bordering northwestern India in southern Asia. The population 113,163,000 and the capital is Islamabad. The early history of Pakistan was largely that of India, and it was not until 1947 that the modern state was created (by the partition of India into Hindu and Muslim homelands). Muslim Pakistan once also included a separate area (East Pakistan), bordering on northeastern India. The two were governed as one nation until 1971, when the eastern part gained independence as Bangladesh. The Indus Valley in Pakistan long served as a route for invading India and was crossed by the Aryans, Huns, Arabs, Mongols, Turks, and Persians. Key dates in the history of Pakistan include:

2500–c1500 BC Indus Valley civilization flourished in Pakistan; succumbed to Aryan invaders.

AD 700–900 Muslim Arabs conquered northwestern India (including Pakistan).

c1200 Turkish invaders occupied Bengal; Sufi mystic saints, over centuries, converted Hindus to Islam.

16TH–19TH CENTS. Eastern (Bangladesh) region controlled by Indian (Muslim) Mughal Empire.

18TH CENT. Afghan Durranis ruled Sind and Punjab in west.

1730s Persia captured western region.

1780–1839 Sikhs (under Ranjit Singh) ruled the Punjab.

1840s British, expanding their domains in India; captured Sind and Punjab but were unable to completely subdue tribes in region.

1901 Britain created North-West Frontier Province of India.

1906 Nationalist Muslim League founded as Indian nationalist movement, dominated by Hindus, failed to hold Muslim support.

1930 Concept of Muslim nation separate from India promulgated by Muhammad Iqbal.

1940 Muhammad Ali Jinnah demanded creation of Muslim state in areas of large Muslim population in India.

1947 Britain created India and Pakistan as separate independent states (Aug. 15).

1947 Capital established at Karachi; Jinnah in office as first governor general (1947–48); Liaquat Ali Khan in office as first prime minister (1947–51).

1947–48 Violence between Hindus and Muslims in India and newly created Pakistani states resulted in migrations by millions between Hindu- and Muslim-controlled lands.

1948–49 India-Pakistan War over Kashmir.

1949 Ceasefire line established in disputed territories of Kashmir and Jammu.

1951 Prime minister Liaquat Ali Khan assassinated.

1955 West Pakistan reorganized into new administrative districts; eastern region officially named East Pakistan.

1956 Constitution adopted; Pakistan became member of the British Commonwealth.

1956–58 Iskander Mirza in office as first president.

1958 President Mirza dissolved legislature and political parties, abrogated the constitution, imposed martial law, and named military ruler (Oct.).

1958–69 Army general Muhammad Ayub Khan held power as head of state; given dictatorial powers (1958) in wake of continuing economic problems and unrest.

1959 Islamabad made capital.

1965 India-Pakistan War (Second) over Kashmir and Rann of Kutch.

1968–69 Strikes and riots in East Pakistan led to Ayub Khan's resignation.

1969–71 Gen. Agha Muhammad Yahya Khan installed as president; declared martial law.

1970 Elections for National Assembly to write new constitution; East Pakistan separatist movement (Awami League) gained majority.

1971 Yahya canceled assembly, banned Awami League.

1971 Bangladesh (East Pakistan) declared independence (Mar. 26).

1971 Bloody civil war (Mar.–Dec.) between Pakistan and Bangladesh; India joined fighting (Dec.) in support of Bangladesh and invaded West Pakistan (Third India-Pakistani War); Pakistan surrendered (Dec. 16).

1971–73 Z. Ali Bhutto, leader of Pakistan People's Party (PPP) in office as president of Pakistan (formerly West Pakistan).

1972 Pakistan withdrew from Commonwealth of Nations.

1973 New constitution adopted (Aug.); Bhutto in power as prime minister.

1973–78 Fazal Elahi Chaudry, former Assembly speaker, in office as president.

1973–75 Baluchistan province torn by tribal fighting; emergency rule imposed.

1974 Pakistan recognized independent state of Bangladesh (Feb.).

1975 Pakhtoonistan separatist movement, supported by Afghanistan, sparked outbreaks of violence in North-West Frontier province.

1976 Pakistan and India resumed diplomatic relations.

1977 Military coup ousted Bhutto (July 5) following contested election and resulting unrest.

1977–78 Gen. Muhammad Zia ul-Haq in office as leader of military government; suppressed political opposition; opposed Soviet occupation of Afghanistan.

1978   Bhutto given death sentence for ordering murder of political opponent's father while in office as president; executed 1979.

1978   President Chaudry resigned; Zia took over as president.

1978–88   Gen. Zia in office as president; his administration was marked by continued repression of opposition and by the growing Islamization of Pakistani society; maintained ties with other Muslim states in Africa and Mideast.

1979   US cut aid to Pakistan over reports Pakistan had nuclear weapons development program.

1979   Soviet invasion of Afghanistan began in support of Soviet-installed Afghan government; refugees fleeing ensuing civil war flooded into Pakistan; Pakistan became conduit for arms being supplied to rebel forces in Afghanistan.

1981   US military and economic aid program renewed.

1981   Movement for Restoration of Democracy (MRD) formed in defiance of government; hundreds of politicians detained or arrested.

1982–88   Pakistan took part in UN-sponsored talks in Geneva to bring an end to fighting in Afghanistan.

1982   Zia continued ban on political activity and postponed scheduled 1982 elections.

1984   Zia administration established system of "prayer wardens" (one in every village), charged with fostering Islamic democracy.

1985   Islamic banking system mandatory throughout Pakistan.

1985   Elections held for new National Assembly; opposition groups won majority of seats; opposition leader Muhammad Khan Junejo appointed prime minister.

1985   Zia introduced constitutional amendment effectively giving president dictatorial powers; Assembly approved amendments.

1985   Pakistan and India agreed to negotiate settlement of disputed border region in northern Kashmir.

1986   Benazir Bhutto, daughter of former President Bhutto, led MRD rallies throughout country calling for Zia's ouster and for free elections; hundreds of thousands attended.

1986   Government crackdown on MRD; rallies banned and leaders arrested, including B. Bhutto (Aug.); moves sparked anti-government riots.

1986   Government signed cooperative agreement on nuclear energy (peaceful uses) with China.

1986   Ethnic rioting in Karachi and elsewhere in the Sindh province (Nov.–Dec.); 170 killed in Karachi.

1987–91   Renewed outbreaks of ethnic rioting in Sind.

1987   Violent clashes between Sunni and Shi'ite Muslims in North-West Frontier province.

1988   Afghan refugees in Pakistan, fleeing the ongoing war in Afghanistan, now numbered some 3.2 million (mostly in North-West Frontier Province).

1988   President Zia dissolved the Assembly (May).

1988   Airplane crash killed President Zia (Aug. 17); cause remains unknown.

1988   Ghulam Ishaq Khan, the Senate chairman, in office as acting president.

1988   Elections held (Nov.); PPP captured largest share of seats.

1988–90   Benazir Bhutto, member of PPP, in office as prime minister (Dec. 1), the first woman leader of a Muslim country; ended state of emergency; her administration marked by economic problems (increasing inflation and taxes), and charges of corruption and nepotism.

1988–   Ghulam Ishaq Khan in office as president.

1988   Pakistan signed Geneva accord (Apr.) for Soviet troop withdrawal from Afghanistan; included non-intervention agreement between Pakistan and Afghanistan, but US and Soviet aid to respective groups in Afghanistan not restricted; fighting in Afghanistan continued following Soviet withdrawal.

1989   Pakistan allowed UN monitors to patrol Afghan border region.

1989   Pakistan rejoined the Commonwealth of Nations.

1989   Muslim separatists in India's Kashmir region mounted campaign for independence or unification with Pakistan; Pakistani opposition parties held nationwide sympathy strikes for separatists.

1990   Some 100 killed in new outbreaks of ethnic rioting in Sind.

1990   Persian Gulf War began (Aug. 2); Pakistan sent some 11,000 troops to help US-led coalition oust Iraq from Kuwait, despite opposition to move.

1990 President Ishaq dissolved the government in wake of increasing dissatisfaction with Bhutto (Aug. 6); declared state of emergency and called for elections.

1990 Bhutto and others arrested on charges of corruption and abuse of power (Sept.).

1990– Mian Nawaz Sharif, leader of Islamic Democratic Alliance, in office as prime minister (Nov.); a Punjabi, he became first Pakistani prime minister from outside Sind; sought to ease tensions with India over unrest in Kashmir region.

1991 Widespread pro-Iraqi protests throughout Pakistan (Jan.) as fighting in Gulf War loomed.

Palaeologus Byzantine ruling dynasty. This Greek family ruled the Byzantine Empire from 1261 to 1453, when the Turks brought the empire to an end. Emperor Michael VIII became the first ruler of the line when he ousted the crusader kings of the Latin Empire of Constantinople and thereby restored the Byzantine Empire. The last ruler of the family, Constantine XI, was killed defending Constantinople against the Turks. The family became extinct in the 16th cent. *Byzantine rulers were:* Michael VIII, 1261–82; Andronicus II, 1282–1328; Michael IX (co-ruler) 1295–1320; Andronicus III, 1328–41; John V, 1341–47; John VI, 1347–54; John V, 1354–76; Andronicus IV, 1376–79; John V, 1379–91; John VII (co-ruler, 1398–1412), 1390; Manuel II, 1391–1425; John VIII, 1425–48; Constantine XI, 1449–53.

Palaeologus, Constantine *See* **Constantine XI.**

Palatinate Historic region located in southwestern Germany, consisting of the Lower Palatinate (in the state of Rhineland-Palatinate) and the Upper Palatinate (in Bavaria). The areas were in the control of the counts palatine, a title given (1156) by Emperor Frederick I to his brother, Conrad, whose descendants became electors palatine (1356) and the leading princes of the Holy Roman Empire. The region passed to the Wittelsbach (*q.v.*) family (1214–1777), underwent many divisions and unifications, and was ravaged during the Thirty Years' War (1618–48) and the War of the Grand Alliance (1689–97). A part of the Palatinate was ceded to France

for a time (1801–15) but was recovered after Napoleon's fall.

pale A specified district that is subject to certain restrictions or to a separate governing body. The Pale in Ireland (12th–16th cents.) centered around Dublin, was ruled by England, and lasted until conquest of Ireland was complete. The Pale of Settlement was created (1792) by Russian empress Catherine II as the only region in which Russian Jews were allowed to settle and travel. It initially consisted of territories ceded by Poland and was greatly enlarged in subsequent years. It was eliminated by the Russian Revolution of 1917.

Pale of Settlement *See* **pale.**

Paleolithic *See* **Stone Age.**

Palermo Stone Inscribed stone, part of a year-by-year record of events of Egyptian dynasties 1st–5th (3d–2d millennium BC). It is an important source of historical information for this period.

Palestine Historic region on the east coast of the Mediterranean, including modern Israel and the part of Jordan west of the Jordan River. Palestine is considered a Holy Land by Jews, Christians, and Muslims, and the religious center of the region is Jerusalem. Palestine, inhabited since very ancient times, is the scene of many of the events recounted in the Bible. The region was controlled by various powers of the ancient world, though it remained a Jewish homeland until late in the Roman era. Palestine fell to the Muslims (7th cent. AD) and Jerusalem, already a holy city to Jews and Christians, became a Muslim holy city as well. Palestine remained under Muslim control until the 20th cent., though toward the end of the 19th cent. Jews were immigrating in large numbers to the region. The movement to create a Jewish state in Palestine after WW I resulted in serious clashes between Arabs and Jews there. After creation of Israel in 1948, the conflict between Arabs and Jews contributed to Mideast instability into the 1990s. (For history of the region after 1948 *see* Israel.) **For more on important persons and major events *see* entries under specific names.** Dates prior to 500 BC are in many cases approximate. Key events in the history of Palestine include:

3D MILLENNIUM BC Formation of towns and cities in region.

c2100 BC Amorites, a Semitic-speaking people, invaded region.

c18TH–16TH CENTS. BC Hyksos invasion; Egypt ruled by Hyksos.

16TH?–13TH? CENTS. BC Hebrews believed to have arrived in Palestine; time of the biblical Patriarchs, Abraham, Isaac, and Jacob [Genesis 11–50]; Hebrews settled in the central region of Palestine (in modern Israel, Jordan, and northeast Egypt).

c1500–c1450 BC Egyptians, led by Thutmose III, conquered Palestine after driving out Hyksos; region known as Canaan.

14TH CENT. BC Egyptians lost control over Palestine during the reign of Ikhnaton.

EARLY 13TH CENT. BC Egyptian king Ramses II reestablished control over Palestine during wars with the Hittites.

c1270?–c1230? BC Exodus; Moses led the Hebrews enslaved in Egypt out of Egypt to the edge of the promised land (Canaan) in Palestine. [Exodus, Leviticus, Numbers, Deuteronomy]

1231 BC Egyptian king Merneptah attacked Hebrews in Canaan.

c1230? Joshua, leading the Hebrews (Joseph tribes), crossed the Jordan River and conquered some Canaanite cities; Jericho believed to be first city they conquered. [Joshua 6]

c1200 BC Sea Peoples occupied Egypt, breaking its hold on Palestine; Philistines, one of the Sea Peoples after whom the land is named, settled on southern coast of Palestine.

11TH CENT. BC Wars between Philistines and Israelites for control of the land.

c1028?–1013? BC Saul became king of the Israelites [1 Samuel 11–12]; formerly led by Judges, tribal leaders, the Israelites were forced to unite by the increasing pressure from the Philistines; after early victories, Saul was defeated and died at Mount Gilboa. [2 Samuel 31]

1013–973 BC David, from the tribe of Judah, reigned; captured Jerusalem and made it "the city of David," the capital; conquered the Philistines, Moabites, Ammonites, and Edomites; established unified kingdom of Israel; put down revolts by his son Absalom and Sheba. [2 Samuel; 1 Kings]

973–933 BC Solomon reigned; kingdom further expanded and a thriving commerce developed; renowned for the splendor of his court, Solomon built many buildings and constructed the first Temple at Jerusalem. [1 Kings 3–11]

933 BC Rehoboam succeeded Solomon; refused to lessen heavy taxes imposed on northern tribes during Solomon's reign.

933 BC Jeroboam led the Ten Tribes of Israel in a revolt against Rehoboam; formed the northern kingdom of Israel; capital at Samaria. [1 Kings 11–14]

933 BC Rehoboam formed the kingdom of Judah (in the south) from the tribes of Judah and Benjamin; conducted wars against kingdom of Israel. [1 Kings 12]

c915 BC Second king of Judah, Abijah, reigned briefly.

c915–875 BC Asa, third king of Judah, ruled.

875 BC Elisha, biblical Hebrew prophet, flourished; said to have succeeded in ending worship of Baal.

c874–853 BC Ahab reigned as king of Israel in the north; his reign marked by wars with Assyria and rise in worship of Canaanite god Baal, promoted by Jezebel, Ahab's wife; time of Elijah's struggle against Baal-worship. [1 Kings 16–22]

850 BC Ancient Moabite stone inscribed with description of Mesha's victory against Israel.

842–816 BC Jehu reigned as king of Israel; led revolt against Baal-worship and slew (843) Ahaziah, king of Judah, and Jehoram, king of Israel; gained control over kingdom of Judah; massacred Baal-worshipers, including Jezebel; paid tribute to Assyrians. [2 Kings 9–12]

780–740 BC Uzziah reigned as king of Judah; kingdom of Judah reached height of its power; time of prophet Isaiah began in last years of Uzziah's reign. [2 Chron. 26]

732?–722 BC Hoshea reigned as last king of Israel; assassinated Pekah and seized power; allied Israel with Egypt and thus brought on the Assyrian conquest at Samaria. [2 Kings 15]

731–727 BC Ahaz reigned in Judah; allied Judah with Assyria against Israel and Syria; lost Judah's independent status. [2 Kings 15–17]

721 BC Kingdom of Israel in north destroyed by Assyrian king Sargon II; capital of Samaria taken after long siege; many Israelites of the north exiled from their lands and thus became known as the Ten Lost Tribes; peoples from the Assyrian empire deported to Samaria; colonies of Aramaeans settled northern kingdom; after intermarriage with native Israelite Samarians, eventually came to be called "Samaritans."

720?–692? BC Hezekiah reigned as king of Judah; rebelled unsuccessfully against rule of Assyrian king Sennacherib. [2 Kings 18:20]

c650–c570 BC Prophet Jeremiah lived.

c640–609 BC Josiah reigned as king of Judah; decline of Assyrian power gave him relative autonomy; Book of Law discovered in the Temple at Jerusalem (c622); gave rise to Deuteronomic Reform, in which foreign cults were purged, the Temple was dedicated solely to worship of Yahweh, and worship was concentrated at Jerusalem. [2 Kings 22–23]

609 BC Josiah killed at the Battle of Megiddo during fighting with the Egyptians; Egyptian king Necho took control of the kingdom of Judah. [2 Kings 23]

605 BC Nebuchadnezzar defeated the Egyptians at the Battle of Carchemish on the Euphrates River; Judah became a Babylonian dependency. [2 Kings 24]

598 BC Judah's revolt against Babylonian rule failed. [2 Kings 25]

597–586 BC Zedekiah reigned as last king of Judah; installed by the Babylonians, he rebelled (588–586) and was defeated; Nebuchadnezzar destroyed the Temple and city of Jerusalem and carried off many of the Judahites to Babylon; kingdom of Judah ceased to exist. [2 Kings 25]

586–538 BC Babylonian Captivity ended by Persian capture of Babylon; Cyrus the Great permitted Jews to return to Palestine, though many remained at Babylon. [2 Chron. 36; Ezra]

538–332 BC Persians ruled Palestine; region administered as part of the satrapy of Syria; districts (under own governors) included Judah, Samaria, and others. [Ezra; Nehemiah]

516 BC Second Temple at Jerusalem completed, formally ending the captivity and reestablishing a center of Jewish worship. [Ezra 6]

458? BC Ezra became religious leader of the Jews; established the Law (Torah) as central to Judaism and the Jewish community. [Ezra 10]

FROM 445 BC Nehemiah, governor of Judaea, rebuilt city and its walls; introduced reforms. [Nehemiah 1–6]

c428 BC Samaritans built their own temple at Mount Gerizim in Samaria, north of Jerusalem, when Jews refused to accept them as true Jews.

332 BC Alexander the Great conquered Palestine.

323–198 BC Ptolemies, Macedonian rulers of Egypt, controlled Palestine; spread Greek language and culture there.

c300–175 BC Hasidim flourished; group strictly observed the Talmud.

198–168 BC Seleucids controlled Palestine, taking it from Egypt in campaigns of Antiochus III.

2D CENT. BC Nabatean Arabs began expanding into Syria as Seleucid power waned; eventually ruled domains that bordered on Palestine; became Roman allies by 1st cent. BC.

EARLY 2D CENT. BC First appearance of Pharisees, who upheld both the written Law of the Torah and traditions of its proper interpretation.

175–163 BC Antiochus IV reigned as Seleucid ruler; prohibited Jewish religious practices and began persecution (168) that sparked revolt by the Maccabees.

168 BC Mattathias, a Jewish priest, began revolt of the Maccabees in Palestine. [1 Mac. 2]

c164 BC Judas the Maccabee expelled the Seleucids from Jerusalem after defeating their armies; rededicated the Temple at Jerusalem (commemorated by Hanukkah).

164–161 BC Judas continued wars, even though Seleucids granted Jews religious freedom; he was killed in fighting. [1 Mac. 5–9]

161–143 BC Jonathan, Judas' brother, Maccabeus continued wars against Seleucids; killed in battle. [1 Mac. 10–12]

142 BC Simon negotiated independence of Judaea from the Seleucids.

142–135 BC Simon served as high priest and governor of the newly independent Jewish state, Judaea; assassinated. [1 Mac. 13–16]

135–104 BC John Hyrcanus reigned; Judaea reached its greatest territorial extent.

104 BC Aristobulus I reigned; adopted title of king and conquered part of (modern) Lebanon.

103–76 BC Alexander Jannaeus reigned; supported the Sadducees and persecuted the Pharisees.

76–67 BC Salome Alexandra reigned; the widow of Alexander Jannaeus, she favored the Pharisees during her reign.

67–63 BC Civil war between Aristobulus II and John Hyrcanus II; Romans under Pompey intervened and took control of Judaea.

63 BC–AD 67 Palestine administered as part of the Roman province of Syria.

63 BC–AD 395 Romans controlled Palestine.

40–37 BC Antigonus, Aristobulus' son, led abortive revolt (with Parthian support) against Roman rule; executed (37 BC).

37–4 BC Herod the Great ruled Palestine under Roman authority; practiced Judaism and promoted Hellenism; became ruthless and cruel toward end of reign.

30 BC–AD 9 Jewish scholar Hillel lived; remembered as great interpreter of Hebrew scriptures.

c20 BC–AD 50 Philosopher Philo lived; established concept of Logos.

8?–6? BC Jesus of Nazareth born; raised as a Jew. [Matthew 2; Luke 3]

4 BC Massacre of the Innocents; Herod ordered all infants in Bethlehem murdered. [Matthew 2]

4 BC–AD 39 Herod Antipas ruled Galilee under Roman authority, married his niece, Herodias, and was thus criticized by John the Baptist; ordered execution of John at behest of Salome. [Matthew 14; Mark 6; Luke 3]

1ST CENT AD Pharisee Johanan ben Zaccai founded the academy at Jabne, thus assuring survival of traditional Judiasm.

AD 6 Jewish zealot leader, Judas of Galilee, sparked revolt against Romans.

AD 26–36 Pontius Pilate, Roman procurator of Judaea, alienated the Jews.

AD 27? Jesus baptized by John the Baptist [Matthew 3; Mark 1]; Jesus began his public ministry in which he spread his teachings and aroused the opposition of the Jewish authorities. [Matthew 4; Mark 1]

AD 30 Last Supper; Jesus arrested at Jerusalem as a threat to religious and political authorities; Herod Antipas refused to pass judgment on Jesus and returned him to Pontius Pilate, who acceded to demands and ordered Jesus' execution. [Matthew 26; Mark 14; Luke 22–23, John 13, 18]

AD 30 Jesus crucified at Jerusalem; his martyrdom, the report of his resurrection, and the subsequent missionary work by his disciples marked the beginning of the Christian era. [Matthew 27; Mark 15–16; Luke 23–24; John 19:20]

AD 36 Pontius Pilate recalled to Rome; subsequent Roman procurators continued to alienate Jews.

c37–c100 AD F. Josephus, historian, lived; wrote *The History of the Jewish Wars.*

AD 66–73 First Jewish revolt; Zealots, a radical Jewish faction, rose against Roman rule; Romans retook Jerusalem and destroyed the Temple (AD 70); Jerusalem destroyed and Jewish state dissolved.

AD 115? Gamaliel of Jabneh died; he helped establish Passover Seder ritual.

AD 132–135 Second Jewish revolt; led by S. Bar Kokba, the Jews failed to end Roman rule; Emperor Hadrian built Aelia Capitolina on site of Jerusalem and refused to allow Jews to live there; thereafter Jews remained centered in Mideast until medieval times, when large numbers of them migrated to Europe.

c135–c220 Patriarch Judah I lived; compiled the Mishna.

4TH CENT. AD Palestine made a center of Christianity after Romans ended persecutions of Christians; many Jews left the region and settled elsewhere in Mideast, in Byzantium, Italy, and North Africa.

AD c330 Emperor Constantine erected the Church of the Nativity in Bethlehem.

5TH–7TH CENTS. Palestine generally under Byzantine rule.

614 Persians conquered Palestine.

628 Byzantine Emperor Heraclius recovered Palestine.

640 Muslim Arabs completed conquest of Palestine; subsequently became Muslim Holy Land.

691 Dome of the Rock built in Jerusalem by Muslims; became site of Muslim pilgrimage.

9TH–11TH CENTS. Palestine controlled by the Fatimids, Muslims based in Egypt and rivaling the Abbasid caliphs for control of the Muslim world; Christians and Jews in Palestine persecuted; control of Palestine contested by other Muslim factions.

11TH–13TH CENTS. Era of the Crusades; European Christians briefly established control over the Palestinian Holy Land.

1099–1291 Latin Kingdom of Jerusalem; Christian kingdom in Palestine founded during the First Crusade; the kingdom ceased to exist after Acre fell (1291) to the Mamelukes (Muslim rulers of Egypt).

13TH–16TH CENTS. Mamelukes controlled Palestine.

16TH–20TH CENTS. Ottoman Turks ruled Palestine; after defeating the Mamelukes (1516) the Ottomans administered Palestine as a part of the province of Syria; general decline of region continued.

c1750 Hasidim evolved in Poland under leadership of Ba'al Shem Tov.

1831 Muhammad Ali, Ottoman viceroy of Egypt, seized Palestine in rivalry with Ottoman sultan; Egyptians held region until 1840; led to period of settlement by Europeans, notably Jews.

1870 European Jews began colonization of Palestine, first Jewish settlement founded (1878).

FROM 1882 Russian Jews, fleeing the pogroms in Russia, began arriving in Palestine.

1897 Zionist movement founded for creation of a Jewish national state in Palestine; Ottoman government turned down Zionist plan, though Zionists actively supported colonization by Jews (from 1906).

1917 British occupied Palestine during the course of their offensive against the Ottoman Turks in WW I.

1917 Balfour Declaration (Nov. 2); British, at the urging of Zionist leaders, declared support for creation of Jewish national state in Palestine.

1920 Britain received preliminary approval from League of Nations for its mandate in Palestine; plan for creation of Jewish state approved.

1921 Anti-Jewish riots by Palestinian Arabs, then the majority population in Palestine.

1922 British League of Nations mandate over Palestine and Transjordan approved.

1922 British White Paper recommended that Jewish state exist within Palestine; proposed limits on immigration by Jews.

1923 Transjordan split off from Palestine; organized as an autonomous state.

1928 Rioting between Arabs and Jews over the Wailing Wall in Jerusalem.

1929 Widespread attacks by Arabs against Jews.

1930 British White Paper recommended limiting Jewish immigration and banning new purchases of land by Jews.

1930s Immigration of Jews to Palestine increased manyfold as Nazi persecutions in Germany began; opposition to British rule in Palestine mounted among Arabs and Jews alike as situation became increasingly intractable.

1936 Widespread riots by Arabs against Jews.

1936–37 Jews formed underground armies in response to Arab attacks; Haganah (1936) adopted solely defensive policy; Irgun Zvai Leumi conducted retaliatory raids (1937) against Arabs and eventually fought British forces as well.

1937 Peel Commission Report; recommended partitioning Palestine into Jewish, Arab, and British sectors.

1937–39 Period of near open war and terrorism with Arabs, Jews, and British battling for control.

1939 British White Paper abandoned partition scheme in favor of limiting Jewish immigration and land purchases; eventual independence to be granted; outbreak of WW II brought temporary halt to serious violence.

1945 Arab League formed.

1945–47 Waves of illegal immigrants entered Palestine as horrors of the Nazi Holocaust created new pressure for creation of Jewish national state; intense fighting between Jews, Arabs, and British.

1947 London Conference; British unable to solve Palestinian problem, put question before UN.

1947 UN approved (Nov.) plan to partition Palestine into Jewish, Arab, and International (Jerusalem) zones; Arabs denounced plan; renewed fighting in Palestine.

1948 State of Israel created as British occupation force completed withdrawal; immediately attacked by Arabs in first Arab-Israeli War.

Palestine Liberation Organization (PLO) Arab political and terrorist organization. Founded in 1964 at an Arab summit as a means of supporting the Palestinians while maintaining Arab control of their political activity, the PLO is now made up of various Arab guerrilla groups dedicated to reclaiming Palestinian homelands now occupied by Israel. The group has been involved in a bitter guerrilla war with the Israelis and their activities have contributed greatly to Mideast instability in past years. Their activities have included airplane hijackings, terrorist bombings, massacres of Israeli civilians, and skirmishes with Israeli military forces. The first head of the PLO was Ahmad Shukayri, who was effectively under the control of his Arab benefactors. Since the 1967 Arab-Israeli War, the PLO has been headed by Yasir Arafat (1929–), whose guerrilla organization (Al Fatah) dominated the PLO. The PLO was formally recognized by the UN in 1974. In the late 1960s and early 1970s, PLO guerrillas clashed with Jordanian troops and were finally forced to leave Jordan. Then in the late 1970s, the PLO used Lebanon as staging area for raids on Israel. The attacks led to the Israeli invasion of Lebanon (1982) and the defeat and forced evacuation of PLO guerrillas from Beirut. In 1988, the PLO declared a government-in-exile of what they proclaimed was the State of Palestine. Arafat, despite increasing dissatisfaction with his leadership, was proclaimed president, and the group officially recognized Israel's right to exist. Ongoing negotiations on Mideast peace that followed the Persian Gulf War sought to address the Palestinian problem.

Pali Indo-European language. Thought to be the language of Buddha, Pali is still employed in the liturgical literature of Buddhists in Sri Lanka, Burma, and Thailand.

Palikao, Charles Guiliaume Cousin-Montauban, count of 1796–1878. French general. His title was bestowed after his victory at Palikao while on an Anglo-French military expedition in China (1860). He briefly served as premier (1870) during the collapse of the French Second Empire.

Palladianism Architectural style developed during the Italian Renaissance by A. Palladio. It incorporated elements of classical Roman architecture. Palladianism was influential in England (17th–18th cents.) and was promoted there by I. Jones.

Palladio, Andrea 1508–80. Famous Italian architect of the Renaissance. Palladio rebelled against excessive ornamentation, adapted classic Roman styles, and created the style known as Palladianism. He is considered the founder of modern Italian architecture.

Palmerston, Henry John Temple, 3d Viscount 1784–1865. British statesman who played an important role in foreign affairs in the 19th cent. He served as secretary of war (1809–28), foreign minister (1830–34, 1835–41, 1846–51), and prime minister (1855–58, 1859–65). A Whig party member, he played a role in arranging Belgian independence (1831), orchestrating European intervention against Muhammad Ali to prevent the break-up of the Ottoman Empire (1841), the Affair of the Spanish Marriages (1846), the Don Pacifico Affair (1850), and the overthrow of French Emperor Napoleon III. His terms as prime minister were marked by British involvement in the Crimean War (1853–56) and the Indian Mutiny (1857–58) and by Britain's neutral support for Italian unification and its stance in the American Civil War.

Palmyra (Tadmor) Ancient Syrian city. Palmyra was supposedly founded by Solomon and was an important trade center after its takeover by Rome. It subsequently became the nucleus of a powerful, quasi-independent eastern empire under Roman domination. The ambitions of its queen, Zenobia, led to destruction of the city (AD 273) by Aurelian.

Palo Alto, Battle of First major battle of the Mexican War (1846–48), fought at this Texas city on May 8, 1846. American forces under Gen. Z. Taylor defeated the Mexican army in the first of several successful engagements against it.

Pan-African congresses International conferences to promote interests of black peoples and nations. Blacks from America and the West Indies met in London in 1900 to protest white oppression in Africa. W.E.B. Du Bois emerged as a leading figure here and in the subsequent meetings of 1919, 1921, 1923, and 1927. The congress in 1945 called for independence of all African states from colonial powers.

Panama (Republic of Panama) Independent state in Central America, located on the Isthmus of Panama that connects Central and South America. The population is 2,243,000 and the capital is Panama City. Panama is bisected by the Panama Canal. Panama was ruled by Spain until 1821 and was part of Colombia until independence was proclaimed in 1903, following a successful revolution. Key events in Panama's history include:

16TH CENT.   Region administered as part of the viceroyalty of Peru; main route to rich Spanish colonies in Peru passed across the Isthmus of Panama.

1502   C. Columbus visited the coastal region on his fourth voyage.

1513   V. de Balboa, Spanish governor, explored the region; crossed the isthmus to the Pacific Ocean.

1519   P. Arias de Ávila founded Panama City.

1717   Administrative control passed to viceroyalty of New Granada.

1821   Joined Colombia in revolt against Spain; was governed subsequently as part of Colombia.

1881   F. de Lesseps began construction of Panama Canal; his French company went bankrupt (1889), however.

1903   Colombia refused US rights to build canal; US backed Panamanian revolt against Colombia, gained Panama its independence.

1903   Hay-Bunau-Varilla Treaty concluded between US and newly independent Panama; established the US–controlled Panama Canal Zone; canal construction began (1904).

1904   Constitution adopted.

1914   Panama Canal opened (Aug. 15).

1939   New treaty provided for equal rights and responsibilities in the Canal Zone.

1941   Pro-German president Harmodio Arias ousted and exiled.

1968   Dr. Arnulfo Arias elected president; overthrown by military coup; two-man junta reigned; overthrown by Gen. Omar Torrijos, head of the National Guard.

1969–78   Demetrio Basilio Lakas Bahas in office as military-backed president; Gen. Torrijos held real power.

1972   New constitution promulgated; National Assembly established.

1977   US and Panama signed treaty (Sept. 7) giving Panama control of canal in 1999.

1978–82   Aristides Royo in office as president.

1978   US Senate approved transfer of Canal Zone to Panama in 1999.

1981   Gen. Torrijos, de facto military ruler, killed in plane crash; military leader M. Noriega alleged to have been behind Torrijos's death.

1982   President Aristides resigned (July) as disunity between factions mounted; Ricardo de la Espriella made president.

1983   New constitution endorsed (Apr.); majority of voters backed a return to civilian rule.

1984   M. Noriega, commander of the National Guard, forced the resignation of President Espriella (Feb. 14).

1984   Nicolas Ardito Barletta, backed by Noriega's National Guard, elected president; Noriega later accused of rigging the election (1986).

1985   President Ardito forced to resign after Dr. Hugo Spadaforo, a critic of the military, was found murdered (Sept. 28).

1985–   Eric Arturo Del Valle in office as president.

1986   US revealed Panamian strongman M. Noriega had been supplying information to both the U.S. and Cuba for years; accused him of involvement with drug smuggling; restricted technology, and money.

1987   Panama Canal failed to make a profit for the second time in eight years.

1987   Demonstrations called to protest increasing power of Noriega's defense forces; vice-president quit after his offices were ransacked (Oct.).

1988   Noriega was indicted by US court for drug trafficking (Feb.).

1988   Congress voted to oust both the president and vice-president.

1988   Manuel Solis Palma became interim head of state; Noriega held real power.

1988   US froze all Panamanian assets (Mar. 4).

1988   US-backed coup attempt (Mar. 16) failed to remove Noriega, effectively consolidating his power.

1988   Presidential elections (May 7) annulled by the government after the main opposition candidate, Guillermo Endara, apparently won.

1989   US ambassador recalled (May), after a brigade-sized force was sent to reassert US rights in the Canal Zone.

1989   Noriega declared head of government (Dec. 15) by Assembly; Assembly then proclaimed state of war with US.

1989   Panamanian troops attacked off-duty American soldiers (Dec. 16); one American killed.

1989   Panama Invasion (Dec.–Feb.): US troops attacked selected targets and hunted down M. Noriega; Noriega brought back to US to stand trial on drug charges (Jan.); later sentenced to prison term (1992).

1989   Guillermo Endara proclaimed himself president on the strength of the May elections.

1989–   President Endara in office.

1990   Endara went on 13-day hunger strike after promised US aid failed to arrive (Mar.).

1991   Pact signed with US for exchange of information about money laundering (Apr.).

1991   Government imposed severe cuts in health, education, and welfare.

1991   Trial of ex-dictator Noriega on drug charges opened in US (Sept.).

1992 Noriega convicted on drug charges in US court; sentenced to 40 years in US prison.

Panama Canal Man-made waterway extending 51 miles across the Isthmus of Panama in Central America. Originally proposed as early as Spanish colonial times and actively pursued by the US since about the mid-1800s, the canal was begun (1881) by F. de Lesseps (builder of the Suez Canal) of France. De Lesseps's firm went bankrupt (1889) as a result of construction problems and outbreaks of tropical disease. The US again took an interest in the project and settled a long dispute with the British over US control of the proposed canal (by the Hay-Pauncefote Treaty, 1901). The US for a time considered a canal through Nicaragua, but under President T. Roosevelt made arrangements to take over the French project in Panama. Colombia (then in control of Panama) refused to ratify a treaty for construction of the canal. The US soon after supported a revolution in Panama. Panama gained independence (Nov., 1903) and on Nov. 17 the US concluded the Hay-Bunau-Varilla Treaty with the new government. Construction work began in 1904 and was completed under the supervision of Col. G. Goethals by 1914. In recent times Panama sought control of the canal and the US agreed (1978) to effect the transfer in 1999.

Panama Canal Zone Area of Panama, extending five miles on either side of the Panama Canal, and administered by the United States from 1903. The US Senate, after a heated controversy, enacted (1978) legislation to dissolve the zone and turn operation of the canal over to Panama in 1999.

Panama Invasion US military action (1989) against Panamanian troops defending the nation's dictator, General M. Noriega. As relations between the US and Panama worsened over Panama's involvement in the drug trade, the US first imposed sanctions (1988) and then broke diplomatic relations with the country. After Panama's National Assembly formally proclaimed Noriega head of the government (Dec. 15, attempts to oust him having failed), the Assembly declared the nation in "a state of war" against the US. The next day, four off-duty US soldiers were attacked by Panamanian troops at a roadblock, and one was killed. US president G. Bush immediately put the 12,000 US troops in Panama on alert (Dec. 17). Another 12,000 US soldiers landed in Panama (Dec. 20) and

attacks on selected targets began soon after. Several days after fighting began, Noriega took refuge in the Vatican's diplomatic mission in Panama City (Dec. 24), which was then surrounded by American troops. Already wanted in the US on drug trafficking charges, Noriega surrendered to US authorities (Jan. 3, 1990) on the condition that he not be given the death penalty. Noriega was transported to Florida (Jan. 4) where he was tried and convicted (1992) for drug trafficking and money laundering. Twenty-six Americans and 697 Panamanians were killed in the invasion. US troops were withdrawn in Feb., 1990.

Panama Scandal Scandal (1892) involving the government of the French Third Republic and the failed French Panama Canal Company. The company, in financial trouble because of mismanagement and corruption, floated a new loan in 1888. To get approval from the Chamber of Deputies for the loan, the company's directors bribed many of the deputies. An investigation some years after the company failed (1889) revealed the bribery and toppled the government.

Pan American conferences (Inter-American ~) Meetings (from 1826) held between various South American states and the US to discuss mutual economic and defense concerns. Conferences up to 1889 (1826, 1847, 1856, 1864) were concerned largely with matters of defense. The First International Conference of American States (1889–90), largely initiated by the US, established what became the Pan-American Union (*q.v.*) and led to treaties covering trade, arbitration of disputes, and international administrative matters. Additional conferences in 1936, 1938, 1939, 1940, and 1945 worked out mutual-defense agreements. In 1948 the Ninth International Conference formed the Organization of American States (*q.v.*).

Pan-American Union Organization founded in 1890 and composed of republics in North and South America. The union promoted technical, commercial, and cultural interchange among its member nations. It became part of the Organization of American States on formation of that body in 1948.

Pandit, Vilaya Lakshmi 1900– . Indian diplomat. Sister of J. Nehru, she led the Indian delegation to the UN and served as ambassador to both Russia and the US.

Pan-Germanism German nationalist movement, organized in 1894. It called for the political unification of all German-speaking people. The movement was used to justify Germany's expansionist policies and after WW I figured in A. Hitler's National Socialist program.

Pangkor Engagement British agreement (Jan., 1874) with the local ruler of Perak, a state in northern Malaya. In exchange for accepting a British resident with authority, the Perak chief was assured of British support. The treaty led to the eventual British domination of the Malay states.

Panic of 1837 US financial panic that began in the spring of 1837, shortly after President M. Van Buren took office. A land speculation boom in the West during A. Jackson's administration was fueled by the many banknotes of inflated value issued by state banks. Jackson's Specie Circular (issued 1836) required payment for public lands (in the West) in hard currency, and thus undermined the value of these notes. A financial collapse followed in 1837, first in the western land market and then spreading to commodities and other markets.

Panic of 1869 *See* **Black Friday.**

Panic of 1873 US financial panic (sometimes also called Black Friday) that began on Sept. 18. It was caused by the failure of Jay Cooke and Company, a financial house that had marketed federal bonds during the Civil War.

Panic of 1893 US financial panic brought on by a withdrawal of British investment capital from the US. British capital had fueled a boom in railroad building in the late 19th cent. A worldwide Depression, however, caused British investors to withdraw from the American market and resulted in a collapse of the railroad boom and a flow of gold out of the US. As a remedy, President G. Cleveland sought repeal of the Sherman Silver Purchase Act (*q.v.*), which he won (1893). The repeal eased pressure on US gold reserves by eliminating the high level of silver purchases required by the act.

Panipat, Battles of Three battles fought by the Mughals at Panipat, in India. 1. On Apr. 20, 1526, Baber and his force of some 2,000 Mughals defeated the Afghans and thus established the Mughal dynasty that ruled until 1761. 2. On Nov. 3, 1556, the third Mughal emperor, Akbar the Great, headed an army of 20,000 and defeated a much larger force of Hindus. 3. On Jan. 14, 1761, the Afghan Emperor Ahmad Shah Durrani defeated an army of Marathas during his invasion of India, left Indian kingdoms weakened and paved the way for the British takeover.

Pankhurst, Emmeline Goulden 1857–1928. British feminist, who founded (1903) the Women's Social and Political Union to promote woman suffrage. A militant, she was frequently jailed. English women received the vote just before her death.

Panmunjom Korean village where peace was negotiated (1951–53) between UN forces and the North Koreans and Chinese during the Korean War (1950–53). The village is located just south of the 38th parallel. The armistice ending the war was signed there July 27, 1953.

Pannonia Ancient Roman province. Pannonia was located south of the Danube River and included parts of what became Austria, Hungary, and Yugoslavia. The territories were conquered by the Roman Empire in AD 9.

Pan-Slavism Slavic unity movement. This movement arose in the 19th cent. and stressed the common culture and history of the various Slavic peoples, then divided between Austrian and Ottoman empires. Pan-Slavism figured in Russian imperial policy, contributed to the outbreak of the Russo-Turkish War (1877–78), and was a factor in Russia's alliance with Serbia against the Austrians in the years before WW I.

Pantaleon, Jacques *See* **Urban IV.**

pantheism Religious term for the belief that God and the universe are one. Pantheism has been a factor in both religion (notably Hinduism, in which Brahman is all things in the universe) and philosophy.

Pantheon Roman temple. Built by Agrippa (27 BC) at Rome to honor all gods, it was rebuilt and restyled as a more spectacular structure (2d cent. AD) by Hadrian. The Pantheon is now a Christian church (from 609).

Paoli, Pasquale 1725–1807. Corsican patriot. Paoli rebelled against Genoese and, later, French domination of Corsica. As governor (1755–69, 1791–93) he instituted political reforms. He drove out the French with British help (1794).

papacy The system of government of the Roman Catholic church, which is headed by the pope (bishop of Rome), who is considered the successor to St. Peter and vicar of Christ. The pope is considered infallible by the Roman Catholic church in matters of faith or morality and is head of independent Vatican City. Early popes played an important role in the spread of the Christian church and in resolving the many doctrinal disputes of that era. In medieval times popes were the central figures in the great struggles for power between the church and European monarchs. Later they instituted the Catholic Reformation (*q.v.*) and, gradually forced to relinquish their secular powers, came to focus on spiritual concerns. In modern times, the popes have been especially active in adapting the church to a rapidly changing world (*see* Second Vatican Council). (*See also* Roman Catholic Church; Papal States.)

Papal States Former territory over which the pope had direct temporal rule (756–1870). The size of the territory varied throughout its history but at its greatest extent it included a wide swath across central Italy. From the 4th cent. the pope had control of estates around Rome (the Patrimony of Saint Peter), but the existence of the sovereign state is dated from the Donation of Pepin (756). Pepin the Short, in return for papal recognition of his accession as king of the Franks, aided the pope against the invading Lombards and donated lands taken from them (around Ravenna) to the pope. The popes remained sovereign during the Middle Ages but real control of the territories was frustrated by feudal nobles and struggles with the Holy Roman emperors (11th–14th cents.). While the papacy was located at Avignon during the Babylonian Captivity, effective control passed to the local nobles. From the 15th to 18th cents., the popes gradually established central authority and brought papal domains to their greatest extent. The Papal States were conquered by Napoleon (1796) and restored to the pope by the Congress of Vienna (1815). Almost all papal domains were lost during the unification of Italy (1860) and, in 1870, Italian king Victor Emmanuel II seized Rome as well. The pope thereupon declared himself a "prisoner" in the Vatican and the Roman Question over rights to the Papal States was not resolved until the signing of the Lateran Treaty (1929).

Papareschi, Gregorio *See* **Innocent II.**

Papen, Franz von 1879–1969. German politician. As P. Hindenburg's chancellor, he facilitated the rise of the Nazi party by lifting the ban on their paramilitary troops and later helped bring A. Hitler to power.

Paphlagonia Ancient country in Asia Minor. Bounded on the north by the Black Sea, it was absorbed by Rome in 65 BC.

Papineau, Louis Joseph 1786–1871. French-Canadian political leader. He stirred his followers in Lower Canada to rebellion against British rule (1837), shortly before the revolt led by W. Mackenzie broke out in Upper Canada. He escaped to the US, returned in 1844, and was pardoned.

Papinian *d.* AD 212. Roman jurist. The friend and counselor of Emperor Severus, he was considered one of the great Roman jurists. He was executed by Caracalla.

Pappus *fl.* AD c300. Greek mathematician. His book *Synagogue (Collection)* records the teachings of earlier mathematicians whose original works have been lost.

Papua New Guinea (*formerly* New Guinea, Territory of) Country consisting of the eastern part of New Guinea and adjacent islands. The population is 3,613,000 and the capital is Port Moresby. Europeans reached New Guinea in the 15th cent. and the southeastern part of the island became (1884) the British protectorate of British New Guinea. It came under control of Australia (1905) and was renamed Papua. The northeastern part of the island was incorporated into the German possession of German New Guinea (1884) and was known as Kaiser-Wilhelmsland. Occupied (1914) by Australia during WW I, it became an Australian mandate (1920) as the Territory of New Guinea. In 1949 Papua and the Territory of New Guinea were merged, and became independent (Sept. 16, 1975) as Papua New Guinea. In 1983 constitutional changes were enacted, giving the national government greater control over provincial governments, some of which had been accused of corruption and inefficiency. Unrest on the island of Bougainville (from 1988) culminated in a declaration of independence by rebels (1990) and an economic blockade by the government. Negotiations failed and incidents of fighting between government troops and the rebels continued into the early 1990s.

papyrus Reed plant once widely cultivated by the ancient Egyptians and used by them to make writing paper (from c3500 BC).

Paracelsus (Hohenheim, Philippus Aureolus Theophrastus Bombastus von) 1493–1541. Swiss alchemist and physician. Paracelsus defied (then) conventional ideas of medicine and introduced the use of particular chemicals to cure specific diseases.

Paraguay (Republic of Paraguay) Landlocked country located in the south-central part of South America. The population is 4,660,000 and the capital is Asunción. Since its independence in 1811, Paraguay has been ruled almost continuously by a succession of dictators. Key dates in Paraguay's history include:

1526–29 Sebastian Cabot explored Paraguay for Spain.

1538 Asunción founded.

1608 Jesuit order established in region.

1617 Hernando Arias de Saavedra set up separate administrations for Paraguay and Argentina.

1721–35 Revolt of the *comuneros;* independence from Spain sought.

1767 Jesuits expelled.

1776 Region became part of the viceroyalty of the Río de la Plata.

1811 Paraguay independent after bloodless rebellion against Spain.

1814–40 J. Francia (El Supremo) in power as first of three early dictators; instituted harsh rule.

1844–62 Carlos Antonio López in power as dictator.

1862–70 Francisco Solano López succeeded his father.

1864–70 War of the Triple Alliance against Uruguay, Brazil, and Argentina; over a million Paraguayans killed.

1870 New constitution promulgated.

1932–35 Chaco War with Bolivia over border region.

1935–38 Buenos Aires Peace Conferences granted most of Chaco region to Paraguay.

1940–48 Higinio Moringio in power as dictator.

1948 Juan Natalicio González elected president.

1949 Revolts (Jan.–Apr.) against Gonzáles and his successor; Frederico Cháves assumed power.

1949–54 Cháves in power.

1953 Cháves reelected.

1954 Cháves ousted by military coup.

1954–89 Gen. Alfredo Stroessner in power; his long reign marked by ruthless suppression of any opposition, widespread smuggling and other forms of corruption, and a pattern of human rights abuses, including illegal arrests, detention, and torture.

1959 Notorious Nazi prison camp doctor, Dr. Josef Mengele, granted citizenship.

1965 Stroessner relaxed siege imposed when he took power; exiles returned.

1967 Constitution revised.

1978 Work begun on Itaipú dam and hydroelectric power plant (the world's largest); joint project with Brazil seen as economic boon to Paraguay, which was expected to earn considerable revenue from exported electric power.

1980 Deposed Nicaraguan president A. Somoza Debayle, who had taken refuge in Asunción, was brutally murdered by unknown gunmen (Sept. 17); police concluded Argentinians were responsible.

1983 Public apathy and human rights violations decried by bishops of Paraguay in annual message to the people.

1983 President Stroessner reelected to fifth consecutive term.

1984 Public anti-government protest held in Asunción for first time in 30 years (Jan. 17).

1984 Itaipú began producing electricity; one turbine on line (Mar.).

1984 Paraguay faced severe economic crisis; national debt climbing rapidly, while planned export of electricity to Brazil frustrated by that country's continuing severe recession.

1984 Government, reacting to mounting opposition, closed the country's top news magazine (Mar. 22).

1985 Investigators hunting Nazi prison camp doctor Josef Mengele discovered he became citizen of Paraguay in 1959; Mengele's remains later discovered in Brazil, where he had lived in hiding.

1985 Government detained leaders of opposition Movimiento Popular Colorado (Jan.).

1985 Opposition group Febreristas staged rally in Asunción (Feb.); Interior Ministry charged with torturing prisoners.

1985 Pro-democracy rally in Asunción (May 14) by coalition of opposition groups.

1986 Some 15,000 demonstrated in Asunción (Feb. 14), calling for return to democratic government.

1987 Febreristas organized anti-government rally in Asunción (Feb. 18) following President Stroessner's decision to run for another term.

1987   Government, seeking to blunt criticism, ended state of siege declared in 1947.

1987   About 15,000 supporters attended Asunción rally (Apr. 25) for return of Coronel Oviedo, exiled leader of the Authentic Radical Liberal Party.

1988   President Stroessner reelected to new five-year term.

1988   Pope John Paul II gave address at Asunción cathedral (May); while he spoke of the need for human rights inside, police brutally attacked crowd gathered outside the cathedral.

1989   Military coup ousted Stroessner (Feb. 3); 17 dead and over 100 former officials arrested on various charges.

1989–   Coup leader Gen. Andrés Rodríguez in office as president; he won election to a full term in May.

1990   Paraguay signed Montevideo Declaration for free passage on Paraguay and Paraná rivers (Mar. 1).

1991   First municipal elections held (May 26).

1991   Ruling Colorado party won clear majority of seats in parliamentary elections (Dec.).

Paramountcy, Doctrine of *See* **Doctrine of Lapse.**

Parentucelli, Tommaso *See* **Nicholas V.**

Pareto, Vilfredo 1848–1923. Italian economist and sociologist. As a professor of political economy, he became known for his analyses of economic problems and for his theories of income and wealth distribution in society. He also researched the nature and formation of social classes (1916). Among his most influential works is the *Manual of Political Economics* (1906).

Paris City, the capital of France and located in north-central France. One of the great cultural and intellectual centers of the world, Paris is the commercial and industrial nub of France. Originally a Gallic village, it was conquered by J. Caesar (52 BC) and prospered under Roman influence. Paris became the capital of several Merovingian kings, notably Clovis I. Hugh Capet, duke of Paris, became king of France (AD 987), and under his influence and that of his successors the city became the capital of France, and a center of trade, learning, and culture. French king Louis XIV moved the capital to Versailles (1682). Paris was a site of struggle between the Armagnacs and Burgundians (*q.v.*) during the Hundred Years' War, and was occu-

pied by the English (1420–36). It was the center of the Massacre of St. Bartholomew's Day (*q.v.*) in 1572. Paris played a major role in the French Revolution and was occupied by allied armies (1814) after the fall of Napoleon. It was also the scene of the revolutions of 1830 and 1848. During the Franco-Prussian War (1870–71) it was occupied by the Germans, and subsequently became the site of the Commune of Paris (*q.v.*). The Germans made an unsuccessful drive to capture Paris during WW I but occupied the city (1940–44) during WW II. In 1968 Paris was the scene of severe political disorder. It was the site of the US-Vietnam peace negotiations (1968–73).

Paris, Commune of *See* **Commune of Paris.**

Paris, Congress of *See* **Congress of Paris.**

Paris, Matthew (~ of Paris) *d.* 1259. Noted English writer of Latin chronicles of the 13th cent. A monk of Saint Albans, he wrote *Chronica Majora,* a history of the world to 1259, and *Historia Anglorum,* a history of England.

Paris, Treaty of 1. Treaty (1229) between French king Louis IX and the nobleman Raymond VII of Toulouse, ending the last of the fighting sparked by the Albigensian Crusade (*q.v.*). Louis gained the county of Toulouse and agreed to certain marriage arrangements. 2. Treaty (Feb. 10, 1763) between Britain, France, and Spain ending the Seven Years' War (1756–63) and the subsidiary French and Indian War in the colonies. The treaty marked the ascendancy of Britain as the leading colonial power. By its terms Britain received French holdings in Canada, America (east of the Mississippi), Grenada, the Grenadines, and Senegal. Britain received Florida from Spain and returned Cuba and the Philippines to Spain, while Spain got all of the Louisiana Territory west of the Mississippi from France. Britain gave France Guadeloupe, Martinique, Miquelon, and St. Pierre. Britain also restored some French possessions in India. 3. Treaty (Sept. 3, 1783, *also sometimes called* Treaty of Versailles) between the US, Britain, and other European powers ending the American Revolution (1775–83). It was negotiated by B. Franklin, J. Jay, and J. Adams for the US. By its terms Britain recognized US independence, US boundaries were fixed (at the Mississippi in the West), Spain reacquired Florida and Minorca from Britain, and France got Senegal and Tobago. The US was granted fishing rights in areas off the

British-Canadian coast and was to prevent abuses against former loyalists. **4.** Treaty (May 30, 1814) between France and the allied powers who had defeated Napoleon. The terms of the treaty were not harsh and included a return of France to her borders of 1792, restoration to France of most of her colonies taken by Britain, and the loss of Malta to Britain. No indemnity was imposed and a congress was to be held at Vienna to work out final arrangements. **5.** Treaty (Nov. 20, 1815) between France and the victorious European allies after Napoleon's defeat at the end of his Hundred Days (*q.v.*). Harsher terms were imposed and included a large indemnity, a return to the borders of 1790, and payment of expenses for an army to occupy northern France. **6.** Treaty (Mar. 30, 1856) between Russia and the allies (Ottoman Turks, Britain, France, and Sardinia) ending the Crimean War. Russia returned Kars and regained Sevastopol, ceded the mouth of the Danube and part of Bessarabia, and abandoned claims to protect Christians within the Ottoman empire. The Black Sea was declared neutral. **7.** Treaty (Dec. 10, 1898) between the US and Spain ending the Spanish-American War (1898). In return for $20 million, Spain gave up Cuba and ceded to the US the territories of the Philippines, Guam, and Puerto Rico.

Paris Peace Conference Conference (1919–20) of Allied leaders at the end of WW I to determine peace terms to be imposed on Germany and the other Central Powers—Austria, Hungary, Bulgaria, and Turkey. It resulted in the Treaty of Versailles (signed, with protest by Germany June 28, 1919), the Treaty of Saint-Germain (signed by Austria, Sept. 10) and the Treaty of Neuilly (signed by Bulgaria, Nov. 27). At the outset of the conference (Jan. 18, 1919) Allied leaders met in the Council of Ten (two representatives for each of five powers) to oversee the activities of a number of commissions charged with various aspects of the settlements (reparations, territorial questions, the League of Nations, etc.). G. Clemenceau served as president of the council. By Mar., 1919, however, a Council of Four had been formed to direct the peace conference. This council consisted of Clemenceau (France), D. Lloyd George (Britain), V. Orlando (Italy), and W. Wilson (US). A major deadlock was broken (Apr. 7) when Wilson threatened to leave the conference, and compro-

mises on such issues as the status of the Rhineland and Danzig were reached. The League of Nations Covenant was approved (as part of the Treaty of Versailles) by the conference Apr. 28, 1919. The conference closed (Jan. 16, 1920), leaving terms of treaties with Hungary and Turkey unresolved.

Park Chung Hee 1917–79. South Korean president (1963–79). He rose to power through the military and participated in the 1961 military coup against the civilian government. Elected president in 1963, he subsequently consolidated his power and instituted a police state in Korea. During his administration, border clashes with North Korea subsided, the economy improved, Korean officials were implicated (1976–77) in charges of attempting to bribe US congressmen, and the US announced plans (1977, never implemented) to withdraw troops stationed there. Park was assassinated (Oct. 26, 1979).

Parker, Dorothy 1893–1967. American writer. Noted for her acerbic wit, she wrote short stories such as *Big Blonde,* screenplays such as *A Star Is Born,* and poetry collections such as *Enough Rope* and *Death and Taxes.*

Parker, Sir Hyde 1739–1807. British admiral. Parker's second-in-command at the Battle of Copenhagen (*q.v.*), H. Nelson, was in charge of actual fighting (1801). In a famous incident during the battle, Nelson ignored Parker's order to withdraw and went on to victory. Nelson replaced Parker as commander soon after.

Parker, Capt. John *See* **Lexington and Concord, Battle of.**

Parkes, Sir Henry 1815–96. Australian statesman. Parkes fought to end the practice of transporting British criminals to Australia. He was also active in promoting free trade and educational and civil service reforms.

Parkman, Francis 1823–93. American historian. Parkman lived with the Sioux, traveled the Oregon Trail, and wrote many works on American history, including *The California and Oregon Trail, A Half-Century of Conflict,* and *Montcalm and Wolfe.*

Parlement A French royal court under the *ancien régime.* There were parlements in Paris and 14 provincial cities. They combined the functions of a department of justice and appellate court, had no legislative powers, but did enjoy a certain "right of remonstrance" against royal acts.

Parlement, Fronde of the *See* **Fronde.**

Parliament Legislative assembly. In Britain, Parliament consists of the reigning monarch, the House of Lords, and the House of Commons. Power rests largely with the House of Commons, the monarch being sovereign in name only and the House of Lords having lost much of its power in 1911. The prime minister is elected from the Commons. British Parliament, the oldest surviving parliament, provided the model for parliaments that were established in British dominions throughout the world. The origins of the British Parliament can be traced to the 13th-cent. royal feudal council, the Curia Regis, which gave rise to the House of Lords and to the irregular assemblages of the knights and burgesses, which gave rise to the House of Commons. Though a forerunner of Parliament (King Edward I's Model Parliament) was convened in 1295, the basic structure of Parliament did not appear until the 14th cent. Thereafter, Parliament began a long struggle for supremacy over the English monarchs, usually relying on its control of finances to force concessions. This struggle resulted in the English Civil Wars (*q.v.*), in which Parliament deposed (and executed) the king and then some years later reinstituted the monarchy. Parliament finally established its supremacy over the monarchs by the Glorious Revolution (*q.v.*) of 1688, and thereafter the monarchs' involvement in government steadily diminished. In the 18th cent., Sir R. Walpole established the prime minister as effective head of government and in the 19th cent. the party system was firmly rooted in Parliament. The ascendancy of the House of Commons came in 1911 when, after a political crisis, the House of Lords lost its veto power over legislation (Parliament Act).

Parliament, An Admonition to the *See* **Admonition to the Parliament, An.**

Parliament Act British act (1911) by which the House of Lords lost its veto power over parliamentary legislation. It was passed amid a political crisis caused by the opposition by the House of Lords to a proposed tax on the wealthy to fund a social insurance program. The bill was advanced (1909) by D. Lloyd George.

Parma, Margaret of *See* **Margaret of Parma.**

Parmenides *fl.* 5th cent. BC. Greek philosopher. Parmenides was a founder and leading member of the Eleatic school. He taught that all being was one reality and that change and motion were but illusions of the senses.

Parnassians French school of poetry prominent during the 19th cent. Parnassians sought technical perfection and emotional detachment in their works, in reaction to the Romantic movement. Noted members of this school include Charles Leconte de Lisle (1818–94), R. Sully-Prudhomme, José-María de Heredia (1842–1905), and P. Verlaine.

Parnassos *See* **Parnassus.**

Parnassus (Parnassos) Mountain located in central Greece. The ancient Greeks believed it to be the favorite haunt of Apollo, the Muses, and Dionysus.

Parnell, Charles Stewart 1846–91. Leading figure in the Irish Home Rule movement in the late 19th cent. He was elected to Parliament (1875) as a Home Rule advocate, became president of the Irish National Land League (1879), and figured prominently in agitation against landlords in Ireland. Though reaction to violent acts by Irish terrorists grew stronger (i.e., Phoenix Park murders), Parnell managed to maintain his position, used his controlling votes to oust and then restore (1886) the Liberals, and forced introduction of the unsuccessful Irish Home Rule Bill (1886). He fell from power after becoming involved in a scandal (1890–91) over an associate's wife.

Parr, Catherine 1512–48. English queen consort, Henry VIII's sixth wife (*m.* 1543). She remained married to Henry until his death and later married T. Seymour (1547).

Parsis (Parses) Followers of Zoroastrianism in India. They migrated to India (c8th cent.) from Persia to escape persecution by Muslims. In modern times they are centered around Bombay.

Parson's Cause Dispute over salaries paid to Anglican ministers in the Virginia colony during the year 1758. In that year, the colony instituted a measure that effectively reduced ministers' pay. It was struck down (1759) by the king, and the ministers subsequently sued for back pay for 1758. In the most famous of these cases, the young lawyer P. Henry defended (1763) Hanover Parish against its minister.

Parthenon Greek temple of the goddess Athena, protectoress of Athens. Built (447–432 BC) during the ascendancy of Pericles, it was one of the greatest works of Greek Doric architecture. The structure was built on the Athenian acropolis by Ictinus and Callicrates, under supervision of the sculptor Phidias. The Parthenon was converted to a Christian church (5th cent. AD) and then to a Muslim mosque (1458). It was damaged (1687) during an attack by the Venetians on the Turks, then in control of the region. Parts of it (the so-called Elgin Marbles) were later removed to the British Museum (1795).

Parthenopean Republic Short-lived Italian republic. The French set up this republic after conquering the kingdom of Naples (Jan. 1799) during the French Revolutionary Wars (1792–1802). It was retaken by the British, under H. Nelson, soon afterward (June, 1799) and the Bourbon rulers were restored.

Parthia Ancient Asian country, located in what is now modern Iran. The territory was part of the Assyrian, Persian, Macedonian, and Seleucid empires before Arsaces founded the Parthian kingdom (247 BC). At its peak (1st cent. BC), the Parthian Empire extended from the Euphrates River to the Indus River and from the Oxus River to the Indian Ocean. Its decline began with attacks by the Romans (39–38 BC). The empire was taken over (AD 226) by Ardashir I, founder of the Sassanidae Empire.

Partisans Yugoslav guerrilla resistance organization that joined the Allies during WW II in fighting the Axis powers. Led by the Yugoslav Communist Tito, the Partisans were an effective fighting force and set up an opposition government in Yugoslavia.

Partition of Poland Three successive divisions of Polish territories in the 18th cent. that resulted in complete dismemberment of Poland. 1. First ~. Russian victories in the Russo-Turkish War of 1768 put it in a position to expand into the region of the Danube, a possibility strongly opposed by Austria. To avert war between Russia and Austria, Prussia proposed that Russia expand into Poland instead. (Poland, torn by a civil war, was unable to resist.) Russia, Austria, and Prussia agreed (Aug. 5, 1772) on the plan and each annexed parts of Poland that together amounted to one-third of Polish domains. 2. Second ~. Liberal reforms enacted in Poland led to the formation of the Confederation of Targowica (1792) by conservative reactionaries. They asked for help to restore conservative rule, and both the Russians and Prussians invaded

Poland. Russia and Prussia then instituted (Jan. 23, 1793) the second partition, leaving only the central part of Poland intact. 3. Third ~. The Poles, led by T. Kosciusko, revolted (1794) against the second partition, and Russia and Prussia put down the rebellion. Austria, Prussia, and Russia thereupon agreed to divide (Oct. 24, 1795) the remaining territory, with the major share going to Russia.

Pascal, Blaise 1623–62. French mathematician, physicist, and religious writer. The son of a noted mathematician, he was contributing to the scientific and philosophical meetings in Paris by the age of 16. He developed the first digital calculator (1642), and invented the syringe and hydraulic press. His studies of properties of fluids (1640s) also led to formulation of Pascal's Law, concerning the distribution of fluid pressure in a closed container. In mathematics, Pascal developed with P. Fermat the modern theory of probability (1657) and also advanced his "theory of indivisibles" (1658–59), the forerunner of modern integral calculus. In 1654, he underwent a powerful religious experience, after which he entered the convent at Port-Royal and wrote several religious works in support of Jansenism.

Paschal II d. 1118. Italian-born pope (1099–1118), successor to Urban II. His reign was marked by continuing struggles over the Investiture Controversy (*q.v.*), first with Holy Roman Emperor Henry IV, then with Emperor Henry V.

Pašić, Nikola (Pashitch, ~) 1846–1926. Serbian statesman. He founded and led the Radical party in Serbia and served several times as premier, pursuing anti-Austrian policies. He was Yugoslavia's first premier (1921–26).

Passarowitz, Treaty of Treaty (July 21, 1718) between the Ottoman Empire and Austria and Venice, ending wars (from 1716) with Austria and Venice. Venice ceded its possessions in the Peloponnesus and Crete to the Ottomans. They in turn ceded the Banat of Temesvar, parts of Bosnia and Serbia, and Lesser Walachia to Austria.

Passchendaele, Battle of *See* **Ypres, Battles of.**

Passy, Frédéric 1822–1912. French economist. Passy was a founder of the International League for Permanant Peace (1867). He was co-winner, with J. Dunant, of the first Nobel Peace Prize (1901).

Pasternak, Boris Leonidovich 1890–1960. Russian author. Pasternak's *Doctor Zhivago* won the

Nobel Prize for Literature (1958) but declined the award in condemnation of Russian Communists. Threatened with exile, he was forced into seclusion.

Pasteur, Louis 1822–95. French chemist and microbiologist, best known for developing the pasteurization process, which bears his name. Pasteur began the work for which he became famous in 1848 when, at the request of a winemaker, he investigated fermentation. He proved that the process involves living microorganisms, and that a certain type, which could be killed by slow heating, caused wine to sour during aging. This was the first use of what became the widely used pasteurization process. Pasteur disproved the theory of spontaneous generation by discovering that dust in the air contains living organisms, which reproduce even in closed containers, and saved the French silk industry by discovering the organism that infected the worms. His work in disease prevention resulted in serums for inoculating sheep against anthrax, fowl against chicken cholera (1881), and most important of all, humans against rabies (1882). As a result of his work, Pasteur developed the germ theory of disease, one of the most important medical theories of all time. The French Pasteur Institute was established (1888) to continue his research.

Paston Letters Correspondence and documents of the English Paston family written during the 15th cent. They are valuable sources of information about English society during that period.

Pastor, Tony (˜, Antonio) 1837–1908. American theater impresario. Pastor helped make vaudeville a respectable family entertainment. Among his star performers were Lillian Russell and Weber and Fields.

Pastry War Brief struggle (1838–39) between France and Mexico over the damages suffered by a French pastrycook during Mexico's civil disturbances. Mexico's refusal to make amends resulted in the French blockade of Vera Cruz and bombardment of San Juan de Ulúa (Oct. 27, 1838). By a treaty (Mar. 9, 1839), Mexico agreed to pay French claims.

Patagonia Located primarily in Argentina, a semi-arid plateau in the southernmost part of South America.

Patay, Battle of Important French victory (June 18, 1429) during the Hundred Years' War (1337–1453). Amid the general French offensive inspired by Joan of Arc, a French force under La Hire surprised and routed some 5,000 English troops under John Talbot, earl of Shrewsbury. This battle, fought at Patay in north-central France, led to the French victory in the north and made possible the crowning of Charles VII at Rheims a month later.

Patel, Vallabhbhai 1875–1950. Indian statesman. A nationalist under M. Gandhi, he took part in organizing the nonviolent demonstrations against British rule and in arranging the independence and partition of British India. He was first deputy minister of independent India (1947–50); his organizational skills were important in molding the diverse elements of India into a unified state.

Pater, Walter Horatio 1839–94. English critic and essayist noted for his devotion to ideal form and beauty, and the technical mastery of his literary style. Among his works are *Studies in the History of the Renaissance,* and *Marius the Epicurean.*

Paterson, William 1658–1719. Scottish financier. He founded and directed the Bank of England (1694–95). He formulated the ill-fated Darien Scheme (*q.v.*).

Pathé, Charles 1863–1957. French film executive. Pathé introduced T. Edison's kinetoscope to French theater audiences and pioneered (1909) the use of newsreels and screen magazines.

Pathet Lao (˜ Country) Laotian Communist political and military organization. Formed in 1950, the group fought the French in the 1950s, later participated in a Laotian coalition government, and, from 1961, fought a bitter civil war against the US–backed Laotian government. With the withdrawal of US forces from Southeast Asia, the Laotian government forces surrendered and the Pathet Lao took control (1975).

Pathfinder, the *See* **Frémont, John Charles.**

Paton, Alan Stewart 1903–88. South African writer and statesman. He wrote *Cry the Beloved Country* about his country's racial problems and helped organize the Liberal party (1953) to oppose apartheid.

patriarch Religious title. The term first referred to such early Old Testament fathers as Abraham, Isaac, Jacob, etc. The word was later used to denote bishops with jurisdiction over other bishops. The early Christian church recognized three original patriarchates, or administrative divisions: Rome, Antioch, and Alexandria. The patriarchates of Constantinople and Jerusalem were added in the 4th and 5th cents.

patricians Members of the Roman upper class, determined by birth. The patricians represented the wealthy, educated, privileged classes of ancient Rome. For many years only they could hold public office. By the 3rd cent. BC, however, this distinction between the patricians and the plebeians was eliminated. Members of the new ruling aristocracy, composed of both patricians and office-holding plebeians, were called nobiles.

Patrick, Saint AD c385–461. Christian missionary and saint. Though much of his life is shrouded in legend, Patrick is credited with converting the Irish from paganism to Christianity. Thus he is called the Apostle of Ireland.

Patrimony of Saint Peter *See* **Papal States.**

patronage *See* **spoils system.**

patroon system *See* **Antirent War.**

Patterson, Eleanor Medill (Gizycka, ~ M.) 1884–1948. American editor, newspaper publisher, and writer. Among the newspapers she had an interest in were the *Chicago Tribune* and the *New York Daily News.*

Patterson, Joseph Medill 1879–1946. American newspaper publisher. In 1919 Patterson founded the *New York Daily News,* the first successful American tabloid.

Patton, George Smith, Jr. 1885–1945. American general, noted tank corps commander during WW II. A controversial figure, he took part in the North Africa campaign, took Palermo (1943) in the invasion of Sicily, and led his Third Army across Europe and into Czechoslovakia. He relieved Bastogne during the Battle of the Bulge (*q.v.*).

Pauker, Ana 1890– . Rumanian Communist leader. She joined the Communist party in 1920 and was influential in the formation of the National Democratic Front (1944) and the Cominform (1947). Pauker served as Rumania's foreign affairs minister from 1947 until 1952, when she was ousted.

Paul 1901–64. Greek king (1947–64), successor to his brother, George II. During his reign, Greece maintained a pro-Western stance and resisted Communist attempts to take over the country.

Paul I 1754–1801. Russian emperor (1796–1801), successor to his mother, Catherine II. On gaining the throne, he reversed many of his mother's reforms, alienated the nobility by tak-

ing steps to centralize power and, by his inconsistent foreign policy, managed to isolate Russia during the period of the French Revolutionary Wars. He was assassinated Mar. 23, 1801.

Paul II (Barbo, Pietro) 1417–71. Italian-born pope (1464–71), successor to Pius II. He quarreled with French King Louis XI over the Pragmatic Sanction of Bourges (*q.v.*) and vigorously opposed Bohemian King George of Podebrad for his toleration of the Hussites. Paul was also a noted patron of the arts.

Paul III (Farnese, Alessandro) 1468–1549. Italian-born pope (1534–49), successor to Clement VII. He sanctioned (1540) the Society of Jesus (Jesuits), initiated the Catholic Reformation (*q.v.*), and called the Council of Trent (1545). He was a noted patron of the arts.

Paul IV (Carafa, Gian Pietro) Italian-born pope (1555–59). Though he succeeded in curtailing church corruption, his extreme orthodoxy and mishandling of political issues during his pontificate did little to advance the cause of the church. He organized the Roman Inquisition and thereby instituted a reign of terror, provoked war between France and the Spanish Habsburgs, denounced the religious accommodation of the Peace of Augsburg (*q.v.*), and instituted the Jewish ghetto in Rome (1555).

Paul V (Borghese, Camillo) 1552–1621. Italian-born pope (1605–21). He put Venice under a papal interdict (1606), though he ultimately lost his attempt to assert papal power there. He also had disputes with the French over Gallicanism (*q.v.*) and the English over King James I's oaths of allegiance to the crown.

Paul VI (Montini, Giovanni Battista) 1897–1978. Italian-born pope (1963–78), successor to John XXIII. Paul continued the Second Vatican Council, begun by John XXIII. But his reaffirmation of the traditional ban on birth control sparked dissension within the church.

Paul, Saint *d.* AD 67. Christian missionary and saint. Originally a Pharisee called Saul of Tarsus, he persecuted Christians until a vision and a miracle converted him. He then became a zealous missionary to the Gentiles and a founder of many churches. His epistles (letters) to his followers are included in the New Testament. He is believed to have been executed in Rome by Nero. His writings greatly influenced subsequent church doctrine.

Paulicians Heretical Christian sect. Centered mostly in Asia Minor (7th–11th cents.), they were gnostic and dualistic in doctrine, and rejected the authority of the Old Testament.

Pauling, Linus Carl 1901– . American biochemist. Pauling won a Nobel Prize in Chemistry (1954) for his theory of chemical bonding and a Nobel Peace Prize (1962) for his opposition to nuclear warfare, making him the first sole recipient of two Nobel prizes. His researches cover a wide range, including investigations into protein structure, antibodies, genetic diseases, inorganic complexes, and crystal structures.

Paullus, Aemilius (Paulus, ˜) c229–169 BC. Roman general and consul during the Third Macedonian War. Paullus conquered the Inguani people of Liguria and later defeated Perseus of Macedonia (168 BC) at the Battle of Pydna, thereby ending the Macedonian War.

Paul of Aegina 7th cent. AD. Alexandrian physician whose great work was a compilation of the medical knowledge of his day.

Paul of Samosata *fl.* AD 260–272. Christian theologian who evolved a theory of monarchianism. He denied the Trinity and held that Jesus was but a mortal man empowered by God. His teachings were subsequently condemned by the church.

Paul the Deacon c725–799? Lombard priest and historian whose history of the Lombards is a valuable source of information about this Germanic people.

Paulus, Aemilius *See* **Paullus, Aemilius.**

Pausanias *d.* c466 BC. Spartan general. He was the victorious commander (479) at the Battle of Plataea (*q.v.*) during the Persian Wars. Later charged with fomenting a scheme to take power in Sparta, he took sanctuary in the temple of Athena, where he was left to starve to death.

Pausanias *fl.* AD 174. Greek geographer. His *Descriptions of Greece* is an important source of information on ancient Greek culture and topography.

Pavia, Battle of 1. Battle (AD 476) in which the German chieftain Odoacer (*q.v.*) defeated the forces defending the last Western Roman emperor Romulus Augustus, at Pavia (now in northern Italy). Odoacer subsequently deposed the emperor (Sept. 4, 476) and thus brought the Western Roman Empire to an end. 2. Siege of the city of Pavia (773–774), then the Lombard capital. Frankish king Charlemagne responded to requests for aid from the pope, then being threatened by the Lombards, and drove the Lombard king Desiderius within the city walls. Desiderius finally surrendered in June, 774, and Charlemagne made himself king of the Lombards. 3. Major defeat for the French (Feb. 24, 1525) during the Italian Wars (1494–1559). The French army of 28,000 soldiers, led by King Francis I, was decimated by some 23,000 troops serving Holy Roman Emperor Charles V (of the Spanish Habsburg line). Francis was captured and later forced to submit to the Treaty of Madrid (*q.v.*).

Pavlov, Ivan Petrovich 1849–1936. Russian physiologist, best known for his studies on conditioning in dogs and other animals. The son of a priest, he entered a theological college but left (1870) to pursue studies in chemistry and physiology at the University of St. Petersburg. His earliest important research concerned the circulatory system (1888–90). He began studies (1890) of the mechanisms involved in digestive secretions, which led to his discovery of the conditioned reflex, for which he became famous. By training a hungry dog to salivate at the sound of a bell (previously associated with food), Pavlov developed his theory, which took into account an unconditioned reflex (salivation), an unconditioned stimulus (food), a conditioned stimulus (the bell), and the "conditioned reflex" (salivation at the sound of the bell). He later applied his discovery to human behavior. Pavlov received the Nobel Prize in Physiology or Medicine, 1904.

Payne-Aldrich Tariff Act American protective tariff. This 1909 bill raised some tariffs on foreign imports to protect American industries. Opposition to it by farmers figured in W. Wilson's victory in the presidential election of 1912.

Paz, Octavio 1914– . Mexican poet, writer, and diplomat. A major Latin American poet, he has published collected poems, including *La estación violenta,* and essays, including *The Labyrinth of Solitude.*

Paz Estenssoro, Victor 1907– . Bolivian political leader and president (1952–56, 1960–64, and 1985–89). A founder of the National Revolutionary Movement (MNR) in 1941, he became president when the MNR took power (Apr. 1952). During his term, he instituted many sweeping reforms, including granting Indians the vote, expropriation of the tin mines, and redistribution of farmlands. He was overthrown by the military

(Nov., 1964), but returned to office again years later in 1985–89. *See also* Bolivia.

Pazzi conspiracy Abortive plot (Apr. 26, 1478) by the Pazzi family to depose Lorenzo de' Medici and family from power in Florence. The plot was backed by Pope Sixtus IV, who wanted to put his nephew in power. The conspirators wounded Lorenzo and killed his brother, Guiliano, but this action provoked a popular uprising against them. Thus the Medicis remained in power.

Peace Commission of 1778 *See* **Carlisle Commission.**

Peace Corps US agency established (1961) by the Kennedy administration. Made up primarily of young, college-age volunteers, the corps sought to improve education, agriculture, and health care in developing countries. The corps suffered recruitment and financial troubles following the Vietnam War and was absorbed (1971) by the larger agency ACTION. President R. Reagan revived the Peace Corps in 1983.

Peace of *See under names inverted, as in* **Pyrenees, Peace of the.**

Peachtree Creek, Battle of *See* **Atlanta Campaign.**

Peale, Charles Willson 1741–1827. American painter and naturalist. Peale is best known for his portraits of G. Washington and other Revolutionary-era figures.

Pea Ridge, Battle of *See* **Elkhorn Tavern, Battle of.**

Pearl Harbor Hawaiian harbor and US naval installation, located on the island of Oahu. A treaty (1887) gave the US rights to the harbor as a coaling port and the naval station was established there (1908). The harbor is best remembered, however, for the Japanese sneak attack there Dec. 7, 1941. While US–Japanese negotiations were under way in Washington, over 100 carrier-based Japanese aircraft conducted a devastating surprise attack on the harbor. With much of the US Pacific fleet moored there, Japanese bombers damaged or sank 19 ships, destroyed almost 200 airplanes, and killed over 2,000 servicemen. The raid brought a declaration of war and US entry into WW II the next day.

Pearse, Patrick Henry 1879–1916. Irish writer and patriot. Pearse promoted the use of the Gaelic language. He commanded rebel forces in the Easter Rebellion (1916) and was named president of the provisional rebel government. He was captured and executed by the British.

Pearson, Lester Bowles 1897–1972. Canadian politician. Actively involved with the UN, Pearson won a Nobel Peace Prize (1957) for his mediation of the 1956 Arab-Israeli War. He served as Canada's Liberal party prime minister (1963–68).

Peary, Robert Edwin 1856–1920. American explorer. Peary led the first expedition to reach the North Pole (Apr. 6, 1909), as well as other earlier expeditions in Greenland. His observations and writings were of considerable scientific importance in the study of arctic regions.

Peasants' Revolt Popular uprising in England (1381) over a variety of grievances, including the poll tax and the Statute of Labourers (1351), which held down wages of a work force then decimated by the plague. Led by Wat Tyler, the rebels marched on London, took the Tower of London and beheaded the archbishop of Canterbury. During a meeting (June 14, 1381) at Mile End, the rebels forced King Richard II to make concessions including an end to forced labor and restrictions on trade. Tyler was killed at London soon afterward, however, and the revolt collapsed. Richard then rescinded the Mile End concessions.

Peasants' War Revolt (1524–26) by the peasants and townsmen in southern Germany and Austria against the repressive policies of the nobles and clergy. Inspired in part by the Reformation and the teachings of such leaders as M. Luther and H. Zwingli, the peasants and poor townspeople formed armies to force religious and political concessions demanded by such rebel leaders as T. Munzer. Luther denounced the movement, and it was ruthlessly crushed (May 1525) in Germany. In Austria the disorders lasted until 1526.

Pease, Edward *See* **Fabian Society.**

Pecci, Gioacchino *See* **Leo XIII.**

Pedersen, Knut *See* **Hamsun, Knut.**

Pedrarias *See* **Arias de Ávila, Pedro.**

Pedro *See also* **Peter.**

Pedro I 1798–1834. First emperor of Brazil (1822–31) and king of Portugal (1826). Pedro declared Brazilian independence from Portugal (Sept. 7, 1822) and accepted a liberal constitution (1824). In 1826, following the death of his father, Portugal's King John VI, he was named king of Portugal in 1826 as Pedro IV, but resigned that year in favor of his daughter Maria II. Later forced to abdicate in Brazil to his son, Pedro II, he returned to Portugal (1831). There he ousted his brother King Miguel and restored Maria II to power (1834).

Pedro II 1825–91. Emperor of Brazil (1831–89), successor to his father, Pedro I. A man of great learning, he worked for reform. The abolition of slavery in Brazil, effected with his support in 1888, was widely opposed by landowners. A republic was declared (Nov. 15, 1889) and he died in exile.

Peel, Sir Robert 1788–1850. British statesman, prime minister (1834–35, 1841–46), and founder of the Conservative party (*q.v.*). A Tory member of Parliament (from 1809) in his early years, he effected a return to the gold standard, instituted criminal law reforms, and established the London police department (called "bobbies" after him). After his first ministry fell, he saw the need for reform, issued his Tamworth Manifesto, and formed the Conservative party. During his second ministry, he introduced an income tax and repealed the Corn Laws (*q.v.*). The latter action brought down his government (1846).

Péguy, Charles 1873–1914. French poet. A noted Catholic supporter of A. Dreyfus, Péguy combined religious and Socialist thought. Among his works are *Le Mystère de la charit de Jeanne d' Arc* (1909) and *Eve* (1913).

Pehlevi *See* **Pahlavi.**

Pei, I. M. 1917– . Chinese-born American architect. Pei studied with W. Gropius (mid-1940s) before starting to work in commercial architecture. Later, in the 1960s, he became known for his large-scale redevelopment and urban renewal projects. Pei designed such buildings as the John F. Kennedy Memorial Library in Boston (completed 1979) and the East Wing of the National Gallery of Art in Washington, D.C. (1979). His work gained him a worldwide reputation.

Peiping *See* **Beijing.**

Peipus, Battle of Lake (Battle of Lake Chudskoye) Decisive battle (1242) between the Russians, led by Prince Alexander Nevski of Novgorod, and the Livonian knights. The invading army of Germanic knights, attempting the conquest of Novgorod, were attacked and defeated by Alexander in a battle fought on the ice-covered Lake Peipus.

Peirce, Charles Sanders 1839–1914. American philosopher. Peirce founded the school of Pragmatism (*q.v.*), later developed by W. James. He regarded logic as the keystone of all philosophy and knowledge.

Peking *See* **Beijing.**

Peking, Treaty of *See* **Beijing, Treaty of.**

Pelagianism Christian heresy (5th cent.) as taught by the British monk Pelagius (AD c354–420?). It held that people can choose good over evil and that there is no original sin, which eliminated the need for baptism. This was in opposition to Saint Augustine's claims for the necessity of grace for salvation, and Pelagius was excommunicated (418).

Pelagius *See* **Pelagianism.**

Pelagius I *d.* 561. Italian-born pope (556–61), successor to Vigilius. Pelagius opposed Emperor Justinian's edict (544) against Nestorianism. Reconciled with Justinian, he then became pope.

Pelopidas *d.* 364 BC. Theban general. Pelopidas recovered Thebes from Spartan control (379 BC), commanded the elite Theban corps, the Sacred Band, at Leuctra and in other battles. He later served with Epaminondas.

Peloponnesian League Confederation of Greek city-states organized and dominated by Sparta (6th cent. BC) as a military alliance.

Peloponnesian War, First *See* **Greece** (461–445 BC).

Peloponnesian War (second ~) (Great ~) War (431–404 BC) between Sparta and Athens (and respective allied city-states) for control of Greece. Before the war Sparta held sway over most of the city-states of inland Greece (through the Peloponnesian League), while Athens controlled the Delian League, a maritime empire extending out over the Aegean. Sparta had a superior land army and Athens had a powerful navy. The two city-states had long been rivals and the intricate system of alliances with other city-states meant that even local conflicts could erupt into a general war. Though Athens entered the war with the riches of the Delian treasury to support its war effort, Sparta ultimately emerged victorious. Athens never regained its former power, and Sparta for a time became the undisputed power in ancient Greece. Key dates in the Peloponnesian War include:

435 BC Dispute between Corcyra and Corinth broke out; Corinthians defeated at the Battle of Leucimne.

433 BC Corcyra formed a defensive alliance with Athens as Corinth, a Spartan ally, prepared to attack.

433 BC Corinthians attacked and Corcyreans were saved from defeat by Athenian intervention; Athenians forced the Corinthians to relinquish control of a colony, Potidaea.

432 BC Trade embargo against Megarians further antagonized members of Sparta's Peloponnesian League (432 BC); Athens accused of breaking Thirty Years' Peace; Sparta reluctantly declared war.

431–421 BC Archidamian War, the opening phase of the war; Athenians planned to avoid land war (by remaining inside city walls) while using their navy to disrupt commerce and raid coastal towns of Peloponnesian League; Sparta planned to invade Attica each year to provoke Athenians to land battle.

431 BC Spartans advanced into Attica.

430 BC Revolt by Potidaea put down by Athenians.

430–428 BC Plague swept Athens, decimating the population and killing the Athenian leader Pericles; Cleon succeeded.

428 BC Athenians suppressed rebellion on Lesbos.

425 BC Athenians occupied Pylos.

424–422 BC Spartans led by Brasidas conquered Amphipolis and other cities in the north (424 BC); Athens decisively defeated in attempt to regain Amphipolis, and both Cleon and Brasidas died.

421 BC Nicias succeeded as ruler of Athens, secured short-lived truce (Peace of Nicias) marking end of first phase of conflict.

418 BC Battle of Mantineia; Sparta victorious over Mantineia, an Athenian ally.

415 BC Alcibiades contested Nicias' rule in Athens; convinced Athenians to mount campaign against the rich city of Syracuse (in Sicily) to resolve local dispute; massive Athenian fleet assembled, to be led by Alcibiades, Nicias, and Lamachus.

415 BC Alcibiades recalled to Athens after the fleet sailed to answer charges of sacrilege; fled to Sparta and helped them against Athens; Nicias in sole command of expedition against Syracuse.

415–413 BC Syracuse decisively defeated Athenians, led by Nicias; staggering losses seriously weakened Athens.

412 BC Alcibiades returned to Athens with (false) promises of Persian aid to Athens, if Athens will agree to change its constitution; led to general uprising and establishment of the Four Hundred, an oligarchy, in Athens (411).

410 BC Alcibiades, having rejoined Athenians at Samos, defeated Spartan fleet at Cyzicus.

407 BC Spartan navy, led by Lysander, defeated Athenian fleet at Notium; led to final exile of Alcibiades from Athens.

406 BC Athenian fleet defeated the Spartans in the Battle of Arginusae.

405 BC Spartans destroyed the Athenian navy at the Battle of Aegospotami, the closing naval battle of the war.

405–404 BC Spartans laid siege to Athens by land and by sea; Athens forced to surrender but was spared total destruction by the Spartans, who confined themselves to tearing down its defensive walls; Delian League broken up and government of the Thirty Tyrants imposed on Athens.

Peloponnesus Peninsula of Greece forming the southern part of the country. It is almost completely separated from mainland (central) Greece by the Gulf of Corinth. In ancient times, its major cities included Sparta and Corinth. The region was also called Morea.

Pemberton, John *See* **Big Black River, Battle of.**

Pembroke, William Marshal, 1st earl of *d.* 1219. English nobleman. He served under the English kings Henry II, Richard I, and John. As regent for Henry III, he ended (1217) the barons' revolt begun when King John revoked the Magna Carta.

penal laws General term for the body of English laws promulgated in the 16th and 17th cents. against Roman Catholics in Britain and Ireland. An outgrowth of the English Reformation, penal laws included acts that denied Catholics the right to worship, hold public office, vote, and own land. Many of the acts were passed during the reigns of Henry VIII and Elizabeth I. The laws were overturned by the Catholic Emancipation Act (1829) and other subsequent acts.

Pendergast, Thomas Joseph 1872–1945. American politician. Pendergast virtually ruled the Democratic party in Missouri and aided the early career of H. Truman. His power was broken by a tax-evasion conviction (1938) and subsequent imprisonment.

Pendleton Civil Service Act US law (Jan. 16, 1883) passed to end political influence and corruption in the hiring of federal government workers. Public pressure for reform had been mounting for some years. After the assassination (1881) of President J. Garfield (by a disgruntled office-seeker), this act, sponsored by Senator George H. Pendleton of Ohio (1825–89), was passed. The act established civil service exams and hiring by merit and created the Civil Service Commission.

Peninsular Campaign Unsuccessful attempt (1862) by Union forces to take Richmond, Virginia, during the American Civil War. Gen. G. McClellan landed his troops on the peninsula between the York and James rivers (Apr. 1862). McClellan, with about 100,000 men, planned to lay siege to Yorktown, the center of Confederate lines across the peninsula. However, Confederate Gen. J. Johnston withdrew (May 3) toward Richmond, and Union armies advanced to positions around White House Landing (May 16), some twenty miles from Richmond. With his forces occupying both sides of the Chickahominy River, McClellan awaited the arrival of I. McDowell, who was to march south overland from Fredericksburg. But Gen. Stonewall Jackson, leading only 18,000 troops, blocked McDowell's forces in the Shenandoah Valley and after defeating them at Winchester, forced McDowell to withdraw back across the Potomac (May 24). On May 31, Gen. Johnston unsuccessfully attacked the south wing of McClellan's forces at Seven Pines (*q.v.*) and he was seriously wounded. Finally, R. E. Lee launched attacks on Union lines for seven straight days (the Seven Days' Battles), striking at Mechanicsville (June 26), Gaines's Mill (June 27), Savage's Station (June 29), Frayser's Farm (June 30), and Malvern Hill (July 1). McClellan withdrew his forces (July 11) soon after, suffering some 16,000 casualties to almost 21,000 for the Confederates.

Peninsular War Series of military campaigns (1808–14) conducted by British, Portuguese, and Spanish forces against the French in the Iberian Peninsula during the Napoleonic Wars. The Peninsular War was prompted by the French invasion of Portugal (Nov. 1807) following Portugal's refusal to join Napoleon's Continental System (*q.v.*). The French army, under Andoche Junot (1771–1813), forced Portuguese king John VI to flee to Brazil. Meanwhile, French forces under J. Murat invaded Spain and occupied Madrid (Mar. 23, 1808). Spanish King Charles IV had been deposed, and the new ruler, King Ferdinand VII, was in turn deposed by Napoleon. A rebellion in Madrid (May 2) was ruthlessly crushed by Murat, and Napoleon named his brother J. Bonaparte king of Spain (June 15). In August a British army landed in Portugal. Under A. Wellesley (later duke of Wellington), the British defeated the French at Vimeiro (Aug. 21), forcing Junot to negotiate the convention of Cintra (Aug. 30), by which the French agreed to evacuate Portugal with British assistance. The British then invaded Spain. They were led by Sir J. Moore. Napoleon returned to Spain and seized Madrid in December, and the French, under Marshal N. Soult, forced Moore's retreat. The British were evacuated at Coruña (Jan. 16, 1809) after a fierce battle in which Moore fell mortally wounded. Saragossa was taken by the French (Feb. 21, 1809). In April, Wellesley again forced the French out of Portugal and invaded Spain. He defeated the French at Talavera (July 28), but was again forced back into Portugal. The contest continued back and forth until 1812, when Wellesley defeated the French at Salamanca (July 22, 1812) and occupied Madrid for several months. Assuming command of all allied forces in the area, Wellesley again defeated the French at Vitoria (June 21, 1813) and began the invasion of France. The British put Bayonne under siege and defeated the French at Toulouse (Apr. 10, 1814). The Peninsular War came to an end with Napoleon's abdication (Apr., 1814).

Penn, William 1644–1718. English religious leader and founder of Pennsylvania. A Quaker, he obtained rights to Pennsylvania (1681), intending to establish a colony based on religious and political freedom. He planned Philadelphia, visited the area, and established friendly relations with the Indians.

Pennsylvania Middle Atlantic state of the US, the 2nd state. Sweden formed the first settlement on Tinicum Island in 1643, but the Dutch (1655) and then the English (1664) took control of the region. The Quaker W. Penn was granted a royal charter in 1681 and established a liberal government guaranteeing religious freedom. Pennsylvania played an important role in the American Revolution and Philadelphia was the center of the new US government (1790–1800). A boundary dispute with Maryland was settled with agreement on the Mason-Dixon line (1784). Pennsylvania became a state in 1787 and adopted its constitution in 1873.

Penry, John 1559–93. Welsh Puritan. He was convicted and executed for writing (under the pseudonym Martin Marprelate) Puritan tracts that caused the Marprelate Controversy (*q.v.*).

Pentapolis In ancient times a group of five city-states.

Pentateuch *See* **Moses.**

Pentecostal churches Protestant fundamentalist churches that profess baptism with the Holy Spirit, a religious experience that may endow one with the ability to prophesy, speak in tongues, or heal by faith.

People's Budget *See* **Lloyd George, David, 1st earl of Dwyfor.**

People's Charter *See* **Chartism.**

People's Council *See* **Volksraad.**

People's Republic of China *See* **China.**

Pepi I *fl.* c2343?–C2294 BC. Ancient Egyptian ruler of the 6th dynasty. He built many monuments and increased trade with the Levant.

Pepi II *fl.* c2294–c2200 BC. Ancient Egyptian king, successor to his father, Pepi I. His reign, the longest in recorded history, was apparently about 94 years. He built a pyramid at Saqqara, near Cairo.

Pepin I *d.* 838. King of Aquitaine (817–838). The son of Louis the Pious, he joined his brother Charles the Bald in wars against their father.

Pepin of Herstal *d.* 714. Mayor of the palace and de facto ruler of the Franks (687–714). He became mayor of the palace (680) of the Frankish kingdom of Austrasia and subsequently defeated the mayor of the palace of Neustria (687). Though he kept the Neustrian king on the throne, Pepin was effectively ruler of both states. He was father of Charles Martel and grandfather of Charlemagne.

Pepin of Landen *See* **Carolingians.**

Pepin the Short 714?–768. First Carolingian king of the Franks (751–768). He and his brother Carloman succeeded their father, Charles Martel. Pepin ruled Neustria as mayor of the palace under Childeric III, who was then nominal king of all Franks. When Carloman retired to

a religious life Pepin forced Childeric into a monastery, and had himself crowned (751) as king of the Franks. In return for papal consent to his crowning, he protected Rome from the Lombards and turned over conquered Italian territories (including the Exarchate of Ravenna) to the pope in what is called the Donation of Pepin (756). These lands formed the basis for the Papal States.

Pepys, Samuel 1633–1703. English administrator and famous diarist. His diary (1660–69) provided a vivid account of the English Restoration society and politics.

Pequot War War (1636–37) between British colonists and Pequot Indians in Connecticut. Friction between colonists and Indians had been building for some years and the murder (1636) of a colonist on Block Island was blamed on the Indians. In retaliation, the colonial militia and their Indian allies raided and burned the Pequot settlement at Mystic, Connecticut, and slaughtered almost all its 600 inhabitants. The few survivors were hunted down and likewise killed.

Percier, Charles *See* **Fontaine, Pierre François Léonard.**

Percy, Algernon, 10th earl of Northumberland 1602–68. English statesman. Percy attempted to reconcile Charles I with the Parliament. Though he eventually supported Parliament in the English Civil War, he opposed Charles's execution.

Percy, Henry, 1st earl of Northumberland 1342–1408. English nobleman. Percy assisted Henry IV in ousting Richard II. However, he later joined with his son Henry (Hotspur) Percy in an attempt to overthrow Henry (1403).

Percy, Sir Henry (Hotspur) 1366–1402. English nobleman. With his father, Henry Percy, 1st earl of Northumberland, he helped bring Henry IV to power and later distinguished himself in battle against the Scots. He fell out with Henry, however, and joined (1403) with his father and others against Henry. He was killed in battle at Shrewsbury.

Percy, Thomas, earl of Worcester c1344–1403. English nobleman. A son of H. Percy, earl of Northumberland, he helped bring Henry IV to power. He then joined his family in revolt (1403) against Henry and was executed.

Percy, Thomas, 7th earl of Northumberland 1528–72. English nobleman. Percy, a Catholic, plotted (1569) to invade England, rescue the Catholic Mary Queen of Scots, and end the Protestant rule of Elizabeth I. The plan failed and he was beheaded.

Perdiccas d. 321 BC. Macedonian general and regent of the empire after the death (323 BC) of Alexander the Great. Perdiccas was killed by his troops while leading a military expedition into Egypt against another of Alexander's generals, Ptolemy. (*See also* Diadochi.)

Pereira, Nuno Álvares 1360–1431. Portuguese general and hero who figured in King John's victory against the Castilians at the Battle of Aljubarrota (*q.v.*).

Péreire, Isaac 1806–80. French financier and writer. He and his brother Émile established themselves as brokers in Paris, purchasing the Paris-to-St. Germain railroad (1835) and founding the Crédit Mobilier (1852), a bank that financed companies to help spur growth in the French economy. Isaac is also known for his writings on French finance and banking.

Peretti, Felice *See* **Sixtus V.**

Pérez, Antonio 1534?–1611. Spanish politician and intriguer, secretary to Spanish King Philip II. He apparently turned Philip against Juan de Escovedo, secretary to the governor of the Spanish Netherlands, and arranged Escovedo's murder. Philip later prosecuted Pérez, who escaped to the Spanish kingdom of Aragon and raised an abortive revolt (1590–91) against Philip.

Pérez de Ayala, Ramón 1880–1962. Spanish writer, one of the leading Spanish novelists of this century. His works include *Balarmino and Apolonio, The Peace of the Path,* and *Tiger Juan.*

Pérez Jiménez, Marcos 1914– . President of Venezuela (1952–58). An army colonel, he took part in the military coup of 1948, was part of the provisional government, and then became president. He ruthlessly suppressed opposition and was later convicted of corrupt practices. He was overthrown (Jan., 1958).

Perga, Apollonius of *See* **Apollonius of Perga.**

Pergamum Ancient city in northern Asia Minor, the capital of the kingdom of Pergamum and one of the greatest cultural centers of the Hellenistic civilization. Pergamum was governed by the Attalid dynasty and under them became the center of a great empire. The rulers Attalus I (*d.* 197 BC), Eumanes II (*d.* 160 BC), and Attalus II (*d.* 138 BC) allied themselves with Rome against the Seleucids and Syrians and thereby expanded the domains of Mysia to include most of Asia Minor. The city flourished as a cultural and commercial center of Asia, and a great library was founded there. Attalus III, who died (133 BC) without heirs, bequeathed Mysia to the Romans. They subsequently reorganized the kingdom into the province of Asia with Pergamum as its capital.

Peri, Jacopo 1561–c1633. Italian composer. Peri participated in writing what is generally considered the first true opera, *Dafne* (c1597). The work is now lost.

Periander d. 585 BC. Tyrant of Corinth (625–585 BC). His reign was harsh, but Corinth enjoyed commercial prosperity and a cultural flowering under his rule. He is one of the Seven Wise Men of Greece.

Pericles c495–429 BC. Athenian statesman, general, and member of the Alcmaeonidae family, who brought Athenian democracy to its fullest flowering. Pericles began his rise to power in Athens as leader of the democratic party after the ostracism of his enemy, Cimon (461). By 453, following the ostracism of his other archenemy Thucydides (son of Melesias), he became the undisputed leader of Athens. He ended war with Persia (449), asserted Athenian domination over member states of the Delian League, and arranged a 30-year truce with Sparta (446). In this period of peace, Pericles strengthened the Athenian navy, instituted reforms that strengthened the Athenian democracy, patronized the arts, and embarked on a great program of building that glorified Athens with such structures as the Parthenon and the Propylaea. He figured in events leading up to the Peloponnesian War (*q.v.*), was ousted from power soon after it began, but was restored (429) shortly before his death. He died in 430 from a plague that swept through Athens.

Perier, Casimir Pierre 1777–1832. French statesman. Perier led the opposition to Charles X, was prime minister (1831–32) to Louis Philippe, and restored order in France following the upheavals of 1830.

Perkins, Frances 1880–1965. Social reformer and US secretary of labor, the first woman cabinet member in the US government. Formerly secretary of the New York State Industrial Commission (1926–33), she was appointed secretary of labor by President F. Roosevelt in 1933. She was one of two cabinet members to remain in office through the entire Roosevelt administration and was instrumental in passage of the Social Security Act (1935) and Fair Labor Standards Act (1938).

Permanent Court of Arbitration *See* **International Court of Justice.**

Permanent Court of International Justice *See* **International Court of Justice.**

Perón, Juan Domingo 1895–1974. Argentine president (1946–55, 1973–74) and nationalist. Peron began his career in the army and became minister of war and vice-president (1945). During the early part of his presidency, he and his wife Eva were popular with the workers and were able to make many economic and political changes, in a reform program called the *peronismo*. His regime became increasingly totalitarian and anticlerical, however, and he was deposed (Sept. 1955). He lived in Spain until his brief return to power in 1973.

Perón, María Estela Martínez de (Isabel Perón) 1931– . President of Argentina (1974–76). The second wife (*m.* 1961) of J. Perón, she was his vice-president (1973–74) and succeeded him after he died in office. She was ousted by a military coup.

Perón, María Eva Duarte de (Evita) 1919–52. Argentine political leader, the wife of President J. Perón (*m.* 1945). Popular with the masses, she wielded great political power during her husband's first term. She effected many reforms, including voting rights for women.

peronismo *See* **Perón, Juan Domingo.**

Perrault, Charles 1628–1703. French poet whose collection of Mother Goose fairy tales for children is world famous. He also precipitated the great literary dispute (called the "quarrel of the ancients and moderns") with his poem *The Age of Louis the Great* (1687) in which he placed authors of his own age above the great figures of classical times.

Perry, Matthew Calbraith 1794–1858. American naval officer. Perry commanded a US naval mission that forced Japan to accept a treaty opening her ports to Western trade (1854).

Perry, Oliver Hazard 1785–1819. American naval officer and hero of the War of 1812. He defeated the British at the Battle of Lake Erie and is remembered for reporting his victory with "we have met the enemy and they are ours."

Persepolis Ancient Persian city, located in what is now southwestern Iran. Persepolis was a capital of the Achaemenid rulers. It was sacked by Alexander the Great (c331 BC).

Perseus c212–166 BC. Macedonian king (191–68 BC), successor to his father, Philip V. His attempts to restore Macedonian hegemony in Greece led to the Third Macedonian War (*q.v.*) with Rome and his defeat at the Battle of Pydna (*q.v.*). He was the last Macedonian king.

Pershing, John Joseph 1860–1948. American general. He won notable victories in the Philippines during the Spanish-American War, led the unsuccessful expedition against F. (Pancho) Villa (1916–17) in Mexico, and commanded the American Expeditionary Force (*q.v.*) during WW I.

Persia Historic empire of ancient origins centered in modern Iran and at times extending well into southwest Asia. The modern successor state to this empire is Iran. Persia began its rise to prominence in about the 7th cent. BC and by the 6th cent. BC had become the dominant power of the ancient Near Eastern world. About this time Zoroastrianism arose in Persia and centuries later became the state religion of Persia (AD 3d cent.). After the 5th cent. BC, the power and fortunes of the empire rose and fell. Persia was conquered variously, notably by the Macedonian Greeks and the Muslims and its vast domains were greatly reduced. Persia nevertheless developed a distinctive culture which drew on Greek, Muslim, and other influences. After a long period of control by Arab Muslims and Turkic peoples, Persia again emerged in the 16th cent. as an independent empire. Modernization began in the early 20th cent., and in 1935 Persia was officially renamed Iran. (For subsequent history, *see* Iran.) Key dates in the history of Persia include:

c1500 BC   Medes and Persians migrated to the Iranian plateau.

c700 BC   Achaemenes founded Persian kingdom and the Achaemenid dynasty of Persian kings; kingdom was dominated by Media until 6th cent. BC.

c628–c551 BC   Zoroaster lived; founded Zoroastrianism, which became the religion of Persia in following centuries.

c600–559 BC   Cambyses I reigned; his son was Cyrus the Great.

558–529 BC   Cyrus (the Great) reigned; established Persian dominance over Media and

Elam and greatly expanded Persian power and territory; borrowed freely from Assyrian and Babylonian cultures.

546 BC Cyrus conquered Lydia in Asia Minor.

539 BC Cyrus conquered Babylonia; Babylonian captivity of the Jews ended.

529–522 BC Cambyses II reigned; murdered his brother Smerdis to secure his power and then pursued successful campaign to conquer Egypt; a false Smerdis seized throne (522) and Cambyses died on return from Egypt.

522–486 BC Darius I (the Great) reigned after seizing power from the false Smerdis; put down revolts within the empire and reorganized domains into satrapies, or administrative districts; instituted effective communications system using horses; extended empire into northern India and ranged into Europe.

499–479 BC Persian Wars; Darius and his successor Xerxes failed in their attempt to subjugate the Greeks, though Persia continued to influence affairs of Greek city-states in subsequent years.

486–465 BC Xerxes I reigned; lost Persian Wars and fell into dissolute life at Susa; decline of empire began; Xerxes assassinated.

464–425 BC Artaxerxes I reigned; put down revolt in Egypt (460–454 BC), permitted Jews to worship at Judaea, kept Persia out of the Peloponnesian War in Greece.

405 BC Egypt successfully revolted against Persian rule.

404–359 BC Artaxerxes II reigned, rule plagued by many revolts; royal palace at Susa rebuilt.

401 BC Great rebellion by Cyrus the Younger, satrap of Asia Minor; led army against Artaxerxes II; Cyrus defeated and killed at battle of Cunaxa; famous retreat by Greek soldiers (under Xenophon) who had fought for Cyrus.

359–338 BC Artaxerxes III again subjugated Egypt (343 BC) after initial unsuccessful campaigns.

336–330 BC Darius III reigned; failed to halt advance of Alexander the Great.

334 BC Darius defeated by Macedonian Greeks under Alexander at Battle of Granicus.

333 BC Battle of Issus: Alexander again defeated Darius.

331 BC Darius decisively defeated at Battle of Gaugamela; long rule of Achaemenid dynasty ended; Darius fled to Bactria.

330 BC Darius assassinated in Bactria.

323–281 BC Wars of the Diadochi; Alexander's generals warred for control of his empire after his death; most of Persia came under Seleucid rule.

312–64 BC Seleucid dynasty, established by Seleucid I, ruled over much of ancient Persian Empire; at its height it included Babylon, Persia, Syria, Bactria, and part of Asia Minor, though control was weak and domains were gradually reduced to Syria; Seleucids introduced Hellenic (Greek) culture to Persia.

3D CENT. BC Bactria overthrew Seleucid rule; became independent kingdom.

247 BC–AD 224 Parthian Empire founded (south of Caspian Sea) by Arsaces I; after overthrowing Seleucid rule, Parthians dealt with nomadic invasions from northeast and successfully blocked eastward advance of Romans; Parthians pushed their empire westward to Mesopotamia.

64 BC Last of Seleucid domains (Syria) conquered by Romans under Pompey; Persia (proper) under Parthian rule.

3D CENT AD Spread of Manichaeism, religious sect based on teachings of Mani.

AD 224–640 Sassanid dynasty reigned in Persia; empire at its greatest extent reached Indus Valley in east and Mesopotamia in west; Persian culture flourished, many buildings and roads constructed.

AD 226–241 Ardashir I reigned; established Zoroastrianism as state religion; built many cities.

AD 241–272 Shapur I reigned; a successful conqueror, he gained parts of Asia Minor and in wars with Rome took Syria and part of Mesopotamia; captured Emperor Valerian.

AD 293–302 Narses reigned; lost substantial territory to the Roman Empire.

AD 309–379 Shapur II reigned; regained much of the territory lost to the Romans by Narses.

AD 399–420 Yazdegerd I reigned; Christians in Persian domains persecuted.

531–579 Khosru I reigned; Sassanid Empire brought to its greatest extent through successful wars against Byzantines (in time of Justinian and Justin II); reformed administration; literature flourished.

590–628 Khosru II reigned; warred against the Byzantines; initially successful, he occupied Egypt and threatened Constantinople;

defeated by the Byzantine Heraclius (622–628).

632–651 Yazdegerd III, last Sassanian ruler, reigned; Persian Empire conquered by the Arabs and absorbed into the Caliphate; Islam introduced into region in place of Zoroastrianism.

819–999 Samanid dynasty in power, native Persian dynasty ruling over Transoxania and Khorasan (in northeast Iran) under nominal control of the Muslim caliphs; Persian culture flourished; Saffaarid dynasty ruled in eastern Iran at about this time.

c940–1020 Firdausi, Persian poet, flourished; wrote *Book of Kings*.

945–1055 Bũyid dynasty ruled over western Iran and Iraq; Buyid state reached its height c980.

999–1186 Ghaznavid dynasty reigned; this Turkish dynasty took control of much of Samanid Empire (west of river Oxus) and extended empire eastward, eventually embracing Afghanistan and part of India.

11TH CENT Poet, astronomer, and mathematician Omar Khayyam flourished.

11TH–14TH CENTS. Seljuks, Muslim Turks, dominated the domains of the Caliphate, including Persia.

c1126–c1189 Poet Anvari lived.

1184–1291 Sadi, mystical and lyric Persian poet, lived; wrote *Gulistan.*

c1207–73 Poet Jalal ad-Din ar-Rumi, founder of order of dervishes, lived.

13TH–16TH CENTS. Mongol conquests; Caliphate fell to the Mongols (1258); there followed a period of rule by Mongols, Timurs, and Turkmen.

1389? Poet Hafiz died; his collected poems published as the *Divan.*

1414–92 Persian poet Jami lived; considered last great Persian poet.

1501–24 Ismail reigned after establishing new Persian Empire; founded Safavid dynasty; established Shi'ite Islam as state religion.

1501–1736 Safavid dynasty in power; engaged in long series of wars with Ottoman Turks and Uzbeks.

1586–1629 Abbas I (the Great) reigned; regained Persian territories lost in wars with Ottoman Turks and Uzbeks; captured Baghdad (1623); encouraged art, trade, and public works.

1722–30 Afghan interlude; Persia under control of Afghans after being defeated by Mir Mahmud.

1724 Russia and Turkey seized portions of Persian Empire.

1730 Nadir Kuli defeated Afghans and forced them from Persia.

1736–47 Nadir Shah reigned; recaptured Persian territories from Russia and Ottoman Empire; invaded India (1738–39).

1794–97 Agha Muhammad reigned as shah; founded Kajar dynasty (ruled 1794–1925); reign noted for its cruelty and repression.

1797–1835 Fath Ali reigned as shah; power of the shah declined as both Russia and Britain sought to dominate Persia; Persia began to lose territories; signed disadvantageous treaty of Gulistan with Russia (1813).

1828 Persia ceded lands in Armenia to Russia by the Treaty of Turkmanchay, following Russo-Persian War of 1826–28.

1856–57 War with Britain; seizure of Persian lands by Afghanistan provoked war with Afghanistan; Britain interceded, defeated Persia, and forced it to recognize Afghan independence.

1863 Baha Allah, religious leader, founded Bahaism.

1901 Britain was granted oil concession; discovery of oil led to increased rivalry between Britain and Russia over Persia.

1906 Shah Muzaffar-ed-Din established first Persian majlis, or national assembly; liberal constitution drawn up.

1907–09 Muhammad Ali reigned as shah; attempted forcibly to overthrow the constitution (1909) and was deposed.

1909–25 Ahmed Shah reigned; last of the Kajar dynasty.

1914–18 WW I; Persia occupied by British and Russian forces.

1919 Persia signed agreement giving Britain control over Persia while recognizing Persian independence; agreement repudiated in 1921.

1920 Became a member of the League of Nations.

1921 British began withdrawing troops from Persia.

1921 Reza Khan became prime minister by a coup (Feb 21).

1921 Treaty with the Soviets; Soviets agreed to withdraw from Persia.

1925 Ahmed Shah deposed by majlis (Oct. 31); Prime Minister Reza Khan made shah (Dec. 13).

1925–41 Reza Shah Pahlavi reigned; began modernization and Westernization of Persia.

1935 Persia renamed Iran (Mar. 21).

Persian Gulf War Brief war in which US-led, UN-sanctioned force crushed the Iraqi army and drove it out of Kuwait (1991). The Iraqi government, saddled with some $75 billion in foreign debt from the Iran-Iraq War (1980–90), saw neighboring oil-rich Kuwait as an easy target: an opportunity to solve its money problems and to enhance its prestige as a military power. After provoking a dispute, Iraq then invaded, occupied, and began to systematically strip the country. Steadfastly refusing all subsequent diplomatic efforts aimed at ending the occupation, and ignoring UN economic sanctions, Iraq brought on fierce counterattack in early 1991 by an international force led by the US. Extensive and touted (by S. Hussein) defensive fortifications were no match for the highly mobile, high-tech armaments the US and allies brought to bear. Enjoying near-complete air superiority, the allies first bombed targets in Kuwait and Iraq and then launched ground attacks on several fronts. Iraqi forces were decimated and within days Hussein was forced to accept humiliating surrender terms. Estimates of Iraqi dead ranged from 50,000 to 100,000 troops killed; Allied losses were put at 223 dead. Key events in the war include:

1989 International concern mounting about Iraq's massive military buildup; subsequently US Congress banned weapons sales to Iraq (July, 1990).

1990 Components for huge cannon barrel, bound for Iraq, seized by customs agents in Britain.

1990 Iraqi government complained about production in excess of OPEC quotas by Kuwait and United Arab Emirates; charged Kuwait with exploiting Iraqi oil reserves along border; declared Kuwait should forgo debts owed by Iraq.

1990 Iraq organized military buildup on frontier with Kuwait as OPEC meeting began (July); Kuwait agreed to lower its oil output.

1990 Talks begun with Kuwait (July) to resolve territorial disputes and the disposition of Iraq's substantial debt to Kuwait; negotiations broke down; Iraqi forces on border now numbered 100,000.

1990 Egyptian president H. Mubarak, acting as intermediary, conveyed to Kuwait Hussein's personal assurances he was not planning an invasion.

1990–91 Iraqi forces quickly invaded (Aug. 2) and occupied Kuwait; Kuwaiti leaders fled to Saudi Arabia and set up government-in-exile; Iraq soon after began stripping the country of virtually everything that could be moved.

1990 UN adopted Resolution 660 (Aug. 2), demanding unconditional Iraqi withdrawal from Kuwait.

1990 Majority of Arab League members condemned the invasion of Kuwait (Aug. 3); however, popular demonstrations in Jordan and northwest African states favored the invasion; PLO opted to back Hussein.

1990 UN imposed economic sanctions against Iraq (Aug. 6), effectively halting export of Iraqi oil; US and British warships blockaded Iraqi ports.

1990 US began sending planes and troops to Saudi Arabia (Aug. 7) in Operation Desert Shield to help secure that country against Iraqi invasion; other nations subsequently sent military forces, creating a multi-national force to defend Saudi Arabia.

1990 Iraq established provisional government in Kuwait (Aug.).

1990 Iraq announced annexation of Kuwait (Aug. 8), claiming Kuwaiti insurgents had requested the Iraqi invasion; soon after began harassing Western diplomats in Kuwait; detained Westerners in Kuwait and Iraq.

1990 Hussein, in bid for Arab support, tried linking resolution of Kuwait invasion to withdrawal of Israelis from occupied territories and to self-rule for Palestinians (Aug. 12); US rejected any such linkage.

1990–91 UN and numerous other intermediaries unsuccessfully attempted to negotiate with Iraqis for withdrawal from Kuwait; Iraqi propaganda meanwhile called on people of Saudi Arabia and Egypt to overthrow their governments (from Sept.).

1990 Iraq held foreign citizens hostage, using them as human shields to prevent attacks on key targets; released all hostages by Dec.

1990 UN passed Resolution 678 (Nov. 29) allowing use of force to drive Iraq out if troops remained in Kuwait past Jan. 15, 1991.

1991 US military buildup in Persian Gulf completed (Jan.); US had 430,000 troops, 2,000 tanks, and 1,300 aircraft against 510,000 troops, 2,000 tanks, and 500 fighter planes for Iraq.

1991 US Congress authorized use of US troops against Iraq (Jan. 12).

1991 Operation Desert Storm commenced with night air attacks on Baghdad (Jan. 16–17); allied air force secured air superiority by end of Jan. and eventually flew over 110,000 sorties over Kuwait and Iraq.

1991 Iraq launched Scud missile attacks on Saudi Arabia and Israel (Jan.–Feb.); bid to draw Israel into war by these Scud attacks, and thereby force Arab states to withdraw from allied effort against Iraq, failed.

1991 Iraqi soldiers briefly captured Saudi border town of Ras al-Khafji (Jan.); troops from US, Saudi Arabia, and Qatar quickly retook town.

1991 Iraqis in Kuwait opened storage tanks, deliberately spilling some 4 million barrels of oil in Persian Gulf (Jan.); set Kuwaiti oil wells on fire.

1991 Iraqi government broke relations with US, UK, France, Italy, and Egypt (Feb.).

1991 Hussein accepted last-minute Soviet peace plans that did not meet UN conditions (Feb.); allies rejected the plans.

1991 US-led, allied ground offensive launched on several fronts against Iraqis (Feb. 23–24); the allies' highly mobile forces quickly rolled over extensive Iraqi defensive works, already softened up by intensive bombing attacks, and pushed deep into Iraq; 150,000 Iraqis taken prisoner.

1991 Scud missile destroyed US military barracks at Dhahran; 28 soldiers killed (Feb.).

1991 US declared ceasefire (Feb. 28); Iraq accepted all terms of UN resolutions, including renunciation of all claims to Kuwait (Mar. 3).

1991 Hussein reshuffled his cabinet in bid to remain in power after humiliating loss (Mar.);

named loyal supporters and family members to key posts.

1991 US troops withdrawn from occupied Iraqi territories (Mar.–May); US troops remained in Kuwait.

1991 US airlifted troops to northern Iraq to halt Iraqi attacks on rebellious Kurds there (May).

Persian Wars Series of military campaigns conducted by the Persians against the Greeks, beginning in 492 BC and ending in 479 BC. Some years before the wars began, the Ionian Greeks revolted against Persian rule (499). The cities of Athens and Eretria aided the Ionian Greeks, but the revolt was crushed (494) by Persian king Darius. Darius then sent a large force to punish Athens and Eretria. The Persians took Macedon and Thrace (492), but their fleet was badly damaged by storms and they were obliged to withdraw. A second expedition occupied Eretria, but while attempting to advance upon Athens, the Persians were defeated at Marathon (*q.v.*) in 490, by an Athenian force led by Miltiades and others. Darius gathered a massive third expeditionary force, but died (486) before it could move against Greece. The expedition was conducted by his son and successor, Xerxes I, who landed in Greece in 480. The Persian land force was delayed at Thermopylae (*q.v.*) by a small Spartan force under Leonidas, and although the Persians subsequently took Athens, their navy was defeated at Salamis (*q.v.*) in 480. Xerxes returned to Persia but left an army in Greece under Mardonius. The Greek victory over Mardonius at Plataea (479) and destruction of the Persian fleet at Mycale that year marked the end of Persia's military campaigns against mainland Greece. After 479, sporadic fighting between the Greeks and Persians continued until a peace was concluded (c449). The Greek victory halted Persian expansionism and ended the threat of Persian invasion.

Persius (Flaccus, Aulus Persius) AD 34–62. Roman satirical poet. Persius was a Stoic whose works attacked the loose moral standards of his day. His works, published posthumously, were a great success.

Peru (Republic of Peru) Country located in western South America. The population is 21,904,000 and the capital is Lima. Peru was the center of the vast Inca Empire conquered (16th cent.) by the Spanish. From the mid-16th cent. until Peru achieved independence, Lima was the seat of Spanish rule in South America. Peru was also a major source of silver and gold. Since independence, Peru has had a history of political instability. Key dates in Peruvian history include:

12TH CENT.   Incas, "people of the sun," settled around Cuzco.

15TH CENT.   Extensive empire carved out by the Incas; included most of Peru and Ecuador and parts of neighboring countries; centered in Cuzco.

1525–32   Huascar succeeded as Emperor of the Incas; murdered by his brother.

c1530–32   Civil war between Atahualpa and Huascar, sons of the Inca ruler Huayna Capac (ruled 1487–1525); Huascar defeated and executed by Atahualpa, who became sole ruler.

1532   Spanish conquistador F. Pizarro arrived; seized and imprisoned Atahualpa and collected a huge ransom in gold and silver.

1533   Atahualpa executed by Pizarro; Cuzco captured; Indian peoples subsequently forced to work in mines and on Spanish lands, under system called *encomienda.*

1535   Lima founded by Pizarro.

1536–44   Manco Capac, new Inca emperor, led unsuccessful revolts against the Spanish.

1537–38   Warfare between the Spanish conquerors; Pizarro defeated forces led by P. Alvarado and Diego de Almagro; Almagro executed.

1539?–1616   Historian Garcilaso de la Vega flourished.

1541   Assassination of Pizarro by supporters of Almagro.

1542   Vaca de Castro, representing the Spanish crown, restored order among the Spanish rulers.

1542   Lima made center of Spanish rule and capital of viceroyalty of Peru, eventually including all of Spanish South America except Venezuela.

1542   "New Laws for the Indies," inspired by B. de las Casas, promulgated; designed to alleviate the hardship of the forced labor imposed on the Indians by the Spanish.

1544–46   Blasco Núñez Vela served as first Spanish viceroy of Peru.

1544–48   Pizarro's brother, Gonzalo, led revolt against the New Laws; though he was defeated, the laws were subsequently not enforced.

1569–81   Francisco de Toledo served as viceroy of Peru.

1586–1617   Saint Rose of Lima, patron saint of South America, lived; first native-born American canonized.

1596–1604   L. de Velasco lived; served as Spanish viceroy of Peru.

1718   Viceroyalty of Peru reduced in size by creation of viceroyalty of New Granada.

1776   Peruvian territory further reduced by creation of the viceroyalty of Río de la Plata.

1781   Tupac Amuru's Incan revolt against Spain failed; he and his family executed.

1796–1859   W. Prescott lived; noted for his histories *The Conquest of Mexico* and *The Conquest of Peru.*

1808   Napoleon conquered Spain; led to rise of independence movements throughout South America.

1821   Peruvian independence proclaimed at Lima (July 28), though Spanish royalist forces had not yet been completely defeated.

1822   Guayaquil Conference (July); S. Bolívar took over leadership of South American independence movement from J. San Martín.

1824   Battle of Ayacucho (Dec. 9); Bolívar secured Peruvian independence by decisively defeating Spanish royalists.

1836–39   Peru and Bolivia united in a confederation; opposed by Chile, the confederation was defeated at the Battle of Yungay and broken up.

1844–62   Gen. Ramón Castilla in office as president (except 1850–55); his administration marked by economic development and stability.

1864–66   War with Spain; Spain attacked Peru after Peru failed to meet financial obligations; Spanish driven out.

1860   Republican constitution adopted.

1879   Peru's independence formally recognized by Spain.

1879–84   War of the Pacific; Peru lost valuable mineral-rich lands to Chile; government nearly bankrupt after war.

1883–1929   Tacna-Arica Controversy; prolonged territorial dispute with Chile; ultimately resolved along lines suggested by US president H. Hoover.

1908–30 Augusto Leguía in power as dictator (except 1912–19); promoted further economic development.

1911 Hiram Bingham discovered ancient Incan city of Machu Picchu.

1924 V. Haya de la Torre founded the radical APRA party.

1933–39 Gen. Oscar Benavides ruled as dictator.

1939–45 Manuel Prado y Ugarteche in office as president.

1945–48 President José Luís Bustamante y Rivero in office after first free elections in many years; overthrown by military after split with APRA party.

1948–56 Gen. Manual Odría in office.

1963–68 Fernando Belaúnde Terry in office after elections run by military.

1968 Belaúnde Terry ousted; inflation and refusal to take over American-owned oil fields blamed.

1968–75 Gen. Juan Velasco Alvarado in power; head of a revolutionary military government aiming at "democratizing" Peruvian society.

1970 50,000 people killed in earthquake in northern Peru.

1975 Military quelled rioting in Lima (Feb.) that resulted from police strike.

1975 Gen. Francisco Morales Bermúdez ousted Gen. Juan Velasco Alvarado from presidency in bloodless coup (Aug. 29).

1978 Unrest resulted from sharp rise in food prices after government imposed austerity measures (May).

1979 Peru's financial situation greatly improved by austerity measures and greater returns on exports (including oil); foreign loans repaid.

1980–85 Fernando Belaúnde Terry in office as president, ending over a decade of military rule.

1980 The Shining Path, a Maoist terrorist group led by Manuel Abimael Guzmán, began terrorist attacks that continued throughout the 1980s; attacks especially heavy in 1989–90.

1981 Strikes broke out to protest price increases and the high rate of inflation (Jan.).

1981 Cease-fire ended border clashes with Ecuador (Feb.); Peru agreed to international arbitration of dispute.

1982 Shining Path raided prison; released 250 inmates (Mar.).

1983 Eight journalists killed (Jan.); dramatic increase in assassinations and human rights abuses.

1984 Government announced a new campaign against terrorism and the drug trade (July).

1985–90 Alan García Pérez in office as president.

1986 Shining Path members held in three prisons around Lima rebelled (June); 254 inmates killed.

1986 APRA candidates gained control of almost all municipalities in local elections (Nov.); the campaign was marked by increasing attempts by Shining Path to disrupt elections.

1987 Plan to nationalize Peru's financial system abandoned amid fierce opposition.

1987 Ten more provinces were placed under direct military control as rebel activity increased.

1989–90 Economic problems, especially spiraling inflation, led to widespread discontent and wave of strikes to demand wage increases.

1989 Two police officers convicted and sentenced to prison terms (Dec.) for the deaths of more than 100 Shining Path prisoners in 1986; 76 others were found not guilty by a military court.

1990 Former Defense Minister, Gen. Enrique López Albujar, assassinated (Jan.); about 15,000 persons arrested for questioning.

1990– Alberto Fujimori in office as president.

1991 Cholera epidemic broke out in the fishing port of Chimbote.

1992 President Fujimori, responding to increased terrorist attacks, seized power (Apr.); dissolved legislature, imposed press censorship, and arrested opponents.

1992 Police captured Guzmán, leader of the Maoist guerrilla group Shining Path (Sept.).

Perugino c1445–1523. Italian painter. Perugino assisted in the decoration of the Sistine Chapel and was the teacher of Raphael.

Peruzzi, Baldassarre 1481–1536. Italian architect and painter. Peruzzi was appointed an architect of St. Peter's Cathedral after Raphael's death. He was noted for his work on the Palazzo Massini at Rome.

Pestalozzi, Johann Heinrich 1746–1827. Swiss educational reformer. Pestalozzi was concerned with the education of deprived children. His use of concrete experience, as opposed to rote learning, in teaching still influences educational theory today.

Pétain, Henri Philippe 1856–1951. French marshal. Though a hero at Verdun in WW I, Pétain collaborated with the Nazis and became head of the French Vichy government during WW II. He was imprisoned for life after the war.

Peter (Simon Peter) *d.* AD 64? Apostle, pope, and saint. According to the Bible Peter, a fisherman of Galilee, was originally known as Simon. He was chosen by Jesus to be the first leader (pope) of his disciples. After Jesus' crucifixion, Peter denied knowing him, an act that Jesus had predicted and that Peter bitterly repented. After word of Jesus' ascension to heaven, Peter actively sought converts, and is believed to have been crucified, head downward, in Rome by Nero. In the Roman Catholic church, he is considered the first pope.

Peter I (Peter the Great) 1672–1725. Russian tsar (1682–1725), successor to his father, Alexis. Peter's reign was dominated by his efforts to modernize and Westernize Russia. He brought Russia into the European sphere, created the first Russian navy, took measures to control the nobility, improved the position of women, reduced the power of the clergy, and imported Western technology. Other events of his reign included Russo-Turkish Wars, and the Northern War with Sweden (1700–21). He also created a new capital city, St. Petersburg, on the Baltic.

Peter I 1844–1921. King of Serbia (1903–18) and king of the Serbs, Croats, and Slovenes (1918–21). Peter supported a constitutional monarchy and expanded Serbian domains in the Balkan Wars (*q.v.*). His son, Alexander, was his regent from 1914.

Peter II 1648–1706. Regent (1668–83) to his mentally impaired brother King Alfonso VI and king of Portugal (1683–1706). After helping Alfonso's wife oust her husband (Nov. 1667), Peter became regent; following annulment of the queen's marriage (1668), he married her. Peter concluded the Treaty of Lisbon (1668), by which Spain recognized Portugal's independence, and failed in his attempt to keep Portugal out of the War of the Spanish Succession.

Peter II 1715–30. Tsar of Russia (1727–30), successor to Catherine I. Only 11 at his accession, he was manipulated by the Dolgoruki family. They arranged the arrest of Catherine's former adviser, A. Menshikov, and moved the capital (1728) to Moscow.

Peter II 1923–70. King of Yugoslavia (1934–45), successor to his father, Alexander, and Yugoslavia's last king. He fled after the Nazi invasion (1941) and while still in exile was deposed (Nov., 1945) in favor of a republic headed by Tito.

Peter III 1717–86. King of Portugal (1777–86). He was crowned with his niece, Maria I, and the two ruled jointly. Both were unfit for rule, however, and the government was run by others.

Peter III 1728–62. Tsar of Russia (1762), successor to his aunt, Elizabeth. Soon after taking power, Peter removed Russia from the Seven Years' War and alienated both the church and the nobles. His wife thereupon conspired in his overthrow (June 9, 1762) and succeeded him as Catherine II (the Great). Peter was killed a short time later.

Peter IV 1319?–87. King of Aragon (1336–87). He put down a revolt by Aragonese nobles and later revoked the privileges granted to them by Alfonso III.

Peter V 1837–61. King of Portugal (1853–61), successor to Maria II. He promoted education and the beginnings of industrialization (Portugal's first telegraph line and first railway were completed in 1856). His reign was troubled by epidemics of cholera and yellow fever.

Peter Lombard c1100–c1160. Italian bishop and theologian. Lombard wrote the *Books of Sentences,* a compilation of early Christian theology that dealt primarily with the nature of the sacraments.

Peterloo Massacre Demonstration that was suppressed at St. Peter's field, in England (Aug. 16, 1819). Some 60,000 demonstrators, petitioning for parliamentary reform and repeal of the Corn Laws (*q.v.*), were dispersed by a cavalry charge. The action killed six and injured more than 400.

Peters, Carl *See* **Tanganyika.**

Petersburg Campaign Concluding action of the American Civil War, fought (June, 1864–Apr. 1865) at Petersburg, Virginia. After the Battle of Cold Harbor, Gen. U. Grant maneuvered around Confederate lines for an attack on Petersburg, which defended the nearby Confederate capital of Richmond. Grant's advance elements were stalled by a small Confederate force under Gen. P. Beauregard, giving Gen. R. Lee time to move up his troops. The battle for Petersburg thereupon degenerated into a long siege and months of grueling trench warfare. Outnumbered, short of supplies and plagued by desertions, the Confederates held out for ten months before their resistance was broken. After their victory at the Battle of Five Forks (q.v.), the Union armies finally breached Confederate lines the next day (Apr. 2). Gen. Lee began his retreat along the Appomattox River that night and the Union forces took both Petersburg and Richmond (Apr. 3). Lee was forced into final surrender at Appomattox Courthouse (q.v.) on Apr. 9.

Peter the Cruel 1334–69.   King of Castile and León (1350–69). Peter was frequently challenged by his illegitimate half-brother Henry of Trastamara, who finally defeated and killed him.

Peter the Great   *See* **Peter I.**

Peter the Hermit c1050–1115.   French religious leader. By his preaching, he won over thousands to the First Crusade (q.v.) and led one of the ill-equipped bands of zealous citizens to Byzantium. His followers were largely wiped out in the early stages of fighting in Asia Minor.

Petite Chouannerie   *See* **Chouans.**

Petition of Right   English parliamentary document (May, 1628), a part of the power struggle between Charles I and Parliament. It was intended to stop abuses of royal power and demanded an end to arbitrary arrest and imprisonment, the quartering of soldiers in civilian homes, taxation without parliamentary approval, and the use of martial law in peacetime. Charles reluctantly agreed to it (June, 1628) in return for money grants he needed to prosecute his foreign wars, then promptly violated it. Nevertheless, the petition is important in English constitutional law.

Petőfi, Sándor 1822–49.   Hungarian poet and national hero. Petőfi's many patriotic poems encouraged the Hungarian revolt (1848). He apparently died in battle during the revolt.

Petra   Ancient city, located in what is now Jordan. Once the capital of the Nabataeans, it was taken by the Romans in AD 106. The city nevertheless continued as a trade center until the rise of Palmyra displaced it.

Petrarch, Francesco (Petrarca, ˜) 1304–74.   Italian Renaissance poet and scholar, Petrarch was one of the greatest scholars and lyric poets of his age and proved to be a major influence in spreading Greek ideals, humanism, and other elements of early Renaissance thought. His sonnets, songs, and madrigals in honor of Laura, his ideal woman, greatly influenced Renaissance poetry.

Petrie, Sir William Matthew Flinders 1853–1942.   British archaeologist. Petrie developed many archaeological research techniques and founded what became the British School of Archaeology in Egypt (1894). He conducted important excavations in Egypt (notably at Memphis), Palestine, and elsewhere.

Petronius (˜ Arbiter) *d.* AD c66.   Roman satirist. His self-indulgent love of luxury made him social arbiter at Nero's court. He is believed to have written *Satyricon,* which humorously depicted the vulgar sensuality of his times.

Petrović, George   *See* **Karageorge.**

phalanx   Greek infantry formation. A phalanx consisted of parallel rows (usually eight) of soldiers in a solid block. It was used with great success for many centuries by the Greeks. The Romans, however, overcame the Greek phalanxes in the Macedonian Wars.

Phansigars   *See* **Thugs.**

Pharaoh   Title of Egyptian kings. The title, meaning "the great house," was bestowed on all kings of ancient Egypt from the time of the New Kingdom.

Pharisees   Ancient Jewish religious and political party that began in the 2d cent. BC. Pharisees emphasized strict observance of the oral as well as the written laws (the Torah), as opposed to their opponents, the Sadducees, who taught only the written law. Reference to them in the New Testament as hypocrites pertains only to those who did not live up to their own strict standards. The Pharisees disappeared after destruction of the Temple (AD 70), but both Orthodox Judaism and Christianity were influenced by their beliefs.

Pharsalus, Battle of   Decisive victory (Aug. 9, 48 BC) for J. Caesar over his rival Pompey at this Greek town in Thessaly. Caesar's force of 20,000 was outnumbered more than two to one, but his tactical genius turned the tide. Pompey had some 15,000 casualties while Caesar's army suffered about 1,200. Pompey fled to Egypt, where he was murdered. This eliminated Caesar's most powerful opponent to his seizing of power in Rome.

Pheidias *See* **Phidias.**

Pheidon *fl.* c670? BC   King of Argos in ancient Greece. Pheidon briefly united the northeast Peloponnese under his rule and is also said to have seized Olympia (672? BC). He introduced a system of measurement used in Argos and elsewhere, but claims that he was responsible for minting the first coins in mainland Greece are apparently unfounded (coins probably appeared in late 7th cent. BC).

phenomenology   Philosophical school developed by E. Husserl. Its followers attempted to suspend preconceived notions about the natural world in order to understand and describe events (phenomena) from within the conscious mind. Phenomenology influenced the development of existentialism.

Phidias (Pheidias) c500–c432 BC.   Famed Athenian sculptor. Phidias was in charge of art and public works in Athens under Pericles. Phidias is believed to have been in charge of sculptures for the Parthenon (*q.v.*) and to have executed three noted statues of Athena and one of Zeus at Olympia.

Philadelphia Convention *See* **Constitutional Convention.**

Philadelphus, Ptolemy II *See* **Ptolemy II.**

Philaret, Vasily Drosdov *See* **Edict of Emancipation.**

Philby, Harold Adrian Russell (Kim Philby) 1912–88.   British intelligence officer who doubled as a Soviet spy (1933–51). As secretary of the British embassy in Washington (1949–1951) he dispatched to the USSR vital information concerning military movements and the US Central Intelligence Agency. In 1963 he escaped to the Soviet Union, eventually becoming a colonel in the KGB.

Philip   Name of two saints of the early Christian Church: Philip the Apostle of Jesus, and Philip who was a deacon and evangelist in Samaria and Ethiopia.

Philip (˜ the Arabian) AD 204?–249.   Roman emperor (244–49). A soldier under Gordian III, Philip executed him, made himself emperor, and ended war with Persia. He presided over the millennial celebration of the founding of Rome. He was overthrown by one of his soldiers, Decius.

Philip (Metacomet) *d.* 1676.   The son of Massasoit, he was the leader of Indians in New England during King Philip's War (*q.v.*). He was killed in battle.

Philip I (of Portugal) *See* **Philip II (of Spain).**

Philip I 1052–1108.   Capetian king of France (1060–1108), successor to Henry I. Throughout his reign Philip struggled to prevent the union of England and Normandy, which would overpower France. He was excommunicated by Urban II for disavowing his first marriage and remarrying. His conflict with the church lasted until 1104.

Philip I (˜ the Handsome) 1478–1506.   Duke of Burgundy, King of Castile (1506), and founder of the Spanish Habsburg line. The son of Holy Roman Emperor Maximilian I, he succeeded (1482) as duke of Burgundy (including the Netherlands) and then married Joanna, daughter of Spanish king Ferdinand II. Later, Philip forced Ferdinand to recognize (1506) his claim to the throne of Castile (as Joanna's husband) but died soon thereafter. Philip's son eventually succeeded in Spain, however, and then became the great Habsburg Holy Roman Emperor Charles V.

Philip II 382–336 BC.   Macedonian king (359–336 BC), whose conquest of Greece laid the foundation for the great Macedonian Empire established by his son, Alexander the Great. From 357 BC, Philip embarked on his program of expansion by war and alliances and defeated his last opponents in Greece (Athens and Thebes) in the Battle of Chaeronea (338 BC). He was killed while preparing to invade Persia.

Philip II (˜ Augustus) 1165–1223.   French king (1179–1223), successor to his father, Louis VII. Philip was the first powerful Capetian king and more than doubled his domains by conquering parts of Flanders and by taking English possessions on the Continent (Angevin domains). Philip at first involved himself in intrigues between English king Henry II and his sons, Richard and John. Next, he and Richard (then king) embarked on the Third Crusade. They quarreled, and Philip returned and unsuccessfully attempted to take Richard's lands on the Continent. During John's reign, however, Philip finally conquered (1204) Normandy, Brittany, Anjou, Maine, and Touraine. Then, by his victory (1214) at the Battle of Bouvines (*q.v.*), he established France as a major power. He also instituted administrative reforms and allowed prosecution of the Albigensian Crusade (*q.v.*).

Philip II 1527–98. King of Spain (1556–98) and Portugal (1580–98, as Philip I). He succeeded his father, Holy Roman Emperor Charles V, to the Spanish throne and had earlier received from him the Spanish Netherlands, Milan, Naples, and Sicily. Philip married English Queen Mary I (1554) and, after her death (1558), was refused by Elizabeth I. Under Philip, Spain emerged as the dominant power in Italy after the Italian Wars (*q.v.*) and enjoyed victories against the Ottoman Turks, notably the Battle of Lepanto (1571). But Philip's efforts to defend Catholicism (sometimes combined with his political aims) led to trouble at home and abroad. Within the empire, persecutions by the Inquisition were increased, resulting in harsh treatment of the Moriscos (*q.v.*) and a revolt in the Spanish Netherlands. The latter ended in the independence of the United Provinces. Philip's conflicts with Protestants in other countries brought war against England and the disastrous defeat of the Spanish Armada (*q.v.*), which resulted in the decline of Spain as a military power. He also involved Spain in the French Wars of Religion, which, combined with his other foreign wars, seriously weakened the finances of the empire.

Philip III (~ the Bold) 1245–85. King of France (1270–85), successor to his father, Louis IX. He died during the retreat from an unsuccessful attack on the Spanish kingdom of Aragon.

Philip III 1578–1621. King of Spain (1598–1621), successor to his father, Philip II. Philip also ruled Naples, Sicily, and Portugal (as Philip II), though he was content to let his favorites do the actual governing. The Moriscos (*q.v.*) were expelled during his reign, in 1609.

Philip IV (~ the Fair) 1268–1314. Capetian king of France (1285–1314), successor to his father, Philip III. Philip's reign was marked by his successful struggle against the church. Early in his reign, Philip's need for money to prosecute foreign wars caused him to impose a tax on the clergy. Pope Boniface VIII opposed the tax (1296) but was soon forced to concede. Philip next arrested a bishop and thereby renewed the dispute with Boniface. To resolve the matter, Philip convened (1302–03) a council of nobles, clergy, and others (the first French States-General). When Boniface answered by threaten-

ing Philip with excommunication, Philip had him arrested. Boniface died soon afterward and Philip secured the election of Pope Clement V. Thereafter, Clement cooperated with Philip, moved the papacy to Avignon (1309, *see* Babylonian Captivity), and condemned the Knights Templars (whose great wealth Philip confiscated). During his reign Philip engaged in wars with England (1294–1303) and Flanders (1302–04).

Philip IV 1605–65. Spanish king (1621–65), successor to his father, Philip III. His reign was marked by his willingness to let his ministers govern and by Spain's decline as a European power. Spain's involvement in the Thirty Years' War (1618–48) proved costly. During the war, Portugal won its independence (1640), Catalonia revolted and was occupied by France, and the Union of Utrecht (*q.v.*) won recognition of its independence (1648). Spanish involvement in the French war of the Fronde, ended by the Peace of the Pyrenees (*q.v.*), cost Spain further losses.

Philip V 238–179 BC. Macedonian king (221–179 BC), successor to Antigonus III. He joined the Achaean League in a successful war against Sparta and the Aetolian League. But his alliance with Hannibal during the Second Punic War against Rome brought Roman retaliation in the First Macedonian War (*q.v.*). Later efforts to expand his domains provoked renewed Roman military action against him and the Second Macedonian War (*q.v.*) ended in his defeat.

Philip V c1294–1322. French king (1316–22) who succeeded on the death of the infant king, John I. The Salic Law (*q.v.*) was invoked to legitimize Philip's succession over the rightful female heir, an infant named Joan. Philip strengthened local militias and instituted other administrative reforms.

Philip V 1683–1746. Spanish king (1700–46), successor to Charles II, and first Bourbon king of Spain. His succession resulted in the War of the Spanish Succession (*q.v.*) and loss of territories by the Peace of Utrecht (*q.v.*). Philip's early attempts to retake lost territories in Italy failed when the Quadruple Alliance (*q.v.*) was formed against him. His later involvement in the Wars of the Polish Succession and Austrian Succession, however, won Naples, Sicily, Parma, and Piacenza for Spain.

Philip VI 1293–1350. French king (1328–50), successor to Charles IV, and first king of the Valois line. The Salic Law (*q.v.*) was invoked to allow Philip to succeed over rival claimants (to prevent succession through females). His reign was marked by the beginning of the Hundred Years' War (1337–1453) and the outbreak of the Black Plague (1348–49) in France.

Philip Augustus *See* **Philip II.**

Philip of Swabia c1177–1208. German king (1198–1208) of the Hohenstaufen line and successor to Holy Roman Emperor Henry VI. Philip was never crowned emperor and his reign was spent overcoming the opposition of his rival for the crown, the Guelph leader Otto IV. He was murdered soon after the struggle had been resolved.

Philippi, Battle of Victory for the Second Roman Triumvirate of Antony, Lepidus, and Octavian (Augustus) over Brutus and Cassius, assassins of Caesar. The battle began on Oct. 27, 42 BC, near the Macedonian city of Philippi, between forces of around 100,000 on each side. Cassius was defeated by Antony and, believing a rumor that Brutus had also lost, committed suicide. The combined triumvirate force then defeated Brutus' forces on Nov. 16, and he committed suicide. The outcome helped ensure Octavian's accession as emperor.

Philippics Two series of historic orations. Demosthenes denounced Philip II of Macedon as a threat to Athens in a series of orations (351–341 BC) known as "philippics." The term was later applied to Cicero's denunciation of M. Antony before the Roman Senate (44–43 BC).

Philippine Insurrection US–Filipino war (1899–1902), an outgrowth of the Philippine Revolution (*q.v.*) and the Spanish-American War. Filipino leader E. Aguinaldo refused to accept the Treaty of Paris (1898), by which Spain ceded the Philippines to the US, and continued to fight for Filipino independence. Aguinaldo was captured (1901) and the war ended a year later.

Philippine Revolution Filipino war for independence from Spain (1896–98). Sparked by the execution of J. Rizal (Dec. 30, 1896), the war was led by E. Aguinaldo. After the outbreak of the Spanish-American War, Aguinaldo helped US Commodore G. Dewey occupy Manila (1898) and established a provisional government. However, the Treaty of Paris (1898) ceded the Philippines to the US, and Aguinaldo led the Philippine Insurrection (*q.v.*) against US control.

Philippines (Republic of the Philippines) Republic composed of over seven thousand islands in the South Pacific. The population is 66,647,000 and the capital is Quezon City. The Philippines were ruled by Spain from the 15th to the late 19th cent. and by the US after the Spanish-American War. The Philippines became fully independent in 1946. Key dates in Philippine history include:

1521   F. Magellan, representing Spain, claimed the Philippines.

1542   Islands named in honor of Prince Philip, later Philip II of Spain.

1564   1571 M. de López de Legaspi completed conquest of islands for Spain.

1571   Manila founded.

1583   Audiencia (colonial supreme court) established.

1600s   Wars with the Dutch, then expanding their East Indies holdings.

1600s–1800s   Moros (native tribe) active as pirates.

1756–63   Seven Years' War in Europe; Manila occupied by British (1762–63).

1763   First Treaty of Paris; Britain returned the Philippines to Spain.

19TH CENT.   Muslims (Moors) raided the Philippines.

1892   Rise of the nationalist movement; secret society, led by Dr. José Rizal, demanded increased native involvement in government.

1896   Existence of Katipunan, society for complete independence, discovered (Aug.); armed revolt against Spanish began.

1896   Dr. Rizal, not associated with Katipunan, executed (Dec.); became martyr.

1896–98   E. Aguinaldo led revolt against Spain.

1898   Spanish-American War between US and Spain; G. Dewey defeated Spain at Manila Bay (May 11); US gained control of Philippines by Treaty of Paris (Dec. 10), ending the war.

1898   US established military rule (Dec.).

1899–1902   Philippine Insurrection; Aguinaldo fought US, headed short-lived rebel government.

1901   Civilian government authorized by Spooner Amendment.

1902–04   William Howard Taft served as governor general; Philippine Commission became governing body.

1903 US resolved Friar Lands Question by purchasing church-owned lands for resale to peasants.

1916 Jones Law provided for elected legislature.

1934 Tydings-McDuffie Act, creating transitional commonwealth government leading to Philippine independence.

1935 Constitution approved by Filipinos.

1935–42 Manuel Quezon y Molina in office as first president; commonwealth established (Nov. 15, 1935).

1942–45 WW II; Philippines occupied by Japan after defeat of US-Filipino forces at Bataan and Corregidor.

1942–45 Tomoyuki Yamashita commanded Japanese forces in the Philippines.

1944 US Gen. D. MacArthur landed (Oct.) at Leyte Gulf.

1945 Manila liberated (Feb.).

1946 Full independence (July 4).

1946–48 Manuel Roxas y Acuna in office as president.

1946–54 Communist-backed Hukbalahap guerrillas, who had fought the Japanese, continued guerrilla warfare; capture of their leader, L. Taruc, broke the rebellion.

1948–53 E. Quirino served as president of the Philippines.

1954 Philippines joined Southeast Asia Treaty Organization (SEATO).

1965–86 Ferdinand Marcos in office as president; his administration continued in power into the 1980s, despite considerable opposition.

1969 Marcos reelected in violent campaign; rioting followed the election.

1972 Martial law instituted (Sept.) to combat terrorism; thousands subsequently killed as government troops attempted to restore order.

1973 Marcos promulgated new constitution; country to be ruled by martial law; Marcos to remain in power indefinitely.

1976 Earthquake hit Mindanao; 8,000 people dead.

1976 Truce reached with Muslim rebels on Mindanao, ending several years of serious rebellion.

1977 Principal opposition leader, Benigno Aquino, sentenced to death (Nov.); Marcos allowed stay of execution; Aquino later exiled from Philippines.

1978 Elections for National Assembly held; first since martial law was imposed.

1981 Martial law ended (Jan.); many restrictions remained in force.

1981 Plebiscite approved constitutional changes.

1981 Marcos won reelection; opposition refused to take part in the election.

1983 Aquino assassinated upon his return to the Philippines after three years in exile (Aug. 21); his death united opposition against Marcos.

1986 Marcos declared the winner in unscheduled presidential election (Feb.); Corazon Aquino, the widow of slain opposition leader, widely believed to be actual winner.

1986 Open revolt against Marcos government; rebels, led by Gen. Fidel Ramos and Defense Minister Juan Enrile, set up headquarters in the Ministry of National Defense (Feb. 22).

1986 Marcos fled to Hawaii (Feb. 25).

1986–92 C. Aquino in office as president; abolished the constitution of 1973, replacing it with interim constitution (Mar. 25).

1986 Government instituted military reforms (Mar.) demanded by supporters of the revolt in February.

1986 Government suppressed pro-Marcos coup; discontent in military heightened by government's conciliatory attitude toward Communist guerrillas (July).

1987 Muslim separatist group MNLF abandoned demands for independent Mindanao (Jan.).

1987 US government blocked F. Marcos's attempt to return to the Phillipines, as part of a coup involving 500 soldiers (Jan.).

1987 New constitution approved (Feb.); provision called for end to US military presence at Subic Bay naval base and Clark air base.

1987 Troops loyal to Aquino quashed coup attempt by rebel officers (Aug. 28).

1988 Vice-President S. Laurel publicly disassociated himself from Aquino and demanded her resignation (Mar.).

1988 Ex-President Marcos and his wife Imelda indicted in the US, charged with transferring over $100 million in funds out of the Philippines.

1989 Pro-Marcos Nacionalista Party revived; Laurel named president and J. Enrile became secretary-general (May).

1989 Marcos died in Hawaii (Sept. 26).

1989 Abortive coup attempt by the Marines and the Scout Rangers (Dec.); Aquino requested US air support.

1990 Protesters demonstrated against the slow implementation of the agrarian reforms of 1988 (May).

1990 Earthquake rocked Luzon; some 1,600 killed.

1990 Brief military revolt on Mindanao; government forced rebels to surrender.

1990 Swiss government, rejecting Marcos family appeals, returned $270 million in Swiss bank accounts to the Philippines.

1991 Massive volcanic eruption of Mt. Pinatubo (June).

1991 Treaty allowing the US to retain Philippine military bases rejected by Philippine Senate (Sept. 16); US agreed to phased withdrawal from Philippine bases.

1992 US turned over Subic Bay Naval Station to Philippines (Nov.).

1992 Gen Fidel Ramos elected president, succeeding Aquino (Apr.).

Philippine Sea, Battle of the Major US victory (June 19, 1944) over the Japanese during WW II. Provoked by the US invasion of the Mariana Islands, the Japanese organized a large naval attack force (including nine carriers) to fight against the US task force protecting the Marianas landing operation. Primarily a battle between carrier-based aircraft, it turned into a rout, known as "the Marianas Turkey Shoot." The Japanese lost 400 planes and three aircraft carriers, and the US firmly established naval superiority in the Pacific.

Philip the Arabian *See* **Philip.**

Philip the Bold *See* **Philip III; Burgundy.**

Philip the Fair *See* **Philip IV.**

Philip the Good 1396–1467. Duke of Burgundy (1419–67). By various means, Philip doubled the size of his holdings and established Burgundy as a powerful kingdom. Involved in rivalry with France, he formed an alliance with England against France by the Treaty of Troyes (1420). He eventually made peace with French king Charles VII in the Treaty of Arras (1435). He founded the Order of the Golden Fleece (*q.v.*).

Philip the Handsome *See* **Philip I.**

Philip the Magnanimous (~ of Hesse) 1504–67. Landgrave of Hesse and German Protestant leader. He was a leader in the struggle against the Catholic Holy Roman Emperor Charles V and organized the Schmalkaldic League (*q.v.*) of German Protestants (1531).

Philistines Ancient people from the Aegean who settled in Palestine (c12th cent. BC). They were skilled iron workers and frequently fought the Israelites, who at the time had no iron. In modern times, "philistine" means an uncultured person.

Phillips, Wendell 1811–84. American reformer. He was associated with W. Garrison in the crusade for the abolition of slavery, and later campaigned for woman suffrage, labor reform, and prohibition.

Philo (~ Judaeus) c20 BC–AD 50. Jewish philosopher. Philo was famous for his synthesis of Greek philosophy with biblical theology. He stressed God's perfection and established the concept of Logos (*q.v.*).

Philo Judaeus *See* **Philo.**

Philometer, Ptolemy VI *See* **Ptolemy VI.**

Philo of Alexandria *See* **Philo.**

Philopater, Ptolemy IV *See* **Ptolemy IV.**

Philopoemen c252–182 BC. Greek general who restored Achaean military power. Formerly a mercenary in Crete, Philopoemen reorganized the Achaean cavalry and in 208–207 adopted heavier armor for the army, as well as new tactics involving the phalanx. He defeated the Spartans at Mantineia (207) and in 192 incorporated Sparta into the Achaean League. He annexed Messene and Elis (191) and demilitarized Sparta (188). Captured during a revolt by Messene, he was killed by poison.

Philosophes Diverse group of literary and scientific figures in France during the 18th-century Enlightenment (*q.v.*). Proponents of rationalism, science, and natural laws, their views frequently challenged religious, political, and social doctrines of their time. *See also* Encyclopedists.

Philostratus (Philostratus the Elder) *fl.* c217. Greek sophist. He wrote the *Life of Apollonius* and *Lives of the Sophists.*

Philostratus the Elder *See* **Philostratus.**

Phips, Sir William 1651–95. Massachusetts colonial governor (1692–94). Phips commanded New England colonial forces during King William's War (*q.v.*). He appointed a commission on witchcraft but disbanded it when his own wife was accused. He was recalled to England.

Phocas *d.* 610 Byzantine emperor (602–610), successor to Maurice by his overthrow. He persecuted the Monophysites and Jews and was overthrown (610) by Heraclius.

Phocis Region of ancient Greece, located in central Greece. The Oracle of Delphi and Mount Parnassus were within its boundaries. It was the focus of the three Sacred Wars (*q.v.*).

Phoenicia Ancient name applied to the narrow coastal region bordering the eastern Mediterranean roughly contiguous with modern Lebanon. The Phoenicians were related to the Canaanites and had established themselves as traders and sailors by the 25th cent. BC. They early came under the influence of the Egyptians, with whom they traded. Although never a unified country, Phoenicia saw the rise of several important cities, notably Byblos, Sidon, Tyre, and Tripoli. Phoenician traders founded settlements throughout the Mediterranean, such as on the islands of Rhodes and Cyprus and at Utica and Carthage. Later Phoenicia gained independence as Egyptian power began to decline around the 12th cent. BC. During this period Phoenician traders ranged widely through the Mediterranean. It is thought they may have also traveled along the western coast of Africa and possibly as far north as Cornwall. The Phoenicians were known for their metalwork and glasswork, woven cloth, and fabric dyed with a color known as Tyrian purple. Their greatest innovation, however, was their alphabet, which was adopted by the Greeks and eventually replaced the older system of hieroglyphic writing. Phoenicia came under Persian domination in the 6th cent. BC and was conquered by Alexander the Great in the 4th cent. BC. Under Macedonian rule much of the region was hellenized and Phoenician culture underwent a decline. Phoenicia ceased to exist when the area was incorporated into the Roman province of Syria (AD 64).

Phoenix Park murders Irish terrorist murders. On May 6, 1882, the British secretary of Ireland, Lord Frederick Cavendish, and his undersecretary, Thomas Henry Burke, were stabbed to death in Dublin's Phoenix Park. The Invincibles, a terrorist offshoot of the Fenians, claimed responsibility. Noted Irish leader C. Parnell was cleared of charges that he was involved in the murders.

Photius c820–891. Byzantine scholar and patriarch of Constantinople (858–867, 877–886).

Photius rose to prominence when he was chosen to replace St. Ignatius during the iconoclastic controversy. When his election was challenged by Pope Nicholas I, Photius retaliated by contesting the pope's right to rule in the East. Though Photius was replaced by Saint Ignatius, he had already created the beginnings of the schism that was to permanently divide the church. Condemned at the Fourth Council of Constantinople (869), Photius was reconciled with the West and was reinstated as patriarch after Saint Ignatius' death. He was, however, forced to resign the office by Byzantine emperor Leo VI.

Phrygia Ancient country of Asia Minor, located in what is now central Turkey. The country prospered from the 8th to 6th cent. BC and two of its kings were supposed to have been the legendary Gordius and Midas. It came under Lydian domination (7th cent.) and thereafter was ruled by various powers.

Phrynichus *fl.* c512–476 BC. Athenian poet and playwright, the first to put women characters in Greek plays. He was fined for writing *Capture of Miletus* (492?) because it reminded Athens of the loss of that city in the Ionian revolt.

Phyfe, Duncan c1768–1854. Scottish-born American furniture maker. His designs were neoclassic (and, later, Empire style) and highly prized for their fine workmanship.

physiocrats French intellectuals (18th cent.) who developed the first complete system of economics. Led by François Quesnay, they emphasized that land was the ultimate source of all wealth, advocated a single tax on it, extolled free trade and laissez-faire, and stressed the importance of natural laws.

Piaget, Jean 1896–1980. Swiss psychologist. Piaget is best known for his studies in child psychology, notably on the sequential stages of a child's intellectual development.

Piast Polish royal dynasty. The Piasts were Poland's first dynasty, ruling from the 11th cent. to 1370, when they were replaced by the Jagiello line. Branches of the family, however, continued to rule in Bohemia for several more centuries.

Picard, Jean 1620–82. French astronomer. Picard accurately measured the degree of a meridian of the earth. He established the Paris Observatory.

Picasso, Pablo Ruiz 1881–1973. Spanish artist and sculptor, one of the most important artists of this century. His early career is generally divided into periods: blue (from 1901), rose (from 1905), and cubist (from 1907). With G. Braque, Picasso is considered the founder of cubism (*q.v.*) and in 1907 painted his famous early cubist work, *Les Demoiselles d'Avignon.* In the 1920s, some of his works took on a surrealistic tone and foreshadowed the agony portrayed in his *Guernica,* commemorating the destruction of the town during the Spanish Civil War. Experimenting with various media and styles in his later years, he continued working until his death.

Piccard, Auguste 1884–1962. Swiss-born Belgian physicist. Piccard is noted for both his balloon ascents into the stratosphere and his deep-sea explorations in a bathyscaphe he designed.

Piccolomini, Aeneas Silvius *See* **Pius II.**

Pichincha, Battle of Ecuadorian victory (May 24, 1822) over Spanish colonial forces. The Ecuadorians, under A. de Sucre, defeated the Spanish at Pichincha volcano, near Quito, and thereby gained Ecuadorian independence.

Pickens, Andrew (Picken, ˜) 1739–1817. American Revolutionary hero. Pickens served notably in the battles of Cowpens and Eutaw Springs, and captured Augusta, Georgia (1781). He later served in Congress (1793–95).

Pickering, Edward Charles 1846–1919. American astronomer and physicist. Pickering invented the meridian photometer and pioneered stellar photometry and spectroscopy at the Harvard Observatory.

Pickering, Timothy 1745–1829. American politician. Pickering served as G. Washington's adjutant general in the American Revolution and later held cabinet posts under Washington and J. Adams. A Federalist and a member of the Essex Junto (*q.v.*), he strongly opposed the War of 1812.

Pickett, George Edward 1825–75. Confederate general in the American Civil War. He is known best for "Pickett's charge" at the Battle of Gettysburg (*q.v.*), a brave but futile charge on Union forces across a half mile of broken ground.

Pico della Mirandola, Giovanni Conte 1463–94. Italian Renaissance philosopher. He published 900 theses that combined Christianity with Platonic thought, and his *Oration on the Dignity of Man* (1486) is considered a characteristic Renaissance work.

Picquart, Georges 1854–1914. French general. Picquart's ardent defense of Capt. A. Dreyfus in the Dreyfus Affair (*q.v.*) led to his own imprisonment. He was later exonerated and became war minister (1906–09) under G. Clemenceau.

Picquigny, Truce of Agreement signed (1475) at Picquigny, France. By its terms English king Edward IV agreed to withdraw his army from France in return for a cash settlement and an annual pension.

Picts Ancient people of Scotland. They frequently invaded Roman-held Britain and established a kingdom in Scotland that flourished in the 8th cent.

Pierce, Franklin 1804–69. US president (1853–57), the fourteenth, successor to M. Fillmore. A Democrat from New Hampshire, he was a US representative (1833–37) and senator (1837–42) and fought in the Mexican War. In 1852, he was nominated for the presidency by the Democrats to break a deadlock. After defeating Gen. W. Scott, the Whig candidate, he sought to reconcile opposing Democratic factions on the slavery issue by appointing cabinet officials from both North and South. Pierce adopted a generally unsuccessful policy of foreign expansion, and his request for a program by which the US could acquire Cuba from Spain resulted in the Ostend Manifesto (*q.v.*). This caused such a furor that his administration disavowed it. During his term of office the US made the Gadsden Purchase (*q.v.*) from Mexico, and the Kansas-Nebraska Act (*q.v.*) was passed (1854). This act, with its doctrine of popular sovereignty and repeal of the Missouri Compromise, led to Bleeding Kansas (*q.v.*), which further strained relations between North and South in the years before the Civil War. Pierce's policies made him vastly unpopular, and he retired to New Hampshire at the close of his term.

Pieria Ancient Greek district, located in north Thessaly. The site of Mount Olympus, it was also the legendary birthplace of Orpheus and the Muses.

Piero della Francesca c1420–92. Italian Renaissance painter. One of the great Italian Renaissance artists, he is renowned for his religious frescoes, including the series *The Story of the True Cross* (1466).

Pietism Religious movement that began in reaction to the doctrinal orthodoxy of German

Lutheranism in the 17th and 18th cents. The leader of this reform was P. Spener, whose book *Pia desideria* encouraged study of the Bible and a spiritual rebirth within the church. Pietism influenced the Moravian and Methodist churches. The movement continued under Spener's successor, August Francke, but declined after Francke's death (1727).

Pietro, Guido di   *See* **Angelico, Fra.**

Pike, Zebulon Montgomery 1779–1813. American general and explorer. Pike explored much of western America and was the first white person to sight Pikes Peak, Colorado. He was killed leading a successful attack on York (now Toronto, Canada) during the War of 1812.

Pilgrimage of Grace Uprising (1536–37) in northern England which began (Oct., 1536) in protest against the abolition of papal authority and suppression of the monasteries by King Henry VIII. Some 35,000 Catholic demonstrators were persuaded to disband. Another uprising followed (Jan. 1537), but its leaders were executed and northern England was placed under martial law.

Pilgrims English religious Separatists, and other dissenters, who sailed aboard the *Mayflower* to Plymouth Rock (Dec. 21, 1620) and founded the first New England colony. Originally, the Separatists opposed the doctrines of the established Church of England and founded an independent congregation. Around 1607 some of them emigrated to Holland to escape harassment and persecution. The experiment in Holland did not prove satisfactory, and the group then negotiated with a London stock company for a charter that would enable them to go to America. In Sept., 1620, 102 passengers embarked on the *Mayflower* for the voyage. Some of the group, including J. Alden and M. Standish, were non-Separatists (called Strangers), hired to protect the stock company's interests. Before landing they signed the Mayflower Compact (*q.v.*), which provided for a government by the will of the majority. The name Pilgrim Fathers, as applied to them, comes from an 1820 commemorative speech by D. Webster.

Pillars of Hercules Mythical name given to the promontories at the Mediterranean (eastern) entrance of the Strait of Gibraltar. They are generally identified with the Rock of Gibraltar in Europe and Jebel Musa in Africa.

Pillnitz, Declaration of Statement issued (Aug. 27, 1791) at Pillnitz, now in Germany, by Austrian emperor Leopold II and Prussian king Frederick William II declaring their willingness to restore French king Louis XVI, provided other European sovereigns agreed. Both monarchs knew that Britain would not agree, so the declaration was empty. However, it caused much resentment in France and helped bring on the French Revolutionary Wars.

Pillow, Gideon Johnson 1806–78. Confederate general in the American Civil War. Pillow's escape from Fort Donelson (*q.v.*) before its surrender to Union forces led to his suspension from command.

Pilsudski, Joseph 1867–1935. Polish general and politician. A lifelong fighter against Russia for Polish independence, he was repeatedly imprisoned and exiled. After declaring Poland a republic (1918) and becoming its first president, he dominated Polish politics under a conservative authoritarian regime, both in and out of office into the 1930s.

Pincherle, Alberto   *See* **Moravia, Alberto.**

Pinckney, Charles 1757–1824. American statesman. As a member of the Constitutional Convention, he submitted a draft of the Constitution, and a number of its elements were incorporated into the final document. He later served in Congress, as governor of South Carolina, and as US minister to Spain.

Pinckney, Charles Cotesworth 1746–1825. American statesman, brother of T. Pinckney. As special envoy to France (1797) he became involved, with E. Gerry and J. Marshall, in the XYZ Affair (*q.v.*). He was twice an unsuccessful Federalist candidate for president (1804, 1808).

Pinckney, Thomas 1750–1828. American politician and diplomat, brother of C. C. Pinckney. As special envoy to Spain (1794–95) he negotiated a treaty (1795) that established American-Spanish borders in North America and secured American navigation rights on the Mississippi River.

Pindar 522?–443 BC. Greek lyric poet who gave his name to the Pindaric ode of English verse. His major works include odes to the victors of the Olympic, Pythian, Isthmian, and Nemean athletic games. Of these, 44 complete odes survive.

Pinel, Philippe 1745–1826. French physician. Pinel advocated humane treatment of the mentally ill. His views and methods completely changed the long-standing approach to mental illness.

Pinkerton, Allan 1819–84. Scottish-born American detective who formed America's first detective agency (1850). Pinkerton foiled an assassination plot against A. Lincoln (1861) and operated an espionage ring against the Confederates.

Pinochet Ugarte, Augusto 1915– . Chilean military leader and president (1973–90). As commander in chief of the army he directed the successful coup against his predecessor, President S. Allende (Sept., 1973). Defeated in the 1990 elections, he retained his military command. *See also* Chile, 1973–90.

Pinter, Harold 1930– . English playwright. Pinter's tense, highly personal work includes the plays *The Birthday Party, The Caretaker,* and *The Homecoming.*

Pinzón, Martín Alonso *d.* 1493. Spanish navigator. Pinzón was co-owner of the ships *Niña* and *Pinta.* He commanded the *Pinta* during C. Columbus's 1492 expedition.

Pinzón, Vicente Yáñez *fl.* 1492–1509. Spanish explorer and navigator. Pinzón commanded the *Niña* on Columbus's first voyage to America (1492). He later voyaged to Brazil and the Amazon estuary (early 1500).

Pippi, Giulio *See* **Romano, Giulio.**

piracy Robbery on the high seas, committed for private gain. In ancient times, Phoenicians preyed on shipping in the Mediterranean. In the Middle Ages, Vikings attacked ships in the Baltic, and Moors also engaged in piracy. The decline of Ottoman power in the Mediterranean led to the rise of the Barbary States (*q.v.*), whose support of piracy led to conflict with European powers and the US (*see* Tripolitan War) in the 19th cent. The formation of standing navies and international laws has eliminated most piracy.

Piraeus Athenian seaport. Built (5th cent. BC) by Themistocles, it is the port of Athens and the leading Greek seaport. It was heavily damaged by the Germans during WW II.

Pirandello, Luigi 1867–1936. Italian dramatist. His powerful, realistic plays, among them *Six Characters in Search of an Author* (1921), had a major influence in 20th-cent. drama. He was awarded the Nobel Prize in Literature in 1934.

Pisa, Council of Roman Catholic church council. It was called (1409) to heal the papal schism that had resulted in the naming of two rival popes, Gregory XII in Rome and Benedict XIII in Avignon. The council deposed both and elected a third pope, Alexander V. Far from ending the schism, the council complicated matters by establishing three papal claimants. The Council of Constance (1414–18) ultimately forced all three to resign and elected Martin V.

Pisa, Leaning Tower of *See* **Leaning Tower of Pisa.**

Pisano, Nicola and **Giovanni** c1220–84; 1245–1314. Italian sculptors. Nicola founded a school of sculpture at Pisa which influenced later Renaissance art. His son Giovanni perpetuated his work in Siena.

Pisistratus c605–527 BC. Tyrant of Athens (560–556, 554–527 BC). Pisistratus established Athenian hegemony in the Hellespont, sponsored extensive public building, passed important land laws, and commissioned a definitive edition of Homer.

Piso, Gaius Calpurnius *d.* AD 65. Roman politician. A prominent plebeian, he was robbed of his wife by the emperor Caligula. He later plotted against the emperor Nero and killed himself when his plot was discovered.

Piso, Lucius Calpurnius Piso Caesoninus *d.* after 43 BC. Roman politician, father-in-law of J. Caesar. As consul (58 BC), he took part in the banishment of Cicero.

Pissarro, Camille 1830–1903. French impressionist painter. One of the most influential impressionists, he is noted for his paintings of street scenes.

Pitman, Sir Isaac 1813–97. English inventor of a shorthand system. His phonetic system of shorthand became one of the world's most used and adaptable systems.

Pitt, William (the Younger) 1759–1806. British prime minister (1783–1801, 1804–06), son of W. Pitt the Elder. Pitt led Britain through the French Revolutionary and early Napoleonic Wars. Pitt entered Parliament in 1781 and by 1783 was in effective control of the government as prime minister. He attempted to reorganize government finances in order to reduce the national debt, lowered customs duties, revised the British East India Company's role in India's government (1784), created Upper and Lower Canada by his Constitution Act (1791), and organized Britain (and various foreign coalitions) for war after the start of the French Revolutionary Wars. Seeking a solution to the Irish problem, he sought a union with Ireland and passage of a Catholic Emancipation Act. The union was effected (1800), but King George III refused to allow passage of the act and Pitt resigned (1801). He returned (1804) to form his second ministry after the outbreak of the Napoleonic Wars and organized the Third Coalition against Napoleon (1805). He died the next year. A revived Tory party formed under his leadership.

Pitt, William (the Elder), 1st earl of Chatham 1708–78. British statesman, and noted orator, called "the Great Commoner." His vigorous foreign policies, during the Seven Years' War (1756–63), led to French defeats in India, Africa, and North America, and to Britain's emergence as the world's greatest colonial power. He entered Parliament in 1735 and, called by George II to serve as secretary of state, he effectively became the prime minister (1756–61) for most of the war in which Britain stripped France of most of its colonial empire. He formed a new ministry (1766–68), but was forced to resign because of poor health.

Pitt-Rivers, Augustus Henry Lane-Fox 1827– 1900. British pioneer archaeologist. A career army officer, he made extensive excavations on his large estate in Wiltshire, emphasizing total site excavation and careful stratigraphic comparisons.

Pittsburg Landing, Battle of *See* **Shiloh, Battle of.**

Pius II (Aeneas Silvius Piccolomini) 1405–64. Pope (1458–64), successor to Calixtus III, a famous Renaissance humanist before becoming a priest. As pope he condemned conciliarism.

Pius IV (Giovanni Angelo de' Medici) 1499– 1565. Pope (1559–65), successor to Paul IV. He convened (1562) the third and most important session of the Council of Trent, and made permanent the Catholic Reformation by ratifying the council's decrees (1564).

Pius V (Ghislieri, Michele) 1504–72. Pope (1566–72), successor to Pius IV, and saint. As pope he put into effect the decrees of the Council of Trent and encouraged the common defense of Christendom against the Turks.

Pius VI (Giovanni Angelo Braschi) 1717–99. Pope (1775–99), successor to Clement XIV. He opposed the assaults on church authority of both Austrian Josephinism and the French revolutionary Civil Constitution of the Clergy. He was taken as a prisoner to France by Napoleon (1798) after Papal domains were conquered in the French Revolutionary Wars.

Pius VII (Barnaba Gregorio Chiaramonte) 1740– 1823. Pope (1800–23), successor to Pius VI. He signed the Concordat of 1801 with Napoleon and took part in his coronation (1804). His later opposition to Napoleon led to French annexation of the Papal States (1809). Pius excommunicated Napoleon but became the emperor's virtual prisoner.

Pius IX (Mastai-Ferretti, Giovanni Maria) 1792– 1878. Pope (1846–78), successor to Gregory XVI. His reign was the longest in Catholic history. During his pontificate the Papal States and Rome passed to Italy (1870). He defined the dogma of the Immaculate Conception (1854) and presided over the First Vatican Council (1869–70).

Pius X (Giuseppe Sarto) 1835–1914. Pope (1903–14), successor to Leo XIII, and saint. His pontificate saw the separation of church and state in France and Portugal. He condemned religious Modernism in his encyclical *Pascendi Dominici Gregis.*

Pius XI (Ambisgio Damians Achille Ratti) 1857–1939. Pope (1922–39), successor to Benedict XV. He was noted for his efforts to secure world peace. As pope he negotiated the Lateran Treaty (1929) with B. Mussolini, which made Vatican City an independent state. He denounced Fascism, Communism, and racism and encouraged missionary work.

Pius XII (Eugenio Pacelli) 1876–1958. Pope (1939–58), successor to Pius XI. Elected pope on the eve of WW II, he worked to relieve the suffering caused by the war. After the Allied victory, however, he was criticized by many for not doing enough to prevent persecution of the Jews. He strongly opposed the rise of Communism and excommunicated several East European leaders.

Pizarro, Francisco c1476–1541. Spanish conquerer of the Incas of Peru. He first went to the New World in 1509, and accompanied V. de Balboa when the latter sighted the Pacific Ocean (1513). With D. de Almagro, he explored (1522–26) the west coast of South America, then returned to Spain (1528) to prepare for the conquest of Peru. In 1531, with fewer than 200 men, he enticed the Inca chieftain Atahualpa into his hands by treachery, extracted an enormous ransom from him, and later had him executed (1533). He then captured the city of Cuzco, and the conquest of Peru was completed. Pizarro founded Lima (1535). In 1537–38, he came into conflict with Almagro and his followers, and he ordered Almagro beheaded. Pizarro was later assassinated by Almagro's followers (1541).

Pizarro, Gonzalo c1506–48.   Spanish conquistador. He was the half-brother of F. Pizarro and was involved in the conquest of Peru. He became governor of Quito, and later led an unsuccessful revolt against the New Laws protecting the Indians.

Place, Francis 1771–1854.   English social reformer. A tailor, he fought successfully against the anti-union Combination Acts. In 1822, he published one of the earliest birth-control tracts.

Plain, the   In the French Revolution, the amorphous, moderate party that occupied the lower seats in the National Convention chamber. It was distinguished from the more radical representatives of the Mountain (*q.v.*), who occupied the higher seats.

Planck, Max 1858–1947.   German physicist, the originator of the quantum theory. Planck earned his doctorate in thermodynamics (1879). Following a lengthy study of the radiation emissions, he formulated a theory (1900) that energy consists of tiny indivisible units called "quanta" (as opposed to waves, as had been believed). The quanta, he postulated, were emitted and absorbed by atoms. This theory, which explained the distribution of radiation, became the foundation of the quantum theory and marked the beginning of modern theoretical physics. Planck won the Nobel Prize for Physics (1918) and became president of the Kaiser Wilhelm Society for the Advancement of Science (1930–35). Planck's Constant is named for him.

Plan de Iguala (Plan of Three Guarantees) Proclamation issued (Feb. 24, 1821) during the Mexican Revolution by the revolutionary Gen. A. Iturbide. It set forth three fundamental objectives of the drive for independence from Spain and was named for the city in which it was issued. Iturbide ignored the plan after he became emperor of Mexico (1822). The objectives were complete independence from Spain, designation of the Roman Catholic church as the state church, and equal rights for all Mexicans.

Plan of Three Guarantees   *See* **Plan de Iguala.**

Planudes Maximus c1260–c1330.   Byzantine scholar. A learned monk, he was noted for this theological work on the procession of the Holy Spirit and for his editing of the *Greek Anthology* of poetry.

Plataea   Ancient city in east-central Greece. It allied itself with Athens against the Persians and was the site of a decisive Greek victory (479 BC) in the Persian Wars (*q.v.*).

Plato 427?–347 BC.   Ancient Greek philosopher, one of the great philosophers of all time. Born to a leading Athenian family, he was originally named Aristocles but was given the name Plato because of his broad shoulders. Little is known of his life. He became a pupil of Socrates, whose ideas and use of the dialectic (Socratic method) in pursuing truth later played an important role in Plato's writings. After Socrates' trial and execution (399 BC), Plato left Athens and traveled to Megara and, it is thought, to Egypt, Italy, and Syracuse. At Syracuse he was unsuccessful in trying to convert Dionysius the Elder to his idea of a state ruled by a philosopher-king. (He later returned to Syracuse to tutor Dionysius the Younger, but did not succeed in instilling his ideas into the youthful ruler.) Plato returned to Athens (388 BC) and founded the Academy (*q.v.*), an institution devoted to the investigation of scientific and philosophical truth, which flourished until the 6th cent. AD, when it was closed by Justinian. Plato taught at the Academy until his death. Among his pupils were Aristotle and Xenocrates. Plato is known best, however, for his writings, among them the *Republic, Apology, Symposium, Phaedo, Meno,* and the *Laws.* All of his writings take the form of dialogues, and many of them contain the character of Socrates as a leading figure. They are noted for their use of the dialectic, the technique of questioning all beliefs and assumptions in an attempt to come to a larger or more general truth or conception of reality. Plato's system of philosophy was based on the concept of a body of unchangeable and archetypal Ideas, of which the world's objects or appearances are mere approximations. The greatest of these Ideas was the Idea of the Good. The quest for the Good would ultimately lead man to harmony with the state and the universe. Plato's writings had enormous influence in the growth of Western civilization, and his writings retain a position of eminence in both Western philosophy and Western literature. In addition, his writings provide the primary source of knowledge of Socrates' teachings.

Platonism Philosophical school or tradition based on the writings of Plato. Platonism is founded on Plato's concept of reality as a body of eternal and unchangeable Ideas. Objects and other things perceived by the senses are only approximations of the more perfect Ideas and, therefore, approximations of ultimate reality. The primary Idea in the Platonic system is the Idea of the Good. Platonic thought attempted to demonstrate the path by which man could come into moral and esthetic balance with society, the state, and the universe. From Plato's writings numerous philosophical schools developed, and Platonism as a general philosophical movement had a major influence on the development of Western culture. It influenced the early Christian church, played a major role in the intellectual life of the Middle Ages, and also helped shape the intellectual and artistic development of the Renaissance.

Platt, Thomas Collier 1833–1910. US senator (1881) and New York State political boss. He helped T. Roosevelt become governor (1898) and vice-president (1900).

Platt Amendment US legislative provisions concerning Cuba, named for Connecticut senator Orville Platt (1827–1905) and added to the army appropriations bill of Mar. 2, 1901. It attempted to govern US relations with Cuba by forbidding Cuba to make any treaty limiting the island's independence or to incur excessive foreign debt. The US was accorded naval-base rights and the right to intervene. To end US occupation, Cuba agreed to these conditions, but abrogated them in 1934.

Plattsburgh, Battle of Important US victory (Sept. 11, 1814) in the War of 1812. Some 14,000 British troops closed on Plattsburgh in a combined land and naval assault (from Lake Champlain) that was the beginning of a British invasion of New York. Heavily outnumbered on land, the Americans attacked with a 14-ship fleet (Sept. 11), led by Commander T. Macdonough. The British fleet was decisively defeated, thus forcing the British to withdraw to Canada and ending the threatened invasion.

Plautus c254–184 BC. Roman writer of comic plays. His comedies, in expressive, idiomatic Latin, greatly influenced later European writers.

plebeians (plebs) In Roman history, the general body of citizens, as opposed to the aristocratic patricians. Originally excluded from all office-holding, by 287 BC (see Rome, 287 BC), they had achieved virtual political equality, although social distinction continued to be maintained.

Plehve, Vyacheslav Konstantinovich 1846–1904. Tsarist Russian official. He pursued forced Russification of minorities, allowed pogroms to be carried out against the Jews, and favored war against Japan to forestall internal tensions. He was finally assassinated.

Pleiad (Pléiade) Name given to several groups of seven poets, including (1) the tragic poets who wrote in Alexandria (c280 BC) under Ptolemy II Philadelphus, and (2) the 16th-cent. French Renaissance poets led by P. de Ronsard.

Plekhanov, Georgi Valentinovich 1857–1918. Russian Marxist theorist and revolutionary leader. A collaborator of N. Lenin up to 1903, Plekhanov later allied himself with the Mensheviks and unsuccessfully attempted reunification with the Bolsheviks.

Plessy v. *Ferguson* See **segregation.**

Plimsoll, Samuel 1824–98. British member of Parliament (1868–80) and social reformer. He worked for the welfare of British sailors and inspired maritime regulations and reforms. The Plimsoll line, marking the limit to which a ship may be loaded, is named for him.

Pliny the Elder AD 23–79. Roman naturalist. His *Historia naturalis,* an encyclopedic study of plant and animal life, was long a standard authority. He died while investigating the eruption of Mount Vesuvius.

Pliny the Younger AD 62?–c113. Roman statesman and author, son of Pliny the Elder. He held various Roman government offices, including that of consul (AD 100), and is noted for a series of letters describing the life of his times.

PLO See **Palestine Liberation Organization.**

Plombieres Agreement Secret alliance (July 20, 1858) formed at Plombieres, France, by Sardinian Prime Minister C. Cavour and French emperor Napoleon III. The two agreed that Sardinia and France would maneuver Austria into war, the hoped-for result being the eviction of Austria from Italy, the strengthening of French influence in Europe, and the annexation of Austrian territories in Italy by Sardinia and France (realized 1859–60).

Plotinus AD c205–270. Neoplatonist philosopher. Plotinus formulated an original philosophy that influenced many later systems of thought, including Christian philosophy and 19th-cent. German idealism.

Plutarch AD 46?–c120. Greek biographer and essayist. He was born in Chaeronea, Boeotia, and spent most of his life there, although he visited Rome and also maintained ties with Delphi, where he was a priest of Apollo (after AD c95). He is known best for his series of parallel biographies, *Parallel Lives*. In each book of this series he eulogized the life of a great Greek and that of a comparable Roman figure. Of these paired biographies, 46 survive, and they are an important source for knowledge of the ancient world. They have greatly influenced modern literature.

Plymouth Brethren Christian sect. Founded (Dec., 1828) in Dublin and (1830) in Plymouth, England, it has spread especially in English-speaking countries. Congregationally organized, the Brethren hold to fundamental Scripture and recognize no special ministry or priesthood.

Plymouth Colony English colony established (1620) on the coast of Massachusetts by the Pilgrims. Originally granted a patent to settle in Virginia, the colonists, upon arrival in New England, drew up the Mayflower Compact, which formed a government based on majority rule and acknowledged the authority of the English crown. The first Thanksgiving Day (1621) was celebrated by the colony in gratitude for a harvest after a winter of terrible privation. The colony joined (1643) the New England Confederation, and became (1691) part of the colony of Massachusetts.

Pobedonotsev, Konstantin Petrovich 1827–1870. Tsarist Russian official. As tutor to tsars Alexander III and Nicholas II and as a jurist and official, he promoted the autocratic form of government in Russia, Russification of minorities, and the supremacy of the Orthodox church.

Pocahontas c1595–1617. Indian woman and American folk heroine. The daughter of Indian chief Powhatan, she befriended colonists at the Jamestown, Virginia, settlement and is said to have prevented the Indians from killing Captain

J. Smith. Her marriage to settler J. Rolfe helped keep peace between the Indians and Virginia settlers.

Podebrad, George of *See* **George of Podebrad.**

Podmore, Frank *See* **Fabian Society.**

Poe, Edgar Allan 1809–49. American writer, one of the leading figures of American literature. He was orphaned in childhood, served in the army, and then was enrolled at West Point (1830). Subsequently expelled, he embarked upon his career as a writer. He became a leading critic as editor of the *Southern Literary Messenger* and other publications, and his stories and poems gained wide notice. Poe's life, however, was marked by tragedy and failure, augmented by poverty and drink, and he died (1849) in Baltimore under mysterious circumstances. Many of his works, among them the poems *The Raven* and *Annabel Lee* and the tales *The Fall of the House of Usher* and *The Murders in the Rue Morgue,* have become classics of American literature. His "tales of ratiocination" have been called the origins of the modern mystery story.

Poggio (Bracciolini, Gian Francesco Poggio) 1380–1459. Italian Renaissance humanist and scholar. Poggio rediscovered numerous manuscripts of Roman authors, among them works by Cicero, Lucretius, and Quintilian.

pogrom Attack on minority groups carried out sometimes with the toleration of the authorities. "Pogrom" is derived from the Russian word for riot or devastation. Pogroms against Jews began in Russia in 1881 following the assassination of Tsar Alexander II and continued sporadically until the Russian Revolution.

Poincaré, Jules Henri 1854–1912. French mathematician and scientist. His work on the theory of functions made advancements possible in physics. He was also well known for explaining science to the public.

Poincaré, Raymond 1860–1934. French president (1913–20) and three times premier (1912–13, 1922–24, 1926–29). He ordered France's occupation of the Ruhr (1923) after Germany failed to pay war reparations.

Poinsett, Joel Roberts 1779–1851. American diplomat and statesman. He represented the US on missions to Latin America, served in Congress (1821–25), and was secretary of war (1837–41) under President M. Van Buren. He opposed nullification and the growing southern movement toward secession.

Point Four Program US foreign-policy program aimed at providing technical assistance to underdeveloped countries. Named for the fourth point in President H. Truman's 1949 inaugural address it was eventually integrated into the over-all US foreign-aid program.

Poison Affair French court scandal. In 1679, an investigation revealed that vast segments of the French population patronized female fortunetellers for black masses and poisons as well as for prophecy. Many such fortune-tellers were arrested and executed, among them one Mme. Monvoison, who was burned in 1680. Her daughter charged that King Louis XIV's mistress, Mme. de Montespan, was one of her mother's clients and had obtained potions to secure the king's love and do away with her rivals. Though the charges were never proved, the executions ceased.

Poitiers, battles of Two decisive battles fought near this city in west-central France. **1.** (Tours, Battle of) Important battle (732) that helped end the Muslim invasion of Frankish domains. The Muslims, led by Abdu-r-Rahman, had overrun Aquitaine and were threatening Tours. To protect the city, the Frankish mayor of the palace, Charles Martel, intercepted the Muslim forces near Poitiers, defeated and killed Abdu-r-Rahman, and thereby forced the Muslims to retreat. **2.** Major victory (Sept. 19, 1356) for the English at the close of the first part of the Hundred Years' War (1337–1453). Edward the Black Prince had been conducting a raid into central France when his force of 7,000 men was intercepted near Poitiers by a 16,000-man army under French king John II. In the subsequent battle, English archers and lightly equipped infantrymen outmaneuvered and badly mauled the superior French force. King John was captured and 2,000 French knights were killed. John was ultimately forced to submit to the Treaty of Brétigny (*q.v.*).

Poitiers, Diane de *See* **Diane de Poitiers.**

Poland (Republic of Poland) Independent state and former Soviet-style people's republic located in Eastern Europe. The population is 38,363,000 and the capital is Warsaw. The Polish state dates to the late 10th cent. kingdom, which reached its height of power and prestige in the 16th cent. Dismembered (18th cent.) by Austria, Prussia, and Russia, it was reestablished as a republic (1918) at the end of WW I, only to be overrun (1939) by Germany and the Soviets at the opening of WW II. After WW II the reconstituted government of Poland fell under Soviet domination and in 1952 a new constitution established Poland as a people's republic, within the Soviet sphere of influence. Labor unrest in the early 1980s coalesced into the Solidarity movement and forced some reforms in Poland's Communist regime. Late in the 1980s, however, chronic economic problems, labor unrest, and the pro-democracy movement sweeping Eastern Europe finally brought down the Communist government. A democratic government and a free market economy succeeded the Communist regime. **For more on important persons and major events,** *see* **separate entries under specific names.** Key dates in the history of Poland include:

c840–1370 Piast dynasty ruled in Poland, after gaining control over Slavs in region.

992–1025 Boleslaus I reigned; first to designate himself Polish king; negotiated the Peace of Bautzen (1018); established Christianity.

1102–38 Boleslaus III reigned; kingdom divided at his death.

1177–94 Casimir II reigned; reunited most territories; established a senate and advanced peasants' rights.

1200s Mongols invaded Poland (1240) and broke up kingdom; Teutonic Knights moved into the north; Germans and Jews began to colonize Polish domains.

1320–33 Ladislaus I reigned; reestablished Polish kingdom and warred against Teutonic Knights.

1333–70 Casimir III, last Piast ruler, reigned; greatly increased Polish power and prestige in Europe, but in instituting elective kingship, strengthened the nobility at the expense of the crown for centuries to come.

1370–82 Polish crown passed to Hungary during reign of Louis I of Hungary.

1386–1434 Ladislaus Jagiello (married to Louis's daughter) reigned as Ladislaus II; founded Jagiello dynasty.

1386–1572 Jagiello dynasty ruled Poland; greatly expanded Polish domains and fostered a period of great cultural flowering.

1401 Treaty of Vilnius with Lithuania laid basis for union in 1569.

1410 Battle of Tannenberg fought by Poles and Lithuanians against Teutonic Knights; halted Knights' eastern advance.

1434–44 Ladislaus III reigned; died fighting the Ottoman Turks at Battle of Varna (1444).

1447–92 Casimir IV reigned; defeated Teutonic Knights in a long war (1454–66) and gained Pomerania and West Prussia.

1467 Casimir IV convened first Polish Sejm (diet).

1505 Nobles forced Polish monarchy to recognize powers of Sejm to legislate; Sejm composed of aristocrats and clergy.

1548–72 Sigismund II, last Jagiello king, reigned.

1558–82 Livonian War fought; S. Báthory gained several victories over Russia; Poland gained territory in Livonia and forced Russia to renounce its claims.

1565 Catholic Reformation began in Poland.

1569 Union of Lublin; Poland and Lithuania united under a single crown; union remained in effect until 18th cent.

1572 Nobles gained complete control of government on the death of Sigismund II; got power to elect monarch; *liberum veto,* giving any member of Sejm right to veto legislation, later weakened government and was finally abolished (1791).

1575–86 Stephen Báthory reigned; conducted war against Russia.

1587–1632 Sigismund III reigned; briefly held Swedish crown (1592–98) and after being deposed began series of wars between Poland and Sweden.

1587–1668 Vasa dynasty reigned.

c1613 Poles invaded Russia during Time of Troubles; marked new attempt to conquer Russia.

1618 Truce of Deulino halted fighting against Russia; Poles retained conquered lands.

1618–48 Thirty Years' War; Poland joined fighting against the Protestants.

1620–21 Poles victorious over the Ottoman Turks at the Battles of Chocim.

1648–68 John II Casimir reigned; Poland, its power declining, faced a Cossack rebellion in the Ukraine, an invasion by Charles X of Sweden (1655), and invasion by the Russians; Poles, however, managed to stave off total defeat.

1655–60 First Northern War with Sweden; by Peace of Oliva (1660) Polish King John II renounced his claim to the Swedish throne, lost northern Livonia.

1667 Treaty of Andrusov ended Thirteen Years' War with Russia; Poland ceded eastern Ukraine.

1682–99 Poland joined Austria in the Austro-Turkish War; Polish King John III Sobieski defeated the Ottoman Turks at Vienna (1683).

1700–21 Northern War; Poland ravaged during war as Russians and Swedes set up rival kings.

1733–35 War of the Polish Succession fought; led to succession of Augustus III as King of Poland.

1764–95 Stanislaus II elected king with the help of Russia and Prussia; dominated by Catherine II of Russia.

1768 Confederation of Bar formed to oppose Russian domination; defeated in 1772.

1772 First Partition of Poland; one-third of Polish domains annexed by Russia, Austria, and Prussia.

1791 New constitution promulgated as Polish national spirit arose; *liberum veto* abolished; kingship became hereditary; gentry admitted to Sejm.

1792 Confederation of Targowica formed by conservative reactionaries.

1793 Second Partition of Poland; Russia and Prussia invaded Poland to restore conservatives to power; annexed further territories, leaving only central Poland.

1794–95 T. Kosciusko led unsuccessful revolt (1794) against partition; Russia, Prussia, and Austria divided the remaining Polish domains in Third Partition and thus eliminated the Polish state.

1807 Napoleon I established grand duchy of Warsaw by Treaty of Tilsit.

1815 Congress Kingdom of Poland created by Congress of Vienna; Russian tsar was king.

1830–31 Russian Tsar Nicholas I suppressed November Revolution, Polish uprising; Poland reduced to Russian province.

1863–64 Unsuccessful January Insurrection against Russian domination of Poland; program of Russification and industrialization begun.

1916 Central Powers established (Nov.) an independent kingdom of Poland during WW I.

1918 Republic of Poland proclaimed (Nov. 11) in wake of Central Powers' defeat in WW I; Joseph Pilsudski named chief of state.

1919 Treaty of Versailles; gave Poland Polish Corridor (strip of land to Baltic) and Polish Prussia; Gdańsk made a free city; Russo-Polish border defined by Lord Curzon but was disputed by Poles.

1920 Russo-Polish War fought (Apr.–Oct.); sparked by Polish advances into the Ukraine.

1921 Treaty of Riga; Russia conceded substantial territories in the Ukraine.

1921 Republican constitution promulgated.

1926 Pilsudski seized power in military coup (May 12); became virtual dictator of Poland until his death in 1935.

1939 Poland joined in partitioning of Czechoslovakia.

1939 A. Hitler demanded cession of free city of Gdańsk and concessions in Polish Corridor to Danzig (Mar.); Germany and Poland entered diplomatic crisis that led to opening of WW II.

1939 Germany invaded Poland (Sept. 1), beginning WW II; USSR attacked Poland (Sept. 17); partition accord signed (Sept. 28) between USSR and Germany.

1939–45 German occupation; six million Poles killed in massacres and extermination camps; Jewish population of three million decimated; millions of others consigned to forced labor.

1941 Germany launched invasion of Russia (June); occupied Russian-held Poland.

1943 Katyn Massacre disclosed by Germans; mass grave of some 15,000 Polish soldiers (captured 1939 and murdered by Soviets, 1940) discovered; Polish government in exile broke off relations with Soviets.

1944 Warsaw Uprising (Aug.–Oct.); Polish underground captured Warsaw but was finally crushed by Germans, as Soviet forces waited outside Warsaw.

1945 Soviets drove remaining German forces out of Poland (Mar.).

1945 Polish Government of National Unity established (June 28) at Lublin.

1945 Old Curzon Line recognized as border with Russia.

1945 Potsdam Conference; former German territory to Oder-Neisse Line (including Gdańsk) put under Polish control.

1945 Poland joined the UN.

1946 Unicameral parliament (the Sejm) adopted by referendum.

1947 Communist leader Boleslaw Beirut elected president (Feb. 5) by Polish Sejm.

1947 Poland established as a people's republic (Feb.); Polish Workers' party, led by Wladyslaw Gomulka, became ruling party.

1948 Gomulka ousted from ruling party and later arrested for "nationalist deviations."

1948 Ruling party became Polish United Workers' party following merger with Socialist party.

1949 Soviet field marshal Konstantin Rokossovski made Polish minister of defense (Nov. 7).

1952 New constitution instituted Soviet-style government.

1953 Cardinal Wyszinski, Polish primate, arrested as government opposition to Roman Catholic church mounted.

1955 Poland became a founding member of the Warsaw Pact.

1956 Poznan Riots (June) by industrial workers suppressed; the riots over food shortages brought Wladyslaw Gomulka to power.

1956–70 Wladyslaw Gomulka (1905–82) in office as head of United Workers' (Communist) party; brought end to repression and persecution of Catholics; denounced Stalinist terrorism and halted collectivization of agriculture; from 1964, he implemented economic reform program, but also began reinstituting repression.

1970 Nonaggression treaty with West Germany signed (Dec. 7) by Polish government.

1970 Workers rioted (Dec. 15) in Gdańsk and other cities over announced sharp increases in food prices.

1970–80 Edward Gierek in power (Dec. 20) as Communist party first secretary, following resignation of Wladyslaw Gomulka.

1976 Workers struck (June 25) to protest plan for major increases in food prices; government delayed increases.

1979 Pope John Paul II, a native of Poland, visited Poland (June 2–11) on first visit by a pope to a Marxist state.

1980 Shipyard strike in Gdańsk quickly spread to other areas in northern Poland (Aug. 14); government reshuffled while negotiations with striking workers continued; government approval of right to strike and right to form unions independent of the Communist party finally ended strike (Aug. 31).

1980 Stanislaw Kania became party secretary, succeeding the ailing Edward Gierek (Sept. 6).

1980 Newly formed independent unions organized into national federation called Solidarity (Sept. 24), led by L. Walesa.

1981 Strike called by Solidarity for five-day work week ended after government agreed to demands (Jan. 31).

1981 100,000 workers in southern Poland went on a ten-day strike to protest corruption in local government (Feb. 6).

1981 Gen. Wojciech Jaruzelski became chairman of the Council of Ministers (Feb. 9); new strikes broke out.

1981 Millions of workers participated in four-hour general strike over various grievances (Mar. 27).

1981 Polish parliament voted (Apr. 10) to ban strikes for two months; Solidarity vowed to strike if its security was threatened.

1981 Polish government narrowly averted bankruptcy when Western nations made new arrangements for repayment of loans (Apr. 27).

1981 Premier Jaruzelski became leader of Poland's Communist party, replacing S. Kania (Oct. 18); he instituted hard-line policy against the labor unrest.

1981 Government declared a state of emergency (Dec. 13); imposed martial law and began a crackdown against Solidarity which included arrests of thousands of union leaders, including L. Welesa; thousands arrested before Solidarity movement was broken and government regained firm control (by early 1982).

1982 Polish parliament disbanded Solidarity (Oct.), banned future national union federations, and limited right to strike; sparked violent protests.

1982 Government released L. Walesa (Nov.) and ended martial law (Dec.).

1983 L. Walesa awarded the Nobel Peace Prize (Oct.); Polish government protested the award.

1984 Government marked 40th anniversary of Poland's People's Republic with general amnesty (July); thousands of prisoners released.

1984 Protests erupted following murder of pro-Solidarity priest by Internal Affairs police (Oct.); four officers later convicted of the killing.

1985 Supporters of banned Solidarity disrupted May Day celebrations nationwide.

1985 Gen. Jaruzelski became head of state (Nov.); formed Consultative Council (1986), which included some former Solidarity members, in hopes of appeasing opposition.

1987 Pope John Paul II visited Poland (June); called for respect for human rights as violent clashes between demonstrators and police broke out.

1988 Sharp price hikes introduced as government attempted to implement economic reforms (Feb.); sparked protests and strikes for higher wages (Apr.–May).

1988 Thousands of workers occupied Lenin Shipyard (May), demanding the government recognize Solidarity.

1988 Widespread unrest followed strike by coal miners demanding reinstatement of Solidarity; government offered to negotiate with Solidarity.

1989 Talks on reinstatement of Solidarity held (Feb–Apr.); government finally agreed to restore Solidarity; free elections to new 100-seat upper house to be held; opposition to be eligible to contest over a third of seats in Sejm; executive presidency to be created and president could be non-Communist.

1989 Roman Catholic church formally recognized by government (May).

1989 Solidarity candidates won all but one seat in new upper house (June).

1989 Soviet leader M. Gorbachev, visiting Germany, publicly reversed long-standing Brezhnev doctrine and declared that states have right to political self-determination (June); later reiterated new Soviet policy of non-interference.

1989– Walesa in office as Poland's first executive president, following elections (July); Communist rule formally ended when Gen. Jaruzelski agreed to formation of Solidarity-dominated coalition government with Communists.

1989 Radical economic reform program introduced; private ownership to be emphasized; privatization began 1990.

1989 Diplomatic relations with Vatican restored (July).

1989 US President G. Bush visited Poland (July); promised increased economic aid.

1989 Warsaw Pact foreign affairs ministers met (Oct.); reasserted end to USSR interventionist Brezhnev Doctrine by which Soviets had justified military intervention in Warsaw Pact countries.

1989 Germany's Berlin Wall, long-standing symbol of Cold War East-West divisions, was torn down (Nov.); collapse of East German government followed soon after.

1989 Polish government changed the country's name to Republic of Poland (Dec.).

1990 Large price increases for consumer goods imposed (Jan.) as part of government's economic stabilization program.

1990 Communist party reconstituted itself as social democratic party, Social Democracy of the Republic of Poland (Jan.).

1990 Foreign creditors agreed to moratorium on foreign debt payments until 1991 (Feb.).

1990 Railway workers' strike called (May) in response to government austerity program; workers sought large pay increases.

1990 Soviet authorities officially acknowledged responsibility for the Katyn massacre for the first time (Apr.); some 15,000 captured Polish troops were massacred by Soviets in 1940.

1990 Center Accord formed by Walesa supporters (May); backed his program of rapid economic reform; opposition, calling for slower shift to market economy, also organized support group, however.

1990 Government signed treaty with Germany that recognized current border along the Oder-Neisse rivers (Nov.).

1990 Walesa elected head of state (president, Dec.), after President Jaruzelski agreed to resign before expiration of his term.

1990– Walesa in office as president.

1990 Economic problems facing Poland's leaders in Dec. included hyperinflation (1,266% in Feb. 1990, reduced to 250% by Dec.), the sudden appearance of high unemployment (6.1% by Dec.), and foreign debt amounting to $46.1 billion.

1991 Warsaw Pact disbanded (Mar.); Soviet troops to be withdrawn from Germany, Hungary, and Czechoslovakia.

1991 Sejm rejected President Walesa's plan to dissolve lower house (Mar.), as opposition to Walesa mounted.

1991 Solidarity led nationwide, one-day strike to protest government's economic policies (May).

1991 Financial scandal (Aug.); central bank president ousted amid revelations of bribery and fraud by senior officials.

1991 Failed coup in the USSR (Aug. 18–21); collapse of former Soviet Union followed soon after.

1992 Widespread strikes sparked by hike in energy prices (Jan.).

1992 Sejm, contravening government's economic reform program, voted retroactive pay increases to public sector employees (May).

Poland, Congress Kingdom of *See* **Congress Kingdom of Poland.**

Poland, Partitions of *See* **Partition(s) of Poland.**

Polano, Pietro Soave *See* **Sarpi, Paolo.**

Pole, Edmund de la, earl of Suffolk c1472–1513. English aristocrat, Yorkist claimant to the throne. He sought Austrian help to make good his claim but was beheaded on the accession of King Henry VIII.

Pole, John de la, earl of Lincoln c1464–87. English aristocrat, Yorkist claimant to the throne. Recognized as heir by his brother-in-law, King Richard III, he led an army from Ireland against Henry VII but was killed.

Pole, Michael de la, 1st earl of Suffolk c1330–89. English chancellor (1383–86). He was a trusted adviser of King Richard II who advanced his family's fortunes and made him earl of Suffolk. He was finally brought down by his enemies and condemned for treason by Parliament.

Pole, Reginald 1500–58. English Catholic cardinal, archbishop of Canterbury (1556–58). A cousin of the Tudors, he broke with King Henry VIII but returned to help Henry's daughter Queen Mary I (Mary Queen of Scots) in her unsuccessful attempt to restore Catholicism.

Pole, William de la, 4th earl and 1st duke of Suffolk 1396–1450. English political leader. He became the principal minister to King Henry VI during the Hundred Years' War, and negotiated Henry's marriage (1445) to Margaret of Anjou.

His attempts to secure peace with France led to his impeachment, exile, and murder.

Polianov, Treaty of *See* **Deulino, Truce of.**

Polignac, Auguste Jules Armand Marie, prince de 1780–1847. French royalist statesman. Strongly Catholic in sympathy, he became the principal minister to King Charles X. His ordinances (1830) dissolving the chamber of deputies and muzzling the press led to the July Revolution (*q.v.*) and Charles's downfall.

polis A Greek city-state (*q.v.*).

Polish Corridor Territory along the Baltic on the west bank of the Vistula awarded to Poland by the Treaty of Versailles (1919). Since it contained many Germans and divided East Prussia from the rest of Germany, it was the cause of great friction between Poland and Germany. During the Nazi regime, the dispute led ultimately to the German invasion of Poland and the opening of WW II.

Polish Succession, War of the War (1733–38) fought to settle the disputed succession to the Polish throne after the death of Polish king Augustus II. Poland, with the support of France, Spain, and Sardinia, sought the succession of Stanislaus I Leszczynski. Russia and Austria supported the accession of Frederick Augustus II, elector of Saxony, as Augustus III. The war ended with the Treaty of Vienna (1735, ratified 1738), by which France acknowledged the accession of Augustus III, and Leszczynski, who abandoned his claim to the throne (1736), received the duchy of Lorraine, which was to revert back to France upon his death. The Spanish ceded Parma and Piacenza to Austria but kept the kingdom of Naples and Sicily.

Politburo Soviet governmental body. The Politburo was the policy-making and administrative arm of the Communist Party of the former USSR and therefore of all Soviet Russia. The first Politburo was created by the Bolsheviks shortly before the 1917 revolution, and included N. Lenin, L. Trotsky, and J. Stalin. After the revolution the Politburo was dissolved, but it was reestablished in 1919. Stalin abolished it in 1952, replacing it with the Presidium. The Politburo was restored in 1966 and abolished in 1991 along with other vestiges of the failed Soviet government. It generally included 11 or 12 members, and its meetings were secret.

Politian, Angelo Ambrogini 1454–94. Italian Renaissance humanist. One of the finest classical scholars of the classical revival, he also wrote outstanding vernacular poetry and the first secular play in Italian (1475).

Polk, James Knox 1795–1849. US president (1845–49), the eleventh, successor to J. Tyler. During his term of office the US fought the Mexican War (*q.v.*) and thereby greatly expanded its territories in the West and Southwest. A Jacksonian Democrat and staunch supporter of American expansionism, Polk was nominated for president as a "dark horse" candidate to break the deadlocked 1844 Democratic convention. Campaigning on the slogan "Fifty-four Forty or Fight" (the Oregon Territory boundary then being disputed with Britain), he defeated H. Clay in a close election. During his term of office, Polk reestablished an independent treasury, lowered tariffs through the Walker Tariff Act (1846), successfully negotiated the Oregon Territory boundary dispute, and acquired the Western and Southwestern territories from Mexico.

Polk, Leonidas 1806–64. American Episcopal bishop and Confederate general. A graduate (1827) of West Point, he resigned his commission to become a missionary and became first bishop of Louisiana (1841–61). When the American Civil War broke out, he became a Confederate general and was killed in action.

Pollaiuolo, Antonio 1429?–98. Florentine Renaissance artist. Especially noted for his bronze statues, Pollaiuolo also pioneered the study of human anatomy through dissection.

Pollock, (Paul) Jackson 1912–56. American painter. Viewing art as expression rather than illustration, he became the leading practitioner of abstract expressionism.

Polo, Marco 1254?–1324? Venetian traveler in China. His book known in English as *The Travels of Marco Polo* was one of the earliest and most important sources of Western knowledge of Asia. Born into a Venetian merchant family, he accompanied (1271) his father and uncle on a trip across central Asia. They reached Beijing and the court of the Mongol emperor Kublai Khan (1275). Polo became a favorite of the emperor and performed missions for him. He returned to Europe via Persia (1292) and arrived in Venice in 1295. Captured by the Genoese in a sea battle and imprisoned in Genoa, he dictated his fabulous memoirs to a fellow prisoner.

Poltava, Battle of Victory (July 8, 1709) of the forces of Russian tsar Peter I over Sweden's king

Charles XII, at Poltava, Ukraine, during the Northern War. An army of some 50,000 Russians destroyed the entire 20,000-man invading Swedish army, except for some 1,500 who fled south into Turkey with Charles. The battle marked the emergence of Russia as a great European power and ended Sweden's position as a military power.

Polyanov, Peace of Treaty (1634) between Russia and Poland. By its terms Poland received Smolensk in return for Polish recognition of Michael as tsar. Michael inaugurated the Romanov dynasty, which ruled Russia until 1917.

Polybius 203?–c120 BC. Greek historian. Deported to Rome, he conceived the idea of his great history, relating in 40 books (of which five survive) the conquest of the Mediterranean world by the Romans.

Polycarp, Saint AD c70–156? Greek bishop of Smyrna, Asia Minor, and martyr. A disciple of Saint John the Apostle and the mentor of Saint Irenaeus, he was a leading figure in the establishment of early Christian theology. He was martyred at age 86.

Polycrates d. c522 BC. Greek tyrant of Samos (c535–522 BC). Polycrates gained for Samos naval eminence in the Aegean. He sent a fleet of 40 ships commanded by his political foes to aid the Persians against Egypt, but they combined with Spartans in an unsuccessful attempt to depose him. He was eventually lured to the mainland and executed by a Persian satrap.

polytheism Belief in many gods, as opposed to the monotheism of Christianity, Judaism, and Islam. In polytheism, each god tends to become identified with a function, such as fire, storm death, etc., and each tends to become personified.

Pombal, Sebastião José de Carvalho e Mello, marquês de 1699–1782. Portuguese statesman. He organized the reconstruction of Lisbon after the great earthquake of 1755. As chief minister (1756–77) he introduced reforms and reduced the power of the Inquisition, but his harsh, authoritarian, and anticlerical rule earned him great enmity.

Pomerania Historic European region on the Baltic Sea. Originally occupied by Slavs, the area has been overrun, split up, and ruled by several countries, including Prussia, Poland, and Sweden. Many of the leading cities, such as Danzig, were once prominent in the Hanseatic League.

Most of Pomerania was restored to Poland after the Potsdam Conference (1945).

Pomerania, Eric of *See* **Eric VII.**

Pompadour, Jeanne Antoinette Poisson, marquise de 1721–64. Royal mistress of French king Louis XV. Through her intelligence and beauty she exercised great influence over the king and French policies. She was an outstanding patron of the arts.

Pompeii Ancient Roman city. Situated at the foot of Mount Vesuvius near modern Naples, it was damaged by an earthquake (AD 63), and then completely covered over by the eruption of Vesuvius (AD 79). Rediscovered (1748), it has become a major source of our knowledge of Roman civilization.

Pompeius, Sextus (Pompey the Younger) c75–35 BC. Roman commander. A son of Pompey the Great, he continued to fight against J. Caesar's forces after Pompey's death (48 BC). He occupied Sicily and attempted to cut off Rome's grain supply. Eventually defeated by Octavian (36 BC), he fled to Asia Minor but was captured and killed.

Pompey 106–48 BC. Roman general and statesman. Pompey, a protégé of Sulla's, gained important victories in Africa, Italy, Spain, and Gaul, and won for himself the title Magnus ("the Great"). After Sulla's death, he defeated Lepidus (77 BC), Sertorius (76 BC), and Spartacus (72 BC). In 70 BC he was elected consul along with Marcus Licinius Crassus. Pompey thereafter cleared the Mediterranean of pirates and consolidated Rome's Asian possessions. Together with Crassus and J. Caesar, he formed the First Triumvirate (60 BC). The rivalry between Caesar and Pompey remained submerged during Pompey's marriage to Caesar's daughter Julia but intensified after her death (54 BC). In 49 BC, Caesar crossed the Rubicon, invaded Italy, and defeated Pompey at Pharsalus (48 BC). Pompey fled to Egypt, where he was murdered.

Pompey the Younger *See* **Pompeius, Sextus.**

Pompidou, Georges Jean Raymond 1911–74. French premier (1962–68) and president of the Fifth Republic (1969–74). A wartime protégé of C. de Gaulle, he later became prominent as both banker and politician, and helped draft the constitution of the Fifth Republic.

Ponce de León, Juan 1460–1521. Spanish explorer. He explored and settled the island of Puerto Rico (1508–09), founding its oldest settlement, Caparra, and was named its governor. Hearing legends about a rejuvenating spring (the "fountain of youth") on the Bahamian island of Bimini, he sailed to the coast of what he named Florida (1513) and landed near the modern city of St. Augustine. His expedition traveled south to the Florida Keys without finding the legendary fountain. Later named military governor (1514) of Florida, he led another expedition there (1521), this time with two ships and 200 men. He was wounded during an Indian attack and died soon after.

Poncelet, Jean Victor 1788–1867. French mathematician. While a war prisoner in Russia following Napoleon I's campaign, he developed the foundations of modern projective geometry.

Pondicherry Former French colony on the southeast coast of India. Founded in 1674, it was the object of fighting during 18th-cent. colonial wars between Britain and France. The colony remained in French hands until 1954 (when it was ceded to India), the last remnant of extensive domains lost by the French to the British in the 18th cent.

Poniatowski, Prince Józef Anton 1763–1813. Polish military leader, and nephew of King Stanislaus II. Poniatowski fought with distinction against Russia (1792) and took part in the Polish revolt (1794) led by T. Kosciusko. He later became minister of war of the duchy of Warsaw (1807) under Napoleon, and fought and died during Napoleon's Russian campaign.

Pontiac c1720–69. Ottawa Indian chief who organized the Great Lakes Indian tribes in a nearly successful uprising known as Pontiac's Rebellion (*q.v.*).

Pontiac's Rebellion (~ Conspiracy) 1763–66. American Indian uprising against the British after the French and Indian Wars. Pontiac, an Ottawa Indian chief, realized that the British were far less friendly to Indians than the defeated French. He enlisted the support of the tribes of the Great Lakes region and conducted a series of raids on British settlements. Though these attacks were brilliantly planned and executed, superior British weaponry forced Pontiac to sue for peace. The uprising was ended by a treaty of amity (July 25, 1766).

Pontius Pilate *fl.* AD 26. Roman prefect of Judaea. By "washing his hands" of ultimate responsibility, he allowed the crucifixion of Jesus.

Pontus Ancient country of northeastern Asia Minor, on the Black Sea, in what is now Turkey. It was founded by Mithradates II (c3d cent. BC) and reached its height under the reign of Mithradates VI. The Pontic Empire was not strong enough, however, to withstand the Romans. Pompey occupied Pontus (66 BC), and made part of it a client kingdom and the rest a Roman province.

pony express US mail delivery system between St. Joseph, Missouri, and Sacramento, California (inaugurated Apr. 3, 1860). The horse and rider system required more than 150 horse-changing stations to enable relay riders to cover the distance in eight to ten days. The pony express was phased out after the first telegraph service to San Francisco began (Oct. 24, 1861).

Poole, William Frederick 1821–94. American librarian. A director of public libraries in Boston, Cincinnati, and Chicago, he devised (1848) the first periodical index, *Poole's Index to Periodical Literature.*

Pop art Art movement (late 1950s to early 1970s) in which subject matter was taken from the popular culture and included reproductions of such things as comic strips and well-known commercial products. It evolved as a reaction against the cultural pretensions Pop artists saw in other art movements. Andy Warhol (1928–87) was one of its leading proponents.

pope *See* **papacy.**

Pope, Alexander 1688–1744. English poet and satirist. A master of the heroic couplet and one of the great poets of his age, Pope expressed the ideas of his time in such graceful and polished works as his *Essay on Man.* Among his other works were *Essay on Criticism, The Rape of the Lock,* and *The Dunciad.*

Pope, John 1822–92. Union general in the American Civil War. Pope fought with distinction on the Mississippi but was disastrously defeated at the Second Battle of Bull Run (1862).

Popish Plot Fictitious English plot fabricated (1678) by T. Oates and Israel Tonge. According to Oates, Catholics had formed a conspiracy to assassinate English king Charles II. The wave of hysteria caused by Oates' allegations led to the persecution and killing of many Catholics.

Popol Vuh Quiché Indian (Mayan) manuscript of the 16th cent. Written by a Quiché and based on traditional Indian documents and lore, it is an important source for ancient Mayan mythology and culture.

Poppaea Sabina *d.* AD 65. Wife (*m.* AD 62) of the Roman emperor Nero. She is said to have persuaded Nero to kill his former wife, his own mother, and the philosopher Seneca. Nero is said to have kicked her to death.

Popular Front Political coalitions in Europe formed by liberals, moderates, Socialists, and Communists during the 1930s. These coalitions were aimed at blocking the then growing Fascist movement, and Popular Front coalitions gained control of governments in France and Spain during the 1930s. (*See also* France, 1936; Second Republic, Spanish.)

popular sovereignty (squatter ~) Pre-Civil War US political doctrine. It held that the settlers of territories had the right to decide whether they would enter the Union as free or slave states. The doctrine was supported by Sen. S. Douglas and was incorporated into the Compromise of 1850 and the Kansas-Nebraska Act (*qq.v.*). Opponents of the plan called it "squatter sovereignty," and it proved to be a failure in settling the slavery question. It led to serious conflicts in the territories, notably Bleeding Kansas (*q.v.*).

Populist party American political party that attempted to challenge the major parties during the 1890s by allying an agrarian coalition with labor and other interests. From the 1870s, when farm prices began to decline, American farmers sought to advance their interests through groups such as the Granger movement, the Greenback party, and the Farmers' Alliances. By 1892 the Populist party was formed. It advocated free coinage of silver and expansion of the currency; lowering of transportation costs by nationalization of the railroads; a graduated income tax; direct popular election of senators; and an eight-hour working day. The party nominated J. Weaver for president in 1892 and he received more than a million votes. The party made further gains in the 1894 congressional elections. Because of a convergence of interests in free silver, the party supported the Democratic candidate, W. Bryan, in 1896. After Bryan's defeat, the party rapidly declined as a political force. Some of the elements of its platform were later enacted by the major parties.

Populists *See* **Narodniki.**

Poquelin, Jean Baptiste *See* **Molière.**

Porphyrogenitus, Constantine *See* **Constantine VII.**

Porphyry (Malchus) AD c233–c304. Greek Neoplatonic philosopher. A disciple and biographer of Plotinus, he also wrote 15 books of anti-Christian polemics, *Adversus Christianos.*

Porson, Richard 1759–1808. English classical scholar. He produced outstanding critical editions of such classical writers as Aeschylus and Euripides.

Porter, Cole 1893–1964. American composer and lyricist. Porter's lyrics and arresting tunes for such musical shows as *Can-Can* and *Kiss Me, Kate* made him one of the leading popular composers of his day.

Porter, David 1780–1843. American naval officer. He served in the Tripolitan War, and, as captain of the *Essex* during the War of 1812, captured the *Alert,* the first British warship taken in the war.

Porter, David Dixon 1813–91. American admiral. Son of D. Porter. During the American Civil War, he commanded Union forces on the Mississippi and in the Atlantic blockade, and he contributed to the Union victories at New Orleans (1862) and Vicksburg (1863).

Porter, Horace 1837–1921. American general and diplomat. During the American Civil War, he served as aide-de-camp to Gen. U. Grant (1864–65). He later served as secretary to President Grant (to 1872), US minister to France (1897–1905), and as a US delegate to the Hague Conference (1907).

Porter, Katherine Anne 1890–1980. American writer, considered a master of the short story. She is also the author of an acclaimed novel, *Ship of Fools.*

Porter, William Sydney *See* **Henry, O.**

Portland, William Bentinck, 1st earl of 1649–1709. Dutch-born English statesman. He negotiated the marriage (1677) of William of Orange (King William III) to Mary, daughter of the duke of York (later James II). He accompanied William to England (1688), was created 1st earl of Portland, and fought for William at the Battle of the Boyne (1690). He negotiated the Treaty of Ryswick (1697).

Porto Rico *See* **Puerto Rico.**

Portsmouth, Treaty of Treaty concluded (Sept. 5, 1905) between Russia and Japan at Portsmouth,

New Hampshire, ending the Russo-Japanese War. By its terms Russia recognized Japan as the dominant power in Korea and ceded Port Arthur, the Liaodong Peninsula, and southern Sakhalin Island to Japan. Both powers agreed to restore Manchuria to China.

Portugal (Portuguese Republic) Country located on the west coast of the Iberian Peninsula in southern Europe. The population is 10,528,000 and the capital is Lisbon. Portugal emerged as an independent state (12th cent.) during the reconquest of the Muslim-held Iberian Peninsula by Spanish Christians. From the 15th to 16th cents., the Portuguese created a formidable overseas colonial empire in Asia, Africa, and South America. The Portuguese were soon eclipsed by the other European powers, however. The monarchy was overthrown in 1910. After a period of unstable republican government, A. Salazar came to power (1932) and began his long dictatorial rule. His death was followed by a period of instability and return to republican government (1976). Key events in Portuguese history include:

5TH–8TH CENTS. AD Region, formerly under Roman control (from 1st cent. BC), was occupied by Visigoths.

711 Muslims conquered Visigoths and took control of entire Iberian Peninsula.

9TH CENT. Gradual reconquest of region from Muslims begun by Spanish Christians.

1095 County of Portugal given to Count Henry of Burgundy by Alfonso VI of Castile; was dowry of his illegitimate daughter Teresa.

1128 Alfonso I Henriques, son of Henry of Burgundy, seized power in the county; had himself crowned king after defeating the Moors at the Battle of Ourique (1139).

1143 Treaty of Zamora granted Portugal independence from Spain; Alfonso I recognized as king.

1179 Pope Alexander III recognized Portugal as an independent kingdom.

1223–48 Alfonso II reigned; he convened first Cortes.

1248–79 Alfonso III reigned, instituted administrative reforms and promoted commerce.

1250 Algarve in the south finally conquered from the Moors, establishing Portugal's present-day borders.

1256 Lisbon, recaptured from the Moors in 1147, became the Portuguese capital.

1276 Pedro Giuliano became Pope John XXI, the only Portuguese to serve as pope.

1294 King Diniz signed a commercial treaty with Edward I, the first of a long series of English-Portuguese pacts.

1325–57 Alfonso IV reigned; ordered murder (1355) of his daughter-in-law I. Castro, thus provoking his son, Dom Pedro (future Peter I), to revolt.

1357–67 Peter I reigned; became known for his harsh administration of justice.

1385 Battle of Aljubarrota ended long series of wars with the Spanish kingdom of Castile; Portuguese victory assured Portugal's continued independence.

1385–1433 John I reigned; marked beginning of Portuguese exploration and colonization; wars against the Muslims in North Africa.

1386 Treaty of Windsor allied Portugal permanently with England; John I married to Philippa, daughter of John of Gaunt.

1415 Conquest of Ceuta in Africa from the Moors; Portuguese subsequently expanded control in Morocco.

1419–60 Prince Henry the Navigator organized voyages of discovery that explored Africa's west coast; provided foundation for what later became Portugal's worldwide colonial empire.

1427 Azores discovered and opened to colonization.

1433–38 Duarte, the "philosopher king," reigned; encouraged Henry the Navigator's efforts to organize voyages of discovery along the coast of Africa.

1438–81 Alfonso V reigned; won important victories against Muslims in North Africa.

1446 African coastal region, later the colony of Portuguese Guinea, settled.

1448 Overseas trading post established by Henry the Navigator, the first such outpost set up by a European power.

1460 Cape Verde Islands and the coast of Guinea became Portuguese colonies; death of Prince Henry the Navigator.

1476 Battle of Toro; King Alfonso V, laying claim to Spanish throne, was decisively defeated by Queen Isabella and King Ferdinand.

1481–95 John II reigned; curbed power of nobles and fostered colonization.

1488 Africa's Cape of Good Hope rounded by Bartholomeu Dias.

1494 Treaty of Tordesillas (June 7) signed with Spain; provided for division of newly discovered lands in Americas, Africa, and Asia; Portugal gained what would become Brazil.

1495–1521 Manuel I reigned; his reign saw Portugal's rise as a major commercial power through its new-found overseas trade.

1496 Jews expelled from Portugal; exodus of middle class and highly educated Jews weakened Portugal.

1497–98 V. da Gama opened up trade route from Portugal to India, providing the foundation for Portuguese Empire; realized strategy proposed by Henry the Navigator, which allowed Portuguese to outflank Muslim traders, then in control of land routes to Indies and Far East.

1500 Brazil claimed by Pedro Alvares Cabral.

1510 A. de Albuquerque occupied Goa, the best port on India's west coast; Goa was a Portuguese colony for over 450 years.

1511 Albuquerque conquered Malacca on Malay Peninsula; Portuguese first of European colonial powers to reach China.

1512–13 Occupation of the Moluccas (islands of Indonesia).

1521 F. Magellan, a Portuguese navigator serving Spain, died in the Philippines; his crew completed what became the first circumnavigation of the world.

1521–57 John III reigned; Portugal reached its height; influence expanded in Brazil, India, Macao, and Moluccas.

1524–80 L. de Camões, considered Portugal's greatest poet, lived; wrote epic poem *The Lusiads.*

1532 First Portuguese settlement founded in Brazil by Admiral M. Sousa.

1536 Inquisition established in Portugal.

1578 Battle of Alcazarquivir in Morocco; Sebastian, son of John III, killed with the flower of Portuguese nobility (Aug. 4); kingdom permanently weakened.

1580 Succession disputed after Sebastian's brother, Cardinal Henry, died; Philip II of Spain invaded and conquered Portugal.

1580–1640 Sixty Years' Captivity saw Portugal ruled as Spanish province; Portuguese seaborne empire weakened.

1580–98 Spanish King Philip II reigned as Philip I.

c1636 Dutch seized Ceylon and Malacca from the Portuguese; other Asian possessions lost.

1640 Portuguese successfully rebelled against Spanish rule and regained independence, though Spanish did not formally recognize Portuguese independence.

1640–56 John IV reigned; founded Braganza line; drove Dutch out of Brazil.

1640–1910 Braganza line in power.

1656–83 Alfonso VI reigned, though in name only due to mental impairment.

1663 Battle of Ameixial (June 8); Portuguese defeated Spanish invaders.

1667 Peter II ousted Alfonso VI; reigned as regent until Alfonso's death in 1683, then succeeded to throne.

1668 Treaty of Lisbon; Spain recognized Portuguese independence.

1701–14 War of the Spanish Succession; Portugal participated after 1703.

1703 Treaty of Methuen (Dec. 27) gave Portuguese wines preference in England in return for preferential treatment of English textiles; began two centuries of Portuguese dependence on the English trade.

1706–50 John V reigned; made peace with France and Spain; gold from Brazil brought period of affluence during John's reign.

1713, 1715 Peace of Utrecht; treaties signed by France and Spain respectively formally ended hostilities with Portugal, following War of Spanish Succession.

1750–77 Marquês de Pombal effectively ruled Portugal as minister to Joseph I; introduced Enlightenment ideas, strengthened monarchy at expense of nobles and church, sought to revitalize declining commerce and agriculture.

1755 Lisbon earthquake destroyed the city and killed thousands; Pombal organized Lisbon's reconstruction.

1777–1816 Maria I reigned (with Peter III until 1786); Pombal's reforms rescinded, bringing on renewed slow decline of the kingdom.

1801 War of the Oranges; Portugal conquered and divided by France and Spain.

1807 Napoleon's armies marched on Portugal; royal family fled to Brazil; Peninsular War began in following year.

1808–14 Peninsular War.

1811 Portugal at last cleared of French troops. Royal family remained in Brazil.

1815 Brazil became a kingdom separate from Portugal, united by the crown.

1816 John VI succeeded to the thrones of both Portugal and Brazil.

1820 Liberal revolution in Portugal created a constitutional monarchy.

1821 John VI returned to Portugal from Brazil; reigned as constitutional monarch (1822–26).

1822 Brazil proclaimed independence; Pedro I established as constitutional monarch there.

1826 Maria II acceded to throne under the regency of Dom Miguel.

1828–33 Civil war, Miguel usurped the throne; Pedro I came to Portugal (1831) and, with the help of European powers, aided the liberals in restoring Maria (1833).

1834–53 Maria II reigned after reaching her majority (with King Ferdinand after 1836); struggle between liberals and conservatives during her reign laid basis for later reforms.

1853–61 Peter V reigned; his reign saw beginnings of industrialization in Portugal.

1861–89 Louis I reigned; legal reforms instituted.

1868 Slavery abolished in Portuguese colonies.

1889–1908 Charles I reigned; assassinated after granting dictatorial powers to his prime minister, João Franco.

1908 Manuel II, last of the Braganzas, succeeded to the throne.

1910 Manuel II deposed by a military coup (Oct. 3–5); republic declared.

1910–11 Poet T. Braga in office as first president of new republic.

1911 Republican constitution instituted; church and state separated; women given vote.

1911–15 M. de Arriaga in office as first elected president; period of economic problems and political unrest continued into 1920s.

1915–18 Portugal fought with the Allies in WW I; pro-German sentiment remained strong in military, however.

1915 Military dictatorship established (Jan.) after National Assembly voted to join Allies against Germany.

1915 Republican government restored following revolt against military (May).

1915–17 President Bernardino Machado in office as president.

1916 Germany declared war on Portugal (Mar.).

1917 Pro-German military leader Sidoni Paes (1872–1918) led uprising that forced republican government to resign (Dec. 9); Sidoni in office as president soon after.

1918 President Paes assassinated (Dec. 15) after only a year in office; period of political instability followed.

1926 Military overthrew the government (May).

1926–51 A. Carmona installed as president.

1926 A. Salazar named finance minister; engineered Portugal's economic recovery.

1927 Government quashed attempted revolt (Feb.).

1931 Military coup attempt failed.

1932–68 Salazar in power as prime minister; thereafter ruled Portugal as dictator.

1933 Salazar-sponsored constitution transformed Portugal into a "corporative state."

1936–39 Salazar supported Fascist Gen. F. Franco in the Spanish Civil War.

1939–45 WW II; Portugal remained neutral; from 1943 allowed Allies use of Azores.

1940 Jews forbidden to travel through Portugal.

1949 Portugal became a founding member of NATO.

1955 Portugal became a member of the UN.

1961 Portuguese Goa forcibly invaded by the Indian army and annexed to India (Dec. 18).

1962 Revolt by independence fighters in Portuguese Angola broke out.

1963, 1964 Revolts for independence broke out in Portuguese Guinea and Mozambique.

1968–74 M. Caetano in office as prime minister; replaced the ailing Salazar; opposition to repressive government mounted.

1969 National Assembly elections held; ruling União Nacional won all seats; opposition parties outlawed immediately afterward.

1970 Salazar, long-time head of Portuguese government, died (July 27).

1970 Ruling party renamed Acção Nacional Popular.

1974 Military coup (Apr. 25) followed government's failure to maintain control over overseas territories in Africa; military junta led by Gen. Antonio de Spinola in power.

1974–76 Gen. Francisco da Costa Gomes in office; replaced de Spinola as president (Sept. 30); his term marked by period of political turmoil.

1974–75 Small and medium-sized farms seized by government in collectivization scheme;

move later rendered illegal by 1977 Land Reform Law.

1974   Independence granted to Guinea-Bissau (Aug. 26).

1975   Gen. de Spinola's followers failed in attempted coup (Mar. 11); government swung to left.

1975   Banks and insurance companies nationalized (Mar. 14–15).

1975   Agreements reached providing independence to Cape Verde Islands (July 5), Mozambique (June 25), São Tomé and Principe (July 12) and Angola (Nov. 11).

1975   Three-man military junta put in charge of country (July 25).

1975   Communist revolt crushed by government troops (Nov. 25–27).

1976   New, pro-Communist constitution adopted to transform Portugal to socialist state; country to be ruled by Council of the Revolution, headed by president of Portugal, in conjunction with legislative Assembly.

1976–86   Moderate Socialist, Gen. Antonio Ramalho Eanes, in office as president following first free elections in decades (June 27); Partido Socialista won largest block of seats in new Assembly; Eanes administration marked by economic problems (rising inflation, trade deficit, and foreign debt, as well as increasing losses by state-run industries); terrorist activity also on rise.

1976   East Timor, once a Portuguese territory, annexed by neighboring Indonesia.

1980   President Eanes reelected (Dec. 8) after death of his principal opponent, Francisco Sá Carneiro.

1982   Assembly approved new constitution; established full civilian government by reducing presidential powers and dissolving the Council of the Revolution.

1984   Demonstration by employees of state-run businesses demanding pay owed them (Apr.); hundreds arrested.

1984   Dozens of suspected terrorists rounded up by police (June), following terrorist campaign by left-wing FP-25 group (Forças Populares de 25 Abril).

1985   Trial of over 70 suspected FP-25 members began amid continued terrorist attacks; some 50 defendants were convicted and sent to prison.

1986   Joined the EEC.

1986–   Dr. Mário Soares, former prime minister and member of the Socialist Party (PSP), in office as first civilian president since 1926; his efforts to reform labor and agrarian laws at first blocked by Assembly, but were soon instituted; his administration marked by privatization program and rapidly improving economy, spurred by foreign investment.

1987   Portugal agreed to turn over to China its overseas territory of Macao in 1999; China to maintain capitalist system in Macao after that time.

1987   Government announced radical reform program, including privatization of state-run industries, sweeping changes in agriculture and education, and reform of labor laws that prevented the government from firing public employees to cut spending.

1988   24-hour general strike by 1.5 million workers protesting government's proposed labor law reform (Mar.); Assembly approved legislation, however; Constitutional Tribunal then rejected new labor law as unconstitutional (May).

1988   Portugal became member of Western European Union (Nov.).

1989   Mass demonstration in Lisbon (Jan.) began a year marked by labor unrest.

1989   Government rocked by charges of financial irregularities against two ministers and by a sex scandal involving wives of high officials.

1989   Constitutional amendments enacted to allow full privatization of Portugal's state-run industries (Aug.).

1990   President Soares won reelection in landslide victory (Jan.).

1990–91   Portuguese-brokered peace talks held in Lisbon between Angolan government and UNITA rebels; peace agreement and ceasefire ending the civil war announced May, 1991.

1991   Talks began with US on renewing lease for US military base in Azores.

Portuguese East Africa   *See* **Mozambique.**

Portuguese Guinea   *See* **Guinea-Bissau.**

Portuguese India   Former Portuguese possessions in India. Comprising Goa, Daman, and Diu, they were the remnants of more extensive possessions and were annexed by India (Dec., 1961).

Porus *fl.* 4th cent. BC.   Ruler of a kingdom in the Punjab region, now divided between modern

India and Pakistan. During Alexander the Great's conquest of the region, Porus fought a great battle against the invading Macedonian armies and though he lost, his valor so impressed Alexander that Porus was reinstated as ruler of the kingdom. He was assassinated some years after Alexander's death.

Poseidonius (Posidonius) c135–c51 BC. Greek Stoic philosopher and historian. He was very successful in promoting Stoicism among the Romans, but none of his voluminous writings has survived.

positivism School of philosophical thought. Positivism holds that all knowledge is based solely on sense experience and denies the possibility of transcendental or metaphysical knowledge. The origins of both the name and the school are usually ascribed to A. Comte.

Posse, Count Arvid *See* **Agrarian party.**

postimpressionism Movement in art dominant in the late 19th and early 20th cents. Going beyond impressionism's preoccupation with light, painters such as P. Cézanne, P. Gauguin, and V. van Gogh combined brilliant colors with studies of angle and form, thus paving the way for the major 20th-cent. movements cubism and fauvism.

Potato War *See* **Bavarian Succession, War of the.**

Potawatomi Indians North American Indian tribe. First settled in northern Wisconsin, they moved to occupy both sides of southern Lake Michigan in the 18th cent. In the 1860s, many moved to Kansas and Oklahoma. The Potawatomi took part in Pontiac's Rebellion (*q.v.*) and fought on the side of the British in the War of 1812.

Potemkin, Grigori Aleksandrovich 1739–91. Russian field marshal and statesman. He helped bring Catherine II to the throne (1762) and remained a powerful and influential favorite of hers. He served with distinction in the Russo-Turkish Wars.

Potidaea Ancient Greek city. Colonized c600 BC, it revolted against Athens (432 BC) and Athens's subsequent treatment of Potidaea helped bring about the second Peloponnesian War. The city was destroyed (348 BC) by Philip II of Macedon.

Potsdam Conference (Berlin Conference) Allied meeting (July 17–Aug. 2, 1945) at Potsdam, near Berlin, after Germany's surrender in WW

II. Present at the conference were US president H. Truman, Russian premier J. Stalin, and Great Britain's prime ministers, first W. Churchill and later C. Atlee (from July 26, 1945, after he had succeeded Churchill as prime minister). The resulting Potsdam Agreement outlawed Nazism in Germany, placed Germany's eastern provinces under the control of Russia and Poland, decentralized the German economy, set terms for reparations, and agreed to try war criminals. The Potsdam Declaration (July 26) called on Japan to surrender unconditionally.

Pottawatomie Massacre Murder of five proslavery settlers on the night of May 24–25, 1856, on Pottawatomie Creek, Kansas. The massacre was carried out by abolitionist J. Brown and his party, and most of the victims were associated with the enforcement of proslavery laws.

Potter, Beatrix 1866–1943. English author of children's stories. She created such classics as the stories of Peter Rabbit and Benjamin Bunny and illustrated them with her own delicate watercolors.

Potter, (Martha) Beatrice *See* **Webb, (Martha) Beatrice.**

Poulenc, Francis 1899–1963. French composer. A member of Les Six, he wrote a variety of sophisticated, often witty songs and is considered a leading composer of this century.

Pound, Ezra Loomis 1885–1972. American poet. A leader in early 20th-cent. modernist literary movements, he created original poetical works, notably his *Cantos,* and was a major influence on US and British literature. His pro-Fascist broadcasts from Italy during WW II led to his incarceration (1946–58) in a mental hospital in Washington, D.C.

Poussin, Nicholas 1594–1665. French painter. Considered the leading 17th-cent. French artist, he painted both religious and mythological scenes in a style that set the standard for French classicism.

Powderly, Terence V. *See* **Knights of Labor.**

Powell, John Wesley 1834–1902. American geologist and ethnologist. Surveyor of the Colorado River system, he was the director of the Smithsonian's Bureau of Ethnology (1879–1902) and of the US Geological Survey (1881–94).

Powers, Hiram 1805–73. American sculptor. He worked in Florence in the predominant neoclassical style and became famous for such works as the highly controversial nude *Greek Slave.*

Powhatan Confederacy   League of North American Indian tribes consisting of some 200 settlements in the Virginia tidewater region and on the east shore of the Chesapeake. The confederacy was formed by Chief Wahunsonacock (called Powhatan by settlers) and for a time had friendly relations with the English colonists at Jamestown. The marriage of J. Rolfe to Pocahontas, the chief's daughter, kept the peace until Wahunsonacock's death. Thereafter, Indian resentment over white encroachment on their lands resulted in the Powhatan War (*q.v.*) and defeat of the confederacy.

Powhatan War   Intermittent struggle of the tidewater Indian tribes of colonial Virginia and Maryland against encroachment of whites seeking new tobacco lands. The marriage of Pocahontas, daughter of the Indian chief Powhatan (1550?–1618), to J. Rolfe had helped keep peace with the English settlers, but after Powhatan's death his successor led an attack (1622) in which some 350 settlers were killed. Settler reprisal was fierce. The next large-scale Indian attack came in 1644, when some 500 settlers were killed. But the tide soon went against the Indians, eventually resulting in the death of three-quarters of the tribes' members and the takeover of most of their lands.

Poynings, Sir Edward   *See* **Poynings's Law.**

Poynings's Law   Acts of the Irish Parliament (1494) secured by the English governor of Ireland, Sir Edward Poynings (1459–1521). The acts sharply limited the power of the Irish Parliament and included statutes putting English laws in force in Ireland and requiring approval of the English king and council for all parliamentary acts.

Poznan Riots   Uprising (June, 1956) in the western Polish city of Poznan. Industrial workers staged a general strike demanding bread and freedom. It was suppressed with military force, leaving 53 dead and over 200 wounded, but it led to a change in Polish Communist party leadership.

Pozzo di Borgo, Carlo Andrea   1764–1842.   Corsican statesman who served in the Russian diplomatic service. An opponent of the Bonapartes, he worked to promote the alliances that eventually defeated Napoleon I and restored the Bourbon dynasty.

praefect   *See* **prefect.**

Praetorian Guard   *See* **Praetorians.**

Praetorians (Praetorian Guard)   Special military force organized (27 BC) by the Roman emperor Augustus to guard the emperor. As the only military force allowed in Rome, they acquired great power, even making and deposing emperors. Septimius Severus reorganized them (AD 193), and Constantine finally abolished them (AD 312).

Praetorius, Michael   1571–1621.   German composer, born Schultheiss. He is remembered for his hundreds of religious choral works as well as for his *Syntagma Musicum,* a history of early 17th-cent. music.

pragmatic sanction   Royal decree on an issue of major importance to the state. The most famous of these sanctions was that issued by Holy Roman Emperor Charles VI in 1713. Lacking male heirs, Charles decreed that succession to the vast Habsburg family domains would be continued through his daughter Maria Theresa and not his older brother's daughters. Charles worked tirelessly to secure acceptance of the sanction by European rulers. Nevertheless, Charles's death (1740) marked the beginning of the War of the Spanish Succession (*q.v.*) over Maria Theresa's accession. The Treaty of Aix-la-Chapelle (1748) ending the war confirmed the Pragmatic Sanction of 1713. (*See also* Pragmatic Sanction of Bourges.) Byzantine Emperor Justinian issued the much earlier Pragmatic Sanction of 554, restoring imperial rule in Italy after the Byzantine conquest there.

Pragmatic Sanction of Bourges   Royal edict issued (July 7, 1438) by French king Charles VII. It supported the Council of Basel, restricted papal authority in France and thus advanced the cause of Gallicanism (*q.v.*), and extended Charles's control over the French church. Louis XI revoked the pragmatic sanction (1461), and it was finally replaced by the Concordat of Bologna (1516).

Pragmatic Sanction of 1713   *See* **pragmatic sanction.**

pragmatism   Important 20th-cent. philosophical school first articulated by C. Peirce (1878) and developed by W. James and others. It stresses experimentation and practical usefulness as major tests of philosophical truths and places actual experience above speculative doctrines. Other pragmatists include the American J. Dewey and the Europeans F. Schiller and H. Bergson.

Prague, Battle of   Prussian victory over Austrian forces before Prague (May 6, 1757) during the

Seven Years' War. Prussian forces of some 64,000 under Prussian king Frederick II defeated an Austrian army of comparable size, forcing some Austrian units to retreat and the balance to retire within the city. The Prussians began a siege of the city.

Prague, Defenestration of *See* **Defenestration of Prague.**

Prague, Jerome of *See* **Jerome of Prague.**

Prague, Peace of Treaty (May 30, 1635) ending hostilities between Holy Roman Emperor Ferdinand II, the elector of Saxony, and other German princes. It closed the Swedish phase of the Thirty Years' War.

Prague, Treaty of Agreement (Aug. 23, 1866) ending the Austro-Prussian War. Austria recognized Prussian hegemony over Schleswig-Holstein and was excluded from the North German Confederation, which O. von Bismarck would later form into a modern, unified Germany.

Praguerie Revolt by French noblemen (Feb., 1440) against King Charles VII. Opposed to the king's military reforms and other measures intended to reduce their power, the nobles arose in imitation of a similar revolt in Prague (hence the name). The dauphin (who later became Louis XI) became the figurehead of the revolt, and the nobles continued to resist royal authority until July, 1440.

Prague Spring Abortive attempt to liberalize the Communist regime in Czechoslovakia (Jan.–Aug., 1968). It began with the ouster of the hardline Czech Communist party leader in favor of liberal Communist A. Dubček, and the movement thereafter became a bold attempt to effect democratic and economic reforms within a Communist country. It was an affront to the USSR, however, and on Aug. 20, 1968, the Soviet dominated Warsaw Pact invaded Czechoslovakia and quickly ended the Prague Spring.

Prairial, coup of 30 *See* **French Revolution, 1799.**

Prajadhipok *See* **Chakkri dynasty.**

Prakrit Family of Indic languages. Developed from the 6th cent. BC as vernacular dialects of Sanskrit, they were occasionally literary languages (as in the Buddhist sacred language Pali and the Jain canonical language, Ardha-Magadhi), but they formed the basis of modern Indo-Aryan languages.

Prasad, Rajendra 1884–1963. First president of the Republic of India (1950–62). A disciple of M. Gandhi, he was three times president of the Congress party and also presided over the Constituent Assembly that drafted India's constitution (1949).

Pratt, Charles, 1st earl Camden 1714–94. British jurist, noted for his decision against the legality of general warrants. He was lord chancellor from 1766 to 1770 and was dismissed for opposing taxation of the American colonies.

Praxiteles *fl.* c370–c330 BC. Ancient Greek sculptor. Considered one of the greatest classical artists, he was famous in antiquity for his nude *Aphrodite of Cnidus.*

predestination Theological doctrine holding that God preordains those who will be saved. Some form of the doctrine was developed in the West by Saint Augustine and was further developed by Calvinism.

Preemption Act US statute (1841) by which squatters occupying government lands could purchase 160 acres from the government at nominal cost provided certain conditions were met. The act was repealed Mar. 3, 1891.

prefect (praefect) In ancient Roman government, a class of officers chosen from the equestrians, to whom authority was delegated. The prefects of the city ruled it in the absence of the consuls, and the Praetorian prefects, commanding the Praetorians, sometimes functioned as virtual prime ministers of the emperors.

Pre-Raphaelites School of English painters and poets, including D. G. Rossetti and J. Millais. The group flourished from 1848 to 1853 and drew its inspiration from the realism of the Italian painters prior to Raphael.

Presbyterianism System of church organization that rose within the Christian church during the Protestant Reformation. It represents a compromise between government by bishops (episcopacy) and congregationalism. Elders assume ministerial and administrative responsibilities within the congregation. Generally Presbyterian churches are governed by a hierarchy of four separate bodies. The session is the governing body of the congregation. Above the session is the presbytery, composed of ministers and elders sent from congregations within a designated area. It is responsible for confirming the congregation's appointment of ministers. Above the presbytery is the synod, which holds some authority over the sessions and presbyteries. The ultimate body is the general assembly, which meets each year to deal with questions involving the entire church. Its head is elected for a term of one year and is the head of the church. Presbyterianism was greatly advanced as a movement by J. Calvin. It spread to the British Isles in the 16th cent. and its doctrinal principles were established by the British Parliament in the 17th cent. Presbyterianism rose in Scotland through the efforts of J. Knox, who founded the Church of Scotland. Other Presbyterian churches included the Presbyterian Church of Ireland and the Calvinistic Methodist Church, in Wales. Presbyterianism also influenced the religious movements in Europe, notably the Huguenots (French Protestants). In America, the Presbyterian church was founded by the Irish Presbyterian leader, Francis Makemie (1658?–1708). Makemie emigrated to America in 1683 and founded the first presbytery in America in 1706. By the mid-18th cent., disputes arose within the movement over evangelical principles and revivals. Presbyterianism in America later branched into numerous groups. Among the leading Presbyterian bodies today are the United Presbyterian Church in the United States of America, Cumberland Presbyterian Church, and Reformed Presbyterian Church of North America.

Prescott, William Hickling 1796–1859. American historian. His fame rests on the histories *The Conquest of Mexico* and *The Conquest of Peru,* both noted for their distinguished literary style.

president Chief executive officer of a body or state. Most modern republics are headed by presidents, sometimes with extensive powers, as in the US and France, or with restricted powers as in Italy and India. (*See also* executive branch; prime minister.)

pre-Socratics Collective name for those Greek philosophers and schools of philosophy that preceded Socrates. Among the schools are the Ionian, Pythagorean, Eleatic, atomist, and Sophist.

Pressburg, Treaty of Treaty (Dec. 26, 1805) between Napoleon I and Austria during the Napoleonic Wars. It was negotiated after Austria's defeat at the battles of Austerlitz and Ulm and eliminated Austria from the Third Coalition against Napoleon. Austria ceded extensive lands in both Italy and Germany to form new Napo-leonic kingdoms and paid a huge indemnity. In return it received Salzburg.

Preston, Battle of Victory (Aug. 17–20, 1648) of O. Cromwell in the English Civil Wars in which the last of the forces supporting King Charles I were defeated. Some 20,000 Scots invaded England but were decisively defeated by Cromwell's force of 8,500 near Preston, Lancashire.

Pretoria Convention Agreement (Aug. 3, 1881) between Britain and the Transvaal, amid the continuing conflict with the Boers. The agreement granted the Transvaal self-government subject to British suzerainty and control over foreign relations. It failed to last.

Pretorius, Andries Wilhelmus Jacobus 1799–1853. Boer leader. He was a leader of the Great Trek (*q.v.*) from the British-dominated Cape Colony to Natal. Continuing to oppose the British, he went into the Transvaal (1848) and was instrumental in establishing Transvaal independence.

Pretorius, Martinus Wessel. 1819–1901 Boer statesman. Son of A. Pretorius. He was elected (1857) first president of the South African Republic (the Transvaal) and (1859) president of the adjoining Orange Free State, but was unable to unite the two.

Prevost, Sir George 1767–1816. British colonial administrator. As governor of Canada (1811–15) he followed a policy of conciliation with the French Canadians. His defeats as commander in Canada in the War of 1812 led to his recall.

Price, Sterling 1809–67. Confederate general in the American Civil War. Price fought in the Mexican War, served as governor of Missouri (1853–57), and led Confederate forces in the West during the Civil War.

Pride, Thomas *See* **Pride's Purge.**

Pride's Purge Incident (Dec. 6, 1648) during the English Civil Wars, in which some 143 members of the House of Commons were removed by force. The members were mostly Presbyterians, believed to be Royalist sympathizers. The purge was led by Capt. Thomas Pride (*d.* 1658), who commanded a Parliamentarian military force. Subsequent sessions of Parliament were known as the Rump Parliament (*q.v.*).

Priestley, John Boynton 1894–1984. British author. A prolific novelist, playwright, and critic, he is especially noted for such expressionist dramas as *Time and the Conways.*

Priestley, Joseph 1733–1804. English chemist, best known for his discovery of oxygen. An ordained Unitarian minister, he worked as a teacher and wrote several noted textbooks before becoming interested in science. He began his studies of gases while living near a brewery, where he noted the "fixed air" (carbon dioxide) which collected above fermentation vats. He succeeded in dissolving the gas in water, producing the first soda water. Priestly found (1772) that a gas necessary to animal life (oxygen) was produced by green plants, and that sunlight was important in plant growth. Next he discovered nitric oxide (1772), sulfur dioxide, ammonia, and then finally identified oxygen itself (1774), which he called "dephlogisticated air." Some years later, his sympathy for the goals of the French Revolution led to the ransacking of his home and laboratories. He emigrated to the US (1794).

Prignano, Bartolomeo *See* **Urban VI.**

prime minister (premier) The head of government in a parliamentary form of government. He serves under the head of state (king or president). In Britain, the prime minister has broad powers, including responsibility for policy making, administrative functions, and appointment of cabinet ministers and other lesser government officers. The prime minister is a member of Parliament and usually is the leader of the majority party. He is responsible to Parliament and must resign in the event that his government cannot carry the majority in Parliament. Under other systems of parliamentary government, the president (as head of state) is invested with the real responsibility of governing and the prime minister has only minor functions.

primitivism In art, the work of an artist who has no formal training in art but who nevertheless has developed a talent far beyond that of a novice. Primitives (now more often called "naive painters") have a fresh but unorthodox style. Among the noted painters of this group are H. Rousseau and Grandma Moses.

Primo de Rivera, José Antonio *See* **Falange.**

Primo de Rivera, Miguel 1879–1930. Spanish general and dictator. After a successful *coup d'état* (Sept., 1923), he became the virtual military dictator of Spain (1923–30). His authoritarian regime provoked widespread opposition and he was forced to resign.

primogeniture In inheritance law, the right of the eldest son to inherit exclusively. In England and Western Europe primogeniture prevented the division of estates and enhanced the power of the landed aristocracy.

Primorski Krai *See* **Maritime Territory.**

Prim y Prats, Juan 1814–70. Spanish general and statesman. He helped overthrow (1868) Queen Isabella, the last Spanish Bourbon queen. He also helped install Amadeus of Savoy as king.

Prince Edward Island A Maritime Province of Canada. Originally inhabited by the Micmac Indians, the island was sighted in 1534 by J. Cartier and named Île St. Jean by S. de Champlain (1603). Settled by the French (early 18th cent.), it was ceded to the British in the Treaty of Paris (1763). It became a crown colony (1769), was renamed in honor of Edward, duke of Kent, in 1789, and entered the Canadian confederation in 1873.

Prince of Wales Title traditionally conferred upon the heir apparent to the British throne. It was first given (1303) to Prince Edward, later King Edward II.

Princes, Fronde of the *See* **Fronde.**

Princeton, Battle of *See* **Trenton and Princeton, Battles of.**

Principality of Antioch One of the most powerful Crusader States (11th–13th cents.). Crusaders conquered the city of Antioch and surrounding territory (located in what is now southeastern Turkey) from the Muslims (1098) during the First Crusade. Bohemond I became its first ruler. It survived until the Mameluke conquest (1268).

Priscian *fl.* AD 500. Latin grammarian. Born in North Africa, he taught at Constantinople. His *Institutiones grammaticae* preserved many otherwise unknown quotations from classical authors and was one of the most popular textbooks of the Middle Ages.

privateering The use of specially commissioned, privately operated ships by belligerents to prey upon enemy shipping in time of war. From the 13th cent. privateering was used to supplement a country's naval strength. The heyday of privateering came in the 16th–17th cents., when such English privateers as J. Hawkins and F. Drake pursued Spanish shipping (late 16th cent.) and the French government commissioned many privateers to prey on English shipping (17th cent.). The US engaged in extensive privateering in the

American Revolution and in the War of 1812, and the last letters of marque authorizing privateers to operate were in fact issued by the Confederate States of America. The practice was proscribed by the Declaration of Paris (1856). The Hague Conference (1907) laid down the conditions under which armed merchant vessels are deemed to be warships.

Privy Council In English history, the council of the monarch's principal advisers. It held executive, legislative, and judicial powers during its heyday. So named during the reign of Henry V (reigned 1413–22), it diminished in importance with the decline of the monarchy's actual political power. Today it remains as a purely formal body.

Probus *d.* 282. Roman emperor (AD 276–282). He defeated the barbarians in Gaul and Illyria, but by allowing barbarian settlements within the empire he set a dangerous precedent. Eventually he was assassinated by his troops.

Proclamation of 1763 British royal proclamation (Oct. 7, 1763) that proscribed further western settlement in the Old Northwest. Conceived as a measure to conciliate the Indians following Pontiac's Rebellion, it fostered a serious Colonial grievance against the mother country.

Proclus AD c410–485. Greek philosopher. A Neoplatonist, he opposed Christianity and attempted to maintain the prestige of pagan philosophy.

proconsul In ancient Roman government, originally a consul whose authority was extended to the completion of a commission, such as a military campaign. Later the office was given to the governor of a Roman province.

Procopius *fl.* 6th cent. Byzantine historian. He served as secretary to the military leader Belisarius and wrote volumes that are leading sources for history during the time of Justinian I.

Procopius the Great 1380–1434. Czech Hussite leader. During the Hussite Wars, he inflicted crushing defeats on the Catholic and imperial forces in 1426 and 1431. Embracing the Taborites, or more extreme Hussite faction, he was killed in the Taborite defeat at Lipany (1434).

Procopius the Little *d.* 1434. Czech Hussite leader. An ally of Procopius the Great, he unsuccessfully commanded the Hussite forces at the siege of Pilsen (1432–34) and died in the battle of Lipany (1434).

Progressive Bloc Alliance of Russian liberals and conservatives in the last Russian duma. From Aug., 1915, it urged reforms on the imperial government to restore confidence and improve Russia's performance in WW I. It advocated strict rule of law and political amnesty. After the February Revolution (1917), members of the bloc helped form a committee that appointed the Provisional Government.

Progressive Conservative party (Conservative party) Major Canadian political party. Like its Liberal party counterpart, it is a broad-based coalition rather than an ideologically oriented party, but it is more fiscally conservative and tends to support business rather than labor interests. The party's base lies in Ontario, Nova Scotia, Manitoba (at times), and other parts of the West. It held power from 1957 to 1963 and from 1984 to the present.

Progressive party Name adopted by three US political parties. 1. Party (also known as Bull Moose party) formed (1912) by Republicans disaffected by the conservative policies of Republican President W. Taft. It arose from the National Republican Progressive League formed (1911) by Senator R. La Follette, ran T. Roosevelt for president, and split the Republican vote, thereby helping W. Wilson to win the 1912 election. 2. Party formed (1924) by Senator R. La Follette in opposition to the conservative policies of both Republican and Democratic parties. La Follette was defeated as its 1924 presidential candidate. 3. Party formed (1948) by dissident Democrats opposed to the policies of Democratic President H. Truman. It called for a more cooperative policy toward Russia. H. Wallace, its 1948 presidential candidate, received only about one million popular votes.

Prohibition In the US, an attempt (1920–33) to legally halt the manufacture, sale, and transportation of alcoholic beverages. The demand for Prohibition grew out of the temperance movements of the 19th and early 20th cents., such as the Prohibition party (*q.v.*) and Anti-Saloon League (*q.v.*), and was aided by a temporary prohibition law instituted during WW I to conserve grain. Prohibition went into force in many states, but it was adopted nationally with passage (1919) of the Volstead Act (*q.v.*) and ratification (1920) of the 18th Amendment. The program was a failure. Citizens found ways to find and consume liquor, notably in establishments called "speakeasies," and gangsters, among them A. Capone, became involved in the manufacture and sale of illegal liquor. Organized crime in the US flourished in the Prohibition era. Prohibition ended (1933) with ratification of the 21st Amendment, which repealed the 18th Amendment.

Prohibition party Minor US political party founded (1869) to work for national prohibition of alcoholic beverages. From 1872 it sponsored a presidential candidate in every national election, but its influence actually declined during national prohibition (1920–33).

Prokofiev, Sergei Sergeyevich 1891–1953. Russian composer. He composed a large body of symphonic, operatic, and ballet music, but is probably known best for his orchestration of *Peter and the Wolf* (1936).

Prokopovich, Feofan 1681–1736. Russian Orthodox prelate, theologian, and reformer. Cooperating with Peter the Great, he refashioned Orthodoxy as an arm of the tsarist state, which endured until the 1917 Russian revolution.

proletariat The working class, without property and living entirely from the sale of their labor. In Marxist theory, the proletariat is believed to be created by the capitalist system. Marxists further hold that the proletariat would, by historical necessity, eventually resort to revolution to seize power from the capitalists.

Propertius, Sextus 50?–15? BC. Roman elegiac poet, a contemporary of Ovid and Vergil. He wrote five books of poems imitating Alexandrian models.

prophet In the Old Testament, a Hebrew spiritual leader who gave guidance to God's people. The role of prophets as moral teachers outweighed their role in foretelling the future. The four major prophets were Isaiah, Jeremiah, Ezekiel, and Daniel. Their writings form a significant part of the Old Testament.

propylaea In ancient Greece, an enclosed entrance hall serving as the gateway to a temple. The most notable example is the propylaea leading to the Acropolis of Athens. It was designed by the Greek architect Mnesicles (*fl.* 5th cent. BC) and construction started in 437 BC.

Protagoras c480–410 BC. Greek philosopher and sophist, adversary of Socrates. He promoted the slogan "Man is the measure of all things,"

i.e., that truth is subjective and relative to the individual.

protectionism System of protecting a nation's domestic industry by levying duty (tariffs) upon competing products imported from abroad. These duties increase the price of the imported goods by comparison with the domestically produced article. They, thus, foster home manufacturers and were imposed in England by Edward III as early as 1337. The first US protective tariff was enacted in 1816 and reached its highest point in US history after WW I. A movement away from protectionism began with British advocacy of free trade in the late 19th cent. and rose as industry in many countries matured. Pres. F. Roosevelt secured from Congress in 1934 the authority to negotiate reciprocal trade agreements lowering tariffs. Protectionism declined after WW II with the formation (1948) of GATT, the General Agreements on Tariffs and Trade, and with the multilateral reductions negotiated in the 1960s, as well as with the creation of the European Common Market (1957).

protectorate In international relations, an arrangement whereby a stronger state undertakes to protect a weaker state, called a protectorate. Theoretically, the protectorate retains its sovereignty, unlike a colony.

Protectorate English government established (1653–59) after the English Civil Wars and the execution (1649) of Charles I. In 1649 England was declared a commonwealth under the rule of the Rump Parliament, although O. Cromwell, controlling the army, wielded real power. Cromwell dissolved the Rump Parliament (1653) and established the Nominated, or Barebones, Parliament. After its failure he accepted the Instrument of Government (*q.v.*), by which he became (1653) lord protector of the Commonwealth of England, Scotland, and Ireland. From then until his death Cromwell was virtual dictator in England (ruling through a system of military districts 1655–56), although he shared nominal power with a council of state and Parliament. In 1657 he accepted the Humble Petition and Advice (*q.v.*), which allowed him to choose his successor. After his death (1658) his son Richard became lord protector. Cromwell's son resigned in 1659 and the Long Parliament was restored. It in turn brought Charles II (1660) to the throne and thus began the Restoration period.

Protestant Episcopal church American Protestant denomination, dating from the 17th cent., when the Anglican church was established in America. The American Revolution (1775–83) caused great disorganization among the Anglican churches in the colonies and, after the war, these churches combined (1789) to form the Protestant Episcopal church, a separate entity within the Anglican Communion. It was again divided during the Civil War (1861–65) but reunited upon the cessation of hostilities.

Protestantism One of the three main branches of Christianity, with Roman Catholicism and Eastern Orthodoxy. Protestantism grew out of the Reformation (*q.v.*) in the 16th cent., and there are numerous Protestant churches that grew out of the reform movement. The two main branches are Lutheranism and Calvinism (*qq.v.*). The characteristic doctrine of the original Protestant movement was justification by faith alone, not by church dispensations or by good works. Renewed emphasis on the teachings of the Bible and a general movement away from liturgy were also characteristic. Protestantism also evolved new forms of church polity, including Congregationalism, Presbyterianism, and Episcopalianism. In the years after the start of the Reformation, new Protestant churches sprang up and existing ones split into diverse sects. The 20th-cent. ecumenical movement (*q.v.*), however, has sought to bring about a reunification of churches. (*See also* Congregationalism, Presbyterianism, Protestant Episcopal church, Church of England, Methodism, Puritanism, Evangelicalism, Great Awakening, Baptists, Anabaptists, Pentecostal churches.)

Protestant Reformation *See* **Reformation.**

Protestant Union Association (1608–21) of German Protestant princes. It was formed to prevent an imperial reimposition of Catholicism and went out of existence after the outbreak of the Thirty Years' War.

Protogenes *fl.* C300 BC. Greek painter, one of the most celebrated of Greek artists of antiquity. None of his paintings has survived.

Proudhon, Pierre Joseph 1809–65. French Socialist and theorist. His theory of "mutualism," in which social groups would bargain within the framework of agreed principles, greatly influenced later radical movements.

Proust, Marcel 1871–1922. French novelist. Author of a vast, panoramic, semi-autobiographical novel, *Remembrance of Things Past* (published 1913–17), Proust is considered one of the greatest authors of the 20th cent.

Provençal Dialect of the Romance languages, once spoken in southern France and notable as the literary language of the medieval troubadors. It is also called *langue d'oc.*

Provisional Government Russian government formed after the fall of the tsar (Mar., 1917). Headed by A. Kerensky, it governed Russia (Mar.–Oct.) until the October Revolution (*q.v.*). (*See also* Russian Revolution.)

Provisions of Oxford Governmental reforms imposed (1258) on English King Henry III by his barons. In need of money to pay for his unsuccessful foreign ventures, Henry convened the Mad Parliament (June 11, 1258) and was forced to accept reforms. Formulated by a special commission headed by S. de Montfort, the Provisions of Oxford included establishment of a 15-man council to advise the king, and reforms of local administration. These were supplemented by the Provisions of Westminster (*q.v.*). Henry later refused to abide by the provisions, however, and this resulted in the Barons' War (*q.v.*).

Prusa *See* **Bursa.**

Prussia Former German state, and one of the most powerful German states, long regarded as the wellspring of German militarism. Its capital was Berlin. At its height it occupied much of north Germany and extended east into what is now Poland. The Teutonic Knights (*q.v.*) conquered the region (13th cent.), and in the 16th cent. Prussia proper (East Prussia) passed to the electors of Brandenburg, though it remained under Polish suzerainty. Polish control was ended in 1660, during the time of Frederick William (the Great Elector). In 1701 the Holy Roman Emperor consented to creation of the Kingdom of Prussia, which included lands gained through expansion to the west. Thereafter Prussia continued to enlarge its domains and, under King Frederick William I (reigned 1713–40), important administrative reforms were effected and a strong army was created. The reign (1740–86) of Frederick II (the Great) brought Prussia to a position of power in Europe by victories in the War of the Austrian Succession and the Seven Years' War (*qq.v.*). Prussia also gained additional lands through the Partitions of Poland (*q.v.*). In the post-Napoleonic period in Europe, Prussia and Austria became rivals for control of the German Confederation (*q.v.*), which had been formed from the remnants of the then defunct Holy Roman Empire. Prussia sought to exclude Austria from the confederation and to unite the other states into a German kingdom under its control. This goal was ultimately achieved (1871) through the efforts of Prussian statesman O. von Bismarck and through Prussian victories in two wars that he helped to provoke, the Austro-Prussian War (1866) and the Franco-Prussian War (1871). Prussian king William I was crowned emperor of Germany and in subsequent years Prussia retained control of the empire. Prussia ceased to exist as a political entity in 1934, when A. Hitler formally abolished the German states. (*See also* Germany, 1815–71.)

Pruth, Treaty of Agreement (July 23, 1711) between Russian tsar Peter the Great and the Ottoman Empire, following Peter's defeat in the third Russo-Turkish War (1710). Peter was obliged to relinquish Azov and demilitarize other forts.

Prynne, William 1600–69. Moderate English Puritan pamphleteer. His attack on the immorality of the theater led to persecution by the government of King Charles I. An implacable opponent of Archbishop Laud, he came back into favor at the Restoration.

Przhevalsky, Nikolai Mikhailovich 1839–88. Russian explorer. His series of expeditions (1870–85) to Mongolia, Tibet, and Singkiang greatly increased the knowledge of the geography and natural history of these areas.

Psamtik I (Psammeticus) *d.* 609 BC. Egyptian pharaoh (663–609 BC), founder of the 26th dynasty. He reunited Egypt, ended Assyrian rule, and opened the country to Greek influence.

Pseudo-Dionysius *See* **Dionysius the Areopagite.**

Ptolemaic system Geocentric cosmological system devised (2d cent. AD) by Ptolemy to explain the apparent movement of celestial bodies against the background of the fixed stars. The theory held sway until the development (16th cent.) of the heliocentric system devised by Copernicus.

Ptolemy (Claudius Ptolemaeus) *fl.* 2d cent. AD. Alexandrian mathematician, astronomer, and geographer. In his 13-volume *Almagest,* he presented his geocentric (earth-centered) theory of the universe, known as the Ptolemaic System, in which the universe, with sun, moon, and planets,

revolves around the Earth and the stars formed a dome of lights beyond the planets. Ptolemy's theory was accepted as fact and was not successfully challenged until the 16th cent. (by Copernicus). Ptolemy also did important work in mathematics, formulating new geometric proofs and theorems. His five-volume *Optica* deals with optical phenomena and describes the first recorded theory of refraction. He also wrote an eight-volume *Guide to Geography* which included detailed, though inaccurate, maps of Asia and Africa, including information on longitude and latitude.

Ptolemy I *d.* 283 BC. Egyptian king (305–285 BC). A Macedonian, Ptolemy was one of Alexander the Great's most successful generals. After Alexander's death (323 BC), he quarreled with other generals (Diadochi, *q.v.*) over the empire's division, and became satrap of Egypt. He engaged in warfare to protect and expand his holdings. Though defeated by Demetrius in a battle at Salamis (306 BC), he named himself Egypt's king and soter (savior) the following year. He established Alexandria as a center of culture and commerce, founded its famed library, planned Egypt's government, and began the Ptolemaic dynasty. He abdicated in favor of his son (285 BC).

Ptolemy II (Philadelphus, Ptolemy II) c308–246? BC. Ancient Egyptian king (285–246 BC), successor to his father Ptolemy I. He helped make Alexandria the center of Hellenistic culture, built the city's famous museum, and commissioned the translation of the Hebrew Bible into the Greek Septuagint.

Ptolemy III (Euergetes, Ptolemy III) *d.* 222? BC. Ancient Egyptian king (246–222? BC), successor to his father, Ptolemy II. He reunited Egypt and Cyrenaica, warred with Syria, and established Egyptian naval supremacy in the eastern Mediterranean.

Ptolemy IV (Philopater, Ptolemy IV) *d.* 205 BC. Ancient Egyptian king (221–205 BC), successor to his father, Ptolemy III. Though he defeated the Seleucids in Syria (217 BC), the loss of Syrian lands and internal rebellions began under his rule. Given to debauchery, he ruled through favorites and had many relatives murdered.

Ptolemy V (Epiphanes, Ptolemy V) *d.* 181? BC. Ancient Egyptian king (205–181? BC), successor to his father Ptolemy IV. During his reign Egypt's Levantine possessions were lost in disastrous wars but peace was finally concluded with his marriage to Cleopatra, daughter of Syrian king Antiochus III. The Rosetta Stone concerns his accession to the throne.

Ptolemy VI (Philometer, Ptolemy VI) *d.* 145 BC. Ancient Egyptian king (180–145 BC), successor to his father, Ptolemy V. Obliged to share power with his brother, later Ptolemy VIII, he helped bring about the first intervention of Rome in Egyptian affairs.

Ptolemy VIII (Physcon, Ptolemy VIII) *d.* 116? BC. Ancient Egyptian king (145–116? BC). Usurping the throne from his brother, he ruled with great cruelty, provoking revolts. He drove the scholars from Alexandria.

Ptolemy IX (Lathyrus, Ptolemy IX) *d.* 81 BC. Ancient Egyptian king (116–81 BC), successor to his father, Ptolemy VIII. He was driven (107) from the throne and returned (88) only after expelling his brother, Ptolemy X Alexander, whose corule his mother had compelled him to accept.

Ptolemy X (Alexander, Ptolemy I) *d.* 88 BC. Ancient Egyptian king (107–88 BC). With the help of his mother, he supplanted his brother, Ptolemy IX, until finally defeated by the latter in a civil war.

Ptolemy XI *d.* 80 BC. Ancient Egyptian king (80 BC). He became ruler upon his marriage to the widow of his predecessor, Ptolemy IX. He murdered her and was in turn murdered by a mob.

Ptolemy XII *d.* 51 BC. Ancient Egyptian king (80–51 BC), an illegitimate son of Ptolemy IX. His misrule brought about his expulsion and he was restored only by force of Roman arms.

Ptolemy XIV *d.* 44 BC. Last Macedonian king of Egypt (47–44 BC). By the order of J. Caesar, he married his sister Cleopatra VII, with whom he co-ruled; She arranged his murder so that her son by Caesar could take the throne.

Ptolemy XV 47–30 BC. Ancient Egyptian king (44–30 BC). He was the son of J. Caesar by Cleopatra VII (daughter of Ptolemy XII), and coruler with his mother. After Cleopatra's suicide (30 BC) he was killed by Octavian. Following his death, Egypt became a Roman province.

Public Safety, Committee of *See* **Committee of Public Safety.**

Public Weal, League of Alliance of French nobles (1465) against French king Louis XI. Led by Duke Philip the Good of Burgundy, it forced concessions from Louis, but Louis eventually used diplomatic means to overcome the league.

Puccini, Giacomo 1858–1924. Italian operatic composer. His major operas, all tragic love stories centering on feminine protagonists, include *La Bohme* (1896), *La Tosca* (1900), and *Madama Butterfly* (1904).

Pudovkin, Vsevolod Illarionovich 1893–1953. Russian film director. A pioneer of film techniques in such classic films as *Mother,* he also wrote the books *Film Techniques* and *Film Acting.*

Puebla, Battle and Siege of Two engagements at Puebla, Mexico, during the French campaign to establish Austrian archduke Ferdinand Maximilian as emperor. In the first battle (May 5, 1862), French forces of 7,500 were thrown back with more than 400 casualties by a defending army of 12,000 Mexicans. In the second battle (May 17, 1863), the city surrendered to a larger French force after the French defeated a Mexican relief column.

***Pueblo* Incident** Seizure of the US Navy intelligence ship *Pueblo* and 83 crewmen off North Korea (Jan. 23, 1968). The US exerted diplomatic efforts to free the crewmen, contending that the vessel had been in international waters. The crewmen were not released by North Korea until Dec. 23, 1968.

Pueblo Indians American Indian tribes inhabiting compact adobe or stone villages in the southwestern US. Of diverse tribal and linguistic backgrounds, they have similar, settled cultures based on agriculture.

Pueblo Rebellion Pueblo Indian rebellion (1680) against Spanish rule in New Mexico. The Pueblo rose against enforced Christianization (Aug. 10, 1680), expelled the Spaniards, and restored ancestor worship. They retained their independence until reconquered in 1692.

Puerto Rico (Porto Rico) West Indian commonwealth (pop 3,336,000) in union with the US. It was discovered by C. Columbus (1493) and settled by Ponce de León (1508). During the Spanish-American War, American troops occupied Puerto Rico, and it was ceded to the US (1898). The Jones Act (1917) gave the Puerto Ricans US citizenship. A movement for independence led to an assassination attempt on President H. Truman (1950), but a 1967 plebiscite elected to keep commonwealth status.

Pueyrredon, Juan Martín de 1776–1850. Argentine general and statesman. As supreme director of the United Provinces of La Plata (1816–19), he provided key support of J. de San Martín in the conquest of Chile (1817).

Pufendorf, Samuel, Freiherr von 1632–94. German jurist and historian. His work *De Jure Naturae et Gentium* maintained that relations between nations ought to be governed by natural law, not by positive law enacted by man.

Pugachev, Emelian Ivanovich 1726–75. Russian leader of the peasant rebellion of 1773–74. Pretending to be Tsar Peter III and to have escaped assassination, he led a formidable but ultimately unsuccessful attempt to abolish serfdom.

Pulaski, Casimir (Pulasi, Kazimierz) c1748–79. Polish aristocrat, patriot, and American Revolutionary leader. Unsuccessful in preventing the First Partition of Poland (1772), he came to America. During the American Revolution he commanded American cavalry with distinction but was killed at Savannah.

Pulitzer, Joseph 1847–1911. Hungarian-born American newspaper publisher. He revitalized old newspapers, pioneered modern journalism, and endowed both the Columbia University School of Journalism and the Pulitzer prizes.

Pulitzer prizes Annual awards for excellence in American literature, music, and journalism. Endowed by J. Pulitzer, they have been awarded annually since 1917.

Pullman Strike US labor dispute (1894). Workers of the Pullman Palace Car Company in Chicago struck (May 11, 1894) to protest a 25 percent wage cut, brought on by the Panic of 1893. The company refused arbitration and that brought in the national union, the American Railway Union, led by E. Debs. Debs called a nationwide boycott and thereby effectively shut down Chicago's rail traffic. However, President G. Cleveland sent 2,000 federal troops to Chicago and broke the strike after considerable violence.

Punctation of Olmütz *See* **Erfurt Parliament; Revolutions of 1848.**

Punic Wars Three major wars between Rome and Carthage resulting in the subjugation of Carthage and Rome's acquisition of territories beyond the Italian Peninsula. **1. First ~.** This war (264–241 BC) was probably brought on by the desire for military aggrandizement by the Roman nobiles. Its immediate cause was a conflict between the Mamertini and forces from Syracuse, on Sicily. Both Carthage and Rome responded to the Mamertini request for aid, and soon after were at war with one another. The Romans built a great fleet, defeated the Carthaginians at the Battle of Mylae (260), and launched an ill-fated invasion of Africa in which the commander, Regulus, was captured (255) by Greek mercenaries. On Sicily, the Carthaginian commander Hamilcar Barca succeeded in thwarting the Romans' attempt at decisive victory. However, the Roman fleet finally destroyed the Carthaginian fleet in the naval battle of Aegates (241) and thereby forced the Carthaginians to accept peace. Rome gained Carthaginian territories on Sicily. Not long after, Rome also annexed Sardinia and Corsica. **2. Second ~.** War (218–201 BC) between Rome and Carthage, sparked by the Carthaginians' conquest of Saguntum, a Spanish city loosely associated with Rome. In the years after the first war, Carthage had greatly expanded its holdings in Spain. With the outbreak of war, the great Carthaginian general Hannibal led his forces on the now famous march from Spain, across the Alps, and into north Italy. He won notable victories at Ticinus (218), Trebia (218), Lake Trasimenus (217) and Cannae (216), but failed to take Rome itself. Although Hannibal gained control of much of southern Italy, Carthage failed to provide him needed support. Finally, the Roman invasion of North Africa by Scipio Africanus Major (204) forced Hannibal to return to Carthage. He was defeated at the Battle of Zama (202), and Carthage itself fell (201). Carthage had to give up its navy and its Spanish territories and never again seriously threatened Roman military superiority. **3. Third ~.** War (149–146 BC) between Rome and Carthage, resulting from Roman fears about a resurgent Carthage and efforts by the Roman, Cato the Elder, to bring about the complete destruction of Carthage. Rome finally declared war and soon after laid siege to Carthage. The Carthaginians refused to surrender, and the Romans, led by Scipio Africanus Minor, were forced to fight in the streets of the city to gain control of it. They then completely destroyed Carthage and organized Carthaginian domains into the Roman province of Africa.

Punjab Historic region of northwest India whose river-delta areas were sites of prehistoric and early Aryan civilizations, The area was conquered by Alexander the Great, and by the Muslims (8th cent.), who converted western Punjab to Islam. The Punjab flourished under the Mughal empire until the 18th cent. when the Sikhs took control. The British made it a province in 1849. In the 1947 partition of India, western Punjab became part of Pakistan, and eastern Punjab became part of India.

Purandhar, Treaty of Treaty (Mar. 1, 1776) between the Marathas of India and the government of the British East India Company, in Calcutta. The company abandoned support of the Maratha pretender Raghunath Rao (*d.* 1783) but retained Salsette Island. The company subsequently disavowed the treaty, and the Maratha Wars (*q.v.*) were resumed.

Purcell, Henry 1659–95. English composer and organist. Noted for his opera *Dido and Aeneas* and his fine religious and ceremonial music, he is considered the outstanding influence in English music before G. Handel.

Pure Land Buddhism School of Mahayana Buddhism, one of the most popular in East Asia. It began in China as early as the 4th cent. and had spread to Japan by the 13th cent.

purge trials Series of political trials (1936–38) in the Soviet Union. The first (Aug., 1936) was held to try several prominent leaders, including G. Zinoviev and L. Kamenev, of complicity in the assassination (Dec., 1934) of S. Kirov, a Communist leader. In fact, it was held to eliminate opponents or potential rivals to the rule of J. Stalin. Subsequent trials (Jan., 1937; Mar., 1938) continued the process, by which Stalin virtually swept away all the old Bolshevik leaders and consolidated his power over every facet of Soviet life, including the Communist party. However, by crippling the party apparatus and eliminating many of Russia's top military leaders, he left Russia vulnerable in the face of the rising power of A. Hitler in Germany. In later years (after Stalin's death) the cases against the trial victims were shown to be complete fabrications.

Puritanism English religious movement (16th and 17th cents.) that sought to reform the Church of England. It began during the reign of Queen Elizabeth I, and sought to purify (hence its name) the English church of Catholic elements. Embracing a sterner form of Calvinism and the authority of the Scriptures, the Puritan movement eventually split into several groups, including the Presbyterians, Congregationalists, and Separatists. Under King James I, the Presbyterians were unable to effect changes within the

Church of England at the Hampton Court Conference (1604). Repression of the Puritans led to the Pilgrim emigration to America (1620) aboard the *Mayflower* (*q.v.*), and to the involvement of Puritans in the English Civil Wars. With the fall of the government of the Commonwealth and Protectorate (and restoration of the monarchy), the Puritan movement in England was thoroughly discredited. It received a final setback with adoption of the repressive Clarendon Code (*q.v.*), aimed at dissenting religious groups. In New England the Puritans established their principles in the Cambridge Platform (*q.v.*) of 1648, and flourished under the leadership of such men as R. Williams, C. Mather, and I. Mather. Though Puritanism largely ceased to exist as a movement after the Restoration, its values of hard work, discipline, education, and thrift had an immense and lasting effect on the development of both English and American society.

Puritan Revolution *See* **English Civil Wars.**

Pusey, Edward Bouverie 1800–82. English theologian and Anglican churchman. With J. Newman he was the principal leader of the Oxford Movement (*q.v.*).

Pushkin, Aleksandr Sergeyevich 1799–1837. Russian poet. Exemplifying the Romantic writer (he was killed in a duel), he is considered one of the greatest of Russian writers, and is noted for such works as the verse novel *Eugene Onegin* (1831) and the play *Boris Godunov* (1831).

Putnam, George Palmer 1814–72. American publisher. He founded (1866) the publishing firm of G.P. Putnam's Sons.

Putnam, Israel 1718–90. American Revolutionary general. During Pontiac's Rebellion (*q.v.*) he relieved Pontiac's siege of Detroit (1764). During the American Revolution he fought at Bunker Hill. He was defeated by the British on Long Island (1776) and on the Hudson (1777).

Putnam, Rufus 1738–1824. American Revolutionary officer, cousin of I. Putnam. He distinguished himself during the American Revolution, helped secure passage of the Northwest Ordinance (1787), and, as a member of the Ohio Company, helped to settle Ohio.

Putney Debates *See* **Levelers.**

Puyi *See* **Xuantong.**

Pydna, Battle of Roman victory (168 BC) over the Macedonians at Pydna, Greece, in the Third Macedonian War. Roman Gen. Lucius

Aemilius Paullus routed Macedonian forces and put their king, Perseus, to flight. After the victory, the Romans divided Macedonia into four republics.

Pylos Harbor in southern Greece. Mythical home of King Nestor, it was the site of an Athenian victory over Sparta (425 BC) and of the Battle of Navarino (1827).

Pym, John 1583?–1643. English statesman. A Puritan, he gave a notable speech (1640) enumerating popular grievances, in the Short Parliament. He was one of the leaders in the Long Parliament whom King Charles I attempted to arrest (1642) in the period leading to the English Civil Wars.

pyramids Great stone structures built by various ancient peoples. The best-known pyramids are in Egypt, especially the three pyramids at Giza (*q.v.*), built during the 3d millennium BC (4th dynasty) as the burial places for pharaohs Khufu, Khafre, and Menkaure (*q.v.*). The first true pyramid was probably that of the last king of the 3d dynasty (Huni), though it may have been completed early in the 4th dynasty by Snefru.

Pyramids, Battle of the Battle fought near Giza (July 21, 1798) between the 36,000-man French expeditionary force under Napoleon I and a 40,000-man Egyptian army under Murad Bey. The French defeated and dispersed the Egyptians and thus gained access to Cairo.

Pyrenees, Peace of the Treaty (Nov. 7, 1659) ending hostilities between France and Spain, which had been renewed during the Fronde of the Princes. Spain ceded lands in Flanders, accepted a border with France at the Pyrenees, and betrothed the daughter of King Philip IV to French king Louis XIV. The treaty is generally thought to mark France's rise as Europe's dominant power.

Pyrrho c360–270 BC. Greek skeptical philosopher. He held that nothing can definitely be known and hence the search for truth is vain.

Pyrrhonism, or absolute skepticism, thus derives from him.

Pyrrhus c318–272 BC. King of Epirus. Pyrrhus was established as coruler of Epirus by Macedonian king Demetrius I. He was overthrown and sent as hostage to Egyptian king Ptolemy I, who befriended him and restored him to his kingdom. Pyrrhus fought costly wars against Macedon and Rome. Although he defeated the Romans at Heraclea (280 BC), Ausculum (279 BC), and Beneventum (275), the great losses incurred gave rise to the term "Pyrrhic victory." He successfully aided Sicily against Carthage and again defeated Macedonia (273 BC), but his attempts to subdue Sparta led to his defeat. He fled to Argos, where he was pursued by a mob and killed.

Pythagoras c582–c507 BC. Greek philosopher and mathematician. Little is known of Pythagoras' life, and none of his writings has survived. However, it is ascertained that he founded a combination school and society at Crotona, Italy, that had great influence on Greek and Roman thought. Pythagoras and his school taught that all relationships could be expressed in numbers, and that numbers were the true essence of life. Many theories developed by the Pythagoreans are still employed today in geometry. Philosophically, the Pythagoreans believed in the transmigration of souls, and that the living of a good life would entitle one to a higher rank on the next turn of the "wheel of birth."

Pythagorean school *See* **Pythagoras.**

Pytheas *fl.* 4th cent. BC Greek navigator and geographer who explored the western coastline of Europe, who was the first Greek to visit the British Isles, and who may have sailed as far north as Iceland.

Pythian Games Ancient Greek games at Delphi. They originally featured musical contests in honor of Apollo; athletic contests were added in imitation of the Olympic Games after 582 BC.

Q

Qadisiyya, Battle of Arab victory (636?) against the Persian Sassanid rulers. The victory resulted in the Arab conquest of all of what became Iraq.

Qatar Small oil-rich Arab state on the Persian Gulf, inhabited primarily by Wahhabi Muslims. The population is 498,000 and the capital is Doha. Qatar was ruled by the Al-Thani dynasty from 1868 until the 1970s. Great Britain made Qatar a dependency in 1916. Oil was discovered in the 1940s, and Qatar became independent in 1971. A coup in 1972 installed Crown Prince Sheikh Khalifa as amir. He adopted social and economic reforms and also limited privileges of the royal family. Qatar, a long-time supporter of Iraq, condemned the invasion of Kuwait and joined the US-led multi-national force against Iraq.

Qianlong (Ch'ien Lung) 1711–99. Chinese emperor (1735–96), fourth emperor of the Qing dynasty. By his military conquests, he brought the Chinese Empire to its greatest territorial extent, adding Xinjiang in the west and establishing Chinese hegemony in Annam and Burma. The government, however, was weakened by rampant corruption.

Qing (Ch'ing; Manchu) Last dynasty of emperors of China (ruled 1644 to 1912). The Qing dynasty was founded (1636) in the Manchurian provinces. Called in (1644) by the Ming emperor to recapture Beijing from the bandit Li Zicheng, the Manchu seized power for themselves and installed Qing emperor Shunzhi. By 1683 all China had been conquered and a government by Manchu and former Ming officials was in complete control. During the dynasty's long reign, China's territory and population were increased threefold. Emperor Qianlong expanded Chinese domains to their greatest point in the 18th cent.,

but, in the 19th cent., incursions by European powers and internal dissent began to weaken the empire. By 1912 the successful Chinese Revolution of 1911 had overthrown Emperor Puyi, last of the Qing rulers. *Qing dynasty rulers were:* Shunzhi 1644–61; Kangxi 1661–1722; Yongzheng 1723–35; Qianlong 1735–96; Jiaqing 1796–1820; Daoguang 1821–50; Xianfeng 1851–61; Tongzhi 1862–75; Guangxu 1875–1908; Xuantong 1908–12.

Quaddafi, Muammar al- 1942– . Radical Arab nationalist, Libyan revolutionist and dictator (1969–). He led the military coup (Sept., 1969) to overthrow King Idris I, and set himself up as ruler of Libya. His reign has been marked by anti-Western policies, the closing of US bases in Libya (1970), government confiscation of Italian and Jewish property (1970), nationalization of foreign-owned oil facilities (1973), a proposed union with Egypt (1973), border wars with Egypt (1977), and an invasion of neighboring Chad (1980). Quaddafi's support for revolutionary and terrorist groups, such as the Black Panthers in the US, the Irish Republican Army in Northern Ireland, the PLO, and Muslim revolutionaries led to the growing isolation of Libya. Responding to suspected Libyan involvement in an anti-American terrorist bombing in Germany, the US launched the Libya bombing (*q.v.*) attack in 1986.

Quadruple Alliance 1. Alliance (1718) formed by Austria, France, Great Britain, and the Netherlands against Spain. The alliance was established after Spanish king Philip V attempted to overturn the terms of the Peace of Utrecht (*q.v.*) by seizing Sardinia and Sicily. Austrian forces landed in Sicily, and British and French forces advanced into Spain. Philip was forced, by the Treaty of the Hague (1720), to abandon his claims in Italy, and the peace settlements made at Utrecht were renegotiated.   2. Alliance (Nov. 20, 1815) formed by Austria, Great Britain, Prussia, and Russia after their defeat of Napoleon. The alliance was made to enforce the conditions of the Treaty of Paris of 1815 and to prevent further French military adventures. In 1818 France was admitted to the alliance. Great Britain gradually turned away from Continental affairs and participation in the alliance.   3. Alliance (1834) formed by France, Great Britain, Portugal, and Spain to support the Spanish constitutionalists and Queen Isabella II against the Carlists in the First Carlist War (1833–39). The alliance was effectively crippled by the Affair of the Spanish Marriages (*q.v.*) in 1846, which led to a serious dispute between France and Great Britain.

Quakers   *See* **Society of Friends.**

Quantrill, William Clarke 1837–65.   Confederate guerrilla leader in the American Civil War. He led a band of marauders in Missouri and Kansas and was responsible for the ruthless pillaging (Aug. 21, 1863) of Lawrence, Kansas, in which some 150 townspeople were killed.

quantum theory   In physics, the theory that energy consists of emissions of discrete particles, or quanta. Pioneered by M. Planck and N. Bohr, the theory is used to explain the behavior of particles on the atomic and subatomic levels and is an essential theory of modern physics.

"quarrel of the ancients and the moderns"   *See* **Perrault, Charles.**

Quartering Act   British parliamentary act passed (Mar., 1765) to defray costs of defending the colonies. It forced the American colonials to pay for British troops stationed in the colonies. The law was bitterly resented because it was enacted without approval of the Colonial legislatures. It was allowed to lapse in 1770, but another Quartering Act was passed (June 2, 1774) after the Boston Tea Party.

Quasimodo, Salvatore 1901–68.   Italian poet and writer, a master of both social and lyrical poetry. He was awarded the Nobel Prize in Literature in 1959.

Quebec   Canadian province. Explored (1534–41) by J. Cartier, and later by S. de Champlain, the region, named New France, became a French colony (1663). The British gained control of it by the Treaty of Paris (1763), and some 35,000 Loyalists settled there during and after the American Revolution. In 1791, the area now known as Ontario was made a separate colony called Upper Canada, and Quebec became known as Lower Canada. Although Quebec and Ontario were subsequently reunited (1841), they entered the confederation of Canada as separate provinces (1867).

Quebec Act   British parliamentary law (June 22, 1774) establishing a permanent government for Canada. The act replaced the temporary administration set up by the Proclamation of 1763, extended Quebec's territory south to the Ohio River, and provided for religious tolerance of Roman Catholics. It also imposed English criminal law in the colony, but continued French civil law. While the act helped to keep Canada loyal to Britain, it angered American colonists and contributed to the outbreak of the American Revolution.

Quebec Campaign   Unsuccessful military expedition (1775–76) by the American colonials against Canada during the American Revolution. Two American contingents were sent against Canada with the ultimate goal of taking Quebec. The force under Gen. B. Montgomery first captured Montreal (Nov., 1775). It later joined a force under Col. B. Arnold in an unsuccessful attack on the strongly fortified Quebec (Dec. 31, 1775). After Montgomery was killed and Arnold was wounded, the Americans broke off the attack. In May, 1776, American forces were withdrawn from Canada.

Quebec Conference   1. Meeting in Quebec, Canada (Oct. 10–27, 1864) that laid the foundations for an independent dominion of Canada. Thirty-three delegates from the various crown colonies of British North America drew up a draft constitution called the Quebec Resolutions, or Seventy-two Resolutions. This formed the basis of the 1867 British North America Act (*q.v.*), creating modern independent Canada.   2. Conference (Aug. 11–24, 1943) attended by US president F. Roosevelt, British prime minister W. Churchill, Canadian prime minister W. L. Mackenzie King, and Chinese foreign minister T. Soong. The conference formulated tentative plans for allied landings in Europe.   3. Meeting between US president F. Roosevelt and British prime minister W. Churchill (Sept. 11–

16, 1944) at which strategy for defeating Germany was discussed. It was decided to advance against Germany on two fronts.

Queen Anne's War American Colonial war (1702–13) between France and England, the American counterpart of the War of the Spanish Succession. The French and their Indian allies waged a bitter war, but the British emerged victorious. The British captured and burned Spanish-held St. Augustine, Florida (1702), the French massacred townspeople of Deerfield, Massachusetts (1704), the British captured the French colony of Acadia (1710), and then unsuccessfully attempted to take Quebec (1711). The war was ended by the Treaty of Utrecht (*q.v.*) and Britain gained Newfoundland, Hudson Bay, and Acadia.

Queipo de Llano, Gonzalo *See* **Fifth column.**

Quesnay, François 1694–1774. French economist and physician. A pioneer in the development of economic theory, he was the leader of the physiocrats (*q.v.*).

Quesnel, Pasquier 1634–1719. French theologian and exponent of Jansenism. One of the principal Jansenist leaders, he was exiled and briefly imprisoned. His teachings were ultimately condemned by Pope Clement XI's papal bull *Unigenitus* (1713).

Quevedo y Villegas, Francisco Gómez de 1580–1645. Spanish poet and writer. He was a brilliant satirist as well as a writer of plays and novels.

Quezon y Molina, Manuel Luis 1878–1944 First president of the Commonwealth of the Philippines (1935–44). Beginning as a rebel against American rule, he turned to tireless lobbying and was instrumental in obtaining the US legislation establishing the commonwealth.

Quiberon Bay, Battle of British naval victory (Nov. 20, 1759) over the French during the Seven Years' War, at Quiberon Bay, Brittany. The decisive British victory forced the French to abandon their plans to invade Scotland.

quietism Type of religious mysticism based on the belief that total passivity of the soul and suppression of all activity, even prayer, can bring communion with God. This type of mysticism is characteristic of a number of religious traditions, notably Hinduism (*q.v.*) and Islamic Sufism (*q.v.*). In the West the doctrine was associated with a Spanish priest, M. de Molinos, and a French mystic, Mme. J. Guyon, both of whom were active in the latter half of the 17th cent.

Quiller-Couch, Sir Arthur Thomas 1863–1944. English man of letters. He edited *The Oxford Book of English Verse* and other anthologies and wrote novels, criticism, essays, and poetry.

Quimby, Phineas Parkhurst 1802–66. American mental healer. Originally a clockmaker, he possessed hypnotic powers and became prominent as a mental healer. One of his patients was M. Eddy. She later founded Christian Science, but denied that Quimby's ideas influenced its principles.

Qin (Ch'in) Fourth dynasty of Chinese rulers (221–207 BC). During this dynasty, warring Chinese states were unified into the first Chinese empire, and the centuries-long tradition of rule by imperial government began with the Qin. Qin, a small independent state in the northwest, began its rise to power under Shang Yang (*d.* 338 BC), who set up a system of rewards and punishments to enforce obedience to the state. Qin thereafter gradually expanded its borders, and by force of arms, Emperor Shi Huangdi (*q.v.*) unified the Warring States under his rule (by 221 BC). As emperor, he ended feudalism and established an administrative system based on imperial rule that became a model for succeeding dynasties. His chancellor, Li Si (280?–208 BC), a student of Hsün-tzu and strong advocate of Legalist philosophy, is generally believed responsible for many of the administrative innovations and for the system of harsh punishments imposed on the populace. Conscription for military service and for massive construction projects (such as the Great Wall, *q.v.*) also resulted in widespread hardship and suffering. Following Shi Huangdi's death, one of his younger sons, Huhai (*d.* 207), was put on the throne. He proved a weak ruler and was overthrown in a rebellion (207). Civil war and the breakup of the Qin empire followed, lasting until the rise of the Han dynasty (202 BC, *q.v.*).

Quincy, Josiah 1744–75. American pamphleteer. Closely associated with J. Adams, he was influential in rallying the American colonies against British policy. He died at sea after pleading the American case in England.

Quine, Willard Van Orman 1908–   . American philosopher and mathematical logician. He refined modern philosophical concepts dealing with language as a logical system.

Quinisext Council (Council in Trullo) Synod of the Orthodox Eastern church convened in Constantinople (692) by Byzantine emperor Justinian II. Pope Sergius I refused to ratify its canons on behalf of the Western church, protesting in particular those allowing clerical marriage below the rank of bishop.

Quintilian (Marcus Fabius Quintilianus) AD c35–c95. Roman writer and rhetorician. A respected teacher of rhetoric, he wrote the *Institutio Oratona,* a major study of rhetoric. His writings were influential in Renaissance times.

Quirino, Elpidio 1890–1956. Filipino statesman. He served as secretary and aide to M. Quezon, and fought in the underground during WW II. Elected (1946) vice-president under M. Roxas, he succeeded Roxas as president of the Philippines (1948–53).

Quisling, Vidkun 1887–1945. Norwegian puppet prime minister (1940–45). A Fascist, he served as prime minister under the German occupation of Norway during WW II. His name became a byword for "traitor." He was tried and executed after the war.

Quran *See* **Koran.**

Qutb ud-Din *See* **Delhi sultanate.**

R

Rabelais, François c1490–1553.   French Renaissance humanist and satirist. After first becoming a monk, he left the monastic life to practice, and teach, medicine. He wrote various works on medicine but is remembered for his literary masterpiece, *Gargantua and Pantagruel* (1532–64), a coarse and witty satire celebrating Renaissance ideals.

Rachmaninov, Sergei Vasilyevich (Rakhmaninov, Sergius Vassilievich) 1873–1943.   Russian composer and piano virtuoso. The last great exponent of Russian romanticism, he wrote his best works for the piano. He spent his later life in the US (after 1917), an expatriate from the Russian Revolution.

Racine, Jean Baptiste 1639–99.   French poet and dramatist, considered a master of French classical tragedy. After a bitter rivalry with J. Molière and P. Corneille, he wrote his greatest works, *Britannicus, Bérénice, Bajazet, Iphigénie,* and *Phèdre.* In 1677, he left the theater, married, and became historiographer to Louis XIV. He later wrote two dramas, *Esther* and *Athalie,* at the request of Mme. de Maintenon.

Radcliffe-Brown, Alfred Reginald 1881–1955.   British social anthropologist who helped establish a scientific basis for social anthropology. He carried out his major studies on the Andaman Islanders.

Radek, Karl Bernhardovich 1885–1939?   Russian Communist politician and journalist. A prominent leader of the Comintern, he was a victim of the Stalinist purge trials (*q.v.*).

Radetzky, Joseph, Count 1766–1858.   Austrian field marshal. He served Austria in wars against the Turks during the 1780s and in most all the wars against France during the era of the French Revolution and Empire. He is best known for his victories in Italy (1848–49), which J. Strauss, Sr., commemorated in the *Radetzky March.*

Radhakrishnan, Sarvepalli 1888–1975.   Indian philosopher and president of India (1962–67). He also served as Indian ambassador and vice-president (1952–62). Primarily an academic, he tried to harmonize Hindu philosophy with modern thought.

Radical Republicans   Wing of the Republican party during the American Civil War and Reconstruction (*q.v.*) periods. Radicals demanded firm adherence to antislavery doctrines and advocated harsh treatment of the South after the war. Under leaders such as T. Stevens, C. Sumner, and B. Wade in Congress, the Radicals passed much important Reconstruction legislation. At the height of their power, they even tried to impeach President A. Johnson (1868). They have been criticized by historians but were also the only consistent upholders of the rights of blacks. They worked for passage of such key legislation as the 14th Amendment to the Constitution.

Radishchev, Aleksandr Nikolayevich 1749–1802.   Russian aristocrat, writer, and liberal. He was exiled to Siberia for denouncing serfdom in what was ostensibly a travel journal, *A Journey from St. Petersburg to Moscow,* published in 1790.

Radom, Confederation of   *See* **Confederation of Radom.**

Radowitz, Joseph Maria von 1797–1853.   Prussian statesman and general. He worked for a German federation under Prussian leadership some 20 years before O. von Bismarck brought it into being.

Radzin, Treaty of   *See* **Russo-Turkish Wars (1).**

Radziwill   Important Polish-Lithuanian princely family that has played a significant role in the history of both countries since the 15th cent.

The first prominent Radziwill became palatine of Vilnius (1492), and others followed him in the post. Several Radziwills in the 16th cent. promoted Calvinism in Poland, but their descendants returned to Catholicism during the Catholic Reformation. In the 18th cent., the Radziwills supported the Saxon monarchs in struggles over the Polish crown.

Raetia *See* **Rhaetia.**

Raffles, Sir Thomas Stamford 1781–1826. British colonial administrator. He was one of the founders of Britain's empire in the Far East and acquired Singapore for Britain in 1819.

Raghunath Rao *See* **Purandhar, Treaty of.**

Rahman, Tunku Abdul *See* **Abdul Rahman, Tunku.**

Raid of Ruthven *See* **Ruthven, William, 4th lord of Ruthven.**

Raikes, Robert 1735–1811. British philanthropist and newspaper publisher. He started a Sunday school in Gloucester, England, to educate poor children, and sparked a nationwide movement to provide such schooling.

Rainalducci, Pietro (Nicholas V) *d.* 1333. Italian churchman and antipope (1328–30). Holy Roman Emperor Louis IV captured Rome and declared Pope John XXII, residing at Avignon, deposed after John had excommunicated him. Louis then named Rainalducci pope as Nicholas V, but Rainalducci soon submitted to John XXII.

Rainbow Division US 42d Infantry Division. It was the first US combat division to arrive in France in WW I, where it distinguished itself (though with heavy losses).

Rainier III *See* **Monaco.**

Rais, Gilles de Laval, seigneur de *See* **Retz, Gilles de Laval, seigneur de.**

Rajagopalachari, Chakravarti 1879–1972. Indian political leader and last governor general of India (1948–50). A disciple of M. Gandhi, he cooperated with Britain once Indian independence was assured. He founded the Swatantra (Freedom) party in 1959.

Rajputs People of northwest India who traditionally considered themselves members of the Hindu warrior class. The Rajputs were organized in a clan system and were powerful from the 7th cent. to the early 17th cent., when they became subjects of the Mughals.

Rakhmaninov, Sergius Vassilievich *See* **Rachmaninov, Sergei Vasilyevich.**

Rákóczy, Francis II 1676–1735. Prince of Transylvania and Hungarian nationalist leader. During the War of the Spanish Succession, he led a nearly successful Hungarian rebellion (1703) against the Habsburg rulers.

Rákóczy, George I 1591–1648. Prince of Transylvania and Hungarian nationalist leader. Pursuing an anti-Habsburg policy, he successfully invaded Hungary and thereby gained concessions and religious liberty for the Hungarians.

Rákosi, Mátyás 1892–1971. Hungarian Communist leader. He came to Budapest as Communist party secretary with the Soviet army in 1944 and consistently followed a Stalinist line, which made him unpopular in Hungary. In and out of office as prime minister (1952–56), he fled the country just prior to the Hungarian Revolution of 1956.

Rakovsky, Khristian Georgievich 1873–? Russian Communist leader and diplomat. He was Soviet ambassador in both London and Paris but was ousted from the Communist party (1927) for opposing Stalin. He was tried during the purge trials and was imprisoned.

Raleigh, Sir Walter (Ralegh, ˜) 1552?–1618. English courtier, adventurer, poet, and favorite of Elizabeth I. Having attended Oxford and taken part in various military adventures during his youth, Raleigh joined Queen Elizabeth's court in 1581 and soon became her favorite. Granted important concessions, he was knighted (1585) and became the captain of the queen's guard in 1587. He organized the ill-fated Roanoke Colony (*q.v.*) in what became Virginia, though Queen Elizabeth refused him permission to join the dangerous voyages to the New World. Raleigh was also involved in other unsuccessful colonizing ventures, which nevertheless resulted in the introduction of potatoes and tobacco to Europe. Conflict with the queen's new favorite, R. Devereux, earl of Essex, resulted in Raleigh's fall from favor (1589). After reestablishing himself at the court, he was imprisoned briefly (1592) and then barred from the court altogether when the queen learned he had secretly married her maid of honor, Elizabeth Throckmorton. Thereafter he gained notoriety as a poet, joined an expedition to South America in search of El Dorado, published a book about the adventure (*Discovery of Guiana*, 1596), and took part in military expeditions against Cádiz and the Azores. Raleigh's downfall came quickly after King James I's succession to the throne (1603). Perceived by the king as an opponent, Raleigh spent the next 13 years in the Tower of London (1603–16) before being released to launch another expedition to South America (1617). But despite the king's express orders, Raleigh attacked a Spanish settlement there. That landed Raleigh in prison again—this time, however, the king ordered him beheaded. Though Raleigh's poetry was widely praised, much of it has been lost.

Rama *See* **Chakkri dynasty.**

Ramakrishna 1836–86. Indian religious seer and mystic, founder of worldwide religious movement based on his belief in a universal religion.

Ramanuja 1017–1137 BC. Hindu religious leader. Rejecting concepts of an exclusive impersonal spirit, he promoted a form of Hinduism emphasizing personal devotion to Vishnu, and was thus influential in the Vaishnava sect.

Rama Tiboti (Ramathibodi I) 1312–69. Thai warrior-king and lawgiver. In 1351, he established a new kingdom (Siam), which his descendants ruled until 1767.

Ramayana With the Mahabharata, one of the two most important Hindu Sanskrit texts. Written c300 BC it chronicles the life of Rama, the ideal man and king.

Rambouillet, Catherine de Vivonne, marquise de 1588–1665. French noblewoman and founder of the first great Parisian literary salon. She received the most distinguished writers and poets of her day and exercised a profound influence on literary taste.

Rameau, Jean Philippe 1683–1764. French composer and music theorist. He wrote influential treatises on harmony and composed harpsichord music, ballets such as *Les Indes Galantes,* and many operas, including *Castor et Pollux.*

Ramée, Pierre de la *See* **Ramus, Petrus.**

Rameses *See* **Ramses.**

Ramillies, Battle of British allied victory (May 23, 1706) over the French in the War of the Spanish Succession (1701–14). Fought at Ramillies, in modern Belgium, the battle pitted some 50,000 British, Dutch, and Danish troops under J. Churchill, duke of Marlborough, against an approximately equal French force. The allies won nearly the whole of the Spanish Netherlands (modern Belgium) by this victory.

Ramiro I *d.* 1063. First king of Aragon (1035–63). He built the kingdom from a base in Navarre, both by appropriating his brother Gonzalo's territories and by conquest of Moorish lands.

Ramsay, Sir William 1852–1919. British chemist, known for his discovery of the family of the noble gases. A professor of chemistry at the University of Bristol and the University of London, he tried to discover why the atomic weight of nitrogen was greater when it was in the atmosphere than in compounds. Suspecting that atmospheric nitrogen was contaminated by a heavy gas, he discovered argon (1894), the first of the noble gases, with British physicist Lord Rayleigh. Next, he succeeded in isolating helium (1895). With British chemist Morris W. Travers, he isolated neon, krypton, and xenon (1898) from air cooled to a liquid state under high pressure. In 1910, he discovered the last of the noble gases, niton (now known as radon), in the radioactive emissions of radium. Ramsay won the Nobel Prize for Chemistry (1904).

Ramses I (Rameses) *d.* 1318 BC. Egyptian pharaoh (1320–18 BC), first king of the 19th dynasty. He made his son Seti I co-regent during his brief reign.

Ramses II (Rameses II) *d.* c1237 BC. Egyptian pharaoh (c1304–c1237 BC), named "the Great." His reign was marked by a period of great prosperity, foreign conquest, and the building of temples at Karnak, Luxor, and Abu Simbel.

Ramses III (Rameses III) *d.* 1167 BC. Egyptian pharaoh (c1198–67 BC) during the 20th dynasty. He defended Egypt against invaders from Libya and the "Sea Peoples," including the original Philistines then colonizing Palestine.

Ramus, Petrus (*orig.* Ramée, Pierre de la) 1515–72. French humanist and the most eminent logician of his time. His reforms of Aristotelian logic were highly regarded in the 16th and 17th cents. A Protestant, he was murdered during a period of religious persecutions in France.

Ranavalona II *See* **Madagascar.**

Ranavalona III *See* **Madagascar.**

Rand, Ayn 1905–82. Russian-born American novelist. Her books exalt her philosophy, called objectivism, which holds that rational self-seeking is a virtue and altruism is a weakness. *The Fountainhead* and *Atlas Shrugged* are among her works.

Randolph, A(sa) Philip 1889–1979. American labor leader and pioneer crusader for black civil rights. He organized the Brotherhood of Sleeping Car Porters and helped end job discrimination against blacks in US defense industries. He was a director of the 1963 March on Washington (*q.v.*).

Randolph, Edmund 1753–1813. American statesman, nephew of P. Randolph. He formulated the Randolph (Virginia) Plan at the Constitutional Convention and later served as US attorney general (1789–94) and secretary of state (1794–95).

Randolph, John 1773–1833. American political leader. He spent most of his career (1799–1829) in Congress, where he was famous for his wit, eloquence, and stubborn defense of states' rights.

Randolph, Peyton c1721–75. American Revolutionary leader and first president of the Continental Congress (1774). He was the uncle of E. Randolph. A longtime member of the Virginia House of Burgesses, he took a leading part in the early events of the American Revolutionary period.

Ranjit Singh (Runjeet ͠) 1780–1839. Maharaja of the Punjab. Making himself the principal leader of the Sikhs (from 1801), he consolidated Sikh rule and conquered Afghan and Pathan territories in northern India.

Ranke, Leopold von 1795–1886. German historian. A votary of carefully researched objective facts, he is considered the father of scientific historiography. He aimed to recreate history as "it actually happened."

Rankin, Jeannette 1880–1973. American congresswoman (1917–19, 1941–43). The first woman member of Congress, she created a furor by casting the only vote against a declaration of war against Japan after Pearl Harbor.

Ranters English religious sect that flourished during the Commonwealth and Protectorate from 1649 to 1660. Its members believed in pantheism, holding that God is coextensive with nature, and appealed to an inner experience, denying the authority of Scripture. The movement was suppressed by Parliament.

Raoul *See* **Rudolph.**

Rapallo, Treaty of Two important treaties signed at Rapallo, Italy. 1. Treaty between Italy and Yugoslavia (Nov. 12, 1920) establishing the Adriatic city of Rijeka (Fiume) as a free city. (It reverted to Yugoslavia after WW II.) 2.

Treaty signed between Germany and the Soviet Union (Apr. 16, 1922) normalizing relations and renouncing mutual war indemnities.

Raphael 1483–1520. Great Italian artist in the High Renaissance style. He studied first with his father, Giovanni Santi, then with Perugino at Perugia, and studied the works of Leonardo da Vinci and Michelangelo. Thereafter, he produced many famous Madonnas and portraits. Summoned to Rome by Pope Julius II (1508), he decorated the Vatican apartment the Stanza della Senatura, and succeeded D. Bramante as chief Vatican architect (1514). His frescoes include the noted *School of Athens* and *Disputa* in the Vatican papal apartment.

Rapp, George *See* **Harmony Society.**

Rappites Christian pietistic community that flourished in the 19th cent. It was founded (1803) by George Rapp in Germany, and the Rappites started other such groups in Pennsylvania and Indiana. Membership dwindled because of rules on celibacy, and the community eventually disbanded.

Rask, Rasmus Christian 1787–1832. Danish philologist. He pioneered the study of the relationships between the Indo-European languages and wrote Icelandic and Anglo-Saxon grammars.

Rasmussen, Knud Johan Victor 1879–1933. Danish explorer and ethnologist. Born in Greenland, he conducted many Arctic expeditions. He is noted for his valuable studies of the North American Eskimos.

Rasputin, Grigori Yefimovich 1872–1916. Russian peasant mystic who had great influence in the court of Tsar Nicholas II. He gained the favor of Tsarina Alexandra because he was able to relieve (1905) the suffering of her hemophiliac son, Alexis. In following years, Rasputin became notorious as a rapacious seducer of women. When Nicholas went to the front during WW I, Rasputin's corrupt influence and scandalous behavior only increased. Thus he hastened the collapse of the tsarist government in the months leading up to the Russian Revolution of 1917. A group of noblemen, including Prince Felix Yusupov, plotted his murder. They poisoned him unsuccessfully, then shot him and drowned him (Dec. 30) in the Neva River.

Ras Tafari *See* **Haile Selassie.**

Rastatt and Baden, treaties of Treaty signed (Mar., 1714) in Rastatt (now in Germany) by which Holy Roman Emperor Charles VI made his personal peace with France in the War of the Spanish Succession. Some months later, in the Swiss city of Baden, he concluded peace on behalf of the states of the empire. These treaties complemented those signed at the Peace of Utrecht (*q.v.*).

Rathenau, Walter 1867–1922. German statesman and industrialist. He organized the German economy for WW I. After the war as foreign minister, he attempted to show that Germany could not pay the excessive war reparations even with good faith efforts ("fulfillment" policy). Rathenau ended the postwar German isolation by helping arrange the Treaty of Rapallo (1922). He was assassinated by nationalist fanatics because he was a Jew and because of his cooperative policy on reparation payments.

Rathlin Island *See* **Robert I.**

rationalism Philosophical doctrine holding that fundamental truths can be deduced by reason alone. It is opposed to empiricism (*q.v.*), the doctrine that such knowledge derives from experiences through the senses. R. Descartes articulated the rationalist doctrine in the 17th cent., and it was further developed by B. Spinoza and G. von Leibnitz. I. Kant formulated a modified form of rationalism, called "critical rationalism," in his work *Critique of Pure Reason.* The rationalist doctrine also affected religious thought, giving rise to the deists (*q.v.*), who denied the truth of religious revelations.

Ravel, Maurice 1875–1937. French composer. An exponent of impressionism, he was both an original composer and a popular one, with such well-known works as *Boléro* (1928) and *La Valse.*

Ravenna Historic city in north-central Italy. Founded in early Roman times, it became the capital of the declining Western Roman Empire (404). It was the Ostrogothic capital (5th–6th cents.), then passed to the Byzantines who created the Exarchate of Ravenna (*q.v.*) as the center of their power in Italy until c750. Conquered by the Franks, Ravenna was given to the pope c756 (the famous Donation of Pepin), and formed the basis of the Papal States (*q.v.*). Ravenna became part of Italy during the unification (1860).

Rawalpindi, Treaty of *See* **Afghanistan, 1919.**

Ray, Man 1890–1976. American painter and photographer. One of the chief exponents of the Dada movement after WW I, he created a variety of experimental works of art, some combining photography and painting.

Ram Mohan Roy (Ray, Rammohan) 1774–1833. Indian thinker and reformer. He advocated a reaffirmation of Hindu culture but supported some aspects of Western culture, notably education. He was a scholar in several Oriental languages, translated Sanskrit classics, and was instrumental in abolishing suttee, or sacrifice of a widow on her husband's funeral pyre.

Rayburn, Samuel Taliaferro 1882–1961. Democrat from Texas, Speaker of the US House of Representatives (1940–47, 1949–53, 1955–61). His 48 years in the House set a record, and he was Speaker longer than anyone before him. He generally supported New Deal and Fair Deal legislation.

Raymond IV *d.* 1105. Count of Toulouse (1093–1105). He was one of the principal leaders of the First Crusade (*q.v.*) and was the key figure in organizing it.

Raymond VI 1156–1222. Count of Toulouse, (c1194–1222). Excommunicated for his tolerance toward the Albigenses of southern France, he later fought S. de Montfort during the Albigensian Crusade (*q.v.*).

Raymond of Tripoli *See* **Baldwin V.**

Razin, Stenka *d.* 1671. Cossack leader, head of the propertyless Cossacks of the Don (1670–71). He raided both Russian and Persian settlements, captured or razed several cities, and was finally defeated and captured by Russian troops at Simbirsk. He was taken to Moscow, tortured, and executed.

Reagan, Ronald Wilson 1911– . US president (1981–89), the 40th, successor to J. Carter. Before entering politics, Reagan enjoyed a long career in movie acting (from 1937) and eventually became host of the television show *General Electric Theater* (1954–62). He married Nancy Davis in 1952, having divorced his first wife (actress Jane Wyman) in 1948. Reagan became a conservative Republican and served two terms as California's governor (1967–75). Twice defeated for the Republican presidential nomination (1968, 1976), Reagan finally won it in 1980. Campaigning on a conservative platform that included tax cuts, reduced federal spending and regulation, and revitalization of the US military, Reagan defeated Democrat J. Carter in a landslide victory. His first term was marked by the end of the hostage crisis (*q.v.*), an assassination attempt (by John W. Hinckley, Jr., Mar. 30, 1981) that resulted in the wounding of President

Reagan and others, passage of the Reagan budget package for reduced federal spending (except defense), breaking of the air controllers' strike, deregulation of the oil and gas and savings and loan industries, successful US efforts in negotiating an end to the Lebanese War, increased US involvement in the war in El Salvador (and opposition to pro-Communist Nicaragua), and the US invasion of Grenada (1983). His economic policies, dubbed Reaganomics, cut inflation and fueled rapid economic growth (from 1983), but this also doubled the national debt (1981–86) and worsened the trade deficit (the US became a debtor nation [1985] for the first time since 1914). Reagan won reelection in 1984, capturing the largest electoral vote majority ever. His new term was marked by passage of the Gramm-Rudman-Hollings Act for a balanced federal budget, four summits with Soviet leader M. Gorbachev (1985, 1986, 1987, 1988), conclusion of the historic Intermediate-Range Nuclear Forces Treaty (INF), passage of the first major income tax reforms in four decades, the bombing of targets in Libya in retaliation for that country's support of terrorists, the politically embarrassing Iran-Contra scandal (*q.v.,* beginning in 1986), the stock market crash of 1987, and the bitter Senate confirmation battle over Supreme Court nominee Robert H. Bork, which Reagan lost. *See also* United States, 1981–89.

realism In philosophy, the theory that things possess a substantive reality independent of the mind that perceives them. It is opposed to philosophical idealism. In literature and art, it is the school that strives for faithful representation of life as it is really lived, without idealization. It was prominent in literature and art, especially in France, from the mid-19th cent. to the early 20th cent. and was opposed to romanticism.

reciprocity The principle or policy by which two or more nations grant each other equal treatment, usually in international trade, which usually results in a mutual lowering of import duties.

Reconquista Name for the drive by Spanish Christians to recapture the Iberian Peninsula from the Muslims. During the Muslim invasions of the early 8th cent., Christians were only able to maintain control over small kingdoms in northern Spain. By the 11th cent. Spanish Christians began an active campaign to expand these domains and retake the peninsula. They had largely succeeded by the 13th cent. The last Muslim stronghold, Granada, was conquered by King Ferdinand and Queen Isabella in 1492.

Reconstruction Period in US history (1865–77) that followed the American Civil War. It was marked by the return of Confederate states to the Union, bitter struggles over political and racial differences, and the failure to effect fundamental social and economic reform of Southern society. President A. Lincoln had already adopted a policy of reconciliation toward the South before his assassination, and President A. Johnson generally attempted to continue it. Radical Republicans in Congress, however, wanted harsher treatment for the South. Their Wade-Davis Bill failed in 1864 and they were enraged when provisional state governments, created by Johnson's executive order (1865), enacted Black Codes (*q.v.*) to restrict Negro rights. Congress responded by passing laws to guarantee Negro rights and to institute harsh reconstruction measures, while the president attempted to veto the legislation. On the national level, the bitter struggle culminated (1868) in the Radical Republicans' (narrowly) unsuccessful attempt to impeach Johnson. The congressional reconstruction program included passage of the 13th Amendment in Dec., 1865, abolishing slavery; the Civil Rights Act (Apr., 1866), countering the Black Codes; the 14th Amendment in June, 1866, guaranteeing Negro rights; legislation sanctioning the Freedmen's Bureau (*q.v.*); the Reconstruction Act (Mar., 1867), dividing Confederate states (except Tennessee) into five military districts; and the 15th Amendment (1869), guaranteeing Negro voting rights. Under the military authorities, there came to power Radical Republican governments composed of carpetbaggers (Northern Republicans and opportunists), scalawags (Southern white Republicans), and former Negro slaves. Rebuilding of the war-torn South began, state constitutions were rewritten to conform to standards set by the Republican Congress, and the states were readmitted (six in 1868, the remaining in 1870). The tenure of the pro-Republican carpetbaggers, however, was highly controversial and deeply resented by white Southerners. It was marked by corruption (although apparently no worse than elsewhere in the country), the rise of bitter sectional and racial hatred among Southerners, and the spread of terrorist groups such as the Ku Klux Klan. Ultimately white Southerners regained control of the state governments, reinstituted discrimination against Negroes, and united to form the one-party, Democratic "solid South." Reconstruction ended with the disputed presidential election of 1876. Republican candidate R. Hayes was awarded the election (which hinged on returns from Louisiana, Florida, and South Carolina), and in 1877 federal troops were withdrawn from the South.

Red Baron *See* **Richthofen, Manfred, baron von.**

Red Cambodians *See* **Khmer Rouge.**

Red Cross International society, today involved in relief efforts in both wartime and peacetime. It was founded (1863) as a result of J. Dunant's call for establishment of a wartime relief agency to provide wounded with medical aid and was sanctioned by the Geneva Convention of 1864. Its functions were later expanded to include peacetime relief work. The American Red Cross was established (1881) by C. Barton.

Red Eyebrows *See* **Han dynasty.**

Redi, Francesco c1626–98. Italian naturalist. A court physician in Tuscany, he proved in one of the first controlled experiments that maggots do not result from spontaneous generation in putrefying meat but come instead from eggs laid by flies.

Red River Settlement British colony in the Red River region of Manitoba, Canada. First established in 1812 it was contested by the Hudson's Bay Company and the North West Company. The Seven Oaks Massacre (1816), in which North West Company agents killed 22 settlers, and other incidents resulted in litigation and the eventual merger of the two companies (1821).

Red Scare *See* **United States, 1920.**

Red Shirt Movement Anti-British movement in the North-West Frontier province of India. It was launched in 1930 by Gaffar Khan (1890–) in support of the Indian National Congress and professed Gandhian nonviolence.

Reed, John 1887–1920. American writer and radical leader. A wealthy Harvard graduate, he embraced communism, witnessed the Russian Revolution, and wrote a famous account of it, *Ten Days That Shook the World.*

Reed, Walter 1851–1902. American army surgeon and bacteriologist. In controlled experiments using human volunteers, he proved conclusively (1901) that yellow fever was transmitted by mosquitoes.

Reform, Catholic *See* **Catholic Reformation.**

Reforma, La Period in Mexican history (1854–76) characterized by liberal reforms directed mainly against special privileges of the army and the church. It began with announcement of the liberals' Plan of Ayutla (Mar. 1, 1854) and the ouster (1855) of the dictator Santa Anna. There followed a succession of liberal presidents (most notably B. Juárez), revolts and civil wars, and the brief restoration of the monarchy under Maximilian. Reform legislation enacted included Ley Juárez (1855), abolishing church and military courts; Ley Lerdo (1856), forcing the sale of church-owned secular lands; a liberal constitution (1857) curtailing military and church power; and Laws of La Reforma (1859), ordering confiscation of church lands.

Reformation Religious reform movement that arose in the 16th cent. It began as a reaction to practices within the Roman Catholic church that some held to be either unsupported by scriptural teaching or simply corrupt and abusive usurpations of authority. The movement ultimately gave rise to the various Protestant churches. Although earlier movements for church reform had arisen in Europe, the Reformation dates from 1517, when Martin Luther issued his Ninety-five Theses. Other Protestants, such as John Calvin, also spread the movement for reform, which was fueled by religious zeal, by the new spirit of Renaissance humanism, and by social changes resulting from the growth of a prospering mercantile class. Key dates in the history of the Reformation include:

14TH CENT. J. Wycliffe led early movement for reform of Roman Catholic church.

1414–18 Council of Constance; attempt made to introduce reforms in the Roman Catholic church.

1415 J. Huss, Bohemian religious reformer, burned at stake for heresy; death led to outbreak of the Hussite Wars in the Holy Roman Empire.

1517 M. Luther posted his Ninety-five Theses at Wittenberg (Oct. 31) in the Holy Roman Empire; the Reformation began.

1518 In Switzerland, H. Zwingli began campaign against sale of indulgences within the church; led growth of Reformation in Swiss cantons.

1519 Luther defended Protestant doctrine in famous Leipzig Debate (July).

1520 Luther excommunicated from the Roman Catholic church.

1521 Luther refused to recant after being called before the Diet of Worms.

1522–23 Knights' War, unsuccessful rebellion by knights to ensure ancient privileges against the Reformation.

1524–25 Peasants' War; Luther condemned violence of peasants' uprising, which was partly inspired by his teachings; peasants savagely repressed.

1526 First Diet of Speyer convened; decreed that German princes could embrace Lutheran teachings.

1529 Colloquy of Marburg; Luther and P. Melanchthon debated against J. Oecolampadius and H. Zwingli on elements of Reformation doctrine.

1529 Second Diet of Speyer overturned ruling of first diet; Lutheran princes issued a protest against its decrees, thereby becoming known as the Protestants.

1530 Diet of Augsburg convened; Melanchthon drew up the Confession of Augsburg, which became the foundation for Lutheranism.

1531 Protestant nobles in the Holy Roman Empire formed the Schmalkaldic League to oppose Emperor Charles V's threats to use force against Lutheranism.

1534 In England, Henry VIII's conflict with the pope over his attempt to divorce Catherine of Aragon (since 1527), came to a climax; excommunicated, he secured the Act of Supremacy, establishing the Church of England. Though Henry maintained Catholic character of church, later rulers introduced Protestant liturgy.

1536 J. Calvin settled in Geneva and issued *Institutes of the Christian Religion,* foundation for Calvinism.

1539 Lutheranism in England suppressed by issuance of Act of Six Articles.

1545 Council of Trent convened, marked beginning of Catholic Reformation; reforms introduced to counter rising tide of Protestantism.

1546–47 Holy Roman Emperor Charles V defeated the Schmalkaldic League in the Schmalkaldic War.

1547–53 Edward VI reigned in England; began reorganization of Church of England into a Protestant church; secured (1547) repeal of Act of Six Articles and issuance (1549) of Book of Common Prayer.

1555 Peace of Augsburg provided formula for ending conflict between Catholics and Protestants within the Holy Roman Empire.

1559 Synod of French Protestant churches held in Paris; led to organization of Huguenot movement in France.

1560 J. Knox secured establishment of Calvinism in Scotland.

1562–98 French Catholics and Huguenots engaged in civil war during Wars of Religion.

1598 French king Henry IV issued the Edict of Nantes, granting religious freedom to the Huguenots.

1618–48 Thirty Years' War; began as a revolt in Bohemia in the Holy Roman Empire and soon became general European war fought between Protestant and Catholic forces.

1648 Peace of Westphalia ended Thirty Years' War and established a measure of religious peace in Europe.

Reformation, Catholic *See* **Catholic Reformation.**

Reform Bills Series of laws that enlarged the British electorate and removed certain voting inequities. A bill in 1832 increased the representation of large towns proportionally and increased the electorate 50 percent by eliminating certain property qualifications. The 1867 act again redistributed parliamentary seats according to population and again doubled the body of eligible voters. The bill in 1884 enabled nearly all males to vote. In 1918, suffrage was extended to all over the age of 30, regardless of sex, and the voting age was lowered to 21 in 1928.

Reformed Church in America Official name since 1867, of the Dutch Reformed church in North America. Both its doctrine and system of church government originated in the Netherlands under Calvinist inspiration. It was transplanted to America as the religion of the Dutch colony of New Amsterdam (New York).

Reform Judaism Religious movement that sought to modernize Judaism. Beginning in Germany (19th cent.) under the leadership of such rabbis as A. Geiger, the movement did away with many Orthodox rituals and practices and stressed instead religious faith and ethics. Since the 1930s, Reform congregations have reinstituted some of the traditional practices.

Reform Movement of 1898 Short-lived reform movement in China during the reign of Emperor Guangxu. China's defeat in the Sino-Japanese War (1894–95) and the attempts by Western powers to exploit China gave rise to sentiment for Westernizing Chinese culture. Scholar and reformer Kang Youwei (1858–1927) gained the emperor's confidence and persuaded him to issue sweeping reforms of traditional Chinese society. The movement was cut short, however, by a coup led by the Empress Dowager Tzu Hsi.

Reims *See* **Rheims.**

Regency British historical and cultural period (1811–20). It spanned the regency of George, prince of Wales, who came to power as regent after his father, George III, went insane. It was marked by the end of the Napoleonic Wars, dissolute courtly life, an interest in antiquity and Oriental artifacts, and a flowering of the arts. Romantic literature, including the work of J. Keats, G. Byron, P. Shelley, and Sir W. Scott, flourished in this period, which also saw the development of distinctive styles in the decorative arts and architecture.

regicides During the English Civil Wars, those who signed the death warrant leading to the execution of King Charles I (1649). Of those still alive at the Restoration of the monarchy (1660), 15 fled abroad and 29 were convicted of treason. Ten were executed.

Regiomontanus (Müller, Johannes) 1436–76. German mathematician, astronomer, and humanist. Involved in the study of Greek manuscripts, he produced the first systematic modern exposition of trigonometry (c1464).

Régnier, Henri de 1864–1936. French poet and writer. One of the foremost members of the symbolist school, he later wrote in a more classical vein.

Regulating Act British parliamentary legislation passed in 1773 reorganizing the British East India Company. Its object was to improve the government of company domains, and it represented the first British government intervention in the company's administration of India. The British government took over complete administrative control by 1858. (*See also* Government of India acts.)

Regulator movement American Colonial society involved in an uprising in the 1760s. Frontier settlers in western North Carolina formed the group to reform corrupt local government and end oppressive taxation. When the Colonial government failed to act, the Regulators refused to pay taxes and ultimately mounted an insurrection. The Regulators were defeated (1771) by the militia under Gov. W. Tryon. Thereafter, many Regulators fled to Tennessee. A similar group in South Carolina succeeded in effecting reforms during the 1760s, then disbanded without serious incident.

Regulus, Marcus Atilius *d.* c250 BC. Roman general in the First Punic War. Captured by the Carthaginians, he was released on parole to persuade the Senate to make peace. Instead he urged the Romans to persist, and then returned, as agreed, to Carthage, where he is said to have been tortured to death.

Rehoboam *d.* c914 BC. Last king of the united kingdom of Israel (933–914) and first king of Judah. During his reign, the 10 northern Hebrew tribes broke away under the leadership of Jeroboam I to form the kingdom of Israel. Rehoboam then ruled the two southernmost tribes. [1 Kings 11–14; 2 Chron 9, 12]

Reichstag Legislative assemblies of the Holy Roman Empire and German successor states. The Holy Roman Emperor began to meet with city representatives c1100. The meetings became formal assemblies after 1250 and exerted legislative power until 1648, playing only a ceremonial role after that date. An elected Reichstag was established by the German Empire from 1871 to 1918, and was continued under the Weimar Republic (1919–33). The Reichstag surrendered its power to A. Hitler by the Enabling Act (1933), and was reduced to ceremonial functions during the Third Reich. It was replaced after WW II by the Bundestag in West Germany.

Reichstag fire The burning of the Reichstag building in Berlin on the night of Feb. 27, 1933. A Dutchman, Marinus van der Lubbe, was convicted for setting the fire. A. Hitler blamed the fire on the Communists, however, and used the incident to justify his assumption of dictatorial powers.

Reign of Terror Period during the French Revolution. Instituted Sept. 5, 1793, and directed by the Committee of Public Safety (*q.v.*), the Terror was intended to crush all opposition to the revolution. Thousands were guillotined or died in prisons. The period also saw the rise of M. Robespierre as virtual dictator of France, enactment of the laws of Maximum (establishing price controls and forbidding hoarding), institution of universal conscription, and reorganization of the army. Toward the end of the Terror, even allies of Robespierre (including followers of J. Hébert and G. Danton) fell victim to the guillotine. Finally, popular reaction against the Terror resulted in the overthrow of Robespierre (July 27, 1794) and the subsequent Thermidorean reaction. (*See also* French Revolution, 1793–94.)

Reimarus, Hermann Samuel 1694–1768. German philosopher. A pioneer thinker of the Enlightenment, he denied the supernatural origins of Christianity and advanced the belief in natural religion of the deists.

Reinhardt, Max (Goldmann, ˘) 1873–1943. Austrian theater director. He originated many modern dramatic techniques and brought new life to productions of classic Greek and Shakespearean drama. Founder of the Salzburg Festival.

Reinsurance Treaty Secret treaty (June 18, 1887) between Germany and Russia replacing the Three Emperors' League. It provided that one party would remain neutral if the other became involved in a war, unless Germany attacked France or Russia attacked Austria. Failure to renew the treaty (1890) led to a Franco-Russian alliance.

relativity Physical theory, advanced by A. Einstein and elaborated by Einstein and others, dealing with the nature and relationship of space and time. Toward the end of the 19th cent., certain anomalies in the system of Newtonian mechanics were discovered. In order to explain them, Einstein advanced the special theory of relativity (1905) and the general theory of relativity (1915), which fundamentally altered the perception of the form and structure of the universe. Fundamental to the theory is the concept that all motion is relative and that space and time are not separate and absolute entities. The theory produced a revolution in mathematics and physics that is continuing today. A unified field theory, which seeks to combine the special and general theories of relativity, has yet to be demonstrated.

Religion, Wars of Series of civil wars (1562–98) in France between the Catholics, led by the powerful Guise family, and the French Protestants, known as Huguenots. The civil wars revolved around religious differences but were further complicated by struggles among the nobility for political power. The wars culminated in the accession of the Huguenot leader, Henry of Navarre (as Henry IV), to the French throne in 1589. In an attempt to resolve the continuing struggle, he converted to Catholicism (1593) and finally ended the wars by the Edict of Nantes (1598), granting religious toleration to the Protestants. Key dates in the history of the wars include:

1560 Conspiracy of Amboise; Huguenots' unsuccessful plot to break influence of Catholic house of Guise over French king Francis II and thereby end persecution of Protestants.

1560–74 Charles IX reigned, following the death of Francis II; a youth at his accession, he was dominated by his mother, Catherine de Médicis, throughout his reign.

1562 Massacre of Vassy; Huguenots massacred by troops of François, duke of Guise.

1562–63 First war fought after Huguenots rebelled against persecution.

1567–68 Second war fought.

1568–70 Third war fought; Huguenots led by Louis I de Bourbon and G. de Coligny; war ended by Treaty of Saint Germain (1570), which granted some freedoms to the Huguenots.

1572 St. Bartholomew's Day Massacre (Aug. 23); brought on by rising influence of Huguenot leader G. de Coligny; resulted in murder of many Huguenots and sparked fourth war.

1572–73 Fourth war fought; ended by Edict of Boulogne.

1574–89 Henry III, another son of Catherine de Médicis, reigned; Catherine continued to exercise considerable influence.

1574–76 Fifth war fought; ended by Peace of Monsieur (1576), by which Huguenots received religious freedom everywhere but in Paris.

1576 Holy League formed by Catholics to oppose Protestantism in France; began alliance with Spain.

1577 Sixth war fought; war sparked by Henry III, who revoked toleration of Protestants at the urging of the Catholic Holy League.

1577 Protestants won favorable terms in the Peace of Bergerac (Sept. 17), ending sixth war.

1580 Seventh war fought after persecution of Huguenots continued; concessions to

Huguenots confirmed by the Treaty of Fleix, ending the war.

1584 French king Henry III designated Henry of Navarre, a Huguenot, as heir to the French throne; Henry of Guise led Catholic Holy League in opposition, resulting in new war.

1585–89 War of the Three Henrys; Henry of Guise took Paris (1588) and deposed Henry III, who fled; Henry of Guise was murdered (1588); Henry III then turned to Henry of Navarre for support and was murdered (1589), thus ending the war.

1589 Huguenot leader Henry of Navarre became King Henry IV.

1589 Spain invaded France to aid the Catholic Holy League against Henry IV.

1589 Battle of Arques; Henry IV defeated Catholics.

1590 Battle of Ivry; Henry IV again victorious in fighting against Catholics.

1593 Henry IV converted to Catholicism.

1594 Henry IV entered Paris.

1598 Henry issued (Apr. 15) the Edict of Nantes, granting Huguenots religious freedom.

1598 Treaty of Vervins (May 2) ended war with Spain.

religious dualism *See* dualism.

Religious Peace of Nürnberg (~ Standstill) Truce (July 23, 1532) that for a time ended religious wars between Holy Roman Emperor Charles V (Catholic) and the Schmalkaldic League (Protestant).

relocation centers WW II internment camps in which Japanese-Americans living in a defined area on the West Coast were forcibly confined between Mar., 1942, and Mar., 1946. Suspected of disloyalty after the Japanese attack on Pearl Harbor, Japanese-Americans were indiscriminately interned in such camps and lost property estimated at some $400 million. This program was later severely criticized and officially deplored by Congress in 1983.

Remarque, Erich Maria 1898–1970. German novelist, best known for his WW I novel *All Quiet on the Western Front*.

Rembrandt (Rijn, Harmenszoon van) 1606–69. Great Dutch painter, noted for his mastery of technique (especially lighting) and for great depth of understanding of his subjects. He spent many years teaching and enjoyed a wide following until the 1640s, when he lost popularity and

began to experience financial problems that continued until his death. He nevertheless produced over 600 paintings, as well as many drawings and etchings, and in the later years of his life created some of his greatest masterpieces. Among his many famous works are *Two Philosophers, The Anatomy Lesson of Dr. Tulp, The Sortie of the Banning Cocq Company, Aristotle Contemplating the Bust of Homer, Bathsheba,* and his series of self-portraits.

Remington, Eliphalet 1793–1861. American arms manufacturer. His firm produced a famous series of rifles and pistols and supplied the US government with small arms from the mid-19th cent.

Remonstrants Dutch Protestants adhering to the liberal Calvinist ideas of J. Arminius. They presented their views to the States General (1610) in a "remonstrance," were condemned by the Protestant Synod of Dort (1618–19), and then were persecuted by the state church until 1625.

Renaissance Transition period in Europe from medieval to modern culture. The Renaissance is generally viewed as a rebirth or reawakening of learning and the arts, which began in Italy in the 1300s and then spread throughout Europe. The Renaissance period may be broadly divided into the Italian Renaissance of the 1300s and 1400s and the Northern Renaissance (centers outside Italy) of the 1400s and 1500s. It may also be divided into Early (c1400–c1490), High (c1490–1520), and Late (1520–1600) periods, though dates of periods vary. Central to the Renaissance period was the rise of Humanism, a movement placing new emphasis on the individual and on the secular (as opposed to spiritual) world. Man became "the measure of all things" and the "universal man," an individual accomplished in a wide variety of pursuits, became a Renaissance ideal. The intellectual "rebirth" of the Renaissance had wide ramifications. There was a greater emphasis on education in areas outside theology, especially the humanities and particularly study of the Greek and Roman classics (the invention of printing helped make this possible). In literature and philosophy, it was man and the world about him that became the center of attention. In the arts, interest began to shift from idealized religious themes to more worldly conceptions, and advances were made in areas of technical concern (perspective, use of color, study of human anatomy). In architecture, Renaissance designers adapted earlier classical forms (as in Palladianism) and medieval Gothic styles were gradually abandoned. Advances in science during the Renaissance helped prepare the way for the 17th-cent. revolution in science. The Renaissance in Italy began in Florence, and thereafter spread to Venice, Rome, and other cities. The great cultural flowering in Italy, as elsewhere, was aided by wealthy patrons, including such families as the Medici, Sforza, Este, and Gonzaga, and Roman Catholic popes such as Julius II and Leo X. Leading figures of the Renaissance are listed by country (and then by birth date) below.

Renaissance in Italy

NICOLA PISANO Founded school of sculpture at Pisa and developed style that influenced Renaissance sculpture in Italy. c1220–84

GIOTTO Florentine artist and architect, departed from the traditional Byzantine forms and created powerful new style of painting, foreshadowing the Renaissance. 1266–1337

PETRARCH Great poet, classical scholar, and Humanist; helped spread interest in classical culture by his researches and poems, thereby laying foundations for the Early Renaissance. 1304–74.

G. BOCCACCIO Poet and storyteller who wrote the *Decameron,* in which the earthly passions of man are portrayed. 1313–75.

F. BRUNELLESCHI First great architect of the Renaissance, he developed systematic rules of perspective and designed the celebrated dome of the cathedral in Florence. 1377–1446.

L. GHIBERTI Leading 15th-cent. Renaissance sculptor famed for his doors for the baptistry of the cathedral of Florence. c1378–1455.

DONATELLO Florentine sculptor, among the greatest Renaissance sculptors; he completed such masterpieces as the bronze statue *David* and *Gattamelata,* a prototype of Renaissance equestrian statuary. c1386–1466.

P. UCCELLO Florentine painter noted for his pioneering use of perspective; masterpiece is cycle of *Noah,* among which is the *Deluge.* 1396–1475

FRA ANGELICO Florentine painter who brought classical stylistic elements to his religious works. c1400–55

L. DELLA ROBBIA Influential Florentine sculptor who did the marble *cantoria* (singing gallery), famous portrayal of children and innocence; founded family studio famous for enameled terracotta works. 1400?–82.

MASACCIO Leading Florentine painter; completed fresco *Trinity,* which marked great advance in understanding of perspective; worked on the historic frescoes of the Brancacci Chapel of Santa Maria del Carmine in Florence. 1401–28.

LEON ALBERTI Early example of universal "Renaissance man," systematized problems of perspective in *Della Pittura,* worked as an architect; wrote poetry; did studies in geography, grammar, and mathematics. 1404–72.

FRA FILIPPO LIPPI Florentine painter noted as a great colorist and draftsman, did *Coronation of the Virgin* and other famous works. c1406–69.

L. VALLA Classical scholar and Humanist; attacked medieval philosophy and did important scholarly and critical works; exposed Donation of Constantine as a forgery. c1407–57.

A. POLLAIUOLO Florentine artist and sculptor, believed first to study human anatomy through dissection. 1429?–98.

G. BELLINI Venetian painter; helped make Venice a center of Renaissance art; taught Giorgione and Titian. c1430–1516.

MANTEGNA Noted for his frescoes, especially in the Camera degli Sposi (wedding chamber) of the Gonzaga Palace. 1431–1506.

M. FICINO Philosopher and leading exponent of Platonism in his time, he translated Greek classics into Latin. 1433–99.

S. BOTTICELLI Florentine painter; *Birth of Venus* among his famous works. c1444–1510.

D. BRAMANTE Painter and architect who pioneered the High Renaissance style in architecture. 1444–1514.

L. DA VINCI Archetypal "Renaissance man," who painted masterpiece *Mona Lisa* and the most famous *Last Supper;* worked as a sculptor, architect, and military engineer; noted also for his scientific studies, especially human anatomy, and for his inventions. 1452–1519.

N. MACHIAVELLI Political philosopher and leading Renaissance figure who wrote the classic on political power, *The Prince.* 1469–1527.

MICHELANGELO A leading figure of the Italian Renaissance who was a painter and sculptor.

Among his many famous works are the *Pietà* and paintings decorating the ceiling of the Sistine Chapel. 1475–1564.

GIORGIONE Venetian painter; leading figure of the 16th-cent. painting in Venice; works include *The Three Philosophers* and *Tempesta*. 1478–1511.

B. PERUZZI Painter and architect who worked in Rome and designed the Palazzo Massini. 1481–1536.

ANTONIO DA SANGALLO THE YOUNGER Leading Florentine architect of his time who built the Farnese Palace at Rome; Sangallo's designs greatly influenced later architects. 1483–1546.

RAPHAEL A great master of the High Renaissance whose many famous works include series of Madonna altar panels and the frescoes *Disputa* and *School of Athens*. 1483–1564.

ANDREA DEL SARTO Noted painter who was influential in Florence and Rome, among his works were frescoes on the life of Saint John the Baptist. 1486–1530.

TITIAN One of the greatest of Renaissance painters; noted for his religious and mythological paintings; works include *Sacred and Profane Love* and the *Pietà*. 1490–1576.

B. CELLINI Sculpted *Perseus with the Head of Medusa* and wrote a famous autobiography; famed as a goldsmith. 1500–71.

A. PALLADIO One of the most influential Renaissance architects; developed architectural style (Palladianism) based on classical Roman forms; wrote famous treatise, *Four Books on Architecture,* and designed villas and church facades. 1508–80.

TINTORETTO A Venetian, leading painter of Late Renaissance Mannerist school; he painted a *Last Supper* and other famous works. 1518–94.

P. VERONESE Great decorative artist of the Venetian school; *Christ in the House of Levi* among his famous paintings. 1528–88.

Renaissance in the Low Countries and German States

ROBERT CAMPIN Early Flemish master; taught Van der Weyden; did *Mérode Altarpiece.* c1378–1444.

J. VAN EYCK Flemish, great Renaissance painter of the 15th cent.; he mastered the technique of painting with oils and made Flanders a center of Renaissance art; his style of realism was widely influential. c1390–1441.

R. VAN DER WEYDEN Flemish painter noted for his treatment of religious themes; *Christ Descending from the Cross* is one of his masterpieces. c1400–64.

HANS MEMLING Leading artist of Bruges in his time; painted *Passion Triptych.* c1430–94.

HUGO VAN DER GOES Greatest Flemish artist of his time; noted for religious works of profound nature; was early influence in northern realism; did masterpiece, *Portinari Altarpiece.* c1440–82.

M. SCHONGAUER Leading engraver of his time, noted for grace and idealistic beauty of his works; works include *Madonna in a Courtyard* and *St. Sebastian.* c1445–91.

H. BOSCH Flemish painter; noted for his imaginative, sometimes bizarre works, famous works include *Garden of Earthly Delights.* c1450–1516.

J. REUCHLIN German scholar and Humanist; he did important studies of classical Greek and Hebrew writings. 1455–1522.

LUCAS CRANACH Leading German painter; his works greatly influenced 16th-cent. German art. 1472–1553.

H. HOLBEIN THE YOUNGER German painter noted for the realism of his portraits; he worked in England from 1532 until his death. 1497–1553.

ERASMUS Leading Renaissance Humanist scholar; his works include an edition of the New Testament, of Latin and Greek classics, critical works, and the satire *The Praise of Folly;* he opposed M. Luther's Protestant reforms. 1466?–1536.

A. DÜRER Great German artist of the Renaissance whose famous works include paintings, altarpieces, engravings, and woodcuts. 1471–1528.

N. COPERNICUS Polish astronomer; leading scientific figure of the Renaissance, he founded modern astronomy by his theory that the earth and other planets revolve around the sun; paved the way for the scientific revolution of the 17th cent. 1473–1543.

MELANCHTHON German theologian, scholar, and Humanist; in addition to his major contributions to the Protestant Reformation, Melanchthon played a significant role in reforming the German educational system. 1497–1560.

M. Grünewald Great German painter; painted religious, often mystical works, including the *Isenheim Altarpiece.* c1475–1528.

P. Brueghel the Elder Leading 16th-cent. Flemish painter noted for his landscapes and peasant scenes, including *Peasant Wedding.* c1525–69.

O. Di Lasso Among greatest of Renaissance composers; noted for his motets. c1530–94.

Renaissance in France

Guillaume de Machaut Poet and great composer in the 14th cent. Ars Nova musical style. c1300–77.

J. Fouquet Leading French painter, famous works include illuminations for the *Book of Hours.* c1415–80.

G. Budé Humanist scholar. Major figure of the Renaissance who established study of the classics in France and who helped organize a great library, which became the Bibliothèque Nationale. 1467–1540.

Jean Clouet A noted portrait painter; he worked in France nearly all his life. c1485–c1540.

F. Rabelais Scholar, Humanist, and author of classic satire, *Gargantua and Pantagruel.* c1490–1553.

Rosso Fiorentino First of several Italians brought to France (1530) by King Francis I and who developed the influential Fontainebleau school of French painting; joined by Primaticcio and others, the school evolved styles of painting and decorative sculpture. 1494–1540.

P. Delorme Great Renaissance architect; introduced a classical style to French architecture; did initial design of Tuileries Palace. c1510–70.

Pierre Lescot Architect who developed decorative style; his work contributed to rise of French classicism; with sculptor Jean Goujon designed part of the Louvre. c1515–78.

P. de Ronsard Great Renaissance poet, he was a leader of the famous group of French Renaissance poets, the Pléiade; other members were Joachim du Bellay, Antoine de Baïf, Étienne Jodelle, Pontus de Tyard, Jean Dorat, and Rémi Belleau. 1525–85.

M. de Montaigne Great essayist, noted for his three books of essays revealing spirit of Humanism and his mastery of style. 1533–92.

Renaissance in England

J. Fisher A noted scholar, Humanist, and theologian, he promoted scholarly study in England; martyred for refusing to yield to King Henry VIII. 1459–1535.

J. Colet Was a leading exponent of scholarly studies and of Humanism. 1467?–1519.

T. More He was an important advocate of Humanism and wrote the classic *Utopia.* 1478–1535.

Roger Ascham Scholar, Humanist, and author who promoted the English vernacular. 1515–68.

E. Spenser One of the greatest Elizabethan poets, he wrote the *Faerie Queene* and other works. c1552–99.

P. Sidney Noted Renaissance courtier and poet wrote the essay *The Defense of Poetry.* 1554–86.

F. Bacon Philosopher and essayist, author of noted works, including *Novum Organum* and *The New Atlantis;* his work in inductive logic proved important to the later advances in scientific thought. 1561–1626.

C. Marlowe Leading poet and dramatist; introduced use of blank verse and psychological themes in English drama. 1564–93.

W. Shakespeare Perhaps the greatest dramatist of all time; his many famous plays mark the culmination of the Elizabethan Age. 1564–1616

I. Jones Architect; he introduced the Renaissance Palladian style in England. 1573–1652

Renaissance in Spain

Cardinal Jiménez Promoted classical studies and founded the University of Alcala. 1436–1517.

Fernando de Herrera Humanist and leading neoclassic poet of 16th-cent. Spain. 1534?–97.

M. de Cervantes Leading figure of the Renaissance in Spain, he wrote the great classic *Don Quixote.* 1547–1616.

L. DE VEGA The virtual founder of Spanish drama, he wrote some 1,800 plays, introduced Italian forms to Spanish poetry. 1562–1635

Renan, Ernest 1823–92. French historian, Orientalist, and writer. He left the seminary after a crisis of faith and afterward wrote about religion from a naturalistic point of view.

René 1409–80. King of Naples (1435–80) and duke of Anjou, Bar, and Lorraine. Involved in the dynastic politics of the time, he was driven out of Naples (1442) by his Aragonese rivals and retired to Provence to devote himself to the arts.

Renewed Church of the Brethren *See* **Moravian church.**

Reni, Guido 1575–1642. Italian painter of the Bolognese school. His works include the *Crucifixion of St. Peter* and his masterpiece, *Aurora and the Hours.*

Renner, Karl 1870–1950. First leader of the Austrian republican government, 1918–20, and president of Austria, 1945–50. A Socialist, Renner held many key positions in the interwar period and advocated the union of Austria and Germany prior to WW II.

Renoir, Jean 1894–1979. French film director. A son of the painter P. Renoir, he is known for his imaginative cinematic effects. His films include the antiwar masterpiece *La Grande Illusion.*

Renoir, Pierre Auguste 1841–1919. French impressionist painter. He was noted for such effects as light filtering through leaves (*Le Moulin de la Galette*). Later in his career he returned to more formal techniques (*Bathers*) and then developed a style marked by its sensuousness. *Girl with Watering Can* (1876) is one of his popular works.

Renville **Agreement** Truce (Jan. 17, 1948) between the Dutch and the Indonesians, signed on the US Navy ship *Renville.* It marked a lull in the fighting between the Dutch and the Indonesian republicans and remained officially in effect, supplementing the Linggadjati Agreement (*q.v.*), until Indonesia obtained independence (1949).

reparations Payments required of a defeated nation for war damages, especially those imposed on Germany after WW I and WW II. German WW I reparations were not specified by the Treaty of Versailles. In 1922, the London Conference set them at $32 billion, though no one expected Germany would ultimately pay that much. The Dawes Plan for repayment was formulated (1924). Economic hardship and the worldwide Depression resulted in the Young Plan (1930), but by 1932 Germany had ceased to make further payments. After WW II, German reparations were officially canceled in 1954.

repartimiento Spanish-American colonial system by which colonists were allowed to recruit specified numbers of Indians for forced labor. The system assumed definite form by 1575 and, though progressively modified, continued in some form until the 19th cent.

republic Form of government in which power is vested in officers who represent the public and who govern in accordance with established laws for the sake of the common good. The government of the United States is a federal republic.

Republic, Council of the Preparliament Russian provisional government (Oct.–Nov., 1917), headed by A. Kerensky. Largely ineffective, it was swept away in the Bolshevik seizure of power.

Republic, Roman *See* **Roman Republic; Rome.**

Republic of *See names inverted.*

Republican party One of the two major US political parties. Founded (1854) by antislavery Whigs and others who were opposed to the Kansas-Nebraska Act (1854) and the extension of slavery into new US territories, it received support from abolitionists, Free-Soilers, Know-Nothings, and others. Its first presidential candidate, J. Frémont, was defeated in the 1856 election, but its second, A. Lincoln, gained the presidency (1860) and thereby precipitated secession of the southern states and, ultimately, the Civil War. During the war, the party split into moderate and radical factions. The radical Republicans favored harsh Reconstruction measures against the South, and their struggle with Lincoln's successor, A. Johnson, led to impeachment proceedings (1868). The Radicals' involvement in corruption and scandals during the administration of U. Grant led to formation of the Liberal Republican party, which unsuccessfully ran H. Greeley against Grant in the 1872 elections. Other breaks in the Republican party occurred in 1884, when the Mugwumps (*q.v.*) abandoned the party to support Democrat G. Cleveland, and in 1912, when the progressive wing of the party formed the Progressive (Bull

Moose) party (*q.v.*). This Republican split secured the election for the Democrat, W. Wilson. The Republican party was hurt in the 20th cent. by corruption in the administration of W. Harding and by the beginning of the Great Depression during the administration of H. Hoover. Hoover was defeated for reelection (1932) by F. Roosevelt, and the Republicans did not regain the presidency until the election (1952) of D. Eisenhower. Subsequent Republican presidents include R. Nixon, G. Ford, R. Reagan and G. Bush.

Republican People's party   Turkish political party. Formed in 1923 by K. Atatürk, it was Turkey's ruling party until 1950. Since then it has been the leading opposition party (to the Democrat party and its successors), with periods of rule. It is republican, secularist, and increasingly leftist in orientation.

Republic of China   *See* **Taiwan.**

Resaca de la Palma, Battle of   Second major battle (May 9, 1846) of the Mexican War (1846–48), fought near present-day Brownsville, Texas. An American force, led by Gen. Z. Taylor, intercepted and defeated the Mexican army, under the leadership of Gen. Mariano Arista, then retreating after the Battle of Palo Alto.

Resistance   Underground political and paramilitary forces that grew inside the countries occupied by Germany during WW II. The French Resistance was notable among them. Its network provided intelligence, published clandestine newspapers, and carried out sabotage, especially after the Allied landings (1944) on the Continent. (*See also* **Partisans.**)

Respighi, Ottorino   1879–1936. Italian composer. His works, such as *The Pines of Rome* (1924) and *The Fountain of Rome* (1916) were influenced by the Russian and German Romantics.

Restoration   1. Period in English history (1660–88) that included the reigns of Charles II and James II. It began with the restoration of the monarchy under Charles after the experiment in republican government failed (*see* **Protectorate**). Growing opposition to the Protectorate (now dominated by the military) prompted one of the military leaders, G. Monck, to take control of London (1659). The royalist Convention Parliament (*q.v.*) was convened, and it made arrangements for Charles's restoration. Charles then issued the Declaration of Breda (*q.v.*), returned to England (1660), and assumed authority. His

subsequent reign was marked by a reaction against Puritans and the policies of austerity they imposed on English life during the Protectorate; enactment of harsh measures by the Cavalier Parliament to ensure religious uniformity with the Church of England (*see* **Clarendon Code**); the rise of anti-Catholic sentiment; the beginnings of the Whig and Tory factions; and a series of misfortunes, including outbreak of the plague (1665), the Great Fire of London (1666), and losses in the Second Dutch War (1664–67). Under James II, anti-Catholic sentiment and reaction against his absolutism brought about (1688) the Glorious Revolution (*q.v.*) and the end of the Restoration period.   2. Period in French history (1814–30) that began with Napoleon's fall from power and restoration of the Bourbon monarchs. Largely through the efforts of C. Talleyrand, Louis XVIII assumed power after Napoleon's first abdication (Apr. 11, 1814), in what is called the First Restoration. His rule was interrupted by Napoleon's Hundred Days (*q.v.*), however, and the Second Restoration began after Napoleon's second abdication (June 22, 1815). The Restoration period included the reigns of Louis and his successor Charles X. It was marked by France's recovery from its defeat under Napoleon and growing friction between the royalist and republican factions. The Restoration was ended (1830) when these tensions culminated in the July Revolution (*q.v.*).

resurrection   Central Christian doctrine holding that the dead will rise in possession of glorified bodies. This expectation is based on the belief in Christ's resurrection from the dead. Resurrection is a facet of other religions, including Islam.

Retz, Gilles de Laval, seigneur de (Rais, ~, ~) 1404–40.   French soldier, nobleman, and marshal of France. A companion of Joan of Arc, he was later convicted of torturing and killing more than 100 children in his castle in Brittany. He thus inspired, it is thought, the Bluebeard legend.

Reuchlin, Johann   1455–1522.   German humanist scholar. He was the first Christian to compose a Hebrew grammar, the *Rudimenta Hebraica,* and he defended the study of Hebrew writings before the Inquisition. He also did important studies in classical Greek.

Reuter, Paul Julius   1816–99.   Founder of the first news wire service, Reuters. Born Israel Beer Josaphat, he developed Reuters from a carrier-pigeon service into a worldwide telegraph network transmitting commercial news.

Reuther, Walter Philip 1907–70. American labor leader. He was a president of the United Automobile Workers (UAW) and helped arrange the merger of the CIO (of which he was also president) with the AFL (1955). He broke with AFL-CIO president G. Meany, however, and took the UAW out of the federation in 1969.

Revere, Paul 1735–1818. American Revolutionary hero, immortalized in the poem by H.W. Longfellow. A Boston silversmith, Revere became involved early in the movement for independence and participated (1773) in the Boston Tea Party. A courier for Boston's Committee of Safety, he started out on what became his legendary ride to warn of the coming of British soldiers (Apr. 18, 1775). He was captured by a British patrol, but his two companions, Samuel Prescott (1751–77?) and William Dawes (1745–99) escaped. Prescott then went on to complete the mission. The Minutemen were thus prepared for the battles of Lexington and Concord (Apr. 19, 1775), which marked the beginning of the American Revolution.

Reversal of Alliances *See* **Diplomatic Revolution.**

reverse lend-lease *See* **lend-lease.**

revival Among Protestant churches, a mass reawakening of religious fervor, especially for intense religious experience. Use of the term dates from the rise of Methodism in England and the Great Awakening (*q.v.*) in the US (18th cent.).

Revocation of the Edict of Nantes *See* **Edict of Nantes.**

Revolt of *See names inverted, as in* **Ciompi, Revolt of the.**

revolution *See under country names (i.e.,* **American, Russian, Chinese**) *and proper names (i.e.,* **Glorious Revolution**).

revolution Fundamental change in political institutions, leadership, and social structure, often accompanied by violence. Classic examples are the American, French, Russian, and Chinese revolutions.

Revolution of 1800 *See* **Adams, John.**

Revolutions of 1848 Revolutions in Europe sparked by the French February Revolution (*q.v.*) of 1848, which overthrew French king Louis Philippe. Soon after the February Revolution, uprisings in Vienna, Prague, Venice, and other cities marked the beginning of a general upris-

ing of national groups within the control of Habsburg Austria. Austrian emperor Ferdinand was forced to make constitutional concessions in Austria, Hungary, and Bohemia, and was faced with a rising movement for independence in Italy. The revolutions led to Ferdinand's abdication (Dec., 1848) and the accession of his nephew as Francis Joseph I. The uprisings in Bohemia and Italy began to fail in 1848. In Aug. 1849, Francis Joseph, with Russian aid, crushed the revolution in Hungary and forced many of its leaders, including L. Kossuth, to flee. In Germany uprisings in Berlin and other cities led to establishment (May 18, 1848) of the liberal Frankfurt Parliament, which sought to reform the German Confederation into a unified state. The Parliament, after much deliberation, adopted a new constitution (Mar. 27, 1849) and offered the crown to Prussian king Frederick William IV, who declined. The Prussians, however, tried to form the Prussian Union, under their domination, but the plan was effectively blocked by Austria by the Punctation of Olmütz (Nov. 29, 1850), which reestablished the old German Confederation. In the meantime, Austria had also reasserted its authority in Italy, Bohemia, and Hungary.

Reyes, Alfonso 1889–1959. Mexican poet, writer, and diplomat, one of the great Mexican literary figures of this century. Among his works are the poem *Visión de Anáhuac* and the essay *Simpatías y diferencias.*

Reyes, Rafael 1850–1921. President of Colombia (1904–09). Elected president, he assumed dictatorial powers and tried to promote the development and modernization of Colombia.

Reynaud, Paul 1878–1966. French statesman. A conservative, he held several ministerial posts under the Third and Fourth French republics, and was prime minister when France fell to the Germans (1940) in WW II.

Reynolds, Sir Joshua 1723–92. English portrait painter. He painted in the "grand style" and dominated the artistic life of the mid-18th cent.

Reza Shah Pahlavi 1877–1944. Shah of Iran (1925–41). An army officer, he led a coup (1921) and later became prime minister (1923). He subsequently assumed dictatorial powers, ousted the shah, Ahmed (1925), and became the shah. He began a program of reform and modernization. He changed the name of his country from Persia to Iran (1935).

Rhaetia (Raetia) Ancient Roman province, added to the empire in 15 BC. It occupied an important position in the Alps between the Danube and the Po. Its principal city was the modern Italian city of Trent.

Rhee, Syngman (Yi Sung-man) 1875–1965. First president of South Korea (1948–60). The first Korean to earn an American Ph.D., he worked for Korean independence, first from China and then from Japan (as an expatriate). He ruled South Korea as a popular but authoritarian president, until forced from office on election-rigging charges.

Rheims (Reims) City in northern France, site of the Gothic cathedral where French kings were traditionally crowned. Clovis, the king of the Franks, was first crowned there in AD 496, and from the 12th to 19th cents. it was used for royal coronations. The cathedral was heavily damaged in WW I but was restored. In WW II, the German surrender (1945) was signed at Rheims.

Rhine, Confederation of the *See* **Confederation of the Rhine.**

Rhineland Region of Germany west of the Rhine River, and a frequent battleground. After WW I the Treaty of Versailles (1919) provided for occupation of most of it by Allied forces and for its eventual demilitarization (reaffirmed 1925 in the Locarno Pact). The last Allied forces (French) left in 1930. In 1936, Hitler remilitarized the region in clear defiance of the treaty and constructed the Siegfried Line (*q.v.*).

Rhode Island Northeastern US state, the 13th state. The Dutch under Adriaen Block explored the region in 1614 and it was settled by R. Williams (1636) after he was exiled from Massachusetts for religious differences. He was granted a charter (1663) by Charles II to forestall claims by Massachusetts and Connecticut. Rhode Island was one of the first colonies to renounce allegiance to England but refused to ratify the Constitution until 1790. Industrial development began (1790) with S. Slater's textile mill in Pawtucket. Rhode Island's constitution was adopted in 1842 after a rebellion led by T. Dorr.

Rhodes Historic Greek city on the island of Rhodes. It was laid out by Hippodamus in 408 BC and was the site of the Colossus of Rhodes (*q.v.*), one of the Seven Wonders of the World. Rhodes flourished as a commercial and cultural center until the 2d cent. BC, when competition

from Delos and tensions with the Romans resulted in its decline.

Rhodes, Cecil John 1853–1902. British South African statesman and financier. He worked for the extension and consolidation of southern African territories under British domination, made a fortune in diamonds, and endowed the Rhodes scholarships at Oxford.

Rhodes, Colossus of *See* **Colossus of Rhodes.**

Rhodesia *See* **Zimbabwe.**

Rhys, Ernest Percival 1859–1946. Welsh writer and critic. He was best known as the editor of nearly all the 1,000 volumes of the world's great books collected in the Everyman's Library series.

Ribalta, Francisco c1555?–1628. Influential Spanish painter, noted for his contrasts of light and dark coloring. His paintings include *Christ Embracing Saint Bernard.*

Ribaut, Jean (Ribault, ˜) c1520–65. French navigator and explorer. He established French forts and early colonies in South Carolina and Florida in the 1560s. He and the settlers were ultimately killed by the Spaniards.

Ribbentrop, Joachim von 1893–1946. German diplomat and Nazi foreign minister (1938–45). He concluded the Russo-German nonagression pact of Aug., 1939, which paved the way for Hitler's attack on Poland (the immediate cause of WW II). He was executed as a war criminal after the war.

Ricardo, David 1772–1823. English economist. He was a pioneer in the development and systematization of economic theory, especially in such areas as value theory, price levels, and free trade.

Ricci, Matteo 1552–1610. Italian Jesuit missionary in China. By mastering the Chinese language and classics, he was able to interpret Christianity and the West for the Chinese literati and thus introduced them to European culture.

Richard I (˜ Coeur de Lion) (˜ Lion-Heart) 1157–99. King of England (1189–99), successor to his father, Henry II, and hero of popular legends. He became duke of Aquitaine (1172), joined his brothers in a rebellion (1173–74) against their father, and defeated him in another clash (1189). He joined (1190) Philip II of France on the Third Crusade, shortly after becoming king. He conquered Cyprus and with Philip took Acre (1191), but was forced into a treaty with Saladin after failing to take Jerusalem. On his way back to England he was captured in Austria and held for ransom (until 1194) by Holy Roman Emperor Henry VI. He then returned to England, put down a revolt by his brother John, and spent the remainder of his reign fighting Philip II in France.

Richard II 1367–1400. King of England (1377–99), successor to Edward III. Conflicts with his barons eventually led to his overthrow by his cousin, Bolingbroke, duke of Lancaster, who became Henry IV. He was the son of Edward the Black Prince.

Richard III 1452–85. Last Yorkist king of England (1483–85). He took the throne from his brother, Edward IV, eliminating the latter's young sons, until he was defeated and killed in the Battle of Bosworth Field (*q.v.*), which ended the Wars of the Roses (*q.v.*).

Richard Coeur de Lion *See* **Richard I.**

Richard Lion-Heart *See* **Richard I.**

Richardson, Dorothy M. 1882–1957. English novelist. She was a pioneer in the stream-of-consciousness technique, employed in her novel *Pilgrimage.*

Richardson, Henry Hobson 1838–86. American architect. He pioneered the Romanesque revival in America, employing the style in such buildings as Boston's Trinity Church, completed in 1877.

Richardson, Samuel 1689–1761. English novelist. His epistolary novel *Pamela: or Virtue Rewarded* (1740) was one of the first true English novels. Richardson's other works include *Clarissa, or the History of a Young Lady.*

Richelieu, Armand Jean du Plessis, duc de 1585–1642. French cardinal and chief minister (1624–42) to Louis XIII. Made a cardinal in 1622, he rose to power as a favorite of Louis' mother, Marie de Médicis. His domestic policy aimed at weakening the power of the nobility and the Huguenots to establish the central absolute authority of the monarchy. His foreign policy sought to end Habsburg power. He formed alliances with Protestants during the Thirty Years' War (1618–48) and finally brought France into it (1635) against the Habsburg powers. The wars wrecked French finances but marked the country's ascendancy as a major power.

Richter, Hans 1843–1916. Hungarian-born conductor. He was a major orchestra conductor in both Germany and England and a noted authority on the operas of his friend R. Wagner.

Richthofen, Manfred, baron von 1892–1918. German pilot in WW I, known as the "Red Baron." He led the German air group known as Richthofen's Circus and was credited with downing 80 Allied aircraft, a record that made him the principal ace of WW I. He was killed in action on Apr. 21, 1918.

Ricimer *d.* AD 472. Roman general of Germanic (Suevian) origin. He defeated the Vandals in 456, and then deposed the Western Roman emperor Avitus. While retaining real power, he subsequently installed and ousted a series of emperors (457–472).

Rickenbacker, Eddie (˜ Edward Vernon) 1890–1973. American pilot, WW I ace and industrialist. He downed a record 26 German planes in WW I and later became president and chairman of Eastern Airlines.

Rickover, Hyman George 1900–86. American admiral. He directed the planning and building of the world's first atomic-powered submarine, the *USS Nautilus,* launched in 1954.

Ridgway, Matthew Bunker 1895–93. American general. He pioneered paratrooper assaults by American forces in Sicily and Normandy during WW II. He later became supreme commander of UN forces in Korea (1951–52) and NATO forces in Europe (1952–53) and served as US chief of staff (1953–55).

Ridley, Nicholas 1500?–55. English bishop, reformer, and Protestant martyr. As bishop of London, he was one of the most effective English reformers. A supporter of the Protestant Lady Jane Grey, he was tried and burned at Oxford with Hugh Latimer after Mary Tudor became queen.

Ridolfi, Roberto 1531–1612. Italian conspirator involved in a plot (1570–71) to restore Catholics to power in England. He planned to murder Queen Elizabeth I and replace her with Mary Queen of Scots, who was to marry the duke of Norfolk. The plan was uncovered when one of the conspirators was captured and confessed. Ridolfi escaped but the duke of Norfolk was beheaded.

Riego y Núñez, Rafael del 1785–1823. Spanish rebel, a leader in the 1820 liberal revolution.

Riehl, Wilhelm Heinrich 1823–97. German writer. He was a novelist, short-story writer, and a distinguished historian of culture.

Riel's Rebellion Brief revolt in western Canada against the government, led by Louis Riel

(1844–85). In 1869–70, Riel organized the Métis (half French, half Indian) of the Red River area into a provisional government, in order to prevent Canada from taking over the land that until then had been administered by the Hudson's Bay Company. The government crushed the revolt, but gave Red River its own provincial government (Manitoba), and Riel escaped to the US. He was the nominal leader of a second revolt (1884–85, actually led by Gabriel Dumont) on behalf of the Métis of Saskatchewan (the Northwest Rebellion), but was captured and hanged.

Riemann, Georg Friedrich Bernhard 1826–66. German mathematician. A highly original thinker, he made many contributions to the science of geometry, some of which were later important to the mathematics of the theory of relativity.

Rienzi, Cola di (Rienzo, ~) 1313–54. Popular leader of the medieval city of Rome. He began as an official under authority of the pope (residing at Avignon) and then conceived his grandiose plan of restoring the Roman Empire. He assumed dictatorial powers over the city for a time but was eventually killed by a mob.

Riga, Treaty of 1. Treaty (Aug. 11, 1920) between Latvia and Russia, at the close of the Baltic War of Liberation (*q.v.*) By it, Russia recognized Latvia's independence.   2. Treaty (Mar. 18, 1921) ending the Russo-Polish War (1919–20). By it, Russia ceded parts of the Ukraine and Belorussia to Poland.

Right Opposition Opponents of J. Stalin in the Central Committee of the Soviet Communist party (1928–29). The former "left-wing Bolshevik" N. Bukharin was sometimes considered the leader of this opposition.

Rights and Grievances, Declaration of *See* **Stamp Act Congress.**

Rights of Man, and of the Citizen, Declaration of the French Revolutionary manifesto. Drafted by E. Sieyès and adopted by the French National Assembly on Aug. 26, 1789, this document outlined inalienable rights of individuals. In 1791, it became the preamble to the French constitution guaranteeing rights of representation, equality before the law, protection of property and from arrest, and freedom of religion, speech, and the press.

Riis, Jacob August 1849–1914. Danish-born American writer and social reformer. He became

famous for his book exposing the conditions in New York tenements, *How the Other Half Lives,* published in 1890.

Rijn, Rembrandt Harmenszoon van *See* **Rembrandt.**

Riksdag Swedish parliament. Formed as a two-chamber body in 1866, it was reduced to a single chamber in 1971. The government is responsible to the Riksdag and, since 1975, the Riksdag speaker has had the right to name the premier. From 1435 to 1865, "Riksdag" was the name of Sweden's states general, which included the peasantry as a fourth estate.

Rilke, Rainer Maria 1875–1926.   Austrian poet. Considered a major 20th-century literary figure, he is best known for his *Duino Elegies* and *Sonnets to Orpheus.*

Rimbaud, Arthur 1854–91.   French poet. He developed a mystical, hallucinatory style in such works as *A Season in Hell* and thereby greatly influenced the later symbolist poets.

Rimini, Golden Bull of *See* **Golden Bull of Rimini.**

Rimsky-Korsakov, Nicolai Andreyevich 1844–1908.   Russian composer. One of the Russian nationalist composers, he is best known for such orchestral works as *Scheherazade* (1888) and such operas as *The Golden Cockerel.*

Ringling, John (*orig.* Rüngeling, John) 1866–1936. American circus impresario. With five brothers, he organized a circus in 1884, bought out Barnum and Bailey in 1907, and, at his death, had sole control of the extensive Ringling Brothers Circus operation.

Río de Janeiro, Treaty of Mutual defense treaty (Sept. 2, 1947) between the US and the Latin American republics. It provided for a united response to attack by outside aggressors and for settlement of disputes between signers.

Rio Salado, Battle of Major victory (Oct. 30, 1340) for Christians over the Muslims (Moors) in Spain. Muslims from North Africa launched their last major invasion of Iberia, and Christians thus faced both Spanish and North African Muslims. King Alfonso XI of Castile and Alfonso IV of Portugal joined forces and routed the Muslims at Seville. The victory marked the beginning of the final phase of the Christian takeover in southern Spain.

Ripley, George 1802–80. American reformer and literary critic. He helped establish the utopian Brook Farm (*q.v.*) experiment and later became an influential book reviewer for the *New York Tribune.*

Risorgimento Italian nationalistic movement resulting in a unified Italian state (1861). In the early 19th cent., during the post-Napoleonic period in Europe, sentiment for unification of Italy, at that time divided and dominated by foreign powers, arose. The Carbonari (*q.v.*), as well as other secret societies, and G. Mazzini's nationalistic movement (Young Italy) were formed and, by the mid-1800s, the unification movement had gained momentum. Abortive liberal republican revolts failed in 1848–49. The Austrians were driven out of north Italy (1859) and G. Garibaldi's successful military campaign (1860) won much of the rest of Italy for the nationalists. Victor Emmanuel was crowned king of Italy in 1861.

Rites Controversy Religious dispute (17th–18th cents.) among Catholic missionaries in China about whether Confucian ancestor veneration was compatible with Christian worship. The Jesuits tended to favor the rites, while the Dominicans and Franciscans tended to oppose them. Pope Clement XI banned all ancestral rites in 1704, making further Jesuit missionary work difficult.

Ritschl, Albrecht 1822–89. German Protestant theologian. His work was a reaction against rationalism and stressed the unique revelation contained in the life and teachings of Jesus.

Rittenhouse, David 1732–96. American astronomer, inventor, and public official. He is said to have built the first telescope in America, and observed the transit of Venus across the sun (1769), concluding the planet had an atmosphere. A surveyor as well, he oversaw the fixing of boundaries between many states in the Northeast, and in the Northwest Territory. Rittenhouse became the first director of the US Mint (1792).

Ritter, Karl 1779–1859. German geographer. One of the founders of modern scientific geography, he was noted for his study of the influence of natural environment on human history.

Rivadavia, Bernardino 1780–1845. Argentine diplomat and statesman, and first president (1826–27) of the United Provinces of La Plata, an Argentine confederation.

Rivera, Diego 1886–1957. Mexican painter. Known for his realistic murals, many on the life and history of Mexico, he identified strongly with populist and leftist causes.

Rivera, José Eustasio 1889–1928. Colombian poet and novelist. He is known for his sonnets and his novel about the rubber gatherers in the Amazon jungle, *The Vortex.*

Rizal, José 1861–96. Philippine writer and nationalist leader. He wrote novels against the Spanish rule in the Philippines. Accused of instigating the revolt against Spain in 1896, he was tried and executed.

Roanoke Colony *See* **Lost Colony.**

Robbe-Grillet, Alain 1922– . French novelist, director, and screenwriter. Originally a trained agronomist, he is considered an originator of "nouveau roman," the French anti-novel of the 1950s, in which structure and external reality dominate the plot and characterization. Among his novels are *The Erasers* (1953) and *Last Year at Marienbad* (1961).

Robber Barons Disparaging term used to describe wealthy 19th-cent. industrialists whose great wealth and success in business were interpreted as a sign of indifference to the workers on whom they depended. The term was popularized as the title of a book that appeared (1934) during the Great Depression, and was used in reference to such notable industrialists as C. Vanderbilt, J. D. Rockefeller, and A. Carnegie, and to financiers such as J. P. Morgan and J. Gould.

Robbins, Frederick Chapman 1916– . American physician. A professor of pediatrics, he shared the 1954 Nobel Prize in Physiology or Medicine with John Enders (1897–85) and Thomas Weller (1915–) for discoveries concerning the polio virus.

Robert I c865–923. Frankish king (922–23). Ruling the land between the Seine and the Loire, he revolted against Charles III, and was made king of the Franks. He was killed in battle soon after. His grandson was Hugh Capet.

Robert I *d.* 1035. Duke of Normandy (1027–35). A strong ruler, he established order in his domains and aided Henry I of France. By his mistress, he fathered William I ("the Conquerer"), whom he legitimized and made his heir.

Robert I (˜ the Bruce) 1274–1329. Scottish king (1306–29) and hero of Scottish independence. Following a struggle with John Comyn (*d.* 1306) for leadership of the Scottish nationalists, Robert was crowned king of Scotland (Mar. 27, 1306) in defiance of the English. He was decisively defeated by the English at the Battle of Methven (June 19, 1306) and was driven into hiding on Rathlin Island, off the Irish coast. There, according to tradition, he renewed his determination to free Scotland after watching a spider persevere in making a web. He returned to Scotland (1307), won new supporters, and ultimately defeated the English at the famous Battle of Bannockburn (*q.v.*). The English recognized Scottish independence by the Treaty of Northampton (1328).

Robert II c970–1031. French King (996–1031), successor to his father, Hugh Capet. Called "the Pious," he was a firm supporter of religious reformers.

Robert II (~ Curthose) c1054–1134. Duke of Normandy (1087–1106). The eldest son of William I ("the Conquerer"), he inherited Normandy while his brother William II took England. Robert was a leader of the First Crusade.

Robert II 1316–90. King of Scotland (1371–90). He was several times regent during the exiles of his uncle, David II. He eventually succeeded him and thus founded the Stuart line of Scottish (and later British) kings.

Robert III c1340–1406. King of Scotland (1390–1406). He ruled (from 1384) for his father, Robert II, until incapacitated by injury in 1388. His brother and his son ruled for him after he became king.

Robert, Henry Martyn 1837–1923. American general and writer. He wrote the famous *Robert's Rules of Order* (1876) for public meetings.

Robert, Saint *See* **Cistercians.**

Robert Curthose *See* **Robert II.**

Robert Guiscard c1015–85. Norman adventurer in Italy and founder of the Kingdom of the Two Sicilies. He was invested by the pope with the rule of southern Italian lands but they remained to be conquered from the Saracens. With his brother Roger I he conquered Sicily, Calabria, Bari, and Salerno. He next took Corfu from the Byzantines (1082). He returned to rescue Pope Gregory VII from Holy Roman Emperor Henry IV, and Robert's troops entered and sacked Rome (1084).

Robert of Courteney *d.* 1228. Latin emperor of Constantinople (1218–28). It was under his ineffective reign that the Latin Empire of Constantinople was reduced to the city and environs.

Robert of Geneva *d.* 1394. Genevan churchman and antipope Clement VII (1378–94). After electing Pope Urban VI, the cardinals reversed themselves and elected Robert, who took up residence at Avignon. This began the Great Schism (*q.v.*).

Roberts, Charles G. D. *See* **Confederation group.**

Roberts, Sir Charles George Douglas 1860–1943. Canadian author. He was noted for his stories set in the Canadian wilderness and his popular *History of Canada* (1897).

Roberts, Owen Josephus 1875–1955. American jurist and associate justice of the US Supreme Court (1930–45). He was prosecutor in the Teapot Dome scandal, followed a generally conservative line as justice, and later headed the commission investigating the Pearl Harbor disaster.

Robert the Bruce *See* **Robert I.**

Robert the Strong *See* **Capetians.**

Robeson, Paul Bustill 1898–1976. Black American actor, singer, and political activist. As a singer, he was best known for his spirituals. He won important acting roles on Broadway and in film, but his resentment over racism in the US led him to embrace Communism in the 1930s. His pro-Communist public attacks on President Truman's Cold War policies forced an end to his acting career and he died in obscurity.

Robespierre, Maximilien François Marie Isidore de 1758–94. French revolutionary. As a lawyer and head of the Jacobins, he was known as "the Incorruptible." He became a member of the National Convention. There, as a leader of the radical Montagnards, he played an important role in ousting (1793) the moderate Girondists from power, and thus in altering the course of the revolution. He next joined (July 27, 1793) and dominated the Committee of Public Safety (*q.v.*) and through it became the leading power behind the Reign of Terror (*q.v.*), which he ultimately used to eliminate even his former allies. He was finally ousted in the coup of 9 Thermidor (July 27, 1794) and was tried and executed the following day.

Robinson, Charles 1818–94. American antislavery leader and first governor of the state of Kansas (1861–63). He was involved in Bleeding Kansas (*q.v.*), was imprisoned for a time by the proslavery forces in the territory, and assumed the governorship after Kansas became a state.

Robinson, Edwin Arlington 1869–1935. American poet. He is best known for his series of poems about the common people of the imaginary Tilbury Town. Among them are *Richard Cory, Miniver Cheevy,* and *Luke Havergal.*

Rob Roy 1671–1734. Scottish freebooter whose name was Robert MacGregor. As head of the MacGregor clan, he led them in cattle-stealing raids and other ventures. His exploits were celebrated in Sir W. Scott's novel *Rob Roy.*

Robusti, Jacopo *See* **Tintoretto.**

Roca, Julio Argentino 1843–1914. Argentine soldier and president (1880–86, 1896–1904). As an army general he opened up Patagonia for settlement. His term as president was marked by rapid development and increased financial speculation.

Roca-Runciman Treaty Trade treaty between Argentina and Britain (signed May, 1933) in which Argentina granted important concessions to the British in return for continued purchases of Argentine beef and grain. Argentina had been hit hard by the worldwide Depression following the US stock market crash of 1929, and meat and grain exports to Britain were crucial to its economy. Thus, the government was forced to make the concessions after members of the British Commonwealth, also suffering from the Depression, won preferential agreements for their meat and grain exports to the United Kingdom.

Rochambeau, Jean Baptiste Donatien de Vimeur, comte de 1725–1807. French general. Having distinguished himself as a commander in Europe, he was sent (1780) with 6,000 troops to America during the Revolution. Accompanying Washington, he was instrumental in winning the Battle of Yorktown (*q.v.*), which ended the American Revolution.

Rochdale Society of Equitable Pioneers First successful consumers' cooperative. It was founded in Rochdale, England, in 1844, on the basis of the ideas of R. Owen. The society began with a grocery store and later expanded to include a textile mill and factory on the same cooperative principles.

Rochefort, Victor-Henri, marquis de Rochefort-Lucay 1830–1913. French journalist. He moved from the extreme left to the extreme right, at first opposing Napoleon III and supporting the Paris Commune (1871). He then turned to G. Boulanger and later the nationalists in the Dreyfus Affair.

Rochester, John Wilmot, 2d earl of 1647–80. English courtier and poet. While personally dissolute he nevertheless fought bravely against the Dutch. He was noted for his satiric poems. Among them were *History of Insipids, Maim'd Debauchee,* and *A Satyr Against Mankind.*

Rockefeller, John Davison 1839–1937. American millionaire industrialist and philanthropist. First employed as a bookkeeper, he later organized (with partners) the Standard Oil Company (1870). Thereafter Rockefeller gained control of the oil industry, built Standard Oil into one of the great trusts, and amassed a huge fortune. His company was the object of government antitrust suits in the early 1900s, and after 1911 Rockefeller turned to philanthropy, notably through his Rockefeller Foundation (established 1913).

Rockefeller, John Davison, Jr. 1874–1960. American industrialist and philanthropist. Heir to his father's vast Standard Oil fortune, he was especially noted for his philanthropies, such as funding the restoration of Colonial Williamsburg and donating the land for the United Nations building.

Rockefeller, Nelson Aldrich 1908–79. Forty-first US vice-president (1974–77) and heir to the vast Rockefeller family fortune. A liberal Republican, he served four terms as New York governor (1959–73) and was nominated to the vice-presidency by G. Ford. He was a noted philanthropist and patron of the arts.

Rockefeller, William 1841–1922. American financier. Associated with his brother J. Rockefeller in the oil business, he also had other stock-market, industrial, and banking interests.

Rockingham, Charles Watson-Wentworth, 2d marquess of 1730–82. British prime minister (1765–66, 1782). He attempted to conciliate the American colonies and repealed the Stamp Act during his first ministry. His second ministry, following the collapse of Lord North's government, saw the repeal of Poynings's Law (*q.v.*) but ended before final peace had been made with the American Colonials.

Rock of Gibraltar *See* **Gibraltar.**

Rockwell, Norman 1894–1978. American painter and illustrator. Best known for his covers for the *Saturday Evening Post* magazine, he painted scenes typical of American life in a realistic style.

rococo Artistic style that succeeded the baroque in Europe. Originating in 18th-cent. France, the rococo style was characterized by highly ornate and decorative designs and lines.

Rodgers, Richard 1902–79. American composer of musical comedies. He produced many outstanding musical shows in collaboration with L. Hart and O. Hammerstein II, winning Pulitzer prizes with the latter for *Oklahoma!* and *South Pacific.*

Rodin, Auguste 1840–1917. Great French sculptor, whose works were executed in a style of Romantic realism. Many of his most famous pieces were studies to be included in the unfinished bronze doors for Paris' Musée des Arts Décoratifs. They include *Adam* (1880) and *Eve* (1881), *The Thinker* (1880), and *The Kiss* (1886). He is noted also for *The Burghers of Calais.*

Rodney, George Brydges, 1st baron Rodney 1719–92. British admiral. Rodney distinguished himself during the Seven Years' War. He became a national hero by defeating the Spanish (thereby relieving Gibraltar, 1780) and the French off Dominica (1782), in fighting related to the American Revolution.

Rodó, José Enrique 1872–1917. Uruguayan writer and philosopher. He upheld spiritual over material values in his most famous essay, *Ariel,* and was considered one of the great Latin American philosophers.

Roebling, John Augustus 1806–69. American civil engineer, born in Germany. He pioneered the use of steel cable in bridge-building, built major suspension bridges at Pittsburgh, Cincinnati, and Niagara, and began the Brooklyn Bridge (completed by his son).

Roebling, Washington Augustus 1837–1926. American civil engineer and bridge builder. The son of J. Roebling, he was associated with his father's firm and completed the building of the Brooklyn Bridge (opened 1883), which had been begun by his father.

Roehm, Ernst *See* **Röhm, Ernst.**

Roemer, Olaus *See* **Rømer, Olaus.**

Roentgen, Wilhelm Konrad 1845–1923. German physicist, the discoverer of X-rays. A professor of physics at several German universities, his scientific studies ranged from elasticity, to properties of gases and heat conduction. He discovered x-rays (1895) while experimenting with a cathode-ray tube. Roentgen discovered that it produced rays that passed through paper, wood, and aluminum, traveled in straight lines, and exposed photographic plates. In publicly announcing his discovery (1896), he exhibited the first X-ray pictures showing the bones of a human hand. His discovery proved an enormous benefit to science and medicine. He was awarded the first Nobel Prize for Physics (1901).

Roe v. Wade US Supreme Court decision (1973) guaranteeing a woman's right to an abortion during the first six months of pregnancy. After that time, the court held the unborn baby was able to survive outside the womb and therefore was subject to state laws. The decision has been one of the most controversial in recent times. During the 1980s and early 1990s, abortion opponents staged protests and helped promote legislative challenges to the court's decision in various states, frequently by limiting abortion rights rather than by an outright ban. Subsequent Supreme Court decisions (as recently as 1992) have allowed some further limits on abortion, but have upheld the basic right.

Roger I c1031–1101. Norman conquerer and count of Sicily. He helped his brother Robert Guiscard conquer southern Italy from the Saracens and Byzantines. He ruled these domains as a papal legate after the death of his brother.

Roger II 1097–1154. Count (1101–30) and then Norman king of Sicily (1130–54). He consolidated the lands conquered by his Norman kinsmen and added Capua, Naples, and the Abruzzi. His rule was one of the most advanced of the times and he brought a period of prosperity. His capital at Palermo became a cultural center.

Roger, Pierre *See* **Clement VI.**

Rogers, John 1500?–55. English Protestant reformer and martyr. He published (under the pseudonym Thomas Matthew) the English-language Matthew Bible of 1537, utilizing mostly the translations of Englishmen W. Tyndale and Miles Coverdale (1488?–1569). This bible was subsequently revised as the Great Bible, which in turn became the basis for the famous King James Version. Rogers was executed after the accession of Catholic Queen Mary I.

Rogers, Will (~, William Penn Adair) 1879–1935. American humorist, writer, and actor. Beginning with a vaudeville act, he went on to write popular columns and books based on his homespun but shrewd and satirical wit. He also appeared in many movies.

Rogers's Rangers British-American Colonial frontier force, composed of some 600 men trained in Indian methods. Commanded by Major Robert

Rogers (1731–95), it carried out numerous daring raids during the French and Indian Wars and Pontiac's Rebellion.

Roget, Peter Mark 1779–1869. English physician and lexicographer. He worked for many years compiling his *Thesaurus of English Words and Phrases* (published in 1852), which has undergone many revisions and remains a standard reference work.

Rohan, Louis René Édouard, prince de 1734–1803. French diplomat and churchman who became a Catholic cardinal. He was French ambassador in Vienna and later was duped into providing security for jewels in the famous Affair of the Diamond Necklace (*q.v.*). He was subsequently banished.

Rohilla War War against the Afghan Rohilla tribe then in India, waged (1774) by the Nawab of Oudh, mainly to recover money owed him by the Rohillas. He crushed the Rohillas with help from a British East India Company brigade provided by W. Hastings, governor of Bengal. The incident later became one of the grounds for Hastings' impeachment.

Röhm, Ernst (Roehm, ˜) 1887–1934. German National Socialist leader. An early Nazi party member and organizer of the storm troops, he was a potential rival to A. Hitler. He was executed without trial on Hitler's orders during the Blood Purge (*q.v.*).

Rojas Pinilla, Gustavo 1900–75. Colombian army leader and president of Colombia (1953–57). He led a coup that ousted the unpopular L. Gómez, but the brutality, ineptitude, and corruption of his own administration led to his ouster by a military junta, backed by both right and left. He was an unsuccessful candidate for president again in 1970.

Roland *d.* 778. A count of the Breton March, Roland provided the basis for the hero of the great French epic poem *The Song of Roland* in which, as part of Charlemagne's rear guard crossing the Pyrenees, he fought valiantly in a great battle against overwhelming numbers of Saracens. The historical Roland was actually cut off and killed by Basques at the Battle of Roncesvalles (*q.v.*), a minor engagement.

Roland de la Platière, Jean Marie 1734–93. French Revolutionary leader and minister of the interior (1792). A prominent member of the moderate Girondist faction, he had to flee Paris during the Reign of Terror. He committed suicide after his wife Manon was arrested and guillotined.

Roland de la Platière, Manon Philipon 1754–93. French woman, the wife of Girondist leader J. Roland de la Platière. She maintained a fashionable revolutionary salon. Arrested during the Reign of Terror, she uttered the words "O Liberty, what crimes are committed in thy name!" just before being guillotined.

Rolfe, John 1585–1622. English colonist in Virginia. He introduced the cultivation of tobacco, which became Virginia's staple crop, and married the Indian woman Pocahontas (*q.v.*). He took her to England (1616), where she died. He was probably killed in the Indian massacre of 1622 after his return to Virginia.

Rolland, Romain 1866–1944. French novelist, biographer, and musicologist. He exalted art, pacificism, and socialism, especially through his 10-volume novel *Jean Christophe,* about a modern genius. He received the Nobel Prize in Literature in 1915.

Rollo (Rou) (Hrolf) c860–c932. Norman chieftain, founder of the duchy of Normandy. He invaded and conquered the land around the mouth of the Seine (now in France). He was granted rule over it (911) by French king Charles III (the Simple) in return for accepting vassalage and baptism.

Rölvaag, Ole Edvart 1876–1931. Norwegian-American writer. He was noted for his portrayal of immigrants in Minnesota, especially in *Giants in the Earth* and the novels that followed it.

Roma *See* **Gypsies.**

Romagna Historical region of north-central Italy. It was the center of Byzantine domains in Italy (6th–8th cents.) and was later incorporated into the Papal States. Its major city was Ravenna (*q.v.*).

Romains, Jules (*pseud.* of Farigoule, Louis) 1885–1972. French writer. He produced a panoramic view of French life in the early 20th cent. in his 27-volume novel, *Men of Good Will.*

Roman Catholic church One of the three major branches of Christianity (with Protestant and Orthodox Eastern churches). It is a worldwide union of churches recognizing the primacy of Rome. The authority of the popes is traditionally believed to derive from the continuous line of popes (bishops of Rome) succeeding Saint Peter.

The church claims to be the one true apostolic Christian church, maintaining its supremacy in doctrinal questions that created other branches of Christianity. The early years of the church, following the crucifixion of Jesus Christ, were marked by the rapid spread of Christianity; persecution and then toleration by the Romans; the growing isolation of Rome and the Western church from the Eastern church (centered at Constantinople) after the end of the Western Roman Empire (AD 476), and finally the alliances between the popes at Rome and the kings of Europe (from the 8th cent.). In following centuries of the Middle Ages, the church became a powerful force in European politics and culture. For a time popes were able to command the submission of the great European monarchs. The struggle between the popes and the Holy Roman emperors, however, gradually eroded that power and, by the 16th–17th cents., papal power was overshadowed by the absolutist monarchs in Europe. Meanwhile the split between the Western and Eastern halves of the Christian world continued to widen, until finally the Schism of 1054 resulted in a complete break and formation of the Orthodox Eastern church (*q.v.*). A second great division of the Christian world occurred in the 16th cent. The Protestant Reformation (*q.v.*) resulted in the creation of a host of new Christian sects and forced the Roman Catholic church to institute the sweeping reforms of the Catholic Reformation (*q.v.*). In modern times the church has been concerned with doctrinal problems raised by modern society and with bridging the divisions within the Christian world. **For more on important persons and events** *see* **entries under specific names.** Key events in the history of the church include:

c8–6? BC Jesus born in Bethlehem; worked as a carpenter until around age 30, when he began his public ministry.

AD c30 Jesus Christ crucified in Jerusalem; disciples claimed he rose from the dead, appeared to them, and commissioned them to preach a Gospel (*lit.* "good news") of eternal salvation through him.

AD c30–44 Disciples of Christ gathered around the Apostle Peter; the nucleus of the new church engaged in preaching the Gospel of Jesus and administering the sacraments.

AD c33 Saul of Tarsus, a Jew, blinded by a vision on the road to Damascus; converted and became St. Paul the Apostle.

AD c43 According to tradition, Apostle St. James ("the Greater") became missionary to Spain; martyred.

AD c45 St. Peter moved to Antioch as first bishop of the church there; St. James left as bishop in Jerusalem.

AD c47–49 St. Paul's first missionary journey (with St. Barnabus and St. Mark) to Cyprus and Asia Minor; began to write the letters, or "epistles" that were the earliest New Testament writings.

AD c50 Council of Jerusalem, proto-council of the church; decided that gentiles converting to Christianity need not observe the full ritual Jewish law.

AD c50–53 Second missionary journey of St. Paul; crossed into Europe (Macedonia) where the church later flourished.

53–57 Third missionary journey of St. Paul; wrote great epistles to the Romans and Corinthians.

c55 St. Peter left Antioch for Rome, where tradition held he became the first bishop (pope).

c59 St. Paul arrested in Jerusalem; sent to Rome for trial.

c62 St. James, bishop of Jerusalem, martyred.

c67 Persecutions of Christians ordered by Nero; Sts. Peter and Paul martyred, according to tradition.

67–79? St. Linus, first of the line of successors to St. Peter, became bishop of Rome (pope).

c95 St. Clement of Rome (fourth pope) wrote "Epistle to the Corinthians," intervening in affairs of a local Greek church.

c107 First mention of the term "Catholic church" (*lit.* "universal church") in an epistle of St. Ignatius of Antioch.

c100–165 St. Justin Martyr, the first Christian apologist, combined Christian belief with Platonic philosophy.

155 Martyrdom of St. Polycarp, Bishop of Smyrna.

177 Large-scale public persecution in the arena at Lyons.

c189 St. Irenaeus of Lyons declared in *Adversus Haereses* that "every church must be in harmony" with the Church of Rome.

249–251 Large-scale persecution under the Emperor Decius.

251 St. Cornelius pope (AD 251–253) and martyr; first schism, resulting in the election of an antipope, Novatian.

258 Edict of persecution of the Emperor Valerian; martyrdom of St. Cyprian of Carthage.

c275 St. Anthony, pioneer of Christian monasticism, retired into Egyptian desert to pursue the ascetic life.

303 Edict of the Emperor Diocletian unleashed ten-year persecution of Christians.

311 Donatist heresy (holding validity of sacraments depended on sanctity of the minister) in North Africa.

313 Edict of Milan: co-emperors Constantine and Licinius established toleration of Christianity within the Roman Empire.

325 First Council of Nicaea (1st ecumenical council): condemned Arianism and issued creed as official profession of faith.

341 St. Julius pope (AD 337–352); defended Nicaea and claimed Roman primacy based on apostolic tradition stemming from Peter.

356 St. Athanasius, Archbishop of Alexandria (AD 328–373), exiled by the Arian emperor Constantius for his defense of Nicaea.

c360 Rise of Macedonianism, the belief that the Holy Spirit was created.

361–363 Emperor Julian ("the Apostate") attempted to reintroduce paganism in the Roman Empire.

c370 St. Basil the Great reorganized monasticism in the East.

378 St. Damasus (pope AD 366–384) condemned Apollinarian heresy.

LATE 4TH CENT. AD Twenty-seven books, constituting the present canon of the New Testament, decreed by Church to be authentic Scripture: Festal Epistle of St. Athanasius of Alexandria (AD 376); Decree of Pope St. Damasus (AD 382); provincial Synod of Carthage (AD 397).

380 Emperor Theodosius the Great decreed Nicene Christianity to be the religion of the Roman Empire.

381 First Council of Constantinople (2nd ecumenical council) condemned Macedonianism; issued creed in substantially the form it is recited today as the "Nicene Creed."

c400 Pelagianism, heresy denying original sin and affirming humans have perfect freedom of the will, introduced in Rome by British monk Pelagius.

410 St. Augustine of Hippo began writing *The City of God.*

417 St. Innocent I (pope AD 402–417) declared that pronouncements of bishops must be confirmed by the Roman See.

431 Council of Ephesus (3d ecumenical council): condemned Nestorianism, which denied Christ's divinity; declared that the Virgin Mary was "the Mother of God"; provoked centuries-long Nestorian schism.

449 St. Leo the Great (pope AD 440–461) condemned unauthorized "robber council" held at Ephesus and issued his famous *Tome* defining the nature of Christ.

451 Council of Chalcedon (4th ecumenical council): rejected Monophysitism; declared Jesus Christ to be true God and true man at the same time; centuries-long schism of Armenian, Egyptian, Ethiopian, and Syrian Monophysite churches stemmed from council's decree.

c495 Gelasius I (pope AD 492–496) wrote to Byzantine emperor Anastasius I denying the right of the state to interfere in church affairs.

c498 Baptism of Clovis, King of the Franks.

529 Monte Cassino abbey founded in Italy by St. Benedict; became center of Western monasticism.

553 Second Council of Constantinople (5th ecumenical council): reiterated condemnation of Nestorianism.

589 Third Council of Toledo: Visigothic King Reccared renounced Arianism and accepted the Roman Catholic faith.

597 St. Gregory the Great (pope 590–604) reformed liturgy; despatched St. Augustine of Canterbury to Christianize England.

610–640 Rise of Monothelite heresy, insisting that Christ had a divine will.

680–681 Third Council of Constantinople (6th ecumenical council): condemned Monothelite heresy.

751 Pepin the Short, King of the Franks, allied Franks with the papacy; marked beginning of Rome's alliance with European powers.

756 "Donation of Pepin"; papal domains constituted as a sovereign entity in central Italy.

787 Second Council of Nicaea (7th ecumenical council) convened by Empress Irene to deal with Iconoclastic controversy; last council considered ecumenical by Eastern Orthodox church.

800 Pope St. Leo III (795–816) crowned Charlemagne emperor of the Romans, strengthening ties with Europe's great monarch.

857 Controversy between Ignatius and Photius and at Constantinople over iconoclasm; Photius challenged right of popes to rule in the East; this resulted in breach between Rome and Constantinople, laying basis for future schism of East and West.

858–867 St. Nicholas the Great reigned as pope.

869–870 Fourth Council of Constantinople (8th ecumenical council): anathematized Photius as a usurper in Constantinople and confirmed decree of Pope Nicholas against him.

910 Monastery of Cluny founded in France.

962 German king Otto I conquered northern Italy and forced the pope to crown him emperor; this marked beginning of Holy Roman Empire.

11–12TH CENTS. Rise of Scholasticism; appearance of the first great medieval philosophers: P. Abelard, P. Lombard, St. Anselm of Canterbury, etc.

1054 Schism of 1054 between Eastern Orthodox and Roman Catholic churches.

1059 Lateran Synod under Pope Leo IX; established papal election procedure, giving cardinals power to elect pope.

1073–85 St. Gregory VII (Hildebrand) pope; well-known for his reforms and insistence on papal authority.

1077 Holy Roman Emperor Henry IV excommunicated, then pardoned as a penitent at Canossa, Italy, by Pope Gregory VII; great struggle between popes and Holy Roman Emperors continued.

1085 Gregory VII finally driven from Rome by Henry IV; died at Salerno.

1085–1122 Investiture Controversy; power struggle between the papacy and the Holy Roman Empire centering on the question of "lay investiture" (appointment of clergy by secular rulers).

1086 Carthusians, strictest monastic order, founded by St. Bruno of Cologne.

11TH–16TH CENTS. The Crusades: medieval holy wars undertaken by European Christians to reconquer the Holy Land from the Muslims.

1098 Cistercian monastic order launched at Cîteaux, France.

1098 Pope Urban II failed to reconcile Eastern and Western churches at the Council of Bari.

1115–35 St. Bernard, Abbott of Clairvaux, France, was principal religious leader in Europe.

1122 Diet of Worms; ended Investiture Controversy.

1123 First Lateran Council (9th ecumenical council) convened; first church council in the West; dealt with church discipline and investiture question, ratifying Diet of Worms.

1139 Second Lateran Council (10th ecumenical council) convened by Innocent II (1130–43); ended schism created by the election of antipope Anacletus II.

1159–81 Alexander III pope; effectively established papal authority over bishops and clergy; excommunicated the Emperor Frederick Barbarossa.

1179 Third Lateran Council (11th ecumenical council): College of Cardinals definitively empowered to elect pope; crusade against Albigenses in southern France proclaimed.

13TH–15TH CENT. Guelphs and Ghibellines were two opposing Italian factions prominent in the struggle for control of Italy; Guelphs usually favored popes, Ghibellines the Holy Roman emperor.

1198–1216 Innocent III pope; height of medieval papacy; preached disastrous Fourth Crusade.

1209 Friars Minor, mendicant order founded by St. Francis of Assisi.

1210 Innocent III excommunicated Holy Roman Emperor Otto IV.

1213 Innocent III forced English King John to acknowledge suzerainty of the pope.

1215 Fourth Lateran Council (12th ecumenical council) convened; doctrine of Transubstantiation defined; Easter duty established.

1216 Dominican Friars, founded by St. Dominic as a preaching order, especially to combat heresy.

1225–74 St. Thomas Aquinas, great theologian and philosopher; his adaptation of Aristotle became official Catholic philosophy in 19th cent.

1232 Inquisition (medieval) established by Pope Gregory IX (1227–41) to oppose spread of such heresies as those of Albigenses and Waldenses.

1245 First Council of Lyons (13th ecumenical council): called by Innocent IV (1243–54) during his struggle with the Emperor Frederick II.

1274 Second Council of Lyons (14th ecumenical council): called by Gregory X (1271–76) to act on pledge of Byzantine Emperor Michael VIII to reunite Eastern and Western churches.

1302 Boniface VIII (1294–1303) issued bull *Unam Sanctam* asserting supreme authority over secular state and "every human creature."

1303 Boniface VIII captured and imprisoned by agents of French King Philip IV; died shortly afterward.

1309–77 Babylonian Captivity of the papacy: Clement V (1305–14) brought it about by moving the seat of the papacy to Avignon.

1311–12 Council of Vienne (15th ecumenical council) convened in France; Knights Templar condemned.

1377 Pope Gregory XI (1370–78) moved the papacy back to Rome, ending the captivity.

1378–1415 Great Schism; Urban VI elected pope (1378–84); then abandoned by a faction of cardinals who elected Clement VII antipope (1378–94); both lines perpetuated.

1414–18 Council of Constance (16th ecumenical council): ended Great Schism by electing Martin V (1417–31) as pope; condemned views of J. Wycliffe and burned J. Huss at the stake (1415).

1431–38 Council of Basel; became embroiled in a struggle with Eugenius IV (1431–37) over Conciliar versus papal authority.

1438–53 Council of Florence (17th ecumenical council); convened to try to end the schism between the Latin and Greek churches.

1483 Spanish Inquisition organized throughout all Spanish possessions.

1492–1503 Alexander VI pope; notoriously corrupt Borgia; successfully resisted invasion of Italy by French King Charles VIII.

1512–17 Fifth Lateran Council (18th ecumenical council) called by Julius II (1503–13) to reform the church; reforms not implemented.

1517 Protestant Reformation: launched by German M. Luther to protest sale of indulgences; nailed Ninety-five Theses on Wittenberg church door challenging Catholic doctrine (Oct. 31); he later developed Lutheranism based on principle of justification by faith alone.

1520 Leo X (1513–21) excommunicated Luther (June 15).

1521 Diet of Worms placed Luther under ban of the Holy Roman Empire (Apr. 17–18).

1523 Adrian VI pope (1522–23); acknowledged guilt of Catholic clergy in helping bring about Protestant Reformation.

1534 Henry VIII secured Act of Supremacy declaring him supreme head of the church in England; Church of England created as organization separate from Rome.

1534–49 Paul III reigned as pope.

1534 Jesuits, or Society of Jesus, founded by St. Ignatius of Loyola; special vow of loyalty to pope taken by Jesuits.

16TH CENT. Catholic Reformation launched in response to Protestant threat.

1545–63 Council of Trent (19th ecumenical council); instituted far-reaching reforms in response to Protestant Reformation; completed comprehensive restatement of Catholic doctrine on the sacraments and instituted radical clerical reforms, including establishment of the modern seminary system for training priests; much important work concluded under Pius IV (1559–65).

1566–72 St. Pius V pope; reformed the missal and promoted the Holy League, which won the victory at sea over the Turks at Lepanto; excommunicated Queen Elizabeth I of England.

1582 Gregorian Calendar instituted (Oct. 15) by Gregory XIII (1572–85).

1621–23 Gregory XV pope; created the Congregation for the Propagation of the Faith to administer church's worldwide missionary effort.

1640 Jansenism, movement emphasizing predestination and denying free will, expounded in *Augustinus,* a book by C. Jansen, Bishop of Ypres.

1643 Bollandists organized: a group of Belgian Jesuits charged with examining and updating lives of the saints.

1653 Five characteristic Jansenist propositions condemned by Innocent X (1644–55).

1713 Clement XI (1700–21) issued Constitution *Unigenitus* against Jansenism.

18TH CENT. Society of Jesus expelled from a number of European countries: Portugal (1759); France (1764); Spain (1767).

1764 Febronianism, belief that all bishops have equal stature, condemned by Clement XIII (1758–69).

1773 Pope Clement XIV (1769–74) dissolved the Jesuit order under pressure from the European Catholic powers.

1790 John Carroll made bishop of Baltimore, first Catholic bishop of the United States.

1790 French Revolution's Civil Constitution of the Clergy subjected the church in France to the National Assembly.

1796 Papal States conquered by Napoleon.

1798 Pius VI taken prisoner by Napoleon.

1809 Napoleon annexed the Papal States to the French Empire and made Pius VII prisoner.

1814 Pius VII restored the Society of Jesus.

1815 Congress of Vienna restored the Papal States to the Pope.

1829 Catholic Emancipation ended persecution of Catholics in Britain.

1846–78 Pius IX pope; defined the dogma of the Immaculate Conception.

1860 Most of Papal States taken from church during the course of Italian unification.

1864 Syllabus of Errors: comprehensive compendium of modern "errors"—"progress, liberalism, and modern civilization"—issued by Pius IX (Dec. 8).

1870 First Vatican Council (20th ecumenical council): declared that God could be known by reason and defined the infallibility of the pope.

1870 German theologian J. Dollinger excommunicated for opposing the doctrine of papal infallibility.

1870 Italian king Victor Emmanuel II seized Rome; pope declared himself a prisoner in the Vatican, marking the beginning of the Roman Question.

1870s Kulturkampf of O. von Bismarck directed against Catholicism in Germany.

1878–1903 Leo XIII pope; pope of social justice and opening to modern democracy.

1879 Encyclical *Aeterni Patris* of Leo XIII made the philosophical and theological system of St. Thomas Aquinas church doctrine.

1891 Encyclical *Rerum Novarum* of Leo XIII emphasized rights of the workingman in modern industrial society (May 15).

1903–14 St. Pius X pope; condemned Modernism as "the resumé of all heresies."

1917 *Codex juris canonici,* revised code of canon law, completed.

1929 Lateran Treaty, agreement between Italy and the papacy settling the Roman Question and establishing the pope as an independent sovereign in Vatican City.

1937 Pope Pius XI (1922–39) condemned Nazism and Communism.

1939–58 Pius XII pope; in Encyclical *Humani Generis* warned that certain modern scientific ideas were incompatible with revealed dogma.

1958–63 John XXIII pope; summoned Vatican Council II (1959).

1962–65 Second Vatican Council (21st ecumenical council) convened by John XXIII; sought to renew spiritual life of all the members of the Church.

1963–78 Paul VI pope; continued Vatican Council II.

1964 Pope Paul VI met Greek Orthodox patriarch Athenagoras in Jerusalem.

1968 Encyclical *Humanae Vitae* of Paul VI reiterating church's traditional condemnation of artificial birth control; caused worldwide controversy and widespread dissent within the church.

1971 International commission of Roman Catholic and Anglican theologians reported agreement on basic teaching concerning the Eucharist (Dec. 30).

1978 John Paul I elected to succeed Paul VI (Aug. 26).

1978 Pope John Paul I died suddenly (Sept. 29); Pope John Paul II elected (Oct. 16); a Pole, he became first non-Italian pope in 455 years.

1979 John Paul II began a series of extensive worldwide missionary journeys by visiting the Dominican Republic, Mexico, US, Poland, Britain, and Spain.

1981 Pope John Paul II seriously wounded by a Turkish terrorist (May 13) in assassination attempt at Vatican City.

1982 Pope John Paul II visited Britain; meetings with Anglican leaders marked a significant step in efforts to reestablish ties between the English church and Rome (May 28).

1983 Pope John Paul II approved revisions to Code of Canon Law, the first revisions since 1917.

1990 Pope reaffirmed church policy of celibacy for priests, in response to calls for allowing priests to marry.

1992 Church condemnation of scientist Galileo reversed by Pope (Oct.); Pope said church erred in 1633 when it condemned Galileo for supporting Copernicus's theory that the earth and other planets revolved around the sun.

Romance languages (Romanic languages) Family of European languages descended from Latin. So called because Latin was the language of the Romans, the principal modern Romance languages are French, Italian, Portuguese, Rumanian, and Spanish.

Roman Empire Name of the Roman state after Augustus assumed imperial powers (27 BC) and thus formally ended the republic. The empire was later divided into the Western Roman Empire (Western Empire) and Eastern Roman Empire (Eastern Empire) in AD 286 by Diocletian. Through much of the subsequent period it was governed by co-emperors of the East and West. The death of Theodosius I marked the beginning of the permanent division (AD 395) of the empire. The Western half consisted of Italy, Gaul, western Illyricum, Africa, Spain, and Britain. The Eastern half primarily consisted of the Balkan Peninsula (including the eastern part of Illyricum) and Asia Minor. The Western Roman Empire, unable to withstand the barbarian invasions (*q.v.*), ceased to exist (AD 476) with the death of Emperor Romulus Augustus. The Eastern Roman Empire survived as the Byzantine Empire, and thus the Carolingian Empire (8th cent.) is sometimes regarded as the successor state to the Western Roman Empire. (*See also* Rome (empire); Byzantine Empire *for detailed history.*)

Romania *See* **Rumania.**

Romanesque Style of medieval art and architecture that reached its height in the 11th and 12th cents. In architecture it was characterized by the use of rounded arches and massive walls. It gave way to the Gothic style (*q.v.*). The Romanesque movement in art, centered in France, represented a fusion of Roman, Carolingian, Byzantine, Teutonic, and other influences and was marked by its concern for powerful imagery and grand conception.

Romanic languages *See* **Romance languages.**

Roman Inquisition *See* **Inquisition.**

Romano, Giulio (*pseud. of* Giulio Pippi) c1492–1546. Italian painter and architect. A favored student of Raphael, he is considered an originator of mannerism (*q.v.*).

Romanov Russian royal dynasty. The Romanovs ruled Russia from 1613 until the revolutions of 1917. They traced their royal lineage to Anastasia Romanovna, first wife (*m.* 1547) of Ivan the Terrible. They came to power after the Time of Troubles (*q.v.*) when Michael Romanov became tsar. The line ended during the Russian Revolution with the assassinations of Nicholas II and his family, including his son and heir Alexis. *Rulers of the Romanov dynasty were:* Michael 1613–45; Alexis 1645–76; Fedor III 1676–82; Ivan V (with Peter) 1682–96; Peter (the Great) 1682–1725; Catherine I 1725–27; Peter II 1727–30; Anna Ivanova 1730–40; Ivan VI 1740–41; Elizabeth 1741–62; Peter III 1762; Catherine II (the Great) 1762–96; Paul I 1796–1801; Alexander I 1801–25; Nicholas I 1825–55; Alexander II 1855–81; Alexander III 1881–94; Nicholas II 1894–1917.

Roman Province of Africa Province created after 146 BC, following the defeat of Carthage in the Third Punic War. Initially it consisted of lands once controlled by Carthage, but, by the 1st cent. AD, it had been greatly expanded east and west to include parts of modern Algeria and Libya. Roman Emperor Septimius Severus later created the province of Numidia from its western end. Diocletian created Tripolitania in the east and Byzacena in the south. A commercially prosperous region under the Romans (1st–3d cents. AD), it fell (AD 424) to the Vandals and declined rapidly thereafter.

Roman Province of Asia Territory of the Roman Empire in western Asia Minor. It was constituted as a province in 133 BC when Rome gained possession of the Kingdom of Pergamum (*q.v.*). The region passed to the Byzantines after the fall of Rome.

Roman Question *See* **Lateran Treaty; Law of Guarantees.**

Roman Republic 1. Name of the ancient Roman state from the time the Romans gained independence (c509 BC) from the Etruscan Tarquin kings to the naming of Octavian as Augustus, traditionally considered the beginning of the Roman empire (27 BC). (For history, *see* Rome [empire].) 2. Republican government established briefly in Rome (1798–99) by the French.

Roman Senate Roman governmental body. Formed in the 6th cent. BC as an advisory council appointed by the kings of Rome, it evolved into a powerful legislative body that lasted until the end of the Roman Empire. Originally composed of patricians, the Senate gradually came to include wealthy plebeians and its membership was determined by previous holding of office. The Senate wielded great power in financial, administrative, military, and religious affairs until the end of the 2d cent. BC, when corruption and the rise of numerous antagonistic political factions within the Senate weakened its ability to govern. The proscription of many members under Sulla further weakened the Senate; by the time of Caesar's assassination (44 BC), it had lost much of its power. Though it survived in the Empire period, the Senate had no real power.

Romanticism Movement in literature and the arts that arose (18th–19th cents.) as a reaction to the extreme rationalism of the Enlightenment (*q.v.*) and the strictures of classicism (*q.v.*) in the arts. The movement began in Germany and England (late 18th cent.) and thereafter spread to other countries. Its aims were various and often conflicting, but generally were characterized by opposition to rationalism and social conventions; belief in the natural man and natural beauty, and in the primacy of human emotions, self-expression, and individualism; and an interest in mystical, medieval, and Oriental themes. The French author and philosopher J. Rousseau is considered an important forerunner of romanticism. The movement gave rise to romantic nationalism and a fondness for experimentation. It declined (from the mid-1800s) and in literature gave way to realism (*q.v.*). Leading Romantic writers include Sir W. Scott, J. W. von Goethe, and V. Hugo; in music, R. Wagner, R. Schumann, F. Liszt, and F. Chopin; in art, J. Turner and F. Delacroix.

Romanus I *d.* 948. Byzantine emperor (920–944). He was regent for Constantine VII, but took the throne himself, fought the Bulgars, and clashed with the great landowners of the empire. He was overthrown by his sons, who were then ousted by Constantine VII.

Romanus II 939–963. Byzantine emperor (959–963), successor to Constantine VII. He was an incompetent profligate under whom imperial affairs were in the hands of his wife and favorite eunuchs. However, his military commander, Nicephorus I, won notable victories against the Arabs and eventually succeeded him.

Romanus III (~ Argyrus) c968–1034. Byzantine emperor (1028–34). He succeeded to the throne by marrying Empress Zöe, the daughter of Constantine VIII. After an irresponsible rule, he was murdered, probably by Zöe and her husband-to-be, Michael IV.

Romanus IV (~ Diogenes) *d.* 1071. Byzantine emperor (1067–71). He married the widow of his predecessor, Constantine X, and reigned as coregent. He was deposed after his total defeat by the Seljuks at the Battle of Manzikert (*q.v.*).

Romanus Argyrus *See* **Romanus III.**

Romanus Diogenes *See* **Romanus IV.**

Romany Indo-European language spoken in a number of dialects by the Gypsy peoples. The language is descended from Sanskrit and began evolving toward its modern form about AD 1000, when the Gypsies migrated out of northwestern India. Romany has a rich oral tradition but no written literature.

Rome Historic city and capital of Italy, located in central Italy. The Vatican City lies within its borders and Rome has long been the seat of the Roman Catholic church. According to Roman tradition, the city of Rome was founded in 753 BC by Romulus. In subsequent years the city grew and came under the influence of the Etruscans (the Tarquin kings). The Romans drove out the Tarquin kings c509 BC and established the Roman Republic. Rome then became the center of an expanding empire which, by the beginning of the 2d cent. AD, encircled the Mediterranean and included much of Europe as well (*for history during this period see* Rome, *below*). Rome remained the capital of the empire until AD 330 when the capital was moved to Constantinople. By the time of the fall of the (Western) Roman Empire in AD 476, Rome had also been supplanted by Ravenna as chief city of the Italian peninsula. During the following centuries, the bishops of Rome gained temporal authority over the city and, after the 8th cent., Rome became the seat of church-controlled domains in central Italy (known as the Papal States, *q.v.*). The history of Rome during the Middle Ages was chaotic. The struggle for power between the popes and the Holy Roman emperors resulted in numerous attacks on the city. Civil strife resulted from attempts to establish a republic at Rome and from the long struggle between Guelphs and Ghibellines (*q.v.*) in Italy. Finally in the 14th and early 15th cents., during the Babylonian Captivity and the Great Schism, Rome sank into chaos and economic ruin. During the 15th cent., the popes reestablished firm control over Rome (and the Papal States). This time also marked the flowering of the Renaissance in Italy, and the popes commissioned the great artists of their time to adorn Rome with magnificent buildings and works of art. Rome again came under attack during the Italian Wars (q.v.) of the 16th cent. But Rome under the popes nevertheless continued its rise as a center of world culture. During the French Revolutionary Wars, Rome was occupied (1798) by Napoleon and a short-lived republic was formed of Italian territories. The popes were restored to control of Rome in 1814, but the seeds of the Italian nationalist movement had been sown. During the Revolutions of 1848, Rome was proclaimed a republic and held out for a short time against the French, who ultimately restored the pope. When the kingdom of Italy was created (1861), its domains did not then include Rome, which remained under papal control. The city was finally occupied in 1870, and in 1871 it was made capital of Italy. The popes, however, refused to recognize the loss of their temporal power and thus began the Roman Question, which was not resolved until 1929. The Fascists came to power through their March on Rome (q.v.) in 1922 and the city was captured (1944) by the Allies during WW II. Rome, which remains the spiritual center of the Roman Catholic world today, was the site of a Catholic pilgrimage in 1950. Modern Rome is a commercial and tourist center of Italy. It is the site of many ancient ruins and historic buildings.

Rome (empire) Great empire of ancient times which for several centuries dominated the Mediterranean world. The history of ancient Rome can be broadly divided into two epochs, the Roman Republic (c509–27 BC) and the Roman Empire (27 BC–AD 476). The rise of Rome began with the subjugation of the Italian peninsula (largely completed by the 3d cent. BC). Acquisition of overseas territories began with the Punic Wars (3d–2d cents. BC) in which the great Carthaginian empire was destroyed and its territories eventually were absorbed by Rome. Thereafter the Romans expanded their domains through various conquests, uniting under their rule an empire that encircled the Mediterranean and extended northward into the British Isles. Roman culture, laws, and customs were spread throughout the empire and greatly influenced the subsequent development of civilization in the West. The decline of the empire began at about the end of the 2d cent. AD and following centuries were marked by the breakdown of authority and political chaos, worsening economic problems, and finally the destructive invasions by various barbarian peoples (probably joined by disaffected Roman subjects). The Western Roman Empire collapsed before the barbarian hordes and is traditionally considered to have ended in AD 476, when the last emperor was defeated and deposed. However, the Eastern Roman Empire continued for many centuries thereafter as the Byzantine Empire (q.v.). (For history of the Italian peninsula after 476, see Italy. See also Rome entry above for history of the city itself.) **For more on important persons and events** see **entries under specific names.** Key events in the history of Rome include:

753? BC Legendary founding of Rome by Romulus.

715?–672 BC Numa Pompilius, according to tradition, succeeded Romulus as king; established religious and civil law.

c616 BC Etruscans, a people of northern Italy, gained control of Rome; ruled as the Tarquin kings: Etruscan civilization greatly influenced Roman civilization.

509 BC Tarquin kings driven out by Romans; uprising caused, according to tradition, by rape of the Roman woman Lucrece; Roman Republic founded.

c509–27 BC Roman Republic; two consuls elected annually; Senate, established as advisory body to the kings, continued and formalized, and finally dominated government during the republic; government first controlled by patricians (aristocrats) with plebeians gaining rights and powers over the centuries.

496 BC Battle of Lake Regillus; Romans defeated neighboring Latins.

c494 BC Plebs seceded to the Sacred Mount to protest oppression by the patricians; tribunate created.

FROM 471 BC Tribunes of the plebs elected in the *Concilium Plebis* (assembly).

458 BC Cincinnatus became dictator; defeated the Aequi.

c450 BC Twelve Tables drawn up as Rome's legal code; plebeian unrest over harsh treatment by patrician magistrates brought about code.

444 BC Election of military tribunes begun after plebs agitated for greater powers.

443 BC Office of censor established, remained part of Roman government until 22 BC.

405–396 BC Romans put the Veii under siege; the town was finally captured and destroyed.

390 BC Rome sacked by the Gauls; Camillus traditionally believed to have brought about the Gauls' withdrawal.

367 BC Tribunes C. Licinus and L. Sextus initiated important reforms; plebs, after years of agitation, permitted to name one consul every year from their ranks; later eligible to hold all other offices and constitutional distinction between patrician and pleb disappeared (except for the plebs' right to hold the tribunate).

367–345 BC Romans variously at war with the Gauls, and neighboring Latin tribes; southern Etruria captured; Hernici, Volsci, and others defeated.

351–341 BC Philippics, orations denouncing Philip II of Macedon, delivered by Demosthenes.

343–341 BC First Samnite War; marked beginning of Rome's move to take control of the Campania.

340–338 BC Latin Wars; Italian cities rebelled for equal status with Rome but were defeated by Roman armies.

339 BC Publilian Laws; plebs, or plebeians, gained further constitutional power by the reforms of Quintus Publilius Philo.

316–304 BC Second Samnite War.

312 BC Construction of Appian Way began.

c300 BC Stoic philosophical school founded by Zeno of Citium; followers included Seneca, Diogenes, and Cato the Younger.

3D CENT. New Roman class of nobile emerged; included both patricians and office-holding plebeians.

3D CENT. Founder of Roman drama, Livius Andronicus, lived.

298–290 BC Third Samnite War; Romans defeated the rebelling tribes, asserting firm control in central Italy.

290 BC Sabines conquered by Rome.

287 BC Reform of the dictator Quintus Hortensius issued after plebeians seceded to the Janiculan hill; *Lex Hortensia* gave plebeians

equal status with patricians by making the *plebiscita* (resolutions) of the plebeians binding on all citizens without the approval of the Senate.

282–272 BC War with the Greek king Pyrrhus who sought to defend the Greek colony of Tarentum (southern Italy) against the Romans; noted Battle of Asculum fought (279 BC); Pyrrhus finally withdrew to Greece.

264 BC–405 AD Gladiators were popular as entertainment in Roman world during this period.

264–241 BC First Punic War against Carthage; Rome won control of Sicily, a valuable grain-producing region.

260 BC Battle of Mylae; important naval victory for Rome over the Carthaginians during the First Punic War.

239–169 BC Father of Latin literature, Quintus Ennius, lived.

238 BC Romans took control of Sardinia, previously a Carthaginian possession.

229–228, 219 BC Illyrian Wars conducted on behalf of Greeks against pirates; marked Rome's first entry into the East.

218–201 BC Second Punic War against Carthage; Hannibal crossed the Alps into Italy and nearly conquered the Romans; Scipio defeated Hannibal in Africa; Rome gained control of Spain and Carthaginian islands in Mediterranean; Carthaginian power broken.

214–205 BC First Macedonian War fought with Macedon; Macedonians, in alliance with Carthage, successful against Rome (Rome settled for a treaty in order to focus on Carthaginians).

c204–149 BC Cato the Elder flourished; noted statesman who advocated return to the traditional Roman ways; urged destruction of Carthage.

203?–c120 BC Historian Polybius lived.

200–196 BC Second Macedonian War fought; Macedonian power reduced; Roman hegemony in Greece established.

171–168 BC Third Macedonian War fought; Romans victorious and Macedon divided into four republics.

160 Comedy *Adelphi* written by Terence.

149–146 BC Third Punic War against Carthage; Carthage captured and completely destroyed; Carthaginian territories made into Roman province of Africa.

149–148 BC Fourth Macedonian War fought; led to Roman annexation of Macedon and complete domination of Greece.

c147–c139 BC Viriatus led successful rebellion against Rome.

c134–132 BC First Servile War, unsuccessful slave uprising against Romans in Sicily.

133 BC Scipio Africanus the Younger finally defeated the Celtiberians in Spain long after their resistance to Roman armies began (from c195).

133 BC Tribune T. Gracchus assassinated by opponents of his land reforms, which sought to improve the peasants' lot and restore the base of the Roman army.

133 BC Kingdom of Mysia (Pergamum) passed to Rome on the death of its king; Romans organized it as the province of Asia.

121 BC C. Gracchus killed; as tribune he had instituted radical reforms, including the land reforms of his brother, T. Gracchus, and a measure forcing government to supply grain at a fair price; reforms reversed after his tribunate and he was killed in subsequent riots.

116–27? BC Scholar Marcus Varro lived.

111–105 BC Romans subdued rebellion in Africa led by King Jugurtha; begun by Marius, completed by Sulla.

105 BC Romans defeated by invading Cimbri and Teutones at the Battle of Arausio in Gaul; the tribes then invaded Italy.

104–100 BC Marius reelected consul each year.

102–101 BC Romans, led by Marius and co-consul Quintus Catulus, defeated the Cimbri at the Battle of Aquae Sextae (102 BC) and Vercellae (101); Marius hailed as a great hero.

c102–99 BC Second Servile War, unsuccessful slave uprising against Romans in Sicily.

1ST CENT. BC Architect Vitruvius lived; known for his work *De architectura.*

c99–c55 BC Lucretius, Roman poet who wrote *On the Nature of Things,* lived.

91 BC M. Drusus advanced reforms, including measure granting citizenship to all Italian peoples subject to Rome; Drusus killed.

c90–88 BC Social War, unsuccessful uprising of Italian tribes against Rome; full citizenship granted to all Italian peoples.

88–87 BC Civil war began; Sulla marched his troops into Rome after tribune Publius Sulpicius Rufus tried to impose reforms by force; Marius, a leader of the popular party, fled and Rufus was executed; Sulla, leader of the optimates (aristocrats) became consul (87 BC) and left Rome to lead armies in First Mithridatic War.

88–84 BC First Mithridatic War; Mithridates of Pontus attempted to seize the Roman province of Asia during the Social War; Roman consul Sulla defeated him but made an incomplete peace in order to speed his return to Rome.

87 BC Cinna, popular party leader, became consul at Rome; attempted to put through Rufus' reforms in Sulla's absence and was driven out of Rome; reentered Rome with Marius' help and massacred many of Sulla's followers.

84?–54? BC Gaius Catullus lived; lyric poet who wrote love poems to woman named Lesbia.

83–82 BC Sulla, returning from the Mithridatic War, defeated supporters of the popular party; ordered proscription of members of the faction.

83–81 BC Second Mithridatic War; Romans attacked Mithridates; restored conquered territory at the end of the war.

82–79 BC Sulla ruled as dictator; instituted conservative reforms to increase power of the Senate and limit that of the tribunes and judiciary; retired after reforms were enacted.

80–72 BC Roman general Sertorius led revolt in Spain against Roman rule.

77 BC Pompey defeated attempt by M. Lepidus to rescind Sulla's reforms by force.

c75–43 BC Cicero flourished; great Roman statesman and orator.

74–63 BC Third Mithridatic War; this war resulted in the complete conquest of Pontus and its annexation to the Roman province of Asia.

73–71 BC Third Servile War, unsuccessful slave uprising in Italy led by Spartacus; slave army defeated by Crassus and Pompey.

70 BC Pompey and Crassus became consuls; rescinded Sulla's reforms, thus restoring power to popular faction.

70–19 BC Vergil lived; considered leading poet of his age.

65–8 BC Horace lived; among the great Latin poets.

64 BC Pompey added domains of Seleucids to the empire as a province; reorganized Rome's province of Asia.

64 BC Palestine brought under Roman control by Pompey.

64–63 BC Conspiracy of Catiline.

60 BC First triumvirate formed by Caesar, Pompey, and Crassus.

59 BC Caesar, as consul, appointed himself to take charge of Gaul for five years (later extended another five years).

59 BC Marriage of Calpurnia to J. Caesar (his last).

59 BC–AD 17 Roman historian, Livy, lived; wrote history of Romans.

58–51 BC Gallic Wars; Caesar's military campaigns led to the conquest of all Gaul and gave him great power and prestige.

c55 BC–AD 40 Seneca the Elder lived.

54?–18? BC Roman elegaic poet Albius Tibullus lived.

53 BC Roman invasion of Parthia halted at Battle of Carrhae; Crassus killed during retreat; first triumvirate ended by his death.

52 BC Pompey, now leader of the optimates, elected sole consul at Rome; engaged in power struggle with Caesar, leader of the popular party.

50 BC Roman historian Sallust expelled from the Senate for his support of J. Caesar; his histories included *Catilina*.

50?–15? BC Poet Sextus Propertius lived.

49 BC Senate ordered Caesar to disband his army in Gaul.

49 BC Civil war (49–46 BC) began; Caesar, refusing to disband his army, led his soldiers in the famous crossing of the Rubicon (Jan. 10–11); marched into Italy against Pompey.

49 BC Caesar laid siege to Pompey's forces at Brundisium, in Italy; Pompey escaped (Mar.) to Greece.

49 BC Caesar entered Rome; did not institute customary proscription of opponents.

49 BC M. Antony made tribune.

49 BC Caesar successful in fighting against Pompey's supporters in Spain.

49 BC Caesar elected consul after renouncing his election as dictator; returned to pursuit of Pompey.

48 BC Caesar defeated by Pompey at Dyrrhachium (now in Albania).

48 BC Battle of Pharsalus, in Greece; Caesar routed Pompey's forces (Aug. 9); Pompey fled to Egypt.

48 BC Pompey killed in Egypt by order of King Ptolemy XII.

48–47 BC Alexandrine War; Caesar, pursuing Pompey, had entered Alexandria, Egypt; found himself under siege by Egyptian forces; dallied with Cleopatra, broke siege and subdued Egypt; installed Cleopatra and Ptolemy XIII on the Egyptian throne.

47 BC Caesar defeated Pharnaces II at the Battle of Zela in brief war in Syria and Pontus; Caesar said of the war, "Veni, vidi, vici" (I came, I saw, I conquered); Caesar next went to Africa.

46 BC Caesar victorious against the last of Pompey's forces at the Battle of Thapsus (Feb. 6); Cato the Younger committed suicide; Roman Senate named Caesar dictator for ten years.

46 BC Back in Rome, Caesar pardoned his enemies and began program of reform aimed at improving lot of the populace; then went to Spain to war against Pompey's sons.

46 BC Caesar instituted the Julian Calendar.

45 BC Caesar defeated Pompey's sons at the Battle of Munda, Spain; was made consul for ten years.

44–43 BC Cicero denounced M. Antony in his philippics.

44 BC Caesar assassinated (Mar. 15) by opponents who feared his growing power; Cassius, Marcus Brutus, and Decimus Brutus among the assassins; M. Antony rose to power in Rome; began to organize against the assassins, who had fled Rome.

44–43 BC Octavian, Caesar's heir, attempted to claim his rights, but was at first opposed by Antony; the two formed an alliance against Caesar's assassins the next year.

43 BC Second Triumvirate formed (Nov.) by Octavian, M. Antony, and Lepidus.

43 BC–AD 17 Ovid lived; wrote classics of Latin poetry.

43 BC Cicero executed on orders from M. Antony, whom he had opposed.

42 BC Forces of Octavian, M. Antony, and Lepidus won decisive victory at the Battle of Philippi (Oct. 27); Brutus and Cassius committed suicide.

42 BC M. Antony began his celebrated love affair with Cleopatra.

40 BC Treaty of Brundisium wed M. Antony to Octavian's sister; Octavian to rule the West, Antony the East; Lepidus to rule Africa.

c39 BC Herod made king of Judaea by M. Antony.

36 BC Octavian defeated Sextus Pompey, a powerful opponent, at the Battle of Mylae.

36 BC Octavian, consolidating his power, deposed Lepidus; M. Antony, meanwhile, renewed his love affair with Cleopatra (unpopular in Rome) and thus aroused opposition in Rome.

35–33 BC Octavian conquered Illyria.

31–30 BC Final struggle between Octavian and Antony; Antony and Cleopatra defeated at the Battle of Actium (31 BC) and the two lovers committed suicide soon after; Octavian became sole ruler of Rome.

30 BC Egypt made a Roman province after Octavian killed King Ptolemy XIV.

29 BC Dionysius of Halicarnassus began his 20-volume history of Rome, *Roman Antiquities.*

27 BC Octavian accepted imperial title, Augustus; marked beginning of Roman Empire.

27 BC–AD 476 Roman Empire; Roman domains reached their greatest extent during this period; first 200 years marked by peace (*Pax Romana*) and prosperity.

27 BC–AD 14 Augustus (Octavian) ruled as first Roman emperor; had complete control of the military and the provinces; reformed both the military and provincial administration, undertook building program and patronized the arts, fostering the "Augustan Age."

c6 BC Jesus of Nazareth born.

3 BC–AD 65 Seneca the Younger, leading literary figure of Rome, lived.

AD 9 Consul Publius humiliated by defeat of Roman troops at hands of German tribes led by Arminius.

1ST CENT. AD Author of pharmacological text *De Materia Medica,* Pedanius Dioscorides, lived.

1ST–2D CENTS. AD Juvenal, Roman satirical poet, lived.

AD 14–c130 Silver Age of Latin literature, literary period following Golden Age; distinguished by authors such as Juvenal, Pliny the Elder and Pliny the Younger, and Seneca.

AD 14–37 Tiberius reigned as emperor, following Augustus' death; Tiberius turned over effective rule to the intriguer, Sejanus (AD 23–31), but finally had him executed.

AD 16 Germanicus Caesar suppressed a revolt by Arminius in Germany.

AD 23–79 Pliny the Elder lived; wrote naturalist encyclopedia *Historia naturalis.*

AD 30 Jesus crucified at Jerusalem.

AD 34–62 Satirical poet Persius lived.

AD c35–c95 Rhetorician Quintilian lived; wrote *Institutio Oratona.*

AD 37–41 Caligula reigned; became insane and ruled as a cruel tyrant.

AD 39–65 Poet Lucan lived; wrote *Bellum Civile (Pharsalia)* describing the civil war between Caesar and Pompey.

AD c40–c104 Poet Martial, writer of epigrams, lived.

AD 41–54 Claudius I reigned, dominated by his wives; added Mauretania (AD 41–42) to the empire and began final conquest of Britain (AD 43).

54–68 Nero reigned; notorious tyrant.

62 Roman empress Octavia, ex-wife of Nero, executed after Nero's third wife, Poppaea, became jealous of her.

64 Rome destroyed by great fire; Nero, suspected of having had it set, blamed the Christians and thereupon began persecutions of Christians; Nero rebuilt Rome.

64? Death of Peter, Christian apostle and saint; traditional first pope (leader of the disciples) believed crucified at Rome on Nero's order.

65 Conspiracy to overthrow Nero discovered.

c66 Roman satirist Petronius died; wrote *Satyricon.*

66–73 First Jewish revolt in Judaea; Jerusalem destroyed (AD 70).

AD 67 Death of Christian Saint Paul; his epistles included in the New Testament and influenced later church doctrine.

68 Nero overthrown; Galba recognized as emperor by Praetorian Guard.

69 Year of the Three Emperors; Galba overthrown; Otho and Vitellius both reigned briefly before Vespasian became emperor.

69–79 Vespasian reigned as emperor following a struggle for power; founded Flavian dynasty.

69–82 Colosseum built.

78–84 Agricola conquered much of Britain; served as governor.

79–81 Titus reigned.

79 Pompeii and Herculaneum buried under volcanic ash during eruption of Mt. Vesuvius.

81–96 Domitian reigned; bought off the army and the Roman mobs and increased the powers of the emperor; unsuccessful in wars in Dacia; assassinated.

90?–99?　Saint Clement I served as pope; believed the author of Epistle to the Corinthians.

96–98　Nerva reigned; introduced legal and tax reforms.

97　Roman historian Tacitus became consul; his historical works included *Histories* and the *Annals.*

98–117　Trajan reigned as emperor; warred against Parthia and Dacia, gaining territories east of the Tigris and Euphrates rivers; empire reached its greatest extent (AD 116).

100　Pliny the Younger, author and statesman, became consul.

2D CENT.　*Attic Nights* written by Gellius.

2D CENT.　Mithraism, the worship of the god Mithras, became popular in the empire until the official adoption of Christianity; beliefs focused on the battle between good and evil.

107　Dacia became a province after a long war against barbarians there (from AD 101).

c107　Saint Ignatius of Antioch executed; Christian bishop first used term "Catholic church."

112　Greek philosopher Dion Chrysostom died.

117–138　Hadrian reigned; undertook considerable building in Rome and the provinces; economic problems, exacerbated by excessive taxation, began to appear.

120　Suetonius, biographer and author of *Lives of the Caesars,* flourished.

132–135　Second Jewish revolt; Jews thereafter forbidden to live in Jerusalem.

138–161　Antoninus Pius reigned; reign marked by general peace and stability.

c155–235?　Dion Cassius, author of an 80-volume *History of Rome,* lived.

161–180　M. Aurelius reigned; despite persecution of Christians, his rule considered wise and humane; he was famous exponent of Stoicism.

166–167　Plague throughout the empire; spread by Roman soldiers returning from war with Parthia (AD 162–165).

180–192　Commodus reigned; gave himself up to dissolute life and some say his reign marked the start of Rome's decline; by arrangement with conspirators, a wrestler named Narcissus strangled Commodus.

193–211　Septimius Severus reigned; his reign began long period of instability in which sol-

diers of the army proclaimed the emperors; Severus reconstituted the Praetorian guard.

3D CENT.　Saints Cispin and Crispinian, Christian martyrs, flourished.

212　Roman citizenship granted to nearly all within the empire by Emperor Caracalla (reigned AD 211–217).

c213–273　Longinus lived; believed author of *On the Sublime.*

FROM AD c214　Alemanni and Goths began attacks on Roman outposts on the northern frontier in Germany.

217–235　Saint Hippolytus reigned as the first antipope, after breaking with Rome over question of heresy.

222　Emperor Heliogabulus killed following short reign marked by debauchery.

3D CENT.　Neoplatonism advanced by Plotinus.

222–235　Emperor Alexander Severus reigned; halted persecutions of Christians; warred against Persia.

250　Decius (reigned AD 249–251) began general persecution of the Christians.

250　Christian heresiarch Noatian lived: antipope and founder of his own religious sect.

253–270　Barbarians broke through Roman frontier defenses; Alemanni advanced to Milan; Franks passed beyond the Rhine; Goths invaded the Balkans and Greece.

260　Emperor Valerian (reigned AD 253–260) captured during wars with Persians.

270　Claudius II (reigned AD 268–270) halted advance of the Goths; allowed them to settle Dacia.

270–275　Aurelian reigned; withdrew from Dacia and drove Alemanni out of Italy.

284–305　Diocletian reigned; instituted wideranging administrative, military, and financial reforms; brought measure of stability to the empire, which by this time, however, was crumbling after a half century of barbarian invasions and continuing political instability, which had seriously disrupted the economy and strengthened the role of the army.

286　Roman Empire divided administratively into the Western and Eastern empires by Diocletian; named Maximian co-ruler, though by adopting him maintained theoretical unity of the empire.

c288　Saint Sebastian, Roman Christian martyr, executed; his death later became a favorite subject of Renaissance art.

293 Diocletian divided the empire into four administrative units (two east, two west); each responsible to respective emperor.

305 Diocletian abdicated.

306 Constantine began his struggle against rivals for control in the Western Empire.

312 Battle of Milvian Bridge; Constantine defeated his last rival for control of the West; a vision he had before the battle led to his conversion to Christianity.

312 Constantine became emperor in the West, Licinius emperor in the East.

312 Praetorian Guard abolished by Constantine.

313 Edict of Milan issued by Constantine and Licinius; established toleration of Christianity throughout empire.

324 Licinius, emperor of the East, defeated by Constantine.

324–337 Constantine reigned as sole ruler; Roman Empire reunited under him; he established his capital at Constantinople (AD 330).

325 Constantine called the Council of Nicaea (1st ecumenical) to resolve question of Arianism; established role of emperor in Eastern church.

333 Donatus flourished; wrote Latin text *Ars grammatica.*

337–361 Constantius II reigned.

361–363 Julian the Apostate reigned; tried to strengthen paganism in the empire, an effort abandoned on his death.

c371 Saint Martin became Bishop of Tours; he founded first monastery in Gaul.

374–392 Saint Ambrose served as bishop of Milan; laid foundations for medieval church relations.

375–379 Theodosius I the Great reigned as emperor in the East; Valentinian II (AD 375–392) and Gratian (375–383) ruled in West.

376 Huns conquered Visigoths in region of modern Rumania, bringing them into contact with Romans.

378 Visigoths decimated Roman forces at the Battle of Adrianople; Eastern emperor Valens killed; Visigoths swept into Europe.

383 Gratian killed in revolt by Maximus; Maximus finally killed by Theodosius (AD 388).

390 Theodosius forced to do penance before Ambrose, bishop of Milan, for massacring

thousands of Greeks; marked a temporary victory of church over temporal power of the emperors.

394 Battle of Frigidus; Theodosius defeated Eugenius, who had usurped and killed Valentinian II; Roman Empire united for last time under Theodosius.

395 Roman Empire permanently divided into Eastern and Western Empires on the death of Theodosius I.

395 Honorius became emperor of the West (ruled AD 395–423), Arcadius emperor of the East (ruled AD 395–408).

396–408 Stilicho, a Vandal and commander of Roman troops in the West, successful against invading barbarians; drove Visigoths out of Greece (AD 397), and blocked attempts to invade Italy; Gaul was meanwhile overrun by barbarians (AD 406).

c404 Ravenna made capital of the West.

407 Romans withdrew from Britain.

408–450 Theodosius II reigned in the East.

409–410 Visigoths under Alaric invaded Italy; sacked Rome (AD 410); subsequently invaded and conquered Spain.

425–455 Valentinian III reigned in the West.

429–431 Vandals crossed from Spain into Africa; conquered Roman territories in North Africa.

441–443 Attila and his brother Bleda led the Huns in invasion of eastern Roman provinces.

450–452 Attila the Hun invaded Gaul and Italy (AD 452).

455 Valentinian III murdered; succession of rulers set up in the West.

455 Gaiseric, king of the Vandals, sacked Rome.

457–474 Leo I reigned as emperor of the East.

474–491 Zeno reigned as emperor of the East; attempted to win control over the Goths.

475–476 Romulus Augustus reigned as last emperor of the West.

476 Odoacer defeated last Roman forces at Battle of Pavia; deposed Emperor Romulus Augustus (Sept. 4), thus ending Western Roman Empire.

Rome, March on *See* **Seven Hills of Rome.**

Rome, treaties of Series of agreements signed in Rome (Mar. 25, 1957), between Belgium, France, Italy, Luxembourg, the Netherlands, and West Germany, that established the European

Economic Community. The treaties eliminated tariffs, established a ruling council of ministers, and also set up the European Atomic Energy Community (Euratom).

Rømer, Olaus (Römer, Ole) (Roemer, ˜) 1644–1710. Danish astronomer. By observing the eclipses of Jupiter's satellites, he was able to prove conclusively (1676) that light travels at a definite speed and not instantaneously. He roughly calculated its speed at 140,000 miles per second.

Rommel, Erwin 1891–1944. German field marshal during WW II. After performing brilliantly in France in 1940, he became the near-legendary German commander of the Afrika Korps in the North Africa Campaign (*q.v.*). He was commander in northern France when the Allies landed in 1944. Rommel was forced to take poison after discovery of his part in the plot against A. Hitler's life.

Romulus Augustulus *fl.* 5th cent. AD. Last Roman emperor of the West, (AD 475–476). He was put on the throne by his father, the Roman general Orestes. He was deposed soon after by the German conquerer Odoacer, who sent him into exile.

Roncalli, Angelo Giuseppe *See* **John XXIII.**

Roncesvalles, Battle of Ambush of the rear guard of Charlemagne's army (Aug. 15, 778) in the Pyrenees Mountains. This minor engagement took place during Charlemagne's return from a military campaign against the Muslims in Spain and provided the inspiration for the epic poem *The Song of Roland.*

Ronsard, Pierre de 1525–85. French poet. Considered one of the greatest poets of the Renaissance, he was a leader of the Pléiade. His works include *Amours de Cassandre, Hymnes,* and the unfinished *La Franciade.*

Röntgen, Wilhelm Conrad *See* **Roentgen, Wilhelm Conrad.**

Roon, Count Albrecht Theodor Emil von 1803–79. Prussian field marshal. As minister of war from 1859, he reorganized the Prussian army and made victories possible in the Austro-Prussian War and in the Franco-Prussian War.

Roosevelt, (Anna) Eleanor 1884–1962. American political figure, humanitarian, and author. As the wife (*m.* 1905) of President F. Roosevelt, she not only worked with her husband but also pursued her own interests as a newspaper and radio commentator and US representative at the UN (1945–52, 1961).

Roosevelt, Franklin Delano 1882–1945. Thirty-second US president (1933–45), successor to H. Hoover, and the only president to win four consecutive elections (1932, over H. Hoover; 1936, over A. Landon; 1940, over W. Willkie; 1944, over T. Dewey). During his long tenure, Roosevelt saw the country through the Depression (*q.v.*) and most of WW II (*q.v.*), vastly increased the power and prestige of the presidency, and firmly committed the federal government to (then) unprecedented direct involvement in promoting the social and economic well-being of American society. A New York Democrat, he first served in state and federal posts, was an unsuccessful vice-presidential candidate (1920), and then was partly paralyzed by polio (1921). He nevertheless persevered, became governor of New York (1928–30, 1930–32), and then won the presidency. He took office (1933) during the worst of the Depression and, in his famous first Hundred Days (*q.v.*) in office, he initiated the first wave of his New Deal (*q.v.*) legislation to counter the Depression. His administration during the rest of the 1930s was marked by still more New Deal legislation (though at a slower pace after 1936), the persisting economic stagnation of the Depression, increasing political opposition, and, finally, concern over the menace of war in Europe. By the late 1930s, Roosevelt had already begun to prepare the nation for war and, with W. Churchill, issued the Atlantic Charter (*q.v.*). After the Pearl Harbor attack (1941) brought the US into the war, he instituted a massive program to put the US economy on a wartime footing and quickly built up American military forces. He then played a prominent role in the Allied wartime conferences (such as Teheran and Yalta) and worked for establishment of the UN. He died shortly before the end of war in the European theater.

Roosevelt, Theodore 1858–1919. Twenty-sixth US president (1901–09), successor to W. McKinley. Roosevelt got his start in politics as a Republican in New York State. After holding both state and federal posts, he became a national hero for his exploits with the Rough Riders (*q.v.*), notably at the Battle of San Juan Hill during the Spanish-American War (1898). Elected vice-president under W. McKinley (1900), he became president a few months later when McKinley was assassinated. He was subsequently elected to a full term in 1904. Roosevelt's administration was marked by his concerted attacks on the business trusts (trust-busting) and passage of reform legislation, including acts to end railroad rebates (Elkins Act, 1903), to create the Department of Commerce and Labor, and to regulate the quality of food and drugs. Roosevelt also actively involved the US in foreign affairs and he played a role in the Venezuela Claims (*q.v.*) dispute; formulated the Roosevelt corollary to the Monroe Doctrine (*q.v.*), using it to interfere in Central American affairs; backed Panamanian revolutionaries and, after they set up a rebel government, arranged a treaty for the building of the Panama Canal (*q.v.*); and mediated at the Portsmouth Conference (1904) to end the Russo-Japanese War. At the end of his term, Roosevelt helped elect his successor, W. Taft, and went abroad for an extended tour. In 1912, after falling out with Taft, he formed the Progressive (Bull Moose) party and attempted to win reelection as president. He lost to W. Wilson. He won the Nobel Peace Prize in 1906.

Roosevelt Corollary *See* **Monroe Doctrine.**

Root, Elihu 1845–1937. US secretary of war (1899–1904) and secretary of state (1905–09). A dedicated internationalist, he negotiated important treaties with Japan (notably the Root-Takahira Agreement, *q.v.*), Britain, and Latin America and consistently promoted disarmament. He received the Nobel Peace Prize in 1912.

Root, John Wellborn 1850–91. American architect. An associate of D. Burnham and leading architect of the Chicago school, he designed buildings that were important in the development of the modern skyscraper.

Root-Takahira Agreement Executive agreement concluded between the US and Japan (Nov. 30, 1908). By its terms, both countries agreed to support an open-door policy in China, maintain the territorial status quo in East Asia, and work for the continued independence and integrity of China. It was named for US Secretary of State E. Root and the Japanese ambassador to the US, Baron Kogoro Takahira (1854–1926).

Rorschach, Hermann 1884–1922. Swiss psychiatrist and neurologist. He devised the famous Rorschach inkblot test for diagnosing mental disorders.

Rosamond *d.* 1176? Mistress of England's Henry II, known as the "Fair Rosamond." The king acknowledged her (1174) after he had imprisoned his wife, Eleanor of Aquitaine. The many legends about her include one that she was murdered by Eleanor.

Rosas, Juan Manuel de 1793–1877. Dictator of Buenos Aires province and ruler of nearly all Argentina (1835–52). A wealthy rancher, he became governor of Buenos Aires province for the first time from 1828 to 1832. On taking office again (1835), he assumed dictatorial powers and extended his control over most of the other Argentine provinces. Thereafter he instituted a reign of terror; alienated foreign powers and thus provoked French and British blockades of Argentina (1838–40, 1845–50); and became involved in a scheme to take over Uruguay. He was overthrown by J. Urquiza, who, with support from Uruguay and Brazil, defeated Rosas' army at Monte Caseros (Feb. 3, 1852).

Rosecrans, William Starke 1819–98. American Civil War general. A successful Union commander at Corinth and Murfreesboro, he was relieved of command after his defeat (1863) at the Battle of Chickamauga Creek (*q.v.*). He later served as a diplomat and congressman.

Rosenberg, Alfred 1893–1946. German Nazi party leader and ideologist. He began as editor of the Nazi paper and provided the party with its anti-Semitic ideology in his *The Myth of the Twentieth Century.* He was hanged as a war criminal after WW II.

Rosenberg, Julius and Ethel (1918–53; 1916–53) First US civilians put to death for espionage. They were tried, then executed on June 19, 1953. They were convicted of transmitting to the Soviet Union secret information about the atomic bomb (1944–45). The information had allegedly been obtained by Ethel's brother, army sergeant David Greenglass, who was an employee of the Los Alamos project. Julius, an Army Signal Corps electrical engineer, was an acknowledged Communist. Many unsuccessful efforts were made to obtain clemency for them.

Rose of Lima, Saint 1586–1617. Peruvian religious mystic. A Dominican, she is the patron saint of South America, and the first native-born South American to be canonized by the Catholic church.

Roses, Wars of the Dynastic wars (1455–85) in England between the houses of York (white rose insignia) and Lancaster (red rose insignia). They fought over rival claims to the English throne. The claimants in both houses were descendants of Edward III, though the Lancastrians had been in power since 1399. However, the Yorkist position was strengthened by discontent over the ineffective rule of Henry VI and his unpopular queen (Margaret of Anjou), English losses in France during the Hundred Years' War (1337–1453), heavy taxes, and disorders such as Cades's Rebellion (*q.v.*). Richard, duke of York, became protector of the kingdom when Henry became temporarily insane (1453–54). The wars began soon after Henry's recovery. Yorkists won the first battle (1455) at St. Albans (*q.v.*). Fighting ceased until 1459, when Yorkists were beaten at the Battle of Ludford Bridge (Oct. 12). But they were victorious at the Battle of Northampton (July 10, 1460) and forced King Henry to name Richard (and Yorkist heirs) as his successor. This disinherited Queen Margaret's son and she then marched an army against the Yorkists. She won a bloody victory at Wakefield (Dec. 30, 1460), in which Richard was slain. She then won (Feb. 17, 1461) the second Battle of St. Albans (*q.v.*) and marched toward London. However, Richard's son, Edward, had already defeated the Lancastrians (Feb. 2) at the Battle of Mortimer's Cross (*q.v.*) and marched into London first. Edward was proclaimed King Edward IV (Mar. 4, 1461), routed Margaret's forces at Towton (*q.v.*), and forced the Lancastrians to flee the country. Edward's reign was undisturbed until 1469, when his brother, George, Yorkist duke of Clarence, and R. Neville, earl of Warwick (a powerful Yorkist) rebelled against him. They were driven out of England (1470) and, in France, formed an alliance with the exiled Lancastrian, Margaret of Anjou, and also won backing from French king Louis XI. They subsequently invaded England (Sept. 1470), briefly restored Henry VI, and put Edward to flight. Edward then formed an alliance with Charles the Bold, duke of Burgundy, and, returning to England (1471), won decisive victories at Barnet (*q.v.*) and Tewkesbury (*q.v.*). His principal opponents either dead or imprisoned (Henry was apparently murdered), Edward lived out the remainder of his life as king. The last phase of the wars broke out soon after Edward's death. Edward's brother, Richard III, seized power (1483) from Edward's son. Henry Stafford, 2d duke of Buckingham, raised an unsuccessful revolt and disaffected Yorkists threw their support to the Lancastrian claimant, Henry Tudor.

Henry Tudor then defeated and killed (Aug. 22, 1485) Richard at the Battle of Bosworth Field (*q.v.*) and was crowned Henry VII. This ended the wars. Henry further cemented the peace by marrying (1486) Elizabeth of York and by quelling the last Yorkist revolts. The wars decimated the ranks of English nobles and they were subsequently unable to oppose the absolutist powers accumulated by Henry and his Tudor heirs.

Rosetta Stone Inscribed basalt stone that provided the key to deciphering ancient Egyptian hieroglyphics. Found (1799) by Napoleon's troops near Rosetta, Egypt, the stone bore inscriptions in Greek, Egyptian demotic, and hieroglyphics. Preliminary discoveries by Thomas Young (1773–1829) concerning the hieroglyphics were used by J. Champollion to finally decipher the ancient writings (1821).

Rosicrucians International society that claims it has the secret knowledge of the ancients. Its doctrine contains elements of occultism and mysticism. The group was first mentioned in 17th-cent. publications.

Ross, Betsy 1752–1836.   American seamstress. Tradition credits her with making the first American flag (adopted by the Continental Congress June 14, 1777).

Ross, Sir John 1777–1856.   British admiral and Arctic explorer. His explorations of Arctic waters failed to find a Northwest Passage (*q.v.*), but the north magnetic pole was located (1831) on one of his expeditions.

Ross, John (Koowescoowe) 1790–1866.   American Indian chief of Scottish and Cherokee parentage. He fought valiantly to prevent the expulsion of his people from Georgia but eventually led them on the long journey (from 1835) to the Indian Territory in Oklahoma.

Rossetti, Christina Georgina 1830–94.   English poet, sister of D.G. Rossetti. A devout Anglican, she spent her later life as a recluse and wrote religious poems. Her works include *Goblin Market and Other Poems* and *Prince's Progress*.

Rossetti, Dante Gabriel 1828–82.   English poet and painter. He was one of the founders of the Pre-Raphaelites, who sought to restore naturalness to painting.

Rossi, Count Pellegrino 1787–1848.   Italian politician, economist, and writer who attempted to form a confederation of Italian states under the leadership of the Papal States. As a young man, he left his native Italy for Switzerland (1816), where he became a professor of law and was active in Swiss politics. He moved to France (1833) and served as French ambassador to Italy (1845). Rossi then was named premier of the Papal States (1848), but was assassinated in Rome that same year.

Rossini, Gioacchino Antonio 1792–1868. Italian composer. Best known as an operatic composer, his comic-opera masterpiece is the still popular *The Barber of Seville* (1816). His best-known dramatic opera is *William Tell* (1829).

Rostand, Edmond 1868–1918. French poet and playwright, best known for his famous play *Cyrano de Bergerac* (1897).

Rothko, Mark (Rothkovich, Marcus) 1903–70. Russian-born American painter. He was a leading exponent of abstract expressionism (*q.v.*). His later works consisted of rectangles of color painted on large canvases.

Rothschild, baron James 1792–1868. French financier and Jewish leader. Raised in a family of international bankers, he settled in Paris (1812) where he was influential in financing of French railway construction.

Rothschild, baron Lionel Nathan de 1808–79. British banker and member of Parliament (1858–74). Son of N. Rothschild, he arranged large international loans such as those for the Irish famine (1847) and the Crimean War (1856). He was the first Jewish member of Parliament.

Rothschild, Mayer Amschel 1743–1812. Founder of the Rothschild banking dynasty. Originally a Frankfurt money-changer, he capitalized on his position as adviser to the landgrave of Hesse-Kassel and, through his sons, founded Rothschild banks in London, Paris, Vienna, and Naples.

Rothschild, Nathan Meyer 1777–1836. Founder of the London branch of the famous Rothschild banking dynasty. He was noted for helping the British subsidize their allies in the fight against Napoleonic France.

Rou *See* Rollo.

Rouault, Georges 1871–1958. French expressionist artist. Employing a "stained-glass" style of bold, vivid colors, he is considered one of the foremost religious artists of this century. Among his works are *Circus* (1906), *Three Clowns* (1917), and *The Old King* (1936).

Rouget de Lisle, Claude Joseph 1760–1836. French army engineer and writer. He wrote (1792) the French national anthem, *La Marseillaise.*

Rough Riders Popular name for the 1st US Volunteer Cavalry in the Spanish-American War (1898). Largely organized by T. Roosevelt and commanded by L. Wood, they mainly fought on foot in Cuba, having been forced to leave their horses behind in Florida. The Battle of San Juan Hill, fought under Roosevelt's command, was their best-known engagement.

Roundheads Pejorative name of the Parliamentarians who opposed Charles I in the English Civil Wars (1642–48). They were so named because of their short haircuts. The Royalists wore their hair long in the then fashionable ringlets.

Rousseau, Henri 1844–1910. French primitivist painter. He painted exotic scenes of jungles, wild beasts, and strange Gypsies in a naive style. His works include *Monkeys in the Orange Trees, Sleeping Gypsy,* and *The Dream.*

Rousseau, Jean Jacques 1712–78. Swiss-born French author and philosopher. A highly controversial figure in his lifetime, he influenced both the development of Romanticism and the political thought of the French Revolution. Rousseau's life was erratic and, after he gained recognition, was marked by bitter quarrels with his friends, flight from one country after another because of hostile reactions to his views, and, finally, at least partial insanity. Among his works were articles for the great French *Encyclopédie; Discourse on Arts and Sciences,* which held that civilization corrupted the essential goodness of man; *Discourse on the Origin of Inequality,* which again treated corruption of the natural man by civilization; the famous *Social Contract* (1762), which postulated both subordination of the individual to the general will of society and the common good toward which society must aim; *Émile,* a novel that influenced educational theory; and *Confessions,* his famous autobiography.

Roussel, Albert 1869–1937. French composer. He combined modern experimental techniques with a basic neoclassical style in such well known works as the ballet *Bacchus and Ariane* (1931).

Rowlatt Acts Legislation passed (Feb., 1919) by the British government of India to extend wartime measures whereby suspected revolutionaries could be tried without juries and even interned without trial. The Indian protests over these measures, led by M. Gandhi, led to the Massacre of Amritsar (*q.v.*).

Rowley, William 1585?–1642? English Jacobean dramatist. He was both an actor and a collaborator on dozens of plays, most notably *The Changeling,* written with T. Middleton. His own best-known play was *All's Lost by Lust.*

Roxana (Roxane) *d.* 311 BC Wife of Alexander the Great, daughter of a local Bactrian chief. Alexander married her (1327 BC) to consolidate his position in Persia and she bore him a posthumous son. Caught in the conflicts between Alexander's generals (Wars of the Diadochi), she and her son were put to death by Cassander.

Roxas y Acuña, Manuel 1892–1948. First president of the independent Republic of the Philippines (1946–48). He was Speaker of the House and senator before independence. During WW II he spied for the Allies while serving in the Japanese occupation government in the Philippines.

Royal Academy of Arts Principal British art organization. It was founded in 1768 by George III, with Sir J. Reynolds as its first president. It has 40 academicians and sponsors studies and biennial exhibitions.

Royal Canadian Mounted Police Canadian federal police force. It was founded (1873) as the Northwest Mounted Police with an original force of 300 men to keep order in the Northwest Territories. Popularly called the Mounties and long celebrated for its dogged pursuit of criminals, the force was given federal status in 1920 and now numbers some 14,000 men and women.

Royal Highlanders *See* **Black Watch.**

Royal Society One of the oldest and most prestigious European scientific societies. Founded in London (1660) as the Royal Society of London for the Improvement of Natural Knowledge, it has counted among its members the most distinguished men of science from its founding down to the present.

Royce, Josiah 1855–1916. American philosopher, an exponent of philosophical idealism. In his works he stressed the importance of individuality and will over intellect.

Ruanda *See* **Rwanda.**

Ruanda-Urundi Former Belgian colonial territory in central Africa, now divided between the independent states of Rwanda and Burundi. Once a part of German East Africa, the region was taken by Belgium in 1916. It was made a UN trust territory in 1946 and was divided in 1962. The Tutsi and the Hutu are the main peoples inhabiting the area.

Rubens, Peter Paul 1577–1640. Flemish painter considered the master of baroque art and noted for the sensuousness and use of color in his works. After studying in Italy, he ran a large workshop in Antwerp and used assistants to help with his many commissioned works, including *Descent from the Cross* and the decoration of France's Luxembourg Palace. Later he became a diplomat and was sent on missions to Spain, where he painted the royal family, and to England, where he did the *Allegory of War and Peace.* Among his many other noted works were *Adoration of the Magi, The Massacre of the Innocents, Venus and Adonis,* and *The Three Graces.*

Rubicon A small stream flowing into the Adriatic. Located in what is now north central Italy it once marked the border between Cisalpine Gaul and Italy. By crossing the Rubicon with his army (Jan. 10–11, 49 BC), J. Caesar irrevocably committed himself to the civil war with the Roman Senate.

Rubinstein, Anton Grigoryevich 1829–94. Russian pianist, a virtuoso esteemed as a master of technique in his time. He was also a respected composer, though his works are rarely performed today.

Rubinstein, Arthur 1886–1982. Polish-born American pianist. Known especially as an interpreter of Chopin, he was one of the most popular of concert pianists for many decades.

Ruby, Jack *See* **Kennedy, John F.**

Rudolf 1858–89. Archduke and heir to the Austro-Hungarian empire. His mysterious death (with his mistress) at Mayerling was officially declared a suicide.

Rudolf I (Habsburg, ~ of) 1218–91. German king (1273–91), and first of the Habsburg kings. His election marked the end of the Interregnum (*q.v.*) in the Holy Roman Empire. His wars against King Ottocar II of Bohemia, a rival for the crown, helped restore eastern German lands, and he consolidated the rule over lands central to his family dynasty (notably Austria).

Rudolf II 1552–1612. Holy Roman emperor (1576–1612), successor to his father, Maximilian II. He reversed his father's policy of toleration of Protestantism and openly supported the Catholic Reformation. However, opposition to his policies (notably a revolt by I. Bocskay in

Hungary) and Rudolf's mental instability made it increasingly impossible for him to rule. By 1606 his brother Matthias had become actual ruler of the empire.

Rudolph (Raoul) *d.* 936. Duke of Burgundy and king of France (923–36), successor to Robert I. His reign was embroiled in a succession of wars against the Normans and Hungarians, fought to consolidate his position.

Rueil, Peace of *See* **Fronde.**

Ruffo, Fabrizio 1744–1827. Roman Catholic cardinal and Neapolitan leader. In 1799 he led a successful insurrection against the Napoleonic regime (Parthenopean Republic) in Naples.

Rufinus *d.* AD 395. Roman statesman. As minister to Theodosius I and his son Arcadius, Rufinus wielded great power in the Eastern Roman empire. He failed in his attempt to marry his daughter to Arcadius and was assassinated by the Goths, probably at the instigation of Stilicho, his rival.

Ruhr District Ruhr River valley (northwest Germany) and one of the world's leading industrial regions. The presence of high-quality coal ultimately led to the region's development (19th cent.) as a center for steel production and other allied industries. It was important to the German war effort in WW I and was occupied (1923–25) by France and Belgium when Germany failed to meet reparations payments after WW I. In WW II the district again supplied much of Germany's war materials and was heavily bombed (1942–45).

Ruisdael, Jacob van (Ruysdael, ˜) c1628–82. Dutch painter of the baroque period. Considered one of the greatest landscapists, he influenced the French and English landscapists of the next two centuries. Among his noted works were *Jewish Cemetery* and *Wheatfields.*

Rum, Sultanate of Former Seljuk kingdom that included much of Anatolia at its height. The Seljuk sultan of Persia, Alp Arslan, won the territory from the Byzantines following the Battle of Manzikert (1071). The Sultanate of Rum emerged as a successor state during the decline of the Seljuk Empire and flourished until being conquered by the Mongols (13th cent.). The region was later taken by the Ottoman Turks (14th cent.) and absorbed into their empire. *See also* Seljuks.

Rumania (Romania; *formerly* Socialist Republic of Rumania) Republic located in southeastern Europe. The population is 23,269,000 and the capital is Bucharest. The area of modern Rumania was largely that of the ancient Roman province of Dacia. With the decline of the Roman Empire the region was subsequently invaded numerous times by Goths, Huns, Slavs, and Bulgars. Though the language is basically derived from Latin, the population is predominantly Slavic. The rise of the principalities of Moldavia and Walachia (14th cent.) was followed by a period of domination (15th–19th cents.) by the Ottoman Empire, and then for a time by the Russian Empire. Proclaimed a kingdom in 1881, Rumania became a people's republic in 1947 and in 1989, as the pro-democracy movement swept through Eastern Europe, the Communist regime was overthrown. Key dates in Rumania's history include:

1330 John Bassaraba founded the independent principality of Walachia.

1349 Bogdan Voda founded the independent principality of Moldavia

EARLY 15TH CENT. Walachia became an Ottoman vassal state.

16TH CENT. Moldavia became an Ottoman vassal state.

1593–1601 Walachian prince Michael the Brave reigned; united Walachia, Moldavia, and Transylvania under his rule (1599–1600); union fell apart after his death.

1711 Moldavia allied with Russia against Ottoman rule; Russian forces sent to region were defeated; Ottomans introduced Phanariot system of rule (rule by governors called Hospodars, who were generally from the Greek quarter in Constantinople).

1768–74 Russo-Turkish Wars; Ottoman Empire defeated by Russia; Treaty of Kuchuk Kainarji marked rise of Russian influence in Moldavia and Walachia, especially as protector of Greek Christians there.

1806–12 Russo-Turkish War fought, Russia defeated the Ottomans and gained Bessarabia.

1822 Ottomans consented to make Rumanians governors of Moldavia and Walachia.

1826 Convention of Akkerman; Russia granted right to oversee the autonomy of Moldavia and Walachia.

1828–29 Russo-Turkish War fought, Russians occupied Moldavia and Walachia; Russia gained virtual protectorates over the principalities through the Treaty of Adrianople (1829), ending the war; both remained technically Ottoman holdings.

1848 Rumanians staged unsuccessful uprising against foreign domination; defeated by combined Russian and Ottoman intervention.

1854–56 Crimean War; Russian forces withdrew from region and Austrian troops moved in; war ended by Treaty of Paris (1856), which established Moldavia and Walachia as principalities under Ottoman suzerainty; Moldavia awarded southern Bessarabia.

1859 Alexander John Cuza became prince of Moldavia and Walachia.

1862 Moldavia and Walachia joined to form the principality of Rumania; capital established at Bucharest.

1866 Cuza deposed; succeeded by Carol I, a member of the House of Hohenzollern-Sigmaringen.

1876–1957 Rumanian sculptor C. Brancusi lived; became a leader of the modern abstract school.

1877–78 Rumania allied with Russia in the Russo-Turkish War; war ended by the Treaty of Berlin, by which Rumania became independent but ceded southern Bessarabia to Russia.

1878 Treaty of San Stefano; Ottoman Turks recognized independence of Rumania.

1881–1916 Queen Elizabeth of Rumania ruled; wrote books under pen name Carmen Sylva.

1881–1955 Composer G. Enesco lived; noted for his Rumanian folk themes.

1881 Rumania became a kingdom (1881); Carol I ruled as first king (1881–1914); modernized the country.

1884 Rumania allied with Austria-Hungary, both for favorable trade concessions and to avoid dependence on Russia.

1907 Peasant uprising in Moldavia against the Jews and against the landed nobles, the Boyars; uprising crushed, but land reforms were subsequently instituted; conflict marked growth of anti-Semitism in Rumania.

1912 First Balkan War against Ottomans; Rumania remained neutral.

1913 Second Balkan War; Rumania allied with Greece and Serbia against Bulgaria and occupied southern Dobruja.

1914 Carol I died (Oct.); succeeded by his nephew Ferdinand I.

1914–27 King Ferdinand reigned.

1914–27 Queen Marie of Rumania reigned; helped convince King Ferdinand to join Allies in WW I.

1914–18 WW I; Rumania initially remained neutral, then joined (June, 1916) the Allies against the Central Powers; after invading Transylvania, the Rumanians were driven back and the kingdom occupied by Austro-German troops; Rumania withdrew from the war by the Treaty of Bucharest (Feb., 1918) but reentered the war (Nov.) on the eve of its ending.

1918–20 At end of WW I Rumania annexed Transylvania, Bessarabia, Bukovina, and part of the Banat; most of its gains were confirmed by the treaties of St. Germain (1919) and Trianon (1920); Russia refused to accept Rumanian annexation of Bessarabia.

1919 Rumania invaded Hungary and overthrew the Communist government of Béla Kun.

1920–21 Rumania joined the Little Entente, an alliance with Czechoslovakia and Yugoslavia for mutual protection.

1922–27 Ion Brătianu, head of the Liberal party, in power; his near-dictatorial authority challenged by both the National Peasants' party under Iuliu Maniu and the Fascist nationalist organization, the Iron Guard, headed by Corneliu Zelea-Codreanu.

1927 King Ferdinand I died; his grandson Michael was made king under a regency.

1930 Carol, Michael's father, assumed the crown as Carol II.

1934 Balkan Entente; joined mutual defense pact with Greece, Turkey, and Yugoslavia.

1938 Carol took control of the government and jailed leaders of the Iron Guard; Zelea-Codreanu and others shot, allegedly while trying to escape.

1939–45 World War II; Rumania and other Balkan nations came under Nazi domination following German offensive in Balkans (1940–41).

1940 Rumania forced by Germany to cede Bessarabia and Bukovina to Russia, Transylvania to Hungary, and southern Dobruja to Bulgaria (Aug.–Sept., 1940); led to severe unrest in Rumania and forced Carol to appoint Ion Antonescu as dictator; Carol then abdicated (Sept. 6).

1941 Rumania joined Germany in its invasion (June, 1941) of Russia; later declared war (Dec., 1941) on the US; occupied (1944) by Russian forces; King Michael led overthrow of Antonescu (Aug. 24); Rumania signed armistice with Russia (Sept. 12, 1944).

1944 Soviet troops, driving Nazis westward before them, entered Rumania.

1945 Soviets installed government dominated by Communists (Mar.).

1945–54 Gheorghe Gheorghiu-Dej in office as Rumanian Communist Party first secretary; as such he was the country's most powerful political figure.

1947 Rumanian Communist party (RCP) merged with Social Democrats, forming Rumanian Workers' Party (RWP); Gheorghiu retained post as party leader.

1947–48 Michael abdicated (Dec. 30, 1947); Rumania proclaimed a people's republic; new constitution, modeled on Russian constitution, adopted (Apr. 13, 1948).

1948 Nationalization of industry and financial institutions began; arrest of opposition politicians began.

1952 New constitution promulgated (July 18), modeled closely on Soviet lines; followed purge of Communist party.

1955–65 Gheorghiu again served as Rumanian Communist Party first secretary; established increasingly independent foreign policy for Rumania from early 1960s.

1955 Rumania became member of Warsaw Pact.

1960 E. Ionesco, Rumanian-born French playwright, wrote *Rhinoceros;* he ranked as leading playwright of the theater of the absurd.

1965 Gheorghiu died (Mar.); Nicolae Ceauşescu, former party official, became party first secretary; RWP renamed Rumanian Communist Party (RCP).

1965 New constitution enacted (Aug.); Rumania renamed Socialist Republic of Rumania; first secretary became general secretary.

1965–89 Ceauşescu in office as RCP general secretary.

1968 Warsaw Pact forces invaded Czechoslovakia; Rumania did not take part.

1974 Ceauşescu became first to hold new office of presidency.

1977 Ceauşescu instrumental in preparations for Egyptian president Sadat's visit to Israel.

1980 Ceauşescu, continuing his independent foreign policy, condemned the Soviet invasion of Afghanistan.

1985 State of emergency declared in Rumania's power industry as ongoing problems reached crisis proportions; military took charge of power generating facilities; energy shortages continued into 1987.

1987 First signs of unrest reported as severe winter led to fuel shortages and energy rationing; strikes called to protest food shortages; by Mar. military in control of mines and important factories.

1987 Rumania scorned by Amnesty International for human rights abuses, particularly in regard to some 2 million ethnic Hungarians living in Transylvania.

1987 Tractor factory workers led protest by thousands in Braşov (Nov.); hundreds arrested after protesters attacked RCP headquarters there; unrest spread to other cities in Dec.

1988 Ceauşescu unveiled radical resettlement plan (Mar.); residents of rural towns (mainly in Transylvania) to be moved to high-rise housing developments that would be part of massive agro-industrial complexes (Mar.); plan called for demolition of 8,000 villages in Transylvania and elsewhere; Ceauşescu rejected storm of criticism against proposal.

1988 Some 50,000 in Hungary demonstrated at Rumanian embassy in Budapest to protest resettlement plan (June).

1989 Four high government officials, including deputy chairman of Council of Ministers and Minister of Finance, sacked following charges of financial irregularities (Mar.).

1989 Former RCP officials criticized Ceauşescu in open letter (Mar.); officials arrested.

1989 Rumania's entire foreign debt eliminated according to Ceauşescu announcement (Apr.).

1989 Ceauşescu arrogantly criticized pro-democracy reforms being enacted in neighboring Communist-bloc countries.

1989 Government declared cereal harvest was 60 million tons (Oct.); records later showed it to be 17 million tons.

1989 Hundreds killed after security police fired on demonstration by thousands at Timişoara, which had been sparked by arrest of outspoken Lutheran clergyman, Father László Tökés (Dec. 17); government sealed borders as protests erupted in other towns.

1989 Ceauşescu called mass rally in Bucharest to demonstrate he was still in control, but was shouted down by crowd (Dec. 21); antigovernment demonstrations broke out that night and the army refused to fire on the crowds; minister of defense shot after refusing to support Ceauşescu; following morning (Dec. 22) army joined crowd as it stormed RCP headquarters; Ceauşescu and his wife escaped by helicopter.

1989 National Salvation Front (NSF), including former Communist officials, dissidents, and army officers, seized power (Dec. 22); fighting against security forces, the Securitate, continued for several days, killing 689 persons.

1989– Ion Iliescu, NSF member and former high Communist official, in office as interim president; government quickly ended food rationing, halted the village destruction program, established military control over security police, ended RCP control of government, and promised free market reforms and free elections in 1990.

1989 Ceauşescu and his wife were captured, tried (Dec. 25), and immediately executed.

1989 Rumania recorded trade surplus for year, largely by increasing exports at a time when shortages of food and consumer goods were widespread; new government halted food exports.

1990 Fighting in Rumania ended (Jan.).

1990 Mounting opposition to Communist-dominated NSF resulted in power-sharing agreement; Provisional National Unity Council (PNUC) established to rule country until elections (Feb.); Iliescu continued as president.

1990 Mass anti-Communist protests held almost daily in Bucharest (Apr.–May).

1990 NSF victorious in election (May 20), but international observers reported voting irregularities; protests continued until June when police began shooting at demonstrators; several killed, thousands arrested.

1990 Violent antigovernment protests resumed (Aug.); strikes and worker unrest began in Nov. as prices rose sharply; protests continued into 1991, forcing government to alter economic policies.

1990 National Agency for Privatization set up (Aug.).

1991 Former Securitate head Gen. Iulian Vlad received three-year sentence (Mar.) for crimes committed during Communist regime; many other ex-officials received similar light sentences or were acquitted.

1991 Riots by miners (Sept.) forced prime minister to resign; unrest continued in Rumania, spurred by frustration over high prices, slow pace of reform, and continued domination of government by Communists.

Rumford, Benjamin Thompson, Count 1753–1814. American-born British physicist. He is best known for his theory that heat is caused by the motion of particles (1798).

Rump Parliament Phase of England's Long Parliament (1640–60) that began following (1648) expulsion of Prebyterian members unacceptable to the army (*see* Pride's Purge). Those expelled were recalled in 1660, restoring the Long Parliament. It voted its own dissolution (Mar. 16, 1660) after providing for the convening of the Convention Parliament (*q.v.*). This paved the way for the English Restoration.

Rundstedt, Gerd von 1875–1953. German field marshal, commander of German forces in Western Europe (1942–45). He was one of the ablest of Hitler's commanders, taking a leading part in the conquest of France, the invasion of Russia, the fortification of Europe, and the Battle of the Bulge.

Runeberg, Johan Ludvig 1804–77. Finnish Romantic poet. He wrote verse epics, and the Finnish national anthem, "Our Land," was adapted from one of his poems.

Rungeling, John *See* **Ringling, John.**

Runjeet Singh *See* **Ranjit Singh.**

Runnymede (Runnimede) Meadow near the Thames River in Surrey, England, where King John was obliged (1215) by his barons to accept the Magna Carta (*q.v.*).

Rupert 1352–1410. German king (1400–10), successor to Wenceslaus and elector palatine of the Rhine (1398–1410). He unsuccessfully attempted to regain the imperial city of Milan which had been taken by the Visconti. Rupert was never crowned Holy Roman Emperor.

Rupert, Prince 1619–82. Count palatine of the Rhine and English Royalist general. A nephew of Charles I, he fought during the Thirty Years' War, and then commanded royalist forces during the English Civil Wars. He won notable victories, but was defeated at the battles of Marston Moor and Naseby. After the restoration of

Charles II, he served as a naval commander in the Dutch Wars and became a founder of the Hudson's Bay Company.

Rupert's Land Canadian territory held by the Hudson's Bay Company from receipt of its charter in 1670 until it was sold to Canada in 1869. Named after Prince Rupert, the company's first president, it included the vast region constituting the drainage basin of Hudson Bay.

Rurik Dynasty of Russian noblemen and tsars that ruled Russia until 1598. The line was founded by Rurik (*d.* 879) and his brothers, Scandinavian adventurers called Varangians, who gained control of Novgorod (c862). Rurik's successor later gained control of the Russian princely states, notably Moscow, and thus came to control the region. Beginning with Ivan III, who ended Tatar control of the region (1480), succeeding members of the line enlarged and consolidated their control over Russian domains. Ivan IV (the Terrible) was the first ruler to proclaim himself tsar and Fëdor I was the last ruler of the Rurik family. He was succeeded by B. Godunov, whose reign ended in the Time of Troubles and the rise of the Romanov dynasty.

Rush, Benjamin 1745?–1813. American physician and politician. He served in the Continental Congress (1776–77), signed the Declaration of Independence, was surgeon general of the Continental Army, and finally treasurer of the US mint.

Rush, Richard 1780–1859. American statesman and diplomat. He negotiated the Rush-Bagot Convention (*q.v.*) that demilitarized the Great Lakes and helped establish the 49th parallel as the border between the US and Canada. He also played a role in preliminary talks with the British that led to formulation of the Monroe Doctrine.

Rush-Bagot Convention Agreement signed between the acting US secretary of state R. Rush and the British diplomat Charles Bagot in 1817. It provided for virtual demilitarization of the US-Canadian border (notably the Great Lakes) and was a basis of subsequent peaceful relations between the US and Canada.

Ruskin, John 1819–1900. British art critic and social thinker, the dominant critic of the Victorian period. He promoted the Gothic Revival movement and later took up the cause of improving the condition of the working class. His critical works included *Modern Painters* and *The Stones*

of Venice. Among his works on social reform were *Time and Tide* and *Fors Clavigera.*

Russell, Bertrand Arthur William, 3d earl Russell 1872–1970. British philosopher, one of the most important of the 20th century. He established a considerable reputation prior to WW I, particularly in the field of mathematical logic, with such works as *Principles of Mathematics* (1903) and *Principia Mathematica* (1910–13). From WW I on, however, he became increasingly involved in pacifism, social reform, and nuclear disarmament. Though his outspoken liberal views sometimes resulted in loss of teaching positions and even arrest, he actively pursued such causes until his last days.

Russell, Charles Taze *See* **Jehovah's Witnesses.**

Russell, Francis, 2d earl of Bedford c1527–85. English courtier and politician. He had to flee the country as a result of his part in the affair of Lady Jane Grey, but returned to hold important posts under Queen Elizabeth I.

Russell, Francis, 4th earl of Bedford 1593–1641. English nobleman who developed the great London market known as Covent Garden.

Russell, Henry Norris 1877–1957. American astronomer. His diagrams showing the relationship between the brightness and spectral class of stars contributed to theories of the evolution of the universe.

Russell, John, 1st earl of Bedford 1486?–1555. English courtier and politician. One of Henry VIII's executors, he was also lord privy seal, and was created earl in 1550.

Russell, John, 4th duke of Bedford 1710–71. English politician. An important opponent of Robert Walpole, he was a Whig leader and served in such posts as first lord of the admiralty, lord lieutenant of Ireland, and ambassador to France.

Russell, John, 1st earl Russell 1792–1878. British statesman and twice prime minister (1846–52, 1865–66). As a member of Parliament, he championed such liberal causes as the Catholic Emancipation Act, the Reform Bill of 1832 (*q.v.*), and the repeal of the Corn Laws.

Russell, Lord William 1639–83. English Whig political leader. As a member of Parliament, he opposed Charles II's pro-French policies. Unjustly accused of being involved in the Rye House Plot (*q.v.*), he was executed and later cleared.

Russell, William, 5th earl and 1st duke of Bedford 1613–1700. English nobleman and Civil War leader. He fought variously for both king and Parliament during the English Civil Wars.

Russia *See* **Commonwealth of Independent States.**

Russia, Orthodox Church of *See* **Orthodox Church of Russia.**

Russia Company *See* **Muscovy Company.**

Russian Civil War War (1918–22) between the Bolshevik Red Army and counterrevolutionary (White Army) forces, variously aided by the Germans, French, British, Japanese, and Americans. The Bolshevik takeover during the Russian Revolution (*q.v.*) coalesced opposition to the Communists (as the Bolsheviks called themselves since 1918) and a number of border territories proclaimed independence. The Red Army, led by L. Trotsky, fought variously in the Ukraine, the Baltic region, northern Russia (against British, French and American forces), the southern Caucasus region, and Siberia (against the Japanese, as well as White Russians). By 1922 most of the former Russian territories had been regained, and with the Communist government in firm control, the Union of Soviet Socialist Republics was proclaimed (Dec. 30). (*See also* Commonwealth of Independent States, 1917–22.)

Russian Federation (*formerly* Russian Soviet Federated Socialist Republic, RSFSR) Independent state, one of the 15 former Soviet constituent republics and now a member of the Commonwealth of Independent States. By far the largest of the former Soviet republics, it stretches from Eastern Europe across northern Asia to the Pacific. The Russian republic embraced about three-quarters of the old USSR (including Siberia) and was home to just over half its population. The history of the Russian Federation is essentially that of the Commonwealth of Independent States (*q.v.*). Following the Bolshevik revolution of 1917, the RSFSR was formally constituted in Jan., 1918, and in 1922 became part of the newly created USSR. During the breakup of the USSR, the RSFSR became a leading force in the drive by constituent republics for greater autonomy from the Communist central government. It became one of the three original Slavic republics to form the CIS (Dec. 8).

Russian Revolution of 1905 Rebellion in Russia that led to the establishment of a constitutional monarchy and paved the way for the Russian Revolution of 1917. Tsar Nicholas II's reign was marked by increased repression and protest against it, calls for reform by the zemstvos (*q.v.*), and widespread discontent over losses in the Russo-Japanese War (*q.v.*). The unrest finally culminated in Bloody Sunday (*q.v.*) in which soldiers fired on a peaceful protest (Jan., 1905). This incident galvanized opposition to the tsarist regime and resulted in widespread strikes and uprisings. By October the revolt had reached a fever pitch and Nicholas was forced to issue the October Manifesto (*q.v.*), in which he acceded to rule by a constitution, promised creation of the Duma (a legislative body), and named Count S. Witte prime minister. Order was restored soon after, though the arrest of rebel leaders provoked some further protests.

Russian Revolution of 1917 Name applied to the political uprising in Russia in which the monarchy was overthrown and the Bolsheviks under N. Lenin came to power. The Revolution of 1917 was actually two revolutions: the February Revolution, which led to the overthrow of the tsar and end of the Romanov dynasty, and the October Revolution, which brought the Bolsheviks (*q.v.*) to power in Russia. The revolution had far-reaching consequences. It brought into being the world's first Communist state and resulted in sweeping reform of Russian society. These reforms did not go unopposed, however, and it was not until 1922 that the Communists brought an end to the Russian Civil War (*q.v.*). (*See also* Commonwealth of Independent States, 1917–22.) Key dates in the history of the revolution include:

1906–11 Nicholas's prime minister Piotr Stolypin attempted unsuccessfully to introduce reforms, while at the same time suppressing the revolutionary movement; assassinated.

1914–18 WW I; severe hardship, failures of Russian government and military reversals contributed to revolutionary movement.

1915 Tsar Nicholas took over command of Russian armies at the front; left Tsarina Alexandra (dominated by the unpopular Rasputin) in charge of the government; her mismanagement of government only caused further political unrest.

1916 Rasputin assassinated (Dec. 30) by angry noblemen; Rasputin's death failed to ease tensions.

1917 February Revolution (Mar. 8, Feb. 23 Old Style); workers in Petrograd (new name of St. Petersburg) went on strike; outbreaks of rioting.

1917 Tsar Nicholas attempted to dissolve the Duma (Mar. 11); his order ignored; soldiers in Petrograd joined the workers in the revolt (Mar. 12).

1917 Strikers organized Petrograd Workers' and Soldiers' Soviet (Mar. 12), which began to assume political power in the capital.

1917 Duma established Provisional Government, headed by Prince Georgi Lvov and including A. Kerensky; Nicholas abdicated in favor of regency of his brother, Grand Duke Michael (Mar. 15).

1917 Grand Duke Michael abdicated (Mar. 16); Romanov dynasty ended; struggle for power between Petrograd Soviet and Provisional Government began.

1917 Provisional Government announced its intention to continue the war against Germany (Mar. 19); Petrograd Soviet gained support among workers and soldiers.

1917 Lenin returned to Russia (Apr.) in "sealed train" provided by Germans. His able supporter, L. Trotsky, arrived in the following month.

1917 Lenin outlined his April theses (Apr. 17) for Bolshevik-dominated government.

1917 Provisional Government foreign minister Pavel Miliukov forced to resign because of his war policies; Kerensky became minister of war (May 18).

1917 First all-Russian Congress of Soviets convened in Petrograd (June 16); delegates largely Mensheviks or Social Revolutionaries; Bolsheviks a minority despite growing support.

1917 Russians launched major military offensive (June 29); its failure (early July) led to growing Bolshevik strength and further weakening of Provisional Government.

1917 Massive demonstrations held in Petrograd (July 16–18); led to resignation of Prince Lvov (July 20); Kerensky became head of Provisional Government.

1917 Provisional Government instituted program of political repression against Bolsheviks and other revolutionary elements (July–Sept.); Lenin forced to flee to Finland.

1917 Gen. Lavr Kornilov led unsuccessful attempt to occupy Petrograd and seize power; arrested (Sept. 14).

1917 Lenin secretly returned to Petrograd (Oct. 20); called for armed insurrection against provisional government.

1917 Provisional government sent troops to close Bolshevik newspapers in Petrograd (Nov. 6), thus sparking revolt.

1917 October Revolution; Bolsheviks seized power in Petrograd (night of Nov. 6–7, Oct. 24–25 Old Style); second all-Russian Congress of Soviets convened (Nov. 7), Bolshevik delegates in majority; most Mensheviks and Social Revolutionaries withdrew; Trotsky announced dissolution of Provisional Government; Kerensky fled; Congress proclaimed Soviets as ruling government bodies throughout Russia; Council of People's Commissars, with Lenin as chairman, created to head government.

1917 Forces of local Soviets fought to take control in ensuing weeks, as Russian Civil War began.

Russian Social Democratic Labor party Russian Marxist political party founded (Mar., 1898) at Minsk by delegates from several revolutionary organizations. Its existence was nominal until its second party congress (1903) in Brussels and London, at which time it divided into two factions, the Bolsheviks (*q.v.*) and the Mensheviks (*q.v.*).

Russo-Finnish War (Winter War) War between Russia and Finland (Nov., 1939–Mar., 1940). Following the outbreak of WW II, Russia began (Nov. 30, 1939) an undeclared war over demands for certain territorial concessions and demilitarization of Finland's defensive Mannerheim Line. While the Soviets bombed Helsinki and shelled Finnish ports, the Finns, under Field Marshal C. Mannerheim, successfully resisted Soviet attacks on the eastern frontier. In early February, however, superior Russian forces began to break Finnish defenses. Ultimately Finland was forced to sign a peace treaty (Mar. 12, 1940) granting Russia the concessions it sought.

Russo-Japanese War Brief war (1904–05) between Russia and Japan, an outgrowth of rivalry over control of Manchuria and Korea. After negotiations failed (largely because of Russian intransigence) to produce a settlement, Japan launched a surprise attack (Feb. 8, 1904) on the Russian stronghold of Port Arthur, defended by Russian Gen. A. Kuropatkin. The Japanese finally took Port Arthur (Jan. 2, 1905) and inflicted a decisive defeat at the Battle of Mukden (Mar. 10, 1905). The final blow came when Russia's Baltic fleet, attempting to relieve Russian forces in the East, was intercepted and destroyed at Tsushima (May 27, 1905) by a Japanese naval force under Adm. H. Togo. The Treaty of Portsmouth (Aug. 29, 1905) ended the war in a humiliating defeat for Russia. Russia conceded territories (including Port Arthur) to Japan, though it retained control of northern Manchuria. The war marked the emergence of Japan as a major power.

Russo-Polish War War between Russia and Poland (Apr. 25–Oct. 12, 1920) caused by Poland's attempt to seize the Russian Ukraine. Allied with Ukrainian nationalists, the Poles entered the Ukraine and occupied Kiev (May 7, 1920). The Russian counteroffensive began in June and by August the Russians had driven the Poles back to Warsaw. On the verge of total defeat, Poland was saved by the intervention of European powers. A military force under French Gen. M. Weygand aided the Poles and forced the Russians to retreat and finally agree to an armistice. The subsequent Treaty of Riga established the Russo-Polish border until WW II.

Russo-Swedish War War (1741–43) between Russia and Sweden, in which Russia emerged victorious after initial Swedish gains. The war was ended by the Treaty of Åbo (*q.v.*), by which Sweden ceded territory in Finland to Russia.

Russo-Turkish Wars Wars fought by Russia and the Ottoman Empire (16th–19th cents.) that resulted in Russian conquest of Ottoman domains between the Black Sea and the Balkans. Concern over Russian expansionism and the general decline of the Ottoman Empire eventually brought direct involvement by other European powers in the 19th cent. (*See also* Eastern Question.) 1. War (1676–81) fought by Tsar Fëdor III of Russia against the Ottomans. He gained most of the Turkish Ukraine by the Treaty of Radzin (1681). 2. War (1695–96) in which Tsar Peter I conquered the Ottoman stronghold of Azov on the Black Sea. Though Peter's European allies made peace with the Ottomans in the Treaty of Karlowitz (1699), he continued hostilities until 1702. 3. War (1710–11) between Peter and the Ottomans, a part of the Northern War (1700–21). Encouraged by France, the Ottomans attacked Russia (1710), defeated

Peter's army at Pruth, and by the Treaty of Pruth (1711) regained Azov. 4. War (1736–39) between the Russians (with their ally, Austria) and the Ottomans, in which the Russians recaptured Azov and overran Moldavia. The Austrians, however, concluded the Treaty of Belgrade (1739), in which Russia acquired only Azov and was forced to agree not to militarize the Black Sea. 5. War (1768–74) declared by the Ottomans (under Mustafa III) on the Russians, under Catherine II. The Russians conquered Moldavia and Walachia and were victorious in the Crimea. The Treaty of Kuchuk Kainarji (*q.v.*) greatly increased Russian influence in the region and established Russia as the protector of Christians within Ottoman domains. 6. War (1787–92) between the Russians under Catherine II (with Austria as ally, 1788–91) and the Ottomans. Following Russia's annexation of the Crimea (1783), tensions increased and finally resulted in war, in which Russia and Austria were generally successful. Austria was forced out of the war (1791) by pressure from Prussia. Russia eventually concluded the Treaty of Jassy (1792), by which it extended its boundary to the Dniestr River and gave up Moldavia and Bessarabia. 7. War (1806–12) between Russia and the Ottomans under Selim III, caused by Selim's removal (1806) of Russian puppet rulers in Moldavia and Walachia. Russian victories in 1811–12 led to the Treaty of Bucharest (1812) and Russia's acquisition of Bessarabia. 8. War (1828–29) between Russia and the Ottomans, an outgrowth of the Greek War of Independence (1821–30). The Russians were successful on the Asian front and penetrated deep into the Balkans (to Adrianople), but were unable to take Constantinople. By the Treaty of Adrianople (*q.v.*), Russia won many concessions. 9. War (1853–56) better known as the Crimean War (*q.v.*). 10. War (1877–78) between Russia and the Ottomans, resulting from the Bosnian Rebellion of 1875. Russia actively encouraged the rebels, and Ottoman attempts to suppress the revolt precipitated a Russian declaration of war (to protect Christians). The Russians decisively defeated the Ottomans, crossed into the Balkans, and halted just outside Constantinople. The resulting Treaty of San Stefano gave Russia so much territory that European powers protested and forced Russia to accept modified terms, as set forth at the Congress of Berlin (*q.v.*).

Rutherford, Ernest, 1st baron 1871–1937. New Zealand—born British physicist, noted for his important studies of radioactivity. He discovered the alpha and beta particles and developed the concept of an atom as a nucleus surrounded by orbiting electrons. He received the Nobel Prize in Chemistry in 1908.

Ruthven, William, 4th lord of Ruthven and 1st earl of Gowrie 1541?–1584. Scottish nobleman. An opponent of Mary, Queen of Scots, he led (1582) the "Raid of Ruthven," in which the boy king James VI of Scotland (later James I of Great Britain) was kidnapped. Ruthven, pardoned for that conspiracy, was executed after yet another plot.

Rutledge, Ann 1813?–35. Supposed object of A. Lincoln's great love. Lincoln's biographer, William Herndon, created the now discredited story of Lincoln's romance with the girl.

Rutledge, John 1739–1800. American political leader. A member of the Continental Congress and the Constitutional Convention, he was instrumental in drafting and ratifying the Constitution.

Rütli Oath (Grütli ~) Traditionally, an oath sworn by representatives of the Swiss cantons of Uri, Schwyz, and Untenwalden, to join in rebellion against Austria. It is regarded as symbolic of Swiss independence.

Ruysdael, Jacob van *See* **Ruisdael, Jacob van.**

Ruyter, Michiel Adriaanszoon de 1607–76. Dutch admiral. He was a lifelong sailor, and his brilliant victories in the Dutch Wars enabled the Netherlands for a time to match British naval power.

Rwanda (Ruanda) East-central African republic. The population is 7,603,000 and the capital is Kigali. An agricultural society, Rwanda is the most densely populated nation in Africa. The minority Tutsi tribe dominated the Hutu majority, until the Hutu rebelled (1959), sending thousands of Tutsi into exile. Formed by the division of Ruanda-Urundi, Rwanda became independent on July 1, 1962. A military coup in 1972 followed unrest between the country's ethnic groups. The government later adopted a new constitution (1978) and held elections for some offices, though the military remained in control. An elected legislature was established in 1988. Constitutional reforms introduced (1991) provided for a multi-party system and in 1992 opposition parties agreed on a transition government pending elections. Some 4,000 rebels invaded Rwanda from Uganda (Oct. 1990) in an unsuccessful effort to topple the government.

Rye House Plot Failed plot (June, 1683) by Whig extremists to assassinate Charles II of England and the duke of York (later James II). It was named for the house where the conspirators met and resulted in the execution of Whig leaders Lord William Russell and Algernon Sidney as suspected conspirators.

Rykov, Aleksey Ivanovich 1881–1938. Russian Bolshevik revolutionary leader. A Politburo member under N. Lenin, he was removed for opposing J. Stalin's collectivization program.

Ryle, Gilbert 1900–74. British philosopher. A leader of the school of rigorous linguistic analysis, he published his noted work, *The Analysis of Mind,* on the mind-body dualism.

Rymer, Thomas 1641–1713. English literary critic and antiquarian. In his *A Short View of Tragedy,* he advocated a return to classicism in drama and attacked such contemporary works as Shakespeare's *Othello.*

Ryswick, Treaty of Treaty (Sept. 27, 1697) between France and the Alliance of Britain, the Netherlands, and Spain. It ended the War of the League of Augsburg. France retained Alsace but acknowledged William III as King of England, and the Dutch gained commercial concessions. Conquests in New France and New England were restored and France returned captured territories in the Netherlands, Luxembourg, and Catalonia to Spain.

S

Saadi *See* **Sadi.**

Saar *See* **Saar Territory.**

Saarinen, Eero 1910–61. Finnish-born American architect, a pioneer of experimental architecture. His works include St. Louis' Gateway Arch, the Dulles Airport terminal in Washington, D.C., and the US embassy in London.

Saarinen, (Gottlieb) Eliel 1873–1950. Finnish-American architect. A leading practitioner of modern architecture as well as a teacher, he collaborated with his son E. Saarinen on several projects. His works include the Music Shed for the Berkshire Music Festival at Tanglewood, Massachusetts.

Saar Territory (Saar) German territory located in Western Germany. A highly industrialized, coal-producing region, it has at various times been ruled by France but became a permanent part of the Federal Republic of Germany in 1957.

Sabbatai Zevi (~ Z'vi) 1626–76. Jewish mystic and sectarian leader. Having proclaimed himself the Messiah, he led an unsuccessful march on Constantinople (1666). Captured, he accepted Islam to save himself.

Sabbatarians (Southcottians) Christians who advocate strict observance of Sunday as the sabbath. Sabbatarians have frequently promoted blue laws to restrict Sunday activities.

Sabellianism Christian heresy. Founded by the Roman theologian Sabellius (*fl.* AD c220), Sabellianism held that the three persons of the Trinity were not three distinct, independent persons but three manifestations of the one Godhead.

Sabellius *See* **Sabellianism.**

Sabine Crossroads, Battle of *See* **Taylor, Richard.**

Sabines Ancient people who lived in the Sabine Hills near Rome. According to legend, the Romans, led by Romulus, captured Sabine women and carried them off to provide wives for themselves. The Sabines were conquered by the Romans (290 BC) and became Roman citizens (268 BC).

Sacajawea (Sacagawea) (Sakakawea) 1787?–1812. American Indian woman who served as an interpreter on the Lewis and Clark expedition (*q.v.*). A Shoshone, she was married to a French-Canadian fur trapper hired by M. Lewis and W. Clark.

Sac and Fox Indians (Sauk Indians) Related North American Algonquin Indian tribes. Inhabiting the Great Lakes area, the Sac and Fox tribes provoked the Black Hawk War (*q.v.*). After their defeat they were eventually pushed west across the Mississippi.

Sacco-Vanzetti case American criminal trial. On Apr. 15, 1920, a factory paymaster and security guard were robbed and killed at South Braintree, Massachusetts. Two Italian immigrants, Nicola Sacco (1891–1927) and Bartolomeo Vanzetti (1888–1927), were arrested, tried, and convicted (July 14, 1921) of the crime. Critics of the trial pointed to lack of concrete evidence and charged there was prejudice against the defendants because of their ethnic origins and political belief in anarchism. Despite international protests and appeals, both men were executed (1927).

Sackville, Thomas, 1st earl of Dorset 1536–1608. British poet, dramatist, and diplomat in service to Queen Elizabeth I. He is remembered today as the author of the first English tragedy in blank verse, *Gorboduc,* written with Thomas Norton (1532–84).

Sacred Band *See* **Pelopidas.**

Sacred War(s) Wars fought by ancient Greek cities in the Amphictyonic League for protection of the Temple of Apollo at Delphi. 1. First ~ (c596–c586 BC). Delphi was located within the territory of the Phocian city of Crisa, and when the city imposed a tax on pilgrims to Delphi, the Amphictyonic League went to war. Crisa was defeated and destroyed and the league took over administration of Delphi. 2. Second ~ (c448 BC). Fought by Athens and Sparta to restore control of Delphi to their respective allies. After the Phocians seized Delphi, the Spartans restored the Delphians. But once the Spartans withdrew, the Athenians intervened and put the Phocians back in control of Delphi. 3. Third ~ (355–346 BC). Phocis, fined by the Amphictyonic League for cultivating sacred grounds, seized Delphi and thereupon came under attack. Phocis, supported by Athens and Sparta, successfully resisted until Philip of Macedon joined forces (352) with the Amphicytonic League. Philip concluded the Peace of Philocrates with Athens (346), defeated Phocis, and became chairman of the league. 4. Fourth ~ (339–338 BC). The league next began a war against Amphissa, which caused Athens to join Thebes against it. Philip of Macedon, leading forces of the league, crushed Athens and Thebes at the Battle of Chaeronea (338) and thereby gained control over Greece.

Sacrosancta *See* **Constance, Council of.**

Sadat, Anwar al- 1918–81. Egyptian president (1970–81) and statesman, noted for securing the first Arab peace treaty with Israel. As an Egyptian army officer, Sadat was imprisoned (1942–44) during WW II for aiding the Germans against the British. He was imprisoned again after the war for acts of terrorism but was acquitted and returned to the military. Following Nasser's 1952 overthrow of King Farouk, Sadat served in several government posts under Nasser. Made vice-president (1969), he succeeded to the presidency on Nasser's death (1970). He ordered Soviet military advisers to leave Egypt and with Syria launched the Arab-Israeli War of 1973 (*q.v.*) against Israel. After the war Sadat engaged in a search for a negotiated peace in the Mideast which led eventually to his historic trip to Jerusalem (Nov., 1977) to address the Israeli Knesset. Peace talks between Israel and Egypt, in which the US took part, led to the Israeli-Egyptian Peace Treaty (Mar., 1979). The Arab world vigorously opposed the treaty and instituted a virtual boycott of Egypt. Opposition within Egypt to Sadat's rule culminated in Sadat's assassination (Oct. 6, 1981) by a group of disaffected Muslim fundamentalists within the army.

Sadducees Ancient Jewish sect. Rivals of the Pharisees from c200 BC, they held to a strict interpretation of the Torah and centered their worship about the Temple. They disappeared as a group after the destruction of the Temple (AD 70).

Sade, marquis de (Donatien Alphonse François, comte de) 1740–1814. French erotic writer. He was several times confined for his cruel sexual perversions, about which he wrote in his novels. The word "sadism" was derived from his name.

Sadi (Saadi) 1184–1291. Classical Persian poet. Mystical and lyric poet, he is known best for his poems *Bustan* (Orchard) and *Gulistan* (Rose Garden).

Sad Night, The *See* **Alvarado, Pedro de.**

Sadowa, Battle of *See* **Königgrätz, Battle of.**

Safavids Persian Muslim dynasty (1501–1736). It was founded by Ismail I, who conquered and subdued large areas of Persia, added several Iraqi territories, and proclaimed Shi'ite Islam as the state religion. Under the military leadership of Abbas I (ruled 1587–1629), the Safavids defeated Turkey, expanded Persia's territories, ended Portuguese encroachment, established trade with the West, and became an international power. The dynasty began a slow decline at the death of Abbas I and ended with the rule (1732–36) of Abbas III, who was overthrown by Nadir Shah.

Sagasta, Práxedes Mateo 1825–1903. Spanish statesman, several times prime minister. He granted autonomy to Cuba (1897) but was blamed for its loss in the Spanish-American War.

Sage, Margaret Olivia Slocum *See* **Sage, Russell.**

Sage, Russell 1816–1906. American financier. He amassed an enormous fortune from his holdings in railroads in association with J. Gould. His widow, Margaret Olivia Slocum Sage (1828–1918), made extensive charitable contributions and established the Russell Sage Foundation.

Saigo Takamori 1828–77. Japanese soldier and statesman. He supported the emperor in the Meiji Restoration but opposed the Westernization of Japan. He eventually led his samurai followers in the unsuccessful Satsuma Revolt (1877), in which he was killed.

saint For names of saints, see under individual names. For places, events, and biographical names beginning with **Saint or St.**, *see below.*

Saint Albans, battles of Battles of the English Wars of the Roses. The first (May 22, 1455), a Lancastrian defeat, resulted in the capture of King Henry VI by Richard, duke of York. The second (Feb. 17, 1461) was a Yorkist defeat, inflicted by Queen Margaret.

Saint Albans Raid Confederate attack from Canada (Oct. 19, 1864) on Saint Albans, Vermont, during the American Civil War. Some 25 Confederate raiders robbed three banks, killing one man, and escaped into Canada. Canada refused to return the raiders, but the money they stole was returned.

Saint Bartholomew's Day, Massacre of *See* **Massacre of Saint Bartholomew's Day.**

St. Clair, Arthur 1734–1818. Scottish-born American Revolutionary general and first governor of the Northwest Territory (1789–1802). He fought at Princeton and Trenton, and was exonerated from blame for the evacuation of Fort Ticonderoga (1778).

Saint Crispin, Knights of *See* **Knights of Saint Crispin.**

Sainte-Beuve, Charles Augustin 1804–69. French literary critic and historian, considered the greatest literary critic of his day. The extent and quality of his work marked a milestone in French intellectual life.

Saint-Exupéry, Antoine de 1900–1944. French airman and writer. A pioneer aviator, he celebrated flying in such books as *Night Flight* and *Wind, Sand and Stars.* His fable *The Little Prince* (1943) is widely read.

Saint-Gaudens, Augustus 1848–1907. American sculptor. The leading sculptor of his time, he is noted especially for his statue of Adm. D. Farragut and the memorial in Washington's Rock Creek Cemetery to Mrs. H. Adams.

Saint George's Day Revolt (Estonian Revolt of 1343) Uprising (1343–45) of Estonian peasants against their Danish overlords. Many Danish and German nobles were killed before the Teutonic Knights quelled the rebellion. Denmark sold Estonia to the order (1346), and they in turn placed it under the rule of the Livonian Knights.

Saint-Germain, Treaty of 1. Treaty (1570) between the Huguenots and Catholics during the French Wars of Religion (*q.v.*). It marked the end of the first phase of the conflict. 2. Treaty (Sept. 10, 1919) between the Allies and Austria which abolished the Austro-Hungarian monarchy and created the new Republic of Austria after WW I. The treaty limited Austria's armed forces and its ability to enter alliances.

St. John, Henry, viscount Bolingbroke 1678–1751. British statesman. A brilliant Tory leader during the reign of Queen Anne, he was compelled to flee to France (1715) after her death and his implication in a Jacobite plot. Pardoned but banned from politics, he became an influential writer.

Saint John Damascene *See* **John of Damascus, Saint.**

Saint-Just, Louis de 1767–94. French revolutionary leader. He was an ardent and pitiless ally of M. Robespierre during the Reign of Terror and was eventually guillotined with him.

Saint Laurent, Louis Stephen 1882–1973. Canadian statesman, Liberal party member, and prime minister (1948–57). A law professor at Laval University, he entered politics in 1941 and subsequently served in the Canadian House of Commons from 1942 until 1958. He served in various posts in government (and as a representative to the UN) before succeeding W. L. Mackenzie King as prime minister. His administration was marked by the entry of Newfoundland to the dominion, by expansion of the social security program, efforts to promote education and the arts, and by efforts to equalize revenues from the provinces.

St. Leger, Barry *See* **Oriskany, Battle of.**

Saint Peter's church Roman Catholic basilica at the Vatican, Rome. The world's largest church, it was built to replace an earlier (4th-cent.) structure. Work began in 1506, and the church was dedicated in 1626. Many Renaissance artists worked on it, among them D. Bramante, Raphael, and Michelangelo. Beneath the altar is the tomb of Saint Peter.

Saint-Saëns, Charles Camille 1835–1921. French composer. A piano and organ virtuoso, he composed symphonies, concerti, and tone poems, but is known best for his opera *Samson and Delilah.*

Saint-Simon, Claude Henri de Rouvro 1760–1825. French social thinker. A great-nephew of L. de Saint-Simon, he formulated an early version of scientific socialism, a precursor of positlvlsm.

Saint-Simon, Louis de Rouvro 1675–1755. French courtier and memoirist. An ardent aristocrat, his *Mémoires,* dealing with the court of King Louis XIV, are considered a major contribution to French literature.

Saionji, Kimmochi, Prince 1850–1940. Japanese statesman and prime minister (1906–08, 1911–12). He participated in the Meiji Restoration, traveled in the West, served in many government posts, and tried to moderate his country's turn toward militarism.

Sakakawea *See* **Sacajawea.**

Saladin 1137?–1193. Muslim sultan and military leader, noted for his chivalry in battle against the Crusaders, founder of the Ayyubid dynasty. An ardent Sunni Muslim, he participated in wars against the Fatimids in Egypt (1164–68), became vizier in Egypt (1169), and formally ended Fatimid control in Egypt (1171). He subsequently extended his control over Damascus, and began to subdue local rulers throughout Syria and Palestine. Saladin then mounted a major campaign against the Latin Kingdom of Jerusalem (*q.v.*) ruled by the Crusaders. He won a signal victory at the Battle of Hattin (July 4, 1187) in Palestine and went on to take Jerusalem (Oct. 2, 1187), thus effectively ending the Latin Kingdom of Jerusalem. This prompted the unsuccessful Third Crusade (*q.v.*), after which Saladin permitted Christians access to Jerusalem. Christian domains in the Holy Land, however, were reduced to a small fraction of their former size.

Salamis, Battle of Naval battle (480 BC) between the Greeks and the Persians during the Persian Wars (*q.v.*). It was fought in the straits between the island of Salamis and the Greek mainland. The Greeks under Themistocles won the battle, one of the most celebrated encounters of history. Themistocles lured the superior Persian navy (600 ships to over 360 Greek vessels) into the narrow straits, and thus made it impossible for the Persians to maneuver. The Greeks subsequently sank 200–300 Persian ships, losing only about 40.

Salazar, António de Oliveira 1889–1970. Dictator of Portugal (1932–68). As minister of finance (1926, 1928–32), Salazar initiated a number of economic recovery programs. Made premier (1932), he instituted a new constitution (1933) which turned Portugal into a corporate state and gave Salazar dictatorial powers. He also served as minister of war (1936–44) and minister of foreign affairs (1936–47). Although a number of Salazar's reform measures were successful, he was unable to substantially reduce poverty and illiteracy in Portugal. He is credited with making the country financially stable.

Salbai, Treaty of Treaty (May, 1782) between the British East India Company and the Marathas ending the first of the Maratha Wars. By its terms, similar to those of the earlier Treaty of Purandhar (*q.v.*), the British withdrew support of the Maratha pretender Ragoba but retained Salsette island.

Salem witch trials Series of witch trials (May–Oct., 1692) in Salem, Massachusetts. The trials were prompted by three young girls who, having heard tales of voodoo, claimed to be possessed by the devil. Their accusations led to hysteria and further accusations. By the time calm had been restored, 19 persons had been executed for witchcraft.

Sales, Saint Francis of *See* **Francis of Sales, Saint.**

Salian dynasty Line of German emperors that ruled the Holy Roman Empire from 1024 to 1125. During its tenure, the investiture controversy (*q.v.*) with the papacy broke out. *Its members included:* Conrad II 1024–39; Henry III 1039–56; Henry IV 1056–1106; Henry V 1106–25.

Salic law Rule of succession in some European royal houses forbidding females to succeed to family titles. Supposedly dating to Frankish times, it was invoked by the French, English, and Spanish monarchies.

Salinger, J(erome) D(avid) 1919– . American writer, known best for his novel *The Catcher in the Rye.*

Salisbury, John of *See* **John of Salisbury.**

Salisbury, Robert Arthur Talbot Gascoyne-Cecil, 3d marquess of 1830–1903. British statesman and prime minister (1885–86, 1886–92, 1895–1902) noted for his advancement of British imperial interests in foreign affairs. Salisbury acted as his own foreign secretary. The Boer War (*q.v.*) was fought during his third ministry.

Salisbury, Robert Cecil, 1st earl of 1563?–1612. English statesman. He succeeded his father, Lord Burghley, as the principal adviser to Queen Elizabeth I, and negotiated the agreement that allowed the Scottish king to succeed peacefully to the British throne as James I. Cecil also served as James's principal minister.

Salk, Jonas 1914– . US physician and microbiologist who developed the first polio vaccine. Born in New York City, he taught at the University of Michigan, where he worked on a vaccine for influenza, and at the University of Pittsburgh, where he developed his vaccine for polio (1954).

He founded the Salk Institute for Biomedical Sciences (1960) and in the early 1980s began researching a vaccine for the AIDS virus.

Sallust (Crispus, Gaius Sallustius) 86–c34 BC. Roman historian. He was expelled from the Senate (50 BC) for immorality and for his support of J. Caesar, and, as governor of Numidia, was accused of extortion. Among his best-known works are the *Catilinae Conivratio,* concerning the conspiracy of Catiline, another monograph, *Bellum Jugurthinum,* and his *Histories,* of which only fragments survive.

Salome Stepdaughter of Herod Antipas (*d.* after AD 40), who was tetrarch of Galilee and Perea. As a reward for dancing before Herod, she demanded the beheading of John the Baptist (*q.v.*). [Matthew 11,14]

Salomon, Haym 1740–1785. American Revolutionary financier and founder of the first Philadelphia synagogue. The principal financial backer of the fledgling American republic, he was impoverished by his loans to the government and to prominent individuals.

Salonica Campaign WW I Allied military expedition (1915–18), originally intended to aid Serbia, then under attack by Bulgaria. The Allied force of some 40,000 tried (Oct., 1915) to link up with the Serbians but was forced to retreat to Salonica in northeastern Greece. With Salonica as their base, the Allies increased forces there to some 250,000 and launched inconclusive attacks against Bulgarian and German forces. In 1917, the Allies forced the pro-German Greek king, Constantine I, to abdicate. The final Allied offensive from Salonica (from Sept., 1918) resulted in Bulgaria's surrender (Sept. 30), liberation of Serbia (Nov. 1), defeat of the Central Powers in Albania and Montenegro (by Nov. 9), and capture of Rumania (Nov. 10). The armistice halted further military action.

Salvation Army Christian and philanthropic organization founded (1878) in England by W. Booth. Organized with military ranks and uniforms, it emphasizes street-corner evangelism and seeks to help satisfy the spiritual and material needs of the poor.

Samanids Persian dynasty that ruled (c819–999) after the Arab Muslim conquest of Iran. The dynasty greatly advanced Persian literature, art, and architecture.

Samaritans Ancient Semitic people settled in Samaria, in the former kingdom of Israel, after its conquest by Assyria (c721 BC). Although they adopted Judaism and the Torah, they were shunned by the Jews returning to Judah after their Babylonian exile.

Samarkand One of the world's oldest cities, now in Uzbekistan. Taken by Alexander the Great (329 BC), it was destroyed (AD 1220) by G. Khan, but recovered and became (1370) capital of the empire of Tamerlane. Samarkand came under Soviet control in 1925.

Samnite War(s) Wars between the Romans and the Samnites, tribes of the mountain region of central and southern Italy. The Romans were ultimately victorious and thereby gained control of central and southern Italy. **1.** First ˜ (343–341 BC) proved indecisive. **2.** Second ˜ (326–304 BC). The Romans, defeated at the Battle of Caudine Forks (321), lost control of Campania (in southern Italy) and in 308, Rome was attacked by various tribes of central Italy. Rome succeeded in gaining the initiative, finally defeated the Samnites, and won firm control of Campania. **3.** Third ˜ (298–290 BC). The Samnites united with other tribes (including the Etruscans and Gauls) against the Romans. Defeated by the Romans at the Battle of Sentinum (295), the tribes were all eventually forced to accept peace.

Samos Greek island near Asia Minor. Colonized (11th cent. BC) by the Ionian Greeks, it became a commercial and cultural center. Pythagoras came from Samos. Under various rulers for a millennium, it reverted to Greece in 1913.

Samos, Aristarchus of *See* **Aristarchus of Samos.**

Samosata, Paul of *See* **Paul of Samosata.**

Samothrace (Samothraki) Greek island in the Aegean, site of the famous statue *Victory* (*Nike*) *of Samothrace,* which was found there in 1863. Samothrace had mainly religious importance in antiquity. It has been part of Greece since 1913.

Sampson, William Thomas *See* **Santiago, Battle of.**

Samsonov, Alexander *See* **Tannenberg, battles of.**

Samudra Gupta *d.* AD c380. Indian emperor (AD c330–c380) of the Gupta dynasty, successor to his father, Chandragupta I. He expanded Gupta control over much of northern India. A poet and musician as well as warrior and conqueror, he was considered a model of the ideal Hindu ruler.

Samuel Last of the judges of ancient Israel and first of the prophets after Moses. A legendary

Israelite hero, he established the Hebrew monarchy anointing first Saul and then David, according to the first Book of Samuel in the Bible.

samurai Former class of military elite in Japan. In the late 12th to 13th cents., samurai referred specifically to a member or horseman in the military band of Minamoto Yoritomo, the shogun who established the Bakufu at Kamakura. Later, as a more general term, "samurai" designated a professional soldier who followed the "way of the bow and arrow." Samurai generally relied on the bakufu and the shogun for leadership, but there were regional loyalties and tensions that made the relationship more complex. During the long, peaceful reign of the Tokugawa shoguns (17th–19th cents.), the samurai gradually moved into bureaucratic posts. After the Meiji Restoration (1868), the class was abolished, and discontented samurai led several unsuccessful revolts, notably the Satsuma Revolt.

Sancho III (~ the Great) c970–1035. King of Navarre (1000–35). He ultimately ruled a unified Spanish state that included Castile, León, Navarre, and Aragon. By his will the kingdom was divided at his death among his four sons.

Sancho the Great *See* **Sancho III.**

Sand, George (Dupin, Barrone Dudevant, Amandine Aurore Lucie) 1804–76. French writer. She wrote some 80 novels celebrating women's freedom and the joys of country life and was notorious for her liaisons with famous men of the day.

Sandburg, Carl 1878–1967. American author whose works are noted for their celebration of America and its people. He gained fame with the poem *Chicago.* His six-volume biography of Abraham Lincoln was awarded a Pulitzer Prize in history in 1940. Among his other volumes of poetry are *Smoke and Steel* and *Good Morning, America.* Sandburg's *Complete Poems* received a Pulitzer Prize in poetry in 1951.

Sand Creek Massacre (Chivington Massacre) Massacre of Cheyenne Indians (Nov. 29, 1864) peacefully encamped on the Sand Creek near Fort Lyon, in Colorado. Some 1,000 raiders led by Col. John Chivington ignored the white flag raised by Cheyenne chief Black Kettle and murdered hundreds. The massacre led to fierce conflict with the Plains Indians in the following years.

Sandino, Augusto 1895–1934. Nicaraguan guerrilla leader. He succeeded in avoiding capture (1927–33) by US marines then occupying Nicaragua, but was murdered during peace negotiations by A. Somoza's troops.

Sandwich, Edward Montagu, 1st earl of 1625–72. English admiral. He supported Parliament in the English Civil Wars but escorted King Charles II from Holland back to England at the Restoration. Ennobled by Charles, he later died in battle against the Dutch.

Sandwich, John Montagu, 4th earl of 1718–92. British politician and three-time British lord of the admiralty (1748, 1763, 1771–82). The Sandwich Islands and the sandwich were named after him. He is said to have devised the latter to eat without having to leave the gaming table.

Sandys, Sir Edwin 1561–1629. English Parliamentarian and colonizer. A prominent opponent of absolute monarchy, he advanced constitutional ideas that later contributed to the overthrow of King Charles I. He was a member of both the Virginia Company and the British East India Company.

San Francisco Conference International conference of 50 nations convened in San Francisco (Apr. 25, 1945) to establish a new international organization following WW II. The conference concluded with the signing of the United Nations Charter (June 26, 1945).

Sanger, Margaret 1879–1976 US social activist and pioneer birth-control advocate. One of 11 children, she eventually became a visiting nurse for the urban poor in New York City. After joining the Socialist Party, she began to advocate birth control openly, especially among the poor, writing and speaking publicly from 1912. She published the *Women Rebel,* a feminist newspaper, and *Family Limitation,* a pamphlet with explicit information on contraceptives. She then set up a birth-control clinic in Brooklyn (1915) and founded the American Birth Control League (1921), which later became Planned Parenthood.

Sanhedrin Ancient Jewish council of elders in Jerusalem which functioned up to the destruction of the Temple (AD 70). According to the Mishna it had academic functions, but according to the Gospels and Flavius Josephus, it also possessed judicial functions, as in the trial of Jesus.

San Ildefonso, Treaty of 1. Treaty (1796) between France and Spain concluded at San Ildefonso, Spain. By its terms the two countries became formally allied against Britain in the French Revolutionary Wars. 2. Secret treaty concluded (1800) between Spain and Napoleon

I, confirmed by later treaties of 1801 and 1802. By its terms Spain retroceded Louisiana to France in return for the newly created kingdom of Etruria in Italy. Napoleon subsequently sold Louisiana to the US against the express terms of this treaty.

San Jacinto, Battle of Battle (Apr. 21, 1836) of the Texas War for Independence, fought at the San Jacinto River near present-day Houston. Some 800 Texans under S. Houston defeated 1,500 Mexicans under Gen. A. de Santa Anna, thereby ensuring Texas' independence.

San Juan Boundary Dispute Dispute between the US and Great Britain over the northwest boundary between the US and British Columbia. Because of the vague wording of the Oregon Treaty of 1846, both Britain and the US claimed the San Juan Islands in the Gulf of Georgia, southeast of Vancouver. Armed conflict (1859) was avoided when both nations decided on joint occupation. By the Treaty of Washington (1871), German emperor Wilhelm I was chosen as arbitrator and awarded the lands to the US (1872).

San Juan Hill, Battle of US victory over the Spanish (July 1, 1898) at San Juan Hill, in Cuba, during the Spanish-American War. Part of the larger Battle of Santiago (*q.v.*), it is celebrated for the part played in it by T. Roosevelt and the Rough Riders (*qq.v.*).

San Marino (Most Serene Republic of ˜) Independent republic located in central Italy. The population is 23,000 and the capital is San Marino. Founded in the 4th cent., San Marino is said to be the oldest republic in Europe and is the smallest in the world. Its independence was recognized (1631) by the pope, and it secured a treaty of friendship with Italy in 1862 (revised in 1971). Twelve years of left-wing rule (1945–57) ended in a bloodless revolution that brought the Christian Democrat party to power. Communists regained control with a left-wing coalition government following elections in 1978, remaining in power until 1986 when they were forced into a coalition with the Christian Democrats. The republic joined the council of Europe in 1988 and the UN in 1992.

San Martín, José de 1778–1850. South American revolutionary leader. He played a major part in the liberation of Argentina, Peru, and Chile from Spanish rule. He led an army across the Andes to defeat the Spanish in Chile (1817) and

deferred to S. Bolívar (1822), who then became the leader of the South American independence movement.

Sannazaro, Jacopo 1458–1530. Italian poet and humanist. He served as court poet in Naples and is known best for his idyll in prose and verse *Arcadia*.

San Remo, Conferenee of *See* Conference of San Remo.

sans-culotte French term meaning "without knee breeches," applied to the more radical supporters of the French Revolution, especially the lower classes. It derived from the long trousers adopted by the lower classes to replace knee breeches, considered aristocratic. (*See also* Hébert, Jacques René.)

Sanskrit Sacred language of the Hindu religion. Long used by Indian religious scholars of the uppermost caste group of Brahmans, it developed from the earlier Vedic language. Though technically a dead language, it continues to be used in scholarly and literary fields. The study of Sanskrit in the 18th cent. led to important archaeological discoveries and also to the development of philology as a science.

San Stefano, Treaty of Treaty (Mar. 3, 1878) between Russia and the Ottoman Turks ending the Russo-Turkish War of 1877–78. The defeated Turks agreed to pay a large indemnity; to recognize the independence of Rumania, Serbia, and Montenegro; to create an autonomous Bulgaria; and to cede large areas to Russia. This treaty was subsequently altered by the Congress of Berlin (1878).

Santa Anna, Antonio López de 1794–1876. Mexican general and statesman. He fought with A. de Iturbide in securing Mexican independence (1821) but helped to overthrow Iturbide in 1823. He followed a policy of supporting, then helping to overthrow, subsequent leaders. His victory over the Spanish at Tampico (Sept., 1829) gave him the title "Hero of Tampico" and helped him gain the presidency (1833). His ruthless treatment of Texans at the Alamo and Goliad aided the Texan independence movement and contributed to Santa Anna's defeat by S. Houston at San Jacinto (*q.v.*) and the loss of Texas. Forced from office (1836), Santa Anna returned to power (1839–44, 1846–47) but was again removed from office after his defeats in the Mexican War (*q.v.*). He returned to power once more in 1853 but was exiled two years later.

Santa Cruz, Andrés 1792–1865. Bolivian military leader and president (1829–39). The son of a Spanish official and a mother who was of Incan descent, Santa Cruz at first served in the royalist army during the wars of independence from Spain. In 1820 though, he joined the revolutionaries, distinguishing himself in battle and eventually earning him the presidency of Bolivia (1829). A staunch conservative, he took office at a time when Bolivia was awash in political and economic chaos, but soon restored order by establishing a harsh dictatorship. Santa Cruz fostered economic progress, strengthened the army, reorganized national finances and introduced new legal codes, oversaw construction of roads, built schools and colleges, and ordered Bolivia's first census and the mapping of the country. Perhaps his most ambitious project was a short-lived confederation with Peru (1936–39), of which he became leader. Perceiving the confederation as a threat, Chile declared war in 1836 and, joined by Argentina the next year, succeeding in breaking up the union by victory at the Battle of Yungay (1839). Santa Cruz was deposed soon after as Bolivian president, and was later exiled to Europe (1843).

Santa Fe Trail Wagon route, some 780 miles long, from Independence, Missouri, to Santa Fe, New Mexico. The trail was a major path of westward migration from the 1820s to 1880, when Santa Fe was connected with the transcontinental rail network.

Santander, Francisco de Paula 1792–1840. Colombian revolutionist and statesman. Associated with S. Bolívar, he governed Great Colombia as vice-president during Bolívar's absences from 1821 to 1828. After Bolívar's death, he was president of New Granada (1833–37).

Santa Sophia *See* **Hagia, Sophia.**

Santayana, George 1863–1952. Spanish-born American philosopher and writer, known best for his four-volume work *The Life of Reason.*

Santiago, Battle of Battle (July 1–3, 1898) of the Spanish-American War, at Santiago de Cuba. In May, 1898, a Spanish fleet under Admiral Pascual Cervera y Topete (1839–1909) was blockaded in the harbor of Santiago de Cuba by a US fleet under Admiral William Thomas Sampson (1840–1902). On July 1, US ground forces attacked the city's defenses, notably in the Battle of San Juan Hill (*q.v.*). On July 3, the Spanish fleet attempted to leave the harbor. In Sampson's absence, Commodore W. Schley engaged and

destroyed the Spanish squadron, suffering one American dead to Spanish losses of some 600. Santiago de Cuba formally surrendered on July 17. Later a controversy arose as to which US commander achieved the American victory— Schley, who opened the naval engagement, or Sampson, commander of the operation.

Santo Domingo Former name for the Dominican Republic (*q.v.*).

Sapir, Edward 1884–1939. Polish-born American linguist and anthropologist. He made major contributions to the study and classification of North American Indian languages.

Sapor *See* **Shapur.**

Sappho *fl.* early 6th cent. BC. Ancient Greek lyric poet of Lesbos. Her lyrics were considered masterly by the ancients, but only a few, mostly fragments, have survived.

Saracens Name applied in the Middle Ages to the Muslim enemies of Christendom. Originally referring to northern Arabian raiders, it eventually was applied to all Muslims, whether Arabs, Moors, or Turks.

Saracoglu, Sukru 1887–1953. Turkish statesman and premier (1942–46). An associate of K. Atatürk in the modernization of Turkey, he served as premier and managed to keep Turkey uninvolved in WW II.

Saratoga, First Battle of *See* **Freeman's Farm, Battle of.**

Saratoga Campaign American military campaign (Sept.–Oct., 1777) during the American Revolution, near Saratoga, New York. The campaign is considered the turning point of the war. On Sept. 19, 1777, some 6,000 British troops under Gen. J. Burgoyne failed to break through the American defense lines of H. Gates, D. Morgan, and B. Arnold in the Battle of Freeman's Farm (*q.v.*). This was followed by a decisive American victory over the British (Oct. 7) in the Battle of Bemis Heights. The Americans subsequently surrounded the British and forced Burgoyne's surrender (Oct. 17). This first major American victory heartened the discouraged patriots, encouraged France to aid the American war effort, and ended British plans to isolate the northern colonies from the rest of America.

Sarbinowo, Battle of (˜ Zorndorf) Prussian victory over Russia (Aug. 25, 1758) in the Seven Years' War. Prussian king Frederick II defeated an invading Russian army and prevented its advance into Brandenburg.

Sardanapalus Assyrian king identified by some, probably mistakenly, with Ashurbanipal. Sardanapalus burned his palace, killing himself and his court, when it appeared Nineveh would be taken.

Sardinia, kingdom of European kingdom formed (1720) for Duke Victor Amadeus II of Savoy after Sicily passed to Austrian control. The kingdom included Sardinia, Savoy, Piedmont, and Nice, and in the 18th and 19th cents. it grew to include other territories. It became the center of the movement to unify Italy in the 19th cent. and was given control of territories conquered by Garibaldi (*q.v.*) in 1860. In 1861, Sardinian king Victor Emmanuel II became king of Italy, and the House of Savoy became the ruling house of Italy.

Sardis Ancient city located near modern Izmir Turkey. As the capital of Lydia, it was the political center of the area and after falling to the Persians (546), became the western terminus for the Persian royal road. Sardis fell to the Ionian Greeks (498 BC) and by inheritance to the Romans (133 BC). Sardis was finally destroyed by Tamerlane (1402).

Sardou, Victorien 1831–1908. French playwright. Immensely popular in his day, he wrote some 70 plays for famous actors and actresses of the time. For S. Bernhardt he wrote the play *La Tosca* (1887), which formed the basis for the opera by G. Puccini.

Sargent, John Singer 1856–1925. American painter. Most of his work was done in London, where he became the most fashionable portrait painter of the day. He also was noted for his murals and landscapes.

Sargon *d.* 705 BC. Ancient Assyrian king (721–705), successor to Tiglath-pileser III. He was also known as Sargon II. He consolidated the Assyrian Empire, defeating and resettling conquered weaker peoples. He conquered Babylon and Samaria and destroyed the northern kingdom of Israel (c721 BC).

Sargon (Sharrukin) *fl.* c2800? BC. Ancient Mesopotamian ruler. From Akkad, he defeated Sumer and established the first great Semitic empire. His empire of Akkad (*q.v.*) included the area later ruled by Babylonia.

Sarmatia Ancient territory between the Vistula and the Caspian Sea inhabited (3d cent. BC–3d cent. AD) by the Sarmatians. An ancient Indo-Iranian nomadic people related to the Scythians, they invaded Roman territory and subdued many neighboring tribes. Eventually they were defeated and settled within the empire (4th cent. AD).

Sarmiento, Domingo Faustino 1811–88. Argentine educator, writer, and first civilian president of Argentina (1868–74). He became known as a writer and educator in exile until the overthrow of J. de Rosas. His presidency was marked by an expansion of democracy and education.

Sarmiento, Félix Rubén García *See* **Darío, Rubén.**

Sarnoff, David 1891–1971. Russian-born American pioneer in the development of commercial radio and television. Beginning as a wireless telegraph operator, he became famous for his reception of wireless signals from the stricken liner *Titanic* (1912). He later was instrumental in forming both the Radio Corporation of America (RCA) and the National Broadcasting Company (NBC).

Saroyan, William 1908–1981. American writer, noted for his fresh, original novels, plays, and stories celebrating life in America. His play *The Time of Your Life* was awarded the Pulitzer Prize for Drama in 1940, but Saroyan declined the honor.

Sarpi, Paolo (Polano, Pietro Soave) 1552–1623. Venetian theologian and historian. In a dispute between Venice and Pope Paul V over papal jurisdiction, he defended the right of the state to ecclesiastical control. He wrote a history of the Council of Trent, attacking it as an exercise of papal absolutism.

Sarto, Andrea del 1486–1530. Florentine painter during the Renaissance. Noted for his craftmanship, he influenced Florentine painting during the High Renaissance. He painted chiefly religious subjects, including *Madonna in Glory* and *Madonna of the Harpies.*

Sarto, Giuseppe *See* **Pius X.**

Sartre, Jean Paul 1905–1980. French philosopher and writer. A major exponent of existentialism, he believed that man is "condemned" to freedom and must rely on his own sense of values and will in life. He wrote the existential treatise *Being and Nothingness* (1943), and such noted works as the play *No Exit* (1944) and the novel *Nausea* (1938).

Sasbach and Altenheim, Battles of Engagements in the Second Dutch War, fought near the Rhine at Sasbach (July 27, 1675) and Altenheim (Aug. 1, 1675). A French army of some 22,000 initially forced a 20,000-man Austrian force into an untenable position at Sasbach, but the French commander, Marshal H. Turenne, was killed. The Austrians subsequently forced the French to retreat, defeated them at Altenheim (Aug. 1), and forced them to withdraw across the Rhine.

Saskatchewan Province of western Canada. Agents of the Hudson's Bay Company first explored (1690) then settled the area (1774) and controlled it until 1869, when it became part of Canada's Northwest Territories. Extension of the railroad (1882) into Saskatchewan brought more settlers, and the last Indian and Métis rebellion was put down in 1885. Saskatchewan became a province in 1905.

Sassanidae (Sassanids) (Sassanians) Last ancient Persian dynasty to rule before the Arab conquest of Persia (651). The dynasty was founded (AD 226) by Ardashir I. The Sassanidae promoted a revival of native Persian arts and letters and made Zoroastrianism the state religion. The last Sassanidae ruler died in exile in 651.

Sassanids *See* **Sassanidae.**

Satie, Erik 1866–1925. French composer and leader of the avant-garde. His spare, satirical musical style, a reaction to romanticism, had considerable influence on the development of 20th-cent. music.

Sato, Eisaku 1901–75. Japanese prime minister (1964–72). He held important government posts during Japan's post-war period. As prime minister, he signed a treaty with the US reestablishing Japan's control over Okinawa. He was awarded the Nobel Peace Prize in 1974.

satrap Name given provincial governors of the ancient Persian Empire. In general, a satrap administered the province, collected taxes, and was the supreme judge.

Satsuma Revolt *See* **Saigo Takamori.**

Saud 1902–69. Saudi Arabian king (1953–64), successor to his father, Ibn Saud. Forced to yield some of his powers to an executive council headed by his brother Faisal (1958), he was deposed by Faisal (1964) and died in exile.

Saudi Arabia (Kingdom of Saudi Arabia) Muslim monarchy (pop. 16,758,000) occupying most of the Arabian peninsula in the Middle East. Its capital is Riyadh. The Muslim holy cities of Mecca and Medina are located in Saudia Arabia, birthplace of Islam. The government remains an absolute monarchy and the society adheres to Islamic traditions. Saudi Arabia, long a US ally, is today one of the world's largest oil-producing nations. Saudi Arabia became a key staging area for the US-led, multi-national force that liberated Kuwait during the Persian Gulf War. (For early history of the region, *see* Caliphate, Empire of.) Key dates in Saudi history include:

18TH CENT. Wahhabi movement, Islamic reform movement, supported by Saud family and Bedouin tribes; they united a Saudi kingdom in Arabia.

c1800 First Saudi reached its height.

1811–18 Wahhabi movement crushed by Egypt; Saud family continued rule in Arabian interior.

1887 Rashid dynasty, rivals of Saudis, captured Riyadh and went on to destroy the Saudi kingdom.

FROM 1902 Ibn Saud revived the Wahhabi movement; seized city of Riyadh; began expanding domains in Arabian peninsula.

1912 Ibn Saud established first Wahhabi colony (*Ikhwan*) in his domains; eventually set up some 100 more colonies to secure control over conquered territories and to spread Wahhabi message of Islamic reform.

1914–18 World War I; Ottoman Empire, which controlled the Mideast and which sided with the Central Powers, collapsed and was broken up after the war.

1915 British signed friendship treaty with Ibn Saud, but later supported Husein ibn-Ali's claim to rule Hejaz.

1916 Husein ibn-Ali, amir of Mecca, rebelled against Ottoman Turkish overlords during World War I; proclaimed himself king of Arabia (1917).

1922 Wahhabi leader Ibn Saud now in firm control of the Nejd.

1924 Husein defeated by Wahhabi leader Ibn Saud; Saud completed conquest of the Hejaz by 1925.

1926 Ibn Saud proclaimed king of the Hejaz and Nejd.

1932 Kingdom of Saudi Arabia formed from Ibn Saud's conquests in Nejd and Hejaz.

1932–53 Ibn Saud reigned as king of Saudi Arabia.

1936 Oil discovered; production began in 1938.

1939–45 World War II; Saudi Arabia remained neutral until Feb. 1945, when it belatedly declared war on Axis.

1945 Saudis joined UN and Arab League.

1946 Large-scale oil exploitation begun by American consortium (Aramco); using revenues, Ibn Saud made massive internal improvements.

1948 Saudi Arabia condemned creation of Israel.

1948–49 First Arab-Israeli War.

1951 New royalty agreement with Aramco, Saudi oil consortium; Saudis receive 50% of net earnings.

1953–64 King Saud reigned, following death of Ibn Saud.

1960 Saudi Arabia became founding member of OPEC; later became leading force in the oil cartel.

1962 Saudis supported royalist forces against victorious republicans during Yemen civil war.

1962 Slavery formally abolished; other reforms enacted.

1964–75 King Faisal reigned after deposing his brother, Saud.

1967 Third Arab-Israeli War.

1973 Fourth Arab-Israeli War (Oct.); Israelis repulsed surpise attack and captured additional territory, including east bank of Suez.

1973 Arab oil embargo established following 1973 war; Saudis led initial OPEC effort to cut off oil to US and other nations to force Israeli withdrawal from occupied territories; Saudis subsequently reaped huge profits as OPEC imposed sharp oil price increases on the world market during the 1970s.

1974 Saudis, demanding participation in Aramco, got 60% ownership of company.

1975 Faisal assassinated by nephew (Mar. 25).

1975–82 King Khalid, brother of Faisal, reigned.

1979 Government broke relations with Egypt to protest Egyptian-Israeli treaty; restored relations in 1987.

1979 Muslim extremists seized the sacred Grand Mosque in Mecca; held it against government troops (Nov. 20–Dec. 4).

1980 Saudi takeover of Aramco completed.

1980 Iran-Iraq war broke out; Saudis aided Iraqis; war heighten Saudi concerns about defense.

1981 US announced sale of Advance Warning and Command Systems (AWAC) planes to Saudi Arabia; deal linked to Saudi agreement to maintain levels of oil production.

1982– Fahd Bin Abdul-Aziz reigned as king after Khalid died (June 13, 1982).

1982 King Fahd presented eight-point "Fahd Plan" for Mideast peace; included recognition of Israel.

1984–89 Government concluded billion-dollar deals for major arms purchases.

1985 Saudis and other OPEC members abandoned production quotas in face of rising oil supplies in world market; adopted "fair share" system in hopes of regaining lost market share.

1985 Terrorists from Iran exploded two bombs in Riyadh (May).

1987 Iranian pilgrims to Mecca fought with Saudi police; 402 killed.

1989 Nonaggression pact signed with Iraq (Mar.).

1990 Iranian terrorists suspected in assassination of three Saudi diplomats in Thailand (Feb.).

1990 Panic-strickened pilgrims at Mecca stampeded a pedestrian tunnel (July), killing 1,426.

1990 Iraq invaded Kuwait (Aug.); susequently built up forces along border with Saudi Arabia; Saudis condemned invasion and provided asylum for Kuwaitis; mobilized entire 67,000-man army.

1990 First US troops sent to Saudi Arabia as part of Operation Desert Shield (Aug. 7), following formal request by Saudis.

1990 Government announced plan to double size of army; massive purchase of US arms planned.

1991 Persian Gulf War; US-led Operation Desert Storm crushed Iraqi military power.

1991 Oil spilled into Persian Gulf by Iraqis occupying Kuwait created enormous ecological damage and threatened Saudi desalinization plants.

1991 Fighting ended in Persian Gulf War by ceasefire (Feb.).

1991 Allied troops began withdrawing from Saudi Arabia (Mar.).

1991 Government granted asylum to 50,000 Iraqi refugees following failed revolt against Iraqi president S. Hussein.

1992 King Faud issued "Basic System of Government" (Mar.), political reforms that decentralized political power and protected some individual rights; established consultative council.

1992 Saudi banker and 60% owner of BCCI, Sheik Khalidbin Mahfouz, indicted in New York on charges of fraud (July) relating to the bank's illegal operations.

Sauk Indians *See* **Sac and Fox Indians.**

Saul First king (11th cent.?) of the ancient Israelites. In the Bible, he was noted for his prowess in battle and for his jealousy of his successor, David, whom he tried to destroy. He committed suicide to escape capture by the Philistines. [1 Samuel 10:31]

Saussure, Ferdinand de 1857–1913. Swiss Sanskrit scholar and linguistic pioneer. His *Course in General Linguistics* is considered one of the foundations of modern linguistics.

Savelli, Cencio *See* **Honorius III.**

Savigny, Friedrich Karl von 1779–1861. German jurist and legal historian. He produced monumental studies of Roman and medieval law and influenced the study of legal history.

Savonarola, Girolamo 1452–98. Italian Dominican religious reformer. He enthralled Florence with his sermons, noted for their moral rigor. He challenged papal authority and later was repudiated and executed by the Florentines.

Savoy, House of European royal dynasty. Founded in the 11th cent. by Humbert I, the White-Handed, it first dominated the French-Swiss-Italian Alpine region, then spread to Piedmont. Made a ducal family of the Holy Roman Empire (1416), it eventually came to rule vast areas of France, Switzerland, and Italy. After receiving the kingdom of Sardinia (1720), their support of Italian unification led to the creation (1861) of the kingdom of Italy, with the house of Savoy as its royal family. The House of Savoy remained the ruling house of Italy until 1946, when a republic was established.

Savoy, Louise of *See* **Louise of Savoy.**

Savoy, Prince Eugene of *See* **Eugene of Savoy, Prince.**

Savoy Conference English ecclesiastical conference (1661) held at the Savoy Palace in London after the Restoration. Twelve bishops of the Church of England and twelve Presbyterians failed to reach agreement on worship and a revision of the Book of Common Prayer.

Saxe, Maurice, comte de 1696–1750. French general and marshal of France. An illegitimate son of the elector of Saxony, he rose to supreme command in the War of the Austrian Succes-

sion. He led the French victory at Fontenoy (1745).

Saxe-Weimar Former duchy in Thuringia, central Germany. United with Eisenach (1741) to form Saxe-Weimar-Eisenach, it became notable under Duke Charles Augustus for its prosperity and its position as a center of the arts. Its capital, Weimar, became an intellectual capital of Europe.

Saxo Grammaticus *fl.* 1188–1201. Danish medieval chronicler. He wrote a history of early Denmark, *Gesta Danorum,* partly legendary, partly factual. Surviving parts of it inspired W. Shakespeare's *Hamlet* as well as the work of Danish Romantic poets.

Saxons Germanic peoples believed to have originated in the area of the Baltic coast that is now Schleswig and the Elbe Valley. First mentioned by Ptolemy (2d cent. AD), their influence grew as the Roman Empire declined. The Saxons conducted numerous raids of piracy along the coasts of northern Germany, Gaul, and Britain, and, with the Angles, many Saxons settled in Britain (5th cent., *see* Anglo-Saxons). On the continent, their constant warfare against the Franks ended with their defeat (9th cent.) and their forced conversion to Christianity by Charlemagne.

Saxony Historic region of northwest Germany once occupied by the Saxons, a Germanic tribe. The Saxons were in firm control of the region by the 5th–6th cents., and in the 5th cent. many of them migrated to Britain. Saxony was conquered by Charlemagne (8th cent.) and incorporated into Frankish domains. It became part of the East Frankish (German) kingdom after 843. Saxony soon became the most powerful of the duchies that emerged during the breakup of the East Frankish kingdom. In 962 the Holy Roman Empire was formed under the leadership of the Saxon duke, Otto (Holy Roman Emperor Otto I).

Saxony, duchy of Medieval German duchy, located in what is now eastern Germany, founded by the early 10th cent. Duke Henry I of Saxony was elected German emperor (919), and his line ruled the Holy Roman Empire until 1024. In 1180, Saxony was seized from Henry the Lion by Frederick Barbarossa and was divided. The ducal title passed to one of the fiefs thus created, and its holder became an elector of the Holy Roman Empire (13th cent.).

Saxony, Electoral Historic territory established along with the title "elector" (13th cent.) after the division (1180) of the duchy of Saxony. Electoral Saxony took part in the Thirty Years' War, first supporting and then opposing the Holy Roman Empire. At the war's end, Saxony emerged as one of the strongest duchies in Germany. In 1697, elector Augustus II became king of Poland. His death led to the War of the Polish Succession (1733–38), after which his son reigned as Polish king Augustus III. During this time Saxony reached its intellectual and cultural golden age, but after the Seven Years' War it began a period of decline. In 1806, it was conquered by Napoleon and made a kingdom.

Saxony, kingdom of Kingdom established (1806) by Napoleon after his conquest of Electoral Saxony. Napoleon raised the electorate to a kingdom and established Frederick Augustus I as its ruler. Saxony's alliance with France contributed to its growth in size and power until Napoleon's downfall. The Congress of Vienna forced Saxony to cede much land to Prussia. In 1830, Saxony was torn by riots, which led to the granting of a constitution the following year. To head off Prussian domination, Saxony sided unsuccessfully with Austria during the Austro-Prussian War and entered the German Confederation in 1866. It became part of the German Empire (1871) and after WW I became a state within the Weimar Republic. Saxony was an important industrial center and became part of East Germany after WW II.

Saxony-Anhalt Former state in Germany consisting principally of the historical German states of Saxony and Anhalt. It was abolished in 1952.

Sayyid dynasty Dynasty that ruled the Delhi region in India from 1414 to 1451. The four sultans of the dynasty were barely able to maintain themselves and eventually gave way to the Lodi dynasty.

Scaevola, Caius Mucius 6th cent.? BC. Legendary Roman hero. Condemned for trying to assassinate Lars Porsena during his siege of Rome (after 509 BC), he so impressed Porsena by thrusting his hand into flame without flinching that he was ordered released and the siege was lifted.

Scaevola, Quintus Mucius *d.* 82 BC. Ancient Roman jurist. He served as tribune (106 BC) and as consul (95 BC) and introduced a law limiting Roman citizenship and the right to vote. This contributed to the outbreak of the Social War (*q.v.*).

Scala, Can Franceseo della (˜, Cane Grande della) 1291–1329. Medieval Italian lord of Verona and member of the prominent Veronese Ghibelline family. He was appointed the imperial vicar of Verona by Holy Roman Emperor Henry VII. He was a patron of the arts, notably of Dante during his exile from Florence.

scalawags American term applied to southern Republicans who supported the federal program of Reconstruction after the US Civil War. A Reconstruction Republican from the North was known as a carpetbagger.

Scaliger, Joseph Justus 1540–1609. Italian-French Renaissance classical scholar. Son of J. C. Scaliger, he produced prodigious linguistic studies and critical editions of the classics. He founded the modern science of chronology by his comparative study of the calendar, *De Emendatione Temporum.*

Scaliger, Julius Caesar 1484–1558. Italian-born French scholar, physician, and philologist, father of J. J. Scaliger. He produced commentaries on the classics and an early study of Latin grammar as well as polemics against such scholars as Erasmus.

Scanderbeg c1404–68. Albanian national hero. Born an Albanian prince, he became a Turkish hostage in childhood and was raised and educated as a Muslim by Sultan Murad II. When the Turks attacked Albania, he escaped (1443) and formed an alliance of Albanian princes to resist the Turks. As commander of Albanian forces, he repulsed 13 Turkish attacks between 1444 and 1466. Soon after his death, the alliance collapsed and Albania fell to the Turks.

Scandinavia Region of northern Europe consisting primarily of Denmark, Norway, and Sweden. The term is usually extended to include neighboring Finland and also Iceland.

Scannabechi, Lamberto *See* **Honorius II.**

Scarlatti, Alessandro 1658/59–1725. Italian composer. Father of D. Scarlatti, he was important in the development of classical harmony and of the opera form. He wrote more than 100 operas, of which the best known is *Il Tigrane.*

Scarlatti, Giuseppe Domenico 1685–1757. Italian composer and virtuoso, son of A. Scarlatti. He is noted for his more than 500 harpsichord sonatas which expanded the sonata form. He composed many while court musician in Madrid.

Scarron, Paul 1610?–60. French writer. He contributed to the development of the drama and the comic burlesque but is remembered for his novel *Le Roman Comique.*

Scaurus, Marcus Aemilius c162–c89 BC. Ancient Roman statesman. According to Cicero, he was a powerful conservative leader in the Roman Senate. He conducted successful Alpine campaigns and controlled the grain supply at Ostia. His daughter married Pompey.

Schacht, Hjalmar Horace Greeley 1877–1970. German financial expert. As president of the Reichsbank (1923–30, 1933–39) he helped halt the ruinous inflation in the 1920s, and as minister of economy (1934–37) he achieved economic stabilization and growth in the early years of Nazi Germany.

Schaff, Philip 1819–93. Swiss-born American Protestant theologian and church historian. He was noted for his studies of ecclesiastical history, *History of the Christian Church* and *The Creeds of Christendom.*

Scharnhorst, Gerhard von 1755–1813. Prussian general. In 1807, he began the reorganization of the Prussian army, transforming it from a mercenary force into a citizen army. He introduced the system by which soldiers were trained and served for a short period, then were replaced by new trainees.

Scheidemann, Philipp 1865–1939. German Social Democratic leader. After WW I and the flight of the kaiser, he proclaimed the Weimar Republic and became its first chancellor (1918). He resigned (1919) in protest against the Treaty of Versailles.

Schelling, Friedrich Wilhelm Joseph von 1775–1854. German philosopher. He contributed to the development of the philosophical movement known as idealism.

Schiller, Friedrich von 1759–1805. German poet and dramatist, one of the leading literary figures of his day. His plays include *The Robbers* and *William Tell.* Schiller's poem *Ode to Joy* was used by L. van Beethoven in the last movement of his Ninth Symphony.

Schirra, Walter Marty, Jr. 1923–   . US astronaut, one of the seven original astronauts. As commander of Gemini 6 he achieved (Dec. 15, 1965) the first successful space rendezvous by linking his craft with Gemini 7. He also commanded the flight (Oct. 11–12, 1968) of Apollo 7.

Schism 1. Schism of 1054. Division of the Christian church into the Roman Catholic (Western) church and the Orthodox Eastern church. Doctrinal and other disputes began separating the two churches (as early as the 5th cent.) and included the question of the filioque (*q.v.*) and the controversy over Photius (*q.v.*). Finally, in 1054, a jurisdictional dispute prompted Pope Leo IX to excommunicate the Patriarch of Constantinople, Michael Cerularius. The patriarch in turn excommunicated the pope and from that point the two churches were considered to be officially separated. 2. Great Schism. Division in the Roman Catholic church (1378–1417) in which two rival lines of popes emerged. Pope Gregory XI died (1378) soon after ending the Babylonian Captivity (*q.v.*) and restoring the papacy to Rome. The Romans demanded election of an Italian pope and Pope Urban VI was elected (1378). However, Urban, by his actions, quickly aroused opposition, and within a few months the cardinals declared his election void. They then elected Clement VII as pope. Urban forced Clement out of Rome and Clement subsequently took up residence at Avignon, France. To end the schism, the Council of Pisa was convened (1409) and declared against the then-reigning popes in Rome and France. In 1410 the council installed John XXIII as pope. John succeeded in winning widespread support and then called the Council of Constance (1414). Gregory XII in Rome resigned and the council deposed both John XXIII and Benedict XIII, then reigning in France. Pope Martin V was elected and the schism was ended.

Schleicher, Kurt von 1882–1934. German general and last chancellor (1932–33) of the Weimar Republic. In an attempt to prevent the rise of A. Hitler, he sought unsuccessfully to receive emergency powers from President P. von Hindenburg. Schleicher left office Jan. 1933, and Hindenburg made Hitler chancellor soon after.

Schleiermacher, Friedrich Ernst Daniel 1768–1834. German Protestant theologian. He opposed both philosophical rationalism and religious dogma. His writings were a major influence in the development of Protestant theology.

Schlesinger, Arthur Meier 1888–1965. American historian, a pioneer in the study of both social and urban history in America. He emphasized the importance of economics in his best-known work, *The Colonial Merchants and the American Revolution.* He edited the notable 13-volume *A History of American Life.*

Schlesinger, Arthur Meier, Jr. 1917– . American historian. His extensive writings on American history include *Age of Jackson* (Pulitzer Prize, 1946), *The Age of Roosevelt, A Thousand Days* (Pulitzer Prize, 1966), and *The Imperial Presidency.* He was elected president of the American Institute of Arts and Letters (1981).

Schleswig-Holstein Historic region and modern German state located in northwest Germany. Denmark gained control of Schleswig in the 12th cent. and Holstein (in fief to the Holy Roman Empire) in the 14th cent. After the collapse of the Holy Roman Empire (early 19th cent.), the German Confederation gained nominal suzerainty over Holstein, while Denmark retained full sovereignty over Schleswig. The rise of nationalism in Denmark and the German states soon created conflict over Schleswig-Holstein, where there was a considerable native-German population. When Danish king Frederick VII moved to annex Schleswig to Denmark, the War of Schleswig-Holstein (1848–50) broke out between Prussia and Denmark. The status of Schleswig-Holstein was unchanged, however. War again broke out in 1864, Denmark was defeated, and Schleswig-Holstein passed to the joint administration of Austria and Prussia. Prussia, then vying with Austria for domination of the German Confederation, used a dispute over the region to start the Austro-Prussian War (1866). Prussia emerged victorious and annexed Schleswig-Holstein. When the unified German Empire was created (1871), the region passed to Germany.

Schley, Winfield Scott 1839–1911. American naval officer. Second in command of the US fleet at the Battle of Santiago (*q.v.*) during the Spanish-American War, Commodore Schley fought the naval engagement that led to the destruction of the Spanish fleet. Later a controversy arose over whether he or his superior, Admiral William Thomas Sampson (1840–1902), should have received credit for the victory.

Schlick, Moritz 1882–1936. German philosopher. He was a leader of the Vienna Circle, a school of logical positivism.

Schlieffen, Alfred, Graf von 1833–1913. German field marshal. As head of the German general staff (1891–1905) he devised the Schlieffen plan (*q.v.*) by 1905, the strategy later attempted by Germany in WW I.

Schlieffen Plan Plan devised by German field marshal A. von Schlieffen to crush French resistance in a war by a massive, lightning attack from the north through Belgian and Dutch territory (ignoring their neutrality). The plan also called for an attack by relatively light forces concentrated in the south against France and in the east against Russia. The plan failed during WW I because it proved impossible to keep to the plan's rigid time schedule and the forces attacking through Belgium and Holland were not strong enough.

Schliemann, Heinrich 1822–90. German archaeologist who discovered and excavated the ruins of ancient Troy. A student of Homer's works, and with independent wealth acquired from business, he devoted himself after early retirement to the search for Troy, and conducted several other excavations, one at Mycenae.

Schmalkaldic League Alliance of Protestant princes and free cities formed at Schmalkalden (1531). Led by Philip of Hesse and John Frederick I of Saxony, it had as its object a common defense against Holy Roman Emperor Charles V's threats to destroy Lutheranism by force. Charles decisively defeated the league at the Battle of Mühlberg (1547).

Schmalkaldic War War (1544–47) waged by Holy Roman Emperor Charles V against the Schmalkaldic League during the Reformation period. Forced to recognize this defensive alliance in 1532, Charles renewed his warfare against it after having made peace with France. He routed the league forces at Mühlberg (1547).

Schmidt, Helmut 1918– . West German chancellor (1974–82) who proved an able and popular statesman. He served with distinction in the German army during WW II and afterward joined the Social Democratic Party. A member of the West German Bundestag from 1953 to 1987 (except for 1962–65), Schmidt served as minister of defense (1969–72) and minister of finance (1972–74). In the latter position he adopted a policy promoting monetary stability, which consolidated West Germany's "economic miracle" (*Wirschaffswunder*) and helped establish the country as one of the world's leading economic powers. He succeeded W. Brandt as chancellor and during his term became an influential leader in European affairs. While remaining a close ally of the US, he worked to improve relations with East Germany, the Communist governments of Eastern Europe, and with the USSR. During a recession in the early 1980s, Schmidt refused to cut social welfare spending and was subsequently forced to step down. H. Kohl replaced him as chancellor.

Schoenberg, Arnold *See* **Schönberg, Arnold.**

Schofield, John McAllister 1831–1906. Union general in the American Civil War. A successful commander in Tennessee and under W. Sherman in Georgia, he went on to become secretary of war (1868–69) and general in chief of the US Army (1888–95).

scholasticism Medieval Christian philosophical and theological movement that arose in the 11th cent. It embraced various schools of thought that were in general terms concerned with questions of reconciling faith and reason and it stimulated a renewed interest in ancient Greek philosophy. Earlier Christian thinkers, notably Saint Augustine (through his writings on Platonism) helped set the stage for medieval scholasticism. In the 11th cent., Saint Anselm founded the movement and in his writings used reason to better understand belief ("faith seeking understanding"). Peter Lombard gave the movement further impetus in the 12th cent. through his work, *The Book of Sentences,* a compilation of the opinions of the church fathers. New works of Aristotle (translated from Arabic) became available for the first time in Christian Europe by the 13th cent. and had a tremendous impact on medieval scholastic thinkers. Albertus Magnus began the synthesis of Aristotelianism and Christian theology, but Saint Thomas Aquinas, one of the greatest thinkers of the Christian church, brought it to full development. Thomism was by no means unopposed, and the theologian Duns Scotus evolved an alternate synthesis. Finally, William of Ockham brought a close to the scholastic tradition (14th cent.) by effectively asserting that there is no rational basis for faith. He thus separated religion and philosophy into two distinct spheres. Thomism, however, experienced a revival in the 15th cent. and in modern times theologians have sought to apply Thomist doctrines to contemporary problems.

Schönberg, Arnold (Schoenberg, ˜)1874–1951. Austrian-born American composer. He revolutionized modern music through his use of a twelve-tone scale and through his influential writing, teaching, and outstanding compositions.

Schönbrunn, Peace of Treaty signed at Vienna (Oct. 14, 1809) following Austria's defeat by France at the Battle of Wagram (*q.v.*) during the Napoleonic Wars. By its terms Austria lost substantial territories to France, Russia, Bavaria, and the Grand Duchy of Warsaw.

Schoolcraft, Henry Rowe 1793–1864. American explorer and ethnologist. He collected much information and lore about American Indian tribes and was one of the pioneers of Indian studies.

School of Alexandria *See* **Alexandrian School.**

Schopenhauer, Arthur 1788–1860. German philosopher. A successor of I. Kant in the idealist school, he saw will rather than mind as the fundamental principle of existence and developed a philosophy based on this idea. His most important work was *World as Will and Idea.*

Schrieffer, John *See* **Bardeen, John.**

Schrödinger, Erwin 1887–1961. Austrian physicist. He formulated the basic wave equation, named for him, describing the motion of subatomic particles—the most widely used tool of quantum mechanics. He was awarded the Nobel Prize in Physics in 1933.

Schubert, Franz Peter 1797–1828. Austrian composer. He is equally celebrated for his more than 500 lieder (art songs) and for his symphonies, including *Symphony in B Flat, Symphony in B Minor,* and *Symphony in C Major.* He is also known for his chamber music, masses, and other compositions. Now considered a musical genius, he achieved little recognition in his lifetime.

Schuman, Robert 1886–1963. French statesman and prime minister (1947–48). As foreign minister (1948–53) he proposed (1950) the Schuman Plan for pooling European coal and steel resources. This move toward European cooperation led eventually to the formation of the European Common Market.

Schumann, Robert Alexander 1810–56. German Romantic composer. In his writing and in his compositions he championed the Romantic movement. A versatile composer, he produced both vocal and orchestral pieces. His *Spring* and *Rhenish* symphonies and his Piano Concerto in A minor are considered among his most outstanding works.

Schuman Plan *See* **Monnet, Jean.**

Schurz, Carl 1829–1906. German-born American statesman, reformer, and journalist. Fleeing Germany after the Revolution of 1848, he distinguished himself in America as politician, diplomat, Civil War general, US senator, and newspaper editor. He was a leader of the mugwumps, opposing J. Blaine in the 1884 presidential campaign.

Schuschnigg, Kurt von 1897–1977. Austrian statesman. As prime minister (1934–38) he strove to prevent Austria's takeover by Germany (1938). He was a German prisoner until 1945.

Schütz, Heinrich 1585–1672. German baroque composer. He introduced Italian-style music and techniques into German music, wrote many outstanding sacred-music pieces, and composed *Dafne,* considered the first German opera.

Schutzstaffel *See* SS.

Schuyler, Philip John 1733–1804. American Revolutionary leader. He served in the Continental Army and was a member of the Continental Congress. As US senator (1789–91, 1797–98) he was a leading Federalist in New York State.

Schwabach, Articles of *See* **Articles of Schwabach.**

Schwann, Theodor 1810–82. German physiologist. He isolated the first enzyme (pepsin) from animal tissue, studied muscle contraction, and identified the cell as the basic unit of plant and animal life.

Schwarzenberg, Felix, Fürst zu 1800–52. Austrian statesman. As prime minister (1848–52) he restored the Austrian Habsburg Empire after its near collapse in the Revolution of 1848. His work was soon eroded by the growth of nationalism.

Schwarzenberg, Karl Philipp, Fürst zu 1771–1820. Austrian field marshal and diplomat. He led the Austrian contingent with Napoleon against Russia (1812) but later commanded the allied forces that defeated Napoleon in 1814.

Schweitzer, Albert 1875–1965. Alsatian theologian and medical missionary in Africa. The son of a Lutheran pastor, Schweitzer won his doctorates in philosophy (1899) and theology (1900) and published *The Quest of the Historical Jesus* in 1906. In 1905, however, he made plans to become a medical missionary, and renouncing fame as a scholar and musician, he took up the study of medicine. In 1913 he and his wife Helene Bresslau (*m.* 1912) left for Africa and subsequently founded Lambaréné Hospital in equatorial Africa. He spent much of the rest of his life there, eventually increasing the hospital's capacity to some 350 patients and adding an associated a leper colony. Schweitzer did not completely abandon his scholarly pursuits, and published his two-volume *Philosophy of Civiliza-*

tion (1923), in which he articulated his philosophical principle of "reverence for life." He was awarded the Nobel Peace Prize in 1952.

Schwenkfeld, Kaspar von 1490–1561. Silesian Protestant religious leader. He tried to chart a middle way between Protestants and Catholics but was persecuted by his fellow Protestants for his views. He founded the sect named for him, the Schwenkfeldians.

Schwerin, Kurt Christoph, Graf von 1684–1757. Prussian field marshal. One of the chief lieutenants of Prussian king Frederick II, he won his greatest victory at the Battle of Mollwitz (1741) in the War of the Austrian Succession.

Scipio Another name for the ancient Roman patrician family Camelii. They were distinguished by their patronage of Greek culture but even more by family members who were outstanding Roman leaders during the 3d and 2d cents. BC. (*See* names below.)

Scipio, Cneius Cornelius *d.* 211 BC. Roman leader. As consul (222 BC) he completed the subjugation of Cisalpine Gaul, and, with his brother P. Scipio, defeated Hasdrubal in Spain (215).

Scipio, Publius Cornelius *d.* c211 BC. Roman leader and general. He was defeated by Hannibal at the Ticino River (218 BC), but his later campaigns in Spain with his brother C. Scipio significantly hindered the Carthaginian efforts. Both brothers were killed in Spain.

Scipio, Quintus Caecilius Metellus Pius *d.* 46 BC. Roman politician and general. He was consul (52 BC) with Pompey and commanded armies for him in Syria and Egypt. In the struggles for control of the Roman state, he lost to J. Caesar at the Battle of Thapsus, and committed suicide.

Scipio Africanus Major 234?–183 BC. Roman general. Sent as proconsul to Spain (210 BC), he conquered the Carthaginians there during the Second Punic War, gained control of the whole country, and pursued the Carthaginians into Africa, where he defeated Hannibal at the Battle of Zama (202 BC). He and his brother Lucius were successful in the war against Syrian king Antiochus III (190 BC).

Scipio Africanus Minor c185–129 BC. Roman consul and general, adopted son of P. Scipio. He ended the Third Punic War (149–146 BC) by conquering and destroying Carthage. He was made consul (147 BC) and censor (142). Reelected consul (134), he crushed a revolt in Spain, destroying the city of Numantia.

Scipio Nasica Serapio, Publius Cornelius *d.* c132 BC. Ancient Roman politician. He violently opposed the reforms of T. Gracchus and personally led the mob that murdered him.

Scopes Trial Celebrated "monkey" trial (July 10–21, 1925) at Dayton, Tennessee. John T. Scopes (1900–70), was charged with violating a 1925 state law by teaching evolution in his high school class. During the trial, C. Darrow, one of Scopes's attorneys, conducted a severe questioning of the fundamentalist beliefs of W. Bryan. Scopes was found guilty and fined. Darrow failed to establish the law's unconstitutionality and it stood until repealed in 1967.

Scotland Former kingdom and now part of Great Britain, located on the island of Great Britain and north of England. Its capital is Edinburgh. Although in union with Britain, Scotland maintains its own system of law and has representation in the British Parliament. Known to the Romans as Caledonia, the region saw the rise (5th–6th cents. AD) of kingdoms established by Picts, Angles, Britons, and Scots; suffered raids (8th–12th cents.) by the Norsemen, and subsequently became embroiled in wars with England, which for centuries sought to establish suzerainty over Scotland. The English and Scottish crowns were joined (1603) under James I, but formal union did not come until 1707. Thereafter the history of Scotland merges with that of Great Britain (*q.v.*). Key dates in the history of Scotland include:

1ST CENT. AD Romans attempted conquest of region, then known as Caledonia.

AD 122 Hadrian ordered construction of military wall to halt continued attacks from Picts in the north (Scotland) on Roman domains in the south.

144 Antonine Wall completed by Antoninus Pius; stone and turf wall rose 10 feet high.

AD 409 Romans withdrew from Britain.

5TH–6TH CENTS. Britons established kingdom of Strathclyde; Picts established kingdom in northern Scotland; Gaelic Scoti from Ireland established kingdom of Dalriada; Angles established kingdom of Northumbria in southern Caledonia and northern England.

563 Saint Columba came to Scotland from Ireland; established monastery and proceeded to spread Christianity.

730 Pictish king Angus MacFergus conquered Dalriada and Strathclyde.

8TH–12TH CENTS. Norsemen made continuous raids on the Scottish coast; gained some holdings in Scotland but generally held little more than the Hebrides, Orkney, and Shetland island groups.

844 Dalriada and kingdom of Picts united under Kenneth MacAlpine; new kingdom known as Alban.

1005–34 Malcolm II reigned; defeated Northumbria at Battle of Carham (1018) and extended kingdom at expense of Northumbrians.

1034–40 Duncan reigned; Strathclyde incorporated into kingdom, which became known as Scotland; severe political turmoil culminated in Duncan's murder by Macbeth.

1040–57 Macbeth reigned; killed and succeeded by Duncan's son Malcolm Canmore, who reigned as Malcolm III.

1057–93 Malcolm III reigned; married Saint Margaret of Scotland, an English princess (1067); reign marked by increasing influence of English and Roman Catholic ideas and practices in both the kingdom and in the Celtic church.

1093 Malcolm III died; leaders of the Scottish clans forced Margaret and her son Duncan II into exile.

1097–1107 Edgar, son of Malcolm III and Margaret, reigned; began the breakup of traditional Scottish clan society and the introduction of a feudal system, which was continued by his successors.

1124–53 David I reigned; lost Northumbrian possessions to England (1149).

1165–1214 William the Lion reigned; sought to regain Northumbria; captured by the English and forced to sign the Treaty of Falaise (1174), by which he swore fealty to English King Henry II.

1189 English king Richard II renounced provisions of Treaty of Falaise in return for a sum of money.

1244–1293 Scottish parliament emerged, beginning with first parliament called by King John Balliol.

1249–86 Alexander III reigned; recaptured the Hebrides Islands from the Norsemen (1266); succeeded by his granddaughter, the infant Margaret of Norway.

1290–92 Margaret died (1290), causing struggle for the succession; English king

Edward I supported the claims of John de Baliol and invaded Scotland; Baliol made king (Nov. 1292).

1295–96 John de Baliol allied with France (1295) in an attempt to end English suzerainty over Scotland; Baliol defeated (Apr., 1296) at Battle of Dunbar; Edward I annexed Scotland, but the Scots continued to rebel against English rule.

1297 Scottish troops under W. Wallace victorious over the English at Battle of Stirling (Sept. 11).

1298 English victorious over the Scots (July 22) at Battle of Falkirk.

1305 Wallace captured and executed by the English; succeeded by Robert the Bruce as leader of Scottish rebellion; Robert was crowned king a year later.

1306–29 Robert the Bruce reigned; established Scottish independence by his victory at the Battle of Bannockburn (June 24, 1314); secured English recognition of Scottish independence by the Treaty of Northampton (1328).

1329–71 David II reigned; rule marked by conflict with Edward de Baliol for the throne and continuing warfare with England.

1346 Invasion of England by David II halted at the Battle of Neville's Cross.

1371–90 Robert II reigned; founded Stuart line in Scotland.

1406–37 James I reigned; held prisoner in England (until 1424); returned to Scotland and attempted to restore order and institute reforms; his rule was resisted by the nobles; he was assassinated.

1488–1513 James IV reigned; married Margaret Tudor, daughter of English king Henry VII, but came into conflict with Henry's son, Henry VIII; led invasion of England but was killed (Sept 9, 1513) along with many Scottish nobles at Battle of Flodden Field.

1513–42 James V reigned; assumed personal rule in 1528; married Mary of Guise (1538), thereby strengthening the alliance formed with France in 1295 and leading ultimately to war with England (1542); James defeated (Nov., 1542) at Battle of Solway Moss; died soon after.

1542–60 Mary, Queen of Scots, daughter of James V, succeeded, under regency of James Hamilton and, later, her mother, Mary of Guise; sent to France (1548), she married the French dauphin (1558), which only fueled resentment against the regency of Mary of Guise; rebellion led by J. Knox (1559–60), aided by English Queen Elizabeth I, led to ouster of Mary of Guise and ascendancy of Scottish Protestants; Scottish Parliament established Presbyterianism as Scottish religion.

1561–67 Mary, Queen of Scots returned to Scotland and assumed rule (1561); instituted Counter-Reformation amid complicated political and religious struggle; Mary ultimately deposed (1567) and imprisoned in England, where she was later executed (1587).

1567–1625 Mary succeeded by her son James VI (1567); James assumed rule of Scotland (1583) and established his authority over the Scottish nobles; on death of English queen Elizabeth I (1603), he became king of both Scotland and England as James I.

1625–49 Charles I reigned in England and Scotland; attempts to introduce Anglican reforms opposed by the Covenanters; Scottish Protestants resisted in the Bishops' Wars (1639–40), which led to the English Civil wars.

1642–49 English Civil Wars; Scottish Covenanters (Presbyterians) had great influence over rebel Parliament until Pride's Purge and ascendancy of the Puritans under O. Cromwell.

1649–60 Scotland ruled under English Commonwealth and Protectorate; rebellions (1649–52) in Scotland in support of royalists put down by Cromwell.

1660–88 Restoration period in England; Presbyterians in Scotland again persecuted by English kings.

1689–1702 Protestants William and Mary reigned after the Glorious Revolution in England; Presbyterianism became Scottish state church.

1702–14 Queen Anne reigned; English and Scottish parliaments passed acts of union that formally united England and Scotland as Great Britain (1707).

Scotland, Church of *See* **Church of Scotland.**

Scotland, Saint Margaret of *See* **Margaret of Scotland, Saint.**

Scotland Yard Name given the criminal investigation division of the London Metropolitan Police. The name comes from the London street on which the first headquarters of the London police was established (1829).

Scott, Robert Falcon 1868–1912. British naval officer and Antarctic explorer. Scott commanded an expedition to the Antarctic (1901–04). On his second expedition (1910–12), Scott's party of five reached the South Pole one month after R. Amundsen, but all died in bad weather during their journey back.

Scott, Sir Walter 1771–1832. Scottish writer, considered the father of the historical novel. Scott's first major work, the ballad collection *Minstrelsy of the Scottish Border,* appeared in 1802–03, but his great success began with the publication of *Waverley* (1814), the first of a number of historical novels known collectively as the Waverley novels. Scott's novels are set in Scotland, England, and Europe, and their popularity made Scott one of the leading authors of his day. Among them are *Guy Mannering, Old Mortality, Quentin Durward,* and *Ivanhoe.*

Scott, Winfield 1786–1866. American politician and general who fought with distinction in the War of 1812. Made commanding general of the US army (1841–61), he captured Vera Cruz (1847) during the Mexican War. He was the unsuccessful Whig candidate for president in 1852. He retired shortly after the outbreak of the Civil War.

Scottish Highlands *See* **Highlands, the.**

Scottsboro Case Notorious US court case (1931) in Scottsboro, Alabama in which nine black men were convicted of raping two white girls. The Supreme Court reversed the decision on procedural grounds and one of the girls recanted her testimony at a second trial. The case became famous as an example of racial prejudice affecting a legal verdict.

scribe Ancient Jewish scholar and teacher of the Old Testament and the Law. By the time of Jesus, scribes were the equivalent of doctors of the law and many conducted classes in the temple precincts for future rabbis. The name may first have been applied to Ezra.

Scriblerus Club English literary club of the early 18th cent., formed to satirize the literary excesses of the period through the writings of a fictitious person, Martinus Scriblerus. Its members included J. Gay, J. Swift, and A. Pope.

Scribner, Charles 1821–71. American publisher. With Isaac Baker (*d.* 1850), he founded (1846) the publishing company that became (1878) Charles Scribner's Sons.

Scribner, Charles 1854–1930. American publisher. Son of C. Scribner, he became president of Charles Scribner's Sons (1879). During his tenure (1879–1928) the firm published the works of some of the most distinguished writers in America.

Scripps, Edward Wyllis 1854–1926. American newspaper publisher. He organized (1895) the first major newspaper chain and established (1907) the United Press news service.

Scrope, Richard *See* **Neville, Ralph.**

scutage Feudal payment to a lord from a vassal in lieu of military service. Scutage existed in Europe, especially in England, but became obsolete by the 14th cent.

Scythia Ancient kingdom, centered in the region north of the Black Sea, but at its greatest extent including territories as far west as the Danube River and as far east as the border of ancient China. The Scythians were nomadic horsemen (among the earliest) skilled in the use of the bow. They flourished from c8th cent. BC, displacing the Cimmerians and largely wiping out their armies in the 7th cent. BC. Also in the 7th cent., they briefly conquered Media, until being driven out. In 612, they joined with the Medes in sacking Nineveh, and in the 6th cent. Persian king Darius checked their expansion into Europe. By 300 BC migrating Celts drove the Scythians out of the Balkans. Nomadic traders, the Scythians developed a flourishing culture influenced by the various peoples with whom they had contact, including the Greeks, Persians, Chinese, and Siberians. Scythia was finally conquered and absorbed by the Sarmatians in the 2d cent. BC.

Seaborg, Glenn Theodore 1912– . American nuclear chemist and chairman of the US Atomic Energy Commission (1961–71). He was the codiscoverer of plutonium (1940) and other elements heavier than uranium (Americium, 1944; Curium, 1944; Berkelium, 1949; and Californium, 1950) and was instrumental in the development of the atomic bomb. He was corecipient of the Nobel Prize in Chemistry in 1951.

Seale, Bobby *See* **Black Panthers.**

"Sealed train" *See* **Lenin, Nikolai.**

sea power Term used to designate those elements including men, ships, shorelines, and industrial capacity that enable a nation to gain control over a portion of the seas. The term was popularized by the American naval officer and historian A. Mahan, especially in his *The Influence of Sea Power Upon History.*

SEATO   *See* **Southeast Asian Treaty Organization.**

Sebastian 1554–78. Portuguese king (1557–78), successor to his grandfather, John III. He led the Portuguese army to a disastrous defeat in Morocco at the Battle of the Three Kings (1578). Popular belief refused to accept his death, and various pretenders and rumors of his return long persisted.

Sebastian, Saint *d.* AD c288.   Roman Christian martyr. According to tradition, he was a Praetorian Guard under Emperor Diocletian. When Sebastian's Christianity was discovered, Diocletian ordered his death by arrows. Sebastian recovered and returned to confront Diocletian, who ordered him beaten to death. His martyrdom was the subject of numerous Renaissance works of art.

secession   Formal withdrawal of a political entity from a larger entity. The term refers especially to the attempt by 11 Southern US states to leave the Union (1860–61), thus precipitating the American Civil War.

Second Coalition, War of the   War (1798–1802) conducted by a coalition of European nations against France, the last phase of the French Revolutionary Wars (*q.v.*). On Dec. 24, 1798, the monarchies of Russia and Britain, in agreement with Naples, Portugal, Austria, and the Ottoman Empire, formed the Second Coalition to oppose Napoleon's expansionism. Russia and Britain agreed to drive France from the Netherlands, Austria was to combat Napoleon in Germany, and Switzerland and combined Austro-Russian forces were to expel the French from Italy. The coalition was only partially successful before Russia withdrew (Oct., 1799), and France subsequently regained some of its earlier losses. The conflict was ended by the Treaty of Amiens (Mar. 27, 1802), which also closed the French Revolutionary Wars.

Second Crusade   *See* **Crusade, Second.**

Second Empire   French government under the rule of Emperor Napoleon III (1852–70). Originally chosen as president of the Second Republic (1848), Napoleon III declared himself emperor in 1852. He followed Napoleon I's tradition of autocratic rule and expansionism, especially in Asia, Indochina, Mexico, and the Crimea. However, France's humiliation in the Franco-Prussian War (1870) led to his overthrow and declaration of the Third Republic. (*See also* France, 1852–70.)

Second Polish Revolution   *See* **January Insurrection.**

Second Punic War   *See* **Punic War(s).**

Second Republic   French government (1848–52) formed after the abdication (Feb. 24, 1848) of King Louis Philippe in the February Revolution (*q.v.*) and establishment of the provisional government. Louis Napoleon, nephew of Emperor Napoleon, was elected president of the republic (Dec. 10). Though the Second Republic had a constitution and a legislature, its rule was brief. Louis Napoleon overthrew his own government, proclaimed himself Emperor Napoleon III (Dec., 1852), and declared the Second Empire.

Second Republic   Spanish republican government (1931–39) formed after the ouster of King Alfonso XIII. A constitution was promulgated and church property was confiscated, but the moderate policies followed by President Niceto Alcalá Zamora (1877–1949) brought attacks from both the right and left. He was ousted in the 1936 elections by the Popular Front (a coalition of republicans, Communists, syndicalists, and Socialistas). Soon after their president, M. Azaña, took office, the Spanish Civil War (*q.v.*) broke out. The Second Republic was replaced by Franco's Nationalist government at the end of the war (1939).

Secret Speech   *See* **de-Stalinization.**

secularism   A movement directed toward concern with the sphere of human existence. In most of its manifestations secularism has set itself in conscious opposition to religion, holding that religion is too concerned with an afterlife, even to the detriment of the potentialities of this world.

Sedan, Battle of   Decisive German victory over France (Sept. 1, 1870) during the Franco-Prussian War, at Sedan, France. It resulted in the surrender (Sept. 2) of Napoleon III and the downfall of the French Second Empire.

Sedgemoore, Battle of   Victory (July 16, 1685) of English king James II over the forces of his nephew James Scott, duke of Monmouth, pretender to the throne. The battle, fought at Somerset, resulted in Monmouth's capture and execution.

Sedgwick, John 1813–64.   American Civil War general. He fought in the battles of Antietam,

Chancellorsville, Fredericksburg, Gettysburg, and in the Wilderness Campaign. He was killed in action at Spotsylvania (May 9, 1864).

Seeckt, Hans von 1866–1936. German general and head of the German army (1920–26). He remolded the limited German army after WW I as a professional force capable of rapid expansion.

Segni, Ugolino di *See* **Gregory IX.**

segregation Separation of the races (especially in reference to whites and blacks) to maintain the social, economic, and political advantages of one over the other. Though by no means restricted to the US, it has been an important factor in its social history. Segregation of whites and blacks was firmly established in the US South by the end of the post–Civil War Reconstruction (*q.v.*). The Supreme Court decision in *Plessy* v. *Ferguson* (1896) upheld the legality of separate but equal facilities (such as schools) and thereby ensured continuation of segregation policies. It was not until the late 1930s and 1940s that the trend toward integration began. Antidiscrimination clauses were included in federal contracts (after 1941) under President F. Roosevelt, and President H. Truman ordered integration of the military (1948). The Supreme Court decision in *Brown* v. *Board of Education of Topeka, Kansas* (1954) began the process of ending school segregation. The 1960s saw the rise of the civil rights movement (*q.v.*) and enactment of landmark civil rights legislation. *See also* apartheid.

Seingalt, Giovanni Jacopo Casanova de *See* **Casanova de Seingalt, Giovanni Jacopo.**

seignorial system *See* **Manorial System.**

Seisachtheia *See* **Solon.**

Sejanus, Lucius Aelius *d.* AD 31. Roman administrator. He was chief adviser for Emperor Tiberius, and may have helped Livilla, wife of the emperor's son Drusus, in Drusus' murder. Tiberius had him executed on suspicion of trying to take power.

Sejm Legislative body of Poland. Polish king Casimir IV summoned the first Polish diet in 1467 and in 1505 the nobles forced the king to recognize the power of the Sejm to legislate. From 1572 until 1791, members of the Sejm had the *liberum veto,* which gave any member the right to veto legislation, and thus weakened the government. In 1919, the Sejm was reorganized into a single, or unicameral, legislature.

Selden, John 1584–1654. English scholar, jurist, and parliamentarian. A leader in English political

life, he was also one of the most erudite scholars of his day. He wrote on the history of English law, religious tithes, and Oriental gods, and in defense of English sovereignty over the seas.

Seleucid Kingdom (˜ Empire) Hellenistic empire of Asia Minor. The Seleucid dynasty (312–64 BC) was centered in Syria and ruled over vast areas of Asia Minor which had been captured by Alexander the Great. The dynasty was founded by the Macedonian Seleucus I, one of Alexander's generals, following Alexander's death. In the division of Alexander's empire, Seleucus was given Babylonia. He rapidly added territories that extended from Syria to the Indus River. Subsequent Seleucid rulers were instrumental in spreading Greek culture throughout Asia Minor. However the empire was gradually reduced and was limited to Syria and Cilicia by the time of its absorption by Rome (64 BC).

Seleucus I *d.* 280 BC. Macedonian general and (from 312 BC) first of the Seleucid rulers of the eastern portions of Alexander the Great's empire. His rule extended over Syria, Asia Minor, Mesopotamia, and Persia. He founded Antioch as his capital.

Selecus II *d.* 226 BC. Syrian king (247–226 BC) successor to his father, Antiochus II. He fought a war with his half-brother Ptolemy III of Egypt as well as against his stepmother Berenice, and eventually lost both Parthia and Asia Minor.

Self-Denying Ordinance *See* **New Model Army.**

Self-Strengthening movement Chinese movement begun (c1861) to adopt elements of Western civilization in order to strengthen the Qing (Manchu) dynasty against both internal forces and further aggression by Western nations. The movement began to decline in the 1870s.

Selim I 1467–1520. Ottoman Turkish sultan (1512–20). He deposed his father, Bajazet II, and killed all who had claims to the throne. He conquered sections of Persia (1514), added Syria and Egypt to the Ottoman domain, and assumed the spiritual authority of the Caliphate.

Selim II c1524–74. Ottoman Turkish sultan (1566–74), successor to his father, Suleiman I. During his reign, Cyprus and Tunisia were added to the empire, but Selim's defeat at the Battle of Lepanto (1571) marked the first major setback to Ottoman expansion.

Selim III 1761–1808. Ottoman Turkish sultan (1789–1807) successor to his uncle Abdu-l-Hamid I. Selim inaugurated a policy of reform and Westernization but was unable to halt the decline in Ottoman power and prestige. Russo-Turkish Wars were fought during his reign. He was overthrown, imprisoned, and murdered.

Seljuks Turkish dynasty that ruled much of western Asia and Asia Minor from the 11th to 13th cents. Originally an Asiatic nomadic people, the Seljuks converted to Islam (11th cent.) and soon created a vast empire after taking power in the Caliphate. Rulers of the dynasty included Togrul Beg, grandson of Seljuk, the founder of the dynasty. Leading the Seljuks eastward, Togrul Beg conquered Persia and entered Baghdad (1055), overthrowing the Buyids (Persians who held power under the caliphs). He thus established the Seljuk sultans as effective rulers in the Caliphate. He was succeeded (1063) by his son Alp Arslan (1029–72), who conquered Syria and Palestine and defeated and captured Byzantine emperor Romanus IV at the Battle of Manzikert (1071). Alp Arslan was succeeded by his son Malik Shah (ruled 1072–92), who brought the Seljuk Empire to its height. After his death (1092), local rulers took over portions of the empire and the Abbasid caliphs gained control of the central government. Continued Seljuk attacks on the Byzantine Empire led to the Crusades (*q.v.*). The Seljuk kingdoms were eventually conquered (13th cent.) by Genghis Khan and his successors. The former Seljuk kingdom of Rum became (14th cent.) the nucleus around which the Ottomans formed their great empire.

Selkirk, Thomas Douglas, 5th earl of 1771–1820. Scottish philanthropist and colonizer. To alleviate hardships of Scottish Highlanders, he established colonies for them on Prince Edward Island and along the Red River, in Rupert's Land (1812).

Sellasia, Battle of *See* **Antigonus III; Cleomenes III.**

Seminole Indians North American Indian tribe. They formed (18th cent.) from the Creek Indians and settled in Florida. Through the early 19th cent. they resisted European encroachment on their lands, notably in the Seminole Wars (*q.v.*), until their defeat and removal (1842).

Seminole Wars Series of wars fought between the US and the Seminole Indians in Florida. 1. The first Seminole War (1817–18) began when Gen. A. Jackson invaded the Spanish-held territory of Florida after a long series of border

skirmishes. He defeated the Seminoles and the war encouraged Spain to sell Florida to the US. 2. The second Seminole War (1835–42) was sparked by attempts of white settlers to remove the Seminoles from their reservation land. The conflict cost 2,000 soldiers and over $20 million and ended only when Seminole leader Osceola (*q.v.*) was betrayed and killed (1842). Most Seminoles were forced to emigrate westward. Those who refused were tracked down and deported during a third conflict (1855–58).

Semite A member of an ethnic group speaking a Semitic language. As early as 2500 BC the Semites began to migrate from the Arabian Peninsula. Semitic peoples include the ancient Akkadians, Assyrians, Aramaeans, Israelites, and Phoenicians, and the modern Arabs and Jews.

Semmes, Raphael 1809–77. American naval officer. As Confederate commander of the Confederate cruiser *Alabama* (1862–64) during the American Civil War, he was able to inflict extensive damage on Union shipping until the *Alabama* was sunk off Cherbourg, France (June 19, 1864).

Sempach, Battle of Decisive Swiss victory (July 9, 1386) over the Austrians at Sempach, Switzerland. The battle secured the independence of the Swiss Confederation from Austrian Habsburg rule.

Senate, Roman *See* **Roman Senate.**

Senenayake, Don Stephen 1884–1952. Prime minister of Ceylon (1947–52). After a distinguished political career in Ceylon under British rule, he became (1948) the first prime minister of independent Ceylon and thus is considered the father of his country.

Seneca, Lucius Annaeus (Seneca the Elder) c55 BC–AD 40. Spanish-born Roman rhetorician and writer of influential works on rhetoric. He was the father of the Roman philosopher Seneca.

Seneca, Lucius Annaeus 3 BC–AD 65. (Seneca the Younger) Roman Stoic philosopher, statesman, and dramatist, considered the leading literary figure of his day. Tutor and adviser to Nero, he held great power during Nero's early reign (54–62). Eventually, conflicts with the emperor led to his retirement, and he was finally ordered to commit suicide by Nero. Seneca's writings included moral essays and nine plays. His works had a profound influence on later literature, notably Elizabethan drama.

Seneca the Elder *See* **Seneca, Lucius Annaeus.**

Senegal West African republic on the Atlantic coast. The population is 7,740,000 and the capital is Dakar. First settled by the Portuguese (15th cent.), Senegal was occupied by the French (17th cent.), became a colony (1895), and then became a member of the French Union (1946). Senegal joined with Mali to form an independent federation (1959–60) but withdrew from the union. L. Senghor was the country's first president (until 1980). Senegal formed (1982) a confederation with the Gambia, called Senegambia, though both countries retained sovereignty. Senegal was among the Central African countries hit by locust swarms in 1988. From 1990 there were armed clashes between rebels and government troops. A peace commission had been established by 1992, but reports of rebel attacks continued.

Senghor, Léopold Sédar 1906– . African poet, writer, and statesman, and president of Senegal (1960–80). He represented Senegal in the French National Assembly and became the country's first president after its independence, working thereafter for African unity. Senghor was inducted into the French National Assembly (1984), the first black member in its history.

Sennacherib *d.* 681 BC. Ancient Assyrian king (705–681 BC), successor to his father, Sargon II. He is noted for the rebuilding of Nineveh, the destruction of Babylon (689 BC), and the siege of Jerusalem (701 BC).

Sennett, Mack (Sinnott, Michael) 1884–1960. Pioneer American filmmaker. His best-known comedies involved the misadventures of the Keystone Kops.

Sentinum, Battle of Roman victory (295 BC) over the Samnites, Etruscans, and Gauls in the third Samnite War (*q.v.*), at Sentinum (now Sassoferrato), in central Italy. The battle established Roman preeminence in the region.

Separatists Factions of English Christians who tried to remove themselves from the authority of the Church of England. The principal Separatists were the Brownists, Pilgrims, Baptists, and the Society of Friends (*qq.v.*).

September Massacres Series of massacres (Sept. 2–6, 1792) carried out in Paris by a mob during the French Revolution (*q.v.*). Some 1,200 jailed prisoners were murdered because of a supposed conspiracy to restore the monarchy.

Septennial Act British parliamentary act (1716) extending the term of a Parliament from three to seven years. It made the dissolution of a Parliament mandatory at the end of seven years. The Whigs secured passage of the act to continue their dominance.

Septimius Severus *See* **Severus.**

Septuagint Oldest existing Greek translation of the Old Testament from the original Hebrew. It was composed in sections from c3d cent. BC to early Christian times. It contains the canonical books of the Bible as well as the Apocryphal or deuterocanonical books. The Septuagint is used by the Greek Orthodox church.

Serbia Constituent republic of Yugoslavia. Settled by Serbs (7th cent.), the region came under Byzantine suzerainty (by 10th cent.). Serbia became the leading kingdom in the Balkan Peninsula under Stephen Dushan (ruled 1331–55). It was a part of the Ottoman Empire from 1459 to 1878 and gained independence (1878) following the Serbo-Turkish War (*q.v.*). Independent Serbia played a prominent role in the Balkan League and in the Balkan Wars (*q.v.*). The assassination of Austrian archduke Francis Ferdinand (1914) by a Serbian nationalist precipitated WW I. After the war, Serbia became part of the united Kingdom of Serbs, Croats, and Slovenes (1918), which formed the basis of modern Yugoslavia. It became a constituent republic of Yugoslavia in 1946 and was a dominant force in Yugoslavian politics in subsequent years. Following the collapse of the Communist government (1990) and final breakup of the Yugoslav federation, Serbia and Montenegro joined to form a Yugoslav successor state, the Federal Republic of Yugoslavia (1992). *See also* Yugoslavia, especially 1980–92.

Serbo-Bulgarian War War (Nov. 13, 1885–Mar. 13, 1886) between Serbia and Bulgaria. After Bulgaria annexed Rumelia, Serbia declared war but was defeated at Slivnitza (Nov. 17–19). Bulgaria was deterred from advancing into Serbia by pressure from the Austro-Hungarian Empire, and peace was made on the basis of the status quo.

Serbo-Turkish War of 1876–78 Balkan conflict between Serbia and its ally Montenegro and the Ottoman Empire. In 1875, the Christian peasants of Herzegovina and Bosnia rebelled against their rulers, the Ottoman Turks. Serbia, an independent principality within the Ottoman Empire, sided with Bosnia and declared war on the Ottomans (June, 1876). Though the Serbs technically lost their war by October, they received support from Russia, which tried to pressure the Ottomans into accepting pro-Christian reforms. When they refused, Russia declared war (1877) on the Ottomans (*see* Russo-Turkish Wars). The Serbs rejoined the conflict and ultimately gained their independence in the Treaty of Berlin (July 13, 1878).

serf In feudalism, a peasant laborer bound to the land owned by a lord. The serf owed payment, usually a portion of crops, and services to the lord in return for protection and use of the land. (*See* feudalism.)

Serra, Junípero (~, Miguel José) 1713–84. Spanish Franciscan missionary in California. Noted for his austere, virtuous life, he accompanied Spanish expeditions and founded nine missions, some of which were the basis of such California cities as San Diego and San Luis Obispo.

Sertorius, Quintus *d.* 72 BC. Roman general. He opposed the constitution imposed on Rome by Sulla. From 80 BC he conducted a rebellion in Spain against Rome and was largely successful until his assassination by one of his soldiers.

Servetus, Michael 1511–53. Spanish Reformation theologian and physician. Attacked by both Catholics and Protestants for his speculative books challenging the Trinity and the divinity of Christ, he was finally burned by order of J. Calvin.

Servile Wars Three slave uprisings against Roman rule. 1. The first Servile War (c134–132 BC) occurred in Sicily. Its leader, Eunus, named himself King Antiochus, and was defeated only with great difficulty. 2. The second Servile War, also in Sicily, raged from c102 to 99 BC. 3. The third Servile War (73–71 BC) was led by the gladiator Spartacus. He conquered much of southern Italy before his defeat by Crassus and Pompey.

Sesostris I *d.* c1926 BC. Ancient Egyptian king of the 12th dynasty (c1970–c1926 BC). Son of Amenemhet I and coregent with him (1980–1970 BC), he led successful expeditions against both Nubia and Libya and brought Egypt to a peak of prosperity.

Sesostris II *d.* 1878 BC. Ancient Egyptian king (1897–1878 BC) of the 12th dynasty, successor to his father, Amenemhet II, with whom he ruled for a time as coregent. His reign was marked by a growth of mining in Nubia and the development of the Faiyum, a fertile area near Cairo.

Sesostris III *d.* 1849 BC. Ancient Egyptian king (1878–1849 BC) of the 12th dynasty, successor to his father, Sesostris II. He reestablished Egypt's southern border at the second cataract of the Nile and increased his power at the expense of the nobles.

Sesshú 1420–1506. Japanese landscape painter and Zen Buddhist monk, considered one of the greatest masters of Japanese painting. He visited China and incorporated styles learned there into his work.

Sethos *See* **Seti.**

Seti I (Sethos) *d.* 1304 BC. Ancient Egyptian king (1318–1304 BC) of the 19th dynasty, successor to his father, Ramses I, and father of Ramses II. He conquered the Libyans, invaded Syria, and built one of the finest tombs in Egypt's Valley of the Kings.

Seti II (Sethos) *d.* 1210 BC. Ancient Egyptian king (1216–1210 BC), who reigned in the last years of the 19th dynasty. After his brief rule, anarchy reigned in Egypt until the accession of Ramses III.

Seton, Elizabeth Ann Bayley 1774–1821. American Roman Catholic, known as Mother Seton. She founded the Sisters of Charity and was the first American-born saint to be canonized (1974).

Settlement, Act of *See* **Act of Settlement.**

Seurat, Georges 1859–91. French neoimpressionist painter. He developed pointillism, a technique of applying paint in tiny individual dots. With this technique he produced masterpieces such as his *Baignade.*

Seven Churches in Asia Seven early Christian churches to which Saint John the Evangelist addressed the Book of Revelation. These seven churches were in the towns of Ephesus, Smyrna, Pergamum, Thyatira, Sardis, Philadelphia (Lydia), and Laodicea (Phrygia).

Seven Days' Battles Series of battles (June 25–July 1, 1862) during the American Civil War by which Confederate forces led by Gen. R. Lee turned back a Union attempt to capture the Confederate capital of Richmond, Virginia, and ended the Peninsular Campaign (*q.v.*). The battles were fought against Union troops under Gen. G. McClellan, and occurred at Mechanicsville (June 26), Gaines's Mill (June 27), Savage's Station (June 29), Frayser's Farm (or Glendale, June 30), and Malvern Hill (July 1).

Seven Hills of Rome The seven hills upon which the city of Rome was built. The original city of

Romulus was built on the Palatine hill. The other hills are: Capitoline (which became the principal one and site of the palaces of the Caesars), Quirinal, Viminal, Esquiline, Caelian, and Aventine.

Seven Oaks Massacre *See* **Red River Settlement.**

Seven Pines, Battle of (Fair Oaks, Battle of) Battle (May 31–June 1, 1862) of the American Civil War, near Fair Oaks, Virginia. The battle was part of the Peninsular Campaign (*q.v.*). Confederate forces under Gen. J. Johnston attacked the Union army, under Gen. G. McClellan, which was advancing toward Richmond. The Confederates inflicted and received heavy losses and were ultimately repulsed. Gen. Johnston was wounded in the battle and was replaced by R. E. Lee soon after.

17th parallel Name applied to the cease-fire line established by the Geneva Conference of 1954 dividing Vietnam in two parts. The line formed the border between North and South Vietnam until reunification of Vietnam (1976).

Seventh Crusade *See* **Crusade, Seventh.**

Seven Weeks' War *See* **Austro-Prussian War.**

Seven Wise Men of Greece List of seven great men of ancient Greece. Sources disagree as to which seven should be included, but one list includes Bias, Chilon, Cleobulus, Periander, Pittacus, Solon, and Thales.

Seven Wonders of the World Seven greatest man-made works of the ancient world. Lists varied but usually included the pyramids of Egypt, the Hanging Gardens of Babylon, the Colossus of Rhodes, the statue of Zeus at Olympia, the Temple of Artemis at Ephesus, the Pharos lighthouse of Alexandria, and the Mausoleum at Halicarnassus.

Seven Years' War War fought (1756–63) in Europe and in colonial domains in other parts of the world. The American phase of the war was called the French and Indian Wars (*q.v.*). The war evolved from two separate ongoing struggles between European powers: the rivalry between Prussia and Austria (which had been humiliated by Prussia in the War of the Austrian Succession, 1740–48) and the colonial rivalry between Britain and France (in Canada, America, India, and elsewhere). The war itself pitted Prussia, Britain, and Hanover against Austria and France. Austria and France were joined variously by Sweden, Russia, Saxony, and Spain. The war began in 1756 and Prussia and Britain eventually emerged victorious. Prussia was confirmed as a leading European power and Britain became the chief colonial power, having stripped France of nearly all its colonial possessions. Key events in the war include:

1748   Austria, humiliated by loss of Silesia to Prussia in the War of the Austrian Succession (1740–48), formed an alliance with Russia.

1754   French and Indian Wars; rivalry between French and British in Ohio Valley region flared into armed clashes; war later merged with Seven Years' War.

1756   Treaty of Westminster (Jan.); George II of England allied with Frederick II of Prussia.

1756   Diplomatic revolution; France allied itself with its traditional enemy, Hapsburg Austria, following the pact between Britain and Prussia.

1756   Frederick II of Prussia invaded Saxony (Aug.); the Saxons surrendered (Oct. 15).

1757   Holy Roman Empire (ruled by the Austrian Hapsburgs) declared war on Prussia (Jan.); alliances with France, Russia, and Sweden formed.

1757   Prussia invaded Bohemia; defeated the Austrians at the Battle of Prague (May 6).

1757   In India, British defeated French at the Battle of Plassey (June 23).

1757   French forces occupied Hanover (Sept.) after defeating the British.

1757   Frederick II of Prussia defeated at Kolin by the Austrians (June), and forced to evacuate Bohemia.

1757   Frederick II defeated the Austrians and French at the Battle of Rossbach, in Saxony (Nov. 5).

1757   Battle of Leuthen, in Silesia (Dec. 5); Prussians under Frederick defeated the Austrians.

1758   British and Hanoverians defeated the French and Austrians at Crefeld (June), after driving the French back across the Rhine in the west.

1758   Frederick II defeated the Russians at Zorndorf (Aug.), halting the Russian advance toward Brandenburg.

1758   Prussians defeated by the Austrians at the Battle of Hochkirch (Oct.), but retained possession of Saxony and Silesia.

1759   Battle of Minden (Aug.); British and Hanoverians defeated a new French offensive in the west.

1759   British captured Quebec, in Canada, in a major victory over France (Sept. 13).

1759   Frederick II badly defeated by the Austrians at Kunersdorf (Aug.) and at Maxen (Nov.).

1759   British naval forces defeated French fleet in the Battle of Lagos, off Portugal (Aug. 7–18); headed off French invasion of England.

1759   French abandoned plans to invade Scotland after being defeated in the naval battle of Quiberon Bay, off Brittany (Nov. 20).

1760   British defeated (Jan. 22) French forces in India at the Battle of Wandiwash, Madras; most important battle of the war in India.

1760   Berlin occupied by the Russians (Oct.), but they were soon forced to withdraw.

1760   Prussians victorious (Nov. 3) over Austrians in bloody battle of Torgau; heavy losses ended fighting for the year.

1761   In India, the British were victorious (Jan.) in fighting at Pondicherry, the French stronghold in southern India.

1761   French defeated by the Prussians at Villinghausen (July 15).

1761   British ended aid to Prussia following accession of George III and the fall of W. Pitt (the Elder).

1762   Spain entered war on the Austrian-French side, in accordance with the Family Compact.

1762   Tsar Peter III succeeded to throne (Jan.) in Russia; an admirer of Prussian king Frederick, he moved to end hostilities with Prussia at a time when Prussia was near defeat.

1762   Treaty of St. Petersburg (May 5); war between Prussia and Russia ended; Sweden made peace with Prussia the same month.

1762   Frederick II defeated the Austrians at Burkersdorf (July 21) and Reichenbach (Aug. 16), recovering Silesia.

1762   British captured Spanish-held Havana, Cuba (Aug. 13), as they continued fighting in the colonies.

1762   Spanish captured fortress of Almeida (Aug. 25) in invasion of Portugal.

1762   Manila, in the Philippines, taken from the Spanish by the British (Oct. 5).

1762   Treaty of Fontainebleau (Nov. 3); preliminary peace between Britain and France.

1763   Treaty of Paris: Britain got French holdings in Canada, America, India, and elsewhere, as well as Spanish Florida; Spain got

Cuba and Philippines back from Britain, Spain got Louisiana Territory from France (Feb. 10).

1763   Treaty of Hubertusberg: Prussia, Austria, and Saxony made peace, leaving Silesia in Prussian hands and confirming Prussian preeminence in Germany (Feb. 15).

Severini, Gino 1883–1966. Italian futurist painter. Influenced by both pointillist neoimpressionism and cubism, he was instrumental in gaining acceptance for futurism (q.v.) in Italy.

Severus, Alexander AD 208?–235. Roman emperor (AD 222–235), successor to his cousin Heliogabalus. Considered a just ruler, he stopped persecution of the Christians during his reign and successfully fought against Persia (232). He was deposed by the army and Maximinus the Thracian in 235.

Severus, Flavius Valerius d. AD 307. Roman emperor of the West (AD 306–307). Named Augustus in the west by Galerius. He marched on Rome against Maxentius, whom he failed to defeat. Severus surrendered and later was executed.

Severus, Lucius Septimius (Septimius Severus) AD 146–211. Roman emperor (AD 193–211). Declared emperor by his legions, he successfully fought several rivals, subdued and annexed Mesopotamia, and used the army to increase imperial authority.

Sevier, John 1745–1815. American frontiersman and first governor of Tennessee (1796–1801, 1803–09). He was active in the American Revolution, represented North Carolina in Congress, and served as governor (1785–88) of the temporary western state of Franklin (q.v.).

Seville, Saint Isidore of *See* **Isidore of Seville, Saint.**

Sèvres, Treaty of Treaty (Aug. 10, 1920) between the Allies and the Ottoman Turks, concluded at Sèvres, France, after WW I but never ratified. By its terms the Ottoman Empire was, among other punishments, forced to renounce all non-Turkish possessions. The Dardanelles were internationalized and demilitarlzed. Palestine and Mesopotamia were to became British mandates, Syria a French mandate, and the Hejaz and Armenia independent kingdoms. The treaty was rejected by the nationalists led by K. Atatürk and was superseded by the Treaty of Lausanne (q.v.) in 1923.

Seward, William Henry 1801–72. American Whig and Republican statesman and secretary of state (1861–69). An uncompromising antislavery politician who spoke of an "inevitable conflict" between slavery and freedom, he failed to gain the 1860 Republican presidential nomination but was A. Lincoln's first cabinet officer. He is known best for the purchase of Alaska from Russia (1867).

Seward's Folly *See* **Alaska.**

Seychelles Republic (*pop.* 71,000) in the Indian Ocean consisting of about 85 islands. The capital is Victoria. First settled by the French (18th cent.), the islands were taken by the British (1794), made a crown colony (1903), and became a republic within the British Commonwealth (1976). A 1977 coup brought about a one-party socialist government and a new constitution was adopted in 1979. Subsequent attempts to overthrow the new government failed, but in 1991 international pressure for democratic reforms resulted in adoption of a multi-party system (1992). A ban on ships carrying nuclear weapons at Seychelles was dropped in 1983.

Seydlitz, Friedrich Wilhelm, Freiherr von 1721–73. Prussian general. Under Frederick II he reorganized the Prussian cavalry and led it in a series of brilliant victories in the War of the Austrian Succession and the Seven Years' War.

Seymour, Edward, 1st duke of Somerset 1506?–52. Protector of England (1547–50). He was virtual ruler of England during the early minority of Edward VI. His moderate religious and land reforms led to his downfall.

Seymour, Horatio 1810–86. American politician. He was governor of New York (1853–55, 1863–65) and an unsuccessful Democratic candidate for president (1868) against U. Grant. As governor during the New York draft riots (1863) he attempted to conciliate the rioters, which led to his defeat for reelection (1864).

Seymour, Jane 1509?–37. Third queen of English king Henry VIII (*m.* 1536), former lady-in-waiting to Henry's two previous queens. She gave birth to his only son (who became King Edward VI) and died a few days later.

Seymour, Thomas, baron Seymour of Sudeley 1508?–1549. English aristocrat. He held high military offices under King Henry VIII after Henry's marriage to his sister J. Seymour and married (1547) Henry's widow, C. Parr. He tried to supplant his brother E. Seymour as protector of Edward VI but was eventually executed for treason.

Sforza, Carlo, Count 1873–1952. Italian diplomat, antifascist leader and minister of foreign affairs (1920–21, 1947–51). He negotiated the Treaty of Rapallo (1922). During B. Mussolini's rule, he lived in exile.

Sforza, Francesco I 1401–66. Italian mercenary. He married (1441) the daughter of F. Visconti, duke of Milan. After Visconti's death (1447), a republic was declared in Milan. Sforza gained control and became duke (1450–66), founding a dynasty that ruled Milan for nearly a century.

Sforza, Francesco II 1495–1535. Last Sforza duke of Milan, son of L. Sforza. He took possession of the duchy (1522) but was deprived of it three years later. Restored as duke (1529), he died without heir.

Sforza, Galeazzo Maria 1444–76. Duke of Milan (1466–76), successor to his father, Francesco I Sforza. He was noted for his cruelty and immorality, and was assassinated.

Sforza, Gian Galeazzo 1469–94. Duke of Milan (1476–80), successor to his father, G. Sforza, under the regency of his mother. The duchy was soon seized from him by his uncle, L. Sforza.

Sforza, Ludovico 1451–1508. Duke of Milan (1494–99), patron of L. da Vinci. Sforza took control of the duchy from his nephew Gian Galeazzo Sforza in 1480 and succeeded officially on his death (1494). He aided French king Charles VIII to invade Naples (1494), then helped to drive him out. He was overthrown by French king Louis XII.

Sforza, Muzio Attendolo 1369–1424. Italian mercenary, founder of the Sforza family. A farmer turned soldier of fortune, he served in the employ of both Naples and Milan. His son Francesco I Sforza became (1450) the first Sforza duke of Milan.

Shackelton, Sir Ernest Henry 1874–1922. British Antarctic explorer. A member of the Royal Naval Reserve, he set out with the ill-fated R. Scott expedition to the Antarctic (1901–03) but returned to England because of poor health. Later he led the British Antarctic Expedition (1908) but was able to get to within 100 miles of the South Pole. The expedition did locate the south magnetic pole, however. In 1914, he set out on another Antarctic expedition, but his ship became icebound and was finally crushed by the ice. Members of his party drifted on ice floes for five months, before escaping by boat to Elephant Island. Shackelton and five others then sailed 800 miles to South Georgia Island, where they got help from a whaling station and rescued the rest of the party.

Shaftesbury, Anthony Ashley Cooper, 1st earl of 1621–83.   English statesman. Shaftesbury supported Parliament in the civil war from early 1644 and as a member of Parliament (1653) helped bring O. Cromwell to power. Breaking with Cromwell in 1654, he became part of the mission sent to ask Charles II to return to the throne (1660). Shaftesbury subsequently served in the royal cabinet council, where he brought about legislation for toleration of Protestant dissenters. He failed in an effort to block the succession of Catholic King James II during a time of anti-Catholic hysteria caused by the T. Oates affair. Soon after he fled to Holland.

Shaftesbury, Anthony Ashley Cooper, 3rd earl of 1671–1713.   English philosopher. A pupil of J. Locke, he rejected rationalism and held that human beings are endowed with a moral sense. His writings influenced later philosophers.

Shaftesbury, Anthony Ashley Cooper, 7th earl of 1801–85.   English social reformer. As a member of the House of Commons (1826–85) he introduced the Coal Mines Act (1842) prohibiting women and children from underground work, sponsored schools and model tenements for the poor, and encouraged the work of F. Nightingale.

Shah Jahan (~ Jehan) 1592–1666.   Fifth Mughal emperor of India (c1628–58). Many great buildings, notably the Taj Mahal, were built during his reign.

Shakers   Christian sect founded (c1747) as an offshoot of Quakerism and transplanted to America (1774) by Mother Ann Lee. She claimed to be the incarnation of God's feminine nature. Shakers believed in celibacy and communal sharing of property. More than 20 Shaker communities existed by around 1830, but the movement declined steadily thereafter.

Shakespeare, William (Shakespere, ~) 1564–1616. English poet and playwright, considered the greatest of all dramatists. Few biographical details of his life are certain. He was born in Stratford-upon-Avon; married Anne Hathaway (1582), who gave him three children; went to London, where he gained a reputation as a playwright and actor with the company the Lord Chamberlain's Men (by 1594); enjoyed sufficient prosperity to buy a house in Stratford (1597) and to become a partner in the Globe Theatre (1599); and lived out his last years as a country gentleman in Stratford (from 1610). Other details of his life have long been a matter of wide speculation and controversy. Even authorship of the plays attributed to him has been questioned, and a few critics have claimed that Shakespeare's works were actually written by someone else (F. Bacon is often cited). But these issues aside, there is little doubt concerning the depth of understanding, mastery of character, eloquence of language, and dramatic intensity revealed in his plays. Although he is known best for his plays, Shakespeare wrote numerous sonnets, collected and published in 1609; two narrative poems, *Venus and Adonis* (1593) and *The Rape of Lucrece* (1594); and the love poem, *The Phoenix and the Turtle* (1601). Shakespeare enjoyed a wide reputation in his own time, but interest in his works declined in the 17th and 18th cents. The Romantic period (18th–19th cents.), however, marked the beginning of renewed appreciation of Shakespeare. Critical works by G. Lessing, S. Coleridge, W. Hazlitt, and many others helped establish Shakespeare's rightful place in literature. Among Shakespeare's many well-known plays are *Hamlet, Macbeth, Romeo and Juliet, King Lear, The Comedy of Errors, A Midsummer Night's Dream, The Merchant of Venice, Julius Caesar, The Taming of the Shrew, Much Ado About Nothing,* and *All's Well That Ends Well.*

Shalmaneser I *d.* 1290 BC.   Assyrian king. He extended Assyria's boundary northward and moved its capital from Assur to Calah, which he had founded.

Shalmaneser III (Shalmaneser II) *d.* 825 BC. Assyrian king (860–825 BC). He made war successfully on Babylonia and Israel and received tribute from King Jehu of Israel.

Shalmaneser V (Shalmaneser IV) *d.* 722 BC. Assyrian king (727–722 BC). He fought King Hosea of Israel but died during the siege of the Israelite capital, Samaria. It was finally taken by his successor, Sargon II.

shamanism   Ancestral religion of such Central Asian peoples as Mongolians, Kirghiz, Tungus, etc. It is based on belief in the powers of shamans who heal the sick and are believed to communicate with and appease the gods through incantations, dreams, and visions. Shamanism is also found among the Eskimos and North American Indians.

Shamil c1798–1871. Muslim leader in the Caucasus. He conducted guerrilla warfare against Russian domination and allied himself with England and France in the Crimean War. After the war he was defeated and captured by Russia (1859).

Shams ud-din Muhammad *See* **Hafiz.**

Shang Chinese dynasty, also called the Yin. The Shang ruled northern China from c1554–1045 BC (c1766 to c1122 by traditional Chinese dating). It is the earliest Chinese dynasty to be historically verified by archaelogical evidence and written inscriptions. The Shang period saw great advances in bronze casting, pottery, weaving, and agriculture. Bronze weapons and spoke-wheeled horse carriages were in use, and Shang rulers mustered armies of 3-5,000 soldiers. Divination, ancestor worship, and human sacrifice (by immolation and decapitation) were practiced and Shang rulers had a highly organized system of government.

Shapley, Harlow 1885–1972. American astronomer. Shapley determined the size of the Milky Way and the sun's position in it. He also contributed to the fields of photometry and spectroscopy.

Shapur I (Sapor I) *d.* AD 272. Persian king (AD 241–272), successor to his father, Ardashir I. He strengthened the Sassanian Empire founded by his father. He captured Roman emperor Valerian at Edessa (AD 260) and imprisoned him, thereby further weakening the Roman Empire.

Shapur II (Sapor II) AD 309–379. Persian king (AD 309–379) from birth. He waged war against the Romans and defeated an invasion (AD 363) by Roman emperor Julian, who died in battle. Shapur received an advantageous peace from Julian's successor, Jovian, and gained control of Armenia.

Sharpsburg, Battle of *See* **Antietam, Battle of.**

Sharrukin *See* **Sargon.**

Shaw, George Bernard 1856–1950. Irish playwright, critic, and political pamphleteer, considered one of the great English playwrights. An outspoken Socialist, he revealed his concern for humanity in such plays as *Mrs. Warren's Profession, Arms and the Man, Major Barbara, Pygmalion,* and *Saint Joan.* His plays helped to revolutionize British theater. He was awarded the Nobel Prize in Literature in 1925.

Shawnee Indians (Shawano ~) North American Indian tribe. Originally inhabiting the Ohio River valley, they migrated to several states before reuniting (18th cent.) in Ohio. Under Tecumseh (*q.v.*), they rose against encroachment on their lands by settlers, but were defeated at Tippecanoe (*q.v.*) and eventually resettled in Oklahoma.

Shawnee Prophet (Tenskwatawa) 1768–1837. Shawnee Indian mystic and leader, brother of Tecumseh. He led the Shawnee at the Battle of Tippecanoe (*q.v.*) in 1811.

Shays' Rebellion American insurrection (1786–87) led by Daniel Shays (1747?–1825). Massachusetts farmers, suffering because of the financial depression after the American Revolution, rose up in hopes of forcing the government to decrease taxes and issue paper money. The revolt was suppressed. Shays was condemned to death but was pardoned.

Sheba (Saba) Biblical country, located in southern Arabia. Its people, the Sabaeans, colonized Ethiopia (10th cent. BC). According to legend, in the same century, Balkis, queen of Sheba, made a visit to the court of Solomon.

Shelburne, William Petty Fitzmaurice, 2d earl of 1737–1805. English statesman. A supporter of W. Pitt, he attempted unsuccessfully to moderate England's course toward its American colonies. He helped conclude the Treaty of Paris (1783).

Shelley, Mary Wollstonecraft Godwin 1797–1851. English writer. The daughter of M. Wollstonecraft and wife of P. Shelley, she is known best as author of the classic novel *Frankenstein.*

Shelley, Percy Bysshe 1792–1822. English poet, one of the leading English Romantic poets, whose work reveals his philosophy and especially his deep concern for political and social reform. The son of a country squire, Shelley went to Oxford (1810) but was expelled after publishing *The Necessity of Atheism* (1811). His first marriage (1811) lasted only until 1814, after which he began a relationship with the woman who was to become his second wife, M. Wollstonecraft Shelley (*née* Godwin, married 1816), with whom he had three children. In 1818 Shelley and his family settled in Italy, where he did his best work, including: *Ozymandias* (1818): *The Cloud, To a Skylark, Ode to the West Wind,* and *The Sensitive Plant* (all 1819); his masterpiece *Prometheus Unbound* (1820); the elegy *Adonais* in memory of

J. Keats and the famous *Defence of Poetry* (1821). Shelley was drowned while sailing off the Italian coast in July, 1822.

Shenandoah Valley Valley in northern Virginia, running north to south between the Allegheny and Blue Ridge mountains. It was a strategic Confederate stronghold and source of supplies during the American Civil War (1861–65) and was the scene of many battles. In 1862, Confederate Gen. Stonewall Jackson, operating in the valley, repulsed troops seeking to reinforce Union Gen. G. McClellan outside Richmond, and thus contributed to the failure of the Union Peninsular Campaign (*q.v.*). Gen. R.E. Lee used the valley as an escape route after offensives against the North failed (notably after Gettysburg, 1863). During 1864, Confederate Gen. J. Early conducted highly successful operations in the valley. Subsequently in that year Union forces under Gen. P. Sheridan began a drive to take control of the valley, completed in 1865.

Shennong The second of China's legendary early emperors, who according to tradition was born in 2800 BC. He was said to have taught the Chinese farming skills and to have established an agricultural society. The discovery of medicinal plants and invention of record-keeping by knotted strings was also credited to him.

Shen Nung *See* **Shennong.**

Shen Yen Huang Ti *See* **Huang Di.**

Sheraton, Thomas 1751–1806. English furniture maker. Sheraton's graceful furniture designs greatly influenced his age and are still popular today.

Shere Ali 1825–79. Emir of Afghanistan (1863–79). His succession was contested by family members, but he gained control wilh British assistance. Later he turned away from Britain and was defeated by the British in the second Afghan War (*q.v.*) in 1878.

Sheridan, Philip Henry 1831–88. Union general in the American Civil War. As commander of the Army of the Shenandoah (1864–65), he defeated Confederate Gen. J. Early and laid waste to the Shenandoah Valley. Early later successfully counterattacked, but Sheridan turned a possible Union disaster into a victory. In Apr., 1865, he cut off Gen. R. Lee's retreat at Appomattox, Virginia, forcing Lee to surrender (Apr. 9).

Sheridan, Richard Brinsley 1751–1816. English dramatist. Among his many plays are *The Rivals*

and *The School for Scandal.* He entered Parliament (1780) and served in several cabinet posts.

Sherman Antitrust Act American law (1890), the first designed to prohibit trusts, monopolies, combinations, and restraint of trade on a national and international level. Supreme Court decisions curtailed its effectiveness until President T. Roosevelt actively enforced it. The law was also strengthened by the Clayton Antitrust Act (1914).

Sherman, James S. 1855–1912. American politician, vice-president of the US under W. Taft (1909–12). He served in the House of Representative 1887–91 and 1893–1909.

Sherman, John 1823–1900. American statesman. As US senator (1861–77, 1881–97) he played a role in Reconstruction after the American Civil War and in formulating the Sherman Antitrust Act (*q.v.*) and the Sherman Silver Purchase Act (*q.v.*). He also served as secretary of the treasury (1877–81) under President R. Hayes.

Sherman Silver Purchase Act American currency law (1890) requiring the American government to buy set amounts of silver each month to be added to the national currency. The mandatory and excessive purchases of silver soon threatened to drain the nation's gold supply and led to the financial Panic of 1893. The act, and consequently the national policy of bimetalism, was repealed (Nov. 1, 1893) and the gold standard was restored.

Sherman's March to the Sea *See* **American Civil War, 1864–65.**

Sherman, William Tecumseh 1820–91. Union general in the American Civil War, noted for saying, "War is hell." A West Point graduate (1840), he resigned from the army (1853), only to rejoin on the outbreak of the Civil War. He fought at the First Battle of Bull Run and afterward was made a brigadier general of volunteers. Transferred to Tennessee, he fought at Shiloh, in the Vicksburg and Chattanooga campaigns, and other battles (1862–63). Already a brigadier general in the regular army, Sherman became supreme commander in the West (Mar., 1864). He then conducted his successful Atlanta Campaign (*q.v.*) and, after capturing the city, began his devastating "March to the Sea" (Nov. 14).

Sherpas *See* **Nepal.**

Sherwood, Robert Emmet 1896–1955. American playwright. His plays, among them *The Petrified Forest, Idiot's Delight,* and *There Shall Be No*

Night, greatly influenced American drama. Sherwood was awarded four Pulitzer prizes (1936, 1939, 1941, 1949).

Sheshonk I *d.* c924 BC. Egyptian king (945–924 BC), founder of the 22d dynasty. Originally a mercenary commander, he usurped the throne, and conducted campaigns in Palestine, apparently in support of Jereboam.

Shidehara, Kijuro, Baron 1872–1951. Japanese diplomat and statesman. As foreign minister (1924–27, 1929–31) he followed a peaceful policy antagonistic to Japanese militarism. After WW II he served briefly (1945–46) as prime minister.

Shi Huangdi (Shih Huang Ti) 255–210 BC. Chinese emperor (247/6–210 BC) who first unified the empire and built the Great Wall of China. Following his accession as king of the Qin Kingdom of northwestern China, he conquered and annexed six other Chinese kingdoms (230–221 BC) to create the Qin Empire. Naming himself Shi Huangdi (First Emperor), he thereupon abolished the old feudal order, divided his empire into 36 military districts, established a centralized administration, and instituted uniform standards in weights and measures, laws, and the written language. He was a builder and, in addition to the Great Wall, ordered construction of roads and canals. His imposition of strict criminal punishments and the struggle with the Confucian scholars (supporters of the old feudal order) during his reign led to the Burning of the Books (213 BC) and the eventual rise of the Han dynasty.

Shih Huang Ti *See* **Shi Huangdi.**

Shi'ites Muslim sect, one of the two major divisions of Islam, the other being the Sunnis (*q.v.*). The Shi'ites originated in Persia as partisans of Ali, son-in-law of Muhammad, after the first Muslim Civil War. They opposed the Umayyad dynasty, supported by the Sunnis. The Shi'ites believe (as do the Sunnis) that a Mahdi will appear. Babism and Bahaism are outgrowths of Shi'ite beliefs. Shi'ism is the official religion of Iran and also has followers in India, Iraq, Yemen, Pakistan, and Lebanon.

Shiloh, Battle of (Pittsburg Landing, ˜) Battle (Apr. 6–7, 1862) of the American Civil War, a Union victory near Pittsburg Landing in southwestern Tennessee. The second major battle of the war; it derives its name from Shiloh church nearby. Here Confederate forces under Gen. A.

Johnston surprised the Union troops under Gen. U. Grant. Bloody fighting ensued, Johnston was killed, and each side suffered more than 10,000 casualties.

Shimabara Rebellion Japanese insurrection (1637–38) in which the predominantly Catholic population of Shimabara rose against unjust taxation. More than 100,000 troops failed to quell the rebellion and a Dutch gunship had to be called in. The rebellion caused further Christian persecution and led Japan's leaders to adopt a policy of isolation.

Shimonoseki, Treaty of Treaty (Apr. 17, 1895) between China and Japan ending the First Sino-Japanese War. By its terms China, who had lost the war, accepted Korean independence and ceded Taiwan, the Pescadores islands, and Port Arthur and the Liaodong Peninsula to Japan. Japan subsequently returned Port Arthur and the Liaodong Peninsula after European protests.

Shinar Biblical region, located between the Tigris and Euphrates rivers and corresponding to southern Babylonia.

Shinran 1173–1262. Japanese Buddhist religious reformer and thinker. He founded the True Pure Land sect, the largest Buddhist sect in Japan today. The sect became prominent in the 15th cent. and descendants of Shinran founded the Ikkō sect, which was involved in religious rebellions (15th cent.).

Shinto Indigenous religion of Japan which is more a way of life than a formal dogma. Its major divinities are Amaterasu, the sun goddess, and her brother Susanowo, the storm god, but all objects contain a holy spirit called kami. Ancestor worship and pilgrimages to shrines are important aspects of Shinto, which literally means "the way of the gods." The Japanese emperor was considered divine as a direct descendent of Amaterasu. This belief was promoted until 1946, when Emperor Hirohito disavowed his divinity.

Shipton, Mother English prophet, believed to have been born Ursula Southiel Shipton (1488–1561). She allegedly predicted events of King Henry VIII's reign and the date of the Great Fire of London (1666).

Shirpuria *See* **Lagash.**

Shivaji *See* **Sivaji.**

Shockley, William *See* **Bardeen, John.**

shogun Military leaders who were the effective rulers of Japan from 1192 to 1867. Shogun was the title of the imperial military commander, and in 1192 the emperor appointed Minamoto Yoritomo shogun. Yoritomo gained control over the government, and in subsequent centuries the shoguns, as well as the warrior class they controlled, ruled Japan. The emperor was sovereign in title only. Under the shoguns, Japan remained locked in a rigid feudal system. The emperor and the imperial court did not again become the focus of power until the Meiji Restoration (1868), which marked the end of feudalism in Japan and the beginning of the movement toward modernization. Beginning in the Ashikaga period, the shogunate itself was hereditary and was held successively by the following families: Ashikaga shogunate 1338–1578; Tokugawa shogunate 1603–1867.

shogunate *See* **shogun; Bakufu.**

Sholes, Christopher Latham 1819–1890. American journalist and inventor. With Carlos Glidden and Samuel W. Soulé, he invented (1868) the first practical typewriter. The machine, with improvements, became (1874) the Remington typewriter.

Sholokhov, Mikhail Alekansdrovich 1905–84. Russian author. He is known best for his trilogy of Russian life: *The Silent Don, And Quiet Flows the Don,* and *The Don Flows Home to the Sea.* He was awarded a Nobel Prize in Literature in 1965.

Shore, Jane *d.* 1527? English mistress to King Edward IV. She had great influence, but after Edward's death, King Richard III forced her into humiliation and poverty.

Short Parliament Fourth English Parliament in the reign of King Charles I. Convened (Apr. 13, 1640) by Charles to provide funds for a war against the Scottish Covenanters, it refused to do so until the king had satisfied to its grievances. It was dissolved (May 5) and followed (Nov. 3) by the Long Parliament.

Shostakovich, Dmitri 1906–1975. Russian composer. He aroused controversy in Russia by following his own musical values, sometimes in conflict with those of Russian politics. He was renowned for his symphonies, notably *Symphony No. 5* (1937), and for his piano and violin concertos.

Shrewsbury, Charles Talbot, duke of 1660–1718. English statesman. He was one of the seven leaders to sign the paper (1688) inviting William of Orange to become English king in the Glorious Revolution. He also played a major part in securing the succession (1714) of the Hanoverian king George I.

Shrewsbury, John Talbot, 2d earl of *See* **Castillon, Battle of.**

Siam *See* **Thailand.**

Sian Incident *See* **Xi'an Incident.**

Sibelius, Jean Julius Christian 1865–1957. Finnish composer and nationalist. A Romantic composer, he brought worldwide attention to Scandinavian music with his symphonies and tone poems, among them *Finlandia.*

Siberia Region of northern Asian Russia stretching from the Urals to the Pacific Ocean and noted for its wealth of natural resources and its harsh climate. It was the site (15th cent.) of the Tatar khanate, which was conquered for Russia (1581) by the Cossacks under Yermak. Russia continued to extend its control over Siberia in the 16th and 17th cents. but relinquished some of its territory to China by the Treaty of Nerchinsk (*q.v.*) in 1689. Settlement increased after construction (1891–1905) of the Trans-Siberian Railway. Siberia was the center of White Russian resistance (1918–20) to Bolshevik rule after the Russian Revolution. Large petroleum reserves have been found in Siberia and it has been greatly developed in the 20th cent.

Sickingen, Franz von 1481–1523. German knight. A free knight, he aided the election of Charles V as Holy Roman Emperor and protected M. Luther and J. Reuchlin. He died fighting in the Knights' War.

Sickles, Daniel Edgar 1819–1914. American politician and Union general in the American Civil War. He fought in the Peninsular Campaign and at Antietam, Chancellorsville, and Gettysburg. He served in Congress (1857–61, 1893–95).

Sicyon Ancient Greek city in the Peloponnesus northwest of Corinth. It rose to power (early 6th cent. BC) under its tyrant Cleisthenes but was later dominated by Corinth or Sparta. It was noted for its artists and art schools.

Sicyon, Butades of *See* **Butades of Sicyon.**

Sidmouth, Henry Addington, 1st viscount 1757–1844. English statesman. As prime minister (1801–04) he concluded the Treaty of Amiens with Napoleon. As home secretary (1812–21) he persecuted the Luddites and helped to bring about the Peterloo Massacre (*q.v.*).

Sidney, Sir Philip (Sydney, ~) 1554–96. English author and courtier. Sidney was influential in the court of Queen Elizabeth I. He is known for his pastoral poems and his prose essay *The Defense of Poetry.*

Siege of   *See under names inverted, as in* **Orléans, Siege of.**

Siegfried Line   Line of fortifications built along Germany's western frontier in the 1930s. It corresponded to the French Maginot Line and succeeded in slowing down the Allied offensive in WW II.

Siena, Saint Catherine of   *See* **Catherine of Siena, Saint.**

Sienkiewicz, Henryk (*pseud.* Litwos) 1846–1916. Polish author. Best known for *Quo Vadis?* (1896), he also worte an historical trilogy, *With Fire and Sword* (1884), *The Deluge* (1886), and *Pan Michael* (1888), about Poland's struggle for political independence. He was awarded the Nobel Prize for Literature (1905).

Sierra Leone   West African republic on the Atlantic Ocean. The population is 4,168,000 and the capital is Freetown. The country's economy is based on agriculture and mining. Sierra Leone was explored (15th cent.) by the Portuguese. Freetown was established privately (1792) as a haven for some 1,000 freed slaves from Nova Scotia. After Britain took control of the region in 1808, tens of thousands more freed slaves were settled there. Sierre Leone became a British protectorate (1896) and achieved independence in Apr. 1961. After a period of prolonged unrest, a one-party government was adopted in 1978. Economic problems continued through the 1980s, however. Constitutional reforms, including a multi-party system, were approved in 1991, but the military seized power (Apr. 1992) and suspended the constitution.

Siete Partidas   *See* **Alfonso X.**

Sieyès, Emmanuel Joseph 1748–1836. French revolutionary statesman. He played a major role in the early years of the French Revolution, drafted the Declaration of the Rights of Man (*q.v.*), and later helped organize the *coup d'état* that overthrew the Directory.

Sigebert I *d.* 575. Frankish king of Austrasia (561–575). His reign was marked by nearly constant warfare with his brother Chilperic I. He defeated Chilperic but was assassinated by order of Fredegunde, Chilperic's wife.

Sigel, Franz 1824–1902. German-born American general. A leader of the Baden insurrections of 1848–49, he fled to America after their failure. He served as a Union general during the American Civil War.

Sigismund 1368–1437. Holy Roman Emperor (1411–37, crowned 1433), last of the Luxembourg emperors. As Hungarian king (1387–1437) he persuaded Pope John XXIII to convene the Council of Constance (1414–18), which ended the Great Schism (*q.v.*). He revoked his guarantee of safe passage to J. Huss, who was condemned for heresy and burned. Huss's death led to the Hussite Wars (*q.v.*).

Sigismund I 1467–1548. Polish king (1506–48), successor to his brother Alexander I. His reign was marked by power struggles with the nobility and warfare with Russia.

Sigismund II (Sigismund Augustus) 1520–72. Polish king (1548–72), successor to his father, Sigismund I. He united Poland with Lithuania and Livonia.

Sigismund III 1566–1632. King of Poland (1587–1632) and Sweden (1592–99). Deposed in Sweden, he engaged in wars to regain his throne. He also invaded Russia and captured Moscow (1610–12).

Sigismund Augustus   *See* **Sigismund II.**

Sigurdsson, Jon 1811–79. Icelandic scholar and statesman. He edited many books of Icelandic literature and history. His efforts contributed to Denmark's granting of self-government to Iceland (1874).

Sikhs   People of northwest India, followers of a religion founded (15th cent.) by Nanak. Fusing Hindu and Muslim beliefs, the Sikhs worship one God and employ meditation and exercise to attain the realization of God. They revere their guru (teacher) and accept as their only religious text the Adi Granth, largely a collection of hymns by the early gurus. They came to control much of the Punjab (15th cent.) but were defeated by the British in the Sikh Wars (*q.v.*) of the 19th cent.

Sikh Wars   Two 19th-cent. wars between the Sikhs and the British.   1. The first Sikh war (1845–46) was sparked by a Sikh invasion into British India and culminated in the defeat of the Sikhs and British annexation of Kashmir.   2. The second Sikh war (1848–49) was caused by an uprising and resulted in a British victory and the annexation of the Punjab.

Sikorski, Wladyslaw Eugeniusz 1881–1943. Polish general and statesman. He fought in WW I, commanded in the Russo-Polish War (1920), and served as prime minister (1922–23). He headed (1939–43) the Polish government in exile during WW II.

Sikorsky, Igor Ivan 1889–1972. Ukrainian-born American aircraft engineer. He is noted for the development (1939) of the first successful helicopter.

Silas (Silvanus) Early Christian missionary. He accompanied the Apostle Paul on his second journey.

Silesia European region situated largely in modern Poland. An industrial and mining center, Silesia was originally part of Poland. It passed to Bohemia (14th cent.), was divided, and was devastated during the Thirty Years' War, after which it passed to Austria (1648). Prussia gained control of much of the region in the Silesian Wars of 1740–45 (*q.v.*). It came under increasing German influence (18th–19th cents.). Partitioned (1921) after WW I, it was seized by Germany in WW II. After the war, most of the region was restored to Poland.

Silesian Wars 1. The first Silesian War (1740–42) was fought between Prussia and Austria for possession of Silesia. It was begun by the invasion of Silesia by Prussian king Frederick II, in alliance with Bavaria, France, and Saxony. Austria was defeated, and by the Treaty of Breslau (1742) Prussia gained possession of much of Silesia. 2. The second Silesian War (1744–45) was begun by Frederick II, who crossed Saxony and invaded Bohemia. He captured Prague but was forced back into Saxony. The war was ended by the Treaty of Dresden (1745) between Austria and Prussia, and Frederick retained possession of Silesia. 3. *See* Seven Years' War.

Siles Zuazo, Hernán 1914– . Bolivian president, 1956–60. A founder of the Movimiento Nacionalista Revolucionario (MNR) in 1941, Siles was elected vice-president in 1951. However, a military junta seized power in 1952, forcing him to join an MNR revolution to gain his post. Siles subsequently served as vice-president under President Paz Estenssoro (1952–56). Succeeding Paz Estenssoro as president in 1956, Siles consolidated reforms begun under the previous administration and imposed measures to halt runaway inflation. Opposed to Paz Estenssoro's bid for a third term, Siles supported an unsuccessful coup against him (1964) and went into exile.

Silk Road (Silk Route) Ancient trade route across Asia from the Roman Empire to China.

Roughly the same route was followed by Marco Polo in his travels.

Silla, kingdom of Ancient kingdom of Korea which arose (1st–2d cents. AD) in southeastern Korea. With the kingdoms of Koguryo and Paekche, it was one of the three early Korean kingdoms and later unified the peninsula under native Korean rule for the first time in 670. An administrative bureaucracy, influenced by Chinese patterns, was set up, and Buddhism flourished. The Silla rulers were supplanted by the Koryo dynasty in 935.

Silvanus *See* **Silas.**

Silva Xavier, José Joaquim da *See* **Tiradentes Conspiracy.**

Silver Age Period in Roman literary history (AD 14–c130) following the Golden Age. It was characterized by the writings of Tacitus, Juvenal, Suetonius, Pliny the Elder and Pliny the Younger, and Seneca.

Sima Guang (Ssu-ma Kuang) 1019–1086. Chinese statesman and historian of the Song dynasty, compiler of the massive *Comprehensive Mirror for Aid in Government,* a history of China from 403 BC to AD 959.

Sima Qian (Ssû-ma Ch'ien) 145–c90 BC. First great historian of China. With his father, he wrote the *Shiji* (*Shih Chi;* Historical Records), a dynastic history of China down to the end of the 2d cent. BC. The 130-chapter work represented a new form of historical literature that was subsequently duplicated in 25 later dynastic histories of China.

Simcoe, John Graves 1752–1806. British soldier and governor. Simcoe fought in the American Revolution and became (1792) the first lieutenant governor of Upper Canada.

Simeon I *d.* 927. Bulgarian prince (893–925) and first tsar of Bulgaria (925–927). Simeon warred successfully against the Magyars, Serbs, and the Byzantine Empire. His court became a center of culture.

Simeon II 1937– . Last tsar of Bulgaria (1943–46), successor to his father, Boris III. Nominal tsar under a regency, he went into exile when the monarchy was abolished.

Simeon Stylites, Saint *d.* AD 459? Syrian Christian ascetic. Simeon lived for thirty years atop a small, high pillar, from which he preached.

Simms, William Gilmore 1806–70. American writer, known for his popular historical romances about life in the South.

Simnel, Lambert 1477?–1534? Pretender to the English throne. Yorkists claimed that Simnel was Edward of Warwick and attempted unsuccessfully to overthrow King Henry VII (1487).

Simon, Théodore *See* **Binet, Alfred.**

Simon Bar Cochba *See* **Bar Kokhba, Simon.**

Simon Commission British commission appointed (Nov., 1927) under the chairmanship of Sir John Simon (1873–1954) to study the working of the Indian constitution established in 1919. It was boycotted by the Indian National Congress for its "all white" composition, and its actions and conclusions aroused great hostility among Indian nationalists.

Simonides of Ceos c556–468? BC. Greek poet, known best for his epitaphs for the dead at Marathon of Thermopylae.

Simon Peter *See* **Peter.**

Simons, Menno *See* **Mennonites.**

Simpson, Sir George 1792–1860. Scottish-born Canadian explorer. Simpson explored Canada for the Hudson's Bay Company and made an overland round-the-world journey (1841–42) by way of the northern regions.

Sims, William Sowden 1858–1936. American naval officer. He commanded US operations in European waters during WW I. With Burton J. Hendrick (1870–1949) he wrote the Pulitzer Prize-winning *The Victory at Sea.*

Sinai Peninsula in northeastern Egypt linking Africa with Asia. It was the scene of battles between Israel and Egypt during the Arab-Israeli Wars.

Sinaitic inscriptions Inscriptions carved on rocks in the Sinai Peninsula. They were discovered (1904–05) by Sir W. Petrie.

Sinan 1489?–1587? Foremost Ottoman architect, who designed and built more than 300 structures. He built the mosques of Suleiman I at Constantinople and Selim II at Adrianople.

Sinclair, Harry F. *See* **Teapot Dome.**

Sinclair, Upton Beall 1878–1968. American writer and reformer. One of the muckrakers (*q.v.*), he is known best for his novel *The Jungle,* an exposé of the meat-packing industry. He was awarded a Pulitzer Prize (1943).

Singapore (Republic of Singapore) Small republic located at the tip of the Malay Peninsula. The population is 2,703,000 and the capital is Singapore. Originally a Malay city, it was destroyed by the Javanese (14th cent.). Sir T. Raffles refounded (1819) the city and under the British East India Company it became a major world port and naval base in the Straits Settlements. The British surrendered Singapore to the Japanese (1942) during WW II but retook the city (1945). Singapore became self-governing in 1959, briefly joined the Federation of Malaysia (1963–65), and became an independent republic (Sept., 1965). Prime Minister Lee Kaun Yew (in office from 1965) ruled the country until he retired in 1990. Constitutional amendments were adopted in 1991 to provide for direct election of the president.

Singer, Isaac Merrit 1811–75. American inventor. He devised and patented (1851) the first continuous-stitch sewing machine. Although he lost a patent-infringement case (1854) to E. Howe, his company soon became the leading manufacturer of sewing machines.

Sinn Fein Irish Nationalist political party of Ireland, whose name means "We Ourselves." Originally a movement founded (1899) by A. Griffith, it sought to gain independence from England. It gathered momentum after the Easter Rebellion (1916) under the leadership of E. De Valera. After De Valera withdrew (1927) to enter the Dáil of the Irish Free State, Sinn Fein declined in importance and eventually became the political arm of the Irish Republican Army (IRA).

Sinnott, Michael *See* **Sennett, Mack.**

Sino-French War Undeclared war (1883–85) between France and China arising from French expansion into Vietnam. China claimed Vietnam as a protectorate, and after France declared a protectorate over Annam (1883), China sent troops to Vietnam. Soon defeated, China was forced (1885) to recognize French interests in Annam and Tonkin.

Sino-Japanese War 1. War (1894–95) between China and Japan over control of Korea. The Japanese, having a modern, well-equipped army, easily invaded Shandong (Shantung) and Manchuria and forced the Chinese to sue for peace. By the Treaty of Shimonoseki (1895), the Chinese agreed to pay a large indemnity, to cede vast areas (including Taiwan) to Japan, to grant trade privileges to Japan, and to recognize the nominal independence of Korea. Japan emerged from the conflict as a major international power. 2. War (1937–45) between China and Japan. Following its occupation of Manchuria (1931–32), Japan pressed the Chinese for further Chinese nationalists and Communists made it all but impossible to resist the growing threat of an invasion by Japan. By the Xi'an Incident (q.v.) in 1936, Nationalists and Communists agreed to form a common front against the Japanese, and in July 1937 hostilities broke out. Japan quickly occupied Beijing and Tianjin, and soon after took Shanghai and the capital of Nanjing. The Japanese continued their rapid advance over the eastern portions of China, taking cities and other strategic points while the Chinese pursued a scorched-earth policy and waged a bitter guerrilla war from within. China declared war on the Axis powers in 1941, after the Japanese attack on Pearl Harbor, and the fighting in China thus became part of WW II. In 1942–44, despite an increase in aid from the US and Britain and the diversion of Japanese forces to fighting elsewhere, the Chinese were unable to gain the initiative though they slowed the Japanese advance and inflicted some serious defeats. In fact, it was not until the spring of 1945, just before the Japanese surrender, that the Chinese were able to mount a successful offensive.

Sinop Turkish seaport on the Black Sea. The destruction of an Ottoman fleet here (1853) by the Russians contributed to the outbreak of the Crimean War (1853–56).

Sino-Soviet Treaty Treaty (Aug. 14, 1945) between China and the USSR. Intended to deter Japanese aggression, it established a joint railway, a joint naval base at Port Arthur, and made Darien a free port.

Sintra, Convention of *See* **Convention of Sintra.**

Sion *See* **Zion.**

Sioux Indians (Dakota Indians) Confederation of American Indian tribes that inhabited large tracts of the Midwest from Lake Superior to beyond the Dakotas. The Sioux concluded several treaties with the US, but after complications following a treaty (1851) involving US acquisition of much of Minnesota, they rose and massacred settlers. Thus began a series of clashes against further encroachment on tribal lands continuing through the 1860s. In 1867 the Sioux moved to Dakota territory, but discovery of gold in the Black Hills (1867) led to further conflict and the Battle of Little Bighorn (q.v.). The last Sioux uprising ended in the massacre at Wounded Knee (q.v.) in 1890.

Siqueiros, David Alfaro 1898–1974. Mexican painter. His murals, such as *March of Humanity* and *Third World,* reflect his ardent socialism and are among Mexico's most celebrated works of art.

Siracusa *See* **Syracuse.**

Sistine Chapel Private papal chapel at the Vatican. Built (1473) by Pope Sixtus IV, it is celebrated for its ceiling and wall paintings by Michelangelo.

Sistova, Peace of Treaty (Aug. 4, 1791) between Austria and the Ottoman empire, concluded at Sistova, Bulgaria. It adjusted mutual borders and returned Belgrade to the Ottomans.

Sitter, William de 1872–1934. Dutch astronomer. He advanced the theory of an expanding universe.

Sitting Bull *d.* 1890. American Indian leader. He led the Sioux in the Battle of the Little Bighorn (q.v.) in 1876. He surrendered (1881), spent his last years on a reservation, and was killed for allegedly resisting arrest.

Sitwell, Dame Edith 1887–1964. English poet. Her poetry reveals a love of beauty and a sense of humanity's sufferings. Among her works are *Clown's Houses, Street Songs,* and *The Canticle of the Rose.*

Sivaji (Shivaji) (Grand Rebel) 1627–80. Indian ruler, founder of the Maratha (q.v.) kingdom. He expanded his domains at the expense of the Mughal Empire.

Siward (Siward the Strong) *d.* 1055. Danish warrior and earl of Northumbria. He supported Edward the Confessor and later defeated Scottish king Macbeth.

Six, Les Group of early 20th-cent. composers who opposed the musical traditions of C. Debussy, C. Franck, and others. They were briefly influential.

Six Acts Acts adopted (Dec. 1819) by the British Parliament to suppress the radical movement for parliamentary reform in England. The acts followed the Peterloo Massacre and greatly curtailed freedom of speech, press, and assembly.

Six Articles, Act of *See* **Act of Six Articles.**

Six-Day War *See* **Arab-Israeli War (Third).**

Six Dynasties Name given to the period in China between the fall of the Han dynasty (AD 220) and the beginning of the Sui (581). The era was marked by political disintegration but such cultural advancements as the introduction of Buddhism and Daoism; medical and scientific study; and the use of coal, tea, and gunpowder. It was named after the six dynasties that ruled during the period: the Shu (221–63), Wu (AD 222–280), Western Jin (265–316), the Eastern Jin (317–419), the Liu-Song (420–479), Northern Wei (387–534). Divided in subsequent years, Northern Wei was conquered in 581 by Yang Jian, who would go onto reunify China under the Sui dynasty (*q.v.*).

Sixteen Kingdoms Name applied to a group of dynasties, all but three non-Chinese, that ruled in northern China from AD 304–439.

Sixth Crusade *See* **Crusade, Sixth.**

Sixtus IV (Francesco delle Lovere) 1414–84. Pope (1471–84), successor to Paul II. A patron of the arts, he built (1473) the Sistine Chapel. He deeply involved the papacy in political intrigues.

Sixtus V (Peretti, Felice) 1521–90. Italian-born pope (1585–90), successor to Gregory XIII. He made many administrative reforms, restored order in the Papal States, and did much rebuilding in Rome.

Sjahrir, Sutan 1909–66. Indonesian prime minister (1945–47). He negotiated the Linggadjati Agreement with the Netherlands, by which the Indonesian government was recognized and plans were made for a permanent independent state.

Skagerrak, Battle of *See* **Jutland, Battle of.**

Skelton, John 1460?–1529. English satirical poet. Tutor to Henry VIII, he wrote sharp verse satires on the morality and people of his day.

skepticism Philosophical position in which either specific knowledge or the ability to know is called into question. Skepticism has been an important aspect of philosophical thought since ancient times (Democritus and the Sophists). In modern times, D. Hume and I. Kant have advanced such theories.

Skinner, B(urrhus) F(rederick) 1904–90. American psychologist and noted exponent of behaviorism (*q.v.*). Among his works are *Walden Two* (1948), *Science and Behavior* (1953), and *Beyond Freedom and Dignity* (1971).

Skobelev, Mikhail Dmitreyevich 1843–82. Russian general. He fought brilliantly in the Russo-Turkish War (1877–78), figuring in the conquest of Russian Turkistan.

Skriabin, Vyacheslav Mikhailovich *See* **Molotov, Vyacheslav Mikhailovich.**

Slater, Samuel 1768–1835. English-born American industrialist. Slater familiarized himself with English cotton-textile machinery and built a similar factory (the first in America) in Rhode Island (1790) from memory.

Slave Coast West African region where European slave traders procured most of their slaves. It includes parts of Nigeria, Dahomey, and Togo.

Slave dynasty First dynasty of the Delhi Sultanate in northern India. It ruled between 1209 and 1290 and was so named because its founder, Qutb-ud-Din Aibak, and most of his successors were once slaves.

slavery Age-old institution of involuntary servitude, now eliminated in nearly every part of the world. Mention of slavery has been found in writings of the Babylonians, Hebrews, Egyptians, and other ancient peoples and it was common among the Greeks and Romans. After the fall of Rome, slavery in the medieval European states was generally replaced by the feudal institution of serfdom. It continued in the Muslim states, however. European involvement in slavery was renewed in the 15th cent. with the beginnings of overseas exploration and colonization, and slaves were used mainly in colonial domains. The Portuguese took the first Negro slaves from West Africa in the 1440s, and in the 16th cent., Spain and England also began trading them (France, Denmark, and American colonials started in the 17th cent.). By the late 17th cent., the English dominated the slave trade. The prime market for slaves was in the New World colonies. The Spanish began importing large numbers of slaves into South America after native Indian slaves proved too rebellious. In North America the first slaves were introduced (1619) at Jamestown, Virginia, and, though slaves were later sent to other British colonies in the Americas, it was in the South that they became an integral part of the plantation economy. Active slave trade by European powers continued throughout the 18th cent. But by the beginning of the 19th cent., abolitionists were already mounting their campaign to bring about its end (*see* abolition).

Slavophile Russian intellectual movement (mid-19th cent.). Slavophiles held that Russian culture was superior to European civilization. The movement declined after the Crimean War.

Slavs Largest ethnic group in Europe, today divided into three main branches: Western, including Poles, Czechs, Slovaks, and Wends; Southern (collectively Yugoslavs), including

Serbs, Croats, and others; and Eastern, including Great Russians, Ukrainians, and Belorussians. The Slavs are thought to have migrated from Asia to Eastern Europe (3d–2d millennium BC). They were then forced eastward beyond the Oder River to their present homelands (5th–6th cents.) by the expansion of the German states.

Slidell, John 1793–1871. US diplomat. Failure of the "Slidell Mission" in Mexico led to the Mexican War (*q.v.*). He also figured in the Trent Affair (*q.v.*).

Slim, William Joseph, 1st viscount 1891–1970. British field marshal. Slim commanded British forces in the reconquest of Burma from the Japanese during WW II.

Sloat, John Drake *See* **Mexican War.**

Slovakia Historic region, a former Czechoslovakian constituent republic, and since 1993 an independent state. Settled by Slovaks (c6th cent.), it became part of the Moravian Empire and was converted to Christianity (9th cent.) by saints Cyril and Methodius. The Magyars conquered Slovakia in 906, and it was ruled by the Hungarians until 1918, when it became part of Czechoslovakia. After the breakup of Czechoslovakia (1938), Slovakia declared its independence (1939) and became allied with Germany for protection. Czechoslovakia was reformed after WW II. The Czech and Slovak republics gained local autonomy under the 1968 constitution. Following the ouster of the Communist regime in 1989, pressure began to mount for an independent Slovakia, and in late 1992, the breakup of Czechoslavakia and creation of independent Slovakia was effected in 1993. *See also* Czechoslavakia.

Slovenia Independent state, formerly a region of northern Yugoslavia, historically united with Croatia. Slovenes settled the region from the 6th cent. AD, and came under Austrian domination from the 14th cent. In 1918 it became part of Yugoslavia. Following the collapse of Communism in Yugoslavia, Slovenia declared independence. *See* Yugoslavia.

Sluis, Battle of (Sluys, ˜) English naval victory (June 24, 1340) over France at the beginning of the Hundred Years' War. Fought near Bruges, the battle resulted in destruction of the French fleet and gave Edward III command of the English Channel for the next generation.

Sluter, Claus *d.* c1406. Flemish sculptor, noted for his sculptures on the tomb of Philip the Bold and at the Carthusian monastery of Champmol.

Sluys, Battle of *See* **Sluis, Battle of.**

Smetana, Bedřich 1824–84. Czech composer, considered the father of Czech national music. Among his noted works were *The Moldau* and the opera *The Bartered Bride.*

Smiles, Samuel 1812–1904. Scottish author. Abandoning a career in medicine, he became a journalist in Leeds, where he edited the progressive *Leeds Times.* A proponent of self-help and hard work, he became known for such books as *Self-Help* (1859), *Character* (1871), *Thrift* (1875), and *Duty* (1880).

Smith, Adam 1723–90. Scottish economist and philosopher. Smith's famous book, *Wealth of Nations* (1776), greatly influenced economic theory. It argued for laissez-faire doctrines such as free trade and held that the "invisible hand" of individual competition would ultimately work to the public benefit.

Smith, Alfred Emanuel 1873–1944. American politician. The governor of New York (1919–20, 1923–28), he was the first Catholic to become a presidential candidate (1928) of a major party (Democrats). He lost to H. Hoover.

Smith, Edmund Kirby (Kirby-Smith, Edward) 1824–93. Confederate general. Smith fought at Bull Run, headed (from 1863) the Trans-Mississippi Department, and was the last general to surrender (May 26, 1865).

Smith, Ian Douglas 1919– . Rhodesian politician. A white supremacist, he became prime minister in 1964 and unilaterally declared Rhodesia's independence (1965) from Britain. His white Rhodesian government subsequently resisted international pressures, including economic boycott, and ruled until 1980, when blacks came to power in the new state of Zimbabwe.

Smith, John 1580–1631. English colonist, a founder of Jamestown, Virginia (1607). He became the effective leader of the colonists soon after their arrival and was named president in 1608. Probably saved by the intervention of the Indian princess Pocahontas, he helped to establish friendly relations with the Indians. An injury in 1609 forced him to return to England.

Smith, Joseph 1805–44. American religious leader, founder of the Mormons (*q.v.*). Some of his religious views, especially those on polygamy, aroused hostility to Mormonism. He was killed by a mob.

Smith, Walter Bedell 1895–1961. American WW II general, Gen. D. Eisenhower's chief of staff (1942–45). He later served as ambassador to the Soviet Union, CIA director, and undersecretary of state.

Smith Act (Alien Registration Act of 1940) US act (June 29, 1940) requiring aliens to register and making it a federal offense to advocate the violent overthrow of the government. This provision was used to prosecute leaders of the American Communist party after WW II.

Smithson, James 1765–1829. English scientist. Smithson bequeathed his fortune to the United States for the purpose of founding the Smithsonian Institution (established 1846).

Smolensk, Battle of Two battles fought at this western Russian city. 1. Victory (Aug. 17, 1812) for Napoleon during his invasion of Russia in the Napoleonic Wars. He later vainly tried to rally his troops there during his retreat. 2. WW II battle (July–Aug. 6, 1941) in which the Germans captured the city during their invasion of the Soviet Union. Russian losses were 100,000 casualties and prisoners.

Smollett, Tobias George 1721–71. Scottish novelist, noted for such comic novels as *The Adventures of Roderick Random, The Adventures of Peregrine Pickle* and *The Expedition of Humphrey Clinker.*

Smoot, Reed 1862–1941. American politician the first Mormon elected senator (1902). He opposed US entry into the League of Nations and coauthored the Hawley-Smoot Tariff (1930).

Smuts, Jan Christiaan 1870–1950. South African soldier and statesman. He fought the British in the Boer War but later was instrumental in forming the Union of South Africa (1910) He was prime minister (1919–24, 1939–48).

Snefru *d.* c2589 BC. First Egyptian king (c2613–2589) of the 4th dynasty. Under his rule Egyptian mining and trade flourished, and government and administration were refined. One of the first true pyramids was built at Dahshur during his reign.

Snow, C(harles) P(ercy), baron 1905–80. English author and physicist. As a novelist he is best known for his *Strangers and Brothers* series of novels, including *The Masters* and *The Affair.*

Snowden, Philip, 1st viscount 1864–1937. English statesman, a Laborite, and several times chancellor of the exchequer. He supported free trade and balanced budgets but was ousted with the Labour government (1931) during the Depression.

Sobhuza II *See* **Swaziland.**

Sobraon, Battle of British victory in the first of the Sikh Wars in northwestern India. Some 25,000 Sikhs were defeated by a 15,000-man Anglo-Indian force. Sikh losses were 8,000 to 2,300 allied deaths.

Soccer War Brief war (July 14–30, 1969) between El Salvador and Honduras. Triggered by tensions over a soccer match between the two national teams, the underlying cause of the war was resentment at the expulsion from Honduras of Salvadoran peasants who had migrated there. About 2,000 soldiers and civilians, mainly Honduran, were killed.

social contract Agreement or bond by which human beings move from a state of nature to form society. This theory was first advanced by T. Hobbes and J. Locke.

Social Credit *See* **Aberhart, William.**

social Darwinism Discredited 19th-cent. social philosophy based on the Darwinian theory of evolution. It held that human societies, like animal species, were subject to the law of "survival of the fittest." Chief exponents were British philosopher H. Spencer and American sociologist William Graham Sumner (1840–1910).

Social Democratic Party of Germany German political party. Founded (1863) as a Marxist workers' party, it became a formidable power in Germany during the early 1900s, and participating in coalition governments of the 1920s, the party became the Weimar Republic's staunchest defender of democratic government. It was suppressed (1933) by A. Hitler and reorganized after WW II. However, it was unable to successfully challenge the coalition of Christian Democrat and other parties until after 1959, when it eliminated Marxist ideology and broadened its appeal as a people's party. Since the 1970s the party has formed coalition governments in Germany under W. Brandt and H. Schmidt.

Social Gospel Movement in American Protestantism (late 19th–early 20th cents.) that sought to apply the principles of the Gospels to the social questions of the day. It advocated a shorter work week, better working conditions, the right to a living wage, the abolition of child labor, etc. The movement declined when organized labor took up many of its causes.

socialism Politico-economic doctrine. Socialism seeks to replace the competitive capitalist system with a cooperative society, in which means of production and distribution are owned either by the government or collectively by the people. A response to the hardships and social injustice bred by the Industrial Revolution, socialism dates primarily from the works of such thinkers as F. Babeuf, C. de Saint-Simon, C. Fourier, and R. Owen (18th–19th cents.). Babeuf, sometimes called the first socialist theorist, sought to advance economic egalitarianism during the French Revolution and this gave rise to the revolutionary movement known as Babouvism. Saint-Simon postulated government control of the economy and industry, while Fourier and Owen believed in decentralizing society into small collectives. Experiments in socialism in the early 19th cent. included founding of utopian communes such as Brook Farm (*q.v.*) and New Harmony (*see* Harmony Society), and L. Blanc's unsuccessful National Workshops (government financed, worker controlled) in France after the 1848 Revolution. New elements of class struggle and the necessity of revolution were added to socialist thought by way of Marx's and Engels' *Communist Manifesto* (1848). For the rest of the 19th cent. and into the early 20th, the doctrinal dispute over revolutionary socialism versus evolutionary socialism divided Socialists and ultimately brought about the permanent split between democratic Socialists (advocates of gradual change) and Communists (advocates of revolutionary change). The disputes were evident in the First and Second International (*q.v.*), the revolutionary sentiment giving rise to anarchism and syndicalism (*q.v.*) in the late 19th cent. Gradualists formed the Fabian Society (*q.v.*) in Britain and Social Democratic parties elsewhere in Europe. Though many other issues divided Socialists in the early 1900s, the triumph of the Bolsheviks in the Russian Revolution of 1917 resulted in the complete separation of revolutionaries (now Communists) from the Socialist movement. Thereafter, democratic Socialists gradually gained power in European countries (especially after WW II), notably in Britain (*see* Labour party), Germany (*see* Social Democratic party of Germany), and, in the 1980s, France. In the US, the Socialist party (*q.v.*) never managed to gain significant power.

Socialist Labor party American Socialist party established in Philadelphia (1876). Founded on Marxist principles, it opposed simple trade unionism. Under the vigorous leadership of

D. De Leon the party reached its zenith in the 1890s and declined thereafter.

Socialist party Former US political party advocating gradual transformation to a Socialist state in the US. Formed (1901) by a merger of the Social Democratic party and moderate elements of the Socialist Labor party, it reached its zenith in the years between 1910 and 1919, under the leadership of E. Debs. Debs ran for president in 1912 and again in 1920 while in prison for opposing US involvement in WW I. The party was seriously weakened (1919) when the radical wing defected to form the US Communist party. Later, during the 1930s, President F. Roosevelt incorporated many of the party's reforms in the New Deal. Led by N. Thomas from the 1920s, the party declined steadily in subsequent years.

Socialist Revolutionary party Russian political party. Founded (1901) by a Populist coalition, it advocated a classless society and agrarian reform and carried out political assassinations. It was suppressed (1922) by the Communists.

Social War (Marsic War) Rebellion (90–88 BC) by tribes in central and southern Italy against Roman rule. The tribes, including the Marsians, Samnites, Pelignians, and Lucanians, had been forced into alliance with Rome in 338 but did not enjoy the privileges of Roman citizenship. The Roman Marcus Livius Drusus proposed extending citizenship (91 BC), but the move was opposed by the Senate and he was assassinated. The tribes then rose in revolt (90 BC) and attempted to form a confederation (Italia) in opposition to Rome. Roman armies (Sulla was a commander) were unable to break the rebellion. It ended after citizenship was offered to all Roman allies and those tribes that ceased hostilities. Eight new gentes (Roman tribes) were created and the new citizens were rapidly assimilated. The Italian peninsula was thus unified under Roman control.

Society of Friends (Quakers) Protestant Christian sect that rejects both formal creed and the need for ministers, holding that they interfere with an individual's communion with the Holy Spirit ("inner light"). Established (c1647) in England under the leadership of G. Fox, the Quakers refused to take oaths, to bear arms, to pay religious tithes, or otherwise conform to the English church. They were persecuted until laws regarding religious toleration were passed (late 17th cent.) and, under W. Penn, founded the

Quaker colony in Pennsylvania (1681). The Friends were early and zealous supporters of abolition of slavery and actively supported pacifism. The American Friends Service Committee (founded 1917) is noted for its support of humanitarian causes.

Society of Jesus (Jesuits)   Roman Catholic religious order, founded (1534) by Saint Ignatius of Loyola and approved (1540) by Pope Paul III. Missionary work, notably by Saint Francis Xavier in the East, began shortly after founding of the order. The Jesuits played an important role in the Catholic Reformation and also established many schools in Europe. However, they aroused opposition from European monarchs, partly because of their loyalty to the pope, and by 1773 Pope Clement XIV was forced to dissolve the order. Pope Pius VII reinstituted it (1814).

Socinianism   Anti-Trinitarian Christian sect founded by Laelius Socinus (1525–62) that flourished in Poland from the 1550s. Socinianists believed Jesus was merely a man, divine only in his function and not his nature. They suffered persecutions and disbanded by the early 17th cent.

Socinus, Laelius   *See* **Socinianism.**

Socrates 470?–399 BC.   Greek philosopher, one of the great philosophers of ancient Greece, whose life and teachings have made a profound impression on Western thought. The son of Sophroniscus, a sculptor, he is thought to have worked in sculpture before turning to philosophy. He fought in the second Peloponnesian War and was noted for his courage and strength. Socrates spent much of his life in the public places of Athens conducting discussions, or dialogues, with his fellow citizens. He developed a mode of inquiry known as the dialectic, or Socratic method, by which the truth of a given statement is tested by a series of questions. His purpose was to gain knowledge, the basis of virtue, or right conduct. He became a well-known figure in Athens and was the subject of mockery in Aristophanes' play *The Clouds.* Eventually he was accused of impiety and corruption of youth and was sentenced to death. With his disciples by his side, he committed suicide by drinking hemlock, as required by his death sentence. Socrates wrote nothing, and our knowledge of his life and teachings comes mainly from the writings of his disciple Plato, notably the *Apology, Crito,* and *Phaedo.*

Soissons, Battle of   *See* **Clovis I.**

Solemn League and Covenant   Agreement (1643) between the Scots and the English Parliamentarians during the English Civil Wars. By it, the Parliamentarians endorsed Presbyterianism for all of England and Scotland in exchange for Scottish military help against the Royalist armies.

Soleri, Paolo 1919– .   Italian-American architect and city planner, known for his futuristic designs of densely populated cities, planned to minimize environmental disturbance.

Solferino, Battle of   Bloody battle (June 24, 1859) fought during the Italian Risorgimento (*q.v.*), or war of unification. King Victor Emmanuel II of Piedmont (later of all Italy) and his allied French forces met the Austrian forces in this indecisive battle in northern Italy. The heavy losses (totaling nearly 30,000 dead) moved the French to a settlement, which resulted in Emmanuel's acquisition of Lombardy.

Solidarity   *See* **Poland, 1980–82.**

Solomon   Great king of ancient Israel (973–933 BC), successor to his father, David, and credited with great wisdom. He encouraged trade and thereby brought on a period of great commercial prosperity. He also built lavish cities, constructed the first Temple at Jerusalem, and (traditionally) was the author of the Song of Solomon, proverbs, and other biblical writings. [2 Samuel 12; 1 Kings 1–11; 2 Chron 1–9]

Solon c638–c559 BC.   Athenian statesman who laid the foundations of democracy in Athens. Elected sole archon (chief magistrate) (594 BC) amid a social crisis caused by the widespread indebtedness of the populace to the aristocracy, he instituted his economic reforms called Seisachtheia. He ended the practice of securing loans with personal liberty (serfdom or slavery resulted from failure to pay), annulled all debts contracted in this manner, restricted exports, and reformed the currency. He also reformed the Athenian constitution, allowing members of the two top census-classes the right to serve as archon (formerly by birthright) and giving the assembly the power to overturn magistrates' verdicts. The power of the Areopagus (*q.v.*) was limited and, according to some sources, the Council of Four Hundred was created to represent the propertied class. Solon also introduced a new law code to modify the harsh Draconian Code.

Solzhenitsyn, Aleksandr Isayevich 1918– . Russian writer and a leading dissident against the excesses of the Soviet system. After receiving the

Nobel Prize for Literature (1970), he was exiled to the West (1974) and settled in the US. Among his works are *The First Circle* (1968), *August 1914* (1971) and *The Gulag Archipelago* (1973).

Somalia (Somali Democratic Republic) Independent state located on the Horn of Africa and bordering the Gulf of Aden and the Indian Ocean. The population is 8,415,000 and the capital is Mogadishu. Key dates in the history of Somalia include:

7TH–10TH CENTS. Arab and Persian traders established in region.

16TH CENT. Ottoman Turks ruled north, Sultan of Zanzibar ruled south.

1862 France established coaling station near Djibouti; Italy settled Eritrea.

1870s–84 Egyptian occupation.

1884 British occupied region formerly held by Egyptians.

1887 Britain established protectorate over its territory.

1888 British and French reached agreement on borders of their respective territories in region.

1889 Italy established protectorate in central region.

1936 Italian Somaliland joined to Ethiopian provinces to form Italian East Africa.

1941 WW II; Britain captured and ruled entire area (until 1950).

1950 Italian Somaliland separated from British territory; came under Italian control as UN trust.

1960 Britain and Italy granted their respective sectors independence; regions joined as Republic of Somalia (July 1).

1964–67 Clashes with Ethiopia and Kenya as Somalis sought to unify large Somali populations in those countries with Somalia.

1969 President Abdi Rashid Ali Shermarke assassinated; parliament replaced by Supreme Revolutionary Council.

1969–91 Maj. Gen. Muhammad Siad Barre in power; marked beginning of his long rule.

1976 Barre dissolved council; named Somali Socialist party only legal political party.

1977 Somalia supported Ethiopian rebels in Ogaden region; led to break with Soviets, who supported the Ethiopian central government; some 11,000 Cuban troops, armed by Soviets, sent to Ethiopia to battle Somalis.

1978 Somalia defeated in war with Ethiopia; US supplied food, relief.

1979 New constitution adopted; People's Assembly elected.

1980 President Barre declared a state of emergency and reinstated the Supreme Revolutionary Council (Oct.).

1982–85 Ethiopian troops continued to hold the border areas captured in 1978; sporadic fighting continued throughout the region.

1982 Anti-government rioting broke out in Hargeisa (Feb.).

1982 Ethiopian-backed rebel forces invaded the central border area of Somalia (July).

1983 Rebels attacked a prison near Berbera (Jan. 2), releasing 724 prisoners.

1984 Somali Airlines flight highjacked by dissidents (Nov. 24), after eight schoolchildren were condemned to death for distributing anti-government leaflets (Oct.).

1986 Barre met with Ethiopians in an attempt to end the hostilities (Jan.).

1988 Rebel forces captured the towns of Hargeisa, Burao, and Berbera (May); after heavy fighting the government recaptured Burao (July) and Hargeisa (Aug.)

1989 Rioting in Mogadishu was brutally suppressed by the military; 400 killed and over 1,000 wounded (July 14); the unrest was precipitated by the arrests of leading Muslim clergymen.

1989 President Barre offered to relinquish power and allow opposition parties to contest elections (Aug.).

1989 Commission appointed to prepare for transition to multi-party elections (Nov.).

1990 President Barre dissolved the government; offered posts in a new government under his leadership to members of the opposition (Jan.).

1990 US cut off most aid to Somalia (Feb.), citing human rights abuses.

1990 Opposition leaders signed declaration demanding President Barre's resignation, appointment of transitional government, and disbanding of security forces (June); Barre had the opposition leaders arrested.

1990 Three main rebel groups joined forces to overthrow Barre (Aug.).

1990 Barre hastily introduced new constitution and electoral reform laws (Oct.).

1991 Fierce fighting in Mogadishu (Jan.) between government troops and rebels of the

United Somali Congress (USC); President Barre fled capital (Jan. 26).

1991 USC leader Ali Mahdi Mohammed seized power (Jan.); his leadership rejected by rebels in north and opposed within his own USC, however.

1991 Somali National Movement (SNM) declared independence in the north; secession opposed by USC and other rebel groups.

1991 Djibouti brokered ceasefire between many rival Somali factions (June), but agreement did not include SNM in the north.

1991 First fighting in the capital since President Mahdi seized control; rival USC factions began vying for control.

1991 US sharply increased emergency aid to Somalia.

1992 New ceasefire negotiated (Feb.); reported taking hold (Mar.).

1992 UN emergency relief supplies began arriving in Somalia (Aug.); US airlift began as hunger and famine became widespread.

1992 UN peacekeeping force arrived (Sept.); unable to gain control of situation however, as continued fighting between rival factions reduced country to state of anarchy; emergency food supplies being stolen by roving groups of bandits.

1992 US sent thousands of troops to Somalia (arrived Dec. 9) to restore order and provide protection for convoys distributing emergency food.

Somaliland Region located on the eastern coast of Africa and extending from the equator north to the Gulf of Aden. It is divided between Afars and Issas (*formerly* French Somaliland) and Somalia (*formerly* British Somaliland and Italian Somaliland).

Somers, John (Sommers, Baron) 1651–1716. English Whig jurist who presided over the framing of the English Bill of Rights (1689) and who was a trusted adviser to William III.

Somerset, Edmund Beaufort, 2d duke of *d.* 1455. English statesman and general. Largely responsible for loss of English territory in France during the Hundred Years' War, he nevertheless held a favored position in Henry VI's government. This provoked the Yorkists and helped precipitate the Wars of the Roses.

Somme, Battle of Two major offensives on the Western Front in northeastern France. 1. First ~:

Allied French and British offensive (July–Nov., 1916), fought to relieve German pressure on Verdun. Allied generals D. Haig and J. Joffre launched repeated attacks against German defensive positions, commanded by P. von Hindenburg and E. von Ludendorff, and gained some territory, but at great cost. Losses were 500,000 Allied troops; 450,000 Germans. 2. Second ~: German offensive (Mar. 21–Apr. 4, 1918) and nearly successful attempt to break through Allied lines. Commanded by Gen. von Ludendorff, the Germans launched a series of major attacks that ultimately drove Allied troops back some 40 miles. Gen. F. Foch, named Allied commander during the battle, halted the offensive by Apr. 4. Losses, nearly 200,000 Allied troops; 180,000 Germans.

Sommers, Baron *See* **Somers, John.**

Somoza, Anastasio 1896–1956. President of Nicaragua (1937–47, 1950–56). As head of the army (from 1933) he ruled the country even when out of office. He established his family's rule in Nicaragua that lasted until 1979.

Sonderbund League (1845) of Catholic cantons of Switzerland. It was formed as a "defense league" against the anti-Catholic movement in the other cantons but was deemed a "separatist league." A brief civil war ensued and ended with the league's defeat in 1847.

Song (Sung) Chinese dynasty and historic period (960–1279), which followed the Five Dynasties (*q.v.*) period. One of the great epochs of Chinese history, it was marked by commercial prosperity, a cultural flowering, administrative reforms, and technological innovations. The dynasty was founded by Taizu (Zhao Kuangyin, reigned 960–976), a general serving the later Chou dynasty ruler. On the emperor's death, Taizu took power and by 976 had largely completed reunification of China. With its capital at Kaifeng, the Song dynasty was not seriously threatened until 1127. At this time, invasions by nomadic Jurchen tribes from the north forced Song rulers to move their capital to Lin'agan in the south. Thus the Song dynasty is usually divided into Northern Song (960–1127) and Southern Song (1127–1279). The Song dynasty was finally conquered (1279) by the invading Mongols under Kublai Khan, who replaced it with the Yuan dynasty. Song rulers instituted administrative reforms (notably those of Wang Anshi, *q.v.*), many of which were aimed at centralizing power (especially to gain firm control over the military) and also fostered the growth of schools and a great government bureaucracy. Commercial prosperity came as a result of increased trade, notably with India, Persia, and the Arabs. The Song period was further marked by the increase in printing (with movable type by the 11th cent.), a revival of Confucianism and the writings of Zhu Xi; the compilation of great encyclopedias and histories; and a golden age of Chinese landscape painting and ceramics. It also saw the use of gunpowder and the magnetic compass for navigation.

Songhai, Empire of Ancient African empire in the Niger Valley of the Sudan. Founded by Berbers (c700) and converted to Islam, the empire reached its height under Askia Muhammad I (c1493–1528) with Timbuktu its chief city. The invasion of Moorish troops from Morocco (1591) destroyed the empire.

Sonni 'Ali *d.* 1492. Ruler (1464–92) of the Songhai Kingdom. He began the expansion of Songhai domains until he controlled much of the Sudan, including Timbuktu (taken 1468).

Sonnino, Sidney, Baron 1847–1922. Italian diplomat who promoted Italy's entry into WW I and who negotiated the secret Treaty of London (*q.v.*) in 1915.

Sons of Liberty Activist patriotic organizations formed in the American colonies from c1765. They organized protests against unpopular British laws such as the Stamp Act. The same name was adopted (1864) by a US Copperhead (*q.v.*) organization seeking a negotiated peace with the Confederacy.

Soong, T. V. 1894–1971. Chinese financier and Guomindang finance minister (1928–31, 1932–31). He reorganized China's financial systems and renegotiated foreign agreements to restore China's control of its tariff rates.

Soong Ch'ing-ling (Sun Yat-sen, Madame) 1892–1981. Chinese political leader. The sister of T. V. Soong and wife (*m.* 1914) of Sun Yat-sen, she was active in the Guomindang until the Communists were expelled.

Soong Mei-ling (Chiang Kai-shek, Madame) 1898– . Chinese political leader, sister-in-law of Sun Yat-sen. A member of the Soong family, she married Chiang Kai-shek (1927) and helped win Western support for the Guomindang.

Sophia 1630–1714. Electress of Hanover, and granddaughter of James I of England. Her son

became George I of England by the Act of Settlement (*q.v.*).

Sophia Alekseyevna 1657–1704. Regent of Russia (1682–89), daughter of Tsar Alexis. She ruled during the minority of her brother Ivan V and half-brother Peter I (Peter the Great).

Sophocles c496–c406 BC. Greek tragedian who is ranked with his contemporaries Aeschylus and Euripides as one of the greatest tragic poets. Active in public life, he served as a treasurer in 442, one of ten generals commanding the military in 440 (and again two other times), as a priest for a religious society (421), and as one of the public officials (413) charged with restoring Athens after its costly defeat at Syracuse. But it was as a dramatist that Sophoclese achieved lasting fame. He made several innovations in Greek drama, including the introduction of a third actor, expansion of the chorus from 12 to 15 members, and the introduction of scene painting. Sophocles wrote over 120 plays and his surviving works include *Antigone, Electra, Trachiniae, Philoctetes, Oedipus at Colonus,* and the most famous, *Oedipus Rex.*

Sophists Greek philosophical movement that flourished from the 5th cent. BC. Skeptical about the possibility of knowing truth, the Sophists opposed philosophical doctrine and instead taught the art of rhetorical persuasion. Protagoras was the first prominent Sophist.

Soranus *fl.* 1st–2d cent. AD. Ancient Greek physician, an authority on gynecology, obstetrics, and pediatrics. His writings were influential through the 15th cent.

Sorel, Agnes c1422–50. French mistress (1444–50) to Charles VII, the first woman to be officially recognized in that capacity in France.

Sorel, Georges 1847–1922. French philosopher, a leading advocate of revolutionary syndicalism (*q.v.*). He wrote *Reflections on Violence.*

Soter (Demetrius) *See* **Demetrius I.**

Soubirous, Marie Bernarde *See* **Bernadette, Saint.**

Soulé, Pierre 1801–70. French-born American politician. As US minister to Spain, he joined with J. Buchanan and John Y. Mason (1799–1859) in writing the controversial Ostend Manifesto (*q.v.*).

Soule, Samuel W. *See* **Sholes, Christopher Latham.**

Soulouque, Faustin Élie (Faustin I) 1785–1867. Haitian dictator. A former slave and soldier, he was elected to the presidency (1847) and made himself emperor (1849–59).

Soult, Nicolas 1769–1851. French marshal. Under Napoleon, he commanded French forces in the Peninsular Campaign and was chief of staff at Waterloo. He later served royalist governments and brought about the French conquest of Morocco.

Sousa, John Philip 1854–1932. Noted American bandmaster and composer. He conducted the US Marine Band and composed many popular marches, including *Stars and Stripes Forever.*

Sousa, Martin Affonso de 1500?–64. Portuguese admiral. He founded the first Portuguese settlement in Brazil (1532) at São Vincente.

South, the US region, comprising the southeastern and south central states. Traditionally, the Mason-Dixon line has been the dividing line between North and South and until recent times marked political, social, and economic differences; it contributed to friction and divisiveness between the two regions. *See also* individual states; Confederacy; American Civil War.

South Africa, Republic of Republic located at the southern tip of Africa. The national capital is Pretoria; the legislative capital is Cape Town. South Africa was first settled by the Dutch, whose descendants, the Boers, developed the Afrikaner language and culture. British settlement and influence increased from the 17th to 19th cent. As a result, the Boers migrated north and east to found Natal, the Transvaal, and the Orange Free State. All eventually were incorporated, after the Boer War (1899–1902), into the Union of South Africa, which became the independent Republic of South Africa in 1961. In the 1980s, South Africa came under international pressure to end its apartheid policies and in the early 1990s finally took steps toward instituting a black majority rule there. Key dates in the history of South Africa include:

1652 Jan van Riebeeck established supply post at Cape of Good Hope for the Dutch East India Company; first permanent European settlement in South Africa.

17TH–18TH CENTS. Descendants of Dutch settlers developed Afrikaner society and culture in region; established new farms and settlements inland.

1815 Cape Colony passed to British control by Congress of Vienna.

1835–43 Great Trek, migration of Boers away from British-controlled territory; Piet Retief, Andres Pretorius, and others led the Boers north and east beyond the Orange River.

1843 British annexed Natal, territory settled by Boers (northeast of Cape Colony).

1852 Boers established independent republic of Transvaal.

1854 Boers established independent republic called the Orange Free State.

1856 Transvaal became known as the South African Republic.

1860s–70s Discovery of diamonds (1867) in Orange Free State and gold (1886) in southern Transvaal led to great influx of British to region and resulting friction with Boers; Britain annexed the Transvaal (1877), but restored its independence in 1881.

1886 Johannesburg founded.

1894 British South Africa Company defeated natives in Matabele War.

1895–1896 L. Jameson led Jameson Raid into Transvaal in attempt to spur uprising of British settlers (Uitlanders) against Boers; raid supported by Cecil Rhodes, prime minister of Cape Colony; raid failed but ultimately contributed to outbreak of Boer (South African) War.

1899–1902 Boer War (South African War) fought between the Boers and British, Boers defeated; Transvaal and Orange Free State made British colonies.

1909 South Africa Act united British colonies into Union of South Africa (Sept. 20).

1910–19 L. Botha in office as first prime minister of the Union of South Africa.

1912 African National Congress Party organized to oppose European domination.

1914–18 Union of South Africa joined Allies in WW I; suppressed revolt (1915) of Boers against support of Britain; occupied (1915) German South-West Africa, which became a League of Nations mandate under South African control after the war.

1919–24 Jan Christiaan Smuts in office as prime minister.

1924–39 J.B.M. Hertzog, leader of the pro-Afrikaner Nationalist party, in office as prime minister; government passed numerous laws advancing segregation of the different racial groups in South Africa.

1927 Immorality Act passed, forbidding sex between members of different races.

1931 British Parliament passed Statute of Westminster; South Africa became self-governing within the British Commonwealth (1934).

1939–48 J. Smuts again prime minister; led South Africa into WW II on Allied side despite pro-German sentiment among many Boers; came under fire by Nationalists over his "liberal" policies; UN opposed to South Africa's racial policies.

1945 South Africa joined the UN.

1945 Government instituted Black Urban Areas Act.

1948–54 D. Malan, member of the National Party, in office as prime minister; established apartheid policies leading to white-run government and segregation of blacks (over 70 percent of population) from whites; National Party remained in power to present day.

1949 Mixed Marriages Act passed, prohibiting marriage between members of different races.

1950s African National Congress (ANC, multi-racial) led opposition to apartheid, mainly through civil disobedience.

1953 Government passed Separate Amenities Act.

1955 Freedom Congress; ANC and other groups issued Freedom Charter, demanding equal political rights for all races.

1958–66 H. Verwoerd prime minister.

1960 ANC and Pan-Africanist Congress (PAC) protested "pass laws"; police killed 67 protesters (Mar.), sparking new demonstrations.

1960 ANC and PAC banned by government; both groups began terror campaigns, mounted from outside South Africa.

1960 South Africa became a republic and left the Commonwealth; white voters approved the move in 1960.

1962 ANC leader Nelson Mandela arrested; later given life in prison on sabotage charges; Mandela later became rallying point for anti-aparteid supporters.

1966–78 B. Vorster in office as prime minister, following assassination of Verwoerd (Sept., 1966).

1966 Group Areas Act passed; races separated into different residential areas; black homelands created (those not working in "white"

South Africa denied South African citizenship); policy forced relocation of hundreds of thousands.

1967 Prohibition of Political Interference Act passed; members of different races not allowed to join same political party.

1974 UN declared its authority over South-West Africa, renamed Namibia; South Africa resisted move; unsuccessful attempt made to expel South Africa from the UN.

1974 South Africa suspended from participation in UN General Assembly.

1976 10,000 black students rioted (June) in Soweto, near Johannesburg; unrest spread to other areas; 600 people killed as government suppressed the demonstrations.

1976 Black homeland of Transkei granted independence by South African government.

1977 Steven Biko, a leading opponent of apartheid, died (Sept. 12) of injuries suffered in prison; death led to renewed protests against South Africa's racial policies.

1977 Government issued new restrictions on political freedoms of blacks (Oct.); activists arrested and black organizations banned.

1977 Black homeland of Bophuthatswana granted independence by South African government.

1978 Prime Minister B. Vorster resigned; denounced UN plan for independence of Namibia.

1978–89 Prime Minister Pieter Willem Botha in office.

1979 Trade unions for African legalized; some minor apartheid rules lifted.

1979 First meeting of AZAPO, formed by African, Colored, and Asian opponents of apartheid.

1979 Black homeland of Venda granted independence.

1980s South African troops launched attacks against SWAPO guerrillas in Namibia.

1981 President's Council on constitutional reform recommended admitting Indians and Coloreds to a three-chamber legislature; Africans excluded; reforms approved in 1983.

1981 Black homeland of Ciskei granted independence.

1983 Africans boycotted local elections to protest exclusion from new parliament.

1984 Violent protests rocked black townships; security police resorted to harsh measures to suppress riots; rival African tribes and political groups also attacked one another.

1984 South Africa agreed to cease-fire with Angola; agreed to withdraw troops from Angola (though some troops remained).

1984 Nkomati accord signed with Mozambique (Mar.); both sides pledged to stop cross-border attacks by opposition forces operating in respective countries.

1984 Bishop Desmond Tutu awarded the Nobel Peace Prize.

1985–86 Various apartheid laws abolished or modified; laws against interracial sex and marriage repealed; controls on residence, employment, and movement ended; blacks granted some property rights in black areas; right-wing opposition to moves mounted.

1985 South African forces raided Lesotho capital to attack guerrilla forces based there (Dec.); relations with Lesotho improved after coup resulted in new government there.

1986 Government declared state of emergency (June) as unrest in black communities continued; some 2,300 persons killed since 1984.

1986 Imposition of sanctions against South Africa by seven Commonwealth nations protesting apartheid; EC and US imposed limited sanctions; legislation in US, however, forced some 200 US companies to withdraw from South Africa; two years later Japan halted direct exports there.

1986 Mozambique president Machel killed in plane crash in South Africa (Oct.); charges of South African involvement in crash never proved.

1987 UN formally demanded South Africa pull its troops out of Angola.

1987 Increasingly militant African trade unions went on long strikes; government continued state of emergency (and again in 1988 and 1989).

1987 Black homeland of KwaNdebele granted independence; widespread violent demonstrations in KwaNdebele broke out.

1988 Agreements reached between all parties for final peace (and independence) in Namibia, and withdrawal of troops (including Cubans) from Angola.

1989 P. W. Botha forced to resign (Aug.).

1989– Frederik Willem de Klerk in office as president; backed further reforms but remained committed to separation of the races.

1989 Mass Democratic Movement organization staged peaceful protest campaign (Aug.–Sept.).

1990 Ban on ANC, PAC and other opposition groups lifted (Feb.); F. W. de Klerk also announced intent to negotiate with Africans for new democratic constitution; promised release of Nelson Mandela and others.

1990 Mandela released from prison (Feb. 11); elected ANC deputy president soon after.

1990 Formal talks between government and ANC held for first time (May).

1990 F. W. de Klerk ended state of emergency (June) everywhere except Natal, where violence between blacks continued; state of emergency lifted in Natal (Oct.).

1990 Ruling National Party ended racial restrictions on its membership (Oct.); Separate Amenities Act repealed (Oct.).

1990 ANC President Oliver Tambo, exiled from South African 30 years ago, returned.

1991 F. W. de Klerk put through repeal of all remaining apartheid laws; reached agreement with ANC on release of prisoners, in return for ANC restrictions on its military activities (Feb.).

1991 Negotiations suspended between ANC and government after ANC, reacting to new violence between blacks, issued ultimatum unacceptable to government (Apr.).

1991 Winnie Mandela, wife of ANC leader Nelson Mandela, convicted on charges of assault and kidnapping (May).

1991–92 Convention for a Democratic South Africa held to determine future form of government.

1992 EC lifted all economic sanctions against South Africa in light of reforms, following similar action by US and Commonwealth nations.

1992 Government began investigation of charges that security forces had caused violence in black townships (Feb.).

1992 White voters overwhelmingly approved referendum on continuing reform program (Mar.).

South Africa Act British act (effective May 31, 1910) that created the Union of South Africa by uniting the British possessions of Cape, Natal, Transvaal, and Orange River. The act also provided a constitution and its provisions established white supremacy there.

South African War *See* **Boer War.**

Southampton, Henry Wriothesley, 3d earl of 1573–1624. Soldier and patron of W. Shakespeare, who dedicated *Venus and Adonis* and *The Rape of Lucrece* to him. Southampton participated in Essex's revolt against Elizabeth I (1601).

Southampton, Thomas Wriothesley, 1st earl of 1505–50. English statesman. He negotiated a treaty between Henry VIII and Holy Roman Emperor Charles V, and was made lord chancellor (1544–47). He supported Henry's antipapal measures but remained a Catholic.

Southampton, Thomas Wriothesley, 4th earl of 1606–67. English nobleman. One of Charles I's close advisers during the English Civil Wars, he became lord high treasurer (1660–67) during the Restoration.

Southampton Insurrection Slave insurrection (Aug., 1831) in Southampton County, Virginia. Led by a rebel slave, N. Turner, who believed he had a divine calling to liberate his brothers, it was quickly suppressed by federal troops.

South Carolina State of southeastern US, the 8th state. Explored by the Spanish, it was first permanently settled by the French (1562). The English claimed the region in 1629, and Charles II granted it to eight noblemen (1663). North and South Carolina were organized as separate colonies (1713), and in 1729 South Carolina became a royal province. During the American Revolution a number of important battles were fought there, and during the American Civil War, South Carolina was the first state to secede (1860). It was readmitted in 1868. The constitution was adopted in 1895.

Southcottians *See* **Sabbatarians.**

South Dakota North-central state of the US, the 40th state. Explored by the French in the mid-18th cent., the area was acquired by the US in the Louisiana Purchase (1803). It was crossed by M. Lewis and W. Clark (1804–6). Fur posts were established in spite of trouble with the Sioux Indians, and farmers began to settle the region in the 1850s. It became part of the Dakota Territory in 1861 and the discovery of gold in the Black Hills (c1874) brought a new influx of settlers. South Dakota became a state and adopted its constitution in 1889.

Southeast Asia Treaty Organization (SEATO) Alliance created by a treaty signed (Sept. 8, 1954) by the US, Australia, France, New Zealand, Pakistan, the Philippines, Thailand, and Britain. It was intended to bolster the region's defenses after the French withdrawal from Indochina. The Vietnam War disrupted the alliance and it held its final joint exercises in 1976.

Southern Rhodesia *See* **Zimbabwe.**

Southern Sung *See* **Sung.**

South Sea Bubble Rush of speculative investment (1720) in the South Sea Company, a trading company founded (1711) in England by R. Harley. The end of the War of the Spanish Succession was expected to result in the company's gaining a monopoly on trade with Spain's American colonies but the treaty of 1713 produced only slightly advantageous terms. With George I as its governor, the company next proposed to assume the British national debt (1720). This brought a rush of speculative investment; company share prices rose from 128.5 to 1,000 pounds in a matter of months. The speculative bubble finally burst in Sept., 1720, bringing the collapse of banks and ruination of thousands of investors.

South-West Africa *See* **Namibia.**

Soutine, Chaim *See* **expressionism.**

Souvanna Phouma 1901–84. Laotian statesman. Of royal descent, he was frequently premier during the years of civil war from 1951. Forced to the right by the gains of the Communist Pathet Lao, he relied heavily on US aid during the Vietnam War years.

soviet Council and basic elective political unit of the former Soviet Union's government. Dominated by the Communist party, soviets were arranged in a hierarchy ranging from local to national jurisdiction and were charged with legislative and executive functions. The first soviets were organized by rebels during the 1905 revolution; during the 1917 revolution the soviets, formed in all of Russia's major cities, rivaled the Russian Provisional Government for power. By taking control (1917) of the powerful Petrograd and Moscow soviets, the Bolsheviks took command of the revolution and ultimately all Russia.

Soviet coup Coup d'état by Communist officials of the USSR (Aug. 18–21, 1991), which ultimately failed because of determined popular opposition mounted by pro-democracy supporters. Hard-line conservative Communists in Moscow, who had been weakened by the failing

Soviet economy and angered by the collapse of Communism in Eastern Europe, suddenly found themselves confronted by the loss of the Baltic States and the threat of a new Union treaty that granted greater autonomy to the Soviet republics at the expense of the central government. The coup leaders decided to strike before the treaty could be signed. On Aug. 18, four officials met with Soviet leader M. Gorbachev at his summer retreat in the Crimea to demand that he declare a state of emergency. When Gorbachev refused, he and his wife were placed under house arrest. The next morning the national news agency Tass announced that Gorbachev was ill and unable to perform his duties. Vice-President Gennadi Yanayev was named acting president, ruling through a committee for the State of Emergency, which included Prime Minister Valentin Pavlov, Defense Minister Dmitri Yazov, Interior Minister Boris Pugo, and KGB Chairman Vladimir Kryuchkov. The committee announced a ban on all political opposition and declared martial law. Within hours, hundreds of tanks moved into Moscow, and troops surrounded the Parliament building where pro-democracy reformer B. Yeltsin began organizing opposition to the coup. Some troops promptly deserted to support Yeltsin. At one point, Yeltsin climbed atop a tank and called for a national strike to restore Gorbachev to power. Thousands of supporters cheered him and began erecting barricades in the streets of Moscow. Seeking international support, Yeltsin also spoke to US President G. Bush and British Prime Minister J. Major by telephone. Meanwhile, European leaders froze more than $1 billion allotted for food and technical aid to the USSR. The turning point came on the night of Aug. 20, when thousands defied a curfew and remained at the Parliament building in anticipation of an attack by pro-coup military forces. Three people were killed during troop movements in Moscow that night (two crushed by tanks and one shot), but widespread opposition to the coup from within the military and the KGB prevented the actual assault. By Aug. 21, the coup collapsed and the tanks withdrew from Moscow. Gorbachev returned to Moscow Aug. 22, fired all who had participated in the coup, and acknowledged Yeltsin's important role in stopping the takeover. One of the coup leaders, Pugo, committed suicide and the others were eventually arrested for treason. Recognizing the Communist Party's role in the attempted coup, Gorbachev resigned as general secretary and called on the Central Committee to disband, marking the end of the party's 74-year rule of the USSR. Soon afterward the constituent republics proclaimed their independence and the USSR collapsed. It was replaced soon after by the Commonwealth of Independent States, a loose confederation of democratic republics effectively led by Yeltsin (as president of the largest republic, the Russian Federation).

Soviet Republic of Hungary   Short-lived Communist government of Hungary that ruled after WW I (Mar. 21–Aug. 1, 1919). After initial successes against the invading Czechs and Rumanians, Communist premier B. Kun was driven out of Hungary, making way for a counterrevolutionary government.

Soviet Union   *See* **Commonwealth of Independent States.**

Spaak, Paul Henri 1899–1972.   Belgian statesman and Socialist. The Belgian foreign minister at various times from 1938 until his death, he served as premier (1938–39, 1946, 1947–50) and was first UN General Assembly president (1946).

space exploration   The age of space exploration began in 1957 with the launching of the first artificial satellite, Sputnik, by the Soviets. Many other "firsts" were recorded in subsequent years as the US and the Soviets engaged in what became known as the "space race." Both nations struggled to gain the lead (and world prestige) on this new frontier. During the 1960s the race focused on landing a man on the moon and in 1969 the US achieved that goal. Enthusiasm for the space race disappeared in the years following the manned moon missions (partly because of the costs). In the 1970s space exploration was carried forward by unmanned space probes sent to the far planets in the solar system (Mars, Jupiter, Saturn). The major advance of the early 1980s was the successful launch of the US space shuttle *Columbia*, the first reusable spacecraft. Key events in space exploration include:

1957   USSR launched Sputnik, inaugurating the Space Age (Oct. 4).
1958   US launched Explorer 1, its first satellite (Jan. 31); Van Allen radiation belts discovered.

1959   Soviet Luna 2 became first spacecraft to make hard landing on the moon (Sept. 12).

1959   Luna 3, Soviet space probe, flew around moon and sent back first pictures of the dark side of the moon (Nov.).

1961   Y. Gagarin, a Russian, became the first man to travel in space, orbited earth inside Vostok I for over an hour (Apr. 12).

1961   Alan Shepard, Jr., became first American in space (May 5), aboard Mercury 3.

1961   Vostok 2; USSR's Gherman Titov made the first space flight lasting more than one day (Aug. 6–7).

1962   Mercury 6; John Glenn became first American to orbit the earth (Feb. 20).

1962   Mariner 2, US space probe, passed by Venus (Dec. 14); sent back scientific data.

1962   Communications satellite Telstar launched by US; provided television pictures between Europe and America (July 1).

1963   Vostok 6; USSR's Valentina Tereshkova became first woman in space (June 16–17).

1965   Aleksei Leonov, Soviet cosmonaut aboard Voskhod 2, became first man to "walk" in space (Mar. 18).

1965   Gemini 4; Edward White became first American to "walk" in space (June 3–7).

1966   Luna 9, Soviet space probe, made first soft landing on moon (Jan. 31).

1966   Venera 3, Soviet space probe, reached Venus (Mar. 1).

1966   Gemini 8; first docking of two spacecraft in outer space (Mar. 16–17).

1966   US space probe, Surveyor 1, made soft landing on moon (June 2).

1966   Pioneer 7, US space probe, launched into orbit around the sun (Aug. 17).

1967   Apollo 1, US manned space capsule, caught fire during testing at Cape Kennedy (Jan. 27); caused first deaths in US space program; astronauts Roger Chaffee, Virgil Grissom, and Edward H. White II were killed.

1968   Apollo 8; Frank Borman, James Lovell, and William Anders orbited the moon, sending back pictures of the lunar surface (Dec. 21–27).

1969   Venera 5, Soviet space probe, landed on Venus; sent back scientific data (May 16).

1969   Mariner 6, US space probe, passed by Mars (July 31); television pictures and data sent back to earth.

1969   Apollo 11; US astronauts Neil Armstrong, Edwin (Buzz) Aldrin Jr., and Michael Collins on historic manned moon-landing mission (July 16–24); Armstrong became first man to set foot on the moon (July 20).

1969   Apollo 12, second lunar landing made by Charles Conrad, Richard Gordon, and Alan Bean (Nov. 14–24).

1970   Apollo 13 moon mission (Apr. 11–18) marred by exploding oxygen tank; astronauts returned safely.

1970   Unmanned Soviet moon probe Luna 16 completed moon landing and return (Sept. 24).

1970   Unmanned Soviet moon probe, Luna 17, landed on moon (Nov. 17).

1971   Apollo 14, Alan Shepard, Jr., Stuart Roosa, and Edgar Mitchell made third US moon landing (Jan. 31–Feb 9).

1971   Soyuz 10 mission; Soviet cosmonauts completed in-space docking with space station, Salyut (Apr. 24).

1971   Soyuz 11 successfully completed (June 7) in-space docking with Salyut; three Soviet cosmonauts found dead in capsule after reentry (June 30).

1971   Apollo 15; fourth manned mission to the moon (July 26–Aug. 7); David Scott, Alfred Worden, and James Irwin aboard.

1971   Mariner 9, US space probe, became first to orbit Mars (Nov. 13); sent back close-up pictures of Mars.

1971   Mars 2, Soviet space probe, passed by Mars (Nov. 27); capsule sent down to surface.

1972   Apollo 16 moon mission (Apr. 16–27); US astronauts stayed over 71 hours on moon; Charles Duke, Thomas Mattingly, and John Young aboard.

1972   Apollo 17; Eugene Cernan, Ronald Evans, and Harrison Schmitt made sixth moon mission (Dec. 7–19); stayed 75 hours on last Apollo moon mission.

1973   Soviets landed unmanned moon vehicle, Lunokhod 2, on moon (Jan. 16).

1973   Salyut 2, Soviet orbital workshop in space (Apr. 3–28).

1973   First US orbiting space station, Skylab 2, launched into space; Skylab damaged during flight (May 25–June 22).

1973   US unmanned space probe, Pioneer 10, passed close to Jupiter (Dec. 3); designed to escape solar system (1986).

1973–74   US Skylab 4 mission (Dec. 16–Feb. 8); last of Skylab series.

1974   Mariner 10, US space probe, passed by Venus (Feb. 5); continued to Mercury.

1974   Mariner 10, US space probe, reached Mercury (Mar. 29).

1974   US Pioneer 11 space probe passed by Jupiter en route to Saturn (Dec. 3).

1975   US Apollo 18 and the Soviet Soyuz 19 linked up in orbit around the earth (July 17–19).

1976   US Viking 1 space probe landed on Mars; photos from surface sent back to earth (July 20).

1976   US Viking 2 space probe landed on Mars (Sept. 3).

1977–78   Soviet cosmonauts aboard Soyuz 27 returned to earth after setting 96-day space endurance record (Dec. 10–Mar. 16).

1979   US Voyager 1 space probe passed by Jupiter; photographs of moons sent back to earth (Mar. 5) continued to Saturn.

1979   US Pioneer 11 space probe passed by Saturn; transmitted scientific data on planet (Sept. 1).

1980   US Voyager 1 passed by Saturn (Nov. 12); sent back valuable scientific data and pictures of Saturn's rings; continued to Uranus (1986).

1981   Soyuz 35; Soviet cosmonauts set record of 185 days in space (Apr. 9–Oct. 11).

1981   World's first reusable spacecraft, the US space shuttle *Columbia*, completed its first flight (Apr. 12–14); three other US space shuttles launched by 1985.

1981   US Voyager 2 passed by Saturn; sent back valuable scientific data (Aug. 25).

1981   US space shuttle *Columbia* returned to earth after completing half of scheduled second mission (Nov 14).

1982   *Columbia* successfully completed its third voyage (July 4).

1982   Two Soviet cosmonauts set new space endurance record (211 days) aboard Salyut 7 (Dec. 10).

1983   First US female astronaut, Sally K. Ride, in space aboard shuttle *Challenger* (June 18–24).

1983   First black American astronaut, Guion Bluford Jr., in space aboard shuttle *Challenger* (Aug. 30–Sept. 5).

1984   First use of rocket propulsion packs for untethered space walks by astronauts, during *Challenger* flight of Feb. 3–7.

1984   Three Soviet cosmonauts establish new record for stay in space (237 days).

1984   Work began on US project to establish permanently crewed space station in orbit by 1995; project subsequently delayed and downsized due to costs and technical problems.

1986   Voyager 2 returned pictures of Uranus and its moons (Jan.).

1986   US space shuttle *Challenger*, on the 25th shuttle mission, exploded after takeoff (Jan. 28); all seven astronauts aboard were killed; faulty booster rocket seals blamed; US shuttle program put on hold until 1988.

1986   Space station Mir launched by Soviets (Feb. 20); two cosmonauts aboard Mir set new record for stay in space (1988, 1 year).

1988   Shuttle program resumed with flight by shuttle *Discovery* (Sept.).

1989   Voyager 2 sent back first closeup pictures of Neptune (Aug.).

1989   Space probe Galileo launched (Oct.); will survey Jupiter and moons in 1995.

1990   Orbiting Hubble Space Telescope launched into space by shuttle *Discovery* (Jan.); flaws in telescope's mirror to be repaired by shuttle crew in 1993.

1991   US space station project reduced in size after Congress balked at $37 billion price tag; station for four crew members to be built between 1995 and 2000.

1992   US astronaut Mae Jemison became first black woman in space aboard shuttle *Endeavour*.

1992   US scientists reported experimenting with "space cannon" to literally shoot durable supplies and equipment into earth orbit.

space shuttle   Spacecraft designed for reuse, developed in the US by the National Aeronautics and Space Administration (NASA). Five shuttle orbiters have been built: *Columbia, Challenger, Discovery, Atlantis,* and *Endeavour.* Launched straight upward like conventional spacecraft, the shuttles glide to earth and land on a runway, much like jet planes, and can be reused as many as 100 times. The first shuttle flight took place on Apr. 12–14, 1981 (the *Columbia*). In 1986, the shuttle *Challenger* exploded shortly after liftoff (Jan. 28), killing all seven astronauts on board and causing the shuttle program to be suspended until 1988. Between 1988 and mid-1992, the remaining shuttles made over 16 successful flights.

Spain (Spanish State)   Country located in Western Europe and occupying the Iberian Peninsula (with Portugal). Its population is 39,623,000; the capital is Madrid. The early history of the modern Spanish state begins with the *Reconquista* (reconquest, 11th–15th cents.), in which Spanish Christians drove the Muslims out of the Iberian Peninsula. Spain remained divided between rival kingdoms until the marriage (1469) of King Ferdinand II and Isabella I began the process of unification by bringing together the two largest kingdoms, Aragon and Castile. Ferdinand and Isabella sponsored Columbus' voyage to the New World (1492) and in the next century Spain gained control over most of the Carribean, and Central and South America. The vast riches in gold that came out of these colonies helped make Spain the leading European power during the 16th cent. Toward the end of the 17th cent., however, Spanish power underwent a decline. By the early 19th cent. its South American colonies were lost in wars for independence. In the 20th cent., Spain was torn by a bloody civil war (1936–39), which brought Gen. F. Franco to power (1939–75). Franco restored order and brought about a long period of stability. **For more on important persons and events** *see* **entries under specific names.** Key events in the history of Spain include:

12TH–11TH CENTS. BC   Phoenicians established colonies on the peninsula (Cádiz, Tartessus).

11TH–5TH CENTS. BC   Basques and Iberians occupied Iberian Peninsula.

6TH CENT. BC   Celts invaded Iberian Peninsula.

3D CENT. BC   Carthaginians, led by Hamilcar Barca, conquered most of the peninsula; established Cartegena as capital.

3D CENT. BC–5TH CENT. AD   Roman occupation of Spain; Rome gained control of Spain from Carthage following the Second Punic War.

134–133 BC   Celt-Iberian War; Rome conquered Celtiberians.

AD 409   Alans, Suevi, and Vandals invaded Spain.

AD 412–419   Visigoths invaded Spain, forcing out Vandals (who invaded North Africa).

AD 419–711   Visigothic kingdom of Toulouse dominated the Iberian Peninsula; Christianity and Roman culture spread.

466–484   Euric ruled much Spain and southern Gaul as king of the Visigoths.

484–507   Visigoth king Alaric II ruled.

557–567   King Athanagild of the Visigoths reigned.

568–586   Leovigild ruled as king of the Visigoths.

711   Muslims, led by Tarik; invaded Spain from North Africa, by 719 conquered all but extreme northern part of Spain, where Christians established kingdom of Asturias (c718).

721–732   Abdu-r-Rahman served as governor of Muslim Spain; killed in the Battle of Tours.

739–757   Christian king Alfonso I ruled in Asturias.

756   Abd er-Rahman I established the Umayyad dynasty in Muslim Spain, after the Abbasid line seized power in the Caliphate.

756–788   Abd er-Rahman served as first Umayyed emir of Córdoba.

788   Spanish March (later called Catalonia) created in northern Spain by Charlemagne out of lands he conquered from Muslims.

866–911   Alfonso III ruled Asturias; greatly extended his domains in wars against Muslims.

905   Independent kingdom of Navarre founded in north.

912–961   Abd er-Rahman III reigned in Muslim Spain; period marked by cultural flowering; Muslim Spain created a caliphate by Abd ar-Rahman (929).

932   Castile founded as an independent kingdom.

934–1002   Mansur served as regent of Muslim Córdoba; warred successfully against the Christians in Spain.

999–1027   Alfonso V gained control of León from the Moors, ruled as king.

1000–35   Sancho III reigned as king of Navarre; briefly united northern Spain under his rule; at his death, Navarre partitioned into kingdoms of Navarre, Aragon, and Castile.

1008–31   Fourth Muslim Civil War; led to elimination of Umayyad caliphate in Spain; Muslim domains broke up into petty kingdoms.

1035–63 Ramiro I, first king of Aragon, ruled.

1035–65 Ferdinand I, king of Castile, reigned; also ruled León from 1037–65.

1065–1109 Alfonso VI reigned as king of Castile and León; El Cid active; Alfonso extended Christian domains to Toledo, only to be driven north by Muslim Almoravides.

1086 Muslim Almoravides invaded Spain and seized power; later conquered by Almohades.

1094 El Cid conquered Valencia.

12TH CENT. Abd-al-Mumin, founder of the Almohade Empire, defeated the Almoravides in North Africa and Spain.

12TH CENT. Hermandad, policelike groups, organized to provide protection against petty criminals and outlaws in Christian kingdoms.

1104–34 Alfonso I ruled Aragon and Navarre.

1135–1204 Spanish-born Jewish philosopher Maimonides lived.

1143 Portugal's independence from Spain recognized by Treaty of Zamora.

1145–51 Muslim Almohades invaded Spain and took control over Muslim domains.

1158 Order of the Knights of Calatrava established by Cistercian monks for protection against the Moors.

1165–1240 Ibn al-'Arabi, Spanish-born Muslim philosopher lived; wrote *The Meccan Revelation.*

1195 Almohades decisively defeated Alfonso VIII of Castile at the Battle of Alarcos.

1212 Alfonso VIII defeated the Muslims in Battle of Navas de Tolosa.

1213–76 King James I ruled Aragon.

1216 Saint Dominic founded the Dominican order.

1217–52 Ferdinand III ruled Castile.

1230 Christian kingdom of Castile united with León; Spain dominated by two great kingdoms, Castile in the west and Aragon in the east.

1238 Kingdom of Granada formed by Muslims.

1252–84 King Alfonso X reigned over Castile and León.

1295–1312 Ferdinand IV ruled Castile and León.

1312–50 King Alfonso XI ruled Castile and León.

1340 Battle of Río Salado, a major victory for Christians over Muslims.

1350–69 King Peter (the Cruel) ruled Castille and León.

1355 Inés de Castro, mistress of future Portuguese King Peter I, murdered on orders of his father, Alfonso IV.

1357 Cardinal de Albornoz wrote constitution for the Papal States.

1369–79 Henry II ruled Castile and León, after killing his half-brother.

1379–90 John I, king of Castile and León, ruled.

1406–54 John II ruled Castile.

1469 Marriage of Ferdinand II of Aragon and Isabella I of Castile; marked beginning of unifiction of Spain, though Ferdinand and Isabella each ruled separately, process of centralizing authority begun.

1474–1566 Missionary and historian, B. de Las Casas, lived; wrote *Historia de las Indias.*

1478 Spanish Inquisition established by King Ferdinand and Queen Isabella; T. de Torquemada, Grand Inquisitor, became notorious for his use of torture and execution.

1479 Treaty of Alcáçovas between Castile and Portugal; Portugal gave up claims to Castilian throne in return for West Africa and Guinea; Castile got the Canary Islands.

1480 Treaty of Alcáçovas concluded by Portugal and Castile.

1486–1546 F. de Vitoria, theologian, lived; championed cause of native peoples in New World.

c1490–c1557 A. Cabeza de Vaca, soldier and explorer, lived; explored American Southwest.

1492 King Ferdinand and Queen Isabella conquered Granada, last Muslim stronghold; Jews expelled from Spain to promote religious unity.

1492 C. Columbus discovered the New World for Spain; established first European contact with this vast realm (which he believed to be part of Asia) and its peoples.

AFTER 1492 Muslims in Spain forced to convert to Catholicism.

1494 Treaty of Tordesillas signed (June 7) with Portugal; provided for division of newly discovered lands in Americas, Africa, and Asia.

1494–1559 Italian Wars for control of Italy; Spanish emerged victorious after years of sporadic warfare; gained southern Italy (Kingdom of Naples) and Milan.

1495   Spain joined the Holy League.

1496   Holy Hermandad created; eventually became national police unit.

16TH CENT.   Spanish "Golden Age"; Spain ranked as the leading European power throughout much of the century; colonization of Spanish domains in the New World and tremendous influx of gold provided the base for this power.

c1500–42   H. De Soto, explorer, lived; believed first European to cross the Mississippi River in America.

1502   Persecution of Muslims in Spain began.

1504   Isabella died; Ferdinand began struggle to gain control of Castile; opposed by Juana (said to be mentally infirm) and her husband Philip.

1506–16   Ferdinand, as regent, gained control of Castile; ruled both kingdoms jointly.

1509–11   Spanish victorious in campaigns against Muslims in North Africa.

1511–22   D. de Velázquez served as first governor of Cuba.

1511–53   Reformation theologian M. Servetus lived.

1512   Ferdinand acquired southern part of kingdom of Navarre; northern part under French hegemony.

1512   Basque kingdom of Navarre fell to Spanish kings.

1513   Ponce de León discovered Florida while searching for the fountain of youth.

1513   V. Balboa discovered the Pacific Ocean.

1516   Francisco J. de Cisneros, prelate and statesman, served as regent of Spain after the death of Ferdinand.

1516–56   Charles I reigned; first of the Habsburg kings of Spain and first king of united Spain.

1516–1700   Habsburgs ruled in Spain.

1519   P. Arias de Ávila founded Panama City.

1519–21   Conquistador H. Cortés conquered Mexico.

1519–56   Charles I became Holy Roman Emperor Charles V; vast Spanish domains joined with those of Habsburg Holy Roman Empire; Charles V thus controlled a great and unwieldy family empire.

1519–22   F. Magellan, in Spanish service, commanded first exploratory voyage around the world; voyage completed by J. Cano, in command after Magellan's death (1521).

1520–21   Revolt of the comuneras; revolt sparked by Charles V's attempts to centralize his authority in Spain.

1523   Conquistador P. de Alvarado conquered Guatemala and El Salvador for Cortés; became governor of Guatemala.

1530s   Conquistador G. Jiménez de Quesada conquered Colombia.

1531   F. Pizarro conquered the Incas of Peru.

1535–50   A. de Mendoza served as first viceroy of New Spain.

1535–1600   Luis Molina, Jesuit, lived; founded Molinism, which sought to recile free will and divine grace.

1536   P. de Mendoza founded Buenos Aires.

1537–42   D. de Irala served as governor of Paraguay, the first in the Americas to be elected by free vote.

1540   Saint Ignatius of Loyola formed the Jesuit religious order.

1540–42   F. Vásquez de Coronado explored American Southwest; his men discovered the Grand Canyon.

1540s   P. de Valdivia conquered Chile.

1542–91   Saint John of the Cross, Doctor of the Church and poet, lived.

1544–46   B. Núñez Vela served as first Spanish viceroy of Peru.

1545–68   Spanish prince Don Carlos de Austria lived.

1548–1617   F. Suárez, Jesuit and Scholastic philosopher, lived.

1550–64   L. de Velasco served as second viceroy of New Spain.

c1555?–1628   Artist F. Ribalta lived; painted *Christ Embracing Saint Bernard.*

1556–98   Philip II reigned as king of Spain; inherited Mediterranean territories, Spanish Netherlands, and overseas empire; an absolutist, Philip vigorously supported Catholicism and the Inquisition.

1559   Treaty of Cateau-Cambresis ended Italian Wars to Spain's advantage.

1561–1627   Poet L. de Góngora y Argote lived.

1562   Saint Teresa of Ávila founded reformed Carmelite order, Discalced Carmelites.

1562–1635   Lope de Vega Carpio, founder of Spanish drama, lived.

1564   M. López de Legaspi conquered Philippines for the Spanish.

1565   Colonizer P. Menendez de Aviles founded St. Augustine, Florida; led the massacre of French Protestants at Fort Caroline, Florida.

1566 Compromise of Breda; protested Spanish rule in the Netherlands.

1567 Netherlands rebelled against Philip's attempts to impose royal authority and Inquisition there; in subsequent war for independence, northern part of Spanish Netherlands won independence as United Provinces.

1567–73 F. de Toledo, duke of Alba, governed the Spanish Netherlands; attempted to crush Dutch revolt for independence.

1571 Battle of Lepanto; Spanish forces joined allied fleet that defeated the Ottoman Turks in a signal naval battle.

1577 Renowned artist El Greco completed *Assumption of the Virgin.*

1580 Portugal united with Spain by Philip, following struggle over succession.

1580–1645 Poet and writer F. de Quevedo y Villegas lived.

1588 Spanish Armada, formed to invade Protestant England, defeated by English and stormy seas.

1589–98 Spain interfered in the Wars of Religion in France.

1598 Treaty of Vervins; halted Spanish support of French Catholic League; helped end Wars of Religion in France.

1598–1621 Philip III reigned.

1598–1607? Explorer J. de Oñate served as first governor of colony in present-day New Mexico.

1598–1618 F. Gómez de Sandoval y Rojas served as prime minister; expelled the Moriscos.

1600–81 Dramatist P. Calderón de la Barca lived.

1605 M. Cervantes published the first part of *Don Quixote;* the sequel was published in 1615.

17TH CENT. Churrigueresque style of architecture introduced by Don José Churriguera.

1609 Christian Moors (Moriscos) exiled from Spain.

1617?–82 Baroque painter B. Murillo lived.

1618–48 Thirty Years' War in Europe; fighting between Spain and France continued to 1659.

1621–65 Philip IV reigned.

1621–43 G. de Guzmán served Philip IV as prime minister.

1634 Artist D. Velázquez painted *Surrender of Breda.*

1640 Portugal regained its independence from Spain after a successful revolt.

1640–59 Province of Catalonia rebelled to maintain autonomy.

1659 Peace of the Pyrenees; ended hostilities stemming from the Thirty Years' War; established border with France.

1665–1700 Charles II reigned as last Spanish Habsburg king; Spain's power continued to decline.

1667–68 War of Devolution, war with France over the Spanish Netherlands.

1672–78 Third Dutch War; Spain lost Franche-Comte and territories in Flanders to France.

1677–79 John of Austria served Charles II as prime minister.

1685 M. de Molinos, priest who founded quietism, condemned by the Inquisition.

1689–97 War of the League of Augsburg; Spain joined this general war against French king Louis XIV.

1692–1766 Elizabeth Farnese, queen of Spain after 1714, lived.

1700 Charles II, just before his death, named Philip V, a Frenchman of the House of Bourbon, as his successor.

1700–46 Philip V reigned.

1700–1868 Bourbon line ruled in Spain (except 1808–13).

1701–14 War of the Spanish Succession; Philip successfully defended his succession, though by the Peace of Utrecht the Spanish Netherlands and Spanish Mediterranean domains passed to Austria; Gibraltar, captured (1704) by British, remained in British hands.

1713 Contract drawn up with the British South Sea Company to provide slaves for New World colonies.

1713–15 Second Peace of Utrecht signed, ending War of Spanish Succession.

1713–84 J. Serra lived; became Franciscan missionary in California.

1714–19 Italian Cardinal G. Alberoni served as de facto prime minister for Spain.

1718 Spain joined the Quadruple Alliance.

1733 Family Compact formed between the Bourbon kings of France and Spain.

1733–38 Spain supported Poland in War of the Polish Succession.

1739–c1743 War of Jenkins's Ear.

1740–48 War of the Austrian Succession.

1746–59 King Ferdinand VI reigned.

1756–63 Seven Years' War; by Treaty of Paris ending war, Spain lost Florida and gained Louisiana Territory.

1759–88 Charles III reigned; considered an enlightened despot, he instituted administrative reforms.

1765–72 J. Gálvez, marqués de la Sonora, served as inspector general to New Spain; reformed colonial administration.

1767 Jesuits exiled in attempt to establish state's supremacy over church.

1776–92 Conde de Floridablanca served as premier of Spain.

1777–83 B. de Gálvez governed Louisiana for Spain; helped Spanish acquire British territories in Florida.

1780–81 Revolt of the communeros in New Granada (Colombia).

1783 Treaty of Versailles, after the American Revolution; Spain, which had sided with the American colonials against Britain, regained Florida.

1786 Artist F. de Goya y Lucientes became court painter to Charles III; painted *Saturn Devouring His Children.*

1788–1808 Charles IV reigned; M. de Godoy and Queen Maria Louisa effectively ruled.

1789 Nootka Sound controversy.

1791–95 F. L. Hector, baron de Carondelet, served as colonial governor of Louisiana and West Florida; increased tensions with US.

1792–1802 French Revolutionary Wars; Spain at first warred against (1793–95) and was defeated by France; later joined France in War of the Oranges (1801), in which Portugal was conquered.

1800 Treaty of Ildefonso; Spain ceded Louisiana territory to French.

1803–15 Napoleonic Wars; Spain was invaded (1808) and occupied by France in Peninsular War. Spain's South American colonies used opportunity to begin movement for independence.

1808 Revolt of Aranjuez (Mar.); sparked by Prime Minister M. Godoy's pro-French policies; resulted in King Charles' abdication.

1808 Charles IV abdicated (Mar. 19); Ferdinand VII succeeded him.

1808 Bayonne Conference (Apr. 6); Napoleon forced Ferdinand to abdicate; Napoleon subsequently named his brother Joseph king.

1808–13 Joseph Bonaparte reigned as king; Spanish resisted his rule, aiding British in the Peninsular War.

1810–26 Spain lost its colonies there as the independence movement spread throughout Spanish New World.

1812 National Cortes met at Cádiz in unoccupied Spain; liberal constitution drawn up.

1814–15 Congress of Vienna convened after Napoleon's defeat; Ferdinand VII formally restored to the Spanish throne.

1814–33 Ferdinand VII reigned; restored after the French were driven out, he rescinded the liberal constitution and instituted conservative, reactionary policies that bred liberal revolt.

1819 Transcontinental Treaty concluded between Spain and US; Spain ceded Florida and the Oregon country to US; US recognized Spanish sovereignty in Texas.

1820–23 Liberal revolution, led by Col. Rafael Riego, failed; French intervened on behalf of the Spanish monarchy.

1821 Mexico's independence from Spain established by Treaty of Córdoba.

1833 Salic Law abolished by Ferdinand VII to allow his daughter Isabella to succeed.

1833 Carlist movement, in support of claim to Spanish throne by Don Carlos and his descendants, began.

1833–68 Isabella II reigned; her succession marked beginning of dynastic struggle with Carlists.

1834 Estatuto Real, royal charter, granted by Isabella, less liberal than 1812 constitution.

1834–39 First Carlist War.

1844–1851 R. M. Navaez served as Queen Isabella's premier.

1846 Affair of the Spanish Marriages.

1854–56 B. Espartero served as prime minister.

1868 Military revolt; growing liberal sentiment and disaffection with Isabella led to proclamation of revolution (Sept. 18) by military officers; government forces were defeated soon after and Isabella was deposed (Sept. 29); provisional government set up.

1869 Constitutional monarchy established by the Cortes.

1870–73   Amadeus reigned as king.

1873   Amadeus abdicated in the face of opposition and increasing political problems.

1873   Spanish Republic established; brought down (1874) by Carlist War.

1873   Virginius affair; Spanish captured US ship *Virginius,* which was smuggling arms to Cuba.

1873–76   Second Carlist War.

1873–1944   Playwright J. Álvarez Quintero lived; collaborated with brother Serafin Álvarez Quintero.

1874–85   Alfonso XII reigned, following restoration of the monarchy.

1874–1931   Bourbon line again ruled in Spain.

1876   New constitution adopted; provided for bicameral legislature.

1876–1973   Cellist and composer P. Casals lived.

1879–1956   P. Baroja y Nessi, Basque-born writer, lived.

1886–1931   Alfonso XIII reigned; Spain was governed under the regency of his mother, Maria Christina, until the early 1900s.

1893–1974   Artist J. Miró lived; painted *Dog Barking at the Moon.*

1896–98   Uprising against Spanish rule in Philippines; led by E. Aguinaldo.

1897   Premier P. Sagasta granted autonomy to Cuba.

1898   Spanish-American War; Spain lost Cuba and the Philippines to the US.

1898   Generation of '98; intellectual movement among Spanish writers and philosophers.

1907   Renowned artist P. Picasso, founder of cubism, painted *Les Demoiselles d'Avignon.*

1912   Spanish Morocco established as a protectorate after agreement with France defining spheres of influence in Morocco.

1914–18   WW I; Spain remained neutral.

1918   Ultraismo poetic movement emerged in post-WW I Spain.

1921   Spanish military defeat (July) at Anul, in Morocco; thousands of Spanish soldiers slaughtered by Moroccan rebel, Abd el-Krim; caused political crisis in Spain.

1921   R. Pérez de Ayala wrote his novel *Balarmino y Apolonio.*

1922   Dramatis J. Benavente y Martínez won the Nobel Prize for Literature.

1923   Military coup (Sept. 13) followed widespread social and political unrest; Primo de Rivera established dictatorship (1923–30).

1930   Rivera forced to resign by mounting opposition to his regime; period of unrest followed his resignation.

1930   J. Ortega y Gasset published *The Revolt of the Masses.*

1931   Surrealist artist S. Dali painted *The Persistence of Memory.*

1931–1939   Second Spanish Republic, established after Alfonso XIII was deposed; monarchy abolished.

1931–36   N. Alcala Zamora, leader of provisional republican government, served as first president of the Spanish Republic; term marked by outbreaks by increasingly radical factions on both the conservative and liberal republican sides.

1933   Falange, Fascist political party, organized.

1934   Catalonia proclaimed independence; revolt put down by government.

1934   Unsuccessful uprising by miners.

1935   F. García Lorca wrote *Lament for the Death of a Bullfighter.*

1936–37   F. Largo Caballero, Socialist leader once called the "Spanish Lenin," served as prime minister of the republic.

1936–39   Spanish Civil War; Gen. F. Franco won control of Spain with aid of Italian Fascists and German Nazis.

1936–39   M. Azaña served as president of Spanish republic during the civil war.

1939–75   Franco ruled Spain as dictator; opposition suppressed and Falange made only legal political party; church and landed aristocracy restored to favor.

1939–45   WW II; Spain remained nominally neutral.

1942   Cortes reestablished.

1953   Spain signed agreement with US providing for US bases in Spain.

1955   Spain admitted to UN.

1956   Spanish Morocco made part of independent Morocco.

1966   New constitution issued by Franco, following period of mounting unrest; introduced liberal reforms, including relaxed censorship, direct election of some members of the Cortes, and religious freedom.

1967   First elections since 1936 held for non-appointive seats in Cortes.

1967   Jews and other non-Catholics allowed to worship openly in Spain, ending centuries-old ban.

1968   Spanish Equatorial Guinea granted independence.

1972   Gen. Franco named Prince Juan Carlos as his successor (to become king).

1973   Franco resigned as premier; retained post as head of state.

1973   Premier Carrero assassinated.

1975   Juan Carlos assumed power (Oct. 30) as head of state; Franco seriously ill.

1975   Franco died (Nov. 20).

1975   King Juan Carlos I succeeded Franco as ruler of Spain (Nov. 22).

1976   Political parties legalized.

1976–81   Adolfo Suárez González in office as prime minister.

1977   Diplomatic relations reopened with the Soviets after nearly 40 years.

1977   Communist Party legalized.

1977   Parliamentary elections held (June); Democratic Center coalition (UCD) victorious.

1978   New constitution providing for constitutional monarchy approved by voters.

1979   Catalonia and Basque provinces granted home rule.

1980   Autonomous parliaments for Catalan and Basques regions elected.

1981–82   Leopoldo Calvo Sotelo in office as prime minister, following Suárez's resignation.

1981   Civil Guardsmen seized the Parliament (Feb. 23) in an abortive coup attempt, which ended the following day; 350 Deputies released unharmed.

1981   Hundreds killed by toxic material in cooking oil.

1982   Socialists won a majority in the elections, bringing them to power in Spain.

1982   Spain became a member of NATO, despite considerable opposition among electorate.

1982–   Socialist Workers' Party (PSOE) leader Felipe González Márquez in office as prime minister; his long administration marked by rise of separatist terrorism, labor unrest, and persistent economic problems (inflation averaged 10 percent throughout the 1980s).

1983   Worker dissatisfaction with government economic restructuring (which eliminated jobs) sparked labor unrest; strikes and other protests continued through much of the 1980s.

1983   Talks with Basque separatist group ETA (Euzkadita Azkatasuna) broke down; government adopted strong anti-terrorist policy.

1983   Anti-terrorist protest marches held in Madrid and Bilbao following ETA bombings and killings.

1984   Reform of military enacted to ensure full civilian control.

1984   Anti-terrorist Grupos Antiterroristas de Liberación (GAL), later branded a death squad, began fighting ETA terrorists; assassinated 23 by 1986.

1984   Mass demonstration by some one million to protest new controls on private schools (Nov.).

1985   Hundreds of thousands demonstrated against government cuts in social security pensions (June).

1985   Bus carrying Civil Guard members in Madrid hit by terrorist bomb (July); 13 killed.

1987   Widespread student protests and strikes by workers signalled growing discontent with government.

1987   ETA bomb wrecked Barcelona supermarket and killed 20; thousands joined demonstration against the terrorists.

1988   Number of Basque parties officially rejected terrorism as means of gaining independence; sporadic negotiations between ETA and government began (Jan.) and continued over next years.

1988   Some 250,000 in Bilbao marched (Mar.), calling for end to terrorism.

1988   Scandal over anti-terrorist GAL; Basque police rumored to have formed the death squad in 1983.

1988   Spain became member of Western European Union.

1988   Government agreed to allow US continued use of bases in Spain but insisted on reduction in force level (Dec.).

1988   One-day general strike by some eight million workers brought country to a standstill (Dec.).

1990   Corruption scandal involving Partido Popular (PP) party finances; treasurer arrested for bribery after he allegedly received money donated by companies seeking government contracts.

1991 Inflation cut to 6 percent, but unemployment topped 15 percent, the highest in Europe.

1992 King Juan Carlos attended historic reconciliation ceremony at Spain's only synagogue (Apr.), five centuries after Jews were expelled from Spain (1492).

1992 Police in France arrested three men believed leaders of the Basque ETA separatist group.

Spangenberg, August Gottlieb 1704–92. German-born American religious leader, founder of the Moravian church in America (1740).

Spanish-American War War (Apr.–Dec., 1898) between the US and Spain. Spain's harsh measures against rebels in Cuba became, in the US, the subject of inflammatory newspaper articles, which aroused American public sentiment for war. It reached a fever pitch after the USS *Maine* (Feb. 15, 1898) was sunk in Havana Harbor. Spanish involvement was never proved but relations between the US and Spain broke down. Although Spain called (Apr. 10) for a cessation of hostilities in Cuba, US president W. McKinley asked Congress for and received (Apr. 11) authority to intervene. Spain declared war (Apr. 24) and the US reciprocated (Apr. 25). On May 1, a US fleet under G. Dewey destroyed the Spanish fleet at Manila Bay in the Philippines. In Cuba the major conflict came in the Battle of Santiago (*q.v.*), in which the Rough Riders under L. Wood and T. Roosevelt fought the Battle of San Juan Hill (July 1) and a US fleet destroyed the Spanish fleet in Santiago Harbor (July 3). In the Philippines, US forces occupied Manila (Aug. 12) a day after signing an armistice. The war was officially ended by the Treaty of Paris (Dec. 10, 1898). By its terms, the US gained control of Cuba, Guam, Puerto Rico, and the Philippines in return for an indemnity of $20 million. The war established the US as a world power.

Spanish Armada (Invincible Armada) Great Spanish war fleet, formed (1588) by King Philip II to invade England and put an end to Protestant rule there (under Elizabeth I). The fleet, under command of the duke of Medina-Sidonia (1550–1615), consisted of about 130 ships. It was anchored at Calais when the English sent fire ships into the anchorage and forced it to scatter. The slow-moving Spanish ships, now out of formation, became easy prey for the English force of 197 smaller and more maneuverable warships and other vessels under the command of C. Howard (of Nottingham). The Armada escaped the English but was further ravaged by storms on the return to Spain. Only half the ships completed the journey and the destruction of the Armada marked Spain's decline as a naval power.

Spanish Civil War War (1936–39) between republican (leftist) and nationalist (rightist) forces in Spain that brought Gen. F. Franco to power in 1939. With the establishment of the Second Spanish Republic in 1931, moderate republicans (liberals, moderate Socialists) gained power. In the first, unsettled years of the republic they were opposed by the nationalists, then consisting of the aristocracy, royalists, the church, military and fascists. However, extremist factions on both sides came to the fore and, after civil war broke out (1936), they played a major role in the continuing struggle. The republican faction was split by conflicts between Communists, anarchists, and radical Socialists. These disputes ultimately contributed to their downfall, despite considerable aid provided by the Soviets. The nationalists, on the other hand, were quickly unified under the leadership of Gen. Franco and were supplied with men and material by Fascist Italy and Nazi Germany. The war devastated Spain, and some 750,000 were killed. Key events in the civil war include:

1931 Monarchy of King Alfonso XIII fell; Second Spanish Republic proclaimed (Apr.).

1931 Republican constitution adopted by the Cortes (legislative assembly) (Dec. 9).

1932 Abortive uprising by royalist faction of the military (Aug. 10); Gen. José Sanjurjo took Seville before rebels were defeated.

1932 Catalonia proclaimed its autonomy (Sept. 25); other local separatist movements arose, weakening republican government.

1933 Nationalists gained majority in elections; liberal reforms negated.

1934 Catalonia unsuccessful in revolt for independence; revolt by Communists put down (Oct.).

1936 Leftist Popular Front won Cortes elections (Feb. 16); nationalists began to consolidate against it.

1936 Spanish Civil War began (July 17–18) when Spanish army, led by Gen. F. Franco, revolted in Morocco; nationalists revolted in Spain.

1936 Nonintervention Pact signed (Aug.) by 27 nations, including Italy, Germany, and Soviets; pact all but ignored by Italy, Germany, and Soviets.

1936 Franco became head of nationalist revolutionary state (Oct. 1), aided by Fascist Italy and Nazi Germany.

1936 Nationalists besieged (Nov.) Madrid; International Brigade (largely Communists) supported republicans.

1937 Málaga fell to Italian troops (Feb. 8).

1937 International Brigade and republicans repulsed nationalists at the Battle of Guadalajara, outside Madrid.

1937 Franco organized (Apr.) fascist Falange and other rightist groups under his command.

1937 German air bombing (Apr.) caused massive destruction and many deaths at Guernica.

1937 Marxists revolted (May) in Barcelona; moderate Socialist premier Largo Caballero ousted; Socialist Juan Negrin led new republican government.

1937 Bilbao, last republican stronghold in the north, fell to the nationalists (June 18).

1937 Republicans won the Battle of Teruel (Dec. 19) during a short-lived offensive; Franco retook Teruel (Feb.).

1938 Nationalist forces split republican territories in two (Mar.–June).

1938 Republicans won Battle of Ebro, but failed to press their advantage (July 24).

1939 Nationalist offensive in Catalonia (Dec.–Jan.); Barcelona fell to Franco (Jan. 26) after heavy fighting; nationalists established control of Catalonia.

1939 Britain and France recognized Franco regime.

1939 Military coup (Mar. 6); Negrin's republican government overthrown; new government sought to end war; Communists rebelled and were defeated; republicans' peace overtures rejected by nationalists.

1939 Nationalists captured Madrid (Mar. 27–28).

1939 Republicans surrendered; civil war ended (Mar 28).

Spanish Guinea *See* **Equatorial Guinea.**
Spanish Inquisition *See* **Inquisition.**

Spanish Main Name (from the 16th cent.) of the coastal region of northern South America and Central America and adjacent Caribbean waters during Spanish colonial times. This region was famous as a haven for buccaneers who raided Spanish treasure fleets.

Spanish March Name of the region in northeast Spain established by Charlemagne in 801 after he conquered it during war against the Muslims. It is part of modern Catalonia.

Spanish Marriages, Affair of the *See* **Affair of the Spanish Marriages.**

Spanish Netherlands *See* **Netherlands, Spanish and Austrian.**

Spanish Sahara Former overseas province of Spain, in northwestern Africa. Spain claimed the region as a protectorate in 1884 and gradually expanded the territory in the 20th cent. It was given up by Spain in 1975 and divided between Mauritania and Morocco.

Spanish Succession, War of the War (1701–14) fought in Europe to determine the succession to the Spanish throne on the death of Spanish king Charles II. (Related fighting in the American colonies was known as Queen Anne's War, *(q.v.)*. French king Louis XIV, seeking to greatly enhance French power on the Continent, supported the accession of his grandson Philip of Anjou. This was opposed by England, which feared French political and economic domination of Europe, and by Holy Roman Emperor Leopold I, who championed the claims of his son, Archduke Charles. A third claimant was Bavarian prince Joseph Ferdinand. Attempts to find a negotiated settlement began after the War of the League of Augsburg (1689–97) with the First and Second Partition treaties. They failed after the death of Charles II and the accession of Philip as Philip V. England then formed the League of Augsburg against France and the war began. Most fighting occurred outside Spain. Key events in the war include:

1698 First Partition Treaty named Bavarian prince Joseph Ferdinand successor in Spain; France and Holy Roman Empire were to receive territories as compensation; treaty opposed by Spain and nullified by death (1699) of Joseph Ferdinand.

1700 Second Partition Treaty; Austrian archduke Charles (later Holy Roman Emperor Charles VI) named heir in Spain; France would receive Milan, Naples, and Sicily in compensation; opposed by Holy Roman Emperor Leopold I.

1700 Spanish king Charles II named Philip of Anjou as his successor; Charles died; France abrogated the Second Partition Treaty and supported Philip's accession (1700) as Philip V.

1701 Britain, alarmed at the union of the French and Spanish crowns and consequent enormous growth of French power, formed the League of Augsburg with the Holy Roman Empire and the Netherlands; France and Spain allied with Bavaria, Savoy, and Portugal against the Alliance; the war began with fighting in Italy and Bavaria.

1703 Savoy and Portugal joined the League of Augsburg.

1704 British and Imperial forces under the duke of Marlborough and Prince Eugene of Savoy defeated the French and Bavarians at the Battle of Blenheim (Aug. 13); French forces obliged to withdraw from Bavaria.

1704 Gibraltar fell to British forces.

1705 Holy Roman Emperor Leopold I died; succeeded by Joseph I.

1706 British and allied forces won a major victory over the French at the Battle of Ramillies, Belgium (May 23); took control of most of Spanish Netherlands.

1706 Eugene of Savoy led allied forces to victory over the French in Battle of Turin (Sept. 7); French forced to retreat from Italy.

1707 French victorious at Battle of Almansa (Apr. 25).

1708 British troops won battle of Oudenaarde (July 11); Britain gained initiative in war.

1709 Allied forces under Eugene of Savoy and the duke of Marlborough defeated the French at Malplaquet (Sept. 11).

1711 Holy Roman Emperor Joseph I died; succeeded by Archduke Charles as Charles VI; Britain withdrew from the alliance because Charles was a claimant to the Spanish throne and an allied victory over France would simply join Spain with the Holy Roman Empire, an equally unacceptable solution to the balance of power in Europe; Charles continued to fight against France.

1713–14 Peace of Utrecht negotiated; series of treaties concluded among European powers ended the war and reorganized European political lines; Philip V's succession confirmed; Britain gained major territorial concessions in Canada from the French.

1714 Treaties of Rastatt and Baden formally ended war between France and Holy Roman Empire.

1720 Treaty of The Hague formally concluded war between Holy Roman Empire and Spain.

Sparta City-state of ancient Greece. Founded c1100 BC by the Dorians, Sparta became, by the 6th cent. BC, one of the most powerful city-states in Greece. Its dominance of the Peloponnesus and support of oligarchies against democracies led to its famous rivalry with Athens. Sparta finally defeated Athens in the Peloponnesian War (*q.v.*) and Sparta became the leading power in Greece. It remained so until its defeat by Thebes at Leuctra (371 BC). Sparta eventually fell under Macedonian, then Roman rule and was destroyed by the Goths (AD 395). In the 18th cent. a new city of Sparta was established near the site of the old one. Key dates in the history of Sparta include:

C11TH CENT. BC Sparta founded by Dorian Greeks.

c800 BC Sparta extended its control over the surrounding region of Laconia.

8TH CENT. BC Earliest known ephors in office; these were Spartan magistrates who served under the Spartan kings and fulfilled executive functions.

735–715 BC First Messenian War; Sparta conquered Messenia, in western Peloponnesus.

c650–c620 BC Sparta put down revolt by Messenians (second Messenian War).

6TH CENT.? BC Lycurgus created Sparta's militaristic society, aimed at producing fierce warriors.

MID-6TH CENT. BC Sparta organized the Peloponnesian League, thereby gaining hegemony over most of the Peloponnesus.

c550 BC Chilon became Spartan ephor; regarded as one of the Seven Wise Men of Greece.

520–490 BC Cleomenes reigned in Sparta; meddled in Athenian politics and maintained Sparta's dominant position in the Peloponnesus.

507 BC Spartans invaded Attica in unsuccessful attempt to oust Cleisthenes and restore aristocracy to power in Athens.

490–479 BC Persian Wars; Sparta joined Athens and other city-states in repulsing invasions of Greece by Persians.

c466 BC Pausanias, Spartan commander accused of treason, took refuge in temple of Athena; Spartans walled him in and left him to starve to death.

464–461 BC Rebellion by helots of Messenia against Sparta.

461–446 BC Sparta fought Athens in the first Peloponnesian War.

431–404 BC Peloponnesian War; Sparta, successful against Athens, emerged as the most powerful city-state in Greece.

c427–400 BC Agis II reigned; led Spartan armies in Peloponnesian War.

395–387 BC Corinthian War; Spartan power in Greece challenged by Athens, Thebes, and other allies.

371 BC Sparta defeated by Thebes at the Battle of Leuctra; Sparta's decline began.

338 BC Philip II of Macedonia gained control of Greece.

338–331 BC Agis III reigned; led unsuccessful revolt against Alexander the Great of Macedonia (333–331 BC).

c266–262 BC Chremonidean War; Sparta and Athens fought against Macedonian rule.

222 BC Sparta defeated by Antigonus III of Macedonia.

146 BC Sparta under Roman rule along with the rest of Greece.

AD 395 City destroyed by Goths under Alaric. the Almoravides in North Africa and Spain.

Spartacus *d.* 71 BC. Thracian-born Roman gladiator who led the slaves in the Servile War (*q.v.*) in Italy (73–71 BC).

Spartacus League Militant German Socialist organization. Protesting against WW I, the Spartacists split from the German Social Democratic party (1916). They later allied themselves with the Russian Bolsheviks (1919) and thus became the German Communist party. Party leaders K. Liebknecht and R. Luxemburg were murdered after they organized a general strike in Berlin (1919).

Spee, Maximillan, graf von 1861–1914. German WW I admiral. He routed a British squadron off the coast of Chile in WW I but was defeated and killed soon after at the Battle of Falkland Islands (1914).

Speer, Albert 1905–81. German architect and Nazi official. He organized German war production, bringing it to its peak (1944). Sentenced to 20 years' imprisonment after the war, he wrote *Inside the Third Reich.*

Speke, John Hanning 1827–64. British explorer. He discovered Lake Victoria, one of the sources of the Nile River.

Spencer, Herbert 1820–1903. English philosopher. An early advocate of evolution, he and T. Huxley helped bring about acceptance of Darwin's theory of evolution. His 10-volume *Synthetic Philosophy* covered the principles of various fields of knowledge.

Spener, Philipp Jacob 1635–1705. German theologian, founder of Pietism (*q.v.*).

Spengler, Oswald 1880–1936. German historian and philosopher. Spengler wrote *The Decline of the West,* in which he likened every culture to a personal cycle of birth, growth, maturity, and inevitable decline. The West, he believed, had reached the last phase.

Spenser, Edmund c1552–99. English poet, considered one of the finest of Elizabethan England. While in the civil service in Ireland, he published (1590) the first three books of his great unfinished epic poem, *Faerie Queene.* The second three books were published in 1596. He also wrote the love sonnet sequence *Amoretti,* which included the wedding poem *Epithalamion,* celebrating his marriage to Elizabeth Boyle.

Speranski, Mikhail Mikhailovich 1772–1839. Russian statesman and reformer. A trusted adviser to Alexander I, he proposed liberal reforms and a constitution (1809) that angered the nobles and brought about his dismissal. Restored by Nicholas I, he compiled a code of Russian law.

Sperry, Elmer Ambrose 1860–1930. American inventor. Best known as the inventor of the gyroscope, Sperry also devised an arc lamp and a searchlight, improved the dynamo and the diesel engine, and founded the Sperry Gyroscope Company.

Speusippus *d.* 339 BC. Athenian philosopher. He succeeded his uncle, Plato, as head of the Academy.

sphinx Mythical creature with a human head and the body of a lion (sometimes winged). Although the image was common to many ancient cultures, the best known is the great stone Sphinx at Giza, Egypt, dating from c2500

BC. In Greek mythology, the sphinx posed a riddle that only Oedipus could answer: What walks on four legs in the morning, two at noon, and three at night? Answer: A human being, who crawls on all fours as a baby, walks on two legs in adulthood, and uses a cane in old age.

Spinoza, Baruch 1632–77. Dutch rationalist philosopher. A lens grinder by trade, he developed a monist philosophy that is a noted example of pantheism (*q.v.*). Among his major works were *Treatise on Religion and Political Philosophy,* and *Ethics.*

Spirit of St. Louis *See* **Lindbergh, Charles A.**

spiritualism (spiritism) Belief in the existence after death of the human spirit or personality, and its ability to manifest itself. Noted advocates have included Madam Blavatsky and A. C. Doyle.

Spode, Josiah 1754–1827. Famous British pottery manufacturer. He developed a new mixture (adding feldspar and bone ash) for his porcelain and popularized many intricate patterns.

spoils system (patronage) In the US, the practice of awarding government jobs to loyal supporters of the party after an election victory. New York Senator W. Marcy coined the term (1832) when he declared that "to the victor belong the spoils." On the national level, the practice became widespread in subsequent years and was eventually curbed by the Pendleton Civil Service Act and other regulations.

Spooner Amendment Amendment to the US Army appropriation bill (Mar. 2, 1901), authorizing the president to abolish the US military government in the Philippines and to establish a civil government.

Spotsylvania Court House, Battle of Bloody American Civil War battle fought in May, 1864, in northeastern Virginia, during the Wilderness Campaign.

Spottiswoode, John 1565–1639. Scottish religious leader. He abandoned his Presbyterianism to support James I's plan to introduce episcopacy in Scotland. Named chancellor of Scotland (1635), he fell out of favor and was ousted in 1638.

Spring and Autumn Period *See* **Ch'un Chiu.**

Spurgeon, Charles Haddon 1834–92. English Baptist preacher, noted for his fundamentalist sermons and the wide following he enjoyed during his lifetime.

Spurs, Battle of the (Guinegate, Battle of) English victory (Aug. 16, 1513) over the French during wars of the Holy League. English king Henry VIII, a member of the league, launched an invasion from Calais into northern France. Reinforced with troops sent by Holy Roman Emperor Maximilian I, the English intercepted a French cavalry force at the village of Guinegate. The French, however, retreated suddenly before serious battle had been joined (thus, Battle of the Spurs).

Sputnik The world's first artificial satellite, launched (Oct. 4, 1957) by the Russians as the first of ten satellites in the *Sputnik* series. The second (Nov. 3, 1957) carried a dog, Laika, into earth orbit.

Spyri, Johanna 1827–1901. Swiss writer. The best known of her many children's books is *Heidi.*

Squanto (Tisquantum) *d.* 1622. American Indian. A member of the Pawtuxet tribe, Squanto assisted the Pilgrims at Plymouth Colony, showing them how to plant and fish. He frequently served as guide, interpreter, and mediator.

Sri Lanka (Democratic Socialist Republic of ˜; *formerly* Ceylon) Island republic in the Indian Ocean, southeast of India. The population is 17,135,000 and the capital is Colombo. The island's ancient inhabitants were conquered (6th cent. BC) by the Sinhalese from India. They introduced Buddhism (3d cent. BC) and established a kingdom that reached its peak in the 4th–6th cents. AD. The island was invaded (11th–12th cents.) by the Tamils from India, who established a kingdom in the north. Much of Ceylon's coastal region was conquered (16th cent.) by the Portuguese and their holdings were seized in turn by the Dutch (17th cent.) and the British (1796). The British established a crown colony (1798) and gained control of the entire island (1815) following the overthrow of the kingdom of Kandy, which had ruled the interior. A nationalist movement, originating in the early 20th cent., led to independence (1948) as a dominion within the British Commonwealth. Ceylon was the site in the 1950s of strife between the country's Sinhalese and Tamil populations, and in 1959 its prime minister S.W.R.D. Bandaranaike (1899–1959) was assassinated. His widow, Mrs. Sirimavo Bandaranaike (1916–) became prime minister (1960), began a program of reforms (including nationalization in 1962 of British and US businesses) and was voted out of office (1965). A more moderate government lasted until 1970, when Bandaranaike again became prime minister as head of a coalition that sought increasingly radical reforms. A Marxist revolt (1971) was crushed in 1972, and that year Ceylon became a republic under the name Sri Lanka. Bandaranaike was voted out of office (1977) and the next year Sri Lanka adopted a presidential form of government. Junius Richard Jayewardene (1906–) became its first president and remained in office until 1989. Tamil rebels seeking an independent state launched a terrorist campaign during the 1980s, killing thousands. India sent a peacekeeping force in 1987, but was obliged to withdraw it (1989) as fighting continued. Government troops subsequently launched a major offensive against rebel forces in 1990 and fighting continued into mid-1992. Indian authorities in Jan. 1992 charged the leader of one Tamil group with involvement in Rajiv Gandhi's assassination.

SS (Schutzstaffel) (Black Shirts) Nazi military corps (formed 1929). Commanded by H. Himmler, it eventually became the instrument of Nazi party control in Germany and occupied territories. By the end of WW II the SS had grown to 35 divisions responsible for domestic and international security and included the Gestapo, the armed Waffen SS units, and concentration camp guards.

Ssŭ-ma Ch'ien   *See* **Sima Qian.**

Ssu-ma Kuang   *See* **Sima Guang.**

St.   *For names beginning with St., see under* **Saint.**

Staël, Madame de (Anne-Louise-Germaine) 1766–1817.   French writer, considered one of the great French women of letters. Her book *De l'Allemagne* (1810) was ordered destroyed by Napoleon, and she was exiled. Reprinted later, it introduced German Romanticism to France.

Stafford, Henry, 2d duke of Buckingham 1454?–1483.   English nobleman, who helped Richard III seize the throne. He later raised an army against Richard, but was captured and beheaded.

Stafford, Humphrey, 1st duke of Buckingham 1402–60.   English nobleman. Stafford served in the Hundred Years' War and supported the Lancasters in the Wars of the Roses. He died at the Battle of Northampton.

Stahl, Georg Ernst 1660–1734.   German chemist. Stahl developed both the phlogiston theory of combustion, and the theory of ani-

mism—that bodily functions are controlled by the soul.

Stair, James Dalrymple, 1st viscount 1619–95.   Scottish judge. A royalist, he was nevertheless appointed judge during the Commonwealth. Ousted during the Restoration he wrote *The Institutions of the Law of Scotland.* He was reappointed under William III.

Stair, John Dalrymple, 1st earl of 1648–1707. Scottish statesman, son of James Stair, lord advocate and secretary of state for William III. His approval of the Glencoe Massacre (*q.v.*) forced his resignation.

Stair, John Dalrymple, 2d earl of 1673–1747. Scottish general and diplomat. He fought for William of Orange (later William III) in Holland and then in England. He served as ambassador to Paris under George I.

Stakhanovism   Movement in the Soviet Union (c1935) to increase industrial workers' output. Aleksey Stakhanov, a coal miner who increased production sevenfold by instituting more efficient techniques, gave his name to the movement. Stakhanovite workers received special pay and privileges.

Stalin, Joseph Vissarionovich 1879–1953. Soviet Communist leader, originally surnamed Dzhugashvili. Stalin joined N. Lenin's Bolshevik faction in 1903 and took part in revolutionary activities. He became (1922) general secretary of the Central Committee after the Bolsheviks came to power in the Revolution of 1917. Shortly before Lenin's death, Stalin and Lenin fell out, but Lenin died before any action was taken. In the ensuing power struggle among Lenin's survivors, Stalin defeated L. Trotsky, G. Zinoviev, L. Kamenev, and N. Bukharin to become virtual dictator of the Soviet Union and the Communist party. In 1928, Stalin instituted a new policy of industrialization and collectivization of agriculture. Resistance by kulaks, or farmers, to collectivization led to untold misery and death. Failures in Stalin's Five-Year Plan (*q.v.*) caused further hardship. The 1930s saw the purge trials (*q.v.*), by which Stalin eliminated all potential opponents, and the signing of a nonaggression pact (1939) with Germany. Stalin's hopes of keeping Russia out of WW II ended with the German invasion of the Soviet Union (June 22, 1941), and his inability to deal at first with the invasion contributed to the Red Army's disastrous early losses. He subsequently acted as commander in chief of the victorious Soviet forces, although his role as military leader is disputed. Stalin's participation in the Teheran (1943) and Yalta (1945) conferences (*q.v.*) established the Soviet Union as one of the major world powers, and led to Soviet domination of Eastern Europe after the war. In the late 1940s and early 1950s he became the leading Communist figure in the Cold War (*q.v.*) and further increased his tyrannical rule. After his death (1953), a power struggle led to the rise of N. Khrushchev, who denounced (1956) Stalin's excesses and the personality cult that had formed around him.

Stalingrad, Battle of   Important turning point of WW II during which the Soviets gained the offensive against the Germans. More than 500,000 Germans under Gen. von Paulus attacked and largely destroyed Stalingrad in Sept., 1942, but the Russians continued to hold out and by Nov., 1942, Gen. G. Zhukov had surrounded the Germans who were forced to surrender (Feb. 2, 1943). Hundreds of thousands were killed and wounded on both sides in this bloody battle.

Stalinism   Doctrines and policies of Soviet dictator J. Stalin. He advocated a pragmatic rather than an ideological approach to creating the socialist state. He abandoned the idea of spreading revolution throughout the world for the sake of creating "socialism in one country" (the Soviet Union). The results of his programs were farreaching: he collectivized agriculture, undertook a massive program to industrialize the nation, and suppressed the church. But by far the most prominent aspect of Stalinism was the "cult of personality." His great success in concentrating power in his own hands and his ruthless measures against dissent in any form made him absolute ruler of the Soviet Union and made his dictates the gospel of the Communist party.

Stalin Line   Soviet defensive fortifications along the border with Poland. Patterned after the Maginot Line (*q.v.*), these defenses failed to prevent the German invasion of WW II.

Stalwarts   Conservative faction of the US Republican party that vied for power in the 1870s and 1880s. Led by New York Senator R. Conkling and by C. Arthur, the Stalwarts opposed the Half-Breeds (*q.v.*). Stalwarts fought the civil-service reforms of President R. Hayes and unsuccessfully tried to nominate U. Grant for a third term.

Stambolov, Stefan 1854–95. Bulgarian politician. Stambolov was a regent after the abdication of Prince Alexander (1886–87) and as prime minister (1887–94) dominated Prince Ferdinand. His strong rule led to his forced resignation and assassination.

Stambuliski, Alexander 1879–1923. Bulgarian politician. Stambuliski headed the Peasants' party, became premier (1919) and dictator. In 1923 he was overthrown and executed.

Stamp Act   British revenue law (1765) intended to raise funds for the defense of the American colonies by selling stamps that had to be used for all newspapers, legal documents, pamphlets, almanacs, cards, etc. Widespread Colonial opposition (sometimes violent) led to the formation of the Stamp Act Congress (*q.v.*) and the Sons of Liberty (*q.v.*). The British Parliament, which had passed the act without consent of Colonial assemblies, repealed it in Mar., 1766. The Stamp Act was one of the Colonial grievances that resulted in the American Revolution.

Stamp Act Congress   Meeting (Oct., 1765) of American colonials to formalize protest against the Stamp Act (*q.v.*). Representatives from New York, New Jersey, Rhode Island, Massachusetts, Pennsylvania, Delaware, South Carolina, Maryland, and Connecticut met in New York City and issued the Declaration of Rights and Grievances, which condemned taxation by the British without Colonial representation in Parliament. Parliament refused to acknowledge the grievances but, under pressure from British merchants, repealed the Stamp Act (Mar., 1766). At the same time Parliament maintained, by the Declaratory Act of 1766, the right to impose taxes within the British Empire.

Standish, Myles c1584–1656. English colonist who sailed to America on the *Mayflower* and served as the military leader and treasurer of Plymouth Colony. He is the subject of a famous poem by H. Longfellow about his supposed unsuccessful courtship of Priscilla Mullins.

Stanhope, Charles, 3d earl Stanhope 1753–1816. British politician and inventor. Stanhope was W. Pitt's brother-in-law and urged conciliation toward America. His many inventions include lenses, calculating machines, a printing press, and fireproof stucco.

Stanford, Leland 1824–93. US senator from California, builder of transcontinental railroads. After successes in the retail business in California, he served as state governor (1861–63). As president of Central Pacific Railroad (1861–93), he influenced railroad development throughout the Southwest. Stanford served as a US senator (1885–93) and founded Stanford University (1885).

Stanhope, Lady Hester 1776–1839. English noblewoman and adventurer, secretary to her uncle, W. Pitt. In 1810 she traveled to the Middle East and, living among the natives, was revered by them as a prophetess.

Stanhope, James, 1st earl Stanhope 1673–1721. English general. He fought in the War of the Spanish Succession and, as George I's secretary of state, negotiated the Triple Alliance (1717) and Quadruple Alliance (1718).

Stanhope, Philip 1805–75. English statesman and historian who served as R. Peel's undersecretary for foreign affairs. He wrote *History of England from the Peace of Utrecht to the Peace of Versailles.*

Stanislaus I (Leszczynski, ˜) Polish king (1704–09, 1733–35). Installed (1704) by the Swedes during the Northern War, he fled Poland after their defeat. His return (1733) after the death of King Alexander II precipitated the War of the Polish Succession (*q.v.*).

Stanislaus II (Poniatowski, ˜ Augustus) 1732–98. Last king of Poland (1764–95), successor to Alexander III. A lover of Catherine II, he was installed by her as king of Poland. Though Russia thereafter dominated Poland, Stanislaus attempted to implement reforms. He was unable to prevent the complete dismemberment of the kingdom in the three Partitions of Poland (*q.v.*).

Stanislavsky, Konstantin (Alekseyev, Konstantin Sergeyevich) 1863–1938. Russian actor, director, and teacher. Stanislavsky co-founded the Moscow Art Theater. His "method acting" theories have profoundly influenced modern acting and directing.

Stanley, Sir Henry Morton 1841–1904. British-born American reporter and explorer. Stanley's diverse activities included fighting for both sides in the American Civil War, newspaper reporting, finding the missing Dr. D. Livingstone in Africa, and colonizing the Congo and Uganda.

Stanley, Wendell Meredith 1904–71. American biochemist. He researched the chemical nature of viruses and was co-winner of the 1946 Nobel Prize in Chemistry.

Stanton, Edwin McMasters 1814–69. American statesman. A Radical Republican, he became sec-

retary of war (from 1862) under President A. Lincoln and later under President A. Johnson. However, Johnson's struggle with Radical Republicans, over control of Reconstruction (*q.v.*) policy, resulted in a presidential order discharging Stanton. Soon after, Radical Republicans in Congress unsuccessfully attempted to impeach President Johnson, saying he had violated the Tenure of Office Act by firing Stanton.

Stanton, Elizabeth Cady 1815–1902. American reformer, a leader of the woman suffrage (*q.v.*) movement. She organized (1848) at Seneca Falls, New York, the first women's rights convention.

Staple, Company of the Merchants of the *See* **Company of the Merchants of the Staple.**

Star Chamber English royal court. An outgrowth of the king's council, it eventually included civil and criminal matters in its jurisdiction, and in the 16th cent. was a popular expedient to common-law courts. Under the Stuart kings (notably Charles I), however, the court became an agency for asserting royal powers. It was abolished (1641) by the Long Parliament.

Starhemberg, Ernst Rüdiger, graf von 1638–1701. Austrian field marshal who successfully defended Vienna against prolonged Turkish attack (1683) during the Austro-Turkish War (*q.v.*).

Starhemberg, Ernst Rüdiger von 1899–1956. Austrian politician. He joined Hitler in the Munich Putsch (1923). Later he formed the Austrian Heimwehr, a Fascist group supporting E. Dollfuss.

Stark, John 1728–1822. American Revolutionary general. Stark participated in fighting at Bunker Hill, Princeton, Trenton, and Saratoga. He defeated J. Burgoyne at Bennington (1777).

Starr, Belle 1848–89. American frontier figure whose fame as a horse thief and outlaw was spread by exaggerated newspaper accounts of her deeds. She was for a time associated with C. Younger and the James gang and later ran a hideout for outlaws.

state Term applied to the political organization of a society, or the form or institution of government ruling the affairs of a society.

States-General (Estates-General) Representative assembly. First established in France as an advisory body to King Philip IV (*q.v.*) in the early 14th cent., it was divided into three "estates": the clergy, the nobility, and the people (third estate). Though it acquired jurisdiction over taxes and other powers, it was eclipsed by the growth of royal power. Thus, the States-General was seldom convened after 1500 and did not meet at all from 1614 to 1789. Finally, Louis XVI was forced by the chaos of royal finances to convene the body in 1789. The meeting resulted in the union of the clergy and the people, the formation of the National Assembly, and the beginning of the French Revolution. The States-General is also the name for the assembly of the Dutch Republic (1579–1795). It was superseded by the National Assembly in 1796.

states' rights Political doctrine prominent in US history. It advocates limitations on federal government powers and is based on the 10th Amendment to the Constitution, which gives the states powers not granted to the federal government or otherwise expressly prohibited. States' rights has figured in many important controversies. The power struggle between Jeffersonian Republicans and the Federalists in the early years of the republic resulted in the drafting of the Kentucky and Virginia Resolutions (*q.v.*), the first statement of states' rights doctrine. In the 1800s, Southern opposition to federal tariff laws fostered the states' rights Nullification Controversy (*q.v.*), and the determination of Southern states to defend slavery led to the bitter American Civil War. This ended the controversy over the states' power to directly oppose federal powers. Nevertheless, states' rights became a factor in opposition to desegregation in the South during the 1950s and 1960s. Finally, limitation of federal powers, which have been expanding for decades, was the basis of R. Reagan's 1980 presidential campaign.

States' Rights Democrats *See* **Dixiecrats.**

Statius, Publius Papinius AD c40–c96. Latin poet. The surviving fragments of his work include the *Achilleid,* the *Silvae,* and *Thebaid.*

Statue of Liberty Statue, now a symbol of the American ideal of liberty. A gift from France in memory of the Franco-American alliance during the American Revolution, it was entitled *Liberty Enlightening the World.* The monument was designed by F.A. Bartholdi and was erected on Liberty Island in New York harbor in 1886.

Statute of Wales English law enacted on Mar. 19, 1284, uniting Wales with England after the conquest of Wales by Edward I.

Stavisky Affair French scandal (1934) that for a time threatened to bring down the Third Repub-

lic. Serge Alexandre Stavisky (1886–1934) had sold great quantities of fraudulent bonds, and discovery of the scandal resulted in his death by either murder or suicide. Rightists charged that it was murder to protect prominent government officials and began agitating to overthrow the republic. The ministries of C. Chautemps and É. Daladier were forced to resign before calm was finally restored.

Steel, Pact of *See* **Pact of Steel.**

Steele, Sir Richard 1672–1729. Noted English writer and dramatist, who wrote essays with J. Addison for the periodicals *Tatler* and *The Spectator.*

Steelyard, Merchants of the *See* **Merchants of the Steelyard.**

Steenkirk, Battle of *See* **League of Augsburg, War of the.**

Steffens, Joseph Lincoln 1866–1936. American journalist. An editor for such periodicals as *McClure's* and *The American,* he was a leading muckraker (*q.v.*) who exposed business and political corruption. He was best known for *The Shame of the Cities* (1904), exposing corruption in the city government.

Steichen, Edward 1879–1973. American photographer. With A. Stieglitz, he founded the Photo-Secession Group (1902) and was among the first to recognize the camera's artistic potential.

Stein, Gertrude 1874–1946. American expatriate writer and a leading avant-garde literary figure in the early 1900s. She lived in Paris from 1903 and influenced such writers as E. Hemingway and F. S. Fitzgerald. Her works include *The Autobiography of Alice B. Toklas* and *Four Saints in Three Acts.*

Stein, baron Heinrich Friedrich Karl vom und zum 1757–1831. Prussian statesman and reformer. He was instrumental in abolishing serfdom and effecting other civil, economic, and military reforms.

Steinbeck, John Ernst 1902–68. Noted American novelist. His works include *The Grapes of Wrath, East of Eden, Of Mice and Men,* and *Tortilla Flat.* He was awarded the Nobel Prize in Literature (1962).

Steiner, Jakob 1796–1863. Swiss-born German mathematician, a pioneer in the study of synthetic geometry.

Steiner, Rudolf 1861–1925. Austrian-German philosopher. Once a Theosophist, he developed his own philosophy of anthroposophy, which stressed spiritual thought without reliance on the senses or material objects.

Steinmetz, Charles Proteus 1865–1923. German-born American electrical engineer. He made important discoveries concerning alternating current and devised a generator to produce artificial lightning.

Steinway, Henry Englehard 1797–1871. German-born American piano manufacturer, and founder of the famous Steinway and Sons piano company. Steinway introduced many innovations into piano construction.

Stendhal (*pseud. of* Marie Henri Beyle) 1783–1842. French writer, one of the great French novelists. His best-known works include the two novels *The Red and the Black* (1830) and *The Charterhouse of Parma* (1839).

Stephen, Saint (Stephen I) 969–1038. First king of Hungary (1001–38). Crowned with the blessings of the pope, he Christianized Hungary. He is called the Apostle of Hungary.

Stephen 1097–1154. King of England (1135–54), successor to Henry I. Forced to acknowledge Henry's daughter, Matilda, as legitimate heir, Stephen nevertheless claimed the throne on Henry's death. Matilda invaded England (1139) and, after capturing Stephen at Lincoln (1141), reigned for six months. Stephen regained the throne and drove Matilda out of England (1148), though he was unable to restore order in his domains.

Stephen I *See* **Stephen, Saint.**

Stephen II *d.* 757. Italian-born pope (752–757). Threatened by the Lombards, he allied the church with the Franks under Pepin the Short, received the Donation of Pepin from him, and thus became the first pope who was also temporal ruler of the Papal States (*q.v.*).

Stephen Báthory 1533–86. King of Poland (1575–86). He successfully fought Russian tsar Ivan the Terrible for control of Livonia. His goal, unfulfilled because of his early death, was the unification of Poland, Muscovy, and Transylvania.

Stephen Dushan c1308–55. King (1331–46) and tsar (1346–55) of Serbia. One of the notable conquerers of European history, he brought Albania, Bulgaria, and Macedonia into a Serbian empire which, however, did not long survive his death.

Stephens, Alexander Hamilton 1812–83. American politician. Though opposed to secession, Stephens served as Confederate vice-president (1861–65). He continually opposed President J. Davis' policies and sought peace with the Union.

Stephens, Uriah S. *See* **Knights of Labor.**

Stephenson, George 1781–1848. English inventor, creator of the first practical railroad locomotive, originally designed for hauling coal in mines. He then built a locomotive for England's first railroad, completed in 1825.

Stepniak, S. 1852–95. Russian revolutionary and author. A Nihilist, he assassinated the tsarist chief of police, and defended his actions in *Life for Life.*

Stern, Otto 1888–1960. German-born American physicist. With German physicist Walther Gerlach (1920–21) at the University of Hamburg, he developed a molecular beam for studying molecules and their characteristics. He also used the device to measure the magnetic moment of a proton (1933). He subsequently settled in the US and was awarded the Nobel Prize for Physics (1943).

Sterne, Laurence 1713–60. British novelist who wrote *A Sentimental Journey* and the famous satirical novel *Tristram Shandy.*

Stesichorus *fl.* c600 BC. Dorian Greek lyric poet. Though only fragments of his work survive, he is thought to have made innovations in Greek poetry and myth.

Steuben, Friedrich Wilhelm, baron von 1730–94. Prussian general in service of American colonials. From 1778, he was responsible for training the American Revolutionary army and organizing it into a conventional military fighting unit. He wrote its first training manual and later was a commander at the Battle of Yorktown.

Stevens, John 1749–1838. American inventor and engineer, a pioneer in steamship design. He built the first American locomotive (1825), and was instrumental in passage of the first US patent laws (1790).

Stevens, Robert Livingston 1787–1856. American engineer and inventor, son of J. Stevens. He invented the T-shape rail and the railroad spike and added the cowcatcher to the front of railroad locomotives.

Stevens, Thaddeus 1792–1868. American statesman. He co-authored the 14th Amendment, was a leader of the Radical Republicans in US Congress during their fight to impose a harsh Reconstruction (*q.v.*) policy, and urged the impeachment of President A. Johnson.

Stevens, Wallace 1879–1955. American poet. An insurance executive, he wrote such poems as *The Man with the Blue Guitar,* and *The Auroras of Autumn.*

Stevenson, Adlai Ewing 1835–1914. American statesman, Stevenson was first assistant postmaster general (1885–89) and vice-president (1893–7) under President G. Cleveland.

Stevenson, Adlai Ewing 1900–65. American statesman, the grandson of Adlai Ewing Stevenson. He served as governor of Illinois (1948–52), was twice the unsuccessful Democratic candidate for president (1952, 1956), and was US ambassador to the UN (1961–65).

Stevenson, Robert Louis 1850–94. Scottish author, renowned for such classic novels as *Treasure Island, The Strange Case of Dr. Jekyll and Mr. Hyde,* and *Kidnapped.*

Stewart *See* **Stuart.**

Stewart, William Morris 1827–1909. American politician, US senator from Nevada (1864–75, 1887–1905). He wrote the final draft of the 15th Amendment, supported silver coinage and won passage of mining laws.

Stieglitz, Alfred 1864–1946. American photographer. With E. Steichen he founded the Photo-Secession Group (1902) and pioneered the development of photography as an art form. He was noted for his photo studies of his wife, Georgia O'Keeffe.

Stilicho, Flavius *d.* AD 408. Roman general. He repulsed invasions by the Vandals (AD 403) and the Goths (AD c406)1. Suspected of plotting against Emperor Honorius, he was beheaded.

Still, Andrew Taylor 1828–1917. American doctor. He founded osteopathy, the theory that diseases can be treated without drugs by massage.

Stilwell, Joseph Warren 1883–1946. American general, commander of US and Nationalist Chinese forces in the Far East during WW II. Forced to retreat during the Japanese invasion of Burma (1942), he led US forces in the reconquest of the region (1943–44).

Stimson, Henry Lewis 1867–1950. American statesman. He was secretary of war (1911–13, 1940–45), serving notably during the WW II years. As secretary of state (1929–33) he formulated the Stimson Doctrine (1932), which proposed the US refuse recognition of territories seized by acts of aggression.

Stimson Doctrine *See* **Stimson, Henry Lewis.**

Stockhausen, Karlheinz 1928– . German composer. Stockhausen's avant-garde techniques include the use of electronic music, improvisation, and simultaneous performances by more than one orchestra.

Stockholm, Treaty of Two treaties signed in Stockholm by Sweden during the Great Northern War (1700–21). In Nov., 1719, Sweden ceded Bremen and Verdun to British king George I, in return for financial and military aid against Russia. In the second agreement (Feb., 1720), Sweden sold sections of Pomerania and the port of Stettin to Prussia.

Stockholm Bloodbath Massacre of over 80 Swedish nobles in Stockholm (Nov. 8, 1520), ordered by Danish King Christian II. The incident temporarily prevented break-up of the Kalmar Union (*q.v.*) but ultimately served to unite Sweden for independence. By 1522 Gustavus I had driven the Danes out of Sweden and dissolved the union.

Stockmar, Christian Friedrich, baron 1787–1863. German physician and diplomat. He helped arrange Prince Albert's marriage to Queen Victoria and later served as their unofficial adviser.

Stoicism Philosophical school founded (c300 BC) at Athens by Zeno of Citium. It arose in opposition to Epicureanism (*q.v.*), spread among the Greeks, and after the 2d cent. BC became influential among the Romans. Stoicism was derived from the teachings of Cynics. Stoics held that all reality is material and that God, or reason, is the universal working force. Thus, living according to nature or reason was to come into harmony with the divine order of the universe. The ideal, virtuous life was to be achieved by exercising wisdom and restraint, by casting off passion and desire, and by right conduct and devotion to duty. Notable adherents of Stoicism include Diogenes of Babylonia, Antipater of Tarsus, Cato the Younger, Seneca, Epictetus, and Emperor Marcus Aurelius.

Stoker, Bram (˜, Abraham) 1847–1912. Irish-born British novelist, best known as the author of *Dracula.*

Stokes, Whitley 1830–1909. Irish jurist. Stokes revised the civil and criminal codes in India (1887).

Stokowski, Leopold 1882–1977. Noted American conductor. Stokowski conducted many contemporary works and unusual orchestrations, and popularized Bach.

Stolypin, Peter Arkadevich 1863–1911. Russian statesman. As prime minister (1906–11), he attempted to control the revolutionary movement by instituting agrarian land reforms and by ruthless use of secret police.

Stolypin Land Reform *See* **Agrarian Reform Act.**

Stone, Harlan Fiske 1872–1946. American jurist, an associate (1925–41) and chief justice (1941–46) of the Supreme Court. He was noted for his dissenting opinions in defense of New Deal legislation.

Stone, Lucy 1818–93. American reformer, a noted public speaker on both abolition and women's rights. With her husband, she helped found the American Woman Suffrage Association.

Stone Age Stage in the development of human culture beginning about 2.5 million years ago and lasting until the beginning of the Bronze Age (*q.v.*), or roughly about 3500 BC (in the Near East). Dating varies widely according to region and particular culture, and an essentially Stone Age culture exists even today among some peoples. The Stone Age is characterized by the use of stone (along with wood and bone) for tools and implements, and is commonly subdivided into the Paleolithic and Neolithic stages. The Paleolithic (Old Stone Age) period is the earliest and lasted until about 8000–6000 BC. The Neolithic (New Stone Age) period is generally taken to begin with the advent of domestication of animals, cultivation of food plants, and development of village culture (although criteria vary). It ends with the appearance of metal weapons and tools. The term Mesolithic (Middle Stone Age) usually refers to a stage of cultural development in northwestern Europe, lasting from about 8000 to 3000 BC.

Stonehenge Famous prehistoric stone structure near Salisbury, in southern England. Built and added to between the 18th and 14th cents. BC, it was apparently used to mark the seasons for agricultural purposes, though not by the Druids, as is popularly believed. The structure is made up of large stones arranged in concentric circles about a central altar stone.

Stones River, Battle of (Battle of Murfreesboro) Battle of the US Civil War, fought (Dec. 31, 1862–Jan. 2, 1863) near Murfreesboro, Tennessee. Union forces under Gen. W. Rosecrans forced the Confederates under B. Bragg to withdraw after a bloody battle.

Storm and Stress *See* **Sturm und Drang.**

Storm, Hans Theodor Woldsen 1817–88. German author, best known for the haunting realism of his novellas, especially *The Rider of the White Horse.*

Storting Norwegian parliament (since 1814). It is divided into an upper house (Lagting) and lower house (Odelsting).

Story, Joseph 1779–1845. American jurist, associate justice of the Supreme Court (1811–45). He generally agreed with Chief Justice J. Marshall and wrote the pivotal court opinion in *Martin* v. *Hunter's Lessee* (1816), which established Supreme Court review of state cases involving constitutional law.

Stowe, Harriet Beecher 1811–96. American writer. The sister of H. W. Beecher, her novel *Uncle Tom's Cabin* (1852) solidified antislavery sentiment in America.

Strabo 63 BC–after AD 21. Greek geographer and historian. His *Geographica* was a compilation of his own observations and the cumulative knowledge of the geography and history of the ancient world.

Stradivari, Antonio (Stradivarius, Antonius) 1644–1737. Italian violin maker, the acknowledged master of his craft.

Strafford, Thomas Wentworth, 1st earl of 1593–1641. English statesman and governor of Ireland. An adviser to Charles I and loyal supporter of his despotic rule, he commanded the king's forces during the second Bishop's War (1640). Following his defeat, Parliamentarians seized the opportunity to eliminate an enemy in their fight with the king. Strafford was impeached and beheaded.

Straits Convention International agreement (July 13, 1841) by which the Ottoman Turks agreed (at the instigation of European powers) to close the Dardanelles to warships during peacetime. The agreement was superseded by the Lausanne Convention (1923), which opened the straits to all warships.

Straits Settlements British colony in Southeast Asia, including the territories of Singapore, Malacca (*q.q.v.*). The colony was broken up in 1946.

Stralsund, Treaty of Agreement (May 24, 1370) by which Denmark made extensive commercial concessions to the Hanseatic League. Defeated (1368) by a coalition the league had formed with Sweden and other powers, Danish king Valdemar IV signed the treaty to regain his throne.

Strang, James Jesse 1813–56. Dissident Mormon leader. He failed in his bid to become leader of the Mormons after J. Smith's assassination (1844), formed his own sect (Strangites), and later established a colony on Beaver Island in Lake Michigan.

Strasbourg, Oath of *See* **Oath of Strasbourg.**

Strasser, Gregor and **Otto** 1892–1934; 1897–1974. German Nazi leaders. These brothers were early supporters of A. Hitler. Otto left the party (1930) to join the Socialist Black Front and his brother, a powerful rival of Hitler's within the party, was assassinated (1934).

Strassmann, Fritz *See* **Meitner, Lise.**

Stratford de Redcliffe, Stratford Canning, Viscount 1786–1880. British diplomat. Stratford served as minister to Ottoman Turkey, and mediated conflicts between that country, Greece, and Russia. He was unable, however, to avert the Crimean War.

Strathclyde Medieval Celtic kingdom in southwestern Scotland, constituted around the 5th cent. Conquered by King Edmund of England in 945, it was annexed by Scotland in 1124.

Strathcona and Mount Royal, Donald Alexander Smith, 1st baron 1820–1914. Canadian financier. Originally a fur trader, he became governor of the Hudson's Bay Company (1889–1914) and was a leading figure in the company that completed the Canadian Pacific Railway.

Straus, Isidor 1845–1912. American merchant. Straus was involved in the family import business, L. Straus and Sons, and, with his brother, N. Straus, took over R.H. Macy and Company. He died aboard the *Titanic.*

Straus, Nathan 1848–1931. American merchant and philanthropist. Straus was associated with the family import business, L. Straus and Sons, and with his brother, I. Straus, took over R.H. Macy and Company. He aided the poor and Zionist charities.

Strauss, Johann 1825–99. Austrian composer noted for his waltzes. Strauss ignored his father's opposition and followed him into a musical career. He composed the waltzes *Blue Danube* and *Tales from the Vienna Woods* and the operettas *Die Fledermaus* and *The Gypsy Baron.*

Strauss, Richard Georg 1864–1949. Famous German composer, noted for his Romantic operas and symphonic poems. The vast body of his work includes the operas *Elektra, Salome,* and *Der Rosenkavalier,* and the orchestral music *Don Juan, Death and Transfiguration, Thus Spake Zarathustra,* and *Till Eulenspiegel's Merry Pranks.*

Stravinsky, Igor Fëdorovich 1882–1971. Russian-born American composer, one of the great composers of the 20th century. He was best known for his ballets, including *The Firebird* (1910), *Petrouchka* (1911), and *The Rite of Spring* (1913).

Streicher, Julius 1885–1946. German Nazi leader, a vicious anti-Semite who used his newspaper, *Der Stürmer,* to spread hatred of the Jews. He joined A. Hitler's Nazi party in the early days and was executed as a war criminal after the war.

Stresemann, Gustav 1878–1929. German statesman. As foreign minister of the Weimar Republic, he succeeded in pursuing a policy of conciliation with Germany's former enemies and arranged Germany's admission to the League of Nations. He shared the Nobel Peace Prize (1926).

Strijdom, Johannes Gerhardus 1893–1958. South African politician. A leader of the Nationalist party (from 1929) and supporter of apartheid he served as prime minister from 1954 to 1958.

strike A collective work stoppage by employees, usually those who are members of a union seeking higher wages or improved working conditions. Strikes in the US were fairly rare until after the Civil War, when a period of rapid industrialization and the organization of workers began. The late 19th and early 20th cents. witnessed many outbreaks of violence in connection with strikes (notably the Homestead and Pullman strikes, *qq.v.*). Since then, however, violence has steadily played less of a role in labor actions. Though uncommon in the US, strikes in support of political causes are common in Europe. Perhaps the most significant were the widespread strikes (1917) in Russia that helped bring down the tsarist government.

Strindberg, Johan August 1849–1912. Swedish playwright and novelist. He is best known for his plays, including *The Father, Miss Julie,* and *The Dance of Death.*

Stroganov Russian merchant family that organized vast colonial enterprises in eastern Russia (16th–17th cents.). They contributed significantly to Russia's expansion into Siberia by organizing entire colonies and military expeditions in pursuit of their commercial expansion. They also provided financial support for tsarist governments.

Stroheim, Erich von 1885–1957.   Austrian-born American film director and actor. He appeared in such classic films as *The Birth of a Nation, Grand Illusion,* and *Sunset Boulevard,* and directed the critically acclaimed *Greed.*

Stroessner, Alfredo 1912–   . Longtime leader and strongman of Paraguay, and its president (1954–89). A hero in the Chaco War, Stroessner became an army general in 1951 and took part in the military coup (1954) that brought him to power. Noted for his brutal suppression of opposition during the 1950s, he steered a more moderate course after the late 1960s. He fostered economic development, built schools and other public facilities, and remained relatively popular until the 1980s, when growing opposition led to his ouster in a military coup (1989). *See also* Paraguay, 1954–89.

Strozzi   Noble Florentine family that opposed the power of the Medici family in Florence. Its members included Filippo Strozzi the Elder (1426–91), Giambattista Strozzi (1488–1538), and Piero Strozzi (*d.* 1558).

Struensee, Johann Friedrich 1737–72.   German-born Danish politician. As physician to the insane Christian VII, he gained control of the government (1770) and assumed dictatorial powers. He was accused of adultery with Queen Caroline and was beheaded.

Stuart (Stewart)   Royal family of Scotland and England (reigned 1603–1714). The family originated in the 11th cent. and from the 12th cent. the Stuarts were hereditary stewards of Scotland. The first Stuart king of Scotland was Robert II (1371–90). The Stuart claim to the English throne stemmed from the marriage of Scottish king James IV to English king Henry VII's daughter, Margaret. Their granddaughter, Mary, Queen of Scots, was mother of Scottish king James VI, who became King James I (1603–25), first Stuart king of England. Thereafter the Stuarts reigned during the tumultuous period of the English Civil Wars and Restoration. The line continued until Queen Anne died without an heir and the Hanoverians came to power (1714, in accordance with the 1701 Act of Settlement). *Stuart rulers of Scotland:* Robert II 1371–90; Robert III 1390–1406; James I 1406–37; James II 1437–60; James III 1460–88; James IV 1488–1513; James V 1513–42; Mary Queen of Scots 1542–67; James VI 1567–1625. *Stuart rulers of England: James 1603–25; Charles I*

1625–49. Commonwealth, Protectorate. *Charles II 1660–85; James II 1685–88; William III 1689–1702; Anne 1702–14.*

Stuart, Arabella 1575–1615.   English noblewoman, a claimant to the throne. Her cousin, King James I, imprisoned her in the Tower of London, where she died.

Stuart, Charles Edward 1720–88.   Claimant to the English throne, a grandson of James II. The hope of the Jacobites, "Bonnie Prince Charlie," The Young Pretender, led them in an abortive revolt (1745) but was defeated at the Battle of Cullodon (1746). He lived abroad thereafter and died in obscurity.

Stuart, Esme, 1st duke of Lennox c1542–83.   Scottish nobleman. A favorite of his cousin King James I of England, he had the earl of Morton executed for Lord Darnley's murder. He was subsequently driven from Scotland for plotting a Spanish invasion of England to rescue Mary Queen of Scots.

Stuart, Frances Teresa, duchess of Richmond and Lennox 1648–1702.   English mistress of Charles II. A great beauty, she is reputed to be the only woman that the king truly loved. She married (1667) Charles Stuart, duke of Richmond, but continued her affair.

Stuart, Gilbert 1755–1828.   American portrait painter, noted for his portraits of G. Washington, J. Adams, T. Jefferson, and J. Madison.

Stuart, Henry Benedict Maria (Cardinal York) 1725–1807.   Last Stuart to claim the English throne. He became the royal pretender as Henry IX on the death of his brother, Charles Edward Stuart (1788). In return for favors granted by King George III, however, he bequeathed the Stuart family jewels to George IV.

Stuart, Jeb (James Ewell Brown) 1833–64.   Confederate cavalry officer in the American Civil War, noted for skillful deployment of his troops in battle and for his daring raids behind Union lines.

Stuart, James Francis Edward (the Old Pretender) 1688–1766.   A Catholic and claimant to the English throne, he was the son of King James II. Styled James III, he was supported by the Jacobites, and French King Louis XIV proclaimed him king of England following the death of James II. France provided him with a fleet to invade Scotland (1708), but English warships turned the invasion force back while still at sea.

Stuart, Mary   *See* **Mary Queen of Scots.**

Sture, Sten c1440–1503.   Swedish patriot. Sture defeated the Danish king Christian I at Brunkeburg (1471) and unsuccessfully attempted to oppose the union of Sweden with Denmark (Kalmar Union, *q.v.*).

Stürghkh, Karl, graf von 1859–1916.   Austrian prime minister (1911–16). He suspended the Parliament (1914) and, an archenemy of liberals and radicals, was assassinated by a Socialist.

Sturm und Drang (Storm and Stress)   German literary movement in the 1770s. It developed as a reaction to rationalism and was the early period of German romanticism. Influenced by J. von Herder, J. Goethe wrote the first major drama produced by the movement, *Götz von Berlichingen* (1773). The following year he published *The Sorrows of Young Werther,* a novel that embodied the movement's concern for character and rebellion against standards (in both contemporary literature and morality). F. Schiller, the other major figure in this movement may be said to have been its last as well. Both Schiller and Goethe went on to become leaders of the classical movement in Germany.

Stuyvesant, Peter 1592–1672.   Dutch administrator, governor of New Amsterdam until its capture (1664) by the English, who renamed it New York.

Suárez, Francisco 1548–1617.   Spanish Jesuit and prominent Scholastic philosopher. Suárez believed in the equality of souls and disputed the divine right of kings in his *Defensio fidei.*

Suckling, Sir John 1609–42?   English poet, one of the Cavalier Poets (*q.v.*). He was best known for his lyrics.

Sucre, Antonio José de 1795–1830.   A South American revolutionary. He was S. Bolívar's chief lieutenant and participated in fighting against the Spanish in Peru, Bolivia, Ecuador, and Colombia and commanded in the Battle of Ayacucho (*q.v.*). He was first president of Bolivia (1826–28).

Sudan (Republic of Sudan)   Republic located in northeastern Africa. Its capital is Khartoum. Northern Sudan, once part of ancient Nubia, was settled by the Egyptians, who were forced out of the region by the 8th cent. BC. Muslims completed conquest of the region in the 16th cent., and Egypt regained control in the early 19th cent. In 1899 the Anglo-Egyptian Sudan, a condominium under British and Egyptian rule, was established. The Sudan became independent in 1956. Key dates in the history of Sudan include:

c3400–2000 BC   Egypt established control over northern Sudan, then part of the ancient region of Nubia.

8TH–4TH CENTS. BC   Cush kingdom flourished, after Nubians revolted successfully against Egypt.

6TH CENT. AD   Christian state of Dongola established; successfully resisted Muslim invasions from Egypt until its fall (15th cent.).

c770   Empire of Songhai founded by Berbers in Niger Valley.

1464–92   Sonni 'Ali ruled Songhai empire; expanded Shonghai domains to include much of modern Sudan; captured Timbuktu (1468).

1591   Muslims from Morocco overran and destroyed the Empire of Songhai.

16TH–19TH CENTS.   Muslim state of Funj flourished in northern Sudan.

1820–22   Region conquered by Egyptians under Muhammad Ali.

1823   Khartoum founded by Egyptians.

1877–80   British officer and administrator C. Gordon served as governor of Egyptian Sudan; streamlined provincial administration and took steps to end the slave trade.

1881–98   Egyptian rule in Sudan challenged by Mahdist revolt led by Muhammad Ahmed, the Mahdi.

1885   Mahdists overran and destroyed Khartoum (Jan.); Gordon killed; Mahdists seized complete control of Egyptian Sudan.

1885   Mahdi died; succeeded by the Khalifa Abdallahi.

1896–98   Joint Anglo-Egyptian expedition to regain Sudan led by British Gen. H. Kitchener; defeated the Khalifa at Omdurman (Sept. 2, 1898).

1898   Fashoda Incident; France nearly sparked war over its claims to the Sudan; renounced claim in return for British concessions in the Sahara.

1899   Anglo-Egyptian Sudan established (Jan. 19); agreement set up joint British and Egyptian rule.

1924   British divided Sudan into separate northern and southern administrative units.

1936   Anglo-Egyptian treaty reaffirmed 1899 agreement for joint rule of Sudan.

1948 Legislative assembly created (June 19); first step in program for Sudanese autonomy.

1953 British and Egyptians signed accord (Feb. 12) calling for Sudanese autonomy within three years.

1955 Predominantly Christian southern Sudanese began revolt against predominantly Muslim northern Sudanese; lasted to 1972.

1956 Sudan became independent (Jan. 1).

1958 Gen. Ibrahim Abboud seized power in army coup; ruled through Supreme Council of Armed Forces.

1964 Parliamentary government restored after civilian revolt.

1964–69 Continuing economic problems and unrest in south resulted in a period of political instability.

1966–67 Sadiq al-Mahdi in office as prime minister.

1969 Col. Gaafar al-Nimeiry seized power (May) in leftist coup.

1969–85 Nimeiry in power as head of state; outlawed political parties and proceeded with nationalization of key industries; maintained close relations with Egypt; economic problems plagued the country throughout his administration; borrowing by government in 1970s set stage for debt problems of 1980s.

1971 Leftist coup by army officers put down (July).

1971 Nimeiry elected president; Sudanese Socialist Union (SSU) formed as the country's one legal political party.

1972 Years of civil war ended (Feb.); southern Sudan granted degree of autonomy by central government, in agreement signed at Addis Ababa.

1973 New constitution adopted; established one-party rule by SSU.

1974 National People's Assembly established; southern Sudan's Regional People's Assembly elected previously in 1973.

1976 Unsuccessful attempt to overthrow Nimeiry; Nimeiry broke diplomatic relations with Libya, suspecting Libyan leader M. Qaddafi of engineering the coup.

1977 President Nemeiry reelected to new six-year term.

1980 System of regional governments, each with own legislative assembly, established.

1982 Signed agreement with Egypt for integration; formed joint parliament with Egypt.

1983 President Nemeiry reelected to third six-year term.

1983 Renewed unrest in south; region divided into thirds, each with own legislative assembly (June).

1983 President Nemeiry abruptly imposed Islamic law throughout the country (Sept.); non-Muslims in north and south opposed move.

1984 Government imposed state of emergency (Apr. 1984) as opposition to Islamic law continued; special courts set up; police powers expanded.

1984 National Assembly rejected president's bid to formally make Sudan an Islamic state; the south now in open revolt (led by insurgent Sudan People's Liberation Movement, SPLM).

1984 Sudan first fell behind on repayment of IMF loans; remained in arrears into the 1990s; had continued borrowing despite trade deficit in early 1980s.

1984–85 Drought in Ethiopia sent some 1 million Ethiopian refugees flooding into the Sudan, adding to those from Chad, Uganda, and Eritrea; meanwhile, Sudan was itself hit by severe drought in east and west.

1985 Nimeiry ousted in bloodless military coup (Apr. 6); SPLM briefly halted, then resumed fighting in south.

1985–86 Gen. Abdel-Rahman Swar al-Dahab, the defense minister, in power as head of state; promised return to civilian government in 1986; political parties legalized; sought closer relations with Libya, Ethiopia, and USSR.

1985 Official name of country became the Republic of Sudan.

1986–89 Sadiq al-Mahdi, head of Umma Party (UP), in office as prime minister; formed coalition government with Democratic Unionist party; efforts at negotiating settlement in south failed; SPLM demanded end to all Islamic laws.

1987 Government imposed state of emergency in face of mounting economic ills; shortages of basic goods and rising prices beset economy.

1988 Some 200–300,000 reported near starvation in south as result of civil war, economic problems, and drought; estimated 3 million throughout Sudan needed food aid.

1989 Government began direct negotiations with SPLM in Ethiopia (Apr.); agreed to suspend all Islamic law pending constitutional conference in Sept.; fighting halted.

1989 Mahdi ousted in bloodless coup (June 30).

1989– Gen. Omar Hassan Ahmad al-Bashir in power as head of state; abolished constitution and dissolved legislature; promised solution to revolt in south.

1989–91 Poor harvests resulting from drought and civil war threatened Sudan with widespread famine; some 7.7 million estimated in danger of starvation.

1989 Fighting in south resumed (Oct.) after negotiations with new, pro-Islamic government failed.

1990 Alleged coup attempts failed (Mar., Apr., Sept., Nov.); meanwhile pro-Islamic faction in government reported increasing.

1990 Sudan, supporting Iraq, refused to condemn the invasion of Kuwait.

1991 Federal system of government instituted; country divided into nine states, each with own government operating under national government; Islamic law to be applied only in northern states.

1992 Government launched offensive against rebels in ongoing civil war (Mar.–May); some 50,000 government troops recaptured much rebel-held territory.

1992 Government began moving Nuba people from homelands in central Sudan; some 50,000 people forcibly relocated in program to isolate rebel sympathizers (Sept.).

Sudetenland *See* **Munich Pact.**

Sue, Eugène (*pseud.* of Marie-Joseph ~) 1804–57. French novelist and journalist. Born to a wealthy family, he worked as a naval surgeon and later used his experiences as the basis for sea stories. He then wrote a number of sensational novels, exposing the social ills that plagued France as a result of the Industrial Revolution. Among his works are *The Mysteries of Paris* (1843) and *The Wandering Jew* (1845). Many of his works first appeared as newspaper serials.

Suetonius (Tranquillus, Gaius ~) *fl.* AD c120. Roman biographer. A private secretary to Hadrian, he is chiefly remembered for his *Lives of the Caesars.*

Sudra caste *See* **caste system.**

Suez Canal Canal in Egypt, an important commercial waterway connecting the Mediterranean Sea and the Red Sea. Built by a private French company (1859–69) under the supervision of F. de Lesseps, the canal was originally financed by a consortium of French interests, which held 52% of the stock, the Egyptian khedive (44%), and others. The British government bought out the khedive's 44% interest in 1875, when financial troubles forced the khedive to raise capital. This, coupled with British control of the Egyptian government in the late 1800s, gave Britain a firm grip on what was then a strategic waterway. Egyptian participation in administration of the canal increased from 1936. After WW II and during the subsequent general withdrawal of the British from Egypt, Britain agreed to pull out all troops, including those based at the canal (by 1954 Anglo-Egyptian Treaty). Egyptian leader G. Nasser nationalized the internationally owned canal company (July 26, 1956), when the US refused to go through with a loan to build his coveted Aswan Dam. The resulting Suez Crisis erupted into war when the Israelis, long denied access to the canal and in collusion with both the British and French, launched the Second Arab-Israeli War (*q.v.*) and invaded Egypt. British and French troops entered the fighting (Oct. 31) to retake the canal. They eventually were replaced by UN troops after a ceasefire was arranged (Nov. 6). The canal was completely blocked during the Third Arab-Israeli War (1967) and was not reopened until June, 1975, following the Fourth Arab-Israeli War (1973).

Suez Crisis *See* **Suez Canal.**

Suffolk, Charles Brandon, 1st duke of *d.*1545. English nobleman. Suffolk was a favorite and brother-in-law of Henry VIII, whom he accompanied to the Field of Cloth of Gold (1520), and for whom he twice invaded France (1523 and 1544).

Suffolk, Henry Grey, duke of *d.*1554. English nobleman. As father of Lady Jane Grey, he joined Northumberland's plot to make her queen. He was spared execution by Mary Tudor, but later joined the T. Wyatt (*q.v.*) uprising and was beheaded.

Suffolk Resolves Resolutions passed (Sept. 9, 1774) at meetings of American colonists in Suffolk County, Massachusetts, to protest the British Intolerable Acts (*q.v.*). They called for disobedience to the acts, nonpayment of taxes, the start of regular militia musters, and an end to trade with Britain. The resolves were forwarded to and endorsed by the Continental Congress.

Sufism Muslim mystical, philosophical, and literary movement. An outgrowth of the Shi'ite sect, it stressed the personal union of the soul with God. Sufism flourished especially in Persia in the 11th cent. and produced the best of the Persian poets. Its greatest exponent was Al-Ghazali.

Sugar Act British law (1764) designed to raise revenue for defense of the American colonies and to put an end to smuggling of molasses and sugar from the French and Dutch West Indies to America. New rules regarding shipment and confiscation of illegal cargoes were especially unpopular among colonists and the act helped foment sentiment for revolution.

Suharto 1921– . President of Indonesia (1967-). A career army officer, he led the army in putting down a Communist-influenced *coup d'état* in 1965. Some 300,000 or more Indonesian Communists were massacred. From then on he effectively controlled the government, though Sukarno remained president. Suharto finally became president in 1967 and has been reelected many times since. While remaining in firm control, Suharto nevertheless faced increasing opposition and separatist unrest. *See also* Indonesia, 1967– .

Sui Chinese dynasty (581–618) that reunited China after the Six Dynasties (*q.v.*) period. The Sui emperors were Wendi (Yang Jian, 541–604) and his son, Yang Guang (*d.* 618). They began construction of a canal system, called the Grand Canal, and refortified the Great Wall. The dynasty was overthrown and the succeeding Tang dynasty adopted many of the Sui governmental systems.

Sukarno 1901–70. Indonesian statesman, president (1949–67), and leader of the nationalists in the fight for independence from the Dutch (1945–49). After becoming president he consolidated his power, dissolved the assembly (1959), and made himself dictator. At the same time, he sought closer relations with the Communists, particularly the Chinese. An attempted Communist coup, however, resulted in a takeover by the Indonesian army and Sukarno's ouster.

Sulayman *See* **Suleiman**.

Suleiman I (Suleyman I) 1494–1566. Sultan of the Ottoman Empire (1520–66), son and successor of Selim I. He was known as "the Magnificent" and "the Lawgiver" for his expansion of the empire, his patronage of the arts, and his many reforms. His conquests include Belgrade (1521),

Rhodes (1522), southern Hungary (at the Battle of Mohacs, 1526), and parts of Persia, Iraq, and Tripoli (by 1551). His navy, under the command of Barbarossa, terrorized the Mediterranean. During his reign, Suleiman also formed what became a long-standing alliance with France against the Habsburg rulers of Europe.

Suleiman II 1642–91. Ottoman sultan (1687–91), successor to his brother, Muhammad IV. Through his minister, Mustafa Kuprili, he introduced liberal reforms. His reign was marked by the Austro-Turkish War (1682–99).

Suleyman I *See* **Suleiman I**.

Sulla, Lucius Cornelius 138–78 BC. Roman general and politician. Sulla fought with distinction in the Social War and served under Marius when Rome fought Jugurtha. But a rivalry with Marius had become a bitter feud and, when Sulla became consul (88 BC), civil war broke out between them. Sulla won that year and then departed for Asia Minor to fight the first Mithradatic War (88–85). Marius subsequently marched on Rome, massacred Sulla's supporters, and took power. Sulla returned to Rome (83), seized power, and defeated Carbo (leader of the Marian party) in the ensuing civil war. He then made himself dictator for life (82) and began the systematic murder of thousands of his opponents. At the same time, he instituted a program of governmental reforms, notably those to restore the power of the Senate. He resigned unexpectedly in 79 BC.

Sullivan, Sir Arthur Seymour 1842–1900. English composer. With lyricist Sir W. Gilbert, Sullivan created such famous operettas as *The Pirates of Penzance, The Mikado,* and *H.M.S. Pinafore.*

Sullivan, John 1740–95. American Revolutionary War general. He saw action at the battles of Long Island, Trenton, Princeton, Brandywine, and Germantown, and fought in the campaign against the Iroquois (1779).

Sullivan, Louis Henry 1856–1924. American architect, considered the father of modernism for his designs of early skyscrapers, especially the Gage Building and the Chicago Stock Exchange. His pupil was F. L. Wright.

Sully, Maximilien de Béthune, duc de 1560–1641. French financier and statesman. A close friend of Henry IV, he became finance minister (by 1598) and restored the royal treasury, which had been seriously depleted by the Wars of Religion.

Sully-Prudhomme, René François Armand 1839–1907. French poet, one of the Parnassians. His poetry was marked by its philosophical concerns. He won the first Nobel Prize for Literature (1901).

sultan Islamic term applied at first to spiritual leaders of the Islamic community and later to Muslim rulers wielding political authority.

Sumatra Treaty *See* **Achinese War.**

Sumer Ancient civilization of southern Mesopotamia from roughly the 4th to 3d millennium BC to the beginning of the 2d millennium BC. Though an extensive village culture existed in the region by the 5th millennium BC, the formation of Sumerian cities and the rise of Sumerian culture did not begin until the 4th to 3d millennium. From that time, such cities as Eridu, Erech, Lagash, Larsa, and Ur flourished as commercial and cultural centers and rivaled one another for control of neighboring lands. In the 24th cent. BC, however, the Semitic people of northern Mesopotamia, the Akkadians (*see* Akkad), conquered Sumeria and made it part of their empire. The Akkadians absorbed and thus spread much of the Sumerian culture (including cuneiform writing) before they were in turn conquered (22d cent. BC) by invaders from the north. Thereafter the Sumerians enjoyed a brief resurgence under the leadership of such cities as Lagash and, notably, Ur. But dynastic struggles and invasions by neighboring peoples brought on their final decline in the 20th cent. BC. During their ascendancy, the Sumerians developed the first writing system (cuneiform) in the Near East, the first written civil law code, commercial and banking systems, skills in pottery-making and metal-working and agricultural and military technology. The fall of Sumerian civilization was followed by the rise of Babylonia (*q.v.*).

Summer Offensive *See* **June Offensive.**

summit conference Meeting by heads of major powers to discuss fundamental issues of mutual interest. These meetings became a prominent feature of East-West diplomacy after WW II. The first (1955) was attended by US president D. Eisenhower, Soviet leader N. Khrushchev, and British prime minister A. Eden and sought to ease Cold War tensions. A 1960 Paris summit between the US, the Soviet Union, and European powers was scuttled by the U-2 incident (*q.v.*). The 1961 Vienna summit between US president J. Kennedy and Khrushchev marked the begin-

ning of further East-West tensions. President R. Nixon's Beijing conference (1972) formally began the process of normalizing US-Chinese relations. Nixon's Moscow conference (1972) marked the first visit to Moscow by a US president.

Sumner, Charles 1811–74. US senator (1851–74) from Massachusetts. A prominent abolitionist, he was attacked and beaten in the Senate by a Southern senator, was a leader of Radical Republicans demanding a harsh Reconstruction policy, and urged the impeachment of President A. Johnson.

Sumter, Thomas 1734–1832. American general. During the American Revolution he commanded (1780) a force of raiders that harassed the British in North and South Carolina. Fort Sumter was named for him.

Sunday, Billy (Ashley, William) 1863–1935. American Christian evangelist and preacher. A former professional baseball player, he gained a wide following (from 1896) for his revival meetings.

Sunday school Program of religious education for the young. The first Sunday school was organized by R. Raikes in England (1780). By 1786 the first one in North America had been organized in Virginia.

Sung *See* **Song.**

Sunga Dynasty that ruled northern India between c185 and c73 BC. It succeeded the Maurya Empire. During the rule of this dynasty Brahmanical Hinduism reemerged as the official state religion, after a temporary eclipse by Buddhism.

Sunnites (Sunnis) Traditional or orthodox sect of Islam, adhered to by over three-quarters of all Muslims. They accept the actual succession of the early Muslim caliphs, while the other major sect, the Shi'ites (*q.v.*), say that Ali (the fourth) was the first true successor of Muhammad. The Sunnites also accept the Sunnah as the legitimate body of Muslim traditions.

Sun Yat-sen 1866–1925. Chinese revolutionary, the father of the Chinese Republic and leader of the Nationalist Guomindang until his death. Sun led an abortive revolt at Guangzhou (Canton) (1895) and for the next 16 years worked in exile to promote revolution in China. He returned to China during the Revolution of 1911 and served for a few months as president of the provisional government (1911–12). Next he led an abortive revolt (1913) against the dictatorial regime of Yuan Shikai and fled China until

1917. Sun became president of the Nationalist government at Guangzhou (1924), formed an alliance with the Chinese Communists, and reorganized the Nationalist Guomindang with the help of Russia. He died before being able to launch his planned Northern Expedition (*q.v.*).

Sun Yat-sen, Madame *See* **Soong Ch'ing-ling.**

Suppiluliumas I *See* **Hittite Empire.**

Supremacy, Acts of *See* **Acts of Supremacy.**

suprematism School of abstract art that began in Russia around 1913. Totally nonrepresentational, it emphasized pure geometric forms. The school was founded by Casimir Malevich (1878–1935) and it influenced modern architecture and industrial design.

Supreme Court Highest court in the US, empowered to interpret treaties, laws, and the Constitution; mediate disputes between states or citizens of different states; and act as the court of final appeal. The Court was established in 1787 by Article 3 of the Constitution. Originally set at six members, its number stabilized at nine in 1869, despite F. D. Roosevelt's efforts to enlarge it in the 1930s. The justices, including one chief justice and eight associate justices, are appointed for life. Justices have generally fallen into two categories: those who strictly interpret the letter of the law, and those whose looser interpretations allow "implied" governmental powers. The first female justice, Sandra Day O'Connor, was appointed to the court in 1981.

Suriname (*formerly* Surinam; Dutch Guiana) Independent republic located on the northeast coast of South America. The capital is Paramaribo and the population is 402,000. Settled by the Dutch and the English, Suriname was granted to the Dutch by the Treaty of Breda (1667), in return for abandonment of Dutch claims to New Amsterdam (New York). Suriname became an autonomous state within the kingdom of the Netherlands (1954) and an independent republic (Nov. 25, 1975). In 1980 the government was overthrown by a military coup. Civil war broke out in 1986. In 1988 though, an elected civilian government took office and reached a settlement to end the war. Following another military coup (Dec. 24, 1990), new elections were held (1991) and Ronald Venetiaan became president.

Surji-Arjungaon, Treaty of Treaty (Dec. 30, 1803) between the British and the Marathas, concluding the second Maratha War. It virtually ended Maratha independence (they agreed to accept a British resident adviser and consolidated British rule over northern Indian territory.

Surprise plot *See* **Bye plot.**

Surprising Treason *See* **Bye plot.**

Surrat, Mary Eugenia 1820–65. American conspirator, who kept the Washington, D.C., boarding house where J. Booth and others planned A. Lincoln's assassination. She was hanged, though her actual guilt is still debated.

surrealism Literary and art movement founded in 1924 by A. Breton. An outgrowth of Dada, it focused on the use of unconscious thought processes and their expression.

Suryavarman II *See* **Angkor Wat.**

Suslov, Mikhail 1902–82. Soviet Communist leader. Suslov held important government positions under J. Stalin, N. Khrushchev, and L. Brezhnev, and was considered a leading spokesman of Soviet Communist ideology. He supported the Russian invasions of Hungary (1956), Czechoslovakia (1968), and Afghanistan (1979), and advocated the imposition of martial law in Poland (1981).

Sussex, kingdom of *See* **Anglo-Saxon Heptarchy.**

Sussex Incident International incident caused by the sinking of the passenger ship *Sussex* by a German submarine (Mar. 24, 1916). Because two of the 80 casualties were American, the US issued the "Sussex Ultimatum" to Germany (Apr. 18 1916). Germany initially agreed to give warning and provide for the safety of those aboard ships being torpedoed, but her resumption of unrestricted submarine warfare (in Feb., 1917) helped bring the US into WW I.

Sussex Ultimatum *See* **Sussex Incident.**

Sutter, John Augustus 1803–80. German-born American pioneer. Gold found (1848) on Sutter's land in the Sacramento, California, Valley set off the Gold Rush (1849). Prospectors overran Sutter's land, killed his cattle, and eventually bankrupted him.

Suttner, Bertha Kinsky, baroness von 1843–1914. Austrian writer and pacifist. Her pacifist novel *Lay Down Your Arms* profoundly influenced many, including A. Nobel. She was the first woman awarded the Nobel Peace Prize (1905).

Suvorov, Aleksandr Vasilievich 1729–1800. Russian general who served Russia in many wars, including the Seven Years' War, Russo-Turkish War (1787–92), and the French Revolutionary Wars.

Sverdrup, Johan 1816–92. Norwegian statesman. A leftist, he was president of the Storting (1871–84) and prime minister (1884–89). He helped institute trial by jury, parliamentary and agrarian reforms, and compulsory military service.

Sverre *d.* 1202. King of Norway (1184–1202), considered one of the great Norwegian kings. He limited the power of the church and aristocracy and increased the power of the monarchy.

Sviatoslav 920–72. Prince of Kiev (945–72) and Rus' national hero. He spent his entire career in conquest, expanding Kiev into an empire that extended from the Volga to the Danube. He was eventually compelled by his onetime Byzantine allies to relinquish his Balkan territories.

Svoboda, Ludvik 1895–1979. Czechoslovakian general and president (1968–75). Svoboda was a military hero in both WW I and WW II. As president, he obtained the release of the political prisoners taken in the Russian invasion of 1968.

Swabia Historic region, now in southwestern Germany. Originally settled by the Suevi and Alamanni, it became a duchy in the 9th cent. and once belonged to the Hohenstaufen family (1105–1254). Thereafter the duchy was divided into smaller land holdings. (*See also* Swabian Leagues.)

Swabian Leagues Protective associations formed at various times in the Middle Ages by cities and other local powers in what is now southern Germany. The most important of them (sometimes called the Great Swabian League) was formed in 1488 by 22 imperial cities, local leagues, and noblemen. It supported Holy Roman Emperor Charles V and its army fought the rebels in the Peasants' War (1524–25). Religious differences during the reformation forced its dissolution in 1534.

Swahili African Bantu people and language. The language shows marked Arabic influence and is spoken in Kenya, Uganda, Tanzania, and Zaire.

Swamp Fox, the *See* **Marion, Francis.**

Swaziland Southeast African kingdom. The population is 779,000 and the capital is Mbabane. The native Swazis migrated to their present homeland (early 19th cent.) under pressure from Zulus and soon afterward granted concessions to European powers. Swaziland became a British territory in 1903, achieved limited self-government in 1963, and became independent on Sept. 6, 1968. King Sobhuza II (reigned 1921–82) dissolved Parliament and assumed personal control of the kingdom in 1973. A new Parliament, with advisory powers only, was created in 1979. Though Sobhuza died in 1982, his successor, King Mswali III, was not named until 1986. Pressure for democratic reform resulted in a committee being established to study possible changes, including restoration of the multi-party system (1991).

sweatshop Term applied to a workplace characterized by unsanitary or dangerous working conditions and by the employment of workers at extremely low pay. Sweatshops flourished in England, the US, and other nations in the 19th cent. and contributed to the rise of unions and passage of labor laws to protect workers.

Sweden (Kingdom of Sweden) Constitutional monarchy (*pop.* 8,407,000) located in northern Europe. Its capital is Stockholm. United with Norway (1319) and Denmark (1397), Sweden came under Danish domination until it gained independence (1523) with Gustavus I as king. By the 17th cent. Sweden had become the greatest power in the Baltic, a position it lost in the Great Northern War (1700–21). During the 19th cent., Norway was united with Sweden. Since the 19th cent. Sweden has maintained a traditional policy of neutrality in all wars. In the early 20th cent., Sweden set up its extensive social welfare system and successfully maintained it until a faltering economy and the need for an economic system compatible with the EEC forced the government to dismantle it. **For more on important persons and events** *see* **entries under specific names.** Key dates in the history of Sweden include:

993–1024 Olaf Skutonung reigned; first Christian king of Sweden.

1150–60 Eric IX reigned, increased Sweden's military and advanced Christianity, began Swedish conquest of Finland, but was killed by Danish Prince Magnus Henrikson.

1240 Invasion of Novgorod (now Russia) halted by defeat in the Battle of the Neva.

1303?–73 Saint Bridget, patron saint of Sweden, lived.

1319–65 Magnus VII reigned; united (1319) Norway and Sweden.

1397 Kalmar Union; Queen Margaret joined Denmark, Norway and Sweden under one crown at Kalmar, Sweden.

1439 King Eric VII deposed from Norway, Sweden, and Denmark.

1450 Sten Sture the Elder expelled Danish-Norwegian king Christian I.

1513–23 Christian II reigned as king of Denmark and Norway (1513–23) and Sweden (1520–23), successor to his father, King John.

1520 Stockholm Bloodbath (Nov. 8); execution of Swedish nobles by Christian II to prevent breakup of Kalmar Union.

1521–23 Swedes rebelled against Christian II and forced Danes from all of Sweden except the southern tip (1521); made Gustavus Vasa king as Gustavus I (1523).

1523–60 Gustavus I reigned; made Lutheranism the state religion, established a hereditary monarchy, and founded the Vasa dynasty.

1558–82 Livonian War.

1560–68 Eric XIV reigned, conquered Estonia (1561).

1569–92 John III reigned, married the sister of Polish king Sigismund II; succeeded by his son, Polish king Sigismund III.

1583–1654 Count A. Oxenstierna lived; ruled Sweden for King Gustavus II during Thirty Years' War.

1592–99 Polish King Sigismund III reigned in Sweden; his rule was opposed by the Swedish Protestants and he was deposed.

1604–11 Charles IX reigned in Sweden.

1611–32 Gustavus Adolphus reigned as Gustavus II; took Ingermanland and parts of Karelia from Russia (1617), conquered most of Livonia from Poland; led Sweden (1630) into the Thirty Years' War.

1611–13 Sweden defeated by Denmark in Kalmar War.

1618–48 Thirty Years' War.

1629 Truce of Altmark between Sweden and Poland.

1631 Treaty of Bärwalde concluded between France and Sweden.

1632–54 Queen Christina reigned; Peace of Westphalia, ending Thirty Years' War, concluded during her rule; Sweden gained substantial territories and the monarch became a prince of the Holy Roman Empire; Sweden became the dominant Baltic power.

1638 New Sweden, Sweden's only American colony, founded in present-day Pennsylvania, New Jersey, and Delaware.

1654–60 Charles X Gustavus reigned following Christina's abdication; waged successful war against Poland (1655–60), the first Northern War; forced Poland to officially cede Livonia by the Treaty of Oliva (May 3, 1660) and won Danish-held territory at southern tip of Sweden.

1660–97 Charles XI reigned; established absolute monarchy.

1668 Sweden, England, and the Netherlands formed Triple Alliance to oppose French King Louis XIV.

1668 First Treaty of Aix-la-Chapelle; ended War of Devolution.

1686 Sweden joined League of Augsburg.

1688–97 War of the League of Augsburg.

1688–1772 E. Swedenborg, scientist and religious leader, lived; his followers formed the Church of New Jerusalem.

1697–1718 Charles XII reigned; presided over Sweden's decline during much of the Great Northern War (1700–21).

1700–21 Great Northern War fought by Sweden against coalition of Denmark, Poland, and Russia; defeated, Sweden was forced to sign the treaties of Stockholm (1720) and Nystadt (1721), by which it lost Estonia, Livonia, and most of its German holdings; war marked the decline of Sweden and the rise of Russia as the dominant power in the region.

1707–78 Botanist C. Linnaeus lived; considered the father of modern botany.

1718–20 Ulrika Eleonora reigned; acceded to a constitution establishing a constitutional monarchy with authority residing in a Riksdag, or parliament.

1741–43 Sweden defeated in Russo-Swedish War; Finnish Territory ceded to Russia.

1742 Astronomer A. Celsius invented the centigrade (Celsius) thermometer.

1743 Sweden and Russia signed the Treaty of Abo.

1756–63 Seven Years' War fought in Europe.

c1770–1810 Swedish Enlightenment.

1771–92 Gustavus III reigned; reimposed (Aug. 19, 1772) absolute monarchy; tyrannical rule led to his murder.

1788–89 Nobles and army officers of the Anjala League unsuccessfully attempted to undermine Gustavus III, then at war with Russia.

1792–1809 Gustavus IV reigned; ruled during French Revolutionary and most of the Napoleonic wars; Russia seized Finland from Sweden (1808) and Gustavus was deposed.

1809 Riksdag adopted new constitution (1809) and made Charles XIII king (reigned 1809–18); Charles ceded (1809) Finland to Russia.

1810 French marshal Jean Baptiste Jules Bernadotte named successor to Charles XIII; Bernadotte soon became leading power in Swedish government.

1814 Sweden and Norway united by Congress of Vienna in Treaty of Kiel.

1814–74 A. J. Ångström, physicist, lived; noted for work in spectrum analysis.

1818–44 Bernadotte reigned as Charles XIV; established Bernadotte dynasty and began period of peace and liberalization in Sweden.

1833–96 A. Nobel, inventor and industrialist, lived; his fortune established the Nobel prizes.

1844–59 Oscar I ruled as king of Norway and Sweden.

1859–72 King Charles XV reigned as king of Sweden and Norway; supported creation of a bicmeral legislature (1866).

1866 Riksdag, Swedish parliament, formed as two-chamber body.

1872–1907 Oscar II reigned as king of Sweden (and Norway to 1905).

1878–79 N. Nordenskjöld of Sweden successfully navigated the long-sought Northeast Passage along the northern coasts of Russia and Siberia to the Pacific.

1880–1932 I. Kreuger, financier who attempted to build world monopoly of the production of matches, lived.

1887 J. Strindberg wrote his play, *The Father.*

1905 Union between Norway and Sweden dissolved.

1907–50 Gustavus V reigned; maintained Swedish armed neutrality through both WW I and WW II.

1911 Old-age pension system established; marked beginning of extensive social welfare system set up in Sweden during subsequent years.

1917 Parliamentary form of government adopted.

1920, 1921–23, 1924–25 H. Branting served as premier; promoted social democracy.

1921 Universal suffrage enacted.

1932–46 Social Democratic leader P. Hansson served as prime minister.

1932–76 Social Democratic party dominated in Swedish government; shared power with opposing parties during WW II (1939–45) but resumed sole control of the cabinet after the war.

1946–68 Tage Erlander in office as prime minister; maintained Sweden's traditional neutrality through much of the Cold War; his administration marked by increased rent subsidies, child welfare benefits, and old age benefits, as well as educational reforms.

1948 Count F. Bernadotte assassinated while serving as UN mediator in Palestine.

1950–73 Gustavus VI reigned; rule was marked by passage of new laws promoting social welfare in Sweden.

1953–61 Swedish statesman D. Hammarskjöld served as UN general secretary.

1955 Biochemist A. Theorell received Nobel Prize for Physiology or Medicine.

1969–76 Olof Palme (Social Democrat) in office as prime minister.

1971 Riksdag, the Swedish parliament, changed from two-house to one-house legislature (Jan.).

1973 Carl XVI became king (Sept. 15), following death of his father.

1974 G. Myrdal awarded the Nobel Prize in Economics.

1976 Forty-year rule of Social Democrats ended; voter dissatisfaction with high tax rates needed to maintain Sweden's elaborate social welfare system brought election victory for Center Party.

1976–78 Thorbjörn Fälldin, Center party leader, in office as prime minister; formed coalition government.

1978–79 Prime Minister Ola Ullsten (Liberal) in office after struggle over increasing number of nuclear power plants.

1979 Center party leader Fälldin returned to office as head of non-Socialist coalition government; rising inflation and unemployment, labor unrest, and a widening budget deficit all troubled the administration in 1980–82.

1980 Voters narrowly approved referendum on continuing nuclear power in Sweden (Mar.); called for eventual phasing out of nuclear plants.

1982–86 Olof Palme, Social Democrat, back in office as prime minister; tried to fight inflationary recession while also keeping public spending down, without cutting social welfare benefits.

1986 Palme assassinated (Feb. 28) by lone gunman while walking unprotected on a quiet street in Stockholm; assassin escaped; police failure to locate killer aroused major controversy.

1986–91 Social Democrat Ingvar Carlsson in office as prime minister; his administration marked by continued economic problems and the dismantling of the social welfare system.

1986 Chernobyl nuclear disaster in USSR; Swedish monitoring stations among first to detect unusual radiation levels from as yet unreported accident.

1987 Scandal over dealings of Swedish arms manufacturer, Bofors AB; Bofors allegedly sold weapons to Mideast country then at war (a violation of Swedish law); secondarily, it was accused of bribing high officials in India to win an arms contract there.

1988 Border dispute with USSR over control of area of Baltic Sea resolved in Sweden's favor (Jan.).

1988 Suspected Palme assassin, middle-aged man with police record and history of mental illness, arrested (Dec.); later convicted and sentenced to life (1989), suspect was acquitted on appeal.

1989 Soviet Union agreed to 40 percent cut in industrial pollution reaching northern Europe by 1993.

1990 Government instituted austerity program as economy slipped into recession (1990–91); abandoned priorities of full employment and maintaining welfare state; ordered government spending cuts and 10 percent cut in government jobs, cuts in health benefits, and partial privatization of state-run businesses.

1991 Income tax abolished for all but wealthiest (Jan.); taxes on goods and services increased to make up for loss of revenues.

1991 Government abolished or reformed regulations limiting competition (Feb.).

1991 Financial industry deregulated (Mar.).

1991 Government declared it would link value of Swedish krona to the ECU.

1991 Carl Bildt elected prime minister (Sept.).

1992 Unemployment rate hit 50-year high (July).

1992 Government and opposition leaders reached accord on austerity budget; spending cuts and new taxes planned for 1993.

Swedenborg, Emanuel 1688–1772. Swedish scientist and religious leader. Swedenborg devoted himself exclusively to religion after 1734. His writings interpreting the Scriptures became the basis for the Church of New Jerusalem, an organization founded by his followers.

Swedish Enlightenment Literary period (c1770–c1810), the flowering of neoclassicism in Sweden. Sometimes called the Gustavian Enlightenment after Gustavus III, the period saw official encouragement of literature through the royal patronage of Gustavus, as well as the founding of the Swedish Academy (1786).

Sweyn (˜ Forkbeard) *d.*1014. King of Denmark (c985–1014). He killed King Olaf I, conquered Norway (1000), and later conquered England (1013). He was the father of Canute.

Swift, Jonathan 1667–1745. Great English satirist. He wrote social and political satires, including *A Tale of a Tub, The Drapier Letters, A Modest Proposal,* and the classic *Gulliver's Travels.*

Swinburne, Algernon Charles 1837–1909. English poet. Swinburne at times offended Victorian sensibilities, but his poems were known for their energy, innovativeness, and mastery of the language. His works include *Atalanta in Calydon, Poems and Ballads,* and *A Song of Italy.*

Swiss Confederation Union of the 22 Swiss cantons that make up Switzerland. The nucleus of the confederation was formed (1291) by the cantons Uri, Schwyz, and Unterwalden (Forest Cantons) to maintain their liberties against encroachments by the Austrian Habsburgs. Other cantons joined in the 14th and 15th cents., and the confederation finally won recognition of its independence in 1648. (*See also* Switzerland.)

Swiss Guards Swiss mercenary soldiers noted for their bravery in the service of European powers, especially France. They were provided (from 1512) by Swiss cantons under agreements called capitulations. The Swiss constitution banned further capitulations (1874).

Swithin, Saint (Swithun, ˜) *fl.* 860. English saint. Swithin was adviser to kings Egbert and Aethelwulf. Traditionally, if there is rain on his feast (July 15), there will be rain for 40 days.

Switzerland (Swiss Confederation) Country located in central Europe and situated in the mountain ranges of the Alps. The population is 6,783,000 and the capital is Bern. The modern state of Switzerland developed from the original "Forest Cantons" that rebelled (13th cent.) against rule of the Austrian Habsburgs. Switzerland was a center of Calvinism during the 16th-cent. Reformation. The neutrality of Switzerland was guaranteed by the Treaty of Paris in 1815 and the country has maintained a tradition of neutrality since then. Such international conferences as the Geneva Conventions have been held there, and organizations such as the International Red Cross and the International Labor Organization have their headquarters there. Key dates in the history of Switzerland include:

58 BC Helvetii, who inhabited what is now Switzerland, conquered by the Romans.

5TH CENT. AD Territory invaded by Germanic tribes (Alemanni and Burgundii).

6TH CENT. AD Area passed under Frankish control.

1033 Area became part of the Holy Roman Empire.

1276 Rudolf of Habsburg, Holy Roman Emperor, attempted to assert feudal rights in Switzerland.

1291 Cantons of Uri, Schwyz, and Unterwalden (around Lake Lucerne) formed defensive league against the Habsburgs; became the basis of the Swiss Confederation.

14TH CENT. Zurich, Glarus, Bern, Lucerne, and Zug joined the Swiss defensive league.

1307 Rutli Oath—traditionally, the alliance of the cantons that became foundation of Swiss independence movement; legend of W. Tell dates from this period.

1315 Austrian invasion repulsed by Swiss Confederation at Battle of Morgarten (Nov. 15).

1386 Swiss routed Austrian Habsburgs at Battle of Sempach (July 9); Swiss hero A. von Winkelried died in battle.

1388 Austrian invaders defeated at the Battle of Nafels, central Switzerland (Apr. 9).

15TH CENT. Fribourg and Solothurn joined the league; Aargau, Thurgau and the valleys of Ticino conquered.

1446 Peace of Constance; ended war over disputed territories between Zurich and neighboring Swiss cantons.

1476 Burgundian invasion repulsed at the Battle of Morat (June 22).

1499 Swiss independence recognized by Emperor Maximilian I in Peace of Basel (Sept. 22).

1493–1541 Alchemist and physician Paracelsus lived; introduced use of specific chemicals to cure specific diseases.

1512 Swiss Guards, mercenery troops, raised by cantons for service to other European powers; practice banned in 1874.

1513 Basel, Schaffhausen, and Appenzell joined the confederation; confederation now composed of 13 cantons.

1515 Battle of Marignano; the French decisively defeated the Swiss.

1516 Alliance with France formed; Swiss adopted what became traditional policy of neutrality; Swiss mercenaries nevertheless served in European wars.

1519 Swiss Reformation launched by H. Zwingli in Zurich.

c1520 Anabaptist movement began in Zurich.

1529, 1531 Kappel Wars; religious wars between Protestants and Catholics.

1531 First Confession of Basel set forth Reformation doctrine.

1536 Geneva, under the influence of J. Calvin, revolted against Savoy and its Catholic bishop; Swiss patriot F. de Bonnivard imprisoned in Chillon castle.

1536 Second Confession of Basel.

1541 Calvin founded theocratic government at Geneva; made Geneva the center of Calvinism.

1562 Second Helvetic Confession written by Heinrich Bullinger; became one the most important statements of Reformation doctrine.

1618–48 Switzerland neutral during the Thirty Years' War.

1648 Peace of Westphalia; Switzerland recognized as a completely independent state.

1654–1705 Mathematician J. Bernoulli lived; helped develop calculus and probability theory.

1667–1748 Jean Bernoulli lived; worked on integral and exponential calculus.

1700–82 Physicist D. Bernoulli lived; worked on mechanical properties of fluids.

1707–83 Mathematician L. Euler lived; called one of the most prolific mathematicians of all time.

1708–77 Physiologist A. von Haller lived; sometimes called the father of experimental physiology.

1730–88 Poet S. Gessner lived.

1746–1827 J. Pestalozzi, educational reformer working with deprived children, lived.

1798 Napoleon conquered Switzerland during the French Revolutionary Wars; established the Helvetic Republic (1798–1803).

1803 Act of Mediation; Napoleon partially restored the traditional Swiss Confederation.

1812 Swiss explorer J. Burckhardt rediscovered ancient city of Petra.

1815 Congress of Vienna; Swiss Confederation restored; nine cantons added.

1815 Treaty of Paris; perpetual Swiss neutrality recognized.

1845 Sonderbund, league of Catholic cantons, established; its existence led to a short civil war and its dissolution (1847).

1848 Constitution adopted; established central federal government, replacing the former confederation.

1864–1949 Geneva Conventions; series of international agreements regulating warfare and treatment of prisoners.

1864 Red Cross established by Swiss philanthropist J. Dunant and others.

1865–1905 Composer E. Jaques-Dalcroze, who developed eurhythmics, lived.

1874 Constitution revised; specified certain federal functions, such as foreign relations and establishing tariffs.

1880–81 World-famous children's story, *Heidi,* published by J. Spyri.

1897 First Zionist council held in Basel; Zionists eventually realized goal of Israeli state.

1902–09 German-born physicist A. Einstein developed his theory of relativity while working in Swiss patent office.

1909–11 Theologian K. Barth held pastorate in Geneva; became one of most influential Protestant theologians of 20th century.

1911–15 Composer E. Bloch taught at the Geneva Conservatory.

1912 Famed psychiatrist C. Jung published *The Psychology of the Unconscious.*

1915 Zimmerwald Conference held by Socialists; N. Lenin denounced conference resolutions against WW I as feeble.

1916 Pioneer linguist F. Saussure published landmark *Course in General Linguistics.*

1921 Inkblot test introduced by psychiatrist H. Rorschach.

1924 Geneva Protocol passed by League of Nations; move for mandatory arbitration of international disputes ignored by major powers.

1925 Locarno Pact signed at Geneva by Germany and other European powers.

1927 Geneva Conference convened; unsuccessful attempt to reduce naval armaments.

1929–54 Child psychologist J. Piaget taught at the University of Geneva.

1932–34 Geneva Conference, unsuccessful attempt to reduce armaments, collapsed when A. Hitler withdrew from conference.

1933 Abstract artist P. Klee returned to Switzerland from Germany.

1954 Geneva Conference led to armistice in the Korean War.

1958 Geneva Conference held between US, USSR, and Great Britain to discuss nuclear test ban.

1959 Switzerland became a member of the European Free Trade Association.

1963 Joined Council of Europe.

1971 Woman suffrage approved (Feb. 7).

1972 Switzerland associated with the European Common Market.

1979 Predominantly French-speaking canton, Jura, created (Jan. 1), bringing total number of cantons to 23 (20 full cantons, 6 half cantons).

1981 Referendum granting women equality with men approved in nationwide vote.

1982 Swiss economy, prospering since the mid-1970s, suffered mild recession; prosperity soon returned and continued to end of 1980s.

1986 Voters overwhelmingly rejected referendum calling for full UN membership; Swiss continued to participate in nonpolitical UN agencies.

1986 Regulations to reduce acid rain adopted by government.

1986 Chemical spill from Basel plant caused devastating pollution in Rhine River.

1987 Referendum to limit number of refugees seeking political asylum approved by voters (Apr.).

1989 Referendum calling for elimination of armed forces in Switzerland turned down by voters.

1990 Riots broke out in Bern during mass demonstration to protest federal prosecutor's office maintaining of secret files on 200,000 persons in Switzerland; government promised to reform system.

1990   Census revealed 7.5 percent population increase in ten years to 6.8 million, largely due to immigration.

1991   Switzerland celebrated 700th anniversary.

1991   Some 500,000 women joined nation-wide strike protesting unequal treatment.

1991   Government signed treaty for creation of European Economic Area (EEA).

1992   Voters approved referendum on joining the IMF and World Bank (May).

Sybaris   Ancient city in what is now southern Italy. Founded by the Achaean Greeks (720 BC), it soon became renowned for its wealth and the decadence of its citizens. It was attacked and destroyed (510 BC) by forces from Croton.

Sybota, Battle of   Naval battle (432 BC) during the Peloponnesian War. A combined force from Corcyra and Athens defeated the Corinthian fleet.

Sydenham, Thomas   1624–1689.   English physician, called the founder of epidemiology and clinical medicine. An Oxford University graduate (1648), he began practicing medicine in London (from 1656). His great care in his observing and recording patients' symptoms eventually earned him the epithet "the English Hippocrates." He named and described scarlet fever and characterized hysteria and St. Vitus' Dance (also known as Sydenham's chorea). Sydenham was the first to use opium for medical purposes and among the first to give iron to patients with anemia. He published *Observationes Medicae* (1676), which became a standard textbook for two centuries.

Sydney, Philip   *See* **Sidney, Sir Philip.**

Sykes-Picot Agreement   Secret agreement concluded by Britain and France (May 9, 1916), regarding partition of the Ottoman Empire after WW I. Britain was to get direct control of southern Mesopotamia and other territories. France was to get Lebanon and parts of Syria. Additional Arab territories (to be a federation of states) were designated as within respective spheres of influence.

Sylvester II (Gerbert d'Avrillaz)   *d.*   1003. French-born pope (999–1003). The first French pope, Sylvester was renowned for his mathematical and scientific expertise. He promoted Christianity in Poland and Hungary.

Symbolists   French literary school of the late 19th cent. A reaction to naturalism and realism, it sought to express universal truths by subjective or symbolic means. Symbolists were followers of P. Verlaine and S. Mallarmé, and their movement spread to other countries, as well as other art forms, notably painting and music.

Symons, Arthur   1865–1945.   British poet and critic. A leading British Symbolist, he helped introduce the movement in Britain.

symposium   In ancient Greece, a drinking party that commenced after dinner. Entertainments included singing, poetry reading, the telling of stories and riddles, and playing of organized games. Paid professionals also provided music and other amusements. A literary genre based on the idea of recounting conversations at a symposium (symposium literature) became popular. Perhaps the greatest work of this type was Plato's *Symposium* (c384).

syndicalism   Theory of government holding that power of the state should be primarily concentrated in the hands of organized labor unions. Influenced by P. Proudhon and G. Sorel, it flourished especially in France, Spain, Italy, and Latin America before WW I. It declined with the spread of Communist-dominated unions.

Synge, John Millington   1871–1909.   Irish poet and playwright. Synge is famous for such studies of Irish life as *Riders to the Sea* and *The Playboy of the Western World.*

Synod of   *See under names in inverted, as in* **Whitby, Synod of.**

Syracuse (Siracusa)   Historic port city in Sicily, Italy. Founded (734 BC) as a Corinthian colony, it became the most powerful city in Sicily under the tyrant Gelon (5th cent. BC) and a Greek cultural center under Hiero, his successor. Syracuse was the scene of major battles (*see* Syracuse, Battle of) during the Peloponnesian and Punic wars, and its conquest by the Romans in 212 BC marked the beginning of its decline. Thereafter it was taken by the Byzantines (AD 535), Arabs (AD 878), and the Normans (1085). It later became part of the Kingdom of the Two Sicilies.

Syracuse, Battle of   1. Protracted battle (415–413 BC) during the Peloponnesian War (431–404 BC). Athens laid siege to the city of Syracuse (now in Sicily) and ultimately committed some 40,000 soldiers and over 200 ships to the action. Syracuse, reinforced by Sparta, eventually killed or captured the entire Athenian force (including the commander Nicias and Demosthenes) and thereby contributed to Athens' defeat in the Peloponnesian War. 2. Battle (387 BC) in which the Carthaginians suffered a decisive defeat after laying siege to Syracuse. 3. Battle (214–212 BC) during the Second Punic War (218–201), in which Rome captured the city. A force of 25,000 Romans under Marcellus attacked the city, defended by Hippocrates. After initial defeats brought about in part by defensive weapons devised by Archimedes, the Romans breached the city's defenses and sacked the city.

Syracuse, Dion of *See* **Dion of Syracuse.**

Syria (Syrian Arab Republic) Country located at the eastern end of the Mediterranean in the Middle East. The population is 12,471,000 and the capital is Damascus. Syria (including Lebanon) was first established as a French mandate after WW I, carved out of territories once controlled by the Ottoman Empire. The French made Lebanon a separate state in 1920, and in 1941 Syria was invaded by British and Free French forces, who ousted the Vichy French government there. As WW II progressed, Syria (and Lebanon) pressed for independence, which came in stages (1941–46) but was not finally complete until nationalist unrest forced the withdrawal of French troops (1946). In more recent times, Syria has played a major role in the Lebanese conflict (*See also* Lebanon). Key events in the history of Syria include:

c2100 BC Amorites (Semites) settled in the area of Syria.

15TH–13TH CENTS. BC Syria part of the Hittite Empire, alternating with Egyptian overlordship.

8TH CENT. BC Most of the area conquered and made part of the Assyrian Empire.

538 BC Persia conquered the region.

333–332 BC Alexander the Great made Syria part of his empire.

312–64 BC Seleucid dynasty in power in Syria and environs; established by Seleucus I following breakup of Alexander the Great's empire.

64 BC Domains of Seleucid Empire (greatly reduced) made into a Roman province by Pompey.

4TH CENT. AD Antioch, a principal center of Christianity, was one of the four ancient patri-

archates, along with Rome, Alexandria, and, later, Constantinople.

5TH CENT. AD Syria remained part of the Byzantine Empire at the dissolution of the Western Roman Empire.

633–640 Arab Muslim conquest of Syria.

661–750 Damascus served as the seat of the Umayyad Caliphate, then the center of the Islamic world.

11TH CENT. Most of Syria under the sway of the Seljuk Turks.

1099 Most of Syria incorporated by the Christian crusaders into the Latin Kingdom of Jerusalem.

1174–87 Saladin, sultan of Egypt, regained Syria for Islam, overthrowing the Latin Kingdom of Jerusalem.

1260 Mongol invasion under Hulagu Khan devastated Syria and almost destroyed Aleppo and Damascus.

1401 The Mongols under Tamerlane again sacked Aleppo and Damascus.

1516 Syria incorporated into the Ottoman Empire for the next four hundred years.

1832–40 Syria annexed to Egypt by Ibrahim Pasha; returned to Ottoman suzerainty (1840).

1920 France granted a League of Nations mandate over Syria, following the breakup of the Ottoman Empire; region included Lebanon.

1926 Lebanon made a separate state by the French.

1936 Syrian autonomy (under the mandate) granted by France; suspended in 1939.

1941 Syria invaded by British and Free French forces, who took it from the Vichy French regime (June).

1941 Syria proclaimed a republic (Sept.).

1943 Rise of Ba'ath party.

1943 French restored Syrian constitution; Shukri al-Kuwatili became first president (1944).

1946 French troops finally withdrew, following unrest caused by continued French military presence; Syrian independence now complete.

1948–49 Arab-Israeli War; Syria joined in attack on newly created Israeli state.

1949 Three military coups, the last led by Col. Adib al-Shishakli (Dec.).

1949–1954 Col. Adib al-Shishakli ruled Syria.

1950 Constitution providing for parliamentary government promulgated; lasted less than a year.

FROM 1954 Ba'ath party became a dominant force in Syrian politics.

1958–61 Syria joined with Egypt in the United Arab Republic (UAR).

1961 Army coup in Syria; Syria withdrew from UAR.

1962 Military coup; constitutional government restored.

1963 Coup by Ba'athists; program of nationalization and social reform adopted; split developed in Ba'ath party.

1966 Coup by radical Ba'athists.

1967 Arab-Israeli War; Israelis victorious in Six-Day War; Golan Heights taken.

1970 Army officers seized power in coup led by Gen. Hafez al-Asad (Nov. 13).

1971– Asad in office as president; remained in office into the early 1990s.

1973 New constitution approved by voters; failure to include provision naming Islam state religion ended in boycott of voting by Sunni Muslims.

1973 First parliamentary elections (May) in over a decade; coalition of Ba'ath, Communist, and Socialist parties secured a substantial majority.

1973 Fourth Arab-Israeli War; Israelis repulsed attacks by Egyptians and Syrians.

1974 Syria signed agreement, mediated by H. Kissinger, with Israel (May); Israel agreed to limited pull-back of its forces in occupied Golan Heights territory.

1974 Syria introduced UN resolution naming Palestine Liberation Organization (PLO) sole representative of the Palestinians.

1976 30,000 Syrian troops sent into Lebanon to help mediate Lebanese civil war.

1980 Formal agreement signed uniting Libya and Syria (Sept. 10).

1980–82 Syrian troops in Lebanon actively supported Muslim factions in Lebanon; clashes with Israelis developed into heavy fighting during the Lebanese War (1982).

1980–87 Dr. Abd ar-Rauf Kassem in office as prime minister; his government was later accused of corruption and inefficiency.

1980–89 Iran-Iraq War; Syria supported Iran, in part due to rivalry between different factions of the Ba'ath party.

1980 Syria signed a 20-year Treaty of Friendship and Cooperation with the USSR (Oct.).

1981 Israel formally annexed the Golan Heights (Dec. 14), captured from Syria during the Third Arab-Israeli War.

1982 Uprising backed by the Muslim Brotherhood brutally suppressed; thousands killed; general amnesty for the Brotherhood was declared in 1985.

1983 Syria rejected Israeli-Lebanonese peace agreement; Asad continued to supply the Shi'ite and Druze militias in Lebanon.

1985 Asad reelected to third seven-year term as president (Feb.).

1986 Series of terrorist bombings killed 144 people in Syria (Apr.); pro-Iraqi, Islamic fundamentalist group claimed responsibility.

1986 Britain accused Syria of complicity in attempted terrorist attack on Israeli airliner; severed diplomatic relations.

1986 European Community imposed strict diplomatic and economic sanctions on Syria.

1986 Syrian troops deployed in Beirut (July) to enforce a cease fire at Palestinian refugee camps.

1987 4,000 Syrian troops deployed in west Beirut following an outbreak of fighting between Shi'ite Amal forces and an opposition alliance (Feb.).

1987 Mahmoud Zuabi became prime minister.

1989 Christian forces headed by Gen. Awn launched futile attempt to expel Syrian forces from Lebanon (Mar.).

1989 Syria and others accepted Taif agreement, Arab sponsored peace plan for Lebanon (Sept.); cease-fire established that month; Syrian forces to help maintain security for new Lebanese government for two years.

1989 Syria and Egypt restored diplomatic relations (Dec.).

1990–91 Persian Gulf War; Syria backed effort to drive Iraq out of Kuwait and sent troops to Saudia Arabia; Syria's relations with the West improved.

1991 Syria and Lebanon signed mutual cooperation treaty (May); Israel denounced treaty as step toward Syrian domination of Lebanon (May).

1991 President Asad reversed his former opposition to regional talks on Mideast problems (July); agreed to direct negotiations with Israel within regional conference framework.

1991–92 Syria attended US–brokered regional Mideast peace conferences, first of which was held at Madrid, Spain (Oct., 1991); five subsequent meetings (to May, 1992) failed to produce substantive progress, however.

1992 President Asad rejected possibility of adopting Western-style democratic reforms, but said new political parties might someday be permitted (Mar.).

1992 Syrian troop withdrawal from Beirut begun (Mar.), in compliance with Taif agreement; troops to pull back to eastern Lebanon by Sept.

1992 Commercial air links with Libya continued (Apr.), despite UN ban ordered after Libya refused to extradite two alleged terrorists.

1992 Syria (with Lebanon) boycotted multilateral talks on Palestinian refugees and other Mideast issues (May), to protest lack of progress in regional peace conferences.

1992 Shiite guerrillas released last two Western hostages held in Lebanon; Syria (with Iran) believed to have engineered this and other hostage releases to improve relations with the US and Europe.

Syrian Orthodox church (Jacobite church) Christian church founded (6th cent.) as a Monophysite sect. Adherents are sometimes called Jacobites after a principal organizer of the church, Jacob Baradaeus, bishop of Edessa (*d.* 578).

Syrian Wars 1. First Syrian War (276–272 BC), between Egypt and the Seleucid Empire. It led to the defeat of Seleucid king Antiochus I and the seizure of Phoenicia and much of Anatolia by Egyptian King Ptolemy II. 2. Second Syrian War (c260–255 BC). It resulted in the defeat of Egypt by Seleucid King Antiochus II, aided by Macedonia. The Seleucids regained much of Phoenicia and Anatolia. 3. Third Syrian War (c245–241 BC), also known as the Laodicean War. It resulted in the Egyptian defeat of Seleucid king Seleucus II, who lost to Egypt parts of Syria and Asia Minor. 4. Fourth Syrian War (221–217 BC). It ended in the victory of Egyptian king Ptolemy IV over Seleucid king Antiochus III, who was forced to cede Coele Syria to Egypt. 5. Fifth Syrian War (c201–195 BC). The Egyptians were defeated by Seleucid king Antiochus III, who regained Coele Syria and parts of southern Asia Minor.

Szilard, Leo 1898–1964. Hungarian-born American physicist. Fleeing the Nazis, he moved to London (1934) and then went to the US where he worked as a nuclear researcher (1942), helped E. Fermi develop the first nuclear reactor (1946), and helped promote the Manhattan Project. Following the war, he advocated peaceful uses for atomic energy, founding the Council for a Livable World.

Szold, Henrietta 1860–1945. American Zionist leader. A teacher, she founded (1912) the Jewish women's group Hadassah.

T

Taaffe, Eduard, graf von 1833–95. Austrian statesman. As premier (1868–70, 1879–93) he attempted to reconcile conflicts between the various national groups comprising the Austro-Hungarian Empire by an "Iron Ring" of conservatives.

Tabari, al- c839–923. Arab historian and writer. He is noted for his commentaries on the Koran and for his *Annals of the Apostles and the Kings,* a compilation of world history from creation to the year 915.

Table of Abydos *See* **Abydos, Table of.**

Table of Tanis *See* **Decree Of Canopus.**

Taborites Most militant wing of the Bohemian Hussites. Named after their fortified city, Tabor, they founded their own sect but were defeated (1452) by a coalition of Catholics and Hussite Utraquists.

Tacitus AD 55?–c117. Roman historian. Tacitus served in many military and governmental posts before becoming consul (AD 97). He quickly gained a reputation as an eloquent speaker, then turned to writing. His works include the *Dialogus,* a book on oratory; *Agricola,* a biography of his father-in-law, Agricola; *Germania,* a history of early German tribes; and two major works on Roman history, the *Histories* and the *Annals.*

Tacna-Arica Controversy Prolonged dispute (1883–1929) over the provinces of Arica and Tacna, which Chile had obtained from Peru at the end of the War of the Pacific (*q v.*). The dispute was finally resolved by the suggestions of US president H. Hoover that Chile should retain Arica but return Tacna, pay an indemnity, and provide Peru with a free port at Arica.

Tafari Makonnen *See* **Haile Selassie.**

Taft, Robert Alphonso 1889–1953. American statesman, son of W. Taft. As US senator from Ohio (1939–53) he was co-sponsor of the Taft-Hartley Labor Act (1947).

Taft, William Howard 1857–1930. US president (1909–13), the 27th, successor to T. Roosevelt. Taft became first civil governor of the Philippines (1901–04), and in 1904, he became secretary of war under Roosevelt. Picked by Roosevelt as his successor, Taft became the Republican candidate for president (1908) and defeated W. Bryan in the election. Taft continued Roosevelt's policy of trust-busting, but he modified Roosevelt's Latin American policy into what came to be known as "dollar diplomacy" (*q.v.*). However, Taft increasingly opposed progressive legislation and policies, and his support of the Payne-Aldrich Tariff (1909) brought much opposition from the progressive wing of the Republican party. He managed to win the 1912 Republican nomination but was now opposed by Roosevelt, who had formed the Progressive (Bull Moose) party (*q.v.*). This split the Republican party and resulted in the election of the Democratic candidate, W. Wilson. Taft subsequently served as chief justice of the US Supreme Court (1921–30).

Taft-Hartley Labor Act US labor relations act passed (1947) over the veto of President H. Truman. It prohibited the closed shop and jurisdictional and secondary strikes and authorized suits against labor unions and government use of 80-day injunctions against some strikes.

Tagalog (Tagal) Filipino people, second-largest ethnic group in the Philippines. They are largely Christian, and their Malayo-Polynesian language, also called Tagalog, is the official language of the Philippines.

Taginae, Battle of *See* **Busta Gallorum, Battle of.**

Tagore, Sir Rabindranath 1861–1941. Indian poet and philosopher. Tagore sought to combine elements of East and West in his works. He was the first Asian to win the Nobel Prize for Literature (1913), for his book-length poem *Gitanjali*.

Taharka (Tirhakah) *d.* 663 BC. Egyptian pharaoh (689–663 BC). The last Nubian king of the 25th (Ethiopian) dynasty in ancient Egypt, he was defeated (671 BC) by the Assyrians in a series of battles and was obliged to abandon Lower Egypt.

Tahmasp I *See* **Ismail I.**

Taine, Hippolyte 1828–93. French critic and historian, one of the leading figures in 19th-cent. positivism. He is noted for his applications of scientific principles to the study of history and humanity.

Taipingdao *See* **Yellow Turbans.**

Taiping Rebellion Uprising (1850–64) against the Manchu dynasty of China, a precursor to the Nationalist and Communist movements. Its leader was Hong Xiuquan (Hung Hsiu-ch'uan, 1813–64) who believed he was the younger brother of Jesus Christ. A new religion was formed around his teachings in the late 1840s and gained support among the peasants and workers in Guangxi (Kwangsi). It was loosely based on Christianity, opposed Confucianism, and advocated (then) radical reforms, such as communal ownership of property and equality of women. Beginning in 1850 with a few thousand followers, the rebels soon gathered support and eventually mustered a highly organized army of a million zealous troops. The rebels succeeded in capturing Nanjing in 1853 and made it their capital. The failure of subsequent expeditions and internal dissent weakened the movement, however. An attempt to take Shanghai (1860) was stopped by the "Ever-Victorious Army" organized by Europeans and later led by C. Gordon. A Manchu army under Zeng Guofang beseiged Nanjing (1862–64) and finally captured the city (July, 1864). Hung committed suicide and the revolt was broken. Nevertheless, it had seriously weakened the Manchu government and paved the way for later rebellions and the final collapse of the Manchu dynasty.

Taira family Japanese military clan, also called Heike. Founded in the 9th cent., it reached the height of its political influence in the 12th cent. but was defeated (1185) by the Minamoto clan in the Gempei War (*q.v.*).

Taira Kiyomori 1118–81. Japanese military leader of the Taira family. As the ally of retired Emperor Go-Shirakawa, he defeated the Minamoto family and led the Taira to high positions in the imperial court. Following the precedent set by Fujiwara regents, his daughter became an imperial consort and his grandson a child emperor.

Taisho (Yoshihito) 1879–1926. Japanese emperor (1912–26). During his reign, Japan joined the Allies in WW I and became firmly established as a great power. His son, the future Emperor Hirohito, became regent in 1921.

Taiwan (Republic of China) (Nationalist China) Island republic located off the coast of China. It includes the island of Taiwan (Formosa) and several smaller islands, such as Quemoy and Matsu. The population is 20,454,000 and the capital is Taipei. First settled (7th cent.) by the Chinese, the island of Taiwan was visited (1590) by the Portuguese, who named it Formosa. The Dutch established a fort (1624) at what is now Tainan, and the Spanish settled in the north. The Dutch forced the Spanish to give up their holdings (1641), and were in turn forced off Taiwan by the Chinese (1662). Chinese immigration into Taiwan increased, and the island was held by the Manchus until after the first Sino-Japanese War, when it passed (1895) to Japan. Japan introduced agricultural and industrial improvements. During WW II, Taiwan was bombed by US planes, and after the war it was returned to China. When the Communists came to power on the mainland (1949), Chiang Kai-shek led millions of his Nationalist Chinese followers to the island and established the Kuomintang government there. The Communists planned to invade (1950), but President H. Truman ordered the US Seventh Fleet to the Formosa Strait to deter any Communist attack. When President D. Eisenhower recalled the fleet (1953), the Communists stepped up their attacks on Quemoy and Matsu, leading to a mutual defense agreement (1955) between Taiwan and the US. Despite continued friction between mainland China and Taiwan, the Nationalists secured tremendous advances in agricultural reform and industrialization. But Chiang's plan to topple the People's Republic of China and return to the mainland proved fruitless. In 1971, Taiwan lost its seat in the UN to the People's Republic of China. In 1978, the US recognized the People's Republic and broke diplomatic ties with Taiwan. In 1991, the government moved to end the technical state of war with Communist China and formally ended the state of emergency imposed in Taiwan 43 years earlier after the Communist victory on the mainland.

Taizong (Tang T'ai Tsung) 600–649. Chinese emperor (626–649), second emperor of the Tang dynasty. Considered the founder of the dynasty, he consolidated the empire, drove out the Turks, and encouraged art and literature.

Taizu *See* **Song.**

Tajikistan (*formerly* Tajik Soviet Socialist Republic). Independent state located north of Afghanistan, and now a member of the Commonwealth of Independent States (CIS). Inhabited by the Tajiks (of Iranian stock) since the 10th cent., the region fell to the Mongols in the 13th and thereafter was ruled variously until Russia gained control in the late 1800s. An unsuccessful revolt was mounted against the Bolsheviks (1917–21), and some years later the region was created a constituent republic of the USSR (1929). The republic declared independence (Sept. 9, 1991) and changed its name during the breakup of the USSR, after which it joined the CIS (Dec., 1991).

Taj Mahal Indian mausoleum in north-central India built (1648) by Shah Jahan in honor of his favorite wife, Mumtaz Mahal. It is considered one of the most beautiful buildings in the world.

Takahira, Baron Kogoro *See* **Root-Takahira Agreement.**

Taliesin (Taliessin) *fl.* 6th-cent. Welsh poet, possibly a mythological figure, to whom is attributed authorship of the poems in the *Book of Taliesin,* a major Welsh work.

tallage In feudalism, a tax levied by a lord on his subjects or their property. Tallage evolved in England to be a tax by the king on estates in royal possession and on chartered towns.

Talleyrand, Charles Maurice de (Talleyrand-Périgord, ˜) 1754–1838. French statesman and diplomat. Originally a cleric in the court of King Louis XVI, Talleyrand was excommunicated (1791) because of his sympathy for radical church and political reform. His persuasive skills brought him high advisory and diplomatic positions under the Directory, Napoleon, Louis XVIII, and Louis Philippe. He represented France at the Congress of Vienna (1814–15), skillfully limiting the demands of other coun-

tries upon France and restoring many European borders to their pre-Napoleonic status.

Tallien, Jean Lambert 1767–1820. French revolutionary. A Jabobin, he supported the Reign of Terror and fell in love with and married (1794) one of his prisoners, T. Tallien. He subsequently led the rebellion of 9 Thermidor which overthrew M. Robespierre.

Tallien, Thérésa Cabarrús (Cabarrus, Jeanne Marie Ignace, Thérésa de) 1773–1835. French political figure. A prisoner of J. Tallien during the French Revolution, she married him (1794) and greatly influenced his political career.

Tallis, Thomas c1505–95. English composer, the first notable writer of church music in the English Reformation. Though he remained a Catholic, he followed the Protestant style of setting English texts to music.

Talmadge, Eugene 1884–1946. American politician. As governor of Georgia (1933–37, 1941–43) he was noted for his opposition to New Deal policies and for firing several professors from the state university for supporting racial equality.

Talmud Written compilation of the oral laws of the Jews, after the Old Testament, the most important Judaic text. It consists of the Mishna (*q.v.*), the text of the laws; and the Gemara, commentary. The two versions of the Talmud are the Palestinian (compiled c5th cent. AD) and the Babylonian (compiled c6th cent. AD). The Babylonian Talmud is much longer and is the authoritative work.

Tamerlane (Timur) c1336–1405. Mongol conqueror. A Muslim and self-proclaimed descendent of Genghis Khan, he gained firm control of the throne of Samarkand (in modern Turkistan) by 1369. Thereafter he led his army of Turks and Mongols in a series of campaigns that vastly expanded his domains. He warred against Persia, and by 1387 had extended his empire to the Euphrates River. Crossing the Euphrates (1392), he advanced northward to conquer the Caucasus region. India was invaded next (1398) and the Delhi Sultanate (*q.v.*) was ruthlessly destroyed, during which time Tamerlane ordered the massacre of tens of thousands. Turning westward again, Tamerlane captured Baghdad (1401), attacked the Egyptian Mamelukes in Syria, and defeated the Ottoman Turks in Asia Minor (Sultan Bajazet I taken prisoner, 1402). Tamerlane died before launching his planned invasion of

China and on his death the empire he had created was divided among his heirs. (*See also* Timurids.)

Tamil Ancient Dravidian language, spoken mainly in Tamilnadu, in southern India.

Tammany Organization that controlled New York City politics through the Democratic party in the 19th and early 20th cents. Under the leadership of W. Tweed, R. Croker, and others, it gained a national reputation for corruption.

Tamworth Manifesto *See* **Conservative party.**

Tanaka Kakuei 1918– . Japanese prime minister (1972–74). A member of the Liberal Democratic Party, he served in the cabinet of E. Sato and succeeded him as prime minister. Tanaka opened diplomatic relations with the People's Republic of China but was forced from office (1974) amid allegations of accepting bribes in the Lockheed scandal. He was convicted (1983) and sentenced to four years in prison.

Tanaka, Giichi, Baron 1863–1929. Japanese prime minister (1927–29) and general who advocated Japanese expansion. The Tanaka Memorial (1927), a plan for Japanese military conquest attributed to him, is now thought spurious.

Tancred *d.* 1194. King of Sicily (1190–94). His short reign was marked by a power struggle with his uncle, Holy Roman Emperor Henry VI, who seized Sicily after Tancred's death.

Taney, Roger Brooke 1777–1864. American jurist, fifth chief justice of the US Supreme Court (1836–64). He handed down the landmark Court decision in the Dred Scott case (*q.v.*) of 1857.

Tang (T'ang) Dynasty of Chinese rulers (618–907). The dynasty was founded after the overthrow of the Sui dynasty by Li Yuan. Tang rulers greatly expanded the empire, and at its height, under Emperor Xuanzong (ruled 712–756), it included parts of Korea, Manchuria, Mongolia, Tibet, and Turkistan. Trade was stimulated, and in the ensuing period of prosperity the arts, particularly poetry and sculpture, flourished. Such masters as Tu Fu, Wang Wei, Li Po, and Hsuan Tsang lived during this period. Confucianism enjoyed a resurgence and was officially adopted by the state. The civil service system was further refined. However, the empire was weakened by an unsuccessful revolt (755–763) led by An Lushan, a Turkish general. In subsequent years, provincial warlords gained power and ultimately overthrew the Tang rulers.

Tanganyika Former republic in eastern Africa, since 1964 part of the republic of Tanzania (*q.v.*).

Capital was Dar-es-Salaam. Tanganyika was already inhabited by the 9th cent. when Arab and Indian traders established towns along the coast. The region was explored by the Portuguese (15th–16th cents.). German colonists, notably Carl Peters (1856–1918), secured agreements (1884–85) for lands with Tanganyikan natives. The German East Africa Company (formed 1887) then administered the area as German East Africa (*q.v.*). The company's inadequate rule led to native resistance and ultimate establishment (1891) of a German protectorate. The area was occupied by the British during WW I and in 1920 part of it became a British League of Nations mandate (as Tanganyika). In 1946, it became a UN trust territory, and on Dec. 9, 1961, it achieved independence. J. Nyerere was its first prime minister. When Tanganyika was made a republic (Dec., 1962), Nyerere became its first president. In 1964, Tanganyika merged with Zanzibar to form Tanzania, and its subsequent history is that of Tanzania.

Tang Hsuan Tsung *See* **Xuanzong.**

Tang T'ai Tsung *See* **Taizong.**

Tannenberg, Battles of 1. Battle (1410) at Tannenberg, Poland, in which the Polish and Lithuanian forces under Polish king Ladislaus II defeated the Teutonic Knights, thus halting their eastward expansion. 2. Major Russian defeat (Aug. 26–30, 1914) by Germany at Tannenberg, Poland, early in WW I. The Russian forces under Gen. Alexander Samsonov (1859–1914) were surrounded and defeated by German forces under generals P. von Hindenburg and E. von Ludendorff. Russian casualties were more than 90,000, and Samsonov committed suicide.

Tannhäuser *fl.* 13th cent. German lyric poet and minnesinger celebrated for his wanderings and thought to have taken part in the Sixth Crusade. His legend is the basis for an opera by R. Wagner.

Tantras Collection of Hindu and Buddhist holy books that include information on such topics as religious rituals, traditions, and the practice of yoga. They date from the 6th or 7th cent.

Tanzania African republic on the east coast of Africa, formed (1964) by the union of Tanganyika and Zanzibar (*qq.v.*). The population is 26,070,000 and the capital is Dar-es-Salaam. The country's history prior to 1964 is that of Tanganyika and Zanzibar. In early 1964, a revolution in Zanzibar toppled that country's government. The new government merged Zanzibar with Tanganyika (Apr., 1964) and J. Nyerere became first president of Tanzania. A new constitution was adopted (1965). Although officially united under one government, Tanganyika and Zanzibar have followed somewhat independent courses. In the 1970s, Tanzania came into repeated conflict with Uganda, headed by I. Amin. In 1979, Tanzanian forces toppled Amin's regime and forced him into exile. Nyerere resigned as president in 1985. The economy, responding to reforms enacted earlier, improved toward the end of the 1980s, and in a move toward more liberal government, authorities released 23,000 political prisoners (1991). Constitutional amendments were drafted in early 1992 to introduce a multi-party political system.

Taoism   *See* **Daoism.**

Tappan, Arthur 1786–1865. American merchant and abolitionist, a founder (1833), with W. Garrison, and first president of the American Anti-Slavery Society. In 1840, he broke with Garrison and established the American and Foreign Anti-Slavery Society.

Tarain, Battles of   *See* **Taraori, Battles of.**

Taraori, Battles of (Tarain, ˜)   Series of battles (1191–92) resulting in the victory of Muhammad of Ghor (*d.* 1206) over the Rajput raja of Ajmer and Delhi. The victory contributed to the Muslim conquest of northern India.

Tarbell, Ida Minerva 1857–1944. American writer and reformer. One of the muckrakers (*q.v.*), she is known best for her *History of the Standard Oil Company* and *Life of Abraham Lincoln.*

Tardieu, André (Villiers, George) 1876–1945. French statesman and writer. He took part in the Paris Peace Conference (*q.v.*) of 1919 and between the world wars held a number of government posts, including that of premier (1929–30, 1930, 1932). He urged a strong stance against rising German militarism.

Tariff of Abominations   *See* **Abominations, Tariff of.**

tariffs   Taxes imposed on imported and sometimes on exported goods, also known as customs duty. Originally used to raise revenue, by the 17th cent. tariffs were used to protect domestic economies. (*See also* protectionism.)

Tarik (˜ ibn Ziyad) *fl.* 711.   Berber general. Tarik led the first Muslim invasion of Spain (711), conquering much of the Iberian Peninsula and firmly establishing Moorish influence there.

Tarkington, (Newton) Booth 1869–1946. American author known for his novels set in small

Midwestern towns. His novels included *Penrod, The Magnificent Ambersons,* and *Alice Adams.* The latter two earned him the Pulitzer Prize for the best American novel in 1919 and 1922.

Tarleton, Banastre   *See* **Cowpens, Battle of.**

Tarpeian Rock   *See* **Capitoline Hill.**

Tarquinius Collatinus *fl.* c509 BC.   Legendary Roman. The rape of his wife, Lucretia, by his cousin, Tarquinius Sextus, led to the fall of the last Tarquin king (509 BC) and establishment of the Roman Republic.

Tarquinius Priscus, Lucius Roman king (c616–578 BC).   He reputedly built the Circus Maximus and the Forum. He was assassinated in a plot to limit the king's power.

Tarquinius, Sextus *fl.* 6th cent. BC.   Etruscan, son of L. Tarquinius Superbus, last king of Rome. Sextus' rape of Lucretia (509 BC) led to the overthrow of the Tarquin line of kings.

Tarquinius Superbus, Lucius   Last Etruscan king of Rome (c534–509 BC). He made Rome powerful and extended its dominions. His cruelty and the rape of Lucretia by his son led to his overthrow.

Tarsus   Ancient Asian city, capital of Cilicia, in southern Turkey. It was the birthplace of the Apostle Paul.

Tartars   *See* **Tatars.**

Tartini, Giuseppe 1692–1770.   Italian violinist and composer. Tartini modified the shape of the bow and wrote hundreds of violin pieces, the best-known being *The Devil's Trill.*

Tartu, Treaty of   Peace treaty (Feb. 2, 1920) between Estonia and Russia, concluded at Tartu, Estonia, at the end of the Baltic War of Liberation. It established Estonian independence.

Tasman, Abel Janszoon 1603?–59.   Dutch navigator. Tasman discovered Tasmania (which he called Van Diemen's Land) and New Zealand (1642).

Tasso, Torquato 1544–95.   Italian poet, considered one of the great Renaissance poets. He is known best for *Ierusalem Delivered,* an epic about the First Crusade.

Tatars (Tartars)   Turkic-speaking peoples of Russia living near the Volga River region and numbering some 6,000,000. The name once referred to Mongols and other Asiatic people who invaded Europe, some of whom merged to form the Golden Horde (*q.v.*), a powerful force in Russia. They adopted Islam (14th cent.) and are Sunni Muslims today.

Tate, John Orley Allen 1899–1979. American poet and critic. He was a founder and editor of *The Fugitive* (1922–25) and a member of the Southern agrarian literary group known as the Fugitives.

Tauroggen, Convention of *See* **Yorck von Wartenburg, Johann David Ludwig.**

Tawney, Richard Henry 1880–1962. British economic historian. Tawney was a leader of numerous social reforms and helped to formulate the Labour party's economic policies. Among his many books is *The Acquisitive Society.*

Taylor, Brook 1685–1731. English mathematician. He formulated Taylor's Theorem, the foundation of differential calculus. He also solved the problem of the center of oscillation.

Taylor, Frederick W. 1856–1915. American industrial engineer. Called the father of scientific management, he developed theories of time management that influenced the development of mass-production techniques. He believed that production efficiency could be improved through time and motion studies of workers.

Taylor, Jeremy 1613–67. English bishop and writer, called the "Shakespeare of the Pulpit" for his moving sermons. They were collected in such volumes as *The Golden Grove.*

Taylor, John 1753–1824. American political philosopher and agriculturalist. Taylor espoused T. Jefferson's contention that democracy was dependent on the farmer. Among his many works are *An Inquiry into the Principles and Policies of the Government of the United States.*

Taylor, Maxwell Davenport 1901–87. American general. He commanded the 82d and then the 101st Airborne divisions during WW II and also commanded the Eighth Army during the Korean War. As chairman of the joint chiefs of staff (1962–64) he advocated US involvement in the Vietnam War.

Taylor, Richard 1826–79. Confederate general in the American Civil War, son of Z. Taylor. His defeat of Gen. N. Banks in the Battle of Sabine Crossroads (Apr. 8, 1864) led to the Union withdrawal from Louisiana and failure of the Red River Campaign, an attempt to gain control of the states of Louisiana, Arkansas, and Texas.

Taylor, Zachary 1784–1850. US president (1849–50), the twelfth, successor to J. Polk. Taylor joined the army in 1808 and fought with distinction in the War of 1812 and in the Black Hawk and Seminole wars against the Indians. His military campaigns earned him the nickname "Old Rough-and-Ready." During the Mexican War (1846–48), he became a national hero by his victories at Palo Alto (*q.v.*) and Resaca de la Palma (*q.v.*) and the capture (Sept., 1846) of Monterrey. In the Battle of Buena Vista (*q.v.*), his decisive victory over a much larger Mexican force ended the war in northern Mexico. Taylor was chosen Whig candidate for president and was elected in 1848. As president he favored the admission of California and New Mexico as free states, even though he himself was a slaveholder. His support of the Wilmot Proviso (*q.v.*), which prohibited the extension of slavery, aroused opposition in the South. Taylor also opposed the key elements of what became the Compromise of 1850 (*q.v.*). During the last days of his administration he was embroiled in a scandal involving members of his cabinet. He planned to reorganize the cabinet but fell ill and died (July 9, 1850).

Tay Son Rebellion Vietnamese uprising (1771–88) led by three brothers from Tay Son, central Vietnam. They overthrew the ruling dynasties gov-erning Vietnam, defeated the Chinese sent to support the rulers, and unified the country. During their brief rule (1788–93) they attempted to introduce social reforms, and are thus regarded as precursors of the 20th-cent. nationalist movements in Vietnam.

Ta Yü *See* **Yü the Great.**

Tchad *See* **Chad.**

Tchaikovsky, Piotr Ilich 1840–93. Russian composer, one of the greatest Russian composers. Noted for the melodic and intensely emotional character of his compositions, he is famous for his scores for ballet, including *Swan Lake* (1877), *The Nutcracker* (1892), and *Sleeping Beauty* (1890). He also composed symphonies, concertos, and other works. Among his best-known works are *Fifth Symphony in F Minor, Sixth Symphony in B Minor, Fourth Symphony in F Minor,* and *Violin Concerto in D Major* (1878).

Tea Act British parliamentary act (May 10, 1773) that gave the British East India Company a virtual monopoly on tea trade in the American colonies. American opposition to the act led to the Boston Tea Party (*q.v.*).

Teach, Edward *See* **Blackbeard.**

Teapot Dome Naval oil reserve in Wyoming that gave its name to the Teapot Dome scandal (1922) during the administration of President

W. Harding. Secretary of the Interior A. Fall, who held jurisdiction over the oil fields, granted exclusive leases to the fields to Harry F. Sinclair (1876–1956) in apparent consideration of a $200,000 "loan." This and a similar arrangement involving assignment of reserves in California to Edward L. Doheny (1856–1935) caused great embarrassment to the Harding administration and led to Fall's conviction for accepting bribes.

technocracy American movement, begun in the early 1930s, advocating the reorganization of society through implementation of technological principles. The movement was short-lived, but some of its ideas remain influential.

Tecumseh 1768?–1813. American Indian leader, chief of the Shawnees. His attempt to form a league of Indian tribes against US encroachment on Indian lands ended with the defeat of his brother at Tippecanoe. He fought with the British in the War of 1812 and died at the Battle of the Thames.

Teheran Conference Allied conference (Nov. 28–Dec. 1, 1943) at Teheran, Iran, during WW II. Attended by US president F. Roosevelt, British prime minister W. Churchill, and Soviet premier J. Stalin, it coordinated strategy involving the Allied invasion of Western Europe.

Teilhard de Chardin, Pierre 1881–1955. French scientist and Catholic theologian. Teilhard's attempts to reconcile Christianity with what he saw as the ongoing social and mental evolution of man gained many supporters but caused him problems with the church. He put forth his theory in *The Phenomenon of Man* (1959).

Telemann, Georg Philipp 1681–1767. German composer. He was a prolific composer whose large body of works includes operas, chamber music, and oratorios.

Teller, Edward 1908– . Hungarian-born American physicist. Teller worked with E. Fermi on the atomic bomb and later supported the movement to build the hydrogen bomb.

Tellez, Gabriel *See* **Tirso de Molina.**

Temesvar, Battle of Austrian victory (Aug. 9, 1849), with Russian support, over the Hungarians. By this victory Austria overthrew the Hungarian republic established by the Hungarian Revolution of 1848.

temperance Movement advocating abstinence from alcoholic beverages. The first temperance group was founded (1808) in Saratoga, New York, and others soon appeared in the US, Great Britain, Ireland, and Scandinavia. The movement was led by churches and women's groups and became a major force in the US through the Woman's Christian Temperance Union (founded 1874) and the Anti-Saloon League (founded 1895). A major result of this movement was ratification (1919) of the 18th Amendment to the US Constitution, which secured Prohibition in the US.

Templars *See* **Knights Templars.**

Temple, Sir William 1628–99. English diplomat. He arranged the Triple Alliance (1688) against France and advanced the marriage plans of William of Orange and Princess Mary of England.

Tempo reforms Japanese reforms implemented (1841–43) by the Tokugawa shogunate in an unsuccessful attempt to restore the financial balance of the shogunate and the political and economic well-being of Japan.

Temujin *See* **Genghis Khan.**

Ten, Council of Venetian tribunal founded (c1310) to investigate plots against the state. It soon gained vast powers in both domestic and foreign matters and existed until abolishment (1797) of the Venetian state by Napoleon.

Tencin, Claudine Alexandrine Guérin de 1685–1749. French writer and literary patron. Her numerous affairs with high political figures brought her wealth and political influence during the reign of King Louis XIV.

Ten Commandments (Decalogue) Ten laws that form the basis of Judaeo-Christian religion. According to the Bible, they were written on two stone tablets and handed down by God to Moses.

Tenentismo Brazilian reform movement of the 1920s. Begun by young army officers seeking social reforms, the movement conducted two revolts (1922, 1924), both of which were quickly crushed. However, it remained an influence into the 1930s.

Teng Hsiao-p'ing *See* **Deng Xiaoping.**

Ten Kingdoms Independent kingdoms that rose in southern China in the period (907–960) between the end of the Tang and the rise of the Sung dynasties.

Ten Lost Tribes of Israel *See* **Lost Tribes of Israel.**

Tennent, Gilbert 1703–64. American Presbyterian clergyman. A powerful preacher, he was a driving force in the Great Awakening (*q.v.*).

Tennis Court Oath Oath sworn (June 20, 1789) by members of the Third Estate during the early stages of the French Revolution. The delegates to the Estates-General had formed (June 17) the National Assembly, and, finding themselves barred from their meeting place, convened at a tennis court, where they swore not to disband until a constitution had been granted the country. Their determination led King Louis XVI to direct the clergy and nobility to join the National Assembly (June 27).

Tennessee Southeastern US state, the 16th state. Its capital is Nashville. First claimed by the French, the Tennessee area was ceded to England after the French and Indian Wars (1763). D. Boone explored the region, and Virginians established the first permanent settlement (1769). After the American Revolution, disgruntled settlers formed the independent state of Franklin (1784–88), and in 1796, Tennessee became a state. Tennessee seceded from the Union (1861) during the Civil War and was the locale of several military engagements, notably the Chattanooga Campaign and the battles of Shiloh and Stones River. Tennessee was readmitted to the Union (1866), and its constitution was adopted in 1870.

Tennessee Valley Authority (TVA) US government agency created by Congress in 1933 to manage development of the Tennessee River Basin. The agency oversaw the construction of some 42 dams, achieving both flood control and cheap electric power. The TVA raised much controversy and was regarded by some as an example of government interference with private industry.

Tennyson, Alfred Lord (˜, Alfred ˜, 1st baron) 1809–92. English poet laureate (1850), considered the leading poet of Victorian England. Born the son of a clergyman, he was educated at Cambridge. When his father died (1831), Tennyson took over responsibility for the family finances and despite difficulties published a book of poems in 1832 (including *The Lotus-Eaters* and *Oenone*). But he did not enjoy widespread acclaim until publishing a new book of poems in 1842, this one containing *Locksley Hall* and *Break, Break, Break,* among others. The year 1850 proved to be a pivotal one for Tennyson: he published *In Memoriam* (recounting his prolonged grief over the untimely death of his friend Arthur Henry Hallam), was named poet laureate, and married Emily Sellwood. Tennyson

completed his famous poem about the Crimean War *The Charge of the Light Brigade* in 1855 and published the first version of *Idylls of the King* in 1859 (last revised by him in 1888). He was created baron in 1883.

Tenochtitlán Capital city of the Aztecs, which stood on the site of present-day Mexico City. Founded c1325, it was captured and largely razed (1521) by H. Cortés.

Tenskwatawa *See* **Shawnee Prophet.**

Tenure of Office Act US act passed over a presidential veto (Mar. 2, 1867) forbidding the removal of certain high government officials without the consent of the Senate. President A. Johnson's removal of secretary of war E. Stanton despite this act led directly to Johnson's impeachment trial.

Ten Years' War Cuban revolt against Spanish rule (1868–78). It was led by Carlos Manuel de Céspedes (1819–74), who called for the gradual emancipation of slaves and universal suffrage. He also favored Cuban independence, although not all the insurrectionists agreed. After 10 years of brutal fighting, which left about 200,000 Cubans and Spanish dead, the insurrection was defeated. The Treaty of El Zanjón (1878) made liberal promises, most of which were not kept.

Tenzing Norgay *See* **Hillary, Sir Edmund Percival.**

Teotihuacán Ancient Mexican city, site of many architectural ruins dating from before the Toltec period.

Terence 185–159 BC. Roman playwright known for his comedies adapted from Greek plays. Six of his comedies survive, among them *Andria, Eunuchus,* and *Adelphi.*

Teresa of Ávila, Saint 1515–82. Spanish Catholic reformer and mystic who contributed significantly to the Catholic Reformation in Spain. She became the first female Doctor of the Church.

Terman, Lewis Madison 1877–1956. American psychologist. Terman gave the term "IQ" (intelligence quotient) to America with his introduction of the Stanford-Binet intelligence tests for schoolchildren.

Territory of Orleans Name given to the area forming the state of Louisiana, from its acquisition in the Louisiana Purchase (1804) to statehood (1812).

Tertullian AD c160–c230. Roman theologian. A convert and a strong defender of Christianity, he later became a Montanist, and still later established his own sect, the Tertullians.

Teruel, Battle of Battle (Dec., 1937–Feb., 1938) of the Spanish Civil War, at Teruel, Spain. Republican forces captured Teruel (Dec., 1937) but were unable to hold it. Teruel was recaptured (Feb., 1938) by the forces under Gen. F. Franco.

Teschen, Treaty of Treaty (May 13, 1779) between Austria and Prussia ending the War of the Bavarian Succession. The treaty made territorial adjustments between the two powers and awarded a cash payment to Saxony, Prussia's ally.

Tesla, Nikola 1856–1943. Croatian-born American inventor noted for his contributions to the development of alternating-current electrical technology.

Test Act English statute (1673). It was established to exclude from public office Roman Catholics and others who refused to support the Church of England and the king's supremacy in ecclesiastical affairs.

Tet Offensive Major offensive (Feb., 1968) by the Vietcong and North Vietnamese regulars during the Vietnam War. The combined Communist forces staged attacks in more than 100 cities throughout South Vietnam (including Saigon), thus proving their continued strength and embarrassing US military leaders. Fighting lasted a month at the city of Hue and Communist losses were heavy, but the offensive proved a major propaganda victory.

tetrarchy In Roman government, any principality, especially in the East, whose rulers retained a degree of sovereignty but were controlled by the Roman Empire. As Tetrarch of Judaea, Herod the Great was "king" under the Romans. The term was also applied to the government created by Diocletian, which was made up of two augusti and two caesars, each one a tetrarch.

Tetzel, Johann c1465–1519. German Dominican monk. His granting of indulgences in return for donations to a building fund for St. Peter's Church sparked M. Luther's initial challenge to the Catholic church.

Teutoburg Forest, Battle of Battle (AD 9) in the Teutoburg Forest, in Germany. There the Germans under Arminius defeated the Roman army under Varus, thus halting Roman expansion east of the Rhine.

Teutonic Knights (German Order) Catholic military order founded (1190) at Acre by German nobles during the Third Crusade. In the 13th cent. the order moved to Europe, became a powerful force, and gained control of Prussia. A branch of the order, the Livonian Knights, expanded its rule to the east. Through the 14th cent., the order expanded its holdings and power, and many of its cities became members of the Hanseatic League. Its continued attacks on Poland and Lithuania led to the order's defeat in the Battle of Tannenberg (1410) and its subsequent decline. The order was dissolved (1525) by Grand Master Albert of Brandenburg, who accepted Protestantism and became duke of Prussia under Polish suzerainty.

Tewfik Pasha 1852–92. Khedive of Egypt (1879–92), successor to his father, Ismail Pasha. Egyptian opposition to Western influence during his rule led to military intervention (1882) by the British, who took virtual control of Egypt.

Tewkesbury, Battle of English battle (May 4, 1471), the final battle of the Wars of the Roses. Here the Yorkists under King Edward IV defeated the Lancastrians led by Margaret of Anjou and Prince Edward.

Texas US state in the Southwest, the 28th state. The Spanish discovered the region (16th cent.), but hostile Indians prevented settlement until the early 18th cent. R. La Salle claimed part of eastern Texas for France (1685), and the French claim was included in the Louisiana Purchase by the US. S. Austin founded the first American settlement in Texas (1821). A province of Mexico, Texas rebelled and declared independence (1836). In the ensuing war, S. Houston defeated the Mexicans at the Battle of San Jacinto (1836), and Texas became an independent republic. US annexation of Texas (1845) led to Texas statehood that year and contributed to the outbreak of the Mexican War. Texas seceded from the Union in 1861 and was readmitted in 1870. The constitution was adopted in 1876.

Texas Rangers Texas military police. They were organized in 1835 to guard the Texas frontier against lawlessness and Indian attacks. In 1935 they became part of the state's highway patrol.

Thackeray, William Makepeace 1811–63. English writer, considered one of the great English novelists. Among his novels are *Vanity Fair, The Paris Sketch-Book,* and *Henry Esmond.*

Thailand (Kingdom of Thailand; *formerly* Siam) Southeast Asian country occupying the western portion of the Indo-Chinese Peninsula. The population is 54,890,000 and the capital is Bangkok. Thailand was the only Southeast Asian country that maintained its independence throughout the entire period of European colonialism. Thailand has generally been pro-Western in its policies. Key dates in the history of Thailand include:

FROM 6TH CENT. AD　Thai peoples began migrating to the area of modern Thailand from the northwest (southeast China, northwest Vietnam, northern Laos).

13TH CENT.　Numerous small Thai kingdoms established in northeastern India, northeastern Burma, and Laos.

1351　Rama Thibodi I established kingdom of Ayutthaya in central Thailand, which ruled until 1767 and gradually eliminated rival Thai states.

1657–88　Narai reigned as king of Siam; established splendid court; established relations with major European and Asian kingdoms.

1782　Phaya Chakkri founded Chakkri dynasty, which has ruled until present day; he reigned as Rama I; moved capital to Bangkok.

1826　Commercial treaty with Britain.

1833　Commercial treaty with the US.

1851–68　King Mongkut reigned; Westernization began.

1855　Bouting Treaty with Britain; Siam opened to foreign trade.

1863–67　France forced Siam to abandon its claims to Cambodia.

1868–1910　Chulalongkorn reigned.

1893　Forced to yield all territory east of the Mekong to France, including all of Laos.

1896　Anglo-French accord guaranteed the country's independence.

1917　Siamese government entered WW I on the side of the Allies (July).

1932　Bloodless coup against King Prajadhipok (reigned 1925–35), forcing him to grant a constitution; constitutional monarchy proclaimed (June 27).

1935–46　Rama VIII reigned.

1938–44, 1947–57　Pibul Songgram in power; long tenure began with appointment as premier; eventually became dictator; renamed country Thailand (1939).

1941　Pibul allowed Japanese to enter the country (Dec. 8).

1942　Thailand declared war on the US and Britain (Jan. 25).

1946　Pridi Phanomyang served as leftist premier in postwar government; Pibul held as war criminal.

1946　King Rama VIII died under mysterious circumstances.

1946–　Rama IX reigned; crowned in 1951 after attaining his majority.

1947　Pridi overthrown (Nov. 9) by Pibul as dissatisfaction with Pridi regime was increasing.

1954　Thailand made the headquarters of the Southeast Asia Treaty Organization (SEATO).

1957　Pibul Songgram overthrown in coup led by Marshal Sarit Thanarat; Thanom Kittakachorn made premier in 1958.

1958–63　Sarit deposed Thanom and ruled by martial law until his death in 1963; political parties banned.

1963　Thanom returned to power; remained in power until 1973; his administration saw massive buildup of US military in Southeast Asia during Vietnam War.

1971　Bloodless coup (Nov. 17); Prime Minister Thanom Kittikachorn seized full power as political unrest and Communist guerrilla attacks mounted.

1972　Interim constitution promulgated; government controls eased (Dec.).

1973　Thanom fled country following student riots (Oct.).

1973　Prime Minister Sanya Dharmasakti installed; return to civilian government.

1974　Political parties legalized under new constitution; new house of representatives established.

1975–76　Political instability followed elections; three right-wing coalition governments failed, the last following student riots.

1976　Military junta seized power amid political crisis and rioting by leftist students (Oct.); declared martial law and outlawed political parties.

1976　New civilian government set up under control of military advisory council; political parties banned.

1976–79　Thanin Kraivixien in office as prime minister, heading an authoritarian regime controlled by the military.

1976　US forces ordered out of Thailand (Mar. 20).

1977 Bloodless coup by council of military advisers ousted prime minister (Oct.).

1977–80 Gen. Kriangsak Chomanan in office as prime minister.

1978–80 Massive influx of refugees from Vietnam, Laos, and Cambodia; Vietnamese invasion of Cambodia sent still more refugees into Thailand; hundreds of thousands of Cambodians subsequently returned to their homeland.

1978 Thai government condemned Vietnamese invasion of Cambodia; incursions by Vietnamese troops fighting rebels in Thailand reported; fears of Vietnamese invasion of Thailand resulted in increased US military aid.

1979 Political parties again legalized; elections held to lower house, while military appointees were named to upper house; military advisory council dissolved.

1980–88 Gen. Prem Tinsulanonda, head of military advisory council, in power as prime minister (Mar.), following Gen. Kriangsak's resignation; his administration marked by improving economy, mass surrender of virtually the last armed guerrilla groups in Thailand; and by continued incursions by Vietnamese troops fighting Cambodian rebels along the Thai border.

1981 Attempted military coup failed (Apr. 3).

1984 Brief border clash between Thai and Laotian troops.

1985 Failed military coup attempt (Sept.); 5 killed and 40 arrested and tried, including the army commander.

1986 Lower house dissolved after it defeated government bill for new tax; Democratic Party won almost one-third the seats in new election; coalition cabinet formed with Prem as prime minister.

1987 Mercenary troops, employed by Thailand's top opium trafficker, driven across border into Burma by Army troops.

1987 Thai Communist party leaders arrested by security forces.

1987 Three-month border clash with Laotian troops; following ceasefire (1988), reached negotiated settlement.

1987 Three-fold increase in number of Vietnamese boat people reported arriving in Thailand; government began refusing to allow boats to land (1988).

1988 Lower house dissolved following new political crisis.

1988–91 Gen. Chatichai Choonhavan, leader of Chart Thai party, in office as prime minister, heading a six-party coalition government; promised to give greater attention to regional problems; opened contacts with Laos, Cambodia, and Vietnam.

1988 Thousands of refugees fled to Thailand from Burma following military coup there (Sept.).

1989–90 Chatichai administration rocked by corruption scandals; Army commander Gen. Chavalit forced to resign (1990).

1989 Rapproachment with Cambodia and Vietnam effectively halted following China's formal opposition to policy.

1990 Leader of failed coups (1981 and 1985), Col. Manoon Roopkachorn, allowed to return to Thailand; appointed to high military post.

1990 Government ordered Cambodian refugee camps controlled by Cambodian resistance groups closed (Mar.); 300,000 Cambodians to be repatriated or resettled in UN-run camps.

1991 Bloodless coup by military (Feb.), ending trend toward more democratic government; Gen. Suchinda Kraprayoon effectively controlled government.

1991 National Peace-keeping Council (NPC) formed by coup leaders to govern Thailand; constitution abolished and legislature dissolved; elections and new government promised.

1991–92 Anand Panyarachun, a businessman, appointed interim prime minister.

1991 New National Legislative Assembly appointed by NPC.

1991 Assembly passed laws banning unions in state enterprises, effectively ending their opposition to privatization program.

1992 Gen. Suchinda Kraprayoon, leader of 1991 coup, in office as prime minister; the fact he was appointed and not elected led to political unrest.

1992 Mass demonstration in Bangkok against Suchinda turned into four-day riot (May); troops fired on protesters in military crackdown; over 50 dead, 600 injured, and 2,000 arrested.

1992 Chaun Leekpai became prime minister (Sept.).

Thaïs *fl.* 4th cent. BC. Athenian courtesan, mistress to Alexander the Great and later to the king of Egypt. A legend, probably false, holds that she induced Alexander to burn Persepolis.

Thakin Shu Maung *See* **Ne Win, U.**

Thales c636–c546 BC. Greek philosopher, considered the first Western natural philosopher. One of the Seven Wise Men of Greece, he held that all things were based on one element—water. According to tradition, Thales made the first prediction of a solar eclipse in 585.

Thames, Battle of the American victory over the British (Oct. 5, 1813) in Ontario, Canada, during the War of 1812. Some 3,000 Americans commanded by W. Harrison defeated 600 British and 1,000 Indian allies under Tecumseh, thereby establishing American control of the Northwest. Tecumseh was killed in this battle.

Thanom Kittikachorn 1911– . Thai army general and prime minister (1963–73). He restored nominal parliamentary democracy, but his seizure of power through a military takeover (1971) led to his ouster (1973).

Thant, U 1909–74. Burmese diplomat. As secretary general of the United Nations (1962–71) he helped find peaceful solutions to the Cuban Missile Crisis (1962) and the conflicts in the Congo (1962) and Cyprus (1964). He was also influential in resolving the India-Pakistan War of 1965.

Thapsus, Battle of Decisive victory (46 BC) for J. Caesar over the remaining supporters of Pompey in North Africa. Thousands were slaughtered, and the opposing commander, M. Scipio, committed suicide. Soon after, Caesar was appointed dictator by the Roman Senate.

Thasos Greek island in the northern Aegean, noted in ancient times for its gold mines.

Thatch, Edward *See* **Blackbeard.**

Thatcher, Margaret (*née* Roberts, ˜) 1925– . Conservative politician and Britain's first woman prime minister (1979–90), serving the longest term (11 years) of any British PM since the early 1800s. Dubbed the "Iron Lady," she imposed tough deflationary economic policies to counter Britain's worsening economic crisis, curbed labor union powers, privatized 45% of state-run industry, promoted social spending cuts, increased defense spending, and maintained close ties with the US. Thatcher was born a grocer's daughter and graduated from Somerville College, Oxford. After marrying Denis Thatcher

(1951), a successful businessman, she became a member of the bar (1953) and entered Parliament (1959). Thatcher served in cabinet posts before becoming Britain's first woman party leader (1975), succeeding E. Heath. Then voter reaction to a wave of strikes brought the Conservatives to office (1979), with Thatcher being elected prime minister. Her first term was marked by creation of black-ruled Zimbabwe (1980) and the British victory in the Falkland Islands War (*q.v.*). Reelected by a landslide in 1983, Thatcher supported Britain's continued nuclear capability and basing of NATO cruise missiles there despite considerable opposition. Other notable events included an agreement returning Hong Kong to China (1984) and a one-year coal miners' strike (1984–85). Thatcher escaped unhurt when an IRA bomb exploded in her hotel at Brighton (Oct., 1984). The following year Ireland was given a consultative role in Northern Ireland (Ulster Plan). Reelected in 1987, Thatcher continued her policies of privatization, tax and spending cuts, and health and education reforms. In 1989 she reluctantly approved Britain's full membership in European Monetary Union, though in 1990 she tried to delay its implementation. With Communist governments collapsing in Eastern Europe and the USSR, she supported German unification and aid to new democracies, but also spoke out for continuing NATO's nuclear capability. From 1989, Thatcher's popularity declined as a result of continuing high unemployment and economic problems tied to her anti-inflationary austerity budget. Bitter opposition to a controversial "poll tax" (enacted 1990 for raising local government revenues) and proposed National Health Service reforms finally forced Thatcher's resignation in Nov. 1990. *See also* Great Britain, 1979–90.

Thaw, Harry K. *See* **White, Stanford.**

Theatre Guild New York production society formed (1919) to present plays of merit from both America and Europe, regardless of commercial acceptability. Among their many successful productions were *Oklahoma!* and *Porgy and Bess.*

Théâtre-Libre Independent theater founded in Paris (1887) by A. Antoine. An important outlet for new naturalist plays, it had a profound influence on later experimental theaters.

theater of the absurd Movement in the drama of the 1950s and 1960s that depicted the human condition as meaningless and absurd. It was characterized by such plays as S. Beckett's *Waiting for Godot* and E. Ionesco's *The Bald Prima Donna.*

Thebes Ancient Egyptian city. Thebes became the religious center of Egypt and rose to political prominence with the 11th dynasty (2130–2000 BC), reaching its peak from the 18th to the 20th dynasties. It was the center of worship of the god Amon and the site of tombs of New Kingdom pharaohs. It declined as cities in the Nile delta became powerful. Thebes was sacked by Assyrians (661 BC), and Romans (29 BC).

Thebes Greek city, the chief city of ancient Boeotia. Founded by Cadmus (according to legend) and settled by Boeotians before 1500 BC, it was involved in numerous struggles with both Athens and Sparta from the 6th to 4th cents. BC. A member of the Peloponnesian League, it nevertheless initially sided with Persia (480–479) during the Persian Wars. Following their victory over the Spartans at the Battle of Leuctra (371 BC) during the Peloponnesian Wars, Thebes gained hegemony over Greece (until 362). Thebes allied itself with Athens against Philip II of Macedonia and he defeated them at Chaeronea (338 BC). The city was destroyed by Alexander the Great (336 BC).

Thebes, Seven Against *See* **Seven Against Thebes.**

Theiler, Max 1899–1972. South African-born American bacteriologist. For his contributions to development of a vaccine for yellow fever, he was awarded the Nobel Prize in Physiology or Medicine in 1951.

theism In theology, belief in a supreme, personal God who is intimately associated with yet apart from the existence of things. Its opposite is Atheism.

Themistocles c525–c460 BC. Athenian statesman and naval commander. Themistocles urged the strengthening of the Greek navy and defeated the Persians at Salamis (480 BC) and was responsible for the rebuilding of Athens' walls after the war. Later he was ostracized (c472) and eventually went to Persia.

theocracy Form of government in which God is the ultimate authority and laws devolve as from God, through priests or clergy. Thus priests act as both spiritual and secular rulers of the state.

Theocritus *fl.* 3d cent. BC. Greek poet considered the originator of pastoral poetry. He brought pastoral poetry to new heights and influenced such later poets as Vergil and E. Spenser.

Theodora AD c500–548. Byzantine empress (AD 527–548), wife of Emperor Justinian (*m.* AD 523). She had great influence during Justinian's rule and played a key role in saving the throne during the Nika riot (AD 532).

Theodore of Mopsuestia AD c350–428. Greek Christian theologian, bishop of Mopsuestia (AD 392–428). He applied scientific and historical criteria to the study of the Bible. He influenced Nestorius and is sometimes considered the real founder of Nestorianism and of the Antiochene school of exegesis (as opposed to the allegorizing Alexandrian School).

Theodoric I (Thierry I) *d.* 534. Frankish ruler, a son of Clovis I. On Clovis' death, Theodoric shared the Frankish kingdom with his brothers Childebert I and Clotaire I.

Theodoric the Great AD c454–526 Ostrogothic king of Italy (493–526). Acting in behalf of Byzantine emperor Zeno, Theodoric led his Gothic army in an invasion of Italy (from 488). By 493 he had captured Ravenna and killed Odoacer, the German chieftain who had overthrown the last Western Roman emperor in 496. He subsequently ruled over Italy as king, though he was nominally in the service of the Byzantines.

Theodosian Code Compilation of Roman laws from the reign of Constantine to that of Theodosius II, under whom it was issued (AD 438). It was later used in compiling the Justinian Code.

Theodosius I (~ the Great) AD 346?–395. Roman emperor of the East (AD 379–395). He defeated the Goths in the East and convened the Second Council of Constantinople (381). He defeated and killed the usurper Maximus (388) and restored Valentinian II to the throne in Italy.

Theodosius II AD 401–450. Roman emperor of the East (AD 408–450), successor to his father, Arcadius. He left the actual ruling to his sister Pulcheria and his wife Eudocia. He authorized the Theodosian Code and negotiated with Attila the Hun.

Theodosius the Great *See* Theodosius I.

Theophilus I (~ the Unlucky) *d.* 842. Byzantine emperor (829–842). The last emperor to advocate the heresy of Iconoclasm, he proved an able administrator and fostered a brief revival of learning and the arts. He suffered major defeats in the near continuous wars against invading Muslims, notably at Amorion (838) in Anatolia, but secured the empire's northern borders in the Black Sea area.

Theophrastus c372–c287 BC. Greek philosopher. He succeeded Aristotle as head of the Peripatetics. He wrote extensively on plants, nature, and ethics.

Theorell, Axel Hugo Teodor 1903–82. Swedish biochemist. He was awarded the Nobel Prize in Physiology or Medicine (in 1955) for his studies of enzyme oxidation.

theosophy Mystical religious philosophy holding that direct knowledge of God is possible and is the means of salvation. Although its concepts date back to early Indian philosophy, modern Theosophy was founded (1875) by H. Blavatsky.

Thermidor Eleventh month of the French Revolutionary calendar. The *coup d'état* of 9 Thermidor (July 27, 1794) brought down M. Robespierre and ended the Reign of Terror. The coup was carried out by a hastily organized coalition of factions in the National Convention, following a speech by Robespierre (July 26) in which he denounced certain unnamed enemies. Robespierre and others were guillotined July 28 and the Thermidorian reaction, as it was called, was swift. The machinery of the Reign of Terror was dismantled, the radical Jacobins were suppressed, and the moderates came into control. Radical reforms were rescinded, among them the Law of Maximums, which set controls on wages and prices (in effect 1793–94). The Thermidorian period ended with the establishment of the Directory (*q.v.*) in 1795. (*See also* French Revolution, 1794–95.)

Thermopylae Historic Greek pass linking northern and southern Greece. Here a small force of Spartans under Leonidas made a heroic but unsuccessful stand (480 BC) against the vastly superior army of Persian king Xerxes during the Persian Wars.

Thermopylae, Battle of *See* **Antiochus III.**

Thespis *fl.* 534 BC. Greek poet, considered the originator of the tragic drama. He was said to have introduced the role of actor to interact with the leader of the chorus, thereby creating dialogue.

Thessaly Ancient Greek region of northern Greece. A fertile plain surrounded by mountains, Thessaly was suited to horse-raising and came under the control of aristocratic families.

Thibault, Jacques Anatole *See* **France, Anatole.**

Thibaw *See* **Burmese War (Third).**

Thiers, Louis Adolphe 1797–1877. French statesman and historian. Thiers served in several ministerial positions under King Louis Philippe, opposed Emperor Napoleon III and the Franco-Prussian War, and after the war became president of the Third French Republic (1871–73). He suppressed the Commune of Paris (1871).

Thierry I *See* **Theodoric I.**

Third Coalition, War of the (1805) Early phase of the Napoleonic Wars fought by a coalition of England, Austria, Russia, and Sweden against France and Spain. Napoleon defeated the Austrians in the Battle of Ulm (*q.v.*), suffered a naval defeat by the British in the Battle of Trafalgar (*q.v.*), and defeated the Austrians and Russians in the Battle of Austerlitz (*q.v.*), thus crushing the coalition.

Third Crusade *See* **Crusade, Third.**

Third Estate In prerevolutionary France, one of the three groups represented in the States-General, the others being the clergy and the nobility. It was composed largely of townsmen, or burghers. Its establishment (June, 1789) of the National Assembly in France marked the beginning of the French Revolution.

Third Punic War *See* **Punic War.**

Third Reich Name given the German government (1933–45) under the rule of A. Hitler and the Nazi party. (*See* Germany, 1933–45; Nazi party.)

Third Republic Name given the French government established (1870) after the fall of the Second Empire in the Franco-Prussian War. It was succeeded (1940) by the Vichy government during WW II. (*See also* France, 1870–1940.)

Third World Term applied to the less developed and often politically nonaligned countries of Africa, Asia, and Latin America.

Thirteen Colonies, the Those original British North American colonies which joined in the American Revolution and became the United States. They were Connecticut, Delaware, Georgia, Maryland, Massachusetts, New Hampshire, New Jersey, New York, North Carolina, Pennsylvania, Rhode Island, South Carolina, and Virginia.

38th parallel Boundary line adopted at the end of WW II to mark the separate areas in Korea where surrender would be made to American and Soviet forces. After the war, a Communist regime was established in North Korea (Democratic People's Republic of Korea), while the

Republic of Korea was established in the south. As a result of the Korean War, South Korea now holds some territory north of the parallel.

Thirty-nine Articles Articles formulating the official doctrines and beliefs of the Church of England. Officially promulgated by the Canterbury Convocation (1571) and approved by Queen Elizabeth I, they were based on 42 articles prepared (1553) by Archbishop T. Cranmer.

Thirty-three Immortals *See* **Lavalleja, Juan Antonio.**

Thirty Tyrants 1. Name given the group of 30 Athenians who ruled Athens (404–403 BC) under Spartan domination after the Peloponnesian War. They were overthrown by Thrasybulus. 2. Name given the group of pretenders to the Roman throne who rose during the reigns of emperors Valerian and Gallienus (AD 253–268).

Thirty Years' War Series of interrelated conflicts (1618–48) that led ultimately to the end of Habsburg dominance in Europe, the crippling of the Holy Roman Empire, and the emergence of France as the leading power in Europe. The war, which left Germany devastated, began in Bohemia as a reaction to imperial repression of Protestantism and quickly spread to other Habsburg domains in the Holy Roman Empire. Denmark and Sweden, each in turn, joined the conflict against the Habsburgs. In the final phase of the conflict, France entered the war in a successful move to break the power of the Holy Roman Empire. Key dates in the history of the Thirty Years' War include:

1576–1612 Holy Roman Emperor Rudolf II reigned; rule marked by repression of Protestants in Germany, disrupting the uneasy truce established between Protestants and Catholics by the Treaty of Augsburg (1555).

1608–09 Protestant leaders established alliance known as the Evangelical Union (1608); Catholics created the Catholic League (1609); stage set for outbreak of warfare between the factions.

1612–19 Matthias reigned; he failed to win peace between Protestants and Catholics.

1618 Defenestration of Prague; began the Bohemian revolt against Habsburg rule.

1618–20 Bohemian phase of the war; began with the Protestant revolt throughout Bohemia that spread into other Habsburg lands.

1619 Bohemians chose Frederick V, elector of the Palatinate, as king; led to split between Lutherans and Calvinists.

1620 Ferdinand II became emperor (Aug.); Catholic League forces under Count Tilly defeated Frederick and the Bohemians at White Hill (Nov. 8); defeat marked end of Bohemian phase of war; Frederick continued the war in the Palatinate.

1620–25 Palatinate phase of the war; Protestants under Frederick at first successful but ultimately defeated by imperial forces led by Tilly; Palatinate passed to Bavarian Duke Maximilian I.

1622 Imperial forces under Tilly defeated (Apr.) at Weisloch; battle marked high point of Protestant fortunes in the Palatinate.

1622 Tilly defeated the Protestants at Wimpfen (May) and Höchst (June); imperial forces began to crush Protestant resistance in the Palatinate.

1622 Protestants victorious at the Battle of Fleurus (now in Belgium).

1623 Protestants defeated at Stadtlohn (Aug.); battle marked virtual end of the struggle in the Palatinate.

1625–29 Danish phase of the war; Danish king Christian IV entered the conflict partly out of religious motives and partly to oppose growing Habsburg influence in northern Germany.

1626 Christian IV advanced into Saxony.

1626 Christian IV defeated (Apr.) by imperial forces under Duke Albrecht von Wallenstein at Dessau.

1626 Imperial forces under Tilly inflicted major defeat on Danes (Aug. 27) at Lutter am Barenberge.

1626–27 Imperial forces under Wallenstein and Tilly forced the Danish army north to the Jutland Peninsula.

1629 Emperor Ferdinand II issued the Edict of Restitution (Mar. 6), canceling Protestant titles acquired through the Peace of Augsburg in 1555.

1629 Treaty of Lübeck (May 12); Denmark withdrew from the conflict, thereby ending the Danish phase; Denmark lost territories.

1630–35 Swedish phase of the war; Swedish king Gustavus II (Gustavus Adolphus), enticed by promises of aid from French minister

Cardinal Richelieu, entered the war against the Habsburgs.

1630 Wallenstein dismissed as commander of imperial army; Tilly assumed command.

MID-1630 Gustavus II advanced his Swedish forces into Pomerania.

1631 Tilly captured Magdeburg (May 20) and destroyed the city; severe reprisals taken against the Protestants who had rebelled.

1631 Swedish and Saxon forces victorious over Tilly (Sept.) at Breitenfeld; Protestant forces advanced south.

1632 Tilly defeated and killed (Apr. 14) at the Battle of the Lech; Protestant forces subsequently captured Munich; Wallenstein returned to command imperial army.

1632 Wallenstein engaged Swedes and Saxons at Battle of Lützen (Nov. 16); Wallenstein defeated, but Gustavus II was killed; Gustavus succeeded by Duke Bernhard of Saxe-Weimar, who advanced into Bavaria.

1633 Wallenstein sought unsuccessfully to secure peaceful settlement to the war; was removed from command; continued to seek peace.

1634 Wallenstein assassinated (Feb. 25).

1634 Gen. M. von Matthias replaced Wallenstein as commander of imperial forces.

1634 Imperial forces defeated Protestants under Bernhard, at Nordlingen (Sept. 6); battle marked virtual end of Protestant alliance with Swedes.

1635 Peace of Prague (May 30) ended Swedish phase of the conflict; its provisions favorable to the Protestants, the treaty formed a groundwork for peace in war-torn Germany.

1635–48 French phase of the war; Cardinal Richelieu, seeking to establish France as leading power in Europe, secured French declaration of war against Habsburg Spain (May 1635); the war evolved into an international struggle between France (and allies) against the Habsburgs and the Holy Roman Empire.

1636 Swedes inflicted heavy casualties on imperial armies at the Battle of Wittstock in Germany (Oct. 4); marked recovery from Nordlingen defeat.

1637 Holy Roman Emperor Ferdinand II died; succeeded by his son Ferdinand III.

1638 Duke Bernhard of Saxe-Weimar defeated imperial forces at Rheinfelden (Mar. 3).

1642–45 Swedish forces under Gen. Lennart Torstensson conquered Denmark; advanced south into Austria and Germany, seriously crippling the Habsburgs' military position.

1642 French minister Cardinal Richelieu died; succeeded by Cardinal Mazarin.

1643 French forces under Prince Louis II de Condé defeated Spanish at Battle of Rocroi (May).

1645 The French under Condé and Viscount Turenne defeated the imperial army at Allersheim (Aug. 3), near Nordlingen.

1645 Matthias ousted as imperial commander.

1647 Treaty of Ulm marked a truce between Bavarian forces and allied French and Swedish armies.

1648 Peace negotiations (1645–48) culminated in the Treaty of Westphalia (Oct. 24), which ended the Thirty Years' War; its terms were favorable to France and Sweden and left the House of Habsburg and the Holy Roman Empire severely crippled; France became the dominant power in Europe.

Thistlewood, Arthur 1770–1820. English revolutionary. He organized (1820) the unsuccessful Cato Street Conspiracy to murder R. Castlereagh and other cabinet members.

Thököly, Emeric (˜, Imre) (Tököly, ˜) 1657–1705. Hungarian patriot. He fought against the Austrian Habsburgs and in 1678 took command of all rebel Hungarian forces. He was allied with the Turks in their unsuccessful assault on Vienna (1683).

Thomas, Dylan Marlais 1914–53. Welsh poet whose work is noted for its originality and brilliant and complicated imagery. Among his writings is the dramatic work *Under Milk Wood.*

Thomas, George Henry 1816–70. Union general in the American Civil War. His actions at the Battle of Chickamauga (1863) saved the Union army from destruction. He later defeated the Confederates at Nashville (1864).

Thomas, John *See* **Christadelphians.**

Thomas, Norman Mattoon 1884–1968. American Socialist leader and Presbyterian minister (1911–31). A leading social reformer, he was six times the Socialist candidate for the presidency from 1928 to 1948.

Thomas, Saint One of the Twelve Apostles of Jesus. His refusal to believe in Jesus' resurrection without evidence led to the term "doubting Thomas." He is thought to have preached in northern Persia and India.

Thomas, Silken *See* **Fitzgerald, Thomas, 10th earl of Kildare.**

Thomas à Becket, Saint 1117–70. English saint, archbishop of Canterbury (1162–70), chancellor of England (1155–62), and onetime friend of King Henry II. Appointed chancellor by Henry and elected archbishop with Henry's aid, Becket infuriated the king by consistently defending church prerogatives and canon law against royal authority. His opposition to the king led to his exile from England (1164–70). Soon after his return, he was murdered by four of the king's knights in Canterbury Cathedral.

Thomas Aquinas, Saint 1225–74. Italian theologian and philosopher whose writings have been officially adopted by the Roman Catholic church. A Dominican, he studied under Albertus Magnus and later taught in Paris and Rome. He successfully opposed the strictly rational interpretation of Aristotelian philosophy advanced by Siger de Brabant (1235?–81?) and the Averroists. He also opposed the teachings of the Augustinians by holding that reason and faith are compatible. His major works are the *Summa Theologica* (c1265–74) and *Summa contra Gentiles* (c1258–64).

Thomson, Sir Charles W. *See* **Challenger Expedition.**

Thomson, Sir Joseph John 1856–1940. English physicist noted for his studies of the electrical conductivity of gases and the charge and mass of the electron. He was awarded the Nobel Prize in Physics in 1906.

Thoreau, Henry David 1817–62. American writer and philosopher. Thoreau was an influential transcendentalist. His works include the journal *Walden* and the essay *On Civil Disobedience.*

Thorfinn Karlsefni *fl.* 1002–10. Icelandic navigator. Thorfinn attempted to establish a colony in North America (probably on an island near Nova Scotia) but abandoned the colony after three years.

Thorndike, Edward Lee 1874–1949. American psychologist. Thorndike devised intelligence and learning-ability tests for children. His works include *Mental and Social Measurements* and *The Psychology of Learning.*

Thornton, William 1759–1828. American architect. His plans (submitted 1793) for the proposed

Capitol in Washington, D.C., were approved by President G. Washington. Much of the central section of the Capitol follows his design, but other elements of the structure were modified.

Thothmes I *See* **Thutmose I.**

Thothmes II *See* **Thutmose II.**

Thousand, Expedition of the *See* **Expedition of the Thousand.**

Thousand Days, War of the Three-year civil war in Colombia between Liberal and Conservative factions (1899–1902). Contributing factors to the start of this Liberal revolt included a faltering economy, Liberal dissatisfaction with the continued rule by Conservatives (since 1886), and the Liberals' mistaken belief that other opponents of the regime (led by Manuel María Sanclemente) would not oppose the revolt. The Liberals won early victories after fighting began (Oct. 17, 1899), and Sanclemente was deposed by Conservatives (July 1900), but his successor, José Manuel Marroquin, succeeded in forcing the Liberals to end the fighting in 1902. Some 80,000 died during the war, and the government and the economy were seriously weakened. The following year the Colombian government proved unable to prevent the secession of Panama.

Thrace Historical European region in the southeastern part of the Balkan Peninsula. Its inhabitants resisted Greek domination, but the Greeks established several colonies in Thrace, notably Byzantium (6th cent. BC). Thrace was taken by Persia (6th cent. BC) and annexed by Rome (1st cent. BC). It passed to the Byzantine Empire, but by AD 1453 the last of Thrace fell to the Ottoman Turks. Thrace was contested by Bulgaria and Turkey in the Balkan Wars (*q.v.*). After WW I, the region was divided among Greece, Bulgaria, and Turkey by the treaties of Neuilly (1919), Sèvres (1920), and Lausanne (1923).

Thrasybulus *d.*c389 BC. Athenian general and statesman. He was banished by the Thirty Tyrants (404 BC) but overthrew them (403 BC) and reestablished democracy in Athens.

Three-Anti Campaign Early campaign (1951–52) by the Chinese Communist party, after its takeover of the Chinese mainland, to eliminate fraud, mismanagement, and corruption.

Three Emperors, Battle of *See* **Austerlitz, Battle of.**

Three Emperors' League Alliance (1873–77, 1881–87) of Germany, Austria-Hungary, and

Russia, originated by German chancellor O. von Bismarck, to preserve peace between Russia and Austria-Hungary and to isolate France. It was disrupted by the Russo-Turkish War of 1877–78 but was secretly renewed in 1881.

Three Feudatories, Revolt of the Rebellion (1673–81) against the Ch'ing (Manchu) dynasty by semi-autonomous areas in Yunnan, Kwangtung, and Fukien, headed by former Ming dynasty generals. They attempted to establish a new dynasty but were defeated.

Three Henrys, War of the French civil war (1585–89), one of the French Wars of Religion. It involved the last Valois king, Henry III; Henry, 3d duke of Guise; and the Huguenot Henry of Navarre (later King Henry IV). Navarre's defeat of the Catholic forces of King Henry III at Coutras (Oct. 20, 1587) led the Catholic Henry of Guise to march on Paris to depose Henry III. The king fled to Blois (May, 1588) and subsequently ordered Guise's assassination (Dec., 1588). This led to a revolt of the Catholics and forced the king to seek refuge with Navarre. While in Navarre's camp the king was murdered (July, 1589). Henry of Navarre continued the struggle to gain the throne.

Three Kingdoms Period in Chinese history (AD 220–280) during which three kingdoms ruled China after the fall of the Han dynasty. They were the Wei, which ruled in the north; the Wu, which ruled in the south; and the Shu Han, which ruled in the west. Wei conquered Shu Han (AD 264) and established the Chin dynasty. The dynasty then conquered the Wu (AD 280) and reunited China. The Three Kingdoms has been characterized as a romantic period, notably in the novel *Romance of the Three Kingdoms.*

Three Kings, Battle of the (Alcazarquivir, Battle of) Moroccan victory (Aug. 4, 1578) over the Portuguese invasion led by Portuguese king Sebastian I. Sebastian supported the Moorish pretender against the king of Fez and was defeated at Alcazarquivir, Morocco. All three kings died in the battle.

Three Mile Island Nuclear-powered electrical generating plant outside Middletown, Pennsylvania. A nuclear accident at the plant, beginning Mar. 28, 1979, resulted in the venting of radioactive gases. Though a full-scale disaster was averted (by Apr. 9, 1979), the crisis resulted in a major reevaluation of the US nuclear energy program.

Three Principles of the People Ideological goals advanced in China by Sun Yat-sen and later claimed by both the followers of Chiang Kai-shek and the Chinese Communists. They included: Nationalism, freedom from imperialism and imperial rule; Democracy, the ability of the Chinese to govern themselves through a form of democratic structure; and Livelihood, a socialist program with primary emphasis on land equalization.

Thucydides c460–400 BC. Greek historian, son of Olores. He was exiled because of his failure (424) as a general in the Peloponnesian War and wrote *The History of the Peloponnesian War* during his exile and after his return to Athens in 404. The work, which is incomplete, covers the years 431–411 and is noted for its accuracy, impartiality, and (then) novel examination of human character in relation to the events of the war.

Thugs (Phansigars) Loosely organized Indian religious sect. Devoted to the goddess Kali, the Thugs dressed as religious mendicants or merchants and killed their victims, usually travelers, as offerings to her. They were suppressed by the British (1830s).

Thule Name given the northernmost known country by the ancient Greeks. The Greek navigator Pytheas (*fl.* 4th cent. BC) reached an island he named Thule. It may have been Iceland, Norway, or one of the Shetland Islands.

Thurber, James Grover 1894–1961. American humorist whose whimsical stories and drawings which appeared regularly in the magazine *The New Yorker,* were noted for their insight into the human condition.

Thuringia Former German state, located in eastern Germany. The region was taken by the Franks in the 6th cent. After 1247, the rule of Thuringia was contested and the land was divided. Most of Thuringia came under the control of Saxony (15th cent.). Its various principalities were reunited (1919) into the state of Thuringia. In WW II, Thuringia was occupied by Russian forces, and in 1952, it was divided among several districts in the former East Germany.

Thutmose I (Thothmes I) *d.* c1512 BC. Egyptian king (c1526–12) during the 18th dynasty. He secured control of the Nile Valley as far as its fourth cataract, on whose rocks he inscribed records of his victories. He also sent military expeditions across the Euphrates River into the land of the Mitanni.

Thutmose II (Thothmes II) Ancient Egyptian king (c1512–04 BC). He married his half-sister Hatshepsut and campaigned in Nubia to put down a revolt there and sent armies into Palestine.

Thutmose III *d.* c1450 BC. Egyptian king (c1504–c1450 BC), successor to his father, Thutmose II. The regency of his aunt, Queen Hatshepsut, ended in c1482, and he began the conquests that made Egypt a great power. He added Syria, Kadesh, Mitanni, and part of the Sudan to his empire. He erected many monuments and temples and brought Egypt great wealth and prosperity.

Thutmose IV *d.* c1417 BC. Ancient Egyptian king (c1425–17 BC) during the 18th dynasty, successor to his father, Amenhotep II. He led successful campaigns in Nubia and Asia Minor. His marriage to the daughter of the Mitanni king in Syria led to a long and advantageous peace.

Thuy, Nguyen Vinh *See* **Bao Dai.**

Tianjin, Treaty of *See* **Opium War** (2).

Tianjin Massacre (Tientsin ˜) Massacre (June 21, 1870) of some 20 French nationals, including the French consul, at Tianjin, China. European warships were sent to Tianjin and war was avoided by Chinese issuance of an official apology.

Tiananmen Square *See* **China, 1989.**

Tiberius 42 BC–AD 37. Second Roman emperor (AD 14–37), successor to his stepfather Augustus. He ruled ably in the early years of his reign but later, under the influence of Sejanus, became a tyrant. He had Sejanus killed (AD 31).

Tibet Autonomous region of China, located in southwestern China. Capital is Lhasa. Tibet was crossed in early times by the trade route from China to India. A Tibetan kingdom rose there (7th cent.) and Buddhism was introduced, which evolved into Tibetan Buddhism (*q.v.*). Its chief religious leaders, the Dalai Lama and Panchen Lama, became the traditional political leaders (until recent times) of Tibet as well. Tibet came under Mongol domination (12th cent.), and then passed to the Chinese Manchu dynasty (1720). Chinese influence in Tibet waned through the 18th and 19th cents. and Tibet was invaded several times by Gurkhas from Nepal. Tibetan resistance to British attempts to open trade relations led to a British invasion (1904) and subsequent concessions. After the fall of China's Manchu dynasty (1912), Tibet again became independent. China invaded it (1950) and restored Chinese control over the country. A rebellion against Chinese rule (1959) was severely crushed and the Dalai Lama fled to India. The Chinese Communists suppressed Tibetan Buddhism, installed a secular government, and in 1965 the country formally became the Tibetan Autonomous Region.

Tibetan Buddhism (*often incorrectly called* Lamaism) Form of Buddhism found in Tibet, Mongolia, and adjacent regions. It began in Tibet (c7th cent. AD) and is derived from Indian Mahayana Buddhism, though it embodies elements of Tantric Buddhism and the native Tibetan religion Bon. The important Yellow Hat Sect was begun (15th cent.) by the lama (monk) Tsong-kha-pa (c1357–1419), who introduced many reforms and established rigorous discipline within the monasteries. In 1641, the Mongols came under the influence of the Yellow Hat Sect and gave control of Tibet to the Dalai Lama, who eventually became secular leader of the country. Spiritual control came to reside with the Paschen Lama. The Dalai Lama was exiled (1959) after an abortive revolt against Chinese domination. Since then the Chinese have actively suppressed Tibetan Buddhism.

Tibullus, Albius 54?–18? BC. Roman elegaic poet. Only two works, *Delia* and *Nemesis,* can be definitely ascribed to him. His patron was Messala.

Ticonderoga, Battle of American victory (May 10, 1775) over the British during the American Revolution at Ticonderoga in northeastern New York. E. Allen and the Green Mountain Boys captured Fort Ticonderoga, at the northern end of Lake Champlain. Artillery from the fort was later used to force the British evacuation from Boston (1776).

Tientsin Massacre *See* **Tianjin Massacre.**

Tiepolo, Giovanni Battista 1696–1770. Italian artist, considered one of the leading Venetian painters of the 18th cent. His massive frescoes are noted for their use of light and color.

Tiffany, Louis Comfort 1848–1933. American decorative artist. He developed and manufactured a form of colored glass known as Tiffany Favrille and produced a great number of works in glass, in the art nouveau style.

Tiglath-pileser I *d.* c1077 BC. Ancient Assyrian king (c1115–c1077 BC). He conquered parts of the former Hittite Empire, invaded Asia Minor and Babylonia, and campaigned west to the Mediterranean.

Tiglath-pileser III *d.* 728 BC. Ancient Assyrian king (745–728 BC). He conquered Syria and invaded Palestine. He also suppressed a revolt in Babylon (729 BC), thereby becoming titular king of Babylon, and launched campaigns as far east as the Caspian Sea. He brought the Assyrian empire to its greatest extent and also proved an able administrator.

Tigranes I the Great c140–55 BC. Armenian king (c95–55 BC). He conquered northern Mesopotamia, Syria, and Cappodocia, but was defeated (69 and 68 BC) by the Romans under Lucullus. He surrendered (66 BC) to Pompey and subsequently ruled Armenia as a Roman vassal.

Tigris and Euphrates Rivers rising in Turkey and flowing through southwestern Asia to join in southern Iraq. The ancient region of Mesopotamia encompassed this river system, and gave rise to such early civilizations as Sumer (*q.v.*), Akkad (*q.v.*), Babylonia (*q.v.*), Assyria (*q.v.*), and Chaldaea (*q.v.*).

Tilak, Bal Gangadhar 1856–1920. Indian nationalist leader. He negotiated the Lucknow Pact (1916), which unified Hindus and Muslims against British rule in India.

Tilden, Samuel Jones 1814–86. American statesman, Democratic presidential candidate (1876) against Republican R. Hayes. Tilden won the popular vote but disputed electoral votes were awarded by a Congressional Commission to Hayes, who thereby won the election.

Tillich, Paul Johannes 1886–1965. German-born American philosopher and theologian. His writings, which sought to blend modern thought with Christianity, include *The Courage to Be* and *My Search for Absolutes.*

Tilly, Johannes Tserklaes, count of 1559–1632. Flemish soldier in Bavarian and imperial service during the Thirty Years' War. As commander of the Catholic League he gained many victories, notably at White Hill (*q.v.*), in 1620. He seized Magdeburg (1631), which was sacked by his troops. He was defeated and killed at the Battle of Breitenfeld (1632).

Tilsit, Treaties of Two treaties signed (July, 1807) by France during the French Revolutionary Wars. 1. By the First Treaty of Tilsit (July 7, 1807), France granted Russia freedom to conquer Finland in return for a Russian attempt to mediate between England and France. If England should refuse mediation, Russia was to ally with France. 2. By the Second Treaty of Tilsit

(July 9, 1807), France gained substantial territory from Prussia, and Prussia was obliged to join the Continental System against Britain.

Time of Troubles Period in Russian history (1604–13) from the rise of the first so-called false Dmitri claimant to the Russian throne to the accession of Tsar Michael and establishment of the Romanov dynasty. In 1598, with the death of Tsar Fëdor I and the end of the Rurik line, B. Godunov was elected tsar. His rule was challenged (1604) by the rise of a pretender in Poland who claimed to be Dmitri, Fëdor's half-brother. He gained much support and at Godunov's death (1605) was made tsar. He was murdered (1606) by the Boyars and succeeded by Basil IV Shuisky (ruled 1606–10), who was confronted by peasant revolts and the rise of new pretenders, including a second false Dmitri. The second Dmitri forced Shuisky to seek aid from Sweden, which in turn prompted a Polish invasion (1609) and occupation of Moscow (1610). Polish king Sigismund III sought the Russian throne for himself and provoked increased Russian resistance after the death (1610) of the second Dmitri. Moscow was relieved by Russian forces (1612) and a national assembly elected (1613) Michael Romanov tsar, thus establishing the Romanov dynasty.

Timoleon of Corinth *d.* c337 BC. Corinthian who freed Sicily from control of the Carthaginians and petty tyrants. When the Greek colony of Syracuse appealed to Corinth for aid against Dionysius II, Timoleon led the invasion of Sicily (344 BC). After defeating armies of Dionysius and a petty tyrant backed by the Carthaginians, he became dictator of Syracuse. In 341, Timoleon defeated an alliance of the Carthaginians and petty tyrants and thereafter fostered a period of prosperity throughout Greek Sicily.

Timon of Athens *fl.* 5th cent. BC. Athenian misanthrope and recluse. Accounts of his life by Lucian and Plutarch formed the basis for the play *Timon of Athens* by W. Shakespeare.

Timothy, Saint d AD c100. Christian disciple, companion to Saint Paul. He is frequently mentioned in the New Testament and two of Paul's letters are addressed to him. According to tradition, he was the first bishop of Ephesus and was martyred there.

Timur *See* **Tamerlane.**

Timurids Turkish dynasty (15th cent.) descended from Tamerlane. Upon Tamerlane's death, the empire, comprising domains extending from India to Persia (modern Iran), was divided into eastern and western sections and distributed between his sons. Shah Rokh (ruled 1405–47), given the eastern half of the empire, quickly reunited much of the territory. He sparked a literary and cultural movement, established a library at his capital Herat, and encouraged trade. After his death, the empire fell into anarchy and eventually disintegrated into local dynasties. Baber, one of these rulers, founded the Mughal (q.v.) Empire in India.

Tinchebrai, Battle of   Battle (Sept. 28, 1106) by which English king Henry I gained control of Normandy.

Tindal, William   *See* **Tyndale, William.**

Tindale, William   *See* **Tyndale, William.**

Tintoretto (Robusti, Jacopo) 1518–94.   Italian painter, one of the great Venetian Renaissance painters of the 16th cent. A leader of the Mannerist school, he was thought to have been a student of Titian. His many works include *Last Supper* (1547), *Susanna Bathing* (1550), *Knight of Malta* (c 1551), *The Finding* (1555), and *Paradise* (1590).

Tippecanoe, Battle of   Victory (Nov. 7, 1811) of US forces led by Gen. W. Harrison over the Shawnee Indians led by Tenskwatawa, brother of Tecumseh. The battle, near the Tippecanoe River in Indiana, broke the power of the Indian alliance formed by Tecumseh and also provided Harrison with the slogan "Tippecanoe and Tyler, Too," for his 1840 presidential campaign.

Tipu Sultan 1753–99.   Indian ruler of Mysore (1782–99). He fought against the British and the Marathas in the Mysore Wars. He was killed in the fourth war and his kingdom was divided.

Tiradentes Conspiracy   A Brazilian movement against Portuguese rule. It was led by José Joaquim da Silva Xavier (1748–92), also called Tiradentes. He was captured (1789) and executed after a lengthy trial.

Tirhaka   *See* **Taharka.**

Tirpitz, Alfred von 1849–1930.   German admiral. As naval secretary from 1897, he built a modern fleet to match the British navy and through the Navy League promoted mobilization of the nationalist movement. He retired (1916) during WW I because of opposition to his policy of unrestricted submarine warfare.

Tirso de Molina (Téllez, Gabriel) 1571?–1648.   Spanish monk and dramatist. A prolific author of some 400 plays, he provided the first literary treatment of the Don Juan legend in *El Burlador de Sevilla.*

Tisquantum   *See* **Squanto.**

Tissaphernes *d.* 395 BC.   Persian satrap. He played a major role in Persia's reconquest of the Ionian Greek cities, and in the Battle of Cunaxa (401 BC).

Tisza, Count Stephen 1861–1918.   Hungarian premier (1930–05, 1913–17). A strong supporter of the Austro-Hungarian dual monarchy, he favored the alliance with Germany and was assassinated for his support of Hungary's WW I role.

Titanic   British ocean liner involved in a major seagoing disaster. Believed to be unsinkable, the liner struck an iceberg during the night (Apr. 14, 1912), while on her maiden voyage. *Titanic* sank the next morning with the loss of more than 1,500 lives.

Titian (*pseud.* of Tiziano Vecellio) 1488–1576.   Italian painter, one of the great Renaissance artists. A member of the Venetian school, Titian painted sumptuous religious and mythological paintings, such as the masterpieces *Sacred and Profane Love* (1515) and *Rape of Europa* (1562). Among his many other famous works are *Worship of Venus* (1518), *Assumption of the Virgin* (1518), and the *Pietà* (1576), his last work.

Tito (Josip Broz) 1892–1980.   President of Yugoslavia (1953–80) and Communist leader. A Russian prisoner during WW I, he participated in the 1917 revolution, then returned to Yugoslavia, becoming leader of the Communist party in 1937. During WW II, he led the Partisans (q.v.) in guerrilla fighting and, from 1945, headed the Yugoslav government. He pursued policies independently of the Soviet Union and was expelled from the Cominform (1948). Thereafter he maintained relations with Western and Communist powers, as well as with nonaligned countries. His regime was one of the most liberal in the Communist world.

Titus *fl.* 1st cent. AD.   Traditional first bishop of Crete and a disciple of Saint Paul. One of Paul's pastoral epistles was addressed to Titus.

Titus AD c39–81.   Roman emperor (AD 79–81), successor to his father, Vespasian. As a general he captured (AD 70) and destroyed Jerusalem and the Temple. As emperor, he rebuilt Rome after a great fire (AD 80) and completed the Colosseum.

Titus Flavius Vespasianus   *See* **Vespasian.**

Titus Lucretius Carus *See* Lucretius.

Tiy *fl.* 1400 BC.   Egyptian queen. She was the mother of Akhenaton and wife of Amenhotep III, over whom she is thought to have exerted great influence.

Tocqueville, Alexis de 1805–59.   French writer and statesman. Tocqueville visited the US in 1831 and wrote the study *Democracy in America,* considered a classic of political literature.

Togliatti, Palmiro 1893–1964.   Italian Communist party co-founder and longtime leader. He advocated liberalization of Communist regimes but never broke with Moscow.

Togo, Heihachiro, Count 1847–1934.   Japanese admiral. In the Russo-Japanese War, he defeated the Russians at Port Arthur (1904) and at the Battle of Tsushima in 1905—the first defeat of a European power by Asians.

Togrul Beg *See* Seljuks.

Tojo, Hideki 1884–1948.   Japanese general and wartime premier (1941–44). Tojo helped instigate the attack on Pearl Harbor (1941) and led Japan's war effort until 1944. He was executed (1948) as a war criminal.

Tokio *See* Tokyo.

Tököly, Emeric *See* Thököly, Emeric.

Tokugawa, Iyeyasu *See* Iyeyasu.

Tokugawa Keiki (Hitotsubashi) 1837–1902. Last Japanese shogun. Made shogun (1867) he surrendered his authority upon the accession (1868) of Mutsuhito as emperor.

Tokugawa   Last shogunate of Japan (ruled 1603–1867). Founded by Ieyasu, who came to power (1603) after the death of Hideyoshi, the shogunate ruled by means of a centralized feudal government. The capital was moved from Kyoto to Edo (now Tokyo) and the reign of the Tokugawa family was marked by a period of peace, prosperity, and cultural flowering. Nearly all foreign trade was ended and Confucianism was promoted. The Tokugawa shoguns were ousted from power during the Meiji (*q.v.*) Restoration.

Tokyo (Tokio) (Edo)   Japan's capital city and its cultural, administrative, and commercial center. Developed as a castle site in the 15th cent., it became the capital of the Tokugawa shogunate (1603) as the city of Edo. During the Meiji Restoration it was made the imperial capital (1868) as Tokyo. It became an industrial center in the 19th cent. and was severely damaged (1923) in an earthquake. During WW II the city was two-thirds destroyed by Allied bombing.

Toledo, Francisco de *d.* 1584.   Spanish colonial administrator and viceroy of Peru (1569–81). He reorganized and stabilized the government of Peru originally set up after the Spanish conquest.

Tolkien, J(ohn) R(onald) R(euel) 1892–1973. British author. An Oxford professor, he is best known as the author of the popular trilogy *The Lord of the Rings.*

Tolstoy, Leo (Tolstoi, Lev Nikolayevich) 1828–1910.   Russian author and philosopher, considered one of the greatest of all novelists. Born into a wealthy family, he attended college for a time and served in the army. He then married (1862) and returned to his country estate, Yasnaya Polyana, where he completed his masterpieces, *War and Peace* (1864–69) and *Anna Karenina* (1873–76). He experienced a religious transformation in 1876 and thereafter dedicated himself to social reform and the development of his new religion, which was a form of Christian anarchism.

Toltec   Ancient people of Mexico, warriors who dominated central Mexico from c900 AD to the rise of the Aztecs (12th–13th cents.). Toltecs were skilled in building, metallurgy, and the arts. They are believed to have worshiped the sun and practiced human sacrifice.

Tombaugh, Clyde William 1906– .   American astronomer. He discovered the planet Pluto (1930) after its existence had been predicted by P. Lowell.

Tompkins, Daniel D. 1774–1825.   American statesman. He was governor of New York (1807–17) and US vice-president (1817–25) under J. Monroe.

Tone, (Theobald) Wolfe 1763–98.   Irish nationalist leader. Tone worked for legislation to free the Irish from Britain and later joined a French military expedition (1798) to Ireland in support of a rebellion. Captured, he committed suicide.

Tong Wars   Violent feuds (1850s–1920s) in US West Coast cities between Chinese immigrants belonging to associations (called tongs) that were dominated by criminal elements.

Tonkin   Historic region in Vietnam, centered in the north around the city of Tonkin (modern Hanoi). Lying on China's southern border, Tonkin came under Chinese domination early in its history and remained under their direct rule from 111 BC to AD 939. Thereafter the region was ruled as part of the early Vietnamese state. French colonials called northern Vietnam Tonkin. *See also* Annam.

Tonkin Resolution, Gulf of *See* **Gulf of Tonkin Resolution.**

Tongzhi (T'ung Chih) 1856–75. Chinese emperor (1862–75) of the Qing dynasty. Most of his reign was spent under the regency of his mother, Cixi. It was a period in which relations with the West were expanded, the Taiping Rebellion was suppressed, and the imperial treasury was restored. Tongzhi died two years after taking full control of the government.

Toombs, Robert 1810–85. American statesman and Confederate general. He was US senator from Georgia (1853–61) and during the American Civil War he saw action at the Second Battle of Bull Run and at Antietam.

Torah Hebrew name for the Pentateuch, the first five books of the Bible. The term is also used more broadly to refer to the entire Hebrew Bible.

Tordesillas, Treaty of Treaty (June 7, 1494) between Spain and Portugal dividing between them the newly discovered lands in the Americas and the East. The treaty generally followed a papal bull, issued by Alexander VI, allotting the Americas to Spain and Africa, and Asia to Portugal. But it fixed the dividing line farther west, giving Portugal a claim to Brazil.

Torgau, Battle of Costly Prussian victory (Nov. 3, 1760) over Austria in the Seven Years' War, fought at Torgau, Germany. Frederick II, leading some 44,000 Prussians, defeated some 65,000 Austrians, commanded by Marshal Count von Daun. Prussian casualties were 13,000.

Tories *See* **Loyalists.**

Torquemada, Juan de 1388–1468. Spanish Franciscan monk and cardinal, an uncle of T. de Torquemada. At the Councils of Basel and Constance, he ably defended papal prerogatives against conciliarism.

Torquemada, Tomas de 1420–98. Spanish Dominican monk. An adviser to King Ferdinand and Queen Isabella, he brought about expulsion of the Jews (1492) from Spain and was named Grand Inquisitor (1493). In this post he promulgated rules for the Inquisition (*q.v.*) and, by his ruthless enforcement of them, made his name synonymous with cruelty.

Torres Vedras, Lines of *See* **Lines of Torres Vedras.**

Torricelli, Evangelista 1608–47. Italian physicist and mathematician who invented the mercury barometer. He wrote *De Motu* (1641), a treatise on movement, and briefly served as Galileo's assistant. After Galileo's death, Torricelli succeeded him as professor of mathematics at Florence and became known for his work in geometry, which contributed to the development of integral calculus. Torricelli also made improvements to the telescope.

Torstensson, Lennart 1603–51. Swedish general. His notable innovations in the use of more mobile field artillery contributed to Swedish success in the Thirty Years' War (1618–48).

Torun, Treaty of Treaty (Oct. 19, 1466) between Poland and the Teutonic Knights. By it Poland obtained the city of Torun and other territories (including Pomerania) from the order and compelled the Teutonic Knights to recognize Polish suzerainty. The treaty restored to Poland lands taken by the order in the 13th cent.

Tory Name of a once-powerful English political party. It was originally applied to Catholic King James II's supporters, who believed in the divine right powers of the king. After the Glorious Revolution (1688), the party represented the rural gentry and some higher aristocracy, and generally favored a powerful monarchy, religious uniformity, and noninvolvement in foreign wars. The party was powerful under Queen Anne (reigned 1702–14) but was virtually eclipsed as a party under George I, because of its ties with the Jacobites (*q.v.*). A new Tory party formed under the leadership of W. Pitt the Younger and remained in power, in one form or another, from 1783 to 1830. However, the party's reactionary domestic policies during this period, coupled with passage of the Reform Bill of 1832, resulted in the collapse of the party in the 1830s. Tory factions reemerged in the Conservative party (*q.v.*).

Toscanini, Arturo 1867–1957. Italian conductor. Considered one of the greatest conductors of all time, he was musical director of La Scala (1898–1907), of the New York Philharmonic (1933–36), and of the NBC Symphony (1937–54).

Tostig d. 1066. Anglo-Saxon earl of Northumbria and brother of England's King Harold II. When his brother sided with Northumbrian rebels against him, Tostig joined Norwegian king Harold III in an unsuccessful invasion of England. Tostig was killed in battle.

totalitarianism Form of authoritarian government in which the state attempts to control every aspect of the life of its citizens. The term was first used to describe the Fascist regime in

Italy, the Nazi regime in Germany, and the Communist regime in the Soviet Union.

Totila (Baduila) *d.* 552. Ostrogothic king. A capable general, he overran most of Italy, briefly reconquering it from the Byzantines (550). He was killed at the Battle of Taginae.

Toulon, Siege of Siege (Aug. 28–Dec. 9, 1793) during the French Revolutionary Wars in which French republican forces succeeded in retaking Toulon. Napoleon, then a young artillery officer, first gained notice there.

Toulouse-Lautrec, Henri de 1864–1901. French artist famous for paintings, lithographs, and posters of Parisian night life, such as *Le Moulin de la Galette* (1891).

Toungoo dynasty Kingdom centered in southern Burma (15th–18th cents.). In the 16th cent. the kingdom was greatly expanded, notably by Bayinnaung, and included all of Burma and parts of neighboring states. Toungoo power began declining after the death (1581) of Bayinnaung.

Tours, Berengar of *See* **Berengar of Tours.**

Tours, Saint Gregory of *See* **Gregory of Tours, Saint.**

Tours, Truce of Truce concluded on May 28, 1444, between the English and French forces in the Hundred Years' War (1337–1453). It lasted until 1449.

Toussaint L'Ouverture, François Dominique c1744–1803. Haitian revolutionary leader. As the leader of a band of Negro rebels, he sided with the French (c1794) and drove out the British and Spaniards. He fell afoul (1801) of Napoleon, however, when he sought greater independence from France.

Tower of Babel Legendary tower. In the Bible, Noah's descendants attempted to build a tower to heaven. But God caused them to suddenly speak different languages, making them unable to understand each other and complete the tower. Thus it was an early explanation for the diversity of language.

Tower of London Historic British fortress located on the Thames River in London. William the Conqueror was said to have begun fortification of the site (c1066). Construction of the central tower, made of white limestone, was begun (c1078). In succeeding centuries, successive encircling walls were added and the fortress was used variously as a royal palace, a jail, and an arsenal. It was the site of the Exchequer, England's central treasury, until the end of the Mid-

dle Ages. But the Tower was also notorious as the place where such historic figures as A. Boleyn, Sir W. Raleigh, and Lady J. Grey were imprisoned or executed.

Townshend, Charles 1725–67. British chancellor of the exchequer. A brilliant but unstable politician, he secured passage of the Townshend Acts (*q.v.*) which aroused opposition in the American colonies.

Townshend, Charles Townshend, 2d viscount 1674–1738. English statesman. He was a participant in Whig governments with his brother-in-law, R. Walpole. His major achievement was the management of British foreign policy between 1721 and 1730.

Townshend Acts British colonial laws (1767) replacing the Stamp Act. The British Parliament passed these four laws (June 15–July 2, 1767), which were designed to reassert its authority over rebellious American colonists. Named for C. Townshend, British chancellor of the exchequer, the acts fixed import taxes on glass, lead, paints, papers, and tea; authorized searches to guarantee compliance; and suspended the New York Assembly's powers until that colony complied with the 1765 Quartering Act. These laws stiffened Colonial resistance, and were repealed (1770), except for the tax on tea. This last provision led to the Boston Tea Party (*q.v.*).

Towton, Battle of Yorkist victory (Mar. 29, 1461) in the English Wars of the Roses (1455–85). Yorkist and Lancastrian forces numbered about 20,000 each, and the battle was fought in a blinding snowstorm. The Yorkists gained the upper hand, massacred the Lancastrians, and forced King Henry VI to flee England. Yorkist king Edward IV then took the throne.

Toynbee, Arnold 1852–83. English economist and sociologist, noted for pioneering settlement work and his economic history, *The Industrial Revolution in England.*

Toynbee, Arnold Joseph 1889–1975. English historian. He produced a notable theory of the rise and fall of civilizations based on the idea of cultural responses to challenges, in the 12-volume *A Study of History.*

Toyotomi Hideyoshi *See* **Hideyoshi.**

trade unions *See* **labor unions.**

Trafalgar, Battle of Naval battle (Oct. 21, 1805) between Britain and France, fought during the Napoleonic Wars, off Cape Trafalgar, Spain. It established British naval superiority for the rest of the century and ended Napoleon's plans to invade England. Twenty-seven British ships under Admiral H. Nelson defeated a fleet of 33 French and Spanish ships commanded by P. de Villeneuve. The French lost 20 ships, the British none. But Nelson was killed by a French sniper.

Trail of Tears   *See* **Cherokee Indians.**

Trajan AD c53–117.   Roman emperor (AD 98–117), successor to Nerva. Born in Spain, he was the first non-Italian emperor. He conquered Dacia and much of Parthia in the east. He encouraged building and constructed Trajan's Forum in Rome and Trajan's Bridge, the first bridge across the Danube.

Tranquillus, Gaius Suetonius   *See* **Suetonius.**

Transcendentalism   New England literary and philosophical movement (c1835–55). Transcendentalists such as R. Emerson and H. Thoreau believed in the goodness and divinity of man and nature. Their beliefs were marked by an emphasis on individuality and opposition to authority.

Transcontinental Treaty (Adams-Onis Treaty) Treaty between Spain and the US, signed on Feb. 22, 1819. Spain gave up claims to Florida and the Oregon Country in return for US recognition of her sovereignty over Texas.

Transvaal   Former independent state and now a South African province, which has the world's richest goldfield. Boers from the Cape Colony began settling there after the Great Trek (*q.v.*) in the 1830s, gaining independence in 1852. They successfully rebelled against the British annexation (1877), but became outnumbered by foreigners (uitlanders) after the discovery of gold in 1886. During the Boer War (1899–1902) the Transvaal was annexed (1900) by Britain, and it became a province of the Union of South Africa in 1909.

Transylvania   Historic region of northwestern and central Rumania. Once part of the Roman province of Dacia, it was conquered by Germanic tribes and became part of Hungary under Stephen I (1003). Control of the region was contested between Austria and the Ottoman Empire (15th–18th cents.), though it enjoyed nearly independent status in the 17th cent. Austria finally gained complete control in 1711 and by 1867 it had become part of Hungary. Rumanian inhabitants, however, were dissatisfied with Magyar domination and supported the seizure (1918) of Transylvania by Rumania. By the Treaty of Trianon (1920), Hungary ceded the territory to Rumania.

Trasimene, Battle of   Carthaginian victory (217 BC) over the Romans in the Second Punic War, near Lake Trasimene in central Italy. The Carthaginian general Hannibal ambushed and totally destroyed a Roman army led by C. Flaminius, who was killed.

Travis, William Barrett 1811–36.   Texas revolutionary hero. He commanded the Texas rebels at the Alamo (*q.v.*) and died in battle there.

Treaty of   *See under names inverted, as in* **Paris, Treaty of.**

treaty ports   Ports specifically designated by treaty as open to trade with foreign nations. In the 19th cent. both China and Japan resisted trade with the West as a matter of policy. To force a change in that policy, Britain precipitated the Opium War (*q.v.*) and, by the resulting Treaty of Nanjing (1842), won trading rights in five Chinese treaty ports. In Japan, Commodore M. Perry used the presence of his US naval fleet (1854) to pressure the Japanese into opening their ports to foreign trade, and soon after treaty ports were established there. Other nations followed and eventually there were over 60 treaty ports in China and 6 in Japan. The system was abolished (1899) in Japan and (1946) in China.

Trebizond, Empire of   Kingdom on the south shore of the Black Sea. After the overthrow of the Byzantine Empire (1204) by the Crusaders, two grandsons of Emperor Andronicus I Comnenus founded this successor state in what is now northeastern Turkey. Located on trade routes with the East, it prospered until taken over by the Ottoman Turks in 1461.

Treitschke, Heinrich von 1834–96.   German historian. A passionate advocate of German nationalism and power, he expounded his ideas in a major work, *History of Germany in the Nineteenth Century.*

Tremblay, François le Clerc du   *See* **Joseph, Father.**

Trent, Council of   Important council of the Roman Catholic Church (19th ecumenical), held in three sessions (1545–47, 1551–52, 1562–63) under two popes, Paul III and Pius IV. It met in response to the Protestant Reformation, and all doctrinal disputes raised by Protestants were answered. The council's far-reaching results were published in the *Catechism of the Council of Trent* (1566) and included reforms and definitions concerning the sacraments, the Scriptures, church dogma, duties of the clergy, and other subjects.

The council marked the beginning of the Catholic Reformation (*q.v.*).

Trent Affair A diplomatic incident during the American Civil War. During the US blockade of the South, the US vessel *San Jacinto,* commanded by Capt. C. Wilkes, seized (Nov. 8, 1861) the British mail steamer *Trent* on the open sea and removed two Confederate commissioners. At the demand of the British, they were released and an international incident was averted.

Trenton and Princeton, battles of American Revolutionary War battles, G. Washington's first victories against the British forces of lords Howe and Cornwallis. Washington made his famous crossing of the Delaware River (Dec. 25, 1776) and captured Trenton by taking 918 Hessians prisoner in a surprise attack. He then eluded some 7,000 British soldiers sent to Trenton and routed a British column near Princeton (Jan. 3, 1777) before moving into winter quarters at Morristown.

Trevelyan, George Macaulay 1876–1962. English historian. He was a champion of "literary" historical writing. His works include *History of England* and *English Social History.*

Trevithick, Richard 1771–1833. English inventor, builder of the first steam railroad locomotive. He obtained a patent (1802) for a high-pressure steam engine of his design and built a steam carriage the following year. Then in 1803 he built the first steam locomotive. In 1805 outfitted a barge with paddle-wheels and his steam engine to create a crude steamboat.

triangular trade In colonial America, a profitable three-way trading system that developed in the 18th cent. between the northern colonies, West Africa, and the West Indies. American colonies, which imported large quantities of supplies and manufactured items from Britain, were barred from exporting surplus fish, meat, and cereals to Britain. To pay for British imports, traders sought markets elsewhere, thus developing what became the triangular, or three-cornered trade. Though trade patterns varied, ships typically sailed from Boston and Newport to West Africa carrying rum, African iron (iron bars used by Africans as currency), staples, and manufactured items. The ships usually left Africa for the West Indies carrying a cargo of slaves, gold dust, spices, and other items. This cargo was in turn sold for a profit in the West Indies, where ships were loaded for the homeward voyage with

molasses, sugar, salt, and bills of exchange, which could be used to buy British goods. British Parliament passed the ineffective Molasses Act in 1733 and the Sugar Act of 1764 to control the trade. The latter act especially helped arouse early sentiment for rebellion in the American colonies.

Trianon, Treaty of Treaty signed at Versailles (June 4, 1920) between the victorious WW I Allies and the new state of Hungary that was created out of Austria-Hungary. The new nation ceded territory to Rumania (Transylvania and part of Banat), Czechoslovakia (Slovakia and Ruthenia), and the Kingdom of Serbs, Croats, and Slovenes (Croatia, Slavonia, and part of Banat). Its army was also reduced to 35,000.

Tribonian *d.* 545? Roman jurist. He headed the commissions that produced the great compilation of Roman law, the *Corpus juris civilis* (*q.v.*) issued by Emperor Justinian.

tribune Name of two different types of government officials in ancient Rome. Military tribunes were originally military commanders, and were either appointed or elected. Tribunes of the plebeians were created, according to tradition, in the 5th cent. BC as a condition for the end of the first secession of the plebs (494 BC). Tribunes of the plebs assumed governmental functions, notably as protectors of the rights of plebeians. Tribunes were required to be plebeians themselves, were elected, were usually 10 in number, and gradually came to play a major role in politics (by their sacrosanctity, right of intercession, and veto power). They had comparatively little power during the Roman Empire.

Trident Conference (Anglo-American Conference) Secret wartime conference of WW II in Washington, D.C. (May 12–25, 1943). President F. Roosevelt, Prime Minister W. Churchill, and their combined chiefs of staff planned the opening of a second front in Europe (Normandy invasion).

Trieste, Free Territory of *See* **Free Territory of Trieste.**

Trilling, Lionel 1905–75. American literary critic and essayist. A Columbia University professor, he was noted for his writings on the American liberal tradition (*The Liberal Imagination* and *Middle of the Journey*), as well as for his literary studies.

Trinidad and Tobago Independent state composed of two tropical islands off the coast of Venezuela. The population is 1,270,000 and the capital is Port of Spain. Trinidad, explored by C. Columbus (1498), was under British rule from 1797. Tobago was settled by the British in 1721 and was combined with Trinidad in 1888. The state won independence Aug. 31, 1962 and became a republic in 1976. Having both offshore oilfields and oil refineries, the country enjoyed economic prosperity during much of the 1980s. In July, 1990, a group of Muslim radicals seized the Parliament, taking the prime minister and some 50 others hostage. The rebels held out for six days before surrendering to authorities.

Trinity Fundamental Christian doctrine about the nature of God. As defined by several early church councils, God has a single divine essence that subsists in three divine persons: the Father, the Son, and the Holy Ghost.

Tripartite Pact *See* **Axis Powers.**

Triple Alliance 1. Alliance formed (1668) by England, the Netherlands, and Sweden to oppose French aggression during the reign of French king Louis XIV. The alliance was short-lived, as Louis soon secured an agreement (Treaty of Dover) with England. 2. Alliance formed (1717) by France, Great Britain, and the Netherlands, primarily to oppose Spain and secure the provisions of the Peace of Utrecht. In 1718 the alliance was joined by Austria, and thus became the Quadruple Alliance (*q.v.*). 3. Alliance formed in the late 19th and early 20th cents. by Germany, Austria-Hungary, and Italy. It was opposed by the Triple Entente. In the late 19th cent. O. von Bismarck sought to strengthen Germany's position against France, following the Franco-Prussian War (1870–71). In 1879, Bismarck secured the defensive Dual Alliance with Austria-Hungary. In 1882, Italy agreed to a defensive alliance with Germany, thus forming the Triple Alliance. The formation of this alliance led first to a series of informal agreements designed to offset the power of the Triple Alliance. By 1891, France had established an informal understanding with Russia. This developed (1893) into a military agreement, which was made public in 1895. In 1898 Théophile Delcassé (1852–1923) became French foreign minister. His policies led to an understanding between France and Great Britain (1904) known as the Entente Cordiale. In 1907 the Anglo-Russian Entente established the set of agreements that completed the Triple Entente. The two power blocs—Triple Aliiance and Triple

Entente—continued to dominate European politics up to the eve of WW I. At that point, Italy was in conflict with Austria-Hungary over the Balkans and refused to enter the war on the side of Germany and Austria-Hungary. This effectively ended the alliance and in 1915, Italy joined the Allies in WW II.

Triple Alliance, War of the War (1865–70) between Paraguay and an alliance formed by Argentina, Brazil, and Uruguay. The war, sparked in part by conflicting interests of Argentina, Brazil, and Paraguay over influence in Uruguay, led to the virtual destruction of Paraguay, the death of a large portion of its population, and loss of much of its territory to Brazil. In 1864–65, Brazil helped establish Venancio Flores (1809–68), a leader of the Colorado faction, as Uruguayan president. Paraguayan president F. López, a supporter of the rival Blanco faction in Uruguay, then declared war on Brazil. He also declared war on Argentina, after it refused to allow Paraguayan forces passage through its territory. Uruguay then joined the alliance with Brazil and Argentina against Paraguay. After initial successes, López withdrew his forces, vastly outnumbered by the Alliance, to Paraguayan territory. By Jan., 1866, the tide had turned against López and, though Paraguayans offered fierce resistance in following years, the Alliance slowly closed in on them. Asunción, the capital, fell in Jan., 1869, and López was captured and executed (Mar. 1, 1870).

Triple Entente *See* **Triple Alliance (3).**

Tripoli Capital of Libya. Founded (c7th cent. BC) by Phoenicians as Oea, it became one of the three major cities of the region called Tripolitania. Captured by the Romans (1st cent. BC), Tripoli was conquered by various peoples after the 5th cent. AD and was in Muslim hands from the 7th cent. It was a noted haven for pirates during this time and the US fought the Tripolitan War (*q.v.*) to suppress them. Tripoli passed to Italy after the Italo-Turkish War (*q.v.*) and later became capital of Libya.

Tripolitania *See* **Roman Province of Africa.**

Tripolitan War Confrontation between the US and the Barbary States (1801–05) resulting from the US refusal to increase payments of tribute to the pasha of Tripoli for his protection from pirate raids. The US blockade of Tripoli (from 1801) was generally unsuccessful against the pirates, and subsequent attempts to negotiate failed. In

1803, the US warship *Philadelphia* was captured by Tripoli and S. Decatur led a famous raiding party that destroyed the ship in the harbor (Feb., 1804). Fighting continued but was unsuccessful until the US organized a land invasion force against Tripoli in 1805. The Tripolitans agreed to a treaty (June 4, 1805) even before the force, under W. Eaton, reached Tripoli. The agreement ended US payments of tribute but acts of piracy continued in subsequent years.

Tripolitan War *See* **Italo-Turkish War.**

trireme Warship used by the Greeks (from c6th cent. BC) which could be used to ram other vessels in battle. A fairly standard design measured 120 feet in length and carried 200 crewmen. The trireme was powered by oarsmen (grouped in threes) and a square sail that could be detached before going into battle.

Trist, Nicholas Philip 1800–74. American diplomat, sent to negotiate an end to the Mexican War. He disregarded orders recalling him and went on to conclude the Treaty of Guadalupe Hidalgo (*q.v.*).

triumph In ancient Rome, a procession through the city celebrating a general's victory in battle. The procession was allowed (during the republic) only for major victories by a magistrate who held supreme and independent command. During the empire, only the emperor or family members he designated were allowed the honor of a triumph and the celebration soon ceased to be connected with military victories. The triumphal procession began at Campus Martius and ended at the temple of Jupiter Capitolinus. Magistrates and Senators led the procession, followed by important captives (usually put to death afterward) and the spoils, sacrificial animals, the *triumphator* riding a four-horse chariot, and lastly the soldiers of his army.

triumvirate In ancient Rome, a board of three government officials appointed to carry out a specified task. The term was applied to the alliance (not legally sanctioned by the government) between J. Caesar, Pompey, and Crassus (formed 60 BC). This is the First Triumvirate. The Second Triumvirate (legally sanctioned) consisted of Octavian (later Augustus), M. Antony, and M. Lepidus, and resulted in reforms that gave the triumvirs dictatorial powers. It was organized in 43 BC.

Trojan War Legendary war between the Greeks, led by Agamemnon, and the city of Troy, de-

fended by Hector and others. It is believed to have had its roots in a real conflict that took place c1275 BC. The mythical battle began when the Trojan prince Paris kidnapped Helen, wife of King Menelaus of Sparta. For 10 years the Trojans and the invading Greeks fought many heroic but inconclusive battles. Finally the Greeks built a large wooden horse, ostensibly a gift for the Trojans. A number of Greek warriors hid inside it and the Greeks returned to their ships, pretending to sail home. The Trojans wheeled the horse inside the city and that night the warriors opened the gates of Troy for their fellow Greeks, who then conquered the city. The war inspired many poems and stories, most notably Homer's *Iliad* and *Odyssey* (*q.v.*).

Trollope, Anthony 1815–82. Noted English Victorian novelist. A chronicler of the ordinary lives of provincial people, he is famous for his series of novels about the fictional county of Barsetshire. Among these novels were *The Warden* and *Barchester Towers.*

Tromp, Maarten Harpertszoon 1597–1653. Dutch admiral. Given supreme command of the Dutch navy, he decisively defeated the Spanish in battle (1639) in the English Channel. He was killed in the Dutch War (1652–54) with the English.

Troppau, Congress of *See* **Congress of Troppau.**

Trotsky, Leon (*pseud. of* Bronstein, Lev Davidovich) 1879–1940. Russian Communist leader. He was a chief theorist, a leader in both the 1905 and 1917 revolutions, and N. Lenin's commissar for foreign affairs. In the latter capacity he arranged the Treaty of Brest-Litovsk with Germany. He next became war commissar, rebuilding the Russian army. Trotsky and his arch-rival, J. Stalin, struggled for power after Lenin's death (1924). Stalin eventually stripped Trotsky of his influence and expelled him from Russia in 1929. Trotsky spent the rest of his life in exile, writing and preaching revolution. Stalin is believed to have masterminded his assassination in Mexico City.

Trotskyism Doctrine of a "permanent revolution" on a worldwide scale advocated by Russian Communist leader L. Trotsky. This doctrine along with Trotsky's advocacy of a greater role for the working class led to his struggle with J. Stalin, who advocated "socialism in one country." Trotsky was ultimately exiled from Russia and assassinated.

Troubadours Medieval lyric poets who composed in the dialect of Provence, *langue d'oc*, in southern France. They flourished between the 11th and the 13th cents. and greatly influenced subsequent European literature.

Trouvère Medieval lyric poets and musicians who composed in the *langue d'ol,* the language of northern France and of the French court centered around Paris. They began writing in imitation of the troubadours, and flourished in the 12th and 13th cents.

Troy Ancient city located along the Hellespont in what is now Asian Turkey. Made famous by the legendary Trojan War (*q.v.*), Troy flourished (3d–2d millennium BC) as the center of Troas. Archaeological evidence indicates it was abandoned from 1100 to 700 BC (after the war). New cities were later built on the site until Roman times. The site was identified as the actual location of the legendary Troy by H. Schliemann, who began archaeological digs there in 1870.

Troyes, Chrétien de *See* **Chrétien de Troyes.**

Troyes, Treaty of Treaty (May 21, 1420) between England and France, an attempt to settle the Hundred Years' War (1337–1453). English king Henry V was to marry the daughter of Charles VI and thereby become successor to the French throne. But the disinherited French dauphin (later Charles VII) resisted the settlement with the aid of Joan of Arc.

Truce of *See under names inverted, as in* **Altmark, Truce of.**

Trucial Coast *See* **United Arab Emirates.**

Trucial Oman *See* **United Arab Emirates.**

Trucial States *See* **United Arab Emirates.**

Trudeau, Pierre Elliott 1919–   . French Canadian Liberal party leader and prime minister (1968–79, 1980–84). He championed liberal domestic programs, won constitutional reforms that included severing Canada's last ties to British Parliament, and steadfastly opposed the French separatist movement. Of French descent, Trudeau won his law degree from the University of Montreal (1943) and practiced law from 1951 to 1961. After teaching law at the University of Montreal (1961–65), he entered Parliament (1965) and served in Liberal government cabinet posts. Trudeau became prime minister (1968) following L. Pearson's retirement. His first term was marked by his opposition to French separatists (though he favored bilingualism), establishment of diplomatic relations with China (1970), and imposition of wage-price controls (1975–78). Continuing economic problems

brought down his government (1979), but Trudeau returned to office (1980) following a short-lived Conservative government. His new term saw the defeat of a French separatist referendum in Quebec (1980) and adoption of a new constitution for Canada (1982), ending the last vestiges of British control of Canada. Continuing economic problems and the failure of his international "peace crusade" led to Trudeau's resignation as prime minister in 1984.

Truffaut, François 1932–84.   French film director and critic. He directed such films as *The 400 Blows* (1959) and *Jules and Jim* (1961). considered typical examples of the "new wave" films.

Trujillo Molina, Rafael Leonidas 1891–1961. General and dictator of the Dominican Republic (1930–61). His rule was marked by ruthless suppression of opposition, which ultimately led to his assassination.

Truman, Harry S 1884–1972.   Thirty-third US president (1945–53), successor to F. Roosevelt. A US senator from Missouri (1935–45), he gained national attention as chairman of a Senate committee investigating defense expenditures. He was elected vice-president under Roosevelt in 1944 and became president on Roosevelt's death (Apr. 12, 1945). Truman participated in the Potsdam Conference (*q.v.*) and ended WW II by ordering the first use of the atomic bombs, dropped on Hiroshima and Nagasaki. Truman's postwar foreign policy was marked by rapidly deteriorating relations with Russia, leading to the Cold War (*q.v.*). He countered Soviet postwar expansion by issuing the Truman Doctrine (*q.v.*), which was intended to contain Communism. It was implemented by the Marshall Plan (*q.v.*), the Point Four Program (*q.v.*), and establishment of NATO (*q.v.*). The Berlin blockade and airlift (*q.v.*) of 1948–49 began during this period. At home, much of his domestic legislation was blocked by Congress, which passed the Taft-Hartley Labor Act (1947) over Truman's veto. Truman received the 1948 Democratic presidential nomination and conducted an energetic whistle-stop campaign. He won the election and outwitted the pollsters who predicted that Republican candidate T. Dewey would become president. His second term was marked by continued Congressional resistance to proposed legislation of his Fair Deal (*q.v.*) program and the outbreak of the Korean War (*q.v.*). During the conflict he aroused a national controversy by dismissing Gen. D. MacArthur from command for insubordination (1951). Truman did not seek reelection in 1952, but supported the candidacy of A. Stevenson.

Truman Doctrine US foreign-policy decision, embodied in a message of President H. Truman of Mar. 12, 1947, calling for military aid to Greece and Turkey to fight Communist rebellions. It signaled US determination to "contain" the further expansion of Communism.

Trumbull, John 1756–1843. Early American painter. He served as an aide to G. Washington in the Revolutionary War and later studied under the painter B. West in London. In 1784 he began his famous series of historical paintings, including *Battle of Bunker's Hill* (1786) and *Death of Montgomery at Quebec* (1788).

Trumbull, Jonathan 1710–85. American patriot. He became governor of Connecticut (1769–84) and during the Revolutionary War supplied G. Washington with war materials and other services.

trust Form of business combine or corporation established to create a monopoly over a particular business or industry. Trusts rose to positions of great power in the US during the late 19th cent. Among the greatest were the oil, steel, sugar, and meat-packing trusts. Their activities led to passage of the Sherman Antitrust Act (*q.v.*) of 1890 and they were vigorously prosecuted during the presidency of T. Roosevelt.

trusteeship Method of governing territories. It was established in 1946 by the UN to replace the former League of Nations mandates (*q.v.*). By the mid-1970s, nearly all the UN trusteeship territories had become independent nations and UN members.

Truth, Sojourner c1797–1883. Former slave and evangelist. Freed in 1827, she embarked on a notable career as a traveling speaker for the Christian Gospels, abolition, and women's rights.

Tryon, William 1729–88. British Colonial governor. As governor of North Carolina, he suppressed the Regulator Movement (*q.v.*). As Governor of New York during the Revolutionary War period, he was at first forced to govern from a British warship.

Ts'ao Ts'ao *See* **Cao Cao.**

Tseng Kuo-fan *See* **Zeng Guofang.**

Tshombe, Moise Kapenda 1919–69. Congolese leader. Tshombe led Katanga in secession (1960–63) from the newly independent Congo Republic, was said to be implicated in the murder of P. Lumumba, and was finally exiled (1963). He returned to become premier (1964–65) of a reunited Congo Republic, but soon after was accused of treason and fled.

Tsin *See* **Jin.**

Tsong-kha-pa *See* **Tibetan Buddhism.**

Tsu Hsi *See* **Tz'u Hsi.**

Tsushima, Battle of *See* **Russo-Japanese War.**

Tubman, Harriet (*orig.* Araminta) c1820–1913. American abolitionist. An escaped slave, she was a principal figure in the Underground Railroad. She aided the Union army during the Civil War.

Tubman, William Vacanarat Shadrach 1895–1971. Liberian president (1943–71). A descendant of freed American slaves, he filled various governmental posts before becoming president. His long tenure was marked by economic progress and social reforms, including granting to women and native Liberians the right to vote.

Tudor Dynasty of English rulers (reigned 1485–1603). The family was of Welsh origins. Its rise to power began with Owen Tudor (*d.* 1461), who fought in the service of Henry V, wed Henry's widow (Catherine of Valois), and supported his Lancastrian stepson, Henry VI, in the Wars of the Roses (*q.v.*). Owen Tudor's grandson (Henry Tudor) became Henry VII after the Lancastrian victory at Bosworth Field (1485) and thus founded the Tudor dynasty. The subsequent Tudor reign saw the rise of England as a naval power, creation of the Church of England, and increased powers of the monarchy. *The Tudor sovereigns were:* Henry VII 1485–1509: Henry VIII 1509–47; Edward VI 1547–53; Mary 1553–58; Elizabeth I 1558–1603.

Tu Fu *See* **Du Fu.**

Tuileries Palace, Storming of the Assault on the French royal palace in Paris (Aug. 10, 1792) during the French Revolution. The attack led to a massacre of the Swiss Guards. French king Louis XVI was suspended from all authority by the Legislative Assembly.

Tully *See* **Cicero, Marcus Tullius.**

Tulunid dynasty *See* **Egypt (868).**

T'ung Chih *See* **Tongzhi.**

Tunisia Republic located in northwestern Africa. The population is 8,094,000 and the capital is Tunis. Once part of Carthage (6th cent. BC), it was conquered (2d cent. BC) by the Romans, then was taken by the Vandals (5th cent. AD), Byzantines (6th cent.), and the Muslims (7th cent.). It thrived under Muslim influence and fell (late 16th cent.) to the Ottoman Turks. Under the rule of Ottoman governors, or beys, Tunisia gained virtual independence within the Ottoman Empire, and became a center for piracy in the 18th and early 19th cents. A French expedition to Tunisia led to establishment (1881) of a French protectorate. The drive for independence began after WW I, and from 1934 H. Bourguiba became a leading figure in the nationalist movement. During WW II, Tunisia was occupied by German and Italian forces and was the site (1943) of fierce fighting between Allied and Axis armies in the North Africa Campaign (q.v.). Following a guerrilla war mounted by rebels against French colonial forces, Tunisia became a republic (July 25, 1957). H. Bourguiba became its first prime minister and first president (1957–87). Bourguiba followed a policy of modernization and agrarian reform and supported a negotiated end to the Middle East crisis between Israel and the Arab nations. During the 1970s his rule was marked by political unrest and by conflict (1980) with Libya. The government sought better relations with Libya following Bourguiba's ouster by Gen. Zine el Abidine Ben Ali (president 1987–   ), and in 1989 the country joined Libya and other African states in an economic organization called the Maghreb Union. Mass pro-Iraqi demonstrations were held (Jan., 1991) by Muslims in Tunisia during the Persian Gulf War.

Tupac Amaru 1742?–81.   Peruvian Indian revolutionary. Taking the name of an ancestral Inca leader, he led Peruvian Indians in a revolt (1780–81) to improve their lot. He was captured and executed.

Tupper, Sir Charles 1821–1915.   Canadian statesman. As premier of Nova Scotia (1864–67), he helped bring that crown colony into the dominion. He was instrumental in promoting the Canadian Pacific Railway and was briefly the federal prime minister (1896) as a Conservative.

Turckheim, Battle of   French victory (Jan. 5, 1675) over the Austrians in the second Dutch War. French marshal H. Turenne led his forces on a winter march across the Vosges, surprised and routed the Austrians under Count Montecuccoli in the Alsace region. France recovered Alsace by this one battle.

Turenne, Henri de la Tour d'Auvergne, vicomte de 1611–75.   Great French military leader. Turenne was created a marshal for his brilliant service in

the Thirty Years' War. Though he sided unsuccessfully with Louis II de Bourbon, Prince de Condé in the Fronde of the Parlement (q.v.), Turenne rejoined the government and defeated the Condé in the Fronde of the Princes (q.v.). He also conducted notable campaigns in the Dutch War (1672–78). He was killed in battle.

Turgenev, Ivan Sergeyevich 1818–83.   Russian novelist. Turgenev chronicled the plight of the serfs in *A Sportsman's Sketches* (1852). He covered the conflict between the older aristocracy and the new, emancipated, nihilistic generation of Russian intelligentsia in *Fathers and Sons* (1862).

Turgot, Anne Robert Jacques 1727–81.   French economist and statesman. A Physiocrat (q.v.), he was controller of finance (1774–76) and attempted by drastic reforms to restore the royal treasury. He was opposed by Queen Marie Antoinette, however, and his ouster continued the financial crisis that contributed to the outbreak of the French Revolution.

Turkestan   *See* **Turkistan.**

Turkey (Republic of Turkey)   Republic located in southwestern Asia (*pop.* 56,549,000). Its capital is Ankara. The modern state of Turkey was created following the collapse of the Ottoman Empire after WW I. A republic was established (1923) by the Nationalists led by Mustafa Kemal (Kemal Atatürk). Atatürk, as the country's first president, embarked on a program of democratization, industrialization, and Westernization that profoundly changed the once Islamic-dominated Turkish life and institutions. For history of the region prior to 1920, *see* Ottoman Empire. Key dates in the history of Turkey include:

1920   Nationalist party, under Mustafa Kemal (later known as Kemal Atatürk), established national government at Ankara (Apr.), in defiance of both the victorious Allied powers and the Ottoman Sultan Muhammad VI.

1920   Treaty of Sèvres (Aug. 10) between Allies and Ottoman sultan; dismembered the Ottoman Empire and established Ottoman successor state in northern Anatolia; treaty opposed by Nationalists.

1920–21   Short-lived Armenian republic established in northeast; Turkish troops retook control by force and expelled surviving Armenians from the region.

1921   Atatürk and Nationalists entered into treaty of friendship with Soviet Union; continued to resist foreign encroachment in Turkey.

1921–22 Greco-Turkish War fought with Greece after Greek invasion of Anatolia; Atatürk drove the Greeks from Anatolia.

1922 Ottoman sultan deposed (Nov. 1) by Nationalist government; his brother assumed the caliphate, but the sultanate ceased to exist.

1923 Republican People's party founded by Atatürk; sole Turkish party until 1946.

1923 Turkish republic proclaimed (Oct. 29); new constitution instituted and Atatürk made first president; government abolished caliphate (1924) and eliminated state support for Islam.

1923 Treaty of Lausanne negotiated with Allies; established borders of modern Turkey, except for contested territory of Alexandretta; Turkey agreed to demilitarization of Dardanelles strait.

1923–38 Atatürk served as president; led successful program of Westernization and industrialization of Turkey; ended religious instruction in schools and abolished Islamic courts; introduced Latin alphabet and Gregorian calendar; adopted democratic reforms but held great personal power.

1928 Turkish state officially secularized, ending traditional Islamic religious dominance.

1932 Turkey admitted to League of Nations.

1934 Women granted right to vote.

1934 Atatürk introduced use of surnames.

1934 Turkey entered Balkan Entente with Greece, Yugoslavia, and Rumania.

1936 Montreux Convention signed; military control of the Dardanelles returned to Turkey.

1938–50 Ismet Inönü served as president, following the death of Atatürk; maintained policy of neutrality through most of WW II.

1939 Territory of Alexandretta ceded to Turkey by France.

1945 Turkey declared war (Feb. 23) on Germany and Japan at end of WW II.

1945 Russia renounced friendship treaty with Turkey (Mar.); demanded cession of Kars and Ardahan (in eastern Turkey) and joint military control of Dardanelles; relations between the two countries broken following Turkish refusal.

1945 Turkey became (June 26) a founding member of the UN.

1946 Opposition political parties legalized, ending one-party system.

1947 US granted (Mar. 24) military and economic aid to Turkey under Truman Doctrine.

1950 Newly formed Democratic party victorious in national elections (May 22); Celal Bayar succeeded Inönü as president; Adnan Menderes made prime minister.

1952 Turkey entered NATO.

1955 Joined Baghdad Pact, which later became CENTO.

1960 Increasing economic problems and rising unrest in the 1950s led to passage of increasingly repressive laws; antigovernment demonstrations (Apr.) broke out and a military coup led by Gen. Cemal Gürsel overthrew government (May); Bayar, Menderes and others arrested; Menderes subsequently executed.

1961 New constitution formulated; Gürsel elected president (Oct.); Ismet Inönü made prime minister.

1961–65 Gürsel in office as president.

1962 Unsuccessful attempt (Feb.) by military officers to overthrow government.

1965–71 Süleyman Demirel served as prime minister; unable to solve country's growing problems.

1966–73 Cevdet Sunay became president following death of Cemal Gürsel.

1971–73 Military in power after widespread student and labor unrest brought down Demirel government.

1973–79 Fahri Korutürk in office as president, marking return to civilian government.

1973 Increase in terrorist attacks by radical Armenian groups directed at Turkish officials abroad.

1974 Bülent Ecevit in office as prime minister.

1974 Turkish forces invaded Cyprus (July 20–22) to protect Turkish Cypriots; invasion came after Cypriot leader Archbishop Makarios was ousted by a pro-Greek military coup.

1975 Süleyman Demirel returned to office as prime minister.

1978 Martial law declared (Dec.) in 13 provinces to counter unrest by Muslim sects.

1979 CENTO dissolved after Pakistan and Iran withdrew.

1980 Turkey signed agreement allowing US use of bases there (Mar.); agreement extended 1987, 1990.

1980 Military coup (Sept. 11) overthrew elected government in wake of growing unrest over economic problems; Gen. Kenan Evren in power; constitution suspended and assembly dissolved.

1980–82 Arrest of some 66,000 terrorists, extremists, and opposition figures as government quashed unrest.

1981 Government dissolved political parties.

1981 Military regime granted unlimited powers (Dec.).

1982 New constitution approved.

1982–89 Gen. Evren in office as president for seven-year term; allowed some loosening of controls, but charges of human rights abuses continued during his administration.

1983 Formation of some political parties allowed, with tight restrictions; conservative Motherland Party won majority of seats to single-house National Assembly.

1983 Turkey recognized newly formed Turkish Republic of Northern Cyprus, the only nation to do so.

1984 Council of Europe readmitted Turkey, rescinding a ban imposed after the 1980 military coup; Turkey readmitted as associate EEC member in 1986.

1984 Guerrilla campaign against government begun by Kurdish Workers' Party, Marxist group advocating creation of Kurdish homeland in southern Turkey.

1986 Turkey, under international pressure to end human rights abuses, agreed to end martial law and to amnesty political prisoners.

1987 Ban on political activity by 200 former politicians (imposed in 1981) ended by national referendum.

1988 State of emergency in Istanbul, invoked in 1980, officially ended.

1988 Over 100,000 Iraqi Kurds fled across border to Turkey, following Iraqi offensive against Kurdish secessionists in Iraq.

1988–89 Fighting between Kurdish guerrillas and government troops intensified; some 2,000 reported killed since 1984.

1989– ANAP leader Turgut Ozal in office as president, following elections.

1990 Urban terrorism by Muslims and left-wing groups reported increasing.

1990 Turkey condemned Iraqi invasion of Kuwait; helped enforce UN economic sanctions against Iraq; allowed coalition forces unrestricted use of NATO bases in Turkey.

1991 General strike by about 1.5 million workers to protest low wages and unsatisfactory working conditions (Jan.); government responded with 60-day ban on strikes.

1991 5,000 political prisoners released following government move toward liberalization.

1991 Some 500,000 Iraqi Kurds fled across Turkish border as Iraqi army put down Kurdish revolt in northern Iraq.

1992 Government to sell holdings in private sector businesses to raise capital (Feb.).

Turkistan (Turkestan) Central Asian region between China, Siberia, and the Caspian Sea. Home of predominantly Turkic peoples, and once dominated by the Mongols, much of it was conquered by the Russians in the 19th cent. It is divided today between the former USSR (Western Turkistan) and China (Eastern Turkistan).

Turkmanchay, Treaty of Treaty (Feb. 22, 1828), between Russia and Persia, ending war with Persia (1826–28). Persia had to cede much of Persian Armenia to Russia and grant the latter extensive commercial and extraterritorial rights.

Turkmenia (*formerly* Turkmen Soviet Socialist Republic) Independent state located north of Iran and Afghanistan; now a member of the Commonwealth of Independent States (CIS). Controlled by various peoples during its early history (the Persians, Arabs, Mongols, and Uzbeks), Turkmenia eventually fell to Russian conquerors (1869–1881). Turkmenia mounted an unsuccessful revolt against the Bolsheviks (1917–19) during the revolution and was made a constituent republic of the USSR (1925). During the collapse of the Soviet Union in 1991, Turkmenia proclaimed its independence (Oct. 27) and joined the CIS on Dec. 21, 1991.

Turks Branch of the Central Asian Turkic people that migrated to the Middle East and Asia Minor between the 11th and the 13th cents. The first wave of Turkish migration was the Seljuks (*q.v.*), who by 1092 controlled Iran, Mesopotamia, Syria, and Palestine. Beginning from a base in the Seljuk sultanate of Rum, the Osmanli Turks began from the 13th cent. to build what became the Ottoman Empire. This later became the basis of modern Turkey.

Turner, Frederick Jackson 1861–1932. American historian. He virtually founded a school of American historical thought with his theory concerning the effect of the Western frontier on American society and government.

Turner, Joseph Mallord William 1775–1851. British artist. Considered the foremost English landscape and seascape painter, Turner was a Romantic whose works anticipated the impressionists.

Turner, Nat 1800–31. American slave leader. Believing he was called by God to emancipate America's black slaves, he led a rebellion by 60 slaves during Aug., 1831, that terrorized rural Virginia and cost the lives of 51 whites. Turner was captured and executed soon after the revolt broke out, but his revolt gave rise to repressive laws for controlling slaves.

Turpin, Richard 1706–39. English robber whose career as a horse thief and highwayman was much romanticized in popular literature.

Tuscany Italian province and historic region located in central Italy. It is centered on what was once the ancient Etruscan kingdom of Etruria and was a center of Italian culture in medieval Renaissance times. Florence and Pisa are among its notable cities.

Tutankhamen (Tutenkhamon) *d.* c1352 BC. Egyptian pharaoh (c1361–52). He restored the polytheistic religion (dominated by the god Amon) after the religious revolution of Akhenaton. His world-famous tomb was discovered in 1922.

Twain, Mark (*pseud. of* Clemens, Samuel Langhorne) 1835–1910. Noted American author who wrote the classics *The Adventures of Tom Sawyer* and *The Adventures of Huckleberry Finn.*

Tweed, William Marcy ("Boss") 1823–78. American politician and New York City "boss." Gaining control of Democratic party patronage, Tweed and his associates (Tweed Ring) made fortunes through their manipulation of city expenditures.

Tweed Ring Conspiracy of politicians, led by W. Tweed, who defrauded New York City of up to $30 million between 1856 and 1872. They controlled city and even some state offices through the Democratic party's Tammany (*q.v.*) machine. In 1871 they were exposed by *The New York Times* and a reform slate was elected to replace them.

Twelve Conclusions *See* **Lollardry.**

Twelve Tables *See* **Rome (450 BC).**

Twelve Tribes of Israel In the Bible, the Hebrew tribes that settled in the Promised Land after the Exodus. The tribes were named after Jacob's offspring. Ten were named after his sons, Reuben, Simeon, Judah, Issachar, Zebulun, Gad, Asher, Dan, Naphtali and Benjamin. Two were named after his grandsons Ephraim and Manasseh. (*See also* Lost Tribes of Israel.)

Twenty-one Demands List of demands presented to China by Japan (Jan., 1915) and backed by threat of invasion. China submitted May 25. The 21 demands included access to China's harbors and islands, control of mineral deposits, the right to colonize Manchuria and Mongolia, and the territorial exclusion of other world powers. China refused, however, to allow Japan to regulate its military, financial, and trade affairs, as was also demanded.

26th of July Movement Rebel movement organized by F. Castro that overthrew (Jan. 1, 1959) the dictatorship of F. Batista during the Cuban Revolution (*q.v.*). It began with Castro's abortive attack (July 26, 1953) with 150 rebels on the Moncada army barracks. Imprisoned after the raid (1953–55), Castro organized a new rebel force in Mexico. He landed in southwestern Cuba (Dec. 2, 1956) with 82 men and was quickly put to flight by government troops. However, he and 11 others managed to establish a base in the Sierra Maestra mountains. With E. Guevara, Castro mounted a guerrilla campaign against Batista that was increasingly successful in the following years. Rebel gains and the withdrawal of US aid to Cuba (1958) finally forced Batista to flee Cuba in 1959.

Two Sicilies, Kingdom of the Name of the kingdoms of Sicily and Naples, which included all of southern Italy below the Papal States and which were variously ruled separately and jointly from the 11th to 19th cents. The Kingdom of Two Sicilies was founded by the Normans, who conquered Sicily and the southern Italian Peninsula (Kingdom of Naples) from the Byzantines, Muslims, and Lombards. The territory passed to the Hohenstaufen Holy Roman emperors (12th cent.). Under them southern Italy became a prosperous commercial center from which Greek and Arab culture spread to Europe. The French nobleman Charles of Anjou conquered Sicily and the kingdom of Naples (1266) after the Hohenstaufen line died out, but he was driven out of Sicily (1282) after the Revolt of the Sicilian Vespers (*q.v.*). The Spanish House of Aragon then took control of Sicily (1302), while the kingdom of Naples remained in the hands of the French Angevin line. A long series of wars between Sicily and Naples ensued, with the Spanish Aragonese finally winning both kingdoms in 1442. Spanish rule was broken by the War of the Spanish Succession (1701–14) and the brief rule of the Austrian Habsburgs. By 1735, however, the Spanish Bourbons were again in firm control of both Sicily and Naples. Napoleon gained Italy at the end of the 18th cent. Spanish rule was restored in 1815, and from 1816 the kingdoms of Sicily and Naples were ruled jointly as the Kingdom of the Two Sicilies. The spread of liberalism and nationalism in the post-Napoleonic period gave rise to revolts by the Carbonari (*q.v.*) and the movement for unification of Italy. The Kingdom of the Two Sicilies was finally conquered (1860) by the Italian nationalist, G. Garibaldi, and was joined with northern states to form the kingdom of Italy (1861).

Tydings-McDuffie Act US legislation (Mar. 4, 1934) that created a Commonwealth of the Philippines. The Commonwealth (effective July 4, 1936) was to last for 10 years. The US continued to control Philippine defense, foreign affairs, and monetary matters during that period. Philippine independence was granted in 1946.

Tyler, John 1790–1862. Tenth US president (1841–45); successor to W. Harrison. Tyler served as US congressman (1817–21), governor of Virginia (1825–27), and US senator (1827–36). A supporter of states' rights and a follower of the ideas of T. Jefferson, Tyler opposed Pres. A. Jackson and became a Whig. His refusal to help expunge a motion censuring Jackson prompted his resignation from the Senate (1836). Tyler was elected vice-president (1841) under W. Harrison and, after Harrison's death (Apr., 1841), Tyler became the first vice-president to succeed to the presidency. His opposition to reestablishment of a national bank led to Tyler's loss of Whig support and the resignation of his cabinet, except for D. Webster, who remained to negotiate the Webster-Ashburton Treaty (*q.v.*) of 1842. Tyler's term of office was also marked by the end of the second Seminole War (1835–43) and by the annexation of Texas (1845). Chosen by a Democratic faction as presidential candidate (1844), Tyler withdrew from the race in favor of J. Polk. In Feb., 1861, Tyler

presided over the Washington Peace Conference, an unsuccessful attempt to avoid the Civil War. When the war came, he served in the provisional Confederate Congress.

Tyler, Moses Coit 1835–1900. American literary historian noted for his *A History of American Literature 1607–1765* and *A Literary History of the American Revolution.*

Tyler, Wat *d.* 1381. English rebel leader. He led the Peasants' Revolt (*q.v.*) in 1381.

Tylor, Sir Edward Burnett 1832–1917. British anthropologist. Often considered the founder of cultural anthropology, Tylor was noted for his theory of cultural evolution.

Tyndale, William (Tindal, ~) (Tindale, ~) *d.* 1536. Pursued by authorities of the English church, he translated the New Testament into English and published (1525) his vernacular edition at Worms. The edition was denounced and Tyndale was captured and burned at the stake some years later. His translation eventually provided the basis for the King James Bible.

Typhoid Mary (Mallon, Mary) *d.* 1938. Notorious "carrier" of typhoid fever. She worked as a cook in New York and caused numerous typhoid outbreaks in places where she worked before she was finally arrested (1915).

tyrant In Greek history, a ruler who usurped or acquired power by illegal means. The term was originally not connected with oppressive rule. Tyrants appeared especially during the 7th through 5th cents. BC and often favored the populace against the aristocrats. Instances of their misrule after the 5th cent. gradually gave the term its modern meaning.

Tyrconnel, Richard Talbot, duke and earl of 1630–91. Irish Jacobite leader. Appointed lord deputy of Ireland (1687) by James II, Tyrconnel attempted to continue ruling Ireland after James was deposed (1688) in the Glorious Revolution. He was defeated at the Battle of the Boyne (*q.v.*) and died shortly thereafter.

Tyre Ancient port city on the Mediterranean Sea and located in what is now Lebanon. It was capital of Phoenicia (11th–6th cents. BC) and a famed commercial center for centuries. It was conquered by Alexander the Great (332 BC), by the Romans (64 BC), and by the Muslims (7th cent. AD). It was destroyed when the Muslims retook it from the Crusaders in 1291.

Tyre, William of *See* **William of Tyre.**

Tz'û Hsi *See* **Cixi.**

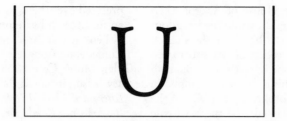

Uccello, Paolo c1396–1475. Florentine painter, noted for his pioneering use of perspective and foreshortening in his works.

Uesugi clan Japanese clan. Founded during the Kamakura shogunate, it rose (15th cent.) to great power in Japan. It challenged (early 17th cent.) the Tokugawa clan for control in Japan but was defeated. It continued to rule in northern Honshu until the fall of the Tokugawa shogunate (1868).

Uffizi Palace in Florence, Italy. Built in the 16th cent., it is now the site of the Uffizi Gallery, one of the greatest art museums in the world.

Uganda (Republic of Uganda) Independent state (*pop.* 17,593,000) located in east-central Africa. Its capital is Kampala. Governed by Britain until 1962, it was under the rule of the notorious dictator I. Amin during the 1970s. Key dates in Ugandan history include:

AD 1100   Bantu-speaking peoples arrived.

FROM c1500   Buganda kingdom established; chief among many kingdoms and tribes occupying present Uganda.

1844   Uganda first visited by Arab traders.

1862   British explorer John Speke was first European in region.

1870s   British and French missionaries arrived.

1880s   Natives slaughtered Christians.

1890   Anglo-German agreement placed Uganda in British sphere of influence.

1894   British protectorate established by British East Africa Company.

1894–1962   British colonial occupation; firm control of countryside established by 1918; small-scale agriculture by native Ugandans developed; Asian immigrants (from Indian subcontinent) controlled commerce.

1962   Uganda became independent (Oct. 9).

1963   Uganda became a republic.

1963–66   Mutesa II, king of Buganda region, in office as president; Dr. Milton Obote, leader of Uganda People's Congress, served as prime minister.

1966   Mutesa overthrown in coup led by Obote (Feb.).

1966–71   Obote in power as head of state.

1967   New constitution instituted by Prime Minister Obote; abolished traditional kingdoms, notably the still-powerful Buganda, and gave central government more power.

1969   Unsuccessful attempt to assassinate Obote (Dec.); Obote subsequently banned opposition political parties.

1970   Banks and import-export businesses nationalized as Obote tried to adopt leftist course.

1971   I. Amin ousted Obote (Jan 25); established dictatorship, dissolving legislature and banning political activity.

1971–79   Amin ruled Uganda; his reign marked by ruthless brutality, including reported deaths of some 300,000 of his opponents, the mass exodus of refugees, and increasing tensions with neighboring states.

1972   Amin expelled all Asians with British passports and all Israeli advisers.

1975   Amin nationalized all lands without compensation.

1976   Entebbe Raid; Israelis rescued passengers of airliner hijacked by Palestinians; airliner had been held in Uganda with Amin's apparent approval.

1976   Hostilities with Kenya ended by formal agreement.

1978   Border clashes with Tanzania; Uganda annexed Tanzanian territory.

1978 Force of Ugandan rebels (Ugandan National Liberation Army, UNLA) and Tanzanian regular troops invaded Uganda (Nov.).

1979 Kampala taken (Apr. 11); Ugandan insurgents aided by Tanzanians deposed Amin, who fled to Libya; provisional government set up.

1979–80 Period of political unrest in which successive provisional governments failed or were ousted.

1980 Military commission under Paulo Muwanga took power.

1980 First elections in years; constitutional government restored; Obote became president.

1980–85 Obote in office as president; his administration marked by increasing guerrilla resistance and institution of harsh measures against opposition.

1981 Antigovernment insurgents reported making frequent terrorist attacks.

1983 National Resistance Army (NRA) launched major offensive (Mar.); many civilians killed and some 100,000 forced to flee.

1985 Obote overthrown in military coup led by UNLA (July 27); military council assumed power.

1985–86 Gen. Tito Okello, army commander, in power as head of state; UNLA soldiers reported continuing human rights abuses.

1985–86 Civil war between NRA troops and forces loyal to Okello; NRA captured Kampala (Jan. 16, 1986) and seized power.

1986– Former defense minister Yoweri Museveni in power as president; formed coalition government; organized system of village government by "Resistance Committees"; banned political activity for five years (extended in 1990).

1986 Government investigated abuses by police over past decades; fired over 80 percent for corruption or unsuitability.

1986–87 "Holy Spirit" rebellion; religious fanatics, led by Alice Lakwena, mounted suicidal attacks on NRA positions in northern and eastern regions; some 5,000 killed before order was restored (Nov. 1987).

1987–88 Inflation, averaging over 100 percent a year since 1980, hit high of 200 percent during this time; by 1990 rate had been reduced to 29 percent, however, following austerity measures enacted by government.

1988 Some 30,000 rebels belonging to various groups surrendered by this time in government amnesty program (Apr.).

1989 National elections held for elective seats to ruling National Resistance Council (NRC).

1989 About 350,000 Ugandan refugees, who fled political unrest and outright war, returned from Sudan by this time.

Ugolino della Gherardesca *d.* 1289. Italian Guelph nobleman who gained control of Pisa (1284). Political intrigues led to his downfall and to a charge of treason. His brutal death by starvation is related by Dante in the *Inferno.*

Uigurs (Uighurs) Turkic people of central Asia. They several times achieved political prominence, and an Uigur Empire flourished in the 8th and 9th cents. Today they are a Sunni Muslim people living mostly in Chinese Xiniang.

Ukraine (*formerly* Ukrainian Soviet Socialist Republic) Independent state and member of the Commonwealth of Independent States. Inhabited as early as c8500 BC, the region lay in the path of various peoples migrating to Europe from central Asia. It fell to the Varangians, invaders from Scandinavia, to establish a distinctly Ukrainian culture there in the 9th cent., centered on the city of Kiev and the surrounding domains controlled by Kievan rulers. From the mid-11th cent., the state of Kiev began to break up, and was finally destroyed in the 13th by the invasion of the Golden Horde. In the 14th cent., Lithuania expanded into the Ukraine. In the 15th the union of Poland and Lithuania brought the Ukraine under Polish control and introduced the feudal system there. But the Poles' harsh rule caused many Ukrainian serfs to flee eastward and southward. These expatriates became known as Cossacks (outlaws, adventurers) and following a revolt (1648–54), the Cossack leader B. Chmielnicki established a short-lived independent state. The Russians soon won control of the eastern Ukraine (1667) and by 1793 controlled the entire region. Nevertheless the movement for Ukrainian independence continued through the 19th cent., and after the Russian Revolution the Ukraine declared its independence (1918). The Soviets recognized it by the Treaty of Brest-Litovsk (1918) but later overran the Ukraine and made it a constituent republic (1922). Stalin's forced collectivization program (early 1920s) resulted in a widespread famine that killed millions of Ukrainians. In 1986, the Ukraine became the site of yet another disaster, the Chernobyl (*q.v.*) nuclear accident in which hundreds were killed outright and thousands of others were exposed to dangerous levels of radiation. Subsequently the Ukraine became one of the leading republics in the fight for greater autonomy from the USSR, and in July, 1990, declared its independence for the first time. Full independence came after a declaration issued on Aug. 24, 1991, making Ukraine the first republic to secede from the USSR in the aftermath of the failed Soviet coup. Ukraine was one of the three original Slavic republics to join the CIS (Dec. 8, 1991).

Ulbricht, Walter 1893–1973. East German Communist leader. A founder of the German Communist party, he became deputy premier of the German Democratic Republic in 1949 and was secretary general of the Social Unity party (1950–71). He ordered the building of the Berlin Wall (1961) and was ousted when the USSR began a policy of rapproachement with West Germany (1971).

Ulm, Battle of French victory (Oct. 20, 1805) over the Austrians at Ulm, Germany, during the War of the Third Coalition. By brilliant maneuvering, Napoleon surrounded the Austrian army led by Baron Karl Mack von Leiberich (1752–1828) and compelled Mack to surrender some 20,000 troops.

Ulm, Treaty of Truce (1647) between the French and Swedish forces and Bavaria toward the end of the Thirty Years' War.

Ulpian (Ulpianus, Domitius) *d.* AD 228. Roman jurist, Praetorian prefect (AD 222–228) under Alexander Severus. His voluminous writings were a major source for the *Digest* of Justinian I.

Ulpianus, Domitius *See* **Ulpian.**

Ulster *See* **Northern Ireland.**

ultraismo Post-WW I poetic movement in Spain and Spanish America. Influenced by the French symbolist and Parnassian movements, it sought to develop poetry beyond its traditional limits.

ultramontanism In the history of the Roman Catholic church, the belief that papal jurisdiction is supreme. It opposed Gallicanism and was upheld by the Vatican Council (1869–70), which promulgated the doctrine of papal infallibility.

Ultraroyalists (Ultras) French reactionary royalist faction that advocated increased monarchial powers following the restoration of King Louis XVIII.

Umar *See* **Omar.**

Umayyad (Omayyad) Muslim dynasty which ruled (661–750) the Caliphate (*q.v.*). The Umayyads held power after the first four orthodox caliphs, so-called because the legitimacy of their reigns is unquestioned. The Umayyads, however, took power after Muawiya, founder of the dynasty, assumed the Caliphate after the death of the caliph Ali in 651. The accession of Muawiya gave rise to the split between the majority Sunni Muslim sect (which does not support Ali and his heirs as the only legitimate successors to the Caliphate) and the Shi'ite sect (supporters of Ali and his successors). The Umayyads established their capital at Damascus, continued the expansion of the Caliphate (Spain, northwest Indian, and the Transcaucasus were conquered), established effective systems of communication, and instituted administrative reforms. Internal unrest mounted toward the end of their reign and a successful revolt (c748) brought the Abbasid dynasty (*q.v.*) to power. Following the revolt, members of the Umayyad family were massacred. Only one is known to have escaped (Abd ar-Rahman I) and he established the Umayyad dynasty in Spain (in power 755–1031). *Umayyad caliphs are:* Muawiya 661–680; Yazid 680–683; Muawiya II 683; Marwan I 683–685; Abd al-Malik 685–705; Walid I 705–715; Sulayman 715–717; Umar II 717–720; Yazid II 720–724; Hisham 724–743; Walid II 743; Yazid III 743–744; Ibrahim 744; Marwan II 744–750.

Umberto I *See* **Humbert I.**

Umberto II *See* **Humbert II.**

Umbria Mountainous region of central Italy. Conquered by the Romans (3d cent. BC), it was part of the Papal States until incorporated into the kingdom of Italy (1860).

UN *See* **United Nations.**

Uncas c1588–c1683. American Indian chief. A Pequot, he broke away and formed the Mohegan Indian tribe. He fought with the British in the Pequot War (*q.v.*) and waged successful war against the Narragansett Indians.

Underground Railroad Secret system in the United States, organized (c1838) by abolitionists, freed slaves, philanthropists, and church leaders, to help Southern slaves escape to freedom in the North and Canada. Until slavery was ended, the organization provided a network of safe havens for escaping slaves on their way to the North. More than 40,000 slaves were said to have been aided by the Underground Railroad. Among the many opponents of slavery who were directly involved in its operation were H. Tubman, a former slave, and H. B. Stowe, the author of *Uncle Tom's Cabin.* The system helped increase Northerners' sympathy for the plight of slaves and also convinced Southerners that the North would never end its opposition to slavery.

Unequal treaties   *See* **China, 1839–43.**

uniformitarianism   *See* **Lyell, Sir Charles.**

Uniformity, Act of   *See* **Church of England** (1549).

Union, Acts of   *See* **Acts of Union.**

union, labor   *See* **labor unions.**

Union League Clubs   Organizations formed in the Northern US states during the Civil War to inspire support for the Union. During Reconstruction the clubs raised support for Republican candidates among newly enfranchised blacks and inadvertently aided the rise of the Ku Klux Klan.

Union of   *See also names inverted, as in* **Utrecht, Union of.**

Union of October 17   *See* **Octobrists.**

Union of Soviet Socialist Republics   *See* **Commonwealth of Independent States.**

unions   *See* **labor unions.**

Unitarianism   Christian denomination. Unitarians deny the doctrine of the Trinity, maintaining that God is one divine, indivisible force. The Unitarian concept has existed under various names since the earliest days of Christianity, but organized Unitarianism had its roots in the Protestant Reformation. Unitarians suffered numerous persecutions, particularly in Poland. They were among America's earliest Colonial settlers and were especially populous in New England and Pennsylvania. The American Unitarian Association was formally established in 1825.

Unitarios   One of the two political groups that sought control of Argentina in the early 19th cent. Favoring strong central government, they opposed the Federalists, who favored greater autonomy in the provinces. The Unitarios came to power during the presidency of B. Rivadavia (1826–27).

Unitas Fratrum   *See* **Moravian church.**

United Arab Emirates   Federation of Arab emirates located on the eastern Arabian Peninsula. The population is 2,250,000 and the capital is Abu Dhabi. Member states include Abu Dhabi, Ajman, Dubai, Fujairah, Ras al-Khaimah, Sharjah, and Umm al-Qaiwain. They were formerly called the Trucial States, Trucial Oman, or the Trucial Coast because of the truces signed by each emirate with Great Britain in 1820. The agreements were later renewed. In the wake of the British withdrawal from the region, the emirates formed the federation in 1971. Ras al-Khaimah chose not to join the federation but reversed its decision in 1972. Oil production (beginning 1962 in Abu Dhabi) has made the United Arab Emirates extremely wealthy on a per capita basis. The government nationalized the Abu Dhabi Petroleum Co. in 1975. More recently, toward the end of the Iran-Iraq war in 1988, Iranian gunboats attacked some United Arab Emirates oil installations in the Persian Gulf. The country has also become a major international banking center, and in 1991 was embroiled in the international BCCI banking scandal. The ruling family of Abu Dhabi held (since 1990) controling interest in the bank, which was shut down in 69 countries.

United Arab Republic   Name designating the political union between Egypt and Syria (1958–61). Yemen also joined the union (1958). Intended to be the nucleus of the United Arab States, it broke up after a coup *d'état* in Syria and Syria's subsequent withdrawal (1961).

United Empire Loyalists   Term applied to those Colonial settlers who supported the British during the American Revolution, especially those who migrated to Canada from the US.

United Front   Union formed twice between the Chinese Communist party and the Guomindang (1924–26, 1936–45). The second alliance was established to achieve a common front against the Japanese invaders.

United Irishmen   (United Irish Society)   Irish political organization founded (1791) by T. W. Tone and others to secure legislative reforms. Suppressed by the British, it became an underground movement and played a key role in the Irish rebellion of 1798.

United Irish Society   *See* **United Irishmen.**

United Kingdom of Great Britain and Northern Ireland   Official name of Great Britain since 1921. The United Kingdom includes England,

Scotland, Wales, Northern Ireland, and several smaller islands. (*See* Great Britain).

United Malays National Organization Malayan political organization. Founded (1946) to oppose British plans for a Malayan union, it played a key role in establishing (Feb. 1, 1948) the Federation of Malaya and also in securing Malayan independence (Aug. 31, 1957).

United Methodist church (United Methodists) US Protestant denomination formed (1968) by the union of the Methodist and the Evangelical United Brethren churches.

United Nations (UN) International body formed during WW II by the nations allied against the Axis. The term was first used by President F. Roosevelt (1941), and the concept of a permanent body to deal with international problems posing a threat to world peace gained momentum with the Moscow Declaration (Oct. 30, 1943), the Dumbarton Oaks Conference (Aug.–Oct., 1944), and the Yalta Conference (Feb., 1945). A meeting of the Allied nations at the San Francisco Conference led to signing (June 26) and ratification (Oct. 24) of the United Nations Charter. The charter provided for several structures within the organization, the leading ones being the Secretariat, the Security Council, and the General Assembly. All members of the UN are represented in the General Assembly, which makes decisions on political, budgetary, trusteeship, and administrative questions. The Security Council includes 15 members, 5 of which—the US, the People's Republic of China, Great Britain, France, and the Russian Federation—are permanent members. The remaining 10 are elected to the council by the General Assembly. The Security Council deals with matters of international security, and in important decisions the affirmative votes of the permanent members are necessary. Hence, frequently UN action has been halted in crises by an effective veto by a member within the Security Council. The Secretariat deals largely with administrative matters involving the UN, but under Secretary-General D. Hammarskjöld, it gained in importance by adopting measures not specifically called for by the Security Council or General Assembly. From the 1950s, the membership of the UN has grown substantially to more than 150 members. Key dates in UN history include:

1942 Declaration of the UN signed by 26 nations supporting aims of the Atlantic Charter (Jan.); later signed by 21 other nations.

1943 Moscow Declaration on General Security (Oct. 30); US, China, Britain, and the USSR approved international organization dedicated to world peace.

1944 Dunbarton Oaks Conference (Aug.–Oct.); US, Britain, USSR, and China planned for international peacekeeping agency; drew up plan for security council on which the four nations (plus France) would be permanent members.

1945 San Francisco Conference (began Apr. 25); 51 nations took part in planning UN organization; UN charter signed (June 26).

1945 UN charter took effect (Oct. 24); day thereafter celebrated as United Nations Day.

1945 World Bank (International Bank for Reconstruction and Development) became a UN agency; to provide financial aid for developing nations.

1945 UNFAO (UN Food and Agricultural Organization) established.

1946–52 Norwegian Trygve Lie served as first UN secretary-general; became outspoken and at times critical advocate for world peace.

1946 UN voted to establish headquarters in New York City (Feb. 14).

1945 First official UN act created the Atomic Energy Commission to oversee and control development of atomic energy.

1946 Human Rights Commission established; promulgated Universal Declaration of Human Rights, which was later approved by all General Assembly members (1948).

1946 UNESCO (UN Educational, Scientific, and Cultural Organization) founded.

1946 UNICEF (UN children's fund) founded.

1946 J. D. Rockefeller, Jr., donated $8.5 million to UN for purchase of 18.5-acre lot in New York City for site of UN permanent headquarters; New York City donated additional acreage (1947).

1947 UN flag adopted.

1947 UN Security Council approved division of Palestine in to Jewish and Arab states (Israel and Jordan); Jerusalem to be administered by UN.

1948 World Health Organization (WHO) became UN agency.

1948 US Congress approved interest-free loan for construction of UN headquarters.

1948–49 UN peace commission sought to end India-Pakistan conflict; arranged cease-fire (1949).

1948 First UN peacekeeping operation approved; unarmed UN observers stationed in Jerusalem, where cease-fire in First Arab-Israeli War was arranged (1949).

1950 Resolution calling for admission of People's Republic of China to the UN introduced—and defeated—for first time; resolution defeated annually until 1971.

1950 Korean War began; Security Council approved military intervention; UN troops (largely US soldiers) turned back unprovoked North Korean invasion of South Korea; war ended by truce (1953).

1951 Office of the UN High Commissioner for Refugees established to provide legal and political protection for refugees; UNHCR awarded Nobel Peace Prize (1954, 1981).

1952 UN headquarters in New York City completed.

1953–61 Swedish diplomat Dag Hammarskjöld served as UN secretary-general; increased UN influence worldwide and involved it in Mideast and African peacekeeping missions.

1956 UN peacekeeping force stationed in Egypt to oversee cease-fire and troop withdrawals following the Suez Crisis.

1960 UN peacekeeping force stationed in the Congo (now Zaire) as civil war broke out after independence from Belgium was declared.

1961 UN Secretary-General Hammarskjöld killed in plane crash while en route to meeting with leader of Congo secessionists (Sept. 17).

1962–71 Burmese diplomat U Thant served as secretary-general; helped mediate Cuban Missile Crisis and unsuccessfully attempted to negotiate an end to the Vietnam War.

1962 World Food Program established to provide emergency food to needy countries.

1963 Britain, US, and USSR signed Partial Test-Ban Treaty; nuclear tests banned in atmosphere, under water, and in outer space.

1964 UN peace-keeping troops stationed in Cyprus amid the crisis between Greek and Turkish Cypriots.

1964 UN Conference on Trade and Development established.

1965 Security Council enlarged from 11 to 15 members.

1965 International Convention on Elimination of All Forms of Racial Discrimination approved by General Assembly; to take effect in 1969.

1965 UN Institute for Training and Research founded; to foster economic and social progress worldwide.

1965 Nobel Prize for Peace awarded to UNICEF.

1966 Economic sanctions against white-ruled Rhodesia approved by Security Council.

1966 UN Capital Development Fund established to provide financial aid to developing countries.

1966 UN Outer Space Treaty signed by 60 nations; limited military use of outer space.

1967 UN Industrial Development Organization approved to help underdeveloped nations.

1967 UN helped arranged cease-fire agreements following Six-Day War in Mideast (June); Security Council called on Israel to give up occupied Arab territory (Nov.), but Israel refused.

1969 Nuclear Nonproliferation Treaty signed by US, USSR, and Britain; prohibited countries from giving nuclear weapons to countries that do not already possess them.

1970 US used Security Council veto for first time, to block resolution against white-ruled Rhodesia.

1971 People's Republic of China finally admitted to UN, its membership having been rejected annually since 1950; Nationalist China (Taiwan) expelled from UN.

1972–82 Austrian diplomat K. Waldheim served as secretary-general.

1972 Office of Disaster Relief Coordinator established to organize international emergency relief efforts.

1972 UN Environmental Program established to promote international cooperation to fight pollution and preserve natural resources.

1974 South Africa ousted by General Assembly because of its apartheid policies.

1974 UN peacekeeping force stationed in Mideast following Fourth Arab-Israeli War.

1974   World Food Conference held at Rome by UN; established World Food Council to coordinate delivery of some 10 million tons of food to needy countries each year.

1976   Resolutions voted against white-ruled South Africa; urged member nations to halt trade, arms shipments, and other contacts with South Africa until apartheid system abolished.

1978   Security Council voted to send peace-keeping forces to southern Lebanon.

1979   Security Council condemned taking of US hostages in Iran; Secretary-General Waldheim unsuccessful in his personal mission to Iran to seek release of hostages (1980).

1982–91   Peruvian Javier Pérez de Cúellar served as secretary-general.

1984   US withdrew from UNESCO in dispute over agency's political and financial activities; Britain withdrew the following year.

1985   UN adopted anti-terrorism resolution.

1988   UN observers stationed in Afghanistan to monitor withdrawal of Soviet troops.

1988   US refused PLO leader Y. Arafat visa to attend UN meeting because of his ties with terrorists; Arafat forced to meet with UN officials in Switzerland.

1988   UN peacekeeping forces awarded the Nobel Peace Prize.

1990–92   UN condemned Iraqi invasion of Kuwait; approved use of force by US-led multi-national military group to drive Iraqis out of Kuwait; imposed severe economic sanctions against Iraq.

1992–   Egyptian Boutros Boutros-Ghali served as secretary-general, the first Arab to hold the post.

United Provinces   Union of provinces in the Low Countries that had rebelled against Spanish rule (1579). It later became the modern state of the Netherlands (*q.v.*).

United Provinces of Central America *See* **Central American Union.**

United States (United States of America) Country located in North America (*pop.* 248,700,000). Its capital is Washington, DC. Originally settled by British colonists (from early 17th cent.), the US achieved independence (18th cent.) by the American Revolution (*q.v.*) and subsequently established a highly successful democratic government under the Constitution. US history in the 19th cent. was marked by the American Civil War (*q.v.*), which threatened to destroy the Union; by westward expansion of US borders to the Pacific coast; by rapid industrialization after the Civil War; and by the emergence of the US as a world power (late 19th cent.). The US joined the Allies toward the end of WW I and, though it refused to enter the League of Nations, subsequently played an increasingly important role in world affairs. Faced with the crippling Depression at home during the 1930s, the federal government enacted sweeping economic and social reforms that greatly increased its involvement in shaping American society (*see* New Deal). In WW II the US played a leading role in the defeat of the Axis Powers. The US emerged as the leading power in the West following WW II and from the late 1940s to about 1990 engaged in the Cold War (*q.v.*) with the USSR. During this period both the US and the USSR, the world's two great superpowers, developed massive nuclear arsenals. US involvement in the Vietnam War during the 1960s and early 1970s seriously eroded US prestige and led to widespread internal unrest. The war, and costly social programs undertaken by the federal government during the 1960s, led to economic problems that lasted throughout the 1970s and into the early 1980s. The 1980s saw a period of economic prosperity under Republican president R. Reagan, as well as a major buildup of US military forces. Reagan and his Republican successor, President G. Bush, both gained important foreign policy successes abroad while struggling with a Democratic-controlled Congress on domestic issues, notably reducing the budget deficit. The election of Democratic president Bill Clinton in 1992 promised a Democratic initiative on deficit reduction. **For more on important persons and major events listed below, *see* separate entries.** Key events in US history include:

c1000   Leif Ericson believed to have landed in North America, the first European to do so.

1170?   Legendary Welshman Madoc said to have landed in America about this time.

1492   C. Columbus made his first landing in the Bahamas (Oct. 12).

1493   Columbus landed in Puerto Rico and Virgin Islands.

1500s   Iroquois Confederacy formed by tribes occupying woodlands from Maine to Great Lakes.

1513   Spaniard Ponce de León arrived in Florida; searched for legendary fountain of youth.

1524   G. Verrazano explored east coast and New York Bay for the French.

1529   Cabeza de Vaca explored American southwest.

1539–42   H. De Soto explored American south; died during expedition.

1540–42   F. Coronado explored southwest; traveled north into what is now Kansas.

1542   J. Cabrillo explored California coast.

1565   St. Augustine, Florida, first permanent European settlement in America, established by Spanish.

1587   Colony established on Roanoke Island, North Carolina; founded under charter granted to Sir Walter Raleigh; settlers mysteriously disappeared.

1587   V. Dare born at the "Lost Colony"; she thus became first child born to English parents in America.

1598–1607   J. de Oñate served as governor of fledgling Spanish colony in American southwest; failed to find riches he sought but explored as far north as Kansas.

1600s   Navaho Indians settled in southwest America.

1607   Jamestown (Virginia) established (May 14) as first permanent English settlement in North America.

1607–08   Unsuccessful attempt to establish colony in Maine.

1609–10   H. Hudson explored the Hudson River and Hudson Bay for the Dutch East India Company.

1612   First tobacco cultivated in Virginia.

1614   Capt. J. Smith traveled north from Virginia and explored New England.

1614   Dutch built trading post at what is now Albany, New York; explored southern New England coast.

1614   Pocahontas, an Indian girl who befriended English settlers at Jamestown, married settler J. Rolfe.

1619   First Negro slaves arrived in Virginia.

1619   Virginia House of Burgesses established.

1620   Pilgrims landed in Massachusetts; established Plymouth Colony.

1621   W. Bradford elected governor of Plymouth Colony; subsequently reelected thirty times.

1622   Pawtuxet Indian Squanto, who had befriended Pilgrims at Plymouth Colony, died.

1622–69   Powhatan War in the south; Virginia and Maryland settlers defeated and killed off most of Powhatan tribe.

1624   Virginia made a royal colony.

1626   P. Minuit of the Dutch New Netherland Company bought Manhattan Island from Indians; established New Amsterdam (later New York City) and settlements in adjacent states.

1630   Massachusetts Bay Colony founded; theocratic government established by the Puritans; thousands of new settlers arrived from England in next decade.

1630s   Colonization of Connecticut begun.

1634   Lord Baltimore (George Calvert) established Maryland Colony as haven for Catholics.

1636   Rhode Island settled by R. Williams.

1636   First American college, what became Harvard University, founded at Cambridge, Massachusetts; Puritan minister I. Mather served as its president 1685–1701.

1636–38   Pequot War in Connecticut; settlers decimated Pequot tribe.

1637   Antinomianism controversy in Massachusetts.

1638   New Sweden founded as Sweden's only colony in America; fell to Dutch under P. Stuyvesant in 1655.

1638   T. Eaton founded New Haven Colony; served as its governor 1639–58.

1640   *Bay Psalm Book,* first book printed in colonies, produced by S. Daye in Cambridge, Massachusetts.

1642–48   Civil war in England, after which the monarchy was abolished for a time.

1643   New England Confederation formed federation of Massachusetts Bay, Plymouth, Connecticut, and New Haven colonies; first such federation in America.

1648–50   War between Iroquois and Huron Indians in Great Lakes region; Huron and neighboring Neutral Nation nearly wiped out.

1651–73   Navigation Acts passed by English Parliament; aimed at Dutch, they sought to control trade between England and the colonies.

1656   Iroquois decimated Erie Indian tribe in the Lake Erie region.

1661   First Bible printed in North America, a special translation for Massachusetts Indians published by missionary J. Eliot.

1652   Maine annexed to Massachusetts.

1662   Half-Way Covenant adopted in New England.

1663   Royal grant for colonization of the Carolinas.

1663–1728   C. Mather lived; became a leading religious and intellectual figure in early America.

1673–74   Frenchmen J. Marquette and L. Jolliet explored region south of Great Lakes, following the Mississippi River southward to the Arkansas River.

1664   New Netherland captured by the English, led by the duke of York; New Amsterdam renamed New York.

1675–76   King Philip's War fought in New England between settlers and Indians led by Metacomet.

1676   Bacon's Rebellion by settlers against colonial government.

1677–79   Culpeper's Rebellion; Carolina colonists rebelled against British taxes and regulations.

1682   R. La Salle claimed Mississippi Valley for France; named it Louisiana.

1682   W. Penn established the Quaker colony of Pennsylvania; Philadelphia founded.

1683   First Mennonite settlement in America founded at what is now Germantown, Pennsylvania.

1684   Massachusetts charter revoked; failure to respect authority of the crown among the charges made against colonists.

1686   Dominion of New England; New England colonies to be united under single colonial government; following Glorious Revolution in England (1688), colonies reverted to separate charter governments.

1689–91   Leisler's Rebellion broke out in New York.

1689–97   King William's War fought; first of series of wars fought between English, French, and their respective Indian allies for control of colonies in North America.

1691   Plymouth Colony became part of Massachusetts Colony.

1692   Salem witch trials in Massachusetts.

1693   College of William and Mary founded at Williamsburg, Virginia, the second college to be established in the colonies.

1700s   Comanche Indians settled in southern Great Plains region.

1700s   Seminole Indians settled in Florida.

1701   A. Cadillac founded Detroit in what is now Michigan.

1701   Yale University became the third college founded in America.

1702–13   Queen Anne's War fought between English and French.

1718   New Orleans founded.

1719   First of German Baptist Dunkards arrived in the colonies, seeking to escape persecution.

1720–60   Great Awakening; religious revival movement in the colonies led by J. Edwards, G. Whitefield, and G. Tennent.

1729   Separate colonies of North and South Carolina established.

1733   Georgia established as the last of the original 13 colonies.

1733   Molasses Act, designed to force American colonists to import more expensive sugar and molasses produced by other British colonies.

1735   P. Zenger acquitted in libel suit; helped establish freedom of press in America.

1737   Walking Purchase, land swindle perpetrated by Pennsylvania officials against the Delaware Indians.

1739   Slave uprisings in South Carolina; 21 whites and 44 blacks killed.

1740   Moravian church in America founded by A. Spangenberg.

1744–48   King George's War; New England colonials successful in fighting against French in Canada.

1746–1800   W. Billings, one of America's earliest composers of hymns, lived.

1748   Lutheran church in America founded by H. Muhlenberg.

1748   Montesquieu's *The Spirit of Laws* published; articulated theory of separation of powers later embodied in US Constitution.

1749   Ohio Company granted land along the Ohio River; company launched first organized effort by Americans to settle lands west of Alleghenies.

1750   British passed Iron Act, which limited American iron industry.

c1750   Smallpox epidemic halved Cherokee Indian population, then living in American southeast.

1753   G. Washington sent into Ohio Valley to tell French to withdraw from region.

1753 Liberty Bell first hung in Independence Hall, Philadelphia.

1754 Contingent of Virginia militia entered Ohio Valley; French forced G. Washington to surrender.

1754 Albany Convention (June 19); called by various colonies for defense against French; B. Franklin's plan for union of colonies rejected.

1754–63 French and Indian Wars; British gained control of French territory in North America.

1755–1828 Painter G. Stuart lived; noted for his portraits of Washington, Jefferson, and others.

1756–1825 Painter J. Trumbull lived; noted for his revolutionary war scenes.

1761 Massachusetts patriot J. Otis led protest against British Writs of Assistance (search warrants); said to have coined expression "Taxation without representation is tyranny."

1763 American painter B. West moved to England, where he enjoyed the patronage of King George III.

1763 Proclamation of 1763 issued by king in attempt to limit further westward settlement.

1763–66 Pontiac's Rebellion in Great Lakes region; unsuccessful uprising of several Indian tribes led by Pontiac.

1764 Sugar Act passed by British Parliament to raise revenue.

1764–71 Regulator Movement by frontier settlers in western North Carolina; opposed corrupt colonial government.

1764–1820 Architect B. Latrobe lived; introduced Greek Revival style in America.

1765 Stamp Act passed by British Parliament; led to establishment of Stamp Act Congress and Sons of Liberty.

1765 Quartering Act passed by British Parliament; caused great resentment in colonies; was allowed to lapse in 1770.

1765 Stamp Act Congress convened (Oct.) to protest British imposition of Stamp Act and other taxes; issued declaration of grievances.

1766 Stamp Act repealed; British Declaratory Act reasserted Parliament's legislative authority in colonies.

1767 Townshend Acts, four acts passed by the British Parliament to raise revenue and reassert its authority in the colonies; led to increased resistance.

1768 Liberty Affair (June 10); British used troops to quell rioting in Boston, after they seized J. Hancock's ship *Liberty.*

1770 Boston Massacre (Mar. 5); British troops, taunted by civilians, fired into a crowd, killing five.

1770 British repealed duties on a number of commodities; tax on tea remained.

1771 Battle of Alamance Creek in North Carolina (May 16); Regulator movement crushed in battle with Colonial militia.

1771–1810 Novelist C. B. Brown lived; sometimes called first professional novelist in America.

1772 British revenue cutter *Gaspee* burned (June) by American colonials in Rhode Island.

1772–74 Committees of Correspondence set up for communications between colonies; figured in spread of independence sentiment for rebellion against British government.

1773 Tea Act passed by British Parliament (May 10).

1773 Boston Tea Party (Dec. 16); colonials dumped shipment of British tea into harbor.

1774 Intolerable Acts passed by Parliament to punish Boston for the Boston Tea Party; increased resentment among colonials and led to convening of First Continental Congress.

1774 Lord Dunmore's War between Virginia militia and Shawnees (Jan.–Oct.).

1774 Suffolk Resolves (Sept.), opposing the Intolerable Acts, passed in Massachusetts; subsequently endorsed by Continental Congress.

1774 First Continental Congress convened (Sept. 5) in Philadelphia; P. Randolph served as president.

1774 Shaker sect established at Watervliet, New York, by English mystic A. Lee.

1774–1821 E. Seton lived; became first native American to be canonized as a saint (1974).

1775 Virginia Convention (Mar.); P. Henry delivered "give me liberty" speech.

1775 Frontiersman D. Boone helped blaze the trail for Wilderness Road, which opened up Kentucky for settlement by Europeans.

1775 P. Revere set out on his famous ride to warn minutemen of impending British raid (Apr. 18).

1775 Crude, human-powered submarine built by American inventor D. Bushnell.

1775   Frontiersman D. Boone helped blaze the Wilderness Road, which became an important route used by settlers moving from Virginia into western Kentucky.

1775–83   American Revolution; colonials, at first fighting for recognition of grievances, soon adopted course for complete independence; under leadership of G. Washington secured defeat of British forces.

1776   Declaration of Independence (July 4) issued by colonials.

1776   First American diplomat, S. Deane, sent to Europe to secure French aid for the Revolution; recruited C. Pulaski, F. von Steuben, and M. Lafayette.

1776   T. Paine published his famous pamphlet *Common Sense* (Jan.).

1777   Articles of Confederation adopted (Nov. 15); established loose federation of the 13 colonies; name United States of America adopted.

1777   Continental Congress adopted first American flag (June 14), which according to tradition was made by B. Ross.

1779   American colonial force defeated Iroquois Confederacy in New York.

1780s   Connecticut Wits flourished about this time at Hartford, Connecticut.

1781   Articles of Confederation in force, following their ratification (Mar. 1).

1782   *Letters from an American Farmer* published by expatriate American M. de Crèvecoeur.

1782   Painter C. Peale opened gallery featuring his portraits of American Revolutionary War heroes.

1783   Treaty of Paris, acknowledging US independence, signed with Britain (Sept. 3).

1784   F. Asbury became first Methodist bishop in the US.

1785–1851   Ornithologist J. Audubon lived; became famous for his drawings of North American birds.

1786–87   Shays's Rebellion in Massachusetts.

1786   Annapolis Convention (Sept.); by this time weaknesses of government under Articles of Confederation had become apparent; discussion of problems at Annapolis led to convening of the Constitutional Convention.

1787   Northwest Ordinance passed (July) to provide for administration of US territories.

1787   Constitutional Convention (May–Sept.); drafted constitution creating strong federal government.

1787–88   Federalist Papers, series of essays written by A. Hamilton, J. Madison, and J. Jay supporting US Constitution.

1787   Constitution signed (Sept. 17); sent to states for ratification.

1788   Constitution of the United States went into effect (June 21) following ratification by ninth state (New Hampshire); established strong central government with a president and bicameral legislature.

1789   Congress convened for first time under US Constitution (Mar. 4).

1789–93   G. Washington elected first US president; inaugurated (Apr. 30), he guided the US through the crucial early years; attempted unsuccessfully to establish government free of partisan politics.

1789   Bill of Rights passed (Sept. 25) by Congress; guaranteed fundamental liberties.

1789   Protestant Episcopal church founded by merger of former Anglican churches in America.

1790   S. Slater built the first cotton textile factory in the US at Rhode Island.

1791   Bank of the United States chartered (Feb. 25); was part of A. Hamilton's aggressive fiscal program as secretary of the treasury.

1791   Vermont admitted as 14th state.

1791   Bill of Rights ratified (Dec. 15).

1792   Republican party, forerunner of the Democratic party, founded by T. Jefferson; opposed Federalist party, led by A. Hamilton and J. Adams.

1792   Kentucky admitted as 15th state.

1792   Tennessee admitted as 16th state.

1792   Financier W. Duer imprisoned for debt, which was said to have contributed to the financial panic that year.

1793   Washington reelected to second term.

1793   French diplomat E. Genêt asked to leave country after attempting to sway popular opinion in favor of revolutionary France against Britain; US passed Neutrality Act (1794).

1793   Cotton gin invented by E. Whitney.

1794   Whiskey Rebellion broke out; Pennsylvania settlers protest federal tax on whiskey.

1794   Battle of Fallen Timbers (Aug. 20); Gen. A. Wayne decisively defeated Indians of Northwest Confederation, ending their resistance to encroachment by settlers.

1794   Jay's Treaty signed (Nov. 19); forestalled war with Britain.

1794 Noted furniture maker D. Phyfe set up his business in New York City.

1794–1877 C. Vanderbilt lived; established family fortune by his successful ventures in shipping and railroads.

1795 Yazoo land claims, land-fraud scheme involving many members of Georgia legislature.

1795 T. Pinckney negotiated treaty settling border between US and Spanish territories in North America.

1795–1840 Roman Catholic D. Gallitzin engaged in missionary work in the frontier of southwestern Pennsylvania.

1796 Washington delivered his Farewell Address (Sept. 18).

1796–1859 Educator H. Mann lived; influenced development of education in US.

1796–1886 Painter A. Durand lived; became a founder of the Hudson River school.

1797–1801 John Adams, Federalist leader, served as second US president; struggle with Jeffersonian Republicans.

1797 XYZ Affair, attempted bribing of American diplomats by French officials; led to undeclared naval war with France.

1798 Alien and Sedition Acts; notorious acts passed by Federalists and aimed at suppressing the Jeffersonian Republicans.

1798 Virginia and Kentucky Resolutions passed in opposition to Alien and Sedition Acts; hinged on doctrine of states' right to nullify federal law.

1799 Fries's Rebellion in Pennsylvania against federal tax.

c1800–01 Great Kentucky revival; wave of evangelical Protestantism spread by camp meetings, featuring hell-fire sermons.

1800 Treaty of 1800; ended US alliance with France.

1800 Washington, D.C., became US capital, replacing Philadelphia.

1800 Election of 1800 ("Revolution of 1800"); Adams lost but tie between T. Jefferson and A. Burr threw the election into the House, which decided on Jefferson as president and Burr as vice-president.

1800s Cheyenne Indians settled in Black Hills region, after being forced out of Minnesota by warfare with other tribes.

c1800–45 Johnny Appleseed (J. Chapman) wandered the western frontier tending apple-tree nurseries he planted in the forests.

1801–09 T. Jefferson served as 3d US president; sought economy in government and less interference in states.

1801 J. Marshall appointed Supreme Court chief justice; served until 1835.

1801 Gabriel's Rebellion in Virginia (Aug. 30); band of few hundred poorly armed slaves failed in attempt to seize Richmond, capital of Virginia, and thus begin a slave revolt throughout the colony; slaves captured and 34 were hung.

1801–05 Tripolitan War against Barbary pirates.

1802 Gunpowder plant built by E. I. Du Pont; from this beginning eventually sprang the massive Du Pont industrial complex.

1802 N. Bowditch published his famous *New Practical Navigator.*

1802–87 Social reformer D. Dix lived; crusaded for humane treatment of inmates in insane asylums and prisons.

1803 Ohio admitted as 17th state.

1803 *Marbury* v. *Madison;* Supreme Court established judicial review of Congressional legislation.

1803 Louisiana Purchase; US purchased territory from France and thereby doubled size of US.

1804 Vice-President A. Burr killed political rival, A. Hamilton, in duel (July).

1804–06 Lewis and Clark expedition explored Louisiana Territory.

1805 President Jefferson's attempt to have Supreme Court Justice S. Chase impeached failed; helped establish Court's independence from political influence.

1805–07 Z. Pike explored western frontier; discovered Pikes Peak (1806).

1807 R. Fulton launched (Aug.) first commercially successful steamboat, the *Clermont.*

1807 Former Vice-President A. Burr tried for treason; acquitted (Sept.).

1807 British ship *Leopard* stopped and searched American frigate *Chesapeake,* removing four crewmen; incident resulted from mutual attempts by Britain and Napoleon of France to blockade shipping; tensions between US and Britain increased.

1807 Embargo Act (Dec.); Jefferson attempted to retaliate against Britain and France for their restrictions, which were hurting US commerce.

1807–73 Scientist J. Agassiz lived; influenced development of natural sciences in 19th cent.

1808 J. J. Astor founded American Fur Company and influenced settlement of the Great Lakes region. His highly successful company eventually monopolized the US fur trade and became the first American trust.

1809–17 President James Madison in office.

1809 Embargo Act repealed after proving more harmful to US commerce than to France or Britain; replaced by Non-Intercourse Act.

1810 Macon's Bill No. 2; another attempt at countering French and British blockades.

1810–12 E. Gerry served as Massachusetts governor; his manipulation of election district lines gave rise to term *gerrymandering.*

1811 Battle of Tippecanoe (Nov. 7); W. Harrison victorious in fighting against the Indians in Indiana.

1811 Construction began on National Road, eventually extending from Cumberland, Maryland, to St. Louis (by 1833).

1812 Louisiana admitted as 18th state.

1812 Boston Manufacturing Co. founded in Massachusetts by F. Lowell and others; company built first factory capable of converting raw cotton into finished cloth.

1812–14 War of 1812 fought with Britain.

1813–14 Creek War fought in Alabama and Georgia; Indians, allied with British during War of 1812, defeated by militiamen led by Gen. A. Jackson.

1813–95 Geologist J. Dana lived.

1814 F. S. Key, watching British attack on Baltimore's Fort McHenry, wrote words to what became the US national anthem, *The Star-Spangled Banner.*

1816 Second Bank of the United States chartered.

1816–25 Construction of Erie Canal in New York; canal, linking port of New York with Midwest, proved commercial success.

1816 American Colonization Society formed to transport freed Negroes to colony in Liberia.

1816 Indiana admitted as 19th state.

1817–25 James Monroe in office as fifth president; his term referred to as "Era of Good Feeling" for relative lack of partisan political struggle.

1817 Rush-Bagot Convention signed with Britain; provided for disarmament of US-Canadian border.

1817–18 First Seminole War; Seminoles in Florida defeated and Spain forced to cede Florida.

1817 Mississippi admitted as 20th state.

1817 Poet W. Bryant wrote *Thanatopsis,* which established him as a leading American poet.

1818 Convention of 1818 established western US-Canadian border at 49th parallel.

1818 Illinois admitted as 21st state.

1818–72 J. Kensett lived; noted as a painter in the Hudson River school.

1819 Transcontinental Treaty (Feb. 22) signed between Spain and US; Spain ceded Florida and the Oregon Country; US recognized Spanish sovereignty in Texas.

1819 In *McCulloch* v. *Maryland,* Supreme Court confirmed congressional powers.

1819 Alabama admitted as 22d state.

1819 Dartmouth College Case; reinforced Constitution's contract clause.

1819 Panic of 1819; financial panic caused by inflation, over speculation in Western lands and other factors; many banks collapsed; South and West hard hit.

1819–20 Writer W. Irving published his famous *Sketch Book.*

1820 Missouri Compromise; to maintain the balance between slaveholding and free states (11 each), Missouri to be admitted without restrictions as to slavery, remainder of Louisiana Purchase north of 30°30′ to be free, and Maine to be admitted as free state; marked rise of North-South sectional conflict over slavery.

1820 Maine admitted as 23d state.

1820s Pioneer S. Austin helped spur settlement in Texas.

c1820–1913 Abolitionist and escaped slave H. Tubman lived; became leading figure in the Underground Railroad.

1821 Missouri admitted as 24th state.

1821 Author J. F. Cooper established himself as a writer with publication of *The Spy;* became famous for his *Leatherstocking Tales* of frontier life.

1823 Monroe Doctrine articulated (Dec. 2) by President Monroe to block attempts to restore colonial control in South America; warned against involvement by European powers in Americas.

1823–27 Frontiersman S. Houston served in Congress; later led Texans in battle for independence.

1823–78 W. "Boss" Tweed lived; became infamous as leader of corrupt Tweed Ring, which controlled New York City's Democratic party and the municipal government.

c1823–96 Pioneering photographer M. Brady lived; noted for his Civil War photographs.

1824 American System proposed by H. Clay for American self-sufficiency.

1824 *Gibbons* v. *Ogden;* Supreme Court decision that reinforced Constitution's commerce clause, giving Congress the right to regulate commerce in the states.

1824 Election of 1824; four-way race finally decided in House in favor of J. Q. Adams, though A. Jackson had won popular vote.

1825 First American steam locomotive built by inventor J. Stevens.

1825 American Unitarian Association founded.

1825–29 J. Q. Adams served as sixth president; embroiled in bitter feud with Jacksonian Democrats.

1825–75 Hudson River school of landscape painters flourished.

1825–94 Artist G. Inness lived; became noted landscape painter.

1826 First of Pan American conferences held between the US and various South American states; conferences held at intervals in subsequent decades.

1826–34 Rise of the Anti-Masonic party.

1826–64 Songwriter S. Foster lived; composed such tunes as *Oh! Susannah* and *Camptown Races.*

1827–31 Frontiersman D. Crockett served his first term in Congress.

1827–41 Statesman D. Webster served his first term in the Senate; known as one of the outstanding orators of his day.

1828 Tariff of Abominations, high tariff on imports, designed to protect developing US industries, raised protests, especially in the South; J. Calhoun advanced his theory of nullification.

1828 N. Webster published *The American Dictionary of the English Language.*

1829 First electric motor built by J. Henry.

1829–37 A. Jackson served as seventh president; spoils system introduced during his administration; Jacksonian democracy ascendant; Jackson's Kitchen Cabinet derided by opposition.

1830 Hayne-Webster debate; Sen. D. Webster refuted doctrine of nullification and defended nationalist view of the Union.

1830 Forerunner of Mormon church organized in New York.

1830 Maysville Road bill vetoed by President Jackson; veto intended as rebuff to H. Clay.

1830 Indian Removal Act implemented by President Jackson.

1830 "T"-shaped railroad rail invented by R. Stevens; Stevens also invented railroad spike and cowcatcher.

1830 Work on US Capitol building completed; final stages supervised by architect C. Bulfinch.

1830 Poet O. W. Holmes wrote *Old Ironsides.*

1830–86 Poet E. Dickinson lived; wrote over 1,000 poems but allowed publication of only a few during her lifetime.

1831 Slave revolt, Southampton Insurrection, in Virginia; led by N. Turner.

1831 Eaton Affair; Washington, D.C., society snubbed wife of secretary of war J. Eaton; led to his resignation, despite President Jackson's attempts to intervene.

1831 McCormick reaper designed by C. McCormick.

1831–65 Abolitionist W. L. Garrison published *The Liberator.*

1832 Tariff of 1832; improved on Tariff of Abominations but failed to quiet opposition in South.

1832 Black Hawk War in what became Wisconsin; marked last major Indian uprising in territory.

1832–33 Nullification controversy; South Carolina attempted to nullify federal tariffs by state ordinance (1832); Vice-President J. Calhoun resigned over the controversy; President Jackson responded with a Force Bill (1833) to allow use of military to collect tariffs; Tariff of 1833, a compromise advanced by H. Clay, ended the controversy.

1832 Jackson, opposed to "monopolistic" practices of the Bank of United States, vetoed bill to recharter (second) Bank of the US; in 1833 transferred federal funds to state banks ("pet banks").

1832 Inventor S. Morse began work on his telegraph apparatus.

1832–99 Novelist H. Alger lived; wrote highly popular series of books in late 1800s.

1833 American Anti-Slavery Society founded by W. Garrison; marked rise of abolitionist movement in US.

1834   Whig party organized by H. Clay to oppose politics of A. Jackson.

1834   Indian Territory formally established; originally included lands west of the Mississippi, later reduced to part of present state of Oklahoma; Indians forcibly relocated (by Indian Removal Act of 1830) from east of Mississippi to Indian Territory.

1835   US public debt retired.

1835   Rise of Locofocos, short-lived faction of radical Jacksonian Democrats; advocated end to the national bank and other monopolies.

1835   S. and A. Grimké publicly opposed slavery for first time; three years later the two sisters called for women's rights as well.

1835   Colt revolver, first successful revolving magazine pistol, invented by S. Colt.

1835–42   Second Seminole War in Florida sparked by attempts to move Seminoles from their lands; Seminoles defeated and forced to move west.

1835–1916   H. Green lived; she became the wealthiest woman in the world during her lifetime.

1836   Texas War for Independence; increased settlement of Texas by Americans led to movement to break away from Mexican rule; despite defeat at the famous Battle of the Alamo (Mar. 6), rebels under S. Houston crushed superior Spanish force at the Battle of San Jacinto (Apr.), thereby gaining independence; formed a republic.

1836   Arkansas became the 25th state.

1836   Specie Circular issued (July) by President Jackson; ordered payment in hard currency for all public lands; designed to halt speculative boom in western real estate; helped precipitate Panic of 1837.

1836   First of series of *McGuffey Readers* published by educator W. McGuffey.

1836–44   Gag rules adopted by US House of Representatives to block antislavery petitions submitted by abolitionists; repealed in 1844.

1836–1902   Writer B. Harte lived.

1836–1910   Artist W. Homer lived; became famous for his seascapes.

1837   Michigan became the 26th state.

1837–41   M. Van Buren in office as eighth president; a Democrat, he attempted to continue former President Jackson's policies.

1837   Senate chose R. Johnson vice-president, breaking electoral college deadlock.

1837   Panic of 1837; financial collapse began in market for western lands and soon spread to commodities markets.

1837   S. Morse successfully demonstrated his telegraph.

1837   Caroline Affair, incident between US and Canada.

1837   Journalist and abolitionist E. Lovejoy killed while defending his printing press against proslavery mob in Illinois.

1837–76   Western frontier lawman J. "Wild Bill" Hickok lived.

1838–39   Aroostook War, US-Canadian border incident.

c1838   Underground Railroad formed by abolitionists to help runaway slaves escape to Canada or free states.

1839   Inventor C. Goodyear discovered process for vulcanizing rubber.

1839–1914   Philosopher C. Peirce founded philosophical school of pragmatism.

1840   Independent Treasury System adopted; won support of President Van Buren after Panic of 1837; had been opposed by Whigs seeking new Bank of the United States.

1840   Author R. Dana wrote *Two Years Before the Mast.*

1840–48   Liberty party formed; first US political party created to promote abolition of slavery.

1841   W. Harrison served (Mar.–Apr.) as ninth US president; first president to die in office (Apr. 4).

1841–45   J. Tyler in office as 10th president, following Harrison's death; first vice-president to succeed to the presidency; opposed Whig effort to establish national bank; his cabinet (except D. Webster) resigned.

1841   Independent Treasury System repealed by Whigs.

1841   Brook Farm, utopian community, founded.

1841, 1844   Two collections entitled *Essays* published by R. W. Emerson.

1842   Webster-Ashburton Treaty settled Northeast Boundary Dispute.

1842   E. A. Poe wrote horror tale *The Pit and the Pendulum,* one of a number for which he is best known.

1842   Ether first used in surgery by physician C. Long.

1843 Newspaper *Mystery* founded by black leader M. Delany.

1843–44 J. Frémont led expeditions to Oregon and California; later helped in conquest of California during Mexican War.

1843–1916 Author H. James lived; lived in England and wrote about European society.

1844 First practical telegraph system set up by S. Morse; Morse sent his famous message "What hath God wrought?" over lines connecting Washington, D.C., and Baltimore.

1845 Texas became the 28th state, following vote by Congress to annex it.

1845 Florida became the 27th state.

1882 Abolitionist and former slave F. Douglass wrote *Narrative of the Life of Frederick Douglass.*

1845–49 J. Polk in office as 11th president; worked vigorously for his programs and supported American expansionism.

1845–48 Mexican War; US, in conflict over territories of the Southwest, invaded and defeated Mexico, Mexico ceded Southwest and California to US by Treaty of Guadalupe Hidalgo.

1845–59 Rise and fall of the Know-Nothing party.

1846 Oregon Treaty negotiated between US and England; settled US-Canadian boundary dispute.

1846 Wilmot Proviso (Aug.); measure (never passed) to prohibit slavery in territories acquired in the Mexican War; aroused bitter opposition in South and contributed to growing North-South sectionalism.

1846 Walker Tariff passed; reduced US tariffs.

1846 Independent Treasury System reestablished.

1846 Iowa admitted as 29th state.

1846 C. Scribner founded what became Charles Scribner's Sons, book publishers.

1846–1911 Temperance crusader C. Nation lived.

1846–48 Mormon migration from Illinois to Salt Lake City led by B. Young.

1847–87 H. W. Beecher served as pastor at Plymouth Congregational Church in New York; noted as influential opponent of slavery and supporter of woman suffrage.

1847–1911 Pioneering newspaper publisher J. Pulitzer lived; endowed Pulitzer prizes, awarded since 1917.

1848 California gold rush began; brought great influx of settlers to California.

1848 Wisconsin admitted as 30th state.

1848 Proslavery Alabama Platform advanced in opposition to the Wilmot Proviso.

1848 *Biglow Papers* published by poet J. R. Lowell.

1848 Free-Soil party formed by antislavery Whigs and Liberty party members; their presidential candidate, M. Van Buren, split the New York vote (1848) and put Z. Taylor in office.

1848 Oneida Community founded by religious reformer J. Noyes.

1848 Seneca Falls Convention, first women's rights convention, held; organized by E. Stanton.

1848–1907 Sculptor A. Saint-Gaudens lived.

1848–1909 Railroad magnate E. H. Harriman lived.

c1849 Icaria commune founded in US by French Socialist E. Cabet.

1849 Riot in New York City's Astor Place opera hall (May 10); 20 killed.

1849 E. Blackwell became first woman to receive medical degree in the US.

1849–50 Z. Taylor (Whig) served as 12th president, died in office (July 9).

1850–53 M. Fillmore (Whig) in office as 13th president, succeeding to the presidency after Taylor's death.

1850 A. Pinkerton formed first US detective agency.

1850 Clayton-Bulwer Treaty; US and Britain agreed to refrain from attempts to dominate Central America; provided for joint control of any canal across the Isthmus of Panama.

1850 California admitted as the 31st state.

1850 Compromise of 1850 (Sept. 9–20); ended heated controversy over extension of slavery into new states, raised by impending admission of California as a free state; established doctrine of popular sovereignty, which led to further crises over slavery issue.

1850 Fugitive Slave Act passed; President Fillmore aroused storm of protest from Northern abolitionists by trying to enforce the act, in keeping with the Compromise of 1850.

1850 Novelist N. Hawthorne published *The Scarlet Letter,* considered the first American psychological novel.

1850–1917 First American saint, F. X. Cabrini, lived.

1851 Western Union emerged as country's dominant telegraph company, as telegraph system spread rapidly nationwide (1850–70).

1851 Sewing machine patented by I. Singer.

1851 Artist E. Leutze painted *Washington Crossing the Delaware.*

1851 Author H. Melville published *Moby Dick,* a classic novel of seafaring life.

1851–1931 M. Dewey, inventor of the Dewey Decimal System for classifying library books, lived.

1852 Wells, Fargo and Company founded; became famous frontier express company.

1852 Author H. B. Stowe published *Uncle Tom's Cabin.*

c1852–1903 Calamity Jane, famous American frontierswoman, lived.

1853–57 F. Pierce (Democrat) in office as 14th president; pursued expansionist foreign policy; failed to head off growing crisis over slavery.

1853 Gadsden Purchase; US bought strip of territory from Mexico along US–Mexican border.

1854 Commodore M. Perry forced Japan to end isolation and sign Treaty of Kanagawa (Mar.).

1854 Kansas-Nebraska Act (May 30); organized separate territories of Kansas and Nebraska; repealed Missouri Compromise of 1820; substituted doctrine of popular sovereignty; pro- and antislavery elements began to settle region.

1854 Republican party formed (July) at Jackson, Michigan; party formed to oppose slavery.

1854 H. D. Thoreau published *Walden.*

c1854 Feminist S. B. Anthony became active in the women's rights movement from about this time.

1854–59 Bleeding Kansas; bitter struggle between pro- and antislavery settlers in Kansas which contributed to the growing national crisis over the slavery issue.

1854 Ostend Manifesto (Oct. 18); called for US to acquire Cuba by purchase or by force; aroused public outcry in North.

1855 Poet W. Whitman published *Leaves of Grass; Familiar Quotations* published by J. Bartlett.

1855 German Pietists founded the Amana communal colonies in east Iowa.

1855–58 Third Seminole War; removal of Seminole Indians to the West completed.

1856 Pottawatomie Massacre (May); five proslavery settlers murdered by J. Brown and followers in Bleeding Kansas.

1856–1915 Educator B. T. Washington lived; known for advocating educational and economic opportunity for blacks.

1856–1919 N. Tesla, Croatian-born inventor, lived; contributed to the development of alternating-current electrical technology.

1857–61 J. Buchanan (Democrat) in office as 15th president; though opposed to slavery, he sought compromise; his policies failed to prevent the secession of Southern states (1860–61), however.

1857 Dred Scott Case; Supreme Court declared Missouri Compromise of 1820 unconstitutional.

1857 Panic of 1857; failure of railroad bonds among causes; many banks failed and widespread unemployment resulted.

1857–1929 T. Veblen, economist and social scientist, lived; coined the term "conspicuous consumption."

1857–1938 Lawyer C. Darrow, lawyer, lived; noted for defending controversial cases.

1857–1947 E. Flagg, architect, lived; designed the Singer Building in New York City.

1858 Minnesota admitted as the 32d state.

1858 Lincoln-Douglas debates (Aug.–Oct.); seven debates between A. Lincoln and S. Douglas during campaign for Senate; Lincoln won national reputation for opposing slavery as immoral; Douglas reelected to Senate.

1858–1942 F. Boas, noted German-American anthropologist, lived.

1859 Oregon admitted as 33d state.

1859 Harpers Ferry Raid (Oct. 16–18), abortive insurrection led by J. Brown; contributed to outbreak of Civil War.

1859 First US oil well drilled at Titusville, Pennsylvania, by E. Drake.

1859–81 Outlaw Billy the Kid lived.

1859–1952 Philosopher and educator J. Dewey lived; wrote *Essays in Experimental Logic.*

1860s Wars against Indians in the West; various tribes (Sioux, Cheyenne, Apache, Navaho) attempted to resist advance of white settlers and were gradually subdued in bloody wars; Indians resettled on reservations.

1860–61 Pony Express in operation.

1860 Election of 1860; Democrats split over slavery issue, Douglas ran as candidate of

Northern Democrats, John Breckinridge as candidate of Southern Democrats; A. Lincoln, Republican candidate, opposed to extension of slavery; Lincoln's victory in the election sparked the secessionist movement in the South.

1860   Ordinance of Secession adopted by South Carolina (Dec. 20); other Southern states soon followed (from Jan., 1861); President Buchanan refused to use force to prevent secession.

1860–1930   Inventor E. Sperry lived; invented the gyroscope.

1861   Union supply ship fired on (Jan. 9) while attempting to relieve Ft. Sumter in Charleston, South Carolina, harbor.

1861   Kansas admitted as the 34th state.

1861   Confederate States of America created (Feb. 4) at meeting of seven (four seceded later) secessionist states; provisional government under J. Davis formed; ordered seizure of all federal property within seceded states.

1861   Washington Conference (Feb.); presided over by J. Tyler, it failed to resolve North-South differences and end secessionist movement.

1861   Crittenden Compromise; unsuccessful, last attempt at preventing civil war; defeated in Senate (Mar.).

1861–65   A. Lincoln served as 16th president; he was inaugurated (Mar. 4) and war broke out the following month; Lincoln succeeded ultimately in preserving the Union and in bringing an end to slavery in the US.

1861   Morrill Tariff enacted (Mar.); first of a series of Civil War–period bills that gradually increased tariffs; established high protective tariff structure.

1861   President Lincoln announced (Apr. 6) he would supply Ft. Sumter in Charleston, South Carolina.

1861   Confederates fired (Apr. 12), on Ft. Sumter and thus began hostilities in the war; Virginia, Alabama, Tennessee, and North Carolina seceded.

1861   Poet H. W. Longfellow wrote his famous narrative poem *Paul Revere's Ride.*

1861–65   American Civil War; bloody conflict culminated long North-South sectional struggle over slavery; South, unable to match North's manpower and supplies, was devastated in fighting and finally defeated.

1862   Legal Tender Act passed; first of series passed to help finance war effort.

1862   Homestead Act passed; encouraged settlement of West.

1862   Morrill Act passed; set aside public lands to create land-grant colleges.

1862   Poet J. Howe wrote *The Battle Hymn of the Republic.*

1862–1910   Short story writer O. Henry lived.

1863   President Lincoln issued the Emancipation Proclamation (Jan. 1), freeing slaves in states currently in revolt against union.

1863   West Virginia became 35th state.

1863   President Lincoln delivered his famous Gettysburg Address (Nov. 19).

1863–64   Navaho Indians subdued by frontiersman K. Carson.

1863–69   Central Pacific Railroad constructed; became important link in transcontinental railroad.

1863–1931   Philosopher G. Mead lived.

1863–1935   Christian evangelist and preacher B. Sunday lived.

1863–1944   L. Baekeland, chemist, lived; invented Bakelite plastic.

1863–1951   W. Hearst lived; built newspaper and magazine publishing empire.

1864   Nevada admitted as 36th state.

1864–1943   G. Carver, agricultural scientist, lived; directed Tuskegee Institute agricultural research.

1865   Gen. R. Lee surrendered at Appomattox Courthouse (Apr. 9), ending Civil War.

1865   President Lincoln assassinated by J. Booth (Apr. 14); died (Apr. 15).

1865–69   A. Johnson in office as 17th president, succeeding on Lincoln's death; attempted to continue Lincoln's policy of reconciliation toward South; engaged in bitter struggle with Radical Republicans in Congress, in attempt to prevent harsh Reconstruction program.

1865   Thirteenth Amendment to the Constitution ratified (Dec. 18); abolished slavery in the US.

1865–77   Reconstruction period; South, ravaged by war, gradually restored; Radical Republicans at first imposed policies designed to guarantee rights of Negroes; but white Southerners gained control of state governments, passed laws establishing segregation; segregation was characteristic of Southern society until the 1960s.

1865–1929   Painter R. Henri lived; member of the "ash can" school.

1866   Civil Rights Act passed over President Johnson's veto; gave blacks full rights as citizens.

1866   Book publishers G.P. Putnam's Sons and Henry Holt and Company founded.

1867   Nebraska admitted as 37th state.

1867   Tenure of Office Act passed (Mar. 2) by Congress; charges of a violation of its provisions by President Johnson were involved in his impeachment (1868).

1867   Congress passed Reconstruction Act (Apr.), dividing former Confederate states (except Tennessee) into five military districts.

1867   Alaska territory purchased from Russia.

1867   Grange organized by Midwest farmers to counter unfair practices by grain-elevator owners and railroads.

1867   Educational reformer H. Barnard named first US commissioner of education.

1868   Impeachment proceedings against President A. Johnson (Feb. 24–May 26), first ever instituted against US president; arose from Johnson's feud with Radical Republicans over Reconstruction policy; Johnson narrowly acquitted (by one vote).

1868   Fourteenth amendment ratified, reaffirming rights of citizens to equal protection under the law.

1868   Burlingame Treaty; treaty of friendship between US and China.

1868   Deere & Company founded by J. Deere in Illinois.

1868   First practical typewriter invented by C. Sholes et al.

1868   Novelist L. M. Alcott published *Little Women.*

1868–1938   Astronomer G. Hale lived; discovered magnetic fields in sunspots.

1869–77   U. Grant in office as 18th president; his term marked by continuing problems of Reconstruction, corruption, and various scandals; era known as the Gilded Age.

1869   Union Pacific Railroad, final link in transcontinental railway, completed (May 10).

1869   Black Friday financial panic (Sept. 24), caused by speculators' attempt to corner gold market.

1869   Knights of Labor, first major US labor organization, formed.

1869   Abolitionist and women's rights activist L. Stone helped found the American Woman Suffrage Association.

1870   Fifteenth Amendment ratified; sought to guarantee Negroes voting rights; along with earlier 14th Amendment and Civil Rights Acts, represented attempts by Republican Congress to guarantee Negroes equal place in post-Civil War society.

1870   J. D. Rockefeller and others formed Standard Oil Co.; Rockefeller subsequently gained control of the oil industry.

1871   Chicago fire (Oct. 8–9); one-third of city destroyed.

1871   Artist J. Whistler painted his famous *Portrait of My Mother.*

1872   Alabama Claims, dispute with Britain, settled by arbitration.

1872   San Juan Boundary Dispute with Great Britain settled; US awarded San Juan Islands southeast of Vancouver.

1872   President Grant reelected despite defection of Liberal Republicans.

1873   Crédit Mobilier of America scandal; arose from corrupt practices in financing of Union Pacific Railroad.

1873   Panic of 1873; financial panic caused by speculative boom.

1873–1900   Carnegie Steel Co. became a leading US steel manufacturer under the stewardship of A. Carnegie.

1874   Women's Christian Temperance Union founded.

1875   Whiskey Ring scandal.

1875   J. Wanamaker founded one of the first department stores, John Wanamaker and Co., in Philadelphia.

1875   Artist T. Eakins painted *The Gross Clinic.*

1876   A. Bell invented the telephone.

1876   Battle of Little Bighorn (June 25); Col. G. Custer and his troops massacred in uprising by Sioux and Cheyenne Indians.

1876   Colorado admitted as the 38th state.

1876   Socialist Labor party founded in Philadelphia.

1876   Election of 1876, Hayes versus Tilden; Hayes needed disputed electoral votes from Florida, South Carolina, Louisiana, and Oregon to win; Hayes awarded the election by Congressional Commission.

1876   Author M. Twain published his classic *The Adventures of Tom Sawyer; Robert's Rules of Order* published by H. Robert.

1877   Inventor T. Edison built first practical phonograph.

1876   Educator F. Adler founded the New York Society for Ethical Culture; also founded the Ethical Culture Movement.

1876–1960   Anthropologist A. Kroeber lived; studied Indians of the US Southwest, Mexico, and Peru.

1877–81   R. Hayes (Republican) in office as 19th president; ended Reconstruction (1877) by withdrawing last of federal occupation forces in South (Florida, South Carolina, Louisiana); adopted policy of reconciliation toward South.

1877   First widespread strikes in US history occurred (July); began with railroad workers in West Virginia, spreading to railroads and other industries around the country.

1877   Surrender of Cheyenne and Sioux Indians responsible for massacre at Little Bighorn; they were removed to Oklahoma.

1878   Bland-Allison Act for free coinage of silver (free-silver movement) passed over President Hayes's veto.

1878–1942   Showman and composer G. Cohan lived; wrote *Over There* and *I'm a Yankee Doodle Dandy.*

1878–1958   J. Watson, behavioral psychologist, lived.

1879   Single-tax system proposed by Henry George in his book *Progress and Poverty.*

1879   T. Edison invented a commercially practical light bulb.

1879   Christian Science founded by M. B. Eddy; she later founded the *Christian Science Monitor* (1908).

1879   Standard Oil trust, first US industry-wide monopoly, controlled 95% of US oil industry by this time.

1879–1928   C. Scribner served as president of Charles Scribner's Sons publishing company; published many distinguished American writers.

1879–1955   Poet W. Stevens lived; wrote *The Man with the Blue Guitar.*

1879–1964   Clergyman J. Holmes lived; helped found the ACLU and NAACP.

1880s   Great buffalo herds of western plains nearly exterminated by this time; Blackfoot Indians, who depended on herds for food, faced mass starvation.

1880   Author L. Wallace published *Ben-Hur.*

1880–1968   H. Keller lived; in spite of blindness and deafness, she became a famous author and lecturer.

1881   J. Garfield (Republican) served as 20th president; shot by disgruntled office-seeker (July 2) and died (Sept. 19).

1881   C. Barton founded American Red Cross.

1881   Barnum and Bailey Circus formed.

1881–85   C. Arthur (Republican) in office as 21st president, succeeding Garfield on his death; backed civil service reform.

1882–94   Chinese Exclusion Acts passed to prohibit immigration of Chinese (particularly laborers) to US.

1882–1907   Railroad magnate J. J. Hill served as president of the Great Northern Railway.

1882–1945   Father of modern rocketry, R. Goddard, lived; built first liquid-fuel rockets.

c1882–1965   Father Divine, black religious leader, lived; known for founding the Peace Mission movement in the Harlem section of New York City.

1882–1977   Conductor L. Stokowski lived.

1883   Pendleton Civil Service Act passed (Jan. 16); established merit system for hiring government workers and ended long fight over civil service corruption.

1883   Wild West Show organized by frontiersman Buffalo Bill.

1883   Brooklyn Bridge built; work completed by W. Roebling.

1884   German-born American inventor, O. Mergenthaler, patented the Linotype machine.

1884   Artist J. Sargent painted *Portrait of Madam X.*

1884–1967   Biochemist C. Funk lived; said to have discovered vitamins.

1885–1939   J. Kern lived; composed music for *Show Boat.*

1885   *Rise of Silas Lapham* published by W. D. Howells.

1885–1952   Psychiatrist K. Horney lived; emphasized social and environmental factors as causes of neuroses.

1885–1959   Swiss-American composer E. Bloch lived.

1885–89   G. Cleveland (Democrat) in office as the 22d president; a reformer, he fought corruption and political bosses; attempted to lower tariffs and lost reelection.

1885–1981   Historian W. Durant lived; wrote *The Story of Civilization* with his wife, Ariel.

1886   American Federation of Labor founded; soon eclipsed the Knights of Labor.

1886 Haymarket Square Riot, Chicago (May 4); anarchist bomb killed and injured many.

1886 Statue of Liberty unveiled (Oct. 28) in New York Harbor.

1886 C. Hall, chemist, discovered first practical process for manufacturing aluminum.

1886 Westinghouse Electric Co. founded by G. Westinghouse.

1886 *Little Lord Fauntleroy* published by F. Burnett.

1886–1924 Labor leader S. Gompers served as president of American Federation of Labor.

1887 Interstate Commerce Commission created to regulate railroads and railroad rates.

1887 *American Journal of Psychology* founded by G. Hall.

1888 Election of 1888; Cleveland won popular vote but lost election to B. Harrison, who won by electoral votes.

1888 G. Eastman, inventor, developed the Kodak camera.

1888–1936 G. Kittredge taught at Harvard; influenced the teaching of English.

1889–93 B. Harrison (Republican) served as 23d US president; administration marked by rising US involvement in international affairs; fiscal policies weakened economy.

1889 Jane Addams opened Hull House in Chicago, one of the first settlement houses in the US.

1889 North Dakota admitted as 39th state; South Dakota, as 40th; Montana, as 41st; and Washington, as 42d.

1890 Sherman Antitrust Act passed (July 2); first US law prohibiting trusts.

1890 Idaho admitted as the 43d state; Wyoming, as 44th.

1890 Sherman Silver Purchase Act passed (July 14); led to financial panic of 1893 and was repealed later that year.

1890 McKinley Tariff passed by Republicans; further increased tariffs.

1890 Sioux Indians massacred at Battle of Wounded Knee (Dec. 29).

1890 Philosopher and psychologist W. James published *The Principles of Psychology;* social reformer J. Riis, *How the Other Half Lives.*

1891 J. Naismith invented the game of basketball.

1891–1970 Logical positivist philosopher R. Carnap lived; known for his works on the philosophy of language.

1891–1971 D. Sarnoff lived; pioneered development of commercial radio and television.

1892 Populist party formed; supported free silver and other policies favoring farmers and labor.

1892 Homestead Strike began (June 30); violence between strikers and Pinkerton detectives hired by Carnegie Steel Company.

1892 Original version of what became Pledge of Allegiance published (Sept.).

1892 Early steel-frame "skyscraper," the Chicago Masonic Temple building, designed by architect D. Burnham.

1892 C. Duryea, inventor and manufacturer, built one of the first successful automobiles.

1893 Anarchist E. Goldman arrested in New York City for inciting a riot.

1893–97 G. Cleveland (Democrat) in office as 24th president (his second term); failed to prevent increase in tariffs and solve continuing economic problems.

1893 Panic of 1893; Pres. Cleveland blamed the Sherman Silver Purchase Act and won its repeal (Oct. 1893).

1894 Coxey's Army of unemployed marched on Washington.

1894 Pullman Strike broken with aid of federal troops.

1894 Wilson-Gorman Tariff passed; continued high protective tariff.

1894 P. Lowell, astronomer, founded the Lowell Observatory in Arizona.

1894 Historian F. Turner wrote *The Significance of the Frontier in American History.*

1894–1964 Mathematician N. Wiener lived; founded cybernetics.

1894–1978 Painter and illustrator N. Rockwell lived; famous for his covers for the *Saturday Evening Post* magazine.

1895 B. T. Washington delivered "Atlanta Compromise" speech, promising blacks would remain cooperative and outside politics if whites would finance vocational training for them.

1895 S. Crane wrote his Civil War novel, *The Red Badge of Courage.*

1895–99 Venezuela Boundary Dispute; US, by virtue of Monroe Doctrine, became involved in finding settlement.

1895–1983 R. (Buckminster) Fuller, architect, lived; known for using geodesic domes in his designs.

1896   Utah admitted as 45th state.

1896   Gold discovered in Klondike, Alaska; gold rush began.

1896   Election of 1896, W. Bryan, Democrat and free-silver advocate, gave famous "Cross of Gold" speech (July 8) attacking Republicans' single gold-standard platform; Bryan won Democratic nomination but lost election to W. McKinley.

1896   *Plessy* v. *Ferguson;* Supreme Court decided in favor of doctrine of "separate but equal" facilities for whites and Negroes; doctrine maintained racial segregation until the 1950–60 period.

1897–1901   W. McKinley (Republican) in office as 25th president; administration marked by period of economic recovery and by expansionsm.

1897   Dingley Tariff imposed high protective tariff.

1897   J. Sousa composed *Stars and Stripes Forever.*

1898   USS *Maine* exploded while in harbor at Havana, Cuba (Feb. 15), leading to Spanish-American War (Apr.–Dec.); US gained Cuba, Philippines, Guam, and Puerto Rico from Spain.

1898   Hawaii annexed by US.

1898–1976   A. Calder, sculptor, lived; originated mobiles.

1899   Austrian-born composer A. Schönberg wrote *Verklärte Nacht.*

1899–1902   Philippine Insurrection; began long struggle by Filipino rebels to gain complete independence from US.

1899   US Open Door policy toward China articulated.

1900   Novelist T. Dreiser wrote *Sister Carrie;* F. Baum, *The Wizard of Oz.*

1900–03   S. Dole became first president of new US Territory of Hawaii.

20TH CENT   Rise of fundamentalist religious movement in the US.

1901   President McKinley shot (Sept. 6) by an anarchist; died (Sept. 14).

1901   W. Reed, army surgeon and bacteriologist, proved that mosquitoes transmitted yellow fever.

1901   F. Norris wrote *The Octopus.*

1901–09   T. Roosevelt (Republican) in office as 26th president, succeeding McKinley; noted for passage of reform legislation, "trust-busting" and other aggressive policies of his administration.

1901   Hay-Pauncefote Treaty with Britain; reversed early Clayton-Bulwer Treaty (1850) and allowed construction of a US-controlled Panama Canal.

1901   Financier J. P. Morgan financed formation of the US Steel Corporation.

1902   President Roosevelt intervened in coal miners' strike.

1902   Photographers A. Stieglitz and E. Steichen founded the Photo-Secession Group.

1902–03   US involved in Venezuela Claims dispute.

1902–32   Justice O. W. Holmes, Jr., served on the Supreme Court; developed "clear and present danger" test in cases involving free speech.

1902–79   R. Rodgers lived; known for his collaborations with L. Hart and O. Hammerstein II, especially *Oklahoma!*

1903   US won favorable settlement in the Alaskan Boundary Dispute with Canada.

1903   Elkins Act passed; ended railroad rebates.

1903   Hay-Bunau-Varilla Treaty (concluded with newly independent Panama), granting US rights to the Panama Canal Zone for construction of the Panama Canal; US backed Panamanian independence fighters after Colombia, then in control of Panama, rejected similar treaty for canal.

1903   W. and O. Wright flew the first successful heavier-than-air, powered airplane at Kitty Hawk, North Carolina (Dec. 17).

1903   Novelist J. London published *Call of the Wild;* K. Wiggin, her novel *Rebecca of Sunnybrook Farm.*

1903–70   Artist M. Rothko, an abstract expressionistic painter, lived.

1904   Construction of the Panama Canal begun.

1904   Roosevelt Corollary to the Monroe Doctrine articulated by President Roosevelt; used to justify subsequent intervention by US in affairs of Latin American nations.

1904   Northern Securities case; Supreme Court ordered giant railroad holding company broken up; paved way for breakup of Standard Oil and other trusts.

1904   Muckraker L. Steffens published *The Shame of the Cities,* exposing urban political corruption; muckraker I. Tarbell published *History of the Standard Oil Company.*

1905   Portsmouth Conference; Roosevelt mediated settlement of Russo-Japanese War of 1905.

1905   *Lochner* v. *New York;* Supreme Court ruled state limits on hours worked violated worker's liberty.

1905   D. De Leon, Communist leader and writer, helped found the Industrial Workers of the World.

1905–6   G. Santayana wrote *The Life of Reason.*

1905–75   L. Trilling, literary critic, lived.

1906   San Francisco, California, destroyed by earthquake (Apr. 18–19).

1906   Hepburn Act passed; extended jurisdiction of Interstate Commerce Commission to other transport industries besides railroads.

1906   Pure Food and Drug Act passed.

1906   U. Sinclair wrote his famous muckraking novel *The Jungle,* exposing conditions in the Chicago meat industry.

1906   Producer O. Hammerstein built the Manhattan Opera House; introduced many European singers in the US.

1907   "Gentlemen's agreement" halted Japanese emigration to US.

1907   Oklahoma admitted as 46th state.

1907   Financial panic.

1907   H. B. Adams published *The Education of Henry Adams.*

1907   Nobel Prize awarded to A. Michelson, physicist.

1907   Newspaper publisher E. Scripps established the United Press news service.

1907   F. Ziegfeld, theatrical producer, introduced the *Ziegfeld Follies* to the American stage.

1907–   J. Barzun, writer and educator, lives.

1908   *Muller* v. *Oregon;* Supreme Court, modifying 1905 decision; cited health concerns as valid reason for upholding Oregon law; case established admissibility of sociological, psychological, and economic data.

1908   H. Ford, auto manufacturer, introduced the Model T car.

1908–   J. Bardeen, physicist, lived; helped develop the transistor and the theory of superconductivity.

1909–13   W. Taft (Republican) in office as 27th president; continued Roosevelt's "trustbusting" policies but came to oppose progressive movement; replaced Roosevelt's aggressive Latin American policy with "Dollar Diplomacy."

1909   National Association for the Advancement of Colored People (NAACP) formed by W.E.B. Du Bois and others.

1909   Payne-Aldrich Tariff adopted; supported by Taft, it maintained protective tariff.

1910   Mann-Elkins Act passed; further strengthened Interstate Commerce Commission and expanded its jurisdiction.

1910   E. A. Robinson wrote his poem, *Miniver Cheevy.*

1910   Russian-born I. Stravinsky composed his ballet, *The Firebird.*

1910–61   E. Saarinen, experimental architect, lived.

1911   Major antitrust rulings issued by the courts; holding company, Standard Oil of New Jersey ordered broken up; American Tobacco Company ordered reorganized; injunction against unfair practices by companies in beef trust.

1911   Novelist E. Wharton published *Ethan Frome.*

1912–25   US troops stationed in Nicaragua, following unsuccessful coup there.

1912   New Mexico admitted as 47th state; Arizona, as the 48th.

1912   Election of 1912; Taft, who had lost support of the progressives and was opposed by T. Roosevelt, nevertheless won Republican nomination; Roosevelt formed insurgent Progressive (Bull Moose) party; this split the vote and enabled W. Wilson to win.

1913   Sixteenth Amendment to Constitution ratified; established national income tax.

1913–21   W. Wilson (Democrat) in office as 28th president; administration noted for passage of progressive reform legislation; Wilson guided US through WW I years, vainly attempting to maintain neutrality.

1913   Seventeenth Amendment to Constitution ratified; provided for direct popular election of senators.

1913   Underwood Tariff enacted, lowering tariffs.

1913   H. Ford developed moving assembly line for mass production of Model T Ford.

1913   Federal Reserve System established.

1913   Composer W. Damrosch wrote the opera *Cyrano de Bergerac.*

1913   W. Cather published her novel *O Pioneers!*

1913   Movie producers C. De Mille and S. Goldwyn made first US feature film, *The Squaw Man.*

1914   US forces landed in Vera Cruz, Mexico amid political crisis there.

1914   WW I began in Europe (Aug.); US initially remained neutral.

1914   Panama Canal opened (Aug. 15).

1914   Federal Trade Commission established.

1914   Clayton Antitrust Act passed.

1915   Mayo brothers founded the Mayo Foundation for Medical Education and Research.

1915   German submarine torpedoed and sank the luxury liner, *Lusitania;* tragedy helped bring the US into WW I.

1915   Poet E. L. Masters published *Spoon River Anthology.*

1915   Movie director D. W. Griffith completed his classic film, *The Birth of a Nation.*

1916   Punitive raid into Mexico following border raid in US by Mexican rebel P. Villa.

1916   US protested German submarine warfare following sinking of *Sussex* (Mar. 24); Germans halted unrestricted submarine warfare.

1916   Federal Farm Loan Act passed.

1916   Short-story writer R. Lardner published *You Know Me, Al.*

1917   US broke relations with Germany (Feb.) after it resumed unrestricted submarine warfare.

1917   Zimmermann Telegram released (Mar. 1).

1917   US declared war on Germany (Apr. 6); participated in war, 1917–18.

1917   G. Barnard sculpted controversial statue of A. Lincoln.

1917–19   J. Rankin served as the first woman member of Congress.

1918   W. Wilson announced (Jan. 8) his Fourteen Points, plan to secure lasting peace after WW I. They contained his proposal for League of Nations.

1918   E. Debs jailed for sedition.

1918   Historian A. Schlesinger wrote *The Colonial Merchants and the American Revolution.*

1918–19   President Wilson participated in Paris Peace Conference (Dec.–June); failed to prevent imposition of harsh terms in Versailles treaty; but won establishment of League of Nations.

1919   Eighteenth Amendment to Constitution ratified; instituted Prohibition.

1919   S. Anderson published his novel *Winesburg, Ohio;* H. L. Mencken, *The American Language;* J. Reed, his account of the Russian Revolution, *Ten Days That Shook the World.*

1919–20   US Senate refused to ratify the Versailles Treaty; Wilson, seeking popular support for the treaty and the League of Nations, went on nationwide campaign but collapsed (Sept., 1919); Senate formally rejected the treaty (Mar., 1920) and the US never joined the League.

1920s–1931   Gangster A. Capone ruled as boss of Chicago's organized crime underworld.

1920   Red Scare ("Red Raids"); Justice Department under A. Mitchell Palmer conducted mass arrests of labor agitators and suspected Communists in wake of Russian Revolution; many deported.

1920   Nineteenth Amendment to Constitution ratified; gave women right to vote.

1920   American Civil Liberties Union founded.

1920   Poet C. Sandburg published *Smoke and Fire;* S. Lewis, his satiric novel, *Main Street.*

1921–23   W. Harding (Republican) served as 29th US president; administration noted for the corruption of Harding's appointees; Harding died (Aug. 2) at outbreak of Teapot Dome scandal.

1921   Sacco-Vanzetti Case; two Italian immigrants convicted in celebrated case.

1922   Fordney-McCumber Tariff enacted by Republicans; raised tariffs again.

1922   Novelist F. S. Fitzgerald published *The Great Gatsby;* R. Flaherty directed *Nanook of the North,* considered the forerunner of documentary motion pictures.

1923–29   C. Coolidge (Republican) in office as 30th president succeeding Harding; restored confidence in government following revelations in Teapot Dome scandal; instituted conservative, pro-business policies and encouraged rampant speculation that led to stock market crash of 1929.

1923   E. Millay published *The Ballad of the Harp Weaver and Other Poems;* K. Gibran, *The Prophet.*

1923   H. Luce co-founded the weekly news magazine *Time.*

1924   Progressive party formed by R. La Follette to oppose both Republican and Democratic parties in presidential elections.

1924   R. Frost received the Pulitzer Prize; known for his poems of rural New England life.

1924   Novelist O. Rölvaag wrote *Giants in the Earth;* G. Gershwin composed *Rhapsody in Blue.*

1924   Inventor C. Birdseye founded what later became the General Foods Corporation.

1924–1972   J. Hoover served as director of the Federal Bureau of Investigation.

1925   Scopes trial conducted in Tennessee; C. Darrow defended teacher charged with teaching theory of evolution.

1925   Poet A. Lowell wrote her poem *Lilacs;* W. C. Williams published *In the American Grain;* E. Pound began serial publication of his epic poem *Cantos* (completed 1968).

1925   Leading Dada painter and photographer M. Ray completed *Clock Wheels.*

1926   E. Hemingway published *The Sun Also Rises;* T. Wilder, *The Bridge of San Luis Rey;* E. Ferber, *Show Boat;* D. Parker published a poetry collection, *Enough Rope.*

1927   C. Lindbergh completed (May 21) first nonstop, solo transatlantic flight in *Spirit of St. Louis;* became national hero overnight.

1927   Sacco and Vanzetti executed (Aug. 22).

1927   *The Jazz Singer,* first sound movie, was released.

1928   Producer W. Disney created his cartoon character, Mickey Mouse; eventually built entertainment empire based on animated cartoons.

1928   Kellogg-Briand Pact concluded; international agreement declared end to war as an instrument of national policy.

1928   Anthropologist M. Mead published *Coming of Age in Samoa.*

1928   S. V. Benét wrote his narrative poem of the Civil War, *John Brown's Body.*

1929–33   H. Hoover (Republican) served as 31st president; continuation of Coolidge's policies brought on the Depression; Hoover, steadfastly opposed to federal action to restore failing economy, took belated steps toward the end of his administration.

1929   Stock market crash began (Oct. 24), beginning the Depression; stocks continued to fall, bringing on widespread unemployment and business failures.

1929–39   Depression; US phase of the worldwide Great Depression brought on by the collapse of the stock market; economic collapse was halted by the mid-1930s but real economic recovery did not come until the beginning of WW II.

1929   W. Faulkner published *The Sound and the Fury;* T. Wolfe, his novel *Look Homeward, Angel;* C. Aiken published *Selected Poems.*

c1930   Physicist E. Lawrence invented the cyclotron.

1930s   F. L. Wright, innovative architect, originated the "prairie style" architecture.

1930   Novelist S. (Dashiell) Hammett published *The Maltese Falcon.*

1930   Astronomer C. Tombaugh discovered Pluto.

1930   Smoot-Hawley Tariff enacted; imposed highest tariffs ever established.

1930   Scientist K. Landsteiner received Nobel Prize in Physiology or Medicine for discovery of human blood types.

1930   Historians H. S Commager and S. E. Morison published *The Growth of the American Republic.*

1931   H. Long, Louisiana political boss and US senator, proposed national "share-the-wealth" scheme; gained national recognition.

1931   J. Addams, social reformer, shared the Nobel Peace Prize with N. Butler.

1931   Humorist O. Nash wrote *Free Wheeling;* P. Buck published *The Good Earth* on life in China.

1931   Mathematician K. Godel formulated Godel's Theorem on mathematical systems.

1932   Reconstruction Finance Corporation established to extend federal credit to banks and other financial institutions (Feb. 2).

1932   Norris–La Guardia Act passed; contracts forbidding workers to join unions ("yellow dog" contracts) made illegal.

1932   Relief and Construction Act, passed to help states finance relief efforts (July 21).

1932   Federal Home Loan Bank Act passed to halt wave of foreclosures (July 22).

1932   Physicist C. Anderson discovered positron.

1932   Bonus Army, thousands of war veterans, forcibly expelled from Washington, D.C. (July).

1932   Protestant theologian R. Niebuhr wrote *Moral Man and Immoral Society.*

1932   A. Earhart became the first woman to fly solo across the Atlantic; she disappeared mysteriously somewhere over the Pacific in 1937.

1932   Author E. Caldwell published *Tobacco Road.*

1933   Twentieth Amendment to Constitution ratified; eliminated lame-duck Congress.

1933   T. Morgan received the Nobel Prize in Physiology or Medicine for proving heredity is controlled by chromosomes and genes.

1933   USS *Ranger,* first US warship designed and built as an aircraft carrier, launched.

1933–45 F. Roosevelt (Democrat) in office as 32d president; responding to the worsening Depression, he put the federal government squarely behind the effort for economic recovery and put through many relief and reform bills to institute his "New Deal"; the only president elected to four terms, he spent the last years of his administration guiding the US through WW II.

1933–34 First New Deal.

1933 Roosevelt inaugurated (Mar. 4) as wave of bank failures reached crisis point.

1933 President Roosevelt declared bank holiday (Mar. 5).

1933 Special session of Congress convened by Roosevelt (Mar. 9); passage of New Deal legislation begun soon after.

1933 Banking Relief Act passed to prevent collapse of US banking system (Mar. 9).

1933 Civilian Conservation Corps (CCC) established (Mar. 31) to provide 250,000 jobs.

1933 Gold standard abandoned (Apr. 19).

1933 Federal Emergency Relief Act passed (May 12), providing funds for local relief efforts.

1933 Agricultural Adjustment Act (AAA) passed, providing farm subsidies (May 12).

1933 Tennessee Valley Authority created (May 18).

1933 Home Owners Loan Corporation (HOLC) created to help prevent foreclosures (June 13).

1933 Home Owners Refinancing Act passed (June 13).

1933 Glass-Steagall Act passed (June 16), creating the Federal Deposit Insurance Corporation (FDIC).

1933 National Industrial Recovery Act (NIRA) passed (June 16).

1933 Civil Works Administration (CWA) established (Nov. 8); eventually provided jobs for millions of unemployed on government projects.

1933 Twenty-first Amendment to the Constitution ratified; repealed Prohibition (Dec. 5).

1933 A. Einstein emigrated to the US and became a member of the Institute for Advanced Study at Princeton.

1934 Dust storms began in the lower Great Plains region of the Midwest; gave rise to the "Dust Bowl" and the westward migration of thousands of farmers.

1934 Securities and Exchange Commission (SEC) created (June 6).

1934 Reciprocal Tariff Act passed (June 12), giving president power to lower tariffs; brought about end of high protective tariffs.

1934 Federal Communications Commission (FCC) created (June 19) to regulate communications industry.

1934 Federal Housing Authority (FHA) created (June 28).

1934 Naturalist and explorer, C. Beebe descended to record depth in the ocean using a bathysphere.

1934 H. Miller wrote *Tropic of Cancer,* banned in the US until the 1960s because of sexual content.

1934 H. Urey received Nobel Chemistry Prize for isolating the heavy-hydrogen isotope deuterium.

1935–39 Second New Deal.

1935 Works Progress Administration (WPA) created (Apr. 8).

1935 Soil Conservation Service established (Apr. 27).

1935 Supreme Court declared National Industrial Recovery Act (NIRA) unconstitutional (May); struggle between court and Roosevelt reached a climax in 1937.

1935 Rural Electrification Administration (REA) created (May 11).

1935 National Labor Relations Act passed (July 5), granting workers right to organize and bargain collectively.

1935 Social Security Act passed (Aug. 14).

1935 Wheeler-Rayburn Act passed (Aug. 28), putting gas and electricity companies under government control.

1935 Wealth Tax Act passed (Aug. 30) to tax incomes over $50,000 at a higher rate.

1935 Neutrality Act passed (Aug. 31); aimed at keeping US out of war.

1935 Louisiana political boss H. Long, who proposed "Share-the-Wealth" scheme, assassinated (Sept. 8).

1935 Forerunner of Congress of Industrial Organization (CIO) established.

1935 C. Odets wrote his play, *Waiting for Lefty;* R. Sherwood, *The Petrified Forest.*

1935 Novelist J. Farrell completed the Studs Lonigan trilogy.

1936   Supreme Court ruled Agricultural Adjustment Act (AAA) unconstitutional (Jan.).

1936   Old Age Revolving Pension scheme advanced by Dr. Francis E. Townsend; plan marked dissatisfaction with New Deal programs; Townsend, Father C. Coughlin, and Rev. Gerald L. Smith subsequently joined forces in opposing the New Deal with "share-the-wealth" plans.

1936   Election of 1936; Republican opposition to Roosevelt's New Deal coalesced around charge that free enterprise had been replaced by regulated monopoly; Roosevelt defeated his Republican opponent, A. Landon.

1936   Pollster G. Gallup successfully predicted the reelection of President F. Roosevelt using a public opinion survey.

1936   Author M. Mitchell published her first and only novel *Gone With the Wind.*

1937   Widespread strikes and labor unrest.

1937   Supreme Court controversy (Feb.–July); Roosevelt, in struggle with Court over New Deal legislation, suggested increasing number of justices; plan denounced as scheme to "pack" the court with supporters and was abandoned.

1937   The *Hindenburg,* a German dirigible, exploded into flames while docking at Lakehurst, New Jersey (May 6); 36 persons died.

1937   Neutrality extended (May); arms sales to belligerents prohibited.

1937   Aviator Amelia Earhart disappeared on flight over South Pacific (July 2).

1937   Nationwide recession began (Oct.); stock prices declined.

1937   J. Dos Passos published the trilogy *U.S.A.;* J. P. Marquand, his novel *The Late George Apley;* poet W. Auden wrote *Letters from Ireland.*

1938   House Un-American Activities Committee formed (May) to investigate Nazis, Communists, and other subversives.

1938   Fair Labor Standards Act passed (June 25), guaranteeing 40-hour work week and minimum wage.

1938   Philosopher W. Quine published *Word and Object.*

1938   T Wilder wrote his play *Our Town;* C. B. Luce, *Kiss the Boys Goodbye.*

1938–58   L. Mies van der Rohe served as professor of architecture at the Illinois Institute of Technology.

1939   US defense appropriations increased as threat of war in Europe mounted.

1939   World War II broke out in Europe; US proclaimed neutrality (Sept. 5).

1939   Artist W. De Kooning, a leading abstract expressionist, painted *Man.*

1939   J. Steinbeck published *The Grapes of Wrath;* N. West, *The Day of the Locust;* R. Chandler, his detective story *The Big Sleep.*

1939   Playwright E. O'Neill wrote *The Iceman Cometh;* W. Saroyan, *The Time of Your Life;* L. Hellman, *The Children's Hour.*

1939   I. Berlin composed *God Bless America.*

1939   Arms embargo established by Neutrality Act repealed to allow France and Britain to purchase munitions.

1939   Ukrainian-born engineer I. Sikorsky developed the first successful helicopter.

1940   Smith Act passed; aliens required to register.

1940s   Artistic movement known as abstract expressionism developed in New York.

1940   Defense appropriation of $18 billion to construct two-ocean navy and raise million-man army (July).

1940   Peacetime draft instituted to raise million-man army (Sept 14).

1940   Nuclear chemist G. Seaborg discovered plutonium.

1940   Advisory Commission to the Council on National Defense set up to mobilize US industry for possible war effort.

1940   Election of 1940; Roosevelt broke tradition (established by G. Washington) of serving only two terms and ran for third term; overwhelmingly defeated Republican opponent, W. Willkie.

1940   Muckraker R. S. Baker received Pulitzer prize for his eight-volume work on W. Wilson.

1941   Roosevelt articulated his policy of Four Freedoms.

1941   Lend-Lease Act passed; program established to supply potential allies (Mar. 1).

1941   Atlantic Charter issued after meeting with British prime minister W. Churchill (Aug.).

1941   Pearl Harbor attacked (Dec. 7) by Japanese; US declared war (Dec. 8).

1941   Critic and essayist E. Wilson published *The Wound and the Bow;* psycholanalyst E. Fromm, *Escape from Freedom.*

1941   O. Welles acted in and directed the film, *Citizen Kane.*

1941–45 US participation in WW II; vast resources of men and matériel available to the US, as well as efficient organization of industry, guaranteed the US both a significant advantage and (eventually) a dominant role in the fighting; with the Allies, US forces fought in both the European and Pacific theaters; the US emerged from the war as a leading world power and, with the Soviet Union, dominated the postwar world.

1942 War Production Board and Office of Price Administration created to manage wartime economy; rationing system instituted.

1942 Internment of Japanese Americans, following Pearl Harbor attack; some 112,000 were forced to move to inland internment centers until 1945.

1942–45 Manhattan Project, US government program to develop atomic bomb; under direction of J. Oppenheimer, scientists on project achieved first sustained nuclear chain reaction (Dec. 2, 1942, by E. Fermi) and exploded world's first atomic bomb in test near Los Alamos (July 16, 1945).

1942 W. Benét awarded Pulitzer Prize for Poetry for *The Dust Which Is God.*

1942 Artist P. (Jackson) Pollock painted *Male and Female;* composer A. Copland wrote *Appalachian Spring.*

1943 Detroit race riot; sparked by competition for housing and high paying defense jobs, as black and white laborers migrated to the city from the South.

1943 A. Moses, known as Grandma Moses, painted *The McDonel Farm.*

1943 O. Stern won the Nobel Physics Prize; his research laid the groundwork for atomic science.

1943 O. Hammerstein, II, collaborated with R. Rodgers on the musical *Oklahoma!*

1943 Novelist A. Rand wrote *The Fountainhead.*

1944 President Roosevelt reelected for unprecedented fourth term, with H. Truman as vice-president; defeated Republican T. Dewey.

1944 Author J. Hersey published *A Bell for Adano.*

1945 President Roosevelt died in office (Apr. 12).

1945–53 H. Truman (Democrat) in office as the 33d president, succeeding Roosevelt; continued many of Roosevelt's policies and brought WW II to a successful conclusion; promoted his Fair Deal domestic policy; instituted programs to rebuild war-torn Europe, and presided over the early phase of the Cold War.

1945 San Francisco Conference held (Apr.–June); UN Charter drafted.

1945 WW II ended with Japan's surrender (Sept. 2).

1945 US joined the newly created UN.

1945 C. Hull, statesman and secretary of state, received Nobel Peace Prize.

1945 Humorist J. Thurber published *The Thurber Carnival.*

c1946 Radioactive carbon-14 dating system developed by W. Libby.

1946 ENIAC, first all-electronic computer, developed.

1946 W. Churchill, former British prime minister, gave famous speech at Fulton Missouri (Mar. 15); warned of the threat of Communism and used the term "Iron Curtain."

1946 Atomic Energy Commission established.

1946 R. P. Warren wrote *All the King's Men;* H. Arendt, political scientist, published *Origins of Totalitarianism.*

1947 Taft-Hartley Labor Act passed by Congress.

1947 Truman Doctrine articulated (Mar. 12) by President Truman; responded to Soviet postwar expansionism.

1947 President Truman issued Loyalty Order (Mar. 22) as fears about Communist subversives in government began to spread ("Red Scare").

1947 National Security Act passed to create a Department of Defense and establish the National Security Council.

1947 J. Michener published *Tales of the South Pacific;* T. Williams wrote his play, *A Streetcar Named Desire.*

1947 Inventor E. Land developed the Polaroid camera.

1948 Marshall Plan; provided massive economic aid for war-torn Europe; brought about rapid economic recovery in Western Europe.

1948 A. Kinsey, zoologist and biologist, published *Sexual Behavior of the Human Male.*

1948–49 US played a leading role in the Berlin airlift.

1948 Election of 1948; opposed by T. Dewey, Republican, and S. Thurmond, candidate of the Dixiecrats, Truman was expected to lose the election; nevertheless conducted vigorous whistle-stop campaign and won the presidency.

1948 Artist A. Wyeth painted *Christina's World.*

1948 N. Mailer wrote *The Naked and the Dead.*

1949 Truman announced (Jan. 5) his Fair Deal program.

1949–52 D. Acheson served as US secretary of state; developed policy of "containment of Communism."

1949 North Atlantic Treaty Organization (NATO) formed (Apr. 4) by nations of Europe and North America.

1949 A. Hiss, accused of being a Communist, convicted of perjury (Nov. 17, 1950); marked beginning of furor over subversives in government.

1949 Point Four Plan instituted to provide technical aid to underdeveloped nations.

1949 A. Miller wrote his play, *Death of a Salesman.*

1949 Evangelist B. Graham began his popular revivalist crusades.

1950 McCarran Act passed by Congress, allowing detention of subversives during national emergencies; law ultimately weakened by Supreme Court decisions and later Congressional amendment.

1950–53 Korean War, pitting Communist East and non-Communist West against each other in armed conflict; US played leading role in what was called UN "police action."

1951 Twenty-second Amendment to the Constitution ratified; presidents limited to serving only two terms.

1951 J. and E. Rosenberg, accused of stealing atomic secrets, convicted; executed in 1953.

1951 Nobel Prize in Physiology or Medicine awarded to M. Theiler for his work in developing yellow fever vaccine.

1951 Novelist J. D. Salinger published *The Catcher in the Rye.*

1952 US exploded first hydrogen bomb.

1952 Election of 1952; A. Stevenson ran as Democratic candidate, D. Eisenhower, Republican; vice-presidential candidate R. Nixon, under attack in campaign, gave famous "Checkers" speech (Sept. 23); Eisenhower won election in landslide and Republicans won control of both houses, ending long period of

government by Democrats. Eisenhower again defeated Stevenson in 1956 election.

1952 E. B. White wrote the children's classic, *Charlotte's Web.*

1953–61 D. Eisenhower (Republican) in office as 34th president; administration marked by period of general peace and prosperity, conservative domestic policy, and Cold War policies of "containment" of Communism and "massive retaliation" in the event of nuclear war.

1953–59 J. F. Dulles served as secretary of state; promoted US Cold War policies and advocated threat of massive nuclear retaliation as deterrent to spread of Communism.

1953 Department of Health, Education and Welfare established.

1953 Biochemist J. Watson, with Sir F. Crick, discovered the molecular structure of DNA.

1953–54 McCarthy hearings; marked height of post-WW II "Red Scare"; ended with censure of senator J. McCarthy by Senate.

1953 Historian B. Catton published *A Stillness at Appomattox.*

1954 *Brown* v. *Board of Education of Topeka, Kansas;* Supreme Court reversed long-standing "separate but equal" doctrine and thus began the desegregation of schools.

1954 Southeast Asia Treaty Organization (SEATO) organized.

1954 L. Pauling won Nobel Prize in Chemistry for theory of chemical bonding; later won Peace Prize for opposing nuclear warfare (1962).

1955 AFL-CIO, major US labor federation, formed by merger of American Federation of Labor and the Congress of Industrial Organizations.

1955 Civil rights movement began; various civil rights groups sprang up after black woman refused to move to back of a bus (Dec. 5) in Montgomery, Alabama; Rev. M. L. King's Southern Christian Leadership Conference (SCLC) among groups that began nonviolent campaign against racial discrimination.

1955 V. Nabokov wrote his novel *Lolita;* J. Baldwin, *Notes of a Native Son.*

1956 Federal Aid Highway Act passed; funded construction of interstate highway system.

1956 Beatnik poet A. Ginsberg wrote *Howl.*

1957 Eisenhower Doctrine enunciated to halt Communism in Mideast.

1957 Civil Rights Act passed; established commission to investigate infringements of Negro voting rights.

1957 Federal troops sent (Sept.) by President Eisenhower to enforce federal court order to desegregate the Little Rock, Arkansas, high school.

1957 Soviets launched (Oct. 4) first earth satellite; US embarrassed by the Soviet "first"; space race began.

1957 Linguist A. (Noam) Chomsky published *Syntactic Structures* on his theory of generative grammar.

1957 Composer L. Bernstein wrote *West Side Story;* novelist J. Kerouac wrote *On the Road.*

1958 Lebanese Crisis; US troops landed in Lebanon.

1958 Economist J. Galbraith wrote *The Affluent Society.*

1959 Alaska became the 49th state.

1959 Hawaii admitted as the 50th state.

1959 Soviet leader N. Khrushchev visited US (Sept.), following visit by US vice-president R. Nixon to the Soviet Union; hopes raised for Cold War "thaw."

1960s Young nonconformist youth movement called counterculture became widespread; hippies and New Left radicals emerged.

1960 US U-2 spy plane shot down (May 1) over Soviet Union.

1960 Presidential election of 1960; Democratic J. Kennedy challenged Republican Vice-President R. Nixon; first election in which television played a significant role, notably in the Kennedy-Nixon debate; Kennedy won by a slim margin, becoming the youngest president ever elected and the first Catholic to hold the post.

1961 Diplomatic relations broken (Jan.) with Cuba; marked beginning of troubles between US and Cuba's revolutionary leader, F. Castro.

1961–63 J. F. Kennedy (Democrat) is in office as 35th president; promoted activist and idealistic climate with his New Frontiers program; gave firm federal support to emerging civil rights movement, began limited US involvement in Vietnam; clashed with Communists in continuing Cold War.

1961 Bay of Pigs Invasion (Apr.); unsuccessful, CIA-backed invasion of Cuba; US deeply embarrassed by incident.

1961 Alliance for Progress established to combat communism in South America. US aid reduced after 1971.

1962 J. Glenn became the first American to orbit the earth (Feb. 20).

1962 Federal troops sent by President Kennedy to enforce integration of the University of Mississippi (Sept.–Oct.).

1962 Cuban Missile Crisis (Oct.); President Kennedy forced Soviets to withdraw missiles from Cuba.

1962 K. A. Porter published her novel, *Ship of Fools;* playwright E. Albee wrote *Who's Afraid of Virginia Woolf?*

1963 US signed Nuclear Test Ban Treaty.

1963 March on Washington, mass demonstration for black civil rights (Aug.).

1963 President Kennedy assassinated (Nov. 22); Warren Commission later investigated shooting to put an end to persistent rumors about various conspiracies.

1963–69 L. Johnson (Democrat) in office as 36th president, succeeding Kennedy; instituted Great Society program and won enactment of legislation for sweeping social reform; made US active participant in Vietnam War; later years of administration marked by widespread antiwar protest and social unrest.

1964 Civil Rights Act of 1964 passed (July 2) to end all discrimination, including religious and sex discrimination.

1964 Gulf of Tonkin Incident; North Vietnam attacked US destroyers (Aug.); Gulf of Tonkin resolution passed by Congress used to justify later massive buildup of US forces in Vietnam.

1964 "War on Poverty" begun by President Johnson with enactment of Economic Opportunity Act (Aug. 30).

1964 Election of 1964, President Johnson ran for first full term against Republican B. Goldwater; Goldwater perceived as dangerously aggressive in foreign-policy thinking; Johnson won landslide victory.

1964 H. Marcuse, political philosopher, published *One Dimensional Man.*

1965–73 US actively involved in Vietnam War; US began bombing North Vietnam (Feb., 1965); sent hundreds of thousands of US troops into battle in unsuccessful effort to block Communist takeover in Vietnam.

1965   Antiwar teach-in held at University of Michigan (Mar.); teach-ins quickly spread to other campuses and thus began the student antiwar movement.

1965   Voting Rights Act of 1965 passed; legislation for Medicare for aged, federal aid to education, and other reform measures passed in this year.

1965   Watts riot in Los Angeles (Aug.); first of race riots by blacks that spread to cities across the country; urban unrest among blacks reached a peak by 1968 and tapered off quickly in following years.

1965   W. Schirra, Jr., successfully rendezvoused in space with Gemini 7.

1965   Militant black leader, Malcolm X, assassinated.

1965   Consumer advocate R. Nader published *Unsafe at Any Speed,* prompting passage of auto safety laws and launching him as a nationally known consumer advocate.

1965   Historian A. Schlesinger, Jr., published *A Thousand Days,* on the Kennedy administration.

1966   Black Panthers, radical-terrorist group, formed; signaled rise of radical militants and end of nonviolent protest in black movement.

1966   NOW (National Organization for Women) founded.

1966   Novelist T. Capote published *In Cold Blood;* writer A. Nin, her seven-volume *Diaries.*

1967   First black Supreme Court justice, Thurgood Marshall, appointed.

1967   Pentagon "siege" by antiwar protesters; marked ascendancy of antiwar protest in US; civil disobedience widespread.

1968   Social unrest reached fever pitch; blacks rioted in cities across the country; rioting by students on various campuses, counterculture, and drug cult within it, widespread among young people.

1968   Pueblo Incident (Jan. 23).

1968   Dr. M. L. King, leading figure of civil rights movement, assassinated (Apr. 4).

1968   R. F. Kennedy assassinated (June 5), while campaigning in Democratic primary.

1968   Election of 1968; widespread opposition to Vietnam War forced Johnson out of presidential race; Democratic National Convention (Chicago, Aug.) marred by rioting by antiwar radicals and subsequent "police riot"; H. Humphrey, Democrat, opposed R. Nixon,

Republican, in presidential campaign; G. Wallace made unsuccessful third-party bid; Nixon, campaigning on conservative law-and-order and honorable peace in Vietnam, won election.

1968   United Methodist church formed by merger of US Methodist church and Evangelical United Brethren church, creating world's largest Methodist body.

1969–74   R. Nixon in office as 37th president; instituted conservative policies, including emphasis on law enforcement and war on widespread drug use; gradually effected US withdrawal from Vietnam; began policy of détente to ease East-West tensions; administration brought down by Watergate scandal.

1969   SALT talks (arms limitation) begun with Soviets.

1969   US landed first man on the moon (July 20).

1969   March on Washington, massive antiwar protest (Nov. 15); demanded immediate, not gradual, withdrawal from Vietnam.

1970   Widespread protest followed US invasion of Cambodia; National Guardsmen fired on protesters at Kent State University (May 4); 100,000 demonstrated in Washington, D.C. (May 9).

1970   SST developmental funding bill defeated in Senate.

1971   Equal Rights Amendment passed by Congress; marked rise of women's rights movement that dominated the 1970s; amendment failed to win ratification after long fight (1982).

1971   US table tennis team visited China (Apr.); marked start of US efforts to normalize relations with China.

1971   Washington shutdown by antiwar protesters failed (May); 7,000 arrested.

1971   Pentagon Papers leaked to press (June); secret government study revealed US had gradually become entangled in Vietnam War.

1971   Voting age lowered to 18 following ratification of the 26th Amendment.

1971   Draft law expired.

1971   President Nixon announced (Aug.) wage and price freeze to combat spiraling inflation; later devalued dollar (1971, 1973, 1974).

1971   Behaviorist B. F. Skinner wrote *Beyond Freedom and Dignity.*

1972 President Nixon visit to China (Feb. 21–27); process of normalization of relations with China continued.

1972 President Nixon on historic first presidential visit to USSR (May 22–June 1); signed SALT I agreement, limiting antiballistic missile systems and missile launchers for offensive weapons.

1972–74 Watergate Scandal; arrest of Watergate burglars (June, 1972) began scandal, which culminated in President Nixon's resignation (Aug. 9, 1974).

1972 SALT II talks began with USSR.

1972 President Nixon signed revenue-sharing bill into law (Oct.).

1972 Election of 1972; Nixon opposed by Sen. G. McGovern; despite recession and continued inflation, Nixon won landslide victory.

1972 G. Wallace partially paralyzed in attempted assassination while campaigning as third-party candidate for the presidency.

1973 Peace agreement "ending" Vietnam War signed at Paris (Jan. 27).

1973 Senate began investigation of emerging Watergate Scandal (Feb.).

1973 Wage and price controls extended (Apr.) to Apr. 30, 1974.

1973 Supreme Court ruled in *Roe* vs. *Wade;* ruling allowed abortions for women up to six months pregnant.

1973 Existence of Nixon tapes revealed (July); long struggle for release of tapes begun by Watergate investigators.

1973 Vice-President S. Agnew resigned (Oct. 10) under pressure from charges of past corruption; pleaded "no contest" to income tax evasion charge.

1973 G. Ford in office as vice-president (Dec. 6).

1973 Poet R. Lowell wrote *The Dolphin.*

1973–77 H. Kissinger served as secretary of state; instituted "shuttle diplomacy" after the 1973 Arab-Israeli War.

1974 Supreme Court ordered President Nixon to release tapes sought by Watergate investigators (July 24).

1974 House Judiciary Committee voted articles of impeachment against President Nixon in Watergate scandal (July 27–30).

1974 President Nixon resigned after admitting involvement in Watergate cover-up; became first president to resign under threat of impeachment (Aug. 9).

1974–76 G. Ford (Republican) in office as 38th president, succeeding Nixon; attempted to restore public confidence in government; recession, inflation, and growing unemployment plagued his administration.

1974 Ford granted Nixon pardon for crimes he allegedly committed in office (Sept. 8).

1974 N. Rockefeller sworn in as vice-president (Dec. 19).

1975 Last Americans evacuated from South Vietnam (Apr. 29) as North Vietnamese completed successful invasion of South; Vietnam united under Communist rule soon after.

1975 Cambodians captured US cargo ship in Mayaguez Incident (May 12).

1975 Novelist S. Bellow published *Humboldt's Gift.*

1976 President Ford ordered sweeping reorganization of US intelligence agencies (Feb. 17).

1976 US Bicentennial celebration (July 4).

1976 Lockheed scandal; firm implicated in payment of bribes to foreign officials to secure contracts.

1976 Election of 1976; President Ford defeated primary challenge by conservative Republican R. Reagan; J. Carter became dark-horse candidate of the Democrats; Carter projected a populist image and, taking advantage of distrust of government, promised sweeping reorganization of executive branch; Carter won election.

1976 Economist M. Friedman won the Nobel Prize in Economics.

1977–81 J. Carter (Democrat) in office as 39th president; his administration marked by growing split with mainstream Democrats, the energy crisis, an economic crisis, the success of Camp David negotiations between Egypt and Israel, and by the hostage crisis in Iran.

1977 House and Senate adopted strict codes of ethics (Mar.–Apr.).

1977 Legislation enacted permitting President Carter to reorganize the executive branch.

1977 Alaska pipeline opened.

1977 US and Panama signed treaty giving Panama eventual control of the Panama Canal; Senate ratified treaty (Apr., 1978).

1978 Camp David Accords signed (Sept. 17) by Israeli prime minister M. Begin and Egyptian president A. Sadat; provided a historic "framework for Mideast peace."

1979 Full diplomatic relations with China established (Jan. 1).

1979 Nuclear accident at Three Mile Island power plant in Pennsylvania (Mar. 28).

1979 President Carter began implementation of oil price decontrol (June 1).

1979 US and USSR signed SALT II agreement on arms limitation (June); ratification held up by Senate opposition and Soviet invasion of Afghanistan; both nations informally observed agreement until 1987, when US abandoned deployment limits.

1979–81 Hostage Crisis in Iran; Muslim militants seized US embassy (Nov. 4) and held 52 Americans hostage, Iranians used incident to humiliate US; finally released hostages (Jan. 20, 1981).

1980 President Carter ordered (Jan. 4) embargo on grain shipments to the Soviet Union in response to Soviet invasion of Afghanistan; later pulled US out of Moscow Olympics.

1980 Six Americans hiding in Iran escaped with help from Canadian diplomats (Jan. 29).

1980 President Carter ordered sharp spending cuts to deal with rising inflation (Mar.); unemployment rate rising; banking industry deregulated.

1980 Attempt to free US hostages in Iran ended in failure (Apr. 28); eight US commandos killed in helicopter crash.

1980 Mount St. Helens, a long-dormant volcano in Washington, erupted with massive force (May 5).

1980 Influx of Cuban "boat people" reached major proportions (May–June).

1980 Election of 1980, President Carter won narrow victory in bitter primary race against rival Sen. E. Kennedy; Republican candidate R. Reagan took advantage of growing disaffection with Democrats' liberal policies and the current economic crisis (inflationary recession); he campaigned on conservative program of tax cuts, less federal spending and regulation, and a strong military; Reagan won landslide victory which swept many Republicans into office and gained them a majority in the Senate.

1980 Prime interest rate rose to 21.5 percent as effort to stem high inflation rate continued (Dec. 19).

1981–89 R. Reagan (Republican) in office as 40th president, the oldest ever elected to the office; on taking office began aggressive pol-icy of cutting federal spending (except defense), while cutting taxes (supply-side economics; "Reaganomics"); Reagan policies cut inflation and brought down high interest rates but at the cost of temporary high unemployment; by 1983, the economy entered period of prosperity.

1981 Americans being held hostage in Iran released (Jan. 20) as President Reagan was being sworn in.

1981 US involvement in El Salvador increased with decision to send additional military advisers; US, charging Nicaragua with aiding Salvadoran rebels, cut off aid (Jan.); Nicaragua countered (1982) by charging US with supporting Contra rebels seeking overthrow of Sandinista government.

1981 President Reagan wounded (Mar. 30) in attempted assassination by John W. Hinckley, Jr.; Hinckley later committed to mental institution.

1981 US launched world's first reusable spacecraft, the space shuttle *Columbia*.

1981 Reagan administration cuts of Social Security benefits blocked by Senate (May).

1981 Strike by federal air traffic controllers (Aug.) broken by President Reagan; striking controllers fired.

1981 Reagan administration abandoned plans for controversial mobile MX missiles (Oct.).

1981 Reagan administration won major victory when Congress approved tax cut package.

1981 S. D. O'Connor sworn in (Oct. 25) as first woman Supreme Court justice.

1981 President Reagan ordered economic sanctions imposed against the Soviets for their part in the crackdown against Solidarity in Poland.

1981 Oil and gas industries deregulated by Reagan; prices rose sharply.

1981 Novelist J. Updike published *Rabbit Is Rich.*

1982 Congress voted to allow savings and loan banks to invest in all areas of business, not just home mortgages; subsequent lack of government oversight and outright fraud led to S&L scandal.

1982 AT&T agreed to breakup sought by US antitrust suit (Jan.); would divest 22 region Bell System telephone companies.

1982 Libyan oil imports banned after US accused country of involvement with terrorism (Mar.).

1982   Demonstration (June 12) in New York City, the largest to-date, in which an estimated 750,000 participated, protesting nuclear arms race.

1982   Provisions of the Civil Rights Act extended for 25 years (June 29).

1982   US successful (Aug.) in its efforts to negotiate withdrawal of PLO guerrillas from Beirut, following Israeli invasion of Lebanon.

1982   Democrats returned majority in House of Representatives in Nov. elections.

1982   Boland amendment passed by Congress, prohibiting military assistance to Contra rebels fighting Nicaragua's pro-Communist government; reversed itself in 1986.

1982   First permanent artificial heart implant completed (Dec. 2); recipient was Barney B. Clark, a dentist.

1983   Strong economic growth in US economy began; inflation and unemployment dropped; period of prosperity, "the go-go years" lasting through much of the 1980s, laid to Reagan policies.

1983   President Reagan proposed his Strategic Defense Initiative (SDI) program, dubbed Star Wars (Mar.).

1983   US blood banks reported taking steps against transmission of AIDS through blood transfusions.

1983   Terrorist bomb in Beirut killed 241 US marines stationed there as part of peacekeeping force (Oct. 25).

1983   US invaded Grenada to counter takeover of moderate leftist government by faction of extremist revolutionary Communists with ties to Cuba (Oct. 31); troops withdrawn after previous government was restored.

1984   Election of 1984; Democratic primary candidate Rev. J. Jackson became first black to launch campaign for major party nomination; W. Mondale won Democratic nomination, selecting as his running mate New York Representative Geraldine Ferraro, the first woman vice-presidential candidate of a major political party; Republican Reagan won landslide victory, capturing largest electoral vote majority ever; Republicans maintained slim majority in Senate (later lost), while Democrats kept their majority in the House.

1985   M. Gorbachev came to power in USSR; marked beginning of closer East-West relations.

1985   Worldwide Live Aid rock concert held in Philadelphia and in London to benefit African famine relief (July).

1985   US became debtor nation for first time since 1914.

1985   World's largest particle accelerator in operation at Fermi Laboratory in Illinois (Oct.).

1985   Geneva summit (Nov.) between Reagan and Gorbachev; marked start of good relations between two leaders; concluded agreement against chemical weapons and resumed cultural exchanges (halted in 1979).

1985   250 US soldiers killed in plane crash at Gander, Newfoundland (Dec. 12).

1985   Gramm-Rudman-Hollings Act passed; ordered budget deficit gradually eliminated by 1991.

1986   Space shuttle *Challenger* exploded (Jan. 31), killing all seven astronauts aboard.

1986   R. Penn Warren named first US poet laureate (Feb.).

1986   Congress overturned Reagan veto of economic sanctions against South Africa's apartheid government.

1986   US warplanes attacked selected targets in Tripoli and Benghazi, Libya (Apr. 21); raid ordered in retaliation for terrorist attack on US military personnel in West Berlin (Apr. 5).

1986   Congress voted $100 million in aid to Contra rebels, reversing itself on 1982 Boland amendment (June); marked major, but temporary, victory for Reagan administration prior to Iran-Contra Scandal.

1986   100th anniversary of Statue of Liberty marked (July).

1986   Congress passed Tax Reform Act, first major overhaul of US tax system in 40 years.

1986   Iceland summit conference (Oct.); Reagan met with Gorbachev on disarmament proposals; Reagan refused to reduce US SDI program; no new agreements reached.

1986   I. Boesky pleaded guilty in Wall Street insider trading scandal (Nov.).

1986–90   Iran-Contra Scandal; Reagan administration embarrassed first by revelations of secret "arms for hostages" deal (Nov.) and then by reports that some of the money had been funneled to Contra rebels fighting in Nicaragua.

1987   Amnesty program for illegal aliens residing in the US began (May) as part of new US immigration policy.

1987 US Navy began providing escorts for Kuwaiti tankers in Persian Gulf (July), following attacks by Iranians.

1987 200th anniversary of US Constitution marked (Sept. 17).

1987 Black Monday (Oct. 19); stock market crashed, heralding end of 1980s bull market and an economic downturn.

1987 Senate refused to confirm nomination of Robert H. Bork as Supreme Court justice; subsequent confirmation of conservative Anthony Kennedy established 5 to 4 conservative majority in the court.

1987 Intermediate Nuclear Forces (INF) Treaty signed at Washington, D.C., summit between Reagan and Gorbachev (Dec.); first treaty to eliminate whole class of weapons (all short and medium range nuclear weapons).

1988 Moscow summit (May–June); INF treaty formally activated; talks on Strategic Arms Reduction Treaty (START) stalled over question of SDI program.

1988 USS Vincennes, pursuing Iranian gunboats that had been harrassing shipping in the Persian Gulf, mistakenly shot down Iranian airbus flying nearby (July 3); 290 civilians killed.

1988 Election of 1988; Massachusetts governor Michael Dukakis, who won the Democratic nomination, turned down runner-up Rev. J. Jackson as his vice-presidential running mate; Republican Vice-President G. Bush, campaigning on Reagan's successful management of economy and US foreign policy, decisively defeated Dukakis; Democrats retained control of both houses of Congress, however.

1988 Soviet leader Gorbachev, speaking at UN, proclaimed end to Cold War; promised USSR would pursue openness (glasnost) and vast program of restructuring of Soviet society (perestroika).

1989–93 G. Bush in office as 41st president; economic recession and rapidly rising national debt ($3 trillion by 1990) proved to be most serious domestic problems, complicated by an ongoing struggle between a Democratic Congress and a Republican president; in foreign affairs, the administration presided over the end of the Cold War and led an international coalition in war against Iraq's invasion of Kuwait.

1989 President Bush proposed expanding discussions on nuclear weapons to include reductions in conventional forces in Europe (June).

1989 President Bush announced anti-drug abuse plan; won cooperation of Colombia, Peru, and Bolivia in fight against drug lords.

1989 Berlin Wall, long-standing symbol of Cold War East-West divisions, was torn down (Nov.).

1989 Malta summit (Dec.); Bush and Gorbachev discussed 50 percent nuclear arms reduction, major reductions in US-USSR conventional forces in Europe, trade deals, and the withdrawal of the USSR from Eastern Europe.

1989 US troops invaded Panama (Dec. 20); sought to halt drug trafficking through the country to US, to capture Panamanian dictator M. Noriega (wanted on drug charges in US), and to restore democracy; Noriega tried and found guilty (1992) in US.

1989 Congress approved S&L bailout fund amounting to $166 billion; final actual cost estimated much higher; additional money approved in 1991.

1990 USSR agreed to exclude US SDI program from START negotiations (Feb.).

1990 Washington summit (May–June); Bush and Gorbachev discussed Soviet blockade of break-away republic of Lithuania; signed trade accord contingent on Soviets' relaxing their emmigration laws; declared Cold War was over.

1990 Bush, breaking campaign pledge, agreed to raise taxes and cut spending as part of compromise deficit reduction plan with Congressional Democrats (July); Democrats agreed to cut Social Security and Medicare entitlement programs.

1990 US and other major Western powers agreed to help Soviets shift to market economy (July); promised economic aid and technical expertise.

1990–91 Persian Gulf War; US vigorously opposed Iraqi invasion of Kuwait (Aug.); led UN–backed moves to bring about Kuwaiti withdrawal, finally resorting to military force; Iraqis driven out of Kuwait and forced to submit to harsh peace terms (Jan.–Feb., 1991).

1990 US, USSR, Britain, and France agreed to reunification of Germany (Sept.); Germany formally reunified.

1990　Treaty on Conventional Armed Forces in Europe (CFE) signed in Paris (Nov.) by NATO and Warsaw Pact members; put limits on conventional forces deployed between Atlantic Ocean and Ural Mountains.

1990　Charter proclaiming end to post-World War II era of confrontation in Europe signed by Bush, Gorbachev, and representatives of 32 other nations (Nov.); set up secretariat for Conference on Security and Cooperation in Europe (CSCE).

1991　US troop strength in Europe to be cut by up to half over next five years, following reorganization of NATO (May).

1991　Some 34 military bases in US to be closed as part of post–Cold War reductions of US military (July).

1991　Historic START treaty signed by President Bush and Soviet leader Gorbachev (July 31); called for first-ever reduction in long-range nuclear arms amounting to 30 percent of stockpiles by 1998.

1991　Soviet coup attempt failed (Aug.); collapse and breakup of Communist-dominated USSR followed soon after, leaving US as world's lone superpower.

1991　House bank scandal; GAO audit of House bank revealed 355 current and former House members had overdrawn their accounts (Sept.).

1991　President Bush ended round-the-clock alert for Strategic Air Command (SAC) long-range bombers armed with nuclear weapons (Sept. 27).

1991　Black justice Clarence Thomas seated on Supreme Court (Oct.) following bitter confirmation battle; televised Senate hearings included charges of sexual harassment by one-time aide Anita Hill; Thomas replaced retiring Justice T. Marshall.

1991　Civil Rights Act of 1991 enacted (Nov.), with provisions making it easier to seek damages in cases of job discrimination.

1991　Gunman killed 23 in worst mass killing in US history (Oct. 16); opened fire in Killeen, Texas, cafeteria and then killed himself.

1992　President Bush pledged to help finance $24 billion aid package for former Soviet Union (Apr.).

1992　Average size of US household reported stabilized for past three years, ending 140-year gradual decline from 5.55 to 2.63 people.

1992　27th Amendment to Constitution ratified (May 7) after languishing for over two centuries since James Madison first proposed it; bars sitting Congress from voting itself pay raises.

1992　Four newly independent Soviet republics agreed to honor cuts in nuclear missiles agreed to in 1991 US-Soviet treaty (May).

1992　US and Russia agreed to cut long-range nuclear missile arsenals by two-thirds (June).

1992　Supreme Court upheld basic right to abortion allowed by *Roe* v. *Wade* but ruled states may impose restrictions (June).

1992　US completed withdrawal of all tactical nuclear weapons from around the world, in accordance with 1991 agreement (July).

1992　Ross Perot, media phenomenon and short-lived independent candidate for president, formally withdrew from race (July), only to reenter late in the campaign.

1992　Race riots broke out in Los Angeles (July), following acquittal of four policemen charged with beating black motorist Rodney King.

1992　Free trade agreement between US, Canada, and Mexico completed (Aug.); created world's largest trading bloc.

United States* v. *E.C. Knight Co.　Supreme Court decision (1895) sharply limiting the federal government's power to regulate trusts. The case was brought by the US government against the E.C. Knight Co., which controlled 98 percent of US sugar-refining operations. But the Court ruled that the Sherman Antitrust Act applied only to interstate commerce and not manufacturing operations. The decision effectively barred the government from direct involvement in regulating the economy for some 40 years.

Universal Declaration of Human Rights　Declaration adopted (Dec. 10, 1948) by the United Nations General Assembly. It proclaimed in general terms the basic social, political, and economic rights that should be accorded to people by governments.

Universalist Church of America　American Protestant Christian denomination. Originating in the late 18th cent., it held that everyone will eventually achieve salvation. Holding similar views to those of the Unitarian church, it merged (May, 1961) with the Unitarians to form the Unitarian Universalist Association.

Untouchables *See* **caste system.**

Upanishads Philosophical commentaries forming the last section of the Hindu Vedas. The Upanishads are the basis for the Vedanta system of philosophy.

Updike, John Hoyer 1932–   . American writer whose novels and stories are noted for their examination and portrayal of modern American life. Among his books are *Rabbit Run, The Centaur,* and *Rabbit Redux.*

Upper Burma Region comprising central and northern Burma, annexed by the British (Jan., 1886) after the third Burmese War. It was partly occupied by the Japanese (1942–45) during WW II and became part of independent Burma (1948).

Upper Canada Named applied (1791 to 1841) to the Canadian region comprising present-day Ontario. Settled primarily by the English-speaking peoples (British and American), it was joined with Lower Canada by the Act of Union (1841) and became known as Canada West. With the confederation of Canada (1867), it became the province of Ontario.

Upper Egypt Region of Egypt, including the entire Nile River valley south of latitude 30 degrees N to Egypt's southern border. In ancient times it was a separate kingdom and was united with Lower Egypt by King Menes (c3100 BC).

Upper Volta *See* **Burkina Faso.**

Ur Ancient Sumerian city once located on the Euphrates River in what is now southern Iraq. One of the earliest cities to rise in Mesopotamia, it was first settled (c4000 BC) and flourished under the 1st (26th–24th cents. BC) and 3d (22d–21st cents. BC) dynasties. The traditional home of Abraham, it was conquered and destroyed several times. Ur was rebuilt (6th cent. BC) by Nebuchadnezzar II but declined and was abandoned (c4th cent. BC), perhaps because of a change in the Euphrates' course. Excavation of the site (begun 19th cent.) has yielded important discoveries.

Urartu Ancient kingdom (13th–7th cents. BC) in what is now eastern Turkey (Armenia). Identified as the biblical Ararat, it reached its greatest extent (ruling northern Syria) in the 8th cent. BC. The kingdom was often attacked by the Assyrians and was finally destroyed by invading Scythians and Medes.

Urban II (Eudes of Lagery) (Odo of Lagery) c1042–99.   Pope (1088–99), successor to Greg-
ory VII. He continued Gregory's reform movement, strengthened the papacy, and, through his preachings, helped to inspire the First Crusade.

Urban IV (Pantaléon, Jacques) *d.* 1264.   Pope (1261–64), successor to Alexander IV. He established the feast of Corpus Christi, opposed the Hohenstaufens, and offered the Sicilian throne to Charles of Anjou.

Urban V (Grimoard, Guillaume de) 1310–70. Pope (1362–70), successor to Innocent VI. Elected pope at Avignon, Urban moved the papacy to Rome (1367). Conflict in Rome and continued war between England and France led him to return to Avignon (1370).

Urban VI (Prignano, Bartolomeo) 1318?–89. Pope (1378–89), successor to Gregory XI. His election and subsequent actions alienated the French cardinals. They denied his election and elected Clement VII, thus beginning the Great Schism.

Urban VIII (Barberini, Maffeo) 1568–1644. Pope (1623–44), successor to Gregory XV. Fearing Habsburg dominance over Rome, he supported the policies of Cardinal Richelieu and the French against Germany in the Thirty Years' War.

Urdu Indo-Iranian language, the official language of Pakistan. Urdu is spoken by more than 25,000,000 people and has a classical literature dating from the 14th cent.

Urey, Harold Clayton 1893–1981.   American chemist. He was awarded the Nobel Prize in Chemistry in 1934 for his isolation of the heavy-hydrogen isotope deuterium, a major step in the development of nuclear fission.

Urquiza, Justo José de 1801–70.   Argentinian soldier and politician. As governor of Entre Ríos province he overthrew the Argentine dictator J. de Rosas (1852). He helped to establish and served as president (1854–60) of the Argentine Confederation.

Ursula, Saint *fl.* 4th cent. AD?   Legendary saint said to have been martyred along with 11,000 virgins at Cologne by the Huns. She is the patron saint of the order of the Ursulines.

Uruguay (Oriental Republic of Uruguay)   Independent state (*pop.* 3,121,000) located on the southeastern coast of South America. Its capital is Montevideo. Uruguay was for a time in the early 20th cent. one of South America's most progressive democracies. Key dates in the history of Uruguay include:

1516 Uruguay explored by Spaniard Juan Díaz de Solis.

1624 Spain established settlement on Rio Negro.

1680 Portugal established colony at Colonia.

c1777 Spain took complete control of region.

1811–14 Uruguay revolted, gained independence from Spain.

1814–20 National hero J. Artigas established control over parts of what are now Uruguay and Argentina; driven into exile by Portuguese.

1816–20 Portuguese invaders from Brazil captured Uruguay.

1825 Thirty-Three Immortals, led by J. Lavalleja, declared independence from Brazil; Argentines sent aid.

1827 Rebel forces defeated Brazilian troops at the Battle of Ituzaingó (Feb. 20).

1830 Republic declared; revolts against government began soon after.

1836 Civil war between Blancos (conservatives) and Colorados (liberals) began 50 years of internal disorder.

1865–70 War of the Triple Alliance; Uruguay allied with Brazil and Argentina against Paraguay.

1872–1917 J. Rodó, noted Uruguayan philosopher, lived.

1880–1958 Ruling Colorado party headed by Batlle family.

1903–07 J. Batlle y Ordóñez became president; instituted progressive, liberal rule; made Uruguay Latin America's first welfare state.

1911–15 Batlle again in office as president.

1919 New constitution; Ordóñez's liberal principles were included.

1931–33 Gabriel Terra in office as president.

1933 Coup by Terra; constitution suspended; Terra ruled until 1938, continuing liberal policies.

1938–43 Alfredo Baldomir (1884–1948) in office as president.

1943–47 Juan José Amézaga in office as president.

1947–51 Luis Batlle Berres in office as president.

1951 Andrés Martínez Trueba in office as president.

1952–66 Presidency abolished by constitutional amendment; Trueba headed nine-member national council.

1958 Colorados, in power for nearly 100 years, overwhelmingly defeated by conservatives (Blancos) in elections.

1967 New constitution; executive commission abolished and strong presidential system established.

1967–72 Jorge Pacheco Areco served as president; rapid increase in living costs sparked labor unrest.

1970 Marxist Tupámaro guerrillas kidnapped and killed US adviser Dan Mitrione.

1972–76 Colorado member Juan María Bordaberry in office as president.

1972–73 Tupámaro guerrilla activities provoked government to institute state of internal war; Tupamaros founder, Raul Sendic (d. 1989), captured in 1972; movement crushed by following year.

1973 "Soft coup"; military revolted (Feb.) as economic problems worsened; Bordaberry remained in office though military held real power.

1973 Constitutional government dissolved by Bordaberry; political activity banned; some 6,000 political prisoners reported being held by 1976.

1974 Military men replaced civilian heads of state-owned businesses.

1976 Bordaberry removed by military (June).

1976–81 Aparicio Méndez in office as president, after being installed by military.

1979 US restored some aid based on relaxing of some repressive measures.

1980 Constitution establishing permanent military rule rejected in plebiscite; continuing economic problems plagued the military regime.

1980–88 Inflation rate averaged 57 percent during this period.

1981 Gen. Gregorio Alvarez Armellino in office as interim president; to rule country until civilian government established; trade unions again legalized.

1983 Economic ills and continued repression resulted widespread unrest; government suspended political activity (Aug.); some 500,000 workers joined in protest (Sept.).

1984 Exiled Blanco candidate Ferreira Aldunate arrested on his return to Uruguay (June 27); mass demonstrations against the government.

1984 Government ended ban on political activity after securing agreement from most parties on transition to democratic government (Aug.).

1985–90 President Julio Maria Sanguinetti, a Colorado member, in office following free elections; political prisoners released and opposition parties legalized; return to democracy hampered by continued economic decline and scores of strikes protesting austerity measures.

1986–87 Strikes by government workers protesting budget cuts and low pay.

1986 Government approved amnesty for officials (military and police) involved in human rights abuses under the past military dictatorships (1973–85); amnesty later affirmed by public referendum.

1988–89 Severe drought resulted in poor harvest and killed considerable livestock.

1989 Price increases imposed in order to meet World Bank conditions for new loan; inflation shot up to 112 percent in 1990; sparked labor unrest.

1990– Blanco party member Luis Alberto Lacalle in office as president, following elections; formed coalition government with Colorado party; pursued economic reforms, including privatization of state-run enterprises, reducing public spending, and renegotiation of foreign debt.

1991 Central bank issued new guidelines to halt flourishing money laundering operations being conducted through Uruguay banks (Apr.).

Uruk *See* **Erech.**

US *See* **United States.**

Ussher, James (Usher, ˜) 1581–1656. Irish scholar and archbishop. He is noted for his biblical chronology, which set the date of Creation at 4004 BC.

USSR (Union of Soviet Socialist Republics) *See* **Commonwealth of Independent States.**

Utah Western US state, the 45th state. The capital is Salt Lake City. First explored (1540) by the Spanish, the region was again visited by J. Bridger, who is credited with discovering the Great Salt Lake (1824). The Mormons under B. Young were the first permanent settlers (1847). The US acquired Utah from Mexico by the Treaty of Guadalupe Hidalgo (1848) at the end of the Mexican War, and Young became governor

of Utah Territory (1850). Conflicts between the Mormons and the US government contributed to the Mountain Meadows Massacre (*q.v.*) and led to the Mormon War (*q.v.*) of 1857–58. The Mormon practice of polygamy was a major stumbling block to Utah statehood. Polygamy was abolished (1890), and Utah was admitted as a state in 1896.

Utah War *See* **Mormon War.**

Uthman (Othman) *d.* 656. Third Muslim caliph (644–56), successor to Omar and son-in-law of Muhammad. He continued Muslim conquest and expanded the power of the Caliphate. He established an official text of the Koran. His assassination marked the start of the first open struggle for leadership of the Caliphate.

utilitarianism Ethical theory holding that the goodness of an act may be judged by its usefulness, or utility. The theory was elaborated by such philosophers as J. Bentham, J. Mill, and J. S. Mill. H. Spencer adapted utilitarianism to the scientific principles of evolution.

utopia Term applied to an imaginary ideal state. As such, the term was first used (1516) by T. More in his book *Utopia.* Later utopian societies were described in books by F. Bacon, E. Bellamy, and others.

Utraquists (Calixtines) Bohemian religious sect of the 15th cent. based on the teachings of J. Huss. Its members held that reception of both bread and wine was necessary for the sacrament of communion. They maintained ties with the Catholic church, opposed the more militant Taborites, and disappeared as a movement with the rise of the Reformation.

Utrecht, Peace of Two series of treaties (1713–15), one between France and other European countries and the other between Spain and other European countries, that ended the War of the Spanish Succession. In the first series France concluded treaties (Apr. 11, 1713) with England, the Netherlands, Savoy, Prussia, and Portugal. By these treaties France acknowledged the accession of Queen Anne to the English throne and ceded to England the Hudson Bay territory, Newfoundland, Nova Scotia, and St. Kitts. The treaties also included French cession of the Spanish Netherlands to Austria by treaty with the Netherlands. France recognized Victor Amadeus II as king of Savoy, recognized the king of Prussia, and signed a peace with Portugal. In the second series of treaties (July, 1713–Feb., 1715), Spain signed treaties with England, Savoy, the Netherlands, and Portugal. Spain ceded Gibraltar and Minorca to England and granted England the right to sell slaves in Spanish America. It ceded Sardinia to Savoy and received acknowledgment of Philip V's succession (the cause of the war); signed a peace with the Dutch; and in 1715 made peace with Portugal. The treaties of Rastatt and Baden (*q.v.*) in 1714, between France and the Holy Roman Empire, completed the settlements.

Utrecht, Union of   Union of provinces in the Low Countries that became independent of Spanish rule (1579) and that later became the modern state of the Netherlands (*q.v.*).

Utrillo, Maurice 1883–1955.   French painter. A prolific artist noted for his independent style, he was known best for his paintings of street scenes of Paris, especially Montmartre.

U-2 affair   Conflict (1960) between US and Russia over the shooting down (May, 1960) of an American U-2 spy plane over the Soviet Union. The affair led to cancellation of a proposed Paris summit meeting between Russia and the Western powers. The U-2 pilot, Francis Gary Powers, was sentenced to prison but was later exchanged for a Russian spy (1962).

Uxmal (Oxmal)   Ancient Mayan city in southeastern Mexico, near Mérida. It flourished (600–900) during the Mayan late classic period and is known for its excellent examples of Mayan architecture.

Uzbekistan (*formerly* Uzbek Soviet Socialist Republic)   Independent state located between Kazakhstan and Turkmenia. It is a member of the Commonwealth of Independent States (CIS). Inhabited from ancient times, the region was conquered by Alexander the Great. Centuries later Muslim Arabs took control (8th cent.), followed by the Mongols (13th cent.). In 1370 Tamerlane made the city of Samarkand his capital. Later the region was ruled by the Uzbeks (16th cent.) and Russia expanded its control over the area beginning in the 1860s. The Uzbeks unsuccessfully attempted to establish their independence during the Russian revolution, and the region became a Soviet republic in 1924. During the collapse of the USSR, the Uzbeks declared independence on Aug. 31, and joined the CIS on Dec. 21.

Uzbeks (Uzbegs)   Turkic people, once a part of the Golden Horde. They occupied parts of Turkistan in central Asia by the 13th cent. and, by the 14th, were ruled by khans of the Golden Horde.

Uzziah (Azariah) *d.* c735 BC.   King of Judah (c780–740 BC). He defeated the Philistines, rebuilt the walls of Jerusalem, and expanded the territory of the kingdom. He was stricken with leprosy toward the end of his reign, supposedly in punishment for his pride.

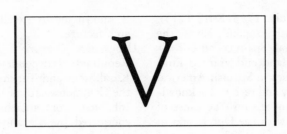

Vaishnavism Form of Hinduism. Its followers worship Vishnu, especially in his incarnation as Krishna or Rama.

Vaisya caste *See* **caste system.**

Valdemar I *See* **Waldemar I.**

Valdemar II *See* **Waldemar II.**

Valdemar IV *See* **Waldemar IV.**

Valdivia, Pedro de c1500–54. Spanish conquistador. He conquered Chile (1540s), founded the city of Santiago (1541) during the conquest, and served as governor of Chile.

Valens AD c328–378. Roman emperor of the East (AD 364–378), appointed by his brother Valentinian I. Valens defeated the Visigoths, then allowed them to settle in the empire. They rebelled and destroyed the Roman army at the Battle of Adrianople (*q.v.*). There Valens was killed and the Eastern Empire was rendered defenseless.

Valentine, Saint *d.* c270. Roman Christian priest who was martyred during the reign of Claudius II. He is associated with Valentine's Day, although the traditional celebration apparently arose from a Roman pagan festival.

Valentinian I AD 321–375. Roman emperor of the West (AD 364–375), successor to Jovian. He appointed his brother Valens emperor of the East and successfully defended the western frontiers of the empire.

Valentinian II AD 371–392. Roman emperor of the West (AD 375–392), successor to his father Valentinian I. He was deposed (AD 387) by Maximus but restored (AD 388) by Theodosius I. He was murdered, possibly by Arbogast.

Valentinian III AD 419–455. Roman emperor of the West (AD 425–455), appointed by his cousin Theodosius II. He allowed the empire to be ruled by others. During his reign Africa was conquered by the Vandals and Gaul and northern Italy were invaded by the Huns.

Valentinus *See* **Gnosticism.**

Valerian *d.* after AD 260. Roman emperor (AD 253–260), successor to Aemilianus. He reimposed persecution of the Christians, appointed his son Gallienus to rule in the West, and was defeated and captured by Persian king Shapur I.

Valéry, Paul 1871–1945. French poet and writer, considered one of the leading French poets of the early 20th cent. His masterpiece is *La Jeune Parque* (1917).

Valla, Lorenzo c1407–57. Italian humanist and scholar. He identified the Donation of Constantine as a fraud, and pointed out the failures of the Latin Vulgate to faithfully translate the Greek Bible.

Valley Forge Village in northeastern Pennsylvania, site of the winter encampment (1777–78) of the Continental Army under G. Washington during the American Revolution. Here Baron F. von Steuben drilled the Continental Army into an efficient military unit.

Valmy, Battle of First important battle (Sept. 20, 1792) of the French Revolutionary Wars, at Valmy, France. Some 36,000 French defeated a force of Austrians and Prussians. Both sides suffered casualties of only a few hundred, but the battle showed that the revolutionary forces were capable of defending France.

Valois French royal house, a branch of the Capetians, who ruled France from 1328 to 1589, beginning with Philip VI. The first half of their reign was marked by the Hundred Years' War and by challenges from the nobility. However, the Valois rulers ably met both threats, consolidated their power, and established their sole right of taxation. The direct line ended with the death of Charles VIII (1498). It continued with the houses of Valois-Orléans and Valois-Angoulême until the advent of Henry IV and the Bourbons (1589). *Valois kings of France included:* Philip VI 1328–50; John II 1350–64; Charles V 1364–80; Charles VI 1380–1422; Charles VII 1422–61; Louis XI 1461–83; Charles VIII 1483–98; Louis XII 1498–1515; Francis I 1515–47; Henry II 1547–59; Francis II 1559–60; Charles IX 1560–74; Henry III 1574–89.

Valois, Catherine of   *See* **Catherine of Valois.**

Valois, Charles of   *See* **Charles of Valois.**

Valois, Elizabeth of   *See* **Elizabeth of Valois.**

Valois, Margaret of   *See* **Margaret of Valois.**

Valparaiso, Treaty of   *See* **Pacific, War of the.**

Vanbrugh, Sir John 1664–1726.   English dramatist and architect. He established himself as one of the leading Restoration dramatists, then turned to architecture. Among his works is Blenheim Palace in Oxfordshire.

Van Buren, Martin 1782–1862.   The 8th US president (1837–41), successor to A. Jackson. A Democrat, he led the Albany Regency (*q.v.*) and served in the US Senate (1821–28), where he supported the policies of A. Jackson. Elected (1828) governor of New York, he soon resigned to become secretary of state (1829–31). In 1832, Van Buren was elected vice-president under Jackson, and in 1836 he won the presidency. His administration was marked by the financial Panic of 1837, passage of legislation establishing an independent treasury system, US neutrality during the Canadian rebellion of 1837 and the Aroostook War (*q.v.*) between settlers in Maine and Canada. Van Buren was defeated in the 1840 presidential campaign, and he was a leader of the Barnburners against the Hunkers (*qq.v.*). In 1848, as the Free-Soil party candidate, he split the Democratic vote and thus helped Z. Taylor win the election.

Vancouver, George 1757–98.   English navigator and explorer. He sailed with Captain J. Cook, and later commanded a detailed survey of the west coast of North America (1792–93). Vancouver Island and Vancouver, B.C., are named for him.

Vandals   Germanic tribe, believed to have originated around Jutland. Fleeing the Huns (early 5th cent. AD), they embarked upon their own campaign of conquest, sweeping through Gaul and into Spain. Led by Gaiseric, they crossed into North Africa (429) and eventually captured Carthage (AD 439). Rome recognized Gaiseric's rule three years later and the Vandals began their pirate attacks upon Mediterranean shipping. From there they raided Sicily and southern Italy, and sacked Rome (AD 455). Arian Christians, they vigorously persecuted other Christian sects. The power of the Vandals declined after Gaiseric's death in the late 5th cent. and was finally broken by the Byzantine general Belisarius (AD 533).

Vandenberg, Arthur Hendrick 1884–1951.   American politician. As US senator (1928–51) he moved from a policy of isolationism to support of the foreign policy of President H. Truman and establishment of the United Nations.

Vanderbilt   American family. Its wealth and position were secured by Cornelius Vanderbilt (1794–1877), who made an immense fortune in shipping and railroads. He gave $1 million to found Vanderbilt University. His son William Henry Vanderbilt (1821–85) succeeded his father in managing the family railroad interests. William's sons included Cornelius Vanderbilt (1843–99) and George Washington Vanderbilt (1862–1914).

Van Dorn, Earl 1820–63.   Confederate general in the American Civil War. Van Dorn received the surrender of Union forces in Texas (1861) and fought at Pea Ridge (Mar., 1862) and Corinth (Oct., 1862). He was murdered in 1863.

Van Dyck, Sir Anthony 1599–1641.   Flemish painter. One of the greatest portrait painters of the 17th cent. He developed a characteristic style that lent an air of dignity and elegance to his subjects and made him extremely popular among the European aristocracy. By 1632 he had become court painter to English King Charles I and spent much of the remainder of his life in England. He painted portraits of many of the leading figures of the English court and greatly influenced later English portrait painters. Van Dyck also painted religious subjects and did etchings and drawings.

Vane, Sir Henry 1589–1655.   English courtier and Parliamentarian, father of H. Vane. He served in every Parliament from 1614 to 1640 and carried out important diplomatic missions for King Charles I. He lost favor with the king and joined the Parliamentary party.

Vane, Sir Henry 1613–62.   English statesman. A Puritan, he served as governor of Massachusetts (1636–37), then returned to England. Siding with the Parliamentarians during the English

Civil Wars, he played a key role in negotiating the Solemn League and Convenant (*q.v.*) and became leader of the House of Commons (1643). During the Commonwealth he served as council of state (1649–53), but left the government in 1653 after opposing Cromwell's dissolving of the Rump Parliament. Vane was executed for his past actions with the Parliamentarians after the restoration of King Charles II.

Van Rensselaer, Stephen 1764–1839. US political leader. He took a prominent part in New York politics, serving as lieutenant governor (1795–1801), major general in the War of 1812, and US congressman (1822–29). He was instrumental in building the Erie Canal.

Vanzetti, Bartolomeo *See* **Sacco-Vanzetti case.**

Varangians Scandinavian conquerers of Russia in the 9th and 10th cents. Also called "Rus," they thus gave Russia its name. They were gradually absorbed by the Slavs. (*See also* **Norsemen.**)

Vardhamana *See* **Mahavira.**

Vargas, Getullo Dornelles 1883–1954. Brazilian statesman, twice president of Brazil (1930–45, 1951–54). He came to power by revolution. Although he encouraged reform and development in industry and agriculture, his rule was dictatorial.

Vargas Llosa, Mario 1936–   . Peruvian expatriate novelist whose sweeping, highly complex novels often centered on Peruvian life. Vargas published his first novel, *The Time of the Hero* in 1962 and secured his reputation with publication of *The Green House* in 1966. Subsequent works included *Captain Pantoja and The Special Service* (1973) and *The War of the End of the World* (1984).

Varna, battles of 1. Ottoman Turkish victory (Nov. 10, 1444) over the Hungarians at Varna, now in Bulgaria. The Turkish forces defeated the Hungarians under J. Hunyadi and killed Ladislaus, king of Poland and Hungary. Eastern Europe remained in Ottoman control. 2. Russian victory (Oct. 12, 1828) over the Ottoman Turkish forces of Sultan Mahmud II during the Russo-Turkish War of 1828. After several months of campaigning, the Russians finally forced the Turks, besieged at Varna, to surrender. The Russians were unable to further prosecute the war, however, and soon took up winter quarters.

Varro, Marcus Terentius 116–27? BC Roman scholar and polymath, one of the most versatile, prolific, and brilliant men produced by Rome.

His writings on history, geography, religion, language, rhetoric, and other subjects filled some 600 books.

Varus, Publius Quintilius *d.* AD 9. Roman general and consul (13 BC). As commander in Germany (AD 6–9) he was totally defeated by Arminius and committed suicide.

Vasa Swedish family that ruled Sweden (1523–1654) and Poland (1587–1668). Established in Sweden by King Gustavus I, it gained the Polish throne through the marriage of Swedish king John III to the sister of Polish king Sigismund II. Their son, a Catholic, became (1587) Polish king Sigismund III. When he attempted to assume the Swedish throne, however, the Protestant Swedes ousted him and installed his uncle, Charles IX (1599). Thereafter, the two Vasa branches fought frequently for domination. The Protestant Swedish Vasas greatly increased Sweden's Baltic influence. The direct Vasa line in Sweden ended with the abdication of Queen Christina and the crowning of her cousin Charles X (1654). In Poland, the ruling line ended with the abdication (1668) of King John II Casimir.

Vasari, Giorgio 1511–74. Italian architect, painter, and art historian. He is noted for his history of Renaissance art and artists, *Vite de' pi eccellenti architetti, pittori e scultori italiani.*

Vasily III 1479–1533. Grand duke of Moscow (1505–33), successor to his father, Ivan III. He continued his father's consolidation of territory by annexing Pskov (1510), Ryazan (1517), and Novgorod-Seversk (1523), and capturing Smolensk (1514).

vassal In feudal society, the holder of a fief, or landed estate granted by an overlord in return for feudal services.

Vassy, massacre of *See* **Guise, François of Lorraine, 2d duke of.**

Vatican City Independent city-state located mostly within the city of Rome. It is the official seat of the pope, head of the Roman Catholic church. Vatican City was established by the Lateran Treaty (Feb. 11, 1929) between Italy and Pope Pius XI. The unification of Italy (1870) had deprived the pope of the former Papal States, by which the popes had endeavored to maintain their independence from any secular ruler. The Lateran Treaty guaranteed papal independence.

Vatican Council 1. The First Vatican Council (1869–70), or 20th ecumenical council of the Catholic church, was convened (Dec. 8, 1869) at the Vatican by Pope Pius IX. It was interrupted by the capture of Rome (Oct. 1870) by Italian troops. The council upheld the pope as supreme leader of the Catholic church and promulgated the dogma of papal infallibility when speaking *ex cathedra* on matters of faith or morals.   2. The Second Vatican Council (1962–65), or 21st ecumenical council of the Catholic church, was convened (Oct. 11, 1962) at the Vatican by Pope John XXIII and continued by Pope Paul VI. The council issued 16 documents through which it sought to promote a spiritual renewal within the Catholic church. It invited representatives from both Protestant and Eastern Orthodox churches to observe the proceedings. Its principal accomplishments included modification of the liturgy of the Mass, support for the spirit of ecumenism, and condemnation of anti-Semitism. Its wide-ranging reforms have had a major impact on the church.

Vauban, Sébastien Le Prestre, marquis de 1633–1707.   French military engineer and marshal of France. He developed a series of parallel trenches at the siege of Maastricht (1673) which revolutionized siege warfare. He also invented the socket bayonet.

Vaucreuil-Cavagnal, Pierre François de Rigaud, marquis de 1698–1765.   Last French governor of New France (1755–60). After the defeat of Gen. L. Montcalm, he surrendered New France to Britain (1760).

Veblen, Thorstein 1857–1929.   American economist and social scientist. He is known best for his book *The Theory of the Leisure Class,* which introduced such phrases as "conspicuous consumption."

Vecellio, Tiziano   *See* **Titian.**

Vedas   Sacred Indian texts. Among the oldest examples of ancient Indian literature, the Vedas include texts of hymns, poetry, and prose that state the essential beliefs, laws, mythology, prayers, and rituals of Hinduism. They originated with the Aryans, who entered India c1500 BC. The Vedas are divided into four primary groupings: the Samhitas, containing hymns and liturgies; the Brahmanas, prose explanations of sacrificial ceremonies; Aranyakas, instructions for sacrifices and meditation; and the Upanishads, mystical and speculative writings.

Vedanta   Term used to describe the philosophy on which modern Hinduism is based. Meaning literally "the end of the Veda," it is based on the knowledge of the final Vedic texts, the Upanishads. Vedanta was developed especially by the Hindu sages Sankara and Ramanuja.

Vega Carpio, Lope Félix de 1562–1635.   Founder of the Spanish drama. He wrote some 1,800 plays and countless other works in prose and verse. His works included "cloak and sword dramas," "heroic comedies," and dramas of domestic life and were immensely popular.

Vehme   *See* **Vehmgericht.**

Vehmgericht (Vehme) (vehmic court)   Special criminal tribunal in medieval Germany. These tribunals flourished in the 14th and 15th cents. but declined with the increased authority exerted by the princes.

vehmic court   *See* **Vehmgericht.**

Velasco, Luis de *d.* 1564.   Spanish colonial administrator, second viceroy of New Spain (1550–64). He improved the condition of the Indians and outfitted the expedition that conquered the Philippines.

Velasco, Luis de 1539–1617?   Spanish viceroy of Mexico (1590–95, 1607–11) and Peru (1596–1604).

Velasco Alvarado, Juan 1910–   .   Peruvian army officer and president (1968–75). A career military man, he rose through the ranks to become army commander in chief under President F. Belaúnde Terry. Following two years of unrest over political and economic matters, Gen. Valasco led the military coup (1968) that ousted Belaúnde and began a long period of military rule. As president, Velasco presided over a revolutionary military government that instituted economic and agrarian reforms, opposed the US and the influence of foreign capital over Peru's economy, and established relations with the former USSR and other Communist-bloc countries. Velasco was himself overthrown in a bloodless military coup.

Velázquez, Diego de 1465?–1522?   Spanish soldier and administrator. He sailed with C. Columbus (1493), was first governor of Cuba (1511–22), and founded Santiago (1514) and Havana (1515).

Velázquez, Diego Rodríguez de Silva y 1599–1660.   Spanish painter, one of the great masters of 17th-cent. art. His mature works, which utilized color, perspective, and light to capture a sense of realism, greatly influenced later painters. His works include portraits of Philip IV and Don Carlos, *Surrender of Breda,* and *Borrachos.*

Vellore Mutiny Sepoy uprising against the British (May 10, 1806) at Vellore, India. The Sepoys seized the fortress in which the family Mysore Sultan Tipu (1753?–99) lived and killed some 130 British soldiers in the effort to free them. Grievances against the British over arbitrary treatment of the Sepoys played a major role in sparking the revolt. The British soon suppressed the mutiny and the family of Tipu Sultan was removed to Calcutta.

Vendée, Wars of the French royalist insurrections. From 1793–1832, the French region of the Vendée frequently attempted counterrevolutions to defeat the French Republic and restore the monarchy. The peasants of the Vendée first rebelled against conscription by the French government (Mar., 1793). They were joined by displaced nobles, who spread the revolt throughout the summer and fall but were defeated at Le Mans (Dec. 12, 1793). The harsh treatment of defeated counterrevolutionaries by the Republicans led to a second Vendée insurrection (1794). Smaller royalist revolts in the Vendée took place in 1799, 1815, and 1832.

Vendôme, César, duc de 1594–1665. French general and politician, a son of French king Henry IV. He participated in conspiracies against King Louis XIII, Cardinal Richelieu, and Cardinal Mazarin.

Vendôme, Louis Joseph, duc de 1654–1712. French general. He fought with distinction in the War of the League of Augsburg and played a major role in the War of the Spanish Succession (1701–14).

Venetia Region of northeastern Italy. Inhabited by the Venetii, it was conquered (2d cent. BC) and made a province by the Romans, ravaged by the Huns (5th cent. AD), and flourished (15th–16th cents.) under the rule of the republic of Venice. Contested by Austria and Italy, it passed to Italy at the close of the Austro-Prussian War (1866) between Austria and Prussia.

Venetian school School of Italian art that flourished in Venice from the 15th through 18th cents. Its artists' works were characterized by their use of color and celebration of light. Among its artists were G. Bellini, Giorgione, Titian, and Tintoretto.

Venezuela (Republic of Venezuela) Independent state located in northern South America on the Caribbean Sea. The population is 19,753,000 and the capital is Caracas. Venezuela is one of the world's major oil-producing nations. Key events in Venezuelan history include:

1498 C. Columbus discovered Venezuela.

1499 Alonas de Ojeda and Amerigo Vespucci explored coast.

1527 First permanent Spanish settlement at Coro.

1567 Caracas founded.

16TH–18TH CENTS. British buccaneers active along coast.

1795 Unsuccessful revolt against Spain.

1810 Revolt against Spain resumed under Francisco Miranda.

1811 Independence declared (July 5).

1821 Independence from Spain established by S. Bolívar's victory at Battle of Carabobo (June 24); Venezuela joined Federation of Greater Colombia.

1830 José Antonio Páez separated Venezuela from federation.

1830–46 Páez in office as first president.

1839–40 British Guiana gained major share of long-disputed territory.

1846–58 José Tadeo Monagas in power.

1864 Short-lived United States of Venezuela formed under Juan Falcon.

1870–88 A. Guzmán Blanco ruled as dictator; overthrown.

1874–1944 Poet Rufino Blanco Fombona lived; became a leader of *Modernismo* literary movement.

1886 British occupied Orinoco River in continuing boundary dispute over British Guiana.

1892–99 Juan Crespo became dictator.

1895 US became involved in ongoing boundary dispute.

1899 Venezuela Boundary Dispute settled in arbitration; most disputed territory awarded to Britain.

1899–1908 Cipriano Castro became president.

1902 Castro's inability to repay long-standing European debts led to Venezuela Claims incident.

1908–35 Dictator J. Gómez in power after deposing Castro; ruled tyrannically; stimulated economic growth.

1935–41 Eleazar López Contrera became president.

1948–58 Military seized power (Nov. 1947) and thereafter installed a series of presidents; military rule ended by popular revolt (1958); democratic government restored.

1958–64 Romulo Betancourt in office as president.

1961 New constitution adopted.

1962 Communist-inspired revolts suppressed as political unrest mounted.

1964–68 Raúl Leoni in power as president.

1966 Leftist terrorists in Caracas suppressed.

1969–74 Rafael Caldera Rodríguez, country's first Christian Democrat president, in office; stabilized economy; legalized Communist Party; established relations with Soviets; wave of political assassinations and kidnappings continued throughout his term.

1970 Venezuela agreed to Port of Spain Protocol, thereby putting aside its claim to a Guyana border region for 12 years.

1974–79 Carlos Peréz, member of Acción Democrática (AD) in office as president; his administration marked by increased agricultural and industrial investment, and nationalization of key industries.

1976 Nationalization (with compensation) of oil companies.

1978 Oil profits declined; austerity measures instituted.

1979–84 Luis Herrera Campíns in office as president; guerrilla attacks and social unrest plagued his administration from 1981, as result of falling oil prices and a declining economy.

1982 Venezuela allowed moratorium to expire on its claim to Guyana border region; dispute put before UN in 1985, but still had not been resolved by early 1990s.

1984–88 Jaime Lusinchi, member of AD, in office as president; promised national campaign to halt corruption; imposed austerity measures in effort to deal with economic problems caused by falling oil prices.

1986 Venezuela rescheduled its public debt.

1987 Student riots broke out.

1988 Minister of Justice resigned amid allegations of connections with drug traffickers (Mar.); Venezuela had become conduit for Colombian drug traffickers by this time.

1988–89 Government agreed to cooperate with Colombia to halt cross-border drug traffic; both countries to increase troops levels along borders.

1988 Widespread protests after police killed 14 fishermen suspected of being drug traffickers (Oct.).

1988– Carlos Pérez back in office as president; instituted measures to counter economic decline, including price increases for gasoline and public transportation.

1989 Widespread rioting broke out in reaction to price hikes (Feb.); 246 killed.

1989 Trade union workers went out on 24-hour general strike calling for government policies favoring labor.

1989 Major financial scandal rocked the government (Aug.); former government minister arrested in connection with fraud case involving loss of some $8 billion in government money.

1990 Riots and looting nationwide (Feb.), following new gasoline price hike and release of government officials arrested on corruption charges.

1991 Government declared all-out war on drug traffickers.

1991 Government lifted price controls on goods and services and cut corporate taxes.

1991 State-run airline privatized (Aug.).

1992 Failed military coup attempt (Feb. 4) by heavily armed soldiers; over 100 killed and more than 1,000 officers and enlisted soldiers arrested.

Venezuela Boundary Dispute Prolonged territorial dispute between Great Britain and Venezuela over the boundary between Venezuela and British Guiana. The disagreement continued through much of the 19th cent. but took on added meaning when gold was discovered in the disputed area. In 1887, the nations broke off diplomatic ties. In 1895, US secretary of state R. Olney invoked the Monroe Doctrine and demanded arbitration. Britain at first refused but eventually yielded to avoid conflict with the US. In 1899, an arbitration panel awarded most of the disputed territory to Britain.

Venezuela Claims Financial claims pressed upon Venezuela in the early 20th cent. During the rule of Venezuelan president C. Castro, Venezuela fell into a complicated financial tangle. In Dec., 1902, France, Great Britain, Germany, and Italy demanded swift repayment of outstanding loans to Venezuela, pressing their claims by sending gunboats to blockade Venezuelan ports. After they bombarded several port cities, the US intervened as unofficial arbitrator. The matter was referred to the Hague Tribunal (1904), which ruled that Venezuela must repay the belligerent countries before settling its debts with neutral nations. Venezuela fulfilled its obligations in 1907.

Venice Italian seaport, capital of Venezia province. Venice was first settled (5th cent. AD) by people fleeing from invasions from the north. It elected its first doge in 697, and by the 9th cent., it began its expansion as a commercial and cultural center. It played a major role in the Fourth Crusade, from which it gained numerous colonial holdings in the eastern Mediterranean, among them Crete and the Ionian Islands. Venice became the leading Italian city after its defeat of its rival, Genoa (1381). An uprising in Venice (1310) led to the rule of the Council of Ten (*q.v.*), which governed Venice until 1797. The rich and powerful Venetian republic in the 15th cent. dominated trade with the East and thus maintained contact between Europe and Asia. With the discovery of the New World and the expansion of the Ottoman Empire (which warred against Venice), Venetian power gradually declined in the 16th and 17th cents. In 1797 the Republic of Venice fell to Napoleon and the region passed to Austrian control. Venice became part of Napoleon's kingdom of Venice (1805–15), returned to Austrian control and became part of Italy (1866) at the end of the Seven Weeks' War between Austria and Prussia.

Venizelos, Eleutherios 1864–1936. Greek statesman. He led the movement in Crete for union with Greece. As Greek prime minister (1910–15, 1917–20) he greatly expanded Greek territory during the Balkan Wars and WW I.

Vera Cruz Incident US occupation of Vera Cruz Mexico (Apr.–Nov., 1914) during the Mexican Revolution. The action was prompted by Mexican seizure of a US ship in Tampico Harbor and led to the fall of V. Huerta.

Vercingetorix *d.* 46 BC. Chieftain of the Arverni tribe in Gaul. He led a great revolt against the Romans (52 BC), was defeated by J. Caesar, exhibited in Rome, and executed.

Verdi, Giuseppe 1813–1901. Italian composer considered the greatest Italian composer of opera in the 19th cent. and perhaps of all time. Among his greatest operas are *Rigoletto* (1851), *Il Trovatore* (1853), and *La Traviata* (1853).

Verdun, Battle of Battle (Feb.–Dec., 1916) fought by French and German forces during WW I for control of the strategic town of Verdun, in northeastern France. The battle began (Feb. 21) when German forces under Crown Prince Wilhelm opened a massive artillery bombardment of French positions around Verdun. The German offensive was calculated to defeat the French army through sheer attrition, as the French were sure to hold Verdun at all costs. After initial German advances, French general H. Pétain assumed command of the Verdun salient, and reinforcements were sent. Through bitter fighting, the Germans continued to advance in the sector but were unable to capture Verdun. Meanwhile the French and British opened the Battle of the Somme (July 1), thus relieving some of the pressure on Verdun. By July 11, the German offensive ground to a halt. The French launched a major counteroffensive (Oct. 24) and by Dec. had regained most of the territory they had lost. The Germans had been unable to crush the French or to break the stalemate on the Western Front. German losses were some 330,000 to French casualties of some 350,000.

Verdun, Treaty of Treaty (843) by which the Carolingian Empire was divided among the three sons and heirs of Emperor Louis I (the Pious). After the death of Louis I (840), the empire was rent by warfare among his sons Louis the German, Charles II (the Bald), and Lothair I. By the treaty, Lothair retained the title of emperor and received the narrow middle parto of the empire, much of what later became Italy, Alsace-Lorraine, Burgundy, and the Low Countries. Louis the German received territory east of the Rhine, which formed the basis for modern Germany. Charles II received the western territory of the empire, which evolved into modern France.

Vereeniging, Peace of Treaty (May 31, 1902) between Great Britain and the Boers ending the Boer War. By its terms, the Transvaal and the Orange Free State accepted British sovereignty and became crown colonies. Britain paid an indemnity for property destroyed and agreed to establish responsible government as soon as possible.

Vergara, Convention of *See* **Convention of Vergara.**

Vergennes, Charles Gravier, comte de 1717–87. French statesman. Appointed foreign minister (1774) by King Louis XVI, he formed the alliance between France and the American colonists during the American Revolution. He negotiated the Treaty of Paris (1783).

Vergil (Virgil) 70–19 BC. Greatest of Latin poets. Born near Mantua, he became a member of the literary circle at the court of Augustus. His works the *Bucolics,* or *Eclogues,* and *Georgics* established him as the foremost poet of his age. His major work, however, remains the *Aeneid.*

Verlaine, Paul 1844–96. French poet, one of the leading poets of the late 19th cent. His works anticipated the poetry of the symbolists.

Vermeer, Jan (~, Johannes) 1632–75. Dutch painter of the baroque period, noted for his landscapes and domestic interiors. He was a master of light and color and one of the giants of 17th-cent. Dutch painting, though he completed only about 35 paintings. They include *Girl Asleep, Young Woman with a Water Jug, The Procuress,* and *Soldier and Laughing Girl.*

Vermont Northeastern US state, the 14th state. Its capital is Montpelier. The area was first explored by S. Champlain (1609), who sailed along the lake named after him. The French made several attempts at settlement (17th–18th cents.), but the first permanent settlement was the British Fort Dummer, near present-day Brattleboro, in 1724. The region was claimed by New Hampshire and New York. New Hampshire's issuance of the New Hampshire Grants (*q.v.*) led to conflicts between the two colonies, and E. Allen formed the Green Mountain Boys to resist New York authority. The Green Mountain Boys played a significant role during the American Revolution, notably at the battles of Ticonderoga and Bennington (*q.v.*). Vermont declared itself an independent state (1777) but was not admitted into the Union until 1791. It took an active role in support of the Union during the American Civil War and was the scene of the St. Albans Raid (1864).

Verne, Jules 1828–1905. French novelist. His extrapolations of contemporary science in fiction had great influence in the development of modern science fiction. Among his works is the classic *Twenty Thousand Leagues Under the Sea.*

Verona, Congress of *See* **Congress of Verona.**

Veronese, Paolo 1528–88. Italian painter, considered one of the greatest decorative artists of the Venetian school. His works are noted for their brilliant use of color.

Verrazano, Giovanni da *See* **New York.**

Versailles, Palace of French royal palace at Versailles, southeast of Paris. Begun (17th cent.) under French king Louis XIV, it was the residence of the French kings (1682–1790) and was the site of the early events of the French Revolution. Here Wilhelm I was proclaimed emperor of Germany (1871) and here were signed the treaties of Versailles (1871, 1919).

Versailles, Treaty of (1783) *See* **Paris, Treaty of** (3).

Versailles, Treaty of Preliminary treaty (1871) ending the Franco-Prussian War, signed at Versailles, France. Negotiators were O. von Bismarck and A. Thiers. France ceded Alsace-Lorraine and agreed to an indemnity of five billion francs.

Versailles, Treaty of Treaty (June 28, 1919) ending WW I. Its provisions, the result of the Paris Peace Conference, were primarily drawn up by US president W. Wilson, British prime minister D. Lloyd George, French premier G. Clemenceau, and Italian prime minister V. Orlando. Germany was not consulted. The treaty also made provision for establishment of the League of Nations. Germany's colonies became mandates of the League of Nations, and Alsace-Lorraine was returned to France. In addition, Germany was forced to accept responsibility for the war, agreed to huge reparations payment and surrender of equipment, limited its army to 100,000 troops, relinquished vast land holdings to Poland (including the Polish Corridor, *q.v.*), and agreed to demilitarization of the Rhineland. The US did not ratify the treaty, but its provisions were implemented and helped to cause the early rise of A. Hitler and Nazism. Hitler subsequently broke the treaty's provisions.

Verucchio, Malatesta da *See* **Malatesta.**

Verus, Lucius Aurelius (Commodus, Lucius Ceionius) AD 130–169. Roman emperor (AD 161–169), coruler with M. Aurelius. Sent to campaign in Parthia (AD 162–165), he spent most of his time in Antioch. He was the first person known to share equally the imperial power.

Vervins, Treaty of Treaty (May 2, 1598) between France and Spain. It helped end the French Wars of Religion by providing for the withdrawal of Spanish support to the Catholic League in France.

Verwoerd, Hendrik Frensch 1901–66. South African political leader. As prime minister of

South Africa (1958–66) he led the establishment of apartheid, or separation of the races, in his country.

Vesalius, Andreas 1514–1564. Belgian physician, a founder of modern anatomy. A lecturer in surgery and anatomy at the University of Padua (1537), he stressed the importance of human dissection, breaking with past methods of using animal dissections to learn about the human body. He is best known for his seven-volume *Fabrica* (1543), which combined extensive descriptions of human anatomy with technical drawings. The work aroused controversy, however, and Vesalius was forced to leave the country (1559).

Vespasian (Titus Flavius Vespasianus) AD 9–79. Roman emperor (AD 69–79), successor to Vitellius. He restored order to the empire, set an example of simple living, built the Colosseum, and founded the Flavian dynasty.

Vespucci, Amerigo 1454–1512. Italian navigator. He explored some 6,000 miles of the east coast of South America, including the mouths of the Amazon River (1499) and the Río del la Plata (1500). Vespucci realized the New World was a new continent, instead of a part of Asia as had been thought. The name "America" is derived from his name. Vespucci also devised a method for figuring longitude with remarkable accuracy and calculated the earth's circumference to within 50 miles of its true measure.

Vestal Ancient Roman priestess who tended the perpetual fires in the Temple of Vesta, goddess of the hearth. The vestal virgins were chosen from prominent Roman families and were bound by a vow of chastity. They enjoyed great privileges and influence in Roman life.

Veterans of Foreign Wars (V.F.W.) American veterans' association founded (1899) after the Spanish-American War and chartered by Congress (1936). It is one of the largest veterans' organizations in the US.

veto Power of the executive to invalidate acts by the legislature. Roman tribunes could veto acts of the Roman Senate. In the US, the president may veto acts of Congress, but Congress can override the veto by a two-thirds vote.

Veuster, Joseph de *See* **Damien, Father.**

viceroy Governor of a province, territory, country by authority of a king or sovereign. Rulers of Spanish territories in the Americas were viceroys, and British viceroys governed Ireland and British India.

Vichy French government headed by Marshal H. Pétain, established during WW II after the French-German armistice (June, 1940). It controlled that part of France not occupied by Germany, and its policies were generally favorable to Germany. The Vichy government lost importance after German occupation (1942) of all France but continued to exist until 1944.

Vicksburg Campaign Successful Union campaign (Nov., 1862–July, 1863) to capture Vicksburg, Mississippi, during the American Civil War. Union capture of the city, last Confederate stronghold on the Mississippi, would effectively have divided the Confederacy in two. Confederate forces under Gen. John C. Pemberton (1814–81) fortified the city and for months successfully repelled Union assaults. In Apr. and May, 1863, Union Gen. U. Grant executed a series of maneuvers by which his forces seized key positions south of the city, crossed the Mississippi, and moved east to halt the advance of Gen. J. Johnston, who had sought to link up with Pemberton's forces. Pemberton, who had moved out of Vicksburg to meet Johnston, was forced back to Vicksburg. Grant began a six-week siege that culminated (July 4, 1863) in Pemberton's surrender of Vicksburg. Union losses were about 10,000 to Confederate losses of some 9,000 casualties and 30,000 prisoners. The campaign was a major defeat for the Confederacy and marked Grant's ascedancy as the Union's leading commander.

Vico, Giovanni Battista 1668–1744. Italian philosopher and historian. He advanced a theory of the cyclical and evolutionary nature of history and urged scientific methods in historical investigation.

Victor Emmanuel I 1759–1824. King of Sardinia (1802–21), successor to his brother Charles Emmanuel IV. He regained a number of Italian territories after the fall of Napoleon, but his autocratic rule led to an uprising and his abdication (1821).

Victor Emmanuel II 1820–78. King of Sardinia (1849–61) and first king of a united Italy (1861–78). As king of Sardinia he appointed Count C. Cavour prime minister and encouraged the efforts of G. Garibaldi (*See* Italy, 1849–78).

Victor Emmanuel III 1869–1947. Italian king (1900–46), successor to his father, Humbert I. He brought Italy into WW I on the side of the Allies. He refused to oppose the rise of Fascism and supported the government of B. Mussolini.

Victoria 1819–1901. Queen of Great Britain and Ireland (1837–1901) and empress of India (1876–1901). Daughter of Edward, duke of Kent, she succeeded her uncle William IV to the English throne, but she was prevented by the Salic law from succeeding to the Hanoverian throne, thus separating the two crowns. Victoria married (1840) her first cousin, Prince Albert of Saxe-Coburg-Gotha, to whom she bore nine children, among them the future Edward VII. Her prime ministers included W. Melbourne, R. Peel, H. Palmerston, B. Disraeli, and W. Gladstone. During her reign, the British Empire reached its peak. Britain established its rule in India, struggled with the question of Home Rule in Ireland, remained neutral during the American Civil War, and fought the Crimean War. Victoria's strict personal moral values greatly enhanced the prestige of the monarchy and gained her enormous popularity. She put her stamp on an entire era of English history, which came to be known as the Victorian Age.

Victorian style Neo-Gothic style of architecture revived in Britain during the reign of Queen Victoria. It began with careful imitation of the Gothic style and gradually developed into a less restricted form. The outstanding buildings designed in the style include the Houses of Parliament and the Manchester Town Hall.

Vidocq, Eugène François 1775–1857. French adventurer and detective who became head of the Police de Sûreté (1809–32, security police) during the rule of Napoleon. He was ousted after being caught as the mastermind of a crime he was investigating.

Vienna, Congress of *See* **Congress of Vienna.**

Vienna, Peace of Treaty (June 23, 1606) that ended the rebellion against the Habsburgs led by the Hungarian leader I. Bocskay. It secured religious toleration for the Hungarian Protestants within the Austrian Empire.

Vienna, treaties of 1. Treaty (Nov. 18, 1738) ending the War of the Polish Succession (*q.v.*). 2. *See* Peace of Schönbrunn. 3. Treaty (Oct. 30, 1864) by which Denmark ceded Schleswig, Holstein, and Lauenburg to Austria and Prussia. 4. Treaty (Oct. 3, 1866) between Austria and Italy following the Seven Weeks' War (1866). By its terms Austria ceded Venetia to Italy.

Vienna Circle Group of intellectuals in the 1920s who met regularly to discuss scientific language and methods. Made up primarily of philosophers, scientists, and mathematicians, the group was associated with logical positivism and was distinguished by its members' adherence to the premise that experience and observation are all-important in establishing meaning. The group disbanded (1938) with the onset of WW II.

Vienne, Council of Fifteenth ecumenical council of the Catholic church (1311–12), at Vienne, France. Convened by Pope Clement V, it dissolved the order of the Knights Templar and condemned the Beghards.

Vieta, François *See* **Vite, François.**

Vietcong (Viet-Nam Cong-San) Communist guerrilla forces that fought in South Vietnam (1954–75) to overthrow the government of South Vietnam and reunify Vietnam under Communist rule. The Vietcong, aided by men and matériel from the North, successfully fought a long and bloody guerrilla campaign against the army of the Republic of South Vietnam and later against the US armed forces sent to aid the South Vietnamese. They formed (1960) the National Liberation Front (*q.v.*), which in turn joined with other groups to form the Provisional Revolutionary Government (PRG). The PRG took part in the cease-fire negotiations in Paris (1973) but, after US withdrawal from Vietnam, the Vietcong and North Vietnamese regular forces completed the conquest of South Vietnam (1975).

Viète, François (Vieta, ~) 1540–1603. French mathematician noted for his contributions to the development of modern algebra.

Viet Minh (Viet Nam Doc Lap Dong Minh) A coalition of Communist and nationalist groups that fought for Vietnamese independence from French rule. It was formed in May, 1941, and led by Ho Chi Minh after his return to Vietnam during World War II. The Viet Minh was dissolved in 1951 after being replaced by the Lao Dong as the ruling party of North Vietnam.

Vietnam Socialist republic located in Southeast Asia. The population is 68,488,000 and the capital is Hanoi. Vietnam's history prior to French occupation in the 19th cent. was that of its three regions: Tonkin, in northern Vietnam; Annam, in central Vietnam; and Cochin China in southern Vietnam. The three regions became part of French Indochina (1887). Vietnam was established as an independent state in 1945. Subsequent attempts by the French to regain authority in the region led to the French Indochina War (1946–54) and division of the country into the

Democratic Republic of Vietnam in the north and the Republic of Vietnam in the south (1954). The country was reunited under Communist rule in 1975 after the long and bloody Vietnam War (*q.v.*). Key dates in the history of Vietnam include:

111 BC Tonkin, inhabited at least since 2d millenium BC, invaded and conquered by Han Chinese; Chinese ruled northern Vietnam as province of Gieo-chi.

2D CENT. AD Champa kingdom in central Vietnam formed by Chams following collapse of Han dynasty in China.

968 Dinh Bo Linh created unified empire of Dai Viet in Vietnam, independent of China.

1407–28 Chinese again ruled Annam following invasion; driven out by Le Loi, who founded Le dynasty.

1535 Region first visited by Portuguese.

1542 Le dynasty effectively split between ruling dynasties in north and south; southern half, ruled by Nguyen lords.

1771–88 Tay Son rebellion; ruling lords in north and south Annam toppled; Vietnam briefly unified, 1788–93.

1802 Nguyen-Anh reunified Vietnam, with French help, under his rule.

1858–62 French won control of southern Vietnam, which they called Cochin China.

1859 Saigon occupied by the French.

1867 France made Cochin China a colony.

1882 French moved troops to northern Vietnam to expand their control of the region; Chinese, who also laid claims to Vietnam, opposed the move.

1883–85 Sino-French War ended in French control of Vietnam and other Indochina domains.

1884 Annam and Tonkin became French protectorates.

1887 French holdings in Vietnam joined with Cambodia to form French Indochina; Laos added in 1893.

1920 Marked increase in nationalist agitation against French rule from this time.

1920 Ho Chi Minh joined French Communist party.

1926–45 Bao Dai reigned as last emperor of Vietnam under French rule.

1930 Communist Party of Indochina founded by Ho Chi Minh.

1932 Ho Chi Minh fled to Moscow to escape French authorities.

1940 Japanese moved into Vietnam (with French consent) while expanding their control over Southeast Asia during the early phases of WW II; Japanese, who held real power, left French in nominal control until Mar., 1945.

1941 Ho Chi Minh formed the Viet Minh to secure Vietnamese independence (May), following his return to Vietnam.

1945 Japanese made Emperor Bao Dai head of new state of Vietnam (Mar.), ending last vestiges of French control in region; Vietnam included Tonkin (in the north), Annam (in central Vietnam), and Cochin China (in the south).

1945 Vietnam occupied by Allied forces at end of WW II; Nationalist Chinese held north and British occupied south.

1945 Ho Chi Minh led Viet Minh into Hanoi (Sept.), after Japan's surrender; proclaimed Democratic Republic of Vietnam (Sept. 2); Ho in office as president.

1946 France reasserted claim to Indochina; reached accord (Mar.) with Ho Chi Minh, recognizing Vietnamese independence within the French Union; however, nationalists continued pushing for full independence.

1946 French Indochina War began (Dec.) following failure of negotiations with Vietnamese nationalists; French colonial forces ultimately defeated after protracted struggle with Vietnamese Communists and nationalists (1954).

1949 State of Vietnam founded in the south by French.

1951 Lao-Dong founded by Ho Chi Minh, who thereupon became chairman; party replaced the Viet Minh as ruling party of the Democratic Republic of Vietnam.

1954 Viet Minh, led by Gen. Vo Nguyen Giap, victorious over French (May 5) at Dien Bien Phu; marked end of French military power in Vietnam.

1954 Geneva Conference divided Vietnam in two along 17th parallel; North Vietnam to be governed by Communists under Ho Chi Minh, south to be governed by Bao Dai regime; French withdrew from South Vietnam; elections to be held (July, 1956) to reunify the country.

1955 Bao Dai government removed (Oct.) by referendum; Ngo Dinh Diem made president of new Republic of South Vietnam (proclaimed Oct. 26).

1955–63 Diem ruled as president; instituted increasingly repressive policies to restore order; promoted further unrest and significant gains in rural areas by Vietcong; overthrown and killed (1963).

1956 Diem government refused to hold elections in south for reunification of Vietnam as scheduled by the Geneva Conference.

1960 National Liberation Front formed by Communist Vietcong and non-Communists seeking overthrow of Diem regime.

1960–75 Vietnam War; Vietnam ravaged and ultimately reunited under Communists, despite massive US commitment to defending South Vietnamese government.

1963 Diem overthrown in military coup (Nov. 1); period of great political instability followed (1963–65).

1964 North Vietnamese army began infiltration of South Vietnam; Gulf of Tonkin Incident (Aug.), attack on US destroyers by North Vietnamese torpedo boats, led to stepped-up US military intervention in Vietnam War.

1965 Gen. Nguyen Van Thieu became head of South Vietnamese government; Nguyen Cao Ky made prime minister.

1967 New constitution promulgated in South Vietnam (Mar.); Thieu elected president and Ky vice-president in elections (Sept.).

1968 Communists staged massive assault in Tet Offensive (Feb.), a turning point in the Vietnam War.

1969 Phased withdrawal of US forces began; massive bombing continued.

1969 Ho Chi Minh died (Sept. 3); Ton Duc Thang became president of North Vietnam.

1971 President Thieu reelected in South Vietnam.

1972 South Vietnamese president Thieu declared martial law (May 10) in the face of Communist advances.

1973 Peace settlement signed (Jan. 27); provided for cessation of all hostilities and withdrawal of all US forces.

1974 Fighting between the South Vietnamese and North Vietnamese intensified in the Central Highlands (Mar.).

1975 North Vietnamese staged massive attack into South Vietnam (Jan.), culminating in toppling of South Vietnamese government.

1975 Evacuation of Americans begun (Apr. 4).

1975 President Thieu resigned (Apr. 21) amid unrest caused by Communist advances in the South.

1975 Last Americans evacuated from South Vietnam (Apr. 29); South Vietnam surrendered to Communists (Apr. 30).

1976 North and south formally reunified (July 2) as Socialist Republic of Vietnam; Saigon renamed Ho Chi Minh City.

1976–86 Le Duan held the office of general secretary of the Communist Party of Vietnam.

1977 Vietnam admitted to UN.

FROM 1978 Mass emigration of ethnic Chinese began as Vietnamese government adopted policy to drive them out; China, after accepting hundreds of thousands of refugees, refused to accept more; Vietnamese "boat people" then tried to escape by sea to other Southeast Asian countries.

1978 Treaty of friendship signed with the Soviets.

1978 Vietnam invaded Cambodia (from Dec.); overthrew harsh regime of Pol Pot (1979) and installed puppet regime before withdrawing troops in 1989 (*See also* Cambodia, 1978–92).

1979 China invaded Vietnam's northern border region (Feb. 17–Mar. 15); claimed action was punishment for Vietnam's invasion of Cambodia; withdrew from region.

1979 Some 200,000 refugees crossed into neighboring countries from Vietnam this year; UN–backed negotiations began in which Vietnam agreed to allow legal emigration.

1984 Government agreed to eventual withdrawal of Vietnamese troops from Cambodia.

1984 Heavy fighting in border clash with Chinese forces (Apr.); sporadic fighting again in 1986–87.

1984 US rejected Vietnamese overtures for normalization of relations, pending return of remains of US MIAs (soldiers missing in action) and resolution of other matters; Vietnamese held talks with US officials in Hanoi on MIAs numbering over 2,200 (1985–86).

1986 Truong Chinh in office as party general secretary, following death of Le Duan.

1986 Nguyen Van Linh named party general secretary; initiated economic reform program called *doi moi* (renovation), which aimed at converting to a market economy.

1987 Foreign-owned companies permitted to operate in Vietnam following reform of foreign investment laws.

1988 Food shortage in north resulted in brief famine there (Apr.–May).

1989 Vietnamese withdrew virtually all remaining troops from Cambodia (Apr.–Dec.); continued to participate in peace talks.

1989 Economic austerity program introduced to meet IMF requirements for loans.

1989 UN–backed conference set criteria for differentiating economic refugees (who could be repatriated to Vietnam) from political refugees (who could claim asylum); Vietnam, USSR, and US opposed forced repatriation.

1989 Unemployment rose sharply as Vietnamese workers abroad, suddenly displaced by events in the USSR, Eastern Europe, and Iraq, were forced to return home.

1990 Anti-corruption campaign; some 18,000 government officials arrested or sacked.

1990 Party Central Committee report, issued in wake of collapse of East European Communist governments, restated government's commitment to both socialism and liberalization of Vietnam's economy; inflation meanwhile reached 1000 percent.

1990–91 Soviets, suffering severe fiscal problems, began sharp cutbacks in aid to Vietnam.

1990 Le Duc Tho, influential member of Politburo, died.

1991 Income tax established to increase government revenues (Jan.).

1991 US proposed program for normalization of US–Vietnamese diplomatic relations (Apr.).

1991– Do Muoi in office as Communist party general secretary.

1992 US ordered 17-year-old trade embargo revised in recognition of Vietnamese government cooperation in locating US MIAs; US to allow sales of medicine, food, and some other basic items.

Viet-Nam Cong-San *See* **Vietcong.**

Viet Nam Doc Lap Dong Minh *See* **Viet Minh.**

Vietnamization US policy during the later stages of the Vietnam War. Implemented by the Nixon administration (early 1970s), it called for a gradual increase in South Vietnamese participation in the war. US military involvement was to be reduced at the same time, until the South Vietnamese took over all fighting.

Vietnam War War fought (1960–75) by Communist and non-Communist forces for control of South Vietnam. It ended in a Communist victory (and in the reunification of North and South Vietnam), despite heavy involvement by US forces (1965–73). The Vietnam War was an outgrowth of the earlier Indochina War (*q.v.*). At the end of that war, Vietnam was divided into Communist North Vietnam and non-Communist South Vietnam by the Geneva accords of 1954. Elections on the question of reunification were to be held in 1956 but South Vietnamese dictator Ngo Dinh Diem refused to hold them. As a result, a Communist insurrection broke out in 1957. At the same time, non-Communist opposition to the Diem regime was mounting. Rampant corruption, government repression and persecutions, and favoritism shown the Vietnamese Catholic minority, all contributed to sentiment for rebellion against Diem. Meanwhile, US aid flowed into South Vietnam to support the Diem regime. US involvement between 1954 and 1960, however, was confined to financial aid, military equipment and a few hundred military advisers. In 1960 guerrilla activity increased markedly and the Communist-dominated National Liberation Front (NLF) was formed by Communist and non-Communist groups in South Vietnam. Open warfare against the South Vietnamese government began. Heavy US involvement in the war started in 1965 and by 1968 over a half million American troops were in Vietnam. In the years of bloody fighting US troops managed to forestall the collapse of the South Vietnamese government, but they were unable to break the strength of the Vietcong forces (aided by North Vietnam, which was in turn supplied by the USSR). The US government, which had lost considerable prestige both at home and abroad because of US involvement in Vietnam, began withdrawing troops in 1969–70, while at the same time attempting to negotiate a settlement. In 1973 a peace treaty was signed and the last US troops were withdrawn. By 1974, the fighting between Communists and South Vietnamese government forces had increased and in 1975 the Communists mounted their final offensive. South Vietnam surrendered (Apr. 30, 1975), ending the war and setting the stage for reunification of Vietnam. Key events in the history of the Vietnam War include:

1960   Guerrilla forces overran a number of outposts (Jan.) maintained by Vietnamese army regulars (ARVN); marked rise of heavy guerrilla activity in South Vietnam.

1960   National Liberation Front (NLF) formed (Dec. 19–20); composed of both Communists and non-Communists and controlled by Communist; called for overthrow of Ngo Dinh Diem and reunification with north; thereafter guerrilla activity increased significantly and open war against Diem regime began.

1961   Vietcong strength reached an estimated 15,000; rapid growth in numbers continued in following years.

1961   South Vietnam signed military and economic aid treaty with US.

1961   Diem proclaimed a state of emergency (Oct.) as his political support dwindled.

1961   US president J. F. Kennedy reasserted US commitment to Diem regime (Dec.); sent 1,500 more advisers; US helicopter units began direct involvement in fighting to support South Vietnamese.

1962   US Military Assistance Command formed; US forces in Vietnam reached 10,000 by year's end.

1962   Vietcong continued to make gains in South Vietnam despite increased US assistance; US strategy of "strategic hamlets" failed; Diem failed to enact promised reforms (especially badly needed land reforms) or to end corruption.

1963   Battle of Ap Bac (Jan. 2) in Mekong Delta; 200 Vietcong repulsed attack by 2,000 well-equipped ARVN soldiers.

1963   Buddhists, demonstrating in Hue against persecution by the Diem regime, fired on by police (May 8); seven Buddhists subsequently resorted to protest by self-immolation (from June 11); martial law proclaimed by Diem (Aug. 21).

1963   Diem overthrown and killed in military coup (Nov. 1); period of prolonged political crisis (1963–65) as nine coups were staged and Vietcong guerrillas rapidly expanded their control in South Vietnam.

1963   US troop levels reached 17,000; Vietcong strength put at about 30,000.

1964   US president L. Johnson reasserted US commitment to South Vietnam (Jan. 1).

1964–68   Gen. W. Westmoreland in command of US troops in Vietnam.

1964   Terrorist bombs exploded (Aug., Dec.) in Saigon hotels where US troops were quartered.

1964   Gulf of Tonkin Incident; US destroyers reported attacks (Aug. 2, 4) by North Vietnamese patrol boats in the Gulf of Tonkin; US bombed North Vietnamese bases.

1964   Gulf of Tonkin resolution passed (Aug. 7) by US Congress; authorized President Johnson to take all steps necessary to protect US forces and prevent further attacks; became important justification for US involvement in war.

1964   Bien Hoa, US air base outside Saigon, attacked by Vietcong (Nov. 1).

1965   US bombing of North Vietnam began (Feb.); attacks on US forces at Pleiku and Quinhon (Feb. 7, 10) first prompted retaliatory bombings of North; President Johnson ordered regular bombing of North Vietnam (Feb. 28) to force negotiations.

1965   First US combat troops sent to Vietnam; 3,500 US marines landed at Da Nang (Mar. 7–9); Vietcong close to taking complete control of the South as the political crisis continued.

1965   First North Vietnamese regulars (about 400–500 troops) infiltrated into South Vietnam (Mar.–Apr.); US bombing (from 1965) of Ho Chi Minh Trail, major Communist supply line to South, failed to halt flow of men and materiel into South.

1965   Nguyen Cao Ky, military strongman, took control of the government (June); his military dictatorship restored order through harsh repressive measures; broke power of Buddhist resistance (by 1966) and arrested political opponents.

1965   US troops in first major offensive against Vietcong (June 28); in subsequent months began taking over major share of the fighting from the ineffective ARVN regulars.

1965   US troop levels reached 175,000 (Dec.); Vietcong (plus North Vietnamese regulars) reached about 150,000.

1966   Heavy bombing raids conducted throughout North Vietnam; Hanoi and Haiphong bombed for first time (June).

1966   Meeting in Honolulu, Hawaii, between President Johnson, Gen. Ky, and leaders of other countries that sent troops to South Vietnam (including Australia, New Zealand, and South Korea).

1967 New South Vietnamese constitution (Mar.).

1967 Invasion of southern parts of the Demilitarized Zone (DMZ) between North and South Vietnam by US and ARVN troops (May).

1967 Gen. Nguyen Van Thieu elected (Sept.) president, Ky elected vice-president; repressive measures continued.

1968 US troop strength reached about 510,000; Vietcong and North Vietnamese regulars numbered about 230,000.

1968 Siege at Khesanh (Jan.–Apr.); 6,000 US marines came under heavy attack.

1968 Tet Offensive (Jan. 30–Feb. 25); Vietcong and North Vietnamese launched surprise attacks on more than 100 cities in South Vietnam, including Saigon; the Communists suffered heavy losses; a major propaganda victory for Communists, it forced US president Johnson to halt escalation in Vietnam and begin peace negotiations.

1968 My Lai Massacre (Mar. 16).

1968 President Johnson announced (Mar.) he would not seek reelection as antiwar movement in US reached major proportions.

1968 Communists launched major offensive, hitting points throughout South Vietnam (May 5–13); Saigon under heavy attack.

1968 Paris Peace negotiations began between US and North Vietnam (May 13).

1968 Vietcong and South Vietnam joined Paris Peace talks after UN halted bombing of the North (Nov.).

1969 R. Nixon took office as US president; US began gradual withdrawal of troops from Vietnam; bombing of North continued as peace talks dragged on; US widened war (1970) to Cambodia and Laos.

1970 US carried out bombing raids inside Cambodia (Feb. 11).

1970 Six-month lull in fighting broken by Communist offensive in South (Apr. 1).

1970 US completed withdrawal of 115,000 troops (Apr.); announced plan to withdraw 150,000 more troops by 1971.

1970 South Vietnamese offensive in Cambodia begun with US support (Apr. 29).

1970 Communist offensive near DMZ successfully repulsed (May 8).

1970 Combined US–South Vietnamese naval force moved up Mekong into Cambodia (May).

1970 US bombers hit targets in North Vietnam, Cambodia, and Laos (Nov.).

1970 US commando raid (Nov. 21) in North Vietnam unsuccessfully attempted to free US POWs.

1971 South Vietnamese troops, backed by US air support, invaded Laos (Jan. 30).

1971 Fire Base 6 in Central Highlands under siege by Communist forces (Apr.).

1971 DMZ defenses taken over by South Vietnamese (July).

1971 Australian and New Zealand forces withdrawn by year's end.

1971 North Vietnamese offensive along Cambodian border (Sept. 26).

1971 South Vietnamese offensive in eastern Cambodia (Nov.–Dec.).

1972 New US troop withdrawals announced (Jan. 13); US strength to be reduced to 69,000 by May 1.

1972 North Vietnamese offensive (Mar.) across DMZ began; South Vietnamese abandoned northern Quang Tri Province (Apr. 2).

1972 North Vietnamese offensive in South Vietnam cut highway from An Loc to Saigon (Apr. 5).

1972 Central Highlands capital of Hoai An overrun by Communist forces (Apr. 19).

1972 Mining of North Vietnamese ports ordered by US president Nixon (May).

1972 Gen. Frederick C. Weyand replaced Gen. Creighton Abrams as commander of US forces in Vietnam (June).

1972 Heavy US bombing raids over the north marked withdrawal of last US combat troops from South Vietnam (Aug.).

1972 Que Son captured by Communists (Aug. 19).

1972 Quang Tri recaptured by South Vietnamese (Sept. 15).

1972 Heavy bombing of North Vietnam ordered by President Nixon (Dec. 15–30); bombing halted as stalled peace talks resumed.

1973 Peace settlement signed (Jan. 27); provided for end to hostilities and withdrawal of all US forces.

1973 International observers stationed in South Vietnam to monitor truce (Feb. 5).

1974 Heavy fighting between South Vietnamese and Communist forces in the Central Highlands (Mar.).

1975 Final North Vietnamese offensive in South Vietnam began (Jan.).

1975 Evacuation of American personnel in South Vietnam began (Apr. 4).

1975 President Thieu forced to resign (Apr. 21) as Communists advanced in South Vietnam.

1975 Last Americans evacuated from South Vietnam (Apr. 29).

1975 South Vietnam surrendered to Communist forces (Apr. 30), ending the war; formal reunification of North and South Vietnam effected (July 2, 1976).

Vietnam Workers' party *See* **Lao-Dong.**

vigilantes American frontiersmen who were members of illegal or extralegal "vigilance committees" formed to establish law in areas where regular judicial systems were lacking or appeared to be inadequate.

Vigilius *d.* 555. Pope (537–555). He became embroiled in the political and religious struggles over Monophysitism. His policies threatened the canons of the Council of Chalcedon and were bitterly opposed in the West.

Vignoles, Étienne de *See* **La Hire.**

Vigny, Alfred Victor, comte de 1797–1863. French poet, dramatist, and novelist, one of France's leading Romantic writers.

Vikings Norse raiders and adventurers who sailed from their homelands in Scandinavia to attack and pillage European coastal settlements (9th–11th cents.). (*See* Norsemen.)

Vikramaditya *See* **Chandragupta II.**

Villa, Pancho (~, Francisco) (Arango, Doroteo) 1877?–1923. Mexican bandit and revolutionary, a leading figure in the revolts against P. Díaz (1910–11) and V. Huerta (1913–14). Villa's raid on Columbus, New Mexico (Mar. 9, 1916), led to the US punitive expedition into Mexico by Gen. J. Pershing.

Villafranca, Peace of June 11, 1859. Armistice ending a war between Austria and France (allied with Sardinia) over Austrian territories in Italy. The armistice followed a decisive victory by Franco-Sardinian forces. The agreement became part of the Treaty of Zurich, signed in Nov. 1859.

Villa-Lobos, Heitor 1887–1959. Brazilian composer considered the leading Latin composer of his day. His works are noted for their merging of classical influences with Brazilian folk music.

Villard, Henry (Hilgard, Ferdinand Heinrich Gustav) 1835–1900. American journalist and financier. A leading figure in rail transportation in the Pacific Northwest, he also formed (1889) the Edison General Electric Company, serving as its president until 1893.

Villars, Claude Louis Hector, duc de 1653–1734. French soldier and marshal of France. He distinguished himself in the War of the Spanish Succession, negotiated the Treaty of Rastatt (1714), and was supreme commander in the War of Polish Succession.

Villehardouin, Geoffroi de c1160–c1213. French historian and crusader who chronicled the Fourth Crusade in his *Conquête de Constantinople*. He is considered the first French historian.

Villehardouin, Geoffroi I *d.* 1218. French crusader and adventurer. Nephew of G. Villehardouin, he conquered part of the Peloponnesus, in Greece, and there established a kingdom that was ruled by his family from 1210 to 1278.

villeinage Aspect of the feudal system by which a villein, or serf, was bound to the land and obliged to perform services to a lord in return for protection and land tenure. The villein was distinguished from the freeholder.

Villèle, Jean Baptiste Séraphin Joseph, comte de 1773–1854. French politician, leader of the French Ultraroyalist faction. As premier (1822–28) he followed conservative policies and stabilized finances.

Villeneuve, Pierre Charles Jean Baptiste Silvestre de 1763–1806. French admiral. He commanded the French fleet and was defeated at the Battle of Trafalgar (1805).

Villeroi, François, duc de 1644–1730. French courtier and marshal of France. A favorite of Louis XIV, he held high military posts in Italy and Flanders but was defeated at the Battle of Ramillies (1706) during the War of the Spanish Succession.

Villiers, George *See* **Tardieu, André.**

Villiers, George William Frederick, 4th earl of Clarendon 1800–70. British statesman, often called the "Great Lord Clarendon." He was three times foreign secretary (1853–58, 1865–66, 1868–70), the first time during the Crimean War (1853–56). During his third term, he helped pave the way for settlement of the Alabama Claims.

Villon, François 1431–1463? One of the greatest French lyric poets. Continually involved in criminal activity, he spent much time in prison and was banished from Paris in 1463.

Vilnius dispute (Vilna dispute) Conflict between Poland and Lithuania over possession of the city of Vilnius. After WW I, Vilnius was ceded to Lithuania, but during the Russo-Polish War of 1920, it was captured (Sept. 9) by Polish forces, and subsequently was annexed by Poland. Occupied by Russian troops (1939), the city was restored to the Lithuanian SSR in 1944.

Vincent de Paul, Saint 1581?–1660. French priest known for his charitable work. He founded the Congregation of the Mission (1625), known as Lazarists or Vincentians, as well as other charitable institutions.

Vincent of Beauvais c1190–c1264. French Dominican priest. He wrote the first three volumes of the *Speculum majus,* an encyclopedic summary of all knowledge, which remained influential for centuries.

Vinci, Leonardo da *See* **Leonardo da Vinci.**

Vinland (Wineland) Region of North America explored and named by Leif Ericson in the 11th cent. Its exact location is not known.

Vinson, Frederick Moore 1890–1953. American jurist, 13th chief justice of the US Supreme Court (1946–53).

Viollet-le-Duc, Eugène Emmanuel 1814–79. French architect and writer, a leader in the Gothic revival movement in France. He restored many medieval structures, including Notre Dame de Paris. His writings stressed the value of function in design.

Virchow, Rudolf 1821–1912. German pathologist. He contributed to many fields of medical science but is known best as a founder of cellular pathology.

Virgil *See* **Vergil.**

Virginia Eastern US state, the 10th state. Its capital is Richmond. The first European settlement in Virginia (1587) was backed by Sir W. Raleigh and located on Roanoke Island. The first successful colony was established (1607) at Jamestown. Virginia Colony established (1619) the first representative assembly (House of Burgesses) in the New World. The colony thrived as a center of the tobacco trade, but corruption and inability of the governor, W. Berkeley, to protect colonists from Indian attack led to Bacon's Rebellion (*q.v.*) in 1676. Importation of slaves led to greater prosperity in the colony and the rise of a wealthy class. Virginia was a leading

force in resistance to British authority and played a major role in the American Revolution, which ended with the Yorktown Campaign (*q.v.*). Virginia was admitted to the Union (1788) and seceded (1861) at the opening of the American Civil War. The northwestern portion of the state broke away (1863) to form West Virginia. Virginia was the scene of several major engagements, notably the first and second battles of Bull Run, Chancellorsville, Fredericksburg, and the Wilderness Campaign. It was readmitted to the US in 1870.

Virginia and Kentucky Resolutions Resolutions passed (Nov., 1798) by the Kentucky legislature and (Dec., 1798) the Virginia legislature. Written by T. Jefferson and J. Madison respectively, they defended states' rights and were passed in protest against the Alien and Sedition Acts of the Adams administration. They contributed to the more radical theory of Nullification.

Virginia and New Jersey Plans In US history, proposed plans for the structure of government offered at the Constitutional Convention (*q.v.*) in 1787. The Virginia Plan, advanced by Edmund Randolph, would have created a strong federal government with a bicameral legislature. The lower house was to be elected by popular vote and would select members of the upper house. The two houses would elect the head of state. The New Jersey Plan, put forward by William Paterson, favored small states and rejected the provision for apportionment by population in both houses. The Connecticut Compromise (adopted July 16) resolved these differences by adopting proportional representation in the lower house and by giving each state an equal vote in the upper house.

Virginia Company 1. Virginia Company of London. Joint-stock company chartered (1606) by English king James I for the purpose of colonizing the New World. The company established the first permanent English settlement in Virginia at Jamestown (1607) and administered it until its charter was revoked in 1624. 2. Virginia Company of Plymouth. Joint-stock company established (1606) by English king James I. It was reorganized (1620) as the Council of New England and established Plymouth Colony (1620).

Virginia Convention American Revolutionary body that met in Virginia (1775, 1776). At the first of these meetings Patrick Henry delivered his "give me liberty or give me death" speech, and at the second he was involved with George Mason in drafting the Virginia Declaration of Rights. This served as a model for the Bill of Rights in the US Constitution.

Virgin Islands Group of islands in the West Indies including the US Virgin Islands (*pop.* 95,000), officially the Territory of the Virgin Islands of the United States; and the British Virgin Islands (*pop.* 10,500), a British colony. The islands were explored (1493) by C. Columbus and subsequently acquired and settled by the English and Danes. The US bought its holdings from Denmark (1917). US Virgin Islanders have held US citizenship since 1927, and in 1972 the islands were granted one representative in the US House of Representatives.

Virginius Affair Crisis (1873) arising from the Spanish capture of the US ship *Virginius,* which was caught smuggling guns to Cuba during the Ten Years' War. The executions of 53 people aboard nearly led to war between the US and Spain.

Viriatus (Viriathus) *d.* 139 BC. Herdsman of Lusitania who successfully led (c147–c139 BC) a rebellion against Rome. The rebellion ended shortly after his assassination.

Visconti Italian family that ruled Milan from the 13th cent. to 1447. The family derived its name from the title viscount. Its members included Giovanni Visconti (*d.* 1354), Gian Galeazzo Visconti (1351–1402), and Filippo Maria Visconti (1392–1447).

Visigoths (West Goths) Germanic tribe, the western branch of the Goths. The Visigoths left the Black Sea region (c3d cent. AD) and harassed the Roman Empire's border region of Dacia. The Visigoths were allowed to settle in Dacia, which had been abandoned, but later, pressed by the Huns, crossed the Danube and petitioned for permission to settle farther south. After suffering abuses for two years, they crushed Emperor Valens at Adrianople (AD 378) and, under Alaric I, sacked Rome (AD 410). They were allowed to rule large areas of Gaul and Spain, and in AD 475, their leader, Euric, declared independence. His son Alaric II was defeated and killed by Clovis (507). The Visigoths then settled around Toledo, and finally capitulated to the invading Muslims (1711).

Vitellius, Aulus AD 15–69. Roman emperor (AD 69). Proclaimed emperor at Cologne, he defeated his rival Otho in Italy and ruled briefly before being defeated by Vespasian.

Vitoria, Francisco de 1486–1546. Spanish theologian. He is known best for his ethical opposition to acts of warfare except in matters of defense. He championed the cause of the subjugated peoples of the New World.

Vitruvius (Marcus Vitruvius Pollio) *fl.* 1st cent. BC. Roman architect, engineer, and writer. He is known for his *De architectura,* a treatise on classical architecture that played a major role in the classical revival.

Vivaldi, Antonio c1675–1741. Italian composer, one of the greatest composers of the Italian baroque period. A gifted violinist, he is known especially for his instrumental pieces, notably *The Four Seasons.* He also composed operas, cantatas, and other works.

vizier In the Ottoman Empire, the most important minister under the sultan. The term was first adopted in the 14th cent. and was applied to provincial, administrative, and military figures.

Vladimir, Saint *See* Vladimir I.

Vladimir I (Saint ~) c956–1015. Grand Prince of Kiev (c980–1015) and first Christian ruler of Rus'. He consolidated Kiev and Novgorod into a single realm and ordered the conversion of his people to Greek Orthodox Christianity.

Volksraad (People's Council) Advisory council established (1916) by the Dutch in Indonesia. It evolved into a legislative body, including both European and Asian members, but was dissolved when the Japanese occupied Indonesia (1942).

Volscians Ancient Italic people known from their wars with the Romans. They participated in the Latin revolt against Rome (340–338 BC) but were conquered by the Romans (late 4th cent. BC).

Volstead Act (National Prohibition Act) Law passed (1919) by the US Congress to enforce the 18th Amendment during Prohibition. It was voided with repeal of the 18th Amendment (1933).

Volta, Alessandro 1745–1827. Italian physicist and inventor of the voltaic pile, the first electric battery. Educated at religious institutions, Volta showed an early interest in science, particularly electricity. In 1775 he invented the electrophorus, a simple device for producing electrostatic charges. Later, he repeated Galvani's experiment with muscle contractions in a frog's leg, except that he discovered the muscle tissue was not needed to produce an electric current. Using silver and zinc disks, separated by cardboard, he created the first voltaic pile (1800), the earliest electrical battery. The volt, a unit of electromotive force, was name for Volta.

Voltaire, François Marie Arouet de 1694–1778. French author and historian, one of the foremost figures of the Enlightenment. Of middle-class origin, he was educated by the Jesuits and soon made his mark as a poet, playwright, and wit. Imprudent talk and witty lampoons against authority brought him first a stay in the Bastille and then exile in England, prompting his *Letters Concerning the English,* which popularized the ideas of I. Newton and J. Locke. An outstanding historian, he is known best today for such books as *Candide* and his *Philosophical Dictionary,* a forceful work supporting the ideas of the Enlightenment.

Vo Nguyen Giap 1912–   . Noted Vietnamese general and government minister. A Communist, he became commander of the Vietminh (1946) and defeated the French at Dien Bien Phu (1954). He played a strategic role in the Tet Offensive (1968) during the Vietnam War and was commander in chief of Communist Vietnam's armed forces until 1975. After Vietnam's reunification, Giap served as minister of national defense (1976–80) and was a member of the Politburo until 1982.

voodoo   A religion in Caribbean areas, particularly Haiti. Dahomeyan in origin (the word is derived from the West African god *Vodun*), it seeks to put its adherents in touch with guardian spirits through ritual and magic.

Voroshilov, Kliment Efremovich 1881–1969. Russian military and political leader. As commissar of defense (1925–40) he helped to rebuild the Red Army on the eve of WW II. He also served as president of the Soviet Union (1953–60).

Vorster, Balthazar Johannes 1915–83. Prime minister of the Union of South Africa (1966–78).

vorticism   Pre-WW I art movement. It sought to simplify forms into an angular, mechanical regularity. Its principal exponents were H. Gaudier-Brzeska and W. Lewis.

Voting Rights Act of 1965   US act passed to ensure the voting rights of blacks previously denied the franchise by literacy tests and other such requirements. The act suspended these tests and empowered federal examiners to certify eligible voters.

Vries, Hugo de 1848–1935. Dutch botanist. He rediscovered the principle of heredity earlier described by G. Mendel and introduced the concept of mutation in plant evolution.

Vuillard, (Jean) Édouard 1868–1940. French artist, a member of the artistic group known as the Nabis. He is known best for his paintings of domestic interiors.

Vulgate   Latin version of the Bible, completed (AD c405) by Saint Jerome and adopted as the standard version by the Roman Catholic church.

Wade, Benjamin Franklin 1800–78. US Senator from Ohio (1851–69). A leader of the Radical Republicans, he was cosponsor of the Wade-Davis Bill (*q.v.*) for Reconstruction, and opposed the policies of A. Lincoln.

Wade-Davis Bill US bill passed (July 2, 1864) before the end of the Civil War, attempting to regulate Reconstruction policies. It never took effect because President A. Lincoln pocket-vetoed it, but it would have required an oath of allegiance to the Union from a majority of a state's citizens, and states would have been required to abolish slavery, repudiate secession, and disqualify from public office anyone who had served the Confederacy. Its principal sponsor was Ohio Senator B. Wade.

Wafd Egyptian nationalist political party founded in 1918. "Wafd" means "delegation," and the name was applied to the party because its founders, including Sa'd Zaghlul, formed a delegation to the British high commissioner to demand a significant change in Egypt's status during the post-WW I peace process, with complete independence as the eventual goal. Although several times declared illegal, the party was Egypt's major organized political force from 1923 until 1952, and it clashed frequently with King Fuad and his successor, Farouk. It came to power with British support during WW II and returned to power again in 1950, this time agitating for further revisions of Anglo-Egyptian treaties. The Egyptian revolution (1952) and dissolution of the political parties brought a temporary end to the Wafd, which was reconstituted in 1983.

Wages and Hours Act *See* **Fair Labor Standards Act.**

Wagner, Richard 1813–83. Famous German composer, whose operas marked the culmination of the German Romantic tradition, and had a great influence on later composers. Among his many works are *The Ring of the Nibelungs, Lohengrin, The Flying Dutchman, Tannhäuser,* and *Tristan und Isolde.*

Wagram, Battle of (Deutsch-Wagram, ˜) Battle fought on July 5–6, 1809, near the Austrian village of Wagram. Napoleon, with some 154,000 troops, defeated an army of some 158,000 under the Archduke Charles. The battle prevented the formation of a new coalition against Napoleon.

Wahhabi Muslim reform movement founded by Muhammad ibn Abd al-Wahhab (18th cent.). It became the religion of the Saudi rulers and is thus an influential sect in modern Saudi Arabia. It is a puritanical movement which advocates living by the Koran and rejects the excesses of luxury and elaborate worship.

Wahunsonacock *See* **Powhatan Confederacy.**

Waiblings *See* **Welfs.**

Wainwright, Jonathan Mayhew 1883–1953. American general, who commanded US forces in the Philippines in WW II. Forced to surrender at Corregidor (1942), he and his troops were held as prisoners of war until 1945.

Wairau Affray (Wairau Massacre) Incident (June 17, 1843) in which 22 English settlers were killed by about 90 Maori natives on New Zealand's South Island. The settlers had tried to arrest the Maori chiefs for resisting land surveys. The British governor took no action against the Maori, but the incident contributed to the outbreak of the Maori Wars.

Waitangi, Treaty of Agreement (Feb. 6, 1840) between the British government and some 500

Maori chiefs. It formed the basis of British annexation and rule of New Zealand. The Maori recognized British sovereignty in return for guarantees of their lands, possessions, and rights as British subjects.

Waite, Morrison Remick 1816–88. American jurist, seventh chief justice of the US Supreme Court (1874–88), best known for his influential interpretations of the 14th and 15th Amendments.

Wakefield, Battle of *See* **Roses, Wars of the.**

Wake Island, Battle of Japanese attack (Dec. 9, 1941) on the American base situated on Wake Island. A force of 377 US marines aided by some 1,000 civilian workers held out until Dec. 23 against a massive Japanese assault.

Walachia (Wallachia) Danubian principality. With neighboring Moldavia, it formed (1859) the modern Balkan state of Rumania. Its inhabitants preserve the ancient Latin speech of Roman Dacia. Walachia was obliged to acknowledge Turkish suzerainty by 1417, became a virtual Russian protectorate in 1774, and became fully independent as Rumania in 1878.

Waldemar I (Valdemar I) (~ the Great) 1131–82. King of Denmark (1157–82). His succession to the Danish throne ended civil war in Denmark. He defeated the Wends, conquered Norwegian lands, and established political ties with Sweden, France, and the Holy Roman Empire.

Waldemar II (Valdemar II) (~ the Victorious) 1170–1241. King of Denmark (1202–41), successor to his brother Canute VI. He conquered a great area in the Baltic but was forced to surrender much of it. He reformed and codified Danish law.

Waldemar IV (Valdemar IV) (~ Atterdag) c1320–75. King of Denmark (1340–75) He regained his kingdom from foreign control and fought against the Hanseatic League. But he was forced to sign the Treaty of Stralsund, which gave the league great influence in Denmark.

Waldemar Atterdag *See* **Waldemar IV.**

Waldemar the Great *See* **Waldemar I.**

Waldemar the Victorious *See* **Waldemar II.**

Waldenses (Waldensians) Religious group centered in Piedmont in Italy and Dauphin in France from the 12th cent. Founded c1170 by a merchant of Lyons, P. Waldo, the Waldenses sought a life of poverty and gospel simplicity. They eventually drifted into what became heresy to the Roman Catholic church, denying purgatory, the

papacy, prayers for the dead, and some of the sacraments. They emphasized a simple biblicism and criticized the ecclesiastical abuses of the day. Often persecuted, they nevertheless continued to survive. Most Waldensians accepted the Reformation and became in effect another Swiss Protestant church (1532). They did not receive full civil and religious rights until 1848.

Waldheim, Kurt 1918– . Austrian president (1986–92) and formerly the fourth secretary general of the UN (1972–82), replacing U Thant of Burma. A career diplomat, he was Austria's UN representative (1965–68), foreign minister (1968–70), and finally Austria's president. An international furor erupted over Waldheim's WW II service as a Nazi intelligence officer during his campaign for the Austrian presidency, but highly publicized charges he participated in abuses against Jews were never proved.

Waldseemüller, Martin *See* **America.**

Waldstein, Albrecht von *See* **Wallenstein, Albrecht von.**

Wales Historic region of Great Britain, located west of England. The home of Celtic tribes known collectively as the Cymry, Wales was invaded by the Romans and later resisted the Anglo-Saxon invasion of Britain (5th cent. AD). Conquered (1276–84) by English king Edward I, Wales was formally joined with England in 1536, after which its history merged with that of England. Key dates in the history of Wales include:

55 BC–1ST CENT. AD Romans advanced into British Isles; occupied areas of Wales, but Welsh tribes continued to resist Roman rule.

5TH CENT. AD Celts fled westward in face of Anglo-Saxon invasion, settling in Wales; subsequent centuries saw the rise of several kingdoms in Wales.

MID-10TH CENT. Hywel Dda reigned in Wales; established unified Welsh legal code.

1062–64 English king Harold led army into Wales (1062–64); defeated Welsh king Gruffydd ap Llewelyn (*d.* 1063).

1136 Welsh forces victorious over English under Henry I.

1158–65 English king Henry II reestablished control in Wales.

1276–84 English king Edward I invaded Wales (1276), defeating Welsh prince Llewelyn ap Gruffydd; Llewelyn staged unsuccessful revolt (1282) and English established control over all Wales; conquest formalized by Statute of Wales (1284).

1301 Edward I named his son (later Edward II) Prince of Wales; first English heir to be so designated; act helped to appease Welsh toward English rule.

1402–c1415 Owen Glendower staged unsuccessful uprising against English.

1536 Wales formally joined with England through the Act of Union.

18TH CENT. Welsh nationalism played key role in establishment of Calvinistic Methodist church in Wales.

19TH CENT. Extensive coal fields opened in the south; Wales became heavily industrialized, but depressed economic conditions in the countryside led to the Rebecca Riots (1843) and mass emigration.

1914 British Parliament ordered disestablishment of Calvinistic Methodist church.

1940s Welsh nationalism showed marked increase in years following WW II; Welsh language introduced (1944) as working language for primary and secondary schools in Wales.

1979 Welsh voters rejected referendum for home rule.

Wales, Prince of   *See* **Prince of Wales.**
Wales, Statute of   *See* **Statute of Wales.**
Walesa, Lech 1943– . Polish labor activist and president of Poland (1990–). An electrician by trade and an avowed labor activist, Walesa organized the 1980 general strike of workers in the Gdansk area (Aug.), centered on the Lenin shipyard. After winning the right to organize from the government, Walesa became head of Solidarity, the first independent union in Poland. In 1981, however, the Polish government imposed martial law, outlawing Solidarity and imprisoning Walesa for nearly a year. In 1988, he began talks with the government, and in 1989 Solidarity and other unions were again legalized. Political reforms including free elections, were also granted. In 1990, following successes of the pro-democracy movement, Walesa won Poland's first direct presidential election by an overwhelming majority. His administration has been marked by severe economic problems resulting from the change from a Communist to free market economy. He won the 1983 Nobel Peace Prize.

Walewska, Countess Marie 1789–1817. Polish noblewoman, mistress to Napoleon I, and mother of Count A. Walewski, a foreign minister of Napoleon III.

Walewski, Comte Alexandre Florian Joseph Colonna 1810–68. French diplomat and a son of Napoleon I and Marie Walewska. He was foreign minister (1855–60) and minister of state (1860–63).

Walker, Robert John 1801–69. American politician. As US Senator (1836–45) he supported westward expansion. He was secretary of the treasury (1845–49) during the Mexican War and helped win passage of the Walker Tariff of 1866, which lowered import duties.

Walker, William 1824–60. American adventurer who led a force to the Mexican state of Lower California (1853–54), briefly establishing a republic. He invaded Nicaragua (1855) and became its president (1856–57).

Walking Purchase Purchase of Delaware Indian lands (1737) in Pennsylvania, in which Pennsylvania Colonial officials cheated the Indians. The Indians determined the size of lands to be sold by the distance a man could walk in a day. Pennsylvania officials, however, cleared a path and secured runners, thereby doubling the size of the tract.

Wallace, Alfred Russel 1823–1913. British naturalist. His studies contributing to the theory of natural selection paralleled, but were independent of, those of C. Darwin.

Wallace, George Corley 1919– . American politician and governor of Alabama (1963–67, 1971–76), noted for resisting school integration in Alabama. A 1968 third-party presidential candidate, he was campaigning for the 1972 Democratic presidential nomination when an assassin's bullet left him partly paralyzed (May 15, 1972).

Wallace, Henry Agard 1888–1965. American agriculturalist, statesman and US vice-president (1941–45). A key figure in the New Deal, he was secretary of agriculture (1933–40) before being chosen for the vice-presidency. He was not renominated because of Southern opposition.

Wallace, Lewis 1827–1905. American author and soldier, best known as author of the historical novel *Ben-Hur*.

Wallace, Sir William c1272–1305. Scottish patriot, a leading figure in the Scottish struggle to win independence from England.

Wallachia *See* **Walachia.**

Wallenstein, Albrecht von (Waldstein, Albrecht von) 1583–1634.   Bohemian noble who served as the chief general to Holy Roman Emperor Ferdinand II during the Thirty Years' War. One of the most famous military men of his time, he commanded imperial forces twice (1625–30, 1632–34), but lost the emperor's trust and was murdered.

Wallis, John 1616–1703.   English mathematician noted for his contributions to the development of the calculus. He wrote on many subjects, including conic sections, logic, grammar, and cryptography.

Wall of Antoninus   Ancient Roman wall stretching 37 miles across southern Scotland. It was built AD c140 by Antoninus Pius as a defense against attacks from the north.

Walloons   French-speaking Belgians. They inhabit mainly the southern provinces of Belgium in contrast to the Dutch-speaking Flemings, who live in the northern provinces.

Walpole, Horace, 4th earl of Orford 1717–97.   English author, noted for his Gothic novel *The Castle of Otranto* (1765), and for his many letters, which are an invaluable source for details about life in Georgian England.

Walpole, Robert 1st earl of Orford 1676–1745.   British statesman and Whig leader, generally regarded as the first British prime minister. Walpole entered Parliament in 1701 and held ministerial posts (1708–11) until being convicted (1712) on dubious charges of corruption by a Tory administration. He supported the succession of the Hanoverian king George I (1714), which restored the Whigs to power, and thereafter began his ascendancy. In 1720 he was called upon to salvage government finances after the disastrous South Sea Bubble (*q.v.*) incident and in 1721 was appointed first lord of the treasury and chancellor of the exchequer. Thereafter he remained in power until 1742, and by his astute handling of Parliament and skillful distribution of royal patronage helped lay the foundations for the office of prime minister. His purge of opposition elements in his ministry (1733) established his firm control over the cabinet. Walpole is especially noted for his accomplishments in the area of finance. He also endeavored to promote trade and reduce tariffs, and sought to keep Britain out of war. Unable to escape involvement in the War of the Austrian Succession, Walpole was ousted from power (1742) after reverses in that war.

Walsh, Thomas James 1859–1933.   American political leader. As US senator from Montana (1913–33), he headed the Senate investigation (1922–23) that exposed the Teapot Dome (*q.v.*) oil-reserve scandal.

Walter, Hubert *d.* 1205.   English archbishop and statesman. He accompanied Richard I on the Third Crusade. As archbishop of Canterbury he raised the ransom to free Richard, and in Richard's absence was the effective ruler of England (1194–98).

Walter, Thomas U.   *See* **Capitol.**

Walter the Penniless *d.* 1096.   French knight, and a leader of a band of soldiers and adventurers known as the Peasants' Crusade. His army plundered eastern Europe in advance of the First Crusade, and was defeated in Asia Minor.

Walther von der Vogelweide c1170–c1230.   German minnesinger (poet musician), considered the greatest lyric poet of medieval Germany.

Wanamaker, John 1838–1922.   American merchant, who founded (1875) in Philadelphia one of the first department stores, John Wanamaker and Company.

Wandiwash, Battle of   British victory over the French (Jan. 22, 1760), near Madras, India. A French force of about 2,000 under the Count de Lally was routed by a British force of about 1,700. The victory was the most significant in India during the Seven Years' War and led to the French withdrawal from India.

Wang Anshi (Wang An-shih) 1021–1086.   Chinese poet, Confucian scholar, and government administrator. As chief minister for the Emperor Shenzong (1048–85), he carried out financial reforms, established an agricultural loan program, levied an income tax, and organized a militia.

Wang Ching-wei   *See* **Wang Jingwei.**

Wang Jingwei (Wang Ching-wei) 1885–1944.   Chinese political leader. He was a supporter of Sun Yat-sen and after Sun's death (1925) challenged Chiang Kai-shek for control of the Guomindang. He served as premier of Japanese-controlled China (1938–44).

Wang Mang 45 BC–AD 23.   Chinese Han dynasty official who seized the throne and ruled as emperor (AD 9–23). He was the only ruler of the Xin dynasty. Wang Mang's many radical governmental and land reforms aroused stiff opposition, and from AD 18, bands of peasant rebels called Red Eyebrows rose against his rule. Finally in AD 23 they attacked the capital city of Chang'an and killed the emperor. Soon after Han dynasty rule was reestablished in China.

Wang Wei 699–759. Chinese poet, painter, and physician of the Tang dynasty. A leading figure in Chinese cultural history, he is noted for his delicate monochrome landscapes and for his poems depicting pastoral scenes.

Wang Yangming 1472–1528. Chinese neo-Confucianist philosopher. He developed a philosophical idealism that conflicted with the realistic Confucianism of the 12th-cent. philosopher Zhu Xi.

Warbeck, Perkin 1474?–99. Flemish impostor and pretender to the English throne. He posed as Richard, the younger brother of Edward V, and sought to usurp the throne of Henry VII. He was defeated, imprisoned, and later executed.

War Communism *See* **New Economic Policy.**

Ward, Artemas 1727–1800. American general, who commanded at the siege of Boston (1775) until G. Washington took over. He later served in the Continental Congress (1780–81) and US Congress (1791–95).

war debts *See* **reparations.**

War Hawks Certain southern and western US Congressmen of the 12th Congress (1811–13) who vigorously promoted war with Britain and who were thus largely responsible for the War of 1812. H. Clay and J. Calhoun were among the War Hawks.

Warhol, Andy *See* **Pop art.**

warlord Regional military commanders in China who, between 1916 and 1949, often functioned as independent rulers in the areas they controlled. Chinese president Yuan Shikai had relied on military force to rule and, after his death in 1916 many of his former generals took control of their military territories, especially in the north. In the south, Chiang Kai-shek consolidated Nationalist rule and by his Northern Expedition regained control over warlords. Many warlords retained local control, however, and were not finally eliminated until the Communist victory in 1949.

Warner, Seth 1743–84. American Revolutionary War officer, a leader of the Green Mountain Boys. He played a major role in the capture of Ticonderoga (1775) and Crown Point (1775).

War of *See under names inverted, as in* **Pacific, War of the.**

Warren, Earl 1891–1974. Chief justice of the US Supreme Court (1953–69) and three-time governor of California, (1943–53). He presided over many controversial Court decisions, notably those outlawing school segregation, establishing the principle of "one man, one vote," and upholding an accused person's rights. He headed the Warren Commission (1963–64), the presidential commission that investigated the assassination of President J. Kennedy.

Warren, Gouverneur Kemble 1830–82. Union general in the Civil War. His defense of Little Round Top during the Battle of Gettysburg helped to secure a Union victory.

Warren, Robert Penn 1905– . American novelist, poet, and critic, identified with the group of Southern writers known as the Fugitives, who celebrated the Southern agrarian traditions. He wrote *All the King's Men.*

Warring States Period (453–221 BC) in Chinese history. This period brought an end to the long reign of the Zhou dynasty (ruled 1122–221 BC) and was marked by the rise of a number of petty kingdoms—Zhou, Jin, Wei, Han, Zhao, Chu, Yan, and Qi. The beginning of the period is usually dated from the end of a long civil war in Jin, when Jin broke up into three smaller states, Han, Wei, and Zhao (453). Corruption was widespread and wars between the states were frequent. Despite the chaotic nature of this period, some of the great thinkers in Chinese history flourished then (notably Mencius) and helped establish doctrines that would later dominate Chinese culture.

Warsaw Ghetto Uprising Full-scale revolt by Jews (Apr. 19–May 16, 1943) against the Nazi program for transporting Polish Jews to death camps. After the Nazis occupied Poland during WW II, the Jewish quarter in Warsaw became a holding area for Jews and by 1942 some 500,000 Jews from the surrounding countryside had been confined in the appallingly overcrowded ghetto. Then from summer 1942, some 5,000 Jews a day were transported to the Treblinka death camp, having been told they were going to labor camps. Jews in Warsaw soon learned the truth from escapees, however. The Jewish Zydowska Organizacja Bojowa (Jewish Combat Organization) put up the first armed resistance on Jan. 18, 1943, eventually forcing the Nazis to halt deportations for a time. The full-scale revolt began Apr. 19, when SS commander H. Himmler launched a major assault on the Warsaw Ghetto. Some 1,500 Jews held off the Nazis for nearly a month before dwindling ammunition supplies and the overwhelming Nazi firepower halted the revolt.

Warsaw Pact *See* **Warsaw Treaty Organization.**

Warsaw Treaty Organization (Warsaw Pact) Now defnunct defensive alliance between the former USSR and its Eastern European satellites, created by a treaty signed in Warsaw (May 14, 1955) to counterbalance NATO. The Warsaw Pact countries consisted of Albania (until 1968), Bulgaria, Czechoslovakia, East Germany, Hungary, Poland, Rumania, and the USSR. The organization was disbanded Mar., 1991, just prior to the collapse of the USSR.

Warsaw uprising Rebellion in which the Polish underground army briefly recaptured and held Warsaw against the Germans (Aug.–Oct., 1944). The Poles were defeated by German reinforcements while the Soviet Army remained idle just across the Vistula. Thus any potential Polish military opposition to postwar Soviet domination of Poland was eliminated.

Warwick, Thomas de Beauchamp, earl of *See* **Beauchamp, Thomas, de, earl of Warwick.**

Washington State in the northwest US, the 42d state. The Spanish, English, and Russians explored the area, but it was American Robert Gray who claimed it for the US (1792). British and US counterclaims were settled in 1846, and Tumwater became the first permanent settlement in 1845. The Washington Territory was created in 1853, and the discovery of gold brought an increase in population. Washington became a state and adopted its constitution in 1889.

Washington, Booker T(aliaferro) 1856–1915. American black educator. Born a slave, he became the moving force in the establishment of Tuskegee (Alabama) Institute and a spokesman for educational and economic opportunity for blacks.

Washington, D.C. *See* **District of Columbia.**

Washington, George 1732–99. First US president (1789–97), known as the Father of His Country. The son of a well-to-do Virginia planter, Washington began his career as a surveyor. He later fought in the French and Indian Wars (1754–63) and served as commander of the Virginia militia (1755–58). A member of the Virginia House of Burgesses (1759–74), he became a leader of the Colonial movement toward self-government. Washington became a delegate to the first Continental Congress (1774–75), and was named by the second Continental Congress as commander in chief of the Continental Army during the American Revolution (*q.v.*). Washington remained in command throughout the Revolutionary War. He turned a disorganized militia into a well-trained army and, despite severe shortages and chaotic communication between the army and the government, led his forces to ultimate victory at the Battle of Yorktown (*q.v.*) in 1781. Washington served as president of the Constitutional Convention (*q.v.*) in 1787, and his efforts to secure adoption of the Constitution led to his election as first president of the US. Washington took the oath of office in New York City (Apr. 30, 1789) and appointed such men as T. Jefferson and A. Hamilton to the government, regardless of their political leanings. Later, Washington sought to remain neutral in the growing political struggle between the Republicans and the Federalists. His term as president was marked by the Whiskey Rebellion (*q.v.*) and the conclusion in 1795 of Jay's Treaty (*q.v.*) with Great Britain. Washington was unanimously reelected (1793), but the bitter political struggle that had developed in the country led him to support the Federalists. His second term was also marked by conflict in the West. Deciding not to accept a third term as president, Washington delivered his celebrated Farewell Address (Sept. 17, 1796), in which he warned against the establishment of permanent alliances. He retired to his estate, Mount Vernon, but returned as commander in chief of the army (1798) when war with France seemed inevitable. War was avoided and Washington died (Dec. 14, 1799) soon after.

Washington, March on *See* **March on Washington.**

Washington Peace Conference *See* **Tyler, John.**

Washington, Treaty of Agreement (May 8, 1871) between Britain and the US that settled the Alabama Claims (*q.v.*) and regulated navigation in the St. Lawrence and the Great Lakes. It was the first treaty in which Canada was recognized as a distinct entity.

Watergate Scandal Major US political scandal (1972–74) involving charges of abuse of power, bribery, official misconduct, and attempts to cover up illegal activities. The scandal forced the resignation of President R. Nixon (1974) and resulted in a period of public distrust of government. The scandal began to unfold (June 17, 1972) when five men were arrested for trying to place an illegal wiretap in the Democratic party headquarters at the Watergate apartment complex in Washington, D.C. With the two others who were arrested in the case, G. Gordon Liddy and E. Howard Hunt, Jr., the group was linked to the White House but nothing could be proved. In the meantime President Nixon was reelected to a second term and the seven involved in the Watergate incident were tried and convicted (Jan., 1973). A Senate committee was formed (Feb., 1973) to investigate. The first break in the scandal came in Mar., 1973, when James McCord, one of the seven convicted, charged that the White House had attempted to cover up the incident. By Apr. 30, 1973, President Nixon was forced to dismiss White House advisers H. R. Haldeman, John D. Ehrlichman, and John Dean. Nixon, however, denied he had any involvement in the Watergate burglary or attempts to cover up the incident. Dean later testified that Nixon had approved the cover-up and implicated Haldeman, Ehrlichman, and former attorney general John Mitchell as well. The major break in the scandal came when it was revealed (July, 1973) that Nixon had taped all conversations in his White House office. The struggle for release of the tapes lasted a year and ended when the Supreme Court ruled against the president (July 24, 1974). The House adopted articles of impeachment against President Nixon (July 27–30) and, after publicly admitting he had been involved in the cover-up, Nixon resigned (Aug. 9). He was succeeded by President G. Ford, who later pardoned Nixon for his involvement in Watergate.

Waterloo, Battle of Final battle of the Napoleonic Wars, fought (June 18, 1815) at this Belgian village south of Brussels, and famous as Napoleon's military demise. After the Battle of Ligny, Napoleon sent a third of his 105,000-man army, under Marshal E. de Grouchy, in pursuit of the retreating 45,000-man Prussian army, under G. von Blücher. He then forced the duke of Wellington's 68,000-man army to withdraw toward Brussels after a battle at Quatre Bras.

With the two forces thus separated, Napoleon attacked Wellington at Waterloo at noon on June 18. However, Napoleon's main attack on Wellington's center was stalled by the British. Later that day Blücher arrived with his Prussian force, after having managed to elude Grouchy. These added reinforcements turned the battle into a rout and Napoleon was compelled to retreat with heavy losses (25,000 French casualties plus those taken prisoner; 23,000 allied casualties). Napoleon abdicated for his second and last time June 22.

Watling Street Ancient Roman road in England, running from London northwest through St. Albans and other points to Wroxeter. It was built as a military road, and parts of it are still in use.

Watson, James Dewey 1928– . American biologist. He and Sir Francis Harry Compton Crick (1916–) discovered (1953) the molecular structure of DNA, one of the most important discoveries this century in the field of genetics. Watson and Crick shared the Nobel Prize for Physiology or Medicine in 1962.

Watson, John Broadus 1878–1958. American psychologist, the leading figure in the establishment of behaviorism.

Watt, James 1736–1819. Scottish inventor, whose improved steam engine helped bring on the steam age and thus became a milestone in the Industrial Revolution. Born the son of a prosperous shipbuilder and merchant, Watt studied to become a mathematical-instrument maker and in 1757 set up his own shop at the University of Glasgow. In 1764 he married his first wife, his cousin Margaret Miller (d. 1773), and that same year began trying to improve on the primitive Newcomen steam engine, work that would ultimately win him fame and fortune. In 1765, Watt invented the steam condenser to reduce excessive heat loss in Newcomen engines. Some years later, Watt entered into a successful partnership with the Birmingham manufacturer Matthew Boulton, to manufacture and sell the improved engine (1775). Watt meanwhile perfected steam engine design through a series of basic improvements, including the sun-and-planet gear (1781) to convert reciprocal motion to rotary motion (thereby vastly increasing possible applications for steam engines); the double-acting steam engine (1782); a centrifugal governor to control engine speed (1789); and a pressure gauge

(1790). Profits from Watt's inventions made him wealthy by 1790, and from 1795 he began devoting his time to travel and other pursuits.

Watteau, Jean Antoine 1684–1721. French painter, considered one of the masters of French painting. His works are noted for their use of color and rendering of natural scenes. Among his works were *Love in the Italian Theater, Love in the French Theater,* and *The Embarkation for Cythera.*

Wattignies, Battle of Battle (Oct. 15–16, 1793) during the French Revolutionary Wars in which inexperienced French levies defeated a professional Austrian army. The 50,000-man French force defeated some 30,000 Austrians in this battle in northern France and thus blocked their drive toward Paris.

Waugh, Evelyn Arthur St. John 1903–66. English author, considered the most gifted satirical novelist of his time. Among his noted works were *Decline and Fall* (1928) and *Brideshead Revisited* (1945).

Way of Five Pecks of Rice *See* **Five Pecks of Rice.**

Weaver, James Baird 1833–1912. American politician. He supported the policies of the Greenback party and was its unsuccessful presidential candidate in 1880. He helped to found the Populist party and was its unsuccessful presidential candidate in 1892.

Webb, (Martha) Beatrice (Potter, ˜) 1858–1943. English writer and social reformer. A social worker in London, she published (1891) *The Cooperative Movement in Great Britain,* and in 1892 married S. Webb, an economist. Members of the Fabian Society, they co-authored *The History of Trade Unionism* (1894) and *Industrial Democracy* (1897), and co-founded the London School of Economics. With her husband, she became influential in the Labour party.

Webb, Sidney James 1858–1947. British social and economic reformer. He and his wife, B. Webb (*née* Potter), were leading figures in the Fabian Society, founded the *New Statesman,* and greatly influenced social reforms in Britain.

Weber, Max 1864–1920. Influential German sociologist and political economist, best known for *The Protestant Ethic and the Spirit of Capitalism,* which explored the role of religious and ethical values in the development of capitalism.

Webern, Anton von 1883–1945. Austrian composer. Taught by A. Schönberg, he wrote 12-tone music, creating a distinctively individual style which led to the development of "atonality." His uniquely modern style was at first unpopular but was taken up (1950s) by a younger generation of composers and musicians.

Webster, Daniel 1782–1852. Noted American lawyer and statesman, considered one of the outstanding orators of his day. He was a vigorous supporter of American nationalism but opposed the annexation of Texas and the Mexican War, and sought to preserve the Union even at the cost of continued slavery. He served as senator (1827–41, 1845–50) and twice as secretary of state (1840–43, 1850–52).

Webster, Noah 1758–1843. American lexicographer, best known for his *Blue-backed Speller* (1783) and for his major work, *The American Dictionary of the English Language* (1828).

Webster-Ashburton Treaty Treaty (Aug., 1842) between Great Britain and the US, settling the northeastern boundary between the US and Canada and providing for suppression of the African slave trade. D. Webster represented the US, and Alexander Baring, 1st Baron Ashburton, represented Britain.

Wedgwood, Josiah 1730–95. English pottery manufacturer, whose scientific and practical approach to the production of pottery was matched by his attention to art and beauty. He was a leading figure in the Industrial Revolution.

Wehlau, Treaty of Agreement (Sept. 19, 1657) by which Poland gave up suzerainty over the Duchy of Prussia. The electors of Brandenburg had inherited ducal Prussia from the Teutonic Knights as a Polish fief. Duke Frederick William, however, won full sovereignty by this treaty, in return for providing military aid for Poland's war against Sweden.

Weidman, Charles Edward, Jr. 1901–75. American dancer and choreographer. His dances are noted for their abstract motions and use of pantomime, and have greatly influenced modern dance.

Weil, Simone 1909–43. French philosopher and mystic, whose writings reflect her social activism and attraction to the Roman Catholic faith.

Weill, Kurt 1900–50. German composer, whose operas are noted for their use of social satire. Best known of these is *The Threepenny Opera,* done in collaboration with B. Brecht.

Weimar Republic German republic (1919–33) created after Germany's defeat in WW I. The new government was created (July 31, 1919) amid social unrest (notably uprisings by Communists) and severe economic problems. In fact Weimar was chosen as the site of the constitutional convention because of the unrest in Berlin. Subsequent years were characterized by chronic parliamentary instability, a period of inflation, and later, mass unemployment, all of which eventually led to A. Hitler's rise to power in 1933. (*See also* Germany, 1919–33.)

Weinstein, Nathan   *See* **West, Nathanael.**

Weismann, August Friedrich Leopold 1834–1914. German biologist. His germ-plasm theory of heredity was a major contribution to the development of modern genetics.

Weiss, Ehrich   *See* **Houdini, Harry.**

Weizmann, Chaim 1874–1952.   Russian-born scientist, Zionist leader, and Israeli statesman. A leader in the Zionist movement, Weizmann helped to negotiate the Balfour Declaration (*q.v.*) and was the first president of Israel (1948–52).

Welfs Ruling family in Bavaria and Saxony which clashed (12th cent.) with their kin in the German royal Hohenstaufen family (called Waiblings). The conflict resulted in the exile of Henry the Lion of Bavaria (a Welf) for failing to help the emperor Frederick I Barbarossa in Italy (1176). Thereafter the Welfs managed to get Henry's son, Otto IV, elected as anti-king to Barbarossa's successor, but their line ended with him. The names for the 13th-cent. Guelphs and Ghibellines (*q.v.*) in Italy were adopted from this earlier rivalry.

Weller, Thomas   *See* **Robbins, Frederick Chapman.**

Welles, Gideon 1802–78.   American statesman. He served as secretary of the navy under A. Lincoln and A. Johnson. He sided with Johnson against the Radical Republicans in the battle over Reconstruction (*q.v.*) policy.

Welles, Orson 1915–85.   American actor, director, and producer. His use of innovative techniques in such films as *Citizen Kane* and *The Magnificent Ambersons* greatly influenced film production.

Wellesley, Richard Colley, marquess 1760–1842. British colonial administrator, brother of Arthur Wellesley, 1st duke of Wellington. As governor general of India (1797–1805) he greatly expanded British rule there.

Wellington, Arthur Wellesley, 1st duke of 1769–1852.   British soldier and statesman. He commanded British, Portuguese, and Spanish forces in the Peninsular War (*q.v.*), defeated Napoleon in the Battle of Waterloo (*q.v.*), and served as prime minister of Great Britain (1828–30). During his tenure, the Test Act (*q.v.*) was repealed and Catholic Emancipation (*q.v.*) was enacted.

Wells, Henry 1805–78.   American expressman. He established (1848) his own express firm, which he later merged with other companies to form the American Express Company (1850). With W. Fargo he formed Wells, Fargo and Company (1852) to handle express service to California.

Wells, H(erbert) G(eorge) 1866–1946.   English author and historian. His novels, romances, and stories are marked by his interests in both scientific and social questions. His works include *The War of the Worlds, The Time Machine, Kipps, Tono-Bungay,* and *Outline of History.*

Wem, George Jeffreys, 1st baron, Jeffreys of   *See* **Jeffreys of Wem, George Jeffreys, 1st baron.**

Wenceslaus 1361–1419.   King of the Germans (1378–1400), and Bohemia (1378–1419). He was successor to his father, Charles IV. Wenceslaus was an ineffective ruler and his reign was marked by religious and political conflicts and widespread rebellion. Amid a war between German nobles and imperial cities (1380s), he eventually sided with the nobles, only to be deposed as German king by them in favor of Rupert in 1400. He also tried and failed to resolve the Great Schism in the Roman Catholic church. After 1400, he retired to his kingdom of Bohemia and was there likewise embroiled in rebellions by nobles who twice imprisoned him (1394, 1402–03). Finally he supported the religious reformer J. Huss against the pope, but was unable to prevent Huss's execution. This led to the Hussite Wars (*q.v.*), which broke out after the execution.

Wenceslaus I *d.* 1253.   King of Bohemia (1230–53), successor to his father Ottocar I. He encouraged Germans to settle in Bohemia, brought Austria under Bohemian control, and was a patron of the arts.

Wenceslaus II 1271–1305.   King of Bohemia (1278–1305), successor to his father Ottocar II. He extended Bohemian control into Poland and Hungary, and was made king of Poland (1300–05).

Wenceslaus III c1289–1306.   King of Hungary (1301–04) and king of Bohemia (1305–06). Son and successor of Wenceslaus II in Bohemia, he renounced his claim to Hungary. He was assassinated after his short reign in Bohemia.

Wenceslaus, Saint *d.* 929. Duke and patron saint of Bohemia. He encouraged Christianity in Bohemia and submitted to the rule of Henry I of Germany. For this he was murdered by his brother, Boleslav I, who succeeded him.

Wendi *d.* 157 BC. Chinese emperor of the Han dynasty (180–157 BC), a son of Gaodi. Highly regarded as a model ruler, Wendi consolidated imperial control of the newly formed Han empire while avoiding the pitfalls of excessive bureacracy and harsh criminal punishments that helped bring down the Qin dynasty.

Wends Slavic people inhabiting East Germany. Also called "Sorbs," they are the remnant of a much more extensive Slavic people, whose lands the Germans conquered (6th–12th cents.).

Wen Wang *fl.* c1150. Reigned as king of the Zhou, a state on China's western frontier. An intelligent and benevolent leader, he became idealized model for later Zhou rulers and greatly extended Zhou domains until Shang rulers recognized him as Count of the West. Arrested (1144) by the last Shang ruler, Zouxin, Wen Wang wrote the Chinese classic *I Ching* (Book of Changes) during his three-year imprisonment, according to traditional accounts.

Wentworth, Benning 1696–1770. American Colonial governor of New Hampshire (1741–67), who made the unauthorized New Hampshire Grants (*q.v.*).

Wentworth, William Charles 1793–1872. Australian statesman. He founded a newspaper, the *Australian* (1824), to advance the cause of self-government and was a leader in the fight for the Australian constitution of 1855.

Werfel, Franz 1890–1945. German poet, playwright, and novelist. After serving in WW I, he espoused anti-military, pacifist themes in his poetry and was jailed because of them. From 1916 he began writing plays and fiction, and is known for *The Forty Days of Musa Dagh* (1934). A Jew, he moved first to France and then the US (1940) to escape Nazism.

Wergeland, Henrick 1808–45. Norwegian writer and patriot. The greatest Norwegian writer of his day, Wergeland was a leading figure in the nationalist movement.

Wertheimer, Max 1880–1943. German psychologist whose studies of the perception of motion

(1910–12) led to the development of Gestalt psychology.

Wesley, Charles *See* **Methodism.**

Wesley, John 1703–91. English evangelist and founder of Methodism (*q.v.*). He was ordained as a priest of the Church of England (1728). At Oxford, he joined a group (1729) of students, called "methodists," who had been organized by his brother Charles (1707–88) and that included G. Whitefield. John later undertook missionary work in colonial Georgia (1735–38). When he returned to London, he experienced a religious awakening during a meeting at Aldersgate St. (May 24, 1738). Thereafter he dedicated himself to evangelical work and conducted numerous missions in England, Ireland, and Scotland. He broke with the established church in 1740, and in 1784 issued a declaration formally constituting the Methodist societies.

Wessex Saxon kingdom, once located in southwestern England, and a part of the Anglo-Saxon Heptarchy. Founded by Saxon invaders in the late 5th cent. AD, it rivaled the other Anglo-Saxon kingdoms for control of territories until the 9th-cent. Danish invasion. Under the leadership of Aethelred I and Alfred the Great, Wessex alone withstood the Danish armies. Then, by reconquering Danish holdings (by 927), the kings of Wessex made themselves masters of all England.

West In US history, the land lying west of the Mississippi River (earlier, west of the original 13 colonies). During the years of westward expansion, the West assumed mythical proportions as the land of unlimited opportunity. (*See also* Manifest Destiny.)

West, Benjamin 1738–1820. American painter of historical scenes. West moved to England in 1763, where George III was his patron. His innovative use of contemporary dress in such paintings as *Death of General Wolfe* influenced later painters.

West, Nathanael (Weinstein, Nathan) 1903–40. American novelist. He had a pessimistic but strangely poetic view of American life, which he depicted in such novels as *Miss Lonelyhearts* and *The Day of the Locust.*

West Berlin *See* **Berlin.**

Western Chin *See* **Jin.**

Western Jin *See* **Jin.**

Western Empire *See* **Roman Empire; Rome.**

Western Reserve Tract of land in Ohio on the south shore of Lake Erie which was held by Connecticut, after it surrendered the rest of its western lands to Congress in 1786. Part of the tract was sold to immigrants whose property had been destroyed during the Revolution. It passed to Ohio in 1800.

Western Roman Empire *See* **Roman Empire; Rome.**

West Florida Controversy Territorial dispute between Spain and the US over western Florida lands on the Gulf of Mexico, roughly located between the Perdido and Mississippi rivers. America claimed the land as part of the Louisiana Purchase, while Spain claimed it under the 1783 Treaty of Paris. American settlers rebelled (1810) and, reinforced by troops sent by President Madison, ended effective Spanish control. Spain relinquished its claims to the area (1819) by the Transcontinental Treaty.

West Germany *See* **Germany.**

West Goths *See* **Visigoths.**

West Indies Islands located between North and South America on the eastern edge of the Caribbean Sea. They include the Greater Antilles, the Lesser Antilles, and the Bahamas. First reached by C. Columbus in 1492, the islands were settled by English, French, Dutch, and their imported African slave labor.

Westinghouse, George 1846–1914. American inventor and manufacturer. He invented the railroad air brake, pioneered the development of alternating current electrical systems, and founded the Westinghouse Electric Company.

Westminster, Statute of English laws, the first three of which were enacted under Edward I. 1. Westminster I (1275) put long-unwritten laws into legal, written forms, most notably equal legal protection for the poor. 2. Westminster II (1285) concerned land tenure and entailments. 3. Westminster III (1290) ended the subinfeudation of land by making a new owner responsible to the prime overlord, not the subholder. 4. Statute, passed by Parliament in 1931, recognizing the autonomy of member nations within the United Kingdom. It created the British Commonwealth of Nations (*q.v.*).

Westminster, Treaties of English treaties signed at Westminster. 1. Treaty (Apr. 5, 1654) ending the First Dutch War (1652–54), which had been fought primarily on the seas. The Dutch agreed to enter a defensive league with England, pay an indemnity, and exclude the House of Orange from the office of stadtholder.

2. Treaty (1662) between England's Charles II and Frederick William, elector of Brandenberg. They granted each other most-favored-nation status. 3. Treaty (Feb. 9, 1674) ending the Third Dutch War (1672–74). The Dutch once again paid an indemnity and returned to England such American Colonial territories as New York, Albany, Long Island, and New Jersey. 4. Covenant of Westminster (Jan., 1756), which established neutrality between Britain and Frederick the Great of Prussia.

Westminster Abbey Church in Westminster, one of the boroughs of Greater London. A leading example of Gothic architecture in England, the abbey is the burial place of numerous national figures, including many English monarchs, and has been the site of virtually every coronation since William I.

Westminster Assembly (Divines at Westminster, Assembly of) Convocation summoned by the Long Parliament to fix the doctrine and practice of the Church of England. It sat between July 1, 1643, and Feb. 22, 1649. Consisting of some 120 clergy and some 30 laity, the assembly was entirely Calvinist. Its *Catechisms* and its *Directory of Public Worship* were accepted in Scotland but not in England.

Westminster Conference Meeting held in London (1866–67) to plan the union of Canadian provinces. Resolutions of the conference were incorporated into the British North America Act of 1867.

Westminster Palace (House of Parliament) Complex of buildings built between 1840 and 1860 to house the British Parliament. It was constructed on the site of the former royal palace built in the 11th cent. That building had been used to house Parliament from the 16th cent., but was destroyed by fire in 1834.

Westphalia Historic province in northwestern Germany. Once a part of the duchy of Saxony, it was administered for centuries by the archbishop of Cologne. Napoleon based a short-lived kingdom for his brother Jerome on part of its territory in 1807. In 1815, after the Congress of Vienna, it became a province of Prussia. The Ruhr district, Germany's industrial center since the late 19th cent., lies within the region.

Westphalia, Peace of Treaty (Oct. 24, 1648) ending the Thirty Years' War. The treaty marked the end of the period of religious wars in Europe that arose from the Protestant Reformation. The major participants in the treaty were Sweden and France on the one side and the Holy Roman Empire and Spain on the other. The treaty seriously weakened the Holy Roman Empire by recognizing the sovereignty of the individual German states within its domains. This was an important victory for France, which had sought to break the power of the Habsburg Holy Roman Emperors. The treaty also recognized the independence of the Netherlands and the Swiss Confederation. Among the various territorial adjustments stipulated in the treaty were those awarding Alsace to France and West Pomerania to Sweden. Other provisions of the treaty related to religious settlements. In general a policy of toleration was instituted in the German states and Calvinism was recognized.

West Virginia State in the east-central US, the 35th state. Originally an uninhabited part of the state of Virginia, West Virginia was settled by European immigrants who came by way of Pennsylvania. Conflicting claims to the area led to the French and Indian Wars (1754–63). Sectional differences, including the dispute over slavery, led to conflicts between western Virginians and the rest of the state. Finally they rejected secession in the Civil War and voted instead to form a new state. West Virginia became a state in 1863 and adopted its constitution in 1872.

Weyden, Roger van der c1400–64. Flemish painter of religious themes, considered one of the most influential painters of his day.

Weygand, Maxime 1867–1965. French general, chief of staff to Marshal F. Foch (1914–23). As French commander in chief (May–June, 1940) during WW II, he was unable to halt the German advance. He later served with the Vichy government.

Weyler y Nicolau, Valeriano 1838–1930. Spanish general. He was captain-general of Spanish forces in Cuba (1896–97), and his harsh treatment of Cuban rebels caused a wave of protest from America just before the Spanish-American War.

Wharton, Edith Jones 1862–1937. American novelist, whose works are noted for their insights into the workings of upper-class American society. Her works include *Ethan Frome* and *The Age of Innocence.*

Wheatstone, Charles 1802–75. British physicist and inventor. With no formal education in science, he entered the family music instrument-making business (1816), where he invented the

concertina (1829) and did studies of acoustics. Eventually appointed professor of physics at King's College in London (1834), he studied optics and electricity and in partnership with William Cooke (1806–1879) developed an early commercial telegraph (1837) and devices that were forerunners of the teleprinter. Wheatsone was also the first to determine the velocity of electricity through a wire. He invented the rheostat, improved the stereoscope and dynamo, and developed the Wheatstone Bridge, a device for measuring electrical resistance.

Wheeler, Joseph 1836–1906. Confederate general in the American Civil War, who opposed Gen. W. Sherman in the Atlanta Campaign. He later served in Congress, and commanded cavalry at Santiago in the Spanish-American War.

Wheeler, William Almon 1819–87. American politician. He served as US vice-president (1877–81) under R. Hayes, after a contested election.

Wheeler-Howard Act *See* **Indian Reorganization Act.**

Whichcote, Benjamin *See* **Cambridge Platonists.**

Whig Name used to denote what was variously a faction and a political party in England (17th–early 19th cents.). The Whig faction emerged in 1679 as a group opposing the succession of the Catholic Stuart king James II. James was finally deposed by Whigs and his former Tory supporters in the Glorious Revolution (*q.v.*) of 1688. Thereafter Whigs became identified with the interests of the wealthy urban and commercial middle class, and by the later 1690s had evolved into a party with clearly defined platform on government, taxation and finance, and war. The Tory faction likewise emerged as a party at this time. Whig leaders, notably Sir R. Walpole, dominated the government during the reign of George I, but the party gradually disintegrated during the 1750s. During the period from 1760 to 1784, Whig and Tory parties ceased to be identifiable as distinct groups and appointments were made on the basis of personal and family influence. In 1784, however, the emergence of a new Tory party (under W. Pitt the Younger) helped coalesce opposition factions into a new Whig party. The Whigs (led by C. Fox) then advanced the interests of industrialists, religious dissenters, and others who favored reforms. The Whig party ceased to exist in the 19th cent. and many of its members joined the emerging Liberal party (*q.v.*), forming the party's conservative wing.

Whig party American political party, organized (1834) by H. Clay in reaction to President A. Jackson. They supported internal improvements, the development of western lands, a regulated currency, a system of weights and measures, a national bank, and high protective tariffs. They also supported compromise on the issue of slavery. Both their elected presidents (W. Harrison and Z. Taylor) died in office, however, and the party grew increasingly divided over slavery. After 1854, many Whigs joined the new Republican party.

Whipple, Abraham 1733–1819. American naval officer. During the American Revolution he captured 11 British merchant ships of the East Indies fleet (1779), one of the greatest captures of the war.

Whiskey Rebellion Name given to the protest (July–Nov., 1794) west of the Alleghenies against an excise tax imposed (1791) by the newly created US government. The western settlers especially resented the tax on whiskey, the distillation of which was an important economic activity. President G. Washington sent troops (Sept.), partly to demonstrate the power of the new federal government, and the rebellion was suppressed without bloodshed.

Whisky Ring Conspiracy by a number of US distillers to deprive the government of tax revenues by bribing officials. The ring was exposed in 1875 and 110 people were convicted. The scandal touched the administration of President U. Grant when his secretary was indicted (though not convicted).

Whistler, James Abbott McNeill 1834–1903. American painter and etcher. Essentially a realist, he pioneered the use of light, form, and color in a way that prefigured abstract art. He is best known for his *Portrait of My Mother.*

Whitby, Synod of Council called by King Oswy of Northumbria (663–664) at Whitby, England, to determine whether the church of Northumbria would follow Celtic or Roman usages. The council's decision to follow Roman usages brought the church closer to European Christian tradition.

White, Edward Douglass 1845–1921. American jurist, associate justice of the Supreme Court (1894–1910) and chief justice (1910–21). He is best known for his "rule of reason" decisions in large antitrust cases, which influenced subsequent antitrust litigation.

White, E. B. (~, Elwyn Brooks) 1899–1985. American writer, humorist, and stylist. For many years as a staffer of *The New Yorker* magazine, he distinguished himself for his light, graceful, and witty style. His numerous works include essays, the children's classic *Charlotte's Web,* and his revision of Strunk's *Elements of Style.*

White, Stanford 1853–1906. American architect. His architectural firm designed the original Madison Square Garden in New York City. He was fatally shot (June 25, 1906) by Harry K. Thaw, the outraged husband of the showgirl Evelyn Nesbit, with whom White was having an affair. The murder was one of the most sensationalized cases of the early 1900s.

White, Walter Francis 1893–1955. American civil rights leader and author, who served (1931–55) as secretary of the NAACP.

Whiteboys Peasant associations formed in Ireland around 1760 to harass landlords, tax collectors, and Protestant clergy. They were so named because they wore white clothing during their nightly forays.

Whitefield, George 1714–70. English evangelist, who helped J. Wesley to establish Methodism. He later broke with Wesley and helped to form the Calvinistic Methodist church. He also preached in America and figured there in the Great Awakening (*q.v.*).

Whitehead, Alfred North 1861–1947. English mathematician and philosopher who collaborated with B. Russell on *Principles Mathematics,* a major study in logic, and who developed a metaphysical theory of reality.

White Hill, Battle of Battle fought on a chalk hill near Prague (Nov. 8, 1620), the first battle of the Thirty Years' War. A German force of some 25,000 under the Count of Tilly defeated a combined Bohemian-Hungarian force of some 15,000 men.

White House Official residence of the president of the US. It is the oldest public building in Washington D.C. (the cornerstone was laid in 1792) and was burned by the British (1814). It was rebuilt by James Hoban in 1817 and was restored between 1949 and 1952.

White Lotus Rebellion Chinese rebellion. The White Lotus was a Buddhist cult that opposed domination by the Manchus of the Qing dynasty. From 1796 to 1804, they conducted a guerrilla revolt in the mountains of central China in protest against their poverty and excessive taxation. The imperial forces were hindered for several years by corruption within the army, but they eventually put down the rebellion. However, the revolt revealed the declining power of the Manchus and paved the way for other revolts in the 19th cent. that ended in the overthrow of the Qing dynasty.

White Plains, Battle of Indecisive battle fought (Oct. 28, 1776) near White Plains, New York, during the American Revolution. British Gen. W. Howe, marching with a force of 20,000 men, engaged a Continental brigade of 14,000, led by G. Washington. After the battle, Washington was forced to withdraw.

White Revolution Reform movement in Iran during the 1960s, instituted by Mohammed Reza Shah Pahlavi and his advisers. It aimed especially at land reforms, and an Office of Land Reform was established on Aug. 20, 1960. Ultimately, however, the "revolution" failed to gain popular support and the shah was forced to abdicate by the Islamic revolution in 1979.

White Russia *See* **Belorussia.**

White Volunteer Army Russian armies formed in the winter of 1917–18 in the peripheral areas of the former Russian Empire to combat the Bolshevik regime established under N. Lenin. Though aided by 14 allied nations, they lacked unified leadership and necessary supplies and were unable to prevail against the Red Army.

Whitgift, John *See* **Marprelate Controversy.**

Whitman, Walt (~, Walter) 1819–92. American poet, one of the great figures in American literature. His major work, *Leaves of Grass,* is noted for its innovative style.

Whitney, Eli 1765–1825. American inventor of the cotton gin (1793). He also pioneered in the use of interchangeable parts in the manufacture of firearms, a major step in the development of mass production.

Whittier, John Greenleaf 1807–92. American poet and abolitionist, best known for his celebration in verse of his native New England and for his antislavery activities in the years before the Civil War.

Whittington, Richard *d.* 1423. English merchant, lord mayor of London, and subject of a popular English legend. According to the story, he was a poor boy who gave his cat to a merchant

to offer in trade. Ultimately the cat was sold for a fortune to a Moroccan ruler plagued by rats.

Wickliffe, John *See* **Wycliffe, John.**

Wiclif, John *See* **Wycliffe, John.**

Widukind (Wittekind) *d.* c807. Leader of the Saxons against Charlemagne. He raided the Rhineland (778), but later submitted and converted to Christianity (785). He is said to have become duke of the Saxons.

Wiener, Norbert 1894–1964. American mathematician, founder of cybernetics, the science of control and communication in animals and machines.

Wiggin, Kate Douglas Smith 1856–1923. American author and educator, best known for her novel *Rebecca of Sunnybrook Farm.*

Wilberforce, William 1759–1833. English politician, humanitarian, and philanthropist, who led in the movement to abolish slavery and the slave trade within the British Empire.

Wilde, Oscar 1854–1900. Irish poet, dramatist, and wit, and a leader of the Aesthetic movement. His works include the novel *The Picture of Dorian Gray* and the play *The Importance of Being Earnest.*

Wilder, Thornton Niven 1897–1975. American author and playwright, whose plays and novels reflected his belief in the universality of human experience. Wilder received Pulitzer prizes for the novel *The Bridge of San Luis Rey* (1927) and the play *Our Town* (1938).

Wilderness, Battle of the American Civil War battle fought (May 5–6, 1864) in Virginia. Some 100,000 Union troops, commanded by Gen. U. Grant, attacked 60,000 Confederate troops, commanded by Gen. R. Lee, but fighting was indecisive in difficult terrain. Grant lost some 18,000 troops (to Lee's 11,000) before moving on to do battle at Spotsylvania. The battle was part of Grant's drive toward Richmond.

Wilderness Road Route followed by American settlers from Virginia into western Kentucky (1790 to 1840). First blazed as a trail by the frontiersman D. Boone c1775, it led from the Shenandoah Valley through the Cumberland Gap to western Kentucky and the Ohio River region.

Wilfrid, Saint (~ of York) 634–709? English churchman, archbishop of York (c665), and one of the leading saints of England. He encouraged the adoption of Roman usages at the Synod of Whitby (*q.v.*), bringing the English church closer to the Roman Catholic church.

Wilfrid of York *See* Wilfrid, Saint.

Wilhelmina 1880–1962. Queen of the Netherlands (1890–1948), successor to her father William III. Forced into exile in Britain during WW II, she encouraged Dutch resistance to German occupation.

Wilkes, Charles 1798–1877. American naval officer and explorer. He explored the region of Antarctica now called Wilkes Land. In 1861 his actions in the Trent Affair (*q.v.*) nearly led to war with Britain.

Wilkes, John 1727–97. English journalist and politician, several times expelled from Parliament for his outspoken attacks in periodicals. He is noted as a champion of freedom of the press.

Wilkins, Roy 1901–81. American black civil rights leader. Long associated with the NAACP, he served as executive secretary (and later director) from 1955 to 1977. He was a principal organizer of the 1963 March on Washington (*q.v.*).

Wilkinson, James 1757–1825. American general. He served in the Revolutionary War, was a member of the Conway Cabal, and was governor of Louisiana Territory (1805–06). He was implicated in the conspiracy of A. Burr.

Willard, Frances 1839–1898. American educator, temperance and women's rights activist. A college administrator, she became corresponding secretary of the newly founded Women's Temperance Union (1874) and later served as its president (1879–98). Committed to the temperance cause, she also supported suffragist S. Anthony and helped bring about the Temperance Union's endorsement of women's suffrage (1882).

William I (William the Conqueror) 1027–87. English king (1066–87) and duke of Normandy (1035–87). The illegitimate son of Robert, duke of Normandy, he succeeded Robert as duke on the latter's death (1035). His early years were marked by continued strife in Normandy. With the help of French king Henry I, he established his rule in Normandy (1047), then later repulsed two French invasions of Normandy (1054, 1058). In 1051, on a visit to his cousin, English king Edward the Confessor, he is thought to have received a promise of the English throne. On Edward's death, however, the crown passed to Harold, earl of Wessex. William secured the pope's support for his claim and raised an army. Invading England (1066) he defeated and killed Harold in the Battle of Hastings (*q.v.*), marched

on London, and was crowned king on Christmas Day. The English resisted his rule and William spent several years crushing rebellions, seizing estates, and redistributing lands to his Norman supporters. He appointed Lanfranc (1005?–89) archbishop of Canterbury, brought the church under his control, and firmly established feudalism in England. In 1072 he forced Scottish king Malcolm to do him homage. William authorized (1085) the compilation of the Domesday Book (*q.v.*), a complete survey of England. His later years were spent largely in Normandy, while Lanfranc conducted William's affairs in England. William suppressed several rebellions led by his son Robert II, and conducted war against French king Philip I. While campaigning he suffered internal injuries in a fall and died at Rouen. His son Robert succeeded him as duke of Normandy, and his son William as king of England. William the Conqueror was an able administrator, a ruthless and intelligent military commander, and one of the greatest leaders of his time. His conquest of England radically altered the history of England and of Western Europe.

William I (~ the Silent, Prince of Orange) 1533–84. Prince of Orange and count of Nassau. In 1568 he led the rebellion of the Netherlands against the rule of Philip II of Spain.

William I 1772–1843. First king of the Netherlands (1815–40). Commerce and industry flourished under his rule, but his heavy-handed treatment of Belgium, then part of the Netherlands, led to its secession in 1830.

William I 1797–1888. King of Prussia (1861–88) and first German emperor (1871–88). Facing a constitutional crisis over army reform, he appointed O. von Bismarck prime minister of Prussia (1862), and thereafter followed a militaristic policy that finally established Prussian dominance over a unified Germany.

William II (~ Rufus) *d.* 1100. King of England (1087–1100), successor to his father William I the Conqueror. His rule was ruthless and he made many enemies. William appointed Anselm archbishop of Canterbury, and later exiled him. He conducted wars in Scotland, Wales, and Normandy, and maintained Norman rule over England.

William II (~ the Good) *d.* 1189. King of Sicily (1166–89). He allied himself with Frederick I Barbarossa and attempted (1185) unsuccessfully to conquer the Byzantine Empire. During the campaign his forces captured Salonika, but the Byzantines turned back the invasion when the Sicilian army approached Constantinople.

William II 1792–1849. King of the Netherlands (1840–49), successor to his father William I. He restored financial stability to the Netherlands and granted constitutional reforms (1848).

William II 1859–1941. King of Prussia and German emperor (1888–1918). An unstable nationalist, he supported Austria-Hungary against Serbia, thereby contributing to the outbreak of WW I and helping to increase military control of the government. With Germany's defeat, he abdicated.

William III (˜ of Orange) 1650–1702. Stadtholder of Holland in the United Provinces of the Netherlands (1672–1702) who became king of England (1689–1702) by the Glorious Revolution (*q.v.*). He ruled jointly with his wife Queen Mary II, promoted Protestantism, and fiscal reform, and led campaigns against Louis XIV in the war of the League of Augsburg. He defeated James II at the Battle of the Boyne in Ireland, thereby ending James's attempt to retake the English throne.

William III 1817–90. King of the Netherlands (1849–90), and grand duke of Luxembourg, successor to his father William II. During his reign, Luxembourg was granted a parliamentary constitution (1867).

William IV 1765–1837. British king (1830–37), successor to his brother, George IV. He opposed parliamentary reform, but reluctantly accepted passage of the Reform Bill of 1832.

William of Ockham   *See* **Ockham, William of.**

William of Orange   *See* **William I; William III.**

William of Tyre c1130–1185. Churchman and historian. He is noted for his *Historia Rerum in Partibus Transmarinis Gestarum,* a history of the Latin Kingdom of Jerusalem from 1095–1184.

William Rufus   *See* **William II.**

Williams, Eric E.   *See* **Trinidad and Tobago.**

Williams, Roger c1603–83. Colonial religious leader. Banished by the Massachusetts Bay Colony for his religious views, he founded the city of Providence (1636) and the colony of Rhode Island. He encouraged religious toleration.

Williams, Tennessee (˜, Thomas Lanier) 1914–83. American playwright, whose works are noted for their insight into the passions and motivations of human beings. Among his many famous plays

are *Cat on a Hot Tin Roof, A Streetcar Named Desire,* and *The Night of the Iguana.*

Williams, Thomas Lanier   *See* **Williams, Tennessee.**

Williams, William Carlos 1883–1963. American poet and physician, whose verse is noted for its use of concise language and of everyday objects and experience. His works include *Pictures from Brueghel, and Other Poems* and *In the American Grain.*

William the Conqueror   *See* **William I.**

William the Good   *See* **William II.**

William the Lion 1143–1214. King of Scotland (1165–1214), successor to his brother Malcolm IV. He attempted unsuccessfully to recover Northumbria from England, and extended his control throughout the Scottish kingdom.

Willkie, Wendell Lewis 1892–1944. American industrialist and political leader. A leading critic of the New Deal, he ran unsuccessfully on the Republican presidential ticket in 1940.

Wilmot Proviso Controversial amendment attached to an 1846 bill presented in the US Congress. The bill sought funds to pay for a negotiated settlement of the US and Mexican boundary dispute that had erupted into the Mexican War. The amendment, authored by Pennsylvania Democrat David Wilmot, contained a ban on extension of slavery into any territories acquired from Mexico. The bill did not pass, but the principle was later adopted by the new Republican party.

Wilson, Charles Thomson Rees 1869–1959. Scottish physicist, inventor of the Wilson cloud chamber. He was awarded, with Arthur C. Compton, the 1927 Nobel Prize for Physics.

Wilson, Edmund 1895–1972. American critic and essayist, considered one of the leading American men of letters in the 20th cent. His many works include *The Wound and the Bow* and *To the Finland Station.*

Wilson-Gorman Tariff Act   *See* **Cleveland, Stephen Grover.**

Wilson, Henry (Colbath, Jeremiah Jones) 1812–75. American politician and abolitionist leader. As US senator (1855–72) he was a leader of the Radical Republicans. He served as vice-president (1873–75) under U. Grant.

Wilson, James 1742–98. American jurist. A signer of the Declaration of Independence, he championed the concept of popular sovereignty at the Constitutional Convention of 1787 and served as associate justice of the Supreme Court (1789–98).

Wilson, Sir James Harold 1916– . British statesman, Labour party prime minister (1964–70, 1974–76). Born the son of an industrial chemist and educated at Oxford, Wilson served in the Ministry of Fuel and Power during WW II. His book *New Deal for Coal* (1945) strongly influenced the Labour Party's plan for nationalizing coal mines. After entering Parliament (1945), Wilson served as Board of Trade president (1947–51) and eventually rose to Labour Party leader in 1963. Taking office as prime minister in 1964, Wilson formed the first Labour government since 1951. His term was marked by signing of the Nuclear Test-Ban Treaty, violence in Northern Ireland, unsuccessful efforts (blocked by C. de Gaulle) to join the European Economic Community (EEC), the scandal over long-time Soviet spy H. (Kim) Philby, unsuccessful attempts to deal with the Rhodesian crisis by means of negotiations and economic sanctions, and nationalization of the steel industry. Wilson stepped down after Labour unexpectedly lost the election in 1970, but returned to office in 1974 amid labor unrest and a fuel crisis. Within a few months the government was rocked by the IRA bombing of Parliament. The following year, Wilson won approval of a referendum on EEC membership and oil began flowing from the newly developed North Sea oilfields. Continuing economic problems forced his resignation in 1976. Wilson was named a life peer in 1983.

Wilson, (Thomas) Woodrow 1856–1924. Twenty-eighth US president (1913–21), successor to W. Taft. A graduate of Princeton University (1879), Wilson joined the faculty of Princeton (1890) and served as its president (1902–10). He resigned and ran successfully for the governorship of New Jersey (1911–13), during which time he became known for his progressive policies. At the 1912 Democratic convention he was nominated for president on the 46th ballot. A split between the regular Republican party and T. Roosevelt's Progressive party helped Wilson win the election. Wilson's first term was marked by the passage of numerous progressive measures, notably the establishment of the Federal Trade Commission (1914) and passage of the Clayton Antitrust Act (1914) and the Federal Farm Loan Act (1916). In for-

eign matters, Wilson opposed the rise of V. Huerta as president of Mexico (1913) and sent US forces to Vera Cruz (1914). He also authorized the punitive expedition into Mexico (1916) led by Gen. J. Pershing (following P. Villa's raid into the US). Wilson sought to keep the US out of war in Europe. The German sinking (1915) of the liner *Lusitania* aroused sentiment for war in the US. However, following the sinking (Mar., 1916) of the *Sussex,* Wilson secured an agreement from Germany to end its policy of unrestricted submarine warfare. Campaigning on the motto "He kept us out of war," Wilson was reelected (1916). He broke diplomatic relations (Feb., 1917) with Germany after it resumed unrestricted submarine activity, and Congress declared war (Apr. 6). In 1918, Wilson announced his famous Fourteen Points (*q.v.*), by which he believed the world could be made "safe for democracy" at war's end. In Dec., 1918, he left for France as head of the US delegation to the Paris Peace Conference. He fought unsuccessfully against the harsh terms of the Versailles Treaty but secured a covenant calling for the League of Nations. Returning to America, he found his proposals rejected by Congress. Wilson began a campaign tour across the US to gain popular support, especially for the League but he suffered a physical collapse (Sept., 1919) and then a stroke (Oct., 1919), from which he never completely recovered. His administration was also marked by passage of the 17th, 18th, and 19th Amendments to the US Constitution. Wilson was awarded the Nobel Peace Prize in 1919.

Wilson's Creek, Battle of Battle of US Civil War, a Confederate victory over Union forces near Springfield, Missouri, on Aug. 10, 1861. A Union force of some 5,400 intercepted an invading force of 11,000 Confederates from Arkansas and after a hard battle was forced to withdraw. The Confederates then took Springfield.

Winckelmann, Johann Joachim 1717–68. German archaeologist, whose *History of the Art of Antiquity* became the basis for modern archaeology.

Winckler, Hugo 1863–1913. German archaeologist and historian whose excavations at Bogazköy, Turkey (1906–12) uncovered the capital of the Hittites and yielded cuneiform tablets that became a main source of information about the Hittite Empire.

Windsor, House of From 1917 the official surname of the royal family of Britain. It replaced the family name of Wettin and dynastic name of Saxe-Coburg-Gotha. This change was effected by George V during WW I.

Windsor, Wallis Warfield, duchess of 1896–1986. American-born wife of the duke of Windsor. Edward abdicated (1936) his throne (as Edward VIII) in order to marry her.

Windsor Castle Castle in New Windsor, Berkshire, England, which has served as the main residence for English monarchs since William I, the Conqueror. The castle stands on a site dating from Celtic times.

Wineland *See* **Vinland.**

Wingate, Orde Charles 1903–44. British general. During WW II he organized and led the Chindits, or Wingate's Raiders, a guerrilla unit that fought against the Japanese in Burma.

Winkelried, Arnold von *d.* 1386. Swiss hero, whose legendary act of self-sacrifice in battle is said to have led to the Swiss victory over Austria in the Battle of Sempach.

Winslow, Edward 1595–1655. Pilgrim leader, one of the founders of the Plymouth Colony. He served as governor (1633–34, 1636–37, 1644–45).

Winslow, Josiah c1629–80. American governor of Plymouth Colony (1673–80), the first native-born Colonial governor in America. He led the colonials in King Philip's War (*q.v.*).

Winstanley, Gerrard 1609–60. English reformer and leader of the Diggers (*q.v.*). A cloth merchant whose business had failed, he became a key figure in organizing the Diggers' first agrarian commune (1649), a response to the high food prices and political upheavals of the Commonwealth period. Winstanley believed the poor should have access to land and after the Digger colonies were broken up (1650) continued to write pamphlets. His work *The Law of Freedom in a Platform* (1652) outlined his vision of a society based on communism.

Winter War *See* **Russo-Finnish War.**

Winthrop, John 1588–1649. English colonist, governor of the Massachusetts Bay Colony 12 times between 1629 and 1648. He greatly influenced the development of this theocratic community and thus affected the subsequent history of Massachusetts.

Wisconsin State in the north-central US, the 30th state. Jean Nicolet of France explored the area (1634), and it was a center of the fur trade in spite of war with the Indians. After 1763, the

British took control, then ceded it to the US after the American Revolution (1783). The Black Hawk War (1832) was the last major Indian uprising, and Wisconsin became a territory in 1836. In 1848, it adopted its constitution and was admitted to the Union.

Wise, Isaac Mayer 1819–1900. American rabbi, founder of many of the Reform Jewish institutions in the US. He was the guiding force in founding Hebrew Union College, the Union of American Hebrew Congregations, and the Central Conference of American Rabbis.

Wise Men of the East *See* **Magi.**

Wishart, George 1513?–1546. Scottish religious reformer and Protestant martyr. His preaching influenced J. Knox. Wishart was convicted and executed for heresy.

Wissman, Hermann von 1853–1905. German explorer of the Congo region (now Zaire) and German East Africa (now Tanzania). He increased knowledge of the area, established outposts, and served as commissioner and governor of German East Africa.

Witenagemot (Witan) King's council that existed in England in Anglo-Saxon times. It consisted mainly of the nobles and bishops, and advised the king on land grants, taxes, and other matters.

Witherspoon, John 1723–94. Scottish-born American clergyman, president of the College of New Jersey (now Princeton University), and signer of the Declaration of Independence.

Witt, Jan de 1625–72. Dutch statesman and patriot. As grand pensionary, he led Holland in the Dutch Wars and was instrumental in forming the Triple Alliance of 1668 and negotiating the Treaty of Aix-la-Chapelle.

Witte, Count Sergei Yulyevich 1849–1915. Russian statesman. As minister of finance (1892–1903), he helped bring about completion of the Trans-Siberian Railway. He served (1905–06) as prime minister after helping to form the Duma.

Wittekind *See* **Widukind.**

Wittelsbach Name of the family dynasty that ruled Bavaria from 1180–1918. In addition to providing Bavarian kings, the line also produced a king of the Germans (Rupert of the Palatinate, 1400–10) and two Holy Roman emperors (Louis IV of Bavaria, 1314–47; Charles VII, 1742–45).

Wittgenstein, Ludwig Josef Johann 1889–1951. Austrian philosopher, one of the major philosophers of the 20th cent. His works deal with the relation of thought and language to the real and metaphysical worlds.

Wittstock, Battle of Swedish victory in the Thirty Years' War. Fought (Oct. 4, 1636) near Berlin, the battle pitted some 22,000 Swedish troops against 30,000 allied troops of the Holy Roman Empire and resulted in imperial losses of 11,000 casualties and 8,000 captured. The Swedes lost about 5,000.

Wobblies *See* **Industrial Workers of the World.**

Wodehouse, P(elham) G(renville) 1881–1975. English author and humorist, best known as creator of Bertie Wooster and his manservant Jeeves in such works as *Much Obliged, Jeeves.*

Wöhler, Friedrich 1800–82. German chemist. His synthesis of urea marked the first time (1828) an organic compound was made artificially from inorganic material.

Wojtyla, Karol *See* **John Paul II.**

Wolfe, James 1727–59. British commander in the French and Indian Wars. He led British forces in the capture of Quebec (1759) from the French, thereby ensuring British dominance in Canada.

Wolfe, Thomas Clayton 1900–1938. American novelist, perhaps best known for his semiautobiographical novel *Look Homeward, Angel,* about a young man's development in a small Southern city.

Wolfram von Eschenbach c1170–c1220. German poet, whose epic poem *Parzifal* is one of the great medieval literary works. Wagner used it as the basis for his opera *Parsifal.*

Wollstonecraft, Mary 1759–97. British writer, women's rights advocate, and mother of writer M. Shelley. Born in London, she became an ardent supporter of equality for women, both social and educational. She was an influential part of a radical group whose members included W. Godwin (whom she married, 1797), T. Paine, W. Wordsworth, and W. Blake. She wrote *A Vindication of the Rights of Women* (1792).

Wolseley, Garnet Joseph, 1st viscount 1833–1913. British field marshal. He worked tirelessly to modernize the British army and from 1895 to 1901 he was commander in chief of the British army. He served in many British campaigns, including the Burma War, the Crimean War, and Riel's Rebellion in Canada, and led the attempt to relieve Gordon at Khartoum.

Wolsey, Thomas c1475–1530. English statesman and Catholic cardinal. As lord chancellor of England (1515–29), he was the leading force in English politics during the early reign of King Henry VIII. He fell from favor after failing to win approval from the pope for the annulment of Henry's marriage.

Woman's Christian Temperance Union (W.C.T.U.) Organization founded (1874) in Cleveland, Ohio, to work against the evils of alcoholic beverages. It was instrumental in the adoption of Prohibition (*q.v.*) in the US and now has branches in many countries.

woman suffrage The right of women to the vote. The movement for woman suffrage arose in many countries in the 19th and 20th cents. In the US, woman suffrage began with a declaration of women's rights issued (July 19, 1848) by L. Mott, E. Stanton, and other feminists. The movement gained momentum with the formation (1869) of the National Woman Suffrage Association, which sought woman suffrage through a constitutional amendment, and the American Woman Suffrage Association, which sought it through state legislation. Both factions merged (1890) to form the National American Woman Suffrage Association. A number of states eventually granted woman suffrage and national woman suffrage was established (1920), by the 19th Amendment to the US Constitution. In Great Britain, the movement for woman suffrage began as a part of the Chartist movement, under such leaders as J. Mill and E. Anderson. In the early 20th cent., the movement became more militant under the leadership of E. Pankhurst and others. Women received equal voting rights with men in Britain in 1928.

Wood, Annie *See* **Besant, Annie.**

Wood, Leonard 1860–1927. American officer. He helped his friend T. Roosevelt form the Rough Riders (*q.v.*), served as military governor of Cuba (1899–1902), chief of staff of the US Army (1910–14), and governor general of the Philippines (1921–27).

Woodhull, Victoria Claflin 1838–1927. American journalist and reformer. She supported such controversial causes as woman suffrage, Socialism, and free love, and in 1872 became the first woman candidate for president.

Woodstock US rock music festival (Aug. 15–17, 1969) held near Bethel, New York. Attended by some 300,000 youths, it marked the high point of the counterculture movement in the US.

Woodville, Elizabeth 1437–92. Wife of King Edward IV of England. After Edward's death, Richard, duke of Gloucester, seized Elizabeth's son, Edward V, and took the throne. Elizabeth's daughter married Henry VII.

Woolf, (Adeline) Virginia 1882–1941. English novelist and critic, whose life and writings had a major impact on 20th-cent. writers. Her home was the center for gatherings of the Bloomsbury Group. Her works include *Mrs. Dalloway* and *To the Lighthouse.*

Woolley, Sir Charles Leonard 1880–1960. English archaeologist. He directed the excavations (1922–34) of the ancient city of Ur, which contributed greatly to knowledge of ancient Mesopotamla.

Woolman, John 1720–72. American Quaker minister, essayist, and abolitionist. Raised in New Jersey, he served as an apprentice tailor before becoming a minister. An early and outspoken critic of slavery, he and other younger Quaker leaders promoted reforms within the Quaker Society that included opposition to slavery. His essays against slavery influenced the antislavery movement, then beginning in the American colonies and in Britain. Among his writings, his *Journal,* published posthumously in 1774, is best known.

Worcester, Battle of Rout (Sept. 3, 1651) of the Scots Royalist forces of Charles II by the Parliamentarians commanded by O. Cromwell. The battle marked the end of Royalist military action following the end of the civil wars.

Wordsworth, William 1770–1850. English poet, a leading English Romantic. Following his graduation from Cambridge University (1791) and a stay in France during the Revolution, he returned to England and published *The Evening Walk* and *Descriptive Sketches* (1793). Settling in Dorset (1795) with his sister Dorothy, he befriended S. Coleridge and the two published their famous *Lyrical Ballads* (1798) anonymously, introducing the Romantic style to England. The work is considered an important turning point in the history of British poetry. A second enlarged edition appeared in 1800. Wordsworth and his sister moved to the Lake District in north England (1799), and in 1802 he married and started a family. During this time, he produced much of his best-known poetry. Among his later volumes were *The Waggoner* (1819) and *The Prelude* (1850), published after his death. Wordsworth was named England's poet laureate in 1843.

Work Projects Administration (*formerly* Works Progress Administration) (WPA) US government agency established in 1935, and originally called the Works Progress Administration (renamed 1939), to create jobs for millions of unemployed during the Depression. It operated until 1943.

World Court *See* **International Court of Justice.**

World Federation of Trade Unions *See* **labor unions.**

World War I Worldwide conflict (1914–18) fought between the Allies (France, Britain, Russia, Italy, US, and others) and the Central Powers (Germany, Austro-Hungarian Empire, Ottoman Empire, and others). The bloodiest, most widespread war the world had known up to that time, WW I resulted in over 30 million casualties, left much of Europe in ruin, and revolutionized modern warfare. Among the causes of WW I were the rise of nationalist movements in Europe (especially in Serbia); hardening of alliances between various European powers (Triple Alliance and Entente, *q.v.*); colonial rivalries in Africa and elsewhere; the continuing instability of the Balkan Peninsular region (Austrian annexation of Bosnia and Herzegovina, 1908); Balkan Wars (1912–13); and the gradual collapse of the Ottoman Empire (Eastern Question, *q.v.*). The spark that touched off WW I was the assassination of Austrian Archduke Ferdinand by a Serbian nationalist in 1914. The war quickly spread to many different fronts and eventually involved all the major Western powers. WW I saw the rise of bloody trench warfare (especially on the Western Front), the mechanization of warfare (tanks, planes, and motorized vehicles used), and the advent of chemical warfare. WW I also brought drastic political changes. Russia's staggering losses on the Eastern Front helped bring down the tsarist government (1917) and led to creation of the first Communist state. The Ottoman Empire, long in decline, finally collapsed under the strains of war and was dismembered. The war also broke up the Austro-Hungarian Empire, giving rise to the independent states of Austria, Hungary, Czechoslovakia, and Yugoslavia (as it was later called). The German surrender finally ended the war in Nov., 1918. Initially, the tremendous destruction caused by the war gave wide support to the newly created League of Nations and international efforts to end wars. But the war had set in motion great social and economic changes. Coupled with German resentment at the harsh peace terms imposed by the Allies, these changes helped pave the way for the outbreak of WW II. Key events in the war include:

1914   Austrian Archduke Francis Ferdinand assassinated (June 28) by a Serbian nationalist in Sarajevo, capital of Bosnia; set in motion chain of events that resulted in outbreak of war.

1914   German Emperor William II promised Austria-Hungary its support in any actions taken against Serbia (July 5).

1914   Austria-Hungary sent Serbia an ultimatum (July 23) pressing demands for suppression of Serbian nationalist groups in Serbia (which threatened to incite rebellion in Austria-Hungary).

1914   Serbia acceded to some demands and rejected others (July 25); Austria-Hungary broke relations with Serbia (which had already begun mobilization of forces) and began its own mobilization (July 25).

1914   Russia, Serbia's ally, unsuccessfully attempted to persuade Austria-Hungary to modify terms of its ultimatum and thereby avoid war (July 25); Russia made initial preparations to mobilize in the event of war.

1914   Britain attempted (July 26) to set up negotiations for a settlement; plan rejected by Germany.

1914   Austria declared war on Serbia (July 28).

1914   Russia ordered partial mobilization against Austria-Hungary (July 29); Germany, promising modification of ultimatum to Serbia, warned Russia against continuing mobilization order; Russian tsar Nicholas II hesitated, then ordered full mobilization (July 31).

1914   British requested recognition of Belgian neutrality (July 30); Germany refused.

1914   Germany declared war on Russia (Aug. 1). Russia, meanwhile, had received French commitment of support; French mobilization begun.

1914   German troops marched into Luxembourg (Aug. 1) to begin implementation of Schlieffen Plan; plan called for quick elimination of France from war to allow concentration

of forces on Eastern Front; France to be attacked from the north (through Low Countries) and by a second (left) flank farther south.

1914   Germans, commanded by Gen. H. von Moltke, invaded Belgium (Aug. 3) after Belgians refused them right of transit.

1914   Germany declared war on France (Aug. 3).

1914   British, protesting Germany's violation of Belgian neutrality, declared war on Germany (Aug. 4).

1914   Strong fortifications at Liège, Belgium, captured by Germans (Aug. 5–16).

1914   French offensive; French attacks, commanded by Gen. J. Joffre, launched into Alsace (Aug. 7–9), Lorraine (Aug. 14–24), and the Ardennes (Aug. 22–25); all failed.

1914   British Expeditionary Force, commanded by Sir J. French, landed at Le Havre (from Aug. 7).

1914   Eastern Front, Russian forces launched invasions of East Prussia (Aug. 13) and the Austrian province of Galicia; Russians, defeated at the Battle of Stallupönen (Aug. 17) in East Prussia, repulsed a counterattack at Gumbinnen (Aug. 20); in Galicia, after two inconclusive battles, the Russians won an important victory at the Battle of Gilna Lipa (Aug. 26–Sept. 1) and threw the Austrians into retreat.

1914   Austrians invaded Serbia (Aug. 16); their first invasion was repulsed, as were the second (Sept.) and third (Nov.).

1914   Western Front, Germans continued their drive through Belgium, capturing Namur after five-day siege (Aug. 19–25); Belgian army withdrew to Antwerp and Germans pushed on to take Antwerp (Aug. 20).

1914   Battle of Charleroi (Aug. 22); Germans defeated French and Belgian forces; continued drive through Belgium.

1914   Battle of Mons (Aug. 23–24); Germans defeated the British Expeditionary Force; Allied forces in Belgium fell into retreat; Germans meanwhile weakened their right flank by sending troops (Aug. 25) to fight Russians on the Eastern Front; strong right flank was crucial element of Schlieffen Plan.

1914   Japan, as a result of alliances with Britain, declared war on Germany (Aug. 23).

1914   British won Battle of Helgoland Bight (Aug. 27), first major naval engagement.

1914   Eastern Front, German general P. von Hindenburg took command in Prussia and, with reinforcements from the Western Front, routed and captured the Russian 2d Army at the Battle of Tannenberg (Aug. 26–29); Russian 1st Army, defeated at the Battle of Mazurian Lakes (Sept. 9–14), barely managed to escape German armies.

1914   First Battle of the Marne (Sept. 5–9); Allied forces had taken up defensive positions on the Marne River in France; German attack faltered and after some days of hard fighting the Germans withdrew (Sept. 10–14) northward to defensive positions on the Aisne River in France.

1914   Gen. E. von Falkenhayn replaced von Moltke as German commander (Sept. 10); opted for victory on Western Front by maintaining defensive positions; opposed efforts for offensives on Eastern Front.

1914   First Battle of the Aisne (Sept. 14–18); Germans held their positions against the British Expeditionary Force.

1914   On the Eastern Front in Galicia the Austrians fell into retreat (Sept. 11–28) following Russian victory at Rawa Ruska (Sept. 5–11); retreated some 100 miles before taking up defensive positions.

1914   German campaigns in Poland; first invasion (Sept. 28–Nov. 1) nearly reached Warsaw before the Germans were driven out; second invasion (Nov. 10) culminated in capture of Lodz (Dec. 6) and retreat of Russian forces to defensive positions.

1914   Germans shifted Western Front offensive operations to north with aim of capturing French Channel ports; captured Antwerp, Belgium (Oct. 9).

1914   Ghent and Bruges captured (Oct. 11, 14) by Germans.

1914   Battle of Yser River, Belgium (Oct. 20–27); Germans advanced against Belgian forces; Belgians halted advance by flooding region (Oct. 27).

1914   Battle of Ypres, Belgium (Oct. 30–Nov. 24); Germans attempted to advance farther south but were held up by the British Expeditionary Force.

1914   Turkish Front, Turkey joined Germans (Oct. 29) against Russia; sultan proclaimed a Muslim holy war (Nov. 14); Turks under Enver Pasha launched invasion of Russian Caucasus in which the Turkish 3d Army was decimated (Battle of Sarikamis, Dec.–Jan.); forces from British India meanwhile occupied points in the Persian Gulf region (Oct.–Dec.).

1914   German cruiser squadron, commanded by Admiral M. von Spee, defeated British naval force (Nov. 1) off Coronel, Chile; British won decisive victory over von Spee at Battle of Falkland Islands (Dec. 8).

1914   Allied offensive along almost entire Western Front (Dec.) failed; war on Western Front shifted to trench warfare and front lines, stretching from Belgian coast to Switzerland, remained largely unchanged until just before war's end.

1915   Abortive Turkish attack on Suez Canal in Egypt (Feb. 3) repulsed by British.

1915   Eastern Front, Second Battle of Mazurian Lakes (Feb. 7–21); Germans inflicted heavy losses on Russians but failed to knock Russia out of the war.

1915–16   Turkish Front, Gallipoli Campaign (Feb. 19, 1915–Jan., 1916); Allies, attempting to open supply route to Russia, launched nearly successful naval bombardment on Turkish installations guarding the Dardanelles strait (Feb. 19–Mar. 18); landings at Helles and Ari Burnu (Apr. 25) ended in disaster, as did Suvla Bay landing.

1915   Western Front, Battle of Neuve Chapelle (Mar. 10–13); British offensive made only small gains.

1915   Second Battle of Ypres (Apr. 22–May 15); Germans released chlorine gas (Apr. 22) in first use of poison gas in war.

1915   Battle of Artois (May 9–June 18); combined British and French offensive, French gained some 2½ miles but were unable to break German lines.

1915   In the East, Austro-German offensive in Galicia (May 4–Oct. 1) sent Russians in Austria into desperate retreat; Russians retreated some 300 miles with heavy losses in men and matériel; Tsar Nicholas II took command of Russian army (Sept. 8) and by month's end established defensive line between Riga and Carpathian Mountains.; much of Poland had been lost.

1915   Passenger liner *Lusitania* sunk by German submarine (May 7), as Germans established (Feb. 17) submarine blockade of Britain; US protested sinking and Germans revised (Sept. 1) submarine policy.

1915 Italy declared war on Austria-Hungary (May 23); ineffective, poorly equipped Italian army, commanded by Count Luigi Cadorna, launched four unsuccessful offensives against the Austrians along the Isonzo River; though Italian front quickly stabilized, it nevertheless tied down Austrian troops.

1915–16 Turkish Front, Armenian massacres; Ottoman government charged ethnic Armenians with aiding Russian forces (June) and ordered them moved away from all strategic points; Armenians subsequently brutalized and marched into desert; some one million killed (1915–16).

1915 On the Western Front, the Battle of Champagne (Sept. 22–Nov. 8); French gained but a few thousand yards in the initial assault; thereafter Gen. Joffre poured more troops into futile effort.

1915 British offensive aimed at Lens (Sept. 25–Oct. 30); British used gas and made more gains but failed to take Lens; British loss heavy, bringing about replacement of Sir J. French by Sir D. Haig as commander.

1915 Battle of Vimy Ridge (Sept. 25–Oct. 30); French offensive failed to take ridge.

1915 Salonica (Greece) Campaign; French and British landed forces in Greece (Oct. 3–5) in attempt to aid Serbia against impending attack; forces unable to link up with Serbians and retired to positions in Salonica; Allies forced overthrow of pro-German Greek king but otherwise remained inactive until end of war.

1915–16 Serbia and Montenegro conquered (Oct. 6–Jan.); Austro-German forces began invasion of Serbia and were joined by Bulgarian forces (entered war Sept. 22) on Oct. 11; Serbs forced into retreat and were later evacuated to Salonica; Montenegro surrendered (Jan. 17).

1915–16 Turkish Front, Allied forces withdrawn from Gallipoli (Dec. 10–Jan. 9), marking end of disastrous campaign; W. Churchill forced to resign as first lord of the admiralty because of the failed campaign.

1916 Turkish Front; Russians began slow advance (Jan. 17) in the Caucasus region; captured Turkish stronghold of Trebizond (Apr.

17), repulsed Turkish counterattacks, and continued slow advance to Oct.

1916 On the Western Front, Battle of Verdun (Feb. 21–Dec. 18); Germans, implementing Falkenhayn's planned war of attrition, attacked French fortifications at Verdun; fighting raged almost whole year, with French taking offensive from Aug.; Germans gained little ground and French retained Verdun; of some 750,000 casualties, 350,000 were French.

1916 Italian Front (Mar. 9–Nov. 14); Italians launched unsuccessful offensive (5th Battle of Isonzo, Mar. 9–17); Austrians attacked at Asiago (May 15–July 7) but were driven back in an Italian counterattack (from June 16); Italians made little gain in 6th–9th battles of Isonzo (Aug.–Nov.).

1916 Russian offensive in the east failed (Mar. 18–28); Russian attack at Lake Naroch had been intended to draw German forces from Verdun.

1916 Sussex Incident (Mar. 24); passenger ship *Sussex* sunk by German submarine; US ultimatum led Germans to halt unrestricted submarine warfare.

1916 Battle of Jutland (May 31); German High Seas Fleet and British Grand Fleet (under Admiral J. Jellicoe) engaged in decisive battle; British suffered greater losses but retained control of North Sea.

1916 Arab revolt in the Hejaz (June 5); revolt, encouraged by British, sought to end Ottoman Turk control over Arabia; Mecca captured (June 10) after Arab leader Hussain ibn Ali declared Hejaz independent.

1916 New Russian offensive in the east (June 4–Sept. 20); Russian Gen. Aleksei Brusilov began successful advance from southwest part of front; broke through Austrian lines and pushed whole front westward before drive ended; offensive cost Central Powers heavy losses; Russians lost about one million men, which left army demoralized.

1916 Battle of the Somme (July 1–Nov. 18) in the west; largely British offensive to help relieve pressure on Verdun; limited gains (125 sq. mi. of territory) of little strategic value and achieved at cost of about 600,000 Allied casualties; German losses totalled 450,000; British made first use of tanks (Sept. 15) in battle.

1916 Field Marshal von Hindenburg replaced Falkenhayn as German commander (Aug.).

1916 Rumania conquered by Central Powers (Aug. 28–Jan. 7); Rumania joined the Allies (Aug. 17) and attacked Austrian Transylvania (Aug. 28); Central Powers invaded Rumania (Sept. 1) and by Nov. had turned the tide; Bucharest captured (Dec. 6) and by Jan. 7 Central Powers had all of Rumania except northeast.

1916 Peace initiatives by US president W. Wilson; Germans agreed (Dec.) to begin negotiations but British refused because of military situation (Rumania had just been lost).

1916 Gen. Robert Nivelle made French commander, replacing Joffre (Dec.).

1917 British campaign in Palestine (Jan.–Dec.); British advance from Egypt toward Ottoman-controlled Palestine began in 1916; British crossed Sinai and fought three battles at Gaza (Mar., Apr., Oct.–Nov.) before dislodging the Turks; crossing into Palestine, they won the Battle of Junction Station (Nov. 13–14) and occupied Jerusalem (Dec. 9).

1917 Germans resumed unrestricted submarine warfare (Feb. 1); expected to be able to win war before US, which sharply opposed unrestricted use of submarines, could enter fighting; US broke diplomatic relations (Feb. 3).

1917 Zimmermann Note released (Mar. 1), secret proposal of alliance between Mexico and Germany; aroused US sentiment for entry into war.

1917 British occupied Baghdad (Mar. 11), a strategic city controlling the region of Mesopotamia; thereafter engaged in operations to clear Turkish forces from region; T. E. Lawrence, meanwhile, played an important role in the continuing Arab revolt against the Turks in Arabia.

1917 Russian Revolution of 1917; demoralized by losses in war and years of repressive tsarist rule, the Russians rose in revolt; Provisional Government established (Mar.) after the overthrow of Tsar Nicholas; Germans transported Bolshevik leader N. Lenin from Switzerland to Russia by famous "sealed train" (Apr.) in hope he would foment new unrest.

1917 US declared war on Germany (Apr. 6), following German submarine attacks on US merchant vessels.

1917 Germans withdrew (Feb.–Apr.) on Western Front to new, stronger defensive positions (the Hindenburg Line).

1917 Allied offensive (Apr.–May) on the Western Front; overall commander was French Gen. Nivelle; began with Battle of Arras (Apr. 9–May 3) in which Canadian forces captured Vimy Ridge (Apr. 12); main attack came in Second Battle of the Aisne (Apr. 16–May 9) in which Germans slaughtered French attackers; exhausted, French army mutinied (May) and many deserted; Gen. H. Pétain replaced Nivelle and restored order (July).

1917 Italian Front (May–Sept.); Italians suffered heavy losses in 10th and 11th battles of Isonzo.

1917 Second Allied offensive on Western Front (June–Nov.); British captured Messines Ridge (June 7–8) in preliminary battle; British launched main assault in Flanders and Third Battle of Ypres (July 31–Nov. 15); this cost almost 300,000 Allied casualties without achieving breakthrough of German lines; French meanwhile made some gains in fighting at Verdun (Aug. 20–26).

1917 Greece joined Allies (July 2) after Allies forced pro-German King Constantine to abdicate (June 11) in favor of his son, Alexander.

1917 July Offensive on the Eastern Front (July 1–Aug.); provisional government mounted attack on Austrian province of Galicia, led by Gen. Brusilov; German counterattack (from July 19) turned back the Russians and large-scale desertions began; Gen. Komilov became Russian commander (Aug. 1).

1917 Germans occupied Riga (Sept. 3) at north end of Eastern Front; Germans advanced eastward as Russians retreated, and took much of Latvia (by Oct. 20), as well as Russian islands in eastern Baltic.

1917 American Expeditionary Force, commanded by Gen. J. Pershing, entered combat on Western Front (Oct.); influx of American combat troops continued, reaching one million by Nov., 1918.

1917 Battle of Caporetto on the Italian Front (Oct. 24–Dec. 26); Austro-German offensive, designed to knock Italy out of the war, sent Italians into retreat from Isonzo River; Italians established new position along Piave River, 70 miles south; Gen. Armando Diaz replaced Gen. Cadorna as Italian commander and Allies sent troops from Western Front.

1917   November Revolution in Russia; Lenin's Bolsheviks seized power (Nov. 7); Lenin soon after sought armistice with Germans; made public secret agreements between Allies at start of war; Russia began negotiations with Central Powers (Dec. 5) for truce.

1917   Battle of Cambrai (Nov. 20–Dec. 3) in the West; British used first massed tank assault but, failing to capitalize on initial gains, were driven back by Germans.

1917   Rumania signed truce with Central Powers (Dec. 6); loss of Russian support made further fighting by remnants of Rumanian army futile.

1917   Russia concluded armistice (Dec. 15), ending fighting on Eastern Front.

1918   President Wilson announced (Jan. 8) his Fourteen Points, plan to secure lasting peace after war's end.

1918   Treaty of Brest-Litovsk (Mar. 3); Russians, after first refusing harsh German terms, accepted when the German armies advanced into Russian domains in the Baltic and Crimean regions; treaty abrogated when Germany surrendered in Nov.

1918   German spring offensive on the Western Front; hoping to split Allied lines, Germans launched Somme Campaign (Mar. 21–Apr. 8) and gained about 40 miles; French Gen. F. Foch named Allied overall commander (Mar. 26) to at last provide coordination of Allied effort.

1918   Second German offensive at Lys (Apr. 9–29); German drive against British in Flanders advanced 15 miles before being stopped.

1918   Red Baron (M. Richthofen), German ace pilot, killed in action (Apr. 21).

1918   Third German offensive near the Aisne River (May 27–June 6); German surprise attack resulted in advance to the Marne River, near Paris; US troops reinforced French forces at Château-Thierry (June 1–4) and halted German advance at the Marne.

1918   Fourth German offensive on the Western Front (June 9–13); Battle of the Metz ended in failure.

1918   Fifth German offensive in the West (July 15–Aug. 6); Second Battle of the Marne began with initial advance by war-weary German troops, who crossed Marne; Gen. Foch turned tide of war with strong counterattack (July 18); Germans, weakened by loss of over three-quarters of a million men in the offensive, withdrew to defensive positions.

1918   Allied offensive in West began (Aug. 8); British broke German lines with surprise attack at Battle of Amiens (Aug. 8–11); Allies won battles of Somme and Arras (Aug. 21–Sept. 3) and Germans retreated behind Hindenburg Line; Americans victorious at the Battle of San Mihiel salient (Sept. 12–13).

1918   Allied offensive from Salonica (Sept. 15–Nov. 10); Bulgaria surrendered (Sept. 29), Serbia liberated (Nov. 1), Albania and Montenegro taken (by Nov. 9) and Rumania captured (Nov. 10).

1918   Battle of Megiddo (Sept. 19) in Palestine; British victory marked beginning of northward drive by British and Arab forces; Damascus, Beirut, and Aleppo captured by Allied forces (Oct.); with Allies advancing from Syria and Mesopotamia, Ottoman Turks signed armistice (Oct. 30).

1918   Last Allied offensive in West (Sept.–Nov.); planned two-prong attack began with US Battle of the Argonne Forest (Sept. 26–Oct. 31); British launched attack in north (Sept. 27) and a broad offensive (with Belgians and French) in the north broke the Hindenburg Line in the following days.

1918   German general E. Ludendorff demanded government begin armistice talks (Sept. 29).

1918   American Army sergeant A. York became a hero after capturing a fortified German position (Oct. 18); took 132 prisoners.

1918   Germans made preliminary contacts with President Wilson to discuss settlement on basis of Fourteen Points (Oct. 4).

1918   Italian offensive (Oct. 24–Nov. 4); following failure of Austrian attack at Battle of Piave (June 15–24), the Italians mounted an attack (Oct. 24); with the Austro-Hungarian Empire collapsing, the Austrians began to withdraw and by Nov. 3 the Italians had begun attacks on Trieste.

1918   Austria sued for peace (Oct. 27) as the Austro-Hungarian Empire crumbled; Poland declared independence (Oct. 15), followed by Czechs, Yugoslavs, and Hungarians.

1918   Austro-Hungarian Empire signed armistice (Nov. 3); empire broken up into independent republics (Nov.).

1918 First meeting between Gen. Foch and German leaders to discuss terms of armistice (Nov 8).

1918 Collapse of the German government (Nov. 9); began with mutiny by German sailors at Kiel (Nov. 3); revolt spreading through Germany forced Emperor William to abdicate (Nov. 9); republic was then proclaimed.

1918 Germany concluded armistice (Nov. 11); acceded to harsh terms, including loss of territory, surrender of most of its navy, and loss of military and transportation equipment.

1919 German warships, to be surrendered to Allies, scuttled at Scapa Flow by German crews (June 21).

1919 Treaty of Versailles signed (June 28); imposed harsh terms on Germany, including heavy reparations, strict limit on size of military, loss of all overseas territories, demilitarization of the Rhineland; Germany was stripped of Alsace-Lorraine and other territories, and had formally placed upon it sole responsibility for the war; treaty also set up League of Nations and made other territorial adjustments.

1919–20 Other separate treaties concluded; included Treaty of Saint Germain (Sept. 10), signed by Austria; Treaty of Neuilly, signed (Nov. 27) by the Bulgarians; Treaty of Trianon, signed (June 4) by Hungary; and the Treaty of Sèvres, signed by the Ottomans (Aug. 10).

World War II Worldwide conflict (1939–45) involving all of the great powers and many of the lesser states as well. The combatants were divided into two opposing groups: the Allies (led by Britain, US, France, and after 1941 the USSR), and the Axis powers (led by Germany, Italy, and Japan). The war resulted in widespread destruction and suffering and cost many millions of lives. In addition, millions of others (notably Jews and Poles) died in Nazi death camps or were made slave laborers. The mechanization of warfare reached new levels in WW II and the airplane emerged as an important weapon in war on land and at sea. Finally, the use of atomic bombs by the US at the end of the war introduced the age of nuclear warfare. The causes of WW II are rooted in the economic, social, and political chaos of Europe following WW I. The economic collapse in Germany after the war and the harsh peace terms imposed by the Allies fostered German resentment and gave birth to A. Hitler's Nazi party. Fascism, under B. Mussolini, was also born of the postwar chaos in Italy. The rise of militaristic, totalitarian regimes was further aided by fear of the Communists and by a new economic collapse in the late 1920s and early 1930s (the Great Depression helped bring Hitler to power in Germany). It was Hitler who, after clearly adopting a militaristic aggressive policy, started WW II by invading Poland (Sept. 1939). Though Hitler quickly conquered Continental Europe, his decision to invade (1941) the USSR (until then an ally) proved to be his undoing. After the Japanese began hostilities in the Pacific theater, the US entered the war and Germany was confronted by the combined forces of the US, the USSR, and the British Commonwealth, as well as resistance fighters from conquered nations. From about 1942, the tide of the war turned against the Axis Powers and the surrender of Nazi Germany (May, 1945) was closely followed by the Japanese surrender (Sept., 1945). Treaties were signed (1947) at Paris by the Allies and Italy, Rumania, Hungary, Bulgaria, and Finland. A peace treaty with Japan was signed (1951). Principal events include:

1938 Germany annexed Austria (Mar.).

1938 Munich Pact signed (Sept.); following policy of appeasement, European powers agreed to formula to allow Germany to take Sudetenland from Czechoslovakia.

1939 Germans occupied all of Czechoslovakia, ignoring terms of Munich Pact and pushing British toward realization he would have to be confronted.

1939 Italy invaded Albania (Apr.).

1939 Allies abandoned appeasement policy in face of aggression by Germans and Italians; began to build up military forces; formed anti-aggression pacts with Turkey, Greece, Rumania, and Poland.

1939 Pact of Steel concluded (May 22); confirmed German-Italian alliance.

1939 Nonaggression Pact between Germany and USSR signed (Aug. 24); Germany no longer threatened with possibility of war on two fronts.

1939 Germany invaded Poland (Sept. 1); WW II began.

1939 Britain and France declared war on Germany (Sept. 3).

1939 German conquest of Poland (Sept. 1–27); Germans learned effectiveness of Blitzkrieg using Panzer tanks, highly mobile mechanized infantry units, and strong air cover; two-pronged German attack advanced eastward, while Soviets launched westward attack beginning Sept. 17; Germans captured Warsaw (Sept. 27) and Poland was partitioned between the victorious Germans and Soviets.

1939–40 Russo-Finnish War (Nov. 30–Mar. 12); Soviets invaded Finland after Finns refused to cede territory; Soviets met unexpectedly stiff resistance at Finnish Mannerheim Line; after months of hard fighting, Finland surrendered.

1939 *Admiral Graf Spee,* German pocket battleship, scuttled (Dec. 17) in Montevideo Harbor; had been badly damaged in battle with British warships off Uruguayan coast.

1940 Britain and France organized military force to aid Finland against the USSR, but Finland sued for peace before it arrived.

1940 Norway conquered by Germans (Apr. 9–June 10); surprise attack began simultaneously in Norway and Denmark; Denmark surrendered (Apr. 9); Norway largely in German hands by mid-May; final victory came with Allied evacuation at Narvik (June 10).

1940 Germans invaded the Netherlands, Luxembourg, France, and Belgium (May 10).

1940 W. Churchill replaced N. Chamberlain as British prime minister (May 10).

1940 The Netherlands conquered by Germans (May 10–14); Germans invaded from south and quickly put Dutch forces into retreat to Antwerp (May 13); German bombing attack on Rotterdam (May 14) brought Dutch surrender.

1940 Invasion of Belgium (May 10–28); two German forces advanced, one to the north took Liège (May 12); the other pushed through the Ardennes and broke Allied defenses at Sedan; this force raced to the English Channel (reached May 20); Germans defeated Allied attempt to break out to the south (May 21–23); Belgium surrendered (May 28).

1940 British evacuation at Dunkirk (June 4); encircled by German forces in Belgium, 200,000 British, 130,000 French, and other Allied forces withdrew by makeshift flotilla to Britain; supplies and equipment lost.

1940 Final German advance into France (June 5–22) began in extreme north, between Abbeville and Sedan and thereby outflanked the French Maginot Line; Germans broke through French defenses at the Aisne and Somme rivers (June 8) and occupied Paris (June 14); defensive fortifications at Verdun captured (June 15) and French sued for peace (June 17); France signed peace terms (June 22); northern France occupied by Germans, southern France run by newly formed Vichy government, a conservative, religious regime that cooperated with Nazi Germany.

1940 Italy declared war on Britain and France (June 10).

1940 C. de Gaulle asked French to join him in resistance to Nazis, but few responded; Free French army formed (June 23) by de Gaulle in London; de Gaulle gradually gains support over next years.

1940 French fleet at Oran sunk by British (July 3).

1940 Vichy government of France forced to allow Japan to occupy French Indochina (July 21).

1940 Latvia, Estonia, and Lithuania absorbed by USSR (Aug.).

1940 Italians conquered British Somaliland (Aug. 6–19); marked beginning of war in Africa.

1940 Battle of Britain begun (Aug. 13); fought entirely in the air, the battle began as preparation for German invasion of Britain; German Luftwaffe failed to knock out British RAF and suffered heavy losses; began bombing London (Sept. 7) and abandoned planned invasion; heavy bombing raids on London continued into 1941.

1940 Italy invaded Egypt (Sept. 13–15) from Libya; British launched counteroffensive (Dec. 8) and drove into Libya; invasions of Italian East Africa begun (Jan. 15, 1941) and completed that year; British advance in Libya continued into Feb., 1941.

1940 Japan concluded Tripartite Pact with Germany and Italy (Sept. 27).

1940–41 Axis offensive in the Balkans (Oct.–May); Italian invasion of Greece (Oct. 28) was repulsed and Greeks invaded Albania (Dec. 3); German troops invaded Yugoslavia and Greece (Apr. 6); Yugoslavia surrendered (Apr. 17); Germans captured Athens (Apr. 27), and drove British off Crete (May 31); Hungary, Bulgaria, and Rumania meanwhile joined Axis powers.

1940 Submarine warfare in the Atlantic; Germans, unable to match Allied surface fleet; organized submarine wolf packs to sink supply convoys; despite implementation of convoy system, loss of Allied shipping increased steadily until Nov., 1942.

1941 US established lend-lease program (Mar. 11) to provide Allies with badly needed supplies; marked increased shift by US from policy of neutrality.

1941 German offensive in North Africa (Apr.–May); Gen. E. Rommel's Afrika Korps launched rapid advance (Apr. 3) against British in Libya; drove British back to Egyptian border by May 29.

1941 R. Hess, close adviser of A. Hitler, flew to Scotland, ostensibly to discuss his plan to end war with British (May 10).

1941 *Bismarck,* German battleship, sunk by British warships while she was on maiden voyage (May 27).

1941 Iraq came under British control (June 4) following brief fight against rebels who had overthrown government there; British and Russian troops later occupied Iran (July 25).

1941 British and Free French occupied Syria, taking control from Vichy French forces (June 8–14).

1941 USSR invaded by Germans (Operation Barbarossa, June 22); three-pronged attack launched, north toward Leningrad, center toward Smolensk and Moscow, and south toward Kiev; rapid German advance caught hundreds of thousands of Soviet troops, but overall numbers of Soviet troops far greater than Hitler anticipated; Stalin proclaimed "scorched earth" policy as Soviets retreated eastward (July 3).

1941 US occupied Iceland (July 7).

1941 Atlantic Charter signed (Aug. 14) by US and Britain; declaration of common war goals even though US still nominally neutral; charter called for freedom to choose form of government.

1941 Russian Front; Germans, advancing rapidly, surrounded Leningrad (Sept. 8) in north and captured Kiev (Sept. 24) in south; German drive on Moscow began (Oct. 2) and Soviets removed to Kuibyshev (Oct. 19);

unable to achieve decisive victory and over-reaching their supply lines, German troops reached outskirts of Moscow (Nov. 15); offensive halted (Dec.) and Russians counterattacked (Nov. and Dec.).

1941 Soviets signed (Oct. 1) agreements with Britain and US; US to provide supplies under lend-lease arrangements; US supply convoys to north Russian ports regularly came under heavy German attacks during war.

1941–42 North Africa Campaign; British launched new offensive into Libya (Nov. 18) and drove Germans back to El Agheila (Jan. 18).

1941–42 Russian winter offensive (Dec.–Feb.); Soviet armies attacked Germans around Moscow (Dec. 6); Hitler ordered troops to hold positions and took direct command of army (Dec. 19); Germans, ill-prepared for Russian winter, forced to withdraw (Jan. 15) to west.

1941 Pearl Harbor (Dec. 7); Japanese surprise attack wrecked US Pacific battleship fleet and marked beginning of Japanese offensive in South Pacific.

1941 US declared war on Japan (Dec. 8); Germany and Italy declared war on the US (Dec. 11).

1941–42 Japanese offensive in Pacific theater; Bangkok, Thailand occupied (Dec. 8); British battleships *Prince of Wales* and *Repulse* sunk (Dec. 10); Guam captured (Dec. 13); Wake Island captured (Dec. 23); Hong Kong surrendered (Dec. 25); in the Philippines, Manila fell (Jan. 2), Bataan (Apr. 9), and Corregidor (May 6); Singapore fell (Feb. 15); conquest of Dutch East Indies completed (Mar. 9), after victory in Battle of Java Sea Mar. 1); Burma conquered (Dec.–May).

1941–42 Arcadia Conference in Washington (Dec. 22–Jan. 14); Roosevelt and Churchill conferred.

1942 Declaration of the United Nations signed (Jan. 1) by Allied leaders; promised to prosecute war until complete defeat of Axis Powers.

1942 Wannsee Conference held in Berlin (Jan. 20); Nazi officials formalized plans to round up and murder Jews.

1942 Gen. D. MacArthur named supreme commander of Allied forces in Southwest Pacific (Mar. 17), following his withdrawal from the Philippines.

1942 US airman J. Doolittle led daring bombing raid against Tokyo and some other targets on Japanese mainland (Apr. 18); bombs from 16 B-25s did little physical damage, but humiliated Japanese high command and boosted morale in US.

1942 Russian Front; abortive Soviet spring offensive halted after a quarter million soldiers were captured in attack (May 12) on Kharkov, in the south.

1942 Anglo-Soviet Agreement (May 26) united Britain and Russia against Nazi Germany.

1942 British launched air attack on Cologne (May 30–31).

1942 Manhattan Project begun by US (June, initially in cooperation with Britain) to develop atomic bomb.

1942 Pacific theater; US naval and air forces turned back Japanese invasion force heading for New Guinea (Battle of the Coral Sea, May 7–8); Japanese invaded Aleutian Islands (June 3), eventually taking Attu; Battle of Midway (June 4–7), US naval air units heavily damaged Japanese fleet sent to take Midway Island.

1942 Czech village of Lidice destroyed by Germans (June 10) after Czech resistance fighters killed high German SS official, R. Heydrich.

1942 US general D. Eisenhower named commander of US forces in European theater (June 25).

1942 Russian Front; German offensive began (June 28), Stalingrad being among its targets; fighting around the city broke out by Aug. 9, as Germans met stiff Russian resistance; heavy fighting continued into fall, when Soviets launched counterattack.

1942 US offensive in the Pacific, troops landed on Guadalcanal (Aug. 7) beginning of fight in Solomon Islands; Japanese naval force heavily damaged in Battle of Eastern Solomons (Aug. 23–25); Guadalcanal secured by US forces (Feb. 1943).

1942 Dieppe Raid (Aug. 19) failed; Allied (experimental landing on French coast cost nearly two-thirds of troops.

1942 Allied offensive in New Guinea began (Sept. 25); Japanese had invaded New Guinea (Mar.) in preparation for attack on Australia; US and Australian forces secured Buna and Gona (Dec.); convoy with Japanese reinforce-

ments sunk by Allied aircraft (Mar. 4, 1943).

1942 British counterattacked Japanese in Burma (Oct.); British gains lost in new Japanese attack (Mar.–May, 1943); Allies meanwhile began building (Dec. 1942) the Ledo Road from India, to provide overland supply route to China.

1942 North Africa Campaign; following new German offensive by Rommel (Jan.), Germans had pushed British back into Egypt; British Gen. B. Montgomery led his forces in crucial Battle of El Alamein (Oct. 23–Nov. 4), in which Germans were driven back into Libya.

1942 US forces, led by Gen. D. Eisenhower, landed in Algeria, Oran, and Casablanca (Nov. 8), beginning second front in North Africa; Vichy French forces ceased all resistance (Nov. 10); Allied forces began eastward advance into Tunisia.

1942 Germans extended their zone of occupation in France to include all of France (Nov. 11); French fleet at Toulon scuttled (Nov. 27) by French.

1942–43 Battle of Stalingrad on the Russian Front (Nov.–Feb.); Soviet offensive began (Nov. 19), and soon encircled 22 German divisions around Stalingrad; these forces reduced to about 90,000 men by the time their commander surrendered (Feb. 2); battle turned tide of war against Germans; meanwhile, long German siege of Leningrad was broken (Jan.).

1943 Casablanca Conference held (Jan. 14–24); Roosevelt and Churchill decided to press for complete German surrender, invasion of France put off; invasion of Sicily planned.

1943 Final Allied offensive in North Africa; US forces advancing east through Tunisia, British driving west from Egypt; British captured Tripoli (Jan. 23); Rommel stung US forces at Battle of Kasserine Pass (Feb. 20), but US soon recovered offensive; British broke through German defensive Mareth Line in Tunisia (Mar.) and Allied forces linked up (Apr. 7), securing the North Africa coast; final Allied offensive (May) resulted in capture of remaining Axis troops.

1943 In the USSR, German counterattack won Kharkov and Belgorod (Mar. 11, 18) and halted Soviet advance after Stalingrad.

1943 Katyn Massacre discovered (Apr. 13); German soldiers discovered mass grave of thousands of Polish soldiers who had been slaughtered by the Soviets in 1940; Soviets denied responsibility.

1943 Warsaw Ghetto Uprising (Apr.–May); some 60,000 Polish Jews rose in desperate and unsuccessful revolt against Nazis; revolt came after Nazis had taken 400,000 to concentration camps.

1943 Trident Conference held (May 12–25); Roosevelt and Churchill planned invasion of Italian Peninsula; put off invasion of France to 1944.

1943 Soviets dissolved (May 22) the Comintern, organization for spread of communism; this marked Stalin's policy of appeasing the Allies.

1943 US forces recaptured Attu in the Aleutian Islands (June 3); ended Japanese threat to North American territories.

1943 Allied invasion of Sicily (July 10–Aug. 18); US, British, and Canadian forces, led by Gen. Eisenhower, landed on south coast; Palermo occupied (July 24); Messina captured (Aug. 18), ending the fight for Sicily.

1943 Sustained Soviet offensive began (July 11); after a weak German attack, the Soviets pushed westward in the region of Orel and Belgorod and by Aug. advance on a broad front was under way; German retreat was confused (by Hitler's intervention) and costly; Soviets crossed Dnieper River in October and recaptured Kiev (Nov. 6); advance continued into 1944.

1943 Allied offensive in the Pacific began (July 1); US and Australian forces advanced in New Guinea, captured Japanese strongholds of Salamaua (July 3) and Lae (Sept. 7); captured New Georgia (Aug. 7), Bougainville (Oct. 31); Gilbert Islands were invaded (Nov. 22).

1943 Fire-bombing of Hamburg (July 24–Aug. 3).

1943 Italy's Fascist leader, B. Mussolini, forced to resign by Fascist Grand Council (July 25) as invasion of Sicily progressed; new government dissolved Fascist party and began peace talks.

1943 Quebec Conference held (Aug. 11–24); Roosevelt and Churchill considered problems related to invasion of France but reached no decisions.

1943 Campaign for Italian mainland; British landed in southern Italy (Sept. 3), US landed at Salerno (Sept. 9); Allies advanced north, taking Naples (Oct. 1); Allies halted by German Gustav Line, south of Cassino, until following spring.

1943 Italy surrendered unconditionally (Sept. 3).

1943 Germans set up Italian puppet state after rescuing the imprisoned Mussolini (Sept. 15); German troops in Italy subsequently put up stiff resistance to Allied forces attempting to take Italian mainland.

1943 Italy declared war on Germany (Oct. 13).

1943 Teheran Conference (Nov. 8–Dec. 1); Roosevelt, Churchill, and Stalin met; Allies to open up second front with invasion of France, in both north and south; agreed on postwar occupation of Germany and redrawing of borders of Germany and Poland.

1944 Morganthau Plan for postwar Germany accepted and then rejected by US and Britain; called for destruction of Germany's industrial base and instituting program to turn Germany into an agricultural society.

1944 Russian offensive continued; Novgorod captured (Jan. 20) and Soviets reached border of Poland (Feb.); in south, reached Rumanian border (Mar. 26); Sevastopol and Crimean region secured (May).

1944 Allied landings at Anzio, Italy (Jan. 22); this attempt to outflank German defensive line failed.

1944 Pacific offensive; US forces invaded Marshall Islands (Feb.), Admiralty Islands (Mar.), and the Marianas (June); US won major victory in Battle of the Philippine Sea (June 19) during Marianas invasion and by it crippled the Japanese navy; Guam secured (Aug.).

1944 Massive bombing raids over Germany (Feb. 20) began.

1944 Allied offensive in Italy; major attack at Cassino (Mar. 15–May 18) finally broke German Gustav Line; Allies pushed north, occupying Rome (June 4) and Florence (Aug. 12); Germans, however, held on to northern Italy until last months of the war.

1944 Normandy invasion; allied landings in France began (June 6) under the command of Gen. Eisenhower; US troops landed at Omaha and Utah beaches, British and Canadian troops at Gold, Juno, and Sword beaches; British reached Caen (July 8) and US forces took Saint-Lô (July 18); meanwhile troops and supplies poured in as largest amphibious operation in history progressed.

1944 Russian front; as Normandy invasion progressed, Soviets launched drives in the east; German armies in Poland collapsed (June–July) before Soviet advance; in south, Soviets entered Balkans, capturing Rumania (Aug. 24), Bulgaria (Sept. 8), Yugoslavia (Oct. 20); met stiff German resistance in Hungary (Nov.); in the north, Finland surrendered (Sept. 19) and Riga, on the Baltic coast, was taken (Oct. 13).

1944 Pro-Soviet government of Poland formed (Lublin Committee); organized in opposition to Polish government-in-exile in London; Lublin Committee became core of Poland's postwar Communist regime.

1944 Hitler narrowly escaped assassination attempt (July 20); Hitler took brutal revenge on all he suspected of complicity.

1944 Saintt-Lô Breakout in France (July 25–27); US forces broke German lines at Saint-Lô, drove southeast to secure Brittany (July–Aug.) and southwest to capture Le Mans (Aug. 8); eastward drive (north of Loire River) next liberated Paris (Aug. 25), which German officers had refused to destroy, and brought the Allies to the Seine River.

1944 Warsaw Uprising (Aug.–Oct.); Polish underground army resistance crushed by Germans; Soviets, meanwhile, halted their advance in Poland just outside Warsaw and refused to aid the pro-West underground army.

1944 Allied landings in southern France, between Marseilles and Nice (Aug. 15); Allied armies moved northward up the Rhône Valley; captured Lyons (Sept. 3) before Germans stalled the advance.

1944 Allied advance eastward; British forces liberated Brussels, Belgium (Sept. 2); Liège captured (Sept. 7), followed by liberation of Luxembourg (Sept. 10) and invasion of German frontier (Sept. 11); Gen. G. Patton's forces crossed the Moselle River to the south (Sept. 7); airborne assault at Arnhem (to outflank German "West Wall" defenses) failed (Sept. 17–26); Allied supply lines now overextended by rapid pace of advance.

1944 Allied invasion force from southern France linked up with northern invasion force at Dijon (Sept. 15).

1944 Hitler issued call-up of all able-bodied males (Sept. 25) for last-ditch defense of Germany.

1944 V-2 rocket attacks on Britain began (Oct. 7).

1944 "Percentage agreement" between Churchill and Stalin; leaders agreed informally that Soviets would dominate Rumania and Bulgaria, British would dominate Greece, and they share influence equally in Yugoslavia and Hungary.

1944 British occupied Greece (Oct.), following withdrawal of German forces; revolt by Communists put down.

1944–45 Philippines Campaign in the Pacific (Oct. 20–Feb. 23); recapture of the Philippines began with landings on Leyte and naval battle of Leyte Gulf; Leyte secured and Luzon invaded by US (Jan.); Manila taken (Feb. 23); resistance by remnants of Japanese forces continued for duration of the war.

1944 US bombers, flying from air bases on Saipan, began regular bombing raids against Japanese cities (Nov.).

1944 Battle of the Bulge in Western Europe (Dec. 16–Jan. 25); Germans mounted surprise attack aimed at breaking overextended Allied lines and capturing Antwerp, Belgium; was last major German offensive.

1945 Russian advance from the east; Warsaw taken by Soviets (Jan. 17), Krakow (Jan. 19); to south, German resistance in Hungary broken and Budapest finally captured (Feb. 13); Soviet units took Vienna, Austria (Apr. 13) and began fight to take Berlin (Apr. 20).

1945 Yalta Conference held (Feb. 4–11); Roosevelt, Churchill, and Stalin discussed plans for occupation of Germany after war, drawing of borders, and plans for European political structures; Soviets agreed to join war against Japan and to become UN member.

1945 Fire-bombing of Dresden (Feb. 13–14).

1945 Battle of Iwo Jima (Feb. 19–Mar. 17) in Pacific; US forces suffered heavy casualties in battle for the strategic island.

1945 Allied offensive into the German Rhineland began (Feb. 23); US forces reached Rhine River (Mar. 2), captured Cologne (Mar. 7); crossed Rhine (Mar. 7) at Remagen; reached Elbe River (Apr. 12). Germans in Ruhr district enveloped (Apr. 1); US forces reached Elbe River (Apr. 12).

1945   Battle of Okinawa (Apr. 1–June 21) fought in Pacific; island provided still closer land base for bombers attacking Japan.

1945   Final Allied offensive in northern Italy (Apr. 9); German resistance broken; last German forces surrendered (May 1).

1945   US president Roosevelt died (Apr. 12).

1945   US and Soviet troops link up at Torgau, along the Elbe River (Apr. 25).

1945   San Francisco Conference held (Apr.–June); wrote United Nations Charter.

1945   Mussolini captured and killed by anti-Fascists (Apr. 28).

1945   Hitler committed suicide (Apr. 30) as Soviet forces closed in on Berlin; K. Doenitz named as his successor.

1945   Berlin capture completed (May 2).

1945   Germany surrendered (May 7); Allied Control Committee formed by Allied military leaders to govern Germany (June 5).

1945   Allies, led by Lord Mountbatten, gained control of Burma (May) after long campaign against Japanese.

1945   Potsdam Conference held (July 17–Aug. 2) by Allies; Roosevelt and Churchill replaced by H. Truman and C. Attlee; conference outlawed Nazism in Germany, established Soviet control of eastern Germany, and called on Japanese to surrender; relations between Allies began to cool, as a result of disagreements over German war reparations, organization of the Polish government, and other questions concerning the postwar world order.

1945   Atomic bomb dropped by US on Hiroshima (Aug. 6); city devastated.

1945   Soviet invasion of Japanese-held Manchuria began (Aug. 8).

1945   US dropped second atomic bomb on Nagasaki (Aug. 9).

1945   Japan surrendered (Aug. 14); signed formal surrender (Sept. 2).

1945–46   Nürnberg Trials held to judge leaders of Nazi party for war crimes; twelve sentenced to death, others to prison.

Worms, Concordat of *See* **Concordat of Worms.**

Worms, Diet of   Imperial diet called (1521) during the Reformation by Holy Roman Emperor Charles V. It was convened at Worms, Germany, to consider action against Protestant reformer M.

Luther. Luther had already been condemned by Pope Leo X and was given safe conduct to appear before the diet (Apr. 17, 1521). There Luther was asked to repudiate his teachings; on the following day he refused. The subsequent Edict of Worms (May 25) declared Luther a heretic and outlaw and forced him to go into hiding for some months.

Worms, Synod of   1. Synod of German Catholic bishops called (1076) at Worms, now in West Germany, by Holy Roman Emperor Henry IV. A high point in Henry's conflict with the pope over lay investiture, the synod declared Pope Gregory VII deposed, in response to Gregory's attempt to impose reforms. Gregory subsequently excommunicated and deposed Henry (1076). 2. Synod of German bishops called (1122) at Worms to settle the Investiture Controversy between Holy Roman Emperor Henry V and Pope Calixtus II. The synod formulated the Concordat of Worms (*q.v.*).

Wounded Knee   Site on the South Dakota Pine Ridge Indian Reservation where US troops massacred some 200 Sioux Indians (Dec. 29, 1890). After the death of Sitting Bull, some of the Sioux were influenced by a seer and fled the reservation. They were rounded up at Wounded Knee by US cavalrymen and while the Indians were being disarmed, a fight broke out. The troops opened fire indiscriminately, massacring men, women, and children.

WPA   *See* **Works Projects Administration.**

Wrangel, Karl Gustaf 1613–76.   Swedish general and naval commander. He distinguished himself during the Thirty Years' War, and in 1646 succeeded L. Torstensson as commander in chief. Under Charles X, Wrangel commanded in wars against Poland, Denmark, and Brandenburg.

Wren, Sir Christopher 1632–1723.   English architect, astronomer, and mathematician. The greatest architect of his day, he designed more than 50 London churches, including St. Paul's Cathedral.

Wright, Frank Lloyd 1869–1959.   American architect whose innovative approach to the design and structure of modern buildings greatly influenced the development of modern architecture. He originated the "prairie style" with lines suggestive of the landscape.

Wright, Horatio Gouverneur 1820–99.   Union general in the American Civil War, who fought at the First Battle of Bull Run, and commanded in the Florida Campaign (1862) and in the defense of Washington, D.C. (1864).

Wright, Orville and Wilbur 1871–1948, 1867–1912. American inventors. Originally bicycle mechanics, the Wright brothers built a biplane kite (1899). They went on to build the first successful heavier-than-air, powered airplane, which they flew for the first time at Kitty Hawk, North Carolina (Dec. 17, 1903). By 1909, they had won the first contract to construct a military plane for the US Army. Wilbur subsequently ran their airplane manufacturing company until his death, while Orville devoted himself to research.

Wright, Richard 1908–1960. Black American author. Embittered by racism in American society, he wrote powerful condemnations of slavery and segregation, as in *Native Son* (1940). He also wrote an autobiography, *Black Boy* (1945), numerous stories, novels, and other works.

Wu Chengen 1506?–82?. Chinese author. He is believed to be the author of *Xiyouji* (*The Journey West*), considered one of the greatest works of comedy in Chinese literature.

Wudi 156–87 BC. Emperor (141–87 BC) of the Chinese Han dynasty. He greatly expanded the empire (into Vietnam, Korea, and the northern and western border regions), instituted administrative reforms to further strengthen imperial authority, set up the Chinese Examination System (*q.v.*), and established Confucianism as the state religion. The end of his reign marked the start of the decline of the Han dynasty.

Wu Hou *See* **Wu Zhao.**

Wundt, Wilhelm 1832–1920. German physiologist and psychologist, considered the father of experimental psychology. He established, at Leipzig, the first laboratory for this discipline.

Wu Peifu 1873–1939. Chinese warlord. He supported Yuan Shikai and the Chinese Republic. From 1916 to 1926 he fought for control of northern China, but his attempt to unify China failed.

Wu Ti *See* **Wudi.**

Wu Wang *fl.* 1122. Founder of the Zhou dynasty and son of Wen Wang. Wu Wang succeeded his father as ruler of Zhou domains on China's western frontier, and after forming a coalition of smaller states, attacked the weak Shang Empire. Following a series of bloody battles, Wu Wang defeated and killed Zouxin. He set up a feudal system of government, dividing up his domains among relatives and nobles willing to acknowledge Zhou suzerainty. Wu Wang died shortly after conquering the Shang.

Wu Zhao (Wu Hou) 625–705. Tang empress of China (684–704). She was a concubine of Emperor Gaozong and ruled first by her influence and then as empress.

Wyandotte Constitution Antislavery constitution prepared (July, 1859) at Wyandotte, Kansas. It marked the culmination of the struggle between slave and antislave forces known as Bleeding Kansas (*q.v.*). The constitution was approved in a popular referendum (Oct., 1859) and Kansas was finally admitted to the Union (Jan. 29, 1861) as a free state.

Wyatt's Rebellion Unsuccessful rebellion against Queen Mary of England by Sir Thomas Wyatt (*d.* 1554) and others in 1554. Though the uprising sparked violence in London, it failed to gain widespread popular support and Wyatt surrendered, was tried, and hanged.

Wycherley, William 1640?–1716? English dramatist, whose plays are noted for their satirical wit. Among his best are *The Country Wife* and *The Plain Dealer.*

Wyclif, John *See* **Wycliffe, John.**

Wycliffe, John (Wyclif, John) (Wickliffe, John) (Wiclif, John) c1320–84. English reformer and theologian whose attacks on church doctrine anticipated the Protestant Reformation. He began the first English translation of the Bible.

Wyeth, Andrew 1917– . American painter. Noted for his precise technique and subtle use of light and color, he paints rural subjects. His best-known work is *Christina's World.*

Wyoming Western US state, the 44th state. The area had been held by Spain, France, and England, but by 1846 the US acquired all of it by purchase or treaty. The fur trade and natural wonders brought explorers, but Indian attacks hindered development until the discovery of gold and the coming of the railroad drew more settlers to the region. The Wyoming Territory was formed in 1868 and was the first to give women the vote. It became a state in 1890 and elected the first US woman governor, Nellie Tayloe Ross (1924). Its constitution was adopted in 1890.

Wyoming Massacre Battle (July 3, 1778) between 1,000 British Loyalists (and Iroquois

Indians) and some 300 American settlers in the Wyoming Valley of Pennsylvania. Most of the settlement men were away with Washington's army. The 300 remaining men and boys ventured out of Forty Fort to meet the British and were massacred by the superior attacking force. The incident outraged American colonials and

led to punitive expeditions against the Iroquois Indians.

Wythe, George 1726–1806. American jurist and statesman. A signer of the Declaration of Independence, he was professor of law at the College of William and Mary (1779–90). He taught T. Jefferson and J. Marshall, among others.

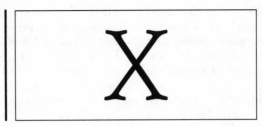

Xanthippe (Xantippe) *fl.* 5th cent. BC. Wife of Socrates, proverbial for her troublesome temper and carping disposition.

Xantippe *See* **Xanthippe.**

Xavier, Saint Francis 1506–52. Catholic missionary priest, called "the Apostle of the Indies." One of the seven original Jesuits (1534), he converted many thousands in India, Ceylon, the Malay Archipelago, and Japan (from 1542).

Xenocrates 396–314 BC. Greek philosopher. A disciple of Plato, he succeeded Speusippus as head of the Greek Academy in 339.

Xenophanes *fl.* 6th cent. BC. Greek philosopher and poet, a member, and once thought to be the founder of the Eleatic school. He asserted the existence of one God closely identified with the material world.

Xenophon c434–c355 BC. Greek military leader and historian who commanded Greek forces in the service of Persian king Cyrus the Younger. His best-known work, the *Anabasis,* recounts the retreat of the Ten Thousand following Cyrus's death at Cunaxa (401 BC).

Xerxes I c519–465 BC. Persian king (486–465 BC), successor to his father, Darius I. He prepared a massive force for the conquest of Greece, but was defeated at Salamis (480 BC). His reign marked the beginning of Persia's decline.

Xia Legendary first dynasty in traditional Chinese history which is said to have reigned c1994–c1523 BC (c2205–c1766 BC, by traditional dating). It was succeeded by the Shang dynasty. Archaeological evidence indicates the existence of an early Xia state in the Yellow River valley in northeastern China. The potter's wheel, bronze weapons, and chariots are believed to have been in use during the Xia period. Yu is the legendary founder of the dynasty.

Xia Gui (Hsia Kuei) *fl.* 1195–1224. Chinese painter during the Song dynasty. Co-founder with Ma Yuan of the Ma-Hsia landscape-painting school, he is regarded as a master of the genre.

Xi'an Incident (Sian ˜) Incident sparked (Dec. 12, 1936) by the arrest of Chinese Nationalist leader Chiang Kai-shek by one of his generals, Zhang Xeuliang, at Xi'an, China. Zhang demanded that Chiang end his war against the Communists and form a united front to fight the invading Japanese. Chiang agreed and was released (Dec. 25). The incident led to a Communist-Nationalistic coalition that lasted through WW II.

Xin, House of *See* **Han dynasty.**

Xiongnu (Hsiung-nu) Asian people who established (3d cent. BC) an empire in Manchuria, Mongolia, and Siberia. They raided northern China for several centuries and established several dynasties, but declined in importance by the 5th cent. AD. The original Great Wall of China was completed (3d cent. BC) to control their advance.

Xuantong (Hsüan tung; Puyi, Henry) 1905–67. Last emperor of China (1908–12). He ruled under the name of Xuantong, and later lived under Japanese protection (1924–31). The Japanese installed him as head of their Manchurian puppet state of Manchukuo (1932–34) and then made him its emperor under the name of K'ang Tê (1934–45).

Xuanzong (Tang Husan Tsung) 685–762. Chinese emperor (712–756), sixth emperor of the Tang dynasty. During his reign China reached the peak of its power and prosperity, though the Tang dynasty's decline began soon after.

Xunzi c298–c230 BC. Chinese philosopher. He systematized the teachings of Confucius and Mencius and thereby played a major role in establishing the Confucian tradition. His great work, *Xunzi,* directly opposed the Confucian tenet that man is innately good, while holding that proper cultural training would enable men to overcome their basic evil nature. He also tutored the renowned opponent of Confucianism, Han Fei.

XYZ Affair Diplomatic incident (1797) between French and US officials that nearly brought the two nations to war. In 1797, US president J. Adams sent C. Pinckney, J. Marshall, and E. Gerry to France to negotiate an end to French interference with US shipping. The commission was not allowed to meet immediately with French foreign minister C. de Talleyrand, but three agents representing France, called X, Y, and Z later by US officials, approached the three US ministers and suggested that the ministers give them a bribe and guarantee to France a large loan. When the affair was made public, American tempers flared and the US and France began an undeclared naval war. The conflict was ended by negotiation of the Convention of 1800 (Sept., 1800). It was during this affair that Pinckney was thought to have said (but probably did not say), "Millions for defense, sir, but not one cent for tribute."

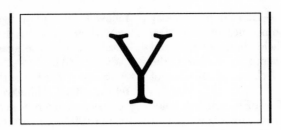

Yahweh Name of God as revealed to Moses. The name is an extension of the original four-letter name YHWH (the Tetragrammaton). From this also came the name Jehovah.

Yakima Indian Wars Series of wars (1855–59) fought by the Yakima Indians in Washington Territory against US encroachment. The Yakima signed (1855) a treaty and agreed to move to a reservation, but under the leadership of Kamiakin, resisted removal. They were eventually defeated and moved.

Yale, Elihu 1649–1721. American-born official of the British East India Company. Yale College (which later developed into Yale University) was named after him.

Yalta Conference Allied conference (Feb. 4–11, 1945) during WW II, at Yalta in the Crimea. Attended by US president F. Roosevelt, British prime minister W. Churchill, and Russian premier J. Stalin, it restated the Allied determination to receive only unconditional surrender in Germany. The conference planned for the postwar occupation of Germany by the four major Allied powers, discussed the postwar reorganization of Europe, and made plans for the San Francisco Conference (*q.v.*) to establish the United Nations.

Yamagata, Prince Aritomo 1838–1922. Japanese soldier and statesman. He played a major role in the modernization of the Japanese army and establishment of Japan as a world power.

Yamamoto, Isoroku 1884–1943. Japanese admiral. He led the attack on Pearl Harbor, thus precipitating US entry into WW II.

Yamasee War Uprising (1715) of the Yamasee Indians against English settlers in South Carolina. Defeated, the Yamasee fled (1716) to Florida and were assimilated into the Creek and Seminole tribes.

Yamashita, Tomoyuki 1885–1946. Japanese general. During WW II he commanded Japanese forces in the conquest of Singapore, Bataan, and Corregidor, and commanded in the Philippines (1942–45). He was hanged for war crimes committed by his troops.

Yancey, William Lowndes 1814–63. American lawyer and politician. A vigorous supporter of slavery, he sponsored the Alabama Platform (1848) and led in the movement for Southern secession.

Yandabo, Treaty of *See* **Burmese War (First).**

Yang Chien *See* **Sui.**

Yang Chu *See* **Yang Zhu.**

Yang Kuang *See* **Sui.**

Yang Zhu (Yang Chu) 440–360? BC. Chinese philosopher. He opposed the philosophy of Confucianism and was later accused of advocating hedonism.

Yankee Term applied by Americans to those who live in New England, by Americans from the South to Northerners, and by non-Americans to Americans. It was probably originally applied to Dutch settlers.

Yarmuk River, Battle of the Arab victory (Aug. 20, 636) over the Byzantine army, on a tributary of the Jordan River. An Arab force of some 25,000 decisively defeated 50,000 Byzantines, thereby breaking Byzantine dominance in the region and paving the way for the Arab conquest of Syria.

Yazid I *See* **Caliphate (680–683); Muslim Civil Wars.**

Yazoo land claims Land scheme in which the Georgia state legislature awarded (Jan. 7, 1795) some 35 million acres of land in present-day Mississippi to four land companies for $500,000. Most of the legislators held shares in the land companies. Congress eventually ordered the lands sold and settled all claims at the cost of some $4 million.

Yeardley, Sir George c1507–1627. British colonial administrator and three times governor of Virginia (1616–17, 1619–21, 1626–27). During his governorship, the first representative assembly in the English colonies was convened at Jamestown (1619).

Yeats, William Butler 1865–1939. Irish poet and playwright. One of the greatest poets of the 20th cent., he was a leading voice in the cause of Irish nationalism. The son of a lawyer turned painter, Yeats published his first poem in 1885 and some years after completed a book of poems called *The Wanderings of Oisin* (1889). About this time he also began a lifelong interest in occultism, which among other things led him to become a devotee of spiritual movements and to marry a spiritualist medium, Georgie Hyde Lees (1917). From about 1896, he was a leader of the Irish Renaissance, which sought to bring about renewed awareness of Irish folk culture, and in the early 1900s he helped found the Abbey Theatre in Dublin, writing such plays as *On Baile's Strand* (1904) for it. Yeats established his reputation as a major poet after publishing *The Wild Swans at Coole* (1917), and what may be his most famous poem, *Easter 1916,* about the Irish revolt against British rule, appeared in 1921. He served in the Irish Senate (1922–28) and in 1923 won the Nobel Prize for Literature. Among Yeats's other poetic works were *The Tower* (1928), *The Winding Stair* (1929), and the posthumously published *Last Poems* (1940).

yellow-dog contract Contract in which an employer extracts as a condition of employment a promise not to join a labor union. Yellow-dog contracts were declared unenforceable by the Norris–La Guardia Act (1932).

Yellow Emperor *See* **Huang Di.**

yellow journalism Journalism emphasizing the sensational through the use of bold headlines, scandal stories, exposés, and the like. Its name arose from a comic strip, *The Yellow Kid,* in the New York *World,* and it figured in the circulation wars of the *World* and the New York *Journal* in the 1880s and 1890s. Yellow journalism contributed to the outbreak of the Spanish-American War.

Yellow Turbans (Taipingdao) Chinese secret society whose members, drawing on the popularity of Daoist cults, rose against the emperor and his advisers (AD 184–204). Their rebellion contributed to the fall of the Han dynasty (AD 220).

Yeltsin, Boris Nikolayevich 1931– . Russian politician and president of the Russian Federation (1990–). After working on construction projects near his home in Sverdlovsk, he joined the Communist party and eventually became the first secretary of the Sverdlovsk District Central Committee (1976). Soviet leader M. Gorbachev appointed Yeltsin (1985) to clean up the corrupt Moscow party organization and also named him to the Politburo (1986). As mayor of Moscow (1985), Yeltsin worked to reform the city but lost favor by his outspoken criticism of party conservatives, who he believed were blocking heeded reforms. Yeltsin's criticisms, extending even to Gorbachev himself, finally brought about his ouster from political posts in 1987–88. But Yeltsin was not finished; he was elected to the Soviet Parliament (1989) and became president of the Russian Federation (1990), the largest of the Soviet republics. Then he quit the Communist party (1990). From his new position he helped lead the campaign for greater autonomy by the Soviet republics, criticized the government bureaucracy (along with his former friend Gorbachev), and advocated both radical economic reforms and a multiparty political system. Yeltsin became an international hero by leading resistance to the Soviet coup (Aug. 1991), and following the collapse of the USSR, he played a major role in creating the Commonwealth of Independent States (CIS). After Gorbachev resigned, Yeltsin emerged as the most powerful political figure in the CIS, and pushed for greater powers in the Russian Federation to speed up badly needed economic reforms. *See also* Commonwealth of Independent States, 1987–92.

Yemen (Republic of Yemen; *formerly* Yemen Arab Republic *and* People's Democratic Republic of Yemen, *or* Southern Yemen) Independent state located at the southwestern tip of the Arabian Peninsula on the east coast of the Red Sea. The population is 11,500,000 and the capital is San'a. Dominated by Egypt and the Ottoman Turks until the early 20th cent., the region was divided into Yemen and Southern Yemen until the two countries were unified in 1990. Key dates include:

12TH–8TH CENTS. BC   Minean kingdom ruled North Yemen.

8TH–2D CENTS. BC   Sabaean kingdom ruled.

1ST CENT. BC   Roman invasion.

4TH CENT. AD   Ethiopian invasions.

6TH–7TH CENTS.   Persia ruled.

628   Region conquered by Muslims; converted to Islam.

10TH-CENT.   Rassite dynasty of Zaidi sect established in the region.

11TH–12TH CENTS.   Fatimids of Egypt ruled the region.

16TH–20TH CENTS.   Ottoman Empire exercised nominal control over the region.

1818–40   Puritanical, nationalistic Wahhabi sect briefly took control of the region.

1839   British East India Company occupied Aden, in what became Southern Yemen.

1854–1914   British East India Company gradually expanded domains around Aden in Southern Yemen through outright purchase and treaties with local rulers.

1913   Northern Yemen granted autonomy by Ottoman Turks after uprisings against their rule.

1918   Northern Yemen gained independence on collapse of the Ottoman Empire.

1934–35   Boundary dispute with Saudi Arabia; Saudi troops invaded Northern Yemen and forced settlement.

1937   Southern Yemen was designated Aden Protectorate by Britain.

1948   Imam Yahaya and two sons assassinated in Northern Yemen by religious leader Sayyid Abdullah ibn-Ahmad el-Wazir; Emir Seif el-Islam Ahmed crowned as successor after revolt was quashed.

1949–50   50,000 Jews in Northern Yemen evacuated to Israel.

1958–61   Northern Yemen joined with Egypt and Syria to form United Arab Republic (UAR).

1962–67   Junta deposed newly crowned Imam Badr in Northern Yemen; republic proclaimed.

1962–69   Civil war in Northern Yemen between forces of new republic and royalist supporters of the imam; Saudi Arabia and Jordan supported royalists; Egypt and Soviet Union supported republicans.

1963–67   Aden Colony made part of Federation of Southern Arabia; terrorist campaign against British rule in Southern Yemen began.

1967   In Southern Yemen, a republic was established (Nov. 30) after Federation of South Arabia collapsed and British withdrew from Aden.

1967–72   Border war between Northern and Southern Yemen.

1969   Southern Yemen president Qahtan Muhammad al Shaabi resigned; replaced by five-man presidential council.

1969–78   Salim Robea Ali chaired presidential council in Southern Yemen; overthrown and executed; Premier Ali Nasser Muhammad replaced him.

1970   Constitution promulgated in Southern Yemen; country's name formally changed to People's Democratic Republic of Yemen.

1972   Agreement providing for unification of Yemen Arab Republic (North) and People's Democratic Republic of Yemen (South) signed, but unification was not completed.

1971   Constitution adopted in North Yemen.

1974   Army took power in North Yemen by bloodless coup; political parties outlawed, constitution suspended.

1974–77   Col. Ibrahim al-Hamidi ruled as head of state in North Yemen; assassinated.

1978   Lt. Col. Ahmed Hussein al-Ghashmi, head of North Yemen Presidential Council, assassinated by bomb carried by envoy from South Yemen (June).

1978–90   Col. Ali Abdullah Saleh in office as president of North Yemen; relected in 1983.

1978   In South Yemen, President Rubayi Ali deposed by opposition and put to death.

1978   Abdul Fattah Ismail elected president of South Yemen; a hard-line Marxist, he reversed policy of reconciliation with North Yemen.

1979   South Yemen signed friendship treaty with the Soviets.

1979   Border clash between North and South Yemen (Feb.–Mar.); discussions in Kuwait resulted in new plan for unification (Mar.).

1980   Ali Nasir Muhammad al-Hasani became president of South Yemen.

1981   Draft constitution for unified Yemen agreed to (Dec.).

1983   First session of the combined council for North and South Yemen (Aug.); to be held on regular basis thereafter.

1986   South Yemen president Ali Nasir Muhammad al-Hasani ordered assassination of opponents in the Political Bureau (Jan. 13); four of six killed; open warfare engulfed country, killing some 5,000 people, before army defeated pro-Muhammad forces; Muhammad fled country.

1986 In South Yemen, Haidar Abu Bakr al-Attas, the former prime minister, named president (Jan. 24); proclaimed general amnesty for former Muhammad supporters (Mar.).

1987 Border clashes between North and South Yemen.

1988 In North Yemen, elections held for new assembly, the Consultative Council; President Saleh reelected for third term.

1989 South Yemen enacted political and economic reforms to shift country to free market economy (July).

1989 Draft constitution for unified Yemen promulgated (Dec. 1) following signing of unification agreement; new government to be multi-party democratic republic.

1990 Travel restrictions between the two countries eliminated (Jan.); South Yemen disbanded government secret police force (Mar.); armed forces of both nations officially dissolved in preparation for unification.

1990 Republic of Yemen created as unification became official (May 22).

1990– Saleh in office as president (from May); promised to focus on economic development and on relations with Arab nations; new assembly created by merging legislatures of two former countries.

1990–91 Persian Gulf War; Yemen denounced Iraqi invasion but opposed use of force against Iraq, on which it depended heavily for trade.

1992 Government representatives boycotted Mideast peace talks in Moscow (Jan.), in gesture of support for PLO.

1992 Israel opened direct dial telephone service to Yemen and nine other Arab states (Mar.).

yeoman In English history, a member of a class between the gentry and simple laborers. The term was also applied to servants or retainers of middle rank and to such units as the Yeomen of the Guard, long the personal bodyguard of the king.

Yeomen of the Guard Personal bodyguard of the sovereign of England, established (1485) by Henry VII. They are often called beefeaters.

Yermak, Timofeyevich (Ermak, Timofeev) *d.* 1584. Cossack leader. He crossed the Urals, conquered the Tatar khanate of Sibir (1582), and brought Siberia under Russian control.

Yersin, Alexandre Émile Jean 1863–1943. Swiss-born French bacteriologist. He discovered, simultaneously with S. Kitasato, the bubonic plague bacillus (1894). He also developed a serum against the disease.

Yiddish Language originally of Central and Eastern European Jews. Developed (12th cent.) from High German and incorporating elements of Hebrew and Slavic, it is celebrated for its rich literature.

Yi dynasty Dynasty of rulers of Korea (1392–1910). The dynasty was founded by Gen. Yi Songgye, who seized power (1392) with aid from China's Ming rulers. The capital was established at Seoul and Chinese cultural influence was strong (Confucianism was adopted by the state). In subsequent years the dynasty repulsed an invasion by the Japanese (1592) but was forced to recognize the Manchus as their overlords after an invasion in 1627. From the 17th to the 19th cents., the Yi rulers imposed a policy of isolationism and it was not until after the Japanese forced them to accept trade relations (1876) that commerce with Western powers began. Soon after, however, the rise of Japanese influence on the mainland resulted in the takeover of Korea. In 1910 Japan ended the Yi dynasty reign by annexing the kingdom.

yin-yang In Chinese philosophy, the two opposite but complementary groups of qualities that form the basis of the world. Yin is represented as earth, dark, female, odd, negative, and passive, and yang is represented as heaven, light, male, even, positive, and active.

Yoga System of spiritual control practiced in both Hinduism and Buddhism. By means of the discipline's techniques of breathing and other exercises—control of the senses, meditation, and withdrawal—the practitioner is led to the blissful union of self with the divine.

Yogacara School of Mahayana Buddhism. Founded in India (4th cent. AD), it flourished especially in the 5th cent. It held that only consciousness was real, not the objects of consciousness.

Yom Kippur War *See* **Arab-Israeli War** (4).

Yongle (Yung-Lo) 1360–1424. Chinese emperor (1403–25), third of the Ming dynasty emperors. He led expeditions against the Mongols, annexed Annam, sent ships as far as East Africa, moved the capital from Nanking to Beijing (1421), and brought the Ming Empire to the point of its greatest power and influence.

Yorck von Wartenburg, Johann David Ludwig (York von Wartenburg, ˘) 1759–1830. Prussian army officer. He led the Prussian forces in Napoleon's invasion of Russia (1812). Yorck signed the Convention of Tauroggen (Dec. 30, 1812) with Russia, neutralizing his forces and preparing the way for Prussia to join the allies against Napoleon.

Yoritomo 1147–99. Japanese warrior of the Minamoto clan. He became the first shogun of Japan (1192) and leader of the Kamakura shogunate. He participated in the rebellion against the Taira clan (1179–85) and then set up the shogunate in 1192.

York, Alvin Cullum 1887–1964. American army sergeant who became one of the most popular heroes of WW I. On Oct. 8, 1918, he advanced on a fortified hill, killing 20 Germans and capturing 132 others, along with 35 machine guns. For this action he won a Croix de Guerre and a Congressional Medal of Honor.

York, Frederick Augustus, duke of 1763–1827. British officer, second son of King George III. He commanded unsuccessful campaigns in the Netherlands during the French Revolutionary Wars. As commander in chief (1798–1809, 1811–27) he helped to modernize the army.

York, House of Royal house of England, a branch of the Plantagenet family. Its members included three kings, Edward IV, Edward V, and Richard III. Its claims to the English throne in opposition to those of the House of Lancaster resulted in the Wars of the Roses (q.v.).

York, Richard Plantagenet, 3d duke of 1411–60. English nobleman and claimant to the throne of England. He served as protector (1454–55 1455–56) during the mental lapses of King Henry VI. His attempts to secure the crown led to the Wars of the Roses (q.v.). He was recognized heir apparent (1460) but was defeated and killed by Margaret of Anjou at the Battle of Wakefield (1460).

Yorktown Campaign Final major campaign (Sept. 28–Oct. 19, 1781) of the American Revolution, at Yorktown, Virginia. It resulted in the surrender of the British army under Gen. C. Cornwallis and secured American independence. After the failure of his Carolina Campaign (q.v.), Cornwallis moved his army north to Yorktown and fortified it. An American force of some 8,000 under the Marquis M. de Lafayette then moved into position and bottled up the British. Cornwallis hoped for relief or reinforcement by sea but soon a French fleet under Count F. de Grasse blocked the harbor and began to bombard the British positions. Generals G. Washington and J. Rochambeau marched south and reinforced Lafayette. In New York a British relief expedition was outfitted by Sir H. Clinton but Cornwallis surrendered (Oct. 19) before it could arrive in Virginia.

York von Wartenburg, Johann David Ludwig *See* **Yorck von Wartenburg, Johann David Ludwig.**

Yoshida, Shigeru 1878–1967. Japanese statesman. He served as prime minister of Japan five times between 1946 and 1954 and oversaw Japan's recovery from WW II.

Yoshihito *See* **Taisho.**

Young, Brigham 1801–77. American Mormon leader. He succeeded J. Smith as president of the Mormon church and led the migration (1846–48) from Illinois to Salt Lake City, Utah.

Young, Thomas *See* **Rosetta Stone.**

Young, Whitney Moore, Jr. 1921–71. American black civil rights leader. As executive director of the Urban League (1961–71) he led the movement to involve private business and the government in programs to aid America's urban poor.

Younger, Cole 1844–1916. American outlaw. He fought with the Confederate guerrilla band of W. Quantrill during the Civil War and after the war joined the outlaw gang of J. James.

Young Germany (Junges Deutschland) German literary movement of the 1830s and 1840s. The movement was in part a reaction to the nationalism and Romanticism as represented by the works of J. Goethe and was influenced by French literature. Among its members was H. Heine.

Younghusband, Sir Francis Edward 1863–1942. British explorer whose travels increased geographical knowledge of central Asia. He secured (1904) a treaty opening Tibet to Western trade.

Young Italy Italian movement that sought establishment of a Republic of Italy. Founded (1831) by G. Mazzini, it was instrumental in the Italian Risorgimento, but declined in importance after 1848.

Young Plan Second plan adopted for payment of German reparations after WW I, succeeding the Dawes Plan. Put into effect in 1930, it was repudiated by A. Hitler and failed by mid-1931.

Young Turks Group of young Turkish revolutionaries who rebelled against Sultan Abdul Hamid II in 1908 and compelled him to restore constitutional government.

Ypres, battles of 1. The First Battle of Ypres (Oct.–Nov., 1914) between Allied and German forces at Ypres, Beigium during WW I, was largely indecisive. The German advance was halted but the Allies suffered more than 100,000 casualties. 2. The Second Battle of Ypres (Apr. 22–May 25, 1915) marked the first time the Germans used poison gas. The German assault failed to unseat the Allies and ground to a halt. 3. The Third Battle of Ypres (July 31–Nov. 10, 1917), also known as the Battle of Passchendaele, began with a massive British artillery bombardment. The Allied advance was crippled by rain and mud, and casualties numbered some 300,000. 4. The Fourth Battle of Ypres (Apr., 1918) was marked by significant German advances but the Germans were again unable to break the Allied hold on the Ypres salient.

Ypsilanti, Alexander 1792–1828. Greek freedom fighter who led an unsuccessful revolt in Moldavia against Turkish rule (1821), but triggered a successful revolution in Greece.

Ypsilanti, Constantine 1760–1816. Greek hospodar (governor) of Moldavia (1799–1801) and Wallachia (1802–07). He encouraged the Serbs to revolt against the Turks. He sought to free Greece but was exiled to Russia.

Ypsilanti, Demetrios 1793–1832. Greek patriot. Son of C. Ypsilanti and brother of A. Ypsilanti, he fought in the war for Greek independence (1821) and was commander in chief of Greek forces (1828–30).

Yuan Mongol dynasty (1260–1368) established (1260) by Kublai Khan. The Yuan made their capital at Beijing, added to the Grand Canal system, constructed a road and canal system linking the country, and developed a postal system. They also encouraged trade with the West. Marco Polo lived at their court and took tales of their culture back to Europe. However, the Yuan never established rapport with the Chinese natives and were soon overthrown by the Ming (1368).

Yüan Shih-kai *See* **Yuan Shikai.**

Yuan Shikai (Yüan Shih-kai) 1859–1916. Chinese imperial official and first president of the Republic of China (1912–16). He ruled harshly and dissolved Parliament in 1914, thus provoking popular revolts. His attempt to establish a new dynasty and restore the empire (1916) led to his downfall.

Yucatán Central American peninsula comprising the southeastern states of Mexico as well as Belize and part of Guatemala. It was the center of Mayan and Toltec civilizations.

Yueh-chih Ancient central Asian people. They ruled a kingdom in Bactria (northern Afghanistan) and northern India (2d cent. BC–5th cent. AD).

Yugoslavia Former Socialist Federal Republic located in southeastern Europe, now a union of two former constituent republics (Serbia and Montenegro) called the Federal Republic of Yugoslavia. The population is 23,664,000 and the capital is Belgrade. Yugoslavia was established (1918) at the close of WW I as the Kingdom of Serbs, Croats, and Slovenes, finally adopting the name Yugoslavia in 1929. The country was invaded (1941) by German forces during WW II and was partitioned among Germany, Bulgaria, Hungary, and Italy. Under Axis occupation, the Yugoslavs carried on bloody ethnic and ideological fighting among themselves, a battle which was won in 1945 by the Communist leader Tito, who became premier of a new Yugoslav government. That same year the Federal People's Republic of Yugoslavia was proclaimed. Until his death in 1980 Tito followed an independent program of Communism and made Yugoslavia a leading force among nonaligned nations. In the 1980s, economic problems and ethnic unrest helped destabilize the country, and as other Communist governments fell in East Europe, the Yugoslav federation began to break up into separate states. The Serb-dominated national government attempted to prevent the secession of constituent republics by force and in mid-1991 a bloody civil war broke out. As breakaway republics (Croatia, Slovenia, and Bosnia-Herzegovina) continued fighting for their independence, Serbia and Montenegro joined to form a successor state to the defunct Yugoslav federation, calling the new state the Federal Republic of Yugoslavia. Fighting, and international efforts at negotiating a solution, continued in the early 1990s. Key dates in the history of Yugoslavia include:

1915 Serbia and Montenegro occupied by Central Powers during WW I; Serbian government-in-exile established on Allied-controlled island of Corfu; joined by representatives of other South Slavic territories.

1917 South Slavic Committee for National Unity issued (July 20) the Corfu Declaration, calling for establishment of a pan-Slavic state under a constitutional monarchy.

1918 Representatives of Montenegro voted (Nov. 26) to join Serbia in movement for unification.

1918 Kingdom of Serbs, Croats, and Slovenes proclaimed (Dec. 4); Serbian Prince Alexander became regent for his father, King Peter I; new kingdom included Serbia and Montenegro as well as the former Austro-Hungarian territories of Bosnia and Herzegovina, Croatia, and Slovenia.

1919–20 New kingdom's borders largely settled by post-WW I Paris Peace Conference; contested area of Fiume seized by Italian iorces during conference (Sept., 1919).

1920 Treaty of Trianon; territory ceded to kingdom.

1920 Treaty of Rapallo signed (Nov. 12) with Italy; Italy received Istria and other territories in return for abandonment of its demand for cession of Dalmatia.

1920–21 Kingdom joined with Czechoslovakia and Rumania in defensive pact known as the Little Entente to counter territorial demands by Bulgaria and Hungary.

1921–26 Nikola Pašić served as premier.

1921 Peter I died (Aug. 16); Alexander succeeded him as Alexander I.

1921 Communist party banned in kingdom; party continued to operate in secret, however.

1924 Italo-Yugoslav Treaty signed.

1928 Stephen Radić, leader of Croatian nationalist movement in the 1920s, assassinated (June 20) by a Serbian representative in the National Assembly; Croatian representatives subsequently walked out and established new Croatian parliament in Zagreb.

1929 Alexander I assumed dictatorial powers (Jan. 6); dissolved parliament and proclaimed the Kingdom of Yugoslavia.

1931 Alexander I declared end to his dictatorial rule (Sept. 3); new constitution reestablished parliament but left the king with great power.

1934 Yugoslavia signed the Balkan Entente, a mutual defense agreement.

1934 Alexander assassinated (Oct. 9) in Marseilles, France, by Croatian extremist; suc-

ceeded by his son Prince Peter under regency led by Alexander's cousin, Prince Paul.

1930s Prince Paul forced to establish ever stronger ties with Germany and Italy during the rising political crisis in Europe.

1937 Josip Broz, later known as Tito, became leader of the Yugoslav Communist party.

1939 Yugoslavian government issued (Aug. 26) new program for national government; Croatia received greater autonomy within Yugoslav federation.

1939–45 World War II broke out in Europe; partisans, guerrilla resistance led by Tito, eventually joined the Allies in fight against Axis.

1941 Yugoslav government joined Axis Tripartite Pact (Mar. 22); government overthrown (Mar. 24) and Prince Peter acceded to the throne as Peter II; new government proclaimed neutrality.

1941 German forces invaded Yugoslavia (Apr. 6) in cooperation with Bulgarian, Hungarian, and Italian forces; country soon overrun; Yugoslav government evacuated Belgrade (Apr. 12); Yugoslav army disbanded into guerrilla units; Serbia and Croatia were organized as puppet states, with the rest of Yugoslavia divided among Germany, Hungary, Bulgaria, and Italy.

1941–44 Draja Mikhailovich led Chetniks, guerrilla group loyal to government-in-exile; Tito led Communist guerrilla forces against both Chetniks and Germans.

1942 Tito established provisional government known as Council for National Liberation.

1944 Exiled King Peter deposed.

1944 Yugoslav government-in-exlle merged (Nov. 24) with Council for National Liberation.

1945 New government installed (Mar. 7) with Tito as premier and Communists in key positions.

1945–80 Tito in power as head of government.

1945 National elections held (Nov. 11); new assembly proclaimed the Federal People's Republic of Yugoslavia (Nov. 29).

1946 New constitution adopted (Jan. 31); established Soviet-style government, a federation of six republics.

1946 Chetnik leader Mikhailovich captured (Mar. 13); found guilty of treason and collaboration, he was executed (July 17) with several other Chetnik leaders.

1947 Allied-Italian treaty (Feb. 10) restored much of Istria to Yugoslavia; port city of Trieste became international territory under UN administration.

1947–48 Tito conducted extensive purge of opposition and followed program of socialization of economy; programs led to increasing criticism by Soviet Communist party.

1948 Relations between Tito and Soviets reached breaking point; Yugoslav Communist party ousted from Cominform; marked beginning of Tito's independent form of Communism.

1950 Government instituted self-management system for state-run businesses.

1952 Ruling party adopted new name, League of Communists of Yugoslavia (Nov.).

1953 New constitutional changes introduced (Jan.); office of president established; Tito elected (Jan. 14) first president of Yugoslavia (remained in office to 1980).

1954 Yugoslavia entered defensive alliance with Greece and Turkey.

1954 Trieste partitioned between Italy and Yugoslavia.

1955 Normal diplomatic relations with the USSR reestablished.

1963 New constitution promulgated; country's name changed to Socialist Federal Republic of Yugoslavia.

1971 Collective leadership system, in which posts were rotated according to schedule, set up by Tito; sought to promote unity among various ethnic groups.

1974 New constitution promulgated (Feb.); Tito sought to shift power from central government to the republics and provinces.

1974 Tito elected president for life (May).

1980 President Tito died (May 4); rotating presidency (president from any given constituent republic served one-year term) established to prevent unrest among Yugoslavia's various ethnic groups; government promised to continue Tito's nonaligned foreign policy.

1981 Ethnic Albanians in Kosovo autonomous province (within Serbia) rioted (Mar.–Apr.); demanded independence as separate republic; more demonstrations, along with terrorist bombings, occurred in 1982; hundreds of Albanians tried and imprisoned for the unrest

in Kosovo, which nevertheless continued in following years.

1983 Muslim unrest in reported on rise in Bosnia-Herzegovina.

1985 23 Croatian terrorists, members of Croatian Militant Togetherness, tried for arms smuggling and terrorist bombings.

1986–87 Serbs and Montenegrins organized mass demonstrations to protest government's failure to halt violence by ethnic Albanians seeking separate state in Kosovo.

1987 Wage rollback and strict price controls imposed by government to check inflation; sparked over 1,500 protest strikes nationwide that year.

1987 Banking crisis followed revelations that major Yugoslav industrial enterprise issued some $900 million in unsecured notes; solvency of 63 banks threatened; similar illegal issues later reported made by 200 other large businesses; over 40 Communist party members expelled.

1988 Communist party called emergency meeting in the face of continuing economic crisis (May); proposed sweeping reforms, including greater democracy and separation of party from state; instituted economic recovery program (June), which in turn led to strikes against continuing price hikes.

1988 Mass anti-government demonstrations in Belgrade (July); demonstrators broke into Federal Assembly (again in Oct.).

1989 Slovenia's legislative assembly voted to declare right to secede from Yugoslavia (Sept.).

1988–89 Serbia and autonomous provinces of Kosovo and Vojvodina all hit by unrest; 100,000 marched in Vojvodina (Oct. 1988), forcing party Presidium to resign; some 100,000 ethnic Albanians marched in Kosovo (Nov.); nearly 1 million Serbs marched in Belgrade to protest mistreatment by ethnic Albanians in Kosovo.

1989 Party Presidium of Montenegro and members of the republic's presidency resigned following continued unrest there (Jan.).

1989 Serb republic amended its constitution to allow greater control over Kosovo and Vojvodina (Feb.); federal troops used to break up hunger strike by thousands of miners in Kosovo; violence between rioters and security police left some 25 dead in Kosovo (Mar.).

1990 Rioting broke out anew in Kosovo over government trials of ethnic Albanians (Jan.); federal troops ordered in to quell disturbances; Serbia subsequently ended autonomy of Kosovo and Vojvodina (July).

1990 Yugoslav Communist party Congress held (Jan.); ended guarantees of Communist party supremacy in country and approved multi-party system.

1990 Slovenia's Communist party formally seceded from national party following feud over greater autonomy (Feb.); Slovenia ended status as socialist republic (Mar.); Croatia followed soon after.

1990 Slovenia and Croatia held multi-party elections (Apr.–May).

1990 Some 35,000 anti-Communist protesters demonstrated in Belgrade (June).

1990 Slovenia formally adopted declaration of sovereignty (July); referendum on secession overwhelmingly approved (Dec.).

1990 Serbs ousted ethnic Albanians from government in Kosovo (Sept.); province paralyzed by general strike called in protest.

1990 Serbian separatist group proclaimed sovereignty for Serbian communities in Croatia (July).

1990 Serbia, Montenegro, Bosnia-Herzegovina, and Macedonia held multi-party elections (Nov.–Dec.); nationalist candidates won in Macedonia and Bosnia, Communist party candidates in Montenegro, and Socialists in Serbia.

1990 Croatia adopted new constitution that asserted its right to secede (Dec.).

1991 National government ordered all paramilitary groups disarmed (Jan.); Croatia and Slovenia refused to comply.

1991 Financial crisis threatened entire Yugoslav monetary system (Jan.); Serbia, seeking to prop up its sagging economy, reportedly had taken 18 million dinars from National Bank.

1991 Unsuccessful negotiations held on Yugoslav federation (Jan.); Slovenia and Croatia refused to attend later sessions.

1991 Macedonia proclaimed its right to withdraw from the federation (Jan.).

1991 Slovenia and Croatia amended constitutions, subordinating federal laws to their own (Feb.); Serb community in Croatia seceded from the republic.

1991 President of national government resigned (Mar.).

1991 Negotiations between presidents of the republics (Mar.); plans put forward for federation of sovereign states and for unified state with democratic government.

1991 Voters in Croatia approved referendum on independence (May).

1991 Macedonia ended status as Socialist republic (June).

1991 Croatia and Slovenia declared full independence (June); national government troops (mainly Serbs) attacked both to reestablish sovereignty.

1991 Serbs in Croatia proclaimed autonomous region of Krajina was to be united with Bosnia-Herzegovina (June).

1991 EC-backed talks brought ceasefire in Slovenia and Croatia (July); fighting resumed in Croatia, however, as Serbian dominated federal troops pressed their offensive.

1991 Voters in Macedonia and Kosovo approved referendums on independence (Sept.).

1991 UN ordered embargo on arms shipments to Yugoslavia in effort to halt fighting (Sept.).

1991 Croatia, still under attack by Serbian national government troops, voided all federal laws (Oct.); Bosnia declared sovereignty.

1991 Slovenia introduced own currency (Oct.).

1991 Croatian forces raided Serb territory (Nov.).

1991 National president announced Yugoslavia had ceased to exist and resigned (Dec.).

1992 Croatia and Slovenia recognized as independent by European Community (Jan.); fighting meanwhile continued and some one million had been forced to leave their homes.

1992 UN peacekeeping force deployed in Yugoslavia.

1992 Bosnia declared independence (Mar.); intense fighting reported in Bosnia between Serbian federal troops and loosely allied Muslim and Croatian forces.

1992 Federal Republic of Yugoslavia created by union of Serbia and Montenegro (Apr.).

1992 Serbian federal government troops launched offensive in Croatia (May).

1992 UN voted harsh trade sanctions against Serbia in effort to force an end to the civil war (June).

1992 Bosnia, Slovenia, and Croatia became UN members (June).

1992   Serbs ended three-month siege of airport in Sarajevo, Bosnia, allowing UN peacekeepers to deliver emergency supplies (June).

1992   Abuses in Serbian detention camps reported (Aug.); two former prisoners accused Serbs of killing 3,000 in one prison camp.

1992   Yugoslavia (Serbia and Montenegro) expelled from UN General Assembly.

Yukawa, Hideki 1907–81.   Japanese physicist. He predicted the existence of the meson (1935) and developed a "nonlocal field" theory for elementary particles. He was awarded the Nobel Prize in Physics (1949).

Yukon (Yukon Territory)   Canadian territory on the Arctic Ocean noted for its mineral resources.

The area was first explored in the 1830s and the Hudson's Bay Company built trading posts there in the 1840s (the first at Francis Lake, 1843). The dominion took control of the region from the company in 1870. In 1896 the Yukon was the scene of a major gold strike and he subsequent gold rush brought tens of thousands of prospectors to the region. The Yukon became a territory in 1898.

Yukon Territory   *See* **Yukon.**

Yu the Great (Ta Yü) *d.* 2197 BC.   Semi-legendary Chinese hero, credited with regulating floods and establishing administrative regulations, and with founding the Xia dynasty, China's first (legendary) dynasty.

Yung-Lo   *See* **Yongle.**

Z

Zabern Affair Incident (1913) involving the conduct of German army officers in Zabern, now Saverne, in Alsace-Lorraine. The imprudent conduct of a German officer led to riots and arrests and caused a controversy in Germany over German military rule in Alsace-Lorraine.

Zacharias (Zachary) 1. *fl.* 6th cent. BC. Prophet of the Old Testament. 2. Book of the Old Testament, also known as Zechariah. 3. Pope (741–52), known as Saint Zacharias (or Zachary).

Zachary *See* **Zacharias.**

Zaghlul Pasha, Saad c1860–1927. Egyptian nationalist leader and statesman. As head of the Wafd party he helped lead the movement for Egyptian independence after WW I.

Zaharoff, Sir Basil 1850–1936. International arms dealer and financier. Born in the Ottoman Empire of Greek parents, he made a fortune selling arms before and during WW I and was suspected of secret political intrigues.

Zahir ud-Din Muhammad *See* **Babur.**

zaibatsu Family-owned Japanese financial and economic combines or cartels. They have played an enormous role in Japan's economic development since the Meiji restoration (1868) and control important segments of Japanese commerce, finance, and industry.

Zaimis, Alexander 1855–1936. Greek statesman, seven times premier between 1897 and 1928 and president of Greece from 1929 to 1935. His presidency was marked by clashes between royalists and republicans. He went into exile in Austria after restoration (1935) of the monarchy.

Zaire (Republic of Zaire; *formerly* Belgian Congo) Independent state located in west-central Africa (*pop.* 35,330,000). Its capital is Kinshasa. Since its independence in 1960, Zaire has been shaken by civil war and by Angolan invasions. Key dates in its history include:

1482 Portuguese visited Zaire; established ties with Kongo tribe.

1860s–90s Muhammad bin Hammad, a Swahili, ruled large areas of eastern Zaire.

1878–84 American reporter Henry Stanley explored the Congo region and established control for King Leopold II of Belgium.

1885 King Leopold II obtained personal title to the area at the Berlin Conference; Leopold created independent Congo under his rule.

1890s Control over countryside established; concessions granted to private companies to exploit the colony.

1908 Belgium formally annexed Congo after reports of brutality against blacks by private companies; named region Belgian Congo; exploitation continued, though treatment of native blacks improved.

1960 Congo granted independence (June 30) after rioting by nationalists; called Republic of the Congo.

1960 Joseph Kasavubu became head of state; Patrice Lumumba became prime minister.

1960 Civil war (July); armed forces mutinied and Katanga province seceded (led by Moise Tshombe) with Belgian support; South Kasai also seceded.

1960 UN and Belgium sent peace-keeping forces.

1960 President Kasavubu staged army coup (Feb.), under leadership of Joseph-Désiré Mobutu; former Prime Minister Lumumba arrested (Dec.); Mobutu stepped down in Feb. 1961.

1961 Lumumba killed under suspicious circumstances (Feb.).

1961 UN Secretary General Dag Hammarskjold died (Sept. 17) in plane crash en route to conference with Tshombe.

1962 Tshombe rejected peace plan of new UN Secretary General U Thant.

1962 UN forces in active fighting against Tshombe's rebel troops in Katanga.

1963 Tshombe surrendered (Jan. 14), ending Katanga secession and civil war.

1963 Coalition government formed; Kasavubu made Tshombe premier.

1965 Kasavubu accused Tshombe of treason, dismissed him; was ousted in turn by Gen. Joseph Mobutu (Nov.).

1965– Mobutu in power; proclaimed "Second Republic"; soon after beginning his long rule, he abolished office of prime minister; restored order and initiated his program of "African Authenticity" by replacing European names of places with African names.

1966 Mobutu nationalized copper mines.

1967 Constitution adopted.

1971 Government changed name from Democratic Republic of the Congo to Zaire.

1974 Constitution amended.

1975 Mobutu nationalized economy; barred religious education in schools; decreed use of African names; changed his name to Mobutu Sese Seko.

1975 Zaire, long a supporter of nationalist FNLA fighting for control of Angola, cut off aid and recognized Angola's central government.

1977–78 Two FNLA invasions from Angola repulsed with aid from France, Belgium, and US.

1977 Direct elections held; Mobutu reelected.

1978 Zaire and Angola agreed to end support of rebel groups trying to overthrow their respective governments.

1982 Second political party, Union pour la démocratie et le progrés social (UDPS), organized.

1983 Mobutu, embarrassed by allegations of human rights abuses, offered amnesty to political exiles.

1984 Government troops recaptured Moba, town taken and held by rebel force for two days (Nov.).

1985 UDPS supporters allegedly arrested and tortured (Nov.–Dec.); President Mobutu admitted in 1986 some accusations were true.

1988 Belgian press reported allegations of corruption in Zaire, including charges Mobutu misappropriated Belgian aid money (Nov.); Mobutu abrogated cooperative treaties with Belgium (Jan. 1989); relations restored following talks (July).

1989 50 students killed in Kinshasa and Lubumbashi after protest against increased school costs turned violent (Feb.).

1990 Mobutu proclaimed "Third Republic" amid increasing unrest and calls for his ouster (Apr.); promised to introduce three-party system and relinquished some of his posts.

1990 Opposition party UDPS legalized (Apr.).

1990 Estimated 50–150 student protesters killed when police cracked down on antigovernment demonstration at Lubumbashi University (May); Belgian government responded to atrocities by freezing aid to Zaire.

1990 Constitution amended; legalized independent trade unions; ended presidential control over National Executive Council and over foreign policy (June).

1990 Multi-party system established.

1990 US ended aid to Zaire following new charges of human rights abuses (Nov.).

1991 Three-day general strike calling for better conditions and ouster of government; hundreds of thousands of government workers participated (Feb.).

1991 Police shot at anti-government demonstrators in central Zaire (Apr.), killing 42.

1992 Loyal troops put down short-lived mutiny by rebellious soldiers (Jan.).

1992 Government troops fired on pro-democracy demonstrators (Feb.), killing about 13 persons.

Zama, Battle of Decisive Roman victory over Carthage (202 BC) during the Second Punic War, at Zama, southwest of Carthage. There the Romans under Scipio Africanus defeated the Carthaginians led by Hannibal.

Zambia (*formerly* Northern Rhodesia) Landlocked republic (*pop.* 8,119,000) located in south-central Africa. Its capital is Lukasa. Formerly the British colony of Northern Rhodesia, Zambia gained independence in 1964. Key dates in its history include:

c1200   Bantu-speaking tribes settled in area.

1851–73   D. Livingstone in Zambia as explorer and missionary.

1855   Livingstone became the first European to sight Victoria Falls.

1889–1924   British South Africa Company ruled area; mining operations and European settlement began.

1911   Territory of Northern Rhodesia formed by joining two British protectorates.

1920s   Rich copper deposits discovered.

1924   British government took over control of territory from British South Africa Company.

1953–64   Northern Rhodesia made part of the Federation of Rhodesia and Nyasaland.

1959   Kenneth Kaunda, black nationalist, formed United National Independence party.

1962   Widespread protest campaign against white rule.

1964   Northern Rhodesia declared independence (Oct. 24); became Republic of Zambia under black African rule.

1964–   K. Kaunda in office as president; Zambia remained in British Commonwealth.

FROM 1965   Zambia's support of UN sanctions against white-ruled (Southern) Rhodesia disrupted Zambia's trade through and with Rhodesia; next years spent developing transport and trade links through other neighboring countries.

1969   Kaunda nationalized (with compensation) foreign copper-mining industry, oil industry.

1972   Kaunda's United National Independence party became only legal party.

1973   New constitution promulgated.

1980   Coup attempt failed (Oct.).

1981   Government forced to impose program of economic austerity as world copper prices fell; national economy declined into recession lasting throughout the 1980s; mounting foreign debt led to further economic ills and civil unrest.

1981   Kaunda reshuffled government in wake of copper miners' strike.

1983–84   Government campaign against corruption and inefficiency.

1985   Ban on strikes imposed following walkout by government employees protesting low wages.

1985–87   Austerity measures imposed by government in response to worsening economy; sparked riots and unrest.

1986   Government restored subsidy on maize after its removal caused a 120 percent increase in price and led to rioting in which 15 were killed.

1986   South African troops attacked suspected ANC bases inside Zambia (May).

1986–87   Zambia Airways personnel charged with smuggling drugs and currency.

1987   Government stopped making full debt-service payments and stopped implementing economic reforms recommended by IMF.

1989   Joint security commission established with Mozambique to end cross-border attacks by rebel groups.

1989   Zambia agreed to end subsidies and price controls, and to devalue currency to regain IMF approval.

1990   Amnesty for political prisoners instituted.

1990   Capital torn by rioting after government imposed new austerity measures (June).

1990   Foreign creditors agreed to refinancing of Zambian foreign debt.

1990   Abortive military coup put down (June 30).

1990   Legislation establishing multi-party system enacted (Dec.).

1991   Zambia credit restored after making arresars payments to World Bank.

1992   Food shortages reported as a result of drought parching much of southern Africa (Mar.).

Zamenhof, Ludwig   *See* **Esperanto.**

Zamolski, Jan (Zamoyski, ~) 1541–1605.   Polish general and statesman. He helped secure the elections of Henry of Anjou, S. Báthory, and Sigismund III as kings of Poland and served as chancellor under each of them. He led Polish forces against the Russians, Turks, and Swedes.

Zamora, Niceto Alcalá   *See* **Second Republic (Spanish).**

Zamora, Treaty of   Agreement (1143) between Castile and Portugal by which Portugal became independent of Spain and Alfonso Henriques, count of Portugal, was recognized as King Alfonso.

Zamoyski, Jan   *See* **Zamolski, Jan.**

Zangi 1084–1146.   Seljuk ruler. He fought successfully against the crusaders, established the Zangid dynasty (1127–1250), and extended his rule over much of Syria, Palestine, and Iraq.

Zanzibar Island region of Tanzania (*q.v.*). Explored by the Arabs (1st cent. AD), it came under Portuguese control (c1505–1698) and then was taken by Arabs from Oman. Under Sayyid Said (1804–56), Zanzibar was a major source for slaves. It became a British protectorate (1890) and joined with Tanganika (1964) to form the United Republic of Tanzania.

Zapata, Emiliano c1879–1919. Mexican revolutionary. An advocate of agrarian reform, he at first supported F. Madero but later opposed Madero and his successors. Zapata's army occupied Mexico City three times in 1914–15.

Zaporozhe Cossacks Ukrainian Cossacks who between the 16th and 18th cents. ruled over a large portion of the Ukraine, defending it against the incursions of Tatars and others. They resisted Polish domination and, in 1654, allied themselves with the Russian tsars. After their alliance with the Swedes against the Russians, Peter the Great virtually ended their independence (1709). Their last fortress was destroyed in 1775.

Zapotec Indian people of Mexico inhabiting the eastern and southern regions of Oaxaca. Once an independent nation centered at Monte Albán, they enjoyed an advanced civilization reflecting Mayan and later Toltec influences. Subsequently allied with the Aztecs, they continued to flourish until the Spanish Conquest.

Zara, Siege of Attack (Nov., 1202) by the armies of the Fourth Crusade on Zara, now in Croatia. Zara had placed itself under the protection of Hungary, and the Venetians, anxious to recover it, persuaded the crusaders to attack.

Zarathustra *See* **Zoroaster.**

Zealots Jewish sect noted for its extreme opposition to Roman rule in Judea. The Zealots played a leading role in the unsuccessful revolt against Rome (AD 66–70).

Zechariah *See* **Zacharias** (2.).

Zedekiah (Mattaniah) *fl.* 6th cent. BC. Last king of Judah (597–586 BC). He allied Judah with Egypt and opposed Babylonian rule. Nebuchadnezzar invaded and destroyed the kingdom (586) and initiated the Babylonian Captivity.

Zeeland, Paul van 1893–1973. Belgian economist and prime minister (1935–37). As prime minister he reaffirmed Belgian neutrality in exchange for German promises of inviolability.

Zelaya, José Santos 1853–1919. President and virtual dictator of Nicaragua (1894–1909). He attempted unsuccessfully to establish by force and revolution the Central American Federation.

Zelle, Margaretha Geertruida *See* **Mata Hari.**

zemstvo A local and provincial assembly in tsarist Russia. Established (1864) as one of the major reforms of Alexander II, the zemstvos produced numerous reforms and improvements before being superseded (1917) by the Soviets after the Bolshevik revolution.

Zen Buddhism Buddhist sect. It was founded (5th cent. AD) by Bodhidharma, who brought it from India to China. From there it spread to Japan. Zen stresses the awakening (satori) of the wisdom (prajna) that lies dormant within each soul. This wisdom is awakened by meditation and by personal instruction of a master to a pupil. Zen came to be a significant influence in many aspects of Chinese and Japanese life.

Zenger, John Peter 1697–1746. American printer and journalist, publisher of the New York *Weekly Journal.* His trial and acquittal (1735) for libel was a landmark in establishing freedom of the press in America.

Zeng Guofang (Tseng Kuo-fan) 1811–72. Chinese general and government administrator under the Qing dynasty. Zeng was successful in suppressing the Taiping Rebellion and conciliating the Western powers. He gave the declining Chinese imperial government a new lease on life.

Zeng He *fl.* 15th cent. Chinese navigator during the Ming period who commanded exploratory voyages to East Africa.

Zeno *d.* AD 491. Roman emperor of the East (AD 474–491), successor to his son Leo II. His rule was marked by internal struggle, and his attempt to reconcile orthodox Christians and Monophysites with his *Henotikon* caused further dissension.

Zenobia *d.* after AD 272. Queen of Palmyra. She greatly expanded her realm through conquest in Asia Minor and Egypt before her defeat and capture by the Roman emperor Aurelian (AD 272).

Zeno of Citium c336–c264 BC. Greek philosopher. Zeno studied under the Cynics before establishing his own school at the Stoa Poikile in Athens, from which evolved the name of his philosophy, Stoicism. Although his writings have not survived, Zeno's teachings were preserved by the philosophical historian Diogenes Laërtius (*fl.* 3d cent. AD).

Zeno of Elea *fl.* 5th cent. BC. Greek philosopher of the Eleatic school. A disciple of Parmenides, he was considered by Aristotle to be the first to use the dialectical method of reasoning.

Zenta, Battle of Austrian victory (Sept. 11, 1697) over the Ottoman Turks at Zenta, now in Yugoslavia. The Ottoman forces were utterly routed by the Austrians under Prince Eugene of Savoy.

zeppelin Name applied to dirigible balloons, especially German military dirigibles and passenger airships. They were so named after Ferdinand Graf von Zeppelin (1838–1917), the airship's inventor and builder. The German dirigible *Graf Zeppelin* completed an around-the-world flight in 1929.

Zerubbabel *fl.* 520 BC. Governor of Jerusalem at the time of the building of the second Jewish Temple.

Zetkin, Clara 1857–1933. German feminist and Communist leader, one of the founders of the German Communist party.

Zeuxis f7. 5th cent. BC. Ancient Greek painter. His works were noted for their use of shading to produce a sense of realism.

Zhang Guotao (Chang Kuo-t'ao) 1897–1979. Chinese political leader, a founding member of the Chinese Communist party. He lost a power struggle with Mao Zedong during the Long March (1935) and defected to the Chinese Nationalists.

Zhang Qian (Chang Ch'ien) *d.* 114 BC. Chinese minister and explorer under Han dynasty emperor Wudi. Sent on official missions into central Asia, he provided the Chinese with knowledge of the cultures in Bactria, Parthia, and India.

Zhang Xueliang (Chang Hsüeh-Liang) 1898– . Chinese warlord of Manchuria (1928–31). Forced to withdraw to China by the Japanese (1931), he was responsible for the Xi'an Incident (1936)

Zhdanov, Andrei Aleksandrovich 1896–1948. Russian Communist leader and general. Made a member of the Politburo (1939), he fought in the Russo-Finnish War and in WW II. A hardline supporter of J. Stalin, he organized (1947) the Cominform, the Communist Information Bureau.

Zhivkov, Todor *See* **Bulgaria,** 1954–89.

Zhou (Chou) Third dynasty of rulers (c1122 BC–c221 BC) in China and the Chinese classical age. The Zhou people, dominant in the Wei River valley, invaded the Shang Kingdom and overthrew (c1122 BC) Zhouxin, the Shang dynasty ruler. Wu Wang became the first emperor and founder of the Zhou dynasty, which lasted for nearly a millennium. The dynasty is traditionally divided into two periods. The *Western* Zhou (c1122–771) lasted until the capital of Hao (near modern Xian) was overrun by local lords and their barbarian allies. The *Eastern* Zhou dynasty (771–221) then established itself at Luoyang. The Eastern Zhou dynasty is subdivided into the Chunqiu (722–481) and the Warring States (481–221) periods, and eventually fell to rulers of the Qin dynasty. The Zhou period was a time of great cultural flowering, in which Bronze Age culture reached its height. The Five Classics were written and Confucius, Lao-tze, and Mencius, among others, spread their teachings. Canals built during this period later became part of the Grand Canal. Feudalism in its Chinese form, begun during the Shang period, was the Zhou system of government.

Zhou Enlai (Chou En-lai) 1898–1976. Chinese Communist leader, premier (1949–76) and foreign minister (1949–58). A founder of the Chinese Communist party, he served (1924–27) with other Communists in the Guomindang's nationalist revolution. During the subsequent civil war (1927–49), in which the Guomindang turned against the Communists, he participated in the Long March. A leading Communist official thereafter, he helped bring the Communists to power in 1949. Later, as foreign minister, he headed delegations to the Geneva and Bandung conferences. He is said to have exercised a moderating influence during the Cultural Revolution and to have been responsible for the Sino-American rapprochement in the 1970s.

Zhou Gong (Chou Kung) *fl.* 12 cent. BC. Chinese statesman, brother of Emperor Wu Wang. A wise and just man, he became the model for Chinese rulers and officials of succeeding generations. He served as regent of the empire on his brother's death, founded the Lu line of nobles, and wrote a code of laws for the Zhou state.

Zhouxin (Chou Hsin) c1154–c1122 BC. Last Shang dynasty emperor of ancient China. He was notorious for his cruelty and debauchery, and his overthrow (1122) brought the Zhou dynasty to power.

Zhu De (Chu Teh) 1886–1976. Leading Chinese Communist general. He participated in the Chinese Revolution of 1911, and, following the break between Nationalists and Communists (1927), he joined with Mao Zedong to form the Communist army. He became general of all Communist forces (1931–54) and, after the Communist victory in China (1949), served in high government posts.

Zhuge Liang (Chu-ko Liang) AD 181–234. Chinese soldier and government minister, credited with helping Liu Pei (161–223) found the Shu Han dynasty (see Three Kingdoms). A military, mathematical, and organizational genius, he is celebrated in Chinese legend and literature.

Zhu Xi (Chu Hsi) 1130–1200. Chinese Neo-Confucian philosopher, one of China's most important commentators on Confucianism. Until 1905, public officials were required to have a thorough knowledge of his works on Confucianism, *The Four Books,* to pass the civil service examination. Though he believed that human nature in reality was less than good, he taught that an individual's essential goodness could be brought out by study of the classics. His teachings were also influential in Japan and Korea.

Zhukov, Georgi Konstantinovich 1896–1974. Russian general and marshal of the Soviet Union. He played a major role in the USSR's defeat of the German offensive in WW II.

Zimbabwe (*formerly* Rhodesia; Southern Rhodesia) Independent, landlocked state located in southern Africa. The population is 10,205,000 and the capital is Salisbury. In the 1960s and 1970s the white minority government of Rhodesia resisted a UN-backed campaign aimed at ending apartheid policies and bringing black Africans into the government. The struggle lasted until 1980, when black Africans formally took control of the government. Key dates in Zimbabwe's history include:

5TH CENT. AD Bantu peoples arrived.

16TH CENT. Portuguese traders arrived.

1889 Colonized by Cecil Rhodes's British South Africa Company.

1890 Salisbury founded.

1893 Rhodes's company defeated Ndebele tribe.

1896–97 Uprisings by the Ndebele and Shona.

1923 Became self-governing colony of Southern Rhodesia under British crown; white rule established.

1933–53 Sir Godfrey Huggins in office as prime minister of Southern Rhodesia.

1953 Southern Rhodesia joined with Northern Rhodesia and Nyasaland to form Federation of Rhodesia and Nyasaland.

1953–56 Huggins in office as first prime minister of federation.

1957 African National Congress (ANC), black nationalist group originally founded in 1934, reactivated with Joshua Nkomo as president.

1959 ANC banned; successor groups also banned, including Zimbabwe African People's Union (ZAPU, formed 1961).

1961 New constitution adopted, providing for nearly complete independence from Britain.

1962–63 Winston Field, leader of the white, pro-segregation Rhodesian Front, in office as prime minister following elections.

1963 Black nationalist Zimbabwe African National Union (ZANU) formed (Aug.) under leadership of Rev. Ndabaningi Sithole.

1963 Federation broke up (Dec.); Northern Rhodesia and Nyasaland, opposed to apartheid policies of new government, voted for independence; Southern Rhodesia chose to remain a colony.

1964 In Southern Rhodesia conservative Ian Smith became prime minister of white-rule government (Apr.); restrictions against blacks tightened.

1965 Talks on independence with Britain broke down over Smith's refusal to meet British requirement for change from minority white rule to majority rule; Smith declared state of emergency.

1965 Rhodesia's white minority government unilaterally declared independence from Britain (Nov. 11); renamed country Rhodesia; British branded independence as illegal and Rhodesia was not recognized by other nations.

1967 Rhodesia became first nation to have economic UN sanctions imposed against it; ZANU and ZAPU began armed revolt against white rule.

1967 South African police sent to Rhodesia following request by Smith for help against black nationalist guerrillas.

1970 Rhodesia became republic (Mar. 2); complete segregation of races instituted.

1972 Terrorist activities by black nationalists increased during the year.

1976 White minority government weakened by economic problems, continuing guerrilla war waged by black nationalists, and end to aid from South Africa; negotiations begun in 1975 continued.

1978 Smith agreed to plan for eventual black majority rule.

1978 Smith, Bishop Abel Muzorewa, Ndabingi Sithole, and Jeremiah Chirau signed agreement to transfer power to black majority; became executive council; transition government opposed by UN and the Patriotic Front (PF), a black nationalist group formed by Nkomo and Robert Mugabe.

1979 New constitution enfranchised all blacks, while maintaining protections for white minority (Jan.); changed name of country to Zimbabwe Rhodesia.

1979 Black majority assumed control (May 31); Muzorewa in office as prime minister; UN sanctions remained in effect; fighting between black nationalist groups.

1979 British-sponsored constitutional conference convened in London (Sept.); PF agreed to reservation of 20 seats in legislature for whites; agreement on transition to black majority rule accepted by all contending parties (Nov.).

1979 Zimbabwe Rhodesian Parliament voted to again become British colony (Dec. 11).

1979–80 Britain's Lord Christopher Soames headed provisional government pending elections for new black majority government; economic sanctions lifted.

1980 Zimbabwe gained formal independence (Apr. 18).

1980–86 Rev. Canaan Banana installed as first president; Mugabe served as first prime minister.

1980 Zimbabwe admitted to UN.

1982 Zimbabwe sent first contingent of troops to Mozambique to aid government against rebels there; maintained troops there through 1980s and into 1990s.

1983 Troops sent to Matabeleland following unrest by followers of Nkomo; some 10,000 troops returned to Matabeleland (1984) in new campaign against guerrillas; estimated 2,000 persons killed in 1983–84.

1984 Formerly all-white RF party dropped racial restrictions and renamed itself Conservative Alliance of Zimbabwe (CAZ).

1985 Many ZANU leaders arrested and questioned concerning links with unrest in Matabeleland; torture allegedly used.

1986 President Banana retired (Dec.); Mugabe became president.

1987 Reservation of seats for white delegates in House of Assembly and Senate abolished; post of prime minister incorporated in executive presidency.

1987 Government balked at imposing economic sanctions against South Africa to protest continued apartheid policy there; decided on more moderate measures (July).

1988 Merger of ZANU and ZAPU approved by both parties; became effective Dec., 1989, under new name ZANU-PF.

1989 Financial scandal resulted in resignations of five cabinet ministers (Mar.–Apr.).

1989 Law passed to abolish Senate and enlarge House of Assembly by 50 percent.

1990 Mugabe reelected as president; ZANU-PF won majority of seats in House.

1990 Official state of emergency, in effect since independence, ended (Aug.).

1990 Legislature approved compulsory land acquisition by government to redistribute farmland owned by white Europeans to black Africans (Dec.).

1991 Ruling party, ZANU-PF, formally abandoned Marxist-Leninist ideology (June).

1992 Parliament passed land reform law (Mar.); would redistribute land from commercial farms to poor.

1992 Government declared national emergency (Mar.), as continuing drought threatened the country with famine.

Zimmermann Telegram (~ Note) Telegram sent (Jan. 16, 1917) by German foreign secretary Arthur Zimmermann to the German ambassador to the US. Zimmermann suggested the possibility of an alliance with Mexico in the event of US entry into WW I against Germany. The telegram, intercepted and made public, helped arouse American sentiment against Germany.

Zimmerwald Conference Socialist conference (Sept. 4–8, 1915) at Zimmerwald, Switzerland, at which the European Socialist parties attempted to forge a common position on WW I. The conference denounced the war as imperialistic, but a faction led by N. Lenin denounced its resolutions as feeble and tepid.

Zinjanthropus *See* **Leakey, Louis Seymour Bazett.**

Zinoviev, Grigori Evseyevich 1883–1936. Russian Communist leader who played a leading role in the Soviet government from 1917 to 1926. With J. Stalin and L. Kamenev he formed the triumvirate that ruled after the death of N. Lenin. He also headed the Comintern (1919–26). He was executed during the Stalinist purges.

Zinoviev letter   Letter, probably a forgery, supposedly written (1924) by G. Zinoviev, then head of the Comintern. The letter called on British Communists to begin a revolution. The publication of the letter helped to bring down Britain's first Labour government.

Zinzendorf, Nikolaus Ludwig, graf von 1700–60. German religious leader who refounded the Moravian church (*q.v.*). His religious views, particularly concerning the importance of emotion in religion, greatly influenced 19th-cent. Protestantism.

Zion (Mount ˜) (Sion) (Mount Sion)   Name originally given to a hill in Jerusalem on which stood the Jebusite city conquered by David. Now the word is symbolic of the Promised Land or of heaven.

Zionism   Jewish movement for the establishment and preservation of a Jewish national state in Palestine. The first Zionist council was held (1897) in Basel, Switzerland under the leadership of T. Herzl. With the advent of WW I, Great Britain lent its support to the movement through the Balfour Declaration (1917), which was incorporated in the British mandate for Palestine and thus helped promote the influx of Jews to Palestine (especially in the early years of the mandate). Though increasing unrest among Arabs in Palestine forced the British to attempt to slow down immigration by Jews, WW II and the Holocaust in Nazi Germany reemphasized the need for a Jewish homeland. The UN plan for the partition of Palestine resulted in the establishment of a Jewish state (May, 1948).

Zipangu   *See* **Japan.**

Ziska, John   *See* **Zizka, John.**

Zita 1892–1989. Last empress of Austria and queen of Hungary (1916–18), wife of Austrian emperor Charles I (*m.* 1911).

Zizka, John (Ziska, ˜) *d.* 1424. Bohemian military leader. He successfully led the Hussites against Holy Roman Emperor Sigismund in the Hussite Wars and introduced modern tactics of warfare, notably the use of mobile artillery.

Zoar   Village in eastern Ohio. Founded (1817) by a group of German Protestant Separatists, it was the site until 1898 of a Separatist experimental communal society.

Zoë c978–1050. Byzantine empress (1028–50), daughter of and successor to Constantine VIII. She married Romanus III, but she had him murdered (1034) and made her lover emperor as Michael IV. Michael V, adopted by Zoë, was deposed after a brief reign (1041–42). Zoë next married Constantine IX.

Zog I (Ahmed Bey Zogu) 1895–1961. President (1925–28) and king of Albania (1928–39). Zog came to power as president after leading a successful uprising against the Albanian provisional government (1924). As president, and then king, he led Albania into military and financial dependence on Mussolini's Italy and was overthrown after the Italian invasion of Albania.

Zola, Émile 1840–1902. French novelist, a leader of the naturalist movement in France and one of the greatest French writers of the 19th cent. He played a leading role in the Dreyfus Affair (*q.v.*).

Zollverein   German customs union. Begun (early 19th cent.) by Prussia, it grew through the 19th cent. to include all the German states. The union became a means by which Prussia isolated Austria from the German Confederation. The union's policies were incorporated (1871) into the German Empire.

Zorndorf, Battle of (Sarbinowo, ˜)   Prussian victory (Aug. 25, 1758) over the Russians at Zorndorf (Sarbinowo), Poland. The Russians lost some 24,000 men to the Austrian casualties of 11,000.

Zoroaster (Zarathustra) c628–c551 BC. Persian religious leader and reformer, founder of Zoroastrianism.

Zoroastrianism   Ancient Persian religion founded (6th cent. BC) by Zoroaster. Its teachings center on Ahura Mazda, a god of righteousness, who would battle the evil spirits led by Ahriman until the ultimate victory over evil is achieved. Zoroastrianism was made the state religion of Persia by the Sassanidae (3d cent. AD) and is believed to have influenced both Judaism and Christianity. Its few remaining adherents are known as Parsees.

Zululand   Historic region, since 1897 a part of the South African province of Natal. Occupied by the Zulus in the 17th cent., the region was the scene of conflicts, notably the Battle of Blood River (*q.v.*), between Zulus and the Boers (then on the Great Trek). By 1840, the Boers were in control of Zululand. Thereafter the British, succeeding the Boers, warred against the Zulus, annexed Zululand in 1887, and made it part of Natal (1897).

Zwingli, Huldreich 1484–1531.   Swiss reformer, the leading figure in the Swiss Protestant Reformation. His opposition to M. Luther's views on the nature of the Eucharist led to great dissension within the Protestant church.

About the Author

Bruce Wetterau is a writer and editor with nearly twenty years' experience in reference publishing. He has written six books, including *The New York Public Library Book of Chronologies* and *The Macmillan Concise Dictionary of World History*. He also helped to compile two trade reference works, *The Pessimist's Guide to History* and *Wise Words and Wives' Tales*. He has contributed to numerous reference books, including *The Random House Dictionary, Second Unabridged Edition*, and to a CD-ROM project on environmental issues. He lives in Charlottesville, Virginia.